WHAT F

"Since being intr
honestly say I ha
All the sadness, t
solve and I know how to help others solve theirs. Studying the book gives you an understanding of the mind, which then leads to helping you reach your goals and the ability to help others."

–**JOHN TRAVOLTA**, *Academy Award–nominated Actor and Cultural Icon*

"I love what I do for a living and *Dianetics* has allowed me to enjoy it even more! Knowing yourself, having trust in yourself and owning your decisions is everything. *Dianetics* made this possible for me."

–**ERIKA CHRISTENSEN**, *Award-winning Actress (Traffic, Parenthood, Will Trent)*

"After using *Dianetics* I had so much more of a deep understanding of the mind and consequently I felt so much more like myself for the first time. I can't imagine any artists not wanting to truly be themselves."

–**STANLEY CLARKE**, *Four-time Grammy Award–winning Bassist and Composer*

"Your health is your real wealth! And your mental health and spiritual health of self is the ultimate wealth! And *Dianetics* gave me tools I can use to strengthen my mind and clear it! And find peace at the same time!"

–**DOUG E. FRESH**, *Hip Hop Legend and Humanitarian*

"*Dianetics* is the only thing that truly handled the mental barriers holding me back, irrational fears, unwanted emotions and self-doubt. It helped me understand and resolve them all."

–**JASON DOHRING**, *Actor (Veronica Mars)*

"As a jazz musician, I fell victim to many of the false solutions that musicians can run into. Nothing positive came out of that. But with *Dianetics*, I was able to get to the root cause of the problems I was experiencing. *Dianetics* made a very dramatic difference in my life."

–**MARK ISHAM**, *Academy Award–nominated Composer and Grammy Award–winning Musician*

"Free from the dark days of the past, free from the uncertainties of the present and free from anxiety about the future. That was my new outlook on life after reading *Dianetics*. Then as I continued to use what I learned from *Dianetics*, my life steadily improved to a bright, secure and worry-free, highly productive and happy life."

–**DAVID CAMPBELL**, *Legendary Composer/Arranger behind over 450 Gold and Platinum Albums, including works of Michael Jackson, Paul McCartney and Taylor Swift*

"After sustaining a knee injury playing football, the mental battle was the hardest part. *Dianetics* fixed all of that. It helped me get past the doubt and trust my body again."

–**NICK FERGUSON**, *10-year NFL Safety and Radio Personality*

"*Dianetics* gave me the tools to strip off the negative, remove the barriers holding me back and unlock my full potential to become the wife, mother, friend and businesswoman I always wanted to be."

–**ELENA CARDONE,** ***Entrepreneur, CEO and Bestselling Author (Build an Empire)***

"*Dianetics* helped me let go of the doubts that were holding me back. I feel clearer, more confident and more in control of my life. And that's been huge for my career and the growth of my business."

–**OMAYMA RAMZY,** ***Award-winning Entertainment Industry Makeup Artist***

"*Dianetics* works–and it works for real. In a very technical, predictable way, it frees us from mental barriers."

–**ROBERT HOGG,** ***Senior Space Robotics Engineer and Mars Mission Manager***

"*Dianetics* helped me understand myself. I realized why I kept repeating the same mistakes and now I have total certainty there won't be any more repeats."

–**ALVIN JOHNSON,** ***CEO of Hope Housing Foundation and Affordable Housing Pioneer***

"*Dianetics* is the owner's manual for the mind. It deepened my understanding of others and profoundly boosted my success in life."

–**CHRIS COLBY,** ***Award-winning Architect, Entrepreneur, Forbes 40 under 40***

"I started reading *Dianetics* out of curiosity about how the human mind works. What I didn't expect was how much it would help me understand myself. I've worked through emotional baggage and strengthened my relationships, both personal and professional."

–**RON DUBOIS**, *(Ret.) US Army Helicopter Pilot*

"*Dianetics* is an incredible book that will change how you relate to others. It's a game-changer."

–**JOY GENDUSA**, *Entrepreneur, Author, Founder of Industry-leading Direct Mail Firm*

"Trauma doesn't just heal with time–it leaves a lasting effect. *Dianetics* offers a way to understand these effects and achieve better mental, emotional and physical well-being."

–**ROHIT ADI, M.D.**, *Emergency Physician and Former Director of Emergency Health Sciences Paramedic Program*

"With *Dianetics*, I found my personal strengths and confidence in my own ideas. I could carve a path forward for myself. I cannot imagine how life would be without *Dianetics*."

–**DR. ANNE DUNEV**, *Naturopathic Practitioner and Clinical Nutritionist*

"*Dianetics* opened a new world for me. It was something I always sensed existed, deep down, and when I finally came across it, it hit me–it was the truth. It revealed reality on how I am, and everyone else is, as a human being and why they do what they do."

–**DR. ALEVTINA MALAKOVA**, *Dentist, Mother, Educator, Inventor*

TO THE READER

Dianetics (from Greek *dia* "through," and *nous* "soul") delineates fundamental principles of the mind and spirit. Through the application of these discoveries, it became apparent that Dianetics dealt with a beingness that defied time–the human spirit–originally denominated the "I" and subsequently the "thetan." From there, Mr. Hubbard continued his research, eventually mapping the path to full spiritual freedom for the individual.

Dianetics is a forerunner and substudy of Scientology which, as practiced by the Church, addresses only the "thetan" (spirit), which is senior to the body, and its relationship to and effects on the body.

This book is presented as it was written in 1950, and is part of L. Ron Hubbard's religious literature and works and is not a statement of claims made by the author, publisher or any Church of Scientology. It is a record of Mr. Hubbard's observations and research into life and the nature of man.

Neither Dianetics nor Scientology is offered as, nor professes to be physical healing, nor is any claim made to that effect. The Church does not accept individuals who desire treatment of physical or mental illness but, instead, requires a competent medical examination for physical conditions, by qualified specialists, before addressing their spiritual cause.

The Hubbard Electrometer, or E-Meter, is a religious artifact used in the Church. The E-Meter, by itself, does nothing and is only used by ministers and ministers-in-training, qualified in its use, to help parishioners locate the source of spiritual travail.

The attainment of the benefits and goals of Dianetics and Scientology requires each individual's dedicated participation, as only through one's own efforts can they be achieved.

We hope reading this book is the first step of a personal voyage of discovery into this new and vital world religion.

This Book Belongs To

____

DIANETICS

THE MODERN SCIENCE
OF MENTAL HEALTH

DIANETICS

THE MODERN SCIENCE OF MENTAL HEALTH

L. RON HUBBARD

new·era®
Publications International ApS
Publications, Inc.

A
HUBBARD®
PUBLICATION

New Era Publications
International ApS
Smedeland 20
2600 Glostrup, Denmark

ISBN 978-87-432-8139-9

Dianetics: The Modern Science of Mental Health–English

DEDICATED TO

Will Durant

Important Note

In reading this book, be very certain you never go past a word you do not fully understand. The only reason a person gives up a study or becomes confused or unable to learn is because he or she has gone past a word that was not understood.

The confusion or inability to grasp or learn comes **AFTER** a word the person did not have defined and understood. It may not only be the new and unusual words you have to look up. Some commonly used words can often be misdefined and so cause confusion.

This datum about not going past an undefined word is the most important fact in the whole subject of study. Every subject you have taken up and abandoned had its words which you failed to get defined.

Therefore, in studying this book be very, very certain you never go past a word you do not fully understand. If the material becomes confusing or you can't seem to grasp it, there will be a word just earlier that you have not understood. Don't go any further, but go back to **BEFORE** you got into trouble, find the misunderstood word and get it defined.

Glossary

A glossary of *Dianetics Terms* is provided at the end of this book. Further, to aid reader comprehension, L. Ron Hubbard directed the editors to provide a glossary for other words and phrases. This is included in the Appendix, *Editor's Glossary of Words, Terms and Phrases.* Words sometimes have several meanings. The *Editor's Glossary* only contains the definitions of words as they are used in this text. Other definitions can be found in standard language or Dianetics and Scientology dictionaries.

If you find any other words you do not know, look them up in a good dictionary.

Synopsis

Dianetics (Greek *dia*, through, and *nous*, mind or soul) is the science of mind. Far simpler than physics or chemistry, it compares with them in the exactness of its axioms and is on a considerably higher echelon of usefulness. *The hidden source of all psychosomatic ills and human aberration has been discovered and skills have been developed for their invariable cure.*

DIANETICS IS ACTUALLY a family of sciences embracing the various humanities and translating them into usefully precise definitions. The present volume deals with Individual Dianetics and is a handbook containing the necessary skills both for the handling of interpersonal relations and the treatment of the mind. With the techniques presented in this handbook, the intelligent layman can successfully treat all psychosomatic ills and inorganic aberrations. More importantly, the skills offered in this handbook will produce the Dianetic *Clear*, an optimum individual with intelligence considerably greater than the current normal, or the Dianetic *Release*, an individual who has been freed from his major anxieties or illnesses. The Release can be done in less than twenty hours of work and is a state superior to any produced by several years of psychoanalysis, since the Release will not relapse.

Dianetics is an exact science and its application is on the order of, but simpler than, engineering. Its axioms should not be confused with theories since they demonstrably exist as natural laws hitherto undiscovered. Man has known many portions of Dianetics in the past thousands of years, but the data was not evaluated for importance, was not organized into a body of precise knowledge. In addition to things known if not evaluated, Dianetics includes a large number of new discoveries of its own about thought and the mind.

The axioms may be found on the end sheets of this volume.* Understood and applied, they embrace the field of human endeavor and thought and yield precision results.

The first contribution of Dianetics is the discovery that the problems of thought and mental function can be resolved within the bounds of the finite universe, which is to say that all data needful to the solution of mental action and Man's endeavor can be measured, sensed and experienced as scientific truths independent of mysticism or metaphysics. The various axioms are not assumptions or theories–the case of past ideas about the mind–but are laws which can be subjected to the most vigorous laboratory and clinical tests.

The first law of Dianetics is a statement of the Dynamic Principle of Existence.

THE DYNAMIC PRINCIPLE OF EXISTENCE IS: SURVIVE!

No behavior or activity has been found to exist without this principle. It is not new that life is surviving. It is new that life has as its entire dynamic urge *only* survival.

---

*See *Fundamental Axioms of Dianetics.*

Survival is divided into four dynamics. Survival can be understood to lie in any one of the dynamics and by faulty logic can be explained in terms of any one dynamic. A man can be said to survive for self alone and by this all behavior can be formulated. He can be said to survive for sex alone and by sex alone all behavior can be formulated. He can be said to survive for the group only or for Mankind only, and in either of these the entire endeavor and behavior of the individual can be equated and explained. These are four equations of survival, each one apparently true. However, the entire problem of the purpose of Man cannot be resolved unless one admits all four dynamics in each individual. So equated, the behavior of the individual can be estimated with precision. These dynamics then embrace the activity of one or many men.

DYNAMIC ONE: The urge of the individual to reach the highest potential of survival in terms of *self* and his immediate symbiotes.

DYNAMIC TWO: The urge of the individual to reach the highest potential of survival in terms of *sex*, the act and the creation of children and their rearing.

DYNAMIC THREE: The urge of the individual to reach the highest potential of survival in terms of the *group*, whether civil, political, or racial and the symbiotes of that group.

DYNAMIC FOUR: The urge of the individual to reach the highest potential of survival in terms of *Mankind* and the symbiotes of Mankind.

Thus motivated, the individual or a society seeks survival and no human activity of any kind has other basis: experiment, investigation and long testing demonstrated that the *unaberrated individual*, the Clear, was motivated in his actions and decisions by *all* the above dynamics and not one alone.

The Clear, the goal of Dianetic therapy, can be created from psychotic, neurotic, deranged, criminal or normal people if they have organically sound nervous systems. He demonstrates the basic nature of Mankind and that basic nature has been found uniformly and invariably to be *good*. That is now an established *scientific fact*, not an opinion.

The Clear has attained a stable state on a very high plane. He is persistent and vigorous and pursues life with enthusiasm and satisfaction. He is motivated by the four dynamics as above. He has attained the full power and use of hitherto hidden abilities.

The inhibition of one or more dynamics in an individual causes an aberrated condition, tends toward mental derangement and psychosomatic illness and causes the individual to make irrational conclusions and act, still in an effort to survive, in destructive ways.

Dianetic technique deletes, without drugs, hypnotism, surgery, shock or other artificial means, the blocks from these various dynamics. The removal of these blocks permits the free flow of the various dynamics and, of course, results in a heightened persistency in life and a much higher intelligence.

The precision of Dianetics makes it possible to impede or release these dynamics at will with invariable results.

The hidden source of all inorganic mental disturbance and psychosomatic illness was one of the discoveries of Dianetics. This source had been unknown and unsuspected, though vigorously sought, for thousands of years. That the discovered source *is* the source requires less laboratory proof than would have been necessary to have proven the correctness of William Harvey's discovery of the circulation of the blood. The proof does not depend upon a laboratory test with complicated apparatus, but can be made in any group of men by any intelligent individual.

The *source of aberration* has been found to be a hitherto unsuspected sub-mind which, complete with its own recordings, underlies what Man understands to be his "conscious" mind. The concept of the unconscious mind is replaced in Dianetics by the discovery that the "unconscious" mind is the *only* mind which is *always* conscious. In Dianetics this sub-mind is called the *reactive mind.* A holdover from an earlier step in Man's evolution, the reactive mind possesses vigor and command power on a cellular level. It does not "remember": it records and uses the recordings only to produce action. It does not "think": it selects recordings and impinges them upon the "conscious" mind and the body without the knowledge or consent of the individual. The only information the individual has of such action is his occasional perception that he is not acting rationally about one thing or another and cannot understand why. There is no "censor."

The reactive mind operates exclusively on physical pain and painful emotion. It is not capable of differentiative thought, but acts on the stimulus-response basis. This is the principle on which the animal mind functions. It does not receive its recordings as memory or experience, but only as forces to be reactivated. It receives its recordings as cellular *engrams* when the "conscious" mind is "unconscious."

In a drugged state, when anesthetized as in an operation, when rendered "unconscious" by injury or illness, the individual yet has his reactive mind in full operation. He may not be "aware" of what has taken place, but, as Dianetics has discovered and can prove, everything which happened to him in the interval of "unconsciousness" was fully and completely recorded. This information is unappraised by his conscious mind, neither evaluated nor reasoned. It can, at any future date, become reactivated by similar circumstances observed by the awake and conscious individual. When any such recording, an engram, becomes reactivated, it has command power. It shuts down the conscious mind to greater or lesser degree, takes over the motor controls of the body and causes behavior and action to which the conscious mind, the individual himself, would never consent. He is, nevertheless, handled like a marionette by his engrams.

The antagonistic forces of the exterior environment thus become entered into the individual himself without the knowledge or consent of the individual. And there they create an interior world of force which exerts itself not only against the exterior world, but against the individual himself. Aberration is caused by what has been done *to*, not done *by* the individual.

Man has unwittingly long aided the reactive mind by supposing that a person, when "unconscious" from drugs, illness, injury or anesthetic, had no recording ability. This permits an enormous amount of data to enter into the reactive bank since none have been careful to maintain silence around an "unconscious" person. The invention of language and the entrance of language into the engram bank of the reactive mind seriously complicates the mechanistic reactions. The engrams containing language impinge themselves upon the conscious mind as commands. Engrams then contain command value much higher than any in the exterior world. Thought is directed and motivated by the irrational engrams. Thought processes are disturbed not only by these engramic commands, but also by the fact that the reactive mind reduces, by regenerating unconsciousness, the actual ability to think. Few people possess, because of this, more than 10 percent of their potential awareness.

The entire physical pain and painful emotion of a lifetime – whether the individual "knows" about it or not – is contained, recorded, in the engram bank. Nothing is forgotten. And all physical pain and painful emotion, no matter how the individual may think he has handled it, is capable of re-inflicting itself upon him from this hidden level unless that pain is removed by Dianetic therapy.

The engram and only the engram causes aberration and psychosomatic illness.

Dianetic therapy may be briefly stated. Dianetics deletes all the pain from a lifetime. When this pain is erased in the engram bank and refiled as memory and experience in the memory banks, all aberrations and psychosomatic illnesses vanish, the dynamics are entirely rehabilitated and the physical and mental being regenerate. Dianetics leaves an individual full memory, but without pain. Exhaustive tests have demonstrated that hidden pain is not a necessity, but is invariably and *always* a liability to the health, skill, happiness and survival potential of the individual. It has *no* survival value.

The method which is used to refile pain is another discovery. Man has unknowingly possessed another process of remembering of which he has not been cognizant. Here and there a few have known about it and used it without realizing what they did or that they did something which Man as a whole did not know could be done. This process is *returning*. Wide awake and without drugs an individual can *return* to any period of his entire life providing his passage is not blocked by engrams. Dianetics developed techniques for circumventing these blocks and reducing them from the status of Powerful Unknown to useful memory.

The technique of therapy is done in what is called a Dianetic *reverie*. The individual undergoing this process sits or lies in a quiet room accompanied by a friend or professional therapist who acts as *auditor*. The auditor directs the attention of the patient to the patient's self and then begins to place the patient in various periods of the patient's life merely by telling him to "go there" rather than "remember."

All therapy is done, not by remembering or associating, but by travel on the *time track*. Every human being has a time track. It begins with life and it ends with death. It is a sequence of events complete from portal to portal, as recorded.

The conscious mind, in Dianetics, is called by the somewhat more precise term of *analytical mind*. The analytical mind consists of the "I" (the center of awareness), all computational ability of the individual and the standard memory banks–which are filled with all past perceptions of the individual, awake or normally asleep (all material which is not engramic). No data are missing from these standard banks, all are there, barring physical organic defects, in full motion, color, sound, tactile, smell and all other senses. The "I" may not be able to reach his standard banks because of reactive data which bar portions of the standard banks from the view of "I". Cleared, "I" is able to reach all moments of his lifetime without exertion or discomfort and perceive all he has ever sensed, recalling them in full motion, color, sound, tone and other senses. The completeness and profusion of data in the standard banks is a discovery of Dianetics, and the significance of such recalls is yet another discovery.

The auditor directs the travel of "I" along the patient's time track. The patient knows everything which is taking place, is in full control of himself and is able to bring himself to the present whenever he likes. No hypnotism or other means are used. Man may not have known he could do this, but it is simple.

The auditor, with precision methods, recovers data from the earliest "unconscious" moments of the patient's life, such "unconsciousness" being understood to be caused by shock or pain, not mere unawareness. The patient thus contacts the cellular-level engrams. Returned to them and progressed through them by the auditor, the patient re-experiences these moments a few times, when they are then erased and refiled automatically as standard memory. So far as the auditor and the patient can discover, the entire incident has now vanished and does not exist. If they searched carefully in the standard banks, they would find it again, but refiled as "Once aberrative, do not permit as such into computer." Late areas of "unconsciousness" are impenetrable until early ones are erased.

The amount of discomfort experienced by the patient is minor. He is repelled mainly by engramic commands which variously dictate emotion and reaction.

In a *Release*, the case is not progressed to the point of complete recall. In a *Clear*, full memory exists throughout the lifetime, with the additional bonus that he has photographic recall in color, motion, sound, etc., as well as optimum computational ability.

The psychosomatic illnesses of the *Release* are reduced, ordinarily, to a level where they do not thereafter trouble him. In a *Clear*, psychosomatic illness has become non-existent and will not return since its actual source is nullified permanently.

The Dianetic *Release* is comparable to a current normal or above. The Dianetic *Clear* is to a current normal individual as the current normal is to the severely insane.

Dianetics elucidates various problems with its many discoveries, its axioms, its organization and its technique. In the progress of its development many astonishing data were thrust upon it, for when one deals with natural laws and measurable actualities which produce specific and invariable results, one must accept what Nature holds, not what is pleasing or desired. When one deals with facts rather than theories and gazes for the first time upon the mechanisms of human action, several things confound him, much as the flutterings of the heart did Harvey or the actions of yeasts did Pasteur. The blood did not circulate because Harvey said it could nor yet because he said it did. It circulated and had been circulating for eons. Harvey was clever and observant enough to find it, and this was much the case with Pasteur and other explorers of the hitherto unknown or unconfirmed.

In Dianetics, the fact that the analytical mind was inherently *perfect* and remained structurally capable of restoration to full operation was not the least of the data found. That Man was good, as established by exacting research, was no great surprise. But that an unaberrated individual was vigorously repelled by evil and yet gained enormous strength was astonishing, since aberration had been so long incorrectly supposed to be the root of strength and ambition according to authorities since the time of Plato. That a man contained a mechanism which recorded with diabolical accuracy when the man was observably and by all presumable tests "unconscious" was newsworthy and surprising.

To the layman, the relationship of prenatal life to mental function has not entirely been disregarded, since for centuries beyond count people were concerned with "prenatal influence." To the psychiatrist, the psychologist and psychoanalyst, prenatal memory had long been an accepted fact since "memories of the womb" were agreed to influence the adult mind. But the prenatal aspect of the mind came as an entire surprise to Dianetics: an unwanted and, at the time, unwelcome observation. Despite existing beliefs–which are not scientific facts–that the fetus had memory, the psychiatrist and other workers believed, as well, that memory could not exist in a human being until myelin sheathing was formed around the nerves. This was as confusing to Dianetics as it was to psychiatry. After much work over some years, the exact influence prenatal life had on the later mind was established by Dianetics with accuracy.

There will be those who, uninformed, will say that Dianetics "accepts and believes in" prenatal memory. Completely aside from the fact that an exact science does not "believe," but establishes and proves facts, Dianetics emphatically does *not* believe in prenatal memory. Dianetics had to invade cytology and biology and form many conclusions by research; it had to locate and establish both the reactive mind and the hidden engram banks never before known before it came upon "prenatal" problems. It had been discovered that the engram recording was probably done on the cellular level, that the engram bank was contained in the cells. It was then discovered that the cells, reproducing from one generation to the next, within the organism, apparently carried with them their own memory banks. The cells are the first echelon of structure, the basic building blocks. They built the analytical mind. They operate, as the whip, the reactive mind. Where one has human cells, one has potential engrams. Human cells begin with the zygote, proceed in development with the embryo, become the fetus and finally the infant. Each stage of this growth is capable of reaction. Each stage in the growth of the colony of cells finds them fully cells, capable of recording engrams. In Dianetics, prenatal memory is not considered since the standard banks which will someday serve the completed analyzer in the infant, child and man are not themselves complete. There is neither "memory" nor "experience" before the nerves are sheathed as far as Dianetic therapy is concerned. But Dianetic therapy is concerned with *engrams*, not memories, with *recordings*, not experience. And wherever there are human cells, engrams are demonstrably possible and when physical pain was present, engrams can be demonstrated to have been created.

The engram is a recording like the ripples in the groove of a phonograph record: it is a complete recording of everything which occurred during the period of pain. Dianetics can locate, with its techniques, any engram which the cells have hidden, and in therapy the patient will often discover himself to be upon the prenatal cellular time track. There he will locate engrams and he goes there only because engrams exist there. Birth is an engram and is recovered by Dianetics *as a recording*, not as a *memory*. By return and the cellular extension of the time track, zygote pain storage can be, and is, recovered. It is *not* memory. It impinged upon the analytical mind and it obstructed the standard banks where memory is stored. This is a very great difference from prenatal memory. Dianetics recovers *prenatal engrams* and finds them responsible for much aberration and discovers that any longing for the womb is not present in any patient, but that engrams sometimes dictate a return to it, as in some regressive psychoses which then attempt to remake the body into a fetus.

This matter of prenatal life is discussed here at length in this synopsis to give the reader a perspective on the subject. We are dealing here with an exact science, precision axioms and new skills of application. By them we gain a command over aberration and psychosomatic ills. And with them we take an evolutionary step in the development of Man which places him yet another stage above his distant cousins of the animal kingdom.

CONTENTS

SYNOPSIS — i

INTRODUCTION

How *to* Read *this* Book — 1

BOOK ONE: *The* GOAL *of* MAN

CHAPTER ONE
The Scope *of* Dianetics — 7

CHAPTER TWO
The Clear — 13

CHAPTER THREE
The Goal *of* Man — 27

CHAPTER FOUR
The Four Dynamics — 45

CHAPTER FIVE
Summary — 51

BOOK TWO: *The* SINGLE SOURCE *of* ALL INORGANIC MENTAL *and* ORGANIC PSYCHOSOMATIC ILLS

CHAPTER ONE
The Analytical Mind *and the* Standard Memory Banks 59

CHAPTER TWO
The Reactive Mind 67

CHAPTER THREE
The Cell *and the* Organism 93

CHAPTER FOUR
The "Demons" 113

CHAPTER FIVE
Psychosomatic Illness 123

CHAPTER SIX
Emotion *and the* Dynamics 147

CHAPTER SEVEN
Prenatal Experience *and* Birth 165

CHAPTER EIGHT
Contagion *of* Aberration 181

CHAPTER NINE
Keying-in *the* Engram 191

CHAPTER TEN
Preventive Dianetics 207

BOOK THREE: THERAPY

CHAPTER ONE
The Mind's Protection 221

CHAPTER TWO
Release *or* Clear 227

CHAPTER THREE
The Auditor's Role 233

CHAPTER FOUR
Diagnosis 241

CHAPTER FIVE
Returning, *the* File Clerk *and the* Time Track 261

CHAPTER SIX
The Laws *of* Returning 277

CHAPTER SEVEN
Emotion *and the* Life Force 305

CHAPTER EIGHT
Some Types *of* Engrams 351

CHAPTER NINE: PART ONE
Mechanisms *and* Aspects *of* Therapy 369

CHAPTER NINE: PART TWO
Mechanisms *and* Aspects *of* Therapy 423

CHAPTER TEN
Dianetics–Past *and* Future 535

Dianetics Terms 549

Fundamental Axioms *of* Dianetics 553

Dianetics *into the* Future 561

APPENDIX

Addresses 590

Editor's Glossary of Words, Terms and Phrases 593

Index 689

How *to* Read *this* Book

Dianetics is an adventure. It is an exploration into *Terra Incognita*, the human mind, that vast and hitherto unknown realm half an inch back of our foreheads.

The discoveries and developments which made the formulation of Dianetics possible occupied many years of exact research and careful testing. This was exploration; it was also consolidation. The trail is blazed, the routes are sufficiently mapped for you to voyage in safety into your own mind and recover there your full inherent potential, which is not, we now know, low but very, very high. As you progress in therapy, the adventure is yours to know why you did what you did when you did it, to know *what* caused those Dark and Unknown Fears which came in nightmares as a child, to know *where* your moments of pain and pleasure lay. There is much which an individual does not know about himself, about his parents, about his "motives." Some of the things you will find may astonish you, for the most important data of your life may be not memory, but engrams in the hidden depths of your mind: not articulate, but only destructive.

You will find many reasons why you "cannot get well" and you will know at length, when you find the dictating lines in the engrams, how amusing those reasons are, especially to you.

Dianetics is no solemn adventure. For all that it has to do with suffering and loss, its end is always laughter–so foolish, so misinterpreted were the things which caused the woe.

Your first voyage into your own *Terra Incognita* will be through the pages of this book. You will find as you read that many things "you always knew were so" are articulated here. You will be gratified to know that you held not opinions, but scientific facts, in many of your concepts of existence. You will find, too, many data that have long been known by all, and you will possibly consider them far from news and be prone to underevaluate them. Be assured that underevaluation of these facts kept them from being valuable, no matter how long they were known, for a fact is never important without a proper evaluation of it and its precise relationship to other facts. You are following here a vast network of facts which, reaching out, can be seen to embrace the whole field of Man in all his works. Fortunately you do not have to concern yourself with following far any one of these lines until you are done. And then these horizons will stretch wide enough to satisfy anyone.

Dianetics is a large subject, but that is only because Man is himself a large subject. The science of his thought cannot but embrace all his actions. By careful compartmenting and relating of data, the field has been kept narrow enough to be easily followed. Mostly this handbook will tell you, without any specific mention, about yourself and your family and friends, for you will meet them here and know them.

This volume has made no effort to use resounding or thunderous phrases, frowning polysyllables or professorial detachment. When one is delivering answers which are simple, he need not make the communication any more difficult than is necessary to convey the ideas. "Basic language" has been used, much of the nomenclature is colloquial; the pedantic has not only not been employed, it has also been ignored. This volume communicates to several strata of life and professions; the favorite nomenclatures of none have been observed since such a usage would impede the understanding of others. And so bear with us, psychiatrist, when your structure is not used, for we have no need for structure here; and bear with us, doctor, when we call a cold a cold and not a catarrhal disorder of the respiratory tract. For this is, essentially, engineering and these engineers are liable to say anything. And scholar, you would not enjoy being burdened with the summation signs and the Lorentz-FitzGerald-Einstein equations, so we shall not burden the less puristic reader with scientifically impossible Hegelian grammar which insists that absolutes exist in fact.

The plan of the book might be represented as a cone which starts with simplicity and descends into wider application. This book follows, more or less, the actual steps of the development of Dianetics. First there was the Dynamic Principle of Existence, then its meaning, then the source of aberration and finally the application of all as therapy and the techniques of therapy. You won't find any of this very difficult. It was the originator who had the difficulty. You should have seen the first equations and postulates of Dianetics! As research progressed and as the field developed, Dianetics began to simplify. That is a fair guarantee that one is on a straight trail of science. Only things which are poorly known become more complex the longer one works upon them.

It is suggested that you read straight on through. By the time you get to the end, you should have an excellent command of the subject. The book is arranged that way. Every fact related to Dianetic therapy is stated in several ways and is introduced again and again. In this way the important facts have been pointed up to your attention. When you have finished the book, you can come back to the beginning and look through it and study what you think you need to know.

Almost all the basic philosophy and certainly all the derivations of the master subject of Dianetics were excluded here, partly because this volume had to stay under half a million words and partly because they belong in a separate text where they can receive full justice. Nevertheless, you have the scope of the science with this volume in addition to therapy itself.

You are beginning an adventure. Treat it as an adventure. And may you never be the same again.

The Goal *of* Man

BOOK ONE

BOOK ONE, CHAPTER ONE

The Scope *of* Dianetics

A SCIENCE OF MIND is a goal which has engrossed thousands of generations of Man. Armies, dynasties and whole civilizations have perished for the lack of it. Rome went to dust for the want of it. China swims in blood for the need of it. And down in the arsenal is an atom bomb, its hopeful nose full-armed in ignorance of it.

No quest has been more relentlessly pursued or has been more violent. No primitive tribe, no matter how ignorant, has failed to recognize the problem as a problem, nor has it failed to bring forth at least an attempted formulation. Today one finds the aborigine of Australia substituting for a science of mind a "magic healing crystal." The shaman of British Guiana makes shift for actual mental laws with his monotonous song and consecrated cigar. The throbbing drum of the Goldi medicine man serves in the stead of an adequate technique to alleviate the lack of serenity in patients.

The enlightened and Golden Age of Greece yet had but superstition in its principal sanitaria for mental ills, the Aesculapian temple. The most the Roman could do for peace of mind for the sick was to appeal to the *Penates*, the household divinities, or sacrifice to *Febris*, goddess of fevers. And an English king, centuries after, could have been found in the hands of exorcists who sought to cure his deliriums by driving the demons from him.

From the most ancient times to the present, in the crudest primitive tribe or the most magnificently ornamented civilization, Man has found himself in a state of awed helplessness when confronted by the phenomena of strange illnesses or aberrations. His desperation in his efforts to treat the individual has been but slightly altered during his entire history and, until this twentieth century passed midterm, the percentages of his alleviations, in terms of individual mental derangements, compared evenly with the successes of the shamans confronted with the same problems. According to a modern writer, the single advance of psychotherapy was clean quarters for the madman. In terms of brutality in treatment of the insane, the methods of the shaman or Bedlam have been far exceeded by the "civilized" techniques of destroying nerve tissues with the violence of shock and surgery–treatments which were not warranted by the results obtained and which would not have been tolerated in the meanest primitive society, since they reduce the victim to mere zombyism, destroying most of his personality and ambition and leaving him nothing more than a manageable animal. Far from an indictment of the practices of the "neurosurgeon" and the ice pick which he thrusts and twists into insane minds, they are brought forth only to demonstrate the depths of desperation Man can reach when confronted with the seemingly unsolvable problem of deranged minds.

In the larger sphere of societies and nations, the lack of such a science of mind was never more evident; for the physical sciences, advancing thoughtlessly far in advance of Man's ability to understand Man, have armed him with terrible and thorough weapons which await only another outburst of the social insanity of war.

These problems are not mild ones: they lie across every man's path; they wait in company with his future. As long as Man has recognized that his chief superiority over the animal kingdom was a thinking mind, so long as he understood that his mind alone was his weapon, he has searched and pondered and postulated in efforts to find a solution.

Like a jigsaw puzzle spilled by a careless hand, the equations which would lead to a science of the mind and, above that, to a master science of the universe, were stirred round and round. Sometimes two fragments would be united; sometimes, as in the case of the Golden Age of Greece, a whole section would be built. Philosopher, shaman, medicine man, mathematician: each looked at the pieces. Some saw they must all belong to different puzzles. Some thought they all belonged to the same puzzle. Some said there were really six puzzles in it, some said two. And the wars went on and the societies sickened or were dispersed, and learned tomes were written about ever-increasing hordes of madmen.

With the methods of Bacon, with the mathematics of Newton, the physical sciences went on consolidating and advancing their frontiers. And like a derelict battalion, careless of how many allied ranks it exposed to destruction by the enemy, studies of the mind lagged behind.

But after all, there are just so many pieces in any puzzle. Before and after Francis Bacon, Herbert Spencer and a very few more, many of the small sections had been put together, many honest facts had been observed.

To adventure into the thousands of variables of which that puzzle was composed, one had only to know right from wrong, true from false, and use all Man and Nature as his test tube.

Of what must a science of mind be composed?

1. An answer to the goal of thought.
2. A single source of all insanities, psychoses, neuroses, compulsions, repressions and social derangements.
3. Invariant scientific evidence as to the basic nature and functional background of the human mind.
4. Techniques (the art of application) by which the discovered single source could be invariably cured, ruling out, of course, the insanities of malformed, deleted or pathologically injured brains or nervous systems and, particularly, iatrogenic psychoses (those caused by doctors and involving the destruction of the living brain itself).
5. Methods of prevention of mental derangement.
6. The cause and cure of all psychosomatic ills, which number, some say, 70 percent of Man's listed ailments.

Such a science would exceed the severest terms previously laid down for it in any age, but any computation on the subject should discover that a science of mind ought to be able to be and do just these things.

A science of the mind, if it were truly worthy of that name, would have to rank in experimental precision with physics and chemistry. There could be no "special cases" to its laws. There could be no recourse to Authority. The atom bomb bursts whether Einstein gives it permission or not. Laws native to Nature regulate the bursting of that bomb. Technicians, applying techniques derived from discovered natural laws, can make one or a million atom bombs all alike.

After the body of axioms and technique was organized and working as a science of mind, in rank with the physical sciences, it would be found to have points of agreement with almost every school of thought about thought which had ever existed. This is again a virtue and not a fault.

Simple though it is, Dianetics does and is these things:

1. It is an organized science of thought built on definite axioms: statements of natural laws on the order of those of the physical sciences.
2. It contains a therapeutic technique with which can be treated all inorganic mental ills and all organic psychosomatic ills, with assurance of complete cure in unselected cases.
3. It produces a condition of ability and rationality for Man well in advance of the current norm, enhancing rather than destroying his vigor and personality.
4. Dianetics gives a complete insight into the full potentialities of the mind, discovering them to be well in excess of past supposition.
5. The basic nature of Man is discovered in Dianetics, rather than hazarded or postulated, since that basic nature can be brought into action in any individual completely. And that basic nature is discovered to be *good.*
6. The single source of mental derangement is discovered and demonstrated on a clinical or laboratory basis by Dianetics.
7. The extent, storage capacity and recallability of the human memory is finally established by Dianetics.
8. The full recording abilities of the mind are discovered by Dianetics with the conclusion that they are quite dissimilar to former suppositions.

9. Dianetics brings forth the non-germ theory of disease, complementing biochemistry and Pasteur's work on the germ theory to embrace the field.
10. With Dianetics ends the "necessity" of destroying the brain by shock or surgery to effect "tractability" in mental patients and "adjust" them.
11. A workable explanation of the physiological effects of drugs and endocrine substances exists in Dianetics and many problems posed by endocrinology are answered.
12. Various educational, sociological, political, military and other human studies are enhanced by Dianetics.
13. The field of cytology is aided by Dianetics, as well as other fields of research.

This, then, is a skeletal sketch of what would be the scope of a science of mind and of what is the scope of Dianetics.

BOOK ONE, CHAPTER TWO

The CLEAR

DIANETICALLY, THE OPTIMUM individual is called the *Clear*. One will hear much of that word, both as a noun and a verb, in this volume, so it is well to spend time here at the outset setting forth exactly what can be called a Clear, the goal of Dianetic therapy.

A Clear can be tested for any and all psychoses, neuroses, compulsions and repressions (all aberrations) and can be examined for any autogenic (self-generated) diseases referred to as psychosomatic ills. These tests confirm the Clear to be entirely without such ills or aberrations. Additional tests of his intelligence indicate it to be high above the current norm. Observation of his activity demonstrates that he pursues existence with vigor and satisfaction.

Further, these results can be obtained on a comparative basis. A neurotic individual, possessed also of psychosomatic ills, can be tested for those aberrations and illnesses, demonstrating that they exist. He can then be given Dianetic therapy to the end of clearing these neuroses and ills. Finally, he can be examined, with the above results. This, in passing, is an experiment which has been performed many times with invariable results.

It is a matter of laboratory test that all individuals who have organically complete nervous systems respond in this fashion to Dianetic clearing.

Further, the Clear possesses attributes, fundamental and inherent but not always available in an uncleared state, which have not been suspected of Man and are not included in past discussions of his abilities and behavior.

First there is the matter of perceptions. Even so-called normal people do not always see in full color, hear in full tone, or sense at the optimum with their organs of smell, taste, tactile and organic sensation.

These are the main lines of communication to the finite world which most people recognize as reality. It is an interesting commentary that while past observers felt that the facing of reality was an absolute necessity if the aberrated individual wished to be sane, no definition of how this was to be done was set forth. To face reality in the present, one would certainly have to be able to sense it along those channels of communication most commonly used by Man in his affairs.

Any one of Man's perceptions can be aberrated by psychic derangements which refuse to permit the received sensations to be realized by the analytical portion of the individual's mind. In other words, while there may be nothing wrong with the mechanisms of color reception, circuits can exist in the mind which delete color before the consciousness is permitted to see the object. Colorblindness can be discovered to be relative or in degrees in such a way that colors appear to be less brilliant, dull or, at the maximum, entirely absent. Anyone is acquainted with persons to whom "loud" colors are detestable and with persons who find them insufficiently "loud" to notice. This varying degree of colorblindness has not been recognized as a psychic factor, but has been nebulously assumed to be some sort of a condition of mind when it was noticed at all.

There are those persons to whom noises are quite disturbing, to whom, for instance, the insistent whine of a violin is very like having a brace and bit applied to the eardrum; and there are those to whom fifty violins, played loudly, would be soothing; and there are those who, in the presence of a violin, express disinterest and boredom; and, again, there are persons to whom the sound of a violin, no matter if it be playing the most intricate melody, is a monotone. These differences of sonic (hearing) perception have, like color and other visual errors, been attributed to inherent nature or organic deficiency or assigned no place at all.

In a like manner, from person to person, smells, tactile sensations, organic perceptions, pain and gravity vary widely and wildly. A cursory check around among his friends will demonstrate to a man that there exist enormous differences of perception of identical stimuli. One smells a turkey in the oven as wonderful, one smells it with indifference, another may not smell it at all. And somebody else may maintain that roasting turkey smells exactly like hair oil, to be extreme.

Until we obtain Clears, it remains obscure why such differences should exist. For in the largest measure, such wild quality and quantity of perception is due to aberration. Because of pleasurable experiences in the past and inherent sensitivity, there will be some difference among Clears and a Clear response should not be assumed automatically to be a standardized, adjusted middle ground, that pallid and obnoxious goal of past doctrines. The Clear gets a maximum response compatible with his own desire for the response. Burning cordite still smells dangerous to him, but it does not make him ill. Roasting turkey smells good to him if he is hungry and likes turkey, at which time it smells very, very good. Violins play melodies, not monotones, bring no pain and are enjoyed to a fine full limit if the Clear likes violins as a matter of taste–if he doesn't, he likes kettledrums, saxophones or, indeed, suiting his mood, no music at all.

In other words, there are two variables at work. One, the wildest, is the variable caused by aberrations. The other, and quite rational and understandable, is caused by the personality.

Thus the perceptions of an aberree* (non-Cleared individual) vary greatly from those of the Cleared (unaberrated) individual.

Now there are the differences of the actual organs of perception and the errors occasioned by these. Some of these errors, a minimum, are organic: punctured eardrums are not competent sound-recording mechanisms. The majority of perceptic (sense message) errors in the organic sphere are caused by psychosomatic errors.

Glasses are seen on noses everywhere around, even on children. The majority of these spectacles are perched on the face in an effort to correct a condition which the body itself is fighting to uncorrect again. Eyesight, when the stage of glasses is entered (not because of glasses), is deteriorating on the psychosomatic principle. And this observation is about as irresponsible as a statement that when apples fall out of trees, they usually obey gravity. One of the incidental things which happens to a Clear is that his eyesight, if it had been bad as an aberree, generally improves markedly and, with some slight attention, will recover optimum perception in time. (Far from an optician's argument against Dianetics, this assures rather good business, for Clears have been known at treatment's end to have to buy, in rapid succession,

***Aberree* is a neologism meaning an aberrated person.

five pairs of glasses to compensate adjusting eyesight, and many aberrees Cleared late in life settle down ocularly at a maximum a little under optimum.)

The eyesight was reduced in the aberree on an organic basis by his aberrations so that the perceptic organ itself was reduced from optimum operating function. With the removal of aberrations, repeated tests have proven that the body makes a valiant effort to reconstruct back to optimum.

Hearing, in addition to other perceptics, varies organically over a wide range. Calcium deposits, for instance, can make the ears "ring" incessantly. The removal of aberrations permits the body to readjust toward its reachable optimum: the calcium deposit disappears and the ears stop ringing. But far and beyond this very specific case, there are great differences in hearing on the organic basis. Organically as well as aberrationally, hearing can become remarkably extended or closely inhibited so that one person may hear footsteps a block away as a normal activity and another would not hear a bass drum thundering on the porch.

That the various perceptions differ widely from individual to individual on an aberrational and psychosomatic basis is the least of the discoveries outlined here. Ability to recall is far more fantastic in its variation from person to person.

An entirely new recall process, which was inherent in the mind but which had not been noticed, came to light in the process of observing Clears and aberrees. This recall process is possible in only a small proportion of aberrees in its fullest sense. It is standard, however, in a Clear. Naturally, no intimation is made here that the scholars of past ages have been unobservant. We are dealing here with an entirely new and hitherto non-existent object of inspection: the Clear. What a Clear can do easily, quite a few people have, from time to time, been partially able to do in the past.

An inherent, not a taught, ability of the remembering mechanisms of the mind can be termed, as a technical word of Dianetics, *returning*. It is used in its dictionary sense, with the addition of the fact that the mind has it as a normal remembering function as follows: the person can "send" a portion of his mind to a past period on either a mental or combined mental and physical basis and can re-experience incidents which have taken place in his past in the same fashion and with the same sensations as before. Once upon a time an art known as hypnotism used what was called "regression" on hypnotized subjects, the hypnotist sending the subject back in one of two ways to incidents in his past. This was done with trance techniques, drugs and considerable technology. The hypnotic subject could be sent back to a moment "entirely" so that he gave every appearance of being the age to which he was returned with only the apparent faculties and recollections he had at that moment: this was called "revivification" (reliving). "Regression" was a technique by which part of the individual's self remained in the present and part went back to the past. These abilities of the mind were supposed native only in hypnotism and were used only in hypnotic technique. The art is very old, tracing back some thousands of years and existing today in Asia as it has existed, apparently, from the dawn of time.

Returning is substituted for "regression" here because it is not a comparable thing and because "regression," as a word, has some bad meanings which would interrupt its use. *Reliving* is substituted for "revivification" in Dianetics because, in Dianetics, the principles of hypnotism can be found explained and hypnotism is not used in Dianetic therapy, as will be explained later.

The mind, then, has another ability to remember. Part of the mind can "return," even when a person is wide awake, and re-experience past incidents in full. If you want to test this, try it on several people until one is discovered who does it easily. Wide awake, he can "return" to moments in his past. Until asked to do so, he probably will not know he has such an ability. If he had it, he probably thought everybody could do it (the type of supposition which has kept so much of this data from coming to light before). He can go back to a time when he was swimming and swim with full recall of hearing, sight, taste, smell, organic sensation, tactile, etc.

A "learned" gentleman once spent some hours demonstrating to a gathering that the recall of a smell as a sensation, for instance, was quite impossible since "neurology had proven that the olfactory nerves were not connected to the thalamus." Two people in the gathering discovered this ability to *return* and, despite this evidence, the learned gentleman continued the dispute that olfactory recall was impossible. A check among the gathering on this faculty, independent of returning, brought forth the fact that one-half of those present remembered a smell by smelling it again.

Returning is the full performance of imagery recall. The entire memory is able to make the organ areas re-sense the stimuli in a past incident. Partial recall is common: not common enough to be normal, but certainly common enough to have merited considerable study. For it again is a wide variable.

Perception of the present would be one method of facing reality. But if one cannot face the reality of the past then, in some part, he is not facing some portion of reality. And if it is agreed that facing reality is desirable, then one would have to face yesterday's reality as well if he were to be considered entirely "sane" by contemporary definition. To "face yesterday" requires a certain condition of recall to be available. One would have to be able to remember. But how many ways are there of remembering?

First there is the *return*. That is new. It gives the advantage of examining the moving pictures and other sense perceptions recorded at the time of the event with all senses present. He can also return to his past conclusions and imaginings. It is of considerable aid in learning, in research, in ordinary living, to be able to be again at the place where the data desired was first inspected.

Then there are the more usual recalls. Optimum recall is by the *return* method of single or multiple senses, the individual himself remaining in present time. In other words, some people, when they think of a rose, see one, smell one, feel one. They see in full color, vividly–with the "mind's eye" to use an old colloquialism. They smell it vividly. And they can feel it even to the thorns. They are thinking about roses by actually recalling a rose.

These people, thinking about a ship, would see a specific ship, feel the motion of her if they thought of being aboard her, smell the pine tar or even less savory odors and hear whatever sounds there were about her. They would see the ship in full-color motion and hear it in full-tone audio.

These faculties vary widely in the aberree. Some, when told to think of a rose, can merely visualize one. Some can smell one but not see it. Some see it without color or in very pale color. When told to think of a ship, some aberrees only see a flat, colorless, still picture such as a painting of a ship or the photograph of one. Some perceive a vessel in motion without color but with sound. Some hear the sound of a ship but fail to see any picture whatever. Some merely think of a ship as a concept that ships exist and that they know about them and fail to see, feel, hear, smell or otherwise sense anything on a recall basis.

Some past observers have called this "imagery," but the term is so inapplicable to sound and touch, organic sensation and pain that *recall* is used uniformly as the technical Dianetic term. The value of recall in this business of living has occupied such scant attention that the entire concept has never been formulated previously. It is therefore detailed at some length here, as above.

It is quite simple to test recalls. If one will ask his fellows what *their* abilities are, he will gain a remarkable idea of how widely varied this ability is from individual to individual. Some have this recall, some have that, some have none but operate on concepts of recall only. And remember, if you make a test on those around you, that any perception is filed in the memory and therefore has a recall which is to include pain, temperature, rhythm, taste and weight with the above mentioned sight, sound, tactile and smell.

The Dianetic names for these recalls are *visio* (sight), *sonic* (sound), *tactile* (touch), *olfactory* (smell), *rhythmic*, *kinesthetic* (weight and motion), *somatic* (pain), *thermal* (temperature) and *organic* (internal sensations and, by new definition, emotion).

Then there is another set of mental activities which can be summated under the headings of *imagination* and *creative imagination*. Here again is abundant material for testing.

Imagination is the recombination of things one has sensed, thought or intellectually computed into existence, which do not necessarily have existence. This is the mind's method of envisioning desirable goals or forecasting futures. Imagination is extremely valuable as a part of essential solutions in any mental problem and in everyday existence. That it is recombination in no sense deprives it of its vast and wonderful complexity.

A Clear uses imagination in its entirety. There is an imagination impression for sight, smell, taste, sound–in short, for each one of the possible perceptions. These are manufactured impressions on the basis of models in the memory banks combined by conceptual ideas and construction. New physical structures, tomorrow in terms of today, next year in terms of last year, pleasure to be gained, deeds to be done, accidents to avoid, all these are imaginational functions.

The Clear has full color-visio, tone-sonic, tactile, olfactory, rhythmic, kinesthetic, thermal and organic imagination in kind. Asked to envision himself riding in a gilded coach and four, he "sees" the equipage moving in full color, he "hears" all the noises which should be present, he "smells" the smells he thinks should be there, and he "feels" the upholstery, the motion, and the presence in the coach of himself.

In addition to standard imagination there is *creative imagination.* This is a very wide undimensional ability, quite variable from individual to individual, possessed in enormous quantity by some. It is included here, not as a portion of the operation of the mind treated as a usual part of Dianetics, but to isolate it as an existing entity. In a Clear who possessed *creative imagination*, even if inhibited, as an aberree, it is present and demonstrable. It is inherent. It can be aberrated only by prohibition of its general practice, which is to say, by aberrating the persistence in its application or encysting the whole mind. But creative imagination, that possession by which works of art are done, states built and Man enriched, can be envisioned as a special function, independent in operation and in no way dependent for its existence upon an aberrated condition in the individual, since the examination of its activity in and use by a Clear possessing it adequately demonstrates its inherent character. It is rarely absent in any individual.

Finally, there is the last, but most important activity of the mind. Man is to be regarded as a sentient being. His sentience depends upon his ability to resolve problems by perceiving or creating and understanding situations. This rationality is the primary, high-echelon function of that part of the mind which makes him a Man, not just another animal. Remembering, perceiving, imagining, he has the signal ability of resolving conclusions and of using conclusions resolved to resolve further conclusions. This is rational Man.

Rationality, as divorced from aberration, can be studied in a Cleared person only. The aberrations of the aberree give him the appearance of irrationality. Though such irrationality may be given the gentler names of "eccentricity" or "human error" or even "personal idiosyncrasy," it is, nevertheless, irrationality. The personality does not depend upon how irrationally a man may act. It is not a personality trait, for instance, to drive while drunk and kill a child on a crosswalk–or even to risk killing a child by driving while drunk. Irrationality is simply that: the inability to get right answers from data.

Now it is a curious thing that although "everybody knows" (and what a horrible amount of misinformation *that* statement lets circulate) it is "human to err," the sentient portion of the mind which computes the answers to problems and which makes man Man is *utterly incapable of error.*

This was a startling discovery when it was made, but it need not have been. It could have been deduced some time before, for it is quite simple and easy to understand. The actual computing ability of Man is never in error, even in a very severely aberrated person. Observing the activity of such an aberrated person, one might thoughtlessly suppose that that person's computations were wrong. But that would be an observer error. Any person, aberrated or Clear, computes perfectly *on the data stored and perceived.*

Take any common calculating machine (and the mind is an exceptionally magnificent instrument far, far superior to any machine it will invent for ages to come) and put a problem on it for solution. Multiply 7 times 1. It will answer, properly, 7. Now multiply 6 times 1 but continue to hold down the 7; 6 times 1 is 6 but the answer you will get is 42. Continue to hold down 7 and put other problems on the machine. They are wrong, not as problems, but as answers. Now fix 7 so that it stays down no matter what keys are touched and try to give the machine away. Nobody will want it because, obviously, the machine is crazy. It says 10 times 10 is 700. But is the calculating portion of the machine really wrong or is it merely being fed the wrong data?

In the same way the human mind, being called upon to resolve problems of a magnitude and with enough variables to confound any mere calculating machine a thousand times an hour, is prey to incorrect data. Incorrect data gets into the machine. The machine gives wrong answers. Incorrect data enters the human memory banks, the person reacts in an "abnormal manner." Essentially, then, the problem of resolving aberration is the problem of finding a "held-down 7." But of that, much, much more, later. Right now we have accomplished our immediate ends.

These are the various abilities and activities of the human mind in its constant task of resolving and putting into solution a multitude of problems. It perceives, it recalls or returns, it imagines, it conceives and then resolves. Served by its extensions – the perceptics and the memory banks and the imaginations – the mind brings forth answers which are invariably accurate, modified only by observation, education and viewpoint.

And the basic purposes of that mind and the basic nature of Man, as discoverable in the Clear, are constructive and good, uniformly constructive and uniformly good, the solutions modified only by observation, education and viewpoint.

Man is good.

Take away his basic aberrations and with them go the evil of which the Scholastic and the Moralist were so fond. The only detachable portion of him is the "evil" portion. And when it is detached, his personality and vigor intensify. And he is glad to see the "evil" portion go because it was *physical pain.*

Later, there are experiments and proofs for these things and they can be measured with the precision so dear to the heart of the physical scientist.

The Clear, then, is not an "adjusted" person, driven to activity by his repressions now thoroughly encysted. He is an unrepressed person, operating on self-determinism. And his abilities to perceive, recall, return, imagine, create and compute are outlined as we have seen.

The Clear is the goal in Dianetic therapy, a goal which some patience and a little study and work can bring about. Any person can be Cleared unless he has been so unfortunate as to have had a large portion of his brain removed or to have been born with a grossly malformed nervous structure.

We have seen the goal of Dianetics here. Let us now inspect the goal of Man.

BOOK ONE, CHAPTER THREE

The GOAL *of* MAN

THE GOAL OF MAN, the lowest common denominator of all his activities, the Dynamic Principle of his Existence, has long been sought. Should such an answer be discovered, it is inevitable that from it many answers would flow. It would explain all phenomena of behavior; it would lead toward a solution of Man's major problems; and, most of all, it should be workable.

Consider all knowledge to fall above or below a line of demarcation. Everything above this line is not necessary to the solution of Man's aberrations and general shortcomings and is inexactly known. Such a field of thought could be considered to embrace such things as metaphysics and mysticism. Below this line of demarcation could be considered to lic thc finite universe. All things in the finite universe, whcthcr known or as yet unknown, can be sensed, experienced or measured. The known data in the finite universe can be classified as *scientific truth* when it has been sensed, experienced and measured. All factors necessary to the resolution of a science of the mind were found within the finite universe and were discovered, sensed, measured and experienced, and became scientific truth. The finite universe contains TIME, SPACE, ENERGY and LIFE. No other factors were found necessary in the equation.

TIME, SPACE, ENERGY and LIFE have a single denominator in common. As an analogy, it could be considered that TIME, SPACE, ENERGY and LIFE began at some point of origin and were commanded to continue to some nearly infinite destination. They were told nothing but *what* to do. They obey a single order and that order is "SURVIVE!"

THE DYNAMIC PRINCIPLE OF EXISTENCE IS SURVIVAL.

The goal of life can be considered to be infinite survival. Man, as a life form, can be demonstrated to obey in all his actions and purposes the one command: SURVIVE!

It is not a new thought that Man is surviving. It is a new thought that Man is motivated *only* by survival.

That his single goal is survival does not mean that he is the optimum survival mechanism which life has attained or will develop. The goal of the dinosaur was also survival and the dinosaur isn't extant anymore.

Obedience to this command SURVIVE! does not mean that every attempt to obey is uniformly successful. Changing environment, mutation, and many other things militate against any one organism attaining infallible survival techniques or form.

Life forms change and die as new life forms develop just as surely as one life organism, lacking immortality in itself, creates other life organisms, then dies as itself. An excellent method, should one wish to cause life to survive over a very long period, would be to establish means by which it could assume many forms. And death itself would be necessary in order to facilitate the survival of the life force itself, since only death and decay could clear away older forms when new changes in the environment necessitated new forms. Life, as a force existing over a nearly infinite period, would need a cyclic aspect in its unit organisms and forms.

What would be the optimum survival characteristics of various life forms? They would have to have various fundamental characteristics, differing from one species to the next just as one environment differs from the next.

This is important, since it has been but poorly considered in the past that a set of survival characteristics in one species would not be survival characteristics in another.

The methods of survival can be summed under the headings of food, protection (defensive and offensive) and procreation. There are no existing life forms which lack solutions to these problems. Every life form errs, one way or another, by holding a characteristic too long or developing characteristics which may lead to its extinction. But the developments which bring about successfulness of form are far more striking than their errors. The naturalist and biologist are continually resolving the characteristics of this or that life form by discovering that need rather than whim govern such developments. The hinges of the clamshell, the awesome face on the wings of the butterfly, have survival value.

Once survival was isolated as the only *dynamic** of a life form which would explain all its activities,

* In order to establish nomenclature in Dianetics which would not be too complex for the purpose, words normally considered as adjectives or verbs have occasionally been pressed into service as nouns. This has been done on the valid principle that existing terminology, meaning so many different things, could not be used by Dianetics without making it necessary to explain away an old meaning to bring forth a new. To remove the step of explaining the old meaning and saying then that one doesn't mean *that*, thus entangling our communications inextricably, and to obviate the ancient custom of compounding ponderous and thundering syllables from the Greek and Roman tongues, this principle and some others have been adopted for nomenclature. *Dynamic* is here used as a noun and will so continue to be used throughout this volume. Somatic, perceptic and some others will be noted, defined when used.

it was necessary to study further the action of survival. And it was discovered that when one considered pain and pleasure, he had at hand all the necessary ingredients with which to formulate the action life takes in its effort to survive.

As will be seen in the accompanying graph,* a spectrum of life has been conceived to span from the zero of death or extinction toward the infinity of potential immortality. This spectrum was considered to contain an infinity of lines, extending ladder-like toward the potential of immortality. Each line, as the ladder mounted, was spaced a little wider than the last, in a geometric progression.

The thrust of survival is away from death and toward immortality. The ultimate pain could be conceived as existing just before death and the ultimate pleasure could be conceived as immortality.

Immortality could be said to have an attractive type of force, and death a repelling force, in the consideration of the unit organism or the species. But as survival rises higher and higher toward immortality, wider and wider spaces are encountered until the gaps are finitely impossible to bridge. The urge is away from death, which has a repelling force, and toward immortality, which has an attracting force; the attracting force is pleasure, the repelling force is pain.

For the individual, the length of the arrow could be considered to be at a high potential within the fourth zone. Here the survival potential would be excellent and the individual would enjoy existence.

From left to right could be graphed the years.

The urge toward pleasure is dynamic. Pleasure is the reward; and the seeking of the reward–survival

*A foldout version of this graph is contained at the back of this book.

Descriptic Graph of Survival

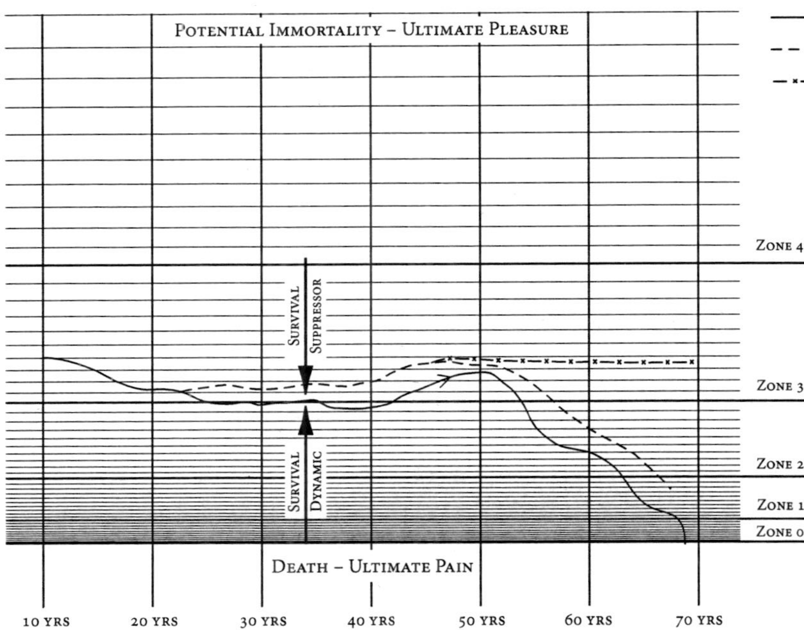

Lines in a geometric progression of spacing, the inner widths being both a quantity of pleasure possible and survival forecast for the organism. Showing lessening degrees of non-survival as immortality is approached.

Survival Suppressor is the effort of other life forms and energy of other kinds to survive.

Survival Dynamic as a level of physical being or mental being. All thrust is upward as a repulsion of pain and an attraction for pleasure.

goals–would be a pleasurable act. And to ensure that survival is accomplished under the mandate SURVIVE! it seems to have been provided that reduction from a high potential would bring pain.

Pain is provided to repel the individual from death; pleasure is provided to call him toward optimum life. *The search for and the attainment of pleasure is not less valid in survival than the avoidance of pain.* In fact, on some observed evidence, pleasure seems to have a much greater value in the cosmic scheme than pain.

Now it would be well to define what is meant by *pleasure* aside from its connection with immortality. The dictionary states that pleasure is "gratification; agreeable emotions, mental or physical; transient enjoyment; opposed to pain." Pleasure can be found in so many things and activities that a catalog of all the things and activities Man has, does and may consider pleasurable alone could round out the definition.

And what do we mean by *pain?* The dictionary states: "physical or mental suffering; penalty."

These two definitions, in passing, are demonstrative of an intuitive type of thought which runs through the language. Once one has a thing which leads to the resolution of hitherto unsolved problems, even the dictionaries are found to have "always known it."

If we wished to make this graph for a life-form cycle, it would be identical except that the value of the years would be increased to measure eons. For there is no difference, it seems, except magnitude, in the scope of the individual and the scope of the species. This inference could be drawn even without such remarkable evidence as the fact that a human being, growing from zygote to adult, evolutes through all the forms which the whole species is supposed to have evolved through.

Now there is more in this graph than has been remarked as yet. The physical and mental state of the individual varies from hour to hour, day to day, year to year. Therefore, the level of survival would form either a daily curve or the curve of a life on a measure of hourly or yearly position in the zones. And there would be two curves made possible by this: the physical curve and the mental curve. When we get toward the back of the book, the relationships between these two curves will be found vital and it will also be seen that, ordinarily, a sag in the mental curve will precede a sag in the physical curve.

The zones, then, can apply to two things: the physical being and the mental being. Therefore, these four zones can be called zones of the states of being. If a person is happy mentally, the survival level can be placed in Zone 4. If the person is extremely ill physically, he might be plotted, on estimation of his illness, in Zone 1 or close to death.

Very unprecise but nevertheless descriptive names have been assigned to these zones:

Zone 3 is one of general happiness and well-being.
Zone 2 is a level of bearable existence.
Zone 1 is one of anger.
Zone 0 is the zone of apathy.

These zones can be used as a Tone Scale by which a state of mind can be graded. Just above death, which is 0, would be the lowest mental apathy or lowest level of physical life, 0.1. A Tone 1, where the body is fighting physical pain or illness or where the being is fighting in anger, could be graded from 1.0, which would be resentment or hostility, through Tone 1.5, which would be a screaming rage, to a 1.9, which would be merely a quarrelsome inclination. From Tone 2.0 to Tone 3.0, there would be an increasing interest in existence, and so forth.

It so happens that the state of physical being or mental being does not long remain static. Therefore, there are various fluctuations. In the course of a single day an aberree may run from 0.5 to 3.5, up and down, as a mental being. An accident or illness could cause a similar fluctuation in a day.

These are, then, figures which can be assigned to four things: the mental state on an acute basis and the mental state on a general, average basis, and the physical being on an acute basis and the physical being on a general basis. In Dianetics, we do not much employ the physical Tone Scale. The mental Tone Scale, however, is of vast and vital importance!

These values of happiness, bearable existence, anger and apathy are not arbitrary values. They are deduced from observation of the behavior of emotional states. A Clear is usually found varying around Tone 4, plus or minus in an average day. He is a general Tone 4, which is one of the inherent conditions of being Clear. A norm in current society, at a wild guess, is probably around a general Tone 2.8.

In this descriptic graph, which is two-dimensional, the vital data for the solution of the problem of the life dynamic are workably combined. The horizontal lines are in terms of geometric progression beginning with the zero line immediately above death. There are ten lines for each zone and each zone denotes a mental or physical state of being, as noted. Geometric progression, so used, leaves ever-increasing spaces between the lines. The width of this space is the survival potential existing at the moment the top point of the survival dynamic arrow is within that space. The further away from death the top point of the survival dynamic arrow is, the better chance the individual has of survival. Geometric progression reaches up toward the impossible of infinity and cannot, of course, reach infinity. The organism is surviving through time from left to right. Survival optimum–immortality–lies in terms of time to the right. Potential only is measured vertically.

The *survival dynamic* actually resides within the organism as inherited from the species. The organism is part of the species as a railroad tie might be said to be part of a railroad as seen by an observer on a train, the observer being always in "now"–although this analogy is not perhaps the best.

Within itself, the organism possesses a repulsive force toward pain sources. The source of the pain is not a driving force any more than the thorn bush which tears the hand was a driving force; the organism repulses the potential pain of a thorn.

At the same time, the organism has at work a force which attracts it to the sources of pleasure. Pleasure does not magnetize the organism into drawing near. It is the organism which possesses the attraction force. It is inherent.

The repulsion of pain sources adds to the attraction for pleasure sources to operate as a combined thrust away from death and toward immortality. The thrust away from death is no more powerful than the thrust toward immortality. In other words, in terms of the survival dynamic, pleasure has as much validity as pain.

It should not be read here that survival is always a matter of keeping an eye on the future. Contemplation of pleasure, pure enjoyment, contemplation of past pleasures, all combine into harmonies which, while they operate automatically as a rise toward the survival potential by their action within the organism physically, do not demand the future as an active portion of the mental computation in such contemplation.

A pleasure which reacts to injure the body physically, as in the case of debauchery, discovers at work a ratio between the physical effect (which is depressed toward pain) and the mental effect of experienced pleasure. There is a consequent lowering of the survival dynamic. Averaging out, the future possibility of strain because of the act, added to the state of being at the moment the debauchery was experienced, again depresses the survival dynamic. Because of this, various kinds of debauchery have been in indifferent odor with Man throughout his history. This is the equation of "immoral pleasures." And any action which has brought about survival suppression or which can bring it about, when pursued as a pleasure, has been denounced at some time or another in Man's history. Immorality is originally hung as a label upon some act or class of actions because they depress the level of the survival dynamic. Future enforcement of moral stigma may depend largely upon prejudice and aberration and there is, consequently, a continuous quarrel over what is *moral* and what is *immoral.*

Because certain things practiced as pleasures are actually pains – and how easy it will be to trace out why when you've finished this volume – and because of the *moral equation* as above, pleasure itself, in any aberrated society, can become decried. A certain kind of thinking, of which more, later, permits poor differentiation between one object and another. Confusing a dishonest politician with all politicians would be an example of this. In ancient times the Roman was fond of his pleasures and some of the things he called pleasure were a trifle strenuous on other species such as Christians. When the Christian overthrew the pagan state, the ancient order of Rome was in a villain's role. Anything, therefore, which was Roman was villainous. This went to such remarkable lengths that the Roman love of bathing made bathing so immoral that Europe went unwashed for some fifteen hundred years. The Roman had become a pain source so general that everything Roman was *evil* and it stayed evil long after Roman paganism perished. Immorality, in such a fashion, tends to become an involved subject. In this case it became so involved that pleasure itself was stigmatized.

When half the survival potential is struck from the list of lawful things, there is a considerable reduction in survival indeed. Considering this graph on a racial scale, the reduction of survival potential by one-half would forecast that direful things lay in wait for the race. Actually, because Man is after all Man, no set of laws, however enforced, can completely wipe away the attraction of pleasure. But in this case, enough *was* removed and banned to occasion precisely what happened: the Dark Ages and the recession of society. Society brightened only in those periods such as the Renaissance in which pleasure became less unlawful.

When a race or an individual drops into the second zone, as marked on the chart, and the general tone ranges from the first zone barely into the third, a condition of insanity ensues. Insanity is irrationality. It is also a state in which non-survival has been so closely approached continually that the race or the organism engages in all manner of wild solutions.

In further interpretation of this descriptic graph, there is the matter of the *survival suppressor*. This, it will be seen, is a thrust downward out of potential immortality at the race or organism represented as the *survival dynamic*. The survival suppressor is the combined and variable threats to the survival of the race or organism. These threats come from other species, from time, from other energies.

These are also engaged in the contest of survival to potential immortality in terms of their own species or identities. Thus there is a conflict involved. Every other form of life or energy could be plotted in a descriptic as the *survival dynamic*. If we were to use a duck's survival dynamic in a descriptic graph, we would see the duck seeking a high *survival* level and Man would be a part of the duck's *suppressor*.

The balance and nature of things do not permit the infinity of the goal of immortality to be reached. In fluctuating balance and in almost unlimited complexity, life and energies ebb and flood out of the nebulous, into forms and, through decay, into the nebulous once more.* Many equations could be drawn concerning this, but it is outside the sphere of our present interest.

In terms of the zones of the descriptic, it is of relative concern what the extent of the force of the suppressor is against the survival dynamic. The dynamic is inherent in individuals, groups and races, evolved to resist the suppressor through the eons. In the case of Man, he carries with him another level of offensive and defensive techniques: his cultures. His primary technology of survival is mental activity governing physical action in the sentient echelon. But every life form has its own technology, formed to resolve the problems of food, protection and procreation. The degree of workability of the technology any life form develops (armor or brains, fleetness of foot or deceptive form) is a direct index of the survival potential, the relative immortality, of that form. There have been vast upsets in the past: Man, when he developed into the world's most dangerous animal (he can and does kill or enslave any life form, doesn't he?), overloaded the suppressor

* The Veda; also Lucretius' *Nature of Things*.

on many other life forms and they dwindled in number or vanished.

A great climatic change, such as the one which packed so many mammoths in Siberian ice, may overload the suppressor on a life form. A long drought in the American Southwest in not too ancient times wiped out the better part of an Indian civilization.

A cataclysm such as an explosion of the core of the Earth, if that were possible, or the atom bomb or the sudden cessation of burning on the Sun would wipe out all life forms *on Earth*.

And a life form can even overload the suppressor on itself. A dinosaur destroys all his food and so destroys the dinosaur. A bubonic plague bacillus attacks its hosts with such thorough appetite that the whole generation of *Pasteurella pestis* vanishes. Such things are not intended by the suicide to be suicide: the life form has run up against an equation which has an unknown variable, and the unknown variable unfortunately contained enough value to overload the suppressor. This is the "didn't know the gun was loaded" equation. And if the bubonic plague bacillus overloads its own suppressor in an area and then ceases to trouble its food and shelter (the animals), then the animals consider themselves benefited.

Reckless and clever and well-nigh indestructible, Man has led a course which is a far cry from "tooth and claw" in every sphere. And so have the redwood tree and the shark. Just as a life form, Man, like every life form, is "symbiotic." Life is a group effort. Lichens and plankton and algae may do very well on sunlight and minerals alone, but they are the building blocks. Above such existence, as the forms grow more complex, a tremendous interdependence exists.

It is very well for a forester to believe that certain trees willfully kill all other varieties of trees around them and then conclude a specious "attitude" of trees. Let him look again. What made the soil? What provides the means of keeping the oxygen balance? What makes it possible for rain to fall in other areas? These willful and murderous trees. And squirrels plant trees. And Man plants trees. And trees shelter trees of another kind. And animals fertilize trees. And trees shelter animals. And trees hold the soil so less well-rooted plants can grow. Look anywhere and everywhere and we see life as an assist for life. The multitude of the complexities of life as affinities for life is not dramatic. But they are the steady, practical, important reason life can continue to exist at all.

A redwood tree may be first out for redwood trees and although it does an excellent job of seeming to exist as redwood alone, a closer glance will show it has dependencies and is depended upon.

Therefore, the dynamic of any life form can be seen to be assisted by many other dynamics and combines with them against the suppressive factors. *None survive alone.*

Necessity has been declared to be a very wonderful thing. But necessity is a word which has been taken rather loosely for granted. Opportunism seems to have been read largely into necessity. What is necessity? Besides being the "mother of invention," is it a dramatic, sudden thing which excuses wars and murders, which touches a man only when he is about to starve? Or is necessity a much gentler and less dramatic quantity? "Everything," according to Leucippus, "is driven by necessity." This is a keynote of much theorizing down through the ages. *Driven*, that is the key to the error. Driven, things are driven. Necessity drives. Pain drives. Necessity and pain, pain and necessity.

Recalling the dramatic and overlooking the important, Man has conceived himself, from time to time, to be an object of chase by necessity and pain. These were two anthropomorphic (manlike) things which, in full costume, stuck spears at him. It can be said to be a wrong concept merely because it does not work to produce more answers.

Whatever there is of necessity is *within* him. Nothing is driving him except his original impetus to survive. And he carries that within himself or his group. Within him is the force with which he fends off pain. Within him is the force with which he attracts pleasure.

It chances to be a scientific fact that Man is a self-determined organism to the outermost limit that any form of life can be, for he still depends upon other forms of life and his general environment. But he is self-determined. This is a matter which will be covered later. But right here it is necessary to indicate that he is not inherently a determined organism in the sense that he is driven on this wonderful stimulus-response basis which looks so neat in certain textbooks and works so completely unworkably in the world of Man. The happy little illustrations about rats do not serve when we are talking about *Man.* The more complex the organism, the less reliably the stimulus-response equation works. And when one reaches that highest complexity, Man, he has reached a fine degree of variability in terms of stimulus-response. The more sentient, the more rational an organism, the more that organism is self-determined. Self-determinism, like all things, is relative. Compared to a rat, however, Man is very self-determined indeed. This is only a scientific fact because it can easily be proven.

The more sentient the man, the less he is a "push-button" instrument. Aberrated and reduced, he can, of course, in a limited degree, be made to perform like a marionette; but then it is understood that the more aberrated a person is, the closer he approaches the intelligence quotient of an animal.

Given this self-determinism, it is interesting to observe what a man does with it. While he can never escape the "didn't know it was loaded" equation in terms of cataclysm or the unexpected gain of some other life form, he operates in a high zone level of survival potential. But here he is, self-determined, rational, his primary weapon, his mind, in excellent working order. What are his necessity instincts?

Necessity, according to that very sentient if rapidly subject-changing article, the dictionary, is "the state of being necessary; that which is unavoidable; compulsion." It also adds that necessity is "extreme poverty," but we don't want *that.* We are talking about survival.

The compulsion mentioned can be re-evaluated in terms of the survival dynamic. That is interior in the organism and the race. And what is "necessary" to survival?

We have seen and can prove clinically that there are two factors at work. The necessity of avoiding pain is a factor because, degree by degree, little things, not much in themselves, can amount to large pains which, compounded in that rapid geometric progression, bring on death. Pain is the sadness of being bawled out for poor work, because that may lead to being fired, which may lead to starvation, which may lead to death. Run any equation into which pain has entered and it can be seen that it reduces down to possible non-survival. And if this were all there were to surviving and if necessity were a vicious little gnome with a pitchfork, it seems rather obvious that there would be scant reason to go on living. But there is the other part of the equation: pleasure. That is a more stable part than pain, Stoics to the contrary, as clinical tests in Dianetics prove.

There is therefore a necessity for pleasure, for working, as happiness can be defined, toward known goals over not unknowable obstacles. And the necessity for pleasure is such that a great deal of pain can be borne to attain it. Pleasure is the positive commodity. It is enjoyment of work, contemplation of deeds well done; it is a good book or a good friend; it is taking all the skin off one's knees climbing the Matterhorn; it is hearing the kid first say daddy; it is a brawl on the Bund at Shanghai or the whistle of amour from a doorway; it's adventure and hope and enthusiasm and "someday I'll learn to paint"; it's eating a good meal or kissing a pretty girl or playing a stiff game of bluff on the stock exchange. It's what Man does that he enjoys doing; it's what Man does that he enjoys contemplating; it's what Man does that he enjoys remembering; and it may be just the talk of things he knows he'll never do.

Man will endure a lot of pain to obtain a little pleasure. Out in the laboratory of the world, it takes very little time to confirm that.

And how does necessity fit this picture? There is a necessity for pleasure, a necessity as live and quivering and vital as the human heart itself. He who said that a man who had two loaves of bread should sell one to buy white hyacinth, spoke sooth. The creative, the constructive, the beautiful, the harmonious, the adventurous, yes, and even escape from the maw of oblivion, these things are pleasure and these things are necessity. There was a man once who had walked a thousand miles just to see an orange tree and another who was a mass of scars and poor-set bones who was eager just to get a chance to "fan another bronc."

It is very well to dwell in some Olympian height and write a book of penalties and very well to read to find what writers said that other writers said, but it is not very practical.

The pain-drive theory does not work. If some of these basics of Dianetics were only poetry about the idyllic state of Man, they might be justified in that. But it happens that out in the laboratory of the world, they work.

Man, in affinity with Man, survives. And that survival is pleasure.

BOOK ONE, CHAPTER FOUR

The Four Dynamics

In the original equations of Dianetics, when the research was young, it was believed that *survival* could be envisioned in personal terms alone and still answer all conditions. A theory is only as good as it works. And it works as well as it explains observed data and predicts new material which will be found, in fact, to exist.

Survival in personal terms was computed until the whole activity of Man could be theoretically explained in terms of *self* alone. The logic looked fairly valid. But then it was applied to the world. Something was wrong: it did not solve problems. In fact, the theory of survival in personal terms alone was so unworkable that it left a majority of behavior phenomena unexplained. But it could be computed and it still looked good.

Then it was that a nearly intuitive idea occurred. Man's understanding developed in ratio to his recognition of his brotherhood with the Universe. That was high flown, but it yielded results.

Was Man himself a brotherhood of Man? He had evolved and become strong as a gregarious being, an animal that hunted in packs. It seemed possible that all his activities could be computed in terms of the survival of the group. That computation was made. It looked good. Man survived, it was postulated, solely in terms of the survival of his group. It looked good, but it left a majority of observed phenomena unexplained.

It was attempted, then, to explain Man's behavior in terms of Mankind alone, which is to say, it was assumed that Mankind survived for Mankind in a highly altruistic way. This was straight down the sylvan path of Jean Jacques Rousseau. It could be computed that Man lived alone for the survival of all Mankind. But when addressed to the laboratory–the world–it did not work.

Finally, it was recalled that some had thought that Man's entire activity and all his behavior could be explained by assuming that he lived for sex alone. This was not an original assumption. But some original computations were made upon it and it is true that, by a few quick twists of the equation, his survival activity can be made to resolve on only the sexual basis. But when this was applied to observed data, again it failed to explain every phenomenon.

An examination was made of what had been attempted. It had been assumed that Man survived only for himself as an individual; it had been computed that he survived only for the group, the pack, for society; it had been postulated that he survived only for Mankind; and finally, it had been theorized that he lived only for sex. *None worked alone.*

A new computation was made on the survival dynamic. Exactly for what was Man surviving? All four of these factors, *self, sex, group* and *Mankind,* were entered into a new equation. And now it was found, a theory was in hand which worked. It explained all observed phenomena and it predicted new phenomena which were discovered to exist. It was a scientific equation, therefore!

From the survival dynamic, in this fashion, were evolved the four dynamics. By *survival dynamic* was meant the basic command "SURVIVE!" which underlay all activity. By *dynamic* was meant one of the four purpose divisions of the entire dynamic principle. The four *dynamics* were not new forces, they were subdivisions of the primary force.

DYNAMIC ONE is the urge toward ultimate survival on the part of the individual and for himself. It includes his immediate symbiotes,* the extension of culture for his own benefit and name immortality.

DYNAMIC TWO is the urge of the individual toward ultimate survival via the sex act, the creation of and the rearing of children. It includes their symbiotes, the extension of culture for them and their future provision.

DYNAMIC THREE is the urge of the individual toward ultimate survival for the group. It includes the symbiotes of the group and the extension of its culture.

DYNAMIC FOUR includes the urge of the individual toward ultimate survival for all Mankind. It includes the symbiotes of Mankind and the extension of its culture.

Life, the atom and the universe and energy itself are included under the symbiotic classification.

It will be seen immediately that these four dynamics are actually a spectrum without sharp division lines.

*The Dianetic meaning of *symbiote* is extended beyond the dictionary definition to mean "any or all life or energy forms which are mutually dependent for survival." The atom depends on the Universe, the Universe on the atom.

The survival dynamic can be seen to sweep out from the individual to embrace the entire species and its symbiotes.

None of these dynamics is necessarily stronger than any of the others. Each is strong. They are the four roads a man takes to survival. And the four roads are actually one road. And the one road is actually a spectrum of thousands of roads contained within the four. They are all in terms of past, present and future in that the present may be a sum of the past and the future may be the product of the past and present.

All the purposes of Man can be considered to lie within this spectrum and all behavior becomes explained.

That Man is selfish is a valid statement when one means an *aberrated* Man. That Man is antisocial is an equally valid statement if one adds the modifier, aberration. And other such statements resolve equally.

Now it happens that these four dynamics can be seen to compete, one with another, in their operation within an individual or a society. There is a rational reason for this. The phrase "social competition" is a compound of aberrated behavior and sentient difficulties.

Any man, group or race may be in contest with any race, group or man and even in contest with sex on an entirely rational level.

The Equation of the Optimum Solution would be that *a problem has been well resolved which portends the maximum good for the maximum number of dynamics*. That is to say that any solution, modified by the time available to put the solution into effect, should be creative or constructive for the greatest possible number of dynamics. The optimum solution for any problem would be a solution which achieved the maximum benefit in all the dynamics. This means that a man, determining upon some project, would fare best if he benefited everything concerned in the four dynamics as his project touched them. He would then have to benefit himself, as well, for the solution to be optimum. In other words, the benefiting of the Group and Mankind Dynamics, but the blocking of the Sex Dynamic and the Self Dynamic would be much poorer than the best solution. The *conduct survival pattern* is built upon this Equation of the Optimum Solution. It is the basic equation of all rational behavior and is the equation on which a Clear functions. It is inherent in Man.

In other words, the best solution to any problem is that which will bring the greatest good to the greatest number of beings, including self, progeny, family associates, political and racial groups, and at length to all Mankind. The greatest good may require, as well, some destruction, but the solution deteriorates in a ratio to the destructiveness employed. Self-sacrifice and selfishness are alike reductive of the optimum action equation and alike have been suspected and should be.

This is entirely a matter of: *does it work?* Even on an unaberrated basis, there are times when one or another of these dynamics has to be dropped from the computation of some activity or other and, indeed, few problems are so entirely intense that they must take into account all the dynamics. But when a problem achieves such intensity, and time is not an important factor, serious errors can follow the omission of one or another of the dynamics from the factors considered.

In the case of a Napoleon "saving France" at the expense of the remainder of Mankind in Europe, the Equation of the Optimum Solution was so far neglected that all the revolutionary gains of the French people were lost. In the case of Caesar "saving Rome," the equation was so poorly done that the survival of Rome was impeded.

But there are special cases when the Equation of the Optimum Solution becomes so involved with time that certain dynamics must be neglected to permit other dynamics to persist. The case of a sailor giving his own life to save his ship answers the Group Dynamic. Such an action is a valid solution to a problem. But it violates the *optimum* solution because it did not answer for Dynamic One: self.

Many examples of various kinds could be cited where one or another of the dynamics must, of necessity, receive priority, all on an entirely rational basis.

On an aberrated basis the equation is still valid, but complicated by irrationalities which have no part of the situation. Many solutions are bad merely because of false educational data or no data at all. But these are still solutions. In the case of aberrated solutions, the dynamics are actually and actively impeded, as will later be outlined in full.

BOOK ONE, CHAPTER FIVE

SUMMARY

THE DYNAMIC Principle of Existence is SURVIVAL.

This survival can be graduated into four zones, each one progressively portending a better opportunity of reaching the potential of immortality. Zone 0 borders from death and includes apathy; Zone 1 borders from apathy and includes violent effort; Zone 2 borders from violence into mediocre but not entirely satisfactory success; Zone 3 borders from the mediocre to the excellent chance. These zones are each occasioned by the ratio of the *suppressor* to the *survival dynamic*. In apathy, Zone 0, the suppressor appears too great to be overcome. In the area of violence, Zone 1, the suppressor more or less overbalances the survival dynamic, requiring enormous effort which, when expended without result, drops the organism into the 0 Zone. In the area of mediocrity, Zone 2, the suppressor and the survival dynamic are more or less evenly balanced. In the area of Zone 3, the survival dynamic has overcome the suppressor and, the chances of survival being excellent, is the area of high response to problems. These four zones might be classed as the zone of no hope, the zone of violent action, the area of balance and the area of high hope. Clinical experiment is the basis of these zones, since they follow a progress of mental or physical being as it rises from the death area into high existence.

The four *dynamics* are subdivisions of the *survival dynamic* and are, in Mankind, the thrust toward potential survival in terms of entities. They embrace all the purposes, activities and behavior of Mankind. They could be said to be a *conduct survival pattern.* The first of these, but not necessarily the most important nor yet the one which will receive priority in various efforts, is the Individual Dynamic, DYNAMIC ONE, which includes the personal survival of the individual as a living person and the survival of his personal symbiotes. DYNAMIC TWO is the thrust toward potential immortality through children and includes all sexual activity as well as the symbiotes of the children. DYNAMIC THREE is survival in terms of the group, which term may include such things as a club, a military company, a city, a state, a nation; this would include the symbiotes of the group. DYNAMIC FOUR is the thrust toward potential immortality of Mankind as a species and the symbiotes of Mankind. Embraced within these classifications are any part of existence, any form of matter and, indeed, the Universe.

Any problem or situation discoverable within the activities or purposes of Mankind is embraced within these dynamics.

The Equation of the Optimum Solution is inherent within the organism and, modified by education or viewpoint and modified further by time, is the operating method of unaberrated individuals, groups or Mankind. The Equation of the Optimum Solution is always present even in severely aberrated individuals and is used as modified by their education, viewpoint and available time. The aberration does not remove activity from the dynamics of survival. Aberrated conduct is *irrational* survival conduct and is fully intended to lead to survival. That the intent is not the act does not eradicate the intent.

THESE ARE THE FUNDAMENTAL AXIOMS OF DIANETICS:

The Dynamic Principle of Existence–SURVIVE!

Survival, considered as the single and sole Purpose, subdivides into four *dynamics*. By *symbiote* is meant all entities and energies which aid survival.

DYNAMIC ONE is the urge of the individual toward survival for the individual and his symbiotes.

DYNAMIC TWO is the urge of the individual toward survival through procreation; it includes both the sex act and the raising of progeny, the care of children and their symbiotes.

DYNAMIC THREE is the urge of the individual toward survival for the group or the group for the group and includes the symbiotes of that group.

DYNAMIC FOUR is the urge of the individual toward survival for Mankind or the urge toward survival of Mankind for Mankind as well as the group for Mankind, etc., and includes the symbiotes of Mankind.

The *absolute goal* of survival is immortality or infinite survival. This is sought by the individual in terms of himself as an organism, as a spirit or as a name, or as his children, as a group of which he is a member or as Mankind and the progeny and symbiotes of others as well as his own.

The reward of survival activity is *pleasure*.

The ultimate penalty of destructive activity is death or complete non-survival, and is *pain.*

Successes raise the survival potential toward infinite survival.

Failures lower the survival potential toward death.

The human mind is engaged upon perceiving and retaining data, composing or computing conclusions and posing and resolving problems related to organisms along all four dynamics and the purpose of perception, retention, concluding and resolving problems is to direct its own organism and symbiotes and other organisms and symbiotes along the four dynamics toward survival.

Intelligence is the ability to perceive, pose and resolve problems.

The *dynamic* is the tenacity to life and vigor and persistence in survival.

Both the *dynamic* and *intelligence* are necessary to persist and accomplish and neither is a constant quantity from individual to individual, group to group.

The *dynamics* are inhibited by engrams, which lie across them and disperse life force.

Intelligence is inhibited by engrams, which feed false or improperly graded data into the analyzer.

Happiness is the overcoming of not unknown obstacles toward a known goal and, transiently, the contemplation of or indulgence in pleasure.

The *analytical mind* is that portion of the mind which perceives and retains experience data to compose and resolve problems and direct the organism along the four dynamics. *It thinks in differences and similarities.*

The *reactive mind* is that portion of the mind which files and retains physical pain and painful emotion and seeks to direct the organism solely on a stimulus-response basis. *It thinks only in identities.*

The *somatic mind* is that mind which, directed by the analytical or reactive mind, places solutions into effect on the physical level.

A *training pattern* is that stimulus-response mechanism resolved by the analytical mind to care for routine activity or emergency activity. It is held in the somatic mind and can be changed at will by the analytical mind.

Habit is that stimulus-response reaction dictated by the reactive mind from the content of engrams and put into effect by the somatic mind. It can be changed only by those things which change engrams.

Aberrations, under which is included all deranged or irrational behavior, are caused by engrams. They are stimulus-response pro- and contra-survival.

Psychosomatic ills are caused by engrams.

The *engram* is the single source of aberrations and psychosomatic ills.

Moments of "unconsciousness" when the analytical mind is attenuated in greater or lesser degree are the only moments when engrams can be received.

The *engram* is a moment of "unconsciousness" containing physical pain or painful emotion and all perceptions and is not available to the analytical mind as experience.

Emotion is three things: engramic response to situations, endocrine metering of the body to meet situations on an analytical level and the inhibition or the furtherance of life force.

The *potential value* of an individual or a group may be expressed by the equation

$$PV = ID^x$$

where I is Intelligence and D is Dynamic.

The *worth* of an individual is computed in terms of the alignment, on any dynamic, of his potential value with optimum survival along that dynamic. A high PV may, by reversed vector, result in a negative worth as in some severely aberrated persons. A high PV on any dynamic *assures* a high worth only in the unaberrated person.

The Single Source *of* All Inorganic Mental *and* Organic Psychosomatic Ills

BOOK TWO

BOOK TWO, CHAPTER ONE

The Analytical Mind *and the* Standard Memory Banks

THIS CHAPTER BEGINS the search for human error and tells where it is not.

The human mind can be considered to have three major divisions. First, there is the *analytical mind;* second, there is the *reactive mind;* and third, there is the *somatic mind.*

Consider the analytical mind as a computing machine. This is analogy because the analytical mind, while it behaves like a computing machine, is yet more fantastically capable than any computing machine ever constructed and infinitely more elaborate. It could be called the "computational mind" or the "egsusheyftef." But for our purposes, the analytical mind, as a descriptive name, will do. This mind may live in the prefrontal lobes–there is some hint of that–but this is a problem of structure and nobody really knows about structure. So we shall call this computational part of the mind the "analytical mind" because it analyzes data.

The *monitor* can be considered part of the analytical mind. The monitor could be called the center of awareness of the person. It, inexactly speaking, *is* the person. It has been approximated by various names for thousands of years, each one reducing down to "I". The monitor is in control of the analytical mind. It is not in control because it has been told to be, but only because it is inherently. It is not a demon who lives in the skull nor a little man who vocalizes one's thoughts. It is "I". No matter how many aberrations a person may have, "I" is always "I". No matter how "Clear" a person becomes, "I" is still "I". "I" may be submerged now and then in an aberree, but it is always present.

The analytical mind shows various evidences of being an organ, but as we know in this age so little of structure, the full structural knowledge of the analytical mind must come after we know what it does. And in Dianetics, we know *precisely* that, for the first time. It is known and can be proven with ease that the analytical mind, be it one organ of the body or several, behaves as you would expect any good computing machine to behave.

What would you want in a computing machine? The action of the analytical mind–or analyzer–is everything anyone could want from the best computer available. It can and does all the tricks of a computer. And over and above that, it directs the building of computers. And it is as thoroughly right as any computer ever was. The analytical mind is not just a *good* computer, it is a *perfect* computer. It never makes a mistake. It cannot err in any way so long as a human being is reasonably intact (unless something has carried away a piece of his mental equipment).

The analytical mind is incapable of error, and it is so certain that it is incapable of error that it works out everything on the basis that it cannot make an error. If a person says, "I cannot add," he either means that he has never been taught to add or that he has an aberration about adding. It does not mean that there is anything wrong with the analytical mind.

While the whole being is, in an aberrated state, grossly capable of error, still the analytical mind is not. For a computer is just as good as the data on which it operates and no better. Aberration, then, arises from the nature of the data offered to the analytical mind as a problem to be computed.

The analytical mind has its standard memory banks. Just where these are located structurally is again no concern of ours at this time. To operate, the analytical mind has to have percepts (data), memory (data), and imagination (data).

There are another data storage bank and another part of the human mind which contain aberrations and are the source of insanities. These will be fully covered later and should not be confused with either the analytical mind or the standard memory banks.

Whether or not the data contained in the standard memory banks is evaluated correctly or not, it is all there. The various senses receive information and this information files straight into the standard memory banks. It does not go through the analyzer first. It is filed and the analyzer then has it from the standard banks.

There are several of these standard banks and they may be duplicated in themselves so that there are several of each kind of bank. Nature seems generous in such things. There is a bank, or set of banks, for each perception. These can be considered racks of data filed in a cross-index system which would make an intelligence officer purple with envy. Any single *percept* is filed as a *concept.* The sight of a moving car, for instance, is filed in the visio-bank in color and motion at the time seen, cross-indexed to the area in which seen, cross-indexed to all data about cars, cross-indexed to thoughts about cars, and so forth and so forth with the additional filing of conclusions (thought stream) of the moment and thought streams of the past with all their conclusions. The sound of that car is similarly filed from the ears straight into the audio-bank and cross-indexed multitudinously as before. The other sensations of that moment are also filed in their own banks.

Now it may be that the whole filing is done in one bank. It would be simpler that way. But this is not a matter of structure, but mental performance. Eventually somebody will discover just how they are filed. Right now the function of filing is all that interests us.

Every percept–sight, sound, smell, feeling, taste, organic sensation, pain, rhythm, kinesthesia (weight and muscular motion) and emotion–is each properly and neatly filed in the standard banks in full. It does not matter how many aberrations a physically intact person has or whether he thinks he can or cannot contain this data or recall it, the file is there and is complete.

This file begins at a very early period–of which more, later. It then runs consecutively, whether the individual is asleep or awake, except in moments of "unconsciousness,"* for an entire lifetime. It apparently has an infinite capacity.

The numbers of these concepts (*concept* means that which is retained after something has been perceived) would stagger an astronomer's computer. The existence and profusion of memories retained were discovered and studied in a large number of cases, and they can be examined in anyone by certain processes.

Everything in this bank is correct insofar as the single action of perception is concerned. There may be organic errors in the organs of perception, such as blindness or deafness (when physical, not aberrational), which would leave blanks in the banks; and there may

* "Unconscious" throughout this work means a greater or lesser reduction of awareness on the part of "I"–an attenuation of working power of the analytical mind.

be organic impairment, such as partial organic deafness, which would leave partial blanks. But these things are not errors in the standard memory banks; they are simply absence of data. Like the computer, *the standard memory banks are perfect, recording faithfully and reliably.*

Now part of the standard banks is audio-semantic, which is to say, the recordings of words heard. And part of the banks is visio-semantic, which is to say, the recordings of words read. These are special parts of the sound and sight files. A blind man who has to read with his fingers develops a tactile-semantic file. The content of the speech files is exactly as heard without alteration.

Another interesting part of the standard memory banks is that they apparently file the original and hand forward exact copies to the analyzer. They will hand out as many exact copies as are demanded without diminishing the actual file original. And they hand out these copies each in kind with color-motion sight, tone-audio, etc.

The amount of material which is retained in the average standard memory banks would fill several libraries. But the method of retention is invariable. And the *potentiality* of recall is perfect.

The primary source of error in "rational" computation comes under the headings of insufficient data and erroneous data. The individual, daily facing new situations, is not always in possession of all the material he requires to make a decision. And he may have been told something on Good Authority which was not true and yet which did not find counter-evidence in the banks.

Between the standard banks, which are perfect and reliable, and the computer, the analytical mind, which is perfect and reliable, there is no irrational concourse. The answer is always as right as it can be made to be in the light of data at hand, and that is all anyone can ask of a computing device or a recording device.

The analytical mind goes even further in its efforts to be right than one would suppose. It constantly checks and weighs new experience in the light of old experience, forms new conclusions in the light of old conclusions, changes old conclusions and generally is very busy being right.

The analytical mind might be considered to have been given a sacred post of trust by the cells to safeguard the colony, and it does everything within its power to carry out that mission. It has correct data, as correct as possible, and it does correct computations on them, as correct as they can be made. When one considers the enormous number of factors which one handles, for instance, in the action of driving a car ten blocks, he can appreciate how very, very busy on how very many levels that analytical mind can be.

Now before we introduce the villain of this piece, *the reactive mind*, it is necessary to understand something about the relation of the analytical mind to the organism itself.

The analytical mind, charged with full responsibility, is far from without authority to carry out its actions and desires. Through the mechanisms of the life-function regulator (which handles all the mechanical functions of living), the analytical mind can effect any function of the body it desires to effect.

In excellent working order–which is to say, when the organism is not aberrated–the analytical mind can influence the heartbeat, the endocrines (such things as calcium and sugar in the blood, adrenaline, etc.), selective blood flow (stopping it in the limbs or starting it at will), urine, excreta, etc. All glandular, rhythm and fluid functions of the body *can* be at the command of the analytical mind. This is not to say that in a Cleared person they always are. That would be very uncomfortable and bothersome. But it does say that the analytical mind can effect changes at desire when it skills itself to do so. This is a matter of laboratory proof, very easy to do.

People have long been intuitive about the "full power of the mind." Well, the full power of the mind would be the analytical mind working with the standard memory banks, the life-function regulator and one other thing.

The last and most important thing is, of course, the organism. It is in the charge of the analytical mind. And the analytical mind controls it in other ways than life function. All muscles and the remainder of the organism can be under the full command of the analytical mind.

In order to keep it and its circuits free of bric-a-brac and minor activities, the analytical mind is provided with a learned training-pattern regulator. Into this, by education, it can place the stimulus-response patterns necessary for the performance of tasks like talking, walking, piano playing, etc. These learned patterns are not unchangeable. Because they are selected by the analytical mind after thought and effort, there is seldom any need to change them; if new situations arise, a new pattern is trained into the muscles. None of these are "conditionings"; they are simply training patterns which the organism can use without attention of any magnitude from the analyzer. An uncountable number of such patterns can be laid into the organism by this method. And they are not the source of any trouble since they file by time and situation, and a very little thought will serve to annul old ones in favor of new ones.

All muscles, voluntary and "involuntary," can be at the command of the analytical mind.

Here, then, is the composite of a sentient being. There is no chance for error beyond the errors incident to insufficient data and erroneous but accepted data (and the last will be used by the analyzer just once if that once proves the data to be wrong). Here is the realm of pleasure, emotion, creation and construction, and even destruction if the computation on the optimum solution says something has to be destroyed.

The dynamics underlie the activities of the analytical mind. The urge toward survival explains all its actions. That we can understand the fundamental simplicity of the functional mechanism does not, however, mean that a man operating this way alone is cold or calculating or intent on "tooth and claw." The nearer Man approaches this optimum in an individual or in a whole society, the quicker and warmer is that society, the more honest may be its moods and actions.

Sanity depends upon rationality. Here is optimum rationality and therefore optimum sanity. And here also are all the things Man likes to think Man should be like or, for that matter, what he has represented his better gods to be like. This is the *Clear*.

This is sanity. This is happiness. This is survival.

Where is the error?

BOOK TWO, CHAPTER TWO

The Reactive Mind

It is fairly well accepted in these times that life in all forms evolved from the basic building blocks, the virus and the cell. Its only relevance to Dianetics is that such a proposition works–and actually that is all we ask of Dianetics. There is no point to writing here a vast tome on biology and evolution. We can add some chapters to those things, but Charles Darwin did his job well and the fundamental principles of evolution can be found in his and other works.

The proposition on which Dianetics was originally entered was evolution. It was postulated that the cells themselves had the urge to survive and that that urge was common to life. It was further postulated that organisms–individuals–were constructed of cells and were in fact aggregations of colonics of cells.

As went the building block, so went the organism. In the finite realms and for any of our purposes, Man could be considered to be a colonial aggregation of cells and it could be assumed that his purpose was identical with the purpose of his building blocks.

The cell is a unit of life which is seeking to survive and only to survive.

Man is a structure of cells which are seeking to survive and only to survive.

Man's mind is the command post of operation and is constructed to resolve problems and pose problems related to survival and only to survival.

The action of survival, if optimum, would lead to survival.

The optimum survival conduct pattern was formulated and then studied for exceptions, and there were no exceptions found.

The survival conduct pattern was discovered to be far from sterile and barren, but was full of rich and most pleasant activity.

None of these postulates outlawed any concept concerning the human soul or divine or creative imagination. It was understood perfectly that this was a study in the finite universe only and that spheres and realms of thought and action might very well exist above this finite sphere. But it was also discovered that none of these factors were needed to resolve the entire problem of aberration and irrational conduct.

The human mind was discovered to have been most grossly maligned, for it was found to be possessed of capabilities far in excess of any heretofore imagined, much less tested.

Basic human character was found to have been pilloried because Man had not been able to distinguish between irrational conduct derived from poor data and irrational conduct derived from another, far more vicious source.

If there ever was a devil, he designed the reactive mind.

This functional mechanism managed to bury itself from view so thoroughly that only inductive philosophy, traveling from effect back to cause, served to uncover it. The detective work which was invested in the location of this arch criminal of the human psyche occupied many years. Its identity can now be certified by any technician in any clinic or in any group of men. Two hundred and seventy-three individuals have been examined and treated, representing all the various types of inorganic mental illness and the many varieties of psychosomatic ills. In each one, this reactive mind was found operating, its principles unvaried. This is a long series of cases and will soon become longer.

The reactive mind is possessed by everyone. No human being examined anywhere was discovered to be without one or without aberrative content in his *engram bank*, the reservoir of data which serves the reactive mind.

What does this mind do? It shuts off hearing recall. It places vocal circuits in the mind. It makes people tone-deaf. It makes people stutter. It does anything and everything that can be found in any list of mental ills: psychoses, neuroses, compulsions, repressions...

What can it do? It can give a man arthritis, bursitis, asthma, allergies, sinusitis, coronary trouble, high blood pressure, and so on down the whole catalog of psychosomatic ills, adding a few more which were never specifically classified as psychosomatic, such as the common cold.

And it is the only thing in the human being which can produce these effects. It is the thing which uniformly brings them about.

This is the mind which made Socrates think he had a demon that gave him answers. This is the mind that made Caligula appoint his horse to a government post. This is the mind which made Caesar cut the right hands from thousands of Gauls, which made Napoleon reduce the height of Frenchmen one inch.

This is the mind which keeps war a thing of alarm, which makes politics irrational, which makes superior officers snarl, which makes children cry in fear of the dark. This is the mind which makes a man suppress his hopes, which holds his apathies, which gives him irresolution when he should act, and kills him before he has begun to live.

If there ever was a devil, he invented it.

Discharge the content of this mind's bank and the arthritis vanishes, myopia gets better, heart illness decreases, asthma disappears, stomachs function properly, and the whole catalog of ills goes away and stays away.

Discharge the reactive engram bank and the schizophrenic faces reality at last, the manic-depressive sets forth to accomplish things, the neurotic stops clinging to books which tell him how much he needs his neuroses and begins to live, the woman stops snapping at her children and the dipsomaniac can drink when he likes and stop.

These are scientific facts. They compare invariably with observed experience.

The reactive mind is the entire source of aberration. It can be proved and has been repeatedly proven that there is no other, for when that engram bank is discharged, all undesirable symptoms vanish and a man begins to operate on his optimum pattern.

If one were looking for something like demons in a human mind–such as those one observes in some inmates of madhouses–he could find them easily enough. Only they are not demons. They are bypass circuits from the engram bank. What prayers and exhortations have been used against these bypass circuits!

If one did not believe in demons, if one supposed that Man were good after all (as a postulate, of course), how would the evil get into him? What would be the source of these insane rages? What would be the source of his slips of the tongue? How would he come to know irrational fear?

Why is it that one does not like his boss although his boss has always been pleasant?

Why is it that suicides smash their bodies to bits?

Why does Man behave destructively, irrationally, fighting wars, killing, ruining whole sections of Mankind?

What is the source of all neuroses, psychoses, insanities?

Let us return to a brief examination of the analytical mind. Let us examine its memory banks. Here we find all the sense concepts on file. Or so it appears at first glance. Let us take another look, a look at the time factor. There is a time sense about these analytical mind banks. It is very accurate, as though the organism were equipped with a fine watch. But there is something wrong here about time–it has gaps in it! There are moments when nothing seems to be filed in these standard banks. These are gaps which take place during moments of "unconsciousness," that state of being caused by anesthesia, drugs, injury or shock.

This is the only data missing from a standard bank. If in hypnotic trance you examine a patient's memory of an operation, these incidents are the only periods in the banks you will not find. You can find these if you care to look and don't care what happens to your patient–of which more, later. But the point is that there is something missing which has always been considered by one and all in any age never to have been recorded.

One and all in every age have never been able to put a finger on insanity either. Are these two data in agreement and do they have relationship? They definitely do.

There are two things which appear to be–but are not–recorded in the standard banks: *painful emotion* and *physical pain*.

How would you go about the building of a sensitive machine upon which the life and death affairs of an organism depended, which was to be the chief tool of an individual? Would you leave its delicate circuits prey to every overload or would you install a fuse system? If a delicate instrument is in circuit with a power line, it is protected by several sets of fuses. Any computer would be so safeguarded.

It happens that there is some small evidence to support the electrical theory of the nervous system. In pain there are very heavy overcharges in the nerves. It may well have been–and elsewhere some Dianetic computations have been made about this–that the brain is the absorber for overcharges of power resulting from injury, the power itself being generated by the injured cells in the area of injury. That is theory and has no place here save to serve as an example. We are dealing now only with scientific fact.

The action of the analytical mind during a moment of intense pain is suspended. In fact, the analytical mind behaves just as though it were an organ to which vital supply was shut off whenever shock is present.

As an example, a man struck in the side by a car is knocked "unconscious" and on regaining "consciousness" has no record of the period when he was "knocked out." This would be a non-survival circumstance. It means that there would be no volition on the part of anyone who was injured, and this is the time when the organism most requires volition. So this is non-survival if the whole mind cuts out whenever pain appears. Would an organism with more than a billion years of biological engineering behind it leave a problem like this unsolved?

Indeed, the organism solved the problem. Maybe the problem is very difficult, biologically, and maybe the solution is not very good, but large provision has been made for those moments when the organism is "unconscious."

The answer to the problem of making the organism react in moments of "unconsciousness" or near "unconsciousness" is also the answer to insanity and psychosomatic illnesses and all the strange mental quirks to which people are liable and which gave rise to that fable "it is human to err."

Clinical tests prove these statements to be scientific facts:

1. The mind records on some level continuously during the entire life of the organism.
2. All recordings of the lifetime are available.
3. "Unconsciousness," in which the mind is oblivious of its surroundings, is possible only in death and does not exist as total amnesia in life.
4. All mental and physical derangements of a psychic nature come about from moments of "unconsciousness."
5. Such moments can be reached and drained of charge with the result of returning the mind to optimum operating condition.

"Unconsciousness" is the single source of aberration. There is no such action as "mental conditioning" except on a conscious training level, where it exists only with the consent of the person.

If you care to make the experiment, you can take a man, render him "unconscious," hurt him and give him information. By Dianetic technique, no matter what information you gave him, it can be recovered. This experiment should not be carelessly conducted because *you might also render him insane.*

A pale shade of this operation can be obtained by hypnosis, either by its usual techniques or drugs. By installing "positive suggestions" in a subject, he can be made to act like an insane person. This test is not a new one. It has been well known that compulsions or repressions can be so introduced into the psyche. The ancient Greek was quite familiar with it and used it to produce various delusions.

There is what is known as a "post-hypnotic suggestion." An understanding of this can assist an understanding of the basic mechanism of insanity. The actions under both circumstances are not identical, but they are similar enough in their essence.

A man is placed in a hypnotic trance by standard hypnotic technique or some hypnotic drug. The operator then may say to him, "When you awaken, there is something you must do. Whenever I touch my tie, you will remove your coat. When I let go of my tie, you will put on your coat. Now you will forget that I have told you to do this."

The subject is then awakened. He is not consciously aware of the command. If told he had been given an order while "asleep," he would resist the idea or shrug, but he would not know. The operator then touches his tie. The subject may make some remark about its being too warm and so take his coat off. The operator then releases his tie. The subject may remark that he is now cold and will put his coat back on. The operator then touches his tie. The subject may say that his coat has been to the tailor's and with much conversation finally explain why he is taking it off, perhaps to see if the back seam had been sewn properly. The operator then releases his tie and the subject says he is satisfied with the tailor and so replaces his coat. The operator may touch his tie many times and each time receive action on the part of the subject.

At last the subject may become aware, from the expressions on people's faces, that something is wrong. He will not know what is wrong. He will not even know that the touching of the tie is the signal which makes him take off his coat. He will begin to grow uncomfortable. He may find fault with the operator's appearance and begin to criticize his clothing. He still does not know the tie is a signal. He will still react and remain in ignorance that there is some strange reason he must take off his coat–all he knows is that he is uncomfortable with his coat on whenever the tie is touched, uncomfortable with his coat off every time the tie is released.

These various actions are very important to an understanding of the reactive mind. Hypnotism is a laboratory tool. It is not used in Dianetic therapy, but it has served as a means of examining minds and getting their reactions. Hypnotism is a wild variable. A few people can be hypnotized, many cannot be. Hypnotic suggestions will sometimes "take" and sometimes they won't. Sometimes they make persons well and sometimes they make them ill–the same suggestion reacting differently in different people. An engineer knows how to make use of a wild variable. There is something which makes it unpredictable. Finding out the basic reason hypnotism was a variable helped to discover the source of insanity. And understanding the mechanism of the post-hypnotic suggestion can aid an understanding of aberration.

No matter how foolish a suggestion is given to a subject under hypnosis, he will carry it out one way or another. He can be told to remove his shoes or call someone at ten the following day or eat peas for breakfast and he will. These are direct orders and he will comply with them. He can be told that his hats do not fit him and he will believe that they do not. Any suggestion will operate within his mind unbeknown to his higher levels of awareness.

Very complex suggestions can be given. One such would be to the effect that he was unable to utter the word "I". He would omit it from his conversation, using remarkable makeshifts without being "aware" that he was having to avoid the word. Or he could be told that he must never look at his hands and he will not. These are *repressions.* Given to the subject when drugged or in a hypnotic sleep, these suggestions operate when he is awake. And they will continue to operate until released by the hypnotic operator.

He can be told that he has an urge to sneeze every time he hears the word "rug" and that he will sneeze when it is spoken. He can be told that he must jump two feet in the air every time he sees a cat and he will jump. And he will do these things after he has been awakened. These are *compulsions.*

He can be told that he will think very sexual thoughts about a certain girl, but that when he thinks them he will feel his nose itch. He can be told that he has a continual urge to lie down and sleep and that every time he lies down he will feel that he cannot sleep. He will experience these things. These are *neuroses.*

In further experiments he can be told, when he is in his hypnotic "sleep," that he is the president of the country and that the secret service agents are trying to murder him. Or he can be told that he is being fed poison in every restaurant in which he attempts to eat. These are *psychoses.*

He can be informed that he is really another person and that he owns a yacht and answers to the name of "Sir Reginald." Or he can be told that he is a thief, that he has a prison record and that the police are looking for him. These would be *schizophrenic* and *paranoid-schizophrenic* insanities respectively.

The operator can inform the subject that the subject is the most wonderful person on earth and that everybody thinks so. Or that the subject is the object of adoration of all women. This would be a *manic*-type insanity.

He can be convinced, while hypnotized, that when he wakes he will feel so terrible that he will hope for nothing but death. This would be the *depressive*-type insanity.

He can be told that all he can think about is how sick he is and that every malady of which he reads becomes his. This would make him react like a *hypochondriac*.

Thus we could go down the catalog of mental ills and by concocting positive suggestions to create the state of mind, we could bring about, in the awakened subject, a semblance to every insanity.

Understood that these are *semblances*. They are similar to insanity in that the subject would *act* like an insane person. He would not *be* an insane person. The moment the suggestion is relieved–the subject being informed that it was a suggestion–the aberration (and all these insanities, etc., are grouped under the heading of *aberration*) theoretically vanishes.*

The duplication of aberrations of all classes and kinds in subjects who have been hypnotized or drugged has demonstrated that there is some portion of the mind which is not in contact with the consciousness but which contains data.

It was the search for this portion of the mind which led to the resolution of the problem of insanity, psychosomatic ills and other aberrations. It was not

*An injunction here: these are tests. They have been made on people who could be hypnotized and people who could not be, but who were drugged. They brought forth valuable data for Dianetics. They can be duplicated only when you know Dianetics, unless you want to actually drive somebody insane by accident. For these suggestions do not always vanish. Hypnotism is a wild variable. It is *dangerous* and belongs in the parlor in the same way you would want an atom bomb there.

approached through hypnotism and hypnotism is just another tool, a tool which is of no use in the practice of Dianetics and is, indeed, not needed at all.

Here we have an individual who is acting sanely, who is given a positive suggestion and who then temporarily acts insanely. His sanity is restored by the release of the suggestion into his consciousness, at which moment it loses its force upon him. But this is only a semblance of the mechanism involved. The actual insanity, one not laid now by some hypnotist, does not need to emerge into the consciousness to be released. There is this difference and others between hypnotism and the actual source of aberration, but hypnotism is a demonstration of its working parts.

Review the first example of the positive suggestion. The subject was "unconscious," which is to say, he was not in possession of complete awareness or self-determinism. He was given something he must do and the something was hidden from his consciousness. The operator gave him a signal. When the signal occurred, the subject performed an act. The subject gave reasons for the act which were not the real reasons for it. The subject found fault with the operator and the operator's clothing, but did not see that it was the tie which signaled the action. The suggestion was released and the subject no longer felt a compulsion to perform the act.

These are the parts of aberration. Once one knows exactly what parts of what *are* aberrations, the whole problem is very simple. It seems incredible at first glance that the source could have remained so thoroughly hidden for so many thousands of years of research. But at second glance, it becomes a wonder that the source was ever discovered. For it is hidden cunningly and well.

"Unconsciousness" of the non-hypnotic variety is a little more rugged. It takes more than a few passes of the hand to cause "unconsciousness" of the insanity-producing variety.

The shock of accidents, the anesthetics used for operations, the pain of injuries and the deliriums of illness are the principal sources of what we call "unconsciousness."

The mechanism, in our analogue of the mind, is very simple. In comes a destructive wave of physical pain or a pervading poison such as ether and out go some or all of the fuses of the analytical mind. When it goes out, so go what we know as the standard memory banks.

The periods of "unconsciousness" are blanks in the standard memory banks. These missing periods make up what Dianetics calls the *reactive mind bank.*

The times when the analytical mind is in full operation plus the times when the reactive mind is in operation are a continuous line of consecutive recording for the entire period of life.

During the periods when the analytical mind is cut out of circuit, in full or in part, the reactive mind cuts in, in full or in part. In other words, if the analytical mind is unfused so that it is half out of circuit, the reactive mind is half in circuit. No such sharp percentages are actually possible, but this is to give an approximation.

When the individual is "unconscious," in full or in part, the reactive mind is cut in, in full or in part. When he is fully conscious, his analytical mind is fully in command of the organism. When his consciousness is reduced, the reactive mind is cut into the circuit just that much.

The moments which contain "unconsciousness" in the individual are contra-survival moments, by and large. Therefore, it is vital that something take over so that the individual can go through motions to save the whole organism. The fighter who fights half out on his feet, the burned man who drags himself out of the fire – these are cases when the reactive mind is valuable.

The reactive mind is very rugged. It would have to be in order to stand up to the pain waves which knock out other sentience in the body. It is not very refined. But it is most awesomely accurate. It possesses a low order of computing ability, an order which is sub-moron, but one would expect a low order of ability from a mind which stays in circuit when the body is being crushed or fried.

The reactive bank does not store memories as we think of them. It stores *engrams.** These engrams are a complete recording, down to the last accurate detail, of every perception present in a moment of partial or full "unconsciousness." They are just as accurate as any other recording in the body. But they have their own *force.* They are like phonograph records or motion pictures, if these contained all perceptions of sight, sound, smell, taste, organic sensation, etc.

The difference between an engram and a memory, however, is quite distinct. An engram can be permanently fused into any and all body circuits and behaves like an entity.

In all laboratory tests on these engrams, they were found to possess "inexhaustible" sources of power to command the body. No matter how many times one was reactivated in an individual, it was still powerful. Indeed, it became even more able to exert its power in proportion to its reactivation.

The only thing which could even begin to shake these engrams was the technique which developed into

*The word *engram* in Dianetics is used in its severely accurate sense as a "definite and permanent trace left by a stimulus on the protoplasm of a tissue." It is considered as a unit group of stimuli impinged solely on the cellular being.

Dianetic therapy, which will be covered in full in the third section of this volume.

This is an example of an engram: A woman is knocked down by a blow. She is rendered "unconscious." She is kicked and told she is a faker, that she is no good, that she is always changing her mind. A chair is overturned in the process. A faucet is running in the kitchen. A car is passing in the street outside. The engram contains a running record of all these perceptions: sight, sound, tactile, taste, smell, organic sensation, kinetic sense, joint position, thirst record, etc. The engram would consist of the whole statement made to her when she was "unconscious": the voice tones and emotion in the voice, the sound and feel of the original and later blows, the tactile of the floor, the feel and sound of the chair overturning, the organic sensation of the blow, perhaps the taste of blood in her mouth or any other taste present there, the smell of the person attacking her and the smells in the room, the sound of the passing car's motor and tires, etc.

These would all be considered something on the order of a "positive suggestion." But there is something else here which is new, something which is not in the standard banks except by context: *pain* and *painful emotion.*

These things are what make the difference between the standard banks and the reactive engram banks: physical pain and painful emotion. Physical pain and painful emotion are the difference between an engram, which is the cause of aberration, *all* aberration, and a memory.*

We all have heard that bad experience is helpful to living and that without bad experience, Man never learns.

* In Dianetics, a *memory* is considered to be any concept of perceptions stored in the standard memory banks which is potentially recallable by the "I". A scene beheld by the eyes and perceived by the other senses becomes a record in the standard memory banks and later may be recalled by "I" for reference.

This may be very, very true. But it doesn't embrace the engram. That isn't *experience*. That is *commanded action*.

Perhaps before Man had a large vocabulary these engrams were of some use to him. They were survival in ways which will be developed later. But when Man acquired a fine, homonymic (words that sound the same but mean different things) language and, indeed, when he acquired any language, these engrams were much more a liability than a help. And now with Man well evolved, these engrams do not protect him at all, but make him mad, inefficient and ill.

The proof of any assertion lies in its applicability. When these engrams are deleted from the reactive mind bank, rationality and efficiency are enormously heightened, health is greatly increased and the individual computes rationally on the survival conduct pattern, which is to say, he enjoys himself and the society of those around him and is constructive and creative. He is destructive only when something *actually* threatens the sphere of his dynamics.

These engrams, then, are entirely negative in value in this stage of Man's development. When he was nearer the level of his animal cousins (who have, all of them, reactive minds of this same kind), he might have had use for the data. But language and his changed existence make any engram a distinct liability, and no engram has *any* constructive value.

The reactive mind was provided to secure survival. It still pretends to act in that fashion. But its wild errors now lead only in the other direction.

There are actually three kinds of engrams, all of them aberrative. First is the *contra-survival engram*. This contains physical pain, painful emotion, all other perceptions and menace to the organism. A child knocked out by a rapist and abused receives this type of engram.

The contra-survival engram contains apparent or actual antagonism to the organism.

The second engram type is the *pro-survival engram.* A child who has been abused is ill. He is told, while he is partially or wholly "unconscious," that he will be taken care of, that he is dearly loved, etc. This engram is not taken as contra-survival, but pro-survival. It seems to be in favor of survival. Of the two, this last is the most aberrative, since it is reinforced by the law of affinity which is always more powerful than fear. Hypnotism preys on this characteristic of the reactive mind, being a sympathetic address to an artificially unconscious subject. Hypnotism is as limited as it is because it does not contain, as a factor, physical pain and painful emotion: things which keep an engram out of sight and moored below the level of "consciousness."

The third is the *painful emotion engram* which is similar to the other engrams. It is caused by the shock of sudden loss, such as the death of a loved one.

The reactive mind bank is composed exclusively of these engrams. The reactive mind thinks exclusively with these engrams. And it "thinks" with them in a way which would make Korzybski swear, for it thinks in terms of full identification, which is to say *identities*, one thing *identical* to another.

If the analytical mind did a computation on apples and worms, it could be stated, probably, as follows: some apples have worms in them, others don't; when biting an apple one occasionally finds a worm unless the apple has been sprayed properly; worms in apples leave holes.

The reactive mind, however, doing a computation on apples and worms as contained in *its* engram bank, would calculate as follows: apples are worms are bites are holes in apples are holes in anything are apples and always are worms are apples are bites, etc.

The analytical mind's computations might embrace the most staggering summations of calculus, the shifty turns of symbolic logic, the computations requisite to bridge building or dress making. Any mathematical equation ever seen came from the analytical mind and might be used by the analytical mind in resolving the most routine problems.

But not the reactive mind! That's so beautifully, wonderfully simple that it can be stated, in operation, to have just one equation: A = A = A = A = A.

Start any computation with the reactive mind. Start it with the data it contains, of course. Any datum is just the same to it as any other datum in the same experience.

An analytical computation done on the woman being kicked, as mentioned, would be that women get themselves into situations sometimes when they get kicked and hurt and men have been known to kick and hurt women.

A reactive mind computation about this engram, as an engram, would be: the pain of the kick *equals* the pain of the blow *equals* the overturning chair *equals* the passing car *equals* the faucet *equals* the fact that she is a faker *equals* the fact that she is no good *equals* the fact that she changes her mind *equals* the voice tones of the man *equals* the emotion *equals* a faker *equals* a faucet running *equals* the pain of the kick *equals* organic sensation in the area of the kick *equals* the overturning chair *equals* changing one's mind *equals*… But why continue? Every single perception in this engram *equals* every other perception in this engram. What? That's crazy? Precisely!

Let us further examine our post-hypnotic positive suggestion of the touched tie and the removed coat. In this we have the visible factors of how the reactive mind operates.

This post-hypnotic suggestion needs only an emotional charge and physical pain to make it a dangerous engram. Actually, it *is* an engram of a sort. It is laid in by sympathy between the operator and subject, which would make it a sympathy engram: pro-survival.

Now we know that the operator had only to touch his tie to make the awakened subject remove his coat. The subject did not know what it was which caused him to remove his coat and found all manner of explanation for the action, none of which was the right one. The engram, the post-hypnotic suggestion in this case, was actually placed in the reactive mind bank. It was below the level of consciousness; it was compulsion springing from below the level of consciousness. And it worked upon the muscles to make the subject remove his coat. It was data fused into the circuits of the body below the command level of the analytical mind and operated not only upon the body, but also upon the analytical mind itself.

If this subject took off his coat every time he saw somebody touch a necktie, society would account him slightly mad. And yet there was no power of consent about this. If he had attempted to thwart the operator by refusing to remove the coat, the subject would have experienced great discomfort of one sort or another.

Let us now take an example of the reactive mind's processes in a lower echelon of life: A fish swims into the shallows where the water is brackish, yellow, and tastes of iron. He has just taken a mouthful of shrimp when a bigger fish rushes at him and knocks against his tail.

The small fish manages to get away, but he has been physically hurt. Having negligible analytical powers, the small fish depends upon reaction for much of his choice of activity.

Now he heals his tail and goes on about his affairs. But one day he is attacked by a larger fish and gets his tail bumped. This time he is not seriously hurt, merely bumped. But something has happened. Something within him considers that in his choice of action he is now being careless. Here is a second injury in the same area.

The computation on the fish reactive level was: shallows equals brackish equals yellow equals iron taste equals pain in tail equals shrimp in mouth, and any one of these equals any other.

The bump in the tail on the second occasion *keyed-in* the engram. It demonstrated to the organism that something like the first accident (identity-thought) could happen again. Therefore, beware!

The small fish, after this, swims into brackish water. This makes him slightly "nervous." But he goes on swimming and finds himself in yellow and brackish water. And still he does not turn back. He begins to get a small pain in his tail. But he keeps on swimming. Suddenly he gets a taste of iron and the pain in his tail turns on heavily. And away he goes like a flash. No fish was after him. There were shrimp to be had there. But away he went anyway. Dangerous place! And if he had not turned away, he would have really gotten himself a pain in the tail.

The mechanism is survival activity of a sort. In a fish it may serve a purpose. But in a man who takes off a coat every time somebody touches a tie, the survival mechanism has long outlived its time. *But it is there!*

Let us further investigate our young man and the coat. The signal for the coat removal was very precise. The operator touched his tie. This is equivalent to any or all of the perceptions the fish received and which made the fish turn back. The touch of the tie could have been a dozen things. Any one of the dozen might have signaled the removal of the coat.

In the case of the woman who was knocked out and kicked, any perception in the engram she received has some quality of *restimulation.* Running water from a faucet might not have affected her greatly. But water running from a faucet *plus* a passing car might have begun some slight reactivation of the engram, a vague discomfort in the areas where she was struck and kicked, not enough yet to cause her real pain, but there all the same. To the running water and the passing car we add the sharp falling of a chair and she experiences a shock of mild proportion. Add now the smell and voice of the man who kicked her and the pain begins to grow. The mechanism is telling her that she is in dangerous quarters, that she should leave. But she is not a fish; she is a highly sentient being, to our knowledge the most complex mental structure so far evolved on earth, organism of the species, Man. There are many other factors in the problem than this one engram. She stays. The pains in the areas where she was abused become a predisposition to illness or are chronic illness in themselves, minor it is true in the case of this one incident, but illness just the same. Her affinity with the man who beat her may be so high that the analytical level, being assisted by a normally high general tone, may counter against these pains. But if that level is low, without much to assist it, then the pains can become major.

The fish that was so struck and received an engram did not disavow shrimp. Shrimp might have made him a little less enthusiastic afterwards, but the survival potential of shrimp-eating made shrimp equal far more pleasure than it did pain.

A pleasant and hopeful life in general – and never think we intimate that the woman stays for food alone whatever the wits say about women–has a high survival potential, and that can overcome a very great deal of pain. As the survival potential diminishes, however, the level of pain (Zone 0 and Zone 1) is more closely approached and such an engram could begin to be reactivated severely.

There is another factor here, however, besides pain–in fact, several more factors. If the young man with the detachable coat had been given one of the *neurotic* positive suggestions, as listed a few pages back, he would have reacted to it on signal.

The engram this woman has received contains a neurotic positive suggestion quite in addition to the general *restimulators* such as the faucet and the car and the overturning chair. She has been told that she is a faker, that she is no good, and that she is always changing her mind. When the engram is restimulated in one of the great many ways possible, she has a "feeling" that she is no good, a faker, and she *will* change her mind.

There are several cases to hand which peculiarly illustrate the sadness of this. One case in particular, which was Cleared, had been beaten severely many times and told a similar thing each time, all derogatory. The content inferred that she was very loose morally and would cohabit with anyone. She was brought in as a case by her father–she had since been divorced–who complained that she was very loose morally and had cohabited with several men in as many weeks. She herself admitted that she was, she could not see how it could be and it worried her, but she just "could not seem to help it." Examination of the engrams in her reactive mind bank brought forth a long series of beatings with this content. Because this was a matter of research, not treatment–although that was given–her former husband was contacted. An examination, independent of her knowledge, demonstrated his rage dramatization to contain these very words. *He had beaten his wife into being a morally loose woman because he was afraid of morally loose women.*

All cases examined in all this research were checked, the patient's engrams against the engrams in the donor. The contents of the incidents were verified wherever possible and were found uniformly to agree. Every safeguard was made to prevent any other method of communication between donor and patient. *Everything found in the "unconscious" periods of every patient, when checked against other sources, was found to be exact.*

The analogy between hypnotism and aberration bears out well. Hypnotism plants, by positive suggestion, one or another form of insanity. It is usually a temporary planting, but sometimes the hypnotic suggestion will not "lift" or remove in a way desirable to the hypnotist. The danger of running experiments with hypnosis on uncleared patients is found in another mechanism of the reactive mind.

When an engram such as our example above exists, the woman obviously was "unconscious" at the time she received the engram. She had no standard bank memory (record) of the incident beyond the knowledge that she had been knocked out by the man. The engram was not, then, an experience as we understand the word. It could work from below to aberrate her thinking processes, it could give her strange pains – which she attributed to something else – in the areas injured. But it was not *known* to her.

The *key-in* was necessary to activate the engram. But what precisely could key it in? At some later time, when she was tired, the man threatened to strike her again and called her names. This was conscious-level experience. It was found to be "mentally painful" by her. And it was "mentally painful" only because there was real, live, physical pain unseen under it, which had been "keyed-in" by the conscious experience. The second experience was a *lock*. It was a memory, but it had a new kind of action in the standard banks. It had too much power and it gained that power from a past physical blow. The reactive mind is not too careful about its time clock. It can't tell one year old from ninety, in fact, when a key-in begins. The actual engram moved up under the standard bank.

She thinks she is worried about what he said in the *lock* experience. She is actually worried about the engram. In this way memories become "painful." But pain doesn't store in the standard banks. There is no place in that bank *for* pain. None. There is a place for the concept of pain and these concepts of what is painful are good enough to keep the sentient organism called Man away from all the pain he believes is actually dangerous. In a Clear there *are* no pain-inducing memories because there is no physical pain record left to ruin the machinery from the reactive mind bank.

The young man with the detachable coat did not know what was worrying him or what made him do what he did. The person with an engram does not know what is worrying him. He thinks it is the *lock* and the *lock* may be a very long way removed from anything resembling the engram. The lock may have similar perceptic content. But it may be on another subject entirely.

It is not very complicated to understand what these engrams do. They are simply moments of physical pain strong enough to throw part or all the analytical machinery out of circuit; they are antagonism to the survival of the organism or pretended sympathy to the organism's survival. That is the entire definition. Great or little "unconsciousness," physical pain, perceptic content and contra-survival or pro-survival data. They are handled by the reactive mind, which thinks exclusively in identities of everything equals everything. And they enforce their commands upon the organism by wielding the whip of physical pain. If the organism does not do exactly as they say (and believe any Clear, that's impossible!), the physical pain turns on. They steer a person like a keeper steers a tiger–and they can make a tiger out of a man in the process, without much trouble, and give him mange into the bargain.

If Man had not invented language or, as will be demonstrated, if his languages were a little less homonymic and more specific with their personal pronouns, engrams would still be survival data and the mechanism would work. But Man has outgrown their use. He chose between language and potential madness and for the vast benefits of the former, he received the curse of the latter.

The engram is the single and sole source of aberration and psychosomatic illness.

An enormous quantity of data has been sifted. Not one single exception has been found. In "normal people," in the neurotic and insane, the removal of these engrams wholly or in part, without other therapy, has uniformly brought about a state greatly superior to the current norm. No need was found for any theory or therapy other than those given in this book for the treatment of all psychic or psychosomatic ills.

BOOK TWO, CHAPTER THREE

The CELL *and* *the* ORGANISM

THE REASON THE ENGRAM so long remained hidden as the single source of aberration and psychosomatic ills is the wide and almost infinitely complex manifestations which can derive from simple engrams.

Several theories could be postulated as to why the human mind evolved exactly as it did, but these are theories and Dianetics is not concerned with structure. A comment or two as a stimulation to future workers in that field might be made, however, wholly as a postulate, that there is a definite connection between any electric-like energy in the body and the energy effusion of cells undergoing injury. A theory could be constructed along the lines that injured cells, further injuring their neighbors by a discharge of electric-like energy, forced the development of a special cell which would act as a conduit to "bleed off" this painful charge. The conduits of cells might have become neurons and the charge might have been better distributed so through the body with less likelihood of local incapacitation at the point of the injury impact. These conduits–neurons–might have been started in formation by impacts at the extremity of the body toward the direction of locomotion. This would make the skull the greatest mass of neurons. Man, walking upright, might have had another new point of impact, the forehead, and so gained his prefrontal lobes. And maybe not. That is just theory, with only a few data to support it which have a scientific value. And it has not been subjected to experiment of any kind whatever.

This much, however, has to be advanced as theory on structure. The cell is one of the basic building blocks of the body. Cells, the better to survive, seem to have become colonies which, in turn, had the primary interest: survival. And the colonies developed or recruited into aggregations which, in turn, were organisms, also with the sole purpose of survival. And the organisms developed minds to coordinate the muscles and resolve the problems of survival. Again, this is still theory and even if it was the track of reasoning which led toward Dianetics, it can be completely wrong. It works. It can be pulled away from Dianetics and Dianetics will remain a science and go on working. The concept of the electronic brain was not vital but only useful to Dianetics and it could be swept away as well–Dianetics would still stand. A science is a changing affair as far as its internal theory goes. In Dianetics, we have our wedge into an enormous scope of research. As Dianetics stands, it works and it works every time and without exception. The reasons why it works will undoubtedly be mulled over and changed here and there to its betterment–if they aren't, an abiding faith in this generation of scientists and the future generations will not have been justified.

Why we talk about cells will become apparent as we progress. The reason we know that past concepts of structure are not correct is because they *don't* work as function. All our facts are functional and these facts are scientific facts, supported wholly and completely by laboratory evidence. Function precedes structure. James Clerk Maxwell's mathematics were postulated and electricity was widely and beneficially used long before anyone had any real idea about the structure of the atom. Function always comes before structure. The astounding lack of progress in the field of the human mind during the past thousands of years is partly attributable to its "organ of thought" lying within a field, medicine, which was and long may be an art, not a science. Basic philosophy to explain life will have to come before that art makes much further progress.

What the capabilities of the cell are, for instance, have been but poorly studied. Some work has been carried on in recent years to find out more, but basic philosophy was absent. The cell was being observed, not predicted.

The studies of cells in Man have been largely done from dead tissue. An unknown quality is missing from dead tissue, the important quality: life.

In Dianetics, on the level of laboratory observation, we discover much to our astonishment that cells are evidently sentient in some currently inexplicable way. Unless we postulate a human soul entering the sperm and ovum at conception, there are things which no other postulate will embrace than that these cells *are* in some way sentient. Entering a new field with postulates which work in all directions–and the basic philosophy of survival is a pilot which leads us on and on into further and further realms, explaining and predicting phenomena on every hand–it is inevitable that data will turn up which does not agree with past theory. When that data is as scientific as the observation that when an apple is dropped under usual conditions on earth, it falls, one cannot help but accept it. Abandoning past theories may do damage to treasured beliefs and one's nostalgic love of the old school tie, but a fact is a fact.

The cells as thought units evidently have an influence, as cells, upon the body as a thought unit and an organism. We do not have to untangle this structural problem to resolve our functional postulates. The cells evidently retain engrams of painful events. After all, they are the things which get injured. And they evidently retain a whip hand of punishment for every time the analyzer fails them. The story of the engram seems to be a story of a battle between the troops and the general every time the general gets some of the troops killed off. The less fortunate this general is in protecting these troops, the more power the troops assume. The cells evidently pushed the brain on an upward evolution toward higher sentience. Pain reverses the process as though the cells were sorry they had put so much power in the hands of a central commander.

The reactive mind may very well be the combined cellular intelligence. One need not assume that it is, but it is a handy structural theory in the lack of any real work done in this field of structure. The reactive engram bank may be material stored in the cells themselves. It does not matter whether this is credible or incredible just now. Something has to be said about it to give one a mental hold on what happens during moments of "unconsciousness."

The scientific fact, observed and tested, is that the organism, in the presence of physical pain, lets the analyzer get knocked out of circuit so that there is a limited quantity or no quantity at all of personal awareness as a unit organism. It does this either to protect the analyzer or to withdraw its power in the belief that an engram is best in an emergency–with which the analyzer, by the way, on observed experience, does not agree.

Every percept present, including physical pain, is recorded during these non-analytical moments.

Whenever pain is present–physical pain, that is–the analyzer gets shut down to a small or large extent. If the duration of the pain is only an instant, there is still an instant there of analytical reduction. This can be proven very easily: just try to recall the last time you were seriously hurt and see if there isn't at least a momentary blank period. Going to sleep under anesthetic and waking up some time later is a more complicated sort of shutdown in that it includes physical pain, but is initially caused by a poison (and all anesthetics are poisons, technically). Then there is the condition of suffocating, as in drowning, and this is a shut-down period to greater or lesser extent. And there is the condition caused by blood, for one cause or another, leaving the area or areas which contain analytical power–wherever they are–and this again causes a greater or lesser degree of analytical shutdown: such incidents include shock (in which the blood tends to lake in the center of the body); the loss of blood by surgery or injury or anemia and the closing of the arteries leading through the throat. Natural sleep causes a reduction of analytical activity, but is actually not very deep or serious. By Dianetic therapy, any experience occurring during sleep can be recovered with ease.

It can now be seen that there are many ways in which analytical power can be shut down. And it can be seen that there is greater or lesser reduction. When one burns one's finger with a cigarette, there is a small instant of pain and a small amount of reduction. When one undergoes an operation, the duration may be in terms of hours and the amount of shutdown may be extreme. The duration and the amount of reduction are two different things, related but quite dissimilar. This is not so very important, but it is mentioned.

We have seen, reading in Dianetics this far, that the principle of the "spectrum" has been quite useful to us. And it can be seen that the amount of reduction in analytical power can be described in the same way that survival potential can be described. There can be a very little bit and there can be a very great deal. Going back and taking a look at the survival-potential range, one can see that there would be death at the bottom and immortality at the top. There is "infinite" survival. Whether or not there can be infinite analytical power is a matter of mysticism. But that there is a definite relationship between individual tone and the amount of analytical shutdown is a scientific fact. Put it this way: with the individual well and happy and enthusiastic, analytical power can be considered to be high (Zones 3 and 4). With the individual under the wheels of a truck, "unconscious" and in agony, the analytical power may be considered to be ranging in Zone 0. There is a ratio between potential survival and analytical power. As one goes down, so does the other. There is more data to be concluded from this than one would think at first glance. It is a very important ratio.

All the percepts are included in an engram. Two of these percepts are physical pain and painful emotion. A third is organic sensation, which is to say, the condition of the organism during the moment of the engram. And how was the organism when the engram was received? Greater or lesser "unconsciousness" was present. This meant that there was an organic sensation of reduced analytical power, since analytical power derives, evidently, from an organ or organs in the body. If an engram is reactivated by a restimulator or restimulators – that is to say, if the individual with an engram receives something in his environment similar to the perceptions in the engram – the engram puts everything it contains (its percepts such as faucets and words) into greater or lesser operation.

There can be greater or lesser restimulation. An engram can be put into force just a little bit by restimulators in the environment of the individual or, with many restimulators present and the body in an already reduced state, the engram can go into a full-force display (which is covered later). But whether the engram is slightly restimulated or greatly restimulated, everything in it goes into effect one way or another.

There is just one common denominator of all engrams, just one thing which every engram has and which is possessed by every other engram. Each contains the datum that *the analyzer is more or less shut down.* There is a shut-down datum in every engram. Therefore, every time an engram is restimulated, *even though physical pain has not been received by the body*, some analytical power turns off, the organ or organs which are the analyzer are fused out of circuit in some degree.

This is highly important to an understanding of the mechanics of aberration. It is a scientific fact, susceptible of proof, and it never varies. This always happens: when an engram is received, the analyzer is shut down by the physical pain and emotion; when the engram is restimulated, the analyzer shuts down as part of the commands of the engram. Actually, this is a very mechanical thing: engram is restimulated, part of the analytical power is shut down. This is as inevitable as turning on and off an electric light. Pull the cord and the light goes off. The reduction of the analyzer is not that sharp–there are grades of light–but it is just as mechanical.

Put a man under ether, hurt him in the chest. He has received an engram because his analytical power was turned off first by ether and then by a chest pain. While he was there on the operating table, the reactive mind recorded the click of instruments, everything said, all sounds and smells. Let us suppose that a nurse was holding one of his feet because he was kicking. This is a complete engram.

The engram will be keyed-in by something in the future, a similar incident. After this, in greater or lesser degree, whenever he hears clicks like instrument clicks, he gets nervous. If he pays attention to what is happening in his body at that minute, he may find that his foot feels slightly as if it were being held. But he is not likely to give any attention to his foot because if he had any attention to give, the chest pain would be found present in some degree. But his analytical ability has been turned off slightly. As the foot felt it was being held, so does the analyzer have the conception of being shut down by ether and pain. The restimulator (the clicking) tended to bring the whole engram slightly into being and part of the engram command is a reduced analytical power.

This is "push-button" in its precision. If one knew another's main restimulators (words, voice tones, music, whatever they are – things which are filed in the reactive mind bank as parts of engrams), one could turn another's analytical power almost completely off, actually render him unconscious.

We all know people who make us feel stupid. There can be two causes for that, but both of them are from engrams, and one of them is the fact that no matter what engram is brought into restimulation, part of the analytical power is turned off.

Engrams can, if environment is uniform, be held in chronic restimulation! This means a chronic partial shutdown of analytical power. The recovery of intelligence by a Clear and the rise of that intelligence to such fantastic heights results in part from the relief of word commands in engrams that he is stupid and in a larger part from the relief of this chronic shut-down condition.

This is not theory. This is scientific fact. It is strictly test tube. The engram contains the percept of a shut-down analyzer; when it is restimulated, the engram puts that datum back into force in some degree.

Engrams, then, being received in "unconsciousness" cause a partial "unconsciousness" to exist every time they are restimulated. The person who has an engram (any aberree) need not receive new physical pain to have a new moment of partial "unconsciousness" take place. Feeling "dopey" or "sleepy" or "dull" results in part from a partially shut-down analyzer. Being "nervous" or in a rage or frightened also carries with it partially shut-off analytical power.

The hypnotist has "success" where he does because he is able, by talking to people about "sleep," to put into restimulation some engram which contains the word *sleep* and shut-down analytical power. This is one of the reasons hypnotism "works."

The whole society, however, is liable to analytical shutdown in greater or lesser degree by the restimulation of engrams.

The number of engrams a person's reactive bank contains may not, however, establish the amount of analytical reduction to which he is subjected. A person may have engrams and they may not have been keyed-in. And if they have been keyed-in, he might not be in an environment which contains any great number of restimulators. Under these conditions, his survival zone position may be high even though he is possessed of a great many engrams. And again, he might have educated himself over and above these engrams to some slight degree.

But a person who has keyed-in engrams and does exist in the area of many restimulators is liable to an enormous amount of restimulation and analytical shutdown. This is a normal condition. If a person has a large number of engrams and they are keyed-in and he lives around many restimulators, his condition can vary from normal to insane. And in a single day–as in the case of a man who experiences moments of rage or a woman who drops into apathies–the condition of a person may vary from normal to insane and back to normal. We take here the word "insane" to mean utter irrationality. So there is temporary or chronic insanity.

The court of law which goes through the lugubrious process of having a man pronounced sane or insane after that man has murdered somebody is itself being irrational. Of course the man was insane *when* he committed the murder. What the court is asking now is whether or not the man is *chronically* insane. This has little bearing on the matter. If a man has gone insane enough to murder once, he will go insane enough in the future to murder again. Chronic, then, means either a chronic cycle or a continuous condition. The law says sanity is the "ability to tell right from wrong." When Man is subject to a mechanism (and all men are) which lets him be rational one minute and restimulated the next, none in the society, if uncleared, can be considered able to always tell right from wrong. This is completely aside from what the law means by "right" and what it means by "wrong."

This is an example of the roller-coaster sanity curve of the aberree. All aberrees possess engrams (the normal number is probably in the hundreds per individual). Analytically, people have a wide latitude of choice and they can deal even with philosophic rights and wrongs. But in aberrated persons the engram bank is always susceptible of restimulation. The "sanest" aberree of

Tuesday may be a murderer on Wednesday if the exactly right situation occurs to trip the exact engram. A Clear is not entirely predictable in any given situation–he has such a wide power of choice. But an aberrated person transcends all predictability for the following reasons:

1. What engrams an aberree has in his reactive engram bank none know, including himself.
2. What situation will contain what restimulators is a matter of chance.
3. What his power of choice will be with the factors in the engrams on a reactive level cannot be established.

The variety of conduct which one can evolve out of these basic mechanics is so wide that it is no wonder that Man was considered to be a rather hopeless case by some philosophies.

The cells, if the engram bank is retained on a cellular level, might be theoretically supposed to have made sure that the analyzer did not get too adventurous in this life-and-death matter of living. They therefore could be considered to have copied down all data contained in every moment of physical pain and emotion resulting in or contained in "unconsciousness." Then when any data similar to this appeared in the environment, they could be wary. And with a large number of restimulators in sight, they could be considered to shut down the analyzer and proceed on reaction. This has a crude safety factor. Obviously, if the organism survived through one period of "unconsciousness," it could be theorized by the cells that the placing of the data and action in effect under circumstances which threatened to be similar would result once more in survival. What's good enough for Grandpa is good enough for me. What was good enough in the bus accident is good enough in a bus.

This moronic "thinking" is typical of the reactive mind. It is just the sort of thinking it does. It is the ultimate in conservatism. It misses the point and important data at every turn, it overloads the body with pain, it is a whirlpool of confusion. If there were just one engram per situation, maybe it would get by. But there may be ten engrams with similar data in them (an *engram lock chain*) and yet the data may be so contradictory that when a new emergency arises which contains the restimulators of the chain, no proper past conduct can be put forth to meet it.

Obviously the *x* factor is language. The cells, if this is a problem in cells (for recall, this part is theory based on data in an effort to explain what happens and a theory can be altered without altering the scientific usefulness of the facts), probably do not understand languages very well. If they did, they wouldn't evolve such "solutions."

Take two engrams about baseball bats. In the first, the individual is hit on the head and knocked out and somebody yells, "Run! Run! Run!" In the second, the individual is knocked out by the bat in the same environment and somebody yells, "Stay there! You're safe!" Now what does he do when he hears a baseball bat or smells one or sees one or hears these words? Run or stay there? He has a similar pain for each action. What actually happens? He gets a headache. This is that thing called conflict. This is anxiety. And anxiety can become very acute indeed, on a purely mechanical level, when one has ninety engrams pulling him south and eighty-nine pulling him north. Does he go north or south? Or does he have a "nervous breakdown"?

The level of brilliance of the reactive mind is about the same as a phonograph. The needle gets put on the record and the record plays. The reactive mind merely puts on the needle. When it tries to select several records out and play them all at once, things happen.

By intentional construction or accident in design or bypass in evolution–where the old, useless organ is still built–the cells managed to hide this engram bank fairly well. Man is conscious in his analytical mind. When he is "unconscious," his analytical mind is unable to monitor the incoming data and the data is not to be found in the thing we call, by analogue, the standard banks. Therefore, whatever came in passed by consciousness. And having passed by, consciousness cannot (without Dianetic process) recall it, since there is no channel for recall.

The engram enters when consciousness is absent. It thereafter operates directly into the organism. Only by Dianetic therapy can the analyzer come into possession of this data. (And the removal of it does not depend upon the analyzer contacting it at all, despite an old belief that the "realization" of something cures it: "realize" an engram and one is in quick trouble without Dianetic technique.) The engram is received by the cellular body. The reactive mind could be the very lowest level of analytical power, of course, but this does not alter the scientific fact that the engram acts as if it were a soldered-in connection to the life-function regulator and the organic coordination and the basic level of the analytical mind itself. By "soldered-in" is meant "permanent connection." This keying-in is the hook-up of the engram as part of the operating machinery of the body. An analytical thought process is not permanently hooked in, but can be thrown in and out of circuit at the will of the analyzer. This is not true of the engram. Thus the term, "soldered-in."

The analytical mind lays down a training pattern; on a stimulus-response basis, this training pattern will work smoothly and well whenever it will do the organism the most good. An engram is a training pattern, all complete in a package, "permanently" hooked into the circuits (without Dianetic therapy) and it goes into operation like a training pattern without any consent whatever from the analyzer.

Influenced itself by the engram in the several ways of reduced analytical power and positive suggestion in the engram, the analytical mind is unable to discover any truly valid reason for the conduct of the organism. It therefore makes up a reason, for its job is to make sure the organism is always right. Just as the young man with the detachable coat gave forth a number of silly explanations as to why he was detaching his coat, so does the analytical mind, observing the body engaged in irrational actions, including speech, for which there seems to be no accounting, justify the actions. The engram can dictate all the various processes incident to living; it can dictate beliefs, opinions, thought processes or lack of them and actions of all kinds, and can establish conditions remarkable for their complexity as well as their stupidity. An engram can dictate anything it contains and engrams can contain all the combinations of words in the entire language. And the analytical mind is forced, in the light of irrational behavior or conviction, to *justify* the acts and conditions of the organism, as well as its own strange blunders. This is *justified thought.*

There are three kinds of thought, then, of which the organism is capable:

1. Analytical thought, which is rational as modified by education and viewpoint.
2. Justified thought, analytical thought attempting to explain reactions.
3. Reactive thought, which is wholly in terms of everything in an engram equals everything in an engram equals all the restimulators in the environment and all things associated with those restimulators.

We have all seen somebody make a blunder and then give forth an explanation of just why that blunder had been made. This is justified thought. The blunder was made, unless out of education or viewpoint, by an engram. The analytical mind then had to justify the blunder to make sure that the body was right and that its computations were right.

Now there are two other conditions which can be caused by engrams. One is *dramatization* and the other is *valence*.

You have seen some child come forth with a tirade, a tantrum. You have seen some man go through a whole rage action. You have seen people go through a whole irrational set of actions. These are *dramatizations*. They come about when an engram is thoroughly restimulated, so thoroughly that its soldered-in aspect takes over the organism. It may come into circuit slightly or wholly, which is to say that there are degrees of dramatization. When it is in full parade, the engram is running off verbatim and the individual is like an actor, puppet-like, playing his dictated part. A person can be given new engrams which will make these old ones take secondary importance. (Society's punishment complex is aimed squarely at giving anti-engram education.)

Dramatization is survival conduct–in the silly, reactive mind way of thinking–based on the premise that the organism, in a "similar" situation, lived through it because these actions were present.

The woman who was knocked down and kicked would dramatize her engram, possibly, by doing and saying exactly the same things done and said to her. Her victim may be her child or another woman. It could or would be the person who gave her the engram if she were strong enough to overcome him. Just because she has this engram does not mean she will use it. She may have a hundred other engrams she can use. But when she dramatizes one, it is as if the engram, soldered-in, were taking over a puppet. As much analytical power as she has left may be devoted to altering the pattern. Therefore, she can make a similar or an identical dramatization.

This aspect of dramatization is strictly "tooth and claw" survival. This is the sort of thing which made observers think that "tooth and claw" was a primary rule.

In went the engram, bypassing rationality and the standard memory banks. Now it is in the organism, but the organism does not know it in the level of consciousness. It is keyed-in by a conscious-level experience. Then it can be dramatized. And far from becoming milder the more it is used, the more an engram is dramatized the more solid is its hold in the circuits. Muscles, nerves, all must comply.

"Tooth and claw" survival. The cells were making sure. And here we come to *valence*. *Valens* means "powerful" in Latin. It is a good term because it is the second half of ambivalent (power in two directions) and exists in any good dictionary. It is a good term because it describes (although the dictionary did not mean it to) the intent of the organism when dramatizing an engram. *Multivalence* would mean "many powerfuls." It would embrace the phenomena of split personality, the strange differences of personality in people in one and then another situation. *Valence in Dianetics means the personality of one of the dramatic personnel in an engram.*

In the case of the woman being knocked out and kicked, there were two valences present: herself and her husband. If another person had been present, the engram would have contained three valences, providing he took any part: herself, her husband and the third person. In an engram, let us say, of a bus accident where ten people speak or act, there would be, in the "unconscious" person, an engram containing eleven valences: the "unconscious" person and the ten who spoke or acted.

Now in the case of the woman beaten by her husband, the engram contains just two valences. Who won? Here is the law of "tooth and claw," the aspect of survival in engrams. Who won? The husband. Therefore, it is the husband who will be dramatized. She didn't win. She got hurt. Aha! When these restimulators are present, the thing to do is to be the winner, the husband, to talk like him, to say what he did, to do what he did. He survived. "Be like him!" say the cells.

Hence, when the woman is restimulated into this engram by some action, let us say, on the part of her child, she dramatizes the winning valence. She knocks the child down and kicks him, tells him he is a faker, that he is no good, that he is always changing his mind.

What would happen if she dramatized herself? She would have to fall down, knocking over a chair, pass out and believe she was a faker, no good and was always changing her mind and she would have to feel the pain of all blows!

"Be yourself" is advice which falls on deaf reactive-mind ears. Here is the scheme. Every time the organism gets punished by life, the analytical mind, according to the reactive mind, has erred. The reactive mind then cuts the analytical mind out of circuit in ratio to the amount of restimulation present (danger) and makes the body react as if it were the person who won in the earlier but similar situation where the organism was hurt.

Now what happens if "society" or the husband or some exterior force told this woman, who is dramatizing this engram, that she must face reality? That's impossible. Reality equals being herself, and herself gets hurt. What if some exterior force *breaks the dramatization?* That is to say, if society objects to the dramatization and refuses to let her kick and yell and shout? The engram is still soldered-in. The reactive mind is forcing her to be the winning valence. Now she can't be. As punishment, the reactive mind, the closer she slides in to being herself, approximates the conditions of the other valence in the engram. After all, that valence didn't die. And the pain of the blows turns on and she thinks she is a faker, that she is no good and that she always changes her mind. In other words, she is in the losing valence. Consistent *breaking of dramatization* will make a person ill just as certainly as there are gloomy days.

A person accumulates, with the engrams, half a hundred valences before he is ten. Which were the winning valences? You will find him using them every time an engram is kicked into restimulation. Multiple personality? Two persons? Make it fifty to a hundred. In Dianetics you can see valences turn on and off in people and change with a rapidity which would be awesome to a quick-change artist.

Observe these complexities of conduct, of behavior. If one set out to resolve the problem of aberration by a system of cataloging everything he observed and were unaware of the basic source, he would end up with as many separate insanities, neuroses, psychoses, compulsions, repressions, obsessions and disabilities as there are combinations of words in the English language. Discovery of fundamentals by classification is never good research. And the unlimited complexities possible from the engrams (and the severest, most thoroughly controlled experiments discovered these engrams to be capable of just such behavior as is listed here) are the whole catalog of aberrated human conduct.

There are a few other basic, fundamental things that engrams do. These will be covered under their own headings: parasite circuits, emotional impaction and psychosomatic ills. With the few fundamentals listed here, the problem of aberration can be resolved. These fundamentals are simple, they have given rise to as much trouble as individuals and societies have experienced. The institutions for the insane, the prisons for the criminals, the armaments accumulated by nations, yes, and even the dust which was a civilization of yesterday exist because these fundamentals were not understood.

The cells evolved into an organism and in the evolution created what was once a necessary condition of mind. Man has grown up to a point where he creates now the means of overcoming that evolutionary blunder. Examination of the Clear proves he no longer needs it. He is now in a position where he can take an artificial evolutionary step on his own. The bridge has been built across the canyon.

BOOK TWO, CHAPTER FOUR

The "DEMONS"

FOR A MOMENT let us leave such scientific things as cells and consider some further aspects of the problem of understanding the human mind.

People have been working on problems related to Man's behavior for a good many millennia. Hindu, Egyptian, Greek, Roman and our own philosophers and researchers of the past few hundred years have been struggling against a superabundance of complexity.

Dianetics could be evolved only by the philosophic compartmentation of the problem into its elements and the invention of several dozen yardsticks such as The Introduction of an Arbitrary, The Law of Affinity, The Dynamic, The Equation of the Optimum Solution, The Laws of the Selection of Importances, The Science of Organizing Sciences, Nullification by Comparison of Authority to Authority and so forth and so forth. All this is fine matter for a tome on philosophy, but here is Dianetics which is a science. It should be mentioned, however, that one of the first steps taken was not invented, but borrowed and modified: that was the Knowable and Unknowable of Herbert Spencer.

Absolutism is a fine road to stagnation and I do not think Spencer meant to be so entirely absolute about his Knowable and Unknowable. Survive! is the demarcation point between those things which can be experienced by the senses (our old friends Hume and Locke) and those things which cannot necessarily be known through the senses, but which possibly may be known, but which one does not necessarily need to solve the problem.

Among those things which one did not necessarily need to know (the Dianetic version of the Unknowable) were the realms of mysticism and metaphysics. Many things, in the evolution of Dianetics, were bypassed solely because they had not yielded solution to anyone else. Therefore mysticism got short shrift despite the fact that the author studied it, not in the little understood, second-hand sources commonly used as authority by some Western mental cults, but in Asia where a mystic who can't make his "astral self" get out and run errands for him is strictly a second-rate character indeed. Well aware that there were pieces in this jigsaw puzzle which were orange with yellow spots and purple with carmine stripes, one found it necessary to pick up only those pieces which were germane. Someday a large number of pieces–about structure with the rest–will come in and there will be answers to telepathy, prescience and so on and on. Understand that there are a lot of pieces in the construction of a philosophic universe. But none of the mystic pieces were found necessary to the creation of a uniformly applicable and aberration-resolving science of mind. No opinion will be delivered at this stage of Dianetics about ghosts or the Indian rope trick beyond the fact they are seen to be multicolored pieces and the only ones we want are white. We have most of the white pieces and it makes a good, solid whiteness where there was blackness before.

Imagine, then, the consternation one must have felt when "demons" were discovered. Socrates had a demon, you'll remember. It told him not what to do, but whether or not he had made the right decision. Here we had been pursuing a course in the finite universe which would have pleased Hume himself for its tenacity to those things which could be sensed. And up popped "demons."

A thorough examination of a number of subjects (14) revealed that every one apparently had a "demon" of some sort. They were randomly selected subjects in various conditions in society. Therefore, the "demon" aspect was most alarming. However, unlike some of the cults (or schools as they call themselves), the temptation to sail off into romantic inexplicable and confounding labels was resisted. A bridge had to be built across a canyon and demons are darned bad girders.

Out in the Pacific Islands – Borneo, the Philippines – I had seen quite a bit of demonology at work. Demonology is fascinating stuff. A demon gets into a person and makes him sick. Or it gets in and talks in lieu of him. Or he goes crazy because he has a demon in him and runs around with the demon shouting. This is demonology in a narrow sense. The shaman, the medicine man, these people deal pretty heavily in demonology (it pays well). But, while not skeptical particularly, it had always seemed to me that demons could be explained a little more easily than in terms of ectoplasm or some such unsensible material.

To find "demons" living in one's civilized fellow countrymen was disturbing. But there they were. At least there were the manifestations which the shaman and medicine man had said were caused by demons. It was found that these "demons" could be cataloged. There were "commanding demons," "critical demons," ordinary "tell-you-what-to-say demons" and "demons" which stood around and yelled or "demons" which simply occluded things and kept them out of sight. These are not all the classes, but they cover the general field of "demonology."

A few experiments with drugged subjects showed that it was possible to set these "demons" up at will. It was even possible to set up the whole analytical mind as a "demon." So there was something wrong with demonology. Without proper ritual, simply by word of mouth, one could make new demons appear in people. *So there are no real demons in Dianetics.* (That's underscored in case some mystic runs around telling people that a new science of mind believes in demons.)

A Dianetic demon is a parasitic circuit. It has an action in the mind which approximates another entity than self. And it is derived entirely from words contained in engrams.

How this demon gets there is not very hard to understand, once you've inspected one close up. Papa, while baby is unconscious, yells at Mama that she's got to listen to him and nobody else, by God. The baby gets an engram. It is keyed-in sometime between babyhood and death. And then, there's the demon circuit at work.

An electronics engineer can set up demons in a radio circuit to his heart's content. In human terms it is as if one ran a line from the standard banks toward the analyzer, but before it got there he put in a speaker and a microphone and then continued the line to the plane of consciousness. Between the speaker and the microphone would be a section of the analyzer which was an ordinary, working section, but compartmented off from the remainder of the analyzer. "I" on a conscious plane wants data. It should come straight from the standard bank, compute on a sub-level and arrive just as data. Not spoken data. Just data.

With the portion of the analyzer compartmented off and the speaker-microphone installation and the engram containing the above words "got to listen to me, by God" in chronic restimulation, another thing happens. The "I" in the upper level attention units wants data. He starts to scan the standard banks with a sub-level. The data comes to him *spoken.* Like a voice inside his head.

A Clear does not have any "mental voices"! He does not think vocally. He thinks without articulation of his thoughts and his thoughts are not in voice terms. This will come as a surprise to many people. The "listen-to-me" demon is common in the society, which is to say, this engram circulates widely. "Stay right there and listen to me" fixes the engram in present time (and fixes the individual in the time of the engram to some extent). After it is keyed-in and from there on, the individual thinks "out loud," which is to say, he puts his thoughts into language. This is very slow. The mind thinks out solutions (in a Clear) at such speed that the word stream of consciousness would be left at the post.

Proving this was very easy. In clearing every case, without exception, one or another of these demons was discovered. Some cases had three or four. Some had ten. Some had one. It is a safe assumption that almost every aberree contains a demon circuit.

The type of engram which makes a "critical demon" is, "You are always criticizing me." There are dozens of such statements contained in engrams, any one of which will make a critical demon, just as any combination of words resulting in a demand to listen and obey orders will make a commanding demon.

All these demons are parasitic. That is to say, they take a part of the analyzer and compartment it off. A demon can think only as well as the person's mind can think. There is no extra power. No benefit. All loss.

It is possible to set up the whole computer (analyzer) as a demon circuit and leave "I" on a tiny and forlorn shelf. This, on the surface, is a pretty good stunt. It makes it possible for the whole analytical mind to work out computations undisturbed and relay the answer to the "I". But in practice it is very bad, for "I" is the will, the determining force of the organism, the awareness. And very soon "I" becomes so dependent upon this circuit that the circuit begins to absorb him. Any such circuit, to last, would have to have pain and be chronic. It would have to be, in short, an engram. Therefore, it would have to be reductive of the intellect and would victimize the owner by eventually making him ill one way or another.

Of all the engram demon circuits found and removed, those which contained a seemingly all-powerful exterior entity which would solve all problems and answer every want were the most dangerous. As the engram keyed-in further and further and was constantly restimulated, it eventually made a spineless puppet out of "I"; because other engrams existed, the sum of the reduction tended toward insanity of a serious sort. If you want a sample, just imagine what you would have to say to a hypnotized person to make him think that he was in the hands of a powerful being who gave him orders and then imagine this as the phrase spoken when an individual had been knocked unconscious one way or another.

There is another full class of demons, the "occlusion demons," the demons who shut things off. These are not properly demons because they don't talk. A bona fide demon is one who gives thoughts voice or echoes the spoken word interiorly or who gives all sorts of complicated advice like a real, live voice exteriorly. (People who hear voices have exterior vocal demons: circuits which have tied up their imagination circuits.)

The occlusion demon doesn't have anything to say. It is what he doesn't permit to be said or done that makes the mental derangement.

An occlusion demon can exist for a single word. For instance, a child receives an engram by falling off her bicycle and losing consciousness; a policeman tries to assist her; she is still unconscious but moving and mutters that she can't move (an old engram at work); the officer says, cheerfully, "Never say can't!" Some time later, she has a conscious-level experience such as another fall, but without injury. (We keep mentioning this second, necessary step, the *lock*, because it is the thing old-time mystics thought was causing all the trouble: it is "mental anguish.") Now she has difficulty saying "can't." Dangerous in any event. What if she had that common engram expression, "Never say no!"?

Occlusion demons hide things from "I". It is as easy for one to mask many words. The individual having one will then omit these words or alter them or misspell them and make mistakes with them. The demon is not the only reason words get altered, but he is a specific case. An occlusion demon can be of a much higher strength and breadth. He can be created with the phrase "Don't talk!" or "Never talk back to your elders" or "You can't talk here. Who said you could talk?" Any of these phrases might produce a stammerer.

Other things besides speech can be occluded. Any ability of the mind can be inhibited by a demon specifically designed to obstruct that ability. "You can't see!" will occlude visual recall. "You can't hear!" will occlude audio recall. "You can't feel!" occludes pain and tactile recall (homonymic stuff, English).

Any perception can be occluded in recall. And whenever it is occluded in recall, it affects actual perception and the organ of perception as well. "You can't see!" may reduce not only recall, but the actual organic ability of the eyes, as in astigmatism or myopia.

One can imagine, with the entire English language (or in other lands with other tongues, any language) susceptible to inclusion within engrams, just how many abilities of the mind's operation can be occluded. An extremely common one is "You can't think!"

So far now "you" has been used in illustrations and examples in order to keep the similarity to hypnotic or drug tests. Actually, sentences which contain "I" are more destructive. "I can't feel anything," "I can't think," "I can't remember." These and their thousands and thousands of variations, when spoken within the hearings of an "unconscious" person, are applicable to himself when he gets the engram keyed-in to circuit.

"You" has several effects. The statement, "You are no good," to an awake person makes that person feel very angry, perhaps, when he has an engram to that effect. Within him he feels, possibly, that people think he is no good. He may have a demon that tells him he is no good. And he will dramatize by telling other people that *they* are no good. It can be sprayed off by being dramatized. A person who has an engram to the effect that he is sexually sterile, for instance, will tell people that they are sexually sterile. ("Don't do as I do, do as I say.") If he has an engram that says, "You are no good, you have to eat with your knife," he may eat with his knife, but he gets excited about people eating with their knives, and he would grow very angry if somebody said *he* ate with *his* knife.

Thus, there are "compulsion demons" and "confusion demons" and so forth and so on.

The engram has a command value. There is a power of choice exercised in the reactive mind about which and what engrams will be used. But any engram, strongly enough restimulated, will come to the surface to be dramatized. And if dramatization is blocked, it will turn on the individual either temporarily or chronically.

The literalness of this reactive mind, in its interpretation of commands and the literalness of their action within the poor, harassed analytical mind is a strange thing in itself. "It is too horrible to be borne" might be interpreted to the effect that a baby was in such bad condition that it had better not be born. There are thousands of clichés in any language which, when literally taken, mean quite the opposite from what the speaker intends.

The reactive engram bank takes them, stores them with pain and emotion and "unconsciousness" and, with moronic literalness, hands them forth to be LAW and COMMAND to the analytical mind. And when the happy little moron who runs the engram bank sees it possible to use up some analytical mind circuits with some of these confounded demons, it is done.

The analytical mind, then, can be seen to be subject to yet another form of attrition. Its circuits, ordinarily intended for smooth, rapid computation, become tied up and overloaded with demon lash-ups. The demons are parasites. They are pieces of analytical mind compartmented off and denied to larger computation.

Is it any wonder that, when these demons are deleted, IQ soars as it can be observed to do in a Clear? Add the demon circuits to the shut-down aspect of restimulation, and truth can be seen in the observation that people run on about one-twentieth of their mental power. Research and scientific tabulation indicate that with the "unconsciousness" aspect and the demon circuits deleted from the engram bank and the data restored into the standard bank as experience, where it should be, about forty-nine fiftieths of the mind have been placed at the service of "I" which he never could use as an aberree.

BOOK TWO, CHAPTER FIVE

Psychosomatic Illness

Psychosomatic illnesses are those which have a mental origin but which are nevertheless organic. Despite the fact that there existed no precise scientific proof of this before Dianetics, an opinion as to their existence has been strong since the days of Greece and in recent times various drug preparations have been concocted and sold which were supposed to overcome these sicknesses. Some success was experienced, sufficient to warrant a great deal of work on the part of researchers. Peptic ulcers, for instance, have yielded to persuasion and environmental change. A recent drug called ACTH has had astonishing but wildly unpredictable results. Allergies have been found to yield more or less to things which depressed histamine in the body.

The problem of psychosomatic illness is entirely embraced by Dianetics and, by Dianetic technique, such illness has been eradicated entirely in every case.

About 70 percent of the physician's current roster of diseases fall into the category of psychosomatic illness. How many more can be so classified after Dianetics has been in practice for a few years is difficult to predict, but it is certain that more illnesses are psychosomatic than have been so classified to date. That *all* illnesses are psychosomatic is, of course, absurd, for there exist, after all, life forms called germs which have survival as *their* goals.

The work of Louis Pasteur formulated the germ theory of disease. With Dianetics is gained the non-germ theory of disease. These two, with biochemistry, complement each other to form the whole field of pathology so far as can be determined at this time – providing, of course, that the virus is included under the germ theory.

Dianetics adds an additional leaf to the germ theory in that it includes *predisposition.* There are three stages of pathology: *predisposition*, by which is meant the factors which prepared the body for sickness; *precipitation*, by which is meant the factors which cause the sickness to manifest itself; and *perpetuation*, by which is meant the factors which cause the sickness to continue.

There are two kinds of illness: the first could be called *autogenetic*, which means that it originated within the organism and was self-generated; and *exogenetic*, which means that the origin of the illness was exterior. Actually, although this is good medicine, it is not quite as precise as Dianetics could desire. Mental illness itself is actually exterior in origin. But medically, we consider that the body can generate its own sicknesses (autogenetic) or that the sickness can come from an exterior source such as bacteria (exogenetic). The Pasteur germ theory would be the theory of exogenetic (exteriorly generated) illness. Psychosomatic illness would be autogenetic, generated by the body itself.

Treatment for accidental injury, surgery for various things such as malformation inherent in the body on a genetic basis, and orthopedics, which actually can be classed under both, remain properly outside the field of Dianetics – although it can be remarked in passing that almost all accidents are to be traced to dramatization of engrams and that Clears rarely have accidents.

Psycho, of course, refers to mind and *somatic* refers to body; the term psychosomatic means the mind making the body ill or illnesses which have been created physically within the body by derangement of the mind. Naturally such diseases, when one has resolved the problem of human aberration, become uniformly susceptible to cure.

Arthritis, dermatitis, allergies, asthma, some coronary difficulties, eye trouble, bursitis, ulcers, sinusitis, etc., form a very small section of the psychosomatic catalog. Bizarre aches and pains in various portions of the body are generally psychosomatic. Migraine headaches are psychosomatic and, with the others, are uniformly cured by Dianetic therapy. (And the word *cured* is used in its fullest sense.)

Just how many physical errors are psychosomatic depends upon how many conditions the body can generate out of the factors in the engrams. For example, the common cold has been found to be psychosomatic. Clears do not get colds. Just what, if any, part the virus plays in the common cold is not known, but it is known that when engrams about colds are lifted, no further colds appear–which is a laboratory fact not so far contradicted by 270 cases. The common cold comes about, usually, from an engram which suggests it and which is confirmed by actual mucus present in another engram. A number of germ diseases are predisposed and perpetuated by engrams. Tuberculosis is one.

The engram itself, as has been covered, follows a cycle of action. The body is predisposed to the conduct and conditions contained in the engram when that engram is first received. Then a conscious-level experience keys-in the engram and other experience or the content of the engram itself may make it chronic. This is predisposition, precipitation and perpetuation in the mental plane.

Engrams and inherited disabilities and accidents and germs are the four ways an organism can be reduced physically from the optimum. Many conditions which have been called "inherited disabilities" are actually engramic. Engrams predispose people to accidents. Engrams can predispose and perpetuate bacterial infections. Therefore, the catalog of ills affected by Dianetics is very long. This is not a book listing effects, but a book stating causes, and so the reader is asked to call upon his own knowledge or consult a medical text to understand just how many thousands and thousands of conditions result from engrams to disturb or derange the body.

At the present time Dianetic research is scheduled to include cancer and diabetes. There are a number of reasons to suppose that these may be engramic in cause, particularly malignant cancer. This is remarked so that attention may be given to the possibility; no tests of any kind have been made on cancer or diabetic patients, and the thought is purely theory and is not to be taken as any kind of an avowal about a cancer cure. Those diseases which were cataloged above, however, have been thoroughly tested and have uniformly yielded to Dianetic therapy.

The mechanism by which the mind is able to cause a physical disability or predispose the body to an illness and perpetuate sickness is, in its basic cause, a very simple thing. The complexity arrives when one begins to combine all the factors possible – then a staggering list of potential illnesses can be written.

A series of simple tests can be made on drugged or hypnotic patients which will prove clinically, in other laboratories, this basic mechanism. A series of these tests was run in the formulation of Dianetics with uniform success.

Let us take, first, something which is only mildly psychosomatic and scarcely an illness at all. A patient is hypnotized. He is given the positive suggestion that he will be able to hear much more acutely. This is "extended hearing." Controlling out other means of his gaining data (including safeguards against telepathy between operator and subject), the hearing can be found to be amplifiable many times over. In fact, there exist all around aberrees who have "extended hearing." By suggestion, the power of the hearing can be tuned down or up so that a person is nearly deaf or can hear pins fall at a great distance. When the suggestion is removed, the subject's hearing returns to its previous normal state.

Similarly, experiments can be performed on the eyes, using light sensitivity. The patient's sight is tuned up or down so that his eyes are much more or much less sensitive to light than is normal for him. This is done entirely on the word suggestion basis, such as "The light will appear very, very bright to you" or "The light will appear so dim it will be hard for you to see." With the former suggestion, the patient can be made to see almost as well as a cat, although other people around might think it impossible to see objects the patient can unerringly point out. In the latter suggestion, the patient can be placed under light almost blinding and yet can read through a glare with apparent comfort.

The tactile sense can likewise be tuned up or down by verbal suggestion until touch becomes painfully acute or so dull it scarcely registers.

So with the various senses. Here we have simply the spoken word going into the mind and causing physical function to change.

Let us now address the heart. By deep hypnosis or drugs, we take a patient into amnesia trance, a state of being wherein the "I" is not in control, but the operator is the "I" (and that's all there is, really, to the function of hypnosis: the transfer of analytical power through the law of affinity from subject to operator, a thing which had a racial development and survival value in animals which ran in packs).

A caution should be observed that a patient who has a very sound heart and no heart-trouble history be chosen for this experiment, which, even above any other hypnotic experiment, can make a patient very ill if he has a heart history. And none of these hypnotic tests should be performed until one has finished this book and knows how to get rid of the suggestions. For hypnosis, as practiced, is strictly live-fuse stuff and the hypnotist who is unacquainted with Dianetics has no more idea how to get rid of a suggestion he has made than he has of how to peel an atom. He has *thought* he had the answer, but Dianetics has treated many, many former hypnotic subjects who were thoroughly, as the engineers interested in Dianetics say, "loused-up." This is no criticism of hypnosis or hypnotists, who are often very able people, but it is a comment that there is more to be known about it.

The heart, by positive suggestion alone, can be speeded up, slowed down or otherwise excited. Here are *words* spoken into the deep strata of the mind which cause *physical* action. Further, blood flow can be inhibited in some area of the body by suggestion alone. (This experiment, it is warned, particularly overloads the heart.) Blood can be denied to a hand, for instance, so that if you were to cut a vein in that hand it would bleed slightly if at all. A fine swami trick, which most amazed the author in India, was the inhibition of blood flow by the awake individual in himself. On command a cut would bleed or not bleed. It looked fantastic and made very good press agentry that here was a swami who had so associated himself with Nirvana that he was in control of all material matters. Awe faded when the author learned that, via hypnosis, he could make his own body do the same thing and no Nirvana involved. The mechanism fades out rapidly and in a few days would have to be renewed: the body has its own optimum operation, and although such a function can be "analytically" handled, it is not an upper echelon analytical job to keep the blood going in the hand. The point here is that blood flow can be interrupted by verbal suggestion. Words connect up with the physical being.

As for how this can come about, we are not so much interested in structure as in function at this stage of the science of mind. Why not, if by knowing function alone we can cure aberrations and psychosomatic ills every time, predict new ills and conditions and generally "work miracles" as such actions were once called before Man knew anything about the mind?

Excreta are among the easiest things to regulate by suggestion. Constipation can be caused or cured by positive suggestion with remarkable speed and facility. The urine can also be so controlled. *And so can the endocrine system.*

It is harder to make tests on some of the more poorly understood functions of the endocrines. Glandular research has not progressed very far at this time. But, by removing engrams and watching the endocrine system rebalance, it has been made obvious that the endocrine system is a part of the control mechanism with which the mind handles the body. The glands are easily influenced. These fluids and secretions–testosterone, estrogen, adrenaline, thyroid, parathyroid, pituitrin, etc.–are the substances the mind uses as one means of controlling the body. They form relay circuits, so to speak. Each one has its own action within the body.

This experiment tends to prove the fallacy of an ancient assumption that the mind was controlled by the glands. An aberree is given a shot of 25 mg of testosterone in oil twice a week. There may be some improvement in his physical status for a short time–his voice may deepen and he may grow more hair on his chest. Now, without suggestion, we simply delete the engrams from his reactive bank so that they can re-form as experience in the standard bank. Before we have completed this task, his body begins to use more of the testosterone. The dose can be markedly reduced and still give more benefit than formerly. Finally, the dose can be eliminated. This experiment has also been performed on people who had not been able to receive benefit from glandular substances, such as testosterone and estrogen, and upon people who were made ill by the administration of these hormones. The deletion of the engrams from the reactive bank uniformly brought about a condition where they could receive benefit from the hormones, but where such artificial administration was not necessary save in cases of extreme age. What this means to gerontology (the study of longevity in life) cannot at this time be estimated, but it can be predicted with confidence that the deletion of engrams from the reactive bank has a marked effect upon the extension of life. A hundred years or so from now this data will be available, but no Clears have lived that long as yet.

Just now, to our purpose, it is easy to demonstrate the effect of positive suggestion upon the endocrine system and the lack of effect of artificial hormones upon aberrees.

This sort of an engram has a terribly reductive effect upon testosterone manufacture: "Sex is horrible, it is nasty, I hate it."

The autonomic nervous system, which has been supposed to run without much connection to the mind, can be shown to be influenced in its parts by the mind. There is a dwindling spiral effect (note the lines on the survival potential chart) whereby the engram starts malfunction in the life-function regulator; this produces malfunction in the mind, which in turn has further effect on the life-function regulator; this again reduces physical activity, and the mind, being part of the organ and, so far as we can tell, organic itself, is further reduced in tone. Mental tone makes body tone go down. Body tone, then being down, makes mental tone go down. This is a matter of inverse geometric progression. A man starts to get sick and, having engrams, he gets sicker. Clears are not subject to this dwindling spiral. Indeed, so entirely superficial is this horrible stuff called psychosomatic illness that it is the first thing which surrenders and can be alleviated without Clearing.

Now the reason why various drug preparations which seek to change psychosomatic illness meet with such uncertain success lies in the fact that the mind, containing these engrams which are "survival" (like a fellow needs a hole in his head), handles the life-function regulator to actively produce illnesses. Something comes to take them away (they're "survival," you see, and these confounded cells moronically insist upon it) and the mind has to rapidly reverse the activity and put an illness back in place again. Try to influence the reactive mind by reason or needles and it is not any easier to convince than a drug-crazed man bent on murdering everybody in a bar. He's "surviving" too.

A concoction like ACTH has a slightly different effect. It is too exclusive to have any research done with it, but on reports about it, it seems to affect engrams in the time sense. That is to say, as will be covered under therapy, the individual's reactive location in time is shifted by it. ACTH and perhaps many others in its category move the individual from one chronic engram into another. This is about as reliable as changing dictators in Europe. The next one may be twice as bad. It may even be a manic and that's horrible despite its apparent "euphoria."

Electric shock treatment, the beatings of Bedlam and other things of their ilk, *including surgical treatment of things psychosomatic in origin*, have another effect, but one not dissimilar to drugs like ACTH, in that they give another shock which transfers the engram pattern to another part of the body and switches around the aberrations (when these things work, it is because the new aberration is less violent than the old one). Shocks, blows, surgery and maybe even things like cobra venom change the effect of the engram bank on the body, not necessarily for the worse, not necessarily for the better; they just change them. Like shooting dice: sometimes one gets a seven.

Then there is the deletion of tissue treatment of psychosomatic ills. This simply removes the area which is busy dramatizing in the physical line. This can be the removal of a toe or the removal of a brain. These things are quite commonly used, as this is being written. The removal of the toe is addressed to one part of the engram content, the *somatic*, and the removal of parts of the brain (as in the transorbital leukotomy and the prefrontal lobotomy or anything else more recent) is addressed mistakenly to "the removal of" the psycho-aberration. There is a surrender system at work in this as well: the surgeon or the patient has an aberration about "getting rid of it," and so bits of the body are cut up or removed. Some patients surrender anatomy on advice or at their own insistence like old-timers shed blood in a phlebotomy. There is a straight parallel between bleeding the patient to make him well and cutting away parts of him to make him well. Both are based on a surrender (get rid of) engram and neither are effective in any way. Barber-basin medicine, it is hoped, will eventually die out as did its patients.

These are the five classes of psychosomatic ills:

1. Those ills resulting from mentally caused derangement in physical fluid flow, which class subdivides into:
   a. Inhibition of fluid flow.
   b. Magnification of fluid flow.
2. Those ills resulting from mentally caused derangement of physical growth, which class subdivides into:
   a. Inhibition of growth.
   b. Magnification of growth.
3. Those ills resulting from predisposition to disease resulting from a chronic psychosomatic pain in an area.
4. Those ills resulting from perpetuation of a disease on account of chronic pain in an area.
5. Those ills caused by the verbal command content of the engrams.

In Class 1a fall such ordinary things as constipation and such extraordinary things as arthritis. Arthritis is a complex mechanism with a simple cause and a relatively simple cure. Remember that there are two things present in an engram: physical pain and verbal command. In arthritis, both must be present (as in the bulk of psychosomatic ills). There must have been an accident to the joint or area affected, and there must have been a command during the "unconsciousness" which attended the injury, which would make the engram susceptible to chronic restimulation. (Such commands as "It is always like this" or "It just goes right on hurting" or "I'm stuck" will produce similar results.) Given this engram and given this engram keyed-in, there is a chronic pain in the area of the injury. It may be minor, but it is a pain just the same. (It can be a pain but not be felt if the engram contains a command which is anesthetic, such as "He'll never feel this," which produces a similar condition but makes one "unconscious" of the pain there.) This pain in the body probably tells the cells and the blood that this area is dangerous. It is therefore avoided. The command permits the mind to influence, let us say, the parathyroid, which contains the secret of the calcium content in the bloodstream. A mineral deposit then begins to be laid down in the area. The mineral deposit is not necessarily the cause of the pain, but it is an organic restimulator so that the more mineral, the more pain, the more the engram keys-in. This is the dwindling spiral. And this is arthritis in action. Understand that the parathyroid and the blood avoidance are theoretical cause; the scientific fact is that when an engram is picked up and deleted about an area containing arthritis, that arthritis vanishes and does not return and this is X-ray plate evidence. It happens every time and does not happen because of any suggestion or medicine; it happens because an engram is picked up and refiled. As the engram goes away, so goes the pain, so vanishes the arthritis. This forms a whole class of ills, of which arthritis is only one. The mechanisms involved vary slightly. All can be headed under "physical derangement caused by reduced body fluid flow."

Class 1b of psychosomatic ills, magnification of fluid flow, contains such things as high blood pressure, diarrhea, sinusitis, priapism (overactivity of the male sex glands), or any other physical condition resulting from a superabundance of fluid.

Class 2a can cause such things as a withered arm, a foreshortened nose, underdeveloped genital organs or any other underdevelopment of a gland having to do with size (which cross-classes this with 1a), hairlessness (which also, like the rest, can be part of the gene pattern and therefore inherent) and, in short, reduction in size of any part of the body.

Class 2b causes such things as oversized hands, a lengthened nose, oversized ears, enlarged organs and other common physical malformations. (Cancer might possibly come under this heading as overhealing.)

Class 3 would include tuberculosis (some cases), liver trouble, kidney trouble, rashes, common colds, etc. (cross-classing with others, as do all of these in one way or another).

Class 4 would include those diseases which, arising without psychosomatic influence, yet fix upon by accident a previously injured area and, by restimulation, keep an engram keyed-in in that area so that a condition becomes chronic. Tuberculosis could be included here. Conjunctivitis, all running sores and any condition which refuses to heal, etc.

This fourth class would also include all bizarre pains and sicknesses which cannot be found to have actual pathology.

Class 5 includes an enormously wide catalog of conditions, any one of which may cross-index to other classes or which arise solely out of engrams which dictate the presence or necessity of an illness. "You always have colds," "I have sore feet," etc., announce a psychosomatic illness and the mechanisms of the body can furnish one.

Any disease whatever can be precipitated by engrams. The disease may be of germ origin; the individual possesses an engram to the effect that he may become sick and on this generalization, becomes sick with whatever is to hand. Further, and even more general, the engram reduces the physical resistance of the body to disease. And when an engram goes into restimulation (perhaps because of a domestic quarrel, an accident or some such thing), the ability of the individual to resist sickness is automatically decreased.

Children, as will be explained, have many more engrams than has been supposed. Almost all childhood illnesses are preceded by psychic disturbance and if psychic disturbance is present–keeping an engram restimulated–such illnesses can be far more violent than they should be. Measles, for instance, can be just measles or it can be measles in company with engramic restimulation, in which case it can be nearly or entirely fatal. A check of many subjects on this matter of childhood illness being predisposed by, precipitated by and perpetuated by engrams causes one to wonder just how violent the diseases themselves really are. They have never been observed in a Cleared child and there is reason to investigate the possibility that childhood illnesses are in themselves extremely mild and are complicated only by psychic disturbance, which is to say, the restimulation of engrams.

In fact, one could ask this question of the entire field of pathology: What is the actual effect of disease minus the mental equation? How serious are bacteria?

The field of bacteriology has been without dynamic principles until now; the dynamic, survival, is applicable to all life forms and "life forms" include germs.

The purpose of the germ is to survive. Its problems are those of food, protection (offense and defense) and procreation. To accomplish these things, the germ survives at its optimum efficiency. It mutates, alters with natural selection and changes dynamically from survival necessity (the missing step of the evolution theory, that last) in order to accomplish the maximum survival possible. It makes errors by killing the hosts, but to have a purpose to survive does not mean that a form necessarily survives.

In pathology, the germ, bent on its purpose, acts as a suppressor to the survival dynamic of the human species. How serious this suppressor is in the absence of engram suppression in the human has not been determined. Enough data exists to indicate that a human individual with his potential in the fourth zone is not, apparently, very subject to disease: the common cold, for instance, if it is a virus or not, passes him by; chronic infections are absent. What antibodies have to do with this or what this factor is, is yet another question. But it remains that a Clear is not easily made ill. In the aberree, illness closely pursues mental depression (depression of the dynamic level).

The aberration of mind and body by engrams leads, then, not only to psychosomatic ills, but also to actual pathology–which has hitherto been considered more or less independent of the mental state. As has been proven by clinical research, clearing of engrams does more than remove psychosomatic illness–potential, acute or chronic. The clearing also tends to proof the individual against the receipt of pathology: to what extent it is not yet known, for such a wide and long-term view is required to establish the actual statistics that the project will require thousands of cases and the observations of medical doctors over a long term.

The amount of aberration which a person manifests, which is to say, the position he would occupy on a sanity scale, has little to do with psychosomatic illness. Such illnesses require only one or two engrams of a specific nature to become manifest. These engrams may not be aberrative in any other way than to predispose the individual to illness. Having a psychosomatic illness is not the same as being "crazy" or having hypochondriacal tendencies. The hypochondriac thinks he has illnesses, a special case of Class 5 above.

Derangement falls sharply into two categories. The first is the mental derangement, any irrational condition, which in Dianetics we call *aberration* in order to avoid constant cataloging of the thousands, the millions of manifestations irrationality can have. The other derangement of the individual is *somatic:* this applies entirely to his physical being and physical ability and health. Both these things are present in every engram: the *aberration* and the *somatic*. But the engram can manifest itself chronically as either a *somatic* (a noun has been made out of an adjective here and it is commonly employed in Dianetics to avoid the use of the word *pain*, which is not embracive and which is restimulative) or as an *aberration* or as both together.

An engram must contain physical pain. When an engram is restimulated in everyday life, that physical pain may appear or it may not. If it does not appear as pain, but as aberration, then the individual is in another valence than his own (the "necessity to manifest his hostilities"). If he is sane enough to be in his own valence, the physical pain will be present. In Dianetics, we say the *somatic* has appeared. When any somatic appears, unless the individual is a preclear in therapy, some of the aberration is also appearing. In short, the aberration can appear by itself or the somatic plus some of the aberration can appear. When a person dramatizes another valence than his own, the aberration is present; when the dramatization, running off the engram phonograph-record-wise in one or another valence, is suppressed by some other factor such as the police or a stronger person or even the individual himself (this has been called *repression*–the term is not used here because it is loaded with other meanings), the somatic most certainly will come into view. The individual is then apparently "better off," as the cells meant him to be, to occupy the survival role in the engram, the winning valence, for he is, at least, not ill. But how many people have been killed, how many banks have been robbed and how many marital partners have been driven mad by these dramatizations? So the health of the individual would be considered by society, in its effort to protect its members, to be a secondary affair. In fact, "society" has not known about this mechanical aspect. The individual who dramatizes the survival valence in his engrams may do violent things to other people. The individual who will not permit himself such a dramatization or who is forced by society away from such dramatization will most certainly become psychosomatically ill. "Heads I win, tails you lose." The answer is in the alleviation or deletion of the engram. For there are many additional aspects to the problem: the man who dramatizes his engrams, society or no society, is not apt to survive; and if he dramatizes them, he is subject to whatever slurs were leveled at the valence he is in by another valence in that same engram.

The combinations of the classes and aspects of psychosomatic illness listed and described here lead to some highly complex situations. It is a scientific fact that no psychosomatic ill exists without an aberration. And it is true that no aberration exists without a potential or actual psychosomatic ill. One of the psychosomatic illnesses one would least expect to find as a psychosomatic affair is the illness of sexual perversion.

The sexual pervert (and by this term Dianetics, to be brief, includes any and all forms of deviation in Dynamic Two such as homosexuality, lesbianism, sexual sadism, etc., and all down the catalog of Ellis and Krafft-Ebing) is actually quite ill physically. Perversion as an illness has so many manifestations that it must be spread through the entire gamut of classes from (1) to (5) above. Overdevelopment of sexual organs, underdevelopment, seminal inhibition or magnification, etc., are found, some in one pervert, some in another. And the sum of it is that the pervert is always a very ill person in one way or another, whether he is conscious of it or not. He is very far from culpable for his condition, but he is also so far from normal and so extremely dangerous to society that the tolerance of perversion is as thoroughly bad for society as punishment for it. Lacking proper means prior to this time, society has been caught between tolerance and punishment, and the problem of perversion has, of course, not been resolved. A bit off the subject here, but it can be remarked about perversion that the best previous explanation for it was something about girls becoming envious of Papa's penis or boys becoming upset about that terrible thing, the vulva, which Mama was incautious enough to show one day. It takes a great deal more than this utter tripe to make a pervert. It is, rather, something on the order of kicking a baby's head in, running over him with a steamroller, cutting him in half with a rusty knife, boiling him in Lysol and all the while with crazy people screaming the most horrifying and unprintable things at him. The human being is a very tough character. He is so confoundedly tough that he has whipped the whole animal kingdom and he can shake the stars. And when it comes to throwing his Second Dynamic out of balance, what that takes is straight out of Dante and Sax Rohmer combined. Hence the pervert, containing hundreds and hundreds of vicious engrams, has had little choice between being dead and being a pervert. But with an effective science to handle the problem, a society which would continue to endure perversion and all its sad and sordid effects doesn't deserve to survive.

Perversion can have other aspects. In one society examined, these aberrations had multiplied so far that a principal mystic cult had sprung up which contended that all mental illness came from sex. This, of course, gave further impetus to aberrations on the Second Dynamic (sex), as such a cultic belief must have been originated by an individual who had severe aberrations across the Second Dynamic. This belief that sex was the only source of human aberration and travail naturally attracted as its practitioners individuals who had similar aberrative patterns. And so the cult further enforced existing aberrative factors in the society, since all their activity was leveled at making sex something ogreish and dreadful by labeling it the society's primary source of mental illness. The prophet of this god was Manichaeus, a Persian of the third century, who taught that all things about the body, especially sex, were evil. The cult of Manichaeus carried on well into the Dark Ages and then vanished, to trouble Man no more.

Any dynamic can be blocked: the Personal Dynamic, the Sex Dynamic, the Group Dynamic or the Mankind Dynamic. Each one has been the target at some time of one cult or another seeking to cure all Man's ills and save him. Dianetics is not interested in saving Man, but it can do much to prevent him from *being* "saved." As an organized body of scientific knowledge,

Dianetics can draw only the conclusion which it observes in the laboratory.

It can be observed that the Church is entirely correct in doing all in its power to prevent blasphemy. Blasphemy can very often be uttered during the "unconsciousness" of a person who has been struck. This would enter sacred names and curses into engrams which, reacting within the individual, give him an unnatural terror and compulsion or repulsion toward God. It is not the religion which is at fault, it is the blaspheming of the religion. Such blasphemy makes the insane zealot and the murderous atheist, both of whom the Church would very gladly do without.

In the realm of psychosomatic illness, any combination of the language is as damaging a factor in an engram as any other factor. The moronic reasoning of the reactive mind, which considers everything in an engram equal to everything in an engram, also considers that everything similar to the engram in the exterior world (the restimulators) is sufficient cause to place an engram in effect. Hence aberration and illness can come about.

There is, however, a peculiarity in psychosomatic illnesses which is chronic: the aberree's reactive mind exercises a power of choice to the extent that *only pro-survival engrams become chronic.* It could be said, on a reactive level, that the aberree will not permit himself to suffer illness from his engrams unless that illness has a "survival" value. This is very important in therapy. The chronic psychosomatic illnesses which a patient displays are those which have a sympathy (pro-survival) background.

It is not possible to "spoil" a child with love and affection. Whoever postulated that it was possible, was postulating out of bad data and no observation. A child *needs* all the love and affection it can possibly get. A test was run in one hospital which tended to show that babies, when left without attention, ran fevers. When given attention, the fevers immediately abated. The test, while not observed personally by the author, seems to have been conducted with proper controls according to report. If this is true, it postulates a mechanism in the human being which uses illness for affection on a genetic basis. There is no reason why not; there have been enough years of engineering–almost two billion–to build anything into the blueprint. These babies, in several groups, were left in the hospital by their parents for the test; they uniformly became ill when not given affection. Here is the law of affinity at work, if these tests were accurately conducted. Their purpose was not to help Dianetics, but to show that the leaving of a baby in the hospital after his birth because he has a slight illness invariably increases that illness.

A series of severely controlled Dianetic experiments over a much longer period demonstrated that the law of affinity, as applicable to psychosomatic illness, was more powerful than fear and antagonism by a very wide margin. So great is this margin that it could be compared as the strength of a steel girder to a straw. It was found, as above, that chronic psychosomatic ills existed only when they had a sympathy engram behind them. The law of affinity might be interpreted as the law of cohesion; "affinity" might be defined as "love" in both its meanings. Deprivation of or absence of affection could be considered as a violation of the law of affinity. Man must be in affinity with Man to survive. The suicide ordinarily commits the act on the computation that the removal of self will some way benefit other selves–this, on the reactive mind level, is a very ordinary computation deriving exclusively from engrams. The violent industrial chieftain with his merciless mien, when he suffers from a psychosomatic ill, ordinarily derives it out of a sympathy engram.

The sympathy engram pretends to be pro-survival. As one preclear said, a man is not victimized by his enemies but by his friends. An engram comes about always from a greater or lesser moment of "unconsciousness." There is no engram without "unconsciousness." It is only when the analyzer is out of circuit that the exterior world can come interior, unrationalized, and work from within. The second the analyzer identifies one of those engrams as such, that engram loses about 20 percent of its value to aberrate and usually 100 percent of its value to cause a psychosomatic illness. Pain is extremely perishable. Pleasure is recorded in bronze. (Not poetry here, science. Physical pain will delete with brief attention. A pleasant or even a media-media experience is so solidly fixed in the mind that no treatment known to Dianetics will shake it and a great deal of effort has been leveled at pleasure recordings just to test them for permanence. They are permanent; physical pain is perishable. Too bad, Schopenhauer, but you were a most mistaken man.)

Exposing a lock (a moment of "mental anguish") to the analyzer once the engram which gave it power is gone, causes that lock to blow away like chaff. The analyzer works on the Doctrine of the True Datum: it has no truck with anything which it once discovers to be false. Just exposing an engram without relieving it has some therapeutic value (20 percent) and this gave rise to a belief that all one had to do was know about his ills and they would vanish. Nice if it were so.

The most aberrative engram, then, is one which is held down by the reactive mind's–that moron's–concept that it is needed in the survival of the individual. This sympathy engram is the one which comes forward and stays chronic as a psychosomatic illness. There are two reasons for this: one is usually in one's own valence when a sympathy engram is received; and one's reactive mind, knowing well the value of affinity, puts forward the psychosomatic illness to attract affinity. There is no volition here on the part of the individual's "I" analytical self. But there is every "volition" on the part of the reactive mind.

A sympathy engram would go something like this: A small boy, much victimized by his parents, is extremely ill. His grandmother attends him and while he is delirious, soothes him and tells him she will take care of him, that she will stay right there until he is well. This puts a high "survival" value on being sick. He does not feel safe around his parents; he wants his grandmother present (she is a winning valence because she orders the parents around) and he now has an engram. Minus the engram there would be no psychosomatic illness. Sickness, "unconsciousness" and physical pain are essential to the receipt of this engram. But it is not a contra-survival engram. It is a pro-survival engram. It can be dramatized in one's own valence.

The psychosomatic illness, in such a case as this, would be a "precious possession." "I" doesn't even know the computation. The analyzer was out when the engram went in. The analyzer cannot recall that engram with anything short of Dianetic therapy. And the engram will not clear away.

Now with this engram, we have a patient with sinusitis and a predisposition to lung infections. It may be that he was luckless enough to marry a counterpart of his mother or his grandmother. The reactive mind cannot tell the difference between grandmother or mother and wife if they are even vaguely similar in speech, voice tone or mannerisms. The wife is not sympathetic. In goes the engram to demand that sympathy. And even if the wife thinks that sinusitis and lung infection are repulsive enough to lead to divorce, the reactive mind keeps that engram keyed-in. The more hatred from the wife, the more that engram keys-in. You can kill a man that way.

The above is a standard sympathy engram. When a therapist tries to get that engram away from the patient, the reactive mind balks. The "I" doesn't balk. The analyzer doesn't balk. These are hopeful that this engram will spring. But the reactive mind keeps it nailed down until the Dianeticist puts a crowbar under it. Then it is gone. (Enough locks may be lifted, by the way, to alleviate this condition. But the patient will dig up another engram!)

Resistance to past therapies has resulted from these sympathy engrams. Yet they lie right there on the surface, fully exposed as chronic psychosomatic illness.

Feeding a patient with a psychosomatic ill any number of drugs can result in only temporary relief. "I" doesn't want the illness. The analyzer doesn't want it. But the body has it and if anybody succeeds in curing it short of removing that engram, the body, at the command of the reactive mind, will find something else to substitute for that ill or develop an "allergy" to the drug or annul the effect of the drug entirely.

Of course, one can always rip living tissue out of the skull with knives, ice picks or shock in wholesale quantities. This will cure a psychosomatic ill. It also, unhappily, cures the personality, the intellect and, all too often, life itself.

In Dianetics, the application of technique to relieve the engrams causing these ills has brought the uniform relief of all patients treated without relapse. In short and in brief, psychosomatic ills can now be cured. All of them.

EMOTION *and* *the* DYNAMICS

EMOTION IS A θ (theta) quantity, which is to say that it is so involved with life forces that Dianetics at this stage handles it with invariable success, but does not attempt to give forth more than a descriptive theory. Much research must be done on emotion; but so long as the therapy embraces it and releases it with success, further data can be dispensed with up to a point.

Emotion would have to be divided sharply into minus emotions and plus emotions. The minus emotion would be non-survival in character, the plus emotion would be pro-survival. The pleasant and pleasurable emotions are not of any great concern to us here. It is believed that all emotion is the same thing. But in its aspects above Zone 1, it can be bypassed as unnecessary to explain at this time for the purpose of this book.

In Zones 1 and 0, emotion becomes very important to therapy. As has been covered earlier, Zones 1 and 0 are the anger and apathy zones respectively. From death up to the border between anger and fear is Zone 0. From this borderline to the beginning of boredom is anger, Zone 1.

It is as if the survival dynamic, in becoming contracted into Zone 1, first began to display hostility. Then on further suppression toward death, anger. On further suppression, rage began to be displayed, then fear as the next lower level, then terror and, finally, just above death, apathy.

And as the dynamic is suppressed, the cells react forcefully to the menace, it could be said, by resisting the menace. The analyzer resists down to the top border of Zone 1, but in ever-decreasing control. From here on down the cells, the actual organism, do the resisting in a last-ditch effort. The reactive mind is thoroughly in command from the top border of Zone 1 straight on down to death, and it is in ever-increasing command of the organism as the dynamic is suppressed.

Emotion seems to be inextricably connected up with the actual force of life. That there is a life force, no engineer could doubt. Man and medicine usually look at the pitcher and forget that the pitcher is only there to hold milk and that the milk is the important quantity. Life force is the helium which fills the free balloon. Out goes the helium, down comes the balloon. When this type of energy is located and isolated as itself–if it *is* just an energy type–then medicine can start moving forward in strides which will make all former steps look like those of a man in a sack race. Medicine doesn't have any spare helium, for one thing.

How high this life force can go on the survival scale is not known. Above Zone 3 is the area of question marks. A Clear goes up into a level of persistence, vigor, tenacity, rationality and happiness. Perhaps someday a Clear will attain the nebulosity the author used to hear about in India which marked the man who was all soul.

How far down it can go is definitely known. A man dies. He doesn't move or think. He dies as an organism, then he dies as cells. There are different periods of "life after death" for the cells and biologists remark that the hair and nail cells do not die for months. So here is a spectrum of death, first the organism and then, colony by colony, the cells.

That is from the bottom of Zone 0 downward. But what we are interested in is the area from Zone 1 down to the bottom of Zone 0. It could be postulated that the analytical mind has its greatest bounce against the suppressor, its highest ability to care for the organism, when it is in the third zone. As the suppressor thrusts downward against it, the analyzer within lower Zone 3 thrusts heavily back. This is *necessity* at work. *The necessity level can rise, in this action, to a point which keys-out all engrams!*

It must be realized that the analyzer considers future suppressors and is continually engaged upon computations which pose problems of the future which the analyzer resolves: this is one of the functions of the imagination. It must further be realized that the analyzer is engaged upon a multitude of computations about the present: for the analytical mind is dealing continually with an enormous number of factors which comprise the suppressor of the present and the suppressor of the future. It computes, for instance, on the alliances with friends and symbiotes, and its greatest victories are achieved by taking some of the suppressor and turning it into an alliance factor.

The individual can be visualized, on the survival spectrum, as being at the tip of the survival dynamic. The suppressor thrusts down, or future suppressors threaten a thrust, and the analytical mind thrusts up with solutions. The level of the individual is determined by how well these suppressors are apparently met.

We speak now of the Clear and, until further mention, we will continue to use the Clear. The Clear is an unaberrated person. He is rational in that he forms the best possible solutions he can on the data he has and from his viewpoint. He obtains the maximum pleasure for the organism, present and future, as well as for the subjects along the other dynamics. The Clear has no engrams which can be restimulated to throw out the correctness of computation by entering hidden and false data into it. No aberration. Hence, the reason we use him here as an example.

The survival dynamic is high, more than balancing the suppressor. Take this as a first condition. This would place the dynamic in Zone 3, Tone 3.9. Now increase the suppressor. The dynamic is pushed back to Tone 3.2. Necessity surges up. The suppressor is thrust back. The dynamic is once more at Tone 3.9. This action could be termed an enthusiastic resurgence. The individual has actually gotten "angry"–that is to say, he has called upon his being to furnish power for thought and action. Mentally, he calls upon whatever constitutes mental energy. Physically, if the suppression was physical, he would call upon his adrenaline. This is proper use of the endocrines, to use them for regaining position in relation to the suppressor. Any and all body function is under analytical (but not necessarily monitored) command.

Now let us suppose that the suppressor surges down against the dynamic and drives the dynamic to 3.0. Necessity level comes up. Action is taken. The full force of the being is thrown against the suppressor. Now let us suppose that a new factor comes into the suppressor and makes it much, much stronger. The individual still attempts to resurge against it. But the suppressor weighs heavier and heavier against him. He is beginning to exhaust his supplies of mental or physical energy (and this suppressor can be on either a mental or physical level). Wearying, the individual drops down to a 2.5. The suppressor again increases. Resurgence is attempted once more. The last supply of available energy or data is thrown out. And another factor comes into the suppressor, increasing its weight. The individual sags down to 2.0.

At exactly this point the analyzer, having failed, finally cuts out. Here is entered the top of Zone 1. Hostility sets in. The suppressor is down, pressing down against actual cellular survival. And it drops lower. The individual goes into anger, recruiting cellularly, but not sentiently, the last forces. Again the suppressor gets new weight. The individual goes into rage. Once more the suppressor drops. The individual goes into fear, Tone 0.9. Again the suppressor lowers, recruiting new factors. The individual is thrust down to 0.6 and here is in terror. Once more the suppressor drops with new force. The individual slides into fear-paralysis, 0.2.

Suppose we parallel this in a very simple, dramatic example so that we do not have to consider a thousand subtle factors. A Clear, inexperienced in hunting, determines to shoot a grizzly. He has a fine rifle. The grizzly appears to be easy game. The man is at 3.9 or above. He feels good. He is going to get that grizzly as the grizzly has been threatening the man's stock. High enthusiasm carries him to the lair. He waits, he finally sees the grizzly. There is a cliff above the man which he could not ordinarily climb. But to get a good shot before the grizzly vanishes, the man has to climb the cliff. Seeing he was in danger of losing the game brought the man down to 3.2. Necessity sends him up the cliff. He fires, but in firing falls back down the cliff. The grizzly is wounded. He starts toward the man. Necessity surges up. The man recovers the gun and shoots again. He is at 3.0 the moment he shoots. He misses. He fires again, but the miss, with the grizzly charging, brought him down to 2.5. He shoots once more. The grizzly takes the ball and keeps on coming. The man shoots again, but he has suddenly realized that his rifle is not going to stop this grizzly. His tone drops to 2.0. He begins to snarl and feverishly work his gun. His bullets go wild. He experiences rage at the gun, the grizzly, the world, and throws the gun away, ready to meet the grizzly, almost upon him, with bare hands. Suddenly the man knows fear. His tone is 1.2. It drops to 0.9 with a smell in his nostrils of the bear. He knows the bear will kill him. He turns and tries to claw up the cliff and get away, but his efforts are frenzied. He is at Tone 0.6, stark terror. The bear strikes him and knocks him from the cliff-side. The man lies still, breathing almost halted, heartbeat slowed to nearly nothing. The bear hits him again and the man lies still. Then the bear decides he is dead and walks away. Shaken, the man eventually comes around, his tone gradually rising up to 2.0, the point where his analyzer shut off. He stirs more and gets up. His tone is back to 2.5, he is analytically afraid and cautious. He recovers his gun. He begins to leave the scene. He feels a great necessity to recoup his own self-esteem and his tone comes to 3.2. He walks away and reaches a safe area. Suddenly it occurs to him that he can borrow a friend's Mauser. He begins to make plans to get that bear. His enthusiasm mounts. But, completely aside from the engram received when the bear knocked him out, he acts on his experience. Three days later, he kills the bear and his tone rises to 4.0 for the space of contemplation and telling the tale and then his mind occupies itself with new matters.

Life is much more complicated than the business of killing grizzlies, usually a lot less dramatic, but always full of situations which cause a fluctuation of the suppressor. The gaining of all pleasurable goals–a bear killed, a woman kissed, a seat in the front row at the opera, a friend won, an apple stolen–are sweeps through various levels of tone. And the individual is generally carrying on three or three thousand computations at once and there are thirty or thirty thousand variables in his computations. Too many unknowns, too many entrances of "didn't know the gun was loaded" factors, all these can throw the analyzer from a direct alignment into the scattered dispersal of non-function. The analyzer can be considered to cut out when Tone 2.0 is reached. From 2.5 down, the computations it makes are not very rational–too many unknowns, too many unexpected factors, too many discoveries of miscalculations.

This is living on a "Clear" basis. When our hunter was hit by the bear, he received an engram. That engram, when it keyed-in, would give him a fear, an apathy attitude, in the presence of certain factors: every perceptic presence–the smell of that ground, twigs, bear-breath, etc. But he killed the bear. The chances of that engram keying-in are remote. Not because he killed the bear, but because he was, after all, a grown man. And, if a Clear, he could have thought back and cleared the whole thing himself.

This is a complete cycle of *emotion*. Enthusiasm and high pleasure are at the extreme top. Fear and paralysis are at the bottom. Feigned death, in Man, is very close to the actual thing on the Tone Scale. It is a valid mechanism. But it is complete apathy.

So long as the analyzer is operating, the receipt of an engram is impossible. Everything files in the standard banks. As soon as the border 2.0 is passed on the way down, "unconsciousness" can be judged to have set in and anything registered, in company with pain or painful emotion, is an engram. This is not a shift of definition. The analyzer cuts out, with surgical anesthetic, at 2.0. The anesthetic may depress the level of awareness further. Pain may depress it even more. But depressing the level of awareness is not necessarily depressing emotion. How much conceived danger or sympathy is present in the environment? This is what depresses the Tone Scale. There can be a reactive engram which contains a Tone 4.0 or one that contains a 1.0 or another that contains a 0.1. This is not, then, quite two-dimensional, this emotion.

The level of depth of consciousness can be affected by painful emotion, poisons or other things which depress awareness. After that, it is all engram and the engrams have their own Tone Scale which runs from 4.0 down to 0.1.

It can be seen now that two things are at work. First is the state of physical being. It is this which tunes down the analyzer. Then there is the mental state of being. This is what tunes down the emotional Tone Scale.

But remember that in engrams there is another factor present: valence. Once its own analyzer is out, the body will assume the evaluation or emotional condition of any other analyzer present. Here we have affinity at work in earnest. "Unconscious" in the presence of other beings, an individual picks up a valence for every other being present. Some of these valences are incidental. He will pick first that valence which is most sympathetic as a desirable future friend (or some similar person). And he will pick that valence which is the top valence (highest survival, the boss, the winner) for his dramatization. He will also take the valence of the winning entity (winning over himself or others) for emotional tone. If the winning valence is also the sympathetic valence, he has an engram which can be utilized to its fullest extent.

Let us make this an example: A man is under nitrous oxide (the most vicious anesthetic ever invented as it is actually *not* anesthetic, but a hypnotic) undergoing exodontistry. As usual, everybody present around the "unconscious" patient chatters and yaps about the patient, the weather, the most popular movie star, or baseball. The exodontist is a tough character, bossy to the nurse, apt to be angry about trifles; he is also very sympathetic toward the patient. The nurse is a blue-eyed blonde who is sexually aberrated. The patient, actually in agony, receiving an engram among engrams which may ruin his life (terrible stuff, nitrous oxide; really hands out a fancy engram as any Dianeticist can attest) is unanalytical. Everything said to him or around him is taken literally. He takes the valence of the exodontist as both the top valence present and the sympathetic valence. But every phrase uttered is aberrative and will be interpreted by that happy little moron, the reactive mind, on the order of Simple Simon who was told he had to be careful how he stepped in the pies, so he stepped in them carefully. These people may be talking about somebody else, but every "I" or "he" or "you" uttered is engramic and will be applied to others and himself by the patient in the most literal sense. "He can't remember anything," says the exodontist. All right, when the engram keys-in, this patient will have an occlusion on memory in greater or lesser degree. "He can't see or feel it": this means an occlusion on sight, pain and tactile. If the patient has his eyes watering in agony at the moment (though completely "under"), he may get actual bad vision as well as poor visual recall from this experience. Now they put him in the hands of this blonde nurse to let him sleep off the drug and recover. She is an aberree among aberrees. She knows patients do weird things when they are still "out" so she pumps him for information about his life. And she knows they are hypnotic (yes, she sure does) so she gives him some positive suggestions. Amusing herself. She says he'll like her. That she'll be good to him. And stay there now for the present.

So the poor patient who has had two wisdom teeth, impacted, taken out, has a full anger-sympathy dramatization. The general tone he takes is the tone the exodontist showed to the others in the room. The exodontist was angry at the nurse. With his recalls all messed up, the patient a few years later meets a woman similar to this nurse. The nurse has given him compulsions toward her. The silly little moron, the reactive mind, sees in this entirely different person enough similarity to create an identity between the nurse and this new woman. So the patient divorces his wife and marries the pseudo-nurse. Only now that he has married the pseudo-nurse, the dental engram begins to key-in in earnest. Physically he gets ill: the two molars adjacent to where the wisdom teeth came out develop large cavities and begin to rot (circulation shutdown, pain in the area, but can't be felt because there's a pain recall shut-off). His memory goes to pieces. His recalls become worse. He begins to develop eye trouble and a strange conjunctivitis. Further (because the dentist leaned on his chest and stomach with a sharp elbow from time to time), he has chest and stomach pains. The nitrous oxide hurt his lungs and this pain is also in chronic restimulation. But most horrible: he believes that this pseudo-nurse will take care of him and he stops to some degree taking care of himself in any way. His energy dissipates and analytically he knows it is all wrong and that he is not himself. For he is now fixed in the valence of the exodontist who is angry with this nurse and so he beats the pseudo-nurse because he senses that from her all evil flows. The girl he married is not and was not the nurse: she sounds something like her and is a blonde. She has her own engrams and reacts. She attempts suicide.

Then, one day, since this is one engram among many, the mental hospital gets our patient and the doctors there decide that all he needs is a good solid series of electric shocks to tear his brain up and, if that doesn't work, a nice ice pick into each eyeball after and during electric shock, the ice pick sweeping a wide arc to tear the analytical mind to pieces. His wife agrees. Our patient can't defend himself: he's insane and the insane have no rights, you know.

Only the cavalry, in this one case, arrived in the form of Dianetics and Cleared the patient and the wife and they are happy today. This is an actual engram and an actual case history. It is a sympathy engram, pro-survival on the moronic reactive mind level.

This is to show the ebb and flow of emotion within this one engram. The physical being is out and in agony. The mental being is given a variety of emotional tones on a contagion principle. The actual emotional tone of the patient, his own, is beaten apathy; hence, he can no longer "be himself."

In passing, it should be mentioned that only absolute silence, utter silence and tomb-like silence, should attend an operation or injury of any kind. *There is nothing which can be said or given as a perceptic in any moment of "unconsciousness" which is beneficial to a patient. Nothing!* In the light of these researches and scientific findings (which can be proven in any other laboratory or group of people in very short order), speech or sound in the vicinity of an "unconscious" person should be punished criminally as, to anyone who knows these facts, such an act would be a willful effort to destroy the intellect or mental balance of an individual. If the patient is complimented, as in hypnosis or during an injury or operation, a *manic* is formed which will give him temporary euphoria and eventually plunge him into the *depressive* stage of the cycle.*

The golden rule could be altered to read: If you love your brother, keep your mouth shut when he is unconscious.

Emotion can be seen, then, to exist in two planes: the personal plane and the extra-valence plane. It is communicable in terms of identical thinking. Rage present when a man is "unconscious" will give him a Tone 1 engram: it will contain rage. Apathy present in the vicinity of an "unconscious" person will give him a Tone 0 engram. Happiness present during an engram is not very aberrative but will give a Tone 4 engram. And so forth. In other words, the emotion of those present around an "unconscious" person is communicated into the person as part of his engram. Any mood can be so communicated.

In dramatizing an engram, the aberree always takes the winning valence and that valence is not, of course, himself. If only one other person is present and the other is talking in terms of apathy, then the apathy is the tone value of the engram. When an apathy engram is restimulated, the individual, unless he wants to be hurt

*The author is well aware that many physicians, in using narcosynthesis, have occasionally accidentally entered "unconscious" periods. They have promptly considered, then, that these areas were equivocal, that the patient was probably not unconscious. In Dianetic research, patients have been rendered "unconscious" to the satisfaction of two doctors, both skeptical (since, no longer skeptical) and have been given material which the Dianeticist knew nothing about. Along with the complete data of the tests, as muttered by the doctors as they took them to make sure, by blood pressure, respiration, etc., that the patient could not be more "unconscious" unless he were dead, the data were recovered in full in every case and for every condition of "unconsciousness." Two patients were for a time severely aberrated by the careless comments of the anesthetizing and examining doctors, a note added to warn those attempting this experiment in the future. This is the stuff of which insanity is made. Be careful with it when manhandling patients.

severely, is apathetic and this tone, being the nearest to death, is the most dangerous one to the individual. The rage emotion communicated to an "unconscious" person gives him a rage engram he can dramatize. This is most harmful to the society. A merely hostile tone present around an "unconscious" person gives him a merely hostile engram (covert hostility). With two people present, each having a different mood, the "unconscious" person receives an engram with two valences other than his own. When this happens, he will first dramatize the winning valence with its mood and, if forced from this, will dramatize the second valence with its mood. Driven from this in a chronic engram, he goes insane.

Nothing here should be construed to mean that a person only uses or dramatizes sympathy engrams. This is very far from the case. The sympathy engram gives him the chronic psychosomatic illness. He can dramatize any engram he has when it is restimulated.

Emotion, then, is communication *and* a personal condition. The cellular-level evaluation of a situation depends upon any other analyzer present, even if that analyzer is thoroughly hostile to it. Lacking such evaluation, the individual takes his own tone for the moment.

There is another condition of emotion which is of extreme and useful interest to the therapist, since it is the first thing with which he will have to deal in opening a case. We do not mean here to start discussing therapy, but to describe a necessary part of emotion.

Great loss and other swift and severe suppressor action dams up emotion in an engram. Loss itself can be a shock to reduce analytical power. And an engram is received. If it is the loss of a sympathetic person on whom an individual has depended, it seems to the individual as if death itself stalks him. When such a suppressor effect occurs, it is as if a strong steel spring had been compressed within the engram. When it releases, it comes with a terrible rush of emotion (if this discharge is, indeed, emotion, though we hardly know what other name to call it).

Life force apparently gets dammed up at these points in life. There may be enormous quantities of that life force available, but some of it becomes suppressed into a loss engram. After that, the person does not seem to possess as much fluid vitality as before. This may be not emotion, but life force itself. The mind then has below it, as in a cyst, a great quantity of sorrow or despair. The more of these charges exist in such an encysted state, the less free are the emotions of the individual. This may be on a basis of suppression to a point from which there is no swift rising. Nothing in the person's future seems to bring him up to any plane like those he occupied before.

The glory and color of childhood vanishes as one progresses into later years. But the strange part of it is that this glamour and beauty and sensitivity to life are not *gone*. They are encysted. One of the most remarkable experiences a Clear has is to find, in the process of therapy, that he is recovering appreciation of the beauty in the world.

Persons, as they live forward from childhood, suffer loss after loss, and each loss takes from them a little more of this θ quantity which may be, indeed, life force itself. Bound up within them, that force is denied them and, indeed, reacts against them.

Only this emotional encysting can, for instance, compartment the mind of a person who is multivalent or who cannot see or hear his past. The analytical mind, worked upon by the reactive bank, compartments and divides with loss after loss until there is no free flow left. Then a man dies.

Thus we could say that emotion, or what has been called emotion, is really in two sections: First, there is the endocrine system which, handled either by the analytical mind in the upper two zones or the reactive mind in the lower two zones, brings emotional responses of fear, enthusiasm, apathy, etc. Second, there would be life force itself becoming compartmented by engrams and being sealed up, little by little, in the reactive bank.

It is possible that a therapy could be formulated which would spring out these various life force charges only and create thereby a full Clear. Unfortunately, to date, this has not been possible.

The odd part of emotion is that it is so ordinarily based on the word content of engrams. If an engram says, "I am afraid," then the aberree is afraid. If an engram says, "I am calm," even if the rest of the engram gives him chattering shakes, the aberree still has to be "calm."

The problem of emotion as endocrine balance and life force has another complication in that the physical pain in an engram is often mistaken for a particular emotion named in the engram. For instance, the engram can say with verbal content that the individual is "sexually excited" and have as a pain content an ache in the legs and have as an actual emotional content (the valence that says, "I'm sexually excited") anger. This, to the aberree dramatizing it, is a complex affair. When he is "sexually excited"–he has an idea what that means as just language–he is also angry and has an ache in the legs. This is actually very amusing in many cases and has led to a standard set of clinical jokes, all of which begin with, "You know, I feel like everybody else."

Dianeticists, having discovered that people evaluate the emotions, beliefs, intelligence and somatics of the world in terms of their own engramic reactions, delight in discovering new concepts of "emotion." "You know how people feel when they're happy; their ears burn." "I feel just like anybody else when I'm happy; my feet and eyes ache." "Of course I know how people feel when they're happy; just pin prickles going all over them." "I wonder how people can stand to be passionate when it makes their noses hurt so." "Of course I know how people feel when they're excited; they have to go to the toilet."

Probably every person on earth has his own peculiar definition for every emotional state in terms of engram command. The command plus the somatics and perceptics make what they call an "emotional state."

Actually, the problem, then, should be defined in terms of the Clear, who can function without engramic orders from the reactive mind. So defined, it breaks down in terms of the endocrine system and the varying level of life force free to resurge against the suppressor.

Laughter, it should be added, is not strictly speaking an emotion, but a relief from emotion. The early Italians had a very definite idea, as represented by their folk tales, that laughter was of therapeutic value. Melancholy was the only mental illness these tales consider and laughter was its only cure. In Dianetics, we have a great deal to do with laughter. In therapy, patients vary in their laughter reaction from the slight chuckle to hilarious mirth. Any engram which really releases may be expected to begin somewhere between tears and boredom and end with laughter; the nearer the engram's tone is to tears at the first contact, the more certainly laughter will appear as it is relieved.

There is a stage of therapy often reached by the preclear when his entire past life seems to be a subject of uncontrollable mirth. This does not mean he is Clear, but it means that a large proportion of the encysted charges have been tapped. A preclear has laughed for two days almost without ceasing. Hebephrenia is not the same thing as this laughter. For the relief of the preclear, on realizing the shadowy aspect and completely knowable character of his past fears and terrors, is hearty.

Laughter plays a definite role in therapy. It is quite amusing to see a preclear, who has been haunted by an engram which contained great emotional charge, suddenly relieve it. For the situation, no matter how gruesome it was, when relieved, is in all its aspects a subject of great mirth. The laughter fades away as he becomes disinterested in it and he can be said to be "Tone 3" about it.

Laughter is definitely the relief of painful emotion.

PRENATAL EXPERIENCE *and* BIRTH

OLD WOMEN LESS than a hundred years ago talked wisely about "prenatal influence" and how a woman marked her child. Many such intuitive thoughts are based, actually, on observed data. It can be observed that the child born out of wedlock is often a luckless creature (in a society which frowns upon such bearings). These tenets have been held in the marketplace for a great many millennia. Just because they have been held is no reason they are true, but they make an excellent beginning for a chapter on prenatal experience and birth.

If Dianetics had worked on obscure theories, such as those of the old women or those of the mystics who believe that "childish delusions" are capable of aberrating a child, Dianetics would not be a science of mind. But it was no obscure theory which brought about the discovery of the exact role prenatal experience and birth play in aberration and psychosomatic ills.

Many schools of mental healing from the Aesculapian to the modern hypnotist were studied after the basic philosophy of Dianetics had been postulated. Much data was accumulated, many experiments were made. The fundamentals about engrams had been formulated and "unconsciousness" had been discovered as being a period of actual recording when the theory began to predict new phenomena not hitherto observed.

There has been, in recent years, a practice called "narcosynthesis." This was actually a branch of "hypnoanalysis" and "deep analysis." It did not produce Clears and it did not even produce alleviation in the majority of its cases, but it was discovered to be an aberrative factor in itself. A thing which aberrates may well lead to something which removes aberrations if it is studied scientifically. Narcosynthesis was so studied. Several cases were examined on which narcosynthesis had been employed. Some of these cases had experienced relief from narcosynthesis. Others had become a great deal worse.

Working with hypnoanalysis, it was discovered that the technique could be varied until it would actually remove the aberrative charge contained in *locks.* In treating schizophrenics with narcosynthesis, it was found that the *locks* (periods of mental anguish not including physical pain or "unconsciousness") would sometimes spring (clear) and sometimes not.

Narcosynthesis is a complicated name for a very ancient process quite well-known in Greece and India. It is drug hypnotism. And it is generally employed either by those practitioners who do not know hypnosis or on those patients who will not succumb to ordinary hypnotism. A shot of sodium pentothal is given intravenously to the patient and he is asked to count backwards. Shortly he stops counting, at which the injection is also stopped. The patient is now in a state of "deep sleep." That this is not *sleep* seems to have missed both narcosynthesists and hypnotists. It is actually a depressant on the awareness of an individual so that those attention units which remain behind the curtain of his reactive bank can be reached directly. These attention units are up against the standard banks. The bypass circuits (demon circuits) which lie between these banks and "I" have themselves been bypassed. In other words, a section of the analytical mind has been exposed which is not aberrated. It is not very powerful and it is not highly intelligent, but it has the advantage of being hard up against the standard banks. This is *basic personality.* The intent and purpose and persistence of these few attention units have the same quality and direction as the whole analytical mind would have if it were Clear. It is a very nice, cooperative group of attention units and it is very useful, for basic personality has all recalls: sonic, audio, tactile, smell, pain, etc. It can get at anything that is in the banks, which is everything perceived or thought in a lifetime, minute by minute. These qualities of basic personality have been very poorly described in hypnotism and it is doubtful, even if it was generally known, that sonic was part of the recall system disclosed by deep hypnotism or the drug hypnotism called narcosynthesis.

A study of basic personality in a multivalent subject who had poor memory, no good recalls and scant imagination disclosed the information that BP (the attention units called *basic personality*) was more able to select out data than AP (*aberrated personality* as represented by the awake subject). It was further discovered that AP could ordinarily *return* better than BP, so far as time-distance went, but that when AP arrived at the earliest place, it was unable to manage recall. But if AP had gone back and established a vague contact with an incident, drug hypnotism or standard hypnotism used on him when he was in *present time* (no longer *returned*) would then permit BP to return. Drug hypnotism has seldom been able to force back very early into a patient's life. But by making the strength of AP go back and then using

BP for the recall, some very early incidents could be reached. This trick was invented to overcome some of the difficulties which had made drug hypnosis relatively uncertain in results.

Then another factor was discovered. All those patients who had been treated by narcosynthesis had become worse every time the people doing the work had crossed over, but left (because "everybody knew" an "unconscious" person didn't record) a period of "unconsciousness." When one of these "unconscious" periods was so probed–by the drug hypnosis called narcosynthesis–the patient usually became worse, not better. Doing a little more probing than had been done by the usual practitioners, Dianetic research entered some of the late-life "unconscious" periods and, with much labor, laid them bare.

Now all drug hypnosis, whether it is called narcosynthesis or a visit from the god Aesculapius, is still hypnosis. Whatever is said to a hypnotized subject remains as a positive suggestion, and these positive suggestions are simply engrams with a somewhat lighter effect and a shorter duration. When a drug is present, the hypnotism is complicated by the fact that hypnotic drugs are, after all, poisons; the body is then possessed of a permanent (at least until Dianetics was discovered) somatic to go along with the suggestion. Drug hypnotism invariably creates an engram. Whatever a practitioner says to a drugged subject becomes engramic in some degree. In the course of Dianetic research it first was supposed, playing back the careless chatter of practitioners out of the minds of patients they had placed under drug hypnosis, that this carelessness in saying so many aberrative things was responsible for some of the failure. But this was found to be true in a very limited sense. Then it was discovered that when the "unconscious" periods were reached by drug hypnosis, they refused to *lift* even when the patient recounted them scores of times. This was blamed on the drug character of the hypnosis.

Straight hypnotism was then used to reach these late "unconscious" periods and these periods still failed to *lift*. Therefore, it was adjudged safe to continue drug use on those patients who refused hypnosis. And the AP-BP alternate trick began to be employed.

It was discovered by drug hypnosis, where it was necessary, and straight hypnosis, where that was possible, that the "schizophrenic" (the *multivalent* aberree) could be made to reach very early periods in every case. And it was further found that an *early* period of "unconsciousness" would often lift. Experimentation brought about a scientific axiom:

THE EARLIER THE PERIOD OF "UNCONSCIOUSNESS," THE MORE LIKELY IT IS TO LIFT.

That is a fundamental axiom of Dianetic therapy.

Manic-depressives who had sonic recall were worked upon, most of them by straight hypnosis, and it was discovered that they also followed this rule. But it was most dramatic in the multivalent aberree: for when the engram did not lift, it impinged against his analytical mind when he was awakened and created a variation in his psychoses and brought with it psychosomatic illnesses as well.

This brought about an understanding of why the multivalent aberree, under narcosynthesis, was made worse whenever some practitioner had glided over (but not entered, of course) a late-life period of "unconsciousness." Now came the problem of applying the axiom. It was postulated that the primary engram must in some way suppress later engrams. In view of other data and postulates, this was an entirely reasonable assumption. The earlier a person went in the life of a multivalent aberree, the less likelihood there was of restimulating him artificially. Often an engram at around two or three years of age would lift entirely and give him a great deal of relief.

The problem of this research was very far from the same problem of those who, not knowing about the reactive mind and "unconsciousness," tried merely to find computing factors on a rational level or incidents of everyday life as aberrative factors in a patient.

When an engram is touched, it is very resistive, particularly above the age of two years. Further, the whole reactive bank was buried deeply under foggy layers of "unconsciousness" and was further safeguarded by a mechanism of the analytical mind which tended to prohibit it from touching pain or painful emotion. The reactive bank was protecting itself all the way through the research, but it was obviously the answer. The problem was how to achieve its relief, if it could be relieved.

Having made several multivalent personalities intensely uncomfortable, a new necessity level was reached whereby something had to be done about the problem. But there was this shining hope, the above axiom. A bridge between insanity and sanity had to be built and there, in the axiom, one had at least a glimmer of a plan. The earlier one had experienced this fog and pain, the lighter these engrams seemed to be.

Then, one day, a multivalent patient, under drugs, went back to his birth. He suffered the pain–and it was very painful with this crude technique, for Dianetics had not yet smoothed down to a well-oiled piece of machinery–and he floundered through the "unconsciousness" of the period and he fought the doctor who had tried to put drops in his eyes and he generally resented the entire proceedings. AP had been sent down first, then later, under drugs, BP had contacted the incident.

This seemed a remarkable day for Dianetics. After twenty runs through birth, the patient experienced a recession of all somatics and "unconsciousness" and aberrative content. He had had asthma. It seemed that this asthma had been caused by the doctor's enthusiasm in yanking him off the table just when he was fighting for his first breath. He had had conjunctivitis. That came from the eyedrops. He had had sinusitis. That had come from the nose swabs used by the pretty nurse.

Rejoicing was held for he seemed to be a new man. A primary psychosis about being "pushed around" had vanished. The subjective reality of this incident was intense. Objective reality did not matter, but this patient had a mother near at hand and objective reality was established simply by returning her in therapy to *his* birth. They had not communicated about it in detail. The recording of her sequence compared word for word with his sequence, detail for detail, name for name. Possibility, even if they had communicated, of such duplication, outside the Dianetic situation, was mathematically impossible. And she had been "unconscious" during his birth and had always supposed that the affair had been quite different and the *return* data collapsed her awake description of it as being so much fable.

In order to make sure that this was no freak (for it is a very poor research man who will base conclusions on a series of one), two manic-depressives were returned to their births and both completed the experience. *But one of these two birth engrams would not lift!*

The postulated axiom was called into play again. If one could find the earliest engram, then the others would lift each in turn. That was the hope.

The manic-depressive whose birth had not lifted was returned to a period before birth in an effort to find an earlier engram.

Structural theories, as fondly held for ages, had thoroughly collapsed already when "unconscious" fog and pain had been penetrated to discover the engram as an aberrative unit. Tests had held up the discovery that all data, awake, asleep and "unconscious," from the moment of conception on was always recorded somewhere in the mind or body. The little matter of myelin sheathing, since it had already been disproven by laboratory research which included the reaching of birth, was discarded. The theory that no recordings can take place in the mind until the nerves are sheathed depends upon a theoretical postulate, has never been subjected to scientific research, and depends for its existence upon Authority alone–and a "science" which depends on Authority alone is a breath in the wind of truth and is therefore no science at all. That babies cannot record until the myelin sheathing is formed has about as much truth, on investigation, as the fact that penis envy is the cause of female homosexuality. Neither theory, when applied, works. For the baby, after all, is composed of cells and it is evidenced now by much research that the cell, not an organ, records the engram.

Thus there was no inhibition about looking earlier than birth for what Dianetics had begun to call *basic-basic* (the first engram of the first chain of engrams). And an earlier engram was reached.

It has since been discovered that a great deal of recording is done by the child in the womb which is not engramic. For a time it was thought that the child in the womb records on the proposition of "extended hearing," where hearing tunes up in the presence of danger and particularly during "unconsciousness." But the first research discovered prenatal engrams to be most easily reached when they contained a great deal of pain. *Cells, not the individual, are evidenced to record pain. And the reactive engram bank is composed only of cells.*

Recourse to nature rather than recourse to Authority is the very building block of modern science. So long as Galen remained an Authority on blood, none but "madmen" like da Vinci, Shakespeare and William Harvey even thought to experiment to find out what truly was the action of blood! So long as Aristotle remained the Authority for All, the Dark Ages reigned. Advance comes from asking free-minded questions of nature, not from quoting the works and thinking the thoughts of bygone years. Recourse to precedent is an assertion that yesterday's mentors were better informed than today's: an assertion which fades before the truth that knowledge is compounded of the experience of yesterdays, of which we have more, most certainly, than the best-informed mentor of yesterday itself.

In that Dianetics was based on a philosophy that used the cell as the basic building block, the fact that recording of engrams was done by cells came with less surprise than it otherwise might have. The engram is not a memory; *it is a cellular trace of recordings impinged deeply into the very structure of the body itself.*

The experience of which cells themselves were capable had already been tested. It had been found that a monocell divided not only its substance, but gave its total experience, as a master disc will make duplicates, to its offspring. Now this is a peculiarity of monocells: they survive as identities. Each is personally its forebear. Cell A divides to a first generation; this generation is also Cell A; the second generation, the second division, creates an entity which is still Cell A. Lacking the necessity of such laborious processes as construction and birth and growth before reproduction, the monocell simply splits. And everything it has learned could be postulated to be contained in the new generation. Cell A dies but through generations from it, the latest generation is still Cell A. Man's belief that *he* is to live in his progeny might possibly derive from this cellular identity of procreation. Another interesting possibility lies in the fact that even neurons exist in embryo in the zygote and neurons do not themselves divide, but are like organisms (and may have the virus as their basic building block).

Dianetics, as a study of function and the science of mind, does not need any postulate concerning structure, however. The only test is whether or not a fact works. If it does work and can be used, it is a scientific fact. And the prenatal engram is a scientific fact. Tested and checked for objective reality, it still stands firm. And as for subjective reality, *the acceptance of the prenatal engram as a working fact alone makes possible the Clear.*

At the end of a series of 270 Clears and alleviations, a short series of five cases was taken to finally settle the argument. These five cases were not permitted to admit anything before birth. They were treated with everything Dianetics, hypnotism and other therapeutics could offer, and no Clear was obtained. This ruled out the "personality of the operator" or "suggestion" or "faith" as factors in Dianetics. These five cases had never been informed of prenatal engrams. Each swerved in toward them, but was restrained without informing him that engrams existed that early. The five were alleviated as to some variety of psychosomatic ills, but the ills were only alleviated, not completely cured. The aberrations remained but little changed. They were extremely disappointed since each had heard something of "the miracles Dianetics could perform." Before them 270 cases had been worked and 270 cases had reached prenatal engrams. And 270 cases had been Cleared or alleviated as the Dianeticist chose and time permitted. All could have been Cleared with an additional average of 100 or so hours for each of the persons who were alleviated. In short, on random cases–and selected cases so that at least two of each classification of neurosis or psychosis were included in the clearing–when prenatal engrams and birth were taken into account and used in therapy, results were obtained. When these factors were not taken into account, results were no more favorable than those attained in the best successes of past schools–which is not nearly good enough for a science of mind.

Dianetics had prenatal and birth engrams wished off on it as facts existing in the nature of things. That past schools have been passing over these engrams and into the prenatal area without success does not mean that prenatals could not be found any more than it means that these past schools found much value in prenatal experience when they considered it at all. The problem is slightly more complex: the difficulty lay in finding the reactive bank which was occluded by "unconsciousness" which had never before been penetrated wittingly as "unconsciousness." The discovery of this reactive bank led to the discovery of *prenatal engrams*, which are quite different from "prenatal memory."

After a few cases had been examined as to objective and subjective reality, Dianetics was forced to accept, if it wished a Clear, the fact that the cells of the fetus record. A few more cases and a little more experience discovered that the embryo cells record. And suddenly it was discovered that recording begins in the cells of the zygote, which is to say, with conception. That the body recalls conception, which is a high-level survival activity, has little to do with engrams. Most patients to date sooner or later startle themselves by finding themselves swimming up a channel or waiting to be connected with. The recording is there. And there's little use arguing with a preclear that he cannot recall being a sperm, engramic or not as the case may be. It must be remarked because any Dianeticist will encounter this.

Anyone postulating that "return to the womb" was an ambition should have examined life in the womb a little more carefully. Even a poor scientist would have at least tried to find out if anybody could recall it before he made a statement that there was a memory of it. But life in the womb does not seem to be the Paradise it has been poetically, if not scientifically, represented. Actuality discloses that three men and a horse in a telephone booth would have but little less room than an unborn baby. The womb is wet, uncomfortable and unprotected.

Mama sneezes, baby gets knocked "unconscious." Mama runs lightly and blithely into a table and baby gets its head staved in. Mama has constipation and baby, in the anxious effort, gets squashed. Papa becomes passionate and baby has the sensation of being put into a running washing machine. Mama gets hysterical, baby gets an engram. Papa hits Mama, baby gets an engram. Junior bounces on Mama's lap, baby gets an engram. And so it goes.

People have scores of prenatal engrams when they are normal. They can have more than two hundred. And each one is aberrative. Each contains pain and "unconsciousness."

Engrams received as a zygote are potentially the most aberrative, being wholly reactive. Those received as an embryo are intensely aberrative. Those received as the fetus are enough to send people to institutions all by themselves.

Zygote, embryo, fetus, infant, child, adult: these are all the same person. Time has been considered the Great

Healer. That can be filed with the things "everybody knew." On a conscious level, it may be true. But on a reactive level, time is nothing. The engram, whenever received, is strong in proportion to the degree it is restimulated.

The mechanism of an engram has an interesting feature. It is not "reasoned" or analyzed nor does it have any meaning until it has been keyed-in. A baby before speech could have an engram in restimulation, but that engram must have been keyed-in by the analytical data the baby has.

The reactive mind steals meaning from the analytical mind. An engram is just so many wave-recordings until it is keyed-in and those recordings, by such restimulation, become effective upon the analytical mind. It may be that the engram never has any reason or meaning in itself, but only thrusts its waves forward as unreasoned things at the body and analyzer, and the body and analyzer, through mechanisms, give them meaning. In other words, the engram is not a sentient recording containing meanings. It is merely a series of impressions such as a needle might make on wax. These impressions are meaningless to the body until the engram keys-in, at which time aberrations and psychosomatics occur.

Thus it can be understood that the prenatal child has no remotest idea of what is being said in terms of words. It does learn, being an organism, that certain things may mean certain dangers. But this is every bit as far as it goes with recording. The mind must become more or less fully formed before the engram can impinge into the analytical level.

The prenatal child can, of course, experience terror. When the parents or the professional abortionist start after it and thrust it full of holes, it knows fear and pain.

It has, however, this prenatal child, an advantage in its situation. Being surrounded by amniotic fluid and dependent for nutrition on its mother, being in a state of growth and easily re-formed physically, it can repair an enormous amount of damage and does. The recovery qualities of the human body are never higher than before birth. Damage which would maim an infant for life or would kill a grown man can be taken in stride by the prenatal child. Not that this damage does not make an engram–it certainly does, complete with all data and speech and emotion–but that this damage does not easily kill it is the point here.

Why people try to abort children is a problem which has its answer only in aberration, for it is very difficult to abort a child. One can say that in the attempt, the mother herself is in more danger of dying than the child, *no matter what method is used.*

A society which suppresses sex as evil and which is so aberrated that any member of it will attempt an abortion, is a society which is dooming itself to ever-rising insanity. For it is a scientific fact that abortion attempts are the most important factor in aberration. The child on whom the abortion is attempted is condemned to live with *murderers,* whom he reactively knows to be murderers, through all his weak and helpless youth! He forms unreasonable attachments to grandparents, has terrified reactions to all punishments, grows ill easily and suffers long. And there is no such thing as a guaranteed way to abort a child. Use contraceptives, not a knitting needle or the douche bag, to hold down population. Once the child is conceived, no matter how "shameful" the circumstances, no matter the *mores,* no matter the income, that man or woman who would attempt an abortion on an unborn child is attempting a murder which will seldom succeed and is laying the foundation of a childhood of illness and heartache.

Anyone attempting an abortion is committing an act against the whole society and the future; any judge or doctor recommending an abortion should be instantly deprived of position and practice, whatever his "reason."

If a person knows he has committed this crime against a child who has been born, he should do all possible to have that child Cleared as soon as possible after the age of eight and in the meantime should treat that child with all the decency and courtesy possible in order to keep the engram out of restimulation. Otherwise, he may send that child to an institution for the insane.

A large proportion of allegedly feebleminded children are actually attempted abortion cases whose engrams place them in fear-paralysis or regressive palsy and which command them not to grow, but to be where they are forever.

However many billions America spends yearly on institutions for the insane and jails for the criminals are spent primarily because of attempted abortions done by some sex-blocked mother to whom children are a curse, not a blessing of God.

Antipathy toward children means a blocked Second Dynamic. Physiological examination of anyone with such blockage will demonstrate a physical derangement of the genitalia or glands. Dianetic therapy would demonstrate attempted abortion or an equally foul prenatal existence and would Clear the individual.

The case of the child who as this is read is not yet born, but upon whom abortion has been attempted, is not hopeless. If he is treated with decency after he is born and if he is not restimulated by witnessing quarrels, he will wax and grow fat until he is eight and can be Cleared, at which time he will probably be much startled to learn the truth. But that startlement and any antagonism included in it will vanish with the finishing of the Clear and his love of his parents will be greater than before.

All these things are scientific facts, tested and rechecked and tested again. And with them can be produced a Clear on whom our racial future depends.

BOOK TWO, CHAPTER EIGHT

CONTAGION *of* ABERRATION

DISEASE IS CONTAGIOUS. Germs, traveling from one individual to another, wander through an entire society, respecting none until stopped by such things as sulfa or penicillin.

Aberrations are contagious. Like germs, they respect none and carry forward from individual to individual, from parents to child, respecting none until they are stopped by Dianetics.

The people of yesterday supposed that genetic insanity must exist, for it could be observed that the children of aberrated parents were often themselves aberrated. There is genetic insanity, but it is limited to the case of actually missing parts. A very small percentage of insanity falls into such a category and its manifestation is mental dullness or failure to coordinate and beyond these has no aberrative quality whatever (such people receive engrams which complicate their cases).

The contagion of aberration is too simple in principle to be much labored here. In Dianetics, we learn that only moments of "unconsciousness," short or long and of greater or lesser depth, can contain engrams. When a person is rendered "unconscious," people in his vicinity react more or less at the dictates of their engrams: in fact, the "unconsciousness" is quite ordinarily caused by somebody's dramatization. A Clear, then, could be rendered unconscious by an aberree who is dramatizing and the aberree's dramatization of his engram would enter as an engram into the Clear.

The mechanics are simple. People under stress, if aberrated, dramatize engrams. Such dramatization may involve the injury of another person and render him more or less "unconscious." The "unconscious" person then receives as an engram the dramatization.

This is not the only way contagion of aberration gets about. People on operating tables, under anesthetic, are subjected to the more or less aberrated conversation of those present. This conversation enters into the "unconscious" person as an engram. Similarly, at the scene of accidents, the emergency nature of the experience may excite people into dramatizations and if a person is "unconscious" because of the accident, an engram is received.

Aberrated parents are certain to infect their children with engrams. The father and mother, in dramatizing their own engrams around sick or injured children, pass them along just as certainly as if those engrams were bacteria. This does not mean that the total reactive bank of a child is composed solely of the parents' engrams, for there are many exterior influences to the home which can enter into the child when it is "unconscious." And it does not mean that the child is going to react to the same engrams the way either parent might react, for the child, after all, is an individual with an inherent personality, a power of choice and a different experience pattern. But it does mean that it is utterly inevitable that aberrated parents will in some way aberrate their children.

Misconceptions and poor data in a society's culture become engrams because not all the conduct around an "unconscious" person is dramatization. If some society believed that fish-eating brought on leprosy, it is quite certain that this false datum would find its way into engrams and sooner or later someone would develop a leprosy-like disease after having eaten fish.

Primitive societies, being subject to much mauling by the elements, have many more occasions for injury than civilized societies. Further, such primitive societies are alive with false data. Further, their practice of medicine and mental healing is on a very aberrative level by itself. The number of engrams in a primitive would be astonishing. Moved out of his restimulative area and taught English, he would escape the penalty of much of his reactive data. But in his native habitat, the primitive is only outside the bars of a madhouse because there are no madhouses provided by his tribe. It is a safe estimate, and one based on better experience than is generally available to those who base conclusions on "modern Man" by studying primitive races, that primitives are far more aberrated than civilized peoples. Their savageness, their unprogressiveness, their incidence of illness all stem from their reactive patterns, not from their inherent personalities. Measuring one set of aberrees by another set of aberrees is not likely to lead to much data. And the contagion of aberration, being much greater in a primitive tribe, and the falsity of the superstitious data in the engrams of such a tribe both lead to a conclusion which, observed on the scene, is carried out by actuality.

Contagion of aberration is very easily studied in the process of clearing any aberree whose parents fought. Mother, for instance, might be relatively unaberrated at the beginning of the marriage. If she is beaten by her husband who is, after all, dramatizing, she will begin to pick up his aberrations as part of her own reactive pattern. This is particularly noticeable when one is clearing a person who was conceived shortly after his parents' marriage or before it. Papa may begin with a certain dramatization which includes beating a wife. Whatever he says in such a dramatization will sooner or later begin to affect the wife and she may–unless extraordinarily well balanced–begin to dramatize these things on her own. Eventually, when the child is born, she will begin to dramatize on the child, thus putting him into a continual state of restimulation.

Birth is one of the most remarkable engrams in terms of contagion. Here the mother and child both receive the same engram which differs only in the location of pain and the depths of "unconsciousness." Whatever the doctors, nurses and other people associated with the delivery say to the mother during labor and birth and immediately afterwards before the child is taken away is recorded in the reactive bank, making an identical engram in both mother and child.

This engram is remarkably destructive in several ways. The mother's voice can restimulate the birth engram in the child and the presence of the child can restimulate the giving-birth engram in the mother. Thus, they are mutually restimulative. In view of the fact that they have all the other restimulators also in common, a later-life situation can cause them each to suffer simultaneously from the engram. If birth included a slammed window, a slammed window may trigger birth dramatization in both, simultaneously, with resultant hostilities or apathies.

Should a doctor become angry or despairing, the emotional tone of birth can be severe. And if the doctor talks at all, the conversation takes on its full reactive literal meaning to both mother and child.

Many cases were Cleared where both mother and child were available. One such case found the mother (as heard by the child in Dianetic clearing) moaning, "I'm so ashamed, I'm so ashamed," over and over. The child had a neurosis about shame. When the mother was Cleared, it was found that *her* mother at birth was moaning, "I'm so ashamed, I'm so ashamed." One can presume that this has been going along, by contagion, since Cheops built his tomb.

In the larger sphere of society, contagion of aberration is extremely dangerous and cannot but be considered as a vital factor in undermining the health of that society.

The social body behaves similarly to an organism in that there are social aberrations which exist within the society. The society grows and may fade like an organism which has people, not cells, for its parts. Where pain is leveled by the head of the society at any member in that society, a source of aberration is begun which will be contagious. The reasons against corporal punishment are not "humanitarian," they are practical. A society which practices punishment of any kind against any of its members is carrying on a contagion of aberration. The society has a social engram, society size, which says punishment is necessary. Punishment is meted. The jails and institutions fill. And then one day some portion of the society, depressed into Zone 1 by a government's freedom with government engrams, jumps up and wipes the government out. And a new set of aberrations is formed from the violence attending the destruction. Violent revolutions never win because they begin this cycle of aberration.

A society filled with aberrees may feel it necessary to punish. There has been no remedy other than punishment. The provision of a remedy for unsocial conduct by members of the group is of more than passing interest to a government for a continuance of its own corporal practices; adding these to the continuing aberrations of the past seriously depresses the survival potential of that government and will someday cause that government to fall. After many governments so fall, its people too perish from this earth.

Contagion of aberration is never more apparent than in that social insanity called war. Wars never solve the need of wars. Fight to save the world for democracy or save it from Confucianism and the fight is inevitably lost by all. War has become associated in the past with competition and it has been believed, therefore, by shifty logic, that wars were necessary. A society which advances into a war as a solution of its problems cannot but depress its own survival potential. No government was ever permitted to enter a war without costing its people some of their liberties. The end product is the apathy of a ruling priesthood, where mystery and superstition alone can band the insane remnants of a people together. This is too easily observed in past histories to need much amplification. A democracy engaging in war has always lost some of its democratic rights. As it engages in more and more wars, it eventually comes under the command of a dictator (rule by a single engram). The dictator, forcing his rule, increases the aberrations by his activity against minorities. Revolt begins to follow revolt. Priesthoods flourish. Apathy awaits. And after apathy comes death. So went Greece, so went Rome. So goes England. So goes Russia. And so goes the United States and with it goes Mankind.

Rule by force is a violation of the law of affinity, for force begets force. Rule by force reduces the self-determinism of the individuals in a society and therefore the self-determinism of the society itself. Contagion of aberration sweeps along like a forest fire.

Engrams beget engrams. And unless the dwindling spiral is interrupted by new lands and mongrel races which escape their aberrative environments, or by the arrival of a means to break the contagion of aberration by clearing individuals, a race will reach downward to the end of the cycle – Zone 0.

A race is as great as its individual members are self-determined.

In the smaller sphere of the family, as in the national scenes, contagion of aberration produces an interruption of optimum survival.

Self-determinism is the only possible way a computer can be built to give rational answers. Holding down 7 in an adding machine causes it to give wrong answers. Entering fixed and not-to-be-rationalized answers into any human being will cause him to compute wrong answers. Survival depends on right answers. Engrams enter from the exterior world into the hidden recesses below rational thinking and prevent rational answers being reached. This is exterior-determinism. Any interference with self-determinism cannot but lead to wrong computations.

In that a Clear is cooperative, a society of Clears would cooperate. This may be an idyllic, Utopian dream and it may not be. In a family of Clears there is observable harmony and cooperation. A Clear can recognize a superior computation when he sees one. He does not have to be slugged and held down and made to *obey* to make him put a shoulder to the wheel. If he *is* made to obey, independent of his thinking, his self-determinism is interrupted to a point where he cannot get right answers; the society which holds him has penalized itself his ability to think and act rationally. The only way a Clear could so be forced would be to give him engrams or turn a neurosurgeon loose upon his brain. But a Clear does not need to be forced. For if the job is important enough to do in terms of general need, he will most certainly do it according to his intelligence and do it as well as possible. One never observes the *forced* individual doing a job well, just as one never observes a *forced* society winning against an equally prosperous free society.

A family which runs on the godhead plan, where somebody must be obeyed without question, is never a happy family. Its prosperity may be present in some material aspects, but its apparent survival as a unit is superficial.

Forced groups are invariably less efficient than free groups working for the common good. But any group which contains aberrated members is likely to become entirely aberrated as a group through contagion. The effort to restrain aberrated members of a group inevitably restrains the group as a whole and leads to further and further restraint.

Clearing one member of a family of aberrees is seldom enough to resolve the problems of that family. If the husband has been aberrated, he will have aberrated or restimulated his wife and children in one way or another, even when he used no physical violence upon them. The parents implant their mutual aberrations in the children and the children, being potentially self-determined units, revolt back to stir up the aberrations of the parents. In that so many of these aberrations, by contagion, have become mutual and held in common with the whole family, the happiness of the family is severely undermined.

The corporal punishment of children is just another facet of the problem of the forced group. If anyone cares to argue over the necessity of punishing children, let him examine the source of the misbehavior of the children.

The child who is aberrated may not have his engrams entirely keyed-in. He may have to wait until he himself is married and has children or a pregnant wife to have restimulators enough to cause him to become, suddenly, one of these things they call a "mature adult" blind to the beauty of the world and burdened by all its griefs. But the child is nevertheless aberrated and has many dramatizations. The child is in a very unlucky situation in that he has with him his two most powerful restimulators–his mother and father. These assume the power of physical punishment over him. And they are giants to him. He is a pygmy. And he has to depend upon them for food, clothing and shelter. One can speak very grandly about the "delusions of childhood" until he knows the engram background of most children.

The child is on the unkind receiving end of all the dramatizations of his parents. A Cleared child is a most remarkable thing to observe: he is human! Affinity alone can pull him through. The spoiled child is the child whose decisions have been interrupted continuously and who is robbed of his independence. Affection could no more spoil a child than the sun could be put out by a bucket of gasoline.

The beginning and end of "child psychology" is that a child is a human being, that he is entitled to his dignity and self-determinism. The child of aberrated parents is a problem because of the contagion of aberration and because he is denied any right to dramatize or counter. The wonder is not that children are a problem, but that they are sane in any action. For by contagion, punishment, and denial of self-determinism, the children of today have been denied all the things required to make a rational life. And these are the future family and the future race.

This is not a dissertation on children nor politics, however, but a chapter on contagion of aberration. Dianetics covers human thought, and human thought is wide ground. When one gazes at the potentialities inherent in the mechanism of contagion, respect for the inherent stability of Man cannot but arise. No "wild animal" reacting with inherent "asocial tendencies" could have built Nineveh or Boulder Dam. Carrying the contagion mechanism like some Old Man of the Sea, we have yet come far. Now that we know it, perhaps we shall truly reach the stars.

BOOK TWO, CHAPTER NINE

KEYING-IN *the* ENGRAM

THE SINGLE SOURCE of inorganic mental illness and organic psychosomatic illness is the reactive engram bank. The reactive mind impinges these engrams upon the analytical mind and the organism whenever they are restimulated after being keyed-in.

There are many known incidents in a lifetime which apparently have a profound influence upon the happiness and mental condition of the individual. The individual remembers these and to them attributes his troubles. In a measure he is right: he is at least looking back at incidents which are held in place by engrams. He does not see the engrams. In fact, unless he is acquainted with Dianetics, he does not know the engrams are there. And even then he will not know their contents until he has undergone therapy.

It can be demonstrated with ease that any moment of "conscious-level" unhappiness which contained great stress or emotion was not guilty of the charge of causing aberration and psychosomatic illness. These moments, of course, played a role in the matter: they were the *key-ins.*

The process of keying-in an engram is not very complex. Engram 105, let us say, was a moment of "unconsciousness" when the prenatal child was struck via mother, by father. The father, aware or not of the child, uttered the words, "Goddamn you, you filthy whore; you're no good!" This engram lay where it was impressed, in the reactive bank. Now it could lie there for seventy years and never become keyed-in. It contains a headache and a falling body and the grating of teeth and the intestinal sounds of the mother. And any of these sounds, post-birth, may be present in large quantities without *keying-in* this engram.

One day, however, the father becomes exasperated at the child. The child is tired and feverish, which is to say that his analytical mind may not be at its highest level of activity. And the father has a certain set of engrams which he dramatizes and one of these engrams is the above incident. And the father reaches out and slaps the child and says, "Goddamn you; you're no good!" The child cries. That night he has a headache and is much worse physically. And he feels both an intense hatred and a fear of his father. The engram has *keyed-in.* Now the sound of a falling body or grating teeth or any trace of anger of any kind in the father's voice will make the child nervous. His physical health will suffer. He will begin to have headaches.

If we take this child who has now become an adult and rake back over his past, we shall discover (though it may be occluded) a lock like the above key-in. And now not only the key-in; we may discover half a hundred, half a thousand such locks just on this one subject. One would say, unless he knew Dianetics, that this child was ruined postnatally by being beaten by the father, and one might attempt to bring the patient's mind back into better condition by removing these locks.

There are literally thousands, tens of thousands of locks in the average life. To take all of these locks away would be a task for Hercules. Every engram a person has, if it has been keyed-in, may have its hundreds of locks.

If conditioning existed as a mechanism of pain and stress, Mankind would be in very bad condition. Fortunately conditioning does not so exist. It appears to exist, but the appearance is not the fact. One would think that if a child were daily thrust around and reviled, he would eventually become conditioned into a belief that this was the way life was and that he had better turn against it.

Conditioning does not, however, exist. Pavlov may have been able to drive dogs mad by repeated experiments: this was simply bad observation on the part of the observer. The dogs might be trained to do this or that. But it was not conditioning. The dogs went mad because they were given engrams if and when they did go mad. A series of such experiments, properly conducted and observed, proves this contention.

The boy who was daily told he was no good and who apparently went into a decline solely because of that, declined only because of the engram. This is a happy fact. The engram may take a while to locate – a few hours – but when it is alleviated or refiled in the standard memory banks, everything which had locked onto it also refiles.

People trying to help others with their aberrations who did not know about engrams were, of course, operating with 2.9 strikes against any success. In the first place, the locks themselves may vanish down into the reactive bank. Thus we get a patient who says, "Oh, my father wasn't so bad. He was a pretty good guy." And we discovered, and the patient discovers, when an engram is sprung, that father was customarily to be found dramatizing. What the patient knows about his past before engrams are sprung is not worth cataloging. In another case we may find a patient saying, "Oh, I had a terrible childhood, a terrible childhood. I was beaten seriously." And we discover, when we get the engrams refiled, that the parents of this patient never laid a hand on him in punishment or wrath in his entire life.

An engram may coast along without being keyed-in for decades. One of the most remarkable types of case is one which spent an entire youth without displaying any aberration. Then suddenly, at the age of twenty-six, we discover him to be so aberrated, so suddenly, that it appears he must have been hexed. Perhaps most of his engrams were concerned with the action of getting married and having children. He has never been married before. The first time he is weary or ill and realizes he has a wife on his hands, the first engram keys-in. Then the dwindling spiral begins to go to work. This one shuts down the analyzer enough so that others can be keyed-in. And finally, we may discover him in an institution.

The young girl who has been happy and carefree to the age of thirteen and then suddenly goes into a decline has not, that moment, received an engram. She has had an engram key-in which let another key-in. Fission reaction. This key-in may have required nothing more than the discovery that she was bleeding from the vagina. She has an emotional engram about this; she becomes frantic. The other engrams, as the days follow, may swing into position to impinge upon her. And so she becomes ill.

The first sexual experience may be one which keys-in an engram. This is so standard that sex has gotten a rather bad name for itself here and there as being an aberrative factor all by itself. Sex is not and never has been aberrative. Physical pain and emotion which incidentally contain sex as a subject are the aberrative factors.

It may be that a patient is urgent in her insistence that her father raped her when she was nine and that this is the cause of all her misery. Large numbers of insane patients claim this. And it is perfectly true. Father did rape her, but it happened she was only nine days beyond conception at the time. The pressure and upset of coitus is very uncomfortable to the child and normally can be expected to give the child an engram which will have as its content the sexual act and everything that was said.

Drug hypnosis is dangerous when one is trying to treat psychotics, as has been mentioned. And there are other reasons it is dangerous. Any operation under anesthetic or any drugging of a patient may bring about the keying-in of engrams. Here is the analyzer shutdown, there is the reactive bank open to be stirred by any comment made by the people around the drugged subject. Hypnotism itself is a condition in which engrams may be keyed-in which have never before been restimulated. The glassy-eyed stare of the person who has been "too often hypnotized," the lack of will seen in people too often hypnotized, the dependence of the subject upon the hypnotic operator–all these things stem from the keying-in of engrams. *Any* time the body is rendered "unconscious" without physical pain, no matter how light the degree of "unconsciousness" is, even if it is only the lightness of weariness, an engram may be keyed-in. And when "unconsciousness" is complicated by new physical pain, a new engram is formed which may gather up with it an entire bundle of old engrams not hitherto keyed-in. Such a late engram would be a *cross-engram* in that it crosses chains of engrams. And if such an engram resulted in a loss of sanity, it would be called a *break engram.*

There are some aspects to various drug "unconsciousnesses" which have been very perplexing in the past. Psychotic women often maintain, after they are awakened from a drugged sleep (and sometimes a hypnotic sleep), that they have been raped. Men occasionally maintain that the operator has tried to perform a homosexual act upon them while they were drugged. Although it occasionally occurs that people *are* raped after being drugged, the largest number of such assertions are merely an aspect of the key-in mechanism. Almost any child has been put through the prenatal discomfort of coitus. Often there was violent emotion other than passion present. Such an engram may stay out of circuit for years until drugged "unconsciousness" or some such thing keys it in. The patient goes to sleep without a keyed-in engram; he wakes up with one. He tries to justify the strange sensations he has (and engrams are timeless things unless they are arranged properly on the time track) and comes out with the "solution" that he must have been raped.

Childhood rapes are very seldom the responsible cause in sexual aberration. They are the key-in.

One looks at the conscious-level locks and sees sadness, mental anguish and misfortune. Some of the experience there seems to be so terrible that it must certainly cause aberration. But it does not. Man is a tough, resilient creature. These conscious-level experiences are at best only guideposts leading toward the actual seat of trouble, and that is not known in any detailed way to the individual.

The engram is never "computed." An example of this, on a lightly aberrative level, can be found in a child's punishment. If one examines a childhood where punishment has been corporal and frequent, he begins to understand the utter futility of the pain-drive theory. Punishment actually and literally and emphatically does no good of any kind whatsoever, but accomplishes quite the reverse, since it occasions a reactive revolt against the punishment source and is likely to cause not only a disintegration of a mind, but also a continual bedevilment of the punishment source. Man reacts to fight sources of pain. When he stops fighting them, he is mentally broken and of little use to anyone, much less himself.

We take a case of a boy who was beaten with a hairbrush every time he was "bad." In researching this case, the most searching inquiry fails to reveal any vivid recall of *why* he was punished, but only *that* he was punished. The progress of the event would go something like this: activity more or less rational, fright at threatened punishment, punishment, sorrow over punishment, renewed activity. The mechanics of the case showed the person to have been engaged in some activity which, whether others would consider it so or not, was nevertheless survival activity to him, giving him either pleasure or actual gains or even the assertion that he could and would survive. The moment punishment is threatened, old punishments go into restimulation as minor engrams, resting usually on major engrams; this shuts down the analytical power to some extent and the recording is now being done on a reactive level. The punishment takes place, submerging analytical awareness so that the punishment records in the engram bank only; the sorrow following is still in the period of analytical shutdown; the analyzer gradually turns on; full awareness returns, and then activity on an analytical plane can be resumed. All corporal punishment runs this gamut and all other punishments are, at best, locks following this same pattern with only the complete shutdown resulting from pain missing.

If the analyzer wants this data for computation, it is not available. There is a reaction in the reactive mind when the matter is approached. *But there are five courses the reactive mind can take with this data!* And there is no guarantee and no method between land and sky of knowing what course the reactive mind will take with the data except knowing the full engram bank–and if that is known, the person could be Cleared with a few more hours work and would need no punishment.

These five ways of handling data make corporal punishment an unstable and unreliable thing. A ratio exists which can be tested and proven in any man's experience: *A man is evil in the direct ratio that destructiveness has been leveled against him.* An individual (including those individuals society is liable to forget as individuals: children) reacts *against* the punishment source whether that source be parents or government. Anything which sets itself forward against an individual as a punishment source will be considered in greater or lesser degree (as it is in proportion to benefits) as a target for the reactions of the individual.

The little accidental milk glass upsets of children, that noise which just accidentally occurs on the porch where the children are playing, that little accidental ruination of Papa's hat or Mama's rug: these are often cold, calculated reactive mind actions against pain sources. The analytical mind may temporize about love and affection and the need of three square meals. The reactive mind runs off the lessons it has learned and devil take the meals.

If one turned an idiot loose on an adding machine to let him audit the company books and let him prevent the auditor from touching equipment and data which has to be his if any answers will be right, one would get very little in the way of correct answers. And if one kept feeding the idiot and made him fat and powerful, the firm would sooner or later go to ruin. The reactive mind is the idiot, the auditor is "I" and the firm is the organism. Punishment feeds the idiot.

The helpless amazement of police about the "confirmed criminal" (and the police belief in the "criminal type" and the "criminal mind") comes about through this cycle. Police, for some reason or other, like governments, have become identified with society. Take any one of these "criminals" and Clear him and the society regains a rational being of which it can use all it can get. Keep up the punishment cycle and the prisons will get more numerous and more full.

The problem of the child lashing back at his parents by "negation" and the problem of Jimmie the Cob blowing a bank guard apart in an armed robbery stem both from the same mechanism. The child, examined on the "conscious level," is not aware of his causes, but will put forth various justifications for his conduct. Jimmie the Cob, waiting for this oh so very sentient society to tie him down with straps in an electric chair and give him an electric shock therapy which will cause him to cease and desist forever, examined for his causes, will pour forth justifications to explain his life and conduct. The human mind is a pretty wonderful computing machine. The reasons it can evolve for unreasonable acts have staggered one and all and particularly social workers. Without knowing the cause and the mechanism, the chances of drawing a correct conclusion by comparing all conducts available are as remote as winning at fan-tan from a Chinese. Hence, the punishments have continued as the muddled answer to a very muddled society.

There are five ways in which a human being reacts toward a source of danger. These are also the five courses he can take on any given problem. And it might be said that this is five-valued action.

The parable of the black panther* is appropriate here. Let us suppose that a particularly black-tempered black panther is sitting on the stairs and that a man named Gus is sitting in the living room. Gus wants to go to bed. But there is the black panther. The problem is to get upstairs. There are five things that Gus can do about this panther:

1. He can go *attack* the black panther.
2. He can run out of the house and *flee* the black panther.
3. He can use the back stairs and *avoid* the black panther.
4. He can *neglect* the black panther.
5. He can *succumb* to the black panther.

These are the five mechanisms: *attack*, *flee*, *avoid*, *neglect* or *succumb*.

All actions can be seen to fall within these courses. And all actions are visible in life. In the case of a punishment source, the reactive mind can succumb, neglect, avoid, flee or attack it. The action is dictated by a complexity of engrams and depends upon which one comes into restimulation. This maelstrom of reaction generally resolves itself, however, in one of the five courses.

If a child is punished and thereafter obeys, he can be considered to have succumbed. And the value of a child who will succumb to punishment is so slight that the Spartans would long since have drowned him, for it means he has sunk into an apathy unless it so happens that he himself has computed the idea, bypassing all reaction, that the thing for which he was punished was not bright (he can't be assisted in this computation if

*In Dianetics considerable slang has been developed by patients and Dianeticists and they call the "black panther mechanism" a neglect of the problem. One supposes this stems from the ridiculousness of biting black panthers.

punishment is entered into the reactive mind by the source trying to assist him). He can flee the punishment source, which at least is not apathy, but merely cowardice, by popular judgment. He can neglect the matter entirely and ignore the punishment source – and would have been called a Stoic by the ancients, but might be called merely dull-witted by his friends. He can avoid the punishment source, which might give him the doubtful compliment of being sly or cunning or pandering. Or he can attack the punishment source either by direct action or by upsetting or fouling the person or the possessions of the source – in which instance, he would be called, on direct action, a valiant fool, taking parental size into account; or in a less direct fashion, he could be called "covertly hostile" or could be said to be "negating." As long as a human being will attack as a response to a valid threat, he can be said to be in fair mental condition – "normal" – and a child is said to be "just acting like any normal child."

Enter punishment into the computation and it no longer computes. It is entirely different in the case of "experience." Life has plenty of painful experience waiting for any human being without other human beings complicating the score. A person who is still unblocked in his dynamics or who has been unblocked by Dianetics can absorb the most amazing amount of hammering in the business of living. Here, even when the reactive mind receives engrams as a result of some of this experience, the analytical mind can continue to cope with the situation without becoming aberrated in any way. Man is a tough, resilient, competent character. But when the law of affinity begins to be broken and such a breaking of affinity gets into the reactive bank, *human beings*, as antagonistic sources of non-survival, become a punishment source. If no contra-survival engrams involving human beings are in the earlier (before five years) content of the engram bank, pro-survival engrams are taken as a matter of course and are not severely aberrative. In other words, it is the breaking of affinity with his fellows on an engramic level which most solidly blocks the dynamics. Man's affinity with Man is far more a scientific fact than it is a poetic and idyllic idea.

The cycle, then, of life which will be "normal" (current average state) or psychotic is an easy thing to draw. It begins with a large number of engrams before birth; it gathers more in the dependent and rather helpless condition post-birth. Punishment of various kinds entering now as locks key-in the engrams. New engrams which will involve the earlier ones enter. New locks accumulate. Illness and aberrated action set in most certainly by the age of forty or fifty. And death ensues sometime afterwards.

Short of the optimum solution of clearing the engrams, there are several things which can be done about aberration and psychosomatic ills. That these methods are uncertain and of only limited value does not mean that they will not occasionally meet with some astonishingly beneficial responses.

Such methods can be classified under the headings of environmental change, education and physical treatment. Taking factors out of the environment of an aberree or taking the aberree out of the environment in which he is unhappy or ineffective can bring about some astonishingly swift recoveries: this is valid therapy; it removes the restimulators from the individual or takes the individual away from the restimulators. It is ordinarily quite hit-or-miss, and more miss than hit, and it will not remove *all* the restimulators by nine-tenths since the individual himself carries the bulk of these around with him or is compelled to contact them. One is reminded of a case which had severe asthma. He had received it in a very severe birth engram; his frantic parents carried him to every mountain asthma resort suggested and spent tens of thousands of dollars in these jauntings. When this patient was Cleared and the engram refiled, it was discovered that the restimulator for his asthma was clean, cold air! The only certainty in the environment approach is that a sickly child will recover when removed from restimulative parents and taken where he is loved and feels safe–for his sickness is the inevitable result of restimulation of prenatal engrams by one or the other or both his parents. Somewhere along the line there is probably a husband or a wife who has descended chronically into the first two zones after marriage, after having married pseudo-mother or pseudo-father or pseudo-abortionist.

In the educational field, new data or enthusiasms may very well key-out engrams by overbalancing the reactive mind in the light of a new analytical surge. If a man can simply be convinced he has been fighting shadows or if he can be persuaded to hang his fears on some indicated cause, whether that cause is true or not, he can be benefited. Sometimes he can be "educated" into a strong faith in some deity or cult which will cause him to feel so invulnerable that he rises above his engrams. Raising his survival potential in any way will raise his general tone to a point where it is no longer on a par with the reactive bank. Giving him an education in engineering or music, where he can receive a higher level of respect, will often defend him from his restimulators. A rise to a position of esteem is actually a change of environment, but it is also educational since he is now taught he is valuable. If a man can be made busy at a hobby or work by personal or exterior education that it is good for him, another mechanism comes into being–the analytical mind becomes so engrossed that it takes to itself more and more energy for its activity and begins to align with a new purpose.

Physical treatment resulting in improved physical condition will bring about hope or change a man's reactions by shifting him on his time track. It may key-out engrams.

These methods are valid therapy: they are also, in reverse, the things which cause aberrations to manifest themselves. There are wrong ways to act and wrong things to do and wrong ways to treat men which, in the light of what we know now, are criminal.

Thrusting a man into an environment which restimulates him and making him stay there is a slice of murder. Making him keep an associate who is restimulative is bad; making a man or a woman stay with a marriage partner who is restimulative is unworkable *mores* unless Dianetic therapy is used; making a child stay in a home where he is restimulated is most certainly inhibitive, not only of his happiness, but of his mental and physical development–a child should have many more rights about such things, more places to go.

On the physical therapy level, anything as violent as surgery or exodontistry in the psychosomatic plane is utter barbarism in the light of Dianetics. "Toothache" is normally psychosomatic. Organic illnesses, enough to fill several catalogs, are psychosomatic. No recourse to surgery of any kind should be had until it is certain that the ailment is not psychosomatic or that the illness will not diminish by itself if the potency of the reactive mind is reduced. Mental-physical therapy is too ridiculous, with the source of aberration now a science, to be seriously mentioned. For no thinking doctor or psychiatrist possessed of this information would touch another electrode for electric shock therapy or even glance at a scalpel or ice pick to perform an operation on the prefrontal lobes of the brain unless that doctor or psychiatrist is himself so thoroughly aberrated that the act springs, not from any desire to heal, but from the most utter and craven sadism to which engrams can bring a man.

BOOK TWO, CHAPTER TEN

Preventive Dianetics

There are many branches in Dianetics. It is actually a family of sciences covered by a single set of axioms. There is, for instance, *Educational Dianetics*, which contains the body of organized knowledge necessary to train minds to their optimum efficiency and to an optimum of skill and knowledge in the various branches of the works of Man. And there is *Political Dianetics*, which embraces the field of group activity and organization to establish the optimum conditions and processes of leadership and intergroup relations. And again there is *Medical Dianetics*. And there is *Social Dianetics*. There are many such subdivisions which are sciences within themselves guided by their own axioms.

We are dealing in this volume, actually, with basic Dianetics and Dianetic therapy as applied to the individual. This is the most immediately important and the most valuable to the individual.

But no book on Dianetic therapy would be complete without a mention of a branch of Dianetics which, some say, is even more important to the race than the therapy. This is *Preventive Dianetics*.

If one knows the cause of something, he can usually prevent the cause from going into effect. The discovery and proof of Ronald Ross that the malaria germ was carried by the mosquito makes it possible to prevent the disease from committing the ravages it once enjoyed at the expense of Mankind. Similarly, when one knows the cause of aberration and psychosomatic illness, he can do a great deal toward preventing them.

While Preventive Dianetics is a large subject, infiltrating the fields of industry and agriculture and other specialized activities of Man, its basic principle is the scientific fact that engrams can be held to minimal content or prevented entirely with large gains in favor of mental health and physical well-being as well as social adjustment.

The engram is actually a very simple thing: it is a moment when the analytical mind is shut down by physical pain, drugs or other means, and the reactive bank is open to the receipt of a recording. When that recording has verbal content, it becomes most severely aberrative. When it contains antagonism on an emotional level, it becomes very destructive. When it is intensely pro-survival in content, it is most certainly capable of thoroughly deranging a life.

The engram, among other things, determines fate. The engram says that a man has to fail to survive and so he contrives numerous ways to fail. The engram commands that he can only experience pleasure among the members of another race and so he goes among them and abandons his own. It commands that he must kill to live and so he kills. And far more subtly, the engram weaves its way from incident to incident to cause the catastrophe which it dictates.

A recent case was plotted out to have actually gone to enormous lengths to break his arm, for with a broken arm he received the sympathy without which the engram said he could not live. The plot covered three years and half a hundred apparently innocent incidents which, when netted together, told the story.

The accident-prone person is a case where the reactive mind commands accidents. He is a serious menace in any society, for his accidents are reactively intentional and they include the destruction of other people who are innocent.

Drivers with several accidents on their records are generally accident-prone. They have engrams which command them to have accidents. When you have run a case, just one, you will see how thoroughly and maliciously disposed this moronic thing, the reactive mind, can be about such things. Cleared drivers could have accidents only through two sources: (a) mechanical failure and, more important, (b) because of accident-prone people. The terrible and awesome death toll taken by our automotive transport is almost all attributable to reactive mind driving rather than learned response driving. The apathy of this society is measured by the fact that it does not act severely to prevent *all* automotive accidents; just one broken windshield is one too many: now that an answer is to hand, action can take place.

The aberree in thousands of ways complicates the lives of others. Preventive Dianetics makes it possible to sort out the aberree who is accident-prone and bar him from activities which will menace others. This is one general aspect of Preventive Dianetics. That the aberrees so isolated can be Cleared is another type of problem.

The other general aspect of Preventive Dianetics, and the more important, is the prevention of engrams and modification of content both on the social and the individual scale. On the social scale, one would delete from the society the causes of aberration in that society as if he were deleting engrams from the individual. In the same way, one can prevent the social causes from occurring in the first place.

In the individual, the prevention of engrams is a very easy matter. Once the source of aberration and illness is known, one can prevent the source from entering a life. If the source has been known to enter, one can prevent the next step, the key-in. Of course, the final answer in all this is therapy to a Clearing, but there is one aspect of the source which is not so answered.

The child cannot be safely Cleared until he is at least five years of age and current practice is to place this figure at about eight years. Improved address to the problem may reduce this figure, but it cannot be reduced below the age of speech unless someone in the future invents a catalyst which simply clears out the reactive mind without further treatment (not as wild as it may sound). But just now, and probably for a long time to come, the child will remain a problem to Dianetics.

Childhood illness is chiefly derived from engrams. It is most likely to be severe before the age of speech and the number of deaths within the first year of life, while medicine may reduce them, is yet a serious thing.

Preventive Dianetics addresses this problem in two phases: first, the prevention of engrams; and second, the prevention of the key-in.

Taking the key-in first, there are two things which can be done to prevent it. The child can be given a calm and harmonious atmosphere which is not restimulative or, if the child appears to be restimulated despite kindly treatment, he can be removed to another environment which will be minus the two most certain sources, his father and mother, and which will contain a source of affection. The test of whether or not a child is restimulated, pre-speech or post-speech, is very simple.

Is he susceptible to illness? Does he eat well? Is he nervous? There can be actual physical things wrong with the child, of course, but these are quickly established by a doctor and they lie in the category of physical derangement.

Quarrels within the hearing of a child, loud noises, frantic conduct, drooling sympathy when he is sick or hurt, these things are some of the key-in catalog. These make a child *ill* physically and aberrated mentally by keying-in his engrams. And nobody can say how many he has!

The primary source of prevention lies in the field, oddly enough, of the regard in which another person is held–his mother.

It is not "biological love" which makes mother play such an enormous role in the life of a human being. It is the simple mechanical truth that mother is a common denominator to all the child's prenatals. The prenatal engram is far more serious than the postnatal. Any such engram a person has contains his mother or his mother and another person, but always his mother. Therefore her voice, the things she says, the things she does, have an enormous and vast effect upon the unborn child.

It is not true that emotion gets into a child through the umbilical cord as people always suppose the moment they hear of prenatals. Emotion comes on another (more electrical than physical) type of wave–what type is a problem for structure. Therefore, anyone who is emotional around a pregnant woman is communicating that emotion straight into the child. And mother's emotion is, in the same manner, so conducted to his reactive mind.

Whether or not the unborn child is "unanalytical" has no bearing on his susceptibility to engrams. The prenatal engram is just another engram. Only when the child is actually struck or hurt by high blood pressure or orgasms or other sources of injury does he become "unconscious." When he becomes "unconscious," he receives all the percepts and words in the area of the mother as engrams. Analytical power has nothing to do with engrams. If the child is "unanalytical," this does not predispose him to engrams. If the child is "unconscious" or hurt, it does. The presence or absence of "analytical power" has nothing to do with whether or not engrams are received.

Morning sickness, coughing, all monologuing (mother talking to herself), street noises, household noises, etc., are all communicated to the "unconscious" child when he is injured. And the child is very easily injured. He is not protected by formed bones and he has no mobility. He is there: when something strikes him or presses him, his cells and organs are injured. A simple experiment to demonstrate how mobility influences this is to lie down in bed and place one's head on a pillow. Then have somebody lean a hand on one's forehead. As there is no mobility, the pressure of the hand is far stronger than it would be if a hand were laid on the forehead when one was standing. The tissue and the water around the child form very slight buffers. In an injury amniotic fluid, as an incompressible medium, presses him, for it cannot compress itself. The child's situation is far from armored. Mother's act of tying her shoes, in the later stages of pregnancy, even may be severe on the child. Mother's strain when lifting heavy objects is particularly injurious. And mother's collision with objects like a table edge might well crush a baby's head. The repair facilities of the unborn child, as mentioned elsewhere, are far above anything ever before discovered. The child may have its head crushed, but the blueprint is still there and the building materials and repair can be made. So it is not a case of the child being "all right" just because it can live through almost anything. It is a case of whether or not these injuries are going to have high aberrative value as engrams.

Attempted abortion is very common – and remarkably lacking in success. The mother, every time she injures the child in such a fiendish fashion, is actually penalizing herself. Morning sickness is entirely engramic, so far as can be discovered, since Clears have not so far experienced it during their own pregnancies. And the act of vomiting because of pregnancy is via contagion of aberration. Actual illness generally results only when mother has been interfering with the child either by douches or knitting needles or some such thing. Such interference causes the mother to become ill and, from an actual physical standpoint, is much harder on the mother than on the child. Morning sickness evidently gets into a society because of these interferences such as attempted abortion and, of course, injury.

The cells know when pregnancy occurs. The reactive mind is acquainted with the fact before the analyzer by process of organic sensation, since the endocrine system is altered. Hence, the mother's discovery of pregnancy has little to do with whether or not she was sick before the discovery.

This entire field has been a subject of considerable research in Dianetics. Much more research must be done. These conclusions are tentative. But the conclusion that the engram is received and that it is as violent as its content, rather than its actual pain, is a scientific fact and not in any way a theory. It is as real a discovery as gravity.

Preventing these engrams is the first consideration. Preventing them from having any content is the second. Women who lead peasant lives, doing heavy labor, are subject to all manner of accident. Perhaps such accidents cannot be prevented because of the purpose these women serve in the society. But when it is known that any injury to the mother can create an engram in the unborn child, it should be the concern of all those present during such an injury, including the mother, to maintain a complete and utter silence. *Any remark is aberrative* in an engram. Even such a statement as "You can remember this when in Dianetic therapy," made toward an unborn child, installs an engram so that every word in this statement means a physical pain just where he received it at the time, and in the future "Dianetic therapy" will be restimulative to him.

The doctor, punching around to find out if mother is pregnant, may say, "Well, it's hard to tell this early." The patient, in Dianetic therapy years later, will *return* into the vicinity of this incident only to draw a blank until the Dianeticist suddenly guesses the content from how the patient describes his reactions. If the doctor is very tough and says, "You had better take good care of yourself, Mrs. Jones. If you don't, you'll be mighty sick!" the child, "unconscious" from the examination no matter how mild it is, will get a mild hypochondria when the engram keys-in and be very concerned over his health.

If the husband uses language during coitus, every word of it is going to be engramic. If the mother is beaten by him, that beating and everything he says and that *she* says will become part of the engram.

If she does not want the child and he does, the child will later react toward him as an ally and perhaps have a nervous breakdown when the father dies. If she wants the child and he doesn't, the ally computation is reversed. This is true when abortion is threatened or attempted, providing the threat is contained in an engram.

Should the mother be injured and the father be highly solicitous, the engram has this for content and the child has a sympathy engram. The way to survive, then, is to be pathetic when injured, and even see to it that one is injured.

A woman who is pregnant should be given every consideration by a society which has any feeling for its future generations. If she falls, she should be helped–but *silently.* She must not be expected to carry heavy things. And she should not have coitus forced upon her. *For every coital experience is an engram in the child during pregnancy.*

An astonishing number of pregnancies must take place which are never realized. The violence of coitus, the use of douches and jellies (used because the woman is still contracepting and does not know she is already pregnant), straining bowel movements, falls and accidents must account for a large number of miscarriages which come about sometime around the first period after conception. For the zygote and embryo forms of the child have a rather frail grip on existence and are very severely injured by things the mother would consider nothing. Once past the first missed period, the chances of miscarriage rapidly grow less and only when the child is a genetic monstrosity or when abortion attempts are made can a miscarriage be expected to take place. The monstrosities are so small a percentage that they are negligible as a possibility.

The amniotic sac can be pierced many times and repeatedly and emptied of all water after the first missed period and the child can still survive. Twenty or thirty abortion attempts are not uncommon in the aberree and in every attempt the child could have been pierced through the body or brain.

The child before birth does not depend upon the standard senses for its perceptions. Engrams are not memories but cellular-level recordings. Therefore, the child needs no eardrums to record an engram. Cases are on hand where whatever hearing mechanism the unborn child had must have been temporarily destroyed by an abortion attempt. And the engram was still recorded. The cells rebuilt the apparatus which was to be the source of sound in the standard banks and stored their own data in the reactive bank.

Release of such engrams means a restoration of rationality to the individual far above the current norm and a stability and well-being greater than Man ever thought Man possessed. These engrams have been confirmed by taking the data from a child, from the mother and the father, and all data checked. So we are dealing here with scientific facts which, no matter how startling, are nevertheless true.

The mother, then, should be extremely gentle on herself during pregnancy and those around her should be entirely informed of the necessity for silence after any jar or injury. And in view of the fact that it is not possible to tell when a woman has become pregnant and in view also of the high potentiality of aberration in the zygote and embryo engrams, it is obvious that society must better its ways toward women if the future health of the child is to be preserved.

The woman has to some degree become considered less valuable in this society than in other societies and times. She is expected to be in competition with men. Such a thing is nonsense. A woman has as high a plane of activity as man. He cannot compete with her any more than she can compete with him in the fields of structure and vigorous activity. Much of the social maelstrom now in existence has as its hub the failure to recognize the important role of the woman as a woman and the separation of the fields of women and men.

The changes which will come about in the next twenty years need no urging here. But with the recent discoveries in photosynthesis which should secure enough food to feed Man better and at less cost, the importance of birth control dwindles. The morality standards have already changed, no matter what moralists do to try to block the change. And woman, therefore, can be freed of many of her undesirable chains.

In the custody of man is the current world and its activity and structure. In the charge of woman is the care of the person of the human being and his children. Almost sole custodian of tomorrow's generation, she is entitled to much more respect than her chattel period of the past gave her.

It is not, then, any wild Utopian thought that woman can be placed above the level hitherto occupied. And so she must be placed if the childhood of tomorrow's generation is to reach any high standard, if homes are to be peaceful and unharassed and if society is to advance.

Preventive Dianetics, in the sphere of the home, must place emphasis on the woman in order to safeguard the child.

As any first step, a mother should be Cleared, for any mother who attempts an abortion is blocked across the Second Dynamic and any block menaces her health as well as her happiness. An antipathy for children has been found to accompany sexual aberration.

Preventive Dianetics, then, on the level of the individual, asks for Cleared parents and then precaution against the aberrating of the child, and further precaution against the keying-in of any aberration the child might have received.

To do this is very easy. Maintain silence in the presence of injury. Do what has to be done for the injured or ill and do it in silence. Maintain silence in the presence of birth to save both the sanity of the mother *and* the child and safeguard the home to which they will go. And the maintaining of silence does not mean a volley of "Sh's," for those make stammerers.

In a wider field, the maintenance of silence around any "unconscious" or injured person is second in importance only to preventing the "unconsciousness" in the first place.

Say nothing and make no sound around an "unconscious" or injured person. To speak, no matter what is said, is to threaten his sanity. Say nothing while a person is being operated upon. Say nothing when there is a street accident. Don't talk!

Say nothing around a sick child or an injured child. Smile, appear calm, but say nothing. Actions do not speak louder than words, but actions are all that can be done around the sick and injured unless one has an active desire to drive them into neurosis or insanity or, at best, to give them a future illness.

And above all, say nothing around a woman who has been struck or jarred in any way. Help her. If she speaks, don't answer. Just help her. You have no idea of whether she is pregnant or not.

And it is a remarkable fact, a scientific fact, that the healthiest children come from the happiest mothers. Birth, for one thing, in a Cleared mother, is a very mild affair. Only birth engrams in the mother made it hard. A Cleared mother needs no anesthetic. And that is well because the anesthetic makes a dazed child and the engram, when it reacts, makes him appear a dull child. A happy woman has very little trouble. And even a few engrams, which arrive despite all precautions, are nothing if the general tone of the mother is happy.

Woman, you have a right and a reason to demand good treatment.

Therapy

BOOK THREE

The Mind's Protection

The mind is a self-protecting mechanism. Short of the use of drugs as in narcosynthesis, shock, hypnotism or surgery, no mistake can be made by an auditor* which cannot be remedied either by himself or by another auditor. Those things which are stressed, then, in this book are ways to accomplish therapy as swiftly as possible with minimal errors; for errors take time. Auditors are going to make errors, that is inevitable. If they make the same error repeatedly, they had better get someone to guide *them* through therapy.

There are probably thousands of ways to get into trouble with mental healing, but all these ways can be classed in these groups:

1. Use of shock or surgery on the brain.
2. Use of strong drugs.
3. Use of hypnosis as such.
4. Trying to crossbreed Dianetics with older forms of therapy.

*The term *auditor* is used in Dianetics to designate anyone skilled in the practice of Dianetic therapy. To *audit* is both to listen and to compute.

The mind will not permit itself to be seriously overloaded so long as it can retain partial awareness of itself; it can only be overloaded when its awareness is reduced to a point where it cannot evaluate anything: it can then be thoroughly upset. Dianetic *reverie* leaves a patient fully aware of everything which is taking place and with full recall of everything which has happened. Types of therapy which do not do this are possible and useful, but they must be approached with the full knowledge that they are not foolproof. Dianetics, then, uses the reverie for the majority of its work and using the reverie, an auditor cannot possibly get himself into any trouble from which he cannot extricate himself and the patient. He is working with an almost foolproof mechanism as long as the mind retains some awareness: a radio or a clock or an electric motor are far more susceptible to injury in the hands of a workman than the human mind. The mind was built to be as tough as possible. It will be found that it is difficult to get it into situations which make it uncomfortable and impossible, with the reverie, to embroil it enough to cause neurosis or insanity.

In the US infantry manual there is a line about decision: "Any plan, no matter how poorly conceived, if boldly executed is better than inaction."

In Dianetics, any case, no matter how serious, no matter how unskilled the auditor, is better opened than left closed. It is better to start therapy if it is to be interrupted after two hours of work than not to start therapy at all. It is better to contact an engram than to leave an engram uncontacted even if the result is physical discomfort for the patient–for that engram will not thereafter possess as much power and the discomfort will gradually abate.

This is scientific fact. The mechanism Dianetics uses is an ability of the brain which Man as a whole did not know he had. It is a process of thought which everyone possesses inherently and which was evidently meant to be used in the overall process of thinking, but which, by some strange oversight, Man has never before discovered. Once a person has learned that he possesses just this one new faculty, he is better able to think than he was before. And he can learn this faculty in ten minutes. Further, when one approaches an engram with this faculty (which, when intensified, is the reverie), some of that engram's sub-level connections are broken and the aberrative factors no longer have as much force either in the physical or mental spheres. Further, the knowledge that there is a solution to mental ills is a stabilizing factor.

Approaching an engram with the reverie is very far from the same as restimulating the engram exteriorly as is done in life. The engram is a powerful and vicious character only so long as it is untapped. In place and active it can be restimulated to cause innumerable mental and physical ills. But approaching it with reverie is approaching it on a new circuit, one that disarms it. The power of the engram is partly the fear of the unknown: knowing brings stability by itself.

Do not think that you will not make patients uncomfortable. That is not true. The auditor's work, when it taps engrams which cannot be lifted, may cause the patient to have headaches, various aches and pains and even mild physical illness, even when the work is carefully done. But life has been doing this to the patient on a much grander scale for years and no matter how badly the case is mauled around, no matter how many aberrations spring into view to plague the patient for a day or two, none are as serious as those which can be occasioned by the environment acting upon the untapped engram.

The auditor can do everything backwards, upside down and utterly wrong and the patient will still be better, provided only that he does not try to use drugs, that he does not use hypnotism and he does not try to cross Dianetics with some older therapy. Once he has used Dianetics, he will not fall back to mystic efforts to heal minds. In short, the point which is offered here is that so long as the auditor takes a relatively simple case at first (to see how the mechanisms of the mind work) and uses only the reverie, he cannot get into trouble. There will be those, certainly, who believe they are so vastly experienced in tom-tom beating or gourd rattling that they won't give Dianetics a chance to work as Dianetics, but will sail in and begin to plague the patient about "penis envy" or make him repent his sins. But the patient who starts to get this will be smart to simply change positions from the couch to the auditor's chair and clear up some of the aberrations of the auditor before work proceeds.

Anybody who has read this book once through and procured a patient with sonic recall for a trial effort will know more about the mind, in those actions, than he has ever known before. And he will be more skilled and able to treat the mind than anyone attempting to do so, regardless of reputation, a very short while ago. This does not mean that men who have had experience with mental patients will not, knowing Dianetics (*knowing Dianetics*), have an edge on those who do not realize some of the foibles of which Man in an aberrated state is capable. And on the other hand, it does not mean that some engineer or lawyer or cook with a few Dianetic cases under his belt will not be more skilled than all other practitioners of whatever background or kind. In this case, the sky is no limit.

One could not say, offhand, that an able hypnotist or an able psychologist, ready and willing to jettison and unlearn yesterday's mistakes, is not better prepared to practice Dianetics. In the field of psychosomatic medicine, the medical doctor, with a vast fund of experience in healing, might very well be far and above other auditors in Dianetic work. But it is not necessarily the case, for in research it has been proven that men and women with most unlikely professional backgrounds have suddenly become auditors superior in skill to those in fields you might suspect were more closely allied. Engineers, particularly, are excellent material and make excellent auditors. Again, Dianetics is not being released to a profession, for no profession could encompass it. It is insufficiently complicated to warrant years of study in some university. It belongs to Man and it is doubtful if anyone could manage to gain a corner on it, for it does not fall within any legislation of any kind in any place. And if Dianetics were legislated into a licensed profession, then it is to be feared that listening to stories and jokes and personal experience would also have to be legislated into a profession. Such laws would put all men of goodwill who lend a sympathetic ear to a friend's troubles inside the barbed wire. Dianetics is *not* psychiatry. It is *not* psychoanalysis. It is *not* psychology. It is *not* personal relations. It is *not* hypnotism. It is a science of mind and needs about as much licensing and regulation as the application of the science of physics. Those things which are legislated against are a matter of law because they may in some way injure individuals or society. Legislation exists about psychoanalysis in some three states in the Union, legislation against or about psychiatry exists everywhere. If an auditor wishes to constitute himself a psychiatrist with the power of vivisecting human brains, if he wants to constitute himself a doctor and administer drugs and medicines, if he wants to practice hypnotism and pour suggestions into a patient, then he must square it with psychiatry, medicine and the local laws about hypnotism, for he has entered other fields than Dianetics. In Dianetics, hypnotism is not used, no brains are operated upon and no drugs are given. Dianetics is not in any way covered by legislation anywhere, for no law can prevent one man sitting down and telling another man his troubles. And if anyone wants a monopoly on Dianetics, be assured that he wants it for reasons which have to do not with Dianetics, but with profit. There are not enough psychiatrists in the country to begin to staff the mental institutions. Surely this generation, particularly with all the iatrogenic* work which has been done, will continue to need those institutions and will need psychiatrists: their field is the treatment of the insane, by definition, and that has nothing to do with thee and me. In psychology, Dianetics drops into line without disturbing anything concerned with staffs or research or teaching posts, for psychology is simply the study of the psyche and now that there exists a science of the psyche it can go ahead with a will. Thus Dianetics is the enemy of none and Dianetics falls utterly outside all existing legislation, none of which anticipated or made any provision for a science of mind.

**Iatrogenic* means illness generated by doctors. An operation during which the doctor's knife slipped and accidentally harmed the patient might cause an iatrogenic illness or injury since the fault would have been with the surgeons.

BOOK THREE, CHAPTER TWO

Release *or* Clear

THE OBJECT of Dianetic therapy is to bring about a *Release* or a *Clear*.

A *Release* (noun) is an individual from whom major stress and anxiety have been removed by Dianetic therapy.

A *Clear* (noun) is an individual who, as a result of Dianetic therapy, has neither active nor potential psychosomatic illness or aberration.

To *Clear* (verb) is to release all the physical pain and painful emotion from the life of an individual or, as in Political Dianetics, a society. The result of this will bring about persistence in the four dynamics, optimum analytical ability for the individual and, with that, all recall. The experience of his entire life is available to the Clear and he has all his inherent mental ability and imagination free to use it. His physical vitality and health are markedly improved and all psychosomatic illnesses have vanished and will not return. He has greater resistance to actual disease. And he is adaptable to and able to change his environment. He is not "adjusted"; he is dynamic. His ethical and moral standards are high, his ability to seek and experience pleasure is great.

His personality is heightened and he is creative and constructive. It is not yet known how much longevity is added to a life in the process of clearing, but in view of the automatic rebalancing of the endocrine system, the lowered incidence of accident and the improvement of general physical tone, it is most certainly raised.

A Release is an individual from whom have been released the current or chronic mental and physical difficulties and painful emotion. The value of a Release, when compared to a Clear, may not at first thought be considered great. But when one understands that a Release is usually in excess of the contemporary norm* in mental stability, it can be seen that the condition is not without great value.

As a standard of comparison, a Clear is to the contemporary norm as the contemporary norm is to a contemporary institutional case. The margin is wide and it would be difficult to exaggerate it. A Clear, for instance, has complete recall of everything which has ever happened to him or anything he has ever studied. He does mental computations such as those of chess, for example, which a normal would do in half an hour, in ten or fifteen seconds. He does not think "vocally" but spontaneously. There are no demon circuits in his mind except those which it might amuse him to set up–and break down again–to care for various approaches to living. He is entirely self-determined. And his creative imagination is high. He can do a swift study of anything within his intellectual capacity, which is inherent, and the study would be the equivalent to him of a year or two of training when he was "normal." His vigor, persistence

* "Norm" is a term in psychology denoting the normal individual, which is to say, an average person. The IQ and behavior of a "norm" would be an averaging out of the current population. There is nothing desirable about being a "norm," for he is badly aberrated.

and tenacity to life are very much higher than anyone has thought possible.

The objection that it is dangerous to create too many Clears in a society is a thoughtless one. The Clear is rational. The acts which damage a society are irrational. That a handful of Clears could probably handle any number of "normals" is within reason, but that the Clear would handle them to their detriment is unreasonable. The more Clears a society possessed, the more chance that society would have to prosper. That a Clear is unambitious is not proven out by scientific observation, for the curve of dwindling ambition follows the curve of reducing rationality; and those who have been Cleared have proven the matter by reactivating all their skills toward goals they had once desired, but had begun to consider unattainable when "norms." That a Clear is in some degree separated from the "norm" is attributable to the gulf between their respective mental abilities, for he has achieved solutions and conclusions before the "norm" has begun to form an idea of what to conclude. This does not make a Clear intolerable to the "norm," for the Clear has none of that superiority attitude which is actually a product of engrams. This is a quick glance at the state of being Clear. But the state cannot be described; it has to be experienced to be appreciated.

A Release is a somewhat variable quantity. Anyone well advanced on the road to Clear is a Release. There is no comparison between a Clear and anything Man has before believed obtainable and there is no comparison between clearing and any therapy hitherto practiced. In the case of the Release only is there a basis of comparison between Dianetics and past therapies such as "psychoanalysis" and any other. A Release can be effected in a few weeks. The resulting condition will be at least equivalent to that following two years of psychoanalysis with the difference that the Release has a guarantee of permanent results and no guarantee of success has ever been made by psychoanalysis. A Release does not relapse into any pattern which has been relieved.

These are the two goals of the Dianetic auditor: *Clear* and *Release*. It is not known at this writing how long is the average time to raise the institutionally insane into the neurotic level: it has been done in two hours, it has been done in ten and in some cases it has required two hundred.*

The Dianetic auditor should determine beforehand in any case whether he wishes to attempt a Release or a Clear. He can achieve either with anyone not organically insane (missing or seared portions of the brain bringing about insanity, mainly genetic or iatrogenic and relatively rare except in institutions). But he should make an estimate of the amount of time he can invest in any one person and regulate his intention accordingly and announce it to his patient. The two goals are slightly different. In a *Release*, one does not attempt entrance into phases of the case which will or may bring about a necessity of long work and gives his attention to the location and release of emotional charge. In a *Clear*, the auditor gives his attention to the location of the *basic-basic* engram, the discharge of emotion and the entire engram bank.

There is a third goal which could be considered a subhead of a Release. This is an *assist*. It is done after injury, or illness following the injury, or illness just sustained, in order to promote more rapid recovery: to *assist* the body in its rehabilitation after injury or illness.

* This present volume is addressed to treatment of the normal person or the neurotic patient not sufficiently violent to be institutionalized. However, with intelligence and imagination these same techniques can be applied with success to any mental state or physical illness. Institutional Dianetics is primarily the reduction of an insanity to a neurosis; the techniques are similar to those described here, but incline more toward heroic measures.

This is specialized therapy which will probably be practiced commonly enough, but is of primary benefit to the medical doctor who, with it, can save lives and speed healing by releasing the engram of that particular illness or injury, thus removing the various engram conceptions which the furtherance of the injury restimulates. Any Dianetic auditor can practice this. The assist has about the same level of usefulness as a faith healing miracle which would work every time.

Estimations of the amount of time the case will require are difficult to attain with any accuracy greater than 50 percent and it should be understood by the patient that the time in therapy is variable. It depends in a measure upon the skill of the auditor, the number of unsuspected engrams never hitherto reactivated, and the amount of restimulation to which the patient is subject during therapy. Therefore, the auditor should not be optimistic in estimating time, but should make his patient understand that greater or lesser time may be consumed in the therapy.

Any person who is intelligent and possessed of average persistency and who is willing to read this book thoroughly should be able to become a Dianetic auditor. When he has Cleared two or three cases, he will have learned far more and understood far more than is contained in this book. For there is nothing which develops an understanding of a machine like handling it in action. This is the instruction book, the machine in question is ready to hand wherever there are men. Contrary to superstition about the mind, it is almost impossible to permanently injure the mechanism. It can be done with an electric shock or a scalpel or an ice pick, but it is almost impossible to do it with Dianetic therapy.

BOOK THREE, CHAPTER THREE

The Auditor's Role

THE PURPOSE OF THERAPY and its sole target is the removal of the content of the reactive engram bank. In a Release, the majority of emotional stress is deleted from this bank. In a Clear, the entire content is removed.*

The application of a science is an art. That is true of any science. The efficacy of its application depends upon the understanding, skill and ability of whoever applies it. The chemist has a science of chemistry and yet the profession of being a chemist is an art. The engineer may have behind him the precision of all the physical sciences and yet the practice of engineering is an art.

Certain rules of procedure can be laid down after the basic axioms of a science are understood. Beyond those rules of procedure are the understanding, skill and ability necessary to application.

Dianetics is extremely simple. This does not mean that cases cannot be extremely complicated. To cover one case for each kind of case in this book would necessitate

*The content of the engram bank is actually *shifted* rather than *removed*, for it refiles under the heading of *experience* in the standard banks. The material, however, appears to vanish in therapy because the therapy is addressed to the engram bank, not the standard banks.

two billion cases and that would only encompass the current population. For each man is a great deal different from every other man. His inherent personality is different. His composite of experience is different. And his dynamics are of different strengths. The only constant is the mechanism of the reactive engram bank and that alone does not vary. The content of that bank is different from man to man, both in quantity and intensity, but the mechanism of operation of the bank and therefore the basic mechanisms of Dianetics are constant from man to man–and were in every age and will be in every future age until Man evolves into another organism.

The target is the engram. It is also the target of the patient's analytical mind and the patient's dynamics as he tries to live his life. It is the target of the auditor's analytical mind and the auditor's dynamics. So bracketed and salvoed, it gives up its store of engrams.

This should be extremely plain to any auditor: the moment he relaxes from the position of auditor and forgets the target, he garners trouble which will consume his time. The moment he makes the error of thinking that the *person*, the *analytical mind* or the *dynamics* of the patient are resisting, trying to stop therapy, or giving up, the auditor has made the fundamental and primary error in the practice of Dianetics. Almost anything that goes wrong can be traced back to this error. It cannot be too emphatically stated that the analytical mind and the dynamics of the patient never, never, never resist the auditor. The auditor is not there to be resisted. He has no concern with resistance from anything except the patient's (and sometimes his own) engrams.

The auditor is not there as the patient's driver or adviser. He is not there to be intimidated by the patient's engrams or be frightened by their aspects. He is there to audit and only to audit. If he feels that he is called upon to be lordly to the patient, then the auditor had better change chair for couch because he has a case of authoritarianism coming into view. The word auditor is used, not "operator" or "therapist," because it is a cooperative effort between the auditor and the patient, and the law of affinity is at work.

The patient cannot see his own aberrations. That is one of the reasons why the auditor is there. The patient needs to be bolstered to face the unknowns of his life. That is another reason the auditor is there. The patient would not dare address the world which has gotten inside him and turn his back upon the world that is outside him unless he has a sentry. That is another reason the auditor is there.

The auditor's job is to safeguard the person of the patient during therapy, to compute the reasons why the patient's mind cannot reach into the engram bank, to strengthen the patient's nerve and *to get those engrams.*

There is a three-way case of affinity at work this moment. I am in affinity with the auditor: I am telling him all that has been discovered and is in practice in Dianetics and I want him to succeed. The auditor is in affinity with the patient: he wants the patient to attack engrams. The patient is in affinity with the auditor because, with minimal work, that patient is going to get better and with persistence lent him by the auditor, plus his own, will become a Release or a Clear. There are even more affinities at work, a vast network of them. This is a cooperative endeavor.

The engram bank is the target, not the patient. If the patient swears and moans and weeps and pleads, those are engrams talking. After a while the engrams that make him swear and moan and weep and plead will be discharged and refiled. The patient, in whatever state, knows full well that the action taken is necessary.

If the auditor is so short of rationality that he mistakes this swearing or moaning as something directed at him personally, that auditor had better change places with the patient and undergo therapy.

The only thing which resists is the engram! When it is being restimulated, it impinges against the patient's analyzer, tends to reduce analytical power, and the patient exhibits a modified dramatization. Any auditor with two brain cells to click together will never be in any slightest danger of his person at the hands of the *prerelease* or *preclear.** If the auditor wants to use hypnotism and try to run late physically painful engrams such as operations when early ones are available, he may find himself targeted. But then he has done something very wrong. If the auditor suddenly gets super-moral and lectures the patient, he may get involved. But again, he has done something very wrong. If the auditor snarls and snaps at the patient, he may get targeted. But once more, a fundamental error has been made.

The target is the engram bank. It is the auditor's job to attack the preclear's engram bank. It is the preclear's job to attack that bank. To attack the preclear is to permit his engram bank to attack the preclear.

We know that there are five methods of handling an engram. Four of them are wrong. To succumb to an engram is apathy, to neglect one is carelessness, but to avoid or flee from one is cowardice. *Attack* and only *attack* resolves the problem. It is the duty of the auditor to make very sure that the preclear keeps attacking engrams, not the auditor or the exterior world. If the auditor attacks the preclear, that's bad gunnery and very poor logic.

---

* The terms *prerelease* and *preclear* are used to designate an individual entered into and undergoing Dianetic therapy. The term *preclear* is used most commonly. The word *patient* is less descriptive because it implies illness, but it is used interchangeably.

The engram bank is best attacked primarily by discharging its emotional charge anywhere it can be contacted. After that it is best attacked by finding out what the preclear, in reverie, thinks would happen to him if he got well, got better, found out, etc. And then it is most and always most important, in any way possible, to contact the primary moment of pain or unconsciousness in the patient's life. This is *basic-basic.* Once an auditor has basic-basic, the case will swiftly resolve. If the preclear's reactive mind is suppressing basic-basic, then the auditor should discharge more reactive emotion, discover the computation now in force and try again. He will eventually get basic-basic. That's important. And that is all that is important in a preclear.

In the prerelease (patient working toward Release only) the task is to discharge emotion and as many early engrams as will present themselves easily. The reduction of locks may be included in prerelease, but only when they lead to basic-basic should locks be touched in a preclear.

There are three levels of healing. The first is getting the job done efficiently. Below that is making the patient comfortable. Below that is sympathy. In short, if you can do nothing for a man with a broken back, you can make him comfortable. If you can't even make him comfortable, you can sympathize with him.

The second and third echelons above are entirely unwarranted in Dianetics. The job can be done efficiently. Making the patient comfortable is a waste of time. Giving him sympathy may snarl up the entire case, for his worst engrams will be sympathy engrams and sympathy may restimulate them out of place. The auditor who indulges in "hand-patting," no matter how much it seems to be indicated, is wasting time and slowing down the case. Undue roughness is not indicated. A friendly, cheerful, optimistic attitude will take care of everything. A preclear sometimes needs a grin. But he has already had more "hand-patting" than the analyzer has been able to compute. *His chronic psychosomatic illness contains sympathy in its engram.*

The next thing the auditor should know and live is the Auditor's Code.* This may sound like something from *When Knighthood Was in Flower* or the *Thirteen Rituals for Heavenly Bliss and Nirvana*, but unless it is employed by the auditor on his patients, the auditor will have some heavy slogging. This code is not for the comfort of the preclear; it is exclusively for the protection of the auditor.

The Auditor's Code should *never* be violated. Practice in Dianetics has demonstrated that violation of the Auditor's Code alone can interrupt cases.

The auditor should be *courteous* in his treatment of all preclears.

The auditor should be *kind*, not giving way to any indulgence of cruelty toward preclears, nor surrendering to any desire to punish.

The auditor should be *quiet* during therapy, not given to talk beyond the absolute essentials of Dianetics during an actual session.

The auditor should be *trustworthy*, keeping his word when given, keeping his appointments in schedules and his commitments to work and never giving forth any commitment of any kind which he has any slightest reason to believe he cannot keep.

* It is interesting that the Auditor's Code outlines, save for its last clause, the *conduct survival pattern* of Man. The Clear operates more or less automatically on this code. Dianetics is a parallel to thought, since it follows the natural laws of thought. What works in Dianetics works as well in life.

The auditor should be *courageous*, never giving ground or violating the fundamentals of therapy because a preclear thinks he should.

The auditor should be *patient* in his working, never becoming restless or annoyed by the preclear, no matter what the preclear is doing or saying.

The auditor should be *thorough*, never permitting his plan of work to be swayed or a charge to be avoided.

The auditor should be *persistent*, never giving up until he has achieved results.

The auditor should be *uncommunicative*, never giving the patient any information whatsoever about his case, including evaluations of data or further estimates of time in therapy.

Various conditions ensue when any of the above are violated. All violations slow therapy and cause the auditor more work. All violations come back to the detriment of the auditor.

For instance, in the last, it is not part of the auditor's work to inform the preclear of anything. As soon as he starts doing so, the preclear promptly hooks the auditor into the circuit as the source of information and so avoids engrams.

The auditor will sec in progress the most violent and disturbing human emotions. He may be moved to sympathy. But if he is, he has overlooked something and hindered therapy: whenever an emotion shows, it is an emotion which will shortly be history. Whatever gyrations the preclear may go through, however much he may move or wrestle around, the auditor must keep firmly in mind that every moan or gyration is one step closer to the goal. For why be frightened or waste sympathy about something which, when it has been recounted a few times, will leave a preclear happier?

If the auditor becomes frightened and pulls that error of all errors when a preclear begins to shake–"Come up to present time!"–he can be sure that the preclear will have a couple of bad days and that the next time the auditor wants to enter that engram it will be blocked.

If an auditor assumes the state of mind that he can sit and whistle while Rome burns before him and be prepared to grin about it, then he will do an optimum job. The things at which he gazes, no matter how they look, no matter how they sound, are solid gains. It's the quiet, orderly patient who is making few gains. This does not mean that the auditor is trying for nothing but violence, but it does mean that when he gets it he can be cheerful and content that one more engram has lost its charge.

The task of auditing is rather much a shepherd's task, herding the little sheep, the engrams, into the pen for slaughter. The preclear isn't under the auditor's orders. But the preclear, if the case runs well, will do whatever the auditor wants with these engrams because *the analytical mind and the dynamics of the preclear want that job done. The mind knows how the mind operates.*

BOOK THREE, CHAPTER FOUR

DIAGNOSIS

ONE OF THE MOST important contributions of Dianetics is the resolution of the problem of diagnosis in the field of aberration. Hitherto, there have been almost unlimited classifications. Further, there has been no optimum standard. As one researches in the field of psychiatric texts, he finds wide disagreement in classification and continual complaint that classification is very complex and lacking in usefulness. Without an optimum goal of conduct or mental state and without knowledge of the cause of aberration, catalogs of descriptions alone were possible and these were so involved and contradictory that it was nearly impossible to sharply assign to a psychotic or neurotic any classification which will lead to an understanding of his case. The main disability in this classification system was that the classification did not lead to a cure, for there was no standard treatment and there was no optimum state to indicate when treatment was at end. And as there was no cure for aberration or psychosomatic illness, there could be no classification which would indicate the direction which was to be taken or what could uniformly be expected of a case.

This is no criticism of past efforts surely, but it is a source of relief to know that the classification of aberration is unnecessary along such complicated lines as have been used and that the cataloging of psychosomatic ills, while necessary to the physician, is unimportant to the auditor. In the evolution of the science of Dianetics there were several stages of classification until it finally became clear that the label on a pathological condition should only be whatever the auditor had to overcome to achieve cure. This system, as now evolved through practice, makes it possible for the auditor to "diagnose" without any more knowledge than is contained in this chapter and his own future experience.

The number of aberrations possible is the number of combinations of words possible in a language as contained in engrams. In other words, if a psychotic thinks he is God, he has an engram which says he is God. If he is worried about poison in his hash, he has an engram which tells him he may get poison in his hash. If he is certain he may be fired from his job any moment, even though he is competent and well-liked, he has an engram which tells him he is about to be fired. If he thinks he is ugly, he has an engram about being ugly. If he is afraid of snakes or cats, he has engrams which tell him to fear snakes and cats. If he is sure he has to buy everything he sees, despite his income, he has an engram which tells him to buy everything he sees. And in view of the fact that anyone not Released or Cleared has upwards of two or three hundred engrams and as these engrams contain a most remarkable assortment of language and as he may choose one of five ways of handling any one of these engrams, the problem of aberration is of no importance *to the auditor* except where it slows therapy.

Most aberrated people talk in a large measure out of their engrams. Whatever the chronic patter of the individual may be – his rage pattern, his apathy pattern, his general attitude toward life – this patter is contained in engrams wherever it departs even in the slightest degree from complete rationality. The man who "cannot be sure," who "does not know" and who is skeptical of everything is talking out of engrams. The man who is certain "it cannot be true," that "it isn't possible," that "Authority must be contacted" is talking out of engrams. The woman who is so certain she needs a divorce or that her husband is going to murder her some night is talking out of either her own or his engrams. The man who comes in and says he has a bad pain in his stomach that feels "just like a #12 gauge copper wire going straight through me" has quite possibly had a #12 gauge copper wire through him in an attempted abortion or talk of such a thing while he was in pain. The man who says *it* "has to be cut out" is talking straight out of an engram either from some operation of his own or his mother's or from an attempted abortion. The man who "has to get rid of it" is again possibly talking out of an attempted abortion engram. The man who "can't get rid of it" may be talking from the same source, but from another valence. People, in short, especially when talking about Dianetics and engrams, give forth with engram talk in steady streams. They have no awareness, ordinarily, that the things they are saying are minor dramatizations of their engrams and suppose that they have concluded these things themselves or think these things. The supposition and explanation are only justified thought: the analyzer performing its duty in guaranteeing that the organism is right no matter how foolishly it is acting.

The auditor can be assured, particularly when he is talking about Dianetics, that he is going to hear in return a lot of engram content; for discussion of the reactive mind generally takes place in language which it itself holds.

Recall that the reactive mind can think only on this equation, A=A=A, when the three As may be respectively a horse, a swearword and the verb "to spit." Spitting is the same as horses is the same as God. The reactive mind is a very zealous Simple Simon, carefully stepping in each pie. Thus, when a man is told he has to delete the content of the reactive bank, he may say that if he did, he is sure he would lose all his ambition. Be assured–and how easily this proves upon therapy and how red-eared some preclears become–that he has an engram which may run something like this:

(*Blow or bump, prenatal*)

FATHER: Damn it, Agnes, you've got to get rid of that goddamned baby. If you don't, we'll starve to death. I can't afford it.

MOTHER: Oh, no, no, no, I can't get rid of it, I can't, I can't, I can't! Honest I will take care of it. I'll work and slave and support it. Please don't make me get rid of it. If I did, I'd just die. I'd lose my mind! I wouldn't have anything to hope for. I'd lose all my interest in life. I'd lose my ambition. Please let me keep it!

What a common one that engram is: and how sincere and "rational" and earnest an aberree can be in supporting his conclusion that he has just "thought up" the "computation" that if he "gets rid of it," he'll lose his mind and ambition, maybe even die!

As this work is written, most of the engrams that will be found in adults come from the first quarter of the twentieth century. This was the period of "Aha, Jack Dalton, at last I have you in my possession!" It was the period of *Blood and Sand* and Theda Bara. It was the period of bootleg whiskey and woman suffrage. It covered the days of "flaming youth" and "The Yanks are coming," and bits of such color will be demanding action in the engram banks. Dianetic auditors have picked up whole passages of the Great Play *The Drunkard* out of prenatal engrams, not as a piece of funny "corn," but as Mama's sincere and passionate effort to reform Papa. Superdrama, Mellerdrammer. And not only that, but also tragedy. The hangover of the Gay Nineties, when the "business girl" had just begun to be "free" and Carrie Nation was saving the world at the expense of bartenders, will be common fare in engrams found in today's adults. Yesterday's clichés and absurdities become, tragically enough, today's engramic commands. One very, very morose young man, for instance, was found to have as the central motif of his reactive mind Hamlet's historic vacillations about whether "to be or not to be, that is the question." Mama (who was what these colloquially minded auditors call a "loop") had gotten it by contagion from an actor-father whose failure to be a Barrymore had driven him to drink and wife beating; and our young man would sit for hours in a morose apathy wondering about life. To classify his psychosis required nothing more than "apathetic young fellow."

Most of engram content is merely clichés and commonplaces and emotional crash dives by Mama or Papa. But the auditor will have his moments. And when he suddenly learns about them, the preclear will have his laughs.

In other words, aberration can be any combination of words contained in an engram. Thus, to classify by aberration is not only utterly impossible, but completely unnecessary. After an auditor has run one case, he will be far more able to appreciate this.

As for psychosomatic ills, as classified in an earlier chapter, these depend also upon accidental or intentional word combinations and all the variety of injury and unbalanced fluid and growth possible. It is very well to call an obscure pain "tendinitis," but more probably and more accurately it is a fall or injury before birth. Asthma comes fairly constantly from birth, as do conjunctivitis and sinusitis, but when these can occur in birth, there is generally prenatal background. Thus, it can be said that wherever a man or woman aches is of minor importance to the auditor beyond using the patient's chronic illness to locate the chain of sympathy engrams, and all the auditor needs to know of that illness is that some area of the body hurts the patient. That, for the auditor, is enough for psychosomatic diagnosis.

It happens that the extent of aberration and the extent of psychosomatic illness are not the regulating factors which establish how long a case may take. A patient may be a screaming lunatic and yet require only a hundred hours to Clear. Another may be a "well-balanced" and moderately successful person and yet take five hundred hours to Clear. Therefore, in the light of the fact that the extent of aberration and illness has only a minor influence on what the auditor is interested in (therapy), classification by these is so much wasted time.

Oh, there are such things as a man being too sick from heart trouble to be worked very hard and such things as a patient worrying so continuously as a manifestation of his usual life that the auditor finds his work difficult, but these are rarities and again have little bearing on the classification of a case.

The rule in diagnosis is that whatever the individual offers the auditor as a detrimental reaction to therapy is engramic and will prove so in the process. Whatever impedes the auditor in his work is identical to whatever is impeding the patient in his thinking and living. Think of it this way: the auditor is an analytical mind (his own) confronted with a reactive mind (the preclear's). Therapy is a process of thinking. Whatever troubles the patient will also trouble the auditor; whatever troubles the auditor has also troubled the patient's analytical mind. The patient is not a whole analytical mind. The auditor will find himself occasionally with a patient who does nothing but swear at him and yet when the appointment time arrives, there that patient is, anxious to continue therapy. Or the auditor may find a patient who tells him how useless the entire procedure is and how she hates to be worked upon and yet if he were to tell her, "All right, we'll stop work," she would go into a prompt decline. The analytical mind of the patient wants to do the same thing the auditor is trying to do: fight down into the reactive bank. Therefore, the auditor, when he encounters opposition, adverse theory about Dianetics, personal criticism, etc., is not listening to analytical data, but reactive engrams. And he should calmly proceed, secure in that knowledge. For the patient's dynamics, all that can be brought to bear, will help him so long as the auditor is an ally against the preclear's reactive mind, rather than a critic or attacker of the preclear's analytical mind.

This is an example:

(*In reverie–prenatal basic area.*)

PRECLEAR: (*believing he means Dianetics*) I don't know. I don't know. I just can't remember. It won't work. I know it won't work.

AUDITOR: (*Repeater Technique, described later*) Go over that. Say, "It won't work."

PRECLEAR: "It won't work. It won't work. It won't work…etc., etc." Ouch, my stomach hurts! "It won't work. It won't work. It won't work..." (*laughter of relief*) That's my mother. Talking to herself.

AUDITOR: All right, let's pick up the entire engram. Begin at the beginning.

PRECLEAR: (*quoting recall with somatics [pains]*) "I don't know how to do it. I just can't remember what Becky told me. I just can't remember it. Oh, I am so discouraged. It won't work this way. It just won't work. I wish I knew what Becky told me, but I can't remember. Oh I wish..." Hey, what's she got in here? Why, Goddamn her, that's beginning to burn! It's a douche. Say! Let me out of here! Bring me up to present time! That really burns!

AUDITOR: Go back to the beginning and go over it again. Pick up whatever additional data you can contact.

PRECLEAR: *Repeats engram, finding all the old phrases and some new ones plus some sounds. Recounts four more times, "re-experiencing" everything. Begins to yawn, almost falls asleep ("unconsciousness" coming off), revives and repeats engram twice more. Then begins to chuckle over it. Somatic is gone. Suddenly engram is "gone." (Refiled and he cannot discover it again. He is much pleased.)*

AUDITOR: Go to the next earliest moment of pain or discomfort.

PRECLEAR: Uh. Mmmmm. I can't get in there. Say, I can't get in there! I mean it. I wonder where...

AUDITOR: Go over the line, "Can't get in there."

PRECLEAR: "Can't get in there. Can't..." My legs feel funny. There's a sharp pain. Say, what the hell is she doing? Why damn her! Boy, I'd like to get my hands on her just once. Just once!

AUDITOR: Begin at the beginning and recount it.

PRECLEAR: (*Recounts engram several times, yawns off "unconsciousness," chuckles when he can't find the engram anymore. Feels better.*) Oh, well, I guess she had her troubles.

AUDITOR: (*Carefully refraining from agreeing that Mama had her troubles, since that would make him an ally of Mama.*) Go to the next moment of pain or discomfort.

PRECLEAR: (*uncomfortable*) I can't. I'm not moving on the time track. I'm stuck. Oh, all right. "I'm stuck, I'm stuck." No. "It's stuck. It's stuck that time." No. "I stuck it that time." Why damn her! That's my coronary trouble! That's it! That's the sharp pain I get!

AUDITOR: Begin at the beginning of the engram and recount, etc.

Each time (it can be seen in this example) that the patient in reverie encountered analytically the engram in near proximity, the engram command impinged itself upon the patient himself who gave it forth as an analytical opinion to the auditor. A preclear in reverie is close up against the source material of his aberrations. An aberree wide awake may be giving forth highly complex opinions which he will battle to the death to defend as his own, but which are, in reality, only his aberrations impinging against his analytical mind. Patients will go right on declaring that they know the auditor is dangerous, that he shouldn't ever have started them in therapy, etc., and still keep working well and efficiently. That's one of the reasons why the Auditor's Code is so important: the patient is just as eager to relieve himself of his engrams as could be wished, but the engrams give the appearance of being a long way from anxious to be relieved.

It will also be seen in the above example that the auditor is not making any positive suggestion. If the phrase is not engramic, the patient will very rapidly tell him so in no uncertain terms and although it still may be, the auditor has no great influence over the preclear in reverie beyond helping him to attack engrams. If the preclear contradicted any of the above, it means that the engram containing the words suggested is not ready to be relieved and another paraphrase is in order.

Diagnosis, then, is something which takes care of itself on the aberration and psychosomatic plane. The auditor could have guessed–and kept it to himself–that a series of attempted abortions were coming up in the above example before he entered the area. He might have guessed that the indecisiveness of the patient was from his mother. The auditor, however, does not communicate his guesses. This would be suggestion and might be seized upon by the patient. It is up to the preclear to find out. The auditor, for instance, could not have known where on the time track the preclear's "coronary pain" was nor the nature of the injury. Chasing up and down looking for a specific pain would be just so much wasted time. All such things will surrender in the course of therapy. The only interest in them is whether or not the aberrations and illnesses go to return no more. At the end of therapy they will be gone. At the beginning they are only complication.

Diagnosis of aberration and psychosomatic illness, then, is not an essential part of Dianetic diagnosis.

What we are interested in is the mechanical operation of the mind. *That* is the sphere of diagnosis. What are the working mechanics of the analytical mind?

1. Perception: sight, hearing, tactile and pain, etc.
2. Recall: visio-color, tone-sonic,* tactile, etc.
3. Imagination: visio-color, tone-sonic, tactile, etc.

These are the mechanical processes. Diagnosis deals primarily with these factors and with these factors can establish the length of time a case should take, how difficult the case will be, etc. And we need only a few of these.

This further simplifies into a code:

1. Perception: over or under optimum.
    a. Sight.
    b. Sound.
2. Recall: under.
    a. Sonic.
    b. Visio.
3. Imagination: over.
    a. Sonic.
    b. Visio.

In other words, when we examine a patient before we make him a preclear (by starting him into therapy), we are interested in three things only: too much or too little perception, too little recall, too much imagination.

In Perception we mean how well or how poorly he can hear, see and feel.

In Recall we want to know if he can recall by sonic (hearing), visio (seeing) and somatic (feeling).

* "Visio" means sight *recall* in Dianetics. "Sonic" means sound *recall*. "Somatic" means pain *recall*. A patient who can *see*, *hear* and *feel* pain stores them. "I", remembering, recalls them as visio, sonic and somatic.

In Imagination we want to know if he "recalls" sonics, visions or somatics too much.

Let us make this extremely clear: it is very simple, it is not complex and it requires no great examination. But it is important and establishes the length of time in therapy.

There is nothing wrong with an active imagination so long as the person *knows* he is imagining. The kind of imagination we are interested in is that used for unknowing "dub-in" and in that kind only. An active imagination which the patient knows to be imagination is an extremely valuable asset to him. An imagination which substitutes itself for recall is very trying in therapy.

"Hysterical" blindness and deafness or extended sight or hearing are useful in diagnosis. The first, "hysterical" blindness, means the patient is afraid to see; "hysterical" deafness means he is afraid to hear. These will require considerable therapy. Likewise, extended sight and extended hearing, while not as bad as blindness and deafness, are an index of *how frightened* the patient really is and is often a straight index of the prenatal content in terms of violence.

If the patient is afraid to see with his eyes or hear with his ears in present time, be assured there is much in his background to make him afraid, for these actual perceptions do not "turn off" easily.

If the patient jumps at sounds and is startled by sights or is very disturbed by these things, his perceptions can be said to be extended, which means the reactive bank has a great deal in it labeled "death."

The recalls in which we are interested in diagnosis are those which are less than optimum only. When they are "*over* optimum," they are actually imagination *dubbed-in* for recall. Recall (under) and imagination (over) are actually, then, one group, but for simplicity and clarity we keep them apart.

If the patient cannot "hear" sounds or voices in past incidents, he does not have sonic. If he does not "see" scenes of past experiences in motion color pictures, he does not have visio.

If the patient hears voices which have not existed or sees scenes which have not existed and yet supposes that these voices really spoke and these scenes were real, we have "*over* imagination." In Dianetics, imaginary sound recall would be *hyper-sonic;* sight recall, *hyper-visio* (hyper = over).

Let us take specific examples of each one of these three classes and demonstrate how they become fundamental in therapy and how their presence or absence can make a case difficult.

A patient with a mild case of "hysterical" deafness is one who has difficulty in hearing. The deafness can be organic, but if organic it will not vary from time to time. This patient has something he is afraid to hear. He plays the radio very loudly, makes people repeat continually and misses pieces of the conversation. Do not go to an institution to find this degree of "hysterical" deafness. Men and women are "hysterically" deaf without any conscious knowledge of it. Their "hearing just isn't so good." In Dianetics this is being called *hypo-hearing* (hypo = under).

The patient who is always losing something when it lies in fair view before him, who misses signposts, theater bills and people who are in plain sight, is "hysterically" blind to some degree. He is afraid he will see something. In Dianetics this is being called, since the word "hysterical" is a very inadequate and overly dramatic one, *hypo-sight.*

Then there is the case of *over*-perception. This is not necessarily imagination, but it can go to the length of seeing and hearing things which are not there at all, which happens to be a common insanity. We are interested in a less dramatic grade in standard operation.

A girl, for instance, who sees something or thinks she sees something, but knows she doesn't and is very startled, who jumps in fright when anyone silently comes into a room and can be so startled rather habitually, is suffering from extended sight. She is afraid she will encounter something, but instead of being blind to it she is too alive to it. This is *hyper-sight.*

A person who is much alarmed by noises, by sounds in general, by certain voices, who gets a headache or gets angry when the people around are "noisy" or the door slams or the dishes rattle, is a victim of extended hearing. She hears sounds far louder than they actually are. This is *hyper-hearing.*

The actual quality of the seeing and hearing does not need to be good. The actual organs of sight and sound can be in poor condition. The only fact of importance is the "nervousness" about reception.

This disposes of the two perceptions in which we are interested in Dianetics. As the auditor talks to people around him and gets their reactions to sights and sounds, he will find wide variety in quality of response.

Recall is the most directly important to therapy, for it is not a symptom, it is an actual tool of work. There are many ways to use recall. The Clear has vivid and accurate recall for every one of the senses. Few aberrees have. The auditor is not interested in other senses than sight and sound because the others will be cared for in the usual course of therapy. But if he has a patient who has no sonic, watch out. And if he has a patient with neither sonic nor visio, beware! This is the multivalent personality, the schizophrenic, the paranoid of psychiatry with symptoms not acute enough to be so classified in normal life. This does not mean, emphatically does not mean, that people without sight and sound recall are insane, but it does mean an above average case and it means a case which will take some time. It does not mean the case is "incurable," for nothing can be further from the truth, but such cases sometimes take five hundred hours. It simply means that such a case isn't any stroll through the park: there is drammer back there in that reactive mind, drammer which says, "Don't see! Don't hear!" Some of the engrams in this case demand reduced or no recall. The organs of sight and sound may be highly extended in their reception. This does not mean that anything need be wrong with the way this person perceives sound or light waves and records them. But it does mean that after he has recorded them, he cannot easily get them back out of the standard bank because the reactive engram bank has set up circuits (occlusion demon circuits) to keep him from finding out about his past. There are, of course, greater or lesser degrees of recall.

The test is simple. Tell the patient wide awake to go back to the time he was entering the room. Ask him what was being said. If he can "hear" it wide awake, he has sonic recall. The auditor knows very well what was said, for if he means to use this test, he utters a certain set of words and notes the actual sounds present. Therefore, if the patient falls into the following category, the *dub-in*, the auditor will be apprised of that.

The sight recall test is equally simple. Show the patient a book with an illustration. After a time interval, ask him to "go back" while he is wide awake and look at that book "in his mind" and see if he can see it. If he can't, this is *hypo-visio*.

More tests similar to this will clearly establish whether or not our patient is recall blind and deaf or whether he falls into the next group.

The over-active imagination which enthusiastically dubs-in sight and sound for the patient without knowledge is something which is definitely a hindrance to fast therapy. There are many demon circuits which snarl up thinking, but these particular dub-in demons mean that the operator is going to get a most awful cargo of what the auditors colloquially call "garbage."* There is, as they further use some of the doubtlessly disgraceful terminology which, despite anything one can do, keeps rising up in this field, something at work in the brain which is a "lie factory."**

The patient asked to recount the conversation as he entered the door by "hearing it" again may confidently start in to give forth all manner of speech which was entirely paraphrase or utterly fictitious. Asked to tell about the picture and page he is shown, he will "see" vividly a lot more than was there or something entirely different. If he is doubtful about it, that is a healthy sign. If he is certain, beware, for it is a demon circuit dubbing-in without his analytical knowledge and the auditor will have to listen to more incidents which never happened than he could begin to catalog and will have to sort out and pick his way through this "garbage" continually to get his preclear to a point where the data is reliable. (And it isn't a matter of grading "garbage" by its improbability–truth is always stranger than fiction; it is a matter of trying to reduce engrams which are not present or bypass engrams which are present and so on in a tangled hash.)

The optimum preclear would be one who had average response to noises and sights, who had accurate sonic and visio and who could imagine and know that he was imagining, in color-visio and tone-sonic. This person,

**Garbage* was technically called *delusion* in the philosophic work of Dianetics, but the term is too harsh and critical, for who has not *some* misconception of a past incident?

***Lie factory* is, technically, a phrase contained in an engram demanding prevarication. It was originally called a *fabricator*.

understand clearly, may have aberrations which make him climb every chimney in town, drink every drop in every bar every night (or try it anyway), beat his wife, drown his children and suppose himself to be a jub-jub bird. In the psychosomatic line, he may have arthritis, gallbladder trouble, dermatitis, migraine headaches and flat feet. Or he may have that much more horrible aberration–pride in being average and "adjusted." He is still a relatively easy case to Clear.

In the case which has sonic and visio shut-off without dub-in, we are dealing with engrams which have shut down some of the primary working mechanisms of the mind. The auditor will have to slog through hours and hours and hours of trying to contact engrams when the patient cannot hear them or see them. A case which merely has a shut-down sonic recall still means that the auditor is going to do a lot more work than on an average case. This case is very, very far from impossible to resolve. That is not the idea here, to frighten off any attempt on such a case. But this case will only be resolved after a great deal of persistent effort. Such a person may be apparently very successful. He may be enormously intelligent. He may have few or no psychosomatic ills. Yet he will prove to have a crammed engram bank, any part of which may come into restimulation at any time and swamp him. Usually, however, this type of case is quite worried and anxious about many things, and such worry and anxiety may put a little more time on the worksheet.

In the case of the *dub-in* who doesn't know it, where circuits are giving him back altered recall, we have a case which may very likely prove to be very long and require artful treatment. For there is a lie factory somewhere in that engram bank. This case may be the soul of truthfulness in his everyday life. But when he starts tackling his engrams, they have content which makes him give out material which is not there.

Sharply and clearly, then, without further reservation or condition, this is Dianetic diagnosis: The aberration *is* the engram content; the psychosomatic illness *is* the former injury. The perceptions of sight and sound, under-optimum recall, over-optimum imagination regulate the length of the case.

If the auditor wants to be fancy, he can list the general Tone Scale position of the individual mentally and physically. The woman who is dull and apathetic is, of course, around Tone 0.5, in the Zone 0 part of the dynamic scale earlier in the book. If the man is angry or hostile, the auditor can mark him down as a 1.5 or somewhere generally in the Zone 1 range of the survival scale. These markings would apply to the probable average tone of the aggregate engrams in the reactive mind. This is interesting because it means that a Zone 0 person is far more likely to be ill and is a slightly harder case than a Zone 1 person. And, as therapy raises tone to Zone 4, the 1.5 is closer to the goal.

It is difficult to estimate time in therapy. As mentioned before, it has several variables such as auditor skill, restimulative elements in the patient's environment and sheer volume of engrams.

The auditor is advised, in his first case, to seek out some member of the family or a friend who is as close as possible to the optimum preclear, which is to say, a person with visio and sonic recall and average perceptions. In clearing this one case, he will learn at firsthand much of what can be expected in the engram banks of any mind; and he will see clearly how engrams behave. If the auditor himself falls into one of the harder brackets and if he means to work with somebody in one of these brackets, that poses no great difficulty. Either case can be

Released in a hundredth the time of any former mental healing technique and they can be Cleared, if any skill at all is used, in five hundred hours of work per case. But if two cases are particularly difficult, before they work on each other, each would be wise to find and Clear a nearly optimum preclear. That way each will be a competent operator when the rougher cases are approached.

Thus, diagnosis. The other perceptions, recalls and imaginations are interesting but not vital in measuring case time. IQ, unless it falls down into the feebleminded level, is no great factor. And even then, the IQ of any patient goes up like a skyrocket with clearing and rises all the while during the work.

There are organic insanities. Iatrogenic psychoses (caused by doctors) are equivocal in Dianetics, for a part of the machinery may have been wrecked. Nevertheless, with many organic psychoses a case can be improved by Dianetics even if an optimum cannot be reached. And so all an auditor can do is try. Insanities caused by missing parts of the nervous system have not been extensively investigated by auditors at this time. The reviving of corpses is not the end of Dianetics; the bringing about of an optimum mind in the normal or merely neurotic person has had the main emphasis. Dianetics can be otherwise used, is being and will be. But with so many potentially valuable people who can be made highly valuable to themselves and society, emphasis has been placed on inorganic aberrations and organic psychosomatic illnesses. Cases which have been subjected to prefrontal lobotomy (which saws a section out of the analytical mind), the topectomy (which removes pieces of brain somewhat as an apple corer cores apples), the transorbital leukotomy (which, while the patient is being electrically shocked, thrusts an ordinary dime store ice pick into each eye and reaches up to rip the analyzer apart) and electric shock "therapy" (which sears the brain with 110 volts), as well as insulin shock and other treatments, are considered by Dianetics to be equivocal. There are ordinary organic insanities such as paresis, but most of these, even so, can be benefited by Dianetics.

BOOK THREE, CHAPTER FIVE

RETURNING, *the* FILE CLERK *and the* TIME TRACK

THERE IS A METHOD of "thinking" which Man did not know he had.

If you would like an illustration of this, ask a small child if she would like to go sleigh riding in memory. She will try to remember the last time she rode her sleigh. She will frown and pucker her brows perhaps. Now tell her to *go back* to the last time she was sleigh riding. Coaxed, she will suddenly come forth with a complete experience and, unless she is badly aberrated, will be able to tell you about the snow getting down her collar and so forth. She is right back there sleigh riding, swimming or whatever you choose.

Man, when and if he thought about this at all, must have mistaken it for imagination. But it is not imagination. Anyone, unless he is very severely aberrated indeed, can be "sent back" wide awake to an experience of the past. In initial tests one should use experiences not long gone and experiences which are pleasant.

This is not *memory* in the way one "remembers something." It is *returning. Remembering* is a far more complicated process than returning. Just why people go around seeking to *remember* some specific or complex datum when they can *return* is something of a mystery when one considers lost articles, things read, conversations had and so forth. *Remembering*, of course, has a very definite role and is an automatic process which provides "I" with conclusions and data in a never-ending stream. But when one wishes a very precise, specific bit of information or when one seeks a past pleasure to contemplate it, *returning* is more to the point.

The hypnotist, with much mumbo jumbo and hand passes et al., has something which he calls "regression." This is a very complicated business which requires being hypnotized. True enough, regression has research value since, by hypnosis, it bypasses occlusions which are not otherwise easy to get around. And regression served Dianetics well when the author was checking his data on memory banks. But it evidently had occurred to none that regression is an artificial use of a natural process.

Undoubtedly some people use *returning* for some of their mental work. And these people probably think that "everybody else" does likewise, which is far from true. But even those people who *return* naturally seldom understand that this is a distinct process, much different from *remembering*.

People also *relive* without being hypnotized or drugged; this is a rarer thing. If a person sits in contemplation of some past glory for a while, he will begin to relive instead of simply return.

In Dianetics, we have had much to do with "spectrums." The spectrum of gradations is a much better mechanism for philosophy than Aristotle's "pendulum," which swung from one extreme to the other. We have the spectrum of the *dynamics*. We call them four dynamics, through which the command SURVIVE! is expressed, and the four are actually a great number of gradations from the cells of "I", through "I", through family and children, through club and city and state, through nation and race and hemisphere and, finally, all Mankind. That is a spectrum: gradations of something which are really the same thing, but which have wider and wider scope or range.

In much the same way as the spectrum of SURVIVE! we have a spectrum of *memory* at work. First there is memory in its most precise, present time sense. Then there is memory of the past. Then there is more memory of the past. And so we move into a part of the spectrum which has been overlooked: part of the "I" returns into the past, then a greater part of "I" returns into the past (at which point we have *return*) and finally, at the extreme, all of "I" is back in the past. First there is *remembering*. This is the furthest from exact data (except in a Clear). Then there is *returning* in which part of the "I" is actually in the past and records appear to be perceptions he is actually experiencing. Then there is *reliving* where a man is so thoroughly in the past for the moment that, while he was recalling an infant experience, if startled he would react just as he would have when a baby.

There is a lot of aberrated notion in this present society about the evils of living in the past. These stem partially from an unwillingness of aberrated people to face and understand yesterday.

One of the prime sources of "bad memory" is mother. Often enough mother has been sufficiently panic-stricken at the thought of Junior's recalling just what she did to Junior that a Mankind-wide aberration seems to have sprung up. The standard attempted abortion case nearly always has an infanthood and childhood full of Mama assuring him that he cannot remember anything when he was a baby. She doesn't want him to recall how handy she was, if unsuccessful, in her efforts with various instruments. Possibly prenatal memory itself would be just ordinary memory and in full recall to the whole race if this guilty conscience in mother had not been rolling along lo! these millennia. In the normal course of work the auditor will have his hands full of Mama screaming objections about her grown son's or daughter's entering into therapy because of what they might find out: Mama has been known, by auditors, to go into a complete nervous collapse at the thought of her child's recalling prenatal incidents. Not all of this, by the way, is based on attempted abortion. Mama often has had a couple of more men than Papa that Papa never knew about; and Mama would very often rather condemn her child to illness or insanity or merely unhappiness than let a child pursue the course of the preclear, even though mother avowedly has no recollection whatever of anything bad ever happening to the child. Under therapy herself, she usually volunteers the truth. Here is the source of why good memory is discouraged in a society and infant and prenatal memory overlooked, to say nothing of the ability to *return* and *relive*.

The index system of the standard bank is a wonderful thing to behold. Everything is there, filed by subject, filed by time and filed by conclusions. All perceptions are present.

With the time file system, we have what is called in Dianetics a *time track*. Going back along this track with part of "I" is *returning*. It is definitely present for both conscious and "unconscious" data. The time track is of vast and interesting concern to the auditor.

The mind is a well-built computer and it has various services. Auditors, backing off from Latin and complexity, call the source of one of these services the *file clerk.** This is not a very dignified name and it is certainly anthropomorphic. There is no small man or woman in there with a green eyeshade. But the action which takes place is a close approximation to what would happen if such an entity did dwell within the mind.

The file clerk is the bank monitor. "He" monitors for both the reactive engram bank and the standard banks. When he is asked for a datum by the auditor or "I", he will hand out a datum to the auditor via "I". He is a trifle moronic when he handles the reactive engram bank, a contagion from the reactive mind, and he will at times hand out puns and crazy dreams when he should be delivering serious data.

The file clerk, if the auditor asks the preclear for the last time he saw a movie, will hand out the movie, the date it was seen, the age and physical being of the person, all perceptics, the plot of the movie, the weather–in short, he hands out everything that was present and connected with the movie.

In ordinary living the file clerk feeds memory to "I" at a rapid rate. A good memory gets its data in split seconds. If the file clerk has to shove the memory around various reactive occlusions, it may take minutes or days for the data to arrive.

If we had a big computing machine of the most modern design, it would have a "memory bank" of punched cards or some such thing and it would have to have a selector and feeder device to thrust out the data the machine wants. The brain has one of these–it could not operate without it. This is the bank monitor, the file clerk.

Keep in mind these two parts of the mind, *the time track* and the *file clerk*, and keep in memory this mechanism

*Technically, the name of the *file clerk* might be "bank monitor units," but the phrase is too unwieldy.

of *returning*. These are the three things we use, with the reactive and standard banks, in the Dianetic *reverie*.

The file clerk is a very obliging fellow. If he has been having trouble getting to the "I" around the reactive occlusions and circuits in general, he is particularly obliging. He cooperates with the auditor.

The monitor system could be considered on the basis of attention units where a man could be supposed to have a thousand. Thus, a thousand possible attention units would be available to a Clear's "I". In the aberree, probably fifty are available to "I", five or six hundred absorbed in the reactive engrams, and the remainder variously used besides composing this mechanism we call the bank monitor, the file clerk.

It seems as if the file clerk in an aberree would rather work with the auditor than with the aberree. That may appear an astonishing fact, but it is a scientific fact. The file clerk works best, then, when he is selecting data out of a preclear's banks to present to the auditor. This is an aspect of the law of affinity. "I's" file clerk and the auditor are a team and they work very often in close harmony without enough consent from the preclear's analyzer to notice.

The *return* is most easily effected, in the aberree, by the auditor's addressing the file clerk, not the patient. This can actually be done with the patient wide awake. The auditor asks him for information, tells him to go back to it. "I" is suddenly in possession of the whole file. Something inside the mind, then, works in close harmony with the auditor and works better for the auditor than it does for the person in whose mind it is. That is the file clerk.

The object of the auditor is to take what the file clerk hands forth and to keep the file clerk from getting swamped by reactive data. Once the data has been given out by the file clerk, it is the business of the auditor to see that the preclear goes over it enough times to take the charge out of it. The mechanism of doing this is extremely simple. In order to help matters and keep the preclear from being distracted, the auditor goes through a routine with every session which disposes the patient to let the file clerk work.

The patient sits in a comfortable chair with arms, or lies on a couch in a quiet room where perceptic distractions are minimal. The auditor tells him to look at the ceiling. The auditor says, "When I count from one to seven your eyes will close." The auditor then counts from one to seven and keeps counting quietly and pleasantly until the patient closes his eyes. A tremble of the lashes will be noticed in optimum *reverie*.

This is the entire routine. Consider it more a signal that proceedings are to begin and a means of concentrating the patient on his own concerns and the auditor than anything else. *This is not hypnotism.* It is vastly different. In the first place, the patient knows everything which is going on around him. He is not "asleep" and he can bring himself out of it any time he likes. He is free to move about (but because it distracts the patient, the auditor does not usually permit him to smoke).

The auditor makes very sure that the patient is not hypnotized by telling him, before he begins to count, "You will know everything which goes on. You will be able to remember everything that happens. You can exercise your own control. If you do not like what is happening, you can instantly pull out of it. Now, one, two, three, four," etc.

To make doubly sure, for we want no hypnotism even by accident, the auditor installs a *canceller*. This is an extremely important step and should not be omitted even when you may be entirely certain that he is in no way influenced by your words. The auditor may inadvertently use restimulative language which will key-in an engram. He may, when he is especially new in Dianetics, use such a thing as a *holder* or a *denyer*, telling the preclear to "stay there" when he is returned on the track or telling him, worst of all things, to "forget it," one of a class of phrases of the forgetter mechanism which is most severe in its aberrative effect, denying the data entirely to the analyzer. To prevent such things from happening, the canceller is vital. It is a contract with the patient that whatever the auditor says will not become literally interpreted by the patient or used by him in any way. It is installed immediately after the condition of reverie is established. A canceller is worded more or less as follows: "In the future, when I utter the word *cancelled*, everything which I have said to you while you are in a therapy session will be cancelled and will have no force with you. Any suggestion I have made to you will be without force when I say the word *cancelled.* Do you understand?"

The word *cancelled* is then said to the patient immediately before he is permitted to open his eyes at the end of the session. It is not further amplified. The single word is used.

The canceller is vital. It prevents accidental positive suggestion. The patient may be suggestible or even in a permanent light hypnotic trance (many people go through life in such a trance). An engram is actually a hypnotic suggestion. It could be said that the purpose of therapy is to awaken a person in every period of his life when he has been forced into "unconsciousness." Dianetics wakes people up. It is not hypnotism, which puts people to sleep. Dianetic therapy wakes them up.

Hypnotism puts them to sleep. Can you ask for a wider difference in polarity? Dianetic therapy removes engrams. Hypnotism installs engrams. Further, Dianetics is a science, an organized body of knowledge. Hypnotism is a tool and an art and is such a wild variable that Man has suspected it as a dangerous thing for centuries and centuries, use it though he did.*

The auditor will inevitably get cases into his hands which will drop into a hypnotic sleep for all he can do to prevent it. Such cases have engrams which make them do this, just as others have engrams which make them stay awake. The auditor then mentions neither "sleep" nor "wake." He takes his cases wherever they drop into their own inversion level and works them from there. Patients will plead to be drugged or put into a trance. *Let them plead!* The reverie has a Clear at its end; drugs and hypnotism have dependency on the auditor and many other undesirable aspects. A case takes longer in amnesia trance than in reverie. The gains in reverie are certain. The patient gets more and more well. When amnesia trance or hypnotism are used instead of reverie, no matter how easily the data seems to come up, the usual run of cases so treated experience little relief until the case is nearly completed, when the patient so long uncomfortable gets suddenly well. Hypnotism carries with it transference, enormous operator responsibility, and other impedimenta with which Dianetics, in long practice, has done without. Hypnotism was used for research, then abandoned.

Hence, install the canceller every time. Never neglect to install it in every session. The patient may be trancing, which is something we don't want, but something which

*An additional difference is that a patient can be *returned* with *no* counting whatever.

we cannot always avoid and which we cannot always detect. Just install the canceller at the beginning of the session. Then after you bring the patient to present time, use the canceller word.

This is a rehearsal, then, of the entire routine:

> AUDITOR: Look at the ceiling. When I count from one to seven your eyes will close. You will remain aware of everything which goes on. You will be able to remember everything that happens here. You can pull yourself out of anything which you get into if you don't like it. All right (*slowly, soothingly*): One, two, three, four, five, six, seven.* One, two, three, four, five, six, seven. One, two, three (*Patient's eyes close and eyelids flicker.*), four, five, six, seven. (*Auditor pauses; installs canceller.*) All right, let us go back to your fifth birthday...(*Work continues until the auditor has worked the patient enough for the period.*)...Come to present time. Are you in present time? (Yes.) (*Use canceller word.*) When I count from five to one and snap my fingers you will feel alert. Five, four, three, two, one. (*Snap.*)

As it can be seen in this example, when work for the day is concluded, the preclear, who may have been *returned* into his past for two hours, *must* be brought back to present time and startled with a finger snap to restore his awareness of his age and condition. Sometimes he is unable easily to come back to present–for which there is quick remedy which we will cover later–so the auditor must always assure himself that the patient feels he actually is in present time.

* If the patient objects to numbers, use letters of the alphabet. He may have been counted down in some past surgical operation so that numbers make him nervous.

This is the reverie. This is all one needs to know about its actual mechanics. Experience will show him a great deal. But these are the basic processes:

1. Assure patient he will know everything that happens.
2. Count until he closes his eyes.
3. Install canceller.
4. Return him to a period in the past.
5. Work with file clerk to get data.
6. Reduce all engrams contacted so that no charge remains.
7. Bring patient to present time.
8. Be sure he is in present time.
9. Give him canceller word.
10. Restore full awareness of his surroundings.

The patient's time track, in the lowest level of attention units, is always in excellent condition. It can be depended upon to reach any date and hour of his life and all the data in it. In the higher levels of awareness, this time track may appear to be in very foul condition. The reactive mind engram circuits stand between these lower levels – right up against the banks – and the higher levels which contain "I". The lower levels contain only a shadow of the force of "I" and appear to be another "I" in a case of multivalent personality.

You can draw this on a piece of scratch paper and it would be helpful if you would do so. Draw a tall rectangle (the standard banks) to the left of the page. Draw half a dozen circles up against the right side of this rectangle for a representation of the file clerk – the bank monitor units. Now draw, about the center of the sheet, a large rectangle. Black it in. This is the area of the reactive engram circuits. It is *not* the reactive bank. It is the circuit pattern from the reactive engram bank which borrows from the analyzer to make demons, vocal thinking, etc. Now, to the right of the page, draw a white rectangle. This is the portion of the analyzer which is "consciousness" and "I".

The whole task of therapy is to get that black rectangle, the reactive engram bank circuits, deleted so that from the standard bank to the left of the sheet to the analyzer portion to the right of the sheet is *all* analyzer. It can't be done with a knife as some people have supposed, evaluating the situation from their own engrams. For that black area you have drawn is *all* analyzer rendered useless by engrams. And when therapy is done, it will all be available for thinking. This increases IQ to an enormous extent.

Now suppose that the bottom of your picture is conception and the top is present time. The vertical route up and down, then, is the time track. In this graph it can be supposed that present time just keeps adding up higher and higher, further and further from conception in the form of new construction (an analogy). For "I" to get data from the standard banks to the left, "I" would have to work through this black rectangle, the reactive mind circuits. To a large extent "I" manages to get data from around this black area. But to a much larger extent it doesn't.

Now suppose that we draw a vertical line at the right of the picture. This line is "awareness." Consider that it can be moved, still vertical, to the left. As the line passes toward the left, we get deeper and deeper "trance." As the line moves into the reactive mind area, it becomes hypnotic trance. Now as it moves even further left and into the circles we are calling "file clerk," it becomes the amnesia trance of hypnotism. Thus, anywhere we place this line we establish a "depth of trance." We want to work over to the right of the reactive bank, nearest the awake level, so that we can keep "I" in contact with his surroundings and keep unwanted data from coming through which will make the patient chronically uncomfortable. If the patient instantly slides from the right all the way to the left so that the attention units, the circles, of the file clerk itself are present, and does so the instant you count from one to seven, he is a hypnotic subject. He may not be aware, when he wakens, of what has taken place, for "I" was out of contact. Work him there, for he will have full sonic, etc., but be very, very careful to work very early in his prenatal area. He might not be able to recall what has taken place and a late engram which, if tapped, will not reduce, may have its full force opened up on "I" when the patient regains possession of himself. Further, you might give him a positive suggestion by accident. Work by preference with trance depth well to the right of the reactive bank.

The characteristics of the units we label "file clerk" are similar in desires to those of the basic individual when he is Cleared. Thus, in any patient, the *basic personality* can be reached, for here is a sample of it. But the auditor should be content to know it is there. As the clearing goes forward, he will see more and more of it. The individual is himself. His personality does not alter, it simply becomes what he wanted it to be all the time at his optimum moments.

The units up against the standard banks can be considered the file clerk. But the file clerk has more than just the standard bank which he can tap. He also has the entire engram bank from which he can pull forth data.

The time track may have several aspects to the preclear. There is actually no track there except time and time is invisible: but the awareness, the "I", can return along it. The track is always there, stretched out. But aberrated ideas of it continually occur and recur in the same patient. It may get all bunched up. It may be very long. It may be that he cannot get on it at all (here's the schizophrenic–he is *off* his time track). But it is there. It is the filing system by *time* and "I" can be returned back along time by the simple request that he do so. If he does not, he is stuck in the present or an engram, which is easy to resolve. And so forth.

Now let us consider the engram bank. It was drawn as a black rectangle in the above sketch. Let us alter that a trifle and draw all this again, with the rectangles represented as triangles with all their points downwards and together, but all else as before: the standard banks, the analyzer (consciousness), and "I". This is a working model now, an analogy, of what the auditor is trying to contact. It is as if the engram bank itself existed in that black triangle. Actually it doesn't, only its circuits, but all we need to visualize is that it does. Therefore, there is a thin point at the bottom. "I" and the file clerk can get together here. This is the bottom of the time track. This is immediately after conception. A little higher up, let's say two and one-half months after conception, it is a little harder for "I" and the file clerk to achieve contact. There is more reactive circuit between them. At seven months after conception it is more difficult. And at twenty years of age it has approached impossibility in most cases without Dianetic technique.

Hence, the auditor will find it expedient to work in the prenatal area and as early in that as possible. If he can clear the time from conception to birth, including birth, his task is nine-tenths complete. To clear the entire reactive bank is his goal.

The reactive bank is like a pyramid which is fairly well armored everywhere but just under the point, and which becomes unarmored when the point is contacted. This is taking the reactive bank in an exposed sector. The effort is to get into the *basic area*, contact early engrams, *erase* the basic-basic engram by recountings and then progress upwards, erasing engrams. These engrams apparently vanish. Actually it takes a hard search to discover them once they are really gone. They exist as memory in the standard bank, but that memory is so unimportant, having been integrated now as experience, that it cannot aberrate. *Nothing in the standard bank can aberrate.* Only the contents of the reactive bank can aberrate–moments of "unconsciousness" and what was recorded within them–and locks. The auditor, in his work, considers an engram erased when it vanishes, when the preclear can no longer contact any part of it, but only after the preclear has thoroughly re-experienced it, complete with somatics.*

This inverted pyramid, in its upper reaches, is effect. In the lower reaches, it is the primary cause of aberration. The cement that holds this inverted pyramid together is physical pain and painful emotion. All the physical pain ever recorded by the organism and all the painful emotion are parts of this inverted pyramid.

The auditor first *discharges* the painful emotion from later life as it was displayed in "conscious moments." He runs these periods as true engrams until the preclear is no longer affected by them. Then he tries to contact *basic-basic:* that first engram. He reduces all engrams he contacts en route to that primary goal. *In every session he tries to reach basic-basic until he is certain he has it.*

*You can contact the file clerk by drugs or hypnotism and gather and reduce engrams. But this is an oversimplified solution. What we are doing in Dianetic therapy is more than this–we are trying to get "I" in contact with the file clerk, not just work the file clerk alone. Hypnoanalysis and narcosynthesis failed because they knew nothing of the engram bank and because they tried, without knowing what it was, to work only the file clerk. The desire of the patient to be worked in amnesia trance or any drugged state is an effort to spare "I" and throw the burden on the file clerk.

Basic-basic is the bottom point. Once it has been gained, an erasure is begun during which engram after engram is "re-experienced" with all somatics until it is gone. Before basic-basic had been reached, the auditor may have had to run engrams twenty times before they reduced. Later he may have found they reduced in five runs. Then he contacts and erases basic-basic. If the patient has sonic by this time – or if he has had it all along – the engrams start erasing with one or two recountings.

The file clerk is smart. The auditor who does not credit the ability of these attention units will involve the case beyond necessity and will lengthen it. The file clerk may hand things out *by phrases*, *by somatics*, *by time*. Whatever he hands out ordinarily will reduce on recountings. By *working with*, not trying to *command*, the file clerk, the auditor will find his case steadily improving until it is Released or fully Cleared. The only time the auditor disregards this is when he uses the Repeater system, which will be described.

We have "I" in a *reverie;* we *return* him to a period in his life along his *time track;* the *file clerk* gives incidents forth which the preclear re-experiences; the auditor makes the preclear recount the *engram* until it is relieved or has "vanished"* (all engrams will eventually "vanish" after *basic-basic* is erased); anything new the file clerk offers, even during the recounting, is addressed by the auditor to make the preclear re-experience it. That is the total sum of activity in Dianetics. There are, as accessories, the Repeater Technique and a few shortcuts. This is therapy. Amplification is needed, of course, and will be found in the ensuing pages to give the auditor all the data he needs. But this is the entire outline of Dianetics therapy.

* The words "vanished" or "erased," when applied to an engram which has been treated, mean that the engram has disappeared from the engram bank. It cannot be found afterwards except by search of the standard memory.

The LAWS *of* RETURNING

THE ENGRAM HAS the aspect of–and is not–a live entity which protects itself in various ways. Any and all phrases in it can be considered commands. These commands react on the analytical mind in such a way as to cause the analytical mind to behave erratically.

Dianetic therapy is parallel to the methods of thought and thinking itself. Anything which reacts against Dianetics and the auditor can uniformly and without exception be found to react in just that way on the patient's analytical mind. Conversely, the patient's problems of thinking in his usual activities are the auditor's problems in therapy.

The bulk of these "commands" the engrams contain are not computable in any way, since they are contradictory or demand unreasonable acts. It is the impossibility of computing them and reconciling them to thought and existence which makes the patient aberrated. Let us take an engram which comes from one of mother's bowel movements. She is straining, which causes compression, which brings about "unconsciousness" in the unborn child. Then, if she habitually talks to herself (a monologuist) as an enormous number of aberrated women do, she may say, "Oh, this is hell. I am all jammed up inside. I feel so stuffy I can't think. This is too terrible to be borne."

This may be in the basic area. The dream mechanism of the mind (which thinks in puns mostly, symbologists to the contrary) may bring forth a dream about hellfire as the engram is approached. The preclear may be sure that he is going to descend into fire if he goes on his time track toward this engram. Further, he may think his time track is all jammed up. This will mean, perhaps, that the incidents are all in one place on it. So much for "This is hell," and "all jammed up inside." Now let us take a look at what happens with "I'm so stuffy, I can't think." The preclear sniffles because he thinks this means a cold in his nose. And as for "This is too terrible to be borne," he is filled with an emotion of terror at the thought of touching the engram, for this command says it is too painful to bear. Additionally, engrams being literal in their action, he may think that *he* was too terrible to be *born.*

The emotional reaction to hell–from some other place on the track, as contained in some other engram–may say that "going to hell" is loud sobbing. Hence, he does not "want" to recount this engram. Further, he is terrified of it because it is "too terrible to be borne." That mother was only discussing with her ambivalent self the necessity of laxatives is never entered into the computation. *For the reactive mind does not reason, it thinks in identities, seeking to command the analytical mind.*

There is only as much data as is in the engram and the analytical reaction to this unthinking thing is utterly literal.

Let us look at another. This is a coitus experience. It has, as its somatic, varying pressure. It is not painful and, by the way, no matter how painful these engrams may be in present time when restimulated, no matter how forceful, when they are actually contacted, their re-experienced pain is very mild, no matter what it was when received. So this is a shaking up of the unborn child, that is all. But it *says*, "Oh, darling, I'm afraid you'll come in me. I'll just die if you come in me. Oh please don't come in me!"

What does the analytical mind do with this? Does it think about coitus? Does it worry about pregnancy? No, emphatically not. The engram that would make one think about coitus would say, "Think about coitus!" and the engram that contained a worry about pregnancy would say, "I am worried about pregnancy." The pain is not severe in this coitus experience, but it specifically states that the engram is not to be entered. "Do not come in me!" He would die if he did, wouldn't he? It says so right there. And the patient finds himself wandering around the track until the auditor uses Repeater Technique (as will be covered).

How about another type of engram? Let us suppose that our poor patient has been unlucky enough to get a Junior tagged on him. Let us suppose his name is Ralph and his father's name is Ralph. (Be careful of these Junior cases, they are unusually complex sometimes.) Mother (see the Kinsey Report, if you've any doubts) is having a quiet affair on the side with Jim. This coitus somatic is no more painful than being gently sat upon, but the patient has a terrible time with it.

MOTHER: "Oh, honey, you are so wonderful. I wish Ralph were more like you but he isn't. He just doesn't seem to be able to excite a girl at all."

LOVER: "Oh, Ralph isn't so bad. I like him."

MOTHER: "You don't know his pride. If Ralph found out about this, it would kill him. He would just die, I know."

LOVER: "Don't worry, Ralph'll never hear."

This little gem of an engram is more common than one would suppose before he begins to get an embryo-eye view of mother. This won't compute in the analyzer as data. Therefore it is a worry. (A *worry* is contradictory engram commands which cannot be computed.) Ralph, Junior, finds that he is very shy sexually. That is the aberrative pattern. Approaching it in therapy, we find we have a sympathy computation with the lover. After all, he said Ralph wasn't so bad, that he liked Ralph. Well, the only Ralph is, of course, to the reactive mind, Junior. This keeps our patient from approaching this engram because he thinks he will lose a friend if he touches it. Further, on the aberrative side, Junior has always worried about people's pride. As we contact this in therapy, he shies violently from it. After all, if he found out about it it would "kill him dead right where he lies." And there is another thing here, a sonic shut-off. It says right there that Ralph will never hear. This is survival stuff. That is what the cells believe. Therefore Ralph never hears *in recall.* There will be more sonic shut-offs. Mother is promiscuous and that generally means blockage on the Second Dynamic. Blockage on the Second Dynamic often means she dislikes children. In short, this would be an attempted abortion case which stabbed Junior full of enough holes to supply a cheese factory for some time. Junior, now a man, may have extended hearing because he is frightened in general of "life." But his sonic recall is zero. This engram, then, would have to be sorted out through the demon circuits as "impressions" which come to the mind. The auditor, taking what the patient says about this, may very soon guess its content and explode it by Repeater Technique.

Now take the case of the mother who, a soul of propriety if a little on the whiny side, discovers she is pregnant and goes to the doctor.

MOTHER: "I think I'm pregnant. I'm afraid I am."

(*Doctor punches her around for a while, knocking the unborn child, who is our preclear thirty years later, into an "unconscious" state.*)

DOCTOR: "I don't think so."

MOTHER: "I'm really afraid I am. I'm sure I'm caught. I just know it."

DOCTOR (*more punching*): "Well, it's hard to tell this early."

It says right there that this man patient of ours is pregnant. If we look, we'll see he has a paunch. That's good survival, that is. And in therapy, we find he is afraid he exists: I am afraid I *am.* And suddenly he isn't moving on the time track. Why? He's caught. That doesn't mean he's pregnant, that means he is *caught.* Further, he won't be able to recount it. Why? Because it is hard to *tell* this early. Consequently, he doesn't speak about it. We free him on the track with Repeater Technique.

Oh this language of ours which says everything it doesn't mean! Put into the hands of the moronic reactive mind, what havoc it wreaks! Literal interpretation of everything! Part of the aberrative pattern of the person who had the above engram was great cautiousness about advancing any opinion. After all, it was hard to tell this early.

Now let us take an engram from a girl patient whose father was badly aberrated. He strikes mother because he is afraid mother is pregnant and father is blocked on Dynamics One, Two, Three and Four.

> FATHER: "Get out! Get out! I know you haven't been true to me! You were no virgin when I married you. I should have killed you long ago! Now you're pregnant. Get out!"

The girl, some five weeks after conception, is knocked "unconscious" by the blow to mother's abdomen. She has a severe engram here because it has painful emotional value which she will never be able to dramatize satisfactorily. The aberrative pattern here demonstrates itself in hysterics whenever a man might accuse her of not being true. She was a virgin when she was married twenty-one years after this engram was received, but she was sure she was not. She has had a "childhood delusion" that her father was likely to kill her. And she is always afraid of being pregnant because it says *now* she is pregnant, which means always, since time is a march of "nows." In therapy, we try to get near this engram. We return the patient to basic area and suddenly find her talking about something which happened when she was five years of age. We return her again and now she is talking about something which happened when she was ten years of age. The auditor, observing any such reaction as this, knows he is handling a *bouncer.* It says, "Get out!" and the patient gets out. The auditor recognizes what is wrong, uses Repeater Technique, and reduces or erases the engram.

Always and invariably, the analytical mind reacts to these engrams as though commanded. It performs on the track as these engrams state. And it computes about the case or about life as these engrams dictate. Healthy things to have around, engrams! Real, good survival! Survival good enough to lay any man in his grave.

The auditor is not much worried by the phrases which assist therapy. An engram received from father beating mother which says, "Take that! Take it, I tell you. You've got to take it!" means that our patient has possibly had tendencies as a kleptomaniac. (Such things are the whole source of the impulses of a thief, the test being that when an auditor erases all such engrams in a patient, the patient no longer steals.) The auditor will find it eagerly recounted because its content offers it to the analytical mind.

The whole species of engrams which say, "Come back here! Now stay here!" as fathers are so fond of saying, account for a snap back to an engram when therapy is entered. The patient goes straight back to it the moment it is exposed. When recounted, the command is no longer effective. But while that engram existed, unentered, it was fully capable of sending people to an institution to lie in a fetal position. Anyone left in institutions who has not been given shocks or prefrontal lobotomy and who suffers from this type of insanity can be released from such an engram and restored to present time simply by use of Repeater Technique. It sometimes takes only half an hour.

Traveling on the track, then, and wandering through the computations the analyzer is compelled by these engrams to attempt is something like playing a child's game which has a number of squares and along which one is supposed to move a "man." A game could actually be composed on the basis of this time track and engram commands. It would be similar to parcheesi. Move so many squares, land on one which says, "Get out!" which means one would go back to present time or toward it. Move so many squares and then lose a move because this square on which we now land says, "Stay here!" and the "man" would stay until the auditor let him out by technique (but because this is struck by therapy, it would have no power to hold long). Then move so many squares to one which said, "Go to sleep," at which the "man" would have to go to sleep. Move so many squares until one was hit which said, "Nobody must find out," and so there would be no square. Move so many until one was reached which said, "I'm afraid," at which the "man" would be afraid. Move again to a square which said, "I must go away," so the "man" would go away. Move once more to a square which says, "I'm not here," and the square would be missing. And so forth and so forth.

The classes of commands which particularly trouble the auditor are only a few. Because the mind actually does some part of its thinking, especially when remembering, by return, even when the individual is not returning, all these commands also impede the thought processes of the mind. In therapy they are particularly irksome and are the constant target of attention of the auditor.

First is the *patient-ejector* species of command. These are colloquially called *bouncers.* They include such things as "Get out!" "Don't ever come back," "I've got to stay away," etc., etc., including any combination of words which *literally* mean ejection.

Second is the *patient-holder* species of command. These include such things as "Stay here," "Sit right there and think about it," "Come back and sit down," "I can't go," "I mustn't leave," etc.

Third is the *engram-denyer* species of command which, literally translated, means that the engram doesn't exist. "I'm not here," "This is getting nowhere," "I must not talk about it," "I can't remember," etc.

Fourth is the *engram-grouper* species of command which, literally translated, means that all incidents are in one place on the time track. "I'm jammed up,"

"Everything happens at once," "Everything comes in on me at once," "I'll get even with you," etc.

Fifth is the *patient-misdirector* which sends the preclear in the wrong direction, makes him go earlier when he should be going later, go later when he should go earlier, etc. "You can't go back at this point," "You're turned around," etc.

The *bouncer* sends the preclear soaring back toward present time. The *holder* keeps him right where he is. The *denyer* makes him feel that there is no incident present. The fourth, the *grouper*, foreshortens his time track so that there is no time track. The *misdirector* reverses the necessary direction of travel.

Contacting any engram causes the preclear to react "analytically." Just as in the case of an engram being restimulated, the commands are impinged upon his analyzer. And although the analyzer may firmly believe it has just computed the reaction all of its own accord, it is actually speaking straight out of the content of an engram or engrams.

This is the method of *Repeater Technique*.

As he goes back along the track contacting engrams, the preclear runs into areas of "unconsciousness" which are occluded by "unconsciousness" or emotion. In most early engrams the preclear can be expected to yawn and yawn. It is not the command "to sleep" which is responsible for this: the "unconsciousness" is releasing (*boiling-off*, the auditors call it). A preclear may, for a space of two hours, fumble around, drop off into "unconsciousness," appear doped, start to go to sleep, without any such command being present.

Part of the engram bundle of data is the analyzer shut-off. When he is returned and an engram is contacted, the preclear then experiences an analyzer attenuation, which means he is much less able to think in the area.

Boiling-off "unconsciousness" is a process very necessary to therapy, for this "unconsciousness" could be restimulated in the everyday life of the individual and, when restimulated, make his wits shut off just a little or a very great deal, slowing down his thought processes.

The aspect of "unconsciousness," then, reduces the preclear's awareness whenever it is contacted. He has dreams, he mumbles foolish things, he flounders. His analyzer is penetrating the veil which kept him from the engram. But it is also highly susceptible, when in this state, to an engram command.

When urged by the auditor to go through the engram and recount it (although the auditor knows it may take minutes for this "unconsciousness" to boil-off enough to let the patient through), the preclear may complain that "I can't go back at this point." The auditor promptly takes note of this. It is an engram command coming through. He does not apprise the patient of this knowledge; the patient usually doesn't know what he's saying. If the patient then continues to have trouble, the auditor tells him, "Say, 'I can't go back at this point.'" The patient then repeats this, the auditor making him go over it and over it. Suddenly the somatic turns on and the engram is contacted.

In interviewing a patient, the auditor notes carefully, without appearing to do so, what phrases the patient chooses and repeats about his ills or about Dianetics. After he has placed the patient in reverie, if he discovers the patient, for instance, insists he "can't go anyplace," the auditor makes him repeat the phrase.

Repetition of such a phrase, over and over, sucks the patient back down the track and into contact with an engram which contains it. It may happen that this engram will not release–having too many before it–but it will not release only in the case it has that same phrase in an earlier engram. So the Repeater Technique is continued with the auditor making the patient go earlier and earlier for it. If all goes on schedule, the patient will very often let out a chuckle or a laugh of relief. The phrase has been sprung. The engram has not been erased, but that much of it will not thereafter influence therapy.

Anything the patient does about engrams and any words he uses to describe the action are contained, usually, in those engrams. Repeater Technique takes the charge off the phrases so that the engrams can be approached.

This technique, of course, can very occasionally land the patient in trouble, but the kind of trouble into which one can get in Dianetics is not very severe. The engram, restimulated in everyday life, can be, and is, violent. Murders, rapes and arsons, attempted abortions, backwardness in school–any aberrated aspect of life–stems from these engrams. But the act of approaching them in Dianetic therapy goes on another channel, a channel closer to the source of the engram. Ordinarily, acting on an unsuspecting individual, the engram has enormous motor and speech power, ties up great numbers of circuits in the mind which should be used for rationality, and generally effects havoc: its contacts are "soldered-in" and cannot be thrown out by the analyzer. In therapy the patient is headed toward the engram: that act alone begins to disconnect some of its "permanent leads." A patient can be gotten into an engram which, unless approached on the therapy route, might have made him curl up like a fetus and get shipped off to the nearest institution. On the therapy route, which is a return down the time track, the most powerful holder has its force limited. A patient can get into a holder which in normal life might be a psychosis. His only manifestation, perhaps, is that when he is told to

"Come up to present time," he simply opens his eyes without actually traversing the interval up the track to present time. He does not suspect he is in a holder until the auditor, watchful for such a manifestation, feeds him Repeater Technique.

AUDITOR: Are you in present time?

PRECLEAR: Sure.

AUDITOR: How do you feel?

PRECLEAR: Oh, I've got a slight headache.

AUDITOR: Close your eyes. Now say, "Stay here."

PRECLEAR: All right. Stay here. Stay here. Stay here. (*several times*)

AUDITOR: Are you moving?

PRECLEAR: No.

AUDITOR: Say, "I'm caught. I'm caught."

PRECLEAR: I'm caught. (*several times*)

AUDITOR: Are you moving on the track?

PRECLEAR: Nope.

AUDITOR: Say, "I'm trapped."

PRECLEAR: I'm trapped. I–Ouch, my head!

AUDITOR: Keep going over it.

PRECLEAR: I'm trapped. I'm trapped. I'm trapped. Ouch! That's worse!

(*His somatic is getting stronger as he approaches the engram holding him on the other side of the "unconsciousness" veil.*)

AUDITOR: Keep going over it.

PRECLEAR: I'm trapped–"Oh, God, I'm trapped. I'll never get out of this place. I'll never get out. I'm trapped!"

AUDITOR: Contact it closely. Make sure there is nothing more in it.

(*A trick to keep the preclear from replaying what he himself has just said and keep running the engram.*)

PRECLEAR: My head hurts! Let me come up to present time!

AUDITOR: Go through it again.

(*If the preclear comes up with this much charge, he'll be unhappy and the incident may be hard to enter next time.*)

PRECLEAR: "Oh, God, I'm trapped. I'm afraid I'm trapped (*new word showed up*). I'll never get out of this place as long as I live. I'm trapped. I'll never get out. I'm trapped." (*aside*) She's crying. "Oh, why did I ever have to marry such a man!"

AUDITOR: How's your head?

PRECLEAR: Hurts less. Say, that's a dirty trick. She's pounding herself on the stomach. That's mean! Why, confound her!

AUDITOR: Re-experience it again. Let's make sure there isn't more in it.

(*Same mechanism to keep the preclear from replaying what he said before rather than what he now gets from the engram. If he* replays *rather than* re-experiences, *the engram won't lift.*)

PRECLEAR: (*Does so, getting some new words and several sounds including the thud of the blows on her abdomen and an auto horn [bulb type] in the street outside.*) Don't tell me I have to run this thing again.

AUDITOR: Recount it, please.

PRECLEAR: Well, so this dame tries to bust my head in and get rid of me. And so I jumped out and beat hell out of her.

AUDITOR: Please re-experience the engram.

PRECLEAR: (*Starts to do so, suddenly finds out that like a piece of string with a loop in it, this engram has straightened out and contains more data where the loops were.*) "I've got to think of something to tell Harry. He'll jump all over me."

(*This was the source of his joking: "jumped out, etc."*)

AUDITOR: Please go over it again. There may be more in it.

PRECLEAR: (*Does so, old parts of it reduce, two new sounds appear: her footsteps and running water. Then he is happy and laughs at it. This engram is* released *because it may not have entirely vanished. Such an engram is in this shape only when it is contacted prior to basic-basic.*)

This is both Repeater Technique and an engram talked into *recession.* This engram may appear again with a very faint additional charge after basic-basic is contacted, but it has lost all power to aberrate or give out a psychosomatic headache or other illness. Yet this engram, not contacted by therapy, was quite enough to make this patient, when a boy, scream with terror every time he found he could not get out of some closed space (claustrophobia).

The Repeater Technique is the one particular phase of Dianetics which requires cleverness from the auditor. Given persistency and patience, any auditor can succeed in the other phases of the science with minimal intelligence. In the Repeater Technique, he must learn how to think–for therapy purposes–like an engram. And he will have to observe how the subject is conducting himself along the time track. And he will have to observe the type of reaction the subject has and draw from this the conclusion as to what sort of command is troubling the subject when the subject himself either does not cooperate or does not know.

This is not to say that the Repeater Technique is hard: it is not. But the ability of the auditor to use it is the principal reason why a case takes longer with one auditor than another. It is a definite ability. It is playing the game mentioned earlier with cleverness. Where is the preclear stuck and with what command? Why has the preclear suddenly stopped cooperating? Where is the emotional charge which is holding up the case? With the Repeater Technique the auditor can resolve all these problems and a clever auditor resolves them much faster than an unclever one.

How does one think like an engram? Ronald Ross, discovering that insects carried germs, considered it necessary to think like a mosquito. Here is a similar menace: the engram. One has to learn to think, for therapy purposes, like an engram.

The auditor could not and does not have to be able to look into a patient's eyes and guess why the patient won't eat anything but cauliflower on Wednesdays. That is an aberration and the auditor does not have to guess at either aberrations or psychosomatic illness sources: they all come out in time and he will learn much about them as he goes. But the auditor must be able to keep his patient straightened out on the track, moving earlier into the basic area, moving upwards from there for a reduction.

The current answer to this is the Repeater Technique. Understand that a whole new art of practice, or many arts of practice, could be evolved for Dianetics: one would be unhappy with his fellow man if such evolution and betterment did not take place. Just now the best that has come forward (and the criterion of best is that it works uniformly in all cases) is the Repeater Technique. The auditor must be able to use it if he expects anything like results from a case at this time. When the auditor–or some auditor–has run a few cases and knows the nature of this beast, the engram, he may–and better had–come forward with improved techniques of his own. The real drawback which Repeater Technique has is that it requires the auditor to be clever.

Being clever does not mean talking a lot. In Dianetics, when one is auditing, that is being very unclever. Indeed auditors, when they begin to work cases, almost invariably so love the sound of their own voices and the feel of their skill that the poor preclear hardly gets a chance to get a word in reactivewise–and it is the preclear who is to be Cleared, who has the only accurate information, who can make the only evaluations.

Being clever in the sense of the Repeater Technique is being able to pick out, from the subject's conversation or action, just what the engrams contain which will prevent his reaching them, progressing through them and so forth. The Repeater Technique is addressed only to *action*, not to aberration.

Here is a case, for instance, which was so "sealed-in" that thirty hours of almost continual Repeater Technique were necessary to break the walls between the analytical mind and the engrams. *It is important to know that an engram would not be an engram if the preclear could contact it easily.* Any engram which can be easily contacted and has no emotional charge is about as aberrative as a glass of soda water.

A young girl with sonic recall, but with extended hearing and such a complete imbalance of the endocrine system that she had become an old woman at twenty-two, was worked for seventy-five hours before she contacted anything in the basic area. This is almost incredible, but it happened. In a patient with sonic shut-off and off his time track, seventy-five hours of work would just about get the wheels greased. But this girl, having sonic recall, should have been well on the road to being Clear and she had yet to touch basic-basic.

By Repeater Technique and Repeater alone, the case was finally resolved. It contained practically no holders or bouncers. It simply appeared that the whole prenatal area was a blank.

Now it happens that an engram, being not a memory with reason in it, is just a set of waves or some other type of recording which impinges itself on the analytical mind and the somatic mind and runs the voice and muscles and other parts of the body. The analytical mind, to justify what it finds going forward, and cut down by the engram in dramatization, may be interjecting data to make this action seem reasonable – to justify it. But this does not make an engram sentient. When an engram is first approached in therapy, it appears to be absent entirely. It may be that three sessions will be required to "develop" this engram. As many are worked, this does not mean three blank sessions, but it means that the "I", in returning, must pass over an engram a few times for the engram to develop. This is important to know. Just as you ask the mind for a datum one week and don't find it (in an aberree) and ask it again the next week and find it, so with engrams. A cardinal principle in therapy is that *if you keep asking for it, you will eventually get the engram.* Returning over and over the prenatal area will, of itself alone, eventually develop the engrams in it so that the analytical mind can attack them and reduce them. This is slow freight. The Repeater Technique – although the engram is still in need of development by several sessions – speeds the process immensely.

In the case of this young girl, it probably would have taken another fifty or sixty hours of work to contact the engrams unless a technique like Repeater had been used. Repeater Technique resolved it when the auditor noted that she kept saying, "I'm sure there's a good reason why I feel bad up in my childhood. After all, my brother raped me when I was five. I'm sure it's up in my childhood, much later. My mother was terribly jealous of me. I'm sure it's later."

This young lady, as might be imagined, had studied some school of mental healing in college which thought sex or eating vitamins caused aberrations of the mind and she had often held forth on the fact that, while she was not averse to what she called "analysis," she did think it dull to expect a fetus to hear anything. She would go into the area before birth and declare she was quite comfortable. *But birth was not in sight.* That is important. The basic engram or engrams in the basic area – around the embryo period – cannot vanish and will not vanish short of therapy. And when birth cannot even be contacted by so much as one somatic, it is certain that something lies before it. If birth were the first engram, everybody could be Cleared in five hours. Birth can even be in sight and there may still remain half a hundred severe prenatal experiences. In her case, nothing was in sight. Her educational pattern had slowed the case: she was always trying to sit in present time and "remember" with a memory so full of occlusions that she couldn't have recalled her mother's right name. (She had acquired this from being in the hands of mental practitioners for ten years who had asked her to do nothing but "remember.") As has been said, she was quite comfortable before birth, sensed the amniotic fluid and was certain that life in the womb was a joyous life for all. The incongruity that she could experience the sensations of this amniotic fluid and floating comfort and warmth and a continued belief that there was no prenatal memory escaped her utterly. The auditor made no slightest effort to convince her. Knowing his business, he merely kept sending her back and forth, trying this mechanism or that.

She finally wanted to know if there *had* to be prenatal experience and was told that what was there was there, that if there was no prenatal memory, then she wouldn't recall any, but that if there was, she might. This is a good, equivocal attitude for an auditor. Dianetics, after all, as one auditor put it, "just shows the yard goods" and makes no sales effort at all.

The auditor had been using Repeater Technique on varieties of phrases. She was moving on the track so there must be a denyer present. And he had utterly run out of ideas when he realized, suddenly, that she was very handy with that phrase, "much later."

AUDITOR: Say, "much later" and return into the prenatal area.

GIRL: Much later. Much later. (*etc.*) (*very bored and uncooperative*)

AUDITOR: Continue please.

(*Never say, "Go ahead" for that means to do just that. Say, "Continue" when you want them to keep on progressing along an engram or repeating and "Return over it" when re-running an engram already run once.*)

GIRL: Much later. Much… I have a somatic in my face! It feels like I am being pushed.

(*This was good news, for the auditor knew she had a mid-prenatal pain shut-off which prevented later somatics from appearing.*)

AUDITOR: Contact it more closely and continue to repeat.

GIRL: Much later. Much later. It's getting stronger.

(*Naturally. On Repeater Technique, the somatic gets stronger until the phrase appears, exactly right. On a non-sonic case it impinges itself indirectly on "I"; in a sonic, the sound comes through as sound.*)

AUDITOR: Continue.

GIRL: Much… I hear a voice! There. That's it. Why, that's my father's voice!

AUDITOR: Listen to the words and repeat them, please.

GIRL: He's talking to my mother. Say, this face pressure is uncomfortable. It keeps going up and down on me. It hurts!

AUDITOR: Repeat his words please.

GIRL: He's saying, "Oh honey, I won't come in you now. It's better to wait until much later to have one." And there's my mother's voice. Say, this pressure is hurting me. No, it's eased up considerably. Funny, the minute I contacted his voice, it got less.

AUDITOR: What is your mother saying, please, if you hear her?

GIRL: She's saying, "I don't want you in there at all then!" She's mad! Say, the somatic stopped.

(*Coitus had ended at this point.*)

AUDITOR: Please return to the start of this and recount.

GIRL: (*Regains the beginning, somatic returns.*) I wonder what they're doing? (*then a pause*) I hear a squishing sound! (*then a pause and embarrassment*) Oh!

AUDITOR: Recount the engram please.

GIRL: There's a sort of a faint rhythm at first and then it gets faster. I can hear breathing. Now it's beginning to bear down harder, but a lot less than it did the first time. Then it eases up and I hear my father's voice, "Oh, honey I won't come in you now. It's better to wait until much later to have one. I'm not too sure I like children that well. Besides, my job..." And my mother must shove at him because there's a sharper somatic here. "I don't want you in there at all then. You cold fish!"

AUDITOR: Return to the beginning and recount it again, please.

GIRL: (*Recounts it several times, somatic finally vanishes. She feels quite cheerful about it but doesn't think to mention that she doubted prenatals existed.*)

This is *Repeater Technique* at work. This particular case had had about two hundred phrases thrown at her for Repeater Technique without finding one of them that would fit. In the first place, there were only a few lower engrams which the file clerk was willing to give out and the auditor was guessing at the whole gamut of denyers. A later incident might have contained–and did, but no somatic appeared–numbers of the phrases he used. But the file clerk was willing to settle for this one, for it was early and could be erased.

The file clerk rarely hands out something in a badly occluded case which cannot be reduced to recession. And an auditor *never* leaves an engram so offered until he has made every effort with many recountings to reduce it. The file clerk, in this case, by the by, would have let down the auditor by putting forth such an engram as birth, which would not have lifted and which would have caused a lot of lost work and given the patient a headache for a few days. The auditor would have let the file clerk down if he had not reduced the engram offered by making the girl go over it several times until the somatic was gone and the voice faded out.

The reason this engram stayed hidden was because its content said so. Actually it was a coitus. As an engram, it seemed to say that the incidents would be found later on in life. Further, as an engram, it said that it was not to be entered.

Repeater Technique will sometimes embroil a patient in trouble of a minor sort by getting him "sucked into" incidents which will not lift. This is not common, but the file clerk occasionally hands out a late incident rather than an early one. However, this is not an error on the part of the file clerk. Remember, he has these engrams filed by subject, somatic and time, and the auditor can use any one of these. When the file clerk responds and hands out a somatic on a repeater phrase the auditor has gleaned from the preclear's chatter or has guessed himself, and yet that somatic will not lift or no voice appears with it (in a sonic case, or merely won't lift with a non-sonic), the file clerk had to unstack a pile of material. Therefore, the auditor, realizing this, finding that a voice does not appear or that the somatic will not lift, has the preclear repeat the same phrase and tells him to go earlier and earlier. Another somatic may turn up in a different place in the body. The file clerk has gotten an even earlier one loose, now that a small amount of trouble has been taken from what he could first get. Now this earlier one is addressed similarly. It may get mediumly strong as a somatic, the preclear repeating the phrase all the while, and still no voice may appear. The auditor then sends the preclear earlier. The file clerk again has managed to get out an even earlier one, now that something has been taken from the second. This time, again, an even earlier somatic turns on, probably down around the basic area in a case which has not previously contacted this area, and this time a voice can be heard. The engram reduces. The file clerk, in short, was willing to risk trouble in order to get several somatics unstacked and let the auditor get a basic incident.

There are variations on this sort of thing. As the filing system is by subject, somatic and time, the auditor can use other things than phrases. He can send a preclear to the "highest intensity of a somatic" and often results may be obtained, though this is not as reliable as by subject nor as foolproof. The preclear, incidentally, does not mind going to any "highest intensity" of somatic because somatics are about a thousandth part as strong as the original agony, though they are quite strong enough. In present time, with the preclear not in therapy, the intensity of one of these somatics can be a drastic affair as witness the migraine headache. Taking the migraine, a preclear can be returned to the very moment of its reception when one would think its intensity would be the highest and yet find a mild, dull ache such as one would get with a hangover. This is part of the principle that any entrance of a case is better than a case not entered at all. For by return with standard reverie technique, the source is approached; and if the source is contacted at all, the power of the engram to aberrate has become reduced in strength no matter how many mistakes the auditor makes.

Returning to "maximum intensity" of a somatic, then, is nothing very painful. *Actual* maximum intensity is when the preclear is awake before the contact with the incident is made. But in returning to "maximum intensity," the incident may often be contacted and reduced. If "maximum intensity," however, contains in its engram the phrases, "I can't stand it!" "It's killing me," or "I'm terrified," then expect our preclear to respond to it in some such way. If he does not respond, then he has an emotional shut-off, which is another problem which will be taken up later.

Similarly, the auditor can handle his preclear in time. There exists a very accurate clock in the mind. The file clerk is very well acquainted with this clock and wherever possible will comply. The auditor who wants the patient to go "six minutes before this phrase is uttered" will generally find that his preclear is now six minutes before it, even though the incident is prenatal. The auditor can bring his preclear forward, then, minute by minute as he desires. He can take a preclear straight through an incident by announcing, "It is one minute later. It is two minutes later. Three minutes have gone by," and so forth. The auditor does not have to wait for those minutes to elapse; he just announces them. He can make a preclear go through time at five minute intervals or hour intervals or day intervals and, unless there is engramic material which holds him or otherwise affects the operation, the auditor can move the preclear on the time track at will. It would be very nice if the auditor could send the preclear to conception and then tell him it is one hour later, two hours later and so forth to pick up the first engram. However, there are more factors involved than time and the plan, though pretty, is not feasible. The time shift is generally used when the auditor is trying to get the preclear ahead of an incident to make sure that he really has a beginning. By returning the preclear by five or ten minute intervals, the auditor may sometimes discover that he is running backwards into a very long and complicated incident and that the headache he has been seeking to alleviate on the preclear was received, actually, hours before the period in which he thought it had initially been received. In such a case there is a second engram appended to an earlier engram and the auditor cannot lift the second one until he has the first one.

Actually, time shift is of limited use. The auditor who tries to go chasing backwards through time will find that he will have on his hands an artificially restimulated case and that the work is much impeded. Repeater Technique works best and is most easily handled by the file clerk. The auditor uses a time shift to get the preclear as close to basic area (early prenatal) as possible and then, generally, if the file clerk doesn't simply go to work handing out engrams which can be washed, one after the other, the auditor uses Repeater Technique. Time shift and "running down a somatic" have some limited use. Some experimentation will show about how much use they have.

The laws of returning are these:

1. A returned patient reacts more, theoretically, to those commands which are earlier than he is on the time track and less to those commands which are later than his point in time.
2. A preclear reacts to those engramic commands:
    a. Which are in chronic restimulation, or
    b. To which he is nearest on the time track.

Thus, if an engram says, "I'm afraid," he is. If it says, "I'd rather die than face this," he would.

If the command to which he is near says, "I'm sleepy," he will be. If it says, "Forget it," he will. Commands in chronic restimulation give a false color to the personality: "I can never be sure of anything," "I don't know," "I can't hear anything" are all possibly in chronic restimulation. If the file clerk won't give them up, then keep working the case anyway around these. They will give up after a while.

3. The action of the preclear on the time track and the condition of the track are regulated exclusively by engramic commands classifiable as *bouncers*, *holders*, *denyers* and *groupers* and *misdirectors*. (These conditions, it is repeated, are quite variable, as variable as language: "I don't know whether I am coming or going," for instance, in an engram makes it very confusing. "I can't go back at this point" makes the preclear keep progressing later and later.)
4. The engramic command manifests itself either in the awake speech of the preclear after a session of therapy or is inadvertently announced as a supposedly "analytical" thought when he nears the vicinity of the command.
5. The engram is not a sentient, rationalized memory but a collection of unanalyzed perceptions and it will develop into contact simply by the process of returning through it, to it, over it or asking for it.
6. The file clerk will give the auditor whatever can be extracted from the engram bank. The auditor must aid the file clerk by reducing in charge or severity everything the file clerk offers. This is done by making the patient recount it. (Otherwise the file clerk gets so

much material piled around that, with this in restimulation, he can no longer get at the files. The auditor who bucks the file clerk is not rare. The file clerk who will buck an auditor except by withholding data which will not reduce has yet to be found.)

The techniques available to the auditor are as follows:

1. *Returning*, in which the preclear is sent as early as possible on his track before therapy itself is engaged upon.
2. *Repeater Technique*, by which the file clerk is asked for data on certain subjects, particularly those affecting the return and travel on the time track, and which aid the ability of the preclear to contact engrams.
3. *Time shift*, by which a preclear can be moved short or long distances on the track by specific announcement of the amount of time forward the preclear is to go or time backwards, or return or progression through intervals of time. (It is also useful to find out if the preclear is moving or which direction he is moving on the time track in order to discover the action some engram may be having upon him.)
4. *Somatic location*, by which the moment of reception of the somatic is located, in an effort to discover whether it is received in this engram or to find an engram containing it.

EMOTION *and the* LIFE FORCE

ONE OF THE LARGEST roles in therapy is played by emotion. In the second book we covered this subject and divided it tentatively, as a theory only, into three divisions:

1. The emotions contained in the command of engrams whereby physical pain became confused with emotions.
2. The emotions contained as endocrine reactions subject to the analytical mind of the Clear and the analytical mind and reactive mind of the aberree.
3. The emotions contained in engrams which bound up free units of life force.

Further work and research on emotion will undoubtedly bring about an even closer understanding of it. But we have a workable knowledge of emotion now. We can use what we know and produce results with it. When we know more, we shall be able to produce much better results, but just now we can produce the Release and the Clear. If we treat emotion as bound-up life force and if we follow these general precepts to release it, we shall obtain a very large gain in any preclear; indeed, we shall produce our largest single gains by so releasing emotion.

In an engineering science like Dianetics, we can work on a push-button basis. We know that throwing a switch will stop a motor, that closing it again will start it and that no matter how many times we open or close that switch our motor will stop or start. We are using here a force which is still as mysterious to us as electricity was to James Clerk Maxwell. Much earlier Benjamin Franklin had observed that electricity existed and had done some interesting things with it, but he had not used it much and he could not control it. A philosopher like Bergson selected out a thing he called élan vital, a life force. Man is alive, there must be a force or flow of something which keeps him alive; when Man is dead, there is no force or flow. This is life force in the Benjamin Franklin stage. As he considered electricity, so did Bergson consider life force. Now we are up, in Dianetics, to the James Clerk Maxwell stage, or very nearly. We know that certain equations can be made about life force and we can use those equations. And we can theorize that "life force" and what has been called a certain kind of "emotion" are either similar or the same thing. We may have the wrong theory, but so might James Clerk Maxwell. Indeed, Maxwell's theories may still be wrong: at least we have electric lights. In Dianetics, we are pretty certain that the majority of tenets are parallels of natural law: these are the big computations. We are not certain that we have emotion properly bracketed, but then we shall not be sure until we have actually taken a dead man and pumped him up with life force again. Short of this extreme, we are on solid ground with emotion as life force.

We can, for instance, take a girl, examine something of her background with, let us say, an electroencephalograph (an instrument for measuring nervous impulses and reactions)* and then proceed on the basis of the information so obtained to do one of two things. The first is inhuman and would not be done, of course, but she could be made sick or insane merely by using this data so obtained. (If the data is obtained in therapy, it is obtained by actual contact with engrams and an engram contacted in reverie has lost its power to aberrate: Dianetic therapy thus makes such an eventuality utterly impossible.) The second and far more important fact to us is that she can be made to recover, with this same data, all the force, interest, persistence and tenacity to life and all the physical and mental well-being possible. If it could not be made to work both ways, we would not have the answer, at least in workable form. (Some fiction writer, by the way, if tempted to horrorize on the first fact, must please recall that the data was obtained with apparatus which would have staggered Doctor Frankenstein for intricacy and skill in use and that Dianetic therapy contacts the data at source: the apparatus is necessary to keep from touching the source, for the instant the source is touched by therapy, its power vanishes like yesterday's headlines. So let's have no *Gaslight* plays about Dianetics, please: they'd be technically inaccurate.)

This is not as simple as electricity in that the switch cannot be turned off and on. So far as Dianetics is concerned, it can only be turned on. We have a rheostat,

*The electroencephalograph, hypnoscopes, intelligence charts, tests for various dynamics and so forth are all mechanical aids to Dianetics. They are primarily used in research. They can be used in practice where available and the skill of the auditor permits, but they have not been generally in such practical use and, at this time and with this therapy, are not needed. Some chemist, one of these days, is going to invent a perfect "trance gas," I hope, which will speed the clearing of a schizophrenic, and some engineer, I trust, will make something to measure nerve impulses cheap enough to be used in general practice. Right now, we can get along without them, no matter how desirable they may be to the future.

then, which will not drop back, but which, when pressed forward, releases more and more dynamic force into the individual and gives him more and more control over its use.

Man is intended to be a self-determined organism. That is to say that as long as he can make evaluations of his data without artificial compulsions or repressions (held-down 7s in an adding machine), he can operate to maximum efficiency. When Man becomes exteriorly determined, which is to say, compelled to do or repressed from doing without his own rational consent, he becomes a push-button animal. This push-button factor is so sharply defined that an auditor, in therapy, who discovers a key phrase in an engram (and does not release it) can use that phrase for a little while to make a patient cough or laugh or stop coughing or stop laughing at the auditor's will. In the case of the auditor, because he got the data at source–contacted the engram itself, which robbed it of some power–the push-button will not last very long, certainly less than two or three hundred pushes. The whole pain-drive effort at handling human beings and most of the data accumulated in the past by various schools has been, unwittingly, this push-button material. If the engram is not touched at source it is good for endless use, its power never diminishing. Touched at source, however, the original recording has been reached and so it loses its power. The "handling of human beings" and what people have been calling, roughly, "psychology" have been actually push-button handling of a person's aberrational phrases and sounds. Children discover them in their parents and use them with a vengeance. The clerk discovers that his boss can't stand a full wastebasket and so always has one full. The bosun on a ship finds out one of his sailors cringes every time he hears the phrase "fancy-pants" and so uses the word to intimidate the man.

This is push-button warfare among aberrees. Wives may find that certain words make the husband wince or make him angry or make him refrain from doing something and so they use these push-buttons. And husbands find their wives' push-buttons and keep them from buying clothes or using the car. This defensive and offensive dueling among aberrees is occasioned by push-buttons reacting against push-buttons. Whole populaces are handled by their push-button responses. Advertising learns about push-buttons and uses them in such things as "body odor" or constipation. And in the entertainment field and the song-writing field, push-buttons are pushed in whole racks and batteries to produce aberrated responses. Pornography appeals to people who have pornographic push-buttons. Corn-and-games government appeals to people who have "care for me" push-buttons and others. It might be said that there is no necessity to appeal to reason when there are so many push-buttons around.

These same push-buttons, because they are 7s held down by pain and emotion (false data forced into the computer by engrams–and every society has its own special patterns of engrams), also happen to drive people insane, make them ill and generally raise havoc. The only push-button the Clear has is whatever his own computer, evaluating on his experience which itself has been evaluated by the computer, tells him is survival conduct along his four dynamics. And so, being no marionette in the hands of careless or designing people, he remains well and sane.

It is not true, however, that a Clear is not emotional, that his reason is cold, and that he is a self-conscious puppet to his own computations. His computer works so rapidly and on so many levels with so many of his computations going on simultaneously, but out of the sight of "I" (though "I" can examine any one of them he chooses), that his *inversion* or acute awareness of self is minimal. *Inversion* is the condition of the aberree whose poor computer is wrestling with heavy imponderables and held-down 7s in his engrams, such as "I must do it. I just have to do it. But no, I'd better change my mind."

The computational difference between the Clear and the aberree is very wide. But there is a much grander difference: life force. The dynamics have, evidently, so much potential force. This force manifests itself as tenacity to life, persistence in endeavor, vigor of thought and act and ability to experience pleasure. The dynamics in a man's cells may be no stronger than those in a cat's cells. But the dynamics in the whole man are easily greater than those in any other animal. Assign this as one will, the man is basically *more alive* in that he has a more volatile response. By *more alive* is meant that his sentient-emotional urge to live is greater than those found in other life forms. If this were not true, he would not now command the other kingdoms. Regardless of what a shark or a beaver does when threatened with final extinction, the shark and the beaver get short shrift when they encounter the dynamics of Man: the shark gets worn as leather or eaten as vitamins and the beaver decks a lady's back.

The fundamental aspect of this is seen in a single reaction. Animals are content to survive in their environments and seek to adjust themselves to those environments. That very dangerous animal–or god–Man has a slightly different idea. Ancient schools were fond of telling the poor demented aberree that he *must* face reality. This was optimum conduct: facing reality. Only it isn't Man's optimum conduct. Just as these schools made the fundamental error of supposing that the aberree was *unwilling* to face his environment when he was actually, because of engrams, *unable* to face it, they supposed that the mere facing of reality would lead to sanity. Perhaps it does, but it does not lead to a victory of Man over the elements and other forms. Man has something more. Some people call it creative imagination, some call it this or some call it that. But whatever it is called, it adds up to the interesting fact that Man is not content merely to "face reality" as most other life forms are. *Man makes reality face him.* Propaganda about "the necessity of facing reality," like propaganda to the effect that a man could be driven mad by a "childhood delusion" (whatever that is) does not face the reality that where the beaver down his ages of evolution built mud dams and keeps on building mud dams, Man graduates in half a century from a stone and wood dam to make a millwheel pond to structures like Grand Coulee Dam, and changes the whole and entire aspect of a respectable portion of Nature's real estate from a desert to productive soil, from a flow of water to lightning bolts. It may not be as poetic as Rousseau desired, it may not be as pretty as some "nature lover" would desire, but it's a new reality. Two thousand years ago the Chinese built a wall which would have been visible from the Moon had anybody been up there to look; three thousand years ago he had North Africa green and fertile; ten thousand years ago he was engaged upon some other projcct; but always he has been shaping things up pretty well to suit Man.

There's an extra quality at work or perhaps just more of it, so much more of it that it looks like a new thing entirely.

Now all this is not any great digression from therapy; it is stated here as an aspect of life force. Where the individual finds himself "possessed of less and less life force," he is losing some of the free units somewhere. And the free units of this life force, in a society or an individual, are the extra surge that is needed to tame North Africa, divide an atom, or reach the stars.

The mechanical theory here–and recall it is but theory and Dianetics can stand without it–is that there are so many units of force per individual. These units may be held in common by a group and may build to higher and higher numbers as "enthusiasm" increases. But for our purposes, we can consider that Man, as an individual or a society–both are organisms–has a ready number to hand for use in any given hour or day. He may manufacture these life units as required and he may simply have a given supply: that is beside the point. What is to the point is that he can be considered, at any hour or day, as just so much *alive*. Consider this as his dynamic potential as we can see on our descriptic earlier.

What happens, then, to this dynamic potential in the aberree? He has a large quantity of engrams in his bank. We know that these engrams *can* sleep for his entire life without being keyed-in, and we know that any or all of them can be keyed-in and thereafter wait for restimulators in the environment to set them into action. We know that his necessity level can suddenly rise and surmount all these keyed-in engrams, and we know that a high survival activity can bring him such a chance of pleasure that the engrams can stay unrestimulated, though keyed-in. And we can suppose that these engrams, from one period of life to another, can actually key-out again and stay out because of some vast change of environment or survival chances.

The usual case, however, is that a few engrams stay keyed-in continually and are restimulated rather chronically by the environment of the individual. And that if he changes environment, the old may key-out, but eventually new ones will key-in.

Most aberrees are in a state of chronic restimulation which, on the average, starts the spiral dwindling down rather rapidly.

As this pertains to life force, the mechanical action of an engram on being keyed-in is to capture so many of these units of life force. Sudden and sweeping restimulation of the engram permits it to capture a great many more units of life force. In the average case, every restimulation captures a greater residue of life force and holds it. When enthusiasm or impetus aligns the purpose of the individual toward a true survival goal (as opposed to a pseudo-goal in the engrams), he recaptures some of these units. But the spiral is dwindling: he cannot capture back, except in very unusual circumstances, as many as he has lost into the engram bank.

Thus it can be said, for purposes of this theory of life force action, that more and more life force units out of an individual's supply are captured and held in the engram bank. Here they are perverted in use to counterfeit themselves as dynamic (as in the manic and the high-euphoria case) and force action upon the somatic and analytical mind. In this engram bank, the life force units are not available as free feeling or for free action, but are used against the individual from within.

An observation here tends to demonstrate this action: the more restimulated an aberree is, the less free feeling he may possess. If caught in a manic (highly complimentary pro-survival engram), his life force is channeling straight through the engram and his behavior, no matter how enthusiastic or euphoric, is actually very aberrated: if he has this much life force to be so channeled, then he can be shown to have even more life force, sentiently directed, when Clear. (This has been done.)

We have demonstrated the parasitic quality of the demon circuits which use pieces of the analytical mind and its processes. This parasitic quality is common to engrams in other ways. If a man has, arbitrarily, 1000 units of life force, he has an ability to channel them, when Clear, into highly zestful existence. In a manic state, with a pro-survival engram in full restimulation, the life force is directed through an aberrated command and gives him, let us say, 500 units of pseudo-dynamic thrust.

In other words, the power is out of the same battery: such an engram has, at best, less power than the whole organism Cleared would have. (This aspect of the manic or super-personality neurotic has misled some of the old schools of mental healing into the thoroughly aberrated and poorly observed belief that insanities alone were responsible for Man's ability to survive, a concept which can be disproven in the laboratory simply by clearing one of these manics or any other aberree.)

The engram uses the same current but perverts it, just as it uses the same analytical mind but usurps it. Not only does the engram have no life of its own, but it is wasteful, as are so many parasites, of the life force of the host. It is thoroughly inefficient. If a comparable device were fitted into an electronic circuit, it would merely lead off and make "unalterable" some of the functions of the equipment which should be left variable and would, in addition, consume, simply by lengthened leads and bad condensers and tubes, power supply vital to the machine.

In the human mind, the engram assumes its most forceful "assist" aspect in the manic, channeling and commanding the organism into some activity of wild violence and monomanic concentration. The "super-salesman," the violently buoyant "gladhander," the fanatical and apparently unkillable religious zealot are classifiable as manics. The abundance of "power" in these people, even when it is as grim as Torquemada's or as destructive as Genghis Khan's, is an object of admiration in many quarters. The manic, as will be later covered, is a "pro-survival," "assist" command in an engram which yet fixes the individual on some certain course. But an engram is capable only of as much "power" as is present in the host, just as it is capable of tying up only as much analyzer as is present.

Let us take a forceful manic who is displaying and functioning on 500 arbitrary units of life force. Let us assume that the entire being is possessed of 1000 arbitrary units of life force. Suppose we have here an Alexander. The dynamics of the average person are unassisted by manics in most cases, but are dispersed as a stream of electrons might be dispersed by a block before them. Here are scattered activity, scattered thoughts, uncomputable problems, lack of alignment. In such a person, with 1000 units present, 950 of those units could be so captured in the engram banks and yet so thoroughly counteractive that the person displays a functioning capacity of only 50 units. In the case of Alexander, it could be assumed, the manic must have been an alignment in a general direction of his own basic purposes. His *basic purpose* is a strong regulator: the manic happens to align with it: a person of great ability and personal prowess becomes possessed of 500 units via a manic engram, believes he is a god and goes out and conquers the known world. He was educated to believe he was a god, his manic engram said he was a god and had a holder in it. Alexander conquered the world and died at thirty-three. He could hold in his manic only so long as it could be obeyed: when it could no longer be obeyed, it changed his valence, became no more a manic and drove him, with pain, into dispersed activities. The engram received from his mother, Olympias, can almost be read even at this late date. It must have said he would be a joyous god who would conquer all the world and must keep on conquering, that he must always strive to rise higher and higher. It was probably a ritual chant of some sort from his mother, who was a high priestess of Lesbos and who must have received some injury just before the ritual. She hated her husband Philip. A son who would conquer all was the answer. Alexander may well have had fifty or a hundred such "assist" engrams, the violent praying of a woman aberrated enough to murder. Thus he could be assumed to have conquered until he could no longer stretch a line of supply for conquering, at which time he, of course, would no longer be able to obey the engram and its force of pain would turn on him. The engrams dictated attack *to conquer*, and they enforced the command with pain: once *conquering* could no longer be accomplished, the pain attacked Alexander. He realized one day he was dying, within the week he was dead, and at the height of his power. Such, on a very large scale, is a manic phrase in an engram at work.

Now let us suppose that Alexander, with only education to turn him against his father, with only prayers to ask him to conquer the world, not engrams, had been Cleared. Answer: given a sufficient and rational reason, he would most certainly have been able to conquer the world and at eighty might well have been alive to enjoy it. How can we assume this?

The manic with 500 units of directed purpose has been Cleared. He now has 1000 units of *sentiently* directed purpose. He is exactly twice as forceful as he was when he was in a forceful manic and his basic purpose may be similar, but now can be realized and will not turn on him the moment he has reached a goal or failed.

This is clinical, the theory behind life force. It was formulated in an effort to explain observed phenomena.

The theory may be wrong, the observed data is not. But the theory must be somewhere close to right because with it could be predicted considerable phenomena which had not been known to exist before: in other words, it is a profitable theory. It followed after Dianetics was well formulated, for a strange fact, vital to the therapist, turned up:

The preclear advanced in therapy in exact ratio to the amount of emotional charge released from his reactive bank.

The purpose and persistency of the aberree was hindered in ratio to the amount of emotional charge within his engram bank. His recovery of survival potential increased in ratio to the amount of energy freed from the engram bank. His health increased in ratio to the amount of energy freed from the engram bank.

The engrams which contained the greatest discharge were those which centered around loss of imagined survival factors.

Hence, this theory of life force was formulated. Any manic Cleared seemed to demonstrate far more actual power and energy than before he was Cleared. And any "normal" Cleared increased in accessible life force units to compare with any manic Cleared.

Undoubtedly further work and observation will refine this theory. At the present moment, however, it serves. It is one of those "scientific theories" thrown in to explain an operation or a long series of observations. In this case, it happens to be squarely aligned with the basic tenets of Dianetics, for it predicts data which can then be found and does not throw out former data predicted by the basic mathematics and philosophy of Dianetics.

Here we are speaking, actually, not of this slippery term, emotion, but, we believe, life force. This life force is considerably enhanced by success and pleasure in general and is, according to this theory, augmented in terms of arbitrary units by pleasure. In other words, pleasure is a thing which recharges the batteries or permits them to be recharged and in a Clear, far from leading to softness, leads to renewed activity since indolence is engramic.

Pleasure is a vitally important factor: creative and constructive endeavor, the overcoming of not unknowable obstacles toward some goal, the contemplation of past goals reached all combine to recharge life force. The person, for instance, who has been an enormous success and then loses that success and so becomes ill is following no rational cycle but an engramic command cycle. In a way he has disobeyed an engramic command and having disobeyed, suffers pain. The "child wonder" who early "burns out" is actually, via therapy, about as burned out as a banked furnace. Any "child wonder" is a forced affair: think of the dreams Mama must have poured through his engrams. She's hurt: "Oh, I'll never forgive myself! If I have ruined my child, I will never forgive myself. My child that's to be the world's greatest violinist!" or "Oh, you brute! You have struck me! You have injured our child. I'll show you. I'll make him the greatest child pianist in all Brooklyn! He's to be a beautiful child, a wonder child! And you've struck him, you brute. Oh, I am going to sit right here until you go away!" (Actual engrams.) The last computes that the way to get even with Papa is to be the greatest pianist in all Brooklyn. The child is a great success: musical ear, practice and great "purpose." He gets this engram restimulated constantly by his mother. But then, one day he loses a contest, he knows suddenly he is no longer a child, that he has failed. His purpose wavers. He gets headaches (Papa's blow) and is at last "neurotic" and "burned out." Cleared, he went back to being a pianist, not as an "adjusted" person, but one of the best paid concert pianists in Hollywood. Music aligned with basic purpose.

Again, in another manic example, a patient who had been some time in therapy–not the first to do this by far–raved that he had been "turned-on" by Dianetics. He was walking about a foot off the earth, chest punched out and so forth. His glasses suddenly would not fit him, his eyes were too good. He was a beaming, powerful case of euphoria. Artificial restimulation had touched a manic engram, had brought it into key for the first time in his life. He felt wonderful. The auditor knew that he was due for a complete comedown within thirty-six hours to three days (the usual time) because an artificial restimulation, by therapy, had tapped the engram. It happened that his grandmother had told her daughter that she must not abort the child because someday it might become a "fine upstanding man or beautiful woman." He was upstanding all right: it almost strained his back muscles. Another glance at the engram in therapy and the manic phase was gone.

This manic, then, as in the case of the boy wonder, can be assumed to have gathered up available life force and suddenly channeled it along basic purpose lines, making a high level of concentration of life force. In the case of the pianist, his Cleared force was well above the manic force. In the other case, currently in process, a level has been reached which is approaching the former level and will surpass it by far.

In the same way, an enthusiasm for a project will channel life force along some purpose line and necessity will suddenly rob back from engrams enough power to carry an individual far, although he has no active manics whatever.

Now we come to the heart of this matter: the *pro-survival engram*. It is pseudo-survival like all engramic "assists," a mirage which dissolves and leaves burning sands.

Formerly we spoke mainly of *contra-survival engrams.* These lie across the dynamics of the individual and his basic purpose.*

The contra-survival engram is, to the dynamics, like a logjam which dams a necessary river. The dynamic is blocked in some degree. Any blockage to any one of the four dynamics (or any section of that spectrum) causes a dispersal of the flow. It does not make less dynamic, particularly, but it does misdirect it in the same order that the river, blocked in its natural flow, might become five streams going in various directions or flood a fertile pasture it should merely have watered.

The pro-survival engram alleges to assist (but does not actually assist) the dynamic on its way. It pretends it *is* the dynamic. In the analogy of the river, the pro-survival engram would be a canal which took the river's force and sent it off in some unintended direction. The pro-survival engram is not a manic; it can and does contain, at times, manic phrases.

A contra-survival engram says, "He's worthless, damn him, let's kill him."

The pro-survival engram says, "I am saving him." If it added, "He is a darling and a very wonder with the ladies," it would then be a pro-survival *with* a manic.

---

*It happens that there is an additional specialization of the dynamics in everyone, a sort of built-in personal dynamic. It is a clinical fact that the basic purpose is apparently known to the individual before he is two years of age. Talent and inherent personality and basic purpose go together as a package; they seem to be part of the genetic pattern. Anyone can be revivified Dianetically in the age of two years and consulted about his purpose in life, and he will come forth with a very specific desire as to what he wishes to accomplish in life (and two year old activity as reviewed confirmed it). It will be discovered that his later life has followed this general pattern wherever he succeeded. Of fifteen persons examined, the basic purpose was found formed at two years of age. And when Cleared, these persons used and pursued that basic purpose.

In terms of the descriptic which defines the survival dynamic and the suppressor, earlier in this book, the contra-survival engram would be part of the suppressor (an aberrated part) and the pro-survival engram would be part of the dynamic thrust (an aberrated part).

Neither one of these things is actually a sentient and computable portion of survival dynamic or suppressor.

The engram (delirium from illness, perhaps) which says, "I will stay with you, darling, so long as you are sick" is an apparent but wholly shadow-stuff part of the survival dynamic. But the reactive mind has no sense of time when restimulated and this engram, keyed-in and constantly restimulated by some concept in it such as an odor or a person's voice who may or may not be the original person, demands that the person who has it be ill just as he was ill when it was said. This way, according to our moron, the reactive mind, lies survival: "I had someone taking care of me when I was ill. I need someone to take care of me. I must be ill." Here is the basic pattern of all sympathy engrams. Here is the basic pattern of the engram which will contain the chronic psychosomatic illness in any patient. The variety is, of course, very large, but all insist that the individual who has them be ill in order to survive.

The suppressor-type engram, always contra-survival, can be cut into restimulation in exactly the same way as the pro-survival engram. An engram is an engram and all the mechanics are the same. The fact that the analytical mind cannot time the engram can make any engram seem omnipresent. Time can "heal" the experiences of the analytical mind, perhaps, but not the reactive mind which has no time–a fact which makes time not the Great Healer, but the Great Charlatan. There may be no actuality at all in this suppressor data. It is false data. Such engrams let an individual, for instance, see a butterfly and then tell him it is dangerous: he then comes to detest spring because that is the time he sees butterflies. This engram may say, "You're all against me. You're against everything I do," which was actually Mama making a stand against her husband and mother-in-law. It contains a concept, a recording of the sound of a sewing machine as well. The individual possessing this engram hears a sewing machine (if this engram has at some time been keyed-in) at a moment when he is weary and dull and, looking toward the machine (he never identifies the actual sound: these engrams protect themselves), sees his wife. She is the *associative restimulator*, something his analytical mind, told to scent danger, picks up as the cause. So he searches around and finds something he is angry about (something almost "rational") and begins to tell her she is against him. Or it can be an engram of such low emotional tone that it is an apathy, and so he sits down and weeps and moans that she is against him. If, during "unconsciousness" at birth, the doctor said he'd have to spank him, the individual possessing this engram howls and gets headaches when he is spanked and when grown spanks his children as the strongest suppressor he can think of.

There is a difference, then, between the pro- and contra-engrams, particularly the real sympathy pro-engram and the contra-engram. And it is a difference, even if we have been long on the road in this chapter, which is of vital interest to the auditor.

All the real reluctance he will see in preclears during therapy will come from these sympathy pro-survival engrams. These add up into some very weird computations. They tell the patient that he had better not "get rid of it" and so the patient struggles to retain his engrams. Such an engram is very common. A typical case is Mama pushing off Papa, who insists he cannot afford a child. The struggle injures the child and in the "unconsciousness" he receives, of course, an engram: Mama is refusing to get rid of it, Mama is on baby's side, therefore baby had better do exactly as Mama says and "not get rid of it." This aligns with purpose, the deepest purpose, to survive. If he gets rid of his engrams, he will die because getting rid of it means death, for Mama said she would die if she got rid of it. Further, on up through life, Mama may have the nasty habit of telling him when he is ill that she will "take care of her baby and protect him from his father," and this makes a new force in the old computation.

Thus we come to the *ally computation.* This will be the chief and number one struggle of the auditor, the thing which will most elusively resist him, the thing which lies down close to the core of a person.

The ally computation is severe enough that an auditor once said that a man is not victimized by his enemies, he is murdered by his friends. Engramically speaking, that is quite true.

The only aberration and psychosomatic ill the patient will continually hold to is a pro-survival engram which is part of an ally computation. That could be written fifty times here without being stressed enough. It is most important, it is the first thing which the auditor is going to buck when he enters a case, the first thing he must discharge if he wishes therapy to go swiftly. He may have to touch and reduce many contra-survival engrams, for they come swiftly enough when called, before he can even get an idea of what the ally computation is. But when he gets an ally computation, he had better run it out and discharge all its emotion or the case will hang fire.

The ally computation is the reactive mind level moronism that survival depends on Grandma or Aunt Sue or some serving maid thirty years dead.

The attendants of the individual when he was ill, the people who begged his pregnant mother to stop trying to abort him, or fed him or otherwise tried to keep him from being hurt: these are the allies.

The reactive mind operates wholly on two-valued logic. Things are life or they are death, they are right or they are wrong, just as the engram wording states. And the personnel of engrams are friends or enemies. The friends, the allies, mean Life! The enemies mean Death! There is no middle ground. Any restimulator or associated restimulator for the pro-survival engram means Life! And any restimulator or associated restimulator for a contra-survival engram means Death!

The auditor, of course, may be a really restimulative person (one who is a pseudo-father, a pseudo-lover of mother before birth, etc.), but he is always an associative restimulator, the person who may take away these terribly, horribly vital things: the pro-survival engrams. The contra-survival engrams outbalance this factor and, of course, the analytical mind of the preclear is always all for the auditor and the therapy.

The trouble comes when the analytical mind is shut down by restimulation and the auditor is seeking the ally computation. Then the preclear's reactive mind dodges and avoids.

The ally computation, however, is simple to trace. And it is very vital to trace it, for this computation may contain the bulk of all the emotional discharge of the case. Freeing the complete ally computation wholly before basic-basic is reached is wholly impossible. But as much life force as possible must be restored to the preclear to make the case work well.

For the ally computation, above all things, encysts the life force of the individual. Here is caught and held the *free feeling*, the very heartbeat of life itself. A preclear is only placed in apathy by ally computations. The body can be almost dead in the presence of antagonism and still rally and fight. But it cannot fight its friends. The law of affinity has been aberrated into an entrance into the reactive engram bank. And that law, even when twisted with the murky shadows of unreason in the reactive mind, still works. It is a good law. It is too good when the auditor is trying to find and reduce engrams which are making the preclear ache with arthritis or bleed internally with stomach ulcers. Why can't he "get rid of" his arthritis? Mama said, when she gracefully fell over a pig, "Oh, I can't get up! Oh, my poor, poor baby. Oh, my baby! I wonder if I hurt my poor, poor baby. Oh, I hope my baby is still alive! Please, God, let him live. Please, God, let me keep my baby. Please!" Only the God to which she prayed was the Reactive Mind, which makes one of its idiot computations on the basis of everything is equal to everything. A holder, a prayer for life, a thoroughly bruised baby's spine, Mama's sympathy, a pig grunt, a prayer to God–all these things are equal to the reactive mind and so we have a fine case of arthritis, particularly since our patient sought "survival" by marrying a girl with a voice just like Mama's sounded when he was in the womb. Ask him to get rid of his arthritis? The reactive mind says, "NO!" Arthritis is a baby is a pig grunt is a prayer to God is wife's sympathy is being poor is Mama's voice and all these things are desirable. He's kept himself poor and he's kept his arthritis and he married a wife who would make a harlot blush and this is pro-survival: wonderful stuff, survival, when the reactive mind computes it! And in the case of the ulcers, here was baby poked full of holes (Mama is having a terrible time trying to abort him so she can pretend a miscarriage, and she uses assorted household instruments thrust into the cervix to do it) and some of the holes are through and through baby's abdomen and stomach: he will live because he is surrounded by protein and has a food supply and because the sac is like one of these puncture-proof inner tubes that seals up every hole. (Nature has been smart about attempted abortion for a long, long time.) It so happens that Mama in this case was not a monologuist, although most of Mama's activity on this line is a dramatization and has conversation with it. But it also so happens that Grandma lives next door and she comes over unexpectedly, shortly after the latest effort to make baby meet oblivion. Grandma may have been an attempted abortionist in her day, but now she is old and highly moral and besides, this baby is not giving her any morning sickness. She therefore finds much to censure when she sees a bloody orangewood stick in the bathroom. Baby is still "unconscious." Grandma berates Mama: "Any daughter of mine who would do such a horrible thing should be punished by the vengeance of God (the principle of 'don't do as I do, do as I say,' for who gave Mama this dramatization in the first place?) and driven through the streets. Your baby has a perfect right to live: if you don't think you can take care of him, *I* certainly will. Now you go right on through with your pregnancy, Eloisia, and when that baby is born, if you don't want him, you bring him to me! The idea of trying to hurt that poor thing!" And so, when our bleeding ulcer case gets born, there is Grandma and there is security and safety. Grandma is here the ally (and she can become an ally in a thousand different ways, any of them based on the principle that she talks sympathetically to baby when he is out like a flounder, and fights Mama in his favor when he is "unconscious"), and when he grows to boyhood he can be found placing a large dependency on Grandma, much to the parental wonder (for *they* never did anything to little Roger, not *they*). And Roger will, when Grandma is dead, develop bleeding ulcers to get her back.

Whoever is a friend is to be clasped to the bosom with bonds of steel, says this great genius, the reactive mind, even though it kills the organism.

The ally computation is a little more than the mere idiot calculation that anyone who is a friend can be kept a friend only by approximating the conditions wherein the friendship was realized. It is a computation on the basis that one can only be safe in the vicinity of certain people and that one can only be in the vicinity of certain people by being sick or crazy or poor and generally disabled.

Show an auditor a child who was easily frightened by punishment, who was not at ease around home and who had allies who seemed more important to him than the parents (grandparents, aunts, boarders, doctors, nurses, etc.) and who was sickly, and the auditor can usually spring into view an attempted abortion background because, more often than not, it is there. Show an auditor a child who showed enormous attachment for one parent and detestation for the other, and the auditor can bring out a background wherein one person wanted to get rid of or hurt the child and the other parent did not.

The ally computation, then, is important. And it is also very secret. Trying to get the real allies in a case is often a great struggle. It may be that a patient had eight or ten of these allies in some cases and tried desperately to hold to them; and when he could not, searched and found mates and friends who were approximations of his allies. A wife, around whom A is continually ill but whom he will not leave under any circumstances, is usually a pseudo-ally, which is to say, she approximates some mannerism of the actual ally, has a similar voice or even a similar first name. B, who will not leave a job and yet who is working far below his ability level in life, may be there because his boss is a pseudo-ally; further, he may be working at this job because an ally had a similar station in life and he is being the ally.

Anything which can so far corrupt a person's life is naturally going to be difficult to some degree in therapy. For when he is asked to get rid of his ally computation, it is as likely that he will give any clue to it as it is that he would have spit in his ally's face.

These pro-survival engrams containing the ally computation can be described as those which contain personnel who defended the patient's existence in moments when the patient conceived that his existence was under attack. This need not be an actual, rational defense: it may only be that the content of the engram seems to indicate it; but it can safely be assumed that the worst ally computations are those when the life of the patient was defended against attackers by the ally. Most ally computations have their genesis in the prenatal area.

The ally computation is sought as the first action in any case and new ally computations are sought throughout a case.

These sympathy pro-survival engrams, which make up the ally computations, vary only in intensity from the standard pro-survival engram. A standard pro-survival engram is bad only because someone has expressed friendship for the patient or another person when he was "unconscious." It is difficult to discover and clear even when it actually has been entirely misread–which is to say that the pro-survival content was intended for another person than the patient, but is only misconstrued by the patient. If the patient is "unconscious" and somebody says, "He is a good guy," actually meaning another person entirely, the egocentric reactive mind takes the phrase to have been meant for oneself. In the sympathy pro-survival engram (the ally computation is composed only of these), there is an actual defense of the person from danger by some ally. This can vary from a dramatic scene wherein somebody has been bent on killing the patient and the ally has arrived, like the cavalry, in the nick of time, to the incident wherein the patient was simply saved (or assumed he was being saved) from destruction such as drowning, being run over, etc. And the sympathy pro-survival engram is only as good as its content in words, for it does not rationalize the action. Engrams have been discovered where the patient was actually being murdered, but the content was such that he was convinced he was being saved. Such a case would include what auditors call a "mutual AA"–a father and mother together attempting an abortion, AA meaning "attempted abortion"–wherein Mama was in utter agreement and disposed herself for the operation, but became frightened and began to scream about "her precious baby" in an effort to save herself from being injured. Patients with this sort of sympathy pro-survival engram can get pretty confused about mother.

The insidious aspects of the sympathy pro-survival engrams are several:

1. They are aligned with the fundamental dynamic of survival in the most literal sense and are therefore aligned with the purpose of the individual.
2. They are like cysts round which contra-survival engrams serve as the outer shell.
3. They most sharply affect the health of the individual and are always the basic factor beneath the psychosomatic illness which the individual displays.
4. They cause the reactive mind (but not the analytical mind) to resist therapy.
5. They are the largest drain upon the life force units.

In (3) above, the pro-survival sympathy engram does more than just carry forward the injury which becomes the psychosomatic illness. Any engram is a bundle of data which includes not only all perceptics and speech present, but also metering for emotion and state of physical being. The last, the state of physical being, would be serious enough. This metering says that *structure* was so and such at the moment this sympathy pro-survival engram was received. In the case of an embryo engram, then, the reactive mind, in forcing the engram back into action, may also force the structural pattern back upon the body: this occasionally results in retarded development, embryo-like skin, embryo-type back curvature, and so forth. The glands themselves, being physical organs, are also sometimes so suppressed in the reactive mind's effort to approximate all conditions. The underdeveloped gonads, the sub-level thyroid, the wasted limb, all these things often come from sympathy pro-survival engrams. This is so observably the case that when an individual is being cleared, growth process begins to bring the body up to genetic blueprint even before the case is completed: the change which takes place in the physical being of the patient is sometimes so remarkable and so marked that it is far more startling than the mere disappearance of a catalog of psychosomatic ills such as coronary, ulcers, arthritis, allergies, and so on.

It would be supposed that anything powerful enough to twist the physical blueprint and keep the body from developing, or make it keep on growing where it should have stopped, would resist any therapy. This is true only in a most limited sense. Once one is aware of what suppresses a case, one can go about vanquishing the suppressors because a pro-survival engram, unlike a contra-survival engram, has an Achilles' heel.

The most workable answer now known to Dianetics lies in the principle of life force units and a technique for throwing them back into circulation. The pro-survival engram collects and holds such units, according to this theory, and collapses when its power to hold units is broken.

Entering a case, then, where one has a chronic psychosomatic illness (and what case doesn't have, even though it is as slight as an occasional fit of sneezing or hiccups), the auditor first scouts it, going through a returning routine to find out how early he can get for material, how the state of the sonic recall is, how occluded is the youth of the person, and so forth. When he has made this survey, he begins to make his computation on the case: First, was the child happy with both father and mother, and if not, where was the child happiest? (There will be where the allies live.) Was either parent an unreasonably powerful factor in shaping the thinking powers of the child? (Here again may be an ally, even if a poor one.) Did the patient have grandparents or other relatives; how did he feel toward them? All this data will be more or less occluded and warped by demon circuits and is about as reliable as the data this patient will inevitably try to get from "loopy" parents or relatives, who not only do not know what happened to him, but might be most anxious not to have anything discovered.

What really did happen? Don't let patients ask relatives or parents anything if you can help it, for these are restimulators in the extreme and never have any data you can use; the patient is just trying to use them as bypass circuits to avoid the pain of recalling things himself. When the case is finished, he will no longer want to hound these people. And if you want a check for research reasons, get one of the relatives and put him through therapy.

The auditor now has some slight idea of who the allies may be. And here comes the Achilles' heel of the ally computation.

Any ally computation may have included the loss of the ally. And the *loss of the ally* may be the trigger which will start chain fission. For what we are going to try to do is blow off or discharge as many life force units as possible from the reactive engram bank and weaken it. Every charge we get from the bank will reinforce the ability of the patient to carry on in existence and will aid his analytical mind to get into the engram bank. Hence, discharging these frozen units is a vital and important part of therapy and the condition of the case will improve in direct ratio to the number of these units so discharged.

Consider these life units as free life energy: an engram capturing them can set itself up, for all intent, as a life force. It is then an entity and only then. The demon circuits, the valence walls (which compartment the analyzer, so to speak, and bring about multivalence), the force and power of the engram itself are all dependent, according to theory and as observed in practice, upon usurped life units.

To free these units is the primary task of therapy; to relieve pain from the engrams is the secondary task; to make the patient comfortable during therapy does not even rank, though there is no need he should be uncomfortable. The dual character of therapy, then, is actually two sections of the same thing: relieving engrams. There is this dual nature in engrams, however, that they have painful emotion (where that means usurped life force) and physical pain (where that means pain of injury, illness, etc.).

To get as early as possible as fast as possible and find basic-basic is the direction and intent of therapy in its first stages. To accomplish this (when it cannot be done immediately merely by returning and finding basic-basic, which can and always should be tried) one relieves the case and robs the engram bank by releasing life units (painful emotion captured them) from the ally computations.

In brief, the entire intent and act of therapy is to find the earliest engram and erase it and then proceed to erase all other engrams, as engrams, so they can no longer be discovered. (They refile in the standard bank, but it takes a genius to find them there and a search of hours and hours: hence, to the auditor they can be said to have "erased," for they are no longer engrams and are now experience.) The first, last and only job of the auditor is to find the earliest engrams available and erase them. That cannot be said too often or too strongly.

The various ways to accomplish this are the techniques and arts of therapy. Anything which brings about this erasure of engrams in place and their refiling as experience is useful and legitimate *whatever it includes*. An engineer intends to remove a mountain which is in the way of a river: his intent and all his effort is directed toward moving that mountain; the ways and means employed by him to move that mountain, by steam shovel, hydraulic rams or dynamite are the art and techniques applied to do the job.

There are three degrees of knowledge in our task:

1. In Dianetics we know the goal: we know the results which come about when that goal is attained.
2. We know the character of the obstructions between us and the goal, but of the *exact character* of the obstruction we can never learn too much.
3. The art and technique of removing the obstruction between us and the goal are legitimate only by the test of whether or not they remove the obstruction.

The method of attack on the problem can always be improved by learning more about the character of the factors in the problem, and by learning new arts and techniques which can be applied to the problem, and by studying to improve our skill in practicing existing arts and techniques. The currently existing art and technique is not to be considered optimum merely because it does the job. The time and ease of work could be shortened by new techniques or advancing skills for old techniques.

All this is interjected so that Dianetics, unlike Aristotelian logic and natural history, will be recognized as an advancing, changing science. It is interjected at this place because no auditor should just sit back with this routine and never try to improve the routine.

Very well, this is the routine. *It works*, but it can never be made to work too quickly or too well:

1. Place the patient in reverie and scout into the prenatal area to see if engrams are available for lifting without further work. If they are there and can be found, take the charge out of them and erase them if possible. Do not try to erase anything as remote from basic-basic as birth unless the file clerk insists on presenting birth. In other words, get the subject into the prenatal area and look for the earliest engrams. Do not ask for specific instances, particularly for something like birth, just take whatever is presented. If you can't get back early, take step two.
2. Scout the patient's life, while he is in reverie (do this in any event sooner or later if the case slows down, but only if it slows down to a point where early engrams are either not reducing or are without any emotion). Establish in this

scout whoever may have been depended upon by the patient and be suspicious always that he has not told you the really important allies, but do not tell him you are suspicious.

3. Find out when the patient lost any ally through death or departure. Approach this moment and one way or another, by getting earlier material and this incident or getting just this incident, discharge the sorrow of loss out of the incidents. Treat any incident in which the ally departs or the patient is separated from the ally as an engram and erase it accordingly or run it until it has no "charge" of sorrow on it. If the "charge" holds, suspect an early moment of sorrow about this ally and find that and treat it as an engram.
4. First, last and always, the job is to get basic-basic and then ever afterwards the currently existing earliest moment of pain or sorrow, and to erase every incident as it is advanced by the file clerk or found by Repeater Technique.
5. Any incident that hangs fire always has a similar incident earlier, and the patient should be taken earlier for the prior incident when an engram will not "reduce" on recounting.
6. At any time the engrams start to become emotionless in tone, even though they reduce, suspect another ally computation and, early or late in the patient's life, get it and reduce it at least until the emotional discharge is gone. Do not get everything in a case restimulated by changing from an unreduced incident to something which looks more fruitful, but reduce everything in view before you go looking for a new sorrow charge.

7. It is better to reduce an emotionless early engram than it is to upset the case by hounding him for an ally computation when a cunning search fails to reveal one in sight. Erasing early emotionless engrams will eventually bring a new ally computation into sight if you occasionally look for it.
8. Consider that any holdup on a case, any unwillingness to cooperate, stems from ally computation.
9. Treat all demon circuits as things held in place by life force units absorbed into the bank and address the problem of demon circuits by releasing charges of sorrow.
10. Consider that loss by death or departure of an ally is identical with a death of some part of the patient and that the reduction of a death or departure of an ally will restore that much life back to the patient. And remember that great sorrow charges are not always death or departure, but merely may be a sudden reversal of stand by the ally.

Always keep in mind that that person who most nearly identifies himself with the person of the patient, such as a sympathetic mother or father or grandparent or relative or friend, is considered by the reactive mind to be a part of the person himself and that anything happening to this sympathetic character can be considered to have happened to the patient. In such a case where an ally has been found to have died of cancer, you may occasionally find the patient to have a sore or scaly place where he supposed the ally's cancer to have been.

The reactive mind thinks in identities only. The sympathetic pro-survival engram identifies the patient with another individual. The death or loss (by departure or denial) of the other individual is therefore a reactive mind conviction that the patient has suffered some portion of death.

Emotional charges may be contained in any engram: the emotion communicates, in the same tone level, from the personnel around the "unconscious" person into his reactive mind. Anger goes into an engram as anger, apathy as apathy, shame as shame. Whatever people have felt emotionally around an "unconscious" person should be found in the engram which resulted from the incident. When the emotional tone of personnel in an engram is obviously angry or apathetic from the word content and yet the patient, recounting, does not feel it, there is something somewhere which has a *valence wall* between the patient and the emotional tone, and that valence wall is nearly always broken down by the discovery of an engram with a sorrow charge sometime earlier or later in a patient's life.

The only legitimate reason for entering later portions of a person's life before the prenatal area has been well exhausted is search for sorrow discharges occasioned by the death, loss or denial by an ally. And by "denial," we mean that the ally turned into an active enemy (real or imaginary) of the patient. The counterpart of the ally, the pseudo-ally, is a person whom the reactive mind has confused with the real ally. The death, loss or denial by a pseudo-ally can contain a sorrow charge.

According to theory, the only thing which can lock up life units is this emotion of loss. If some method existed of doing nothing but freeing all life units, the physical pain could be neglected.

A Release is brought about, one way or another, by freeing as many life units as possible from periods of loss with minimal address to actual engrams.

The loss of an ally or pseudo-ally need contain no other physical pain or "unconsciousness" than the loss itself occasions. This is serious enough. It makes an engram.

Any person who is suddenly discovered to be occluded in a patient's life can, with some reliability, be considered an ally or pseudo-ally. If, either while *remembering* or *returning*, large sections of a patient's association with another person are missing, that person can be called an occluded person. It is a better guarantee of ally status if the occlusion surrounds the death of the person or a departure from or a denial by that person. It is possible for occlusion to take place, also, for punishment reasons, which is to say, the occluded person may also be an arch enemy. In such a case, however, any memory present will concern the death or defeat or illness of the occluded person. Occlusion of a person's funeral in the memory of a patient would theoretically label that person an ally or pseudo-ally. Recollection of the funeral of a person but occlusion of pleasant association might tend to mean that the person was an enemy. Such rules are tentative. But it is certain that any occlusion means that a person had a vast and unrevealed significance in a patient's life which should be explained.

It may be remarked at this point that the recovery of the patient will depend in large measure on the life units freed from his reactive bank. This is a discharge of sorrow and may be quite violent. The usual practice is to "forget" such things and the "sooner forgotten, the sooner healed." Unfortunately this does not work: it would be a happy thing if it did. Anything forgotten is a festering sore when it has despair connected with it. The auditor will find that every time he locates that arch denyer, "forget it," he will get the engram it suppressed; when he can't locate the engram and yet has found a somatic, a "forget it" or "don't think about it" or "can't remember it" or "don't remember it" or some other denyer will be sitting there in the context of the engram. Forgetting is such unhealthy business that when a thing has been "put out of mind," it has been put straight into the reactive engram bank and in there it can absorb life units. This "loopy" computation, that forgetting things makes them bearable, is incredible in view of the fact that the hypnotist, for instance, gets results with a positive suggestion when he puts one of these denyers on the end of it. That has been known now for a great many eons: it was one of the first things the author was taught when he studied Asiatic practices: from India it long ago filtered to Greece and Rome and it has come to us via Anton Mesmer: it is a fundamental principle in several mystic arts: its mechanics were known even to the Sioux medicine man. Yet people at large, hitherto unguided about it, and perhaps because they lacked any real remedy, believed that the thing to do with sorrow was to "forget it." Even Hippocrates remarks that the whole of an operation is not finished until the patient has recounted the incident to all of his friends in turn. And while this is inadequate therapy, it has been, like the confessional, a part of popular knowledge for lo, these many ages: yet people persist in suppressing sorrow.

The auditor will many times in his activity be begged by a patient "not to talk to me about so-and-so's death." If he is foolish enough to heed this tearful plea when the patient is in reverie, then the auditor is actively blocking a Release. *That* is the first incident he should get!

Perhaps it would be bad, without Dianetic technique, to approach such things, but with our art it is easy not only to enter the actual moment of the incident, but to then recount it until the tears and wailings are but echoes in the casebook. Treating that loss like an engram, recounting it until it is no longer painful emotionally, is to give back to the patient vitality he has not had since the incident took place. And if the incident does not ease on a dozen recountings, slide back down its sorrow track, just as you would with any other engram, and find earlier and earlier moments. A patient starting to discharge sorrow at the age of fifty may find himself, two hours later, down in the basic area recounting the primary moment of sorrow, at the moment when the lost ally first became an ally. If the auditor can get the whole chain on any one ally, exhausting sorrow from it from later to earlier, taking all the sorrow he can get from every incident and stripping the entire series of engrams of their charge, he may, in a few hours work, rid the case of enough emotional charge to then begin an orderly erasure.

Please observe this difference: The Achilles' heel of the ally computation can be considered late on the chain of incidents which concern that ally, which is to say that we have a funnel here, upright in time, which can be entered late and followed early. The Achilles' heel of the contra-survival engram chain is in the earliest incidents, exactly the reverse of the emotionally painful engrams.

To regain out of the engram bank life units so that enough free emotion is available to Release or Clear a case, start with late ally or pseudo-ally losses and work back earlier.

To release the physical pain of the individual from the engram bank, start early (as close to conception as you can get) and work through to late.

Physical pain in the contra-survival chain can suppress painful emotion in the pro-survival chain.

Painful emotion in the pro-survival chain can suppress physical pain in the contra-survival engrams.

If you were to draw a picture of the prenatal area of the reactive engram bank, it would appear somewhat as follows: A long line drawn horizontally, representing time, would have dark blots on it representing engrams; one end of the line would represent conception, the other end birth: above this line would lie a dark area, like a heavy mist, extending from one end of the line to the other and dropping down almost to it: above this dark mist would lie another horizontal line, the *apparent* time track along which the patient returns. The first long line is the actual time track; the mist is painful emotion; the uppermost dark line is what the patient mistakes and uses for his time track.

The painful emotion is, of course, occasionally tapped in the prenatal area itself, and the opportunity of dispersing it by so discovering prenatal emotional charges should never be overlooked by the auditor: indeed, once much of the later-life painful emotion is discharged, a great deal of painful emotion can be found among the early engrams. The better part of this mist, and the first part the auditor often contacts, is in late life: although it originates, as charge, in late life, it can be said to lie on this prenatal area.

Moments of loss, the loss by death or departure of any of the patient's allies, and the loss of an ally because he turns against the patient, trap these emotional charges and intervene them between the patient and actuality. Although the moment of loss was post-birth, in infanthood, childhood, adolescence, adulthood, it was retroactive in suppressing early engrams.

This aspect of painful emotion is a key-in of the early incidents by the moment of loss. In other words, a moment of great loss suppresses the individual on the Tone Scale to a point where he approximates the level of early engrams and these, keyed-in, hold the units of charge thereafter.

Life units so seized are held and are the life of engrams. As in electricity, a positive charge glances away from a positive charge: like charges repel each other. The analyzer operating, it can be said for analogy, on the same kind of charge as that contained in the engram, glances away from the engram, which remains thereby unknown and intact.

As the individual returns into the area of the early engrams–which are held keyed-in by virtue of the seized charges from late incidents–he can quite comfortably pass by enormous quantities of aberrative material without even suspecting it is present. However, when the late moments of painful emotion are released, the auditor can go immediately into the early area and find engrams of physical pain which he had not hitherto been able to uncover.

Actually the late moments and the early moments are both engrams: the news or observation of loss shuts down the analyzer and everything which then enters it is engramic and is filed in the reactive mind. Because of sight and a memory of activity which is connected to the present, all of which serves to keep an individual oriented, a person can often recall the moment of loss–whereas he cannot recall prenatal material, for he lacked in that area any connection with orienting factors which would impinge themselves on the analyzer. While the prenatal infant definitely, especially in the late stages, has an analyzer, experience and memory are not coordinated and the existence of engrams is not then suspected by the analytical mind. This is not true of the later periods of life, particularly those after speech has been learned and is being used. The fact of the matter is that this later-life ability to recall surrounding circumstances without feeling any extremity of pain also serves to hide here the existence of an actual engram: a person feels that he knows all about such a moment of loss analytically; actually he has no contact with the engram itself, which contains a moment of "unconsciousness" of a lesser depth than that, for instance, of the anesthetic variety. *Childhood losses of allies, however, can be so entirely occluded that the allies themselves are not remembered.*

The auditor will find very late engrams easy to contact. And he will also discover something else. The patient may not be, as he is returning to such a moment of loss, occupying his own body. This "phenomenon" has been known for several thousand years and even the latest mention of it merely said that it was "interesting" without making any further effort to find out *why* a person, returned to an area in hypnotic regression, sometimes could be found within himself (which is to say, seeing things as though he were himself) and sometimes saw things there and himself included as part of the scenery (as though he had a detached view). Because we have discovered that a natural function of the mind is to return in an awake state to past incidents does not alter the fact that we encounter aspects hitherto known as mysterious "phenomena" of drug dreams and hypnotism. We are not by any means practicing hypnotism: so this means that hypnotism and Dianetics use similar abilities of the mind; it does not mean that such abilities belong in the field of hypnotism. And one of the various aspects of the *return* is that it occasionally–or, in some patients, continually–encounters areas where the patient is "outside" his body. These exteriorized views of self have two explanations: one of them is *valence*, whereby the patient has taken unto himself the identity of another person and sees the scene through that other person's eyes; the other is *exteriorization*, in which painful emotion is present in such quantity that the patient cannot occupy himself. That painful emotion may stem from past or future incidents to the moment when the patient is witnessing a scene to which he has been Dianetically returned. On several recountings of the scene, the patient will come nearer and nearer to an occupation of his body until at last he sees the scene from within his body. At times no emotional discharge (tears, etc.) takes place until the patient has gone over the incident several times and until he is within his own body. It is as though, returned, he had to scout the ground to find out if it was safe to occupy himself. If, after a few recountings, no discharge such as tears takes place, then the emotion is suspended elsewhere, earlier or later, but usually much later. *Exteriorization* because of emotion is the same as exteriorization because of physical pain to all intents and purposes of the auditor. When he encounters a case which, all the way up and down the track, is continually exterior, he should address his skill to the release of moments of painful emotion.

All patients seem to have the idea that time heals and that some incident of ten or twenty years ago no longer has any effect upon them. Time is a Great Charlatan, not a Great Healer, as has been remarked. Time by the processes of growth and decay alters, and environment introduces new faces and activities and thus alters the restimulators: a moment of painful emotion in the past has, like any other engram, its own restimulators and is, in addition, holding keyed-in all the early engrams which relate to it so that their restimulators also work: every restimulator has a set of restimulators which are associated to it by the analytical mind, which cannot see the real restimulator. All this makes a complex pattern, but complex in therapy only if one does not know the source of aberration. If the auditor returns the patient to any moment of painful emotion in the past and runs it as an engram, he will discover that all its original charge is present and will discharge.

He will usually find the patient shying away from any thought of going into the actual engram: the preclear may attempt to detail all manner of bric-a-brac, his own thoughts, the reasons why it no longer is painful to him, and so forth. These thoughts and data before the fact or after it are about as much use in running an engram as a dissertation about "childhood illusions" was to the problem of removing aberrations from the human mind. The auditor who will listen to these "reasons" and "I remembers" in lieu of running the engram itself will not get his patient well and will waste valuable hours of therapy. An auditor who will do this belongs to the hand-patting school of thought which believes sympathy has value. He does not belong in an auditor's chair. It is wasted time, wasted valuable time, to listen to anything the patient thought or said or did or believed when the patient should be going into the engram and running it as an engram. Certainly there is a necessity to find out, from the patient's talk, where that engram is, but once it is located, all else is dross.

Take a moment when a child is notified of his parents' deaths. The auditor learns that the parents died when the child was two years of age. He can then deduce, without further trouble or questions, that somebody must have told his patient about the death of the parents, that there was a precise moment when the patient, then an infant, learned about that death. Recounting the matter in present time, without being returned, the patient is using all the intervening years as buffers against the painful emotion. The auditor returns the patient, without further preamble than the usual routine of putting the patient into reverie, to the moment when the patient learned of the death of the parents. The patient may do a little fumbling to orient himself in the past, but shortly he will have a contact with the instant somebody informed him. Be assured, if that child loved his parents at all, that an engram exists here. The engram starts at the first moment the child is informed, when the analyzer can be expected to have shut down. The end of the engram is a moment, an hour, a day or even a week later when the analyzer again turned on. Between the first moment of analytical attenuation and a regain of analytical power is the engram. The first minutes of it are the most severe. Running an hour of it (an hour of incident, not of therapy) should be more than ample. Most auditors run only the first few minutes several times to get a test of whether or not there is going to be any emotional discharge. Run such a period of loss which must contain painful emotion exactly as you would run a period of physical pain and "unconsciousness" with another source. For the period of painful emotion is an "unconscious" period just as certainly as if the patient had been struck with a club. If the emotion in this period can be contacted with four or five recountings (each time starting at the beginning, making sure the patient is returned and in contact with *all* perceptics of the incident, and running it for what it is, an engram), then the engram should be recounted until the emotion in it is *gone*, until the patient is bored with it or even cheerful about it. If after four or five recountings the patient is still well exteriorized, still has not contacted any emotion, then the charge is suspended elsewhere, either earlier or later, and tries should be made in terms of other losses, no matter how many years from the unyielding incident, to get a discharge. After a discharge is blown off elsewhere, the incident first addressed, as in the case of the two-year-old who lost his parents, may discharge. It is certain that sooner or later such an incident will discharge and it is also certain that the case will not make much progress in getting any bulk of physically painful engrams until such a severe incident *is* well discharged.

Discharges are contacted, often, in very unlikely places. Somewhere they contact the surface enough so that a touch by the returned patient will permit the units to free, permit engrams to key-out and come into view on the time track in their proper places.

The engram bank becomes severely distorted by painful emotion and the areas of painful emotion become severely distorted by physical pain elsewhere. The filing system of the reactive mind is bad. The file clerk is able to recover and deliver to the auditor only so many painful emotion engrams or physical pain engrams at a time. They may be disordered in their positions on the track, which is to say, the auditor may contact an early physically painful engram (always his most important job), then contact one in mid-prenatal, then one post-birth, and thereafter no other engrams of the physical pain variety seem to be present (engrams of the physical variety which contain knock-outs by accidents, illnesses, surgery or injury). This does not mean that the case is stalemated or that the patient is Cleared. It more likely means that there are incidents of the other engram variety (painful emotion, stemming from loss by death, departure or reversal of allies) which can now be contacted. The auditor then looks for and exhausts the emotional discharge from the loss engrams, usually later in life. These, with the units freed back in circulation, allow earlier physical pain engrams to appear and the auditor reduces each one of these he can contact. As soon as he can no longer find physically painful engrams, he goes back to a search for painful emotion engrams and so forth alternately as necessary. The mind, being a self-protecting mechanism, will sooner or later block the patient from physical pain engrams if painful emotion engrams are ready, and it will block him from painful emotion engrams as soon as physical pain engrams are ready.

Start late to get painful emotion and work back early. Start early to get physical pain engrams and work toward late. And whenever any engram is contacted, run it until it is no longer troublesome in any way to the patient or is entirely gone (refiled, but gone for all the auditor and patient will be able to tell at the moment). If an incident, after many recountings, shows no signs of lightening (somatic not decreasing or emotion either not expressed or not decreasing), only then should the auditor seek another incident. In a painful emotion engram, the charge is often later. In a physical pain engram, the suspension is invariably caused by the existence of the same phrase in an earlier physical pain engram which can be contacted and, in such case, the auditor should go back over the phrases which brought him to the somatic until he finds a contact and a lift of the engram.

It should be extremely clear by this time that rationalization* about action or conduct or conditions does not advance therapy and is of no use beyond occasional aid in locating engrams. It should be equally clear that no amount of explanation or hand-patting or evaluation by the auditor is going to advance the erasure of the engrams themselves. It should be plain that what a person thought at the time of the incident was not aberrative. It should be clear that painful emotion puts the compartments and demon circuits into the mind and that the physical engrams hold the aberration and physical pain in the body.

**Rationalization* means justified thought–the excuses one makes to explain his irrational behavior.

This entire operation is mechanical. It has nothing to do with justified thought or shame or reasons. It has only to do with exhausting the engram bank. When the bulk of painful emotion is gone, the person is *Released;* when the engram bank is exhausted of content, the person is *Cleared.*

The mind is like a fine piece of equipment: as itself and as a mechanism it is almost impossible to destroy except by removing some of its parts: engrams do not remove parts of the mind, they add unnecessary things to it. Envision a beautiful, streamlined machine, operating perfectly: that would be the mind without the additions of pain and painful emotion. Now envision this beautiful machine in the hands of a crew of moronic mechanics: they start to work around it and do not know that what they do affects the machine at all. Now they see that something is wrong with the machine and are all unwitting that they have placed various assorted monkey wrenches, hatpins, old cigar butts and yesterday's garbage into it and around it. Their first thought is to put something new on or in the machine to correct its operation and they add arbitrary gadgets to it in order to patch up the machine's operation. Some of these gadgets appear to help the machine (sympathy engrams) and can be used, in the presence of the remaining bric-a-brac, by the machine itself to help its stability. The morons interrupt the fuel supply (painful emotional engrams) or, like the person who beat the car with a switch when it would not go, try to goad the machine (punishment drive) and so add more trouble. At last this machine appears to be a hopeless wreck, being almost hidden beneath everything added to it and thrust into it, and the moron mechanics shake their heads and say, "Let's put something else on it or it will stop!" They do and the machine appears to stop (goes insane).

In Dianetics, a workmanlike job of clearing away the debris in and around the machine is performed. It is not done by adding any more debris. The moron mechanics (the content of the reactive mind) seem dismayed at this action, but the machine itself, suddenly aware that something is being done for it which will actually bring it into good running operation again, begins to help. The more debris which is cleared, the better it runs and the less force the moron mechanics have. The course of improvement should be and is rapid. We can stop when the machine is running at least as well as the "normal" machine (a Release) or we can stop when we have all the debris out of the machine (a Clear). When we have effected a Clear, we behold something which has never been beheld before because it never before existed in a debris-free state: a perfect machine, streamlined, powerful, shining, able to adjust and care for all its own operations without further therapeutic assistance of any kind.

Some Types *of* Engrams

Two examples of each kind of engram are given, so that the auditor can clearly understand their differences.

Contra-survival Engram

This is any kind of engram which lies across the dynamics and has no alignment with purpose.

Fight between mother and father shortly after conception. Father strikes mother in stomach. She screams (first percepts are pain, pressure, sound of blow and scream) and he says, "Goddamn you, I hate you! You are no good. I'm going to kill you!" Mother says, "Please don't hit me again. Please don't. I'm hurt. I'm hurt. I'm frantic with pain!" Father says, "Lie there and rot, damn you! Goodbye!"

In this engram, we have a severe aberrative situation: first, because it is early; second, because its content says the person who has it is hurt and frantic; third, because it has a *holder* and is therefore apt to become chronic ("Lie there"); fourth, because it can produce disease ("and rot"); fifth, because it has religious connotation about God and being damned; sixth, because it gives the individual a feeling other people are no good ("you" applies to other people, ordinarily); seventh, because it has an emotional tone, by content, of hostility ("I hate you"); and eighth, because the individual, post-birth, has to live with these restimulative persons, his father and mother. It has other additional effects, giving, like all engrams, two additional and unnecessary *valences* to the individual, one of which, the mother's, is a coward valence and the other, the father's, a bully valence. The individual may dramatize this in several ways: if he does not dramatize it, he feels the pain (as he would then be in his own valence) whenever it is restimulated; if he dramatizes the mother, he will feel the pain *she* received, which is a blow in the stomach (whereas his own was on his head and heart); if he dramatizes the father, he will be in trouble with society, to say nothing of his own wife and children. There is no winning with any engram of any kind, but so long as a person has engrams, some kinds, the sympathy engram particularly, serve to hold away antagonistic engrams.

The second contra-survival example is a morning sickness engram where the mother is vomiting so violently that the compression on the child is severe and renders it "unconscious." The mother is vomiting and gasping and saying to herself between spasms, "Oh, why was I ever born! I knew I shouldn't have let him come in me. I knew it, I knew it. It was wrong but he had to do it anyway. Ugh, how nasty. Sex is nasty. It's horrible. I hate sex. I hate men. I hate them. Oh, ugh, it won't come up, it won't come up. I am so sick at my stomach and it won't come up."

In this engram, we have something a woman might dramatize if she were pregnant, but which a man could never dramatize as pregnancy but only by being sick at his stomach. Much morning sickness seems to be an aberration stemming from engrams: somewhere back in time some mother may have vomited from food poisoning and started the whole thing, perhaps in the days when Man was still in trees. Now note that the mother *is* throwing up, that the content of her stomach *is* being regurgitated: the engram, however, says that it *won't* come up; when this is dramatized with the individual in his own valence, he experiences pressure on him and "unconsciousness" and thus such a dramatization is impossible; when this is dramatized it must be dramatized as the mother, but the *action* is not dramatized so much as the *command* and we get a condition where the individual with such an engram, when he is sick, cannot vomit. The *command* of the engram is more important than the *action* people take in it. On a reactive level there is no rationality. If this were on a conscious level, where it would not be aberrative, of course, the action could be mimicked and then would contain actual vomiting, the action on the conscious level being more important than the word content.

In therapy, when we encounter this engram, we may have difficulty entering it because it says that "I shouldn't have let him come in me," which is a *denyer*. We also find, with the "It won't come up," a *holder*. The engram will most certainly lift the moment these words and the somatic lift, and these words could not interrupt the engram. If the engram does not lift, it is because there is a previous engram with much the same content (the aberree has a pattern of dramatization which he repeats over and over and over, giving people around him many incidents which are more or less alike except in their point in time). This could be restimulated in the environment (but not in therapy) to a point where it would cause madness, for "it" may also refer to the child who, identifying himself with the word "it," then cannot rise to present time. In therapy, the engram is somewhat drained of power just by being touched with the returned analytical mind; further, the auditor discovers the patient is not moving on the track and a scout of the situation soon discovers the holder, for the patient will sooner or later say he "can't come up" even if the auditor has not guessed it.

In the aberrative sphere, this engram would probably put a heavy block across the Second Dynamic and we would find the person in whose reactive mind it was being frigid, prudish and sharp with children (all of which go together in various combinations). Further, we would find an apprehension that "he" was going to have to do something when he found out it was wrong. In the psychosomatic sphere, it might cause headaches during or because of coitus or a tendency to nausea whenever coitus was performed. Any of the phrases of this engram, like any other phrases in any other engram, would tend to give him both the somatic and the aberration, providing, of course, the individual was in a state of low analytical power as found in weariness or slight illness. Thus, this one is waiting until somebody says during a future "unconsciousness" period, preferably in a voice like the mother's would sound through the walls of the abdomen and womb, "Ugh, how nasty!" or some other phrase to key it in. "Nastier," by the way, would not key it in; "Ugly" despite a similar syllable to "Ugh" would not key it in. The sound of vomiting itself probably would key it in.

Pro-survival Engram

This could be any engram which, by content only, not by any real aid to the individual containing it, pretended to assist survival.

Let us take a coitus engram: Mother and father are engaged in intercourse which, by pressure, is painful to the unborn child and which renders him "unconscious" (common occurrence, like morning sickness, usually present in any engram bank). Mother is saying, "Oh, I can't live without it. It's wonderful. It's wonderful. Oh, how nice. Oh, do it again!" and father is saying, "Come! Come! Oh, you're so good. You're so wonderful! Ahhhh!" Mother's orgasm puts the finishing touch on the "unconsciousness" in the child. Mother says, "It's beautiful." Father, finished now, says, "Get up," meaning she should take a douche (they do not know she is pregnant) and then begins to snore.

Obviously, this is a valuable incident because one "cannot live without it." Furthermore, "it's beautiful." Also, "it's wonderful." But it is also extremely painful. It cannot be followed because it has first something which beckons part of the mind back, "Come!" and then, later, tells it to "Get up." Things that are "beautiful" and "wonderful" can cause our patient, not in therapy, to have an orgasm when she looks at beautiful and wonderful things, providing they have been so labeled.

Dramatization of this can be in either the father valence or the mother valence: to dramatize it in the personal valence would mean physical pain. Thus, the individual holding this will be found, varied only by his other coitus engrams, to be, as father, disgusted after the act and telling his partner to "Get up." The emotion is contained in *how* the words "Get up" were spoken: this is a telegraphed emotion out of voice tones, not word content: engrams always contain both.

In therapy, we find the reactive mind very chary of letting this one come to view because, after all, one "cannot live without it." There are whole classes of these *favorable evaluation* phrases in engrams and wherever he comes upon one the auditor will find the preclear's reactive mind holding out on him. "I don't want to lose you," "Hold onto this," "I can't let go of this, I'd fall," and so forth. But this is, after all, just another engram and "pleasant" or not is aberrative.

Masochistic and sadistic impulses often stem from coital engrams which contain those specific things. So the auditor is not to infer that merely because this coitus is painful to the child, it will make the child a masochist or a sadist. If masochism or sadism is present in the patient, it is caused by engrams which contain rapes, beating for sexual gratification, enjoyment of pain, etc., and engrams which homonymically seem to state that sex and pain are alike, such as a "normal" coitus which says, "It hurts so good! Hurt me again, Bill. Hurt me again! Oh, shove it in me, way up! Make it hurt so I can come." Dramatized by a boy, this might very well bring about sodomy because the engram is not an observed action but a series of commands, literally taken.

Thus, our pro-survival coitus engram, as the first example of one here, is relatively innocent in a person's aberrative pattern. But by an accident of words, it could be very different in its aberrative effect.

The second pro-survival example concerns another prenatal engram. (One auditor commented, while he was being cleared, that "I had thought of my life B.D.–before Dianetics–as a graph of years, in which the time from conception to birth occupied one-fiftieth of the linear distance between conception and present time, but now think of the prenatal period as occupying two-thirds of the distance between the beginning and now." The prenatal area, cleared, at last went back to being one-fiftieth.)

The mother, subject to high blood pressure, continually brought about a condition of great pain in the unborn infant, particularly when she was agitated. (This is a prime source of migraine headache.) Whatever it was which agitated her into high blood pressure at the moment this engram was received was unknown–and much of the "plot" of prenatal life may remain unknown, for the explanatory data may come before the pain and the engram and a complete recording only happens after the instant of pain when some degree of "unconsciousness" comes about. The mother, at the beginning of the engram, when pressure began to build up and stiffen out the unborn child, was weeping. She was by herself. "Oh, how am I ever going to get out of it. Everything looks so drab and colorless to me. Oh, why did I ever start it; I can't possibly go through with it. But I have to, I have to. I would be sick if I didn't. Oh, Lord, everything comes in on me at once. I am utterly trapped. But there, I will go through with it, I'll feel better. I'll be brave and do it. I've got to be brave. I am brave. I am the bravest person in the world. I have to be and I am." The pressure receded.

Exactly what this was about will remain a mystery to the auditor who reduced it, the patient who had it, the author and the reader: such is often the case with an engram. They are conceived in misunderstanding and they aren't to be understood, save mechanically, and only deleted from the engram bank.

This is a particularly dangerous engram to have, for it contains a manic in the words, "bravest person in the world." "I", of course, is ordinarily used by the unborn child to be himself, when the engram is at last able to effect an analyzer in which there is speech. Before that moment, of course, there is just a recording without word meaning, although even before the words are given meaning, the engram can be aberrative. This is further dangerous because it says, "I'm trapped," and because it says, "Everything comes in on me at once." "Trapped" is our enemy, the *holder*. But "everything comes in on me at once" is a *grouper*. Further, the remainder of the content, as an engram, will not compute in the analyzer. It says one "must go through with it," but that one "cannot go through with it," that one "would get sick if I didn't go through with it," but that "it is impossible." Everything being equal to everything, as our moronic enemy, the reactive mind computes, this engram both repels and attracts therapy: it brings about a condition of indecision in the analytical mind which is insufferable.

The individual holding this engram might find himself–as it acted as aberration–first in the manic portion of being the bravest person in the world and then, regressed a trifle by a slight change of restimulators such as his migraine headache getting bad, find himself utterly undecided about any course of action and with the telegraphed emotion, contained in the tears, of being very depressed. But this is pro-survival because it apparently dictates a way out of a situation. As an additional factor, it brings–with its phrase about "everything being drab and colorless"–colorblindness, at least in recall, so that the recalled images of the past are "seen" in the mind as having no color. It can bring about, if added to by enough subsequent dramatizations, actual perceptic colorblindness. The whole engram is very likely, when combined with other factors, to place the individual in an institution with all of his somatic turned on (migraine) and, because of the grouper, all other pain he felt in his life turned on as well. This grouper bunches the track of the engram bank all into one place and then puts the individual squarely in that place.

In therapy, when this was contacted, a case which had been classified as "insane" came into a Release state of "normal." The patient had been institutionalized, was in the fetal position and had regressed physically. That she kept screaming these exact words and weeping had been placed on her record as the manifestation of a childhood delusion. The case was opened by Repeater Technique, using the words she kept screaming, after she had had her attention fixed upon the auditor by loud, monotonous noise. There were some former incidents containing these words which had to be reached before the incident in dramatization would ease. However, engrams like this are commonly contacted in more or less "normal" people and are relieved as routine. A very high degree of restimulation had been experienced by this patient and several severe loss engrams had occurred which had kept earlier content keyed-in.

It might also be remarked in re all these "trapped," "caught," "can't get out of it" cases (which is to say, where there are several holders and also a high quantity of painful emotion) that certain fetal aspects are visible even when the case is "normal." A shiny skin, a spinal curvature, only partial development of the gonads – all are common and one or many such signs may be present.

SYMPATHY ENGRAM

The first example is an illness suffered by a patient when he was a small boy. At two years and a half he was taken ill with pneumonia. He had a considerable background of attempted abortion and the usual engram cargo received from aberrated parents. He was extremely worried about the quarrels and upsets of his own home; numbers of his engrams had been keyed-in and among them was his pneumonia. His grandmother came and took him to her home because, whenever he was ill, his mother would go away and leave him. The incident was extremely occluded and was only reached after several late-life, painful emotion engrams had been discharged and after almost a hundred prenatal physical pain engrams had been released. The grandmother, when he was crying in delirium, mistook his activity as demonstrating that he was "conscious," which he was not, and she sought to reason with him. She said, "Those people don't really mean to be so bad to you, honey. I know they have good hearts really. You just do what they say and believe what they tell you and you'll be all right. Now promise you'll do that, won't you, honey." The child, in the last depths of reaction, responded and promised her he would believe them and do what they said. "I love you very much," the grandmother continued, "and I will take care of you. Now don't worry, honey. Forget it now. Just get a little rest."

The phrases contained in this engram, because they were on a trance level and because they could be held in place by his fever and pain, produced a very profound effect on the child. He had to believe whatever was said. This means *literal* belief and cost him, for one thing, much of his sense of humor. Because he wanted to be all right, he had to believe what his parents said; the things they had said, prenatally, contained every kind of a bad datum possible about who was the boss and how much fun it was to beat the mother and so forth. All this, then, was made into "true data" which, because his sympathy engram said so, he had to *believe.* No more horrible curse could ever be laid on anyone than those in sympathy engrams which say, "Believe what is said," "Believe what is read," "Believe people," because that engram means literally that the poor old analyzer will now never be able to evaluate its own data unless, by utter rebellion, the individual negates against the whole world, which can occasionally be done. Let this individual, however, as this one did, marry a woman who has characteristics similar to his grandmother's (a pseudo-grandmother) and he becomes prey to: (a) the pain and illness, chronic, which he experienced in his grandmother sympathy engrams (necessary to get and keep her sympathy); and (b) all his prenatals, since the pseudo-grandmother throws him into his own valence. This makes him quarrel, which makes his wife fight back, and suddenly this woman is not pseudo-grandmother but pseudo-mother. Exit sanity.

In therapy, when we encounter this sympathy engram at last, it is discovered to have been buried in two ways:

1. It was aligned with purpose.
2. It had a *forgetter mechanism* on it.

Because of (1) the self-protection of the mind permitted it to give up the engram only when enough tension was taken off the case to permit the mind to get along without this engram.

In (2) we have a device which is common in engrams. Whenever we try to run an engram which has somatics enough even to make the preclear roll around on the couch, but which contains no word content, we suspect a *forgetter mechanism*. There are evidently people in this world who think that the panacea for all mental discomfort is to forget: "Put it out of my mind," "If I remembered it I would go mad," "Junior, you never remember a thing I tell you," "Nobody can remember anything," "Can't remember," and just plain "I don't know," as well as the master of the family of phrases, "Forget it!" all bar information from the analyzer. A whole case, freshly opened, may keep answering everything with one of these denyers (there are many other kinds of *denyers*, if you recall). Repeater Technique will eventually begin to release the phrase from various engrams and begin to show up incidents. To have a grandmother who says, "Forget it" continually every time a child gets hurt is to be cursed beyond Macbeth. A forgetter, used by an ally, all by itself and with practically no pain or emotion present, will submerge data which in recall would not be aberrative, but which so buried–by a forgetter–makes things said just before it aberrative and literal.

Hence, this engram remained utterly out of sight until the case was almost finished and as soon as it was contacted, the already de-intensified reactive bank collapsed and the patient was Cleared.

The second example of the sympathy engram concerns a childhood experience of a patient who, at the beginning of therapy, was a remarkably confused individual. Here is an example of a sympathy engram which is not uncommon. (It will not be primary in any ally computation, but because it is often repeated in the same case, becomes aberrative.) This incident occurred when the child had been badly hurt in an accident. He had received a fractured skull and concussion and was for many days in a coma. He had never learned that such an incident happened to him although examination afterwards disclosed evidence of the fracture and disclosed also that while he had known there was a ridge in his skull, he had never wondered about it for an instant. His father and mother were, at the time, on the verge of divorce and, in the presence of the only partly conscious child, quarreled several times in these few days, evidently upset by his accident and recriminative as to whose fault it was. The first part of the series of engrams within this one large engram are unimportant as an example, save that they brought about a condition where the mother put herself forward as a defender of the child who was *not* under attack by the father. The mother's conversation aberratively indicated that the father was attacking the child (and the words in an engram, rather than the action, are important as aberrative factors). Finally, the father left the house and home. The mother sat down by the boy's trundle bed and, weeping, told him she would keep him from dying, that she would "work and slave and wear her fingers to the bone" to keep him alive and "I am the only reason you are alive. I have defended you against that beast and monster. If it were not for me, you would have died long ago and I am going to care for you and protect you. So don't pay any attention to anything people tell you. I am a good mother. I have always been a good mother. Don't listen to them. Please, baby, stay here and get well, please!"

This remarkable piece of nonsense came, of course, straight out of her reactive mind. She did not feel guilty about the way she was taking care of the baby, though she had done her cyclic worst for this child since conception. (There is no such thing as guilt nor a guilt complex that is not straight out of an engram that says, "I am guilty" or some such similar phrase.)

Here is *ambivalence* at work. By ambivalent is meant power on two sides. It had better be called *multivalence*, for it is demonstrable that people have many valences, twenty or thirty not being unusual for a "normal." This mother, with her wild pleas and her mawkish sentimentality, shifted around in valences like a whirling dervish. She was capable of being viciously cruel, torturing her child with, as the Navy calls them, "capricious and unusual punishments": yet one of these valences which, unfortunately for the patient, only turned on when he was ill, was one of savage protection for the child and assurances to him that she loved him and would never leave him to starve, etc. She formed in this child, because of her own reactive pattern and her inabilities, close to a thousand engrams before he was ten. This particular specimen given was fairly standard.

The aberrative aspect of this engram was a "conviction" that if one's mother were not around and if one were not on good terms with her, one would starve, die or suffer generally. Also it meant, because of the time it was given, having a bad headache if one wanted to live. The whole series of these engrams made a highly complex pattern of psychosomatic ills including sinusitis, a chronic rash, allergies and numerous other actual physical ills, despite the fact that the patient had always tried to be as forthright in his physical being as possible and was not in any way a hypochondriac.

In therapy, the entire chain of fights in this area, much of the prenatal area and most late-life, painful emotion engrams were relieved before this sympathy engram displayed itself.

As a note on the subject of sympathy engrams, these are in nowise exclusively found in childhood: they exist prenatally and postnatally, and sometimes late in life. Any persons who defend the child against further abortion attempts become part of the sympathy engram chains and, of course, they are allies whose loss is something to be dreaded. Late sympathy engrams have been discovered at fifty years of age. One, discovered at thirty, consisted of a nymphomaniac nurse who, during the period when the patient was still under ether and still in pain, talked to him obscenely, played with his genitals and still managed, by the content of her remarks, to plant a sympathy engram which produced a very serious psychic condition in the patient. (It is in nowise true that many cases of sexual play exist while the patient is under anesthetic or drugged, but because this is a standard psychotic reaction of delusion is no reason to rule that the incident cannot occasionally happen.)

The sympathy engram only has to sound like a sympathy engram to become one: there is no evaluation of actual intent by the reactive mind.

PAINFUL EMOTION ENGRAM

Three of these are given to illustrate a type of each. They can happen at any period, including prenatally, but are most easily tapped in more recent life, when they will then lead back to early incidents of physical pain, sympathy engrams and the like.

The first example is a case of loss by death of an ally. A girl, at the age of eighteen, was given a painful emotion engram by being told by her parents that her aunt was dead. The aunt was a prime ally. The patient, treated at the age of thirty-one, recalled the death of her aunt, but attributed her sorrow to other things such as a restimulation of what she called her own "death instinct" (which was, in reality, engramic chatter by mother about wanting to die and get it all over with). Actually, the aunt had been a large factor in dissuading the mother from "getting rid of" the child and had made the mother promise that she would not. The aunt had also tended the child, postnatally, through illnesses and was, in fact, the only refuge for the girl when a termagant mother and a religiously bigoted father would converge on her. For neither had wanted her and there had been a number of efforts to terminate the pregnancy pre-term.

Her father communicated the information to the girl with a sonorous voice and appropriately long face. "I want you to be very respectful at the funeral, Agatha." ("What funeral?") "Your aunt just passed to the great beyond." ("She's dead?") "Yes, death must come to us all and we must all be prepared someday to meet the fate which waits for us at the end of the road. For it is a long path, life, and God and flaming hell wait at its other end and someday we all must die. Be sure you are very respectful at the funeral." She had begun to pale at the word "funeral," she was to all purposes "unconscious" when she heard the first mention of "death" and she remained "unconscious," if moving about, for two whole days. The case had been very slow until this engram was discovered and run. An enormous discharge of grief took place, which had never before manifested itself. It was reduced to boredom in eight recountings, at which the first moment of the aunt's intervention in the abortion attempts was automatically contacted and released. Thereafter the case made progress in the prenatal area, prohibition against "getting rid of it" having been removed and, according to theory, free units being available, the charge had come off the prenatal area. There were five other allies in this case, the girl (with parents who had been so wicked to her) having attached herself to anyone who would show her interest and refuge. As lower physical pain came into view, more allies showed up and more painful emotion engrams were discharged, permitting new physically painful engrams to display themselves.

The next example is an engram from a patient who had all his life been reared and cared for by "moneyed parents." He had a very severe prenatal area which yet would not lift to view. It was discovered at length that his nurses had been his only source of love and affection and that his mother, being a woman who liked to unsettle the household as often as possible, would discharge a nurse every time she found the child had grown fond of her, even though the mother herself made it plain that she considered the child "nasty."

The engram: The boy sees his nurse coming out of the house with her suitcase in her hand. He stops playing in the yard and runs to her to "scare her." She is quite angry from the scene she has just had–an Irish girl–and yet she smooths her face and kneels down beside him.

"I am leaving, Buddy. I can't stay here anymore. No, I can't be your nurse now. But there, there, you'll have another one. Don't cry. It's not good for little boys to cry. Goodbye, Buddy. I love you." And she goes off out of sight.

He was stunned from the first instant she said she was leaving. The prohibition against crying was from an ally: whatever an ally says must be good and must be believed because allies are survival and one must survive: allies therefore must be believed. He had not cried except on rare occasions of enormous sorrow in all the years thereafter. Eight of these departures were touched without result, but with this one, they all loosened and discharged, one after the other.

Any departure of or from an ally contains an emotional charge which, if it will not display itself, is elsewhere suppressed.

The third example of the painful emotion engram is the third type, loss of an ally by reversal. A wife loved her husband very dearly. They had gotten along well together until his parents came into the vicinity and began to malign his wife. He was furious with them for it and quarreled with them. His wife was a pseudo-ally and unfortunately that ally had told the child to believe his parents. (This is fairly chronic with allies: if they would give the child correct data when he is emotionally disturbed or ill, there would be less trouble. A remark such as, "Well, you'll grow up someday and be able to care for yourself," is much better than a hatful of Emersonian platitudes.) This brought about a tragic reversal. The reactive mind, restimulated at the sight of his wife (the husband was emotionally disturbed, very restimulated already by his parents), threw in the data that one must believe one's parents. This made his wife no good, as per their aberrative chatter. He went into his father's valence to escape this imponderable situation and that valence beat women. He struck his wife repeatedly, dramatizing one of his father's engrams: "I hate you. You are no good. I should have listened to them sooner. You're no good."

The wife was in therapy. This charge suppressed itself, not out of shame for her husband's actions, but for the mechanical reason that the early area had to be relieved before this one would discharge (smart file clerk). Her case had slowed down to a point where the board looked entirely clear although somatics (which she attributed to natural causes) and aberrations (which she said were reasonable reactions) still manifested themselves. Suddenly this incident appeared when Repeater Technique was used on the auditor's random guess, "I hate you," for it was known that she said this now and then to her husband. Three recountings discharged this painful emotion despite its violence (it made her weep until she almost choked). Immediately twelve prenatals, all fights between her mother and father (an ally, of which her husband was the pseudo-ally) wherein the mother beat her abdomen and cursed the child, appeared and were erased and the case progressed to Clear.

Loss of dogs, dolls, money, position, even the threat of a loss, anything may bring about a painful emotion engram so long as it is loss. It may be loss by death, loss by departure, loss by reversal. Anything connected with the life of the patient and associated by him with his own survival seems to be capable of locking up life units when lost. A condition of such painful emotion is that it has early physically painful engrams upon which to append. The physically painful engram is still the villain, but it has an accomplice in the painful emotion engram.

BOOK THREE, CHAPTER NINE: PART ONE

MECHANISMS *and* ASPECTS *of* THERAPY

THE CASE ENTRANCE

EVERY CASE PRESENTS a new problem of entrance. No two human beings are exactly alike and no two cases will follow the exact pattern. However, this presents no problem to Dianetics since the mechanics are always the same.

There are three case classifications: the *sonic recall*, the *non-sonic recall*, and the *imaginary recall* (what auditors call a *dub-in recall*).

In the sonic recall case, the entrance is very easy. But in all cases the basic procedure is the same. Put the patient in reverie (and don't worry too much if he doesn't go into a very deep reverie because reverie only serves to fix his attention on himself and the auditor, and you can at least accomplish that). Install a canceller. Return him to childhood to pick up a pleasant incident and then find a minor pain incident such as a slap in the face. Run him through this a few times just to let him get the idea. If he doesn't respond well, put him into yesterday and let him ride to work and ask him about sounds and sights, then send him to childhood again.

The object of finding a minor incident such as a slapped face is to find out if the patient has a pain shut-off. A pain shut-off is not particularly difficult in Dianetics. You can get back before the command which installed the anesthesia, but it is interesting to know about it because you want to look for it early in the case. See then if the patient has an emotional shut-off. This again is not particularly embarrassing, but again is data you want to find eventually.

Test now to find out if the patient is within himself or if he is outside himself, watching himself. If he is exteriorized, you are working a case which has considerable walled up emotion in it which must be discharged.

Now make a try to basic-basic. You might surprise yourself and get it. And you might work fifty hours for it, releasing the case the while. Get whatever the file clerk will give you in the prenatal area and what you get, *reduce*.

Whether basic-basic is contacted or not, locate as many prenatals as will present themselves without much coaxing and reduce each one.

If you find no prenatals, bring the patient up to present time but remind him to keep his eyes closed. Now ask him a few questions about his family, his grandparents, his wife or, if the preclear is a woman, her husband. Ask about any former husbands or wives. Ask about children. And ask particularly about death. You are looking for a painful emotional engram, an instant of loss which will discharge.

Finding out about one, even if it is just the death of a favorite dog, return the preclear to it and run it from the first moment he hears the news of it and for the ensuing few minutes of it. Then start it again. Reduce the moment as an engram. You want an emotional discharge. Run it several times. If you don't get a discharge, find some other moment of loss, some failure, something, anything which will discharge: but do it all quietly as if with sympathy. Lacking any success, start in with Repeater Technique, never for a moment giving any intelligence that you are anything but calmly concerned for his welfare (even if some of his gyrations worry you). Try such phrases as "Poor little____" using his or her childhood name.

When the preclear has repeated this several times (the auditor at the same time stating that the somatic strip will return to any incident containing the phrase to assist the "suck down"), he may find himself in a high tension incident which will discharge. If nothing discharges yet, keep calm (all this work will pay dividends in the next session or the next or next), keep searching, keep observing. There is emotional charge here somewhere which will discharge. Try other combinations of words such as those which would be said to a sick and worried child; make the preclear repeat them.

If you have had no success as yet, make another test, without saying it is a test, to see if the preclear is actually leaving present time. Don't let him "try to remember"–you want him to *return* and that is another process, although it is just as natural to the brain. If he is stuck in present time, start him on Repeater Technique again, suggesting bouncers: "Get out and never come back!" "You can't ever return!" etc., which would account for his being still in present time. If he is not returning after some of this, start in with holder phrases: "I'm stuck!" "Don't move!" and so forth.

Stay calm, never appear anxious. If you get neither a discharge nor an engram with Repeater Technique in this first session and if you get no motion on the track, read this manual again and try your patient not later than three days after this first session. At that time some of the data you have asked for may be available.

Ordinarily, however, you will receive either a prenatal or a discharge and if you get a discharge, then ask the somatic strip to go back for the prenatal it was sitting on. Reduce everything you can find. If birth turns up and seems to be in full recall, try to reduce that, but do so in the knowledge that it probably will not lift very far and in the knowledge that you had better run it over and over and over to de-intensify it all you can.

Sometimes the preclear will go into a deeper reverie than you wish. But do not try to wake him into a higher level. Work him where he is. But if he seems to be in something approaching hypnotic trance, be very careful of your language. Never tell him, for instance, to go back there and stay there until he finds something. That's a holder. Don't use holders and bouncers and groupers et al., on anyone in Dianetics. "Will you please return to the prenatal area?" "Let's see if the somatic strip can locate an early moment of pain or discomfort." "Please pick up the somatic at the beginning and roll the engram." "What do you hear, please?" "Continue" (when you want him to keep on going from the point of the engram where he is to the later end of the engram). "Recount that again, please."

There's nothing to be nervous about. If you get nervous, then he'll get nervous.

Sometimes you run into a pain shut-off. This has a tendency to put the pain into the muscles and the muscles will jump and quiver and the patient may sense this and still feel nothing more. Once in a great while a patient will have such a thorough pain shut-off that he bounces about, all unconscious of the action, and almost falls from couch to floor. If you run into this, do not be alarmed: the pain is locked in somehow. Get early enough and you'll locate a somatic he can feel, or go late and find an emotional charge.

Don't be misled if he tells you, with regard to emotion, that he has worked it all out in psychoanalysis or some such thing. He may have walled in the death of his wife or sweetheart or child, but the whole engram is still there, crammed with captured units, ready to be run exactly as an engram.

If you run into a heavy emotional charge, simply let the patient weep, keep him at the business of running the engram in a soft, sympathetic voice, have it recounted until there is no charge left in any of it and then run him early into the prenatal area or early childhood to get a physical pain engram that must have been below that emotional charge and held it in place.

The extravagance of emotional discharge is nothing to be alarmed about. Bringing the patient out of it and to present time suddenly would cause him unhappiness about it. Running the painful emotion engram will discharge, in a few recountings, sorrow which society has believed could never be countered or relieved except by repression. Get the moment he first heard the news or observed the thing which made him feel so bad. Run it far enough from its beginning to make sure that you have the initial shock–a few minutes of engram time will do–and then get him to recount it again. He may observe himself to be far outside himself when you start. The moment may not discharge until you have run it several times. Remember, he is *returned* to the incident, he is not running it as a memory, a thing which would do no good whatever.

Do not let him replay anything, ever. *Replay* is a bad habit some preclears have of playing over what they remember they said the last time instead of progressing through the engram freshly on each recounting and contacting what is contained in the engram itself. Tell the preclear there may be some more in it, ask him what color the bed in the room he is returned to is, keep his attention, by any quiet mechanism, upon the scene. And do not let him replay ever, not on any engram at any time: he could replay forever without therapeutic value, each time saying what he remembered he said the last time. There is a difference between this and the repeated re-experiencing of the engram to gather additional data and to get rid of the charge.

Discharge emotion, reduce incidents of physical pain as early prenatally as possible. If you can't get into the prenatal area at first, it has many bouncers in it and Repeater Technique will take you there.

If the patient keeps saying such a thing as "I can't remember," be patient–always follow the code. Have him start running that phrase as Repeater Technique. If he gets a somatic but contacts nothing else, send him earlier. If he gets another and still can't contact on "I can't remember," send him earlier; his whole engram bank must be strewn with them, poor fellow. Somebody really didn't want him to know what had happened to him. Eventually you will get back to an engram which will release a phrase. When he has gone over the phrase a few more times, he will smile or chuckle or perhaps merely feel relieved. Now you can either run the engram in which you found the earliest phrase, which is best, or you can come back toward present time, lifting the phrase as it later appeared. Or you can start on something else which may block the case.

The goal and the whole goal is to place the standard bank in entire conscious reach of the individual by deleting:

1. Early and subsequently all physical pain engrams.
2. All demon circuits (which are merely contained in engrams and come up more or less automatically).
3. All painful emotion engrams.

The process of work is to get as early as you can, preferably prenatal and very early in that, and try to find and reduce an engram, complete with all somatics (pain) and perceptics (words and other sensations). If you fail in this, you go late, any time from birth forward to present time, and find a moment of loss or threatened loss from which you can get an emotional charge. Then you go back early, early, early and find the engram on which it rested. You try always, until you are certain you have it, to get basic-basic, the earliest engram. You reduce as many early engrams as you can find, using the file clerk and Repeater system, and when you seem to run out of material, you go later into life and try to find another emotional charge.

The physically painful engrams cover up later emotional charges. Emotional charges cover up physically painful engrams. Back and forth, back and forth. Run as much as you can get early: when it seems to be running out or getting too unemotional, get some later material.

This is the way you work a case. No matter what kind of a case it is, no matter what the state of its recall, no matter if the case is normal, psychotic or neurotic or what, this is the way.

These are the tools:

1. Reverie or fixed attention if you cannot get reverie.
2. Return.
3. Repeater Technique.
4. A knowledge of bouncers, holders, groupers, misdirectors, denyers.
5. A knowledge of the painful emotion engram.
6. The reduction or the erasure.
7. The flash answer.
8. The valence shift.

This is all you need to do:

1. Keep the patient mobile, able to move on the track.
2. Reduce or erase everything you get your hands on.
3. Deduce from the remarks of the patient, in or out of therapy, what must be his bouncers, holders, groupers, misdirectors, denyers.
4. Keep it solidly in mind that the number one goal is basic-basic, the earliest moment of pain and "unconsciousness."
5. Keep in mind that the patient may have "computations" which make his illness or his aberrated state "valuable" to him and discover whence those "computations" come by flash answer to your questions.
6. Keep the case progressing, gaining, work only for progress and gain, not for sudden, soaring results. Worry only when the case remains static and worry then in terms of finding the engram which is balking everything. Its content will be a close approximation to the way the

patient says he feels about it and will contain the same or similar words.

7. Get the patient back to present time each time you work and feed him the canceller. Test him with an *age flash*, get his first reply to how old he is, find the holder at that age if he is not at present time.
8. Keep your temper no matter what the patient says.
9. Never try to tell him what his data means: he knows and he alone knows what it means.
10. Keep your nerve and run Dianetics; like Farragut said, "Damn the torpedoes! Go ahead."
11. Wife, son, whatever you may be to the preclear, *you* are the auditor when you are auditing. He cannot compute his own engrams to find them; if he could, they would not be engrams. You can compute them. Do what you think a good auditor would do, never what the patient says save only when he accidentally concurs in his opinion that a good auditor would do that. Be the auditor, not a recording device. You and the file clerk in his mind are running the case: what his engrams and his analytical mind believe should have no force in any of your computations. You and his file clerk know. He, as "I", doesn't know.
12. Be surprised at nothing. Audit.

These are the things you must not do:

1. Dilute Dianetics with some practice or belief of yesteryear; you will only slow or sidetrack a case. Analyzing data received on any other basis than getting more engrams leads to delay and

confusion for the preclear. It is a temptation to use this material for other reasons than getting engrams if one has been trained in another field than Dianetics. Yielding to that temptation before one knows how Dianetics works is a very unfair test of Dianetics, completely aside from the way it snarls a case. The temptation is great because, with Dianetics, you get such a wealth of data.

2. Do not bully the patient. If the case is not progressing, then the fault lies with the auditor. Do not surrender to an old practice of getting mad at a patient just because he doesn't get well. *You* may be *sure* the engram you have just reduced out of his reactive engram bank is the reason he won't take baths, but if he still refuses to bathe, be certain there is an earlier reason.
3. Don't assume grandly that you have a "different" case just because it doesn't resolve swiftly. They are all "different" cases.
4. Don't run for help to somebody who does not know Dianetics if your nerve fails you. The reason the case did not progress or became involved is right there: your nerve failed you. Only Dianetics can work a problem in Dianetics.
5. Do not listen to a patient's complaints as complaints; use them as data to get engrams.
6. Do not suppose that just because you cannot reach prenatal engrams in a case that they are not there. There are scores and scores of them in every case. Remember that an engram isn't a memory; it has to be developed to become within recall. There is no human being walking

on earth today who does not have a plenitude of prenatals.

7. Do not allow the patient to use his mother or his memory of what he has been told as a bypass of prenatals. *Every time you find a patient talking in past tense instead of present tense he is not returned to an incident.* Unless he is returned, the engram will not lift.
8. Do not suppose that because a patient does not feel bad today about a sorrow of yesterday that a despair charge is not located back on his track when he received the impact of that despair. Time may encyst, it does not heal.
9. Do not think in terms of "guilt complexes" or "shame" unless you think of them as engram content, for there they will be found. Never suggest to a patient that he may be at fault in an engram.
10. Any departure from optimum behavior or conduct or rationality on the part of the patient is engramic: don't make "allowances for human nature" any more than you, as a mathematician, would make allowances for an adding machine which brought up wrong answers. Sexual fears, repressions, defenses are not "natural" as they have been regarded in the past.
11. Don't worry about the patient's aberrations. Work to contact and reduce and erase engrams. You will find, in any patient, enough aberrations to fill a dictionary.
12. Don't fret if your patient does not become a Clear in an evening or a month. Just keep working. You'll have him above normal so quickly you won't realize when you passed it. Above that you are shooting for a very high goal.

"Stuck in Present Time"

Cases, when they are entered, are found in various positions and situations on the time track; sometimes they are off the time track entirely and sometimes the time track is all snarled up in a ball. Now and then the time track is found to be in good condition and the engrams available, but this is not ordinary.

No case can be said to be more difficult than another except in the matter of recalls, dub-ins and shut-offs. But the case which seems to be stuck in present time and on whom no repeater phrase works is very often quite puzzling to an auditor. The preclear will not return to engrams. Ordinarily there may be pain and emotional shut-offs and the painful emotion cannot be quickly discharged. Sometimes somatics will turn on, but no content can be gained. Sometimes there is no somatic, but content. The situations are quite various.

There are several things an auditor can do. The first of them is to use his wits. The next is to indoctrinate the patient into returning. This indoctrination is quite simple. The auditor takes the patient back a few hours and has the patient tell what he sees. The sonic and visio may be occluded, but the patient may have some idea of what is taking place. The auditor then takes him back a few days, then a few months and finally several years, each time getting the patient to describe his "surroundings" as best he can. The patient now has the idea of returning. He can travel at least along portions of his life which are not occluded by engrams.

When the patient is returned to some early moment in his life, begin to use Repeater Technique on him, aiming toward obvious things such as feeling shut-offs (going over the word "feel") or forgetter mechanisms (such as "forget"). An engram may then be contacted and reduced.

If Repeater Technique still does not work and still does not get data, diagnose by his behavior in therapy and his statements what must be troubling him or occluding his recalls and again use these guesses as repeater. For instance, he may have no recollection of some member of his family. Have him repeat the familiar name. Or have him repeat his own childhood nickname until an incident is contacted.

Should this still fail, then find some light locks, incidents which contain minimal pain, and run those. Such things as falls from a tricycle, getting sent from the table, getting spanked or scolded, being kept after school and so forth will serve. After he has reduced several locks, again try to find an engram.

The running of locks will not bring about any great recovery and there are thousands and thousands of locks in any case, most of which will vanish without assistance from the auditor once the severe engrams are located. But locks may be used to indoctrinate the patient into returning and therapy in general and may even bring about an improved condition in him by demonstrating to him that he *can* face his past.

The foremost things to do in any case at the beginning are to:

1. Attempt to locate and erase basic-basic.
2. Discharge painful emotion. The sooner emotion can be released, the better, and there is always emotion on a case just as there are always plenty of prenatal incidents.

But when a case is stuck in present time, either when it is opened or during progress, it is highly charged with occluded emotion and it is obeying a restimulated engram to the effect that it must go all the way to *now* and stay there. The wording of this engram will generally be expressed by the patient himself in complaining of his trouble. Repeater Technique is used with this clue. That failing, indoctrinate the patient by taking him back to what he can contact and when indoctrination is done, as above, start using Repeater Technique again.

There is one motto which applies to all therapy: "If you keep asking for it, you'll get it." Any and all engrams surrender on the basis of returning the patient to the area time and again, session after session. The engram bank may be balky, but enough asking will bring forth any data in it sooner or later. Just keep asking, keep the routine of therapy running. Even a "stuck in present time" case will eventually begin to return on the sole principle of Repeater Technique.

There are certain things that the auditor may be doing which are wrong. He may be trying to work the case on data taken from parents or relatives, which is usually fruitless in view of the fact that it undermines the preclear's faith in his own data (all the data will check with the relatives; just don't worry about checking it until the case is finished). Or he may be trying to work the case in the presence of other people. Or he may be violating the Auditor's Code. A list of these deterrents to progress is to be found elsewhere in this volume.

Basic-Basic

The first goal of the auditor is basic-basic and after that always the earliest moment of pain or discomfort which he can reach. He may have to go late for emotional charges and these themselves may be physically painful. Emotion may bar the patient from basic-basic. But always that first turn-off of the analyzer is important and when it is gained, subsequent engrams are much more easily reduced.

Basic-basic is the vital target for two reasons:

1. It contains an *analyzer shut-off* which itself is restimulated every time a new engram is received. The common denominator of all engrams is analyzer shut-off. Turn it on the first time it was shut off and a vast improvement takes place in the case, for thereafter analyzer shut-off is not as deep.
2. An *erasure* (which is to say, an apparent removal of the engram from the files of the engram bank and refiling in the standard bank as memory) of basic-basic widens the track beyond it markedly and brings many new engrams into view.

Basic-basic is occasionally found weeks before mother's first missed period, which would place it much earlier than any examination for pregnancy or an attempted abortion. Sometimes in a non-sonic case, sonic is discoverable in basic-basic, but far from always.

Considerable material may be erased before basic-basic appears.

Sometimes basic-basic gets erased without either the auditor or the preclear knowing that it has been reached, basic-basic being merely another engram in the basic area. Sometimes much painful emotion must be discharged in the later-life areas before basic-basic discloses itself.

Always, however, basic-basic is the target and until he has a good idea that he has reached it, the auditor, once every session, makes an effort to get it. Thereafter he tries to get the earliest moment of pain or discomfort he can reach *every session*. If he can reach nothing early, he seeks to discharge a late emotional engram. When it is completely discharged–*reduced* or *erased* as an engram–then he goes down into the earliest material the file clerk will give him.

Whatever comes up, the auditor seeks to take all the charge out of it, whether that charge is pain or emotion, before he proceeds on his way to new material. This is done merely by returning the patient back over the incident many times until it no longer affects him either painfully or emotionally, or until it seems to vanish.

The Reduction and the Erasure

These two terms are highly colloquial. Serious effort has been made to deter their use and substitute for them something sonorous and wonderfully Latin, but no progress has been made to date. Auditors insist on using colloquial terms such as "AA" for attempted abortion, "louse up" for engrams which seriously aberrate, "aberree" for a person not Released or Cleared, "zombie" for an electric shock or neurosurgical case and so forth. It is feared that a tendency exists in them to be disrespectful to the hallowed and sacred tomes of yesteryear, to the dignity of past Authorities which labeled much and did little. However this may be, "reduction" and "erasure" are in such common use that to change them is hardly necessary.

To reduce means to take all the charge or pain out of an incident. This means to have the preclear recount the incident from beginning to end (while returned to it in reverie) over and over again, picking up all the somatics and perceptions present just as though the incident were happening at that moment. To reduce means, technically, to render free of aberrative material as far as possible to make the case progress.

To erase an engram means to recount it until it has vanished entirely. There is a distinct difference between a reduction and an erasure. The difference depends more upon what the engram is going to do than upon what the auditor wants it to do. If the engram is early, if it has no material earlier which will suspend it, that engram will erase. The patient, trying to find it again for a second or sixth recounting, will suddenly find out he has no faintest idea what was in it. He may ask the auditor who, of course, will give him no information whatever. (The auditor who prompts is slowing down therapy by making himself the patient's memory.) Going through it and trying to find it may cause the patient some amusement when he cannot. Or it may make him puzzled, for here was something which had, on first contact, a painful somatic and a highly aberrative content which now no longer seems to exist. That is an erasure. Technically the engram is not erased. If the auditor cares to spend some time solely for purposes of research, he will find that engram in the standard banks now, labeled "formerly aberrative: rather amusing: information which may be useful analytically." Such a search is not germane to therapy. If the incident had a somatic, was recounted a few times and then, when its last new material was found, vanished, it is erased so far as the engram bank is concerned. It will no longer be "soldered" into the motor circuits, will no longer be dramatized, it no longer blocks a dynamic and is no longer an engram but a memory.

The reduction has some interesting aspects. Let us take a childhood incident (age of four, let us say) which had to do with a scalding. This is contacted while much data remains in the basic area. It has many things below it which will hold it in place. Nevertheless, it has emotional charge and therapy is slowed by that charge. The file clerk hands out the scalding. Now it will not erase, but it will reduce. Here is a job which will take more time than an erasure. And there may be several aspects to that job.

The somatic is contacted, the incident is begun as close to the beginning as the auditor can get and is then recounted. This scalding, let us say, has apathy as its emotional tone (Tone 0.5). The preclear slogs through it apathetically, well exteriorized, watching himself be scalded. Then suddenly, perhaps, an emotional discharge may come off, but not necessarily. The preclear returns to the beginning and recounts (re-experiences) the whole thing once more. Then again and again. Soon he begins to get angry at the people involved in the incident for being so careless or so heartless. He has come up to anger (Tone 1.5). The auditor, although the patient would like to tell how vicious his parents are or how he thinks laws ought to be passed about scalding children, patiently puts the preclear through the incident again. Now the preclear ceases to be angry and finds that he is bored with the material. He has risen up to boredom on the Tone Scale (Tone 2.5). He may protest to the auditor that this is a waste of time. The auditor puts him back through the incident again. New data may show up. The somatic may or may not be still present at this period, but the emotional tone is still low. The auditor puts the preclear through the incident again and the preclear may, but not always, begin to be sarcastic or facetious. The incident is again recounted. Suddenly the preclear may be amused about it, but not always, and the incident, when it obviously has reached a high tone, may be left. It will probably sag in a few days. But that is a matter of no great importance, for it will be erased wholly on the return from basic-basic. In any case, it will never be as aberrative as it was before the reduction.

A reduction will sometimes result in the whole engram's apparently disappearing. But it is obvious when this will occur. Without much lifting in the Tone Scale, the incident, by repetition, simply goes out of sight. This is reducing to recession. In a few days that incident will be back in force again, almost as strong as ever. There is material before it and emotional charge after it which make it unwieldy.

Several things can happen, then, to an engram in the process of work. It can reduce, which is to say, discharge emotionally and somatically and be of no great aberrative power thereafter. It can reduce to recession, which is to say, it merely goes out of sight after several recountings. It can erase, which is to say, vanish and cease to be thereafter so far as the engram bank is concerned.

A little experience will tell an auditor what engrams are going to do after he has contacted them. Erasure takes place, ordinarily, only after basic-basic has been reached or, for that matter, when the basic area is being worked. The reduction occurs with an emotional discharge. The reduction to recession happens when there is too much in the engram bank suppressing the incident.

Every now and then even the best auditor will get hold of an engram and decide to grind it out now that it has been contacted. It is a sorry job. Perhaps it is better to grind it out than to merely restimulate it and let the patient be irritated by it for a couple of days. Perhaps not. But in any case that engram which reduces only to recession was better not contacted in the first place.

New auditors are forever charging at birth as an obvious target. Everybody has a birth: in most patients it can be located rather easily. But it is a painful incident and until the basic area has been thoroughly worked and until late-life painful emotion has been discharged and until the file clerk is ready to hand up birth, the incident is better left in place. It will usually reduce to recession and afterwards keep popping up to plague the auditor. The patient gets obscure headaches, gets sniffles, feels uncomfortable afterwards unless birth is taken on the return (from the basic area). The auditor is wasting time, of course, by trying to remove these headaches and sniffles because birth, with the whole prenatal life before it, will not properly reduce or erase but only recede. It is too often the case that birth, if prematurely contacted, will give the patient a headache and a cold. These discomforts are minor and of no great importance, but the work the auditor may have invested in working an incident which will only reduce to recession is lost work. True, the file clerk occasionally hands out birth: if he does, there is an emotional charge on it which will discharge and the incident will reduce properly. The auditor by all means should take it. True, a case sometimes stalls down and the auditor runs birth anyway just to see if he can speed things up. But merely going back to birth to put one's hands on an engram because he knows it is there will bring about discomfort and lost time. Go prenatal as far as you can and see what the file clerk will hand forth. Try Repeater Technique in the basic area. You may get incidents which will erase. If there is nothing there, find out about a painful emotion engram in late life, the death of a friend, the loss of an ally, a failure of a business, something. Blow a charge from it and reduce it as an engram and then go back prenatally as early as possible and see what has turned up. If the file clerk thinks you need birth, he'll give it out. But do not ask for birth just to have an engram to work, because it may prove to be a thoroughly uncomfortable and fruitless endeavor. Birth will come up when it will come up and the file clerk knows his business.

Charging into any late period of "unconsciousness" such as surgical anesthetic, where physical pain is present in large quantities, can bring about this needless restimulation. You can, of course, fare better with such things in reverie than in hypnosis or narcosynthesis where such a restimulation might bring about severe results. In reverie the effect is light.

HANDLING THE SOMATIC STRIP

There are "two little men" on each side of the brain, a set for each lobe, "hanging by their heels." The outer one is the *motor strip*, the inner one, the *sensory strip.** If you wish to know more about the structure of these pairs, Dianetic research will have the answer in a few more years. Currently there is something known about them, a description. To an engineer who knows Dianetics, the current description which will be found in the library is not entirely reasonable. These are, possibly, switchboards of some sort. Readings can be taken in the vicinity of them – just aft of the temples – if you have a very sensitive galvanometer, a galvanometer more sensitive than any on the public market today. Those readings show emanations of a field of some sort. When we have established the precise type of energy flowing here, we can probably measure it with better precision. When we know exactly where the thinking is done in the body, we will know more about these strips. All Dianetic research has established to date is that, beneath a welter of labels, nothing is actually known which is worth recounting about these structures beyond the fact that they have something to do with coordination of various parts of the body. We do, however, refer to them for lack of something better, in the course of therapy. Now that we know something about function, further research certainly cannot help but yield precision answers about structure.

The auditor can turn somatics on and off in a patient like an engineer handles switches. More aptly, he can turn them on and off in the body like a conductor runs a streetcar along a track. Here we have the game referred to previously when we talked about the time track.

*The sensory strip could be considered the "mental" side of the switchboard; the motor strip, the physical side.

In a patient who is working well, the somatic strip can be commanded to go to any part of the time track. Day by day, hour by hour, in normal life the somatic strip ranges up and down this track as engrams are restimulated. The auditor, working a patient, may find his own somatic strip obeying his own commands and some of his own somatics turning on and off, a fact which is at worst mildly uncomfortable. The whole body, the cells, whatever it is that is moving we do not really know. But we can handle it and we can assume that it at least passes through the switchboard of the little men who hang by their heels.

"The somatic strip will now go to birth," says the auditor.

The patient in reverie begins to feel the pressure of contractions thrusting him down the birth canal.

"The somatic strip will now go to the last time you injured yourself," says the auditor.

The preclear feels a mild reproduction of the pain of, perhaps, a bumped knee. If he has sonic and visio recall, he will see where he is and suddenly realize that it was in the office: he will hear the clerks and typewriters and the car noises outside.

"The somatic strip will now go into the prenatal area," says the auditor.

And the patient finds himself in the area, probably floating along, not uncomfortable.

"The somatic strip will now go to the first moment of pain or discomfort which can now be reached," says the auditor.

The patient drifts around a moment and suddenly feels a pain in his chest. He begins to cough and feels depression all over him. Mama is coughing (often source of chronic coughs).

"Roll the cough," says the auditor.

The patient finds himself at the beginning of the engram and begins to run it. "Cough, cough, cough," says the patient. *He then yawns.* "It hurts and I can't stop," he quotes his mother.

"Go to the beginning and roll it again," says the auditor.

"Cough, cough, cough," begins the patient, *but he is not coughing as badly now. He yawns more deeply.* "Ouch. It hurts, it hurts, and I can't seem to stop," quotes the preclear, *listening directly if he has sonic, getting impressions of what's said if he does not. He has picked up words now that were suppressed in it by "unconsciousness." "Unconsciousness" is beginning to come off with the yawns.*

"Roll it again," says the auditor.

"I can't stop," says the preclear, *quoting all that he finds this time. The somatic is gone. He yawns again. The engram is erased.*

"The somatic strip will now go to the next moment of pain or discomfort," says the auditor.

The somatic does not turn on. The patient goes into a strange sleep. He mutters about a dream. Suddenly the somatic gets stronger. The patient begins to shiver.

"What occurs?" says the auditor.

"I hear water running," says the preclear.

"Somatic strip will go to the beginning of the incident," says the auditor. "Roll it."

"I keep on hearing water," says the preclear. *(He must be stuck, the somatics did not move. This is a holder.)*

"Somatic strip will go to whatever it is that is holding," says the auditor.

"I'll hold it in there a while and see if it does some good," quotes the preclear.

"Pick up the beginning of the incident now and roll it," says the auditor.

"I feel myself being jostled," says the preclear. "Ouch, something bumped me."

"Pick up the beginning and roll it," says the auditor.

"I'm sure I must be pregnant," quotes the preclear. "I'll hold it in there a while and see if it does some good."

"Is there anything earlier?" says the auditor.

The preclear's strip goes to the earlier moment where he feels pressure as she tries to get something into the cervix. Then he rolls the engram and it erases.

This is handling of the somatic strip. It can be sent anywhere. It will pick up the somatic first, usually, and then pick up the content. Using Repeater Technique, the somatic strip is "sucked down" to the incident and the somatics turn on. Then the incident is run. If it does not lift, find an earlier incident simply by telling the somatic strip to go to the earlier incident.

If the somatic strip does not move, which is to say, if somatics (physical sensations) do not turn on and off, then the patient is stuck somewhere on the track.

He can be stuck in present time, which would mean he has a bouncer thrusting him all the way up the track. Use Repeater Technique or merely try to send the somatic strip back. If it won't go, get various bouncer phrases like "Can't go back," "Run a mile," etc., and with them suck the somatic strip down to the incident and run it.

The somatic strip may move through an incident with full sensation and yet, returning over the same ground several times, will not bring out data. Time after time this can be done without result in some engrams: the somatics remain almost the same, undulating through the incident each time, but with no other content. Then the auditor is "bucking" a denyer, a phrase such as "This is a secret," "Don't let him know," "Forget it," etc. In such a case, he sends the somatic strip to the phrase which denies the data:

> "Go to the moment a phrase is uttered denying this data," says the auditor.
>
> *After a moment,* "If he found out about this, it would kill him," quotes the preclear, *either from sonic or from impressions.*

Then the auditor sends the somatic strip back to the start of the incident and it goes on through it, this time with other perceptic content. The somatics, unless the incident is very late prenatal with basic area full of material, undulate (fluctuate according to the action of the engram) and diminish to either reduction or erasure on consecutive recountings.

The auditor tells the somatic strip to go earlier, sometimes it goes later. This is a misdirector. "Can't tell which way I am going," "Going backwards," "Do just the opposite," these are the type of phrases of the misdirector. The auditor recognizes that he has one in the preclear, guesses it or discovers it from the preclear's wording of the complaint about the action, and by repeater or direct command of the strip, picks up the phrase and the engram, reduces or erases it and continues.

If the somatic strip does not respond according to command, then a bouncer, a holder, a misdirector, or a grouper has been restimulated and should be discharged. The somatic strip will be where the command is which forbids it to function as desired.

There are good and bad conductors of this somatic strip. The good conductor works closely with the file clerk, using such broad orders as "The somatic strip will pick up the earliest moment of pain or discomfort which can be reached" or "The somatic strip will go to the highest intensity of the somatic you now have" (when a somatic is bothering the patient). The bad conductor picks out specific incidents which he thinks might be aberrative, bullies the somatic strip into them and somehow beats them down. There are moments when it is necessary to be quite persuasive with the strip and moments when it is necessary to pick out incidents of physical pain, but the auditor is the best judge of what should take place. As long as the strip will work smoothly, finding new incidents and running over them, he should not tamper with it beyond making sure that he reduces everything the strip contacts.

A very fine way to thoroughly wreck a case is to put the somatic strip into an incident, decide something else is more important and go rushing off to it, get that half lifted and go off to something else. By the time three or four incidents have been so touched, but not reduced, the strip stalls down, the track starts to bunch up and the auditor has a snarl which may take him many hours of therapy or a week or two of rebalancing (letting the case settle) to bring back to a workable state.

The patient will sometimes want a somatic turned off. It has been bothering him. That means that the strip is somehow hung up in some incident which therapy or the patient's environment has restimulated. Ordinarily it is not worth the time and trouble to locate the incident. It will settle out of its own accord in a day or two and it may be an incident which cannot be reduced because of the earlier engrams.

The somatic strip is handled in a late incident just as it is sent to an earlier one. Despair charges are contacted in the same way.

If you want a test to see if the strip is moving, or to test recall, send it back a few hours and find out what you get. While the prenatal area is easier to reach than yesterday in many cases, some idea will be gained of how the patient is working.

PRESENT TIME

The beginning is conception. Your patients sometimes have a feeling that they are sperms or ovums at the beginning of the track: in Dianctics this is called the *sperm dream*. It is not of any great value so far as we know at this time. But it is very interesting. It does not have to be suggested to the preclear. All one has to do is send him to the beginning of the track and hear what he has to say. Sometimes he has an early engram mixed up with conception.

At the late end of the track is, of course, now. This is present time. It happens now and then that patients are not getting back to present time because they have struck holders en route. Repeater Technique with holders will generally free the strip and get it to present time.

A patient may get a trifle groggy with all the things which have been happening to him in the course of a therapy session. And he may have reduced resistance to engrams as he comes back up the track and may thus trip a holder. The auditor should be very sure the patient is up in present time. Occasionally the patient will be so thoroughly stuck and the hour so advanced that the effort to bring him all the way up is not feasible at the time. A period of sleep will generally accomplish it.

There is a test whereby the auditor can tell if the preclear is up to present time. He snaps a question at the preclear, "How old are you?" The preclear gives him a "flash answer." If it is the preclear's right age, the preclear is in present time. If it is an earlier age, there is a holder there and the patient is not in present time. There are other methods of determining this, but it is not very important, by and large, if the patient does fail to make it.

Snapping questions at people, asking how old they are, elicits some surprising answers. Being stuck on the track is so common in "normal" people that a day or two or a week or two of failure to reach present time in a preclear is far from alarming.

Anyone who has a chronic psychosomatic illness is definitely stuck somewhere on the time track. Snap questions about it get "Three" or "Ten years" or some such answer quite ordinarily even when asked of people who suppose they are in good health. Reverie reveals to them where they are on the track. Sometimes, in the first session, a preclear shuts his eyes in reverie to find himself in a dentist's chair at the age of three. He has been there for the last thirty years or so because the dentist and his mother both told him to "stay there" while he was shocky with pain and gas–so he did, and the chronic tooth trouble he had all his life is that somatic.

This doesn't happen very often, but you can find someone you know, it is certain, who would flash answer "Ten years" and, being put in reverie, would find himself, as soon as the engram came to view, lying flat on his back in a ball park, or some such situation, with somebody telling him not to move until the ambulance came: that's his arthritis!

Try it on somebody.

THE FLASH ANSWER

A device in common use in therapy is the *flash answer*. This is done in two ways. The first mentioned here is the least used.

> "When I count to five," says the auditor, "a phrase will flash into your mind to describe where you are on the track. One, two, three, four, five!"

> "Late prenatal," says the preclear, or "yesterday" or whatever occurs to him.

The flash answer is the first thing which comes into a person's head when a question is asked him. It will come from the engram bank, usually, and will be useful. It may be "demon talk," but it is generally right. The auditor merely asks a question, such as what is holding the patient, what denies him knowledge, etc., prefacing the question with the remark, "I want a flash answer to this."

> "I want a flash answer to this," says the auditor. "What would happen if you became sane?"

> "Die," says the patient.

> "What would happen if you die," says the auditor.

> "I'd get well," says the patient.

And with this data, they then make an estimate of the current computation on allies or some such thing. In this case, the ally said to the preclear when he was ill, "I'd die, just die if you didn't get well. If you're sick much longer I'll go insane." And a former engram said the preclear had to be sick. And this is, after all, just an engram. So Repeater Technique is used on the word "die" and an ally is uncovered that the preclear never knew existed and a charge is blown.

Much valuable data can be recovered by clever use of the flash answer. If there is no answer at all, it means that the answer is occluded and that is almost as good a reply as actual data since it means some kind of a cover-up.

Dreams

Dreams have been used considerably by various schools of mental healing. Their "symbology" is a mystic foible forwarded to explain something which the mystics did not know anything about. Dreams are crazy house mirrors by which the analyzer looks down into the engram bank.

Dreams are puns on words and situations in the engram bank.

Dreams are not much help, being puns.

Dreams are not much used in Dianetics.

You will hear dreams from patients. Patients are hard to shut off when they start telling dreams. If you want to waste your time, you will listen.

Valence Shift

A mechanism used in Dianetics is the *valence shift*.

We know the way a patient gets into valences when he dramatizes his engrams in life: he becomes a winning valence and he says and does rather much what the person in the winning valence did in that engram.

The theory behind it is this: returned to a time the patient may consider too painful to enter, he can be shifted into a valence which felt no pain. A dull way to persuade him is to tell him he does not have to feel the pain or the emotion and let him go through it. This is very bad Dianetics because it is a positive suggestion and every safeguard must be taken to keep from giving suggestions to the patient, for he may be very suggestible even when he pretends not to be. But there is the valence shift and this permits the patient to escape the pain and still remain in the engram until he can recount it.

Example: father beating mother, unborn child knocked "unconscious." The data is available in the father valence with no pain, in the mother valence with her pain, in the child's valence with his pain.

The way to handle this, if the patient positively refuses to enter it although he has somatics, is to shift him in valence.

The auditor says, "Go into your father's valence and be your father for the moment."

After some persuasion the patient does so.

"Bawl your mother out," says the auditor. "Give her a fine talking-to."

The patient is now on that circuit which contains no "unconsciousness" and approximates the emotion and the words his father used to his mother. The auditor lets him do this a couple or three times until the charge is somewhat off the engram. Then he turns the patient's valence into the mother:

"Be your mother for the moment now and talk back to your father," says the auditor.

The patient shifts valence and is his mother and repeats his mother's phrases.

"Now be yourself," says the auditor, "and recount the entire incident with all somatics and emotion please."

The patient is able to re-experience the incident as himself.

This works very well when one is trying to get at an ally.

"Shift valence," says the auditor to the returned patient, "and plead with your mother not to kill the baby."

"Now be a nurse," says the auditor, with the preclear returned to some incident he seems very fearful about entering, "and plead with a little boy to get well."

The patient will correct the auditor's concept of the script and usually will proceed.

The patient will often refuse to go into a valence because he hates it. This means there must be considerable charge in the person he refuses to be.

This mechanism is rarely used, but is handy when a case is stalling. The father did not obey the holders or commands, he uttered them. The nurse would not obey her own commands. And so forth. Thus many holders and denyers can be flushed to view. It is useful in the beginning of a case.*

* Valence shift is seldom used except where an engram is suspected which will not otherwise be approached by the patient. He will often approach the engram with valence shift when he will not approach it as himself. Valence shift is somewhat undesirable when employed on a suggestible subject since it violates the Dianetic rule that no positive suggestion be used beyond those absolutely necessary in returning and recounting and uncovering data. Therefore valence shift is seldom employed and rarely on a suggestible person. It should be considered a last resort and practiced only when the preclear is entirely and completely unable to confront and attack an engram which the auditor is certain is present: and this is rare.

TYPES OF CHAINS

Engrams, particularly in the prenatal area, are in *chains*. That is to say, there is a series of incidents of similar types. This is useful classification because it leads to some solutions. The chains one can most easily contact in a preclear are the least charged. The most aberrative chains will usually be the hardest to reach because they contain the most active data. Remember the rule that what the auditor finds hard to reach, the analyzer of the patient found hard to reach.

Here is a list of chains–not all the possible chains by any means–found in one case which had passed for "normal" for thirty-six years of his life.

COITUS CHAIN, FATHER. 1st incident zygote. 56 succeeding incidents. Two branches, father drunk and father sober.

COITUS CHAIN, LOVER. 1st incident embryo. 18 succeeding incidents. All painful because of enthusiasm of lover.

CONSTIPATION CHAIN. 1st incident zygote. 51 succeeding incidents. Each incident building high pressure on child.

DOUCHE CHAIN. 1st incident embryo. 21 succeeding incidents. One each day to missed period, all into cervix.

SICKNESS CHAIN. 1st incident embryo. 5 succeeding incidents. 3 colds. 1 case grippe. One vomiting spell, hangover.

MORNING SICKNESS CHAIN. 1st incident embryo. 32 succeeding incidents.

CONTRACEPTIVE CHAIN. 1st incident zygote. 1 incident. Some paste substance into cervix.

FIGHT CHAIN. 1st incident embryo. 38 succeeding incidents. Three falls, loud voices, no beating.

ATTEMPTED ABORTION, SURGICAL. 1st incident embryo. 21 succeeding incidents.

ATTEMPTED ABORTION, DOUCHE. 1st incident fetus. 2 incidents. 1 using paste, 1 using Lysol, very strong.

ATTEMPTED ABORTION, PRESSURE. 1st incident fetus. 3 incidents. 1 father sitting on mother. 2 mother jumping off boxes.

HICCUP CHAIN. 1st incident fetus. 5 incidents.

ACCIDENT CHAIN. 1st incident embryo. 18 incidents. Various falls and collisions.

MASTURBATION CHAIN. 1st incident embryo. 80 succeeding incidents. Mother masturbating with fingers, jolting child and injuring child with orgasm.

DOCTOR CHAIN. 1st incident, 1st missed period. 18 visits. Doctor examination painful but doctor an ally, discovering mother attempting an abortion and scolding her thoroughly.

PREMATURE LABOR PAINS. 3 days before actual birth.

BIRTH. Instrument. 29 hours labor.

In that mother was a sub-vocal talker, this made a sizable quantity of material to be erased, for the remainder of the patient's life was in addition to this. This was a 500-hour case, non-sonic, imaginary recalls which had to be cancelled out by discovering lie factories before the above data could be obtained.

There are other chains possible, but this case was picked because it contains the usual ones found. Mother's lover is not very unusual, unfortunately, for he puts secrecy into a case to such an extent that when the case seems very, very secret, then a lover or two will seem indicated. But don't suggest them to a preclear. He may use them for an avoid.

TYPES OF SOMATICS

There are two kinds of somatics, those which properly belong to the patient and those which belong to his mother or some other person. The first actually happened, so did the second. But the patient should not have his mother's somatics. If he does, if he is found complaining of headaches whenever his mother has a headache, there is an engram, very early, which says he must have whatever she has: "The baby is part of me," "I want him to suffer as I suffer," etc. Or the phrase may be some entirely misunderstood thing literally taken. However, all this "comes out in the wash" and should be no great concern of the auditor's.

"UNCONSCIOUSNESS"

While "unconsciousness" has been covered elsewhere in various ways, in therapy it has two special manifestations. The *yawn* and the *boil-off.*

The engram of physical pain contains deep "unconsciousness" and if it is going to lift, particularly in the basic area, it comes off in yawns. After a first or second recounting, the patient starts to yawn. These yawns are turning on his analyzer.

In a very extreme engram–a prenatal electric shock which mother received–five hours of "unconsciousness" boil-off have taken place during therapy. The shock lasted for less than a minute, but so close did it bring the individual to death that when the incident was first contacted in therapy, he swam and floundered and had strange dreams, muttered and mumbled for five hours. That is a record. Forty-five minutes of this boil-off is rare. Five or ten minutes of it is not uncommon.

The auditor will take a patient into an area. No somatic turns on. But the patient begins to drowse into a strange kind of sleep. He rouses from this from time to time, mutters something, usually idiotic, rouses again with a dream and generally makes no progress to all appearances. But progress is being made. A period when he was almost dead is coming up to the surface. Soon a somatic will turn on and the patient will run an engram a few times on command, will yawn a little and then brighten up. Such a quantity of "unconsciousness" was, of course, sufficient to keep his analyzer about nine-tenths shut off when he was awake, for if it was near basic, it was part of every other engram. Such an engram, with such deep "unconsciousness," when released produces a marked improvement in a case, as much as a painful emotion engram at times.

It is up to the auditor to sit it through no matter how long it takes. It may make an uncleared auditor very sleepy to watch all this, but it should be done. He will rarely strike one that lasts an hour, but every case has such a period lasting from ten minutes to a half-hour.

He should stir the patient up once in a while and try to make him go through the engram. There is a very special way to stir a patient into life: *don't touch his body*, for it may be highly restimulative and make him very upset. Touch only the bottoms of his feet with your hand or your own feet and touch them just enough to jog him into attention for a moment. That keeps the boil-off in progress and does not permit the patient to sag into ordinary sleep.

The boil-off can be confused, by an inexperienced auditor, with an engram command to sleep. However, if the auditor will observe the patient closely, he will find that in the boil-off the patient gives every appearance of being drugged; while in a sleep command, he simply goes to sleep and does it very smoothly. The boil-off is a trifle restless, full of mutterings and flounderings and dreams. The sleep is smooth.

An engramic command to go to sleep, acting on the returned preclear, is broken by sending the somatic strip to the moment when the sleep command is given. If the preclear contacts it and goes over it, he will quickly awaken on the track and continue with therapy.

The boil-off may be full of yawns, mutterings or grunts. Sleep is usually quiet and gentle.

Just why this is called a "boil-off" and just why auditors are fond of the term is obscure. It was originally and sedately named "comatic reduction," but such erudition has been outvoted by the fact that it has never been used.

If you are fond of listening to dreams, you will find them in plenty in the boil-off. As images on the desert are distorted by the glass snakes of heat waves, so are the engramic commands distorted to the analyzer through the veil of "unconsciousness."

LOCKS

It is one of the blessings of nature that the *lock* is something which needs minor attention. A lock is an incident which, with or without charge, is in conscious recall and which *seems* to be the reason the aberree is aberrated. Perhaps this was another way the bank protected itself. A lock is a moment of mental discomfort containing no physical pain and no great loss. A scolding, a social disgrace: such things are locks. Any case has thousands and thousands of locks. The auditor will discover them in plenty if he cares to waste time looking for them. The treatment of these locks was the main goal of an old art known as "hypnoanalysis." Most of them can be reduced.

The key-in of an engram takes place at some future date from the time the engram was actually received. The key-in moment contains analytical reduction from weariness or slight illness. A situation similar to the engram, which contained "unconsciousness," came about and keyed-in the engram. This is a *primary lock.* Breaking it, if it can be found, produces the effect of keying-out the engram. But it can be considered a waste of time even if it has some therapeutic value and was used, without understanding, by some past schools.

If an auditor wants to know how the case was reacting to life, he can find some of these thousands and thousands of locks and look them over. But that is probably all the interest he has in them, for locks discharge. They discharge automatically the moment the engram holding them is erased. A whole life rebalances itself when the engrams are gone and the locks need no treatment. Neither does the preclear now Cleared need education as to how to think: like the blowing of locks, this is an automatic process.

These locks lie down among the engrams sometimes. The preclear may be deep in the prenatal area and suddenly think about a time when he was twenty or, as is common in therapy, think about an engram he heard from somebody else. This is a good clue. Pay no further heed to the lock: find the engram to which it attached itself, for there is an engram immediately with it. In dreams, these locks in distorted form come swimming up out of the bank, complicating the dream.

THE JUNIOR CASE

Do not take on a Junior for your first case if you can avoid it. If father was named George and the patient is called George, beware of trouble. The engram bank takes George to mean George and that is identity-thought de luxe.

Mother says, "I hate George!" "That means Junior," says the engram though mother meant father. "George is thoughtless." "George must not know." "Oh, George, I wish you had some sex appeal, but you haven't." And so go the engrams. A Junior case is seldom easy.

It is customary to shudder, in Dianetics, at the thought of taking on a Junior case. An auditor can be expected to slave his hardest when he has a case with non-sonic, which is off the time track, and which is named after father or mother. Such cases resolve, of course, but if parents knew what they did to children by giving them any name which might appear in the engram bank, such as that of parents or grandparents or friends, it is certain the custom would vanish instanter.

RESTIMULATING THE ENGRAM

"Ask often enough and you will receive," is always true when working the engram bank. Simply by returning into an area enough times, engrams will appear. If it is not there today, it will be there tomorrow. But if it is not there tomorrow, it will be there the day after and so forth. Emotional discharges are most certainly located by asking for them time after time, returning the patient over the part of the track where the charge is expected to lie. What Repeater Technique will fail to do can be done by returning the patient, session after session, to a portion of his life. Sooner or later it will come into view.

Occluded Life Periods and People

Whole areas of the time track will be found occluded. These contain suppressors by way of engram command, ally computations and painful emotion. Persons can vanish utterly from sight for these reasons. They come to view after a few engrams have been lifted in basic or the area has been developed as above.

Animosity toward Parents

It always happens, when one Clears a child or adult, that the preclear goes through stages of improvement which bring him up the Tone Scale and cause him, of course, to pass through the second zone, anger. A preclear may become furious with his parents and other offenders in the engram bank. Such a situation is to be expected. It is a natural byproduct of therapy and it cannot be avoided.

As the case progresses, the Tone Scale, of course, rises and places the preclear in a state of boredom toward the villains who have wronged him. At last he reaches Tone 4, which is the tone of the Clear. At this time he is very cheerful and willing to be friends with people whether they have wronged him or not: of course he has the data about what to expect of them, but he nurses no animosity.

If a parent feels that the child, knowing all, would turn against him, then the parent is mistaken. The child has already, as an aberree, turned very thoroughly against the parent whether his analyzer knows all or not and the most uncertain and unlovely conduct may result from further hiding of the evidence.

It is a matter of continual observation that the good Release and the Clear feel no animosity whatever toward their parents or others who had caused their aberrations and indeed stop negating, defending and fighting so irrationally. The Clear will fight, certainly, for a good cause and he will be the most dangerous opponent possible. But he does not fight for irrational reasons like an animal and his understanding of people is very much enlarged and his affection can at last be deep. If a parent wishes love and cooperation from a child, no matter what he has done to that child, permit therapy and achieve that love and cooperation with the child self-determined and no longer secretly in apathy or rage. After all, the Clear has learned the source of his parents' aberrations as well as his own; he recognizes that they had engram banks before he did.

PROPITIATION

In the process of work a stage will be passed, in the upper range of apathy, of propitiation. This conciliation is an effort to feed or sacrifice to an all destructive force. It is a state wherein the patient, in deep fear of another, offers expensive presents and soft words, turns the other cheek, offers himself as a doormat and generally makes a fool out of himself.

Many, many marriages, for instance, are marriages not of love, but of that shabby substitute, propitiation. People have a habit of marrying people who have similar reactive minds. This is unfortunate, for such marriages are destructive to both partners. She has a certain set of aberrations: they match his. She is pseudo-mother; he is pseudo-father. She had to marry him because father tried to murder her before she was born. He had to marry her because mother beat him when he was a child. Incredible as it may seem, these marriages are very common: one or the other partner becomes mentally ill, or both may deteriorate. He is unhappy, his enthusiasms crushed; she is miserable. Either, with another partner, might be a happy person yet, out of fear, they cannot break apart. They must propitiate each other.

The auditor who finds a marriage in this condition and attempts to treat one of the partners, had better treat both simultaneously. Or such partners had better treat each other and soon. Tolerance and understanding are almost always fostered by mutual help.

Propitiation is mentioned here because it has a diagnostic value. People who start bringing the auditor expensive gifts are propitiating him and it probably means that they have a computation which tells them, engramically, that they will die or go crazy if they become sane. The auditor may enjoy the gifts, but he had better start looking for a sympathy engram not yet suspected or tapped.

Love

Probably no single subject in the concerns of Man has received as much attention as Love.

It is not untrue that where one finds the greatest controversy, there he will also find the least comprehension. And where the facts are least precise, there one can also find the greatest arguments. And so it is with Love.

Without doubt Love has ruined more lives than war and made more happiness than all the dreams of Paradise.

Entangled with a thousand songs a year and submerged beneath a solid tonnage of poor literature, Love should have a proper chance to be defined.

It has been discovered that there are three kinds of Love between woman and man: the first is covered under the law of affinity and is the affection with which Mankind holds Mankind; the second is sexual selection and is a true magnetism between partners; the third is compulsive "Love" dictated by nothing more reasonable than aberration.

Perhaps in the hero and heroine legends there have been cases of the second kind; and surely as one looks about him in this society, he can discover numbers of happy partnerships based on a natural and strongly affectionate admiration. The third kind we find in plenty: tabloid literature is devoted to it and its travails; it crams the courts with urgent pleas for divorce, with criminal acts and civil suits; it sends children weeping into the corner away from quarrels and it launches from its broken homes broken young women and men.

Dianetics classifies this third kind of love as "reactive mind partnership." Here is a meeting of minds, but the minds are on the lowest computational level possessed by Man. Driven together by compulsion, men and women mate who will find in that mating nothing but sorrow and reduction of their hopes.

He is pseudo-brother who beat her regularly or he is pseudo-father whom she had to mind. Maybe he is even pseudo-mother who screamed ceaselessly at her, but whom she had to placate. And he might be the doctor who hurt her so savagely. She may be his pseudo-mother, his pseudo-grandmother whom he had to love despite the way she undermined his decision; she may be a pseudo-nurse in some operation long gone or the pseudo-teacher who kept him after school to whet her sadism upon him.

Before the marriage takes place, they only know there is a compulsion that they must be together, a feeling that each must be extremely nice to the other. And then the marriage takes place and more and more restimulation of ancient pain is felt until at last each is ill and life, complicated now perhaps by unhappy children, is an unhappy ruin.

The mechanism of propitiation carries with it covert hostility. Gifts given without cause and beyond the ability to expend, self-sacrifices which seem so noble at the time compose propitiation. Propitiation is an apathy effort to hold away a dangerous "source" of pain. Mistaken identity is one of the minor errors of the reactive mind. To buy off, to nullify the possible anger of a person, perhaps long since dead but living now again in the partner, is the hope of propitiation. But a man is dead who will not sometimes fight. The hostility may be masked, it may be entirely "unknown" to the individual who indulges it. Certainly it is always justified in the mind of the person who exerts it and is supposed to be a natural consequence of some entirely obvious offense.

The wife who makes inadvertent blunders before the guests and by them accidentally gives away the truth of her husband's favorite myth, the wife who forgets the little favors he has asked, the wife who suddenly stabs him with a "logical" pin in the region of his hopes: these are wives who live with partners whom they must, out of some wrong done years before the courtship and by some other man, propitiate; and these are wives who, propitiating, numb the hopes and misunderstand the sorrows of their mates.

The husband who sleeps with another woman and "accidentally" leaves the lipstick on his tie, the husband who finds her excellent cooking bad and idleness in her days, the husband who forgets her letters he must mail, the husband who finds her opinions silly: these are husbands who live with partners whom they must propitiate.

A soaring, roller-coaster curve of peace and war in the home, failures to understand, mutual curtailment of liberty and self-determinism, unhappy lives, unhappy children and divorce are caused by reactive-mind marriages. Compelled by an unknown threat to marry, repelled by fear of pain from trust, this "meeting of minds" is the primary cause of all marital disaster.

The law lacked definition and so invoked great difficulty in the path of those involved in such marriages. The track of it is the dwindling spiral of misery which accompanies all chronic restimulation and leads only down to failure and to death. Someday there will, perhaps, exist a much more sentient law that only the unaberrated can marry and bear children. The present law only provides that marriages must be at best most difficult to part. Such a law is like a prison sentence for the husband, the wife and the children–all and every one.

A marriage can be saved by clearing its partners of their aberrations. An optimum solution would include this in any case since it is most difficult for a wife or a husband to rise, even when divorced, to any future plane of happiness: and where there are children, if clearing is not effected, a great injustice has been done.

It is usually discovered that when both partners in a reactive-mind marriage are cleared of aberration, life becomes considerably more than tolerable; for human beings often have a natural liking even when no sexual selection has been present. The restoration of a marriage by clearing the partners may not bring about one of the great loves that poets strummed about, but it will at least bring a high level of respect and cooperation toward the common goal of making life worthwhile. And in many marriages so Cleared it was discovered that the partners, beneath the dirty cloth of aberration, loved each other well.

A major gain to such a clearing is for the children's sake. Nearly all marital discontent has as its major factor aberration on the Second Dynamic, sex. And any such aberration includes a nervous disposition toward children.

Where there are children, divorce does not answer, clearing does. And with clearing comes a fresh new page of life on which happiness can be written.

In the case of the reactive-mind marriage, turn-about clearing is often complicated by the concealed hostilities which lie below the propitiative mechanism. It is wise for the partners to look outside the home, each interesting a friend in a therapy turn-about. If such mutual clearing is begun, with the partners working on each other, much restraint of anger and exertion of patience must be practiced and the Auditor's Code must be most severely followed. It requires a saintly detachment to bear the Tone 1 of the partner who, returned to a quarrel, seasons the recountings with further recrimination. If it must be done, it can be done. But when many quarrels and travails have beset a couple, it is easier if they each look without the home for a therapy partner.

Additionally, there is a kind of "rapport" established between any auditor and preclear. And after the therapy session is done, a strengthening of the natural affinity is such that a small deed or word may be taken as a savage attack, with the result of a quarrel and the inhibition of therapy.

Men can be considered to be best audited by men and women by women. This condition is changed when one deals with a woman who has such severe aberrations about women that she is in fear around them, or when one is auditing a man who has deep fear of men.

The dynamics of men and women are somehow different and a wife, particularly if there have ever been quarrels of any magnitude, sometimes finds it difficult at times to be sufficiently insistent to audit her husband. The husband may audit, in the usual case, without great difficulty, but when in therapy himself, his feeling that he must rise superior to the situation forces him to attempt auto-control, a thing which is impossible.

THE ERASURE

Sooner or later–if you keep trying–you will get basic-basic, the earliest moment of "unconsciousness" and physical pain. You will know when you have it, perhaps, only because things start to erase rather than reduce. If the patient still has a sonic shut-off, you can still erase: sooner or later that sonic will turn on, perhaps not even until the case is almost finished. You will reach basic-basic sooner or later.

The erasure, then, is more or less the same procedure as the entrance. You erase all the early engrams, always the earliest you can find, and you keep discharging painful emotion engrams either in the basic area or in the later periods after birth and later in life. You erase as much as you can find in the early part of the case, then you release all the emotion you can find later in the case (erase everything in each engram you touch) and then you come back and find early material.

The reactive engram bank is a hurrah's nest. The file clerk must have a great deal of trouble with it. For things are keyed-in early and late; sometimes all he can get is material under certain topics; sometimes all he can get is material under certain somatics (all teeth, for instance); sometimes he can go in an orderly parade forward in time and give consecutive incidents: this last is the most important proceeding.

Not until you have worked out every moment of physical pain and discharged all the moments of painful emotion will the case be Cleared. There will be times when you are sure that you are almost to the goal only to discover, going into the prenatal area again, a new series of material uncovered by the later life painful emotion you have released.

One day you will find a case which will not have any occlusions anywhere on the track, which will no longer be interested in engrams (apathy cases aren't interested at the start; Clears, at the top level, are not interested either, making a cycle, though the Clear is a long way from apathetic), which will have all recalls, which will compute accurately and make no errors (within the limitations of the data available) and which, in short, has an exhausted engram bank. But do not be too optimistic, ever. Keep looking until you are sure. Observe the case to make certain no aberrations are displayed about anything, that dynamics are high in it and that life is good. If this person now feels he can solve all the problems of life, lick the world with one hand tied behind him and feel a friend to all men, you have a Clear.

The only way you can go wrong is to compute with the idea that human beings are full of error and evil and sin and that if you have made a person less unhappy and above normal, he is to be judged a Clear. This is a *Release*.

In gold panning, it is true that every tenderfoot mistakes iron pyrites (fool's gold) for gold. The tenderfoot will crow with delight over a bright bit of something in his pan which, actually, is worth a few dollars a ton. And then he sees real gold! The moment he sees real gold in that pan, he knows what gold really looks like. It cannot be mistaken.

Aside from the fact that psychometry would show a Clear phenomenally intelligent, would show his aptitude and versatility wide, there is another quality: the human quality of a freed man. You take a Release through psychometry and show him to be above normal, too.

But a Clear is a Clear and when you see it, you will know it with no further mistake.

That a Clear is no longer interested in his extinct engrams does not mean he is not interested in the troubles of others. That a person is not interested in his own engrams does not necessarily argue a Clear, but may well be another mechanism: the apathy of neglect. To have engrams and neglect them is a common aberration with the reactive mind on a Tone Scale of apathy. To have no engrams and neglect them is another thing. Every apathy case, neglecting his engrams as an answer to his woe, insisting he is happy, insisting, as he racks himself to pieces, that there is nothing wrong with *him*, will, in work, particularly after basic-basic is lifted, become interested in his engrams and more interested in life. It is easy to tell the apathy case from the Clear, for the two are at opposite ends of the spectrum of life: the Clear has soared up toward victory and triumph; the apathy knows victory and triumph are not for him and explains they are not worth it.

What the life span of a Clear is cannot be answered now; ask in a hundred years.

How can you tell a Clear? How close does the man measure to optimum for Man? Can he adjust to his environment smoothly? And far more important, can he adjust that environment to him?

Sixty days and again six months after a Clear has apparently been effected, the auditor should again make a search for any neglected material. He should question the possible Clear carefully as to the events of the past interval. In such a way, he can learn of any worries, concerns or illnesses which may have taken place and attempt to trace these to engrams. If he cannot then find engrams, the Clear is definitely and without question Cleared. And he will stay that way.

If a case merely stalls, however, and while aberration seems to be present, engrams cannot be found, the cause probably lies with thoroughly masked despair charges: painful emotional engrams. These are not necessarily postnatal, they can be within the prenatal period and involve circumstances which are very secret—or so the engrams announce. Also, some cases have stalled and proven "impenetrable" because of a current or immediately past circumstance the patient has not revealed.

There are two reasons which can delay a case:

1. The person may be so aberratedly ashamed of his past or so certain of retribution if he reveals it that he does nothing but avoid.
2. The person may be in fear because of some existing circumstance or threat.

The auditor is not interested in what the patient does. Or in what the patient has done. Dianetics treats of what has been done *to* the person, exclusively, in therapy. What has been done *by* a patient is of no concern. The auditor who would make it any concern is practicing something other than Dianetics. However, a patient, because of his engrams, may become obsessed with the idea that he must hide something in his life from the auditor. The two general classes above cover the general conditions.

These active reasons, as under (1), may be such a thing as a prison sentence, a murder hitherto unknown (although many people think they have done murder who have not even threatened it to anyone), abnormal sexual practices, or some such circumstance. The auditor should promise not to reveal any confidential matter, purely as a matter of routine, and explain the principle of "done *to*, not done *by*." And no auditor would taunt or revile a patient for having been victimized by his engrams. As under (2), there may exist some person, even the wife or husband, who has cowed the patient into secrecy. One case is at hand where no advance was made although there were many incidents contacted: the incidents would not reduce or erase no matter where they were. It was discovered that this case, a woman, had been beaten savagely and often by her husband and that she had been threatened with death if she told the auditor a word of these acts; and yet these acts contained the whole despair charges of the case and had to be released. Seeing this, finally suspecting, the auditor was able to gain her confidence and locate the despair charges. Even if he had not gained her confidence, by constant restimulation of late-life areas he would have provoked her tears. In another case, that of a small child, dub-in recall was so obvious and lie factories were so busy that the auditor at last realized that he was attempting to penetrate not just the secrecy on an engram, but the secrecy imposed upon a child by someone at hand. The mother, in this case, out of the idea that she would be apprehended, had furiously threatened the child to say nothing about his treatment at home. There was more than this behind the case; there were eighty-one attempted abortions, an incredible number.

Anything is the business of an auditor if it has become an engram. If society has jailed a man, if all is not well in the home, these are things done *to* a person. What the person did to "deserve" this treatment is of no concern.

THE FOREIGN LANGUAGE CASE

Now and again an auditor will encounter a strange sort of holdup in a case. He will be unable to get anything to clear or make sense in the prenatal area and sometimes in childhood as well as the prenatal area. He may be encountering a "foreign language case." Occasionally the child did not know he was born to other parents (who may have spoken a foreign tongue) than those he has known as his parents. This is a special sort of mix-up of its own which is rather easily resolved simply by running engrams. It is always possible for the patient to forget that his parents spoke some other tongue in the home. Another tongue than the one the patient is using or other than that of the country in which the patient resides is, in one way, an asset: it gives a prenatal area which is very difficult to restimulate although it may still be acting upon the patient's mind. But it is no asset to the auditor, who must now deal with a patient who does not know the language, who may not have sonic recall and yet has an engram bank full of data which once had meaning and really is his basic language.

The best remedy for such a case is to get an auditor who knows both the language used in the prenatal area and the present tongue. Another remedy is to take a dictionary to the case and figure out the bouncers et al., from the dictionary. Another way is to return the patient often enough into the infant period that he begins to pick up the language again (making the file drawer of it come forth) and then ask the patient for phrases which, in the foreign tongue, would mean this or that. Gradually, he may recover the language and so exhaust the bank. This is an extremely difficult case only when there was no childhood use of the other tongue. Given childhood use of that tongue, the auditor simply keeps returning the patient to childhood when he knew the tongue and then returning him into the prenatal area: the patient can translate what is happening. The clichés of other tongues than that the auditor speaks are often quite productive of other literal meanings than comparable clichés in the auditor's tongue. This difference of cliché is a very responsible agent in the social aberrations of one nation as they differ from those of another. "I have hot," says the Spaniard. "I am hot," says the Englishman. Engramically, they mean different things, even if they mean the same to the analyzer.

BOOK THREE, CHAPTER NINE: PART TWO

MECHANISMS *and* ASPECTS *of* THERAPY

EXTRASENSORY PERCEPTION

EVERY TIME THE AUDITOR has a case with dub-in recall or which is highly charged with emotion, the case may return into the prenatal area and start describing scenery. This is the awe and wonder of some beholders. There is the patient in the womb and yet he can "see" outside. The patient tells about father and mother and where they are sitting and what the bedroom looks like, and yet there he is in the womb. Some pretty theories can be advanced for this: one of them is that the tortured fetus develops extrasensory perception in order to see what is coming next. ESP is an excellent theory and some observation may confirm it, *but not in the fetus.*

One must recall that the fetus, even if it has highly developed and clever cells, is yet not a truly rational organism. The presence of the engram does not necessarily mean that the fetus could think. The engram became most severely aberrative when the child finally learned speech. The engram is not a memory, but a recording of pain and percepts.

Returning a grown man or a child into the prenatal area returns there an experienced mind which, connecting with these engrams, forms conclusions. To listen to some preclears one would think they read Keats and drank lemonade every afternoon at four throughout the prenatal period.

To return *reason* and analytical power back into a period when neither reason nor analytical power existed, of course, impinges upon the returned individual many ideas. All he is supposed to run are the engrams and their contents. He may additionally, by dream mechanisms and current computation, try to fashion in a whole technicolor picture of the scenery.

This prenatal ESP does not in fact exist. It has been proven, after considerable test, that whenever the returned preclear thinks he sees something, the scenery itself is mentioned in the engrams and gives him an imaginary picture of it. There is no prenatal ESP, in other words. There are only descriptions and actions which suggest scenery, and these suggestions, operating now upon the imagination, bring about the supposed visio.

This is most chronic with patients who have high-powered lie factories. When the auditor sees this, he begins to form a notion of the case he is engaged upon, he knows dub-in sonic may be used and he should find and discharge all painful emotion he can reach, for it is this painful emotion which so disposes a case to avoid. He can find, then, the lie factory itself, not the lie factory of the lie factory which produces lie factories, but the actual engram which causes all this delusion.

However, never bring a preclear up short on this material. Don't tell him it is imaginary, you'll drive the lie factory into higher effort. For there are sympathy computations here, despairful losses, great prenatal pain and childhood neglect. And it would take little to shatter what self-confidence this patient has managed to assemble. Therefore walk softly, look for despair charges, allies, sympathy engrams and get the lie factory. Then the case will settle down and progress to Clear.

ELECTRIC SHOCK

It has been found important, in entering a case, to locate and relieve all engrams caused by electric shock of whatever kind. These seem to produce a grouping of engrams, whether they are received prenatally (as some have been), accidentally, or at the hands of psychiatrists. Any electric shock seems to have more than usual force in the engram bank and apparently deranges the memory files of both past and future events surrounding the shock area. Further, electric shock injury contains a great depth of "unconsciousness" which thereafter holds the analytical mind in a reduced state.

TACIT CONSENT

In the case of two preclears working on each other, each one assuming in his turn the auditor's role, a condition can arise where each prevents the other from contacting certain engrams.

For example, preclear A has an ally computation concerning a dog. He unknowingly seeks to protect this "pro-survival" engram within himself although, of course, failure to release it will hinder therapy. As he audits preclear B, he has a tendency to project his own problems into preclear B, which is to say, he has some slight confusion of identity. If preclear B is known to have some "pro-survival" engram about a dog, then preclear A, auditing, will actually avoid making preclear B contact B's own engram. This is a mistaken idea that by letting B keep his dog engram, A can retain his dog engram.

This is "tacit consent." It might be summed as a bargain: "If you don't make me get well, I won't make you get well." This should be guarded against: once known that such a condition exists and that such reluctance to Clear the other is manifested, "tacit consent" ceases.

It may also happen that a husband and wife may have a mutual period of quarrels or unhappiness. Engaged upon Clearing each other, working alternately as auditor, they avoid, unknowingly but by reactive computation, the mutual period, thus leaving in place painfully emotional engrams.

Tacit consent is not easily recognized by the individuals so involved and preclears, alternating as auditors, should be very wary of it, for it cannot do other than slow a case.

Emotion and Pain Shut-offs*

A case which manifests no emotion or cannot feel pain when emotion and pain should be present in some incident is suffering from a "feeling" shut-off: this most likely will be found in the prenatal area. The word "feeling" means both pain and emotion: thus the phrase, "I can't feel anything," may be an anesthetic for both.

If an exteriorized view of the incident (where the patient sees himself and is not in himself) or what pretends to be prenatal "ESP" is present, the emotional shut-off probably stems from painful emotion engrams in late life or at least post-birth. If there is no exteriorized view and the patient is within himself, and yet no sharpness of pain or emotion manifests itself while he is running through an engram, an early emotional shut-off or an early pain shut-off should be suspected and should be

*The somatic strip works in all shut-offs whether the patient *feels* it or not. The somatic strip also obeys, but no somatic turns on when the incident is occluded by "unconsciousness," the somatic appearing after the boil-off.

located by Repeater Technique. Run the words "No emotion" until a paraphrase is obtained: run the words "I can't feel," or some other phrase meaning the same thing and the patient, if the engrams are available and are not suppressed by others, will eventually respond.

It may happen that a case may "work" very well, which is to say that engrams present themselves and can be run and reduced, without emotion manifesting itself as part of the content and with somatics which are dull and not so much pain as simply pressure. If the pain and emotion shut-offs do not yield at first to Repeater Technique, many engrams may have to be run in the basic area without pain or emotion, but only with pressure and word content. In such a case, pain and emotion can eventually be contacted, after which therapy is more beneficial.

EXTERIORIZED VIEWS

Whenever you find a patient, returned, outside himself and seeing himself, that patient is off the track. He should not be told so, but the despair charges, which is to say, the painful emotion engrams, should be found as soon as possible and discharged. This is something of the same mechanism as the ESP described above.

TELEPATHY

Every few cases, some preclear may try to palm off telepathy as an aberrative factor. This is more rainbow chasing. There may be telepathy. But so far as research has shown the fetus doesn't receive any and even if he receives it, it is not aberrative in any way.

Exhaustive tests were made on telepathy and ESP, and in every case an explanation was found which did not need to go into mind reading or radar sight.

When a patient tries to tell the auditor that he is reciting mother's thoughts received prenatally, be certain that somewhere around there is an engram in which she says these exact words aloud. Mothers, especially when aberrated severely and especially when aberrated severely enough to attempt abortion, have many engrams they dramatize. The power of the dramatization commonly manifests itself as monologues. Some mothers have a very great deal to say to themselves when alone. All of this speech is, of course, transmitted to the child when he is injured, and he may be injured without mother being injured as in an attempted abortion. For considerable time after such an injury the child is usually "unconscious" and in pain; he therefore records in engrams these monologues (and often the voice is quite loud). He doesn't hear it: it is simply cellularly recorded. All such monologuing is aberrative, of course, and produces some remarkable patterns of insanity and neurosis.

But of telepathy, there is none that is aberrative so far as we know at this time. So the auditor should not accept telepathy any more than he would accept ESP.

Prenatal Living Conditions

It is very noisy in the womb. A person may think he has sonic and yet hear no "womb" sounds, which means that he does not have sonic, but only dub-in. Intestinal squeaks and groans, flowing water, belches, flatulation and other body activities of the mother produce a continual sound.

It is also very tight in later prenatal life.

In a high blood pressure case, it is extremely horrible in the womb.

When mother takes quinine, a high ringing noise may come into being in the fetal ears as well as her own–a ringing which will carry through a person's whole life.

Mother gets morning sickness, has hiccups and gets colds, coughs and sneezes.

This is prenatal life.

The only reason anybody "wanted" to "return to the womb" was because somebody hit mother and yelled "Come back here!" so the person does.

THE ENGRAM FILING SYSTEM

Engrams are not filed in the orderly fashion managed by a Cleared standard bank. Engrams are filed in a way which would defy Alexander. Hence, it is difficult to know when the proper consecutive item will appear.

Time, topic, value, somatic and emotion are the methods of filing.

The return from basic-basic may be an apparent orderly progress into late life. Suddenly a despair charge is triggered and discharged. The auditor looks back at the prenatal area and finds a whole new series of incidents in view. Progress is then begun back to present time, step by step, another discharge is triggered and another series of prenatals come into sight. These are erased and progress is made back toward present time when still another despair charge is released and still more prenatals come to view. These are erased and so forth and so on.

The engram filing system gives out data by somatic, time, topic, value or emotion. Usually the file clerk hands out material on the basis of time and topic. Emotion in the bank keeps the file clerk from getting at a certain series of incidents; when the emotion is discharged, the incidents become available and incidents are brought out until another emotional charge stops the file clerk. The wit of the auditor is most used, not in getting prenatals, but in finding these later-life emotional charges and discharging them.

All in all the engram filing system is very poor, unlike the standard bank. But it is also very vulnerable, now that we understand it.

The engram filing system data can be erased. Standard bank data cannot be erased. Pain is perishable; pleasure endures.

Alleviation

The psychoanalyst or general counselor in human relations is occasionally faced with a type of problem which Dianetics, applied in small quantity, can resolve easily.

It is possible, when a person has been too disturbed by an event of the day to address himself to the problem at hand, to alleviate his disturbance with a few minutes of work.

A sudden change in the aspect of a patient, a sudden deterioration of his serenity, generally stems from some incident which has caused him mental anguish. Although this change of mind has its source in the restimulation of an engram, the moment of restimulation, which is a lock, may be addressed and alleviated with success.

Using reverie or merely asking the patient to close his eyes, the analyst can request him to return and be in the instant wherein he was disturbed. That instant may be in the same day or the same week as the office call. A moment of analytical shutdown will be discovered wherein some restimulative person or circumstance upset the equilibrium of the patient. This moment is a lock. It can be recounted, ordinarily, as an engram and the latest source of tension will relieve so that work can be continued. The engram itself, upon which the lock depended, may not be accessible without a full Dianetic address to the problem.

The auditor, finding a patient much disturbed, can often save time by relieving the lock which caused the immediate disturbance of the preclear.

Locating locks on a wholesale basis is unremunerative from a Dianetic viewpoint since there are thousands and thousands of them in every case. Locating the last lock, which is hindering work, may be of benefit.

THE TONE SCALE AND REDUCTION OF ENGRAMS

Because it is very important, the mechanism of the reduction of a late painful emotion engram must be specifically detailed.

The uses of reduction on late engrams are wide and various. When the auditor gets into trouble with his preclear by some violation of the Auditor's Code, he can treat the violation as a painful emotion engram and reduce it, at which moment the effect of his blunder will be gone in the preclear. The auditor merely returns the preclear back to the blunder and runs the error itself as an engram. When the husband has quarreled with his wife or she has found out some unpleasant thing about his activities, he can treat the quarrel or the discovery as a painful emotion engram and release it with the result of no further worry about it by his wife. When the little boy's dog has just been run over, the incident can be treated as a painful emotion engram and released. When the preclear's wife has just left him, treat the leaving as a painful emotion engram and release it. Whatever the shock or upset, it can be reduced in an individual by regular reduction technique and the individual will cease to be troubled by it in the painful emotion sense.

It does not matter whether the engram occurred two hours or ten years ago, painful emotion can be reduced from it. It is run exactly like any other engram, beginning at the beginning of the first shock with the patient returning to it and continuing far enough along it to adequately embrace its first impact.

The aspect of this reduction is a pattern which does not much vary. If the news struck the individual into apathy, then as he recounts, he will (unless there is a severe emotional shut-off elsewhere) progress through the incident a time or two, perhaps, before he contacts it properly. Then there will come the tears and despair of apathy. Another two or three runs should bring up anger. Then further recounting (always from beginning to end as re-experience) brings the tone up into boredom. Further recounting should bring it to Tone 3 or 4 release or, most favorably, laughter.

This progress of the tones is the clue which led to the establishment of the Tone Scale from 0 to 4. A Tone 4 is laughter.

There is sometimes a stage in the Tone 2 area where the patient begins to be offhand and flippant. This is not Tone 4, it denotes more data present. He may resist recounting at this point, saying the incident is released. The auditor must insist on further recounting whenever he finds the preclear unwilling to recount again, for here is data being suppressed and more charge is present. The flippancy is generally found to be an escape mechanism and is sometimes uttered in the very words which are yet concealed. More recounting (without the auditor insisting any certain words be found) is then done until the patient reaches Tone 4.

Here we have, in vignette, the behavior of the whole engram bank in the process of therapy. The entire bank rises from its initial tone level eventually up to Tone 4, higher and higher as more and more engrams are erased or reduced. The bank's rise is not, however, a smooth upward curve, for new engrams will be contacted with apathy in them and some have manics in them. The painful emotion engram, however, does a rather smooth rise. If it is going to release at all, it will rise up the scale. If it does not rise up the scale – apathy to anger, anger to boredom, boredom to cheerfulness or at least no concern – then it is suppressed by an incident with similar content.

An engram may begin at Tone 1 – anger – and rise from there. If it is found to be in Tone 2 at the start – boredom – it is hardly an engram.

It may, however, be in a false Tone 2 and suppressed by other data so that the patient merely appears bored and careless about it. A few recountings may bring about release of it, at which moment it will sag instantly to apathy – Tone 0 – and then come on up the scale of the tones. Or another engram may have to be contacted.

The whole physical being follows this Tone Scale throughout a course of therapy. The mental being follows this Tone Scale. And painful emotion engrams follow it.

On an erasure down in the basic area or when returning from basic-basic, two or three runs will erase an engram of whatever kind unless it is the basic on a new chain of similar incidents. But engrams which show no emotion anywhere on the track are suppressed by emotional or feeling shut-offs, late painful emotion or early engrams which simply shut off the pain or emotion in so many words.

A case should be kept "live." There must be variability of emotion. A monotone recounting, which is to say, one which does not vary the engramic tone but merely reduces, is necessary in the basic area at times. But anytime a patient becomes orderly and "well-drilled" and expresses no concern over his engrams as he recounts them, there is late painful emotion to be tapped or early emotional shut-off. Conversely, if the patient is too continuously emotional about all and anything, if he weeps awhile and then laughs hysterically, therapy is being done. But one should be alert for something engramic in the prenatal area which says he has to be "too emotional," which is to say, he has engrams which make him emotional by their command content.

The Tone Scale is very useful and is a good guide. It will be most prominent in reducing post-speech engrams, but will also appear earlier.

Any painful emotion engram can be run. If it is properly reducing and not suppressed elsewhere, it follows the Tone Scale upward to Tone 4.

If the Patient Does Not Work Well on Repeater Technique

If, when the patient repeats a line the auditor has given him, the patient does not move to an incident, three things can be wrong: first, the patient cannot move on the track; second, the phrase may be sensibly withheld by the file clerk until such time as it can be cleared; or third, the phrase does not exist as engramic material.

The patient may also have strong "control yourself" engrams which manifest themselves by his snatching control from the auditor, being very bossy or simply refusing cooperation. Repeater Technique, when directed at "control yourself" and "I've got to operate" and allied phrases, can then work.

The usual reason Repeater Technique does not work is that the patient is in a holder. If he is returned but does not shift on the track when Repeater Technique is given him, use Repeater Technique on the holders.

Remember that a "feeling" shut-off can deny all somatics so that the patient does not feel them. If the patient seems insensible to trouble on the track, be sure that he has a feeling shut-off.

A large emotional charge may also inhibit Repeater Technique.

The somatic strip does not go well into emotional charges (painful emotion engrams) and Repeater Technique is therefore indicated.

If Repeater Technique does not work, although it is seldom necessary, one may request the patient to imagine "the worst thing that could happen to a baby" and so forth, and from his conversation may be garnered new phrases for repeater work which will take the patient into an engram.

SINGLE WORD TECHNIQUE

Words as well as engrams exist in chains. There is always a first time for the recording of each word in a person's life. The whole common language may lie within the engram bank. The possible combinations of that common language may well approach infinity. The ways various denyers, bouncers, et al., can be phrased are always beyond count.

Two "happy" facts exist, however, to reduce the auditor's labors. First, the dramatis personae of his engrams are at this date aberrated. Each aberree has standard dramatizations which he repeats over and over in restimulative situations. The reaction, for instance, of the father to the mother is repetitious: if he utters a set of phrases in one engramic situation, he will utter it in subsequent similar situations. If the mother, for example, has an accusative attitude toward the father, then that attitude will be expressed in certain terms and these terms will appear in engram after engram. The second fact is that where the father or mother is abusive to the other, the other will eventually begin to suffer contagion of aberration and will repeat the other's phrases. In a first-born child, where parental brutality is present, one can observe the parents through the engrams of the patient and see one or the other gradually take up the other's phrases either to worry about themselves or to re-deliver them. All this tends to make the engrams appear in chains of incidents, each incident much like the next. When one has the basic on each type of chain, the subsequent incidents on that chain are sufficiently similar to permit many incidents to be reduced or erased immediately after the first is found. The *first* incident on the chain, the basic for that chain, holds the others more or less in place and out of sight; therefore, the basic of the chain is the goal.

Each word in the bank can be discovered to have been delivered to the bank for the first time. Words also reduce in chains with the virtue that each subsequent appearance of the word in the bank locates automatically a new engram which, of course, is reduced or erased as soon as it is contacted or as soon as its basic can be located.

Single word technique is very valuable and useful. It is a special kind of Repeater Technique. On most patients, the repetition, by themselves, of one word will cause the associated words to suggest themselves. Thus, one asks the patient to repeat and return on the word *forget.* He starts repeating the word *forget* and shortly has an associated set of words making a phrase such as "You can never forget me." Here we have a phrase in an engram and the remainder of the engram can then be run.

When a late engram has had to be contacted to progress a case and yet will not relieve, it is possible to take each word or phrase of that late engram and run it back with Repeater Technique. Thus, the earlier engrams which hold this late engram in place can be located and reduced, and eventually one will have reduced the late engram itself. This, by the way, is a common and useful practice.

There is a law about this: *When any phrase or word in an engram will not reduce, the same phrase or word occurs in an earlier engram.* One may have to discharge late emotion to get the earlier phrase, but ordinarily single word repeater or phrase repeater will attain it.

There are only a few dozens of words necessary to get almost any engram. These would be the key single word repeaters. They are such words as these: *forget, remember, memory, blind, deaf, dumb, see, feel, hear, emotion, pain, fear, terror, afraid, bear, stand, lie, get, come, time, difference, imagination, right, dark, black, deep, up, down, words, corpse, dead, rotten, death, book, read, soul, hell, god, scared, miserable, horrible, past, look, everything, everybody, always, never, everywhere, all, believe, listen, matter, seek, original, present, back, early, beginning, secret, tell, die, found, sympathy, mad, crazy, insane, rid, fight, fist, chest, teeth, jaw, stomach, ache, misery, head, sex, Anglo-Saxon four-letter words of sex and profanity, skin, baby, it, curtain, shell, barrier, wall, think, thought, slippery, confused, mixed, smart, poor, little, sick, life, father, mother, familiar names of parents and any others of household during prenatal and childhood period, money, food, tears, no, world, excuse, stop, laugh, hate, jealous, shame, ashamed, coward,* etc.

Bouncers, denyers, holders, groupers, misdirectors, et al., each have their common single words and these are few.

The bouncer would contain: *out, up, return, go, late, later,* etc.

The holder would contain: *catch, caught, trap, trapped, stop, lie, sit, stay, can't, stuck, fixed, hold, let, lock, locked, come,* etc.

The grouper would contain: *time, together, once, difference,* etc.

The single word technique shines nowhere brighter than in the Junior case, where the patient carries the name of one or another parent or grandparent. By clearing out the patient's name from the prenatal engrams (where it is applied to another person, but misinterpreted by the patient as himself) the patient can regain his own definition and valence. Always use the patient's first name and last name (separately) as repeater, Junior or not.

If the engram bank is blank on a phrase, it probably is not blank on a common word. Any *small* dictionary will provide an ample fund for single word technique. Use also any list of familiar first names, male and female, and you may discover allies or lovers not otherwise contactable.

The painful emotion engram sometimes yields slowly by simply directing the somatic strip to it. Sometimes the patient finds it difficult to approach an overcharged area. Single word technique using the name of the ally, if known, or words of sympathy, endearment, death, rejection or farewell and the love name of the patient as a child, in particular, will often yield swift results.

By the way, in using Repeater Technique, word or phrase, the auditor *must* not stir the case up too much. Get what shows and reduce that. Reduce the somatic the person manifests when he goes into reverie and always try to find it for a while, even if you don't succeed. If you stir up something en route down a chain which won't reduce, mark it to be reduced when you have the basic.

Using single word technique one often obtains phrases which would otherwise remain hidden, but which come into view when the key word is tapped. Using "hear" as a single word, for instance, the following phrases came to light which had thoroughly impeded the progress of the case. No effort was being made to contact such an engram in the prenatal area. Indeed, the "fight" chain had never been suspected since the patient had never dramatized it; and because such a violent prenatal fight chain existed, the fact that his parents fought violently in the home was utterly struck from the standard banks so that he would have denied such a thing with shocked surprise had it been suggested. The somatic was unusually severe, caused by the father kneeling on the mother and choking her.

Patient repeated "hear" several times, the auditor asking him to return to an incident containing that word. The patient continued to repeat and then suddenly sank into a stupor when he reached the prenatal area. He remained in this boil-off for about thirty minutes and then, the auditor rousing him occasionally to make him repeat the word "hear," manifested a strong somatic. "Hear" became "Stay here!" The somatic became stronger and "Stay here" was repeated until the patient could move freely on the track through the engram. He contacted his father's voice and was most reluctant to carry on with the engram, due to its intense emotional violence. Coaxed and edged into it by the auditor, the engram was recounted:

> FATHER: "Stay here! Stay down, damn you, you bitch! I'm going to kill you this time. I said I would and I will. Take that! (*Intensified somatic as his knee ground into the mother's abdomen.*) You better start screaming. Go on, scream for mercy! Why don't you break down? Don't worry, you will! You'll be blubbering around here, screaming for mercy! The louder you scream the worse you'll get. That's what I want to hear! I'm a punk kid, am I? You're the punk kid! I could finish you now but I'm not going to! (*Auditor suddenly has trouble, patient taking last phrase literally and stopping his recounting; auditor starts him again.*) This is just a sample. There's a lot more than that where it came from! I hope it hurts! I hope it makes you cry! You say a word to anybody and

I'll kill you in earnest! (*Patient now running ahead with such an emotional surge that commands are less active on him. This command to remain quiet disregarded.*) I'm going to bust your face in. You don't know what it is to be hurt! (*Somatic lessened by removal of the knee.*) I know what I'm going to do to you now! I'm going to punish you! I'm going to punish you and God is going to punish you! I'm going to rape you! I'm going to stick it into you and tear you! When I tell you to do something, you've got to do it! Get up on the bed! Lie down! Lie still! (*Crack of bones as she is struck in the face with a fist. Blood pressure coming up and hurting baby.*) Lie still! You'll always be here! I'm going to finish this! You're unclean! You are dirty and diseased! God's punished you and now I'm going to punish you! (*Coitus somatic begins, very violent, further injuring child.*) You've got something terrible in your past. You think you've got to be mean to me! You try to make me feel like nothing! You're the one that's nothing! Take it, take it!" (*String of sexual banalities screamed for about five minutes.*)

The patient recounted this three times and it erased. It was basic-basic! Three days after conception, as nearly as could be judged by the subsequent days to the missed period. It threw into view almost all the other important data in the case, which then resolved and was Cleared.*

*Apropos of this text, it crossed the "fight chain" with the "coitus chain," occluding both. Wherever this engram originated or where the engrams which are compounded into it came from is, of course, a matter of antiquity. This was home conduct for Papa, a character confirmed by the fact that both his wife and child were almost psychotic. Papa was not "psychotic." He was a "bold, forceful" and "forthright" man, president of a bank and renowned for his hardheadedness. The son was a drunkard, a soapbox atheist, and negated against everything his father represented, including money. The son, while still in therapy, incautiously told his father of this engram and the father raved wildly against Dianetics for two days and then came down with "rheumatic fever," in which state he sent for the auditor in the case to Clear him, which was done. Both cases were sonic shut-offs, pain and emotion shut-offs.

The single word might have landed the patient on some other of the "hears" in the case. In this event it would be necessary to pick it up at its earliest moment or the remainder of the engram might not erase or reduce.

The word "hear" might also have landed the patient later on the track, in which case the engrams would have had to have been traced back earlier until one was found which would erase, reducing each one as it was encountered until the earliest was reached when all would erase.

In using single word repeater as in phrase repeater, the auditor should not permit a rapid, unmeaning repetition, but a slow repeat, the auditor requesting the somatic strip to return the while and asking the patient to contact anything else which might associate with the word.

> CAUTION: If the patient is not moving on the track, do not give him repeater words or phrases at random as these will pile up engrams where the patient is stuck. Use only efforts to get the patient moving on the track by discovering and reducing the phrase that is holding him.

> CAUTION: Basic-basic does not always have words in it, often being only painful and accompanied with womb sounds. It will, nevertheless, hold everything in place by its perceptics.

SPECIAL CLASSES OF COMMANDS

There are several distinct classes of commands. They are outlined here for ready reference with some samples of each.

Aberrative commands can contain anything. The auditor does not much concern himself with them. Refer back to our young man and the coat in Book Two and there we find, in the guise of hypnotic commands, some idea of what aberrative commands are. "I am a jub-jub bird," "I can't whistle Dixie," "The world is all against me," "I hate policemen," "I am the ugliest person in the world," "You haven't any feet," "The Lord is going to punish me," "I always have to play with my thing," may be very interesting to the patient and even amusing to the auditor and may have caused a considerable amount of trouble in the patient's life. Where Dianetic therapy is concerned, these all come up in due course. Looking for a specific aberration or a specific somatic is sometimes of interest and sometimes of some use, but it is not usually important. These aberrative commands may contain enough data to make the patient a raving zealot, a paranoid or a catfish, but they are nothing to the auditor. They come up in due course. Working on them or about them is secondary and less.

The primary business of the auditor in any case is to keep the patient moving on the track, keep his somatic strip free to come and go and *reduce engrams*. The moment the patient acts as though or responds as though he was not moving, or the moment the file clerk will not give forth data, then something is wrong and that something has to do with a few classes of phrase: there are thousands of such phrases contained in engrams, variously worded, but only five classes.

DENYERS

"Leave me alone," which means, literally, that he must leave the incident alone.

"I can't tell" means he can't tell you this engram.

"It's hard to tell" means it is *hard* to tell.

"I don't want to know" means he has no desire to know this engram.

"Forget it" is the classic of the sub-class of denyer, the forgetter mechanism. When the engram simply won't come to view, but there is a somatic or a muscle twitch, send the somatic strip to the denyer. It is often "Forget it" or "Can't remember" as a part of the engram. "I don't know what's going on" may be Mama telling Papa something, but the preclear's analyzer, impinged, then doesn't know what's going on.

"It's beyond me" means he is right there, but he thinks he isn't.

"Hold onto this, it's your life!" makes the engram "vital" to existence.

"It can't be reached," "I can't get in there," "Nobody must know," "It's a secret," "If anybody found out, I'd die," "Don't talk" and thousands more.

HOLDERS

The holder is the most frequent and the most used since whenever the preclear can't shift on the track or come to present, he is in a holder. A holder combined with a denyer will still hold: if it can't be found, look for the denyer first, then the holder.

"I'm stuck" is the classic phrase.

"That fixed it" is another.

"I'm caught" doesn't mean to the preclear what Mama meant when she said it. It may mean to her that she is pregnant, but it tells the preclear he is caught on the track.

"Don't move," "Sit there until I tell you to move," "Stop and think." (On this last phrase, when it is uttered on a first recounting, the auditor may have to start him going again, for he does just that: he stops and thinks and he would stop there and think for some time. The auditor will see this strange obedience to this literal nonsense as he works a case.)

And thousands more. Any way words literally understood can stop a person or keep him from moving.

BOUNCERS

The bouncer could best be demonstrated by a curve. The preclear goes back into prenatal and then finds himself at ten years of age or even present time. That's a bouncer at work. He goes early on the time track: it says come back up.

When the preclear can't seem to get earlier, there is a bouncer ejecting him from an engram. Get a comment from him on what's happening. Take the comment or some phrase which would be a bouncer and use Repeater Technique until he settles back down on the engram. If he contacts it easily, it won't bounce him again.

"Get out" is the classic bouncer. The patient usually goes toward present time.

"Can't go back at this point" may mean Mama has decided she will have to have the baby after all or finish the abortion, but to the preclear it means he must move on up the time track or that he can't get any earlier period.

"Get up there."

"Run a mile." ("Beat it" would not be a bouncer; it would mean the preclear should beat the engram.)

"I must go far, far away," so he does.

"I'm growing up," "Blow you higher than a kite," "Batter up."

And thousands more.

GROUPERS

The grouper is the nastiest of all types of command. It can be so variously worded and its effect is so serious on the time track that the whole track can roll up into a ball and all incidents then appear to be in the same place.

This is apparent as soon as the preclear hits one. The grouper will not be discovered easily. But it will settle out as the case progresses and the case can be worked with a grouper in restimulation.

"I have no time" and "Nothing makes any difference" are the classic groupers.

"Everything comes in on me at once" means just that.

"They're all in there together," "Screwed up," "Balled up," "It's *all* right here."

"You can remember all this in present time" (a serious auditor error if he uses this to a suggestible patient, for it will gloriously foul a case).

"You associate everything."

"I am tangled up," "Jam everything in there at once," "There's no time," and thousands more.

MISDIRECTORS

This is an insidious character, the misdirector. When it appears in an engram, the patient goes in wrong directions, to wrong places, etc.

"You're doing it all backwards."

"All up now" is a grouper and a misdirector.

"Always throwing it up to me" puts the preclear up the track some distance and from there he tries to pick up engrams.

"You can't go down" is partly bouncer, partly misdirector.

"We can't get to the bottom of this" keeps him off from basic-basic.

"You can start over again" keeps him from finishing the recounting, whereupon he goes back to the beginning of the engram instead of running it.

"Can't go through that again" keeps him from recounting.

"I can't tell you how it began" keeps him starting his engrams in the middle and they will not then reduce. There are many such phrases.

"Let's settle down" and all "settlings" make him drift backwards down the track.

"I am coming down with a cold" puts the aberree in a common cold engram. This can be counted upon to make every cold much worse.

"Come back here" is really a *call back*, but it directs him away from where he should be. A patient who reaches present time with difficulty and then begins to go back has a "Come back here" or a "Settle down."

"Down and out" misdirects him not only away from present time, but to the bottom of the track and off it. This is a misdirector and a derailer all at once.

"Can't get past me" is a misdirector on the order of a reverser.

"You don't know down from up" is the classic phrase.

"I'm all turned around."

A special case is the *derailer* which "throws him off the track" and makes him lose touch with his time track. This is a very serious phrase since it can make a schizophrenic and something of this sort is always to be found in schizophrenia. Some of its phrases throw him into other valences which have no proper track, some merely remove time, some throw him bodily out of time.

"I don't have any time" is a derailer as well as a grouper.

"I'm beside myself" means that he is now two people, one beside the other.

"I'll have to pretend I am somebody else" is a key phrase to identity confusion.

"You're behind the times" and many more.

There is another special case of the misdirector. The auditor says to go to "present time" and the file clerk throws out a phrase with "present" in it. It does not matter if the "present" in the phrase was a Christmas present; if it is in the prenatal area, the preclear goes there, ignoring what the auditor meant.

"That's all at present," is a vicious phrase, putting everything in present time.

"It's a lovely present."

And others. "Now" is sometimes confused with present time but not often. The auditor should not say, "Come to now," because if he did, he would find more "nows" than he could comfortably handle. "Present" is a rarer engramic word and is therefore used. "Now" appears too frequently.

SUMMARY

Several severely aberrated persons who had little memory of the past have been found to be entirely off their time tracks, regressed into the prenatal area and stuck when the case was entered. As far as their wits were concerned, they had only a few months of past from where they were back to conception. And yet these people had managed somehow to function as normals.

Emotional charges usually hold the person off his track and, indeed, are the only things which give these engram commands any power according to current findings.

DIFFERENCES

There arc two axioms about mind function with which the auditor should be familiar.

I. THE MIND PERCEIVES, POSES AND RESOLVES PROBLEMS RELATING TO SURVIVAL.

II. THE ANALYTICAL MIND COMPUTES IN DIFFERENCES. THE REACTIVE MIND COMPUTES IN IDENTITIES.

The first axiom is of interest to the auditor in his work because with it he can clearly establish whether or not he is confronting a rational reaction. The seven-year-old girl who shudders because a man kisses her is not computing; she is reacting to an engram since at seven she should see nothing wrong in a kiss, not even a passionate one. There must have been an earlier experience, possibly prenatal, which made men or kissing very bad. All departures from optimum rationality are useful in locating engrams, all unreasonable fears and so forth are grist to the auditor's mill. The auditor, with the above law, should study as well, the Equation of the Optimum Solution. Any departure from optimum is suspect. While he cares little about aberrations, at times a case will stall or seem to have no engrams. He then can observe the conduct of his patient and his patient's reactions to life in order to gain data.

The second law is Dianetics' contribution to *logic.* In the philosophic text this is more fully entered. Aristotle's pendulum and his two-valued logic were abandoned, not because of any dislike of Aristotle, but because broader yardsticks were needed. One of these yardsticks was the spectrum principle, whereby gradations from zero to infinity and infinity to infinity were used, and Absolutes were considered utterly unobtainable for scientific purposes.

In the second axiom, the mind can be conceived to recognize differences very broadly and accurately in its nearest approach to complete rationality and then, as it falls away from rationality, to perceive less and less difference until at last it achieves a near approach to utter inability to compute any difference in time, space or thought, and so can be considered completely insane. When this follows one thought only, such as a sweeping statement that "All cats are the same," it is either careless or insane since all cats are not the same, even two cats who look, act and sound alike. One could say, "Cats are pretty much the same," and still be dealing with rather irrational thought. Or one could recognize that there was a species *Felis domesticus*, but that within it cats were decidedly different, not only from breed to breed, but cat to cat. That would be rationality, not because one used Latin, but because he could tell the difference among cats. The fear of cats has as its source an engram which usually does not include more than one cat and that is a very specific cat of a specific breed with a certain (or perhaps uncertain) personality. The preclear who is afraid of all cats is actually afraid of one cat and a cat which is most likely dead these many years at that. Thus as we swing from complete rationality down to irrationality, there is a narrowing of differences until they nearly vanish and become similarities and identities.

Aristotle's syllogism, in which two things equal to the same thing are equal to each other, simply does not begin to work in logic. Logic is not arithmetic, which is an artificial thing Man invented and which works. To handle a problem in logic the mind flutters through an enormous mass of data and computes with dozens and even hundreds of variables. It does not, and never did, think on the basis that two things equal to the same thing are equal to each other, except when employing mathematics it had conceived, the better to resolve abstract problems. It is an abstract truth that two and two equal four. Two what and two what equal four? There is no scale made, no yardstick or caliper or microscope manufactured, which would justify the actuality, for instance, that two apples plus two apples *equal* four apples. Two apples and two apples are four apples now if they are the same apples. They would not equal four other apples by any growth or manufacturing process ever imagined. Man is content to take approximations and call them, loosely, exactitudes. There is no Absolute anything save in abstract terms set up by the mind to work out exterior problems and achieve approximations. This may seem to be a stretched conception, but it is not. The mathematician is very well aware that he is working with digit and analog approximations set up into systems which were not necessarily here before Man came and will not necessarily be here after he is gone. Logic, even the simple logic of wondering about the wisdom of going shopping at ten, is handling numerous variables, indefinites and approximations. Mathematics can be invented by the carload lot. There is no actual Absolute, there is only a near approach. Our grammarians alone, much behind the times, insist, probably in memory of the metaphysician, on Absolute Reality and Truth.

This is here set down partly because it may be of interest to some, but mainly because the auditor must realize that he has an accurate measuring stick for sanity. *Sanity is the ability to tell differences.* The better one can tell differences, no matter how minute, and know the width of those differences, the more rational he is. *The less one can tell differences and the closer one comes to thinking in identities (A = A), the less sane he is.*

A man says, "I don't like dogs!" Spot it, auditor: he has an engram about one or two dogs. A girl says, "All men are alike!" Spot it, auditor: here's a *real* aberree. "Mountains are so terrible!" "Jewelers never go anyplace!" "I hate women!" Spot them: those are engrams right out in broad daylight.

Those engrams which inhibit the analytical mind in differentiating are those engrams which most seriously inhibit thinking.

"You can't tell the difference," is a common engram. "There is no difference," "Nothing will ever make any difference to me again," "People are all bad," "Everybody hates me." This is insanity bait, as the auditors say, and puts a man "spin-bin bound."

There is another class of identity-thought and that is the group which destroys time differentiation. "You don't know when it happened!" is a classic phrase. "I don't know how late it is" and others have a peculiar effect on the mind, for the mind is running on a precision chronometer of its own and the engrams can thoroughly misread the dial. On a conscious level one goes along fairly well on analytical time. The engrams slide around back and forth according to when they are keyed-in or restimulated. An engram may underlie today's action which belonged forty years ago on the time track and should be back there. It is not remarks about time difference so much that aberrate; it is the untimed character of engrams. Time is the Great Charlatan: it heals nothing, it only changes the environmental aspects and a man's associates. The engram of ten years ago, with all its painful emotion, may be encysted and "forgotten," but it is right there, ready to force action if restimulated today.

The reactive mind runs on a dime store wristwatch; the analytical mind runs on a battery of counterchecking chronometers of which a liner could be proud. The cells think that wristwatch is a pretty fair gimmick–and it was, it was, back there in the days when Man's ancestor was washed in by the waves and managed to cling to the sand.

Thus, a primary test for aberration is similarity and identity, the primary test for rationality is differentiation and the minuteness or largeness with which it can be done.

"Men are all alike," she says. And they are too! To her. Poor thing. Like the fellow who raped her when she was a kid, like her detested father who said it.

Relative Importances and "Believe" and "Can't Believe"

The auditor will find himself confronted with two arch enemies in "you must believe it" and "I can't believe."

The mind has its own equilibrium and ability and it is aided no more by engrams than an adding machine is aided by a held-down 7.* One of the most important functions of the mind is the computing of the relative importances of data.

In discovering and conducting research on Dianetics, for instance, there were billions of data about the mind accumulated throughout the last few thousand years. Now, with a six-foot rear vision mirror, we can look back and see that here and there people had expressed opinions or turned up unevaluated facts which are now data in some of the axioms of Dianetics or parts of its discoveries. These facts existed in the past, some exist now in Dianetics, but with a tremendous difference: they are evaluated. *Evaluation* of the data for its importance was vital before the information was of value. Dr. Sententious might have written in 1200 A.D. that he believed actual demons did not exist in the mind; Goodwife Sofie in 1782 was heard to say that she was certain that prenatal influence had warped many a life; Dr. Zamba might have written in 1846 that a hypnotized patient could be told he was crazy and that he would thereafter act crazy. Dr. Sententious might have said *also* that angels, not demons, caused mental illness because the patient had been evil; Goodwife Sofie also might have said that punk water poultices cured "ravings"; Dr. Zamba might also have declared that hypnotized patients needed only a few

*(Or a 5, as in the recent case at Harvard where a spot of solder held down 5 in an electronic computer, much to the dismay of the gentlemen who depended upon it for answers.)

more positive suggestions to make them well and strong. In short, for every datum which approached truth, there were billions which were untrue. The missing part of each datum was a scientific evaluation of its importance to the solution. The selection of a few special drops of water from an ocean of unspecial drops is impossible. The problem of discovering true data could be resolved only by jettisoning all former evaluations of humanity and the human mind and all "facts" and opinions of whatever kind and starting fresh, evolving the entire science from a new highest common denominator. (And it is true that Dianetics borrowed nothing, but was first discovered and organized; only after the organization was completed and a technique evolved was it compared to existing information.)

The point here is that monotone importance in a class of facts leads to nothing but the most cluttered confusion. Here is evaluation: opinions are nothing, authority is useless, data is secondary: establishment of relative importance is the key. Given the world and the stars as a laboratory and a mind to compute the relative importance of what it perceives, and no problems can remain unsolved. Given masses of data with monotone evaluation and one has something which may be pretty but isn't useful.

The stunned look of fresh-caught ensigns of the Navy when they first see in the metal the things about which they have so laboriously read is a testimony to more than the faulty educational system currently employed: the system seeks to train something which is perfect, the memory; it aligns little or nothing with purpose or use and ignores the necessity of personal evaluation of all data, both as to need for it and its use. The stunned look comes from the overwhelming recognition that whereas they have thousands of data about what they see, they do not know whether it is more important to read the chronometer when they take a sextant sight or use only blue ink in writing a logbook. These gentlemen have been wronged educationally, not because they have not been given thousands of data relative to ships, but because they have not been told the relative importance of each datum and have not experienced that importance. They know more facts than the less educated, but they know less about factual relation.

More pertinent to the auditor, there are two species of engramic commands which give monotone evaluation to data. The persons who have either of these as a major content in the engram bank will be similarly aberrated even if each manifests the aberration with opposite polarity.

Every now and then some unfortunate auditor finds a "Can't believe it" on his hands. This case is extremely trying. Under this heading come the "I doubt it," the "I can't be sure" and the "I don't know" cases.

Such a case is easy to spot, for when he first comes into therapy he begins by doubting Dianetics, the auditor, himself, the furniture and his mother's virginity. The chronic doubter is not an easy case because he cannot believe his own data. The analyzer has a built-in judge which takes in data, weighs it and judges it right, wrong or maybe. The engramic doubter has a "held-down 7" to the effect that he has to doubt everything, something much different from judging. He is challenged to doubt. He must doubt. If to doubt is divine, then the god is certainly Moloch. He doubts without inspecting, he inspects the most precise evidence, and he still doubts.

The auditor will return this patient to a somatic which tears half his head off, which is confirmed by scars, which is confirmed by aberration, and which is doubted as an incident.

The way to handle this case is to take his pat phrases and feed them to him in reverie or out of reverie with Repeater Technique. Make him go over and over them, sending his somatic strip back to them. Shortly a release of the phrase will take place. Feed all doubter phrases which the patient has used in this manner. Then continue the case. The object is not to make him a believer, but to place him in a situation where he can evaluate his own data. Don't argue with him about Dianetics: arguing against engrams is senseless since the engrams themselves are senseless.

In ten or twenty hours of therapy, such a patient will begin to face reality enough so that he no longer doubts the sun shines, doubts the auditor or doubts that he had a past of some sort. He is only difficult because he requires these extra hours of work. He is usually, by the way, very aberrated.

The "Can't believe it" finds difficulty in evaluation because he has difficulty giving credence to any fact more than any other fact: this produces an inability to compute relative importances among data with the result that he may be as concerned with the shade of his superior's tie as with the marriage he himself is about to undertake. Similarly, the "You must believe it" case finds difficulty in differentiating among importances of various data and may hold equally firmly the idea that paper is made from trees and that he is about to be fired. Both cases "worry," which is to say, they are unable to compute well.

Rational computation depends upon the *personal* computation of the relative importances of various data. Reactive "computation" deals exclusively with the equation that widely different objects or events are similar or equal. The former is sanity, the latter is insanity.

The "Must believe it" case will present a confused reactive bank, for the bank embraces the most unlikely differences as close similarities. The "Must believe it" engram command can dictate that one person, a class of persons, or everyone must be believed, no matter what is written or said. The auditor, returning the patient, will find major aberrations held in place by a lock containing only conversation.

When father is the actual source and is an ally of the patient, the auditor will discover that almost everything father said was accepted *literally* and unquestioningly by his child. The father may not have been aware of having established this "Must believe it" condition and he may even be a jocular man, given to jokes. Every joke will be found to be literally accepted unless the father carefully labeled it a joke, which meant it must not be literally accepted. One case folder is to hand here where father was the source of "Must believe": one day the father took his daughter, three years of age, down to the seacoast and, through the fog, pointed to a lighthouse. The lighthouse gave an eerie aspect in the foggy night. "That's Mr. Billingsly's place," said the father, meaning that Billingsly, the lighthouse keeper, lived there. The child nodded faithfully, if a little frightened, for "Mr. Billingsly" threw around a mane of hair–shadows–glared to seaward with one eye sweeping the water and stood a hundred feet tall and "Mr. Billingsly" let out moans which sounded quite ferocious. His "place" was a ledge of rock. As a preclear twenty years later, the daughter was discovered to be frightened of any low moaning sound. The auditor patiently traced down the source and found, much to the delight of himself and the daughter, "Mr. Billingsly." Vast quantities of aberration, peculiar conceptions and strange notions were found to derive from casual statements the father had made. Being skilled in his task, the auditor did not bother to try to locate and erase everything the father had said, a task which would have taken years and years: he located, instead, the prenatal "You must believe me" and its engramic locks, and all the non-engramic locks, of course, disappeared and were automatically re-evaluated as experienced data rather than "held-down 7s." Of course, there is always much more wrong with a case than a mere "You must believe me," but the change of viewpoint which the patient experienced immediately afterwards was startling: she was now at liberty to evaluate her father's data, which she had not been before.

Because they teach in terms of altitude* and Authority, educational institutions themselves form a social "You must believe it" aberration. It is impossible to reduce an entire university education, even if it sometimes appears desirable, but by addressing the moments when the patient was hammered into *believing* or accepting school, from kindergarten forward, many a fact-clogged mind can again be made facile which was not so before; for the facts will be re-evaluated automatically by the mind for importances, not accepted on monotone evaluation as is the case in "formal education."

The "Can't believe it" is a subject so weary and dreary to the auditor that he may find himself, after a few finished cases, running adroitly away from one. The "I don't know" and the "I can't be sure" cases are not as bad as the "I can't believe it." The prize case in difficulty

* By *altitude* is meant a difference of level of prestige – one on a higher altitude carries conviction to one on a lower altitude merely because of altitude. The auditor may find himself unable to gain sufficient *altitude* with some patients to work them smoothly and he may have so much altitude with others that they believe everything he says. When he has too little altitude, he is not believed; when he has too much, he is believed too well.

in Dianetics is a patient who is a Junior named after either father or mother, who has not only shut-down pain, emotion, visio and sonic recall, but also dub-in for them on a false basis, with a lie factory working full blast, who is uncooperative and who is a "Can't believe it."

Monotone evaluation hinders the "Can't believe it's" acceptance of all facts. Any case may have a few "Can't believe its." But some cases are so thoroughly aberrated by the phrase that they disbelieve not only reality, but also their own existence.

The mind has a "built-in doubter" which, unhindered by engrams, rapidly sorts out importances and, by their weights, resolves problems and arrives at conclusions. The rational mind applies itself to data presented, compares it to experience, evaluates its veracity and then assigns it relative importance in the scheme of things. This is done by a Clear with a rapidity which sometimes requires the splitting of seconds. By a normal, the time required is extremely variable and the conclusions are more apt to be referred to another's opinion or compared to Authority rather than to personal experience. That is the fundamental effect of contemporary education which, through no particular fault of its own and despite every effort it has made to free itself, yet through lack of tools, is forced to follow scholastic methods. These, by contagion of aberration, persist against all efforts of advanced educators. The normal is taught on one hand to *believe* or else he'll fail and on the other to *disbelieve* as a scientific necessity: belief and disbelief cannot be taught, they must be personally computed. If a mind could be likened to a general served by his own staff, it could be seen to have a G-2 which, as a combat intelligence center, collected facts, weighted them for importance and formed an estimate of a situation or the value of a conclusion. As the intelligence officer would fail if he had a signed order to disbelieve everything, so does the mind fail which has a reactive command to disbelieve. Certainly a military organization would lose to every puny enemy if it had, conversely, a command to believe everything, and a man will fail if he has a reactive mind order to believe all information in the world around him.

The *believe* and *disbelieve* engrams present different manifestations, and while one cannot be said to be either more or less aberrative than the other, it is certain that the disbelieve engram, by and large, seems to make the less sociable man.

Disbelief occurs in various degrees, of course. There is, for instance, a social disbelief engram which promotes a class of literature which is as insincere as it is unwitty. Insincerity, shame of emotional demonstration, fear of praising may stem from other things than merely a disbelief engram, but a disbelief engram is most certainly present in the majority of such cases.

The auditor will find, when he is trying to enter a very strong "Can't believe it" case, that experience is disbelieved, the auditor is disbelieved, hope of results is disbelieved and that the most ridiculous and unreasonable insults and arguments may be presented. The patient may squirm in a veritable snake pit of somatics and still disbelieve that he is re-experiencing anything.

It is a sadly chronic fact that an aberree has a certain set of clichés from out of his engram bank. He will repeat these clichés for all occasions and circumstances. Mother, having an engram bank of her own and father having his, will be found to be uttering pretty much the same sort of statement time after time. These are dramatizations. One of the parents may have had an "I don't know" ready to precede everything he or she said, which makes a whole "stack" of "I don't knows" in the engram bank which much undermines understanding.

In the same way, "You must believe!" or "You can't believe!" may become "stacked" in the engram bank. Once one has heard a few engrams from a patient, he knows he will have many, many more similar engrams from that source. Once an auditor has listened to the personnel in the patient's engram bank for a very short time, he knows pretty much what he will have in many, many more engrams. Hence, any phrase is liable to be much repeated in the engram bank, with varying somatics and accompanying perceptics. If mother is troubled with high blood pressure and it is raised by father–to the intense discomfort of the child and a degree which often produces a later migraine headache–she is apt to utter, "I can't believe you would treat me this way." Privately, she must have been hard to convince (one doesn't convince much against engramic "reasoning"), for he treated her this way about every three days, and every three days she was saying, "I can't believe you" or "I can't believe you would do this to me" or "I can't believe anything you say" or some such thing.

The "Can't believe" is apt to be rather hostile since "Can't believe" is often hostile conversation. "You've got to believe me" is more apt to be a pleading or whining sort of an engram. "Believe what I tell you, goddamn it," is, however, fully as hostile as an auditor might expect.

An auditor who finds a case intensely and unreasonably skeptical should expect a "Can't believe" stack in the engram bank. If he finds a patient incapable of holding an opinion of his own, but weather-vaning to each new person or quoting an Authority (all authorities get easily identified with father in the reactive bank), he should suspect a "Must believe" in some form as well as other things. There are many manifestations of either case. The chronic aspect in therapy is that the "Can't believe" suspects his own data so strongly that he alters it continually and the engrams–which, after all, have just one, exact package of content–will not properly reduce; the "Must believe" takes up every engram he hears about as his own and that does *him* little good.

Do not suppose that any case has a standard aspect, however. The language contains many words and combinations of words, and aberrees are not unusual who have the entire basic language and all its idioms securely connected up to some somatic or other. Cases ordinarily contain "Can't believe" and "Must believe" phrases in the same bank. Only when these phrases become top-heavy does the person respond in a set pattern. When the set pattern is of either species of phrase, then the auditor confronts a patient who must have had, at best, a most unhappy life. But either case Clears. They all Clear, even Juniors.

PHYSICAL PAIN AND PAINFUL EMOTION COMMANDS

Besides visio and sonic, another vital recall to therapy is the somatic, which is to say, the physical pain of the incident. Running a physically painful incident without a somatic is worthless.

If physical pain is present, it may come only after considerable "unconsciousness" has been "boiled-off." If the incident contains pain, but the somatic is not turned on, the patient will wriggle his toes and breathe heavily and nervously or he may have jumping muscles. The foot wriggling is an excellent clue to the presence of any somatic turned on or not turned on. Breathing heavily and jumping muscles and various twitches without pain denote two things: either a denyer is in the incident and the content isn't being contacted or, if the preclear is recounting, the somatic may be shut-off in the incident or elsewhere, either earlier by command or late by painful emotion. The patient who wriggles a great deal or who does not wriggle at all is suffering from a pain or emotion shut-off or late painful emotion engrams or both.

There is a whole species of commands which shut off pain and emotion simultaneously: this is because the word "feel" is homonymic. "I can't feel anything" is the standard, but the command varies widely and is worded in a great many ways. The auditor can pick up his own book of these from patients who, describing how they feel or rather, how they don't feel, give them away. "It doesn't hurt" is a class of phrases specifically shutting off pain, a class which includes, of course, such things as "There isn't any pain," etc. Emotion is shut off by a class of phrases which contain the word "emotion" or which specifically (literally translated) shut off emotion.

The auditor should keep a book of all denyers, misdirectors, holders, bouncers and groupers which he discovers, each listed under its own heading. In this way, he adds to material he can use for Repeater Technique when he sees something is wrong with the way the patient is moving on the track. But there are four other classes of phrases which he should also study and list: *shut-offs*, *exaggerators*, *derailers* and *lie factories*. He can also add to his classes.

He will discover enormous numbers of commands in engrams which can accomplish these various aspects. And he should be particularly interested in the pain and emotion *shut-offs* and the *exaggerators*, which is to say, those engramic commands which give the aspect of too much pain and too much emotion. There is no reason to give large numbers of them here. They are quite various, language being language.

Many combinations are possible. A patient can be found to weep over the most trivial post-speech things and yet have few or no somatics. Several things can cause this. Either he had a mother or a father who wept for nine months before he was born, or he has an exaggerator at work which commands that he be emotional about everything: "Too much emotion." In combination with this, he can have something which says he can feel no pain or can't hurt or even can't feel.

A patient who aches and suffers and yet cannot weep would have a reverse set of commands: he has a "no emotion" command early on the track or a long chain of them and yet has commands which dictate pain to excess: "I can't stand the pain," "The pain is too great," "I always feel I'm in agony," etc. "I feel bad," on the other hand, is a shut-off because it says there is something wrong with the mechanism with which he feels and implies disability to feel.

Both pain and emotion can be commanded into exaggeration. But it is a peculiar thing that the body does not manufacture pain to be felt. All pain felt is genuine, even if exaggerated. Imaginary pain is non-existent. A person "imagines" only pain he has actually felt. He cannot imagine pain he has not felt. He may "imagine" pain at some time later than the actual incident, but if he feels pain, no matter how psychotic he is, that pain will be found to exist somewhere on his time track. Scientific tests have been carefully conducted in Dianetics to establish this fact and it is a valuable one. You can test it yourself by asking patients to feel various pains, "imagining them" in present time. They will feel pains for you so long as you ask them to feel pains they have had. Somewhere you will find the patient unable to actually feel the pain he is trying to "imagine." Whether he is aware of it or not, he has had pain wherever he "imagines" it and is simply doing a somatic strip return for you on a minor scale.

This aspect of pain is quite interesting in that many patients have, at one time or another in their lives, pretended to the family or the world that they had a pain. The patient thought, when he asserted this "make-believe" pain, that he was lying. In therapy, the auditor can use these "imaginings," for they lead straight to sympathy engrams and actual injury. Further, these "imaginary" pains are generally displayed to the person or pseudo-person who was the sympathy ally present in the engramic moment. Thus, if a small boy always pretended to his grandmother, and thought he was pretending, that he had a bad hip, it will be discovered eventually that sometime in his early life he hurt that same hip and received sympathy during the engramic moment which is now eclipsed from the analyzer. Patients often feel quite guilty over these pretenses. Sometimes soldiers in the recent war have come home pretending they had been wounded and, when in therapy, are afraid the auditor will find out or give them away to their people. This soldier might not have been wounded in the war, but an engram will be found which contains sympathy for the injury of which he complains. He is asking for sympathy with a colorful story and believes he is telling a lie. Without informing him of this Dianetic discovery, the auditor can often flush into view a sympathy engram which might otherwise have to be arduously hunted down.

"Cry baby" is a phrase against which the preclear will negate in an engram, thus inhibiting tears. It is quite ordinary to find the preclear confusing himself with older brothers and sisters who are in his prenatal life: their jeers, mother's orders and so forth then all register. If the preclear knows of any older children, the auditor should look for them in the engrams of prenatal life, for children are quite active and often bounce up and down on mother's lap or collide with her. Any childish phrases of derision are then not always post-birth.

It has been said during Dianetic research that if one could release all the painful emotion of a lifetime, he would have 90 percent of the clearing done. However, the painful emotion is only a surface manifestation of the physical pain engrams and would not be painful if the physical pain did not co-exist or exist priorly.

When emotion and pain shut-offs exist in a case, the patient is normally tense of muscle and nervous, given to twitching or merely tension. When pain and emotion are exaggerated by commands, one has a highly dramatizing case on his hands.

THE ALLY VERSUS THE ANTAGONIST

It is necessary for the auditor to know the reactive mind's evaluation of importances. Moronic or not, the reactive mind distinguishes violently between friend and foe, about the only piece of differentiation it does.

There is a prime test for an ally. And recall that the ally is a part of sympathy engrams, the things which are most likely to produce psychosomatic illnesses, immaturities and confusion on a grand scale. As long as it can rebel and negate, the reactive mind takes care of the enemies so far as it is able. It can, of course, be twisted by circumstance into the valence of the enemy and so cry havoc and abreact in general if this was a winning valence. But it will not ordinarily use the data of the enemy contained in a contra-survival engram, save to negate against it. When the general tone nears Zone 1, of course, the reactive mind starts picking up and obeying antagonistic commands. Thus, if father is the villain of the piece, an antagonist, father's commands are not the reactively obeyed commands, but the commands the aberree will usually negate against or avoid.

This is not the case, however, with the ally. The ally, the person from whom sympathy came when the patient was ill or injured, is heeded and obeyed since his "purpose" is apparently aligned with the purpose of the individual to survive. If one thing about a person is right, then, according to our moronic little friend, the reactive mind, everything about that person is right, everything that person says and does is right and particularly is right whatever that person said in the engram.

The chronic psychosomatic illness is ordinarily from a sympathy engram. This is quite important, for the sympathy engram will be the last or hardest to reach, being aligned with survival purpose.

A "Must believe" from an ally means that the person *must* believe. A "Must believe" from an antagonist ordinarily brings about a circumstance that the person must *not* believe.

Here, in the ally and the antagonist, we have the age-old tale of the hero and the villain, the heroine and the villainess, Mazda and Ahriman, the cowboy in the white hat and the cowboy in the black. The Hindu trinity is found, as source, in father, mother and unborn baby. But the war of "good and evil" is found as reactive data in the engram bank in the form of the ally and the antagonist.

The very best logic of which the reactive mind is capable is two-valued, white and black, and two-valued logic finds its response only in the reactive bank. And the reactive mind works out all problems in absolutes, bringing about logical monstrosities, for there is the absolute of good, the absolute of evil and the absolute of identity-thought. Any rational computation demonstrates an absolute to be impossible from a standpoint of truth or workability: but the reactive mind never quibbles, it just reacts. It knows a champion when it sees one (it thinks) and it knows a villain (it supposes). The ally, the champion, is everybody who has any characteristic of the ally; and the antagonist, the villain, is everyone who has any characteristics of the antagonist. Further, anything associated with the ally is a champion and everything associated with the antagonist is villainous. If the ally is an aunt, then aunts are good. If the antagonist is a sign painter, then sign painters are all evil. Further, the doilies Auntie crocheted mean that doilies are good and that all lacework is good and that anything on which lacework sits is good and that anything which looks like lacework is good and so on in the *ad absurdum* which only the reactive mind can manage without a qualm. And the signs the painter painted were evil and where they sit is evil and paint is evil and the smell of paint is evil and brushes are evil so hairbrushes are evil so the dresser on which hairbrushes sit is evil and so on.

There is an axiom here which it is well not to slight in working a patient:

> ANY CHRONIC PSYCHOSOMATIC ILLNESS HAS AT ITS SOURCE A SYMPATHY ENGRAM.

And another:

> A REACTIVE MIND WILL NOT PERMIT AN INDIVIDUAL TO BE ABERRATED OR CHRONICALLY PSYCHOSOMATICALLY ILL UNLESS THE ILLNESS HAS SURVIVAL VALUE.

This does not mean that the individual has a power of choice analytically. It does mean that the reactive mind, working quietly and hitherto hidden so well, chooses, on identity computation, physical and mental conditions to match any circumstance even remotely similar to any concept in the engram bank.

There is such a thing as *necessity level.* This rises and keys-out engrams and can key-out the control of the reactive mind itself. Necessity level often rises. The individual can force it to rise analytically whether or not actual cause exists. A person may have no engram about going to the electric chair for murder and yet have an engram about murdering people. Necessity level rises and analytically overwhelms all impulse to kill, for the analyzer knows all about electric chairs. When the necessity level cannot rise, then one is dealing with a low-dynamic individual. An artist, terribly aberrated about his work through the kind efforts of obligingly caustic critics, can yet boost himself by his necessity bootstraps to do another piece of work and damn the aunt who said he gave her too many chins in her portrait and ripped the work to shreds, or damn the critics who said he was too new and his work too swift. Necessity level can soar above the reactive mind by, as the marine sergeant said, "Sheer guts." Given too many current restimulators, used too hard by life, an individual, caught in the dwindling spiral of reactivated engrams, may come at last to a point where he cannot longer remain well. If this is his first serious sag and if the sag is deep, a psychosomatic illness will appear and become more or less chronic and, this is important, it will stem directly from a sympathy engram.

All psychosomatic ills carry with them, if less obvious, aberrative commands which mean that a person suffering from psychosomatic illness, whether he relishes the idea or not, is also suffering from the aberration which is part of the same engram.

If the auditor wants to find the *real* holders, the *real* reasons his case appears to resist getting well, the *real* aberrative factors and illnesses, he will look to the ally or allies, for any case may have many. He will exhaust from them the painful emotion of loss or denial and backtrack immediately to find the underlying engrams.

Remember too that the reactive mind is not bright enough to realize that two sides of the same person are the same person. Hence, we can have Mother-the-white-angel and Mother-the-howling-harridan. As the white angel, she is implicitly followed; as the harridan, she is negated against. Father may be Father-the-beneficent and Father-the-baby-killer. And so with all allies. But only the pure, the absolute, the never changing ally who, resolute and firm, stayed the cold sharp hand of death and placed tenderly in the expiring hand of the wistful child the strong and flaring torch of life (or at least said, "Poor baby, you feel so bad; please don't cry,") is the model, the paragon, the gold-footed idol with free access to the gods. (This was Grandpop: he drank too much and he cheated at cards, but the reactive mind doesn't see it that way because Grandpop hauled baby through pneumonia and was darned sure baby got well: good acts if he hadn't been so melodramatic about it and if he hadn't talked so much while the poor kid was "unconscious.")

Question the patient adroitly about father and mother: if he isn't much disturbed by their deaths (if they are dead) or if he is simply careless of them or if he bares his teeth, they are antagonists; the allies are elsewhere. If the mother and father are indifferently or angrily or propitiatively regarded, be very sure then that the patient had a rough time of it between conception and birth and later; and be sure, if this is the case, that there will be allies in plenty, for the child will have sought them out in every scrape or injury. But you will not find the allies, usually, by mere questions. The reactive mind considers them to be pure gold even if the engrams in which they appear have somatics enough to wreck a person for life. It hides allies. The auditor has to look for them through discharging painful emotion. The death, departure or denial by an ally is a certain painful emotion engram. One way or another, working at it from later painful emotion or earlier physically painful engrams, the ally will eventually uncover and can be entered as memory in the standard banks and erased as illness out of the engram bank.

The solution of chronic psychosomatic ills lies largely in the field of sympathy engrams. These will not erase early, however, for they are the inner bastion behind which the reactive mind crouches and observes the storming of the outer defenses by antagonists. The painful emotion of ally losses masks, at times, not only allies, but antagonists as well. The sympathy engram is not the only source of psychosomatic illness by far, but it is the source of the *chronic* psychosomatic ill.

By the way, nothing in this dissertation about allies should be construed to mean that one should not show love to a child. Observers in the past have jumped at questionable conclusions when they felt that demonstrated affection aberrates a child. Lack of affection may kill him, but the reverse is not true. The only way an ally can aberrate a child *is by talking to and sympathizing with a child who is very ill or "unconscious" from injury*. If he does this, he alloys the child's personality with his own, creates an eventual possibility of psychosomatic illness and aberration and may generally disable the child for life (except for Dianetics, of course). Love a child best and do for him best when he is well. Do anything you please with him when he is well, say what you please. When he is sick or hurt, it is best to, as the bosun said, "Patch him up and keep goddamned quiet!"

TOKENS

The tale of the magic amulet, the lucky talisman, the belief in the charm and the long catalog of fetishes, the objects and mannerisms which one keeps as sakes are the "dearly beloveds" of the reactive mind.

There is nothing wrong with a man keeping llamas in the parlor or wearing purple and green suspenders or rubbing fireplugs for luck, nor is there anything wrong with sighing over a stolen lady's slipper or smoking Pittsburgh stogies. Any *Rights of Man* should provide for such eccentricities. But the auditor can use this data to detect vital information.

In Dianetics, the term *token* is defined to embrace the objects and habits which an individual or society keeps by not knowing they are extensions of an ally.

By identity-thought there are *associative restimulators* for every restimulator in the environment: those things connected with the restimulator. Being blank on the subject, the analytical mind, apprised by physical reaction that a restimulator of something is nearby, then picks up the associative restimulator, but does not select the actual restimulator. (In Book Two, the young man's signal to remove his coat was a touch of the tie: he did not cite the tie in his complaint; the nearest he came to it was the person and clothing of the hypnotic operator. These were *associative restimulators.*)

A restimulator for a contra survival engram might be an electric light; the aberree looks to the shade, the pull chain, the room or the person under the light to be a source of annoyance, and not only does he not know that a restimulator is present, but supposes that the associated objects have some evil in themselves.

The associative restimulator for a contra-survival engram needs no name other than that, *associative restimulator*. The pain is the thing, the things associated in any way with the thing are the thing, are other things, etc., is the reactive equation which fills the world of the aberree full of fear and fills him full of anxiety. Leave a child in a place or a room where he has been unhappy and he may become ill, for he is confronted with some restimulator and he can at best explain, like the adult, his fear in terms of things not rationally connected to the restimulator. This is the mechanism of engramic restimulation.

It is mostly terribly uncomfortable to any aberree who, try as he might, cannot say why he does not like some person or object or locale and who cannot connect any of the three with the actual item which is the restimulator and does not know he has an engram about it. This method of detecting engrams leads nowhere quickly since one cannot select objects, persons or locales and know they are restimulators. They may be only associative restimulators to the actual restimulator item in the environment. (Words contained in engrams, by the way, and any other precise restimulator can "push-button" the aberree into action or apathy if they are used upon him. In words it has to be the exact word; for instance, paint*ed* will not do when paint*er* is in the engram. What is paint*ed*, however, may be an associative restimulator and the aberree may declare he does not like it; that he does not like it does not mean that it will "push his buttons" and make him cough or sigh or get angry or get sick or whatever the engram containing the word dictates he should do.)

The token is a very special kind of restimulator. While the auditor may not find much use for the associative restimulator as applied to contra-survival engrams, he can employ the token as a means of detection to locate allies.

The token is any object, practice or mannerism which one or more allies used. By identity-thought, the ally is survival; anything the ally used or did is, therefore, survival. The valence of the ally is that one most frequently employed by the aberree. While the Clear can shift himself into valences he imagines or beholds at will and convenience and out of them at will and can stabilize in his own at will, the aberree skids around into valences without his knowledge or consent and is most likely to be in any valence but his own. The person who seems to be a different person every time he is met or a different person to each person he meets, with special valences manifesting here and others manifesting there, is shifting into various winning valences; interfered with in his shifts, he goes into secondary valences; if forced into his own valence, he becomes ill. It is understood, of course, that all valences manifest something of himself.

Shifting into ally valences is the fundamental practice of the aberree. He will feel most at ease when his own valence is alloyed to some degree with an ally valence. So long as the ally or the pseudo-ally is not available, the aberree reminds himself of the ally valence with tokens. These tokens are the things the ally possessed, practiced or did.

An aberree will often inextricably associate himself with a pseudo-ally, as in marriage, and then make the astonished discovery that he is not partnered with the optimum ally conduct. (Mother was an ally; mother baked bread. Wife is pseudo-mother, though neither she nor he knows it; wife does not bake bread. Mother frowned on lipstick; wife wears lipstick. Mother gave him his way; wife has a bossy attitude. Wife is pseudo-mother because she has similar voice tones only.) The aberree then reactively and unknowingly attempts to coax wife or partner into the ally valence by assuming that the moment of the sympathy engram is present time–a mechanical shift caused only by the restimulation of the sympathy engram because of voice tones or some such thing–and proceeds to manifest the ghost of the engram illness or injury or operation as a psychosomatic sickness. The computation of the reactive mind is simple–just like Simple Simon–one forces the ally into being by manifesting the somatic with which the ally sympathized. This can also be an effort to turn a partner, in which the reactive mind thinks it has discovered an ambivalent friend-enemy, into the sympathy valence. Wife is cruel. Mother was cruel until the injury, then she was nice. Manifest the injury as a chronic psychosomatic illness and wife will be nice. Actually, wife isn't nicer, so the computation gets stronger, the illness gets stronger, and down into the dizzy dwindling spiral we go. The psychosomatic illness is also a denial of dangerousness, a plea of helplessness–a shade of opossum playing, fear-paralysis: "I'm no menace to you. I'm sick!"

The aberree goes into his own valence of the time of the sympathy engram in his bid for sympathy and his denial of his own dangerousness. The valence of himself, of course, is complicated by the age-tab and somatic of the engram in which he was immature and not well.

The psychosomatic illness is, as well, a token, which is to say, it is a reminder of a time when he once had love and care and was told so. He needs it about as much as he needs to be atom bombed, of course, but this is good, solid reactive mind "survival" and the reactive mind is going to make it so he can survive if it kills him.

This is all mechanical and is actually merely restimulation of an engram, but it is better understood as a low order computation.

In the absence of an ally, and even in the presence of the ally, he uses reactive mimicry. Conscious mimicry is a wonderful way to learn. Reactive mimicry is most alloying to the personality. Reactively, he once had an ally and imitates the ally. Consciously, he may not even recall the ally or the habits of the ally.

The ally, remember, is somebody who has entered the interior world of the mind when the analyzer was shut down by illness or injury or an operation and gave forth sympathy or protection. The ally is part of the sympathy engram. If a child had grandparents he liked and was lucky enough not to be ill around them or be talked to by them in sympathetic terms when he was ill or injured, the grandparents would still be much loved. In Dianetics, an ally is only someone who has offered sympathy or protection in an engram. We don't have to have engrams to be loved or to love: quite the contrary, one is better loved and loves more without engrams.

The token applies, Dianetically, only to the ally and is an object, practice or mannerism similar to an object, practice or mannerism of the ally.

The ally smoked Pittsburgh stogies, so the aberree may smoke Pittsburgh stogies no matter what they do to his throat or his wife. The ally wore bowlers; the lady aberree dotes on riding habits but has never ridden a horse. The ally knitted; the aberree specializes in wearing knit things, or a lady at least makes a pretense of knitting and sometimes wonders why she ever took it up, she is so bad at it. The ally used profanity; the aberree uses the same profanity. The ally wiped his nose on his sleeve and picked his nose; the aberree wipes his nose on a dinner jacket and fiddles with his nostrils.

The token may be a reminder of pure ally or it may be a reminder of the friend side of an ambivalent friend-enemy. And it may be a winning valence that was also ambivalent toward the aberree. The token is never an associative restimulator in the meaning that it reminds of some antagonist, for associative restimulators are abhorred.

The most chronic token, the most constant habit, practice or mannerism of the preclear is a direct arrow to the pure ally. And the pure ally is the one the reactive mind will guard to its highest level of the beset dungeon keep. And that is the target of the auditor. He may have to relieve the majority of the engram bank before he can erase the engram which is most likely to aberrate the individual, to saddle him with strange practices and to make him chronically ill.

Observe your preclear and see what he does and says that are strange to his personality, things he does but does not much seem to enjoy. See what he uses and what his mannerisms are. Among this collection you may, by asking discreet questions, jog an ally into his memory which he had forgotten and, so jogging, reach swiftly toward the sympathy engram in which that ally is contained; or reach toward an emotional discharge, the painful emotion engram of the loss of that ally, his illness or incidents concerning him.

Another but special token is that which stems from a "die if you don't" command. Fathers, for instance, suspicious of paternity, sometimes claim while trouncing or upsetting mothers that they will kill the child if it isn't just like father. This is a very unhappy type of token, to say nothing of being, usually, a bad engram; it can go to the extent of remodeling structure, of making noses long or hair absent; it may compel an aberree into a profession he does not admire and all out of the engramic command that he must be like the parent. As this type of command is usually given before birth, it is often addressed, unknowingly, to a girl, fathers not being gifted ordinarily with clairvoyance; in such a case it will bring about a most remarkable structural change in a woman and form some unusual mannerisms, "ambitions" (like the dog that gets whipped if he doesn't fetch the duck) and some habits which, to say the least, are astonishing. Father, post-birth, to accomplish the reactivation of such an engram, must be quite ambivalent so that the friend-enemy compute comes into being. Not to be like father is to die: to force father into his sympathy-engram self, the reactive mind must manifest the token of illness. Token and likeness are the answer to such a computation. And recall, all such computations are not simple, but are made further complex by the addition of dozens of other engramic computations.

The friend-enemy is rather easy to find as an enemy, not too hard to find as a friend. Standard technique with its repeater and return et al., would in themselves at last locate any engram and erase the bank so that it properly refiles. The use of the token facilitates the auditing.

In the case of the pure ally, the champion of the right, standard technique also at last arrives. But here how smooth the use of the token sometimes makes the road! For the token may be as alarmingly strange as an elephant in a bird cage. It takes a *real* ally to keep some of these odd habits around.

Measure the preclear against his environment and education and his society and profession. See what doesn't seem to belong amid the things he uses, the objects he adores and the mannerisms his friends find so strange. Then find out if he or the spouse knew of anyone who did those things or liked those things.

Do not suppose from all this that our Clear has jettisoned all strange mannerisms. Self-determinism is individuality in the extreme; personality is inherent and, revealed by Clearing, looms up high above the aberree. The engrams compress a man and make him small and afraid. Released, his power comes into play.

The sympathy engram is to a man like a crutch when he has two sturdy legs. But oh, the preclear sobs where he loses old Uncle Goston, whose habit of spitting on the floor, as transplanted, so astonished our preclear's friends and business associates. But the grief is brief, usually the half-hour it takes to run the sympathy engram out. Suddenly the preclear recalls Uncle Goston, recalls a thousand things Uncle Goston and he used to do, for the engram had Uncle Goston occluded and among those missing from the sight of "I". Although it might have said in the engram, "All right, there, there, there, Billy. I'll take care of you. Don't thrash around so. You'll be all right. There, there, there. Poor little fellow. Poor little fellow. What a terrible rash you've got. How feverish. There, there, there, Billy. You'll be all right as long as I am here. I'll take care of my Billy. Go to sleep now. Go to sleep and forget it." And Billy was all the time "unconscious" and never "knew" about it. Afterwards, he got a partner who looked like Uncle Goston (but happened to be a fool), and when bankrupt somehow developed a rash and a chronic cough and got very "feverish" about his business affairs. He took to spitting on the floor no matter where he was and his health got worse and he got worse, but if you had asked him about any uncles before he went into therapy, he would have been very vague.

"Give me a flash reply," says the auditor. "Who used to spit on the floor?"

"Uncle Goston," answers the preclear. "Gosh, that's funny (hawk, spit), I hadn't thought of him for years. He was never around much, though *(not more than ten years constantly, the auditor may discover)*. Don't suppose he's important. Let's take up Mrs. Swishback, that teacher I had..."

"Let's return now to the time Uncle Goston helped you," says the auditor, "The somatic strip will now go back to the time your Uncle Goston helped you."

"I feel like my skin's on fire!" complains the preclear. "This must be...hey, it's my allergy! But I don't see anybody. I don't... Wait, I get an impression of somebody. Somebody... Why, it's Uncle Goston!" *And he runs it and the rash goes away.*

But maybe the auditor had to get a hundred engrams before he got this one. And then the preclear suddenly remembers about him and Uncle Goston and the time – but get on with therapy.

Complete remembering seems to be a synonym for complete sanity. But don't suppose that just because a Clear gets rid of his Uncle Gostons and his habit of spitting on the floor that he will not now indulge in any eccentricity. The difference is, he is not compelled into eccentricity without his consent. Good Lord, what a Cleared mind can think up to keep itself from being bored!

WHAT TO DO IF A CASE STOPS PROGRESSING

Even in the easiest cases there will come times when progress seems to stop. Here is a list of possibilities of why:

1. The preclear is not moving on the track despite appearances, but is being subject to one of the five types of commands which can inhibit his free motion or information. The commonest of these is a holder and the preclear may be found to be in an engram and in a strange valence.

2. There is an emotional or pain shut-off. These can always be detected even at the beginning of a case. The patient's muscles will tremble or twitch when he is in an engram, but he will not feel the somatic: this is inevitably a pain shut-off. Out of therapy the patient may be very tense, his neck muscles in particular may be tight: this is often an emotional shut-off. Either of these conditions can be observed in many aberrees before beginning therapy. If they appear while therapy is in progress, look for pain or emotional shut-offs.
3. There is an exaggerator of emotion and a pain shut-off so that the patient weeps over anything, but wriggles and twists when asked to approach pain. He is feeling emotion without feeling the pain.
4. There is an emotional charge in some area which has not been discharged, but which is ready to discharge. Or, conversely, if you have been trying to get an emotional discharge in a late painful emotion engram and have had no success, there is a feeling shut-off early in the prenatal area.
5. The Auditor's Code has been broken. Change auditors or reduce the moments when the code was broken.
6. There is an emotional upset in the patient's life current with therapy. Question him closely and remove the charge, if possible, of the emotional upset as an engram.
7. The auditor has missed an important point in this book. Study it.

If a Case "Refuses" to Get Well

It has long been a popular idea, if an erroneous fact, that people desire to retain their neuroses. In any case which "resists" therapy, you may be certain that the engrams are resisting, not the patient; do not, therefore, attack the patient but the engrams.

There are many computations which give the appearance of resistance. The commonest of these is the ally computation, which derives from engrams containing allies who seem to plead that the patient is not to rid himself of anything. An ordinary situation is one in which some relative or friend of the mother's is advising the mother against aborting the child. The ally is pleading, "Do not get rid of it!" The preclear knows this person to be a friend of his of the highest order. The preclear may interpret this to mean that he is not to get rid of his engrams.

Another computation is the stupidity of computation, wherein the preclear begins to believe he will be stupid or lacking a mind if he gives up engrams. This stems, for example, from the mother saying she will lose her mind if she loses the child: she calls the child "it." A whole chain of these may appear in a case, giving the preclear the idea that if he parts with any engrams, he will lose his mind. This is the primary reason why past schools believed that the mind was composed of neuroses instead of an inherent personality. The engrams, even though unknown, appeared very valuable, which they are not–none of them.

Yet another computation is one of secrecy. It seems to the preclear that his life depends upon holding some secret. This is common in a case where the mother has had a lover. Mother and the lover both enjoin secrecy.

The preclear, obeying engramic commands, believes that he has much to lose if he tells this secret, even though those who enjoined it were not even aware that he was present or, if they knew, that he was "listening." One secrecy computation stems from the mother's fearing to tell the father that she is pregnant: if the mother is an ally of the child, then the child will be extremely tenacious of this type of engram.

All cases have one or more computations which inhibit a delivery of engrams. Some have all the above and more. This is no great worry to the auditor for, by Repeater Technique, he can open the engram bank.

Drugs

The so-called hypnotics have no great use in Dianetics except, on occasion, when a patient is psychotic and narcosynthesis is employed. By hypnotic is meant such preparations as phenobarbital, hyoscine, opium and so on. These sleep-producing drugs are undesirable save only as a sedative and would be administered as sedatives by a medical doctor. Any patient who *needs* a sedative already has a medical doctor whose business it is. The auditor should not, then, concern himself with hypnotics or anything producing sleep. Some preclears will beg to be given sleeping drugs to "facilitate therapy," but any such drug is an anesthetic and shuts down somatics, inhibiting therapy. Further, none but the insane should be worked in amnesia trance, particularly a drug trance, for the work is longer than necessary and the results slow, as elsewhere explained. Dianetics wakes people up; it does not try to drug them or hypnotize them. Hence, the hypnotic drug is worthless to the auditor.

Patients who wish to be knocked over the head with lead pipes or otherwise put into a deep trance should not be allowed to have their way even when they humorously present their own lead pipes.

The trick is to put "I" in contact with the file clerk. All hypnotics work to shut down "I". While the file clerk can be reached and sonic and visio are available and even while, with much labor, a Clearing can be so effected, even the most "hopeless" case is better worked in contact; the work is faster, more satisfactory and less troublesome.

When one discovers the science of mind, he inevitably discovers numerous other things not properly in his province. Among these is the confusion which has unwittingly existed about hypnotics. Those things labeled "hypnotics," as named above, are not hypnotics at all, but anesthetics. And those things labeled anesthetics are not anesthetics, but hypnotics. This will become brilliantly clear to the auditor when he finds himself tangling with his first "anesthetic" nitrous oxide engram in some preclear. Perhaps there will have been another engram wherein morphine was administered for days and even weeks, leaving the patient in a stupor which, by the definition "hypnotic," should have been a trance: the aberrative material will be there, but it will be found to be slight compared to a chloroform or nitrous oxide engram.

Ether, chloroform and nitrous oxide–the "anesthetics" place the patient in a deep hypnotic trance: the reactive bank is wide open and all reception is sharp, clear and aberrative in the extreme. Of the three, nitrous oxide is easily the worst, being no anesthetic which would dull pain at all, but a first-class hypnotic. In nitrous oxide, the pain is filed and the content is filed with high and brilliant fidelity. Some years ago some investigator wondered if nitrous oxide did not make the brain decay. Fortunately brains do not decay that easily; but nitrous oxide does bring into being particularly severe engrams. The serious late-life engrams which the auditor will encounter may include, at the list's top, a nitrous oxide dental or surgical or obstetrical engram. Nitrous oxide engrams are particularly bad when they involve exodontistry; they often form the most severe late-life engram. Aside from the fact that all exodontists have in the past talked too much and have offices which are far too noisy with street sounds, running water and flapping drill belts, nitrous oxide is not at all anesthetic and sharpens rather than dulls pain.

In reverse, nitrous oxide makes an excellent hypnotic for institutional therapy. It is far from the best obtainable from the chemists, that is certain, for some brilliant chemist will certainly be able to bring out a good gas hypnotic now that Dianetics is known and the need of it in institutions is realized.

There are some drugs which assist reverie, however. The commonest and most easily obtainable is plain, strong coffee. A cup or two of this occasionally alerts the analyzer enough so that it can reach through deeper layers of "unconsciousness." Benzedrine and other commercial stimulants have been used with some success, particularly on psychotic patients. These bring the mind enough awake to permit it to overcome engramic commands. Such commercial stimulants have the disadvantage of exhausting a "Q" quantity in the mind.

This Q quantity has not been much studied. It is as though the brain burns a certain amount of Q when it is exhausting engrams. For instance, therapy every day may bring results more rapidly, but it will also bring some stale sessions. Therapy every two or three days produces the best results as observed. (Therapy once a week permits the engrams to sag and slows a case, one week being too long.) Benzedrine burns up Q. After a few sessions with Benzedrine, the current stock of Q is exhausted and the work has been observed to deteriorate either until a higher dosage was administered – and there is a close limit to that – or until more Q was manufactured.

Here, with all this, must be included an important and vital fact. It should be on a page by itself and underscored.

ALL PATIENTS IN THERAPY SHOULD BE GIVEN A DOSAGE OF VITAMIN B_1 ORALLY OR BY INJECTION AT THE MINIMUM OF 10 MG PER DAY.

Reducing engrams exhausts Q which seems to depend in some measure on B_1. You can be absolutely certain of nightmares in a patient who is not taking his B_1. Taking liberal doses of that, he will have no nightmares. D.T.'s are probably caused by a similar exhaustion of Q quantity. D.T.'s are best treated by B_1 and Dianetics. Something like D.T.'s on a very minor scale has been observed to develop in occasional patients who were negligent about their B_1. With it, in therapy, they thrive.

Alcohol is rarely an assist to the auditor. In fact, alcohol is rarely an assist to anyone. A depressant, classifiable at best as a poison, alcohol has the single virtue of being highly taxable. *All* alcoholics are alcoholic because of their engrams. All alcoholics, unless they have injured their brains – which case is cited only because it is possible, not because research in Dianetics demonstrated any real evidence of it – can be Released. Alcoholism is engramic. It has become, in some very understandable way, a class of contagious aberration whereby the reactive mind confuses alcohol and "being a good sport" or "having fun" or "forget your troubles." Some of these things can also be obtained by strychnine and cyanide. Alcohol has its uses: one can put specimens of frogs and such in it, one can clean the germs off needles with it, it burns well in rockets. But one would not consider preserving his stomach in a glass jar and, unless insane, does not think of himself as a needle. While some drunks think they act like rockets, few have been observed to reach an altitude of more than the floor. It is not only a poor stimulant-depressant, it is also an hypnotic in the finest sense: what is done to a drunk becomes an engram.* The chronic alcoholic is physically and mentally ill. Dianetics can Clear him or even merely Release him without too much trouble, for alcohol is apparently not physiological in its addictive effect. With the whole range of chemistry to choose stimulants and depressants from, why the government chooses a superiorly aberrative and inferiorly stimulative compound to legalize is a problem for the better mathematicians, possibly those who deal exclusively in tax income problems. Opium is less harmful, marijuana is not only less physically harmful, but also better in the action of keeping a neurotic producing, phenobarbital does not dull the senses nearly as much and produces less aftereffect, ammonium chloride and a host of other stimulants are more productive of results and hardly less severe on the anatomy. But no, the engrams, contaging unpleasantly along from the first crude brew which made one of our ancestors drunk, decree that alcohol is the only thing which is to be drunk if a person wants to "forget it all" and "have a good time." There is really nothing wrong with alcohol, save that it depends mainly on engrams and other advertising for its effect and is otherwise remarkably inferior in performance: that it makes such aberrative engrams is probably its main claim to fame and infame. Making one drug immoral and another one taxable is a sample of the alcohol engram in society. However, although it is immensely legal, it is doubtful if the auditor will find any use for it in therapy.

And speaking of drugs, that three thousand cycle note in your ears came either from a nitrous oxide engram

* I am not being paid by the WCTU to write this; it is only that I have had to Clear too many alcoholics.

or mother taking lots of quinine before you were born in the hope that she would not be a mother, saying the while, "It makes my ears ring so: it just keeps on and on and on and will not stop!"

AUTO-CONTROL

Since the beginning of Dianetics research twelve years ago, patients have, in the majority, had some belief that they could run their cases in "auto-control."

Not understanding that an auditor is only interested in what has been done *to*, not done *by* a patient, some shyness or imagined guilt often prompts this vain hope that one can accomplish therapy alone.

It cannot be done. That is a flat statement and it is a scientific fact. The auditor is necessary for a large number of reasons. He is not there to control or order the preclear about, but he is there to listen, to provide insistence, to compute the trouble the preclear is having and remedy it. The work is done on these equations:

THE DYNAMICS OF THE PRECLEAR ARE LESS THAN THE FORCE IN HIS REACTIVE BANK.

THE DYNAMICS OF THE PRECLEAR PLUS THE DYNAMICS OF THE AUDITOR ARE GREATER THAN THE FORCE IN THE PRECLEAR'S REACTIVE BANK.

THE ANALYTICAL MIND OF THE PRECLEAR IS SHUT DOWN WHENEVER HE REACHES AN ENGRAM AND HE IS THEN UNABLE TO PURSUE IT AND RECOUNT IT ENOUGH TIMES TO DISCHARGE IT WITHOUT AUDITOR ASSISTANCE.

THE ANALYTICAL MIND OF THE PRECLEAR PLUS THE ANALYTICAL MIND OF THE AUDITOR CAN DISCOVER ENGRAMS AND RECOUNT THEM.

There is another equation, not elsewhere mentioned, but germane to the Auditor's Code, which demonstrates mathematically the necessity of that code:

THE FORCE OF THE PRECLEAR'S ENGRAM BANK PLUS THE FORCE OF THE AUDITOR'S ANALYTICAL MIND IS GREATER THAN THE ANALYTICAL MIND AND THE DYNAMICS OF THE PRECLEAR.

This explains the necessity of never attacking the preclear personally. It also explains the behavior of the aberree under attack in usual life and why he grows angry and apathetic, for this equation overwhelms his analyzer.

These equations demonstrate actual natural laws.

Auto-control finds the preclear attempting to attack something which has never been overcome by his analyzer, although his analyzer has never been trying, interiorly, to do anything else but attack that bank so long as the analyzer would operate. The fact that the preclear's analyzer shuts down whenever he comes into an area of "unconsciousness" was why the engrams could take him over and use him as a puppet when they were restimulated–they simply shut down the analyzer.

Many efforts by many patients have been made to put Dianetics on an auto-control level. They have all failed and thus far it is believed to be utterly and completely impossible. The preclear in auto-control reverie may be able to reach some locks: he can certainly reach pleasant experiences and achieve data recall by return, but he cannot attack his own engrams without a standard auditor-preclear arrangement.

Aside from Dianetic reverie, some preclears have been foolish enough to attempt auto-hypnosis and thus reach their engrams. Hypnotism in any form is unwarranted in Dianetics. Auto-hypnosis used in Dianetics is probably as close to fruitless masochism as one can get. If a patient places himself in auto-hypnosis and regresses himself in an effort to reach illness or birth or prenatals, the only thing he will get is ill. Of course, people will try. None are ever convinced until they have tried once they begin to agitate about auto-control. But be sure to have a friend and this book handy so that he can audit away the headaches and such that suddenly turn on.

Dianetic reverie, which means with an auditor present, is not dangerous or severe. Auto-control is often very uncomfortable and often fruitless. It should not be attempted.

The Clear alone can auto-control his whole time track back to conception and does when he wants specific data from anywhere in his life. But he is Clear.

ORGANIC MENTAL ALTERATIONS

There are several things which can happen to the nervous system, including the brain, which can cause structural change. These are called, in Dianetics, *organic mental alterations*. They are not called "organic neuroses" or "organic psychoses" because the alteration of structure does not necessarily produce aberrations. There has been a confusion in the past between behavior caused by organic differences and behavior caused by engrams: this confusion came about because the engram bank and the reactive mind were not known.

Any human being with an organic mental alteration also has engrams. The behavior dictated by the engrams and the action caused by alteration are different things. Engrams carry dramatizations, delusions, tantrums and various inefficiencies with them. Alterations establish inabilities to think or perceive or record or recall. For instance, the radio set may have new filters and circuits added to it which change and vary its performance and reduce it from optimum; these would be engrams. The radio set might have original tubes or circuits deleted from it or it might have some of the wires crossed; this would be organic mental alteration.

The sources of organic mental alteration are as follows:

1. Variation of the blueprint of structure by reason of a changed gene pattern. Some parts of the body would grow too much or too little to establish any alteration of structure. This is usually so gross a change that it is obvious. The feebleminded and so on may suffer either from engrams or an altered blueprint, but usually both.
2. Alteration of the nervous system by disease or growths which divides into two classes:
    a. Disease destruction as in paresis.
    b. Additional construction as in the case of tumors.
3. Alteration of the nervous system by drugs or poisons.
4. Alteration by physical disorder as in the case of a "paralytic stroke" wherein certain tissues are inhibited or destroyed.
5. Physical change in structure due to injury as in the case of a head wound.
6. Alteration of structure by surgery as a necessity to remedy injury or disease.
7. Iatrogenic alterations (caused by doctors) undertaken under a misapprehension of brain function. These can be divided into two classes:
    a. Surgical, to include such things as the transorbital leukotomy, prefrontal lobotomy, topectomy and so forth.

b. Shock "therapies" of all kinds including electric shock, insulin shock, etc., etc., etc., etc., etc., etc., etc., etc., etc., etc., etc., etc., etc.

The first six sources of organic mental alteration are much less common than has been supposed. The body is an extremely hardy mechanism and its repair facilities are enormous. If an individual can be made to speak or follow orders at all, it is conceivable that the techniques of Dianetics can be applied to reduce the engrams in the engram bank, bringing about considerable improvement in the condition and mental ability of the individual. When these various sources are so severe that they inhibit any use of therapy, and when it is certain that no recourse to therapy is possible and that it is utterly impossible to reach the engram bank by standard technique, trance or drugs,* such cases can be considered beyond the help of Dianetics.

Category 7 presents another problem. Here we have selective experimentation at work and it would be flatly impossible to conceive, without months of study of their experimental subjects, how many brands and varieties of operation have been performed and how many odd and bizarre shocks have been used.

All iatrogenic alterations of the nervous system can be considered under the heading of "reduced ability," in other words, inability. In each case something has been done to reduce the ability of the individual to perceive, record, recall or think. Any of these complicate a case for Dianetics, but they do not inevitably bar Dianetics from working.

In shock cases, such as electric shock, tissue may have been destroyed and the memory banks may in some way

* See later, Advice to the Auditor.

have been scrambled, the time track may be altered and other conditions may exist.

In all such iatrogenic alterations, the results of Dianetics must be considered equivocal.

BUT IN ALL SUCH CASES, PARTICULARLY THOSE OF ELECTRIC SHOCK, DIANETICS SHOULD BE USED IN EVERY POSSIBLE WAY IN AN EFFORT TO IMPROVE THE PATIENT.

All shocks and operations should be picked up for what they are: engrams.

NO PERSON WHO CAN PERFORM ROUTINE TASKS OR WHOSE ATTENTION CAN BE ATTRACTED AND FIXED SHOULD FEEL DESPAIR OR BE CONSIDERED HOPELESS.

Any person who has been subjected to such treatment may not be able to reach optimum mental efficiency, but he may be able to reach a level of rationality even yet in excess of the current normal. The thing to do is try. In spite of what has happened or what has been done, in the large majority of cases there may be a chance of excellent recovery.*

Organic Derangement

A standard class of prenatal engrams has as its content the worry of the parents that the child will be feebleminded if not now aborted in earnest. This adds an emotional overload to such engrams and it adds, as importantly, an aberrative condition in the now grown patient that he is "not right," "all wrong," "feebleminded" and so forth.

*Attempted abortion sometimes may do strange things to a brain. This can be considered under the heading of injury. Most sonic recalls can be recovered. If various recalls cannot be recovered, engrams can still be removed. Intelligence in such cases will rise and is often already extremely high.

The difficulty of aborting the child is nearly always underestimated: the means used are often novel or bizarre; the worry because the child has not come out of the womb after the abortion attempt is acute; and the concern that he is now damaged beyond repair – all combine to make severely aberrative engrams and, because of their content, engrams which are difficult to reach.

The aberrative quality of the "feebleminded" species of remark is, of course, high. The worry that the child may be born blind or deaf or otherwise incapacitated is common. The former class of engramic remarks can bring about actual feeblemindedness; the latter concern over blindness and so on bring about, at best, impaired visio and sonic recall.

The shut-off of the recalls is occasioned, as well, by an engramic belief in the society at large that the unborn child is blind, unfeeling and not alive. This belief is introduced into AA (attempted abortion) engrams by people's self-justification remarks while attempting an abortion: "Well, he can't see, feel or hear anyway." Or "It doesn't know what's going on. It's blind, deaf and dumb. It's a sort of growth. It isn't human."

The greater part of all sonic and visio recall shut-off has as its source the remarks made at such times or by painful emotion and other engramic data. Hundreds of hours of therapy may pass before these recalls turn on.

The bulk of all shut-offs will turn on in the course of therapy. There are thousands of engramic remarks and emotional situations which will deny the preclear his recall and that recall can be expected ordinarily to restore.

A very low-dynamic patient (for people have various native strengths of the dynamic) may have recalls shut-off rather easily. A high-dynamic patient would require much more aberration before the recalls are closed down.

These recalls can be turned on simply by running out the physically painful and painful emotion engrams.

It must not pass unremarked, however, that the abortion attempts actually can, if rarely, derange the brain and nervous mechanisms beyond the fetal ability to repair. The result of this is actual, physiological disability.

Children and adults now classified as feebleminded may then be separated into two groups: the actual, physiological class and the aberrated class. Further, recall shut-offs must be classified into two classes as well, regardless of the dynamic and intelligence of the individual: those occasioned by brain damage received during an attempted abortion and those which are solely aberrational and derived from engramic commands and emotion.

The ability of the fetus to repair damage is phenomenal. Brain damage can ordinarily be repaired perfectly regardless of how many foreign substances were introduced into it. Just because the brain was touched in an attempted abortion is no reason to suppose that the recall shut-off has this as a source, for this is the rarer of the two causes.

It is understood that this is being read by many with recall shut-offs and it is understood that it may well produce a considerable upset. But remember this: *sonic and visio recall are not vital to a nearly full Release.* This comment about organic damage does not mean that a Release cannot be effected which will leave the person more competent and happier, for this can always be done regardless of the recalls. And remember this: *recalls almost always turn on even if it takes five hundred hours or more.* This condition is only remarked because it will be found in some few cases.

The "tests" and "experiments" with human brain vivisection in institutions are not, unfortunately, valid.

For all the pain and trouble and destruction caused by these "experiments," they were done without a proper knowledge of aberration and mental derangement. None of such data is of any value beyond showing that the brain can be cut in various ways without entirely killing the man. For the patients used responded both to engramic disorder and the physical disorder caused by the psychiatrist, and there is no way to differentiate between these after the operation except by Dianetics. Conclusions drawn from this data are then invalid conclusions, for the response of the patient after the operation might have stemmed from a number of sources: engramic, the engram of the operation itself, attempted abortion damage early in life, brain disability on account of the operation and so forth. Hence, draw no conclusions that impairment of conceptual thinking, for instance, results only when a part of the brain is removed, that recall is shut off only when the brain is vivisected and so on. From a scientific standpoint, no such "findings" were conclusive of anything except that the brain can be damaged late in life without entirely killing a man and that surgery of any kind often brings about a mental change in the patient. True, it may have been discovered that this or that portion of the switchboard called the brain, when removed, removed also some ability to perform.

DIANETIC FIRST AID

It will be of interest to those associated with emergency hospital work, particularly, that the healing and recovery of any patient can be enormously benefited and the term of illness shortened by removing the engram occasioned at the moment of injury.

The accident case sometimes dies in a few days from shock, or does not recover and will not heal swiftly. In any injury–a burn, cut, a bruise of whatever kind–a trauma lingers in the injured area. The moment of the injury created an engram. This engram inhibits the release of the trauma. The fact that the injured part still hurts is an organic restimulator which depresses the ability of the patient to recover.

Using reverie, or merely working the patient with his eyes closed, and working the patient as soon after the injury as possible, the doctor, nurse or relative can return the injured person to the moment when the injury was received and usually recover and exhaust the incident as a usual engram. Once the engram of the injury is reduced, the general mental tone of the patient improves. Further, the injured area is no longer inhibited from healing.

Some experimental work on this demonstrated that some burns would heal and disappear in a few hours when the engram which accompanied their reception was removed. On more serious injuries, tests showed definite and unmistakable acceleration of the rate of healing.

In operations, when anesthetics have been used, Dianetics is useful in two ways:

1. As a preventive measure.
2. As a recovery measure.

In the first, no conversation of any kind should be held around or with the "unconscious" or semiconscious patient. In the second, the trauma of the operation itself should be recovered and relieved immediately afterwards.

A Problem in Mutual Therapy

R and his wife C Cleared each other in eight months with Dianetics, working four hours a night, four nights a week, each of them auditing the other for two hours of the four.

This mutual arrangement had been complicated by the fact that whereas R was very eager to be Cleared, his wife was quite apathetic about the work: he had managed only after much persuasion to get the cases started.

He was a high-dynamic case with much emotion encysted; she was an apathy case who entirely neglected her troubles (black panther mechanism). He was troubled with a chronic ulcer and anxieties about his job; she was troubled with a general allergic condition and a chronic carelessness in domestic affairs. They were not to any great degree mutually restimulative, but they had problems about tacit consent, avoiding the subjects which had most upset them while together, such as a miscarriage she had had and the loss of their home by fire many years before, as well as other shocks. Further, they were faced by R's intensity on the one hand and his introversion, which caused him to slight her therapy; and C's apathy on the other hand, which at once aided R's effort to take more time as the preclear than she and which made her less interested in being a good auditor.

Further complication took place because C did not understand the Auditor's Code or its use and on several occasions had become angry and impatient with R when he was in session and returned, an attitude which tended to force R into an anger valence.

Along this uncertain course, therapy had been continuing. R was then informed of tacit consent and told he had better release some of their mutual painful emotion. He thereafter addressed the engram of the burning home and suddenly found himself able to audit some early sympathy engrams of his wife's which had not heretofore been available. It was discovered that her allergies stemmed from a father sympathy compute and that R was the pseudo-father. This resulted in a marked improvement in C's case. She began to suffer less from her allergies and a chronic heart pain she had had so long that she no longer heeded it vanished as well. She became interested in being a good auditor and studied the subject. She became slightly annoyed with R when he demanded more than his share of therapy time. (This increase of interest is always true of any apathy case which began with neglect of engrams.)

R, however, was much inhibited by her periods of anger and found that he now operated almost exclusively under auto-control, a condition wherein *he* decided what should be run and what should not be run in himself. This auto-control is, of course, useless, since if he knew about his aberrations and the data in his engrams, they would not be engrams. He, therefore, started on a period of refusing to display any emotion since she had mocked him about it, would not follow her directions and was, in short, obeying the engrams which she had given him when angry with him during past sessions. C was advised to pick up the moments of anger she had displayed as an auditor during therapy and when these were reduced, it was found that R worked well again and cooperated.

His ulcer stemmed from an attempted abortion. His father, an extremely aberrated individual, had sought to abort the baby when it was seven months in the womb. The mother remonstrated that the baby might be born alive. The father said that if it were alive when born, he would kill it as soon as it came out. He had said, further, that the mother had to hold still while he operated. On another occasion the father had said that he would lock the mother in a closet until she decided to abort the child. (This case was much complicated because the mother had been afraid to tell the father and had pretended not to be pregnant for three months, giving the husband the belief that the child, seven months along, was actually only four months along. Therefore, there was much secrecy in the case, much confusion and conflicting data.) This meant that R had a severe *holder* in the prenatal area: he was held by the engram which included a penetration of his stomach. This was the *key* engram, which is to say, other engrams, by the mechanism of similar somatic and content, had gathered around it to suppress it. This was the tangle of incident which C was confronting unknowingly: it had become more tangled by her anger. R would now cooperate, but his time track had wound into a ball around the holder engram, the key. Two exodontistries for the removal of wisdom teeth with nitrous oxide anesthesia were also suppressing the prenatals.

C worked for some time trying to get at the late extraction engrams, which contained an enormous amount of conversation between the dentist and his assistants and R's mother, who, unfortunately for his sanity, had accompanied him to the dentist's office.

R was made intensely uncomfortable by the continual restimulation of engrams which yet could not be reached. He was no more uncomfortable than he had often been in the past and his discomfort would have been absent had C understood and followed the Auditor's Code. The case made no progress for several weeks.

C's therapy was progressing. It was intensely restimulative to R to work upon her and increased his discomfort, but the more he worked on her, the better auditing she did and the more intelligent she was (her IQ went up about fifty points after five weeks of therapy). C desired to know how she could break the impasses in his case and was informed that she was now practicing tacit consent; for she had many times been needlessly thoughtless of R, long before therapy was undertaken, and she now realized what she had done to him and yet could not bring herself to face the fact that she was a responsible party to so much of his unhappiness. She had quite ordinarily used angry language to him which she well knew would "push-button" him into doing something or into retreating from a quarrel, which language had been restimulative to him long before therapy.

C thereupon entered into painful emotional engrams late in R's life and, by working early physically painful engrams which said R could "feel nothing" alternately with late engrams when he was feeling intensely on an emotional plane but could not exhibit it, began to release the emotion in the case. R then showed steady improvement. Late painful emotion was released and early prenatals would show to be reduced, at which more late emotion would be visible for reduction.

It was suddenly disclosed in the case that the reason R was so easily upset by C lay in the person of a nurse who had attended R during his tonsillectomy when he was five years of age. C had some similarity of mannerism to this nurse. This was a sympathy engram and when it was released, the time track began to straighten out and the abortion engrams could be more easily contacted.

It so happened that R had been well off his time track most of his life, his memory occluded, his recall in poor condition. This was found to lie in the hidden key engram: the abortion attempt wherein his father had vowed to kill him if he came out and had added that the child could not see, feel or hear anything anyway, engramic material which was demonstrated by R's inability to move on his time track.

The moment the key was found–two hundred and eighty hours of therapy had elapsed–R came back on the time track, could move on it, and the erasure of his engrams proceeded in an orderly fashion.

C had been Cleared about two months before R reached the final engram. C's allergies, however, disappeared long before her case was Cleared completely, and R's ulcer and some other psychosomatic difficulties also vanished well before his case was finally Cleared.

A Problem in a Restimulated Case

G was Cleared in ten months of sporadic sessions. His case had the initial diagnosis of non-sonic, non-visio, pain and emotional shut-off, permanent light trance, permanent "regression" at the age of three years. This is to say that the instant he went into reverie, he was startled and frightened to find himself in a dental chair, three years old and having a tooth pulled, an engram in which he had been situated, unknowingly, about half of his ensuing life. It had been the partial cause of his chronic tooth decay and his inability to sleep as negation against the anesthetic. The situation was obvious since he immediately began to wrestle about and lisp, which condition was instantly remedied by running the engram so that he could come to present time, which he did.

He had had considerable difficulty in life, was a high dynamic but manifested apathy. It was discovered after seventy-five hours, at which time Release took place, that his wife was sometimes his pseudo-grandmother and also, by ambivalence, was his pseudo-mother. As his sympathy computation demanded that he be ill so that his grandmother would stay with him and as his contra-survival engrams demanded that his mother was only nice to him when he was ill, the reactive computation added up to the fact that he must be ill continually, which demand had been obeyed by his body for twenty-three years. All this was recovered and remedied, of course, only by reducing engrams.

The erasure began to take place at the end of about two hundred hours of therapy and was proceeding when the case suddenly stopped all progress. For fifty or more hours of therapy, few engrams could be located, those which were located could not be reduced, no painful emotion could be reached and whatever engrams were reached and reduced were located and treated only because the auditor in this case used highly skilled forcing techniques, which are almost never necessary and should not be employed save in psychotic cases. Such endeavor had not been necessary at the beginning of the case. Something was obviously wrong.

On close questioning, it was discovered that G's wife was violently opposed to Dianetics, that she never lost any chance of leveling the most scathing attacks against it to G and particularly when he was in the company of friends. She derided him as being psychotic. She sought a lawyer to give her a divorce (announcing it after he had entered therapy, but actually having had continual consultation on it with a lawyer for two years past) and generally agitated and disturbed G to such an extent that he was continually receiving painful emotional engrams even though he did not display any emotion against her.

They had a child, nine years of age, a boy. G was very fond of the boy. The child had had an unusual number of childhood illnesses and suffered from eye trouble and chronic sinusitis; he was backward in school. The wife was somewhat sharp with the child. Anything he did made her nervous.

The auditor in the case, on learning the facts about her attitude toward her husband in general and Dianetics in particular, held a conference with her about her husband. She was found to be unopposed to therapy for herself. Shortly after the conference, G and this woman had a brief quarrel in which G made the remark that she must be aberrated. She took intense affront at this and said that he must be the one who was crazy, since he was interested in Dianetics. He countered with the fact that of the two, he must be the least aberrated, since he was taking steps to do something about it. Further, he pointed out that she must be aberrated or she would not be as quarrelsome with the child as she was, a fact which definitely indicated that she must have a block on her Second Dynamic, sex.

The following day, he came home from work and found she had withdrawn the money from the bank and gone to another town, taking the boy with her. He followed and found her staying with some of her relatives. She had told them that he beat her and had gone so crazy that he had to have therapy. The truth of the matter was that he had never touched her brutally in his life. In this meeting, before witnesses, she began to rave and revile any "system of psychiatry" which believed in pre-speech memory. He pointed out to her that many schools of the past had believed in pre-speech memory, that the whole background of psychiatry had long talked about "memories of the womb" without knowing what they were, and so forth.

Her relatives, seeing him so calm about it, forced her to return home with him. En route she made a dramatic gesture, although in no way threatened, of committing suicide by leaping out of the car.

The auditor in the case had a private conversation with her on her return. He had somewhat belatedly deduced the fact that there was something in her life which she was afraid her husband would find out and that, confronted with a science which could recover all memory, she had become wildly emotional about it. She at length admitted, under close questioning, that this was the case, that her husband must never know. She was so disturbed that the auditor, with her consent, gave her a few hours of therapy.

It was instantly discovered that her father had many times threatened to kill her mother and that her father had not wanted her. Further, it was found that her father's name was Q and that her engram bank was strewn with remarks such as "Q, please don't leave me. I will die without you." Additionally, when she was no longer in session, she suddenly volunteered what was to her a hysterically humorous fact that all her life she had been having affairs with men named Q no matter what their shape or size or age. This was far from a Release, but in view of the fact that his other patient, G, was jeopardized by all this unnecessary hubbub and that therapy was being stalled, the auditor further questioned her. She divulged that she had tried many times to abort their son because she was terribly frightened that he would be a blond whereas she and her husband had dark hair. Further, the engrams of that child, she knew, contained data which she considered incriminating beyond mere abortion: while pregnant she had had intercourse with three men other than her husband.

The auditor pointed out to her that this guilt feeling, no matter how real, was still engramic in her and that it was doubtful if her husband would kill her on receipt of these tidings. He told her that she was condemning a child to a second-rate existence and that she was reducing her husband to apathy by her fears and causing the auditor far more work than was necessary. In her husband's and the auditor's presence she confessed her infidelity and learned with some amazement that her husband had known about it for years. He had not known about her attempts on their child.

She was requested to study a therapy manual and Clear the child which, with her husband's help, she did. The auditor continued G on to Clear, who then Cleared his wife.

ADVICE TO THE AUDITOR

The hidden source of human aberration was hidden for a number of very specific reasons. The auditor will encounter all of these and although, with these techniques, the ability of the reactive engram bank to deny him is precisely nil, he should know the nature of the beast he has under attack.

The mechanisms of protection which the engram bank had – although they are not very good now that we know how to penetrate this armor of insanity's cause – are as follows:

1. Physical pain.
2. Emotion in terms of captured units.
3. "Unconsciousness."
4. The delayed character of the key-in.
5. Delay between restimulation and illness.
6. Utter irrationality.

Of the physical pain, we know much – that the mind, in memory, sought to avoid it just as the mind in life seeks to avoid it as an outside source: hence, memory blockage.

Emotion of loss piles up to make a buffer between the individual and the reality of death.

"Unconsciousness" is not only a mechanism of hiding data, it is also a block to memory which cannot jump the gaps of past moments when the fuses were blown.

An engram might slumber for the better part of a lifetime and then, given the correct set of restimulators in the right moment of physical weariness or illness, manifest itself, making an *apparent* cause of insanity or lesser aberration many years after the actual incident had taken place.

Another aspect of the bank protective mechanism was the restimulator lag, which is to say that when a keyed-in engram was restimulated, it often required two or three days for action to take place. (Example: Say a migraine headache has as its restimulator a rhythmic bumping sound; that sound is heard by the individual who has the engram; three days later he suddenly has a migraine.) Given this lag, how could one locate the cause of a specific restimulation of a sporadic illness?

The utter irrationality of an engram, the ultimate in irrationality, that everything equals everything else in the engram and that these are equal to things in the exterior environment which are only vaguely similar is a feat of idiocy which any sentient man might be expected to overlook as a "thought process."

Man has been looking for this source for some thousands of years, but he was looking for something which was complicated on the grounds that anything which could be so harrowing, so destructive, so vicious and so capable of producing complex manifestations must therefore have a complex source; on examination it is remarkably simple.

The auditor will have very little to do with trying to draw a line between sanity and insanity, they are such relative terms. He will be asked to compare Dianetics with old standards such as the complex classifications of Kraepelin: it can be done, but it has the usefulness of Aristotelian natural history, of interest only to the historian.

If an individual is incapable of adjusting himself to his environment so as to get along with or obey or command his fellows, or more importantly, if he is incapable of adjusting his environment, then he can be considered to be "insane." But it is a relative term. Sanity, on the other hand, closely approaches, with Dianetics, a potential absolute meaning: for we know the optimum mind. Modifications of education and viewpoint may make the rational action of one person appear irrational to another, but this is not a problem of sanity; it is a problem of viewpoint and education, with which the auditor will have but small concern.

Thus, the patients the auditor will encounter will fall into the three general Dianetic classes of non-sonic recall, imaginary recall and sonic recall. The question of sanity does not arise: the question of how difficult or how long the case may be is fairly well determined by the degree of these three conditions.

However, the auditor will find that he may have in his hands a truly "insane" case, one which is "psychotic." The treatment of such a case depends on which of the three above classes the psychotic patient may be entered. The problem is to de-intensify the engrams of the patient as swiftly as possible.

The conditions and mechanisms which hide the engram bank do not vary: they are uniformly present in every patient, in every human being. The techniques of Dianetics may be improved upon–and what scientific technique, particularly in its first few years of existence, cannot be–but they also do not perform selectively but are applicable to all individuals.

Hence, if we have an "insane" patient, the fundamental problem does not change and Dianetic technique works as in any other case. The task is to reduce the intensity of charge in the case so that it can be resolved by standard technique.

Insane patients are often found stuck on the time track, in which case a holder is fed to them, one kind after another, until they are moving again. If the patient is regressed, he has become so thoroughly stuck that he has lost touch with the present time. Any patient can begin to *relive* instead of merely return and the auditor, as the remedy for this, merely snaps at them that they can remember this, which places them in a *returned* status again. Insane patients are often found listening to one engram over and over, in which case it is again only necessary to fix attention and feed them holders until they are once more moving on the track. Insane patients are sometimes discovered completely off the time track, listening to demons or seeing illusion. The problems are always the same: use Repeater Technique when, by one means or another, their attention has been fixed and then either get them moving on the track or get them back on the time track. The schizophrenic is usually a long way off his time track.

The best way to de-intensify a case so that it can be entered in routine therapy is to discover and discharge painful emotion engrams. If ordinary means fail, get the help of a medical doctor, place the patient under nitrous oxide or sodium pentothal and reach a deep level of trance where the patient will be found, ordinarily, to be capable of moving on his track even though he was off his track when awake. Find a late despair engram and discharge it as described in the chapter on emotion (Book Three, Chapter Seven, Emotion and the Life Force). The technique for deep trance is no different except that very cautious safeguards must be taken to say nothing which will aberrate the patient further, but to limit all conversation to therapy patter, being very careful to include the canceller.

The insane patient is obeying some engramic command, perhaps many, no matter what he is doing. That command may dictate, by the patient's misinterpretation, some strange action; it may dictate demons; it may dictate anything. But diagnosis merely consists of observing the patient in order to discover, by his actions, what the engramic command might be.

This volume does not cover Institutional Dianetics beyond these few remarks, but an auditor who knows the fundamentals in this volume and with any understanding can bring about a "sanity" in patients in a short time which the boards of these institutions normally consider a miraculous recovery. The patient, however, is very far from a Release and many more hours should be spent in discharging further painful emotion and reducing engrams before an auditor should consider it safe to permit him to leave therapy.

The auditor should be extremely cautious, at least for the next twenty years, about any case which has been institutionalized, for he may be getting a case with iatrogenic psychosis–caused by doctors–in addition to the patient's other engrams. Dianetics may help a mind a little in which the brain has been "ice picked" or "apple cored," but it cannot cure such insanity until some clever biologist finds a way to grow a new brain. Electric shock cases are equivocal: they may or may not respond to treatment, for brain tissue may have been burned away to a point where the brain cannot function normally. In entering any such case, the auditor will be perplexed by the scrambled condition of the standard bank, to say nothing of the circuits by which he should be able to reach the engram bank. Syphilis and other brain erosions should be similarly classified and should be approached or undertaken only with the full knowledge that Dianetics may not be able to help the dismembered machine at all. There have been many thousands of these brain "operations" and hundreds of thousands of electric shock treatments: thus the auditor should be alert not to engage upon what may be a hopeless cause when there exist so many cases which can better be helped. Any case which has been institutionalized should be suspected.

And if anything unusual in the way of memory scramble or lack of coordination is observed, searching inquiry may reveal hidden institutionalization. Further, an auditor called upon to assist a case which is about to be institutionalized should always be wary. The case which is being sent to an institution may be a case which has been in one before, regardless of the protestations of relatives or friends that such is not the circumstance.

Similarly, combat exhaustion cases should be warily undertaken; for the case was probably processed before quitting the service, at which time electric shock or brain operation or narcosynthesis may have been applied without the knowledge or consent of the patient.

These warnings are given not because the auditor will be in any particular physical danger–patients seldom do anything but cooperate, sane or insane, when Dianetics is applied, even if they snarl about it–but because much work may be expended only to discover that the entire mental machinery has been wrecked beyond repair.

If the auditor undertakes an electric shock case, he should address his primary attention to the release of that shock as an engram; for there is all manner of careless chatter contained in these institutional engrams, which may further inhibit treatment. This is aside from the fact that any electric shock, anywhere in the body, has a tendency to derange the engram bank and bind it so that its incidents are more than usually snarled.

For no other reason than the advance of Dianetics and the conservation of an auditor's time, it should also be remarked that the third-degree methods of some police departments and general police abuse of criminals or ordinary citizens may have to be released in a case before it can be further treated. Prison terms may contain large despair charges sufficient to derange the mind and yet may be hidden by the patient under the mistaken idea that the auditor is interested or will be disappointed in his "character."

Various other things enter into the engram bank which would not be suspected as obstacles to therapy unless mentioned. Hypnotism can be extremely aberrative and may hold up a case. An auditor should have some working knowledge of it so that he can release the engrams it makes, not so he can work Dianetics. Hypnotism is the art of implanting positive suggestions in the engram bank. Here they may append themselves to engrams and become locks on those engrams. As most engram banks contain a sample of most common words, hypnotism is almost certain to be aberrative. The reduction of analytical power by artificial means places the subject in an optimum condition for the receipt of an engram. The hypnotist uses the forgetter mechanism with most of his suggestions and most people have similar engramic remarks which make it impossible for the hypnotist's suggestion to release. Hypnotism can be considered as a "high-powered" lock and may be a serious obstacle in the patient's engram bank. With clearing, the suggestions having no anchors of pain below them in engrams, vanish as locks. But hypnotic suggestions may have to be found and cleared before a case can proceed. Hypnotism is very commonly used in this society and it is very often the case that, with the forgetter mechanism, the patient is unable to recall whether he had ever been hypnotized or not. Return Technique will discover it; Repeater Technique, making the patient return with repetition of hypnotic patter (by the patient) such as "Go to sleep, go to sleep, go to sleep," can be depended upon to locate it.

Not all hypnotism is in the parlor. Perverts quite commonly use it despite the fact that the "moral" nature is supposed to rise in a hypnotized subject. Incidents, even with people of repute, have been found in patients when examining their childhood. These incidents were often entirely occluded to the patient, so thoroughly cowing were the commands contained in the hypnotic suggestion.

Dianetics and hypnotism can be combined, but so can Dianetics and astronomy. The auditor will find himself working with hypnotic patients and will have to be very careful with patter in order to install minimal words of his own in the engram bank so as not to turn Dianetics into hypnotism.

Any benefit derived from hypnotism is in the field of research or the installation of a temporary manic engram. The latter has far more harm than value. Hypnotic anesthetic is vastly overrated. And hypnotism as a parlor game is a thing which no society should tolerate, for it may be sufficiently destructive to cause the engrams to restimulate to a point of insanity. And the hypnotist never knows the content of the engram bank. Any good hypnotist, if he can conquer his desire to talk, should make a good auditor: but if he tries to combine Dianetics and hypnotism, he will find himself with a very thoroughly sick patient on his hands. *Never install a positive suggestion of any kind in a patient no matter how much he may beg for one. It has proven nearly fatal.*

An entire case can be worked in deep amnesia trance. It is often possible to waken a sleeping person into a deep trance simply by speaking to him quietly several nights in succession at the same hour and finally getting him to respond to the invitation to talk. Dianetic therapy can then be entered upon and pursued and will succeed, particularly if the auditor is not careless enough to artificially restimulate a late physical pain engram, treating in the post-birth life mainly engrams of painful emotion. If the person on whom the therapy is being done is aware of the action, he can be put into reverie so that earlier data can be reached, "I" being more powerful than the weak, if wise, attention units which constitute basic personality. He is alternately worked in amnesia trance and then in reverie. The case will resolve eventually even if reverie is not used. But there are grave responsibilities with amnesia trance: a canceller must always be installed and used in every session. Minimal conversation must be employed. All auditor desires should be stated as questions, if possible, as these are not aberrative to the degree that commands are. This method has been successful and can be used. But reverie, even if it appears slower, even if sonic is not present, is far more satisfactory for the excellent and incontrovertible reason that the patient recovers more swiftly and recovers on a steady upgrade whereas amnesia trance may incapacitate him for days together, when incidents are apparently lifted in deep trance, but nevertheless "hung up" in the awake state. Amnesia trance is definitely not advised: it has been subjected to much research and has been found to be both uncomfortable for the patient and harassing to the auditor. However, if other methods cannot be used for one reason or another (and none of those reasons include the desire of the preclear who, if the auditor would let him, might crave drugs, hypnotism and positive suggestion in an effort to escape his engrams and who, if allowed, would have himself a wonderfully messy case for the auditor to unsnarl), amnesia trance can be employed, but always with the greatest caution and always with the full knowledge that the patient's recovery is retarded by as much as a factor of three, for working on a level with the engram bank leaves the analyzer circuits unused in the discharge. Reverie is best.

External Problems with Patients

It may happen that a patient who has made progress suddenly ceases to make further progress. The answer may lie elsewhere than therapy. The environment of the preclear may be so intensely restimulative that he is distracted, always in restimulation and thus works slowly. It may be discovered, in such a case, that the preclear (as in one case) has made a bargain with a wife or husband who desires divorce that he or she wait until the preclear is Cleared. Other situations of a life nature can place an environmental value on not being Cleared. The auditor has no business with the private lives of his preclears, but in a case where therapy itself is made difficult by existing situations, the auditor, with his time at stake, has every right to discover the reason. All these reasons will compute into some environmental advantage in not being Clear. Removing the preclear temporarily from his home, for instance, may change his environment and advance therapy. The auditor has a right to ask that, Clear or not, the patient resolve the problem on his own initiative. It is common with preclears that they do not realize that they are Releases. For so glittering is the goal of Clear that they cease to compare themselves to the normal, which they have already overpassed.

A patient can commonly be expected to introvert to a very marked degree in the course of Dianetic therapy. As the case progresses, this introversion reaches an acute stage about three-quarters or thereabouts through and thereafter recedes. Ambiversion is a marked characteristic of the Clear. When introversion has been marked, a fairly good gauge of the advance of the case is in the preclear's interest in exterior things.

Nearly all preclears talk a great deal about their engrams up to the point when they are very solid Releases.

If they don't or won't talk about their engrams in common conversation, the auditor can suspect something highly protected in the engram bank concerning the necessity to hide something: the auditor can act accordingly. Although the auditor may weary of such conversation, it nevertheless reveals much new material to him if he observes the phrases which the preclear uses about engrams.

It is very, very true that aberration is caused by what has been done *to*, not what has been done *by* the patient. The actions of the patient in dramatizing, in committing crimes and so forth are not aberrative to the patient. Therefore, the preclear's activities need be no concern whatever of the auditor's. Whole cases have been completed without the auditor's knowing what the preclear did for a living. While responsibility for his actions is necessarily demanded of him by an aberrated society, antisocial activity is the result of engrams which dictate it. The patient is not responsible for what he himself has done. Cleared, the matter is different. A Clear can be considered entirely responsible for his own actions, for he can compute rationally on the basis of his experience. But the aberree has little or no real control over his actions. Therefore, the auditor should make it plain that he does not care what the aberree who becomes a preclear has done in life. The problem on hand between the auditor and the preclear is an engram bank which contains, exclusively, what other people have done in life and what has been done to the preclear in moments when he could not protect himself. This approach is not only truth, it has a therapeutic value. For in so explaining himself, an auditor can often obtain cooperation which would otherwise be denied.

The auditor should never violate the Auditor's Code with a patient. Extended terms of therapy inevitably result from such violations.

Restimulation

The mind is a self-protecting mechanism–but so is Dianetics. A science of thought which works would so closely approximate the working principles of the mind that it would follow in parallels the injunctions and provisos of the mind itself. Such is the case with Dianetics: the mind is diagnosed by its reaction to therapy, therapy is improved by the reactions of the mind to it. This is a working principle of great value since it explains much observed phenomena and predicts most of the remainder. Part of this parallelism is the self-protection feature.

It is almost impossible to injure a mind: it is an extremely tough organism. Of course, when one begins to hew and saw upon it with metal or poison it with drugs or bacteria or throw its natural armor aside as with hypnotism, unfortunate things can occur.

Charlatanism is almost impossible where Dianetics in any of its principles is being practiced. One either practices all Dianetics and gets results or practices himself into a decline: that is a mechanical, scientific fact. Dianetics, as a self-protecting science, demands practice by Clears or at least good Releases. A Clear very closely follows in all his conduct the better aspects of the Auditor's Code: his ethical level is very high. Hence, anyone starting a practice of Dianetics is going to find himself, no matter what his original intention, thrust toward the goal of being a Clear.

There is an excellent reason for this. There is a principle known as restimulation of the auditor. We have an understanding now of what makes an engram come into restimulation. When it comes into restimulation, it forces the pain or the action of the engram into being in the organism. The observation of some percept in the environment which approximates a recording–sound or sight or organic sensation–in the engram, brings the engram into greater or lesser play. Similarly, when an auditor is not Cleared himself or when he is not in therapy himself working toward the goal of a Clear, he becomes restimulated. He is, after all, listening constantly to engramic material in a patient. This engramic material is the very stuff of which insanity is made. Anyone has engrams: sooner or later a patient is going to start going over an engram of his own which will approximate the auditor's own engrams. This leads to great discomfort for the auditor unless the auditor is in therapy and can have the discomfort so brought forth released. So long as one is merely working late locks, this is not so much the case and has made it possible for practitioners and mental healers of the past to escape much of the penalty of their own aberrations. But when one deals with the root material of these aberrations, a constant hammering by restimulators can bring about a serious condition. This is the mechanism which causes people in asylums to fall prey themselves to psychoses, although one must have had them in the first place for them to have been restimulated.

The auditor may run one or two cases without any serious repercussion: indeed, no matter what the repercussion, it can be eliminated by Dianetics. To save his own comfort, however, he should himself be Cleared or Released as soon as possible. He can work as a Release without too much trouble, and this makes it possible for him to make a mutual compact where he is worked on while he is working the other. A condition can then come about where two preclears are each auditors. This alternation between the couch and the auditor's chair will usually work very well.

Two persons, however, after they have begun work, may discover that they are mutually restimulative, which is to say, each is a pseudo-person in the other's engrams or one is restimulated (voice tone, incidents) by the other. This should be no bar to therapy. It has been overcome and therapy has gone forward despite the most severe restimulative circumstances. A common avoidance technique on the part of a subject is to claim the auditor restimulates him: it is not sufficiently important to stop therapy. It may be, however, that two people can enter a third into the chain and, by one clearing the next, considerably ease the tension. The triangular work plan, where no person is working on the person who is working him, is quite successful.

A husband and wife who have quarreled long and often may find it too restimulative to Clear each other. It is possible to do if other arrangements cannot be made and it is often done: but if therapy does not go well, he should find a therapy partner and so should she. Mothers who have attempted abortion on their children or otherwise maltreated them can accomplish therapy on those children: but in any case of restimulative circumstance such as this, the greatest precaution must be taken by the auditor to adhere severely to the Auditor's Code – to do otherwise might bring much more stress into therapy than is necessary. In such a case, the mother had better herself have at least a Release accomplished upon her before she attempts to Clear her children – and she should not touch those children until they are at least eight.

The subject of auditor restimulation, where the auditor restimulates the preclear or the preclear restimulates the auditor, does not include the routine aspect of therapy that the preclear is always being artificially restimulated via standard therapy. An engram can be restimulated by being touched several times and so it will lift. The auditor restimulation problem is a specific one where the auditor is a pseudo-enemy, a similarity to a person who has harmed the patient. Wild antagonism on the part of a patient to an auditor is usually traced to this. Some patients have such a hatred of men that only women can work them, some have such a hatred of women that only men can work them. But even when there is a wild antipathy, if there exists no other auditor or person who can be trained quickly as one, therapy can proceed anyway: and it will accomplish results.

REBALANCING A CASE

Any case dropped out of therapy will rebalance itself in a few weeks, which is to say, it will settle to a new high for the individual. Unless drug hypnotism or some other Dianetically illegal method is used, all cases will so rebalance, much benefited. Restimulations can be expected to die down if they are due to therapy. The patient will gradually find his own level in the Released state. Cases do not have to be carried forward to Clear if auditor time is short. But it is, of course, better if they are and, indeed, the majority of patients will insist that they be.

WORKING TIME IN THERAPY

The usual period of a Dianetic treatment is two hours. In these two hours, with the usual patient, everything is going to be accomplished which can be accomplished on that day. Working every day is not necessary, but working every two days or every three days is desirable. Working with periods a week apart is not optimum, for the case tends to rebalance. Further, there is a sag in a case, usually every fourth day, when it is not worked in periods as short as three days. The fourth-day sag is a natural mechanical thing: an engram, keyed-in, when it is restimulated in life, takes about four days to cut in sharply. In therapy, three days is sometimes required to develop an engram. This does not mean that three days have to elapse before it is available and it does not mean that work has to stop for three days; but it does mean that engrams, not being memories and articulate as such, take three days, sometimes, to come to the surface.

To be more clear, an engram can be asked for on day one and will be found on day three. Meanwhile the auditor is getting other engrams. This process is so automatic that it requires no attention and will not come to notice except in cases that are being worked once a week. The engram is asked for on day one, is ready to reduce on day three, sags on day four and is rebalanced by day seven.

The three-day aspect is interesting in another sense. This time of three days is just an observation of the average behavior of preclears. Precision investigation may fix it at 2.5 days or 3.6 days (it varies in individuals), but three days is close enough for our purposes. When one is doing just a Release on a case, he will sometimes find that it is necessary to take a late engram and run it: the physical pain engram of later life (post-birth) will appear to rise, will remain constant for three days and then will sag. When it sags, the auditor will have to go back to it and run it again. Taking out these sags will eventually make the later-life engram stay in a recessed state.

Euphoria often sets in on a case when the auditor touches an engram which contains a manic. The patient will then go around saying how wonderful Dianetics is because he is now in magnificent condition and is so happy. Watch out. In three or four days this manic will have sagged back to a depressive state. Be wary if somebody experiences one of these skyrocket "recoveries," for it is about as permanent as the fire of a burning match. It goes out and leaves very cold ashes. The auditor, seeing this euphoria, had better enter the case again and reduce the engram it contains more thoroughly or get a more basic engram.

The length of time it takes to Clear a person is quite variable. By blowing despair charges and working a few early engrams, an auditor can get a better state of being in the patient than in any past therapy in twenty or thirty hours: this is a Release. It compares to two or three years of past therapeutic work. The length of time it takes to get a Clear cannot be compared to any past standard because a Clear is something no past standard ever dreamed about.

In a sonic case, where recall is in good condition, a Clear can be obtained in a hundred hours. In a case which has thoroughly shut-down recalls, anything can happen up to, in extremity, a thousand hours. Similarly the imaginative case, which has things which never happened, may be long.

Look at it this way: we can get the results of two or three years of psychoanalysis in a score or two of hours of Dianetics and what we accomplish with Dianetics does not have to be done again, which is not true with psychoanalysis. This is the Release. He can go about his business in a far more competent fashion, his emotional charges being largely freed. In the Clear, we are attempting and can achieve a supernormal state of mind. Thousands and thousands and thousands of hours were spent in the education of a man: the expenditure of two or even ten thousand hours of work to make him rank above what would formerly have been possible for him is work well spent. But we do not have to spend anything like this amount of time. People have been Cleared in anything from thirty hours, when they had sonic and little volume, to five hundred hours when they had shut-down recall plus imaginary recall. What an auditor can do with his first few cases by way of time is a question mark. He will get to the Clear eventually and certainly in less than twelve hundred hours in a severe case. All the time he is working toward a Clear, he is achieving a higher and higher Release which, after at least fifty hours, rises well above the current norm and keeps right on soaring. Improvement is such that from week to week the change is physiologically noticeable and psychologically startling. If one thinks the reach for Clear is a short jump and a small gain, then he has no conception of just how high that goal is.

Most auditors will try for Release at first and are wise if they do. When their own case is finally Cleared, only then will they suddenly realize that the state was worth far more time than was expended to attain.

It is impossible to forecast, with a new auditor, just how much time he will consume in making errors, learning his tools, attaining skill. It is therefore impossible to estimate for him how long it will take him to gain a Clear in a patient. A well-trained auditor never takes more than eight hundred hours with the worst of cases: five hundred is high.

Data from Relatives

The auditor will always be plagued by the anxiety of the patient to get data from relatives or friends. The request for this data itself is restimulative, both to the preclear and the relative. Mothers have been made very ill by being given the restimulators of their own past illnesses by the child who has "suddenly found out."

It is a uniform experience that the data obtained from relatives, parents and friends, by the preclear, is absolutely and utterly worthless. Here we are depending upon an aberree's memory when we have at hand, with Dianetics, a reliable source of accurate material. Auditors have had cases progress very smoothly and then suddenly stop progress: on inquiry it is discovered that the preclear has been running around to his parents and relatives for material and they, wanting nothing more than that he forget all about what they have done to him, throw him red herrings which have to be carefully eliminated. These are the villains of the piece, the people who have done the things to the preclear which made him an aberree. If one expects accurate data from them, one might as well expect the moon to be green cheese.

If the auditor wants data from these people and requests it, bypassing the preclear, he may get somewhere. But any data so received has a value which, in intelligence, is used to label "Incompetent Source–Improbable Material."

Warn a preclear not to bother his relatives and parents and explain to him that he can make them ill by asking for data, on the restimulator principle. If we want confirmation of the data received, the only way to get it is put the parent or relative in therapy. At such time, we shall get the basic dramatization sources: in the prenatal life and childhood of the parent. This is a problem of research, not of therapy.

If the auditor has Mama available, he can run off the child's birth and then Mama giving birth, keeping the two apart, and get his check on the accuracy of therapy. And there are other data that can be so compared, using proper safeguards.

The subjective reality, not the objective reality, is the important question to the auditor. First, last and always, *does the patient get well?*

Stopping Therapy

The woman scorned has a violent rival in the preclear on whom therapy has been stopped by the auditor's decision.

Keeping the preclear in therapy, no matter how seldom are the sessions, satisfies in some measure the effort his basic personality makes to fight clear of the aberrations.

The basic personality, the file clerk, the core of "I" which wants to be in command of the organism, the most fundamental desires of the personality, may be considered synonymous for our purposes. There is an enormous surge of this basic self–which is really the individual himself–to conquer the engrams. The engrams, borrowing life from their host, appear as things which do not want to be conquered. As mechanistic as all this actually is, the auditor will often find himself wondering at the resistance the engrams can make and marveling at the efforts of the basic personality to conquer the engrams. He works *with* the basic personality, the individual himself, and ignores the engramic efforts to interfere. But there is a situation in which the basic personality seems to give free play to the engrams in an effort to accomplish therapy.

In work a "patient" might have been skeptical, sarcastic or even vicious to the auditor. Or the patient may have been thought to be completely neglectful of his engram bank. Or the patient may even rage that he hates therapy. For some of these reasons, the auditor may injudiciously decide to cease working the patient. The patient is so informed. For a short while, perhaps, the patient may manifest no reaction. But in a few minutes, a few hours or a few days, basic personality, denied a route out, may begin to use every weapon to hand to compel the auditor to resume therapy.

Disturbed by cessation of therapy, even though he may have insisted upon its being stopped, the ex-patient may begin either to rapidly decline or to attack to his face or behind his back the auditor and even therapy itself. The woman scorned has rarely made such thorough upsets as ex-patients who have been refused continuance of therapy. Auditors have been personally reviled, have had other preclears searched out and undermined by violent attacks upon therapy itself, have been targeted by all manner of accusations and whispering campaigns and have been made most uncomfortable by preclears who have had further therapy denied to them before a Release had taken place. Even solid, legitimate Releases, whose psychosomatic ills have disappeared and who should be quite cheerful, have been observed to create turbulence when the auditor would not take them through to Clear. Any number of mechanisms may be used by the ex-patient, as many mechanisms as men use to force other men into action. One of the mechanisms is a resumption of apathy and a "swift decline." Another is wild campaigning against therapy. Another is personal attack of the auditor. Each has, as its provable intention, the resumption of therapy.

The mind knows how the mind works. And the mind which has tasted a way out of pain and unhappiness may be expected, if that way is blocked, to use all methods to cause therapy to be resumed.

No matter how thoroughly disagreeable the ex-patient has been, the moment the auditor starts therapy upon him again, the attitude alters. No further destructive efforts are made against the auditor or therapy, but all is almost as well as it was before the cessation was declared.

Do not suppose, however, that the preclear, if he has been neglectful, recalcitrant or generally uncooperative before, will now embrace therapy as a chastened patient.

Far from the case, he is now at least as difficult to work as he was before *plus* some additional antagonism engendered by the cessation order.

In such a case, the auditor is damned if he does and double-damned if he doesn't. But there is a way out of this. The phenomenon of "transference," where the patient simply transfers his griefs to the practitioner, is not the mechanism here at work; transference is a different thing, bred of a thirst for attention and a feeling of needed support in the world. Transference can be expected to keep up forever if permitted; the patient of a doctor, for instance, may go on and on having illnesses just to keep the doctor around. Transference may occur in Dianetic therapy, the patient may lean on the auditor solidly, beg the auditor for advice, appear to hold out engrams in an effort to keep the auditor working hard and available and interested; all this is the result of a sympathy computation and is aberrated conduct. The clever auditor will not give advice or attempt to run anyone's life, for a person works well only as a self-determined organism. In Dianetic therapy, no matter what the attitude of the patient, no matter how great his "desires to be ill" or his transference of burden, no matter about even his vicious remarks to the auditor during sessions, the condition cannot obtain forever. Basic personality is trying to get through; "I" is trying to integrate self. Even indifferent work will eventually release enough charge from a case and reduce enough engrams to bring a higher stability to the patient. Basic personality gets stronger and stronger and therefore more self-reliant. The introversion occasioned by continual effort to reach the interior world of the engram bank de-intensifies and extroversion comes more and more into being as the case advances. The way out is to work the patient smoothly and well and one day he will be well Released or Clear. But meanwhile, if you stop therapy on anyone, don't be surprised at anything that happens; you can only remedy it by resuming the case.

AUDITOR EVALUATION

The auditor must do much evaluation to himself. *He does not evaluate or force upon his preclear any computation.* If the preclear computes that this was what was making him ill, then this is what the auditor accepts. Explaining to the preclear what it was in the engram which affected him so and so, is not only a waste of time, but also makes the preclear confused. The reason an auditor evaluates is to make sure he is not accepting imagined data or incomplete data as engrams.

An incident will not lift unless the data in it is correct: this is automatic. Change just one syllable in the incident and it will stick. Or if it seems to go away, it will be back. So there is no fear that any incident which decreases with recounting is incorrect. The data in it must be more or less correct or it would not so reduce. Thus the auditor who challenges incidents, data or otherwise plays God is going to have a thoroughly fouled-up case on his hands before he goes very far, and he is going to have a subject who is not progressing. If the subject begins to run an engram where Mama is having intercourse with five Eskimos, let him run it and never, never, never, never tell him that you feel it was untrue. If you tell the subject you think he is imagining things, you may give him a serious setback. Tell him you think Mama had her reasons and you have sided with the opposition: you are not attacking the engram, you are helping Mama attack the subject. To criticize, correct or otherwise judge the preclear has no slightest part in Dianetics and will do more to slow up a case than any other single action. An auditor who challenges the material given him may be practicing witchcraft or Chinese acupuncture or shamanism or voodoo, but he is not practicing Dianetics. And he will not get results. One remark to the subject such as, "I think that you are mistaken in believing your mother would try to abort you" or "I feel that you are imagining it," may set your preclear back fifty hours. The auditor does not criticize or judge the preclear, nor does he evaluate for the preclear that person's material.

Auditing is all done privately and to oneself. If the patient has just recounted his fifth prenatal train wreck, you may be sure you have run into a lie factory in some engram. The wrong way to go about correcting this is communicating it to the preclear. The right way to go about it is to find the lie factory, an engram containing such a remark as, "Tell me anything! Tell me anything. I don't care so long as you say something. But for God's sakes don't tell me the truth, I can't stand it!" Or "You can't tell him the truth. It would hurt too much." There are a thousand forms of lie factory. And they are not too uncommon.

Never tell the preclear why you are looking for anything. If you say you want a lie factory, the lie factory will make up a lie factory. If you say you want an emotional charge, you will inhibit any emotional charge from discharging. Simply make a quiet estimate of the situation, reduce everything which seems valid and keep on trying to get the reason why the case is not functioning as well as possible.

The test for validity of an engram is not *plot.* Plot is worthless. Engrams are just collections of remarks contained in periods of "unconsciousness." It makes no difference whatever whether these remarks agree with the way the auditor thinks a life should be run or the way a preclear should look up to his parents. Plot is something writers put in stories. Auditors have nothing to do with it.

An engram is basically illogical and irrational; don't try to read rationality into one! If the parents were known to be fine, upstanding members of the community and the engrams seem to indicate that Mama nightly played the prostitute, accept the engrams.

Validity is very simply established. Ask these questions of the engram:

1. Does it have a somatic?
2. Does the somatic undulate, which is to say, undergo a running change?
3. Does it reduce? (If it does not, the content the preclear is running is wrong or the engram is way up the chain and has others before it.)
4. Does the engramic content agree with the patient's aberration?
5. Does the somatic agree with psychosomatic ills the patient is known to have had?
6. Does it bring relief to the patient? And this last is more important than all the rest.

Because mental healers of the past have grandly said, "Oh, this does not fit with *my* idea of how life is run," is no reason an auditor should run Dianetics off the rails. Mental healers of yesteryear did not get results. Dianetics gets results: and one of the most important reasons why Dianetics gets results is that it is not trying to warp life to fit Dianetics, but is applying Dianetics to life. Many new and startling things will come to the notice of the auditor. His motto, as seen on an ancient English crest where a ninety-foot raven stood upon a castle, could read, "Be surprised at nothing."

The Kinsey Report did not begin to tell the story you, as an auditor, will get in Dianetics. Because the mother, by herself, is neither the face she showed Junior or the face she showed society and because mother and father, by themselves, do not conduct themselves as they might be supposed to have done in society is insufficient reason to force a preclear to go on being an aberree.

Continually in the psychiatric texts we come upon patients who tried to tell psychiatrists about prenatal life and who were told, with droll solemnity, that the incidents were imaginary. Patients who had been given up on all fronts by all existing schools because their data was not tailored to fit the belief of those schools have recovered fully and achieved optimum mental condition, well above that of their former mentors, with Dianetics, partially because Dianetics does not set itself above the facts of life. The Dianeticist not only requires the patient to face reality by running the engrams, but he also requires himself to face reality by accepting the fact that whatever the content, if it fits *any* of the above conditions listed, it is valid in therapy.

Auditing means to listen; it also means to compute. Computing on a case consists of establishing where the patient departs from optimum rationality in his conduct of life, but more important, where physically painful and painful emotion engrams exist and how they can be approached and reduced.

Patients discover some astonishing things about their parents and relatives when they are in therapy. Often they discover, like one patient who had believed he had daily been beaten by his father, that life was actually much better than it had seemed.

Premarital conception cases are very common, with the patient yet unborn discovering himself at his parents' wedding. And these cases are often very difficult to resolve since they contain so much secrecy in their engrams.

The lie factory mechanisms will often try to give Mama extra lovers and try to make Papa into a raving beast, but a lie factory is very easy to detect: the incidents brought forth do not run like engrams: the second time over their content is widely changed, they do not have somatics and their content is not aberrative.

In short, the test is whether or not one has an actual engram, not whether or not the engram makes sense. For father could well have been a raving beast in a boudoir and mother could well have had coitus with the boarders: and father could well have been a tame lamb for all the reputation mother gave him post-birth and mother could well have been a frigid prude despite the wild tales the preclear might have heard. The truth will come out in the reduction, but its truth is no concern of the auditor's beyond getting up engrams.

First, last and always, get engrams, get them as early as possible for pain, later for emotion, get them, erase them, discharge them, clear them! That they did not compute as true data was what drove the aberree into being an aberree. Leave plot to writers: our task is therapy.

But don't "buy garbage": ask for the somatic, see if it varies as the preclear utters the words. Test for engrams. And devil take the plot.

DIANETIC DON'TS

Don't give any patient a positive suggestion as therapy in itself or to assist therapy.

Don't fail to give a canceller at every session's beginning and use it at every session's end.

Don't ever tell a patient he can "remember this in present time" because the somatic will come to present time and that is very uncomfortable.

Don't ever, ever, ever, ever tell a patient that he can "remember everything that ever happened to him in present time" because that groups everything in present time if the patient has slid into a deep trance. And that makes it necessary to unsnarl a whole case. Want to waste two hundred hours?

Don't ever retaliate in any way when a patient in reverie gets angry at you. *Follow the Auditor's Code.* If you get angry with him, you may throw him into an apathy which will take you many hours to undo.

Don't evaluate data or tell a patient what is wrong with him.

Don't crow. If the preclear is your wife or husband or child, don't rub it in that the favorite argument phrase was out of an engram. Of course it was!

Don't question the validity of data. Keep your reservations to yourself. Audit the information for your own guidance. If the patient doesn't know what you think, the engrams will never get a chance to evade.

Don't ever snap a patient to present time just because he begs for it. If he is in the middle of an engram, the only way out of it is *through* it. The power of the engram is slight when the patient is returned to it. It turns on hard when the patient comes to present time. The patient will have a nervous shock if he is snapped to present.

Don't ever get frightened, no matter what kind of squirming or squalling a patient may do. It isn't serious, any of it, although it is sometimes dramatic.

Don't ever promise to Clear a case: promise only to Release it. You may have to go away or work on something more urgent. And a broken promise to a preclear will be taken very hard.

Don't interfere with the private life of a preclear or give him guidance. Tell him to make up his own mind about what he should do.

Don't break the Auditor's Code. It is there to protect *you*, not just the preclear. Therapy can't hurt him if you do but half a job on it and do half of that wrong; breaking the code can make you very uncomfortable because it will make you a target of the preclear and cost you considerable extra work.

Don't leave engrams half-reduced when you are given them by the file clerk.

Don't get inventive about Dianetics until you have worked at least one case out. And don't get too inventive until you have worked a case which has sonic, a case which has shut-off sonic and a case which has imaginary sonic. Clear these and you will know. And you will have met enough engrams to get some ideas that can be of great benefit to Dianetics. If you don't get ideas after that and after you yourself are in therapy and Cleared, there's something wrong. Dianetics is an expanding science, but don't expand it until you know which way it travels.

Don't mix gasoline and alcohol or Dianetics and other therapy, except purely medical, dispensed by a professional *medical* doctor.

Don't get a case snarled up and then take it to a psychiatrist who knows no Dianetics. Only Dianetics can unsnarl Dianetics and yesterday's methods won't help your patient one slightest bit when all he needs is another run through the one you snapped him out of too fast. Take a cinch on your nerve and send him back through the incident again. In Dianetics, today's obvious nervous breakdown is tomorrow's most cheerful being.

Don't quit, don't balk. Just keep running engrams. And one day you'll have a Release. And another day you'll have a Clear.

DIANETICS—PAST *and* FUTURE

THE HISTORY OF DIANETICS

THE HISTORY of Dianetics would be the history of a voyage of discovery, of an exploration into new and nearly uncharted realms, *Terra Incognita*, the Human Mind, a land which lies an inch behind your forehead.

The voyage has taken twelve years and the labor has been long, but we have charts now and can go and return at will.

Observations of savage and civilized races in this and far climes formed the foundation for the anthropological research: the writings of a few men in the last four thousand years formed the scholarly pilots. The ancient Hindu writings, the work of the early Greeks and Romans including Lucretius, the labors of Francis Bacon, the researches of Darwin and some of the thoughts of Herbert Spencer compose the bulk of the philosophic background. Inevitable absorption from our current culture provided much unnoticed information. The remainder has been what the navigator calls "off the chart."

In 1935 some of the basic research was begun; in 1938 the primary axioms were discovered and formulated. For the next several years these axioms were tested in the laboratory of the world. The war interrupted the work, as wars will, being chaos, but shortly after the cessation of actual hostilities, research was renewed. Within a year the fundamentals of this science as they applied to the human mind had been integrated. They were tested on a long series of random patients and each test further refined the work, but each application brought specific results.

Five years after the initial resumption of labor, in 1950, the work was prepared for release, all tests having brought forth the conclusion that Dianetics *is* a science of mind, that it *does* disclose hitherto unknown laws about thought and that it has worked on every type of inorganic mental and organic psychosomatic illness. Further, in the refinement of form attained, it was proven possible for the work to be used easily by people not lengthily trained.

The goal we have here reached is a science which is workable and which can be worked with success by briefly taught individuals. This goal has not hitherto been attained or even approached.

Once one has gained a foothold on unknown lands, more things become known to him and with each new datum his horizon further widens, including broader bodies of knowledge. Dianetics cures, and cures without failure. And there are further goals.

Education, medicine, politics and art and, indeed, all branches of human thought are clarified with Dianetics. And even so that is not enough.

Dianetics has as yet a brief history: it has a strong youth: it forecasts a better tomorrow. Before it is much older it will have included even more within its scope. The history of Dianetics is scarce begun.

Plan A included the perfection of the science, its testing on patients of all kinds and, finally, the dissemination of Dianetics as pertaining to therapy. That plan ends with the release of this book.

Plan B includes a further research into life force, an attempt at resolution of some of the ills not yet embraced such as cancer and diabetes, and the perfection of techniques discovered and their dissemination. That will end Plan B.

Plan C includes an effort to discover a higher echelon of universal origin and destination, if the problem is one of origin and destination, and the factors and forces involved to the end of securing a better understanding and useful application of the knowledge so gained, if gained, and if so gained, its dissemination.

A portion of Plan B is the organization of a foundation so that the research can be more swiftly accomplished.

The history of Dianetics has just begun. What other things begin with the origin of a science of mind only tomorrow can tell.

JUDICIARY DIANETICS

This brief summary of Judiciary Dianetics is included in this present work as an aid to the auditor.

Judiciary Dianetics covers the field of adjudication within the society and among the societies of Man. Of necessity, it embraces jurisprudence and its codes and establishes precision definitions and equations for the establishment of equity. It is the science of judgment.

Jurisprudence and its adjudications are constructed on the cornerstones of *right* and *wrong*, *good* and *evil*. Definition of these is inherent in Dianetics: by these definitions a correct solution can be reached with regard to any action or actions of Man.

The fundamental test of rationality is the ability to differentiate right from wrong. The fundamental factors in establishing censure are good and evil. Without precision definition of these four factors, any structure of law or judgment is rendered forceless and becomes involved through its introduction of arbitrary factors which seek to adjudicate by introducing errors to nullify errors. Penal codes which will answer all needs can only be written when precision, scientific definitions exist for the four factors, and civil equity which will not lead to injustice can only then be established and formulated.

The problems of jurisprudence and, indeed, all judgment are inextricably interwoven with the problems of behavior.

An ideal society would be a society of unaberrated persons, Clears, conducting their lives within an unaberrated culture: for either the person or the culture may be aberrated. The aberrations of the culture enter into the equations of conduct as irrational factors both from the door of education and of social customs and jurisprudence. It is not enough that an individual be himself unaberrated, for he discovers himself within the confines of a society which itself has compounded its culture into many unreasonable prejudices and customs.

The establishment of actual source for wrong and evil is a fundamental problem of all jurisprudence. The actual source unfortunately lies in the irrationalities of those in past generations who, working with limited knowledge and oppressed by their environs, sought solutions with equations which contained false and indefinite factors. These generations, long entombed, cannot be brought to bar. We are the heirs to all the ages of the past and that is good: but we are heirs as well to all the irrationalities of the past and that is evil. Under such circumstances and in the absence of broad reason, adjudication by the auditor of the preclear as relates to evil or wrong actions cannot be performed with accuracy. The criminal and the insane, the hypochondriac and the wife-beater, the merciless dictator who seeks to shake the world and the street cleaner who only sits and weeps are all, each one, gripped and driven by their own sources of unreason, by the world which has entered into the hidden depths of their pain-wracked minds and which, in the form of social aberration, pounds against them from without.

The auditor is interested in what has been done *to*, not done *by* his patient; for whatever the patient has done is forever beyond recall and was not the source, but was only the manifestation of his griefs.

Given a society of unaberrated persons, given a culture from which has been deleted all unreason, then and only then can Man be truly responsible for his acts, then and only then. But we must take the shadow of the responsibility now for the fact of it. A man does not *have* to surrender to his engrams.

Perhaps at some distant date only the unaberrated person will be granted civil rights before law. Perhaps the goal will be reached at some future time when only the unaberrated person can attain to and benefit from citizenship. These are desirable goals and would produce a marked increase in the survival ability and happiness of Man.

Even now the codes of jurisprudence can be reformed and it can be ascertained with precision whether the act which brought the individual before law was an aberrated act, or stemmed from an aberration of culture, or was an act which was committed to the detriment of another or of society. Surely the process of punishment can be refined so as to sentence the individual, not to further aberration as a prisoner or a ruined man, but to a higher plane of reason through the deletion of the aberration.

The past acts of an individual who has been Cleared should be stricken from his record even as his illnesses have been, for with the cause removed there can be no point in retribution unless society itself is so aberrated that it desires to operate on sadistic principles.* There is more than idealism here, for it can be shown that aberration in individuals and the society rise in progressive ratio to the amount of punishment employed.

Efforts to resolve problems of jurisprudence which yet did not embrace precision definitions for *right* and *wrong*, *good* and *evil*, had recourse only to a principle known in Dianetics as the Introduction of an Arbitrary. Broad, unchangeable rules were thrust into problems in an effort to resolve them and yet each new rule further drove reason aside so that more rules were needed. An arbitrary structure is one in which one error has been observed and an effort has been made to correct it by introducing another error. In progressive complexity, new errors must be introduced to nullify the evil effects of old errors. A culture, to say nothing of jurisprudence, grows complex and unwieldy in progressive ratio to the number of new evils it must introduce in an effort to nullify old evils. At last there can be no reason; there can be but force and where there lives no reason and yet lives force, there is naught but the maelstrom of an insane rage. Where there dwells an insane rage, still unresolved, there must at length come apathy; and apathy, dwindling down, inevitably reaches death.

We are here at a bridge between one state of Man and a next. We are above the chasm which divides a lower

* Our present society is not aberrated in this respect: the insane man is not held guilty or responsible for his acts. Lacking definition of a precise scientific nature for insanity and failing to recognize that all irrational acts are temporary insanity, the society has not been able to carry out its fundamental intention.

from a higher plateau and this chasm marks an artificial evolutionary step in the progress of Man.

The auditor is at that bridge. When Cleared, he will be at its higher end. He will watch much traffic cross. He may see customs, laws, organizations and societies attempt to avoid the bridge, but being swept along, tumble into a nothingness below.

In his attitude toward his preclears or toward society at large, he can gain nothing by reprimanding and judging past error in the light of current sentience. Not only can he gain nothing, but he can inhibit progress. It is a remorseless fact that the attack upon unreason has begun. Attack unreason, not the society or the man.

DIANETICS AND WAR

The social organisms which we call states and nations behave and react in every respect as though they were individual organisms. The culture has its analytical mind, the combined sentience of its citizens in general and its artists, scientists and statesmen in particular. The social standard memory bank is the data accumulated along the generations. And the social organism has as well its reactive mind as represented by the prejudices and irrationalities of the entire group. This reactive mind is served by an engram bank wherein lie past painful experiences and which dictates reactive action on certain subjects whenever those subjects are restimulated in the society. This, all too briefly, is an analogy used in Political Dianetics.

The social organism behaves in a manner which can be graphed on the Tone Scale; it has its survival dynamic and its suppressors, its internal suppression due to engrams and its urge toward an infinity of optimum duration. Criminals, traitors and zealots constitute, for instance, internal engrams which suppress the survival potential on the Tone Scale.

There is a precision definition for each social level as related to the Tone Scale. A free society, working in complete cooperation toward common goals would be a Tone 4 society. A society hindered by arbitrary restrictions and oppressive laws would be a Tone 2 society. A society managed and dictated to by the whims of one man or a few men would be a Tone 1 society. A society governed by the mystery and superstition of some mystic body would be a Tone 0 society. The potential of survival in each case can be seen anywhere in history. Any Golden Age is a Tone 4. Oppressive practices, individual greeds and miscalculation in general reduce the society by introducing into it dissatisfied elements. To cope with these, in the past, further oppression has been used. The survival of the society reduced further. With more oppression came new engrams and so down the Tone Scale slipped the chances of long survival. And with this reduction of potential came pain as the lower zones were entered.

Societies rise and fall on the Tone Scale. But there is a danger point below which a society cannot go without reacting as would an individual so suppressed: the society reaches a break point and goes mad. This point is around 2.0.

The quarrel of society with society, nation with nation, has many causes, all of them more or less irrational. There have been many times when one society was forced to crush another less sentient than itself. But with each clash, new engrams were born both in the international scene and within the societies themselves.

War is an international Tone 1. It is no more rational than any individual who, reaching a general and chronic

Tone 1, is placed in an institution or, temporarily Tone 1, commits some crime and is thereafter imprisoned. But there is no jailer to societies, there is at this time only death and so they die and so they have died.

Before this time no tool could be employed by a nation but force when faced with another nation gone mad. By contagion of aberration, both nations then went mad. No nation ever fully won a war. No nation ever finally triumphed by force of arms. No nation ever averted war by posing threat or exhibiting defense.

Man is now faced, by these pyramiding hatreds, with weapons so powerful that Man himself may vanish from the Earth. There is no problem in the control of these weapons. They explode when and where Man tells them to explode. The problem is in the control of Man.

There is no national problem in the world today which cannot be resolved by reason alone. All factors inhibiting a solution of the problem of war and weapons are arbitrary factors and have no more validity than the justified explanations of a thief or murderer.

The farmer of Iowa has no quarrel with the storekeeper of Stalingrad. Those who say such quarrels exist *lie.*

There are no international concerns which cannot be resolved by peaceable means, not in the terms of supranational government, but in the terms of reason.

Jockeying with indefinable ideologies, playing with mass ignorance, non-existent entities like nightmares march the world in the form of the Gods of Ism.

No self-interest can be so great as to demand the slaughter of Mankind. He who would demand it, he who would not by every rational means avert it, is insane. There is *no* justification for war.

Behind the curtains of language and different customs populaces are taught to recognize no kinship with other populaces. Taught by their own terrors and governed by their own aberrations, leaders hold up other isms as detestable things.

There is no perfect political state on earth today, there is not even a good definition of a perfect political creed. States are the victims of internal and external aberrations.

Dianetics addresses war because there is in fact a race between the science of mind and the atom bomb. There may be no future generation to know which won.

Rationality alone can guide Man past these threats to his extinction.

Insanity does not exist without a confusion of definitions and purpose. The solution to the international problem does not lie in the regulation or curtailment of weapons nor yet in the restraints of men. It lies in the definition of political theory and policy in such terms that there can be no mistaking the clear processes; it lies in the establishment of rational goals toward which societies can collectively and individually work; and it lies in an inter-social competition of gains so great that none become dispensable to any other.

Man's primary fight is not with Man: that is insanity. Man's primary fight is with those elements which oppress him as a species and bar his thrust toward high goals. Man's fight is with the elements, with space and time, and with species which are destructive to him. He has hardly begun his conquest. He is just now armed with tools enough and science enough to make good his conquest of the Universe. He has no time to bicker and indulge in tantrums and yah-yah across back fences about atom bombs.

The harnessing of atomic power puts other worlds within his reach. Why haggle for this one? The late discoveries in the field of photosynthesis bid fair to feed and clothe him royally even though he number a thousand times his present billions on Earth. For what reason can he quarrel? Why?

Two rational men will enter into a contest of gain and worth and production. Are these mighty nations, these powerful, fearful, thundering "giants," actually small and poorly educated, barely sane little boys screaming insults at each other over the possession of a dead cat? What of armies? Armies die. If might makes right, then Rome still rules the world. Who fears now this archaeological curiosity that was Rome?

There is a higher goal, a better goal, a more glorious victory than gutted towns and radiation-burned dead. There is freedom and happiness and plenty and a whole Universe to be won.

He who would not see it is far from worthy to rule. He who would indulge his hates is too insane to advise.

How much can Man conquer? He loses if he conquers Man. He wins if he conquers his own fears and conquers then the stars.

Attack the natural enemies of Man, attack them well, and war of Man with Man cannot thereafter be a problem. This is rationality.

Dianetics is not interested in saving the world, it is interested only in preventing the world from being saved. One more time would be fatal! Dianetics is not against fighting; it defines what may be fought. Those things include the sources of Man's travail within the individual, within the society and the enemies of all Mankind. Man, bewildered, has not known his enemies. They are visible now: attack!

THE FUTURE OF THERAPY

In twenty or a hundred years the therapeutic technique which is offered in this volume will appear to be obsolete.

Should this not prove to be the case, then the author's faith in the inventiveness of his fellow Man will not have been justified. We have here something which has not before existed, an invariably working science of mind. The application methods cannot but be refined.

All sciences begin with the discovery of basic axioms. They progress as new data is discovered and as the scope of the science is widened. Various tools and techniques rise up continually, improved and re-improved. The basic axioms, the initial discoveries of Dianetics are such solid scientific truths that they will be altered but little. The data discovered by those axioms is already large and daily expanding. The techniques of using that data as represented in this volume will, before much more time elapses, be modified and improved. Their virtue just now is that these techniques work and produce good, solid, scientific results.

Once upon a time somebody set up the basic principles which had to do with fire. There had not been controlled fire before. Cooking, heating and finally metallurgy made a new culture. The basic principles of fire are not much altered. The techniques employed in handling fire soon after it was discovered by Man would be considered somewhat obsolete to us now. We have matches and lighters and fuels today, but just after fire was understood and began to be used, the bow-drill fire maker and flint and steel would have been considered marvelous inventions: even so, Man was already using fire and had been using it with profit for some time both as a weapon and as a household utility when the bow-drill and flint and steel were discovered or invented.

In the case of the wheel, basic principles were laid down which have not altered to this day. The first workable wheel must have been a rather unwieldy affair. But compared to *no* wheel, it was a miracle.

Thus with Dianetic therapy. The basic principles, axioms and general discoveries of Dianetics form an organization not before possessed by Man. Not unlike the first fires and the first wheels, the therapy technique can be enormously improved. It works now; it can be used now with safety and effectiveness.

There are two definite drawbacks to this present technique. It demands more skill of the auditor than should be necessary and it is not as swift as it could be. The auditor should not be required to do any computing whatever and, indeed, a therapy technique could be envisioned where no auditor at all was necessary, for he is vital at the present time. A complete Clear should take but a handful of hours. The problems here are those of improvement in terms of less skill required and less work.

One might say that it is an imposition upon a mathematician and philosopher to require him to resolve all the problems himself and to put forth all improvements. Indeed, it is an imposition that he be required to develop any technique of application at all, for there should be in any society an apportionment of labor.

When the basic axioms and computations were finished, it was impossible to release them for there were none to whom such research could be released for application. Thus the work had to be carried out to its furthest extent of not only experimentation, but the development and proof of the techniques of application.

One might here use an analogy of bridge engineering. Let us suppose that two plateaus exist, one higher than the other, with a canyon between them. An engineer sees that if the canyon could be crossed by traffic, the hitherto unused higher plateau, being much more fertile and pleasant, would become the scene of a new culture. He sets himself the task of building a bridge. It had been supposed that no bridge could be built across the canyon and, indeed, since those on the lower plateau could not see the higher level, the existence of the higher plateau itself was denied. The engineer, by evolving new principles of bridge building and discovering new significance in his materials, manages to throw a bridge across the canyon. He himself crosses and he inspects the plateau carefully; others cross over his bridge and examine the new terrain with delight. Still more and more cross the bridge. The bridge is solid and, if not wide, can yet safely be negotiated. It has not been built for heavy, fast traffic. But it contains the basic principles and axioms by which the canyon can be spanned again and again. Many people begin to approach the canyon and look up.

What sort of an opinion would you have of the society on the lower plateau if they but moaned and wept and argued and gave no hand at all in the matter of widening the bridge or making new bridges?

In this handbook we have the basic axioms and a therapy which works.

For God's sake, get busy and build a better bridge!

Dianetics Terms

ABERRATION: Any deviation or departure from rationality. Used in Dianetics to include psychoses, neuroses, compulsions and repressions of all kinds and classifications.

ABERREE: Dianetic neologism for any aberrated individual.

ANALYTICAL MIND: That mind which computes–the "I" and his consciousness.

AUDITOR: The individual who administers Dianetic therapy. To audit means "to listen" and also "to compute."

BASIC: The first engram on any chain of similar engrams.

BASIC-BASIC: The first engram after conception, the basic of all chains by sole virtue of being the first moment of pain.

BOUNCER: Any engram command which, when approached by the analytical mind on the time track, makes the patient move back toward present time.

CHAINS: Any series of incidents in the engram bank which have similar content.

CLEAR: The optimum individual; no longer possessed of any engrams.

Dictionary: Bright; unclouded, hence, serene; clean; audible; discriminating; understanding; free from doubt; sure; innocent; net, as profit over expenses; free from debt; free from any entanglement. *v.t.* To make clear, as of dirt or obstruction; to enlighten; to free from guilt, blame, etc.; to open for passage; to disentangle. *v.i.* To become clear and bright. *n.* A clear space or part.

DEMON: A bypass *circuit* in the mind, called "demon" because it was long so interpreted. Probably an electronic mechanism.

DENYER: Any engram command which makes a patient believe that the engram does not exist.

DIANETICS: (Greek *dia*, through, and *nous*, mind or soul); what the mind (or soul) is doing to the body.

DYNAMIC: The urge, thrust and purpose of life–SURVIVE!–in its four manifestations: self, sex, group and Mankind.

ENGRAM: Any moment of greater or lesser "unconsciousness" on the part of the analytical mind which permits the reactive mind to record; the total content of that moment with all perceptics.

ENGRAM BANK: The storage place in the body where engrams, with all their percepts, are recorded and retained and from which engrams act upon the analytical mind and the body.

ENGRAM COMMAND: Any phrase contained in an engram.

ERASE: To cause an engram to "vanish" entirely by recountings, at which time it is filed as memory and experience.

GROUPER: An engram command which makes the time track or incidents on it become tangled in such a way that the track appears shortened.

HOLDER: Any engram command which makes an individual remain in an engram knowingly or unknowingly.

MEMORY: Anything which, perceived, is filed in the standard memory bank and can be recalled by the analytical mind.

MISDIRECTOR: Any engram command which makes the patient move in a way or direction on the track which is contrary to instructions of the auditor or the desires of the analytical mind of the patient.

PERCEPTIC: Any sense message such as a sight, sound, smell, etc.

PRECLEAR: Any person who has been entered into Dianetic therapy.

PRERELEASE: Any patient who is entered into therapy to accomplish a Release from his chief difficulties, psychosomatic or aberrational.

PSYCHOSOMATIC: Any physical disorder or ill generated by the body itself.

REACTIVE MIND: The cellular-level mind which is not "unconscious" but is always conscious–the hidden mind, hitherto unknown.

REDUCE: To render an engram free from somatic or emotion by recountings.

RELEASE: Any person who has been advanced to a state approximating 1950 normal by Dianetic therapy, whether advanced from a psychotic or neurotic condition. The act of releasing by therapy.

SOMATIC: Dianetic neologism for pain, any body condition experienced when contacting an engram; the pain of a psychosomatic illness.

SONIC: Recall by hearing a past sound with the "mind's ear."

STANDARD MEMORY BANK: The storage place in the mind where all consciously perceived data (sight, sound, hearing, smell, organic sensation, kinesthesia, tactile as well as past mental computations) are recorded and retained and from which they are relayed to the analytical mind. Includes all data of a conscious nature from conception to "now."

SUPPRESSOR: The exterior forces which reduce the chances of the survival of any form.

SYMBIOTE: Any entity of life or energy which assists an individual or Man in his survival.

TIME TRACK: The timespan of the individual from conception to present time on which lies the sequence of events of his life.

VISIO: Recall by seeing a past sight with the "mind's eye."

Fundamental Axioms *of* Dianetics

The Dynamic Principle of Existence—SURVIVE!

Survival, considered as the single and sole Purpose, subdivides into four *dynamics*. By *symbiote* is meant all entities and energies which aid survival.

DYNAMIC ONE is the urge of the individual toward survival for the individual and his symbiotes.

DYNAMIC TWO is the urge of the individual toward survival through procreation; it includes both the sex act and the raising of progeny, the care of children and their symbiotes.

DYNAMIC THREE is the urge of the individual toward survival for the group or the group for the group and includes the symbiotes of that group.

DYNAMIC FOUR is the urge of the individual toward survival for Mankind or the urge toward survival of Mankind for Mankind as well as the group for Mankind, etc., and includes the symbiotes of Mankind.

The *absolute goal* of survival is immortality or infinite survival. This is sought by the individual in terms of himself as an organism, as a spirit or as a name, or as his children, as a group of which he is a member or as Mankind and the progeny and symbiotes of others as well as his own.

The reward of survival activity is *pleasure*.

The ultimate penalty of destructive activity is death or complete non-survival, and is *pain*.

Successes raise the survival potential toward infinite survival.

Failures lower the survival potential toward death.

The human mind is engaged upon perceiving and retaining data, composing or computing conclusions and posing and resolving problems related to organisms along all four dynamics and the purpose of perception, retention, concluding and resolving problems is to direct its own organism and symbiotes and other organisms and symbiotes along the four dynamics toward survival.

Intelligence is the ability to perceive, pose and resolve problems.

The *dynamic* is the tenacity to life and vigor and persistence in survival.

Both the *dynamic* and *intelligence* are necessary to persist and accomplish and neither is a constant quantity from individual to individual, group to group.

The *dynamics* are inhibited by engrams, which lie across them and disperse life force.

Intelligence is inhibited by engrams, which feed false or improperly graded data into the analyzer.

Happiness is the overcoming of not unknown obstacles toward a known goal and, transiently, the contemplation of or indulgence in pleasure.

The *analytical mind* is that portion of the mind which perceives and retains experience data to compose and resolve problems and direct the organism along the four dynamics. *It thinks in differences and similarities.*

The *reactive mind* is that portion of the mind which files and retains physical pain and painful emotion and seeks to direct the organism solely on a stimulus-response basis. *It thinks only in identities.*

The *somatic mind* is that mind which, directed by the analytical or reactive mind, places solutions into effect on the physical level.

A *training pattern* is that stimulus-response mechanism resolved by the analytical mind to care for routine activity or emergency activity. It is held in the somatic mind and can be changed at will by the analytical mind.

Habit is that stimulus-response reaction dictated by the reactive mind from the content of engrams and put into effect by the somatic mind. It can be changed only by those things which change engrams.

Aberrations, under which is included all deranged or irrational behavior, are caused by engrams. They are stimulus-response pro- and contra-survival.

Psychosomatic ills are caused by engrams.

The *engram* is the single source of aberrations and psychosomatic ills.

Moments of "unconsciousness" when the analytical mind is attenuated in greater or lesser degree are the only moments when engrams can be received.

The *engram* is a moment of "unconsciousness" containing physical pain or painful emotion and all perceptions and is not available to the analytical mind as experience.

Emotion is three things: engramic response to situations, endocrine metering of the body to meet situations on an analytical level and the inhibition or the furtherance of life force.

The *potential value* of an individual or a group may be expressed by the equation

$$PV = ID^{x}$$

where I is Intelligence and D is Dynamic.

The *worth* of an individual is computed in terms of the alignment, on any dynamic, of his potential value with optimum survival along that dynamic. A high PV may, by reversed vector, result in a negative worth as in some severely aberrated persons. A high PV on any dynamic *assures* a high worth only in the unaberrated person.

DIANETICS *into the* FUTURE

Since exploding into a darkening world in May of 1950, Dianetics has changed lives for countless millions, opening the doors wide to personal well-being and achievement.

Dianetics brings an understanding of the human mind that exists nowhere else. One's potentials appear greater, yet more attainable. Life's hidden barriers fall away. And one becomes more and more oneself.

Dianetics is incomparable. It stands on workability and fact, tested in the proving grounds of public application for three-quarters of a century. Its ultimate impact may yet be unknown, but this much is certain: It will continue to elevate our culture and uplift its people for all the years to come.

In the pages which follow you will discover the greater story of this extraordinary and timeless book—its reach, its influence and its enduring legacy.

DIANETICS
L. RON HUBBARD
DIANETICS

DIANETICS *into the* FUTURE

THE HISTORY of Dianetics has just begun. What other things begin with the origin of a science of the mind only tomorrow can tell.

Thus L. Ron Hubbard prepared his readers for advancements he knew would surely follow, and thus we present this follow-up history of Dianetics in the 21st century.

Appropriately, that history begins with the May 9th 1950 publication of *Dianetics: The Modern Science of Mental Health*, and what was rightfully described as a national Dianetics storm. Among other barometers of the day were 750 auditing groups spontaneously forming across America, and many thousands more embarking into *Terra Incognita* as the title continued topping a *New York Times* bestseller list. Also forming in a whirlwind of enthusiasm beyond the spring of 1950 were the far-flung Dianetics Research Foundations where L. Ron Hubbard lectured, instructed and otherwise met a staggering popular demand. Nevertheless, and precisely as promised in his own closing chapter of this book, further research was most definitely soon underway–and expressly in accord with what he enumerated as Plan B: a concerted investigation into the life force.

TEN STAR

Daily N…

…S ANGELES 54

…ESDAY, SEPT. 5, 1950

…IDENT NEWSPAPER FOR INDEPENDEN…

DIANETICS SERIES TODAY DAILY NEWS

…e of the most controversial sub-…f recent months–the new sci-…f Dianetics–is comprehensively …ed in the language of the lay-… …tarting today in the Daily News. …Daily News staff writer, with …tions to keep an open mind on …bject and make a thorough study …ead L. Ron Hubbard's best-sell-…ook, interview the author and …ed classes of instruction.

…at he read, what he saw and …e heard he reports today in the …f a series of articles offering an …ive analysis of Dianetics.

…be well informed on this popu-…bject, start reading the series …on Page 2.

…ess-Telegram

Best Sellers

…TION

…IANETICS, by Hubbard.

…W I RAISED MYSELF FROM …ILURE TO SUCCESS IN SELLING, … Bettger.

…ORLDS IN COLLISION, by Velikovsky.

…OOK YOUNGER AN…y Hauser.

…E YOUR REAL SEL…

…ON

THE CARDINAL, by…

THE KING'S CAVA…

THE WALL, by Her…

THE BIG FISHERM…

EACH BRIGHT RI…

Hubbard's di… they've all …

(This is the first of a daily ser… newly formulated science of Di… known as Dianetic processing,… impartial report on the claims … mulator of scientific axioms of … attracted millions of adherents.

WED, SEPT. 6, 1950 • DAILY NEWS, LOS ANGELES • 2

Dianetics: A study of the mind–fastest growing 'm…

L. RON HUBBARD LAUGHS READILY

Because "Dianetics is no solemn adventure"

HE EXPLAINS, DOES NOT DEFEND

"A science of mind was a goal ... of Man"

ALL OF LIFE WAS FASCINATI…

"I began to think of men as basic…

Dianetics – taking U. S. by storm

(continued from page 2)

was obvious that mind meters body function." He was later to conclude that "what has been called emotion is really in two sections: first, there is the endocrine system which, handled either by the analytical mind... or the reactive mind...brings emotional responses of fear, enthusiasm, apathy, etc." Glands were an instrument of body control!

Hubbard confesses he finally tired of listening with half an ear to lectures repeating the dictums of authority while he was doing his own thinking on other planes, and he left the university sans degree.

He went on a cruise to the West Indies aboard a four-masted schooner. This was at the depth … 1930s and upon his return he encountered the necessity of nourishing the body as well as the mind.

During his student days he had begun to write pulp fiction and he turned to this as a means of livelihood. His first stock in trade were flying stories, to be followed by travel and adventure yarns and by science fiction.

When he married his economic problem was doubled, so he doubled his output. He became one of the most prolific and most successful writers in his field.

"I got pretty good at it. I wrote 100,000 words a month to support myself."

A note to critics here. Do not expect any apology from Hubbard today for Hubbard's past. As for trappings, he regards higher education as now administered as mere surface scratchings.

Neither will he offer any excuses for popular identification of him solely as a pulp author. Hacking out potboilers was a living and a means to an end. He regarded himself first and always the scholar and scientist.

By 1935 he was ready to begin some of the basic research, and by 1938 the primary axioms of Dianetics had been discovered and formulated. Hubbard at that time was so nearly tempted to send up a trial balloon that he wrote a book embracing the principles of his science, but he allowed the book to languish unpublished.

"I knew what the principles…

Au… sci…

(Th… the new… therapy… objectiv… Ron H… process…

L. … pher, N… space s… literatu…

He … account… and as… Authori…

He … blocky … hair, la… seemin… ready h… Ene…

ws

EOPLE

lay

ce a year
and the fall
ty is all set

own stores
for months
registers are
gs have all
the rest is up

ay your dollar
rchants have
it, or else their
e.

geles Transit
tric railway are
and equipment
are the restau-

in on dozen bar patrons

Too much overhead forced the Keith Jones cocktail lounge at 727 South Hill street to close its doors today, but the management was philosophical about it—there's no use crying over spilled liquor.

Twelve patrons were quietly imbibing their grog, said bartender Robert Keegan, 30, of 810 South Alvarado street, when the roof fell in.

It isn't exactly the roof, but three tons of overhang that broke loose from its anchorage over the bar. Everyone escaped serious injury, but Keegan suffered painful cuts of the hands when the mirror behind the bar was smashed.

Damage was estimated at $15,000, including destruction of a considerable supply of liquor stock.

Mrs. Opal Brownstein, 40, of 527 Carondelet street, was pinned by one arm to the fallen wreckage and was released by her husband, Irving, 39.

Dianetics believed key to increased zest for living

(Continued from Page 3)

I'd be a lot happier," commented this seemingly very happy man.

Dianetics' list of positives, on the other hand, is a lengthy one, by its composer's own recital.

It can remove the aberrations which make man a selfish and anti-social creature.

It can put an end to his psychosomatic illnesses, such as the common cold, arthritis, migraine, ulcers, allergies, asthma, sinusitis, bursitis, (hysterical) paralysis and (non-pathological) eye trouble, to mention only a few, and possibly a whole host of other ailments which up to now have not been recognized by medicine as psychosomatic in origin. As an example of the latter he reports:

"A number of germ diseases are predisposed and perpetuated by engrams. Tuberculosis is one."

Dianetics can rid society of the costly curse of alcoholism: "All alcoholics are alcoholic because of their engrams. Discharge the reactive engram bank... and the dipsomaniac can drink when he likes and stop."

It can largely discourage the "criminal" practice of abortion, a "crime committed against a child," and it can decimate crimes of violence where the penal system has failed.

It holds hope that man may at last dispense with the ugly institution of war, because wars are the end product of social aberrations at the national level: "By contagion of aberration, both nations (go) mad. Rationality alone can guide man past these threats to his extinction."

It can stamp out homosexuality, which is attributed to attempted abortion: "... with an effective science to handle the problem, a society which would continue to endure perversion... doesn't deserve to exist."

Linked with psychosomatic illnesses, chronic mental derangements, be they cyclical or continuous, can be wiped out.

Dianetics can rectify the mental short circuits which bring accidental death, can increase longevity, minimize the pain of child bearing and present mankind with vast new intellectual vistas by freeing him from the fetters imposed by Precedent and Authority.

"Advance comes from asking free-minded questions of nature, not from quoting the works and thinking the thoughts of bygone years," Hubbard argues. "So long as Aristotle remained the Authority for All, the Dark Ages reigned."

But best of all, he says Dianetics is available to all.

The technique of Dianetic thera py, he insists, is basically simp and can be understood and applie to each other by any two reaso ably intelligent people.

"No previous background in p choanalysis or psychology is n essary."

That claim is the target on w professional men have trained beaviest critical guns.

(Concluded tomorrow)

Federal agents today picked San Jose beauty on a secret p complaint growing out of the tigation of the murder 1st Feb dope runner Abe Davidian.

Charged with having pe herself was Georgia described as the sweeth Russell (Rusty) Deane, on 15 persons indicted in th million dollar narcoti blowup which resul Davidian's slaying.

AAst. U.S Atty, Norma said the complaint, f before U.S. Commission Calverley, was based on Miss Martin gave the Fe jury covering Doane's the day of the murder in

Neukom said she pla her apartment at t moment of the killing, ernment has proof where.

The judge particul the jurors not to allow t influenced by their toward Communism tance or refusal of any testimony.

Dr. Weinbaum wa court at the end of the his blond wife, Lina.

He is charged w perjury and one of fr his denial to an Am last year that he wa the Communist par lent overthrow of government.

Following the the top-ranking p

y about 30,000 of these.

DIANETICS: Husbands are auditing their wives; neighbors form discussion groups

(This is the third of a daily series published by the Daily News on the newly formulated science of Dianetics and the technique of mental therapy known as Dianetic processing. The series will continue an objective and impartial report on the claims and accomplishments of L. Ron Hubbard, formulator of scientific axioms of human thought processes which already have attracted millions of adherents.)

By JOHN CLARKE
(Daily News Staff Writer)

National headquarters of the Hubbard Dianetic Research Foundation ... but, like popula-

Yet even before the Foundation's local branch was opened and before Hubbard came here to lecture and conduct demonstrations of therapy before the initial class of paying students, the movement had fanned out at an epidemic rate.

Dianetics clubs blossomed like wild flowers in the spring, organized by people who merely had read the book, "Dianetics: The Modern Science of Mental Health," urgently recommended to them by other people who had read the book.

Neighbors formed discussion groups, husbands began to "audit" their wives and wives their husbands, and seminars on such vaguely comprehended topics as "Survival Dynamics" and "The Optimum Individual" became ... cultural fare on college cam-

... in July that the ...ened its doors, ...3950 West Sixth ... courses opened ...y building hous- ...and 20 "process- ...South Park View

...tly acquired was a ...t Hoover street and ...evard. This is the ...e," where advanced ... receive intensified ... guidance from ...nts. ... of practical laborato-

ry, where aspiring auditors themselves are audited as well as auditing, or processing, preclears. It is something akin to the pre-graduation cramming of students everywhere. These are seeking to be certified by the Foundation as professional auditors.

Much of this type of training is performed on a team basis, with student A and student B alternating as auditor and pre-clear, as practitioner and patient.

Also much favored in polishing up students is the triad system, whereas student A audits student B, B audits C and C audits A.

Regarded as the "ideal" tryad is one in which all three members are of the same sex, the same general cultural level and whose relationships each to the others is friendly but not intimate.

Still another project involves the reservation of 20 to 30 rooms each weekend at the country club Hotel-Villa at 445 North Rossmore Avenue, where what is obscurely described as "intensive auditing with chemical assist" is conducted on a continuous 4 hour basis.

Participating in these seminars of concentrated therapy each week are 40 student auditors and 30 pre-clears. For each four students there is a professional auditor. He is present not only for purposes of instruction but presumably to supervise the administration of the chemical "assists."

(continued on Page 12, Col 5)

...ement' in America

RESEARCH WAS HIS INSTRUMENT
"I knew what the principles were but ..."

...or tells birth of ...tific brainchild

(...second of a daily series published by the Daily News on ...ulated science of Dianetics and the technique of mental ... as Dianetic processing. The series will continue an ...partial report on the claims and accomplishments of L. ... formulator of scientific axioms of human thought ... already have attracted millions of adherents.)

By JOHN CLARKE
(Daily News Staff Writer)

...bard is a onetime engineer, mathematician, philoso- ...ficer and prolific producer of science fiction of the ...antastic, school of

...re, by his own ...dependent thinker ... a rebel against ...Orthodoxy.

...an of 39 years, ...shocks of very red ... mobile features, ...dless energy and

... humor stand him

motivated out of ignorance (of Dianetics) which is deplorable, or (economic) self-interest, which is even more deplorable.

But if medical men, the book trade, the literary critics, contemporaries in the writing craft, economists, politicians and observers of human phenomena generally have been astounded, appalled or puzzled by the instan-

...er rising slowly ... California is ...d morning low ... afternoon clear... slightly below ...s. Weather Bureau ..., with temperatures ...y Sunday. ... case you're on ... persons a b... ... said has called to in...

DIANETICS
New mental science helps to rationality, zest for living, clai...

(This is the fourth of a daily series published by the Daily News on the newly formulated science of Dianetics and the technique of mental therapy known as Dianetic processing. The series provides an objective and impartial report on the claims and accomplishments of L. Ron Hubbard, formulator of scientific axioms of human thought processes which already have attracted millions of adherents.)

By JOHN CLARKE
(Daily News Staff Writer)

Spectacular success, particularly the sudden variety, does not bring rewards wholly unadulterated by tribulations, irritations and complications previously unexperienced.

L. Ron Hubbard has learned this lesson, if he did not know it before, in he is pleased with explaining what it is.

Almost hourly, by way of illustration, he is called upon to rebuke the misconception that his theories and his conclusions constitute a new religion.

This is the most common of all the false notions about Dianetics which he is called upon to confront and attempt to batter down.

Although he asserts that all human behaviorisms can be accounted for without resort to metaphysics or mysticism, and although he does have a great deal to say about human morals and mores, Hubbard rejects and considers unfair the attempts which have been made to identify or confuse his (scientific) concepts with organized religions, religious philosophies, spiritual be... faiths, cults or deitific venerations

L. Ron Hubbard delivered 155 public lectures in 1950 alone, to meet a nationwide demand for Dianetics.

EVENING ★ ★ ★ EDITION

DAILY MAIL

ON INSIDE PAGES
State - A-12 Regional B-8
Local - B-1 Business - C-1
Sports - D-1 Theater - D-14
Comics - D 16 Weather - D-16

Dianetics-Overnight Whirlwind Success

A Mental Science That Unleashes the Mind

Los Angeles Times

BEST SELLERS

Nonfiction Leaders

1. "Dianetics" — Hubbard
2. "The Mature Mind" — Overstreet
3. "Look Younger, Live Longer" — Ha
4. "Courtroom" Reynolds
5. "Betty Crocker's Picture Cook Book" Crocker
6. "The Little Princesses" — Crawfo
7. "Behind the Flying Saucers" — Sc
8. "Behind Closed Doors" — Zacha
9. "The Effects of Atomic Weapons" Combat Forces Press
10. "Roosevelt in Retrospect" — Gu

PIC

DIANETICS SERIES TODAY IN DAILY NEWS

ontroversial subjects of
science of Dianetics—is
d in the language of the
the Daily News.
iter, with instructions
he subject and make
d L. Ron Hubbard's
ed the author and
n.
and what he heard
series of articles
f Dianetics

The subject is immense and the research trail exhaustive. But suffice it to say, within the space of twelve months, L. Ron Hubbard had indeed identified an animating force within every living thing. This he called *Theta*, and distinguished it as energy existing separate and distinct from the physical universe as we know it. In that regard, Theta was a chink in a wall beyond which lay another realm entirely of *Terra Incognita*. It was also a signpost to a most intriguing statement in his discussion of The Cell and the Organism (Book Two, Chapter Three). That is:

> "Unless we postulate a human soul entering the sperm and ovum at conception, there are things which no other postulate will embrace than that these cells *are* in some way sentient."

The first leg of such research culminated in mid-1951 with the publication of L. Ron Hubbard's next book on Dianetics, *Science of Survival*. That the book is built upon a Hubbard Chart of Human Evaluation by which one can unerringly predict human behavior and pinpoint proper case entrance is also, of course, significant; for here were the first of the technical refinements postulated through previous pages.

L. Ron Hubbard personally demonstrating Dianetics techniques with an early E-Meter.

L. Ron Hubbard in his office at one of the first Scientology organizations.

Meanwhile, and likewise as discussed on an earlier page in this volume, L. Ron Hubbard most definitely succeeded in developing a "very sensitive galvanometer" with which to measure then unknown human energy output. In fact, this was the first in a long line of developing electropsychometers, better known today as the *E-Meter*, and measuring mental state or change of state. Thus, in Dianetics terms, E-Meters were soon employed to pinpoint engrams with unimaginable speed and precision.

Yet the farthest ends of L. Ron Hubbard's research beyond the spring of 1950 followed from that larger Plan C:

> "An effort to discover a higher echelon of universal origin and destination."

Needless to say, the subject is commensurately vast, and ultimately involved no less than an actual measurement of that postulated human soul. (For the record, the first such valuation was conducted with an electropsychometer in Wichita, Kansas through late 1951 with additional tests in Phoenix, Arizona through 1952.) Also needless to say,

L. Ron Hubbard ultimately gave more than 3,000 lectures to delineate discoveries relating to the human mind and spirit.

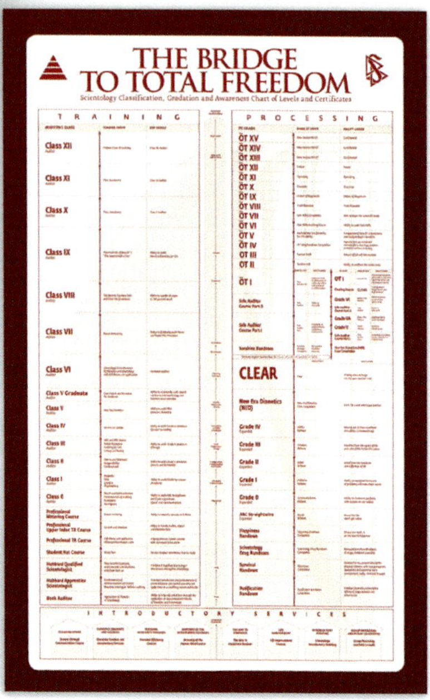

The Scientology Classification, Gradation and Awareness Chart of Levels and Certificates is the chart that shows the step-by-step route to Clear and beyond. There are now tens of thousands of Clears across more than a hundred nations.

the results of those tests would fill many another L. Ron Hubbard volume, but the long and short is this: Within two years of authoring the book you now hold in your hands, L. Ron Hubbard became the first to scientifically isolate and identify the human spirit.

This, then, is the subject of *Scientology* as founded by L. Ron Hubbard in 1952. It literally means "knowing how to know," and is defined as "the study and handling of the spirit in relationship to itself, universes and other life." It both extends from and embraces the central truths of Dianetics, and is thus a fully practical religion. In point of fact, just as you have now glimpsed the State of Clear, so Scientology presents a step-by-step route to even higher states–states not even previously imagined, but nonetheless absolutely real. In that regard, Scientology is that better Bridge L. Ron Hubbard called for when concluding this book. Scientology is that wide and solid route to a vastly higher plateau.

In no way, however, did the story of Dianetics conclude with the founding of Scientology. For as L. Ron Hubbard further predicted:

> "The application methods cannot but be refined."

Accordingly, and specifically toward still faster preclear progress he developed advanced Dianetics procedures. Those procedures are now available in Churches of Scientology world over and, in consequence, there are now tens of thousands of Clears across more than a hundred nations.

Negative Comments by Surgeons Can Harm Unconscious Patients

Patients can hear during operations

Dianetics was the first publication to state that speech during surgery has a negative effect on the unconscious patient.

Also in consequence to the greater advancement of Dianetics is all that now stands as "conventional wisdom" as regards the human mind: the universally standard medical dictionary enjoining physicians, "Nothing [should be] said in the patient's presence that the patient should not hear, because the unresponsive patient is still aware of surroundings and can hear what is said," or the *London Sunday Times* similarly cautioning medicos, "Anesthetized patients often hear subconsciously everything that is said during operations and can suffer ill effects as a result." Then there is the Natural Childbirth Movement recommending silent birthing, while whole schools of medical thought are at last subscribing to the fact that prenatal experience significantly shapes personality.

Finally–and herein lies the other side of the Dianetics story beyond the spring of 1950–there is all this book has come to represent as a worldwide movement unto itself. In a word, there has been no more popular handbook of its kind in history. Since original publication, *Dianetics* has seen translation into more than fifty languages and appeared on some 600 bestseller lists.

Dianetics' unrelenting popularity is additionally measured in more than 600 bestseller lists worldwide.

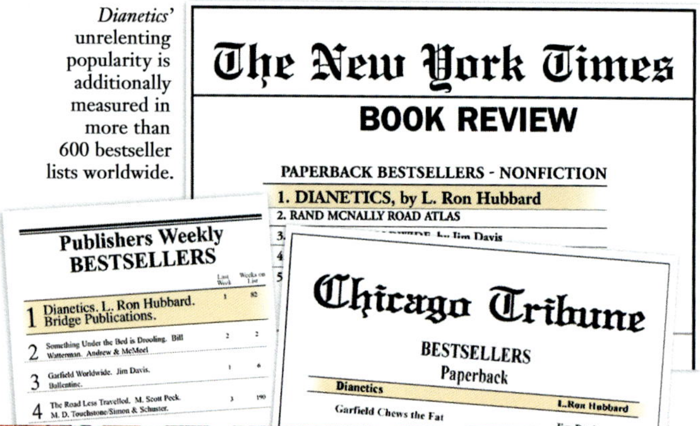
The New York Times

BOOK REVIEW

PAPERBACK BESTSELLERS - NONFICTION

1. DIANETICS, by L. Ron Hubbard
2. RAND MCNALLY ROAD ATLAS

Publishers Weekly BESTSELLERS

		Last Week	Weeks on List
1	Dianetics. L. Ron Hubbard. Bridge Publications.	1	82
2	Something Under the Bed is Drooling. Bill Watterman. Andrew & McMeel	2	2
3	Garfield Worldwide. Jim Davis. Ballentine.	1	6
4	The Road Less Travelled. M. Scott Peck. M. D. Touchstone/Simon & Schuster.	3	190

Chicago Tribune

BESTSELLERS

Paperback

Dianetics — L.Ron Hubbard

Garfield Chews the Fat

There are Dianetics groups in thousands of cities across six continents with new groups forming every week.

Decades after its first publication, it not only earned the *Publishers Weekly* Century Award for an unprecedented 100 weeks on its bestseller list, it also returned to the *New York Times* bestseller list. Moreover, that popularity is entirely universal, with Dianetics Foundations, organizations and grass-roots groups from Asia to Africa and all across the Americas and Europe. To cite but a few representative examples: there are Tibetan monasteries where Dianetics now replaces introspective meditation, and universities where Dianetics has all but supplanted psychology. There are additionally hundreds of state and city offices now proclaiming May 9th as "Dianetics Day," and the Random House Modern Library Reader's poll ranking this book among the ten most significant nonfiction works of the 20th century. While as we continue into this 21st century, a new reader picks up a copy somewhere in the world every 60 seconds, and so embarks upon the journey you yourself have now begun.

How far and how fast one progresses on that journey is, of course, the reader's choice. But there are now Dianetics seminars and courses in thousands of Dianetics groups now established world over, not to mention every Scientology church and mission – and all to speed you towards the personal realization of everything you have just read.

A new reader picks up a copy of *Dianetics*, somewhere in the world, every 60 seconds.

The Church of Scientology Flag Organization – home of upper level services

Today, Dianetics is thriving as part of the
fastest growing religion in the world.

Los Angeles, California, Scientology Headquarters for the United States

Inglewood, California

South Los Angeles, California

San Fernando Valley, California

Pasadena, California

Ventura, California

Silicon Valley, California

San Francisco, California

Los Gatos, California

Denver, Colorado

Portland, Oregon

Las Vegas, Nevada

Orange County, California

San Diego, California

San Jose, California

Sacramento, California

Chicago, Illinois

Columbus, Ohio

Austin, Texas

Atlanta, Georgia

Greater Cincinnati, Ohio

Dallas, Texas

Seattle, Washington

Phoenix, Arizona

Nashville, Tennessee

CHURCH OF
SCIENTOLOGY
Kansas City, Missouri

SCIENTOLOGY
SCIENTOLOGY
Salt Lake City, Utah

Ybor Square
Tampa, Florida

Twin Cities, Minnesota

Washington, D.C.

Orlando, Florida

Miami, Florida

Detroit, Michigan

Harlem, New York

Buffalo, New York

New York, New York

Hundreds of Churches of Scientology with Hubbard Dianetics Centers exist worldwide.

Québec, Canada

Bogotá, Colombia

Mexico City, Mexico

Paris, France

London, United Kingdom

Copenhagen, Denmark

Rome, Italy

Madrid, Spain

Berlin, Germany

Johannesburg, South Africa

Sydney, Australia

Auckland, New Zealand

Kaohsiung, Taiwan

Tokyo, Japan

Dianetics is the solution to the problems we face personally and as a society. In a world where race is pitted against race and nation against nation; where sudden violence shatters lives; where friends and family suffer pain, confusion and unhappiness, this book reveals the one common source and Man's true natural enemy—the reactive mind. And it provides the only technology to get rid of it.

It has stood the test of time, changing lives everywhere for three-quarters of a century.

The time has come for you to start the adventure. Contact your local Dianetics Center or the Church of Scientology and begin walking the road to a better life today.

And may you never be the same again.

Scan the QR code
to find your local Dianetics Center
or the Church of Scientology nearest you
or visit ***dianetics.org/locator***

APPENDIX

Addresses 590

Editor's Glossary of Words, Terms and Phrases 593

Index 689

Addresses

Dianetics is a forerunner and substudy of Scientology, the fastest-growing religion in the world today. Dianetics Centers exist in Churches of Scientology throughout the world, and new ones are continually forming.

Dianetics Centers offer introductory services and can help you begin your journey, or get you started on the adventure of Dianetics auditing. To obtain more information or to locate the Dianetics Center nearest you, visit the Dianetics website:

dianetics.org
e-mail: info@dianetics.org

Every Church of Scientology offers both introductory services as well as formalized training in the subject of Dianetics. They can also provide further information about Mr. Hubbard's later discoveries on the subject of Scientology.

To obtain more information, visit the Scientology website:

scientology.org
e-mail: info@scientology.org

To locate the Center or Church nearest you, visit:

scientology.org/locator

You can also write to the Publications Organizations, listed below, who can direct you to one of the thousands of Centers and Churches world over:

New Era Publications International ApS
United Kingdom
Europe
newerapublications.com
New Era Publications
International ApS
Smedeland 20
2600 Glostrup
Denmark
Tel: (45) 33 73 66 66
Toll-free: 800-8088-8008
E-mail: books@newerapublications.com

Bridge Publications, Inc.
North & South America
Australia, New Zealand & Oceania
Africa & Asia
bridgepub.com
Bridge Publications, Inc.
5600 E. Olympic Blvd.
Commerce, CA 90022
United States
Tel: (323) 888-6200
Toll-free: 1-888-885-5005
E-mail: info@bridgepub.com

L. Ron Hubbard's books and lectures may be obtained from any Church of Scientology or direct from the publishers.

EDITOR'S GLOSSARY
OF WORDS, TERMS AND PHRASES

Words often have several meanings. The definitions used here only give the meaning that the word has as it is used in this book. Technical terms appear in bold type. Beside each definition you will find the page on which it first appears, so you can refer back to the text if you wish.

This glossary is not meant to take the place of standard language or Dianetics and Scientology dictionaries, which should be referred to for any words, terms or phrases that do not appear below.

—The Editors

aberrated: affected by *aberration,* any deviation or departure from rationality. Page iv.

ABERRATION: ANY DEVIATION OR DEPARTURE FROM RATIONALITY. USED IN DIANETICS TO INCLUDE PSYCHOSES, NEUROSES, COMPULSIONS AND REPRESSIONS OF ALL KINDS AND CLASSIFICATIONS. (From *Dianetics Terms.*) From the Latin, *aberrare,* to wander from; Latin, *ab,* away, *errare,* to wander. It means basically to err, to make mistakes, or more specifically to have fixed ideas which are not true. The word is also used in its scientific sense. It means departure from a straight line. If a line should go from A to B, then if it is "aberrated" it would go from A to some other point, to some other point, to some other point, to some other point, to some other point and finally arrive at B. Taken in its scientific sense, it would also mean the lack of straightness or to see crookedly as, in example, a man sees a horse but thinks he sees an elephant. Page i.

ABERREE: DIANETIC NEOLOGISM FOR ANY ABERRATED INDIVIDUAL. (From *Dianetics Terms.*) Page 16.

abiding: continuing without change; enduring; lasting. Page 94.

abreact: express or act out an impulse, emotion, etc., such as one previously forgotten or repressed. Page 465.

Absolute Reality: in some schools of thought, a concept used to explain existence by stating that there is an ultimate reality that is above or goes beyond the laws of nature or is more than physical. Such schools propose an Absolute Reality conceived of as existing in and by itself without relation to anything else. Page 450.

absolutism: the belief that absolutes exist and are obtainable, such as absolute wrong or absolute right. Page 114.

abstract: thought of apart from concrete realities, specific objects or actual instances. An abstract idea is based on general or nonspecific ideas rather than on actual things and events. Page 449.

account: to regard; consider as, as in *"society would account him slightly mad."* Page 85.

Achilles' heel: a vulnerable spot, portion or area. From the story of the Greek warrior Achilles, who was dipped in a magical river soon after birth in an attempt to give him god-like invulnerability. The waters did make him invulnerable, except for the heel by which he was held. During a war he was killed by a poison arrow in that spot. Page 330.

ACTH: *adrenocorticotropic hormone*, a hormone used as a drug in treating allergies, arthritis, asthma and several other disorders. It also stimulates the production of other hormones in the body. Page 123.

acupuncture: a Chinese medical practice or procedure that is said to cure illness or provide local anesthesia by the use of needles inserted at specified points of the body. Page 528.

acute: 1. brief or having a short course as opposed to chronic (long-lasting). Page 34.

2. intense or severe. Page 104.

3. of the senses or nervous system, keen, sharp, quick in catching or responding to impressions; sensitive (to impressions). Page 127.

ad absurdum: in the condition of being to the point of absurdity (utterly or obviously senseless, illogical; contrary to all common sense). Page 467.

address: the aiming or directing of words to a particular person, often characterized as being made with a particular attitude as *"a sympathetic address."* Page 83.

adjudged: determined in one's own judgment; considered, regarded or judged (a thing to be so and so or that it is so and so). Page 169.

adjudication: the act of making a decision, forming an opinion or estimate of, such as by a judge in a court of law. Page 537.

adrenaline: a chemical substance secreted by the adrenal glands, which increases heart rate, blood pressure, etc. Page 64.

adroitly: in a skillful manner; expertly. Page 457.

Aesculapian: having to do with *Aesculapius,* the god of medicine in ancient Greece and Rome, whose descendants, priest-physicians, practiced their art in magnificent temples. Because it was supposed that a visit from Aesculapius brought about a cure of the sick in dreams, patients were put to sleep (using drugs and/or hypnosis) and their dreams interpreted. Page 7.

affront: offense (to one's dignity), as from what is viewed as a deliberate act or display of disrespect. Page 503.

aft (of): in a position behind something, as in *"just aft of the temples."* Page 389.

agent: an active cause. Page 421.

aggregations (of colonies): groups of organisms formed together into a connected structure and living or growing in close association with each other. *Colonies* in this sense means groups or masses of individual animals or plants, of the same kind, living or growing in close association. *Aggregation* is used in its biological sense, the act or process of organisms coming together to form a group. Page 67.

agitate: to stir up feeling, interest, support and the like about something that one feels should be done. Page 489.

Ahriman, Mazda and: *Ahura Mazda,* the supreme deity and creator of all things in Zoroastrianism (an ancient religion of Iran) and *Ahriman,* an evil spirit and arch rival of the deity Mazda. Page 466.

Alexander: Alexander the Great (356–323 B.C.), military general and king of Macedonia (an ancient kingdom in northern Greece), who conquered much of what was then considered the civilized world, stretching from present-day Greece to India. *See also* **defy Alexander.** Page 315.

algae: simple organisms that live in oceans, lakes, rivers, ponds, etc. Algae look like, but differ from, plants by not having leaves, roots or stems and include seaweed. Algae use sunlight as energy to produce their own food. Page 39.

alloys: mixes with something else and lowers in degree; corrupts by mixture. An *alloy* is a metal that is formed by mixing two

Glossary

types of metal together, or by mixing metal with another substance. Page 470.

altruistic: unselfishly concerned for or devoted to the welfare of others. Page 46.

ambivalent: the co-existence of opposing attitudes or feelings, such as love and hate, toward an object, idea, etc. Page 108.

ambiversion: a state of balance between introversion and extroversion. *Introversion* is a directing one's interest inward or to things within self and *extroversion* is a directing one's interest outward or to things outside of self. Page 514.

ammonium chloride: a colorless, crystalline substance used in many cold medicines and cough remedies. Page 486.

amnesia trance: a deep trance of a person as if asleep, making him susceptible to commands. *Amnesia* in this sense refers to the fact that the person normally does not remember what took place during the deep trance state. Page 128.

amniotic: relating to the *amnion*, a sac which forms around the embryo and is filled with a fluid in which the embryo floats, thus absorbing jolts or shocks. Page 177.

amour: a French word meaning love or affection. Page 43.

amulet: an object worn on the body with supposed magical power to protect against injury or evil. Page 471.

analog: representing data by measurement of a continuously varying value that corresponds proportionally to the thing being measured, such as temperature. For instance, in a thermometer, a column of liquid expands or contracts to give an approximate measurement of temperature. Because the liquid can move in a continuous or uninterrupted flow, rather than in the fixed steps or values of numerical digits, the measurement is said to be analog as opposed to digital. Page 450.

analogue: something having analogy to something else. An *analogy* is a comparison between two things that are similar in some respects, often used to help explain something or make it easier to understand. Page 79.

analogy: a comparison between two things that are similar in some respects, often used to help explain something or make it easier to understand. Page 28.

ANALYTICAL MIND: THAT MIND WHICH COMPUTES—THE "I" AND HIS CONSCIOUSNESS. (From *Dianetics Terms.*) Page viii.

anemia: a condition of the blood in which there are too few red blood cells, resulting in breathlessness, weakness, etc. Page 97.

Anglo-Saxon: plain and simple English, especially language that is blunt, short and often rude or vulgar. Page 437.

anguish: extreme distress, suffering or pain. Page 119.

anthropological: pertaining to the science that deals with the origins, physical and cultural development, biological characteristics and social customs and beliefs of humankind. Page 535.

anthropomorphic: described or thought of as having human form or attributes. From Greek *anthropo*, human and *morpho*, form or structure. Page 41.

antibodies: proteins produced by certain blood cells as a primary immune defense to attack specific viruses, bacteria or foreign substances that enter the body. Page 137.

antipathy: a feeling of disgust toward something usually together with an intense desire to avoid or turn from it. Page 179.

antiquity: ancient times; times long since past. Page 440.

AP: aberrated personality as represented by the awake subject. Page 167.

appended: attached or affixed. Page 301.

apportionment: the act of dividing and assigning something among people or groups. Page 547.

apprehended: arrested for having done something illegal. Page 419.

apprise(d): inform or advise. Page 255.

approximation(s): a fact, object or description which is similar to something else, but which is not exactly the same. Page 79.

apropos of: with regard to; concerning. Page 440.

aptitude: a natural ability for something, as for learning; capability; intelligence. Page 416.

aptly: to the point. Page 389.

arch: chief; most important; most extreme; greatest, especially most hostile. Page 69.

arduously: requiring great exertion, energy, etc.; strenuously. Page 464.

Aristotelian logic: the method of logic of Greek philosopher Aristotle, based on a pair of propositions that, taken together, give a new conclusion. For example: "All trees have roots. An oak is a tree. Therefore an oak tree has roots." The data and

Glossary

conclusions of Aristotelian logic can be evaluated only as yes or no, true or false. Page 334.

Aristotle: (384–322 B.C.) Greek philosopher, educator and scientist who believed that the Earth is the center of a spherical universe, that the soul does not exist separate from the body, that knowledge is based only in sense experience, and that something is either true or false, yes or no, with no middle point. Page 173.

Aristotle's pendulum: Greek philosopher Aristotle's principle which states that there is no middle ground and that something is either true or false, yes or no, is or is not the same as something else. Page 262.

armaments: the weapons and supplies of war with which a military unit is equipped. Page 111.

arsenal: an establishment for the manufacture and storage, or for storage alone, of weapons and ammunition of all kinds, for the military and naval forces of the country. Page 7.

arthritis: inflammation of the joints, causing pain, swelling and stiffness. Page 69.

articulate(d): 1. expressed distinctly; given utterance vocally or with distinct, audible sounds. Page 1.

2. expressed, formulated or presented with clarity and effectiveness. Page 2.

artificial restimulation: restimulation by therapy as contrasted to that taking place in the environment. Page 319.

Asiatic: belonging or relating to Asia or its people, practices and beliefs. Page 339.

aside: a remark made that is not part of the actual dialogue but given to impart information on what is happening. Taken from the theater where an actor makes a remark, usually to the audience, that the other characters on stage supposedly cannot hear. Page 289.

asocial: antagonistic to society or social order; avoiding or hostile to other people. Page 190.

aspect(s): 1. one side or part of something; a facet, phase or part of a whole. Page xi.

2. the appearance of something to the mind or eye; a particular appearance or quality. Page 234.

assertion: something declared or stated emphatically (as being true). Page 82.

astigmatism: a visual defect caused by the unequal curving of the surface of the eye. It prevents light rays from coming to a focus, thus producing blurred vision. Page 120.

astral self: *astral body*, a belief in mystical thought in the existence of a sort of spirit body or a "double" of the physical body. It was believed this astral body could be separated from the physical body. Page 114.

at length: 1. in detail. Page xii.
2. after some time. Page 1.

attain to: get, reach or arrive at. Page 539.

attenuated: weakened or reduced in force, intensity, effect, quantity or value. Page 55.

attrition: a gradual wearing or weakening. Page 121.

AUDITOR: THE INDIVIDUAL WHO ADMINISTERS DIANETIC THERAPY. TO AUDIT MEANS "TO LISTEN" AND ALSO "TO COMPUTE." (From *Dianetics Terms.*) Page viii.

auditor: a person whose job it is to officially examine company financial records. Page 198.

authoritarianism: the doctrine or theory that favors absolute obedience to a person or group of persons (authority), as against individual freedom. The ending *-ism* means a doctrine, theory, system, etc. Page 235.

Authority: a supposed expert or collection of experts whose views and opinions on a subject are likely to be accepted without question and in disregard of observable facts. Page 10.

auto-control: *automatic control*, in which something controls itself, without having to be handled or operated by something exterior. For example, an aircraft can operate on automatic pilot, in which the altitude and course are maintained without the pilot's hands on the control mechanisms of the aircraft. The relationship of auto-control to Dianetics is described in Book Three, Chapter Nine: Part Two, section entitled "Auto-Control." Page 415.

auto horn (bulb type): an instrument attached to early vehicles and sounded as a warning, consisting of a horn-shaped tube at one end and a flexible rubber bulb at the other. Compression of the bulb drives air out through the horn-shaped end, emitting a characteristic sound. Page 290.

auto-hypnosis: the act or process of hypnotizing oneself; also, a self-induced hypnotic state or condition; self-hypnosis. *Auto* means self. Page 488.

autonomic nervous system: that part of the nervous system that regulates involuntary and seemingly automatic activities such as heart rate, breathing and digestion. Page 131.

avert(ed): prevent the occurrence or unfortunate, dangerous and disastrous effects of. Page 543.

avowal: an open declaration asserting something is true. Page 126.

awed: filled with *awe*, an overwhelming feeling of mixed wonder and fear produced by something thought of as mysterious, powerful or the like. Page 8.

axioms: statements of natural laws on the order of those of the physical sciences. Page i.

bacillus: a rod-shaped *bacterium* (plural is *bacteria*), which is an individual single-cell microscopic organism, some of which cause disease. From Latin "little rod." Page 39.

backward(ness): slow to learn or behind in progress. Page 287.

Bacon: Francis Bacon (1561–1626), influential English philosopher who believed that any bias or prejudice in scientific thinking must be abandoned and that accurate observation and experimentation were vital to science. He helped develop the scientific method of solving problems. Page 9.

bacteria: single-cell organisms, some of which cause disease. Page 124.

balks: stops short, as at an obstacle, and refuses to go on or to do something specified. Page 146.

ball: a solid, usually spherical projectile for a rifle, pistol, etc. Page 152.

banalities: statements that are overused and consequently lacking in interest or originality or that are boringly ordinary. Page 440.

bank(s): a storage place for information, as in early computers where data was stored on a group or series of cards called a bank. Page vi.

banked: (of a fire) covered over, as with ashes or fresh fuel, to ensure continued low burning. Page 318.

bar: obstruct, prevent, hinder or impede. Page viii.

Bara, Theda: (1890–1955) American silent film star who became famous for playing an irresistibly beautiful woman who lured men into dangerous or disastrous situations. Page 244.

barber-basin medicine: a reference to the crude medical services that barbers delivered for many hundreds of years, such as bloodletting. During this period, a broad assortment of ailments were believed to be caused by an overabundance of blood or by impurities in the blood. The patient would be cut at the bend of the elbow to allow "extra" or "impure" blood to flow out of the body and into a basin, hence the term "barber-basin medicine." Page 133.

bar, brought to: taken to trial; brought to justice. The bar is the railing in a courtroom that separates the judges, lawyers, jury, people on trial, etc., from the general public. Page 538.

bargain, into the: in addition, besides. Page 91.

Barrymore: John Barrymore (1882-1942), American actor who established himself as one of the most outstanding actors of his generation, well known for his portrayal of Hamlet, from the play of the same name by English playwright William Shakespeare. Page 245.

Glossary

BASIC: THE FIRST ENGRAM ON ANY CHAIN OF SIMILAR ENGRAMS. (From *Dianetics Terms.*) Page 247.

BASIC-BASIC: THE FIRST ENGRAM AFTER CONCEPTION, THE BASIC OF ALL CHAINS BY SOLE VIRTUE OF BEING THE FIRST MOMENT OF PAIN. (From *Dianetics Terms.*) Page 172.

basic personality: the individual himself. The person, minus his pain, dramatizations and reactive mind and its content. Page 167.

bastion: any fortified place or strong defense. Used figuratively. Page 470.

battalion: a military unit of approximately five hundred to eight hundred soldiers. Page 9.

batteries: whole arrays or groupings of similar things used together. Page 309.

batter up: in baseball, the batter is the player who uses a long cylindrical wooden stick (bat), which he swings to hit the ball that is thrown to him. Each batter in turn tries to hit the ball and when the phrase "Batter up!" is called out, the next batter moves into position so that play can start. Used in this context with a double meaning as a sexual pun in reference to a male. Page 444.

bawl(ed) (someone) out: reprimand or scold (someone) loudly or severely. Page 42.

bear down: to press or weigh down on someone or something; put pressure onto. Page 297.

bearings: instances, actions or ways of conducting or carrying oneself or of behaving. Page 165.

bears out: shows to be true; supports or confirms. Page 89.

beat it: a slang phrase demanding that one go away, depart. Page 444.

beckons: directs or signals something (such as the mind) to come to a particular place. Page 355.

bedevilment: a tormenting or deliberately causing harm or pain by harassing, as with doubts, distractions or worries. Page 197.

Bedlam: an old insane asylum (in full, *St. Mary of Bethlehem*) in London, known for its inhumane treatment of its inmates. Page 8.

behind the times: old-fashioned in regard to ideas, methods, etc.; outdated; unfashionable; old. Page 446.

behold: hold in view; look at or observe. Page 264.

belt: a band of strong flexible material used in machinery to transmit motion or power. A *drill belt* would be a belt used to drive a dentist drill. Page 484.

belt, under one's: done, experienced or acquired something that will be of benefit to one in the future. Page 224.

beneficent: one who performs kind or good deeds. Page 469.

Benzedrine: brand name of a drug that increases physical and mental activity, prevents sleep and decreases appetite. Page 484.

berates: scolds (someone) vigorously or lengthily. Page 326.

Bergson: Henri Bergson (1859-1941), French philosopher who defined the mind as pure energy, the élan vital, or life force, responsible for all organic evolution. Page 306.

beset: 1. plagued or troubled. Page 414.
2. being attacked from all sides. Page 476.

bicker: argue in a bad-tempered way about something unimportant. Page 544.

bid fair: seem likely or probable. Page 544.

bigoted: utterly intolerant of any creed, belief or opinion that differs from one's own. Page 365.

biochemistry: the science dealing with the chemistry of living matter. Page 12.

black-tempered: having a mood that is full of anger or hatred. Page 200.

blasphemy: something done or said that shows disrespect for God. Page 142.

bleed off: to drain or draw sap, water, electricity, etc., off or away from (something). Page 93.

blithely: in a manner without thought or regard; heedlessly. Page 176.

Blood and Sand: a reference to the 1922 story and film of the same name. A handsome bullfighter, after being unfaithful to his wife, is fatally wounded in the ring by a bull. Carried away, leaving a trail of blood in the sand, he dies in her arms, saying, "I love only you." Page 244.

blubbering: weeping noisily and without restraint. Page 439.

bluff, game of: a reference to playing a game in which one uses boastful language, not intended to be carried out, but merely tried with the purpose of influencing another who allows himself to be affected by it. It alludes to a game of cards where one places a bet or challenges an opponent, pretending to hold a better hand of cards than one actually does. Page 43.

boarders: persons who pay for regular meals, or room and meals, at others' homes. Page 327.

boil-off: the manifestation of former periods of unconsciousness, accompanied by grogginess. In its English usage, *boil-off* refers to the reduction of quantity of a liquid by its conversion to a gaseous state, such as steam. Boil-off is described in Chapter Nine: Part One, Mechanisms and Aspects of Therapy. Page 286.

bona fide: authentic and genuine in nature. Page 118.

bootleg: made, sold or transported illegally; so called from the practice of hiding a liquor bottle in the leg of one's boot. Page 245.

bootstraps, boost himself by his necessity: by sheer necessity, improve or strengthen himself as a result of his own efforts; a variation of *pull oneself up by one's own bootstraps,* meaning better oneself by one's own efforts. *Bootstraps* are loops at the back of boots for pulling them on. Page 468.

borne: endured or tolerated. Page 43.

Borneo: the third largest island in the world, located about 400 miles (640 kilometers) east of Singapore in the East Indies near the Philippines. Page 115.

bosun: an officer on a ship whose job is to supervise maintenance of the ship and its equipment. Page 308.

boudoir: a small, elegantly furnished room, where a lady may retire to be alone or to receive her intimate friends. Page 531.

Boulder Dam: a dam (now called Hoover Dam) located on the Colorado River at the Arizona-Nevada border in the United States. A major engineering achievement, it is 726 feet (221 meters) high. Page 190.

BOUNCER: ANY ENGRAM COMMAND WHICH, WHEN APPROACHED BY THE ANALYTICAL MIND ON THE TIME TRACK, MAKES THE PATIENT MOVE BACK TOWARD PRESENT TIME. (From *Dianetics Terms.*) Page 282.

bound up: literally, tied in the same bundle. Hence, confined with or as if with bonds of some kind so as to deprive of liberty; made captive. Page 160.

bow-drill fire maker: an ancient device consisting of a wooden bow with a string tied to each end and a pointed stick (or bone) to be used as a drill. The string is wrapped around the upright drill and the bow is moved from side to side while the drill's point stays in one place against another piece of wood. The resulting friction created by the twisting point makes the wood hot enough to start burning. Page 546.

bowlers: stiff felt hats with a round crown and curved brim. Page 475.

boy wonder: a talented and bright young man. Page 319.

BP: the attention units called basic personality. Page 167.

brace and bit: a tool for boring, consisting of a removable drill (bit) fitted into a rotating handle (brace). Page 15.

bracketed: fired both beyond and short of a target in order to find the range. Used figuratively. Page 234.

brackets: classes; groupings; classifications. Page 258.

brackish: somewhat salty, especially from being a mixture of fresh and salt water. Page 85.

brawl: a rough and noisy fight, usually in a public place and one involving a large number of people. Page 43.

bric-a-brac: small ornamental objects or articles that are of interest, sentimental or decorative value but of little monetary value; by extension, anything nonessential, resembling bric-a-brac. Page 65.

bring up short: cause a sudden and unexpected halt or pause. Page 424.

British Guiana: former name of *Guyana*, an independent republic on the northeast coast of South America. Page 7.

bronc, fan a: wave or flap a hat against the sides of a bucking horse that is trying to get a rider off its back, as in a rodeo (a public exhibition of cowboy skills, as bronco riding and calf roping). A *bronc* or *bronco* is a wild untrained horse of North America; using a hat in this way serves to balance the rider and further enliven the horse. Page 43.

brought to bar: taken to trial; brought to justice. The bar is the railing in a courtroom that separates the judges, lawyers, jury, people on trial, etc., from the general public. Page 538.

bubonic plague: a highly contagious and often fatal epidemic disease transmitted by fleas from infected rats, prevalent throughout Europe and Asia in the fourteenth century. Also known as Black Death. Page 39.

buck(s): 1. resists or opposes directly and stubbornly; goes against. Page 303.

2. come up against; find oneself opposed to. Page 323.

buffers: things that lessen or absorb the shock of an impact. Page 212.

(bulb type), auto horn: an instrument attached to early vehicles and sounded as a warning, consisting of a horn-shaped tube at one end and a flexible rubber bulb at the other. Compression of the bulb drives air out through the horn-shaped end, emitting a characteristic sound. Page 290.

bullies: forces one's way aggressively or by domination; forces into submission or compliance. Page 394.

Bund: a famous landmark in Shanghai, China, a boulevard along the Huang-p'u River lined with parks and European-style buildings. Page 43.

buoyant: lighthearted; cheerful. Page 314.

bursitis: inflammation of a fluid-filled sac (bursa) that reduces friction between bones where they join, particularly at the elbow, knee or shoulder. Page 69.

business girl: a term used by prostitutes to describe themselves, especially for those working independently and thus retaining all money earned. Page 245.

but: no more than; just; only, as in *"The enlightened and Golden Age of Greece yet had but superstition."* Page 7.

by and large: in general; considering everything. Page 79.

bypass circuits: a reference to paths for diverting part or all of an electric current so it skips one or more elements of a circuit. Used to describe demon circuits, which lie between "I" and the standard banks, bypassing the normal route. Page 70.

by the by: by the way; incidentally. Page 298.

by virtue of: by reason of; as a result of. Page 342.

Caesar: Julius Caesar (ca. 100-44 B.C.), Roman general and statesman who considered the government of Rome to be rotten and intended to "save" Rome from decay. Between 58 and 50 B.C. Caesar conquered and subdued the Gauls. Ending the war at a town where resistance was strong, he waited for their water supply to run out and cut off the right hands of all those who fought against him. This served as an example for all others who would resist Rome. In 46 B.C. Caesar was appointed Roman dictator for life, but was assassinated two years later. Page 49.

calculus: a branch of mathematics used for determining such quantities as the area of an irregularly shaped object. Page 84.

Caligula: (A.D. 12-41) Roman emperor (A.D. 37-41). An insane and vicious tyrant, he had most of his relatives murdered, declared himself a god, made his favorite horse a chief administrator of the Roman government and was finally assassinated by officers of his guard. Page 69.

caliper: a precise measuring instrument having two curved legs or jaws that can be adjusted to determine thickness, diameter and distance between surfaces. Page 449.

call: a short visit to a place (such as a doctor's office, one's office of employment, etc.). Page 430.

call(ed) upon: 1. ask or require, as in "*the human mind, being called upon to resolve problems.*" Page 24.
2. make a demand upon, as in "*the reader is asked to call upon his own knowledge.*" Page 126.

capricious: tending to change unpredictably or abruptly with no apparent reason; erratic. Page 363.

cardinal: of main importance; principal; chief. Page 293.

carload lot: a *carload* is the amount carried by a railroad freight car. *Lot* refers to numerous articles forming a group that is regarded or handled as one item. Hence, used figuratively in this context, a *carload lot* means a large quantity of items viewed as being grouped together, as if in the space of a railroad freight car. Page 450.

carmine: a deep red color tinged with purple. Page 114.

casebook: a record or account of facts, circumstances, etc., connected with a person or subject available for study or as a historical record. Page 339.

cataclysm: a sudden and violent physical action producing changes in the Earth's surface, such as an earthquake or devastating flood. Page 39.

catalyst: something that acts as the stimulus in bringing about or hastening a result. Page 210.

catarrhal: marked by inflammation of the membranes in the nose and throat, causing an increase in the production of mucus, as happens in the common cold. From Greek *cata*, down and *rhein*, to flow. Page 3.

caught: to become pregnant. Page 281.

caustic: cutting or sarcastic; bitter or sharp. Page 468.

cavalry: mounted soldiers traditionally portrayed in American movies as coming to the rescue of those in need at the last critical moment. Page 157.

cease and desist: stop doing something; discontinue or make something come to an end. Page 199.

censor: in Freudian theory, that restraining force which keeps undesirable and distasteful ideas, impulses and feelings in the unconscious of an individual. Page v.

censure: 1. find fault with; express strong disapproval of. Page 326. 2. a sentence of punishment by civil or military authority. Also, opinion, judgment; the act of blaming, finding fault with or condemning sternly. Page 538.

cervix: a neck-like opening at the bottom of the womb which leads into the vagina. Page 325.

cessation: a temporary or complete stopping. Page 39.

chaff: the dry, inedible outer covering of wheat or other grain. Page 144.

chain fission: same as *fission reaction*, a reference to the chain reaction that takes place when the center portion of an atom (the nucleus) is split (fissioned) into smaller parts, with these smaller parts ejecting outward and splitting other atoms, which in turn split others in an ever-widening reaction. Page 332.

CHAINS: ANY SERIES OF INCIDENTS IN THE ENGRAM BANK WHICH HAVE SIMILAR CONTENT. (From *Dianetics Terms.*) Page 104.

champion: a person who fights for or defends any person or cause. Page 467.

chances: happens or comes about. Page 41.

charge: 1. a store or accumulation of energy. Literally, charge is an accumulation of electricity. Charges are either positive or negative. Positive charges repel positive charges and negative charges repel negative charges, while positive and negative charges attract each other. Page 73.

2. suffusion (gradual spreading through or over), as with emotion, such as hopelessness. Page 85.

charlatan: one who pretends to have expert knowledge or skill; fake. Page 321.

chary: cautious or careful; wary. Page 355.

chastened: made more restrained or cautious; subdued. Page 525.

chattel: of or characteristic of being a chattel (a personal possession). Women were once considered chattel. Page 217.

cheek, turns the other: accepts injuries or insult without seeking revenge; refuses to retaliate. Page 409.

Cheops: Egyptian king (reigned in twenty-sixth century B.C.), and builder of the largest pyramid in the world, known as the Great Pyramid, in which he was buried. Page 185.

chieftain: the leader or head of a group (often referring to a tribe or clan). Page 143.

chloroform: a colorless toxic liquid once used as an anesthetic. Page 483.

chronic: long-lasting or happening continually, as of an illness, medical condition, etc. Page 87.

chronometer: an instrument for measuring time precisely; highly accurate kind of clock, as for use in navigation. Page 451.

cinch: a firm grip. Page 533.

circuits: in electricity, complete routes traveled by an electrical current and which carry out specific actions. In Dianetics the term is used to describe parts of the mind acting as circuits do, performing various functions. Page 14.

circumventing: finding a way around (an obstacle). Page vii.

clairvoyance: the apparent power of perceiving things or events in the future or beyond normal sensory contact. Page 476.

class of literature: a reference to American magazines of the early to mid-1900s that featured supposedly true stories about the lives, problems, romances, etc., of everyday people, emphasizing sensationalized crime and love confessions. Much of the material for these stories reportedly came from women who had access to actual case histories. Page 459.

clause: a distinct section of a legal document, usually separately numbered, that says a particular thing must or must not be done. Page 238.

CLEAR: THE OPTIMUM INDIVIDUAL; NO LONGER POSSESSED OF ANY ENGRAMS. DICTIONARY: BRIGHT; UNCLOUDED, HENCE, SERENE; CLEAN; AUDIBLE; DISCRIMINATING; UNDERSTANDING; FREE FROM DOUBT; SURE; INNOCENT; NET, AS PROFIT OVER EXPENSES; FREE FROM DEBT; FREE FROM ANY ENTANGLEMENT. *v.t.* TO MAKE CLEAR, AS OF DIRT OR OBSTRUCTION; TO ENLIGHTEN; TO FREE FROM GUILT, BLAME, ETC.; TO OPEN FOR PASSAGE; TO DISENTANGLE. *v.i.* TO BECOME CLEAR AND BRIGHT. *n.* A CLEAR SPACE OR PART. (From *Dianetics Terms.*) Page i.

clime: a region or realm. Page 535.

coach and four: a coach with the four horses which pull it. Page 22.

Cob, Jimmie the: a made-up name for a leader of a gang of criminals. *Cob* is a British term for leader or chief. Page 199.

cognizant: fully aware of or having knowledge of something. Page vii.

cohesion: (of objects) the state of sticking together, or (of people) being in close agreement and working well together. Page 143.

coitus: sexual intercourse. Page 195.

cold fish: used to describe someone who is emotionless or devoid of strong feeling (such as sexual desire). Page 297.

colloquial: characteristic of or appropriate to ordinary or familiar conversation rather than formal speech or writing; informal. Page 3.

comatic: of or pertaining to a coma (a state of mental or physical sluggishness). From the Greek *koma,* deep sleep. Page 405.

combat exhaustion: a condition characterized by anxiety, irritability, depression, etc., occurring after prolonged or severe battle experience. Page 510.

Glossary

comedown: a decline from a higher to a lower state or quality. Page 319.

come forth: broadcast, originate, make. Page 107.

commentary: a fact or piece of evidence that explains or illustrates a condition or characteristic. Page 14.

compact: a contract made between two parties; a mutual agreement or understanding. Page 517.

company: a military unit consisting of approximately sixty to one hundred ninety troops. Page 52.

compartmenting: dividing into separate aspects, functions or the like. Page 2.

complex: in psychoanalysis, a *complex* is a set of impulses, ideas and emotions that compel habitual patterns of behavior. Page 107.

compound: 1. a combination of things that have been added together. Page 48.

2. a substance containing two or more elements (substances that themselves cannot be broken down into simpler substances) in exact proportions. A compound can be made up of many elements and usually has properties unlike those of the elements it is made up of. Page 486.

compounding: forming new words by joining together words or syllables (for example, cookbook, blackbird, etc.). Page 29.

compulsions: irresistible impulses that are irrational or contrary to one's own will. Page 10.

conciliation: an attempt to establish harmony and goodwill; the act of soothing the anger of; making friendly. Page 409.

concocting: creating or devising. Page 77.

concourse: an act or instance of combined action; cooperation. Page 63.

condensers: devices for accumulating (from *condensing* which means to make more dense or compact) and holding electrical charge. A condenser consists of two equally but oppositely charged conducting surfaces held apart by insulating material. Page 314.

conditioning(s): a process of supposedly changing behavior by rewarding or punishing a subject each time an action is performed until the subject associates the action with pleasure or distress. Based on the dog experiments of Ivan Petrovich Pavlov (1849-1936) who presented food to a dog while he sounded a bell. After repeating this procedure several times, the dog (in anticipation) would salivate at the sound of the bell whether or not food was presented. Pavlov concluded that all acquired habits, even the higher mental activity of Man, depended on conditioned reflexes. A *conditioned reflex* is a response (for example, secretion of saliva in a dog) brought about by a secondary stimulus (for example, the ringing of a bell) repeatedly associated with an original stimulus (for example, the sight of meat). Page 65.

conduit: something that forms a pathway for channeling a flow, as of electricity, enabling it to pass from one place to another. Page 93.

confirmed: firmly settled in a particular habit and unlikely to change, as a "*confirmed criminal.*" Page 199.

confound: 1. to make feel confused; bewilder. Page x.

2. throw (something) into confusion. Page 24.

3. a word used to express anger at something or somebody; damn. Page 289.

confounded: damned, cursed, blasted; used as a mild oath. Page 121.

Confucianism: the system of ethics, education and statesmanship taught by Chinese philosopher Confucius (ca. 551–479 B.C.) stressing love for humanity, ancestor worship, respect for parents and harmony in thought and conduct. During the communist takeover in the early 1900s, Confucianism fell into disfavor since it stressed upholding and respecting the government that the communists wanted to overthrow. Page 186.

conjunctivitis: inflammation of the *conjunctiva*, a delicate membrane that covers the inner lining of the eyelid and the white part of the eyeball. This condition is known informally as *pinkeye*, so called from the pink or red color of the infected eye and eyelid. Page 135.

consecrated: set apart as holy; made or declared sacred for religious use. Page 7.

conservation: wise utilization of something so as to prevent waste or loss. Page 510.

consternation: confused and distressing excitement; dismay. Page 115.

constitute: appoint; give a certain office or function to. Page 225.

construed: interpreted or taken in a specified way. Page 159.

content: that which is contained within something else; subject matter; the substance or details of a particular event, discourse, etc. Page 55.

contention: a point advanced or being proved. Page 193.

contrives: thinks up; devises; schemes; plans. Page 208.

controlling: a reference to the specialized meaning of control in scientific experiments. In this sense, a *control* is a standard or comparison for checking or verifying the results of an experiment. *Controlling out* refers to excluding (controlling) certain factors so as to ensure they do not influence the results. Page 127.

controls: things that provide a set standard of comparison or means of verification, as in a scientific experiment. Page 143.

conversely: introducing a statement or idea that reverses one that has just been made or referred to. Page 277.

cordite: a smokeless, explosive powder used to propel ammunition out of guns. The name refers to the cord-like lengths in which it was made. Page 15.

corn: something tiresomely or ridiculously old-fashioned or sentimental. Page 245.

corn-and-games: describing a government that provides mass entertainment to the population to prevent it from causing trouble. This phrase refers to the practices of ancient Rome of supplying official public amusement (games) and distributing free food as a means of keeping the people happy. Page 309.

corner: possession of the whole amount or supply of something. Page 225.

cornerstones: the chief foundations on which things are constructed or developed. From the stone that unites two masonry walls at an intersection. Page 537.

coronary: of or pertaining to the human heart, with respect to health. Page 69.

corporal: of the human body (*corporal punishment* would be punishment inflicted directly on the body). Page 185.

cosmic: relating to the universe as a whole, in contrast to the Earth alone. Page 32.

counter-: a word used in combination with another with the meaning of: in opposition or response to; opposite; against. Page 63.

counterchecking: checking again; confirming by a second check. Page 451.

counterfeit: to fake the appearance of; pretend. Page 313.

cowboy in the black hat: a reference to a law-breaking villain as portrayed in Western movies who characteristically wore a black hat. Page 466.

cowboy in the white hat: a reference to a law-abiding good guy or hero as portrayed in Western movies who characteristically wore a white hat. Page 466.

cowed: frightened with threats, violence, etc., into submission or obedience. Page 419.

cowing: frightening into submission or obedience. Page 512.

craven: so cowardly as to be considered worthy of disgust or hatred. Page 205.

crazy house mirror: a reference to a mirror built to give a distorted image, found in an amusement park fun house (an attraction consisting of a series of rooms and passages, sloping or moving floors, distorting mirrors and other devices designed to surprise or amuse). Page 398.

credence to, giving: accepting (a statement, etc.) as true; believing, crediting. Page 455.

credible: capable of being believed or accepted (as true). Page 96.

creed: any system of beliefs or principles in general. Page 544.

crest: a symbolic object that sits upon the top of a coat of arms (a group of emblems and figures usually arranged on and around a shield and serving as the special insignia of some person, family or institution). Page 529.

criterion: a standard of judgment; a rule or principle for evaluating or testing something. Page 292.

crocheted: produced by needlework done with a needle having a small hook at one end for drawing the thread or yarn through intertwined loops. Page 467.

cross-index system: a method wherein subject matter is noted at one place and refers one to another place, such as an index at the back of a reference book that notes all places certain subjects can be found in that book. Page 61.

crow: boast in triumph. Page 416.

cry baby: a person, especially a child, who cries easily for very little reason. Page 464.

cry havoc: cause destruction or confusion. Originally an order given to an army (havoc!) as a signal for the seizing of goods, properties, etc. Page 465.

culpable: deserving blame, as being wrong, evil, improper, etc. Page 140.

cults: groups marked by great or excessive devotion to some idea or thing; especially, such devotion regarded as offbeat and odd or temporary. Page 114.

cunning(ly): showing skill and cleverness in a way that is intended to deceive. Page 78.

cure: solve a problem or deal with a situation in a way that rectifies (makes or sets right, remedies) or eliminates it. Page 8.

cursory: performed rapidly with little attention to detail. Page 15.

curtailment: a cutting short; reducing in area or amount; shortening in duration or scope. Page 412.

custodian: one that guards and protects or maintains; one entrusted with safekeeping, care and guardianship. Page 217.

cyanide: a lethal chemical compound utilized as a poison since ancient times. Page 485.

cyclic: of or pertaining to a cycle or cycles, or characterized by recurrence in cycles. A *cycle* is a period of time during which a characteristic, often regularly repeated event or sequence of events occurs. *See also* **manic** and **manic-depressive.** Page 363.

cyst: a closed, protective sac containing fluid or semisolid material. Page 160.

cytology: the branch of biology dealing with the structure, function and life history of cells. Page xi.

Dalton, Jack: the hero of an old-fashioned play, *Curse You, Jack Dalton!* written by Wilbur Braun in 1930. Jack is in love with his family's maid but the villain of the story plots with a Spanish adventuress (who wants to marry Jack) to get the maid drugged and shipped to a lunatic asylum. Jack foils the plot and ends up with his love. Page 244.

Dante: Italian poet (1265–1321) who in his best-known work, *The Divine Comedy*, describes his imaginary journey through hell and heaven and presents the horrors of hell in poetic detail. Page 141.

Dark Ages: the period in European history from the A.D. 400s to the early 1300s. The term refers to the intellectual darkness, such as lack of learning and schooling during this period, the loss of many artistic and technical skills and the virtual disappearance of the knowledge of the previous Greek and Roman civilizations. Page 37.

Darwin: Charles Darwin (1809-1882), English naturalist and author who originated the theory of evolution by natural selection which holds that all species of plants and animals developed from earlier forms and that the forms which survive are those best adapted to the environment. Page 67.

da Vinci: Leonardo da Vinci (1452-1519), Italian painter, draftsman, sculptor, architect and engineer who discovered that blood circulated and traced with some accuracy the blood vessels of the body. Page 173.

dearly beloveds: things that are regarded with love and affection. Page 471.

debauchery: excessive and unrestrained indulgence of one's appetites, especially for sensual pleasures. Page 36.

decks: covers or clothes in a fine, elegant manner. Page 310.

decried: strongly disapproved of, openly criticized or condemned. Page 36.

deduced: formed as a conclusion from things already observed or known. Page 23.

deed: something that is done, performed or accomplished; an act. Page 22.

deep analysis: in psychoanalysis, a practice of supposedly discovering hidden data and then evaluating it for the patient. Page 166.

defy Alexander: a reference to a story wherein Alexander the Great (356-323 B.C.), marched into the ancient city of Gordium in Asia Minor. In the city square was a wagon fastened so ingeniously to a beam with a rope that no one could untie it. Alexander was told that whoever could untie the knot would rule all of Asia. To this he took his sword and with one stroke severed the rope and went on to conquer much of Asia. *Defy* means to confront a person with something that baffles him. Page 429.

de-intensify(ied): remove any acute or strong sensations, feelings, emotions, etc. Page 362.

delirium(s): a state of extreme mental excitement, marked by restlessness, confused speech and hallucinations. Page 8.

de luxe: of special elegance or fineness; of a luxurious standard and surpassing all others in its class. By extension, to a high degree or amount. Page 407.

demarcation, line of: that which marks the boundaries or limits of, or divides something so that its divided parts are separate and identifiable. Page 27.

democracy: a system of government in which power is given to the people, who rule either directly or through freely elected representatives. Page 186.

DEMON: A BYPASS *CIRCUIT* IN THE MIND, CALLED "DEMON" BECAUSE IT WAS LONG SO INTERPRETED. PROBABLY AN ELECTRONIC MECHANISM. (From *Dianetics Terms.*) Page 113.

denominator: something common to or characteristic of a number of things, people, etc. Page 27.

DENYER: ANY ENGRAM COMMAND WHICH MAKES A PATIENT BELIEVE THAT THE ENGRAM DOES NOT EXIST. (From *Dianetics Terms.*) Page 268.

deranged: put out of order, disordered, disarranged. Also, disturbed mentally; insane. Page iv.

derelict: guilty of neglect of duty. Page 9.

derided: laughed at or made fun of someone; ridiculed. Page 502.

derision: unkind laughter or remarks that ridicule someone. Page 465.

dermatitis: inflammation of the skin resulting in redness, swelling, itching or other symptoms. Page 125.

descriptic: 1. of or relating to something that describes, explains or gives the characteristic details of. Page 31.

2. a graph which describes, explains or gives the characteristic details of something. Page 38.

designing: acting in a deceitful way; making secret plans for personal benefit. Page 309.

desist, cease and: stop doing something; discontinue or make something come to an end. Page 199.

detachment: the act of being disconnected, separated or removed from association with. Specifically, in the sense used here it means a disinterest in or remoteness from the concerns of others, as in "*professorial detachment.*" Page 2.

deterrent(s): a thing or factor that serves to prevent, check or arrest something from occurring. Page 382.

detriment: damage, disadvantage or injury. Page 229.

devil take the (meals, plot): used to wish evil on something, or as a negation or rejection of something, as if the devil should come and take such a thing away. Page 198.

diabetes: a disease in which a person's system cannot properly absorb normal amounts of sugar. It is characterized by excessive production of urine and abnormal thirst and some forms can be life threatening. Page 126.

diabolical: extreme or exceedingly great in degree. Page x.

DIANETICS: (GREEK *DIA*, THROUGH, AND *NOUS*, MIND OR SOUL); WHAT THE MIND (OR SOUL) IS DOING TO THE BODY. (From *Dianetics Terms*.) Page i.

digit: a reference to numbers (such as 0 through 9) used in counting or measuring systems. Page 450.

digression: the act of deviating or wandering away from the main topic or purpose in speaking or writing. Page 311.

dime store: a term used to describe something inexpensive. A *dime store* is a store offering a wide assortment of low-priced items for personal and household use, formerly costing five or ten cents. Page 259.

dipsomaniac: a person with an uncontrollable craving for alcoholic drink. Page 70.

direful: dreadful; terrible. Page 37.

disavow: deny any association with somebody or something. Page 87.

discharge: release charge (anger, fear, grief or apathy); unburden. Page 70.

dismembered: mangled or mutilated; cut or broken in pieces. Page 509.

disposes: 1. deals with conclusively; settles. Page 254.
2. puts into a willing or receptive frame of mind; makes willing; inclines. Page 267.

dissertation: a written communication about a subject, in which it is discussed at length. Page 189.

dividends: returns or rewards resulting from activities, efforts or undertakings. Page 371.

divulged: disclosed or revealed (something private, secret or previously unknown). Page 504.

Dixie: an inspirational song about the southern United States written in 1859 by American composer Daniel Decatur Emmet (1815-1904). Page 442.

doilies: small mats, as of lace, put under dishes, vases or the like as decorations or to protect surfaces. Page 467.

doormat: a mat for people to wipe their shoes on before entering a house, room, etc. Hence, a person who submits to being a habitual object of abuse or humiliation by another. Page 409.

dotes on: shows extreme fondness for something. Page 475.

down and out: completely without resources or a means of livelihood, such as having no money, no home and living on the street. Page 446.

dramatis personae: in Dianetics, the people present in an engram. It is Latin and literally means people (or persons) of a drama, used to refer to the actors or characters in a drama or play or those who are part of an actual event. Page 435.

dramatization: a whole irrational set of actions. They come about when an engram is thoroughly restimulated. When it is in full parade, the engram is running off verbatim and the individual is like an actor, puppet-like, playing his dictated part. Dramatization is fully described in Book Two, Chapter Three, The Cell and the Organism. Page 88.

drammer: a variation of the word *drama*, a situation or a series of events involving vivid characters or intense conflict of forces, suggesting a play. Here referring to instances of *dramatizing*, of acting out whole sets of irrational actions. Page 255.

dreary: dull and uninteresting; tiresome. Page 457.

driven through the streets: carried in a cart through the streets, by way of punishment or public exposure. Page 326.

droll: amusingly odd. Page 530.

drooling: performed with exaggerated desire, emotion such as sentimentality. Page 211.

dross: waste matter; worthless stuff; rubbish. Page 345.

Dr. Sententious: a made-up name. *Sententious* means inclined to state wise sayings and to often make judgments about moral questions. Page 452.

Drunkard, The: popular drama by William H. Smith (1806-1872) about the evils of alcohol and the virtues of abstaining from it. Written in 1844, it had numerous revivals, becoming one of the longest-running plays in America. Page 245.

D.T.'s: abbreviation for *delirium tremens*, a condition induced by excessive and prolonged use of alcohol and characterized by hallucinations, mental confusion, restlessness, sweating and trembling. Page 485.

dub-in: a term used to characterize vision or recall which is imaginary. The term comes from the motion-picture industry. To "dub," in moviemaking, is to create and add sounds to a picture after filming is complete. This process ("dubbing") results in a fabricated soundtrack that *seems* to the audience like it actually took place when filmed, but much or *all* of it was created in the studio long after filming was finished and then "dubbed in." In Dianetics, "dub-in" indicates altered recall, where the person "sees" more than was there or something entirely different. It is imaginary, but he is certain that he saw it. What is happening is that without the person's analytical knowledge, part of his mind is throwing in data which isn't true, and the person will tell you lies. Page 252.

dull(ness): somewhat unintelligent or stupid. Page 181.

dungeon keep: the main inner tower of a medieval castle that served as the living place for a lord and his family and which was used as the final defensive stronghold when the castle was under siege. Page 476.

Durant, Will: William (Will) James Durant (1885–1981), American historian and author of popular philosophy. In the mid-1920s, Durant wrote *The Story of Philosophy*, a book covering the lives and works of the world's greatest philosophers. Written so the average man could understand it, the book sold millions of copies. *Dedication.*

dwindling spiral: the worse an individual gets, the more capacity he has to get worse. (*Spiral* here refers to a progressive downward movement, marking a relentlessly deteriorating state of affairs, and considered to take the form of a spiral. The term comes from aviation where it is used to describe the phenomenon of a plane descending and spiraling in smaller and smaller circles, as in an accident or feat of expert flying, which if not handled can result in loss of control and a crash.) Page 131.

DYNAMIC: THE URGE, THRUST AND PURPOSE OF LIFE—SURVIVE!—IN ITS FOUR MANIFESTATIONS: SELF, SEX, GROUP AND MANKIND. (From *Dianetics Terms.*) Page ii.

Glossary

dynamic: from the Greek *dunamikos*, powerful. Hence, motivating or energizing force (of existence or life), as in *Dynamic Principle of Existence*. Page iii.

dynasties: prominent and powerful families or groups of people whose members retain their power and influence through several generations. From the Greek *dynasteia*, "lord." Page 7.

earnest, in: a phrase used to intensify something already stated; with full seriousness, as of intention or purpose. Page 154.

ebb and flood: a decline and increase; constant fluctuation, as the outward and inward movement of ocean tides. Page 38.

echelon: a level, as in a step-like arrangement or order. An *echelon* is one of a series in a field of activity. Page i.

ectoplasm: a material that supposedly oozes from spirits or ghosts, making it possible for them to materialize and perform physical feats such as lifting objects. It is also believed by some to be an airy, whitish substance which allegedly spreads out from a medium during a trance and takes on a human form or face. (A *medium* is a person through whom the spirits of the dead are said to be able to contact the living.) Page 115.

edged: advanced gradually or cautiously. Page 439.

efficacy: the capacity for producing a desired result or effect; effectiveness. Page 233.

effusion: the action of giving off, radiating or emanating. Page 93.

egocentric: viewing everything in relation to one's self; self-centered. Page 328.

egsusheyftef: a made-up word with no meaning. Page 59.

Einstein: Albert Einstein (1879-1955), German-born American physicist whose theories on the nature of mass and energy led to development of the atomic bomb. Page 3.

electroencephalograph: an instrument for recording the electrical activity of the brain. Page 306.

elicits: draws out, causes or produces something as a reaction or response. Page 396.

Ellis: Havelock Ellis (1859-1939), English writer and physician who conducted studies in the psychology of sex. Page 140.

elucidates: makes clear, explains. Page x.

elusively: cleverly or skillfully escape (one's notice or attention). Page 323.

embarrassing: making something difficult or complicated; hampering or impeding some action, as by being a block that hinders or obstructs. Page 370.

embroil: throw into confusion, disorder or the like; cause to become entangled. Page 222.

embryo: the unborn young of a human in the earliest stages of development, specifically from conception to about the eighth week. Page xi.

embryo, in: in an undeveloped stage. Page 174.

Emersonian: related to Ralph Waldo Emerson (1803-1882), American essayist and idealist. His writings, a series of loosely related impressions, maxims, proverbs and parables, cover topics such as self-reliance, friendship, manners, character and similar subjects. Page 367.

encyst(ing): enclose or encapsulate something in, or as if in, a resistant covering. From *en*, to bring or put into a certain state or condition; *cyst*, a closed, protective sac. Page 22.

endearment: something that manifests affection. A word of endearment is one that would be said to a person one loves. Page 438.

endeavor: activity or effort. Page ii.

endocrine: of or having to do with the system of glands which secretes hormones (chemical substances) from certain organs and tissues in the body. These glands and their hormones regulate the growth, development and function of certain tissues and coordinate many processes within the body. For example, some of these glands increase blood pressure and heart rate during times of stress. Page 12.

endocrinology: the branch of biology dealing with the endocrine glands and their secretions, especially in relation to their processes or functions. Page 12.

engendered: brought about; produced. Page 526.

ENGRAM: ANY MOMENT OF GREATER OR LESSER "UNCONSCIOUSNESS" ON THE PART OF THE ANALYTICAL MIND WHICH PERMITS THE REACTIVE MIND TO RECORD; THE TOTAL CONTENT OF THAT MOMENT WITH ALL PERCEPTICS. (From *Dianetics Terms.*) Page v.

ENGRAM BANK: THE STORAGE PLACE IN THE BODY WHERE ENGRAMS, WITH ALL THEIR PERCEPTS, ARE RECORDED

AND RETAINED AND FROM WHICH ENGRAMS ACT UPON THE ANALYTICAL MIND AND THE BODY. (From *Dianetics Terms.*) Page vi.

ENGRAM COMMAND: ANY PHRASE CONTAINED IN AN ENGRAM. (From *Dianetics Terms.*) Page 100.

enjoin: urge or impose with authority; enforce. Page 481.

ensigns: in the United States Navy, commissioned officers of the lowest rank. (A *commission* is a document granting authority to military officers issued by the president of the United States.) Page 453.

entity: a thing that has real individual existence; something that exists as a particular unit. Page 22.

entombed: placed in a tomb, buried; figuratively, no longer existing, gone. Page 538.

environs: environments or surroundings. Page 538.

equated: put in the form of an equation. Page iii.

equation: 1. a mathematics term showing that two things are of the same value or equal each other. Also, by extension, any situation or problem with several variable factors that has been calculated and proven with mathematical precision. Page iii.
2. a set of factors, such as different facts or ideas, that all affect a situation and must be considered together. Page 28.

equilibrium: mental or emotional balance. Page 430.

equipage: a carriage and all that accompanies it, such as horses, attendant servants, etc. Page 22.

equity: the quality of being fair or impartial; fairness; impartiality. Page 537.

equivocal: 1. of doubtful nature or character; questionable; dubious; suspicious, as in *"They have promptly considered, then, that these areas were equivocal."* Page 158.
2. allowing the possibility of several different meanings, as in *"This is a good, equivocal attitude for an auditor."* Page 295.

ERASE(D): TO CAUSE AN ENGRAM TO "VANISH" ENTIRELY BY RECOUNTINGS, AT WHICH TIME IT IS FILED AS MEMORY AND EXPERIENCE. (From *Dianetics Terms.*) Page vii.

erosion: a gradual destruction or weakening of something over a period of time. Page 509.

erudition: exhibition or use of scholarly knowledge or learning. Page 405.

ESP: abbreviation for *extrasensory perception. See* **extrasensory perception.** Page 423.

estrogen: a hormone that develops and maintains feminine characteristics in the body. Page 129.

et al.: abbreviation for the Latin phrase *et alia*, meaning "and others." Page 262.

ether: a colorless liquid having an aromatic odor and sweet, burning taste, formerly used as an inhalant anesthetic to produce unconsciousness and insensibility to pain. Page 79.

euphoria: a feeling of well-being or elation, especially one that is groundless or inappropriate to current circumstances. Page 132.

evolutes: develops by *evolution*, the natural process from an early or partially developed stage to a more highly organized condition by gradual modification. Page 32.

exclusive: available or belonging only to particular people or groups, and not shared with any others, as ownership or the like. Page 132.

excreta: waste matter expelled from the body. Page 64.

exhaustive: leaving no part unexamined or unconsidered; complete; thorough. Page vii.

exhortations: urgings, advisings or earnest cautionings; urgent appeals or warnings. Page 70.

exodontistry: that branch of dentistry concerned with extracting teeth. Page 154.

expedient: suitable, practical or efficient in achieving a particular end; fit, proper or advantageous under the circumstances. Page 274.

expend(ed): to lay out, spend (labor, time, effort, etc.) for a given purpose; to lay out (money) for specific items. Page 51.

extrasensory perception: perception or communication outside of normal sensory capability, as in telepathy. Page 423.

extravagance: unrestrained excess of emotion, conduct, opinion, etc. Page 373.

extricate: free or release (someone or something) from a confining, difficult or undesirable condition or situation. Page 222.

eyeshade, green: a type of headgear consisting of a strap to which is attached a green colored beak or visor (shade) which prevents light from directly hitting the eyes, such as from a bare light bulb. Green eyeshades were traditionally associated with people working hard at a task, such as newspaper editors, accountants, clerks, etc. Page 265.

fable: a false statement of belief. Page 73.

facetious: joking or trying to be humorous, especially at an inappropriate time. Page 386.

facile: moving, acting, working, proceeding, etc., with ease. Page 457.

facility: readiness or ease due to skill, aptitude or practice. Page 129.

faculty: an inherent capability of the mind or body, such as the sense of smell. Page 18.

fair: plainly visible; distinct. Page 253.

faith healing: of or pertaining to *faith healing*, a healing or cure believed to have been accomplished through religious faith, prayer, etc. Page 231.

false data: items of information that do not correspond with truth or reality. Page 150.

familiar: of or having to do with a family. Page 381.

fan a bronc: wave or flap a hat against the sides of a bucking horse that is trying to get a rider off its back, as in a rodeo (a public exhibition of cowboy skills, as bronco riding and calf roping). A *bronc* or *bronco* is a wild untrained horse of North America; using a hat in this way serves to balance the rider and further enliven the horse. Page 43.

fancy-pants: someone (usually a man or boy) who is overly elegant, overdressed and sometimes weak and effeminate. Page 308.

fan-tan: a Chinese gambling game in which an unknown number of coins or objects are placed under a bowl. Bets are made on how much will be left after the coins or objects are removed four at a time until there are four or less remaining. Page 199.

far cry: quite some distance; a long way; hence only remotely related; very different. Page 39.

fare: 1. get along; experience good or bad fortune, treatment, etc. Page 48.

2. material such as that provided for use, consumption, etc. Page 245.

Farragut: David Glasgow Farragut (1801-1870), American naval officer and hero of the American Civil War (1861-1865). During a battle, after witnessing a ship strike a mine (called a torpedo at the time) and sink, Farragut shouted the famous words, "Damn the torpedoes! Full speed ahead!" and led his ships through to victory. Page 377.

fashion in: fit or accommodate into (something). Page 424.

fat: (having) many desirable elements or qualities; thriving. Page 179.

Febris: in Roman mythology, *Febris* (fever) was the goddess who protected people against fevers. Page 7.

feebleminded: lacking normal mental powers; stupid, unintelligent. Page 179.

feigned: pretended; imitated; made a false show of. Page 153.

Felis domesticus: a domestic cat. *Felis* is the overall family name of cats including domestic cats and wild cats, as lions, tigers, etc. Page 449.

festering: generating pus (a yellowish fluid consisting of the liquid part of blood plus dead cells, bacteria, etc.) due to infection. Figuratively, producing continual irritation. Page 338.

fetishes: natural or artificial objects (as animal teeth or wood carvings) believed among some primitive people to have power to protect or aid their owners. Page 471.

fetus: the unborn human in the womb, from after the second month of pregnancy until birth. Page xi.

fidelity: adherence to fact or detail. Page 483.

field: 1. a sphere of activity, interest, action or operation, etc. Page ii.

2. a space where a specific, measurable force exists. Page 389.

fiendish: very cruel and wicked. Page 213.

file clerk: the bank monitor. "He" monitors for both the reactive engram bank and the standard banks. When he is asked for a datum by the auditor or "I", he will hand out a datum to the auditor via "I". The file clerk is covered in Book Three, Chapter Five, Returning, the File Clerk and the Time Track. Page 261.

filters: in radios, electronic components which block out unwanted radio waves traveling through the air so that the radio receives a specified, correct signal. Page 489.

fireplugs: another name for fire hydrants. Page 471.

fission reaction: a reference to the chain reaction that takes place when the center portion of an atom (the nucleus) is split (fissioned) into smaller parts, with these smaller parts ejecting outward and splitting other atoms, which in turn split others in an ever-widening reaction. Page 194.

flaming youth: a reference to young people and their vigorous, colorful and unrestrained behavior, particularly during the 1920s in America. Page 245.

flash answer: see Book Three, Chapter Nine: Part One, section entitled "The Flash Answer." Page 376.

flat: absolute, downright or positive; without qualification. Page 487.

fleetness of foot: the ability to run fast. Page 38.

flint and steel: a method of starting a fire from the sparks given off by flint (a hard stone) when it is struck with iron or steel. Page 546.

flippant: lacking in seriousness; disrespectful. Page 432.

floundered: struggled clumsily or helplessly or in a confused manner. Page 170.

flounder, out like a: unconscious. A *flounder* is a flatfish that lives on the bottom of the ocean, habitually rests on one side and is often partially buried in the mud or sand giving the appearance of being dead or unconscious. Page 326.

flutters: moves unsteadily, backward and forward, here and there, with quick sometimes irregular movements. Page 449.

foible(s): 1. a minor flaw or shortcoming in personal character or behavior; failing; weakness, as in "*who do not realize some of the foibles of which Man in an aberrated state is capable.*" Page 224. **2.** an odd or eccentric interest in something; a fad, as in "*Their 'symbology' is a mystic foible.*" Page 398.

for all: in spite of the fact. *For all* implies that something is true even though there are some obstacles or opposing conditions. Page 2.

forebear: ancestor, forefather. Page 173.

foreshortens: reduces, contracts or makes shorter. Page 285.

forlorn: deserted or abandoned and showing signs of neglect. Page 118.

formulated: expressed in precise form; stated definitely or systematically. Page iii.

forthright: straightforward or direct; proceeding on a straight course with nothing unusual entered in. Page 364.

fostered: promoted or encouraged, as in terms of growth, development or the like. Page 410.

foul: 1. notably unpleasant or distressing; morally degraded. Page 179.
2. cause (something) to become entangled or muddled. Page 445.

Frankenstein, Doctor: a character in a novel by English novelist Mary Shelley (1797-1851). Frankenstein creates a monster in his laboratory by assembling parts of dead bodies and activating the creature with electricity. Page 307.

Franklin, Benjamin: (1706-1790) American philosopher, diplomat and scientist. In 1747, he began studying electricity and later became famous for his kite experiment, in which he flew a homemade kite during a thunderstorm and proved that lightning is electricity. Page 306.

freight, slow: something that moves slowly. *Freight*, short for *freight train*, refers to a train that transports cargo, usually a much slower train than those carrying passengers. Page 294.

fresh-caught: newly acquired, arrived or obtained, likened to fish that are just caught. Page 453.

fret: to be anxious or worried. Page 379.

frigid: inhibited in the ability to experience sexual excitement during sexual activity. Page 354.

frowning: contracting the brow, as an expression of concentration or deep thought. "*Frowning polysyllables*" refers to the delivery of large words (polysyllables) with a look of concentration or deep thought in order to impress someone. Page 2.

full parade: the full show, displaying everything; complete in all respects; including everything. This phrase alludes to the formal parade in which soldiers, sailors or other military personnel march in full dress uniform, complete in all details. Page 107.

furtherance: helping something to develop or to be successful; advancement; assistance. Page 56.

fuse: figuratively, a device to protect against shock, overload, etc. From the field of electricity, where in an electric circuit a strip of easily melting metal is inserted, which melts (or "blows") and thus interrupts the electrical flow to prevent damage should the electrical current increase beyond a certain safe level. Page 72.

futility: lack of usefulness or effectiveness; pointlessness. Page 196.

Galen: (ca. 129-200) Greek physician who believed that the liver converted food into blood which then flowed into the rest of the body and was absorbed. His undisputed authority in medicine discouraged original research and inhibited medical progress until the sixteenth century when British physician William Harvey (1578-1657) discovered that blood circulated throughout the body and was propelled by the heart, thus refuting Galen's theories. Page 173.

gallbladder: a pear-shaped muscular sac attached to the undersurface of the liver, in which fluid produced by the liver and used in digestion of fats is stored and concentrated. *Gallbladder trouble* refers to the formation of small, hard masses in the gallbladder, causing pain and difficulties with digestion of fats. Page 257.

galvanometer: an instrument for measuring small electrical currents. Page 389.

gamut: the entire scale or range of something. Page 140.

garners: gets or acquires; picks up or accumulates. Page 234.

Gaslight: a stage suspense thriller by English playwright and novelist Patrick Hamilton (1904-1962). In the play, a Victorian wife is deliberately being driven insane by her murderous husband, who is secretly searching for jewelry belonging to the wife's deceased aunt (whom he murdered). His various schemes, such as dimming the gaslights and pretending only his wife notices ("proving" she is hallucinating) are obstructed when a suspicious detective discovers the plan to kill the wife and the murder of her aunt. Page 307.

gasoline and alcohol: a reference to the mixing of gasoline and alcohol. As alcohol is cheaper than gasoline and can also be burned in a car engine, attempts have been made to mix the two. However, alcohol readily absorbs water directly from the air and when attempting to mix alcohol with gasoline, this alcohol/water combination separates out from the gasoline and can cause damage to the parts of an engine. Thus, gasoline mixed with alcohol is considered harmful. Page 533.

gauge: a standard measure or scale of measurement such as for the thickness or diameter of an object. For instance, a piece of #12 gauge copper wire is approximately the thickness of a wire coat hanger. Page 243.

Gauls: inhabitants of an ancient region in Western Europe consisting of what is now mainly France and Belgium. The Gauls were conquered by the Romans in the 50s B.C. Page 69.

gave (given) rise to: originated; produced; caused. Page 73.

Gay Nineties: in United States history, the period of the 1890s remembered for its success and great wealth based on growth in business and industry. Members of the expanding workforce, hoping for a better life in the cities, found instead long hours and unhealthful working conditions in many businesses and factories. Page 245.

gem: something likened to or prized as a precious stone, because of its beauty or worth. Used sarcastically. Page 280.

genesis: the coming into being of something; the initial stage of a developmental process; origin. Page 328.

Genghis Khan: (ca. 1162-1227) Mongol conqueror who founded the largest land empire in history and whose armies, known for their use of terror, conquered many territories and slaughtered the populations of entire cities in the face of any resistance. Page 315.

geometric progression: a series of numbers, such as 1, 2, 4, 8, 16, 32, 64, 128, 256, 512, 1024, etc., where each number is multiplied by a constant quantity (in this example, by 2), in order to arrive at the next number. This results in each next number changing by greater and greater amounts as the progression advances. Page 30.

germane: closely or significantly related; pertinent. Page 114.

gilded: covered with or as if with a thin layer of gold. Page 22.

gimmick: a clever mechanism or object. Page 451.

girder: a large iron or steel beam used as a main supporting element in building bridges and large buildings. Page 115.

gladhander: someone who greets or welcomes (everyone) warmly, especially with an excessive or insincere appearance of warmth. Page 314.

glass snakes: referring to snake-like forms, such as heat waves seen rising from a landscape during the heat of the day. Page 405.

gleaned: learned, discovered or found out, usually bit by bit or slowly. Page 298.

gnome: in folklore, any of a race of small, misshapen, dwarf-like beings, supposed to dwell in the earth and guard its treasures. Page 42.

goad: to drive or urge on, as if with a sharp pointed stick used to drive cattle. Page 349.

godhead: the state or quality of being God or a god. Page 188.

golden rule: a rule of ethical conduct, usually phrased "Do unto others as you would have them do unto you." Page 158.

gold-footed idol: a superior being without fault; someone who can do no wrong. A figurative reference alluding to, and contrasting with, the Biblical idol with head of gold and feet of clay, that is, something that appears strong and admirable, but that will be destroyed because of an underlying weakness or fault. Page 469.

Goldi medicine man: medicine man of the Goldi people, traditionally hunters and fishermen, who inhabit a valley in southeastern Siberia. In the ceremonies of their medicine men, the drum is employed to communicate with spirits. Page 7.

gold panning: washing (gravel, sand, etc.) in a pan in search of gold. Page 416.

gonads: organs or glands that produce reproductive cells; sex glands. Page 330.

good sport: a sociable, pleasant person who agrees without complaint to do what is asked by a companion. Page 485.

Goodwife: a title of respect for a woman. Page 452.

gourd rattling: a reference to the use of a rattle by a medicine man for the purpose of frightening demons away in religious rituals, etc. A *gourd* is hard-shelled fruit of various plants whose dried shell is used for musical instruments, utensils, etc. Page 224.

grammarians: those who are knowledgeable in grammar or in language generally, such as its structure, spelling, etc. Also, more generally, those who write on the basic elements or principles of any science, art, discipline or practice. Specifically, the reference here is to such words as *Absolute Reality* and *Truth*, where their capitalization (grammar) transforms them from their usual meaning to something absolute and without gradation of meaning. Page 450.

Grand Coulee Dam: a dam on the Columbia River in Washington State, USA. It is one of the largest concrete structures in the world and a major source of electric power. Page 311.

green eyeshade: a type of headgear consisting of a strap to which is attached a green colored beak or visor (shade) which prevents light from directly hitting the eyes, such as from a bare light bulb. Green eyeshades were traditionally associated with people working hard at a task, such as newspaper editors, accountants, clerks, etc. Page 265.

gregarious: living in communities; given to association with others of one's kind. Page 45.

grim: fierce, cruel, savage or harsh in state of mind or action. Page 314.

grind it out: to work at something laboriously to bring it to a point or state of extinction or depletion, etc. Page 387.

grippe: an infectious disease commonly called the flu. Page 401.

grist to one's mill: something that is to one's advantage or profit. *Grist* is grain which is to be ground up. Page 448.

grizzly: a reference to a *grizzly bear*, a large brown bear of North America. Page 151.

ground, giving: yielding to force or forceful argument; retreating. Page 239.

GROUPER: AN ENGRAM COMMAND WHICH MAKES THE TIME TRACK OR INCIDENTS ON IT BECOME TANGLED IN SUCH A WAY THAT THE TRACK APPEARS SHORTENED. (From *Dianetics Terms.*) Page 284.

G-2: a designation for the military intelligence section of the United States Army or Marine Corps. Page 458.

guideposts: things that serve as guides; guidelines. Page 196.

guilt complex: in psychoanalysis, a *complex* is a set of impulses, ideas and emotions that compel habitual patterns of behavior, in this case causing the feeling of guilt. Page 363.

gunnery: the firing of heavy guns or projectiles. Used figuratively. Page 236.

gun was loaded, didn't know the: from a defensive statement used to explain an accidental shooting which has come to mean an act committed which has destructive consequences but with a lack of foreknowledge, prediction or observation. Page 39.

gutted: that has had the contents (resources, goods, etc.) removed, as by force. Page 545.

gyrations: motions in a circle or spiral; turning round, wheeling or whirling. Page 239.

habit, riding: an outfit typically worn by a horseback rider, including jacket, special pants that are wide at the hips and narrow around the calves, and a hat with a round crown and a small visor. Page 475.

hallowed: regarded as holy. Page 384.

Hamlet: the central figure of a tragedy of the same name by William Shakespeare, first published in 1603. Wavering over whether to live or die, Hamlet delivers the famous lines: "To be or not to be, that is the question..." Page 245.

hand-patting: striking or clapping gently with the inner surface of the fingers as an expression of sympathy or soothing. Used figuratively, showing sympathy for someone. Page 237.

hang fire: stall or delay. The phrase literally refers to the delayed firing of a gun that doesn't go off when the trigger is pulled or which goes off late. Page 323.

hardy: capable of enduring difficult conditions; sturdy and of good health. Page 491.

harlot: a disreputable woman; a prostitute. Page 325.

harridan: a scolding, vicious woman. Page 469.

harrowing: extremely distressing or painful; disturbing. Page 506.

Harvey: William Harvey (1578-1657), English physician who, using scientific procedures and experimentation, discovered that blood circulates and that the heart propels it through the body, thus refuting the theories of Galen. Page v.

hash: 1. a dish made of cooked potatoes or other vegetables, usually combined with chopped-up pieces of cooked meat and normally reheated by frying until golden brown. Page 242.
2. a mess or jumble. Page 256.

hatful: a considerable quantity, from the amount that can be contained in a hat. Page 367.

hatpin: a long, ornamental pin for fastening a woman's hat to her hair. Page 349.

havoc, (something) wreaks: causes or produces harm, damage, etc. Page 281.

hawk: clear the throat noisily. Page 478.

hazarded: proposed as a guess. Page 11.

heads I win, tails you lose: I win whatever happens. From the phrase *head(s) or tail(s)*, used in tossing a coin, where someone is asked to announce which side of the coin will be facing up when it comes to rest. If he is correct, he wins. *Head(s)* is the side of a coin containing the image of a head and *tail(s)* is the reverse side. Page 139.

hebephrenia: in psychiatry, a form of insanity characterized by inappropriate reactions, such as excessive silliness. Page 163.

heed: give attention; have regard for. Page 339.

heed, pay no: give something no notice or consideration. Page 406.

Hegelian grammar: a reference to the correct usage of certain terms by Georg Wilhelm Friedrich Hegel (1770-1831), German philosopher who determined that the world contained absolutes. Hegel's use of language reflected this view. For example, in the use of the word "accurate" and the omission of "very accurate" or "not quite accurate," the latter two being considered "bad grammar." Page 3.

held forth: spoken out (publicly) at length on a particular subject. Page 294.

helium: a very light colorless gas used to inflate balloons, airships, etc. Page 148.

Hercules: in ancient Greek and Roman mythology, a hero of enormous strength and courage who was commanded by a king to accomplish twelve seemingly impossible tasks. Page 193.

heroic: having, displaying or characteristic of the qualities appropriate to somebody who commits an act of remarkable bravery or who has shown great courage, strength of character or other admirable qualities (a hero); courageous. Page 230.

hew: make rough, heavy cutting blows, as with an ax. Page 516.

hexed: affected as if by an evil spell. Page 194.

high flown: being high above the ordinary level of thought. Page 45.

hinder: prevent or make it difficult for something to happen; stop. Page 239.

Hindu: of or related to *Hinduism*, a religion of India that emphasizes freedom from the material world through purification of desires and elimination of personal identity. Hindu beliefs include reincarnation. The sacred writings of Hinduism include the Veda. Page 113.

Hindu trinity: a reference to the three great gods in Hinduism: Brahma, the creator of the universe; Vishnu, the preserver of the universe; and Shiva, who personifies both the destructive and the procreative forces of the universe. A *trinity* is a combination or set of three individual things (as gods, persons, things, etc.) that form a unity or are closely connected to one another. Page 466.

Hippocrates: (ca. 460-377 B.C.) Greek physician known as the "father of medicine" and famous for his medical writings including an oath which served as a model for the ethical practice of medicine. Page 339.

histamine: a substance released in the body in response to an allergy; it helps the body fight infections by increasing the supply of blood and other fluids to affected areas, but it also produces uncomfortable reactions such as sneezing, watery eyes, runny nose, itching and swelling of body tissues. Page 123.

hitherto: up to this time; until now. Page ii.

HOLDER: ANY ENGRAM COMMAND WHICH MAKES AN INDIVIDUAL REMAIN IN AN ENGRAM KNOWINGLY OR UNKNOWINGLY. (From *Dianetics Terms*.) Page 268.

hole in his head, like a fellow needs a: to emphatically have no need for something. Literally it means, needs something in the same way as (like) a person needs an actual hole in his head. Page 131.

hormones: chemical substances secreted by glands or tissues in the body that regulate growth and development, control the function of various tissues, support reproductive functions, and regulate metabolism (the process used to break down food to create energy). Page 130.

hub: a center around which other things revolve or from which they radiate; source. Page 216.

hubbub: confusion or uproar. Page 504.

Hume: David Hume (1711-1776), Scottish philosopher who believed that all human thought and knowledge was based on direct experience of the world through the senses and who attempted to analyze the workings of the mind to show this. Page 114.

hurrah's nest: a state of confusion or disorder; a chaotic heap or mess; a disorderly mass. Page 415.

hyacinth, buy white: a reference to a line of poetry by American writer James Terry White (1845-1920) which reads: "If thou of fortune be bereft/And in thy store there be but left/Two loaves–sell one, and with the dole/Buy hyacinths to feed thy soul." (*Bereft* means deprived or stripped of. *Dole* means a small portion. *Hyacinths* are plants having fragrant clusters of bell-shaped flowers in different shades.) Page 43.

hydraulic ram: a ram operated by liquid pressure, such as water. A *ram* is any of various devices for battering, crushing, driving or forcing something. Page 333.

hyoscine: a drug used as a sedative or hypnotic. Page 482.

hypnoanalysis: a method of psychoanalysis in which a patient is hypnotized in an attempt to reach analytic data and early emotional reactions. Page 166.

hypnoscopes: instruments used to determine whether a person is a hypnotic subject, such as a hollow magnet that is said to cause a person certain "sensations" when placed on their finger if they are a "good" hypnotic subject. Page 307.

hypochondriac: one who suffers excessive anxiety over his health, often with imaginary illnesses. Page 77.

"I": (in philosophy and other fields) the source of thinking; the person himself, as distinct from the body, who is aware of being self; the soul. Page viii.

idealism: the cherishing or pursuit of high or noble principles, purposes, goals, etc. Page 540.

identities: exact samenesses in qualities or characteristics; equivalents or equals. Page 55.

identity-thought: the type of thought of the reactive mind. It thinks in terms of full identification, which is to say *identities*, one thing *identical* to another. This can be stated as everything equals everything, or A=A=A=A=A. The analytical mind thinks in differences and similarities. The better one can tell differences, no matter how minute, and know the width of those differences, the more rational he is. The less one can tell differences and the closer one comes to thinking in identities, the less sane he is. Page 86.

ideologies: systems of ideas, doctrines, opinions, etc., or ways of thinking of an individual, class, etc., especially as a basis of economic or political theories or systems. Page 543.

idiosyncrasy: a characteristic, habit, mannerism or the like that is peculiar to an individual. Page 23.

idyllic: serenely beautiful; untroubled and happy. Page 44.

ilk: kind, sort or class. Page 132.

imagery: the formation of mental images, figures or likeness of things, or of such images collectively. Page 19.

impacted: pressed tightly together, as a tooth wedged between the jawbone and another tooth and unable to emerge properly because of its abnormal position, lack of space, etc. Page 156.

impaction: the action of becoming packed in, firmly fixed, dammed up. Page 110.

impasses: points or situations, etc., from which further progress is blocked; difficulties without solution; literally referring to a road that has no exit. Page 499.

impedimenta: things that impede or hinder one's progress. Page 269.

impetus: driving force or motive; impulse. Page 41.

implicitly: without reservation, question or doubt. Page 469.

imponderables: things that cannot be figured out or solved by thinking. Page 310.

imposition: an excessive, unwarranted or uncalled-for requirement or burden. Page 547.

incapacitation: incapability of normal activity; the act of making something incapable or unfit. Page 93.

incidence: the occurrence, rate or frequency of a disease, crime or something else undesirable. Page 183.

incidental: happening in an unplanned or unpredictable way, along with something else. Page 16.

incident to: naturally accompanying or pertaining to. Page 65.

incongruity: something that is not consistent with other factors of a situation. Page 295.

incontrovertible: not open to question or dispute; undeniable. Page 513.

index system: a method of sequential arrangement of material, extremely detailed, by alphabetical listing of names, places, subjects, etc., or by specific categories, dates, times, events, etc. Page 264.

Indian rope trick: a magic trick, Oriental in origin, in which a magician suspends a rope in midair which a person climbs up and then seemingly disappears. Page 114.

indictment: any charge, accusation or serious criticism. Page 8.

indifferent: 1. rather poor or bad; not good at all. Page 36. 2. neither good nor bad; average; mediocre. Page 526.

indoctrinate: instruct in a principle, procedure, subject, etc.; teach. Page 380.

indolence: laziness and inactivity; a tendency to avoid exertion. Page 318.

inductive: of or concerned with reaching a conclusion based on observation (of facts, phenomena, etc.). Page 68.

indulgence: yielding to or satisfying desires, feelings, etc. Page 54.

indulges: gives way to, allows; gives oneself up to. Page 237.

inextricably: beyond all possibility of being disentangled. Page 29.

infame: infamy, the disgrace to somebody's reputation caused by a dishonorable act or behavior. Page 486.

inherently: in a manner that is existing in someone's or something's internal character as a permanent and inseparable element, quality or attribute. Page x.

injudiciously: unwisely or in a manner lacking judgment. Page 524.

injunction(s): **1.** an earnest warning. Page 77.
2. an emphatic order or command. Page 516.

in kind: with the same thing; in something of the same kind or in the same way as that received or borne. Page 22.

inorganic: not belonging to the body or its parts (such as its organs) or physical things. Page i.

in re: with regard to; concerning. Page 359.

insensible: incapable of perceiving through the senses or the mind. Page 435.

insidious: operating or proceeding in an inconspicuous or seemingly harmless way but actually with grave effect. Page 329.

instanter: instantly; at once, immediately. Page 407.

instrument: a reference to any of various instruments or tools used in childbirth, such as scissors, clamps, syringes, etc. Page 402.

insufferable: difficult or impossible to endure; intolerable. Page 358.

insulin shock: a form of psychiatric shock treatment introduced in the 1930s. The purported treatment consists of a series of shots, injecting an excessive amount of insulin into the body, thereby inducing convulsions and a coma. Page 260.

intelligence officer: a military officer responsible for collecting and processing information (such as on hostile forces) especially through secret means. Page 61.

intent: something planned or the purpose that accompanies a plan. Page 53.

intent, for all: for all practical purposes. Page 332.

intent on: with full attention concentrated or focused on one thing. Page 66.

in the stead of: in the place of a person or thing as occupied by a successor or substitute. Page 7.

intimate: to suggest or hint that something is a certain way. Page 87.

Glossary

intimation: something suggested or implied. Page 17.

introversion: a directing of one's interest inward or to things within the self. Page 497.

intuitive: known directly and instinctively, without being discovered or consciously perceived. Page 32.

inversion: a reversal of position; a change to the opposite state or condition. Page 269.

invoked: called forth; caused. Page 413.

involved: included in or participating in something as a necessary element, condition or circumstance, as in *"no Nirvana involved."* Page 129.

IQ: *Intelligence Quotient,* a number arrived at by tests and intended to indicate a person's intelligence. (*Quotient* means the result of division, and refers to the way the test is calculated to obtain the average for the age group.) Page 121.

irksome: annoying; irritating; exasperating. Page 284.

irresolution: wavering in decision as to a course of action. Page 70.

Ism: a distinctive doctrine, theory, system or practice. Page 543.

jauntings: journeys or trips, especially short ones, normally thought of as for pleasure. Page 203.

jeers: remarks expressing contempt or scorn. Page 464.

jettison: throw away, reject, get rid of (an obstacle or burden). Page 224.

Jimmie the Cob: a made-up name for a leader of a gang of criminals. *Cob* is a British term for leader or chief. Page 199.

jockeying: skillfully managing for the purpose of gaining an advantage. Page 543.

jocular: joking; humorous. Page 456.

jostled: pushed or bumped against roughly. Page 392.

jub-jub bird: an imaginary bird, noted for its ferocious nature, created by and appearing in the works of English author Lewis Carroll (1832–1898). Page 257.

Junior: **1.** a male child; son, as in "Ask Junior to help you with that." Page 176.

2. younger (usually designating the younger of two men bearing the same full name, as a son named after his father). Page 279.

jurisprudence: the science or philosophy of law; the systematic knowledge of the laws, customs and rights of men in a state or community necessary for the due administration of justice. Page 537.

Keats: John Keats (1795-1821), English poet whose works are known for their dignity, melody and rich imagery. Page 424.

keep, dungeon: the main inner tower of a medieval castle that served as the living place for a lord and his family and which was used as the final defensive stronghold when the castle was under siege. Page 476.

key, brought it into: activated, as if operating a key, a small manual device for opening, closing or switching electronic contacts. Page 319.

keyed-in: literally, a *key* is a small manual device for opening, closing or switching electronic contacts. *Key-in* is used here to describe a dormant engram that has activated and is now thrown into circuit. Page 86.

keynote: the central or most important point or theme of something. Page 40.

key-out: literally, a *key* is a small manual device for opening, closing or switching electronic contacts. *Key-out* is used here to describe the action of engrams being deactivated and going out of circuit. Page 149.

kinetic: pertaining to motion. Page 81.

Kinsey: Alfred Charles Kinsey (1894-1956), American biologist who investigated human sexual behavior, interviewed some 18,000 people, and published his findings in 1948 and 1953. Page 279.

kinship: relationship; close connection. Page 543.

kleptomaniac: someone with an obsessive urge to steal, especially when there is no economic necessity. Page 283.

Knighthood Was in Flower, When: title of a novel by Charles Major (1856-1913) that captured the chivalry (courteous conduct) of twelfth- and thirteenth-century England when knights were at their height of fame and prominence. Page 238.

Knowable and Unknowable of Herbert Spencer: a reference to the philosophy of Herbert Spencer (1820-1903), English philosopher known for his application of the scientific doctrines of evolution to philosophy and ethics. Spencer claimed that knowledge was of two kinds: (1) knowledge gained by the individual, and (2) knowledge gained by the race. He also believed that there is a basic and final reality beyond our knowledge, which he called the "Unknowable." Page 113.

Glossary

Korzybski: Alfred Korzybski (1879-1950), Polish-American scholar and founder of general semantics, a highly organized philosophical approach to language. Korzybski believed the imprecise use of language affected human behavior (people react mentally and physically to the meaning of words), causing confusion and miscommunication among people. Korzybski believed that the fundamental to thinking was the ability to distinguish and that the literal identification of one thing with another (when in fact it was not identical) is what causes difficulties and even insanity in Man. Page 83.

Kraepelin: Emil Kraepelin (1856-1926), German psychiatrist who developed a classification system for mental illness. Page 506.

Krafft-Ebing: Baron Richard von Krafft-Ebing (1840-1902), German psychiatrist and author of works on sexual deviations. Page 140.

laid in(to): set, placed or deposited (in or into); placed in position (inside something). Page 65.

lash-ups: the actions of being tied up with ropes, cords, etc. Here, used to describe how the circuits of the mind ordinarily intended for smooth, rapid computation are tied up or caught up with parasitic demons. Page 121.

last-ditch: made, done, etc., in a final, often desperate, act of resistance or opposition. Page 148.

late: at a time period in or near the present time. Page ix.

Law of Affinity: the Law of Affinity might be interpreted as the Law of Cohesion (a force that binds or unites). Deprivation of or absence of affection could be considered as a violation of the Law of Affinity. Man must be in affinity with Man to survive. Page 113.

lead (off): to guide or channel something (away). Page 314.

leads: literally, flexible electrical conductors, used to connect two points in an electrical path. Used here to describe mental connections. Page 287.

leaf: a sheet of paper or page in a book; also the written or printed matter on it. By extension, an event or sequence of events worthy of being written and recorded, as in the pages of history. Page 124.

leprosy: an infectious skin and nerve disease characterized by white scaly scabs, deformities and the eventual loss of sensation. Page 183.

Lesbos: a mountainous Greek island in the Aegean Sea, off the coast of Turkey. Page 316.

Leucippus: Greek philosopher (fourth century B.C.) who believed that all matter was made up of atoms, that all observable properties of an object result from the behavior of these atoms, and that this behavior of atoms was completely determined in advance. He held that everything came about for a reason and by necessity. Page 40.

leveled: aimed or directed at or towards. Page 139.

lichens: gray, green or yellow plants appearing in often flat patches on rocks and other surfaces. Page 39.

lick: overcome or defeat. Page 416.

lieu of, in: in place of; instead of. Page 115.

light of, in the: with the help given by knowledge of (some fact); taking into account; considering. Page 63.

line: a series of individual things (such as bodies) following one after the other, as "*in the physical line.*" Page 132.

line of demarcation: that which marks the boundaries or limits of, or divides something so that its divided parts are separate and identifiable. Page 27.

liner: a large ship for passengers, mail, cargo, etc., especially one on a regular route. Page 451.

lisp: pronounce or speak with a *lisp*, a speech defect consisting in pronouncing *s* and *z* like or nearly like the *th* sounds of *thin* and *this*. Page 501.

"little men hanging by their heels": *see* **"two little men...hanging by their heels."**

live-fuse: of or like a lit fuse or explosive. A *fuse* is a cord of material that burns easily, lit at one end to carry a flame along its length to set off an explosive at the other end. Page 128.

lo: look! see! Used to call attention to something. Page 264.

lobe(s): a rounded projection or subdivision of an organ of the body. Page 59.

Locke: John Locke (1632-1704), English writer, philosopher and political theorist who argued that the human mind is a "blank slate" at birth until experience begins to "write" on it. He believed that one can know nothing unless it has been part of one's experience. Page 114.

locomotion: the action of moving from one place to another. Page 93.

logbook: a book in which details of a trip made by a ship or aircraft are recorded. Page 454.
logjam(s): an immovable pileup of logs causing blockage in a river. Page 320.
looms up: rises into view as something massive, impressive or of importance. Page 477.
loop: someone who is crazy or nutty. Page 245.
loopy: a slang term meaning crazy or nutty. Page 331.
lordly: acting toward others as though one is better or more important than they are. Page 235.
Lorentz-FitzGerald-Einstein equations: a reference to the equations of Hendrik Lorentz (1853-1928) and George Francis FitzGerald (1851-1901) who concluded that a moving body exhibits a contraction or shrinking in the direction of its motion by an amount that depends on how closely it approaches the speed of light. These findings later contributed to the work of Albert Einstein (1879-1955). Page 3.

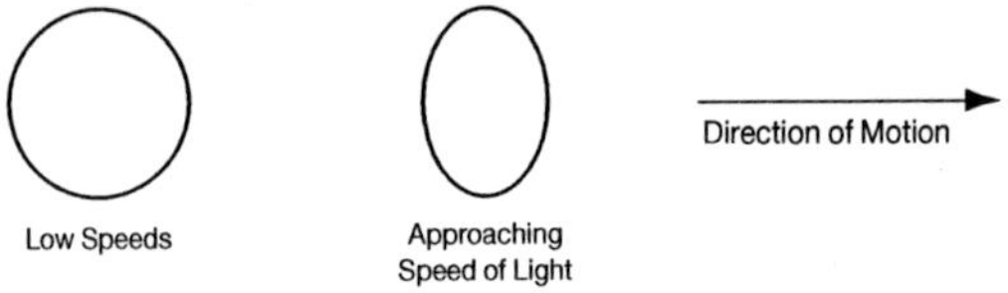

lot, carload: a *carload* is the amount carried by a railroad freight car. *Lot* refers to numerous articles forming a group that is regarded or handled as one item. Hence, used figuratively in this context, a *carload lot* means a large quantity of items viewed as being grouped together, as if in the space of a railroad freight car. Page 450.
loud: offensively bright. Page 14.
loused-up: made (someone or something) worse rather than better. Page 128.
love name: an additional, informal name used affectionately, as when speaking to a child. Page 438.
Lucretius: (ca. 98-55 B.C.) Roman poet and author of the unfinished instructional poem *On the Nature of Things*, published in six volumes, which sets forth in outline a complete science of the universe. Page 38.

lugubrious: extremely dismal or gloomy, especially in a slow, serious or ridiculous manner. Page 102.

Lysol: a brand name for a liquid disinfectant. Page 140.

Macbeth: the title character of a play by William Shakespeare. Macbeth meets three witches who predict that he will be king of Scotland but that his descendants will not hold the throne. Macbeth secures and holds the throne through multiple murders but fails to change the remainder of the prediction and is killed in battle. His wife and accomplice, crazed with remorse, also dies. Page 361.

maelstrom: a large, powerful or violent whirlpool; hence a restless, disordered state of affairs. Page 200.

magic healing crystal: a type of crystal considered to have the power to heal, as is found among certain primitive medicine men in Australia who are said to believe that healing crystals were placed on Earth by gods of the sky. *Crystal* is a transparent rock-like substance resembling ice. Page 7.

makeshifts: temporary substitutes. Page 76.

makes shift: temporarily substitutes something of an inferior kind or uses inferior means. Page 7.

malady: an illness, condition or situation that is problematic and requires a remedy. Page 77.

malaria: an infectious disease transmitted by the bite of infected mosquitoes, common in hot countries and characterized by severe chills and fever. If not treated it can cause death. Page 208.

malignant: (of a tumor) characterized by uncontrolled growth. Page 126.

maligned: spoken harmfully or untruthfully about; spoken evil of. Page 68.

mammoths: large extinct mammals related to the elephant, that had hair and long curved tusks, existed mainly in the Northern Hemisphere and died out more than 10,000 years ago. Page 39.

Man: the human race or species; humankind; Mankind. Page ii.

man: 1. a human being, without regard to sex or age; a person. Page iii. 2. any of the pieces used in a board game, such as chess or checkers. Page 283.

mandate: an order or command. Page 32.

mange: an infectious skin disease of animals, and sometimes humans, resulting in hair loss, scabs and itching. Page 91.

manic: 1. a manic engram, a highly complimentary pro-survival engram. If an individual is caught in a manic, his life force is channeling straight through the engram and his behavior, no matter how enthusiastic or euphoric, is actually very aberrated, as in *"It may even be a manic and that's horrible despite its apparent 'euphoria.'"* Page 132.

2. a phrase in a manic engram, such as *"If it added, 'He is a darling and a very wonder with the ladies,' it would then be a pro-survival* with *a manic."* Page 320.

manic: 1. characterized by mania, abnormal excitability, exaggerated feelings of well-being, etc., as in *"This would be a* manic-*type insanity."* Page 77.

2. a person characterized by *mania*, as in *"as in the manic and the high-euphoria case."* Page 313.

manic-depressive: a person alternating between extremes of excitement and depression. Page 70.

march: a steady forward movement or progression. Page 282.

marionette: a puppet manipulated from above by strings attached to its jointed limbs. Page vi.

marketplace: the everyday world. Page 165.

masochistic: marked by pleasure gained (sometimes sexual) from pain, degradation, etc., inflicted or imposed on oneself, either as a result of one's own actions or the actions of others. Page 356.

master disc: the original (master) of a phonograph record, made out of metal and used to make duplicate phonograph records (flat vinyl discs with grooves, on which music, voice or other sounds are recorded). The master disc has a series of grooves and when impressed upon hot, softened vinyl, these grooves are duplicated so the phonograph record contains a copy of the original sound. Page 173.

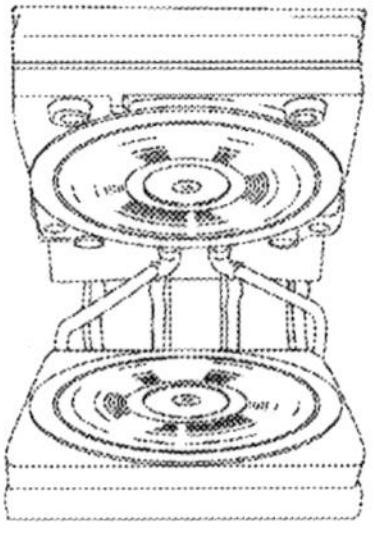

Matterhorn: a famous mountain peak in the Alps rising 14,692 feet (4,478 meters). It is located on the border of Switzerland and Italy. Page 43.

mauled (around): handled or dealt with in a rough manner. Page 223.

mauling: rough or careless handling. Page 183.

Mauser: the name of a German military rifle, from the last name of the inventor, Peter Paul Mauser (1838-1914). Page 152.

maw: anything that seems like a gaping hole that devours things or people. Page 43.

mawkish: filled with sickly sentimentality; weakly emotional. Page 363.

Maxwell, James Clerk: (1831-1879) Scottish physicist and mathematician who in 1864 described the relationship between electricity and magnetism and whose work laid the foundation for later advances in the use of electricity. Page 95.

Mazda and Ahriman: *Ahura Mazda*, the supreme deity and creator of all things in Zoroastrianism (an ancient religion of Iran) and *Ahriman*, an evil spirit and arch rival of the deity Mazda. Page 466.

measure, in a: to some extent or degree. Page 191.

mechanical: 1. concerned with or involving material objects or physical conditions or forces, as in "*which handles all the mechanical functions of living.*" Page 64.

2. of or relating to *mechanics*, the procedural or operating details (of something). When applied to theories, *mechanics* means the explanation of phenomena by the assumption of mechanical action; the explanation of how something works, as in "*that is a mechanical, scientific fact.*" Page 516.

mechanical processes: processes that operate with definite, specific actions, producing an unvarying result; processes whose actions can be explained by the assumption of mechanical actions or of how something works. Page 251.

mechanics: the procedural or operating details (of something). When applied to theories, *mechanics* means the explanation of phenomena by the assumption of mechanical action; the explanation of how something works. Page 99.

mechanism(s): 1. a structure or system (of parts, components, etc.) that together perform a particular function as would occur in a machine, as in "*gazes for the first time upon the mechanisms*

Glossary

of human action" or *"a man contained a mechanism which recorded with diabolical accuracy."* Page x.

2. the agency or means by which an effect is produced or a purpose is accomplished, likened to the structure or system of parts in a mechanical device for carrying out some function or doing something, as in *"he is the optimum survival mechanism which life has attained."* Page 28.

mechanistic: of or pertaining to a *mechanism*, a structure or system (of parts, components, etc.) that together perform a particular function as would occur in a machine. Page vi.

media-media: a coined term used to mean average or regular; intermediate or halfway. *Media* is from a Latin word meaning middle. Page 144.

medium: a substance or the environment in which an organism naturally lives or grows. Page 212.

melancholy: sadness and depression of spirits; tendency to be sad, gloomy or depressed. Page 162.

mellerdrammer: a humorous variation of *melodrama*, a dramatic piece characterized by exaggerated emotions and sensational incidents. Page 245.

MEMORY: ANYTHING WHICH, PERCEIVED, IS FILED IN THE STANDARD MEMORY BANK AND CAN BE RECALLED BY THE ANALYTICAL MIND. (From *Dianetics Terms.*) Page v.

men of goodwill: people (irrespective of sex or age) who are well-wishing and have a desire to do good to others. Page 225.

Mesmer, Anton: (1734–1815) Austrian physician who pioneered the practice of hypnotism in medicine. Page 339.

metal, in the: a coined term for in reality or as something actually exists, such as the metal instruments and equipment on a ship. Page 453.

metallurgy: the technique or science of working or heating metals so as to give them certain desired shapes or properties. Page 546.

metaphysician: a person who specializes or is versed in metaphysics. *See also* **metaphysics.** Page 450.

metaphysics: the branch of philosophy concerned with the ultimate nature of existence or the nature of ultimate reality that is above or goes beyond the laws of nature or is more than physical. First applied to writings of Aristotle (384–322 B.C.), the term literally means "after physics," as these writings followed his works entitled *The Physics.* Page ii.

meted: dealt out. Page 185.

metering: 1. supplying (a fluid) in a measured or regulated amount. Page 56.

2. measuring or recording the quantity or quality of something. Page 330.

midterm: the midpoint or approximate midpoint of a period of time. Page 8.

mien: a person's appearance, bearing or posture, especially facial expressions, as an indication of mood or character. Page 143.

militate: to operate or work against, or have a substantial effect or influence on something, especially a negative one. Page 28.

millennia: the plural form of *millennium,* a period of 1,000 years. Page 113.

millwheel pond: a pond that drives the machinery of a mill through the force of moving water. (A *mill* is a building equipped to grind or crush solid substances.) Page 311.

mind: listen to and obey someone. Page 411.

mind's eye: the ability to imagine or remember images or scenes, to "see" things with the mind; the ability of seeing a mental vision consisting of an imaginary or recollected sight, as opposed to one actually seen at the time. Page 20.

mirage: something that falsely appears to be real. Literally, a *mirage* is an optical illusion of a sheet of water appearing in the desert or on a hot road, caused by light being distorted by alternate layers of hot and cool air. Page 319.

mirror, crazy house: a reference to a mirror built to give a distorted image, found in an amusement park fun house (an attraction consisting of a series of rooms and passages, sloping or moving floors, distorting mirrors and other devices designed to surprise or amuse). Page 398.

mirth: joyfulness, gaiety or merriment, especially when characterized by laughter. Page 162.

misconstrued: misunderstood as to the meaning; taken in the wrong sense. Page 328.

MISDIRECTOR: ANY ENGRAM COMMAND WHICH MAKES THE PATIENT MOVE IN A WAY OR DIRECTION ON THE TRACK WHICH IS CONTRARY TO INSTRUCTIONS OF THE AUDITOR

OR THE DESIRES OF THE ANALYTICAL MIND OF THE PATIENT. (From *Dianetics Terms.*) Page 285.

mocked: treated someone with ridicule or contempt. Page 498.

molars: large back teeth in humans used for chewing and grinding. Page 156.

Moloch: a god worshiped throughout the countries of the ancient Middle East and to whom violent child sacrifices were supposed to have been made. Page 454.

mongrel: of mixed race, origin, character, nationality, etc. Page 187.

monitor: a device or system that supervises, regulates, controls or directs the performance of something. Page 59.

monkey wrenches: wrenches with one movable jaw, adjusted by a screw to fit various sizes of a nut, etc. Page 349.

monocell: an organism composed of a single cell. Page 173.

monologuist: a person who delivers *monologue*, a drama in which a single actor speaks alone. Used here to mean speaks to oneself. Page 277.

monomanic: characterized by *monomania*, such concentration on a single object or idea as to suggest mental derangement. Page 314.

monotone: characterized by an uninterrupted sameness, due to complete lack of distinction in emphasis, importance, quality, etc. Literally, a *monotone* is a vocal utterance or series of speech sounds in one unvaried tone. Page 15.

monstrosity(ies): 1. a person that is abnormally developed, formed contrary to the ordinary course of nature; deformed. Page 215.

2. an excessively bad or shocking example. Page 466.

moored: fixed firmly; secured. Page 83.

Moralist: a teacher or student of morals; a thinker or writer concerned with moral principles and problems, specifically any of the Christian Moralists of the Middle Ages (fifth through fourteenth centuries). In their writings, the Moralists dictated that a person should follow certain virtues (qualities of goodness) in determining whether actions are right or wrong, good or evil, and that evil people deserved an unhappy life. Page 25.

mores: heavily agreed-upon, policed codes of conduct of a society. Page 178.

morning sickness: nausea and vomiting sometimes accompanied by dizziness, headache, etc., that affects some women during the first months of pregnancy. Page 212.

moronic: marked by extreme deficiency in judgment or sense. Page 104.

morose: gloomy; depressed; sour-tempered. Page 245.

morphine: a powerful drug used in medicine to relieve severe pain; prolonged use can lead to addiction. The name comes from *Morpheus,* the Roman god of sleep and dreams. Page 483.

mother of invention: from the saying "necessity is the mother of invention" which means that an urgent need often prompts one to work out a new solution. Page 40.

motif: a dominant idea or theme. Page 245.

motor: of, pertaining to or involving muscular movement. Page vi.

motor strip: a long narrow area of the brain, which is believed to control the movement of the various muscles and movements of the body. *Motor* means of, relating to, or being a nerve that passes from the nervous system to a muscle, conducting an impulse that causes movement. (See text for further description.) *See also* **"two little men...hanging by their heels."** Page 389.

mulled over: thought about carefully; considered at length. Page 94.

multitudinously: in many numerous ways. Page 62.

mumbo jumbo: complicated and sometimes purposeless activity or language intended to obscure; also meaningless talk; nonsense. Page 262.

mutates: undergoes *mutation. See* **mutation.** Page 137.

mutation: a sudden structural change in the hereditary material of an organism's cells resulting in a new trait or characteristic not found in the parents, as distinguished from a variation resulting from generations of gradual change. *Hereditary* means having to do with traits or characteristics transmitted from generation to generation through reproduction. Page 28.

myelin sheathing: a whitish material that surrounds some nerve cells and that aids transmission of nerve impulses. Prior to 1950, prevailing theory held that the human child was incapable of recording memory until the formation of myelin sheathing after birth. Page xi.

myopia: defective vision of distant objects; nearsightedness. Page 70.

mysticism: the belief that personal communication or union with truth or the divine (God, gods or goddesses) is achieved through direct perception or sudden insight rather than through rational thought. Page ii.

Napoleon: Napoleon Bonaparte (1769-1821), French general who crowned himself emperor of France in 1804. His constant wars to expand French territory left the country smaller than before he took power, with a half a million men dead. The statement that he reduced the height of Frenchmen one inch refers to his action of placing French military personnel who were tall (whereas he was short) in dangerous situations where they were more likely to be killed. Page 49.

narcosynthesis: hypnotism brought about by drugs whereby a patient undergoes psychotherapy while affected by such drugs and in a "deep sleep." *Narco* is short for narcotic and means a drug that produces hypnosis. *Synthesis* in this sense means the combination of separate elements of sensation or thought into a whole. The name was created by psychiatrists using drugs during World War II attempting to "rebuild (synthesize) the disintegrated or broken-down" soldier. Page 158.

Nation, Carrie: (1846-1911) American reformer who advocated avoidance of alcoholic drinks. She was famous for raiding saloons and demolishing bottles of liquor and barroom furniture with a hatchet. Page 245.

natural history: a branch of knowledge embracing the study, description and classification of natural objects such as animals, plants and minerals. Page 334.

naturalist: a person who studies nature, especially by direct observation of animals and plants. Page 29.

natural selection: the process by which forms of life having traits that better enable them to adapt to specific environmental pressures, such as predators, changes in climate, competition for food or mates, will tend to survive and reproduce in greater numbers than others of their kind, thus ensuring the survival of those favorable traits in succeeding generations. A *predator* is an animal that hunts, kills and eats other animals to survive, or any other organism that behaves in a similar manner. Page 137.

Nature: the creative and regulative physical power which is conceived of as operating in the material world and as the immediate cause of all of its phenomena. Often represented as having human qualities or character, i.e., Mother Nature. Page x.

nature of the beast: the essential character or inherent qualities of a thing, person, etc. *Nature* means the innate or inseparable combination of properties something has that give it its fundamental character. *Beast* means a thing or person of a particular kind. Page 505.

naught: nothing. Page 540.

nebulosity: a faint and indistinct glow, as from an inner source of light. Page 148.

nebulously: in a hazy, vague, indistinct or confused manner. Page 15.

nebulous, the: the formless matter supposed to have existed before the creation of the universe, characterized as hazy, vague, lacking definite form or feature. From a Latin word *nebula*, meaning a mist, vapor or cloud. Page 38.

necessity level: the degree to which an individual feels the need or necessity to take a certain course of action. Page 149.

negate: deny the truth, existence or fact (of something). Page 201.

negotiated: moved through or over in a satisfactory manner. Page 548.

neologism: a recently coined word or a recently extended meaning of an existing word. Page 16.

nerve failed you, your: a variation of *lost your nerve*, lost one's confidence, courage or control. *Failed* means having lost one's power or strength, or broken down under power or strength of opposition. *Nerve* refers to one's courage, coolness and firmness of mind in dangerous circumstances. Page 378.

neurology: the scientific study or knowledge of the anatomy, functions and diseases of the nerves and the nervous system. Page 19.

neuron: a cell that transmits nerve impulses and is the basic functional unit of the nervous system; also called *nerve cell.* Page 93.

neuroses: plural of *neurosis*, an emotional state containing conflicts and emotional data inhibiting the abilities or welfare of the individual. Page 10.

neurosurgeon: one who practices surgery on any part of the nervous system, including the brain. Page 8.

Newton: Sir Isaac Newton (1642-1727), English scientist and mathematician whose discoveries and theories about the laws of gravitation and motion laid the foundation for much of the scientific progress since his time. Page 9.

nick of time, in the: just before it is too late; just before something bad happens. The word *nick* is from an obsolete definition meaning the critical moment. Page 329.

Nineveh: the oldest and most populous city (ca. 700 B.C.) of the ancient Assyrian empire (now northern Iraq). It had an elaborate system of canals and aqueducts, wide streets, gardens and palaces and a wall some 7.5 miles (12 kilometers) in circumference surrounding it. Page 190.

Nirvana: the goal of the Hindus. Hindu beliefs are that "Reality is One" (Brahma) and that ultimate salvation, and release from the endless cycle of birth to death, is achieved when one merges or is absorbed into the "one divine reality," with all loss of individual existence. Page 129.

nitrous oxide: a sweet-smelling, sweet-tasting gas used in dentistry and surgery to render the patient unconscious. Page 154.

nomenclature: a set or system of names or terms, as those used in a particular science or art. Page 3.

nostalgic: characterized by *nostalgia*, a mixed feeling of happiness, sadness and longing when recalling a person, place or event from the past or the past in general. From Greek *nostos*, a returning home and *algos*, pain. Page 95.

nowise, in: in no way, manner or degree. Page 364.

nurses: keeps a feeling in the mind or heart for a long time and allows it to grow or deepen. Page 408.

nymphomaniac: affected with *nymphomania*, abnormally excessive and uncontrollable sexual desire in a woman. Page 364.

object of chase: something that is attacked or hunted, such as an animal or bird that is hunted by Man or by another animal for food. Page 40.

oblivion: the state or condition of being forgotten or unknown. Page 43.

obscure: 1. not easily understood. Page 15.

2. not well-known to many people. Page 165.

3. indistinctly or imperfectly felt; not clearly perceived by the senses. Page 246.

obstetrical: pertaining to the care and treatment of women in childbirth and during the period before and after delivery. Page 484.

obtain: to be in force or effect; prevail. Page 526.

obviate: to do away with or prevent by effective measures. Page 29.

occasioned: brought about or caused something. Page 16.

ocularly: relating to the eyes or eyesight. Page 17.

odor: (of good or bad) repute, favor or estimation. Page 36.

offhand: 1. without previous thought or preparation. Page 224.
2. so casual or informal as to appear impolite or uncaring. Page 432.

ogreish: resembling or characteristic of an *ogre,* a man-eating monster in folklore and fairy tales, usually represented as a hideous giant. Page 141.

Old Man of the Sea: a character in the story of Sinbad the Sailor, the Old Man of the Sea (a sea god) forces Sinbad to carry him on his shoulders for days until Sinbad gets the old man so drunk he falls off. The phrase has come to mean an intolerable, heavy burden that is hard or impossible to get rid of. Page 190.

old school tie: a tie of characteristic pattern worn by former students of a particular school, especially an English school. The term is used figuratively to denote the wearer of such a tie and the behavior and attitudes usually associated with those wearing such a tie, especially conservatism and group loyalty. Page 95.

olfactory: of or pertaining to the sense of smell; used in smelling. Page 19.

Olympian: characteristic of *Mount Olympus,* the highest mountain in Greece, believed to be the home of the gods. Page 43.

omnipresent: present in all places at the same time. Page 321.

operate: do something; perform a work or labor. Used in this context with a double meaning (as an example of a statement in an engram) of perform surgery on a person. Page 434.

opium: an addictive drug prepared from the juice of a poppy (a plant with large red, orange or white flowers). Page 482.

opossum playing: pretending to be dead, ill, asleep, unaware, etc. An *opossum* is a small, tree-dwelling American animal that is active at night and habitually pretends death when endangered. Page 474.

Glossary

opportunism: the art, policy or practice of taking advantage of opportunity or circumstances, especially with little regard for principles or ultimate consequences. Page 40.

orangewood stick: a slender, rounded stick with tapered ends of hard, fine-grained wood from the orange tree, used for manicuring the nails. Page 326.

order of, on the: resembling to some extent; like. Page ii.

organic: of or belonging to the body or body parts. Page viii.

organic sensation: the condition of the organism (or organs in the body) during the moment of the engram. Page 14.

organ of thought: the brain. Page 95.

ornamented: furnished with *ornaments,* accessories, articles or details used to beautify the appearance of something to which it is added or of which it is a part, as in "*the most magnificently ornamented civilization.*" Page 8.

orthopedics: the branch of medicine dealing with the treatment of deformities, diseases and injuries of the bones, joints, muscles, etc. Page 124.

ovum: a female reproductive cell. Page 95.

pagan: characterized by the worship of many gods, as in the religions of the ancient Romans and Greeks. Page 36.

pain-drive theory: the psychological practice of inflicting pain, deprivation (the action of removing or withholding something from the enjoyment or possession of someone) or other unpleasant consequences on an individual to make them avoid what is considered by the practitioner undesirable action or behavior. Page 44.

pallid: lacking sparkle or liveliness; dull. Page 15.

palm off: cause (something) to be accepted as genuine, true, etc., by trickery; impose (a thing) fraudulently (on or upon a person). Page 427.

palsy: muscular inability to move part or all of the body, sometimes accompanied by involuntary tremors of the limbs. Page 179.

panacea: a remedy for all ills or difficulties. Page 361.

pandering: doing everything another wants, often to get some advantage for oneself. Page 201.

parable: a simple story illustrating or teaching a truth, moral lesson, etc. Page 200.

paragon: (said of a person or thing) a model of excellence or perfection of a kind. Page 469.

paralytic stroke: a blockage of a blood vessel to the brain causing inadequate oxygen supply, leading to paralysis of parts of the body. Page 490.

paranoid-schizophrenic: a person suffering from schizophrenia and in whom hallucinations, delusions of greatness, magnificence, etc., or delusions of persecution are prominent. *See also* **schizophrenic.** Page 76.

parathyroid: 1. a reference to the hormone secreted by the parathyroid gland. Page 129.
2. the *parathyroid gland*, consisting of four tiny glands that function as one gland. These glands lie in the front of the neck close to the thyroid gland. The parathyroid secretes a substance (hormone) into the blood that helps regulate the amount of calcium and other minerals in the body. These minerals are necessary for a number of important body processes, including bone growth and muscle and nerve function. Page 134.

parcheesi: a board game played by four or less people where the movement of pieces along a track composed of squares is determined by throws of dice. Page 283.

paresis: psychosis caused by widespread destruction of brain tissue occurring in some cases of syphilis (a serious disease that is transmitted sexually). Page 260.

parlor: a room in a house used primarily for receiving and entertaining guests. Page 77.

par, on a: on an equal level with. Page 203.

passes of the hand: in hypnotism, the actions of moving the hand over or along the body of a subject, supposedly resulting in a hypnotic state. Page 79.

Pasteur: Louis Pasteur (1822–1895), French chemist who in the late 1800s formulated *the germ theory of disease*, that disease was spread by germs attacking the body. He was noted for his discovery that the desired production of alcohol in the process of fermentation is indeed due to yeast (a small single-celled organism). He found that wine turns bitter because of germs that enter the wine while it is being made and showed these germs can be killed by applying controlled heat. This became known as *pasteurization* and was also applied to killing the

Glossary

germs in milk. (*Fermentation* is a chemical process that breaks down organic materials, such as when the microscopic organism yeast breaks down sugar into alcohol and carbon dioxide gas.) Page x.

Pasteurella pestis: the name for the bacteria that causes bubonic plague. *See also* **bubonic plague.** Page 39.

pat: so easily and readily produced as to suggest lack of proper thought. Page 455.

paternity: the fact or state of being the father of a child. Page 476.

pathologically: through or by disease. Page 10.

pathology: 1. the science or study of the causes and nature of disease. Page 124.

2. any condition that is a deviation from the normal healthy condition, such as a disease. Page 124.

patter: 1. what someone says; talk or chatter. Page 242.

2. talk, discussion or speech associated with a particular situation, group of persons or profession. Page 508.

paunch: a large and protruding belly. Page 281.

Pavlov: Ivan Petrovich Pavlov (1849-1936), Russian physiologist, noted for his dog experiments. Pavlov presented food to a dog while he sounded a bell. After repeating this procedure several times, the dog (in anticipation) would salivate at the sound of the bell, whether or not food was presented. Pavlov concluded that all acquired habits, even the higher mental activity of Man, depended on conditioned reflexes. A *conditioned reflex* is a response (for example, secretion of saliva in a dog) brought about by a secondary stimulus (for example, the ringing of a bell) repeatedly associated with an original stimulus (for example, the sight of meat). Page 193.

pedantic: things that show unnecessary stress on minor or trivial points of learning, displaying a scholarship lacking in judgment or sense of proportion. Page 3.

penal codes: a body of laws dealing with various crimes or offenses and their legal penalties. Page 538.

Penates: in ancient Roman religious belief, the gods of a household or state. Page 7.

pendulum, Aristotle's: Greek philosopher Aristotle's principle which states that there is no middle ground and that something is either true or false, yes or no, is or is not the same as something else. Page 262.

penicillin: a powerful drug used to treat infections and serious diseases caused by bacteria. Page 181.

penis envy: in psychoanalysis, the supposed hidden, unexpressed longing by a female for a penis, leading to feelings of inferiority. Page 172.

peptic ulcer: a sore formed on the lining of the stomach or adjacent organs due to secretion of excess digestive acid, sometimes causing chronic stomach pain. *Peptic* means pertaining to or associated with digestion. Page 123.

PERCEPTIC: ANY SENSE MESSAGE SUCH AS A SIGHT, SOUND, SMELL, ETC. (From *Dianetics Terms.*) Page 16.

percepts: impressions or mental results of perceiving by the senses; things that are perceived. Page 61.

permanent leads: literally, *leads* are flexible electrical conductors which connect two points in an electrical path and used here to describe mental connections. "*Permanent leads*" refer to the apparent soldered-in nature of engrams which cannot be thrown out by the analyzer except through Dianetics techniques. Page 287.

personal pronouns: pronouns that show by their form whether they refer to the person speaking, such as "I" in *I shall eat;* the person spoken to, such as "you" in *you work hard;* or the person or thing spoken of, such as "he" in *he is walking.* A *pronoun* is used in place of a noun, such as "he" instead of Joe. Page 91.

persuasion: a method of treating something, consisting essentially in rational conversation and re-education. Page 123.

phenobarbital: a bitter crystalline acid used as a sedative, hypnotic and anticonvulsant. An *anticonvulsant* counteracts violent muscular contractions. Page 482.

phlebotomy: the act or practice of opening a vein to let "impure" or "extra" blood out of the body as a therapeutic measure. From Greek *phlebo,* vein, and *tomos,* cutting. Page 133.

phonograph record: a vinyl disc (normally 12 inches in diameter) with grooves (indentations) in it, on which music, voice or other sounds are recorded. A needle is lowered upon the disc which is spinning on a rotating, round table. The needle fits in the grooves of the record and transfers the sound recorded in the grooves to speakers for playback. Page xii.

photosynthesis: the process by which green plants and certain other organisms use the energy of light to convert carbon dioxide and water into food. Page 216.

physics: the science that deals with matter, energy, motion and force, including what these things are, why they behave as they do and the relationship between them. Page i.

piece: a product of creative work, such as a theatrical production. *See also* **villain of the (this) piece.** Page 64.

pilloried: held up to public contempt, ridicule or scorn. Page 68.

pilot: something which leads, guides or conducts, as through unknown places, etc. Page 95.

pine tar: a thick sticky brown to black substance obtained from pine wood, with a distinct odor and used in paints and varnishes. Page 20.

Pittsburgh stogies: long, thin, roughly made and inexpensive cigars from the city of Pittsburgh, in southwest Pennsylvania, USA. Page 471.

pituitrin: a reference to the hormones produced by the *pituitary gland,* a small gland about the size of a pea lying under the brain near the center of the skull. The pituitary gland secretes hormones that control or influence a wide range of bodily functions, including the activities of certain other glands. Page 129.

placate: make someone less angry or hostile, usually by doing or saying things to please him or her. Page 411.

plane: a level of existence, consciousness or development. Page iv.

plankton: a collection of small microscopic organisms, including algae, that float or drift in great numbers in fresh or salt water at or near the surface and serve as food for fish and other larger organisms. Page 39.

platitudes: dull, unoriginal or empty statements on a moral theme, especially those expressed as if they were important or helpful. Page 367.

Plato: (427–347 B.C.) Greek philosopher noted for his works on law, mathematics, philosophy and natural science. Plato believed that artists and poets do not create because they possess some special knowledge but rather they are seized by irrational inspiration, a sort of "divine madness." Page x.

polarity: that quality or condition in a physical body or system that manifests opposite or contrasting properties, as in a magnet where one end is positive and the other negative. Hence, opposite or different polarity would be the condition of having opposite properties or powers from something else. Page 269.

polysyllables: words consisting of several (poly), especially four or more *syllables,* a word or part of a word pronounced with a single sounding of the voice. For example: simplicity (sim plic i ty). "*Frowning polysyllables*" refers to the large words sometimes employed by those who act very learned and serious. Page 2.

ponderous: of grave importance, seriousness, weightiness (used figuratively) and unpleasantly dull. Page 29.

portal: a doorway or gateway that is large or elaborate in construction; the entrance, with the immediately surrounding parts of a building, church, etc. Hence poetically, a "door" or "gate"; a means of entrance. Page viii.

portends: forecasts, predicts. Page 48.

positive suggestion(s): in hypnosis, a suggestion or command which is given to a hypnotized subject who then obeys it unknowingly. Also, any phrase or command in the mind acting like one given to a hypnotized person. Page 74.

post, left at the: left way behind. *Post* refers to the pole on a racetrack marking the point where a race starts. Page 117.

postnatally: during the time period after birth; especially of the period immediately after birth. Page 192.

postulates: things that are suggested or assumed to be true as a basis for reasoning. Page 3.

poultices: hot, soft, moist masses, as of flour, herbs, mustard, etc., sometimes spread on cloths, applied to sore or inflamed parts of the body. Page 452.

preamble: an introductory statement, fact, event, etc.; a preliminary. Page 345.

precedent: a previous instance or case which is or may be taken as an example or rule for subsequent cases, or by which some similar act or circumstance may be supported or justified. Page 173.

precepts: rules, instructions or principles that guide somebody's actions, especially ones that guide moral behavior. Page 305.

PRECLEAR: ANY PERSON WHO HAS BEEN ENTERED INTO DIANETIC THERAPY. (From *Dianetics Terms.*) Page 138.

predisposition: a condition which renders its possessor inclined or liable to disease, illness, etc. Page 87.

prefrontal lobes: lobes situated at the front or forepart of the brain. A *lobe* is a roundish projection or subdivision of an organ of the body. Page 59.

prefrontal lobotomy: a psychiatric operation carried out by boring holes into the skull, entering the brain and severing the nerve pathways in the two frontal lobes, resulting in the patient becoming an emotional vegetable. Page 132.

PRERELEASE: ANY PATIENT WHO IS ENTERED INTO THERAPY TO ACCOMPLISH A RELEASE FROM HIS CHIEF DIFFICULTIES, PSYCHOSOMATIC OR ABERRATIONAL. (From *Dianetics Terms.*) Page 236.

prescience: knowledge of things before they exist or happen. Page 114.

press agentry: promotion or publicity. A *press agent* is a person employed to promote the interests of an individual, organization, etc., by obtaining favorable publicity through news stories, mentions in columns, events and the like. Page 129.

prestige: standing or estimation in the eyes of others; influence; reputation. Page 457.

presumable: capable of being taken for granted; entitled to belief without examination or direct evidence. Hence, something that is assumed to be correct or workable without close inspection. Page x.

pre-term: before the end of the normal period of pregnancy. Page 365.

pretty: inventive, cleverly made or originated. Page 300.

prevarication: the act of speaking falsely or misleadingly; deliberately misstating or creating an incorrect impression; lying. Page 256.

priesthood: a group of people who claim or obtain special and exclusive knowledge, understanding or power in a specific field or area. Page 186.

prize: (in describing undesirable qualities) outstanding of its kind; unrivaled. Page 457.

processed: put through the steps of an official procedure for purposes of registration or examination, prior to the beginning or end of a period of military service. Page 510.

profusion: a great quantity or amount. Page viii.

progeny: children, descendants or offspring considered as a group or collectively. Page 49.

prompts: reminds someone about something that they have forgotten; provides or supplies information to help someone remember something. Page 385.

propitiation: a low emotion below anger and close to apathy. *Propitiation* is the act of trying to please or satisfy someone in a way calculated to win their favor in order to defend or protect oneself against their disapproval, attack, etc. Page 409.

proposition: something proposed or offered for consideration, acceptance or adoption. Page 67.

propriety, soul of: somebody who is a perfect example of socially correct and appropriate behavior. *Soul* here means a person who perfectly represents some quality or attribute. Page 281.

protoplasm: the colorless, jelly-like liquid that is present in the cells of all living plants, animals and humans and consists of the living matter of plant and animal cells. Page 80.

province: the range of one's proper duties and functions; sphere or field of activity or authority. Page 483.

provisos: conditions, qualifications or limitations. Page 516.

prowess: exceptional or superior skill, strength, bravery, etc. Page 315.

pseudo-: a word combined with other words to mean "false" or "pretended." Also, apparently similar to (a specified thing) as in *pseudo-nurse, pseudo-mother, pseudo-father,* etc. Page 156.

psyche: the mind. Page 69.

psychic: of or pertaining to the human mind; mental. Page 14.

psychometry: testing of individuals to find out their intelligence, aptitude, various personality traits, etc. Page 416.

psychoses: conflicts of commands which seriously reduce the individual's ability to solve his problems in his environment to a point where he cannot adjust himself to some vital phase of his environmental needs. Page xii.

PSYCHOSOMATIC: ANY PHYSICAL DISORDER OR ILL GENERATED BY THE BODY ITSELF. (From *Dianetics Terms.*) Page i.

pucker: to draw or gather a part of the face into wrinkles or irregular folds, as in *worry puckered his brow.* Page 261.

pull chain: a chain which operates a mechanism when pulled, such as to turn a light on or off. Page 471.

pull the cord: the action of pulling on a *light cord,* a cord which hangs from a ceiling or lamp stand and operates an electric light. Page 99.

punishment complex: in psychoanalysis, a *complex* is a set of impulses, ideas and emotions that compel habitual patterns of behavior, in this case causing the action of punishment. Page 107.

Glossary

punk: an offensive term for a young man regarded as worthless, lazy or arrogant. Page 439.
punk water: a reference to *spunk water*, rainwater that collects in hollow tree stumps, popularly thought to be a remedy, especially for warts. Page 452.
puns: words used in such a way as to suggest two or more meanings or different associations, or two or more words of the same or nearly the same sound with different meanings. Page 265.
puristic: characterized by *purism*, rigid adherence to or insistence upon purity or correctness, especially in language or style. Page 3.
pygmy: a small person; one small in size, capacity or power. Page 189.
pyramiding: increasing at a steady and progressive rate. Page 543.
pyrites: a shiny compound of iron and sulfur, found in many places and often mistaken for gold and sometimes called "fool's gold." The name *pyrite* comes from the Greek word for fire. Page 416.
Q quantity: a factor or agency that is not named or is of an unknown identity. Page 484.
qualm: a feeling of uneasiness about a point of conscience or the correctness of an action. Page 467.
quarters: 1. living spaces. Page 8.
2. a particular but unspecified person, group of people or area. Page 315.
quibbles: argues or objects over small or minor matters. Page 467.
quick-change artist: a performer or other person who is skilled at changing quickly from one costume or character to the next. Page 110.
quinine: a bitter-tasting drug used to relieve pain and fevers and once the only drug treatment available for malaria. Page 428.
quivering: having a light, rapid motion; vibrating, as something alive might do. Page 43.
racial: concerning all Mankind; the human race. Page 37.
rack(s): a framework of bars, wires or pegs on which articles are arranged or deposited. Used figuratively. Page 61.
racks: causes to suffer trouble, stress, anxiety, etc. Page 417.
radar sight: the ability of an individual to "see" things in remote locations, as radars do. A *radar* is an electronic device designed

to detect or identify remote objects by sending out radio waves and measuring the time for the radio wave to return to the sending device. Page 427.

railroad tie: any of the parallel crossbeams to which the rails of a train track are fastened. Page 35.

rainbow chasing: following after something that is pointless; from the old story that a pot of gold can be dug up by anyone reaching the end of a rainbow, where it touches the earth. Page 427.

raise havoc: cause widespread damage, destruction or disruptive chaos. Page 309.

rake over (something): to examine something that happened in the past in great detail. Page 192.

ranges: moves or passes, as if by traveling along or through an area. Page 390.

rapport: a harmonious relationship in which the people concerned understand each other and communicate well. Page 414.

REACTIVE MIND: THE CELLULAR-LEVEL MIND WHICH IS NOT "UNCONSCIOUS" BUT IS ALWAYS CONSCIOUS—THE HIDDEN MIND, HITHERTO UNKNOWN. (From *Dianetics Terms.*) Page v.

read (largely) into: introduce an additional idea or element or significance into something, frequently implying that the insertion is unwarranted or erroneous. Page 40.

realized: presented or brought before the mind with vividness and clarity. Page 14.

realm: any sphere or region. Page 1.

recalcitrant: resisting control; defying authority or guidance. Page 525.

recesses: concealed or inner areas or parts of something. Page 187.

recession: a condition of an incident being out of sight after several recountings, as in "*an engram talked into* recession." Page 290.

recession: 1. a diminishing or declining in terms of prosperity, artistic and technical skills and learning (as from the virtual disappearance of the knowledge of the previous Greek and Roman civilizations during the Dark Ages). Page 37.

2. the action of falling back, declining, in character, value or amount, as in "*the patient experienced a recession of all somatics.*" Page 171.

Glossary

record: a vinyl disc (normally 12 inches in diameter) with grooves (indentations) in it, on which music, voice or other sounds are recorded. A needle is lowered upon the disc which is spinning on a rotating, round table. The needle fits in the grooves of the record and transfers the sound recorded in the grooves to speakers for playback. Page xii.

recount: tell someone about something; give a description of an event or experience. Page 169.

recoup: regain or recover. Page 152.

recourse to: the act or instance of turning to something for aid, use or help. Page 10.

recriminative: bringing counter-accusations against a person. Page 362.

recruited: increased in natural population as the offspring grow and become members. Page 94.

red herring: something that draws attention away from the central issue; literally, a smoked herring (a small food fish of the North Atlantic) having a reddish color. The phrase derives from the use of such fish to distract hunting dogs from the trail. Page 523.

REDUCE: TO RENDER AN ENGRAM FREE FROM SOMATIC OR EMOTION BY RECOUNTINGS. (From *Dianetics Terms.*) Page 256.

redwood: a giant tree, native to California and Oregon, remains of which existed between 180 million and 135 million years ago. Redwoods are among the oldest and largest of living things, some reaching over 2,000 years of age and with heights of 350 feet (106.68 meters) and trunk diameters of as much as 30 feet (9.14 meters). Page 39.

refined: 1. free from crudeness or coarseness; cultivated; elegant. Page 80.

2. made finer, purer and more precise. Page 536.

regressive: 1. of or pertaining to returning in one's mind to an earlier period or stage of life as a result of mental illness. Page xii.

2. moving back into a worse condition; declining. Page 179.

re-improved: brought into a more desirable, valuable or excellent condition again. Page 546.

RELEASE: ANY PERSON WHO HAS BEEN ADVANCED TO A STATE APPROXIMATING 1950 NORMAL BY DIANETIC THERAPY, WHETHER ADVANCED FROM A PSYCHOTIC OR NEUROTIC

CONDITION. THE ACT OF RELEASING BY THERAPY. (From *Dianetics Terms*.) Page i.

remonstrated: stated or pleaded in protest, objection or disapproval. Page 498.

remorseless: marked by a continuation without lessening in strength or intensity; characteristic of something that never stops or that is impossible to stop. Page 541.

Renaissance: the period in European history from the early 1300s to the 1600s marked by a revival of art, literature and learning. During this period, many scholars and artists rejected the culture of the Dark Ages and recaptured the spirit of the Greeks and Romans in their own artistic works. *Renaissance* is from a Latin word for "reborn." Page 37.

render: cause to be or become; make. Page v.

repression(s): the actions, processes or results of suppressing into the unconscious or keeping out of the conscious mind unacceptable memories or desires. Page 10.

resilient: able to recover quickly, from illness, injury, mental pain, etc. Page 196.

resolute: motivated by or displaying determination and purposefulness. Page 469.

resounding: expressed in a rich, full or impressive manner. Page 2.

restimulation: a condition in which an approximation of the reactive mind's content or some part thereof is perceived in the environment of the organism. Page 87.

resultant: something occurring as a result or following as a consequence. Page 184.

resumption: the act or an instance of picking something back up again or continuing with something, as after a temporary stop; to resume. Page 525.

retribution: punishment caused or inflicted for evil done. Page 418.

retroactive: extending in scope or effect to matters which have occurred in the past. Page 341.

return to the womb: a reference to the psychiatric theory that people have a hidden desire to return to the "safety" and "comfort" of the womb. Page 176.

reverie: a light state of "concentration" not to be confused with hypnosis; in reverie the person is fully aware of what is taking place in the present. Page viii.

reviled: criticized in an abusive or angrily insulting manner. Page 193.

rheostat: a device that operates in an electric circuit to gradually increase or decrease the flow of current, as with lights that can be varied in brightness. Page 307.

rheumatic fever: a serious disease characterized by fever, swelling and pain in the joints, and a sore throat, and frequently resulting in permanent damage to the valves of the heart. Page 440.

riding habit: an outfit typically worn by a horseback rider, including jacket, special pants that are wide at the hips and narrow around the calves, and a hat with a round crown and a small visor. Page 475.

Rights of Man: a reference to any document or legislation (law) that might be drawn up to serve as a guarantee of basic rights of individuals, the principles of human liberty, etc. Page 471.

Rohmer, Sax: pen name of British writer Arthur Sarsfield Ward (1883?–1959), creator of the mysterious Dr. Fu Manchu. Rohmer portrayed the famed criminal genius in a series of novels published between 1913 and 1959. Dr. Fu's plots often failed as he employed female spies who fell in love with the wrong man. Page 141.

roll: figuratively, an indication to start something moving or into action. *Roll* means to begin, commence, to put into operation. The word is used in the movie industry as an order from a director or an assistant director to start the camera and sound equipment into action. Page 372.

roller-coaster: with reference to a situation or condition characterized by sudden, extreme and often repeated changes, or persistent or violent ups and downs, as one fluctuating between conflict and harmony or great happiness and despair. The term comes from an amusement park, where a roller coaster is a train with open cars that moves along a high, sharply winding track built with steep inclines that produce sudden, speedy plunges for thrill-seeking passengers. Page 102.

Ross, Ronald: (1857–1932) British physician noted for establishing the connection between mosquitoes and malaria. Page 208.

Rousseau, Jean Jacques: (1712–1778) French writer and influential political philosopher whose best-known theory was the "natural man," a belief that Man was essentially good and equal in his natural state but had been corrupted by civilization.

He proposed "spiritual refreshment" for Man through a return to nature. Page 46.

running down: to search out and locate the moment of reception of a somatic. Page 301.

running out: exhausting the negative influence of something; erasing. Page 494.

running sore(s): a painful open skin infection (a sore) that is discharging pus (a yellowish fluid consisting of the liquid part of blood plus dead cells, bacteria, etc.). Page 135.

run off: same as *run out*, meaning to exhaust the negative influence of something; to erase. Page 523.

sack race: a race in which contestants have their legs restricted in a sack and move by jumping. Page 148.

sadism: a type of behavior in which pleasure is obtained from hurting others and making them suffer physically or mentally. Page 140.

sag: lower in tone; also, sink down or decline, as from a higher to a lower emotional state. Page 151.

sakes, keeps as: keeps things for the memories they call to mind. From the term *keepsakes.* A *keepsake* is a small item kept in memory of the person who gave it or originally owned it. Page 471.

salvoed: fired on, with several guns all at once. Used figuratively. Page 234.

sanitaria: plural of *sanitarium*, an institution for the treatment and recuperation of the mentally ill or those with chronic illnesses. Page 7.

sarcastic: characterized by words that mean the opposite of what they seem to say and make fun of or insult something or someone. Page 386.

scalding: a getting burned or injured by hot liquid or steam. Page 385.

scaly: covered or partially covered with *scales*, thin flakes of shedding skin. Page 336.

scant: barely sufficient or adequate. Page 21.

scent: perceive by the mind. Page 322.

schizophrenic: a person with two (or more) apparent personalities. *Schizophrenia* means "scissors" or "two," plus "head." Literally, *splitting of the mind*, hence, *split personality*. Page 70.

scholarly: of or having to do with *scholars*, those who have a great deal of knowledge in a particular branch of learning, especially in the field of literature or philosophy; those who have engaged in advanced study and acquired detailed knowledge in some special field and who engage in the analysis and interpretation of such knowledge. Page 535.

Scholastic: a person involved in *Scholasticism*, a system of Christian thought extending from the beginning of the ninth century to the latter part of the fifteenth century (end of the Middle Ages). Scholasticism was an effort to coordinate and bring into alignment the religious beliefs of Christian faith with philosophic reason and thus to give a rational content to and deeper understanding of that faith. In so doing, Scholastics discussed and wrote about such matters as Man's relationship to God, evil, sin, etc. Page 25.

Schopenhauer: Arthur Schopenhauer (1788-1860), German philosopher known for his philosophy of pessimism who believed that the will to live is the fundamental reality and that this will, being a constant striving, cannot be satisfied and only causes suffering. Page 144.

science: knowledge; comprehension or understanding of facts or principles, classified and made available in work, life or the search for truth. A science is a connected body of demonstrated truths or observed facts systematically organized and bound together under general laws. It includes trustworthy methods for the discovery of new truth within its domain and denotes the application of scientific methods in fields of study previously considered open only to theories based on subjective, historical or undemonstrable, abstract criteria. The word *science* is used in this sense–the most fundamental meaning and tradition of the word–and not in the sense of the *physical* or *material* sciences. Page i.

science of (mind): in such uses as *science of art, science of mind*, the application of scientific methods in fields of study formerly considered open only to theories based on opinion or abstract data which cannot be proven or demonstrated. Page i.

scores: a great many. From the word *score*, meaning twenty. Page 169.

script: a series of (changing) events, actions, dialogues, likened to the written text of a play, film, etc. Page 400.

seared: burned, charred or scorched (as from electric shock). Page 230.

secret: a reason or explanation not immediately or generally apparent; answer. The parathyroid secretes a hormone which in turn controls the concentration of calcium in the blood. Hence, the parathyroid contains the answer as to how the concentration of calcium in the blood is maintained. Page 134.

secret service: a branch or department of a government, such as the Secret Service in the United States, whose duty it is to protect the president or head of state. Page 76.

sedately: in a quiet and rather dignified manner. Page 405.

semantic: of, pertaining to or arising from the different meanings of words or other symbols; of or relating to meaning in language. Page 63.

seminal: of or pertaining to *semen*, the impregnating fluid of men and male animals. Page 140.

sensory strip: a long narrow area of the brain, which is believed to monitor the senses of the body such as sight, smell, touch and hearing. *Sensory* means connected with the reception and transmission of sense impressions. (See text for further description.) *See also* **"two little men…hanging by their heels."** Page 389.

Sententious, Dr.: a made-up name. *Sententious* means inclined to state wise sayings and to often make judgments about moral questions. Page 452.

sentient: conscious or capable of perceptions; consciously perceiving. Page 23.

sentry: one who or something which keeps guard or watches over something, like a military *sentry*, a soldier stationed to keep watch over something or to control access to a place. Page 235.

seven, sometimes one gets a: a reference to a game of chance called *craps*, a game in which two dice are thrown and in which a first throw of 7 (or 11) wins, a first throw of 2, 3 or 12 loses, and a first throw of 4, 5, 6, 8, 9 or 10 can be won only by throwing the same number again before throwing a 7. If he throws a 7 he is unsuccessful (craps out). Page 132.

sextant: a tool used by navigators to determine the position of the stars. From the Latin *sextant*, sixth part, so called because the instrument's arc is a sixth of a circle. Page 454.

shadow-stuff: *stuff* is something regarded as an unspecified substance or material. *Shadow-stuff* is that which has the nature of a *shadow*, an unreal appearance or image. Page 321.

Glossary

Shakespeare: William Shakespeare (1564-1616), English dramatist and poet, considered the greatest playwright of all time. Several passages of his plays include reference to the fact that the heart controls the function of blood circulation. Page 173.

shaman: a priest or priestess who is said to relay messages between the natural and supernatural worlds and to use magic to cure ailments, predict the future and to contact and control spiritual forces. One technique for the cure of the sick involved singing special songs and blowing tobacco smoke over the person, as tobacco was believed to have magical powers. Page 7.

sheer: the most complete and utter (used to emphasize the unlimited extent of something). Page 258.

shifty: having, displaying or suggestive of deceitful character; tricky. Page 84.

shocky: affected with shock (a state of reduced mental awareness and physical functioning due to the effects of an impact, injury, drug, etc.). Page 396.

shooting dice: in a game of chance called craps, throwing a pair of dice. *See also* **seven, sometimes one gets a.** Page 132.

short shrift: little attention or consideration in dealing with a matter. Page 114.

shoulder to the wheel, put a: set to work vigorously; strive energetically toward achieving an objective. Page 187.

side, on the (condition specified): rather more than less; tending toward (the quality or condition specified). For example, saying someone is *"on the whiny side"* means that they tend to spend a lot of their time whining or complaining. Page 281.

signal: remarkable; notable. Page 23.

Simple Simon: a reference to the children's story which tells of a young boy whose mother instructs him to "Watch out when you go outside to play. I've got six pies cooling on the doorstep and you be careful how you step on those pies." Taking his mother's directions literally, the boy goes out onto the porch and steps, very carefully, right in the middle of each pie. Page 155.

sinusitis: an inflammation of a sinus or the sinuses (any of the hollow cavities in the skull connecting with the nasal cavities). Page 69.

Sioux: a group of Native American peoples inhabiting the northern plains of North America, now mainly living in the north central part of the United States. Page 339.

situation: place or location. Page 177.

skills: acquires the ability, as by knowledge, practice, etc., to do something; trains. Page 65.

sky is no limit, the: a variation and intensification of the phrase, *the sky's the limit*, meaning there is no limit to what somebody can achieve, do, earn, etc. Page 224.

sleigh: a child's sled, a small vehicle consisting of a platform mounted on runners, for coasting down snow-covered hills. Page 261.

slice: a figurative use of *slice*, as in a fragment, sliver or piece, meaning an aspect or form of. Page 204.

slight: treat as of small importance or with indifference; pay little or no attention to; to disregard. Page 467.

slip(s) of the tongue: a mistake in speaking, unintentionally made. Page 71.

slog: work hard for long hours. Page 257.

slogging: working steadily and carefully for long hours. Page 238.

slow freight: something that moves slowly. *Freight*, short for *freight train*, refers to a train that transports cargo, usually a much slower train than those carrying passengers. Page 294.

slumber: be in a state of inactivity. Page 505.

slurs: insulting remarks. Page 139.

smooths: changes the facial expression to one that is pleasant, calm or peaceful, as in "*she smooths her face.*" Page 366.

snake pit: among primitive peoples, a large pit containing poisonous snakes into which victims are thrown for execution or as a test of endurance. Used figuratively to mean an intensely chaotic or disagreeable place or situation. Page 459.

snarl up: complicate or confuse, mess up. Page 237.

so and so: in a certain but unspecified manner or way, as in "*what it was in the engram which affected him so and so.*" Page 527.

soapbox: describing one who makes informal, often impassioned speeches to street audiences from any improvised platform (such as a soapbox). Page 440.

society: companionship or association with one's fellows; friendly or intimate connection. Page 82.

Socrates: (ca. 470–399 B.C.) Greek philosopher, said to believe in a "demon" (meaning here, an inner voice). The demon supposedly forbade Socrates to do things, but never gave any positive encouragement, only predictions of good or bad luck, or cautions when he was about to make an incorrect decision. Page 69.

sodium pentothal: a substance used as a general anesthetic and in psychotherapy as a hypnotic. Page 166.

sodomy: anal or oral intercourse with a member of the same or opposite sex. Page 356.

soldered: fastened with *solder,* any of various metals that melt at low temperatures and which when heated will flow into a joint between metal parts to unite them. *Soldering* is used in electronics to firmly unite two parts so that electricity will flow between them. Hence, joined, fastened or cemented (to something). Page 105.

solemnity: marked by serious or dignified feeling, character or appearance. Page 530.

solicitous: anxious or concerned. Page 214.

SOMATIC: DIANETIC NEOLOGISM FOR PAIN, ANY BODY CONDITION EXPERIENCED WHEN CONTACTING AN ENGRAM; THE PAIN OF A PSYCHOSOMATIC ILLNESS. (From *Dianetics Terms.*) Page 21.

somatic strip: in Dianetics, a mechanism of the mind that locates moments of time for the individual. It is under the orders of the auditor and under such orders can relocate incidents. In the field of medicine, it is what is known as a motor strip and sensory strip, two strips of the brain that are thought to control motor function (physical movement) and sensory function. Since Dianetics does not depend on structural discoveries or conclusions and since it is not firmly established that these strips in the brain perform such functions, the term *somatic strip* is used in Dianetics to describe the *function* of what the medical field calls motor and sensory strips. *See also* **"two little men...hanging by their heels."** Page 371.

SONIC: RECALL BY HEARING A PAST SOUND WITH THE "MIND'S EAR." (From *Dianetics Terms.*) Page 15.

sonorous: of sounds or voice having a full, rich, loud and deep sounding character. Page 365.

sooth: truth, reality or fact. Page 43.

sorry job: a difficult, dismal or troublesome affair. Page 387.

soul (of): a person who perfectly represents some quality or attribute such as truthfulness. Page 257.

spanned: extended or reached across from one point to another. Page 548.

Spartans: the citizens of Sparta, one of the cities of ancient Greece, who in wanting to build a war-like people, killed children considered too weak to become warriors, and sent boys at age seven to military camps where they learned to endure harsh conditions and severe discipline. Page 200.

specious: seeming to be good, sound, correct, logical, etc., without really being so. Page 40.

spectrum: the entire range or extent of something, arranged by degree, with opposite values at its limits. Page 30.

Spencer, Herbert: (1820-1903) English philosopher known for his application of the scientific doctrines of evolution to philosophy and ethics. Spencer claimed that knowledge was of two kinds: (1) knowledge gained by the individual, and (2) knowledge gained by the race. He also believed that there is a basic and final reality beyond our knowledge, which he called the "Unknowable." Page 9.

spin-bin: a colloquial term for a mental institution; a lunatic asylum. Page 451.

sport, good: a sociable, pleasant person who agrees without complaint to do what is asked by a companion. Page 485.

sprayed off: scattered broadly as with a spraying action. Page 120.

spring: clear, as if with the rapid motion of a spring uncoiling. Page 146.

squalling: crying or screaming loudly and harshly. Page 532.

square: cause to correspond to or harmonize with. Page 225.

square meals: nourishing or filling meals. Page 198.

squirm: feel or display discomfort or distress. Page 459.

stalemated: put into a situation where progress is impossible. The term comes from the game of chess describing the situation where one player is unable to make any move without his most important piece, the king, being in a position to be captured. When this happens the game is ended in a tie. Page 347.

Stalingrad: the former name for Volgograd, an industrial and port city in southwestern Russia on the Volga River. Page 543.

stammerer: one who speaks with difficulty, repeating sounds or words and often stopping, before saying things correctly. Page 119.

Glossary

standard memory bank: THE STORAGE PLACE IN THE MIND WHERE ALL CONSCIOUSLY PERCEIVED DATA (SIGHT, SOUND, HEARING, SMELL, ORGANIC SENSATION, KINESTHESIA, TACTILE AS WELL AS PAST MENTAL COMPUTATIONS) ARE RECORDED AND RETAINED AND FROM WHICH THEY ARE RELAYED TO THE ANALYTICAL MIND. INCLUDES ALL DATA OF A CONSCIOUS NATURE FROM CONCEPTION TO "NOW." (From *Dianetics Terms.*) Page viii.

station: the position someone holds in society or in an organization, etc., in terms of rank; social standing. Page 327.

staved in: crushed in; broken inward. Page 176.

stayed the cold sharp hand of death: stopped, halted or checked the process of someone dying. Page 469.

stiff: difficult, requiring persistence. Page 43.

stigma: a mark of disgrace, something that detracts from the character or reputation of a person, group, etc. Page 36.

stigmatized: characterized or marked as disgraceful or very bad. Page 37.

stimuli: plural of *stimulus*, any action or agent that causes or changes an activity in an organism, organ or part, as something that starts a nerve impulse, activates a muscle, etc. Page 15.

stock: livestock; the horses, cattle, sheep and other useful animals kept or raised on a farm or ranch. Page 151.

Stoics: members of an ancient Greek (300 B.C.) school of philosophy or their followers who acted unaffected by joy, grief, pleasure or pain. The school believed in the calm acceptance of all occurrences as the unavoidable result of unalterable destiny. From the Greek *stoa* (a porch), the place where this philosophy was taught. Page 42.

stream of consciousness: the continuous, uninterrupted flow of thoughts and feelings through the mind. Page 117.

strewn: have something scattered over an area. Page 374.

strikes, 2.9: a reference to a strike in baseball–a player trying to hit the ball and missing. When a player does so three times he loses his turn and must leave the field of play. Because in baseball a batter can only have 1, 2 or 3 strikes against him, *2.9 strikes* is used figuratively to refer to someone or something that has little chance of success. Page 193.

struck: encountered or hit; come upon. Page 284.

strummed: a figurative reference to poetry accompanied by a stringed musical instrument, such as a guitar, harp, etc., which is strummed (played by brushing the strings with the fingers). Page 413.

strychnine: a bitter, poisonous drug obtained from the seeds of certain trees and plants found in such places as India, China and northern Australia. Page 485.

stupor: a state of grogginess or apparent sleep. Page 439.

sub-vocal: characterized by the occurrence of spoken words with barely audible sound. Page 402.

suffrage: the right to vote, especially in a political election. Page 245.

sulfa: a reference to *sulfa drugs*, any of a group of drugs once used to treat a range of bacterial infections. Page 181.

summated: added together, summed up. Page 21.

summation signs: symbols used in higher mathematics to show the total amount of things added together. Page 3.

summations of calculus: *calculus* is a branch of mathematics used for determining such quantities as the area of an irregularly shaped object (as opposed to a square or circle). In making such calculations, many figures are added together (summation). Page 84.

super-: above or beyond, more or higher than, above the range, capacity, scope, etc. Page 236.

superabundance: more than a sufficient amount; excessive. Page 113.

super-moral: overly concerned with judging the goodness or badness of human action and character. Page 236.

SUPPRESSOR: THE EXTERIOR FORCES WHICH REDUCE THE CHANCES OF THE SURVIVAL OF ANY FORM. (From *Dianetics Terms.*) Page 31.

supranational: outside or beyond the authority of one national government. Page 543.

susceptible of: capable of submitting successfully to an action, process or operation. Page 99.

sustained: experienced or suffered (injury, loss, etc.). Page 230.

swab(s): a piece of soft material used by a doctor, nurse, etc., for cleaning out an opening in the body (such as a nose). Page 171.

swami: an honorary title given to a Hindu religious teacher. Page 128.

switch: a slender flexible rod, stick or twig, especially one used for whipping or disciplining. Page 349.

syllogism: a type of argument consisting of three statements such that the first two imply the conclusion. For example, "All trees have roots. An oak is a tree. Therefore an oak tree has roots," or "Only trees have roots. A bird is not a tree. Therefore a bird does not have roots." Page 449.

sylvan: characteristic of, associated with or belonging to a woods or forest; typical of the natural and pleasing simplicity of the countryside. Page 46.

SYMBIOTE: ANY ENTITY OF LIFE OR ENERGY WHICH ASSISTS AN INDIVIDUAL OR MAN IN HIS SURVIVAL. (From *Dianetics Terms.*) Page iii.

symbolic logic: the use of the concepts and techniques of mathematics to solve situations in logic. *Symbolic logic* uses those parts of logic that can be modeled mathematically and manipulates these in attempting to solve problems of logic. One is manipulating meanings instead of numbers. Page 84.

symbologists: a reference to psychiatrists who believe that dreams symbolically represent one's waking experience and "repressed desires." Page 278.

synopsis: a brief or condensed statement giving a general view of something. Page i.

syphilis: an infectious disease, usually sexually transmitted, that progresses in three stages. In its final stage the disease may attack the brain, spinal cord and other parts of the body, causing blindness, deafness, mental illness, heart failure, paralysis and bone deformities. Page 509.

tab: a small projection from a card, paper or folder used as an aid in filing. Used figuratively. Page 474.

tabloid: of or pertaining to a *tabloid*, a newspaper, usually half the ordinary size, with many pictures and short, often sensational, news stories. Page 411.

tacit: not expressed or declared openly, but implied or understood. Page 425.

tactile: the sense of touch. Page viii.

tagged: given a nickname or assigned a verbal label (such as Junior, in Sam Smith, Junior). Page 279.

talisman: an object marked with magic signs and believed to give its bearer supernatural powers or protection. Page 471.

talking-to: a scolding given to somebody, especially by somebody in authority. Page 399.

tangling (with): becoming involved with or attempting to deal with something difficult, confusing, problematic or the like. Page 483.

tapped: penetrated, opened up, reached into, etc., for the purpose of using something or drawing something off; began to use. Page 162.

taunt: state unkind or insulting things to someone, especially about their weaknesses or failures. Page 418.

technicolor: having bright, intense colors. This term comes from the commercial film process called *Technicolor*, used in making color motion pictures. Page 424.

telepathy: communication directly from one person's mind to another's without speech, writing or other signs or symbols. Page 114.

temporize: act to suit the time or occasion; adapt to a situation; bow to practical necessities. Page 198.

tenacity: the quality or property of being tenacious (persistently continuing, keeping a firm hold on); toughness. Page 54.

tended: cared for or looked after. Page 365.

tenderfoot: a raw, inexperienced person such as a newcomer to the ranching and mining regions of the western United States, unused to hardships. Page 416.

tendinitis: inflammation of a tendon, tough tissue that connects muscle and bone. Page 246.

tension: mental or emotional strain; intense, suppressed suspense, anxiety, or excitement. Page 361.

tentative: of the nature of or made or done as a trial, experiment; not final. Page 213.

termagant: an overbearing, quarrelsome, scolding, nagging woman. Page 365.

Terra Incognita: an unknown or unexplored region. Latin "unknown land." Page 1.

testosterone: a hormone that develops and maintains masculine characteristics in the body. Page 129.

thalamus: a relay center in the brain for sensory information. Page 19.

therapy: the administration and application of Dianetics techniques and procedures to resolve problems concerning human behavior and psychosomatic illness. Page iv.

θ (theta): the symbol for the eighth letter of the Greek alphabet. Page 147.

third-degree: involving intensive questioning or rough treatment by police, which inflicts mental or physical suffering, in order to obtain information or a confession. Page 510.

Thirteen Rituals for Heavenly Bliss and Nirvana: a made-up name for a book. Page 238.

three thousand cycle note: a high-pitched sound. *Cycle* refers to a vibration. The more vibrations a sound wave has, the higher the pitch. Page 486.

thunderous: of or related to powerful and persuasive language using long words to impress others. Page 2.

thwart: oppose; prevent from accomplishing a purpose. Page 85.

thyroid: **1.** a reference to the hormones secreted by the thyroid gland. Page 129.

2. the *thyroid gland*, which regulates body growth and metabolism (how fast cells convert oxygen and nutrients into energy and heat for the body's use). The thyroid gland is located in the front of the neck. Page 330.

tidings: news or information. Page 504.

TIME TRACK: THE TIMESPAN OF THE INDIVIDUAL FROM CONCEPTION TO PRESENT TIME ON WHICH LIES THE SEQUENCE OF EVENTS OF HIS LIFE. (From *Dianetics Terms.*) Page viii.

tomes: books, especially very heavy, large books. Page 9.

tom-tom: any of various drums, as of Indian or African tribes, usually beaten with the hands and sometimes used by a medicine man or tribal societies to drive demons or evil spirits out of someone's body. Page 224.

tonnage: a large amount or weight. A *ton* is equivalent to 2,000 pounds. The suffix *-age* means "collection of." Page 410.

tonsillectomy: an operation for the removal of the tonsils (small round pieces of flesh at the sides of the throat near the back of the tongue). Page 500.

tooth and claw: marked by fierce or savage struggle, such as in a jungle. *Tooth and claw* is a variation of *tooth and nail*, often used in the phrase *to fight with tooth and nail*, with the use of one's teeth and nails as weapons. Page 39.

topectomy: an operation in which parts of the brain are removed. Page 259.

Torquemada: Tomás de Torquemada (1420-1498), Catholic monk and chief official of the Spanish Inquisition for fifteen years during which time 2,000 people were executed for beliefs different from those of the Church. His name has become synonymous with cruelty. Page 314.

tract: a system of organs or body parts that work together to provide for the passage of something such as air, food or bodily waste products. Page 3.

tractability: the condition of being tractable (easily managed or controlled). Page 12.

trail is blazed: the path has been laid out and the route marked for others to follow. Literally, to *blaze a trail* is to lay out as a path by marking trees with white by chipping off a piece of bark. Page 1.

trance: a half-conscious state seemingly between sleeping and waking in which ability to function voluntarily may be suspended. Page 18.

transcends: goes beyond the limit or range of. Page 103.

transference: in psychotherapy, the process whereby somebody, such as a patient, unconsciously redirects feelings, fears or emotions onto someone else, often the analyst. The theory is that the feelings of the patient do not originate in the present situation but merely repeat earlier feelings he or she had for another (such as a parent) at some former time. Page 269.

transient: lasting only a short time; existing briefly; temporary. Page 32.

transorbital leukotomy: a psychiatric operation in which an ice pick is forced through the back of the eye sockets, piercing the thin bone that separates the eye sockets from the frontal lobes. The tip of the ice pick is then inserted into the frontal lobes and the nerve fibers connecting these to the rest of the brain are severed, resulting in the patient becoming an emotional vegetable. Page 132.

travail(s): pain, extreme anxiety or emotional torment or suffering resulting from mental or physical hardship. Page 141.

traversing: traveling or moving across, over or through an area or place. Page 288.

treatment: the practice of Dianetics techniques and procedures to resolve problems concerning human behavior and psychosomatic illness. Page i.

treats (of): addresses or deals with. Page 418.

trifles: things that have little or no importance. Page 155.

trinity: a combination or set of three individual things (as gods, persons, things, etc.) that form a unity or are closely connected to one another. Page 466.

trinity, Hindu: a reference to the three great gods in Hinduism: Brahma, the creator of the universe; Vishnu, the preserver of the universe; and Shiva, who personifies both the destructive and the procreative forces of the universe. A *trinity* is a combination or set of three individual things (as gods, persons, things, etc.) that form a unity or are closely connected to one another. Page 466.

tripe: nonsensical rubbish; anything worthless. Page 140.

trouncing: beating or thrashing severely. Page 476.

truck with, has no: has no dealings or communication with. Page 144.

trundle bed: a low bed on small wheels, that can be rolled under another bed when not in use. Page 363.

Truth: in some schools of thought, that which is thought of as true, real or actual in a general or abstract sense, a truth that has no shades of gray but is complete and total in itself. The view of such schools is that this "Truth" lies beyond the realm of human experience and therefore cannot actually be known by anyone. Page 450.

tuberculosis: a serious infectious disease in which swellings appear on the lungs and other parts of the body, once ranked among the most common causes of death in the world. Page 125.

tubes: a reference to *vacuum tubes,* devices once broadly used in electronics to control flows of electrical currents. They are called vacuum tubes because they are sealed glass tubes or bulbs from which almost all the air has been removed in order to improve electrical flow. Page 314.

tuned down (or up): adjusted or prepared for operating in a specific way. Page 127.

turned-on: made interested, excited with enthusiasm, likened to flipping a switch such as one that allows electricity to flow. Page 319.

#12 gauge copper wire: wire that is approximately the thickness of a wire coat hanger. *Gauge* refers to a standard measure or scale of measurement such as for the thickness or diameter of an object. Page 243.

"two little men...hanging by their heels": reference to the motor strip and sensory strip of the brain. The *motor strip* is a long narrow area of the brain which is believed to control the movement of the various muscles and movements of the body. The *sensory strip* is a long narrow area of the brain which is believed to monitor the senses of the body such as sight, smell, touch and hearing. The medical term for these strips of the brain is *homunculus*–a Latin word meaning "little man," to describe the function of each part of these strips which are believed to correspond to the shape of the human body, with the top of the strips monitoring the feet, the middle monitoring the torso and the bottom monitoring the head, hence "upside down." To illustrate the function of the strips, medical publications use illustrations of two little men hanging by their heels (see illustration). Page 389.

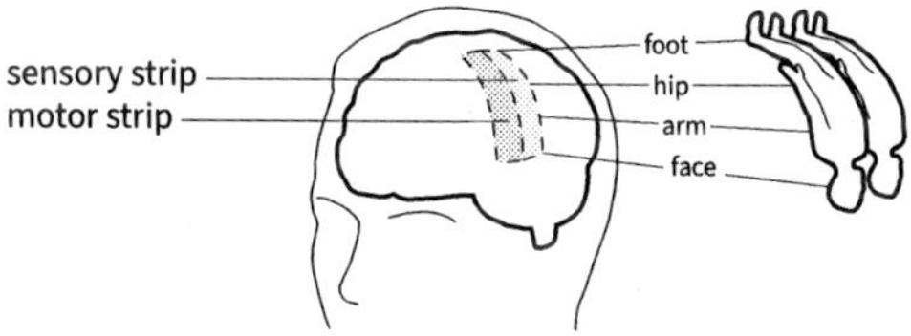

2.9 strikes: a reference to a strike in baseball–a player trying to hit the ball and missing. When a player does so three times he loses his turn and must leave the field of play. Because in baseball a batter can only have 1, 2 or 3 strikes against him, *2.9 strikes* is used figuratively to refer to someone or something that has little chance of success. Page 193.

two-valued logic: a system of logic based on the principle that there is no middle ground: something is either right or wrong, true or false, yes or no. Page 324.

uncharted: not shown or located on a map; unexplored; unknown, as a place or region. Page 535.

undermine: attack by indirect, secret or underhanded means, often by degrees, somewhat comparable to the action of wearing away a base or foundation. Page 188.

undimensional: not having specified dimensions. Hence, unrestricted, unbounded or limitless. Page 22.

undulating: fluctuating (according to the action of an engram). Page 393.

Union, the: the United States. Page 225.

universe: everything that exists everywhere; the whole space time continuum in which we exist, together with all the matter and energy within it, as opposed to the observable universe only. Page 9.

unremunerative: not giving back any helpful result in exchange for work or effort that has been put in to some activity. Page 431.

unwieldy: not mentally manageable; not useful or workable; impractical. Literally, *unwieldy* means difficult to carry or manage because of bulk or shape. Page 265.

unwittingly: unknowingly; unconsciously; without awareness. Page vi.

unyielding: not surrendering or giving way, as to some force, influence, pressure or the like. Page 346.

upstanding: honest and socially responsible; honorable. Page 319.

usurps: takes over or seizes (without authority or right); employs wrongfully. Page 314.

Utopian: of or like Utopia, an ideal and perfect place or state. The word "Utopia" was first used in a book of the same name by English writer Thomas More in 1516. *Utopia* is an account of an ideal society, with justice and equality for all citizens. Page 187.

vacillations: acts of wavering in mind, will or feeling; hesitations in choice of opinions or courses. Page 245.

valence shift: see Book Three, Chapter Nine: Part One, section entitled "Valence Shift." Page 376.

valiant: 1. worthy; excellent. Page 17.

2. boldly courageous; brave. Page 201.

variable(s): something subject to change. The term is most commonly used in mathematics and science where it represents something unknown or unpredictable. A *variable* is often contrasted with a *constant* which is known and unchanging. Page 9.

vector: something which has both a direction and quantity. For example, force would be a vector as it has a direction and an amount but mass is not a vector as it has no direction. Page 56.

Veda: the earliest learned writings of which there is any record. The most ancient sacred literature of the Hindus, telling about evolution, about Man coming into this universe and the curve of life which is birth, growth, degeneration and decay. The word *veda* means knowledge. Page 38.

vengeance: punishment that is given in return for a wrong; revenge. Page 326.

vengeance, with a: to an extreme degree; in an intense manner. Page 308.

veracity: correctness or accuracy. Page 458.

veritable: possessing all of the distinctive qualities of the person or thing specified. Page 459.

vignette, in: in one description of a person, place, situation, etc., that captures the features of the broader picture. Literally, a *vignette* is a small illustration that fades into its background without a definite border. Page 432.

villain of the (this) piece: the person or thing that is guilty or responsible for what is harmful or wrong in some activity or situation. A *piece* is a theatrical play and the *villain* is the character whose evil motives or actions form an important element in the plot and is blamed for a particular evil or difficulty. Page 64.

virtue of, by: by reason of; as a result of. Page 342.

virus: a minute organism only capable of reproducing inside another living organism. Viruses are lifeless by themselves, cannot reproduce and unlike living organisms, they are not made up of cells. Page 67.

VISIO: RECALL BY SEEING A PAST SIGHT WITH THE "MIND'S EYE." (From *Dianetics Terms.*) Page 21.

vivisecting: cutting apart a living body to examine the structure, relation of parts or the like. Page 225.

volatile: having an energetic liveliness. Page 310.

volition: the power of choosing, deciding, exercising the will. Page 72.

volley: a burst or outpouring of many things at once or in quick succession. Page 217.

voodoo: a body of beliefs and practices originally from Africa that includes magic and the supposed exercise of supernatural powers through the aid of evil spirits. Page 528.

wash, comes out in the: is eventually resolved satisfactorily or put right. Page 403.

washed: gotten rid of; removed. Page 301.

wax: increase gradually in size and strength, said of human beings. Page 179.

WCTU: Women's Christian Temperance Union, an organization founded in 1874 which campaigns against alcohol use. *Temperance* means the practice of not consuming alcoholic drinks. Page 486.

weary: 1. physically or mentally exhausted by hard work, exertion, etc.; worn out; tired. Page 194.
2. characterized by or causing impatience or dissatisfaction. Page 457.
3. become impatient or dissatisfied with something. Page 515.

wearying: becoming tired. Page 150.

weather-vaning: constantly changing one's mind, like a weather vane which changes direction with the wind. A *weather vane* is a plate of metal, usually of an ornamental form, placed high on top of a building on a vertical rod so as to turn freely with the wind and show the direction from which it is blowing. Page 460.

well-nigh: very nearly; almost. Page 39.

well, would be: would be suitable, proper or appropriate under the circumstances. Page 32.

welter: a confused mass; jumble. Page 389.

whence: from what source, origin or cause. Page 376.

When Knighthood Was in Flower: title of a novel by Charles Major (1856-1913) that captured the chivalry (courteous conduct) of twelfth- and thirteenth-century England when knights were at their height of fame and prominence. Page 238.

whet: to make a feeling, sense or desire more keen or intense, as by indulging in some activity to a small degree, in order to make a feeling more pleasurable. Hence, "*to whet her sadism upon him*" refers to a person (a teacher) increasing the enjoyable intensity of her sadism by acting cruelly to her student. Page 411.

while, the: during the time, in the meantime; meanwhile, as in "*And you might work fifty hours for it, releasing the case the while.*" Page 370.

whip hand: a position of advantage or control. Literally, a hand that holds a whip, especially one used to drive horses. Page 96.

whirling dervish: a member of a Turkish religious order of monks. As part of their worship they spin around and dance to music. *Dervish* is a word of Turkish origin meaning "beggar." Page 363.

whispering campaign: the organized spreading of rumors to destroy the reputation of a person, organization, etc. Page 525.

whistle while Rome burns: a variation of *fiddle while Rome burns*, a saying alluding to a legend of Roman emperor Nero Claudius Caesar who in July A.D. 64 was said to have played a fiddle while a great fire burned and destroyed most of the city of Rome. The saying is often used to describe people who can remain indifferent and detached while all hell is breaking loose around them. Page 240.

wholesale: extensive; performed on a large scale or affecting large numbers or amounts. Page 146.

wielding the whip: exercising power or authority (through pain). Page 91.

wild variable: a factor in a situation or problem that behaves in an uncontrolled, strange or unpredictable fashion. Variable is most commonly used in mathematics and science where it represents something unknown or unpredictable. A variable is often contrasted with a constant which is known and unchanging. Page 75.

wince: to make an expression of pain with the face because of seeing or thinking of something unpleasant or embarrassing. Page 309.

wisdom teeth: one of the four teeth at the back of each side of the upper and lower jaw of human beings. They are the last teeth to emerge. Page 156.

wished off on: forced or imposed on someone. Page 175.

wistful: having or showing a feeling of vague or regretful longing. Page 469.

with a vengeance: to an extreme degree; in an intense manner. Page 308.

without: at, to, or on the outside of; exterior to, as in *"it is easier if they each look without the home for a therapy partner."* Page 414.

wits: 1. persons having or noted for saying smart or brilliant things, sometimes so as to amuse others. Used here sarcastically. Page 88.

2. mind; understanding or intelligence. Page 286.

woe: deep distress or misery; misfortune. Page 2.

woman scorned: a reference to the phrase *Hell hath [has] no fury like a woman scorned,* meaning no one has more fury or wrath than a woman whose love has been rejected, or who thinks her worth or dignity has been insulted, ignored, etc. Page 524.

word of mouth, by: by speaking, as distinguished from writing or other methods of expression; orally. Page 116.

worksheet: a sheet of paper on which work schedules, working time, etc., are recorded. Page 257.

wracked: subjected to extreme mental or physical suffering; tortured. Page 539.

wreaks, havoc (something): causes or produces harm, damage, etc. Page 281.

wriggle: make repeated twisting and turning motions. Page 461.

x: in the equation $PV = ID^x$, it is the symbol for an unknown power. (A *power* in mathematics is the number of times something is multiplied by itself. For example 3^3 is 3 times 3 times 3 = 27.) Here, the "x" indicates that a person's dynamic (D) could be multiplied by itself an unknown number of times. This was written to encourage discovery of what the power of the dynamic might be and conclude some means of establishing potential value by psychometry. Page 56.

***x* factor:** a relevant but unknown element or circumstance. Page 104.

yah-yah across back fences: talk of a critical or ridiculing nature with one's neighbors or associates. *Across back fences* refers to the tradition of neighbors speaking (or complaining) across a fence that separates their properties. *Yah* is an exclamation of disgust or ridicule. Page 544.

Yanks are coming, the: reference to a line from "Over There," a patriotic song by American composer George M. Cohan (1878–1942) about American men going to Europe (1917) to fight in World War I. (*Yank* is an abbreviation for *Yankee,* a native of the United States of America.) Page 245.

yard goods: literally, fabrics sold by the yard (three feet or approximately one meter). *Goods* refer to articles for sale, especially fabric. Hence, in reference to auditing, "*just shows the yard goods*" means that the auditor lets the preclear find out about himself or herself without suggestion or evaluation. Page 295.

yardsticks: any tests or standards used in measuring, judging, etc. Page 113.

yeast: a microscopic single-celled organism capable of converting sugar into alcohol and carbon dioxide and hence used for producing alcohol in beer and wine, and for making bread rise. Page x.

yesteryear: the past. Page 377.

yet: though the case be such; nevertheless; in spite of that, as in "*The enlightened and Golden Age of Greece yet had but superstition.*" Page 7.

yield(ed): **1.** produce or give forth (results, products, etc.). Page ii. **2.** give up further resistance; surrender. Page 123.

Zamba, Dr.: a made-up name. Page 452.

zealot: a person who shows excessive enthusiasm for a cause, particularly a religious cause; fanatic. Page 142.

zombie: literally, a dead body brought back to life again. Hence anyone who lacks the ability to think independently and lacks energy, enthusiasm, etc. Page 384.

zombyism: the state of lacking energy, enthusiasm or the ability to think independently, likened to a *zombie,* a dead body brought back to life again. Page 8.

zygote: a female reproductive cell that has been fertilized by a male reproductive cell. Page xi.

Index

A

AA
see **attempted abortion**
A=A=A, 84, 244, 450
aberrated conduct, 52
aberrated personality (AP), 167
aberration, vii, 13
attempted abortions and, 179
caused by engrams, 55, 555
classification of, 241-245
contagion of, *see* **contagion of aberration**
definition, 55, 138, 549, 555
diagnosis, 250, 258
done *to*, not done *by*, vi, 515
educational institutions and, 457
extent of, 246
held-down 7, 24
hypnotism and, 89
inorganic, i
marrying pseudo-mother, 211
mechanics of, 99
nature of data offered and, 61
number of, 242
parts of, 76-78
patient cannot see his own, 235
patterns of, 182
personality versus, 16
prevention of social causes, 210
primary test of, 451
psychosomatic illness and, 138
source of, v, 55, 70, 73, 91, 555
sudden display, 194-195
suggestions and, 75, 77
aberrative commands, 442
aberree, 16, 34, 102
definition, 549
family of, 188
perceptions of, vary, 16
purpose and persistency, 317
see also **aberration; preclear**
ability
computational, ix
Dianetics and, 11
aborigine, 7
abortion, *see* **attempted abortion**
absolute goal, 53, 553
absolutes, 114, 448-449, 466
accidents, 79, 125-126, 182, 209
accident-prone, 209
aches, 125
ACTH, 123, 132
action
commanded, 74
forced on somatic and analytical mind, 313
types of, 199
adrenaline, 64, 129, 150
adventure, 1, 4

Aesculapian, 165, 168
  temple, 7
affinity
  breaking of, 201
  definition, 143
  law, *see* **law of affinity**
  Man and survival, 44, 143
  restimulation and, 87
  strengthening of, 414
  three-way case of, 235
  see also **emotion**
age flash, 377
aging
  see **gerontology**
Ahriman, 466
alcohol, 485-486
  alcoholics and engrams, 485
Alexander the Great, 315-316
allergy, 69, 125, 364
  case history, 498
alleviation, 430
  so that work can be continued, 430
ally, 473
  antagonist versus, 465-470
  childhood losses of, 343
  definition, 475
  denial by, 337
  departure of or from, 338, 367
  loss of, 332, 338
    finding out, 335
    retroactive in suppressing early engrams, 341
  occlusion and, 338
  prime test for, 465
  pseudo-ally, 327
    see also **pseudo-ally**
  reversal, 336, 367
  tokens and, 471, 473, 475-476
ally computation, 323-330
  Achilles' heel, 331, 340
  definition, 323
  description, 326
  genesis of, 328
  resistive case and, 481
  suppressor on time track, 408
  tacit consent and, 425
  threatened or attempted abortion, 214
  when to suspect, 335
altitude
  definition, 457
ambivalence
  definition, 363
  see also **multivalence; valence**
ambiversion, 514
ammonium chloride, 486
amnesia, 73
amnesia trance, 128, 482, 512-513
  definition, 128
  "depth of trance," 272
  effort to spare "I" and, 275
  versus reverie, 269
amniotic fluid
  injury and, 212
  sac, 215
analytical mind, 59-65
  attenuated, 55, 556
  basic personality and, 167
  body and, 64-65, 154
  cells and, xi
  computation, 83
  computer and, 60
  computes in differences, 447
  consciousness and, 79

data and, 54, 59, 61, 63, 105, 144, 555
definition, viii, 54, 549, 555
dynamics and, 66
incapable of error, 60
justification and, 293
mechanics of, 251
monitor and, 59
necessity level and, 149
never resist the auditor, 234
non-analytical moments and, 96
parasitic demon and, 118
preclear's plus auditor's, 487
reactive mind and, 177
remaining unaberrated, 201
shutdown, 430
standard memory banks, 61
time sense, 71
training pattern and, 65

analytical power, 97-101
engrams and, 212
prenatal area and, 424
reduction, 97
restimulation of engram and, 99
Zones and, 98

analytical shutdown, 97-98, 102
tone and, 98

analytical thought, 106
justification and, 106

analyzer, 60, 97-100, 149-153
attenuation, 283, 285
reduction of, 99
set up as demon circuit, 118
shut-down, 101, 195
see also **analytical mind**

anesthetics
hypnotics, 483
in operations, 79, 182, 496
poisons, 97
shuts down somatics, 482

anger, 33
Zone 1, 147
suppressor and, 150

anger-sympathy dramatization, 156

animal
life force, versus man's, 310

animosity toward parents, 408

answers
mind and, 25
wrong, 24

antagonism, 465-470, 519

antagonist, 465-470

anti-engram education, 107

anxiety, 104, 227, 257, 472, 522

AP (aberrated personality), 167

apathy, 33
ally computations and, 325
case history, 497
in engram, 158, 386
interest in engrams, 416
neglecting engrams, 417
propitiation and, 409, 412
succumbing to engram, 236
Zone 0, 147

apples and worms, 83

arbitrary
introduction of, 113, 540
structure, 540

Aristotle, 173, 262
pendulum, 448
two-valued logic, 448

art, 233

arthritis, 69, 125, 133, 257, 397
example, 325

Index

artificial restimulation, 319
assist
description, 230
"assist" engram, 316
see also **engram; manic**
associative restimulator, 322, 324, 471-475
example, 471
identity-thought, 471
asthma, 69, 125, 171, 202
astigmatism, 120
atheist, 142
atom bomb, 7
attack, 200, 236
auditor or therapy, 525
engram, 527
preclear, 488
attempted abortion, 178-180, 213-215, 243, 327, 383, 402
brain and, 492
mutual AA, 329
physiological disability and, 494
shut-offs and, 493
sympathy engram chains and, 364
attention units, 266
audio-bank, 62
audio-semantic, 63
auditing
definition, 530
do's and don'ts, listed, 376-379
goal, 375
routine, 267, 270, 334-336
shepherd's task, 240
ten basic steps, 271
ten-step procedure, 334-336
tools, 376
auditor, viii-ix, 234
advice to, 222, 258, 505-513
ally against preclear's reactive mind, 247
associative restimulator, 324
attitude, 238, 295
confidential matter, 418
definition, 221, 549
don'ts, 372, 377, 527
do's and don'ts, listed, 376-379
duty, 236
equivocal, 295
errors of, 221, 234, 240, 382, 431
evaluation, 527-531
first goal of, 382
four techniques available to, 303
gifts to, 410
goals of, 230, 274
job, 235
necessary, 487
physical pain versus painful emotion engrams, 347
preclear and, equations, 487
primary error of, 234
professional backgrounds, 225
relative to preclear, 377
Repeater Technique and cleverness, 291-293
restimulation of, 390
of auditor, 516
role, 233-239
stopping therapy, 524-526
suggestion and, 250
sympathy and, 238
temper, 377
tools of, 376

well-trained, 522
whatever impedes the auditor in his work, 246
who can become, 231
Auditor's Code, 238-239, 532-533
break, remedy for, 431, 480
Clear and, 238, 516
courageous, 239
courteous, 238
equation demonstrating necessity of, 488
evaluation, 239
kind, 238
patient, 239
persistent, 239
quiet, 238
thorough, 239
trustworthy, 238
uncommunicative, 239
violation of, 382
why important, 250
auditor's role, 233-239
Australia aborigine, 7
Authority, 172-173, 457
Good Authority, 63
Nullification by Comparison, 113
science of mind, 10
auto-control, 415, 487-489
autogenetic
definition, 124
illness, 124
auto-hypnosis, 488
autonomic nervous system, 131
avoid, 200
awareness
center of, viii, 59
mind and, 222
10 percent of potential, vii
axioms, ii, 547
chronic psychosomatic illness, 467
definition, 11
earlier period of "unconsciousness," 169
mind function, 447
sciences and, 546
Axioms of Dianetics, Fundamental, 553-556

B

B_1, 485-486
nightmares and, 485
Bacon, Francis, 9, 535
bacteria, 136
bank monitor
definition, 265
units, 265
banks, 61-63
for each perception, 61
see also **engram bank; reactive mind; standard (memory) banks**
Bara, Theda, 244
barber-basin medicine, 133
Barrymore, 245
basic, 436
definition, 549
basic area, 275, 278, 301, 387
basic-basic, 275-276, 382-383
auditor and, 415
auditor tries to reach, 332, 335
case opening and, 370
case resolution and, 237
caution, 441

Index

definition, 172, 237, 549
every session, 275
foremost thing to do at beginning of case, 381
number one goal, 376
return from, 429
basic engram, 294
basic personality
definition, 167, 524
file clerk and, 273
basic purpose, 315, 320
beauty
appreciation of, 160
Bedlam, 8, 132
behavior
dynamics and, 48
irrational, 55, 555
"Believe" and "Can't Believe," 452-460
Benzedrine, 484
Bergson, 306
biochemistry, 12, 124
"biological love," 211
birth, xii
engram of, 171-175, 202, 203
file clerk, 388
in a Cleared mother, 218
prematurely contacted, 388
prenatal experience and, 165
reduction of, 372
same engram for mother and child, 184
step one of routine and, 334-335
black panther mechanism, 200
child and, 200
blasphemy, 142
blindness, 62, 493
colorblindness, 14
hysterical, 252-253
Blood and Sand, 244
blood flow, 128
blood pressure
high, 69, 135, 428
body
analytical mind and, 64-65, 154
boiling-off, 285
changing effect of engram bank on, 132
don't touch patient's, 404
effect of sympathy engram, 329
patient "outside" his body, 343
see also **exteriorization**
reactive mind and, vi
resistance to disease, 136
boil-off, 285-286, 403-405, 461
description, 405
jogging preclear into attention, 404
origin of term, 405
somatic and, 426
Borneo, 115
Boulder Dam, 190
bouncer, 285
definition, 284-285, 549
description, 444
examples, 282-283, 444
phrases, 393
track regulated by, 302
words contained in, 437
BP, *see* **basic personality**
brain, 132
vivisection, 494
break engram, 195

bridge, 540, 547-548
build a better, 548
built across the canyon, 111
British Guiana, 7
bubonic plague bacillus, 39
bursitis, 69, 125
bypass circuits, 70, 167

C

Caesar, Julius, 49, 69
calcium deposits, 17
calculating machine, 24
Caligula, 69
canceller, 267, 531
description, 268
every session, 269
cancer, 126
"Can't Believe," 452-460
case
basic-basic and, 237
chronic doubter, 454
classifications, 369
combat exhaustion case, 510
computing on a, 530
de-intensifying a, 508
delay, 418, 505
don't promise to Clear, 532
entrance, *see* **case opening**
hopeless, 492
improvement ratio, 332
institutionalized, 509
kept "live," 433
length of, 258
opening, *see* **case opening**
rebalancing, 395, 519
"refuses" to get well, 481-482
running the, 377
stalled, 418
stops progressing, what to do, 479
tools to work, 376
type
"death instinct" case, 365
"different" case, 378
foreign language case, 419
high-euphoria case, 313
institutionalized, 509
manic case, 313
psychotic case, 502
sonic and visio, 257
stuck in present time, 380-382
case histories
birth engram, 171-172
by type of engram, 351-366
drunkard son of "bold, forceful" man, 438-439
imposed secrecy, 419
"insane" in fetal position, 358
manic
fine upstanding man, 319
pianist, 318
mutual therapy, 496-500
restimulated case, 501-504
sympathy engram, exodontistry, 154-157
use of Repeater Technique, 292-297
case opening, 331, 381
cells, xi, 67, 93, 111, 173
Charles Darwin, 67
engram and, 96, 172
engram bank and, 103
recording pain, 173
thought units, 96
unit of life, 67
cellular engrams, v
cellular intelligence, 96

censor, v
chain
cross-engram and, 195
definition, 401, 550
first incident on, 436
types of, 401-403
words in chains, 436
charge
aberree and emotional, 317
analogy to electrical charge, 342
auditor running into, 373
drained, 73
electric-like energy and, 93
somatic strip and, 435
see also **emotional charge**
child, 188-189
accidental mishaps of, 198
antipathy toward, 179
child wonder, 318
Clearing and, 188, 210
Dynamic Two, iii
engrams, 136
feebleminded, 179
glory and color of, 160
healthiest, 218
illnesses, 136, 178, 210
is a human being, 189
losses of allies, 341-342
love and, 142, 470
cooperation from, 409
marriage of unaberrated people and, 413
nervous disposition toward, 413
only way an ally can aberrate, 470
Preventive Dianetics, 210-217
punishment of, 188, 200
rape, 195
reaction to engrams and, 182
restimulation, 204
restimulators and, 189, 203, 472
self-determined, 189
"spoil" a, 142, 189
"child psychology," 189
China, 7
chloroform, 483
Christians, 36
chronic, 100
definition, 102
only pro-survival engrams, 142
sympathy engram and, 144
chronic illness, 246
Church, 142
circuit, 14, 70, 271
containing "I", 120
containing "you," 120
drawing, 271
overloaded with demon lash-ups, 121
parasitic, 116
verbal, 118
vocal, 69
see also **demon circuits**
claustrophobia, 290
Clear, iv, ix, 13-24, 148, 227-231, 349, 416-418
ambiversion, 514
attributes of, 14
compared to contemporary "norm," 228
debris-free state, 350
definition, i, 13, 149, 550
and description, 227
dictionary, 550

description, iv
dwindling spiral and, 131
dynamics and, iv
Equation of the Optimum Solution and, 49
ethical level, 516
eyesight and, 16
goal in Dianetic therapy, 25
imagination and, 22
inversion and, 309
length of time to Clear a person, 521
life force, 310
mannerisms, 477
no mental voices, 117
operates on Auditor's Code, 238, 516
past acts of, 540
perceptions in, 14
prenatal engram and, 174
rendered "unconscious," 182
responsibility and, 515
sanity and, 66
self-determinism, 25
society and, 187
tests, 13
Tone 4 and, 34
tone of, 408
without ills or aberrations, 13

clearing
turn-about, 414

clichés, 420, 459
engramic commands and, 245

clock in the mind, 300

coffee, 484

cohesion, law of, 143

coitus
chain types, 401
during pregnancy, 196, 214-215, 278
engram, 354
example, 355
language during, 214

cold
birth and, 388
common cold, 69, 125

colorblindness, 14

comatic reduction, 405
see also **boil-off; "unconsciousness"**

combat exhaustion, 510

commanded action, 82

command phrase
classes of, 284-285
phrasing of, 435, 437
use in Dianetics, 372

commands, engramic, ix, 277
anesthesia and, 370
boil-off, 285
command value of engram, 120, 121
definition, 551
effect on preclear, 302
examples, 277-282
importance, 353
laws concerning, 301
physical pain and painful emotion commands, 461-464
special classes of, 441
suppressors, 408
time track, 302
yesterday's clichés, 245
see also **command phrase**

compulsion, 76, 85
Clear and, 13

compulsive "love," 411
reactive mind and, 69
compulsion demons, 120
computation
analytical versus reactive mind's, 83
analyzer and, 149
apples and worms example, 83
perception *equals* every other perception, 84
rational, 455
primary source of error, 63
secrecy and, 481
stupidity, 481
valuable, 376
see also **ally computation**
computer
analytical mind and, 60
computing machine, 59, 199
computing on a case, 530
concept
definition, 62
percept filed as a, 61
conception, 172
conditioning, 193
conduct pattern, 82
conduct survival pattern
Equation of the Optimum Solution, 49, 52, 238
Confucianism, 186
confusion, 544
identity, 425, 446
confusion demons, 120
conjunctivitis, 135, 156, 171
birth and, 246
consciousness
analytical mind and, 79
depth of, 154
engram and, 105
post-hypnotic suggestion, 85
constipation, 401
positive suggestion and, 129
contagion of aberration, 181-189, 436
birth and, 184
definition, 181
family and, 188
nations and, 543
social effects, 185
war and, 186
contemplation, 35
"Continue," 295, 372
contraceptive, 178, 402
contra-survival engram, 145, 201, 320-323, 329-330, 340
Achilles' heel of, 330
definition, 82, 351
examples, 351-354
restimulator, 471-472
"unconsciousness" and, 79
cooperative effort, 235
coronary trouble, 69
corporal punishment, 188
counting, 267
courageous
Auditor's Code, 239
courteous
Auditor's Code, 238
covert hostility, 412
creative imagination, 21, 68, 311
Clear and, 22
description, 22
criminal, 199, 541
critical demon, 117
criticism, 242
cross-engram
definition, 195

cross-index system, 61
cult, 114
culture
analytical mind, 541
engrams and, 183
growing complex and unwieldy, 540
cyanide, 485
cycle of aberration, 185
cycle of life, 202
cyclic aspect of life, 29
cytology, 12

D

Dalton, Jack, 244
danger
reaction toward source of, 199
Dante, 141
Dark Ages, 37
Darwin, Charles, 67, 535
data
analytical mind and, 54, 59, 61, 63, 105, 144, 555
ask again, 293
computation and, 24
Doctrine of the True Datum, 144
engram filing system and, 429
evaluation of, 452-457
file clerk and, 265, 429
flash answer and, 376
from relatives, 522
held-down 7, 24
insufficient and erroneous, 63, 65
intelligence and, 54, 554
da Vinci, 173
deafness, 62
hysterical, 252
death
ally, loss of, 336-337
"death instinct" case, 365
failures and, 54, 554
patient begging not to talk about, 339
spectrum of, 149
urge away from, 30
"death instinct" case, 365
debauchery, 36
deep analysis
faulty, 166
definition, 285
aberration, 55, 138, 549, 555
aberree, 549
affinity, 143
ally, 475
ally computation, 323
altitude, 457
ambivalence, 363
amnesia trance, 128
analytical mind, viii, 54, 549, 555
auditing, 530
auditor, 221, 549
autogenetic, 124
axioms, 11
bank monitor, 265
basic, 549
basic-basic, 172, 237, 549
basic personality, 167, 524
bouncer, 284, 549
chain, 401, 550
chronic, 102
Clear, i, 13, 149, 227, 550
concept, 62
contagion of aberration, 181

Index

contra-survival engram, 82, 351
cross-engram, 195
demons, 116, 550
denyer, 284, 285, 550
Dianetics, i, 550
dramatization, 107
dynamic, 47, 550
electroencephalograph, 306
emotion, 56, 556
engram, xii, 55, 80, 90, 173, 177, 208, 302, 550, 555-556
engram bank, 550
engram command, 551
erase, 333, 384, 551
erasure, 276, 383
exogenetic, 124
exteriorized view, 426
exteriorly determined, 308
file clerk, 265
flash answer, 397
genetic insanity, 181
gerontology, 130
grouper, 284, 551
habit, 55, 555
happiness, 42, 54, 555
holder, 443, 551
homonymic, 82
hyper-hearing, 254
hyper-sight, 254
hypnosis, 128
hypo-hearing, 253
hypo-sight, 253
"hysterical" blindness, 252
"hysterical" deafness, 252
"I", viii
iatrogenic, 10, 490
imagination, 21
insanity, 37, 455
inversion, 310
irrationality, 23
Judiciary Dianetics, 537
justified thought, 348
kinesthesia, 62
lie factory, 256
life-function regulator, 64
lock, 119, 144, 166, 405
manic, 313
memory, 81, 551
misdirector, 285, 551
mutually restimulative, 517
norm, 228
occluded person, 338
organic insanity, 230
organic sensation, 98
painful emotion engram, 83
perceptic, 551
perception, 14
perpetuation, 124
pleasure, 32
precipitation, 124
preclear, 236, 551
predisposition, 124
prerelease, 236-237, 551
present time, 395
pro-survival engram, 83, 320, 354
pseudo-ally, 337
psychosomatic, 125, 551
psychosomatic ill(ness), 123-124
reactive mind, 55, 551, 555
rebalancing, 395
reduce, 384, 552
regression, 18
Release, i, 227, 416, 552
Repeater Technique, 511
replay, 374
restimulator, 98-99
restimulator lag, 505

returning, 18-19, 261, 263, 303
revivification, 18
sanity, 450
schizophrenic, 169
shut-off, 462
soldered-in, 105
somatic, 251, 552
somatic mind, 55, 555
sonic (sound), 251, 552
spectrum, 263
standard (memory) banks, 61, 552
suppressor, 552
symbiote, 47, 552
tacit consent, 425
time track, viii, 264, 273, 552
token, 471, 473, 475
training pattern, 55, 555
"unconsciousness," 55, 556
valence, 108
vanished, 276
visio (sight), 251, 552
worry, 280, 455
deletion of tissue treatment, 132
delirium
illness, 79
delusion
childhood, 189, 311
engrams and, 424, 489
misconception of past incident, 256
democracy, 186
demon circuits
analyzer set up as, 118
auditing goal and, 375
bypassed in narcosynthesis, 167
Clear and, 228
dub-in, 256
handling of, 336
life force units and, 336
parasitic quality, 313
valence walls and, 332
see also **circuit; demons**
demonology
description, 115
demons, 70, 113-120
classes of, 115
compulsion, 120
confusion, 120
critical, 117
definition, 116, 550
description, 121
discovery of, 115
occlusion, 118
take a part of the analyzer, 117
see also **circuit; demon circuits**
denyer, 339
action on time track and, 302
canceller and, 268
definition, 284, 285, 550
examples, 284, 353, 442
Repeater Technique on, 295
departure, 368
of or from ally, 338
depression, 137, 391
depressive
manic and, 158
depressive-type insanity, 77
derailer, 446, 462
derangement, 73
of body, 133
two categories, 138
dermatitis, 125, 257

Descriptic Graph of Survival
description, 30-34
further interpretation, 37-38
despair charges, 419
case stalling and, 418
detachable coat, *see* **"touch my tie" example**
diabetes, 126
diagnosis, 241-258
computing on a case, 530
description of Dianetics, 258
factors in, 251
IQ and, 259
perceptions and, 251
rule in, 246
Dianetics
adventure, 1, 4
auditing, goal, 25
belongs to, 225
branches of, 207
definition, i, 550
development of, 3
diagnosis, described, 258
don'ts, 531
see also **Auditor's Code**
equations of, 45
first aid, 495-496
fundamental and primary error in practice of, 234
future of therapy, 545-548
goal of therapy, 13, 25
history of, 535-537
hypnotism and, 269
Individual Dianetics, i
in the 21st century, 561
legislation and, 226
main emphasis of, 259
other practices and, 224-225, 377, 533
parallel to thought, 238
past and future, 535
philosophic background, 535
preventive, 496
research on, 168, 452, 465
routine in, 270
science of mind and, 11, 225
scope of, 7-11
simplicity of, 233
talking about, 243
ten-step procedure, 334-336
terminology, 29
therapy
don'ts, 531
tools, 376
wakes people up, 482
war and, 541-545
what it does and is, 11
works, 94
yardsticks, 113
dictator, 186
differences, 447-450
sanity and, 450
differentiation, 451, 465, 538
disabilities
inherited, 126
discharge, 275, 346, 370-373
disease, 136-137
germ and non-germ theory of, 12, 124
70 percent psychosomatic, 123
see also **illness**
doctor
Dianetics and, 533

misapprehension of brain function by, 490
recommending abortion, 179
Doctrine of the True Datum, 144
done *to*, not done *by*, vi, 418, 487, 515, 539
don'ts
auditor, 372, 377, 527
dopey
feeling dopey, 101
see also **boil-off**
do's and don'ts
listed, 376-379
doubter, 454
douche, 178, 215, 401
dramatic personnel, 108
dramatis personae, 435
dramatization, 107-108
accidents and, 125
anger-sympathy, 156
blocked, 121
breaking a, 110
caused by engrams, 107
contagion of, 182-183
definition, 107
each aberree has standard, 435
example of, 107, 353
people under stress and, 182
valence and, 107-108, 158
drawing, 271-274
prenatal area of the reactive engram bank, 341
dream, 278, 398, 404
drive, 40
drug(s), 482-486
causing organic mental alterations, 490
hypnosis, 195
hypnotic
poisons, 168
mind's protection and, 221
patients who plead for, 269
psychosomatic ill and, 146
reason for uncertain effects, 131
drug dreams, 343
drug hypnotism, 166-167, 195
engram and, 168
see also **narcosynthesis**
drug trance, 482
***Drunkard, The*,** 245
D.T.'s, 485
dub-in, 256, 419
demons, 256
imagination, 252, 369
lie factories and, 257
prenatal scenery, 423
testing recall for dub-in, 255
dub-in case, 380
dwindling spiral, 134, 194, 313
ally computation and, 474
chronic restimulation and, 413
Clears and, 131
dynamic(s), 47-50, 52, 113
analytical mind and, 66
assisted by other dynamics, 40
behavior, 48
blocked, 141, 179, 202, 320, 354
resilience of individual, 201
contest with other dynamics, 48
definition, 47, 550
description, iii, 47-50

Index

Dianetics and, iv
emotion and, 147-148
four dynamics, 45-49
inherent, 38
inhibited by engrams, 54, 554
intelligence and, 54, 554
never resist auditor, 234
preclear's less than force in reactive bank, 487
preclear's plus auditor's greater than force in preclear's bank, 487
spectrum of, 262
strength of, 48
survival, 29
see also **survival dynamic**
unblocked by, 201
various native strengths of, 493
Dynamic Four, iii, 47, 52-53, 553
see also **Mankind**
Dynamic One, iii, 47
Dynamic Principle of Existence, ii, 3, 53, 553
Dynamic Three, iii, 52
see also **group; Group Dynamic**
Dynamic Two, iii, 47, 52
blocked, 179, 354
see also **child; sex**

E

ears ringing, 17, 487
education
analytical surge and, 203
analytical thought and, 106
valid method of therapy, 202
Educational Dianetics
description, 207
educational institutions, 457
Einstein, 10
ejection, 284
élan vital, 306
electrical theory of the nervous system, 72
electric-like energy, 93
electric shock, 132, 157, 199, 204, 260, 403, 425
case, 510
effects of, 509
memory banks and, 491
mental alteration, 491
electroencephalograph, 307
definition, 306
Ellis, 140
embryo, 176, 215
emotion, 147-161, 305
bound up life force, 305
charge
location of, 364, 407
complete cycle of, 153
content of engrams and, 161
definition, 56, 556
dynamics and, 147
grizzly hunter, example, 151-152
laughter and, 162
life force and, 147-148, 317
loss and, 159, 337, 505
minus emotions and plus emotions, 147
painful emotion commands, 461-464
recall and, 21
role in therapy, 305
shut-offs, 300, 426, 462

somatic strip and emotional charge, 435
theta quantity, 147
three things, 56, 556
two sections, 161
see also **painful emotion**

emotional charge
best attack on engram bank and, 237
departure of or from an ally, 367
engram and, 293, 337
file clerk and, 429
if you run into a heavy, 373
orderly erasure and, 340
painful emotion engram and, 480
pain shut-off and, 372
physically painful engrams and, 375
prenatal, 341
Release and, 230
Repeater Technique and, 435
see also **charge**

emotional encysting, 160

encysting
emotional, 160
life force, 324
time and, 379
whole mind, 22

endocrine, 129, 161
analytical mind and, 64
emotion and, 161

energy, 28-29

engineers, 225

England, 186

engram, v, vi, xi
aberration and, 55, 379, 555
all the percepts, 98
analytical mind
justification of engram and, 293
reaction of analyzer to engrams, 283, 285
analytical power and, 212
apathy case and, 417
approach to, 223
"assist" aspect, 314
believe and disbelieve, 459
break engram, 195
cells and, 96
chronic, 142
coitus engram, 354
commands in engrams
classes of phrase, 442
in chronic restimulation, 301
more important than action in engram, 353
physical pain and painful emotion, 461-464
sleep commands, 405
special classes, 441
see also **commands, engramic**
command value, 120
common denominator of, 383
complete recording, 80
contagion of aberration, *see* **contagion of aberration**
contra-survival, *see* **contra-survival engram**
cross-engram, 195
cycle of action, 125
definition, xii, 55, 80, 90, 173, 177, 208, 302, 550, 555-556
description, xii-xiii, 177

Index

develop, 293
three days, 520
difference between a memory and, 80
discovery of, 168-170
disease, 136
dramatization and valence, 158
dynamics inhibited by, 54, 554
emotion and word content of, 355
emotionless, 335
establishing validity, 529
examples of, 81, 351-366
baseball bats, 104
birth engram, 171
ether, 99
exodontistry, 154-157
restimulation, 87
see also **woman knocked out and kicked**
filing system of, 429
greatest discharge and, 317
habit and, 55, 555
hypnotic suggestion, 268
illness, precipitated by, 136
intelligence inhibited by, 54, 554
interest in, 416
Junior case engram, 279
keep asking for the, 294
keying-in the, 191-203
language and, 281
late engrams, 431
loss of ally and, 338
memory and, 80, 275, 378
must contain physical pain, 138
necessity level and, 149
neglect of, 417
only way out of it is *through* it, 532
organic functions and, 135
parent's death, description of running, 346
perception *equals* every other perception, 84
percepts and, 98
physical pain and verbal command, 133
physical pain engram, start early and work toward late, 348
power of, 223, 308, 332
power of choice and, 120
prevention, 210, 213
primary engram, 169
pro-survival, *see* **pro-survival engram**
received as a zygote, 176
recession and, 387
restimulating the, 407
shocks and operations are, 492
shut-down datum, 99
single source of aberrations, 55, 555
special case, 446
surrender engram, 133
talking out of, 243, 285
test for validity of, 528
therapy and, vii
things that can happen to, 387
three-day aspect of, 520
three kinds, 82
tone value of, 159, 337
training pattern, 105

two hours or ten years ago, 431
two or three runs will erase, 433
types of, 82, 351-366
uncontacted, 222
when consciousness is absent, 105

engram bank, 69
attack, 236
definition, 550
difference between standard banks and, 81
dreams and, 398
effect on body, change, 132
hypnotism and, 511
mechanisms of protection, 505
see also **reactive mind**

engram chains
see **chain**

engram-denyer, 284, 353
see also **denyer**

engram filing system, 429

engram-grouper, 284
see also **grouper**

engram lock chain, 104

environment
adjusting to, 310
approach on asthma case, 202
change of, 202
danger or sympathy in, 154
restimulative, 202

equation(s)
auditor and preclear, 487
of Dianetics, 45
of immoral pleasures, 36
of survival, iii
$PV = ID^x$, 56, 556

Equation of the Optimum Solution, 52, 113, 448
Clear and, 49

erase, 376, 384-388, 415
basic-basic and, 387
definition, 333, 384, 551
description, 415
two or three runs, 433

erasure
definition, 276, 383

error
analytical mind and, 60
human error, 23, 59
Man incapable of, 23
primary source in "rational" computation, 63

ESP, *see* **extrasensory perception**

estrogen, 129

ether, 99, 483

euphoria, 132, 313, 520

evaluation, 453
auditor and, 292, 527-531
Auditor's Code, 239
Dianetic Don'ts, 532
of a fact, 2
of data, 452-457

evil
good and evil, 537
Man and, 25, 198

evolution, 67

exaggerator, 462, 480

excreta, 64, 129

Existence
Dynamic Principle of, ii, 3, 53, 553

exodontistry, 154, 484

exogenetic
definition, 124
illness, 124

Index

exorcists, 8
experience, bad, 81
extended hearing, 127, 172, 252
extended sight, 252
exterior-determinism, 187
exteriorization, 343
painful emotion and, 343
exteriorized view, 343, 426-427
case opening and, 370
definition, 426
exteriorly determined
definition, 308
external problems with patients, 514
extrasensory perception, 423-424
extroversion, 526
eyes, 120, 125-126
eyesight, 16

F

fabricator, 256
facing
reality, 14, 19, 310, 530
fact, evaluation of, 2
failures
death and, 54, 554
faith healing, 231
family of aberrees, 188
Farragut, 377
fate, 208
favorable evaluation phrases, 355
fear, 147, 151-153, 161
Dark and Unknown Fears, 1
delay in case and, 418
paralysis, 151, 179
Febris, 7
feebleminded, 179, 490, 492-493
feeling shut-offs, 426, 435, 480
Felis domesticus, 449
fetishes, 471
fetus, 423
ability to repair damage, 494
high blood pressure and, 356
physical aspects and, 359
records in womb, 175
recovery qualities of, 178
file clerk, 265, 273-276
auditor and, 266, 297, 301, 347
bank monitor, 265
basic personality and, 273, 524
definition, 265
drawing, 271
emotion and, 429
"I" and, 275
late incident and, 298
Laws of Returning, 302
working with, 276
finger snap, 270
finite universe, 27
first aid
Dianetics, 495-496
fish, 87
example of reactive mind's processes, 85-86
flash answer, 376, 396-398
definition, 397
flee, 200, 236
flippancy, 432
fluid flow, 133
force
forced groups, 188

forced individual, 188
rule by, 186
foreign language case, 419
forgetter mechanism, 268, 361
hypnotist and, 511
see also **command phrase**
forgetting, 338-339
fourth-day sag, 519
Franklin, Benjamin, 306
friend-enemy, 474-475, 477
function
structure and, 95, 129, 389
word causing physical function to change, 127
Fundamental Axioms of Dianetics, 553-556
funeral
occlusion or recollection of, 338
fuse system, 72
future
analyzer and, 149

G

Galen, 173
gallbladder trouble, 257
galvanometer, 389
"garbage," 256-257
Gay Nineties, 245
genetic insanity
definition, 181
Genghis Khan, 315
geometric progression, 34
inverse, 131
germ, 124, 136-137, 181
theory of disease, 124
gerontology
definition, 130
"getting rid of it," 132
glands, 129, 330
glasses, 16
"Go ahead," 295
goal of life, 28
goal of Man, 27-42
goal of survival, 53, 553
Golden Age, 542
golden rule, 158
Goldi medicine man, 7
good
greatest, 49
Man is, 25
Goston, Uncle, 478-479
government, 186
gradations, 448
Grand Coulee Dam, 311
Great Charlatan, 321, 344, 451
greatest good, 49
Great Healer, 344
time and, 321
Greece, 186, 339
Golden Age of, 7, 9
grind, 387
grizzly, 151
group
Dynamic Three, iii, 47
potential value, 56, 556
survival of, 46
Group Dynamic, 47, 50, 52
grouper, 285, 437
definition, 284, 551
description, 444
don't use on preclear, 372
examples, 444
time track and, 284, 302
growth
derangement of physical, 133

guilt complex, 363, 379
gun
"didn't know it was loaded," 39, 42, 153

H

habit
definition, 55, 555
Hamlet, 245
happiness, 33
definition, 42, 54, 555
Tone 4 engram, 158
Harvey, William, v, x, 173
headache
birth and, 388
migraine, *see* **migraine headaches**
healing
mental, 221
three levels of, 237
health
energy freed from the engram bank, 317
hearing, 15-16, 172, 252-256
extended, *see* **extended hearing**
see also **sonic (sound)**
heart, 128-129
heartbeat, 64
heels
little men hanging by their, 389-390
held-down 7, 24, 187
adding machine, 308
example, 454
Hindu
trinity, 466
writings, 535
Hippocrates, 339
holder
action of time track and, 302
canceller and, 268
definition, 443, 551
description, 284, 285
examples, 351, 392, 443
Repeater Technique and, 287
use on preclear, 372
words contained in, 437
homonymic
definition, 82
homosexuality, 140
hormones, 130
hostility, 33
Hume, 114
hyoscine, 482
hyper-hearing
definition, 254
hyper-sight
definition, 254
hyper-sonic, 253
hyper-visio, 253
hypnoanalysis, 166, 275
locks and, 406
hypnosis
aberration and, 89
auditor and, 224
dangerous, 77
definition, 128
description, 511
Dianetics and, 269, 343
drug, *see* **drug hypnotism**
experiment, 128
forgetting and, 339
key-in of engrams and, 195
laboratory tool, 75
manic formed during, 157
plants by positive suggestion, 89

reactive mind and, 83
revivification and, 18
semblances of insanity and, 77
sleep and, 101, 166
"touch my tie" example, 74-75, 78, 84, 86, 471
unwarranted in Dianetics, 488
used for research, then abandoned, 269
wild variable, 75, 77
hypnotic drugs
poisons, 168
hypnotics, 482, 483
hypnotic trance, 74, 268
hypochondriac, 77, 138, 364
hypo-hearing
definition, 253
hypo-sight
definition, 253
hypo-visio
test, 255
"hysterical" blindness, 252-253
definition, 252
"hysterical" deafness, 253
definition, 252

I

"I", 60, 119, 128, 483
definition, viii
demon circuits and, 118
iatrogenic, 10, 230, 490
alterations, 491
insanity, 230
psychoses, 259, 509
work, 226
ice pick, 8, 157, 204
identification, 83
identity(ies), 451
associative restimulators and identity-thought, 471
confusion, 446
narrowing of differences and, 449
reactive mind computes in, 55, 278, 447, 555
thought, 83-84, 278
Junior case and, 279, 407
identity-thought, 86, 407
Absolute of, 466
ally and, 473
associative restimulators, 471
time differentiation and, 451
idiosyncrasy, 23
illness
breaking dramatizations and, 110
childhood illness, 136, 178, 210
delay between restimulation and, 505
delirium of, 79
depression of the dynamic level, 137
kinds of, 124
precipitated by, 136
survival value and, 467
imagery recall, 19
imaginary recall, 369
imagination, 21, 251
Clear and, 22-23
creative, 21-22, 68, 311
definition, 21
diagnosis and, 251-252
function of, 149
use of in therapy, 464

immoral pleasures, equation of, 36
immortality, 53, 553
attractive force, 30
survival and, 51
importances, 452
computing of the relative, 452-460
Laws of the Selection of Importances, 113
India, 339
Indian rope trick, 114
individual
location on survival spectrum, 149
optimum, 13
potential value, 56, 556
scope of, 32
self-determined, 187
worth of, 56, 556
Individual Dianetics, i
infinite survival, 28
inherited disabilities, 126
injury
pain of, 79
prenatal injuries, 212
silence and, 157, 214-216
insanity
chronic, 102
confusion and, 544
court of law and, 102
definition, 37, 455
genetic insanity, 181
guilt and, 540
organic, 259
definition, 230
semblance of, 77
temporary, 102
treatment of, 8
"unconsciousness" and, 73
Institutional Dianetics, 230, 509
insulin shock, 491
intelligence, 54, 554
aberrated person and, 41
cellular, 96
Clear and, 13
inhibited by engrams, 54, 554
see also **IQ**
interest
in engrams, 416
Tone Scale, 34
Introduction of an Arbitrary, 113, 540
introversion, 514, 526
inversion
definition, 310
IQ, 121, 228, 259, 272
irrationality, 23, 138, 505
definition, 23
sources of irrational conduct, 68

J

Jimmie the Cob, 199
Judiciary Dianetics, 537-540
Junior case, 279, 407, 438, 457
description, 407
see also **case; valence**
jurisprudence, 537-540
justified thought, 106, 243
definition, 348

K

key-in, 89, 191-203
delay in action, 505
description, 191-192

example, 192, 354
hook-up of engram, 105
low analytical level, 192
mechanics of, 100
moments of loss and, 341
of an engram, 406
preventing, 210-211
primary lock, 406
key-out, 203, 312, 468
physical treatment and, 204
kicked, *see* **woman knocked out and kicked**
kind
Auditor's Code, 238
kinesthesia
definition, 62
kinesthetic (weight and motion), 21
Kinsey Report, 279, 529
kleptomaniac, 283
Knowable and Unknowable, 113-114
knowledge
line of demarcation, 27
three degrees of, 333
Korzybski, 83
Kraepelin, 506
Krafft-Ebing, 140

L

language, vi, 91
engramic thinking, examples of, 281
engrams and, 82
foreign language case, 419
in engrams, 142, 302
in this book, 3
potential madness and, 91
word combinations and aberrations, 242
x factor, 104
laughter, 162, 432
description, 162
relief of painful emotion, 163
law
reactive engram bank and, 121
sanity and, 102
law of affinity, 113, 128, 325
auditor and patient, 235
break of, 201
description, 143-144
file clerk and, 266
love and, 410
more powerful than fear, 83
violation of, 186
law of cohesion, 143
laws of returning, 301
Laws of the Selection of Importances, 113
legislation, 225
lesbianism, 140
Leucippus, 40
lie factory, 256, 257, 402, 424, 462
definition, 256
detection, 530
right way to handle, 528
life, 28
cyclic aspect of, 29
goal of, 28
group effort, 39
spectrum of, 30
life force, 305-317
ally computation and, 324
emotion, 147-148
engrams disperse, 54, 554

largest drain upon, 329
losses and, 160
manic and, 313-316
painful emotion and, 332
Plan B and, 537
theory of, 306, 317
therapy and, 161, 311
theta quantity, 160
units, 313
life forms, 28, 39
life-function regulator, 64, 105
definition, 64
engram and, 131
literalness
reactive mind and, 121
lock, 90, 119, 405-406
alleviation of, 430
definition, 119, 144, 166, 405
engram lock chain, 104
example, 192
hundreds for one engram, 193
hypnoanalysis and, 166
key-in and, 406
locating, 431
primary lock, 406
vanish down into the reactive bank, 193
Locke, 114
logic, 324, 448-449
reactive mind and, 466
two-valued, 324
Lorentz-FitzGerald-Einstein equations, 3
loss, 159, 335-337, 339-346, 364-365, 367-368
description of running, 345
find moment of, 371
of the ally, 332
loss engram, 160, 359
exhausting emotional discharge from, 347
love, 410-414
"biological love," 211
children and, 142, 470
propitiation and, 409
see also **affinity**
Lucretius, 38, 535
Lysol, 140

M

magic healing crystal, 7
Man
affinity with, 44, 143
animal kingdom and, xiii
basic nature of, 11
behavior of, 46, 48
evil portion of, 198
goal of, 27
good, x
incapable of error, 23
inherent stability of, 190
is good, 25
life force, animal and, 310
only detachable portion, 25
primary fight, 544
self-determined organism, 41-42
tomorrow's generation, 217
see also **Dynamic Four**
manic, 157, 313-316
basic purpose, 315
Cleared, 317
definition, 313

euphoria and, 313, 520
examples, 315, 318-319, 357
installed in hypnotism, 77
old schools of mental healing and, 314
sagged back, 520
manic-depressive, 157, 169
Manichaeus, 141
cult of, 141
Mankind
basic nature, iv
Dynamic Four, iii, 47, 52-53, 553
survival of, 46
Mankind Dynamic, 49, 141
see also **Mankind**
mannerism, 471, 473, 475-476
Clear and, 477
marriage
clearing its partners, 413
contagion of aberration in, 183
propitiation in, 409
reactive mind partnership and, 411
see also **Dynamic Two**
masochism, 356
mathematician, 9
mathematics, 449-450
Maxwell, James Clerk, 95, 306
Mazda and Ahriman, 466
mechanical aids, 307
Medical Dianetics, 207
medicine
life force and, 148
medicine man, 9, 115
melancholy, 162
memory
definition, 81, 551
deranged by electric shock, 425
engrams and, 80, 275, 378
index system, 264
spectrum of, 263
memory banks, 24
electric shock and, 491
"men hanging by their heels," 389-390
mental alterations, 491
organic, 489
sources of, 489-491
mental anguish, 119
mental conditioning, 73
mental curve, sag in, 33
mental healing, 221
mental illness
ancient treatments for, 7
inorganic and organic, 191, 259
mental voices, 117
Mesmer, Anton, 339
metaphysics, 27, 114
migraine headaches, 125, 299, 357
mimicry, 474
mind
abilities and activities, 24
basic purposes of, 25
can return, 19
command post of operation, 68
extremely tough organism, 516
fine piece of equipment, description, 349

full power of, 65
function of, 54, 447, 554
knows how the mind operates, 240, 525
most important activity, 23
protection, 221-226
records continuously, 73
science of, *see* **science of mind**
self-protecting mechanism, 221
three major divisions, 59
time, 300
"unconsciousness" and, 71-72
"mind's eye," 20
minus emotions, 147
misdirector, 285, 393, 437
definition, 285, 551
examples, 445
time track and, 302
Moloch, 454
monitor
description, 59
monologuing, 212, 277, 428
morning sickness, 212-213, 401
moronic "thinking," 104
morphine, 483
mother
Preventive Dianetics, 211-218
motor controls
reactive mind and, vi
motor strip, 389
see also **somatic strip**
motto, 382
multivalence, 108, 169, 363
"Must believe," 456-460
case, 456
from ally or antagonist, 466
myelin sheathing, xi, 172
myopia, 120
mysticism, 27, 114

N

Napoleon, 49
narcosynthesis, 158, 166-167, 275, 510
description, 166
Nation, Carrie, 245
natural selection, 137
Nature, x, 173
necessity, 40-42, 137
necessity level, 149-151, 312, 468
low-dynamic individual and, 468
neglect, 200, 236
of engrams, 417
nervous system, 131
electrical theory of, 72
neurons, 93
neuroses, 70
clearing and, 13
example of, 76
Institutional Dianetics and, 230
organic, 489
reactive mind and, 69
working a neurotic case, 375
neurotic, 91, 241, 318
positive suggestions, 88
Newton, 9
nightmares, 1
B_1 and, 485
Nineveh, 190
Nirvana, 129
nitrous oxide, 154, 483, 486
nomenclature, 29

non-germ theory of disease, 12
Dianetics and, 124
non-sonic recall, 369
norm, 91, 228-229
around Tone 2.8, 34
definition, 228
Release versus, 522
North Africa, 311-312
Nullification by Comparison of Authority to Authority, 113
nymphomaniac, 364

O

occlusion, 155, 408
ally or pseudo-ally, 338
occluded emotion, 381
occluded person, definition, 338
occlusion demons, 118
olfactory (smell), 19, 21
operation
anesthetics used in, 182, 496
contagion of aberration in, 182
silence and, 157
surgical
should be run as engrams, 492
sources of mental alteration, 490
opium, 482, 486
optimum individual, 13
optimum solution, 48-49, 52, 413
see also **Equation of the Optimum Solution**
organic
derangement, 492-494
functions, engram and, 135
insanity
definition, 230
internal sensations, 21
mental alterations, 489-491
sensation, *see* **organic sensation**
organic restimulator, 134
organic sensation, 14
definition, 98
pregnancy and, 213
organism, 35
analytical mind and, 65
cells and, 93
complexity, stimulus-response and, 41
dramatizing an engram, 108
four ways it can be reduced, 126
in presence of physical pain, 96
social and individual, 541
organs, 135
orthopedics, 124
over-perception, 253

P

pain, vii
analytical mind and, 72, 97
analyzer knocked out, 96
cells and, 96
death and, 30
description, 32, 54, 554
difference between standard banks and reactive engram banks, 81
engram contains, 90, 138

engramic commands
and, 461
"imaginary," 464
necessity of avoiding, 42
organism and, 35
pain-drive theory, 40, 44, 196
physical pain and painful
emotion commands,
461-464
pleasure and, 35-36
pretended, 464
reaction to sources of, 197
reactive mind and, 55, 555
repelling force, 32
shut-off, 370, 372, 426, 480
wriggles and twists when
asked to approach, 480
pain-drive theory, 40, 44, 196
painful emotion, vii, 71
description of running an
engram, 345
difference between
standard banks and
reactive engram
banks, 81
engram bank severely
distorted by, 347
engramic commands
and, 461
exteriorized views and,
344, 426
laughter and, 163
prenatal and later-life, 341
start late and work back
early, 348
surface manifestation of the
physical pain engrams, 465
two hours or ten years
ago, 431
painful emotion engram, 83,
365-368, 431-434
alternate as necessary, 347
case history, 500
auditing goal and, 375
case stalling and, 418
definition, 83
emotional charge and, 480
examples, 365
losses and, 368
opening case and, 370
single word technique, 438
palsy, 179
paralysis, fear, 151, 179
paralytic stroke, 490
paranoid-schizophrenic, 76
parasitic circuit, 116
see also **circuit**
parathyroid, 129
parcheesi, 283
parent
animosity toward, 408
contagion of aberration
and, 182
data from, 523
see also **child**
paresis, 260, 490
past
what patient knows
about, 194
Pasteur, x, 124
past tense
patient talking in, 379
pathology, 124, 137
effects of disease, 136-137
three stages of, 124
patient, 235
Auditor's Code, 239
cannot see his own
aberrations, 235

classes of, 507
cooperative effort between auditor and, 235
external problems with, 514-516
low-dynamic, 493
offhand and flippant, tone level of, 432
opposition by, 247
preclear and, 251
shut-offs exist, 465
somatic strip and, 390
will hold to pro-survival engram, 323
see also **preclear**

patient-ejector, 284
see also **bouncer**

patient-holder, 284
see also **holder**

patient-misdirector, 285
see also **misdirector**

Pavlov, 193

Penates, 7

penicillin, 181

percept
filed as a concept, 61
listing of, 62

perceptic
definition, 551

perception, 14-17
definition, 14
diagnosis and, 251
engram contains all percepts, 98
equals every other, in engram, 84
extrasensory, 423
occluded in recall, 119
sonic, differences of, 15

perpetuation, 133
definition, 124

persistent
Auditor's Code, 239

personality, 16, 108, 167
see also **basic personality**

perversion, 140-142

phenobarbital, 482, 486

phonograph, xii, 80, 104, 139

photosynthesis, 216, 544

phrases, 277
classes of, 442-446
favorable evaluation, 355
file clerk and, 276
Repeater Technique and, 287
repetition of, 286

physical curve, sag in, 33

physical pain and painful emotion commands, 461-464

physical pain engrams
alternate with painful emotion, 500
auditing goal and, 375
emotional charge and, 375
see also **engram**

physical treatment, 204

pituitrin, 129

Plan A, 537

Plan B, 537

Plan C, 537

pleasure, 30, 32, 35-37, 42-43, 53, 144, 554
attracting force, 30
definition, 32
description, 43
life force, 317
pain and, 32

plot, 528, 531

plus emotions, 147
pneumonia, 359
Political Dianetics, 227, 541
description, 207
"Poor little __," 371
positive suggestion, 127, 129, 168
auditor and, 250
denyer and, 339
endocrine system and, 130
engram and, 81
heart and blood flow, 128
hypnosis and, 74
insanity and, 78
justified thought and, 106
neurotic, 88
never install, 512
prevention of, 268
valence shift and, 400
post-hypnotic suggestion, 74-75, 85
postnatal
versus prenatal, 211
potential value
individual or group, 56, 556
Powerful Unknown, viii
power of choice, 103
aberree and, 103
child, engrams and, 182
reactive mind exercises a, 142
which engram used, 120
precipitation
definition, 124
preclear
auditor and, equations, 487
contacting engram, 285
criticize, correct or otherwise judge the, 527
definition, 236, 551
emotional upset in patient's life current with therapy, 480
exteriorized views and, 344
indicators and manifestations
ally computation, 336
ashamed of his past, 418
laughter, 162
introversion of, 514
never attack the, 488
optimum, 256
patient and, 251
private life of, 532
relative of auditor, 377
reluctance, 322
responsibility of, 515
see also **patient**
predictability
Clear versus aberree, 103
predisposition, 87, 124, 133
definition, 124
prefrontal lobotomy, 132, 259, 490
pregnancy, 212
coitus during, 196, 214-215, 278
prenatal, xi
ally computations and, 328
conditions in the womb, 428
describing scenery, 423
non-engramic recordings, 172
prenatal engram
Clear and acceptance of, 174
different from prenatal memory, 175
ESP and, 423-424
examples of verbal contents, 245

more serious than
postnatal, 211
running of
example, 247-249
prenatal experience, 165-178
past schools and, 175
prenatal injuries, 212
prerelease
definition, 236-237, 551
present tense
patient talking in, 379
present time, 395-396
bouncer and, 285
definition, 395
misdirector and, 446
stuck in present time, 371, 380-382, 393
test of preclear being in, 396
Preventive Dianetics, 207-217, 496
children, 210
description, 208
on the individual scale, 209
on the social scale, 209
women and, 217
priesthood, 186
primary engram, 169
primitivc
societies, 8, 183
tribe, 7
principle of the spectrum, 97
prize case in difficulty, 457
prompting, 385
propitiation, 409-411
pro-survival background, 145
pro-survival engram, 83
ally computation and, 328
become chronic, 142
definition, 83, 320, 354
description, 320
examples, 354, 359
insidious aspects of, 329
patient will hold to, 323
pseudo-survival, 319
see also **engram**
protoplasm, 80
pseudo-ally, 327, 473
definition, 337
occlusion and, 338
psychiatrist, 204
psychiatry, 225, 503
classification and diagnosis, 241
psychoanalysis, i, 225, 229, 373, 521
psychology, 225, 226, 308
psychoses
Clear and, 13
iatrogenic, 259, 509
not organic, 489
organic, 489
produced by hypnosis, 76
reactive mind and, 69
psychosomatic
definition, 125, 551
psychosomatic ill(ness), vii, 123-143, 474
aberration and, 139
alleviation of, 174
autogenetic illness, 124
cataloging of, 242
caused by engrams, 55, 555
chronic, 142, 159, 321
source, 467
classification, 246

Clear and, ix, 227
clearing and, 13
definition, 123-124
deletion of tissue treatment, 132
Dianetics and, i
drug preparations, 131
dynamics and, iv
extent of, 246
five classes of, 133
fluid flow and, 133
former injury, 258
hidden source, iv
holding to, 323
key-in, 177
"precious possession," 145
pro-survival background, 142
reactive mind and, 69
Release and, ix
70 percent of Man's ailments, 10
source of, 55, 91, 191, 555
sympathy background, 142

psychotherapy
single advance of, 8

psychotic, 507

punishment, 196-201
children, 188
contagion of aberration and, 185
does no good, 196
society and, 107, 185
succumbing and, 200

puns, 278, 398

purpose
basic, 315, 320

push-button, 100, 308, 472
factor, 308

PV = ID^x, 56, 556

pyramid, 274

Q

Q quantity, 484-485

quiet
Auditor's Code, 238

quinine, 428, 487

R

race
great as self-determined, 187

Ralph, 279

rape, 195

rapport
between auditor and preclear, 414

rationality, 23, 449
Dianetics and, 11
Equation of the Optimum Solution and, 49
fundamental test, 538
in Cleared person, 23
irrationality and, 505
sanity and, 66
self-determinism and, 187
test of, 451
what rational computation depends upon, 455

rationalization, 348
action, conduct or conditions and, 348

reaction
toward a source of danger, 199

reactive bank, *see* **reactive mind**

reactive engram circuits, 271

reactive mind, v, 59, 67-88
A=A=A, 84, 244

analytical mind and, 177
bank, periods of "unconsciousness," 79
cells and, xi, 96, 173
combined cellular intelligence, 96
composed of engrams, 83
computes in identities, 447
definition, 55, 551, 555
description, v
discussion of the, 243
example of
apples and worms, 83
fish, 85
file clerk and, 265, 302
five courses in handling data, 198-200
habit and, 55, 555
identification, 83
identities, 55, 278, 555
impinges engrams upon the analytical mind and the organism, 191
literalness of, 121
moronic "thinking," 104
possessed by everyone, 69
power of choice and, 142
punishment feeds, 199
rugged, very, 80
Simple Simon, 155, 244, 474
social organism has its, 541
source of psychosomatic ills, 191
survival and, 467
two-valued logic, 324
works in absolutes, 466
Zones and, 148
see also **engram bank**

reactive thought, 106

reality
facing, 14, 19, 310, 530
importance to auditor, 523
Man and, 311
perception and, 14, 19

reason, 538-539
national problems and, 543

rebalancing
a case, 519
definition, 395

recall, 251, 254
ability, variations in, 17, 20-21
basic personality and, 167
classes of, 507
diagnosis and, 251
Dianetic names for, 21
imagination and, 251
kinesthetic (motion and weight), 21
olfactory (smell), 19, 21
optimum, 20
organic, 21
perception occluded in, 119
potentiality of, 63
Release and, 494
rhythmic, 21
shut-off of, 493
low-dynamic patient and, 493
somatic (pain), 21
sonic (sound), 21
standard banks and, 63
tactile (touch), 21
testing, 21, 255
thermal (temperature), 21
three case classifications, 369
visio (sight), 21

recession, 290, 387
file clerk and, 298
reducing to, 386
recording(s), xii
cellular level, xi
cellular trace of, 173
of the lifetime are available, 73
reduce, 370
definition, 384, 552
when any phrase or word in an engram will not reduce, 437
reduction, 376, 384, 386-388
erasure and, 384
example, 385
Tone Scale and, 386, 431
re-experience, 18-19
refiling, vii-ix, 134, 233, 235, 333, 348, 383
arthritis and, 134
everything locked onto engram, 193
regression, 18, 262
definition, 18
description, 18
relative importances, 452
relatives
data from, 522
Release, ix, 227-231, 349, 533
at least as well as "normal," 350
brought about by, 337
definition, i, 227, 416, 552
sonic and visio recall, 494
value of, 228
reliving, 18, 263, 507
reluctance, 322
remember, 371, 479, 531
everything that happens, 267
returning and, 261
ways to, 20
Renaissance, 37
Repeater Technique, 285, 303, 361, 371, 392
addressed only to action not to aberration, 292
auditor's cleverness and, 290-292
case history, 292-297
definition, 511
demonstration of, 288-290, 295-297
description, 286-287
handling shut-offs with, 380
if the patient does not work well on, 434
present time and, 395
routine and, 335
shut-offs and, 427
single word technique, 435-436
use of, 508
when used, 285
examples, 279-282
replay, 374
definition, 374
repressions, 76, 139
Clear and, 13
reactive mind and, 69
resentment, 33
resilience
blocked dynamics and, 201
resistance, 481
to disease, 136

resolution
of unsolved problems, 32
responsibility, 515
restimulation, 516-519
affinity and, 87
analytical power and, 99
artificial, 319
auditor asking for engram, 407
canceller and, 268
childhood illness and, 136
chronic, 100, 301, 313
dramatization and, 107
escaping of, 183
example and description, 87
greater or lesser, 99
illness and, 505
marriage and, 411
mechanism of, 472
mutually restimulative, definition, 517
of auditor, 390
pain, restimulative word, 138
problem in a restimulated case, 501 504
restimulator lag, definition, 505
restimulator
associative, 322, 471
see also **associative restimulator**
child lives with, 189
definition, 98-99
examples of, 88, 98-99, 189
handled by environmental change, 202
matter of chance and, 103
organic, 134
restimulator lag
definition, 505
returning, vii, 261
advantage, 20
data, 171
definition, 18-19, 261, 263, 303
exteriorized views and, 343-344
file clerk and, 265
full performance of imagery recall, 19
indoctrinating patient into, 380
laws of, 301
remembering and, 261, 371
send a portion of the mind, 18
test for ability to, 19
"Return over it," 295
Return Technique, 511
reverie, viii, 222-223
auditor present, 489
basic processes, 271
deeper than you wish, 372
description, 267
example, 270
reveals where preclear is stuck on track, 396
routine to bring about, 267
scouting for material when preclear is in, 334
serves to fix attention on self and auditor, 369
three things we use, 266
use of, on lock, 496
reversal, 336, 367
revivification, 18
definition, 18
rhythmic, 21
right, 537

Index

Rohmer, Sax, 141
Rome, 7, 36, 186, 339
Ross, Ronald, 208
malaria germ, 291
Rousseau, Jean Jacques, 46, 311
routine, 267, 334-336
rehearsal, 270
rule by force, 186
Russia, 186

S

sadism, 140, 356
sag
in a case, 519
physical and mental curves, 33
psychosomatic illness and, 468
sanity
break engram and, 195
bridge between insanity and, 170
definition, 450
law and, 102
rationality and, 66
remembering and, 479
see also **rationality**
schizophrenic, 76
definition, 169
narcosynthesis and, 166
time track and, 274, 446, 508
scholastic, 25
Schopenhauer, 144
science
application of, 233
science of mind, i, 7-11
composed of, 10
Dianetics and, 11
history of Dianetics, 536
legislation and, 225
Science of Organizing Sciences, 113
scientific truth, ii, 27
scope
of the individual, 32
of the species, 32
Second Dynamic, 141
see also **Dynamic Two**
secrecy, 419-420, 481, 530
sedatives, 482
self
Dynamic One, 47
survival in terms of, 45
self-determinism, 41-42, 186, 308, 477
child is entitled to, 189
Clear and, 25
Man and, 41
of individuals, 186
of the society, 186
selfishness, 48, 49
self-sacrifice, 49
senses, 127, 254
sensory strip, 389
see also **somatic strip**
sentience, 23, 41
session
basic-basic and, 275
see also **ten steps**
7, held-down, 24-25
sex, iii, 46, 141, 194
Dynamic Two, 47
pain and, 356
sexual perversion, 140-142
society and, 178

Sex Dynamic, 47, 52
Shakespeare, 173
shaman, 7-9
demons and, 115
shame, 379
shock, 97, 491
accident, shock of, 79
electric, *see* **electric shock**
shutdown
analytical, 97-101
of analytical mind, 195, 430
shut-off, 462
analyzer shut-off, 383
case with, 257
definition, 462
emotion shut-off, 300, 426, 462
feeling, 426, 435
handling with Repeater Technique, 380
indicators of, 462, 465
occlusion demon and, 118
pain shut-off, 370, 372, 426, 480
recall shut-off, 493
low-dynamic patient and, 493
somatic shut-off, 461
somatic strip and, 426
sonic shut-off, 293, 415
examples, 280
sight, 16, 127, 251
extended sight, 252
see also **visio (sight)**
silence, 157, 214, 216
in the presence of injury, 217
similarities, 449, 451
Simple Simon, 155, 244, 474
reactive mind, 155, 244
simplicity, 3
single word repeaters, 437
single word technique, 435-439
case history, 438
sinusitis, 69, 125, 364
birth and, 246
sleep
analyzer shut-down, 101
boil-off and, 285, 404
experience occurring during, 97
hypnotism and, 101, 269
smell (olfactory), 14, 19
snap fingers, 270
Social Dianetics, 207
society, 183, 185
break point, 542
Clears and, 187
contagion of aberration in, 183, 185
deleting causes of aberration, 209
ideal society, 538
pleasure and, 36
Political Dianetics, 227, 541
primitive, 183
punishment complex and, 107
self-determinism of, 186
sex and, 178
woman and, 217
Socrates, 69
sodium pentothal, 166

soldered-in, 105
definition, 105
thorough restimulation and, 107
solution
Equation of the Optimum, *see* **Equation of the Optimum Solution**
greatest good, 49
somatic, 21, 138
anesthetics and, 482
boil-off and, 426, 461
clue to the presence of any, 461
definition, 251, 552
file clerk and, 276
"highest intensity" of, 299
reduction of, 385
types of, 403
validity of engram and, 529
somatic location, 303
somatic mind, 59
definition, 55, 555
somatic strip, 389-395
description, 390
emotional charges and, 435
good and bad conductors of, 394
handling of, 371, 389
Repeater Technique and, 392
shut-offs and, 426
sonic (sound), 15, 21, 253
definition, 251, 552
erasure and, 415
recall, 369, 507
Release and, 494
shut-off, 293, 415
examples, 280
soul, 68, 95
sound, 251
space, 28-29
species
scope of, 32
spectrum, 262, 448
definition, 263
of memory, 263
principle of, 97
Spencer, Herbert, 9, 113, 535
sperm dream, 395
split personality, 108
stability
inherent, 190
stammerers, 217
standard (memory) banks, viii, 61-63
are perfect, 63
auditing goal and, 375
basic personality and, 167
content of, 61, 275
definition, 61, 552
difference between reactive engram banks and, 81
drawing, 271
file clerk monitors, 265
filing system described, 61
potentiality of recall, 63
refiled in, ix
stimulants, 484
stimulus-response, v, 41
complexity of organism and, 41
training pattern, 105
stopping therapy, 524
stream of consciousness, 117
stress, 182, 191, 193, 227, 233, 518
stroke, paralytic, 490

structure, 60
alteration of, 490
body structure and pro-survival engram, 330
Dianetics and, 93
function and, 94-95, 389
theory, 94
strychnine, 485
stuck in present time, 371, 380-382, 393
stuck on the track, 396
stupidity computation, 481
sub-mind, v
successes, 54, 554
succumb, 200, 236
suck down, 371, 393
suggestion, 74-87
auditor and, 250, 512
example of, 74
hearing, sight, tactile tuned down or up, 127
kinds of aberration and, 76-78
post-hypnotic, 74-75, 85
sympathy engram and, 85
"take" or not, 75
see also **positive suggestion**
suicide, 143
sulfa, 181
superstition, 186, 542
suppression
emotions and, 148
suppressor, 51, 149-152, 321
dams up emotions in engram, 159
definition, 552
Descriptic Graph of Survival, 37
engram type, 321
germ acts as, 137
occlusion and, 408
overloaded by life form, 39
survival suppressor, 31, 37
survival zones and, 51
suppressor-type engram, 321
example, 321
surgery, 124, 132, 204, 221, 490, 495
surrender engram, 133
survival, 51
aberrated conduct and, 53
absolute goal of, 53, 553
ally and, 473
conduct pattern, 49, 52, 68, 82, 238
depends on right answers, 187
dynamic, *see* **survival dynamic**
Dynamic Principle of Existence, 28, 51
dynamics and, 45-47
entire dynamic urge, ii
illness and, 467
loss of imagined survival factors, 317
Man in affinity with Man, 44, 143
methods of, 29
mind and, 117
none survive alone, 40
only dynamic of a life form, 29
optimum, 49
pleasure and, 30
potential, 54, 317, 554
primary technology of, 38
reward of, 53, 554

survival suppressor, 37
tooth and claw, 108
see also **SURVIVE!**
survival conduct pattern, 49, 52, 68, 82, 238
survival dynamic, 31, 35-38, 42, 51
embracing species and symbiotes, 48
emotions and, 147
four dynamics, subdivisions of, 52
four factors, 46
individual and, 149
lowering of, 36
suppressor(s) and, 37, 149, 321, 541
survival necessity, 137
survival scale, 148
see also **Descriptic Graph of Survival**
survival suppressor, 31, 37
see also **suppressor**
SURVIVE!, 47, 114
Dynamic Principle of Existence, 53, 553
dynamics, 262
mandate, 32
single common denominator, 28
spectrum of, 263
see also **survival**
swami, 128
syllogism, 449
symbiote, 47, 53, 553
definition, 47, 552
symbiotic, 39
sympathy, 237
auditor and, 345
chronic psychosomatic illness and, 238
ESP and, 424
sympathy background, 142
sympathy engram, 143-144
basic pattern of, 321
buried, 361
chronic psychosomatic illness and, 467-468, 470
description, 144
dramatization, 145, 159, 474
effects of, 329
examples, 145, 322, 359-364, 478
illness and, 143, 145
post-hypnotic suggestion and, 85
pretends to be pro-survival, 144
psychosomatics and, 246
reluctance of preclear and, 322
synopsis
Dianetics, i
syphilis, 509

T

tacit consent
definition and description, 425
example, 497
tactile (touch), 14, 21, 127
talisman, 471
target, 234-235
technique
Repeater Technique, 435
single word technique, 435-440

steps of, 334-336
types of, 303
telepathy, 427
ten steps, 271
routine, 334-336
terminology, 29
Terra Incognita, 1-2
terror, 148, 151
test
aberration, 451
ally, 465
Clear, 13
engram, 529
hypo-visio, 255
present time, preclear and, 371, 396
rationality, 451
recall, 21, 255
for dub-in, 255
testosterone, 129
theory on structure, 94
therapy, 272
briefly stated, vii
description, viii
entire outline of, 270
every two or three days, 484
fundamental axiom of, 169
future of, 545 548
goal of, iv, 13
intent and act of, 333
keep asking for engram, 293
motto, keep asking for it, 382
mutual, 496-500
process of thinking, 247
purpose of, 233, 268
routine, 267, 270, 334-336
starting, 222
stopping, 524-526
task of, 332
time in therapy, 319, 519-522
estimation of, 231, 521
Tone Scale and, 433
valid methods of, 202-203
thermal (temperature), 21
θ (theta), 147, 160
think, thinking, thought, vi
analytical thought, 106
imagination and, 21
justified, 106, 348
reactive mind's moronic "thinking," 104
reactive thought, 106
three kinds of thought, 106
thorough
Auditor's Code, 239
thought stream, 61
three days, 506, 520
thyroid, 129, 330
time, 321, 379
analytical mind's time sense, 71
conscious versus reactive levels, 176
Equation of the Optimum Solution and, 48
file clerk and, 276
Great Charlatan, 341, 451
handling preclear in time, 300
in therapy, 319, 519-522
estimation of, 231, 521
time shift, 300, 303
time track, 204, 264-265, 271-272, 276
aberrated ideas of, 273
action of the preclear on, 302
condition of, 271, 302
definition, viii, 264, 273, 552

derailer and, 446
grouper and, 284
late end of, 395
moving on, 462
occluded areas of, 408
off the track, 427, 508
prenatal, 341
reverie and, 396
somatic strip and, 390
stuck in present time, 371, 380-382, 393
stuck on the track, 395
caution, 441
tissue, deletion of, 132
token, 471-479
ally and, 471, 473, 475-476
definition, 471, 473, 475
examples, 475
psychosomatic illness, 474
tone
acute, 34
amount of analytical shutdown, 98
cycle of, 150, 151
emotional tone of birth, 184
engrams and, 159, 337
example, man and bear, 151
general, 34
patient in Tone 2 area, 433
personal, extra-valence or dramatized, 158
reactive mind and, 148
Tone 0, 33, 542
Tone 0.2, fear-paralysis, 151
Tone 0.5, apathy, 386
Tone 0.6, terror, 151-152
Tone 0.9, fear, 151
Tone 1, 33, 542
Tone 1.5, 33
Tone 1.9, 33
Tone 2, 33
analyzer shuts off, 152
patient in Tone 2 area, 433
society in Tone 2, 542
Tone 2.5, boredom, 152, 386
Tone 2.8, 34
Tone 3, 33
Tone 4, 34, 432, 542
use in diagnosis, 258
war and, 542
zones of, 33
tone-deaf, 69
Tone 4 engram
happiness, 158
Tone Scale, 33
depresses, 154
great loss and, 341
position of the individual, 258
reduction of engrams and, 386, 431-434
social levels, 542
social organism graphed on, 541
therapy and, 433
use in diagnosis, 259
toothache, 204
tooth and claw, 108-109
topectomy, 259, 490
Torquemada, 314
touch, *see* **tactile (touch)**
"touch my tie" example, 74-75, 78, 84, 86, 471
associative restimulator, 471
track, *see* **time track**
training pattern, 65, 105
definition, 55, 555

trance, 268-269, 372, 482, 513-514
deep hypnotic, 483
depth of, 272
effort to spare "I" and, 275
see also **amnesia trance; hypnotic trance**
transference, 269, 526
transorbital leukotomy, 132, 259, 490
triangular work plan, 518
trustworthy
Auditor's Code, 238
truth
Doctrine of the True Datum, 144
scientific, ii, 27
tuberculosis, 125
turn-about clearing, 414
"two little men hanging by their heels," 389-390
two-valued logic
reactive mind and, 324, 466

U

ulcers, 125
case history, 497
example, 325
uncommunicative, 239
Auditor's Code, 239
"unconscious," 62, 71-73
boil-off and, 285, 403, 461
contagion of aberration and, 183
emotions around "unconscious" person, 158
keep mouth shut when one is, 158
loss of ally and, 366
mind, v
periods
exactness of everything found, 89
single source of aberration, 73
time track and, 264
total amnesia, 73
"unconsciousness," vi, ix, 403, 405
block to memory, 505
contagion of aberration and, 182
definition, 55, 556
drug, 196
earlier period of, 169
insanity-producing variety, 79
manifestations of, 403
mechanism of protection, 505
partial, 101
preclear's awareness and, 286
yawning and, 248, 285, 391, 403
see also **"unconscious"**
United States, 186
universe, 9, 27, 47, 52, 544-545
urine, 64, 129

V

valence
ally, 473
caused by engrams, 107
definition, 108
derailer and, 446

Index

dramatization of, 139, 158
exteriorized views and, 343
most frequently employed, 473
multivalence, 108, 169, 363
picking up a, 154
shift, 376, 398, 473
tokens and, 473
winning valence, 109-110, 139, 154, 159
valence shift, 376, 398-400
example, 399
valence wall, 332, 337
vanished
definition, 276
variables, 16
Veda, 38
villain
reactive mind, 64
violin, 15-16
virus, 137, 174
Charles Darwin, 67
visio (sight), 21, 251-252
definition, 251, 552
recall, 494
see also **sight**
visio-bank, 61
vitamin B_1, 485
nightmares and, 485
vivisection, 494

W

war, 9, 186, 542-544
Dianetics and, 544
international Tone 1, 542
no justification for, 543
winning valence, 109, 139, 154, 159
woman knocked out and kicked, 81, 87, 89
analytical computation, 84
dramatization, 107-109
key-in, 89
lock, 90
positive suggestion, 88
reactive mind computation, 84
valences, 108-109
womb, 428
life in, 176
longing for, xii
memories of the, xi
most aberrative stages, 176
return to, 176
"see" outside, 423
women, 216-217
patient with hatred of, 519
Preventive Dianetics and, 217
psychotic women, 196
word
aberrations and, 242
chains, 436
contained in engrams can "push-button" aberree, 472
feel, homonymic word, 462
"I", used in engrams, 120
occlusion demon and, 119
pain, as a word, 138
single word technique, 435
"you," used in engrams, 120
worry
definition, 280, 455

worth
of an individual, 56, 556
wrong, 537

Y

yawning
"unconsciousness" releasing, 248, 285, 391, 403

Z

zombyism, 8
Zones
analytical power and, 98
auditor locating preclear in, 258
description, 33
Zones 0-4, 33, 51
emotion and, 147
level of pain, 88
of the states of being, 33
survival zones, 51
Zone 1, 151
society in, 185
Zone 3, 150
zygote, 32, 175-176, 215

Index

Ready to put Dianetics into action?

EXPERIENCE THE

POWER OF DIANETICS

Enroll in a life-changing seminar at your local Dianetics Center and unlock the ultimate power of Dianetics. Watch exclusive films that teach precise techniques you can apply right away to begin overcoming barriers and making real change. Guided by trained Dianetics specialists, you'll gain tools to:

- Overcome stress, self-doubt and past traumas
- Take a vital step toward becoming Clear
- Start living life with greater confidence and control

No experience needed–just a desire to transform your life. Reserve your seat today.

Attend the

DIANETICS SEMINAR

To find the seminar nearest you visit

dianetics.org/seminar

Heribert Meffert / Christoph Burmann / Martin Koers (Hrsg.)

Markenmanagement

Heribert Meffert / Christoph Burmann /
Martin Koers (Hrsg.)

Marken-management

Identitätsorientierte Markenführung
und praktische Umsetzung

Mit Best Practice-Fallstudien

2., vollständig überarbeitete
und erweiterte Auflage

GABLER

Bibliografische Information Der Deutschen Bibliothek
Die Deutsche Bibliothek verzeichnet diese Publikation in der Deutschen Nationalbibliografie; detaillierte bibliografische Daten sind im Internet über <http://dnb.ddb.de> abrufbar.

Prof. Dr. Dr. h.c. mult. Heribert Meffert Ist Professor der Betriebswirtschaftslehre, insbesondere Marketing, und emeritierter Direktor des Instituts für Marketing am Marketing Centrum der Universität Münster (MCM).
Er ist Vorsitzender des Vorstands der Bertelsmann Stiftung Gütersloh.

Prof. Dr. Christoph Burmann ist Inhaber des Lehrstuhls für innovatives Markenmanagement (LiM) an der Universität Bremen.

Dr. Martin Koers ist Assistent des Vorstandsvorsitzenden der Ford AG, Köln.

1. Auflage März 2002
2. Auflage April 2005

Lektorat: Barbara Roscher / Ute Grünberg

Der Gabler Verlag ist ein Unternehmen von Springer Science+Business Media.
www.gabler.de

Umschlaggestaltung: Regine Zimmer, Dipl.-Designerin, Frankfurt/Main
Satz: FROMM MediaDesign GmbH, Selters/Ts.
Druck und buchbinderische Verarbeitung: LegoPrint, Lavis
Gedruckt auf säurefreiem und chlorfrei gebleichtem Papier
Printed in Italy

ISBN 3-409-21821-1

Vorwort zur 2. Auflage

Trotz großer Erstauflage können wir schon nach gut zwei Jahren eine zweite Auflage drucken. Das freut uns sehr und spornt an für die Arbeit an diesem Buch. So sehr, dass mit der nun vorliegenden zweiten Auflage fast ein ganz neues Buch entstanden ist. Warum? War der erste Wurf so schlecht? Keineswegs. Ganz im Gegenteil.

Die erste Auflage hat zu einem umfassenden Feedback von Managern, Wissenschaftlern und Studenten geführt und uns gezeigt, dass wir mit unserem innovativen, identitätsorientierten Ansatz der Markenführung genau richtig liegen. Hätten wir uns damals entschieden, der unüberschaubaren Vielzahl an Monographien und Readern zur Markenführung lediglich ein Werk hinzuzufügen, welches das Thema mit allseits bekannten Analysen und Konzepten traktiert, wäre die Reaktion aus dem Lesermarkt wohl kaum so umfassend ausgefallen. Fazit: Wer sich differenziert, regt zur Auseinandersetzung an. Das gilt für Marken und für Markenbücher.

Innovationen sind jedoch selten schon beim ersten Entwurf fehlerfrei. Innovationen verlangen beim Käufer in der Regel Veränderungen beim Kauf- und Nutzungsverhalten, führen zu intensiven Interaktionen zwischen Erstkäufern und Anbieter, zu umfassendem Lernen voneinander und letztlich zur Optimierung der Innovation. So verstehen wir auch den Prozess von der Erst- zur Zweitauflage dieses Buches. Was haben wir dabei optimiert, ergänzt und vertieft?

Zunächst haben wir das theoretische Fundament des identitätsorientierten Ansatzes weiterentwickelt. Das Konstrukt der Markenidentität wird dabei in sechs konstitutive Elemente zerlegt und damit einer Steuerung durch das Markenmanagement besser zugänglich gemacht. Auch deshalb, weil wir einen umfassenden Managementprozess zur identitätsorientierten Führung von Marken neu entwickelt, in der Praxis erprobt und theoretisch verankert haben. Besondere Aufmerksamkeit haben wir in diesem Zusammenhang der innengerichteten Markenführung gewidmet. In einem eigenen Kapitel haben wir hierzu den aktuellen Stand der Forschung zusammengetragen und berichten über erste empirische Ergebnisse eines großen Forschungsprojektes zur innengerichteten Markenführung an der Universität Bremen.

Aufgrund der in den letzten Jahren stark gewachsenen Relevanz von Markenportfolios haben wir das Kapitel zum Management von Markenarchitekturen neu verfasst. Ebenfalls neu hinzugekommen ist ein Kapitel über Markenevolutionsstrategien, um den dynamischen Aspekten der Markenführung in stärkerem Maße als bisher Rechnung zu tragen.

Erheblich erweitert haben wir auch den Bereich des Markencontrollings. Hier befasst sich ein neues Kapitel beispielsweise mit der Analyse und Steuerung der Markenkannibalisierung innerhalb von Markenportfolios. Darüber hinaus wurde der Bereich der Bewertung und Bilanzierung von Marken vertieft und erweitert.

Ferner haben wir ein neues Kapitel über Sponsoring und Event-Management als Instrumente der Markenprofilierung aufgenommen und die Kapitel zur Gestaltung der Markenpersönlichkeit und den Markenausdehnungsstrategien erheblich überarbeitet. Die drei Kapitel zur Führung von Marken in der Politik, bei Städten und bei Regionen wurden durch die Ergebnisse von drei breit angelegten empirischen Studien ergänzt und dadurch erheblich aussagekräftiger gestaltet. Schließlich haben wir im Fallstudienteil des Buches zahlreiche neue Best Practice Cases integriert (zum Beispiel Germanwings, Lufthansa Passage, DHL, Ford Galaxy, Bertelsmann Stiftung) und dafür einige ältere Fälle herausgenommen.

Die Errichtung des ersten Lehrstuhls an einer Universität im deutschsprachigen Raum, der sich ausschließlich dem Markenmanagement widmet und dessen Besetzung durch einen der drei Herausgeber, hat den Innovationsprozess von der ersten zur zweiten Auflage maßgeblich gefördert. Die Studenten der Universität Bremen, die in ihrem Hauptstudium die spezielle Betriebswirtschaftslehre „Innovatives Markenmanagement" als Vertiefungsfach gewählt haben, konnten sich mit zahlreichen Ideen in die Überarbeitung des Buches einbringen. Ebenso die Marketingstudenten an der Universität Münster. Dafür gebührt ihnen unser Dank.

Darüber hinaus konnte das Konzept der identitätsorientierten Markenführung in zahlreichen Forschungstransferprojekten an den Universitäten in Bremen und Münster harten Praxistests unterzogen und dabei weiterentwickelt werden. Nicht zuletzt haben zahlreiche ehemalige und aktuelle Mitarbeiter am Marketing Centrum Münster (MCM) der Universität Münster und am Lehrstuhl für innovatives Markenmanagement (LiM) der Universität Bremen ihr Know-how aus der Arbeit mit dem identitätsorientierten Markenmanagementansatz eingebracht. Damit dies so bleibt, ist ergänzend zu diesem Buch vom Gabler-Verlag und dem Deutschen Universitätsverlag eine Schriftenreihe zum „Innovativen Markenmanagement" aufgelegt worden, in der aktuelle Forschungsergebnisse publiziert werden sollen. Der erste Band zur Steigerung des Customer Equity als einem Oberziel des Markenmanagements ist soeben erschienen.

Besonders freut uns schließlich, dass zahlreiche renommierte Manager aus der Markenführungspraxis großer Unternehmen nicht nur für Diskussionen bereitstanden, sondern selber Fallstudien aus ihren Unternehmen für unser Buch verfasst haben. Wir glauben, dass die Kombination eines in sich geschlossenen, theoretisch fundierten Managementkonzeptes mit „Best-Practice" Fallstudien für den Leser einen wichtigen Mehrwert bietet, den er in dieser Form anderswo nicht erhält. Wir würden uns freuen, lägen wir mit dieser Einschätzung richtig und müssten schon bald die Arbeit an der dritten Auflage starten.

Dieses Buch wäre ohne die umfassende Unterstützung vieler Personen nicht möglich gewesen. Dafür möchten wir uns herzlich bedanken. Besonders hervorzuheben sind hier die Diplom-Kaufleute Lars E. Blinda (M.A.), Axel Nitschke, Philip Maloney (M.A.) und Jan-Philipp Weers vom Lehrstuhl für innovatives Markenmanagement der Universität Bremen sowie Dipl.-Kfm. Sebastian Dettmers vom Institut für Marketing des Marketing Centrums Münster an der Universität Münster. Darüber hinaus möchten wir Frau Barbara Roscher vom Gabler-Verlag herzlich danken, die sich in der seit vielen Jahren bewährten und immer wieder vorbildlichen Art und Weise für unser Werk eingesetzt hat.

Bremen und Münster
im Februar 2005

Prof. Dr. Dr. h.c. mult. Heribert Meffert
Prof. Dr. habil. Christoph Burmann
Dr. Martin Koers

Vorwort zur 1. Auflage

Marken sind seit jeher ein Schlüsselthema der marktorientierten Unternehmensführung. Vielfach ist die Erfolgsgeschichte des Marketing mit der Entwicklung und Durchsetzung starker Marken verbunden. Sie stehen für hohe Kundenzufriedenheit, Loyalität und wirtschaftlichen Erfolg. Derzeit ist der „Erfolgsfaktor Marke“ in aller Munde. Die Markenführung erfährt eine ungeahnte Renaissance. So werden an der Börse selbst in schwierigen Zeiten Milliardenbeträge für die Akquisition etablierter Marken ausgegeben. Durch geschickten Markentransfer gelingt es, mit etablierten Marken in fremden Märkten schnell starke Wettbewerbspositionen aufzubauen. Das parallele Angebot mehrerer Marken für ein und dieselbe Zielgruppe trägt dazu bei, die Marktanteile auf den hart umkämpften Märkten zu steigern. Mit Hilfe innovativer, von aktuellen Lifestyletrends geprägter Markenkonzepte lassen sich in kurzer Zeit neue Märkte schaffen und verteidigen. Im Internet entstehen innerhalb weniger Jahre neue „virtuelle“ Marken, die etablierte Anbieter außerhalb des Internets bedrängen oder sogar übernehmen.

Andererseits steht bei wachsender Dynamik und Komplexität wirtschaftlicher Entwicklungen die Markenführung vor zahlreichen Herausforderungen. So wurden im deutschen Lebensmittelhandel die bisher führenden Markenartikel erstmals von billigeren Handelsmarken von ihrer Marktführerposition verdrängt. Der Anteil der reinen Preiskäufer wächst in diesem Bereich bei sinkender Markenloyalität. Darüber hinaus zwingen Fusionen und strategische Allianzen zur Neugestaltung von Markenarchitekturen. Alt eingeführte Firmenmarken werden eliminiert und neue Namen mit erheblichen werblichen Investitionen am Markt eingeführt. Selbst traditionell starke Marken schützen nicht vor wirtschaftlichem Mißerfolg beziehungsweise einer „plötzlichen“ Insolvenz.

Vor diesem Hintergrund gewinnen Fragen nach einem effektiven und effizienten Markenmanagement für Praktiker, Wissenschaftler und Studenten gleichermaßen eine neue Aktualität. Eine einfache Fortschreibung traditioneller Markenführungsansätze erscheint angesichts durchgreifender Veränderungen der Märkte nicht mehr zeitgemäß. Die **identitätsorientierte Markenführung**, ein seit Mitte der 90er Jahre parallel am Institut für Marketing und an den Universitäten in Berkeley (USA) und Paris entwickeltes Konzept, bietet in dieser Situation einen erfolgversprechenden Ansatz zur Neuorientierung des Markenmanagements. Dieses Konzept wurde in den vergangenen Jahren im Rahmen zahlreicher Forschungsprojekte des Instituts für Marketing in der Praxis erprobt und weiter entwickelt. Aus diesen Projekten sind einige der hier publizierten Fallstudien entstanden. Die mittlerweile vorliegenden theoretischen Erkenntnisse zur identitätsorientierten Markenführung bilden die Grundlage des vorliegenden Buches. Das Konzept der identitätsorientierten Markenführung liefert gleichzeitig den verbindenden Rahmen für alle Einzelbeiträge dieses Werkes.

Das Buch wäre ohne die tatkräftige Mithilfe zahlreicher Personen nicht möglich gewesen. Zuerst möchten wir den beteiligten Unternehmen für ihre Mitwirkung am Buch und an der Weiterentwicklung des identitätsorientierten Markenführungsansatzes danken. Darüber hinaus gilt unser besonderer Dank allen Mitarbeitern des Instituts für Marketing an der Westfälischen Wilhelms-Universität Münster für ihre vielfältige Unterstützung bei der Fertigstellung dieses Buches.

Besonders hervorzuheben ist Herr Dipl.-Kfm. Michael Ahrens, der sich in der Phase der Drucklegung besonders engagiert und gründlich um die technische Endredaktion des Buches gekümmert hat. Nicht zuletzt bedanken wir uns bei Frau Roscher vom Gabler-Verlag für die gewohnt außerordentlich professionelle, flexible und jederzeit angenehme Art der Zusammenarbeit.

Münster

Prof. Dr. Dr. h.c. mult. Heribert Meffert
Dr. Christoph Burmann
Dr. Martin Koers

Inhaltsverzeichnis

Vorwort zur 2. Auflage ___ V

Vorwort zur 1. Auflage ___ IX

Kapitel 1: Grundlagen der Markenführung

Christoph Burmann, Heribert Meffert und Martin Koers

Stellenwert und Gegenstand des Markenmanagements **3**

1. Stellenwert der Markenführung in Wissenschaft und Praxis ___ 4
2. Definition des Markenbegriffs ___ 5
3. Grundlagen der Markenbildung ___ 9
4. Nutzen der Marke aus Nachfrager- und Anbietersicht ___ 10
5. Ausblick ___ 15

Heribert Meffert und Christoph Burmann

Wandel in der Markenführung –
vom instrumentellen zum identitätsorientierten Markenverständnis **19**

1. Verändertes Markenverständnis im Zeitablauf ___ 20
2. Entwicklungsstufen der Markenführung ___ 22
2.1 Marke als bloßes Eigentumszeichen ___ 22
2.2 Marke als Merkmalskatalog: Instrumenteller Ansatz der Markenführung ___ 22
2.3 Angebotsbezogenes Markenverständnis: funktionsorientierter Ansatz der Markenführung ___ 24
2.4 Nachfragerbezogenes und wettbewerbsorientiertes Markenverständnis ___ 25
2.41 Verhaltens- beziehungsweise imageorientierter Ansatz der Markenführung ___ 26
2.42 Technokratisch-strategieorientierter Ansatz der Markenführung ___ 27
2.5 Marke als sozialpsychologisches Phänomen ___ 27
2.51 Fraktaler Ansatz der Markenführung ___ 29

2.52 Identitätsorientierter Ansatz der Markenführung 30
3. Fazit 32

Christoph Burmann und Heribert Meffert
Theoretisches Grundkonzept der identitätsorientierten Markenführung 37
1. Markenwert und Markenstärke als Leitgrößen der Markenführung 38
2. Theoretische Grundlagen der identitätsorientierten Markenführung 39
2.1 Paradigmen der Unternehmensführung als Basis der Markenführung 39
2.11 Der market-based view 39
2.12 Der resource-based view 40
2.2 Integration der markt- und ressourcenorientierten Sichtweise im Konzept der identitätsorientierten Markenführung 42
2.3 Interpretationsformen der Markenidentität 43
2.31 Sozialwissenschaftliche Ansätze der Identitätsforschung 43
2.32 Wirtschaftswissenschaftliche Interpretation der Markenidentität 49
3. Konzeptionelle Ausgestaltung der identitätsorientierten Markenführung 51
3.1 Perspektiven und Gegenstand der Markenidentität 51
3.11 Das Fremdbild der Markenidentität als Akzeptanzkonzept der Marke 53
3.12 Die Markenidentität als Aussagekonzept der Marke 56
3.121 Markenherkunft *58*
3.122 Markenkompetenz 59
3.123 Art der Markenleistungen 60
3.124 Markenvision 61
3.125 Markenwerte 62
3.126 Markenpersönlichkeit 63
3.2 Zusammenhang zwischen Markenidentität, Markenimage und Markenpositionierung 65
4. Fazit 67

Christoph Burmann und Heribert Meffert
Managementkonzept der identitätsorientierten Markenführung 73
1. Spannungsfelder im Rahmen des Identitätsmanagements 74
2. Identitätsorientierte Markenführung als Managementprozess 75
2.1 Strategisches Markenmanagent 77
2.11 Situationsanalyse 77
2.12 Unternehmens- und Markenziele 78
2.13 Konzeption der Markenidentität 79
2.14 Entwicklung der Markenarchitektur 80
2.15 Festlegung der Markenidentitäten für die übrigen Unternehmensmarken 81
2.16 Auswahl der Markenevolutionsstrategie 83

2.17 Identitätskonforme Markenorganisation 84
2.2 Operatives Markenmanagement 86
2.21 Umsetzung der Markenidentität in Markenleistungen 86
2.22 Umsetzung der Markenidentität im Markenpricing 90
2.23 Umsetzung der Markenidentität in der Markenkommunikation 91
2.24 Umsetzung der Markenidentität in der Markendistribution 95
2.25 Sicherung der Ganzheitlichkeit der Markenidentität durch Markenintegration 97
2.26 Absicherung der Markenidentität durch rechtlichen Markenschutz 97
2.3 Marken-Controlling 101
2.31 Definition und Abgrenzung 101
2.32 Markenberichtswesen 103
2.33 Markenerfolgsmessung 105
3. Fazit 112

Christoph Burmann und Sabrina Zeplin

Innengerichtetes identitätsbasiertes Markenmanagement 115
1. Innengerichtetes identitätsbasiertes Markenmanagement als Voraussetzung für die Schaffung starker Marken 116
2. Brand Citizenship Behavior: Was bedeutet „die Marke leben"? 117
3. Brand Commitment als Auslöser von Brand Citizenship Behavior 120
4. Ein ganzheitliches Modell für das innengerichtete identitätsbasierte Markenmanagement 122
4.1 Drei Hebel zur Generierung von Brand Commitment 124
4.11 Sicherstellung des Personen-Markenidentitäts-Fit durch HR-Aktivitäten 124
4.12 Generierung von Markenverständnis durch interne Kommunikation 125
4.13 Förderung von markenorientierter Führung auf allen Ebenen 129
4.2 Abstimmung der Kontextfaktoren: Kultur- und Struktur-Fit 131
5. Fazit 134

Kaptel 2: Strategien des Markenmanagements

Heribert Meffert und Andreas Bierwirth

Corporate Branding – Führung der Unternehmensmarke im Spannungsfeld unterschiedlicher Zielgruppen 143
1. Herausforderungen an das Corporate Branding 144
2. Theoretische Grundlagen für die Führung von Unternehmensmarken 146
2.1 Unternehmensmarke im Lichte des sozialpsychologischen Markenverständnisses 146
2.2 Betrachtungsperspektiven der Führung von Unternehmensmarken 147
2.21 Unternehmensmarke als Vermögensgegenstand 147

2.22	Unternehmensmarke als psychologischer Zusatznutzen	151
3.	Implikationen für die Führung von Unternehmensmarken	155
3.1	Zielgruppenspezifische Markenführung durch die Gestaltung der Markenarchitektur	155
3.2	Identitätsorientierte Markenführung als Grundkonzept zur zielgruppenübergreifenden Führung von Unternehmensmarken	158
4.	Ausblick	160

Christoph Burmann und Heribert Meffert

Gestaltung von Markenarchitekturen **163**

1.	Wachsende Herausforderungen an die Führung von Markenportfolios	164
2.	Die Markenarchitekturgestaltung als Grundlage der strategischen Führung von Markenportfolios	165
2.1	Unternehmens- und Markenhierarchien	166
2.2	Strategische Markenrollen	168
2.3	Eindimensionale Strukturierungsansätze für Markenarchitekturen	169
2.4	Mehrdimensionaler Strukturierungsansatz für Markenarchitekturen	173
2.41	Vertikale Dimension	175
2.42	Horizontale Dimension	175
2.43	Handelsgerichtete Dimension	178
3.	Fazit	181

Christoph Burmann, Heribert Meffert und Lars Blinda

Markenevolutionsstrategien **183**

1.	Markenevolution als dynamische Weiterentwicklung von Marken	184
2.	Markenkonsolidierungsstrategien	185
2.1	Sofortige Elimination	186
2.2	Abgestufter Rückzug	187
2.21	Abschöpfungsstrategien	187
2.22	Migrationsstrategie	188
2.3	Fokussierungsstrategie	190
3.	Markenexpansionsstrategien	192
3.1	Geografische Expansionsstrategien	193
3.11	Multinationale Markenstrategie	194
3.12	Globale Markenstrategie	195
3.13	Internationale Markenadaptionsstrategie	196
3.2	Markenerweiterungsstrategien	196
3.21	Markenausdehnungsstrategie	200
3.22	Markentransferstrategie	201
3.23	Lizenzierungs- und Franchisestrategie	203
3.24	Co-Branding-Strategie	206
3.25	Autarkiestrategie	208
4.	Fazit	210

Heribert Meffert und Jesko Perrey
Mehrmarkenstrategien – identitätsorientierte Führung von Markenportfolios **213**
1. Stellenwert der Mehrmarkenstrategie 214
2. Gegenstand von Mehrmarkenstrategien 217
2.1 Charakteristika von Mehrmarkenstrategien 217
2.2 Chancen und Risiken im Marktauftritt 219
3. Planungsprozess von Mehrmarkenstrategien 227
3.1 Marktstrategische Standortbestimmung als Ausgangspunkt 229
3.2 Strategische Rahmenplanung 230
3.21 Gestaltung der Markenportfolios und Festlegung markenspezifischer Rollen 231
3.22 Marktstrategische Positionierung und Leitbilder der Marken 231
3.3 Ausgestaltung der Instrumentalstrategien 234
4. Organisatorische Verankerung von Mehrmarkenstrategien 236
5. Zusammenfassung und Fazit 239

Mirko Caspar und Christoph Burmann
Markenerweiterungsstrategien **245**
1. Relevanz der Markenerweiterung für das Markenmanagement 246
2. Gegenstand und konzeptionelle Grundlagen der Markenerweiterung 247
2.1 Definition des Markenerweiterungsbegriffes 247
2.2 Chancen und Risiken der Markenerweiterung 249
2.3 Bestehende Ansätze zur Analyse und Erklärung von Markenerweiterungen 253
2.31 Einstellungstheoretische Ansätze 254
2.32 Gedächtnispsychologische Ansätze 258
3. Bestimmungsfaktoren der nachfragerseitigen Beurteilung von Markenerweiterungen 259
3.1 Bestimmungsfaktoren der Beurteilung des Erweiterungsproduktes 259
3.11 Stärke und Struktur der Ursprungsmarke 260
3.12 Charakteristika der Transferkategorie 261
3.13 Beziehung zwischen Ursprungsmarke und Transferprodukt 262
3.14 Kommunikationspolitik 263
3.2 Bestimmungsfaktoren des Rücktransfers auf die Ursprungsmarke 263
4. Implikationen für das Management der Markenerweiterung 264
4.1 Strategische Standortbestimmung 265
4.2 Positionierung des Transferproduktes 266
4.3 Marktstrategische Instrumenteausgestaltung 266
5. Fazit 267

Kapitel 3: Controlling des Markenmanagements

Heribert Meffert und Martin Koers

Identitätsorientiertes Markencontrolling – Grundlagen und konzeptionelle Ausgestaltung **273**

1. Stellenwert des Markencontrolling 274
2. Theoretische Grundlagen des Markencontrolling 275
2.1 Begriffliche Abgrenzung des Markencontrolling 275
2.2 Ziele und Aufgaben des Markencontrolling 276
3. Anforderungen und Zielgrößen des Markencontrolling 278
3.1 Anforderungen an das Markencontrolling 278
3.2 Zielgrößen des Markencontrolling 279
4. Konzeptionelle Ausgestaltung eines identitätsorientierten Markencontrolling auf Basis der Balanced Scorecard 282
4.1 Das Konzept der Balanced Scorecard 282
4.2 Grundstruktur einer Markenscorecard 284
4.3 Identifikation von Steuerungsgrößen für eine Markenscorecard 285
4.31 Berücksichtigung markenbezogener Anspruchsgruppen bei der Ermittlung von Steuerungsgrößen 286
4.32 Bestimmung von Steuerungsgrößen durch Operationalisierung des Markenleitbildes 289
4.33 Steuerungsgrößen in Markenportfolios 291
5. Fazit 294

Heribert Meffert und Martin Koers

Markenkannibalisierung in Markenportfolios **297**

1. Markenkannibalisierung als zentrale Herausforderung bei der Verfolgung von Mehrmarkenstrategien 298
2. Grundüberlegungen zur Wanderungsanalyse bei der Verfolgung von Mehrmarkenstrategien 299
3. Erfassung interner und externer Wanderungsbewegungen in Mehrmarkenstrategien 303
3.1 Erfassung interner Wanderungsbewegungen: Substitutions- versus Kannibalisierungsanalyse 305
3.11 Substitutionsanalyse 305
3.12 Kannibalisierungsanalyse 307
3.2 Erfassung externer Wanderungsbewegungen: Partizipationsanalyse 311
4. Integration interner und externer Wanderungsbewegungen im Rahmen von Wanderungsbilanzen 313
5. Zusammenfassung 315

Christoph Burmann, Marcel Kranz und Jan-Philipp Weers

Bewertung und Bilanzierung von Marken – Bestandsaufnahme und kritische Würdigung **319**

1. Markenbewertung als Herausforderung an die marktorientierte Unternehmensführung 320
1.1 Die Marke als Treiber des Unternehmenswertes 320
1.2 Bilanzierung von Markenwerten 321
1.3 Steuerungswirkungen des Markenwertes 322
1.4 Markenwert und Markenstärke als Gegenstand der Markenbewertung 324
2. Verfahren der Markenbewertung 326
2.1 Klassisch finanzorientierte Verfahren 327
2.2 Verfahren unter Berücksichtigung der Markenstärke 331
3. Zweckbezogene und methodische Markenbewertungsunterschiede 335
3.1 Zweckbezogene Unterschiede der Verfahren 336
3.2 Methodische Unterschiede 338
3.21 Erfassung der Markenstärke 339
3.22 Monetäre Abbildung des Markenwertes 340
3.3 Anforderungen an die Markenbewertung aus Sicht der identitätsorientierten Markenführung 342
4. Fazit 343

Heribert Meffert und Christoph Burmann

Abnutzbarkeit und Nutzungsdauer von Marken **347**

1. Problemstellung 348
2. Abnutzbarkeit von Marken 349
2.1 Rechtliche versus wirtschaftliche Abnutzbarkeit von Marken 349
2.2 Abnutzbarkeit aus verhaltenstheoretischer Perspektive 350
3. Nutzungsdauer von Marken 352
3.1 Lebenszyklusanalyse als Grundlage zur Nutzungsdauerbestimmung 352
3.2 Konzeption einer allgemeinen Nutzungsdauerverteilungsfunktion 352
3.3 Determinanten der Nutzungsdauer von Marken 355
3.31 Determinanten zur Klassifikation der Markennutzungsdauer 355
3.32 Determinanten eines andauernden Werteverzehrs bei Marken 357
4. Zusammenfassung und Ausblick 360

Kapitel 4: Ausgewählte Problemfelder des Markenmanagements

Fabian Hieronimus und Christoph Burmann

Persönlichkeitsorientiertes Markenmanagement **365**

1. Die Markenpersönlichkeit im Rahmen des strategischen Markenmanagements 366
1.1 Herausforderungen an das Markenmanagement 366
1.2 Bedeutung der Markenpersönlichkeit für das strategische Markenmanagement 367
2. Konzeption und Operationalisierung der Markenpersönlichkeit 369
2.1 Abgrenzung der Markenpersönlichkeit 369
2.2 Relevante Grundlagen der Persönlichkeitspsychologie 371
2.3 Messansätze der Markenpersönlichkeit 372
3. Steuerung der Markenpersönlichkeit 376
3.1 Determinanten der Markenpersönlichkeit 376
3.2 Wirkung der Markenpersönlichkeit 379
4. Bedeutung der Markenpersönlichkeit für die Unternehmenspraxis 381
5. Fazit 382

Christoph Burmann und Axel Nitschke

Profilierung von Marken mit Sponsoring und Events **387**

1. Relevanz von Sponsoring und Event-Kommunikation für das Markenmanagement 388
2. Theoretische Grundlagen 389
2.1 Abgrenzung und Typologisierung von Sponsoring und Event-Kommunikation *389*
2.2 Wirkungsprozess von Sponsoring und Event-Kommunikation *392*
2.3 Sponsoring und Event-Kommunikation im Kontext der identitäsorientierten Markenführung 393
3. Erfolgsfaktoren für die Profilierung von Marken durch Sponsoring und Event-Kommunikation 395
3.1 Planung der Kommunikationsmaßnahmen 395
3.2 Durchführung der Kommunikationsmaßnahmen 397
3.3 Controlling der Kommunikationsmaßnahmen *399*
4. Fallbeispiel zur Profilierung der Stadtmarke Bremen durch Werder Bremen 401
5. Zusammenfassung und Ausblick 407

Christoph Burmann, Michael Schleusener und Jan-Philipp Weers

Identitätsorientierte Markenführung bei Dienstleistungen **411**

1. Herausforderungen an die Führung von Dienstleistungsmarken 412
1.1 Besonderheiten von Dienstleistungsmarken 412
1.2 Vertrauensfunktion von Dienstleistungsmarken 415

1.3 Differenzierung im Wettbewerb durch Dienstleistungsmarken 416
2. Dienstleistungsmarken im Rahmen des identitätsorientierten Markenmanagements 417
2.1 Identitätsverständnis als Ausgangspunkt 417
2.2 Interaktion zwischen Nachfrager und Mitarbeitern als Besonderheit des Markenmanagements bei Dienstleistungen 419
2.21 Sicherung der Qualitätskonstanz von Markenleistungen 419
2.22 Mitarbeiterführung im Interaktionsprozess zur Vermittlung der Markenidentität 421
2.23 Sicherung des Fits zwischen Marken-, Mitarbeiter- und Kundenidentität 423
2.3 Kundenidentität als Determinante des Markenwahlverhaltens bei Dienstleistungen 425
3. Ausgewählte Aspekte des identitätsorientierten Managements von Dienstleistungsmarken – ein Beispiel aus Assekuranz 426
4. Fazit 429

Michael Bongartz, Christoph Burmann und Philip Maloney
Marke und Markenführung im Kontext des Electronic Commerce 433
1. Entwicklung des Electronic Commerce als Ausgangspunkt 434
2. Begriffliche Abgrenzungen und Klassifizierungen von Marken im Electronic Commerce 435
2.1 Abgrenzung des Markenbegriffes im Electronic Commerce 435
2.2 Klassifizierungen von Marken im Electronic Commerce 438
2.3 Überprüfung der Klassifikationsmerkmale anhand der Konsumentenverhaltensforschung 440
3. Stellenwert und Herausforderungen der Markenführung im Electronic Commerce 442
3.1 Nutzerbezogene Bedeutung und Funktionen der Marke im Electronic Commerce 442
3.2 Wettbewerbsbezogene Bedeutung und Funktionen der Marke 447
3.3 Anforderungen an den Markenmanagementprozess im Electronic Commerce 448
3.31 Strategisches Markenmanagement im Electronic Commerce 448
3.32 Operatives Markenmanagement im Electronic Commerce 450
3.33 Marken-Controlling im Electronic Commerce 451
4. Implikationen für die Markenführung im Electronic Commerce 451
4.1 Implikationen für das strategische Markenmanagement 451
4.11 Festlegung der Markenleistungen 451
4.12 Festlegung der Markenarchitektur 453
4.2 Implikationen für das operative Markenmanagement 457
4.21 Intra-mediale und inter-mediale Markenintegration 457

4.22 Internetbasierte und klassische Maßnahmen der Markenkommunikation ___ 458
4.3 Implikationen für das Marken-Controlling ___ 460
5. Zusammenfassung ___ 462

Ingo Lasslop
Identitätsorientierte Führung von Luxusmarken **469**
1. Zunehmende Bedeutung von Luxusmarken als Herausforderung an das Markenmanagement ___ 470
2. Der Luxusbegriff im Kontext der Markenführung ___ 472
3. Das Identitätssystem von Luxusmarken ___ 475
3.1 Besonderheiten des Selbstbilds von Luxusmarken ___ 475
3.2 Besonderheiten im Fremdbild von Luxusmarken: Selbstkongruenz und Wertausdruck ___ 477
4. Management von Luxusmarken ___ 481
4.1 Strategische Optionen für Luxusmarken ___ 481
4.2 Besonderheiten des operativen Managements von Luxusmarken ___ 484
4.21 Markenbildung durch überragende Qualität und Design ___ 484
4.22 Markenbildung durch konstante Preispolitik ___ 485
4.23 Markenbildung durch Flagship-Stores und selektiven Vertrieb ___ 486
4.24 Markenbildung durch symbolische Kommunikation ___ 488
5. Fazit ___ 491

Michael Welling
Markenführung im professionellen Ligasport **495**
1. Bedeutungszuwachs der Markenführung im professionellen Ligasport als Folge einer veränderten Aufgabenumwelt ___ 496
2. Bedingungen und Herausforderungen einer identitätsorientierten Markenführung im Ligasport ___ 500
2.1 Leistungsbündelspezifische Besonderheiten des professionellen Ligasports als Ausgangspunkt ___ 500
2.2 Multiple Zielgruppen der Markenführung als Konsequenz leistungsbündelspezifischer Besonderheiten ___ 504
2.21 Leistungsabsatzbezogene Zielgruppen: Zuschauer als konsumtive und Sponsoren als investive Nachfrager ___ 504
2.22 Leistungsaufteilungsbezogene Zielgruppen: Medien- und Agenturpartner sowie Netzwerkpartner im Dienstleistungszentrum Stadion ___ 506
2.23 Leistungspotenzialbezogene Zielgruppen: Mitarbeiter im sportlichen und außersportlichen Bereich ___ 508
3. Adaption des GAP-Modells der identitätsorientierten Markenführung für Ligasportklubs ___ 510
3.1 Harmonisierung von Selbst- und Fremdbildern als Leitidee für die Entwicklung eines GAP-Modells ___ 510

3.2 Konzeption eines GAP-Modells für die Markenführung im Ligasport 511
3.3 Anwendung des GAP-Modells – ausgewählte Ergebnisse am Beispiel VfL Bochum 1848 e. V. 514
4. Fazit 518

Helmut Schneider
Ausgestaltung einer identitätsorientierten Markenführung in der Politik **523**
1. Von der politischen Propaganda zur Markenführung – Entwicklungslinien und Perspektiven des Politikmarketing 524
2. Relevanz und Funktionen von Marken in der Politik 526
3. Identitätsorientierte Führung von Politikmarken 531
3.1 Das GAP-Modell als Bezugsrahmen der identitätsorientierten Führung von Politikmarken 532
3.2 Ausgestaltung einer identitätsorientierten Führung von Politikmarken – dargestellt am Beispiel der SPD 536
4. Fazit 557

Christian Ebert
Identitätsorientiertes Stadtmarketing **563**
1. Markenführung als Herausforderung an das Stadtmarketing 564
2. Identität einer Stadt als inhaltlicher Referenzpunkt der Markenführung im Stadtmarketing 565
2.1 Inhaltliche Präzisierung des Begriffs der Stadtidentität 565
2.2 Nutzenpotenziale stadtbezogener Identität 567
3. Stadtbezogene Modifikation des identitätsorientierten Markenführungsansatzes 569
4. Empirische Fundierung des identitätsorientierten Stadtmarketing 574
4.1 Tragfähigkeit der „Marke Münster“ als Untersuchungsobjekt 574
4.2 Ableitung eines Markenkerns als strategischer Ausgangspunkt des identitätsorientierten Stadtmarketing 575
4.3 Identifikation von Maßnahmenprioritäten 579
4.4 Zusammenfassung des identitätsorientierten Anpassungsprozesses 582
5. Zusammenfassung und Implikationen 585

Manfred Kirchgeorg
Identitätsorientierter Aufbau und Gestaltung von Regionenmarken **589**
1. Stellenwert von Regionenmarken und Regionenmarketing 590
1.1 Profilierung von Regionen im Wettbewerb 590
1.2 Funktionen und Besonderheiten von Regionenmarken 594
1.3 Gestaltung von Marken für Regionen 598
1.4 Erfassung von Einstellungen gegenüber Regionen und Regionenmarken 601
2. Empirische Analyse von Markennamen für Regionen 604

2.1 Markenbildung für die Region „Mitteldeutschland“ 604
2.2 Analyse der Assoziationen zum Regionennamen „Mitteldeutschland“ 605
2.3 Bekanntheitsgrad von Aktivitäten der Region „Mitteldeutschland“ 607
2.4 Räunliche Identifikation der Region „Mitteldeutschland“ 607
2.5 Einstellungen zur Region „Mitteldeutschland“ im Vergleich zum „Ruhrgebiet“ 610
3. Implikationen für markenstrategische Entscheidungen im Regionenmarketing 612

Kapitel 5: Best Practice im Markenmanagement

Klaus Morwind, Jörg P. Koppenhöfer und Peter Nüßler
Markenführung im Spannungsfeld zwischen Tradition und Innovation: Persil – Da weiß man, was man hat 621
1. Persil: Die bestimmende Marke im deutschen Waschmittelmarkt 623
2. Persil – von 1907 bis heute 626
2.1 Die Produkte 626
2.2 Die Kommunikation 628
2.3 Die Packung 629
2.4 Die Promotion 630
2.5 Der Vertrieb 631
3. Systematik einer erfolgreichen Produkteinführung – Der Launch von Persil Megaperls® 1994 631
3.1 Das System 631
3.2 Strategische Ausgangslage 633
3.3 Der Prozess der Neuproduktentwicklung und Einführung von Persil Megaperls® 635
3.31 Die Identifikation des Verbraucherbedürfnisses 635
3.32 Abgleich mit dem Markenimage und der Markenpositionierung 635
3.33 Entwicklung der Selling Proposition 636
3.34 Überprüfung der Produktleistung vor dem Hintergrund der Selling Proposition 637
3.35 Definition der Kommunikationsziele 639
3.36 Die Kommunikation 639
3.37 Überprüfung des gesamten Marketing-Mix und Ableitung des Marktpotenzials 641
3.4 Die Erfolgskontrolle nach der Produktneueinführung 642
3.41 Standardmarktbeobachtung 642
3.42 Effizienz- und Abweichungsanalysen 645
4. Es gibt nur ein Persil: Die Erfolgsfaktoren einer einzigartigen Marke 646
5. Grenzenloses Persil. Die internationale Verbreitung der Marke 647

Jürgen Plüss

Markenmonopol für Qualität – Das Beispiel Miele **649**

1. Einleitung 650
2. Das Umfeld der Markenführung im Hausgerätemarkt 650
2.1 Hohe Marktsättigung 650
2.2 Distribution im Wandel 651
3. Die Miele Position: Qualitative und quantitative Marktführerschaft 651
4. Miele: Die Erfolgsfaktoren 654
4.1 Einzelmarkenstrategie 654
4.2 Markencode Qualität 655
4.3 Premiumposition in der Preispolitik 656
4.4 Innovation 657
4.5 Langlebiges Design 658
4.6 Guter Service beziehungsweise Kundendienst 660
4.7 Breite Distribution 661
4.8 Kommunikation: Kreativität reduziert auf das Produkt 662
4.9 Erfolgsfaktor „Erfolg“ 664
4.10 Kontinuität 664
5. Ausblick 665

Jürgen Althans und Gerd Brüne

Markenführung und Markentransfer der Zeitschrift GEO **667**

1. Konzeptionelle Grundlagen der Markenführung von Zeitschriften 668
2. Markenführung von GEO 669
2.1 Markenführung im Lesermarkt 669
2.11 Produktpolitik 669
2.12 Kontrahierungspolitik 672
2.13 Distributionspolitik 672
2.14 Kommunikationspolitik 673
2.2 Markenführung im Anzeigenmarkt 674
2.21 Produktpolitik 674
2.22 Kontrahierungspolitik 675
2.23 Distributionspolitik 676
2.24 Kommunikationspolitik 676
3. Markentransferstrategien von GEO 677
3.1 Transfer auf neue Zeitschriften im Inland 677
3.2 GEO-Nebenprodukte 681
3.3 Internationalisierung 683
3.4 Fernsehen und Internet 684
4. Erfolgskontrolle von Markenführung und Markentransfer bei GEO 685
4.1 Messkriterien 685
4.2 Ökonomische Erfolgskontrolle 685
4.3 Erfolgskontrolle im Hinblick auf den Markenwert 686
4.4 Verbundeffekte 690
5. Zusammenfassung 691

Michael Lambertz

Management von komplexen Markenportfolios – Markenführung in der World of TUI **693**

1. Herausforderungen und Trends bei der Markenführung im Touristik-Markt 694
1.1 Herausforderung der Markenführung im Tourismus 694
1.2 Zentrale Entwicklungstrends im Touristik-Markt 694
2. Ausgangssituation TUI AG 697
3. Management von komplexen Markenportfolios über die touristische Wertschöpfungskette 700
3.1 Ansatz einer mehrdimensionalen Markenführung 700
3.11 Horizontale Markenführung auf Veranstalterebene 700
3.12 Vertikale Markenführung über die Wertschöpfungskette 703
3.13 Internationale Markenführung über die Ländermärkte 706
3.2 Integration der Markenführung 709
4. Erfolge infolge der Einführung der Dachmarke „World of TUI" 710
5. Ausblick 713

Heribert Meffert und Ingo Lasslop

Erfolgreiche Markenführung bei homogenen Verbrauchsgütern – Das Beispiel JET **715**

1. Die Ausgangsposition der Marke JET 716
2. Der deutsche Tankstellenmarkt 716
2.1 Historische Branchenentwicklung 716
2.2 Veränderungen im Konsumentenverhalten 718
2.3 Veränderungen im Wettbewerbsumfeld 719
2.4 Die Bedeutung der Marke 723
3. Das Konzept zur Profilierung der Marke JET 724
3.1 Die strategische Rolle der Markenpolitik für JET 724
3.2 Das Markenleitbild von JET 727
3.3 Durchsetzung des Markenleitbildes in der Preis-, Produkt- und Distributionspolitik 728
3.4 Durchsetzung des Markenleitbildes in der Kommunikationspolitik 728
3.5 Durchsetzung des Markenleitbildes nach Innen 732
4. Erfolg der Markenprofilierung bei JET 733

Martin Koers und Wolfgang Booms

Herausforderungen an die Markenführung bei produktpolitischer Standardisierung – Der Fall Ford Galaxy I und II **735**

Teil 1: Segmenteinstieg und -eroberung durch Produktstandardisierung im noch jungen Markt für Großraumlimousinen (Ford Galaxy I 1990–2000) 737
1. Zur Ausgangssituation bei der Entwicklung des Ford Galaxy 737
2. Ziele der horizontalen Kooperation zwischen Ford und Volkswagen 739

3. Maßnahmen im Rahmen des Badge Engineering auf Herstellerseite 742
3.1 Positionierung des Ford Galaxy: Room Needing, Image Concerned 742
3.2 Operative Maßnahmen im Rahmen des Badge Engineering-Projekts 743
3.21 Produktpolitik 743
3.22 Preispolitik 744
3.23 Kommunikationspolitik 746
3.24 Distributionspolitik 748
4. Zentrale Ergebnisse 749
Teil 2: Segmentbehauptung und -abgrenzung durch zunehmende Differenzierung im reifenden Markt für Großraumlimousinen (Ford Galaxy II 2000–2004) 752
1. Erfahrungen aus Galaxy I sowie Marktsituation Ende der 90er Jahre 752
2. Strategische Implikationen für den Galaxy II: horizontale Differenzierung bei verstärkter vertikaler Integration 754
3. Auswirkungen der strategischen Umorientierung auf den Marketing-Mix des Galaxy II 755
3.1 Produkt- und Preispolitik 755
3.2 Kommunikations- und Distributionspolitik 758
4. Zentrale Ergebnisse 760

Andreas Bierwirth und Volker Scheible
High-speed-Aufbau einer neuen Marke – Das Beispiel Germanwings 763
1. Einleitung 764
2. Die unternehmensstrategische Entscheidung: Einstieg in das Low-Cost-Segment 764
3. Das Geschäftskonzept: Konsequente Umsetzung der Erfolgsfaktoren 766
3.1 Preisstrategie: Königsdisziplin im preisdominierten Low-Cost-Segment 767
3.2 Marktstrategie und Streckennetz: Volumen und Vielfalt 768
4. Die Marke Germanwings als Fundament und Rahmen des unternehmerischen Vorgehens 770
4.1 Identitätsorientierte Markenführung bei Germanwings 770
4.2 Die Positionierung der Marke Germanwings 770
4.3 Die Entwicklung und Gestaltung der Marke Germanwings 772
5. Produkt und Service an Bord und Boden: Qualität trotz „no-frills“ 773
6. Germanwings Vertrieb: Ein E-Commerce-Unternehmen 774
7. Marketingkommunikation: Beschleuniger des Markenaufbaus 776
8. Der Erfolg in Zahlen 777
9. Ausblick 779

Wolfgang Giehl und Christoph Baumgarten

Markenmanagement als Motor der neuen Markenidentität DHL im Konzern Deutsche Post World Net **781**

1. Einleitung 783
2. Die Markenstrategie 783
2.1 Ausgangslage 783
2.2 Von der Akquisition zur Integration 784
2.3 DHL wird zum Komplettanbieter 786
2.4 Corporate Design und Rebranding 787
2.41 Die Basics: DHL im Zeichen des Konzerns 787
2.42 Der Außenauftritt: Rebranding im großen Stil 789
2.43 Die Unternehmenskleidung: Marke hautnah 791
2.44 Die weltweite Umsetzung 793
2.5 Die Markenkampagne 794
2.6 Der Claim 794
2.7 Der Rollout-Plan 795
3. Die Markenkampagne im Detail 796
3.1 TV-Spot international 796
3.2 Anzeigen international 798
3.21 Eine Botschaft geht um die Welt 798
3.22 Die Integration der Partner 800
3.23 Die Anzeigenschaltung 802
3.3 TV und Print speziell für Deutschland 802
3.4 Die Follow-up-Kampagne 803
3.5 Internet 804
3.6 Direktmarketing 805
3.7 Broschüren 805
3.8 Veranstaltungen 806
4. Das Ergebnis: Mehr Wirkung 807
5. Die interne Kommunikation 808
5.1 Information und Emotion 808
5.2 Printmedien und -maßnahmen 809
5.3 DHL zum Anfassen 812
6. Situation und Ausblick 813
6.1 Brand Dynamics 813
6.2 Nonstop zur weltweiten Top-Marke 815

Harald W. Eisenächer

Lufthansa – Excellence in Branding **819**

1. Einführung 820
2. Historie des Unternehmens und der Marke Lufthansa 820
2.1 Historie des Unternehmens 820
2.2 Markenhistorie und Entwicklung der Corporate Identity 821
3. Prozess und Modell zur optimierten Markenführung 826

4. Die Lufthansa Kommunikation im Zeichen des 11. September 829
5. Neuer Markenauftritt und zunehmende Emotionalisierung 832
6. Zusammenfassung und Konklusion 835

Heribert Meffert
Markenführung in Stiftungen – Beispiel Bertelsmann Stiftung 837
1. Einführung 838
2. Mission der Bertelsmann Stiftung – Leitbild als Fundament 838
3. Bedeutung der Marke für die Arbeit der Bertelsmann Stiftung 840
4. Genese des Markenkerns der Bertelsmann Stiftung 843
4.1 Ausgangssituation 843
4.2 Entwicklung des Markenkerns 844
4.21 Inhaltlicher Markenkern 844
4.22 Definition der Arbeitsweise und des Anspruchs 846
4.3 Notwendigkeit einer Dachmarke 848
5. Fazit 851

Kapitel 6: Ausblick

Christoph Burmann
Kritische Reflektion zum Markenmanagement 855

Stichwortverzeichnis 861

Marken- und Firmenverzeichnis 873

Die Autoren 879

KAPITEL

1 Grundlagen der Markenführung

Stellenwert und Gegenstand des Markenmanagements 3

Christoph Burmann, Heribert Meffert und Martin Koers

Wandel in der Markenführung – vom instrumentellen zum identitätsorientierten Markenverständnis 19

Heribert Meffert und Christoph Burmann

Theoretisches Grundkonzept der identitätsorientierten Markenführung 37

Christoph Burmann und Heribert Meffert

Managementkonzept der identitätsorientierten Markenführung 73

Christoph Burmann und Heribert Meffert

Innengerichtetes identitätsbasiertes Markenmanagement 115

Christoph Burmann und Sabrina Zeplin

Stellenwert und Gegenstand des Markenmanagements

Christoph Burmann, Heribert Meffert und Martin Koers

1.	Stellenwert der Markenführung in Wissenschaft und Praxis	4
2.	Definition des Markenbegriffs	5
3.	Grundlagen der Markenbildung	9
4.	Nutzen der Marke aus Nachfrager- und Anbietersicht	10
5.	Ausblick	15

1. Stellenwert der Markenführung in Wissenschaft und Praxis

Fragestellungen der Führung von Marken stellen bereits seit geraumer Zeit ein Schlüsselthema der marktorientierten Unternehmensführung dar. In den letzten Jahren sind wohl zu kaum einem anderen Thema mehr Veröffentlichungen erschienen. Die publizistische Bedeutung spiegelt sich auch ganz real in monetären Größen wieder. Im Jahr 2002 investierten allein deutsche Unternehmen circa 30 Milliarden Euro in den Aufbau und die Führung von Marken (Perrey/Riesenbeck 2003). Diese beeindruckende Zahl lässt sich auf den Nutzen einer Marke für die Nachfrager und den daraus resultierenden ökonomischen Wert der Marke für ein Unternehmen zurückführen. So wird beispielsweise der Wert der Marke Coca-Cola in Abhängigkeit von der eingesetzten Berechnungsmethode auf Beträge zwischen 48 Milliarden US-Dollar und 83 Milliarden US-Dollar geschätzt und repräsentiert damit etwa 50 Prozent des gesamten Unternehmenswertes. Der hohe Wert des immateriellen Vermögensgegenstandes Marke macht die Notwendigkeit einer bilanziellen Erfassung des Markenwertes deutlich, die mittlerweile auch vom Gesetzgeber nachvollzogen wird. Gleichzeitig zeigt die Schwankungsbreite der errechneten Markenwerte die Problematik einer den Grundsätzen ordnungsgemäßer Buchführung entsprechenden Evaluierung auf (vgl. hierzu auch den Beitrag zur Markenbewertung in diesem Buch).

Abbildung 1: Wirkung von Marken auf die Präferenzbildung der Konsumenten

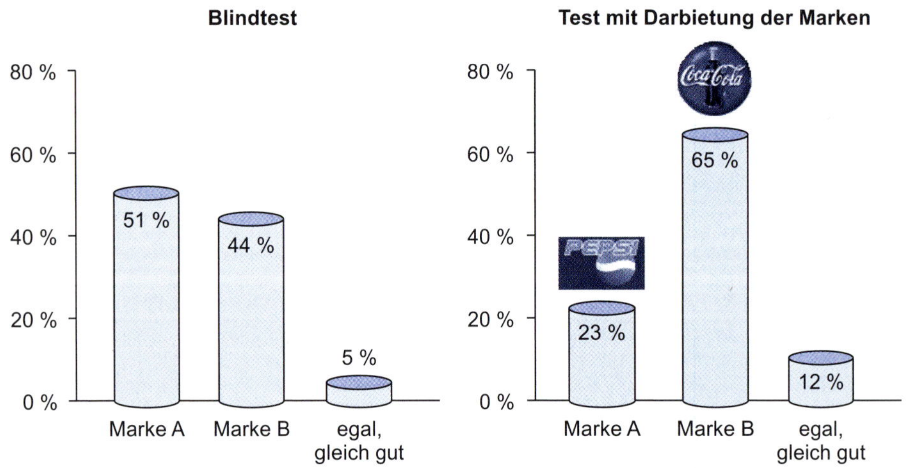

GABLER GRAFIK

Unbeschadet der Problemstellung der bilanziellen Bewertung, ist die Grundlage des finanziellen Wertes einer Marke ihre Wirkung bei Kauf- und Auswahlentscheidungen von Nachfragern. Sehr anschaulich kann diese Wirkung anhand des bekannten „Cola-Tests" gezeigt werden (vgl. Abbildung 1). Während bei einem Blindtest der Marken Pepsi und Coca-Cola 51 Prozent der Teilnehmer die Marke Pepsi vorzogen und nur 44 Prozent Coca-Cola wählten, änderte sich dieses Bild merklich, als der Test mit Darbietung der Marke durchgeführt wurde. In diesem Fall wählten nur noch 23 Prozent der Probanden Pepsi, während 65 Prozent Coca-Cola bevorzugten (Chernatony/McDonald 2003, S. 14 f.). Anhand dieses Präferenztests bei quasi homogenen Produkten lässt sich der Nutzen erkennen, den eine Marke für den Nachfrager stiftet.

2. Definition des Markenbegriffs

Bei der Untersuchung von Marken wird in der Regel zwischen der Marke als einem gewerblichem Schutzrecht, der Marke als markiertem Produkt und der „eigentlichen" Marke unterschieden. Ein Produkt wird in diesem Zusammenhang als technisch-funktionales Eigenschaftsbündel interpretiert, welches Sachgüter und Dienstleistungen umfassen kann (Brockhoff, 1999, S. 12 ff.). Über die Jahre wurde der Terminus Marke sowohl in der Wissenschaft als auch in der Praxis je nach Verständnis und Verwendungssituation sehr unterschiedlich definiert (vgl. für eine begrenzte Aufzählung Tabelle 1). Diese Begriffsvielfalt hält bis zur heutigen Zeit an.

Tabelle 1: Markendefinitionen

Domizlaff (1939)	Ein(e) Marke(nartikel) ist eine Fertigware, die mittels eines Zeichens markiert ist und die dem Konsumenten mit konstantem Auftritt und Preis in einem größeren Verbreitungsraum dargeboten wird.
Ogilvy (1951)	The brand is the consumer's idea of a product.
Mellerowicz (1963)	Marken(artikel) sind [...] für den privaten Bedarf geschaffene Fertigwaren, die in einem größeren Absatzraum unter einem besonderen, die Herkunft kennzeichnenden Merkmal (Marke) in einheitlicher Aufmachung, gleicher Menge sowie in gleich bleibender und verbesserter Güte erhältlich sind und sich dadurch, sowie durch die für sie betriebene Werbung, die Anerkennung der beteiligten Wirtschaftskreise (Verbraucher, Händler und Hersteller) erworben haben (Verkehrsgeltung).
American Marketing Association (vor 2004), Kotler (1991, 2000), Keller (1993)	A name, term, sign, symbol, or design, or a combination of them intended to identify the goods or services of one seller or a group of sellers and to differentiate them from those of competition.

Aaker (1992)	Eine Marke ist ein charakteristischer Name und/oder Symbol.
Kapferer (1992)	Die Marke ist für den potenziellen Käufer ein Erkennungszeichen.
Weinberg (1993)	Unter Marken(artikeln) versteht man übereinstimmend Güter, die durch ein Markenzeichen gekennzeichnet sind und sich durch einen zeitlich relativ stabilen und prägnanten Eigenschaftskatalog auszeichnen.
MarkenG § 3 Abs. 1 (1995)	Als Marken können [...] alle Zeichen, insbesondere Wörter einschließlich Personennamen, Abbildungen Buchstaben, Zahlen, Hörzeichen, dreidimensionale Gestaltungen einschließlich der Form einer Ware oder ihrer Verpackung sowie sonstiger Aufmachungen einschließlich Farben und Farbzusammenstellungen geschützt werden, die geeignet sind, Waren oder Dienstleistungen eines Unternehmens von denjenigen anderer Unternehmen zu unterscheiden.
Baumgarth (2001)	Eine Marke ist ein Name, Begriff, Zeichen, Symbol, eine Gestaltungsform oder eine Kombination aus diesen Bestandteilen, welches bei den relevanten Nachfragern bekannt ist und im Vergleich zu Konkurrenzangeboten ein differenzierendes Image aufweist, welches zu Präferenzen führt.
Adjouri (2002)	Eine Marke ist ein Botschafter zwischen Unternehmen und Zielgruppen [...], ein Zeichen, das mittels von Bedeutungen Produkte bzw. Dienstleistungen eine Identität gibt und diese bei den Zielgruppen erfolgreich vermittelt.
Keller (2003)	A brand is [...] a product, but one that adds other dimensions that differentiate it in some way from other products designed to satisfy the same needs.
Bruhn/GEM (2003)	Als Marke werden Leistungen bezeichnet, die neben einer unterscheidungsfähigen Markierung durch ein systematisches Absatzkonzept im Markt ein Qualitätsversprechen geben, das eine dauerhaft werthaltige, nutzenstiftende Wirkung erzielt und bei der relevanten Zielgruppe in der Erfüllung der Kundenerwartungen einen nachhaltigen Erfolg im Markt realisiert bzw. realisieren kann.
Welling (2003)	Eine Marke ist ein individuelles und schutzfähiges Zeichen bzw. Zeichenbündel, das ein Marktteilnehmer im Wettbewerb verwenden kann, um angebotene bzw. anbietbare Leistungsbündel durch Kennzeichnung von denen anderer Marktteilnehmer zu unterscheiden und durch die Verwendung zugleich in seinen Sinne positive, d. h. tauschrelevante Wirkungen bei aktuellen und potenziellen Tauschpartnern bzw. Tauschbeeinflussern zu entfalten, die seine Zielsetzungen zu erreichen helfen.
American Marketing Association (2004)	A name, term, design, symbol, or any other feature that identifies one seller's good or service as distinct from those of other sellers. The legal term for brand is trademark. A brand may identify one item, a family of items, or all items of that seller.

GABLER GRAFIK

Auf der Grundlage des ganzheitlich ausgerichteten identitätsorientierten Markenmanagements wird die „Marke“ in Anlehnung an Keller (2003, S. 3 f.) als

„ein Nutzenbündel mit spezifischen Merkmalen, die dafür sorgen, dass sich dieses Nutzenbündel gegenüber anderen Nutzenbündeln, welche dieselben Basisbedürfnisse erfüllen, aus Sicht relevanter Zielgruppen nachhaltig differenziert“
(Burmann/Blinda/Nitschke 2003, S. 3)

definiert. Dieses Markenverständnis unterscheidet sich zunächst von den Markendefinitionen im Markengesetz (MarkenG § 3) und der American Marketing Association (AMA). Dort wird ausgehend von der Marke als rechtlich geschütztem Warenzeichen oder markiertem Produkt lediglich auf verschiedene Erscheinungsformen und Funktionen einer Marke (zum Beispiel Herkunfts- oder Garantiefunktion) abgestellt, ohne zuvor die **Substanz der Marke** bestimmt zu haben. Demgegenüber wird hier ebendiese Substanz der Marke in den Mittelpunkt der Betrachtung gerückt.

Das **Nutzenbündel Marke** konstituiert sich stets aus materiellen und immateriellen Komponenten. Es handelt sich in zweifacher Weise um eine Bündelung. Einerseits werden bei der Marke **physisch-funktionale Nutzenkomponenten**, andererseits verschiedenartige Zeichen als **symbolische Nutzenkomponenten** gebündelt. Die physisch-funktionalen Nutzenkomponenten sind ein Ergebnis der Innovationsfähigkeit der die Marke tragenden Institution. Das Bündel aus symbolischen Nutzenkomponenten umfasst neben den schutzfähigen Zeichen wie Namen, Logos, Musik-Jingles, Herkunftsbezeichnungen etc. auch nicht schutzfähige Zeichen, die den Auftritt und das Wesen der Marke charakterisieren. Die symbolischen und die physisch-funktionalen Nutzenkomponenten der Marke können in unterschiedlicher Weise zur nachhaltigen Differenzierung und damit zur Entstehung und Stärke einer Marke beitragen. Das Ausmaß und die Nachhaltigkeit der Differenzierung sind immer dann besonders groß beziehungsweise lange andauernd, wenn sich sowohl die physisch-funktionalen als auch die symbolischen Nutzenkomponenten einer Marke von konkurrierenden Angeboten unterscheiden. Das gesamte Nutzenbündel sendet dabei unternehmensextern wahrnehmbare Signale aus, die sich im Markenimage der externen Zielgruppen widerspiegeln (vgl. Abbildung 2).

Das Markenverständnis des identitätsorientierten Markenmanagements grenzt sich so mit von anderen Ansätzen aus der Markenliteratur ab, welche die Marke lediglich als ein Zeichenbündel (Welling 2003), als ein gewerbliches Schutzrecht (Schröder 2001), als ein Vorstellungsbild im Kopf der Konsumenten oder als markiertes Produkt definieren (Mellerowics 1963; für einen Überblick über verschiedene Auffassungen vgl. Sattler 2001, S. 39 f.; Esch 2004, S. 19 ff.). Das obige Markenverständnis unterscheidet sich auch von einschlägigen Produkt- und Dienstleistungsdefinitionen aus der Marketingwissenschaft, welche die symbolischen Nutzenkomponenten, die hier als konstitutive Bestandteil der Marke interpretiert werden, nicht umfassen.

Eine **Verkürzung des Markenverständnisses** auf markierte Produkte und Dienstleistungen oder ein Zeichenbündel beziehungsweise Schutzrecht erscheint nicht zweckmäßig, weil der Managementprozess der Entwicklung und Stärkung von Marken auf die nachhaltige Beeinflussung des Kunden- und Mitarbeiterverhaltens ausgerichtet sein muss. Er darf sich somit weder auf das Technologie- und Innovationsmanagement, noch auf rein juristische oder Grafikdesign- und Werbeaktivitäten beschränken. Die angestrebten Wirkungen und der darauf ausgerichtete, integrierte Managementprozess determinieren demzufolge das Markenverständnis.

Abbildung 2: **Die Marke als Bezugsobjekt des identitätsorientierten Markenmanagements**

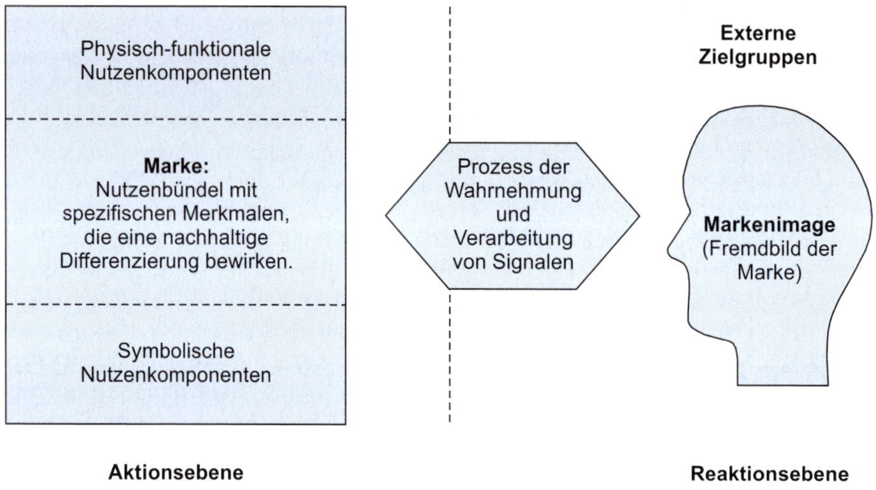

GABLER GRAFIK

Das Konzept des identitätsorientierten Markenmanagements geht über die einseitige Ausrichtung auf die Wahrnehmung der Marke beim Nachfrager **(Markenimage)** weit hinaus, denn diese „klassische" Outside-in-Perspektive der Marke wird um eine Inside-out-Perspektive ergänzt. Diese analysiert das Selbstbild der Marke aus Sicht der internen Zielgruppen innerhalb derjenigen Institution, die die Marke trägt (zum Beispiel Mitarbeiter, Management, Eigentümer, Absatzmittler). Dieses Selbstbild wird als die **Identität einer Marke** bezeichnet.

Gemäß dieses Verständnisses wird das **Markenmanagement** als ein integrativer, funktionsübergreifender Bestandteil der Unternehmensführung verstanden, welcher auf der hierarchisch höchsten Führungsebene im Unternehmen verankert sein sollte. Der identitätsorientierte Ansatz stellt damit eine Erweiterung gegenüber anderen Markenführungsansätzen dar, die ausschließlich absatzmarktbezogen sind. Die Ursachen beziehungsweise Quellen für das Entstehen der komparativen Konkurrenzvorteile einer Marke werden bei diesen Ansätzen ausgeblendet.

3. Grundlagen der Markenbildung

Die Marke beeinflusst nur dann das Kaufverhalten positiv, wenn sie mit einem **„added value“** verbunden ist. Dieser Mehrwert ist das Ergebnis eines vom Nachfrager vollzogenen Vergleichs zu einem konkurrierenden markenlosen Angebot, welches dieselben Basisbedürfnisse erfüllt. Der wahrgenommene Nutzenvorteil einer Marke repräsentiert den Markenwert aus Konsumentensicht oder, synonym, den **psychografischen Markenwert** (Farquhar 1990). Er schlägt sich unmittelbar in der Kaufbereitschaft des Nachfragers nieder.

Die Marke ist dabei das Ergebnis einer Vielzahl über einen längeren Zeitraum durchgeführter Maßnahmen und der hierauf basierenden Erfahrungen der Nachfrager. Der Managementprozess der Planung, Koordination und Kontrolle dieser Maßnahmen kann als **Markenführung** bezeichnet werden (vgl. in diesem Zusammenhang auch den Beitrag zum Managementkonzept der identitätsorientierten Markenführung in diesem Buch). Für den Markeneigner, gemeint ist hier der Besitzer des gewerblichen Schutzrechtes, besteht das Ziel der Markenführung in der Steigerung des ökonomischen Markenwertes (Aaker 1992, Irmscher 1997; Sattler 2002), welcher auf dem von den Nachfragern wahrgenommenen Nutzenvorsprung basiert. Der **ökonomische Markenwert** wird häufig operationalisiert über die Preisprämie, die der Nachfrager für ein Markenprodukt im Vergleich zu einem markenlosen Produkt zu zahlen bereit ist (Sander 1994; Schweiger 1998; vgl. auch den Beitrag zur Markenbewertung in diesem Buch). Das markenlose Produkt steht dabei stellvertretend für den Basisnutzen eines Produktes. Es kann jedoch auch ohne die Zahlung einer Preisprämie ein ökonomisch relevanter Markenwert bestehen, der sich in einem Absatzmengeneffekt niederschlägt. Dies ist der Fall, wenn der wahrgenommene Nutzenvorteil einer Marke in der Abwägung gegenüber preisgleichen Wettbewerbern zum Kauf der Marke führt. Ein gutes Beispiel hierfür ist die Marke „Aldi“, die sich im Lebensmitteleinzelhandel als preisgünstigste Marke positioniert, sodass sich der Markenwert primär aus der realisierten Mengenprämie und einer hohen Kundenbindung speist.

Grundlage des ökonomischen Markenwertes ist somit die **Stärke der Marke**. Eine starke Marke verfügt extern neben einer ausreichenden **Eroberungsrate** vor allem über eine hohe **Markentreue**. Insoweit definiert sich die Markenstärke zunächst anhand der tatsächlichen **Kaufverhaltensrelevanz** einer Marke. Von Treue beziehungsweise Loyalität gegenüber einer Marke kann dann gesprochen werden, wenn der Nachfrager eine positive Einstellung gegenüber der Marke besitzt und diese wiederholt kauft. Zur Entstehung von Markenloyalität reicht es nicht aus, dass sich der Nachfrager an eine Marke erinnert, denn einerseits kann die Markenerinnerung mit einem diffusen Vorstellungsbild einhergehen. Trotz der Erinnerung an den Markennamen verfügt der Nachfrager in diesem Fall nicht über ein klares Markenimage (Herzig 1991). Damit besitzt die Marke nur eine sehr begrenzte Kaufverhaltensrelevanz. Andererseits kann der erinnerte Markenname mit einem klaren, aber negativen Vorstellungsbild verbunden sein, sodass es nicht zu wiederholten Käufen der Marke kommt und die Markenloyalität nur gering ausfällt. Die **Markenbekanntheit** ist somit eine notwendige, aber keine hinreichende Bedingung für die

Stärke der Marke. Markenstärke in diesem Sinne korreliert in hohem Maße mit dem ökonomischen Wert der Marke. Die Unterscheidung zwischen Markenloyalität und Markenerinnerung ist vor allem im Zusammenhang mit alten Marken von Bedeutung, an die man sich zwar noch erinnert, die für das eigene Kaufverhalten jedoch keine oder nur noch eine geringe Relevanz besitzen.

Markenstärke hat im Konzept der identitätsorientierten Markenführung darüber hinaus eine **innengerichtete Dimension**. Bezug nehmend auf die Verhaltensrelevanz beschreibt es das Ausmaß an **Markencommitment** der Mitarbeiter (psychologische Bindung gegenüber der Marke), das deren Bereitschaft zu zusätzlichen, freiwilligen Arbeitsanstrengungen zur Erreichung der Markenziele determiniert (siehe dazu auch den Beitrag zu den konzeptionellen Grundlagen des identitätsorientierten Markenmanagements als auch den Beitrag zum innengerichteten Markenmanagement in diesem Buch).

Die Markenbildung setzt umfangreiche **Lernvorgänge** voraus. Lernen bezeichnet die systematische Änderung des Verhaltens aufgrund von Erfahrungen. Damit ist der Begriff zwischen Informationsverarbeitung und -speicherung angesiedelt (Meffert 1992, S. 62). Der Nachfrager muss das in der Positionierung zum Ausdruck kommende Nutzenversprechen einer Marke lernen. Er muss lernen, worin im Vergleich zu konkurrierenden Produkten der Mehrwert der Marke liegt, und schließlich muss er lernen, wo er die Marke erwerben kann. Unabhängig von der Vielzahl an Lerntheorien, die in der Literatur diskutiert werden (Kroeber-Riel/Weinberg, 2003, S. 324 ff.), besteht Einigkeit darin, dass Lernen in der Regel mit einem **hohen Zeitbedarf** einhergeht. Dies trifft auch auf die Internalisierung der Markenidentität bei den Mitarbeitern zu. Um die Früchte erfolgreicher Markenführung „ernten" zu können, bedarf es somit eines hohen Maßes an Geduld beziehungsweise eines langen Planungshorizontes. Stehen kurzfristig zu realisierende Erfolge im Mittelpunkt des Managementinteresses, verkommt Markenführung schnell zum „Labeling" und die Wirkung der Marke verpufft.

4. Nutzen der Marke aus Nachfrager- und Anbietersicht

Die Analyse der Markenbildung verdeutlicht, dass die Marke wichtige Funktionen für den Nachfrager und andere Bezugsgruppen der Marke erfüllt (vgl. Abbildung 3). So stellt die Marke aus verhaltenstheoretischer Sicht eine Orientierungshilfe dar. Die Marke erhöht die Markttransparenz, wodurch es dem Nachfrager schneller ermöglicht wird, das gewünschte Produkt **zu identifizieren**. Marken kommen damit dem Bequemlichkeitsstreben der Menschen entgegen, das heißt, der Suchaufwand wird reduziert. Die kognitive Entlastung durch Marken geht jedoch über den verringerten Suchaufwand hinaus. Kaufentscheidungen finden in der Regel auf Basis unvollkommener Informationen statt. Durch die Wahrnehmung einer Marke und die sich direkt anschließende Aktivierung des zugehörigen Markenimages werden gespeicherte Informationen verfügbar, die eine **Bewertung und Entscheidungsfindung** erleichtern. Wurde der Kunde beim Erstkauf einer Marke zufrieden gestellt, erreicht er mit dem Wiederkauf eine erhebliche Beschleunigung und Vereinfachung seines Kaufentscheidungsprozesses. Marken fungieren als so genannte „information chunks“ und führen zu einer Komplexitätsreduktion (Kroeber-Riel/Weinberg 2003, S. 265).

Abbildung 3: Nutzen der Marke aus Nachfragerperspektive

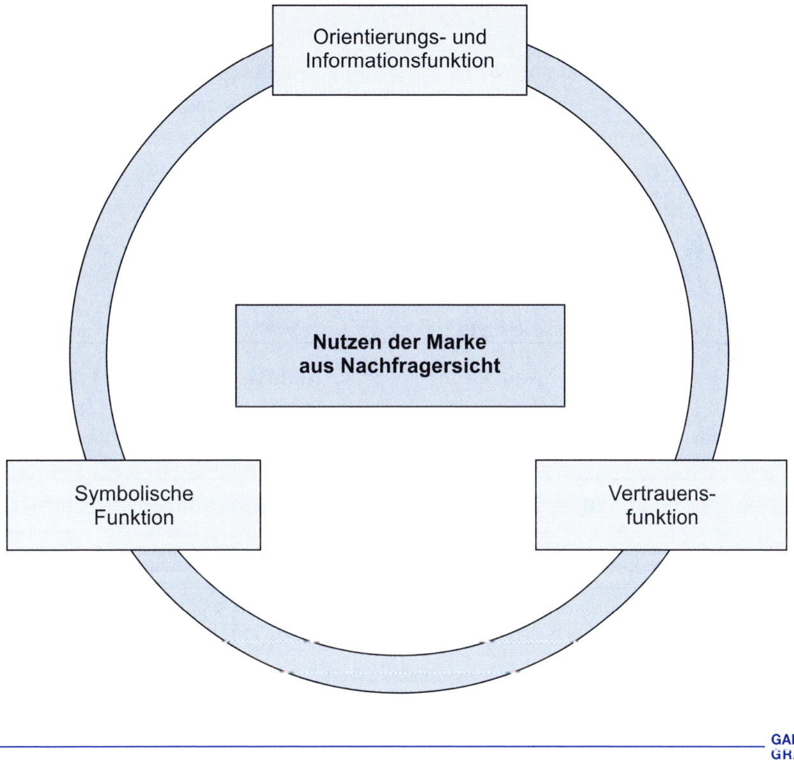

Aus transaktionskostentheoretischer Sicht verringern sich durch Marken die Such- und Informationskosten. Eine Marke kann für den Nachfrager damit „günstiger“ sein als ein markenloses Produkt. Kaufverhaltensrelevant ist letztlich die Summe aus Preis- und Transaktionskosten (Kaas 1990, S. 543). Marken übernehmen somit zunächst einmal eine **Orientierungs- und Informationsfunktion**.

Ferner wird der Marke aufgrund ihrer Bekanntheit, Kompetenz und Identität Vertrauen entgegengebracht **(Vertrauensfunktion)**. In der Informationsökonomie wird in diesem Zusammenhang unterstellt, dass bei Transaktionsprozessen zwischen Anbietern und Nachfragern Informationsasymmetrien und damit Verhaltensunsicherheiten auftreten. Dabei wird die Höhe der Informationsdefizite und das Maß an Verhaltensunsicherheit eines Nachfragers von den Beurteilungsmöglichkeiten eines Leistungsangebots determiniert. Es wird eine Unterscheidung von Leistungsmerkmalen nach Such-, Erfahrungs- und Vertrauenseigenschaften vorgenommen. Vor allem bei Produkten mit einem hohen Anteil an Vertrauenseigenschaften, die auch nach dem Kauf und Konsum eines Produktes nicht zweifelsfrei beurteilt werden können (zum Beispiel technischer Wartungszustand und Sicherheit eines Flugzeuges im Rahmen eines Pauschalurlaubs; Leistungsqualität einer Risikolebensversicherung), besteht beim Nachfrager ein hohes Risikoempfinden. Aufgrund des vom Nachfrager empfundenen Risikos ergibt sich für den Anbieter die Notwendigkeit, beim Nachfrager Vertrauen aufzubauen. Die Marke kann hier als Signal für eine bestimmte Leistungsqualität aufgefasst werden und trägt zu einer **Minderung des subjektiv empfundenen Risikos** bei. Eine Marke erbringt somit für die Nachfrager oft den Nachweis von Sicherheit während der Gebrauchs-, Verbrauchs- und Entsorgungsphase durch Abgabe eines Qualitätsversprechens.

Darüber hinaus kann die Marke für den Nachfrager eine **Prestigefunktion** in seinem sozialen Umfeld erfüllen. Bereits William James hat im 19. Jahrhundert erkannt, dass Menschen Güter über die funktionale Bedürfnisbefriedigung hinaus zum Ausdruck ihrer Persönlichkeit benutzen: *„A man's self is the sum total of all that he can call his, not only his body and his psychic power, but his clothes and house, his wife and children, his ancestors and friends, his reputations and works, his lands and yacht and bank account. All these things give him the same emotions."* (James 1890, S. 291). Marken können damit zu einem Mittel der Kommunikation der eigenen Persönlichkeit gegenüber anderen Menschen werden **(Identitätsvermittlung)**.

Neben dieser Identitätsvermittlung können Marken **identitätsstiftende Wirkung** entfalten, indem der Nachfrager Attribute der Marke auf sich selbst überträgt und damit sein Eigenbild definiert. Neben der reinen Selbstverwirklichung kann hierdurch soziale Gruppenzugehörigkeit zum Ausdruck gebracht werden. Der Nachfrager kommuniziert mit Hilfe der Marke in seinem sozialen Umfeld. In diesem Zusammenhang wird der Marke als Mythos (Kehrer 2001) in jüngster Zeit gar eine „Religionsfunktion" oder, etwas abgeschwächt, eine **sinnstiftende Wirkung** zugeschrieben (Kunde 2000). Marken stehen hier stellvertretend für bestimmte Wertvorstellungen oder Lebensstile. Marken können symbolhaft auch mit persönlich wichtigen, angenehmen oder unangenehmen Erlebnissen verknüpft werden, diese aktualisieren und damit Verhalten beeinflussen.

In allen diesen Fällen steht die Marke symbolhaft für wichtige Motivatoren des Verhaltens der Nachfrager. Dieser **symbolischen Funktion der Marke** kommt bezüglich der Beeinflussung des Verhaltens interner und externer Bezugsgruppen der Marke oft die größte Bedeutung zu.

Aus dem nachfragerseitigen Nutzen der Marke ergeben sich zahlreiche Chancen für die Unternehmen im Rahmen der Markenführung. Die Marke soll durch ihre absatzfördernde Wirkung vor allem zu einer Steigerung des ökonomischen Markenwertes führen (vgl. Abbildung 4). Ein professionelles Markenmanagement soll **Präferenzen** für das eigene Leistungsangebot schaffen und es damit gleichzeitig von konkurrierenden Angeboten **differenzieren**. In diesem Zusammenhang wird synonym auch von **Profilierung** gesprochen.

Abbildung 4: **Nutzen der Marke aus Anbieterperspektive**

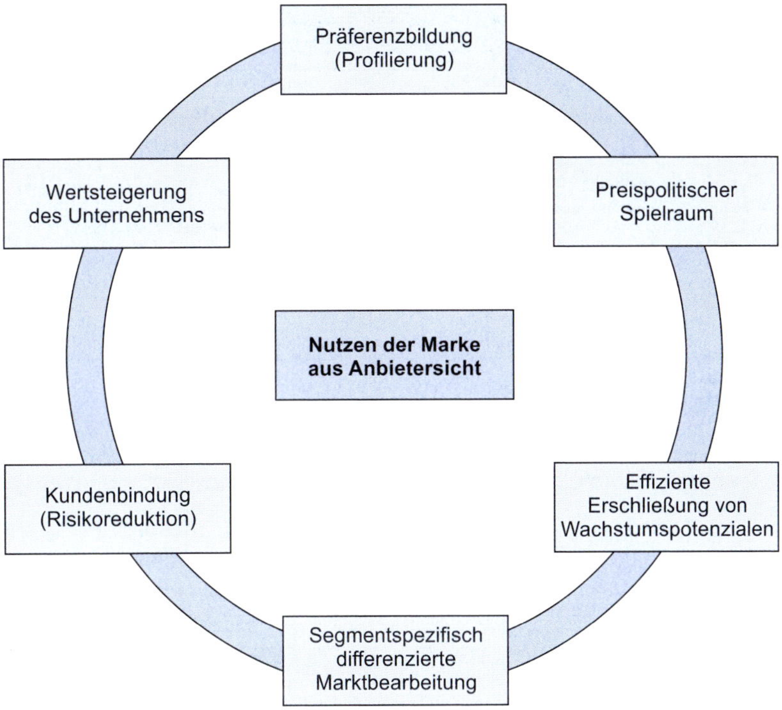

GABLER GRAFIK

Darüber hinaus kann durch ein professionelles Markenmanagement die Planungssicherheit erhöht werden. Im Laufe der Zeit sollen immer mehr Nachfrager die Marke aufgrund ihrer Zufriedenheit und ihrer gefühlsmäßigen Verbundenheit wiederkaufen und weiterempfehlen. Dadurch soll eine **hohe Kundenbindung** erreicht werden, die ihrerseits die Volatilität der Absatzentwicklung eines Unternehmens reduziert. Diese **Risikoreduktion** führt zu niedrigeren Zinssätzen bei der Diskontierung zukünftiger Einzahlungsüberschüsse und damit zu einer **Unternehmenswertsteigerung**. Darüber hinaus kann auf diese Weise die Aufnahme von Fremdkapital erleichtert und die Fremdkapitalkosten gesenkt werden. Durch die Umsetzung der neuen, verschärften Anforderungen an die risikoadäquate Eigenkapitalausstattung der Banken („Basel II") hat dieser anbieterseitige Nutzen gut geführter Marken an Bedeutung gewonnen.

Abbildung 5: Die 25 wertvollsten Marken der Welt

Rang 2004	Rang 2003	Name	Wert in Milliarden Dollar 2004	Wert in Milliarden Dollar 2003
1	1	Coca-Cola	67,394	70,453
2	2	Microsoft	61,372	65,174
3	3	IBM	53,791	51,767
4	4	General Electric	44,111	42,340
5	5	Intel	33,499	31,112
6	7	Disney	27,113	28,036
7	8	McDonald's	25,001	24,699
8	6	Nokia	24,041	29,440
9	11	Toyota	22,673	20,784
10	9	Marlboro	22,128	22,183
11	10	Mercedes	21,331	21,371
12	12	Hewlett-Packard	20,978	19,860
13	13	Citibank	19,971	18,571
14	15	American Express	17,683	16,833
15	16	Gillette	16,723	15,978
16	17	Cisco	15,948	15,798
17	19	BMW	15,866	15,106
18	18	Honda	14,874	15,625
19	14	Ford	14,475	17,066
20	20	Sony	12,759	13,153
21	25	Samsung	12,553	10,846
22	23	Pepsi	12,066	11,777
23	21	Nescafé	11,892	12,336
24	22	Budweiser	11,846	11,894
25	29	Dell	11,500	10,367

GABLER GRAFIK

Quelle: Interbrand 2004

Ebenso wird durch die Markenpolitik eine **differenzierte Bearbeitung mehrerer Marktsegmente leichter möglich**. Einzelne Marktsegmente können mit verschiedenen zielgruppenspezifischen Marken optimal bedient werden (vgl. in diesem Zusammenhang den Beitrag zur Mehrmarkenstrategie in diesem Buch). Ebenso eröffnet die Markenpolitik langfristig **attraktive Wachstumspotenziale** durch Markenexpansionsstrategien (vgl. hierzu den Beitrag zu Markenevolutionsstrategien in diesem Buch). Starke Marken erleichtern hier die Erschließung geografisch neuer Absatzregionen und erhöhen die Erfolgswahrscheinlichkeit bei der Einführung neuer Produkte und Dienstleistungen. Letztere können mit den bislang unter einer Marke angebotenen Produkten und Dienstleistungen verwandt sein (so genannte Markenausdehnung) oder völlig neuartige Leistungen repräsentieren (so genannter Markentransfer).

Die Marke soll dem Unternehmen weiterhin einen **preispolitischen Spielraum** verschaffen. Je besser es gelingt, eine Marke im Vergleich zu konkurrierenden Angeboten als „etwas Einzigartiges“ darzustellen, desto größer ist dieser Spielraum. Ein professionelles Markenmanagement führt somit auch aus diesem Grund zu einer Wertsteigerung des Unternehmens.

Diese und weitere betriebswirtschaftliche Argumente zu Gunsten der Führung von Marken haben in den letzten Jahren eine breite Akzeptanz gefunden und dazu geführt, dass Marken als mit Abstand wichtigste **immaterielle Vermögenswerte** immer stärker in den **Mittelpunkt des Interesses** von Wissenschaft und Praxis gerückt sind. Wie bedeutsam das Management dieses „intangible assets“ mittlerweile geworden ist, verdeutlicht Abbildung 5, in der abschließend die Markenwerte der 25 weltweit wertvollsten Marken im Jahr 2004 dargestellt sind.

5. Ausblick

Um das beschriebene Potenzial von Marken auszuschöpfen, müssen Unternehmen ein modernes und professionelles Markenmanagement betreiben. Stellt man jedoch der hohen praktischen Relevanz der Markenführung die Forschungsbemühungen und Entwicklungen in der wissenschaftlichen Diskussion zum Markenverständnis und der Markenführung gegenüber, so zeigt sich ein eher heterogenes und manchmal diffuses Bild.

So finden sich in der marketingwissenschaftlichen Literatur die unterschiedlichsten Interpretationen sowohl zum Markenverständnis als auch zu der Art und Weise, wie Marken erfolgreich geführt werden sollten. Marken werden unter anderem als Personen, als Beziehung, als Mythos und Religion, als Wertesystem, als Logo oder als bloßes Herkunftszeichen aufgefasst. Diese Ausuferung des Markenverständnisses lässt sich auch anhand der Vielzahl objektbezogener Markenkonzepte aufzeigen. Ausgehend von den klassischen Konzepten der Konsumgüter-, Dienstleistungs- und Investitionsgütermarke hat sich ein regelrechter Begriffsdschungel gebildet, der von Öko- und Kultmarken bis hin zu Online-Marken oder digitalen Marken reicht.

Das Spannungsfeld zwischen der unbestrittenen Relevanz von Marken für den Unternehmenserfolg auf der einen Seite und dem ausufernden Begriffsverständnis und höchst heterogenen Führungskonzepten auf der anderen Seite macht es somit erforderlich, ein theoretisches Fundament und klares Verständnis für die Markenführung aufzubauen. Vor diesem Hintergrund erscheint es sinnvoll, zunächst die unterschiedlichen Entwicklungsstufen der Markenführung und des Markenverständnisses zu systematisieren und anhand ihrer zentralen Merkmale zu kennzeichnen, um darauf aufbauend ein integriertes Konzept der Markenführung theoretisch begründet abzuleiten.

Literatur

Aaker, D. (1992), Management des Markenwertes, Frankfurt/M.

Adjouri, N. (2002), Die Marke als Botschafter: Markenidentität bestimmen und entwickeln, Wiesbaden.

Baumgarth, C. (2001): Markenpolitik: Markenwirkungen, Markenführung, Markenforschung, Wiesbaden.

Brockhoff, K. (1999), Produktpolitik, 4. Aufl., Stuttgart [u.a.].

Bruhn, M. (2003), Was ist eine Marke?: Aktualisierung der Markendefinition, in: Jahrbuch der Absatz- und Verbrauchsforschung, Vol. 50, 2004, S. 4–30.

Burmann, Ch., Blinda, L., Nitschke, A. (2003), Konzeptionelle Grundlagen des identitätsbasierten Markenmanagements, Arbeitspapier Nr. 1 des Lehrstuhls für innovatives Markenmanagement (LiM), Burmann, Ch. (Hrsg.), Universität Bremen, Bremen.

Chernatony, L. de, McDonald, M. H. (2003), Creating Powerful Brands, 3. Aufl. Oxford.

Domizlaff, H. (1939), Die Gewinnung öffentlichen Vertrauens. Ein Lehrbuch der Markentechnik, 1. Aufl., Hamburg.

Esch, F. -R. (2004), Strategie und Technik der Markenführung, 2. Aufl., München.

Farquhar, P. H. (1990), Managing Brand Equity, in: Journal of Advertising Research, Aug./Sept., S. 7–12.

Herzig, O. A. (1991), Markenbilder – Markenwelten: Neue Wege in der Imageforschung, Wien.

Irmscher, M. (1997), Markenwertmanagement, Frankfurt/M.

James, W. (1890), The Principles of Psychology, New York.

Kaas, H. P. (1990), Marketing als Bewältigung von Informations- und Unsicherheitsproblemen im Markt, in: DBW, 50. Jg., Nr. 4, S. 539–548.

Kapferer, J. N. (1992), Die Marke – Kapital des Unternehmens, Landsberg/Lech.

Kehrer, R. (2001), Marke und Mythos – Eine kulturwissenschaftliche Betrachtung des betriebswirtschaftlichen Phänomens Marke, in: Bruhn, M. (Hrsg.), Die Marke – Symbolkraft eines Zeichensystems, , Bern u.a., S. 197–218.

Keller, K. L. (1993), Conceptualizing, Measuring, and Managing Customer-Based Brand Equity, in: Journal of Marketing, Vol. 57, Januar, S. 1–22

Keller, K. L. (2003), Strategic Brand Management, 2. Aufl., Upper Saddle River.

Kotler, Ph. (2000), Marketing Management: Analysis, Planning, Implementation, and Control, Millennium ed. – Upper Saddle River, NJ Prentice-Hall.

Kunde, J. (2000), Corporate Religion, Wiesbaden.

Meffert, H. (1992), Marketingforschung und Käuferverhalten, 2. Aufl., Wiesbaden.

Meffert, H., Bongartz, M. (2000), Marktorientierte Unternehmensführung an der Jahrtausendwende aus Sicht der Wissenschaft und Unternehmenspraxis – eine empirische Untersuchung, in: Deutschsprachige Marketingforschung – Bestandsaufnahme und Perspektiven, im Auftrag der Wissenschaftlichen Kommission Marketing im Verband der Hochschullehrer für Betriebswirtschaft e.V, Backhaus (Hrsg.), Stuttgart, S. 381–405.

Mellerowicz, K. (1963): Markenartikel – Die ökonomischen Gesetze ihrer Preisbildung und Preisbindung, 2. Aufl., München [u.a.].

Ogilvy, D. (1951), Speech to American Marketing Association, Chicago, AMA Procedings.

Perrey, J., Riesenbeck, H. (2003), Starke Marken sind kein Zufall, in: Marketing Journal, Nr. 3, Mai/Juni, S. 46–48.

Sander, M. (1994), Die Bestimmung und Steuerung des Wertes von Marken. Eine Analyse aus Sicht des Markeninhabers, Heidelberg.

Sattler, H. (2001), Markenpolitik, Stuttgart.

Sattler, H. (2002), Monetäre Bewertung von Markenstrategien für neue Produkte, Stuttgart.

Schröder, H. (2001), Neuere Entwicklungen des Markenschutzes. Markenschutz-Controlling vor dem Hintergrund des Markengesetzes, in: Köhler, R.; Majer, W.; Wiezorek, H., (Hrsg., im Auftrag der GEM Gesellschaft zur Erforschung des Markenwesens e.V., Wiesbaden), Erfolgsfaktor Marke: Neue Strategien des Markenmanagements, München.

Schweiger, G. (1998), Markenwertforschung: Die Konsumenten bestimmen den Wert einer Marke, in: Werbewissenschaft und Marktforschung, Leistungsbericht, Wien, S. 20–23.

Weinberg, P. (1993), Markenartikel und Markenpolitik, in: Wittmann, W.; Kern, W.; Köhler, R.; Küpper, H.-U.; v. Wysocki, K. (Hrsg.), Handwörterbuch der Betriebswirtschaft, Teilband 2 (I-Q), 5.,völlig neu gestaltete Aufl., Stuttgart, S. 2679–2690.

Welling, M. (2003), Bausteine einer integrierten image- und identitätsorientierten Markenführung als Beitrag zur Markentheorie, Schriften zum Marketing Nr. 47, Ruhr Universität Bochum, Bochum.

Wandel in der Markenführung – vom instrumentellen zum identitäts-orientierten Markenverständnis

Heribert Meffert und Christoph Burmann

1.	**Verändertes Markenverständnis im Zeitablauf**	**20**
2.	**Entwicklungsstufen der Markenführung**	**22**
2.1	Marke als bloßes Eigentumszeichen	22
2.2	Marke als Merkmalskatalog: Instrumenteller Ansatz der Markenführung	22
2.3	Angebotsbezogenes Markenverständnis: Funktionsorientierter Ansatz der Markenführung	24
2.4	Nachfragerbezogenes und wettbewerbsorientiertes Markenverständnis	25
2.41	Verhaltens- beziehungsweise imageorientierter Ansatz der Markenführung	26
2.42	Technokratisch-strategieorientierter Ansatz der Markenführung	27
2.5	Marke als sozialpsychologisches Phänomen	27
2.51	Fraktaler Ansatz der Markenführung	29
2.52	Identitätsorientierter Ansatz der Markenführung	30
3.	**Fazit**	**32**

1. Verändertes Markenverständnis im Zeitablauf

Seit der Entstehung des klassischen Markenartikelkonzeptes zu Beginn dieses Jahrhunderts hat sich das Verständnis vom Wesen einer Marke aufgrund tiefgreifender Änderungen in den Markt- und Umweltbedingungen gewandelt. Auf der Suche nach dem „richtigen" Weg der Markenführung wurde dabei immer wieder der Ruf nach einem „Paradigmenwechsel", nach einer Neuorientierung im Markenmanagement laut. Die veränderten Rahmenbedingungen haben somit nicht nur unterschiedliche Markenbegriffe, sondern auch verschiedene **Ansätze der Markenführung** hervorgebracht.

Stark vereinfacht lassen sich in diesem Zusammenhang **fünf Phasen in der Markenentwicklung** voneinander abgrenzen und deren Implikationen für die Markenführung aufzeigen. Im Folgenden wird auf den Gegenstand moderner Markenführung und seine historische Entwicklung näher eingegangen. Hierzu werden die einzelnen Entwicklungsstufen entsprechend der Abbildung 1 dargestellt, wobei die Herausbildung der einzelnen Phasen durch wesentliche Veränderungen in der Aufgabenumwelt der Unternehmen (Makroebene) und dem Wandel der Beziehungen zwischen Hersteller und Handel (Mikroebene) erklärt wird.

Abbildung 1: **Entwicklung des Markenverständnisses und der Markenführungsansätze im Zeitablauf**

Zeitraum	Mitte 19. Jahrhundert bis Anfang 20. Jahrhundert	Anfang 20. Jahrhundert bis Mitte 60er	Mitte 60er bis Mitte 70er	Mitte 70er bis Ende 80er	90er Jahre
Aufgabenumwelt	■ Industrialisierung und Massenproduktion ■ Qualitätsschwankungseffekt ■ Anonyme Ware (Stapelware) vorherrschend	■ Wirtschaftliches Wachstum „Nachfragesog" ■ Zahlreiche technische Innovationen ■ Verkäufermärkte	■ Rezession/ 1. Ölkrise ■ Aufhebung der Preisbindung (1967) ■ Käufermärkte	■ Gesättigte Märkte ■ Hohe Imitationsgeschwindigkeit ■ „Information Overload" ■ Qualität als K.O.-Kriterium	■ Informationsgesellschaft, Markenführung im Internet ■ Positionierungsenge ■ Verantwortungsverlagerung von Einzel- zu (Unternehmens-) Dachmarken

Handels-hersteller-Beziehungen	■ Persönliche Kundenbeziehungen der Hersteller und des Handels ■ Starke Stellung des Handels	■ Handlanger-funktion des Handels ■ Meinungs-monopol der Hersteller-marken ■ Produktivitätssprünge im Handel ■ Starke Ausbreitung klassischer Hersteller-marken	■ Einführung von Handelsmarken ■ „Popularisierung des Marketing" ■ Marken-Know-how Asymmetrie zu Gunsten des Herstellers	■ Wachsende Handels-macht und Konfliktverschärfung ■ Einführung von Geltungs-marken ■ Steigendes Marken-Know-how des Handels	■ Informationsmonopol des Handels ■ Intensivierung des Direktkanals Hersteller – Kunden ■ Marketing-führerschaft des Handels in vielen Bereichen ■ Handels-marken verdrängen Hersteller-marken
Marken-verständnis	■ Marke als Eigentums-zeichen und Herkunfts-nachweis	■ Warenfokus ■ Marke als Merkmals-katalog	■ Produktions- und Vertriebs-methode ■ Vermarktungsform	■ Nachfrager-gewinnung ■ Subjektive Markenbestimmung	■ Nutzen-bündel mit nachhaltiger Differenzierung ■ Marken-identität als Selbstbild der Marke ■ Marken-image als Fremdbild der Marke
„Modernes" Marken-management		■ Instrumenteller Ansatz „Markentechnik"	■ Funktions-orientierter Ansatz	■ Verhaltens- und image-orientierter Ansatz ■ Technokratisch, strategieorientierter Ansatz	■ Integriertes identitäts-orientiertes Markenmanagement ■ Fraktales Markenmanagement

GABLER GRAFIK

2. Entwicklungsstufen der Markenführung

2.1 Marke als bloßes Eigentumszeichen

Die einsetzende **Industrialisierung** und mit ihr die **Massenproduktion** vieler bis dato handwerklich erzeugter Konsumgüter führten ab Mitte des 19. Jahrhunderts zu einem Verlust der persönlichen Geschäftsbeziehungen zwischen produzierenden Unternehmen und dem Endverbraucher (Leitherer 1955; Leitherer 2001). An ihre Stelle trat der anonyme Massenmarkt. Die Hersteller verloren den direkten Kontakt zum Verbraucher. Die in vielen Branchen noch unausgereifte Produktionstechnik hatte einerseits zur Folge, dass die Qualität industrieller Fertigwaren oftmals erheblichen Schwankungen ausgesetzt war. Darüber hinaus begrenzte das erst rudimentäre Produktions- und Koordinations-Know-how die Betriebsgröße der Hersteller. Die Struktur des Warenangebotes blieb somit stark regional geprägt. Anonyme Waren beherrschten das Bild in fast allen Produktgruppen.

In den Anfängen des vergangenen Jahrhunderts zeichnete sich im Handel ein wachsender Preiswettbewerb durch Warenhäuser, Filialisten und Konsumvereine als innovative Betriebsformen ab (Berekoven 1978, S. 36). Die Markierung von Waren diente in dieser Zeit in erster Linie als Eigentumskennzeichnung und Herkunftsnachweis (Linxweiler 2001, S. 49). Das Markenverständnis war durch den bloßen Vorgang der Kennzeichnung beziehungsweise Markierung geprägt. **Markenführung als betriebswirtschaftliches Managementkonzept existierte noch nicht**.

2.2 Marke als Merkmalskatalog: instrumenteller Ansatz der Markenführung

Vor dem Hintergrund dieser Rahmenbedingungen sind die Entstehung und rasche Verbreitung des vor allem von Domizlaff geprägten klassischen Markenartikelkonzeptes zu sehen (Domizlaff 1951). Dieses Konzept bot den **Konsumgüterherstellern** die Chance, indirekt wieder mit dem Verbraucher in Kontakt zu treten und ihren Einfluss auf den Verkauf ihrer Waren im Handel deutlich zu vergrößern. Diese Ziele der Hersteller sollten durch eine hohe und vor allem konstante Warenqualität, eine gleichartige Aufmachung, den Vertrieb in einem größeren, überregionalen Markt und insbesondere den Vorverkauf der Waren durch klassische Werbung erreicht werden. Die zahlreichen im Zuge der Industrialisierung und Massenproduktion entstehenden technischen Innovationen bildeten zumeist den Kern für erfolgreiche Markenkommunikation und Markenbildung. Das starke wirtschaftliche Wachstum und die in den meisten Warengruppen vorherrschende Situation des Verkäufermarktes förderten die schnelle Diffusion des klassischen Markenartikelkonzeptes. Unter diesen Marktbedingungen waren die Zusicherung einer zuverlässig hohen Qualität, eine durch die Werbung aufgebaute hohe Bekanntheit und eine bislang unbekannte Convenience (Preisgleichheit und Verfügbarkeit in allen wichtigen Handelsgeschäften) die Schlüsselfaktoren für den Markterfolg.

Auch im **Handel** stieß das klassische Markenartikelkonzept zunächst auf Gegenliebe, denn die Preis- und Vertriebsbindung des Markenartikels verhinderte einen ruinösen Preiswettbewerb. Darüber hinaus ließen sich bei den Betriebsabläufen im Handel erhebliche Produktivitätsfortschritte durch Einführung der Selbstbedienung und den weitgehenden Verzicht auf Dimensionierungs-, Verpackungs-, Qualitätssicherungs- und Informationsfunktionen realisieren. Die Übernahme dieser Funktionen durch die Hersteller (Meffert/Burmann 1991, S. 57) in Verbindung mit deren Betriebsgrößenwachstum durch Massenproduktion resultierte schließlich in einer starken Machtposition der Markenartikelhersteller. Immer öfter wurden der Vorwurf des „Meinungsmonopols der Markenartikel" und die Klage über die zum Erfüllungsgehilfen degenerierte Funktion des Handels laut (Berekoven 1978, S. 37).

In dieser zweiten Entwicklungsphase waren das Verständnis vom **Wesen der Marke** durch einen **konsumgüterorientierten Warenfokus** und die Suche nach konstitutiven Eigenschaften gekennzeichnet. Der Markenbegriff wurde durch einen **Merkmalskatalog** gekennzeichnet, der sich stets auf physisch fassbare Konsumgüter bezog. Dienstleistungen, Investitionsgüter oder gar Vorprodukte waren nach damaligem Verständnis keine Marken (Mellerowicz 1963, S. 39). Konsequenterweise sprach man im unternehmerischen Alltag, in der Wissenschaft und sogar auf seiten des Gesetzgebers ausschließlich von **Markenartikeln** oder **Markenwaren**. So definiert Mellerowicz Marken als *„... für den privaten Bedarf geschaffene Fertigwaren, die in einem größeren Absatzraum unter einem besonderen, die Herkunft kennzeichnenden Merkmal (Marke) in einheitlicher Aufmachung, gleicher Menge sowie in gleichbleibender und verbesserter Güte erhältlich sind und sich dadurch sowie durch die für sie betriebene Werbung die Anerkennung der beteiligten Wirtschaftskreise (Verbraucher, Händler und Hersteller) erworben haben (Verkehrsgeltung)"* (Mellerowicz 1963, S. 39). Wird mindestens eine Anforderung von einem Produkt nicht erfüllt, liegt bei strenger Auslegung des merkmalsorientierten Verständnisses kein Markenartikel vor (Leitherer 1954).

In der **Markenführung** herrschte ein instrumentell geprägtes Verständnis vor (Findeisen 1925, S. 32; Goldack 1948, S. 22; Domizlaff 1951, S. 27 f.; Mellerowicz 1963, S. 12 f.; Hartmann 1966, S. 12 f.). Dieser **instrumentelle Ansatz** fand seinen Niederschlag in dem Begriff der **Markentechnik**, die sich vor allem mit der Namensfindung und -gestaltung, der Verpackungsform und dem Einsatz der klassischen Werbung beschäftigte (Hartmann 1966, S. 15). Einem naturgesetzlichen Zusammenhang vergleichbar wurden unabhängig von der Unternehmens- und Marktsituation feste Grundregeln aufgestellt, bei deren Befolgung sich quasi automatisch der Erfolg einstellen sollte (Domizlaff 1951, S. 27 f.). So formulierte Domizlaff – der als einer der Väter der professionellen Markenpolitik gelten kann – im Jahre 1939 „22 Grundgesetze der natürlichen Markenbildung", die als Grundsätze für den Markenerfolg gelten sollten. In diesen Grundgesetzen werden die konstitutiven Merkmale der Marke aufgegriffen und Instrumente zu ihrem Aufbau und ihrer Pflege beschrieben.

hauptung gegenüber einem im Markenbereich zusehends selbstbewusst auftretenden Handel eingesetzt.

Die wachsende Konzentration im **Handel** ließ die Absatzmittler zu „gate-keepern“, das heißt zu einem Nadelöhr auf dem Weg des Markenartikels vom Hersteller zum Verbraucher, werden (Lewin 1963, S. 206 f.). Dem gestiegenen Preisbewusstsein der Verbraucher kam der Handel durch die Einführung von Gattungsmarken entgegen (Meffert/Bruhn 1984, S. 7 f.). Der knappe Regalplatz und die Handelsforderung nach Listungsgebühren und anderen versteckten Rabatten bei der Aufnahme neuer Marken in das Sortiment hatten eine Verschärfung der Konflikte zwischen Handel und Herstellern zur Folge.

Das **Markenverständnis** wurde in dieser Phase von einer nachfragebezogenen, subjektiven Begriffsauffassung geprägt. Danach waren diejenigen Produkte oder Dienstleistungen als Markenartikel zu bezeichnen, welche von den Konsumenten als solche wahrgenommen werden (Berekoven 1978, S. 43; Meffert 1979, S. 23 f.). Dieses Markenverständnis löste sich damit bewusst von objektiv bestimmbaren Wareneigenschaften oder bestimmten Produktions- und Vertriebsmethoden. Es zielte vielmehr auf die Gewinnung von Kunden ab und stellte die **Wahrnehmung der Marke durch den Konsumenten** in den Mittelpunkt der Betrachtung. Nur vor dem Hintergrund dieses subjektiven Markenverständnisses ist die Entstehung des Begriffes „Gattungsmarke“ zu erklären.

2.41 Verhaltens- beziehungsweise imageorientierter Ansatz der Markenführung

Das subjektive Markenverständnis spiegelte sich auch in der Markenführung wider. In dieser Phase fand der verhaltens- beziehungsweise imageorientierte Ansatz der Markenführung in Wissenschaft und Praxis größere Verbreitung (Berekoven 1978, S. 43 f.; Murphy 1987, S. 1 f.; Aaker/Keller 1990, S. 27 f.; Trommsdorff 1992, S. 458 f.). Dieser Ansatz basiert auf den Ergebnissen der umfangreichen Forschung zur Bedeutung, Entstehung und den Komponenten des **Markenimages** (Keller 1993). Auf der Grundlage dieser Arbeiten wurden Handlungsempfehlungen zur zielgerichteten Beeinflussung des von den Nachfragern wahrgenommenen Markenimages entwickelt.

Im Gegensatz zum funktionsorientierten Ansatz, der die Markenführung lediglich als Teil des Markenartikel-Marketings verstand, fordert der imageorientierte Ansatz eine Gleichstellung von Marketing und Markenführung. Dieser Auffassung liegt die Überzeugung von der grundsätzlichen Imagerelevanz aller Marketingparameter eines Markenartikelherstellers zugrunde. Trotz dieses grundsätzlich breiten Aufgabenspektrums der Markenführung führte der **ausgeprägte Imagefokus** dieses Ansatzes zu einer Überbetonung von methodischen Aspekten (Operationalisierung des Markenimages, Determinanten des Markenimages, Einflussstärke der Determinanten etc.) und zu einer **Vernachlässigung des Integrationsaspektes**. Die spezifischen Stärken und Schwächen des

Markenunternehmens und die funktionsübergreifende Abstimmung und Vernetzung einzelner Maßnahmen zur Imagegestaltung blieben als Folge der zumeist partialanalytisch-methodischen Vorgehensweise unberücksichtigt.

2.42 Technokratisch-strategieorientierter Ansatz der Markenführung

Parallel zum imageorientierten Ansatz entwickelte sich ein **technokratisch-strategieorientierter Ansatz der Markenführung** (Voss 1983, S. 17 f.; Meffert 1988, S. 115 f. und 289 f.; Brandmeyer/Schulz 1989; Franzen/Trommsdorff/Riedel 1994; Haedrich/Tomczak 2003). Dieser Ansatz versuchte, die Integrationsdefizite des imageorientierten Ansatzes zu beseitigen. Hierzu wurde ein Wechsel in der Betrachtungsweise von der **Verhaltenskonstruktebene** zur **Unternehmensführungsebene** vollzogen. Die Planung, Steuerung und Koordination aller auf den Absatzmarkt gerichteten Maßnahmen der Markengestaltung standen im Mittelpunkt des Interesses. Die in den 80er Jahren einsetzende intensive Beschäftigung mit dem Markenwert führte zu einer weiteren Popularisierung des strategischen Ansatzes der Markenführung. Allerdings mündete die stark formalisierte Darlegung der Markenbildung in der Folge in ein technokratisch-mechanistisches Vorstellungsbild von den Zielen und Aufgaben der Markenführung.

2.5 Marke als sozialpsychologisches Phänomen

Die **fünfte Entwicklungsphase**, ab dem Beginn der 90er Jahre, ist bezüglich der **Aufgabenumwelt** der Unternehmen von einer weiteren Angleichung der Produktqualitäten gekennzeichnet. Dies ist vor allem eine Folge der zunehmenden Modularisierung von Produktkonzepten, beispielsweise bei Computern, Haushaltsgeräten oder Automobilen, und der damit einhergehenden Standardisierung. Das aus Kosten- und Flexibilitätsgesichtspunkten zunehmende Outsourcing trägt aufgrund der Nutzung identischer Lieferanten und Einbauteile durch direkte Wettbewerber, welche in der Vergangenheit unabhängig voneinander Teile entwickelten, ebenfalls zu einer wachsenden Qualitätshomogenität der Markenartikel bei.

Die wachsende internationale Verflechtung und Globalisierung des Wettbewerbs führten zu einer immer schnelleren Verbreitung neuen technologischen Know-hows. Diese Entwicklung fördert zusätzlich die Angleichung der technisch-objektiven Produkteigenschaften konkurrierender Marken. Die zunehmende Qualitätsangleichung und Substituierbarkeit der Angebote erstrecken sich nicht nur auf Konsumgüter, sondern auch auf Dienstleistungen und Investitionsgüter. Dies erklärt, warum auch Dienstleister, Investitionsgüterhersteller und Zulieferer in den vergangenen Jahren in verstärktem Maße auf die Entwicklung eigener Marken zur Differenzierung ihrer Leistungen zurückgegriffen haben (Simon 1994).

Vor diesem Hintergrund ist auch das **Vordringen von Dachmarkenstrategien** zu sehen. Es erklärt sich einerseits aus der Tatsache, dass Dachmarken bei Dienstleistungsunternehmen gegenüber Einzelmarkenstrategien in der Regel vorteilhafter sind (Meffert/Bruhn 2003, S. 405). Andererseits erleichtern Dachmarken die Durchsetzung und Positionierung im „Dschungel" der Markeninflation. Die **Positionierungsenge** und die aufgrund des hohen Mindestwerbedrucks gestiegenen Kosten der Markenführung lassen die Unternehmen immer häufiger bei Neueinführungen von Einzelmarkenkonzepten Abstand nehmen. Dieses Vorgehen entspricht auch den Anforderungen der Verbraucher, weil aufgrund des größeren Wissens über wirtschaftliche Zusammenhänge die Verantwortung von Unternehmen vom Kunden heute wesentlich breiter definiert wird und eine **Verantwortungsverlagerung** von Einzelmarken zum Gesamtunternehmen beziehungsweise **zur Firmendachmarke** zu beobachten ist (Goodyear 1994, S. 66).

Eine weitere für die Markenpolitik wichtige Rahmenbedingung liegt im Zusammenwachsen der Informations- und Kommunikationstechnologien und der schnellen Verbreitung weltweiter Kommunikationsnetze. Weltweite Netzwerke wie das Internet in Verbindung mit den neuen Multimediatechnologien ermöglichen in vielen Bereichen eine deutliche Erhöhung der Markttransparenz. Sie bieten dem Konsumenten zumindest das Potenzial, sich vor einer Kaufentscheidung ohne große Mühen einen umfassenden Marktüberblick zu verschaffen und dabei vor allem Preisvergleiche anzustellen und Leistungen von Anbietern zu beziehen, die bislang aufgrund ihrer räumlichen Entfernung nicht zum „evoked set" des Konsumenten gehörten.

Analysiert man die markenrelevanten Veränderungen in den **Hersteller-Handels-Beziehungen**, dann fällt der enorme Zugewinn an Einfluss und Know-how auf Seiten des Handels auf. Das Vertrauen der Kunden gegenüber großen Einzelhandelsketten und die Margenvorteile selbstmarkierter Produkte nutzt der Handel für den Ausbau seiner Handelsmarkenprogramme insbesondere im Lebensmittelbereich. Die problemlose Verfügbarkeit freier Produktionskapazitäten auf Seiten der Hersteller unterstützt diese Entwicklung massiv. Die fortschreitende Verbreitung von Scannerkassen und die auf diesem Wege gewonnenen Kundendaten versetzen den **Handel** gegenüber den Herstellern zusehends in die Lage eines **Informationsmonopolisten**. Diesen Informationsvorsprung versucht der Handel durch den Ausbau des eigenen Marken-Know-hows, teilweise durch Abwerbung von Markenspezialisten bei den führenden Markenartikelherstellern, für die Stärkung der Eigenmarken zu nutzen. Nicht zuletzt ist die Einführung des Category Managements Ausdruck dieser Entwicklung.

Mit wachsendem Marken-Know-how geht der Handel verstärkt dazu über, bislang beim Hersteller angesiedelte Funktionen zu übernehmen (Meffert/Burmann 1991, S. 57). Die weiter zunehmende Konzentration im Einzelhandel tut ein Übriges, die Markenwünsche der Händler gegenüber den Herstellern durchzusetzen. Vor diesem Hintergrund dürften zukünftig nur die stärksten Herstellermarken einer Warengruppe (so genannte **A-Marken**) eine realistische Listungschance im Handel besitzen.

Die skizzierten Veränderungen in den Rahmenbedingungen haben seit den 90er Jahren wiederum zu einem veränderten Markenverständnis geführt. Die Marke wird heute vor allem unter sozialpsychologischen Aspekten betrachtet. Ging mit dem („harten") technokratisch-strategieorientierten Ansatz der Markenführung eine stark formalisierte Vorstellung von der Markenbildung einher, welche der oftmals von subjektiven Einflüssen und emotionalen Aspekten geprägten „weichen" Führung von Marken nur unzureichend gerecht wurde, werden diese vor allem im Rahmen des identitätsorientierten Ansatzes der Markenführung stärker betont.

2.51 Fraktaler Ansatz der Markenführung

Der fraktale Ansatz der Markenführung (Gerken 1994a) trennt sich von allen Grundprinzipien der Markenführung (zum Beispiel Nutzenversprechen, Positionierung, Zielgruppenorientierung, Prägnanz, Kontinuität), wie sie in den übrigen, bereits dargestellten Ansätzen enthalten sind. Vielmehr soll bei der „fraktalen Marke" der Markenkern durch einen **Mythos** ersetzt werden. Die Mythosdimension umfasst dabei das nicht direkt beschreibbare „Faszinosum" der Marke. Durch bestimmte (zum Beispiel kommunikative) Rituale soll der Mythos auf Dauer mit der Marke verbunden werden und ihr damit Festigkeit und Zeitlosigkeit verschaffen. Neben dem Mythos beinhaltet die Marke zudem die Komponenten „Kairos" und „Logos" (Gerken 1994b). Unter **Kairos** versteht Gerken dabei die Zeitgeistkomponente, in der sich die unterschiedlichen und zum Teil gegensätzlichen Strömungen und Trends der Zeit zusammenfinden. Der **Logos** umfasst schließlich die sachlichen Informationen einer Marke. Er spiegelt das Interesse des Nachfragers wider, neben den spirituellen Komponenten auch faktische Kenntnisse über die Marke zu erwerben.

Aufgabe der Markenführung ist es nach diesem Ansatz, Risiken zu produzieren und die Nachfrager in diese Risiken hineinzuführen. Dies soll über *„mitwandernde Markenoberflächen geschehen, die kurzfristig neue Trends wiedergeben und sich im Fluss des Zeitgeistes selbst organisieren"*. Im ständigen Wechsel der Kommunikationsthemen und der Markengestalt soll sich eine Profilierung der Marke ergeben (Gerken 1994b). Gerken bezeichnet den Zustand der Marke, bei dem radikale Brüche der Marke absichtlich herbeigeführt werden, als **„homogene Inhomogenitäten"** (Gerken 1994a). Den zielgruppenfokussierten Einsatz der Marketing-Mix-Instrumente im Rahmen der klassischen Markenführung hält er dabei für verzichtbar.

Das fraktale Markenverständnis weist somit einen **fundamentalen Unterschied zu den klassischen Verständnissen** der Marke auf, bei denen die Wiedererkennbarkeit sowie die Balance von Kontinuität und Anpassung an neue Bedürfnisse eine große Rolle spielen. Der fraktale Ansatz der Markenführung unterliegt vor diesem Hintergrund vielfältiger **Kritik** aus Wissenschaft und Praxis (Paulus 1995). Vor allem der Verstoß gegen die Kontinuitätsforderung der Markenführung und der bewusste Verzicht auf bewährte Markenführungsregeln bieten Anlass zu Kritik und haben eine Verbreitung dieses Ansatzes letztlich verhindert.

Gerken fordert eine gänzliche Verabschiedung von Zielgruppen und bezeichnet diese als *„Scheinwirklichkeiten"* (Gerken 1990, S. 46). In diesem Zusammenhang stellt Gerkens Ansatz jedoch in zweifacher Hinsicht keine geeignete Alternative dar. Zum einen beruht die Überlegung *„mit den Konsumentenbedürfnissen wandernder Markenoberflächen"* auf einem **Denkfehler**. Während die absatzmarktgerichteten Aktivitäten im klassischen Zielgruppenkonzept auf bestimmte Segmente ausgerichtet sind und demzufolge einzelne Nachfrager erreichen können, wenn diese dem entsprechenden Segment angehören, zielt im Konzept Gerkens eine „springende" Marketing-Konfiguration auf ebenfalls „springende" Nachfragerbedürfnisse. Die **Gefahr eines Misfits zwischen Leistungsspektrum und Nachfragerbedürfnissen** ist in diesem Fall allerdings deutlich höher als im klassischen Marketing (Perrey 1998, S. 233). Zum anderen lässt sich die von Gerken propagierte Szenen- und Trendorientierung allenfalls für stark personalisierte Dienstleistungen umsetzen, in denen unmittelbar auf die veränderten Nachfragerbedürfnisse reagiert werden kann. In vielen, insbesondere fixkostenintensiven Märkten ist eine solche unmittelbare Reaktion jedoch nahezu ausgeschlossen.

Das Verdienst des fraktalen Markenverständnisses liegt vor allem im **Aufbrechen starrer Denkmuster** der Markenführungsdebatte. Im Vergleich zum strategieorientierten Ansatz betont der fraktale Ansatz die kaum fassbaren Aspekte der Marke, die ihren Mythos ausmachen. Letztlich ist dieser Aspekt fraktaler Markenführung jedoch allenfalls Gewinn bringend in bestehende Ansätze der Markenführung zu integrieren und kann nicht über die aufgezeigten Gefahren und **Operationalisierungsdefizite** des gesamten fraktalen Markenführungskonzeptes hinwegtäuschen. In der Summe spricht somit vieles dafür, dass die fraktale Markenführung eher zu einem Verfall denn zu einer Stärkung der Marke führt.

2.52 Identitätsorientierter Ansatz der Markenführung

Auf Basis der vorhergehenden Ansätze und zeitlich parallel zum fraktalen Ansatz der Markenführung hat sich das **identitätsorientierte Markenverständnis** herausgebildet. Im Rahmen dieses Verständnisses wird die Kaufverhaltensrelevanz von Marken primär auf deren **Identität** zurückgeführt (Kapferer 1992, S. 39 f.; Meffert 1994a, S. 480; Meffert/Burmann 1996). Eine konsistente und relevante Markenidentität bildet dabei die Voraussetzung für das **Vertrauen der Nachfrager** in die Marke. Das Vertrauen in die Marke wiederum ist die Grundlage einer langfristigen Kundenbindung und Markentreue. Auch bei der Marke gilt, nur wem man vertrauen kann, bleibt man treu.

Die Betrachtung der Marke aus sozialpsychologischer Perspektive bedeutet nicht, dass hier ökonomische Aspekte in den Hintergrund treten. Vielmehr kann die hohe **ökonomische Relevanz des Identitätskonstruktes** durch Rückgriff auf die Neue Institutionenökonomie belegt werden (Bonus 1995, S. 2 f.). Bezüglich des Vertrauenskonstruktes zeigen Untersuchungen, dass sich das Vertrauen des Kunden als Wettbewerbsvorteil nutzen lässt und darüber hinaus Transaktionskosten eingespart werden können (Kaas 1990, S. 545; Plötner 1995, S. 50 f.; Kenning 2003).

Die zentrale Bedeutung der Identität einer Marke hat zum **identitätsorientierten Ansatz** der Markenführung geführt (Kapferer 1992, S. 39 f.; Schmitt/Pan 1995; Upshaw 1995;

Aaker 1996; Meffert/Burmann 1996; Schmitt/Simonson 1997). Die wesentlichen Unterscheidungsmerkmale zum technokratisch-strategieorientierten Ansatz liegen dabei in der Erweiterung der absatzmarktbezogenen um eine **innengerichtete Ressourcen- und Kompetenzperspektive** und dem durch die sozialpsychologische Ausrichtung nicht deterministischen und **dynamisch ausgerichteten Denkansatz**. Im Mittelpunkt der Betrachtung stehen die Wechselseitigkeit von unternehmensinterner Markenidentität und unternehmensexternem Markenimage sowie die Betonung einer über Funktions- und Unternehmensgrenzen hinweg greifenden Vernetzung aller markenbezogenen Aktivitäten im Sinne einer Ganzheitlichkeit der Markenführung.

Die identitätsorientierte **Neuorientierung der Markenführung** erscheint auch deshalb notwendig, weil der imageorientierte Ansatz durch seine methodisch-partialanalytische Vorgehensweise (Schweiger/Wust 1988; Huber 1990; Theis 1992; Mayerhofer 1995) den Anforderungen eines modernen Markenmanagements nur mehr unzureichend gerecht wird. Die Imagemessung und die gezielte Beeinflussung der Wahrnehmung konzentrierten sich vornehmlich auf einzelne Produkteigenschaften. Hinter vielen Marken, insbesondere im Gebrauchsgütersektor, standen in den früheren Entwicklungsphasen selbstständige, oftmals durch Eigentümerunternehmer geprägte Unternehmen. Die eindeutige Zuordnung einer Marke zu einer Firma beziehungsweise einem Unternehmer machte früher die Markenwerte und -eigenschaften transparent und erleichterte Mitarbeitern und Nachfragern die Identifikation mit der Marke.

Demgegenüber hat sich die Situation heute grundlegend verändert. Vorherrschend sind Konzerne, deren **Markenportfolio** durch zahlreiche, ehemals selbstständige und später akquirierte Marken gekennzeichnet ist. Beispielhaft sei hier auf den Volkswagen-Konzern mit den Marken Audi, Bentley, Bugatti, Lamborghini, Seat, Skoda, Volkswagen oder den Electrolux-Konzern mit den Marken AEG, Juno, Electrolux, Zanussi und Zanker verwiesen. Die Motivation zur Übernahme von Marken hat sich dabei grundlegend geändert. Stand früher der Erwerb des Anlage- und Umlaufvermögens unter Einschluss des Mitarbeiterstamms im Mittelpunkt des Interesses, geht es heute in erster Linie um die Übernahme der Rechte an eingeführten Markennamen. Dies hat zur Folge, dass es oft bereits kurz nach der Akquisition zur Zusammenlegung zahlreicher Funktionsbereiche bis hin zur Stilllegung von Betriebsteilen oder sogar des gesamten Betriebs des übernommenen Unternehmens kommt. Dies führt zur Erosion bis hin zum Totalverlust der **Identität der gekauften Marken**. In diesem Zusammenhang bestätigt sich das Bonmot *„Marken sterben nie, sie werden ermordet (vom Management)“*.

Darüber hinaus sind heute, wiederum vor allem im Gebrauchsgütersektor, häufig so genannte **Gleichteile- beziehungsweise Plattform-Strategien** zu beobachten, die zur Standardisierung und einheitlichen Verwendung ganzer Baugruppen und Module über die Markengrenzen hinweg führen (Bliss 2000). Außerdem wird zur Verbesserung der eigenen Kostensituation heute in erheblich stärkerem Maße als in der Vergangenheit vom **Outsourcing** Gebrauch gemacht. Dies begünstigt die weitere **Erosion der substanziellen Elemente einer Marke und ihrer Identität**. Auch die stark gewachsene Produkt- und Variantenvielfalt als Antwort der Industrie auf die Fragmentierung der Nachfrage (Büchelhofer 2002) hat heute zu einer Situation geführt, in der ein Aufbau starker Marken ohne eine klare Fokussierung auf die Identität einer Marke und der ihr zugrunde liegenden Ressourcen und Kompetenzen kaum noch möglich ist.

Vor dem Hintergrund dieser Entwicklungen kann die identitätsorientierte Markenführung heute als ein **Managementprozess** verstanden werden, der die Planung, Koordination und Kontrolle aller Maßnahmen zum Aufbau starker Marken bei allen relevanten Zielgruppen umfasst. Ziel ist eine funktions- und unternehmensübergreifende Integration (inklusive Absatzmittlern) aller mit der Marke zusammenhängenden Entscheidungen und Aktivitäten zum Aufbau von langfristig stabilen und werthaltigen Marke-Kunden-Beziehungen im Sinne des Oberziels einer Maximierung des Markenwertes.

3. Fazit

Betrachtet man die verschiedenen Ansätze der Markenführung in einer Gesamtschau, so ist ähnlich wie im Marketing einerseits eine Vertiefung („deepening“) und andererseits eine Verbreiterung („broadening“) der Markenführung festzustellen (vgl. Abbildung 2).

Ausgehend von einer lediglich auf bestimmte Warenmerkmale und später auf einzelne Instrumente ausgerichteten Markenführung ist zunächst eine **Vertiefung** durch die Einbeziehung der Wirkungen auf den Absatzmärkten festzustellen. Demzufolge beschäftigte sich die Markenführung verstärkt mit Aspekten des Konsumentenverhaltens. Beschränkte sich dies zunächst auf das beobachtbare Verhalten und klassische Kaufentscheidungskriterien, wurden später auch ökologische und gesellschaftliche Aspekte sowie sozialpsychologische Phänomene in die Markenführung integriert. Eine weitere Vertiefung stellte schließlich die Ergänzung der absatzmarktgerichteten durch die innengerichtete Perspektive der Markenführung und damit eine Fokussierung auf Ressourcen und Kompetenzen dar. Organisations- und Führungsaspekte werden auf diese Weise in die Aufgaben der Markenführung integriert und die Erkenntnisse der Ressourcen- und Kompetenztheorie können für das Markenmanagement nutzbar gemacht werden.

Abbildung 2: Entwicklung des Markenverständnisses und der Markenführungsansätze im Zeitablauf

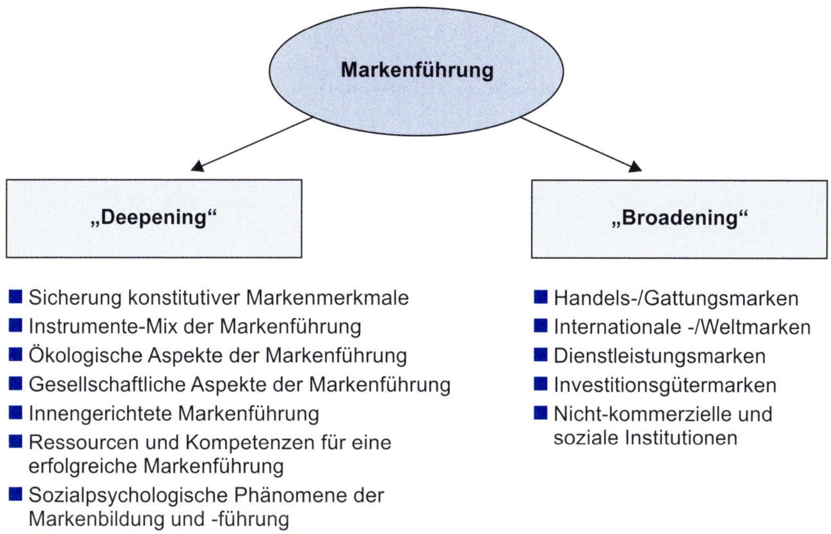

GABLER GRAFIK

Im Zuge der **Verbreiterung** der Markenführung erweiterte sich der Gegenstandsbereich schließlich von einer klassischerweise auf qualitativ hochwertige Konsumgüter beschränkten Betrachtung auf generische Produkte, Dienstleistungen, Investitionsgüter, Künstler, Vereine und Wohlfahrtsorganisationen bis hin zu Städten und Regionen (unter anderem Niedner 1994, S. 1645; Strobl 1994, S. 1659).

Literatur

Aaker, D. A. (1996), Building Strong Brands, New York u.a.

Aaker, D. A., Keller, K. L. (1990), Consumer Evaluations of Brand Extensions, in: Journal of Marketing, Vol. 54, Januar, S. 27–41.

Alewell, K. (1974), Markenartikel, in: Tietz, B. (Hrsg.), Handwörterbuch der Absatzwirtschaft, Wiesbaden, Sp. 1217–1227.

Angehrn, O. (1969), Handelsmarken und Herstellermarken im Wettbewerb, Stuttgart.

Berekoven, L. (1978), Zum Verständnis und Selbstverständnis des Markenwesens, in: Markenartikel heute. Marke, Markt und Marketing, Schriftenreihe Markt und Marketing des Gabler-Verlags, Wiesbaden, S. 35–48.

Bliss, Ch. (2000), Management von Komplexität – Ein integrierter, systemtheoretischer Ansatz zur Komplexitätsreduktion, Wiesbaden.

Bonus, H. (1995), Europäische Identität aus ökonomischer Sicht, Volkswirtschaftliche Diskussionsbeiträge des Instituts für Genossenschaftswesen der Westfälischen Wilhelms-Universität Münster, Beitrag Nr. 216, Münster.

Brandmeyer, K., Schulz, R. (1989), Die „Markenbilanz“, in: Marketing Journal, 22. Jg., S. 360–363.

Büchelhofer, R. (2002), Markenführung im Volkswagen-Konzern im Rahmen der Mehrmarkenstrategie, in: Meffert, H., Burmann, Ch., Koers, M. (Hrsg.), Markenmanagement. Grundfragen der identitätsorientierten Markenführung, 1. Aufl., Wiesbaden.

Dichtl, E. (1978), Grundidee, Entwicklungsepochen und heutige wirtschaftliche Bedeutung des Markenartikels, in: Gabler-Verlag (Hrsg.), Markenartikel heute. Marke, Markt und Marketing, Wiesbaden, S. 17–34.

Domizlaff, H. (1951), Die Gewinnung öffentlichen Vertrauens. Ein Lehrbuch der Markentechnik, 2. Aufl., Hamburg (1. Aufl. 1939).

Dubber, D. (1969), Die Bedeutung des Markenartikels im Prozeß der industriellen Entwicklung, Schriftenreihe zur Industrie- und Entwicklungspolitik, Voigt, F. (Hrsg.), Band 2, Berlin.

Findeisen, F. (1925), Die Markenartikel im Rahmen der Absatzökonomie der Betriebe, Berlin.

Franzen, O., Trommsdorff, V., Riedel, F. (1994), Ansätze der Markenbewertung und Markenbilanz, in: Markenartikel, Nr. 8, S. 372–387.

Gerken, G. (1990), Abschied vom Marketing. Interfusion statt Marketing., Düsseldorf.

Gerken, G. (1994a), Die fraktale Marke, Düsseldorf.

Gerken, G. (1994b), Die moderne Marke wird zum Fraktal, in: Horizont, Nr. 15, S. 14.

Goldack, G. (1948), Der Markenartikel für Nahrungsmittel, Nürnberg.

Goodyear, M. (1994), Marke und Markenpolitik, in: Planung und Analyse, Nr. 3, S. 60–67.

Haedrich, G., Tomczak, T. (2003), Strategische Markenführung: Planung und Realisierung von Marketingstrategien für eingeführte Produkte, Bern, Stuttgart.

Hansen, P. (1970), Der Markenartikel, Betriebswirtschaftliche Schriften, Leitherer, E. (Hrsg.), Band 36, Berlin.

Hartmann, V. (1966), Markentechnik in der Konsumgüterindustrie, Mellerowicz, K. (Hrsg.), Schriftenreihe des Forschungsinstituts für das Markenwesen, Band 10, Freiburg i.Br.

Huber, B. (1990), Strategische Marketing- und Imageplanung: Theorie, Methoden und Integration der Wettbewerbsstrukturanalyse aus Imagedaten, Berlin.

Kaas, K. P. (1990), Marketing als Bewältigung von Informations- und Unsicherheitsproblemen im Markt, in: Die Betriebswirtschaft, 50. Jg., Nr. 4, S. 539–548.

Kapferer, J. N. (1992), Die Marke – Kapital des Unternehmens, Landsberg/Lech.

Keller, K. L. (1993), Conceptualizing, Measuring, and Managing Customer-Based Brand Equity, in: Journal of Marketing, Vol. 57, Januar, S. 1–22.

Kenning, P. (2003), Customer Trust Management. Ein Beitrag zum Vertrauensmanagement im Lebensmitteleinzelhandel, Wiesbaden.
Leitherer, E. (1954), Die Entwicklung des Markenwesens. Von den Ursprüngen bis zum Beginn der fünfziger Jahre, Neuauflage 1988, Nürnberg.
Leitherer, E. (1955), Die Entwicklung moderner Markenformen, in: Markenartikel, 17. Jg., S. 539–566.
Leitherer, E. (2001), Geschichte der Markierung und des Markenwesens, in: Bruhn, M. (Hrsg.), Die Marke – Symbolkraft eines Zeichensystems, Bern [u.a.], S. 55–74.
Lewin, K. (1963), Feldtheorien in Sozialwissenschaften. Ausgewählte theoretische Schriften, Bern/Stuttgart.
Linxweiler, R. (2001), BrandScoreCard: ein neues Instrument erfolgreicher Markenführung, Groß-Umstadt.
Mayerhofer, W. (1995), Imagetransfer – Die Nutzung von Erlebniswelten für die Positionierung von Ländern, Produktgruppen und Marken, in: Schweiger, G. (Hrsg.), Schriftenreihe Empirische Marketingforschung, Band 13, Wien.
Meffert, H. (1979), Der Markenartikel und seine Bedeutung für den Verbraucher, Gruner + Jahr AG & Co. (Hrsg.), Hamburg.
Meffert, H. (1988), Strategische Unternehmensführung und Marketing, Wiesbaden.
Meffert, H. (1994a), Markenführung in der Bewährungsprobe, in: Markenartikel, Nr. 12, S. 478–481.
Meffert, H. (1994b), Marketing-Management. Analyse – Strategie – Implementierung, Wiesbaden.
Meffert, H., Bruhn, M. (1984), Markenstrategien im Wettbewerb, Wiesbaden.
Meffert, H., Bruhn, M. (2003), Dienstleistungsmarketing, Wiesbaden.
Meffert, H., Burmann, Ch. (1991), Umweltschutzstrategien im Spannungsfeld zwischen Hersteller und Handel – Ein Beitrag zum vertikalen Ökomarketing, in: Meffert, H., Wagner, H., Backhaus, K. (Hrsg.), Arbeitspapier Nr. 66 der Wissenschaftlichen Gesellschaft für Marketing und Unternehmensführung e.V., Münster.
Meffert, H., Burmann, Ch. (1996), Identitätsorientierte Markenführung – Grundlagen für das Management von Markenportfolios, Meffert, H., Wagner, H., Backhaus, K. (Hrsg.), Arbeitspapier Nr. 100 der Wissenschaftlichen Gesellschaft für Marketing und Unternehmensführung e.V., Münster.
Mellerowicz, K. (1963), Markenartikel – Die ökonomischen Gesetze ihrer Preisbildung und Preisbindung, 2. Aufl., München [u.a.].
Niedner, M. (1994), Markenpolitik für Städte und Regionen, in: Bruhn, M. (Hrsg.), Handbuch Markenartikel, Stuttgart, S. 1645–1658.
Paulus, J. (1995), Fraktale Marke: Verbrauchter Mythos, in: Werben & Verkaufen, Nr. 10, S. 80 86.
Perrey, J. (1998), Nutzenorientierte Marktsegmentierung: ein integrativer Ansatz zum Zielgruppenmarketing im Verkehrsdienstleistungsbereich, Wiesbaden.
Plötner, O. (1995), Das Vertrauen des Kunden. Relevanz, Aufbau und Steuerung auf industriellen Märkten, Wiesbaden.
Schenk, H. O.(1994), Handels- und Gattungsmarken, in: Bruhn, M. (Hrsg.), Handbuch Markenartikel, Stuttgart, S. 57–78.
Schmitt, B. H., Pan, Y. (1995), Managing Corporate and Brand Identities in the Asia-Pacific Region, in: California Management Review, Winter, S. 15–31.
Schmitt, B.H., Simonson, A. (1997), Marketing aesthetics. The Strategic Management of Brands, Identity, and Image, New York [u.a.].
Schweiger, G., Wust, C. (1988), Neue Wege in der nonverbalen Imagemessung am Beispiel der Länderimageforschung, in: Werbeforschung & Praxis, 33. Jg., S. 32–44.
Simon, H. (1994), Markenpolitik auf dem Vormarsch (Teil 1), in: Markenartikel, Nr. 12, S. 578 581.

Strobl, H. (1994), Markenpolitik für Natur- und Umweltschutzorganisationen, in: Bruhn, M. (Hrsg.), Handbuch Markenartikel, Stuttgart, S. 1659–1679.

Theis, H.J. (1992), Einkaufsstättenpositionierung, Wiesbaden.

Trommsdorff, V. (1992), Wettbewerbsorientierte Image-Positionierung, in: Markenartikel, Nr. 10, S. 458–463.

Upshaw, L. B. (1995), Building Brand Identity: A Strategy for Success in a Hostile Marketplace, New York [u.a.].

Voss, W. D. (1983), Modellgestützte Markenpolitik. Planung und Kontrolle markenpolitischer Entscheidungen auf der Grundlage computergestützter Informationssysteme, in: Meffert, H., Steffenhagen, H., Freter, H. (Hrsg.), Schriftenreihe Unternehmensführung und Marketing, Band 16, Wiesbaden.

Theoretisches Grundkonzept der identitätsorientierten Markenführung

Christoph Burmann und Heribert Meffert

1.	**Markenwert und Markenstärke als Leitgrößen der Markenführung**	**38**
2.	**Theoretische Grundlagen der identitätsorientierten Markenführung**	**39**
2.*1*	Paradigmen der Unternehmensführung als Basis der Markenführung	39
2.*11*	Der market-based view	39
2.*12*	Der resource-based view	40
2.*2*	Integration der markt- und ressourcenorientierten Sichtweise im Konzept der identitätsorientierten Markenführung	42
2.*3*	Interpretationsformen der Markenidentität	43
2.*31*	Sozialwissenschaftliche Ansätze der Identitätsforschung	43
2.*32*	Wirtschaftswissenschaftliche Interpretation der Markenidentität	49
3.	**Konzeptionelle Ausgestaltung der identitätsorientierten Markenführung**	**51**
3.*1*	Perspektiven und Gegenstand der Markenidentität	51
3.*11*	Das Fremdbild der Markenidentität als Akzeptanzkonzept der Marke	53
3.*12*	Die Markenidentität als Aussagekonzept der Marke	56
3.*121*	Markenherkunft	58
3.*122*	Markenkompetenz	59
3.*123*	Art der Markenleistungen	60
3.*124*	Markenvision	61
3.*125*	Markenwerte	62
3.*126*	Markenpersönlichkeit	63
3.*2*	Zusammenhang zwischen Markenidentität, Markenimage und Markenpositionierung	65
4.	**Fazit**	**67**

1. Markenwert und Markenstärke als Leitgrößen der Markenführung

Aus der Perspektive der Unternehmensführung kann der Erfolg einer Marke anhand ihrer Markenstärke, im Sinne der Verhaltensrelevanz der Marke, und ihres Markenwertes gemessen werden. Die Markenstärke wird dabei üblicherweise als Voraussetzung zur Entstehung des ökonomischen Markenwertes betrachtet. Der Markenwert wird von vielen Autoren demzufolge als die wesentliche Leitgröße der Markenführung in den Mittelpunkt der Forschung gerückt. Insbesondere in der amerikanischen Marketingforschung wird der Untersuchung des Markenwertes seit Mitte der 80er Jahre breiter Raum gewidmet (vgl. zum Überblick Srivastava/Shocker 1991; Sattler 2001; Keller 2003; Schimansky 2004). Die Heterogenität der jeweiligen Forschungszwecke hat jedoch einerseits zu einer schwer überschaubaren Vielfalt an Begriffsdefinitionen geführt (Sander 1994, S. 236) und andererseits ganz unterschiedliche Einzelaspekte des Markenphänomens in den Mittelpunkt der Betrachtung gerückt (Tauber 1988; Farquhar/Han/Ijiri 1992; Rossiter/Lawrence 1993; Schmitt/Pan 1995). Dies erschwert in zunehmendem Maße die wissenschaftliche Forschung zur Markenführung und zum Markenwert.

Grundsätzlich können zwei verschiedene Motive für die Erforschung des Markenwertes unterschieden werden (vgl. auch den Beitrag zur Bewertung und Bilanzierung von Marken in Kapitel 3). Der **finanzwirtschaftlich orientierten Forschung** (vgl. unter anderem Kern 1962; Herp 1982; Kaas 1990; Simon/Sullivan 1991 und 1993) geht es um die Bestimmung des Geldwertes einer Marke zum Zwecke der Bilanzierung, der Lizenzierung, der Akquisition oder der Schadensbemessung bei Markenpiraterie. Die **verhaltenswissenschaftlich geprägte Forschung** (Andresen 1991, Keller 1993 und 2003; Aaker 1996, Esch/Geus 2001, S. 1025 ff.) verfolgt demgegenüber primär das Ziel, die langfristige Effektivität und Effizienz von Markenführungsmaßnahmen zu verbessern.

Basis der verhaltenswissenschaftlichen Arbeiten ist die Überlegung, dass alle Markenführungsaktivitäten eines Unternehmens beim Nachfrager zu einem markenspezifischen Vorstellungsbild führen. Diese Markenrepräsentation in der Psyche des Nachfragers beeinflusst wiederum die Wirkung aller zukünftigen Markenführungsaktivitäten (Berekoven 1978, S. 43 f.; Kapferer 1992, S. 10; Keller 1993, S. 2; Dacin/Smith 1994). Die Zielsetzung dieser Arbeiten besteht in der Regel darin, theoretisch und empirisch diejenigen zentralen Verhaltenskonstrukte zu bestimmen, welche die Stärke einer Marke erklären.

Daneben gibt es Modelle, die eine **Integration der finanzwirtschaftlichen und verhaltenswissenschaftlichen Arbeiten** versuchen (Franzen/Trommsdorff/Riedel 1994; Sattler 1995; Bekmeier-Feuerhahn 1998; Sattler/Högl/Hupp 2002). Im Gegensatz zu den finanzwirtschaftlichen Arbeiten, deren Beitrag sowohl zur Erklärung der Markenstärke als auch zu deren Aufbau begrenzt ist, vermitteln die verhaltenswissenschaftlichen Arbeiten wertvolle Hinweise für die identitätsorientierte Markenführung. Der Ansatzpunkt zum Aufbau einer starken Marke wird dabei seit etwa der Mitte der 90er Jahre vor allem **in der Identität der Marke** gesehen. (Kapferer 1992, S. 39 f.; Upshaw 1995, S. 25; Meffert/Burmann 1996; Aaker/Joachimsthaler 2000, S. 31 ff.; Burmann/Blinda/Nitschke 2003).

Die Markenidentität ist letztendlich das bestimmende Konstrukt, welches eine Marke authentisch werden lässt und sie nachhaltig differenziert. Ein wesentliches Defizit der verhaltenswissenschaftlich geprägten Forschung zur Markenführung ist, dass sich die meisten Untersuchungen aufgrund ihrer Zielsetzung zumeist auf ausgewählte Einzelaspekte des Markenphänomens konzentrieren (Wiswede 1978; Unger 1986, S. 18 f.; Schmitt/Dube 1992; Smith/Park 1992; Trommsdorff 1992; Reddy/Holak/Bhat 1994; Chajet/Shachtman 1995). Eine nachhaltig erfolgreiche Markenführung bedingt jedoch ein ganzheitliches, in sich konsistentes und integriertes Konzept. Im Folgenden soll daher versucht werden, ein **ganzheitliches, integriertes Konzept der identitätsorientierten Markenführung** zu entwickeln.

2. Theoretische Grundlagen der identitätsorientierten Markenführung

Im Gegensatz zum „Entweder-oder" älterer Markenführungsansätze strebt die identitätsorientierte Markenführung im Sinne eines Gesamtkonzepts eine umfassende **Integration der angebots- und nachfragerorientierten Betrachtungsperspektiven** an. Denn Meffert folgend zeichnet „[...] langfristig erfolgreiche Unternehmen [...] neben Marktorientierung auch Ressourcenausrichtung aus. In Zukunft werden Unternehmen somit die Inside-out- und die Outside-in-Perspektive stärker dialogisch entwickeln müssen" (Meffert 1998, S. 709 ff.).

In diesem Zusammenhang ist angesichts der bislang oft zu beobachtenden Theoriedefizite der Markenführung zunächst zu überprüfen, welche betriebswirtschaftlichen Forschungsansätze einen Beitrag zur Schaffung eines Theoriefundaments der Markenführung zu leisten vermögen. Hierzu erscheinen sowohl der „market-based-view" als auch der „ressource-based-view" aus der strategischen Managementforschung geeignet. Die wesentlichen Aussagen beider Konzepte werden im Folgenden kurz skizziert.

2.1 Paradigmen der Unternehmensführung als Basis der Markenführung

2.11 Der market-based view

Aufbauend auf der Industrial-Organization-(IO-)Theorie nach Mason (1939) und Bain (1959) sowie dem daraus abgeleiteten Structure-Conduct-Performance-(S-C-P-)Paradigma unterstellt der market-based view (MBV), dass ein dauerhafter Unternehmenserfolg zum einen durch die Struktur der Produktmärkte, in denen ein Unternehmen tätig ist, und zum anderen durch das strategische Verhalten des Unternehmens in seinen Produktmärkten determiniert wird.

Insbesondere Porter zeigt, wie sich die Überlegungen der IO-Forschung für das strategische Management nutzen lassen. Nach Porter ist ein Unternehmen in der Lage, durch eine **geeignete Positionierung in attraktiven Produkt-Markt-Segmenten** eine dauerhafte, verteidigungsfähige Wettbewerbsvorteilsposition zu erlangen, um so einen nachhaltigen Unternehmenserfolg zu sichern (Porter 1996, S. 61 ff.). Attraktive Branchen sind zum Beispiel solche mit geringer Wettbewerbsintensität. Zur Beurteilung der Attraktivität von Branchen beziehungsweise Märkten hat Porter sein Konzept der fünf Wettbewerbskräfte entwickelt (Porter 1999, S. 32).

Allerdings wird diese ausschließlich marktorientierte Sichtweise im strategischen Management auch kritisiert. So wird angeführt, dass der MBV die wechselseitige Beeinflussung von Marktstruktur, -verhalten und -erfolg ignoriert und sich das Verhalten von Unternehmen auf reines Anpassen an Marktstrukturveränderungen beschränkt (Proff 1998, S. 31). Die Marktstruktur wird als gegeben interpretiert, obwohl sie von Unternehmen verändert werden kann. Darüber hinaus **vernachlässigt der MBV unternehmensinterne Ressourcen und organisationale Fähigkeiten** als Grundlage von Wettbewerbsvorteilen, sodass das Unternehmen selbst eine „black box“ bleibt. Vor allem jedoch unterstellt der MBV eine vollständige Homogenität aller Unternehmen einer Branche im Hinblick auf ihre Ressourcenausstattung.

2.12 Der resource-based view

Ursprünglich als Gegenkonzept zur marktorientierten Forschungsrichtung gibt der resource-based-view (RBV) die Betrachtung von Unternehmen als black box bei der Analyse von Wettbewerbsvorteilen auf (vgl. umfassend zum Beispiel Freiling 2001). Auf Basis empirischer Ergebnisse wird argumentiert, dass die klassischen Branchenstrukturvariablen der IO-Forschung nicht ausreichen, um Unterschiede in der Profitabilität von Geschäftseinheiten zu erklären (Hansen/Wernerfelt 1989; Rumelt 1991). Der RBV bezweifelt insbesondere die Dominanz externer Faktoren und **unterstellt, dass der Unternehmenserfolg durch unternehmensspezifische und einzigartige Ressourcen und Fähigkeiten determiniert wird**. Entsprechend wird teilweise auch vom Resource-Conduct-Performance (R-C-P-)Paradigma gesprochen. Um dauerhafte Wettbewerbsvorteile zu erreichen, wird auf Basis der unternehmensspezifischen Ressourcenausstattung das adäquate strategische Verhalten des Unternehmens abgeleitet.

Barney definiert **Ressourcen** zunächst sehr allgemein als „all assets, capabilities, organizational processes, firm attributes, information, knowledge etc. controlled by a firm that enable the firm to conceive of an implement strategies.“ (Barney 1991, S. 101). Dabei können von allen grundsätzlich auf Märkten beschaffbaren **Inputgütern** nur solche tatsächlich als Ressourcen angesehen werden, die unternehmensintern „veredelt“ wurden und damit den langfristigen Erfolg eines Unternehmens im Markt, zumindest teilweise, zu erklären vermögen (Freiling 2001, S. 19). **Organisationale Fähigkeiten** sind eine Teilmenge dieser Ressourcenausstattung des Unternehmens. Sie können als „the organization's collective capacity for undertaking a specific type of activity"(Lieberman/Montgomery 1998, S. 1112) definiert werden. Die spezifischen Aktivitäten beziehen sich dabei auf die Kombination von Ressourcen zur Generierung eines Wettbewerbsvorteils. Ein dauerhafter Unternehmenserfolg basiert somit auf der „richtigen" Nutzung der verfügbaren Ressourcen zur Generierung eines wettbewerbsüberlegenen Kundennutzens. Um als Quelle eines Wettbewerbsvorteils geeignet zu sein, müssen Unternehmensressourcen

- wertvoll (valuable),
- knapp (rare),
- nicht vollkommen imitierbar (imperfectly imitable) und
- nicht substituierbar (no strategically equivalent substitutes)

sein (Barney 1991, S. 105 f.). Sind diese Ressourcen vorhanden, liegen die Aufgaben des Managements primär darin, die Ressourcen derart miteinander zu kombinieren, dass sie den Anforderungen der Märkte gerecht werden. Die sich von anderen Unternehmen unterscheidenden organisationalen Fähigkeiten werden auch als **Kompetenzen** oder Kernkompetenzen bezeichnet (Prahalad/Hamel 1990; Teece/Pisano/Shuen 1997). Sie beziehen sich auf die Fähigkeit einer Institution, Inputgüter und insbesondere deren Teilmenge der Ressourcen zielgerichtet so zu kombinieren, dass daraus ein der Konkurrenz ebenbürtiger oder sogar überlegener Kundennutzen entsteht. Ein **dauerhaft überlegener** Kundenutzen basiert auf **Kernkompetenzen**, wohingegen zur „einfachen" Behauptung im Markt die Verfügbarkeit von Kompetenzen ausreichend ist (Freiling 2001, S. 36). Da sich auch eine Marke und ihr Leistungsprogramm aus der „richtigen" Kombination von Ressourcen ergeben, lässt sich eine erfolgreiche Markenführung letztlich auf spezifische organisationale Fähigkeiten eines Unternehmens zurückführen. **Die Identifikation und zielgerichtete Gestaltung dieser Fähigkeit(en) stellt aus ressourcentheoretischer Perspektive den Kern der Markenführung dar.**

Sony besaß beispielsweise in den 80er Jahren die Kernkompetenz der Miniaturisierung und hat auf dieser Basis im Markt für Hifi-Geräte zahlreiche neue Produkte herausgebracht. Ebenso wird IBM aufgrund langjähriger Kumulation spezifischer Erfahrungen eine besondere Forschungskompetenz zugeschrieben. Dies zeigt sich in der hohen Anzahl der bei IBM entstehenden Patente. Zwischen 1993 und 2002 meldeten die Forscher und Erfinder von IBM insgesamt 22.357 Patenten in den USA an. In dieser Zeit erhielt IBM mehr Patente als die zehn größten US-Unternehmen zusammengenommen, darunter Hewlett-Packard/Compaq, Intel, Sun, Microsoft, Dell, Apple, EMC, Oracle und EDS (IBM Deutschland 2004). Diese Beispiele machen jedoch deutlich, dass über die ökonomische Relevanz von Ressourcen und Fähigkeiten letztlich immer der Markt entscheidet, sodass der RBV nicht auf die Marktperspektive verzichten kann. Marktrelevant sind Ressourcen nur dann, wenn sie durch Kompetenzen beziehungsweise Kernkompetenzen zu Nutzenbündeln kombiniert werden, die einen überlegenen Kundennutzen stiften.

Die Schwäche des RBV liegt in der Vernachlässigung dynamischer Aspekte, das heißt der Notwendigkeit des Wechsels vorhandener Ressourcen und Fähigkeiten bei sich wandelnden Marktbedingungen (Burmann 2002, S. 170 ff.). Diese Kritik wird im **Dynamic Capability-Ansatz** und dem competence-based view (CBV) aufgegriffen, bei dem neben der Ressourcenausstattung eines Unternehmens die Entwicklung spezifischer Fähigkeiten im Zeitablauf in die Betrachtung einbezogen werden (Teece/Pisano/Shuen 1997). Unternehmen mit dauerhaft überdurchschnittlichen Kapitalrenditen zeichnen sich demnach vor allem durch überlegene Replikations-, Lern- und Rekonfigurationsfähigkeiten, das heißt die Fähigkeit zur schnellen Multiplikation vorhandener und Aneignung neuer Ressourcen aus (Burmann 2002).

Zusammenfassend sind somit die frühzeitige Identifikation neuer Kunden-Nutzen-Potenziale und der Aufbau aller hierfür notwendigen Ressourcen und Kompetenzen erfolgsentscheidender, als eine einseitige Beschäftigung mit dem wettbewerbsstrategischen Gedankengut Porter'scher Prägung. Vor dem Hintergrund des Dynamic Capabilities-Ansatzes und des competence-based views wird stattdessen die Notwendigkeit einer ganzheitlich ausgerichteten Markenführung deutlich und die Befruchtung zwischen Inside-out- und Outside-in-Perspektive betont.

2.2 Integration der markt- und ressourcenorientierten Sichtweise im Konzept der identitätsorientierten Markenführung

Vergleichbar mit der Synthese des markt- und ressourcenorientierten Ansatzes in der strategischen Unternehmensführung, lässt sich auch die Notwendigkeit zu einer Neuausrichtung der Markenführung begründen. Basierten die Aussagen der Marketingwissenschaft zur Markenführung bisher dominant auf der Outside-in-Perspektive (Nachfrage- beziehungsweise Imageorientierung), so ist diese Sicht heute um eine Inside-out-Betrachtung zu ergänzen. Letztlich kann erst durch die Verfolgung beider Perspektiven den Ansprüchen an eine **ganzheitliche Markenführung** Rechnung getragen werden. Diesem Anspruch wird der Ansatz der identitätsorientierten Markenführung gerecht.

Im Vergleich zu älteren Markenführungsansätzen erweitert der identitätsorientierte Ansatz der Markenführung die bisher vorherrschende absatzmarktbezogene Sichtweise um eine innengerichtete Perspektive. Der Ansatz interpretiert die **Identität** und als Kernbestandteil dieser die **Kompetenz** einer Marke als wichtige Voraussetzung für die Gewinnung des Vertrauens der Nachfrager. Ältere Markenführungsansätze verstehen Markenkompetenz demgegenüber als Qualität der markierten Produkte, ignorieren dabei allerdings sowohl die Beziehung der Marke zu den Ressourcen und Fähigkeiten des Markeninhabers als auch die Wechselwirkungen zwischen den verschiedenen internen und externen Anspruchsgruppen der Marke.

Im Gegensatz dazu konstituiert sich die **Markenidentität** über einen längeren Zeitraum als Folge der Wechselwirkungen von marktorientierten Handlungen eines Markenartikelherstellers und der Wahrnehmung dieser Handlungen durch die Nachfrager. Im Mittelpunkt der Betrachtung stehen somit die Wechselseitigkeit von Markenimage (externe

Wahrnehmung) und Identität einer Marke (interne Reflektion des eigenen Tuns) sowie die Betonung einer über Funktions- und Unternehmensgrenzen hinweggreifenden Vernetzung aller markenbezogenen Aktivitäten.

Eine Ausrichtung der Markenführung an der Identität einer Marke setzt ein klares **Verständnis vom Gegenstand, der Entstehung und den einzelnen Komponenten der Markenidentität** voraus. Obwohl der Identitätsbegriff in der sozialwissenschaftlichen, der institutionenökonomischen und der unternehmenskulturellen Literatur kontrovers diskutiert wird, lassen sich unabhängig vom jeweiligen Forschungszweig konstitutive Merkmale der Identität identifizieren.

2.3 Interpretationsformen der Markenidentität

2.31 Sozialwissenschaftliche Ansätze der Identitätsforschung

Etymologisch rührt der Begriff *Identität* vom lateinischen Wort „idem" her, welches „dasselbe" bezeichnet. Aus diesem Grund wird der Begriff oftmals auch als „völlige Gleichheit" und „Wesenseinheit" beschrieben (Duden 2001, S. 488; Welling 2003, S. 13). In der sozialwissenschaftlichen Forschung wird der Begriff abhängig vom jeweiligen Forschungszweck sehr heterogen verwendet. Demzufolge gibt es in diesem Bereich bislang keine allgemein anerkannte Begriffsdefinition (Frey/Haußer 1987; Achterholt 1988, S. 29 f.; Conzen 1990; Gugutzer 2002). Das Begriffsverständnis ist vielmehr geprägt von den jeweiligen Forschungszwecken und den betrachteten Untersuchungsobjekten. So wird der Identitätsbegriff in der Soziologie zur Kennzeichnung eines Bündels typischer Rollen eines Individuums verwendet. In der Psychologie steht der Identitätsbegriff für das Selbstkonzept von Personen (Rosenberg 1979; Hogg/Cox/Keeling 2000), während die Moraltheologen und Philosophen mit Identität ein über die Zeit relativ stabiles Set persönlicher Werthaltungen und ethischer Prinzipien beschreiben. Die Psychiatrie schließlich beschreibt mit Identität die Unversehrtheit und Funktionsfähigkeit aller Organisationsleistungen des Nervensystems (Conzen 1990).

Häufig werden in der Umgangssprache die Termini *Identität* und *Persönlichkeit* synonym verwendet. Allerdings handelt es sich bei der Identität um ein umfassenderes Konstrukt als die Persönlichkeit. In der Psychoanalyse repräsentiert die Identität die Ganzheit der Persönlichkeitseigenschaften, die zu mehr als der Summe ihrer Teile verschmelzen und unabhängig von der Veränderung und der Weiterentwicklung einzelner Persönlichkeitseigenschaften es erlauben, den Menschen beziehungsweise die Marke als „denselben" zu identifizieren und als im Zeitverlauf gleich bleibendes Wesen stets wieder zu erkennen (Conzen 1990, S. 69 f.).

Dabei gehen viele wesentliche Untersuchungen zum Identitätsbegriff in der sozialwissenschaftlichen Forschung auf John Locke zurück. Dessen Forschungserkenntnisse zur personalen Identität sind für die identitätsorientierte Markenforschung von hoher Relevanz, da sie als Basis vieler sozialwissenschaftlicher und betriebswirtschaftlicher Weiterentwicklungen der Identitätsforschung dienen (vgl. zu Lockes Verständnis von Identität beispielsweise ausführlich Thiel 2001). Locke unterscheidet zwischen der „Identität als Mensch“ und der „Identität als Person“. Die „Identität als Mensch“ bezieht sich allein auf die Existenz des materiellen Körpers und ist somit als gegeben anzusehen. Die Identität konstituiert sich nach diesem Verständnis allein durch die Existenz des Körpers bzw. des Objektes. Daher würde beispielsweise ein Verstorbener zunächst allein durch die Fortexistenz seines Körpers seine Identität behalten. Erst durch die Auflösung seines Körpers würde auch seine Identität aufhören zu existieren. Die „Identität als Person“ konstituiert sich dagegen erst durch die Existenz eines Bewusstseins und des Denkens (Welling 2003, S. 13 ff.) Nach Locke bedarf die letztere Identitätsauffassung eines selbstreferenziellen Bewusstseins, um reflektierend durch die Verknüpfung von Vergangenheit und Gegenwart die Identität der eigenen Person festzustellen. Es handelt sich daher um eine subjektive Konstruktion der Identität, häufig auch als so genannte „Ich-Identität“ bzw. „persönliche Identität“ bezeichnet, die beim Menschen erst durch einen Prozess des selbstreflexiven Denkens entsteht. Das heißt die Person bildet ihre Identität, indem sie ihr Wissen und ihre Erfahrungen über sich selbst in der Vergangenheit und Gegenwart verarbeitet. In diesem so genannten Selbstkonzept vereinen sich das Identitätssubjekt und -objekt in einer Person (Frey/Haußer 1987, S. 20).

Weitere Forschungsbemühungen, und hier insbesondere die Forschung von Erik Erikson, greifen dieses bewusstseinsorientierte Verständnis des Identitätsobjektes als Gegenstand der Identitätszuschreibung auf und erweitern es. Erikson, der als Wegbereiter der psychoanalytischen Identitätsforschung gilt (Haußer 1995, S. 75), betrachtet explizit die Perspektive der Identitätsfeststellung und das Bezugsobjekt der Identität (vgl. Tabelle 1).

Tabelle 1: Systematisierung von Identität und Image in Anlehnung an Erikson

Perspektive der Identitätsfeststellung / Bezugsobjekt der Identität	**Interne Perspektive (Selbstbild)**	**Externe Perspektive (Fremdbild)**
Individuen	Identität einer Person (Persönliche Identität)	Image einer Person (Soziale Identität)
Gruppen von Menschen	Identität von Gruppen (Wahrgenommene Identität der Gruppenmitglieder von ihrer eigenen Gruppe)	Image von Gruppen (von Nichtgruppenmitgliedern wahrgenommene Identität einer fremden Gruppe)
Andere Objekte, z. B. Marken (hier verstanden als Personenkollektive)	Internes Selbstbild der Marke = Markenidentität	Externes Fremdbild der Marke = Markenimage

GABLER GRAFIK

Erikson differenziert zum einen zwischen der Identität von Individuen und der Identität von sozialen Gruppen (Bezugsobjekt der Identität). Zum anderen differenziert er zwischen der „persönlichen Identität" und einer „sozialen Identität", welche von anderen Personen zugeschrieben werden kann (Perspektive der Identitätszuschreibung). Die „soziale Identität" ist somit ein Fremdbild der persönlichen Identität und wird deswegen nachfolgend als Image bezeichnet.

Individuen als Gegenstand der Identitätszuschreibung

Die persönliche Identität (Ich-Identität) kennzeichnet das Vorhandensein eines Bildes des Individuums von sich selbst (Conzen 1990, S. 72 f.). Es dient einem Menschen als Abgrenzung von anderen Personen und als Orientierungsrahmen für sein Verhalten. Mit anderen Worten kann auch von einem individuellen Konzept der eigenen Person gesprochen werden (Müller 1987, S. 1098). Die persönliche Identität beruht auf der „unmittelbaren Wahrnehmung der eigenen Gleichheit und Kontinuität in der Zeit, und der damit verbundenen Wahrnehmung, dass auch andere diese [eigene] Gleichheit und Kontinuität erkennen." (Erikson 1973, S. 18).

Tabelle 2: Konstitutive Merkmale der Identität von Menschen und Marken

Konstitutive Merkmale	Individuen	Marken
Wechselseitigkeit	Identität entsteht erst durch die In-Beziehung-Setzung der eigenen Person zu anderen Menschen.	Die Markenidentität entsteht erst durch Abgrenzung zu konkurrierenden Leistungsangeboten und durch die Interaktion mit den Nachfragern.
Kontinuität	Beibehaltung essenzieller Merkmale über die Zeit zur Identifikation der Person. Diese Merkmale beschreiben die Art und das Wesen der Person. Akzidenzielle Merkmale der Identität können sich im Zeitverlauf verändern.	Beibehaltung der so genannten essenziellen Markenmerkmale im Zeitablauf.
Konsistenz	Widerspruchsfreie Kombination von Persönlichkeitsmerkmalen (zeitpunktbezogen).	Vermeidung von Widersprüchen im Markenauftritt und Führungsverhalten. Laufende Abstimmung der essenziellen und akzidenziellen Merkmale.
Individualität	Biologisch und soziologisch bedingte Einzigartigkeit des Individuums.	Einzigartigkeit wesentlicher Identitätsmerkmale im Vergleich zu konkurrierenden Leistungsangeboten.

GABLER GRAFIK

Im Vordergrund dieses Verständnisses von Erikson steht demnach neben der Selbstreflexion die Wechselseitigkeit einer Innen- und Außenperspektive. Die Wahrnehmung der Außenperspektive manifestiert sich in der **„sozialen Identität“** (vgl. Tabelle 1), das heißt, dem Individuum wird von anderen Personen ein Image im Sinne eines Merkmalsbündels zugeschrieben (Frey/Haußer 1987, S. 3). Die persönliche Identität wird laufend mit der Wahrnehmung dieser persönlichen Identität durch Dritte verglichen und gegebenenfalls angepasst (Weidenfeld 1983, S. 19). Hier unterscheidet sich Eriksons Verständnis der Identität von Locke. Nach Erikson kann eine Identität nur festgestellt werden, wenn zwei Menschen beziehungsweise Dinge in Relation zueinander gesetzt werden (Haußer 1995, S. 3 f.). Die Interdependenz zwischen der persönlichen Identität und dem von Außen zugeschriebenen Image einer Person ist demnach ein konstitutives Merkmal der Identität und lässt diese sich fortentwickeln. Unabhängig von der im Einzelfall gewählten Identitätsdefinition lassen sich aus den Arbeiten von Erikson zur psychoanalytischen Identitätsforschung vier grundlegende, konstitutive Merkmale des Identitätsbegriffs ableiten (vgl. Tabelle 2).

- Die **Wechselseitigkeit** kennzeichnet den Tatbestand, dass Identität nur in der Wechselwirkung zwischen Menschen entstehen kann. Diese Wechselseitigkeit der Identität wird auch als „Paradigma der Identitätsforschung“ bezeichnet (Frey/Haußer 1987, S. 17). Ähnlich verhält es sich mit Marken, die nicht in einer Konkurrenzbeziehung zu anderen Leistungsangeboten stehen, auch in diesem Fall wäre die Markenidentität von untergeordneter Bedeutung.

- Das Merkmal der **Kontinuität** kennzeichnet die Beibehaltung wesentlicher Merkmale einer Person oder einer Gruppe über einen Zeitraum mehrerer Jahre. Dieses Set **essenzieller Merkmale** beschreibt das Wesen dessen, dem Identität zugeschrieben wird. Gehen diese essenziellen Merkmale verloren, erlöscht die Identität. Diese essenziellen Merkmale kennzeichnen die Identität als Institution im Sinne der Neuen Institutionenökonomie. Im Gegensatz zu essenziellen Merkmalen können sich die **akzidenziellen Merkmale** eines Identitätsgegenstandes verändern, ohne dass die Person oder Gruppe ihre Identität verlieren (Böhm 1989, S. 48 f.). Für den Aufbau einer klaren Identität ist somit eine Kontinuität der akzidenziellen Merkmale nicht erforderlich. Allerdings üben auch akzidenzielle Merkmale einen Einfluss auf die konkrete Gestalt der Identität aus.
  Zu den essenziellen Identitätsmerkmalen einer Person gehören demnach beispielsweise das Geschlecht, Datum und Ort der Geburt oder bestimmte Körpermerkmale. Ein Mensch kann anhand seiner essenziellen Merkmale während des gesamten Lebens als ein und dieselbe Person identifiziert werden. Demgegenüber gehören unter anderem die berufliche Stellung, die wirtschaftliche Situation oder der Kleidungsstil zu den akzidenziellen Merkmalen der Identität, die sich im Laufe der Zeit verändern können, ohne dass ein Individuum damit zwingend seine Identität verändert.

- Das Identitätsmerkmal der **Konsistenz** bezieht sich im Gegensatz zur Kontinuität nicht auf einen Zeitraum, sondern auf einen Zeitpunkt. Es kennzeichnet die Vermeidung von Widersprüchen (Wiedmann 1994, S. 1041), denn nur eine in sich und nach außen widerspruchsfreie Kombination einzelner Persönlichkeitsmerkmale führt zu einer klaren Identität. Mit anderen Worten, erst eine integrierte, innen- und außengerichtete Abstimmung aller Markeneigenschaften kann zu einer klaren Markenidentität führen.

- Das vierte Identitätsmerkmal, die **Individualität**, beschreibt schließlich die Einmaligkeit eines Identitätsobjektes. Diese Einzigartigkeit kann auf ein einzelnes, individuelles Merkmal oder die individuelle Kombination auch anderweitig vorzufindender Merkmale zurückzuführen sein. Bei einem personenbezogenen Begriffsverständnis der Identität ist das Merkmal der Individualität beziehungsweise Einzigartigkeit bereits aus biologischen Gründen automatisch erfüllt. Demgegenüber ist die Identität vieler Marken gerade deshalb so schwach, weil den Marken in der Wahrnehmung der Nachfrager und der eigenen Mitarbeiter jede Individualität fehlt. In diesen Fällen kann nicht von echten Marken, sondern bestenfalls von „Labeln" im Sinne einheitlich markierter Produkte gesprochen werden.

Im Rahmen der Wechselseitigkeit bei der Konstitution und Weiterentwicklung der Identität sind für einen Menschen die Rollenerwartungen der Umgebung von hoher Bedeutung. Da ein Individuum selten alle Rollenerwartungen der Gesellschaft und der persönlichen Umgebung erfüllen kann und damit in Rollenkonflikte gerät, benötigt es eine starke persönliche Identität (Ich-Identität), also ein sicheres Gefühl von sich selbst, um durch diese Konflikte nicht zermürbt zu werden (Bonus 1994, S. 3). Die persönliche Identität zeichnet sich durch eine hohe zeitliche Konstanz aus. Ein Persönlichkeits- beziehungsweise Identitätswandel vollzieht sich somit stets sehr langsam. Die Wurzeln der persönlichen Identität sind immer in der Biografie des Menschen verankert (Krappmann 1988).

Eine starke persönliche Identität ist dabei die Voraussetzung der Verlässlichkeit einer Person nach außen. Vertrauen kann man nur derjenigen Person, die eine Identität besitzt. An dieser Stelle wird die Verbindung zwischen dem Identitäts- und dem Vertrauenskonstrukt deutlich. **Vertrauen setzt Identität voraus** (Luhmann 1973).[1] Die Identität verschafft Glaubwürdigkeit, weil sie klare Erwartungen generiert und diese später auch einzulösen vermag. Kompetenz als Bestandteil von Identität sichert dabei die **Leistungsfähigkeit**, die übrigen Identitätskomponenten dagegen die **Leistungsbereitschaft.** Erst eine klare Markenidentität hat das Vertrauen der Nachfrager in die Leistungsfähigkeit und Leistungsbereitschaft der Marke zur Folge.

Vertrauen hat in diesem Zusammenhang nicht nur eine sozialwissenschaftliche Bedeutung. Für Anbieter und Nachfrager ergibt sich vielmehr auch eine konkrete ökonomische Bedeutung (Ripperger 1998). In **volkswirtschaftlicher Betrachtung** stellt das Ausmaß zwischenmenschlichen Vertrauens eine wichtige Bestimmungsgröße für die Ausprägung nationaler Wirtschaftsstrukturen und die Bildung von Institutionen dar (Fukuyama 1995). Damit beeinflusst das Ausmaß zwischenmenschlichen Vertrauens auch die Wettbewerbsvorteile von Regionen und Nationen. In **betriebswirtschaftlicher Betrachtung** führt das Vorliegen von Vertrauen zur Einsparung von Transaktionskosten beim Anbie-

1 Nach Luhmann ermöglicht Vertrauen „mehr Möglichkeiten des Erlebens und Handelns [...], weil im Vertrauen eine wirksame Form der Reduktion von Komplexität zur Verfügung steht." Luhmann (1973), S. 7.

ter, die dieser anderweitig zur Anbahnung von Geschäftsabschlüssen insbesondere im Bereich der Kommunikation und zur Risikoabsicherung aufwenden müsste. Darüber hinaus stellt das Vertrauen des Nachfragers einen wesentlichen Wettbewerbsvorteil dar, der sich für den Anbieter in entsprechenden ökonomischen Erfolgsgrößen niederschlägt (Kenning 2003). Für den Nachfrager reduziert sich mit wachsendem Vertrauen das wahrgenommene Risiko, vom Anbieter und dessen angebotenen Leistungen enttäuscht zu werden. Damit kann der Nachfrager diejenigen Kosten einsparen, die anderweitig zur Reduzierung des Risikos anfallen würden (Plötner 1995, S. 11 f.). Hierbei sind beispielsweise an Kosten durch den Abschluss von Versicherungen, Informationskosten durch die Suche nach geeigneten, oder auch an die Kosten der Bildung von finanziellen Reserven zur Abdeckung möglicher Risiken zu denken.

Gruppen als Gegenstand der Identitätszuschreibung

Gruppen von Menschen bilden die zweite Kategorie der Identitätsbezugsobjekte. Die Gruppenidentität kann somit auch zur Beschreibung der Identität sozialer Systeme (zum Beispiel Kulturen, Vereine, Städte, Regionen, Unternehmen, Abteilungen) verwendet werden. Konstituierend ist dabei die Selbstreflexion der Gruppenmitglieder. Die Gruppenidentität umfasst diejenigen Eigenschaften einer Gruppe, die konstant bleiben, auch wenn einzelne Gruppenmitglieder die Gruppe verlassen (Werthmöller 1994, S. 39). Die Gruppenidentität drückt sich in gemeinsamen Werten, Überzeugungen, Eigenschaften und Verhalten aus, die aus gemeinsamen Erfahrungen und Lernen entstehen. Sie grenzt die Gruppe von anderen Gruppen ab (Schein 1985, S. 185 f.). Dagegen manifestiert sich eine gruppenexterne Identitätszuschreibung, das heißt eine Zuschreibung einer Identität durch Personen, die dieser Gruppe nicht angehören, in einem Gruppenimage (vgl. Tabelle 2). Eine starke Gruppenidentität wird zu einem Bestandteil der persönlichen Identität und wirkt wie eine Klammer für den Zusammenhalt der Gruppe.

Auch Unternehmen und Marken als Gruppen von Menschen weisen in der Form der Corporate beziehungsweise Brand Identity eine solche Form der Identität auf. Bereits Domizlaff konstatierte in den 30er Jahren des vergangenen Jahrhunderts, dass jede Marke über ein eigenes „Gesicht" verfügt (Domizlaff 1994, S. 701). Damit verwies er auf eine Analogie zur menschlichen Identität, die sich letztlich aus verschiedenen, im Zeitverlauf konstanten Merkmalen konstituiert und für jeden Menschen einzigartig ist.

Da im sozialwissenschaftlichen Verständnis Identität grundsätzlich als Ergebnis menschlicher Interaktion und Reflexion betrachtet wird, wäre eine Übertragung des sozialwissenschaftlichen Identitätsbegriffs aus Tabelle 1 und Tabelle 2 auf „Marken", verstanden als Schutzrechte oder leblose „Zeichenbündel", unzulässig.[2] Die Markenidentität ist somit auch aus diesem Grunde als Gruppenidentität zu interpretieren. Das die Marke tragende Personenkollektiv verfügt somit über eine eigene, selbstreflexive Identität. Die Markenidentität lässt sich vor diesem Hintergrund definieren als (Burmann/Blinda/Nitschke 2003, S. 16):

2 Vgl. die Kritik an älteren identitätsorientierten Markenführungsansätzen von Welling (2003), S. 10 f.

„diejenigen raum-zeitlich gleichartigen Merkmale der Marke, die aus Sicht der internen Zielgruppen in nachhaltiger Weise den Charakter der Marke prägen."

Hinsichtlich der Betrachtungsperspektive (vgl. Tabelle 1) kann zwischen der Markenidentität als **Selbstbild** aus Sicht der internen Zielgruppen (zum Beispiel Eigentümer, Führungskräfte, Mitarbeiter) und dem Markenimage als **Fremdbild** aus der Sicht der externen Zielgruppen (zum Beispiel Kunden, Lieferanten, Verbraucherverbände, Umweltschutzgruppen, Behörden, Anwohnern) unterschieden werden. **Die Markenidentität konstituiert** sich daher in zweifacher Weise durch:

- einen kollektiven, selbstreferenziellen Prozess des sich bewusst Machens bei allen für eine Marke arbeitenden Personen. Hierbei handelt es sich um die interne Zielgruppe des Markenmanagements;
- durch die Interaktion mit markenexternen Personen und Personengruppen und deren Wahrnehmung der eigenen Marke und anderer Leistungsangebote.

Markenimage und Markenidentität stehen somit in einem permanenten Austauschprozess, der im Zeitablauf aus sich heraus zu Veränderungen bei der Identität und dem Image einer Marke führen kann.

Genauso wie sich die persönliche Identität und die Identität von Gruppen aus verschiedenen Merkmalen konstituiert, setzt sich aus der Perspektive des identitätsorientierten Markenmanagements auch die Markenidentität aus verschiedenen Komponenten zusammen. Die Markenidentität wird jedoch wie die Identität einer Person ganzheitlich wahrgenommen. Die Ausprägung und Kombination der einzelnen Identitätskomponenten einer Marke muss somit eine in sich widerspruchsfreie, schlüssige „Gestalt" ergeben, die sich letztendlich von anderen Leistungsangeboten im relevanten Markt differenziert (Meffert/Burmann 1996, S. 36 f.).

2.32 Wirtschaftswissenschaftliche Interpretation der Markenidentität

Die umfassende Analyse der sozialwissenschaftlichen Identitätsforschung könnte Zweifel an der ökonomischen Relevanz des Identitätskonstruktes aufkommen lassen. Auf der Grundlage der **Neuen Institutionenökonomie** (zum Beispiel Erlei/Leschke/Sauerland 1999) kann die ökonomische Bedeutung der Identität jedoch belegt werden (Dörtelmann 1997). Voraussetzung hierfür ist die Überwindung des Paradigmas vom homo oeconomicus durch die Neue Institutionenökonomie und insbesondere die Arbeiten des Nobelpreisträgers Douglas C. North. Durch die Einführung von **mentalen Modellen** als interne, subjektive Repräsentation der Außenwelt beim Individuum und so genannte pfadabhängiger Prozesse, das heißt der Berücksichtigung von Zufällen und Ungleichgewichtszuständen (North 1992, S. 96 f.), konnten auch komplexere Probleme der Nationalökonomie, beispielsweise der politischen Ökonomie oder der wirtschaftlichen Entwicklung, einer Lösung nähergebracht werden (Denzau/North 1994, S. 10 f.; Bonus 1995, S. 2).

Unter einer **Institution** wird „ein System von Werten und Normen verstanden, das für den Fall von Verstößen mit Sanktionen bewährt ist“ (Bonus 1995, S. 4). Institutionen schaffen **Rahmenbedingungen für menschliches Handeln**. Institutionen sind mentale Modelle des Individuums (Denzau/North 1994, S. 4). Durch ihre zeitliche Konstanz dienen sie dem Menschen zur Orientierung. In diesem Zusammenhang wird zwischen fundamentalen und sekundären Institutionen unterschieden (Dietl 1993, S. 71 f.).

Fundamentale Institutionen sind beispielsweise in der Geschichte einer Nation verankert und wandeln sich nur sehr langsam. Sie können vom Menschen nicht direkt verändert werden. Demgegenüber können sekundäre Institutionen bewusst gestaltet werden. Sekundäre Institutionen sind immer nur dann „wirksam“, wenn sie in das Werte- und Normensystem der fundamentalen Institutionen eingebettet sind. Beispielsweise kann das Rechtsempfinden der Bevölkerung als fundamentale Institution, die konkreten Gesetze und die Justizverwaltung als sekundäre Institution aufgefasst werden. Gesetze und Justizverwaltungen können nur dann ihren Zweck erfüllen, wenn sie mit dem Rechtsempfinden der Bevölkerung harmonieren (Bonus 1995, S. 5).

Das Identitätskonstrukt kann ebenfalls eine Art **Werte- und Normensystem** von hoher zeitlicher Konstanz interpretiert werden, welches dem Menschen als Rahmenbedingung seines Handelns dient. Auch die Identität stellt wie die Institution eine subjektive Repräsentation bestimmter Vorgänge aus der Außenwelt des Individuums dar. Vor diesem Hintergrund kann die Gruppenidentität aller Mitarbeiter eines Unternehmens (Identität der Corporate Brand beziehungsweise Corporate Identity) ebenso wie die Identität einzelner Marken als sekundäre Institution verstanden werden. Sowohl die Unternehmens- als auch die Markenidentität können sich nur dann entwickeln und Einfluss auf das Verhalten von Mitarbeitern und Nachfragern ausüben, wenn sie in das Werte- und Normengefüge der sie umgebenden Gesellschaft eingebettet sind. Insoweit stellt die regionale beziehungsweise nationale Kultur, in der das Unternehmen beziehungsweise die Markenorganisation angesiedelt ist, für die Unternehmens- und Markenidentität eine fundamentale Institution im Sinne der Neuen Institutionenökonomie dar.

Der Identität kommt somit zur Erklärung und Beeinflussung ökonomischer Sachverhalte eine hohe Bedeutung zu. Darüber hinaus kann festgehalten werden, dass sich die Corporate Identity und die Markenidentität der Mitarbeiter nur langsam wandeln und vom Management nicht kurzfristig und direkt im Sinne einer deterministischen Mittel-Zweck-Beziehung beeinflusst werden kann. Wichtig ist ferner, dass sich eine klare Markenidentität nur dann etabliert, wenn sie schlüssig in die Unternehmensidentität eingebettet wird und mit dieser harmoniert.

Neben der Neuen Institutionenökonomie hat sich auch die **Betriebswirtschaftslehre** mit dem Identitätskonstrukt beschäftigt. Dies geschah insbesondere im Zusammenhang mit Untersuchungen zur Unternehmenskultur sowie zur Unternehmensphilosophie und Corporate Identity. Die Analyse der entsprechenden Publikationen zeigt zunächst, dass viele Autoren eine weitgehende Gleichsetzung zwischen dem Kultur- und dem Identitätsbegriff vornehmen (Deal/Kennedy 1982, S. 137; Schein 1985, S. 44; Heinen 1987, S. 31; Bonus 1994, S. 9). Danach ist eine starke Unternehmenskultur vor allem durch eine starke Gruppenidentität aller Unternehmensmitglieder geprägt. Vice versa lässt sich die

Identität eines Unternehmens „kultivieren“ und durch geeignete Rituale und gemeinsam gelebte Werte und Normen sichtbar machen (Deal/Kennedy 1982, S. 59; Schein 1985, S. 14; Bonus 1994, S. 15). Zur Beantwortung der Frage, aus welchen Merkmalen sich Markenidentität ergibt, liefern die Ergebnisse der Unternehmenskulturforschung erste Hinweise. Demnach müsste sich die Markenidentität auf für Nachfrager und Mitarbeiter „beobachtbare und erlebbare Artefakte“, wie charakteristische Merkmale der Produktion und der Produkte, besonderen Merkmalen der Sprache und der Kommunikation, spezifischen Verhaltensweisen der Mitarbeiter und markentypischer Symbole, zurückführen lassen (Schein 1985, S. 14 f.).

Die über praxisorientierte Handlungsempfehlungen hinausgehenden Publikationen führen hinsichtlich der Strukturelemente der Corporate Identity zu dem Ergebnis, dass hier zwischen Unternehmensphilosophie als Kern der Corporate Identity und dem Verhalten, der Kommunikation und dem Erscheinungsbild des Unternehmens unterschieden wird (Achterholt 1988, S. 42; Meffert 1994b, S. 85 f.; Birkigt/Stadler/Funck 1998). Daneben wird zwischen dem formulierten Selbstbild der Corporate Identity (Vision, Philosophie), dem realisierten Selbstbild (Kommunikation, Erscheinungsbild, Verhalten) und dem Fremdbild der Corporate Identity differenziert (Achterholt 1988, S. 42). Dies verdeutlicht zweierlei, die starke Bezugnahme auf die sozialwissenschaftliche Identitätsforschung und die Inkonsistenz der verschiedenen Ansätze und Begriffe, die häufig von den jeweiligen Autoren nicht oder nur vage definiert werden.

Die Analyse der betriebswirtschaftlichen Literatur verdeutlicht letztlich, dass es trotz der umfassenden Auseinandersetzung mit dem Markenphänomen bislang keine Ansätze gibt, die sich systematisch und stringent mit den Komponenten, der Entstehung und der Beeinflussung der Markenidentität und ihrem Verhältnis zum Markenimage und zur Marke befassen.

3. Konzeptionelle Ausgestaltung der identitätsorientierten Markenführung

3.1 Perspektiven und Gegenstand der Markenidentität

Das Konzept des identitätsorientierten Markenmanagements geht über die einseitige Ausrichtung auf die Wahrnehmung der Marke beim Nachfrager (Markenimage) hinaus. Die „klassische“ Outside-in-Perspektive der Marke wird um eine Inside-out-Perspektive ergänzt. Diese analysiert das Selbstbild der Marke aus Sicht der internen Zielgruppen innerhalb derjenigen Institution, die die Marke trägt. Dieses Selbstbild wird als Markenidentität bezeichnet (vgl. Abbildung 1).

Abbildung 1: Grundidee des identitätsorientierten Markenmanagement

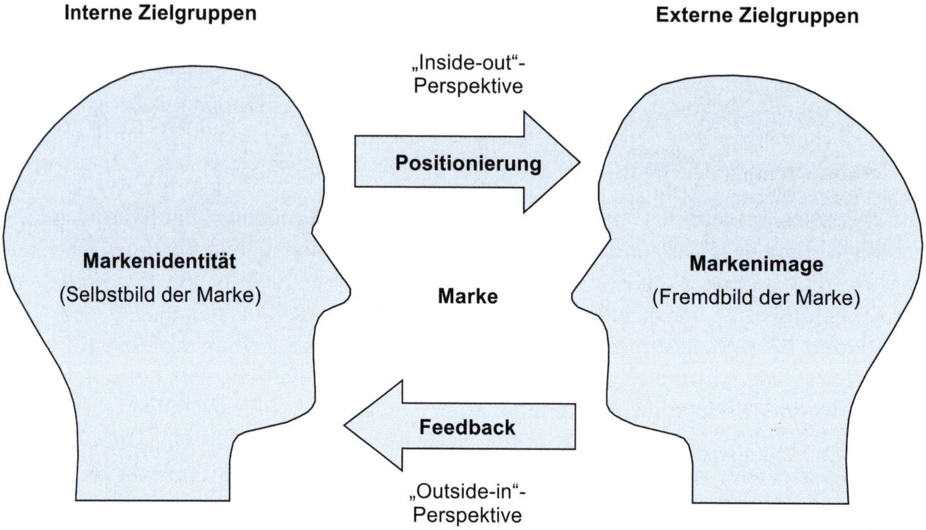

GABLER GRAFIK

Die Markenidentität bringt die wesensprägenden Merkmale einer Marke, für welche die Marke zunächst nach innen und später auch nach außen stehen soll, zum Ausdruck. Demnach handelt es sich um ein Aussagenkonzept (Kapferer 1992, S. 44 f), welches sich jedoch erst durch die Beziehung der internen Zielgruppen untereinander und der Interaktion zwischen internen und externen Zielgruppen der Marke konstituiert (Burmann/Blinda/Nitschke 2003, S. 5). Im Mittelpunkt der Markenidentität steht die Formulierung eines Kundennutzens, den die Marke aus Sicht des Anbieters erfüllen soll, und der in der spezifischen (Kern-)Kompetenz der Marke verankert ist.

Während sich die Markenidentität im Unternehmen aktiv konstituiert, formt sich das Fremdbild bei den verschiedenen externen Zielgruppen erst später und über einen längeren Zeitraum (vgl. Abbildung 2). Es schlägt sich letztlich im Image der Marke nieder (Meffert/Burmann 1996, S. 34). Das Markenimage ist somit als ein **Akzeptanzkonzept** der Nachfrager bezüglich deren Beurteilung der Marke zu interpretieren. Es stellt kein Managementkonzept dar, denn „um akzeptiert zu werden, muss die Marke zunächst konzipiert sein." (Kapferer 1992, S. 45).

Abbildung 2: **Beziehung zwischen Marke, Markenidentität und Markenimage**

Die Markenidentität ist die Ganzheit derjenigen raum-zeitlich gleichartigen Merkmale der Marke, die aus **Sicht der internen Zielgruppen** in nachhaltiger Weise den Charakter der Marke prägen.

Eine Marke ist ein **Nutzenbündel mit spezifischen Merkmalen**, die dafür sorgen, dass sich dieses Nutzenbündel gegenüber anderen Nutzenbündeln, welche dieselben Basisbedürfnisse erfüllen, aus Sicht relevanter Zielgruppen nachhaltig differenziert. (Quelle: in Anlehnung an Keller 2003)

Das Markenimage ist ein in der Psyche relevanter **externer Zielgruppen** fest verankertes, verdichtetes, wertendes **Vorstellungsbild** von einer Marke.

GABLER GRAFIK

Quelle: Burmann/Blinda/Nitschke 2003, S. 6

3.11 Das Fremdbild der Markenidentität als Akzeptanzkonzept der Marke

Beim Markenimage handelt es sich um ein mehrdimensionales Einstellungskonstrukt (Trommsdorff 2003, S. 150 f.; Kroeber-Riel/Weinberg 2003, S. 168 ff.; Foscht/Swoboda 2004, S. 171 f.), welches das in der Psyche relevanter externer Zielgruppen fest verankerte, verdichtete, wertende Vorstellungsbild von einer Marke wiedergibt. Das Markenimage ist das Ergebnis der individuellen, subjektiven Wahrnehmung und Dekodierung aller von der Marke ausgesendeten Signale. Insbesondere bezieht sich dies auf die subjektiv wahrgenommene Eignung dieser Marke zur Befriedigung der Bedürfnisse des Individuums.

Grundvoraussetzung für die Bildung eines Markenimages bei den externen Zielgruppen ist die Bekanntheit einer Marke (vgl. Abbildung 3). Die Markenbekanntheit (Brand Awareness) misst die Fähigkeit potenzieller Nachfrager, sich an ein Markenzeichen zu erinnern (Brand Recall) oder es nach akustischer und/oder visueller Stützung wieder zu erkennen (Brand Recognition) und diese Kenntnisse einer Produktkategorie zuzuordnen (Aaker 1991, S. 61). Da die Markenbekanntheit die notwendige Voraussetzung für die Entstehung eines Vorstellungsbildes im Kopf der Zielgruppen ist, kann sie definitorisch keine Komponente des Markenimages sein. Im Rahmen der Markenwertforschung kommt dem Bekanntheitsgrad zur Bestimmung des Markenwertes zwar eine besondere Bedeutung zu (Keller 1993, S. 7). Bei der Analyse der Markenidentität und des Markenimages kann auf diesen Aspekt jedoch verzichtet werden, weil das konstitutive Identitätsmerkmal der Wechselseitigkeit die Bekanntheit der Marke beim Nachfrager voraussetzt.

Abbildung 3: Komponenten des Markenimage

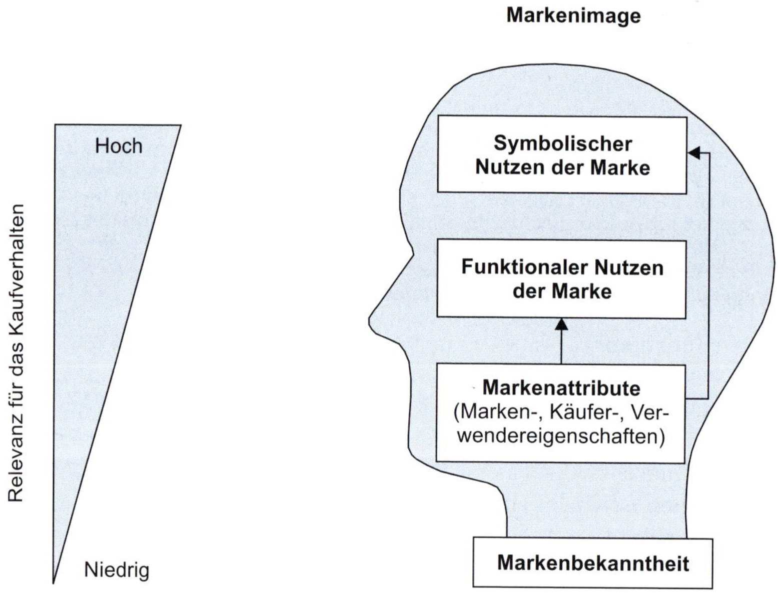

GABLER GRAFIK

Quelle: Burmann/Blinda/Nitschke 2003, S. 7

In Anlehnung an Vershofen und Keller unterteilt der identitätsoreintierte Markenführungsansatz das Markenimage in drei Komponenten: den Markenmerkmalen (Brand Attributes), dem aus diesen Merkmalen abgeleiteten funktionalen Nutzen der Marke und dem symbolischen Nutzen der Marke für den jeweiligen Nachfrager (Vershofen 1940, Keller 1993, S. 17). Die Relevanz dieser drei Imagekomponenten für das Kaufverhalten nimmt von der Markenbekanntheit bis zum symbolischen Nutzen einer Marke in der Regel zu.

Die **Markenattribute** repräsentieren sämtliche vom Nachfrager wahrgenommene Eigenschaften einer Marke. Hierunter fallen sowohl sachlich-rationale Eigenschaften als auch bildhafte und emotionale Eigenschaften. Es kann sich sowohl um Attribute, die mit der physischen Beschaffenheit (zum Beispiel Farbe, Form, Duft, technische Eigenschaften etc.) in Verbindung stehen, als auch um immaterielle Attribute (zum Beispiel Preis, Garantie, Herkunftsland etc.) handeln. Auch die Wahrnehmung typischer Käufer oder Verwender der Marke ist Bestandteil der Markenmerkmale und prägt potenziell das Markenimage. Die Gesamtheit aller Markenattribute wird vom Nachfrager verdichtet und bewertet. Das Ergebnis dieser Verdichtung und Bewertung ist der wahrgenommene funktionale und symbolische Nutzen einer Marke.

Im Marketing bezeichnet der Terminus *Nutzen* den Grad der Befriedigung von Bedürfnissen, den ein Objekt aus all seinen Merkmalen für den Nachfrager erbringt (Diller 1992, S. 826; Perrey 1998, S. 12; Meffert 2000, S. 333). Der **funktionale Nutzen** in Abbildung 3 umfasst sämtliche Nutzendimensionen, die sich aus den physikalisch-funktionellen Merkmalen der Marke sowie aus der Informationsfunktion und der Vertrauensfunktion der Marke ergeben. Der Nachfrager nimmt die Marke als eine Art Hilfe in seiner Informationsbeschaffung wahr, die ihn entlastet (Kroeber-Riel/Weinberg 2003, S. 268). Sie verringert die wahrgenommene Komplexität des Marktangebotes und führt so zu einer Senkung der Transaktionskosten im Kaufprozess. Beispielsweise zeigt sich der funktionale Nutzen eines Fahrzeuges der Marke BMW in seiner Fähigkeit, die Fahrzeuginsassen von Ort A nach Ort B zu transportieren, aber ebenso in den spezifischen Eigenschaften des Wagens, wie zum Beispiel seiner Fahrdynamik.

Ebenfalls dem funktionalen Nutzen einer Marke zuzuordnen ist deren Eignung zur Risikoreduktion. Marken können die von Nachfragern wahrgenommenen Risiken, beispielsweise im Bereich der Produktsicherheit (zum Beispiel Crashsicherheit eines Autos, Gefahr von Krankheitserregern in Nahrungsmitteln), der langfristige Ersatzteilversorgung, des Angebots technischer Kundendienstleistungen, des finanziellen Risikos oder des sozialen Risikos (zum Beispiel mangelnde Akzeptanz im Freundeskreis) verringern. Der Erfolg der Mehrzahl der Marken baut jedoch nicht allein auf dem funktionalen Markennutzen auf, sondern beruht immer stärker auf der symbolischen Bedeutung, die die Marke beim Nachfrager evoziert.

Ein **symbolischer Nutzen** entsteht immer dann, wenn eine Marke neben ihrer funktionalen Nutzenstiftung dem Nachfrager einen zusätzlichen Nutzen stiftet.[3] Hier ist beispielsweise an die:

- Vermittlung von Prestige (= Geltungsnutzen),
- Vermittlung eines Gefühls der Gruppenzugehörigkeit,
- Wahrnehmung der Marke als Mittel zur Selbstverwirklichung,

---

3 Der Begriff des Zusatznutzens geht auf den Gründer der Gesellschaft für Konsumforschung (GfK AG) in Nürnberg, Wilhelm Vershofen, zurück. Vgl. Vershofen (1940), S. 71 sowie Meffert (2000), S. 333.

- Verknüpfung der Marke mit individuell wichtigen Erlebnissen und Erinnerungen (zum Beispiel Urlaubserlebnisse, erste Liebe, enge Freunde),
- Marke als Mittel zur Generierung von Beziehungsvorteilen (zum Beispiel aufgrund enger persönlicher Beziehungen an bestimmte Markenrepräsentanten),
- Marke als Sinnbild individuell wichtiger Werte oder Lebensstile,

zu denken. In allen diesen Fällen steht die Marke symbolhaft für wichtige Motivatoren des Verhaltens der Nachfrager.

3.12 Die Markenidentität als Aussagekonzept der Marke

Identität entsteht immer aus einer Kombination mehrerer Merkmale oder Eigenschaften, die aufeinander abgestimmt sein müssen und letztlich ein und dieselbe Person widerspiegeln. Ebenso wie die Identität einer Person erst im Laufe mehrerer Jahre heranwächst (Wiedmann 1994, S. 1045), kann sich auch eine klare Markenidentität nur über einen längeren Zeitraum entwickeln.

Aus diesem Grund sollten die **essenziellen Merkmale** der Markenidentität von der Markenführung nicht oder zumindest nur geringfügig verändert werden. Ansonsten besteht die Gefahr, die Identität der Marke nachhaltig zu beschädigen. Dagegen können die **akzidenziellen Merkmale** der Markenidentität verändert werden. Kapferer (Kapferer 2001, S. 35) führt entsprechend an, dass sich mit der Entwicklung der Technologie, der Produktpalette und der Käufer einer Marke die akzidenziellen Merkmale im Sinne eines stilistischen Codes der Marke durchaus ändern können, wenn der Ursprung und mithin der Kern der Markenidentität, er bezeichnet diesen als genetischen Code der Marke, bewahrt wird. Die Differenzierung zwischen essenziellen und akzidenziellen Merkmalen der Markenidentität basiert auf der sozialwissenschaftlichen Identitätsforschung. Obwohl eine Übertragung auf die Markenidentität konzeptionell schlüssig ist, stehen vertiefende Untersuchungen über die minimal notwendige beziehungsweise maximal zulässig Veränderung der Markenidentität und ihrer einzelnen Komponenten im Zeitablauf noch aus. Eine klare und generalisierbare Abgrenzung zwischen essenziellen und akzidenziellen Merkmalen der Markenidentität ist daher (noch) nicht möglich.

Das Spannungsfeld von Veränderung und Kontinuität kann am Beispiel Volkswagen verdeutlicht werden. Für die Marke Volkswagen war über lange Jahre hinweg der Name Sinnbild für eine klare Markenidentität. Die Aufgabe des Herstellers war es, ein „Auto für das Volk" zu entwickeln, wobei die Gründungsidee in der Solidarität (ein Volk, ein Wagen) lag. Später stand der Hersteller vor dem Problem, die Marke, die mit dem VW-Käfer anfangs auf nur einem Produkt basierte, an die soziologische Evolution, die technologischen Entwicklungen und die wachsenden Ansprüche der Autofahrer anzupassen. Es galt somit, die Markenidentität an die neuen Erfordernisse anzugleichen, ohne den

Kern der Marke zu verändern. Entsprechend wurde verstärkt der sparsame Verbrauch, die Werthaltigkeit, Robustheit und Sicherheit des Autos betont, ohne jedoch den Identitätskern der Marke Volkswagen wirklich zu verändern (Kapferer 1992, S. 110 f.).

Auf der Grundlage der sozialwissenschaftlichen und psychologischen Identitätsforschung lassen sich sechs konstitutive Komponenten identifizieren, welche eine umfassende Beschreibung der Markenidentität im Sinne ihrer raum-zeitlich gleichartigen Merkmale ermöglichen (vgl. Abbildung 4). Die **Markenherkunft** stellt die Basis der Markenidentität dar. Die **Markenkompetenz**, welche auf den Ressourcen und organisationalen Fähigkeiten einer Unternehmung beruht, begründet den spezifischen Wettbewerbsvorteil der Marke und sichert diesen ab. Die grundsätzliche **Art der Markenleistungen** determiniert, wie eine Marke für den Nachfrager nutzbar wird. Die Gestaltung der Identität wird langfristig geleitet durch die **Markenvision**. Die **Markenwerte** geben wieder, woran die Marke und ihre Repräsentanten glauben. Die **Markenpersönlichkeit** determiniert den Kommunikationsstil der Marke. Durch die spezifische Ausprägung ausgewählter oder aller dieser Komponenten wird die Identität einer Marke für den Nachfrager wahrnehmbar und erlebbar.

Abbildung 4: Komponenten der Markenidentität

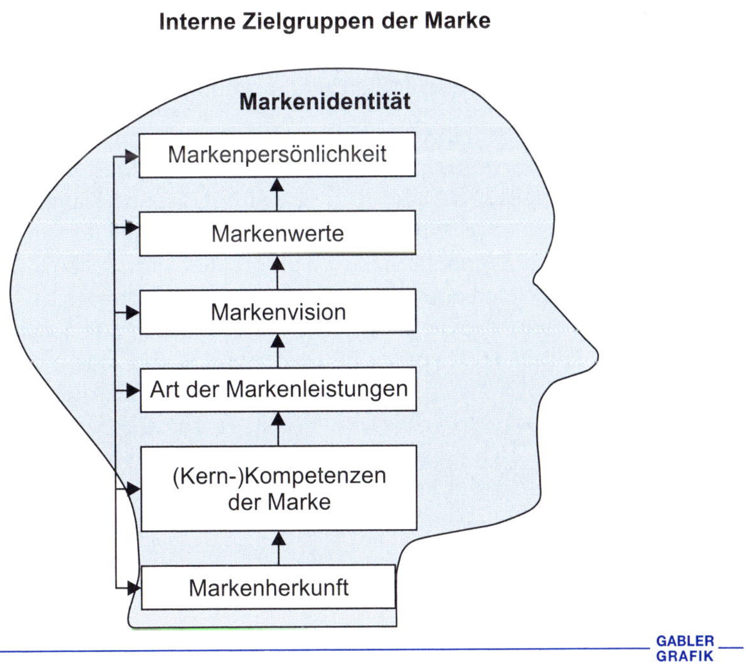

Quelle: Burmann/Blinda/Nitschke 2003, S. 7

3.121 Markenherkunft

Die **Herkunft der Marke** bildet das Fundament der Markenidentität. Die Markenherkunft ist für die Markenführung von hoher Relevanz, da eine Marke von den internen und externen Zielgruppen zunächst im Kontext ihres **Ursprungs** wahrgenommen und interpretiert wird. So konstatieren beispielsweise Aaker und Joachimsthaler: „Knowing the roots of a person, place, or firm can help create interest and a bond. The same is true for a brand." (Aaker/Joachimsthaler 2000, S. 249). Die Markenherkunft ist eng mit der Historie einer Marke verbunden. Während jedoch die Markenherkunft einzelne Facetten der Markenhistorie herausgreift und in besonderer Weise betont, umfasst die Markenhistorie sämtliche Ereignisse der Vergangenheit, die mit der Marke in Verbindung gebracht werden. Die Markenherkunft ist daher im Gegensatz zur Markenhistorie eine durch das Markenmanagement **langfristig gestaltbare Identitätskomponente**. Im Idealfall verleiht sie allen weiteren Aktivitäten des Markenmanagements ein hohes Maß an Glaubwürdigkeit und Authentizität. Sie umfasst drei Facetten: die regionale Herkunft, die kulturelle Herkunft und die institutionelle Herkunft (Blinda 2003, S. 38 f. und 51 ff.).

Untersuchungen aus dem Bereich der Country-of-origin-Forschung belegen, dass Nachfrager Produkte und Marken oftmals anhand ihrer **nationalen beziehungsweise regionalen Herkunft** bewerten (Hausruckinger 1993; Papadopoulos 1993; Lebrenz 1996; Baumgarth 2004, S. 187 ff.). Beispielsweise wird die Biermarke Foster's weltweit mit ihrer australischen Herkunft assoziiert. Foster's Markenidentität baut auf dieser Herkunft auf und das Markenmanagement setzt in der Markenkommunikation die australische Herkunft aktiv ein, um sich vom Wettbewerb zu differenzieren.

Die identitätsorientierte Markenherkunft bezieht sich jedoch nicht ausschließlich auf die regionale Herkunftsdimension. Aufbauend auf Erkenntnissen der Culture-of-brand-origin-Forschung kann auch die **kulturelle Herkunft** die Identität einer Marke in signifikanter Weise prägen. Da es Nachfragern durch die heute vorherrschende internationale Konfiguration von Unternehmensaktivitäten oftmals schwer möglich ist, einzelne Länder als das Herkunftsland einer Marke zuzuordnen, greifen sie eher auf „cultural cues" bei der Identifizierung der Herkunft einer Marke zurück. Nach Lim/O'Cass sind Nachfrager diese „cultural cues" wesentlich verfügbarer als Informationen zum spezifischen Herkunftsland (Lim/O'Cass 2001). Beispielsweise kann allein der Name der Automobilmarke Hyundai bereits asiatische Herkunftsassoziationen evozieren, ohne das der Nachfrager weiß, dass es sich hierbei um eine koreanische Marke handelt. Die Biermarke Paulaner kann daher als eine durch die bayerische Kultur geprägte Biermarke und nicht lediglich als deutsches Bier identifiziert werden. Die regionale und die kulturelle Herkunft einer Marke umfassen demnach sämtliche Einflüsse, die sich aus den Herkunftsländern und -regionen für die Markenidentität ergeben und diese stärken können (Charmasson 1988; Leclerc/Schmitt/Dube 1994, S. 263 f.).

Die **institutionelle Herkunft** als dritte Dimension der Markenherkunft umfasst den Ursprung einer Marke in einer bestimmten Branche oder Organisation, häufig als so genannte „Made-by"-Herkunft bezeichnet, und die daraus resultierenden Einflüsse auf die Identität einer Marke. Wichtige Determinanten in diesem Zusammenhang sind die Branchenusancen, die Unternehmenskultur und die Unternehmensgründer (Burmann/ Maloney 2004, S. 3). Insbesondere die Unternehmensgründer und -führer können die Markenidentität des Unternehmens und auch die Identitäten einzelner Produktmarken entscheidend prägen. Beispielsweise haben die Unternehmensgründer von Aldi, Theo und Karl Albrecht, die auf Sparsamkeit und Effizienz ausgerichtete Unternehmenskultur des Konzerns entscheidend geprägt. Ebenso steht Dr. Claus Hipp als Unternehmensführer und Nachfahre des Firmengründers „mit seinen Namen" für den biologischen Anbau der Zutaten und die Qualität der Produkte der Babynahrungsmarke Hipp (Blinda 2003, S. 66). Andererseits wird die Wahrnehmung von Uhren, Handtaschen, Sonnenbrillen, Parfum und Schuhen der Marke Gucci von der institutionellen Herkunft der Marke aus der Bekleidungsindustrie geprägt.

Das Markenmanagement kann durch eine Betonung einzelner Herkunftsfacetten die **wahrgenommene Herkunft** einer Marke langfristig verändern. Ebenso kann die Markenherkunft durch Kooperationen und Unternehmensfusionen erweitert, angereichert aber auch erodiert werden. Darüber hinaus können sich Outsourcing-Entscheidungen oder die Verlagerung wichtiger Unternehmensteile ins Ausland langfristig signifikant auf die Wahrnehmung der Markenherkunft und letztlich der Markenstärke auswirken.

3.122 Markenkompetenz

Neben der Markenherkunft basiert die Identität einer Marke vor allem auf den jeweiligen **Kompetenzen** der die Marke führenden Institution. Sie repräsentieren die spezifischen **organisationalen Fähigkeiten** eines Unternehmens zur marktgerechten Kombination von Ressourcen. Ältere Markenführungsansätze verstehen unter der Kompetenz einer Marke in erster Linie die **Produktqualität**. Hierbei handelt es sich jedoch um ein stark verkürztes Verständnis des Begriffes, welches die Interdependenzen zwischen der Marke und ihrer Entstehung und Weiterentwicklung, das heißt den organisationalen Fähigkeiten eines Unternehmens, außer Acht lässt. Diese Interdependenzen sind jedoch bedeutend, da der identitätsorientierte Markenführungsansatz die Marke letztlich als das Ergebnis der richtigen Kombination von Unternehmensressourcen versteht. Wurde in diesem Sinne eine Marke geschaffen, kann sie selbst wiederum als Ressource des Unternehmens interpretiert werden.

Markenkompetenzen können in diesem Zusammenhang als das Handlungspotenzial eines Unternehmens interpretiert werden, verschiedene Ressourcen des Unternehmens so zu kombinieren, dass eine an den Marktanforderungen ausgerichtete Marke entsteht. Die Behauptung oder sogar Dominanz gegenüber Wettbewerbern ist dabei nur möglich, wenn die Marke einen der Konkurrenz ebenbürtigen oder sogar überlegenen Kundennutzen stiftet (Freiling 2001, S. 27). Ein dauerhaft überlegener Kundenutzen basiert auf den **Kernkompetenzen einer Marke**, wohingegen zur „einfachen" Behauptung im Markt die Verfügbarkeit von Markenkompetenzen ausreichend ist (Freiling 2001, S. 26). Die Existenz von Kompetenzen und Kernkompetenzen bemisst sich aus der Perspektive des identitätsorientierten Markenmanagementansatzes somit stets an der Erzeugung von **mit Preisbereitschaften verknüpften Kundennutzens** durch die die Marke tragende Institution.

Da die Kompetenzen und Kernkompetenzen einer Marke auf Wissensvorsprüngen gegenüber dem Wettbewerb basieren, sind sie stets temporär. Es bedarf somit **permanenter Investitionen in die Erneuerung von Kompetenzen**, um Wissensvorsprünge und die mit ihnen verknüpften Wettbewerbsvorteile der Marke zu verteidigen. Ebenso bedarf es kontinuierlicher Investitionen in die Bindung derjenigen Humanressourcen, die für die Entstehung der Kompetenzen und Kernkompetenzen einer Marke verantwortlich sind, denn alle organisationalen Fähigkeiten basieren letztlich auf der Verknüpfung des Know-hows von Individuen.

3.123 Art der Markenleistungen

Die Festlegung der grundsätzlichen Form und Art der **Markenleistungen** basiert direkt auf der Markenkompetenz. Die grundsätzliche Art der Markenleistungen determiniert, wie eine Marke für den Nachfrager nutzbar wird. Es muss die grundsätzliche Form und Ausstattung von Produkten und Dienstleistungen, die eine Marke anbieten soll, festgelegt werden. Ebenso wie ein Mensch im Rahmen seiner persönlichen Identität für sich bestimmt, welche Rolle und Funktion er in der Gesellschaft erfüllen möchte (zum Beispiel in Form seines ausgeübten Berufes), wird bei der Markenidentität festgelegt, welchen funktionalen Nutzen eine Marke dem Nachfrager bieten soll.

Im negativen Sinne sei hier „beispielhaft" auf die Marke Jaguar verwiesen (vgl. Abbildung 5). Eine bewusste, professionelle Festlegung der Markenleistungen, die zu den übrigen Komponenten der Markenidentität passt, hat hier offenkundig nicht stattgefunden. Anders ist die jüngste Erweiterung des Produktprogramms von Jaguar um einen vergleichsweise preiswerten „Einstiegskombi" nicht zu erklären. Der Identitätsfit dieses Fahrzeuges ist derart schwach, dass es nahe liegend erscheint, die geringe Marktakzeptanz dieses Produktes und die Schwierigkeiten der Marke Jaguar insgesamt auch auf ein verfehltes Markenidentitätsmanagement zurückzuführen.

Abbildung 5: Vergleich typischer Jaguar-Modelle mit dem neuen Jaguar-Estate

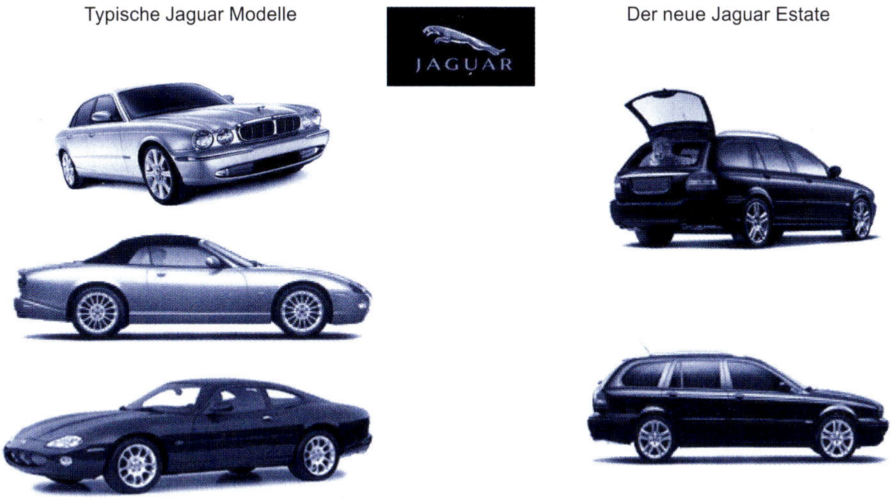

GABLER GRAFIK

3.124 Markenvision

Ein weiterer, wesentlicher Bestandteil der Markenidentität ist die **Markenvision**. Sie gibt die langfristige Entwicklungsrichtung (fünf bis zehn Jahre) einer Marke vor. Die Markenvision sollte allen internen Zielgruppen eine wichtige Motivation sein. Ind spricht in diesem Zusammenhang von einer so genannten „Ideologie", welche in der Lage ist, allen Mitarbeitern ein gemeinsames Credo zu bieten, an das diese glauben und mit dem sie sich identifizieren können (Ind 2003, S. 395). Mittels bildhaft-emotionaler Leitlinien sollen die Bedeutung und die Funktion der Marke bei der Realisierung der langfristigen, strategischen Unternehmensziele dargestellt werden. Im Vergleich zur Markenvision sind Markenziele jedoch durch einen höheren Konkretisierungsgrad und einen kürzeren Zeithorizont gekennzeichnet. Die Markenvision übernimmt somit eine Koordinationsfunktion und dient der Sicherstellung eines unternehmensweiten, mit den Markenzielen konformen Handelns. Sie sollte sowohl die anvisierten Marktsegmente, als auch die grundlegenden Differenzierungsmerkmale gegenüber Wettbewerbern beinhalten. Die Markenvision muss dabei eine langfristig realisierbare Wunschvorstellung zum Ausdruck bringen, um intern Motivations- und Identifikationskraft entfalten zu können (Kapferer 1992, S. 110 f.).

3.125 Markenwerte

Die **Markenwerte** repräsentieren die Grundüberzeugungen von Management und Mitarbeitern oder, mit anderen Worten, woran die Marke „glaubt". Sie sollen vor allem wichtige emotionale Komponenten der Markenidentität sowie die Wünsche der relevanten Zielgruppen an eine ideale Marke zum Ausdruck bringen. Fokussiert auf wenige Aussagen, sollen sie einen Bezug zu dem durch die Marke versprochenen, vor allem symbolischen Kundennutzen aufweisen (Burmann/Blinda/Nitschke 2003, S. 22).

Die Markenwerte spielen für die Authentizität der Marke eine wichtige Rolle. Sie sollten daher von den Mitarbeitern „gelebt" werden. Denn erst durch ein konsequentes, aktives „Leben" seitens der Mitarbeiter einer Marke können die Markenwerte ein integraler Teil der Markenidentität werden und die Marke emotional aufladen. In einem solchen Fall werden derartige Glaubenssätze eine wichtige Komponente dessen, was sich in den Köpfen der externen Zielgruppen als Markenimage herausbildet.

Abbildung 6: Die Markenwerte von „The Body Shop"

THE BODY SHOP™

TIERSCHUTZ: The Body Shop setzt sich aktiv für ein Verbot von Tierversuchen in der Kosmetikindustrie ein. Als eines der ersten Unternehmen hat The Body Shop das internationale Humane Cosmetic Standard-Logo erhalten.

HILFE DURCH HANDEL: Mit seinem „Hilfe durch Handel" Programm baut The Body Shop langfristige Handelsbeziehungen zu Partnern in allen Teilen der Welt auf und bezahlt den Produzenten faire Preise für hervorragende natürliche Inhaltsstoffe und Accessoires.

SELBSTACHTUNG: Jeder Mensch ist schön – jeder auf seine eigene Weise. The Body Shop glaubt, dass Make-up, Düfte und Feuchtigkeitscremes zwar die Persönlichkeit und Individualität von Menschen untersteichen, sie aber nicht einem festgelegten Schönheitsideal entsprechen sollten.

MENSCHENRECHTE: Mit Kampagnen für die Rechte von Menschen will The Body Shop das öffentliche Bewusstsein aufrütteln und Betroffenen helfen. The Body Shop ist überzeugt, dass Unternehmen die Macht haben, Veränderungen in Gang zu bringen.

UMWELTSCHUTZ: The Body Shop nimmt Umweltschutz sehr ernst. Deshalb enthalten die Verpackungen kein PVC und ein Großteil der Flaschen basiert auf einem hohen Anteil an recyceltem Kunststoff. Außerdem hat die Unternehmenszentrale sowie viele Filialen auf erneuerbare Energie umgestellt.

MADE WITH PASSION™ | AGAINST ANIMAL TESTING | SUPPORT COMMUNITY TRADE | ACTIVATE SELF ESTEEM | DEFEND HUMAN RIGHTS | PROTECT OUR PLANET

GABLER GRAFIK

Quelle: Burmann/Maloney 2004, S. 9

Ein geeignetes Beispiel einer Marke mit besonders ausgeprägten Markenwerten ist „The Body Shop". Die Markenführenden von „The Body Shop" haben für ihre Marke klare Werte wie beispielsweise „against animal testing," „defend human rights" oder „protect our planet" formuliert und konsequent bei der Führung der Marke umgesetzt (vgl. Abbildung 6).

3.126 Markenpersönlichkeit

Azoulay und Kapferer definieren die **Markenpersönlichkeit** als „the set of human personality traits that are both applicable and relevant for brands." (Azoulay/Kapferer 2003, S. 151). Diese Auffassung der Markenpersönlichkeit wird durch Gilmores „Theorie des Animismus" gestützt (Gilmore 1919). Sie besagt, dass Menschen grundsätzlich dazu neigen, Artefakte durch die Verleihung menschlicher Eigenschaften zu „beseelen." Hieraus ergibt sich eine Vereinfachung der Interaktion mit Objekten. Aus dieser Perspektive verfügen auch Marken über „menschliche Merkmale" im Sinne einer eigenen Persönlichkeit (Aaker 1997; Fournier 1998; Huber/Herrmann/Weis 2001; Hermann/Huber/Braunstein 2001).

Diese für Marken relevanten Persönlichkeitsmerkmale finden ihren Ausdruck im verbalen und non-verbalen Kommunikationsstil einer Marke. Der markenspezifische Kommunikationsstil wird sowohl von den typischen Repräsentanten einer Marke, als auch von der Herkunft der Marke geprägt (Aaker 1997, S. 348; Burmann/Blinda/Nitschke 2003, S. 23). Nach der Markteinführung einer Marke kann die Persönlichkeit der Marke auch durch die typischen Verwender und Käufer der Marke beeinflusst werden. Beispielhaft kann hier auf die Produktmarke Opel Manta oder die Marke Harley Davidson verwiesen werden, deren Persönlichkeit in besonderer Weise durch eine über einen längeren Zeit raum hinweg homogene Käufergruppe geprägt werden. Diese Prägung der Markenpersönlichkeit durch typische Käufer- und Verwender kann bewusst geplant und zum Beispiel in der Markenkommunikation ausgelobt werden. Sie kann sich jedoch auch ungeplant einstellen und gegebenenfalls negativ auf die Marke wirken, wie im Fall des Opel Manta. Vor allem über die Markenpersönlichkeit und die Markenwerte kann die Beziehung zwischen der Marke und den Nachfragern emotional aufgeladen und dadurch gefestigt werden. Sie beeinflussen in starkem Maße, ob die Marke von den Zielgruppen gemocht beziehungsweise als sympathisch wahrgenommen wird (Moser 2003, S. 67 ff.).

Beispielsweise hat Mini als Lifestyle-Marke eine junge, moderne Persönlichkeit, die unkonventionell auftritt und versucht, in ihrer Kommunikation die Zielgruppen mit Witz zu überraschen. Dies spiegelt sich in einem entsprechenden Charakter der Markenkommunikation wider (vgl. Abbildung 7).

Abbildung 7: Die Markenpersönlichkeit am Beispiel der Marke Mini

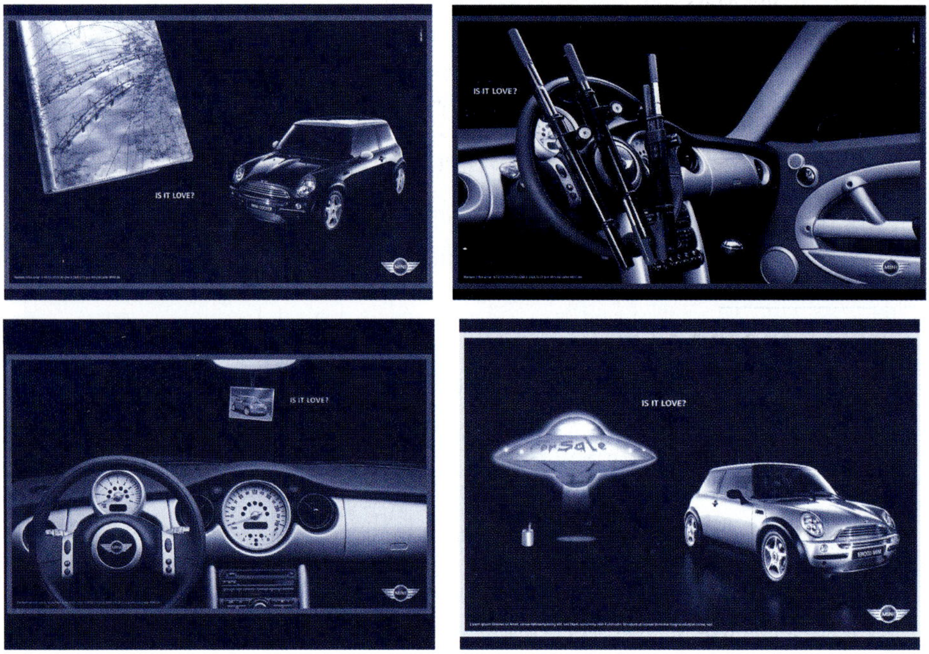

GABLER GRAFIK

Zusammenfassend ist festzuhalten, dass Aussagen über die Bedeutung der verschiedenen hier diskutierten Identitätskomponenten für die tatsächliche Ausprägung der Markenidentität nur unter Berücksichtigung der jeweiligen Rahmenbedingungen im Einzelfall zu treffen sind. Aaker/Joachimsthaler führen in diesem Zusammenhang fünf Fragen an, die bei der Identifikation relevanter Identitätskomponenten helfen können (Aaker/Joachimsthaler 2000, S. 57):

1. „Does it capture an element important to the brand and its ability to provide the customer value or support customer relationships?
2. Does it help differentiate the brand from its competitors?
3. Does it resonate with the customer?
4. Does it energize employees?
5. Is it believable?"

Der Stellenwert der einzelnen Identitätskomponenten hängt letztlich auch von der betrachteten Produktkategorie ab (Dienstleistungen, Investitionsgüter, Convenience-, Shopping-, Specialty Goods etc.). Darüber hinaus stellen die Zielgruppenstruktur, die Art des zentralen Markennutzens, die Markenidentität der Hauptwettbewerber und die Struktur des Markenportfolios eines Unternehmens wesentliche Determinanten dar. Die generelle Bedeutung der Markenidentität für das Verhalten gegenüber der Marke wird darüber hinaus von der Stärke der persönlichen Identität des Individuums beeinflusst. Personen mit eher schwacher Ich-Identität werden sich eher in der Identität einer Marke wiederfinden und sich mit dieser identifizieren als Personen mit einer starken Ich-Identität (Goodyear 1994, S. 65).

3.2 Zusammenhang zwischen Markenidentität, Markenimage und Markenpositionierung

Den Zusammenhang zwischen der Gestaltung der Markenidentität und den intendierten Wirkungen im Markt bezüglich des Markenimages zeigt zusammenfassend Abbildung 8.

Die Ausgestaltung der Markenpersönlichkeit, der Markenwerte und der Markenvision determiniert primär die Wahrnehmung des symbolischen Markennutzens, wohingegen die Ausgestaltung von Art und Form der Markenleistungen die Wahrnehmung des funktionalen Markennutzens bestimmt. Der Fit dieser vier Identitätskomponenten mit den (Kern-)Kompetenzen und der Herkunft einer Marke determiniert die Glaubwürdigkeit der intendierten Markenpositionierung.

Die Glaubwürdigkeit hat direkte Auswirkungen auf das der Marke entgegengebrachte Vertrauen. Diese wird ferner durch die **Interaktionsintensität** zwischen externen und internen Zielgruppen der Marke beeinflusst (Petermann 1992). Dies ist unter anderem darauf zurückzuführen, dass eine hohe Interaktionsintensität in der Regel zu einer Annäherung und im Idealfall zur Übereinstimmung von Ist-Markenidentität und Ist-Markenimage führt (Krappmann 1988). Mit diesem höheren Fit gewinnt die Identität der Marke an Prägnanz. Diese Annäherung von Ist-Identität und Ist-Image der Marke sagt jedoch noch nichts über die Soll-Identität und das Soll-Image der Marke und damit den Zielerreichungsgrad der Markenführung aus.

Aus dem Markenidentitätskonzept ergibt sich die Positionierung der Marke, im Rahmen derer bestimmt wird, wie die Markenidentität zu zentralen Eigenschaften mit engem Bezug zu den Kaufentscheidungskriterien der relevanten, externen Zielgruppen verdichtet werden kann. Mit Hilfe der Positionierung wird versucht, eine im Vergleich zu Wettbewerbern vorteilhafte Stellung (Position) in der Psyche der externen Zielgruppen aufzubauen. Als erstes sind hierzu die **Positionierungsdimensionen** zu identifizieren. Diese bilden den so genannten Positionierungsraum und sind aus den zentralen Kaufentscheidungskriterien der Zielgruppe herzuleiten (Homburg/Krohmer 2003, S. 410 ff.) Mittels der Idealposition eines Produktes beziehungsweise einer Dienstleistung und den bereits existierenden Wettbewerbsangeboten lassen sich in diesem Raum anschließend erfolgsversprechende **Positionierungsstrategien** für die eigene Marke identifizieren. Grundsätzlich stehen dabei zwei Basisoptionen zur Verfügung. Bei einer **Points-of-Difference-Strategie** wird versucht, die Marke möglichst weit weg von den Wettbewerbern aufzustellen. Bei einer **Points-of-Parity-Strategie** wird die Imitation eines Wettbewerbers angestrebt (Keller 2003, S. 131 ff.). Beide Strategien können bezüglich der verschiedenen Nutzenkomponenten einer Marke kombiniert werden. Bei einzelnen Nutzenkomponenten der Marke werden dann Konkurrenten imitiert, bei anderen hingegen eine Differenzierung angestrebt.

Abbildung 8: Zusammenhang zwischen Identität und Image der Marke

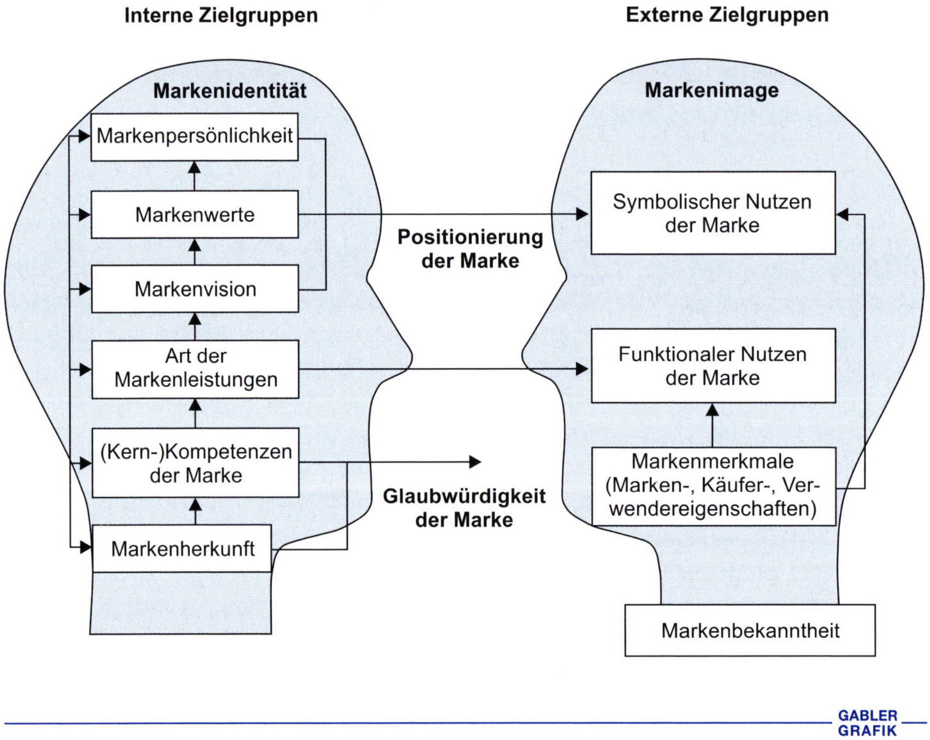

Quelle: Burmann/Blinda/Nitschke 2003, S. 25

4. Fazit

Vor dem Hintergrund einer ansteigenden Produktvielfalt und der Informationsüberlastung der Nachfrager ist die klassische Markenartikelkonzeption heute aktueller als jemals zuvor. Dabei erscheint eine stärkere Ausrichtung der Markenführung an der Markenidentität als strategischem Kern jeder Marke geeignet, die bei vielen Marken in den letzten Jahren erodierende Beziehung zum Nachfrager wieder zu stärken.

Grundlage jeder dauerhaften Kundenbeziehung ist das der Marke entgegengebrachte Vertrauen. Die Bedeutung des Vertrauens für den Aufbau starker Marken ist beileibe nicht neu. Bereits 1939 hat Domizlaff die Gewinnung von Vertrauen in den Mittelpunkt seiner markentechnischen Überlegungen gestellt. Die seit dieser Zeit entstandenen Ansätze der Markenführung haben dieser frühen Erkenntnis jedoch nur unzureichend Rechnung getragen. Stattdessen konzentrierten sich diese Ansätze, wie in weiten Teilen seiner Ausarbeitungen auch Domizlaff selbst, auf instrumentelle, funktionelle oder marketingtechnokratische Aspekte der Markenführung. Die Untersuchung der Voraussetzungen und Einflussfaktoren der Vertrauensbildung im Rahmen der Markenführung wurde demzufolge vernachlässigt.

Vertrauen kann nur auf der Basis von Glaubwürdigkeit und Verlässlichkeit entstehen. Die subjektiv wahrgenommene Sicherheit, sich auf jemanden hinsichtlich der Einhaltung bestimmter Zusagen verlassen zu können, lässt Vertrauen entstehen. Ein im Zeitablauf widerspruchsfreies, konsistentes und damit zuverlässiges Verhalten ist nur dann möglich, wenn eine Person ein klares Bild von sich selbst hat. Mit anderen Worten, eine Person muss eine Identität besitzen, um von anderen als verlässlich und vertrauenswürdig anerkannt zu werden. Einem Menschen ohne Identität kann man nicht vertrauen. Die Stärke der Identität ist dabei vor allem auch von dem Grad der Übereinstimmung zwischen dem Selbstbild und dem von anderen zugeschriebenen Fremdbild der Identität (Image) abhängig. Diese Überlegungen sind auf Marken übertragbar.

Ebenso wie die Identität einer Person über viele Jahre hinweg entsteht, entwickelt sich auch die Identität einer Marke nur über einen längeren Zeitraum. Dementsprechend ist die gezielte Beeinflussung einer Markenidentität durch die Markenführung nur langfristig möglich. Ebenso wie die Identität einer Person setzt sich auch die Markenidentität aus einer Vielzahl einzelner Komponenten zusammen. Die Komplexität der sich ergebenden Wirkungsbeziehungen stellt hohe Anforderungen an die Markenführung und ist nur durch die Entwicklung entsprechender organisationaler Fähigkeiten dauerhaft zu meistern.

Die Hauptaufgabe des identitätsorientierten Markenmanagements liegt daher in der Schaffung einer eigenständigen Markenidentität durch eine aufeinander abgestimmte, im Zeitablauf im Wesentlichen stabile Gestaltung und Vermittlung aller Komponenten der Markenidentität und der Durchsetzung eines gemeinsamen Vorstellungsbildes von der Marke in den Köpfen aller internen und externen Zielgruppen. Dies erfordert einen Managementprozess, der sämtliche Aktivitäten zur Steuerung einer Marke erfasst und zweckmäßig strukturiert. Dieser Managementprozess soll im nächsten Kapitel dargelegt werden.

Literatur

Aaker (1991), D. A., Managing Brand Equity: Capitalizing on the value of a brand name, New York, NY [u.a.].
Aaker (1996), D. A., Building Strong Brands, New York.
Aaker (1997), J., Dimensions of Brand Personality, in: Journal of Marketing Research, Vol. 34, August, S. 347–356.
Aaker (2000), D. A., Joachimsthaler, E., Brand Leadership, New York [u.a.].
Achterholt (1988), G., Corporate Identity. In zehn Arbeitsschritten die eigene Identität finden, Wiesbaden.
Andresen (1991), T., Innere Markenbilder: MAX – wie er wurde, was er ist, in: Planung und Analyse, 18. Jg., Nr. 1, S. 28–34.
Azoulay A., Kapferer J.-N. (2003), Do brand personality scales really measure brand personality, in: Journal of Brand Management, 11. Jg., Nr. 2, November, S. 143–155.
Bain, J. (1959), Industrial Organization, New York.
Barney, J. B. (1991), Firm Resources and Sustained Competitive Advantage, in: Journal of Management, Vol. 17, No. 1, S. 99–120.
Baumgarth, C. (2004), Markenpolitik: Markenwirkungen, Markenführung, Markenforschung, 2. Aufl., Wiesbaden.
Bekmeier-Feuerhahn, S. (1998), Marktorientierte Markenbewertung: eine konsumenten- und unternehmensbezogene Betrachtung, Wiesbaden.
Berekoven, L. (1978), Zum Verständnis und Selbstverständnis des Markenwesens, in: Markenartikel heute. Marke, Markt und Marketing, Schriftenreihe Markt und Marketing des Gabler-Verlags, Wiesbaden, S. 35–48.
Birkigt, K., Stadler, M. M. (1998), Corporate Identity – Grundlagen, in: Corporate Identity: Grundlagen, Funktionen, Fallbeispiele, Birkigt, K., Stadler, M. M., Funck, H. J., 9. Aufl., Landsberg/Lech, S. 11–64.
Blinda, L. (2003), Relevanz der Markenherkunft für die identitätsbasierte Markenführung, Arbeitspapier Nr. 2 des Lehrstuhls für innovatives Markenmanagement (LiM), Burmann, Ch. (Hrsg.), Universität Bremen, Bremen.
Böhm, B. (1989), Identität und Identifikation. Zur Persistenz physikalischer Gegenstände, Frankfurt/M.
Bonus, H. (1994), Das Selbstverständnis moderner Genossenschaften, Tübingen.
Bonus, H. (1995), Europäische Identität aus ökonomischer Sicht, Volkswirtschaftliche Diskussionsbeiträge des Instituts für Genossenschaftswesen der Westfälischen Wilhelms-Universität Münster, Beitrag Nr. 216, Münster.
Burmann, Ch. (2002), Strategische Flexibilität und Strategiewechsel als Determinanten des Unternehmenswertes (zugl. Habilitationsschrift Universität Münster), Wiesbaden.
Burmann, Ch., Blinda, L., Nitschke, A. (2003), Konzeptionelle Grundlagen des identitätsbasierten Markenmanagements, Arbeitspapier Nr. 1 des Lehrstuhls für innovatives Markenmanagement (LiM), Burmann, Ch. (Hrsg.), Universität Bremen, Bremen.
Burmann, Ch., Maloney, P. (2004), Vertikale und horizontale Führung von Marken, Arbeitspapier Nr. 9 des Lehrstuhls für innovatives Markenmanagement (LiM), Burmann, Ch. (Hrsg.), Universität Bremen, Bremen.
Chajet, C., Shachtman, T. (1995), Image Design. Corporate Identity für Firmen, Marken und Produkte, Frankfurt/M.
Charmasson, H. (1988), The Name is the Game, Homewood/Illinois.
Conzen, P. (1990), E. H. Erikson und die Psychoanalyse. Systematische Gesamtdarstellung seiner theoretischen und klinischen Positionen, Heidelberg.

Dacin, P. A., Smith, D. C. (1994), The Effect of Brand Portfolio Characteristics on Consumer Evaluations of Brand Extensions, in: Journal of Marketing Research, Vol. 31, Mai, S. 229–242.
Deal, T., Kennedy, A. (1982), Corporate Cultures – the Rites and Rituals of Corporate Life, Reading/Mass. u. a. (deutsch: Unternehmenserfolg und Unternehmenskultur, Bonn 1987).
Denzau, A. T., North, D. C. (1995), Shared Mental Models: Ideologies and Institutions, in: Kyklos, Vol. 47, S. 3–31 (zitiert nach Bonus, H., Europäische Identität aus ökonomischer Sicht, Münster).
Dietl, H.(1993), Institutionen und Zeit, Tübingen.
Diller, H. (Hrsg.) (1992), Stichwort: „Nutzen“ in: Diller, H.: Vahlens großes Marketinglexikon, S. 826, München.
Domizlaff, H. (1994), Grundgesetze der natürlichen Markenbildung, in: Bruhn, M. (Hrsg.): Handbuch Markenartikel, Bd. 2, Stuttgart, S. 689–724.
Dörtelmann, Th., (1997) Marke und Markenführung – eine institutionentheoretische Analyse, Gelsenkirchen.
Duden (2001), Stichwort: „Identität“, in: Duden – Die deutsche Rechtschreibung, Bd. 1, 22. Aufl., Mannheim, S. 488.
Erikson, E., Ich-Entwicklung und geschichtlicher Wandel, in: Erikson, E. (Hrsg.) (1973), Identität und Lebenszyklus, Frankfurt/M., S. 11–54 (engl. Original von 1959).
Erlei, M., Leschke, M., Sauerland, D. (1999), Neue Institutionenökonomik, Stuttgart.
Esch, F.-R., Geus, P. (2001), Ansätze zur Messung des Markenwertes, in: Esch, F.-R. (Hrsg.), Moderne Markenführung, 3. Aufl., Wiesbaden, S. 1025–1058.
Farquhar, P. H., Han, J.Y., Ijiri, Y. (1992), Brands on the Balance Sheet, in: Marketing Management, No. 1, S. 16–22.
Foscht, T., Swoboba, B. (2004), Käuferverhalten, Wiesbaden.
Fournier, S. M. (1998), Consumers and their Brands : Developing Realationship Theory in Consumer Research, in : Journal of Consumer Research, Vol. 24, March, S. 343–373.
Franzen, O., Trommsdorff, V., Riedel, F. (1994), Ansätze der Markenbewertung und Markenbilanz, in: Markenartikel, Nr. 8, S. 372–387.
Freiling, J. (2001), Resource-based View und ökonomische Theorie – Grundlagen und Positionierung des Ressourcenansatzes, Wiesbaden.
Frey, H. P., Haußer, K. (1987), Entwicklungslinien sozialwissenschaftlicher Identitätsforschung, in: Frey, H.P., Haußer, K. (Hrsg.), Identität. Entwicklungslinien psychologischer und soziologischer Forschung, Stuttgart, S. 3–26.
Fukuyama, F. (1995), Trust: The Social Virtues and the Creation of Prosperity, New York.
Gilmore, G. W. (1919): Animism, Boston .
Goodyear, M. (1994), Marke und Markenpolitik, in: Planung und Analyse, Nr. 3, , S. 60–67.
Gugutzer, R. (2002), Leib, Körper und Identität – Eine phänomenologisch-soziologische Untersuchung der personalen Identität, Wiesbaden.
Hansen, G. S., Wernerfelt, B. (1989), Determinants of Firm Performance: The Relative Importance of Economic and Organizational Factors, in: Strategic Management Journal, Vol. 10, S. 399–411.
Hausruckinger, G. (1993): Herkunftsbezeichnungen als präferenzdeterminierende Faktoren – Eine internationale Studie bei langlebigen Gebrauchsgütern, Diss., Frankfurt am Main 1993.
Haußer, K. (1995), Identitätspsychologie, Berlin.
Heinen, E. (1987), Unternehmenskultur, München.
Hermann, A., Huber, F., Braunstein, C. (2001), Gestaltung der Markenpersönlichkeit mittels der „means-end-“Theorie, in: Esch, F.-R. (Hrsg.), Moderne Markenführung, Wiesbaden, S. 103–134.
Herp, T. (1982), Der Marktwert von Marken des Gebrauchsgütersektors, Frankfurt/M.
Hogg, M. K., Cox, A. J., Keeling, K. (2000), The impact of self-monitoring on image congruence and product/brand evaluation; in: European Journal of Marketing, No.5/6, S. 641–666.

Homburg, Ch., Krohmer, H. (2003), Marketingmanagement, Wiesbaden.
Huber, F., Herrmann, A., Weis, M. (2001), Markenloyalität durch Markenpersönlichkeit – Ergebnisse einer empirischen Studie im Automobilsektor, in: Marketing ZFP, Nr. 7, S. 5–15.
IBM Deutschland (2003), IBM meldet zum 10. Male hintereinander die meisten US-Patente an, Pressemeldung vom 13.01.2003, http://www-5.ibm.com/de/pressroom/presseinfos/2003/030114_1.html, Abruf: 25.08.2004.
Ind, N. (2003), Inside out: How employees build value, in: Journal of Brand Management, No. 6, Vol. 10, S. 393–402.
Kaas, K. P. (1990), Langfristige Werbewirkung und Brand Equity, in: Werbeforschung und Praxis, Nr. 3, S. 48–52.
Kapferer, J. N. (1992), Die Marke – Kapital des Unternehmens, Landsberg/Lech.
Keller, K. L. (1993), Conceptualizing, Measuring, and Managing Customer-Based Brand Equity, in: Journal of Marketing, Vol. 57, January, S. 1–22.
Keller, K. L. (2003), Strategic brand management: building, measuring, and managing brand equity, 2. Aufl., Upper Saddle River, NJ [u.a.].
Kenning, P. (2003), Customer Trust Management. Ein Beitrag zum Vertrauensmanagement im Lebensmitteleinzelhandel, Wiesbaden.
Kern, W. (1962), Bewertung von Warenzeichen, in: Betriebswirtschaftliche Forschung und Praxis, Nr. 1, S. 17–31.
Krappmann, L. (1988), Soziologische Dimensionen der Identität: Strukturelle Bedingungen für die Teilnahme an Interaktionsprozessen, 7. Aufl., Stuttgart.
Kroeber-Riel, W., Weinberg, P. (2003), Konsumentenverhalten, 8. Aufl., München.
Lebrenz, S. (1996): Länderimages: Einflussfaktor und Bedeutung für das Konsumentenverhalten – eine empirische Studie bei langlebigen Gebrauchsgütern, Diss., Köln 1996.
Leclerc, F., Schmitt, B. H., Dube, L. (1994), Foreign Branding and its Effects on Product Perceptions and Attitudes, in: Journal of Marketing Research, Vol. 32, Mai, S. 263–270.
Lieberman, M. B., Montgomery, D. B. (1998), First-Mover (Dis)Advantages: Retrospective and Link with the Resource-based View, in: SMJ, Vol. 19, S. 1111–1125.
Lim, K., O'Cass, A. (2001), Consumer brand classifications: an assessment of culture-of-origin versus country-of-origin, in: Journal of Product and Brand Management, Vol. 10, No. 2, S. 120–136.
Luhmann, N. (1973), Vertrauen – ein Mechanismus der Reduktion sozialer Komplexität, 2. Aufl., Stuttgart.
Mason, E. C. (1939), Price and Production Policies of Large-Scale Enterprises, in: American Economic Review, Vol. 29, S. 61–74.
Meffert, H. (1994), Marketing-Management. Analyse – Strategie – Implementierung, Wiesbaden.
Meffert, H., Burmann, Chr. (1996), Identitätsorientierte Markenführung – Grundlagen für das Management von Markenportfolios, Arbeitspapier Nr. 100 der Wissenschaftlichen Gesellschaft für Marketing und Unternehmensführung e.V., Meffert, H., Wagner, H., Backhaus, K. (Hrsg.), Münster.
Meffert, H. (1998), Herausforderungen an die Betriebswirtschaftslehre – Die Perspektive der Wissenschaft, in: DBW, 58. Jg., Nr. 6, S. 709–730.
Meffert, H. (2000), Marketing – Grundlagen marktorientierter Unternehmensführung. Konzepte – Instrumente – Praxisbeispiele, 9. Aufl., Wiesbaden.
Moser, M. (2003), United we brand: how to create a cohesive brand that's seen, heard, and remembered, Boston.
Müller, W. R. (1987), Identität und Führung, in: Handwörterbuch der Führung, Kieser, A., Reber, G., Wunderer, R. (Hrsg.), Stuttgart.
North, D. C. (1992), Institutionen, institutioneller Wandel und Wirtschaftsleistung, Tübingen (Original New York u. a. 1990).

Papadopoulos, N. (1993): What Product and Country Images Are and Are Not, in: Papadopoulos, N./Heslop, L. A. (Hrsg.): Product-Country Images – Impact and Role in International Marketing, Binghampton, NY 1993, S. 3–38.

Perrey, J. (1998), Nutzenorientierte Marktsegmentierung – Ein integrativer Ansatz zum Zielgruppenmarketing im Verkehrsdienstleistungsbereich, Wiesbaden.

Petermann, F. (1992), Psychologie des Vertrauens, 2. Aufl., München.

Plötner, O. (1995), Das Vertrauen des Kunden. Relevanz, Aufbau und Steuerung auf industriellen Märkten, Wiesbaden.

Porter, M. E. (1996), What is Strategy, in: Harvard Business Review, No. 6, Nov.-Dez., S. 61–78.

Porter, M. E. (1999), Wettbewerbsvorteile: Spitzenleistungen erreichen und behaupten, 5. Aufl., Frankfurt/M., New York.

Prahalad, C. K., Hamel, G. (1990), The Core Competence of the Corporation, in: Harvard Business Review, Vol. 68, May-June, S. 79–91.

Proff, H. (1998), Mikroökonomische Wurzeln eines strategischen Managements zwischen Markt- und Ressourcenorientierung, in: Strategien für die Automobilindustrie: Ansatzpunkte im strategischen Management und in der Industriepolitik, Proff, H., Proff, H. V., (Hrsg.), Wiesbaden, S. 23–45.

Reddy, S. K., Holak, S. L., Bhat, S. (1994), „To Extend or Not to Extend: Success Determinants of Line Extensions", in: Journal of Marketing Research, Vol. 31, May, S. 243–262.

Ripperger, T. (1998), Ökonomik des Vertrauens – Analyse eines Organisationsprinzips, Tübingen.

Rosenberg , M. (1979)., Conceiving the Self, New York,

Rossiter, J. R., Lawrence, A. (1993), Brand Equity Building for New Brands via Appropriate Advertising Symbol Selection, in: European Advances in Consumer Research, Vol. 1, S. 125–132.

Rumelt, R. P. (1991), How much does Industry matter?, in: Strategic Management Journal, Vol. 12, S. 168 ff.

Sander, M. (1994), Die Bewertung internationaler Marken auf Basis der hedonischen Theorie, in: Marketing ZFP, 16. Jg., Nr. 4, S. 234–245.

Sattler, H. (1995), Markenbewertung, in: Zeitschrift für Betriebswirtschaft, 65. Jg., Nr. 6, S. 663–682.

Sattler, H. (2001), Markenpolitik, Stuttgart.

Sattler, H., Högl, S., Hupp, O. (2002), Evaluation of the financial value of brands, No 7, Research Papers on Marketing and Retailing, University of Hamburg.

Schein, E. H. (1985), Organizational Culture and Leadership, San Francisco.

Schimansky, A. (2004), Der Wert der Marke, München.

Schmitt, B. H., Dube, L. (1992), Contextualized Representations of Brand Extensions: Are Feature Lists or Frames the Basic Components of Consumer Cognition?, in: Marketing Letters, No. 3, S. 114–126.

Schmitt, B. H., Pan, Y. (1995), Managing Corporate and Brand Identities in the Asia-Pacific Region, in: California Management Review, Winter, S. 15–31.

Simon, C. J., Sullivan, M. W. (1991), The Measurement and Determinants of Brand Equity: A Financial Approach, Chicago.

Simon, C. J., Sullivan, M. W. (1993), The Measurements and Determinants of Brand Equity a Financial Approach, in: Marketing Science, Vol. 12, Winter, S. 28–52.

Smith, D., Park, C. (1992), The Effects of Brand Extensions on Market Share and Advertising Efficiency, in: Journal of Marketing Research, Vol. 29, No. 1, S. 296–313.

Srivastava, R. K., Shocker, A. D. (1991), Brand Equity: A Perspective on its Meaning and Measurement, Marketing Science Institute (Hrsg.), Report Nr. 91–124, Cambridge/Mass.

Tauber, E. M. (1988), Brand Leverage: Strategies for Growth in a Cost Control World, in: Journal of Advertising Research, Vol. 28, S. 26–30.

Teece, D. J., Pisano, G., Shuen, A. (1997), Dynamic Capabilities and Strategic Management, in: Strategic Management Journal, Vol. 18, S. 509–533.

Thiel, U. (2001), Personen und persönliche Identität in der Philosophie des 17. und 18. Jahrhunderts, in: Sturma, D. (Hrsg.): Person: Philosophiegeschichte – Theoretische Philosophie – Praktische Philosophie, Paderborn, S. 79–101.

Trommsdorff, V. (1992), Wettbewerbsorientierte Image-Positionierung, in: Markenartikel, Nr. 10, S. 458–463.

Trommsdorff, V. (2003), Konsumentenverhalten, 5. Aufl., Stuttgart.

Unger, F. (Hrsg.) (1986), Konsumentenpsychologie und Markenartikel, Heidelberg u. a.

Upshaw. L. B. (1995), Building Brand Identity: A Strategy for Success in an hostile Marketplace, New York u.a.

Vershofen, W. (1940), Handbuch der Verbrauchsforschung (Bd. 1), Berlin.

Weidenfeld, W. (1983), Die Identität der Deutschen – Fragen, Positionen, Perspektiven, in: Die Identität der Deutschen, Weidenfeld, W. (Hrsg.), Schriftenreihe der Bundeszentrale für politische Bildung, Band 200, Bonn, S. 13–49.

Welling, M. (2003), Bausteine einer integrierten image- und identitätsorientierten Markenführung als Beitrag zur Markentheorie, Schriften zum Marketing Nr. 47, Ruhr Universität Bochum, Bochum.

Werthmöller, E. (1994), Räumliche Identität als Aufgabenfeld des Städte- und Regionenmarketing, Schriften zu Marketing und Management, Meffert, H. (Hrsg.), Bd. 24, Frankfurt/M.

Wiedmann, K. P. (1994), Markenpolitik und Corporate Identity, in: Bruhn, M. (Hrsg.), Handbuch Markenartikel (Bd. 2), Stuttgart, S. 1033–1054.

Wiswede, G. (1978), Psychologie der Markenbildung, in: Markenartikel heute. Marke, Markt und Marketing, Gabler Verlag (Hrsg.), Wiesbaden, S. 135–158.

Managementkonzept der identitätsorientierten Markenführung

Christoph Burmann und Heribert Meffert

1. **Spannungsfelder im Rahmen des Identitätsmanagements** **74**

2. **Identitätsorientierte Markenführung als Managementprozess** **75**
2.1 Strategisches Markenmanagent 77
2.11 Situationsanalyse 77
2.12 Unternehmens- und Markenziele 78
2.13 Konzeption der Markenidentität 79
2.14 Entwicklung der Markenarchitektur 80
2.15 Festlegung der Markenidentitäten für die übrigen Unternehmensmarken 81
2.16 Auswahl der Markenevolutionsstrategie 83
2.17 Identitätskonforme Markenorganisation 84
2.2 Operatives Markenmanagement 86
2.21 Umsetzung der Markenidentität in Markenleistungen 86
2.22 Umsetzung der Markenidentität im Markenpricing 90
2.23 Umsetzung der Markenidentität in der Markenkommunikation 91
2.24 Umsetzung der Markenidentität in der Markendistribution 95
2.25 Sicherung der Ganzheitlichkeit der Markenidentität durch Markenintegration 97
2.26 Absicherung der Markenidentität durch rechtlichen Markenschutz 97
2.3 Marken-Controlling 101
2.31 Definition und Abgrenzung 101
2.32 Markenberichtswesen 103
2.33 Markenerfolgsmessung 105

3. **Fazit** **112**

1. Spannungsfelder im Rahmen des Identitätsmanagements

Die Hauptaufgabe des identitätsorientierten Markenmanagements liegt in der Schaffung einer eigenständigen Markenidentität durch eine integrierte Gestaltung aller Identitätskomponenten und der Sicherstellung eines hohen Fits zwischen Identität und Image der Marke. Im Rahmen von Markenportfolios vervielfachen sich die sich hieraus ergebenden Abstimmungsprobleme. In diesem Fall liegt das besondere Problem in der Überbrückung eines vierfachen Spannungsfeldes (vgl. Abbildung 1):

1. dem Spannungsfeld zwischen der Identität und dem Image jeder Marke,
2. dem Spannungsfeld zwischen den verschiedenen Markenidentitäten innerhalb des Portfolios,
3. dem Spannungsfeld zwischen den Markenidentitäten und der Unternehmensidentität (Wiedmann 1994, S. 1033 f.) und
4. dem Spannungsfeld zwischen den international unterschiedlichen Identitätswahrnehmungen in verschiedenen Ländermärkten.

Abbildung 1: Spannungsfelder des identitätsorientierten Markenmanagements

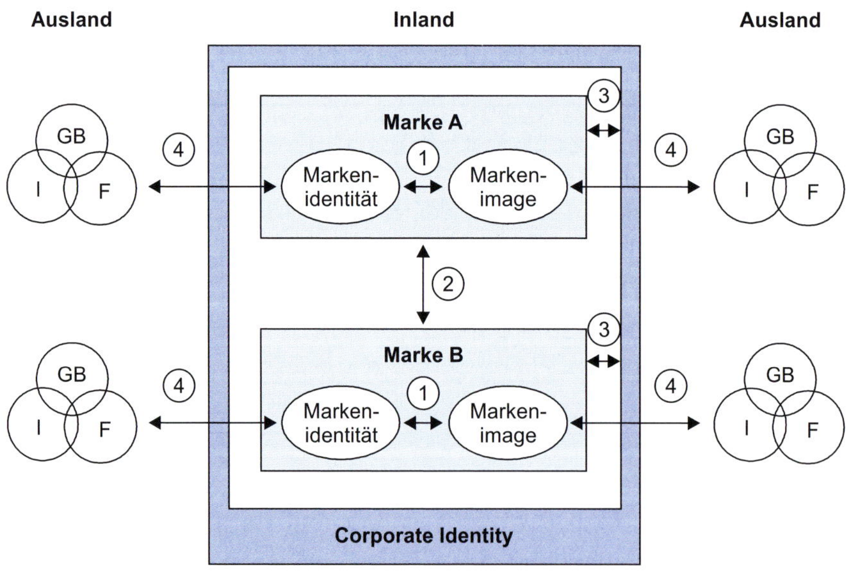

GABLER GRAFIK

Zur Überbrückung dieser Spannungsfelder ist eine Systematisierung der komplexen Aktivitäten im Rahmen der identitätsorientierten Markenführung erforderlich. Da vom Management das Markenimage nicht direkt, sondern lediglich indirekt über die Markenidentität gesteuert werden kann, stellt die Identität den Ausgangspunkt des Managementprozesses der Markenführung dar. Obwohl die identitätsorientierte Markenführung nachfolgend als ein sequentieller Managementprozess dargestellt wird, können sich zwischen den einzelnen Schritten zeitliche Überschneidungen und Feedbackschleifen ergeben.

2. Identitätsorientierte Markenführung als Managementprozess

Der Managementprozess der identitätsorientierten Markenführung dient der Planung, Koordination und Kontrolle aller Maßnahmen zum Aufbau starker Marken bei allen relevanten Zielgruppen. Ziel ist eine funktions- und unternehmensübergreifende Integration aller mit der Markenführung zusammenhängenden Entscheidungen und Aktivitäten zum Aufbau von langfristig stabilen und werthaltigen Marke-Kunden-Beziehungen. Die identitätsorientierte Markenführung ist dementsprechend dem Oberziel einer Maximierung des **Customer Equity** (Kundenstammwert) verpflichtet (Burmann/Hundacker 2003a/b). Der Managementprozess setzt sich aus drei Teilprozessen zusammen, die in Abbildung 2 im Überblick dargestellt sind.

Aufbauend auf der Situationsanalyse werden zunächst im **strategischen Markenmanagement** die Grundsatzentscheidungen über die konkreten Ziele und den inhaltlichen Gegenstand der Marken eines Unternehmens getroffen sowie die grundlegenden Verhaltenspläne zur Erreichung dieser Ziele festgelegt. Das **operative Markenmanagement** hat die Aufgabe, im Rahmen von Detailentscheidungen die konkrete Ausgestaltung der Markenführungsinstrumente und deren rechtliche Absicherung durchzuführen. Die Ausgestaltung leitet sich aus den Vorgaben des strategischen Markenmanagements ab und basiert im Wesentlichen auf den bekannten Marketinginstrumenten (Meffert 2000). Den dritten Teilbereich stellt das **Marken-Controlling** dar. Dessen Aufgabe ist die Informationsversorgung aller an der Markenführung beteiligten Personen und die Beurteilung aller Markenführungsaktivitäten hinsichtlich deren Effektivität und Effizienz.

Abbildung 2: **Prozess des identitätsorientierten Markenmanagements**

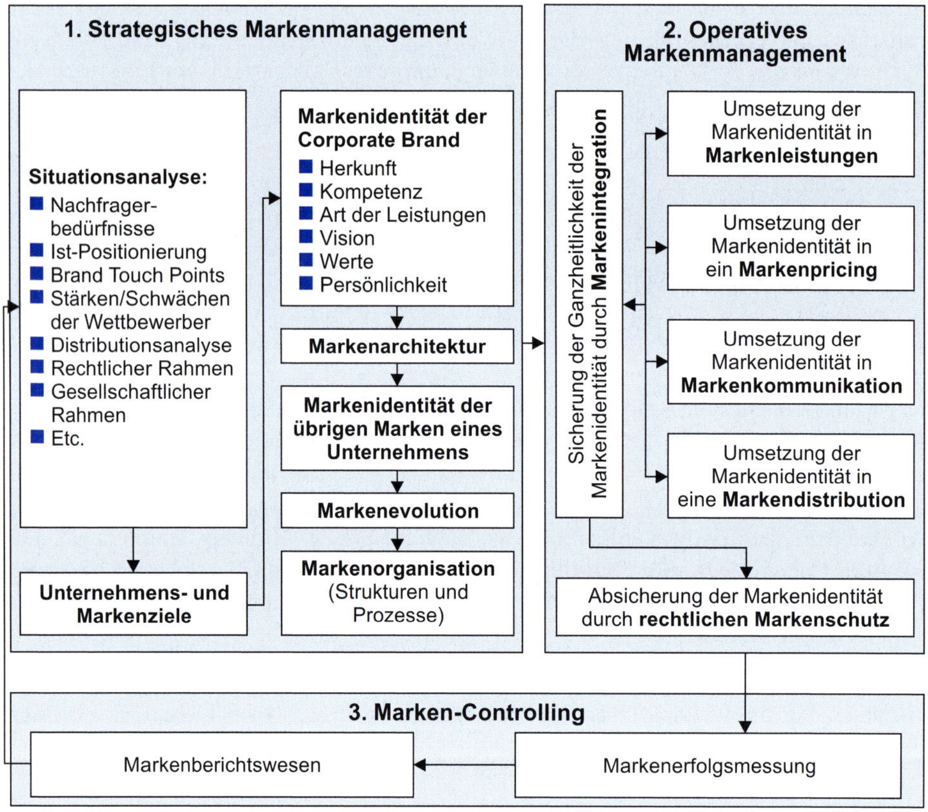

GABLER GRAFIK

Quelle: Burmann/Blinda/Nitschke 2003, S. 10

2.1 Strategisches Markenmanagement

2.11 Situationsanalyse

Ausgangspunkt des identitätsorientierten Markenmanagements ist eine fundierte **Analyse der Rahmenbedingungen** und der **Ausgangssituation** der eigenen Marke(n). Hierzu gehört eine umfassende Erfassung der aktuellen Kundenbedürfnisse und Nachfragetrends. Im Rahmen der Situationsanalyse ist auch zu untersuchen, wo und in welcher Erscheinungsform die relevanten Zielgruppen die Marke erleben und mit dieser in Berührung kommen (Brand Touch Points). Des Weiteren ist zu analysieren, wie die Marke aus Sicht der Zielgruppen im Vergleich zu Wettbewerbern wahrgenommen wird (Ist-Positionierung).

Abbildung 3: Beispielhaftes Ergebnis einer Situationsanalyse

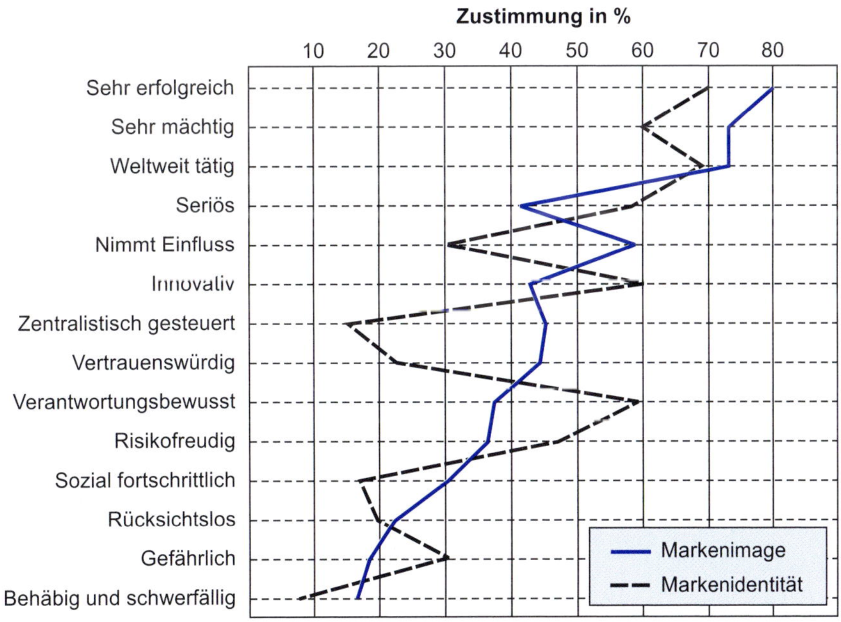

GABLER GRAFIK

Parallel zur Analyse der externen Unternehmensumwelt (Outside-in-Perspektive) muss eine ebenso detaillierte und umfassende Analyse der **internen Rahmenbedingungen** erfolgen (Inside-out-Perspektive). Dies beinhaltet vor allem eine Analyse der Ressourcen, der organisationalen Fähigkeiten und der Unternehmenskultur. Erst ein hoher Fit dieser drei Elemente mit der Markenidentität ermöglicht eine hohe Glaubwürdigkeit der Marke nach innen und außen sowie ein wettbewerbsüberlegenes Lernen der Marke, beziehungsweise der sie tragenden Institution. Erste Hinweise auf einen solchen Fit können die Ergebnisse einer so genannten **GAP-Analyse** liefern (Parasuraman/Zeithaml/Berry 1985, S. 46 ff.). GAP-Analysen werden primär im Marken-Controlling verwendet, liefern zugleich aber auch wichtige Informationen im Rahmen der Situationsanalyse.

In diesem Zusammenhang zeigt Abbildung 3 GAPs zwischen den Ausprägungen der Markenidentität und des Markenimages bei einem international tätigen Medienunternehmen. Hier wird deutlich, dass die interne Markenidentität der befragten Top-Manager zum Teil erheblich vom wahrgenommen Markenimage der hier befragten unternehmensexternen Meinungsführer abweicht. Diese identifizierten Schwachpunkte sind als Informationsgrundlage für das identitätsorientierte Markenmanagement von hoher Bedeutung.

2.12 Unternehmens- und Markenziele

Auf Basis der in der Situationsanalyse identifizierten internen und externen Rahmenbedingungen lassen sich konkrete **markenpolitische Zielsetzungen** festlegen. Beispielsweise kann das in Abbildung 3 identifizierte GAP in der Dimension „sozial fortschrittlich" zu der Formulierung eines Zieles zur Reduzierung dieses GAPs führen. Die Markenziele sind durch einen ein- bis fünfjährigen Zeithorizont gekennzeichnet und lassen sich in psychografische und ökonomische Zielkategorien einteilen. Bei der Definition der Markenziele ist eine operationale Formulierung zu wählen. Ziele sind dann operational formuliert, wenn sie nach Inhalt, Ausmaß, Zeitbezug und Segmentbezug präzise definiert wurden (vgl. hierzu und den Zielkategorien umfassend Meffert 2000, S. 680 f.). Eine operationale Markenzielsetzung kann beispielsweise für den deutschen Markt in einer zehnprozentigen Steigerung der Markenbekanntheit in der Zielgruppe 18- bis 39-jähriger Männer innerhalb eines Jahres liegen. Die **ökonomischen Markenziele** sind eng mit den Unternehmenszielen (zum Beispiel Unternehmenswert, Kapitalrentabilität, Umsatz, Absatz, Marktanteil, Arbeitsplatzsicherung etc.) verbunden. Bei den ökonomischen Markenzielen handelt es sich um Kernergebnisgrößen wie beispielsweise das Customer Equity einer Marke, das Preispremium der Marke, die Akquisitions- und Kundenbindungskosten der Marke oder die Umsatzrendite. **Psychografische Zielgrößen** sind beispielsweise die Markenbekanntheit, die Marken- und Händlerloyalität (Burmann 1991), die Eroberungsrate, die Zufriedenheit, die Weiterempfehlungsrate oder die Markensympathie. Die Markenziele bilden Vorgaben für die Konzeption der Markenidentität. Oberstes Markenziel ist eine Steigerung des Customer Equity einer Marke und damit ihres ökonomischen Wertes. Dies begründet sich damit, dass der ökonomische Markenwert nicht nur im aktuellen Kaufverhalten der Konsumenten, sondern auch im zukünftigen Markenpotenzial zum Ausdruck kommt. Die Bestimmung des Customer Equity einer Marke liefert somit wichtige Informationen bei markenstrategischen Entscheidungen wie der Markenausdehnung oder dem Markentransfer (vgl. hier auch den Beitrag zur Markenbewertung in diesem Buch).

2.13 Konzeption der Markenidentität

Die Konzeption der Markenidentität stellt den bedeutendsten Schritt im Rahmen des strategischen Markenmanagements dar. Wie im vorangegangenen Beitrag dieses Buches beschrieben, lassen sich auf der Grundlage der sozialwissenschaftlichen und psychologischen Identitätsforschung sechs konstitutive Komponenten identifizieren, welche eine umfassende Beschreibung der Markenidentität ermöglichen (Burmann/Blinda/Nitschke 2003):

- Die **Markenherkunft** stellt die Basis der Markenidentität dar. Diese bildet gewissermaßen die Wurzel der Markenidentität, da die Marke zunächst im Kontext ihres Ursprungs wahrgenommen und interpretiert wird. Die Markenherkunft umfasst „die Gesamtheit aller geografischen, kulturellen und institutionellen Einflüsse, die festlegen von wo, wem oder was eine Marke entstammt" (Blinda 2003, S. 38).
- Die **Markenkompetenz** begründet den spezifischen Wettbewerbsvorteil der Marke und sichert diesen ab. Sie repräsentiert die spezifischen organisationalen Fähigkeiten eines Unternehmens zur marktgerechten Kombination von Ressourcen.
- Die grundsätzliche Art der **Markenleistungen**, welche direkt auf der Markenkompetenz aufbauen, determiniert, wie eine Marke für den Nachfrager nutzbar wird. Sie bestimmt somit die grundsätzliche Form und Ausstattung von Produkten und Dienstleistungen der Marke.
- Die Gestaltung der Identität wird geleitet durch die **Markenvision**. Sie gibt die langfristige Entwicklungsrichtung (fünf bis zehn Jahre) einer Marke vor und erfüllt eine wichtige Motivations-, Identifikations- und Koordinationsfunktion.
- Die **Markenwerte** geben wieder, woran die Marke und ihre Repräsentanten glauben. Sie repräsentieren vor allem wichtige emotionale Merkmale der Markenidentität sowie die Wünsche der relevanten Zielgruppen an eine ideale Marke.
- Die **Markenpersönlichkeit** determiniert den Kommunikationsstil der Marke. Der markenspezifische Kommunikationsstil wird sowohl von den typischen Repräsentanten einer Marke, als auch von der Herkunft der Marke geprägt (Aaker 1997, S. 348).

2.14 Entwicklung der Markenarchitektur

Während bei den bisherigen Schritten im Managementprozess eine singuläre Markenbetrachtung im Fokus stand, geht es bei der Gestaltung der **Markenarchitektur** um die Koordination eines Portfolios an Marken. Die Markenarchitektur ist in der Praxis oft eher das „zufällige" Ergebnis internen und vor allem externen Wachstums. Eine identitätsorientierte und mit der Unternehmensstrategie konforme Gestaltung von Markenarchitekturen findet hingegen bei vielen Unternehmen bislang kaum statt.

Die Markenarchitektur eines Unternehmens kann unter Zuhilfenahme von **drei Dimensionen** differenziert erfasst und gestaltet werden (vgl. zur Gestaltung der Markenarchitektur ausführlich den Beitrag in diesem Buch): einer vertikalen Dimension zur Gestaltung des Integrationsgrades über die verschiedenen hierarchischen Organisations- und Markenebenen hinweg (zum Beispiel Ebene des Gesamtunternehmens, der strategischen Geschäftsbereiche, der Produkte etc.), einer horizontalen Dimension zur Gestaltung der Anzahl von Marken auf der jeweiligen Hierarchieebene und eine handelsgerichtete Dimension zur Gestaltung des Auftritts der Marken im Handel.

Der **vertikale Integrationsgrad** bezieht sich auf die Intensität der Verknüpfung der Marken unterschiedlicher organisationalen Ebenen des Unternehmens. Dies umfasst nicht nur die Intensität der Verknüpfung der Corporate Brand mit Marken auf hierarchisch untergeordneten Organisationsebenen (zum Beispiel die mögliche Verknüpfung der Corporate Brand Henkel mit der Produktmarke Persil, in unterschiedlichen Intensitätsstufen), sondern zum Beispiel auch die Intensität der Verknüpfung von Marken der strategischen Geschäftseinheiten (SGE) mit Marken auf der Produktebene (zum Beispiel Verwendungsintensität der Marke dit als Marke der Geschäftseinheit Wertpapierfonds der Dresdner Bank auf einzelnen Fondprodukten, zum Beispiel dit-Europazins, dit-Kapital-Plus oder INTERGLOBAL). Allgemein kennzeichnet der vertikale Integrationsgrad der Markenarchitektur die Intensität der Verknüpfung organisationshierarchisch übergeordneter mit untergeordneten Marken zur Markierung von Leistungen eines Unternehmens.

Ein maximaler vertikaler Integrationsgrad liegt vor, wenn alle Leistungen eines Unternehmens unter der Unternehmensmarke geführt werden. Hier wird von einem so genannten **„Branded House"** gesprochen (Aaker/Joachimsthaler 2000, S. 118). Exemplarisch für diese Form der Markenarchitektur kann auf Unternehmen wie McDonald's, Nokia, IBM oder Rolex verwiesen werden. In diesem Fall ist das Kosteneinsparpotenzial durch Synergieeffekte am höchsten. Bei einem minimalen vertikalen Integrationsgrad treten nicht die Corporate Brand sondern ausschließlich die Produktmarken gegenüber dem Endnachfrager in Erscheinung. Die Unternehmensmarke ist hier für die Endnachfrager nicht wahrnehmbar. Diese Option wird als **„House of Brands"** bezeichnet (zum Beispiel Procter & Gamble, Unilever). Synergieeffekte können hier, wenn überhaupt, nur in sehr geringem Ausmaß verwirklicht werden, da bei dieser Markenarchitektur die Eigenständigkeit der Produktmarken im Vordergrund steht.

Dazwischen gibt es zwei Markenarchitekturoptionen, bei denen sowohl die Unternehmensmarke, als auch die Marken auf untergeordneten organisationalen Ebenen des Unternehmens gemeinsam zur Markierung von Leistungen verwendet werden (Laforet/ Saunders 1999, S. 51 ff.). Beim so genannten **Sub-Branding** (Baumgarth 2004, S. 178) dominiert die Unternehmens- oder SGE-Marke gegenüber der Produktmarke (zum Beispiel United Airlines Express, HP Deskjet). Beim **Endorsement-Branding** dominiert dagegen die Produktmarke gegenüber der Unternehmens-/SGE-Marke (Aaker 1996, S. 243 ff.). Beispiele hierfür sind Magnum von Langnese und Spee von Henkel.

Die Gestaltung der **horizontalen** Markenarchitektur bezieht sich auf die Anzahl der von einem Unternehmen angebotenen Marken pro Marktsegment. Bei einer **Einzelmarkenstrategie** wird jeweils eine Marke exklusiv auf ein Marktsegment ausgerichtet. Einzelmarkenstrategien bieten sich insbesondere für kleinere Märkte an. Wird ein Marktsegment parallel von zwei oder mehr Marken eines Unternehmens bearbeitet, spricht man von einer **Mehrmarkenstrategie**. Sie ist vor allem zur Bearbeitung größerer und heterogener Marktsegmente empfehlenswert (vgl. zu dieser Strategie den Beitrag über Mehrmarkenstrategien in diesem Buch). Die Mehrmarkenoption ist mit einer Branded House-Markenarchitektur nicht sinnvoll kombinierbar.

Die **handelsgerichtete Dimension** der Markenarchitektur betrachtet die Positionierung eines Unternehmens im vertikalen Wettbewerb. Zu entscheiden ist, ob ein Unternehmen seine Produkte ausschließlich als klassischer Markenhersteller anbietet oder ob es darüber hinaus beziehungsweise stattdessen die Absatzmittler (Groß- und/oder Einzelhandel, Importeure, Exporteure) mit Produkten für deren Eigenmarken (so genannte private label) beliefert. In diesem Fall wird teilweise auch von einer „dualen Markenstrategie" gesprochen (Esch 2004, S. 479 f.) Im letzteren Fall muss entschieden werden, in welchem Qualitätsniveau die Absatzmittler beliefert werden sollen (Meffert 2000, S. 873). Dies ist umso bedeutender, da Kannibalisierungseffekte sowie eine Imageschädigung der eigenen Herstellermarken vermieden werden müssen.

2.15 Festlegung der Markenidentitäten für die übrigen Unternehmensmarken

Auf Basis der Markenarchitektur werden im nächsten Schritt die Markenidentitäten für die SGE- und Produktmarken (soweit vorhanden) festgelegt. Diese Identitäten werden mithilfe der sechs bereits beschriebenen Markenidentitätskomponenten (Markenherkunft, Markenkompetenz, Markenleistungen, Markenvision, Markenwerte, Markenpersönlichkeit) operationalisiert.

Auf Basis der Markenidentität gilt es, Entscheidungen hinsichtlich der angestrebten **Markenpositionierung** zu treffen. Das Ziel der Positionierung von Marken besteht darin, mit bestimmten Produkteigenschaften sowohl eine dominierende Stellung in der Psyche der Konsumenten (die eigene Markenposition ist näher an den Idealvorstellungen der Nachfrager als Konkurrenzangebote) als auch eine hinreichende Differenzierungsfähigkeit gegenüber Konkurrenzprodukten zu erreichen. Folglich dient die Festlegung der

Markenidentitäten dem Erreichen einer **Dominanzposition** sowie einer Positionierung, welche gegenüber den relevanten Wettbewerbern das größte **Differenzierungspotenzial** besitzt.

Für die zielgerichtete Ausgestaltung der Markenidentität müssen die Nachfrager durch eine Marktsegmentierung zu möglichst homogenen Zielgruppen zusammengefasst werden. Für jede Zielgruppe, die ein ausreichendes Absatzpotenzial bietet, kann entsprechend den Idealanforderungen der jeweiligen Zielgruppe eine Marke geschaffen werden. Diese Analyse ist vor dem Hintergrund der im Unternehmen verfügbare Ressourcen und Fähigkeiten kritisch auf ihre Implementierbarkeit zu überprüfen.

Die Idealanforderungen der externen Zielgruppen (im Sinne eines Soll-Markenimages) sind jedoch mit den klassischen Marktforschungsmethoden häufig nicht valide zu erfassen. In diesem Zusammenhang ist die Äußerung eines TOP-Managers eines großen, weltweit tätigen Automobilkonzerns zu verstehen:

„Grundsätzlich gilt, dass die Manager und besonders die Top-Manager der einzelnen Marken noch am besten über die wünschbare und mögliche Zukunft der Marke Bescheid wissen und daher ein Soll-Image viel klarer und deutlicher festlegen können als dies auch gut informierten Kunden möglich wäre. […] Es hätte zum Beispiel nie einen [das Modell X, Anm. d. Verf.] gegeben, wenn das Soll-Image vom Markt her bestimmt worden wäre." Und weiter: „Die Menschen sind eben nicht in der Lage zu artikulieren, was sie wirklich fasziniert. […] Es gilt festzuhalten, dass große wirtschaftliche Erfolge häufig gegen große Widerstände durchgesetzt werden mussten und dass sie trotz eines großen Fehlschlag-Risikos zustande kamen. Hier gilt nach wie vor die Auffassung des österreichischen Nationalökonomen Schumpeter: „Der Markt ist immer schon voll, was neu hinzukommt, muss sich gegen die Logik des Marktes durchsetzen." (Koers 2001, S. 168).

Im Rahmen der Bestimmung der Markenpositionierung ist insoweit eine Balance zwischen

- einer **reaktiven Positionierung**, bei der sich die Positionierung insbesondere an den artikulierten Wünschen der Konsumenten orientiert (primär Outside-in-Betrachtung), und
- einer **aktiven Positionierung**, bei der dem Kunden bisher unbekannte, für seine Kaufentscheidung aber wichtige Eigenschaftsdimensionen besetzt werden (primär Inside-out-Betrachtung) sicherzustellen.
- Ferner kann der Aufbau von Begeisterung und Loyalität gegenüber Marken nur über die **Fokussierung auf wenige Markenkompetenzen** erfolgen. Bei diesen Markenstärken muss zudem auf eine hinreichende Anpassungsfähigkeit (strategische Flexibilität) gegenüber neuen Werten, Trends und Bedürfnissen geachtet werden.

Wie aufgezeigt, entsteht die Markenidentität erst durch eine wechselseitige Beziehung zwischen internen und externen Zielgruppen der Marke, sodass sie nicht isoliert aus der Perspektive des Marktes oder des Unternehmens betrachtet werden darf, sondern im Spannungsfeld zwischen dem Unternehmen und seiner Umwelt steht. Zur Sicherstellung einer starken Markenidentität besteht ungeachtet reaktiver oder aktiver Positionierung somit langfristig das Ziel einer Übereinstimmung zwischen dem Idealimage der Konsumenten und der Identität der Marke.

2.16 Auswahl der Markenevolutionsstrategie

Im Rahmen der **Markenevolutionsstrategien** wird die zeitpunktbezogene Perspektive der Markenarchitektur um eine zukunftsgerichtete, **dynamische Perspektive** ergänzt. Es handelt sich jedoch nicht um die Betrachtung eines Portfolios von Marken, sondern um eine **singuläre Analyse** jeder einzelnen Marke. Allerdings haben diese markenspezifischen Entscheidungen mittelfristig Auswirkungen auf die Gestaltung der Markenarchitektur. Eine Markenevolutionsstrategie ist *ein langfristiger, bedingter und globaler Verhaltensplan, der die Entwicklungsrichtung einer Marke hinsichtlich ihrer Expansion beziehungsweise Konsolidierung für die kommenden zwei bis fünf Jahre festlegt* (vgl. den Beitrag zu Markenevolutionsstrategien in diesem Buch).

Bei einer **Markenkonsolidierungsstrategie** werden Unternehmensressourcen von einzelnen Marken abgezogen beziehungsweise desinvestiert, um sie effizienter für andere Verwendungszwecke einzusetzen. Zur Markenkonsolidierung stehen die Optionen **sofortige Elimination, abgestufter Rückzug und Fokussierung** zur Verfügung. Ein **abgestufter Rückzug** ist dadurch gekennzeichnet, dass sich die Marke in mehreren Schritten, über einen Zeitraum von mehreren Monaten oder sogar Jahren aus einzelnen Teilmärkten und schließlich vollständig aus dem bislang bearbeiteten Markt zurückzieht. Hierbei kann zwischen einer **Migrations-** und einer **Abschöpfungsstrategie** differenziert werden. In letzterem Falle wird die Marke ohne weitere Investitionen so lange am Markt gehalten, wie sie positive Cashflows generiert. Bei einer **Migrationsstrategie** bleibt das vorhandene Angebotsprogramm (Produkte und/oder Dienstleistungen) einer Marke meist weitestgehend unverändert am Markt erhalten, aber die bislang verwendeten Markenzeichen werden durch eine andere Markierung ersetzt. Hier kann beispielsweise auf die Migration der Marke Arthur Andersen zur Marke Accenture und die Migration von Texaco zu DEA und später zu Shell verwiesen werden. Bei der dritten möglichen Konsolidierungsstrategie, der **Fokussierungsstrategie**, wird das Leistungsprogramm einer Marke signifikant verkleinert. Hiermit geht in der Regel ein Rückzug aus einzelnen Marktsegmenten einher. Durch das stärker fokussierte Leistungsprogramm können vor allem Komplexitätskosten reduziert und das Markenimage gestärkt werden, weil die Marke ein klareres Profil bekommt. Beispielhaft kann hier auf die Investitionsgütermarke Schmitz Cargobull verwiesen werden (Bliss 2000, S. 225 ff.).

Markenexpansionsstrategien werden bei Marken umgesetzt, die aufgrund ihrer Stärke über noch nicht ausgeschöpfte Umsatz- und Ertragspotenziale verfügen. Diese können zum einen in neuen, geografischen Absatzräumen **(geografische Expansion)** und zum anderen in neuen Produkten liegen **(Markenerweiterung)**. Im Rahmen einer geografischen Expansion wird das Absatzgebiet einer Marke erweitert. Bei einer Markenerweiterungsstrategie wird die Anzahl der unter einer Marke angebotenen Produkte und Dienstleistungen vergrößert. Sie kann weiter in Markenausdehnungs- und Markentransferstrategien differenziert werden. Bei einer **Markenausdehnungsstrategie** (Line Extension) wird die Expansion einer Marke in gleichen oder verwandten Produktkategorien verfolgt; bei einer **Markentransferstrategie** (Category Extension) die Expansion in neue, nicht verwandte Produktkategorien. Alle drei Markenexpansionsstrategien können als **Lizenzierungs- bzw. Franchisingstrategie**, als **Co-Branding** oder als **Autarkiestrategie** umgesetzt werden (vgl. den Beitrag zu Markenevolutionsstrategien in diesem Buch).

2.17 Identitätskonforme Markenorganisation

Die Entscheidung über die **identitätskonforme Markenorganisation** als letzter Schritt des strategischen Markenmanagements legt die organisationale Verankerung einer Marke im Unternehmen fest. Dazu gehört die Definition der für die Führung einer Marke notwendigen Strukturen, Prozesse, sowie Informations- und Anreizsysteme. Die Markenidentität geht letztlich auf die Entscheidungen aller an der Konzipierung der Marke (das heißt sämtlicher Geschäftsprozesse, die zur Entstehung der Marke beziehungsweise der Markenleistungen durchlaufen werden müssen) beteiligten Personen zurück. Dies schließt neben der Unternehmensleitung und den Mitarbeitern alle Personen in den Vertriebskanälen sowie das Kundendienstpersonal mit ein. Die Geschäftsprozesse müssen daher so strukturiert werden, dass sie die effiziente Zusammenarbeit der Mitarbeiter fördern und die Markenidentität unterstützen.

Von hoher Relevanz ist die **Verankerung der Markenführung im Management**. Die schnelle Beförderung und Versetzung junger Brand Manager hat hier in den letzten Jahren bei vielen Unternehmen zu einer hohen Fluktuation der direkt für die Marke verantwortlichen Personen geführt. Teilweise sind Brand Manager nur noch ein bis zwei Jahre für eine Marke direkt verantwortlich, bevor sie wieder andere Positionen übernehmen. Diese „Rotation" führt schnell zu einer inneren Aushöhlung und Erosion der Markenidentität (Klante 2004), weil sie meist mit einer an kurzfristigen Erfolgen orientierten Führung der Marke einhergeht. Der langfristige Aufbau einer starken Marke ist unter solchen organisatorischen Rahmenbedingungen kaum möglich. Darüber hinaus ist darauf zu achten, dass die Identität der für die Marke verantwortlichen Führungskräfte einen möglichst hohen Fit zur Identität der Marke aufweist. Dies erhöht das **Markencommitment** und kann zu **Brand Citizenship Behavior** führen, das heißt zu einem hohen freiwilligen Engagement für die Marke beitragen, andere Mitarbeiter und Kunden für die Marke begeistern und auf diese Weise die Marke von innen heraus stärken (vgl. den Beitrag zur innengerichteten Markenführung in diesem Buch). Letztlich stellt nur eine Verankerung des strategischen Markenmanagements und des Marken-Controllings auf höchster organisationaler Ebene die für den Markenaufbau notwendige Konstanz in der Führung von Marken sicher.

Eine identitätskonforme Markenorganisation kann selbst zu einer wesentlichen Quelle der Markenidentität werden. Der persönliche Kontakt des Nachfragers mit den die Marke repräsentierenden Personen, dem Verkäufer im Handel, dem Kundendienstmitarbeiter oder dem Markenvertreter auf Messen oder Sponsoringveranstaltungen kann eine entscheidende Basis für die Entstehung einer dauerhaften Beziehung zwischen Marke und Kunden im Sinne einer langfristigen Kundenbindung darstellen. Der Stellenwert, den die Mitarbeiter einer dauerhaften, persönlichen Kundenbeziehung beimessen, manifestiert sich in der **Serviceorientierung einer Marke**. Diese Servicementalität der Mitarbeiter hat einen hohen Einfluss auf die vom Kunden wahrgenommene Markenidentität, weil sie das ernsthafte Bemühen zum Ausdruck bringt, auf die individuellen Bedürfnisse des Kunden einzugehen und echte Wertschätzung für den Kunden signalisiert (Schmitt/Pan 1995, S. 28).

Diese „menschliche", **emotional intensiv erlebbare Dimension der Markenführung** wird in den nächsten Jahren für die Profilierung von Marken erheblich an Bedeutung gewinnen. Hierfür ist einerseits der Verlust an menschlichen Beziehungen im Alltag aufgrund gesellschaftlicher Veränderungen verantwortlich. Dieses Vakuum kann von professionell geführten Marken teilweise ausgefüllt werden. Andererseits bietet die Profilierung der Marke über ihre Serviceorientierung einen erfolgversprechenden Ansatz, um die Imitation durch Wettbewerber nachhaltig zu erschweren. Gerade weil die Stärkung der Marke von innen heraus über eine Steigerung des Markencommitments eine schwierige und langwierige Managementaufgabe ist, schafft sie wirkungsvolle **Barrieren gegenüber der Konkurrenz**, die nur mit großer Zeitverzögerung überwunden werden können. Daher sollte die Markenorganisation so aufgebaut werden, dass die beteiligten Personen die Markenidentität internalisieren können und sie so unterstützen und fördern.

Die anzustrebende **Einzigartigkeit jeder Marke** legt es daher nahe, die organisatorischen Einheiten als Träger der Marke so selbstständig wie möglich zu führen. Gleichzeitig ist jedoch eine möglichst hohe **Ausschöpfung von Synergien** zwischen den verschiedenen Unternehmensbereichen und -marken sicherzustellen. Können Synergien nicht oder nur in geringem Umfang realisiert werden, sollte konsequent geprüft werden, ob die jeweils betroffene Marke durch einen Verkauf nicht in höherem Maße zur Wertsteigerung des Gesamtunternehmens beitragen kann, als durch eine Fortführung im eigenen Unternehmen. Auf der anderen Seite muss bei der Realisierung von Synergien zwischen mehreren Marken darauf geachtet werden, dass diese die externe Wahrnehmung der Marken durch die Nachfrager und das interne Markencommitment nicht negativ beeinflussen. Die umfassende, für die Kunden sichtbare Verwendung von Teilen der Massenmarke Ford im Y-Type von Jaguar kann diesbezüglich als Negativbeispiel gelten.

Besondere Schwierigkeiten ergeben sich in diesem Zusammenhang bei der identitätsgerechten Ausgestaltung der Führung und Organisationsstrukturen einer Marke im Rahmen von **Markenportfolios** (vgl. hier auch den Beitrag zur Markenarchitektur in diesem Buch). Die Zugehörigkeit aller Marken eines Portfolios zu demselben Unternehmen erschwert hier die Ausprägung von markenspezifischen Denk- und Verhaltensmustern bei den Mitarbeitern, die sich letztlich in unterschiedlichen und einzigartigen Markenidentitäten manifesteren sollten.

Von besonderer Bedeutung ist die Konzipierung einer identitätskonformen Markenorganisation bei **Dienstleistungsmarken** (vgl. hierzu den Beitrag zur identitätsorientierten Markenführung bei Dienstleistungen in diesem Buch). Mehr noch als im Konsum- und Investitionsgütersektor wird die Markenidentität im Dienstleistungssektor mangels anderweitiger materieller Wahrnehmungsanker durch die Mitarbeiter, vor allem diejenigen im direkten Kundenkontakt, beeinflusst. Aufgrund der herausgehobenen Bedeutung der Verhaltenskomponente für die Markenidentität sollte der Gestaltung der Markenorganisation und -kultur hier besondere Aufmerksamkeit gewidmet werden. Stellvertretend für Marken, deren Identität in starkem Maße durch ein vergleichsweise homogenes Verhalten der Mitarbeiter geprägt ist, sei hier auf die Deutsche Bank, Cathay Pacific Airlines und insbesondere auf McKinsey&Company verwiesen.

Bei großen, divisionalisierten Unternehmen kann auch die **Unternehmens- beziehungsweise Konzernzugehörigkeit** eine wesentliche Stütze der Markenidentität sein und prägend auf die zu gestaltende Markenorganisation wirken. Dies trifft dann zu, wenn das Unternehmen traditionell durch ein starkes Zusammengehörigkeitsgefühl der verschiedenen Unternehmensbereiche und Tochtergesellschaften geprägt ist.

2.2 Operatives Markenmanagement

Im zweiten Teil des Managementprozesses werden die strategischen Vorgaben durch die Ausgestaltung der Markenführungsinstrumente in konkrete Maßnahmen umgesetzt. Von zentraler Bedeutung für den Erfolg von Marken ist dabei die inhaltliche, formale und zeitliche Integration aller im Rahmen der Markenführung eingesetzten Instrumente.

2.21 Umsetzung der Markenidentität in Markenleistungen

Das Umsetzen der Markenidentität in die **Markenleistungen** stellt einen zentralen Bereich des operativen Markenmanagements dar. Dies umfasst zum einen die technisch-qualitative Gestaltung der Produkte beziehungsweise Dienstleistungen einer Marke. Sie können eine wichtige Komponente der Markenidentität darstellen. Allerdings umfasst die Markenleistungspolitik mehr als die technisch-qualitative Gestaltung der Marke. Sie beinhaltet vielmehr alle Entscheidungstatbestände, die sich auf die marktgerechte Gestaltung der von einer Marke im Absatzmarkt angebotenen Produkte und Dienstleistungen beziehen. Die Markenleistungen unterliegen dabei einem ständigen Anpassungsprozess durch sich ändernde Kundenerwartungen. Kundengerichtet geht es bei der Gestaltung der Markenleistungen letztlich um den Nachweis **echter Problemlösungsfähigkeit** in der Gebrauchs-, Verbrauchs- und Entsorgungsphase. Diese Problemlösungsfähigkeit muss bereits in der Formulierung der Markenidentität zum Ausdruck kommen.

Die Stärke einer Marke wird dabei langfristig vor allem durch die **Innovationsfähigkeit** der sie tragenden Institution determiniert. Innovationsfähigkeit ist in diesem Zusammenhang als Kompetenz zur nachhaltigen Generierung, Entwicklung und Markteinführung unternehmenssubjektiv neuer Markenleistungen zu verstehen. Kompetenz wiederum beschreibt als Begriff die dauerhafte, marktgerechte Kombination von materiellen und immateriellen Ressourcen, die einer Institution zur Verfügung stehen. Am Beispiel der Marke Audi wird der Zusammenhang zwischen Innovationsfähigkeit einer Institution, hier der Audi AG, und der Stärke der Corporate Brand Audi besonders deutlich (vgl. Abbildung 4).

Abbildung 4: **Innovationsfähigkeit am Beispiel der Marke Audi**

1980:
Einführung des permanenten Allradantriebes „Quattro“.

1982:
Einführung des neuen Audi 100 mit dem mit Abstand geringsten cW-Wert (= 0,30) seiner Klasse.

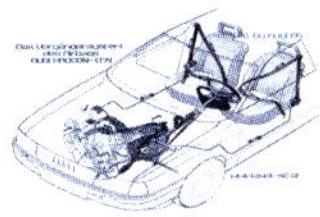

1985:
Einführung der Sicherheitstechnologie ProCon zum Schutz des Fahrers vor einem Aufprall auf das Lenkrad.

1986:
Einführung der vollverzinkten Karosserie mit zehnjähriger Garantie.

1989:
Einführung des Turbo-Diesels mit Direkteinspritzung im Pkw-Bereich.

1994:
Einführung der Aluminiumleichtbauweise (Space-Frame) einer kompletten Karosserie beim Audi A8.

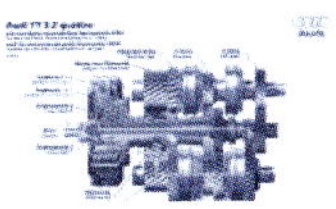

1997:
Einführung eines Sechs-Gang-Getriebes bei Modellen mit Allradantrieb Quattro.

2003:
Einführung des DSG Direktschaltgetriebes in Serienfahrzeugen.

GABLER GRAFIK

Audi hat durch ständige Innovationen seine Positionierung „Vorsprung durch Technik" auf dem Automobilmarkt technologisch untermauert und damit glaubwürdig werden lassen. Weitere Beispiele für technische Innovationen, die in besonderer Weise die Markenpositionierung unterstützen sind das Sonnenschutzspray von Nivea oder gekühlte (nicht gefrorene) Fertiggerichte von Hilcona. Jedoch hat die in den letzten Jahren wachsende **technisch-qualitative Angleichung** der Produkte in vielen Branchen zu einem relativen Bedeutungsverlust der rein technologischen Innovationsfähigkeit geführt. In den Vordergrund treten heute oftmals Vermarktungsinnovationen beziehungsweise Innovationen in der Markenführung. Dennoch repräsentiert die Markenleistungspolitik nach wie vor den Kern vieler Marken. Dies auch deshalb, da sie aufgrund ihrer einfachen Nachvollziehbarkeit durch die Nachfrager zur Rechtfertigung von Preisprämien besonders geeignet ist. Sie trägt damit zur Steigerung der wahrgenommenen „Ehrlichkeit" von Marken bei.

Die **Innovationskraft** einer Marke (= hohe Innovationsfähigkeit) spiegelt sich ebenfalls in der Entwicklung und Gestaltung der **Markenverpackung** wieder, die ebenfalls im Bereich der Markenleistungspolitik angesiedelt ist. Verpackungen vermögen insbesondere bei homogenen Produktinhalten einen direkten und wesentlichen Beitrag zur Markenprofilierung zu leisten (Koppermann 2002). Dieser Zusatznutzen kann kaufentscheidend sein. Beispielsweise führte die Einführung der so genannten „Squeeze-it"-Flasche zu einer wesentlich einfacheren Verwendung von Ketchup, mit der Einführung der PET-Flasche bei Bier konnte das 2003 eingeführte Dosenpfandproblem für viele Markenhersteller gelöst werden und die Einführung der neuen 24er Kiste der Biermarke Beck's erhöhte den Tragekomfort der Kisten für den Nachfrager erheblich (vgl. Abbildung 5).

Entscheidend ist in diesem Zusammenhang nicht die technische Neuheit als solche, sondern die Frage, was von den Nachfragern als Nutzen stiftende Innovation und damit als Differenzierungsmerkmal wahrgenommen wird.

Eng verbunden mit der Verpackungsgestaltung, sind die **Gestaltung und das Design von Marken und ihrer Zeichen** (Zec 2001; Vatter 2003). Beispielweise ist die Coca-Cola-Flasche sowohl Verpackung als auch eingetragenes Markenzeichen. Die visuelle Gestaltung kann dabei, wie das Beispiel der Marke Rolls-Royce verdeutlicht, mit einer außergewöhnlichen technisch-qualitativen Gestaltung zusammenfallen, ist jedoch grundsätzlich unabhängig von dieser zu betrachten. Bang & Olufsen, Braun, Alfa-Romeo, Citroen oder jüngst Renault sind gute Beispiele für Marken, die sich zu einem wesentlichen Teil mithilfe eines ungewöhnlichen Designs zu profilieren versuchen. Insbesondere im asiatischen Kulturkreis sind das Design und damit der ästhetische Gehalt einer Marke für den Erfolg einer Marke von großer Bedeutung (Schmitt/Pan 1995, S. 26). Das hervorstechende Design kann sich auf das Produkt, die Verpackung und das Markenlogo beziehen. Die Verpackung kann dabei neben ihren klassischen Funktionen (zum Beispiel Schutz beim Transport) auch das Wiedererkennen der Marke unterstützen. Konsequent an der Markenidentität ausgerichtet, können die Verpackungsgestaltung und die Markenzeichen die Vermittlung positionierungsrelevanter Markeninhalte unterstützen. Dabei sind die **Prägnanz** und die **Diskriminationsfähigkeit** der Verpackung, des Produktdesigns und des Markenlogos von wesentlicher Bedeutung.

Abbildung 5: Verpackungsinnovationen am Beispiel von Heinz Tomaten-Ketchup sowie Beck's und Holsten Bier

Heinz-Tomaten-Ketchup in der Squeeze-it-Flasche

Beck's-24er-Kasten mit gummierten Griffen und in neuem internationalem Design

Holsten Premium-Pils in der PET-Flasche

GABLER GRAFIK

Quelle: Burmann/Blinda/Nitschke 2003, S. 36

Klassische Beispiele für die einzigartige Gestaltung von Verpackungen sind die Marken Odol, Maggi oder auch Coca-Cola. Die Gestaltung des „Single-Frame"-Kühlergrills bei Audi, der seit 2003 als die wesentliche, modellübergreifende Designkomponente für neue Modelle eingesetzt wird, ist als markenprägendes Erkennungszeichen ebenfalls der Markenleistungspolitik zuzuordnen (siehe Abbildung 6).

Abbildung 6: Der „Single-Frame"-Kühlergrill als übergreifendes Markenleistungselement der Fahrzeugmodelle von Audi

Audi A3 Audi A6

Audi A4 Audi A8

GABLER GRAFIK

2.22 Umsetzung der Markenidentität im Markenpricing

Die Markenidentität muss sich ebenfalls in einer der Marke angemessenen Preispolitik widerspiegeln. Der Rahmen für das **Markenpricing** wird bereits über die grundsätzliche Art der Markenleistungen im Rahmen der Identitätsgestaltung gesetzt. Innerhalb der Gestaltung des Markenpricings wird festgelegt, zu welchen Konditionen und welchen Lieferbedingungen eine Marke am Markt angeboten werden soll. Eine hohe Preisstellung geht dabei in der Regel auch mit einer niedrigen Verbreitung einher, die zu einer höheren Exklusivität der Marke führt. Vice versa führt eine sehr niedrige Preisstellung zu einer „Vermassung" der Marke. Dies hat über die Markenverwender wiederum Einfluss auf das Markenimage und durch dessen wechselseitige Beziehung zur Identität dann auch auf die Markenidentität.

Wie die anderen Markenführungsinstrumente trägt das Markenpricing zur Erreichung der übergeordneten strategischen Markenziele bei. Spezifikum dieses operativen Markenmanagementbereichs ist jedoch, dass eine Veränderung des Markenpreises sich unmittelbar auf die Ertragskraft der Marke auswirkt. Eine wesentliche Zielgröße des Markenpricing ist daher die **Preisbereitschaft** der Nachfrager und die intendierte **Preisprämie** einer Marke. Diese Prämie ist ein direkter Indikator für die Stärke der Marke. Je stärker die Marke ist, das heißt, je mehr sie in der Lage ist, das Kaufverhalten ihrer Nachfrager positiv zu beeinflussen, desto höher ist die erzielbare Preisprämie.

Die Bedeutung des Markenpricings hat in den letzten Jahren stark zugenommen. Der steigende Wettbewerbsdruck drängt viele Herstellermarken in einen über den Preis geführten Verdrängungswettbewerb. Vor allem schwache B- und C-Marken, für welche die Nachfrager nicht bereit sind, (hohe) Preisprämien zu bezahlen, werden durch Handelsmarken stark bedrängt und teilweise substituiert. Der Preiskampf setzt darüber hinaus auch starke A-Marken zunehmend unter Druck. Deren kostenintensive Forschung & Entwicklung und andere markenspezifische Investitionen werden durch schmalere Markenrenditen in Frage gestellt. Ein Beispiel hierfür ist die Lebensmittelbranche. Unternehmen wie Unilever, Procter & Gamble oder auch Nestlé reduzieren zurzeit radikal ihre Markenportfolios, um ihre Finanzmittel auf die so genannten **„Brand Champions“** (starke A-Marken) einer Produktkategorie konzentrieren zu können. Die „Brand Champions“ können sich dem Aktionismus und Preisdruck im Handel besser entziehen und sich so die wirtschaftliche Grundlage für zukünftige Investitionen in die Markenunterstützung erhalten. Hierbei sind sie oft auf eine enge Kooperation mit dem Handel angewiesen. Die Implementierung eines **Category Managements** auf Handelsseite unterstützt diese Entwicklung (Ballhaus 2004, S. 38 ff.).

Allgemein ist zwar die Preisstellung einer Marke kurzfristig im Rahmen von Preisaktionen oder in Reaktion auf Wettbewerbsmaßnahmen (nach unten) veränderbar, allerdings ist bei größeren Anpassungen mittelfristig mit erheblichen Identitätsproblemen zu rechnen.

2.23 Umsetzung der Markenidentität in der Markenkommunikation

Bei der Diskussion identitätsbestimmender Faktoren war in der Vergangenheit häufig eine alleinige Konzentration auf die **Markenkommunikation** zu beobachten (vgl. unter anderem Antonoff 1983; Chajet/Shachtman 1995; Birkigt/Stadler/Funck 1998). Trotz der unbestritten hohen Bedeutung der Kommunikationspolitik für die Markenidentität haben die vorangegangenen Ausführungen gezeigt, dass eine alleinige Konzentration auf die Kommunikation bei der Umsetzung der Markenidentität in keiner Weise ausreichend ist. Dennoch spielt die Markenkommunikation bei der Vermittlung der Markenidentität eine nicht zu unterschätzende Rolle.

Die **Markenkommunikation** greift bei der Ansprache der Kunden auf die gängigen Instrumente der Marketingkommunikation (Meffert 2000, S. 678 ff.) zurück (klassische Werbung, Sponsoring, Event-Kommunikation, Verkaufsförderung, Direktkommunikation, Public Relations, Messen und Ausstellungen, Internet etc.). Die besondere Herausforderung in der Markenkommunikation liegt in einer **inhaltlich** und **formal konsistenten Gestaltung** der Markenbotschaft bei allen gewählten Kommunikationsinstrumenten im Sinne einer konsequent auf die Vermittlung der Markenidentität fokussierten Kommunikation. Die notwendige Bedingung für den Aufbau des intendierten Markenimages ist die Bekanntmachung der Marke bei den relevanten Zielgruppen. Darüber hinaus hat die Markenkommunikation die Aufgabe, die Identität der Marke gegenüber den externen Zielgruppen zu vermitteln und bei der Markenimagebildung in den Köpfen der Zielgruppe vor allem die intendierten funktionalen und symbolischen Nutzenassoziationen zu erzeugen. Die Identität der Marken Beck's, Red Bull und Jägermeister werden beispielsweise in besonderer Weise durch die Markenkommunikation geprägt. Ein weiteres Beispiel ist die stark auf Aktualität ausgerichtete Kommunikationspolitik von Coca-Cola. Das flächendeckende, nationale, regionale und lokale Engagement im Sponsoring- und Eventbereich trägt erheblich zur Markenidentität von Coca-Cola bei.

Vor dem Hintergrund der wachsenden technisch-funktionalen Austauschbarkeit vieler Markenprodukte kommt der **emotional-symbolischen „Sinnstiftung“** von Marken eine hohe Bedeutung in der Markenkommunikation zu. Dies sollte jedoch – wo immer möglich – von klaren technisch-funktionalen Leistungsvorteilen der Marke begleitet werden, um in nachhaltiger Weise zu einem verhaltensrelevanten Markenimage zu führen. Vor allem die **Fragmentierung** vieler Märkte macht dabei die gezielte Ansprache der markenrelevanten Zielgruppen zunehmend schwerer. Vor diesem Hintergrund werden auch neue Kommunikationsinstrumente wie das Sponsoring, die Event-Kommunikation oder auch die Nutzung des Internet für die Entwicklung der Markenidentität zunehmend wichtiger (vgl. hierzu auch die Beiträge zur Profilierung von Marken durch Sponsoring und Event-Kommunikation und zur Markenführung im E-Commerce in diesem Buch).

> Zur Neupositionierung der Marke Adidas zu Beginn der 90er Jahre wurde 1992 mit dem Adidas Streetball Challenge eine Eventkommunikation eingesetzt. Dabei handelt es sich um Streetball-Turniere, die von Adidas an zentralen Plätzen von Städten veranstaltet wurden. Merkmal dieser Kommunikation war die aktive Teilnahme sowohl der beteiligten Teams als auch der Zuschauer. Die Streetball-Turniere fanden europaweit statt. Nach fünf Jahren wurde in Berlin mit 3.200 Teilnehmern und 40.000 Zuschauern eine Finalveranstaltung durchgeführt. Insgesamt nahmen über 500.000 Menschen an den Streetball-Turnieren teil. Die Event-Kommunikation wurde durch die Co-Sponsoren Sprite, Lufthansa, Siemens, SAT 1, MTV und Sport Bild finanziell unterstützt. Adidas setzte diese Form der Event-Kommunikation auch in weiteren Sportarten, wie Fussball und Outdoor-Sportarten, um (vgl. Aaker/Joachimsthaler 2000, S. 190 ff.).

Darüber hinaus kommt in Branchen, die durch eine hohe Austauschbarkeit der Produkte und somit einen Mangel an objektiv-technischen Differenzierungskriterien gekennzeichnet sind (zum Beispiel Zigaretten, Waschmittel, Bier, Universalbanken, Airlines) dem Aufbau **markenspezifischer Erlebniswelten** im Rahmen der Identitätsbildung eine herausgehobene Bedeutung zu.

Im Mai 2000 wurde vom Volkswagen-Konzern die Autostadt eröffnet. Neuwagenkäufer haben hier die Möglichkeit, ihren Wagen persönlich vom Werk abzuholen. Weiterhin kann auf dem Gelände ein Zeithaus mit einer Ausstellung zum Thema Mobilität besucht werden. Zusätzlich beherbergt die Autostadt Markenpavillons der Konzernmarken Seat, Skoda, Audi, Volkswagen, Bentley und Lamborghini. Abgerundet wird das Angebot auf dem circa 25 ha großen Areal durch Erlebnisgastronomie, zahlreichen temporären Sonder-Events, einem fünf Sterne Ritz-Carlton Luxushotel sowie dem Konzern-Forum. Ziel der Autostadt ist die Intensivierung der Marke-Kunden-Beziehung durch den Aufbau einer Erlebniswelt rund um das eigentliche Produkt. Der Erfolg dieser innovativen Form der Markenkommunikation spiegelt sich in mehr als fünf Millionen Besuchern seit Eröffnung der Autostadt wider.

Neben der Schaffung realer Erlebniswelten wie der VW-Autostadt spielen in der Markenkommunikation visuelle **Schlüsselbilder** (zum Beispiel Marlboro's Cowboys, grünes Beck's Segelschiff, amerikanische Harley-Davidson Highways) und akustische Schlüsselmelodien (zum Beispiel Beck's Song Sail away von Joe Cocker, Jingle der Deutschen Telekom), als so genannte Brand Icons für eine Profilierung einer Marke eine bedeutende Rolle (vgl. Abbildung 7).

Abbildung 7: **Schlüsselbilder in der Kommunikation der Marken Marlboro, Harley Davidson und Beck's**

GABLER GRAFIK

Die **Brand Icons** stellen die für den Nachfrager direkt erlebbaren, visuellen, akustischen, haptischen (zum Beispiel Coca-Cola Flasche), olfaktorischen (zum Beispiel Geruch des Connolly-Leders in einem Jaguar) und gustatorischen (zum Beispiel Zartheit und Süße einer Milka-Tafelschokolade) Repräsentationen der Marke dar (Moser 2003, S. 91). Brand Icons können im Rahmen der Markenkommunikation zu Ankerpunkten mit hoher Wiedererkennungskraft aufgebaut werden. Sie sollten multisensual angelegt sein, das heißt möglichst alle Sinne des Menschen ansprechen und damit auch auf diese Weise den Anspruch der ganzheitlichen Markenkommunikation einlösen. Als ein prägnantes Beispiel kann in diesem Zusammenhang Philip Morris angeführt werden. Hier hat es das Markenmanagement durch kontinuierliche und konsistente Kommunikation über die Jahre verstanden, die Marke Marlboro eng mit der Landschaft des „Wilden Westens" der USA und einer spezifischen Art Cowboy zu verbinden. Heute reicht es aus, Nachfragern ein Bild einer Prärie-Landschaft oder den Ausschnitt eines Cowboy-Gesichtes zu zeigen, um bei ihnen die Assoziation zu Marlboro abzurufen. Dies repräsentiert den höchsten Zielerreichungsgrad, den ein Unternehmen mit dem Einsatz von Schlüsselbildern in der Markenkommunikation erreichen kann und verdeutlicht die „Macht" von Brand Icons.

Tabelle 1: Slogans als identitätsprägendes Brand Icon

Slogan	Marke	Richtige Markenzuordnung
„... macht Kinder froh und Erwachs'ne ebenso"	Haribo	93 %
„... Dir Deine Meinung!"	Bild	93 %
„Wenn's um Geld geht ..."	Sparkasse	93 %
„Die zarteste Versuchung seit es Schokolade gibt"	Milka	92 %
„Bitte ein ..."	Bit(Burger)	91 %
„Hoffentlich ... versichert"	Allianz	90 %
„... Das einzig Wahre ..."	Warsteiner	87 %
„Waschmaschinen leben länger mit ..."	Calgon	87 %
„... räumt den Magen auf"	Rennie	87 %
„... Schöne Ferien"	TUI	85 %
Basis: Jeweilige Kenner des Slogans (unbranded) in der dt. Bevölkerung ab 16 Jahren, n = 1.000		

GABLER GRAFIK

Quelle: Kirschhofer 2000, S. 9

Die meisten Marken verwenden in ihrer Kommunikation Claims und Slogans. Hierbei handelt es sich um kurze Phrasen, die in der Kommunikation deskriptive oder emotionale Informationen über eine Marke transportieren und dazu dienen, das Wiedererkennen sowie die Positionierung einer Marke zu unterstützen. Tabelle 1 zeigt die Ergebnisse einer Studie zur Gedächtniswirkung von Slogans, die häufig von Jingles als akustischem Brand Icon unterstützt werden. In diesem Zusammenhang integrieren direkte Jingles den Markennamen (zum Beispiel Ei-Ei-Ei Verpoorten), indirekte Jingles hingegen weisen keinen direkten Bezug zum Namen auf (zum Beispiel Sail away-Song bei Beck's Bier). Die in den letzten Jahren in Deutschland vermehrt zu beobachtende Verwendung englischsprachiger Slogans (zum Beispiel „Come in and find out" von Douglas) ist oft nicht zielführend. Empirische Studien zeigen, dass häufig nur ein Bruchteil der Zielgruppe die verwendeten englischen Begriffe übersetzen kann und ein noch geringerer Anteil der Zielgruppe diese dann auch im Sinne des Markeninhabers interpretiert (vgl. zu englischen Claims in Deutschland ausführlich die Trendstudie von Endmark AG 2003). Hier wird Markenkommunikation offenkundig „aus dem Bauch" der Verantwortlichen heraus statt auf der Basis fundierter Informationen über die eigene Zielgruppe betrieben.

Im Vergleich zu den sonstigen identitätsprägenden Brand Icons weisen Slogans und Jingles als akzidenzielle Merkmale der Markenidentität eine höhere zeitliche Flexibilität auf.

Der **Kommunikation und Präsentation der Marke am Point of Sale** (PoS) kann für die Umsetzung der Markenidentität ebenfalls eine hohe Bedeutung zukommen (Roediger 1993, S. 60). Der Kontakt zum Absatzmittler stellt für den Konsumenten häufig die einzige Möglichkeit zum Aufbau einer persönlichen Beziehung zur Marke dar. Der Auftritt der Marke beim Absatzmittler determiniert die Wahrnehmung dieser Kontaktaufnahme. Neben dem konkreten Verhalten der Verkaufs- oder Kundendienstmitarbeiter prägen auch andere Merkmale des Point of Sale, zum Beispiel Gebäudearchitektur, Innenausstattung, Zugänglichkeit beziehungsweise Standort, Lichtverhältnisse, Parkmöglichkeiten, Öffnungszeiten, Gerüche oder Farben die Wahrnehmung der Marke. Vor allem die **Erlebnisqualität einer Marke** wird durch das Umfeld am PoS in hohem Maße beeinflusst. Die Bedeutung der Markenpräsentation am PoS für die Markenidentität wird vor allem in der Automobilindustrie (zum Beispiel BMW versus Lada oder Kia) und im Bekleidungsbereich (zum Beispiel Boss und Escada versus Daniel Hechter) sichtbar.

2.24 Umsetzung der Markenidentität in der Markendistribution

Generell befasst sich die **Markendistribution** mit der Übermittlung von materiellen und immateriellen Leistungen vom Verkäufer zum Käufer. Dabei kann der Aufgabenkreis der Markendistribution in zwei Bereiche aufgeteilt werden. Zum einen müssen Entscheidungen über die **Wahl der Absatzkanäle** getroffen werden. Zum anderen befasst sich die Markendistribution mit dem **logistischen System**, das für die physische Übermittlung der Markenleistungen zum Endkunden zuständig ist (Meffert 2000, S. 600 ff.). Das Markenmanagement sollte versuchen, eine systematische Durchdringung des Zielmarktes zu erreichen sowie ein konsistentes Erscheinungsbild der Marke durch die Auswahl, Steuerung und Kontrolle der Absatzkanäle und Handelsbetriebsformen (Geschäftsniveau, Sortimentsstruktur, Ausstattung, Service etc.) sicherzustellen. Zentrales Entscheidungskriterium ist dabei der Fit zur **Markenidentität**. Beispielsweise wäre es für die Luxusuhrenmarke Rolex wenig geeignet, für ihre Uhren als Absatzkanal die Warenhäuser zu wählen, da dieser Absatzkanal negative Ausstrahlungswirkungen auf die Wertanmutung der Marke hervorrufen würde. Dagegen kann sich eine Marke durch die Besetzung spezifischer Absatzkanäle Wettbewerbsvorteile gegenüber Konkurrenzmarken verschaffen (z. B. Vertrieb von Getränken des Coca-Cola-Konzerns bei McDonald's).

Bei der Markendistribution müssen insbesondere starke Marken, die potenziell über eine hohe **Pull-Wirkung** verfügen und daher für den Handel kaum verzichtbar sind, den Aufbau von **vertrauensvoll-kooperativen Hersteller-Handels-Beziehungen** sicherstellen. Sie besitzen gegenüber dem Handel aufgrund ihrer Pull-Wirkung, die Nachfrager auch längere Einkaufswege in Kauf nehmen lässt, zwar eine größere Verhandlungsmacht, allerdings macht sie ihre besondere Marktstellung auch für einen Missbrauch durch den Handel attraktiv. Dies begründet sich in einer stark aktionistisch ausgerichteten Marketingpolitik des Handels, der die Sogwirkung von Preisaktionen bei starken Marken nutzt, um Kunden in seine Filialen zu locken. Dieser **Preis- und Promotionaktionismus** führt auf Dauer jedoch zur Markenerosion und schadet den Herstellern und dem Handel (Diller 2001, S. 122). Letzterer beraubt sich damit wichtiger Referenzartikel zur Beurteilung der hohen Preiswürdigkeit seiner eigenen (niedrigpreisigeren) Handelsmarken durch den Kunden.

Ein Ausweg aus dieser Situation bieten gemeinsame Investitionen in das Category Management (Holzkämper 1999; Ballhaus 2004) und ECR, Efficient Consumer Response (Seifert 2004). Beide verfolgen das Ziel einer möglichst effektiven und effizienten Kooperation zwischen Herstellern und Handel. Ein gutes und vertrauensvolles Verhältnis ist insbesondere bei Marken mit niedrigem Involvement der Nachfrager (zum Beispiel Taschentücher, Kaugummis etc.) von Relevanz. Hier werden die Kaufentscheidungen zugunsten einer Marke in der weit überwiegenden Zahl der Fälle erst in der Einkaufsstätte getroffen und sind somit stark durch PoS-Aktivitäten beeinflussbar. Diese Marken sind daher sehr auf die Kooperation mit dem Handel angewiesen.

Eine wesentliche Grundlage der Markenidentifikation der Absatzmittler stellt in diesem Zusammenhang das Angebot hinreichender ökonomischer Anreize dar, die den Absatzmittlern langfristig eine Sicherung ihrer wirtschaftlichen Existenz erlauben.

2.25 Sicherung der Ganzheitlichkeit der Markenidentität durch Markenintegration

Eine langfristig starke Marke kann nur dann aufgebaut werden, wenn sich alle operativen Markenmanagementmaßnahmen an der zuvor definierten Markenidentität ausrichten. So gehören beispielsweise der Niedrigpreis der Swatch-Uhr zusammen mit der unkonventionellen Kommunikation und dem außergewöhnlichen Design der Uhren zum unabdingbaren Bestandteil der Marke Swatch. Diese Konsistenz ist im Rahmen der **Markenintegration** sicherzustellen. Hierfür ist in den meisten Fällen **organisatorisch** eine **eigenständige Stelle** erforderlich, die zum einen mit der Markenidentität und den Markenmaßnahmen vertraut ist und zum anderen durch ihre Unabhängigkeit und Interdisziplinarität eine Integration der Markenmaßnahmen sicherstellt. Diese Stelle ist klassischerweise diejenige des Markenmanagements. Die Sicherung der langfristigen Kontinuität im Markenauftritt, ohne die eine starke Marke nicht aufgebaut werden kann, ist jedoch mit einem im Zyklus weniger Jahre wechselnden Markenmanager nicht vereinbar. Daraus resultiert die Notwendigkeit einer Verankerung der Markenführung im Top-Management des Unternehmens. Die Markenintegration dient letztendlich dem Durchsetzen eines gemeinsamen Vorstellungsbildes von der Marke bei allen internen und externen Zielgruppen.

2.26 Absicherung der Markenidentität durch rechtlichen Markenschutz

Der rechtliche Schutz von Marken und Markenzeichen hat in den letzten Jahren aufgrund des wachsenden Konkurrenzkampfes sowie der zunehmenden Intensität der Markenpiraterie stark an Bedeutung gewonnen. Schätzungen des Counterfeiting Intelligence Bureau besagen, dass Markennachahmungen inzwischen circa sechs Prozent des Welthandels ausmachen (ICC Counterfeiting Intelligence Bureau 2003, S. 138). Jedoch wird die rechtliche Absicherung der Marken von vielen Unternehmen nach wie vor vernachlässigt. Dies hat erhebliche Konsequenzen für die betroffenen Unternehmen. Wird darauf verzichtet, die Marke und ihre wichtigsten Brand Icons in das Markenregister einzutragen, verfügt das Unternehmen über keine **Ausschließlichkeitsrechte**, die es Wettbewerbern verbieten würden, Zeichen zu übernehmen oder sich eng an ihnen anzulehnen. Die hohe Bedeutung des **rechtlichen Markenschutzes** drückt sich daher in einem separaten Ablaufschritt des identitätsorientierten Managementprozesses aus.

Tabelle 2: Überblick über markenrelevante Rechtsordnungen

	MarkenG	PatG	GebrMG	GeschmMG
Schutzgegenstand	Schutz der Kennzeichnungsmittel (zwei- und dreidimensionale Zeichen, Hörzeichen), mit deren Hilfe Waren und Dienstleistungen mehrerer Wettbewerber voneinander unterscheidbar sind	Technische Erfindungen, die neu sind, auf einer erfinderischen Tätigkeit beruhen und gewerblich anwendbar sind	Technische Erfindungen, die neu sind	Muster und Modelle mit ästhetischem Zweck bzw. Wirkung für die Herstellung gewerblicher Erzeugnisse (Design)
Formale Entstehungsvoraussetzungen	■ Eintragung beim DPMA ■ Nicht eingetragene Marke, Benutzung/Verkehrsgeltung, notorische Bekanntheit; bekannte Marke		Anmeldung/Eintragung beim DPMA	
Materielle Voraussetzungen	Kennzeichnung von Waren und Dienstleistungen, Unterscheidungskraft des Zeichens, Selbstständigkeit des Zeichens	Weltneuheit und Erfindungshöhe	Erfinderischer Schritt	Neuheit und Eigentümlichkeit
Schutzdauer	■ Zehn Jahre mit unbegrenzter Verlängerungsmöglichkeit ■ Nicht eingetragene Marke: solange sie benutzt wird bzw. notorische Bekanntheit vorliegt	20 Jahre	Zehn Jahre	20 Jahre
Zivilrechtliche Ansprüche	■ Unterlassung ■ Schadensersatz ■ Vernichtung ■ Auskunft hinsichtlich Dritter			

GABLER GRAFIK

Quelle: Baumgarth 2004, S. 19

Die Aufgabe des rechtlichen Markenschutzes besteht darin, alle schutzfähigen Brand Icons (zum Beispiel Name, Logo, markenspezifischer Melodien in der Markenkommunikation etc.) vor dem Zugriff und Missbrauch durch die Konkurrenz rechtlich abzusichern, um einer Erosion des Markenwertes vorzubeugen (Schröder 2001; Baumgarth 2004, S. 18 ff.). Dabei sollte die **Schutzfähigkeit** einzelner Brand Icons so früh wie möglich überprüft werden, um späteren, kostspieligen Veränderungen vorzubeugen. Darüber hinaus sollte im Rahmen eines institutionalisierten Prozesses der **Markenüberwachung** laufend analysiert werden, ob Dritte die eigene Marke oder einzelne Brand Icons in unzulässiger Weise verwenden. Diese Dienstleistung wird unter anderem von spezialisierten Rechtsanwaltskanzleien angeboten. Ausgewählte für den Markenschutz relevante Rechtsordnungen sind in Tabelle 2 dargestellt.

Neben dem Markengesetz und den in Tabelle 2 aufgeführten Rechtsordnungen sind unter anderem das Bürgerliche Gesetzbuch, das Handelsgesetzbuch, das Gesetz gegen den unlauteren Wettbewerb sowie auf internationaler Ebene das Madrider Markenabkommen und die Pariser Übereinkunft zum Schutz geistigen Eigentums zu beachten. Laut dem zum 1. Januar 1995 in Kraft getretenen Markengesetz (MarkenG) sind beim Deutschen Marken- und Patentamt ins Markenregister eingetragene Marken und Markenzeichen allgemein schutzfähig, wenn sie über **Unterscheidungskraft** verfügen und auf **Selbstständigkeit** beruhen (MarkenG § 3 Abs. 2). Schutzfähige Zeichen sind Wort-, Bild- und Hörzeichen oder eine Kombination aus diesen.

Allerdings können auch Marken und Markenzeichen, die nicht im Markenregister des Deutschen Marken- und Patentamt oder anderen Rechtsinstitutionen eingetragen sind, über einen juristischen Markenschutz verfügen. Zu diesen zählen zum einen Marken mit so genannter **Verkehrsgeltung**. Die Anforderungen an das Maß der Verkehrsgeltung sind allerdings nicht explizit festgelegt und hängen unter anderem von den Verkehrskreisen der Marke ab (MarkenG § 4 Abs. 2 sowie MarkenG § 8 Abs. 3). Zum anderen zählen hierzu notorisch bekannte Marken im Sinne der Pariser Verbandsübereinkunft zum Schutz des geistigen Eigentums (PVÜ). Hierbei handelt es sich um Weltmarken wie beispielsweise Nokia, Coca-Cola, Microsoft oder BMW, auch wenn sie in einem spezifischen Land noch nicht vermarktet werden (vgl. MarkenG § 4 Abs. 3). Bei rechtlichen Markenkonflikten wird das Schutzrecht in der Regel nach Zeitrang zugesprochen (Baumgarth 2004, S. 19).

Die Schutzrechte eingetragener Marken können durch fünfjährige Nicht-Benutzung verfallen (MarkenG § 43) oder erlöschen, wenn der Markenname zum allgemeinen Sprachgebrauch gehört (vgl. Insert 1). Eine konsequente Ausschöpfung der rechtlichen Markenschutzmöglichkeiten minimiert den potenziellen Schaden an einer Marke durch den Missbrauch Dritter. Diese Absicherung trägt zur Sicherung der Wettbewerbsposition bei und bildet durch ihren juristischen Kontrollcharakter eine Brücke zum Marken-Controlling.

INSERT 1 **Süddeutsche Zeitung vom 19. Januar 2004**

Die Deutsche Post kämpft um ihren Namen

Zählt das Wort „Post“ zum allgemeinen Sprachgebrauch – oder gehört es fest zum Unternehmen Deutsche Post?

Dieser Streit zum Markenrecht muss juristisch geklärt werden. Die Deutsche Post will „Post“ prinzipiell als ihren Markennamen für alle Postdienstleistungen, Paket- und Kurierdienste gegen die Konkurrenz geschützt wissen.

Mit Wirkung von Dezember 2003 ist der Name auch beim Deutschen Marken- und Patentamt (München) eingetragen und damit gültig, wie Unternehmenssprecher Dirk Klasen am Montag in Bonn bestätigte.

Löschungsantrag

Dem Unternehmen komme es vor allem darauf an, dass Konkurrenten mit der Nutzung des Wortes „Post“ nicht zugleich auch den guten Namen der Deutschen Post für sich nutzten.

Inzwischen wurde jedoch ein so genannter Löschungsantrag beim Patentamt eingereicht, mit dem die neue Konkurrenz den vom früheren Staatsmonopolisten verfochtenen Anspruch wieder zu Fall bringen will.

Als Antragsteller verweist der Bundesverband internationaler Express- und Kurierdienstleister (BIEK) darauf, das Wort „Post“ sei Teil des allgemeinen Sprachgebrauchs“.

Die Beförderung von Briefen, Paketen, Kurier- und Expresssendungen würden auch von BIEK-Mitgliedsfirmen angeboten.

„Nachträgliche Monopolisierung“

„Die Eintragung einer Marke mit der Bezeichnung „Post“ für derartige Leistungen widerspricht daher der Entwicklung des Postmarktes und stellt den Versuch dar, innovative und privatwirtschaftlich entwickelte Dienstleistungen nachträglich zu monopolisieren“, betonte der BIEK-Vorsitzende Ralf Wojtek.

Das Briefmonopol dürfe nicht durch die Hintertür wieder eingeführt werden. Die Eintragung der Marke widerspreche zudem der Zielsetzung des Postgesetzes, den Wettbewerb zu fördern.

Bis zu einer Entscheidung, die sich voraussichtlich über Jahre hinziehen dürfte, kann die Post laut Klasen die Wortmarke weiter für sich nutzen und wie schon bisher gegen andere Firmen mit Unterlassungsklagen vorgehen. Sie war hier bereits in Fällen wie Regiopost, Citypost oder Post2 erfolgreich.

Im jüngsten Einzelfall zog der Bonner Platzhirsch allerdings den Kürzeren. Der EP Europost, einer Tochter der niederländischen Royal TPG, die zusammen mit der Hermes Logistik Gruppe auf dem deutschen Versandmarkt aktiv ist, gelang es bereits in zweiter Instanz gegen den Einspruch der Deutschen Post, bei Patentamt den Namen „TPG Post Deutschland“ zu verteidigen. Eine Verwechslungsgefahr bei diesem Namen mit der Deutschen Post bestehe nicht, befand die Behörde.

Mehrere Abmahnungen

Dieses Urteil sei allerdings gefällt worden, bevor die Marke der Post eingetragen worden sei, erläuterte Klasen. Die Deutsche Post werde diese Einzelfall-Entscheidung auch vor dem Bundespatentgericht anfechten.

Die Deutsche Post versuche Wettbewerber „auf der Spielweise des Markenrechts in die Enge zu treiben“, erklärte der Vorstandsvorsitzende der EP Europost, Alex Eglseer.

„Wir wissen, dass die Deutsche Post bereits mehrere kleine und mittelgroße Postdienstleister mit Abmahnungen einzuschüchtern versucht hat und mit rechtlichen Schritten droht.“ Vor allem regional tätige kleine Unternehmen könnten sich langjährige Verfahren nicht leisten und mieden deshalb die juristische Auseinandersetzung. „Die EP Europost scheut diese Auseinandersetzung nicht.“

Die Deutsche Post hatte bereits im Februar 2000 die Wortmarke „Post“ angemeldet, bevor sie nun nach langer Behördenprüfung eingetragen wurde. Sie legte dazu eine Umfrage vor, die nachweisen sollte, dass „Post“ eine schützenswerte Marke ist.

Rund 85 Prozent der Befragten hätten dabei den Begriff „Post“ der Deutschen Post und mit ihr verbundenen Unternehmen zugeordnet, sagte Klasen. Der Deutschen Post gehe es darum, dass es keine „Verwechslungsgefahr“ gebe. „Wir wollen nicht, dass Trittbrettfahrer mit unserem guten Namen Deutsche Post werben oder von ihm profitieren.“

2.3 Marken-Controlling

2.31 Definition und Abgrenzung

Den dritten Teilbereich des Managementprozesses bildet das **Marken-Controlling** (vgl. zum Marken-Controlling auch ausführlich den Beitrag in diesem Buch). Die Aufgaben des allgemeinen Controllings umfassen die Beschaffung und Aufbereitung von Führungsinformationen, die Ausrichtung der unternehmerischen Handlungen auf das Ergebnis, die Gestaltung des Informations- und Planungssystems (Systembildung) sowie die Abstimmung des Informations- und Planungssystems (Systemkopplung) (Meffert 2000, S. 1123 ff.). Hieraus ergeben sich die spezifischen Aufgaben des Marken-Controllings. Im Kontext des Markenmanagement umfasst ein Marken-Controlling die **Informationsversorgung und Beratung** aller mit dem Markenmanagement befassten Stellen, verbunden mit einer übergeordneten **Koordinationsfunktion** (Kriegbaum 2001, S. 66 ff.).

Ziel ist die **Rationalität und Ergebnisorientierung** der Markenführung sicherzustellen und eine zielgerichtete Entscheidungsvorbereitung zur Erhaltung und Verbesserung der Reaktionsfähigkeit des Markenmanagements zu gewährleisten. Ein effektives Marken-Controlling unterstützt das strategische und operative Markenmanagement in allen Planungsschritten. Die Implementierung der operativen Maßnahmen wird durch eine regelmäßige Kontrolle des Zielerreichungsgrades in den einzelnen Teilbereichen begleitet, um gegebenenfalls rechtzeitige Steuerungsmaßnahmen einleiten zu können. Somit ist das Marken-Controlling zugleich der Abschluss eines Zyklusses des identitätsorientierten Markenmanagements, sowie der Ausgangspunkt für die Situationsanalyse im Rahmen eines neuen Prozesszyklus.

Auf übergeordneter Ebene ist das **zentrale Objekt** des identitätsorientierten Marken-Controllings die **Marke-Kunde-Beziehung**. Die Stärke der Marke-Kunde-Beziehung wird durch den **Grad der Kundenbindung** gemessen (vgl. Abbildung 8). Kundenbindung wird in diesem Zusammenhang als *Grad der subjektiv wahrgenommenen, kognitiven und affektiven Verbundenheit eines Nachfragers (als potenzieller, aktueller oder ehemaliger Kunde der Marke) gegenüber einer Marke* definiert. Die Kundenbindung verändert sich im Verlauf des Lebenszyklusses eines Nachfragers. Den Maximalwert, und somit die für die markenführende Institution in der Regel höchste Profitabilität, erreicht die Marke-Kunde-Beziehung während der Ausweitung in der Phase der Kundendurchdringung. Da sich die adäquaten Kundenbindungsmaßnahmen in den verschiedenen Phasen des Nachfragerlebenszyklusses unterscheiden, ist eine Kenntnis des Kundenbindungsgrades der verschiedenen Nachfragergruppen notwendig. Nur so können die zur Festigung der Beziehung geeigneten Maßnahmen bestimmt werden.

Abbildung 8: Dynamik der Marke-Kunde-Beziehung

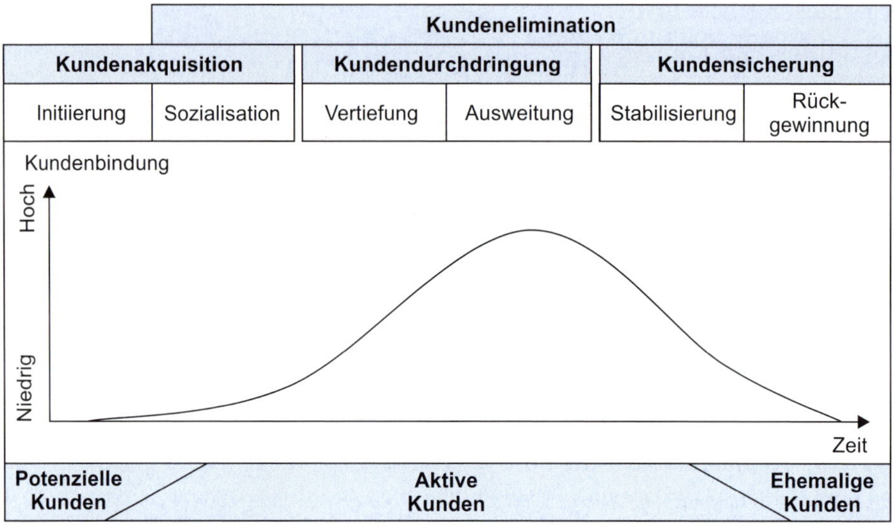

GABLER GRAFIK

Quelle: Burmann/Blinda/Nitschke 2003, S. 45

Das Marken-Controlling kann in die zwei Unterbereiche Markenerfolgsmessung und Markenberichtswesen eingeteilt werden. Die **Markenerfolgsmessung** soll eine **Evaluation** der Ergebnisse des Markenmanagements und eine **Diagnose** der hinter den ermittelten Ergebnissen stehenden Ursachen ermöglichen. Die Markenerfolgsmessung umfasst die Gesamtheit der mittels verschiedener Tools erhobenen Daten aus unternehmensinternen und -externen Quellen. Das **Markenberichtswesen** hat die Aufgabe, die umfassenden und komplexen Ergebnisse der Markenerfolgsmessung in einer zur Entscheidungsunterstützung geeigneten Form aufzubereiten. Dies erfordert eine Strukturierung und Verdichtung der zahlreichen im Rahmen der Markenerfolgsmessung erhobenen Daten.

Im Folgenden wird zuerst das Markenberichtswesen mit der Markenscorecard als übergeordneter Rahmen für die Markenerfolgsmessung vorgestellt. Im Anschluss wird auf ausgewählte Konzepte zur Markenerfolgsmessung eingegangen, mittels derer die Markenscorecard gefüllt werden kann.

2.32 Markenberichtswesen

Um für das Markenmanagement entscheidungsrelevante Informationen bereit zu stellen, müssen sowohl **quantitative ökonomische Ergebnisgrößen** (mit Vergangenheitsbezug), als auch **qualitative psychografische Ergebnistreiber** beziehungsweise Vorsteuergrößen (mit Zukunftsbezug) erfasst werden. Für ein systematisches Marken-Controlling ist es notwendig, die einzelnen Kennzahlen in ein übergeordnetes System zu integrieren. Der Aufbau des nachfolgend vorgestellten identitätsorientierten Marken-Controllings orientiert sich an der Grundstruktur der Balanced Scorecard (BSC) nach Kaplan und Norton (Kaplan/Norton 1996). Die Balanced Scorecard hat seit Mitte der 90er Jahre in Theorie und Praxis eine weite Verbreitung gefunden. Sie berücksichtigt sowohl die interne, als auch die externe Perspektive des Unternehmens. Sie entspricht somit in einem wesentlichen Aspekt dem Konzept der identitätsorientierten Markenführung.

Eine **markenspezifische Scorecard** (vgl. Abbildung 9) sollte sowohl die evaluativen, als auch die diagnostischen Elemente der Markenerfolgsmessung abbilden. Hierzu werden die externe Markt- und die interne Unternehmensperspektive mit qualitativen und quantitativen Indikatoren abgebildet. Erst diese ganzheitliche Herangehensweise generiert ein umfassendes Bild über die Effektivität und Effizienz der Markenführung (Klein-Bölting/ Maskus 2003, S. 64 ff.; Riesenbeck/Perrey 2004, S. 229 ff.). Darüber hinaus garantiert sie, dass eine gegebenenfalls auf kurzfristige Ertragssteigerungen ausgerichtete, verkürzte Shareholder Value-Philosophie den langfristigen Aufbau einer starken Markenidentität nicht gefährdet. Ein Ansatz für die Ausgestaltung eines Markenberichtwesens für das identitätsorientierte Markenmanagement ist die **LiM®-Marken-Scorecard**. Ihre Grundstruktur ist in Abbildung 9 dargestellt.

Die LiM®-Marken-Scorecard berücksichtigt sowohl die Markenidentität, als auch das Markenimage. Die vier Dimensionen bauen hierarchisch aufeinander auf und stehen in einem **Ursache-Wirkungs-Verhältnis**. Die Ursachen werden durch Key-Performance Indikatoren in der Dimension „Markenidentität“ abgebildet. Die Messindikatoren auf der Identitätsebene können entsprechend ihrer Steuerungswirkung als **zukunftsgerichtet** (leading) bezeichnet werden, da ihre Ausprägungen den zukünftigen Markenerfolg beeinflussen. Die aus den Potenzialen und Prozessen resultierenden **Wirkungen** drücken sich in den unternehmensexternen Dimensionen Markenimage und Kundenverhalten sowie letztendlich in den finanziellen Ergebnissen aus. Während die Dimension des Markenimages ebenfalls noch zukunftsgerichtete Indikatoren enthält, sind die Messgrößen der beiden oberen Dimensionen vergangenheitsgerichtete (lagging) Kennzahlen.

Basis der Markenscorecard sind die Kennzahlen der **internen** Sichtweise, das heißt der Dimension der **Markenidentität**. Diese wird durch die zwei Bereiche Prozesse und Potenziale repräsentiert und bildet somit die Lern- und Wachstumsperspektive der Unternehmung ab.

Abbildung 9: Grundstruktur der LiM®-Marken-Scorecard

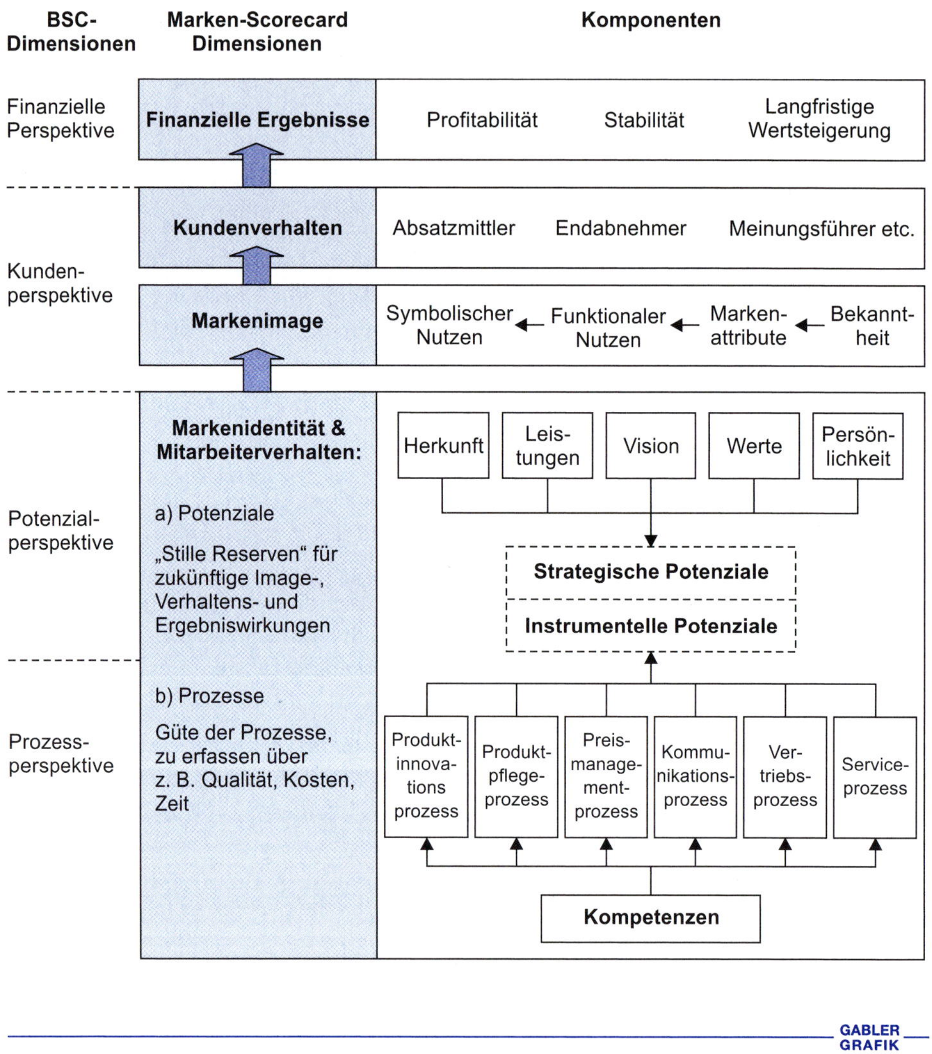

Quelle: Burmann/Blinda/Nitschke 2003, S. 47

Mittels geeigneter Indikatoren werden in der **Prozessperspektive** die für die Befriedigung der Kundenbedürfnisse **zentralen Prozesse** erfasst und hinsichtlich ihrer Güte (zum Beispiel Qualität, Kosten, Zeit) beurteilt. Generell sind dieses der Produktinnovations-, Produktpflege-, der Preismanagement-, der Kommunikations-, der Vertriebs- sowie der Serviceprozess. Entsprechend den Spezifika einer Unternehmung können darüber hinaus weitere Prozesse relevant sein. Die Prozesse basieren auf den Kompetenzen der Unternehmung. Diese kompetenzbasierten Prozesse können auch als instrumentelle Potenziale der Unternehmung interpretiert werden.

Die **Potenzialperspektive** der Markenidentität repräsentiert die durch die Markenidentität aufgebauten „stillen Reserven“ für zukünftige Image-, Verhaltens- und Ergebniswirkungen. Neben den bereits erwähnten instrumentellen Potenzialen werden hier die strategischen Potenziale erfasst, die sich durch eine konsequente Verankerung der Markenidentität bei allen internen Zielgruppen der Marke abrufen lassen. Diese leiten sich direkt aus den Komponenten der Markenidentität ab. Insofern erfasst die Potenzialperspektive die Güte des innengerichteten Markenmanagements. Demgegenüber erfasst die Prozessperspektive die Güte der (Kern-)Kompetenzen der die Marke tragenden Institution und überwacht zugleich den Fit dieser Kompetenzen zu den übrigen Komponenten der Markenidentität.

Die **Kundenperspektive** umfasst die Dimensionen Markenimage und Kundenverhalten. Analog zu den zu Beginn dieses Buches bereits ausführlich erläuterten Komponenten des **Markenimages** werden hier die Bekanntheit, die Markenattribute, der funktionale Nutzen sowie der symbolische Nutzen erfasst.

Dem Markenimage ist im Sinne einer Ursache-Wirkungs-Beziehung das **Kundenverhalten** über- beziehungsweise nachgeordnet. Mittels verschiedener Kennzahlen werden Aspekte des Kundenverhaltens wie beispielsweise Kommunikationsverhalten, Neukundengewinnung (Eroberungsrate), Wiederkaufrate, Kannibalisierungsgrad, Verbrauchsintensität etc. abgebildet. Diese Kennzahlen werden differenziert für die verschiedenen Nachfragergruppen gebildet.

Die **finanzielle** Perspektive einer Markenscorecard erfasst Kennzahlen der finanziellen Leistungsfähigkeit der Marke. Sie repräsentiert die höchste Zielebene, auf der sich die Ergebnisse der unteren Ebenen widerspiegeln. Die Kennzahlen beziehen sich hier beispielsweise auf den Customer Equity der Marke, die Kapitalrentabilität oder Umsatzsteigerungsraten (vgl. hierzu ausführlich den Beitrag zur Markenbewertung in diesem Buch).

Die Kennzahlen der vier Perspektiven der LiM® Marken Scorecard können durch verschiedene Analysen ermittelt werden. Neben den klassischen Analysen und Instrumenten auf Basis interner Rechnungswesen- und externer Marktforschungsdaten sind hier insbesondere die GAP-, die Markenstärke- und die Image- und Positionierungsanalyse zu nennen.

2.33 Markenerfolgsmessung

Bei der Markenerfolgsmessung werden grundsätzlich alle mit der Marke in Verbindung stehenden Leistungskennziffern analysiert. Hierbei handelt es sich sowohl um eine Kontrolle der **Effektivität** als auch der **Effizienz**. Die Effektivitätsmessung beurteilt lediglich den Erreichungsgrad der gesetzten Ziele, ohne diese mit den eingesetzten Ressourcen in Beziehung zu setzen. Dies erfolgt in der Effizienzmessung, anhand derer eine wirtschaftliche Beurteilung der Markenzielerreichung erfolgen kann. Während bei der evaluativen Markenerfolgsmessung Ergebnisgrößen für verschiedene Aspekte des Markenmanagementprozesses ermittelt werden, versucht die diagnostische Markenerfolgsmessung die dahinter stehenden Ursachen transparent zu machen. Wichtigster Schritt im Rahmen der evaluativen Markenerfolgsmessung ist die **Erfassung der Markenstärke**.

Voraussetzung für den Aufbau einer starken Marke ist eine möglichst hohe Übereinstimmung der Markenidentität und des Markenimages. Unter Markenstärke wird die interne und externe **Verhaltensrelevanz einer Marke** verstanden (vgl. zur externen Verhaltensrelevanz Fischer/Hieronimus/Kranz 2002, S. 9 ff. und Kranz 2004). Je mehr eine Marke das tatsächliche Verhalten von Menschen prägt, desto größer ist die Markenstärke. Die Verhaltensrelevanz wird für die externen Zielgruppen vor allem durch das Image der Marke, für die internen Zielgruppen durch die Identität der Marke determiniert (vgl. Abbildung 10).

Abbildung 10: Grundstruktur einer Markenstärkeanalyse

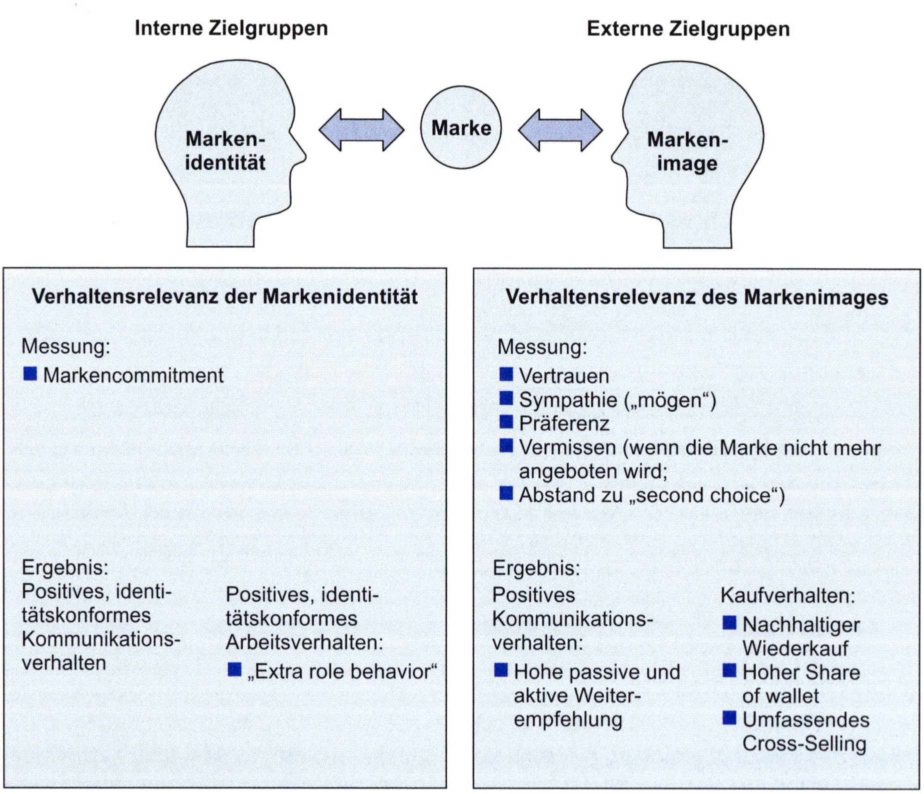

GABLER GRAFIK

Quelle: Burmann/Blinda/Nitschke 2003, S. 50

Die Markenstärke bei den **internen Zielgruppen** kann durch das Konstrukt **Markencommitment** gemessen werden. Das Markencommitment beschreibt den Grad der psychologischen Bindung der Mitarbeiter gegenüber der Marke. Ein hohes Markencommitment resultiert in einer überdurchschnittlichen, freiwilligen Arbeitsanstrengung der Mitarbeiter (extra role behavior) die Markenziele zu erreichen. Diese besondere Arbeitsleistung wird als **Brand Citizenship Behavior** bezeichnet. Sie führt zu einer höheren Güte unternehmensinterner Prozesse und zu einem positiven, identitätskonformen Kommunikationsverhalten der Mitarbeiter (Burmann/Zeplin 2004, S. 59 f.). Insoweit kann die interne Stärke einer Marke auch über das Ausmaß von Brand Citizenship Behavior operationalisiert werden.

Die Markenstärke bei den **externen Zielgruppen** kann indirekt anhand des Markenvertrauens, der Markensympathie, der Markenpräferenz, des Grades an Markenvermissens (bei Elimination einer Marke) und der Distanz der Marke zur zweitbesten, subjektiv präferierten Marke (second choice distance) gemessen werden. Eine hohe Markenstärke kommt jedoch letztlich in einem positiven Kommunikations- und Kaufverhalten zum Ausdruck und kann demzufolge auch nur über die Erfassung dieser Verhaltensweisen direkt gemessen werden (vgl. Abbildung 10). Die Schwierigkeiten und der hohe Aufwand bei der direkten Messung führen jedoch oft zu einem Rückgriff auf die indirekte Messung. Wie bereits im Kapitel zur Grundkonzeption der identitätsorientierten Markenführung erläutert, wird die Markenstärke bei den externen Zielgruppen ganz wesentlich von der Markenstärke bei den internen Zielgruppen determiniert.

Ergibt sich bei der Evaluation der Markenstärke ein unbefriedigendes Bild, sind die Ursache zu diagnostizieren. Hierfür stehen im Rahmen des identitätsorientierten Markenmanagements vor allem zwei Instrumente zur Verfügung: die Marken-GAP-Analyse (vgl. zur GAP-Analyse allgemein Parasuraman/Zeithaml/Berry 1985, S. 46 ff.) und die Image- und Positionierungsanalyse. Für eine Marken-GAP-Analyse ist es notwendig, sowohl das Selbstbild als auch das Fremdbild einer Marke in ihre jeweilige Soll- und Ist-Komponente zu zerlegen:

- Das **Soll-Selbstbild (Soll-Identität)** der Marke beschreibt den Kern der anzustrebenden Zielidentität im Rahmen des unternehmerischen Aussagenkonzepts.
- Das **Ist-Selbstbild (Ist-Identität)** hingegen repräsentiert die tatsächliche interne Umsetzung der vorgegebenen Inhalte einer Marke.
- Während das **Ist-Fremdbild (Ist-Image)** im Rahmen des Akzeptanzkonzepts die externe Wahrnehmung des tatsächlichen Auftritts einer Marke bei den relevanten Zielgruppen umfasst,
- beinhaltet das **Soll-Fremdbild (Soll-Image)** das von den externen Zielgruppen als ideal empfundene Image einer Marke.

Das Markenmanagement muss sich an den Erwartungen der Nachfrager orientieren, welche sich im Ideal-Markenimage (Soll-Markenimage) manifestieren. Durch die Zerlegung der Markenidentität und des Markenimages in SOLL- und IST-Zustände können mittels der **GAP-Analyse** vier wesentliche Konsistenzlücken identifiziert werden, die eine Marke schwächen (vgl. Abbildung 11).

Abbildung 11: GAP-Modell einer evaluativen Markenerfolgsmessung

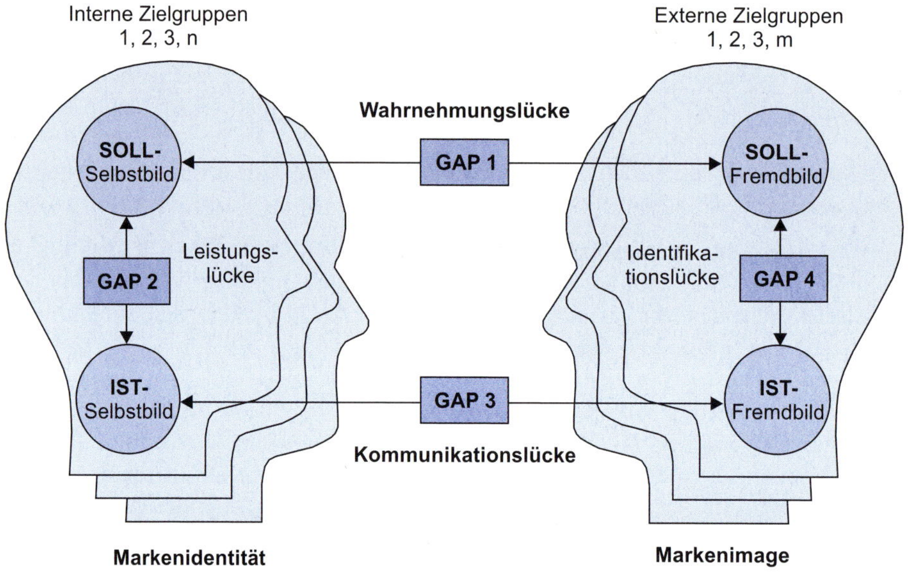

Quelle: in Anlehnung an Meffert/Burmann 1996, S. 62

GAP 1 kennzeichnet als **Wahrnehmungslücke** die Abweichung zwischen den Erwartungen der Nachfrager gegenüber einer Marke (Ideal-Image) und der Wahrnehmung dieser Erwartung auf Seiten des Markenmanagements. Die Entstehung des Ideal-Images wird dabei von den Bedürfnissen, Erfahrungen und der Mund-zu-Mund-Kommunikation der Nachfrager beeinflusst. Vielfach ist diese Abweichung der Ausgangspunkt einer Marken-GAP-Analyse. Zur Sicherstellung einer starken Markenidentität gilt es – wie bei allen GAPs – eine Schließung der Lücke herbeizuführen. Vor diesem Hintergrund liefert die Identifikation der Ideal-Images der Konsumenten wichtige Anhaltspunkte zur Formulierung des Selbstbildes. Maßnahmen, die zur Schließung der Divergenz zwischen den von den Nachfragern implizit (latent) oder explizit erwarteten und vom Anbieter wahrgenommenen Erwartungen beitragen, sollten auf fundierter Marktforschung basieren.

Eine Diskrepanz zwischen dem unter Beachtung der Kundenerwartung formulierten Selbstbild durch das Management und seiner tatsächlichen Realisierung zeigt eine **Leistungslücke (GAP 2)**. Dabei lassen sich zwei Probleme identifizieren:

- Diskrepanz zwischen dem durch die Unternehmensleitung formulierten Markenselbstbild (Planung) und seiner Spezifikation hinsichtlich konkreter Markenmerkmale. Beispielsweise ist in der Automobilindustrie die Spezifikation der im Selbstbild formulierten Merkmale „Sportlichkeit und Dynamik" in konkrete Markeneigenschaften hinsichtlich Höchstgeschwindigkeit, Beschleunigung, Fahrwerksabstimmung oder Innenausstattung etc. mit Schwierigkeiten verbunden.

- Diskrepanz zwischen den geplanten und korrekt spezifizierten Markenmerkmalen und den tatsächlich erbrachten Markenleistungen auf operativer Ebene. So kann es beispielsweise trotz spezifizierter Markenmerkmale im Entwicklungs-Lastenheft eines Automobilherstellers in Bezug auf die Markenqualität zu Fahrzeugmängeln bei der Auslieferung kommen.

Bei den hier aufgeführten Abweichungen handelt es sich somit um **unternehmensinterne GAPs**. Anhand der Ausprägung von GAP 2 kann zusammenfassend die Güte des innengerichteten Markenmanagements abgelesen werden. Ursachen für die aufgeführten GAPs sind insbesondere unzureichende Potenzialfaktoren, die in Form mangelnder Mitarbeiterqualifikation oder einer ungeeigneten unternehmensinternen Infrastruktur verhindern, dass formulierte Markenmerkmale für den Kunden erlebbar umgesetzt werden. Zur erfolgreichen Umsetzung des formulierten Selbstbildes in eine tatsächlich erlebbare Marktleistung sind neben der Sicherstellung einer geeigneten Infrastruktur bestimmte Voraussetzungen bei den Mitarbeitern zu erfüllen (Burmann/Zeplin 2004). So ist die Kenntnis („Kennen") und das „Verstehen" des Soll-Selbstbildes zu gewährleisten und die Betroffenen sind mit der entsprechenden Kompetenz („Können") auszustatten. Überdies ist mit der Akzeptanz („Wollen") des Selbstbildes bei den internen Anspruchsgruppen die Voraussetzung für die Leistungs- und Einsatzbereitschaft der Mitarbeiter zu erreichen (Kolks 1990, S. 110 ff.).

GAP 3 des Modells bezieht sich auf die Abweichung zwischen der tatsächlich erstellten und der in der marktgerichteten Kommunikation versprochenen Leistung (relevant sind hier alle Brand Touch Points). So kann beispielsweise die besondere Wirtschaftlichkeit eines Automobils als wesentliches Kennzeichen der Marke herausgestellt werden, ohne dass der Kunde dies bei seinem tatsächlichen Benzinverbrauch oder den Ersatzteilpreisen nachvollziehen kann. Eine **Kommunikationslücke** tritt somit immer dann auf, wenn Erwartungen bei dem Kunden aufgebaut werden, die später aus Sicht der Nachfrager von der Marke nicht erfüllt werden.

Das **GAP 4** kennzeichnet schließlich eine Abweichung zwischen dem SOLL-Markenimage und dem IST-Markenimage und entsteht aus der subjektiven Bewertung der Marke aus Sicht der externen Zielgruppen. Ursache für diese **Identifikationslücke** sind entweder die GAPS 1 bis 3 oder der Nachfrager ist nicht in der Lage, die tatsächliche Eignung der Marke zu beurteilen. Existiert ein solches GAP, wobei auch eine positive Lücke möglich ist (die Erwartungen des Nachfragers werden übertroffen), so ist zu unterscheiden, ob die Abweichung noch im Toleranzbereich des Nachfragers liegt oder ob er diese Diskrepanz als unakzeptabel einstuft.

Schließlich können die Absatzmittler verstärkend oder abschwächend auf mögliche GAPs zwischen Selbst- und Fremdbild einwirken. So können unterschiedliche Auffassungen von Hersteller und Händler über die Ausprägung der die Markenidentität beeinflussenden Produkt- und PoS-Merkmale existieren (zum Beispiel abweichende Einschätzung der Ideal-Images aus Handels- und Herstellerperpektive). So beeinflussen in der Automobilindustrie die Vertragshändler unmittelbar das Fremdbild der externen Anspruchsgruppen durch konkrete PoS-Standards, erbrachte Serviceleistungen vor und nach dem Kauf oder aber die handelseigene Markenkommunikation, welche abweichend bzw. inkonsistent von der des Herstellers erfolgen kann (zum Beispiel Verwendung konfliktärer Bildwelten im Print-Bereich, Abweichung von den markenspezifischen Farbcodes etc.). Letztlich sind diese Abweichungen zwischen Hersteller und Absatzmittlern Ausdruck einer mangelhaften Verankerung der Markenidentität nach innen.

Tabelle 3 stellt die angeführten GAPs zusammenfassend dar und konkretisiert diese nochmals am Beispiel der Automobilindustrie aus Hersteller und Händlerperspektive.

Tabelle 3: Beschreibung und Beispiele des GAP-Modells

GAP	Beschreibung	Beispiel
Wahrnehmungslücke	Abweichung zwischen den Erwartungen der Konsumenten gegenüber einer Marke (Soll-Fremdbild) und der Wahrnehmung dieser Erwartung auf Seiten des Herstellers und Händlers	■ Bedeutung von umweltverträglichen Ausstattungsmerkmalen (Hersteller) oder vom Service am PoS (Händler)
Leistungslücke	Abweichung zwischen dem formulierten Markenselbstbild und seiner Spezifikation hinsichtlich bestimmter Markenmerkmale Abweichung zwischen den geplanten Produktmerkmalen (Soll-Selbstbild) und der tatsächlich erbrachten Markenleistung (Ist-Selbstbild)	■ Realisierung der Imagedimensionen Sportlichkeit (Hersteller) und Kundennähe (Händler) ■ Abweichung zwischen Lastenheft und Ist-Produkt (Hersteller); Diskrepanz zwischen PoS-Standard und tatsächlichem Händlerservice (Händler)
Kommunikationslücke	Abweichung zwischen der tatsächlich erstellten und der in der marktgerichteten Kommunikation versprochenen Leistung	■ Herstellerseitige Qualitätsgarantie wird durch zahlreiche Fahrzeugmängel untergraben; Mobilitätsgarantie aus der Werbung wird vom Händler nicht eingelöst
Identifikationslücke	Abweichungen zwischen Ideal-Image einer Marke und tatsächlichem Markenimage	

GABLER GRAFIK

Zu beachten ist, dass die Komplexität der Gap-Analyse noch durch die explizite Berücksichtigung **verschiedener interner und externer Zielgruppen** gesteigert wird. Dies wird in Abbildung 11 durch die hintereinander gelegten Köpfe angedeutet. So können beispielsweise voneinander abweichende Markenidentitätsvorstellungen beim Top-Management, dem Vertrieb und der Forschung- und Entwicklungsabteilung existieren. Das Markenimage kann sich zum Beispiel auf Handelsebene von den Images bei Bestandskunden und Altkunden unterscheiden, woraus weitere GAPs resultieren.

Je kleiner im Rahmen der Marken-GAP-Analyse die identifizierten Lücken ausfallen, desto stärker ist in der Regel eine Marke. Aufbauend auf den Ergebnissen der Marken-GAP-Analyse können im nächsten Schritt zur Diagnose einer unzureichenden Markenstärke das Markenimage und die Markenidentität noch differenzierter analysiert werden. Die Analyse der Defizite bei der Markenidentität und damit auch der innengerichteten Markenführung kann anhand der Komponenten der Markenidentität strukturiert werden. Die Untersuchung der Defizite bezüglich des Markenimages kann durch eine Image- und Positionierungsanalyse unterstützt werden. Mit Hilfe dieses diagnostischen Instrumentes können Rückschlüsse auf mögliche Ursachen eines mangelhaften Images gezogen werden (vgl. Abbildung 12).

Abbildung 12: **Grundstruktur einer Image- und Positionierungsanalyse**

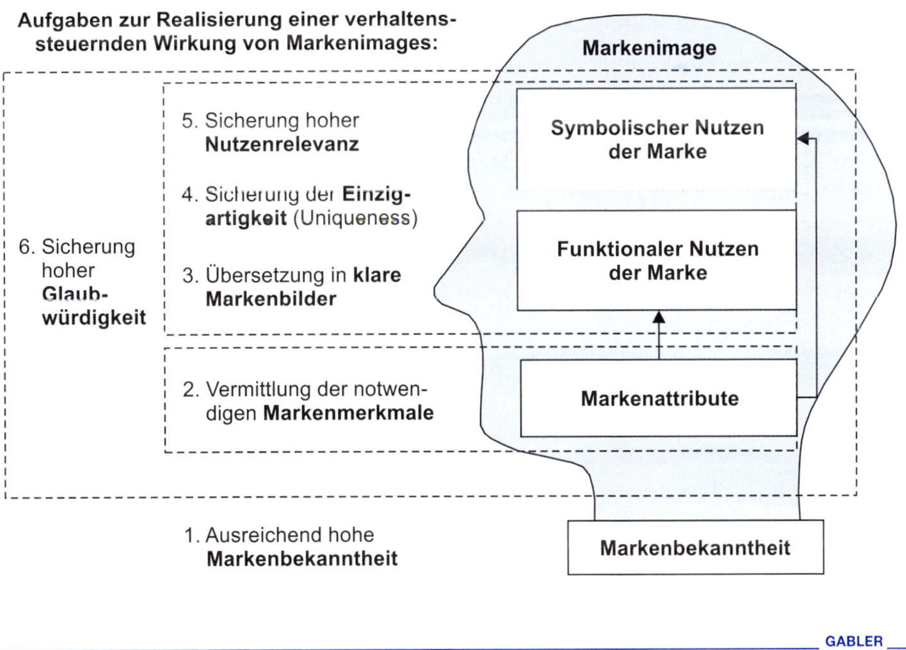

Quelle: Burmann/Blinda/Nitschke 2003, S. 53

Als erstes muss eine **ausreichende hohe Markenbekanntheit** in der relevanten Zielgruppe vorhanden sein, da diese die Grundvoraussetzung für die Existenz eines Markenimages ist. Als zweites bedarf es einer **Vermittlung der relevanten Markenmerkmale**. Die dritte, vierte und fünfte Voraussetzung beziehen sich auf die Nutzendimensionen des Markenimages. Der funktionale und der symbolische Nutzen der Marken müssen in **klare Markenbilder** übersetzt werden. Zudem ist die **Einzigartigkeit** und die **Nutzenrelevanz** des Markenimages sicherzustellen. Als sechstes muss das Markenmanagement eine hohe Glaubwürdigkeit des gesamten Markenimages sicherstellen. Die Glaubwürdigkeit ist vor allem davon abhängig, wie die externen Zielgruppen den Fit zwischen der Herkunft und den Markenkompetenzen auf der einen Seite und den Kernleistungen, der Vision, den Werten und der Persönlichkeit der Marke auf der anderen Seite beurteilen. Dieser Fit wird ganz wesentlich durch das Verhalten aller Mitarbeiter beeinflusst.

Darüber hinaus determiniert das Ausmaß der Markenintegration, das heißt die formale und inhaltliche Konsistenz des externen Markenauftritts die wahrgenommene Glaubwürdigkeit der Marke. In wie weit diese Faktoren erfüllt sind, kann der Image- und Positionierungsanalyse ermittelt werden, welche auch die relevanten Wettbewerbsmarken einschließen muss.

3. Fazit

Aufgabe der identitätsorientierten Markenführung ist die ganzheitliche, aufeinander abgestimmte Gestaltung aller für die Markenidentität relevanten Komponenten. In diesem Sinne muss eine innen- und außengerichtete, funktionsübergreifende Integration aller Markenführungsmaßnahmen angestrebt werden. Der Erreichung dieses Ziels dient der hier entwickelte Managementprozess einer identitätsorientierten Markenführung. Er stellt insbesondere deshalb eine geeignete Basis für das Markenmanagement dar, weil er der nachfragerorientierten Perspektive (Outside-in) gleichberechtigt eine innengerichtete Perspektive des Markenmanagements (Inside-out) gegenüberstellt.

Literatur

Aaker, D. A. (1996), Building Strong Brands, New York.

Aaker, J. (1997), Dimensions of Brand Personality, in: Journal of Marketing Research, Vol. 34, August, S. 347–356.

Aaker, D. A. (2000), Joachimsthaler, E., Brand Leadership, New York [u. a.]

Antonoff, R. (1983), Corporate Identity, Frankfurter Allgemeine Zeitung (Hrsg.), o.O.

Ballhaus, J. (2004), Category Management: Mit den Augen des Kunden sehen, in: Absatzwirtschaft, 47. Jg., Nr. 9, S. 38–42.

Baumgarth, C. (2004), Markenpolitik: Markenwirkungen, Markenführung, Markenforschung, 2. Aufl., Wiesbaden.

Birkigt, K., Stadler, M. M. (1998), Corporate Identity – Grundlagen, in: Birkigt, K., Stadler, M. M., Funck, H. J. (Hrsg.), Corporate Identity: Grundlagen, Funktionen, Fallbeispiele, 9. Aufl., Landsberg/Lech, S. 11–64.

Blinda, L. (2003), Relevanz der Markenherkunft für die identitätsbasierte Markenführung, Arbeitspapier Nr. 2 des Lehrstuhls für innovatives Markenmanagement (LiM), Burmann, Ch. (Hrsg.), Universität Bremen, Bremen.

Bliss, Ch. (2000), Management von Komplexität – Ein integrierter, systemtheoretischer Ansatz zur Komplexitätsreduktion, Wiesbaden.

Burmann, Ch. (1991), Konsumentenzufriedenheit als Determinante der Marken- und Händlerloyalität. Das Beispiel der Automobilindustrie, in: Marketing ZFP, 13. Jg., Nr. 4, S. 249–258.

Burmann, Ch., Blinda, L., Nitschke, A. (2003), Konzeptionelle Grundlagen des identitätsbasierten Markenmanagements, Arbeitspapier Nr. 1 des Lehrstuhls für innovatives Markenmanagement (LiM), Burmann, Ch. (Hrsg.), Universität Bremen, Bremen.

Burmann, Ch., Hundacker, S. (2003a), Customer Equity Management – Modellkonzeption zur wertorientierten Gestaltung des Beziehungsmarketings, Arbeitspapier Nr. 3 des Lehrstuhls für innovatives Markenmanagement (LiM), Burmann, Ch. (Hrsg.), Universität Bremen, Bremen.

Burmann, Ch., Hundacker, S. (2003b), Customer Equity Management bei kontinuierlichen Dienstleistungen – Eine empirische Anwendung, Arbeitspapier Nr. 4 des Lehrstuhls für innovatives Markenmanagement (LiM), Burmann, Chr. (Hrsg.), Universität Bremen, Bremen.

Burmann, Ch., Zeplin, S. (2004), Innengerichtetes identitätsbasiertes Markenmanagement – State-of-the-Art und Forschungsbedarf, Arbeitspapier Nr. 7 des Lehrstuhls für innovatives Markenmanagement (LiM), Burmann, Ch. (Hrsg.), Universität Bremen, Bremen.

Chajet, C., Shachtman, T. (1995), Image Design. Corporate Identity für Firmen, Marken und Produkte, Frankfurt/M.

Diller, H. (2001), Preis- und Distributionspolitik starker Marken vor dem Hintergrund fortschreitender Handelskonzentration, in: Köhler, R., Majer, W., Wiezorek, H. (Hrsg.), Erfolgsfaktor Marke – Neue Strategien des Markenmanagements, München, S. 117–133.

Endmark Trendstudie (2003), Englische Claims in Deutschland, Endmark AG (Hrsg.), Köln.

Esch, F.-R. (2004), Strategie und Technik der Markenführung, 2. Aufl., München.

Fischer, M., Hieronimus, F., Kranz, M. (2002), Markenrelevanz in der Unternehmensführung – Messung, Erklärung und empirische Befunde für B2C-Märkt, in: Backhaus, K. et. al. (Hrsg.), MCM/McKinsey & Company Arbeitspapier Nr. 1, Münster.

Holzkämper, O. (1999), Category Management. Strategische Positionierung des Handels, Göttingen.

ICC Counterfeiting Intelligence Bureau (Hrsg.) (2003), The International Anti-Counterfeiting Directory 2003, Barking.

Kapferer, J. N. (2001), Reinventing the brand, London.

Kaplan, R., Norton, D. (1996), The balanced scorecard: translating strategy into action, Boston.

Kirschhofer, A. V. (2000), Die Slogans mit der besten Markenintegration, in: planung & analyse, o. Jg., Nr. 2, S. 9.

Klante, O. (2004), Identifikations- und Erklärungsansätze für Markenerosion, Wiesbaden.

Klein-Bölting, U., Maskus, M. (2003), Value Brands. Markenwert als zentralen Treiber des Unternehmenswertes, Stuttgart.

Kranz, M. (2004), Die Relevanz der Unternehmensmarke – Ein Beitrag zum Markenmanagement bei unterschiedlichen Stakeholdern, in: Meffert, H. (Hrsg.), Schriften zu Marketing und Management, Bd. 48, Frankfurt/M.

Kriegbaum, C. (2001), Markencontrolling: Bewertung und Steuerung von Marken als immaterielle Vermögenswerte im Rahmen eines unternehmenswertorientierten Markencontrolling, Vahlen, München.

Koers, M. (2001), Steuerung von Markenportfolios, Ein Beitrag zum Mehrmarkencontrolling am Beispiel der Automobilwirtschaft, Frankfurt/M.

Kolks, V. (1990), Strategieimplementierung: Ein anwendungsorientiertes Konzept, Wiesbaden.

Koppermann, U., (2002), Design und Verpackung, in: Albers, S., Hermann, A. (Hrsg.), Handbuch Produktmanagement: Strategientwicklung, Produktplanung, Organisation, Kontrolle, 2. Aufl., Wiesbaden, S. 124–143.

Laforet, S., Saunders, J. (1999), Managing Brand Portfolio: Why leaders do what they do, in: Journal of Advertising Research, Nr. 39, January/February, S. 51–66.

Meffert, H. (2000), Marketing – Grundlagen marktorientierter Unternehmensführung. Konzepte – Instrumente – Praxisbeispiele, 9. Aufl., Wiesbaden.

Meffert, H., Burmann, Ch. (1996), Identitätsorientierte Markenführung – Grundlagen für das Management von Markenportfolios, Arbeitspapier Nr. 100 der Wissenschaftlichen Gesellschaft für Marketing und Unternehmensführung e.V., Meffert, H., Wagner, H., Backhaus, K. (Hrsg.), Münster.

Moser, M. (2003), United we brand: how to create a cohesive brand that's seen, heard, and remembered, Boston.

Parasuraman, A., Zeithaml, V., Berry, L. L. (1985), A Conceptual Model of Service Quality and its Implications for Future Research, in: Journal of Marketing, Vol. 49, S. 41–50.

Riesenbeck, H., Perrey, J. (2004), Mega-Macht Marke – Erfolg messen, machen, managen, Augsburg.

Roediger, R. (1993), Markenführung: Europäisches Pflaster, in: Absatzwirtschaft, Nr. 2, S. 56–60.

Schmitt, B. H., Pan, Y. (1995), Managing Corporate and Brand Identities in the Asia-Pacific Region, in: California Management Review, Winter, S. 15–31.

Schröder, H. (2001), Neuere Entwicklungen des Markenschutzes, in: Köhler, R., Majer, W., Wieczorek, H. (Hrsg.), Erfolgsfaktor Marke – Neue Strategien des Markenmanagements, München, S. 309–322.

Seifert, D. (2004), Efficient Consumer Response, Category Management, Supply Chain Management und CPFR als neue Strategieansätze, 3. Aufl., Mehring.

Vatter, Ch. (2003), Competitve Aesthetics: Complexity and Logo Design, Arbeitspapier der Abteilung für angewandte Kognitionspsychologie und Medienpsychologie des Psychologischen Instituts, Universität Tübingen.

Wiedmann, K. P. (1994), Markenpolitik und Corporate Identity, in: Bruhn, M. (Hrsg.), Handbuch Markenartikel (Bd. 2), Stuttgart, S. 1033–1054.

Zec, P. (2001), Die Rolle des Design bei der Entwicklung von Markenartikeln, in: Bruhn, M. (Hrsg.), Die Marke – Symbolkraft eines Zeichensystems, Bern [u. a.], S. 227–250.

Innengerichtetes identitätsbasiertes Markenmanagement

Christoph Burmann und Sabrina Zeplin

1. **Innengerichtetes identitätsbasiertes Markenmanagement als Voraussetzung für die Schaffung starker Marken** **116**

2. **Brand Citizenship Behavior: Was bedeutet „die Marke leben"?** **117**

3. **Brand Commitment als Auslöser von Brand Citizenship Behavior** **120**

4. **Ein ganzheitliches Modell für das innengerichtete identitätsbasierte Markenmanagement** **122**

4.1 Drei Hebel zur Generierung von Brand Commitment 124
4.11 Sicherstellung des Personen-Markenidentitäts-Fit durch HR-Aktivitäten 124
4.12 Generierung von Markenverständnis durch interne Kommunikation 125
4.13 Förderung von markenorientierter Führung auf allen Ebenen 129
4.2 Abstimmung der Kontextfaktoren: Kultur- und Struktur-Fit 131

5. **Fazit** **134**

1. Innengerichtetes identitätsbasiertes Markenmanagement als Voraussetzung für die Schaffung starker Marken

Wenn es um Markenmanagement geht, denken die meisten Fachleute – aus der Praxis wie aus der Wissenschaft – an Marktforschung, Entscheidungen über Markenarchitektur und Markenpositionierung und das Management von Werbe- und Media-Agenturen.[1] Im Optimalfall führt dies alles zu einer hohen Markenbekanntheit in der angestrebten Zielgruppe und zu einem Markenversprechen, von dem sich die Zielnachfrager zunächst angezogen fühlen. Doch dies ist nicht genug, um **Vertrauen** in eine Marke oder gar **Loyalität** gegenüber einer Marke zu erzeugen. Michael Maskus, Leiter Group Marketing der Allianz Group, stellt fest: *„Man muss halten, was man verspricht."*

Wenn das Markenversprechen, das in der Werbung gemacht wird, nicht über alle Kunden-Marken-Kontaktpunkte hinweg konsistent erfüllt wird, leidet die Glaubwürdigkeit und letztlich die Stärke der Marke. Dieser Mangel an Konsistenz führte zum Beispiel zu einer Krise der Marke C&A. Im britischen Markt wurden TV-Werbespots mit der Aufforderung „Discover the difference at C&A today" gesendet. Doch konnten die Kunden, die der Aufforderung gefolgt waren, lediglich einen negativen Unterschied zu vergleichbaren Bekleidungshandelsketten feststellen: schlecht gestaltete Ladenflächen, unmoderne Kleidungsstücke von schlechter Qualität und unfreundliches Personal. Als Resultat verfremdeten enttäuschte Kunden den Markennamen C&A zu „Cheap & Awful". Im Jahr 2000 wurden alle 113 C&A-Geschäfte in Großbritannien geschlossen (Craik 2000). In Deutschland beging C&A denselben Fehler: Diejenigen, die aufgrund der trendorientierten, preisgekrönten Kinowerbung, die sich an junge, modeorientierte Zielgruppen richtete, in die Geschäfte kamen, wurden durch das veraltete Ladendesign aus den 80ern und durch unmodisches Ladenpersonal der älteren Generation gleich wieder verschreckt. Nach einer langen Zeit der Markenschädigung und des Verlustes von Marktanteilen, achtet C & A heute auf Konsistenz der Werbung und der Kundenerlebnisse mit der Marke.[2]

Dieses Beispiel zeigt, dass eine starke Marke mehr benötigt als eine ansprechende Markenkommunikation. Ebenso wie eine Person braucht eine Marke eine konsistente Identität, um Vertrauen und Loyalität zu erzeugen. Auf dieser Erkenntnis beruht der identitätsbasierte Ansatz des Markenmanagements. Gemäß Burmann, Blinda und Nitschke (2003, S. 5) umfasst die **Markenidentität** „diejenigen raum-zeitlich gleichartigen Merkmale ei-

---

1 Eine Befragung von 105 Entscheidungsträgern in Marketing und Vertrieb zeigte, dass 50 Prozent mit Markenführung nur externe Kommunikation verbinden, 25 Prozent reduzieren Markenführung sogar nur auf Logo, Design und Name einer Marke. Vgl. o. V. (2004).

2 So wurde einerseits massiv in die Modernisierung der Filialen investiert, die nun ein Durchschnittsalter von nur drei Jahren aufweisen, und andererseits ein neuer Claim („Preise gut, alles gut.") eingeführt, der die Markenidentität stützt statt sie zu leugnen. Mit Erfolg: „Reader's Digest" hat C&A jüngst zur vertrauenswürdigsten Marke Deutschlands erklärt, und die Gewinne wachsen wieder. Vgl. Dierks (2004); Kohlbrück (2004).

ner Marke, die aus Sicht der internen Zielgruppen in nachhaltiger Weise das Wesen und den Charakter der Marke prägen." Sie setzt sich aus den sechs Komponenten Markenherkunft, Markenkompetenz (organisationale Fähigkeiten), Markenleistungen, Markenvision, Markenkernwerte und Markenpersönlichkeit zusammen (Burmann, 2004). Die Konsistenz dieser sechs Komponenten determiniert neben anderen Einflüssen die Stärke einer Marke. Die Markenwahrnehmung der Nachfrager wird durch die tatsächlichen Markenleistungen entlang aller **Kunden-Marken-Kontaktpunkte** geprägt, für die zu einem signifikanten Anteil die Mitarbeiter und deren Verhalten verantwortlich sind. Dies betrifft nicht nur Mitarbeiter der Marketing-Abteilung, sondern alle Mitarbeiter, die direkt oder indirekt zu den Produkten oder Dienstleistungen der Marke und/oder zur formellen oder informellen Außenkommunikation beitragen.

Aus diesem Grund müssen die Mitarbeiter die Markenidentität kennen, sie nach innen und außen vertreten und in ihr eigenes Verhalten übernehmen. Sonst kann es passieren, dass sie durch ihr Verhalten die Erwartungen, die durch die Kommunikation generiert werden, enttäuschen. Das folgende Beispiel illustriert dies: Das Telekommunikationsunternehmen O2 mit seinem Claim „O2 can do" versucht sicherzustellen, dass jeder Mitarbeiter denkt „I can do", damit die Kunden sagen „O2 really can do". Nicolas Georghiou, Leiter Corporate Culture & Events bei O2 erläutert: „Wenn die Kunden zu viele negative Erlebnisse hätten, würden sie ganz schnell anfangen, sich über den Claim ‚O2 can do' lustig zu machen". Um eine starke Marke aufzubauen und zu erhalten, muss das absatzmarktgerichtete Markenmanagement also um ein fest **institutionalisiertes innengerichtetes Markenmanagement** ergänzt werden, das die entsprechenden internen Voraussetzungen für eine konsistente Markenidentität schafft. In der Praxis ist dies vielfach noch nicht geschehen, obgleich die Bedeutung des innengerichteten Markenmanagements in den letzten Jahren von einer zunehmenden Zahl von Markenforschern (de Chernatony 1999, Brexendorf/Tomczak 2004; Esch/Vallaster 2004) und Praktikern (Joachimsthaler 2002; Mitchell 2002; Ind 2003) betont wird.

2. Brand Citizenship Behavior: Was bedeutet „die Marke leben"?

Die zentrale Rolle von Mitarbeitern für die Markenbildung liegt darin begründet, dass die Markenidentität letztlich erst durch die Entscheidungen und Handlungen der Mitarbeiter „zum Leben erweckt" wird. Besonders deutlich wird dies in dienstleistungsintensiven Branchen. Diese Aussage ist nicht auf das Kundenkontaktpersonal beschränkt. Gummesson (1987) prägte den Begriff **„Part-time Marketer"** für Mitarbeiter außerhalb der Marketing- und Vertriebsbereiche, um zu betonen, dass sie durch ihre Verantwortung für die Qualität der Produkte und Dienstleistungen beziehungsweise durch ihre interne Lieferantenrolle für die Mitarbeiter im Kundenkontakt einen bedeutenden indirekten Einfluss auf die Erfahrungen der Nachfrager und damit die Markenwahrnehmung haben.

Einige Unternehmen haben diese Einsicht sehr gut umgesetzt. Die Coffee Shop-Kette Starbucks ist ein hervorragendes Beispiel: Sie gibt sehr wenig für traditionelle Werbeaktivitäten aus, erwartet jedoch, dass ihre Mitarbeiter für den Kunden ein außergewöhnliches Erlebnis schaffen. Howard Schultz, CEO von Starbucks erinnert sich stolz an eine Unterhaltung mit einem Mitarbeiter: *„One of our store partners made an amazing discovery this week. He said that we are not, as he once thought, in the coffee business serving people. He said we are in the people business serving coffee."* (Bedbury 2003, S. 50)

Vielfach wird verlangt, dass die Mitarbeiter „die Marke leben" (Ind 2001). Welche konkreten Erwartungen an die Mitarbeiter damit verbunden sind, lässt sich durch das Konstrukt des **Brand Citizenship Behavior** – zu Deutsch „Markenbürgertum" – operationalisieren. Es ist adaptiert vom Organizational Citizenship Behavior (OCB), einem Konstrukt aus der Organizational Behavior Forschung, dem seit den 80er Jahren viel Aufmerksamkeit gewidmet wird. OCB beschreibt individuelle, freiwillige Verhaltensweisen außerhalb von Rollenerwartungen (so genanntes nicht erzwingbares funktionales Extra-Rollenverhalten), die nicht direkt oder explizit durch das formale Entlohnungssystem anerkannt werden, und die in Summe die Leistungsfähigkeit der Organisation steigern (Smith et al. 1983; Organ 1988; Podsakoff et al. 2000). Wir betrachten Brand Citizenship Behavior als ein aggregiertes Konstrukt, das bestimmte generische (marken- und branchenunabhängige) Mitarbeiterverhaltensweisen umfasst, die die Markenidentität stärken. Diese generischen Verhaltensweisen können analog zur OCB-Forschung zu Dimensionen verdichtet werden.

Für OCB haben Podsakoff et al. (2000) in einer umfassenden Literaturauswertung sieben **Dimensionen** identifiziert: (1) „helping behavior" (anderen freiwillig bei arbeitsbezogenen Problemen beziehungsweise deren Vermeidung helfen), (2) „organizational compliance" (gewissenhafte Befolgung der organisationalen Regeln, Vorschriften und Verfahrensweisen, auch ohne Beobachtung oder Überwachung), (3) „individual initiative" (Durchführung von aufgabenbezogenen Verhaltensweisen mit einem Engagement, das weit über das hinausgeht, was minimal notwendig ist oder generell erwartet wird), (4) „sportsmanship" (Bereitschaft, unvermeidbare Schwierigkeiten und lästige Pflichten der Arbeit klaglos zu ertragen), (5) „organizational loyalty" (Vermittlung eines positiven Bildes und Verteidigung der Organisation nach außen), (6) „self-development" (Weiterentwicklung der persönlichen, arbeitsrelevanten Kenntnisse, Fähigkeiten und Fertigkeiten aus eigenem Antrieb), (7) „civic virtue" (Interesse an der Organisation als Ganzes und aktive Mitwirkung an ihrer Steuerung, Beobachtung des Umfeldes und positiver Weiterentwicklung).

Diese Dimensionen sind auf das Brand Citizenship Behavior übertragbar, allerdings mit einem etwas anderen Fokus. Während die erste Dimension des OCB innengerichtet ist („helping colleagues"), sollte sie sich beim Brand Citizenship Behavior ebenso an Nachfrager richten – der Fokus ist breiter. Bei den anderen sechs Dimensionen ist der Fokus des Brand Citizenship Behavior enger – sie beziehen sich nur auf die Marke und nicht auf die gesamte Organisation. Nachfolgend haben wir den Gegenstand und die Bezeichnungen der sieben Dimensionen für das Bezugsobjekt des Brand Citizenship Behaviors angepasst:

1. **Hilfsbereitschaft** (positive Einstellung, Freundlichkeit, Unterstützung und Empathie gegenüber internen und externen Nachfragern; Übernahme von Verantwortung für Aufgaben außerhalb des eigenen Verantwortungsbereichs, falls notwendig, zum Beispiel in der Verfolgung von Beschwerden oder Reklamationen),
2. **Markenbewusstsein** (Befolgung von markenbezogenen Verhaltensleitlinien und Berücksichtigung der Auswirkungen von Aussagen und Verhaltensweisen auf die Marke in allen Situationen, auch ohne Beobachtung oder Überwachung, zum Beispiel in privaten Situationen),
3. **Markeninitiative** (besonderes Engagement bei markenbezogenen Tätigkeiten, das weit über das von internen und externen Nachfragern geforderte oder erwartete Maß hinausgeht, zum Beispiel Inkaufnahme unbezahlter Überstunden zur termingerechten Fertigstellung eines Kundenauftrags),
4. **Sportsgeist** (keine Klagen über Schwierigkeiten und lästige Pflichten des Engagements für die Marke; ausgeprägte Absicht, das Engagement für die Marke auch bei hohen Opportunitätskosten fortzusetzen, zum Beispiel wenn ein Konkurrenzunternehmen ein höheres Gehalt bietet),
5. **Markenmissionierung** (Empfehlung der Marke gegenüber anderen, auch in nicht arbeitsbezogenen Situationen, zum Beispiel Freunden; Weitergabe der Markenidentität an neue Mitarbeiter, zum Beispiel durch Übernahme einer Mentorenrolle),
6. **Selbstentwicklung** (Bereitschaft, kontinuierlich markenbezogene Kenntnisse, Fähigkeiten und Fertigkeiten weiterzuentwickeln, zum Beispiel durch Teilnahme an Trainings in Eigeninitiative) und
7. **Markenentwicklung** (Beitrag zur Weiterentwicklung der Markenidentität, zum Beispiel durch Weitergabe von Kundenfeedback oder durch innovative Ideen).

Die Verantwortlichen der Deutschen Bank hatten vermutlich einige dieser Verhaltensweisen im Hinterkopf, als sie den Claim „Leistung aus Leidenschaft“ entwickelten. Sie wollten erreichen, dass ihre Mitarbeiter nicht wie „Verkaufsroboter“ arbeiten, sondern mehr Empathie für die Nachfrager zeigen. Allerdings ist es deutlich einfacher, solche Erwartungen auf dem Papier an die Mitarbeiter zu stellen als sie tatsächlich dazu zu bewegen, sich entsprechend zu verhalten. Befragungen zeigen, dass die Deutsche Bank diesbezüglich noch Defizite aufweist, denn die Kunden sind mit der Servicequalität der Deutschen Bank und damit ihrem Markenerlebnis nicht zufrieden (o. V. 2003b). Infolgedessen sind die Glaubwürdigkeit und Image-Werte für die Marke vergleichsweise niedrig (Machatschke 2004). In einer britischen Studie konnte gezeigt werden, dass der Anteil der Mitarbeiter, die die Marke wirklich leben, unternehmens- und branchenübergreifend sehr niedrig ist, obwohl knapp die Hälfte der 925 Befragten angibt, dass das Verhalten der Mitarbeiter entscheidenden Einfluss auf Wiederkauf und Weiterempfehlung der Marke hat (MCA Communicates 1999; MORI 1999). Wie also können Mitarbeiter dazu bewegt werden, das gewünschte Brand Citizenship Behavior zu zeigen?

3. Brand Commitment als Auslöser von Brand Citizenship Behavior

Wir argumentieren, dass **Brand Commitment** der zentrale Auslöser von Brand Citizenship Behavior ist. Wir definieren Brand Commitment als das Ausmaß der psychologischen Verbundenheit eines Mitarbeiters mit der Marke, die zu einer Bereitschaft des Mitarbeiters führt, Brand Citizenship Behavior zu zeigen. Der Begriff Commitment wurde in den letzten Jahren bereits im Kontext des innengerichteten Markenmanagements verwendet (Thomson et al. 1999; de Chernatony 1999; Ind 2001; Joachimsthaler 2002; Vallaster 2004). Dies geschah jedoch in fast allen Fällen, ohne den Begriff theoretisch zu fundieren. Mit Blick auf die Corporate Brand eines Unternehmens ist das Konstrukt des Brand Commitment synonym zum organisationalen Commitment zu interpretieren. Letzteres wird üblicherweise als psychologische Bindung zwischen Mitarbeiter und Organisation definiert (Mowday/Deers/Porter 1979; Salancik 1982; Allen/Meyer 1990a; Mathieu/Zajac 1990). Es konnte empirisch gezeigt werden, dass organisationales Commitment Mitarbeiter zu funktionalem Extrarollenverhalten veranlasst (O'Reilly/Chatman 1986; Allen/Meyer 1996). Unsere Hypothese ist, dass dies auch für Brand Citizenship Behavior gilt. Brand Commitment könnte in diesem Falle als eine latente Variable interpretiert werden, die den sieben Dimensionen beziehungsweise typischen Verhaltensweisen zugrunde liegt, die wir unter dem Begriff Brand Citizenship Behavior zusammengefasst haben.

Vor diesem Hintergrund stellt sich die Frage, wie die Entstehung von Brand Commitment erklärt werden kann? In Übereinstimmung mit O'Reilly/Chatman (1986) und basierend auf den frühen Arbeiten von Kelman (1958) unterscheiden wir in diesem Zusammenhang drei psychologische **Determinanten des Brand Commitment**: Fügsamkeit, Identifikation und Internalisierung.

Fügsamkeit in Bezug auf die Markenidentität beschreibt die Aneignung bestimmter Verhaltensweisen, die konsistent mit der angestrebten Markenidentität sind, nur um spezifische, extrinsische Belohnungen zu erhalten oder Bestrafungen zu vermeiden. Die Fügsamkeits-Determinante basiert auf der **Austausch-Theorie** von Adams (1965), laut derer Individuen ihre geleisteten Beiträge rational gegen erzielte Belohnungen abwägen. Es ist leicht nachvollziehbar und wurde von O'Reilly und Chatman empirisch nachgewiesen, dass auf Fügsamkeit basierendes Brand Commitment kein Verhalten hervorruft, das über Rollenerwartungen hinausgeht. Es bewirkt allerdings eine Einhaltung von Regeln, die als Grundvoraussetzung für Brand Citizenship Behavior angesehen werden kann. Fügsamkeit wird einerseits durch die Unternehmensstrukturen beeinflusst, insbesondere durch Anreizsysteme mit formalen Belohnungen und Sanktionen (Farrell/Rusbult 1981), und andererseits durch die Unternehmenskultur mit informellen Belohnungen und Sanktionen durch soziale Kontrolle (O'Reilly/Chatman 1996).

Identifikation mit der Markenidentität bezieht sich auf die Akzeptanz sozialen Einflusses aufgrund eines Zugehörigkeitsgefühls zu der Gruppe, die die Marke trägt, und der Wahrnehmung, mit dem Schicksal dieser Gruppe untrennbar verbunden zu sein. Die

Identifikationsdimension stützt sich auf die Interpretation der Markenidentität als Gruppenidentität. Sie ist von der **Theorie der sozialen Identität** abgeleitet, laut derer die Identität eines Individuums nicht nur aus der persönlichen Identität, sondern auch aus einer sozialen Identität besteht, die ausgeprägte Gruppenklassifikationen umfasst. Diese Klassifikationen können entweder selbstinduziert sein („self-stereotyping"), wenn das Individuum von ihnen erwartet, dass sie sein Selbstwertgefühl heben, oder sie können von anderen vorgenommen werden. Entsprechend kann die Stärke der Identifikation bei unterschiedlichen Klassifikationen variieren (Ashfort/Mael 1989; Albert/Eshforth/ Dutton 2000). Eine starke Identifikation führt zu Brand Citizenship Behavior durch das Gefühl einer persönlichen Verpflichtung gegenüber der Marke als Gruppe, das heißt gegenüber den eigenen Mitarbeitern, den Kollegen, dem CEO oder dem direkten Vorgesetzten. Identifikation kann gefördert werden durch die Betonung der Besonderheit der Marke und der Unterscheidung vom Wettbewerb, durch charismatische Führung und individuelle Förderung (Mael/Ashforth 1992) sowie durch eine starke Unternehmenskultur mit gemeinsamen Ritualen und Symbolen (Mayrhofer/Strunk/Meyer 2003).

Internalisierung der Markenidentität umschreibt die Übernahme von Kernwerten der Marke in das eigene Selbstkonzept als Leitprinzipien des eigenen Handelns. In seiner Extremform bedeutet Internalisierung eine vollständige Übereinstimmung der persönlichen Identität und der Markenidentität. Das **Selbstkonzept** ist *„die Gesamtheit der Gedanken und Gefühle eines Individuums in Bezug auf sich selbst"* (Rosenberg 1979, S. 7) einschließlich seiner Charakterzüge, Kompetenzen und Werte (Leonard/Beauvais/ Scholl 1999). Es entspricht weitgehend der persönlichen Identität[3]. Ein Individuum strebt nach Selbstkongruenz und verhält sich daher aufgrund von intrinsischer Motivation konsistent zu seinem Selbstkonzept. Internalisierung entsteht durch **organisationale Sozialisation**, falls nicht schon vor Eintritt des Individuums in die Organisation eine hohe Kongruenz zwischen seiner persönlichen und der Markenidentität bestanden hat (van Maanen/Schein 1979). Der Sozialisationsprozess besteht dabei sowohl aus der informellen Übermittlung der Markenidentität durch Kollegen als auch der formalen Kommunikation.

Die drei beschriebenen Determinanten des Brand Commitment sind nicht voneinander abhängig. Das Brand Commitment eines jeden Individuums kann sowohl auf einer als auch auf mehreren Determinanten gleichzeitig, in unterschiedlich starker Ausprägung, beruhen. Vor dem Hintergrund der aktuellen Forschung ist davon auszugehen, dass Identifikation und insbesondere Internalisierung ein hohes Brand Commitment erzeugen, wohingegen Fügsamkeit negativ auf das Brand Commitment wirkt, weil es lediglich zu opportunistischem Verhalten führt.

3 Mit dem Selbstkonzept einer Person beschäftigt sich die sozialpsychologische Forschung. In der Terminologie der psychoanalytischen Forschung entspricht es weitgehend der „persönlichen Identität"; vgl. Frey/Haußer (1987). Das Konstrukt der Markenidentität basiert auf der psychoanalytischen Identitätsforschung und kann als eine Ausprägungsform der Gruppenidentität oder synonym auch als soziale Identität interpretiert werden.

4. Ein ganzheitliches Modell für das innengerichtete identitätsbasierte Markenmanagement

Hinsichtlich des Brand Commitment bestehen in der Praxis erhebliche Defizite. Diverse empirische Studien bestätigen dies: Die Befragungen der Gallup Organization (2003) in Deutschland und von Towers Perrin (2003) in den USA zeigen, dass weniger als ein Fünftel der befragten Mitarbeiter sich stark für die Corporate Brand engagiert und freiwillig zusätzliche Anstrengungen unternimmt. Etwa dieselbe Anzahl zeigt keinerlei Engagement – sie machen lediglich „Dienst nach Vorschrift".

Wie kann dieses auch für andere Länder zu konstatierende Defizit behoben werden? Wir haben, basierend auf Experteninterviews[4] und dem aktuellen Stand der Forschung zum organisationalen Commitment und zum innengerichteten Markenmanagement, ein ganzheitliches Modell entwickelt, das drei zentrale Ansatzpunkte und vier Kontextfaktoren für die Generierung von Brand Commitment und Brand Citizenship Behavior aufzeigt (siehe Abbildung 1).

Das Modell stellt unseres Erachtens einen wesentlichen Fortschritt für die Forschung zum innengerichteten Markenmanagement dar. Die bisher entwickelten Modelle decken nur Teilaspekte ab oder sind sehr generisch. So leitet Wittke-Kothe (2001) auf Basis von verhaltenswissenschaftlichen Grundlagen aus der Personalforschung und insbesondere dem „Change Management" ein Phasenmodell der internen Markenführung ab. Sie reduziert innengerichtetes Markenmanagement jedoch auf ein einmaliges Veränderungsprojekt, durchzuführen im Rahmen einer Projektorganisation, und beschreibt somit eher einen einmaligen Prozess der (Marketing-)Strategieimplementierung beziehungsweise des Turnaround- oder Change-Management denn einen kontinuierlichen innengerichteten Managementprozess.

Vallaster und de Chernatony (2004) entwickeln auf Grundlage von Expertengesprächen das Modell des „leadership based brand building" für Dienstleistungsmarken. Sie argumentieren, dass markenorientiertes Mitarbeiterverhalten durch die Führungskräfte ausgelöst wird, die eine klare Markenvision entwickeln müssen und die soziale Interaktion der Mitarbeiter untereinander fördern sollten. Unklar bleibt jedoch, weshalb das Modell nur das Führungsverhalten betrachtet und andere Aspekte des innengerichteten Markenmanagements ausklammert.

4 Von April bis Juni 2004 wurden elf semistrukturierte Experteninterviews durchgeführt. Interviewpartner waren zwei unabhängige Markenexperten und neun Führungskräfte mit Verantwortung für die Corporate Brand oder das innengerichtete Markenmanagement in den Branchen Finanzdienstleistungen, Telekommunikation, Elektronik und Transport/Tourismus. Die Interviewpartner wurden aufgrund ihrer Expertise und Erfahrung im innengerichteten Markenmanagement ausgewählt. Die betrachteten Unternehmen sind alle in dienstleistungsintensiven Branchen tätig, in welchen dem innengerichteten Markenmanagement eine besonders hohe Bedeutung zukommt. Ihre Größe reicht von 3.500 bis zu 400.000 Mitarbeitern.

Abbildung 1: Ein ganzheitliches verhaltensorientiertes Modell für das innengerichtete Markenmanagement

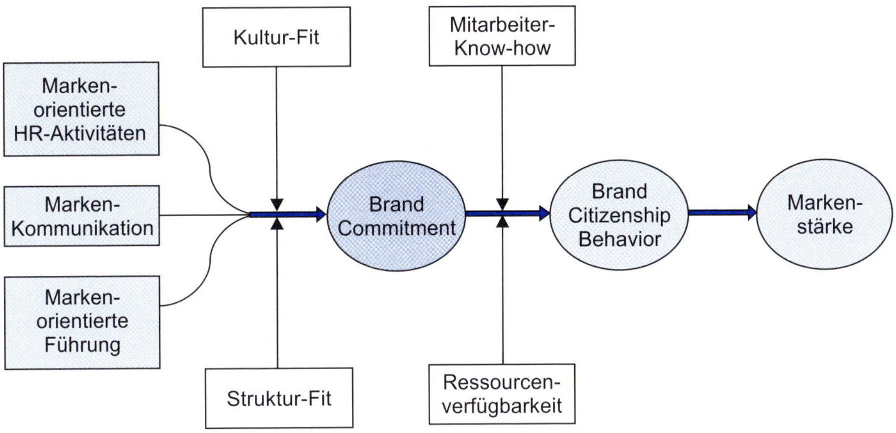

GABLER GRAFIK

Ein weiteres Modell zum innengerichteten Markenmanagement wurde von Brexendorf und Tomczak (2004) entwickelt. Sie betrachten interne Markenführung als Managementprozess mit den sieben Stufen (1) Situation analysieren, (2) Ziele der internen Markenführung festlegen, (3) Markenidentität entwickeln und Markenversprechen festlegen, (4) Markencommitment aufbauen und markenfokussierte Unternehmenskultur gestalten, (5) Markenidentität und Markenversprechen vermitteln, (6) Markenidentität und Markenversprechen leben und (7) Markenidentität und Markenversprechen sowie Ziele der internen Markenführung kontrollieren. An dem Modell sind jedoch die fehlende theoretische Fundierung und die geringe Spezifität zu kritisieren. Brexendorf und Tomczak beschreiben einen allgemeinen Prozess des Markenmanagements statt einen spezifisch auf die innengerichtete Markenführung hin ausgelegten Prozess. Ferner ist zu kritisieren, dass sie sich bei der konkreten Ausgestaltung der innengerichtet besonders relevanten Schritte (4) bis (6) nahezu ausschließlich mit der formellen internen Kommunikation beschäftigen. Alle anderen Handlungsparameter und Einflussfaktoren des innengerichteten Markenmanagements werden vernachlässigt oder nur kurz am Rande erwähnt.

4.1 Drei Hebel zur Generierung von Brand Commitment

Die Experteninterviews haben gezeigt, dass es nicht einen einzigen Treiber für Brand Commitment gibt. Eine große Anzahl von Maßnahmen müssen parallel durchgeführt und koordiniert werden. Wir haben diese Maßnahmen im ersten Schritt zu drei Hebeln zusammengefasst: markenorientierte Human-Resource-Management Aktivitäten (HR-Aktivitäten), interne Marken-Kommunikation und markenorientierte Führung. Die theoretische Basis und praktische Anwendung dieser drei Hebel für das innengerichtete Markenmanagement wird im Folgenden dargestellt. Von den Experten wurde übereinstimmend darauf hingewiesen, dass diese Hebel nur dann zum Erfolg führen, wenn die Kontextfaktoren im Einklang mit der Markenidentität sind: Kultur- und Struktur-Fit sind notwendige Voraussetzungen für die Entstehung von Brand Commitment, und Brand Commitment führt nur dann zu Brand Citizenship Behavior, wenn jeder einzelne Mitarbeiter über das notwendige Know-how und die entsprechenden Ressourcen verfügt, um ein konsistentes Markenerlebnis zu gewährleisten.

Die Abstimmung der Kontextfaktoren alleine garantiert keine Identifikation oder Internalisierung der Markenidentität, sondern lediglich Fügsamkeit. Auf Identifikation basierendes Brand Commitment lässt sich insbesondere durch markenorientierte Führung erzielen, während die Internalisierung der Markenidentität vor allem durch HR-Aktivitäten und interne Kommunikation erreicht werden kann.

4.11 Sicherstellung des Personen-Markenidentitäts-Fit durch HR-Aktivitäten

Unter den Experten herrschte Uneinigkeit in Bezug auf die Frage, ob einige Mitarbeiter eine natürliche Prädisposition für ein höheres Brand Commitment haben, während andere sich aufgrund ihrer Persönlichkeit nie an irgendetwas binden. In dieser generalisierten Form müssen wir der These widersprechen. Dennoch ist anzunehmen, dass einige Personen eine höhere Kongruenz zwischen ihrer persönlichen Identität und der Markenidentität haben als andere, schon bevor sie in das Unternehmen eintreten. In diesem Fall sind beispielsweise die Markenwerte schon Teil des Selbstkonzepts dieser Personen.

Dies bedeutet, dass ein markenorientiertes HR Management sicherstellen muss, dass Bewerber mit einem hohen **Personen-Markenidentitäts-Fit** rekrutiert und selektiert werden, und dass die Mitarbeiter mit einem hohen Personen-Markenidentitäts-Fit bevorzugt befördert werden (c. p.). Dies bedeutet, dass das Markenidentitätskonzept die Basis für das **Arbeitgebermarketing,** die **Personalauswahl** und die **Beförderungskriterien** sein muss. Ind (1998, S. 325) drückt das folgendermaßen aus: *„Recruitment is a branding exercise, it's part of the management of the corporate brand."* So selbstverständlich diese Forderung scheint, in der Realität findet die erforderliche Abstimmung zwischen Marken- und HR-Management häufig nicht statt. Es existieren jedoch Methoden, die erfolgreich eingesetzt werden (Chatman 1989; O'Reilly/Chatman/Caldwell 1991). Unabhängig von diesen Methoden kann Personen-Markenidentitäts-Fit durch Selbstselektion erzielt werden, indem einerseits Eigenschaften erfolgreicher Mitarbeiter aufgezeigt werden und andererseits den Bewerbern ermöglicht wird, vor ihrer Entscheidung Zeit mit Mitarbeitern zu verbringen (Chatman 1991).

Eine zweite Möglichkeit für das HR-Management, zur Internalisierung der Markenidentität beizutragen, besteht in der Einführung neuer Mitarbeiter in die Organisation. Normalerweise organisiert die HR-Abteilung eine Art Einstiegstraining oder -veranstaltung für neue Mitarbeiter. Dies hat großen Einfluss auf den anfänglichen **Sozialisationsprozess** und muss deshalb die Markenidentität mit ihrer Herkunft und Vision, ihren Kernwerten, Fähigkeiten und ihrer Persönlichkeit vermitteln. In späteren Phasen der Karriere eines Mitarbeiters kann dies durch Führungsnachwuchsprogramme ergänzt werden, die wiederum die Markenidentität beleuchten. Zusätzlich zu formellem Training können Events und ein Mentorenprogramm die informelle Weitergabe der Markenidentität fördern. Mehrere Studien haben gezeigt, dass institutionalisierte Sozialisation einen signifikanten positiven Einfluss auf die Generierung von organisationalem Commitment, organisationaler Identifikation und Personen-Organisations-Fit hat (Allen/Meyer 1990b; Chatman, 1991; Ashforth/Saks 1996; Klein/Weaver 2000). Dasselbe dürfte für das Brand Commitment gelten.

4.12 Generierung von Markenverständnis durch interne Kommunikation

Die Sicherstellung eines guten Personen-Markenidentitäts-Fit durch entsprechende HR-Maßnahmen allein reicht jedoch nicht aus. Alle Mitarbeiter – Neueinstellungen und „Alt"-Mitarbeiter – müssen die Markenidentität verstanden und verinnerlicht haben. In vielen Unternehmen – insbesondere bei Ex-Monopolisten oder „ingenieursgetriebenen" Unternehmen – ist es hier zunächst notwendig, ein **Bewusstsein für die Relevanz der Marke** zu schaffen. In vielen Fällen wird die Verantwortung für die Marke an die Marketing-Abteilung delegiert, und der Rest des Unternehmens fühlt sich nicht verantwortlich. Nicholas Georghiou, Leiter Corporate Culture & Events bei O2 unterstreicht dies: *„Die größte Herausforderung ist es, den Mitarbeitern in Bereichen wie dem Einkauf, die weiter weg vom Kunden sind, ein Gefühl für die Marke zu geben."*

Erst wenn jeder einzelne Mitarbeiter erkennt, dass er oder sie persönlich einen signifikanten Einfluss auf das Markenerlebnis und die Markenwahrnehmung der Nachfrager hat, kann versucht werden, den Mitarbeitern ein **Verständnis für die Markenidentität** zu vermitteln. Dies erfordert eine Verbalisierung des Markenidentitätskonzepts, die sowohl verständlich als auch ansprechend für alle Mitarbeiter ist, vom Vorstandsmitglied bis hin zum Pförtner. Einige Unternehmen besitzen zwar ein „Identity Statement", meist sind diese Erklärungen jedoch viel zu generisch und daher für die Mitarbeiter weder verständlich noch handlungsrelevant. Diese Statements sind häufig das Ergebnis eines aufwendigen, unternehmensweiten Meinungsbildungsprozesses, bei dem es durch die im Mittelpunkt stehende Konsensbildung nahezu unmöglich wird, die Markenidentität zu definieren und prägnant zu verdichten. Die Entwicklung und Vermittlung der Markenidentität ist eine wichtige Führungsaufgabe des Top-Managements und sollte nicht als basisdemokratischer Prozess missverstanden werden.

In diesem Zusammenhang ist auch auf Keller und sein **„Brand Mantra“** zu verweisen. Brand Mantras sind kurze Aussagen mit drei bis fünf Wörtern *„that capture the irrefutable essence or spirit of the brand“* (Keller 1999, S. 45). Sie sind ein leicht zu merkendes Stenogramm für das komplexe Markenidentitätskonzept und können als „Leitplanken“ für die Entscheidungen und das Verhalten der Mitarbeiter dienen. Nike hat das Brand Mantra „authentic athletic performance“ als Orientierungshilfe für ihre Markenaktivitäten eingeführt. Dies hat sie davor bewahrt, ihre Produktlinie in Bereiche auszudehnen, die nicht zur Markenidentität gepasst hätten. In ähnlicher Weise hat Disney das Brand Mantra „fun family entertainment“ geholfen, nicht markenidentitätskongruente Kooperationsangebote abzulehnen. Beispielsweise eine Kooperation mit einer Investmentgesellschaft, die ein Produkt für Familien, die für die Ausbildung ihrer Kinder sparen, offerieren wollte. Investmentgesellschaften und der für sie relevante Markt haben aus Sicht der meisten Familien üblicherweise nur wenig mit „fun“ und „entertainment“ zu tun und sind daher für Disney eher unpassend.

Laut Keller muss ein Brand Mantra drei Kriterien erfüllen: es muss kommunizieren, vereinfachen und inspirieren. Die Basis für ein Brand Mantra ist die Markenidentität. Es muss daher die sechs Komponenten der Markenidentität – Markenherkunft, Markenkompetenz, Markenleistungen, Markenvision, Markenwerte und Markenpersönlichkeit – widerspiegeln. Idealerweise wird es von einer kleinen Gruppe entwickelt, wobei Konsens in der Geschäftsführung essenziell ist, damit es wirklich als Basis für Entscheidungen dient und nicht nur auf dem Papier existiert. Als SIEMENS ihre Werbeagentur gebeten haben, ein solches Brand Mantra für ihre Corporate Brand zu entwickeln, hat der Vorstand alle Vorschläge abgelehnt, da sie sich durch sie eben nicht inspiriert fühlten. Schließlich hat der Vorstandvorsitzende von Pierer selber den Anstoß zu dem Brand Mantra „global network of innovation“ gegeben, an dem sich nun alle SIEMENS Aktivitäten – einschließlich M&A-Entscheidungen – orientieren. Hierbei muss jedoch kritisch angemerkt werden, dass hier ein „Brand Mantra“ formuliert wurde, ohne zuvor ein vollständiges Konzept für die angestrebte Markenidentität zu entwerfen.

Zwischen der Entwicklung einer Markenidentität und eines Brand Mantra auf der Geschäftsleitungsebene und der täglichen Arbeitsroutine der Mitarbeiter klafft allerdings meist noch eine erhebliche Lücke. Das Brand Mantra muss für die Mitarbeiter folglich operationalisiert, das heißt greifbar gemacht werden. Das bedeutet, dass spezifische **Verhaltensleitlinien** und **Vorgaben** entwickelt werden müssen – entweder top-down oder partizipativ. Eine umfassende Mitarbeiterpartizipation dürfte hier zu einem stärkeren Brand Commitment (Identifikation und Internalisierung) führen. Demgegenüber werden ausschließlich top-down verkündete Verhaltensleitlinien eher ein schwächeres Brand Commitment, basierend auf Fügsamkeit, erzeugen. Unter den Praktikern besteht hier jedoch kein Konsens: Bei einem großen deutschen Kreditinstitut werden Leitlinien von den Mitarbeitern dezentral entwickelt und anschließend in Zielvereinbarungen mit Vorgesetzen aufgenommen. Bei Tchibo hingegen werden detaillierte Verhaltensrichtlinien für das Verkaufspersonal zentral entwickelt und ihre Einhaltung von „Mystery Shoppers" alle drei Wochen kontrolliert.

Neben den eher rationalen Verhaltensleitlinien müssen die Mitarbeiter auf der **emotionalen Ebene** angesprochen werden, um Brand Commitment zu erzeugen (Thomson et al. 1999). Um dies zu erreichen, ist eine professionelle interne Kommunikation rund um das Markenidentitätskonzept unerlässlich. Interne Kommunikation kann in drei Formen unterteilt werden, die sich ergänzen und die aufeinander abgestimmt werden müssen: zentrale Kommunikation, Kaskadenkommunikation und laterale Kommunikation (vgl. Abbildung 2).

Abbildung 2: **Drei Formen interner Kommunikation**

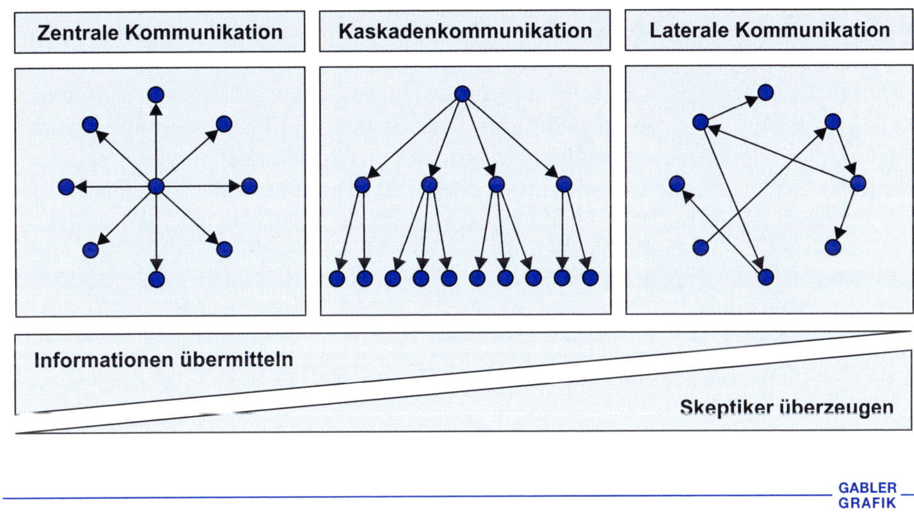

Zentrale Kommunikation geht von einer zentralen Abteilung, üblicherweise der Kommunikationsabteilung, aus. Die häufigste Art der zentralen Kommunikation folgt dem **Push-Prinzip**: meist schriftliche Materialien (zum Beispiel Mitarbeiterzeitungen, Newsletter) werden verteilt, ohne Rücksicht darauf, ob die Inhalte bei den Mitarbeitern auch tatsächlich ankommen. Dies sollte durch Kommunikation nach dem **Pull-Prinzip** ergänzt werden, zum Beispiel über das firmeneigene Intranet. In diesem Fall suchen Mitarbeiter aktiv nach Informationen, statt sie ungefragt zu erhalten, was leicht zu einem „information overload" führen kann. Zentral organisierte Events sind ein drittes Medium für zentrale Kommunikation. Sie ergänzen das Pull- und Push-Prinzip um **interaktive Kommunikation**. O2, die sich selbst als „mitarbeiter- und eventgetriebene Organisation" beschreiben, organisieren regelmäßig sogenannte „Blue Events" (in Anlehnung an ihre Firmenfarbe) für alle Mitarbeiter, bei denen markenbezogene Themen aufgearbeitet werden. Zentrale Kommunikation ist sinnvoll, um Aufmerksamkeit für die Marke zu erzeugen und aktuelle Information rund um die Marke weiterzugeben. Natürlich wirkt dabei auch **externe Kommunikation** auf die Mitarbeiter. Wolfgang Dötz, Vice President Brand&Design bei Siemens, illustriert dies: *„Manchmal lassen sich einige Dinge im Unternehmen durch einen Artikel im ‚Manager Magazin einfacher erreichen als durch Vorstandsschreiben."*

Kaskadenkommunikation beginnt weit oben im Unternehmen, idealerweise bei der Geschäftsführung, und wird dann nach unten durch die Hierarchie weitergegeben. Sie ist ebenso wie die zentrale Kommunikation geeignet, um Informationen an alle Mitarbeiter weiterzugeben, aber weit aufwendiger. Der Vorteil der Kaskadenkommunikation liegt darin, dass sie für skeptische Mitarbeiter wesentlich überzeugender ist, weil Informationen vom direkten Vorgesetzten als relevanter und glaubwürdiger wahrgenommen werden als Informationen von einer zentralen Stelle. Um das Markenidentitätskonzept in der Organisation zu kommunizieren, wurde in einigen Unternehmen von den Markenverantwortlichen eine **Toolbox** entwickelt, die Führungskräfte in der täglichen Kommunikation und bei der Vorbereitung von Markenworkshops unterstützen soll. Häufig noch effektiver als Markenworkshops, die vom Vorgesetzten durchgeführt werden, sind Teamworkshops ohne Vorgesetzten. Diese selbstlernenden Gruppen von ungefähr zehn Mitarbeitern wählen einen Moderator aus ihrer Mitte und können durch ein Visualisierungstool unterstützt werden, dass als **Lernlandkarte** bezeichnet wird. Lernlandkarten sind grafische Repräsentationen eines Themas – in diesem Falle des Markenidentitätskonzepts – in Poster-Größe. Sie stellen Informationen in einer sehr anschaulichen Art und Weise zur Verfügung und regen die Mitarbeiter dazu an, über die Markenidentität und ihre Implikationen für die eigene Tätigkeit nachzudenken und zu diskutieren. Als Ergebnis entwickelt die Gruppe ohne hierarchischen Druck, sondern aus eigenem Antrieb persönliche und gruppenbezogene Umsetzungspläne. Ein großes deutsches Kreditinstitut hat Lernlandkarten eingesetzt, um auf allen Ebenen ein Verständnis für ihr Markenidentitätskonzept zu erreichen. Der Verantwortliche ist sehr zufrieden mit den Ergebnissen: *„Für die Mitarbeiter wirkt es nicht wie Indoktrination von oben. Da sie die Implikationen für ihr eigenes Verhalten selbst entwickelt haben, sind sie von den gemeinsam entwickelten Zielen überzeugt und werden mit großen Commitment versuchen, sie zu erreichen."*

Laterale Kommunikation beschreibt die informelle Weitergabe von Informationen unter Mitarbeitern unabhängig von ihrer Hierarchieebene oder Abteilungszugehörigkeit, umgangssprachlich auch als „Gerüchteküche" oder „Flurfunk" bezeichnet. Dies ist die wirkungsvollste Kommunikationsform um Skeptiker zu überzeugen, da Informationen von seinesgleichen am ehesten angenommen wird. Es ist jedoch sehr schwierig, diese Form der Kommunikation zu kontrollieren und für die Zwecke der internen Kommunikation aktiv zu nutzen. Ein vielversprechender Ansatz ist das **organisationale Storytelling**. Schein (1985, S. 80) beschreibt die Wirkungsweise folgendermaßen: *„Stories and myths about how the organization dealt with key competitors in the past, how it survived a downturn in the economy, how it developed a new and exciting product, how it dealt with a valued employee, and so on, not only spell out the basic mission and specific goals (and thereby reaffirm them) but also reaffirm the organization's picture of itself, its own theory of how to get things done and how to handle internal relationships."* Storytelling kann genutzt werden, um ein Gemeinschaftsgefühl und eine gemeinsame Ausrichtung rund um das Markenidentitätskonzept zu erzeugen (Boyce 1995). Geschichten entstehen dabei nicht nur ungeplant, sondern können auch bewusst eingesetzt werden, um das Markenidentitätskonzept zu kommunizieren (Martin et al. 1983; Dennehy 1999; Denning 2004). Nike versucht, das organisationale Storytelling zu professionalisieren, indem es ausgewählte Führungskräfte zu „Corporate Storytellers" ernannt hat, die zur Aufgabe haben, Legenden zu verbreiten, die das „just do it" unterstützen (Ind 2001; Mitchell 2002, S. 158 ff.). Ebenso O2: sie stellen „can do"-Stories in ihr Intranet, die besonders gut das erwünschte Mitarbeiterverhalten beschreiben.

Obwohl unsere Hypothese ist, dass laterale Kommunikation am effektivsten ist, um Brand Commitment zu erzeugen, müssen alle drei Formen parallel eingesetzt werden, da sie einander ergänzen. Fünf Kriterien wurden in den Experteninterviews als erfolgskritisch für die interne Markenkommunikation angesehen: Zunächst muss das Unternehmen offen mit seinen Mitarbeitern kommunizieren, sodass sie sich informiert fühlen. Außerdem müssen die übermittelten Informationen klar, spezifisch und relevant für die entsprechenden Empfänger sein. Schließlich darf nicht vergessen werden, dass viel Geduld vonnöten ist: im Normalfall braucht es mehrere Kommunikationsrunden, bis die Markenidentität wirklich von den Mitarbeitern verstanden und verinnerlicht wird.

4.13 Förderung von markenorientierter Führung auf allen Ebenen

Der dritte zentrale Hebel zur Generierung von Brand Commitment ist Führung. Ohne markenorientierte Führung werden die größten Kommunikationsanstrengungen zu nichts führen, da ihnen Glaubwürdigkeit und Dringlichkeit fehlt. Grundsätzlich können zwei Ebenen der Führung unterschieden werden: Die Makro-Ebene bezieht sich auf die Rolle des CEO und der Geschäftsführung im Markenmanagement-Prozess, während es auf der Mikro-Ebene um die Mitarbeiterführung der Führungskräfte in der gesamten Organisation geht.

Auf der **Makro-Ebene** haben die Geschäftsführung und insbesondere der CEO einen großen Einfluss auf die interne wie auch die externe Markenwahrnehmung. Rolke (2004) konnte empirisch nachweisen, dass in der Außenwahrnehmung eine Korrelation zwischen dem CEO-Image und dem Corporate Brand Image besteht. Dasselbe gilt nach innen. Mitarbeiter nehmen innengerichtete Markenmanagement-Aktivitäten nur dann ernst, wenn sie durch die Worte und Taten des CEO unterstützt werden. Daher muss innengerichtetes Markenmanagement „ganz oben" ansetzen und zunächst den CEO beziehungsweise die Geschäftsführung von der Relevanz der Marke und vom Markenidentitätskonzept überzeugen, sodass sie sich als Vorbilder verhalten. Michael Maskus unterstützt dies: *„Bei der Allianz Group fühlt sich der CEO verantwortlich für die Marke."* Entsprechend wird der CEO Michael Diekmann in einem Presseartikel über die Hauptversammlung der Allianz Group mit dem Satz „Wir halten, was wir versprechen" zitiert – sehr nah am Werbeversprechen *„The power behind the promise"*.

Die Kehrseite dieser herausgehobenen **Rolle des CEO** ist, dass wenige unbedachte Worte oder Taten des CEO das Markenimage nachhaltig schädigen können. Dies geschah beispielsweise durch den Deutsche Bank CEO Josef Ackermann, der als Angeklagter im Mannesmann-Prozess vor dem Gerichtssaal ein von der Presse als sehr arrogant wahrgenommenes Verhalten zeigte. Eine weitere Gefahr liegt darin, dass die Markenidentität so abhängig von der Persönlichkeit des CEO werden kann, dass sie nach einem Wechsel des CEO substanzlos und zu einer leeren Hülle wird. Dies war zum Beispiel bei Easyjet nach dem Abgang des charismatischen Gründers Stelios Haji-Ionnou der Fall. Deshalb ist es dringend notwendig, dass der CEO die Markenidentität stützt und nicht umgekehrt. Ein CEO mit Charisma und innerer Stärke kann die Markenidentität stärken, jedoch nur, wenn er bereit ist, seine Persönlichkeit der Markenidentität unterzuordnen (Pälike 2000). Josef Hattig, früherer CEO der Brauerei Beck & Co. formuliert dies so: *„Ist die Marke der Boss oder der Boss die Marke?* [...] *Der Verbraucher spricht mit der Marke, nicht mit dem Unternehmen und so ist auch die eingangs gestellte Frage beantwortet: Die Marke ist der Boss!"*

Auf der **Mikro-Ebene** muss jede Führungskraft ebenso ein Vorbild für das Leben der Markenidentität sein. Gemäß der **sozialen Lerntheorie** (Bandura 1977) lernen Menschen neue Einstellungen und Verhaltensweisen insbesondere durch Beobachtung der Verhaltensweisen anderer. Sie lernen durch die Imitation dieser Verhaltensweisen oder durch die Beobachtung der Konsequenzen. Soziales Lernen kann als informeller Teil des Sozialisationsprozesses interpretiert werden, durch den die Mitarbeiter die Markenidentität übernehmen. Zusätzlich zur Vorbildfunktion kann angenommen werden, dass bestimmte Arten von Führungsverhalten eher zu einem hohen Brand Commitment führen als andere. Das Führungsverhalten, welches aus unserer Sicht am effektivsten zur Generierung von hohem Brand Commitment ist, wird am besten durch die Theorie der transformationalen Führung von Burns (1978) und Bass (1985) beschrieben.

Transformationale Führung in Bezug auf die Markenidentität kann verstanden werden als Verhaltensweisen, die die Wertesysteme und Ambitionen der einzelnen Mitarbeiter so beeinflussen, dass sie ihre eigenen Interessen hinter die Markenziele zurückstellen (Yukl 1989). Sie ergänzt transaktionale Führung, die auf sozialen Tauschprozessen aufbaut und höchstwahrscheinlich nur schwaches Brand Commitment auf Basis von Fügsamkeit verursacht. Transformationale Führung hingegen hat signifikant positiven Einfluss auf organisationales Commitment und OCB (Podsakoff/Mackenzie/Bommer 1996). Es wird auch vermutet, das sie organisationale Identifikation fördert (Mael/Ashforth 1992, S. 117), sodass wir annehmen, dass durch diese Art der Führung Brand Commitment basierend auf Identifikation erzeugt werden kann.

In quantitativen Untersuchungen konnte Bass (1985) vier Faktoren identifizieren, die charakteristisch für transformationale Führer sind: **Charisma, Inspiration, intellektuelle Stimulation und individuelle Aufmerksamkeit**. Charismatische Führungskräfte zeigen eine Vision und den großen Zusammenhang auf, schaffen Stolz bei ihren Mitarbeitern und gewinnen Respekt und Vertrauen von ihnen. Inspiration drückt sich darin aus, dass Führungskräfte hohe Erwartungen kommunizieren, Symbole nutzen, um die Anstrengungen zu fokussieren und dass sie wichtige Ziele in einfacher Art und Weise kommunizieren. Führungskräfte sind dann intellektuell stimulierend, wenn sie Intelligenz, Rationalität und sorgfältige Problemlösungen fördern. Individuelle Aufmerksamkeit geben sie ihren Mitarbeitern, indem sie jeden Mitarbeiter individuell behandeln ihn coachen und ihm persönliche Ratschläge geben.

Die ersten zwei Faktoren wurden auch von den interviewten Experten als Erfolgsfaktoren mehrfach ungefragt genannt, während die Bedeutung der anderen beiden Faktoren für das innengerichtete Markenmanagement noch unklar ist. Alle vier Faktoren können in Executive Trainings und durch Coaching erlernt werden, sogar Charisma (Bass 1990, S. 27 ff.; Gardner/Avolio 1998; Nerdinger/von Rosenstiel 1999). Mehrere Praxisexperten betonen im Zusammenhang mit Führung im innengerichteten Markenmanagement auch die Notwendigkeit des **Empowerments** von Mitarbeitern, das sich sehr gut mit transformationaler Führung verbinden lässt, jedoch nach Bass keine Voraussetzung ist (Bass 1990, S. 23 f.). Empowerment passt zu unserem theoretischen Modell, da Mitarbeiter mit Brand Commitment basierend auf Identifikation und Internalisierung mehr Gestaltungsfreiraum haben können und müssen als solche, die nur ein geringes Brand Commitment auf Basis von Fügsamkeit haben.

4.2 Abstimmung der Kontextfaktoren: Kultur- und Struktur-Fit

Die drei Hebel markenorientierte HR-Aktivitäten, Markenkommunikation und markenorientierte Führung resultieren nur dann in einem hohen Brand Commitment, wenn die Unternehmenskultur und -struktur auf das Markenidentitätskonzept abgestimmt sind. Unter Unternehmenskultur ist die Gesamtheit gemeinsamer Grundannahmen, Werte und Normen zu verstehen, die von den Unternehmensmitgliedern geteilt und auf neue Mitglieder übertragen werden sowie Denken und Verhalten der Unternehmensmitglieder prägen (Schein 1985; Heinen/Dill 1990, S. 17). Aufgrund ihres starken Einflusses auf die Einstellungen und Verhaltensweisen der Mitarbeiter, ist ein **Markenidentitäts-Kultur-Fit** von entscheidender Bedeutung für den Erfolg des innengerichteten Markenmanagements (Scholz 1987; Piercy/Peattie 1988; de Chernatony 1999; Hatch/Schultz 2001). Bestünde dieser Fit nicht, würde die Markenidentität von den Mitarbeitern nicht akzeptiert. Eine starke Markenidentität, die von den Mitarbeitern gelebt wird, basiert daher immer auf Werten, die kongruent zu denen der Unternehmenskultur sind.

Dies bedeutet, dass die Unternehmenskultur schon bei der Entwicklung der Markenidentität berücksichtigt werden muss. Generell fördert eine starke Unternehmenskultur die Konsistenz der Markenidentität aufgrund ihres informellen Koordinationseinflusses (O'Reilly/Chatman 1996). Sollte ein Misfit zwischen der angestrebten Markenidentität und der Unternehmenskultur entdeckt werden, bestehen drei Möglichkeiten (Schwartz/Davis 1981): Anpassung der Markenidentität, Management um die Kultur herum oder Anpassung der Kultur. Die erste Option ist die einfachste und wird in der Regel die sinnvollste sein. Da die Unternehmenskultur die Markenhistorie und -herkunft widerspiegelt, garantiert diese Option die Kontinuität in der Entwicklung der Markenidentität. Das Management um die Kultur herum kann unter bestimmten Umständen sinnvoll sein. DaimlerChrysler hat beispielsweise für die Marke Smart eine komplett neue Organisation geschaffen, da die angestrebte Markenidentität von Smart nicht zur Mercedes-Kultur gepasst hätte. In manchen Fällen ist es notwendig, eine Kulturanpassung zu versuchen, zum Beispiel wenn die Kultur über einen langen Zeitraum unverändert geblieben ist, während sich Kundenbedürfnisse und die Positionierung der Wettbewerber gewandelt haben.

Eine Anpassung der Unternehmenskultur ist jedoch sehr schwierig, da sie aus sozialer Interaktion entsteht und durch das Management nicht vollständig kontrollierbar ist. Ein manchmal propagiertes „Kulturmanagement" ist daher nur begrenzt möglich; Kultur kann höchstens aktiv beeinflusst werden (Lundberg 1985; Nord 1985). Dies bringt es mit sich, dass eine Anpassung der Unternehmenskultur ein langwieriger Prozess ist, der viel Geduld erfordert. Es gibt aus unserer Sicht zwei vielversprechende Ansätze für die zielgerichtete Beeinflussung der Unternehmenskultur. Der Ansatz des **symbolischen Managements** (Berg 1985; Trice/Beyer 1985; Homburg/Pflesser 1999) macht sich die Tatsache zunutze, dass Kultur in einem zirkulären Prozess entsteht (Hatch 1993). Symbole sind sichtbare Ausprägungen von Bedeutungszusammenhängen, die durch kulturspezifische Regeln bestimmt werden. Sie sind auf der einen Seite Ergebnis von Unternehmenskultur, auf der anderen Seite beeinflussen sie die Unternehmenskultur durch ihre Interpretation. Durch die bewusste Kreation von neuen Symbolen oder durch Veränderung bestehender Symbole kann Kultur verändert werden. Gemäß Homburg und Pflesser (1999) gehören Erzählungen, Sprache, Rituale sowie Architektur/Bürogestaltung in diesem Sinne zu typischen Symbolen. Der **Counter-Cultures-Ansatz** von v. d. Oelsnitz (2000) basiert auf der Beobachtung, dass sich unterhalb der Unternehmenskultur üblicherweise Subkulturen bilden. Er schlägt vor, insbesondere die Subkulturen zu fördern, die näher an der angestrebten Markenidentität liegen als die Unternehmenskultur. Nach einer gewissen Zeit verändert sich durch den Einfluss der Subkultur dann die Gesamtunternehmenskultur in die gewünschte Richtung.

Die **Unternehmensstrukturen** sind der zweite Kontextfaktor, der angepasst werden muss. Unternehmensstrukturen umfassen Anreizsysteme, Infrastruktur und Organisationsstruktur. Der erste Schritt der Anpassung von **Anreizsystemen** besteht darin sicherzustellen, dass sie den gewünschten markenidentitätskonsistenten Verhaltensweisen nicht widersprechen (Kerr/Slocum Jr. 1987). Um explizit bestimmte erwünschte Verhaltensweisen zu fördern, können diese als Vorgabe in Zielvereinbarungen übernommen werden, sodass sie überwacht und bei erfolgreicher Umsetzung entsprechend belohnt werden können. Da Mitarbeiter ihr Brand Commitment nur dann in Brand Citizenship Behavior umsetzen können, wenn sie über die notwendigen Ressourcen und entsprechendes Know-how verfügen, müssen eine geeignete **Informationsinfrastruktur, Planungs-, Budgetierungs- und Controlling-Systeme** vorhanden sein.

Außerdem können Mitarbeiter nur dann Brand Citizenship Behavior zeigen, wenn sie über die entsprechenden Entscheidungskompetenzen und organisatorische Unterstützung verfügen. Daher muss die **Organisationsstruktur** die Markenidentität unterstützen. Schwierigkeiten in diesem Bereich entstehen insbesondere in Unternehmen mit mehreren **Divisionen**, die integrierte Produkte oder Dienstleistungen liefern sollen. Bei der Deutschen Telekom beispielsweise war die Autonomie der vier Divisionen dazu gedacht, den internen Wettbewerb zu fördern. Sie führte jedoch zu erheblichen Service-Problemen, da Verantwortlichkeiten für Kunden und Kompetenzen nicht klar abgegrenzt waren. Vor dem Hintergrund dieser markenschädigenden Probleme hat der Vorstand nun mehrere divisionsübergreifende Initiativen eingerichtet und arbeitet an einer neuen, stärker markenzentrierten Organisationsstruktur. Die Probleme divisionaler Organisationsstrukturen sind umso gravierender, wenn es sich bei den Divisionen um vormals eigenständige Unternehmen mit eigener Marke und Kultur handelt, die durch Akquisitionen oder Fusionen zu einer Division unter einer Marke geworden sind, wie es zum Beispiel bei der Allianz Group der Fall ist. Ganz anders sieht die Situation aus, wenn die Divisionen ihre eigene Marke haben. Dann sollten sie bewusst getrennt werden, um ihre eigene Markenidentität ausbilden zu können, ohne jedoch auf mögliche Synergien zu verzichten. Die BMW Group hat dies Anfang 2004 umgesetzt, indem sie ihren Marken BMW, Mini und Rolls-Royce mehr Autonomie im Markenmanagement gegeben hat (o. V. 2003a).

Eine weitere organisatorische Herausforderung liegt in der Einbindung **externer Partner** in das innengerichtete Markenmanagement. Dies ist besonders wichtig, wenn Kundenkontaktpersonal, beispielsweise Call Center Mitarbeiter, ausgelagert sind. Ein hohes Brand Commitment zu erreichen ist für einen externen Call Center Mitarbeiter oft schwierig, da die emotionale Distanz zur Markenorganisation in der Regel hoch ist. Vodafone hat dieses Problem vermieden, indem sie ihr Call Center intern belassen haben. Christian Böing, Head of Proposition Management Vodafone Office sagt dazu: *„Unsere Call Center Agenten repräsentieren die Marke, also möchten wir die besten Mitarbeiter haben, die committed sind und die Art, wie Vodafone denkt, leben. Wenn bei denen eine Frage auftaucht, die sie nicht beantworten können, ist es wirklich so, dass sie sich innerhalb von drei Stunden durch die ganze Organisation gewühlt haben und den Kunden mit einer Lösung zurückrufen, der dann völlig überrascht von der Kompetenz des Mitarbeiters ist."*

Die Organisationsstruktur muss nicht nur die Markenidentität stützen, das innengerichtete Markenmanagement selber braucht eine Verankerung in der Organisationsstruktur, das heißt eine **Institutionalisierung**. Dies beginnt auf der obersten Ebene der Organisation. Wenn einer der Geschäftsführer beziehungsweise Vorstände, idealerweise der CEO, die formale Verantwortung für die Marke übernimmt, signalisiert dies die Bedeutung des Markenmanagements. Da die Hebel des innengerichteten Markenmanagements verschiedene organisationale Funktionen betreffen, kann die operationale Koordination der Aktivitäten weder allein bei der Marketing- noch bei der HR-Abteilung liegen. Eine Projektorganisation ist ebenso wenig geeignet, da innengerichtetes Markenmanagement eine kontinuierliche Aufgabe ist. Ein vielversprechender Ansatz scheint die Einrichtung eines **„Executive Brand Council"** zu sein, der alle funktionalen und divisionalen Vorstände umfasst und der regelmäßig zusammenkommt, um innen- und außengerichtete Markenmanagement-Themen zu diskutieren und Entscheidungen zu treffen. Ein solcher Council arbeitet erfolgreich bei 3M und Kodak (Dunn/Davis 2003a; Dunn/Davis 2003b) und wurde kürzlich auch bei Opel (Elsen 2002) und der Deutschen Bahn eingeführt.

Innengerichtetes Markenmanagement kann auf dezentraler Ebene durch die Ernennung von **„Brand Ambassadors“** in jeder Division und jedem geografischen Standort unterstützt werden. Sie fungieren als Multiplikatoren, die die Markenidentität an ihre Kollegen kommunizieren und sie zu aktivem Engagement anregen. Sie geben der Zentrale Empfehlungen in Bezug auf Markenthemen und tauschen in schriftlicher Form oder bei Treffen mit anderen Brand Ambassadors Best Practices aus (Ind 2001, S. 124). SIEMENS hat dieses Konzept angewendet. Bei diesem großen, diversifizierten Unternehmen mit über 400.000 Mitarbeitern in circa 600 Tochterunternehmen und 190 Ländern hat es sich als zielführend erwiesen.

5. Fazit

In diesem Beitrag wurde ein Modell für das innengerichtete Markenmanagement vorgestellt, das auf der Forschung zum organisationalen Verhalten und auf der Beobachtung von Best Practices in Unternehmen basiert. Ausgangspunkt unseres Beitrages sind starke Marken. Die Stärke einer Marke beruht auf der Konsistenz aller Markenerlebnisse der Kunden entlang aller Kontaktpunkte mit der Marke. Diese Konsistenz kann nur dann sichergestellt werden, wenn alle Mitarbeiter Brand Citizenship Behavior zeigen, das durch ein starkes individuelles Brand Commitment hervorgerufen wird.

Die hier erarbeiteten Erkenntnisse zum innengerichteten identitätsorientierten Markenmanagement sollen abschließend in Form einer Metapher zusammengefasst werden. Marken werden dabei als Regatta-Segelboote (inklusive Besatzung) interpretiert. Erfolgreich ist ein Segelboot bei einer Regatta dann, wenn es die Winde besser auszunutzen vermag, als die Konkurrenz. Hierzu braucht die Besatzung in der Vertikalen einen stabilen Mast, in der Horizontalen einen stabilen Mastbaum. Dem innengerichteten identitätsorientierten Markenmanagement geht es ebenso. **Es ist nur dann erfolgreich, wenn es die vertikale mit der horizontalen Führungsdimension verbindet** (vgl. Abbildung 3).

Die vertikale Dimension umfasst die Entwicklung der verschiedenen Identitätskomponenten mit fester Verankerung im Bootsrumpf, die hier als Unternehmenshistorie und -kultur interpretiert werden kann. Die horizontale Dimension das erfolgreiche Transportieren der Markenidentität in die „Köpfe und Bäuche“ aller Mitarbeiter. Damit steht dann Mast und Mastbaum einer starken Marke, in die dann der Wind hineingreifen kann um die Marke nach vorne zu schieben.

Abbildung 3: **Metapher eines erfolgreichen innengerichteten identitätsorientierten Markenmanagements**

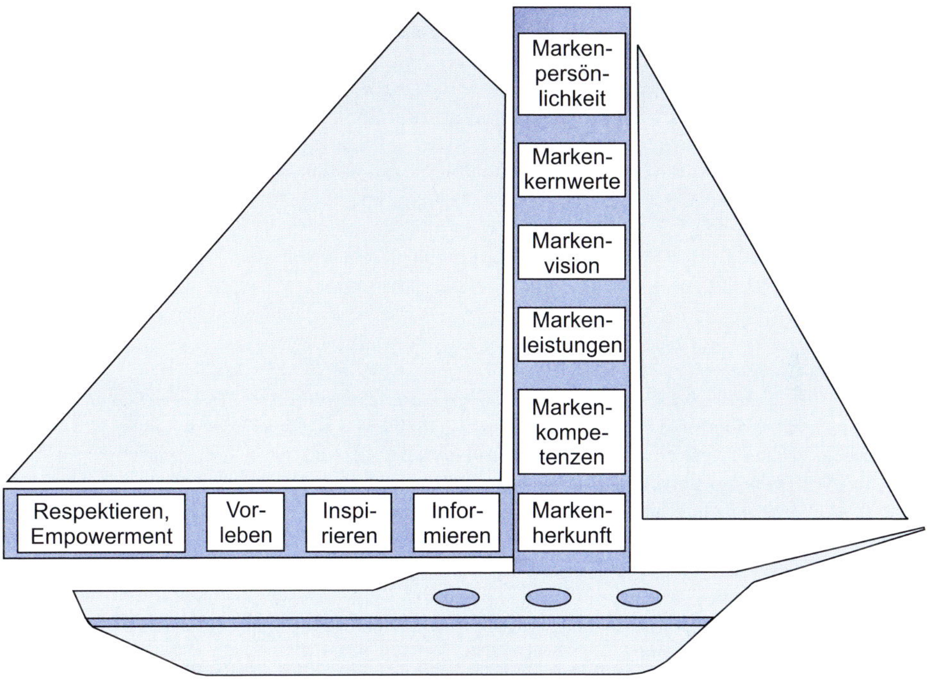

Der differenzierteren Ausgestaltung der horizontalen Dimension haben wir uns im vierten Kapitel dieses Beitrags ausführlich gewidmet. Zwei Aspekte sind in diesem Beitrag nicht betrachtet worden, die für die erfolgreiche Umsetzung des innengerichteten Markenmanagements jedoch unerlässlich sind: der Ablauf der einmaligen **Implementierung** eines innengerichteten Markenmanagements und das kontinuierliche **Controlling**. Ihre Ausgestaltung wird im Rahmen eines laufenden Dissertationsprojektes der Co-Autorin untersucht.

Literatur

Adams, J. S. (1965), Inequity in Social Exchange, in: Berkowitz, L. (Hrsg.), Advances in Experimental Psychology, New York, S. 267–299.
Albert, S., Eshforth, B. E., Dutton, J. E. (2000), Organizational Identity and Identification: Charting New Waters and Building New Bridges, in: Academy of Management Review, Jg. 25 (1), S. 13–17.
Allen, N. J., Meyer, J. P. (1990a), The Measurement and Antecedents of Affective, Continuance and Normative Commitment to the Organization, in: Journal of Occupational Psychology, Jg. 63, S. 1–18.
Allen, N. J., Meyer, J. P. (1990b), Organizational Socialization Tactics: A Longitudinal Analysis of Links to Newcomers' Commitment and Role Orientation, in: Academy of Management Journal, Jg. 33 (4), S. 847–858.
Allen, N. J., Meyer, J. P. (1996), Affective, Continuance, and Normative Commitment to the Organization: An Examination of Construct Validity, in: Journal of Vocational Behavior, Jg. 49, S. 252–276.
Ashforth, B. E., Mael, F. (1989), Social Identity Theory and the Organization, in: Academy of Management Review, Jg. 14 (1), S. 20–39.
Ashforth, B. E., Saks, A. M. (1996), Socialization Tactics: Longitudinal Effects on Newcomer Adjustment, in: Academy of Management Journal, Jg. 39 (1), S. 149–178.
Bandura, A. (1977), Social learning theory, Englewood Cliffs, NJ.
Bass, B. M. (1985), Leadership and Performance Beyond Expectations, New York.
Bass, B. M. (1990), From Transactional to Transformational Leadership: Learning to Share the Vision, in: Organizational Dynamics, Jg. 18 (Winter), S. 19–31.
Bedbury, S. (2003), A New Brand World: 8 Principles for Achieving Brand Leadership in the 21st Century, New York.
Berg, P.-O. (1985), Organization Change as a Symbolic Transformation Process, in: Frost, P. J. et al. (Hrsg.), Organizational Culture, Beverly Hills, S. 281–299.
Boyce, M. E. (1995), Collective Centring and Collective Sense-making in the Stories and Storytelling of One Organization, in: Organization Studies, Jg. 16 (1), S. 107–137.
Brexendorf, T. O., Tomczak, T. (2004), Interne Markenführung, in: Albers, S. et al. (Hrsg.), Verkauf – Kundenmanagement, Vertriebssteuerung, E-Commerce, Digitale Fachbibliothek, Sektion 03.15 Personal und Führung, Düsseldorf,
Burmann, Ch. (2004), Marken brauchen Führung, in: Gesellschaft zur Erforschung des Markenwesens e.V. (G.E.M.) (Hrsg.), Marke: Erfolgsfaktor auch in Zukunft, Wiesbaden, S. 75–93.
Burmann, Ch., Blinda, L., Nitschke, A. (2003), Konzeptionelle Grundlagen des identitätsbasierten Markenmanagements, Arbeitspapier Nr. 1, Lehrstuhl für innovatives Markenmanagement, Universität Bremen.
Burns, J. M. (1978), Leadership, New York.
Chatman, J. A. (1989), Improving Interactional Organizational Research: A Model of Person-Organization-Fit, in: The Academy of Management Review, Jg. 14 (3), S. 333–349.
Chatman, J. A. (1991), Matching People and Organizations: Selection and Socialization in Public Accounting Firms, in: Administrative Science Quarterly, Jg. 36 (3), S. 459–484.
Craik, L. (2000), Left behind in the race for style and value, in: The Guardian vom 16. Juni 2000.
de Chernatony, L. (1999), Brand Management Through Narrowing the Gap Between Brand Identity and Brand Reputation, in: Journal of Marketing Management, Jg. 15 (1-3), S. 157–179.
Dennehy, R. F. (1999), The Executive as Storyteller, in: Management Review, Jg. 88 (March), S. 40–43.
Denning, S. (2004), Telling Tales, in: Harvard Business Review, Jg. 82 (5), S. 122–129.

Dierks, B. (2004), Konservativer Modernisierer, in: Financial Times Deutschland vom 8. Juni 2004.
Dunn, M., Davis, S. (2003a), Building Brands from the Inside, in: Marketing Management, Jg. 22 (May/June), S. 32–37.
Dunn, M., Davis, S. (2003b), 'Operationalizing' the Brand: Bringing It to Life Internally Strengthens Brand and Business, in: The Business to Business Marketer, Jg. 8 (8), S. 1–3.
Elsen, M. (2002), Vollgas mit Handbremse, in: W&V, Jg. 40 (Oktober), S. 24–28.
Esch, F.-R., Vallaster, C. (2004), Mitarbeiter zu Marken-Botschaftern machen, in: Markenartikel, Jg. 66 (2), S. 8–12; 46–47.
Farrell, D., Rusbult, C. (1981), Exchange Variables as Predictors of Job Satisfaction, Job Commitment, and Turnover: the Impact of Rewards, Costs, Alternatives and Investments, in: Organizational Behavior and Human Performance, Jg. 28, S. 78–95.
Frey, H.-P., Haußer, K. (1987), Entwicklungslinien sozialwissenschaftlicher Identitätsforschung, in: Frey, H.-P./Haußer, K. (Hrsg.), Identität: Entwicklungen psychologischer und soziologischer Forschung, Stuttgart, S. 3–26.
Gardner, W. L., Avolio, B. J. (1998), The Charismatic Relationship: A Dramaturgical Perspective, in: Academy of Management Review, Jg. 23 (1), S. 32–58.
Gummesson, E. (1987), The New Marketing – Developing Long-Term Interactive Relationships, in: Long Range Planning, Jg. 20 (4), S. 10.
Hatch, M. J. (1993), The Dynamics of Organizational Culture, in: Academy of Management Review, Jg. 18 (4), S. 657–693.
Hatch, M. J., Schultz, M. (2001), Are the Strategic Stars Aligned for Your Corporate Brand?, in: Harvard Business Review, Jg. 79 (2), S. 128–132.
Heinen, E., Dill, P. (1990), Unternehmenskultur aus betriebswirtschaftlicher Sicht, in: Simon, H. (Hrsg.), Herausforderung Unternehmenskultur, Stuttgart, S. 12–24.
Homburg, C., Pflesser, C. (1999), „Symbolisches Management" als Schlüssel zur Marktorientierung: Neue Erkenntnisse zur Unternehmenskultur, Arbeitspapier Nr. M43, Institut für Marktorientierte Unternehmensführung; Universität Mannheim.
Ind, N. (1998), An Integrated Approach to Corporate Branding, in: Journal of Brand Management, Jg. 5 (5), S. 323–329.
Ind, N. (2001), Living the Brand: How to Transform Every Member of Your Organization into a Brand Champion, London.
Ind, N. (2003), Inside Out: How Employees Build Value, in: Journal of Brand Management, Jg. 10 (6), S. 393–402.
Joachimsthaler, E. (2002), Commitment: Mitarbeiter – Die vergessene Zielgruppe für Markenerfolge, in: Absatzwirtschaft, Jg. 50 (11), S. 28–34.
Keller, K. L. (1999), Brand Mantras: Rationale, Criteria and Examples, in: Journal of Marketing Management, Jg. 15, S. 43–51.
Kelman, H. C. (1958), Compliance, Identification, and Internalization: Three Processes of Attitude Change, in: Journal of Conflict Resolution, Jg. 2 (1), S. 51–60.
Kerr, J., Slocum Jr., J. W. (1987), Managing Corporate Culture Through Reward Systems, in: Academy of Management Executive, Jg. 1 (2), S. 99–108.
Klein, H. J., Weaver, N. A. (2000), The Effectiveness of an Organizational-level Orientation Training Program in the Socialization of New Hires, in: Personnel Psychology, Jg. 53 (1), S. 47–66.
Kohlbrück, O. (2004), C&A macht alles besser – Textilkette formuliert Sprichwort zum aktuellen Claim um, in: Horizont vom 20 Mai 2004.
Leonard, N. H., Beauvais, L. L., Scholl, R. W. (1999), Work Motivation: The Incorporation of Self-Concept-Based Processes, in: Human Relations, Jg. 52 (8), S. 969–998.
Lundberg, C. C. (1985), On the Feasibility of Cultural Intervention in Organizations, in: Frost, P. J. et al. (Hrsg.), Organizational Culture, Beverly Hills, S. 169–185.

Machatschke, M. (2004), Imageprofile: Olympiade der Konzerne, Manager Magazin, http://www.managermagazin.de/unternehmen/imageprofile/0,2828,282735,00.html.
Mael, F. A., Ashforth, B. E. (1992), Alumni and Their Alma Mater: A Partial Test of the Reformulated Model of Organizational Identification, in: Journal of Organizational Behavior, Jg. 13, S. 103–123.
Martin, J., Feldman, M. S., Hatch, M. J., Sitkin, S. B. (1983), The Uniqueness Paradox in Organizational Stories, in: Administrative Science Quarterly, Jg. 28 (3), S. 438–453.
Mathieu, J. E., Zajac, D. M. (1990), A Review and Meta-Analysis or the Antecedents, Correlates and Consequences of Organizational Commitment, in: Psychological Bulletin, Jg. 108 (2), S. 171–194.
Mayrhofer, W., Strunk, G., Meyer, M. (2003), Gruppenidentität, in: Martin, A. (Hrsg.), Organizational Behaviour – Verhalten in Organisationen, Stuttgart, S. 197–209.
MCA Communicates (1999), The Brand Ambassador Benchmark: A survey of staff attitudes and behaviours and their impact on customer loyalty.
Mitchell, C. (2002), Selling the Brand Inside, in: Harvard Business Review, Jg. 80 (1), S. 99–105.
MORI (1999), Consumers Voting With Their Feet: Nearly One in Six Say Poor Dealings with Staff Put Them Off from Purchasing, http://www.mori.com/polls/1999/mca99.shtml.
Mowday, R. T., Deers, R. M., Porter, L. W. (1979), The Measurement of Organizational Commitment, in: Journal of Vocational Behavior, Jg. 14, S. 224–247.
Nerdinger, F. W., von Rosenstiel, L. (1999), Die Umgestaltung der Führungsstrukturen im Rahmen der Implementierung des Internen Marketing, in: Bruhn, M. (Hrsg.), Internes Marketing: Integration der Kunden- und Mitarbeiterorientierung; Grundlagen – Implementierung – Praxisbeispiele, 2., überarb. und erw. Aufl., Wiesbaden, S. 175–190.
Nord, W. R. (1985), Can Organizational Culture Be Managed?, in: Frost, P. J. et al. (Hrsg.), Organizational Culture, Beverly Hills, S. 187–196.
o.V. (2003a), BMW gibt seinen Automarken mehr Eigenständigkeit, in: Berliner Zeitung vom 20. November 2003.
o.V. (2003b), Keine Fortschritte im Service: Kunden fühlen sich durch Unternehmen nicht angemessen behandelt, in: Frankfurter Allgemeine Zeitung vom 10. November 2003.
o.V. (2004), Das Missverständnis Marke, in: Frankfurter Allgemeine Zeitung vom 12. Juli 2004.
O'Reilly, C. A., Chatman, J. A. (1986), Organizational Commitment and Psychological Attachment: the Effects of Compliance, Identification; and Internalization on Prosocial Behavior, in: Journal of Applied Psychology, Jg. 71, S. 492–499.
O'Reilly, C. A., Chatman, J. A. (1996), Culture as Social Control: Corporations, Cults and Commitment, in: Research in Organizational Behavior, Jg. 18, S. 157–200.
O'Reilly, C. A., Chatman, J. A., Caldwell, D. S. (1991), People and Organizational Culture: A Profile Comparison Approach to Assessing Person-Organization Fit, in: The Academy of Management Journal, Jg. 34 (4), S. 487–516.
Organ, D. W. (1988), Organizational Citizenship Behavior: The Good Soldier Syndrome, Lexington, MA.
Pälike, F. (2000), „Die Manager-Marke kommt! Persönlichkeit ist ein Added Value.“ in: Absatzwirtschaft, Jg. 43 (Sondernummer Oktober), S. 16–18.
Piercy, N. F., Peattie, K. J. (1988), Matching Marketing Strategies to Corporate Culture: The Parcel and the Wall, in: Journal of General Management, Jg. 13 (4), S. 33–44.
Podsakoff, P. M., Mackenzie, S. B., Bommer, W. H. (1996), Transformational Leader Behaviors and Substitutes for Leadership as Determinants of Employee Satisfaction, Commitment, Trust and Organizational Citizenship Behaviors, in: Journal of Management, Jg. 22 (2), S. 259-298.
Podsakoff, P. M. Mackenzie, S. B., Paine, J. B., Bachrach, B. G. (2000), Organizational Citizenship Behaviors: A Critical Review or the Theoretical and Empirical Literature and Suggestions for Future Research, in: Journal of Management, Jg. 26 (3), S. 513–563.

Rolke, L. (2004), Wie das Image von Geschäftsführern und Vorständen den Unternehmenswert beeinflusst, unveröffentlichtes Vortragsmanuskript.
Rosenberg, M. (1979), Conceiving the Self, New York.
Salancik, G. R. (1982), Commitment and the Control of Organizational Behavior and Belief, in: Staw, B. M./Salancik, G. R. (Hrsg.), New Directions in Organizational Behavior, Nachdruck (Erstausgabe 1977), Malabar, S. 1–54.
Schein, E. H. (1985), Organizational Culture and Leadership, Washington.
Scholz, C. (1987), Corporate Culture and Strategy – The Problem of Strategic Fit, in: Long Range Planning, Jg. 20 (4), S. 78–87.
Schwartz, H., Davis, S. M. (1981), Matching Corporate Culture and Business Strategy, in: Organizational Dynamics, Jg. 10 (Summer), S. 30–48.
Smith, C. A. et al. (1983), Organizational Citizenship Behavior: It's Nature and Antecedents, in: Journal of Applied Psychology, Jg. 68 (4), S. 653–663.
The Gallup Organization (2003), Das Engagement am Arbeitsplatz in Deutschland sinkt weiter, Pressemeldung vom 30. Oktober 2003
Thomson, K. et al. (1999), The Buy-in Benchmark: How Staff Understanding and Commitment Impact Brand and Business Performance, in: Journal of Marketing Management, Jg. 15 (8), S. 819–835.
Towers Perrin (2003), Working Today: Understanding What Drives Employee Engagement – The 2003 Towers Perrin Talent Report
Trice, H. M./Beyer, J. M. (1985), Using Six Organizational Rites to Change Culture, in: Kilmann, R. H. et al. (Hrsg.), Gaining Control of the Corporate Culture, San Francisco, S. 370–399.
Vallaster, C. (2004), Action Research for Studying Internal Branding, in: Buber, R. et al. (Hrsg.), Applying Qualitative Methods to Marketing Management Research, Houndmills, S. 194–205.
Vallaster, C., de Chernatony, L. (2004), Internationalisation of Service Brands: The Role of Leadership During the Internal Brand Building Process, in: Journal of Marketing Management, noch nicht erschienen.
van Maanen, J., Schein, E. H. (1979), Toward a Theory of Organizational Socialization, in: Research in Organizational Behavior, Jg. 1, S. 209–264.
von der Oelsnitz, D. (2000), Marketingimplementierung durch „Counter-Cultures", in: Marketing ZFP, Jg. 22 (2), S. 109–118.
Wittke-Kothe, C. (2001), Interne Markenführung: Verankerung der Markenidentität im Mitarbeiterverhalten, Wiesbaden
Yukl, G. (1989), Managerial Leadership: A Review of Theory and Research, in: Journal of Management, Jg. 15 (2), S. 251–289.

KAPITEL

2 Strategien des Markenmanagements

Corporate Branding – Führung der Unternehmensmarke im Spannungsfeld unterschiedlicher Zielgruppen 143
Heribert Meffert und Andreas Bierwirth

Gestaltung von Markenarchitekturen 163
Christoph Burmann und Heribert Meffert

Markenevolutionsstrategien 183
Christoph Burmann, Heribert Meffert und Lars Blinda

Mehrmarkenstrategien – identitätsorientierte Führung von Markenportfolios 213
Heribert Meffert und Jesko Perrey

Markenerweiterungsstrategien 245
Mirko Caspar und Christoph Burmann

Corporate Branding – Führung der Unternehmensmarke im Spannungsfeld unterschiedlicher Zielgruppen

Heribert Meffert und Andreas Bierwirth

1.	**Herausforderungen an das Corporate Branding**	**144**
2.	**Theoretische Grundlagen für die Führung von Unternehmensmarken**	**146**
2.1	Unternehmensmarke im Lichte des sozialpsychologischen Markenverständnisses	146
2.2	Betrachtungsperspektiven der Führung von Unternehmensmarken	147
2.21	Unternehmensmarke als Vermögensgegenstand	147
2.22	Unternehmensmarke als psychologischer Zusatznutzen	151
3.	**Implikationen für die Führung von Unternehmensmarken**	**155**
3.1	Zielgruppenspezifische Markenführung durch die Gestaltung der Markenarchitektur	155
3.2	Identitätsorientierte Markenführung als Grundkonzept zur zielgruppenübergreifenden Führung von Unternehmensmarken	158
4.	**Ausblick**	**160**

1. Herausforderungen an das Corporate Branding

Die Unternehmensmarke steht unter dem Schlagwort des „Corporate Branding“ im aktuellen Fokus der Wissenschaft und Praxis. Ursache hierfür sind ihre spezifischen Potenziale zur Profilierung einer Unternehmung vor dem Hintergrund immer komplexer werdender Herausforderungen.

Diese liegen zunächst in einer **Ausweitung des Wettbewerbs auf die Beschaffungsmärkte**. Insbesondere im Kapital- und Finanzmarkt sind Unternehmen gefordert, den auftretenden Engpässen durch eine Differenzierung vom Wettbewerb unter gleichzeitiger Herausstellung der eigenen Vorteile zu begegnen. Hierbei hat die Unternehmensmarke insofern eine profilierende Wirkung, als die bekannten Funktionen einer Marke auf die Zielgruppen in den Beschaffungsmärkten transferierbar sind (Demuth 2000, S. 14). So kann sie durch eine Entfaltung ihrer Vertrauensfunktion Aktionären eine sichere Geldanlage signalisieren oder gegenüber potenziellen Mitarbeitern als Anker für die Identifikation mit einem faszinierenden Unternehmen fungieren. Hinzu kommt ein wachsendes Interesse der Nachfrager an den hinter den einzelnen Produkten oder Leistungen stehenden Unternehmen, welche gerade durch die Unternehmensmarke abgebildet werden.

Eine besondere Herausforderung ergibt sich ferner durch die **Zunahme von Unternehmenskäufen und Fusionen**. Dabei stellt die Auswahl des Namens für das neu geschaffene Unternehmen (zum Beispiel E.ON) aufgrund der einhergehenden, hohen Signalwirkung eine zentrale Aufgabe dar (Langner/Esch 2004, S. 103). So verdeutlicht die neue Unternehmensmarke nicht nur den Charakter einer Übernahme oder Fusion, sondern lässt auch Aussagen über die zukünftige Unternehmensidentität zu. Beides kann sowohl zu erheblichen Reaktanzen als auch positiven Impulsen im Rahmen der Unternehmensintegration führen.

Ein weiterer Treiber für die hohe Bedeutung der Unternehmensmarke ist in der **Internationalisierung** vieler Unternehmen zu sehen. Insbesondere bei global agierenden Unternehmen ersetzen die durch eine Unternehmensmarke symbolisierten Eigenschaften („made by“) die bislang mit dem Herkunftsland verbundenen Erwartungen („made in“).

Schließlich führt das zunehmende Bewusstsein um den **ökonomischen Wert** einer Unternehmensmarke zu einer steigenden Relevanz für die Entscheidungen vieler Führungskräfte. So wird die Entwicklung des Markenwertes einer Unternehmensmarke als ein weiterer Bewertungsmaßstab für die Leistung des Managements herangezogen. Tabelle 1 zeigt in diesem Zusammenhang die zehn wertvollsten deutschen Unternehmensmarken exemplarisch auf.

Die Führung einer Unternehmensmarke sieht sich angesichts der skizzierten Herausforderungen vor einer wachsenden **Komplexität**. Ein wesentlicher Treiber hierfür ist die Erweiterung der Zielgruppen einer Marke vom Kreis der Nachfrager auf die Gesamtheit der unternehmerischen Anspruchsgruppen. So nimmt die Varianz der durch eine Marke zu berücksichtigenden Interessen deutlich zu. Im vorliegenden Beitrag sollen vor dem Hintergrund einer theoretischen Interpretation der Unternehmensmarke Implikationen für ihre zielgruppenorientierte Führung aufgezeigt werden.

Tabelle 1: **Markenwerte von deutschen Unternehmensmarken**

Rang	Unternehmensmarke	Markenwert 2003 (in Milliarden Euro)
1	DaimlerChrysler	25.229
2	Deutsche Telekom	20.019
3	Allianz	15.758
4	Deutsche Bank	15.719
5	Volkswagen	15.699
6	BMW	15.697
7	SIEMENS	15.370
8	RWE	10.878
9	E.ON	10.790
10	Deutsche Post	8.791

GABLER GRAFIK

Quelle: Göttgens/Leach/Wirtz 2004, S. 12

2. Theoretische Grundlagen für die Führung von Unternehmensmarken

2.1 Unternehmensmarke im Lichte des sozialpsychologischen Markenverständnisses

Aufgrund des hohen Interesses an der Unternehmensmarke, insbesondere in populärwissenschaftlichen Veröffentlichungen, ist die Fragmentierung des Begriffsverständnisses zur Unternehmensmarke wenig verwunderlich. Tabelle 2 zeigt beispielhaft die Vielfalt existierender Definitionen einer Unternehmensmarke. Daher ist es notwendig, zunächst eine definitorische Abgrenzung des Untersuchungsgegenstandes vorzunehmen. Ausgangspunkt ist eine Zerlegung der Unternehmensmarke in ihre beiden semantischen Bestandteile des „Unternehmens" und der „Marke".

Die Marke ist *„ein Nutzenbündel mit spezifischen Merkmalen, die dafür sorgen, dass sich dieses Nutzenbündel gegenüber anderen Nutzenbündeln, welche dieselben Basisbedürfnisse erfüllen, aus Sicht relevanter Zielgruppen nachhaltig differenziert"* (Burmann/Blinda/Nitschke 2003, S. 3). Auch die Corporate Brand kann ein solches Nutzenbündel darstellen und somit Markencharakter aufweisen. Allerdings bezieht sich dies nicht allein auf die angebotenen Produkte oder Dienstleistungen, sondern auf die Unternehmung als Ganzes.

Tabelle 2: **Unterschiedliche Definitionsansätze der Unternehmensmarke**

Autor	Definitionen der Unternehmensmarke
Merbold (1994)	Symbolische Verdichtung von Unternehmenskultur und -identität
Ind (1997)	Beziehung zwischen Unternehmen und Anspruchsgruppen
Halliday (1998)	Informationsträger unternehmensbezogener Werte
Heinlein (1999)	Zusammenfall von Unternehmensname und Marke

GABLER GRAFIK

In diesem Zusammenhang ist eine Unternehmung als „zielgerichtetes Sozialsystem" aufzufassen und koalitionstheoretisch interpretierbar. So besteht die Zusammensetzung eines solchen Systems aus freiwilligen, zielorientierten Zusammenschlüssen mehrerer Personen oder Gruppen, die auch als Anspruchsgruppen eines Unternehmens aufzufassen sind (Cyert/March 1963, S. 17). Der Begriff der Unternehmensmarke beziehungsweise deren anglizistisches Synonym der Corporate Brand erfordert kein neues Begriffsverständnis. Es handelt sich bei ihr letztlich um eine „normale" Marke. Der Unterschied zu beispielsweise einer Produktmarke liegt lediglich im Objekt der Markierung, welches im Falle der Unternehmensmarke die Unternehmung in ihrer Gesamtheit ist. Daher kann eine Unternehmensmarke wie folgt definiert werden:

Eine Unternehmensmarke ist „ein **gesamtunternehmerisches** Nutzenbündel mit spezifischen Merkmalen, die dafür sorgen, dass sich dieses Nutzenbündel gegenüber anderen **gesamtunternehmerischen** Nutzenbündeln, welche dieselben Basisbedürfnisse erfüllen, aus Sicht relevanter Zielgruppen nachhaltig differenziert".

Hiervon ist der Begriff des **„Corporate Branding"** abzugrenzen. Während Kircher Corporate Branding allein auf die Vergabe des Unternehmensnamens für bestimmte Subjekte, Objekte oder Leistungen beschränkt, wird an dieser Stelle mit Corporate Branding die **Führung der Unternehmensmarke** gekennzeichnet (Kircher 1997, S. 60 f.). Diese stellt einen Prozess dar, welcher die Phasen der zielgerichteten Planung, Koordination und Kontrolle aller Aktivitäten beziehungsweise Gestaltungsparameter der Unternehmensmarke beinhaltet.

2.2 Betrachtungsperspektiven der Führung von Unternehmensmarken

Die Formulierung von Zielen für die Führung einer Unternehmensmarke wird in hohem Maße durch die jeweils eingenommene Betrachtungsperspektive determiniert. So ist eine Unternehmensmarke einerseits als Vermögenswert oder transferierbares Vermögensrecht anzusehen. Im Fokus dieser Betrachtung steht somit ihr ökonomischer Wert. Ferner kann sie als sozialpsychologisches Phänomen verstanden werden, welches den relevanten Zielgruppen einen Zusatznutzen stiftet. Beide Perspektiven stehen in einem Ursache-Wirkungs-Verhältnis: der psychologische Zusatznutzen ist wesentliche Grundlage für die Entstehung des ökonomischen Wertes.

2.21 Unternehmensmarke als Vermögensgegenstand

Mit dem ökonomischen Wert einer Unternehmensmarke geht die Maximierung des **Markenwertes** und damit letztlich die Maximierung des **Customer Equity** als entsprechendes Oberziel ihrer Führung einher (vgl. den Beitrag zur Bewertung und Bilanzierung von Marken in diesem Buch). Er ist Ausgangspunkt für die Bewertung aller Maßnahmen zur

Abbildung 1 : **Zielgruppenspezifische Wertbeiträge zum Markenwert einer Unternehmensmarke**

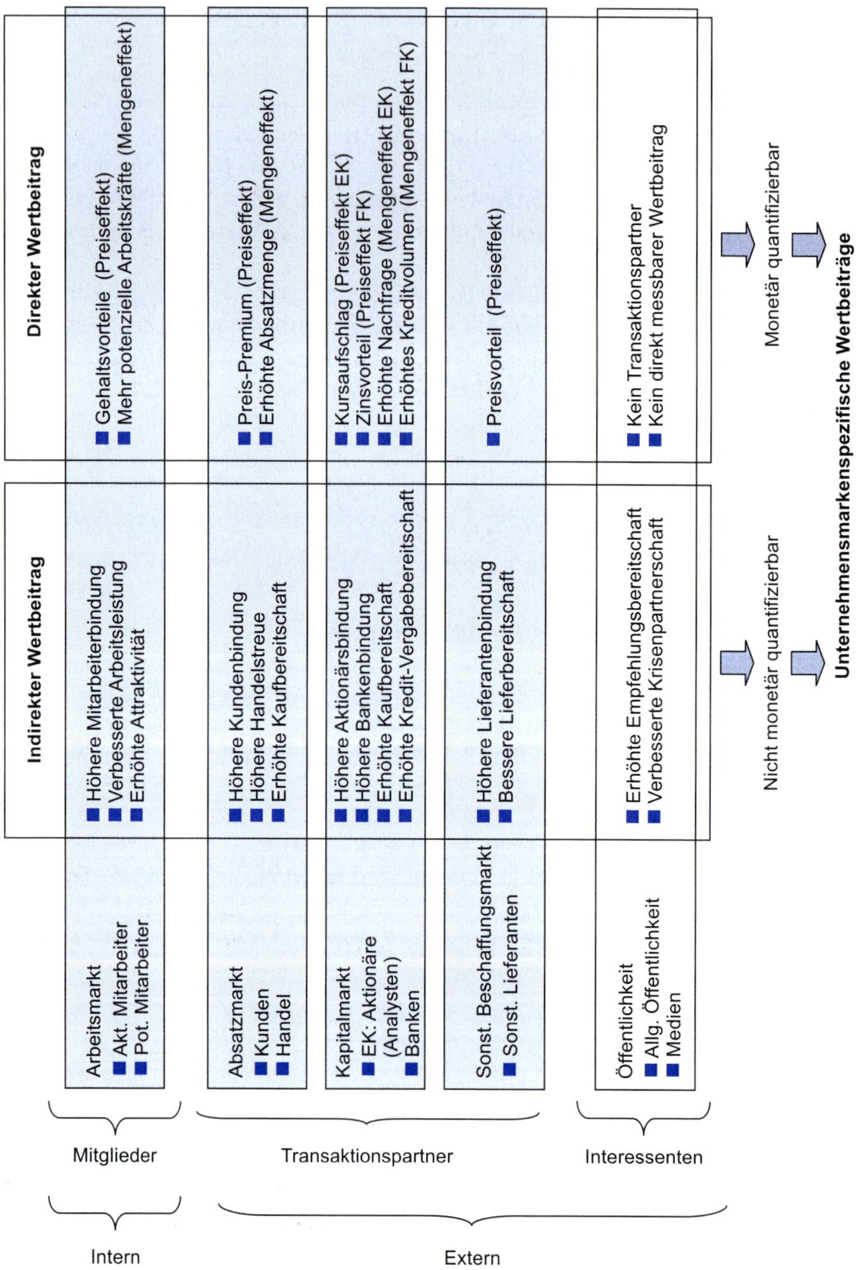

GABLER GRAFIK

Quelle: Meffert/Bierwirth 2001, S. 6

Gestaltung der Unternehmensmarke. Wenngleich die valide Messung des Markenwertes bereits bei Produktmarken methodisch mit großen Schwierigkeiten verbunden ist, eignen sich die mit ihm verbundenen Gedanken zur Ableitung einer entsprechenden Führungsphilosophie. Diese wird seit einigen Jahren unter dem Begriff der „wertorientierten Markenführung" herausgestellt (Jenner 2001, S. 145 ff.; Sattler 2001, S. 60 ff.).

Die Besonderheit des Markenwertes einer Unternehmensmarke im Vergleich zu beispielsweise einer Produktmarke resultiert aus seiner komplexeren Zusammensetzung. So beschränken sich die Beiträge zum Markenwert nicht allein auf den Kreis der Nachfrager in Absatzmärkten. Auch bei den übrigen Zielgruppen der Unternehmensmarke lassen sich entsprechende Beiträge generieren. Abbildung 1 gibt einen Überblick ausgewählter Beitragsquellen in unterschiedlichen Zielgruppen.

Abbildung 2: **Die komplexe Zusammensetzung des Markenwertes einer Unternehmensmarke**

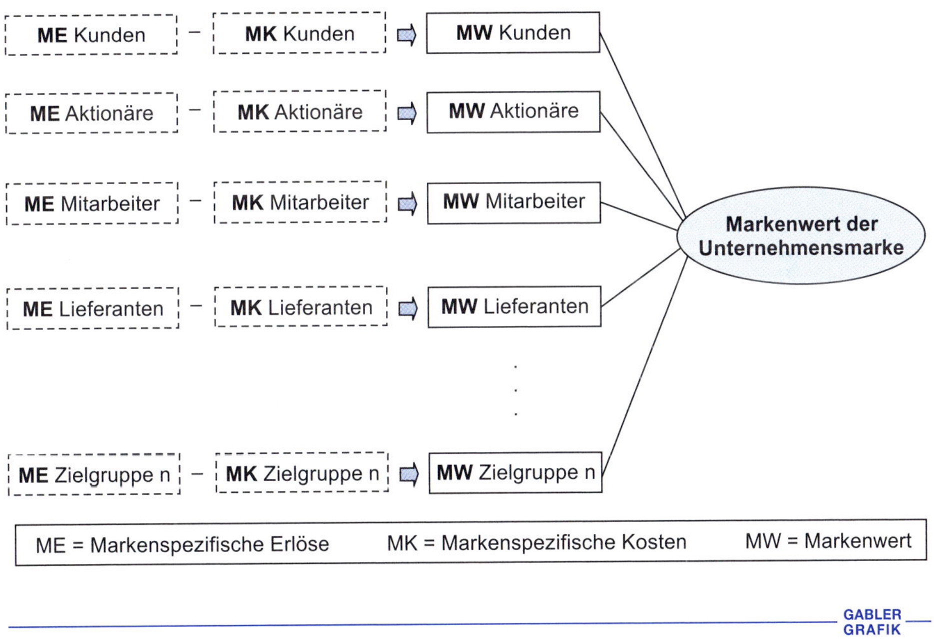

Quelle: Bierwirth 2003, S. 54

Der Markenwert einer Unternehmensmarke resultiert demnach zum einen aus der Aggregation aller zielgruppenspezifischen Wertbeiträge. Ferner haben die skizzierten Wertbeiträge ausschließlich Erlöscharakter. Sie können daher auch als **unternehmensmarkenspezifische Erlöse** bezeichnet werden. Der Markenwert einer Unternehmensmarke wird jedoch ebenso durch die Kosten beeinflusst, die zur Generierung dieser zusätzlichen Erlöse notwendig sind (Farquhar/Ijiri 1993, S. 77; Kapferer 2000, S. 398). Derartige Kosten sind als **unternehmensmarkenspezifische Kosten** interpretierbar. Erst die Differenz dieser beiden Größen ermöglicht eine Aussage hinsichtlich des effektiven Wertbeitrages einer Zielgruppe zum Markenwert der Unternehmensmarke. Der Gesamtmarkenwert einer Unternehmensmarke ergibt sich somit aus der in Abbildung 2 veranschaulichten Aggregation aller Teilwerte in den verschiedenen Zielgruppen der Unternehmensmarke.

Abbildung 3: Treiber für die Interdependenz der Markenbilder im Wahrnehmungsprozess der Unternehmensmarke

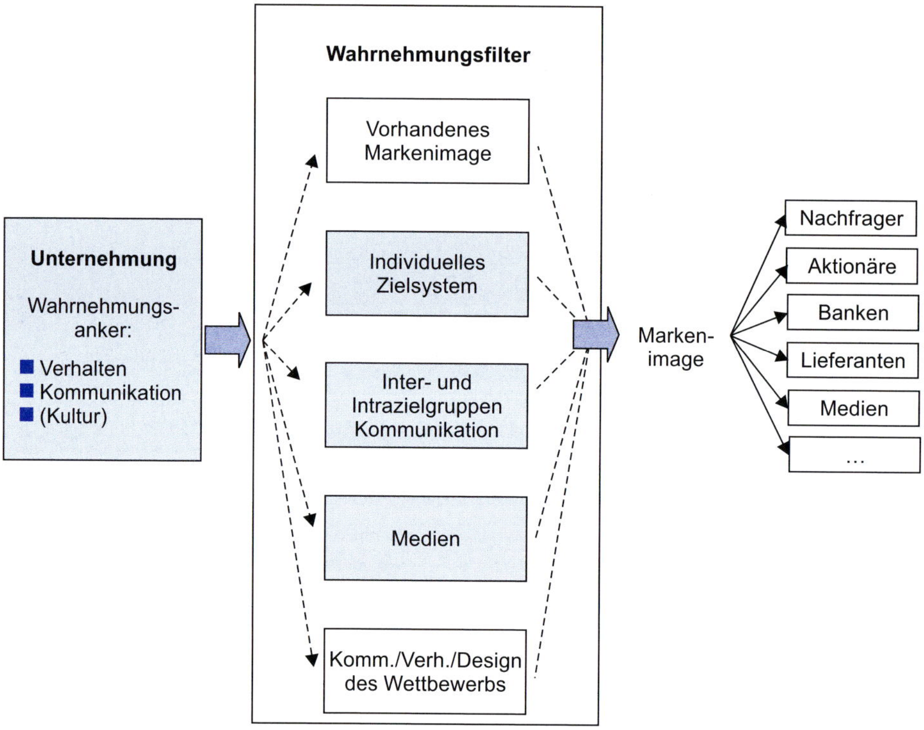

GABLER GRAFIK

Quelle: in Anlehnung an Cornelissen 2000, S. 120

Die Zielsetzung der Maximierung des Gesamtmarkenwertes ist vor diesem Hintergrund auf die einzelnen Zielgruppen herunterzubrechen. Als besonders problematisch erweisen sich in diesem Zusammenhang die existierenden **Interdependenzen** der zielgruppenspezifischen Wertbeiträge. Diese sind begründet durch eine gegenseitige Abhängigkeit der aus dem Wahrnehmungsprozess resultierenden Markenimages. So führen beispielsweise die Kommunikation zwischen den Zielgruppen oder intrapersonale Rollenüberschneidungen zu einer gegenseitigen Beeinflussung der Markenimages. Ebenso ist in der Unternehmensmarke nur eine einzige Unternehmensidentität verankert, die zwischen den einzelnen Zielgruppen nicht beliebig variieren kann. Die Treiber der skizzierten Interdependenz sind im Rahmen des in Abbildung 3 dargestellten Wahrnehmungsprozesses einer Unternehmensmarke blau schraffiert herausgestellt.

Aus diesem Grund kann mit der Maximierung des Markenwertes der Unternehmensmarke die nur suboptimale Ausschöpfung der Beitragspotenziale einzelner Zielgruppen einhergehen. Die Analyse der ökonomischen Zielsetzung führt somit zur Forderung nach einer zielgruppenorientierten Koordination, deren Aufgabe in der Abstimmung der einzelnen Wertbeiträge hin zu einem aggregierten Gesamtmaximum zu sehen ist.

2.22 Unternehmensmarke als psychologischer Zusatznutzen

Die Definition einer Marke als ein aus Sicht der relevanten Zielgruppen nachhaltig differenziertes **Nutzenbündel** mit spezifischen Merkmalen knüpft an den eigentlichen Ursachen für die zielgruppenspezifischen Wertbeiträge der Unternehmensmarke an. Grundsätzlich lassen sich zwei unterschiedliche Erklärungsansätze ableiten, die einerseits die zielgruppenspezifischen Wertbeiträge theoretisch begründen und andererseits einen Ausgangspunkt zur Ableitung von Zielen der Führung von Unternehmensmarken darstellen.

Einen ersten Erklärungsansatz liefert die **Neue Institutionenökonomie**. Hierbei erklärt sich der ökonomische Wert der Unternehmensmarke aus ihrem Transaktionskostensenkungspotenzial (Kaas 1995, S. 3 ff.). Ausgangspunkt ist die begrenzte Rationalität und die damit verbundene Unsicherheit bei Entscheidungen als Dimension der jeweiligen Transaktionskosten (Erlei/Leschke/Sauerland 1999, S. 69 ff.; Picot/Dietl/Franck 2002, S. 67 ff.). Die Unsicherheit ist bei **Vertrauenseigenschaften** grundsätzlich und bei Erfahrungseigenschaften zumindest vor dem Zeitpunkt ihrer Überprüfbarkeit durch nicht verfügbare Informationen begründet. Die Unternehmensmarke fungiert jedoch als Surrogat dieser Information. So stellt sie einen **„Information Chunk“** dar, der die infolge einer verdichteten Wahrnehmung des Unternehmens entstandenen Schlüsselinformationen verkörpert. Diese Schlüsselinformationen werden als Indikator für eine Beurteilung der real komplexeren Umweltsituationen herangezogen.

Dies setzt allerdings die Glaubhaftigkeit der Unternehmensmarke beziehungsweise der durch diese symbolisierten Informationen voraus. Ist diese gegeben, wirken die symbolisierten Informationen wie Sucheigenschaften. Sie treten somit an die Stelle der den Wahrnehmenden ursprünglich interessierenden Erfahrungs- und Vertrauenseigenschaften. Aus der Tatsache, dass sich die Wahrnehmenden unter der Prämisse der Glaubwürdigkeit auf den symbolisierten Inhalt einer Unternehmensmarke verlassen, ergibt sich die **Vertrauensfunktion** einer Unternehmensmarke. Eine wesentliche Herausforderung für die Markenführung ist daher die Schaffung eines hohen Maßes an Glaubwürdigkeit. Diese wird im Rahmen der Informationsökonomie durch die Existenz einer entsprechenden Reputation begründet, die dem Unternehmen einen Vertrauensvorschuss verschafft.

Das Konstrukt der **Reputation** wurde insbesondere in der anglo-amerikanischen Forschung näher beleuchtet. Die Reputation eines Unternehmens resultiert aus einer ganzheitlichen Bewertung eines Unternehmens im Zeitablauf. Den existierenden Operationalisierungsansätzen ist gemein, dass die Reputation einer Unternehmung aus der Aggregation von Bewertungen entsteht, in denen das Unternehmen aus unterschiedlichen Perspektiven beurteilt wird (Fombrun 1996, S. 115). Diese spiegeln die unterschiedlichen Interessen der verschiedenen Zielgruppen eines Unternehmens wider. Die in Abbildung 4 durch unterschiedliche Linienstärken (dick, durchgezogen, gestrichelt, gepunktet) dargestellte Gewichtung der Reputationsdimensionen unterscheidet die einzelnen Zielgruppen voneinander. Gavin und Fombrun sprechen vor diesem Hintergrund von einem integrierten Ansatz der Anspruchsgruppenberücksichtigung (Gavin/Fombrun 2000, S. 18). Letztlich ermöglichen jedoch alle in der Literatur vorliegenden Operationalisierungen der Reputation keine trennscharfe Abgrenzung vom Imagekonstrukt. Das **Image der Corporate Brand** auf der Basis der im ersten Kapitel dieses Buches vorgenommenen Konstruktdefinition umfasst somit auch die Reputation.

Abbildung 4: Zielgruppenübergreifende Interpretation der Reputation

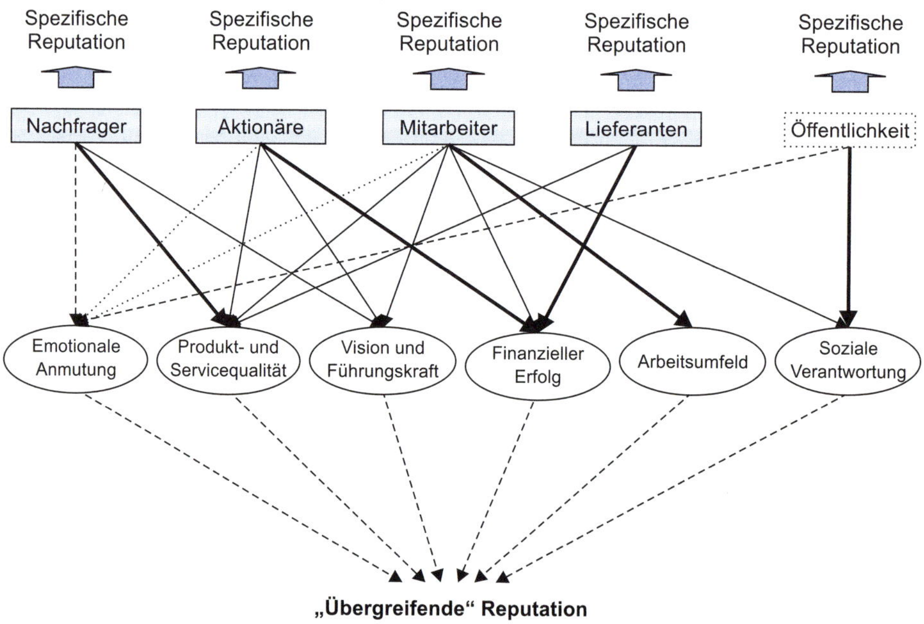

GABLER GRAFIK

Quelle: in Anlehnung an Fombrun 1996, S. 50 ff.

Eine weitere Funktion der Marke ergibt sich durch das Symbolisieren von **Sucheigenschaften**. Da diese Informationen jedoch auf der Grundlage einer entsprechenden Recherche verfügbar beziehungsweise überprüfbar sind, beschränken sich die Möglichkeiten zur Reduzierung der bei einer Transaktion vorherrschenden Unsicherheit nicht ausschließlich auf die Unternehmensmarke. Vielmehr werden die in der Unternehmensmarke verdichtet abgebildeten Informationen bewertet und mit den vergleichbaren Kosten zur Recherche entsprechend sicherer Informationen verglichen. Der Nutzen einer Unternehmensmarke resultiert somit aus ihrer Fähigkeit, die für eine Transaktion notwendige Informationsrecherche zu substituieren. Durch die entsprechende Reduzierung des Informationsbedarfes trägt sie zu einer Entlastung der Transaktionskosten bei. Daraus folgt die **Rationalisierungsfunktion** der Unternehmensmarke. Da sich die Unternehmensmarke in einem wettbewerbsähnlichen Verhältnis zur Informationsbeschaffung über andere Wege befindet, erfolgt eine Bewertung der symbolisierten Inhalte hinsichtlich ihrer Qualität und Quantität. Die Qualitätsbeurteilung der verdichteten Informationen erfolgt insbesondere hinsichtlich ihrer Glaubhaftigkeit.

Mit der Herausstellung der **Vertrauenswürdigkeit** eines Unternehmens ist bereits eine erste Zielsetzung für die Markenführung gekennzeichnet. Darüber hinaus hat eine Unternehmensmarke die sich aus den institutionenökonomischen Eigenschaften ihrer angebotenen Leistungen ergebenden Unsicherheiten zu kompensieren. Dies sollte zielgruppenspezifisch erfolgen. Abbildung 5 gibt einen Überblick über die durch eine Unternehmensmarke zu symbolisierenden, zielgruppenspezifischen Inhalte. Auch hier verdeutlicht sich die Notwendigkeit einer zielgruppenorientierten Koordination zur Sicherstellung eines zwischen den Zielgruppen widerspruchsfreien Markenauftrittes.

Neben der Neuen Institutionenökonomie leisten auch verhaltenspsychologische Theorien einen hohen Erklärungsbeitrag für die Relevanz der Unternehmensmarke. Einen hohen Stellenwert hat in diesem Zusammenhang die **Theorie des Selbstkonzeptes**. Diese differenziert unterschiedliche Perspektiven des Selbst, wobei zwischen dem vorhandenen und dem idealen Selbst sowie der Eigen- und Fremdwahrnehmung unterschieden wird (Filipp 1993, S. 50 ff.). Der besondere Nutzen jeder Marke liegt in ihrem Beitrag, die Entwicklung einer Person hin zum idealen Selbst zu unterstützen (Sommer 1998, S. 80). So erfolgt auch durch die Identifikation mit der Unternehmensmarke ein Transfer der Dimensionen der Markenidentität auf die jeweilige Humanpersönlichkeit. Voraussetzung hierfür ist, dass die Unternehmensmarke selbst über eine klare Identität verfügt. Die Unternehmensmarke wird als Identifikationsanker gerade seitens aktueller oder potenzieller Mitarbeiter genutzt. So tragen zum Beispiel prestigeträchtige Arbeitsplätze wie McKinsey oder Lufthansa dazu bei, dass sowohl die Mitarbeiter hinsichtlich des Empfindens über ihre eigene Identität, aber auch in ihrer jeweiligen Fremdwahrnehmung entsprechend beeinflusst werden.

Für die Führung der Unternehmensmarke lässt sich aus diesem Erklärungsansatz ableiten, dass ihre spezifische Identität besonders herauszustellen ist. Umso klarer und intensiver die Markenidentität empfunden wird, desto höhere Identifikationspotenziale werden dem Wahrnehmenden geboten.

Abbildung 5: Inhaltsdimensionen einer Unternehmensmarke

		Übergeordnete Vertrauenseigenschaften	Vertrauenseigenschaften	Erfahrungseigenschaften	Sucheigenschaften
Nachfrager	Produkt-/Leistungsfokussierung	Dauerhafter Fortbestand des Unternehmens	■ Einhaltung des Leistungs-/Produktversprechens ■ Kundendienst/Service	■ Produkt-/Leistungsqualität	■ Leistungs-/Produktmerkmale ■ Bewertungen von neutralen Instanzen ■ Medienberichte
Aktionäre	Finanzfokussierung		■ Dauerhafte Wertsteigerung ■ Ansprechende Dividendenpolitik/Kurspflege ■ Kompetentes Management	■ Informationsverhalten des Unternehmens	■ Historische Kursverläufe ■ Geschäftsberichte ■ Bewertungen von neutralen Instanzen ■ Medienberichte
Banken			■ Dauerhafte Unternehmensbonität ■ Kompetentes Management	■ Informationsverhalten des Unternehmens ■ Zahlungsweise/Liquidität	■ Bonitätsmerkmale (z. B. Bilanzen)
Lieferanten			■ Dauerhafte Unternehmensbonität ■ Abnahmesicherheit	■ Partnerschaftliches Verhältnis	■ Bonitätsrankings ■ Bankauskünfte
Führungskräfte	Sozialfokussierung		■ Persönliche Entwicklungschancen ■ Dauerhaft adäquate Bezahlung	■ Unternehmenskultur ■ Förderungsmaßnahmen	■ Bezahlung ■ Imagerankings ■ Publikationen ■ Leitbilder als Grundlage von Verhalten und Entscheidungen
Mitarbeiter			■ Sicherer Arbeitsplatz	■ Unternehmenskultur	■ Entlohnung ■ Leitbilder als Grundlage von Verhalten

Übergeordnete Vertrauenseigenschaften – Interessengetriebene Eigenschaften

Vertrauensfunktion – Rationalisierungsfunktion

GABLER GRAFIK

Quelle: Meffert/Bierwirth 2001, S. 6

3. Implikationen für die Führung von Unternehmensmarken

3.1 Zielgruppenspezifische Markenführung durch die Gestaltung der Markenarchitektur

Die Führung der Unternehmensmarke befindet sich in einem Spannungsfeld zwischen der Berücksichtigung möglichst vieler zielgruppenspezifischer Interessen sowie der Notwendigkeit einer zielgruppenübergreifenden Koordination. Eine der in diesem Zusammenhang bedeutendsten Gestaltungsoptionen stellt die Bestimmung der **Markenarchitektur** dar (vgl. den Beitrag zur Markenarchitektur in diesem Buch).

Vor diesem Hintergrund sind aus verschiedenen Alternativen zur Markierung von Hierarchieebenen drei alternative Markenarchitekturtypen ableitbar, die ein jeweils unterschiedliches Eingehen auf die verschiedenen Interessen der einzelnen Zielgruppen ermöglichen. Im Rahmen einer **„undifferenzierten Zielgruppenansprache"** tritt in allen Hierarchieebenen und damit auch gegenüber allen Zielgruppen nur eine einzige Marke – die Unternehmensmarke – auf. Demnach sind durch die Unternehmensmarke zielgruppenübergreifend alle Interessen abgewogen zu berücksichtigen. Wenngleich im Rahmen einer solchen Markenstrategie die Unternehmensmarke eine besonders hohe Bekanntheit erlangt und durch die zwischen den Zielgruppen und Hierarchieebenen realisierbaren Transfereffekte zu vergleichsweise geringen Kosten zu führen ist, erscheint das Potenzial aller realisierbaren Wertbeiträge unausgeschöpft, da die Standardisierung der Aussagen zu einer geringeren Profilierung in den Teilmärkten führt.

Reziprok hierzu verhält sich die Bewertung der **„differenzierten Zielgruppenansprache"**. Hierbei beschränkt sich der Auftritt der Unternehmensmarke allein auf die Top-Ebene. Auf der Unternehmensbereichebene erfolgt eine Einführung von zusätzlichen Unternehmensbereichsmarken (Company- oder SBU-Brands), auf der Produktebene möglicherweise auch noch verschiedener Produktmarken. Hierdurch werden jene Zielgruppen, die nicht zu den Fokuszielgruppen der Unternehmensmarke zählen, von dieser markentechnisch getrennt. Die zwischen den Zielgruppen existierenden Interdependenzen in der Wahrnehmung werden zerschnitten beziehungsweise reduziert. Somit können die einzelnen Marken in den Hierarchieebenen auf die entsprechend verbliebenen Fokuszielgruppen ausgerichtet und das Potenzial der erzielbaren Wertbeiträge besser ausgeschöpft werden. Allerdings sind mit dieser Markenstrategie höhere Kosten verbunden, da jede Marke isoliert aufgebaut und gepflegt werden muss.

Schließlich ist auch die **„gemischte Zielgruppenansprache"** anzuführen. Abgeleitet aus der Strategie des „Endorsement-Branding" wird der dominierende Auftritt der Unternehmensbereichs- oder Produktmarken durch einen oft nur unauffälligen Zusatz, wie zum Beispiel „by XY" oder „ein Unternehmen der XY-Gruppe", ergänzt. Die Unternehmensmarke kann sich dabei mit ihren symbolisierten Inhalten auf ihre Fokuszielgruppen in der Top-Ebene konzentrieren. Zugleich wird durch den Hinweis auf die Zugehörigkeit zum Unternehmen in den unteren Hierarchieebenen ein Imagetransfer der Unternehmensmarke zu den übrigen Marken des Unternehmens stattfinden. Dieser Imagetransfer ist nicht in allen Fällen zielführend. Im positiven Fall gelingt es beispielsweise, die Zugehörigkeit zu einer „finanzstarken Unternehmensgruppe“ oder einer „faszinierenden Unternehmenswelt“ zu symbolisieren, ohne auf eine spezifischere Ansprache der Zielgruppen mittels Unternehmensbereichs- oder Produktmarken zu verzichten.

Eine exemplarische Darstellung der Strategietypen ist in Abbildung 6 enthalten. Die Begrenzung der Darstellung auf eine einzige Unternehmensbereichsmarke deutet bereits darauf hin, dass die skizzierten Typen idealisierte Formen darstellen.

Abbildung 6: Optionen für die Gestaltung von Markenarchitekturen

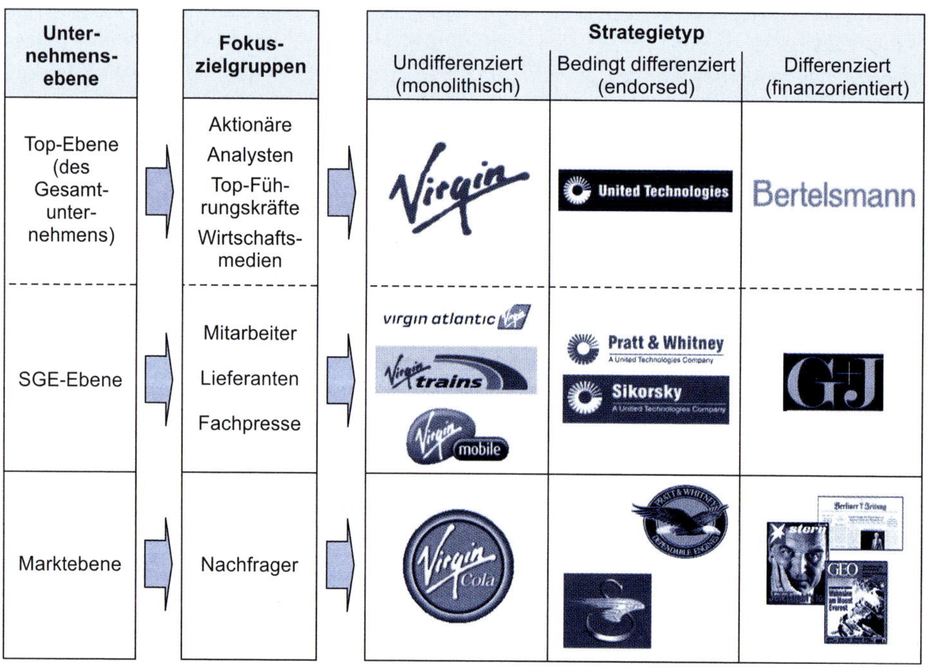

GABLER GRAFIK

Quelle: in enger Anlehnung an Bierwirth 2003, S. 135 f.

Abbildung 7: Markenwertorientierte Analyse der zielgruppenbezogenen Markenarchitekturtypen

	Auswirkungen auf markenspezifische *Erlöse*	**Auswirkungen auf markenspezifische *Kosten***
***Undifferenzierte* Zielgruppenansprache** ➢ Markenwert der Unternehmensmarke: **hoch** ➢ Markenwert der Unternehmensbereichs- und Produktmarken: **nicht vorhanden**	■ Geringere zielgruppenspezifische Wertbeiträge, da nur bedingt auf die differenzierten Interessen eingegangen werden kann (Notwendigkeit der unternehmensweit einheitlichen Positionierung). ■ Identifikation auf eine einzige Markenpersönlichkeit beschränkt. ■ Positive Imagetransfereffekte zwischen den Zielgruppen determinieren starke Unternehmensmarke.	■ Zielgruppenspezifische Koordinationskosten vergleichsweise hoch, da die Konsistenz über viele Zielgruppen herzustellen ist. ■ Markenvielfaltsbezogene Koordinationskosten vergleichsweise gering, da nur eine Marke existiert. ■ Kostensynergien hoch, da sich alle Ausgaben auf nur eine Marke fokussieren (zum Beispiel Synergien in Kommunikation etc.).
***Differenzierte* Zielgruppenansprache** ➢ Markenwert der Unternehmensmarke: **gering** ➢ Markenwert der Unternehmensbereichs- und Produktmarken: **hoch**	■ Nahezu vollständige Ausschöpfung der zielgruppenspezifischen Beitragspotenziale, da durch die unterschiedlichen Marken auf die differenzierten Interessen der ZG eingegangen wird (unternehmensweit differenzierte Positionierung möglich). ■ Schaffung vielfältiger Markenpersönlichkeiten denkbar mit einhergehenden umfangreichen Identifikationspotenzialen. ■ Geringe Imagetransfereffekte führen zu einer vergleichsweise schwachen Unternehmensmarke (dafür aber werthaltige Unternehmensbereichs- und Produktmarken).	■ Zielgruppenspezifische Koordinationskosten vergleichsweise gering, da durch Zerschneidung von Interdependenz die Notwendigkeit der Koordination entfällt. ■ Markenvielfaltbezogene Koordinationskosten durchschnittlich, da zwar viele Marken existieren, diese jedoch nicht miteinander verbunden werden. ■ Wenig Kostensynergien, da jede Marke einzeln profiliert werden muss.
***Bedingte differenzierte* Zielgruppenansprache** ➢ Markenwert der Unternehmensmarke: **relativ hoch** ➢ Markenwert der Unternehmensbereichs- und Produktmarken: **relativ hoch**	■ Hohe, aber nicht vollständige Ausschöpfung der zielgruppenspezifischen Beitragspotenziale, da durch die unterschiedlichen Marken zwar auf die differenzierten Interessen der ZG eingegangen wird, die Positionierungsfreiräume jedoch durch den Auftritt der Unternehmensmarke begrenzt sind. ■ Vielfalt der Markenpersönlichkeiten ist durch die Persönlichkeit der Unternehmensmarke eingeengt. Somit eine begrenzte Ausweitung der Identifikationspotenziale. ■ Mögliche Imagetransfereffekte führen sowohl zu einer relativ starken Unternehmensmarke bei gleichzeitiger Existenz starker Unternehmensbereichs- und Produktmarken.	■ Zielgruppenspezifische Koordinationskosten vergleichsweise hoch, da die Konsistenz über viele Zielgruppen herzustellen ist. ■ Markenvielfaltbezogene Koordinationskosten sehr hoch, da Fit zwischen den Marken herzustellen ist. ■ Kostensynergien in geringem Ausmaß vorhanden, jedoch sind auch die weiteren Marken entsprechend zu profilieren.

GABLER GRAFIK

Quelle: Bierwirth 2003, S. 148 und 154

Als besonders problematisch erweist sich die konkrete Auswahl einer geeigneten Markenarchitektur. So müsste sich diese nicht nur an einer Maximierung des ohnehin schon komplexen Markenwertes einer Unternehmensmarke orientieren, sondern an einer Maximierung der gesamten Markenwerte aller in einer Unternehmung vorhandenen Marken. Eine derartige Bewertung ist jedoch nur schwer umsetzbar. Einige Tendenzaussagen sind allerdings in Abbildung 7 dargestellt. Demzufolge scheint gerade die „gemischte Zielgruppenansprache" mit dem Endorsed-Branding der Unternehmensmarke besonders vorteilhaft.

Aufgrund der existierenden Bewertungsdefizite hinsichtlich des Markenwertes sind kontingenztheoretisch abgeleitete Bewertungskriterien zu beachten, die als Eignungsgrößen für eine spezifische Markenarchitektur fungieren (vgl. hierzu auch den Beitrag über Markenarchitekturen in diesem Buch). Einige solcher Kriterien haben Laforet und Saunders herausgestellt (Laforet/Saunders 1999, S. 64). Von ihnen wird der Architekturtyp einer „undifferenzierten Zielgruppenansprache" insbesondere für traditionsreiche, marktführende Unternehmen mit einem überschaubaren Angebotsportfolio empfohlen, die zugleich über eine einheitliche Positionierung möglichst im Premium-Segment verfügen. Eine „differenzierte Zielgruppenansprache" eignet sich hingegen für Unternehmen, die dezentralisiert in unterschiedlichen Märkten mit möglicherweise heterogenen Positionierungen agieren und hierdurch mit divergierenden Interessen konfrontiert werden. Die gemischte Markenarchitektur wird schließlich für effizienzorientierte Unternehmen mit ausgeprägten Images bei den Unternehmensbereichs- oder Produktmarken empfohlen.

Durch die Gestaltung der Markenarchitektur kann die partielle Trennung einiger Zielgruppen von der Unternehmensmarke und somit eine zielgruppenspezifischere Markenführung ermöglicht werden. Letztlich bedarf es für die Führung einer Unternehmensmarke eines Konzeptes zur simultanen, zielgruppenübergreifenden Markenführung. Die identitätsorientierte Markenführung wird diesen Herausforderungen in besonderem Maße gerecht.

3.2 Identitätsorientierte Markenführung als Grundkonzept zur zielgruppenübergreifenden Führung von Unternehmensmarken

Ein wesentliches Fundament der identitätsorientierten Markenführung bilden die Erkenntnisse in der sozialpsychologischen Forschung, nach der die Identität einer Person erst durch eine wechselseitige Wahrnehmung von weiteren Personen entstehen kann (Weidenfeld 1983, S. 19). Die Stärke einer Humanidentität resultiert aus der Übereinstimmung der Wahrnehmung dieser Identität aus eigener und fremder Sicht (vgl. den Beitrag zum theoretischen Grundkonzept der identitätsorientierten Markenführung in diesem Buch). Diese Erkenntnis wird im Kontext der **identitätsorientierten Markenführung** auf das Konstrukt einer Marke übertragen.

So resultiert die Stärke einer Marke aus der Übereinstimmung ihres von außen wahrgenommenen Fremd- sowie des unternehmensintern analog existierenden Selbstbildes. Hiermit einher geht die Notwendigkeit, im Rahmen der Führung einer Marke sowohl die internen als auch die externen Zielgruppen zu berücksichtigen. Damit findet sich der für die Unternehmensmarke besonders relevante Aspekt einer zielgruppenübergreifenden Markenführung in den Gedanken der identitätsorientierten Markenführung entsprechend wieder (Bickmann 1999, S. 32 f.; Heinlein 1999, S. 283 ff.).

Ziel der identitätsorientierten Führung einer Unternehmensmarke ist daher die Gewährleistung einer starken Unternehmensmarkenidentität. Hierzu sind jene zielgruppenübergreifend akzeptierten Identitätsdimensionen als gemeinsame Klammer zu identifizieren, die das Unternehmen in den unterschiedlichen Absatz- und Beschaffungsmärkten wettbewerbsrelevant positionieren. Die Berücksichtigung der unterschiedlichen Zielgruppen erfolgt im Rahmen der identitätsorientierten Markenführung dabei weniger durch ein Eingehen auf die spezifischen Interessen als vielmehr durch die Durchsetzung einer gemeinsamen Basis. Abbildung 8 verdeutlicht diese Vorgehensweise.

Abbildung 8: **Koordination von internen und externen Zielgruppen mit dem Konzept der identitätsorientierten Markenführung**

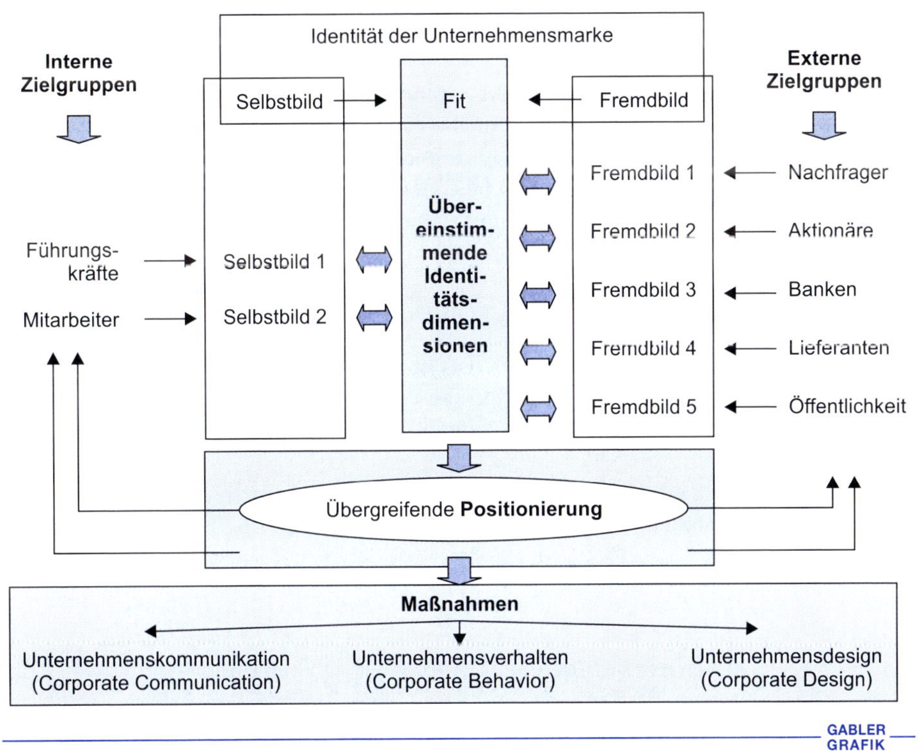

Quelle: in enger Anlehnung an Bierwirth 2003, S. 168

Die besondere Leistung der identitätsorientierten Markenführung für das Management einer Unternehmensmarke ist vor diesem Hintergrund in der Bereitstellung eines konzeptionellen Rahmens zu sehen, der eine Verwässerung der Unternehmensmarke durch die Gewährleistung einer konsistenten Wahrnehmung zwischen den Zielgruppen verhindert.

4. Ausblick

Im Rahmen des Beitrags wurde die hohe Komplexität der Markenführung von Unternehmensmarken aufgrund der Existenz unterschiedlicher Zielgruppen aufgezeigt. So steht die Markenführung in einem Spannungsfeld zwischen der Anpassung an ihre spezifischen Interessen und der Notwendigkeit einer zielgruppenübergreifenden Koordination.

Eine besondere Schwierigkeit ergibt sich hinsichtlich der integrativen Sicht von Zielgruppen vor allem durch die häufig vorzufindende funktionale Trennung des Finanz-, Personal- und Absatzmarketing. Die Aktivitäten dieser Bereiche beeinflussen in nicht unerheblichem Maße die Unternehmensmarke. Deshalb bedarf es entsprechender Kompetenzen für die Sicherstellung einer ganzheitlichen Koordination. Die Wissenschaft ist in diesem Zusammenhang gefordert, entsprechende Instrumente für die zielgruppenbezogene Koordination zu entwickeln.

Darüber hinaus wird die ohnehin hohe Komplexität der Führung einer Unternehmensmarke durch die Zunahme von Unternehmensfusionen weiter gesteigert. So ist häufig innerhalb nur kurzer Zeit eine Entscheidung über die neue Namensgebung eines „Gemeinschaftsunternehmens“ zu treffen. Der neue Unternehmensname hat eine hohe Aussagekraft über den Charakter einer Fusion und generiert Implikationen für die zu erwartende Unternehmensidentität. Somit kommt der Auswahl des neuen Markennamens eine große Bedeutung zu. Auch hier ergeben sich mit der Validierung von Bewertungskriterien Herausforderungen für weitere wissenschaftliche Forschungsarbeiten.

Vor diesem Hintergrund scheint die Beschäftigung mit der Unternehmensmarke als eigenständigem Untersuchungsgegenstand eine wertvolle Erweiterung im Rahmen des oftmals kritisierten Deepening und Broadening der Markenführung darzustellen. Die aufgezeigten Forschungsdefizite verdeutlichen letztlich die Notwendigkeit, der Unternehmenspraxis durch eine Intensivierung der Forschung innovative Lösungsvorschläge für diese zweifellos aktuelle Herausforderung aufzuzeigen.

Ein Erfolg versprechender Ansatz ist insbesondere in der weiteren Zusammenführung von Erkenntnissen aus der Corporate-Identity(CI-)- und der Markenforschung zu sehen. In beiden Forschungsrichtungen hat das Konstrukt der „Identität“ eine zentrale Bedeutung. Die Perspektiven auf die Identität unterscheiden sich hingegen. So bezieht sich die CI-Forschung auf eine ganzheitliche Betrachtung des Unternehmens, während sich die Markenforschung mit den Aspekten der Marke befasst. Mit der Unternehmensmarke kommt es jedoch zu einer Verschmelzung der Betrachtungsobjekte. Aus diesem Grund können die von langjähriger Forschungstradition geprägten Forschungsrichtungen bei einer integrativen Vorgehensweise innovative Problemlösungen für die Unternehmensmarke generieren.

Literaturhinweise

Bickmann, R. (1999), Chance: Identität, Berlin u.a.

Bierwirth, A. (2003), Die Führung der Unternehmensmarke – Ein Beitrag zum zielgruppenorientierten Corporate Branding, Frankfurt/M.

Burmann, Ch., Blinda, L., Nitschke, A. (2003), Konzeptionelle Grundlagen des Identitätsbasierten Markenmanagements, LiM Arbeitspapiere, Nr. 1, Bremen.

Cornelissen, J. (2000), Corporate Image: an audience centred model, in: Corporate Communications: An international Journal, Vol. 5, No. 2, S. 119–125.

Cyert, R. M., March, J. G. (1963), A Behavioral Theroy of the Firm, Englewood Cliffs.

Demuth, A. (2000), Das strategische Management der Unternehmensmarke, in: Markenartikel, Nr. 1, S. 14–20.

Erlei, M., Leschke, M., Sauerland, D. (1999), Neue Institutionenökonomik, Stuttgart.

Farquhar, P. H., Ijiri, Y. A. (1993), Dialogue on Momentum Accounting for Brand Management, in: International Journal of Research in Marketing, Vol. 10, No. 1, S. 77–92.

Filipp, S.-H. (1993), Selbstkonzept-Forschung – Probleme, Befunde, Perspektiven, 3. Aufl., Stuttgart.

Fombrun, C. J. (1996), Reputation: Realizing Value from the Corporate Image, o.A.d.O.

Gavin, S., Fombrun, C. J. (2000), Foundations for good reputations, in: Star Tribune, v. 27.4.2000, S. 17–18.

Göttgens, O., Leach, M., Wirtz, B. (2004), Regelmäßiges Markenwert-Benchmarking – Markenbewertung der DAX 30 und Euro Stoxx 50 Unternehmen mittels BEES, www.bbdo.de/de/home/presse/publikationen_vortraege.Par.0012.Link1Download.tmp/Rcgclmacssigcs%20Markenwert-Benchmarkingv3.pdf, (Abruf: 30. August 2004).

Halliday, A. (1998), Corporate Branding, in: Urban Land, February 1998, S. 96–97.

Heinlein, M. (1999), Identität und Marke: Brand Identity versus Corporate Identity?, in: Bickmann, R. (Hrsg.), Chance: Identität, Berlin u.a., S. 282–310.

Ind, N. (1997), The Corporate Brand, Ebbw Vale.

Jenner, Th. (2001), Markenführung im Zeitalter des Shareholder-Value, in: Harvard Business Manager, H. 3, S. 54–63.

Kaas, K. P. (1995), Marketing und Neue Institutionenökonomik, in: Kontrakte, Geschäftsbeziehungen, Netzwerke, Kaas, K. P. (Hrsg.), Düsseldorf u. a., S. 1–17.

Kapferer, J.-N. (2000), Strategic Brand Management, 3. Aufl., London.

Kircher, S. (1997), Corporate Branding – mehr als Namensgebung, in: planung & analyse, Nr. 1, S. 60–61.

Laforet, S., Saunders, J. (1999), Managing Brand Portfolios: Why Leaders do what they do, in: Journal of Advertising Research, January-February, S. 51–66.

Langner, T., Esch, F.-R. (2004), Corporate Branding auf Handlungsoptionen abstimmen, in: Esch, F.-R., Tomczak, T., Kernstock, J., Langner, T. (Hrsg.), Corporate Brand Management – Marken als Anker strategischer Führung von Unternehmen, Wiesbaden, S. 101–128.

Meffert, H., Bierwirth, A. (2001), Stellenwert und Funktionen der Unternehmensmarke – Erklärungsansätze und Implikationen für das Corporate Branding, in: Thexis, 18 Jg., Nr. 4, S. 5–11.
Merbold, C. (1994), Unternehmen als Marken, in: Bruhn, M. (Hrsg.), Handbuch Markenartikel, Stuttgart, S. 107–119.
Picot, A., Dietl, H., Franck, E. (2002), Organisation – eine ökonomische Perspektive, 3. Aufl., Stuttgart.
Sattler, H. (2001), Markenpolitik, Frankfurt/M.
Sommer, R. (1998), Die Psychologie der Marke. Die Marke aus der Sicht des Verbrauchers, Frankfurt/M.
Weidenfeld, W. (1983), Die Identität der Deutschen – Fragen, Positionen, Perspektiven, in: Weidenfeld, W. (Hrsg.), Die Identität der Deutschen, Schriftenreihe der Bundeszentrale für politische Bildung, Band 200, Bonn, S. 13–49.

Gestaltung von Markenarchitekturen

Christoph Burmann und Heribert Meffert

1. **Wachsende Herausforderungen an die Führung von Markenportfolios** **164**

2. **Die Markenarchitekturgestaltung als Grundlage der strategischen Führung von Markenportfolios** **165**

2.1 Unternehmens- und Markenhierarchien 166
2.2 Strategische Markenrollen 168
2.3 Eindimensionale Strukturierungsansätze für Markenarchitekturen 169
2.4 Mehrdimensionaler Strukturierungsansatz für Markenarchitekturen 173
2.41 Vertikale Dimension 175
2.42 Horizontale Dimension 175
2.43 Handelsgerichtete Dimension 178

3. **Fazit** **181**

1. Wachsende Herausforderungen an die Führung von Markenportfolios

Die Markenportfolios vieler Unternehmen, also die Gesamtheit der von einem Unternehmen geführten Marken (Aaker 2004, S. 16), sind in der Vergangenheit stetig angewachsen. Diese Entwicklung ist neben zahlreichen Marken-Neueinführungen auch in der Globalisierung der Märkte begründet. Hier ist ein deutlicher Konsolidierungstrend durch nationale („within-border“) und internationale („cross-border“) M & A-Aktivitäten zu beobachten, der sich in einer Vergrößerung bestehender Markenportfolios niedergeschlagen hat (vgl. Abbildung 1).

Abbildung 1: Entwicklung der „cross-border" Merger & Acquisition Aktivitäten der G10-Länder (Belgien, Deutschland, Frankreich, Großbritannien, Italien, Japan, Niederlande, Schweden, Schweiz und Vereinigte Staaten) inklusive Australien und Spanien

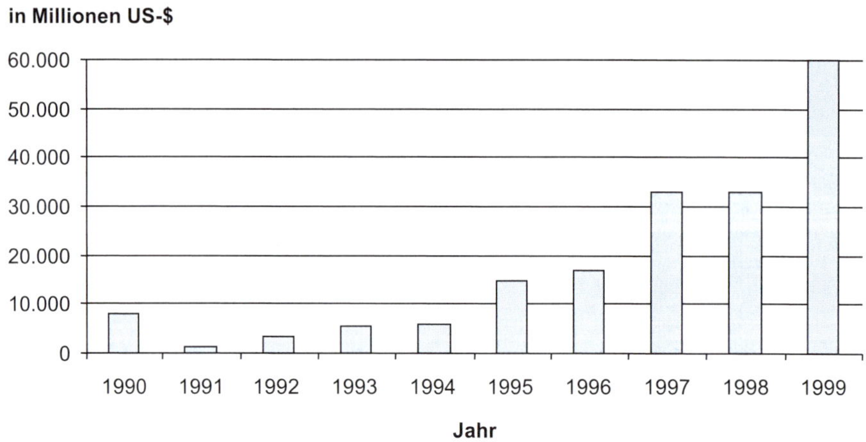

GABLER GRAFIK

Quelle: o. V. 2001, S. 336

Auf diese Weise angewachsene Markenportfolios stellen die Markenverantwortlichen vor ein breites Spektrum an Führungsherausforderungen. Hierbei sind insbesondere steigende Komplexitätskosten durch einen erheblich gewachsenen Koordinationsbedarf relevant. Ferner droht durch die Vielzahl der Marken in einem Portfolio eine Erosion ehedem klarer Markenprofile und damit eine Auflösung bestehender Präferenzmuster bei den Nachfragern. Ein entsprechendes Beispiel für die wenig erfolgreiche Führung eines

Markenportfolios liefert der Konsumgüterhersteller Unilever: Durch Marken-Neueinführungen beziehungsweise Akquisitionen war Unilevers Markenportfolio bis Ende der 90er Jahre auf annähernd 2.000 Marken angewachsen, was Effizienzeinbußen und den Verlust von Profilschärfe der einzelnen Marken zur Folge hatte. Im Jahr 2000 identifizierte Unilever diese Entwicklung als eine der Kernursachen für die unbefriedigenden Geschäftsergebnisse und antwortete mit harten Einschnitten in das Markenportfolio, das bis 2004 auf 400 Marken reduziert werden soll (Riesenbeck/Perrey 2004, S. 260 ff.).

Was aber sind die richtigen Instrumente und Orientierungsgrößen für die Führung eines Markenportfolios? Zur Restrukturierung und erfolgreichen Führung von Markenportfolios können die meisten der bislang vorliegenden Publikationen über das Markenmanagement nur einen eingeschränkten Beitrag leisten, weil sie die Interdependenzen innerhalb eines Markenportfolios nicht explizit berücksichtigen. Stattdessen sind sie auf die „optimale" Führung **einer** ausgewählten Marke ausgerichtet. Vor diesem Hintergrund stellt die Gestaltung der Markenarchitektur einen Ansatz zur (Re-)Integration der strategischen Markenführung dar.

2. Die Markenarchitekturgestaltung als Grundlage der strategischen Führung von Markenportfolios

Durch die Festlegung der Markenarchitektur wird die oftmals historisch begründete Zusammensetzung des Markenportfolios mit einer inneren Logik ausgestattet, strukturiert und dadurch einer systematischen Steuerung zugänglich gemacht. Den **Gegenstand** der Markenarchitekturgestaltung bildet die Bestimmung der auf den einzelnen Unternehmensebenen zu verwendenden Marken, ihrer spezifischen Rollen und Positionierungen sowie der zwischen den Marken gewünschten Beziehungen (Aaker/Joachimsthaler 2000, S. 135). Die Markenarchitektur eines Unternehmens liefert einen langfristigen Verhaltensplan für die Markenführung und dient in der Umsetzung als Grundlage zur Festlegung von Markenevolutionsstrategien und operativen Markenentscheidungen (vgl. Abbildung 2). Im Ergebnis soll die systematische Markenarchitekturgestaltung zur Ausprägung starker Markenidentitäten führen, bei gleichzeitig hoher Effizienz und Effektivität der Markenführung durch Vermeidung unnötiger Komplexität des Markenportfolios und Ausnutzung bestehender Synergiepotenziale.

Abbildung 2: Organisation von Markenarchitektur, Markenevolutionsstrategien und operativen Markenentscheidungen

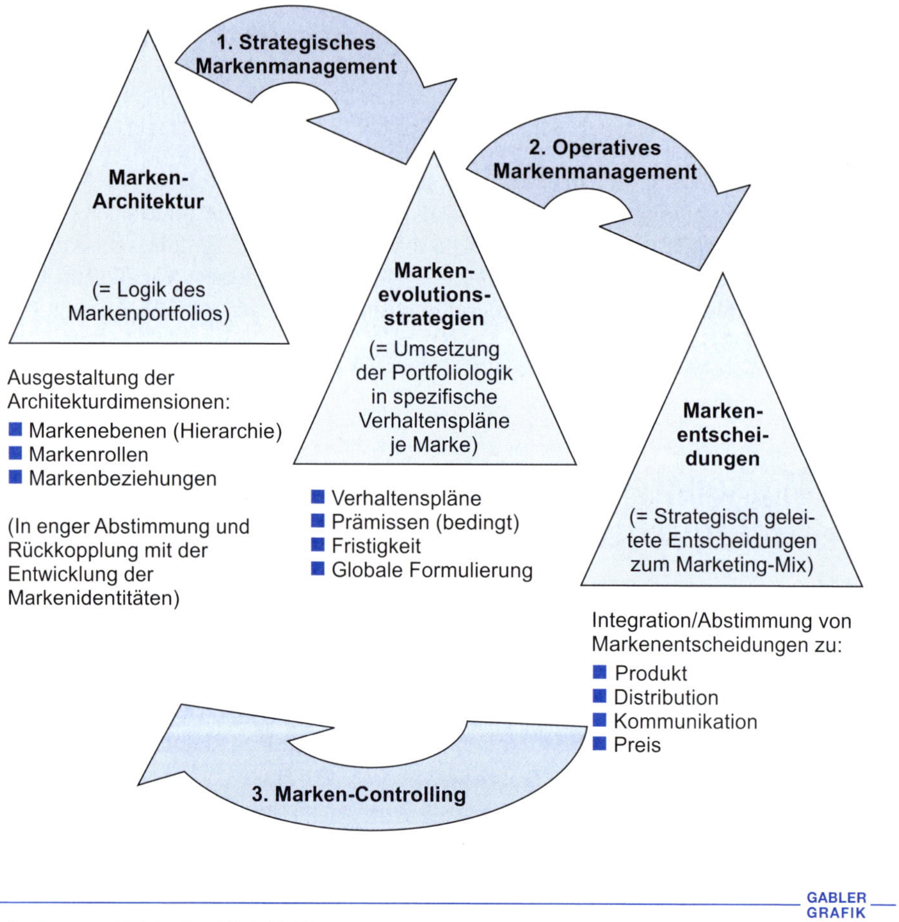

Quelle: Burmann/Spickschen 2004, S. 26

2.1 Unternehmens- und Markenhierarchien

Die Systematisierung der unterschiedlichen Marken eines Unternehmens in einem hierarchischen Ordnungsrahmen sowie die Analyse ihrer Zusammenhänge wird in der anglo-amerikanischen Markenforschung sowohl unter den Begriffen „brand hierarchy" (Keller 2003) als auch „brand architecture" (Aaker/Joachimsthaler 2000; Kapferer 2000) beleuchtet. Ausgangspunkt ist die Überlegung, dass die organisatorischen Ebenen eines

Unternehmens zugleich Ursprung spezifischer **Markenformen** sind. Dieser Zusammenhang lässt sich beispielhaft an einem Unternehmen mit drei Hierarchieebenen – der Top-Management Ebene, der Ebene strategischer Unternehmensbereiche oder Tochtergesellschaften und der Ebene der Produkte beziehungsweise Dienstleistungen – verdeutlichen (vgl. Abbildung 3). Auf der Top-Management-Ebene eines Unternehmens sollte die Führung der **Corporate Brand** angesiedelt sein. Auf der Ebene der strategischen Unternehmensbereiche sind **SBU-Brands** (Strategic Business Units) oder auch **Company-Brands** (sofern es sich um Marken rechtlich eigenständiger Unternehmen innerhalb des Portfolios handelt) anzutreffen. Diese sind hierarchisch der Unternehmensmarke untergeordnet.

Exemplarisch ist diese Differenzierung anhand der Marken Bertelsmann (Unternehmensmarke) und Gruner&Jahr (Unternehmensbereichsmarke) oder EADS (Unternehmensmarke) und Airbus (Unternehmensbereichsmarke) zu belegen. Auf der dritten Ebene der hier beispielhaft betrachteten Unternehmenshierarchie sind schließlich Produktmarken angesiedelt. Hierbei spielt es terminologisch keine Rolle, ob **Produktmarken** für die Vermarktung von Sachgütern oder Dienstleistungen eingesetzt werden. Stellvertretend für andere Produktmarken können hier die Produktmarke Golf von Volkswagen, Persil von Henkel, Nivea von Beiersdorf, dit als Produktmarke der Unternehmensbereichsmarke Dresdner Bank oder ICE bei der Deutschen Bahn genannt werden. Der Zusammenhang zwischen Unternehmens- und Markenhierarchie wird in Abbildung 3 veranschaulicht.

Abbildung 3: Der Zusammenhang von Unternehmens- und Markenhierarchie

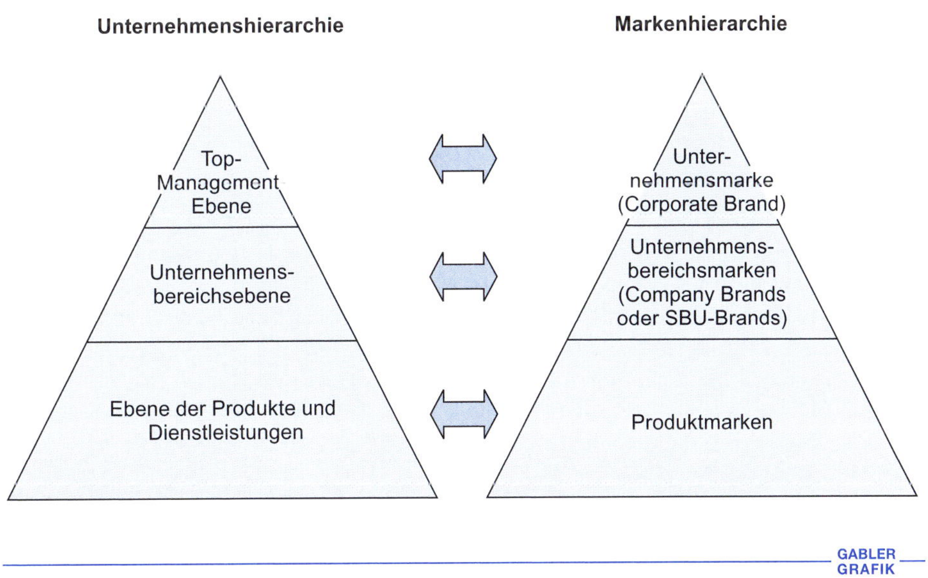

Quelle: in Anlehnung an Keller 2000, S. 536

Von besonderem Interesse für die Führung von Markenportfolios ist die Beziehung zwischen den dargestellten Markenebenen sowie den daraus ableitbaren Handlungsoptionen für die Gestaltung der Markenarchitektur. Eine erste Aussage zur Beziehung zwischen den Markenhierarchieebenen ergibt sich bezüglich der Markenassoziationen. So kann beispielsweise zwischen **organisationalen** (Unternehmensmarke) und **produktbezogenen Markenassoziationen** (Produktmarke) differenziert werden. Vor diesem Hintergrund definiert Aaker die Rolle der Unternehmensmarke als Anker für organisationale Assoziationen (Aaker 2004, S. 264 ff.). Sie soll die Kultur und Werte einer Organisation zum Ausdruck bringen. Darüber hinaus soll die Unternehmensmarke ein möglichst hohes Maß an Glaubwürdigkeit für die Produktmarken erzeugen. Die Rolle der Produktmarken zielt hingegen auf die Verankerung überwiegend produktspezifischer Assoziationen in der Psyche der Nachfrager. Damit wird offensichtlich, dass die Unternehmensmarke eine unterstützende Wirkung für die Wettbewerbsfähigkeit der übrigen Marken im Portfolio hat. Die Unternehmensmarke trägt zur übergreifenden Profilierung gegenüber allen Anspruchsgruppen bei, während Produktmarken an den Interessen einzelner Nachfragersegmente oder spezifischer Leistungsvorteile ausgerichtet sind.

Eine Analyse der **Beziehung zwischen der Unternehmensmarke und den Unternehmensbereichsmarken** ist in der Literatur bislang noch nicht unternommen worden. Dies mag zunächst an der Schwierigkeit liegen, daß beide Markenformen gleichermaßen durch organisationale Assoziationen gekennzeichnet sind. Die Rolle der Unternehmensbereichsmarken besteht zunächst in der Vertiefung bestimmter Assoziationen der Unternehmensmarke. Dadurch kann die Markenkompetenz präziser auf einzelne Märkte zugeschnitten werden, ohne dabei sofort sehr enge Kompetenzassoziationen wie bei einer Produktmarke hervorzurufen. Bei der Kombination beider Markenformen ist aufgrund der Überschneidung der Assoziationen auf eine Vermeidung von Widersprüchen zu achten. Die Kenntnis der Beziehungen zwischen den verschiedenen Markenhierarchieebenen ist die Basis zur Ableitung der Markenarchitektur.

2.2 Strategische Markenrollen

Die Definition der strategischen Rolle jeder Marke im Portfolio ist eine zentrale Aufgabe bei der Gestaltung von Markenarchitekturen. Sie sollte auf Grundlage einer gründlichen Situationsanalyse des Marktes, der Wettbewerber und des eigenen Unternehmens erfolgen. Im Ergebnis sollten alle Zielsetzungen der Markenführung durch vorhandene oder neu aufzubauende Marken umgesetzt werden können und keine Marke ohne zielführende Rolle und Aufgabe im Portfolio verbleiben (Aaker 2004, S. 23 ff.). In der Literatur liefert Keller einen entsprechenden Strukturierungsansatz für strategische Markenrollen in einem Portfolio (Keller 2003, S. 531 ff.):

- Die Rolle der **„Flagship-Brand“** zeichnet sich durch hohe Ergebnisbeiträge und besondere Marktbedeutung (Marktführerschaft) aus (zum Beispiel Persil von Henkel). Sie werden auch als A-Marken bezeichnet.

- **„Flanker-" oder „Fighter-Brands"** dienen der Verteidigung wichtiger und profitabler Marken des Portfolios (zum Beispiel Flagship-Brands), insbesondere gegen Preisdruck durch andere Herstellermarken und vor allem Handelsmarken. Sie werden oft auch als B-Marken bezeichnet. Die Festlegung des Leistungsangebotes dieser Marken bedarf einer gründlichen Analyse, weil der Einsatz von Marken mit dieser Rolle gleichzeitig das Risiko birgt, die profitablere – und laut Rollenbeschreibung zu schützende Marke – zu kannibalisieren (zum Beispiel Spee von Henkel oder HUGO von Boss).
- **„Cash Cow-Brands"** zeichnen sich durch stagnierende beziehungsweise leicht rückläufige Umsätze aus. Sie sind langjährig etabliert und bewegen sich Dank ihres vorhandenen Markenprofils und loyaler Nachfrager in der Profitabilitätszone, obwohl sie wenig bis gar keine Marketingunterstützung erhalten (zum Beispiel Lux-Seife von Unilever oder Weißer Riese-Waschmittel von Henkel). Sie werden auch als C-Marken bezeichnet.
- **„Low-End Entry-Level-Brands"** und **„High-End Prestige-Brands"** werden als Ergänzungen zu einer bestehenden Marke eingesetzt. Sie sollen von den positiven Assoziationen der Nachfrager mit der bestehenden Marke profitieren und zugleich neue Käuferschichten durch Preisvorteile oder einen klaren symbolischen Nutzen erschließen. Trotz der wahrgenommenen Nähe unterscheiden sie sich von der bestehenden Marke in den Schwerpunkten ihres Leistungsspektrums. Boss-Selection im Bekleidungsbereich beziehungsweise United Airlines Express, Hapag-Lloyd Express und GEXX von Germania im Luftfahrtbereich sind Beispiele für High-End Prestige- und Low-End Entry-Level-Brands. In den meisten Praxisbeispielen für Low-End Entry-Level Brands zeigte sich jedoch die große Gefahr dieser speziellen Markenrolle: Sie führt langfristig entweder zum Verschwinden der Muttermarke, zu deren Ergänzung sie ursprünglich gedacht war, oder wird vom Markt nicht akzeptiert (zum Beispiel Lufthansa Express in den 90er Jahren). Dieses Risiko besteht in abgemilderter Form auch für High-End Prestige-Brands (zum Beispiel StyleLab by Diesel).

2.3 Eindimensionale Strukturierungsansätze für Markenarchitekturen

Eine Reihe von Wissenschaftlern hat in den letzten Jahren Ansätze zur Strukturierung von Markenarchitekturen entwickelt (Olins 1989, S. 78; Laforet/Saunders 1994, S. 68 f.; Laforet/Saunders 1999, S. 51 ff.; Aaker/Joachimsthaler 2000, S. 104 ff.; Esch/Bräutigam 2001; Aaker 2004). Als Grundlage zur Bestimmung der Markenarchitektur dient diesen Autoren die Festlegung des vertikalen Integrationsgrades. Unterschiede ergeben sich lediglich im Detail in Abhängigkeit von der jeweils eingenommenen Analyseperspektive.

Der **vertikale Integrationsgrad** bezieht sich auf die Intensität der Verknüpfung der Marken unterschiedlicher organisationalen Ebenen des Unternehmens. Dies umfasst nicht nur die Intensität der Verknüpfung der Corporate Brand mit Marken auf hierarchisch untergeordneten Organisationsebenen (zum Beispiel die mögliche Verknüpfung der Corporate Brand Henkel mit der Produktmarke Persil, in unterschiedlichen Intensitätsstufen), sondern auch die Intensität der Verknüpfung von Marken der strategischen Geschäftseinheiten (SGE) mit Marken auf der Produktebene (zum Beispiel Verwendungsintensität der Marke dit als Marke der Geschäftseinheit Wertpapierfonds der Dresdner Bank auf einzelnen Fondprodukten, zum Beispiel dit-Europazins, dit-Kapital-Plus oder Thesaurus).

Für ein Unternehmen bestimmt sich die Anzahl der hier zu treffenden Entscheidungen durch die Anzahl der Unternehmens- und Markenhierarchieebenen. Basierend auf der Struktur aus Abbildung 3 mit drei verschiedenen Hierarchieebenen ergeben sich zwei Entscheidungstatbestände. Es ist zunächst festzulegen, inwieweit eine Marke auf der Top-Management Ebene und auf der Unternehmensbereichsebene zu verwenden ist. Darauf aufbauend ist zu bestimmen, in welcher Intensität die auf der Unternehmensbereichsebene geführte(n) Marke(n) auf der Produktebene eingesetzt werden. Diese beiden Entscheidungen bestimmen die vertikale Dimension der Markenarchitektur. Die Allianz hat beispielsweise in den ersten Jahren nach der Akquisition ihre Corporate Brand Allianz nicht in ihrem Unternehmensbereich Banken eingesetzt. Dort wurde vielmehr ausschließlich die erworbene Company Brand Dresdner Bank verwendet. Bei der Bertelsmann AG wird die Unternehmensbereichsmarke Gruner + Jahr nicht auf der Produktebene eingesetzt. Hier kommen stattdessen die Produktmarken wie Stern oder GEO zum Einsatz.

Abbildung 4: **Eindimensionale Strukturierung von Markenarchitekturoptionen („Brand Relationship Spectrum")**

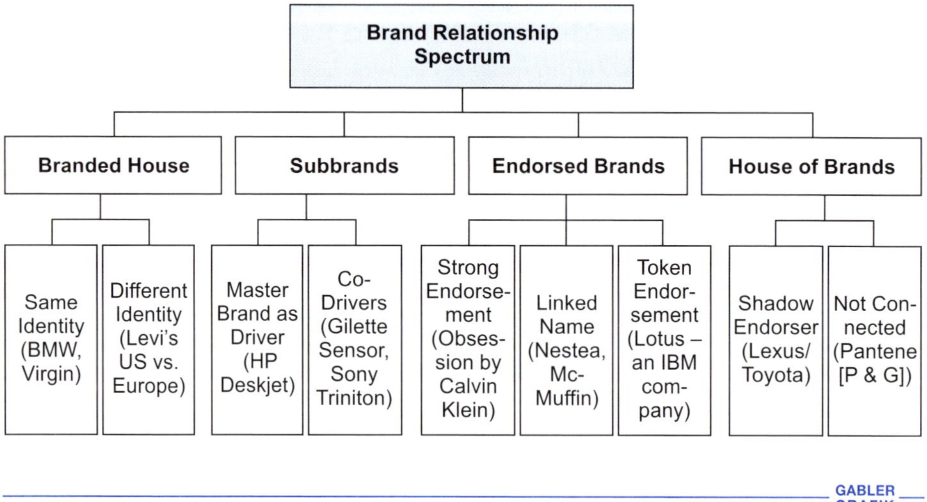

Quelle: Aaker/Joachimsthaler 2000, S. 106

Aufbauend auf dem Ansatz von Laforet und Saunders (1994, S. 68 ff.) unterscheiden Aaker und Joachimsthaler in ihrer eindimensionalen Strukturierung möglicher Handlungsoptionen vier Architekturtypen (vgl. Abbildung 4). Sie spannen dabei ein Kontinuum auf zwischen einer **House of Brands**-Architektur und einer **Branded House**-Architektur. Diese beiden Optionen bilden die Endpunkte des Kontinuums, welches den Grad der vertikalen Integration einer Markenarchitektur beschreibt. Sie werden ergänzt durch die zwei gemischten Architekturtypen **Sub-Branding** und **Endorsement Branding**. Diese vier Grundtypen unterteilen sie weiter in neun Unterformen, deren klare, überschneidungsfreie Abgrenzung ihnen jedoch nicht gelingt (Aaker/Joachimsthaler 2000, S. 104 ff.; Aaker 2004, S. 48).

Abbildung 5: **Ausgewählte Beispiele für die vier Basisoptionen der Gestaltung von Markenarchitekturen nach Aaker/Joachimsthaler**

Unternehmens-ebene	Branded House	Subbrand	Endorsed Brands	House of Brands
Unternehmens-ebene	Virgin Lufthansa	hp invent	Nestlé Good Food, Good Life	Procter&Gamble ↕
Unternehmens-bereichs-ebene	Virgin trains Virgin mobile	hp invent	Nestlé Good Food, Good Life	Procter&Gamble
Produkt-ebene	Virgin Cola	HP Deskjet HP Officejet HP Designjet HP LaserJet	Nestlé Nesquik Nestea Nescafé	Luvs.com Pampers

GABLER GRAFIK

Die vier Basisoptionen bei der Gestaltung einer Markenarchitektur nach Aaker/Joachimsthaler lassen sich folgendermaßen charakterisieren (vgl. Abbildung 5):

- **Branded House Option**: Bei dieser Strategie liegt ein maximaler vertikaler Integrationsgrad vor. Es werden alle Leistungen eines Unternehmens unter der Corporate Brand geführt. Diese ersetzt den eigenständigen Auftritt von Unternehmensbereichs-

und Produktmarken. Diese Markenarchitektur ist sowohl bei Güterherstellern als auch bei Dienstleistungsunternehmen anzutreffen, zum Beispiel bei Virgin, Nokia, IBM oder McDonald's.

- **House of Brands Option**: Es tritt nicht die Corporate Brand, sondern ausschließlich Produktmarken oder Unternehmensbereichsmarken gegenüber den Endnachfragern in Erscheinung. Der vertikale Integrationsgrad ist also minimal. Auf der Produktebene wird typischerweise eine Einzel- oder Mehrmarkenstrategie verfolgt. Gerade bei Konsumgüterherstellern mit dem Bedarf nach unterschiedlichen Positionierungen ihrer Produkte findet diese Option häufig Verwendung (zum Beispiel bei Procter & Gamble oder Unilever).

Zwei weitere Basisoptionen zur Gestaltung der Markenarchitektur ergeben sich durch Kombinationen aus zwei Marken eines Unternehmens, die in einem hierarchischen Über-/Unterordnungsverhältnis stehen. Laforet und Saunders konnten in einer empirischen Studie für die Lebensmittelindustrie zeigen, dass diese beiden Basisoptionen dort in 52 Prozent der untersuchten Fälle verwendet wurden (Laforet/Saunders 1999, S. 52 ff.). Die Über- beziehungsweise Unterordnung bezieht sich nicht nur auf die Verwendung von Unternehmens- und Produktmarken, sie kann sich beispielsweise ebenso auf Unternehmensbereichs- und Produktmarken beziehen. In jedem Falle ergibt sich hier ein mittlerer Integrationsgrad. Dabei kann hinsichtlich der dominierenden Rolle im jeweiligen Auftritt der zwei Marken differenziert werden:

- **Sub-Branding Option**: Hier dominiert zumeist die Corporate Brand beziehungsweise die Unternehmensbereichsmarke. Sie wird durch spezifische Zusätze im Sinne von Untermarken (Sub-Brands) ergänzt. Diese Zusätze beziehen sich oft auf ausgewählte Leistungsmerkmale. Exemplarisch sei auf den Zusatz „Deskjet" bei Druckern von Hewlett & Packard hingewiesen. Als spezielle Erscheinungsform dieser Option können beide Marke auch gleichberechtigt zur Markierung beitragen, wie dies beispielsweise bei Gilette (Gilette Sensor) der Fall ist.
- **Endorsement Branding Option**: Hier dominiert die Produktmarke. Sie wird durch einen dezenten, kleinen Hinweis auf die Zugehörigkeit der Produktmarke zu einem übergeordneten, größeren Unternehmen oder Unternehmensbereich unterstützt (endorsed). Der Nutzen der Endorsement Option und ihre präferenzfördernde Wirkung ist unter anderem durch Saunders und Guoqun (1996) empirisch nachgewiesen worden. Wichtig ist hier die Abgrenzung zwischen Endorsement und Produktmarke hinsichtlich ihrer spezifischen Rollen. Das Endorsement (Unternehmens- oder Unternehmensbereichsmarke) dient primär zur Vermittlung von Glaubwürdigkeit und damit zur Absicherung des Leistungsversprechens der Produktmarke, welche wiederum die spezifische Leistungskompetenz zum Ausdruck bringen soll. Weil das Endorsement eine Klammerfunktion für die Produktmarken einnimmt, ist bei seiner Führung auf die Herausstellung bestimmter, übergreifender Inhaltsdimensionen zu achten. Eine Endorsement-Markenarchitektur findet sich beispielsweise bei Nestlé. In diesem Zusammenhang ist eine **Sonderform** der Endorsement-Architektur zu erwähnen, bei der die gemeinsam auftretenden Marken eines Unternehmen auf derselben Hierarchieebene des Unternehmens angesiedelt sind. Beispielsweise ist auf der

Verpackung der Toilettenpapiermarke Charmin von Procter & Gamble (P&G) der Hinweis zu lesen „Vom Hersteller der Tempo Taschentücher". Hier werden also mehrere Produktmarken gemeinsam zur Markierung verwendet, wobei die für die Endorsement Option typische Dominanz einer Produktmarke, hier Charmin, erhalten bleibt.

Schließlich können alle vier **Basisoptionen miteinander kombiniert** auftreten. So könnte beispielsweise ein multinational orientiertes Unternehmen mit starker Marktposition im Heimatmarkt und schwacher Marktposition in den Auslandsmärkten im Inland eine House of Brands Architektur, in den Auslandsmärkten hingegen eine Branded House Architektur wählen.

2.4 Mehrdimensionaler Strukturierungsansatz für Markenarchitekturen

Die eindimensional auf den vertikalen Integrationsgrad abzielenden Markenarchitekturansätze in der Literatur werden der Entscheidungskomplexität in der Praxis nicht gerecht. Vor dem Hintergrund der oben beschriebenen Ziele und Gegenstande der Markenarchitekturgestaltung ergeben sich mehr als eine Entscheidungsdimension. Es liegt bislang erst ein mehrdimensionaler Gestaltungsansatz vor, der nachfolgend näher beschrieben werden soll.

Abbildung 6: Gestaltungsdimensionen von Markenarchitekturen

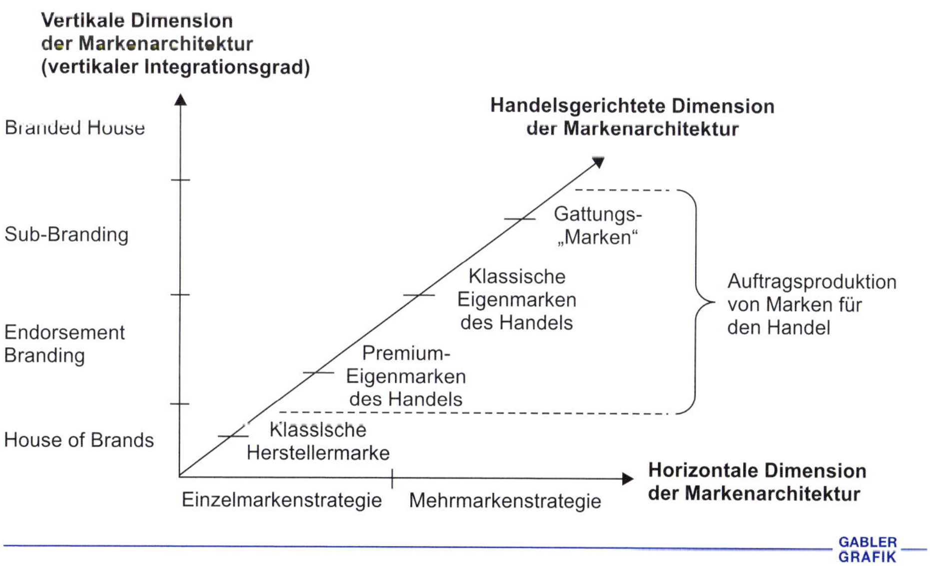

Quelle: Burmann/Blinda/Nitschke 2003, S. 26

Burmann, Blinda und Nitschke (2003, S. 26 ff.) schlagen zur Erfassung und Analyse von Markenarchitekturen eine Erweiterung der vertikalen um eine horizontale und eine handelsgerichtete Dimension vor (vgl. Abbildung 6).

Abbildung 7: Bewertungskriterien für die Auswahl der vertikalen Basisoption bei der Gestaltung von Markenarchitekturen

	Gestaltungsoptionen			
Kriterien	**Branded House**	**House of Brands**	**Endorsement**	**Sub-Branding**
Interne Kriterien				
Risikoausgleich	– –	+	++	O
Synergienutzung	++	O	+	++
Kosten/Marktinvestionen	++	++	O	++
Interne Akzeptanz bei Mitarbeitern	++	O	++	++
Managementakzeptanz	[illegible]	[illegible]	O	++
Implementierungsdauer	[illegible]	[illegible]	+	– –
Koordinierungsbedarf	– –	+	[illegible]	O
Externe Kriterien				
Strategieflexibilität	++	O	++	++
Positionierungs- und Aktionsflexibilität	++	O	++	++
Marktausschöpfung	++	+	O	++
Akzeptanz bei Allianz- und Kooperationspartnern	++	O	++	++
Akzeptanz bei Nachfragern	++	++	O	++
Akzeptanz bei Shareholdern	++	O	+	++
Cross-Selling-Potenziale	++	++	O	++

GABLER GRAFIK

Quelle: Burmann/Spickschen 2004, S. 39

2.41 Vertikale Dimension

In der vertikalen Dimension der Markenarchitektur verwendet dieser Ansatz die von Aaker und Joachimsthaler vorgestellten und bereits beschriebenen vier Basisoptionen. Zur Beurteilung und Auswahl der geeigneten Basisoptionen kann auf die in Abbildung 7 dargestellten Kriterien zurückgegriffen werden, die hier an einem anonymisierten praktischen Beispiel exemplarisch angewendet wurden. In Abhängigkeit von dem zu analysierenden Unternehmen sollten die Kriterien gewichtet werden, um im Sinne eines Scoring-Modells die Entscheidungsfindung zweckmäßig zu unterstützen. Die Bewertungskriterien berücksichtigen sowohl unternehmensinterne Aspekte wie interne Akzeptanz, Synergieausschöpfung, Implementierungskosten oder Koordinationsbedarf, als auch unternehmensexterne Aspekte wie externe Akzeptanz, Spielraum für Markenstrategieänderungen oder auch Aktivierungspotenzial für ein Cross-Selling.

2.42 Horizontale Dimension

In der horizontalen Dimension der Markenarchitektur gibt es zwei Gestaltungsoptionen, die Einzelmarken- und die Mehrmarkenstrategie. Die Markenfamilienstrategie (Meffert 2002, S. 142) wird hier sachlogisch nicht der Markenarchitektur, sondern dem Bereich der Markenevolutionsstrategien zugeordnet (vgl. den Beitrag zu den Markenevolutionsstrategien in diesem Buch). Im Rahmen der Gestaltung von Markenarchitekturen geht es um die Festlegung der grundsätzlichen Positionierungen und strategischen Rollen der Marken eines Unternehmens. Beides ist von der konkreten Anzahl der von einer Marke angebotenen Produkte, als einzigem Unterscheidungsmerkmal zwischen Einzelmarke und Familienmarke, unabhängig. Darüber hinaus ist ausgehend von einer Einprodukt-marke eine Abgrenzung von Familienmarken gegenüber Markenerweiterungen nicht möglich. Aus diesem Grunde wird auf Familienmarken hier und im Rahmen der Markenevolutionsstrategien nicht eingegangen.

Mit der Entscheidung für eine Einmarken- oder Mehrmarkenstrategie legt ein Unternehmen fest, ob die ausgewählten Marktsegmente mit ausschließlich einer Marke oder mit mehreren konkurrierenden Marken bearbeitet werden.

Bei der **Einzelmarkenstrategie** wird jedes Produkt eines Unternehmens unter einer eigenen Marke angeboten (Meffert 2002, S. 138 ff.). Jedes Marktsegment wird dabei von nur einer Marke bearbeitet. Eine Einzelmarkenstrategie verfolgt beispielsweise das Unternehmen Ferrero mit seinen Marken Nutella, Duplo, Giotto oder Raffaelo.

Ein wesentlicher **Vorteil** dieser Strategie besteht in der Möglichkeit, für jede Marke eine unverwechselbare Markenidentität mit spezifischen Markenleistungen aufbauen zu können. Das Bedürfnisprofil der Nachfrager und das Nutzenprofil der Marke können optimal aufeinander abgestimmt werden, wobei der Koordinationsbedarf zwischen den Marken eines Unternehmens gering ist.

Mit dem Aufbau einer individuellen Markenidentität ist auch die Bildung eines eigenständigen Markenimages verbunden. Dies verhindert negative Ausstrahlungseffekte zwischen den verschiedenen Einzelmarken, unterbindet gleichzeitig aber auch eine mögliche gegenseitige Stärkung. So würde beispielsweise ein potenzieller Imageeinbruch bei Pampers (Windeln) nicht zwangsläufig zu negativen Ausstrahlungseffekten bei Tempo (Papiertaschentücher) oder Blend-a-Med (Zahnpasta) führen, obwohl beide Einzelmarken zum Unternehmen Procter & Gamble gehören.

Der **Nachteil**, dass die Einzelmarke in allen Lebenszyklusphasen die gesamten Markenführungsaufwendungen allein zu tragen hat, spricht gegen diese Strategie. Bei der Markteinführung und dem Markenaufbau entstehen dem Unternehmen dadurch vergleichsweise hohe Kosten. Da es sich um eine komplette Neueinführung der Marke handelt, kann nicht auf bestehende Bekanntheit und Akzeptanz im Markt oder Händlergoodwill zurückgegriffen werden. Sind auf Dauer für notwendige Produktmodifikationen nicht genügend Finanzmittel vorhanden, kann sich die Lebensdauer der Einzelmarke verkürzen, welches unter Umständen eine Amortisation der aufgewendeten Marketingkosten verhindert. Die, aufgrund der Informationsüberlastung der Nachfrager und der hohen Wettbewerbsintensität vieler Märkte, stark gestiegenen Mediaaufwendungen zur Profilierung von Marken sprechen ebenfalls gegen eine Einzelmarke. Auch der Aufbau echter Leistungsvorteile ist bei einer Vielzahl von Einzelmarken im Unternehmen schwierig zu realisieren, weil die meisten Unternehmen nur über ein enges Set an Kompetenzen verfügen, mit denen sich in glaubwürdiger Weise Markenidentitäten aufbauen lassen.

Im Gegensatz zur Einzelmarkenstrategie werden bei der **Mehrmarkenstrategie** von einem Unternehmen mindestens zwei Marken in demselben Produktbereich parallel geführt (vgl. den Beitrag zur Mehrmarkenstrategie in diesem Buch). Diese sprechen nicht getrennte, sondern identische Marktsegmente an. Die einzelnen Marken unterscheiden sich dabei in den Produkteigenschaften, im Preis oder auch im kommunikativen Auftritt. Beispielsweise bietet der Volkswagenkonzern im Marktsegment der Kompaktwagen drei Marken an (VW, Skoda, SEAT), deren Produkte sich technisch weitgehend gleichen.

Als **Vorteil** dieser Strategie ist zunächst die breitere Marktabdeckung zu nennen, welche durch die Schaffung von „Konkurrenz im eigenen Hause" in der Lage ist, Markenwechsler mit dem eigenen Produktprogramm zu bedienen. Darüber hinaus kann durch mehrere Marken der interne Wettbewerb verschärft und dadurch Leistungen optimiert werden.

Die **Nachteile** dieser Strategie liegen zum Beispiel in den vergleichsweise geringeren Umsatzzuwächsen bei einer Markenneueinführung (Meffert 1999) oder dem Anstieg von Komplexitätskosten, welcher die Rentabilität trotz eines Umsatzanstiegs oft verschlechtert (Quelch/Kenny 1995; Bliss 2000). Daneben besteht die Gefahr der Kannibalisierung der Marken (vgl. den Beitrag zur Markenkannibalisierung in diesem Buch). Tabelle 1 fasst die Chancen und Risiken der Einzel- und Mehrmarkenstrategie zusammen.

Tabelle 1: Vergleich der Einzel- und Mehrmarkenstrategie

Strategietyp / Aspekte	Einzelmarke	Mehrmarke
Merkmal	■ Führung eines jeden Produkts unter einer Marke	■ In jedem Produktbereich parallele Führung von mindestens zwei auf den Gesamtmarkt ausgerichteten Marken
Chancen	■ Gezielte Ansprache einzelner Kundensegmente ■ Spezifische Markendifferenzierung durch optimale Abstimmung von Bedürfnisprofilen ■ Aufbau eines unverwechselbaren Produktimages ■ Kaum Gefahr negativer Ausstrahlungseffekte auf andere Marken ■ Geringerer Koordinationsbedarf bei den unterschiedlichen Marktanteils- und Kostendegressionseffekten	■ Bessere Marktausschöpfung ■ Halten von potenziellen Markenwechslern durch Produktdifferenzierung ■ Erhöhte Markteintrittsbarrieren für Konkurrenzmarken dank breiterer Regalflächenabdeckung ■ Schutz der übrigen Produkte vor Preiskampf durch Einführung von „Kampfmarken"
Risiken	■ Zurechnung der Markenkosten allein auf ein Produkt ■ Ungenügende Amortisation der aufgewendeten Kosten bei kurzer Lebensdauer der Einzelmarke ■ Trend des Markennamens zur Bezeichnung der Produktgattung und Verlust der differenzierenden Markenpersönlichkeit ■ Fehlende Stützung der Produktmarke durch angrenzende Marken	■ Suboptimale Verwendung der finanziellen und personellen Unternehmensressourcen ■ Gefahr der Übersegmentierung ■ Kannibalisierung der eigenen Monomarke durch gegenseitige Substitution der Marktanteile
Zentrale Anforderungen	■ Möglichkeit des Aufbaus einer eigenständigen Markenpersönlichkeit	■ Existenz von Finanzkraft und Management-Know-how in ausreichendem Maße. Glaubwürdige Markendifferenzierung

GABLER GRAFIK

2.43 Handelsgerichtete Dimension

Die handelsgerichtete Dimension der Markenarchitektur erfasst die Positionierung eines Unternehmens im vertikalen Wettbewerb. Hierbei gilt es festzulegen, ob ein Unternehmen seine Produkte ausschließlich als klassischer Markenhersteller anbietet oder ob es stattdessen beziehungsweise darüber hinaus die Absatzmittler (Groß- und/oder Einzelhandel, Importeure, Exporteure) mit Produkten für deren Eigenmarken (so genannte private label) beliefert (vgl. Abbildung 6). Im letztgenannten Fall ist ferner festzulegen, welches Qualitätsniveau diese Produkte haben sollen (Premiumeigenmarken des Handels, klassische Eigenmarken des Handels oder Gattungsmarken). Dies ist umso bedeutender, da Kannibalisierungseffekte sowie eine Imageschädigung der eigenen Herstellermarken vermieden werden müssen.

Die **Imageerosion und der Relevanzverlust vieler Herstellermarken** aus Sicht der Endnachfrager in den vergangenen Jahren ist ganz wesentlich auf Managementdefizite der Industrie bei der Ausgestaltung der handelsgerichteten Dimension der Markenarchitektur zurückzuführen. Die parallele Belieferung der Absatzmittler mit qualitativ (nahezu) identischen Produkten für deren Handelsmarken hat den „Geiz ist geil"-Trend erst ermöglicht und den eigenen (Hersteller-)Marken langfristig die Existenzgrundlage entzogen. In überzogener Wachstumseuphorie und Selbstüberschätzung aufgebaute Produktionskapazitäten sind hier oft die Ursache vieler Entscheidungen zu Gunsten der vermeintlich attraktiven Produktion von „private labeln". Die häufig mehrjährige Verzögerung beim Auftreten der Probleme für die eigenen Marken macht deren Identifikation und Verhinderung in einem auf kurzfristige Erfolge ausgerichteten Unternehmen nahezu unmöglich. Hier ist mancherorts eine Neuorientierung der Führungsphilosophie erforderlich.

Die zunehmende Produkthomogenität und der Aufbau von Markenführungskompetenz im Handel haben den Relevanzverlust bei vielen Herstellermarken in jüngster Zeit noch beschleunigt. Dies ist in vielen Fällen auf das Fehlen spezifischer Markenkompetenzen auf Seiten der Herstellermarken beziehungsweise Industrie zurückzuführen (Burmann 2003). In Ermangelung spezifischer Kompetenzen, die allein in der Lage sind, den Herstellermarken in nachhaltiger Weise Einzigartigkeit zu verleihen, ist eine Behauptung gegenüber dem Handel langfristig nahezu unmöglich. In einem solchen Fall befriedigt eine Herstellermarke wenig mehr als Basisbedürfnisse und austauschbare Zusatzbedürfnisse und ist vom Absatzmittler leicht durch eine Handelsmarke zu ersetzen.

Als **Handelsmarken** werden in diesem Zusammenhang Waren- oder Firmenkennzeichen definiert, mit denen eine Handelsorganisation ihre Waren markiert. Mit dieser Definition ist jedoch keine explizite Beschreibung der Marken verbunden, sondern lediglich der Handel als Träger der Marke festgelegt. Lange Zeit herrschte **Uneinigkeit darüber, ob es sich bei Handelsmarken überhaupt um echte Marken handelt**. Wendet man die konstitutiven Merkmale der Marke nach Mellerowicz (1963) an, ist leicht ersichtlich, dass die Handelsmarke zum Beispiel das Kriterium der Ubiquität nicht erfüllen kann, da die Marke zumeist nur in den Geschäftsstätten eines Handelsunternehmens erhältlich ist. Unter Verwendung der modernen Markendefinition aus dem ersten Kapitel dieses Buches können Handelsmarken jedoch durchaus den Rang einer echten Marke erreichen. Dies trifft bislang vor allem auf die Corporate Brands im Einzelhandel zu, wohingegen vielen „Marken" des Handels auf der Produktebene aufgrund ihrer vollständigen Austauschbarkeit ein Markenstatus nicht zuzusprechen ist. Im Folgenden soll auf die drei wichtigsten Erscheinungsformen von Handelsmarken auf der Produktebene näher eingegangen werden, um die einzelnen Optionen auf der handelsgerichteten Dimension der Markenarchitektur zu konkretisieren.

Gattungsmarken erfüllen in ihrer Produktkategorie jeweils nur die qualitativen **Mindestanforderungen** und besetzen das Preiseinstiegssegment. Dabei liegen sie nicht selten circa 50 Prozent unter dem Preisniveau der Herstellermarkenartikel (Ahlert/Kenning/Schneider 2001, S. 46). Da sie oft in weißer Verpackung auftreten und nur die Gattungsbezeichnung (zum Beispiel Mehl, Zucker etc.) auf der Verpackung führen, werden sie auch als „no names", „generics" oder „weiße Ware" bezeichnet. Dabei ist es keineswegs so, dass Gattungsmarken unmarkiert sind. In ihrer gewollten Schlichtheit besitzen sie vielmehr eine sortimentseinheitliche Gestaltung mit einem eindeutigen Wiedererkennungssymbol und Namen. Slogans wie „gut und billig" oder „attraktiv und preiswert" dienen darüber hinaus der Orientierung der Nachfrager. Das Handelsunternehmen selbst tritt im Markennamen selten in Erscheinung, um einen negativen Imagetransfer zu vermeiden. Die Marken-Tipp von Extra, AS von Schlecker und SmartPrice von Wal Mart sind einige der bekanntesten Gattungsmarken in der deutschen Handelslandschaft.

Die Gattungsmarken beschränken sich zumeist auf Produktgruppen, bei denen auf Nachfragerseite ein geringes Einkaufsrisiko wahrgenommen wird und auf Produzentenseite eine einfache Produktgestaltung vorherrscht. Dies ist häufig bei Verbrauchsgütern des täglichen Bedarfs der Fall. Dementsprechend ist in diesen Segmenten der Anteil der Gattungsmarken besonders hoch.

Bei der Einführung der Gattungsmarken in den 60er Jahren hatten diese vor allem die Aufgabe, die klassischen Handelsunternehmen im Preiskampf mit den aufkommenden Discounthandelsformen zu stärken. Heute dienen die Gattungsmarken primär zur **Abrundung des Sortiments** der Handelsunternehmung und als Signal für die Preiswürdigkeit der Einkaufsstätte im Wettbewerb (Becker 2002, S. 219 ff.). Eine direkte Konkurrenz zum klassischen Herstellermarkenartikel wird nicht angestrebt.

Die **klassischen Eigenmarken** des Handels streben ein Qualitätsniveau an, welches mit den klassischen Herstellermarken etwa vergleichbar ist (Dumke 1996, S. 123). Allerdings zeichnen sie sich bei ähnlichen Ausstattungs- und Qualitätsmerkmalen durch einen **deutlichen Preisvorteil** gegenüber den Herstellermarkenartikeln aus. Beispiele aus der Praxis sind die Marke Milsani für Milchprodukte von Aldi oder die Marke Salto für Tiefkühl- und Fertiggerichte von REWE. Diese klassischen Eigenmarken sind primär in Produktkategorien mit geringem Innovationsgrad zu finden. Häufig stellen sie Nachbildungen von Herstellermarken dar und treten als Folger in bereits erschlossene, reife Märkte ein.

Ihre Qualität soll denen der Herstellermarken möglichst ebenbürtig sein, damit der Verbraucher den niedrigen Preis im Sinne eines guten Preis-Leistungs-Verhältnisses wahrnimmt und eine Präferenz für diese Marken aufbaut. Die Verpackungsgestaltung nimmt für diese Marken eine wichtige Stellung ein, da durch sie am Point of Sale (PoS) die im Vergleich zu Herstellermarken geringere Endverbraucherwerbung kompensiert werden muss. Oft wird die Verpackung einer bekannten Marke als Vorbild für die Gestaltung der Eigenmarke verwendet, um an deren Imagebonus teilhaben zu können. Dementsprechend hat beispielsweise die englische Handelskette Sainsbury ihr Cola-Getränk gemäß dem Design des bekannten Marktführers Coca-Cola gestaltet.

Abbildung 8: Imagebonus durch Adaption des Designs von Herstellermarken

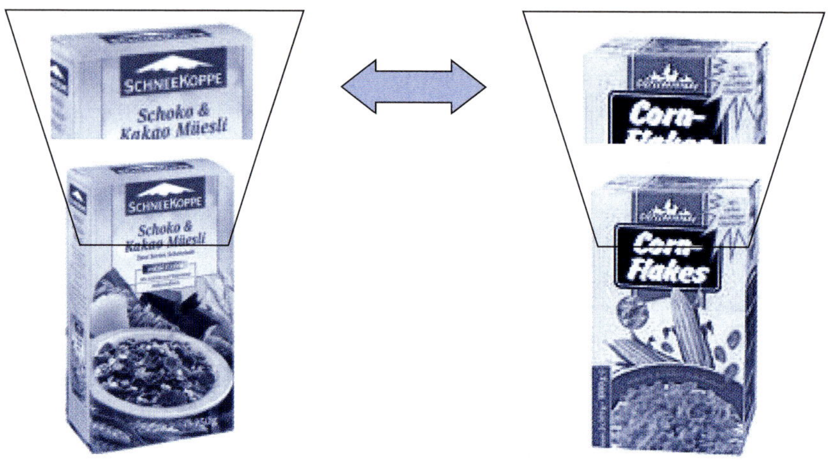

Schneekoppe **Gletscherkrone (Aldi)**

GABLER GRAFIK

Um erfolgreich am Markt agieren zu können, ist für diese Form der Handelsmarken ein professionelles Marketing und ein kontinuierliches **Handelsmarkenmanagement** unerlässlich. Die relativ hohe und beständige Qualität, die möglichst hohe Bekanntheit und Verbreitung sowie die werbliche Unterstützung sind ebenfalls von großer Bedeutung für den Erfolg der klassischen Eigenmarken des Handels. Auf der finanziellen Seite sollen diese Eigenmarken durch günstige Bezugsbedingungen und niedrigere Vertriebskosten bessere Spannen für den Handel erwirtschaften als die Herstellermarken. Der Beitrag der Handelsmarken zur Profilierung des Handels ist im Vergleich zur Herstellermarke bisher allerdings nur ansatzweise erforscht. Nach einer Studie von Ahlert, Kenning und Schneider (2001, S. 252 f.) stellen jedoch die Profilierung, die Kundenbindung sowie die Renditeverbesserung die Hauptziele der klassischen Handelsmarkenpolitik dar (Zellekens/Horbert 1998).

Die **Premium Eigenmarken des Handels** streben eine im Vergleich zum Durchschnitt der Herstellermarken in einer Warengruppe überlegene Qualität an. Sie stellen somit nicht wie die anderen Handelsmarkentypen „Me-too"-Produkte dar (Horbert 2000). Durch die Zurverfügungstellung eines einzigartigen Zusatznutzens wollen sie eine höhere Kundenzufriedenheit und damit eine höhere Kundenbindung erreichen. Die erhöhte Qualität soll dabei den Preis als Entscheidungskriterium in den Hintergrund treten lassen und dem Handel einen preispolitischen Spielraum verschaffen. Das englische Unternehmen Marks & Spencer beispielsweise vertreibt unter seinem Handelsmarkenlabel St. Michael ein Nahrungsmittelsortiment, welches die qualitativen Ansprüche vieler Herstellermarken übertrifft und damit eine erhöhte Preisbereitschaft beim Nachfrager erzeugt (Dunne/Narasimhan 1999, S. 95 ff.). Eine ähnliche Preisprämie erreicht die Marke Füllhorn von REWE, die den Nachfragern durch die Herausstellung der Ökologieorientierung der Lebensmittel einen Zusatznutzen kommuniziert. Die Premium-Handelsmarken zeichnen sich generell durch eine eigenständige und individuelle Produktgestaltung aus und sind zumeist in Segmenten mit hoher Innovationsrate angesiedelt. Für den Erfolg der Premium-Handelsmarken sind die überlegene Qualität und der Einsatz kommunikationspolitischer Maßnahmen unabdingbar. Ohne die Bereitstellung der spezifischen Kompetenzen der Herstellermarkenproduzenten dürften sie jedoch nur in den seltensten Fällen ihre Marktposition nachhaltig verteidigen können. Die kooperierende Industrie ermöglicht somit den Premium-Eigenmarken des Handels erst ihre Existenz.

Letztlich ist die Entscheidung zu Gunsten einer der handelsgerichteten Markenarchitekturoptionen nur vor dem Hintergrund der im Unternehmen verfügbaren Ressourcen und Kompetenzen, eines langfristigen Rentabilitätsvergleichs und einer sorgsamen Analyse der Risikoexposition und Risikoneigung des jeweiligen Unternehmens zu treffen.

Aufgrund zahlreicher **Interdependenzen** handelt es sich bei der Gestaltung der einzelnen Dimensionen der Markenarchitektur nicht um ein sequentielles, sondern um ein simultan zu lösendes Entscheidungsproblem. Die Entscheidungen zur Markenarchitektur müssen dabei im Kontext der Markenevolutionsstrategien betrachtet werden.

3. Fazit

Während die Entscheidungen im Rahmen der Markenarchitekturgestaltung eine zeitpunktbezogene Analyse unterstellen, steht bei der Festlegung der Markenevolutionsstrategie die zukunftsgerichtete, dynamische Entwicklung des Markenportfolios im Mittelpunkt (vgl. hierzu den Beitrag zu Markenevolutionsstrategien in diesem Buch). Darüber hinaus rückt die Markenevolutionsstrategie von der Betrachtung des Markenportfolios in seiner Gesamtheit ab und legt die zukünftige Entwicklung und Position einer jeden einzelnen Marke fest. Die Analyse und Gestaltung der Markenarchitektur ist insoweit eng mit der Festlegung der Markenevolutionsstrategie und der Konzeption der Identitäten aller Marken eines Unternehmens abzustimmen.

Literatur

Aaker, D. A. (2004), Brand Portfolio Strategy – Creating Relevance, Differentiation, Energy, Leverage and Clarity, New York u.a.

Aaker, D. A., Joachimsthaler, E. (2000), Brand Leadership, New York.

Ahlert, D., Kenning, P., Schneider, D. (2001), Das Wachstum der Handelsmarken – Ursachen und Zukunftsperspektiven, in: Bruhn, M. (Hrsg.), Handelsmarken – Entwicklungstendenzen und Zukunftsperspektiven der Handelsmarkenpolitik, 3. Aufl., Wiesbaden, S. 243–260.

Becker, J. (2002), Marketing-Konzeption, 7. Aufl., München.

Bliss, Ch. (2000), Management von Komplexität – Ein integrierter, systemtheoretischer Ansatz zur Komplexitätsreduktion, Wiesbaden.

Burmann, Ch. (2003), Kompetenz entscheidet – Worauf es bei einem erfolgreichen Markenmanagement ankommt, in: Verlagsbeilage „Marken" der Frankfurter Allgemeinen Zeitung (FAZ) vom 25. Juni 2003, S. B3.

Burmann, Ch., Blinda, L., Nitschke, A. (2003), Konzeptionelle Grundlagen des Identitätsbasierten Markenmanagements, LiM Arbeitspapiere, Nr. 1, Bremen.

Burmann, Ch., Spickschen, J. (2004), Die Relevanz der Corporate Brand in der Markenarchitekturgestaltung internationaler Finanzdienstleister, LiM Arbeitspapiere, Nr. 8, Universität Bremen, Burmann, Chr. (Hrsg.), Bremen.

Dumke, St. (1996), Handelsmarkenmanagement, Hamburg.

Dunne, D., Narasimhan, Ch. (1999), Neue Gewinnchancen mit Eigenmarken, in: Harvard Business Manager, No. 6, S. 95–101.

Esch, F.-R., Bräutigam, S. (2001), Analyse und Gestaltung komplexer Markenarchitekturen, in: Esch, F.-R. (Hrsg.), Moderne Markenführung, 3. Aufl., Wiesbaden, S. 711–732.

Horbert, C. (2000), Handelsmarken 2000 – Strategien, Potenzial, Perspektiven, Köln.

Kapferer, J.-N. (2000), Strategic Brand Management, 3. Aufl., London.

Keller, K. L. (2003), Strategic Brand Management: building, measuring and managing brand equity, 2. Aufl., Upper Saddle River.

Laforet, S., Saunders, J. (1994), Managing Brand Portfolios, in: Journal of Advertising Research, Vol. 34, Nr. 5, S. 64–76.

Laforet, S., Saunders, J. (1999), Managing Brand Portfolios: Why Leaders do what they do, in: Journal of Advertising Research, January-February, S. 51–66.

Meffert, H. (1999) Mehrmarkenstrategien – immer die beste Option?, in: Absatzwirtschaft, Sondernummer Oktober, S. 82–87.

Meffert, H. (2002), Strategische Optionen der Markenführung, in: Meffert, H.; Burmann, Ch.; Koers, M. (Hrsg.), Markenmanagement – Grundfragen der identitätsorientierten Markenführung, Wiesbaden, S. 135–165.

Mellerowicz, K. (1963), Markenartikel – Die ökonomischen Gesetze ihrer Preisbildung und Preisbindung, 2. Aufl., München u. a.

o.V. (2001), Report on consolidation in the financial sector, January.

Olins, W. (1989), Corporate Identity: making business strategy visible through design, Boston.

Quelch, J. A., Kenny, D. (1995), Markenpolitik I: Lieber den Gewinn steigern als die Zahl der Varianten, in: Harvard Business Manager, No. 1, S. 94 – 101.

Riesenbeck, H, Perrey, J. (2004), Mega-Macht Marke, Frankfurt.

Saunders, J., Guoqun, F. (1996), Dual Branding: how corporate names add value, in: Marketing Intelligence & Planning, No. 14/7, S. 29 – 34.

Zellekens, H.-J., Horbert, C. (1998), Marken 1998 – Das neue Verhältnis von Handels- und Herstellermarken im Lebensmittelhandel – Ergebnisse einer Untersuchung des EHI, Köln.

Markenevolutionsstrategien

Christoph Burmann, Heribert Meffert und Lars Blinda

1.	**Markenevolution als dynamische Weiterentwicklung von Marken**	**184**
2.	**Markenkonsolidierungsstrategien**	**185**
2.1	Sofortige Elimination	186
2.2	Abgestufter Rückzug	187
2.21	Abschöpfungsstrategien	187
2.22	Migrationsstrategie	188
2.3	Fokussierungsstrategie	190
3.	**Markenexpansionsstrategien**	**192**
3.1	Geografische Expansionsstrategien	193
3.11	Multinationale Markenstrategie	194
3.12	Globale Markenstrategie	195
3.13	Internationale Markenadaptionsstrategie	196
3.2	Markenerweiterungsstrategien	196
3.21	Markenausdehnungsstrategie	200
3.22	Markentransferstrategie	201
3.23	Lizenzierungs- und Franchisestrategie	203
3.24	Co-Branding-Strategie	206
3.25	Autarkiestrategie	208
4.	**Fazit**	**210**

1. Markenevolution als dynamische Weiterentwicklung von Marken

Während bei Entscheidungen zur Gestaltung der Markenarchitektur eine zeitpunktbezogene Perspektive im Fokus steht, wird diese im Rahmen der **Markenevolutionsstrategien** um eine zukunftsgerichtete, **dynamische Perspektive** ergänzt. Diese zeitliche Entwicklungsperspektive ist notwendig, weil das Markenmanagement aufgrund sich ändernder Markt- und Unternehmensbedingungen Marken über die Zeit weiterentwickeln muss. Eine Markenevolutionsstrategie ist ein langfristiger, bedingter und globaler Verhaltensplan, der die Entwicklungsrichtung einer Marke hinsichtlich ihrer Expansion beziehungsweise Konsolidierung für die kommenden zwei bis fünf Jahre festlegt.

Abbildung 1: Markenevolutionsstrategien

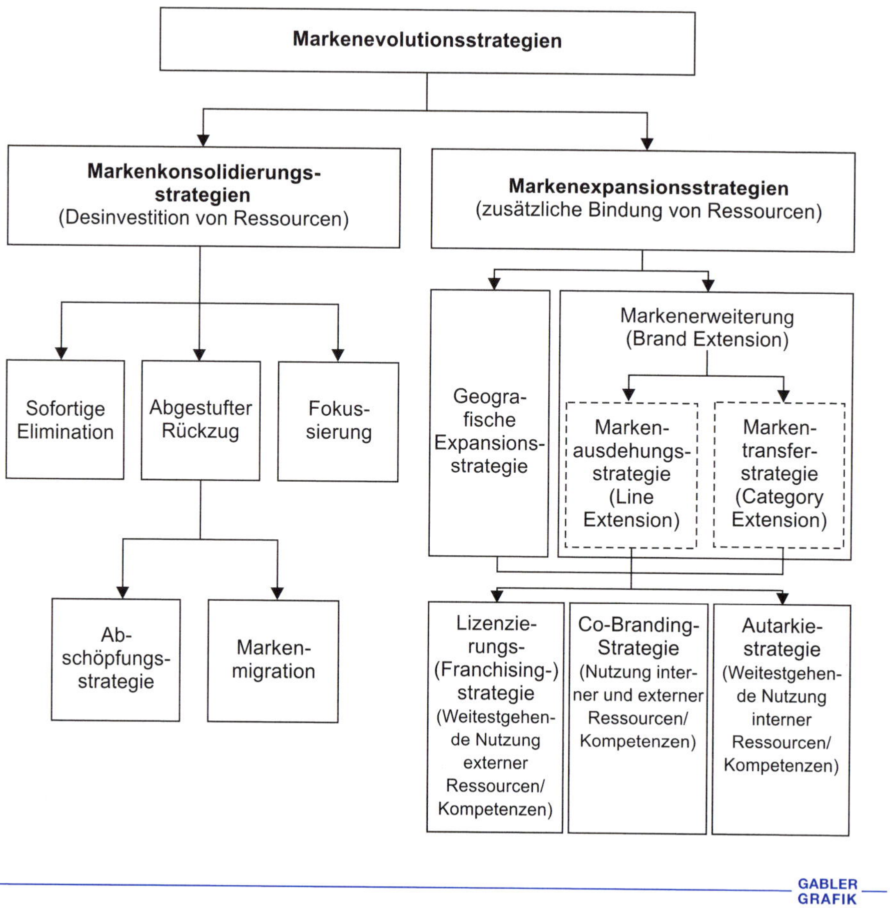

Im Gegensatz zur Festlegung der Markenarchitektur, die sich auf alle Marken des Portfolios bezieht, handelt es sich bei einer Markenevolutionsstrategie zunächst um eine **singuläre Analyse** für jede einzelne Marke. Allerdings haben diese markenspezifischen Entscheidungen Auswirkungen auf die Gestaltung der Markenarchitektur. Die Handlungsoptionen bei der Gestaltung von Markenevolutionsstrategien lassen sich grundsätzlich in Konsolidierungs- und expansive Strategien klassifizieren (vgl. Abbildung 1).

2. Markenkonsolidierungsstrategien

Unternehmen sehen sich insbesondere in den Triade-Märkten verstärkt der Problematik stagnierender und schrumpfender Märkte gegenüber (Meffert 2000, S. 259). Schätzungen zufolge weisen 50–70 Prozent aller Branchen in Westeuropa, Japan und den USA nur noch geringe, keine oder sogar negative Wachstumsraten auf (Harrigan 1999). Diese Entwicklung hat zur Folge, dass Unternehmen seit den 90er Jahren immer häufiger ihr Markenportfolio verkleinern. Bei diesen Markenkonsolidierungsstrategien werden Unternehmensressourcen von einzelnen Marken abgezogen beziehungsweise desinvestiert, um sie für andere Verwendungszwecke einzusetzen. Eine Markenkonsolidierungsstrategie sollte immer dann eingesetzt werden, wenn die in einer Marke gebundenen Ressourcen eines Unternehmens effizienter für andere Aktivitäten eingesetzt und die langfristige Wettbewerbsposition des Unternehmens verbessert werden kann.

Die nicht zielführende **Komplexität vieler Markenportfolios** resultiert oftmals aus Mergers & Acquisitions (M&A). Sie behindert häufig die Expansion des Unternehmens stärker, als sie nachhaltiges Wachstum generiert (Sachs 2002, S. 9). Seit Mitte der 90er Jahre konsolidieren daher viele Unternehmen ihre Portfolios. Unilever verfolgte beispielsweise unter dem Titel „Path to Growth" eine Markenportfoliokonsolidierungsstrategie, die das Portfolio von 1.600 Marken im Jahr 2000 bis Ende 2004 auf rund 400 Marken reduzieren sollte. Die Gründe für diesen „Konsolidierungstrend" können vier Bereichen zugeordnet werden:

- **Marktsättigung**: In den westlichen Ländern weisen viele Branchen, insbesondere der Bereich der kurzlebigen Konsumgüter, Marktsättigungstendenzen auf. Es wird dadurch für Unternehmen immer schwieriger, ihren Marktanteil auszubauen. Dies ist nur durch die Verdrängung von Wettbewerbern möglich. Eine Erhöhung des Wettbewerbsdrucks und steigende Ausgaben für die Markenführung, die von schwachen Marken nicht mehr getragen werden können, sind die Folge. Darüber hinaus wird auch die klare Positionierung von Marken aufgrund der hohen Zahl angebotener Marken immer schwieriger (Positionierungsenge). Ohne eigenständige Positionierung verlieren Marken jedoch langfristig Marktanteile und erhöhen damit die Notwendigkeit zur Markenkonsolidierung.
- **Rentabilitätsdruck**: Durch den steigenden Wettbewerbsdruck, kürzere Produktlebenszyklen und wachsende Anforderungen der globalen Kapitalmärkte steigt der Rentabilitätsdruck auf die Markenportfolios der Unternehmen. Empirische Untersu-

chungen haben ergeben, dass Unternehmen mit einem fokussierten Markenportfolio stärker wachsen als Unternehmen, die eine Vielzahl ähnlicher Marken aufweisen (Sachs 2002, S. 9).

- **Handelsmarkendruck**: Die zunehmende Konzentration im Einzelhandel und die anbieter- wie nachfragerseitige Popularisierung von Handelsmarken führen zu einer sinkenden Bedeutung so genannter B- und C-Marken der klassischen Markenartikelunternehmen. Immer öfter verbleiben heute lediglich starke A-Marken der Markenartikelhersteller im Sortiment des Einzelhandels. Diese werden dann durch verschiedene Handelsmarken mit mittlerem und niedrigem Preisniveau ergänzt. Besonders ausgeprägt ist diese Entwicklung beispielsweise bei Bau- und Heimwerkermärkten. Diese Entwicklung verstärkt den Konsolidierungsdruck auf Seiten der Markenartikelhersteller.
- **Globalisierungsdruck**: Die zunehmende Globalisierung führt in vielen Bereichen zu sich angleichenden Bedürfnissen, Verbrauchertrends und Lifestyles. Dies eröffnet global ausgerichteten Marken zusätzliche Chancen. Die Implementierung einer globalen Markenstrategie stellt jedoch hohe Anforderungen an die Ressourcenausstattung des Unternehmens. Ebenso wird die Verteidigung etablierter Marktpositionen gegenüber neu in einen Markt eindringenden globalen Marken immer aufwendiger. Beide Globalisierungseffekte erhöhen die Notwendigkeit zur Markenkonsolidierung.

Marken, die in den letzten Jahren in Deutschland eliminiert wurden, sind beispielsweise Nixdorf Computer, Attika (Zigaretten), Atari Computer, Amiga Computer, Lipobay (Medikament), Heisse Tasse (Trockenfertiggericht), Spüli (Haushaltsreiniger), BfG Bank AG, Texaco und DEA (Tankstellen). Unternehmen stehen im Rahmen einer Markenkonsolidierungsstrategie im Wesentlichen drei Optionen zur Verfügung: die sofortige Elimination der Marke, ein abgestufter Rückzug und eine Fokussierungsstrategie.

2.1 Sofortige Elimination

Bei der sofortigen Elimination wird versucht, die Marke so schnell wie möglich vom Markt zu nehmen. Diese Strategie sollte dann gewählt werden, wenn die Marke einen hohen negativen Cash Flow aufweist und sich darüber hinaus negativ auf das Image der Unternehmensmarke auswirkt. So wählte beispielsweise das Chemie- und Pharmaunternehmen Bayer diese Strategie, um seine Produktmarke Lipobay nach dem Auftreten mehrerer Todesfälle durch die Einnahme dieses Medikamentes, vom Markt zu nehmen. In einigen Fällen wird angestrebt, die betroffene Marke an Dritte zu veräußern. Zur Implementierung einer Strategie der sofortigen Elimination sind erhebliche **sachliche und personelle Barrieren** zu überwinden, die eine sofortige Elimination erschweren können oder nicht sinnvoll erscheinen lassen. Zum einen können durch eine schnelle Veräußerung oftmals nur geringe Erlöse aus den Vermögenswerten der Marke realisiert werden. Darüber hinaus entstehen gegebenenfalls hohe Kosten für die Auflösung der die Marke betreuenden strategischen Geschäftseinheit (Schneider 1990, S. 71 ff.). Zum anderen müssen bei einer sofortigen Elimination oftmals Ausstrahlungseffekte auf andere Marken des Unternehmens in Kauf genommen werden, die sich insgesamt negativ für das Gesamtunternehmen auswirken. So kann die Umsetzung einer Markenkonsolidierung negativ auf die Motivation der gesamten Belegschaft wirken, wenn beispielsweise die Gründe für die Konsolidierung mangelhaft vom Top-Management an die betroffenen internen und externen Anspruchsgruppen kommuniziert werden.

2.2 Abgestufter Rückzug

Ein abgestufter Rückzug ist dadurch gekennzeichnet, dass sich die Marke in mehreren Schritten, über einen Zeitraum von mehreren Monaten oder sogar Jahren, aus einzelnen Teilmärkten und schließlich vollständig aus dem bislang bearbeiteten Markt zurückzieht. Hierfür werden die Marketingaktivitäten Schritt für Schritt eingestellt. Bei einem abgestuften Rückzug kann zwischen einer **Abschöpfungs- und einer Markenmigrationsstrategie** differenziert werden.

2.21 Abschöpfungsstrategie

Bei einer Abschöpfungsstrategie sind die Zahl der loyalen Kunden und das Kosteneinsparpotenzial noch groß genug, um kurz- bis mittelfristig eine ausreichende Kapitalrentabilität zu gewährleisten. Zu diesem Zweck werden gezielte Desinvestitionen vorgenommen. Dies beginnt in der Regel mit einem Abbau des Kommunikationsbudgets der Marke und einer Reduktion der abverkaufsunterstützenden Maßnahmen im Bereich der Markendistribution. Darüber hinaus wird oft die Anzahl der Produkte und Produkttypen unter der Marke reduziert und das Serviceniveau im Kundendienst verringert. Im letzten Schritt können Einsparungen durch eine Verschlechterung der Produktqualität (zum Beispiel Umstellung auf minderwertigere Zutaten beziehungsweise Vorprodukte) realisiert und Preiserhöhungen durchgesetzt werden. Alle diese Maßnahmen senken die Kosten für die Markenführung. Die Marke lebt bei dieser Strategie von Ihrer Substanz, die sich ohne Unterstützung langsam abbaut. Sie wird ohne weitere Investitionen so lange am Markt gehalten, wie sie positive Cashflows zur Erfüllung der Ziel-Kapitalrentabilität generiert.

2.22 Migrationsstrategie

Bei einer **Migrationsstrategie** bleibt das vorhandene Angebotsprogramm (Produkte und/oder Dienstleistungen) einer Marke meist weitestgehend unverändert am Markt erhalten, aber die bislang verwendeten Markenzeichen werden durch eine andere Markierung ersetzt. Synonym wird daher auch von einer Substitutionsstrategie gesprochen (Burmann/Blinda 2004). Diese Migration fällt zum einen häufig mit dem Verkauf von Unternehmensteilen zusammen, um auf diese Weise in größerem Umfang Aktiva freisetzen zu können. Zum anderen wird sie häufig im Rahmen einer Internationalisierungsstrategie eingesetzt, um nationale durch internationale Marken zu substituieren. Letzteres war ausschlaggebend für die Substitution des vom amerikanischen Unternehmen Mars Inc. nur in Deutschland verwendeten Markennamens Raider durch die international verwendete Markierung Twix (für einen Schokoriegel). Für eine erfolgreiche Migrationsstrategie sollte die Marke folgende Vorraussetzungen erfüllen (vgl. auch Sachs 2002):

- Die Nachfrager müssen gewillt sein, die Leistungen der Ursprungsmarke unter einer anderen Markierung zu akzeptieren beziehungsweise besser erfüllt zu sehen. Die Kundenbindung gegenüber der Ursprungsmarke sollte also primär auf dem funktionalen und nicht auf dem symbolischen Nutzen der Ursprungsmarke beruhen, denn zumeist bleiben die funktionalen Leistungsmerkmale durch eine Migrationsstrategie unangetastet.
- Die essenziellen Merkmale der Markenidentität der Ursprungsmarke müssen zur Identität der aufnehmenden Marke passen. Ein Mis-Fit könnte die aufnehmende Marke ansonsten beschädigen.
- Die Assoziationen der externen Zielgruppen bezüglich der neuen Markierung müssen zum Image der alten Markierung passen.
- Die Migration muss zu einer langfristigen Stärkung der aufnehmenden Marke führen.
- Die Kosteneinsparungen aus der Standardisierung der Markierung und der Markenführung als Folge einer Migrationsstrategie müssen die gegebenenfalls entfallenden Deckungsbeiträge aufgrund von Kundenabwanderungen überkompensieren.
- Die internen Zielgruppen (Management, Mitarbeiter) müssen von der Migration überzeugt sein. Dies sollte vor allem durch eine offene top-down Kommunikation der Notwendigkeit beziehungsweise den strategischen Beweggründen für die Markenmigration gewährleistet werden.

Beispielhaft für Markenmigrationen der letzten Jahre kann auf die zweimalige Migration von Texaco zu DEA und einige Jahre später zu Shell, die Migration der Marke PriceWaterhouseCoopers Consulting zu IBM Business Consulting Services oder auch die Migration von der Marke BASF (im Markt für Ton- und Datenträger) auf EMTEC verwiesen werden.

Eine Markenmigration kann grundsätzlich sukzessiv oder ad-hoc erfolgen. Bei einer **sukzessiven Migration** werden die Markenzeichen schrittweise über einen Zeitraum mehrerer Monate oder sogar Jahre durch die Zeichen der neuen Marke substituiert. Dabei kommt es für eine Übergangszeit zu einem parallelen Auftritt der alten und neuen Markierung. Dies ist bei Migrationen im Zusammenhang mit Fusionen und Akquisitionen besonders ausgeprägt, weil hier oft Unklarheit bezüglich der strategischen Ziele des neuen Markeneigentümers besteht. Sukzessiv treten jedoch die alten Markenzeichen in den Hintergrund und werden schließlich vollkommen durch die neuen Markenzeichen ersetzt. Diese Form der Markenmigration weist ein hohes Maß an Kontinuität auf, da sich Mitarbeiter und Kunden langsam auf den Wechsel der Markenzeichen einstellen können. Darüber hinaus können die notwendigen Investitionen für die Markenmigration über einen längeren Zeitraum gestreckt und damit leichter finanziert werden. Ein Beispiel für die Umsetzung dieser sukzessiven Vorgehensweise bei einer Markenmigration ist die Migration der Marke D2-Mannesmann zu Vodafone.

Auf der anderen Seite kann die **Ad-hoc-Migration** gewählt werden. Hierbei werden die Markenzeichen der zu substituierenden Marke umgehend durch die neue Markierung ausgetauscht, ohne dass es zu einem parallelen Auftreten von alten und neuen Markenzeichen kommt. Diese Umsetzungsform ist vor allem dann zu bevorzugen, wenn die substituierende Marke über eine andere Positionierung als die zu ersetzenden Marke verfügt. Darüber hinaus sollte diese Form der Markenmigration gewählt werden, wenn ein klarer Bruch zur Vergangenheit und Herkunft der alten Marke angestrebt wird. Dies war beispielsweise bei der Migration der Marke Arthur Andersen zu Accenture gewollt, um ein Umdenken und den Abschluss zur skandalreichen Vergangenheit des Beratungsunternehmens zu signalisieren (vgl. Abbildung 2). Der wesentliche Nachteil dieser Migrationsoption ist die weitgehende Vernichtung des über die Zeit aufgebauten Markenkapitals der substituierten Marke und die hohen Investitionen innerhalb eines sehr kurzen Zeitraums.

Abbildung 2: **Markenmigration am Beispiel der Marken D2-Mannesmann/Vodafone und Arthur Anderesen/Accenture**

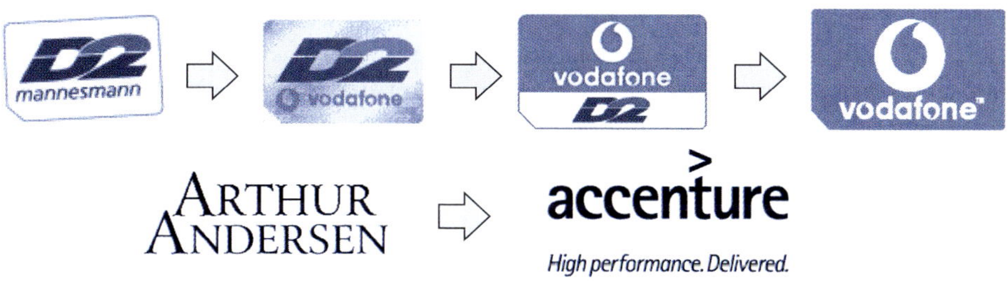

GABLER GRAFIK

3. Markenexpansionsstrategien

Markenexpansionsstrategien werden bei Marken umgesetzt, die aufgrund ihrer Stärke (im Sinne einer positiven Beeinflussung des Kunden- und Mitarbeiterverhaltens) über noch nicht ausgeschöpfte Umsatz- und Ertragspotenziale verfügen. Diese können zum einen in neuen, geografischen Absatzräumen und zum anderen in neuen Produkten liegen (Markenerweiterung).

Durch den weltweiten Abbau von Handelsbarrieren und die internationale Angleichung von Nachfragerbedürfnissen stellt die geografische Expansion von Marken für Unternehmen seit geraumer Zeit eine wesentliche Wachstumsmöglichkeit dar. Insbesondere die Öffnung der ehemaligen Ostblockländer in den 90er Jahren sowie die Integration zahlreicher dieser Länder in die Europäische Union im Jahr 2004 haben viele Markenartikler dazu genutzt, mit ihren Marken in geografisch neue Märkte zu expandieren.

Abbildung 3: **Die Marke Nivea als Beispiel einer erfolgreichen expansiven Markenevolutionsstrategie**

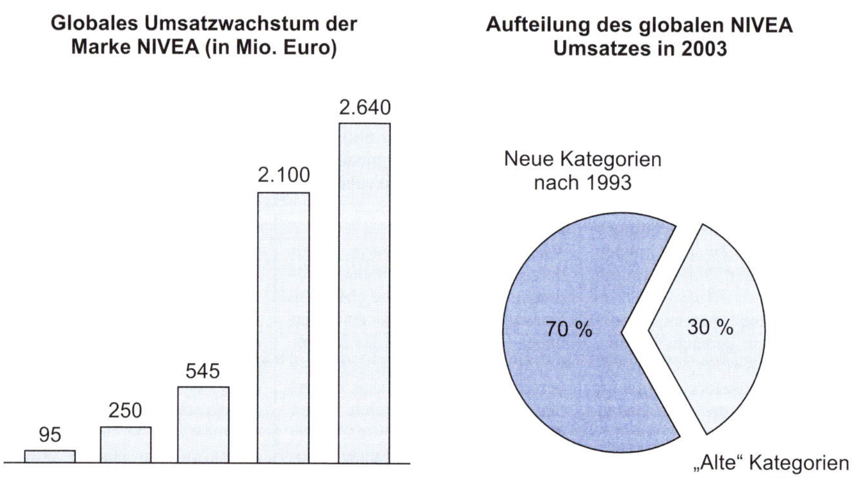

GABLER GRAFIK

Quelle: nach Angaben der Beiersdorf AG, 2004 sowie Schätzung des LiM

Daneben haben auch die klassischen Markenerweiterungen (Markenausdehnungs- und Markentransferstrategien) stark an Bedeutung gewonnen, da unter den heutigen Marktbedingungen (Markeninflation, Positionierungsenge, hoher Preisdruck, hohe Imitationsgeschwindigkeit etc.) die **Markteinführungskosten** und das **Floprisiko** von Produktlaunches mit einem völlig neu entwickelten Markennamen (Neumarkenstrategie) sehr hoch sind. So werden je nach Studie und Autor die Kosten für Markenneueinführungen auf 25 bis 50 Millionen Euro (Aaker 1990, S. 47) und das Risiko eines Flops auf ca. 80 bis 95 Prozent geschätzt (Köhler 1994, S. 435; Sattler/Völckner/Zatloukal 2003, S. 147). Markteinführungskosten und Floprisiko können durch den Einsatz von Markenerweiterungsstrategien signifikant gesenkt werden. Bei einer **Markenerweiterungsstrategie** soll die Stärke einer etablierten Marke helfen, Wissensstrukturen (Markenbekanntheit, -imagekomponenten), die Nachfrager von einer Marke in der Vergangenheit gesammelt haben, auf das neue Produkt zu transferieren (Sattler 2001, S. 141). Dies steigert die Akzeptanz des Neuproduktes und damit die Effizienz von Produktlaunches, da die anfänglichen Investitionskosten und die fortlaufenden Markenführungskosten reduziert werden können.

Marken wie Camel, Joop, Boss und Nivea und andere haben in den letzten zehn Jahren jeweils mehrfach erfolgreich Markenexpansionsstrategien umgesetzt und damit Umsatz- und Ertragssteigerungen erzielen können. Insbesondere das Unternehmen Beiersdorf hat es erfolgreich verstanden, die Marke Nivea auf neue Produkte und Produktkategorien auszuweiten und gleichzeitig international zu expandieren (vgl. Abbildung 3).

3.1 Geografische Expansionsstrategien

Stellt eine Unternehmung in anderen nationalen Märkten ein erhebliches Umsatz- und Ertragspotenzial für eine Marke fest, kann im Rahmen einer **geografischen Expansion** das Absatzgebiet dieser Marke erweitert werden. Eine geografische Markenexpansionsstrategie umfasst die Ausweitung des Absatzraumes einer Marke auf bisher nicht bearbeitete Absatzmärkte.

Beispielsweise expandierte die in der ehemaligen DDR in der Stadt Werningerode am Harz ansässige Biermarke Hasseröder (1872 als Brauerei „Zum Auerhahn" im Werningeroder Stadtteil Hasserode gegründet) Anfang der 90er Jahre zunächst stark in den neuen Bundesländern, wo sie schnell zu einer der beliebtesten Biermarken aufstieg. Mitte der 90er Jahre wurde die Marke dann verstärkt national vermarktet und insbesondere durch ihr starkes Sponsoring-Engagement im Boxsport in ganz Deutschland bekannt. Parallel verzeichnete die Marke ein kontinuierliches Absatzwachstum (vgl. Abbildung 4). Heute gehört Sie zu den größten und stärksten Biermarken Deutschlands.

Der Großteil der geografischen Expansionsstrategien verfolgt jedoch die Ausweitung des Absatzraumes über den Heimatmarkt auf andere Länder. In diesem Fall steht einer Marke generell die Verfolgung einer **multinationalen Markenstrategie, einer globalen Markenstrategie** oder einer **internationalen Markenadaptionsstrategie** offen (Meffert 1988; Waltermann 1989; Güldenberg 2000, S. 25 ff.; Kapferer 2000, S. 336 ff.).

Abbildung 4: **Absatzentwicklung der Marke Hasseröder von 1991 bis 2003 in Deutschland**

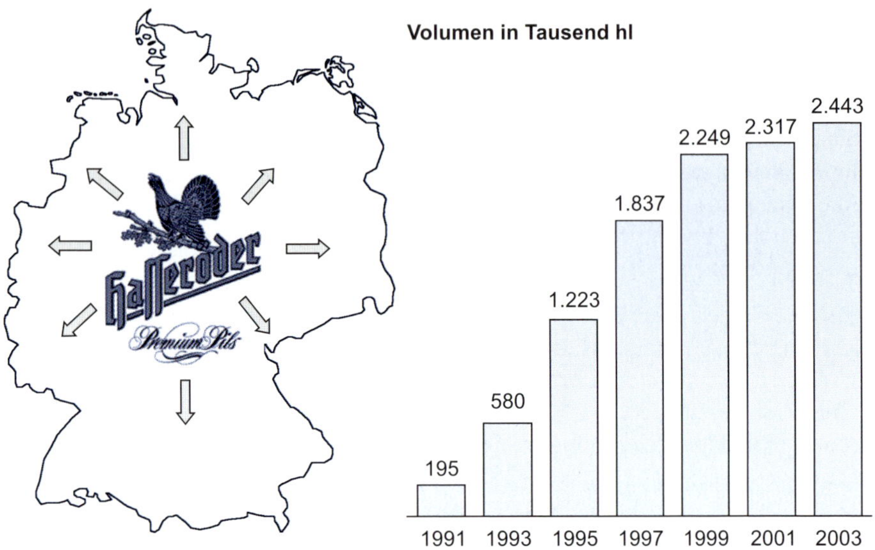

Quelle: nach Angaben von Hasseröder, 2004

3.11 Multinationale Markenstrategie

Bei der **multinationalen Markenstrategie** verfolgt ein Unternehmen in jedem neuen nationalen Absatzgebiet ein individuelles Markenkonzept. Das ursprüngliche Markenkonzept aus dem Heimatmarkt wird so angepasst, dass es als so genanntes „local brand" eine optimale Anpassung an die länderspezifischen Bedürfnisse der Nachfrager und die Berücksichtigung nationaler Spezifika in den Kommunikations-, Preis- und Distributionsgegebenheiten sowie bei gesetzlichen Bestimmungen erlaubt. Im Extremfall kann dies bis zu einer vollständigen Neuentwicklung einer Marke führen. Nestlé beispielsweise verfolgt mit der Babynahrungsmarke Alete diese Strategie erfolgreich.

Unter strategischen Gesichtspunkten einer globalen Markenportfolioführung kann eine multinationale Markenstrategie sinnvoll sein. Dies ist allerdings meist nur dann der Fall, wenn Unternehmen Marken zusätzlich erwerben, die sich in bestimmten Auslandsmärkten durchgesetzt haben und dort gut positioniert sind. Die mangelnde Nutzung von Synergien im Marketing und im Extremfall sogar fehlende Degressionseffekte im gesamten Geschäftssystem stellen zentrale **Nachteile** der multinationalen Markenpolitik dar. Ferner wird das Goodwill-Potenzial der Ursprungsmarke auf neuen internationalen Märkten nicht beziehungsweise nur unzureichend genutzt.

3.12 Globale Markenstrategie

Im Gegensatz zur multinationalen Markenstrategie versuchen Unternehmen im Rahmen der globalen Markenstrategie, ein einheitliches Markenkonzept ausgerichtet an der ursprünglichen Markenidentität ohne Anpassungen und Rücksicht auf nationale Unterschiede global durchzusetzen. Im Idealfall wird die Marke weltweit mit identischer Markierung, Qualität, Positionierung, Verpackung sowie übereinstimmender Kommunikations-, Preis- und Distributionspolitik vertrieben (Aaker/Joachimsthaler 2000, S. 301 ff.).

Ein wesentlicher **Vorteil** einer globalen Markenstrategie liegt im Aufbau einer über alle Länder hinweg einheitlich auftretenden Marke. Aus diesem Grund achtete das Unternehmen Unilever bei der Neuordnung seiner Markenstrategie darauf, dass seine langfristig fortzuführenden A-Marken, beispielsweise Knorr, Bertolli und Lipton, international geschützt waren beziehungsweise werden konnten und keine sprachlichen Schwierigkeiten oder negative Assoziationen zum Markennamen existierten. Der Aufbau einer globalen Marke führt im Vergleich zu einer multinationalen oder einer internationalen Adaptionsstrategie vor allem zu erheblichen Kostenvorteilen.

So können häufig Kostensenkungspotenziale im Produktions- und Kommunikationsbereich ausgeschöpft werden. Beispielsweise hat Coca-Cola allein durch die Standardisierung der Werbemittelproduktion innerhalb von 20 Jahren 90 Millionen Dollar eingespart. Die Einführung von Diet-Coke erfolgte deshalb weltweit mit gleicher Konzentratformel, Positionierung und werblicher Argumentation (Quelch/Hoff 1986). Weiterhin lassen sich Lern- und Know-how-Effekte der einzelnen Niederlassungen nutzen, wodurch F & E- und Markteinführungserfahrungen schneller übertragen werden können.

Die **Nachteile** einer globalen Markenstrategie liegen vor allem in der Vernachlässigung lukrativer Nischen und länderspezifischer Bedürfnisse sowie in der wenig auf die jeweilige Kultur angepassten Kundenansprache. Problematisch ist dies vor allem dann, wenn die Markenidentität aufgrund ihrer Werte und Persönlichkeit in den einzelnen Ländern Konflikte auslöst. Beispielsweise war dies in Italien bei Starbucks der Fall oder in Saudi-Arabien bei Coca-Cola. Darüber hinaus ergibt sich die Gefahr des Entstehens von Konflikten zwischen Mutter- und Tochtergesellschaften durch eine zentral gesteuerte Markenpolitik. Aufgrund der immer noch existierenden Unterschiede in der Bedarfsstruktur der Nachfrager und den wettbewerbsbezogenen Rahmenbedingungen bleibt das globale Markenkonzept eher standardisierbaren Dienstleistungen (zum Beispiel McDonald's, Ikea), High-Tech-Produkten (zum Beispiel IBM, Sony, Microsoft), Prestigeartikeln (zum Beispiel Perrier, Chanel, Bogner) und wenig kulturgebundenen Gütern (zum Beispiel Coca-Cola, Levi's) vorbehalten. Dennoch lassen sich selbst bei solchen Marken länderspezifische Anpassungen im Markenauftritt nicht völlig verhindern. Die Coca-Cola Company muss zum Beispiel bei ihrer Marke Fanta durch lebensmittelrechtliche Spezifika in Deutschland, Spanien und Italien Unterschiede im geschmacklichen und farblichen Erscheinungsbild in Kauf nehmen und passt ebenfalls den Marketing-Mix ihrer Top-Marke Coca-Cola leicht den länderspezifischen Unterschieden an (Kreutzer 1989, S. 281).

3.13 Internationale Markenadaptionsstrategie

Die Mehrzahl der Unternehmen verfolgt aufgrund länderspezifischer Unterschiede eine **internationale Markenadaptionsstrategie**, die synonym auch als gemischte Markenstrategie bezeichnet wird. Bei dieser Strategie wird ein möglichst hoher Standardisierungsgrad bei gleichzeitiger Anpassung an ausgewählte Länderspezifika angestrebt. Hierbei wird versucht, unter Beibehaltung der essenziellen Markenidentitätsmerkmale bei leichten Anpassungen der akzidenziellen Identitätsmerkmale an individuelle Ländergegebenheiten Kosten- und Nutzenvorteile auszuschöpfen. Zentrales Problem der internationalen Markenadaptionsstrategie ist die Bestimmung des **optimalen Adaptionsgrades** der Marke in den einzelnen Ländermärkten. Dabei muss beachtet werden, inwieweit etwa Anpassungen der Qualität oder des Preises in den verschiedenen Ländern vorgenommen werden können, ohne dass die Markenidentität gefährdet wird und bei international mobilen Konsumenten Irritationen auftreten.

3.2 Markenerweiterungsstrategien

Markenerweiterungsstrategien **(Brand Extensions)** stellen die zweiten Kategorie der expansiven Markenevolutionsstrategien dar. Die **Markenerweiterung** ist als eine Unternehmensaktivität zu verstehen, bei der die positiven Imagekomponenten einer existierenden Marke auf ein neues Produkt aus einer bereits bearbeiteten, verwandten oder völlig neuen Warengruppe übertragen werden (Aaker 1990; Meffert/Heinemann 1990; Kapferer 1992; Sattler 1998; Esch/Fuchs/Bräutigam 2001; Keller 2001; Günther 2002; Zatloukal 2002). Durch die Übertragung positiver Konsumerfahrungen von Produkten der bereits etablierten Marke auf das neue Produkt werden die Nachfrager beim Markenwahlprozess kognitiv entlastet. Die **Vorteile** der Markenerweiterung für Unternehmen liegen dabei vor allem in der Möglichkeit, schnell und relativ kostengünstig einen hohen Bekanntheitsgrad und ein positives Image für ein neues Produkt aufbauen zu können (Wölfer 1994, S. 529 ff.).

Markenerweiterungsstrategien haben über die letzten Jahre konstant an Bedeutung gewonnen. Sie werden von Unternehmen daher vor allem bei Produktneueinführungen angewendet. So belegt eine Anfang der 90er Jahre in den USA durchgeführte Studie, dass bei Produkteinführungen in Fast Moving Consumer Goods (FMCG) Märkten, der Einsatz von Markenerweiterungsstrategien gegenüber Neumarkenstrategien im Zeitraum von 1977 bis 1991 von 40 Prozent auf circa 90 Prozent gestiegen ist (Rangaswamy/Burke/Oliva 1993, S. 61). Die hohe Relevanz von Markenerweiterungen hat auch in der Wissenschaft zu verstärkten Forschungsbemühungen in diesem Bereich geführt.

Zwar herrscht bei einer Markenerweiterungsstrategie prinzipiell eine singuläre Markenbetrachtung vor, allerdings verändert sich durch die Implementierung von Markenausdehnungs- und Markentransferstrategien auch die Markenarchitektur. Das Management der sich hieraus ergebenden Interdependenzen stellt die Markenführung vor erhebliche Probleme.

In der Marketingliteratur ist der Begriff der **Markenerweiterung** durch eine starke terminologische Heterogenität gekennzeichnet. Abhängig von der jeweiligen Situation werden Begriffe wie Markentransfer, Brand-Stretching, Brand-Extension, Markendehnung, Markenausweitung teilweise synonym verwendet, teilweise mit völlig anderen Inhalten belegt. Gemeinsam haben alle Begriffe, dass

- die Identität einer etablierten Marke
- für neue Produkte
- durch die Verwendung eines gemeinsamen Markenkonzeptes für das Stamm- und das Erweiterungsprodukt
- mit dem Ziel einer Übertragung positiver Imagebestandteile bei den Nachfragern

verwendet wird (Aaker 1990, S. 47; Hätty 1994, S. 563; Meffert 1994, S. 185; Sattler 1998, S. 2; Günther 2002, S. 5 f.; Zatloukal 2002, S. 1; Völckner 2004, S. 74).

Mehrere Studien belegen in diesem Zusammenhang die hohe Bedeutung von **vier Erfolgsfaktoren** für das Gelingen beziehungsweise Scheitern von Markenerweiterungen (Sattler/ Völckner/Zatloukal 2003; Völckner 2003). Diese sind der **Fit des neuen Produktes zur Muttermarke** (auch als globale Ähnlichkeit zwischen Ursprungsmarke und Erweiterungsprodukt bezeichnet), die **Marketingunterstützung für das neue Produkt**, die davon stark beeinflusste **Handelsakzeptanz** für das neue Produkt sowie das **Involvement der Nachfrager gegenüber der Muttermarke** (vgl. Abbildung 5 sowie Völckner 2003 und den Beitrag über Markenerweiterungsstrategien und ihren Erfolgsfaktoren in diesem Buch). Andere in den letzten Jahren identifizierte Faktoren, wie beispielsweise die Breite der Produktpalette der Muttermarke, die Qualitätseinschätzung der Muttermarke durch Nachfrager, der Erfolg vergangener Erweiterungen sowie die allgemeine Einstellung der Nachfrager gegenüber neuen Produkten etc. weisen in neueren Untersuchungen einen geringeren Erfolgsbeitrag auf (Sattler 1997; Sattler/Völckner/ Zatloukal 2003; Völckner 2003).

Abbildung 5 zeigt wesentliche Erfolgsfaktoren von Markenerweiterungen und ihren Einfluss auf den abschließenden Erfolg der Erweiterung. Die an den Pfeilen in der Abbildung angegebenen Koeffizienten geben das unmittelbare Maß für die relative Stärke der einzelnen Beziehungen wieder. Sie können maximal Werte zwischen –1 und +1 annehmen. Die durchgezogenen Linien in Abbildung 5 kennzeichnen bedeutende Einflüsse von Faktoren auf den Erfolg von Markenerweiterungen. Beispielsweise hat die Marketingunterstützung für das neue Produkt einen hohen positiven Einfluss auf die Handelsakzeptanz. Die Handelsakzeptanz wiederum hat einen hohen Einfluss auf den Markenerweiterungserfolg, der nur vom Fit des neuen Produktes zur Muttermarke übertroffen wird. Dieser Fit wird ebenfalls stark positiv durch die Marketingunterstützung für das neue Produkt beeinflusst.

Abbildung 5: Erfolgsfaktoren von Markenerweiterungen und ihre Beziehung

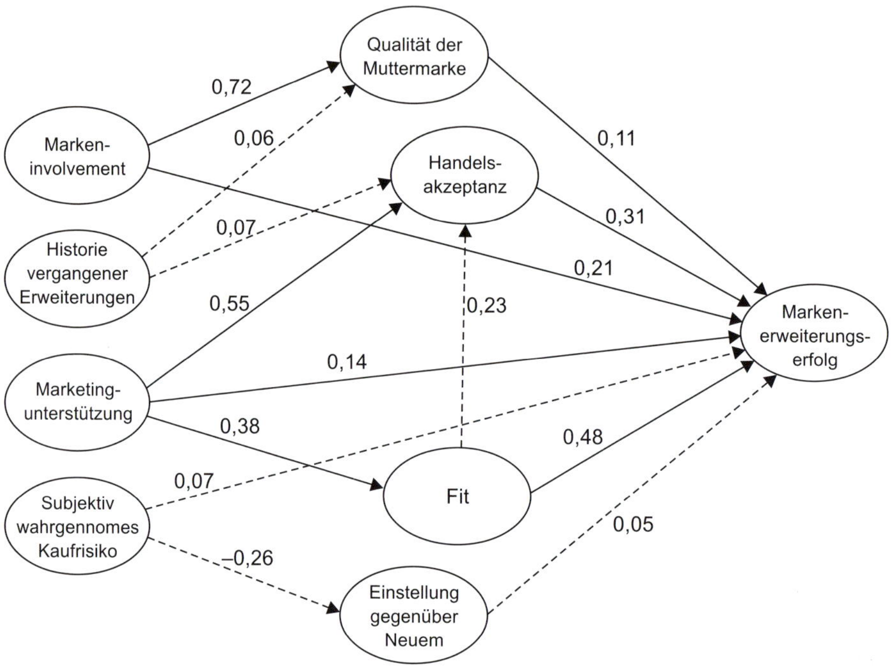

GABLER GRAFIK

Quelle: Völckner 2004, S. 76

Die Positionierung des neuen Produktes sollte auf der Identität der Ursprungsmarke basieren. Im Zeitverlauf können sich Markenerweiterungsprodukte von der Ursprungsleistung beziehungsweise den Ursprungsassoziationen der Muttermarke durchaus weiter entfernen. Wichtig für den dynamischen Erfolg einer Markenerweiterung im Zeitablauf ist in diesem Zusammenhang zweierlei.

Einerseits muss den internen und externen Zielgruppen der Marke **genügend Zeit** gegeben werden, die jeweilige Erweiterung der ursprünglichen Marke zu erlernen. Dies erfordert Geduld beim Markeninhaber. Andererseits sollten die jeweiligen Erweiterungen stets **in kleinen Schritten** erfolgen, um auf diese Weise ein effektives und schnelles Lernen der verschiedenen Markenzielgruppen zu unterstützen. Es ist daher ratsam, Markenerweiterungen „in Kreisen" um die Positionierung der Ursprungsmarke vorzunehmen (Kapferer 1992, S. 139). Ein gutes Beispiel für eine „geduldige", behutsam in kleinen Schritten vorgehende Markenerweiterung ist die Marke Nivea (vgl. Abbildung 6), die zunächst ihre Produktpalette auf weitere Cremeprodukte ausweitete, danach in verwandte

Pflegeprodukte und schließlich in pflegende und dann sogar in dekorative Kosmetikprodukte expandierte, ohne bei den meisten dieser Schritte den Kern der Markenidentität, die (bezahlbare) Pflege zu verwässern (Prick 1989).

Abbildung 6: Markenerweiterungen am Beispiel der Marke Nivea

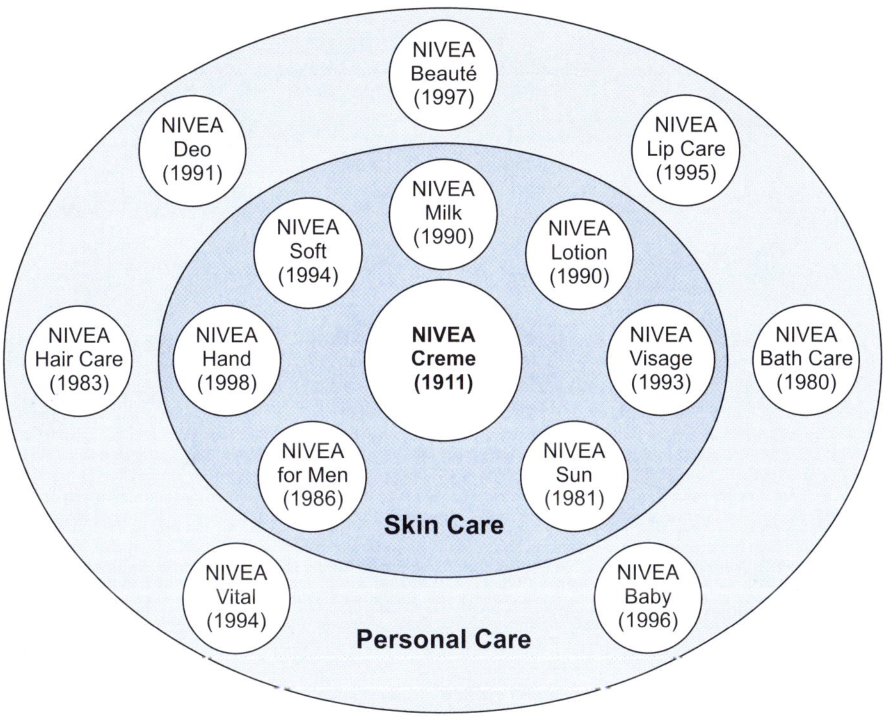

GABLER GRAFIK

Quelle: nach Angaben der Beiersdorf AG, 2004

Markenerweiterungsstrategien können weitergehend in Markenausdehnungs- und Markentransferstrategien differenziert werden. Beide Strategieoptionen erfüllen die oben beschriebenen Merkmale. Die **Markenausdehnungsstrategie** (Line Extension) beschreibt die Expansion einer Marke in **gleichen oder verwandten Produktkategorien,** die **Markentransferstrategie** (Category Extension) demgegenüber die Expansion in **neue, nicht verwandte Produktkategorien**. Beispielsweise handelt es sich bei der Expansion der Automobilmarke Porsche in das Segment der Sport Utility Vehicle (SUV) um eine Markenausdehnungsstrategie, bei der Expansion der Marke in modische Accessoires hingegen um eine Markentransferstrategie (in diesem Fall durch Anwendung einer Markenlizenzierungsstrategie) (vgl. Abbildung 7).

Abbildung 7: Differenzierung von Markenausdehnungs- und Markentransferstrategien am Beispiel der Marke Porsche

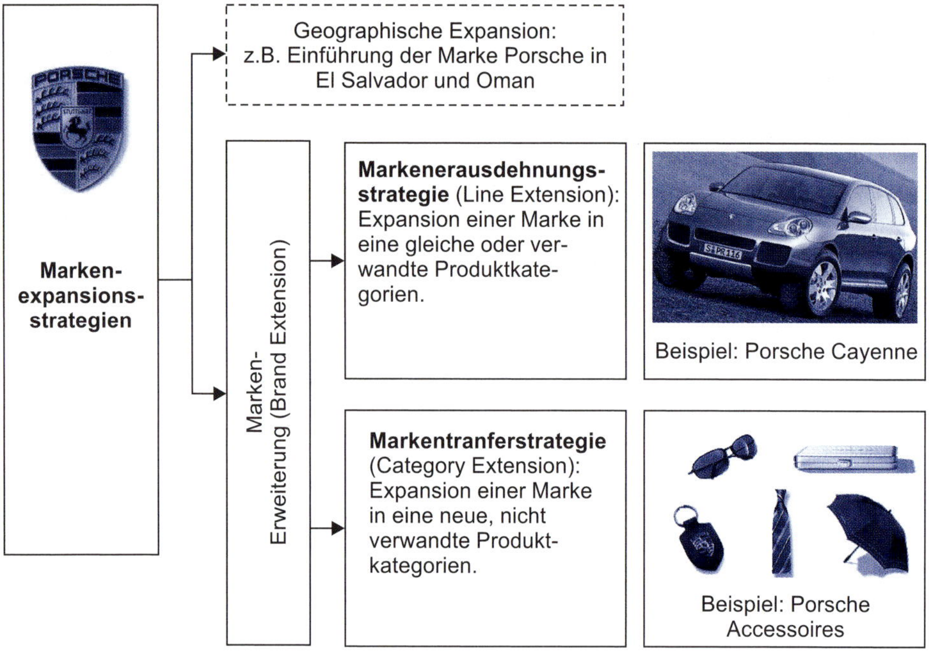

GABLER GRAFIK

3.21 Markenausdehnungsstrategie

Bei einer Markenausdehnungsstrategie **(Line Extension)** wird die Anzahl der unter einer Marke angebotenen Produkte und Dienstleistungen innerhalb der bisher bearbeiteten Produktkategorie vergrößert. Circa 80 bis 90 Prozent der Produktneueinführungen fallen unter die Kategorie der Line Extensions (Keller 2003, S. 581). Der wesentliche Vorteil der Markenausdehnungsstrategie liegt in der Möglichkeit zu einem schnellen und kostengünstigen Aufbau eines Images für das Neuprodukt (Wölfer 1994, S. 528 ff.). Diese Ausdehnung kann in dreifacher Weise realisiert werden.

Erstens kann in einem **„klassischen Brand Stretch"** eine Marke durch das zusätzliche Angebot von technisch-funktional ähnlichen Leistungen innerhalb der Produktkategorie und in Marktsegmenten, die an den bislang bedienten Ursprungsmarkt angrenzen, ausgedehnt werden. Exemplarisch ist hier die Markenausdehnung von Nivea-Creme auf

Nivea-Milk und andere Hautcreme-Produkte zu nennen oder auch die Ausdehnung der Tafelschokolade-Marke Milka auf weitere Schokoladeprodukte wie Milka Montelino, I love Milka, Naps und M-Joy.

Zweitens kann die Ausdehnung der Marke in preislich und qualitativ höher beziehungsweise niedriger positionierte Marktsegmente (**Trading-up** beziehungsweise **Trading-down**) erfolgen. Ein Beispiel für einen Trading-up in der Mode- und Textilbranche ist die Marke Boss mit der Einführung der „Super-Brand" Baldessarini sowie als Trading down die Einführung der jüngeren und preisaggressiveren Marke Hugo.

Drittens kann die Markendehnung durch die Ausweitung des Leistungsangebotes einer Marke in vor- und/oder nachgelagerten Stufen der Wertschöpfungskette (**Rückwärtsintegration** beziehungsweise **Vorwärtsintegration**). Als Beispiel können hier die Ausdehnung der HiFi-Marke Bang & Olufson (B&O) in den Einzelhandel durch den Aufbau markenexklusiver Einzelhandelsgeschäfte im Besitz von B&O oder die Ausdehnung der Reiseveranstaltungsmarke TUI in den Endverbrauchervertrieb durch Aufbau der Reisebürokette TUI ReiseCenter angeführt werden (in beiden Beispielen handelt es sich um eine Vorwärtsintegration in Richtung auf den Endkunden der Marke).

3.22 Markentransferstrategie

Die Markentransferstrategie **(Category Extension)** stellt die zweite Stufe einer Markenerweiterungsstrategie dar. Hierbei handelt sich um eine weitergehende Markenerweiterung als bei der Markenausdehnung, da im Rahmen einer Markentransferstrategie die Marke in grundlegend **neue Märkte** übertragen wird, die **keinen technisch-funktionalen Zusammenhang** mit dem Ursprungsmarkt der Marke aufweisen.

Auf diese Weise dehnte Camel seine Produktpalette, ausgehend vom klassischen Bereich der Tabakmarke, erfolgreich aus. Heute werden unter der Marke Camel zum Beispiel auch Herrenbekleidung und Uhren angeboten, die mittlerweile einen erheblichen Teil des Gesamtumsatzes ausmachen. Im Dienstleistungsbereich hat beispielsweise das Reiseunternehmen Club Mediterranée einen Markentransfer auf Konsumgüter wie Freizeit- und Kosmetikartikel sowie Uhren, Brillen und Fahrräder vorgenommen (Hätty 1989, S. 247) und im Jahr 2003 weitete die Marke Dextro Energy (Traubenzucker) ihre Produkte auf die Produktkategorien Energy Drinks und Müsli-Riegel aus.

Eine wesentliche Voraussetzung für den Erfolg des Markentransfers bildet erneut die Ähnlichkeit zwischen der Marke und dem Transferprodukt (Park/Milberg/Lawson 1991, S. 185 ff.; Keller 2001, S. 705 ff.; Zatloukal 2002, S. 59 ff.). Aufgrund des nicht existenten technisch-funktionalen Zusammenhanges zwischen Ursprungs- und Transferprodukt, muss das Markenmanagement diese Ähnlichkeit über andere sachbezogene (Denotationen) und insbesondere über symbolhafte, oft stark gefühlsgeprägte Assoziationen (Konnotationen) herstellen (Hätty 1989, S. 82; Meffert/Heinemann 1990). So lassen sich mit einem Sportwagen zum Beispiel denotative Assoziationen wie Schnelligkeit, Verarbeitungsqualität und Preis verbinden, während Luxus, Exklusivität und Erotik mögliche Konnotationen darstellen. Bei dem Automobilhersteller Jaguar, der ausgehend vom Stammsegment Pkw unter anderem Bekleidung, Brillen, Reisegepäck und Schreibgeräte entwickelte, bilden eher emotionale Assoziationen wie Exklusivität und Prestige eine gemeinsame Klammer zwischen Haupt- und Transferprodukt. Wie bedeutend diese Sicherung der Ähnlichkeit ist, kann an dem Misserfolg von Levis Ende der 80er Jahre verdeutlicht werden. In diesem Fall verfehlte das Markenmanagement von Levis die Herstellung einer Verbindung zwischen seinem Image als Jeanshersteller und einer neu, unter der Marke Levis auf den Markt gebrachten Herrenanzugslinie (Aaker 1990, S. 50).

Die Herausstellung eines übereinstimmenden Verwendungsumfeldes oder gemeinsamer Erlebniswelten und Lebensstile kann ebenfalls Grundlage eines erfolgreichen Markentransfers auf der Basis einer hohen Ähnlichkeit sein. Michelin-Autoreifen und der Guide-Michelin mit dem gleichen Verwendungsumfeld des Autofahrens, Marlboro-Zigaretten und Marlboro-Freizeitkleidung mit der gemeinsamen Erlebniswelt Freiheit können hier als Beispiele genannt werden (Mayer/Mayer 1987, S. 109 ff.).

Mit der Nutzung einer vorhandenen Marke und ihres so genannten „Goodwills" im Rahmen der Markentransferstrategie sind eine Reihe von **Chancen** verbunden, die sich zum Teil aus den allgemeinen Vorteilen von Markenerweiterungen ableiten. Geringere Markteintrittsbarrieren reduzieren das Floprisiko und erleichtern den Eintritt in völlig neue Produktbereiche. Dies erlaubte beispielsweise dem amerikanischen Unternehmen Mars Inc., welches ursprünglich nur Schokoladenriegel anbot, ab Ende der 90er auch Speiseeis in „Riegelform" anzubieten. Resultat war die Gewinnung zusätzlicher Käufergruppen und die Erschließung eines neuen strategischen Geschäftsfeldes. Durch die Übertragung positiver Konsumerfahrungen entlastet der Markentransfer den Nachfrager beim Kaufprozess und bietet Orientierung.

Neben den Vorteilen für das Transferprodukt kann allerdings in umgekehrter Richtung auch ein **Image-Rücktransfer** auf die Stamm-Marke erfolgen. Dies stärkt und erweitert potenziell das Markenimage der Stamm-Marke. So konnte die Mövenpick Holding durch den Erfolg der Transfermarken im Eiscreme-, Kaffee- und Saucenbereich nicht nur diese Felder erfolgreich ausbauen, sondern auch das traditionelle Restaurant- und Hotelgeschäft stärken. Weitere Vorteile der Markentransferstrategie sind die Verringerung der Kosten für die Markenbildung sowie die Abschwächung beziehungsweise Umgehung von Werbebeschränkungen beispielsweise im Bereich alkoholischer Getränke und Tabakwaren.

Diesen Chancen stehen aber auch erhebliche **Risiken** des Markentransfers gegenüber. Es ist mit einer **Erosion der Markenidentität** und nachfolgend dem Verlust der Glaubwürdigkeit der Marke zu rechnen, wenn die Stamm- und Transferprodukte sich in ihrer Positionierung zu sehr voneinander entfernen, zu unterschiedliche Zielgruppen ansprechen (Loken/Roedder 1993) und/oder zu viele oder zu schnell aufeinander folgende Markentransfers vorgenommen werden. Ein typisches Beispiel hierfür stellte in der Vergangenheit die Marke Gucci mit circa 14.000 verschiedenen Produkten dar. Die Diversifikation in neue Produktbereiche, vor allem über Lizenzvergabe, führte hier zu einem hohen Koordinationsbedarf der markenpolitischen Maßnahmen von Hauptmarke und Transferprodukten. Eine ungenügende Koordination führte schließlich zu sehr unterschiedlichen Qualitätsniveaus und Marketingkonzepten für die Gucci-Produkte und in der Folge zu einem massiven Glaubwürdigkeits- und Kompetenzverlust der Marke.

Die aufgezeigten Risiken machen deutlich, dass zum Erfolg einer Markentransferstrategie eine Analyse des Transferpotenzials von Marken und eine Ähnlichkeitsmessung von Stamm- und Transferprodukt unerlässlich sind (Mayer/Mayer 1987, S. 82 ff.; Hätty 1989, S. 139 ff.; Meffert/Heinemann 1990; Sattler 1998, S. 2; Zatloukal 2002, S. 6).

Die drei im Rahmen der Markenevolution beschriebenen Expansionsstrategien (geografische Expansion, Markenausdehnung und Markentransfer) können als Lizenzierungs- beziehungsweise Franchisingstrategie, als Co-Branding oder als Autarkiestrategie implementiert werden (vgl. Abbildung 1).

3.23 Lizenzierungs-und Franchisestrategie

Identifiziert ein Unternehmen ein Erweiterungspotenzial für eine seiner Marken, gilt es festzustellen, ob es über die notwendigen Ressourcen und Kompetenzen (organisationale Fähigkeiten) verfügt, die Markenerweiterung eigenständig durchzuführen (Autarkiestrategie). Sind die notwendigen Ressourcen und Kompetenzen nicht in ausreichendem Maße intern vorhanden, so kann das Unternehmen dennoch Erweiterungspotenziale ausschöpfen, indem es eine **Lizenzierungs- oder Franchisestrategie** verfolgt. Dies bedeutet, dass es als Markeninhaber einem anderen Unternehmen das Recht zur Nutzung seiner Marke gewährt (Böll 1999). Es bedient sich bei dieser Form der Markenexpansionsstrategie nahezu ausschließlich oder weitgehend der Ressourcen und Kompetenzen der jeweiligen Lizenznehmer oder Franchisepartner. Die Markenlizenzierung kann sich dabei auf die **Vermarktung neuer Produkte** beziehen oder auf die Vermarktung **bestehender Produkte in neuen Märkten** beziehungsweise Regionen (Binder 2001, S. 400). Insbesondere im letzteren Fall (geografische Expansion) können Markenlizenzierungen oftmals sogar der einzige Weg sein, in einen ausländischen Markt zu expandieren. Dies ist der Fall, wenn beispielsweise der Aufbau von Produktionsanlagen vor Ort zu kostenintensiv wäre, jedoch gleichzeitig hohe Transportkosten oder die Verderblichkeit der Produkte einen Export verhindern. Darüber hinaus können die rechtlichen Rahmenbedingungen im Zielland eine Lizenzierung unumgänglich machen. Beispielsweise lizenzieren viele international tätige Brauereien die Bierproduktion in vielen Ländern an kooperierende Brauereien vor Ort.

Markenlizenzierungen haben jedoch auch in den Heimmärkten an Bedeutung gewonnen. Nach Schätzungen gab es im deutschsprachigen Raum im Jahr 1999 circa 750 Markenlizenzverträge im Bereich der Markenerweiterungen durch neue Produkte mit einem geschätzten Gesamtumsatz von 6,7 Milliarden Euro (exklusive Vertriebslizenzen, Binder 2001, S. 387 f.). Manche Marken, wie beispielsweise Joop, Aigner oder Natreen, erwirtschaften durch Markenlizenzierungen höhere Umsätze als durch ihre selbsterstellten Produkte. Dies verdeutlicht, dass Markenlizenzen ein durchaus erfolgreiches Instrument der Markenexpansion sein können.

Aufgrund der finanziellen und personellen Restriktionen vieler Unternehmen und der allgemeinen Entwicklung, sich in der Unternehmensführung auf **Kernkompetenzen und Kerngeschäftsfelder**, in denen man über nachhaltige Wettbewerbsvorteile verfügt, zu konzentrieren, erscheint eine Lizenzierungs-/Franchisestrategie heute in besonderer Weise attraktiv. Für den Markeninhaber ergeben sich dabei eine Reihe von **Vorteile,** die sich sieben Kategorien zuordnen lassen (Binder 2001, S. 395 ff.).

Durch den stärkeren Marktauftritt (höherer Kommunikationsdruck) ist eine **Steigerung der Markenbekanntheit** möglich. Insbesondere Modemarken nutzen Markenlizenzen, um ihre Markenbekanntheit zu steigern. Beispielhaft können hier die Marken Calvin Klein, Joop oder Boss angeführt werden. Bei der Beurteilung von Marken durch die Nachfrager spielt die wahrgenommene **Markenkompetenz** eine wesentliche Rolle. Diesbezüglich ist es ein weiterer Vorteil von Markenlizenzen, dass Unternehmen durch sie das Leistungsangebot ihrer Marke schnell und kostengünstig um zusätzliche Problemlösungen erweitern können. Durch den Rückgriff auf externe Ressourcen und Kompetenzen der Kooperationspartner kann die von den Nachfragern wahrgenommene Markenkompetenz vertieft und gestärkt werden, ohne dabei in einem langfristigen und aufwendigen Prozess unternehmensinterne Kompetenzen aufbauen zu müssen. Das breitere Kompetenzimage der Marke lässt die Marke als einen umfassenden Problemlöser erscheinen. Beispielsweise betreibt die Sportartikelmarke Head das Geschäft mit Sportbekleidung ausschließlich über Lizenznehmer und fokussiert sich dadurch auf ihre Kernkompetenzen im Bereich von Tennisschlägern und Skiern.

Durch die Ausweitung der wahrgenommenen Markenkompetenz und eine verstärkte kommunikative Unterstützung, kann das **Markenimage** beeinflusst und gestärkt werden. Insbesondere bei Parfum- und Modeprodukten, deren Werbung oftmals ausschließlich auf Emotionen beruht, kann das Markenimage in seiner symbolischen Dimension aufgeladen werden. Markenlizenzen können daher zu einer Steuerung des Markenimages in bestimmte Richtungen beitragen (zum Beispiel Prestige, Sportlichkeit, Leidenschaft, Weiblichkeit etc.). So haben die Zigarettenmarken Camel und Marlboro ihr Image als Marken für Abenteuer und Freiheit beispielsweise durch Lizenzvergabe an Bekleidungshersteller im Bereich Outdoor und Sportswear gestärkt.

Langfristig können Markenlizenzierungen zu einer **Steigerung der Markenloyalität** beitragen. Durch die Erweiterung der Produktpalette erhöht sich potenziell die Kontakt- und Verwendungshäufigkeit der Marke. Dies hat langfristig über die Markenbekanntheit und Markenzufriedenheit Auswirkungen auf die Markenloyalität (Weinberg/Diehl 2001, S. 28). So können insbesondere Hersteller von FMCG-Marken durch das Angebot von längerlebigen Produkten die Markenloyalität stärken. Beispielsweise bietet die Biermarke Beck's in ihrem Merchandisingsortiment verschiedene langlebige Gebrauchsgüter an (zum Beispiel Badehandtücher, Aschenbecher, T-Shirts etc.).

Durch die Vergabe von Lizenzen erzielt der Markeninhaber **Einnahmen aus Lizenzgebühren**. Diesen stehen üblicherweise keine wesentlichen Ausgaben gegenüber. So machen Lizenzgebühren bei Marken wie beispielsweise Mövenpick, Jil Sander, Boss oder Adidas einen erheblichen Teil des gesamten Unternehmensgewinns aus. Diese finanziellen Ressourcen können von den Herstellern genutzt werden, um sie in die weitere Stärkung ihrer Marke zu investieren. Die Höhe der Lizenzgebühren liegt je nach Einsatz der eingesetzten Bemessungsregel in der Regel zwischen drei und 12,5 Prozent vom Umsatz des Lizenznehmers (Binder 2001, S. 404 ff.).

Markenlizenzen führen zu einer Verbesserung des Umfanges und der Intensität des **rechtlichen Markenschutzes**. In den meisten Fällen beschränkt sich der rechtliche Markenschutz lediglich auf die Warengruppen, in denen tatsächlich Produkte unter der Marke angeboten werden. Marken ohne „notorische Bekanntheit“ (MarkenG § 4 Abs. 3) verfügen außerhalb ihrer Stammbereiche somit in der Regel über keinen Markenschutz und sind daher für andere Unternehmen rechtmäßig verfügbar. Eine Lizenzvergabe, die sich auf neue Warengruppen erstreckt, weitet demnach den Schutz der Marke auf diese Bereiche aus. Darüber hinaus, gehen Lizenznehmer verstärkt gegen Produktpiraterie und Plagiate vor und erhöht dadurch die Intensität des Markenschutzes.

Der Einsatz von Markenlizenzen beziehungsweise Franchiseverträgen eröffnet die Chance, die Nachfrager durch **neue Vertriebswege** anzusprechen. Hierdurch erhöht sich die Anzahl der Kontaktpunkte, ohne dass der Lizenzgeber wesentliche Investitionen in die neuen Vertriebskanäle tätigen muss. Hier sind insbesondere Franchiseverträge von Bedeutung.

Bei **Franchiseverträgen** handelt es sich im Kern um Vertriebslizenzen, das heißt um eine sehr enge Kooperation zwischen Markeninhaber (Franchisegeber) und einem beziehungsweise in den meisten Fällen vielen Vertriebspartnern (Franchisenehmer). Den Franchisenehmern wird gegen eine Franchisegebühr das Recht eingeräumt, Produkte und Dienstleistungen unter den Marken- und Warenzeichen und der Ausstattung des Franchisegebers anzubieten (Meffert 2000, S. 639 f.). Beispiele hierfür sind bekannte Fast-Food-Marken wie McDonald’s und Burger King aber auch Foto Quelle, Essanelle Friseursalons und Sunpoint Sonnenstudios. Der Markeninhaber erhält in der Regel eine fixe Eintrittsgebühr zu Vertragsbeginn sowie umsatzabhängige Zahlungen.

Bei dieser Form der Markenerweiterung behält der Markeninhaber in erheblichem Umfang die Kontrolle über die Verwendung seiner Marke. Der Umgang mit der Marke wird durch Ergebnis- und Verhaltenskontrollen überprüft. Ferner schränkt der Markeninhaber in der Regel die wirtschaftliche Selbstständigkeit durch direkte Weisungsbefugnisse über den Franchisenehmer stark ein. Die besonderen **Vorteile** eines Franchisesystems auf Seiten des Markeninhabers liegen neben den teils erheblichen Einkünften aus Franchisegebühren in der Kontrolle über die Franchisenehmer und den Marktauftritt der eigenen Marke. Das in der Regel standardisierte Auftreten der Marke am Markt führt zu einem konsistenten Markenimageaufbau bei den Nachfragern. Darüber hinaus spart der Markeninhaber die erheblichen Investitionskosten in neue Filialen und realisiert dadurch ein vielfach höheres Wachstums- beziehungsweise Expansionstempo.

Trotz ihrer zahlreichen Vorteile beinhalten Markenlizenzierungsstrategien auch einige **Risiken** für den Markeninhaber. Die Risiken beziehen sich vor allem auf die Beeinträchtigung der **Konsistenz der Markenidentität**. Wird bei der Selektion ein Partner gewählt, der eine grundsätzliche Divergenz in der Unternehmenskultur und Markenführung aufweist, kann dies zu Missverständnissen und Spannungen führen, die die Marke beschädigen können. Darüber hinaus erwirbt der Lizenznehmer das Recht zur Entwicklung und Herstellung von Lizenzprodukten. Existiert dabei ein Mis-Fit zwischen den neuen Produkten und der Markenidentität und werden sie durch unzureichende Koordination zwischen Lizenznehmer und Markeninhaber falsch im Markt positioniert, so besteht die Gefahr, die Marke zu schwächen und langfristig zu gefährden. Dieses Risiko ist umso größer, je umfassender der Markeninhaber die Kommunikation der Produkte dem Lizenznehmer überlässt. Ein Lizenzprogramm sollte daher als ein integriertes Instrument des Markenmanagements gesehen werden. Daher sind die Partnerselektion, die Betreuung und die Koordination der Lizenznehmer wesentliche Erfolgsfaktoren, um mit einer Marke durch Lizenzierungen nachhaltig zu expandieren (Binder 2001, S. 409).

3.24 Co-Branding-Strategie

Im Gegensatz zur Lizenzierungs- und Autarkiestrategie, bei denen immer nur eine Marke in Erscheinung tritt, wird das Leistungsangebot bei einer Co-Branding-Strategie durch zwei oder mehr Marken im Verbund markiert (Aaker/Joachimsthaler 2000, S. 141 f.). In der Regel bringen alle Kooperationspartner ihre Ressourcen und Kompetenzen in größerem Umfang ein. Co-Branding zeichnet sich durch vier wesentliche Merkmale aus (Baumgarth 2003, S. 22 f.):

- Verbindung von mindestens zwei Marken,
- die für den Nachfrager wahrnehmbar kooperieren,
- um durch die Kooperation der Marken ein gemeinsames Leistungsbündel zu schaffen
- und sowohl vor als auch nach der Co-Branding Kooperation aus Sicht der Nachfrager selbstständig sind.

Co-Branding Strategien haben in der jüngsten Vergangenheit an Bedeutung gewonnen, da viele Hersteller sich von diesen Kooperationen eine Imageverbesserung sowie eine Verbreiterung ihrer Markenkompetenz aus Sicht der Nachfrager erhoffen. Die Besonderheit des Co-Branding besteht in der Problematik, mindestens zwei Identitäten eigenständiger Marken unter Berücksichtigung der zugrunde liegenden gemeinsamen Leistung verbinden zu müssen, ohne dass es zu Konflikten zwischen den Markenidentitäten kommt.

Bekannte Beispiele für **horizontale Co-Brandings** sind unter anderem der Otto Versand und die Baumarktkette Obi, die ein gemeinsames Online-Portal unter der Marke Obi@Otto betreiben, McDonald's und Smarties mit dem Eis McFlurry Smarties oder

Milka und Kellogg's mit der Schokoladen-Sonderedition Crispy Joghurt. Als Sonderform des Co-Branding ist die Schaffung einer neuen (zusätzlichen) Markenidentität für die gekennzeichnete Kooperation (so genanntes Mega-Brand) unter Einschränkung der individuellen markenbezogenen Handlungsfreiheiten anzusehen (Rao/Ruekert 1994, S. 87 ff.; Blackett/Boad 1999). Exemplarisch ist hier die Star Alliance als Zusammenschluss mehrerer Luftverkehrsdienstleister (Lufthansa, US Airways, United, Spainair, Singapore Airlines, Scandinavian Airlines, Polish Airlines, bmi, Austrian, Asiana Airlines, ANA, Air New Zealand, Thai Airways, Varig, Air Canada) zu nennen, wobei die beteiligten Marken auch nach der Kooperationsvereinbarung weiterhin als eigenständige Marken existent bleiben (vgl. Abbildung 8 sowie Netzer 1999, S. 158 ff.).

Abbildung 8: **Co-Branding am Beispiel der Marken Milka/Kellogg's, Häagen-Dazs/Baileys, SonyEricsson und Star-Alliance**

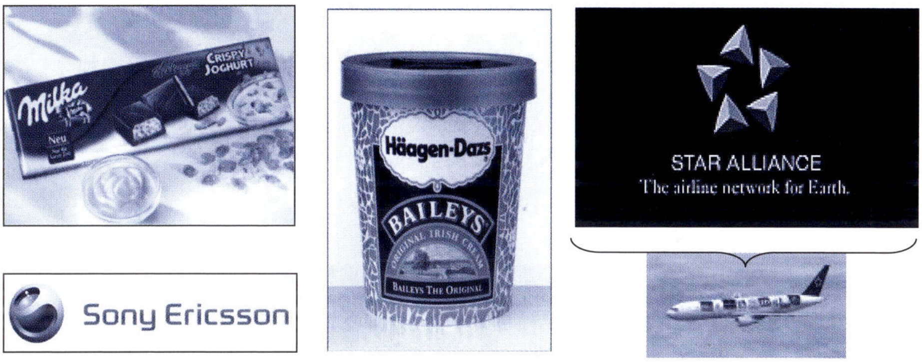

GABLER GRAFIK

Im Gegensatz zur horizontalen Ausgestaltungsform bezieht sich bei der **vertikalen Form des Co-Brandings** die Zusammenarbeit auf vor- und nachgelagerte Wertschöpfungsstufen. Diese Form des Co-Branding wird auch als **Ingredient Branding** bezeichnet. So arbeitet die Computerfirma IBM mit dem Chip-Hersteller Intel zusammen und Coca Cola verwendet die künstliche Süßstoffmarke NutraSweet für Cola Light (Baumgarth 1998, S. 11; Freter/Baumgarth 2000, S. 289 ff.).

Der Erfolg des Co-Branding wird durch zwei wesentliche Faktoren determiniert (Baumgarth 2004, S. 180 ff.):

1. **Komplementarität der Markenidentitäten** – die Identitäten der kooperierenden Marken sollten in hohem Maße komplementär zueinander sein. Ein Zusatznutzen wird sowohl für die Nachfrager als auch für die Markenmitarbeiter nur dann geschaffen, wenn die kooperierenden Marken sich ergänzende Identitäten, vor allem sich ergänzende Kompetenzen in die Co-Brand einbringen (Park/Jun/Shocker 1996,

S. 453 ff.). Ein hoher Fit im Sinne von vollständiger Deckungsgleichheit ist hier demgegenüber nicht erstrebenswert.

2. **Fit der Zielgruppen** – ohne eine Überlappung der Zielgruppen ist das jeweilige Markenimage des Kooperationspartners für die eigenen Kunden nur bedingt verhaltensrelevant. Das immer auf die Beeinflussung von Kaufverhalten abzielendes Co-Branding wäre dann nicht zielführend.

Die **Chancen** beziehungsweise Vorteile des Co-Branding liegen vor allem in der Möglichkeit des gegenseitigen Imagetransfers und der Nutzung eines vorhandenen Vertrauensbonuses des Partners (Baumgarth 2003). So kann das Co-Branding zu positiven Spill-over-Effekten für die beteiligten Individualmarken führen (Simonin/Ruth 1998). Darüber hinaus lassen sich durch Co-Branding zusätzliche Umsatzpotenziale und Preisprämien ausschöpfen sowie neue Märkte erreichen, die für die einzelnen beteiligten Marken durch hohe Eintrittsbarrieren schwer zugänglich sind. Durch das Co-Branding lässt sich für die Nachfrager ein Zusatznutzen generieren, der lediglich durch die Kooperation der Marken erzielt werden kann.

Das Co-Branding ist jedoch auch mit **Nachteilen** verbunden. Den Chancen eines positiven Imagetransfers stehen in gleicher Weise die Gefahren negativer Ausstrahlungen zwischen den beteiligten Marken gegenüber. Des Weiteren wächst durch die Kombination von Marken die Gefahr der Verwirrung von Kunden und Mitarbeitern durch eine Erosion vormals klarer Positionierungen. Der gemeinsame Auftritt erfordert zudem eine enge Abstimmung zwischen den Beteiligten im Hinblick auf ihre markenbezogenen Aktivitäten (Koordinationskosten) und engt die individuellen Positionierungsspielräume ein.

In Tabelle 1 sind abschließend die wesentlichen Chancen und Risiken der Markentransferstrategie und des Co-Branding zusammenfassend dargestellt.

3.25 Autarkiestrategie

Bei allen Markenexpansionsstrategien wirken die Ressourcen und Kompetenzen der Unternehmung als begrenzender Faktor. Dies kann es notwendig machen, für eine Expansion Kooperationen einzugehen. Verfügt jedoch ein Unternehmen über alle erforderlichen Ressourcen und Kompetenzen, so kann die Markenexpansion autark realisiert werden.

Dies hat vor allem den Vorteil, dass alle Rechte beim Markeninhaber verbleiben, sämtliche Entscheidungen ausschließlich von ihm getroffen werden (vollständige Kontrolle der Markenführung) und die Erträge der Markenexpansion nicht mit Lizenznehmern oder anderen Kooperationsunternehmen geteilt werden müssen. Darüber hinaus verbleiben alle im Rahmen des Markenmanagements gesammelten Erfahrungen und Lerneffekte im Unternehmen und erschweren damit die Imitation durch Konkurrenten. Die Autarkiestrategie schafft somit in besonderer Weise die Voraussetzung zur Schaffung nachhaltiger Wettbewerbsvorteile.

Tabelle 1: Kennzeichnung der Markentransferstrategie und des Co-Branding

Strategietyp / Aspekte	Markentransferstrategie	Co-Branding
Merkmal	■ Übertragung positiver Imagekomponenten von einer etablierten Marke auf ein Transferprodukt einer neuen Produktkategorie	■ Gemeinsamer Auftritt von selbstständigen Marken im kooperativen Verbund
Chancen	■ Besetzen strategischer Geschäftsfelder ■ Gewinnung neuer Zielgruppen in neuen Märkten ■ Senkung der Markeneintrittsbarrieren ■ Reduzierung der Markenbildungskosten ■ Erweiterung des Assoziationsfeldes der Stammmarke ■ Stärkung der Hauptmarke durch Rückfluss positiver Imagebestandteile ■ Abschwächung bzw. Antizipation von Werbebeschränkungen	■ Vermeidung hoher Anfangsinvestitionen für Neumarken ■ Schnell hohe Bekanntheit ■ Vertrauensbonus ■ Gegenseitiger Imagetransfer
Risiken	■ Markenerosion durch zu viele oder zu schnelle aufeinanderfolgende Markentransfers ■ Verlust der Markenidentität durch Ansprache unterschiedlicher Zielgruppen ■ Negative Ausstrahlungseffekte bei geringer Imageaffinität zwischen Haupt- und Transfermarke ■ Wachsender Koordinationsaufwand durch horizontale Abstimmung in der Markenführung von Hauptmarke und Transferprodukten	■ Fehlende Positionsfreiräume ■ Hoher Koordinationsbedarf ■ Diffuse Markenidentität ■ Gefahr negativen Imagetransfers
Zentrale Anforderungen	■ Sicherstellung eines starken imagemäßigen Zusammenhangs von Haupt- und Transfermarke	■ Fit zwischen beteiligten Marken sowie eindeutiger Leistungsbezug der Co-Brands

GABLER GRAFIK

4. Fazit

Neben der Konzipierung der Markenidentitäten und der Gestaltung der Markenarchitektur für das gesamte Markenportfolio eines Unternehmens stellt die Bestimmung der Evolutionsstrategie für jede einzelne Marke des Portfolios die wichtigste Führungsentscheidung im Rahmen des identitätsorientierten Markenmanagements dar. Sie wird im Wesentlichen von der Ressourcen- und Kompetenzausstattung eines Unternehmens determiniert.

Obwohl die Ressourcentheorie der strategischen Unternehmensführung (Resource-based-view) erste Hinweise zur Identifikation und dem gezielten Management von Ressourcen und Kompetenzen liefert (Burmann 2002), bestehen in diesem Bereich noch erhebliche Wissensdefizite (Freiling 2000). Angesichts dieser Lücken in der Wissenschaft erscheint verständlich, warum in der Markenpraxis zahlreiche Missmanagementbeispiele bezüglich der hier diskutierten Evolutionsstrategien, insbesondere mit Blick auf die oben ausführlich dargestellten Markenerweiterungsstrategien, zu beobachten sind. Oftmals scheint aber auch ein zu kurzfristig und ausschließlich auf die Generierung von Zusatzumsätzen ausgerichtetes Markenmanagement für den Misserfolg so mancher Markenevolutionsstrategie in der Vergangenheit verantwortlich zu sein. Hier liefert der vorliegende Beitrag erste Hinweise für eine Professionalisierung der zu treffenden Entscheidungen.

Literatur

Aaker, D. A. (1990), Brand Extensions: The Good, the Bad, and the Ugly, in: Sloan Management Review, Summer, S. 47–56.

Aaker, D. A., Joachimsthaler, E. (2000), Brand Leadership, New York et al.

Baumgarth, C. (1998), Ingredient Branding: Begriff, State of the Art & Empirische Ergebnisse, Arbeitspapier des Lehrstuhls für Marketing an der Universität Siegen, Siegen.

Baumgarth, C. (2003), Wirkungen des Co–Brandings, Habil., Wiesbaden.

Baumgarth, C. (2004), Markenpolitik – Markenwirkungen – Markenführung – Markencontrolling, 2. Aufl., Wiesbaden.

Binder, Ch. (2001), Lizenzierung von Marken, in: Esch, F.–R. (Hrsg.), Moderne Markenführung–Grundlagen, Innovative Ansätze, praktische Umsetzung, 3. Aufl., Wiesbaden, S. 385–411.

Blackett, T., Boad, B. (1999), Co–Branding , Houndmills.

Bliss, Ch. (2000) Management von Komplexität – Ein integrierter, systemtheoretischer Ansatz zur Komplexitätsreduktion, Wiesbaden.

Böll, K. (1999), Merchandising und Licensing, München.

Burmann, Ch., Blinda, L. (2004), Identitätsbasiertes Markenmanagement, in: Wirtz, B., Göttgens, O. (Hrsg.), Integriertes Marken– und Kundenwertmanagement, Wiesbaden.

Burmann, Ch. (2002)., Strategische Flexibilität und Strategiewechsel als Determinanten des Unternehmenswertes (zugl. Habilitationsschrift Universität Münster), Wiesbaden.

Esch, F.-R. (2004), Strategie und Technik der Markenführung, 2. Aufl., München.

Esch, F.-R., Fuchs, M., Bräutigam (2000), Konzeption und Umsetzung von Markenerweiterungen, in: Esch, F.-R. (Hrsg.), Moderne Markenführung: Grundlagen – Innovative Ansätze – Praktische Umsetzung, Wiesbaden, S. 669–704.
Freiling, J. (2000), Entwicklungslinien und Perspektiven des Strategischen Kompetenz–Managements, in: Hammann, P., Freiling, J., (Hrsg.), Die Ressourcen– und Kompetenzperspektive des Strategischen Managements, Wiesbaden, S. 14–45.
Freter, H., Baumgarth, C. (2000), Ingredient Branding – Begriff und theoretische Begründung, in: Esch, F.-R. (Hrsg.), Moderne Markenführung: Grundlagen – Innovative Ansätze – Praktische Umsetzung, Wiesbaden, S. 289–315.
Güldenberg, H. G. (2000), Markenführung im Spannungsfeld zwischen lokalen und globalen Anforderungen, in: Markenführung im Spannungsfeld zwischen Rationalität, Emotionalität und Mythos – Aktuelle Herausforderungen und Erfolgsfaktoren, in: Meffert, H., Backhaus, K., Becker J. (Hrsg.), Dokumentationspapier Nr. 140 der Wissenschaftlichen Gesellschaft für Marketing und Unternehmensführung e. V., Münster, S. 22–32.
Günther, S. (2002), Wahrnehmung und Beurteilung von Markentransfers – Erfolgsfaktoren für Tranferprodukte und Markenimage, Dissertation, Wiesbaden.
Harrigan, K. R. (1999), Unternehmensstrategien für reife und rückläufige Märkte, Frankfurt/M.
Hätty, H. (1989), Der Markentransfer, Heidelberg.
Kapferer, J. N. (1992), Die Marke – Kapital des Unternehmens, Landsberg/Lech.
Kapferer, J. N. (2000), Strategic Brand Management, London.
Keller, K. L. (2003), Strategic brand management – building, measuring, and managing brand equity, 2. Aufl., Upper Saddle River, NJ [u.a.].
Keller. K. L. (2001), Erfolgsfaktoren von Markenerweiterungen, in: Esch, F.-R. (Hrsg.), Moderne Markenführung: Grundlagen – Innovative Ansätze – Praktische Umsetzung, Wiesbaden, S. 705–719.
Köhler, R. (1994), Planungs- und Entwicklungsprozess neuer Markenartikel und Markteinführung, in: Bruhn, M. (Hrsg.): Handbuch Markenartikel, Bd. 1, Stuttgart, S. 433–462.
Kreutzer, R. (1989), Markenstrategien im länderübergreifenden Marketing, Markenartikel, Nr. 11, S. 569–572.
Loken, B., Roedder, J. D. (1993), Diluting Brand Beliefs: When do brand extensions have a negative impact?, in: Journal of Marketing, Vol. 57, July, S. 71–84.
Mayer, A.,Mayer, R.U. (1987), Imagetransfer, Hamburg.
Meffert, H. (1988), Strategische Unternehmensführung und Marketing, Wiesbaden.
Meffert, H. (1994), Marketing-Management. Analyse – Strategie – Implementierung, Wiesbaden.
Meffert, H. (2000), Marketing, 9. Aufl., Wiesbaden.
Meffert, H., Heinemann, G. (1990), Operationalisierung des Imagetransfers, in: Marketing ZFP, Nr. 1, 1. Quartal, S. 5–10.
Netzer, F. (1999), Strategische Allianzen im Luftverkehr: nachfragerorientierte Problemfelder ihrer Gestaltung, Frankfurt/M.
Park, C. W., Milberg, S., Lawson, R. (1991), Evaluation of Brand Extensions: The Role of Product Feature Similarity and Brand Concept Consistency, in: Journal of Consumer Research, Vol. 18, September, S. 185–193.
Park, C., Jun, S. Y., Shocker, A. D. (1996), Composite Branding Alliances, in: Journal of Marketing Research, Vol. 33, No. 4, S. 453–466.
Prick, H.-J. (1989), Nivea-Markentransfer: von der Marke für die Hautcreme zur Dachmarke für die Hautpflege, in: Markenartikel, Nr. 10, S. 504–509.
Quelch, J. A., Hoff, E. (1986), Globales Marketing – nach Maß, in: Harvardmanager, No. 4, S. 107–110.
Rangaswamy, A., Burke, R. , Oliva T. (1993), Brand Equity and the Extendibility of Brand Names, in: International Journal of Research in Marketing, Vol. 10, S. 61–75.

Rao, A. R., Ruekert, R. W. (1994), Brand Alliances as Signals of Product Quality, in: Sloan Management Review, Vol. 36, No. 1, S. 87–97, Fall 1994.

Sachs, A. (2002), Portfolio–Management bei Unilever, in: Marketingjournal, Nr. 2, S. 8–17.

Sattler, H. (1998), Beurteilung der Erfolgschancen von Markentransfers, in: Zeitschrift für Betriebswirtschaft (ZfB), 68. Jg., Nr. 5, S. 475–495.

Sattler, H. (2001), Brand Stretching: Chancen und Risiken, in: Köhler, R., Majer, W., Wieczorek, H. (Hrsg.): Erfolgsfaktor Marke – Neue Strategien des Markenmanagements, München, S. 141–149.

Sattler, H., Völckner, F., Zatloukal, G. (2003), Erfolgsfaktoren von Markentransfers, in: Marketing ZFP, 25. Jg., Nr. 3, S. 147–168.

Simonin, B. L., Ruth, J. A. (1998), Is a company known by the company it keeps?, in: Journal of Marketing Research, 35. Jg., Nr. 1, S. 30–42.

Völckner, F. (2003), Neuproduktererfolg bei kurzlebigen Konsumgütern: Eine empirische Analyse der Erfolgsfaktoren von Markentransfers, Dissertation, Wiesbaden.

Völckner, F. (2004), Fünf Faktoren entscheiden über den Erfolg von Markentransfers, in: Absatzwirtschaft, September, S. 74–79.

Waltermann, B. (1989), Internationale Markenpolitik und Produktpositionierung: Markenpolitische Entscheidungen im europäischen Automobilmarkt, Wien.

Weinberg, P., Diehl, S. (2001), Aufbau und Sicherung von Markenbindung unter schwierigen Konkurrenz– und Distributionsbedingungen, in: Köhler, R., Majer, W., Wiezorek, H. (Hrsg.): Erfolgsfaktor Marke – Neue Strategien des Markenmanagements, München, S. 26–35.

Wölfer, U. (1994) Produktlinienerweiterungen (Line extension), in: Bruhn, M. (Hrsg.) Handbuch Markenartikel, Bd. 1, Stuttgart, S. 527–541.

Zatloukal, G. (2002), Erfolgsfaktoren von Markentransfers, Dissertation, Wiesbaden.

Mehrmarkenstrategien – identitätsorientierte Führung von Markenportfolios

Heribert Meffert und Jesko Perrey

1.	**Stellenwert der Mehrmarkenstrategie**	**214**
2.	**Gegenstand von Mehrmarkenstrategien**	**217**
2.1	Charakteristika von Mehrmarkenstrategien	217
2.2	Chancen und Risiken im Marktauftritt	219
3.	**Planungsprozess von Mehrmarkenstrategien**	**227**
3.1	Marktstrategische Standortbestimmung als Ausgangspunkt	229
3.2	Strategische Rahmenplanung	230
3.21	Gestaltung der Markenportfolios und Festlegung markenspezifischer Rollen	231
3.22	Marktstrategische Positionierung und Leitbilder der Marken	231
3.3	Ausgestaltung der Instrumentalstrategien	234
4.	**Organisatorische Verankerung von Mehrmarkenstrategien**	**236**
5.	**Zusammenfassung und Fazit**	**239**

Abbildung 2: Mehrmarkenstrategien in der Automobilindustrie

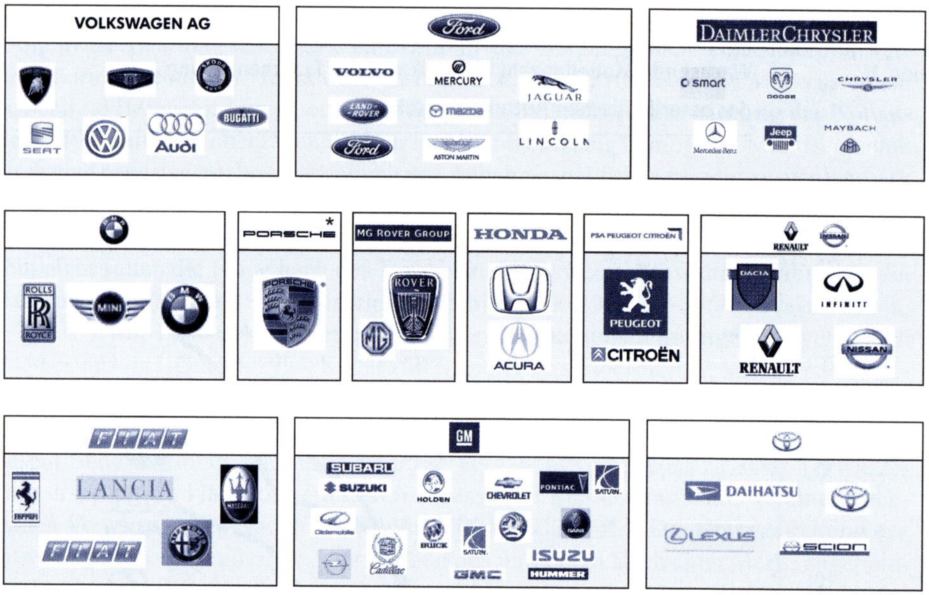

* Einzelmarkenstrategie

GABLER GRAFIK

Quelle: McKinsey; Motorpresse Stuttgart 2004

Die aus der Akquisition vormals selbstständiger Marken oder aus internen Wachstumsüberlegungen hervorgehende Führung von Markenportfolios ist schließlich auch im Dienstleistungssektor verstärkt anzutreffen. So offeriert die TUI AG ihre touristischen Leistungen neben der Stammarke TUI über Marken wie Airtours, Dr. Tigges, 1-2-Fly, Wolters Reisen, l'tur und Robinson Club. Im Flugdienstleistungsbereich tritt Hapag Lloyd mit der zusätzlichen Discount-Marke HLX an, und auch die Lufthansa AG ist über ihre 50prozentige Tochter Thomas Cook mit der Marke Condor parallel im Billigflugsegment aktiv (Genger 2004, S. 6). Seit der Einführung eines Direktzugs unter der Marke Metropolitan lässt sich schließlich auch die Deutsche Bahn AG als Mehrmarkenanbieter bezeichnen (o. V. 1997, S. 58). Allerdings wurde jüngst beschlossen, den Metropolitan einzustellen. Dies zeigt die besonderen Schwierigkeiten einer erfolgreichen Mehrmarkenpolitik bei Dienstleistern.

2. Gegenstand von Mehrmarkenstrategien

Die Mehrmarkenstrategie lässt sich als Instrument zur Profilierung von Markenportfolios im horizontalen Wettbewerb charakterisieren (Meffert 1992, S. 137). Im Vergleich zu alternativen Strategien der Markenprofilierung ist die Ausübung dieser Strategie mit spezifischen Chancen und Risiken verbunden.

2.1 Charakteristika von Mehrmarkenstrategien

Im Gegensatz zum Management eines Produktportfolios mit Hilfe einer Dach- oder Familienmarkenstrategie setzt die Mehrmarkenstrategie die Führung mehrerer selbstständiger Marken voraus. Eine Mehrmarkenstrategie lässt sich dabei anhand der folgenden, konstitutiven Merkmale charakterisieren (Kapferer 1992, S. 211 ff.):

Parallele Führung mehrerer selbstständiger Marken,

- die auf **denselben Produktbereich** ausgerichtet sind,
- deren Produkte und Dienstleistungen sich anhand zentraler Leistungsmerkmale beziehungsweise der Ausgestaltung der Marketinginstrumente **unterscheiden**,
- deren voneinander **getrennter Marktauftritt** von den Nachfragern als solcher **wahrnehmbar** ist und
- die innerhalb der Gesamtunternehmung **organisatorisch abgegrenzte** und mit der Markenführung betraute Einheiten darstellen.

Die Ausrichtung mehrerer Marken auf **denselben Produktbereich** kann in einer angebotsorientierten Interpretation mit einer parallelen Bearbeitung des Gesamtmarktes gleichgesetzt werden. Da sich die Angebote der verschiedenen Marken allerdings gewöhnlicherweise in ihren Leistungsmerkmalen, dem Preis, dem kommunikativen Auftritt oder in ihrem Vertrieb unterscheiden, liegt der Mehrmarkenstrategie in einem nachfragerbezogenen Verständnis zumeist die Philosophie einer differenzierten Ansprache verschiedener Käufersegmente des Gesamtmarktes und damit einer segmentspezifischen Ausrichtung der unterschiedlichen Marken auf denselben Produktbereich zugrunde.

Dabei lassen sich einzelne Produktbereiche in der Praxis nicht immer scharf voneinander abgrenzen, sodass nicht selten Interpretationsspielräume hinsichtlich der von Unternehmen verfolgten Markenstrategien aufkommen. Beispielhaft können die Marken Duplo, Rocher, Giotto, Mon Chérie, Ferrero Küsschen und Raffaello angeführt werden, die vom Anbieter Ferrero verschiedenen Produktbereichen zugeordnet werden und dementsprechend als Einzelmarken gelten (Meffert 2000, S. 856). Bei Zugrundelegung des Verständnisses einer subjektiv empfundenen Substituierbarkeit von Produkten (Dichtl et al. 1977) müsste hier indes vom selben Produktbereich und damit von einer Mehrmarkenstrategie gesprochen werden.

Wichtig ist in diesem Zusammenhang auch die Frage, ob die Mehrmarkenstrategie quasi homogene, in der Qualitätswahrnehmung **kaum unterscheidbare Konsumgüter** zum Gegenstand hat (zum Beispiel Benzin, Zigaretten, Waschmittel) oder eine Differenzierung im Bereich **langlebiger Konsumgüter** (zum Beispiel Automobile oder Waschmaschinen) anstrebt. Während die erste Kategorie von Mehrmarkenstrategien sich insbesondere im kommunikativen Bereich des Marketing-Mix bewegt, erfordert letztere eine umfassendere Differenzierung auch in den übrigen Komponenten des Marketing-Mix, insbesondere dem Leistungsangebot, den Vertriebswegen und in der Preispolitik.

Die Existenz einer abgegrenzten Einheit, die für die Führung einer einzelnen Marke verantwortlich ist, lässt sich schließlich als **innerorganisationales Merkmal** einer Mehrmarkenstrategie bezeichnen. Die Ausgestaltung der organisationalen Einheiten auf Markenebene sowie das markenübergreifende Zusammenspiel dieser Einheiten stellen eine zentrale Herausforderung an das Management von Markenportfolios dar. Hier gilt es, den optimalen Grad an Autarkie der einzelnen Markeneinheiten entlang der Wertschöpfungskette zu bestimmen. Im Einzelfall wird diese Aufgabe in hohem Maße von den mit einer Mehrmarkenstrategie verfolgten Zielsetzungen auf Unternehmensebene determiniert.

Abbildung 3: Mehrmarkenstrategie des Volkswagen-Konzerns

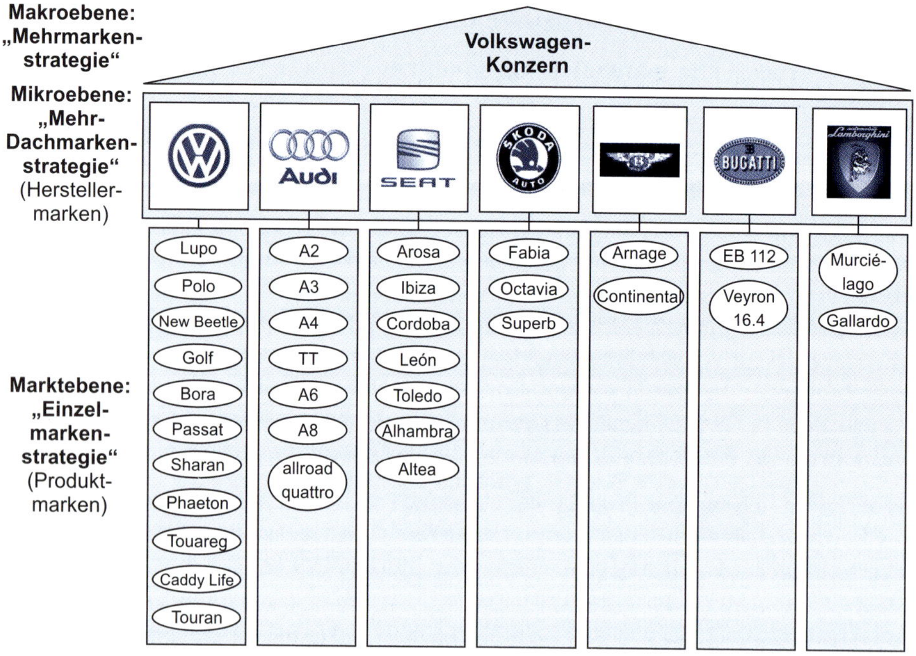

GABLER GRAFIK

Die Mehrmarkenstrategie tritt in der Praxis **nur selten in „Reinform“** auf. Vorherrschend sind vielmehr Unternehmen, deren Marktauftritt durch eine **Kombination** verschiedener markenstrategischer Optionen gekennzeichnet ist. Beispielhaft sei an dieser Stelle die Mehrmarkenstrategie des Volkswagen-Konzerns genannt (vgl. Abbildung 3). Die Herstellermarken Volkswagen, Audi, Seat, Skoda etc. umfassen dabei ihrerseits Dachmarken, die im Markt mit verschiedenen, auf die unterschiedlichen Bedürfnissegmente ausgerichteten Fahrzeugen operieren. Exakterweise müsste somit an dieser Stelle von einer Mehr-Dachmarkenstrategie gesprochen werden. Dabei stehen die Dachmarken letztlich im Fokus der Strategieüberlegungen, da von diesen die markenprägenden Leistungen offeriert werden, die den Ausgangspunkt der Markenwahrnehmung durch die Nachfrager bilden.

2.2 Chancen und Risiken im Marktauftritt

Die wirksame Ausübung einer Mehrmarkenstrategie setzt eine sorgfältige Abwägung der mit dieser Form des Marktauftritts verbundenen Chancen und Risiken voraus. Eine derartige Analyse bildet die Grundlage zur Formulierung der in Abhängigkeit des situativen Kontextes im Rahmen von Mehrmarkenstrategien verfolgten Ziele.

Die grundsätzlichen Ziele von Mehrmarkenstrategien lassen sich aus den allgemeinen Unternehmens- und Marketingzielen ableiten und stehen in einer engen Beziehung zueinander (Meffert 1994, S. 93 ff.; Becker 2002, S. 13 ff.). Zur Sicherstellung des Oberziels der Ertrags- und Renditesteigerung stellt der **Markenwert** die relevante ökonomische Größe dar. In Mehrmarkenstrategien gilt es dabei, den Markenwert des Gesamtportfolios zu maximieren. Zu diesem Zweck fungieren wettbewerbs- und nachfragergerichtete ebenso wie innengerichtete Zielsetzungen als Subziele.

Im Rahmen der **wettbewerbsgerichteten** Ziele von Mehrmarkenstrategien nehmen die Erhöhung des Absatzvolumens beziehungsweise die Ausweitung der Marktanteile des gesamten Markenportfolios eine zentrale Bedeutung ein. Durch eine differenzierte Positionierung der Marken besteht die Chance, eine breite Marktabdeckung zu erzielen und auftretenden Nischenbedürfnissen mit entsprechenden Leistungen zu begegnen. Sind die verschiedenen Marken des Portfolios durch eigenständige und nachfragerseitig wahrgenommene Identitäten geprägt, lässt sich zudem eine gezielte und bedarfsgerechte Konsumentenansprache vornehmen, die zu einer zusätzlichen Verbesserung der **Marktdurchdringung** beiträgt. Als Beispiel für diese Vorgehensweise kann die sukzessive Einführung von zehn Marken in den amerikanischen Waschmittelmarkt durch Procter & Gamble angeführt werden. Obwohl jedes hinzugekommene Produkt Umsatzeinbußen bei den etablierten Marken verursachte, stieg der Gesamtumsatz aller Marken durch Hinzugewinnung von speziell angesprochenen Konsumentengruppen an (Kotler 1988, S. 469).

Eine eng mit der breiten Marktabdeckung verbundene, wettbewerbsgerichtete Zielsetzung von Mehrmarkenstrategien stellt die Absicherung der Wettbewerbsposition beziehungsweise die Schaffung von Markteintrittsbarrieren dar. Eine derartige **Marktabsi-**

cherung nimmt in Portfolios mit einer „starken Marke“ beziehungsweise Referenzmarke eine besondere Bedeutung ein (Kapferer 1997, S. 283). Die Mehrmarkenstrategie bietet dabei die Chance, durch Einführung von „Kampfmarken“ die Referenzmarke vor einem Preiskampf zu schützen. Eine derartige „Schutzschild-Funktion“ kommt etwa im Waschmittelmarkt den Marken Weißer Riese und Spee für Persil, im Automobilsektor den Marken Skoda und Seat für Volkswagen oder im Tourismusmarkt der Marke 1-2-Fly für TUI beziehungsweise im Nahrungsmittelbereich der Kaffee-Marke Onko für Kraft Foods zu. Eine ähnliche Zielsetzung verfolgte auch Reemtsma bei der Einführung der preisaggressiven Marke West, die damals die etablierten Marken Stuyvesant, R6 und R1 vor einem aufkommenden Preiskampf im Tabakmarkt bewahren sollte. Handelsgerichtet bietet die Erweiterung des Markenportfolios die Chance einer Ausweitung der **Regalplatzfläche** und damit der Schaffung einer zusätzlichen Markteintrittsbarriere für die potenzielle Konkurrenz. Auf diese Weise decken die Marken Rama, Sanella, Bertolli, Du Darfst, Becel und Lätta von Unilever das Margarine-Sortiment weitestgehend ab.

Eine weitere wettbewerbsgerichtete Zielsetzung von Mehrmarkenstrategien stellt die **Streuung des Marktrisikos** beziehungsweise **die Erhöhung der Aktionsflexibilität** im Wettbewerb dar. So bietet sich im internationalen Wettbewerb die Chance zur **Markterschließung** mit den jeweils bestgeeigneten Marken, womit das Risiko im Marktaufbau reduziert werden kann. Diese Überlegungen bildeten etwa für den Volkswagen-Konzern eine wichtige Grundlage bei der Akquisition der Marken Seat und Skoda. Konnte mit Seat über eine breite Präsenz im spanischen Heimatmarkt eine verbesserte Wettbewerbsposition auf den südeuropäischen beziehungsweise durch mediterrane Bedürfnisse geprägten Automobilmärkten erzielt werden, diente die Integration Skodas vorwiegend der Erschließung der wachsenden osteuropäischen Absatzareale (Burmann 1995). Die Chancen einer erhöhten Aktionsflexibilität im internationalen Wettbewerb lassen sich nahtlos auf die Bearbeitung des Heimatmarktes übertragen. So kann etwa entstehenden Nachfragetrends durch eine Ausweitung des Leistungsspektrums einzelner Marken mit einem überschaubaren Marktrisiko begegnet werden. Eine ähnliche Intention verfolgte Mercedes-Benz mit der Beteiligung am Kleinwagenprojekt Smart. Die Befriedigung des aufkommenden Wunsches nach Kleinstfahrzeugen mit der Premiummarke Mercedes wäre dabei durch die dann in ihrem Nutzenversprechen kaum noch übereinstimmende Produktpalette mit der Gefahr einer Verwässerung der eigenen Markenidentität einhergegangen. Mit einer Vermarktung dieses innovativen Fahrzeuges unter der Marke Smart sollen hingegen der Fit zwischen Angebot und Nachfrage (junge, umweltfreundliche und modisch-aufgeschlossene Käuferschichten) sichergestellt und das Risiko eines negativen Imagetransfers auf die Marke Mercedes minimiert werden.

Gleichmaßen versucht Toyota seit Juni 2003, mit der Einführung der Marke Scion auf dem US-amerikanischen Markt die spätestens seit dem Auslaufen der Produktion der „Kult-Marke“ VW-Käfer in Mexiko existierende Marktnische zu schließen, ohne dass das eher konservative Image der Marke Toyota verwässert werden würde (siehe auch Insert 1). So werden neben den im Niedrigpreissegment angesiedelten zwei Basisversionen xA und xB eine Reihe modischer Accessoires (so genannte „Scion Ware“) wie beleuchtete Getränkehalter, farbige Lenkräder und Schaltknüppel oder blaue LED-Innenbeleuchtung angeboten, welche insbesondere junge Käufer ansprechen und die Marke mit emo-

INSERT 1 **Handelsblatt vom Dienstag, 14. Oktober 2003**

Toyota soll Accessoire für coole Typen werden

Die neue Marke „Scion“ kopiert ein Konzept, das schon den VW Käfer zum US-Kult machte

HANDELSBLATT, 14.10.2003

je PORTLAND. Wie gewinnt man als Autohersteller mit solidem Mittelklasse-Image Kunden, die mehr Luxus wollen und lieber Mercedes oder BMW kaufen? Man erfindet am besten eine völlig neue Marke – wie Toyota mit Lexus vorgemacht hat.

Seit Juni versuchen die Japaner diesen Trick nun am anderen Ende des Markenspektrums – offenbar wieder mit Erfolg. Mit dem „Scion“, zu deutsch „Spross“, will der Autohersteller sich eine Kundenschicht erschließen, für die Toyotas Autos sind, die von älteren Männern mit Hut knapp unter der Geschwindigkeitsbegrenzung gefahren werden.

Scion soll dagegen die coolen Typen mit persönlichem Stil anziehen. Sie sehen aus wie Rapper, fahren Skateboard und haben genügend Kohle für ihr erstes Auto – die image-, mode- und technologiebewussten Internetfreaks zwischen 16 und 26. Scion soll für sie werden, was der VW-Käfer als „Herbie“ und „Love Bug“ für die Marihuana rauchenden Väter und Großväter war: Ausdruck eines Lebensgefühls, Kult.

Foto: Toyota

„A“ sagen – oder doch lieber „B“? Der ungewöhnlich gestylte Scion xB (li.) ist doppelt so beliebt wie das Modell xA.

Und für dieses Lebensgefühl ist bei Scion die Markenerweiterung bereits geplant – nach dem Vorbild etwa von Harley-Davidson und Ferrari, deren Fans eine breite Palette von Accessoires kaufen können, von T-Shirts über Jacken bis zu Reisetaschen. Bei Toyota heißt das „Scion Ware“ und kommt schon in Kürze auf den Markt – coole, übergroße Kleidung für den gepflegten Web-Surfer.

Der Verkauf der Autos ist in den USA gut angelaufen. Zielgruppengemäß testet Toyota im Internet, ob jugendliche Käufer die neue Marke annehmen – während VW mit dem Auslaufen der Produktion in Mexiko den alten Käfer der Väter endgültig begraben hat. Zu kaufen gibt es den Scion vorläufig nur in Kalifornien. In den ersten vier Monaten bis Ende September setzte Toyota 6 414 Einheiten ab. „Selbst aus Deutschland reiste ein Käufer an“, sagt Scion-Vizepräsident Jim Farley.

Scions gibt es in zwei Geschmacksrichtungen: xA und xB. Beide kosten unter 15 000 $, mit einer langen Liste von Sonderausstattungen, mit denen der Käufer seinen Wagen individueller gestalten kann. Der Renner ist der xB – zur Überraschung selbst von Toyota. Das Auto sieht aus wie ein zu heiß gewaschener Kastenlieferwagen mit stumpfer Schnauze. „Ungewöhnliches, unverwechselbares Styling, viel Stauraum und gutmütiges Fahrverhalten“, sagen Tester. „Wir waren geschockt, dass wir vom xB doppelt soviel verkaufen können wie vom xA“, sagt Toyota-Manager Farley. „Cool“, sagen kalifornische Fans.

Der xA ist deutlich verwechselbarer: eine Kreuzung zwischen VW Golf und Minivan mit einem Schuss Mini Cooper. „Niedlich“ sei er, aber nicht „cool“, findet Autotester Paul Lienert. Für die Generation Y sei das Auto „einfach zu langweilig“.

Genug gibt es offenbar von beiden nicht. „Wir haben eine Warteliste“, sagt Edwin Tan, Verkaufsmanager des einzigen Scion-Händlers in San Francisco. Die Kunden machten reichlich Gebrauch von den 40 Optionen, um ihre Autos ganz auf sich zuschneiden zu können. Toyota denke jetzt an eine nur grundierte Version, die der Käufer mit Farben nach eigenem Gusto spritzen kann. Die Ähnlichkeit mit den wild bemalten Flower-Power-Käfern ist nicht zufällig.

Im September verkauften Toyota-Händler 1631 Scions – wenig, verglichen mit fast 60 000 Einheiten der Brot-und-Butter-Modelle Corolla und Camry. Aber die Japaner haben große Pläne. Ab Februar 2004 wird es die neue Marke auch entlang der Ostküste bis nach Texas geben. Ab Juni, wenn die Produktpalette um einen zweisitzigen Sportwagen erweitert wird, will Toyota Scions landesweit anbieten. Für 2005 peilt der Hersteller den Absatz von 100 000 Scions in den USA an.

tionalen Eigenschaften aufladen sollen. Aufgrund des großen Erfolgs der ersten zwei Modelle xA und xB wurde im Juli 2004 der Scion tC eingeführt, der – im Stile der 3er-Reihe von BMW – ebenfalls auf eine junge Käuferschicht abzielt. Die präzise Positionierung der Marke sowie die scharfe Abgrenzung gegenüber Toyota spiegelt sich in einer Käufergruppe wider, die zu über 70 Prozent aus Männern unter 30 Jahren besteht (Wilson 2004, S. 2) – und mit der Marke Toyota kaum zu erreichen gewesen wäre.

Nachfragergerichtet bieten sich mit Hilfe der Mehrmarkenstrategie vorwiegend Chancen in der Kundengewinnung und Kundenbindung, die aus der Breite und Tiefe der Marktabdeckung durch das Markenportfolio resultieren. Insbesondere zur Erhöhung der **Kundenbindung** lassen sich Vorteile durch den Marktauftritt mit mehreren Marken erzielen. Gerade in Märkten mit niedriger Markentreue eröffnet die Mehrmarkenstrategie Möglichkeiten, Markenwechsler innerhalb des eigenen Unternehmens zu halten. Auf einer übergeordneten Perspektive wird damit die Zielsetzung des Aufbaus von Loyalität zur einzelnen Marke durch die Maximierung der Markenportfolio- beziehungsweise Unternehmensloyalität erweitert. Mit Hilfe einer differenzierten Positionierung der einzelnen Marken bietet sich gar in zahlreichen Produktbereichen die Chance einer ganzheitlichen Kundenbetreuung während des gesamten Lebenszyklus („Customer-Life-Cycle"-Konzept, Meffert 2000, S. 895). Als Beispiel sei hier der Automobilkäufer genannt, der von einem Kleinwagen zu einem Fahrzeug der Mittelklasse und schließlich zu einem Automobil des Premiumsegments wechselt und dabei möglicherweise wiederholt innerhalb des Markenportfolios wandert, der Gesamtunternehmung mithin treu bleibt. **Innengerichtet** soll die Mehrmarkenstrategie schließlich den „Wettbewerb im eigenen Haus" fördern und so die Leistungsmotivation und Effizienz der Mitarbeiter der separaten Markeneinheiten erhöhen.

Vor dem Hintergrund eines wachsenden Kostendrucks treten die mit der Ausübung von Mehrmarkenstrategien verfolgten Ziele häufig hinter die übergeordnete, innengerichtete Zielsetzung der **Nutzung von Synergiepotenzialen** zurück. So steht die in der Praxis zu beobachtende Akquisitions- und Fusionswelle weniger im Zeichen markenstrategischer Überlegungen als vielmehr im Fokus von Größenbestrebungen zur Sicherung einer Führungsposition im globalen Wettbewerb – selbst wenn sich die Suche nach Übernahmekandidaten zumeist auf „seelenverwandte Unternehmen" konzentriert (o. V. 1998, S. 52). Entlang der Wertschöpfungskette bieten sich im Rahmen von Mehrmarkenstrategien zahlreiche Ansatzpunkte zur Ausschöpfung von Synergieeffekten durch Gleichteile oder Plattformen (Dudenhöffer 1998, S. 22 ff.). Die Möglichkeit zur Nutzung innerbetrieblicher Synergien kann somit als zentrale Chance einer Mehrmarkenstrategie angesehen werden (vgl. zusammenfassend Abbildung 4), zeigt allerdings gleichzeitig den Übergang zu den wesentlichen **Risiken** dieses markenstrategischen Instrumentariums auf.

Abbildung 4: Chancen von Mehrmarkenstrategien

GABLER GRAFIK

Insbesondere im Bereich langlebiger Gebrauchsgüter verleiten die in den Wertschöpfungsketten des Markenportfolios vorhandenen Synergien nicht selten zu einer intensiven Verfolgung von Gleichteile-Strategien, die zu einer **Standardisierung** und einheitlichen Verwendung ganzer Baugruppen über Markengrenzen hinweg führen. Im Zielkonflikt zwischen Kostenreduktion und Produktdifferenzierung gewinnt die Nutzbarmachung von „Economies of Scales“ häufig derart an Bedeutung, dass den einzelnen Marken durch die Verwendung von Gleichteilen, gemeinsamen Markenplattformen bis hin zum Angebot baugleicher Produkte die Differenzierungsbasis entzogen wird. Die Erosion dieser substanziellen Elemente der Marken führt in der Folge zu einer Schwächung der Markenidentitäten. Aus dem Automobilsektor seien in diesem Zusammenhang beispielhaft die baugleichen Fahrzeuge Ford Fiesta und Mazda 121 des Ford-Konzerns oder VW Sharan und Seat Alhambra des Volkswagen-Konzerns genannt. Das Risiko **negativer Imagetransfereffekte** zwischen den Marken des Portfolios, welches im Rahmen von Mehrmarkenstrategien durch den getrennten Markenauftritt grundsätzlich minimiert werden soll, kann somit durch eine markenübergreifende Angebotsstandardisierung leicht erhöht werden. Bei der Verfolgung einer Mehrmarkenstrategie stellt daher eine **übermäßige Synergienutzung** aufgrund der hierdurch induzierten **Erosion der Markenidentitäten** des Portfolios ein zentrales Risiko dar.

Im Zusammenhang mit der Plattformstrategie in der Automobilindustrie drängt sich die bekannte Geschichte vom Haarschneideautomaten auf. Der Friseur weist den Anbieter dieses Automaten auf unterschiedliche Kopfformen seiner Kunden hin, wobei dieser bemerkt, dass dies zwar zutreffe, nach Einsatz des Automaten jedoch alle Kopfformen gleich seien. Man könne – so lässt sich die Geschichte fortsetzen – die notwendige Unterscheidbarkeit der Kunden durch verschiedenartige Hüte wieder herstellen. Wenn auch diese Geschichte erfunden ist, so kennzeichnet sie doch ein Kernproblem der Mehrmarkenstrategie im Bereich langlebiger Konsumgüter. Einerseits führt wachsende Differenzierung zu steigenden Komplexitätskosten. Andererseits sind bei der Plattformenplanung für jede Marke entsprechend dem Kundenprofil maßgebliche Unterscheidungsmerkmale festzulegen (Meffert 1999).

Die grundsätzliche Identifikation und Nutzbarmachung von Synergien sind indes im Rahmen von Mehrmarkenstrategien als unabdingbare Voraussetzung zur Sicherstellung der übergeordneten Rentabilitätsziele anzusehen (siehe auch Insert 2). So werden die personellen und finanziellen Unternehmensressourcen bei der Ausübung von Mehrmarkenstrategien auf mehrere Marken verteilt und somit zersplittert. Im Vergleich zu alternativen markenstrategischen Varianten, wie etwa der Einzel- oder Dachmarkenstrategie, birgt die Mehrmarkenstrategie somit das Problem einer **suboptimalen Ressourcenverwendung** (so können die vorhandenen Ressourcen oftmals zu wenig auf starke Marken konzentriert werden). Dabei entsteht vielfach eine Duplizierung von Anstrengungen, die zwar insbesondere in Forschung und Entwicklung sowie produktionsseitig – wie oben beschrieben – durch die Nutzung von Synergien reduziert, allerdings nicht vollständig abgebaut werden kann. Aufgrund der markenindividuellen Profilierungsnotwendigkeit lassen sich in diesem Zusammenhang vor allem im Marketing beziehungsweise den betrieblichen Funktionen mit unmittelbarem Kundenkontakt (Vertrieb und Kundendienst) nur wenige Ansatzpunkte zur Bündelung der Ressourcen identifizieren. Da die einzelnen Marken den erforderlichen Profilierungsaufwand hier in der Regel alleine tragen müssen, sind im Rahmen von Mehrmarkenstrategien oft **hohe Kosten** durch die parallele Marktbearbeitung die Folge. Es vermag daher kaum zu überraschen, dass sich die Rentabilität bei Mehrmarkenstrategien mit wachsender Anzahl an Marken trotz eines Umsatzanstiegs oft verschlechtert (Quelch 1994, S. 153).

Dieser Zusammenhang verdeutlicht, dass die Mehrmarkenstrategie prinzipiell nicht mit der Strategie der Kostenführerschaft vereinbar ist, da die hierfür erforderliche Nutzung von **Economies of Scale** durch die parallelen Markenführungskosten konterkariert wird (Kapferer 1997, S. 281 f.). Gleichwohl sind Unternehmen (mit Ausnahme von Luxusgüterherstellern) gezwungen, auf den gestiegenen Kostendruck zu reagieren und ebenfalls zu möglichst geringen Kosten zu produzieren. Insofern sehen sich Markenartikelhersteller einem Spannungsfeld zwischen Standardisierung und Differenzierung ausgesetzt.

INSERT 2 **Frankfurter Allgemeine Zeitung vom 6. September 2004**

Autokonzerne mit wenigen Marken sind die Gewinner

„Fokussierte" Hersteller verdienen deutlich mehr als breit aufgestellte Unternehmen

kön. FRANKFURT, 5. September. Automobilunternehmen, die sich auf wenige Marken konzentrieren, haben sich in den vergangenen Jahren bei Absatz und Ertragskraft besser entwickelt als breit aufgestellte Hersteller. Während fokussierte Konzerne in den Jahren 1998 bis 2003 ihre Produktion deutlich um durchschnittlich 37 Prozent ausgeweitet hatten, mußten die Voll-Anbieter in diesem Zeitraum einen leichten Rückgang hinnehmen. In der Umsatzrendite zeigt sich ebenso eine Diskrepanz: Unternehmen wie Honda und Toyota erzielten im Durchschnitt 7,7 beziehungsweise 7,6 Prozent, General Motors hingegen nur 1,2 Prozent. Dies ist das Ergebnis einer Studie von Willi Diez vom Institut für Automobilwirtschaft (IFA).

„In der Vergangenheit haben Full-Line-Konzerne ihre Größe offensichtlich nicht in gleicher Weise in Wachstum und Profitabilität umsetzen können wie die fokussierten Unternehmen", sagt Diez. Er definiert Hersteller als „strategisch fokussiert", die sich auf eine oder auf maximal drei Marken konzentrieren wie Toyota mit der Luxuswagen-Marke Lexus, BMW mit Rolls-Royce und Mini oder Renault mit Nissan. Die Studie kommt in einer Zeit, in der angesichts der schwachen Nachfrage das Überangebot auf den Automobilmärkten offensichtlich und mehr denn je den Abbau von Kapazitäten notwendig macht. In der vergangenen Wochen haben mehrere Hersteller in Europa und in den Vereinigten Staaten Produktionskürzungen angekündigt, da sie in den nächsten Monaten entgegen der ursprünglichen Erwartung nicht mit einer steigenden Nachfrage rechnen.

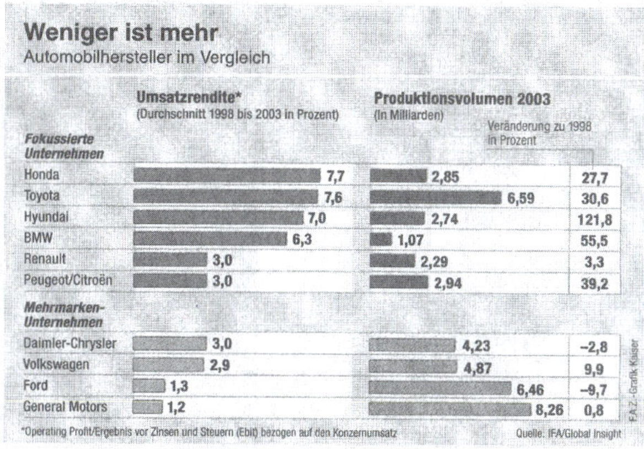

Der als Automobilexperte in der Branche anerkannte Professor der Fachhochschule Nürtingen nennt mehrere Faktoren, die zu der unterschiedlichen Entwicklung führen. Erstens würden die erhofften Synergie-Effekte – die durch höhere Produktionsvolumen realisierbaren Kostenvorteile – überschätzt. In der Industrie gelte ein Kostensenkungspotential von 2,5 Prozent bei einer Verdoppelung der Absatzmenge als Durchschnitt. In Mehrmarken-Konzernen mit einem Angebot im Premium-, Nischen- und Massensegment falle dieser Effekt geringer aus als bei den stärker fokussierten Herstellern. Denn der positive Einfluß aus vereinheitlichten Komponenten, Aggregaten (Getriebe, Motoren) oder kompletten Plattformen sei begrenzt.

Hinzu käme, daß wegen der rückläufigen Fertigungstiefe und der Verlagerung von Arbeiten nach außen ein großer Teil der Synergien bei den Zulieferern anfallen würde. Die Synergieeffekte durch zusammengefaßte Produktionsumfänge kämen also vielmehr kleineren Herstellern zugute.

Zweitens wird der Unternehmenserfolg mehr durch eine höhere Durchdringung und bessere Erschließung der Märkte erreicht als durch Synergien. Fokussierte Hersteller würden ihre Märkte besser ausschöpfen. Diez nennt BMW als Beispiel, die in relativ kurzer Zeit den Markt im Premiumsegment in Asien ausgebaut hätten. Drittens sei die Komplexität bei einem umfassenden Markenangebot mit zusätzlichem Planungs-, Abstimmungs- und Umsetzungsaufwand verbunden, was gegen einen beschleunigten und vereinfachten Entscheidungsprozeß spreche.

Diez betont aber auch, daß die Mehrmarken-Konzepte nicht grundsätzlich unterlegen sein müssen. Unternehmen mit einem breiten Angebot hätten den Vorteil mehrerer strategischer Optionen, um die Profitabilität zu erhöhen. So könnten sie über Premiumautos die durchschnittliche Wertschöpfung je Fahrzeug erhöhen und das Markenimage verbessern, dabei gleichzeitig Kostenvorteile über die Volumenmarken erzielen. Schließlich würde ja auch Toyota dazu übergehen, den derzeit zwei Marken eine dritte mit dem Namen „Scion" in Nordamerika hinzuzufügen, um sich in zunehmend differenzierten Märkten zu etablieren. Umgekehrt müsse General Motors darüber nachdenken, ob nicht eine weitere Markenbereinigung sinnvoll sei.

Der Erfolg des jeweiligen Geschäftsmodells hänge vor allem von der konsequenten Umsetzung ab, die Unternehmensorganisation an die strategischen und operativen Aufgaben anzupassen. Daher, so Diez, sei es unwahrscheinlich, daß sich nur ein Modell langfristig durchsetze. Vielmehr gebe es Anzeichen, daß beide Strategien angesichts der durchgeführten und noch zu erwartenden Marktbereinigungen aufeinander zugingen.

Im Marktauftritt stellt schließlich die **„Kannibalisierung"** der Marken durch gegenseitige Marktanteilssubstitution ein zentrales Risiko von Mehrmarkenstrategien dar (siehe auch den Beitrag zur Markenkannibalisierung in diesem Buch). Werden die charakteristischen Unterschiede zwischen den Marken von den Nachfragern nicht mehr differenziert wahrgenommen oder wird der Marktauftritt zunehmend homogenisiert, steigt die Gefahr einer Bearbeitung der gleichen Nachfragersegmente. Die Mehrmarkenstrategie setzt somit stets eine genaue Abwägung der mit zusätzlichen Marken erzielbaren Mehrerlöse einerseits und der zusätzlichen Kosten andererseits voraus. Eine derartige Analyse wird indes durch die innerbetrieblichen Verbundbeziehungen der Marken und die damit verbundenen Schwierigkeiten einer eindeutigen **Zurechnung der Kosten** erschwert. Durch die in der Praxis zunehmend zu beobachtende Verschiebung der Kostenstrukturen zugunsten von Fixkosten gewinnt dieses Problemfeld zusätzlich an Komplexität und erscheint insbesondere im fixkostendominanten Dienstleistungsbereich allenfalls approximativ lösbar (Backhaus 1997, S. 6).

Wettbewerbsgerichtet ist die Verfolgung einer Mehrmarkenstrategie zudem mit der Gefahr einer **„Übersegmentierung"**, das heißt einer zu feinen Parzellierung des Gesamtmarktes, verbunden (Becker 2002, S. 291). Die Abzielung auf zu viele Teilsegmente mit separaten Marken ist überdies wenig zweckmäßig, wenn deren Bearbeitung nicht eine hinreichende Profitabilität garantiert oder andere wettbewerbsstrategische Funktionen (zum Beispiel Gewinnung der Technologieführerschaft) für das Markenportfolio erfüllt. Im Kontext der Bildung von Zielsegmenten für die einzelnen Marken ist ferner das Problem der mangelnden **zeitlichen Stabilität** der Segmentlösung zu berücksichtigen (Perrey 1998, S. 227 ff.). Treten im Markt veränderte Präferenzen oder strukturelle Nachfrageverschiebungen auf, kann dies zu einem Verlust an wahrgenommener Trennschärfe zwischen den einzelnen Marken führen und damit die ursprünglich differenzierte Positionierung und daraus resultierend letztlich den Grad der Marktabdeckung des Portfolios gefährden.

Die **Konzentration des Handels** und die Zunahme an eigenen Handelsmarken schwächen zudem die Position der Hersteller und können vor dem Hintergrund begrenzten Regalplatzes zur Verdrängung von Herstellermarken führen. Dabei ist zu beobachten, dass ein zu weit diversifiziertes Markenportfolio insbesondere die Platzierung umsatzschwacher Marken gefährdet. Im Bereicht der Fast Moving Consumer Goods konnte festgestellt werden, dass allein von 1998 bis 2001 der wertmäßige Marktanteil umsatzschwächerer Herstellermarken um vier Prozentpunkte auf gut 33 Prozent zurückging, während Handelsmarken etwa im gleichen Maße Marktanteile hinzugewinnen konnten (Wübbenhorst/Wildner 2002, S. 19). Eine Konzentration vieler Hersteller auf ihre A-Marken ist daher vermehrt zu beobachten.

Schließlich birgt eine zu starke Einschränkung der **markenspezifischen Handlungsfreiräume** durch übergreifende, das gesamte Markenportfolio betreffende Entscheidungen ein weiteres Risiko bei der Mehrmarkenstrategie. So ist der eigenständige Marktauftritt durch zentrale Entscheidungen und die vielfach bestehende Notwendigkeit, auf vorhandene Strukturen und Systeme zurückzugreifen, gefährdet und schränkt die einzelnen Marken etwa im Hinblick auf ihre Positionierungsfreiräume oder die Konfiguration ihrer Leistungen ein. Auf diese Weise lassen sich Chancen im Wettbewerb (zum Beispiel die

Wahl kostengünstigerer Lieferanten) durch die einzelnen Marken oftmals nicht aufgreifen beziehungsweise kann Risiken nicht rechtzeitig durch entsprechende Handlungsweisen begegnet werden (etwa einem verstärkten Preisbewusstsein bei Bindung an markenübergreifende Produktionstechniken). Abbildung 5 fasst die zentralen Risiken der Mehrmarkenstrategie nochmals zusammen.

Abbildung 5: Risiken von Mehrmarkenstrategien

GABLER GRAFIK

3. Planungsprozess von Mehrmarkenstrategien

Angesichts der aufgezeigten Chancen und Risiken von Mehrmarkenstrategien setzt die wirksame Umsetzung dieser markenstrategischen Profilierungsform einen systematischen und dynamischen Planungsprozess voraus (vgl. Abbildung 6). Zur Sicherstellung der Präferenzbildung bei den Nachfragern sowie zur Differenzierung der Marken gegenüber dem Wettbewerb und innerhalb des Portfolios gilt es in diesem Zusammenhang, die Planung des **Marktauftritts** für das Markenportfolio vorzunehmen und kontinuierlich zu aktualisieren (Meffert 1992, S. 130 ff.; Meffert/Burmann 1996a, S. 50 ff.). Aufbauend auf einer marktstrategischen Standortbestimmung durch eine umfassende Analyse der Umfeldbedingungen sind dabei auf der Ebene der strategischen Rahmenplanung markenübergreifende Ziele zu formulieren sowie daran ansetzend markenspezifische Rollen, Positionierungen und Leitbilder zu fixieren. Auf der Grundlage dieser übergeordneten Stoßrichtungen des Marktauftritts erfolgt auf der Ebene der marktstrategischen Instrumenteausgestaltung die Planung des zielgerichteten und auf die relevanten Absatzmärkte abgestimmten Einsatzes der absatzpolitischen Instrumente. Als Koordinations- und Steuerungsinstrument der Mehrmarkenstrategie fungiert schließlich das Mehrmarkencontrolling. Nach dem Prinzip des „feed back/feed forward" ist hier eine kontinuierliche Überwachung und Aktualisierung des Marktauftritts sowie der Planungsprämissen vorzunehmen.

Abbildung 6: Planungsprozess von Mehrmarkenstrategien

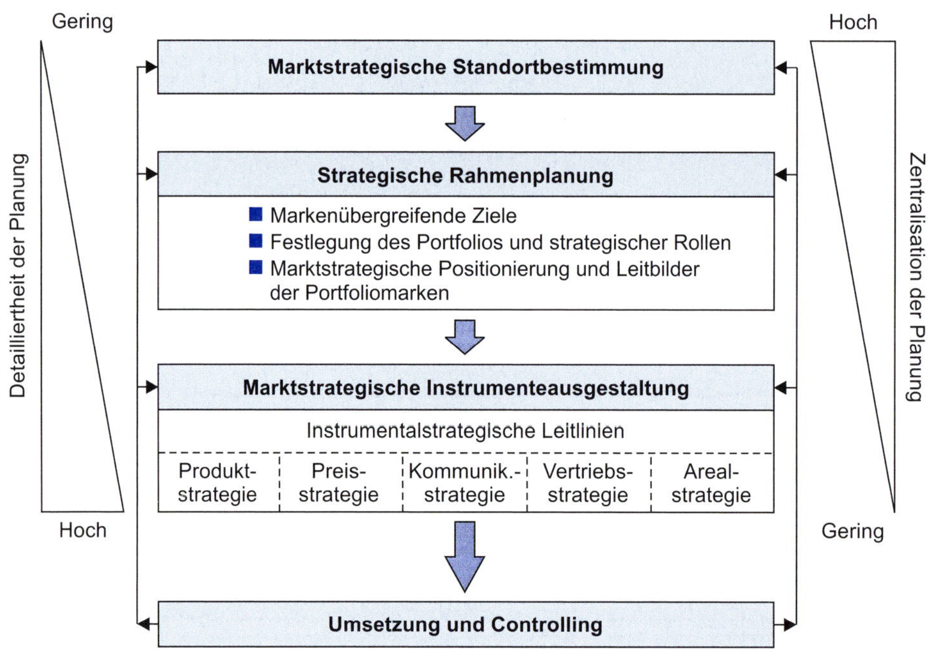

GABLER GRAFIK

Insgesamt ist der Planungsprozess von Mehrmarkenstrategien nicht als streng sequentielle Abfolge verschiedener Planungsstufen zu interpretieren (Haedrich/Tomczak 1994, S. 930). In einem rückgekoppelten und dynamischen Planungsverlauf sind hier vielmehr mehrere interdependente Teilprobleme fortlaufend zu lösen und aufeinander abzustimmen. Die **institutionelle Verankerung** der Planung verlagert sich dabei gewöhnlicherweise mit zunehmender Detailliertheit dieser Teilprobleme auf die Ebene der dezentralen Markeneinheiten.

3.1 Marktstrategische Standortbestimmung als Ausgangspunkt

Ausgangspunkt des Planungsprozesses von Mehrmarkenstrategien stellt eine ausführliche Analyse des **internen und externen Unternehmensumfelds** dar. Zur Ableitung einer tragfähigen Mehrmarkenstrategie ist es im Rahmen der marktstrategischen Standortbestimmung Aufgabe, eine Abgleichung der unternehmens- beziehungsweise markenspezifischen Stärken und Schwächen mit den umfeldbedingten Chancen und Risiken vorzunehmen. Im Mittelpunkt steht dabei eine fortlaufende Identifikation der Kundenbedürfnisse, auf deren Basis die Gestaltung beziehungsweise Aktualisierung zielgruppenspezifischer Problemlösungen mit Hilfe geeigneter Marken vorgenommen werden kann. In diesem Zusammenhang sind die Nachfrager in regelmäßigen Abständen anhand geeigneter Segmentierungskriterien zu intern möglichst homogenen sowie extern möglichst heterogenen Zielgruppen zusammenzufassen. Aufgrund ihrer geringen prognostischen Relevanz für das Wahlverhalten verlieren die klassischen soziodemografischen Segmentierungskriterien zu diesem Zweck zunehmend an Bedeutung, sodass zur **Zielgruppenbildung** verstärkt psychografische Kriterien wie Nutzenerwartungen oder Lebensstilmerkmale verwendet werden (Meffert 2000, S. 192 ff.). Es ist jedoch zu beachten, dass bei vergleichsweise geringem Involvement der Konsumenten nicht immer ein hinreichender Zusammenhang von psychografischen Kriterien wie Einstellung oder Lebensstil und dem tatsächlichen Verhalten besteht (Kroeber-Riel/Weinberg 2003, S. 175; Esch 2003, S. 364 f.). Insofern gilt es, im Vorfeld mögliche Segmentierungskriterien hinsichtlich ihrer Kaufverhaltensrelevanz zu prüfen (zu weiteren Anforderungen an die Segmentierungskriterien siehe Meffert 2000, S. 186 ff.).

Da verschiedene Segmentierungsansätze zumeist mit divergierenden Zielgruppenlösungen einhergehen (Stegmüller/Hempel 1996, S. 25 ff.), macht die Gewinnung eines möglichst differenzierten Abbildes der Nachfragestrukturen häufig eine alternative Identifikation von Zielsegmenten anhand verschiedener Segmentierungskriterien erforderlich. In Produktbereichen, in denen ein hohes Involvement der Nachfrager unterstellt werden kann, lassen sich etwa mit Hilfe von Lebensstil-Segmentierungen zusätzliche Erkenntnisse hinsichtlich der durch emotionale Bedürfnisse geprägten Käuferstrukturen aufdecken, die dann als geeignete Ergänzung zu den Ergebnissen der vorwiegend auf rationale Bedürfnisse ausgerichteten Nutzensegmentierung fungieren können (Koers 2001, S. 211). Eine mögliche Anpassung des Marktauftritts – etwa durch Elimination oder Neuausrichtung vorhandener Marken beziehungsweise Akquisition oder eigenständige Kreation neuer Marken – lässt sich dann auf Basis einer Abstimmung der Bedürfnisstrukturen der so ermittelten Zielgruppen mit den internen Unternehmensressourcen sowie der Wahrnehmung und Akzeptanz des Markenportfolios durch die Nachfrager vornehmen.

Dabei setzt die Identifikation der **Wahrnehmung und Akzeptanz** der von einer Unternehmung offerierten Marken eine sorgfältige Analyse hinsichtlich deren Verankerung in der Psyche der Nachfrager voraus. Da die präferenzbildende und damit absatzfördernde Wirkung von Marken in besonderer Weise durch Vertrauen und Kompetenz geprägt ist, sind im Rahmen einer markenstrategischen Standortbestimmung spezifische verhaltenswissenschaftliche Konstrukte zu analysieren. Neben einer regelmäßigen Ermittlung der ungestützten **Markenbekanntheiten** (Share of Mind), die als notwendige Bedingung markenspezifischer Assoziationen durch die Nachfrager und somit letztlich als Grundvoraussetzung für den möglichen Kauf der Markenprodukte fungieren, ist insbesondere eine dezidierte Analyse der **Markenimages** vorzunehmen. So ist im Rahmen disaggregierter Imageanalysen zu überprüfen, ob sich die angestrebte Kompetenzdifferenzierung im Wettbewerbsumfeld sowie im internen Markenvergleich in entsprechenden Detailimages der Marken widerspiegelt. Beispielsweise sollte die Reisemarke 1-2-Fly des TUI-Konzerns über ein preisorientiertes Image verfügen, während dies für die etablierte Marke TUI keine notwendige Voraussetzung darstellt und für die Premiummarke Airtours eher hinderlich wäre.

Insgesamt sind im Rahmen der marktstrategischen Standortbestimmung sämtliche psychografischen Größen sowie die in Situationsanalysen üblicherweise herangezogenen ökonomischen Kriterien (Marktanteile, Umsätze, Erträge etc.) zu analysieren (vgl. hierzu auch die Ausführungen zum Markencontrolling in diesem Buch). Als Resultat der markenspezifischen Investitionen fungieren schließlich die **Markenloyalitäten** beziehungsweise die **Loyalität gegenüber dem Gesamtportfolio**, aus deren Entwicklungen wertvolle Hinweise zur zukünftigen strategischen Ausrichtung des Markenportfolios (Anzahl der Marken, Zielsegmente etc.) abgeleitet werden können. Da von einer Unternehmung durchaus mehrere Markenportfolios in unterschiedlichen Produktbereichen geführt und damit mehrere Mehrmarkenstrategien verfolgt werden können, ist diese „Portfolioloyalität“ begrifflich von der übergeordneten Unternehmensloyalität zu trennen.

3.2 Strategische Rahmenplanung

Die strategische Rahmenplanung nimmt im Planungsprozess von Mehrmarkenstrategien eine Schlüsselstellung ein. In diesem Zusammenhang ist es zentrale Herausforderung, den Bezugsrahmen für einen intern wie extern differenzierten Marktauftritt des vorhandenen beziehungsweise in Abhängigkeit der Anfordernisse des Marktes neu zu gestaltenden Markenportfolios zu schaffen (Traylor 1986, S. 73). Hierzu stellt die Formulierung und Präzisierung übergreifender Zielsetzungen des Marktauftritts die strategische Grundlage dar.

Im Rahmen von Mehrmarkenstrategien ist insbesondere die dezidierte Zielkonkretisierung im Hinblick auf die zu bearbeitenden Absatzareale von großer Bedeutung, da hieraus eine möglichst eindeutige Präzisierung der auf die einzelnen Märkte auszurichtenden Marken (insbesondere im Rahmen der Markterschließung) abzuleiten ist. Länderspezifische Besonderheiten lassen zudem oftmals eine grundlegende Anpassung des Markenportfolios erforderlich werden.

3.21 Gestaltung des Markenportfolios und Festlegung markenspezifischer Rollen

Hier bieten sich grundsätzlich die Möglichkeiten eines eigenständigen Aufbaus neuer Marken, der **Akquisition** fremder Marken sowie eines kooperativen Vorgehens (Meffert/ Burmann 1996a, S. 55). In der Praxis wird dabei zunehmend auf eine gezielte Akquisition von Fremdmarken zurückgegriffen, da mit diesen – aufgrund des häufig starken Markennamens – eine unmittelbare Erschließung ausgewählter Käufersegmente und damit eine Abrundung des Markenportfolios erzielt werden kann. Im Vergleich zum eigenständigen Aufbau präferenzfördernder Marken, der insbesondere im Bereich langlebiger Konsumgüter zumeist viele Jahre in Anspruch nimmt, lässt sich auf diese Weise ein erheblicher Zeitvorteil generieren. Der Erfolg der Übernahme der Marke Mini durch BMW mag ein Beispiel für diese Vorgehensweise darstellen (Buchenau 2004, S. 13). Praxisbeispiele lassen sich indes auch für den eigenständigen Aufbau neuer Marken – etwa die zahlreichen selbstgeschaffenen Marken von Ferrero im Süßwarenbereich – oder ein kooperatives Vorgehen – zum Beispiel die Kooperation zwischen Mercedes-Benz und der Schweizerischen Gesellschaft für Mikroelektronik und Uhrenindustrie (unter anderem Eigner von Swatch) im Rahmen des angesprochenen Kleinwagenprojekts Smart – anführen.

Nicht zuletzt stellt auch die **Elimination** einzelner Marken eine mögliche Maßnahme zur Restrukturierung des Markenportfolios dar (Aaker 2004a, S. 295 ff.). Insbesondere bei einer großen Anzahl parallel geführter Marken in einem Markt kann dabei durch die Elimination umsatz- und ertragsschwacher Marken die Gesamtrentabilität des Portfolios gesteigert werden, da Kostensenkungspotenziale genutzt und Kannibalisierungseffekte vermieden werden (Kumar 2003, S. 88).

Auf Basis der festgelegten Portfoliostruktur sind dann die Ziele und Aufgaben der einzelnen Marken im Wettbewerbsumfeld und innerhalb des Portfolios zu präzisieren, die jedoch geeignet operationalisiert werden müssen, um die markenspezifischen Aktivitäten in gewünschter Weise zu kanalisieren und damit zu einer Sicherstellung der Effektivität und Effizienz des Gesamtsystems beizutragen (Aaker 2004a, S. 85 ff.). Dieser Forderung kann mit einer Definition von **strategischen Rollen** für die Marken des Portfolios in geeigneter Weise Rechnung getragen werden (vgl. den Beitrag zur Markenarchitektur in diesem Buch).

3.22 Marktstrategische Positionierung und Leitbilder der Marken

Mit der marktstrategischen Positionierung soll im Rahmen von Mehrmarkenstrategien sowohl eine dominierende Stellung der Marken in der Psyche der Nachfrager als auch eine hinreichende Differenzierung gegenüber den Marken des Wettbewerbs und des eigenen Portfolios erzielt werden (Becker 2002, S. 217 ff.). Dabei sind Marktpositionen festzulegen, in denen die Bedürfnisse ausgewählter Zielsegmente mit maßgeschneiderten Angeboten in der subjektiven Wahrnehmung der Konsumenten dauerhaft besser als von anderen Anbietern befriedigt werden (Tomczak/Roosdorp 1996, S. 26). Aufbauend auf den strategischen Rollen der Marken sind diese Marktpositionen derart zu formulieren, dass für jede Marke eine positive Alleinstellung im Verhältnis zum Wettbewerb und den übrigen Marken des Portfolios und damit die Basis für den Aufbau einer **„Unique Selling Proposition"** geschaffen wird (Riesenbeck/Perrey 2004, S. 133 f.). Bei der Verfolgung von Mehrmarkenstrategien lassen sich folgende Voraussetzungen für die dauerhafte Erreichung dieser angestrebten Soll-Positionen im Wahrnehmungsraum der Nachfrager anführen (Haedrich/Tomczak/Kaetzke 2004, S. 46 f.):

- Ein zielgruppenspezifischer Nutzen ist anzusprechen (Zielgruppenbezug),
- der Nutzen muss für die Nachfrager deutlich wahrnehmbar sein (Wahrnehmbarkeit),
- dem angesprochenen Nutzen muss eine hohe Bedeutung im Rahmen der Auswahlentscheidung der Nachfrager zukommen (Dominanz),
- der Nutzen muss durch die Marke in ein physikalisch funktionales Angebot oder im Rahmen der werblichen Umsetzung in eine „Unique Advertising Proposition" transformiert werden können (Realisierbarkeit),
- der Nutzen muss die einzelne Marke vom Wettbewerb und innerhalb des Portfolios abgrenzen (Inter- und Intradiskriminanz) und
- der Nutzen sollte möglichst lange Gültigkeit besitzen (zeitliche Stabilität).

Insgesamt besteht die Herausforderung im Rahmen der Positionierungsentscheidungen in Mehrmarkenstrategien darin, eine **bestmögliche Abdeckung des Gesamtmarktes** sicherzustellen und zu diesem Zweck möglichst für jede Marke eine differenzierte Stellung im Wahrnehmungsraum der Nachfrager zu besetzen, die es ermöglicht, einen komparativen Wettbewerbsvorteil zu erzielen. Die Festlegung erfolgswirksamer Marktpositionen setzt dabei unmittelbar an den in den strategischen Rollen definierten Zielsegmenten für die verschiedenen Marken an. Der als Grundlage der Positionierung fungierende und von den einzelnen Marken angesprochene Nutzen kann bei diesen Zielsegmenten sowohl auf physikalisch funktionale Leistungsmerkmale rekurrieren als auch einen **symbolischen Zusatznutzen** darstellen (Nommensen 1990, S. 13 ff.).

Zur Abbildung des von den verschiedenen Marken angesprochenen Nutzens im Wahrnehmungsraum der Konsumenten wird im Rahmen von Positionierungsentscheidungen häufig auf **analytische Verfahren** zurückgegriffen (Meffert 2000, S. 356 ff.; Backhaus et al. 2003, S. 480 ff.). So können die verschiedenen Marken sowie die relevanten Wettbewerber mit Hilfe der Multidimensionalen Skalierung, der Faktorenanalyse oder der Diskriminanzanalyse entsprechend der nachfragerseitig wahrgenommenen Markenähnlichkeit in einem mehrdimensionalen Raum eingeordnet werden. Auf Basis dieser „Ist-Positionierungen" lassen sich dann unter Zuhilfenahme zusätzlicher Präferenzdaten oder aufgrund strategischer Überlegungen die „Soll-Positionen" der einzelnen Marken festlegen, um eine bestmögliche Marktabdeckung durch das gesamte Portfolio sicherzustellen. In Abbildung 7 ist exemplarisch ein diskriminanzanalytisches Positionierungsmodell im Automobilsektor auf der Grundlage von Einstellung zum Automobil dargestellt. Die Positionierung der Automobilmarken wurde hier über die Diskriminanzachsen der in die Analyse einbezogenen Einstellungsdimensionen ermittelt. Je näher eine Marke an der Spitze eines Pfeiles eingeordnet ist, desto mehr stimmen die Fahrer dieser Marke der entsprechenden Aussage zu. Damit wird in diesem Zusammenhang das Problem der zur Bildung des Wahrnehmungsraumes heranzuziehenden Kriterien beziehungsweise Nutzendimensionen und deren Messung deutlich.

Abbildung 7: Positionierungsmodell im Automobilsektor

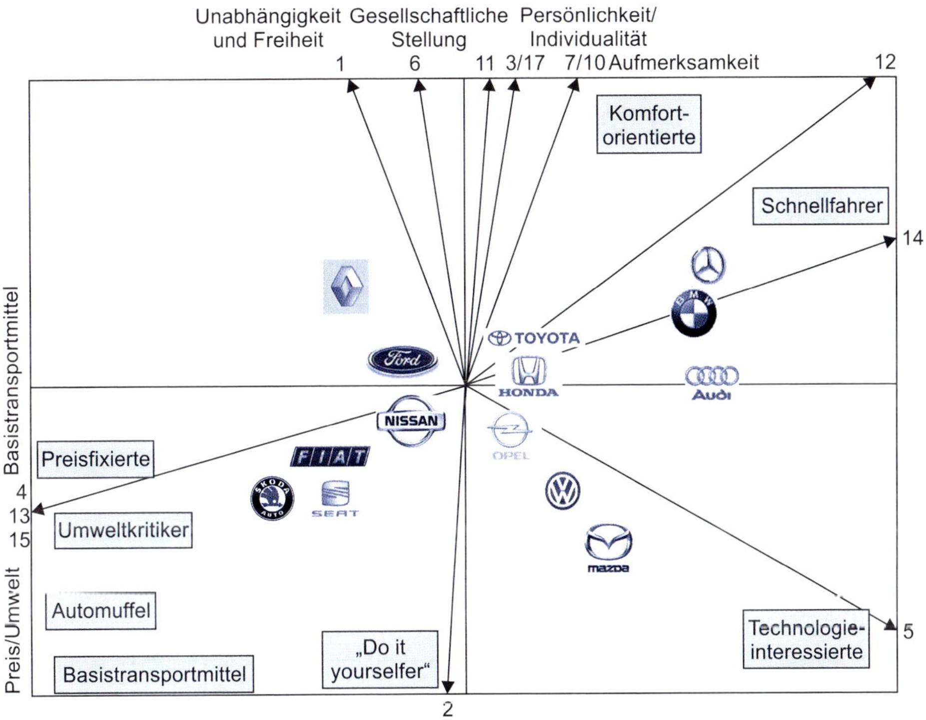

GABLER GRAFIK

Quelle: Volkswagen 1996

Ungeachtet der zur Ableitung von Positionierungsentscheidungen verwendeten Kriterien setzt die wirksame Ausübung von Mehrmarkenstrategien eine fortlaufende Aktualisierung und Anpassung der Markenpositionierungen voraus. Im Einzelfall sind somit sowohl Umpositionierungen als auch Neupositionierungen vorzunehmen (Haedrich/Tomczak/Kaetzke 2004, S. 63 f.). Die Erfolgswirksamkeit der einzelnen Markenpositionierung steigt indes mit deren Kontinuität, die zum Aufbau eines klaren Markenimages bei den Nachfragern beiträgt und damit eine wesentliche Voraussetzung zur Erzielung dauerhafter Wettbewerbsvorteile darstellt (Esch/Andresen 1996, S. 78). Eine konsequen-

le Verhaltensweisen zur Schaffung einer gemeinsamen Vermarktungsphilosophie und der damit einhergehenden Standardisierung des Vermarktungsprozesses (zum Beispiel die Festlegung von Preisabständen zwischen den Marken anhand einheitlicher Kriterien) gerichtet. Auf diese Weise lassen sich die Interdependenzprobleme im Markenportfolio geeignet transparent machen und damit die markenübergreifenden Abstimmungen der Instrumentalstrategien durch eine Vereinheitlichung des Vermarktungsprozesses erleichtern. Ein derartiges Vorgehen trägt überdies zu einer wirksamen und identitätssichernden Ausschöpfung vorhandener Synergien zwischen den Marken bei.

4. Organisatorische Verankerung von Mehrmarkenstrategien

Die Planung von Mehrmarkenstrategien ist eng mit der organisatorischen Verankerung dieses markenstrategischen Profilierungsinstruments verknüpft. Die Schaffung eigenständiger und innerhalb des Markenportfolios klar abgegrenzter Markenidentitäten erfordert eine **institutionelle Koordination** aller an der Prägung einzelner Markenidentitäten mitwirkenden Personen in separaten organisatorischen Einheiten. Die anzustrebende Individualität jeder Marke legt es nahe, diese organisatorischen Einheiten als Träger der Marken so selbstständig und von den anderen Marken beziehungsweise deren Organisationseinheiten so getrennt wie möglich zu führen. Auf diese Weise lässt sich der Unternehmergeist („Entrepreneurship") jeder Marke fördern und damit die zur Schaffung eigenständiger Markenpersönlichkeiten erforderliche Kreativität und Flexibilität sowie die markenspezifische Nähe zu den Bedürfnissen der Nachfrager und zum Wettbewerb erhöhen. Die daraus resultierende Lücke in der Organisationskontrolle kann jedoch vor dem Hintergrund divergierender Eigeninteressen der jeweiligen Markenverantwortlichen zu Suboptimierungen im Sinne des Gesamtportfolios führen (Aaker 2004b, S. 26 f.). Die Einführung immer neuer Marken und Blockaden gegen Eliminierung wenig rentabler Marken sind denkbare Konsequenzen.

Verstanden als die Führung eines komplementären, synergetischen Portfolios zielt die Mehrmarkenstrategie jedoch weniger auf die **Optimierung des Marktauftritts** einzelner Marken als vielmehr des internen Zusammenspiels der verschiedenen Marken zur bestmöglichen Marktbearbeitung durch das gesamte Portfolio und damit zur Sicherstellung der übergeordneten Gesamtzielsetzungen ab. Dies macht eine **Vernetzung** der organisatorisch selbstständigen Markeneinheiten und deren Geschäftsprozesse erforderlich und schränkt den Grad der markenspezifischen **Autarkie** entlang der vollständigen Wertschöpfungskette ein (Ghoshal/Bartlett 1995, S. 148). Die damit oftmals einhergehende Zentralisierung von Entscheidungen (etwa bei der Festlegung der Positionierungen der Marken) sowie die verbindliche Nutzung gemeinsamer Ressourcen (zum Beispiel Plattformen) dürfen jedoch die einzelnen Markenidentitäten nicht untergraben (Meffert/Burmann 1996a, S. 56).

Abbildung 9 zeigt in diesem Zusammenhang ein Kontinuum der Mehrmarkenführung zwischen Zentralisation und Dezentralisation mit entsprechend differierenden Autonomiegraden der markenspezifischen Einheiten beziehungsweise Eingriffstiefen der Portfolioleitung (vgl. hierzu ausführlich Koers 2001, S. 71 ff.). Die idealtypischen Portfolioausprägungen können entsprechend der Position auf dem Kontinuum anhand der Eingriffstiefe der Portfolioleitung in die Markeneinheiten klassifiziert werden. Während die Unternehmensleitung in dem hier als **operatives Portfoliomanagement** bezeichneten Markenportfolio auch operative Aufgaben der Markenführung wahrnimmt beziehungsweise diese notfalls direktiv durchsetzt, beschränkt sich das **strategische Portfoliomanagement** auf die Schaffung des strategischen Rahmens, innerhalb dessen die einzelnen Portfoliomarken weitgehend autonom agieren. In einem reinen **Finanzportfolio** fungieren die einzelnen Marken schließlich ausschließlich als Investitionsobjekt des Unternehmens, wobei das Portfoliomanagement keinerlei Einfluss auf markenspezifische Strategien und deren Durchsetzung ausübt, sondern lediglich Renditeaspekte fokussiert. Bei nicht hinreichender Erfüllung der Renditeerwartung werden die Marken in Analogie zum Wertpapierportfolio veräußert.

Abbildung 9: Ausprägungen alternativer Zentralisationsgrade und Eingriffstiefen im Markenportfolio

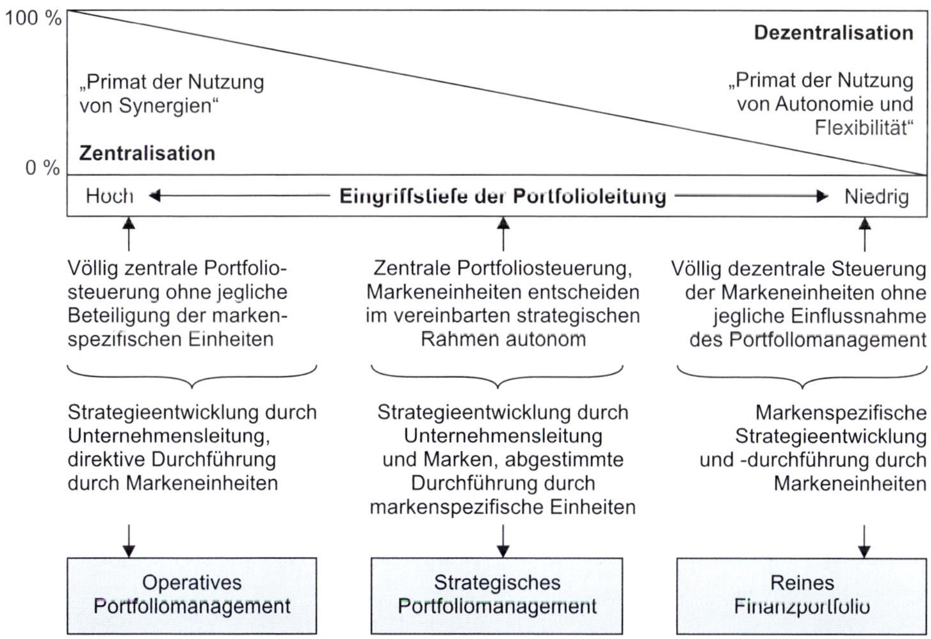

GABLER GRAFIK

Quelle: Koers 2001, S. 75

Die rein dezentrale Führung eines Markenportfolios als Finanzportfolio stellt indes primär ein theoretisches Konzept dar, da die zentrale Festlegung strategischer Rollen und Positionierungen sowie die Realisierung markenübergreifender Synergien als Notwendigkeit einer gleichermaßen effektiven wie effizienten Mehrmarkenstrategie zu interpretieren sind. Demgegenüber geht ein rein operatives Portfoliomanagement je nach Größe des Markenportfolios vielfach mit einer Überlastung der Unternehmensleitung einher.

Unter der grundsätzlichen **Mehrmarkenführungs-Maxime** „so viel Dezentralität wie möglich, so wenig Zentralität wie nötig" sollte die organisatorische Verankerung von Mehrmarkenstrategien letztlich auf eine Optimierung des Autarkiegrades der selbstständigen Markeneinheiten im Rahmen eines strategischen Portfoliomanagements ausgerichtet sein. Als Schnittstelle der untereinander vernetzten Markenorganisationen fungiert dabei eine übergeordnete Koordinationsstelle, die hierarchisch auf der Ebene der Unternehmensleitung beziehungsweise der Leitung des Markenportfolios angeordnet oder dieser als Stabsstelle unmittelbar unterstellt ist. Die Führung des Markenportfolios erfolgt dann im Gegenstromverfahren, wobei die Portfolioleitung im Sinne einer Top-Down-Planung die Formulierung der Stoßrichtungen des Marktauftritts dominiert, während die dezentralen Markeneinheiten mit der konkreten Ausgestaltung der Instrumentalstrategien und damit der Umsetzung dieser Rahmenplanung auf der Grundlage spezifischer Zielvereinbarungen betraut sind. Abweichungen von diesen Zielvereinbarungen können dann nach dem Prinzip der Bottom-Up-Planung in einer Anpassung der strategischen Rahmenplanung resultieren. Das organisatorische Zusammenspiel der verschiedenen Marken und der Portfolioleitung lässt sich in verschiedenen Abstimmungsgremien (zum Beispiel Preisgremium) institutionalisieren.

Zur konkreten Festlegung der **markenspezifischen Freiheitsgrade** und damit zur Sicherstellung einer an den übergeordneten Unternehmenszielsetzungen orientierten Optimierung der Mehrmarkenstrategie bietet sich schließlich eine **Formulierung übergreifender Leitsätze** des Marktauftritts an. Im Rahmen derartiger Leitsätze sind die zentralen Grundsätze der Führung des Markenportfolios sowie des innerorganisationalen Zusammenspiels der dezentralen Markeneinheiten zu definieren. Die als grundsätzliche Prinzipien der Mehrmarkenführung zu interpretierenden Leitsätze sollten insbesondere in Bezug auf folgende Aspekte ausgestaltet werden:

- Zusammensetzung des Markenportfolios,
- Grad des eigenständigen Marktauftritts der Unternehmung (unter eigener Markierung),
- Grad der Eigenständigkeit der Marken im Marktauftritt (eigenständige versus kombinierte Markierung),
- Grad der innerorganisationalen Eigenständigkeit der Marken (insbesondere hinsichtlich der funktionalen Organisationsstruktur),
- Grad der eigenständigen Ergebnisverantwortung der Marken,
- Grad der Markenbindung an innerorganisationale Ressourcen (Technologien, Plattformen, Lieferanten etc.),

- übergeordnete Steuerungs- und Koordinationsinhalte (zum Beispiel zentrale Positionierungsvorgaben),
- Steuerungs- und Koordinationsinhalte zwischen den Marken sowie
- Prozess und Instrumente der Zielvereinbarung.

5. Zusammenfassung und Fazit

Vor dem Hintergrund der verstärkten Polarisierung des Konsumentenverhaltens und eines wettbewerbsinduzierten Kostendrucks stehen Anbieter von Markenartikeln vor der zentralen Herausforderung, einer zunehmenden Fragmentierung bislang homogener Marktsegmente durch eine bedarfsgerechte Ausweitung des Angebotsspektrums gerecht zu werden und gleichzeitig die Wirtschaftlichkeit der Marktbearbeitung sicherzustellen. Unter dem Bewusstsein, dass eine ausgeprägte Markenidentität die unabdingbare Voraussetzung für die Schaffung des Vertrauens der Nachfrager in die Marke bildet, erscheinen die mit einer Erweiterung des Leistungsspektrums durch eine Ausdehnung der Marke verbundenen Deprofilierungsrisiken vielfach zu hoch, sodass eine Marktbearbeitung mit mehreren, parallel auf den Absatzmarkt ausgerichteten Marken und damit die Verfolgung einer Mehrmarkenstrategie zunehmend an Bedeutung gewinnen.

Die wirksame Ausübung von Mehrmarkenstrategien setzt indes eine sorgfältige Analyse der mit dieser Form des Marktauftritts verbundenen Chancen und Risiken voraus. Diese können im Einzelfall in Inhalt und Ausmaß variieren und lassen Schlussfolgerungen hinsichtlich der Vorteilhaftigkeit von Mehrmarkenstrategien im Vergleich zu alternativen Markenprofilierungsstrategien somit nur vor dem Hintergrund des spezifischen situativen Kontextes zu. Zusammenfassend können die Chancen und Risiken von Mehrmarkenstrategien auf **drei wesentliche Spannungsfelder** reduziert werden:

- Im **Spannungsfeld zwischen Kannibalisierung und Partizipation** gilt es, eine bestmögliche Marktabdeckung unter Minimierung von Substitutionseffekten innerhalb des Markenportfolios sicherzustellen (vgl. zur Kannibalisierungsanalyse den Beitrag in diesem Buch).
- Darüber hinaus sieht sich eine Unternehmung bei der Verfolgung von Mehrmarkenstrategien dem Optimierungsproblem zwischen der **Ausschöpfung vorhandener Synergien** im Markenportfolio und der Notwendigkeit eines auf die Eigenprofilierung aller Marken abzielenden und damit möglichst **differenzierten Marktauftritts** ausgesetzt (vgl. Insert 3).
- Schließlich ist der optimale Grad der Eigenständigkeit jeder einzelnen Marke im Marktauftritt sowie im innerorganisationalen Zusammenspiel zu bestimmen und damit das Spannungsfeld zwischen einer **Zentralisierung** und **Dezentralisierung** von Entscheidungen zu überbrücken.

INSERT 3 **Handelsblatt vom Freitag, 26. August 2003**

Vor VW ist keine Nische mehr sicher

Pischetsrieder setzt auf Produktvielfalt

HANDELSBLATT, 26.8.2003

hof WOLFSBURG. Einen Super-Sportwagen gibt es bei Ferrari oder beim VW-Konzern (Lamborghini), eine Edellimousine bei Rolls Royce oder bei VW (Bentley), einen Geländewagen bei Range Rover oder VW (Touareg), einen Transporter bei Mercedes oder VW: Die Liste ließe sich lange fortschreiben, doch VW-Konzernchef Bernd Pischetsrieder ist sie noch immer nicht lang genug: „85 Prozent aller Segmente" will er bis 2005 abdecken. Das heißt: Für fast jede Spielart eines Autos will der VW-Chef potenziellen Käufern ein Angebot machen. Vom Stadtflitzer à la Drei-Liter-Lupo bis zum schweren Lastwagen, wie sie derzeit nur in Südamerika gebaut und angeboten werden, vom Spaßauto wie dem Audi TT bis zum Familienbus. Kein Konkurrent soll sich vor VW sicher fühlen können.

So wird ein neuer Bruder des Golfs, ein kleiner und preiswerter Roadster als Konkurrent für die Mazdas, Fiats und Peugeots dieser Welt bereits am 1. September der Öffentlichkeit vorgestellt – wenn auch nur als Studie, die an die glorreichen Zeiten eines Karmann Ghia auf Käfer-Basis erinnert. Außerdem hat Pischetsrieder kürzlich angekündigt, die große Lücke zwischen der Luxuslimousine Phaeton und dem Passat zu füllen. Konkurrent dieses Modells, „das keine klassische Stufenheck-Limousine sein wird", so Pischetsrieder, ist der BMW 5er und die Mercedes C-Klasse.

Doch nicht nur mit der Marke VW will Pischetsrieder angreifen. Mit Skoda soll den preisgünstigen Anbietern aus Fernost das Leben schwer gemacht werden, Audi wildert erfolgreich im Revier der sportlichen Autos von BMW & Co., Seat soll den südeuropäischen Charme verkörpern – ein Attribut, das bislang von der italienischen Fiat-Tochter Alfa Romeo besetzt ist.

Wie ehrgeizig die Pläne des VW-Chefs sind, zeigen zwei Zahlen: So wurden 1987 innerhalb der Automobilindustrie neun Segmente gezählt, heute sind es 33. Die Wolfsburger wollen in 28 davon vertreten sein. Das kostet Geld, das bei bestimmten Nischenmodellen „eigentlich im Marketing-Etat verbucht werden müsste", wie Analysten mit Seitenhieb auf den Phaeton geschrieben haben. Verdient werden muss das Geld weiter mit den Brot- und Butter-Autos – allen voran dem Golf.

Dass die Entwicklungskosten bei dieser Auffächerung der Palette nicht in den Himmel schießen, soll die Modulstrategie verhindern: Sie bedeutet, dass immer mehr Autos auf einer ähnlichen Bodengruppe konstruiert werden und gleiche Bauteile nicht nur in einer Fahrzeugkategorie, sondern auch segmentübergreifend eingesetzt werden können. „Auf diese Weise profitiert der Golf-Kunde schon heute vom Einstieg des Konzerns in die Luxusklasse", verkündet Pischetsrieder – vielleicht auch, um die hohen Entwicklungskosten für den Phaeton zu rechtfertigen.

Eine gleichermaßen effektive wie effiziente Ausübung von Mehrmarkenstrategien setzt einen dynamischen Planungsprozess voraus. Im Mittelpunkt dieses, die Lösung interdependenter Teilprobleme umfassenden und damit rückgekoppelten Planungsverlaufs steht die strategische Rahmenplanung von Mehrmarkenstrategien. Die präzise und auf eine konturierte Markenabgrenzung abzielende Ausgestaltung der strategischen Rollen, Positionierungen und Leitbilder der Marken kanalisiert die markenspezifischen Aktivitäten in gewünschter Weise und bildet die zentrale Voraussetzung zur Schaffung differenzierter Markenidentitäten. Zur Steuerung und Koordination von Mehrmarkenstrategien bedarf es darüber hinaus eines Mehrmarkencontrolling, welches durch Generierung zentraler Steuerungsgrößen einen Beitrag zur Optimierung des externen Marktauftritts sowie des internen Zusammenspiels der Portfoliomarken zu leisten vermag.

Literaturverzeichnis

Aaker, D. A. (1990), Brand Extensions: The Good, the Bad, and the Ugly, in: Sloan Management Review, Vol. 31, No. 4, Summer, S. 47–56.

Aaker, D. A. (1998), Mit der Marke in einen neuen Markt, in: Harvard Business Manager, Nr. 3, S. 43–52.

Aaker, D. A. (2004a), Brand Portfolio Strategy, New York.

Aaker, D. A. (2004b), Warum sich Unternehmen selbst im Weg stehen, in: Absatzwirtschaft, Nr. 7, S. 26–29.

Aaker, D. A., Joachimsthaler, E. (2000), Brand Leadership, New York.

Backhaus, K. (1997), Fixkostenintensität und Unternehmenspolitik, in: Meffert, H., Backhaus, K. (Hrsg.), Kostenstruktur und Fixkostenmanagement als Herausforderungen an die Unternehmensflexibilität, Dokumentation des 31. Münsteraner Führungsgespräches der Wissenschaftlichen Gesellschaft für Marketing und Unternehmensführung e.V., Münster, S. 6–22.

Backhaus, K. (2003), Industriegütermarketing, 7. Aufl., München.

Backhaus, K., Erichson, B., Plinke, W., Weiber, R. (2003), Multivariate Analysemethoden, 10. Aufl., Berlin u. a.

Baumgarth, C. (2004), Markenpolitik. Markenwirkungen – Markenführung – Markencontrolling, 2. Aufl., Wiesbaden.

Becker, J. (2002), Marketing-Konzeption – Grundlagen des strategischen Marketing-Managements, 7. Aufl., München.

Bruhn, M. (2003), Marketing, 6. Aufl., Wiesbaden.

Büchelhofer, R. (2002), Markenführung im Volkswagen-Konzern im Rahmen der Mehrmarkenstrategie, in: Meffert, H., Burmann, C., Koers, M. (Hrsg.), Markenmanagement – Grundfragen der identitätsorientierten Markenführung, 1. Aufl., Wiesbaden.

Buchenau, M.-W. (2004), Der Mini gibt BMW den notwendigen Schwung, in: Handelsblatt vom 4.5.2004, S. 13.

Burmann, G. (1995), Marktarealstrategien der internationalen Automobilhersteller, in: Hünerberg, R., Heise, G., Hoffmeister, M. (Hrsg.), Internationales Automobilmarketing, Wiesbaden, S. 121–141.

Dichtl, E., Andritzky, K., Schobert, R. (1977), Ein Verfahren zur Abgrenzung des „relevanten Marktes“ auf der Basis von Produktperzeptionen und Präferenzurteilen, in: Wirtschaftswissenschaftliches Studium, 6. Jg., Nr. 6, S. 290–301.

Dudenhöffer, F. (1998), Abschied vom Massenmarketing – Systemmarken und Beziehungen erobern Märkte, Düsseldorf, München.
Dudenhöffer, F. (2001), Systemmarken – Vernetzung produktnaher Angebote um Marken, in: Esch, F.-R. (Hrsg.), Moderne Markenführung. Grundlagen – Innovative Ansätze – Praktische Umsetzungen, 3. Aufl., Wiesbaden, S. 413–433.
Esch, F.-R. (1992), Positionierungsstrategien – konstituierender Erfolgsfaktor für Handelsunternehmen, in: Thexis, 9. Jg., Nr. 4, S. 9–15.
Esch, F.-R. (2003), Strategie und Technik der Markenführung, München.
Esch, F.-R., Andresen, Th. (1996), 10 Barrieren für eine erfolgreiche Markenpositionierung und Ansätze zu deren Überwindung, in: Tomczak, T. et al. (Hrsg.), Positionierung – Kernentscheidung des Marketing, St. Gallen, S. 78–94.
Genger, J. (2004), Condor mischt Billigfluggeschäft auf, in: Financial Times Deutschland vom 27.5.2004, S. 6.
Ghoshal, S. S., Bartlett, Ch. (1995), Building the entrepreneurial Corporation: New Organizational Processes, New Managerial Tasks, in: European Management Journal, Vol. 13, No. 21, June, S. 139–155.
Haedrich, G., Tomczak, T. (1994), Strategische Markenführung, in: Bruhn, M. (Hrsg.), Handbuch Markenartikel – Anforderungen an die Markenpolitik aus Sicht von Wissenschaft und Praxis, Bd. II: Markentechnik, Markenintegration, Markenkontrolle, Stuttgart, S. 925–948.
Haedrich, G., Tomczak, T., Kaetzke, P. (2004), Strategische Markenführung, 3. Aufl., Bern, Stuttgart, Wien.
Kapferer, J.-N. (1997), Strategic Barnd Management, 2. Aufl., London.
Kapferer, J.-N. (1992), Die Marke – Kapital des Unternehmens, Landsberg/Lech.
Keller, K. L. (2003), Strategic brand banagement – building, measuring and managing brand equity, Upper Saddle River, N. J.
Koers, M. (2001), Steuerung von Markenportfolios: Ein Beitrag zum Mehrmarkencontrolling am Beispiel der Automobilwirtschaft, Frankfurt/M.
Kotler, P. (1988), Marketing Management, 6. Aufl., Englewood Cliffs, N. J.
Kroeber-Riel, W., Weinberg, P. (2003), Konsumentenverhalten, 8. Aufl., München.
Kumar, J. (2003), Kill a Brand, Keep a Customer, in: Harvard Business Review, December, S. 86–95.
Laforet, S., Saunders, J. (1994), Managing Brand Portfolios: How the Leaders do it, in: Journal of Advertising Research, Vol. 34, No. 5, September/October, S. 64–76.
Meffert, H. (1992), Strategien zur Profilierung von Marken, in: Dichtl, E., Eggers, W. (Hrsg.), Marke und Markenartikel als Instrumente des Wettbewerbs, München, S. 129–156.
Meffert, H. (1994), Marketing-Management – Analyse, Strategie, Implementierung, Wiesbaden.
Meffert, H. (1999), Mehrmarkenstrategie – immer die beste Option? in: Absatzwirtschaft, Sondernummer Oktober, S. 82–87.
Meffert, H. (2000), Marketing – Grundlagen marktorientierter Unternehmensführung, 9. Aufl., Wiesbaden.
Meffert, H., Burmann, Ch. (1996a), Identitätsorientierte Markenführung – Grundlagen für das Management von Markenportfolios, in: Meffert, H., Wagner, H., Backhaus, K. (Hrsg.), Arbeitspapier Nr. 100 der Wissenschaftlichen Gesellschaft für Marketing und Unternehmensführung e.V., Münster.
Meffert, H., Burmann, Ch. (1996b), Towards an Identity-Orientated Approach of Branding, University of Cambridge, Research Papers in Management Studies, No. 18.
Menzel, S. (1999), Volkswagen bekommt in diesem Jahr den Deutschen Marketing Preis / Mehrmarkenstrategie als Erfolgsrezept, in: Handelsblatt vom 3.8.1999, S. 43.

Michael, B. M. (1999), Laudatio Deutscher Marketing-Preis 1999 an Volkswagen AG, in: Kongressdokumentation vom Deutschen Marketing Verband des 27. Deutschen Marketing-Tag am 29. Oktober 1999 in Frankfurt unter dem Thema „Chancen im 3. Jahrtausend. Information managen – Zukunft gestalten", S. 47.

Nommensen, J. N. (1990), Die Prägnanz von Markenbildern, Heidelberg.

o. V. (1997), Fahrt ins Ungewisse, in: Wirtschaftswoche, Nr. 19, S. 56–62.

o. V. (1998), Völlig neue Regeln, in: Wirtschaftswoche, Nr. 21, S. 51–59.

o. V. (2004), autofahren in deutschland 2004, Motor-Presse Stuttgart (Hrsg.), Stuttgart.

o. V. (2004), Die Zukunft bringt neue und weniger Marken, in: Handelblatt vom 2.3.2004, S. 17.

Perrey, J. (1998), Nutzenorientierte Marktsegmentierung – Ein integrativer Ansatz zum Zielgruppenmarketing im Verkehrsdienstleistungsbereich, Wiesbaden.

Pischetsrieder, B. (2003), Marken, Märkte und Prozesse – Volkswagen AG, in: Gottschalk, B., Kalmbach, R. (Hrsg.), Markenmanagement in der Automobilindustrie, Wiesbaden, S. 409–421.

Quelch, J. A. (1994), Extend Profits, Not Product Lines, in: Harvard Business Review, September/October, S. 153–160.

Reinking, G. (2001), Die Modelle der VW-Marken sollen einander weniger gleichen, in: Financial Times Deutschland vom 27.8.2001, S. 3.

Riesenbeck, H., Perrey J. (2004), Mega-Macht Marke, Wien.

Sattler, H. (2003), Markentransferstrategien, Research Papers on Marketing and Retailing, No. 12, Hamburg.

Schobinger, N. (2002), Markenintegrationsmanagement bei Fusionen und Akquisitionen, in: Handelblatt vom 29.4.2002, S. b6.

Schulz, H. (1997), Mannheimer: für jede Zielgruppe eine Marke, in: Bank und Markt, Nr. 9, S. 23–24.

Smith, D. C., Park, W. C. (1992), The Effects of Brand Extensions on Market Share and Advertising Efficiency, in: Journal of Marketing Research, Vol. 29, No. 1, S. 296–313.

Stegmüller, B., Hempel, P. (1996), Empirischer Vergleich unterschiedlicher Marktsegmentierungsansätze über die Segmentpopulation, in: Marketing ZFP, 18. Jg., Nr. 1, S. 25–31.

Tomczak, T., Roosdorp, A. (1996), Positionierung – Neue Herausforderungen verlangen neue Ansätze, in: Tomczak, T. et al. (Hrsg.), Positionierung – Kernentscheidung des Marketing, St. Gallen, S. 6–42.

Traylor, M. B. (1986), Cannibalism in Multibrand Firms, in: Journal of Consumer Marketing, Vol. 3, No. 2, Spring, S. 69–75.

Waldinger, C. (2003), Auf der Bremse, in: werben und verkaufen, Nr. 1–2, S. 6–7.

Wilson, R. (2004), Entry Level Luxury, in: Automotive Industries, July, S. 2.

Wübbenhorst, K. L., Wildner, R. (2002), Die Schwäche der Marke ist die Schwäche schwacher Marken, in: Planung & Analyse, 29. Jg., Nr. 2, S. 17–21.

Markenerweiterungsstrategien

Mirko Caspar und Christoph Burmann

1.	**Relevanz der Markenerweiterung für das Markenmanagement**	**246**
2.	**Gegenstand und konzeptionelle Grundlagen der Markenerweiterung**	**247**
2.1	Definition des Markenerweiterungsbegriffes	247
2.2	Chancen und Risiken der Markenerweiterung	249
2.3	Bestehende Ansätze zur Analyse und Erklärung von Markenerweiterungen	253
2.31	Einstellungstheoretische Ansätze	254
2.32	Gedächtnispsychologische Ansätze	258
3.	**Bestimmungsfaktoren der nachfragerseitigen Beurteilung von Markenerweiterungen**	**259**
3.1	Bestimmungsfaktoren der Beurteilung des Erweiterungsproduktes	259
3.11	Stärke und Struktur der Ursprungsmarke	260
3.12	Charakteristika der Transferkategorie	261
3.13	Beziehung zwischen Ursprungsmarke und Transferprodukt	262
3.14	Kommunikationspolitik	263
3.2	Bestimmungsfaktoren des Rücktransfers auf die Ursprungsmarke	263
4.	**Implikationen für das Management der Markenerweiterung**	**264**
4.1	Strategische Standortbestimmung	265
4.2	Positionierung des Transferproduktes	266
4.3	Marktstrategische Instrumenteausgestaltung	266
5.	**Fazit**	**267**

Markenerweiterungsstrategien können weitergehend in Markenausdehnungs- und Markentransferstrategien differenziert werden. Die **Markenausdehnungsstrategie** (Line Extension) beschreibt die Expansion einer Marke in gleichen oder verwandten Produktkategorien, die **Markentransferstrategie** (Category Extension) demgegenüber die Expansion in neue, nicht verwandte Produktkategorien (Keller 2003, S. 578 f.). Beide Strategieoptionen erfüllen die oben beschriebenen Merkmale (vgl. den Beitrag zu Markenevolutionsstrategien in diesem Buch). Voraussetzung für die Nutzung einer existierenden Marke und somit der Generierung von Synergie-Effekten ist dabei, dass neue und alte Produkte der Marke als eine Einheit wahrgenommen werden (Park/Milberg/Lawson 1991, S. 185 ff.; Keller 2001, S. 705 ff.; Zatloukal 2002, S. 59 ff.).

Abbildung 1: Abgrenzung der Markenerweiterungsbegriffe

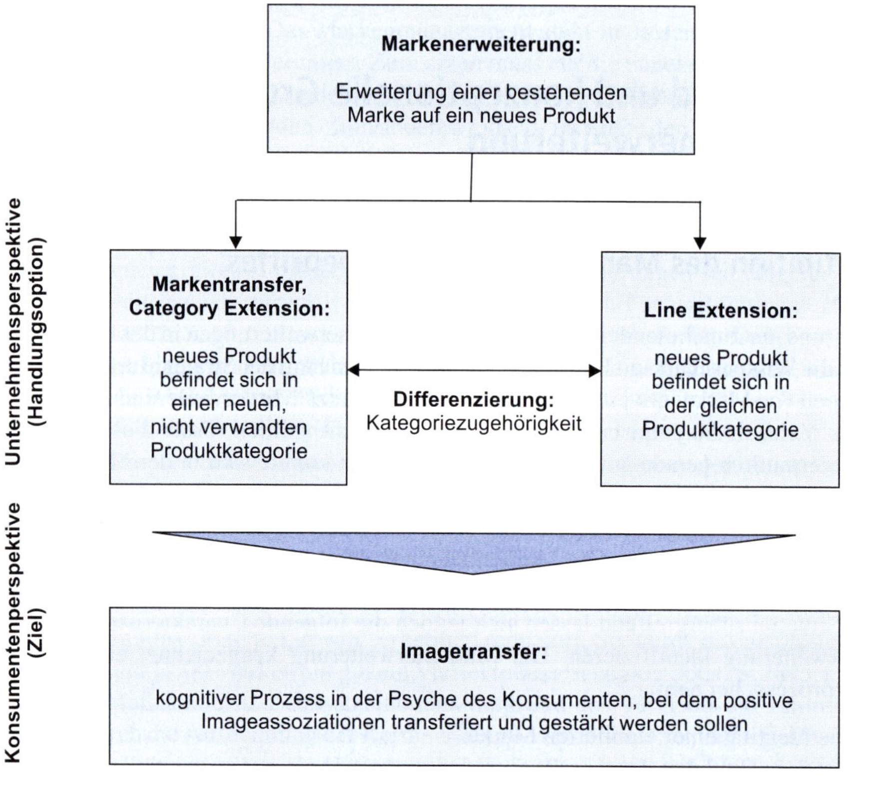

Quelle: in Anlehnung an Caspar 2002, S. 29

Der Definition der Markenerweiterung liegt implizit eine Unternehmensperspektive zugrunde und sie bezeichnet dementsprechend einen Managementprozess. Der Begriff **Imagetransfer** kennzeichnet im Unterschied zur Markenerweiterung nicht den Managementprozess, sondern den angestrebten kognitiven und emotionalen Prozess der Assoziations- und Vorstellungsübertragung im Kopf der Nachfrager (unter anderem Caspar 2002, S. 27). Dabei handelt es sich beim Markenimage um ein mehrdimensionales Einstellungskonstrukt (Trommsdorff 2003, S. 150; Kroeber-Riehl/Weinberg 2003, S. 168 ff.), welches das in der Psyche relevanter externer Zielgruppen fest verankerte, verdichtete, wertende Vorstellungsbild von einer Marke wiedergibt. Das Markenimage ist das Ergebnis der individuellen, subjektiven Wahrnehmung und Dekodierung aller von der Marke ausgesendeten Signale (vgl. hierzu auch den Beitrag zur Grundkonzeption des identitätsorientierten Markenmanagements in diesem Buch). Die Abgrenzung der unterschiedlichen Begrifflichkeiten der Markenerweiterung ist in Abbildung 1 im Überblick dargestellt.

Die folgenden Ausführungen beziehen sich zwar im Kern auf Markentransfers, also Erweiterungen in neue Produktkategorien, gelten aber auch für Line Extensions. Daher sollen die Begriffe Transferprodukt und Erweiterungsprodukt sowohl für Produkte, die in eine neue Produktkategorie eingeführt werden, als auch für solche, die das Produktportfolio innerhalb der bestehenden Kategorie erweitern, verwendet werden. Diese Aggregierung steht im Einklang mit anderen verhaltenswissenschaftlichen Untersuchungen aus diesem Forschungsbereich, die beide Erscheinungsformen der Markenerweiterung ebenfalls gemeinsam analysieren (Sattler 1997; Zatloukal 2002; Völckner 2003). Darüber hinaus werden die Begriffe Ursprungsmarke und Muttermarke als Bezeichnung für die bereits etablierte Marke, welche der Ausdehnung zugrunde liegt, ebenfalls als Synonyme zur Anwendung kommen.

2.2 Chancen und Risiken der Markenerweiteurng

Mit der Markenerweiterungsstrategie sind eine Reihe von allgemeinen **Chancen und Risiken** verbunden, die anhand der Tragfähigkeit der Marke und entsprechend dem Vorliegen und der Ausprägung unterschiedlicher Bestimmungsfaktoren der Markenerweiterung abgewogen werden müssen.

Die grundsätzlichen Ziele der Markenstrategien lassen sich als Konkretisierung der Oberziele wie Rendite-, Gewinn- und/oder Wertmaximierung der Unternehmung verstehen (Meffert 1994, S. 93 ff.; Becker 2002, S. 13 ff.). Dabei stellt der **Customer Equity** als spezifische Ausprägung des ökonomischen Markenwertes die zentrale markenspezifische Erfolgsgröße zur Sicherung der Oberziele der Unternehmung dar. Im Sinne einer Mittel-Zweck-Beziehung liegen diesen ökonomischen Zielgrößen der „psychografische Markenwert" beziehungsweise synonym die **Markenstärke** zugrunde.

Die Markenstärke ist extern gerichtet im Sinne einer positiven Beeinflussung des Kaufverhaltens gegenüber der Marke zu verstehen (Burmann/Blinda/Nitschke 2003, S. 50 f.). Sie erklärt sich aus einem hohen Fit zwischen Markenidentität und Markenimage sowie durch die Vermittlung eines für die Zielgruppe relevanten, einzigartigen Markennutzens (Keller 1993, S. 13; Burmann/Blinda/Nitschke 2003, S. 53). Die Markenbekanntheit stellt dabei die conditio sine qua non für die Entstehung von Markenstärke dar. **Die effiziente, effektive und schnelle Übertragung der Markenstärke** auf das neue Produkt durch Rückgriff auf die verwendeten Markierungen der etablierten Marke ist das Kernziel jeder Markenerweiterung (Caspar 2002, S. 46). Dieses Kernziel begründet positive Wirkungen auf **Konsumenten-** und **Handelsebene**.

Auf **Konsumentenebene** soll die Übertragung eines etablierten Markenimages die sofortige Markenwahrnehmung und Präsenz des neuen Produktes unterstützen und den Lernaufwand für die Konsumenten reduzieren (Aaker 1990; Meffert/Heinemann 1990; Kapferer 1992; Sattler 1998; Esch/Fuchs/Bräutigam 2001; Keller 2001; Günther 2002; Zatloukal 2002; Völckner 2003). Zudem sollen der Bekanntheits- und Vertrauensvorsprung der etablierten Marke die Risikoreduktionsfunktion stärken. Etablierte Marken können so die Informations- und Suchkosten des Nachfragers senken. Unter Umständen können „Beziehungsvorteile" für die Kunden in Form von personalisierten und kundenspezifischen Angeboten realisiert werden, wenn Anbieter auf bereits gesammelte Erfahrungen und kundenspezifische Informationen aus bestehenden Kanälen zurückgreifen und diese für ein entsprechendes Angebot nutzen können (Court/Leiter/Loch 1999, S. 102).

Mit Bezug auf den **Handel** soll die etablierte Marke bei der Durchdringung etwaiger Handelsbarrieren gegen die Einführung neuer Produkte helfen sowie für eine verbesserte PoS-Präsenz und Regalplatzsicherung sorgen. Die Listungsbereitschaft soll insgesamt erhöht und der Akquisitionsaufwand verringert werden (Esch 2004, S. 282). Neuere Untersuchen haben gezeigt, dass die Handelsakzeptanz gegenüber einem neuen Produkt durch Markenerweiterungen signifikant erhöht werden kann, wenn die Markenerweiterung durch Marketingaktivitäten unterstützt wird (Völckner 2003).

Für das **Unternehmen** resultiert aus den positiven Effekten auf Konsumenten- und Handelsebene, dass die Marketingeffektivität und -effizienz durch die Nutzung der Ursprungsmarke erhöht werden können. Marktseitig sollen so vor allem eine Steigerung der Kaufbereitschaft und Erstkaufrate und die Durchsetzung eines Preispremiums erzielt werden (Aaker 1990, S. 49). Zudem können die Ausweitung der Zielgruppen, die Besetzung neuer Geschäftsfelder und die Senkung der Markteintrittsbarrieren unterstützt werden (Meffert 2000, S. 867). Innengerichtet kann außerdem die Ausnutzung interner Synergien zur Kostenreduktion beitragen (Court/Leiter/Loch 1999, S. 102 ff.; Sattler 2003, S. 4). Durch die Steigerung von Marketingeffektivität und -effizienz wird insgesamt eine Reduktion des Floprisikos angestrebt.

Neben den Chancen der Unterstützung des neuen Produktes durch eine Markenerweiterung bestehen auch **Chancen für die Ursprungsmarke**. So kann durch eine Erweiterung zum Beispiel die Revitalisierung oder die Umpositionierung der Marke unterstützt werden. Außerdem ist eine Verlängerung des Lebenszyklus der Marke möglich (Hätty 1989, S. 576; Sattler 2003). Generell besteht die Chance, dass die angestrebten Bekanntheits- und Imageeffekte für das Transferprodukt im Sinne eines Spill-Over-Effektes auch auf die Ursprungsmarke zurückwirken und diese stärken (Hätty 1989, S. 299 ff.; Smith/Park 1992, S. 298). Abbildung 2 zeigt zusammenfassend die Chancen beziehungsweise Ziele von Markenerweiterungen.

Abbildung 2: Zielsystem der Markenerweiterung

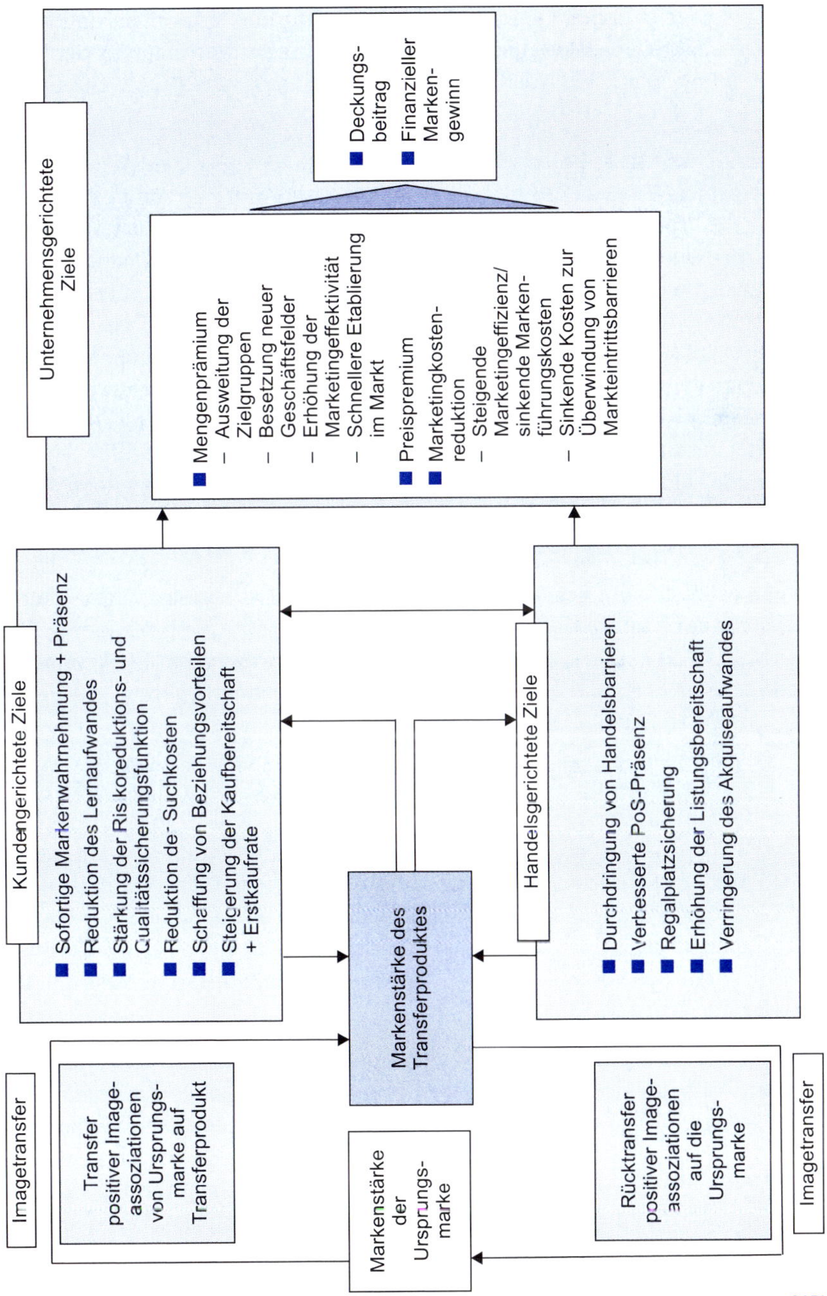

GABLER GRAFIK

Quelle: Caspar 2002, S. 50

Mit der Markenerweiterung sind neben den Chancen jedoch auch einige **Risiken** verbunden. Diese beziehen sich allgemein auf das Risiko der Verringerung der aktuellen oder potenziellen Markenstärke und einen daraus folgenden Verlust an Markenwert. Die Gefahr kann entweder in hohen Opportunitätskosten aufgrund eines nicht optimalen Fits des Transferproduktes zur Markenidentität liegen oder in der Verringerung der Markenstärke der Ursprungsmarke aufgrund von Kannibalisierungs- oder negativen Imageeffekten.

Ein grundsätzliches Risiko besteht in der **mangelnden Akzeptanz** des neuen Angebots. Dies kann beispielsweise auf eine zu schwache Ursprungsmarke zurückzuführen sein, welche das neue Produkt nicht ausreichend unterstützen kann. Das neue Produkt hätte im Falle eines zu schwachen oder neutralen Einflusses der Ursprungsmarke aber wahrscheinlich auch ohne die Unterstützung der Ursprungsmarke Probleme gehabt, sich am Markt zu etablieren. Schlimmer ist es jedoch, wenn die transferierten Assoziationen der Ursprungsmarke aufgrund fehlender Relevanz oder neuer, situationsspezifischer Konnotationen negative Affekte im neuen Kontext hervorrufen. Im schlimmsten Fall kann durch die Erweiterung die Markenidentität der Ursprungsmarke durch **Rücktransfer** neu gebildeter, negativer oder widersprüchlicher Assoziationen angegriffen werden. Bei zu häufigen und heterogenen, vom Konsumenten nicht mehr nachvollziehbaren Erweiterungen kann es zu einer schleichenden Erosion der Ursprungsmarke kommen (Aaker 1990, S. 52 ff.; Swaminathan/Fox/Reddy 2001; Zatloukal 2002).

Selbst wenn es zu keinem negativen Transfer zurück zur Ursprungsmarke kommt, besteht das Risiko der **Kannibalisierung** der Ursprungsprodukte (Cravens/Piercy/Prentice 2000, S. 382 ff.; Aaker 2004, S. 213). Im Medienmarkt wurde zum Beispiel bei vielen Ausdehnungen von Printmarken befürchtet, durch Angebote im Internet oder Fernsehen das Kerngeschäft zu kannibalisieren. Daher scheuten sich unter anderem viele traditionelle Medienunternehmen, ein vollwertiges Angebot ihrer etablierten Marken ins Internet zu stellen. Allerdings sollte sich das Markenmanagement dabei immer auch die Frage stellen, ob bei Unterlassung der Markenerweiterung das Umsatzvolumen nicht durch neue Wettbewerbsangebote bedroht wird. Gerade in von Konvergenz und der Erosion der klassischen Wertschöpfungsketten geprägten Industrien wie Telekommunikation, Medien und IT ist die Bedrohung der Ursprungsmarken durch andere, oft neue Wettbewerber nicht zu unterschätzen. In diesem Fall ist die eigene Kannibalisierung der durch die Wettbewerber natürlich vorzuziehen (vgl. zur Markenkannibalisierung auch den Beitrag in diesem Band).

Schließlich können bei Markenerweiterungen auch Opportunitätskosten durch den Verzicht auf den Aufbau einer neuen Marke entstehen. Denn sollte es gelingen, eine neue Marke erfolgreich im Markt zu etablieren, kann unter Umständen ein erhebliches neues Wertpotenzial geschaffen werden. Dieses könnte sich zum Beispiel auch in neuen Markenerweiterungen, bei denen die neue Marke als Erweiterungsplattform dient, manifestieren. Der Verzicht auf die Option, eine neue Markenplattform zu schaffen, muss daher im Sinne von Opportunitätskosten ebenfalls ins Kalkül mit einbezogen werden (Aaker 1990, S. 54; Sattler 1999, S. 15). Die Risiken der Markenerweiterungen sind in Tabelle 1 noch einmal zusammengefasst.

Tabelle 1: Risiken des Markentransfers

Risikenfür das Transferprodukt	Risiken für die Ursprungsmarke
■ Mangelnde Akzeptanz des Erweiterungsproduktes durch - zu schwache Muttermarke - mangelnde Relevanz der Assoziationen - kontextspezifische, negative Bewertung transferierter Assoziationen ■ Opportunitätskosten aufgrund Verzicht auf Aufbau einer neuen starken Marke	■ Verlust der Glaubwürdigkeit und Qualistätsanmutung durch Rücktransfer negativer Assoziationen bei Scheitern der Markenerweiterung ■ Langfristige Erosion des Markenimages durch inkonsistente, inkongruente Erweiterung ■ Kannibalisierung der Ursprungsmarke

GABLER GRAFIK

2.3 Bestehende Ansätze zur Analyse und Erklärung von Markenerweiterungen

Die Forschungsbemühungen zur Markenerweiterungen können allgemein in finanzwirtschaftliche und verhaltenswissenschaftliche Ansätze unterteilt werden.

Finanzwirtschaftliche Ansätze führen eine finanzielle Bewertung einer Markenerweiterung durch. Sie ermitteln die spezifischen, diskontierten Einzahlungsüberschüsse, die bei Übertragung einer etablierten Marke auf das neue Produkt erzielbar sind. Dieser Barwert wird dann mit dem Barwert der Einzahlungsüberschüsse, die bei Etablierung einer völlig neuen Marke zu erzielen wären, verglichen. Neben allgemeinen Problemen bei der Ermittlung der markenerweiterungsspezifischen Einzahlungsüberschüsse ist hier im Hinblick auf die Markenführung die fehlende Einbeziehung von Verhaltenskonstrukten zu bemängeln. Finanzwirtschaftliche Ansätze sind daher für die Ableitung von Hinweisen für erfolgreiche Markenerweiterungen nicht geeignet (vgl. auch den Beitrag zur Bewertung und Bilanzierung in diesem Buch).

Die große Mehrzahl der Forschungsansätze und empirischen Untersuchungen zu Markenerweiterungen ist daher **verhaltenswissenschaftlich geprägt** (Sattler 1997, S. 483 ff.). Die verhaltenswissenschaftlichen Ansätze können danach unterschieden werden, ob sie auf Image- beziehungsweise Einstellungstheorien oder gedächtnistheoretischen Schema- und Kategorisierungstheorien aufbauen. Der Vorteil der Kategorisierungs- und Schematheorien ist, dass sie die kognitiven und emotionalen Prozesse bei der Imageübertragung abbilden und so den Einfluss unterschiedlicher Bestimmungsgrößen auf den Imagetransfer sehr anschaulich theoretisch erklären können. Sie stehen aber nicht im Widerspruch zu den einstellungstheoretischen Konzepten, sondern stellen nur die gedächtnispsychologische Sichtweise dar, welche auch als theoretische Grundlage der Einstellungstheorien dienen kann (Grunert 1982, S. 13 und 20). Abbildung 3 zeigt noch einmal die Ansätze zur Untersuchung von Markenerweiterungen im Überblick.

Abbildung 3: Ansätze zur Untersuchung von Markenerweiterungen

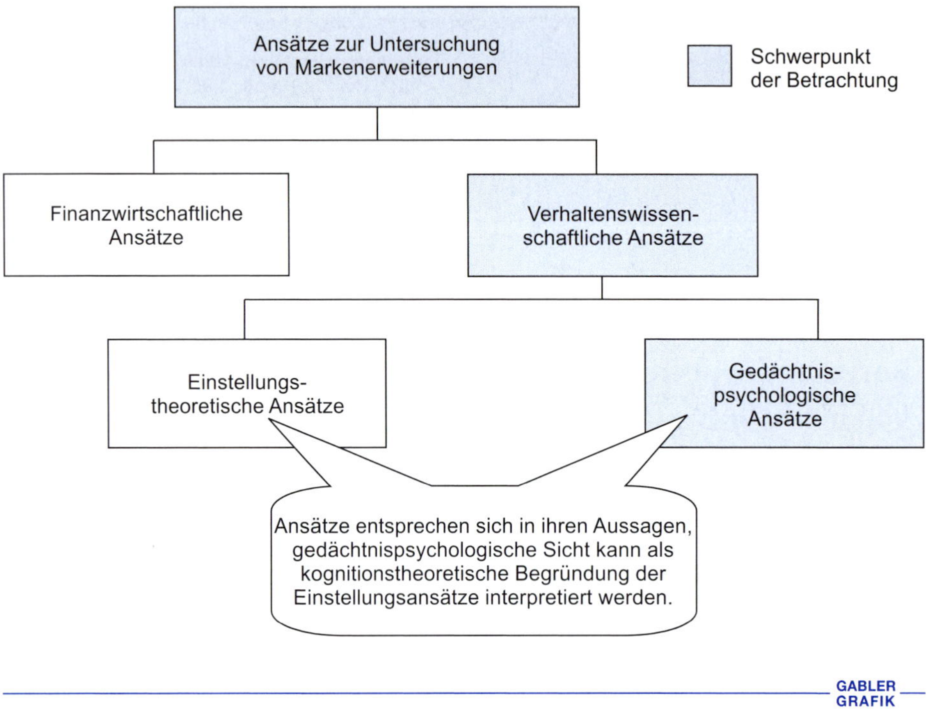

2.31 Einstellungstheoretische Ansätze

Die einstellungstheoretischen Ansätze sehen die Einstellung als gelernte Prädispositionen eines Individuums, auf bestimmte Stimuli konsistent positiv oder negativ zu reagieren (Meffert 1992b, S. 55). Dabei wird die Einstellung im Allgemeinen als eindimensionale Größe interpretiert (Hätty 1989, S. 81). Das Image der Marke wird als ein mehrdimensionales, mit subjektiven Werten versehenes, komplexes psychisches Konstrukt definiert (Trommsdorff 2003, S. 150; Kroeber-Riehl/Weinberg 2003, S. 168 ff.). Es ist der Einstellung insofern verwandt, als dass es die mehrdimensionale Struktur der unabhängigen Eindruckswerte, welche der eindimensionalen Einstellung zugrunde liegen, abbildet (Berekoven/Eckert/Ellenrieder 2004, S. 82 f.). Die Erklärung des Phänomens des Imagetransfers kann bei einstellungstheoretischer Sicht unter anderem über den speziellen Lernprozess der Reizgeneralisation erfolgen (Hätty 1989, S. 100). Die Reizgeneralisation beschreibt das Verhalten, eine zu einem bestimmten Stimulus gehörende, gelernte Reaktion nicht nur bei identischen, sondern auch bei ähnlichen Reizen hervorzurufen. Übertragen auf die Einstellung gegenüber einer Marke kann dies bedeuten, dass bei einem ähnlichen Stimulus, also einem neuen Produkt mit gleicher Markierung, die gelernte Einstellung bezüglich der Ursprungsmarke auch durch das neue Produkt hervorgerufen wird (Hätty 1989, S. 98 ff.). Entscheidend für diesen Effekt ist damit die Ähnlichkeit der Stimuli beziehungsweise des neuen Transferproduktes mit dem etablierten Vorstellungsbild von der Marke.

Im Folgenden sollen mit den Modellen von Schweiger und Meffert/Heinemann zwei der bekanntesten einstellungstheoretischen Modelle zur Markenerweiterung vorgestellt werden. Im Anschluss daran werden die Grundzüge der Schema- und Kategorisierungstheorien kurz beschrieben. Diese bilden die theoretische Grundlage für die Beschreibung der Kernbestimmungsfaktoren der nachfragerseitigen Beurteilung von Markenausdehnungen im nächsten Kapitel.

Das Modell von Schweiger

Schweiger entwickelte eines der ersten und bekanntesten Modelle zum Imagetransfer auf Basis der Einstellungstheorie (Schweiger 1982, S. 321–323; vgl. Abbildung 4).

Er versteht dabei unter Images ein System **rein konnotativer Eigenschaften**. Dabei sind unter konnotativen Eigenschaften die nichtsachhaltigen, emotionalen Produkteigenschaften zu verstehen (Meffert/Heinemann 1990, S. 5). Der Ansatz von Schweiger steht damit im Widerspruch zur Konzeptualisierung des Markenimages im Rahmen des identitätsorientierten Markenmanagements, nach der dem Markenimage sowohl denotative (sachhaltige) als auch konnotative Dimensionen zugrunde liegen. Schweigers Konzeptualisierung hat sich in der Markenforschung bisher nicht durchsetzen können.

Um letztlich auch denotative Ähnlichkeiten der Produkt-Markenkombinationen erfassen zu können, werden von Schweiger neben dem Markenimage die technologischen Eigenschaften der Produkte separat in die Betrachtung einbezogen. Schweiger ermittelt in seinem Modell die Eignung einer Produktklasse für einen Transfer sowie das Transferpotenzial einer Marke durch ein Distanzmaß in einem mehrdimensionalen Raum. Die räumliche Nähe innerhalb des Wahrnehmungsraumes wird dabei sowohl durch die emotionale Affinität von Marke und Erweiterungsprodukt als auch durch die technologische Affinität von bestehendem Produkt und Erweiterungsprodukt bestimmt. Je näher sich die Produkt-Markenkombinationen sind, desto vorteilhafter wird die Erweiterung wahrgenommen. Die wahrgenommene Distanz erklärt so die Prädisposition zum Versuchs- und Wiederkauf.

Abbildung 4: **Imagetransfermodell von Schweiger**

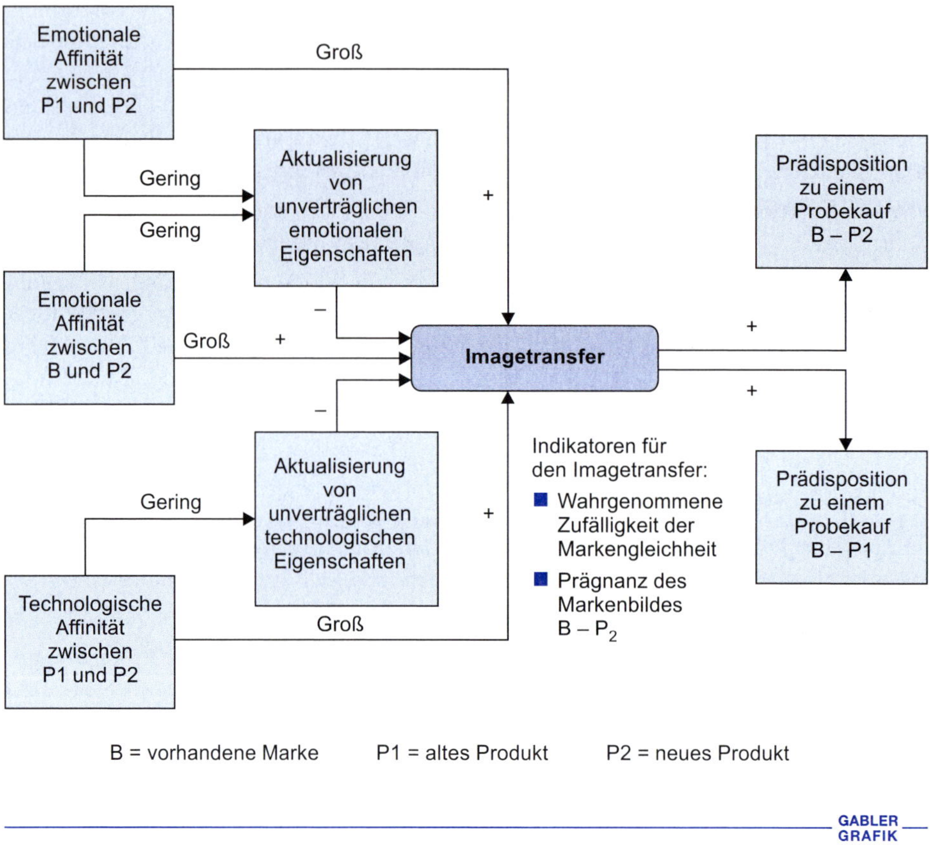

Quelle: Schweiger 1982, S. 322

Aus dem unmittelbar entscheidungsorientierten Modell von Schweiger lassen sich unter anderem folgende Implikationen für das Marketing ableiten (Meffert/Heinemann 1990, S. 6):

- Konsumenten sollten möglichst in beiden Produktklassen Verwender sein.
- Emotionale und technologische Affinität sollte einen Mindestwert überschreiten, damit ein Transferpotenzial gegeben ist.
- Zwischen dem Markennamen und dem neuen Produkt sollte eine psychologische Affinität bestehen.

Kritik erfährt das Modell jedoch vor allem aufgrund der mangelnden verhaltenswissenschaftlichen Fundierung des Operationalisierungsansatzes, der Vernachlässigung der Integriertheit des Images von Produkt und Marke sowie der mangelnden empirischen Bestätigung (Hätty 1989, S. 170; Esch/Fuchs/Bräutigam 2001, S. 779 f.).

Das Modell von Meffert/Heinemann

Meffert und Heinemann adaptieren das Modell von Schweiger, indem sie die Operationalisierung der Konstrukte verhaltenswissenschaftlich fundieren und die Integriertheit des Images von Marke und Produkt zugrunde legen (Meffert/Heinemann 1990, S. 7 ff.). Sie strukturieren den Imageraum entsprechend der Einstellungstheorie nach zwei Dimensionen (denotativ und konnotativ), innerhalb derer sich die Images aus affektiven und kognitiven Komponenten aufbauen. Der Imagetransfer wird auch in diesem Modell durch die wahrgenommene Ähnlichkeit zwischen Ursprungsmarke und Transferprodukt erklärt, die sich aufbauend auf bestehenden Distanzmodellen (Trommsdorff 1975) als Distanzmaß zwischen einem bestehenden Produkt-Markenimage und einem hypothetischen Expansionsprodukt folgendermaßen ermitteln lässt:

Abbildung 5: Imagetransfermodell von Meffert/Heinemann

$$IT_{ijN} = \sum_{K=1}^{n} I_{ijkA} - H_{ijkN}$$

IT_{ijN} = Imagetransfertauglichkeit des neuen Produktes N in Bezug auf das positive Image der Marke j, ermittelt beim Käufer i.

Je kleiner IT, desto besser die Imagetransfertauglichkeit, desto größer das transferierbare Volumen an Imagebestandteilen.

I_{ijkA} = Als Eindrucksideal ermittelte, positive Einstellung des Käufers i in Bezug auf die Marke j beim einstellungsrelevanten Merkmal k des bisherigen Produktes A.

H_{ijkN} = Die von demselben Konsumenten i in Bezug auf das Merkmal k eingeschätzte Ausprägung beim hypothetischen neuen Produkt N gleichen Markennamens j.

GABLER GRAFIK

Quelle: Meffert/Heinemann 1990, S. 8

Die Ähnlichkeit beziehungsweise Affinität lassen sich danach als Summe der Differenzbeträge zwischen den wahrgenommenen Ausprägungen der einstellungsrelevanten Merkmale von Muttermarke und hypothetischem Transferprodukt ermitteln. Hervorzuheben ist die Möglichkeit, durch das Modell die Transfertauglichkeit getrennt nach denotativen und konnotativen Merkmalen zu erheben. So lassen sich Hinweise auf kognitive

(Vorstellungsbeeinflussung) und emotionale Beeinflussungsmöglichkeiten (Präferenzbeeinflussung) zur Erhöhung des Imagetransferpotenzials ableiten (Meffert/Heinemann 1990, S. 8).

Ungeachtet der theoretischen Modellfundierung liegen auch zu diesem Modell bisher keine empirischen Überprüfungen beziehungsweise Anwendungen mit einer validen Erfassung der beteiligten Variablen vor. Auch bleiben Rückübertragungen von Imagebestandteilen auf die Ursprungsmarke unberücksichtigt. Ein weiterer Kritikpunkt ist, dass offensichtlich alle im Modell berücksichtigten Eigenschaften der Marke in die Beurteilung der Ähnlichkeit einfließen und eine geringe Distanz zwischen Ursprungsmarke und Transferprodukt aufweisen müssen. Es ist jedoch in den letzten Jahren gezeigt worden, dass einzelne markenspezifische Assoziationen einen besonders großen Einfluss auf das Transferpotenzial haben und sogar den Effekt der globalen Ähnlichkeit dominieren können (Murphy/Medin 1985; Broniarczyk/Alba 1994, S. 215). Zudem wird mit dem Modell nur die durch die Ähnlichkeit von Marke und hypothetischem Expansionsprodukt bestimmte, wahrscheinlich transferierbare Menge an Imagebestandteilen ermittelt. Dies sagt aber noch nichts darüber aus, ob und in welchem Ausmaß die Imagebestandteile der Ursprungsmarke im neuen Kontext überhaupt vorteilhaft beurteilt werden. Angestrebt werden muss letztendlich nur der Transfer positiver Bestandteile des Images der Ursprungsmarke, denn nur diese können die positive Verhaltensrelevanz des Erweiterungsproduktes erhöhen. Zur Bestimmung der wahrgenommenen Vorteilhaftigkeit der Erweiterung reicht die reine Affinitätsmessung also noch nicht aus. Ungeachtet der Kritikpunkte liefert das Modell jedoch wertvolle Hinweise zur Operationalisierung der globalen Ähnlichkeit als einem zentralen Bestimmungsfaktor der Beurteilung von Markenausdehnungen.

2.32 Gedächtnispsychologische Ansätze

Zur theoretischen Fundierung der Ableitung zentraler Bestimmungsgrößen der nachfrageseitigen Wahrnehmung und Beurteilung von Markenerweiterungen soll der schema- und kategorisierungstheoretische Ansatz kurz dargestellt werden (vgl. zu den Kategorisierungstheorien allgemein: Barsalou 1983; Murphy/Medin 1985; in Zusammenhang mit der Markenausdehnung vgl. Sujan/Bettman 1989; Aaker/Keller 1990; Boush/Loken 1991; Bridges 1992). Gemäß diesem Ansatz wird das Markenimage im Gedächtnis durch mentale Schemata beziehungsweise mentale Kategorien repräsentiert. Schemata können als große, komplexe Wissenseinheiten verstanden werden, die typische Eigenschaften und feste, standardisierte Vorstellungen von bestimmten Objekten, Personen oder Ereignissen umfassen (Esch/Wicke 2001, S. 47). Sie dienen dazu, Lernprozesse durch Denkschablonen zu vereinfachen. Stimmen etwa eingehende Informationen über ein Objekt mit dem Konzept eines bestehenden Schemas überein, so kann das Objekt diesem Schema zugeordnet und somit „schematisch“ bearbeitet werden. Diese Funktion wird auch als Kategorisierungsfunktion bezeichnet (Boush/Loken 1991, S. 18).

Genau auf diese Funktion beziehen sich zahlreiche Theorien zur Erklärung der Informationsverarbeitung bei Imagetransfers. Wenn neue Objekte – in diesem Fall Erweiterungsprodukte – wahrgenommen beziehungsweise bewertet werden, können aus schematheoretischer Sicht folgende Effekte auftreten: Ist das Erweiterungsprodukt einem bestehenden Markenschema sehr ähnlich und nicht mit inkongruenten Informationen verbunden, so kann das Objekt „problemlos" dieser bestehenden mentalen Kategorie zugeordnet werden, ohne das bestehende Markenschema signifikant zu verändern (Gürhahn-Canli/Maheswaran 1998, S. 466). So werden die Attribute des bestehenden Images auch mit dem neuen Produkt assoziiert – das Erweiterungsprodukt „erbt" die Assoziationen und damit das Image der bestehenden Marke (Boush/Loken 1991, S. 18).

Ist das Erweiterungsprodukt dagegen sehr atypisch und hat keine konzeptionellen Gemeinsamkeiten mit einer bestehenden Kategorie, wird ein solcher Imagetransfer nicht gelingen und für das Erweiterungsprodukt bildet sich ein neues, eigenständiges Image. Mit dem neuen Produkt werden dann bestimmte Merkmale und Nutzenvorstellungen assoziiert, die letztlich zu einem neuen Schema führen. Dieser Verarbeitungsprozess, der auf der Wahrnehmung der einzelnen Marken- und Produktmerkmale basiert, wird auch als stückweiser Prozess oder als Piecemeal Processing bezeichnet (Fiske 1982).

Die beschriebenen Arten kognitiver Verarbeitung dürfen allerdings nicht als sich gegenseitig ausschließende alternative Prozesse verstanden werden. Vielmehr können beide Prozesse gemeinsam auftreten und sich auch gegenseitig beeinflussen (Smith/Shoben/Rips 1974; Fiske/Pavelchak 1986). Die Kategorisierungstheorien können aufgrund ihrer großen Erklärungsrelevanz als Grundlage zur Ableitung der zentralen Bestimmungsfaktoren der nachfragerseitigen Beurteilung von Markenerweiterungen dienen. Im Folgenden sollen solche Bestimmungsfaktoren erläutert werden, die sowohl entsprechend den kategorisierungstheoretischen Ansätzen fundierbar sind, als auch empirisch überprüft und bestätigt wurden.

3. Bestimmungsfaktoren der nachfragerseitigen Beurteilung von Markenerweiterungen

3.1 Bestimmungsfaktoren der Beurteilung des Erweiterungsproduktes

Die Bestimmungsfaktoren der nachfragerseitigen Beurteilung von Markenerweiterungen haben sowohl einen Einfluss auf die Wahrnehmung des Erweiterungsproduktes als auch der Muttermarke. Zunächst sollen die Bestimmungsfaktoren und ihr Einfluss auf das Erweiterungsprodukt dargestellt werden, bevor der Effekt auf das Image und die Stärke der Ursprungsmarke dargestellt wird. In der bisherigen Forschung werden als zu erklärende beziehungsweise abhängige Variable hauptsächlich die Einstellung gegenüber dem Transfer (sowohl affektiv als auch konativ), die wahrgenommene Qualität und die Markenstärke untersucht.

3.11 Stärke und Struktur der Ursprungsmarke

Einer der stärksten und auch empirisch am häufigsten untersuchten Einflussfaktoren auf die Beurteilung des Erweiterungsproduktes durch die Nachfrager ist die Qualitätseinschätzung oder **Stärke der Ursprungsmarke** (Smith/Park 1992, S. 198 ff.). Der Transfer positiver Imagekomponenten setzt voraus, dass überhaupt positive Assoziationen in einem existierenden Markenschema vorhanden sind und dieses Schema stark genug ist, um durch das neue Objekt hervorgerufen zu werden. Erst dann kann die erwünschte schematische Bewertung des Erweiterungsproduktes erzielt werden. Mit zunehmender Markenstärke der Ursprungsmarke, das heißt steigender Bekanntheit sowie stärkeren, positiveren und einzigartigeren Assoziationen, steigt demnach die Wahrscheinlichkeit einer positiven Beurteilung des Erweiterungsproduktes. Dabei ist der Einfluss der Ursprungsmarke umso stärker, je größer der wahrgenommene Fit beziehungsweise die Ähnlichkeit zwischen Muttermarke und Erweiterungsprodukt ist (Hätty 1994, S. 572 ff.; Sattler/Völckner/Zatloukal 2002, S. 4 ff.; Caspar 2002, S. 225), denn je stärker die Verbindung zwischen neuem Produkt und bestehender Marke ist, desto stärker und umfangreicher ist die Übertragung der Assoziationen der Ursprungsmarke und damit ihr Einfluss auf das neue Produkt.

Zudem hat sich gezeigt, dass auch ein **breites Produktportfolio** unterhalb einer bestehenden Marke, bei hoher Qualität und geringer Qualitätsvarianz, einen positiven Einfluss auf die Erweiterungsbeurteilung hat. Eine Historie erfolgreicher Markenerweiterungen kann also zum Erfolg weiterer Markenerweiterungen beitragen (Dacin/Smith 1994; Court/Leiter/Loch 1999). Allerdings haben Untersuchungen gezeigt, dass der Einfluss dieses Faktors zur Erklärung des Erfolgs einer Markenerweiterung relativ gering ist (Völckner 2004, S. 75).

Neben der Markenstärke und der Charakteristika des Produktportfolios hat auch die **Art des Images** der Ursprungsmarke Einfluss auf den Erfolg des Imagetransfers. Unter der Annahme, dass Markenimages unterschiedlich stark von einzelnen Assoziationen geprägt werden, das heißt einige Assoziationen hervorstechen und das Markenimage dominant prägen, können unterschiedliche Imagetypen unterschieden werden. Nach der Salienz und Stärke von Imageassoziationen kann grob zwischen produktgeprägten Images (Dominanz physisch-technischer Merkmale) und nutzen- konnotativ geprägten Images unterschieden werden (Meffert/Heinemann 1990; Bridges 1992; Park/Milberg/Lawson 2001). Als salient werden hervorstechende imageprägende Assoziationen bezeichnet (Meffert/Heinemann 1990, S. 7; Bridges 1992, S. 3 ff.).

Je stärker nutzenorientiert/konnotativ die salienten Assoziationen der Ursprungsmarke sind, desto größer ist die Wahrscheinlichkeit, dass die Marke auch als zum neuen Objekt passend wahrgenommen werden kann und desto positiver fällt die Beurteilung des Transferproduktes aus (Rangaswamy/Burke/Oliva 1993, S. 65; Reddy/Holak/Bhat 1994, S. 246). Danach wären zum Beispiel von zwei hypothetischen Kosmetikmarken für Gesichtscreme, bei der eine durch sehr produktnahe Nutzenassoziationen wie: „zieht schnell ein, nicht fettend, riecht gut" geprägt wäre, die andere durch abstraktere Assoziationen wie: „pflegend, benutzen die großen Stars, entwickelt mit Hilfe der besten Forscher", die Tragfähigkeit beziehungsweise das Potenzial zur Ausdehnung der zweiten Marke entsprechend der beschriebenen Forschungsergebnisse als höher einzuschätzen.

3.12 Charakteristika der Transferkategorie

Die Charakteristika des Transferproduktes beziehungsweise der Erweiterungskategorie können ebenfalls einen Einfluss auf die Beurteilung der Markenerweiterungen durch die Nachfrager haben. Zu nennen ist hier unter anderem die von den leistungsspezifischen Besonderheiten des Transferproduktes abhängende **Art der Leistungsbeurteilung**. Im Allgemeinen wird zwischen Such-, Erfahrungs- und Vertrauensgütern unterschieden. Kann der Konsument mittels sensorisch wahrnehmbarer Attribute die Qualität der Leistung abschätzen, wird von einem Suchgut gesprochen. Ist eine beziehungsweise Qualitätsbeurteilung ausschließlich über den Gebrauch möglich, handelt es sich um Erfahrungsgüter. Im Extremfall ist selbst durch den Gebrauch die Qualität der Leistung durch den Konsumenten nicht bestimmbar, und es wird von Vertrauensgütern (zum Beispiel bei Beratung, medizinischer Versorgung, Informationsdienstleistungen etc.) gesprochen. Es hat sich gezeigt, dass Erfahrungs- und Vertrauensgüter im Wesentlichen über weiche Imagefaktoren im Gegensatz zu „harten" Fakten beworben werden können und dass für den Konsumenten gerade bei Erfahrungsgütern und Vertrauensgütern glaubwürdige Markenidentitäten aufgrund mangelnder objektiver Kriterien von entscheidender Bedeutung für das Kaufverhalten sind (Smith/Park 1992, S. 300). Daher ist davon auszugehen, dass die allgemeine Relevanz einer bereits etablierten Marke mit hohem Vertrauenspotenzial in diesen Produktkategorien besonders hoch ist. Denn wenn ein Unternehmen eine bereits bestehende Marke als Faustpfand einsetzt, kann die Markierung als besonders guter Qualitätsindikator verstanden werden, da das Unternehmen auch die bereits aufgebaute Reputation in den bestehenden Produktkategorien der Ursprungsmarke riskiert.

Mit einer ähnlichen Begründung werden auch der Einfluss des **Kenntnisstandes der Konsumenten** in der neuen Produktkategorie und der Einfluss der **wahrgenommenen Schwierigkeit der Herstellung** von Produkten als Bestimmungsfaktor genannt. Je weniger die Nachfrager die Produkte beurteilen können und je schwieriger die Herstellung eines Produktes scheint, desto stärker vertrauen die Nachfrager den etablierten Marken auch in der neuen Produktkategorie (Aaker/Keller 1990, S. 30; Smith/Park 1992, S. 301; Zatloukal 2002, S. 54 f.). Die theoretische Begründung ist in diesem Fall allerdings nicht so schlüssig, die empirischen Überprüfungen dieser Bestimmungsfaktoren demzufolge bisher nicht eindeutig (Zatloukal 2002, S. 47 f.).

3.13 Beziehung zwischen Ursprungsmarke und Transferprodukt

Von besonderer Relevanz für den Erfolg eines Markentransfers ist der wahrgenommene **Fit zwischen Muttermarke und Transferprodukt** (Zatloukal 2002; Caspar 2002; Völckner 2003). Extensive Untersuchungen zu diesem Erfolgsfaktor haben gezeigt, dass der Fit zwischen Muttermarke und Transferprodukt neben der Marketingunterstützung für das Transferprodukt den bedeutendsten Einflussfaktor für den Erfolg einer Markenerweiterung darstellt (Völckner 2003). Entsprechend der Ausführungen zur Kategorisierungstheorie können Imagebestandteile nur transferiert werden, wenn zwischen der Ausgangsmarke und dem Erweiterungsprodukt ein glaubwürdiger Zusammenhang, das heißt konzeptkonsistente Gemeinsamkeiten bestehen. Sonst ist keine Verknüpfung des Erweiterungsproduktes mit beziehungsweise keine Einordnung in das bestehende Markenschema möglich. Zudem kann die Tatsache, dass Produkte mit demselben Markennamen keine erkennbaren Ähnlichkeiten aufweisen, zu Irritationen und negativen Assoziationen oder Bewertungen führen.

Der wahrgenommene Fit kann zum einen entsprechend dem Modell von Meffert/Heinemann durch die umfassende Ähnlichkeit von Attributen und Assoziationen erklärt werden. Zum anderen kann die wahrgenommene Ähnlichkeit aber auch auf einige wenige saliente und besonders relevante Assoziationen zurückzuführen sein. Das heißt, es kann schon ausreichen, wenn sich Ursprungsmarke und Transferprodukt nur entlang weniger, das Marken- und Produktkonzept definierender Eigenschaften oder Assoziationen ähneln (Murphy/Medin 1985). Diese ähnlichkeitskonstituierenden, gemeinsamen Attribute beziehungsweise Assoziationen werden auch als **Transferklammer** bezeichnet. So kann beispielsweise eine relevante symbolische Nutzenassoziation, wie soziales Prestige, als Transferklammer ausreichen, um einen Imagetransfer bei einer Markenausdehnung in eine in Bezug auf die physischen Produktattribute vollkommen unähnliche Produktkategorie zu ermöglichen. Denn im Hinblick auf die Erreichung des persönlichen Ziels der sozialen Anerkennung können beide Produkte in dieselbe mentale Kategorie eingeordnet werden. In diesem Fall kann von einer so genannten Konzeptkonsistenz gesprochen werden (Murphy/Medin 1985).

Welche Assoziationen beziehungsweise Attribute der Ursprungsmarke als Transferklammer herangezogen werden sollten, richtet sich neben der Vorteilhaftigkeit und Stärke der Assoziation der Ursprungsmarke nach der **Relevanz der Assoziation** für das neue Angebot beziehungsweise die neue Produktkategorie (Nakamoto/McInnis/Jung 1993; Broniarczyk/Alba 1994; Völckner 2003). Es reicht also nicht aus, dass sich Ursprungsmarke und Transferprodukt in irgendeiner Dimension ähnlich sind, sondern diese Dimension muss auch im Kontext der neuen Produktkategorie relevant sein, um positiv wahrgenommen zu werden. Ansonsten können die transferierten Imageassoziationen für das neue Produkt keine unterstützende Wirkung entfalten und es droht sogar eine situationsspezifisch negative Bewertung. Neben der Relevanz ist gemäß dem allgemeinen Positionierungsansatz zudem die **Einzigartigkeit** der Assoziationen in der neuen Produktkategorie anzustreben, damit eine Differenzierung vom Wettbewerber in der neuen Produktkategorie möglich ist (Meffert 1992a, S. 131; Caspar 2002, S. 220 ff.).

3.14 Kommunikationspolitik

Hat sich das Marketingmanagement für eine Markenerweiterung entschieden, kann durch die **Kommunikationspolitik** aktiv Einfluss auf die Wahrnehmung der Erweiterung genommen werden.

So kann versucht werden, die Transferklammer beziehungsweise die konzeptionellen Gemeinsamkeiten zwischen Ursprungsmarke und Transferprodukt in der Kommunikationspolitik herauszustellen. Neben der Betonung der Gemeinsamkeiten besteht die Möglichkeit, die Relevanz der Assoziationen deutlich zu machen beziehungsweise zu stärken, um die Erweiterung zu unterstützen. Die Kommunikationspolitik kann so den wahrgenommenen Fit entscheidend beeinflussen, besonders wenn Marke und Erweiterungsprodukt gemeinsame, physische Eigenschaften haben, das Markenimage oder -schema jedoch eher über intangible und extrinsische Kriterien bestimmt wird (Bridges 1992). Die kommunikative Unterstützung der Relevanz und Salienz dieser extrinsischen Attribute kann die ansonsten eher physische Transferklammer in diesem Fall noch ergänzen und stärken.

3.2 Bestimmungsfaktoren des Rücktransfers auf die Ursprungsmarke

Wie bereits geschildert, sind neben der positiven Beurteilung der Markenerweiterung auch die Stärke oder der Wert der bestehenden Ursprungsmarke als Zielgröße relevant. Der Wert beziehungsweise **die Stärke der Ursprungsmarke** sollten im Rahmen der Ausdehnung mindestens erhalten bleiben, bestenfalls noch erhöht werden. Eine Gefährdung des Wertes der Ursprungsmarke ist dagegen zu verhindern. Die Bestimmungsfaktoren für die Beurteilung der Ursprungsmarke beziehungsweise den Rücktransfer von Images entsprechen denen des Transfers von Assoziationen auf das Transferprodukt. So wird der Transfer von Imageassoziationen zurück auf die Ursprungsmarke von der Markenstärke und Struktur des Transferproduktes und dem Fit zwischen Transferprodukt und Ursprungsmarke beeinflusst. Je positiver, einzigartiger und stärker sich das **Image des Transferproduktes** in der neuen Produktkategorie etablieren kann, desto höher ist die Wahrscheinlichkeit positiver Rücktransfers. Auch hier gilt: je **ähnlicher die Konzepte** und je **relevanter** die neuen Assoziationen des Transferproduktes für die Muttermarke sind, desto stärker und positiver sind die zu erwartenden Effekte. Misslingt jedoch die Ausdehnung und wird der Transfer nicht akzeptiert beziehungsweise negativ beurteilt, so kann dies das Image der Muttermarke gefährden.

Selbst bei erfolgreichen Transfers kann eine übermäßige Erweiterung die Ursprungsmarke langfristig negativ beeinflussen. Wie bereits erläutert, kann die Markenstärke über einen hohen Fit zwischen Markenidentität und Markenimage sowie positive, einzigartige und starke Assoziationen erklärt werden. Die Stärke der Assoziationen äußert sich unter anderem darin, wie schnell und in welchen Situationen die Assoziationen hervorgerufen werden. Bei sehr breiter, eher inkonsistenter, aber nicht vollkommen inkongruenter Erweiterung kann eine Erweiterung des Markenschemas der Ursprungsmarke durch Zuordnung neuer Transferprodukte zwar unter Umständen ermöglicht werden. Da aber eine starke Transferklammer und eine gemeinsame Markenwelt der Erweiterung fehlen, kann dann eine schleichende Erosion des Images eintreten. Bei der Ergänzung und Verknüpfung der unterschiedlichen Schemata droht bei Dissonanzen beziehungsweise inkongruenten Assoziationen, dass bestehende Assoziationen ergänzt, in den Hintergrund gedrängt, eingeschränkt, aufgelöst oder unterdrückt werden (Loken/Roedder John 1993).

Wie beim Transfer positiver Komponenten hängen das Ausmaß der Übertragung und damit der Einfluss auf die Ursprungsmarke davon ab, wie stark die Schemata von Ursprungsmarke und Transferprodukt verknüpft werden. Ist das Ursprungsmarkenimage fest verankert und gibt es eine eindeutig unterschiedliche Positionierung des Transferproduktes, so scheint die Ursprungsmarke relativ gut geschützt zu sein. Je stärker jedoch die Beziehung zwischen den Konzepten und damit der Fit ist, desto größer ist auch die Gefährdung der Ursprungsmarke bei einem Misserfolg des Transferproduktes.

Im Allgemeinen wird davon ausgegangen, dass die Erweiterung der Marke Gucci auf über 14.000 Produkte sowie die Ausdehnung der Marke Cadillac zu einem zu hohen Koordinationsaufwand, unterschiedlichen Qualitätsniveaus und divergierenden Markenkonzepten der Produkte geführt haben. Dies hat bei beiden Marken einen signifikanten Verlust an Glaubwürdigkeit und Kompetenzanmutung verursacht (Aaker 1990, S. 53 f.; Meffert 2000, S. 869).

Obwohl die genannten Beispiele inkonsistenter Erweiterungen aus der Praxis den oben beschriebenen Zusammenhang anschaulich verdeutlichen, konnten diese Erkenntnisse in Experimenten bisher nur teilweise belegt werden (Loken/Roedder John 1993). Es ist dazu jedoch anzumerken, dass die Erosion eines bestehenden Images im Allgemeinen sehr lange dauert und damit experimentell nur schwer zu belegen ist. Insgesamt weisen die theoretischen und praktischen Erkenntnisse recht eindeutig darauf hin, dass die Gefahr der Erosion oder Verwässerung des Markenimages besteht und diese bei der Planung von Markenerweiterungen unbedingt zu berücksichtigen ist, denn zumindest langfristig kann das durch eine starke Markenidentität aufgebaute Vertrauenskapital durch inkonsistente Markenbilder und eine Erosion des Images aufs Spiel gesetzt werden.

4. Implikationen für das Management der Markenerweiterung

Bei der Entscheidung über eine potenzielle Markenerweiterung zur Unterstützung einer Produktinnovation oder Produktdifferenzierung spielen zahlreiche Aspekte eine Rolle. Wird die generelle ökonomische Vorteilhaftigkeit der Produkteinführung in einen neuen Markt vorausgesetzt, stellt sich vor dem Hintergrund der aufgezeigten markierungsspezifischen Chancen und Risiken die Frage, wie die Positionierung des neuen Produktes sowie die Ausgestaltung der marktstrategischen Instrumente im Falle einer Markenerweiterungsstrategie aussehen sollten.

4.1 Strategische Standortbestimmung

Zunächst müssen die **Stärke und Struktur des Images** der potenziell zu erweiternden Marke detailliert erhoben und im Vergleich zu Wettbewerbsmarken bewertet werden. Hierfür stehen zahlreiche unterschiedliche qualitative und quantitative Verfahren zur Verfügung. Wichtig ist jedoch hervorzuheben, dass gerade qualitative, indirekte Erhebungsverfahren – wie zum Beispiel die freie Assoziation oder projektive Verfahren – besonders gut geeignet sind, die interne Struktur der Images und die strukturprägenden, spezifischen Imagekomponenten zu erfassen (Keller 2001, S. 1064 f.). Wie bei der Erläuterung der Bestimmungsfaktoren ausgeführt, können der Strukturtyp des Images und spezifische Assoziationen entscheidenden Einfluss auf die Beurteilung des Markenerweiterung haben. Um die Auswertbarkeit und die Verlässlichkeit der Aussagen zu erhöhen, sollten Markenimage und Markenstärke zusätzlich, aber auch auf jeden Fall quantitativ und multiattributiv untersucht werden. Auch hierfür steht eine Vielzahl von Verfahren und Skalen zur Verfügung.

Neben einem soliden Verständnis der Ursprungsmarke und deren Hauptwettbewerbern ist im Anschluss die **potenzielle Erweiterungskategorie** zu untersuchen. Hierbei kommt es darauf an, Bedürfnisstrukturen, Motive, Einstellungen und Nutzungsgewohnheiten der Konsumenten in der potenziell neuen Kategorie zu ermitteln. Diese Informationen bilden gemeinsam mit zu erhebenden soziodemografischen Daten die adäquaten Kriterien zur **Segmentierung des Marktes** in homogene Zielgruppen.

Auf Basis dieser Informationen können nun Analysen zu den erläuterten zentralen Bestimmungsfaktoren durchgeführt werden. Hierbei gilt es vor allem herauszufinden, welche Attribute, Nutzen sowie globale Assoziationen der Muttermarke in der neuen Produktkategorie als relevant, vorteilhaft und einzigartig wahrgenommen werden können. Diese Analysen bilden die Grundlage für die Positionierungsentscheidung bezüglich des neuen Erweiterungsproduktes in der Produktkategorie. Besondere Aufmerksamkeit sollte dabei darauf gerichtet sein, dass sämtliche für die Untersuchung der oben genannten Bestimmungsfaktoren der Markenerweiterung relevanten Nutzenbedürfnisse, Nutzungsmotive sowie Einstellungen erfasst werden und zwar so, dass ein Bezug zu den Ausgestaltungsparametern des Marketingmixes hergestellt werden kann. So sollte etwa bei einer Untersuchung der Affinität von Ursprungsmarke und Transferprodukt deutlich werden, welche Produktattribute, Nutzendimensionen und globale Assoziationen eine wahrgenommene Ähnlichkeit begründen können, sodass dies bei der Positionierung und Ausgestaltung des Marketingmixes beachtet werden kann.

Stehen unterschiedliche potenzielle Produktkategorien zur Auswahl, können die Informationen über die Relevanz und Nutzenpotenziale der Ursprungsmarke in den Zielkategorien auch für eine erste qualitative Bewertung der Vorteilhaftigkeit unterschiedlicher Erweiterungskategorien verwendet werden.

4.2 Positionierung des Transferproduktes

Bei der Positionierung geht es generell darum, mit bestimmten Markeneigenschaften sowohl eine starke und vorteilhafte Stellung in der Psyche des Konsumenten **(Dominanz)** als auch eine Differenzierung gegenüber dem Wettbewerb zu erlangen **(Differenzierung)**. Die im Rahmen der Positionierung angestrebten Eigenschaften müssen dabei einen eindeutigen **Zielgruppenbezug** haben, **wahrnehmbar** und möglichst **dauerhaft gültig** sein (Meffert/Perrey 1998, S. 24 f.). Auf Basis der strategischen Standortbestimmung werden demnach die Eigenschaften des neuen Transferproduktes entlang der verschiedenen Nutzendimensionen so festgelegt, dass sie die Bedürfnisse der Zielgruppe möglichst gut treffen (Vorteilhaftigkeit) und eine Differenzierung vom Wettbewerber möglich ist (Einzigartigkeit).

Diese allgemeinen Anforderungen an die Positionierung von Marken sind jedoch auf Basis der Analysen zu den Bestimmungsfaktoren der Beurteilung der Markenerweiterung zu ergänzen. Die Positionierung ist dergestalt vorzunehmen, dass ein ausreichender Fit von Assoziationen des Transferproduktes und der Ursprungsmarke erzielt wird. Zudem ist anzustreben, dass sich das Images der **Ursprungsmarke** in den Kerneigenschaften des neuen Produktes spiegelt. Bestenfalls entsprechen für einen hohen Fit gerade die **imageprägenden, salienten Assoziationen** der Ursprungsmarke den relevanten, bedürfnisbefriedigenden Nutzenfunktionen des neuen Produktes. Zudem ist darauf zu achten, dass auch die neu ausgewählten beziehungsweise zusätzlichen Markeneigenschaften des Erweiterungsproduktes zu den bestehenden Markenassoziationen der Ursprungsmarke passen, um auf jeden Fall negative Rücktransfers zu vermeiden.

Für den Aufbau einer wettbewerbsfähigen Position des Erweiterungsproduktes bieten sich folgende zwei Möglichkeiten (Meffert 1992a, S. 133 ff.). Kann die wahrgenommene Markenkompetenz der Ursprungsmarke aufgrund ihres Imageprofils einen relevanten **funktionalen oder symbolischen Nutzenaspekt** des Erweiterungsproduktes unterstützen und ist dieser bisher von Wettbewerbern noch ungenügend bearbeitet worden, so bietet sich das Besetzen dieser **strategischen Nische** an. Alternativ besteht die Möglichkeit, das Transferangebot mit einer neuen Eigenschaftsdimension zu ergänzen, solange diese für das Kaufverhalten der Transferprodukt-Zielgruppe relevant ist und keine negativen Assoziationen im Verwendungskontext der Ursprungsmarke erzeugt.

4.3 Marktstrategische Instrumenteausgestaltung

Auf Basis der im Rahmen der Positionierung festgelegten einzigartigen und vorteilhaften Eigenschaften des Erweiterungsproduktes sowie der Attribute, die als Transferklammer die Übertragung positiver Imagekomponenten auf das neue Produkt sicherstellen sollen, werden im Rahmen der marktstrategischen Instrumenteausgestaltung alle weiteren Marketing-Mix-Instrumente abgestimmt. Hierbei gilt es, im Rahmen der Produkt-, Preis-, Kommunikations- und Distributionspolitik immer auch auf die Koordination mit der

Ausgestaltung der Ursprungsmarke zu achten, um die Etablierung einer relevanten, konsistenten Transferklammer zu sichern, das Potenzial zur Übertragung von Imagekomponenten auszuschöpfen und negative Rücktransfers zu verhindern. Insgesamt sollte so eine widerspruchsfreie Umsetzung des Markenbildes von Ursprungsmarke und Transferprodukt sowie der verbindenden Transferklammer gewährleistet werden, um die Glaubwürdigkeit der Marke langfristig zu schützen.

5. Fazit

Vor dem Hintergrund des wettbewerbsinduzierten Absatz- und Preisdrucks in zunehmend fragmentierten und oftmals stagnierenden Märkten stehen viele Unternehmen vor der Herausforderung, ihr Produktangebot den ausdifferenzierenden Kundenwünschen auf wirtschaftliche Art und Weise anzupassen und zu erweitern. Die Markenerweiterung stellt dabei eine viel versprechende Strategie dar.

Um das Potenzial der Ursprungsmarke optimal auszunutzen und sie gleichzeitig vor negativen Rücktransfers zu schützen, bedarf es allerdings einer sorgfältigen Planung, welche auf der genauen Kenntnis der Bestimmungsfaktoren der nachfragerseitigen Transferbeurteilung aufbaut. Auf Basis einer robusten und umfassenden Analyse von Ursprungsmarke und möglicher Transferkategorie gilt es, folgende Faktoren bei der Strategie sicherzustellen:

- Die Ursprungsmarke sollte **stark** genug sein, den Transfer tragen beziehungsweise unterstützen zu können, das heißt, sie sollte ausreichend bekannt sein und durch starke, vorteilhafte und einzigartige Vorstellungsbilder geprägt sein.
- Bei der **Positionierung und Ausgestaltung des Erweiterungs- beziehungsweise Transferproduktes** sollte sichergestellt werden, dass die Eigenschaften und Nutzenversprechen des Transferproduktes die imageprägenden Assoziationen der Muttermarke widerspiegeln und so ein ausreichender **Fit** und **Konzeptkonsistenz** zwischen Ursprungsmarke und Transferprodukt gewährleistet ist, damit in der Summe eine **starke** und **vorteilhafte** sowie **differenzierende Verankerung** des neuen Produktes im Wahrnehmungsraum der Zielgruppe durch die Ursprungsmarke unterstützt werden kann.
- Das Transferprodukt sollte in der neuen Transferproduktkategorie nur mit solchen neuen, das Markenschema erweiternden Eigenschaftsdimensionen in Verbindung gebracht werden, die **konsistent** mit der bestehenden **Markenidentität der Ursprungsmarke** sind.
- Nutzenversprechen und Markenassoziationen sollten **relevant** und **einzigartig** im Kontext der Transferproduktkategorie sein.

- Die Markenerweiterung sollte mit einer ausreichenden Ressourcenunterstützung der Produkteinführung durchgeführt werden. Dies erhöht zum einen die Handelsakzeptanz der Markenerweiterung signifikant, als auch die Akzeptanzwahrscheinlichkeit seitens der Konsumenten.

Diese Anforderungen sind über eine Koordination und Kontrolle sämtlicher Marketingmixausgestaltungen über alle Produkte der Marke hinweg sicherzustellen. Diese Koordination und Kontrolle muss auf Grundlage der aus der Markenidentität abgeleiteten Vorgabe erfolgen, um die Glaubwürdigkeit und Stärke der Marke langfristig zu sichern und eine Erosion der Identität und des Images zu verhindern.

Literatur

Aaker, D. A. (1990), Brand Extensions: The Good, the Bad and the Ugly, in: Sloan Management Review, Vol. 31, No. 4, Summer, S. 47–56.

Aaker, D. A. (2004), Brand Portfolio Strategy, New York.

Aaker, D. A., Keller, K. L. (1990), Consumer Evaluations of Brand Extensions, in: Journal of Marketing, Vol. 54, No. 1, January, S. 27–41.

Barsalou, L. (1983), Ad Hoc Categories, in: Memory and Cognition, Vol. 11, No. 3, S. 211–227.

Becker, J. (2002), Marketing-Konzeption – Grundlagen des strategischen Marketing-Managements, 7. Aufl., München.

Berekoven, L., Eckert, W., Ellenrieder, P. (2004), Marktforschung – Methodische Grundlagen und praktische Anwendung, 10. Aufl., Wiesbaden.

Boush, D. M., Loken, B. (1991), A Process-Tracing Study of Brand Extension Evaluation, in: Journal of Marketing Research, Vol. XXVII, No. 1, February, S. 16–28.

Bridges, S. (1992), A Schema Unification Model of Brand Extension, in: Marketing Science Institute, Report No. 92–123.

Broniarczyk, S. M., Alba, J. W. (1994), The Importance of the Brand in Brand Extensions, in: Journal of Marketing Research, Vol. XXXI, No. 2, May, S. 214–228.

Burmann, Ch., Blinda, L., Nitschke, A. (2003), Konzeptionelle Grundlagen des identitätsbasierten Markenmanagements, in: Burmann, Ch. (Hrsg.), Arbeitspapier Nr. 1 des Lehrstuhls für innovatives Markenmanagement (LiM), Universität Bremen, Bremen.

Caspar, M. (2002), Cross-Channel-Medienmarken, Frankfurt/M.

Court, D. C., Leiter, M. C., Loch, M. A. (1999), Brand Leverage, in: McKinsey Quarterly, No. 2, S. 100–110.

Cravens, D. W., Piercy, N. F., Prentice, A. (2000), Developing market-driven product strategies, in: Journal of Product & Brand Management, Vol. 9, No. 6, S. 369–388.

Dacin, P. A., Smith, D. C. (1994), The Effect of Brand Portfolio Characteristics on Consumer Evaluations of Brand Extensions, in: Journal of Marketing Research, Vol. XXXI, No. 2, May, S. 229–242.

Deutsches Patent- und Markenamt (Hrsg.) (2004), DPMA Jahresbericht 2003, München.

Ernst & Young, Nielsen (1999), New Product Introduction: Successful Innovation/Failure: A Fragile Boundary, o. O.

Esch, F.-R. (2004), Strategie und Technik der Markenführung, 2. Aufl., München.

Esch, F.-R., Fuchs, M., Bräutigam, S. (2001), Konzeption und Umsetzung von Markenerweiterungen, in: Esch, F.-R. (Hrsg.), Moderne Markenführung: Grundlagen – Innovative Ansätze – Praktische Umsetzungen, 3. Aufl., Wiesbaden, S. 755–791.

Esch, F.-R., Wicke, A. (2001), Herausforderungen und Aufgaben des Markenmanagements, in: Esch, F.-R. (Hrsg.), Moderne Markenführung: Grundlagen – Innovative Ansätze – Praktische Umsetzungen, 3. Aufl., Wiesbaden, S. 3–55.

Fiske, S. T. (1982), Schema-Triggered Affect: Applications to Social Perception, in: Clark, M. S., Fiske, S. T. (Hrsg.), Affect and Cognition: the 17th Annual Carnegie Symposium on Cognition, Hillsdale, N.J., S. 171–190.

Fiske, S. T., Pavelchak, M. A. (1986), Category-Based Versus Piecemeal-Based Affective Responses: Developments in Schema-Triggered Affect, in: Sorrentino, R. W., Higgins, T. E. (Hrsg.), Handbook of Motivation and Cognition: Foundation of Social Behavior, New York, S. 167–203.

Grunert, K. G. (1982), Informationsverarbeitungsprozesse bei der Kaufentscheidung: ein gedächtnispsychologischer Ansatz, Frankfurt/M.

Günther, S. (2002), Wahrnehmung und Beurteilung von Markentransfers – Erfolgsfaktoren für Transferprodukte und Markenimage, Wiesbaden.

Hätty, H. (1989), Der Markentransfer, Heidelberg.

Hätty, H. (1994), Markentransferstrategien, in: Bruhn, M. (Hrsg.), Handbuch Markenartikel, Bd. 1, Stuttgart, S. 561–581.

Keller, K. L. (1993), Conceptualizing, Measuring, and Managing Customer-Based Brand Equity, in: Journal of Marketing, Vol. 57, No. 1, January, S. 1–22.

Keller, K. L. (2001), Kundenorientierte Messung des Markenwerts, in: Esch, F.-R. (Hrsg.), Moderne Markenführung: Grundlagen – Innovative Ansätze – Praktische Umsetzungen, 3. Aufl., Wiesbaden, S. 1059–1079.

Keller, K. L. (2003), Strategic brand banagement – building, measuring and managing brand equity, Upper Saddle River, N. J.

Kroeber-Riel, W., Weinberg, P. (2003), Konsumentenverhalten, 8. Aufl., München.

Loken, B., Roedder John, D. (1993), Diluting Brand Beliefs: When Do Brand Extensions Have a Negative Impact?, in: Journal of Marketing, Vol. 57, No. 3, July, S. 71–81.

Meffert, H. (1992a), Strategien zur Profilierung von Marken, in: Dichtl, E., Eggers, W. (Hrsg.), Marke und Markenartikel, München, S. 129–156.

Meffert, H. (1992b), Marketingforschung und Käuferverhalten, 2. Aufl., Wiesbaden.

Meffert, H. (1994), Entscheidungsorientierter Ansatz der Markenpolitik, in: Bruhn, M. (Hrsg.), Handbuch Markenartikel, Bd. 1, Stuttgart, S. 173–197.

Meffert, H. (1994), Marketing-Management – Analysen, Strategie, Implementierung, Wiesbaden.

Meffert, H. (2000), Marketing – Grundlagen marktorientierter Unternehmensführung, 9. Aufl. Wiesbaden.

Meffert, H., Heinemann, G. (1990), Operationalisierung des Imagetransfers, in: Marketing ZFP, Nr. 1, 1. Quartal, S. 5–10.

Meffert, H., Perrey, J. (1998), Mehrmarkenstrategien – Ein Beitrag zum Management von Markenportfolios, Meffert, H., Wagner, H., Backhaus, K. (Hrsg.), Arbeitspapier Nr. 121 der Wissenschaftlichen Gesellschaft für Marketing und Unternehmensführung e.V., Münster.

Murphy, G. L., Medin, D. L. (1985), The Role of Theories in Conceptual Coherence, in: Psychological Review, Vol. 92, No. 3, July, S. 289–316.

Nakamoto, K., McInnis, D. J., Jung, H.-S. (1993), Advertising Claims and Evidence as Bases for Brand Equity and Consumer Evaluations of Brand Extensions, in: Aaker, D. A., Biel, A. L. (Hrsg.), Brand Equity and Advertising: Advertising's Role in Building Strong Brands, Hillsdale, N. J., S. 218–297.

Park, C. W., Milberg, S., Lawson, R. (2001), Beurteilung von Markenerweiterungen, in: Esch, F.-R. (Hrsg.), Moderne Markenführung, 3. Aufl., Wiesbaden, S. 825–842.

Rangaswamy, A., Burke, R. R., Oliva, T. A. (1993), Brand Equity and the Extendibility of Brand Names, in: International Journal of Research in Marketing, Vol. 10, No. 1, S. 61–75.

Reddy, S. K., Holak, S. L., Bhat, S. (1994), To extend or not to extend: Success determinants of line extensions, in: Journal of Marketing Research, Vol. XXXI, No. 2, May, S. 243–262.

Reich, I. (2003), Nahrungsmittel-Multis bieten derzeit kaum Kurschancen, in: Handelsblatt vom 13.10.2003, S. 33.

Ries, A., Trout, J. (1986), Positioning: The battle for your mind, 2. Aufl., New York.

Sattler, H. (1997), Monetäre Bewertung von Markenstrategien für neue Produkte, Stuttgart.

Sattler, H. (1998), Beurteilung der Erfolgschancen von Markentransfers, in: Zeitschrift für Betriebswirtschaft (ZfB), 68. Jg., Nr. 5, S. 475–495.

Sattler, H. (1999), Entscheidung: Neue Marke oder Markentransfer, in: Markenartikel, Nr. 1, S. 14–18.

Sattler, H. (2003), Markentransferstrategien, Research Papers on Marketing and Retailing, No. 12, Hamburg.

Sattler, H., Völckner, F., Zatloukal, G. (2002), Erfolgsfaktoren von Markentransfers, Research Papers on Marketing and Retailing, No. 2, Hamburg.

Schweiger, G. (1982), Imagetransfer, in: Marketing Journal, Nr. 4, S. 321–323.

Simon, C. J., Sullivan, M. W. (1993), The measurement and determinants of brand equity: A financial approach, in: Marketing Science, Vol. 12, No. 1, Winter, S. 28–52.

Smith, D. C., Park, C. W. (1992), The Effects of Brand Extension on Market Share and Advertising Efficiency, in: Journal of Marketing Research, Vol. XXIX, No. 3, August, S. 296–313.

Smith, E. E., Shoben, E. J., Rips, L. J. (1974), Structure and Process in Semantic Memory: A Featural Model for Semantic Decisions, in: Psychological Review, Vol. 83, No. 3, S. 214–241.

Sujan, M., Bettman, J. R. (1989), The effects of brand positioning strategies on consumer's brand and category perceptions: some insights from schema research, in: Journal of Marketing Research, Vol. XXVI, No. 4, November, S. 454–467.

Swaminathan, V., Fox, R. J., Reddy, S. K. (2001), The Impact of Brand Extension Introduction on Choice, in: Journal of Marketing, Vol. 65, No. 4, October, S. 1–15

Trommsdorff, V. (1975), Die Messung von Produktimages für das Marketing, Köln [u. a.].

Trommsdorff, V. (1992), Wettbewerbsorientierte Image-Positionierung, in: Markenartikel, Nr. 10, S. 458–463.

Trommsdorff, V. (2003), Konsumentenverhalten, 5. Aufl., Stuttgart.

Völckner, F. (2003), Neuprodukterfolg bei kurzlebigen Konsumgütern – Eine empirische Analyse der Erfolgsfaktoren von Markentransfers, Wiesbaden.

Völckner, F. (2004), Fünf Faktoren entscheiden über den Erfolg von Markentransfers, in: Absatzwirtschaft, September, S. 74–79.

Zatloukal, G. (2002), Erfolgsfaktoren von Markentransfers, Wiesbaden.

KAPITEL

3 Controlling des Markenmanagements

Identitätsorientiertes Markencontrolling – Grundlagen und konzeptionelle Ausgestaltung 273
Heribert Meffert und Martin Koers

Markenkannibalisierung in Markenportfolios 297
Heribert Meffert und Martin Koers

Bewertung und Bilanzierung von Marken – Bestandsaufnahme und kritische Würdigung 319
Christoph Burmann, Marcel Kranz und Jan-Philipp Weers

Abnutzbarkeit und Nutzungsdauer von Marken 347
Heribert Meffert und Christoph Burmann

Identitätsorientiertes Markencontrolling – Grundlagen und konzeptionelle Ausgestaltung

Heribert Meffert und Martin Koers

1.	**Stellenwert des Markencontrolling**	**274**
2.	**Theoretische Grundlagen des Markencontrolling**	**275**
2.1	Begriffliche Abgrenzung des Markencontrolling	275
2.2	Ziele und Aufgaben des Markencontrolling	276
3.	**Anforderungen und Zielgrößen des Markencontrolling**	**278**
3.1	Anforderungen an das Markencontrolling	278
3.2	Zielgrößen des Markencontrolling	279
4.	**Konzeptionelle Ausgestaltung eines identitätsorientierten Markencontrolling auf Basis der Balanced Scorecard**	**282**
4.1	Das Konzept der Balanced Scorecard	282
4.2	Grundstruktur einer Markenscorecard	284
4.3	Identifikation von Steuerungsgrößen für eine Markenscorecard	285
4.31	Berücksichtigung markenbezogener Anspruchsgruppen bei der Ermittlung von Steuerungsgrößen	286
4.32	Bestimmung von Steuerungsgrößen durch Operationalisierung des Markenleitbildes	289
4.33	Steuerungsgrößen in Markenportfolios	291
5.	**Fazit**	**294**

1. Stellenwert des Markencontrolling

Für eine erfolgreiche Führung von Marken im Sinne der Unternehmensoberziele ist eine rein intuitive oder gar „spirituelle Markenführung" im Sinne Gerkens (Gerken 1994) nicht ausreichend. Marken stellen keinen Selbstzweck dar, sondern dienen der Realisierung unternehmerischer Oberziele. Auch erfordert der Aufbau einer starken Markenidentität erhebliche Investitionen in die Marke, sodass eine verstärkte „Rationalität" im Rahmen der Markenführung – gerade vor dem Hintergrund vergangener Marken-Fehlinvestitionen – unumgänglich ist.

So haben beispielsweise in der jüngsten Vergangenheit auch Energieversorger das Thema Marke für sich entdeckt und mehrere Millionen Euro in Markenaufbaukampagnen investiert. Entsprechend erreichen Commodity-Marken wie Yello oder E.ON mittlerweile Bekanntheitsgrade, die den klassischen Konsumgütern in keiner Weise nachstehen. Fraglich ist jedoch, ob sich der Aufwand jemals in ökonomischem Erfolg niederschlägt. So berichtete die Presse im März 2002, dass E.ON mit seiner „Mix-it, Baby" – Kampagne nur 1.100 Kunden zum Markenwechsel animieren konnte. Bei Werbeausgaben von ungefähr 22,5 Millionen Euro betragen die Akquisitionskosten somit 20.500 Euro pro Neukunde. Liefert dieser einen durchschnittlichen Jahresumsatz von geschätzt circa 600 Euro, dürften sich diese Ausgaben wohl kaum amortisieren.

Zur Sicherstellung der **Rationalität unternehmerischen Handelns** bedarf es somit leistungsfähiger Controllingsysteme auch im Rahmen der Markenführung, welche sowohl quantitative als auch qualitative Daten berücksichtigen und den Ergebnisbeitrag der Markenführung offen legen. Wiedmann weist in diesem Zusammenhang prägnant auf die Notwendigkeit eines auf die jeweilige Unternehmenssituation zugeschnittenen Mischungsverhältnisses zwischen „harter und weicher" Markenführung hin: *„Dort, wo etwa die Markenführung in praxi bereits stark mystizistische Züge trägt, muss Controlling mittels rationaler Planung, Steuerung und Kontrolle ein Stück weit zur ‚Entzauberung der magischen Markenwelt' beitragen. Dort, wo allein das Primat der ‚harten Fakten' regiert, ist für mehr Spiritualität und Emotionalität Sorge zu tragen."* (Wiedmann 1994, S. 1307; vgl. hierzu auch Meffert/Koers 2004).

Zwar wird auf die **Notwendigkeit von Controllingsystemen** im Rahmen der Markenführung sowohl in der wissenschaftlichen Literatur als auch in der Unternehmenspraxis immer wieder hingewiesen (Tomczak/Reinecke 1998; Franzen 1999; Kriegbaum 2001; Esch 2004). Bisherige Ansätze des Markencontrolling beschränken sich jedoch vielfach noch immer auf Insel- beziehungsweise Bereichslösungen wie etwa Konzepte zur Messung des Markenwertes, Verfahren der Markenwahrnehmungsanalyse oder Ansatzpunkte zur Markenloyalitätsbestimmung (siehe beispielhaft die verschiedenen Beiträge zur Markenkontrolle bei Esch 2001). Dabei steht häufig die reine „Messung" im Sinne einer „Markenkontrolle" im Fokus der Untersuchungen. Ein umfassendes Markencontrolling bedeutet jedoch nicht nur Markenmessung beziehungsweise -kontrolle. Vielmehr muss das Markencontrolling durch Berücksichtigung verschiedener Steuerungsgrößen der gesamthaften Markensteuerung dienen.

Vor diesem Hintergrund verfolgt der vorliegende Beitrag das Ziel, mithilfe der **Balanced Scorecard** ein Konzept des Markencontrolling zu skizzieren, welches eine umfassende Integration sowohl weicher als auch harter Faktoren der Unternehmensführung erlaubt. Dabei soll der Schwerpunkt nicht auf die Art und Weise der Generierung spezifischer Kennzahlen und Steuerungsgrößen gelegt werden, sondern vielmehr auf ihre sinnvolle Integration in ein Gesamtkonzept. Hierzu sollen zuvor sowohl die theoretischen Grundlagen als auch die allgemeinen Anforderungen und Zielgrößen des Markencontrolling eingehend beleuchtet werden.

2. Theoretische Grundlagen des Markencontrolling

2.1 Begriffliche Abgrenzung des Markencontrolling

Obwohl das Controlling mittlerweile zum festen Bestandteil der betriebswirtschaftlichen Praxis und damit zu einem wichtigen Erkenntnisobjekt der Betriebswirtschaftslehre geworden ist, liegt eine unumstrittene inhaltliche Festlegung des Begriffs nicht vor. Noch immer liefert das Schrifttum zum Controlling eine Fülle von kontroversen Beiträgen mit im Detail heterogenen terminologischen Interpretationen. Betrachtet man darüber hinaus die unterschiedlichen Definitionsansätze der Marke, so kann bei dem Versuch einer definitorischen Abgrenzung eines Markencontrolling zweifelsohne von einer doppelten Begriffsheterogenität gesprochen werden.

Trotz abweichender Begriffsauffassungen besteht in der Literatur Konsens darüber, dass Controlling weit mehr als buchhaltungsorientierte ex-post Kontrolle bedeutet, sondern sich vielmehr als anwendungsorientierter Zweig der Betriebswirtschaftslehre zukunfts- und aktionsorientiert mit Aufgaben der Informationsversorgung, Planung und Kontrolle sowie der Koordination befasst und – um eine klare Trennung zwischen Führung und Controlling zu gewährleisten – primär als **Führungsunterstützungsfunktion** in eine ganzheitliche Unternehmensführung eingebunden ist. Die existierenden definitorischen Ansätze unterscheiden sich letztlich darin, welcher Stellenwert den einzelnen Aufgaben im Rahmen des Controlling zukommt. Einen mittlerweile weit akzeptierten Raum nimmt das in den Arbeiten von Horváth zugrunde gelegte führungssystem- beziehungsweise koordinationsorientierte Grundverständnis ein, das auch von Küpper und Weber in unterschiedlichen Ausprägungen aufgegriffen wird (Küpper 2001; Horváth 2003; Weber 2004). Bei diesem Konzept wird das gesamte Aufgabenspektrum des Controlling unter die Metaebene der Koordination des Führungssystems gestellt. Bei dem älteren, vorrangig informationsorientierten Grundverständnis wird die Koordination hingegen als gleichrangig mit der Informationsversorgung, Planung und Kontrolle angesehen (Reichmann 1995). Einen weiteren Typus von frühen Definitionen stellt das Controlling auch als Teilbereich der Unternehmensführung heraus, welcher für die konsequente Zielausrichtung des Unternehmens Sorge zu tragen hat und als führungsphilosophiebezogener Ansatz interpretiert wird (Siegwart 1986).

Den folgenden Ausführungen wird ein primär **koordinationsorientiertes Verständnis des Controlling** zugrunde gelegt, wobei Koordination auch den Bereich der Informationsversorgung umfassen soll, da es sich hier letztlich um eine Abstimmung zwischen Management und dem Informationsversorgungssystem handelt. Durch Beschaffung und Aufbereitung von Führungsinformationen soll das Controlling das Entscheiden und Handeln in der Unternehmung ergebnisorientiert ausrichten. Dabei hat das Controlling das Informationsversorgungs- sowie Planungs- und Kontrollsystem sowohl zu gestalten (Systembildung beziehungsweise -gestaltung) als auch innerhalb des konzipierten Systemzusammenhangs laufend Abstimmungen vorzunehmen sowie Störungen zu beseitigen (Systemkopplung beziehungsweise Systemnutzung). Vor dem Hintergrund dieser Überlegungen wird das Controlling somit als ein führungsunterstützendes Konzept zur informationellen Sicherung ergebnisorientierter Planung, Steuerung und Kontrolle verbunden mit einer übergeordneten Koordinationsfunktion verstanden, dessen Aufgabenspektrum sowohl systemgestaltende als auch systemnutzende Aktivitäten umfasst (Meffert 2000, S. 1123 ff.). Anders ausgedrückt steht Controlling somit nach Weber für die Sicherstellung von Rationalität der Unternehmensführung (Weber/Schäffer 2001).

Die in der Praxis mit der Arbeitsteilung beziehungsweise Spezialisierung einhergehenden Organisationslösungen weisen unmittelbar auf die Sinnhaftigkeit beziehungsweise Notwendigkeit unternehmensbereichsbezogener **Controlling-Teilgebiete** hin. Die damit zusammenhängende Spezialisierung des Controlling führt zu speziellen Controllingansätzen und Ausprägungen mit jeweiliger Modifikation und Anpassung der „typischen" Controlling-Instrumente. Vor diesem Hintergrund lässt sich das Markencontrolling als spezielle Ausprägung des Controlling interpretieren, das die Informationsversorgung und Beratung aller mit der Markenführung befassten Stellen verbunden mit einer übergeordneten Koordinationsfunktion zur Unterstützung und Ergänzung der markenspezifischen Planungs-, Steuerungs- und Kontrollprozesse im Unternehmen umfasst.

2.2 Ziele und Aufgaben des Markencontrolling

Primäres Ziel des hier verwendeten Controllingbegriffs ist die Erreichung „optimaler Zustände" im Rahmen der Markenführung. Die umfassende Unterstützung im Hinblick auf eine Ergebnisoptimierung der Markenführung kann somit als Kardinalziel des Markencontrolling interpretiert werden. Aus diesem Oberziel lassen sich weitere Subziele ableiten:

- Sicherstellung der **Rationalität** sowie Erhaltung der **Reaktions- und Adaptionsfähigkeit** der Markenführung durch Versorgung mit markenrelevantem Wissen sowie
- Verbesserung der **Wirksamkeit der verfolgten Markenpolitik** durch Koordination und Ausrichtung aller markenbezogenen Aktivitäten auf die Ziele der Markenpolitik.

Aus den Zielen ergeben sich unmittelbar die Aufgaben des Markencontrolling. Dabei kann zwischen systemgestaltenden und systemnutzenden Aktivitäten differenziert werden. Die **systemgestaltende Funktion** umfasst primär die Sicherstellung einer ex-ante Koordination der Markenführung durch Schaffung geeigneter Rahmenbedingungen, die koordinierte Entscheidungen überhaupt erst ermöglichen. Dem Markencontrolling kommt hier die Aufgabe zu, an der Entwicklung und Implementierung von Informationssystemen, organisatorischen Richtlinien und Prozessstrukturen sowie Planungs- und Kontrollinstrumenten für die Markenführung mitzuwirken.

Zu den **systemnutzenden Funktionen** gehören die Unterstützung des Markenmanagements auf allen Ebenen der Planung, die regelmäßige Kontrolle der Umsetzung strategischer und operativer Pläne und die Sicherstellung der Informationsversorgung aller an der Markenführung Beteiligten innerhalb des durch die systemgestaltende Funktion geschaffenen Rahmens.

Während das Informationsmanagement die Infrastruktur aus IT-Sicht gestaltet, verantwortet das Markencontrolling eine betriebswirtschaftlich sinnvolle inhaltliche Gestaltung der Informationen und stellt diese den jeweiligen mit der Markenführung betrauten Stellen art-, zeit- und mengengerecht zur Verfügung. In diesem Sinne leistet das Markencontrolling eine Planungsunterstützung des Markenmanagements bei der Aufstellung des strategischen Gesamtplanes der Markenführung und dessen Aufspaltung in operative Teilpläne (wie Zielplan, Ressourcenplan, Terminplan). Um veränderten Anforderungen an die Markenführung möglichst frühzeitig durch eine Anpassung der Planung Rechnung zu tragen, ist im Rahmen von Kontroll- beziehungsweise Abweichungsanalysen ein kontinuierlicher und systematischer Vergleich von Sollvorgaben und Ist-Zuständen hinsichtlich der verfolgten Zielsetzungen durchzuführen. Dabei hat das Markencontrolling zum einen nach dem Feed-back-Prinzip eine Ex-post-Überwachung durch eine Bestandsaufnahme der Markenführung hinsichtlich ökonomischer, psychografischer und verhaltensbezogener Größen vorzunehmen. Zum anderen hat es als „Frühwarnsystem" feed-forward im Sinne einer Ex-ante-Überwachung Soll-Ist-Abweichungen zu antizipieren und damit ihr Eintreten zu verhindern. Die in einer übergeordneten Sichtweise zu betrachtende Koordinationsfunktion des Markencontrolling beinhaltet schließlich die Abstimmung der markenpolitischen Handlungen einzelner dezentraler Organisationseinheiten im Hinblick auf die mit der Markenpolitik verfolgten Ziele. In diesem Zusammenhang kann auch von einer Zielausrichtungsfunktion des Markencontrolling gesprochen werden. Neben der vertikalen Koordination einzelner Hierarchieebenen und der horizontalen Koordination durch Abstimmung der markenbezogenen Aktivitäten benachbarter Abteilungen kommt der Koordination in zeitlicher Hinsicht durch Abstimmung der kurz-, mittel- und langfristigen Markenplanung im Rahmen des Controlling eine entscheidende Bedeutung zu.

Die **Ergebnisperspektive** zeigt, ob die verfolgte Markenstrategie ex-post zu einer Ergebnisverbesserung beiträgt. Kennzahlen, die dieser Perspektive zugrunde liegen, nehmen dabei eine Doppelrolle ein: Zum einen definieren sie die Leistung, die von der Strategie erwartet wird, zum anderen fungieren sie als Endziele für die weiteren Perspektiven der Scorecard. Denn jede für eine Scorecard gewählte Kennzahl ist Teil einer Ursache-Wirkungskette, die ihr Ende in der Ergebnisperspektive und damit in einem Ergebnisziel findet. Scheinbar sinnvolle Zielwerte bei den anderen Perspektiven erweisen sich auf Dauer wenig nützlich, wenn angestrebte ökonomische Ergebnisgrößen zur Befriedigung der Kapitalgeber nicht erreicht werden.

Die **externe Marktperspektive** bildet die Markenleistung so ab, wie sie vom Nachfrager wahrgenommen wird und sich vom Wettbewerb differenziert und umfasst damit alle nachfrager- und wettbewerbsentscheidenden Größen, welche die marktseitige Akzeptanz und Wettbewerbsfähigkeit der Marke widerspiegeln. Im Rahmen der **internen Perspektive** geht es darum, die Kernkompetenzen einer Marke so abzubilden, dass die vom Nachfrager gewünschten beziehungsweise vom Management intendierten Leistungen marktgerecht erfüllt werden können. Hierzu sind die für die markenspezifische Leistungserstellung kritischen Prozesse zu identifizieren (vgl. in diesem Zusammenhang auch die Ausführungen zur GAP-Analyse im Rahmen des Managementkonzeptes der identitätsorientierten Markenführung in diesem Buch). Im „Innovationsprozess" sind die artikulierten beziehungsweise latent vorhandenen Wünsche der Nachfrager zu erforschen, um darauf aufbauend Leistungen zu schaffen, die diesen Wünschen entsprechen. Im „Erstellungsprozess" als zweiter Stufe der internen Wertkette werden die angestrebten Leistungen produziert. In der dritten Stufe erfolgt schließlich der „Markttransfer" der erstellten Leistung, wobei Abweichungen zwischen tatsächlich erstellter und der in der marktgerichteten Kommunikation versprochenen Leistung des Herstellers Kommunikationsgaps anzeigen. Störungen im Prozess der Markenerstellung liegen unter anderem in einer unzureichenden internen Identifikation der Beteiligten mit der Marke begründet. Als Indikator einer innengerichteten Markenidentifikation lässt sich analog zur Hersteller-Handels-Identifikation eine hohe Mitarbeiterzufriedenheit anführen.

Die Verbindung der hier genannten Perspektiven im Rahmen der Markenscorecard stellt letztlich sicher, dass die Inside-out- und Outside-in-Perspektive der Markenführung über Ursache-Wirkungsketten interagieren und damit nicht isoliert betrachtet werden. Die Innenperspektive und damit auch innengerichtete Leistungstreiber beeinflussen die Außenperspektive, welche wiederum Auswirkungen auf das Unternehmensergebnis hat.

Die bisher betrachteten Kennzahlen und Steuerungsgrößen sind noch allgemeiner Natur und grundsätzlich im Rahmen eines jeden Markencontrolling zu reflektieren. Jede Marke verfügt jedoch auch über spezifische Besonderheiten und Andersartigkeiten, die es im Markencontrolling zu beachten gilt. Diese Besonderheiten und Andersartigkeiten einer Marke drücken sich verdichtet in der Identität einer Marke aus.

4.32 Bestimmung von Steuerungsgrößen durch Operationalisierung des Markenleitbildes

Ein Markenleitbild kann die zentralen Elemente der Markenidentität in Form einer plastischen, für jeden verständlichen Darstellungsform vermitteln und die spezifischen Kompetenzen einer Marke zum Ausdruck bringen. Als Beispiel lässt sich das weiterentwickelte Leitbild der Marke Ford mit dem Markenslogan „Besser ankommen" und den Markenwerten „Verlässlichkeit", „Zeitgemäß" und „Fahrvergnügen" anführen, das durch seine neue Konkretisierung nunmehr „mit Leben gefüllt" wird und damit die in Abbildung 3 angeführte Reaktion beim Nachfrager hervorrufen kann (Mattes/Stackmann/Koers 2003).

Abbildung 3: **Markenleitbild am Beispiel Ford**

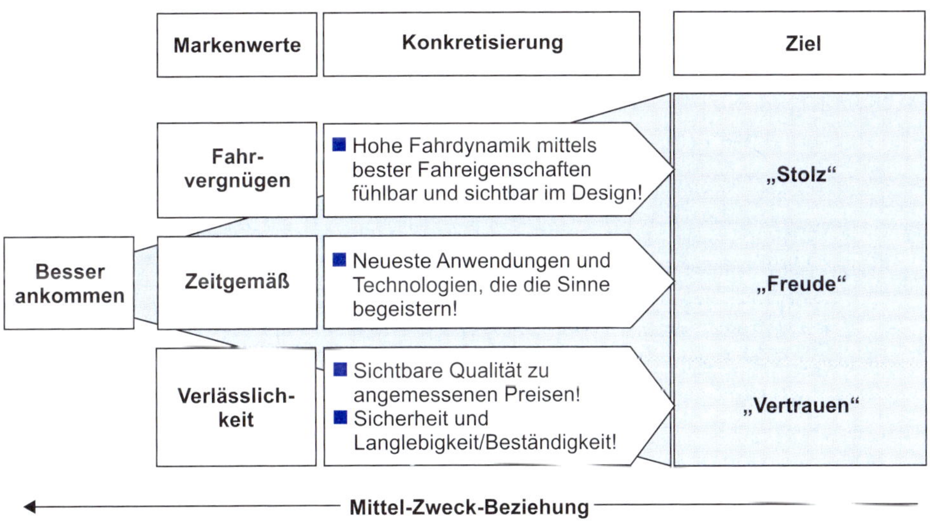

GABLER GRAFIK

Zur Bestimmung von Leistungstreibern in einer Scorecard kann auf ein solches Markenleitbild und seine Konkretisierung zurückgegriffen werden. Während die generischen Größen der Ergebnisperspektive (zum Beispiel Marktanteil) für alle Marken Gültigkeit besitzen, sollten die Leistungstreiber als Frühindikatoren die Besonderheiten der Marke widerspiegeln, mit der sich diese von Fremdmarken unterscheiden möchte. Die Leistungstreiber sollten somit die Einzigartigkeit einer Marke reflektieren.

Abbildung 4: **Operationalisierung der Leitbilddimension Verlässlichkeit der Marke Ford**

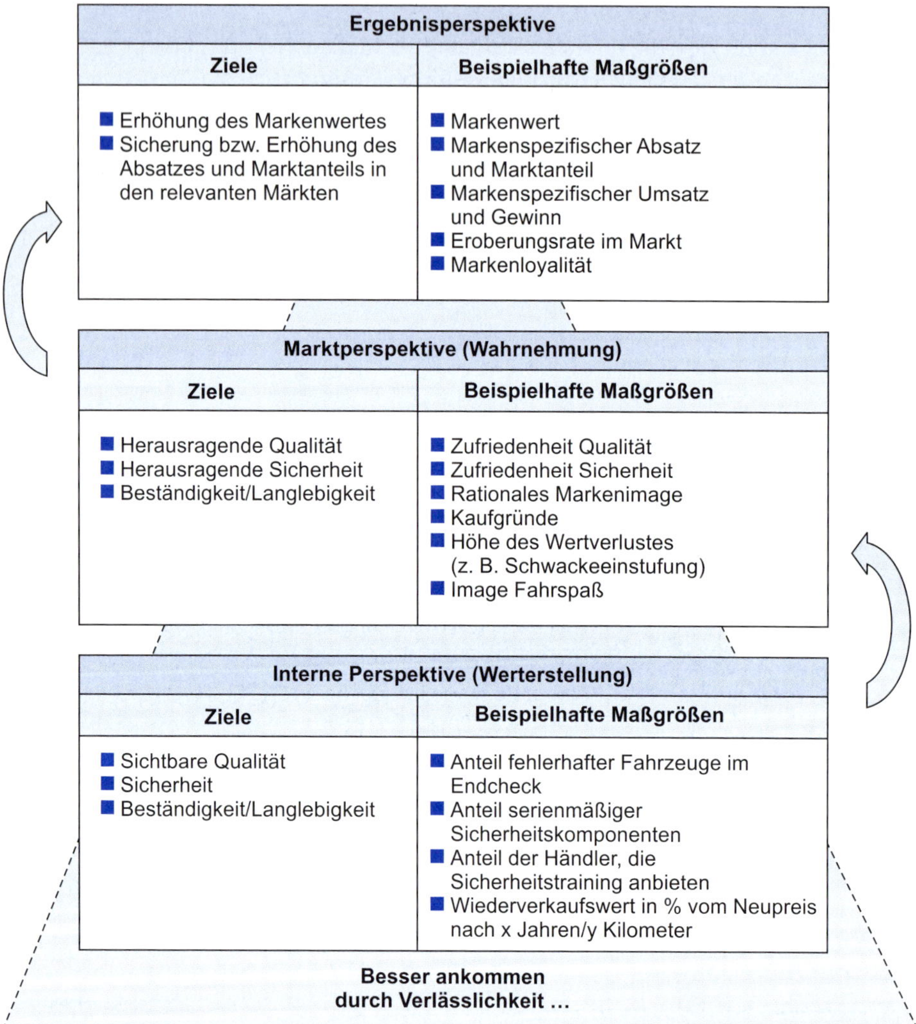

GABLER GRAFIK

Abbildung 4 zeigt exemplarisch die Behandlung der Leistungstreiber „Sichtbare Qualität", „Sicherheit" und „Langlebigkeit beziehungsweise Beständigkeit" als Treiber der Verlässlichkeitsdimension der Marke Ford, welche das Unternehmen als Fundament ihrer intendierten Markenwahrnehmung interpretiert. Diesen Leistungstreibern sind Maßgrößen zuzuordnen, die den Zielerreichungsgrad der jeweiligen Markendimension widerspiegeln. Beispielsweise lässt sich das Ziel „Sichtbare Qualität“ des Markenwertes „Verlässlichkeit“ intern und damit im Aussagenkonzept der Marke über den „Anteil fehlerhafter Fahrzeuge im Endcheck“ messen, während extern im Rahmen des Akzeptanzkonzepts diese Dimension über Zufriedenheitswerte und Imageitems abgebildet werden kann. Ein geringer Anteil fehlerhafter Fahrzeuge im Endcheck soll sich in einer Erhöhung der Qualitätszufriedenheit niederschlagen und damit den Markenwert „Verlässlichkeit“ in der Wahrnehmung der Nachfrager weiter aufladen. Ziel ist es, langfristiges Vertrauen in die Marke Ford zurückzugewinnen bzw. weiter aufzubauen. Wird die Marke Ford als verlässlich wahrgenommen, soll sich dies in einer Erhöhung der Markenloyalität respektive Marktanteils im Rahmen der Ergebnisperspektive widerspiegeln. Interne Perspektive, Marktperspektive und Ergebnisperspektive sind folglich über eine vermutete Ursache-Wirkungsbeziehung miteinander verknüpft.

4.33 Steuerungsgrößen in Markenportfolios

Da Unternehmen in der Praxis häufig nicht isoliert mit einer einzelnen Marke, sondern mit komplexen Markenportfolios agieren, sind im Rahmen des Markencontrolling auch **Wechselbeziehungen zwischen den Marken** zu erfassen (Koers 2001). So ist die Ford Motor Company in nahezu allen Fahrzeugklassen vertreten und verfolgt eine klar definierte Mehrmarkenstrategie mit entsprechenden Positionierungen der einzelnen Marken (vgl. Abbildung 5). Neben den Dachmarken Ford, Mazda, Mercury und Lincoln umfasst der Konzern die Premiummarken Aston Martin, Jaguar, Volvo und Land Rover im Rahmen seiner Premier Automotive Group. Unter dem Dach der Automotive Consumer Service Group sind überdies verschiedene Dienstleistungsmarken vereint (Mattes et al. 2003).

Analog zum bisher beschriebenen Vorgehen sind im Rahmen der Steuerung von Markenportfolios für sämtliche Marken im Portfolio in Abhängigkeit ihrer Markenidentität eigenständige Scorecards zu entwerfen. Wichtig ist dabei schon im Rahmen der Festlegung der Markenarchitektur, dass sich die Markenwerte in einem Portfolio nicht überschneiden, sondern möglichst heterogen ausfallen. Stehen bei Ford die Markenwerte „Verlässlichkeit“, „Zeitgemäß“ und „Fahrvergnügen“ im Vordergrund, betont die Marke Volvo unter dem Markenleitbild „Safety for Life“ vor allem Sicherheitsaspekte beziehungsweise hebt die Marke Lincoln als „American Luxury“ den Ursprung der Marke im amerikanischen Raum sowie den Anspruch, luxuriöse Fahrzeuge anzubieten, besonders hervor. Analog zum Vorgehen bei der Marke Ford gilt es auch bei diesen Marken, eine weitere Operationalisierung der Leitbilder vorzunehmen.

Abbildung 5: Markenportfolio im Rahmen der Mehrmarkenstrategie der Ford Motor Company

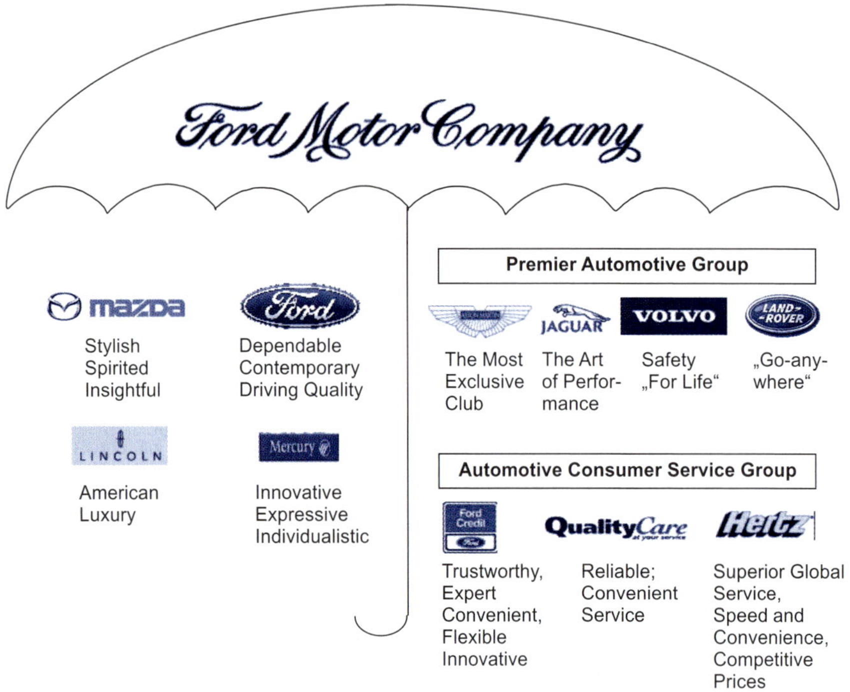

Da in einem komplexen Markenportfolio die operative Führung der Marken vielfach bei den dezentralen Markeneinheiten liegt, beschränkt sich die Portfolioleitung zumeist auf eine strategische Rahmenplanung des Gesamtportfolios. Hier werden die entsprechenden Markenidentitäten definiert. Eine Scorecard der Portfolioleitung führt die dezentralen Markenscorecards zusammen und ergänzt sie um Kennzahlen, die sich aus der Gesamtbetrachtung des Markenportfolios ergeben (zum Beispiel Wanderungs- beziehungsweise Kannibalisierungssalden zwischen den Marken im Gesamtportfolio; vgl. hierzu auch den Beitrag zur Markenkannibalisierung in diesem Buch). Im Ergebnis entsteht dabei ein „Netz“ von über die Portfolioscorecard miteinander verwobenen Markenscorecards, wobei die vertikale Scorecard-Ausdehnung auch weiter auf Modellebene beziehungsweise sonstige nachgelagerte Ebenen erfolgen kann (Wiese 2000). Der konzeptionelle Aufbau einer solchen **Scorecard-Hierarchie** ist abschließend der Abbildung 6 am Beispiel des Markenportfolios der Ford Motor Company zu entnehmen.

Abbildung 6: **Hierarchisierung von Markenscorecards**

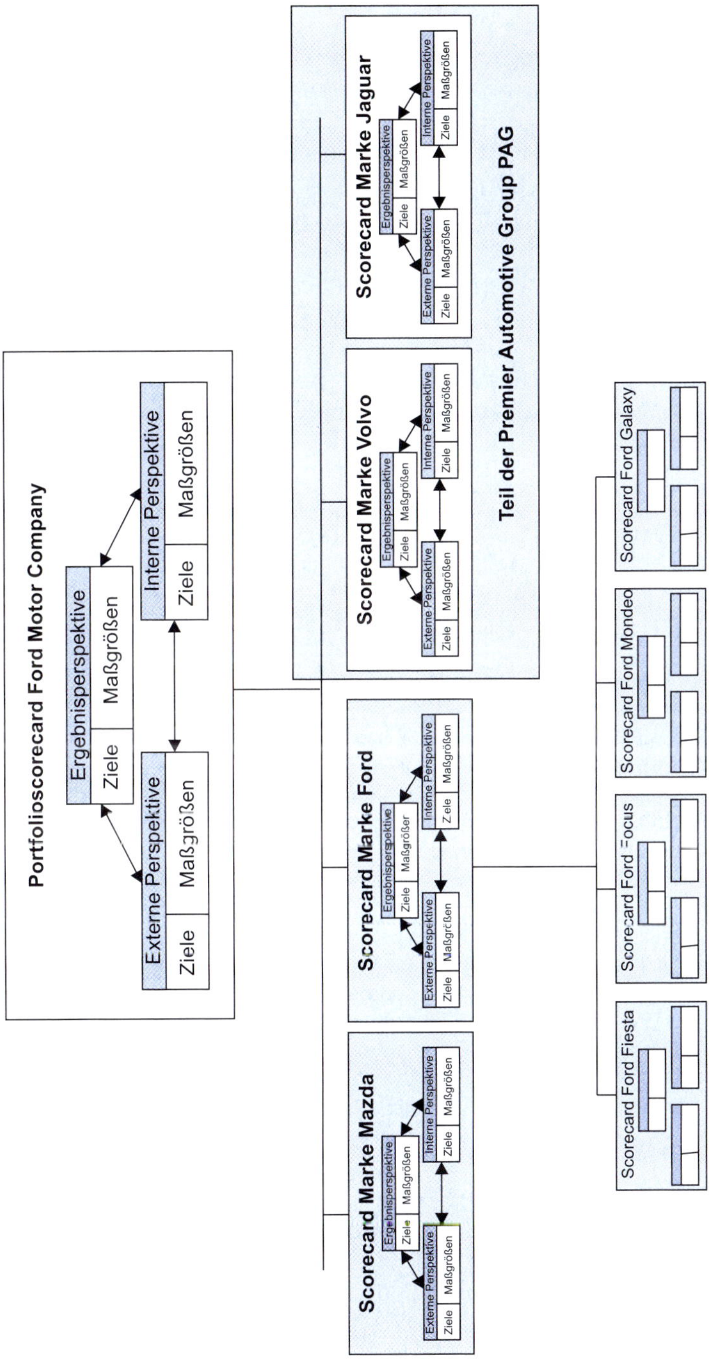

GABLER GRAFIK

5. Fazit

Damit auch das Markencontrolling dem Wechselspiel zwischen Inside-out- und Outside-in-Perspektive der identitätsorientierten Markenführung Rechnung trägt, ist es zweckmäßig, mit einer internen Unternehmensperspektive, einer externen Marktperspektive und einer Ergebnisperspektive drei Scorecard-Perspektiven im Rahmen der Erstellung einer Markenscorecard zu unterscheiden. Während die interne Perspektive Informationen im Rahmen des Aussagenkonzepts der Markenführung erfasst, betrachtet die Markt-Perspektive notwendige Kennzahlen des Akzeptanzkonzepts der Markenführung und die Ergebnisperspektive schließlich die angestrebte Ergebniswirkung der Markenstrategie. Um im Falle eines Markenportfolios die Wechselwirkungen zwischen verschiedenen Marken zu erfassen, bietet es sich überdies an, das Portfolio aus vor- und nachgelagerten Scorecards zu betrachten, da ein solches Vorgehen eine konsistente Informationsversorgung unterschiedlicher Aggregationsebenen des Portfolios und damit eine hierarchische Informationsintegration gewährleistet.

Literatur

Ahlert, D. (1998), Anforderungen an Handelsinformationssysteme aus Nutzersicht – Auswertungspotenziale für das Handels- und Wertschöpfungsprozeß-Management, in: Ahlert, D. et al. (Hrsg.), Informationssysteme für das Handelsmanagement: Konzepte und Nutzung in der Unternehmenspraxis, Berlin u. a.

Bekmeier-Feuerhahn, S. (1998), Marktorientierte Markenbewertung, Wiesbaden.

Burmann, Ch. (1991), Konsumentenzufriedenheit als Determinante der Marken- und Händlerloyalität – Das Beispiel der Automobilindustrie, in: Marketing ZFP, Nr. 4, S. 249–258.

Crimmins, J. C. (1992), Better Measurement and Management of Brand Value, in: JoAR, No. 4, S. 11–19.

Esch, F.-R. (2001), Moderne Markenführung: Grundlagen – innovative Ansätze – praktische Umsetzung, Esch, F.-R. (Hrsg.), 3. Aufl., Wiesbaden.

Esch, F.-R. (2004), Strategie und Technik der Markenführung, 2. Aufl., Stuttgart.

Fournier, S. M. (1998), Consumers and Their Brands: Developing Relationship Theory, in: Journal of Consumer Research, Vol. 24, March, S. 343–373.

Franzen, O. (1999), Strategisches Marken-Controlling für Finanzdienstleistungen, in: Planung und Analyse, Nr. 6, S. 22–26.

Gerken, G. (1994), Die fraktale Marke, Düsseldorf.

Güldenberg H. G., Franzen, O. (1994), Operatives Markencontrolling, in: Bruhn, M. (Hrsg.), Handwörterbuch Markenartikel, Band 2, Stuttgart, S. 1337–1351.

Homburg, Ch., Giering, A. (1999), Messung von Markenzufriedenheit und Markenloyalität, in: Esch, F.-R. (Hrsg.), Moderne Markenführung: Grundlagen – innovative Ansätze – praktische Umsetzung, Wiesbaden, S. 1089–1100.

Horváth, P. (2003), Controlling, 9. Aufl., München.
Horváth P. (2004), Die Strategieumsetzung erfolgreich steuern, Stuttgart.
Horváth & Partner (Hrsg.) (2004), Balanced Scorecard umsetzen, 2. Aufl., Stuttgart.
Kaplan, R. S., Norton, D. P. (1997), Balanced Scorecard: Strategien erfolgreich umsetzen, aus dem Amerikanischen übersetzt von P. Horváth, Stuttgart.
Köhler, R. (1998), Marketing-Controlling: Konzepte und Methoden, in: Reinecke, S., Tomczak, T., Dittrich, S. (Hrsg.), Marketingcontrolling, St. Gallen, S. 10–21.
Koers, M. (2001), Steuerung von Markenportfolios, Ein Beitrag zum Mehrmarkencontrolling am Beispiel der Automobilwirtschaft, Frankfurt/M.
Kriegbaum, C. (2001), Markencontrolling: Bewertung und Steuerung von Marken als immaterielle Vermögenswerte im Rahmen eines unternehmenswerteorientierten Controlling, München.
Küpper, H.-U. (2001), Controlling, 3. Aufl., Stuttgart.
Küpper, H.-U., Weber, J., Zünd, A. (1990), Zum Verständnis und Selbstverständnis des Controlling, in: ZfB, Nr.: 3, S. 281–294.
Linxweiler, R. (2001), BrandScoreCard: ein neues Instrument erfolgreicher Markenführung, Groß-Umstadt.
Mattes, B., Stackmann, J., Koers, M. (2003), Besser ankommen: Stellenwert und Gegenstand der Markenführung zur Repositionierung und Profilierung der Marke Ford, in: Ebel, B., Hofer, M., Al-Sibai, J. (Hrsg.), Automotive Management – Strategie und Marketing in der Automobilwirtschaft, Berlin, S. 591–613.
Mattes, B., Meffert, H., Landwehr, R., Koers, M. (2003), Trends in der Automobilindustrie: Paradigmenwechsel in der Zusammenarbeit zwischen Zulieferer, Hersteller und Händler, in: Ebel, B., Hofer, M., Al-Sibai, J. (Hrsg.), Automotive Management – Strategie und Marketing in der Automobilwirtschaft, Berlin, S. 13–38.
Mayer, R. (2004), Die Balanced Scorecard, in: Bensberg, F., Brocke, J. v, Schultz, M. B. (Hrsg.), Trendbericht zum Controlling, Festschrift für Heinz Lothar Grob, Heidelberg, S. 81–95.
Meffert, H. (2000), Marketing: Grundlagen marktorientierter Unternehmensführung: Konzepte – Instrumente – Praxisbeispiele, 9. Aufl., Wiesbaden.
Meffert, H., Koers, M. (2004), Markenführung versus Controlling? – Ansatzpunkte zur Verbindung „weicher" und „harter" Erfolgsfaktoren mithilfe der Balanced Scorecard, in: Bensberg, F., Brocke, J. v., Schultz, M. B. (Hrsg.), Trendbericht zum Controlling, Festschrift für Heinz Lothar Grob, Heidelberg, S. 53–79.
Müller-Hagedorn, L. (1999), Bausteine eines Management-Informationssystems: Balanced Scorecard – Benchmarking – Betriebsvergleich, in: Beisheim, O. (Hrsg.), Distribution im Aufbruch – Bestandsaufnahme und Perspektiven, München, S. 729–754.
Reichmann, Th. (1995), Controlling mit Kennzahlen und Managementberichten: Grundlagen einer systemgestützten Controlling-Konzeption, 4. Aufl., München.
Siegwart, H. (1986), Controlling-Konzepte und Controller-Funktionen in der Schweiz, in: Mayer, E., v. Landsberg, G., Thiede, W., (Hrsg.), Controlling-Konzepte im internationalen Vergleich, Freiburg i. Br., S. 105–131.
Tomczak, T., Reinecke, S. (1998), Aufgabenorientiertes Marketingcontrolling – Auf dem Weg zu einem managementorientierten Marketingcockpit, in: Reinecke, S., Tomczak, T., Dittrich, S. (Hrsg.), Marketingcontrolling, St. Gallen, S. 90–109.
Tolle, E., Steffenhagen, H. (1994), Kategorien des Markenerfolges und einschlägige Meßmethoden, in: Bruhn, M. (Hrsg.), Handwörterbuch Markenartikel, Band 2, Stuttgart, S. 1283–1303.
Weber, J. (2004), Einführung in das Controlling, 9. Aufl., Stuttgart.
Weber, J., Schäffer, U. (1999), Entwicklung von Kennzahlensystemen, WHU- Forschungspapier Nr. 62, Koblenz.

Weber, J., Schäffer, U. (2000), Balanced Scorecard und Controlling, 3. Aufl., Wiesbaden.
Weber, J., Schäffer, U. (2001), Marketingcontrolling: Sicherstellung der Rationalität in einer marktorientierten Unternehmensführung, in: Reinecke S., Tomczak, T., Geis, G. (Hrsg.), Handbuch Marketingcontrolling, St. Gallen, S. 32–49.
Wiedmann, K-P. (1994), Strategisches Markencontrolling, in: Bruhn, M. (Hrsg.), Handwörterbuch Markenartikel, Band 2, Stuttgart, S. 1305–1336.
Wiese, J. (2000), Implementierung der Balanced Scorecard: Grundlagen und IT-Fachkonzepte, Wiesbaden.

Markenkannibalisierung in Markenportfolios

Heribert Meffert und Martin Koers

1. **Markenkannibalisierung als zentrale Herausforderung bei der Verfolgung von Mehrmarkenstrategien** **298**

2. **Grundüberlegungen zur Wanderungsanalyse bei der Verfolgung von Mehrmarkenstrategien** **299**

3. **Erfassung interner und externer Wanderungsbewegungen in Mehrmarkenstrategien** **303**

3.1 Erfassung interner Wanderungsbewegungen: Substitutions- versus Kannibalisierungsanalyse 305

3.11 Substitutionsanalyse 305

3.12 Kannibalisierungsanalyse 307

3.2 Erfassung externer Wanderungsbewegungen: Partizipationsanalyse 311

4. **Integration interner und externer Wanderungsbewegungen im Rahmen von Wanderungsbilanzen** **313**

5. **Zusammenfassung** **315**

1. Markenkannibalisierung als zentrale Herausforderung bei der Verfolgung von Mehrmarkenstrategien

Die Verfolgung einer Mehrmarkenstrategie wird in jüngster Zeit vielfach als unternehmerisches Erfolgsrezept sine qua non gesehen. Vor allem in schwach wachsenden und gesättigten Märkten des Konsumgüter- und Dienstleistungsbereichs nimmt die aus der Fusion beziehungsweise Akquisition fremder Marken oder aus internen Wachstumsüberlegungen hervorgehende Führung von Markenportfolios mittlerweile eine dominierende Stellung ein (Mattes et al. 2003). Im Spannungsfeld zwischen Effektivität und Effizienz werden die verschiedenen Marken eines Portfolios dabei zumeist intern unter dem Primat der größtmöglichen Synergienutzung, im Marktauftritt jedoch unter der Maxime einer möglichst deutlichen Differenzierung geführt.

Eine übermäßige Synergienutzung bei wesentlichen Merkmalen einer Marke kann jedoch zu einer Schwächung der Markenidentitäten des Portfolios und damit zur Erosion vormals klar konturierter Marken führen. Hierdurch erhöht sich die Austauschbarkeit der Marken in der Wahrnehmung der Nachfrager, welche grundsätzlich durch den getrennten Markenauftritt minimiert werden soll. Werden in der Folge die charakteristischen Unterschiede zwischen den verschiedenen Portfoliomarken nicht mehr differenziert wahrgenommen, steigt die Gefahr der Bearbeitung gleicher Nachfragersegmente. Den Vorteilen einer Mehrmarkenstrategie, wie einer breiten Marktabdeckung oder einer erhöhten Effizienz in Kundengewinnung und Kundenbindung durch Halten von Markenwechslern im Portfolio, stehen somit auch zentrale Nachteile gegenüber (Quelch/Kenny 1994, S. 153 ff.; Meffert 1999; Koers 2001, S. 39 ff.).

Im externen Marktauftritt stellt die **Kannibalisierung** der Marken das zentrale Risiko von Mehrmarkenstrategien dar. In diesem Fall gehen die Absatzerfolge einer Marke zu Lasten der Absätze anderer Marken im Portfolio. Diesen Sachverhalt verdeutlicht Abbildung 1. Laut Pressebericht (o. V. 2000, S. 12) ging die fehlende technische Differenzierung der Marken im Volkswagen-Konzern vor einigen Jahren aufgrund der intensiven Verwendung von Gleichteilen mit einer zunehmenden Homogenisierung des Marktauftritts einher. Dies hatte zur Konsequenz, dass die Marke VW zunehmend Käufer an die preislich niedriger positionierten Marken Skoda und Seat verlor. Insbesondere gegenüber der preisaggressiv auftretenden Marke Skoda hatten sich die Verluste in 1999 gegenüber 1997 nahezu verfünffacht.

Im Gegensatz zur Markenkannibalisierung, welche auch als Markensubstitution bezeichnet wird, kann die portfolioübergreifende Gewinnung von Käufern anderer Marken als **Partizipationseffekt** bezeichnet werden (Gutenberg 1979, S. 548; Jacob 1988). Die Untersuchung beziehungsweise Überlagerung von Partizipations- und Substitutionseffekten im Rahmen von Wanderungsanalysen stellt somit einen zentralen Ansatzpunkt zur Analyse der Wirksamkeit einer Mehrmarkenstrategie dar. Im Spannungsfeld zwischen Substitution und Partizipation gilt es, eine bestmögliche Marktabdeckung unter Minimierung von Kannibalisierungseffekten innerhalb des Markenportfolios sicherzustellen.

Abbildung 1: **Kannibalisierung im Volkswagen-Konzern**

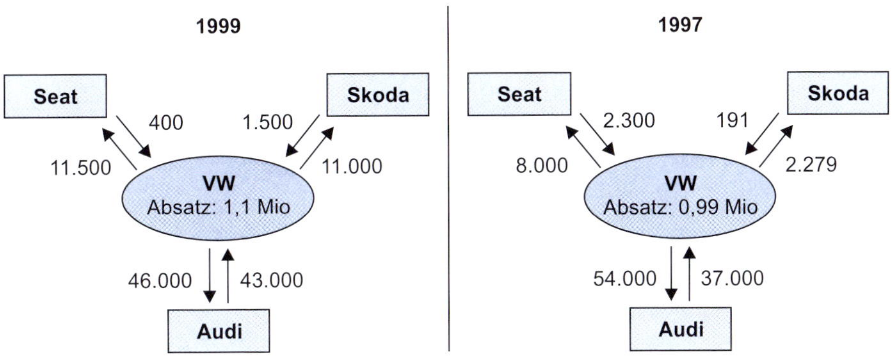

GABLER GRAFIK

(Lesebeispiel: in 1997 sind 2.279 bisherige VW-Käufer zur Marke Skoda gewechselt, wohingegen 191 von der Marke Skoda zu VW wechselten)
Quelle: o. V. 2000, S. 12

2. Grundüberlegungen zur Wanderungsanalyse bei der Verfolgung von Mehrmarkenstrategien

Im Gegensatz zu Positionierungs- und Markenwahrnehmungsanalysen kann die **Wanderungsanalyse** als quantitatives „Herzstück" eines Controlling von Markenportfolios bezeichnet werden. Denn das strategische Controlling von Mehrmarkenstrategien hat zumeist weniger den Charakter eines quantitativen Kennzahlenmonitoring, sondern greift verstärkt auf strategische Analysetechniken wie Positionierungs- und Markenwahrnehmungsanalysen zurück, um damit auch der „kreativen" beziehungsweise „weichen" Komponente der Markenführung Rechnung zu tragen (Wiedmann 1994; Franzen 1995).

Demgegenüber ist im Rahmen von Wanderungsanalysen eine (wertmäßige) Gegenüberstellung von Wanderungsbewegungen innerhalb des Markenportfolios mit solchen zwischen den eigenen Portfoliomarken und dem Wettbewerb vorzunehmen. Durch eine Gegenüberstellung von Substitutions- und Partizipationseffekten wird letztlich das Ergebnis der markenpolitischen Aktivitäten als „harte" Komponente der Markenführung offenbart. Detaillierte Untersuchungen zum Thema Partizipation und Substitution im Rahmen der Mehrmarkenführung sind indes nicht vorhanden, gleichwohl die Begriffe häufig genannt werden. Im Folgenden wird daher zunächst der Grundgedanke der Analyse in Anlehnung an Mason und Milne vereinfacht erläutert (Moorthy/Png 1992, S. 345 ff.; Mason/Milne 1994, S. 163 ff.; Lomax 1997, S. 27 ff.).

Mason und Milne gehen bei ihren Überlegungen zweckmäßig von einer festen Position einer jeden Portfoliomarke im Wahrnehmungsraum der Nachfrager aus. Dies verdeutlicht Abbildung 2 anhand eines fiktiven Marktes mit drei Marken, wobei die Marken A und B von dem gleichen Hersteller produziert werden und somit dem gleichen Markenportfolio angehören.

Abbildung 2: **Grundmodell der Substitution und Partizipation**

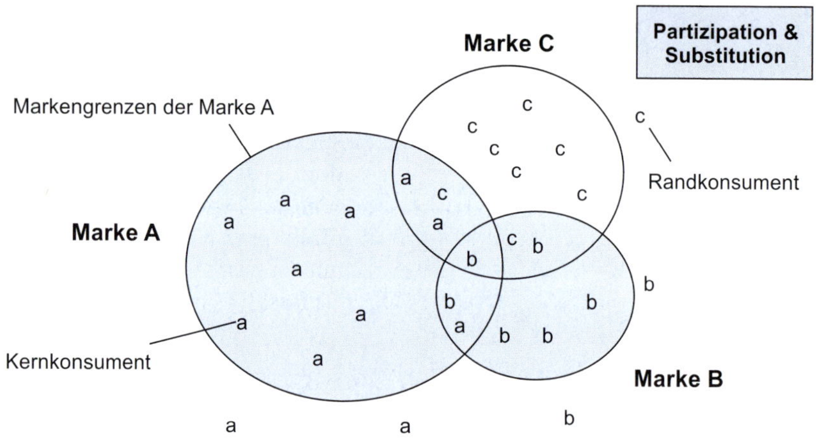

	Marke A	Marke B	Marke C
Kernkonsumenten	10	6	8
Markenpotenzial	13	8	12
Substitution	1/10 = 10 %	2/6 = 33 %	0
Partizipation	2/10 = 20 %	2/6 = 33 %	(1+1)/8 = 25 %
Potenzialausschöpfung	10/13 = 77 %	6/8 = 75 %	8/12 = 67 %

GABLER GRAFIK

Quelle: in Anlehnung an Mason/Milne 1994, S. 165

Die Kleinbuchstaben kennzeichnen einzelne Konsumenten und verdeutlichen, welche Marke erworben wurde. Je zentrierter sich ein Konsument in einem bestimmten Markenbereich befindet (ausgedrückt durch die Nähe zum Mittelpunkt eines jeden Kreises), desto eher entspricht dieser Konsument der Zielgruppe der Marke beziehungsweise kann dieser als „typisch“ für die Marke bezeichnet werden.

So kaufen etwa die meisten Konsumenten der im Markenbereich A vorzufindenden Konsumenten die Marke A, andere jedoch die Marken B und C. Die tatsächlichen Markenkäufer einer Marke innerhalb der zugehörigen Markengrenze können als Kernkonsumenten bezeichnet werden (also a-Konsumenten im Markenbereich A), die Gesamtzahl der Konsumenten innerhalb der Markengrenze als Markenpotenzial (also a, b und c-Konsumenten im Markenbereich A). Der Quotient aus tatsächlichen Käufern (hier 10 Konsumenten) und dem Potenzial der Marke A (hier 13 Konsumenten) kann somit als Potenzialausschöpfung definiert werden (10/13 = 77 Prozent). Die Buchstaben außerhalb der einzelnen Markenbereiche beschreiben schließlich Konsumenten, die zwar eine spezifische Marke kaufen, sich allerdings nicht im Zielmarkt der Marke entsprechend der gewünschten Positionierung befinden und somit als Randkonsumenten bezeichnet werden können.

Alle Konsumenten, die in Abbildung 2 im Bereich der Marke A liegen, diese aber nicht gekauft haben, sind entweder durch die portfolioeigene Marke B substituiert worden oder zur Konkurrenzmarke C gewandert (Partizipation der Konkurrenz). Marke A hat somit einen Konsumenten von Marke B substituiert (ein „a" liegt im Überschneidungsbereich zur Marke B) und zwei Konsumenten von der Fremdmarke C gewonnen (Partizipation: zwei „a" liegen im Überschneidungsbereich mit der Marke C). Die Ergebnisse der Substitution und Partizipation des fiktiven Beispiels lassen sich der Tabelle aus Abbildung 2 entnehmen.

Letztlich sind bei der Einführung einer neuen Marke B – also bei einem Übergang von einer „Ein"-Markenstrategie zu einer „Zwei"-Markenstrategie – neben dem in der Realität vorherrschenden gleichzeitigen Substitutions- und Partizipationseffekt theoretisch sämtliche Szenarien denkbar (Abbildung 3; Traylor 1986, S. 72):

- **vollständige Substitution** – sämtliche Käufer der neuen Marke B gehen zu Lasten der portfolioeigenen Marke A,
- **teilweise Substitution** – ein Teil der Käufer geht zu Lasten der Marke A, ansonsten zieht die Marke B neue Konsumenten an, sodass die neue Marke das Marktvolumen des Portfolioinhabers erweitert,
- **teilweise Partizipation** – ein Teil der Käufer geht zu Lasten der Marke C, ansonsten erweitert die Marke B das Marktvolumen,
- **vollständige Partizipation** – sämtliche Käufer der Marke B gehen zu Lasten der Fremdmarke C etc..

Hohe Substitutionsraten deuten dabei auf eine starke portfoliointerne Konkurrenz zwischen den Portfoliomarken, hohe positive Partizipationsraten auf eine hohe Wettbewerbsstärke der Portfoliomarken hin.

Ein wesentlicher **Grund hoher Substitutionsraten** kann in der mangelnden Differenzierung und der damit einhergehenden hohen Austauschbarkeit der Portfoliomarken in der Wahrnehmung der Konsumenten liegen. Verdeutlicht an Abbildung 2 bedeutet dies, dass sich letztlich zu viele Konsumenten im Überschneidungsbereich der Marken befinden (etwa zu viele a-Konsumenten im Bereich der Marke B).

Abbildung 3: Vollständige und teilweise Substitution beziehungsweise Partizipation

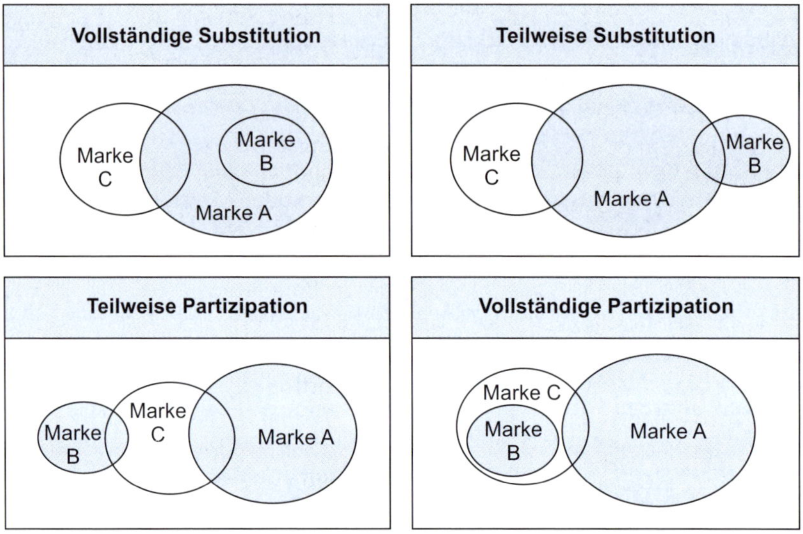

GABLER GRAFIK

Das Ausmaß der Substitution hängt dabei wesentlich von der Stellung der Marken im Preis- und Qualitätsfeld des Marktes ab. Es kann davon ausgegangen werden, dass der Substitutionseffekt in einem Portfolio umso geringer sein wird, je größer der Preis- und gleichzeitige Qualitätsunterschied zwischen den Marken des Portfolios ist. Umgekehrt wird der Substitutionseffekt in einem Portfolio umso größer sein, je geringer der Preis- und Qualitätsunterschied zwischen den Marken des Portfolios ist. Denn bei gleicher wahrgenommener Qualität wird es ceteris paribus nur schwer möglich sein, höhere Preise durchzusetzen. Vor dem Hintergrund der Verwendung von Gleichteilen, Plattformen etc. lässt sich jedoch in vielen Branchen eine Qualitätsangleichung feststellen. Gleichzeitig wird eine Preisdifferenzierung vorgenommen, die stärkere Substitutionseffekte zugunsten von Preismarken und zu Lasten von Premiummarken erwarten lässt. In diesem Zusammenhang führt Diez treffend an, „mit dem Argument „Audi-Technik zu Skoda Preisen“ lässt sich besser Geschäfte machen als gegen den Vorwurf „Skoda-Technik zu Audi-Preisen“ (Diez 1999, S. 32).

Nach Porter ersetzt ein Produkt ein anderes, wenn es dem Abnehmer unter Berücksichtigung seiner Substitutionsneigung einen **Substitutionsanreiz** bietet, der stärker ist als die **Substitutionskosten** (Porter 1999, S. 361). Eine Alternativmarke bietet dabei einen Substitutionsanreiz, wenn sie im Vergleich zu ihrem Preis dem Abnehmer einen höheren Wert als die bislang bezogene Marke bietet. Die Substitutionskosten sind hingegen eine

Analogie zu den Kosten, die beim Wechsel von einer Marke zu einer anderen entstehen. In dem von Diez beschriebenen Falle liegt der Substitutionsanreiz darin, dass die vergleichbare Qualität einer Marke zu niedrigeren Preisen erworben werden kann.

Mikroökonomisch kennzeichnet die Wirtschaftswissenschaft den Begriff **„enge Substitutionsprodukte“** auch als Produkte mit hoher Kreuzpreiselastizität der Nachfrage. Analog kann von engen Substitutionsmarken gesprochen werden. Wenn, bei Unveränderlichkeit aller übrigen Einflussfaktoren der Nachfrage, der Preis einer Marke steigt und dies zu einer Erhöhung der Nachfrage für eine andere Marke führt, sind die beiden Marken enge Substitutionsmarken (Bultez et al. 1989, S. 155).

Allerdings kann in Markenportfolios durchaus eine **gewisse Substitution erwünscht** sein: Unter der Prämisse ansteigender Einzeldeckungsbeiträge sowohl entlang der Portfoliomarken (zum Beispiel von der Marke Ford zur Premiummarke Volvo im Ford-Konzern) als auch der Modelle innerhalb einer Marke (vom Kleinwagen Ford Ka zum Ford Mondeo) ergibt sich eine gewünschte Substitution entlang der ansteigenden Einzeldeckungsbeiträge, da sich hierdurch letztlich der Portfoliogesamtgewinn erhöhen lässt. Folglich ist Traylor zuzustimmen, wenn er sagt: *„The real task of management, then, is* ***not to avoid cannibalism*** *[Hervorhebung d. Verf.], but to know when and where it happens, be aware of its likely competitive and profitability effects, and take the appropriate marketing action that serves the best strategic interests of the enterprise.“* (Traylor 1986, S. 74).

3. Erfassung interner und externer Wanderungsbewegungen in Mehrmarkenstrategien

Um zu wissen *„when and where it happens“* sind Partizipations- und Substitutionseffekte im Rahmen von Wanderungsbilanzen zusammenzuführen. Das Grundschema der Wanderungsanalyse ist Abbildung 4 zu entnehmen (Koers 2001). Während im Rahmen der **Partizipationsanalyse** sowohl die Zuwanderungen der neu hinzugewonnenen Käufer, die bislang Konkurrenzmarken erworben haben als auch die Abwanderungen aktueller Käufer zu den Wettbewerbern untersucht werden, kommt der **Substitutionsanalyse** die Aufgabe zu, Wechsel der Kunden von einer Marke des Portfolios zu einer anderen Marke des Portfolios aufzudecken und mithin eine mögliche „interne Konkurrenz“ der Marken innerhalb des Markenportfolios zu analysieren. Hierbei wird im Folgenden noch zwischen „echter“ Substitution einerseits sowie Loyalitätsgewinnen aufgrund „erwünschter“ Substitution im Portfolio andererseits unterschieden. Die Ergebnisse der Partizipations- und Substitutionsanalyse und damit der Effekt der Mehrmarkenstrategie lassen sich schließlich in einer Wanderungsmatrix beziehungsweise -bilanz zusammenfassen.

Abbildung 4: Grundschema der Wanderungsanalyse

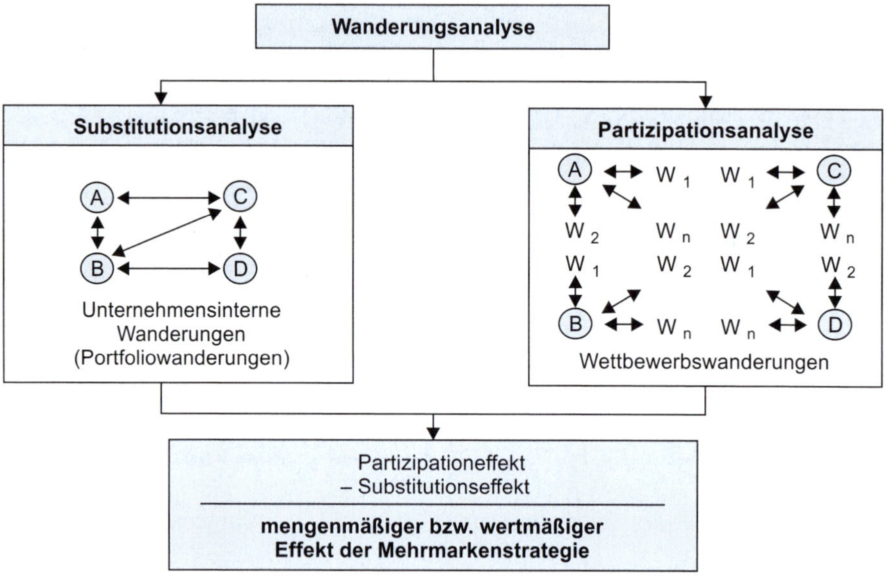

Legende:
A, B, C, D: Portfoliomarken
W_1, W_2, W_n: Fremdmarken

GABLER GRAFIK

Bei der im Folgenden vorzunehmenden **Wanderungsanalyse** zur Erfassung von Partizipations- und Substitutionseffekten *„to know when and where it happens"* wird zur besseren Veranschaulichung auf ein Markenportfolio eines Automobilherstellers mit mehreren Marken zurückgegriffen. Da im Rahmen der Analyse jedoch weniger die Darstellung konkreter Zahlen als vielmehr die grundsätzliche konzeptionelle Vorgehensweise von Interesse ist, werden die Markennamen durch Buchstabenbezeichnungen (Marken A-D) benannt. Bei den quantitativen Angaben handelt es sich überdies um fiktive, aber im richtigen Verhältnis stehende Daten. Zum besseren Verständnis der intendierten Portfoliostruktur sind die strategischen Rollen der hier betrachteten Marken (Marken A-D) in Tabelle 1 dargestellt.

Tabelle 1: Struktur des betrachteten Markenportfolios

Marke	Auftrag im Markenportfolio	Ausrichtung der Marke
A	Hauptmarke	Befriedigung der breiten Volumensegmente [Absicherung und Ausbau]
B	Trendmarke	Emotions- und trendorientierte Käufer [Angreifer Trendsegmente]
C	Preismarke	Funktions- und preisorientierte Käufer [Verteidiger Preissegmente]
D	Premiummarke	Befriedigung gehobener Ansprüche [Eroberung Premium-/Aufsteigersegmente]

GABLER GRAFIK

3.1 Erfassung interner Wanderungsbewegungen: Substitutions- versus Kannibalisierungsanalyse

3.11 Substitutionsanalyse

Die Analyse der Markensubstitution kann auf der Grundlage unterschiedlicher Messkonzepte erfolgen. Grundsätzlich besteht die Möglichkeit, Informationen über das tatsächliche Markenwechselverhalten als Grundlage zur Beurteilung der Austauschbeziehungen heranzuziehen. Hierzu bietet es sich an, regelmäßig die Vorbesitz- und Abwanderungsstrukturen einer Marke zu erheben. Dabei gibt die **Vorbesitzstruktur** im vorliegenden Fall Auskunft darüber, welchen Vorwagen die Besitzer einer bestimmten Marke gefahren haben. Im Gegensatz dazu zeigt die **Abwanderungsstruktur**, zu welchem Modell die ehemaligen Besitzer einer Marke überwechseln (Bauer/Hannig 1987, S. 5 ff.). In Abbildung 5 sind die portfoliointernen Wanderungen der vier betrachteten Marken mit fiktiven Daten beispielhaft dargestellt.

Abbildung 7: Erwünschte versus unerwünschte Substitution

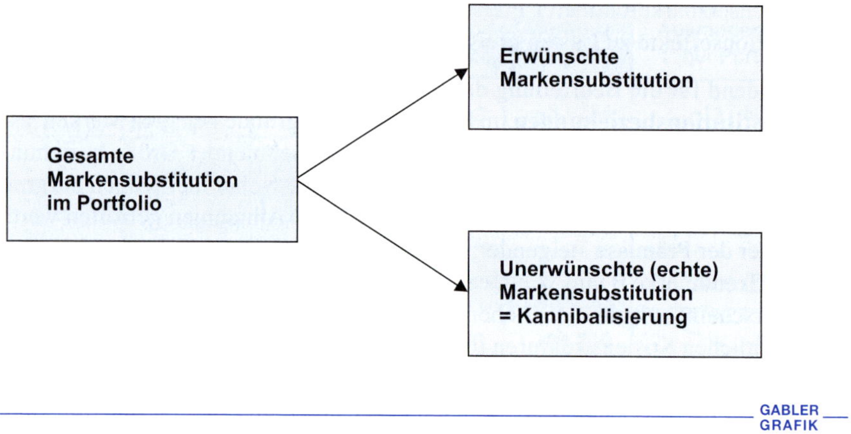

Echte Substitution umfasst von den berechneten Wanderungen von einer Marke A zu einer Marke B im gleichen Portfolio nur diejenigen Konsumenten, die als Alternative für den Kauf der Marke B auch die frühere Marke A tatsächlich erwogen haben (so genannter Second-Choice-Ansatz):

- Denn streng genommen lässt sich im Markenportfolio nur bei solchen Wanderbewegungen von **echter, „unerwünschter" Substitution** – im Folgenden als **Kannibalisierung** bezeichnet – sprechen, bei denen Nachfrager von einer Marke des Portfolios zur anderen wechseln, dabei jedoch als Alternativmarke die vorher besessene – und damit die Marke des Portfolios – und nicht eine Wettbewerbsmarke in Betracht gezogen haben. Relevant sind somit die **Erwägerraten**. Zur Bestimmung der Erwägerrate wird der Käufer eines Produkts unmittelbar nach seiner Kaufentscheidung gefragt, für welche Marke er sich entschieden hätte, wenn das tatsächlich erworbene Modell beziehungsweise Produkt der jeweiligen Marke nicht erhältlich gewesen wäre.
- Markenwechsler innerhalb des Portfolios ohne Präferenz für die vorher besessene Marke können hingegen den **Loyalitätsgewinnen des Portfolios** zugerechnet werden, das heißt, ohne Präsenz weiterer Marken im Portfolio wären sie zu Fremdmarken abgewandert. Letztlich ist es besser, Käufer – trotz Markensubstitution – im eigenen Portfolio zu halten, als sie an den Wettbewerber zu verlieren. Hier handelt es sich somit um „erwünschte" Substitution im Markenportfolio.

Dabei gilt:

- Je höher die Erwägerraten zwischen den Portfoliomarken, als desto austauschbarer werden diese empfunden beziehungsweise
- je höher der Loyalitätsgewinn und damit die erwünschte Substitution, desto effektiver ist die Mehrmarkenstrategie trotz Substitution, da Markenwechsler nicht zu Fremdmarken, sondern zu portfolioeigenen Marken abwandern.

Abbildung 8 veranschaulicht diesen Sachverhalt, indem die portfoliointernen Wanderungsbewegungen aus Abbildung 5 um Erwäger und Nicht-Erwäger ergänzt werden.

Abbildung 8: **Kannibalisierungseffekt einer Mehrmarkenstrategie**

von \ zu	Marke A	Marke B	Marke C	Marke D	Σ Abwanderungen* (* nur Portfolio)	Σ Absatz
Marke A	—	+20.194 davon: A-Erwäger +11.866 Nichterwäger +8.308	+14.142 davon: A-Erwäger +8.200 Nichterwäger +5.942	+83.284 davon: A-Erwäger +45.186 Nichterwäger +38.098	**-117.620**	**1.248.072**
Marke B	+6.012 davon: B-Erwäger +1.108 Nichterwäger +4.904	—	+1.832 davon: B-Erwäger +492 Nichterwäger +1.340	+768 davon: B-Erwäger +380 Nichterwäger +388	**-8.612**	**121.862**
Marke C	+250 davon: C-Erwäger +122 Nichterwäger +128	+504 davon: C-Erwäger +236 Nichterwäger +268	—	+258 davon: C-Erwäger +130 Nichterwäger +128	**-1.012**	**76.924**
Marke D	+94.494 davon: D-Erwäger +54.646 Nichterwäger +39.848	+2.540 davon D-Erwäger +418 Nichterwäger +2.122	+2.886 davon: D-Erwäger +1.392 Nichterwäger +1.494	—	**-99.920**	**466.704**
Σ Zuwanderungen (* nur Portfolio)	**+100.756**	**+23.238**	**+18.860**	**+84.310**	**-227.164** **-227.164**	**Σ 1.913.562**
Σ Kannibalisierung	**+55.876**	**+12.540**	**+10.084**	**+45.696**	**Σ +124.196**	
Σ Loyalitätsgewinn	**+44.880**	**+10.698**	**+8.776**	**+38.614**	**Σ +102.968**	

Lesebeispiel: Marke A zu Marke C durch A-Erwäger = Kannibalisierung, durch Nichterwäger hingegen Portfolio-Loyalitätsgewinn (5.942 Konsumenten Marke A nicht erwogen: für die Marke A verloren, aber im Portfolio gehalten)

GABLER GRAFIK

So haben beispielsweise von den 14.142 Markenwechslern, die von der Marke A zu C gewandert sind (siehe auch Wanderung von Marke A zu Marke C in Abbildung 6 und 7), 5.942 Konsumenten die vorher besessene Marke A nicht mehr als Kaufalternative erwogen, wohl aber eine Fremdmarke. Diese Konsumenten könnten deshalb theoretisch als verloren gelten, wären sie nicht von einer anderen Portfoliomarke – in diesem Fall von C – aufgefangen und im eigenen Portfolio gehalten worden. Diese Konsumenten sind somit durch die Marke C dem Portfolio loyal geblieben. Hier handelt es sich somit um erwünschte Substitution.

Dagegen hätten sich im vorliegenden Beispiel 8.200 Konsumenten wieder für die Marke A entschieden, wäre das tatsächlich erworbene Modell der Marke C nicht erhältlich gewesen. Diese Konsumenten können damit als kannibalisiert durch die Marke C bezeichnet werden. Nur hier ist somit von wahrer Kannibalisierung zu sprechen. Würde die Marke C nicht existieren, hätten diese Konsumenten abermals die Marke A gekauft.

Summiert über die Marke C ergibt sich bei einer Zuwanderung von den Marken A, B und D in Höhe von 18.860 eine Kannibalisierung von 10.084 und ein Loyalitätsgewinn von 8.776. Von 227.164 Wanderungen im Markenportfolio insgesamt sind somit theoretisch 124.196 als echte Kannibalisierung, hingegen 102.968 als Loyalitätsgewinn des Portfolios zu interpretieren. Folglich eröffnet die Mehrmarkenstrategie die Möglichkeit, den Aufbau von Loyalität zur einzelnen Marke durch die Maximierung der **Portfolioloyalität** zu erweitern, um so der zunehmenden Fragmentierung des Automobilmarktes und der damit einhergehenden wachsenden Markenwechselbereitschaft zu begegnen.

Betrachtet man den Gesamtabsatz des Portfolios in Höhe von 1.913.562 Einheiten, lässt sich der **Substitutionsindex** im Portfolio berechnen als

$$\text{Substitutionsindex} = \frac{\text{Portfoliointerne Wanderungen}}{\text{Neuwagenkäufer insgesamt}}$$

Damit ergibt sich ein Index in Höhe von 11,9 Prozent (227.164/1.913.562), das heißt, 11,9 Prozent des Gesamtabsatzes beruhen auf portfoliointernen Wanderungen. Je höher letztlich der Substitutionsindex, desto mehr gehen die Umsatzerfolge einer Marke zu Lasten anderer Marken im Portfolio. Analog zum Substitutionsindex lassen sich der **Kannibalisierungs-** sowie der **Loyalitätsindex** berechnen:

$$\text{Kannibalisierungsindex} = \frac{\text{Summe der Erwäger („echte" Substitution)}}{\text{Neuwagenkäufer insgesamt}}$$

$$\text{Loyalitätsindex} = \frac{\text{Summe der Nichterwäger (Loyalitätsgewinn)}}{\text{Neuwagenkäufer insgesamt}}$$

Entsprechend ergibt sich ein Kannibalisierungsindex in Höhe von 6,5 Prozent (124.196/1.913.562), das heißt, 6,5 Prozent des Gesamtabsatzes beruhen auf echter Substitution und damit Kannibalisierung sowie ein Loyalitätsindex des Gesamtportfolios in Höhe von 5,4 Prozent (102.968/1.913.562). Die Summe aus Kannibalisierungs- und Loyalitätsindex ergibt wiederum den Substitutionsindex (6,5 Prozent + 5,4 Prozent = 11,9 Prozent).

Je höher der Kannibalisierungsindex, desto eher kann eine Marke aus dem Portfolio eliminiert werden, da als Alternativmarken jeweils andere Marken des Portfolios genannt werden und keine Fremdmarken. In diesem Zusammenhang ist insbesondere eine dynamische Veränderung der Kennzahl im Zeitablauf von Interesse: Sinkt der Kannibalisierungsindex im Zeitablauf bei steigendem Substitutionsindex, so stellt dies ein Indiz einer effektiven, **Life-Cycle-gerichteten Mehrmarkenstrategie** dar, da Markenwechsler entsprechend der Zielsetzung der Mehrmarkenstrategie nicht zu Fremdmarken abwandern, sondern im Markenportfolio gehalten werden (Loyalitätsgewinn). Konsumenten wandern also im Idealfall von niedrigpreisigen Einsteigermarken zu hochpreisigen Premiummarken im Portfolio anstatt zum Wettbewerber abzuwandern.

Eine weitere Analyse der markenspezifischen Wanderungssalden lässt sich vornehmen, indem der Beitrag der einzelnen Modelle zu den Markensalden, das heißt die Substitutionsbeziehungen zwischen den einzelnen Modellen der Marken, nach dem gleichen Vorgehen bestimmt werden. Die Summe der einzelnen Modellsalden erklärt dabei die Markensalden. Insbesondere aus **zeitlich-dynamischer Perspektive** bietet eine disaggregierte Analyse auf Modell- beziehungsweise Produktebene einen hohen Erkenntniswert zur Erklärung der markenspezifischen Wanderungssalden. Neue Modelle beziehungsweise Produkte bringen Bewegung und Unruhe in den Markt, da sie Nachfrage auf sich ziehen. Da nahezu alle Innovationsprodukte einen Substitutionsprozess auslösen, indem sie eine bisherige Lösung ganz oder teilweise substituieren, ist auch davon auszugehen, dass neue Modelleinführungen einer Marke positive Substitutionseffekte zu Lasten der sonstigen Portfoliomarken bewirken. In der Regel werden sich die Modelle der einzelnen Portfoliomarken dabei in verschiedenen Produktlebenszyklusphasen befinden. Die Erzielung eines ausgewogenen „Life-Cycle-Mixes" der Modelle nimmt somit einen zentralen Stellenwert bei der Mehrmarkenführung ein und ist weitgehend kongruent mit der Realisierung eines gut ausbalancierten Markenportfolios.

3.2 Erfassung externer Wanderungsbewegungen: Partizipationsanalyse

In Analogie zur Berechnung der Substitutions- und Kannibalisierungbeziehungen im Markenportfolio kann der Partizipationseffekt der Mehrmarkenstrategie durch Bestimmung der Wanderungen zwischen den Portfolio- und den Wettbewerbsmarken ermittelt werden. Hier erweist sich eine getrennte Analyse der Wanderungsbewegungen zwischen den eigenen Marken und den im Rahmen der Ausgestaltung der Mehrmarkenstrategie definierten strategischen und operativen Wettbewerbern als zweckmäßig. Während operative Wettbewerber solche Hersteller darstellen, die eine Homogenität von Leistungsspektrum, Marketingstrategie und arealstrategischer Präsenz aufweisen, orientiert sich die Definition strategischer Wettbewerber am langfristigen, visionären Kompetenzanspruch der Marken im Wettbewerbsumfeld (Clef 1999, S. 72 ff.). Eine Unterscheidung der Wanderungsrichtungen zu operativen und strategischen Wettbewerbern ermöglicht somit

Aussagen über das Konkurrenzverhalten der einzelnen Portfoliomarken im Wettbewerb. Da sich die Definition strategischer Wettbewerber am langfristigen, visionären Kompetenzanspruch der Marken im Wettbewerbsumfeld orientiert, ermöglichen die Wanderungsstrukturen zwischen den strategischen Wettbewerbern und den einzelnen Portfoliomarken im Zeitablauf auch eine Überprüfung der Realisation eines solchen Kompetenzanspruchs.

Abbildung 9 zeigt in Analogie zu den Substitutionssalden in Abbildung 6 den Partizipationseffekt in Form von Partizipationssalden für die im Beispiel betrachteten Marken (strategische sowie primäre und sekundäre operative Wettbewerber durch Kleinbuchstaben gekennzeichnet). Hier wird deutlich, dass in der Summe sämtliche Marken des Portfolios mit Ausnahme von Marke A eine Absatzpartizipation und damit einen Wettbewerbsgewinn zu Lasten anderer Anbieter im Markt erzielen. Über alle Marken hinweg ergibt sich jedoch aufgrund der hohen Abwanderungen der Marke A zu ihren strategischen und vor allem operativen Wettbewerbern ein Verlust in Höhe von 70.244 ME.

Abbildung 9: Partizipationssalden der Mehrmarkenstrategie

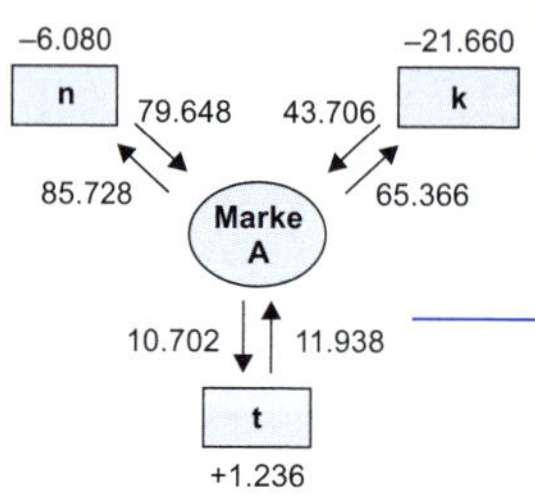

Wettbewerber	Marke A	Marke B	Marke C	Marke D
Strategisch Σ	m −19.024*	e −68	s +264 q +14	f +4.894
Operativ Primär Σ	n −6.080 k −21.660 t +1.236 **−26.504**	p −606 i +3.550 **+2.944**	i +966 o +1.840 u +602 **+3.408**	m −6.662 s −2.256 **−8.918**
Sekundär Σ	i −9.206 p −40.914 f −2.614 **−52.734**	k −914 o +1.760 h +516 **+1.362**	k +3.592 p +1.544 v +2.118 **+7.254**	n +11.680 o +1.688 **+13.368**
Sonstige Σ	**−7.934**	**+764**	**+14.530**	**−3.864**
Gesamt Σ	**−106.196**	**+5.002**	**+25.470**	**+5.480**

Σ −70.244

GABLER GRAFIK

* Gesamtsalden aus Gewinnen (+) und Verlusten (–) in 1998 in Deutschland

Analog zum Substitutionsindex lässt sich der **Partizipationsindex** berechnen als

$$\text{Partizipationsindex} = \frac{\text{Portfolioexterne Zuwanderungen}}{\text{Neuwagenkäufer insgesamt}}$$

Dabei gilt: Je höher der Partizipationsindex, desto mehr gehen die Absatzerfolge der Portfoliomarken zu Lasten von Fremdmarken. Ein hoher Partizipationsindex ist somit Indiz einer hohen Wettbewerbsfähigkeit der Portfoliomarken.

4. Integration interner und externer Wanderungsbewegungen im Rahmen von Wanderungsbilanzen

Der Gesamteffekt der Mehrmarkenstrategie lässt sich unter Zusammenführung des Substitutions- und Partizipationseffektes im Rahmen einer Wanderungsbilanz (oder synonym Wanderungsmatrix) ermitteln (Abbildung 10). Dabei wird zwischen dem Bruttoeffekt und dem Nettoeffekt der Mehrmarkenstrategie unterschieden.

Abbildung 10: Brutto- versus Netto-Effekt der Mehrmarkenstrategie

	Marke A	Marke B	Marke C	Marke D	Σ
Gesamt Σ Substitution	–16.864	+14.626	+17.848	–15.610	0
Gesamt Σ Partizipation	–106.196	+5.002	+25.470	+5.480	–70.244
Wanderung Σ ohne LG	**–123.060**	**+19.628**	**+43.318**	**–10.130**	**–70.244**
Loyalitäts-gewinn Σ	**+44.880**	**+10.698**	**+8.776**	**+38.614**	**+102.968**
Gesamt Σ Partizipation	–106.196	+5.002	+25.470	+5.480	–70.244
Wanderung Σ mit LG	**–61.316**	**+15.700**	**+34.246**	**+44.094**	**+32.724**

	Brutto-Effekt Mehrmarkenstrategie (ohne Loyalitätsgewinn)	Netto-Effekt Mehrmarkenstrategie (mit Loyalitätsgewinn)
Wanderungssaldo	**–70.244**	**+ 32.724**

GABLER GRAFIK

Der hier als **Bruttoeffekt der Mehrmarkenstrategie** bezeichnete Wanderungssaldo der Mehrmarkenstrategie berechnet sich als Summe von portfoliointerner Substitution und portfolioexterner Partizipation über alle Marken. Der Bruttoeffekt umfasst somit Substitutions- und Partizipationseffekt, wobei beim Substitutionseffekt nicht zwischen „erwünschter“ Substitution (welche aus Portfolioperspektive als Loyalitätsgewinn bezeichnet werden kann) und Kannibalisierung unterschieden wird. Er weist ein negatives Ergebnis in Höhe von 70.244 ME aus, wobei die Marken A und D einen negativen, B und C hingegen einen positiven Ergebnisbeitrag leisten. Wie ersichtlich, entspricht der Gesamtsaldo des Portfolios somit der Summe der Partizipationseffekte, da sich gesetzmäßig die Substitutionssalden im Portfolio gegenseitig aufheben.

Der Partizipationseffekt allein hat allerdings nur eine vergleichsweise geringe Aussagekraft bezüglich der Wirksamkeit der Mehrmarkenstrategie. Zentrales Ziel der parallelen Markenführung ist es, Markenwechsler innerhalb des eigenen Portfolios zu halten. Der Bruttoeffekt der Mehrmarkenstrategie ignoriert jedoch eine Differenzierung der Substitution in „Kannibalisierung“ einerseits und „Loyalitätsgewinn“ durch erwünschte Substitution andererseits und nimmt somit eine „verkürzte“ Bewertung vor.

Vor diesem Hintergrund errechnet sich der **Nettoeffekt der Mehrmarkenstrategie** als Partizipation plus Loyalitätsgewinn, das heißt 102.968 – 70.244 = 32.724. Dieser gibt entsprechend dem Second-Choice-Ansatz somit einen Wanderungssaldo unter Berücksichtigung derjenigen Markenwechsler an, welche die in t_0 besessene Portfoliomarke nicht mehr erwogen haben und damit für das Portfolio als verloren gelten würden, wären sie nicht tatsächlich im Portfolio von einer anderen Marke in t_1 aufgefangen worden. Letztlich stellt somit der Loyalitätsgewinn die zentrale Größe zur Bewertung von Wanderungsbewegungen im Portfolio dar: Je größer der Loyalitätsgewinn, desto effektiver ist die Mehrmarkenstrategie, da Markenwechsler nicht zu Fremdmarken abwandern, sondern zu portfolioeigenen Marken und damit dem Gesamtportfolio erhalten bleiben.

In Bezug auf das Markenwahlverhalten findet letztlich sowohl beim Substitutionseffekt als auch beim Partizipationseffekt ein Markenwechsel statt. Substitutions- und Partizipationseffekte zeigen somit unmittelbare Auswirkungen auf den markenspezifischen Absatz einer Marke. Je höher die markenspezifischen positiven Substitutions- und Partizipationssalden, desto höher erweist sich der markenspezifische Absatz. Hier offenbart sich letztlich das **„Dilemma der Mehrmarkenführung“**: Stellen positive Substitutionssalden aus Sicht einer Marke grundsätzlich anzustrebende Vorzugszustände dar, da sie letztlich die Wettbewerbsstärke der Marke indizieren und ihren Absatz positiv beeinflussen, sind sie aus Gesamtportfolioperspektive insbesondere bei Wanderungen von deckungsbeitragsstarken zu deckungsbeitragsschwachen Marken negativ zu beurteilen, deuten sie doch vor allem auf eine hohe Austauschbarkeit der Marken im Portfolio hin.

5. Zusammenfassung

Die Wanderungsanalyse fungiert als quantitatives „Herzstück“ eines Mehrmarkencontrolling. Hier ist eine Gegenüberstellung der Wanderungsbewegungen innerhalb des Markenportfolios (Substitutionseffekte) mit den Wanderungen zwischen den eigenen Marken und dem Wettbewerb (Partizipationseffekte) vorzunehmen.

In diesem Zusammenhang erscheint eine getrennte Ermittlung der Loyalitätsgewinne im Markenportfolio sinnvoll, wobei dazu auf so genannte „Second-Choice Daten“ zurückzugreifen ist, welche über die in Erwägung gezogene Alternativmarken der Nachfrager Auskunft geben. So lässt sich streng genommen nur bei solchen Wanderbewegungen von Kannibalisierung und damit echter Substitution sprechen, bei denen Nachfrager von einer Marke des Portfolios zur anderen wechseln, dabei jedoch als Alternativmarke die vorher besessene – und damit die Marke des Portfolios – und nicht eine Wettbewerbsmarke in Betracht gezogen haben. Markenwechsler innerhalb des Portfolios, ohne Präferenz für die vorher besessene Marke, können hingegen den Loyalitätsgewinnen des Portfolios zugerechnet werden. Unter Zusammenführung des Substitutions- und Partizipationseffektes lässt sich der Gesamteffekt der Mehrmarkenstrategie im Rahmen einer Wanderungsbilanz erfassen.

Abbildung 11 gibt zusammenfassend einen Überblick zentraler Kennzahlen und Indizes mit entsprechenden Interpretationen im Rahmen des Controlling von Markenportfolios.

Abbildung 11: Zentrale Kennzahlen des Mehrmarkencontrolling

Kennzahl	Definition	Interpretationen
Substitutions-index	Ausmaß der portfoliointernen Wanderungsbewegungen.	Je höher der Substitutionsindex, desto mehr gehen die Umsatzerfolge einer Marke zu Lasten anderer Marken im Portfolio. Zu vermeiden: Substitutionseffekte entlang sinkender Deckungsbeiträge.
Kannibalisierungsindex	Ausmaß der portfoliointernen Wanderungsbewegungen, bei denen Nachfrager von einer Portfoliomarke zur anderen wechseln, dabei jedoch als Alternativmarke die vorher besessene angeben.	Je höher der Kannibalisierungsindex, als desto austauschbarer werden die Portfoliomarken aus Sicht der Konsumenten wahrgenommen. Folglich gilt: bei hohem Kannibalisierungsindex kann eine Marke umso eher aus dem Portfolio eliminiert werden, da als Alternativmarken jeweils andere Portfoliomarken genannt werden.
Loyalitäts-index	Ausmaß der portfoliointernen Wanderungsbewegungen, bei denen Nachfrager von einer Portfoliomarke zur anderen wechseln, dabei jedoch nicht als Alternativmarke die vorher besessene angeben, sondern eine Fremdmarke. Letztlich also portfoliointerne Wanderungen minus Kannibalisierung.	Je höher der Loyalitätsindex, desto effektiver ist die Mehrmarkenstrategie, da Markenwechsler nicht zu Fremdmarken abwandern, sondern zu portfolioeigenen Marken.
Partizipations-Index	Ausmaß der portfolioexternen Zuwanderungen.	Je höher die portfolioexternen Zuwanderungen (Abwanderungen), desto stärker (schwächer) erweist sich das Portfolio im Wettbewerbsumfeld, d. h. desto positiver ist c. p. die Mehrmarkenstrategie.
Erwäger-Rate	Gibt an, inwieweit eine Marke von Fremdmarkenbesitzern als Kaufalternative in Erwägung gezogen wurde (sog. Second-Choice-Ansatz).	Je höher die Erwägerrate, desto höher der potenziell mögliche, aber unrealisierte Absatz einer Marke; dabei gilt: ■ je höher die Erwägerraten zwischen den Portfoliomarken, desto austauschbarer werden diese empfunden; ■ je höher die Erwägerraten zwischen den Portfoliomarken und Fremdmarken, desto höher erweist sich der potenzielle Absatz des Portfolios.
Marken-Loyalitätsrate	Gibt (vereinfacht) an, wie viele Marken-Besitzer bei einem Folgekauf wieder die entsprechende Marke erwerben.	Je höher die ML, desto unveränderter sollte die Marke im Portfolio geführt werden.
Marken-Eroberungs-rate	Gibt an, wie viel Prozent der Folgekäufer mit einer Fremdmarke im Vorbesitz durch die Marke erobert werden konnten.	Je höher die ER, desto höher die Wettbewerbsstärke der betreffenden Portfoliomarke.

GABLER GRAFIK

Literatur

Bauer, H. H., Hannig, U. (1987), Die Erfassung der Substitutionswirkung eines neuartigen Elektrowerkzeuges für den Heimwerker-Markt, in: Marketing ZfP, Nr. 1, S. 5–15.

Bultez. A. et al. (1989), Asymmetric Cannibalism in Retail Assortements, in: Journal of Retailing, Vol. 65, Nr. 2, Summer, S. 153–192.

Clef, U. (1999), Mehrmarkenstrategie für die Pole-Position, in asw, Sondernummer Oktober, S. 72–80.

Copulsky, W. (1976), Cannibalism in the Marketplace, in: Journal of Markting, October, S. 103–105.

Diez, W. (1999), Plattform-Strategien: Irrweg oder Königsweg in der Modellpolitik, Arbeitspapier Nr. 2 des Instituts für Automobilwirtschaft, Gelsenkirchen.

Fisher, J. C., Pry, R. H. (1971), A Simple Substitution Model of Technological Change, in: Technological Forecasting and Social Change, Vol. 2, May, S. 75–88.

Franzen, O. (1995), Marken-Controlling effizient gestalten, in: Markenartikel, Nr. 2, S. 57–62.

Gutenberg, E. (1979), Grundlagen der Betriebswirtschaftslehre, Zweiter Band, Der Absatz, 16. Aufl., Berlin, Heidelberg, New York.

Jacob, H., Der Absatz, in: Allgemeine Betriebswirtschaftslehre: Handbuch für Studium und Prüfung, Jacob, H. (Hrsg.), 5. Aufl., Wiesbaden 1988.

Koers, M. (2001), Steuerung von Markenportfolios: Ein Beitrag zum Mehrmarkencontrolling am Beispiel der Automobilwirtschaft, Frankfurt/M.

Lomax, W. et al. (1997), The measurement of cannibalization, in: Journal of Product & Brand Management, Vol. 6, No. 1, S. 27–39.

Lomax, W., McWilliam, G. (2001), Consumer Response to Line Extensions: Trial and Cannibalisation Effects, in: Journal of Marketing Management, S. 391–406.

Mason, Ch. H., Milne, G. R. (1994), An Approach for Identifying Cannibalization within Product Line Extensions and Multi-Brand Strategies, in: JoBR, S. 163–170.

Mattes, B., Meffert, H., Landwehr, R., Koers, M. (2003), Trends in der Automobilindustrie: Paradigmenwechsel in der Zusammenarbeit zwischen Zulieferer, Hersteller und Händler, in: Ebel, B., Hofer, M., Al-Sibai, J. (Hrsg.), Automotive Management – Strategie und Marketing in der Automobilwirtschaft, Berlin, S. 13–38.

Meffert, H. (1999), Mehrmarkenstrategie – immer die beste Option? in: asw, Sondernummer Oktober, S. 82–87.

Moorthy, K. S., Png, I. P. L. (1992), Market Segmentation, Cannibalization and the Timing of Product Introduction, in: Management Science, 38. Jg., Nr. 3, S. 345–359.

o.V. (2000), Piechs Sündenbock, in: Wirtschaftswoche vom 1.6.2000, Nr. 23, S. 12.

Porter, M. E. (1999), Wettbewerbsvorteile: Spitzenleistungen erreichen und behaupten, 5. Aufl., Frankfurt/M., New York.

Quelch, J. A., Kenny, D. (1994), Extend Profits, Not Product Lines, in: Harvard Business Review, September/October, S. 153–160.

Traylor, M. B. (1986), Cannibalism in Multibrand Firms, in: Journal of Consumer Marketing, Vol. 3, No. 2, Spring, S. 69–75.

Wiedmann, K-P. (1994), Strategisches Markencontrolling, in: Bruhn, M. (Hrsg.), Handwörterbuch Markenartikel, Band 2, Stuttgart, S. 1305–1336.

1. Markenbewertung als Herausforderung an die marktorientierte Unternehmensführung

1.1 Die Marke als Treiber des Unternehmenswertes

Während in der Industriegesellschaft materielle Vermögensgegenstände wie beispielsweise der Maschinenpark, Gebäude und die Roh-, Hilfs- und Betriebsstoffe den Wert einer Unternehmung bestimmten, zeigt sich heutzutage, in der Transformationsphase zur Dienstleistungs- und Informationsgesellschaft, ein anderes Bild. Analysiert man in diesem Zusammenhang den Wert der im Standard & Poor 500 Index zusammengefassten 500 größten börsennotierten amerikanischen Unternehmen, so zeigt sich, dass sich seit Beginn der 90er Jahre der an der Börse bezahlte Marktwert des Eigenkapitals immer weiter von dessen bilanziellem Buchwert entfernt hat (vgl. Abbildung 1).

Abbildung 1: **(Eigenkapital-) Tobin's q der im S&P 500 notierten Unternehmen**

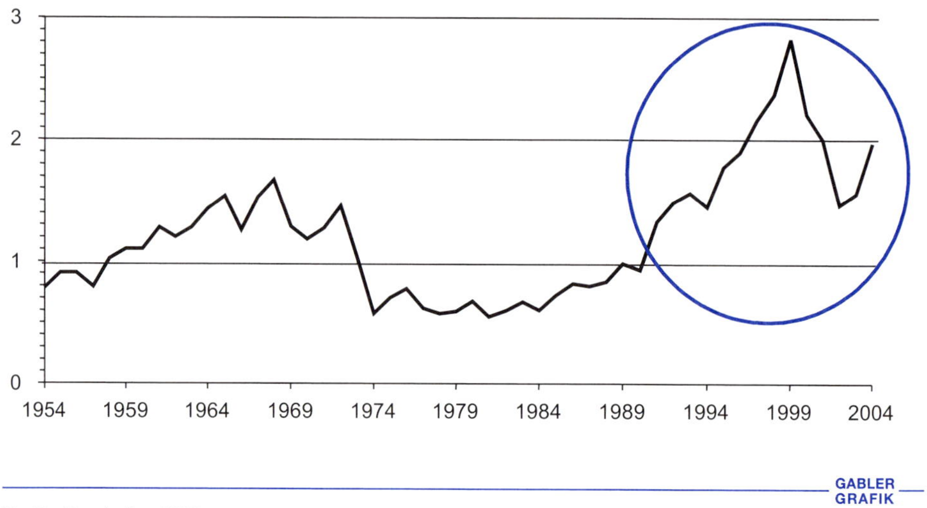

Quelle: Hundacker 2005

Dieses auch als **Tobin's q** bezeichnete Verhältnis aus Markt- zu Buchwert des Eigenkapitals, liegt trotz mehrjähriger Börsenkrise mittlerweile bei einem Wert von zwei. Damit ist der Marktwert vieler Unternehmen doppelt so hoch wie ihr Buchwert. Untersuchungen von Sattler et al. und Burmann zeigen, dass eine ähnliche Situation auch für den deutschen Markt zu konstatieren ist (Sattler/Högl/Hupp 2002, S. 482 f.; Burmann 2002, S. 4 f.).

Das „Auseinanderlaufen" von Markt- und Buchwert kann auf die Existenz von **immateriellen Vermögenswerten**, die nicht in den Bilanzen erfasst sind, zurückgeführt werden. Der mit Abstand wichtigste immaterielle Vermögensgegenstand ist dabei zumeist die Marke. Ein weiterer wichtiger immaterieller Vermögenswert, das Wissen beziehungsweise das spezifische Know-how eines Unternehmens und seiner Mitarbeiter, lässt sich in den Markenwert überführen. Im Rahmen des identitätsorientierten Markenführungsansatzes ist die **Markenidentität** die Voraussetzung für die Entstehung eines ökonomischen Markenwertes. Kernbestandteil der Markenidentität wiederum ist die Markenkompetenz, die sich als emergente Eigenschaft aus dem Wissen und Know-how der Mitarbeiter eines Unternehmens formt (Burmann 2002, S. 184 ff.). Ohne eine klare und bei allen Mitarbeitern fest verankerte Markenidentität kann kein wettbewerbsüberlegenes Markenimage und damit kein ökonomischer Markenwert entstehen. Erst ein entsprechendes Markenimage ist in der Lage, das Kaufverhalten der relevanten Zielgruppen positiv zu beeinflussen und damit die Substanz für eine ökonomische Markenbewertung zu liefern (vgl. den Beitrag zu den konzeptionellen Grundlagen der identitätsbasierten Markenführung in diesem Buch).

1.2 Bilanzierung von Markenwerten

Die asymmetrische Entwicklung von Buch- und Marktwert hat den Gesetzgeber dazu veranlasst, die Vorschriften bezüglich der bilanziellen Behandlung von Marken grundlegend zu überdenken.

Nach deutschem Bilanzrecht besteht aktuell ausschließlich für erworbene, nicht selbst erstellte Marken eine Ansatzpflicht. Im Falle des Unternehmenserwerbs gilt nach § 246 I in Verbindung mit § 248 II HGB aufgrund des Vollständigkeitsgebotes eine Ansatzpflicht der Markenwerte. Dabei ist zu beachten, dass eine Abgrenzung des sich auf die Marke beziehenden Entgeltes eindeutig gegeben sein muss (Hammann/von der Gathen 1995, S. 204). Kann eine solche Abgrenzung nicht vorgenommen werden, sieht der Gesetzgeber keinen expliziten Ausweis der erworbenen Markenwerte vor, sondern nach § 255 IV HGB lediglich den Ansatz eines Geschäftswertes. Der Markenwert wird folglich undifferenziert im Goodwill ausgewiesen. Der Ansatz von selbst geschaffenen Markenwerten ist nach deutschem Bilanzrecht gemäß § 248 II HGB (noch) generell verboten.

Anders verhält es sich jedoch bei den internationalen Bilanzierungsvorschriften der Vereinigten Staaten oder Großbritanniens. Bei Merger & Acquisitions gemäß den amerikanischen Rechnungslegungsvorschriften US-GAAP muss das erwerbende Unternehmen neben den übrigen erworbenen Vermögensgegenständen und Schulden auch immaterielle Vermögensgegenstände im Rahmen einer so genannten Purchase Price Allocation einzeln identifizieren und monetär bewerten (Pfeil/Vater 2002, S. 67). Damit sollen dem Kapitalmarkt entscheidungsrelevante Informationen zur Verfügung gestellt werden, die verhindern, dass wichtige Unternehmenswerttreiber wie die Marke in der undifferenzierten Restgröße des Goodwill aufgehen. Sofern von einer zeitlich unbestimmten Nutzungsdauer der Marke ausgegangen werden kann (dies dürfte in der Markenpraxis den Regelfall darstellen), ist die Marke nicht planmäßig abzuschreiben. Stattdessen darf nur abgeschrieben werden, wenn im Rahmen einer regelmäßigen Überprüfung (Impairment-Test) nachgewiesen wird, dass der Buchwert der Marke über deren Marktwert liegt (Meisner 2003, S. 118).

Aktuelle Entwicklungen deuten darauf hin, dass diese Regelungen auch in die International Financial Reporting Standards (IFRS) aufgenommen werden sollen. Damit wird ab 2005 für börsennotierte Unternehmen, die ihre Konzernabschlüsse nach IFRS aufstellen, diese Praxis verpflichtend. Gleichzeitig erwägt der Deutsche Standardisierungsrat § 248 II HGB aufzuheben. Damit würde auch nach deutschem Handelgesetzbuch, wie bei den US-GAAP, für selbst erstellte immaterielle Vermögensgegenstände ein faktisches Ansatzwahlrecht gelten (Gerpott/Thomas 2004; Hanser 2004).

Neben der Bilanzierung hat der ökonomische Markenwert auch im Rahmen der Lizenzierung, dem Kauf und Verkauf von Markenrechten und der Verletzung dieser Markenrechte mit den daraus resultierenden Schadensersatzansprüchen hohe Bedeutung (Binder 2000, S. 359).

1.3 Steuerungswirkungen des Markenwertes

Es wird deutlich, dass die **Evaluierung des Wertes einer Marke** in zahlreichen Einsatzfeldern des Wirtschaftslebens notwendig wird. Bei den hier exemplarisch aufgeführten externen Markenbewertungsanlässen muss die Bewertung in einer **monetären Größe** erfolgen. Insbesondere bei der Verwendung von Markenwertinformationen im Jahresabschluss wird die zwingende Quantifizierung in Geldeinheiten offensichtlich.

Neben den externen Bewertungsanlässen existiert interner Bedarf an zuverlässigen Informationen über den Wert der Marke. Zum einen stellt die Bewertung an sich einen Wert dar, da von dieser eine Signalwirkung ausgeht (Quelch/Austin/Laidler-Kylander 2004, S. 23 f.). Sie vereinfacht es dem Markenmanagement, funktionsbereichsübergreifend ein Bewusstsein für die Rolle der Marke als Treiber des Unternehmenswertes zu schaffen (Lehmann 2004, S. 74). Insbesondere in wirtschaftlich angespannten Zeiten hat das Markenmanagement so eine bessere Argumentationsbasis, auf den Investitionscharakter von Markenausgaben hinzuweisen. Unabhängig von der Entscheidung über eine Transformation in eine monetäre Größe liefert der Markenwert wichtige Entscheidungsgrundlagen in den einzelnen Phasen der Planung, Steuerung und Kontrolle des Managementprozesses der Markenführung.

Beispielsweise ist die strategische Allokation von finanziellen Ressourcen ein wichtiger Punkt in der Planungsphase. Insbesondere im Rahmen von Markenportfolios ist die Budgetallokation von Bedeutung. Unternehmen mit einer Vielzahl von Marken stehen in periodisch wiederkehrenden Entscheidungsprozessen vor der Frage, in welche der verschiedenen Marken investiert oder de-investiert werden soll.

Bei der Planung von markenbezogenen Unternehmensaktivitäten stellt sich weiterhin die Frage des Ursprungs der Stärke einer Marke. Es gilt zu diagnostizieren, auf Basis welcher Komponenten die Marke positive Erfolgsbeiträge für das Unternehmen generiert. Zur Steuerung von Marken und Markenportfolios bedarf es klarer Aussagen über die aktuelle und potenzielle Stärke von Marken, mit deren Hilfe notwendige Markenführungsmaßnahmen identifiziert und Transferpotenziale von Marken auf andere Länder oder Produktbereiche analysiert werden können. Die Ergebnisse der Markenbewertung können überdies als eine Komponente in die Entwicklung von Anreizsystemen eingehen. Eine Beurteilung der Markenverantwortlichen mittels dieser Informationen würde der Forderung nach einer stärkeren Fokussierung des Markenmanagements auf wertorientierte Erfolgsgrößen gerecht werden (Esch/Wicke 2000, S. 55).

Abbildung 2: **Anlässe der Markenbewertung**

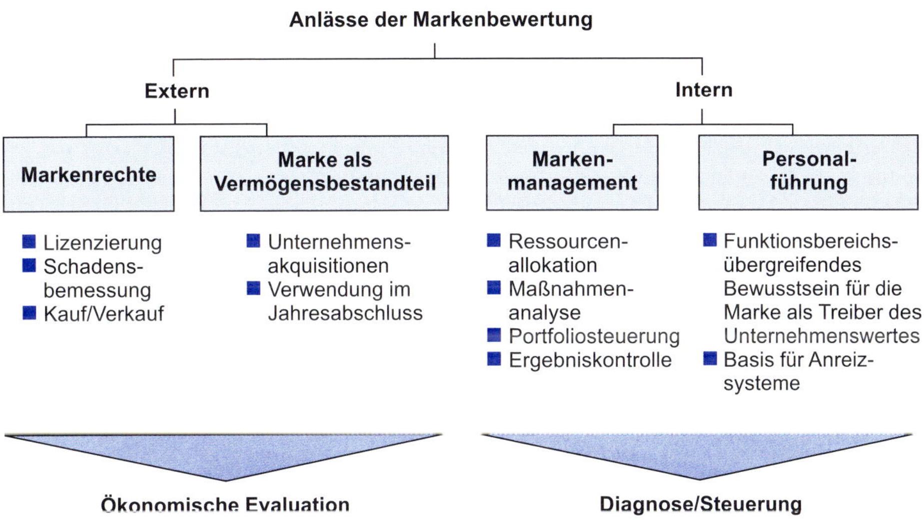

GABLER GRAFIK

Die dargestellten internen Anlässe der Markenbewertung zeigen, dass eine Quantifizierung des Markenwertes in monetären Einheiten nicht zwingend erforderlich ist. Ausnahme ist einzig die zu erwartende kommunikative Signalwirkung eines monetären Markenwertes. Prinzipiell stehen bei den internen Bewertungsanlässen die **Analyse der Stärke der Marke** und die Generierung von Maßnahmen zu ihrer Steigerung im Mittelpunkt. Hierbei werden Referenzgrößen benötigt, die Aussagen über die relative Position der Marke im Vergleich zu einer Bezugsgröße liefern. Diese Bezugsgröße kann

- die Marke im Zeitablauf,
- eine andere Marke im Unternehmensportfolio,
- die Marke eines Wettbewerbers oder
- die Marke in unterschiedlichen Marktbedingungen

sein (Franzen/Trommsdorff/Riedel 1994, S. 1378 f.). Eine zusammenfassende Übersicht der Anlässe der Markenbewertung liefert Abbildung 2.

1.4 Markenwert und Markenstärke als Gegenstand der Markenbewertung

Im Zusammenhang mit der Bewertung von Marken hat die Literatur eine Vielzahl von Begriffen und Perspektiven hervorgebracht. So finden sich Begriffe wie Markenstärke, Markenwert, Markenkraft, brand equity, customer value, customer equity, brand assets und viele weitere (Bekmeier-Feuerhahn 1998, S. 30 ff.). Insgesamt kann festgehalten werden, dass sich diesbezüglich in der Wissenschaft keine einheitlichen Begriffdefinitionen und -verwendungen durchgesetzt haben. Die gemeinsame Klammer für nahezu alle Begriffe bildet jedoch die Markenbewertung. Die Markenbewertung greift dabei prinzipiell auf einen finanzorientierten, einen verhaltensorientierten oder einen erweiterten Markenwertbegriff zurück (vgl. Abbildung 3).

Der finanzorientierte, investitionstheoretisch geprägte Markenwertbegriff beinhaltet zwingend eine monetäre Perspektive des Markenwertes. Schon 1962 beschrieb Kern *„den Wert von Warenzeichen als die Summe der auf den gegenwärtigen Zeitpunkt diskontierten Zusatzgewinne“* (Kern 1962, S. 18). Durch die Zielgröße „Gewinn“ als Resultante des Rechnungswesens wird die monetäre Ausrichtung dieses Verständnisses deutlich. Ähnlich, jedoch auf Basis von Zahlungsströmen, definieren auch Simon/Sullivan und Kaas den Markenwert als *„Barwert aller zukünftigen Einzahlungsüberschüsse, die der Eigentümer aus der Marke erwirtschaften kann“* (Kaas 1990, S. 48; Simon/Sullivan 1993, S. 29). Die Vertreter dieses klassischen Markenwertbegriffs nehmen dabei eine primär unternehmensbezogene Perspektive im Sinne einer Rechenwerkorientierung ein. Das Ergebnis der Markenbewertung ist mit der Dimension Geldeinheit ratioskaliert und erlaubt alle arithmetischen Operationen.

Der verhaltensorientierte, psychografische Markenwertbegriff setzt bei der Wirkung der Marke auf das Verhalten der internen und externen Zielgruppen einer Marke, der Markenstärke, an. Die **Markenstärke** bezeichnet demzufolge die **Verhaltensrelevanz** einer Marke. Diese Verhaltensrelevanz wird für die externen Zielgruppen durch das Markenimage und für die internen Zielgruppen durch die Markenidentität determiniert (vgl. Abbildung 3). Bei der Berechnung des verhaltensorientierten Markenwertes greifen die bislang vorliegenden Verfahren jedoch nur auf die Verhaltensrelevanz für externe Zielgruppen zurück. Nach diesem einseitig verkürzten, auf den Absatzmarkt reduzierten Verständnis, definiert Kriegbaum Markenstärke als Konstrukt, das die derzeitige und zukünftige Markenwahl des Konsumenten determiniert und auf Basis von Informationsverarbeitungsprozessen entsteht (Kriegbaum 2001, S. 75). Die Markenstärke ist eine der finanziellen Markenbewertung vorgelagerte Stufe, bei der eine Quantifizierung in Geldeinheiten weder notwendig, noch üblich ist. Die Markenstärke ist damit eine dimensionslose Größe, welche über ihre Verhaltenswirkung die finanziellen Erfolgsbeiträge der Marke generiert.

Abbildung 3: Strukturierung des Begriffsverständnisses bei der Markenbewertung

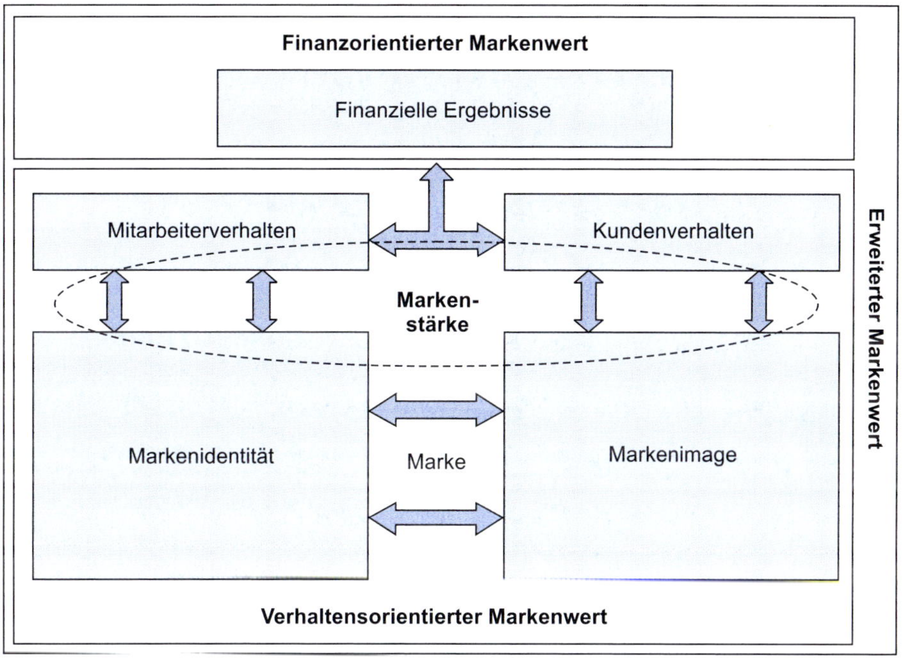

GABLER GRAFIK

Der **erweiterte Markenwertbegriff** nimmt eine integrative Sicht ein. So definieren Schulz/Brandmeyer den Markenwert als *„die Gesamtheit aller positiven und negativen Vorstellungen, die im Konsumenten ganz oder teilweise aktiviert werden, wenn er das Warenzeichen wahrnimmt und die sich in ökonomischen Daten des Markenwettbewerbs spiegeln“* (Schulz/Brandmeyer 1989, S. 365). Auch Bekmeier-Feuerhahn betont die monetäre Dimension, bezieht jedoch explizit auch die Konsumenten ein. Sie definiert den Markenwert *„als die durch die Markierung ausgelösten gegenwärtigen und zukünftigen Wertsteigerungen von Leistungen auf Konsumenten- und Unternehmensseite, die öko-*

nomisch nutzbar und in monetären Maßeinheiten zu bewerten sind" (Bekmeier-Feuerhahn 1998, S. 46). Dieser erweiterte Markenwertbegriff beinhaltet die externe, nachfragerbezogene Markenstärke und eine monetäre Ergebnisgröße, vernachlässigt jedoch nach wie vor die interne, mitarbeiterbezogene Markenstärke.

2. Verfahren der Markenbewertung

Die verschiedenen Systematisierungsansätze von Verfahren zur Bewertung einer Marke gibt Tabelle 1 wieder. Der Überblick zeigt, dass analog zu den vorgestellten Begriffsdefinitionen des Markenwertes ein zentrales Unterscheidungskriterium darin liegt, welche Art von Daten in die Verfahren eingehen und welche Form von Ergebnisgröße ermittelt wird.

Tabelle 1: Systematisierung von Markenbewertungsverfahren

Systematisierungskriterium	Ausprägungen	Systematisierungskriterium verwendet von (z. B.)
Perspektive **Analyseverfahren**	Finanzorientiert versus verhaltensorientiert und kompositionell versus dekompositionell	Bekmeier-Feuerhahn (1998), Meisner (2003), Franzen/Trommsdorff/Riedel (1994) und Calderon/Cerverva/Mollá (1997); Irmscher (1997), Sattler (2001)
Markenwirkung	Cause versus Effect	Calderon/Cerverva/Mollá (1997)
Herkunft	Theorie versus Praxis	Berndt/Sander (1994)
Aggregationsgrad	Globalmodelle versus Indikatormodelle	Franzen/Trommsdorff/Riedel (1994), ähnlich Keller (2003)
Stufigkeit	Einstufig-direkt versus mehrstufig-indirekt	Kriegbaum (2001)
Problemfokus	Isolation von Ist- versus Prognose zukünftiger markenspezifischer Zahlungen	Sattler (2000)

GABLER GRAFIK

So rekurriert die Unterscheidung in finanz- und verhaltensorientierte Verfahren auf eine Berücksichtigung beziehungsweise einen Verzicht auf monetäre Größen. Ähnlich zu begründen ist die Einteilung in Wirkungen starker Marken (effects) und Ursachen starker Marken (causes). Hier steht die Analyse der Markenstärke im Mittelpunkt. Wenn die ermittelte Markenstärke als Basis für die Transformation in eine monetäre Größe genutzt wird, hat dies eine Mehrstufigkeit der Verfahren zur Folge. Entsprechend wird eine Unterscheidung in ein- und mehrstufige beziehungsweise in globale und indikatorgestützte Verfahren vorgenommen.

Im Vergleich hierzu ist die Systematisierung von Sattler problemorientiert. Die Zuordnung der Verfahren anhand ihrer Lösungsbeiträge bedingt jedoch, dass die Systematisierung nicht überschneidungsfrei geschieht. Darüber hinaus werden die Verfahren in kompositionelle und dekompositionelle Ansätze untergliedert (Sattler 2001, S. 136 ff.). Die Unterscheidung nach Herkunft der Verfahren erscheint wenig zweckmäßig, weil Markenbewertungsansätze heute immer häufiger in Kooperationen zwischen Theorie und Praxis entwickelt werden (vgl. zum Beispiel Andresen/Esch 2000, S. 991).

Zusammenfassend kann festgehalten werden, dass die Berücksichtigung beziehungsweise der Verzicht auf die Markenstärke im Rahmen der Markenbewertung das wichtigste Kriterium zur Systematisierung von Markenbewertungsverfahren ist. Danach bestimmt sich der mögliche Einsatzzweck und Aussagegehalt einer Markenbewertung. Diesem Gedanken Rechnung tragend, soll im Folgenden eine Unterscheidung in klassisch finanzorientierte Verfahren einerseits und die Markenstärke berücksichtigende Verfahren andererseits, vorgenommen werden.

2.1 Klassisch finanzorientierte Verfahren

Die klassischen Verfahren der Markenbewertung orientieren sich gemäß dem finanzorientierten Markenwertbegriff an Größen der Unternehmensrechnung. Bei der Ermittlung von Markenwerten auf Basis des internen Rechnungswesens wird von **kostenorientierten Verfahren** gesprochen. Diese gehen auf die Vorgehensweise im Rahmen der Unternehmensbewertung zurück und setzen den Markenwert mit einem zu ermittelnden Substanzwert gleich. Dieser ermittelt sich aus den Kosten, welche den Aufbau der Marke begründen. In Abhängigkeit vom Zeitpunkt der Betrachtung wird zwischen Wiederbeschaffungskosten und historischen Kosten der Marke unterschieden (Barwise et al. 1989). Folglich ergibt sich der Markenwert auf Basis historischer Kosten/Wiederbeschaffungskosten als Summe aller angefallenen Kosten, die durch den Aufbau und den Erhalt der Marke verursacht wurden/würden (Stobart 1989, S. 26).

Preisorientierte Verfahren legen die Annahme zugrunde, dass jede Marke eine Preisprämie im Vergleich zu nicht markierten Konkurrenzangeboten erzielen kann (Sander 1994a, S. 78). Crimmins ermittelt beispielsweise die Preisprämie gegenüber Konkurrenzmarken indirekt aus dem erfragten Markenwahlverhalten (Crimmins 1992, S. 5 ff.). Andere Ansätze versuchen, die Preisprämie mittels direkter Befragungen zu quantifizie ren (Argwal/Ro 1996; Park/Srinivasan 1994). Durch Multiplikation der Preisprämie mit der Absatzmenge wird der Wert der Marke bestimmt. Konsequent angewendet bedeutet dies, dass alle preisaggressiv auftretenden Marken (z. B. Aldi) über keinen Markenwert verfügen. Die beschriebene Ermittlung der Preisprämie ist darüber hinaus immer an die Verfügbarkeit eines unmarkierten Produktes gebunden, was in der Praxis häufig zu Problemen führt. Ferner kann die Marke auch über einen reinen Mengeneffekt oder einen Kundenbindungseffekt (geringeres Risiko der Zahlungsströme), also ohne die Existenz einer Preisprämie, signifikante ökonomische Werte schaffen.

Ein um Kostengrößen erweiterter preisorientierter Ansatz ist das Verfahren zur Markenbewertung von Sander (Sander 1994b). Im Rahmen der **„hedonistischen Theorie"** werden Produktpreise durch individuell bewertete Produkteigenschaften erklärt, wobei der Markenwert als eine spezifische Produkteigenschaft gesehen wird. Dieser lässt sich je Produkt bestimmen und mit der Absatzmenge multiplizieren. Der Endwert der Marke wird über die Subtraktion des so ermittelten Markenwertes mit den markenspezifischen Kosten quantifiziert.

Die **kapitalmarktorientierten Verfahren** sehen in der Bewertung eines Unternehmens am Kapitalmarkt die Grundlage für die Ermittlung des Markenwertes. So separieren Simon/Sullivan den Marktwert des Unternehmens, der aus der Multiplikation des Aktienpreises mit der Anzahl der ausgegebenen Aktien resultiert, in materielles und immaterielles Vermögen. Die immateriellen Vermögensbestandteile werden dann wiederum in markenbezogene und nicht-markenbezogene Werte aufgeteilt (Simon/Sullivan 1993, S. 30 ff.). Das Verfahren setzt die zentrale Prämisse, dass über den Kapitalmarkt mit einer quasi-vollkommenen Marktstruktur der „wahre" Marktwert eines Unternehmens bestimmt wird und die Aufspaltung auf markenbezogene Werte vorgenommen werden kann. Das hat zur Folge, dass eine Bewertung von Unternehmen an deren börsliche Notierung geknüpft ist.

Der Grundgedanke, dass der Markenwert auf einem Markt über Angebot und Nachfrage bestimmt wird, schlägt sich auch in den **Analogieverfahren** nieder. Eine Marke wird hier durch die Zahlungsbereitschaft eines Abnehmers bewertet. Die Zahlungsbereitschaft manifestiert sich im Fall des vollständigen Erwerbes der Marke im Kaufpreis, im Fall des Teilerwerbes von Rechten in der Lizenzgebühr. Für Marken, die weder verkauft noch in Lizenz veräußert werden sollen, werden als Näherungsgrößen für deren Wert die in der Branche üblichen Lizenz- oder Transaktionspreise herangezogen (Barwise et al. 1989, S. 51 ff.).

Die zukünftige Ertragskraft einer Marke ist zentraler Bestandteil der **ertragswertorientierten Bewertungsverfahren** (Kaas 1990, S. 49 ff.). Das Ergebnis dieser Verfahren ist der auf den Bewertungszeitpunkt diskontierte Barwert einer Marke. Notwendige Voraussetzung für den Einsatz dieser Verfahren ist die Quantifizierung zukünftiger markenspezifischer Zahlungen und die Bestimmung des Kapitalisierungszinsfußes. Ein klassischer ertragswertorientierter Ansatz ist das Modell von Kern (Kern 1962). Als Basis für die Diskontierung werden markenspezifische Umsätze herangezogen. Dadurch soll eine Einbeziehung von Kosten vermieden werden, die nicht durch die Marke induziert worden sind (Kern 1962, S. 25; Franzen/Trommsdorff/Riedel 1994, S. 1379 f.). Die markenspezifischen Umsätze werden durch Multiplikation der erwarteten Gesamtumsätze mit einem branchenüblichen Lizenzsatz ermittelt. Der Diskontierungszinssatz orientiert sich ebenfalls an der Branche und soll eine durchschnittliche Umsatzrendite widerspiegeln. Aus der Formel zur Ermittlung des Markenwertes wird der investitionstheoretische Charakter des Verfahrens deutlich:

$$W = \sqrt[3]{U^2} \cdot L \cdot \frac{q^n - 1}{q^n \cdot (q-1)}$$

W = Markenwert
U = durchschnittliche Umsatzerwartung pro Jahr
L = Lizenzsatz in Prozent
n = Zeitraum der Umsatzerwartungen (Lebensdauer der Marke)
q = Rentenbarwertfaktor

Kern differenzierte 1962 bezüglich der Lebensdauer der Marke zwischen starken und schwachen Marken, ohne diese genauer zu kategorisieren. Für starke Marken soll demnach eine Lebensdauer von drei bis zehn Jahre, für schwache hingegen von nur drei bis sechs Jahre angesetzt werden (vgl. hierzu auch den Beitrag zur Nutzungsdauer von Marken in diesem Buch). Aus der Formel wird ersichtlich, dass der Markenwert einem degressiven Verlauf folgt und mit steigendem Umsatz andere Faktoren als die Marke auf den Umsatzzuwachs wirken (Kern 1962, S. 27).

Auch der **Ansatz von Herp** orientiert sich an den Umsatzwirkungen der Marke (Herp 1982). Die Marke generiert einen bestimmten Anteil des erzielten Umsatzes, der als Markenwert definiert wird (Herp 1982, S. 31). Mittels der Conjoint-Analyse (Backhaus et al. 2003, S. 543 ff.) werden aus der Präferenz (Gesamtnutzen) der Nachfrager Teilnutzenwerte für verschiedene Produkteigenschaften und die Marke ermittelt (Bekmeier-Feuerhahn 1998, S. 87). Die Multiplikation dieses Wertes mit der Absatzmenge ergibt dann den Markenwert. Dieser Wert ist wegen des notwendigen Vergleichs unterschiedlicher Marken durch die Befragten immer ein relativer Markenwert ohne natürlichen Nullpunkt (Sander 1994b, S. 91 ff.).

Der aktuellste finanzorientierte Ansatz zur Markenbewertung stammt von der internationalen Unternehmensberatung **McKinsey (Brand Equity Meter)**. Dieser Ansatz stützt sich auf eine Cashflow basierte Ertragswertberechnung des die Marke führenden Unternehmens (Riesenbeck/Perrey 2004, S. 295 ff.). Es setzt den Schwerpunkt ferner auf allgemein zugängliche Marktdaten und ergänzt diese durch drei globale konsumentenorientierte Größen. Dieser Ansatz wurde als Reaktion auf die sich abzeichnenden neuen Bilanzierungsregeln entwickelt. Entsprechend soll die Markenwertberechnung unter Beachtung der allgemeinen Grundsätze der Rechnungslegung, insbesondere dem Prinzip konservativer, vorsichtiger Bewertung, erfolgen. Die Objektivität und jederzeitige externe Überprüfbarkeit der Markenwertberechnung steht im Vordergrund des Brand Equity Meters.

Auf der Basis des Umsatzes der Marke, der EBITDA-Marge des die Marke führenden Unternehmens oder Unternehmensbereiches, des Grenzsteuersatzes des Unternehmens, der Erhaltungsinvestitionen des Unternehmens und des gewichteten Gesamtkapitalkostensatzes des Unternehmens, jeweils bezogen auf die vergangenen drei Jahre, wird entsprechend der bekannten Discounted Cash Flow Methode (DCF) der Unternehmensbewertung ein sogenannter „Customer Equity" berechnet. Diese Bezeichnung ist irreführend, weil hier keinesfalls der aus der betriebswirtschaftlichen Forschung bekannte Customer Equity im Sinne eines Kundenstammwertes berechnet wird (Burmann 2003; Rust/Lemon/Zeithaml 2004), sondern lediglich der DCF-basierte Unternehmenswert.

Da der McKinsey-spezifische „Customer Equity" nicht ausschließlich auf die Wirkung der Marke zurückzuführen ist, wird in einem zweiten Schritt der durch die Marke induzierte Anteil an diesem Wert ermittelt. Er bestimmt sich durch das allgemeine Gewicht von Marken bei der Kaufentscheidung, dem Bekanntheitsgrad der betrachteten Marke und dem Quadrat der spezifischen Imagestärke der Marke in Relation zum Wettbewerb. Zur Ermittlung dieser Faktoren wird auf die Primärmarktforschung zurückgegriffen. Der Markenwert ergibt sich schließlich als Produkt des „Customer Equity" mit dem Anteilswert der Marke (vgl. Abbildung 4). Ein wesentliches Problem ist die Tatsache, dass an dieser Stelle ein branchenübergreifend standardisierter Anteilswerte berechnet wird. Darüber hinaus ist dieses Vorgehen vergangenheitsorientiert. Hat es in der Vergangenheit keine gut geführten Marken in einer Branche gegeben, schließt der McKinsey-Ansatz die Möglichkeit zum Aufbau erfolgreicher Marken kategorisch aus. Dies steht den Erfahrungen in der Praxis diametral gegenüber. Gerade in fragmentierten Branchen, in denen sich bislang kein Anbieter mit einer Marke erfolgreich profilieren konnte, ergeben sich für innovative Marken besondere Chancen.

Abbildung 4: Das McKinsey „Brand Equity Meter" – Bestimmung des Anteils der Marke am Customer Equity

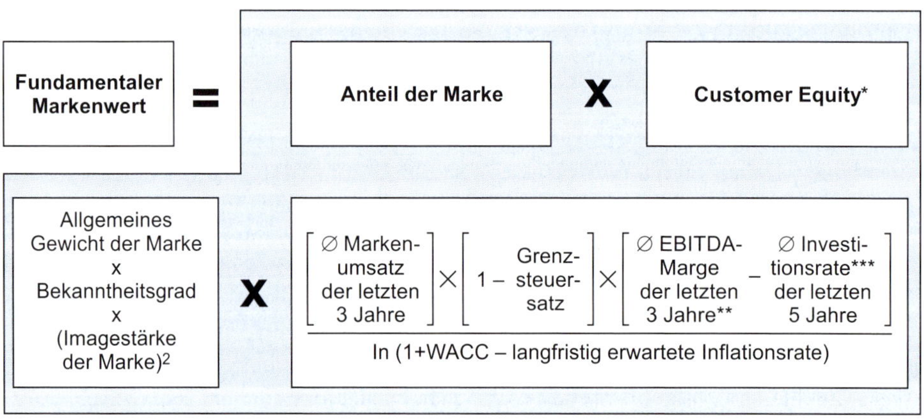

* Customer-Equity-Berechnung weicht bei Banken und Versicherungen ab
** EBITDA der jeweiligen Markensequenz bzw. Businessunits/Unternehmen
*** Investitionsrate der Erhaltungsinvestitionen in Prozent vom Umsatz

GABLER GRAFIK

Quelle: Riesenbeck/Perrey 2004, S. 315

2.2 Verfahren unter Berücksichtigung der Markenstärke

Im Gegensatz zu den finanzorientierten Verfahren steht bei den im Folgenden vorgestellten Verfahren die Markenstärke im Mittelpunkt des Interesses. Eine Transformation in ein monetäres Ergebnis wird teilweise vorgenommen, ist aber nicht notwendiger Bestandteil der Verfahren.

Das 1989 von der Markenberatung Interbrand publizierte Modell berechnet den Markenwert **kompositionell** in zwei Stufen. In einem ersten Schritt werden im Rahmen eines Punktbewertungsverfahrens sieben verschiedene Hauptkategorien bewertet, die je nach Branchenzugehörigkeit des markenführenden Unternehmens durch 80 bis 100 Unterkategorien beschrieben werden (Riedel 1996, S. 48). Die Hauptkategorien umfassen die in Tabelle 2 dargestellten Kriterien (Bekmeier-Feuerhahn 1998, S. 79; Heider/Strehlau 2000, S. 508). Interbrand bezeichnet den resultierenden Punktwert der ersten Bewertungsstufe stark verkürzt als „Markenstärke". Da hier jedoch nur in dem mit 15 Prozent gewichteten Faktor „Markenstabilität" ansatzweise konsumentenorientierte Größen (Markenbekanntheit) betrachtet werden, entspricht die „Markenstärke" nach Interbrand in keiner Weise dem hier vertretenen Verständnis des Begriffes Markenstärke. Interbrand verwendet den Begriff Markenstärke stattdessen in einem sehr allgemeinen, umgangssprachlichen Sinne. Über eine S-förmig verlaufende Marktindexkurve wird der Punktwert in einen Multiplikator transformiert, der wiederum mit dem gewichteten, marktbezogenen Durchschnittsgewinn der letzten drei Jahre multipliziert wird.

Tabelle 2: Kategorien und Gewichte des Ansatzes von Interbrand

Hauptkategorie	Beispielhafte Indikatoren	Gewicht
Marktposition/ -führerschaft	Marktanteil, Breite der Kundenbasis, Distributionsdichte	25 %
Markenstabilität	Alter der Marke, Bekanntheitsgrad, Konstanz der Kommunikation	15 %
Markt	Größe, Stabilität, Konkurrenzstruktur	10 %
Internationalität	Internationale Präsenz, Markteintrittsposition	25 %
Trend der Marke	Umsatzentwicklung, Wachstumspotenzial	10 %
Marketing – Unterstützung	Werbeaufwendungen, Einsatz von Kommunikationsinstrumenten	10 %
Rechtlicher Schutz	Eintragung, Verkehrsgeltung	5 %

GABLER GRAFIK

Ähnlich dem Vorgehen von Interbrand bilden auch bei der von Schulz/Brandmeyer entwickelten „Marken-Bilanz" 19 gewichtete Indikatoren, die sich wiederum in sechs Hauptkategorien unterteilen lassen, das Fundament der Markenbewertung (Schulz/Brandmeyer 1989, S. 361). Die Hauptkategorien richten sich nach Leitfragen wie „Was gibt der Markt her?" oder „Wie stark sind die Konsumenten mit der Marke verbunden?". Die herangezogenen Kennziffern werden in Skalenwerte transformiert, wobei über alle 19 Kriterien eine Maximalpunktzahl von 500 Punkten erreicht werden kann. Der resultierende Punktwert, die „Markenstärke" gemäß Schulz/Brandmeyer, geht in die Monetarisierung des Markenwertes ein. Mit Hilfe des Ertragswertverfahrens werden die geschätzten zukünftigen Erträge der Marke diskontiert, wobei sich der Diskontierungsfaktor aus der „Markenstärke" ergibt. Hohe Punktwerte führen zu einem niedrigen Diskontierungsfaktor und so zu hohen Markenwerten (Berndt/Sander 1994, S. 1362 f.). Die Marken-Bilanz wurde in den 90er Jahren zu einem modular aufgebauten Markencontrollingsystem weiterentwickelt, dem „Nielsen Brand Performancer". Das relevante Bewertungsmodul, der „Brand Monitor", verdichtet die Indikatoren der Marken-Bilanz in:

- Marktattraktivität (Volumen und Wachstum des Marktes) Gewicht ca. 15 %
- Durchsetzungsstärke im Markt (Marktanteil in Menge und Wert) Gewicht ca. 35 %
- Nachfragerakzeptanz (Markenbekanntheit, Relevanz der Marke) Gewicht ca. 40 %
- Verbreitungsgrad (numerische und gewichtete Distribution) Gewicht ca. 10 %

(Franzen/Trommsdorff/Riedel 1994, S. 1395; A. C. Nielsen Konzept & Markt, 2001). Die Markenstärke als Ergebnis der Bewertung im Brand Monitor wird in Beziehung zu den Werten der relevanten Wettbewerber gesetzt und so in eine „relative Markenstärke" überführt, die im „Brand Value System" in Anlehnung an die Vorgehensweise in der Marken-Bilanz monetarisiert wird.

Ein ebenso komplexes wie mehrstufiges Verfahren der Markenbewertung stellt Bekmeier-Feuerhahn vor (Bekmeier-Feuerhahn 1998, S. 111 ff.). Innerhalb dieses Ansatzes wird auf der ersten Stufe die Markenstärke als Antriebskraft gemessen, die aus der subjektiven Wertschätzung der Marke entsteht. Grundlage für die Messung der Markenstärke bilden die kognitiven Prozesse des Käuferverhaltens auf Basis der Imagery- und Hemisphärenforschung. Im Einzelnen werden die Indikatoren „Einzigartigkeit", „Qualität", „Zugriffsfähigkeit" und „Intensität" für die zu untersuchende Marke sowie für ein unmarkiertes Produkt erhoben. Über eine multiplikative Verknüpfung der unterschiedlichen verbalen und bildlichen Assoziationen und deren Logarithmierung ergibt sich eine Kennzahl, welche die Markenstärke abbildet. Das Ergebnisintervall liegt dabei zwischen Werten von –3,999 und +3,999. So charakterisieren Ergebnisse von –3,999 bis 0 schwache Marken, Werte darüber starke Marken. Neben der Markenstärke wird aus den markenbezogenen Erlösen und Kosten der monetäre Markengewinn ermittelt. Die Informationen hierzu liefern Branchenanalysen und Expertenurteile. Im Anschluss daran werden Marktpreise für die Komponenten „Markenstärke" und „Markengewinn" auf einem simulierten Testmarkt mittels Experteneinschätzungen generiert. Eine Zusammenführung der Ergebnisse ergibt den Markenwert. Das Modell enthält somit Elemente der indikatorgestützten-, der kostenorientierten- sowie der Analogieverfahren.

Abbildung 5: **Positionierung von Waschmittelmarken im Modell der GfK (1999)**

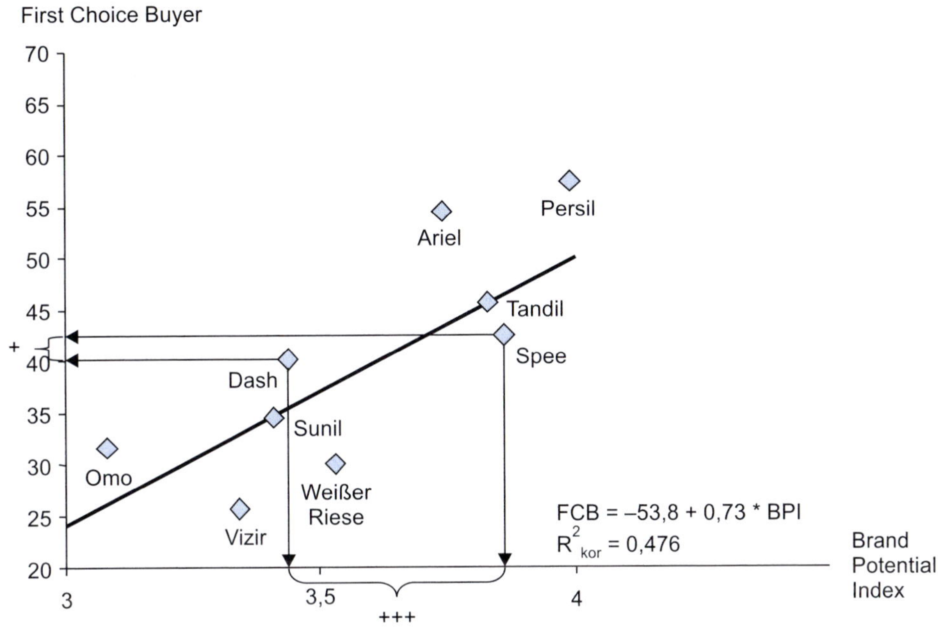

GABLER GRAFIK

Quelle: GfK Studie 2000 „Key Driver starke Marken"

Eine Fusion von Informationen aus Paneldaten und Verbraucherbefragungen stellt das im Jahr 2000 vorgestellte Markenbewertungsmodell der Gesellschaft für Konsumforschung (GfK) **„BASS – Brand Assessment System"** dar (Twardawa/Hupp 2000; Hupp 2000a). Das Modellergebnis ist keine monetäre Größe, sondern eine relative Bewertung von Marken. Über eine Analyse von Paneldaten können Käufe von „Fast Moving Consumer Goods (FMCG)" verschiedenen Käufergruppen zugeordnet werden. Die Gruppe der „First Choice Buyer" sind diejenigen Käufer einer Marke, die sie als erstpräferierte Marke kaufen. Der Umsatzanteil, den die „First Choice Buyer" zum Gesamtumsatz der Marke beitragen, ist der „First Choice Value". Mit diesen Maßen sollen in dem Verfahren das Erlöspotenzial und die Stabilität der zu bewertenden Marke abgebildet werden. Sie setzen folglich am beobachtbaren Verhalten der Konsumenten an. Die Markenstärke wird mit Hilfe des „Brand Potential Index" erfasst, der sich aus zehn Komponenten, beispielsweise der Markensympathie, -bekanntheit oder Mehrpreisakzeptanz, zusammensetzt. Die einzelnen Komponenten werden direkt abgefragt und gewichtet. Aus der Zusammenführung der Erlöskomponente „First Choice Buyer" und dem „Brand Potential Index" werden Aussagen über den Status und die zukünftige Entwicklung der Marken getroffen (vgl. Abbildung 6).

Das Beispiel zeigt, dass, obwohl die Waschmittelmarken „Dash“ und „Spee“ einen ähnlich hohen Anteil an „First Choice Buyern“ haben, „Spee“ die deutlich höhere Markenstärke aufweist. Der Markenwert ist somit insgesamt höher einzuordnen, da ein höherer „Brand Potential Index“ in dem Modell auf zukünftig steigende Marktanteile schließen lässt. Diese Aussage wurde durch eine Analyse der Paneldaten im Zeitvergleich von 1999 und 2000 bestätigt (GfK, Studie „Key Driver starke Marken 2000).

Abbildung 6: Der Brand RATING-Ansatz zur Markenbewertung

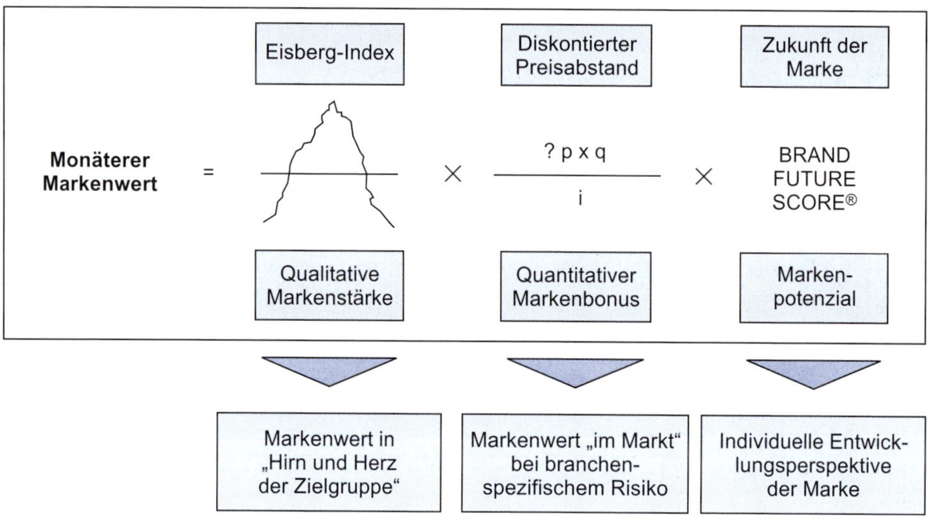

GABLER GRAFIK

Quelle: Musiol et al. 2004, S. 386

Eine dynamische Sichtweise der Komponenten des Markenwertes nimmt schließlich auch der **„Markeneisberg“** der Unternehmensberatung „icon brand navigation“ ein (vgl. zum Beispiel Esch/Andresen 2001, S. 1081 ff.). Die gemessene Markenstärke ergibt sich hier aus den beiden Komponenten „Markenbild“ und „Markenguthaben“, wobei dem Markenbild eine kurzfristige, dem Markenguthaben eine langfristige Perspektive zugrunde liegt. Der Beitrag der Komponenten zum Gesamtergebnis ist dabei vom Alter der Marke abhängig. Ein Markenguthaben kann nur langfristig und über die Beeinflussung des Markenbildes aufgebaut werden. Bei der praktischen Anwendung werden für eine zu bewertende Marke standardisierte Befragungen durchgeführt. Die erhobenen Werte werden dann mit der „Icon-Datenbank“ abgeglichen. Die Datenbank enthält Referenzgrößen der Branche beziehungsweise des Produktbereiches bezüglich der untersuchten Werte. Aus den resultierenden Abweichungen können Aussagen über die Bewertung der Marke im Branchenvergleich gezogen werden.

Der **Brand-Rating Ansatz** von icon brand navigation und Dr. Wieselhuber & Partner baut auf dem Markeneisberg-Modell auf. Er ermittelt den Markenwert entsprechend der in Abbildung 6 dargestellten Kombination von finanzorientierten und verhaltensorientierten Komponenten. Der Markenwert setzt sich hier neben den Komponenten aus dem Markeneisberg aber auch aus der Komponente „quantitativer Markenbonus“ und „Markenpotenzial“ zusammen. Der quantitative Markenbonus ergibt sich aus der realisierten Preisprämie der Marke und der abgesetzten Menge. Das Markenpotenzial ergibt sich aus den Vermutungen über die zukünftigen Entwicklungspotenziale der Marke sowie Art und Ausmaß des rechtlichen Markenschutzes (Musiol et al. 2004, S. 374 ff.).

3. Zweckbezogene und methodische Markenbewertungsunterschiede

Die vorgestellten Verfahren geben einen Eindruck von den verschiedenartigen Vorgehensweisen bei der Bewertung einer Marke sowie von der Komplexität dieser Aufgabenstellung. Marktforschungsunternehmen, Werbeagenturen und Unternehmensberater bieten inzwischen eine Fülle weiterer Markenbewertungsverfahren an. In der Literatur sind mittlerweile bis zu 500 verschiedene Verfahren zu finden (Strelau/Heider 2000, S. 150). Die Vielfalt spiegelt gleichzeitig auch das Ausmaß der Uneinigkeit über den „richtigen Weg“ in der Markenbewertung wider. Dies umso mehr, als dass verschiedene Verfahren am Beispiel ein und derselben Marke zu höchst unterschiedlichen Ergebnissen kommen. Besonders deutlich sind die Unterschiede bei der monetären Bewertung. So haben beispielsweise in einer aktuellen Studie neun Unternehmen eine fiktive Marke bewertet (Hanser/Högl/Maul 2004). Trotz exakt gleicher Datenbasis lagen die ermittelten Markenwerte in einer Bandbreite von 173 Millionen Euro bis 958 Millionen Euro (vgl. Abbildung 7).

Bei den Verfahren aus Abbildung 7 lassen sich zum Teil systematische Unterschiede feststellen, die sich aus der unterschiedlichen **Zweckeignung** der Verfahren ergeben. Sofern unterschiedliche Bewertungszwecke verfolgt werden, sind unterschiedliche Markenwerte nicht nur zulässig, sondern zwingend (Seiwert 2004, S. 37). Allerdings bestehen auch unsystematische Unterschiede, die sich nur auf unterschiedliche **methodische Vorgehensweisen** zurückführen lassen. Im Folgenden sollen ausgewählte Aspekte zweckbezogener und methodischer Markenbewertungsunterschiede vorgestellt werden.

Abbildung 7: **Ergebnisse der Markenbewertungsstudie von Hanser/Högl/Maul 2004**

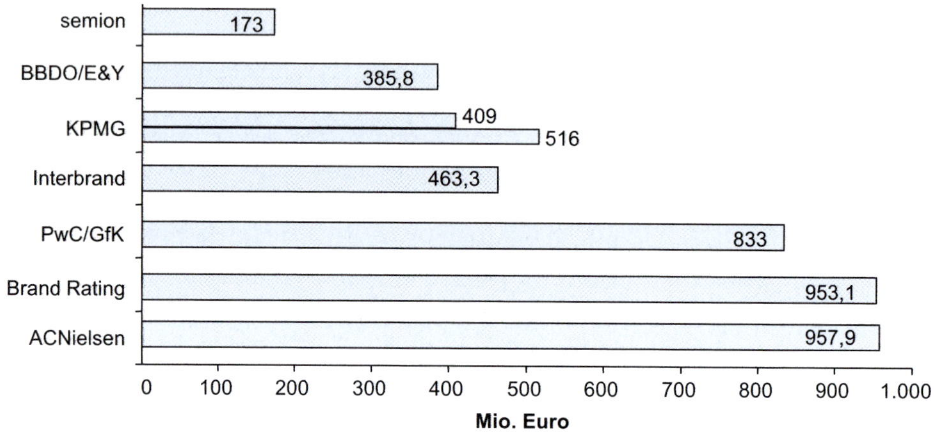

3.1 Zweckbezogene Unterschiede der Verfahren

Einen wesentlichen Einfluss auf das Ergebnis der Markenbewertung hat die Zugrundelegung von **„Fair Values"** versus **„Values in Use"**. Der Fair Value wird dann verwendet, wenn handels- oder steuerliche Vorschriften einzuhalten sind, also der Zweck der Unternehmensbewertung einen bilanziellen Hintergrund hat. Der Fair Value abstrahiert von der Perspektive des markenführenden Unternehmens und legt damit einen objektivierten, marktübergreifenden Wertmaßstab zugrunde. Beispielsweise ermittelt der Ansatz von KPMG und der **Advanced Brand Valuation** Ansatz von PriceWaterhouseCoopers und der GfK auf Basis einer Fair-Value Bewertung die abschreibungsbedingte Steuerersparnis, die ein Erwerber einer Marke als Folge der bilanziellen Aktivierung erwarten kann (Hanser/Högl/Maul 2004, S. 225). Der Ausweis dieser Steuerersparnis führt entsprechend auch zu einem höheren Markenwert.

Nach einer von Sattler/PriceWaterhouseCoopers durchgeführten Studie werden bislang gerade einmal elf Prozent der Verfahren zum Zweck der unternehmensexternen Berichterstattung innerhalb des Jahresabschlusses verwendet (vgl. Abbildung 8).

Im Gegensatz dazu wird bei unternehmensinternen Anlässen der Value in Use verwendet, der eine Evaluierung aus subjektiver Perspektive des markenführenden Unternehmens ermöglicht und damit zur internen Entscheidungsunterstützung des Markenmanagements grundsätzlich besser geeignet ist.

Abbildung 8: **Verwendungszwecke bisher durchgeführter Markenbewertungen**

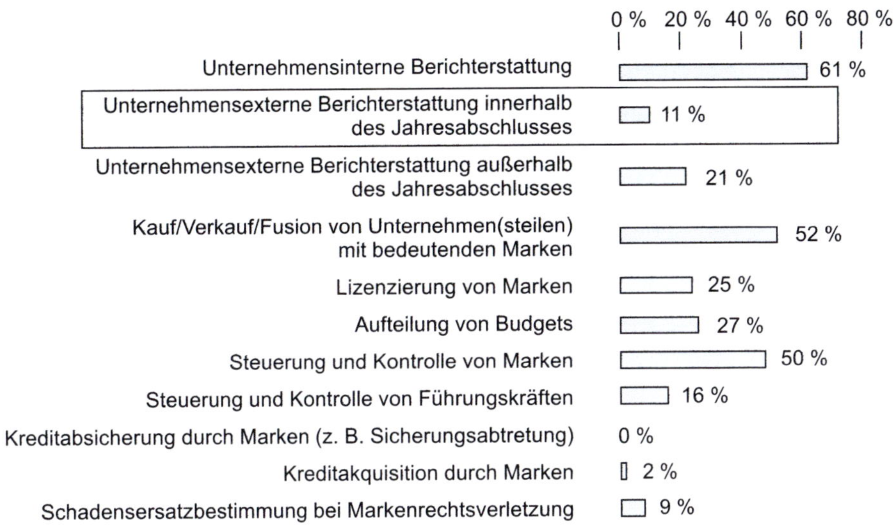

Quelle: Sattler/PriceWaterhouseCoopers 2001, S. 23

Zur Entscheidungsunterstützung ermitteln einige Verfahren neben dem Fortführungswert (Going-Concern-Markenwert) auch den Wert markenstrategischer Optionen. Verfahren, die den Wert markenstrategischer Optionen ermitteln, taxieren diesen, insbesondere bei Fast Moving Consumer Goods, häufig auf bis zu 50 Prozent des Gesamtmarkenwertes (Sattler 2004, S. 32). Der Wert markenstrategischer Optionen speist sich insbesondere aus der Möglichkeit der Markenausdehnung in Form von Line Extensions oder Category Extensions (vgl. den Beitrag zu Markenevolutionsstrategien in diesem Buch). Abbildung 9 gibt beispielhaft die Ermittlung eines „Brand Stretching Scores" auf Basis eines Strukturgleichungsmodells wieder, mittels dessen die Erfolgswahrscheinlichkeit einer Markenausdehnung bewertet wird (Sattler/Högl/Hupp 2002, S. 25 ff.).

Abbildung 9: **Modell zur Ermittlung des Wertes von zukünftigen markenstrategischen Optionen**

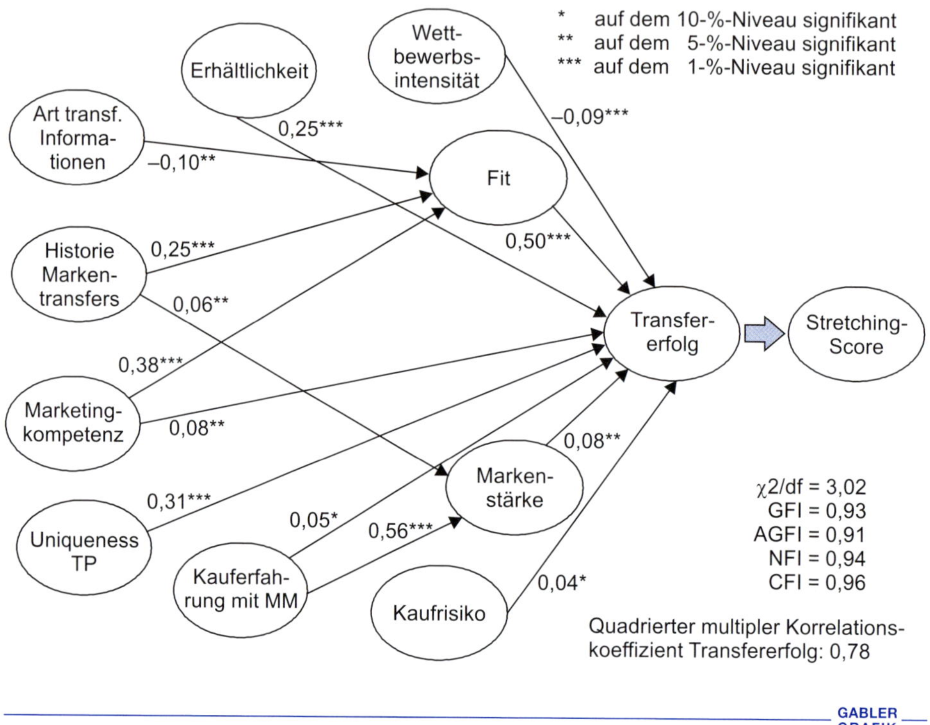

Quelle: Sattler/Högl/Hupp 2002, S. 16

3.2 Methodische Unterschiede

Die Markenbewertung steht wie jedes Messverfahren vor grundsätzlichen Problemen, die auf messtheoretische und umsetzungsbezogene Überlegungen zurückgehen (vgl. zum Beispiel Bekmeier-Feuerhahn 1998, S. 63 ff.; Riedel 1996, S. 50; Irmscher 1997, S. 98 ff.). **Messtheoretische Problemfelder** sind zum Beispiel Probleme bei der Objektivität, Reliabilität und Validität. Unter **Objektivität** wird die möglichst große Freiheit von subjektiven Einflüssen des Messenden verstanden. Das Ergebnis muss intersubjektiv vergleichbar sein. Die **Validität** bezieht sich auf die Abbildung des tatsächlichen Sachverhaltes. Wenn etwa die Markenstärke mittels des Indikators „Wiederholungskäufe" aus Warenkorbanalysen operationalisiert wird, so muss die Validität in zweierlei Hinsicht überprüft werden. Zum einen ist zu fragen, ob Paneldaten tatsächlich Auskunft über die Wiederholungskäufe geben und ob diese das Konstrukt „Markenstärke" faktisch abbilden (Kroeber-Riel/Weinberg 2003, S. 32). **Reliabilität** bezeichnet die formale Genauigkeit des Messinstrumentes, so dass die Messergebnisse zu unterschiedlichen Zeitpunkten und bei unterschiedlichen Personen gleich bleiben. Neben diesen grundsätzlichen Problemfeldern birgt die Erfassung der Markenstärke einige spezielle Schwierigkeiten, die bei der Bewertung von Marken berücksichtigt werden müssen.

3.21 Erfassung der Markenstärke

Ein erstes Problem bei der Erfassung der Markenstärke liegt in den unterschiedlichen Definitionen dieses Begriffs begründet. Hier hat der vorliegende Beitrag auf der Basis des identitätsorientierten Markenführungsansatzes eine klare Position bezogen. Markenstärke als Verhaltensrelevanz der Marke für die internen und externen Zielgruppen ist jedoch in der Regel nicht direkt messbar, sondern muss anhand von Indikatoren erfasst werden. Die Auswahl der Indikatoren ist angesichts der in der Literatur vorgeschlagenen bis zu 100 Indikatoren ein nicht zu unterschätzendes Entscheidungsproblem (Kriegbaum 2001, S. 81; Steinwartz 2001, S. 64 ff.).

Ein weiterer Kritikpunkt richtet sich auf die häufig verwendeten Punktbewertungsansätze, zum Beispiel bei der Marken-Bilanz, dem Brand-Rating Ansatz und bei Interbrand und die dort höchst subjektive Auswahl der Indikatoren (Hammann 1992, S. 222; Berndt/Sander 1994, S. 1368). Darüber hinaus unterstellen Punktbewertungsmodelle, dass die verwendeten Kriterien im statistischen Sinne unabhängig sind. Für die Verfahren von Interbrand und Schulz/Brandmeyer lassen sich jedoch zahlreiche, zum Teil erhebliche Korrelationen feststellen (Herreiner 1994, S. 45 ff.). Der Grund hierfür liegt in der Tendenz von Scoring Modellen begründet, mit zunehmender Anzahl von Indikatoren Korrelationen auszubilden. Damit eng verbunden ist das Problem der Gewichtung der Indikatoren. Hier ergibt sich ein Spannungsfeld zwischen branchenabhängiger Variation der Gewichte versus konstanter Gewichtung. Letzteres hat eine bessere Vergleichbarkeit der Ergebnisse zur Folge. Da die Bewertungsverfahren häufig in der Beratungspraxis eingesetzt werden, sind die Gewichtungen der Verfahren darüber hinaus oft nicht zugänglich.

Die Kritik an der subjektiven, auf Erfahrungen der Modellentwickler basierenden Auswahl und Gewichtung der Indikatoren hat dazu geführt, dass mit Hilfe von Kausalanalysen die Einflussgrößen der Markenstärke validiert werden (vgl. zum Beispiel Riedel 1996, S. 106 f., Bekmeier-Feuerhahn 1998, S. 141 ff.). Dabei lassen sich jedoch ebenfalls erhebliche Unterschiede bezüglich der grundlegenden Modellformulierung feststellen, was zu großen Teilen durch differierende Begriffsverständnisse und Zielsetzungen der Modelle erklärt werden kann. So bemerkt Bekmeier-Feuerhahn zu Recht, dass die von Riedel genutzten Indikatoren eng mit dem Kaufakt verbunden sind, was bei einem psychischen, dem Kaufakt vorgelagerten Konstrukt wie der Markenstärke nicht sinnvoll erscheint (Bekmeier-Feuerhahn 1998, S. 85).

Ein weiterer Ansatz zur Validierung der Markenstärke ist der Einsatz der konfirmatorischen Faktoranalyse. Dieses Instrument wurde bei der Entwicklung des „Brand Potential Index" eingesetzt (Hupp 2000b, S. 47). Ähnlich wie bei der Kausalanalyse ist es auch hier notwendig, ex ante ein Strukturmodell zu formulieren, dessen Beziehungsstruktur mittels der erhobenen Daten überprüft wird. Da die unterschiedlichen Strukturmodelle auf Basis einer spezifischen Datengrundlage, wie etwa einem bestimmten Markt oder einer bestimmten Branche, bestätigt werden, ist die Generalisierbarkeit der ermittelten Ergebnisse kritisch zu hinterfragen.

3.22 Monetäre Abbildung des Markenwertes

Eine zentrale Quelle unterschiedlicher monetärer Bewertungsergebnisse ist das Problem der **Isolation von Erfolgsbeiträgen der Marke** von denjenigen des die Marke führenden Unternehmens (Kapferer 2000, S. 402; Sattler 2000, S. 225 f.). Die vorgestellten Verfahren generieren markenspezifische Erfolgsgrößen aus allgemeinen Marktbeurteilungen, aus Konsumenten– oder Expertenurteilen oder aus dem Rechnungswesen. Alle diese Ansätze sind letztlich nicht befriedigend, weil nicht valide. Die Bestimmung des Geldwertes einer Marke über die geäußerte Zahlungsbereitschaft eines Investors stellt hier zwar eine idealtypische Vorgehensweise dar, die aber nur in den seltensten Fällen in der Praxis anwendbar sein dürfte. Bei der Annäherung über den Kapitalmarkt oder den Cashflow-Ertragswert (bei McKinsey) tritt das Problem der Separation von Unternehmens- und Markenwert in besonderer Schärfe auf, weil zumeist nur sehr grob und oberflächlich mit dem Isolationsproblem umgegangen wird. Auch eine Schätzung über Experten ist methodisch als wenig valide abzulehnen.

Einer Isolation der Erfolgsbeiträge durch Konsumentenurteile sind vor allem bei direkter Abfrage von Zahlungsbereitschaften oder Präferenzen Grenzen gesetzt. Die dekompositionelle Vorgehensweise der Conjoint-Analyse ohne Vorgabe von zu bewertenden Einzelkriterien stellt hier einen Fortschritt dar. Die Kritik verbirgt sich in den Prämissen des Verfahrens. Darüber hinaus werden auch hier **markenspezifische Auszahlungen**, Aufwendungen oder Kosten zur Ermittlung des Markenwertes benötigt. Die Nutzung von Daten aus dem Rechnungswesen führt schließlich zu dem Problem der Vergangenheitsorientierung. So würden letztlich hohe Kosten einen hohen Markenwert bedingen et vice versa, was höchst zweifelhaft erscheint (Sander 1994, S. 98; Keller 2003, S. 477 ff.).

Ein weiteres schwerwiegendes Problem vieler monetärer Markenbewertungen liegt in der **Verwendung von Gewinnen, Deckungsbeiträgen, EBITDA-Margen oder Zahlungsüberschüssen** einer oder mehrerer Bezugsperioden. Damit wird vernachlässigt, dass Marken durch (temporäre) Probleme beim internen Kostenmanagement keineswegs weniger wertvoll werden. Schließlich sei erwähnt, dass sich in diesem Zusammenhang auch bilanzpolitische Maßnahmen auf den berechneten Markenwert auswirken und diesen massiv verzerren können.

Eine zukunftsorientierte Bewertung von Marken beinhaltet eine Prognose über die zukünftigen Erfolgswirkungen der Marke. Unabhängig von der Isolation der Zahlungsgrößen ergibt sich dadurch ein **Prognoseproblem**. Bei der Errechnung des Ertragswertes muss die Anzahl der Perioden vorgegeben werden. Das bietet erhebliches Potenzial für willkürliche Entscheidungen bei der Einschätzung des Bewertungszeitraums oder der erwarteten Lebensdauer der Marke (Kruschwitz 1998, S. 140 f.). Neben der Vorgabe der Nutzungsdauer ist ebenfalls der Diskontierungszinssatz zu benennen, dessen Höhe ebenfalls ein Problem darstellt (Perridon/Steiner 1998, S. 84 f.). Prognostiziert man beispielsweise gemäß Abbildung 11 für die ersten sechs Jahre steigende und ab dem siebten Jahr konstante jährliche Zahlungsüberschüsse (Brand Earnings), ergibt sich bei einem unterstellten risikoadjustierten Zinsfuß von sieben Prozent ein Markenwert von 30 Millionen Euro. Unterstellt man hingegen, dass der risikoadjustierte Zinsfuß nicht sieben, sondern zwölf Prozent beträgt, sinkt der Markenwert rapide auf nur noch 16,8 Millionen Euro (Sattler/Högl/Hupp 2002, S. 12).

Abbildung 10: Einfluss des Diskontierungssatzes auf den Markenwert

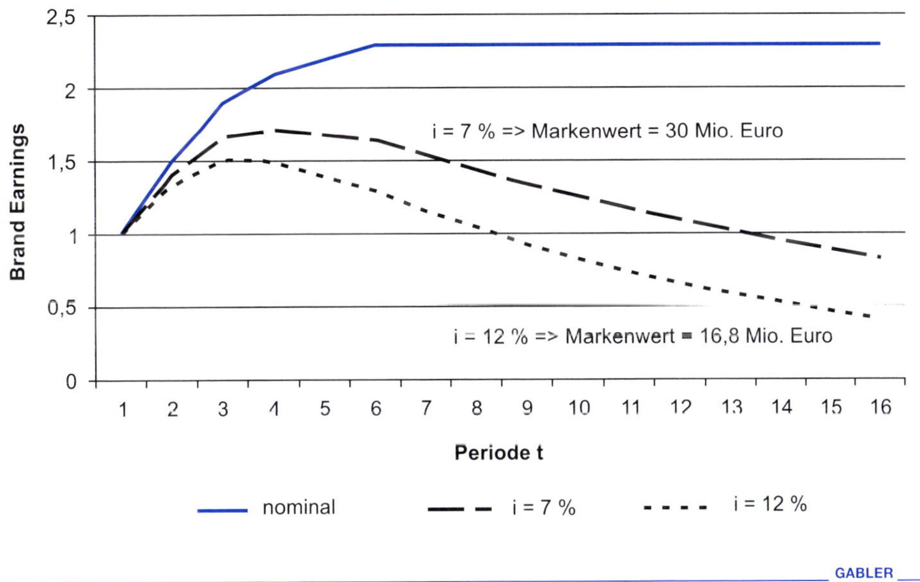

Quelle: Sattler/Högl/Hupp 2002, S. 12

Da die Marke ein dynamisches Phänomen ist, fallen Maßnahmen der Markenführung und deren Wirkung zeitlich auseinander (Kapferer 2000, S. 52). Die Berücksichtigung dieser time-lags stellt ein weiteres Problem bei der Markenbewertung dar.

1. Problemstellung

Nach § 253 Abs. 2 Satz 1 und 2 HGB sind die Anschaffungs- und Herstellungskosten von Vermögensgegenständen des Anlagevermögens, **deren Nutzung zeitlich begrenzt ist,** um planmäßige Abschreibungen zu vermindern. Gemäß § 6 Abs. 1 Nr. 1 Satz 1 EstG haben sich die Abschreibungen an der **betriebsgewöhnlichen Nutzungsdauer** des Wirtschaftsgutes zu orientieren. Planmäßige Abschreibungen für entgeltlich erworbene Marken sind somit nur dann möglich, wenn deren Nutzungsdauer begrenzt ist beziehungsweise Marken der Abnutzung unterliegen. Der zweite Senat des Bundesfinanzhofes hat diesbezüglich mit Beschluss vom 04.09.1996 festgestellt, *„dass entgeltlich erworbene Warenzeichen, die auf Dauer betrieblich genutzt werden, keinem Wertverzehr unterliegen"*. Diese Auffassung wird vor allem damit begründet, dass *„es doch weder eine gesetzliche Regelung, noch einen allgemeinen Erfahrungssatz (gibt (Anmerkung des Verfassers)), wonach sich der Wert von Warenzeichen generell innerhalb einer bestimmten Nutzungsdauer verbraucht und diesem Umstand durch eine planmäßige Abschreibung Rechnung zu tragen ist"*. Auch die Diskussion über den International Accounting Standard 38 (IAS 38.79 – 38.90) zur zukünftigen Bilanzierung immaterieller Vermögensgegenstände hat gezeigt, dass eine Reihe von Bilanzierungsexperten die Auffassung vertritt, Marken seien nicht abnutzbar (IASC, Basis for Conclusions, IAS 38.45 (a. i)). Demgegenüber hat jedoch der der Bundesfinanzhof in einer Stellungnahme vom 27.02.1998 Marken aus ertragssteuerlicher Sicht als abnutzbare Wirtschaftsgüter bezeichnet und damit implizit die Notwendigkeit kontinuierlicher Marketinganstrengungen zur Aufrechterhaltung beziehungsweise Steigerung des Markenwertes unterstrichen. Vor diesem Hintergrund soll der Frage nachgegangen werden, **ob und in welcher Form auf Dauer genutzte Marken einem Werteverzehr unterliegen**.

Neben der Gewinnermittlung aufseiten des Markenkäufers ist diese Frage **auch im Rahmen der Markenführung von hohem Interesse**. Marken werden dabei als Investitionsobjekte betrachtet. Dem Markenmanager obliegt die Vorteilhaftigkeitsbestimmung für alternative Markeninvestitionen und das Controlling dieser Investitionen. Zur Bestimmung der Vorteilhaftigkeit von Investitionen in verschiedene Marken oder in unterschiedliche Markenstrategien für eine bestimmte Marke müssen der Zahlungsstrom und damit die Nutzungsdauer der Markeninvestitionen bestimmt werden. Ausgehend von diesen beiden Interessenlagen soll herausgearbeitet werden, dass es aus theoretischer und empirischer Betrachtung zahlreiche Anhaltspunkte zur Bestimmung von Erfahrungssätzen gibt, wonach sich der Wert verschiedener Klassen von Marken generell innerhalb bestimmter Nutzungsdauerintervalle verbraucht. Nachfolgend wird dabei auf der Grundlage des geltenden Rechts argumentiert (de lege lata).

Dabei ist bei der Untersuchung von Marken grundsätzlich zwischen der Marke als gewerblichem Schutzrecht, dem markierten Produkt und der „eigentlichen" Marke zu unterscheiden (vgl. in diesem Zusammenhang auch den Beitrag zum Stellenwert und Gegenstand des Markenmanagements in diesem Buch). Die präzisierte Fragestellung lautet somit: Welche **betriebsgewöhnliche Nutzungsdauer** hat

- das gewerbliche Schutzrecht,
- das markierte Produkt und
- die Marke?

Während die Nutzungsdauer des gewerblichen Schutzrechtes faktisch unbegrenzt ist, trifft dies auf das markierte Produkt und die Marke nicht zu. Beim **markierten Produkt** ist in der Regel von einer auf wenige Jahre beschränkten Lebensdauer auszugehen (Simon 1982, S. 188). In der Automobilindustrie sind zum Beispiel Produktlebenszyklen von fünf bis sieben Jahren üblich, bei Personalcomputern 1,5 bis zwei Jahre und bei modischer Damenoberbekleidung drei bis sechs Monate. An dieser Stelle wird der Unterschied zwischen dem markierten Produkt und der **Marke** deutlich. Während zum Beispiel unter der Marke „VW Golf" circa alle sechs Jahre ein vollständig neu konstruiertes Produkt angeboten und unter der Damenoberbekleidungsmarke „Gerry Weber" circa alle sechs Monate eine komplett neue Kollektion vorgestellt wird, weisen beide Marken eine längere Lebensdauer auf.

2. Abnutzbarkeit von Marken

2.1 Rechtliche versus wirtschaftliche Abnutzbarkeit von Marken

Die Frage der Abnutzbarkeit von Marken kann sich auf die rechtliche oder wirtschaftliche Abnutzbarkeit beziehen. Die Begriffsauffassung des Bundesfinanzhofes in seinem Beschluss vom 4.9.1996 bezieht sich auf die **rechtliche Abnutzbarkeit** im Sinne **der Geltungsdauer von Warenzeichenrechten**. Laut § 47 MarkenG beträgt die Schutzdauer eingetragener Marken zehn Jahre. Sie ist beliebig oft um weitere zehn Jahre verlängerbar. Aus dieser rechtlichen Sicht stehen Marken dem Unternehmen faktisch dauerhaft zur Verfügung. Eine Abnutzbarkeit wäre dann abzulehnen. Dieser Argumentation liegt jedoch ein **verkürztes Markenverständnis** zugrunde, denn es wird ausschließlich der Frage nachgegangen, wie lange das **gewerbliche Schutzrecht** vom Unternehmen genutzt werden darf. Vernachlässigt wird, dass der Wert einer Marke nicht primär durch das gewerbliche Schutzrecht als solches begründet wird, sondern durch die Loyalität der Nachfrager gegenüber einer Marke als Folge eines überlegenen **Markennutzens**.

Um den für die tatsächliche Werthaltigkeit einer Marke beziehungsweise deren Werteverzehr verantwortlichen Bestimmungsfaktoren gerecht zu werden, muss auf die **wirtschaftliche Abnutzbarkeit** von Marken abgestellt werden. Die alleinige Relevanz der wirtschaftlichen Abnutzbarkeit kann aus den Zwecken der Handels- und Steuerbilanz abgeleitet werden. *„Primärzweck der Handelsbilanz ist die vorsichtige Ermittlung eines ausschüttungsfähigen Vermögenszuwachses. Dieser deckt sich mit dem Zweck der Steuerbilanz, einen nach Maßgabe der wirtschaftlichen Leistungsfähigkeit steuerbaren*

Gewinn zu ermitteln" (Barth/Kneisel 1997, S. 474). Ebenso wie die Nutzungsdauer von Maschinen nicht technisch, sondern lediglich wirtschaftlich bestimmt werden kann (Leffson 1938, S. 308), ist auch die Nutzungsdauer von Marken nicht rechtlich, sondern wirtschaftlich zu bestimmen.

Aufgrund der in Handels- und Steuerbilanz deutlich werdenden Fokussierung auf die wirtschaftliche Leistungsfähigkeit eines Unternehmens wird hier ebenfalls auf eine wirtschaftliche Betrachtungsweise abgestellt. Die Bestimmung der Markennutzungsdauer aus rein wirtschaftlicher Perspektive ist jedoch mit hoher Unsicherheit und dementsprechend **großen Ermessensspielräumen** verbunden. Zur **Objektivierung** wird bei materiellen Vermögensgegenständen vorgeschlagen, eine Normierung der wirtschaftlichen Nutzungsdauer entsprechend den steuerlichen AfA-Tabellen verbindlich vorzugeben (Baetge 2003, S. 201 f.). Dieses Vorgehen erscheint auch im Zusammenhang mit der Abnutzung von Marken sinnvoll.

2.2 Abnutzbarkeit aus verhaltenstheoretischer Perspektive

Die Entstehung eines psychografischen Markenwertes setzt umfangreiche **Lernvorgänge** aufseiten der Nachfrager voraus. Der Verbraucher muss das Nutzenversprechen einer Marke lernen, er muss lernen, worin im Vergleich zu konkurrierenden Produkten die bessere Leistung der Marke liegt, und schließlich muss er lernen, wo er die Marke erwerben kann. Unabhängig von der Vielzahl an Lerntheorien, die in der Literatur diskutiert werden (Aaker/Keller 1990; Kroeber-Riel/Weinberg 2003, S. 324 ff.), besteht Einigkeit darin, dass Lernen in der Regel mit einem hohen Zeitbedarf einhergeht. Erlernte Verhaltensmuster werden im Langzeitgedächtnis abgespeichert. Die Inhalte des Gedächtnisses unterliegen jedoch **Vergessenswirkungen**. Ebenso wie das Lernen erfolgt jedoch auch das Vergessen über einen längeren Zeitraum. Das Vorstellungsbild von aus dem Markt ausgeschiedenen Marken wird im Laufe der Jahre diffuser und von immer weniger Nachfragern erinnert, womit diese Marken letztlich ihre Kaufverhaltensrelevanz und Werthaltigkeit verlieren. Überträgt man die Erkenntnisse der lerntheoretischen Forschung auf die Markenführung, so ist davon auszugehen, dass bei einer Reduzierung der markenpolitischen Aktivitäten verstärkt Vergessenseffekte beim Nachfrager eintreten.

Abbildung 1 zeigt am Beispiel einer PKW-Marke, dass bereits zwölf Wochen nach dem Ende einer die Marke stärkenden Werbekampagne die Erinnerung der Befragten an das in dieser Kampagne ausgelobte Nutzenversprechen der Marke und die Penetration positiver Markeneinstellungen (hier der Sympathie) um über ein Drittel zurückgegangen sind. Diese Vergessenswirkungen sind nicht linear fortzuschreiben. Sie verdeutlichen jedoch, dass selbst bei einer nur vorübergehenden Einstellung der werblichen Unterstützung von Marken mit einer Schwächung der Verhaltensrelevanz und damit der Werthaltigkeit einer

Marke zu rechnen ist. Im Durchschnitt über alle 60 untersuchten Marken aus 24 Warengruppen ergab sich nach zwölf Wochen ein Rückgang der Erinnerungsleistung um zehn Prozent[1].

Abbildung 1: Rückgang der Erinnerungsleistung und der Penetration positiver Markeneinstellungen nach dem Ende einer Markenkampagne

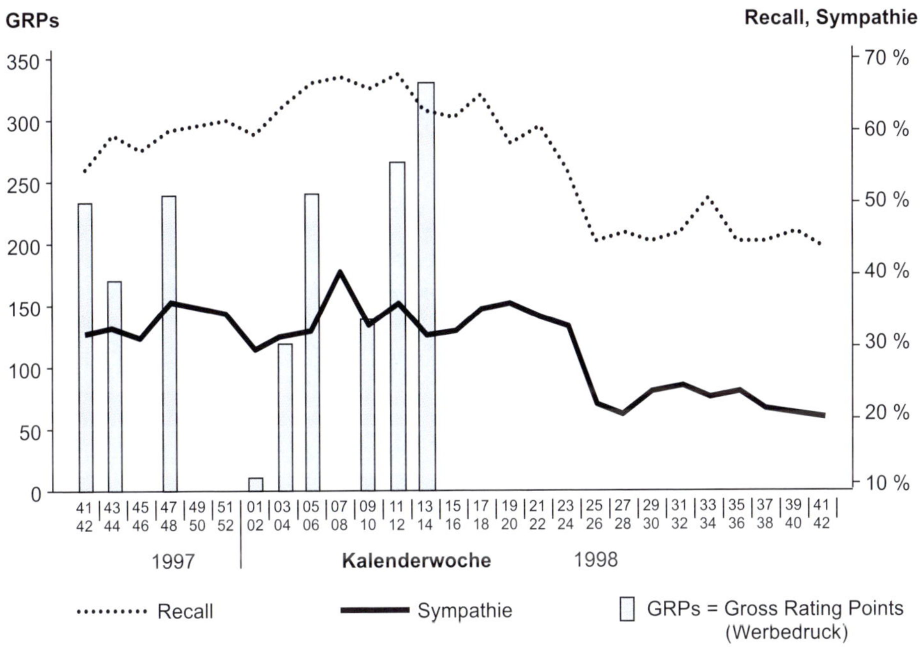

GABLER GRAFIK

Problematisch erscheint vor diesem Hintergrund somit nicht die Frage, **ob** beim Nachfrager Vergessenswirkungen auftreten (Frage der Abnutzbarkeit von Marken), sondern **in welcher Form**, das heißt in welcher Intensität und in welchem zeitlichen Verlauf, diese Vergessenswirkungen einsetzen.

1 Im Rahmen dieser Studie wurden zwischen dem 7.10.1997 und dem 19.10.1998 wöchentlich 300 Personen (insgesamt 15.631) zwischen 14 und 64 Jahren telefonisch befragt (repräsentative Zufallsstichprobe).

3. Nutzungsdauer von Marken

Vor diesem Hintergrund soll der Frage nachgegangen werden, **innerhalb welcher Nutzungsdauer sich der Wert bestimmter Typen von Marken gewöhnlich verbraucht**. Angesichts des noch rudimentären Forschungsstandes kann es hier lediglich das Ziel sein, erste Anhaltspunkte zu generieren und dabei im Wesentlichen den Such- und Aufgabenraum für die weiterführende Forschung zu strukturieren.

3.1 Lebenszyklusanalyse als Grundlage zur Nutzungsdauerbestimmung

Das „Werden und Vergehen" von Produkten wird in Lebenszyklusmodellen durch im Zeitablauf veränderte Wettbewerbskonstellationen und Nachfragerbedürfnisse erklärt. Empirisch konnte das Lebenszykluskonzept in zahlreichen Einzelfällen, insbesondere auf hoch aggregierter Ebene, bestätigt werden. Bei stärker disaggregierter Analyse wurde das Lebenszykluskonzept jedoch auch falsifiziert, sodass es bislang keine hinreichende prognostische und normative Relevanz besitzt (Höft 1992). Ihm kommt jedoch der Verdienst zu, die Endlichkeit der Lebensdauer von Marken zu verdeutlichen. Dementsprechend kann das Lebenszyklusmodell als Basis zur weiteren deduktiven Ableitung der Nutzungsdauer von Marken verwendet werden.[2]

3.2 Konzeption einer allgemeinen Nutzungsdauerverteilungsfunktion

Zur **induktiven Ableitung** der Nutzungsdauer von Marken wird in einem zweistufigen Vorgehen auf unterschiedliche empirische Untersuchungen zurückgegriffen. Im ersten Schritt werden Studien, die sich mit dem Erfolg und damit mittelbar der Lebensdauer neu in den Markt eingeführter Marken beschäftigen, ausgewertet. Diese empirischen Arbeiten haben oftmals lediglich den Charakter von Fallstudien, können aber, bei einer größeren Zahl untersuchter Marken, zumindest eine Indikatorfunktion übernehmen. Sie kommen in der Regel zu dem Ergebnis, dass lediglich **ein bis 15 Prozent aller Markenneueinführungen sich mittel- bis langfristig zu erfolgreichen Marken entwickeln** (Aaker 1991, S. 24; Interbrand 1992, S. 16 f.). Betrachtet werden dabei ausschließlich neu eingeführte Marken. Die Einführung eines neuen Produktes unter einer bekannten, bereits

2 Vgl. Enis/La Garce/Prell, 1977 und Simon, 1978, die als Bezugsobjekt für Lebenszyklusanalysen ebenfalls auf die besondere Eignung von Marken verweisen.

etablierten Marke wird hier ausgeschlossen. Die große Schwankungsbreite dieser „Überlebensrate“ von Marken verdeutlicht die **Notwendigkeit einer branchenspezifischen Betrachtung**, die jedoch aufgrund der bisher sehr lückenhaften empirischen Datenlage kaum möglich ist.

Um ein vollständigeres Bild von der Markenlebensdauer zu erhalten, können die empirischen Untersuchungen über Produktlebenszyklen herangezogen werden. Droege, Backhaus und Weiber kommen in einer 1993 (S. 54) durchgeführten Untersuchung für den Industriegüterbereich zu dem Ergebnis, dass sich die durchschnittliche Produktlebensdauer in diesem Wirtschaftszweig von elf in den 70er Jahren auf nur noch sechs Jahre in diesem Jahrzehnt reduziert hat. Eine Studie des Fraunhofer Instituts für Arbeitswissenschaft und Organisation aus dem Jahr 1990 (S. 34) untersucht ebenfalls die Entwicklung der Lebenszyklen von Produkten im Industriegüterbereich. Für die Branche Elektrotechnik und Computer wurde eine durchschnittliche Produktlebensdauer von vier Jahren ermittelt. Eine sich auf zahlreiche Industrie- und Konsumgüter des verarbeitenden Gewerbes beziehende Studie des Münchener Ifo-Instituts ermittelte über alle Produktgruppen eine durchschnittliche Produktlebensdauer von 4,3 Jahren (1986, S. 5). Auch bei der Vorteilhaftigkeitsanalyse von Investitionsobjekten ist eine Bestimmung der wirtschaftlichen Nutzungsdauer notwendig. Auf der Grundlage zahlreicher empirischer Erfahrungswerte ist dabei zum Beispiel für die Metall verarbeitende Industrie eine durchschnittliche wirtschaftliche Nutzungsdauer von fünf Jahren ermittelt worden (Suckut 1992, S. 85), die als Indikator für die **durchschnittliche (wirtschaftliche) Produktlebensdauer** in dieser Branche interpretiert werden kann.

Im Vergleich zu Industriegütern liegt die Nutzungsdauer von Konsumgütern in der Regel unterhalb der oben zitierten vier bis sechs Jahre. Auf der anderen Seite ist zu berücksichtigen, dass in den zitierten Studien nicht explizit Marken-, sondern Produktlebenszyklen untersucht wurden. Obwohl Marken- und Produktlebenszyklen konzeptionell weitgehend identisch sind, ist angesichts der oben bereits genannten Gründe davon auszugehen, dass die absolute Lebensdauer von Marken länger ist als diejenige von Produkten. Zur weitergehenden Spezifizierung der Nutzungsdauer von Marken kann auf die im Rahmen der Innovationsforschung ermittelten Ergebnisse zu „Flopraten“ von Neuprodukteinführungen zurückgegriffen werden (Loch 1997). Dabei ist jedoch zu berücksichtigen, dass sich die „Flopraten“ oft auf Produkt und nicht auf Markenneueinführungen beziehen und insoweit Korrekturen vorzunehmen sind. Wägt man alle genannten Argumente gegeneinander ab, so ist die induktive Herleitung einer allgemeinen Nutzungsdauerverteilung von Marken zwar grundsätzlich möglich, hinsichtlich ihres Aussagegehaltes jedoch mit Einschränkungen behaftet.

In **deduktiver Betrachtung** basiert der in Abbildung 2 dargestellte Funktionsverlauf auf den theoretischen Grundaussagen des Lebenszykluskonzeptes. Induktiv wurde der Funktionsverlauf aus zahlreichen Fallstudien zur Lebensdauer einzelner Marken sowie der durchschnittlichen Produktlebensdauer in verschiedenen Branchen abgeleitet (Meffert/Burmann 1998). Trotz dieses ersten Versuches einer induktiven und deduktiven Fundierung ist der Funktionsverlauf aus Abbildung 2 lediglich als eine **grobe, branchen- und länderübergreifende Approximation der realen Lebensdauerverteilung von Marken** zu interpretieren. Für weiterführende empirische Untersuchungen kann der dargestellte Funktionsverlauf als Basishypothese dienen.

Abbildung 2: Verteilungsfunktion der Nutzungsdauer von Marken

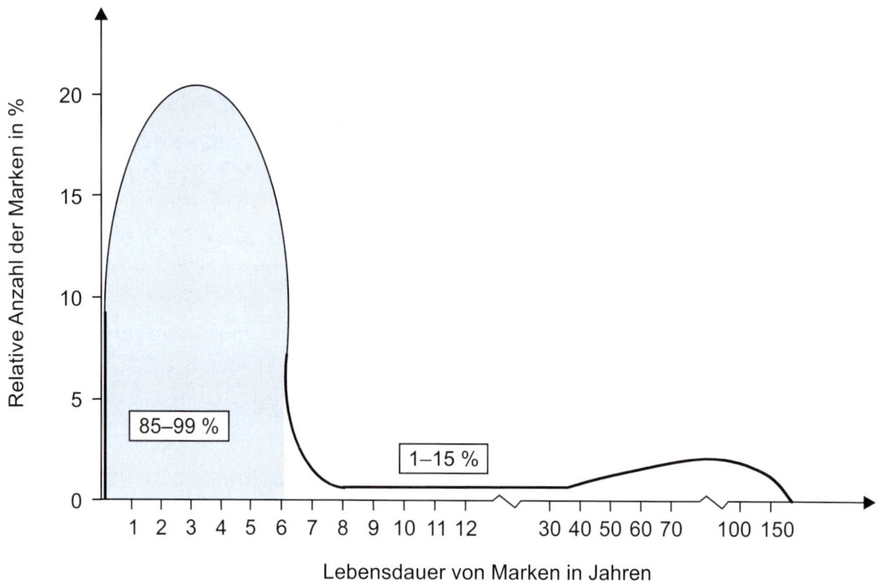

GABLER GRAFIK

Unbeschadet von dem noch lückenhaften Erkenntnisstand wird deutlich, dass die große Mehrheit der Marken eine relativ kurze Nutzungsdauer hat. Dieses Ergebnis erscheint zunächst überraschend, weil sich die subjektiven Assoziationen zum Stichwort „Marken" zumeist auf sehr langlebige Marken beziehen (zum Beispiel Maggi, Dr. Oetker, Persil, Nivea) und intuitiv eine längere Lebensdauer erwarten lassen. Diese **subjektive Wahrnehmungsverzerrung** erklärt sich dadurch, dass es die wenigen sehr erfolgreichen Marken durch ihre jahrzehntelange Marktpräsenz und ihre massiven Investitionen in die Kommunikation (in kumulativer Betrachtung) geschafft haben, sich dauerhaft im Gedächtnis der Nachfrager zu verankern.

3.3 Determinanten der Nutzungsdauer von Marken

Im Folgenden werden zunächst solche Determinanten der Markennutzungsdauer untersucht, die vor der Markteinführung einer Marke zur groben Klassifikation der zu erwartenden Markenlebensdauer verwendet und vom Markeninhaber gestaltet werden können. Im nächsten Abschnitt (4.3.2) werden dann Einflussfaktoren analysiert, die **nach** der Markteinführung zu einer andauernden Gefahr der Abnutzung des Markenwertes führen. Diese Faktoren können als **Ursachen für planmäßige Abschreibungen des Markenwertes** interpretiert werden. Diese Determinanten sind vom Markeninhaber nur sehr begrenzt zu kontrollieren.

3.31 Determinanten zur Klassifikation der Markennutzungsdauer

Zu den von Anfang an bedeutsamen Determinanten der Markennutzungsdauer zählen insbesondere der Gütertyp, die Markenstrategie und die rechtliche Absicherung der Marke (vgl. Abbildung 3).

Abbildung 3: Determinanten zur Klassifikation der Nutzungsdauer von Marken

	Markenlebensdauer	
	... eher länger	**... eher kürzer**
Branchenzugehörigkeit/ Gütertyp	■ Marken bei (langlebigen) Gebrauchsgütern ■ Dienstleistungen ■ Investitionsgüter ■ High-Involvement-Produkte	■ Marken bei (kurzlebigen) Verbrauchsgütern ■ Low-Involvement-Produkte
Markenstrategie: – Strategieoption – Markierungsobjekt – Markteintrittszeitpunkt – Art des Wettbewerbsvorteils	■ Dachmarken ■ Erstmarken ■ Pioniermarken ■ Marken mit Leistungs- (Qualitäts-)vorteil	■ Einzelmarken ■ Zweit-, Drittmarken ■ Me-too-Marken ■ Marken mit Preisvorteil
Rechtliche Absicherung der Marke	Wettbewerbsvorteile der Marke durch Patente, Lizenzen, Konzessionen oder durch (künstliche) Monopole/ Regulierung abgesichert	Wettbewerbsvorteile der Marke rechtlich nicht/kaum abgesichert

GABLER GRAFIK

Der **Gütertyp** beeinflusst die Nutzungsdauer einer Marke über die Lebensdauer der markierten Leistung. Gebrauchsgütermarken weisen demzufolge zumeist eine längere Lebensdauer auf als Verbrauchsgütermarken. Hierfür ist vor allem das in der Regel höhere Involvement bei Gebrauchsgütern verantwortlich. Dieses reduziert Vergessenswirkungen und beeinflusst das markenspezifische Wahrnehmungsverhalten positiv (Kroeber-Riel/Weinberg 2003). Je größer der Anteil hoch-involvierter Kunden unter allen Markenverwendern ist, desto länger ist tendenziell die Lebensdauer einer Marke.

Die Lebensdauer von Marken fällt bei Dienstleistungen und Investitionsgütern tendenziell höher aus als bei Konsumgütern. Dies ist im Wesentlichen auf den **in der Regel höheren Anteil an Vertrauenseigenschaften bei vielen Dienstleistungen und Investitionsgütern** zurückzuführen. Die bei vielen Dienstleistungen und Investitionsgütern fehlende Möglichkeit zur ex ante Überprüfung der anbieterseitig zugesagten Leistungseigenschaften lässt den Nachfrager umfassender als bei Konsumgütern auf die Marke als Surrogat für die Produktqualität zurückgreifen. Dies fördert die Markenloyalität und damit die Werthaltigkeit und Lebensdauer der Marke.

Neben dem Gütertyp kommt der **Markenstrategie** eine herausgehobene Bedeutung für die Abschätzung der Markenlebensdauer zu (vgl. in diesem Zusammenhang auch den Beitrag zu den strategischen Optionen der Markenführung in diesem Buch sowie Meffert 1992). Hinsichtlich der markenstrategischen Optionen ist zu konstatieren, dass Dachmarken tendenziell eine längere Lebensdauer aufweisen als Einzelmarken. Mehr- und Familienmarkenstrategien sind zwischen der Dach- und der Einzelmarkenstrategie einzuordnen. Die längere Markenlebensdauer bei Dachmarken ist vor allem auf die größere Flexibilität in der Markenführung und die breitere Zielgruppe einer Dachmarke zurückzuführen.

Im Allgemeinen ist davon auszugehen, dass die Lebensdauer einer Marke mit zunehmender Disaggregation des Markierungsobjektes sinkt. Die Markenlebensdauer wird ferner vom **Markierungsobjekt** beeinflusst. Von der Erst- über die Zweit- bis hin zur Drittmarke ist von einer abnehmenden Lebensdauer auszugehen. Ein ähnliches Ergebnis zeigt sich beim **Markteintrittszeitpunkt**. Auch hier nimmt die Lebensdauer von Marken in der Regel mit wachsender Verzögerung des Markteintrittszeitpunktes ab. Der Markteintritt als Pionier bietet den wahrnehmungspsychologischen Vorteil, sich als erste Marke einer neuen Produktkategorie im Gedächtnis der Nachfrager zu verankern. Auch die Art des Wettbewerbsvorteils einer Marke beeinflusst deren Lebensdauer. Echte Leistungsvorteile von Marken sind durch Wettbewerber schwieriger und nur mit größerem Aufwand zu kopieren als Preisvorteile.

Schließlich determiniert auch die **rechtliche Absicherung einer Marke** deren Lebensdauer. Sind die Wettbewerbsvorteile einer Marke durch Patente, Lizenzen, Konzessionen oder staatliche Regulierungen abgesichert, verlängert sich die Lebensdauer einer Marke.

3.32 Determinanten eines andauernden Werteverzehrs bei Marken

Im Folgenden werden solche Determinanten kurz skizziert, die eine andauernde Gefahr für die Werthaltigkeit von Marken darstellen und in der Regel nur in begrenztem Maße vom Markenmanagement beeinflusst werden können. Die weite Verbreitung dieser die Nachhaltigkeit des Markenwertes bedrohenden Faktoren macht es erforderlich, planmäßige Abschreibungen auf den Markenwert vorzunehmen (IAS 38.80). Dies auch deshalb, weil Zeitpunkt und Umfang des Werteverzehrs mit vertretbarem Aufwand nicht präzise bestimmbar sind. Daher ist eine näherungsweise Verteilung der eintretenden Abnutzungseffekte über den Zeitraum der voraussichtlichen Markennutzung notwendig. Abbildung 4 kann demnach als **Systematik wichtiger Ursachen für eine planmäßige Abschreibung von Marken interpretiert werden**.

Abbildung 4: Systematik von Abschreibungsursachen für den Markenwert

Horizontaler Wettbewerb	■ Laufende Markteintritte neuer Wettbewerber ■ Wachsender Globalisierungsdruck ■ Zunehmender Kommunikationswettbewerb („Markeninflation") ■ Steigende Homogenität und Austauschbarkeit von Marken ■ Zunehmende Markenpiraterie
Vertikaler Wettbewerb	■ Ansteigender Filialisierungs- und Internationalisierungsgrad der Absatzmittler ■ Zunehmender Konzentrationsgrad der Absatzmittler (Preisdruck) ■ Kontinuierliche Verbesserung des Marketing Know-hows der Absatzmittler
Konsument	■ Steigende Markenwechselbereitschaft, sinkendes Markenbewusstsein ■ Wachsendes Preisbewusstsein ■ Kontinuierlicher Wandel der Bedürfnisstrukturen ■ Laufende Vergessenswirkungen
Technologie	■ Regelmäßige Produkt- und Prozessinnovationen ■ Neue Informations- und Kommunikationstechnologien

GABLER GRAFIK

Eine wichtige Abschreibungsursache ist der zunehmende **horizontale Wettbewerb**. Die Deregulierung vieler Branchen, die Öffnung von Ländergrenzen unter anderem aufgrund von Freihandelsabkommen und technologische Innovationen führen in vielen Märkten zum **Eintritt neuer Wettbewerber und Marken**. Reagiert das Markenmanagement heute zu langsam auf Veränderungen der internationalen Faktorpreis- und Wettbewerbsstrukturen, so verliert die Marke als Folge des hohen **Globalisierungsdrucks** schnell Marktanteile und sieht sich der Gefahr einer Erosion ihres Wertes ausgesetzt.

Zudem hat die schnelle und problemlose Verfügbarkeit leistungsfähiger Produkt- und Prozesstechnologien zu einer wachsenden technisch-objektiven **Produkthomogenität** in vielen Märkten geführt (Diekhof 1998, S. 77). Dies hat bei vielen Marken zu einem empirisch nachweisbaren Anstieg der vom Nachfrager wahrgenommenen Austauschbarkeit geführt (BBDO 1993). Mit wachsender Austauschbarkeit verliert die Marke – bei allem rechtlichen Schutz der formalen Markierung – zunehmend ihren Wert.

Die Inflation „neuer“ Marken hat zu einer Verschärfung des Kommunikationswettbewerbs geführt. So wurden zum Beispiel im amerikanischen Lebensmitteleinzelhandel 1994 über 20.000 neue Marken eingeführt (Quelch/Harding 1996). In Deutschland wurden 1998 circa 54.000 Marken beworben, davon circa 3.500 mit einem Kommunikationsbudget von über eine Million DM p. a. (Keller 1998). Der intensivere Kommunikationswettbewerb wird auch an der Entwicklung der Aufwendungen für klassische Kommunikation in Deutschland deutlich, die im Zeitraum 1986 bis 1996 von elf auf über 26 Milliarden DM p. a. gestiegen sind. Dies hat dazu geführt, dass 1997 im deutschen Fernsehen über 1,5 Millionen Werbespots zu sehen waren (o. V. 1997). Damit wachsen die notwendigen Aufwendungen zur Profilierung von Marken, wohingegen deren Wirkungseffizienz tendenziell sinkt. Mit Blick auf den verschärften Kommunikationswettbewerb ist jedoch auch zu berücksichtigen, dass bereits eingeführte, fest etablierte Marken im Vergleich zu neu eingeführten Marken relative Vorteile verbuchen können. Nicht zuletzt hat auch die steigende Zahl der Fälle von **Markenpiraterie** zu einer Erhöhung des horizontalen Wettbewerbsdruckes geführt.

Die wachsende Wettbewerbsintensität im vertikalen, **absatzstufenübergreifenden Marketing** führt ebenfalls zu einem andauernden Abwertungsrisiko auf den Markenwert. Dies betrifft vor allem Herstellermarken. Der in den vergangenen Jahren kontinuierlich gestiegene **Filialisierungs- und Internationalisierungsgrad im deutschen Einzelhandel** hat die Fähigkeiten der Handelsunternehmen, durch eigene Marken mit den Herstellern in Wettbewerb zu treten, deutlich verbessert. Dies geht mit einem **wachsenden Marketing-Know-how des Handels** einher.

Im Einzelhandel ist ferner ein bis heute ungebremster **Konzentrationsprozess** zu beobachten (M&M Eurodata 1997). Die als Folge der steigenden Nachfragemacht sinkenden Handelsabgabepreise der Markenhersteller schwächen die Ertragskraft insbesondere der Herstellermarken. Der starke Preisdruck im vertikalen Markenwettbewerb wird durch die laufenden Marktanteilsgewinne preisaggressiver Betriebsformen weiter verstärkt.

Auch das Verhältnis der **Verbraucher** zur Marke hat sich gewandelt. In vielen Bereichen ist heute ein **Anstieg der Markenwechselbereitschaft** zu beobachten (Dekimpe et al. 1996). Trotz hoher Zufriedenheit mit den bis dato verwendeten Marken kommt es aufgrund des **„variety seeking behavior“** der Nachfrager zum Kauf „fremder“ beziehungsweise neuer Marken. Die damit einhergehende **sinkende Markentreue** reduziert c. p. den Markenwert.

Eine rückläufige Markentreue, in empirischen Untersuchungen zumeist vereinfacht über den Wiederkauf einer Marke operationalisiert, lässt sich in vielen Warengruppen empirisch belegen. So hat sich zum Beispiel die Zahl der von jedem Haushalt für den Einkauf von Gütern des täglichen Bedarfs im Durchschnitt aufgesuchten Geschäfte von 1984 bis 1997 von 9,8 auf 10,8 erhöht (Twardawa 1998, S. 12). Da sich gleichzeitig die Nachfrage nach Gütern des täglichen Bedarfs nicht signifikant verändert hat, ist die Markentreue gegenüber Einzelhandelsgeschäften gesunken. Auch im deutschen Pkw-Markt ist in den vergangenen Jahren eine sinkende Markentreue zu verzeichnen gewesen (vgl. Abbildung 5).[3]

Abbildung 5: Entwicklung der Markentreue im deutschen Pkw-Markt

Marken	1992 (in Prozent)	1997 (in Prozent)	Veränderung (in Prozent)
Deutsche Marken (VW, Audi, Ford, Opel, Daimler-Benz, BMW)	65,9	62,5*	–5,2
Italienische Marken (Fiat, Lancia, Alfa)	53,2	47,7	–10,3
Französische Marken (Citroen, Peugeot, Renault)	62,9	58,6	–6,8
Japanische Marken (Toyota, Nissan, Mazda, Mitsubishi, Honda, Suzuki, Daihatsu, Subaru)	66,5	56,2	–15,5

* Lesebeispiel: Im Modelljahr 1997 kauften im Durchschnitt 62,5 Prozent aller Besitzer eines Pkws mit deutscher Marke, die sich einen neuen Pkw kauften, wieder die Marke ihres bisherigen Fahrzeugs.

GABLER GRAFIK

Quelle: Volkswagen AG

3 Die Markenloyalitätsraten in Abbildung 5 wurden auf Basis der jährlich von den Automobilherstellern durchgeführten Neuwagenkäufer-Studie berechnet. In dieser Gemeinschaftsstudie werden jährlich 41.000 Pkw-Käufer vier bis sechs Monate nach der Fahrzeugübernahme schriftlich befragt.

Das Kaufverhalten der Verbraucher ist darüber hinaus seit vielen Jahren durch ein **zunehmendes Preisbewusstsein** gekennzeichnet (Bott/Jung/Link 1999). Dies ist ein Indikator für die nachlassende Anziehungskraft vieler Marken, denn der Preis wird bei der Kaufentscheidung umso wichtiger, je weniger der Nachfrager mit einer Marke ein klares, nutzenorientiertes Vorstellungsbild verbindet. Die **Instabilität der Bedürfnisstrukturen** der Nachfrager stellt für den Wert etablierter Marken eine Gefahr dar, ist aber auch die Grundlage für den Erfolg neuer Marken. Die sich laufend in ihrer Bedeutung verändernden Konsumtrends legen eine planmäßige Abschreibung des Markenwertes nahe.

Der **technologische Fortschritt** führt bei etablierten Marken zu einer permanenten Gefahr, durch neue Marken mit technisch besseren Produkten verdrängt zu werden. Während Innovationen unter kurzfristiger Perspektive als ein diskontinuierliches Phänomen erscheinen (und damit durch außerplanmäßige, einmalige Wertberichtigungen buchhalterisch abgebildet werden könnten), ist bei langfristiger Betrachtung näherungsweise von einem relativ **kontinuierlichen Prozess** auszugehen. Aus diesem Grunde erscheint eine Berücksichtigung der Gefahren des technologischen Fortschritts für den Wert etablierter Marken durch eine planmäßige Markenwertabschreibung zweckmäßig. Ferner verbessern **neue Informations- und Kommunikationstechnologien** die Markttransparenz für Nachfrager und Einkaufsmanager sowie die Diffusionsgeschwindigkeit neuer Marken. Dies wird den Preisdruck für viele Marken weiter erhöhen und die Erosion der Marktposition etablierter Marken verstärken. Auch hieraus ergibt sich ein steigender „Abwertungsdruck" für Marken.

4. Zusammenfassung und Ausblick

Der vorliegende Beitrag befasst sich aus marketingwissenschaftlicher Sicht mit der wirtschaftlichen Abnutzbarkeit und Nutzungsdauer von Marken. Die dargelegte Argumentationslinie führt zu der Schlussfolgerung, dass Marken einer Abnutzung unterliegen. Die Untersuchung legt je nach situativem Branchenkontext eine Abschreibungsperiode von etwa drei bis acht Jahren nahe (Gold 1998).

In seiner Stellungnahme vom 27.2.1998 ist das Bundesministerium der Finanzen (BdF) im Grundsatz der obigen Argumentationslinie gefolgt. Eine planmäßige Abschreibung des Markenwertes erscheint darüber hinaus auch deswegen geboten, weil die außerplanmäßige Teilwertabschreibung des derivativen Markenwertes nach den Plänen des Gesetzgebers weitestgehend abgeschafft werden soll. Das Problem der konkreten Nutzungsdauerbestimmung wird damit in besonderer Weise virulent, bleibt jedoch sowohl aus Sicht des BdF als auch des IASC weitgehend ungelöst. Der Abschreibungszeitraum von 15 Jahren, beziehungsweise 20 Jahren nach IAS 38, stellt eine widerlegbare Höchstgrenze dar. Die vorliegende Analyse zeigt demgegenüber zahlreiche Ansatzpunkte für eine erheblich kürzere Nutzungsdauer auf. Für eine hinreichend präzise und valide wissenschaftliche Analyse und Prognose der Nutzungsdauer von Marken bleibt freilich eine Reihe von Fragen offen. Das betrifft einmal das komplexe Zusammenspiel der zahlreichen, hier identifizierten Determinanten der Nutzungsdauer und ihre empirische Absicherung im konkreten Kontext. Weiterführende typologische Ansätze unter besonderer Bezugnahme auf die Marktleistung und die verfolgte Markenstrategie sind erforderlich. Letztlich könnte eine in dieser Weise fortgeführte Markenforschung in der Konzeption von „AfA-Tabellen für Marken" münden und damit zu einer Objektivierung sowohl des Jahresabschlusses als auch des Investitionscontrolling im Rahmen der Markenführung beitragen.

Literatur

Aaker, D. (1991), Managing Brand Equity, New York [u.a.].
Aaker, D., Keller, K. L. (1990), Consumer Evaluations of Brand Extensions, in: Journal of Marketing, Vol. 54, Jan., S. 27–41.
Baetge, J. (2003), Bilanzen, 7. Aufl., Düsseldorf.
Baldinger, A. L., Rubinson, J. (1996), Brand Loyalty: The Link Between Attitude and Behavior, in: Journal of Advertising Research, Nov.-Dec., S. 22–34.
Barth, T., Kneisel, H. (1997), Entgeltlich erworbene Warenzeichen in der Handels- und Steuerbilanz, in: Die Wirtschaftsprüfung, Nr. 14, S. 473–479.
BBDO (Hrsg.) (1993), Brand Parity Study II, Düsseldorf.
Beike, P. (1998), SAT.1 AdTrend, SAT.1 GmbH (Hrsg.), Berlin.
Beschluß des Bundesfinanzhofes vom 4.9.1996, in: Deutsches Steuerrecht (DStR), Wochenschrift für Steuerrecht, Wirtschaftsrecht und Betriebswirtschaft, München, S. 1770.
Bott, H., Jung, A., Link, O. (1999), „Ich bin doch nicht Blöd", in: Der Spiegel, Nr. 33 v. 16.8.1999, S. 80–84.
Bundessteuerblatt, Teil I, 1998, Nr. 5, S. 252.
Dekimpe, M. G., Mellens, M., Steenkamp, J. B., Vanden Abeele, P. (1996), Erosion and Variability in: Brand Loyalty, Working Paper No. 96-114, Marketing Science Institute (Hrsg.), Boston.
Diekhof, R. (1998), Kosmopoliten sind gefragt, in: Werben & Verkaufen, Nr. 38, S. 74–77.
Droege, W., Backhaus, K., Weiber, R. (1993), Strategien für Investitionsgütermärkte: Antworten auf neue Herausforderungen, Landsberg/Lech.
Enis, B. M., La Garce, R., Prell, A. E. (1977), Extending the Product Life Cycle, in: Business Horizonts, June, S. 46–56.
Fraunhofer-Institut für Arbeitswissenschaft und Organisation (1990), F & E heute, Industrielle Forschung und Entwicklung in der Bundesrepublik Deutschland, München.
Gold, G. (1998), Steuerliche Abschreibungsmöglichkeit für Marken?, in: Der Betrieb, S. 956–959.
Höft, U. (1992), Lebenszykluskonzepte, Berlin.
IAS International Accounting Standard 38: Intangible Assets, IASC (Hrsg.), September 1998.
IASC (Hrsg.) (1998), Basis for Conclusions IAS 38, IAS 22 and Summary of Changes to E60 and IAS 22, London.
Ifo-Institut für Wirtschaftsforschung (Hrsg.) (1986), Innovationsbericht, Ergebnisse des Ifo-Innovationstests 1984/85, München.
Interbrand Group (Hrsg.) (1992), The world's greatest brands. An international review by Interbrand, New York u.a.
Keller, V. v. (1998), Macht des Namens, in: Wirtschaftswoche, Nr. 45 v. 29.10.1998, S. 100–103.
Kroeber-Riel, W., Weinberg, P. (2003), Konsumentenverhalten, 8. Aufl., München.

Leffson, U. (1938), Die wirtschaftlichen Wirkungen des technischen Fortschritts, in: Zeitschrift für Nationalökonomie, S. 238–320 und 414–449 (zitiert nach Baetge 1996, S. 231).

Loch, C. (1997), Disziplin oder Flexibilität, in: Arthur D. Little (Hrsg.), Management von Innovation und Wachstum, Wiesbaden, S. 184–201.

Meffert, H. (1992), Strategien zur Profilierung von Marken, in: Dichtl, E., Eggers, W. (Hrsg.), Marke und Markenartikel als Instrument des Wettbewerbs, München, S. 129–156.

Meffert, H., Burmann, Ch. (1998), Abnutzbarkeit und Nutzungsdauer von Marken – Ein Beitrag zur steuerlichen Behandlung von Warenzeichen, Arbeitspapier Nr. 118 der Wissenschaftlichen Gesellschaft für Marketing und Unternehmensführung e.V., Meffert, H., Backhaus, K. (Hrsg.), Münster.

M & M Eurodata (Hrsg.) (1997), M & M Topfirmen, Strukturen, Umsätze und Vertriebslinien des Lebensmitteleinzelhandels Food/Nonfood in Deutschland, Frankfurt/M.

o.V. (1997), Täglich 27 Stunden Werbung im Fernsehen, in: Frankfurter Allgemeine Zeitung v. 9.10.1997, S. 21.

Quelch, J. A., Harding, D. (1996), Brands Versus Private Labels: Fighting to Win, in: Harvard Business Review, No. 1, S. 99–109.

Simon, H. (1978), Produktlebenszyklus und Preisstrategie, in: WiST, Nr. 3, S. 116–123.

Simon, H. (1982), Preismanagement, Wiesbaden.

Suckut, S. (1992), Unternehmensbewertung für internationale Akquisitionen: Verfahren und Einsatz, Wiesbaden.

Twardawa, W. (1998), Neueste Daten zur Marken- und Einkaufsstättentreue, in: Strategien zur Schaffung und Erhaltung von Markenloyalität, G.E.M. Gesellschaft zur Erforschung des Markenwesens e.V. (Hrsg.), Frankfurt/M., S. 10–21.

KAPITEL

4 Ausgewählte Problemfelder des Markenmanagements

Persönlichkeitsorientiertes Markenmanagement 365
Fabian Hieronimus und Christoph Burmann

Profilierung von Marken mit Sponsoring und Events 387
Christoph Burmann und Axel Nitschke

Identitätsorientierte Markenführung bei Dienstleistungen 411
Christoph Burmann, Michael Schleusener und Jan-Philipp Weers

Marke und Markenführung im Kontext des Electronic Commerce 433
Michael Bongartz, Christoph Burmann und Philip Maloney

Identitätsorientierte Führung von Luxusmarken 469
Ingo Lasslop

Markenführung im professionellen Ligasport 495
Michael Welling

Ausgestaltung einer identitätsorientierten Markenführung in der Politik 523
Helmut Schneider

Identitätsorientiertes Stadtmarketing 563
Christian Ebert

Identitätsorientierter Aufbau und Gestaltung von Regionenmarken 589
Manfred Kirchgeorg

Persönlichkeitsorientiertes Markenmanagement

Fabian Hieronimus und Christoph Burmann

1. **Die Markenpersönlichkeit im Rahmen des strategischen Markenmanagements** **366**
1.1 Herausforderungen an das Markenmanagement 366
1.2 Bedeutung der Markenpersönlichkeit für das strategische Markenmanagement 367

2. **Konzeption und Operationalisierung der Markenpersönlichkeit** **369**
2.1 Abgrenzung der Markenpersönlichkeit 369
2.2 Relevante Grundlagen der Persönlichkeitspsychologie 371
2.3 Messansätze der Markenpersönlichkeit 372

3. **Steuerung der Markenpersönlichkeit** **376**
3.1 Determinanten der Markenpersönlichkeit 376
3.2 Wirkung der Markenpersönlichkeit 379

4. **Bedeutung der Markenpersönlichkeit für die Unternehmenspraxis** **381**

5. **Fazit** **382**

1. Die Markenpersönlichkeit im Rahmen des strategischen Markenmanagements

1.1 Herausforderungen an das Markenmanagement

Marken stellen wichtige Vermögensgegenstände für Unternehmen dar. Wohingegen in früheren Jahren häufig die Produktqualität durch die Markierung hervorgehoben wurde, hat sich die Zeit gewandelt. Neben diesen marktseitigen Herausforderungen setzen **nachfragerseitige Entwicklungen** das Markenmanagement vermehrt unter Druck (Meffert/Twardawa/Wildner 2000). So hat sich mit der gesicherten Grundversorgung und dem zunehmenden Wohlstand in der Gesellschaft die Funktion des Konsums verändert. Die ursprünglich im Vordergrund stehende Befriedigung von Grundbedürfnissen tritt zunehmend in den Hintergrund. Der Zusatznutzen, also Nutzenelemente, die nicht durch den technisch-funktionalen Grundnutzen repräsentiert werden, gewinnt eine stärkere Bedeutung für die Kaufentscheidung. Der Argumentation von Maslow folgend (Maslow 1975) treten soziale Bedürfnisse, Prestigebedürfnisse und das **Bedürfnis nach Selbstverwirklichung** in den Vordergrund. Hieraus erschließt sich ein Chancenpotenzial für Marken, entgegen der durch die schleichend fortschreitende Produkt- und Qualitätshomogenisierung neues Differenzierungspotenzial in der Emotions- und Erlebniswelt der Konsumenten realisieren zu können.

Marken übernehmen somit zunehmend sozialpsychologische Funktionen (Bolz/Bosshart 1995). Die Nachfrager „instrumentalisieren Produktbesitz (Markenkauf) zur **Selbstinszenierung** auf der Bühne des sozialen Lebens“ (Bauer/Huber 1997, S. 3). Um Marken somit heutzutage erfolgreich zu führen, müssen diese aktiv im täglichen Leben der Konsumenten positioniert und etabliert werden. Der Motorradhersteller Harley-Davidson hat dies bereits auf eindrucksvolle Weise erreicht: So ist das Harley-Davidson-Logo das in den Vereinigten Staaten am häufigsten tätowierte Motiv. Ein Verantwortlicher des Motorradherstellers meint dazu: „Wir verkaufen einen Lebensstil und verschenken Motorräder dazu“ (Belz 1999). Für Harley-Davidson ist dies ein untrügliches Zeichen lebenslanger Markenloyalität, für die Motorradfahrer Ausdruck eines kompletten – durch die Marke transportierten – Lebensgefühls (Schouten/McAlexander 1995).

Sowohl Theorie als auch Praxis bieten zu diesen Zwecken eine **Vielzahl von Führungskonzepten** zum Management von Marken an. Ein bloßer Blick auf die im deutschsprachigen Raum erschienenen Veröffentlichungen der letzten Jahre zeigt die Vielfalt an eingenommenen Perspektiven, die zur Steuerung und zum Verständnis des Konstrukts Marke geliefert werden: Ob nun die Marke als System (Otte 1993), als Botschafter (Adjouri 2002) oder als Frame (Herrmann 1998) verstanden wird oder der Wert (Bauer/Huber 1997), die Zukunft (Herrmann 1999), die Macht (Roth 1999) oder das Geheimnis (Simon 2001) der Marke Gegenstand der Untersuchung ist – aus unzähligen Blickwinkeln lassen sich, den Autoren zufolge, Impulse für die Markensteuerung liefern (vgl. auch den Beitrag zum Wandel in der Markenführung in diesem Buch).

Jedoch besitzt nicht jede Markenkonzeption automatisch Bedeutung für die Markensteuerung. Grundsätzlich erfährt eine Markenkonzeption ihre Relevanz aus der kontextspezifischen Markt- und Konsumentensituation und kann hinsichtlich ihrer Erfüllung dieser Anforderung als mehr oder weniger geeignete **Steuerungsperspektive** bezeichnet werden. Als eine auf Fehleinschätzungen in der Markt- und Konsumentensituation basierende Konzeption muss beispielsweise das von Gerken propagierte Marktbearbeitungskonzept der **fraktalen Markenführung** (Gerken 1994; Reeb 1998) bezeichnet werden. Gerkens Forderung zur „gänzlichen Verabschiedung von Zielgruppen" (Gerken 1990) kann aus heutiger Sicht als **Fehleinschätzung des Markt- und Konsumentenumfeldes** gedeutet werden (vgl. zum Beispiel Perrey 1998). Die Auswahl einer Markenkonzeption muss folglich den Besonderheiten der Markt- und Konsumentensituation gerecht werden. Eine in diesem Zusammenhang vermehrt diskutierte Facette der Markenführung ist die Persönlichkeitsorientierung.

1.2 Bedeutung der Markenpersönlichkeit für das strategische Markenmanagement

Eine geeignete Perspektive, den im einführenden Abschnitt aufgezeigten Herausforderungen der Emotionalisierung sowie Differenzierung gerecht zu werden, wird durch eine stärker **persönlichkeitsorientierte Markenführung** bereitgestellt. Dabei wird die Marke vor allem entlang ihrer Persönlichkeit gesteuert. Im Zentrum des Interesses steht somit die **Markenpersönlichkeit,** die die Gesamtheit aller menschlichen Assoziationen, die Konsumenten mit einer Marke verbinden, umfasst (Aaker/Fournier 1995).

Dieses spezifische Verständnis ermöglicht es, die **emotionalen Nutzenpotenziale der Marke** besser auszuschöpfen. Diese üben bei Kaufwahlhandlungen eine immer größere Bedeutung aus. So werden aufgrund der ausreichenden Befriedigung von Grundbedürfnissen Kaufentscheidungen von Nachfragern vermehrt zu Zwecken der **sozialen Demonstranz** getätigt. Hierdurch tritt die funktionale Leistungserbringung zugunsten emotionaler Wertschöpfung in den Hintergrund. Durch eine stärkere Fokussierung auf die Persönlichkeit können Marken entsprechend ihres Beitrages zur Präsentation der Nachfrager-Persönlichkeit effektiver gesteuert werden (vgl. den Beitrag zur theoretischen Grundkonzeption der identitätsorientierten Markenführung). So hat sich der Sportartikelhersteller Nike durch eine von Leistung, Leidenschaft und Lässigkeit geprägte Markenpersönlichkeit eine starke Beziehung zum Konsumenten aufgebaut und diese optimal zum Aufbau seiner Frauenlinie genutzt.

Neben der bloßen Nutzung von Marken zur sozialen Demonstranz gewinnen in zunehmendem Maße **beziehungstheoretische Aspekte** für die Markenführung an Bedeutung (Fournier 1998). Auch hierbei ist die Markenpersönlichkeit von großer Hilfe für eine effektive Markensteuerung: Erst wenn die Markenpersönlichkeit verstanden wird, kann die Kunden-Marken-Beziehung fundiert analysiert werden. Diese Erkenntnis erlaubt wiederum, Erklärungen zu finden, warum Nachfrager zu bestimmten Marken eine emotionale Beziehung aufbauen und diese als Freund, Ratgeber oder Partner begreifen (Rozanski/Baum/Wolfsen 1999).

Weiterhin gewährleistet die Markenpersönlichkeit eine langfristige **Differenzierung vom Wettbewerb**. Untersuchungen haben gezeigt, dass Assoziationen mit der Markenpersönlichkeit im Vergleich zu Produktattributen eine stärkere Differenzierung erlauben (Biel 1993). Hat eine Marke erst einmal eine Alleinstellung erreicht, wie das bei der Marke Marlboro durch die Erlebniswelt des Cowboys der Fall ist, so ist es schwer, von dieser Position verdrängt zu werden. Diese Alleinstellung manifestiert sich in einer klaren Markenpersönlichkeit und lässt sich von Wettbewerbern nur schwer imitieren. Aaker/Batra/Myers kommen sogar zu dem Schluss, dass der Versuch eines Wettbewerbers, die Markenpersönlichkeit zu kopieren, dem Markeninhaber häufig kostenlose Werbung beschert (Aaker/Batra/Myers 1992).

Auch in der **Marketingpraxis** wird die Markenpersönlichkeit als ein immer wichtigeres Paradigma der Markensteuerung erachtet (Halliday 1996; Matthies 1997). Beispielsweise zeigt der Zigarettenmarkt, wie trotz eines nahezu identischen Produkt- und Verpackungsdesigns eine **präferenzerzeugende Alleinstellung durch die Markenpersönlichkeit** erreicht werden kann (Domizlaff 1996). Auch in der Automobilbranche wird versucht, über den Aufbau einer Markenpersönlichkeit die Kaufentscheidung zu beeinflussen. So zielt BMW sowohl bei der Einführung der 5er-Reihe als auch der 7er-Reihe auf die Betonung menschlicher Eigenschaften ab, auch die Einführungskampagne des Mini bedient sich durch die Thematisierung von Liebe zum Mini des Konstrukts der Markenpersönlichkeit. Jedoch erfreut sich die Markenpersönlichkeit nicht nur bei Gütern der sozialen Demonstranz besonderer Beliebtheit, auch für Küchen- und Haushaltsgeräte, die Güter des privaten Konsums darstellen, besitzen Persönlichkeitsmerkmale eine Kaufverhaltensrelevanz (Govers/Hekkert/Schoormans 2002).

Neben einer stärkeren Emotionalisierung und einer klaren Differenzierung der Marke ermöglicht die persönlichkeitsorientierte Betrachtungsweise, zusätzlich Impulse hinsichtlich der **langfristigen Pflege der Marke** zu liefern. Während Produktattribute einem ständigen Wandel unterliegen, sind die Vorstellungen eines Konsumenten von einer Markenpersönlichkeit von Dauer und verändern sich im Zeitablauf nur graduell (Aaker/Batra/Myers 1992). Diese langfristigen Assoziationen bilden die Basis für die strategische Ausrichtung der Marke und dienen somit als **Grundlage der Markenidentität**.

Obwohl der Markenpersönlichkeit erst in letzter Zeit hohes Interesse sowohl aus der Forschung als auch aus der Praxis zuteil wurde, ist die grundsätzliche **Relevanz der Markenpersönlichkeit** für das Markenmanagement schon seit geraumer Zeit unbestritten. Domizlaff, der Begründer der Markentechnik, wusste früh um die Bedeutung des Konstrukts und schrieb bereits Ende der 30er Jahre in seinen Grundgesetzen der natürlichen Markenbildung: „Eine Markenware ist das Erzeugnis einer Persönlichkeit und wird am stärksten durch den Stempel einer Persönlichkeit gestützt“ (Domizlaff 1982, S. 141). Rieger fügte hinzu, dass „Marken ohne Persönlichkeit zum Tode verurteilt [sind], von Geburt an“ (Rieger 1985, S. 56).

2. Konzeption und Operationalisierung der Markenpersönlichkeit

Der Grund einer bislang unzureichenden Verankerung der Markenpersönlichkeit im Markenmanagement liegt in der **fehlenden Steuerbarkeit** des Konstrukts. Lange Zeit gelang es nicht, ein valides und reliables Messinstrumentarium zu entwickeln. Mit der Vorlage der faktorenanalytisch begründeten Brand Personality Scale veröffentlichte Jennifer Aaker im Jahr 1997 eine Skala, die dieses Problem zu lösen versuchte (Aaker 1997). Sie entwickelte ein über alle Produktkategorien anwendbares Messinstrument, welches eine **validere und reliablere Messung des Konstrukts Markenpersönlichkeit** ermöglichte, als dies in der Vergangenheit möglich war. Auch wenn zwischenzeitlich am Konzept von J. L. Aaker erhebliche Kritik geübt wird (Azoulay/Kapferer 2003), soll im Folgenden auf dem Gedankengut von J. L. Aaker aufgebaut werden.

Aufbauend auf der Brand Personality Scale von J. L. Aaker lässt sich das Konstrukt Markenpersönlichkeit systematisch erforschen. So fordert J. L. Aaker **weitere Forschungsaktivitäten,** um die Determinanten und Konsequenzen der Markenpersönlichkeit besser zu verstehen: „The brand personality framework and scale developed in this research also can be used to gain theoretical and practical insight into the antecedents and consequences of brand personality, which have received a significant amount of attention but little empirical testing“ (Aaker 1997). Auch Batra/Lehmann/Singh haben im Jahr 1992 bereits eine tiefere Erforschung der Markenpersönlichkeit gefordert: „More academic research is needed on the inferential processes through which the nonverbal elements of an advertisement shape a brand's perceived personality“ (Batra/Lehmann/Singh 1992, S. 94).

2.1 Abgrenzung der Markenpersönlichkeit

Das Konstrukt der Markenpersönlichkeit steht in der Tradition des wirkungsorientierten Markenverständnisses wie es durch die Arbeiten von Berekoven und Thurmann begründet und von Kapferer, Aaker und Keller in den letzten Jahren geprägt wurde. Es stellt die soziologischen und psychologischen Wirkungskomponenten in den Vordergrund der Markenführung und kann somit einen Erklärungsbeitrag zu der Fragestellung liefern, warum sich Personen bei der Produktwahl „irrational“ verhalten und zu Marken teilweise dauerhafte Beziehungen aufbauen. So wurde bei der Einführung der New Coke auf dem US-amerikanischen Markt trotz erfolgreicher Blindtests, die für die Einführung von New Coke gesprochen hatten, das Produkt vom Markt vehement zurückgewiesen. Ursächlich hierfür war keinesfalls das Produkt, sondern die Assoziationen und Verbindungen mit der „alten“ Coke (Schindler 1992). Das Konstrukt der Markenpersönlichkeit greift somit die Gedanken der wirkungsorientierten Markenführung auf und betont, die Terminologie Vershofens verwendend, die Zusatznutzenkomponente eines Leistungsangebotes.

Die Idee, dass Marken genauso wie Menschen eine Persönlichkeit besitzen, ist nicht neu. Schon im Jahr 1919 gelangte Gilmore in seiner **Theory of Animism** zu der Erkenntnis, dass der Mensch eine Neigung hat, das Unbeseelte zu beseelen (Gilmore 1919). Der Vorgang, unbelebten Objekten menschliche Charakterzüge zu verleihen, ist praktisch in allen menschlichen Gesellschaften immer wieder unternommen worden (Brown 1991). Dieses Verhalten lässt sich auch beim Umgang mit Marken beobachten (Aaker 1996).

Die Theorien zum Animismus legen die Annahme nahe, dass ein natürliches Bedürfnis besteht, Objekten menschliche Eigenschaften zu verleihen, um Interaktionen mit der nichtmateriellen Welt zu vereinfachen (McDougall 1911; Nida/Smalley 1959). Selbst wenn Konsumenten ihren Produkten in der Regel keine Namen geben, so verleihen sie ihnen jedoch menschliche Züge. Folglich ist es nicht ungewöhnlich, wenn Leute sagen: „Mein Computer fühlt sich viel besser, wenn ich ihm etwas Ruhe gönne." Oder: „Mein Auto springt nur nicht an, um mich zu ärgern." Menschen denken demnach über Marken, als seien sie menschliche Charaktere (Levy 1959; Plummer 1984). Diese Erkenntnis war für Meffert und Burmann (1996) die Grundlage für die Entwicklung ihres identitätsorientierten Markenführungsansatzes und schlägt sich heute in der Konzeptualisierung des Konstruktes der Markenidentität nieder, bei der die **Markenpersönlichkeit eine von sechs Bestandteilen der Markenidentität** ist (vgl. den Beitrag zur theoretischen Grundkonzeption des identitätsorientierten Markenmanagementansatzes in diesem Buch).

Im Folgenden wird die **Definition** von J. L. Aaker übernommen, die die Markenpersönlichkeit als „the set of human characteristics associated with a brand" definiert (Aaker 1997, S. 347). Sie sind im Wesentlichen das Ergebnis der Markenführungsaktivitäten der jeweils betrachteten Marke und deren Wettbewerber. Die Markenpersönlichkeit kann demnach sowohl demografische Merkmale wie Geschlecht, Alter oder Klassenzugehörigkeit als auch klassische Persönlichkeitswesenszüge, wie zum Beispiel Intelligenz oder Aufrichtigkeit umfassen. Die Markenpersönlichkeit von Volvo aus Sicht amerikanischer Konsumenten kann beispielsweise beschrieben werden als ein verlässlicher und vertrauenswürdiger Mann mit europäischem Akzent, der jedoch etwas schwerfällig und ohne rechten Humor ist (Aaker 1994, S. 33). Die Markenpersönlichkeit verkörpert somit eine Facette der Marke. Sie stellt keinen ganzheitlichen Anspruch an die Erklärung des Phänomens Marke; vielmehr beschränkt sie sich auf den psychologischen und soziologischen **Teilbereich der Marke**.

2.2 Relevante Grundlagen der Persönlichkeitspsychologie

Zur Konzeptualisierung der Markenpersönlichkeit bedarf es zunächst eines Ausfluges in die menschliche Persönlichkeitspsychologie. Diese befasst sich mit den **individuellen Unterschieden von Menschen** und zielt darauf ab, Individuen in ihrer Einzigartigkeit zu erfassen (Pervin 2000). Dieses Ziel schließt den Versuch ein, Individuen voneinander abzugrenzen, sodass häufig die von William Stern geprägte Bezeichnung **„Differenzielle Psychologie“** synonym verwendet wird (Fisseni 1998). Dabei bezieht sich die differenzialpsychologische Betrachtung nicht nur auf Unterschiede zwischen Personen zu einem gegebenen Zeitpunkt (Querschnittsbetrachtung **interindividueller Unterschiede**), sondern auch auf Unterschiede innerhalb einer Person in Abhängigkeit von bestimmten Situationen (Längsschnittbetrachtung **intraindividueller Unterschiede**).

Im Rahmen der Persönlichkeitstheorie existieren **zahlreiche Theorieansätze**, die abstrakt oder konkret, strukturiert oder komplex Antworten auf Fragen geben, welche die Struktur des Organismus, den Prozess des Funktionierens der Persönlichkeit sowie das Wachstum und die Entwicklung dieser Strukturen und Prozesse betreffen. So geht Kelly beispielsweise so weit, dass er grundsätzlich jeden Menschen als Persönlichkeitsforscher sieht, entwickelt er doch Möglichkeiten, Informationen über Menschen zu ordnen, und trifft Voraussagen, wie sich Menschen verhalten werden (Kelly 1955). Die Explikation dieser Vorstellungen, die Ausformulierung und Konzeptualisierung führen schließlich zu der Mannigfaltigkeit verschiedener Persönlichkeitstheorien. Eine umfassende Darstellung der Persönlichkeitstheorien kann somit an dieser Stelle nicht erfolgen (vgl. hierzu Pervin 2000; Fisseni 1998).

Nicht zuletzt durch ihre einfache Operationalisierbarkeit hat die **faktorenanalytische Forschungsrichtung** eine erhebliche Anzahl von Arbeiten hervorgebracht. Die faktorenanalytische Persönlichkeitstheorie verfolgt dabei das hochgesteckte Ziel, der Persönlichkeit als **Gesamtheit** gerecht zu werden, und bietet sich somit als geeignetes Theoriekonzept sowohl für die Erforschung der Persönlichkeit als auch der Markenpersönlichkeit an (Eysenck 1967).

Die faktorenanalytische Persönlichkeitsforschung wurde maßgeblich von Guilford, Cattell und Eysenck geprägt und macht sich folgende Hauptannahme zu Eigen: Menschen besitzen ein weites Spektrum von Eigenschaften, um auf jeweils besondere Weise zu reagieren. Solche Dispositionen werden als **Persönlichkeitswesenszüge** bezeichnet (Guilford 1974). Die Ausprägung eines Persönlichkeitswesenzuges bei einem Individuum ermöglicht somit eine Vorhersage darüber, wie sich jemand in einer gegebenen Situation wahrscheinlich verhalten wird (Cattell 1979). Die Vertreter dieser faktorenanalytischen Theorie stimmen somit darin überein, dass Wesenszüge die Grundbausteine der menschlichen Persönlichkeit sind. An dieser Stelle und auch bezüglich der zahlreichen Definitionen und Forschungstraditionen zeigen sich **Parallelen zwischen der Persönlichkeits- und der Identitätsforschung**. Je nach Standpunkt sind beide Konstrukte einmal synonym, ein anderes Mal klar voneinander zu trennen. Die einzelnen Vertreter der faktorenanalytischen Theorie unterscheiden sich untereinander darin, welche Merkmale sie unter den die Persönlichkeit bestimmenden Wesenszügen subsumieren. Auch hier gleichen sich Identitäts- und Persönlichkeitsforschung.

Vor diesem Hintergrund verwundert es nicht, dass alle drei Forscher mit Hilfe der Faktorenanalyse zu jeweils unterschiedlichen Lösungen kamen: Guilford postuliert eine Sieben-Faktoren-Lösung, Cattell schlägt 16 und Eysenck lediglich drei Faktoren zur Beschreibung der menschlichen Persönlichkeit vor (Fisseni 1998). Obwohl die unterschiedlichen Lösungen nicht grundsätzlich konfliktäre Standpunkte abbilden, galt diese Situation ob der vielen Forschungsarbeiten hinsichtlich einer Einigung bei der Dimensionalität der menschlichen Persönlichkeit als relativ ernüchternd.

Seit Beginn der 90er Jahre scheint jedoch eine **Konvergenz der unterschiedlichen Forschungsarbeiten** zu erfolgen. Vermehrt setzt sich die Überzeugung durch, dass die menschliche Persönlichkeit mit fünf Persönlichkeitsdimensionen beschrieben werden kann. In weiteren Arbeiten, die sich über beide Forschungsströme erstreckten, konnten Fünf-Faktoren-Lösungen mehrfach extrahiert werden, sodass die Fünf-Faktorenstruktur allgemeine Anerkennung erfuhr. Aufgrund inhaltlich unterschiedlicher Ausgestaltungen dieser Skalen stellt sich jedoch die Frage, welche fünf Faktoren die tatsächliche Abbildung der menschlichen Persönlichkeit gewährleisten. Zur empirischen Beantwortung dieser Frage führte John eine Expertenbefragung durch: Zehn Fachleute mussten acht Taxonomien mit Hilfe von 300 Adjektiven der Adjective Check List charakterisieren (John 1990).

Die resultierende Fünf-Faktoren-Lösung entsprach der Fünf-Faktoren-Struktur von Norman mit geringfügigen Abweichungen im fünften Faktor „Culture“, der wohl etwas zu eng gefasst ist. So kann McCrae und John zugestimmt werden, dass heute sehr viel für die Arbeitshypothese spricht, dass das **Fünf-Faktoren-Modell der Persönlichkeit** in seiner Repräsentation der Wesensstrukturen stimmig ist (McCrae/John 1992). Die Bedeutung dieser Fünf-Faktoren-Lösung erschließt sich hauptsächlich aus ihrer Generalisierbarkeit, die sie aus unterschiedlichen Studien zur Vorhersage affektiver, kognitiver sowie konativer Einstellungskomponenten erlangte. Weitere Unterstützung erfährt das Konstrukt dieser so genannten „Big Five“ durch die Übertragbarkeit auf verschiedenste Kulturen, was nach McCrae/Costa die biologische Basis aller Menschen reflektiert (McCrae/Costa 1997).

2.3 Messansätze der Markenpersönlichkeit

Ähnlich wie bei der Entwicklung der Fünf-Faktoren-Lösung der menschlichen Persönlichkeit brachten sowohl Wissenschaft als auch Praxis unterschiedliche Ansätze zur **Messung der Markenpersönlichkeit** hervor. Im Mittelpunkt stand dabei die Klärung der Frage, welche die menschliche Persönlichkeit beschreibenden Eigenschaftswörter auch tatsächlich zur Beschreibung der Markenpersönlichkeit geeignet sind.

Wells et al. versuchten bereits 1957, **„Produktpersönlichkeiten“** mit **Adjektivlisten** zu beschreiben. Als Grundlage diente ihnen dazu „The teacher's word book of 30,000 words“ von Thorndike/Lorke. Hieraus suchten sie alle Eigenschaftswörter, die bei einer Million befragter Menschen mindestens 50-mal genannt worden waren, und reduzierten diese in einem zweiten Schritt um all diejenigen Begriffe, die sich mehr auf die Beschreibung von Objekten als auf die Beschreibung von Personen bezogen, die zweideutig oder zur Beschreibung im Rahmen von Kaufprozessen nicht geeignet waren (wie zum Beispiel „tot“). Schließlich ergab sich eine Liste von **108 Adjektiven**, mit der die Persönlichkeit unterschiedlicher Automobilmarken ermittelt wurde (Wells et al. 1957). Hierbei wurde von den Autoren vereinfacht angenommen, dass Produkt- und Markenpersönlichkeit identisch sind. Des Weiteren muss angemerkt werden, dass das Vorgehen nicht empirisch validiert wurde und es sich somit um eine **rein subjektiv generierte Attributliste** handelt, was die Autoren in ihrem Fazit selbst einräumen (Wells et al. 1957, S. 317).

In der folgenden Zeit wurden durch Plummer, Alt und Griggs sowie Batra, Lehmann und Singh weitere Ansätze zur faktorenanalytischen Messung der Markenpersönlichkeit entwickelt (Hieronimus 2003). Diese zeichneten ein ähnlich **verwirrendes Bild der Messung von Markenpersönlichkeiten** wie die Anfänge der faktorenanalytischen Beschreibung der menschlichen Persönlichkeit. Einerseits wurden Ad-hoc-Skalen benutzt, die jedoch nur für spezifische Forschungsabsichten sinnvoll waren und denen aufgrund ihrer willkürlichen Item-Auswahl immer der Makel der möglichen Unvollständigkeit anhaftete. Auf der anderen Seite kamen Skalen zum Einsatz, die der Persönlichkeitspsychologie entliehen waren und unzureichend im Kontext von Marken validiert wurden. Allein schon aufgrund der Tatsache, dass die Markenpersönlichkeit einem **anderen Entstehungsprozess** unterliegt als die menschliche Persönlichkeit, kann diese nicht mit einer Skala aus der menschlichen Persönlichkeitspsychologie gemessen werden. Folgerichtig forderte Kassarjian ein eigenes Untersuchungsdesign für die Messung der Markenpersönlichkeit (Kassarjian 1971).

Dieser Forderung kam J. L. Aaker im Jahr 1997 mit der **Entwicklung der Brand Personality Scale (BPS)** nach (Aaker 1997). Basierend auf der Arbeit von Malhotra, die einen Prozess zur Skalenentwicklung für Selbst-, Persönlichkeits- und Produktkonstrukte beinhaltet (Malhotra 1981), entwickelte die Forscherin ein Konstrukt, das dem „Big Five“-Konstrukt der menschlichen Persönlichkeitsforschung sehr ähnlich ist. Hierbei differenziert sie insbesondere die breite **empirische Datenbasis** sowie die exakte **methodische Vorgehensweise** von den zuvor veröffentlichten Arbeiten. Die sehr breit angelegte Konzeptualisierung brachte Aaker jedoch den berechtigten Vorwurf ein, ihr Markenpersönlichkeitskonstrukt nicht klar von anderen Konstrukten abgrenzen zu können und sich darum auch nicht zu kümmern (Azoulay/Kapferer 2003).

Zunächst stellte J. L. Aaker aus allen relevanten Quellen eine **Adjektivliste** zusammen. Hierzu verwendete sie die Skalen der Persönlichkeitspsychologie, die vorgestellten Skalen bisheriger Forschungsarbeiten sowie zusätzlich Listen von Marktforschungsinstituten und Werbeagenturen. Als Resultat konnten **309 Persönlichkeitswesenszüge** festgehalten werden. In einem nächsten Schritt wurde die Liste im Rahmen einer schriftlichen

Für den deutschsprachigen Raum wurde im Jahr 2003 die bisher einzige Skala zur Messung der Markenpersönlichkeit vorgelegt, bei der zwei Faktoren extrahiert werden konnten, die einer kausalanalytischen Überprüfung Stand halten (Hieronimus 2003). Diese „aggregierte" Lösung unterteilt die Markenpersönlichkeit in eine auf „Temperament & Leidenschaft" basierende Dimension sowie auf einen auf „Vertrauen & Zuverlässigkeit" begründeten Faktor. Abbildung 2 zeigt die Skala.

3. Steuerung der Markenpersönlichkeit

3.1 Determinanten der Markenpersönlichkeit

Nachdem gezeigt wurde, wie die Markenpersönlichkeit auf Basis der faktorenanalytischen Vorgehensweise gemessen werden kann, wird in diesem Abschnitt auf die Gestaltungsmöglichkeiten der Markenpersönlichkeit eingegangen. Hierbei lassen sich der direkte und der indirekte Transfer von Attributen unterscheiden. Direkte Persönlichkeitstransfers zeichnen sich durch einen unmittelbaren Transfer eines Wesenszuges von einer mit dem Unternehmen assoziierten Person (zum Beispiel Vorstandsvorsitzender) auf die Markenpersönlichkeit aus, während indirekte Transfers nicht von einer Person ausgehen, sondern über die Wahrnehmung der verschiedenen Ausprägungen der Markenführung (zum Beispiel Preissetzung, Kommunikation) die Markenpersönlichkeit prägen. Dabei gilt es zu beachten, dass die Wahrnehmung der Markenpersönlichkeit durch jede direkte oder indirekte Erfahrung mit der Marke beziehungsweise dem Unternehmen geprägt wird. Diese Berührungspunkte im Sinne der „Brand Touch Points" von Burmann und Meffert (vgl. den Beitrag zur theoretischen Grundkonzeption in diesem Buch) sind vielfältig und decken nicht nur die komplette Bandbreite der Instrumente der Markenführung ab, sondern erstrecken sich zusätzlich weit über das institutionalisierte Marketing hinaus und liegen teilweise nicht mehr im unmittelbaren Einflussbereich des Unternehmens.

Zu den direkten Determinanten zählen das Image des typischen Verwenders, der Vorstandsvorsitzende, die Mitarbeiter sowie reale als auch künstliche Testimonials. Das Image des **typischen Verwenders** kann einerseits als das Image von tatsächlichen Verwendern der Marke konzeptionalisiert werden und andererseits als eine idealisierte Form, wie sie in der Werbung dargestellt wird. So wird die Markenpersönlichkeit von Harley-Davidson, die hauptsächlich auf der Dimension „Ruggedness" basiert, durch die tatsächlichen Harley-Davidson-Fahrer geprägt und erfährt zusätzlich durch die in der Werbung idealisierte Form von Freiheit und Männlichkeit Unterstützung (Schouten/Alexander 1995). Konsumenten identifizieren sich mit dieser Verwendergruppe und werden durch Erlangung von sozialer Konformität positiv in ihrer Kaufentscheidung beeinflusst. In manchen Fällen kann die idealisierte Form jedoch **negative Wirkungen** hervorrufen. Untersuchungen zeigen beispielsweise, dass die Markenwahrnehmung negativ beeinflusst werden kann, wenn die in der Werbung dargestellten Persönlichkeiten **zu weit vom tatsächlichen Selbstkonzept des Konsumenten entfernt** sind. So kann beispielsweise die steigende Attraktivität von weiblichen Models die Produktwahrnehmung von Frauen negativ beeinflussen (Bower 2001).

Dem **Vorstandsvorsitzenden** kommt in einigen Fällen ebenfalls eine zentrale Rolle in der Gestaltung der Markenpersönlichkeit zu. Insbesondere wenn die Markenkommunikation auf den Kapitalmarkt ausgerichtet ist, wird die Markenpersönlichkeit stark durch das leitende Management beeinflusst. General Electric, jahrelang als Liebling der Börsen gehandelt, verdankt den Erfolg seiner Wahrnehmung als innovativer Konzern seinem langjährigen CEO Jack Welch. Auch Jürgen Schrempp, Vorstandsvorsitzender der DaimlerChrysler AG, prägt durch sein Verhalten die Markenwahrnehmung seines Konzerns. Diese Wahrnehmung besitzt durchaus eine hohe Relevanz für die Anlageentscheidung von Investoren: Eine Studie von Burson-Marsteller belegt, dass 50 Prozent der Befragten sich bei ihrer Anlagestrategie von einem hohen Ansehen des CEO leiten lassen (Burson-Marsteller 2001). Allerdings wirkt die **oft fehlende Kontinuität und Konsistenz im Verhalten des Top-Managements** negativ auf die Wahrnehmung der Markenpersönlichkeit und kann damit zur Erosion einer Marke beitragen.

Auch **Mitarbeiter** können in Abhängigkeit der Branche wichtige Treiber der Markenpersönlichkeit sein. Insbesondere in vertriebsnahen Branchen beeinflusst die tägliche Interaktion des Mitarbeiters mit dem Kunden die Wahrnehmung des Gesamtunternehmens. In der Versicherungswirtschaft prägen beispielsweise die Versicherungsvertreter zu einem beachtlichen Teil die Markenwahrnehmung (vgl. den Beitrag zum identitätsorientierten Markenmanagement bei Dienstleistungen in diesem Buch). Ähnlich wie beim Verwenderimage kann auch hier die Werbung genutzt werden, eine idealisierte Form der Mitarbeiter in den Köpfen der Konsumenten zu verankern. So hat die Versicherung Hamburg-Mannheimer durch die Einführung des fiktiven Versicherungsvertreters Herrn Kaiser einen idealisierten Vertreter kreiert, der die positive Wahrnehmung der Markenpersönlichkeit verstärken soll.

Weiterhin ermöglicht der Einsatz von **Testimonials**, die Markenpersönlichkeit direkt zu beeinflussen. Diese Art der Steuerung von Markenpersönlichkeiten erfreut sich in der Praxis zunehmender Beliebtheit. Über 200 Marken integrieren mittlerweile Prominente in ihre Kommunikationskampagnen, und auch Werbepraktiker sehen im Einsatz Prominenter eine sinnvolle Strategie, der Reizüberflutung beim Konsumenten zu entgegnen. Der Einsatz von Prominenten kann zu beachtlichen Erfolgen führen, birgt jedoch auch das Risiko, durch ein Fehlverhalten des Prominenten die Marke zu schädigen oder kann bei mehreren Markenengagements des Prominenten zu geringerer Assoziationsstärke zu führen.

Schließlich ist, insbesondere in letzter Zeit, die Verwendung von künstlichen beziehungsweise erschaffenen Personen zu beobachten. **Selbstkreierte Testimonials** haben den großen Vorteil starker Anpassungsfähigkeit und hundertprozentiger Kontrolle durch den Werbetreibenden. Es kann sich hierbei um die Verwendung von realen oder künstlich erschaffenen Personen handeln. Auch ist es möglich – wie beispielsweise bei der Schokoladenmarke M&M – durch **Anthromorphisation** das ganze Produkt zu vermenschlichen.

Der **indirekte Transfer** von Attributen lässt sich entlang der Instrumente der Markenführung kategorisieren. Im Bereich der **Produktpolitik** beeinflussen die Produktkategorie, das Produktdesign, die Verpackung sowie der Markenname beziehungsweise das Markenlogo die Markenpersönlichkeit. So fanden die niederländischen Forscher Govers, Hekkert und Schoormans heraus, dass es möglich ist, durch eine Vorgabe an die Produktentwicklung die Wahrnehmung der Markenpersönlichkeit durch das Produktdesign zu steuern (Govers/Hekkert/Schoormans 2002). Die Verpackung kann durch ihre Haptik, Optik, Olfaktorik und ihr Gewicht die Markenpersönlichkeit kommunizieren. So löst beispielsweise die Verpackung der Rocher-Kugel von Ferrero durch ihre Exklusivität positionierungsrelevante Assoziationen aus, die sich auf die Wahrnehmung der Markenpersönlichkeit auswirken (Esch/Langner 2001).

Abschließend ist im Rahmen der Produktpolitik noch die Art der Markierung, das heißt der **Markenname** und das **Markenlogo**, aufzuführen, die ebenfalls zum Aufbau der Markenpersönlichkeit beitragen kann. So konstatiert Keller: „Clearly, logos have meaning and associations that change consumer perceptions of the company" (Keller 1998), jedoch wurde diese Aussage bis heute nicht umfassend empirisch analysiert. Allgemein lässt sich jedoch bemerken, dass die Gestaltungsfaktoren von Markenlogos wie Form, Farbe und die Interaktion von Form und Farbe einen direkten Einfluss auf die Markenpersönlichkeit haben. Der Einfluss des Markennamens kann zum Beispiel an den vielen Neumarken, die der Internet-Boom hervorgebracht hat, illustriert werden: So wies zu Boom-Zeiten des E-Commerce eine Marke, die durch den Zusatz „.com" oder „.de" gekennzeichnet war, auf eine fortschrittliche Markenpersönlichkeit hin. Heutzutage haftet solchen Marken eher Erfolglosigkeit an, die sich folgerichtig auch in einer weniger attraktiven Markenpersönlichkeit manifestiert.

Das zweite wesentliche Instrument zum Aufbau einer Markenpersönlichkeit stellt die **Kommunikationspolitik** dar. Batra, Lehmann und Singh vertreten die Meinung, dass der Werbung die größte Bedeutung für den Aufbau einer Markenpersönlichkeit zukommt (Batra/Lehmann/Singh 1993). Neben den bereits dargelegten Einflüssen durch Prominente oder andere Testimonials kann Werbung auch in einem weiten Sinne zum Aufbau einer Markenpersönlichkeit genutzt werden. Untersuchungen zeigen, dass sich der **Werbestil** auf die Wahrnehmung der Markenpersönlichkeit auswirkt. So beeinflusst beispielsweise **vergleichende Werbung** die Wahrnehmung der Markenpersönlichkeit negativ, wie John Hegarty, Chairman und Creative von Bartle Bogle Hegarty, beschreibt: „We often talk about brands as personalities, yet we usually do not like people who have a go at other people. We generally prefer those who have the confidence to be themselves" (o. V. 1995).

Die **Preispolitik** zeichnet sich ebenfalls über ihre indirekte Wirkung auf die Markenpersönlichkeit aus. Aaker argumentiert, dass eine hochpreisige Marke als arrogant und mondän gesehen wird (Aaker 1996). Theoretische Unterstützung erfährt Aaker aus den Erkenntnissen der Preispsychologie: Der so genannte **Snob-Effekt** besagt, dass sich durch die Verteuerung eines Produktes ein positiver Nutzen für den Konsumenten dadurch ergibt, dass er in seiner sozialen Umwelt Exklusivität und Einzigartigkeit demonstrieren kann. Auch aus beziehungstheoretischer Perspektive lässt sich dieses Wahlverhalten erklären: So neigen Konsumenten dazu, sich in bestimmten Situationen zu belohnen. Da der Belohnungseffekt mit der Wertigkeit der Marke steigt, wirkt sich die Verteuerung der Marke positiv auf das Kaufverhalten aus.

Wie die anderen Instrumente des Marketing-Mix beeinträchtigt auch der **Distributionskanal** die Wahrnehmung der Markenpersönlichkeit. So kann durch die Wahl des Vertriebskanals die Innovationskraft der Marke unterstützt werden (Internet versus Einzelhandel). Ebenfalls spielen das Design und die Gestaltung von Filialen und Vertretungen eine zunehmend bedeutende Rolle und werden mehr und mehr auf die gewünschten Markenassoziationen abgestimmt. Schließlich wirkt sich insbesondere die Wahrnehmung der Vertriebsmitarbeiter durch den Nachfrager auf die wahrgenommene Markenpersönlichkeit aus.

3.2 Wirkung der Markenpersönlichkeit

Die Wirkung der Markenpersönlichkeit und somit ihre Relevanz entfaltet sich durch drei grundsätzliche Wirkungsmodelle (Aaker 1996). Das dominante Wirkungsmodell stellt hierbei das **Self-Expression Model** dar. Hierbei wird unterstellt, dass Menschen ein Bedürfnis haben, ihr **Selbstkonzept** auszudrücken (Sirgy 1986). Bezogen auf Marken besagt die **Kongruenztheorie,** dass durch eine größtmögliche Übereinstimmung zwischen der angestrebten Identität und Persönlichkeit eines Individuums und der Identität und Persönlichkeit der konsumierten Marke eine **präferenzerzeugende Wirkung beim Konsumenten** entsteht (Aaker 1996).

Forschungsarbeiten der letzten zehn Jahre zeigen, dass dieses Bedürfnis dynamischer Natur ist und das angestrebte Selbstkonzept situativ schwankt (Aaker 1996). So kann beispielsweise ein Buchhalter von seinen Kollegen als humorvoll, kreativ und fleißig empfunden werden, während seine Golfpartner ihn als entspannt und guten Verlierer schildern und ihn seine Freunde als wahren Hedonisten erleben (Aaker 1996). McCracken bestätigt mit seiner Aussage die Relevanz von Marken für diesen Prozess: „All of us are constantly constructing and reconstructing the self. This calls for new meanings or new ways of defining or presenting the self. There are several sources for these meanings, including consumer goods and brands." (McCracken 1993, S. 127). An dieser Stelle wird ein wesentlicher Unterschied zwischen Markenpersönlichkeit und Markenidentität deutlich: **Die Markenidentität ist das zeitlich stabilere Konstrukt.** Die Markenpersönlichkeit, als eine von mehreren Facetten der Markenidentität, kann demgegenüber flexibler an veränderte Umstände angepasst werden. Die permanente Suche vieler Nachfrager nach immer neuen Darstellungsmöglichkeiten bietet dem Markenmanagement somit die Möglichkeit, durch die Bereitstellung vorgefertigter Markenpersönlichkeiten dem Bedürfnis nach Persönlichkeitstransfer nachzukommen.

Abbildung 3: **Wirkungsansätze der Markenpersönlichkeitsforschung**

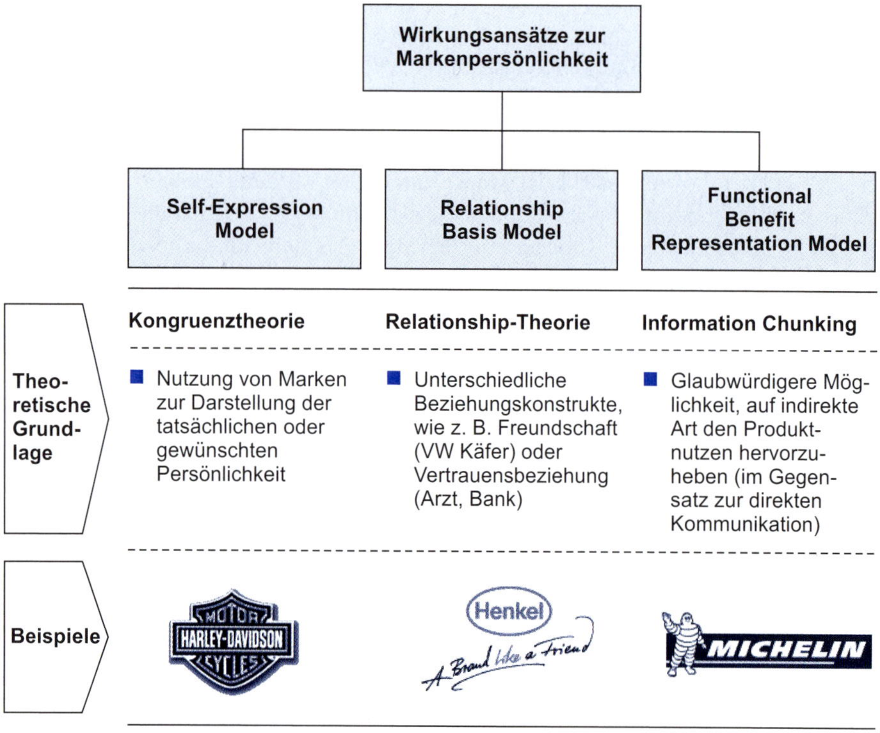

GABLER GRAFIK

Das **Relationship Basis Model** versucht, die Erkenntnisse der Beziehungstheorie der Markenpolitik zugänglich zu machen. Während das Self-Expression Model die Nutzung der Marke zur Selbstdarstellung als Wirkungshypothese postuliert, steht im Relationship Basis Model die Beziehung zur Marke im Zentrum der Untersuchung. So grenzt Fournier das Relationship Basis Model eindeutig zur Kongruenztheorie des Self-Expression Models ab: „Consumer-brand relationships are more a matter of perceived goal compatibility than congruence between discreet product attributes and personality trait images" (Fournier 1998, S. 366). Anders als beim Self-Expression Model **stellt die Marke hier ein aktives Element dar**. Die Marke wird nicht als Instrument zur Selbstinszenierung betrachtet, sondern wird zu einem „lebendigen" Beziehungspartner (Blackston 2000).

Als dritter Erklärungsansatz zur Wirkungsweise von Markenpersönlichkeiten dient das **Functional Benefit Representation Model**, welches den **funktionalen Nutzen** der Marke in den Vordergrund stellt. Aakers Argumentation folgend dient die Markenpersönlichkeit als **Strukturierungshilfe** zur Repräsentierung und zum Abruf von funktionalem Markenwissen. Demnach beschreibt das Markenimage im Gedächtnis der Konsumenten Wissensstrukturen beziehungsweise Schemata in Form von Assoziationen und verknüpfenden Verbindungen (Cohen/Basu 1987). Unter Schemata können dabei große, komplexe Wisseneinheiten verstanden werden, die typische Eigenschaften und feste, standardisierte Vorstellungen von bestimmten Objekten, Personen oder Ereignissen (in diesem Fall Marken) umfassen (Rumelhart 1980). Diese Schemata werden häufig durch **semantische Netze** dargestellt, die im Allgemeinen gespeichertes Wissen beziehungsweise Konzepte als Knoten und assoziative Verbindungen zwischen diesem Wissen (Konzepten) als Kanten beziehungsweise Verknüpfungen erfassen (Grunert 1982). Der Prozess der **Abbildung** und **Abrufung von Markenwissen** wird durch die Markenpersönlichkeit positiv verstärkt. So bestätigt Biel, dass die Markenpersönlichkeit eine aktivere Verarbeitung von Markenwissen erlaubt, was sich wiederum positiv in der Relevanz der Assoziationen für das Individuum niederschlägt (Biel 1993). Die **Zugänglichkeit von Wissen** spielt zudem eine wichtige Rolle in kognitiven Verarbeitungsprozessen von Konsumenten: Je leichter abrufbar eine Information gespeichert ist, desto eher wird sie für die Entscheidungsfindung herangezogen (Dick/Chakravati/Biehal 1990). Diese Vereinfachungsprozesse beziehen sich auch auf Speicherung und Abrufung von Markenwissen. Je stärker die Markenpersönlichkeit demnach in der Lage ist, **assoziative Netzwerke** zu formieren, desto wertvoller ist sie im Rahmen des Functional Benefit Representation Model.

4. Bedeutung der Markenpersönlichkeit für die Unternehmenspraxis

Für die Managementpraxis bietet sich durch das Konstrukt der Markenpersönlichkeit somit ein wichtiger und relevanter Entscheidungsrahmen. Im Rahmen eines fünfstufigen Prozesses kann die Markenpersönlichkeit optimiert werden.

Zunächst muss mittels der **Ist-Analyse** die Markenpersönlichkeit gemessen und verstanden werden. Dies kann beispielsweise im Rahmen des von der Unternehmensberatung McKinsey und der GfK Kommunikations- und Markenforschung entwickelten Tool „Brand Personality Gameboard" geschehen – ein Instrument zur Messung und Darstellung der Markenpersönlichkeit (Fanderl/Hölscher/Hupp 2003). Hier wird auf Basis des faktorenanalytischen Ansatzes die Markenpersönlichkeit gemessen und in einem zweidimensionalem Raum dargestellt. Vor dieser quantitativen Verortung der Markenpersönlichkeit können qualitative Verfahren (zum Beispiel Fokusgruppen) helfen, die qualitativen Aspekte des Markenimages besser zu verstehen.

Nachdem die Wettbewerbssituation berücksichtigt ist, hilft in einem zweiten Schritt eine Möglichkeitsanalyse der Produktkategorie, den möglichen Lösungsraum einzugrenzen. Wie schon im Rahmen der Wirkungsanalysen gezeigt wurde, kann die Wirkung der Markenpersönlichkeit aus der Kongruenztheorie oder auch der Beziehungstheorie erklärt werden. Produkte die der **sozialen Demonstranz** unterliegen (zum Beispiel Bekleidung), lassen sich besser über das Self-Expression Model steuern, andererseits kann über die Beziehungstheorie eine geeignete Markenpersönlichkeit für Dienstleistungsmarken (zum Beispiel Asset Management) definiert werden.

In einem dritten Schritt müssen die Bedürfnisse der einzelnen **Kundensegmente** berücksichtigt werden, die im Rahmen der Nutzungssituation ermöglicht werden. Hierbei können Lebenswelt-Segmentierungen helfen, die es erlauben, wünschenswerte Selbstkonzepte verschiedener Segmente besser zu verstehen. Auf Basis eines holistischen Segmentverständnisses können dann Segmente ausgewählt werden, die ökonomisch sinnvoll sind und deren ideales Selbstkonzept verstanden ist.

Schließlich gilt es, in einem vorletzten Schritt den **Wettbewerbsbezug** herzustellen. So können sich verschiedene Markenpersönlichkeiten als relevant erweisen, jedoch ist es die Einzigartigkeit einer Positionierung (und somit einer Markenpersönlichkeit) die den ökonomischen Erfolg determiniert. So kann eine „schwächere" Markenpersönlichkeit aufgrund ihrer Unbesetztheit durch den Wettbewerb eine sinnvolle Position sein.

Letztendlich gilt es in einem abschließenden Schritt, eine Markenpersönlichkeit auszuwählen, die das **Wertversprechen der Marke** widerspiegelt. Wenn man beispielsweise eine vergleichsweise schwache Beratungsleistung im Vertrieb hat und gleichzeitig eine intelligente Markenpersönlichkeit transportiert entsteht ein Konflikt, welcher beim Konsument präferenzmindernde Wirkung besitzt.

5. Fazit

Die in diesem Beitrag herausgestellten Möglichkeiten einer Übertragung des Persönlichkeitskonzeptes auf die Markenführung haben gezeigt, dass wertvolle Impulse aus dieser Forschungsrichtung abgeleitet werden können. Sowohl das Bedürfnis, Marken zur Demonstranz des Selbst zu verwenden als auch die Möglichkeit, die Beziehung zum Konsument auszugestalten, machen das Konstrukt der Markenpersönlichkeit heute zu einem unverzichtbaren Instrument einer modernen Markenführung.

Literatur

Aaker, D. A. (1994), Wie eine Markenpersönlichkeit erfolgreich aufgebaut wurde, in: Harvard Business Manager, 16. Jg., Nr. 4, S. 28–39.

Aaker, D. A. (1996), Building Strong Brands, New York.

Aaker, D. A., Batra, R., Myers, J. (1992), Advertising Management, Englewood Cliffs, N. J.

Aaker, J. L. (1997), Dimensions of Brand Personality, in: Journal of Marketing Research, Vol. XXXIV, No. 3, August, S. 347–356.

Aaker, J. L., Benet-Martínez, V., Garolera, J. (2001), Consumption Symbols as Carriers of Culture: A Study of Japanese and Spanish Brand Personality Constructs, in: Journal of Personality and Social Psychology, Vol. 81, No. 3, S. 492–508.

Aaker, J. L., Fournier, S. (1995), A Brand as a Character, a Partner and a Person: Three Perspectives on the Question of Brand Personality, in: Advances in Consumer Research, Vol. 22, No. 1, S. 391–392.

Adjouri, N. (2002), Die Marke als Botschafter – Markenidentität bestimmen und entwickeln, Wiesbaden.

Alt, M., Griggs, S. (1998), Can a Brand be Cheeky?, in: Marketing Intelligence and Planning, Vol. 6, No. 4, S. 9–16.

Azoulay, A., Kapferer, J.-N. (2003), Do brand personality scales really measure brand personality, in: Journal of Brand Management, Vol. 11, No. 2, November, S. 143–155.

Batra, R., Lehman, D. R., Singh, D. (1993), The Brand Personality Component of Brand Goodwill: Some Antecedents and Consequences, in: Aaker, D. A., Biel, A. L. (Hrsg.), Brand Equity and Advertising, Hillsdale, N. J., S. 83–95.

Bauer, H. H., Huber, F. (1997), Der Wert der Marke, Arbeitspapier Nr. 120 des Instituts für Marketing, Universität Mannheim, Mannheim.

Belz, C. (1999), Trends in Kommunikation und Marktbearbeitung, in: Belz, C., Tomczak, T. (Hrsg.), Thexis: Fachbericht für Marketing, Nr. 3, St. Gallen.

Biel, A. L. (1993), Converting Image into Equity, in: Aaker, D. A., Biel, A. L. (Hrsg.), Brand Equity and Advertising: Advertising's Role in Building Strong Brands, Hillsdale, N. J., S. 67–82.

Blackston, M. (2000), Observations: Building Brand Equity By Managing the Brand's Relationships, in: Journal of Advertising Research, Vol. 40, No. 6, November/December, S. 101–105.

Bolz., N., Bosshart, D. (1995), Kult-Marketing: die neuen Götter des Marktes, 2. Aufl., Düsseldorf.

Bower, A. B. (2001), Highly Attractive Models in Advertising and the Women Who Loathe them. The Implications of Negative Affect for Spokesperson Effectiveness, in: Journal of Advertising, Vol. 30, No. 3, Fall, S. 51–63.

Brown, D. E. (1991), Human Universals, New York.

Cattell, R. B. (1979), Personality and Learning Theory, New York.

Cohen, J. B., Basu, K. (1987), Alternative Models of Categorization: Toward a Contingent Processing Framework, in: Journal of Consumer Research, Vol. 13, No. 4, March, S. 455–472.

Dick, A., Chakravarti, D., Biehal, G. (1990), Memory-Based Inferences During Consumer Choice, in: Journal of Consumer Research, Vol. 17, No. 1, June, S. 82–93.

Domizlaff, G. (1996), Der Kommunikationswert der Marke als Voraussetzung erfolgreicher Markenführung, in: Markenartikel, 58. Jg., Nr. 7, S. 303–306.

Domizlaff, H. (1982), Die Gewinnung des öffentlichen Vertrauens, Hamburg.

Esch, F.-R., Langner, T. (2001), Branding als Grundlage zum Markenaufbau, in: Esch, F.-R. (Hrsg.), Moderne Markenführung – Grundlagen, innovative Ansätze, praktische Umsetzungen, 3. Aufl., Wiesbaden, S. 407–420.

Eysenck, H. (1967), The Biological Basis of Personality, Springfield, IL.

Fisseni, H.-J. (1998), Persönlichkeitspsychologie – Auf der Suche nach einer Wissenschaft, 4. Aufl., Göttingen.

Fournier, S. (1998), Consumers and Their Brands: Developing Relationship Theory in Consumer Research, in: Journal of Consumer Research, Vol. 24, No. 4, March, S. 343–373.

Gerken, G. (1990), Abschied vom Marketing – Interfusion statt Marketing, Düsseldorf.

Gerken, G. (1994), Die fraktale Marke, Düsseldorf.

Gilmore, G. W. (1919), Animism: or, Thought Currents of Primitive Peoples, Boston.

Govers, P., Hekkert, P., Schoormans, J. (2002), Happy, Cute and Tough: Can Designers Create a Product Personality that Consumers Understand?, in: McDonagh, D., Hekkert, P., Erp, J. v., Gyi, D. (Hrsg.), Design and emotion: The experience of everyday things, New York, 345–349.

Grunert, K. G. (1982), Informationsverarbeitungsprozesse bei der Kaufentscheidung: ein gedächtnispsychologischer Ansatz, Frankfurt/M.

Guilford, J. (1974), Persönlichkeit – Logik, Methodik und Ergebnisse ihrer quantitativen Erforschung, 6. Aufl., Weinheim.

Halliday, J. (1996), Chrysler brings out brand personalities with '97 ads, in: Advertising Age, Vol. 67, No. 40, S. 3.

Herrmann, C. (1998), Die Marke als Frame: Versuch einer entscheidungsorientierten Theorie der Marke, Witten-Herdecke.

Herrmann, C. (1999), Die Zukunft der Marke: mit effizienten Führungsentscheidungen zum Markterfolg, Frankfurt/M.

Hieronimus, F. (2003), Persönlichkeitsorientiertes Markenmanagement, Frankfurt/M.

John, O. P. (1990), The Big Five Factor Taxonomy: Dimensions of Personality in the Natural Language and in Questionnaires, in: Pervin, L. (Hrsg.), Handbook of Personality, New York, S. 66–100.

Kassarjian, H. H. (1971), Personality and Consumer Behavior: A Review, in: Journal of Marketing Research, Vol. IIX, No. 4, November, S. 409–418.

Keller, K. L. (2003), Strategic brand banagement – building, measuring and managing brand equity, Upper Saddle River, N. J.

Kelly, G. A. (1955), The Psychology of Personal Constructs, New York.

Levy, S. (1959), Symbols for Sale, in: Harvard Business Review, Vol. 37, No. 4, S. 117–124.

Malhotra, N. (1993), Marketing Research: An Applied Orientation, Englewood Cliffs, N. J.

Maslow, A. M. (1975), Motivation and Personality, in: Levine, F. M. (Hrsg.), Theoretical Readings in Motivation, Chicago, S. 358–379.

Matthies, W. (1997), Perspectives on Product Personality, in: Twice, Vol. 12, No. 23, S. 20.

McCracken, G. (1993), The Value of the Brand: An Anthropological Perspective, in: Aaker, D. A., Biel, A. L. (Hrsg.), Brand Equity & Advertising, Hillsdale, N. J., S. 125–139.

McCrae, R. R., Costa, P. T. (1997), Personality Trait Structure as a Human Universal, in: American Psychologist, Vol. 52, May, S. 509–516.

McDougall, W. (1911), Body and Mind: A History and Defense of Animism, New York.

Meffert, H., Burmann, Ch. (1996), Identitätsorientierte Markenführung – Grundlagen für das Management von Markenportfolios, Meffert, H., Wagner, H., Backhaus, K. (Hrsg.), Arbeitspapier Nr. 100 der Wissenschaftlichen Gesellschaft für Marketing und Unternehmensführung e.V., Münster.

Meffert, H., Twardawa, T., Wildner, R. (2000), Aktuelle Trends im Verbraucherverhalten – Chancen und Risiken für den Markenartikel, Meffert, H., Backhaus, K., Becker, J. (Hrsg.), Arbeitspapier Nr. 137 der Wissenschaftlichen Gesellschaft für Marketing und Unternehmensführung e. V., Münster.

Nida, E., Smalley, W. (1959), Introducing Animism, New York.

Otte, T. (1993), Marke als System, ihre Eigenkräfte regeln den Markt, Hamburg.
Perrey, J. (1998), Nutzenorientierte Marktsegmentierung: Ein integrativer Ansatz zum Zielgruppenmarketing im Verkehrsdienstleistungsbereich, Wiesbaden.
Pervin, L. (2000), Persönlichkeitstheorien, 4. Aufl., München.
Plummer, J. (1984), How Personality Makes a Difference, in: Journal of Advertising Research, Vol. 24, No. 6, S. 27–31.
Reeb, M. (1998), Lebensstilanalysen in der strategischen Marktforschung, Wiesbaden.
Rieger, B. (1985), Zum Tode verurteilt, von Geburt an: Marken ohne Persönlichkeit, in: Markenartikel, 47. Jg., S. 56–60.
Roth, F. (1999), Die Macht der Marke, Frankfurt/M.
Rumelhart, D. E. (1980), Schemata: The Building Blocks of Cognition, in: Spiro, R. J., Bruce, B. C., Brewer, R. J. (Hrsg.), Theoretical Issues in Reading Comprehension, Hillsdale, N. J., S. 33–58.
Schindler, R. (1992), The Real Lesson of New Coke: The Value of Focus Groups for Predicting the Effects of Social Influence, in: Marketing Research, Vol. 4, No. 4, December, S. 22–27.
Schouten, J., McAlexander, J. (1995), Subcultures of Consumption: An Ethnography of the New Bikers, in: Journal of Consumer Research, Vol. 22, No. 1, June, S. 43–61.
Simon, H.-J. (2001), Das Geheimnis der Marke, ABC der Markentechnik, München.
Sirgy, M. J. (1986), Self-Congruity: Toward a Theory of Personality and Cybernetics, New York.
Smit, E., van den Berge, E., Franzen, G. (2002), Brands Are Just Like Real People!: The Development of SWOCC's Brand Personality Scale, International Research in Advertising Conference, Kopenhagen Business School, Denmark, 2.–3. Mai.
Wells, W. et al. (1957), An Adjective Check List for the Study of ‚Product Personality', in: Journal of Applied Psychology, Vol. 41, No. 5, S. 317–319.

Profilierung von Marken mit Sponsoring und Events

Christoph Burmann und Axel Nitschke

1. Relevanz von Sponsoring und Event-Kommunikation für das Markenmanagement **388**

2. Theoretische Grundlagen **389**

2.1 Abgrenzung und Typologisierung von Sponsoring und Event-Kommunikation 389

2.2 Wirkungsprozess und Funktionsweise von Sponsoring und Event-Kommunikation 392

2.3 Sponsoring und Event-Kommunikation im Kontext der identitätsorientierten Markenführung 393

3. Erfolgsfaktoren für die Profilierung von Marken durch Sponsoring und Event-Kommunikation **395**

3.1 Planung der Kommunikationsmaßnahmen 395

3.2 Durchführung der Kommunikationsmaßnahmen 397

3.3 Controlling der Kommunikationswirkungen 399

4. Fallbeispiel zur Profilierung der Stadtmarke Bremen durch Werder Bremen **401**

5. Zusammenfassung und Ausblick **407**

1. Relevanz von Sponsoring und Event-Kommunikation für das Markenmanagement

Während die Werbeaufwendungen im Bereich der klassischen Kommunikationsinstrumente 2004 gegenüber dem Vorjahr stagnierten, legte **Sponsoring** auf drei Milliarden Euro in Deutschland zu. Bis zum Jahr 2006 wird ein weiterer Anstieg des Gesamtvolumens auf 4,4 Milliarden Euro erwartet (pilot checkpoint 2004, S. 5). Für die **Event-Kommunikation** lag das Marktvolumen im Jahr 2004 bereits bei 3,7 Milliarden Euro und für die nächsten Jahre erwartet die Branche weitere **Zuwächse** (Braun 2004, S. 28), nicht nur aufgrund der Fußball Weltmeisterschaft 2006 in Deutschland.

Vielmehr ist die **nachlassende Wirkung klassischer Kommunikationsinstrumente** die wesentliche Ursache für die steigende Relevanz von Sponsoring und Event-Kommunikation für die Markenführung. Die Konsumenten leiden an einer Informationsüberlastung durch Werbung. Von 1992 bis 2002 hat sich alleine die TV-Werbung in Deutschland von elf Stunden auf 45 Stunden täglich mehr als vervierfacht (S&P 2002). Dabei wird eine wachsende Anzahl von Marken bei gleichzeitig homogener werdenden Produkten beworben. Marken werden in vielen Bereichen austauschbar. Sie verlieren gegenüber dem Preis an Relevanz für das Kaufverhalten und die Loyalität der Konsumenten gegenüber Marken sinkt. Die Beziehung zwischen den Marken und ihren Nachfragern erodiert und damit der oft wertvollste Vermögensgegenstand von Markenartiklern.

Um diese Entwicklung aufzuhalten oder gar umzukehren wird vielfach versucht **Marken über einen symbolischen Zusatznutzen im Wettbewerb zu differenzieren**. Mit zunehmender technisch-funktionaler Homogenität von Produkten nimmt die Bedeutung affektiver gegenüber kognitiver Faktoren im Kaufentscheidungsprozess zu. Diesem Zusammenhang wird durch die **Emotionalisierung von Marken** Rechnung getragen (Esch 2004, S. 27 ff.). Auf diesem Wege soll eine positive Veränderung des Markenimages, eine unverwechselbare Positionierung und eine Stärkung der **Marke-Kunde-Beziehung** realisiert werden.

Ein Weg zur Schaffung eines symbolischen Zusatznutzens ist eine **erlebnisorientierte Markenführung**, welche sich an den emotionalen Bedürfnissen der Zielgruppen ausrichtet. Neben produktpolitischen Maßnahmen, wie beispielsweise einem emotionsauslösenden Produktdesign (Koppelmann 2003), können Marken vor allem durch kommunikative Maßnahmen emotional aufgeladen werden. Hier eignen sich insbesondere die stark erlebnisorientierten Instrumente Sponsoring und Event-Kommunikation, da die Nachfrager in einer ihrem Lebensgefühl entsprechenden, emotionalen Kontaktsituation direkt angesprochen werden (Burmann/Nitschke 2004).

2. Theoretische Grundlagen

2.1 Abgrenzung und Typologisierung von Sponsoring und Event-Kommunikation

Sponsoring bezieht sich auf die Nutzung fremdinitiierter Events (Institutionen, Mannschaften, Person) als Trägermedium eigener Kommunikationsbotschaften in einem realen emotionalen Kontext. Dabei steht die Kommunikationsbotschaft nicht im Mittelpunkt des Besucherinteresses, weshalb beim Sponsoring die Besucher vor Ort (direkte Zielgruppe) zwar ein hohes Situations-, aber nur ein niedriges Botschaftsinvolvement aufweisen. Unter Involvement wird der Grad der Ich-Beteiligung einer Person verstanden (Trommsdorff 2002, S. 56). Die Informationswahrnehmung erfolgt hier peripher. Bei der direkten Zielgruppe kann durch Sponsoring daher eine mittlere Kontaktqualität erreicht werden (Lardinoit/Debaix 2001, S. 169; Lasslop 2003, S. 15). Die Kontaktquantität ist in der Regel höher als bei einer hinsichtlich des Budgets vergleichbaren Event-Kommunikationsmaßnahme. Die Kontaktkosten können bei Berücksichtigung der indirekten Zielgruppe (indirekter Kontakt mit der Sponsoringmaßnahme durch die Medienberichterstattung) als niedrig bezeichnet werden.

Unter einem **Event** wird allgemein ein Ereignis verstanden, welches sportlicher, kultureller oder gesellschaftlicher Natur sein kann. **Event-Kommunikation** ist die Nutzung eigenständig initiierter Veranstaltungen (so genannter Marken-Events) als Trägermedium eigener Kommunikationsbotschaften in einem inszenierten emotionalen und interaktionsfähigen Kontext. Dabei steht die Kommunikationsbotschaft der Marke im Mittelpunkt des Interesses der Event-Teilnehmer, weshalb eine hohes Situations- und ein hohes Botschaftsinvolvement realisiert wird. Die Informationswahrnehmung erfolgt zentral. Bei der direkten Zielgruppe wird eine hohe Kontaktqualität realisiert, die starke Imagetransferwirkungen ermöglicht (Ueding 1994, S. 59; Nickel 1998, S. 7; Zanger 2001, S. 833). Die Quantität der Kontakte ist dagegen in der Regel gering, woraus relativ hohe Kontaktkosten resultieren.

Wird die Zielsetzung zugrunde gelegt, dass Sponsoring einen positiven Beitrag zum Markenwert leisten soll, und nicht aus altruistischen Motiven durchgeführt wird, können die Nachfrager einer Marke als Hauptzielgruppe identifiziert werden. Generell können, insbesondere durch Sponsoring-Engagements (Sponsorships) im Profisport, große Zielgruppen mit niedrigen Kontaktkosten über die Medien erreicht werden. Gleichzeitig ist die Kommunikationsbotschaft im Wesentlichen auf die Darstellung des Markennamens begrenzt. Hieraus resultiert, dass Sponsoring einen wesentlichen Beitrag zur **Erhöhung der Markenbekanntheit** liefern kann.

Darüber hinaus kann zwischen den Kommunikationszielen der Induzierung eines **symbolischen Zusatznutzens** und der **Absatzförderung** unterschieden werden. Beispielsweise konnte Adidas als Co-Sponsor und Ausrüster zahlreicher Fußball Nationalmannschaften bei der Europameisterschaft 2004 ca. 1,3 Millionen Fan-Trikots und sechs Millionen EM-Fußbälle verkaufen. Dagegen stand beim Olympiaengagement 2004 in Athen eine Imageverbesserung im Vordergrund (Riering/Seidel 2004, S. 16). Dementsprechend ist zwischen einem „absatzorientierten Sponsoring", bei dem die direkte Erzeugung von Kaufabsicht (konative Einstellungskomponente) im Vordergrund steht, und einem „markenorientierten Sponsoring", mit der Dominanz einer stark affektiv geprägten Imageprofilierung, zu unterscheiden (vgl. Abbildung 1). Da diese affektiven Prozesse wesentlich für die Emotionalisierung von Marken sind, soll nachfolgend nur das **„markenorientierte Sponsoring"** betrachtet werden.

Abbildung 1: Typen von Sponsoring

GABLER GRAFIK

Im Bereich der Event-Kommunikation lassen sich in Abhängigkeit von den Kommunikationsinhalten und Zielgruppen **vier Grundtypen von Events** unterscheiden (vgl. Abbildung 2). Auf der horizontalen Achse kann eine Differenzierung zwischen internen und externen Zielgruppen erfolgen. Als zweites ist zu bestimmen, welches dominante Kommunikationsziel mit dem Event verfolgt werden soll. Es kann zwischen einer primären Verbesserung des Wissens über die Markenmerkmale, beziehungsweise den funktionalen Nutzen und einer Fundierung von symbolischen Nutzendimensionen unterschieden werden (Lasslop 2003, S. 20 ff.).

Durch die stark emotionale Prägung des Eventtyps „externes Marken-Event" eignet sich dieser Typ besonders zur Bewältigung der anfangs aufgezeigten Herausforderung, dem Aufbau einer stabilen Marke-Kunde-Beziehung. „Externe Marken-Events" richten sich primär an die externen Zielgruppen einer Marke und wirken auf die symbolische Nutzenkomponente des Markenimages. Generell sind sie durch eine starke Erlebnisorientierung gekennzeichnet. Durch die Induzierung emotionaler Prozesse bei der Zielgruppe wird eine starke Kommunikationswirkung erreicht, die in der Regel durch Sponsoring in diesem Ausmaß nicht möglich ist (Weinberg/Nickel 1998). Nachfolgend sollen deshalb **externe Marken-Events** im Vordergrund der Betrachtung stehen.

Abbildung 2: Typen von Marken-Events

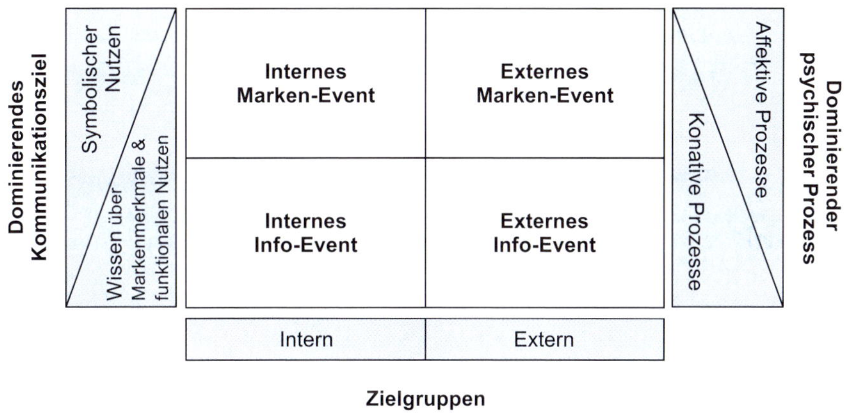

GABLER GRAFIK

Quelle: in Anlehnung an Lasslop 2003, S. 23

Sowohl Sponsoring als auch Event-Kommunikation haben das Ziel, die Präferenz der anvisierten Zielgruppe zu Gunsten einer bestimmten Marke positiv zu beeinflussen und so eine kaufverhaltensrelevante Wirkung zu entfachen. Aus den obigen Definitionen und Abgrenzungen ist ersichtlich, dass beide Instrumente Unterschiede hinsichtlich der Qualität und Quantität der Kontakte mit der direkten Zielgruppe aufweisen. Beide Kommunikationsmaßnahmen ermöglichen jedoch die Nachfrager in einer **emotionalen und erlebnisorientierten Kommunikationssituation** zu kontaktieren. Da diese Charakteristika der Kontaktsituation ausschlaggebend für die Emotionalisierung von Marken sind, werden zum einfacheren Verständnis nachfolgend die **Begriffe Event-Kommunikation und Sponsoring synonym verwendet**. Dies gilt nur, sofern eine sachliche Differenzierung zwischen beiden Instrumenten nicht notwendig ist. Ebenso wird nur der Fall eines Sponsorings von Veranstaltungen betrachtet, wobei die Ausführungen ebenso Gültigkeit für das Sponsoring von Institutionen, Mannschaften oder Einzelsportlern haben.

2.2 Wirkungsprozess und Funktionsweise von Sponsoring und Event-Kommunikation

Generell sind Sponsoring und Event-Kommunikation im Gegensatz zu klassischen Kommunikationsinstrumenten durch eine bessere Informationsaufnahme bei den Rezipienten gekennzeichnet. Beide Instrumente genießen bei den Rezipienten ein besseres Ansehen als klassische Werbung mit der Folge einer fehlenden oder nur schwachen Reaktanz bei den Zielgruppen (Meenaghan 2001a, S. 193 ff.; Sportfive 2003, S. 21). Hierdurch wird eine bessere Kontaktqualität realisiert. Reaktanz kennzeichnet den Prozeß der Beeinflussungsabwehr. Reaktanz tritt auf, wenn Personen sich durch einen Beeinflussungsversuch in ihrer Meinungs- und Entscheidungsfreiheit bedroht fühlen. Die Folge von Reaktanz ist das Verharren einer Person auf ihrem Meinungsstandpunkt (Trommsdorff 2002, S. 281).

Die vom Unternehmen gesendete Kommunikationsbotschaft soll mittels des Botschaftsträgers Event die anvisierten Zielgruppen erreichen. Die Besucher eines Events werden dabei direkt erreicht, die Öffentlichkeit über Medien und Mund-zu-Mund Propaganda indirekt (vgl. Abbildung 3). Bei den Empfängern sind **vier Wirkungsstufen** zu unterscheiden. Auf der ersten Stufe wird die Kommunikationsbotschaft wahrgenommen (Bekanntheitswirkung). Darauf aufbauend kann zwischen affektiven und kognitiven Wirkungen differenziert werden, welche zusammen als Imagewirkungen bezeichnet werden können. Die vierte Stufe des Wirkungsprozesses sind konative Wirkungen, beispielsweise die der Absicht zum Kauf oder zur persönlichen Kommunikation über die Marke (Kroeber-Riel/Weinberg 2003, S. 614).

Abbildung 3: **Wirkungsprozess von Sponsoring und Event-Kommunikation**

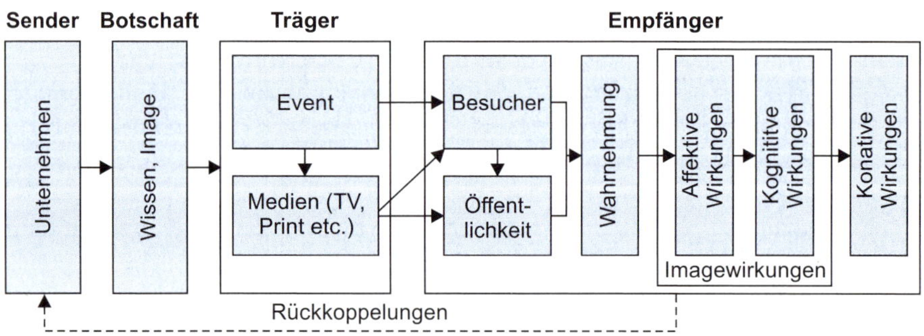

GABLER GRAFIK

Insbesondere affektive Wirkungen können durch erlebnisorientierte Kommunikation induziert werden. Dies erfolgt über einen Imagetransfers zwischen Stammobjekt (Event) und Transferobjekt (Marke). Unter **Imagetransfer** wird die **Übertragung von Assoziationen zwischen einem Stammprodukt und einem Transferprodukt** verstanden (Zentes 1996, S. 67 f.). Im Gegensatz zu klassischen Kommunikationsinstrumenten wie Werbung lässt sich der Einfluss von Medium und Botschaft bei der Wahrnehmung der Kommunikationsbotschaft im Sponsoring- oder Event-Kontext nicht trennen. Das emotionale Erlebnis bei einem Event und die Informationen über eine Marke werden so vom Rezipienten gemeinsam wahrgenommen. Hierdurch können **Assoziationen vom Stammobjekt** (dem Event oder dem Gesponsertem) **auf das Transferobjekt** (Marke) **übertragen** werden. Bekanntheitssteigerungen und Imagewirkungen durch Sponsoring (Gwinner/ Eaton 1999; Harvey 2001; Lardinoit/Derbaix 2001; Grohs/Wagner/Vstecka 2004) und durch Events konnte mehrfach empirisch belegt werden (Zanger/Drengner 1999; Nufer 2002; Lasslop 2003). Eine **gemeinsame Wahrnehmung** von Event und Marke ist jedoch nicht alleine ausreichend für die anvisierten affektiven Wirkungen in der Psyche der Zielgruppen. Vielmehr muss darüber hinaus eine gedankliche **Verbindung** zwischen Stamm- und Transferobjekt existieren (Gwinner 1997; Meenaghan 2001b; Nufer 2002, S. 192). In diesem Zusammenhang wird auch vom **Fit zwischen Event und Marke** gesprochen. Diese Frage wird ausführlich in Kapitel 3.1 bei der Auswahl der spezifischen Event-Maßnahme diskutiert.

2.3 Sponsoring und Event-Kommunikation im Kontext der identitätsorientierten Markenführung

Im Konzept des identitätsorientierten Markenmanagements wird die Stärke einer Marke durch die Markenidentität, das Markenimage und demzufolge der Beziehung zwischen den Nachfragern und der Marke determiniert (Keller 1993, Fournier 1998) In diesem Kontext kann eine Marke als *„ein Nutzenbündel mit spezifischen Merkmalen, die dafür sorgen, dass sich dieses Nutzenbündel gegenüber anderen Nutzenbündeln, welche dieselben Basisbedürfnisse erfüllen, aus Sicht relevanter Zielgruppen nachhaltig differenziert"* definiert werden (Burmann/Blinda/Nitschke, S. 3). Voraussetzung aller festen Beziehungen (im Zwischenmenschlichen wie bei Marken) ist eine klare und verlässliche Vorstellung über die Persönlichkeit des Beziehungspartners, das heißt seiner Identität.

Unter der **Markenidentität** werden *„diejenigen raum-zeitlich gleichartigen Merkmale einer Marke [verstanden], die aus Sicht der internen Zielgruppen in nachhaltiger Weise den Charakter der Marke prägen"* (Burmann/Blinda/Nitschke 2003, S. 16). Die Wahrnehmung der Marke bei den externen Zielgruppen drückt sich im **Markenimage** aus, welches das in der Psyche relevanter Zielgruppen fest verankerte, verdichtete Vorstellungsbild von einer Marke darstellt (in Anlehnung an Kroeber-Riel/Weinberg 2003, S. 197).

Aufgrund der gemeinsamen Wahrnehmung von Event und Marke tritt das Event als Filter in die Beziehung zwischen Markenidentität und Markenimage ein (vgl. Abbildung 4). Durch die Verdeutlichung der Markenwerte und der Markenpersönlichkeit in der erlebnis- orientierten Event- und Sponsoring-Kommunikation wird versucht, die Positionie rung der Marke mittels einer Akzentuierung ihrer symbolischen Nutzendimensionen zu verbessern. Das **direkte und/oder interaktive Erleben der Markenwerte und Markenpersönlichkeit** bei einem Event induziert eine **starke Identifikation der Nachfrager mit der Marke** und fördert somit den Aufbau einer Beziehung. Gleichzeitig erfolgt ein Imagetransfer vom Event auf die Marke.

Abbildung 4: Events und Sponsoring im Kontext des identitätsoridentierten Markenmanagements

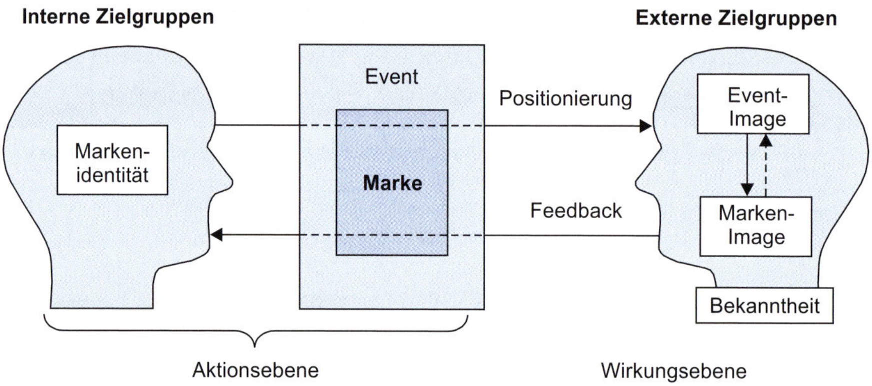

GABLER GRAFIK

Durch seine Interaktivität offenbart Event-Kommunikation neben der Positionierung noch eine zweite, gegenwärtig oft vernachlässigte Funktion von Events für das Markenmanagement. Durch den direkten Kontakt mit der Zielgruppe können die internen Zielgruppen ein **Feedback** über die Glaubwürdigkeit und Relevanz der Marke bei den externen Zielgruppen bekommen. Hierfür ist ein systematisches Erfassen und Weiterleiten der Feedback-Informationen erfolgskritisch. Insbesondere vor dem Hintergrund, dass die Markenmitarbeiter vor Ort bei Events heute oftmals durch externe Dienstleister gestellt werden, ist ein systematisches Event-Controlling unabdingbar, damit das vorhandene Informationsgewinnungspotenzial genutzt werden kann.

Um die oben erläuterten Potenziale der erlebnisorientierten Kommunikationsinstrumente optimal für das Markenmanagement zu nutzen, müssen die wesentlichen **Wirkungsdeterminanten** von Sponsoring und Event-Kommunikation berücksichtigt werden. Bei der **Auswahl** der spezifischen Kommunikationsmaßnahme sind der Fit zwischen Event, Marke und Zielgruppe sowie die Dauer der Kommunikationsmaßnahme zu berücksichtigen (Fischer/Mäder 2002; Roy/Cornwell 2003). Bei der **Durchführung** der Kommunikationsmaßnahme sind eine Wahrnehmung der Marke bei den Zielgruppen und eine positive Bewertung sicherzustellen. Als Letztes ist ein systematisches Kommunikations-**Controlling** sicherzustellen, um ein zielgerichtetes Lernen zur kontinuierlichen Verbesserung der Effektivität und Effizienz sicherzustellen (Burmann 2002, S. 93 ff.).

3. Erfolgsfaktoren für die Profilierung von Marken durch Sponsoring und Event-Kommunikation

3.1 Planung der Kommunikationsmaßnahmen

Bei der Zusammenstellung des Kommunikations-Mixes bedarf es einer grundsätzlichen Analyse, ob die anvisierten Kommunikationsziele mit Sponsoring oder Event-Kommunikation effektiv und effizient zu erreichen sind. Hierbei sind die in Kapitel 2.1 diskutierten Charakteristika wie die Qualität, Quantität und die Kosten der realisierten Kontakte zu berücksichtigen. Bei gegebener Mittelkonformität und einer Entscheidung für eines der beiden Instrumente ist die konkrete Auswahl des Event-Typs oder Sponsoringobjekts zu treffen. Hierbei sind der so genannte Event-Marken-Fit und die Event-Zielgruppen-Kongruenz wesentliche Determinanten.

Zur Analyse des **Event-Marken-Fits** wurde das allgemeine Modell von **von Weizäcker** (1974) von Burmann/Nitschke (2005) weiterentwickelt. Dieses stellt den Zusammenhang zwischen Fit und Kommunikationswirkung dar. Der Fit zwischen einem Event und einer Marke wird danach durch die Art der vom Event auf den Rezipienten ausgehenden Informationen beziehungsweise Reize determiniert. Diese Reize können entweder bekannt sein, und so lediglich das beim Rezipienten vorhandene Markenschema **bestätigen**, oder neu und damit **erstmalig** für den Rezipienten sein. Nach der Lerntheorie führen weder vollständig bekannte, noch vollständig neue Reize zu einer Kommunikationswirkung, welche im vorliegenden Fall als differenzielle Veränderung des Images verstanden wird (vgl. Abbildung 5). Eine optimale Wirkung wird beim „richtigen" Verhältnis von bekannten und neuen Reizen erreicht.

Ist der **Fit** zwischen Event und Marke **zu gering**, also im Bereich zwischen F_0 und F_{kritU}, erhält der Rezipient zu viele erstmalige Reize. Diese kann er nicht mit seinem bestehenden Markenschema verknüpfen. Es kommt daher zu keiner Imageveränderung, sondern lediglich zu einer Erhöhung der **Bekanntheit**.

Im Bereich zwischen F_{kritO} und F_{max} ist der **Fit zu groß**, das heißt, der Rezipient ist einer zu großen Anzahl bekannter Reize durch das Event ausgesetzt. Es setzt schnell Langeweile ein. Neben einer Erhöhung der **Bekanntheit** wird in diesem Fall das bestehende **Markenimage bestenfalls intensiviert**. Eine Veränderung des Images im Sinne von neuen Imagedimensionen findet daher nicht statt.

An Hand des stufenförmigen Verlaufs der Kurve bei einer dichotomen Interpretation des Wirkungszusammenhangs ist zu erkennen, dass bei einem **mittleren oder auch gutem Fit** im Bereich zwischen F_{kritU} und F_{kritO} die größte Wirkung erzielt werden kann. Hier ist ein ausreichender Teil neuer Reize vorhanden, um das Image zu verändern, und darüber hinaus ausreichend bekannte Reize, die das „Andocken" der neuen Impulse an das vorhandene Imageschema ermöglichen. Ein mittlerer, beziehungsweise guter Event-Marken Fit ist die **hinreichende Bedingung** für einen Imagetransfer. Ist diese Bedingung erfüllt, kann eine **Imageveränderung** durch einen Imagetransfer vom Stammprodukt, dem Event, auf das Transferprodukt, die Marke, realisiert werden. Zusätzlich erhöht sich die Bekanntheit. Je nach dem Verhältnis von neuen und alten Reizen kann zusätzlich eine Intensivierung des vorhandenen Images erreicht werden. Bei der Messung des Event-Marken-Fits sollten sowohl funktionale als auch symbolische Affiniäten zwischen dem Event und der Marke berücksichtigt werden.

Abbildung 5: Zusammenhang zwischen Event-Marken-Fit und Kommunikationswirkung

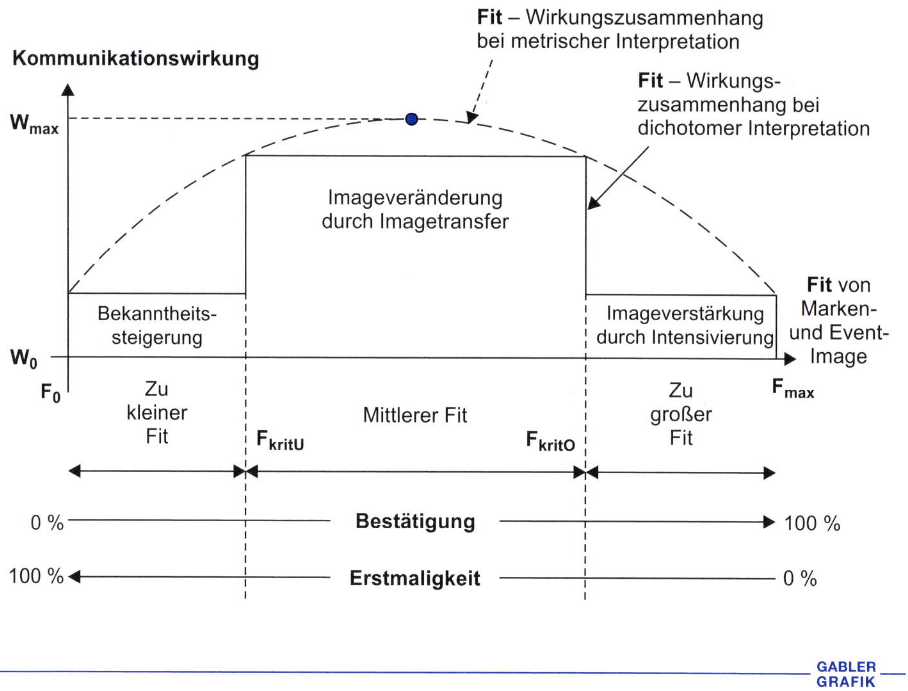

Quelle: Burmann/Nitschke 2005, S. 21.

Als weitere wesentliche Wirkungsdeterminante ist der **Fit zwischen der Zielgruppe und dem Event** zu berücksichtigen. Eine positive Einstellung der Zielgruppen und ein hohes Involvement bezogen auf das Event wirken sich positiv auf die Kommunikationswirkungen aus (Quester/Farrelly 1998; Lasslop 2003). Um eine weitestgehende Kongruenz zwischen von Event und Zielgruppe zu realisieren, sind bei der Auswahl und Gestaltung der erlebnisorientierten Kommunikationsmaßnahme der Lebensstil der Zielgruppen zu berücksichtigen (Weinberg/Nickel 1998, S. 62).

Neben einem, dem primären Kommunikationsziel (Stärkung vorhandener oder Bildung neuer Imagedimensionen) entsprechenden Fit, sind in der Konzeptionsphase die Integration des Events oder Sponsorships in die Markenkommunikation sowie die umfassende

Vernetzung mit begleitenden Kommunikationsinstrumenten zu berücksichtigen. Empirische Studien belegen, dass durch begleitende Werbung vor, während und nach dem Event sowohl die Bekanntheits- als auch die Imagewirkungen wesentlich gesteigert werden kann (Lardinoit/Quester 2001; Grohs/Wagner/Vstecka 2004). Gleichzeitig ist eine unzureichende Vernetzung einer der häufigsten Ursachen für einen mangelnden Erfolg erlebnisorientierter Kommunikation. So hatte das Sponsorship des Automobilherstellers Hyundai bei der Fußball Europameisterschaft 2004 einen geringeren Erfolg als die Maßnahmen der anderen Hauptsponsoren, weil das Budget für begleitende Kommunikationsmaßnahmen zu gering war. Experten schätzen, dass das Budget für begleitende Kommunikation mindestens das Dreifache der Lizenzkosten eines Sponsorships betragen sollte (Hermanns/Bob Bomlitz Group 2004, S. 39; Janke/Zils 2004; Nöcker 2004, S. 15).

Als letzte Determinante für den Kommunikationserfolg ist die **Dauer eines Sponsorships** oder einer Serie von Events bei der Planung zu berücksichtigen. Einmalige oder kurzfristige Maßnahmen wirken sich oft gar nicht oder lediglich vorübergehend auf die Markenbekanntheit und das Markenimage aus. Im Sinne einer kontinuierlichen Markenführung, mit dem Ziel der Etablierung einer langfristigen Marke-Nachfrager-Beziehung, ist eine nachhaltige Imageveränderung nur über langfristig angelegte und kontinuierliche Sponsorships oder Serien von Events möglich. Dies bedingt mehrjährige Event- und Sponsoring-Engagements, die eher auf fünf bis zehn als auf zwei bis drei Jahre angelegt sein sollten.

3.2 Durchführung der Kommunikationsmaßnahmen

Bei der Implementierung erlebnisorientierter Kommunikationsinstrumente müssen drei wesentliche Faktoren sichergestellt werden, um die anvisierten Wirkungen bei den Nachfragern zu realisieren (vgl. Abbildung 6).

Als erstes muss die **Event-Attribution** sichergestellt werden. Diese bezieht sich auf die gemeinsame Darbietung und Wahrnehmung von Event und Marke. Bei der direkten Zielgruppe kann die Event-Attribution durch die Darbietung markentypischer visueller, akustischer, olfaktorischer, gustastorischer, haptischer und somatischer Reize im Wahrnehmungsbereich der Event-Besucher erreicht werden (Lasslop 2003, S. 100 ff.). Darüber hinaus besteht bei Marketing-Events die Möglichkeit, durch die inhaltliche Gestaltung der Kommunikationsbotschaft, Assoziationen zu bereits existentem Markenwissen zu schaffen. Bei der indirekten Zielgruppe ist eine ausreichende Event-Attribution schwieriger zu realisieren, da die Kommunikationsbotschaft nur über Dritte (Medien, Teilnehmer/Besucher) die Ziel-Rezipienten erreicht. Neben einer Darbietung der visuellen Markenzeichen im Wahrnehmungsfeld der Medien sind die Medienvertreter mit gezielten PR-Maßnahmen zu informieren. Mit der Event-Attribution ist die notwendige Bedingung für einen Imagetransfer vom Event auf die Marke erfüllt (Nufer 2002, S. 192).

Abbildung 6: **Aktions- und Wirkungsebene erlebnisorientierter Kommunikationsinstrumente**

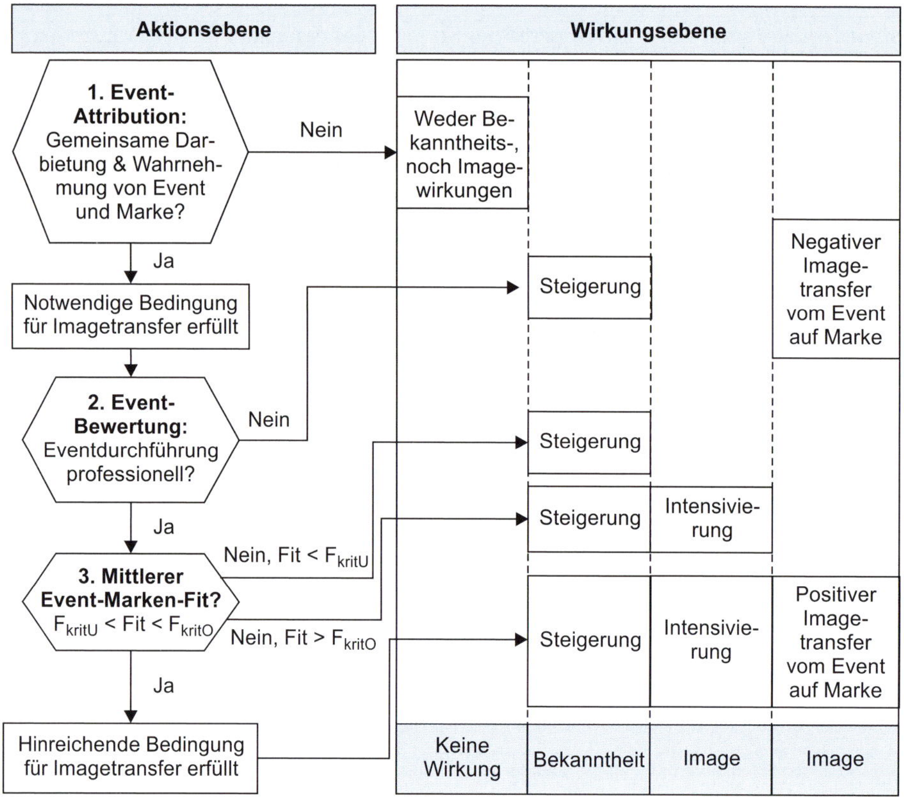

GABLER GRAFIK

Als zweites ist eine **professionelle Durchführung** des Events sicher zu stellen. Defizite in diesem Bereich führen zu einer negative Bewertung des Events und somit auch der Marke durch die Rezipienten. Folge wäre zwar eine Erhöhung der Markenbekanntheit, aber auch eine negative Imageveränderung der Marke. Die besondere Relevanz einer positiven Event-Bewertung zeigt sich in den starken negativen Kommunikationswirkungen als Folge von Unzufriedenheit (Michalski 2002, S. 134).

Der **Event-Marken-Fit** wurde bereits weitestgehend durch die Auswahl eines spezifischen Events auf übergeordneter Ebene determiniert. Im Rahmen der Implementierung ist der anvisierte mittlere Fit durch die spezifische Ausgestaltung des Events sicherzustellen.

3.3 Controlling der Kommunikationswirkungen

Aufgrund der hohen Bedeutung von Sponsoring und Event-Kommunikation im Kommunikations-Mix der Markenartikelindustrie und den steigenden Kosten für den Einsatz dieser Instrumente ist eine **systematische Erfolgsmessung** von hoher Relevanz für die Unternehmen (Hermanns/Bob Bomliz Group 2004). Dabei steht die Frage der Effektivität und Effizienz von Sponsoring und Event-Kommunikation im Vordergrund. **Effektivität** bezieht sich auf die Kommunikationswirkung im Verhältnis zu einem vorab definierten Zielniveau. Mit der **Effizienz** wird die Frage nach dem notwendigen Aufwand zur Realisierung der Kommunikationswirkung diskutiert. Event-Kommunikation kann als effizient bezeichnet werden, wenn sie ein besseres Output/Input-Verhältnis im Vergleich zu alternativen Kommunikationsinstrumenten aufweißt (Scholz 1992, S. 533 ff.; Lasslop 2003, S. 10 ff.). Die Notwendigkeit eines standardisierten Erfolgsnachweises für erlebnisorientierte Kommunikationsinstrumente hat auch die Organisation der Werbetreibenden im deutschen Markenverband erkannt. Gemeinsam mit dem Zentralverband der deutschen Werbewirtschaft soll zukünftig eine Kontaktdefinition für direkte und indirekte Zielgruppen sowie ein Intermedia-Vergleich entwickelt werden (Janke 2004).

Ansatzpunkt des Event-Controllings ist der Wirkungsprozess erlebnisorientierter Kommunikation (vgl. Abbildung 3). Die Effektivität einer Maßnahme kann direkt durch eine Messung der Kommunikations- und Verhaltenswirkungen bei den Empfängern der Kommunikationsbotschaft erfasst werden. Bei dieser direkten wirkungsorientierten Bewertung eines Events ist allerdings das Problem der **fehlenden Isolierbarkeit der eventspezifischen Kommunikationswirkung** virulent. Event-Kommunikation wird in der Regel komplementär zu anderen Kommunikationsinstrumenten eingesetzt. Hieraus entstehen sachliche Interdependenzen inhaltlicher Art zwischen den einzelnen Kommunikationsinstrumenten. Die nach der Durchführung einer erlebnisorientierten Kommunikationsmaßnahme gemessenen Wirkungen sind somit auch ein Resultat des Einsatzes anderer Kommunikationsinstrumente.

Gleiches gilt für die **mangelnde Zurechenbarkeit von finalen Verhaltenswirkungen**: Diese werden von den übrigen Markenführungsinstrumenten, insbesondere der Preispo litik, erheblich mit beeinflusst und können in der Regel nicht exakt auf den Einsatz von bestimmten Kommunikationsinstrumenten, beziehungsweise deren isolierter Kommunikationswirkung, zurückgeführt werden. Neben dem Zurechnungs- beziehungsweise Isolationsproblem ist nicht auszuschließen, dass die Kommunikations- und Verhaltenswirkungen von **externen Störeinflüssen** verzerrt werden, die außerhalb des Einflussbereiches des Unternehmens liegen (zum Beispiel Konkurrenzaktivitäten, Wertewandel, Wirtschaftsklima). Darüber hinaus stellt sich die Herausforderung, die Kommunikations- und Verhaltenswirkungen von Sponsoring- und Event-Kommunikation im Vergleich zu klassischen Kommunikationsinstrumenten (monetär) zu bewerten, um eine Aussage über die Effizienz treffen zu können.

Ein Event-Controlling muss demzufolge versuchen, die Wirkung interner- und externer Störgrößen von der eigentlichen Eventwirkung zu trennen. Nur dann kann die Eventwirkung beurteilt und ein monetarer Wert ausreichend valide ermittelt werden. Im Gegensatz zur sonstigen kommunikativen Wirkungsforschung ist die Durchführung von Labor- und Feldexperimenten bei Events und Sponsoring aufgrund der Zielgruppenheterogenität und weiterer schwer zu kontrollierender Wirkungsdeterminanten (Expositionsdauer, Atmosphäre) nur bedingt möglich. Nach dem aktuellen Stand der Wirkungsforschung ist eine **direkte, wirkungsorientierte** Vorgehensweise (das heißt die Kommunikations- und Verhaltenswirkungen explizit berücksichtigenden) **nicht ausreichend valide möglich**.

Abbildung 7: Kompositionelles und holistisches Vorgehen zur Wertbestimmung von Sponsoring und Event-Kommunikation

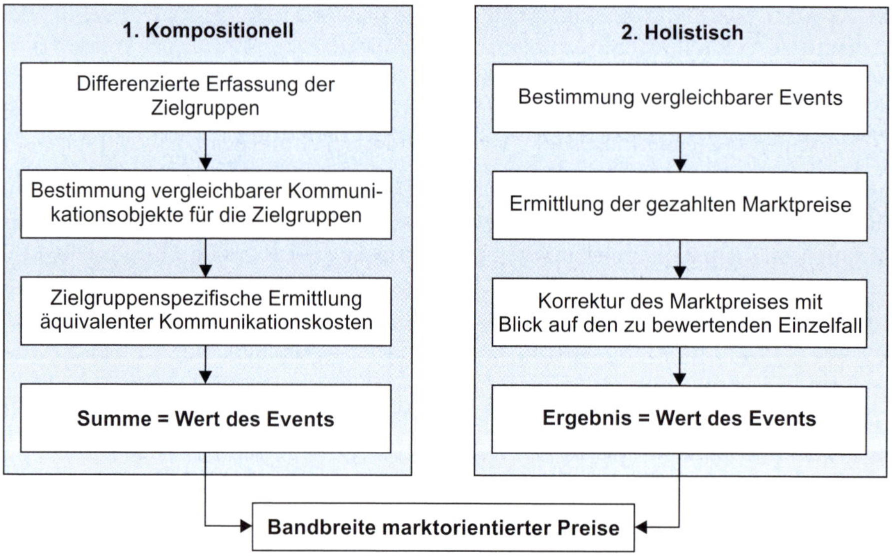

GABLER GRAFIK

Aus diesem Grund haben sich anstelle einer direkten Berücksichtigung von Kommunikations- und Verhaltenswirkungen in Wissenschaft und Praxis Ansätze herausgebildet, welche die **Wirkungen implizit im Rahmen von Opportunitätskalkülen zu erfassen versuchen**. Der Grundgedanke dieser Ansätze besteht in der Annahme, dass die existierenden Marktpreise für Kommunikationsmaßnahmen das Ergebnis einer Beurteilung der jeweiligen Kommunikations- und Verhaltenswirkung durch Marktteilnehmer (Verlage, Media-Agenturen, Rechtehändler, Agenturen) darstellen. In den verschiedenen realisierten Marktpreisen von Printanzeigen, TV-Spots, Messen und auch Sponsoringrechten drückt sich somit implizit die **Einschätzung des Marktes hinsichtlich der Qualität der einzelnen Kommunikationsmittel** aus.

Ausgehend von der Prämisse, dass die einzelnen Marktpreise einen validen Wertmaßstab für Kommunikations- und Verhaltenswirkungen bilden, kann der angemessene Preis eines nicht am Markt gehandelten Kommunikationsobjektes entweder **kompositionell** durch Summierung der kommunikativen Teilwirkungen oder **holistisch** durch die Analyse vergleichbarer Event-Preise bestimmt werden (vgl. Abbildung 7). Durch Anwendung beider Methoden zur Wertermittlung wird eine Bandbreite möglicher Marktpreise gebildet, die hinsichtlich ihrer Angemessenheit und Validität dann auf mehreren Säulen ruht. Dieses Vorgehen hat empirisch bereits mehrfach bewährt (Burmann/Nitschke 2005) und wird nachfolgend an Hand eines Praxisbeispiels verdeutlicht. Dabei werden die Imagewirkungen des Fußball-Bundesligisten Werder Bremen auf die Stadt Bremen erfasst und monetär bewertet. Die Profilierung der Stadt Bremen wird dabei als Markenprofilierung interpretiert (zur Bedeutung und Anwendung des identitätsorientierten Markenmanagements auf Städte und Regionen vgl. die beiden Beiträge in diesem Buch).

4. Fallbeispiel zur Profilierung der Stadtmarke Bremen durch Werder Bremen

Ziel der Untersuchung war es, die Wirkungen des Fußballbundesligisten Werder Bremen (Werder) auf das Image der Stadt Bremen als Marke (Bremen) zu messen und finanziell zu bewerten. Damit behandelt das vorliegende Beispiel den Sonderfall der Analyse von Imagewirkungen eines Dauer-Events auf dessen Standort. Hierbei standen nicht die direkten Effekte, beispielsweise die durch Werder geschaffenen Arbeitsplätze oder induzierten Steuereinnahmen, sondern **indirekten Effekte**, welche nicht zu unmittelbaren finanziellen Einnahmen führen, im Mittelpunkt. Dabei ergab sich das Problem, dass eine gezielte empirische Untersuchung über Image- und Verhaltensänderungen nicht möglich war, da die Saison 2003/04 ex-post bewertet werden sollte. Zur Bewertung des Dauer-Events Werder konnte lediglich auf das in der Vergangenheit erhobene Datenmaterial über die Medienpräsenz und Zielgruppenkontakte zurückgegriffen werden.

Hierzu wurde ein **Grundmodell zur Evaluation der Event-Wirkungen** entwickelt, welches zwischen den verschiedenen durch das Event erreichten Zielgruppen und Evaluationsstufen differenziert (vgl. Abbildung 8). Es ergab sich ein **Vier-Quadranten-Schema,** welches auf der Vertikalen nach den verschiedenen Zielgruppen, auf der Horizontalen zwischen den Evaluationsstufen der Erfassung und der Bewertung der Kommunikationswirkungen differenziert.

Die **direkte** Zielgruppe (Stadionbesucher vor Ort) wird entsprechend ihres Referenzpotenzials für Bremen strukturiert. Dabei wird eine weitestgehende Kongruenz der Gruppen Unternehmer/Investoren mit den VIP's, der Bürger Bremens mit den „normalen“ Heimfans sowie der Touristen mit den auswärtigen Fans unterstellt. Die **indirekte** Zielgruppe (Medienöffentlichkeit) unterteilt sich in die Subgruppen Unternehmer/Investoren, qualifizierte Arbeitskräfte und potenzielle Touristen. Die **Erfassung** der Kommunikationswirkung richtet sich an den drei Wirkungsdeterminanten Event-Attribution, professionelle Event-Bewertung und mittlerer Event-Marken-Fit aus (vgl. Abbildung 6). Die **Bewertung** erfolgt anschließend sowohl nach der kompositionellen, als auch nach der holistischen Methode (vgl. Abbildung 7).

Abbildung 8: Grundmodell zur Erfassung von Kommunikationswirkungen

2. Evaluationsstufe / 1. Zielgruppen	2.1 Erfassung der Kommunikationswirkung	2.2 Bewertung der Kommunikationswirkung
1.1 Direkte Zielgruppe - Investoren (VIPs) - Bürger (Heimfans) - Touristen (Gästefans)		
1.2 Indirekte Zielgruppe - Investoren, qualifizierte Arbeitskräfte - Touristen		

GABLER GRAFIK

Im ersten Schritt wurde im Rahmen einer Analyse der **Event-Attribution** untersucht, in wie weit das Event Werder und die Stadt Bremen gemeinsam wahrgenommen werden. Während bei der **direkten Zielgruppe** eine Wahrnehmung Bremens durch den Aufenthalt in der Stadt und im Weserstadion als **gegeben** angenommen werden konnte, war dieses bei der indirekten Zielgruppe nicht automatisch der Fall. Bei der Erfassung der Kommunikationswirkungen mit der indirekten Zielgruppe wurde in einer Inhaltsanalyse überprüft, in wie weit die Stadt durch die Berichterstattung über Werder vom Mediennutzer prinzipiell wahrgenommen werden konnte. Hierbei wurde sowohl der inhaltliche Bezug des Artikels, also die Art der gemeinsamen Darbietung von Werder und der Stadt Bremen, als auch die Prominenz des Hinweises auf die Stadt Bremen überprüft.

Der zweite Prüfschritt war die **Event-Bewertung**. Diese hängt bei der **direkten Zielgruppe** von der **Event-Gestaltung**, der **Stimmung** der Besucher, sowie vom Event-**Umfeld** ab und ist vom Professionalisierungsgrad der Event-Durchführung abhängig. Auch ohne eine breite quantitative Marktforschung über die Zuschauerzufriedenheit konnte anhand von Expertengesprächen eine hinreichend valide Aussage hinsichtlich der Frage einer **professionellen Event-Durchführung** getroffen werden. Sowohl die Rahmenbedingungen im Stadion, als auch die sportliche Leistung der Mannschaft führten zu einer **positiven** Bewertung hinsichtlich des Professionalisierungsgrades des Events. Die Medienvertreter als Sub-Zielgruppe der Eventbesucher führen die Event-Bewertung stellvertretend für die **indirekte Zielgruppe** (Öffentlichkeit) aus und kommunizieren ihre persönlichen Bewertung durch die **Tonalität ihrer Berichterstattung**. Bei der Medienresonanzanalyse wurden die einzelnen Berichte daher entsprechend ihrer Tonalität verschiedenen Wirkungskategorien zugeordnet, um die unterschiedlichen Kommunikationswirkungen einer positiven gegenüber einer neutralen oder negativen Berichterstattung zu berücksichtigen.

Der **Fit zwischen dem Bundesligisten Werder und der Stadt Bremen** wird durch die Art der von Werder auf die Rezipienten ausgehenden Informationen determiniert. Auf Grundlage der gemeinsamen langen Historie der Stadt Bremen und Werders kann der Event-Marken-Fit generell als „zu groß“ bezeichnet werden (vgl. Abbildung 5). Wegen des außergewöhnlichen Erfolges von Werder in der Saison 2003/04 haben die Assoziationen wie „erfolgreich“ und „professionelles Management/Führung“ in der jüngeren Vergangenheit jedoch so stark zugenommen, dass tendenziell von einem **guten Event-Marken-Fit** ausgegangen werden kann. Dieser ungewöhnliche Erfolg kann im Sinne des Modells aus Abbildung 5 als „neue Information“ für die Rezipienten der Werder Berichterstattung interpretiert werden. Erst durch diese neuen Informationen werden Kommunikationswirkungen und damit Imagetransfereffekte für die Stadt Bremen ausgelöst. Der Imagetransfer wird dabei durch die funktionalen (zum Beispiel geografische und semantische Nähe) und symbolischen Gemeinsamkeiten (zum Beispiel hanseatisch) zwischen Werder und der Stadt Bremen positiv beeinflusst (Quester/Farrelly 1998; Gwinner/Eaton 1999, S. 53; Johar/Pham 1999, S. 305 ff.).

Basis der **kompositionellen Bewertung** war die Anzahl der realisierten Zielgruppenkontakte eines Events. Die Bewertung der Zielgruppenkontakte des Events Werder wurde mittels vergleichbarer Kommunikationskontakte anderer Events vorgenommen. Die Auswahl geeigneter Vergleichsobjekte orientierte sich an der Kontaktqualität des Events Werder. Die Kontaktqualität bei der **direkten Zielgruppe** zeichnet sich durch ein hohes situatives und mittleres Botschaftsinvolvement sowie eine hohe Kontaktdauer mit der Stadt Bremen aus. Durchschnittlich besuchten die Werder-Fans in der Saison 2003/04 6,6 Heimspiele und verweilte dabei pro Spiel knapp über drei Stunden in der Stadt. Diese Merkmale der Kontaktqualität bestimmen die Auswahl der für die Bewertung notwendigen Vergleichsobjekte.

Als Vergleichsobjekte für die direkte Zielgruppe werden das fünfmonatige Expo-Event der Firma Bertelsmann aus dem Jahr 2000 („Planet m“, Planet der Medien), das Dauer-Event „Autostadt“ des Volkswagen-Konzerns in Wolfsburg sowie das einwöchige Tennis Turnier „Gerry Weber Open“ des gleichnamigen Damenbekleidungsherstellers in Halle/Westfalen verwendet.

Die **Wertigkeit** der durch Kommunikationsmaßnahmen erreichten Zielgruppen ist **von den Zielen des Senders abhängig**. Da für die Stadt Bremen nur vom Globalziel einer generellen Imageverbesserung bei standortexternen Zielgruppen ausgegangen werden konnte, wurde für die Kommunikationskontakte mit der Gruppe der Heimfans der im Vergleich zu anderen Zielgruppen niedrigste Wert angesetzt. Unter Berücksichtigung von Kontaktdauer, -qualität und -häufigkeit wurden die auswärtigen Fans entsprechend den normalen Besuchern des „planet m“ und der Gerry Weber Open mit zehn Euro bewertet. Die Bewertung der VIP's orientiert sich ebenfalls am „planet m“. Ein Werder-VIP wurde demzufolge in Abhängigkeit von der Kontaktqualität mit ca. 140 Euro bewertet. Somit ergibt sich für die **direkte Zielgruppe** ein Kommunikationswert in einer Höhe von 1,7 Millionen Euro (vgl. Abbildung 9).

Abbildung 9: **Bewertung von Kontakten mit der direkten Zielgruppe**

	Anzahl Personen pro Saison	Bewertung je Kontakt in Euro	Gesamter Kontaktwert in Euro
VIPs	4.160	140 Euro	582.376 Euro
Gast-Fans (Auswärtige)	88.500	10 Euro	885.000 Euro
Bremer Heimfans	95.687	2 Euro	191.374 Euro
		Σ:	1.658.750 Euro

GABLER GRAFIK

Die Kontaktwerte für die **indirekte Zielgruppe** errechnete sich aus dem Vergleich der redaktionellen Print-, TV- und Radio-Berichterstattung über Werder mit dem Preis einer klassischen Werbemaßnahme in der gleichen Größe (Länge) und an der gleichen Stelle (zum gleichen Zeitpunkt beziehungsweise mit der gleichen Reichweite). Im ersten Schritt wurden **unkorrigierte Äquivalenzwerte** berechnet, bei denen die unterschiedliche Wirkung von klassischer Werbung und der redaktionellen Berichterstattung über Werder noch nicht berücksichtigt wurde.

Diese unterschiedlichen Wirkungen wurden anschließend im zweiten Schritt bei der Berechnung der **korrigierten Äquivalenzwerte** mit einbezogen. Die Wirkungsunterschiede werden durch Multiplikatoren abgebildet, welche auf Basis von drei Korrekturfaktoren gebildet wurden (Inhaltsbezug der Werderberichterstattung zur Stadt Bremen, Tonalität der Berichterstattung und Prominenz, Wahrnehmbarkeit des Hinweises auf die Stadt Bremen in der Berichterstattung). Die Berechnungen wurden getrennt für die Print-, die TV- und die Radio-Berichterstattung durchgeführt. Für die Print-Berichterstattung ergibt sich nach Anwendung der Multiplikatoren ein monetärer Wert von ca. 850.000 Euro, für die TV-Berichterstattung ein Wert von ca. 3 Millionen Euro. Für das Radio wurde ein Wert von ca. 155.000 Euro berechnet (vgl. Abbildung 10).

Über die Medienpräsenz im Internet und in internationalen Medien waren leider keine Marktforschungsdaten verfügbar. Die mediale Präsenz von Werder in diesen Bereichen konnte deshalb lediglich als „stille Wirkungsreserve“ berücksichtigt werden.

Nach der **kompositionellen Methode** ergibt sich somit für Bremen aus dem Imagetransfer von Werder in der Saison 2003/04 insgesamt ein **äquivalenter Werbewert von ca. 5,7 Millionen Euro** (Burmann/Nitschke 2005).

Abbildung 10: **Zusammenfassung der Wertermittlung nach der kompositionellen Methode**

Saison 2003/2004		
Direkte Zielgruppe	Besucher Weser-Stadion	1.658.750 Euro
Indirekte Zielgruppe	Print-Berichterstattung (nur Inland)	847.173 Euro
	TV-Berichterstattung (nur Inland)	3.069.141 Euro
	Radio-Berichterstattung (nur Inland; nur ARD-Bundesliga-konferenz)	155.033 Euro
	Σ korrigierter äquivalenter Werbewerte für die Stadt Bremen:	5.730.097 Euro

GABLER GRAFIK

Im zweiten Schritt wurde die Wertbestimmung nach der **holistischen Vorgehensweise** durchgeführt. Als geeignete Vergleichsobjekte kamen nur andere Dauer-Events aus dem Sportbereich in Frage. Die auszuwählenden Benchmarks müssen eine möglichst hohe Vergleichbarkeit hinsichtlich der Zielgruppe und der Kommunikationswirkung aufweisen. Die ermittelten Marktpreise sind dann, aufgrund einer in der Regel nicht gegebenen 100-prozentigen Vergleichbarkeit (zum Beispiel verschiedene Standorte, Teilnehmerzahlen, Übertragungszeiten), nachträglich durch Korrekturfaktoren anzupassen.

Als Vergleichsobjekt für den Wert des Wortes „Bremen" im Vereinsnamen von Werder wurden die so genannten **„Naming Rights"** von Profi-Sport Mannschaften gewählt. Diese existieren in Deutschland bislang primär im Basketball- und Eishockeysport. Der Wert eines Namin Rights (inklusive Trikot-Sponsorship) beträgt in der Basketball Bundesliga (BBL) durchschnittlich 1 Millionen Euro. In der Deutschen Eishockey Liga (DEL) konnte die Düsseldorfer EG für ihr Naming Right 0,6 Millionen Euro pro Saison erlösen. Aufgrund der unterschiedlichen Bedeutung von Basketball, Eishockey und Fußball in Deutschland wurde eine Korrektur beziehungsweise Umrechnung der Marktwerte für „Naming Rights" in der Basketball-Bundesliga und der Deutschen Eishockey Liga in solche für die Fußball-Bundesliga (Deutsche Fußball Liga = DFL) vorgenommen. Diese Umrechnung basiert auf den Kriterien Größe der direkten Zielgruppe, Größe der indirekten Zielgruppe (nur im TV) und Dauer von TV-Übertragungen (vgl. Abbildung 11).

1. Herausforderungen an die Führung von Dienstleistungsmarken

1.1 Besonderheiten von Dienstleistungsmarken

Die Bedeutung von Dienstleistungen steigt seit einigen Jahren kontinuierlich an. Wachsende Anteile an der Wertschöpfung und der Beschäftigung dokumentieren den in modernen Volkswirtschaften eingeleiteten Strukturwandel von der Industrie- zur Dienstleistungsgesellschaft. Auch die Transformation des Angebotsspektrums etablierter Sachgüterproduzenten weist auf den gewachsenen Stellenwert von Dienstleistungen hin. So ist nicht selten der Service rund um das materielle Kernprodukt zum differenzierenden Faktor industrieller Wertschöpfung geworden. Um Wettbewerbsfähigkeit in einer globalisierten Welt zu sichern, gilt es, diesen Transformationsprozess nicht nur nachzuvollziehen, sondern aktiv mitzugestalten. Dies führt zu einer verstärkten Auseinandersetzung mit den Besonderheiten des Dienstleistungsmarketing.

Konsequenterweise stellt sich auch im Hinblick auf die Markenführung die Frage, in wie weit die Besonderheiten des Dienstleistungsmarketing (Meffert/Bruhn 2003, S. 50 ff.) eine Modifikation bestehender Markenführungsansätze notwendig machen. Die Bedeutung von Marken für Dienstleistungsunternehmen ist dabei kaum zu übersehen. Letztlich gibt es so gut wie keine nicht markierten Dienstleistungen. Während Unternehmensdachmarken (Corporate Brands) im Dienstleistungssektor weiterhin die bekanntesten Marken darstellen, ist bei vielen Unternehmen festzustellen, dass für einzelne Dienstleistungsangebote ebenfalls Marken und markenähnliche Bezeichnungen eingeführt werden. So lässt sich beispielsweise bei der Deutschen Bahn AG eine Fülle von Servicebezeichnungen identifizieren, die zu einem großen Teil als Marken eingetragen sind. Einen Auszug für den Personenverkehr der Deutschen Bahn AG gibt Abbildung 1 wieder.

Vor diesem Hintergrund ist eine Abgrenzung der bloßen Servicebezeichnungen oder „Labels" von echten Marken notwendig, die über eine Definition der Markencharakteristika bei Dienstleistungen erfolgen kann. Der Abgrenzung und **Definition von Dienstleistungsmarken** kommt in der Literatur ein vergleichsweise hoher Stellenwert zu. Als erster Anhaltspunkt werden unter anderem die Kategorisierung der amtlichen Statistik oder des Markenrechts herangezogen (Bruhn 2001, S. 216 f.). Diese Überlegungen beruhen im Kern auf der Existenz einer rechtlichen Schutzmöglichkeit für die Verwendung von Dienstleistungsmarken, die oft als Voraussetzung für ihre ökonomische Bedeutung genannt wird. Mit dem Markenrecht von 1995 (Pascual 1998; Stauss 2001, S. 552 ff.) ist diese Fragestellung zumindest juristisch insofern beantwortet, als dass Marken für Dienstleistungen nunmehr Sachgütermarken gleichgestellt sind.

Auch aus neuerer betriebswirtschaftlicher Perspektive ist für die Definition des Terminus „Marke" eine Bezugnahme auf die stoffliche Beschaffenheit des markierten Objektes nicht notwendig. In Anlehnung an Keller (Keller 2003) definieren Burmann et al. (Burmann/Blinda/Nitschke 2003, S. 3) die „Marke“ als *„ein Nutzenbündel mit spezifischen Merkmalen (in Form von Kommunikation, Kundendienst, technischen Innovationen etc.), die dafür sorgen, dass sich dieses Nutzenbündel gegenüber anderen Nutzenbündeln, welche dieselben Basisbedürfnisse erfüllen, aus Sicht relevanter Zielgruppen nachhaltig differenziert“.*

Abbildung 1: Auszug der Marken und markenähnlichen „Label" des Personenverkehrs der Deutschen Bahn AG im Jahr 2004 (Kategorisierung der Autoren)

Produktmarken und -„labels“	Servicemarken und -„labels“	Angebotsmarken und -„labels“
■ InterCityExpress (ICE)	■ UmsteigeService	■ Sparpreis 25
■ ICE Sprinter	■ KurierGepäck	■ Sparpreis 50
■ InterCity/EuroCity (IC/EC)	■ GepäckträgerService	■ Bayern-Ticket
■ DB NachtZüge	■ Moonlight-Check-in	■ Rail & Fly
■ CityNightLine (CNL)	■ ServicePoint	■ Sommer Spezial
■ DB AutoZug	■ DB Lounge	■ City Ticket
■ RegionalExpress (RE)	■ InfoRiese	■ BahnCard 25
■ RegionalBahn (RB)	■ Park+Ride	■ BahnCard 50
■ S-Bahn	■ Park&Rail	■ BahnCard 100
■ UrlaubsExpressZüge	■ DB Service Store	
■ Metropolitan	■ bahn corporate	
	■ bahn.comfort	
	■ ReiseZentrum	
	■ Call a Bike	

GABLER GRAFIK

Unbeschadet der definitorischen Gleichstellung von Dienstleistungs- und Sachgütermarken sollen im folgenden auf Basis eines gütertypologischen Ansatzes (Engelhardt/Kleinaltenkamp/Reckenfelderbäumer 1993) die Besonderheiten der Markenführung für Dienstleistungen herausgearbeitet werden. Als **zentrale Abgrenzungsmerkmale** werden in diesem Zusammenhang die weitgehende Intangibilität beziehungsweise Immaterialität von Dienstleistungen sowie die notwendige Kundenbeteiligung in Form einer Integration des externen Faktors genannt (Meffert/Bruhn 2003, S. 60).

So wird bezüglich der **Immaterialität**, als Grundproblem der Markenführung bei Dienstleistungen, die physische Markierung respektive Kennzeichnung angeführt (Bruhn 2001, S. 215). Eine nähere Analyse der Eigenschaften von Sachgütern und Dienstleistungen führt zu der Erkenntnis, dass aus theoretischer Sicht die Schwierigkeit einer Markierung bei Dienstleistungen aufgrund ihrer Immaterialität nicht gegeben ist. Ein Sachgut als physisch präsentes Produkt bedarf streng genommen keiner Markierung, da sich jeder von der physischen Beschaffenheit am Gut selbst überzeugen kann. Das Vorzeigen des Gutes reicht aus, um sich darüber zu verständigen, was gemeint ist. Dies ist bei Dienstleistungen nicht der Fall. Da die Leistung erst mit dem Erstellungsprozess Realität wird, erfordert eine der Leistung vorgelagerte Verhandlung zwischen Transaktionspartnern – die Voraussetzung für das Zustandekommen einer ökonomischen Transaktion ist – bereits eine Benennung der auszutauschenden Leistungsbestandteile (Küpers 1999, S. 121 ff.). Eine hinreichende Spezifizierung erfährt die Dienstleistung jedoch erst mit der Nennung desjenigen, der die Leistung erbringt, da ohne diesen beziehungsweise seine Potenzialfaktoren die Dienstleistung nicht erstellt werden kann. Damit ist die Bezeichnung Voraussetzung einer Markierung und insofern als grundsätzliche Bedingung für das Zustandekommen von Dienstleistungstransaktionen anzusehen.

Die Immaterialität stellt zwar weiterhin eine Herausforderung für das **Anbringen einer Markierung** dar, für die jedoch mittlerweile zahlreiche Ansatzpunkte gefunden werden konnten (Tomczak 1999, S. 8; Meffert/Bruhn 2003, S. 399). So lassen sich beispielsweise die Potenzialfaktoren, die für die Erstellung der Dienstleistung benötigt werden, markieren. Darin eingeschlossen ist auch das Kundenkontaktpersonal, das häufig beispielsweise mittels Uniform die Markierung trägt. Darüber hinaus bieten tangible Elemente im Rahmen der Dienstleistungsproduktion viele Möglichkeiten, das Markenzeichen anzubringen. Beispiele sind die Seifenverpackung im Hotel oder das Geschirr an Bord eines Linienflugzeuges. Schließlich lassen sich auch materielle Elemente nutzen, um über den flüchtigen Dienstleistungsprozess hinaus den Kontakt zur Marke nicht abreißen zu lassen, sondern die Phase des Leistungsprozesses zu verlängern.

Gegenüber dem Aspekt der Immaterialität wurden in der Literatur die aus der **Integration des externen Faktors** resultierenden Probleme in der Markenführung vernachlässigt. Der Dienstleistungsnachfrager muss entweder sich selbst oder seine Verfügungsobjekte in den Dienstleistungsprozess einbringen, um die Dienstleistung vornehmen zu lassen. So ist es beispielsweise bei einem Flug der Nachfrager selbst, an dem die Ortsveränderung vorgenommen wird, während für eine Autoreparatur der Nachfrager lediglich sein Verfügungsobjekt, in diesem Fall seinen Pkw, zur Dienstleistungserstellung einbringen muss.

Die sich aus der Kundenintegration als Schlüsselproblem eines Dienstleistungsanbieters ergebenden Implikationen für das identitätsorientierte Markenmanagement stehen daher im Mittelpunkt dieses Beitrags. Bevor hierauf näher eingegangen wird, sollen zunächst kurz die Funktionen von Dienstleistungsmarken erläutert werden.

1.2 Vertrauensfunktion von Dienstleistungsmarken

Die vielfältigen Funktionen von Dienstleistungsmarken lassen sich grundlegend in nachfragergerichtete und eher wettbewerbsgerichtete Funktionen unterscheiden (vgl. Abbildung 2).

Abbildung 2: Grundfunktionen der Marke im Dienstleistungsbereich

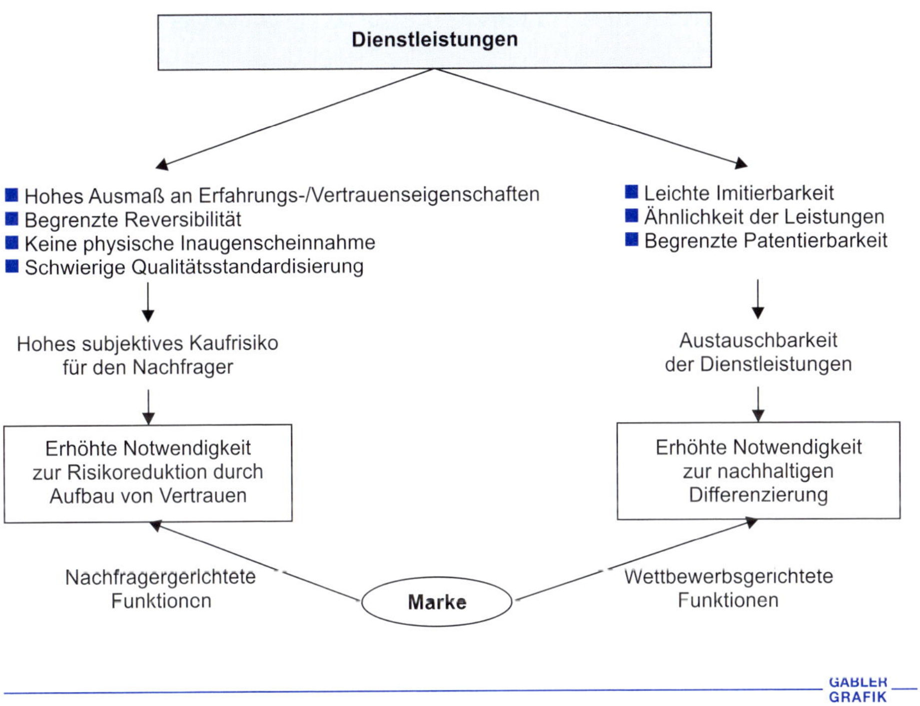

Quelle: in Anlehnung an Tomczak/Brockdorff 2000, S. 491

Aus Nachfragersicht kommt der Marke primär eine **Vertrauens- und Orientierungsfunktion** zu. Diese Markenfunktion hat bei Dienstleistungsmarken eine besondere Relevanz. Sie resultiert vor allem aus informationsökonomischen Leistungsbesonderheiten; so weisen Dienstleistungen einen höheren Anteil an Erfahrungs- und Vertrauenseigenschaften auf als Sachgüter. Da Erfahrungs- und Vertrauenseigenschaften vor dem Kauf nicht überprüfbar sind und der Nachfrager somit gezwungen ist, auf Ersatzindikatoren auszuweichen, besitzt die Marke einen besonderen Stellenwert bei der Reduktion des wahrgenommenen Risikos. Dieser Vertrauensfunktion kann eine Marke jedoch nur gerecht werden, wenn das dahinter stehende Leistungsversprechen durch den Anbieter auch eingehalten werden kann. Aus diesem Grund ist die Qualitätskonstanz in der Leistungserstellung und damit das **Qualitätsmanagement** im Dienstleistungsbereich besonders bedeutend. Dies trifft grundsätzlich auch auf den Sachgüterbereich zu, jedoch kann das Qualitätsmanagement dort zumeist nur noch eine geringe Wettbewerbsdifferenzierung bewirken und ist deshalb im Rahmen der Markenführung in den Hintergrund getreten.

Wichtig ist in diesem Zusammenhang, dass bei Dienstleistungen die weitgehende **Gleichzeitigkeit von Produktion und Absatz** (das Uno-actu-Prinzip) eine nachträgliche Kontrolle und Verbesserung einmal produzierter Qualität verhindert. Dienstleistungsqualität muss in den meisten Fällen in der direkten Interaktion mit dem Kunden erzeugt werden, ohne dass die Möglichkeit einer nachgelagerten Qualitätskontrolle besteht. Darüber hinaus übernimmt teilweise der Kunde die Funktion einer Kontrollinstanz in der direkten Interaktion mit dem Kundenkontaktpersonal (Lehmann 1998, S. 35 ff.). Zentral für das Leistungsergebnis ist weiterhin die erfolgreiche Integration des Nachfragers in den Leistungserstellungsprozess. Dies betrifft nicht nur seine eigene Problemlösungskompetenz, sondern auch sein Bemühen um eine aktive Mitarbeit am Zustandekommen des gewünschten Leistungsergebnisses (Corsten 2000). Die hohe Bedeutung der Dienstleistungsqualität hat zu umfangreichen Forschungsbemühungen im Bereich der Kundenzufriedenheit und des Qualitätsmanagements bei Dienstleistungen geführt (Bruhn/Stauss 2000; Homburg 2003). Die Vertrauensfunktion der Marke und damit die Frage nach dem entsprechenden Qualitätsmanagement im Dienstleistungsbereich zeigt die Notwendigkeit einer **integrierten Betrachtung der Marke**.

1.3 Differenzierung im Wettbewerb durch Dienstleistungsmarken

Der Differenzierungsfunktion von Marken kommt im Dienstleistungssektor eine besondere Bedeutung zu. **In der Praxis** wird die besondere Notwendigkeit zur Differenzierung bei Dienstleistungsmarken nicht ausreichend beachtet. Oftmals sind innerhalb ganzer Dienstleistungsbranchen kaum Unterschiede in der Positionierung und dem Management von Marken zu erkennen. Von dieser Situation profitieren, wenn überhaupt, nur die Marktführer, da sie durch eine solche Erstarrung im status quo ihre Marktposition absichern können. Beispielhaft kann hier auf Finanzdienstleistungsbranchen und in der Assekuranz speziell auf die Marke Allianz verwiesen werden. Für die konkurrierenden Marken kann es letztlich nur Erfolg versprechend sein, aus dem gleichförmigen Verhalten auszuscheren und eine eigenständige Markenidentität aufzubauen, um auf diese Weise den etablierten Marktführern Marktanteile abnehmen zu können.

Eine professionelle, identitätsbasierte Markenführung ermöglicht es darüber hinaus, trotz grundsätzlich geringer Eintrittsbarrieren in einen Dienstleistungsmarkt, **hohe Marktzugangsschranken** aufzubauen und damit den Markteintritt von Neuanbietern zu unterbinden oder zu erschweren. Eine Verteidigung des eigenen Leistungsvorsprungs lässt sich so auch bei fehlender oder eingeschränkter Patentierbarkeit realisieren.

2. Dienstleistungsmarken im Rahmen des identitätsorientierten Markenmanagements

Im Dienstleistungsbereich ist die **identitätsorientierte Markenführung** aufgrund der hohen Bedeutung der **personellen Komponente** sowohl auf Mitarbeiterseite als auch im Hinblick auf die Integration der Nachfrager als externe Faktoren ein viel versprechender Ansatz, der bereits wiederholt im Dienstleistungszusammenhang Anwendung gefunden hat (Ludwig 2001, S. 34 f.; C. Meffert 2002; Eckert 2004). Dabei wurde jedoch primär die allgemeine Vorgehensweise des Ansatzes auf die Markenführung bei Dienstleistungen übertragen, ohne vertiefend die konstitutiven Dienstleistungsmerkmale zu berücksichtigen.

In Theorie und Praxis besteht weitgehend Einigkeit darüber, dass das Markenmanagement als **integrativer Bestandteil der Unternehmensführung** zu verstehen ist und die Markenführung nicht auf kommunikationspolitische Maßnahmen beschränkt werden kann. Der identitätsorientierte Ansatz greift die Forderung der funktionsübergreifenden, ganzheitlichen Ausrichtung des Markenmanagements auf und erweitert gleichzeitig die vorherrschende absatzmarktbezogene Sichtweise um eine innengerichtete, mitarbeiterbezogene Perspektive. Wie bereits bei den mitarbeiterbezogenen Ausführungen zum Qualitätsversprechen einer Marke und den damit sich ergebenden Anforderungen an das Qualitätsmanagement deutlich wurde, muss diesem Aspekt bei der Unternehmensführung im Dienstleistungssektor höchste Bedeutung zugemessen werden.

2.1 Identitätsverständnis als Ausgangspunkt

Grundlegend für den Ansatz der identitätsorientierten Markenführung ist das Verständnis des **Identitätskonstruktes** (vgl. auch den Beitrag zum theoretischen Grundkonzept der identitätsorientierten Markenführung in diesem Buch). Die persönliche Identität oder Ich-Identität bezeichnet die Tatsache, dass ein Individuum ein Bild oder ein Konzept von sich selbst besitzt (Epstein 1993). Demgegenüber bezieht sich die Gruppenidentität auf ein Kollektiv an Subjekten, die neben ihrer jeweiligen persönlichen Identität eine gemeinsame Identität als Gruppe aufweisen, die auch in dieser Weise von den Gruppenmitgliedern empfunden wird.

Im Dienstleistungsbereich tritt die Identität des **Subjektes** weitaus stärker in den Vordergrund als bei Sachgütern, weil die Mitarbeiter mit ihrer Ich-Identität im Erstellungsprozess gegenüber den Nachfragern meist direkt in Erscheinung treten. Die demzufolge stärker von einzelnen Personen geprägte Identitätszuschreibung auf die Dienstleistungsmarke ist bei personellen Dienstleistungen eine wichtige Besonderheit des Markenmanagements (vgl. Abbildung 3).

Abbildung 3: Bedeutung der unterschiedlichen Identitätskonstrukte bei Dienstleistungen

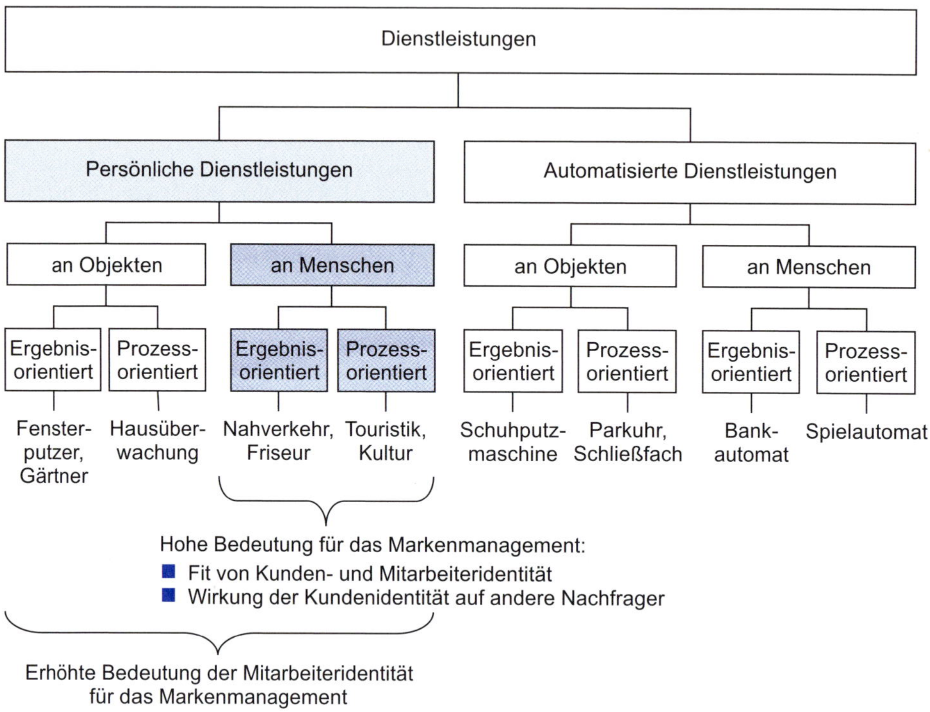

Quelle: in Anlehnung an Meffert/Bruhn 2003, S. 41

Der Bezug zur Ich-Identität des Nachfragers wird in diesem Zusammenhang unmittelbar ersichtlich, da sein eigenes Selbstverständnis mit der Identität des Dienstleistungspersonals als direkt erlebbare Repräsentanten der Dienstleistungsmarke und damit letztlich der Identität der Dienstleistungsmarke selbst konfrontiert wird (Küpers 1999, S. 135 ff.). Es ist somit notwendig, die **Interaktion Mitarbeiter-Nachfrager**, die **Nachfragerintegration im Leistungserstellungsprozess** und **die Wirkung der Kundenidentität auf andere Nachfrager** im Hinblick auf ihre Implikationen für die Markenführung bei Dienstleistungen zu untersuchen.

Diese drei Aspekte prägen stark den prinzipiell sehr hohen Individualisierungsgrad von Dienstleistungen und führen damit gleichzeitig zu der Frage, wie die für die Markenführung so wichtige Qualitätskonstanzbedingung bei Dienstleistungen sichergestellt werden kann.

2.2 Interaktion zwischen Nachfrager und Mitarbeitern als Besonderheit des Markenmanagements bei Dienstleistungen

2.21 Sicherung der Qualitätskonstanz von Markenleistungen

Bei personellen Dienstleistungen, vor allem gegenüber Menschen, findet eine **Interaktion** der Mitarbeiter des Dienstleistungsanbieters mit dem Nachfrager statt, in der die Akteure als Persönlichkeiten zueinander in Beziehung treten und **soziale Handlungen** vollführen (Nerdinger 2001). Aufgrund der Integration des externen Faktors hängt die Qualität des Dienstleistungsergebnisses dabei stark von der Kooperationsbereitschaft des Nachfragers während der Dienstleistungserstellungsphase ab. Für eine erfolgreiche Bewältigung der Dienstleistungsaufgabe ist es daher förderlich, wenn die Mitarbeiter bei den Nachfragern bestimmte Gefühle auslösen, die die Kooperationsbereitschaft steigern (Hochschild 1990). In den meisten Fällen versuchen die Mitarbeiter das Selbstwertgefühl des Nachfragers zu steigern, beispielsweise durch höfliches oder achtungsbezeugendes Verhalten. Situationsabhängig kann es aber auch notwendig sein, autoritär oder sehr bestimmend aufzutreten. Eine Flugbegleiterin beispielsweise ist nicht nur **Gastgeberin**, sie ist auch gleichzeitig **Ordnungsmacht** und muss neben der Sicherstellung des allgemeinen Wohlbefindens auch Sorge für ein den Sicherheitsvorschriften entsprechendes Verhalten der Passagiere tragen (Nerdinger 2001).

Das Beispiel zeigt, dass die Steuerung von Dienstleistungsinteraktionen hohe soziale Anforderungen an die Mitarbeiter stellt. Gleichzeitig ist für den Nachfrager das Auftreten des Kundenkontaktpersonals oftmals zentraler Indikator für die Qualitätswahrnehmung des Dienstleistungsangebotes (Stauss 2000). In der persönlichen Kontaktsituation materialisiert sich für den Nachfrager die abstrakte, immaterielle Dienstleistung und damit zugleich die Marke.

Aus Sicht des identitätsorientierten Markenmanagements ist in dieser Situation die Gewährleistung von Konstanz der essenziellen Identitätsmerkmale ein zentraler Aspekt für den Aufbau einer starken Marke. Damit steht weniger das Eingehen auf individuelle Kundenwünsche als vielmehr die Durchsetzung einer standardisierten Markenleistung im Vordergrund. Aufgrund der hohen Bedeutung der personellen Interaktion ist demnach die Gewährleistung von konsistentem und konkordantem Mitarbeiterverhalten eine conditio sine qua non für den Markenaufbau im Dienstleistungsgeschäft.

Ein Beispiel möge dies verdeutlichen: macht der Kunde den Besuch bei seinem bevorzugten Friseursalon von der Verfügbarkeit eines bestimmten Mitarbeiters abhängig, ist es dem Dienstleistungsanbieter nicht gelungen, über seine Dienstleistungsmarke Kaufverhalten zu beeinflussen. Stattdessen ist die Ich-Identität des Mitarbeiters und, daraus resultierend, das Verhalten des Mitarbeiters Präferenz stiftend. Die Mitarbeiteridentität gehört aber in der subjektiven Wahrnehmung des Kunden nicht zu den konstitutiven Elementen der Gruppenidentität aller Mitarbeiter und damit zur Marke. Denn Kennzeichen der Gruppenidentität ist, dass diese auch dann erhalten bleibt, wenn einzelne Mitglieder der Gruppe wechseln.

In praxi versuchen Dienstleistungsanbieter daher oftmals, Verhalten zu standardisieren. Gleichförmiges Verhalten durch Vorschrift und Anweisung wird allerdings den hohen sozialen Anforderungen zur Steuerung der Dienstleistungsinteraktion nur sehr ungenügend gerecht (Stauss 2000). Derselbe Kunde kann, je nach seiner persönlichen Befindlichkeit, ein bestimmtes Verhalten des Mitarbeiters in einer Situation als freundlich, in einer anderen Situation als aufgesetzt empfinden (Nerdinger 2001). Auch situative Einflüsse des Umfeldes machen eine Adaption des Mitarbeiterverhaltens notwendig. Von Verkäuferinnen im Supermarkt wird beispielsweise ein freundliches Verhalten erwartet, bilden sich allerdings Schlangen vor den Kassen, sollten die Verkäuferinnen eher geschäftig wirken, da die Kunden die Wartezeit ansonsten auf ein schlechtes Zeitmanagement der Verkäuferinnen zurückführen (Sutton/Raffaeli 1988).

Damit wird deutlich, dass im Dienstleistungsbereich die Mitarbeiter vor folgender Herausforderung stehen: Auf der einen Seite gilt es, die zentralen Identitätskomponenten der Marke in der Kundenkontaktsituation durch einheitliches Auftreten in der Gruppe erfahrbar werden zu lassen. Auf der anderen Seite muss der Mitarbeiter stark individualisiert handeln, um den hohen sozialen Anforderungen, die sich aus der jeweiligen Kontextsituation während der Kundeninteraktion ergeben, gerecht zu werden und dem Nachfrager das Gefühl einer persönlich-individuellen Wertschätzung zu geben.

Nach dem Ansatz des identitätsorientierten Markenmanagements stehen beide Anforderungen allerdings nicht im Widerspruch zueinander. Einheitliches Auftreten wird hiernach nicht verstanden als strikte Gleichförmigkeit sozialen Handelns, sondern als einheitliche Vermittlung der wichtigsten Komponenten der Markenidentität gegenüber dem Nachfrager als geschlossen auftretende Gruppe. Die sozialen Handlungen der Mitarbeiter müssen folglich der jeweiligen Kontextsituation angepasst sein, also einen hohen Individualitätsgrad aufweisen. Bedingung ist dabei nur, dass in der Dekodierung der sozialen Interaktionsprozesse durch den Nachfrager am Ende ein kundenübergreifend einheitliches Verständnis der Markenidentität steht. Das Bild, welches sich jeder Kunde über die Marke macht, muss also deren Identität entsprechen. Eine Gleichförmigkeit sozialer Handlungen kann aufgrund der Individualität der Nachfrager und der Kontaktsituation dabei sogar hinderlich sein.

Es zeigt sich, dass die Anforderungen an das innengerichtete Markenmanagement im Dienstleistungsbereich wesentlich höher sind als im Sachgüterbereich, wo die Markenidentität zumeist ohne Berücksichtigung der persönlichen Kontaktsituation dem Kunden über unpersönliche Medien vermittelt wird. Die Führung der Marke zeichnet sich insofern im Sachgüterbereich durch einen geringeren Komplexitätsgrad aus.

2.22 Mitarbeiterführung im Interaktionsprozess zur Vermittlung der Markenidentität

Die Ausführungen zum Interaktionsprozess zeigen, dass ein institutionalisiertes, innengerichtetes Markenmanagement für Dienstleister von entscheidender Bedeutung ist. Zur markenadäquaten Gestaltung der Interaktionsprozesse ist es notwendig, dass die Mitarbeiter ein ausgeprägtes **Brand Citizenship Behavior** zeigen. Voraussetzung dieses Brand Citizenship Behaviors ist ein hohes **Brand Commitment** der Mitarbeiter, also eine starke psychologische Verbundenheit mit der Marke (vgl. den Beitrag zum innengerichteten Markenmanagement in diesem Buch). Dem Management stehen zur Förderung von Brand Commitment **drei zentrale Stellhebel** – markenorientierte Human Resource Aktivitäten, Marken-Kommunikation und die bewusst markenorientierte Führung – zur Verfügung (vgl. Abbildung 4).

Abbildung 4: Ganzheitliches Modell für das innengerichtete Markenmanagement im Dienstleistungsservice

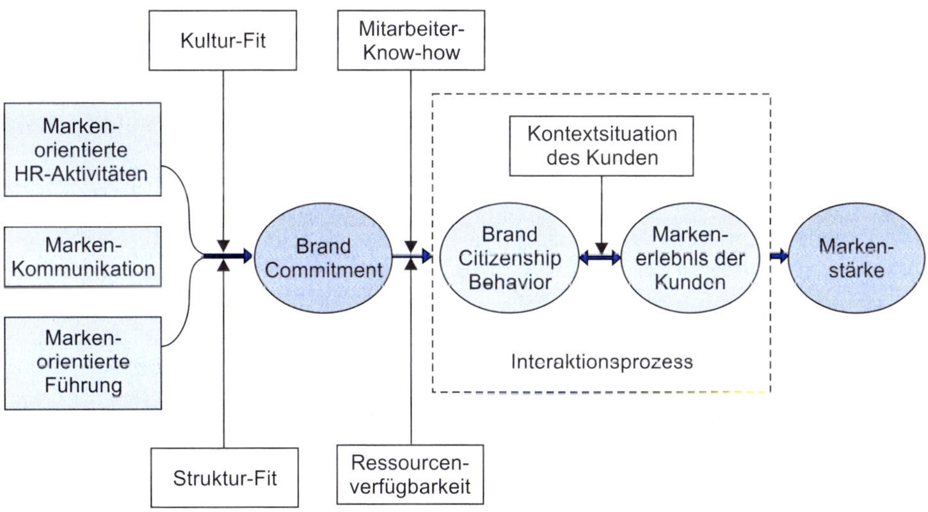

GABLER GRAFIK

Für die **Personalauswahl** im Rahmen der markenorientierten Human Resource Aktivitäten ergeben sich zentrale Implikationen aus dem identitätsorientierten Ansatz der Markenführung (Gebert/von Rosenstiel 1996, S. 213 ff.). Im Mittelpunkt der Betrachtung steht dabei zum einen die Markenidentität, zum anderen die Identität des neu einzustellenden Mitarbeiters (Crisand 2000). Hier ist ein größtmöglicher Fit zwischen der Markenidentität und der Identität des potenziellen Mitarbeiters anzustreben. Bei dauerhafter Diskrepanz bezüglich der essenziellen Merkmale kann der Mitarbeiter die Markenidentität gegenüber dem Nachfrager nicht erkennbar werden lassen, da er sich ständig im Widerspruch zu seinem eigenen Selbst-Konzept befinden würde (Fischer 1993, S. 57 ff.). Eine Adaption der zentralen Werte der Marke kann so gar nicht oder nur mit sehr großem und lang andauerndem Lernaufwand erfolgen. Darüber hinaus sollte der neue Mitarbeiter durch die ihm eigenen Besonderheiten möglichst einen Beitrag zur dynamischen Weiterentwicklung der Markenidentität leisten können. Es ist nicht das Ziel, ausschließlich „stromlinienförmige" Mitarbeiter zu beschäftigen, sondern durch neue Merkmale der zukünftigen Mitarbeiter eine Evolution der Markenidentität zu erreichen. Die herausragende Qualität, die Dienstleistern wie beispielsweise der Disney Company attestiert wird, ist nicht zuletzt Resultat eines klaren innengerichteten Markenmanagements, dass seinen Ausgangspunkt bei der Personalauswahl nimmt (Moores 1991, S. 446).

Aus diesem Gedanken heraus kommt nach der Personalauswahl auch der **Integration des neuen Mitarbeiters** in die Gruppe eine hohe Bedeutung zu (Nerdinger 1994, S. 289 ff.). Dieser Anpassungsprozess ist vor dem Hintergrund der Ausführungen zur Personalauswahl so zu gestalten, dass zwar die einheitliche Identität der Marke kommuniziert und weitervermittelt wird, darüber hinaus jedoch auch die neuen Impulse, die der neue Mitarbeiter der Marke möglicherweise geben kann, nicht verloren gehen, sondern erkannt und gefördert werden (Gebert/von Rosenstiel 1996, S. 88 ff. sowie zum responsiv-organisationalen Lernen der Dienstleistungsorganisation Küpers 1999, S. 207 ff.). Dies ist eine besondere Herausforderung an das Management und die Personalführung, da neben die Bewahrung des Bestehenden noch das Erkennen neuer, bislang unbekannter Entwicklungsmöglichkeiten tritt. Schließlich ist auch die **Personalentwicklung** in den aufgespannten Rahmen einzuordnen.

In Bezug auf die Vertiefung der Markenidentität über die Zeit ist der zweite Stellhebel, die **Marken-Kommunikation**, zentrales Instrument (vgl. Abbildung 4). Im Mittelpunkt steht die kontinuierliche Vermittlung und dialogische Verinnerlichung der Markenidentität auf einer für die Mitarbeiter handlungsrelevanten Ebene. Dotzler (1995) zeigt am Beispiel einer Bank die hier einsetzbaren Instrumente wie beispielsweise Mitarbeitergespräche, Konferenzen und Abteilungsleitertreffen. Die Ritz-Carlton Hotel Company verteilt an ihre Mitarbeiter kleine Faltblättchen, auf denen allgemeine Verhaltensgrundsätze niedergeschrieben sind. Die Hotelkette macht dabei gegenüber den Mitarbeitern deutlich, dass über ihre Dienstleistungsfunktion hinaus die Entwicklung und Einbringung einer eigenen Persönlichkeit in den Dienstleistungserstellungsprozess erwünscht ist. Die schriftlich fixierte Handlungsmaxime bei Ritz-Carlton lautet: *„We are Ladies and Gentleman serving Ladies and Gentleman"* (Meffert/Bruhn 2003, S. 635). Damit werden den Mitarbeitern sehr plastisch die Markenwerte beschrieben, in deren Rahmen die Befriedigung individueller Kundenwünsche erfolgen soll. Gleichzeitig wird den Mitarbeitern in der Interaktion mit den Bedienten so viel Handlungsspielraum eingeräumt, dass sie flexibel auf die individuelle Kontextsituation des Nachfragers eingehen können.

Dritter Stellhebel ist die **Führung** (vgl. Abbildung 4). Als Besonderheit für den Dienstleistungsbereich soll hier auf einen Aspekt eingegangen werden, der als **„substitute for leadership"** bezeichnet wird (Kerr/Jermier 1987). Damit wird ausgedrückt, dass der Nachfrager nicht nur in seiner Qualitätswahrnehmung und seinem Handeln durch den Mitarbeiter beeinflusst wird, sondern der Kunde auch sozialen Einfluss auf das Mitarbeiterverhalten ausübt. Dabei kann es zu der Situation kommen, dass der Kunde mehr oder weniger bewusst führungsähnliche Aufgaben übernimmt (Meyer/Blümelhuber/ Pfeiffer 2000, S. 65). Zwischenmenschliche Anerkennung und Förderung des Selbstwertgefühls durch verbale Äußerungen (Lob), das Zeigen von Gefühlen (Lachen, Heiterkeit) oder finanzielle Zuwendungen (Trinkgeld) des Kunden können zu einer derart starken Quelle von Selbstachtung, Arbeitszufriedenheit und Motivation werden, dass der unmittelbare Einfluss und das Verhalten des hierarchisch Vorgesetzten nahezu vollständig durch das Kundenfeedback überlagert wird (Lehmann 1998, S. 38). Das Feedback und die Expertise des Kunden sind grundsätzlich positiv zu bewerten, da sie einen Beitrag zu kundenorientiertem Mitarbeiterverhalten leisten können, allerdings kann es auch zu nicht markenkonformen Handlungen anstiften. Illustriert werden kann dieser Fall anhand einer interessanten Beobachtung von Normann (Norman 1984, S. 53). So neigen Stewards von Fluggesellschaften oftmals dazu, beim Check-in eher Passagiere der Economy Class zu bedienen und ihnen einen weitaus höflicheren und zuvorkommenderen Service zu Teil werden zu lassen als den Reisenden aus der First Class. Dieses Verhalten lässt sich unmittelbar aus dem Interaktionsverhalten der Nachfrager erklären. So neigt das Klientel aus der First Class zu einem stärker distanzierten bis überheblicheren Verhalten gegenüber den Stewards als dies bei Passagieren aus der Economy Class der Fall ist, die sich für erhaltene Hilfestellungen und Ratschläge des Flugpersonals wesentlich erkenntlicher zeigen und entsprechend positiveres Kundenfeedback geben. In solchen Fällen, in denen die Ich-Identität des Nachfragers nicht markenkonforme Steuerungswirkung entfaltet, handelt es sich um ein weiteres dienstleistungsspezifisches Problem des Markenmanagements, welchem durch entsprechende Führungsmaßnahmen zu begegnen ist.

2.2.3 Sicherung des Fits zwischen Marken-, Mitarbeiter- und Kundenidentität

Einen unmittelbaren Eindruck von der Markenidentität erhält der Kunde nicht allein über die Mitarbeiterinteraktion. Prinzipiell können sämtliche wahrnehmbaren Elemente im Leistungserstellungsprozess die Markenwahrnehmung des Nachfragers prägen. Die Integration des Kunden in den Leistungserstellungsprozess sollte der Dienstleistungsanbieter deshalb nutzen, um bestimmte Ereignisse fest in der Wahrnehmung der Nachfrager zu verankern. So bietet es sich beispielsweise an, die Markenwahrnehmung durch das Setzen von kommunikativ wiederholbaren und leicht erlernbaren „Clues" wie Symbolen, Markennamen und Slogans während des Leistungserstellungsprozesses zu steuern. Die rein optische Vermittlung kann durch weitere, beispielsweise haptische oder olfaktorische Elemente ergänzt und dem Nachfrager mehrfach kodiert dargeboten werden. Neben bewusst gesetzten Einzelsignalen muss auch die Funktionalität und Anmutung der physischen Umgebung als ein Einflussfaktor der Markenwahrnehmung gezielt gesteuert werden (Stauss 2000, S. 325). Die für die Qualitätswahrnehmung besonders wichtigen Kontaktsituationen mit der Dienstleistung werden auch als **„moments of truth“** (Zeithaml/Bitner 2003, S. 99) bezeichnet. Sie sollten vom Dienstleistungsanbieter im Rahmen einer Kontaktpunktanalyse ermittelt und hinsichtlich ihrer markenadäquaten Ausgestaltung überprüft und realisiert werden (Stauss 2000, S. 327 ff.).

Bei der Analyse des Leistungserstellungsprozesses hinsichtlich des Fits der einzelnen Phasen zur Markenidentität muss ein enger Bezug zur Kundenidentität hergestellt werden (Fischer 1993, S. 57 ff.). Dies gilt insbesondere für die Phasen, in denen die Kunden einen Teil der Leistungserstellung selbst übernehmen müssen (Corsten 2000). Die amerikanische Fluglinie Southwest Airlines beschränkt beispielsweise ihr Serviceangebot im Rahmen eines so genannten „No-Frill“-Konzeptes auf die absolut notwendigen Dienstleistungen. So muss die Gepäckbeförderung zum Flugzeug vom Kunden selbst vorgenommen werden. Personen, die nicht über die notwendigen Fähigkeiten verfügen, um sich in den Dienstleistungsprozess einzubringen, müssen deshalb aufgrund des Misfits der Markenidentität mit der Kundenidentität von der Inanspruchnahme der Dienstleistung ausgeschlossen werden.

Neben den physischen und psychischen Fähigkeiten sollte ebenfalls eine gewisse Kompatibilität der übrigen Identitätskomponenten sichergestellt werden, um eine aus Nachfragersicht zufrieden stellende Einbindung in den Leistungserstellungsprozess und das intendierte Markenerlebnis gewährleisten zu können. Dieser Aspekt wird in der Dienstleistungspraxis häufig vernachlässigt. Bei Inkompatibilitäten oder zumindest nur schwachem Fit der Markenidentität mit der Kundenidentität in einzelnen Phasen des Dienstleistungserstellungsprozesses kann beispielsweise im Rahmen einer Externalisierungsstrategie (Corsten 2000) das Aktivitätsniveau der Marke bewusst zurückgefahren werden. Externalisierungsstrategien sind zwar in praxi häufig anzutreffen, ihre Initiierung ist allerdings zumeist kostengetrieben (zum Beispiel Übertragung von Kontoführungsaufgaben vom Schalterpersonal auf die Bankkunden mittels des Einsatzes von Bankautomaten). Anders dagegen beim Shouldice Hospital – eine Klinik, die sich auf Leistenbruch-Operationen spezialisiert hat und als eines der erfolgreichsten Krankenhäuser der Welt gilt. Hier werden die zu operierenden Patienten von ehemaligen Patienten in die Operationsabläufe eingewiesen. Aufgrund deren Erfahrungen können glaubwürdigere und authentischere Informationen übermittelt werden als durch das Pflege- beziehungsweise Arztpersonal, welches womöglich niemals selbst eine Leistenoperation durchstehen musste (Meyer/Blümelhuber/Pfeiffer 2000, S. 66). Einzelne Kundenidentitäten können damit die Wahrnehmung des Dienstleisters prinzipiell genauso stark prägen wie die Identitätszuschreibung auf das Pflegerpersonal von außen. Der Einfluss von typischen Verwendern auf das Markenimage soll deshalb im folgenden Kapitel eingehender untersucht werden.

2.3 Kundenidentität als Determinante des Markenwahlverhaltens bei Dienstleistungen

Gemäß der „Image-Kongruenz"-Hypothese ist die Präferenz und Kaufabsicht für eine Marke abhängig von deren Image und dem Bild, das der Nachfrager von sich selbst hat und anderen vermitteln möchte. Dieses reflexive Bild von sich selbst wird auch als Selbstkonzept bezeichnet (Rosenberg 1979, S. 7). Es entspricht im Wesentlichen der Ich-Identität beziehungsweise persönlichen Identität. Die Übereinstimmung zwischen dem Selbstkonzept eines Individuums und dem Markenimage determiniert neben anderen Einflüssen die Markenwahlentscheidung. Nach dieser Theorie liegt der Nutzen einer Marke somit primär darin, das tatsächliche Selbstkonzept eines Kunden zu bestätigen oder die Entwicklung hin zu einem gewünschten Selbstkonzept zu fördern (Sirgy 1982, S. 289). Auch wenn keine Einigkeit darüber herrscht, welche Teile des Selbst in welcher Weise zur Wahrnehmung der Kongruenz beitragen, ist diese Hypothese durch mehrere empirische Studien in ihrer Substanz gut bestätigt worden (Strebinger/Otter/Schweiger 1997). Überführt man die „Image-Kongruenz"-Hypothese in das identitätsorientierte Markenkonzept, ist sowohl ein Fit zwischen Identität und Image der Marke, als auch zwischen dem individuellen Selbstkonzept des Nachfragers und des von ihm wahrgenommenen Markenimages herzustellen (C. Meffert 2002, S. 93 ff.).

Als dienstleistungsspezifische Besonderheit ist dabei zu beachten, dass der Kunde durch die Integration in den Erstellungsprozess mit seiner Identität nicht nur in sehr engen Kontakt mit der Markenidentität tritt, sondern, sofern er innerhalb des Leistungserstellungsprozesses wahrgenommen wird, seine Identität die Marke auch in der Außenwahrnehmung (Markenimage) nachhaltig prägt. Er nimmt somit Einfluss auf die Markenwahlentscheidung Dritter (Fischer 1993, S. 63 ff.; Nerdinger 1994, S. 243 ff.). Beispielhaft sei hier auf besonders luxuriöse Hotels oder Restaurants verwiesen, bei denen das dort verkehrende Publikum einen Großteil der Faszination der jeweiligen Marke ausmacht. Dies kann soweit gehen, dass ein Teil der Nachfrager, bei denen es sich beispielsweise um Prominente handelt, zum wichtigsten Grund einer Inanspruchnahme dieser Leistung wird. Gleichzeitig ist für die Prominenten das Zusammensein mit Ihresgleichen beziehungsweise das Ungestörtsein wichtigster Grund für ihre Wahlentscheidung. Bei Aufnahme dieser Hotels oder Restaurants in einen Reiseführer wird jedoch oftmals nicht mehr das distinguierte Klientel, sondern der Tourist typischer Nachfrager, mit der Folge, dass die Identität der Marke Schaden nimmt. In der Außenwahrnehmung prägen dann die Identitäten der Touristen das Markenimage, welches mit dem Selbstkonzept des ehemals dort verkehrenden Publikums nur noch sehr wenig gemein hat. Der mangelnde Fit des durch Touristen geprägten Markenimages mit deren Selbstkonzept wird gemäß der Image-Kongruenz-Hypothese längerfristig zu einem Fernbleiben dieses Publikums führen mit entsprechender Konsequenz auch für andere Nachfrager, deren Erwartungen gegenüber der Marke enttäuscht werden.

Es bedarf somit eines „Fits" zwischen der Markenidentität und der Identität der betroffenen Nachfrager, um eine starke Marke aufzubauen. Ein Beispiel für das Vorliegen eines solchen Fits lässt sich bei genossenschaftlich organisierten Anbietern wie den Volksbanken identifizieren. Die Kunden können gleichzeitig Mitglieder in der Genossenschaft sein, wodurch über das entstehende Wir-Gefühl eine recht weit gehende Integration stattfindet (Meyer/Maier 1998, S. 87 ff.).

Ein strategisch ausgerichtetes Markenmanagement sollte daher zunächst berücksichtigen, welche **Kundensegmente** zur Markenidentität passen. Durch eine Vernachlässigung dieses Aspektes kann die Attraktivität einer Dienstleistungsmarke entscheidend beeinträchtigt werden, wenn Nachfrager entgegen ihrer Erwartung nicht die gewohnten Kunden antreffen. Aus Sicht des identitätsorientierten Markenmanagements ist somit das Management des Kundenzugangs von entscheidender Bedeutung.

Bezüglich der **Steuerung des Kundenzugangs** ist zunächst zu entscheiden, ob diese auf Basis einer Selbstselektion der Nachfrager, beispielsweise nach Preisbereitschaften, erfolgen soll, oder ob der Anbieter aktiv eine Auswahl der Kunden vornimmt. Ein Beispiel für letztere Vorgehensweise ist das Vorschreiben einer verbindlichen Kleiderordnung (beispielsweise für den Einlass in ein Casino) oder die Beschränkung des Zugangs auf Mitglieder. Dies führen Fluggesellschaften durch, die den Zugang zu bestimmten Wartebereichen (Lounges) auf die Inhaber bestimmter Statuskarten einschränken. Eine andere Form der Steuerung des Kundenzugangs kann durch die Konzentration auf ausgewählte Vertriebskanäle erfolgen. Alle Vorgehensweisen sind davon abhängig, dass sich zielführende und operationalisierbare Indikatoren für die Kundenidentitäten finden lassen.

3. Ausgewählte Aspekte des identitätsorientierten Managements von Dienstleistungsmarken – ein Beispiel aus der Assekuranz

Eine Dienstleistungsbranche, für die der Ansatz der identitätsorientierten Markenführung eine steigende Relevanz besitzt, ist die Assekuranz. Denn der ehemals sehr stark regulierte deutsche Versicherungsmarkt befindet sich seit Umsetzung der 3. EG-Richtlinie im Jahre 1994 im Umbruch. Steigender Wettbewerbsdruck durch fallende Prämien bei wachsender Angebotsvielfalt und gleichzeitig nur sehr moderatem Wachstum kennzeichnen die neue Marktsituation. Neben zahlreichen Fusionen und Unternehmensübernahmen (Allianz/AGF/DresdnerBank, AXA/UAP, Zürich/Agrippina/BAT/Deutscher Herold, DeutscheBank/ScudderVermögensverwaltung, Winterthur/DBV/Credit Suisse, Gernali/AMB, ERGO, ...) haben Markteintritte ausländischer Versicherer dem Verdrängungswettbewerb zusätzliche Schärfe verliehen (Dill 2001, S. 271–272; Görgen et al. 2003, S. 42–45).

Traditionell ist die Branche geprägt von der Auffassung, dass allein Vertriebsstärke den Geschäftserfolg sichert (Klein-Bölting/Maskus 2003, S. 96). Dies hängt sicherlich zum einen mit der vor der Deregulierung auf strikten Vorsichtsprinzipien aufbauenden Aufsichtspolitik der Bundesanstalt für Finanzdienstleistungen zusammen, die durch regulierende Eingriffe in die Produkt-, Preis- und Finanzpolitik der Versicherer kaum Spielraum für den Aufbau nachfrageinduzierter Sogwirkungen durch ein professionelles Markenmanagement bot (Jara 2000, S. 84), zum anderen allerdings sicherlich auch mit den so wenig absatzfreundlichen Eigenschaften von Versicherungsprodukten (Delisle 1981, S. 46). Versicherungen bieten finanziellen Schutz gegen Negativereignisse wie beispielsweise Krankheit, Unfall, Diebstahl oder Berufsunfähigkeit. Damit berühren sie Themen, mit denen sich Kunden nur ungern auseinander setzen. Versicherungen führen ferner zu längerfristigen Vertragsbindungen, und im Zeitpunkt des Kaufs bieten sie keinen konkreten Gegenwert. Der Wettbewerb der Versicherer beschränkte sich daher primär auf den Aufbau eigener Vertriebsnetze: Versicherungsprodukte ließen sich nach allgemeiner Auffassung nur in den Markt „hineindrücken". Und je mehr Personen am „hineindrücken" waren, desto besser. Der juristisch und wirtschaftlich selbstständige, faktisch jedoch an ein Versicherungsunternehmen gebundene Ausschließlichkeitsvertreter (Einfirmenvertreter) erwies sich hierfür als das ideale Instrument und verdankt nicht zuletzt den geschilderten Umständen seine in Deutschland marktbeherrschende Stellung (Görgen et al. 2003).

Nach der Deregulierung werden Versicherungsprodukte nun aber nicht mehr nur über Ein-, sondern auch über Mehrfirmenvertreter distribuiert. Mehrfirmenvertreter wie Makler und Strukturvertriebler sind nicht nur juristisch und wirtschaftlich, sondern auch faktisch unabhängig, sodass den Versicherern die Bezugsbasis zur Ausübung von Angebotsdruck am Point of Sale bei diesen Distributionskanälen abhanden gekommen ist. Auch die für die Versicherer durch technische Innovationen neu hinzugewonnenen unpersönlichen Distributionskanäle wie beispielsweise das Internet sind ungeeignet zur Ausübung von Angebotsdruck, da die Initiative für deren Nutzung von den zunehmend besser informierten Nachfragern ausgeht. Konsequenz dieser Entwicklung ist, dass aus Sicht der Versicherer Produkte nicht mehr nur „verkauft", sondern zunehmend auch „gekauft" werden. Eine starke Marke zur Induzierung eines Nachfragesogs für die eigenen Produkte ist damit zu einem strategischen Erfolgsfaktor im Multi-Kanal-Vertrieb des umkämpften Versicherungsmarktes avanciert (Dill 2001, S. 274).

Zugleich erschwert der Multi-Kanal-Vertrieb die konsistente Führung der Marke über alle Verkaufsstellen hinweg, da er zu einer Multiplikation markenidentitätsprägender Faktoren führt (Böing/Huber 2003, S. 74). Erfüllt die Marke in der Kommunikation geweckte Erwartungshaltungen in den Vertriebsstellen nicht, entstehen kognitive Dissonanzen auf Seiten des Versicherungsnachfragers und die Marke verliert sehr schnell an Relevanz und Wert (Kroeber-Riel/Weinberg 2002, S. 182 ff.).

Die Abstimmung stellt sich insbesondere dort problematisch dar, wo die Einflussnahme des Versicherungsunternehmens auf die Distributionsstellen nur begrenzt ist. Dies ist insbesondere bei den von Mehrfirmenvertretern geführten Absatzkanälen der Fall. Der in der deutschen Assekuranz noch immer umsatzstärkste Absatzkanal, der Ausschließlichkeitsvertrieb, weist aufgrund der faktischen Abhängigkeit vom Versicherungsunternehmen daher die besten Voraussetzungen zur Durchsetzung der eigenen Markenpolitik auf. Über diesen Absatzkanal bietet es sich daher an, insbesondere solche Produkte zu distribuieren, bei denen nicht einzelne Dienstleistungsangebote mit ihren Leistungselementen, sondern deren Integration in eine umfassende Beratungs- und Betreuungsleistung im Vordergrund stehen (Lehmann 1998, S. 191 ff.). Denn je kundenspezifischer und komplexer das Dienstleistungsangebot, desto wichtiger ist es für den Versicherer, Einfluss auf das Verhalten des Kundenkontaktpersonals nehmen zu können.

Anders als beim Verkauf einer Ware zu einem bestimmten Preis, handelt es sich bei diesen Leistungen um komplexe Lösungsbündel, deren Vertragsausgestaltung nur in engem Bezug zur Person des Versicherungsnehmers erfolgen kann. Die Ausgestaltung der Beratungs- und Betreuungsleistung bestimmt wesentlich die differenzierende Individualisierung der Marktleistungen. Dabei hat in der subjektiven Wahrnehmung des Nachfragers die Qualitätsbeurteilung der Versicherungsleistung nicht nur einen sachlichen Hintergrund. Sie wird entscheidend durch in der Identität des Versicherungsvertreters verankerte Werte wie Hilfsbereitschaft und Freundlichkeit geprägt. Der Versicherungsvertreter steht dabei vor der Herausforderung, kundenübergreifend den **Interaktionsprozess** an den Markenwerten auszurichten. Die Markenidentität wird dabei für den Nachfrager durch die Ich-Identität des Versicherungsvertreters erfahrbar. Weist diese beziehungsweise in Gesamtsicht die zahlreichen Ich-Identitäten der Versicherungsvertreter keinen Fit mit der Markenidentität auf, wird es der Versicherung nicht gelingen, sich gegenüber dem Wettbewerb zu konturieren beziehungsweise im Markt zu positionieren.

Aufgabe des Versicherungsvertreters ist es ferner, während der Vertragsverhandlungen mit den künftigen Versicherungsnehmern eine Risikoselektion vorzunehmen. Neben im Antrag aufgeführten objektiven Risikomerkmalen müssen auch subjektive Risikomerkmale, die sich fast nur durch Befragung ermitteln lassen, festgestellt werden. Ein Kunde mit einer subjektiv hohen Schadeneintrittswahrscheinlichkeit könnte dabei versuchen, diese gegenüber dem Versicherungsvertreter zu verbergen, um eine Deckung seiner Risiken zu nur durchschnittlichen Bedingungen zu erhalten (Lehmann 1998, S. 150). Dem **Management des Kundenzugangs** kommt damit gerade im Versicherungsgeschäft große Bedeutung zu, weniger aufgrund einer unmittelbaren Außenwirkung einzelner Kundenidentitäten, als vielmehr durch das in der Kundenidentität verankerte Risikoprofil, welches mittelbar Einfluss auf die Prämiengestaltung der übrigen Kunden nimmt. Aus einer so veränderten Preisstellung kann ein wesentlicher Imageschaden der Marke resultieren.

Sofern es zum Eintritt des Schadenfalls kommt, ist dies der zentrale Kristallisationspunkt der Kundenbeziehung zum Versicherer. In ihm zeigt sich, ob das in den Versicherer gesetzte Vertrauen gerechtfertigt war oder ob es im entscheidenden **„moment of truth“** der Kundenbeziehung enttäuscht wird (Herrmann 1994, S. 219). Die Schadenregulierung sollte daher nicht allein auf Basis juristischer Ansprüche des Nachfragers erfolgen, sondern in engem Bezug zu den sozial-psychischen Bedürfnissen des Geschädigten stehen (Jara 2000, S. 104). Anstatt lediglich dem finanziellen Ausgleich von vertraglich abgedeckten Schadenereignissen bürokratisch nachzukommen, gilt es also in der angespannten Wettbewerbssituation die Chancen wahrzunehmen, die sich aus einem Schadenfall für die Profilierung der Marke ergeben. Unerwähnt soll allerdings nicht bleiben, dass bei Übernahme von Schadenregulierungsaufgaben durch den Versicherungsvertreter nicht selten das **„Substitute-for-leadership“**-Phänomen virulent wird, indem die Nachfrager den Versicherungsagenten zu allzu umfassender Regulierung verleiten. Herausforderung ist demnach, die Schadenregulierung als Profilierungsraum für die Marke zu nutzen, ohne damit einen finanziellen Mehraufwand zu verursachen. Die amerikanische Versicherungsunternehmung „The Progressive Transportation Group" ist ein gutes Beispiel, wie Versicherer die schwierige Bewährungsprobe Schadenfall als Chance nutzen können. Speziell ausgebildete Katastrophenteams können mittels einer 24-Stunden-Hotline angefordert werden und leisten innerhalb kürzester Frist in den ganzen USA sofortige Hilfe bei Transportschäden. Auf diese Weise wird für die Nachfrager der Markenwert „schnelle Hilfe" unmittelbar erfahrbar. Durch den Verzicht auf bürokratisches Vorgehen, welches häufig langwierige Verhandlungen mit den Geschädigten unter Hinzuziehung von Anwälten nach sich zog, konnten gleichzeitig die Schaden- und Schadenbearbeitungskosten gesenkt werden (Lehmann 1992, S. 410).

Die genannten Aspekte zeigen den potenziellen Handlungsspielraum, den Versicherer nutzen können, um sich der neuen Marktsituation zu stellen. Geschäftserfolg wird deutlich weniger durch intensive Vertriebsaktivitäten als vielmehr durch ein umfassendes Markenmanagement gesichert. Es gilt, ein System der gemeinsamen Wertschöpfung zwischen Versicherer und Nachfrager in Gang zu setzen. Komparative Konkurrenzvorteile sind dabei weniger durch das eigentliche funktionale Leistungsangebot als vielmehr durch die kundenorientierte Gestaltung des Leistungserstellungskonzeptes zu erzielen, bei der es gilt, die Beziehungsdimension kundenübergreifend am Markenkonzept auszurichten. Dabei spielt, wie gezeigt, insbesondere das Personal eine herausragende Rolle. Zahlreiche Versicherungsunternehmen betreiben ihre Personalpolitik allerdings noch immer unter dem Primat der Vertriebsstärkenmaximierung, mit der Folge einer sträflichen Vernachlässigung des **innengerichteten Markenmanagements**. Bei einigen Versicherern zu beobachtende Fluktuationsraten bei Außendienstmitarbeitern in den ersten zwei Jahren von nahezu 50 Prozent (Jirsa/Ochmann/Etzel 2004, S. 339) machen eine konsistente und konkordante Vermittlung der Markenidentität im Wettbewerbsumfeld unmöglich. Eine Situation, von der einzig große Versicherer mit marktbeherrschender Stellung profitieren.

4. Fazit

Mit den vorhergehenden Ausführungen konnte gezeigt werden, dass das Konzept der identitätsorientierten Markenführung auch und insbesondere für das Markenmanagement von Dienstleistungen höchste Relevanz besitzt. Im Sinne des entscheidungsorientierten Ansatzes der Betriebswirtschaftslehre vermag der Ansatz nicht nur Handlungsbedarfe aufzuzeigen, sondern bietet gleichzeitig das konzeptionelle „Rüstzeug" für deren systematisches Management.

Ausgewählte untersuchte Aspekte waren in diesem Zusammenhang die Mitarbeiter-Kunden Interaktion, die Kundenintegration im Leistungserstellungsprozess und die Wirkung der Kundenidentität auf andere Nachfrager. Es zeigte sich dabei, dass der Erfolg des

Markenmanagements im Dienstleistungssektor stark „von innen" ausgeht. Im Sachgüterbereich, wo die Markenidentität zumeist anonymisiert über Massenmedien vermittelt wird, die Kundenidentität nicht in den Leistungserstellungsprozess integriert wird und damit die Außenwahrnehmung der Mitarbeiter- als auch Kundenidentität nicht so unmittelbar ist, sind die Anforderungen an das innengerichtete Markenmanagement wesentlich geringer.

Der identitätsorientierte Ansatz, der in Abgrenzung zu anderen Markenführungskonzeptionen die absatzmarktgerichtete mit der innengerichteten Perspektive vernetzt, erweist sich damit als geeignet, um die in der Einleitung aufgestellte Forderung, den Transformationsprozess von der Industrie- zur Dienstleistungsgesellschaft nicht nur nachzuvollziehen, sondern aktiv mitzugestalten, zu erfüllen. Für die deutsche Assekuranz als klassische Dienstleistungsbranche wurde die Bedeutung der identitätsorientierten Markenführung im Hinblick auf die nach der Deregulierung verschärfte Wettbewerbssituation hin exemplifiziert.

Literatur

Böing, Ch., Huber, A. D. (2003), Markenmanagement im Multikanalvertrieb – identitätsorientierte Markenführung über alle Absatzkanäle, in: Ahlert, D., Hesse, J., Jullens, J., Smend, P. (Hrsg.), Multikanalstrategien. Konzepte, Methoden und Erfahrungen, Wiesbaden.

Bruhn, M. (2001), Die zunehmende Bedeutung von Dienstleistungsmarken, in: Köhler, R., Majer, W., Wiezorek, H. (Hrsg.), Erfolgsfaktor Marke, München, S. 213-225.

Bruhn, M., Stauss, B. (Hrsg.) (2000), Dienstleistungsqualität. Konzepte, Methoden, Erfahrungen, 3. Aufl., Wiesbaden.

Burmann, Ch., Blinda, L., Nitschke, A. (2003), Konzeptionelle Grundlagen des identitätsbasierten Markenmanagements, in: Burmann, Ch. (Hrsg.), Arbeitspapier Nr. 1 des Lehrstuhls für innovatives Markenmanagement (LiM), Universität Bremen, Bremen.

Corsten, H. (2000), Der Integrationsgrad des externen Faktors als Gestaltungsparameter in Dienstleistungsunternehmungen – Voraussetzungen und Möglichkeiten der Externalisierung und Internalisierung, in: Bruhn, M., Stauss, B. (Hrsg.), Dienstleistungsqualität, 3. Aufl., Wiesbaden, S. 145–168.

Crisand, E. (2000), Psychologie der Persönlichkeit, 8. Aufl., Heidelberg.

Delisle, E. (1981), Marketing in der Versicherungswirtschaft, 2. Aufl., Karlsruhe.

Dill, C.-M. (2001), AXA – am Anfang war die Kraft, in: CONSART Management Consultants (Hrsg.), Strategisches Marken-Management für Banken. Branding – der Erfolgsfaktor im Retailgeschäft, Wiesbaden, S.269–288.

Dotzler, H.-J. (1995), Gestaltung der internen Kommunikation als Grundlage marktorientierter Veränderungsprozesse – am Beispiel der HYPO-Bank, in: Bruhn, M. (Hrsg.), Internes Marketing, Wiesbaden, S. 221–235.

Eckert, D. (2004), Digitale Marken. Analyse der Markenpolitik für digitale Leistungsbündel, Dissertation Universität Bochum, Wiesbaden.

Engelhardt, W. H., Kleinaltenkamp, M., Reckenfelderbäumer, M. (1993), Leistungsbündel als Absatzobjekte, in: zfbf, 45. Jg, Nr. 5, S. 395–426.

Epstein, S. (1993), Entwurf einer Integrativen Persönlichkeitstheorie, in: Filipp, S.-H. (Hrsg.), Selbstkonzept-Forschung, 3. Aufl., Stuttgart, S. 15–45.

Fischer, M. (1993), Phänomenologische Analysen der Person-Umwelt-Beziehung, in: Filipp, S.-H. (Hrsg.), Selbstkonzept-Forschung, 3. Aufl., Stuttgart, S. 47–66.
Gebert, D., von Rosenstiel, L. (1996), Organisationspsychologie, 4. Aufl., Stuttgart.
Görgen, F., Müller-Reichart, M., Lünzer, M., Neumann, M. (2003), Marketing- und Vertriebsstrategien im internationalen Versicherungsgeschäft, in: Zeitschrift für Versicherungswesen, 54. Jahrgang, 15.01.2003.
Herrmann, H. (1994), Ein „Grundgesetz" für die optimale Schadenregulierung – Was für die Qualität einer Versicherung entscheidend ist, in: Versicherungswirtschaft, Nr. 4, S. 218–224.
Hochschild, A. R. (1990), Das gekaufte Herz, Frankfurt/M.
Homburg, Ch. (Hrsg.) (2003), Kundenzufriedenheit. Konzepte, Methoden, Erfahrungen, 5. Aufl., Wiesbaden.
Jara, K. M. (2000), Zielorientierte Neugestaltung des Schadenmanagements in Versicherungsunternehmen – Ansätze für die Sach- und Haftpflichtsparten des Privatkundengeschäfts, Dissertation der Universität St. Gallen, Gossau.
Jirsa, V., Ochmann, H., Etzel, S. (2004), Was tun gegen die Fluktuation im Außendienst?, in: Versicherungswirtschaft, Nr. 5, S. 339–340.
Keller, K. L. (2003), Strategic brand management: building, measuring, and managing brand equity, 2. Aufl., Upper Saddle River, NJ u.a.
Kerr, S., Jermier, J. M. (1987), Substitutes for Leadership: Their Meaning and Measurement, in: Organizational Behavior and Human Performance, Nr. 22, S. 375 – 404.
Klein-Bölting, U., Maskus, M. (2003), Value Brands, Ulm.
Kroeber-Riel, W., Weinberg, P. (2003), Konsumentenverhalten, 8. Aufl., München.
Küpers, W. (1999), Phänomenologie der Dienstleistungsqualität, Wiesbaden.
Lehmann, A. P. (1998), Qualität und Produktivität im Dienstleistungsmanagement. Strategische Handlungsfelder im Versicherungs- und Finanzdienstleistungswettbewerb, Wiesbaden.
Lehmann, A. (1992), Total Quality Management made in USA: Amerika skizziert neue Wege zur Qualität, in: Versicherungswirtschaft, Nr. 7, S. 405–410.
Ludwig, E. (2001), Management von Markensystemen am Beispiel von Tourismusunternehmen, Dissertation an der Universität St. Gallen.
Meffert, C. (2002), Profilierung von Dienstleistungsmarken in vertikalen Systemen. Ein präferenzorientierter Beitrag zur Markenführung in der Touristik, Dissertation an der Universität St. Gallen.
Meffert, H., Bruhn, M. (2003), Dienstleistungsmarketing. Grundlagen – Konzepte – Methoden, 4. Aufl., Wiesbaden.
Meyer, A., Blümelhuber, C., Pfeiffer, M. (2000), Der Kunde als Co-Produzent und Co-Designer – oder: die Bedeutung der Kundenintegration für die Qualitätspolitik von Dienstleistungsanbietern, in: Bruhn, M., Stauss, B. (Hrsg.), Dienstleistungsqualität, 3. Aufl., Wiesbaden, S. 49–70.
Meyer, A., Maier, M. (1998), Markenpolitik für Banken – Einige Anregungen und Beispiele, in: Tomczak, T., Schögel, M., Ludwig, E. (Hrsg.), Markenmanagment für Dienstleistungen, St. Gallen, S. 78–92.
Moores, B. (1991), Lessons from some of Americas most respected service providers, in: van der Wiele, T., Timmers, J. G. (Hrsg.), Proceedings of the „Workshop on Quality Management in Services", Booklet 3, Brussels, S. 437–450.
Nerdinger, F. (1994), Zur Psychologie der Dienstleistung, Stuttgart.
Nerdinger, F. (2001), Psychologische Aspekte der Tätigkeit im Dienstleistungsbereich, in: Bruhn, M., Meffert, H. (Hrsg.), Handbuch Dienstleistungsmanagement, 2. Aufl., Wiesbaden, S. 243–261.
Normann, R. (1984), Service Management: Strategy and Leadership in Service Businesses, Chichester [u.a.].

Pascual, G. O. (1998), Marken – und insbesondere Dienstleistungsmarken – aus rechtlicher Sicht, in: Tomczak, T., Schögel, M., Ludwig, E. (Hrsg.), Markenmanagement für Dienstleistungen, St. Gallen, S. 148–160.

Rosenberg, M. (1979), Conceiving the self, New York.

Sirgy, J. M. (1982), Self-Concept in Consumer Behavior: A Critical Review, in: Journal of Consumer Research, Vol. 9, S. 287–300.

Sutton, R. I. (1988), Raffaeli, A., Untangling the Relationship Between Displayed Emotions and Organizational Sales: The Case of Convenience Stores, in: Academy of Management Journal, Vol. 31, No. 3, S. 461–489.

Stauss, B. (2000), Internes Marketing als personalorientierte Qualitätspolitik, in: Bruhn, M., Stauss, B. (Hrsg.), Dienstleistungsqualität, 3. Aufl., Wiesbaden, S. 203–222.

Stauss, B. (2001), Markierungspolitik bei Dienstleistungen – Die „Dienstleistungsmarke", in: Bruhn, M., Meffert, H. (Hrsg.), Handbuch Dienstleistungsmanagement, 2. Aufl., Wiesbaden, S. 549–571.

Strebinger, A., Otter, T., Schweiger, G. (1997), Selbstrelevante Wirkungen der Markenpersönlichkeit bei einem Produkt des täglichen Bedarfs: Die moderierende Rolle von Motivation und Fähigkeit zu zentraler Verarbeitung, Arbeitspapier Abteilung Werbewissenschaft und Marktforschung, Wirtschaftsuniversität Wien.

Tomczak, T. (1999), Markenführung bei Dienstleistungen aus Sicht der Wissenschaft, in: Meffert, H., Backhaus, K., Becker, J. (Hrsg.), Markenführung bei Dienstleistungen, Dokumentationspapier Nr. 129 der Wissenschaftlichen Gesellschaft für Marketing und Unternehmensführung e. V., Münster, S. 5–12.

Tomczak, T., Brockdorff, B. (2000), Bedeutung und Besonderheiten des Markenmanagements für Dienstleistungen, in: Belz, C., Bieger, T. (Hrsg.), Dienstleistungskompetenz und innovative Geschäftsmodelle, St. Gallen, S. 486–502.

Tomczak, T., Ludwig, E. (1998), Strategische Markenführung für Dienstleistungen, in: Tomczak, T., Schögel, M., Ludwig, E. (Hrsg.), Markenmanagement für Dienstleistungen, St. Gallen, S. 48–65.

Zeithaml, V. A., Bitner, M. J. (2003), Service Marketing: Integrated Customer Focus Across the Firm, 3. Aufl., London.

Marke und Markenführung im Kontext des Electronic Commerce

Michael Bongartz, Christoph Burmann und Philip Maloney

1.	**Entwicklung des Electronic Commerce als Ausgangspunkt**	**434**
2.	**Begriffliche Abgrenzungen und Klassifizierungen von Marken im Electronic Commerce**	**435**
2.1	Abgrenzung des Markenbegriffes im Electronic Commerce	435
2.2	Klassifizierungen von Marken im Electronic Commerce	438
2.3	Überprüfung der Klassifikationsmerkmale anhand der Konsumentenverhaltensforschung	440
3.	**Stellenwert und Herausforderungen der Markenführung im Electronic Commerce**	**442**
3.1	Nutzerbezogene Bedeutung und Funktionen der Marke im Electronic Commerce	442
3.2	Wettbewerbsbezogene Bedeutung und Funktionen der Marke	447
3.3	Anforderungen an den Markenmanagementprozess im Electronic Commerce	448
3.31	Strategisches Markenmanagement im Electronic Commerce	448
3.32	Operatives Markenmanagement im Electronic Commerce	450
3.33	Marken-Controlling im Electronic Commerce	451
4.	**Implikationen für die Markenführung im Electronic Commerce**	**451**
4.1	Implikationen für das strategische Markenmanagement	451
4.11	Festlegung der Markenleistungen	451
4.12	Festlegung der Markenarchitektur	453
4.2	Implikationen für das operative Markenmanagement	457
4.21	Intra-mediale und inter-mediale Markenintegration	457
4.22	Internetbasierte und klassische Maßnahmen der Markenkommunikation	458
4.3	Implikationen für das Marken-Controlling	460
5.	**Zusammenfassung**	**462**

Tabelle 1: Markenbegriffe im Internet-Kontext

Begriff	Autor(en)	Definition/Beschreibung
„Online-Marke“	Pätzmann 2001, S. 5	„Online-Marken existieren nur im Netz“ (als Beispiel werden angeführt: Amazon, eBay und Yahoo)
„Internet-Marke“	Baumgarth 2004, S. 332	„Internet-Marken“ werden implizit definiert als: alle Marken, die das Medium Internet in irgendeiner Form nutzen.
„E-brand“	Specht 2001, S. 258 f.	Als „E-Brands“ bezeichnet Specht solche Marken (Leistungsangebote), die für das Internet geschaffen wurden und im Internet gepflegt werden. Betroffen ist hierbei der gesamte Marketing-Mix. Überdies stellt die Präsenz im Internet den Kern aller Markenaktivitäten dar.
	Baumgarth 2004, S. 334	„Bei E-Brands“ handelt es sich um Marken, die überwiegend im Internet aufgebaut wurden.
„Digitale Marke“	Eckert 2004, S. 88	„Eine digitale Marke ist ein Zeichen, welches zur Kenntlichmachung eines digitalen Meinungsgegenstandes dient.“

GABLER GRAFIK

Hinsichtlich der Verwendung und Abgrenzung des Begriffs „Online-Marke“ von Pätzmann ist zunächst zu konstatieren, dass diese nicht trennscharf ist (Pätzmann 2001 S. 5). Es ist nicht eindeutig abzugrenzen, wann eine Marke *„nur im Netz“*, womit augenscheinlich das Internet gemeint ist, „existiert“ und was genau unter dem Terminus „existieren“ zu subsumieren ist. Unklar ist hier, ob beispielsweise die Marke Amazon tatsächlich *„nur im Netz“* existiert, wenn die Auslieferung der mit einem markierten Karton verpackten Produkte in der „realen Welt“ vollzogen wird. Dieses Problem kann auch durch einen Zusatz wie „reine“ oder „pure“ „Online-Marken“ (Eckert 2004, S. 86) nicht gelöst werden, da auch diese Abgrenzung nur schwer möglich ist. So wird insbesondere in der Zukunft eine Trennung von ausschließlich im Internet aktiven und im Internet explizit nicht aktiven Marken immer weniger möglich sein (Manschwetus/Rumler 2002, S. 229; Eckert 2004, S. 86). Entsprechend kann festgehalten werden, dass es immer weniger Marken gibt, die das Internet konsequent *nicht* nutzen und andererseits aber auch nur sehr wenige „Online-Marken“ keine Ressourcen in der „realen Welt“ in Anspruch nehmen.

Eine weitere gängige Bezeichnung für „Online-Marken“ ist der Terminus „Internet-Marken“. Baumgarth subsumiert unter der Bezeichnung „Internet-Marken“ zwei Formen von im Internet aktiven Marken, ohne hierbei jedoch den Begriff der „Internet-Marke“

präzise zu definieren (Baumgarth 2004, S. 332). Implizit versteht er „Internet-Marken" als solche Marken, die das Medium Internet verwenden, heutzutage also nahezu **alle** Marken. Die erste Form von „Internet-Marken" bezeichnet er als „reale-Marken", die das Internet in verschiedenen Intensitätsgraden nutzen. Hierbei verändert die Intensität der Internetnutzung nicht die Bezeichnung als „Internet-Marke". Diese Bezeichnung gilt sowohl für eine geringe als auch für eine hohe Nutzungsintensität. Eine „reale Marke", welche das Medium Internet lediglich zu Kommunikationszwecken verwendet, ist demzufolge eine „Internet-Marke" mit einer geringen Nutzungsintensität. Auf einen allgemeinen Medienkontext übertragen würde dies bedeuten, dass eine Marke, die das Medium „Radio" zu Kommunikationszwecken verwendet, zu einer „Radio-Marke" wird.

Die zweite Form von „Internet-Marken" bezeichnet Baumgarth als „e-brands" und definiert diese als *„Marken, die überwiegend im Internet aufgebaut wurden"* (Baumgarth 2004, S. 334). Zunächst erscheint die Bezeichnung einer „Internet-Marke" als „e-brand" pleonastisch und insbesondere angesichts der auch im allgemeinen Sprachgebrauch häufig inhaltsgleichen Verwendung der Bezeichnungen „Internet" und „E" keine Klarheit schaffen zu können. Darüber hinaus muss bezüglich der Beschreibung des Terminus „e-brand" angemerkt werden, dass diese durch den Einschub *„überwiegend"* einen großen Ermessungsspielraum bestehen lässt. Demgegenüber bietet der Aspekt des ursprünglichen Aufbaus (der Herkunft) einer Marke einen besseren Hinweis zur Begriffsdefinition. So stellt die **„Markenherkunft"** ein wichtiges Merkmal dar, welches zur Generierung einer Klassifizierung herangezogen werden sollte. Dieses Merkmal ist bedeutend, da eine Marke eng mit ihrer Historie verbunden ist und *„im Kontext ihres Ursprunges wahrgenommen und interpretiert wird"* (Burmann/Blinda/Nitschke 2003, S. 18).

Die Bedeutung dieses Merkmals wird auch durch den ersten Teil der Beschreibung von „e-brands" durch Specht bestätigt. Dieser erachtet die ursprüngliche Bestimmung einer Marke als ein wichtiges Kriterium ihrer Einordnung (Specht 2001, S. 258 f.). Darüber hinaus sieht Specht für die Klassifizierung als reine „e-brand" eine hohe Bedeutung des Internet für den gesamten Marketing-Mix und die Fokussierung aller Markenaktivitäten auf das Internet vor. Auf die Definition der Marke als ein Nutzenbündel mit spezifischen, differenzierenden Merkmalen zurückgreifend, muss hierbei zunächst berücksichtigt werden, dass das Nutzenversprechen einer Marke das zentrale Element aller Markenführungsaktivitäten darstellt. Eine Fokussierung *aller* Markenführungsaktivitäten auf das Internet ist daher lediglich im Zusammenhang mit einem internetspezifischen Nutzenversprechen denkbar. Da das Nutzenversprechen einer Marke wiederum auf den spezifischen Kompetenzen der Marke basieren muss, um nachhaltig differenzierend zu sein (Burmann/Maloney 2004, S. 3), ist darüber hinaus eine internetspezifische Markenkompetenz für die Fokussierung aller Markenaktivitäten auf das Internet erforderlich. Der Begriff der „Markenkompetenz" meint hierbei die *„spezifischen organisationalen Fähigkeiten eines Unternehmens zur marktgerechten Kombination von Ressourcen"* (Burmann/Blinda/Nitschke 2003, S. 20). Eine Marke kann in der „virtuellen Welt" nur bestehen, wenn sie internetspezifische Kompetenzen aufweist. Es lässt sich hieraus die Anforderung ableiten, dass als zweites Merkmal die **„Markenkompetenz"** zur Generierung eines Begriffsverständnisses und einer Klassifizierung zu berücksichtigen ist.

Unter besonderer Berücksichtigung des Objektes der Markierung verwendet Eckert den Begriff der „digitalen Marke“ und definiert diese als *„Zeichen, welches zur Kenntlichmachung eines digitalen Meinungsgegenstandes dient“* (Eckert 2004, S. 88). Der Zusatz „digital“ beschränkt hierbei den Geltungsbereich dieser Definition auf solche Marken, die eine im Binärcode darstellbare Leistung markieren (Eckert 2004, S. 28 und 88). Die Schwierigkeit dieses Begriffsverständnisses ergibt sich dadurch, dass Marken wie beispielsweise Amazon oder ebay, welche gemeinhin als durch das Internet entstanden angenommen werden, eine nicht vollständig digitalisierbare Leistung markieren und somit von dieser Definition nicht erfasst werden (Eckert 2004, S. 34). Darüber hinaus stellt eine Beschränkung auf „digitale Meinungsgegenstände“ einen schwer abgrenzbaren Geltungsbereich dar. Trotz dieser Einschränkung gibt jedoch auch dieses Begriffsverständnis durch den berechtigten Hinweis auf den Leistungsfokus einer Marke einen wichtigen Anhaltspunkt zur Ableitung eines dritten Merkmals. Dies ist das Merkmal der **„Markenleistung“**.

Hierbei gilt es zu beachten, dass nicht die Gesamtheit der markierten Leistungen, sondern der Kern der Markenleistung zu berücksichtigen ist. Der Kern bestimmt sich durch die „grundsätzliche Art der Markenleistungen“, also *„wie eine Marke für den Nachfrager nutzbar wird“* (Burmann/Blinda/Nitschke 2003, S. 21). Auf das Beispiel von Amazon übertragen, besteht die Markenleistung nicht in den angebotenen Produkten. Die Markenkernleistung von Amazon besteht in der Sammlung, Systematisierung und Aufbereitung von mehreren Millionen Produkten verschiedener Kategorien und in der kundenfreundlichen Darbietung und Verfügbarmachung dieser Produkte im Internet (Wirtz 2001b, S. 424 ff.). Diese Leistung ist in digitaler Form erhältlich.

Zusammenfassend ergeben sich drei Merkmale, die für ein Begriffsverständnis und eine darauf aufbauende Klassifizierung von Marken im Kontext des Electronic Commerce heranzuziehen sind: die **„Markenherkunft“**, die **„Markenkompetenz“** und die **„Markenleistung“**.

2.2 Klassifizierungen von Marken im Electronic Commerce

Klassifizierungen von Marken im Internet-Kontext versuchen, diese auf Basis eines oder mehrerer Merkmale hinsichtlich des Grades ihrer Internetnutzung einzuordnen. Betrachtet man diese Klassifizierungen, so kann festgestellt werden, dass sich alle Klassifikationen auf die drei obigen Merkmale „Markenherkunft“, „Markenkompetenz“ und „Markenleistung“ zurückführen lassen.

So nehmen beispielsweise Kernstock, Brockdorff und Schubiger eine Klassifizierung vor, welche primär das Merkmal der **„Markenherkunft“** verwendet (Kernstock/Brockdorff/Schubiger 2002, S. 584 ff.). Sie gehen dabei zunächst von so genannten *„On- und Offline-Performern“* aus. Also von Marken, die ihren Ursprung im „On- oder Offline-Bereich“ haben und dort stark sind. Darüber hinaus berücksichtigen sie „Potential Brands“. Dies sind keine Marken, sondern lediglich Produkte oder Dienstleistungen im

„On- oder Offline-Bereich". Schließlich führen sie den Begriff „Crossover Brands" ein. Eine Marke, bei welcher ein Ursprung nicht mehr erkennbar ist und die nachhaltig erfolgreich medien- und kanalübergreifend etabliert ist. Als hierfür beispielhaft werden von den Autoren die Marken AOL Time Warner, Sixt und e-Sixt, oder DER SPIEGEL und Spiegel-Online genannt.

In ähnlicher Weise stellt Kastenmüller eine Klassifizierung vor, bei welcher er, vergleichbar der „Crossover Brand", eine Konvergenz der Geltungsbereiche einer Marke vorsieht (Kastenmüller 2002 S. 597 ff.). Entsprechend nimmt er eine Unterteilung in „klassische"- und „dotcom-Marken" vor und bezeichnet die sich aus deren Annäherung ergebenden Marken als „Konvergenz-Marken". Den Prozess der Konvergenz bezieht er dabei auf zwei Ebenen. Die erste Ebene ist die der Anpassung und Erweiterung der Geschäftsmodelle hin zu einer medienübergreifenden Geschäftstätigkeit. Die zweite Ebene bezieht Kastenmüller auf die Nutzung aller zur Verfügung stehenden Medien im Rahmen der Markenkommunikation. Die Veränderungen auf beiden Ebenen müssen mit der Entwicklung von entsprechenden Prozesskompetenzen einhergehen, da sie ansonsten substanzlos und langfristig nicht erfolgreich sind (Birkhofer/Schögel 2002, S. 407 ff.; Bauer/Herrmann 2004). Es lässt sich bei der von Kastenmüller vorgenommenen Klassifizierung demzufolge das Merkmal der **„Markenkompetenz"** wiederfinden.

Schließlich stellt Eckert eine Klassifizierung vor, welche nicht auf der Ebene der Marken, sondern des zu markierenden Leistungsbündels ansetzt (Eckert 2004, S. 29 ff.). Das entscheidende Merkmal ist dabei der Digitalisierungsgrad der angebotenen Leistungen. Hierzu geht Eckert davon aus, dass ein Leistungsbündel grundsätzlich in „Primär-" und „Sekundärleistungen" zu unterteilen ist. Eine „Primärleistung" definiert er als den *„Teil des Leistungsbündels, der dem Nachfrager besonders wichtig ist"* (Eckert 2004, S. 29). Hinsichtlich der Unterteilung räumt Eckert ein, dass „Primär-" und „Sekundärleistungen" nicht allgemeingültig abzugrenzen sind, da die Nachfrager individuell entscheiden, welche Leistungsbestandteile sie als „primär" und welche sie als „sekundär" wahrnehmen. Entscheidend für die Klassifizierung eines Leistungsbündels ist letztlich, inwieweit Leistungsbestandteile in digitaler Form angeboten werden können. Den höchsten Digitalisierungsgrad erreichen demzufolge die Anbieter von solchen Leistungsbündeln, bei welchen sowohl die „Primär-" als auch die „Sekundärleistung" vollständig digitalisierbar ist. Als ein Beispiel führt Eckert Anbieter von im Internet downloadbarer Software an. Auf die oben identifizierten, konstitutiven Merkmale bezogen, ist bei der von Eckert vorgenommene Klassifizierung das Merkmal der **„Markenleistung"** entscheidend.

Betrachtet man die hier vorgestellten Klassifizierungen so fällt zunächst auf, dass zwei der drei Klassifizierungen von einer Annäherung einst klar getrennter „On-" und „Offline-Marken" ausgehen. Auch Eckert trägt diesem Tatbestand Rechnung, indem er einräumt, dass es schwierig sei, ein Beispiel für ein in keiner Weise digitalisierbares Leistungsbündel zu finden und dass inzwischen nahezu alle Marken in irgendeiner Form im Internet aktiv sind (Eckert 2004, S. 30 und 86). Es ist daher in Frage zu stellen, ob der Versuch, Marken dichotom in „On- und Offline-Marken" zu unterteilen sinnvoll und durchführbar ist (Wirtz 2001a, S. 477). Da eine solche Unterteilung auf Basis des gegenwärtigen Standes der Forschung nicht trennscharf vorgenommen werden kann, soll sie im Folgenden unterbleiben.

Entgegen einer dichotomen Unterteilung in „On- und Offline-Marken“ ist mit Blick auf die drei konstitutiven Merkmale davon auszugehen, dass die Identität einer Marke in unterschiedlichem Ausmaß durch das Medium Internet geprägt sein kann (Internetprägung der Markenidentität). Je stärker die Merkmale „Markenherkunft“, „Markenkompetenz“ und „Markenleistung“ auf das Medium Internet ausgerichtet sind, umso stärker ist die Identität der betrachteten Marke durch das Internet geprägt.

Hierbei erscheint das Vernachlässigen der übrigen drei Komponenten der Markenidentität (die Markenvision, die Markenwerte und die Markenpersönlichkeit; vgl. den Beitrag zur Grundkonzeption der identitätsorientierten Markenführung in diesem Buch) in diesem Zusammenhang zulässig, da diese im Wesentlichen unabhängig von den verwendeten Medien sind. Dies drückt sich unter anderem dadurch aus, dass die empirische Konsumentenverhaltensforschung bislang keine Ansatzpunkte für ihre Kaufverhaltensrelevanz im Electronic Commerce liefert. Die Kaufverhaltensrelevanz der drei hier identifizierten konstitutiven Merkmale des Grades der Internetprägung einer Markenidentität kann demgegenüber durch die Konsumentenverhaltensforschung belegt werden (vgl. Kapitel 2.3).

Abschließend kann festgehalten werden, dass die Notwendigkeit einer Differenzierung des Markenbegriffes nicht existiert, da ein *neues* Markenverständnis für den Electronic Commerce nicht erforderlich ist. Darüber hinaus ist auch eine Klassifizierung nur in begrenztem Ausmaß realisierbar, da eine trennscharfe Unterteilung von Marken gegenwärtig kaum möglich ist und überdies unzweckmäßig erscheint. Es ist jedoch möglich, den Grad der **„Internetprägung“** einer Markenidentität anhand der Merkmale „Markenherkunft“, „Markenkompetenz“ und „Markenleistung“ festzulegen.

2.3 Überprüfung der Klassifikationsmerkmale anhand der Konsumentenverhaltensforschung

Wie aktuelle empirische Untersuchungsergebnisse zum Konsumentenverhalten im Internet zeigen, sind die zur Festlegung des Grades der „Internetprägung“ einer Markenidentität herangezogenen Merkmale „Markenherkunft“, „Markenkompetenz“ und „Markenleistung“ für die **„Marktakzeptanz“** eines Electronic-Commerce-Angebots relevant. So spielt insbesondere die Markenherkunft für den Erfolg von Electronic-Commerce-Angeboten eine entscheidende Rolle. Eine Untersuchung von Brynjolffson und Smith belegt, dass Marken, die ihre Herkunft in der „realen Welt“ haben, in der Lage sind, ein Preispremium von bis zu neun Prozent gegenüber Marken, die ihre Herkunft in der „virtuellen Welt“ haben, zu erzielen (Brynjolffson/Smith 2000). Die Gründe sind darin zu suchen, dass in der „realen Welt“ etablierte Marken bereits über eine hohe Markenbekanntheit und einen Vertrauensvorsprung verfügen und diese beiden Merkmale den Vertrauensmangel gegenüber dem Medium Internet auszugleichen vermögen (Esch et al. 2001, S. 567).

Auch die Bedeutung der **„Markenkompetenz“** lässt sich anhand der Konsumentenverhaltensforschung belegen. So zeigt eine Untersuchung der Kundenfreundlichkeit von 47 Web-Auftritten namhafter deutscher Unternehmen, dass viele Anbieter die grundlegenden Anforderungen an einen Web-Auftritt nicht beherrschen. Die meisten Web-Auftritte der betrachteten Marken weisen hinsichtlich der für Nachfrager wichtigen Aspekte der Kundenkommunikation und Benutzerfreundlichkeit erhebliche Schwächen auf. Sie sind daher nicht in der Lage, die potenziellen Vorteile, die das Internet gegenüber anderen Kommunikations- und Absatzkanälen besitzt, zu nutzen (Englbrecht/Hippner/Wilde 2004a, S. 83 ff.) Die mangelhafte Umsetzung der Web-Auftritte der betrachteten Unternehmen kann auf das Fehlen organisationaler Prozessfähigkeiten zurückgeführt werden (Bauer/Herrmann 2004). Erst durch den Aufbau der für das Medium Internet und den Electronic Commerce relevanten Kompetenzen kann eine Marke Nachfrager binden und sich langfristig erfolgreich in der „virtuellen Welt“ etablieren.

Abbildung 1: **Internetprägung und Markterfolg eines Electronic-Commerce-Angebotes**

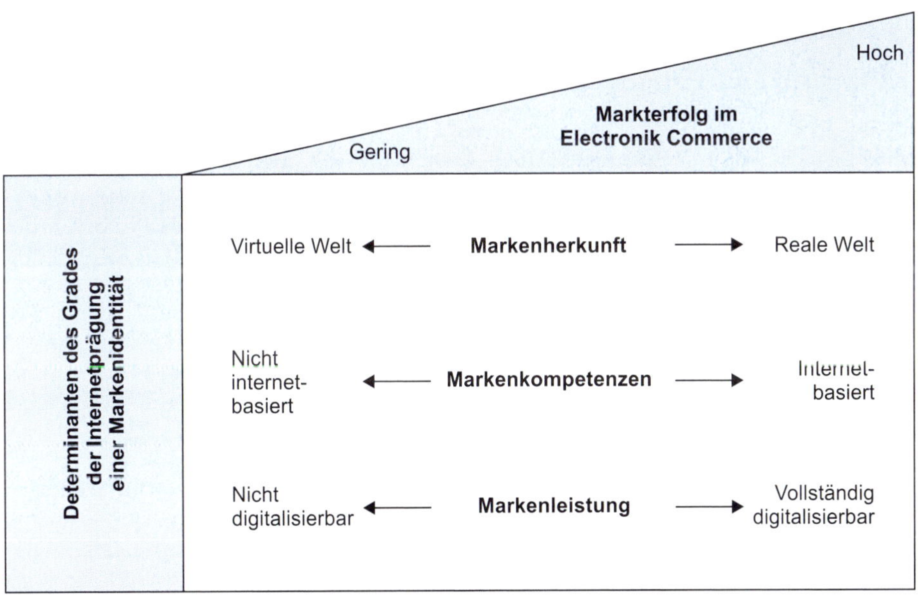

GABLER GRAFIK

Schließlich weisen auch die angebotenen **„Markenleistungen“** eine enge Beziehung zu der nachfragerseitigen Akzeptanz des Electronic-Commerce-Angebots auf. So sind bezüglich der Akzeptanz von im Internet angebotenen Produkten und Dienstleistungen deutliche Unterschiede zu erkennen. Während viele Nachfrager Güter mit geringem Digitalisierungsgrad beziehungsweise „E-Share“ (Bliemel/Fassott 2002, S. 676) wie etwa

Möbel und Bekleidung vor dem Kauf „real“ sehen oder anprobieren möchten, genügt beim Erwerb von Software oder Büchern häufig die Beschreibung des Angebotes (Bauer/ Sauer 2004, S. 39).

Die Relevanz der zur Beurteilung des Grades der „Internetprägung“ einer Markenidentität herangezogenen Merkmale lässt sich also durch die empirische Konsumentenverhaltensforschung untermauern. Hierbei ist es jedoch nicht möglich, den Grad der Internetprägung einer Markenidentität mit dem Markterfolg im Internet gleichzusetzen. So steigert einerseits das Vorhandensein von internetspezifischen Markenkompetenzen und für das Internet geeigneter Markenleistungen die Internetprägung einer Markenidentität und auch die Akzeptanz eines Electronic-Commerce-Angebotes. Andererseits verhält es sich jedoch mit der Markenherkunft genau umgekehrt. Bezüglich des Merkmals der Markenherkunft ist der Ursprung einer Marke in der „realen Welt“ für die Akzeptanz des Angebotes vorteilhaft, wohingegen dieser jedoch den Grad der „Internetprägung“ senkt (vgl. Abbildung 1).

3. Stellenwert und Herausforderungen der Markenführung im Electronic Commerce

Im Mittelpunkt der folgenden Betrachtungen steht die Relevanz der Marke für das Informations- und Kaufverhalten im Electronic Commerce, also der durch Marken wahrnehmbare Zusatznutzen für den Internetnutzer. Den Ausgangspunkt der weiteren Betrachtung bilden daher die nutzenstiftenden Funktionen, die eine Marke aus Sicht der Internetnutzer im Electronic Commerce erfüllen kann.

3.1 Nutzerbezogene Bedeutung und Funktionen der Marke im Electronic Commerce

Aus der Perspektive der Internetnutzer kommt Marken im Kontext des Electronic Commerce neben einer Orientierungsfunktion insbesondere eine Risikoreduktionsfunktion zu (Klein-Bölting/Busch 2001, S. 148 ff.).

In ihrer Eigenschaft als **Orientierungshilfen** entfalten Marken ihre nutzenstiftende Wirkung für Internetnutzer, indem sie das Auffinden eines geeigneten Angebotes im Electronic Commerce durch die Reduktion von Suchkosten erleichtern. So ist als Folge der Aufhebung räumlicher beziehungsweise geografischer Einkaufsrestriktionen im Internet die Anzahl möglicher Alternativen, die zur Befriedigung eines spezifischen Kundenbedürfnisses in Frage kommen, in der Regel wesentlich stärker ausgeprägt als dies in traditionellen Marktumgebungen der Fall ist (Meffert 2000, S. 2).

Angesichts der kaum überschaubaren Angebotsvielfalt im Internet werden die Nutzer vor besondere Probleme bei der Informationsselektion, -verarbeitung und -speicherung gestellt. Vollständige Informationen über die Eignung der alternativen Electronic Commerce-Angebote zur individuellen Bedürfnisbefriedigung sind in der Regel nur zu unvertretbar hohen Suchkosten erhältlich. Ward und Lee weisen in diesem Zusammenhang empirisch nach, dass unerfahrene Internetnutzer aufgrund der im Vergleich zu erfahreneren Nutzern höheren Kosten eigener Informationsaktivitäten signifikant häufiger auf Marken als Informationssubstitute bei ihrer Navigation im Internet zurückgreifen. Der Orientierungsnutzen von Marken im Internet wird demnach vor allem durch nutzerspezifische Eigenschaften, wie die Interneterfahrung und die damit in Verbindung stehenden Kosten eigener Informationsaktivitäten im Internet, bestimmt (Ward/Lee 2000, S. 14 f.). Der Orientierungsnutzen von Marken wird auch durch Preisagenturen und Suchdienste im Internet nicht geschmälert, weil auch hier Markenpräferenzen eine Vorselektion und damit eine erleichterte und verbesserte Suche ermöglichen.

Über die auf effektiverer und effizienterer Informationsverarbeitung basierende Orientierungsfunktion hinaus bieten Marken im Electronic Commerce eine **Risikoreduktionsfunktion** für die Nachfrager. Die besondere Bedeutung der risikoreduzierenden Wirkung von Marken ergibt sich aus dem höheren wahrgenommenen Risiko beim Internet-Shopping gegenüber stationären Einkaufssituationen (Tan 1999, S. 165 ff.). Dies ist auf verschiedene medieninduzierte Ursachen zurückzuführen:

- Eine Überprüfung physischer Produkteigenschaften beziehungsweise die Beurteilung der Potenzialfaktoren des Anbieters bei Dienstleistungen vor dem Kauf sind im Electronic Commerce in der Regel nicht möglich (Van den Poel/Leunis 1999, S. 250).
- Ebenso wie Katalogbestellungen zeichnen sich auch Kaufsituationen im Internet durch fehlenden persönlichen Kontakt zwischen Anbieter und Nachfrager aus. Daher ist von einer erhöhten nachfragerseitigen Risikowahrnehmung auszugehen (Jasper/Ouellete 1994, S. 23).
- Bei Transaktionen, die eine physische Auslieferung des Produktes erfordern, erhöht sich das wahrgenommene Risiko, zum Beispiel durch mögliche Transportschäden sowie unpünktliche oder falsche Lieferungen.
- Neben psychischen, physischen, sozialen, funktionalen und finanziellen Risiken ergeben sich durch die Notwendigkeit des Datenaustauschs zwischen den Transaktionspartnern im Electronic Commerce zusätzlich informationelle Risiken (Dudenhöffer 2000, S. 13; Kuhlen 2000, S. 220). Diese Risiken lassen sich zum einen in Gefahren des Datenmissbrauchs durch Dritte aufgrund mangelnder Sicherheit bei der Datenübertragung und zum anderen in Gefahren hinsichtlich der missbräuchlichen Verwendung der übermittelten Daten durch den Transaktionspartner selbst unterteilen (Hoffman/Novak/Peralta 1998, S. 2).

Diese medienbedingten Risikotreiber im Electronic Commerce korrespondieren eng mit den am häufigsten genannten Barrieren des Online-Einkaufs aus Konsumentensicht (vgl. Abbildung 2).

Abbildung 2: Barrieren des Online-Einkaufs

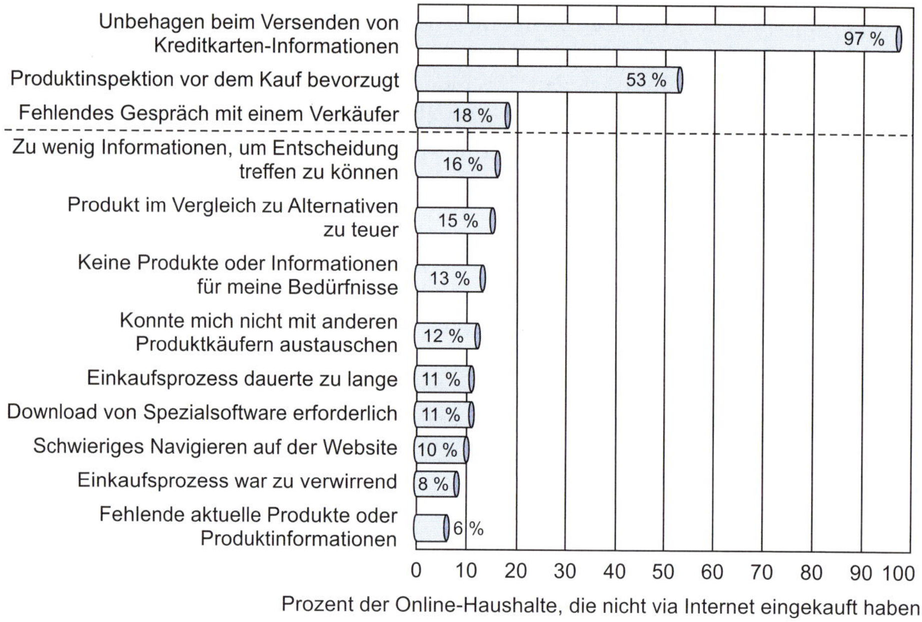

GABLER GRAFIK

Quelle: Ernest & Young 1999, S. 11

Das Potenzial von Marken zur Reduktion des wahrgenommenen Risikos und damit zur Überwindung von Einkaufsbarrieren im Electronic Commerce konnte bereits empirisch nachgewiesen werden. Van den Poel und Leunis stellen in einer Befragung zum Kauf eines kleinen Radiogerätes sowie eines hochwertigen Fernsehgerätes fest, dass die generelle Akzeptanz des Internet als Transaktionsmedium durch das Vorhandensein einer etablierten Marke in Verbindung mit weiteren risikoreduzierenden Maßnahmen gesteigert wird (Van den Poel/Leunis 1999, S. 253 f.). Ebenso belegt Tan in einer Studie mit 179 Teilnehmern die risikoreduzierende Wirkung des Markenimages und der Anbieterreputation im Electronic Commerce, die insbesondere für Produktkategorien mit hohem wahrgenommenem Risiko stark ausgeprägt ist (Tan 1999, S. 171 ff.).

Das Konstrukt des wahrgenommenen Vertrauens der Nachfrager steht in engem Zusammenhang zu der risikoreduzierenden Wirkung einer Marke. Unter **Vertrauen** ist dabei die Einstellung des Vertrauensgebers zu verstehen, dass der Vertrauensempfänger – in diesem Fall der Absender der Markenbotschaft – über die Bereitschaft und Fähigkeit verfügt, die an ihn gerichteten positiven Erwartungen zu erfüllen (Bouncken 2000, S. 5). Ob hierbei das vom Nachfrager wahrgenommene Risiko eine Konsequenz, eine Determinante oder ein Antagonismus von Vertrauens darstellt, ist umstritten (Bauer et al. 2004b, S. 7, Bauer/Neumann/Jöst 2004, S. 262). Diese Fragestellung kann jedoch im Folgenden vernachlässigt werden, weil die Maßnahmen zum Aufbau von Vertrauen mit denen zur Reduktion des wahrgenommenen Risikos weitestgehend deckungsgleich sind. Für diese Arbeit soll daher davon ausgegangen werden, dass das wahrgenommene Risiko eine Konsequenz des Vertrauens gegenüber einer Marke ist. Die Relevanz dieser Vertrauensfunktion einer Marke wird nicht zuletzt dadurch untermauert, dass Vertrauensmangel vielfach als Hauptursache für die bislang nicht ausgeschöpften Wachstumspotenziale im Electronic Commerce identifiziert wird (Reichheld/Schefter 2000; Lee/Turban 2001).

Die nutzenstiftende Wirkung der Marke ergibt sich dadurch, dass der Internetnutzer aufgrund seines Vertrauens in die Marke diejenigen Kosten einsparen kann, die ansonsten zur Reduzierung seines Risikos anfallen würden (Plötner 1995, S. 11 f.). Im Kontext des Electronic Commerce ist dabei unter anderem an Kosten durch den Abschluss von Rücktritts- oder Transportversicherungen, durch zusätzliche telefonische oder persönliche Kontaktaufnahme mit dem Anbieter oder durch die Einholung ausführlicher Informationen über die Sicherheits- und Datenschutzstandards des Anbieters zu denken. Damit wird das Vertrauen der Nachfrager in die Marke des Anbieters zu einem entscheidenden Wettbewerbsfaktor im Electronic Commerce (Kuhlen 2000, S. 221).

Eine von Ernest & Young durchgeführte Untersuchung zum **Einkaufsverhalten** im Internet unterstreicht in diesem Zusammenhang den Stellenwert von Marken für Kauf- und Auswahlentscheidungen. So betonen 82 Prozent der Befragten, dass eine bekannte Produktmarke und 79 Prozent, dass eine bekannte Anbietermarke für ihre Kaufentscheidung im Internet wichtig oder sehr wichtig ist (Ernest & Young 1999, S. 11). In ähnlicher Weise zeigt ein von Bauer, Neumann und Jöst durchgeführtes Online-Experiment, dass sich das einem Online-Shop entgegengebrachte Vertrauen positiv durch den Einsatz von Vertrauensintermediären beeinflussen lässt. Es konnte ferner belegt werden, dass der Grad der Vertrauensübertragung mit der Markenstärke des vertrauensgebenden Intermediäres positiv korreliert (Bauer/Neumann/Jöst 2004, S. 267 ff.). Tabelle 2 gibt einen zusammenfassenden Überblick der empirischen Studien zur nutzerbezogenen Kaufverhaltensrelevanz von Marken im Electronic Commerce.

Während bislang die Relevanz von Marken für Kauf- und Auswahlentscheidungen im Electronic Commerce aufgrund ihrer nutzenstiftenden Orientierungs- und Risikoreduktionswirkungen dargestellt wurde, soll im Folgenden die Differenzierungsfunktion der Marke im Electronic Commerce analysiert werden.

Tabelle 2: Empirische Untersuchungen zur Relevanz von Marken im Electronic Commerce

Autoren	Untersuchungsgegenstand	Empirische Basis/ Datenauswertung	Zentrale Ergebnisse
Ernest & Young (1999)	■ Analyse des Einkaufsverhaltens beim Online Shopping	■ Telefoninterviews von Nutzern ■ n = 1.362	■ 82 Prozent der Befragten erklären, dass die Produktmarke beim Einkauf via Internet wichtig oder sehr wichtig ist. ■ 79 Prozent der Befragten erklären, dass die Anbietermarke beim Einkauf via Internet wichtig oder sehr wichtig ist.
Tan (1999)	■ Konsumentenseitige Risikowahrnehmung beim Internet-Shopping und Effektivität von Risikoreduktionsstrategien	■ Business Undergraduates der Nat. University of Singapore ■ n = 179 ■ Conjoint-Analyse	■ Konsumenten nehmen beim Internet-Shopping ein höheres Risiko als beim stationären Einkauf wahr. ■ Risikoaverse Konsumenten kaufen signifikant weniger oft im Internet ein. ■ Der Referenzgruppenansatz ist insgesamt die bevorzugte Risikoreduktionsstrategie, gefolgt von der Anbieterreputation, dem Markenimage und Gewährleistungen. Bei Produkten mit hohem wahrgenommenen Risiko ist das Markenimage die wichtigste Risikoreduktionsstrategie.
Boston Consulting Group (2000)	■ Markenvorteile von Multichannel- gegenüber reinen Electronic-Commerce-Anbietern	■ Analyse des Nutzungsverhaltens beim Online-Shopping	■ 61 Prozent der Nutzer von Multichannel-Anbietern und 46 Prozent der Nutzer von reinen Electronic-Commerce-Anbietern gelangen durch direkte Eingabe der URL – also des Markennamens – auf die Website.
Davis/Buchanan-Oliver/Brodie (2000)	■ Rolle der Marke in Electronic-Commerce-Umgebungen	■ Fokus-Gruppen-Interviews mit 26 Konsumenten	■ Marken dienen als Ausgangspunkt zur Bildung von Vertrauensbeziehungen zwischen Konsumenten und Online-Anbietern im Electronic Commerce.
Degeratu/Rangaswamy/Wu (2000)	■ Einfluss von Markennamen auf die Kaufentscheidung in Online- und traditionellen Supermärkten	■ Peapod Panel: n = 300 ■ IRI Panel: n = 1.039 ■ Zweistufiges Schätzmodell (1) binär/(2) multinomial	■ Der Einfluss der Marke auf Kaufentscheidungen hängt vom Ausmaß der verfügbaren Informationen in den jeweiligen Einkaufsumgebungen ab. ■ In den jeweiligen Einkaufsumgebungen herrschen unterschiedliche Informationsverhältnisse für verschiedene Produktkategorien. Der Einfluss der Marke auf Kaufentscheidungen variiert daher mit der betrachteten Produktkategorie.
Van den Poel/Leunis (2000	■ Bedeutung risikoreduzierender Elemente in unterschiedlichen Einkaufsumgebungen	■ E-Mail-Befragung registrierter Nutzer ■ n = 93 ■ ANOVA	■ Die Akzeptanz des Internets als Transaktionsmedium wird durch das Vorhandensein risikoreduzierender Elemente (Geld-zurück-Garantie, bekannte Marke, Preisreduktion) gesteigert.

Ward/Lee (2000)	■ Marken als Informations-substitute bei Kauf- und Aus-wahlentschei-dungen im Elec-tronic Commerce	■ 8th GVU's WWW User Survey (October 1997) ■ Branding Sample: n = 1.987 ■ Kreuztabellierung/ logistische Regression	■ Erfahrenere Internetnutzer sind schneller und erfolgreicher bei der Informations-suche im Electronic Commerce. ■ Mit zunehmender Interneterfahrung der Nutzer sinkt der Rückgriff auf Marken als Informationssubstitute.
Bongartz (2002)	■ Erfolgswirkungen des internetbezo-genen Marken-führungsverhal-tens	■ Multivariate Analyse-methoden ■ n = 225	■ Es existieren direkte Effekte der internet-bezogenen Markengestaltung auf den Markenbekanntheits-, Markenimage- und Markenbindungserfolg. Ein zentraler Erfolgsfaktor ist die medienübergreifende Abstimmung der Markenaktivitäten.
Bauer/Neu-mann/Jöst (2004)	■ Einfluss des Einsatzes von Vertrauensinter-mediären auf das Vertrauen von Nachfragern	■ Online-Experiment ■ n = 862	■ Der Einsatz von Vertrauensintermediären wirkt sich positiv auf das Vertrauen in den Anbieter eines Online-Shops aus. ■ Das Ausmaß der Vertrauensübertragung korreliert positiv mit der Markenstärke des Vertrauensintermediärs.

GABLER GRAFIK

3.2 Wettbewerbsbezogene Bedeutung und Funktionen der Marke

Die **Differenzierungsfunktion** der Marke basiert auf einem Vergleich zu Wettbewerbsangeboten. Die wachsende Bedeutung der Differenzierungsfunktion von Marken ist zum einen auf die steigende Anzahl konkurrierender Angebote im Electronic Commerce und zum anderen auf die zunehmende Austauschbarkeit dieser Angebote im Hinblick auf technische und funktionale Eigenschaften zurückzuführen. Die Gründe hierfür sind unter anderem in der Verwendung von standardisierten Softwarelösungen sowie im Rückgriff auf zum Teil identische Content-Provider zu sehen (Meffert 2000, S. 2 f.). Zudem können innovative Zusatzfunktionen von Wettbewerbern innerhalb kürzester Zeit imitiert werden und stellen somit keinen dauerhaften Vorteil für den Innovator dar (Reimerdes 2000, S. 33). Gerade bei standardisierten Electronic Commerce-Angeboten kann die Marke oft einen symbolischen Zusatznutzen vermitteln, durch den sie sich von konkurrierenden Angeboten unterscheidet.

So ermöglicht das Internet durch die Einbindung von Datenbankanwendungen und Feedbackmöglichkeiten den effizienten Aufbau einer interaktiven und individualisierten Kommunikation mit potenziellen Nachfragern (Fritz 2001, S. 142). Die Nachfrageransprache ist somit nicht mehr auf eine eindimensionalen Kommunikation mit einer anonymen Kundenmasse reduziert, sondern kann die Form eines personalisierten Dialoges mit potenziellen Nachfragern annehmen (Walter 2000, S. 67 f.). Derartige Direktkommunikationsmaßnahmen mit personalisierter Kundenansprache werden in der Zukunft stark an Bedeutung gewinnen (Holtrop/Döpfner/Wirtz 2003, S. 127). So wird argumentiert, dass internetbasierte Direktkommunikationsmaßnahmen in der Lage sind, ein beinahe „persönliches" Verhältnis zwischen Nachfrager und Marke zu evozieren, durch welches eine höhere Kundenbindung im Internet erreicht werden kann (Lihotzky 2003, S. 218 f.). Ob eine Personalisierung der Nachfrageransprache tatsächlich das Vertrauen in die Marke stärkt, ist indes durchaus umstritten (Licharz 2002, S. 233 ff.).

Mit dieser Entwicklung einhergehend ist eine zunehmende Individualisierung der Nachfrager-Marke-Beziehung (Meyer/Pfeiffer 2002, S. 563), welche ihrerseits sehr spezifische Anforderungen an das Marken-Controlling stellt. Dies gilt umso mehr, als dass das Internet nicht nur die Nachfrageransprache seitens des markenführenden Unternehmens erleichtert, sondern auch die Kommunikation unter den Nachfragern etwa in Form von Online Brand Communities (Meyer/Pfeiffer 2002, S. 564 ff.) erheblich effizienter werden lässt. Die Markenwahrnehmung einzelner Nachfrager kann dadurch wesentlich durch andere Nachfrager geprägt werden (Lederer/Hill 2001). Angesichts dieser Entwicklung gewinnt das Management der **horizontalen Markenkommunikation**, also der Kommunikation zwischen den Nachfragern einer Marke, immer mehr an Bedeutung (Meyer/Pfeiffer 2002, S. 573 ff.).

3.3 Anforderungen an den Markenmanagementprozess im Electronic Commerce

3.31 Strategisches Markenmanagement im Electronic Commerce

Die Analyse der Bedeutung und Funktionen von Marken im Electronic Commerce hat gezeigt, dass mit

- der Etablierung der Marke als Orientierungsanker im Internet,
- der Überwindung der aus Nutzersicht wahrgenommenen Vertrauensdefizite sowie
- der Besetzung von Alleinstellungsmerkmalen aufgrund der zunehmenden Anzahl und Homogenisierung der Angebote im Wettbewerb

drei zentrale Anforderungen an die Markenführung im Electronic Commerce existieren.

Vor diesem Hintergrund erlangt die Etablierung einer starken **Markenidentität** einen besonderen Stellenwert für die Markenführung im Electronic Commerce (vgl. in diesem Zusammenhang auch den Beitrag zum theoretischen Grundkonzept der identitätsorientierten Markenführung in diesem Buch). Eine ausgeprägte Markenidentität ist die Grundlage der wahrgenommenen Einzigartigkeit und Unverwechselbarkeit einer Marke und bildet die Voraussetzung für das Entstehen und die Festigung des Vertrauens der Internetnutzer in die Marke. Die identitätsorientierte Markenführung bietet somit einen Erfolg versprechenden Ansatz zur Profilierung eines Anbieters im Electronic Commerce.

Die identitätsorientierte Markenführung strebt die Erschaffung einer in ihrem Gesamtauftritt konsistenten Markenidentität durch die Koordination aller mit der Marke in Verbindung stehenden Entscheidungen an (Meffert/Burmann 2002, S. 30). Dieses Bestreben erfordert eine die Markenidentität in den Mittelpunkt stellende, holistische Herangehensweise. Der identitätsorientierte Markenmanagementprozess versucht, diesen Anforderungen gerecht zu werden (vgl. Abbildung 3). Besondere Herausforderungen dieses Prozesses im Electronic Commerce sind dabei zum einen in der inhaltlichen Erweiterung der einzelnen Prozessschritte um internetspezifische Aspekte und zum anderen in der Berücksichtigung medienübergreifender Interdependenzen zu sehen.

Abbildung 3: Der identitätsorientierte Markenmanagementprozess

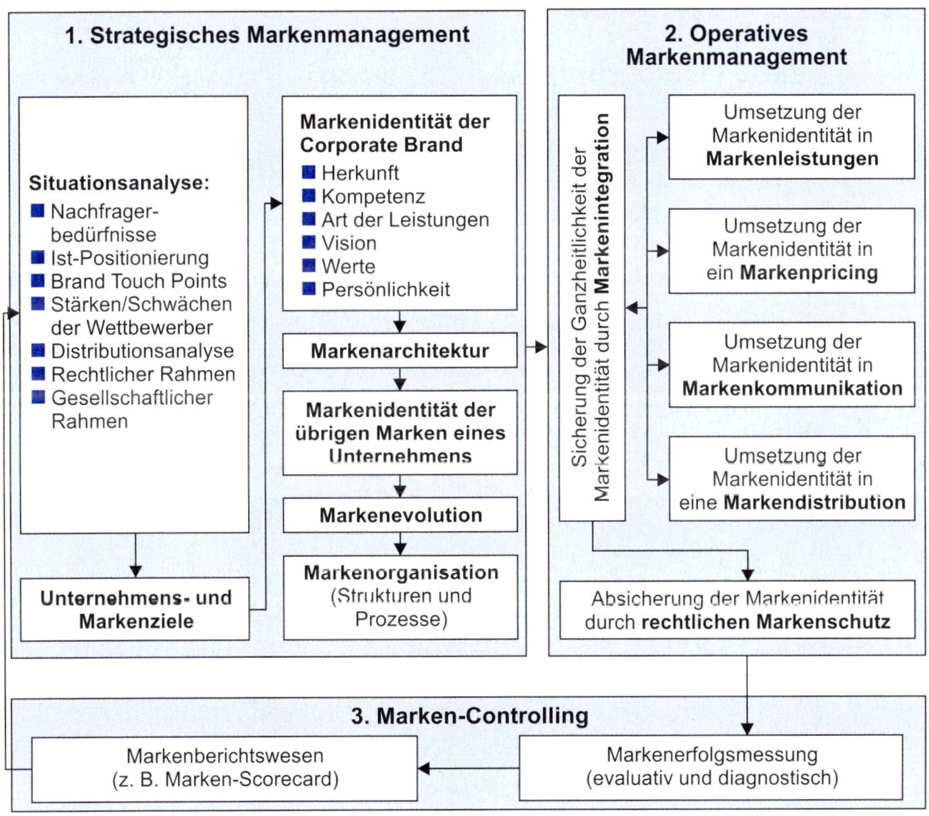

GABLER GRAFIK

Quelle: Burmann/Blinda/Nitschke 2003, S. 10

Das strategische Markenmanagement sieht zunächst die Festlegung aller Entscheidungen über die wesentliche Ausrichtung der Marke beziehungsweise des Markenportfolios eines Unternehmens vor. Die Definition der Markenidentität bildet dabei den Kern des strategischen Markenmanagements. Aufbauend auf den organisationalen Fähigkeiten des markenführenden Unternehmens sind hierbei insbesondere die Formulierung der Markenkernleistung und damit verbunden die Identifikation eines **schwer-imitierbaren, internetspezifischen Kundennutzens** für das Markenmanagement im Electronic Commerce elementar (Bliemel/Eggert 2002, S. 631). So ist im Kontext des Electronic Commerce der Aufdeckung von solchen Problemlösungsideen besondere Beachtung zu widmen, die sowohl gegenüber internetbasierten (intra-mediale Konkurrenz) als auch gegenüber nicht-internetbasierten Angeboten (extra-mediale Konkurrenz) eine dominierende Stellung in der Wahrnehmung der Nutzer einnehmen und somit über ein hohes Differenzierungspotenzial im Wettbewerb verfügen.

3.32 Operatives Markenmanagement im Electronic Commerce

Im Rahmen des operativen Markenmanagements gilt es, einen integrierten und auf die Markenidentität abgestimmten Einsatz aller Marketinginstrumente sicherzustellen. Hierbei sind in einem ersten Schritt die identitätsbestimmenden, **internetspezifischen Gestaltungselemente** einer Marke im Electronic Commerce herauszuarbeiten. Hier ist insbesondere die durch das Internet gegebene Möglichkeit der Personalisierung aller Marketing-Mix Aktivitäten zu prüfen. Neben diesen medienspezifischen Besonderheiten bei der Gestaltung des Markenauftritts ergeben sich in Abhängigkeit vom parallelen Einsatz von On- und Offline-Medien besondere Anforderungen hinsichtlich der Abstimmung aller Maßnahmen auf die Markenidentität. Neben der **intra-medialen Markenintegration** gilt es zusätzlich, eine **inter-mediale Integration** aller markenpolitischen Maßnahmen zu gewährleisten (Esch/Hardiman/Langner 2000, S. 12).

Der **Markenkommunikation** kommt hierbei die Aufgabe zu, den internetspezifischen Markennutzen nach innen und außen zu vermitteln. So setzt die Erfüllung der Orientierungsfunktion durch die Marke nicht zuletzt eine ausreichende Markenbekanntheit und Verankerung der Markenbotschaft bei den anvisierten Zielgruppen des Electronic Commerce-Angebotes voraus. Neben dem Einsatz klassischer Maßnahmen der Markenkommunikation sind hierbei in Abhängigkeit von den Inhalten und Zielgruppen vor allem internetbasierte Aktivitäten zu berücksichtigen (Mohn 2000, S. 45 f.; Schnetkamp/Kenning 2000, S. 27). Diesbezüglich stellt besonders die individualisierte Nachfrageransprache eine bedeutende Form der Markenkommunikation im Bereich des Electronic Commerce dar. Durch die Möglichkeit der **Individualisierung** lässt sich die nutzerspezifische Relevanz der Markenleistungen noch eindeutiger herausstellen (Lihotzky 2003, S. 151). Letztendlich gilt jedoch auch für die Markenkommunikation im Electronic Commerce, dass diese nicht durch das verwendete Medium bestimmt werden sollte, sondern an der Markenidentität auszurichten ist (Kastenmüller 2002, S. 597).

3.33 Marken-Controlling im Electronic Commerce

Dem **Marken-Controlling** obliegt die Aufgabe der Sicherstellung von Rationalität und Ergebnisorientierung aller mit dem Markenmanagement verbundenen Entscheidungen (Meffert/Koers 2002, S. 407). Hierfür sind insbesondere die Entwicklungen im Unternehmensumfeld sowie entsprechende Frühaufklärungskennzahlen und -indikatoren zu analysieren (Kühn/Fasnacht 2001, S. 90 ff.). Der Beobachtung des marktlichen Umfeldes wird dabei im Bereich des Electronic Commerce eine besondere Bedeutung zuteil. So ist durch die horizontale Markenkommunikation zwischen den Nachfragern in Form von Chats oder Foren ein rascher Meinungsaustausch und in der Folge eine schnelle Meinungsbildung möglich (Meyer/Pfeiffer 2002, S. 573). Diese innovativen Möglichkeiten der schnellen Meinungsbildung führen zu einer erhöhten Volatilität der Kundenwünsche und Markenpräferenzen im Electronic Commerce. Darüber hinaus birgt das Medium Internet die Gefahr der schnellen, nicht kontrollierbaren Verbreitung von nicht markenidentitätskonformen Markenbotschaften (Meyer/Pfeiffer 2002, S. 567). Insgesamt ergeben sich somit für das Marken-Controlling durch die medienspezifischen Besonderheiten des Internet neue Anforderungen. Zu deren Lösung bieten internetbasierte Verfahren, wie beispielsweise die Auswertung von Logfiles, erweiterte Möglichkeiten, um zu schnelleren und präziseren Ergebnissen für die Anpassung markenpolitischer Aktivitäten zu gelangen.

4. Implikationen für die Markenführung im Electronic Commerce

4.1 Implikationen für das strategische Markenmanagement

4.11 Festlegung der Markenleistungen

Den Ausgangspunkt des Planungsprozesses des strategischen Markenmanagements bildet die Analyse der aktuell und potenziell relevanten Nachfragerbedürfnisse sowie der unternehmensinternen Kompetenzen. Grundlage der Identifikation relevanter internetspezifischer Nachfragerbedürfnisse ist hierbei die Synthese der Outside-in- und Inside-out-Perspektive. Hierbei dient die **Outside-in-Perspektive** dazu, latent vorhandene Kundenwünsche zu ergründen, wohingegen die **Inside-out-Perspektive** das Aufspuren kompetenzbasierter, innovativer Problemlösungsansätze innerhalb des Unternehmens ermöglicht (Tomczak/Roosdorp 1996, S. 27 ff.). Beide Perspektiven weisen im Kontext des Electronic Commerce eine besondere Relevanz auf. So ist einerseits das Aufspüren latent vorhandener Bedürfnisse aufgrund des hohen Grades an Interaktivität im Bereich des Electronic Commerce (Meyer/Pfeiffer 2002, S. 566 ff.) mit relativ geringerem Aufwand möglich. Andererseits ist auch die Inside-out-Perspektive im Kontext des Electronic Commerce von großer Bedeutung (vgl. Abbildung 1). Die identifizierten Nachfragerbedürfnisse müssen schließlich mit den vorhandenen (oder den zukünftig zur Verfügung stehenden) unternehmensinternen Kompetenzen in der Form vereinbar sein, dass diese auch glaubwürdig erfüllt werden können.

Letztlich soll die Verknüpfung beider Perspektiven zur Festlegung ebenso marktrelevanter wie nachhaltig erfolgreicher Markenleistungen führen, die vom Wettbewerb aufgrund des Einsatzes unternehmensspezifischer Kompetenzen nur schwer imitiert oder substituiert werden können. Im Zentrum der Markenkernleistung steht hierbei die **Formulierung eines internetspezifischen Kundennutzens** (Dayal/Landesberg/Zeisser 2000, S. 46 f.), welcher den gemeinsamen Bezugspunkt aller weiteren Schritte des Markenmanagements darstellt.

Im Kontext des Electronic Commerce lassen sich mit dem funktionalen, dem prozessualen und dem beziehungsorientierten Nutzen drei Dimensionen aufzeigen, die zur Definition der Markenleistung und des internetspezifischen Kundennutzens herangezogen werden können (Court et al. 1999, S. 13):

- **Funktionale Kundennutzenvorteile** einer Marke im Electronic Commerce kommen in überlegenen objektiv-technischen Leistungen der Marke zum Ausdruck. Hierzu zählen beispielsweise die generelle Funktionsfähigkeit und Sicherheit der markierten Leistungen im Electronic Commerce. Gerade für funktionale Nutzenbestandteile einer Marke, die im Electronic Commerce oftmals auf dem Einsatz innovativer Softwarelösungen beruhen, ist jedoch zu beobachten, dass diese in kürzester Zeit durch Konkurrenten imitiert werden. Das Potenzial für die Schaffung von Wettbewerbsvorteilen durch funktionale Nutzenversprechen der Marke ist im Electronic Commerce dementsprechend als gering einzustufen.
- **Prozessuale Kundennutzenvorteile** einer Marke im Electronic Commerce bestehen in einer einfacheren, schnelleren, günstigeren und angenehmeren Abwicklung von Transaktionen zwischen der Marke und ihren Nachfragern (Court et al. 1999, S. 7). Die besonderen Eigenschaften des Internet bieten hier neue Ansatzpunkte, um internetbasierte Marken gegenüber klassischen Marken mit überlegenen prozessualen Nutzenattributen zu versehen (Convenience-Vorteile). So kann beispielsweise die Annehmlichkeit von Einkäufen via Internet durch die räumliche und zeitliche Unabhängigkeit und Unmittelbarkeit des Mediums betont werden, da die Nutzer ihre Bedürfnisse von zu Hause aus rund um die Uhr befriedigen können, ohne Wartezeiten in Kauf nehmen zu müssen (Swinka 2000, S. 30).
- Demgegenüber besteht in der Formulierung und Implementierung eines **beziehungsorientierten Kundennutzenvorteils** der Marke das größte Potenzial zu einer Abgrenzung sowohl gegenüber konkurrierenden Angeboten im Electronic Commerce als auch gegenübert nicht-internetbasierten Marken. Dieser ist eine spezifische Ausprägungsform des symbolischen Nutzens einer Marke und als solches stark emotio-

nal geprägt. Vorteile aus Beziehungen können dabei in sozio-emotionale sowie instrumentelle Vorteile differenziert werden (Fournier 2001, S. 143). Das Internet bietet aufgrund der Interaktivität des Mediums und der Möglichkeit zur **Personalisierung von Angeboten** eine besondere Chance zur Schaffung instrumenteller Beziehungsvorteile. Diese ergeben sich zum Beispiel. durch Erleichterungen oder Vergünstigungen bei der Abwicklung von Transaktionen im Electronic Commerce, die sich erst aufgrund wiederholter Interaktionen zwischen Nutzer und Marke entfalten können. Beispielhaft sei an dieser Stelle die Bereitstellung von individuellen Buch- oder Musikempfehlungen durch den Anbieter Amazon genannt, die auf vergangenen Kontakten zwischen dem Markenanbieter und dem Nutzer beruhen. Derartige instrumentelle Nutzenvorteile münden in einer verbesserten Stabilität der Marken-Nachfrager-Beziehung und einer verstärkten Bindung des Nachfragers an die Marke. Beides reduziert die Volatilität der markeninduzierten Zahlungsströme und damit deren Risiko aus Sicht von Kapitalgebern. Letztlich steigt damit der Markenwert.

Ebenso ermöglichen Interaktivität und Personalisierungsoptionen die Schaffung sozio-emotionaler Vorteile, indem die Marke als aktiver Beziehungspartner auftritt und damit für Nachfrager **„quasi-soziale Kompetenz"** erlangt (Hamm 1997, S. 46; Kastenmüller 2001, S. 223 f.). Der auf einer informationstechnologischen Basis beruhende Aufbau personalisierter Beziehungen bietet dabei insbesondere gegenüber nicht-internetbasierten Marken aus anonymen Massenmärkten enorme Profilierungspotenziale. Gleichzeitig stellt die Etablierung von Beziehungsvorteilen einen wirksamen und schwer-imitierbaren Schutz gegenüber konkurrierenden Marken im Electronic Commerce dar, da ihr Aufbau wiederholte Interaktionen in der Vergangenheit voraussetzt.

4.12 Festlegung der Markenarchitektur

Die Eingangs dargestellten, orientierungserleichternden und risikoreduzierenden Wirkungen einer Marke werden wesentlich durch die Gestaltung der Markenarchitektur beeinflusst.

Den Ausgangspunkt für die Wahl der Markenarchitektur bei der Nutzung des Internet bildet die Frage, ob eine autonome oder eine fremdbestimmte Markenführung gewählt wird. Bei der **fremdbestimmten Markenführung** verzichten Unternehmen auf die eigenständige Führung einer Marke für ihre Aktivitäten im Electronic Commerce, indem sie ihre Angebote beispielsweise in Electronic Shopping-Malls oder Portale integrieren und sich im Wesentlichen den markenpolitischen Aktivitäten dieser Partner unterordnen. Auf diese Weise können die Wirkungen der Marke eines übergeordneten Partners genutzt werden, ohne Investitionen für den Aufbau einer eigenständigen Marke im Electronic Commerce in Kauf nehmen zu müssen. Demgegenüber stehen jedoch die fehlenden Einflussmöglichkeiten auf die markenpolitischen Aktivitäten sowie die Abhängigkeit vom ausgewählten Kooperationspartner. Der Verzicht auf die autonome Führung einer Marke im Electronic Commerce soll deswegen im Folgenden nicht weiter betrachtet werden.

Bei der **eigenständigen Markenführung** im Electronic Commerce wird der Entscheidungsspielraum hinsichtlich der Markenarchitektur durch die Verfügbarkeit einer etablierten Marke aus der „realen Welt" bestimmt. Während Electronic-Commerce-Anbieter mit fehlenden Aktivitäten in traditionellen Märkten gezwungen sind, eine eigenständige internetbasierte Marke aufzubauen, eröffnen sich für Unternehmen, die bereits über eine etablierte Marke verfügen, weitere markenstrategische Möglichkeiten. Diese lassen sich anhand des Integrationsgrades zwischen der bereits vorhandenen Marke und dem internetbasierten Markenauftritt systematisieren (Boston Consulting Group/Gruner + Jahr AG & Co. 2000, S. 26 f.; Meffert/Schleusener 2001, o. S.):

- Im Rahmen einer **Virtuellen Markenstrategie** wird eine unabhängige, internetspezifische Marke für die Aktivitäten im Electronic Commerce geschaffen, die keine Verbindungen zu bereits vorhandenen Marken aus klassischen Marktumgebungen aufweist. Bekannte Beispiele für die Verfolgung einer Virtuellen Markenstrategie sind das europäische Netzwerk von Online-Marktplätzen Scout 24 oder das Auktionshaus ebay. Diese markenstrategische Option steht sowohl reinen Electronic-Commerce-Anbietern offen als auch Unternehmen, die bereits über eine Marke in klassischen Marktumgebungen verfügen.
- Einen höheren Integrationsgrad weist eine **Duale Markenstrategie** auf, bei der, ausgehend von einer existierenden Marke, durch die Verbindung vorhandener Markenelemente mit neuen internetspezifischen Komponenten (zum Beispiel durch die Verwendung von Namenszusätzen beziehungsweise -bestandteilen oder einer ähnlichen visuellen Gestaltung des Markenauftritts) eine quasi-neue Marke für die Aktivitäten im Electronic Commerce geschaffen wird. Beispiele hierfür stellen die Marken Spiegel-Online – als Internet-Angebot des Magazins DER SPIEGEL – oder E-Sixt, das Online-Angebot des Autovermieters Sixt, dar.
- Im Fall einer sehr umfassenden Abstimmung zwischen der internetbasierten und der vorhandenen Marke kann von einer **vollständig integrierten Markenstrategie** gesprochen werden. Hier wird die zugrunde liegende markierte Leistung unter Verwendung eines einheitlichen Markennamens sowohl über das Internet als auch über klassische Transaktionskanäle angeboten. Beispielhaft können das Kaufhaus Karstadt oder der Babynahrungshersteller HiPP angeführt werden.

Abbildung 4 fasst die markenstrategischen Alternativen bei der Gestaltung einer Markenarchitektur für den Electronic Commerce zusammen. Mit Blick auf den oben abgeleiteten Stellenwert sowie die Anforderungen an die Markenführung im Kontext des Electronic Commerce lassen sich die alternativen Markenstrategien einerseits hinsichtlich ihrer außengerichteten Wirkungen und andererseits hinsichtlich ihrer innengerichteten Steuerungserfordernisse und -spielräume bewerten.

Abbildung 4: Strategische Optionen der Markenarchitekturgestaltung für den Electronic Commerce

Fremdbestimmte Markenführung	Eigenständige Markenführung		
	Bedingung: ---	Bedingung: Existenz einer Marke aus klassischer Marktumgebung	
Strategietyp	**Virtuelle Markenstrategie**	**Duale Markenstrategie**	**Vollständig integrierte Markenstrategie**
Definition	Unabhängige, internetspezifische Marke ohne Verbindung zu Marken aus klassischen Marktumgebungen	Verbindung vorhandener Elemente einer Kernmarke mit neuen internetspezifischen Bestandteilen zu Kombinierter Marke	Verwendung eines einheitlichen Markennamens für Electronic Commerce und weitere Transaktionskanäle
Integrationsgrad	Keine Integration	Teilweise Integration	Vollständige Integration
Beispiele	■ Ebay ■ Scout 24	■ Spiegel-Online ■ E-Sixt	■ Karstadt ■ HiPP

GABLER GRAFIK

Bezüglich der **orientierungserleichternden, risikoreduzierenden und differenzierenden Wirkungen von Marken** im Electronic Commerce ist der vollständigen Integrationsstrategie das größte Potenzial zu konstatieren. Durch die Verwendung einer bereits etablierten Marke können gegenüber der Virtuellen Markenstrategie Bekanntheits- und Vertrauensvorsprünge genutzt werden, die sich in einer größeren Nutzungsbereitschaft beim Internet-Shopping niederschlagen (Ahlert/Kenning/Schneider 2000, S. 210 f.; Gruner + Jahr AG & Co. 2000, S. 12 ff.). Ebenso belegen Untersuchungen, dass voll integrierte Marken aufgrund ihrer Mehrkanalpräsenz in der Wahrnehmung der Internetnutzer über ausgeprägtere Differenzierungsmerkmale verfügen, die sich in deutlich höheren Wiedererkennungsraten widerspiegeln (Wirtz 2001a, S. 484 ff.; Eierhoff 2002, S. 344 ff.). Allerdings ist bei der Verfolgung dieser Markenstrategie aufgrund der engeren Wechselwirkungen zwischen der „virtuellen" und „realen Welt" im Vergleich zu einer Virtuellen Markenstrategie auch von einer Gefahr negativer Ausstrahlungseffekte auszugehen. In einem ähnlichen Spannungsfeld zwischen orientierungserleichternden, risikoreduzierenden und differenzierenden Wirkungen einerseits sowie den Gefahren negativer Ausstrahlungseffekte andererseits, bewegen sich duale Markenstrategien.

Hinsichtlich der **Steuerungs- und Gestaltungsfreiräume im Rahmen des Prozesses des identitätsorientierten Markenmanagements** (vgl. Abbildung 3) bestehen bei der Verfolgung einer Virtuellen Markenstrategie tendenziell größere Spielräume, da in der Regel nicht an Traditionen oder Verpflichtungen aus der Vergangenheit angeknüpft werden muss (Felsenberg 2000, S. 62). Demgegenüber dürfen bei einer voll integrierten Markenstrategie die konstitutiven Elemente der bereits existierenden Marke – die Markenherkunft, die organisationalen Fähigkeiten, die Markenvision, die Markenleistung, die Markenwerte und die Markenpersönlichkeit – durch die Aktivitäten im Electronic Commerce nicht wesentlich verändert werden, um eine Erosion der Markenidentität und damit des aufgebauten Vertrauens bei den Bezugsgruppen der Marke zu vermeiden. Darüber hinaus existiert ein im Vergleich zur Virtuellen Markenstrategie erweiterter Koordinationsbedarf zur Sicherstellung eines konsistenten Erscheinungsbildes zwischen der „virtuellen -" und der „realen Präsenz" einer voll integrierten Marke, da neben einer kommunikativen auch eine leistungsbezogene Abstimmung zu erfolgen hat.

Abbildung 5: **Bewertung strategischer Optionen der Markenarchitekturgestaltung im Electronic Commerce**

	Kriterium \ Strategietyp	Virtuelle Markenstrategie	Duale Markenstrategie	Vollständig integrierte Markenstrategie
Wirkungsebene	Orientierungspotenzial	○	◑	●
	Risikoreduktionspotenzial	○	◑	●
	Differenzierungspotenzial	○	◑	●
	Gefahr von Ausstrahlungseffekten	○	◑	●
	Gefahr der Verwässerung des Markenimages	○	●	◑
Gestaltungsebene	Flexibilität	●	◑	○
	Koordinationsbedarf	◑	◑	●
	Nutzung von Synergiepotenzialen	○	◑	●
	Kosten der Markenetablierung	●	◑	○

● stark ausgeprägt ◑ mittel ausgeprägt ○ gering ausgeprägt

GABLER GRAFIK

Den **Flexibilitätsvorteilen** Virtueller Markenstrategien stehen jedoch erhebliche Nachteile vor allem bei den notwendigen Investitionen zur Erzeugung einer ausreichenden Markenbekanntheit gegenüber. Synergiepotenziale – beispielsweise im Rahmen der Markenkommunikation in unterschiedlichen Medien – können im Gegensatz zu voll integrierten Markenstrategien nicht ausgeschöpft werden. Duale Markenstrategien nehmen wiederum eine Mittelstellung ein. Mit wachsender Entfernung der Markenführungsaktivitäten im Internet von denjenigen in der „realen Welt" ist einerseits die Erweiterung der Kompetenzbereiche der Marke denkbar, andererseits folgen daraus sinkende Synergiewirkungen. Abbildung 5 gibt einen abschließenden Überblick über die Vor- und Nachteile der unterschiedlichen markenstrategischen Optionen für den Electronic Commerce.

4.2 Implikationen für das operative Markenmanagement

4.21 Intra-mediale und inter-mediale Markenintegration

Im Kontext des Electronic Commerce ist an dieser Stelle zwischen intra-medialen und inter-medialen Integrationsbemühungen zu unterscheiden. Das Ziel der **intra-medialen Markenintegration** besteht in der Gewährleistung der inhaltlichen und formalen Konsistenz der identitätsbestimmenden Gestaltungselemente auf allen Ebenen des Markenauftrittes im Internet. Dies bedeutet zum einen, dass dem Nutzer im Rahmen seines Einkaufsvorganges im Electronic Commerce, das heißt vom ersten Kontakt mit der Website über die Produktsuche bis hin zum Bestell- und Bezahlvorgang, ein konsistentes und der Markenidentität entsprechendes Bild vermittelt werden muss (Reimerdes 2000, S. 41). Zum anderen ist sicherzustellen, dass jede Ebene und Verzweigung des Markenauftritts für sich allein genommen keine Widersprüche zu den identitätsbestimmenden Merkmalen der Marke erzeugt, da die Nutzer mit Hilfe von Suchfunktionen, gespeicherten Bookmarks oder sonstigen Links unmittelbar in tief verzweigte Ebenen des Markenauftritts eintauchen können, ohne der vom markenführenden Unternehmen intendierten Strukturierung der Website zu folgen (Esch/Hardiman/Langner 2000, S. 12).

Die **inter-mediale Markenintegration** bezieht sich hingegen auf die medienübergreifende Abstimmung aller Markenführungsmaßnahmen. Hierzu bedarf es zunächst einer markenspezifischen Analyse aller Verbindungslinien zwischen den Online- und den Offline-Aktivitäten der betrachteten Marke. Der sich aus diesen Verbindungen ergebende Integrationsbedarf kann von einer rein kommunikativen Abstimmungsnotwendigkeit zwischen klassischen und neuen Medien bis hin zu einem umfassenden, den gesamten Marketing-Mix betreffenden Koordinationserfordernis zwischen den Marketingmaßnahmen in klassischen und digitalen Marktumgebungen reichen. Er wird vor allem durch die Wahl der Markenarchitektur für den Electronic Commerce determiniert.

Die entlang der funktionalen, prozessualen und beziehungsorientierten Dimension konzipierten Markenleistungen sind schließlich in ein konkretes Erscheinungsbild der Marke im Electronic Commerce zu transferieren. Zur Bestimmung der relevanten Identitätskomponenten des Internetauftrittes kann dabei auf verschiedene Untersuchungen zur Wahrnehmung und Akzeptanz von Electronic-Commerce-Angeboten zurückgegriffen werden. Als prägende Einflussfaktoren wurden im Rahmen dieser Studien

- der wahrgenommene Informationsgehalt der Website,
- die Qualität der auf der Website dargebotenen Informationen,
- das Angebot risikoreduzierender Leistungen,
- die Nutzerfreundlichkeit der Website,
- die gestalterische Aufmachung der Website,
- die Dialogorientierung der Website,
- und die Aktivierungswirkung einer Website, insbesondere durch bildliche Stimuli,

identifiziert (Bongartz 2002, S. 61 ff.; Bauer et al. 2004b, S. 18; Englbrecht/Hippner/Wilde 2004a, S. 86 ff.; Bauer/Grether 2004, S. 122; Bauer/Mäder/Fischer 2004, S. 288 ff.). Darüber hinaus stellen insbesondere die Form sowie der Grad der Personalisierung der Markenleistungen und der Markenkommunikation ein für den Electronic Commerce wesentliches Instrument zur Gestaltung des Internetgestützten Markenauftrittes dar. Hinsichtlich der Personalisierung kann zwischen einer impliziten- und einer expliziten Personalisierung unterschieden werden. Während die implizite Personalisierung auf durch vorherige Nutzung des Online-Angebotes generiertes Datenmaterial zum Beispiel in Form von Logfiles, zurückgreift, basiert die explizite Personalisierung auf vom Nachfrager geäußerten Präferenzen bezüglich der angebotenen Information und Inhalte (Graßmann 2004, S. 464). Hierbei ist jedoch stets die Markenidentität als die Gestaltungsspielräume definierendes Element zu berücksichtigen.

4.22 Internetbasierte und klassische Maßnahmen der Markenkommunikation

Ziel der Markenkommunikation ist die Vermittlung der Markenpersönlichkeit und des zentralen Nutzenversprechens der Marke gegenüber außenstehenden Bezugsgruppen, insbesondere den aktuellen und potenziellen Internetnutzern. Dabei sollen Sympathie, Präferenzen und Vertrauen gegenüber der Marke und damit eine erhöhte Kauf-, Wiederkauf- und Weiterempfehlungsabsicht erreicht werden. Darüber hinaus wird innengerichtet die Förderung eines markenadäquaten Verhaltens der Mitarbeiter auf Basis eines klaren Markenverständnisses und einer hohen Identifikation mit der Marke angestrebt. Im Rahmen der innen- und außengerichteten Markenkommunikation für Electronic-Commerce-Angebote können internetbasierte und klassische Maßnahmen differenziert werden.

Die **internetbasierten Maßnahmen der Markenkommunikation** lassen sich in direkt steuerbare und lediglich indirekt steuerbare Kommunikationsmaßnahmen unterteilen (Eckert 2004, S. 168 ff.):

- Im direkten Einflussbereich des markenführenden Electronic Commerce Unternehmens liegen zunächst **Maßnahmen auf der eigenen Website beziehungsweise im Intranet-Bereich**. Diese stellen den Kern der internetbasierten Markenkommunikation dar. Besonders zu beachten sind hierbei die Konformität des Web-Auftrittes mit der Identität der Marke (Meffert/Bongartz 2003, S. 579 f.) sowie die Nutzerfreundlichkeit der Website (Göldi 2002, S. 720). Ferner nimmt die Einrichtung eines nur für Organisationsmitglieder zugänglichen Intranet-Bereiches eine besondere Stellung im Rahmen der innengerichteten Markenkommunikation ein. Hier können beispielsweise für die Mitarbeiter detaillierte markenbezogene Informationen oder konkrete Gestaltungs- und Verhaltensrichtlinien zugänglich gemacht werden. Um eine hohe Relevanz der internen Kommunikationsmaßnahmen für das Mitarbeiterverhalten sicherzustellen ist es notwendig, eine dialogische Form der Kommunikation zu verfolgen und die Anregungen und Wünsche der Mitarbeiter zu berücksichtigen (Joachimsthaler 2002, S. 32). Auch hierfür eignet sich das Intranet in ausgezeichneter Weise. Durch die Öffnung von Teilen oder des gesamten Intranet für externe Zielgruppen können darüber hinaus die Transparenz und Glaubwürdigkeit der Marke nach außen erhöht werden, indem zum Beispiel unternehmensinterne Informationen über den Lieferstatus oder den Umgang mit persönlichen Daten für Betroffene offen gelegt werden (Aaker/Joachimsthaler 2000, S. 238 ff.).

- Ebenfalls vom markenführenden Unternehmen direkt steuerbar sind Maßnahmen, die außerhalb der eigenen Website angesiedelt sind und auf eine **Zugriffsreaktion** der Nutzer abzielen. Diese Maßnahmen sind dazu geeignet, die Besucherfrequenz auf der eigenen Electronic Commerce Website zu steigern. Hierzu zählen unter anderem das Platzieren von Schlüsselwörtern in Suchmaschinen, das Design der Vernetzung durch das Platzieren von Links, das Versenden von E-Mails etwa in Form von Newslettern oder der Einsatz von Bannerwerbungen (Kania 2001, S. 181 ff.; Klein-Bölting/Busch 2001, S. 153 f.; Specht 2001, S. 260; Eckert 2004, S. 169 f.). Insbesondere hinsichtlich des Versendens von E-Mails sowie des Einsatzes von Bannerwerbungen sind jedoch die Akzeptanz seitens der Nachfrager und die Wirkungen auf deren Verhalten umstritten (Gleich 2003, S. 291 ff.; Bauer et al. 2004a).

- Nicht direkt durch das markenführende Unternehmen steuerbar ist die **Kommunikation auf horizontaler Ebene**, also die Interaktion zwischen Nachfragern (Eckert 2004, S. 171). Diese findet vor allem in Chats und Foren (giga.de), Communities (smart-forum) oder Meinungsportalen (ciao.com) statt (Algesheimer/Herrmann/Dimpfel 2004, S. 174). Eine empirische Untersuchung der Motive des Lesens von Artikulationen in Meinungsportalen ergab, dass die Interaktion unter den Nachfragern vor allem dem Informations- und Erfahrungsaustausch dient (Hennig-Thurau 2004, S. 189 ff.). Eine Kontrolle dieses Austausches unter den Nachfragern ist praktisch nicht möglich. Einen Versuch stellt der von Coca-Cola praktizierte Einsatz von so genannten „Brand Cops" dar, die versuchen, negative Diskussionen über die Marke oder Markenrechtsverletzungen zu unterbinden (Meyer/Pfeiffer 2002, S. 573). Neben solchen retrospektiven Kontrollansätzen stellt insbesondere der proaktive Aufbau von Virtuellen Communities eine Form der mittelbaren Einflussnahme dar. **Virtuelle Communities** sind Gruppen, denen ein spezifischer Interessenschwerpunkt zugrunde liegt und bei denen die verwendeten Inhalte von den Mitgliedern der Virtuellen Community bereitgestellt werden (Hagel III/Armstrong 1997, S. 23 f.; Bennemann/Schröder 1999, S. 261 ff.). Werden diese vom markenführenden Unternehmen als Kommunikationsplattform zur Verfügung gestellt, so spricht man hierbei auch von „Marken- oder Brand Communities" (Ernst 2002, S. 62 ff.). Im Idealfall sind derartige „Markengemeinden" in der Lage, ein mit der Markenidentität konformes, soziales Netzwerk von markentreuen Internetnutzern aufzubauen (McWilliam 2000, S. 43 ff.; Muniz/O'Guinn 2001, S. 427).

Die internetbasierten Maßnahmen sind durch **klassische innen- und außengerichtete Maßnahmen der Markenkommunikation** zu ergänzen. Neben der Nennung der Internet-Adresse auf allen Produkten, Verpackungen und Publikationen bietet sich insbesondere der Einsatz reichweitenstarker klassischer Werbemedien zur Steigerung der Bekanntheit der Internetaktivitäten und zur Erzeugung positiver Markenassoziationen an (Esch et al. 2001, S. 570 f.; Schneider/Gerbert 1999, S. 121 f.).

4.3 Implikationen für das Marken-Controlling

Das zentrale Objekt des identitätsorientierten Marken-Controllings ist die **Marke-Kunde-Beziehung**. Die Stärke der Marke-Kunde-Beziehung spiegelt sich im Grad der Übereinstimmung von Markenidentität und Markenimage wider und determiniert die Stärke einer Marke. Zur Erfolgskontrolle der Marke-Kunde-Beziehung bieten sich verschiedene internetbasierte Datenerhebungsmethoden an.

Allgemein wird die Erhebung und Aufbereitung von Informationen über Nachfrager und deren Verhalten durch das Medium Internet begünstigt. Dies liegt daran, dass viele Informationen im Verlauf des Datenaustausches zwischen Webseiten und Nachfragern automatisch generiert werden und ohne weiteren Aufwand permanent und im Zeitablauf dynamisch ausgewertet und genutzt werden können (Buxel 2001, S. 29 f.). Die Erhebungsmethoden lassen sich hierbei anhand des Grades der Nachfragerintegration in reaktive und nicht-reaktive Erhebungsmethoden differenzieren. Während reaktive Erhebungsmethoden dadurch gekennzeichnet sind, dass der Nachfrager sich über die Erhebung der Daten bewusst ist und diese gegebenenfalls aktiv zur Verfügung stellt, es sich also um eine Form der Erlaubnisbasierten Datenerhebung handelt (Permission Marketing), ist sich der Nachfrager bei den nicht-reaktiven Erhebungsmethoden der Datenerhebung nicht bewusst (Wiedmann/Buxel 2004, S. 300). Die nicht-reaktiven Erhebungsmethoden sehen sich aufgrund der potenziell vom Nachfrager nicht autorisierten Datenerhebung daher häufig dem Vorwurf ausgesetzt, mit ethisch-moralischen Ansprüchen nicht konform zu sein (Buxel 2004, S. 480 ff.).

Eine bedeutende **nicht-reaktive Erhebungsmethode** stellt die Logfile-Analyse dar. Logfiles sind Textdateien, welche den Austausch von Daten zwischen Server und Client protokollieren und somit bestimmte Abläufe der Rechnertätigkeit automatisch festhalten (Wiedmann/Buxel 2004, S. 302; Englbrecht/Hippner/Wilde 2004b, S. 357). Die Logfile-Analyse dient der systematischen Auswertung von Nutzungsvorgängen des Electronic Commerce-Angebotes (Ifsen 2004, S. 263 f.). Mit Hilfe der Logfile-Analyse lassen sich Aussagen über die Nutzung des Electronic-Commerce-Angebot generieren, beispielsweise die:

- „durchschnittliche Anzahl der Besuche pro Tag/Woche/Monat,
- durchschnittliche Verweildauer,
- durchschnittliche Anzahl der Page-Impressions (Seitenaufrufe) pro Besuch,
- Herkunft der Besucher,
- benutzten Programme und Einstellungen der Besucher“ (Worzyk/Löhdefink 2004, S. 410 ff.).

Bezüglich der Logfile-Analyse ist kritisch zu bemerken, dass Logfiles die eindeutige Zuordnung von Nachfragern nicht erlauben, da lediglich der zugreifende Client-Rechner identifiziert wird, nicht jedoch der Benutzer des Rechners (Englbrecht/Hippner/Wilde 2004a, S. 357). Überdies werden wesentliche Kennzahlen, wie etwa die Zufriedenheit oder der Erwerb der Electronic-Commerce-Angebote nicht berücksichtigt (Reinecke/Köhler 2002, S. 883).

Die Nachteile nicht-reaktiver Erhebungsmethoden können durch **reaktive Erhebungsmethoden** ausgeglichen werden. Bei reaktiven Erhebungsmethoden ist insbesondere an die Erhebung von Benutzer- oder Kundenstammdaten zu denken (Englbrecht/Hipner/Wilde 2004a, S. 359). Diese Daten werden von den Nachfragern selbst verwaltet und müssen von diesen oftmals in regelmäßigen Abständen aktualisiert werden, wodurch ein stets aktuelles Nachfragerprofil generierbar ist. Zur Erhebung solcher Daten bieten sich Fragebögen mit offenen- oder geschlossenen Formularfeldern sowie Wahlmenüs an (Wiedmann/Buxel 2004, S. 306 f.). Geschlossene Formularfelder sind beispielsweise solche zur Erhebung von Namen oder Kontaktadressen, bei welchen hinsichtlich der Eingabe keine Freiheitsgrade auf thematischer Ebene bestehen. Demgegenüber bieten offene Formularfelder die Möglichkeit der Erfassung von inhaltlich nicht festgelegten Daten. Wahlmenüs erlauben dem Nachfrager schließlich die Auswahl aus fest vorgegebenen Angebots- oder Inhaltskategorien ohne Freiheitsgrade (Wiedmann/Buxel 2004, S. 306 f.). Darüber hinaus bieten sich im Rahmen reaktiver Erhebungsmethoden zur Erfolgskontrolle der Marke-Kunde-Beziehung sämtliche Befragungs- und Marktforschungsmethoden an, die auch bei der Markenführung in der „realen Welt“ verwendet werden.

5. Zusammenfassung

Im schnell wachsenden Markt des Business-to-Consumer Electronic Commerce besitzen Marken aufgrund ihrer differenzierenden, orientierungserleichternden und risikoreduzierenden Wirkungen eine sehr hohe Relevanz für Kauf- und Auswahlentscheidungen der Nutzer. Aufgrund dieser Bedeutung von Marken hat sich das Markenmanagement zu einem zentralen Erfolgsfaktor für Unternehmen im Electronic Commerce entwickelt (Aaker 2000, S. 148; Meffert/Böing 2000, S. 20).

Wie aufgezeigt werden konnte, ist es weder sinnvoll noch in eindeutiger Weise möglich, eine internetspezifische Ausprägungsform einer Marke im Sinne von Internet-/E-/Online- oder Digital-Brands zu definieren. Allerdings kann die Identität einer Marke in unterschiedlichem Ausmaß durch das Medium Internet geprägt sein. Das Ausmaß der Internetprägung der Markenidentität lässt sich an den Merkmalen „Markenherkunft", „Markenkompetenz" und „Markenleistung" festmachen.

Die identitätsorientierte Markenführung hat sich als adäquater Ansatz zur Profilierung und Positionierung eines Electronic-Commerce-Angebotes erwiesen. So ist es auf der Basis einer im Markenauftritt konsistenten und im Zeitablauf kontinuierlich geführten Markenidentität möglich, den Vertrauensmangel gegenüber der „virtuellen Welt" durch den Aufbau von Markenvertrauen zu kompensieren. Hierbei sind insbesondere die durch das Internet gegebenen Möglichkeiten der Individualisierung und Personalisierung der Nachfrageransprache hervorzuheben. Darüber hinaus stellt die Wahl der Markenarchitektur einen entscheidenden Ansatzpunkt für die Gestaltung des internetbasierten Markenmanagements dar. Mit der Virtuellen Markenstrategie, der Dualen Markenstrategie und der vollständig integrierten Markenstrategie wurden drei strategische Optionen der Gestaltung der Markenarchitektur für den Electronic Commerce vorgestellt. Die Darlegung der unterschiedlichen nutzer- und wettbewerbsbezogenen Wirkungen kann dabei als Basis einer systematischen Vorauswahl dienen.

Die durch das Internet gegebenen Möglichkeiten der Kommunikation mit den Nachfragern sind schließlich im Rahmen der Markenkommunikation ebenso zu berücksichtigen und konsistent in den Markenauftritt zu integrieren, wie die Interaktion zwischen den Nachfragern. Hierbei erweist sich besonders die horizontale Kommunikation zwischen den Nachfragern als eine schwer zu beeinflussende, neue Herausforderung für das Marken-Controlling.

Schließlich muss konstatiert werden, dass sich durch die Verwendung des Mediums Internet weder die Begrifflichkeiten der Markenführung wandeln müssen, noch die grundlegenden „Gesetze" der Markenführung außer Kraft gesetzt werden. Das Internet erfordert nicht mehr aber auch nicht weniger als die Beachtung einiger medienspezifischer Anpassungserfordernisse.

Literatur

Aaker, D. A. (2000), „Rezept für Mittelmäßigkeit", in: Wirtschaftswoche, Nr. 11, 9.3.2000.

Aaker, D. A., Joachimsthaler, E. (2000), Brand Leadership, New York.

Ahlert, D., Kenning, P., Schneider, D. (2000), Markenmanagement im Handel – Von der Handelsmarkenführung zum integrierten Markenmanagement in Distributionsnetzen: Strategien – Konzepte – Praxisbeispiele, Wiesbaden.

Algesheimer, R., Herrmann, A., Dimpfel, M. (2004), Konsumenteninteraktionen – Relevanz und Implikationen, in: Bauer, H. H., Rösger, J., Neumann, M. M. (Hrsg.), Konsumentenverhalten im Internet, München, S. 173–188.

Angehrn, A. (1997), Designing Mature Internet Business Strategies: The ICDT Model, in: European Management Journal, Vol. 15, No. 4, S. 361–369.

Bauer, H. H., Grether, M. (2004), Flow – Gebannt im Internet surfen, in: Bauer, H. H., Rösger, J., Neumann, M. M. (Hrsg.), Konsumentenverhalten im Internet, München, S. 107–131.

Bauer, F., Herrmann, T. (2004), Eine tolle Website allein ist nicht genug – erst die dahinter liegende Prozessqualität bindet Kunden, in: Wiedmann, K.-P., Buxel, H., Frenzel, T., Walsh, G. (Hrsg.), Konsumentenverhalten im Internet – Konzepte – Erfahrungen – Methoden, Wiesbaden, S. 363–377.

Bauer, H. H., Sauer, N. E. (2004), Internetnutzungs- und Online-Kaufverhalten in Deutschland und den USA, in: Wiedmann, K.-P., Buxel, H., Frenzel, T., Walsh, G. (Hrsg.), Konsumentenverhalten im Internet – Konzepte – Erfahrungen – Methoden, Wiesbaden, S. 35–55.

Bauer, H. H., Mäder, R., Fischer, Ch. (2004), Effektive Gestaltung von Online-Markenkommunikation, in: Bauer, H. H., Rösger, J., Neumann, M. M. (Hrsg.), Konsumentenverhalten im Internet, München, S. 275–296.

Bauer, H. H., Neumann, M. M., Jöst, Ch. (2004), Der Einsatz von Vertrauensintermediären im elektronischen Handel, in: Bauer, H. H., Rösger, J., Neumann, M. M. (Hrsg.), Konsumentenverhalten im Internet, München, S. 255–273.

Bauer, H. H., Görtz, G., Haber, T. E., Hartmann, A. (2004a), Die Akzeptanz des Werbe-Newsletters als Instrument der Online-Verkaufsförderung, in: Bauer, H. H., Rösger, J., Neumann, M. M. (Hrsg.), Konsumentenverhalten im Internet, München, S. 217–232.

Bauer, H. H., Neumann, M. M., Huber, F., Hölzing, J. A. (2004b), Relevanz und Kausalitäten von Konsumentenvertrauen im Internet, in: Bauer, H. H., Rösger, J., Neumann, M. M. (Hrsg.), Konsumentenverhalten im Internet, München, S. 3–21.

Baumgarth, C. (2004), Markenpolitik – Markenwirkungen – Markenführung – Markencontrolling, 2. Aufl., Wiesbaden.

Bennemann, St., Schröder, J. (1999), Virtuelle Communities als Instrument des Internet-Marketing, in: Fritz, W. (Hrsg.), Internet-Marketing, Stuttgart, S. 258–278.

Birkhofer, B., Schögel, M. (2002), Gestaltung marktorientierter Geschäftsmodelle im Electronic Commerce, in: Schögel, M., Tomczak, T., Belz, Ch. (Hrsg.), Roadm@p to E-Business – Wie Unternehmen das Internet erfolgreich nutzen, St. Gallen, S. 400–429.

Bliemel, F., Eggert, A. (2002), Kundenbindung mit Electronic Commerce, in: Schögel, M., Tomczak, T., Belz, Ch. (Hrsg.), Roadm@p to E-Business – Wie Unternehmen das Internet erfolgreich nutzen, St. Gallen, S. 620–633.

Bliemel, F., Fassott, G. (2002), Produktpolitik im Electronic Business, in: Weiber, R. (Hrsg.), Handbuch Electronic Business, 2. Aufl., Wiesbaden, S. 673–688.

Böing, Ch. (2001), Erfolgsfaktoren im Business-to-Consumer-E-Commerce, Wiesbaden.

Bongartz, M. (2002), Markenführung im Internet – Verhaltenstypen – Einflussfaktoren – Erfolgswirkungen, Wiesbaden.

Boston Consulting Group, Gruner + Jahr AG & Co. (Hrsg.) (2000), eBranding – Kernfusion in der Markenführung, Köln.

Bouncken, R. (2000), Vertrauen – Kundenbindung – Erfolg? Zum Aspekt des Vertrauens bei Dienstleistungen, in: Bruhn, M. (Hrsg.), Dienstleistungsmanagement – Jahrbuch 2000, Wiesbaden, S. 4–22.

Bruhn, M. (2002), Electronic Services – Eine Einführung in den Sammelband, in: Bruhn, M., Stauss, B. (Hrsg.), Dienstleistungsmanagement Jahrbuch 2002 Electronic Services, Wiesbaden, S. 3–41.

Brynjolffson, E., Smith, M. D. (2000), Frictionless Commerce? A Comparison of Internet and Conventional Retailers, in: Management Science, 46. Jg., Nr. 4, S. 563–585.

Burmann, Ch., Maloney, Ph. (2004), Vertikale und horizontale Führung von Marken, Arbeitspapier Nr. 9 des Lehrstuhls für innovatives Markenmanagement (LiM), Burmann, Ch. (Hrsg.), Universität Bremen.

Burmann, Ch., Blinda, L., Nitschke, A. (2003), Konzeptionelle Grundlagen des Identitätsbasierten Markenmanagements, Arbeitspapier Nr. 1 des Lehrstuhls für innovatives Markenmanagement (LiM), Burmann, Ch. (Hrsg.), Universität Bremen.

Buxel, H. (2001), Customer Profiling im Electronic Commerce: Methodische Grundlagen, Anwendungsprobleme und Managementimplikationen, Achen.

Buxel, H. (2004), Kunden- und geselschaftspolitische Problemfelder biotischer Beobachtungen in der Online-Marktforschung, in: Wiedmann, K.-P., Buxel, H., Frenzel, T., Walsh, G. (Hrsg.), Konsumentenverhalten im Internet – Konzepte – Erfahrungen – Methoden, Wiesbaden, S. 469–485.

Court, D., French, T. D., McGuire, T. J., Partington, M. (1999), Marketing in 3-D, in: The McKinsey Quarterly, Nr. 4, S. 6–17.

Davis, R., Buchanan-Oliver, M., Brodie, R. J. (2000), Retail Service Branding in Electronic CommerceEnvironments, in: Journal of Service Research, Vol. 3, No. 2, S. 178–186.

Dayal, S., Landesberg, H., Zeisser, M. (2000), Building digital brands, in: The McKinsey Quarterly, Nr. 2, S. 42–51.

Degeratu, A. M., Rangaswamy, A., Wu, J. (2000), Consumer chioce behavior in online and traditional supermarkets: The effects of brand name, price, and other search attributes, in: International Journal of Research in Marketing, Vol. 17, S. 55–78.

Dudenhöffer, F. (2000), Herausforderungen an die Markenführung im Zeitalter des Internet aus wissenschaftlicher Perspektive, in: Meffert, H., Backhaus, K., Becker, J. (Hrsg.), Markenführung im Internet, Dokumentationspapier Nr. 141 der Wissenschaftlichen Gesellschaft für Marketing und Unternehmensführung e. V., Münster, S. 6–25.

Eckert, D. (2004), Digitale Marken – Analyse der Markenpolitik für digitale Leistungsbündel, Wiesbaden.

Eierhoff, K. (2002), Medienprodukte über alle Kanäle für mehr Kunden – die Click-and-Mortar-Strategie der Bertelsmann AG, in: Schögel, M., Tomczak, T., Belz, Ch. (Hrsg.), Roadm@p to E-Business – Wie Unternehmen das Internet erfolgreich nutzen, St. Gallen, S. 344–360.

Englbrecht, A., Hippner, H., Wilde, K. D. (2004a), Aufzeichnung und Analyse des Konsumentenverhaltens im Internet – Einsatzpotenziale des Web Mining, in: Bauer, H. H., Rösger, J., Neumann, M. M. (Hrsg.), Konsumentenverhalten im Internet, München, S. 353–370.

Englbrecht, A., Hippner, H., Wilde, K. D. (2004b), Kundenorientierung als Determinante des Käuferverhaltens im Internet – Eine Analyse ausgewählter Websites deutscher Unternehmen, in: Bauer, H. H., Rösger, J., Neumann, M. M. (Hrsg.), Konsumentenverhalten im Internet, München, S. 81–105.

Ernest & Young (Hrsg.) (1999), The Second Annual Ernest & Young Internet Shopping Study – The Digital Channel Continues to Gather Stream, New York.

Ernst, A. (2002), Zum wachsenden Einfluss von Communities und gesellschaftlichen Entwicklungen auf die Marke, in: Meyer, A. (Hrsg.), Arbeitspapier zur Schriftenreihe Global Branding, Bd. 6, München.

Esch, F. R., Hardiman, M., Langner, T. (2000), Wirksame Gestaltung von Markenauftritten im Internet, in: Thexis, Nr. 3, S. 10–16.

Esch, F.-R., Roth, S., Kiss, G., Hardiman, M. (2001), Markenkommunikation im Internet, in: Esch, F.-R., Moderne Markenführung – Grundlagen – Innovative Ansätze – Praktische Umsetzungen, 3.Aufl., Wiesbaden, S. 565–597.

Felsenberg, A. (2000), Die Marken des Internet, in: HORIZONTmagazin, Nr. 1, S. 62.

Fournier, S. M. (2001), Markenbeziehungen – Konsumenten und ihre Marken, in: Esch, F.-R. (Hrsg.), Moderne Markenführung: Grundlagen – innovative Ansätze – praktische Umsetzungen, 3. Aufl., Wiesbaden, S. 135–166.

Fritz, W. (2001), Intenet-Marketing und Electronic Commerce – Grundlagen – Rahmenbedingungen – Instrumente, 2. Aufl., Wiesbaden.

Gleich, U. (2003), Onlinewerbung und ihre Wirkungen, in: Media Perspektiven, Nr. 6, S. 290–298.

Göldi, A. (2002), Web-Design und Content Management, in: Schögel, M., Tomczak, T., Belz, Ch. (Hrsg.), Roadm@p to E-Business – Wie Unternehmen das Internet erfolgreich nutzen, St. Gallen, S. 704–721.

Graßmann, B. (2004), Erforschung des Konsumentenverhaltens als Baustein für die Entwicklung neuer Geschäfts- und Marketingstrategien bei T-Online, in: Wiedmann, K.-P., Buxel, H., Frenzel, T., Walsh, G. (Hrsg.), Konsumentenverhalten im Internet – Konzepte – Erfahrungen – Methoden, Wiesbaden, S. 455–468.

Gruner + Jahr AG & Co. (Hrsg.) (2000), Stern Trendprofile 10/00 – Markenstatus der Online-Marken, Hamburg.

Hagel III, J., Armstrong, A. G. (1997), Net Gain – Profit im Netz: Märkte erobern mit virtuellen Communities, Wiesbaden.

Hamm, I. (1997), Electronic Branding, in: planung & analyse, Nr. 1, S. 45–49.

Hauptverband des Deutschen Einzelhandels (Hrsg.) (2004), E-Commerce-Umsatz 2004, http://www.einzelhandel.de/servlet/PB/menu/1021965/index.html, Abruf vom 21.07.2004.

Hennig-Thurau, Th. (2004), Motive des Lesens von Kundenartikulationen im Internet: Theoretische und empirische Analyse, in: Wiedmann, K.-P., Buxel, H., Frenzel, T., Walsh, G. (Hrsg.), Konsumentenverhalten im Internet – Konzepte – Erfahrungen – Methoden, Wiesbaden, S. 171–193.

Hermanns, A., Matzdorf, S., Riedmüller, F. (2001), Marken im Internet – die virtuelle Herausforderung, in: Hermanns, A., Sauter, M. (Hrsg.), Management-Handbuch Electronic Commerce: Grundlagen, Strategien, Praxisbeispiele, 2. Aufl., München, S. 193–209.

Hoffman, D. L., Novak, T. P., Peralta, M. (1998), Building Consumer Trust in Online Environments: The Case for Information Privacy, http://www2000.ogsm.vanderbilt.edu/, Vanderbilt University.

Holtrop, T., Döpfner, M., Wirtz, B. W. (2003), Deutschland Online – Entwicklungsperspektiven der Medien- und Internetmärkte, Wiesbaden.

Ifsen, D. (2004), Kundenverhalten im Internet – Messinstrumente und Analyseverfahren als Basis einer kundenorientierten Webseitengestaltung, in: Wiedmann, K.-P., Buxel, H., Frenzel, T., Walsh, G. (Hrsg.), Konsumentenverhalten im Internet – Konzepte – Erfahrungen – Methoden, Wiesbaden, S. 257–272.

Jasper, C. R., Ouellete, S. J. (1994), Consumers' Perception of Risk and the Purchase of Apparel from Catalogs, in: Journal of Direct Marketing, Vol. 8, Spring, S. 23–36.

Joachimsthaler, E. (2002), Commitment: Mitarbeiter – Die vergessene Zielgruppe für Markenerfolge, in: Absatzwirtschaft, 50. Jg., Nr. 11, S. 28–34.

Kania, D. (2001), Branding.com: online branding for marketing success, Lincolnwood (Chicago).

Kastenmüller, S. (2001), Markenbildung im Internet, in: Hermanns, A., Sauter, M. (Hrsg.), Management-Handbuch electronic commerce: Grundlagen, Strategien, Praxisbeispiele, 2. Aufl., München, S. 211–226.

Kastenmüller, S. (2002), Die Marke im Spannungsfeld der Konvergenz, in: Schögel, M., Tomczak, T., Belz, Ch. (Hrsg.), Roadm@p to E-Business – Wie Unternehmen das Internet erfolgreich nutzen, St. Gallen, S. 596–618.

Kernstock, J., Brockdorff, B., Schubiger, N. (2002), Crossover Branding®–Ein Bezugsrahmen zur medien- und kanalübergreifenden Markenführung, in: Schögel, M., Tomczak, T., Belz, Ch. (Hrsg.), Roadm@p to E-Business – Wie Unternehmen das Internet erfolgreich nutzen, St. Gallen, S. 582–594.

Klein-Bölting, U., Busch, O. (2001), Markenführung im Digital Age, in: Merten, K., Zimmermann, R. (Hrsg.), Das Handbuch der Unternehmenskommunikation 2000/2001, Köln.

Kuhlen, R. (2000), Vertrauenssicherung auf elektronischen Märkten, in: WISU, Nr. 2, S. 220–226.

Kühn, R., Fasnacht, R. (2001), Strategische Frühwarnung als Aufgabe des Marketingcontrollings, in: Reinecke, S., Tomczak, T., Geis, G. (Hrsg.), Handbuch Marketingcontrolling, St. Gallen, Wien, S. 90–105.

Lederer, C., Hill, S. (2001), See Your Brand Through Your Customers' Eyes, Vol. 79, June, S. 3–11.

Lee, M. K. O., Turban, E. (2001), A Trust Model for Consumer Internet Shopping, International Journal of Electronic Commerce, Vol. 6, S. 75–91.

Licharz, E.-M. (2002), Vertrauen in B2C, Köln.

Lihotzky, N. (2003), Kundenbindung im Internet – Maßnahmen und Erfolgswirksamkeit im Business-to-Consumer-Bereich, Wiesbaden.

Manschwetus, U., Rumler, A. (2002), Markenführung im Internet, in: Manschwetus, U., Rumler, A., Strategisches Internetmarketing – Entwicklungen in der Net-Economy, Wiesbaden, S. 227–244.

McWilliam, G. (2000), Building Stronger Brands through Online Communities, in: Sloan Management Review, Spring, S. 43–54.

Meffert, H. (2000), Einführung in die Themenstellung, in: Meffert, H., Backhaus, K., Becker, J. (Hrsg.), Markenführung im Internet, Dokumentationspapier Nr. 141 der Wissenschaftlichen Gesellschaft für Marketing und Unternehmensführung e. V., Münster, S. 1–5.

Meffert, H., Böing, Ch. (2000), Erfolgsfaktoren und Eintrittsvoraussetzungen im Business-to-Consumer-E-Commerce – ausgewählte Ergebnisse einer empirischen Analyse, in: Meffert, H., Backhaus, K., Becker, J. (Hrsg.), Arbeitspapier Nr. 138 der Wissenschaftlichen Gesellschaft für Marketing und Unternehmensführung e. V., Münster.

Meffert, H., Bongartz, M. (2003), Einsatz neuer Medien im Markenmanagement, in: Wirtz, B. W. (Hrsg.), Handbuch Medien- und Multimediamanagement, Wiesbaden, S. 575–597.

Meffert, H., Burmann, Ch. (2002), Wandel in der Markenführung – vom instrumentellen zum identitätsorientierten Markenverständnis, in: Meffert, H.; Burmann, Ch.; Koers, M. (Hrsg.), Markenmanagement – Grundfragen der identitätsorientierten Markenführung, Wiesbaden, S. 17–33.

Meffert, H., Koers, M. (2002), Identitätsorientiertes Markencontrolling – Grundlagen und konzeptionelle Ausgestaltung, in: Meffert, H.; Burmann, Ch.; Koers, M. (Hrsg.), Markenmanagement – Grundfragen der identitätsorientierten Markenführung, Wiesbaden, S. 404–428.

Meffert, H., Schleusener, M. (2001), Markenführung im Dienstleistungsbereich – klassisches und E-Branding im Spannungsfeld, in: Festschrift zum 60. Geburtstag von Matthias Haller, St. Gallen.

Meyer, A., Pfeiffer, M. (2002), Meine Marke, deine Marke, unsere Marke? Interactive Branding als Herausforderung für die Markenführung im E-Business, in: Schögel, M., Tomczak, T., Belz, Ch. (Hrsg.), Roadm@p to E-Business – Wie Unternehmen das Internet erfolgreich nutzen, St. Gallen, S. 558–581.

Mohn, Ch. (2000), Internet als Plattform neuartiger Geschäftsmodelle – Markenaufbau im Spannungsfeld von Zeit, Qualität und Vertrauen, in: Meffert, H., Backhaus, K., Becker, J. (Hrsg.), Markenführung im Internet, Dokumentationspapier Nr. 141 der Wissenschaftlichen Gesellschaft für Marketing und Unternehmensführung e. V., Münster, S. 42–46.

Muniz Jr., A. M, O'Guinn, T. C. (2001), Brand Community, in: Journal of Consumer Research, Vol. 27, March, S. 412–432.

Pätzmann, J. (2001), E-Branding – Erfolgsfaktoren für die Markenführung im Internet, in: Marketing, Zeitschrift für Forschung und Praxis der Markenführung, Nr. 1, S. 4–8.

Plötner, O. (1995), Das Vertrauen des Kunden. Relevanz, Aufbau und Steuerung auf industriellen Märkten, Wiesbaden.

Reichheld, F., Schefter, P. (2000), Warum Kundentreue auch im Internet zählt, Harvard Business Manager, 41. Jg., S. 70–80.

Reimerdes, G. (2000), Innovative Markenkonzepte als Herausforderung für traditionelle Geschäftsmodelle, in: Meffert, H., Backhaus, K., Becker, J. (Hrsg.), Markenführung im Internet, Dokumentationspapier Nr. 141 der Wissenschaftlichen Gesellschaft für Marketing und Unternehmensführung e. V., Münster, S. 33–41.

Reinecke, S., Köhler, S. (2002), Marketing Performance Measurement im Internet, in: Schögel, M., Tomczak, T., Belz, Ch. (Hrsg.), Roadm@p to E-Business – Wie Unternehmen das Internet erfolgreich nutzen, St. Gallen, S. 880–905.

Schneider, D., Gerbert, Ph. (1999), E-Shopping: Erfolgsstrategien im electronic commerce: Marken schaffen, Shops gestalten, Kunden binden, Wiesbaden.

Schnetkamp, G., Kenning, P. (2000), Wie Ihre Website zur Marke wird, in: EinzelHandelsBerater spezial, Nr. 1, S. 26–28.

Specht, U. (2001), Markenführung und Internet – Eine Analyse aus der Perspektive der Fast Moving Consumer Goods Branche, in: Die Betriebswirtschaft, 61. Jg., Nr. 2, S. 257–263.

Swinka, St. (2000), Transfer klassischer Marken in das Internet – Ansatzpunkte und Ausgestaltungsformen, in: Meffert, H., Backhaus, K., Becker, J. (Hrsg.), Markenführung im Internet, Dokumentationspapier Nr. 141 der Wissenschaftlichen Gesellschaft für Marketing und Unternehmensführung e. V., Münster, S. 26–32.

Tan, S. J. (1999), Strategies for reducing consumers' risk aversion in Internet shopping, in: Journal of Consumer Marketing, Vol. 16, No. 2, S. 163–180.

TNS Infratest (2004), Monitoring Informationswirtschaft – 7. Faktenbericht 2004, München.

Tomczak, T., Roosdorp, A. (1996), Positionierung – Neue Herausforderungen verlangen neue Ansätze, in: Tomczak, T., Rudolph, T., Roosdorp, A., (Hrsg.), Positionierung: Kernentscheidung des Marketing, St. Gallen, S. 26–42.

Van den Poel, D., Leunis, J. (1999), Consumer Acceptance of the Internet as a Channel of Distribution, in: Journal of Business Research, Vol. 45, S. 249–256.

Walter, F. (2000), Die Zukunft des Online-Marketing, Mering.

Ward, M. R., Lee, M. J. (2000), Internet shopping, consumer search and product branding, in: Journal of Product and Brand Management, Vol. 9, No. 1, S. 6–20.

Welling, M. (2003), Bausteine einer integrierten image- und identitätsorientierten Markenführung als Beitrag zur Markentheorie, Schriften Zum Marketing, Nr. 47, Bochum.

Wiedmann, K.-P., Buxel, H. (2004), Konsumentenverhaltensforschung im Internet mittels Profilbildungstechniken: Methodische Grundlagen, in: Wiedmann, K.-P., Buxel, H., Frenzel, T., Walsh, G. (Hrsg.), Konsumentenverhalten im Internet – Konzepte – Erfahrungen – Methoden, Wiesbaden, S. 291–326.

Wirtz, B. W. (2001a), Electronic Business, 2. Aufl., Wiesbaden.

Wirtz, B. W. (2001b), Medien- und Internetmanagement, 2. Aufl., Wiesbaden.

Worzyk, T., Löhdefink, M. (2004), Die Logfile-Analyse als Instrument der Messung und Auswertung von Kundenverhalten im Rahmen der Erfolgskontrolle von Websites – Hintergrund, Möglichkeiten und Lösungen, in: Wiedmann, K.-P., Buxel, H., Frenzel, T., Walsh, G. (Hrsg.), Konsumentenverhalten im Internet – Konzepte – Erfahrungen – Methoden, Wiesbaden, S. 403–417.

Identitätsorientierte Führung von Luxusmarken

Ingo Lasslop

1. Zunehmende Bedeutung von Luxusmarken als Herausforderung an das Markenmanagement **470**

2. Der Luxusbegriff im Kontext der Markenführung **472**

3. Das Identitätssystem von Luxusmarken **475**

3.1 Besonderheiten des Selbstbilds von Luxusmarken 475

3.2 Besonderheiten im Fremdbild von Luxusmarken: Selbstkongruenz und Wertausdruck 477

4. Management von Luxusmarken **481**

4.1 Strategische Optionen für Luxusmarken 481

4.2 Besonderheiten des operativen Managements von Luxusmarken 484

4.21 Markenbildung durch überragende Qualität und Design 484

4.22 Markenbildung durch konstante Preispolitik 485

4.23 Markenbildung durch Flagship-Stores und selektiven Vertrieb 486

4.24 Markenbildung durch symbolische Kommunikation 488

5. Fazit **491**

1. Zunehmende Bedeutung von Luxusmarken als Herausforderung an das Markenmanagement

Der Vermarktung von Produkten und Dienstleistungen, die in qualitativ und preislich gehobenen Marktsegmenten angesiedelt sind, kommt seit geraumer Zeit ein steigendes Interesse zu. Eine besondere Herausforderung liegt dabei im Bereich der Markenpolitik, da die Marke als Kristallisationspunkt die einzigartigen Nutzenversprechen verkörpert, die mit Luxus- und Premiumgütern verbunden werden. Diese Einschätzung spiegelt sich in einer **zunehmenden Anzahl wissenschaftlicher Beiträge** wider, in denen Aspekte der Führung von Luxus- und Premiummarken intensiv diskutiert werden (Nueno/Quelch 1998; Kisabaka 2001, Kapferer 2001; Dietz 2001; Meffert/Lasslop 2004).

Als Auslöser des gestiegenen wissenschaftlichen Interesses an Luxusmarken lassen sich verschiedene Entwicklungen ausmachen. Aus einer volkswirtschaftlichen Perspektive zeigt sich zunächst, dass das Volumen und damit die **wirtschaftliche Bedeutung** der wichtigsten Teilmärkte des Luxussektors im vergangenen Jahrzehnt stetig gestiegen ist.

So sind die Top-Segmente in den Branchen Schuhe, Porzellan, Silberwaren, Uhren, Schmuck, Parfüm, Kosmetika, gehobene Mode und Accessoires in den 90er Jahren um durchschnittlich drei bis zehn Prozent pro Jahr gewachsen (Arnauld 2000). Für die Zukunft wird mit einer Fortsetzung des Wachstums gerechnet, das wie in den Jahren zuvor deutlich über dem der Weltwirtschaft liegen wird.

Zurückzuführen ist dieser Trend zunächst auf den gestiegenen Wohlstand innerhalb der westlichen Industrienationen. In Deutschland zeigt sich beispielhaft ein Anstieg des verfügbaren Einkommens der privaten Haushalte von 980 Milliarden Euro in 1991 auf 1.386 Milliarden Euro im Jahr 2002 (Deutsche Bundesbank 2003, S. 146). Damit wurde die materielle Voraussetzung für eine „Demokratisierung" des Luxus geschaffen, die eine steigende Anzahl von Nachfragern in die Lage versetzt, höherpreisige Luxusmarken zu erstehen. Zusätzlich förderte der Wirtschaftsboom in Asien zu Beginn der 90er Jahre die Nachfrage nach Luxusgütern und -marken ebenso wie die Entstehung der „New Economy" und der damit verbundene schnelle finanzielle Aufstieg breiter Mitarbeiterschichten am Ende des letzten Jahrzehnts. Für die mittelbare Zukunft werden weitere Wachstumsimpulse von den aufstrebenden Volkswirtschaften Chinas, Indiens und Osteuropas erwartet (LVMH 2004).

Aus einer soziologischen Perspektive erscheint die grundsätzlich **gewandelte Funktion des Konsums** eine weitere Erklärung für die zunehmende Bedeutung von Luxus zu liefern (Nueno/Quelch 1988, S. 81 ff.; Haseloff 1992; McCracken 1992). So erfüllt der Konsum oder Besitz spezieller Marken vor dem Hintergrund zunehmend verschwindender Schicht- und Klassenunterschiede über die reine Befriedigung von Grundbedürfnissen hinaus eine soziale Funktion: Die Wahl einer Marke dient in dieser Interpretation dem Ausdruck der eigenen Persönlichkeit und des eigenen Wertesystems (Haseloff 1982, S. 150 ff.; Karmasin 1993, S. 237 ff.). Dieses hat sich im Zuge des gestiegenen Wohlstands ebenfalls auf breiter gesellschaftlicher Ebene gewandelt. So lassen sich exemplarisch mit der Genussorientierung bzw. dem Hedonismus einerseits und dem Streben nach

Selbstverwirklichung und Authentizität andererseits zwei zentrale Entwicklungen ausmachen (Wiswede/Engelmann 1999, S. 7), die für das Kaufverhalten wichtiger geworden sind und insbesondere das Streben nach höherwertigen Gütern und Marken fördern.

Aus Anbietersicht erklärt sich die Attraktivität der Premiumsegmente neben dem gesteigerten motivationalen „Wollen" und dem vermehrten materiellen „Können" der Nachfrager noch aus weiteren Faktoren. So ist die **Wettbewerbsintensität** in den Premium- und Luxussegmenten vermeintlich geringer, was insbesondere auf eine **geringere Bedeutung des Preises als Wettbewerbsinstrument** zurückgeführt wird. In vielen niedrig- bis mittelpreisigen Produktkategorien erscheint eine Positionierung als Premiummarke damit als „Königsweg" (Braun 2000), um sich der direkten Konkurrenz durch ständig stärker werdende Handelsmarken zu entziehen. Aus ökonomischer Perspektive steht dahinter die strategische Überlegung, auf Basis eines überlegenen Gesamtnutzens des Angebots gegenüber generischen Marken ein Preispremium zu generieren, das bei vergleichsweise geringeren Volumina überdurchschnittliche Renditen verspricht. Tatsächlich zeigen empirische Ergebnisse, dass die Renditen in übermäßig von Premiummarken dominierten Produktfeldern bei relativ niedrigeren Marktanteilen der einzelnen Anbieter wesentlich höher ausfallen als in vergleichbaren Kategorien, die von generischen- und Handelsmarken dominiert werden (Vishvanath/Mark 1997). Zudem verspricht der Aufbau einer profilierten Markenwahrnehmung in Zeiten vielfach austauschbarer Kernleistungen und kürzerer Innovationszyklen eine von der Produktsubstanz zumindest kurz- bis mittelfristig unabhängige Möglichkeit zur Absicherung der eigenen Wettbewerbsfähigkeit.

Allerdings ist die Führung einer Premium- oder Luxusmarke auch mit **zunehmenden Herausforderungen** verbunden: Der vermeintlich geringe Wettbewerbsdruck für Luxusmarken nimmt durch preisaggressive und qualitativ oft gleichwertige generische Marken ständig zu. Um die besondere Führungsrolle innerhalb eines Marktes zu verteidigen, bedarf es daher ständiger technischer oder stilistischer Weiterentwicklungen. Dieser **Innovationsdruck** erfordert erhebliche finanzielle und personelle Ressourcen. Gleiches resultiert aus dem zur Erreichung effizienter Stückzahlen ableitbaren **Globalisierungsdruck** vieler Luxusmarkenhersteller und der damit einhergehenden Herausforderung, Distributionssysteme bei Beibehaltung hoher qualitativer Standards weltweit auszudehnen. Durch die vermehrte globale Ausdehnung insbesondere der „großen" Luxuskonzerne (zum Beispiel LVMH, Vendome) steigt gleichzeitig der Konkurrenzdruck für die mittelständischen Hersteller von Luxusmarken, die lediglich auf regionalen Märkten tätig sind und sich dort nun intensiver Konkurrenz gegenübersehen. Zusätzlich bedroht gerade in den Hauptwachstumsmärkten Asiens eine steigende Zunahme von Plagiaten, die zu einem Bruchteil des Originalpreises angeboten werden, das exklusive Image und die Umsätze von Luxusmarken.

Die steigende Dynamik in den Rahmenbedingungen erfordert sowohl von global operierenden Luxuskonzernen als auch den mittelständischen Luxusherstellern vermehrte Anstrengungen zur systematischen Profilierung ihrer Marken. Dabei zeigt sich allerdings, dass gerade die Unternehmen im Luxussegment einer systematischen Markenführung in der Vergangenheit zu wenig Bedeutung beigemessen haben (Dubois/Duquesne 1993, S. 36).

Vor diesem Hintergrund erscheint es zunächst notwendig, den vielschichtigen Begriff Luxus im Kontext der Markenführung zu konkretisieren. Darauf aufbauend werden die Besonderheiten im Identitätssystem von Luxusmarken analysiert, die sowohl in den Dimensionen des Markenselbstbilds, als auch im Markenfremdbild und dessen spezifischen Nutzenkategorien liegen. Aus den hier gewonnenen Einsichten über den Wirkungsmechanismus von Luxusmarken können schließlich die Besonderheiten des Managements von Luxusmarken dargestellt werden.

2. Der Luxusbegriff im Kontext der Markenführung

Der Begriff Luxus wird abhängig von zeitlichen Epochen, dem jeweiligen politisch-ökonomischen Umfeld und moralisch-ethischen Standpunkt des Betrachters differenziert und teilweise unterschiedlich konzeptualisiert.[1] Aus ökonomischer Perspektive wird Luxus objektorientiert zur Abgrenzung von Gütern und Marken und verhaltensorientiert hinsichtlich deren Konsumption diskutiert.

Obgleich bereits in der Antike die Güterausstattung und -verwendung schichtspezifisch unterschiedlich war, beginnt die **verhaltensorientierte Begriffsverwendung** von Luxus in breiter Form erst bei der Kennzeichnung des Konsums der herrschenden Schichten im 17. und 18. Jahrhundert (Pöll 1980, S. 9). Luxus besteht demnach in einem hohen Aufwand, der über das Lebensnotwendige, sozial Angemessene oder den „normalen" Lebensstandard hinausgeht (Mühlmann 1975, S. 69 ff.). Der damit gemeinte, vornehmlich **quantitativ geprägte Konsumbegriff** wird aus ethisch-religiöser Sicht als unsittlich und unmoralisch verurteilt. Die zu dieser Zeit mit dem Begriff Luxus assoziierten Inhalte sind dementsprechend überwiegend negativ (zum Beispiel Übermäßigkeit, Prunk, Protzerei, Ausschweifung oder Zügellosigkeit). Dies ändert sich im Zuge der industriellen Revolution, die es einer steigenden Anzahl von Menschen ermöglicht, vormals unerreichbare Luxusgüter zu konsumieren. Der damit verbundene Wandel zu einem **qualitativen Luxusverständnis** spiegelt sich in positiven Wertungen und Assoziationen wider: Luxus wird nun vermehrt mit gutem Geschmack, Klugheit, Eleganz und Wohlstand verbunden (vgl. die umfassende Darstellung bei Mühlmann 1975).

In der **objektbezogenen Begriffsverwendung** wird Luxus dichotomisch als Gegenpol zu notwendigen Gütern des täglichen Gebrauchs für Produktkategorien benutzt, die zur Grundversorgung des Konsumenten notwendig sind (Bearden/Etzel 1982; Berry 1994; Chaudhuri 1998; Kemp, 1998). Dabei lassen sich Luxusgüter **interkategorial** durch eine tendenziell weniger automatisierte Fertigung, geringere Produktionsvolumina, höhere Produktqualität und ein höheres Preisniveau der Produktgruppe kennzeichnen. Ein damit zusammenhängender Bestimmungsfaktor des Luxusgrades einer Produktkategorie ist

1 Bereits im Jahre 1801 weist Krünitz darauf hin, dass „die Begriffe vom Luxus so vielfach als die Meinungen über dessen Schädlichkeit und Unschädlichkeit sind". Vgl. Krünitz (1801), S. 40.

der Diffusions- beziehungsweise Knappheitsgrad (Bearden/Etzel 1982, S. 184). Aus dieser Definition wird ebenfalls deutlich, dass es sich bei Luxusgütern tendenziell eher um Gebrauchs- als um Verbrauchsgüter handelt.

Anhand der genannten Kriterien zeigt sich bereits die Relativität des Luxusbegriffs: Ein TV-Gerät galt vor 50 Jahren als Luxusgut; es wurde nur in kleinen Stückzahlen produziert, war damit exklusiv und hatte einen hohen Preis, während heute praktisch jeder Haushalt einen Fernseher besitzt. Neben dieser zeitlichen Relativität hängt die Einschätzung des Luxusgrades ebenfalls stark von der persönlichen Situation des Betrachters, vor allem von dessen persönlichen Lebensbedingungen und kulturellem Umfeld, ab (zum Beispiel der Besitz eines TV-Geräts in Europa versus Zentralafrika).

Während der Begriff Luxusgut zu einer Abstufung von Produktkategorien benutzt wird, kennzeichnet die Luxusmarke **intrakategorial** primär die herausgehobene Stellung markierter Produkte innerhalb einer Produktkategorie. So werden Herrenanzüge, Armbanduhren und auch Automobile seit geraumer Zeit eher zu Alltags- denn zu Luxusgütern gezählt (Bearden/Etzel 1982); trotzdem handelt es sich bei Armani, Rolex oder Rolls-Royce um Luxusmarken. Werden Luxusmarke und Luxusgut synonym verwendet, so hat dies zur Folge, dass die Klassifizierung einer Marke primär von der Produktkategorie abhängt. So sind für Kapferer „Marken wie Dior für einen Teil ihrer Aktivitäten ein Luxusunikat, für einen weiteren Teil eine Luxusmarke und schließlich für einen dritten Teil eine gehobene Marke“ (Kapferer 2001, S. 351).

Diese explizite Unterscheidung von Marke und der unter ihr vermarkteten Produkte unterbleibt in einer **wirkungsorientierten Perspektive**, welche auch diesem Beitrag zugrunde gelegt wird. Die Einstufung als Luxusmarke erfolgt holistisch und unabhängig von der Produktkategorie. Statt auf das einzelne Produkt wird auf den abstrakten Markenkern als Klammer abgestellt, die sich in jedem Produkt widerspiegelt. Dieser Gedanke knüpft an das Konzept der identitätsorientierten Markenführung an und findet sich für den Bereich der Luxusmarken bereits explizit bei Dubois/Paternault: „Whatever their nature and price, all products under the same brand name share a symbolic identity and a core of values expressing the quintessence of the brand. Whether they are automobiles, wristwatches, writing instruments or sunglasses, all Porsche items express the Porsche Legend and are clearly identified as such.“ (Dubois/Paternault 1995, S. 71).

Der von den Nachfragern **wahrgenommene Kern einer Luxusmarke** zeigt sich dabei nach einer breit angelegten empirischen Untersuchung von Dubois/Laurent/Czellar in **sechs Facetten** (Dubois/Laurent/Czellar 2001):

- **Hoher wahrgenommener Preis**, sowohl interkategorial (absoluter Preis) als auch intrakategorial (relativer Preis im Vergleich mit anderen Marken der selben Produktkategorie);
- **Exzellente Qualität**, sowohl hinsichtlich der eingesetzten Materialien als auch der wahrgenommenen oder vermuteten hohen Sorgfalt und Expertise im Herstellungsprozess;

- **Einzigartigkeit**, die sich im Eindruck einer schweren Erhältlichkeit beziehungsweise Knappheit widerspiegelt;
- **Ästethik** in Form eines mit allen Sinnen wahrgenommenen Produkterlebnisses;
- **Historie** durch eine wahrgenommene Kontinuität im Auftritt und Design;
- **Nicht-Notwendigkeit**, die sich in einer dominierenden Wahrnehmung symbolischer gegenüber technisch-funktionalen Eigenschaften niederschlägt.

Abbildung 1: **Abgrenzung der Optionen im vertikalen Markenwettbewerb**

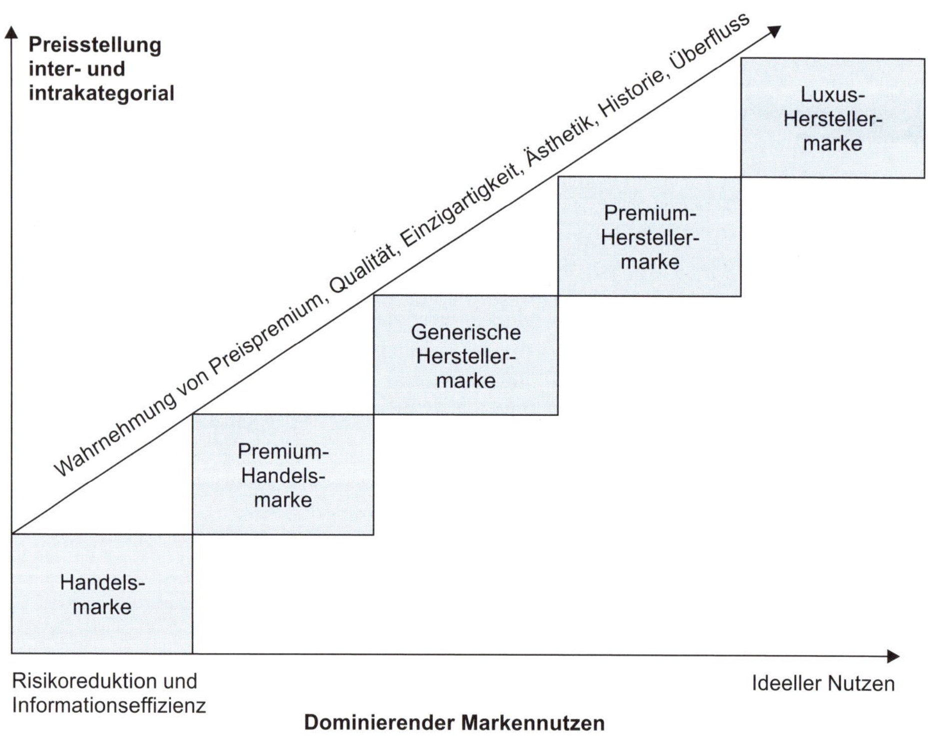

GABLER GRAFIK

Zusammengenommen schaffen diese spezifischen Wahrnehmungsmuster einen herausragenden **ideellen Nutzen** für den Nachfrager, der sich in der Möglichkeit äussert, durch den Kauf und Besitz von Luxusmarken eigene Wertvorstellungen sowie die Zugehörigkeit zu einer sozialen Klasse oder Gruppe zu demonstrieren. Dagegen treten die bei generischen Marken dominierenden Markenfunktionen der Informationseffizienz (Nutzen in Form entscheidungsrelevanter, einfach zugänglicher Informationen) und Risikoreduktion (Nutzen in Form der Verminderung entscheidungsimmanenter Risiken) in den Hintergrund.

Die Luxusmarke lässt sich auf Basis der vorangegangenen Ausführungen vereinfacht durch die angebotsorientierte Dimension „Preisstellung“ sowie die wirkungsorientierte Dimension „Dominierende Markenfunktion“ gegenüber alternativen Optionen im vertikalen Markenwettbewerb, wie (Premium-)Handelsmarken und (Premium-)Herstellermarken, abgrenzen (vgl. Abbildung 1).

Zusammenfassend kann eine Luxusmarke definiert werden als ein Nutzenbündel mit spezifischen Merkmalen (insbesondere objektiv höhere Qualität, Preisstellung und Knappheit), die zu einem weit überdurchschnittlich differenzierten Vorstellungsbild im Kopf des Konsumenten, einer Dominanz der ideellen Markenfunktion und in Konsequenz zu einem weit überdurchschnittlich hohen wahrgenommenen Gesamtnutzen, einer weit überdurchschnittlichen Begehrlichkeit sowie einer weit überdurchschnittlichen Preisbereitschaft führen. Die Kategorisierung als Luxusmarke ist dabei stets relativ, das heißt interpersonell und situativ unterschiedlich sowie zeitlich nicht konstant.

3. Das Identitätssystem von Luxusmarken

3.1 Besonderheiten des Selbstbilds von Luxusmarken

Die Markenidentität stellt diejenigen raum-zeitlich gleichartigen Merkmale dar, die aus Sicht der internen Zielgruppen in nachhaltiger Weise den Charakter der Marke prägen (Burmann/Blinda/Nitschke 2003, S. 5). Eine Markenidentität entsteht immer erst aus einer wechselseitigen Beziehung zwischen internen (Selbstbild) und externen (Fremdbild) Zielgruppen einer Marke (vgl. in diesem Zusammenhang auch den Beitrag zur theoretischen Grundkonzeption der identitätsorientierten Markenführung in diesem Buch). Eine wichtige Komponente der Markenidentität sind dabei die spezifischen Ressourcen und Kompetenzen, die der Marke ihre Einzigartigkeit verleihen. Hier zeigen sich bei der Betrachtung von Luxusmarken einige Besonderheiten.

Den Kern der Markenidentität bildet das Nutzenversprechen der Marke. Dieses ist bei Luxusmarken weniger auf konkrete technisch-funktionale Eigenschaften einzelner Leistungen, sondern tendenziell stärker auf die Verwirklichung **abstrakter, oftmals ästethisch-kultureller Nutzenversprechen** ausgerichtet (Vukelic 2000, S. 40 ff.). Dies ermöglicht eine für Luxusmarken typische Übertragung der Identität auf ein breites Produktspektrum, ohne dass Widersprüche aus konkreten Produktassoziationen das Kompetenzfeld der Markenidentität einschränken.

Der stärkste Einfluss auf die Identität von Luxusmarken ist in der **Markenherkunft/-historie („Pedigree")** zu sehen (Braun 1997, S. 281). Hier zeigt sich, dass der Aufbau einer Luxusmarke nicht kurzfristig erfolgen kann, sondern ein oftmals mehrere Jahrzehnte dauernder Prozess ist. Die Entwicklung einer Luxusmarke führt somit aus ressourcentheoretischer Perspektive zu einem Wettbewerbsvorteil, da die zugrundeliegenden Ressourcen nicht unmittelbar von Konkurrenten imitiert werden können (Dierickx/Cool 1989). Viele der international führenden Luxusmarken, wie zum Beispiel Rolls-Royce (Automobile, gegründet 1904), Hermes (Lederwaren, gegründet 1837), Rolex (Uhren, Einführung der Marke 1908) oder Chanel (Mode, gegründet 1912) besitzen bei aller unterschiedlichen Branchenzugehörigkeit eine sehr lange Tradition. Das durchschnittliche Alter der 75 Unternehmen, die im Comitée Colbert (Vereinigung der französischen Luxusindustrie) zusammengeschlossen sind, betrug im Jahre 1995 über 100 Jahre (Braun 1997, S. 279 f.). Dieser „Zeitanker" verleiht den Marken den Status einer Institution und stellt für potenzielle neue Wettbewerber eine schwer zu überwindende Markteintrittsbarriere dar.

Einen wesentlichen Teil dieser Tradition und damit auch der Markenidentität stellen gerade bei Luxusmarken die **Gründerpersönlichkeiten** dar. Dies zeigt sich zum Beispiel bei Marken wie Chanel, Lagerfeld, Louis Vuitton oder Yves Saint Laurent, bei denen die Unternehmensgründer zugleich Namensgeber und bestimmendes Element der Markenidentität sind. In Deutschland wird die starke Verankerung mit der Gründerpersönlichkeit beispielhaft bei den Luxusmarken Joop und Jil Sander deutlich, die auch lange nach ihrem Ausscheiden das prägende Element der jeweiligen Markenpersönlichkeit bleiben.

Diese Persönlichkeiten stellen oftmals nicht nur als Namensgeber eine Schlüsselressource für ihre Marke dar, sondern haben vielfach auch durch ihre eigene Designkompetenz die für Luxusmarken bestimmende Kreativität und Stilbildung gefördert. Die bei Luxusmarken besonders ausgeprägte **Adaptions- und Innovationsfähigkeit** ist die Voraussetzung, um modische Trends selbst aktiv bestimmen zu können. Damit einher geht oftmals eine ganzheitliche und starke Unternehmenskultur, welche die erforderliche Konsistenz, Kontinuität und Authentizität der Marke über viele Produktfelder hinweg im Rahmen des ständigen Innovationsprozesses sichern.

Eine weitere zentrale Identitätsquelle stellt das **Herkunftsland** dar, das gerade für Luxusmarken eine besondere Bedeutung aufweist (Piron 2000, S. 317). Dieser Country-of-Origin-Effekt kann sich sehr spezifisch auf eine einzelne Marke (zum Beispiel Lange & Söhne aus Glashütte) oder abstrakt auf eine ganze Markenklasse (französischer Champagner, russischer Kaviar, italienische Herrenmode) beziehen. Obgleich der Einfluss des Country-of-Origin-Effektes auf die Markenidentität länderspezifisch variiert, erweist sich besonders Frankreich als identitätsprägend für viele der bekannten Luxusmarken (Dubois/ Paternault 1997, S. 79 ff.).

Gerade bei Luxusmarken stellen neben dem bereits erwähnten Markennamen weltweit bekannte **Symbole** ein weiteres bestimmendes Element der Markenidentität dar (Braun 1997, S. 281). So wird die „Spirit of Ecstasy" ebenso untrennbar mit Rolls-Royce assoziiert wie die ineinander verschränkten Buchstaben mit Chanel. Während bei generischen Marken die visuellen Gestaltungselemente oftmals eine reine Orientierungsfunktion erfüllen, vermitteln die genannten Symbole darüber hinaus den speziellen Mythos einer Luxusmarke.

Schließlich wird die Identität von Luxusmarken stark von **Besonderheiten im operativen Vermarktungssystem** geprägt. Hierzu zählen neben einer überragenden Produktqualität und einem selektiven Vertrieb vor allem die Preisstellung. Dies zeigt sich zum Beispiel in einer McKinsey-Studie, in der die Fähigkeit, über einen Zeitraum von mehr als fünf Jahren einen substanziell höheren Preis als eine Marke mit vergleichbaren tangiblen Eigenschaften zu erzielen, als objektivierbares Kriterium für eine Luxusmarke herausgestellt wird (McKinsey 1990).

3.2 Besonderheiten im Fremdbild von Luxusmarken: Selbstkongruenz und Wertausdruck

Im Rahmen der identitätsorientierten Markenführung ist das Image einer Luxusmarke als Fremdbild der Markenidentität zu interpretieren. Es stellt damit das Ergebnis einer Allokation der Ressourcen dar, die das Selbstbild der Markenidentität prägen.

Die Besonderheiten im Fremdbild einer Luxusmarke basieren auf den spezifischen Assoziationen, die das Image im Wahrnehmungsraum der Nachfrager bestimmen. Dabei lässt sich Luxus beziehungsweise luxuriös selbst als eine mögliche Imageausprägung charakterisieren, die neben den bereits in Kapitel 2 genannten Spezifika von verschiedenen Subitems wie zum Beispiel edel, stilvoll, teuer, geschmackvoll, excellent oder wertvoll geprägt wird. Im Gegensatz zu generischen Marken dominieren emotionale, abstrakte Assoziationen gegenüber rationalen, auf konkrete Produkteigenschaften bezogene Vorstellungen. Bei der Kaufentscheidung treten damit funktionale Nutzendimensionen gegenüber emotional-symbolischen Eigenschaften der Marke zurück: „More than other products, luxury items are bought for what they mean, beyond what they are" (Dubois/Paternault 1995, S. 71).

Einen theoretisch fundierten Rahmen für die Analyse des symbolischen Konsums von Marken liefert die Selbstkonzeptforschung. Das **Selbstkonzept beziehungsweise das Selbstimage** eines Menschen umfasst nach Rosenberg „the totality of the individual's thoughts and feelings having reference to himself as an object" (Rosenberg 1979, S. 9). Es handelt sich um ein System aus Werten, Zielen und Regeln, das es dem Individuum erlaubt, seine Wahrnehmung und Handlungen im Kontext seiner Umwelt zu organisieren und somit eine eigene Wirklichkeit zu konstruieren. Zentral für die Entstehung und Entwicklung des Selbstkonzepts ist dabei die Interaktion mit der sozialen Umwelt des Individuums (Familie, Freunde, sonstige Referenzgruppen). Dabei werden Verbindungen zwischen eigenen Handlungen und den Reaktionen der relevanten Umwelt auf diese Handlungen hergestellt und im Kontext des Selbstkonzeptes interpretiert.

Eine besondere Bedeutung kommt dabei neben den beteiligten Subjekten (das Individuum und seine soziale Umwelt) den Objekten der Interaktionen zu, wenn mit ihnen signifikante soziale Bedeutungsmuster verbunden werden. Produkte, Dienstleistungen, Einkaufstätten und insbesondere Marken können in dieser Perspektive als **Symbole** interpretiert werden, deren Konsumption als Instrument der indirekten Kommunikation zwischen Individuen und deren sozialer Umwelt fungieren können (Levy 1959; Grubb/Grathwohl 1967; Sirgy 1982; Lee 1990).

Die **Anforderungen an symbolische Kommunikationsobjekte** werden dabei von Luxusmarken besonders gut erfüllt:

- **Hohe soziale Aufmerksamkeit** beziehungsweise hohe Aufmerksamkeit beim Kauf oder Gebrauch der Marke als notwendige Bedingung, um symbolische Werte für eine Vielzahl von Personen darstellen zu können (Holman 1980; Belk/Bahn/Mayer 1982, S. 24 ff.; Sirgy 1982, S. 287 f.).
- Soziale und persönliche **Relevanz der assoziierten Bedeutung** für das Selbstkonzept der Nachfrager. Gerade Luxusmarken weisen erstrebenswerte Assoziationen beziehungsweise Werte auf, die als sozial relevant erachtet werden können, zum Beispiel in Form von Status und Prestige (Adlwarth 1983, S. 49 ff.).
- Ein hoher Grad an **Spezifität**, der es dem Nachfrager erlaubt, auf verschiedene Marken aus einem Produktfeld zum Ausdruck seines Selbstkonzeptes zurückgreifen zu können. Die intendierten Wirkungen können demnach nur durch spezielle, unterscheidbare Marken erfolgen, nicht jedoch durch allseits gebrauchte Massenmarken (Kroeber-Riel/Trommsdorff 1973, S. 69).
- Die Existenz einer **starken Markenpersönlichkeit** als Summe der mit dem Markenimage assoziierten relevanten Eigenschaften (Grubb/Hupp 1968, Holmann 1980). Hier ist bei Luxusmarken besonders an Gründerpersönlichkeiten zu denken, die für die Marke stehen (zum Beispiel Joop, Sander, Armani).

Der letztgenannte Punkt verweist bereits auf den **Mechanismus der symbolischen Kommunikation,** der durch einen Vergleich der Persönlichkeit des Markenrezipienten mit der aus der Markenidentität abgeleiteten Persönlichkeit der Marke gekennzeichnet ist. Dieser Vergleich kann sich auf das reale Selbstbild der Nachfrager oder auf dessen Idealbild des eigenen Selbst, das heißt auf eine Wunschvorstellung der eigenen Persönlichkeit, beziehen. Die Markenpersönlichkeit wird dabei analog zu einer Humanpersönlichkeit aufgefasst und gleichsam beseelt, wodurch ein Vergleich der beiden Persönlichkeiten und als Folge ein Transfer relevanter Merkmale der Markenpersönlichkeit auf die eigene Persönlichkeit erleichtert wird. Gelingt diese „symbolische Selbstergänzung“ (Buß 1998), kann die Luxusmarke die in Abbildung 2 dargestellten Funktionen erfüllen (Grubb/Grathwohl 1967): Wird das Image der Luxusmarke von der relevanten Umwelt der Nachfrager geteilt, kann die Marke die **extrinsische Funktion** eines indirekten Kommunikationskanals zwischen Individuum und dessen sozialer Umwelt erfüllen. Die Markenwahl führt zu einer vom Nachfrager intendierten Reaktion seiner sozialen Umwelt, die zum Beispiel in einer Einordnung des Individuums als stilvoll oder mächtig bestehen kann. Erfolgt die Reaktion in der intendierten Weise, kommt es letztlich zu einer Bestätigung oder Erhöhung des Selbstkonzepts (Dubois/Laurent/Czellar 2001).

Darüber hinaus erfüllt die Marke auch eine **intrinsische Funktion**, indem der Konsument die der Marke sozial beigemessenen Eigenschaften direkt auf seine eigene Persönlichkeit überträgt. Beispielsweise kann ein Konsument seine Selbsteinschätzung, er sei elegant und stilvoll, durch den Kauf eines Anzuges einer italienischen Luxusmarke bestätigen. Die Marke dient damit als Symbol in einem internen Kommunikationsprozess und trägt auf diese Weise ebenfalls zu einer Festigung oder Erhöhung des Selbstkonzepts bei.

Abbildung 2: Der Zusammenhang von Selbstkonzept, Markenidentität und symbolischem Konsum

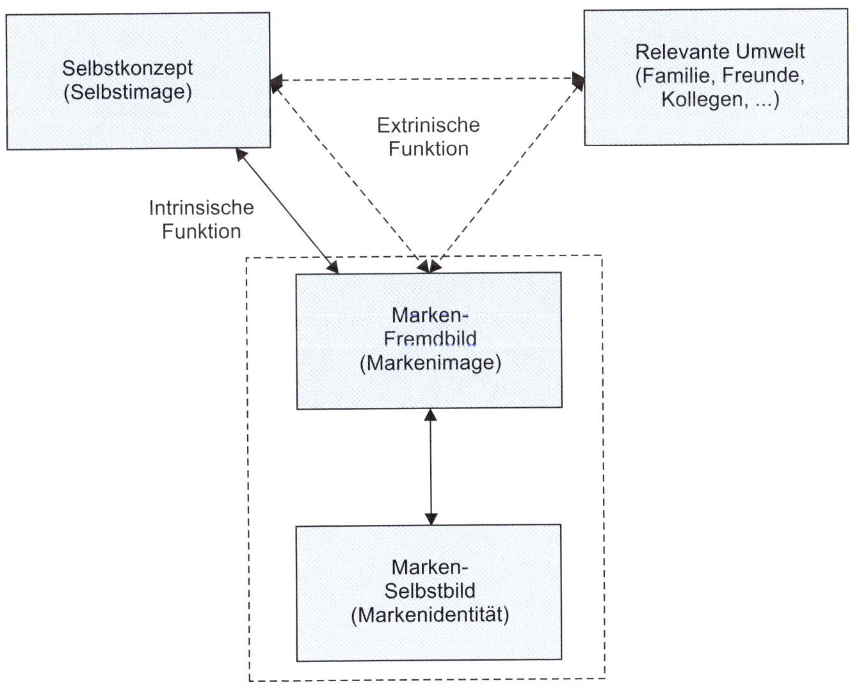

GABLER GRAFIK

Quelle: in Anlehnung an Grubb/Grathwohl 1967

In einer Erweiterung dieses Modells lässt sich die Wahl von Luxusmarken auf drei zentrale Motive zurückführen, die wiederum auf situativ unterschiedlich dominante Facetten des Selbstkonzepts zurückzuführen sind: Das private, distinktive oder öffentliche Selbstkonzept (vgl. Abbildung 3 beziehungsweise zur Struktur des Modells Hogg/Cox/Keeling 2000).

Abbildung 3: **Motive der Luxusmarkenwahl**

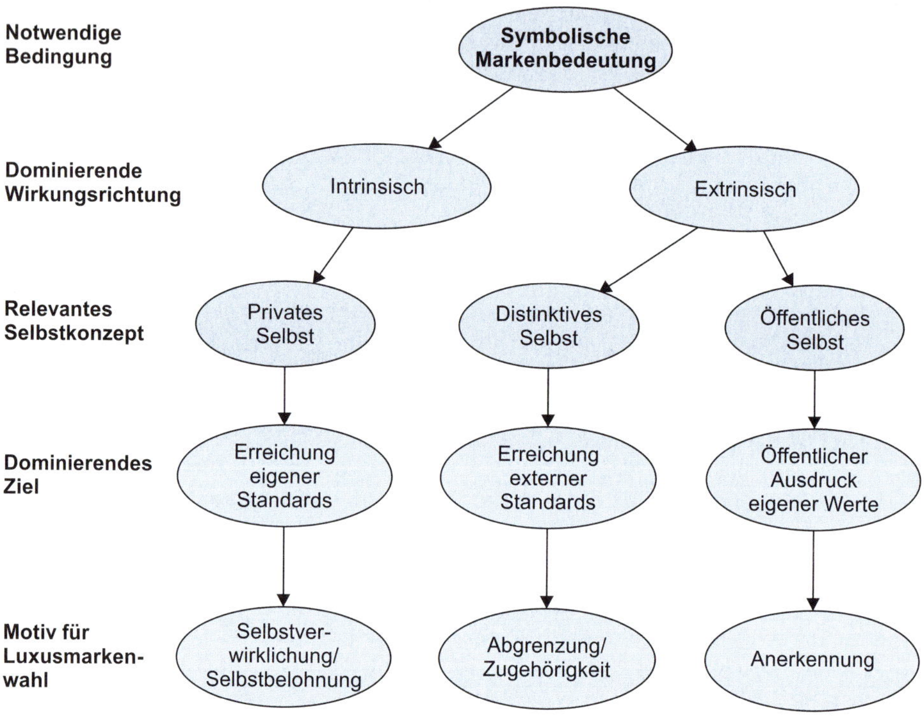

GABLER GRAFIK

Das **private Selbstkonzept** der Nachfrager moderiert den bereits beschriebenen Prozess, in dem der Konsument durch den Besitz und die Verwendung von Luxusmarken die eigenen, internalisierten Wertestandards zu erreichen sucht. Es dominieren nicht außengeleitete Motive, sondern das Bestreben, das Image der Luxusmarke auf seine eigene Persönlichkeit zu übertragen sowie der primär intrinsische Wunsch, sich selbst gut zu behandeln (Mayer 1998, S. 49). Die dahinter stehenden Motive der **Selbstverwirklichung** und **Selbstbelohnung** sind als intrinsisch zu klassifizieren, weil sich die zur Motivbefriedigung zentrale ideelle Nutzendimension der Marke hier grundsätzlich ohne direkten Kontakt zur Außenwelt entfalten kann. Voraussetzung für diese Wirkungen ist allein eine konkrete Vorstellung über die reale und ideale Komponente des Selbst und der Markenpersönlichkeit. Diese Wirkungskette bietet eine Erklärung für die Nachfrage nach qualitativ hochwertigen, aber weniger auffälligen Luxus- beziehungsweise Kennermarken (Diez 2001, S. 20).

Die Orientierung am **distinktiven Selbstkonzept** zielt primär auf die Erreichung von externen Standards ab, die von den relevanten sozialen Einflussgruppen der Nachfrager gesetzt werden. Durch die Wahl einer Luxusmarke soll damit mehr oder minder bewusst das Motiv befriedigt werden, eine horizontale **Abgrenzung** beziehungsweise **Zugehörigkeit** zu bestimmten Gruppen sowie eine vertikale Abgrenzung beziehungsweise Zugehörigkeit zu bestimmten, in der Regel unteren Schichten auszudrücken. Dieser Wirkungsmechanismus verdeutlicht ebenfalls die Relevanz der ideellen Nutzendimension von Luxusmarken. Besonders stark wird die distinktive Funktion von hochpreisigen Luxusmarken erfüllt, da deren Besitz direkt auf den intendierten wirtschaftlichen Status des Besitzers schließen lässt.

Das **öffentliche Selbstkonzept** ist gleichsam auf die Stellung des Individuums in seiner sozialen Umwelt bezogen. Es zielt aber nicht primär auf den Aus- oder Einschluss des Individuums von oder zu bestimmten Gruppen und Schichten ab, sondern vielmehr auf eine generell positive Beurteilung eigener Wertvorstellungen durch die relevante soziale Umwelt. Damit liefert dieser Wirkungspfad eine Erklärung für das Streben nach ästhetisch-kulturellem Luxus, der eher als schön und stilvoll denn als status- und prestigeträchtig angesehen wird. Die Eigenschaft einer Luxusmarke, als Beweismittel für den eigenen guten Geschmack, Stil und andere als wichtig erachtete Persönlichkeitswerte dienen zu können, stellt hier das zentrale Auswahlmotiv dar.

4. Management von Luxusmarken

4.1 Strategische Optionen für Luxusmarken

Unter strategischen Gesichtspunkten ergeben sich für die Führung von Luxusmarken zwei sequentielle Problemfelder: Zunächst gilt es, eine Positionierung im Luxussegment aufzubauen. Hier stehen neben dem Aufbau einer neuen Marke der Erwerb fremder Luxusmarken sowie die Revitalisierung traditionsreicher Marken zur Verfügung. In der zweiten Phase gilt es dann, für die einzelne Luxusmarke oder ein Luxusmarkenportfolio strategische Optionen zur Absicherung und weiteren Entwicklung der Wettbewerbsposition beziehungsweise Wachstum, zu identifizieren, zu bewerten und zu nutzen. Eine profilierte Position kann aus Sicht des gesamten Markenportfolios insbesondere durch weitere Akquisitionen gefestigt werden. Beim Management einer einzelnen Luxusmarke kann diese zunächst in der bestehenden Produktkategorie im Rahmen der Line Extension ausgeweitet werden. Zudem lassen sich insbesondere bei Luxusmarken die Dehnung der

4.2 Besonderheiten des operativen Managements von Luxusmarken

4.21 Markenbildung durch überragende Qualität und Design

Die Besonderheiten der Produktpolitik bestehen bei Luxusmarken vor allem hinsichtlich Design, Fertigung und Programmpolitik. Die Sicherstellung und Vermittlung einer **überragenden Qualität** sowohl in funktionaler als auch kulturell-ästhetischer Hinsicht bildet die Grundlage, um die spezifische Symbolkraft einer Luxusmarke auch in den übrigen Instrumentalbereichen gewährleisten zu können. Kurzfristig erscheint es zwar durchaus möglich, mangelnde Produktsubstanz – und damit mangelnden technisch-funktionalen Nutzen – mit einem überragenden Markenimage beziehungsweise dem daraus resultierenden ideellen Nutzen zu kompensieren (zum Beispiel verfehltes Design in einer Haute-Couture-Show). Mittel- bis langfristig ist aber aufgrund des engen Zusammenhangs zwischen Substanz und Image eine überragende Substanzqualität unabdingbar für den dauerhaften Erfolg einer Luxusmarke.

Im Bereich **Produktdesign** kommt bei Luxusmarken der Anmutungswirkung besondere Bedeutung zu. Diese kann im Wesentlichen durch die Dimensionen Formgebung (zum Beispiel Bang&Olufsson), Farbgebung (zum Beispiel die Farbe Rot bei Ferrari), Geruch (zum Beispiel Chanel No. 5) und grafische Elemente (zum Beispiel der Polospieler bei Ralph Lauren) stilisiert werden. Daneben ist die Auswahl der verarbeiteten Materialien von hoher Bedeutung, da sie entscheidend für die Sinneswahrnehmung und damit symbolische Bedeutung einer Luxusmarke sein kann (zum Beispiel visuelle, olfaktorische und taktile Wirkungen von Wurzelholz und edlem Leder in der Innenausstattung eines Rolls-Royce). Neben der Gestaltung des eigentlichen Produktes kommt der **Verpackungsgestaltung** bei Luxusmarken besondere Bedeutung zu, insbesondere in den Bereichen Parfüms und hochwertige Alkoholika. Hier werden zur Vermittlung von Luxus vermehrt wertvolle Flakons oder Geschenkboxen aus hochwertigen Materialien wie Samt, Seide, Glas, Holz und Metall eingesetzt. In der Kombination dieser Materialien kann sich der hohe Anspruch einer Luxusmarke ausdrücken (Tonbridge 1995, S. 17).

Neben der durch das Design primär vermittelten ästhetischen Anmutung muss eine Luxusmarke dauerhaft höchste funktionale Anforderungen hinsichtlich Zuverlässigkeit und Haltbarkeit erfüllen. Bei Luxusuhren macht zum Beispiel die Eigenkonstruktion und handwerkliche Fertigung eines mechanischen Uhrwerks den wesentlichen Nutzen der Marke aus. Neben diesem **handwerklichen Geschick** („Craftsmanship") bei kleineren Serien sind insbesondere die im Zuge von vertikalen Markendehnungen entstehenden hohen Produktionsvolumina einer strengen und rigiden Qualitätskontrolle zu unterziehen (Braun 1997, S. 84). Die Einführung umfassender **Qualitätssicherungssysteme** wie zum Beispiel TQM kann daher vor allem bei Luxusmarken als wichtiges Element der Markenführung angesehen werden.

Eine vergleichsweise hohe Bedeutung hat im Rahmen der Programmpolitik die Ausgabe von zeitlich und mengenmäßig limitierten **Sondereditionen** (Braun 1997, S. 85). Neben Sondereditionen ohne bestimmtes Thema kann es sich hierbei zum einen um ein speziell für einen bedeutenden, zumeist in der Öffentlichkeit stehenden Kunden angefertigtes Einzelstück (zum Beispiel die von den Haute-Couture-Marken zur jährlichen Oscar-Verleihung angefertigten Kleidungsstücke für bekannte und öffentlichkeitswirksame Schauspieler) beziehungsweise um eine begrenzte Serie unter direkter Bezugnahme auf eine öffentliche Persönlichkeit (zum Beispiel Edition Schumacher von Omega) handeln. Daneben kann mit der Wiederauflage eines schon einmal gefertigten Produktes (zum Beispiel die Wiederauflage des Uhrenmodells FHF durch die Luxusmarke Maurice Lacroix nach zehn Jahren) die besondere Bedeutung der Tradition für die Luxusmarke herausgestellt werden. Alle Formen der Sondereditionen betonen durch ihre limitierte Verfügbarkeit den einer Luxusmarke inhärenten Knappheitsaspekt und können so zu einer Erhöhung der Begehrlichkeit beitragen.

4.22 Markenbildung durch konstante Preispolitik

Im Rahmen der Preispolitik beruhen die Besonderheiten von Luxusmarken auf **spezifischen Funktionen des Preises**, die sich vor allem auf die Rabatt- und Konditionenpolitik der Anbieter auswirken.

Die gesamten mit einer Marke verbundenen tangiblen und intangiblen Eigenschaften wurden bereits in Kapitel 2 als Leistungsbündel interpretiert, das für den einzelnen Nachfrager einen bestimmten Gesamtnutzen aufweist. In der Regel ist dabei der Preis als wahrgenommenes Äquivalent dieses Leistungsbündels mit einem negativen Nutzenbeitrag verbunden (Schneider 1999, S. 3). Im Bereich von Luxusmarken kann dagegen der Preis einen **positiven Nutzenbeitrag** stiften, was sich in einer positiven Korrelation zwischen Preisniveau und Absatzmenge manifestiert. Dabei lassen sich zwei unterschiedliche Effekte voneinander abgrenzen (Diller 2000, S. 163). Im Rahmen der **preisorientierten Qualitätsbeurteilung** wird der Preis als Indikator für die Qualität einer Marke herangezogen. Als Resultat werden teurere Marken qualitativ besser eingeschätzt als billigere Marken. Während der Preis hier primär zur Risikoreduktion – bei Luxusmarken besonders zur Reduktion des sozialen Risikos – dient und somit als Qualitätsindikator fungiert, kann der Preis einer Marke auch direkt als positives Element zum Gesamtnutzen einer Luxusmarke beitragen. Bei diesem als **Veblen-Effekt** bezeichneten Verhalten wählen Nachfrager höherpreisige Luxusmarken aufgrund ihrer inhärenten Öffentlichkeitswirksamkeit aus, um damit bewusst finanziellen Wohlstand, Prestige und Status zu demonstrieren. Die dahinter stehende Wirkungslinie des distinktiven Selbstkonzepts zeigt sich dabei insbesondere in den Produktkategorien Mode, Uhren und Automobile.

Die Auswirkungen dieser Besonderheiten der Preisfunktion von Luxusmarken zeigt sich in einer **zurückhaltenden Rabatt- und Konditionenpolitik**. Da wahrgenommene Preissenkungen zu einer Abwertung des Gesamtnutzens der Luxusmarke und zu einer Zerstörung des Preisvertrauens führen können, erweisen sich die Abgabe- und Endverbraucherpreise von Luxusmarken über den Produktlebenszyklus vergleichsweise konstant im Vergleich zu unteren Segmenten (Diez 2001, S. 128 ff.). Auch gilt es, den **Preisabstand** zu den in der gleichen Produktkategorie angebotenen Nicht-Luxusmarken konstant zu halten, um die preisbedingte Aura der Luxusmarke nicht zu gefährden. Einen entscheidenden Beitrag hierzu kann insbesondere die Distributionspolitik liefern.

4.23 Markenbildung durch Flagship-Stores und selektiven Vertrieb

Im Bereich der Distributionspolitik lässt sich mit steigendem Luxusgrad der Marke und der Produktkategorie eine tendenziell **steigende Selektivität der Distributionspolitik** feststellen. So wird die aktuelle Designerkollektion von Chanel von einer wesentlich geringeren Anzahl an Outlets vertrieben als die Parfums oder Deodorants der gleichen Marke, deren Distribution wiederum deutlich selektiver als die Massenmarken der gleichen Güterkategorie vertrieben wird. Bei einer zunehmenden vertikalen Ausweitung der Luxusmarken steigt der Druck, breitere Distributionskanäle zu nutzen. Gleichzeitig darf das Luxusimage der Marke nicht beschädigt werden. Die Distributionsstruktur vieler Luxusmarken ist daher in drei Bereiche aufgeteilt (vgl. Abbildung 4), die sich insbesondere hinsichtlich der Sortimentsbreite, strategischen Ziele und Zielgruppen sowie den Verkaufsvolumina unterscheiden. Zudem differieren die einzelnen Kanäle bezüglich der Kontrollmöglichkeiten imagerelevanter Faktoren wie Standort, Ladengestaltung, und der Qualität des Verkaufspersonals (vgl. im Folgenden Nueno/Quelch 1997, S. 66 ff.; Braun 1997, S. 91 f.; Vukelic 2000, S. 138 ff.).

Die unter dem Aspekt der Markenführung höchste Priorität kommt eigenbetrieben, exklusiven Filialen **(„Flagship-Stores“)** zu. Diese bieten das komplette Sortiment der unter der Marke vertriebenen Produkte an, vermitteln die Identität und den Lifestyle der Luxusmarke und tragen oft selbst zum luxuriösen Image der Marke bei. Eng damit zusammenhängend ist die zusätzliche Aufgabe, die qualitativen Standards für die weiteren Distributionskanäle zu setzen. Die primäre Zielgruppe bilden die Stammkunden der Marke, denen die komplette Markenwelt präsentiert werden soll. Obgleich das volle Sortiment angeboten wird, ist der Anteil am gesamten Umsatzvolumen vergleichsweise gering, da relativ wenige Outlets dieser Art betrieben werden. Die bekanntesten Beispiele von Flagship-Stores finden sich in den internationalen Metropolen New York (Ralph Lauren auf der Madison Avenue), Paris (Louis Vuitton in Saint-Germain des Prés) und Tokyo (Espace TAG Heuer in Omotesando).

Abbildung 4: Vertriebskanäle von Luxusmarken

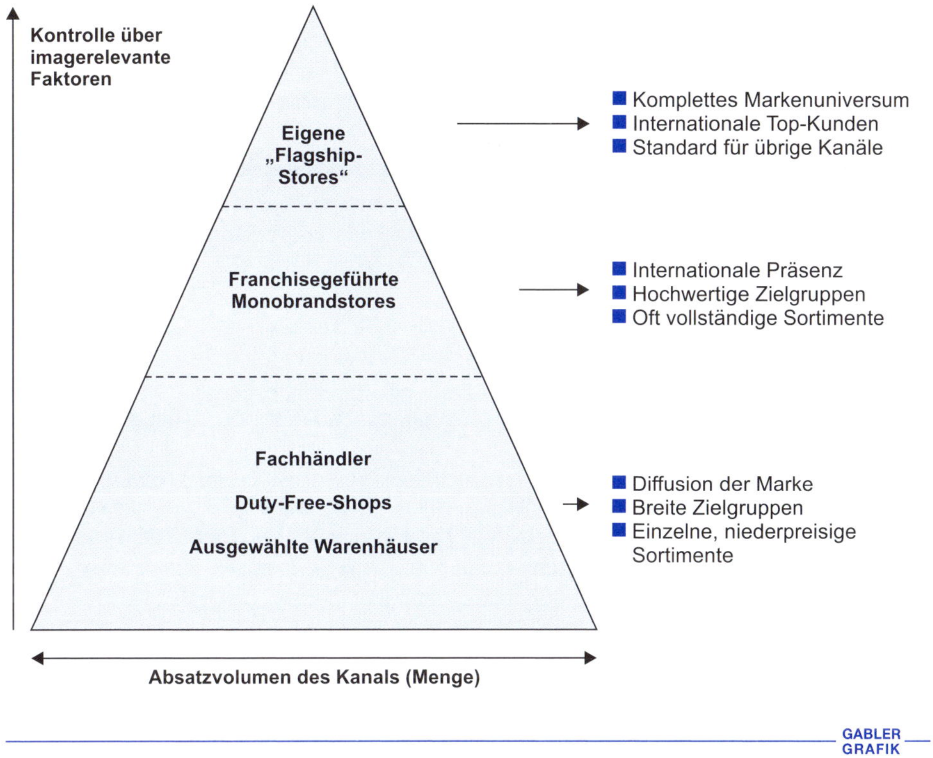

Quelle: in Anlehnung an Nueno/Quelch 1997

Eine Ebene unter den Flagship-Stores sind die zahlreichen **Franchise-betriebenen Verkaufsstätten** angesiedelt. Hierbei werden ebenfalls ausschließlich Produkte der eigenen Luxusmarke verkauft. Primäres strategisches Ziel ist die internationale Ausdehnung der Luxusmarke unter Sicherstellung der Markenidentität, mit der die gehobene, jedoch nicht nur die internationale Spitzenzielgruppe der Marke angesprochen werden soll. Franchisenetzwerke eignen sich besonders dort, wo das lokale Vertriebs-Know-how nicht die Qualitätsstandards der Marke erfüllt.

Breitere Massensegmente werden schließlich durch ausgewählte **Fachhändler, Duty-Free-Shops und gehobene Warenhäuser** bedient. In diesen Vertriebskanälen werden jeweils nur einzelne, meist weniger exklusive und teure Sortimentsbausteine angeboten. Die Gefahr negativer Einflüsse auf das Markenimage ist hier am höchsten, da die Marke in der Regel weniger kontrolliert im direktem Wettbewerbsumfeld angeboten wird. Allerdings können durch diese Kanäle breitere Zielgruppen – sowohl hinsichtlich der sozialen Schicht als auch bezüglich der regionalen Ausdehnung – angesprochen werden. Die

Sicherstellung der Kontrolle über das gesamte Distributionssystem auch im Rahmen anhaltenden Wachstums ist damit stärker noch als bei generischen Marken einer der entscheidenden Erfolgsfaktoren bei der Führung von Luxusmarken.

4.24 Markenbildung durch symbolische Kommunikation

Besonderheiten der Kommunikation für Luxusmarken ergeben sich hinsichtlich der unterschiedlichen Bedeutung einzelner Kommunikationskanäle im Vergleich zu anderen Marken und der inhaltlichen Ausgestaltung der Markenkommunikation. Zurückhaltung in klassischen Massenmedien ist das herausragende Merkmal. Dabei fällt besonders die weit unterdurchschnittliche Gewichtung klassischer TV-Werbung im Kommunikationsmix von Luxusmarken auf (Braun 1997, S. 34). Dies lässt sich auf die nicht ausreichende Möglichkeit der vertikalen Kundendifferenzierung in diesem Medium zurückführen. Die im Luxusbereich dominierenden Kommunikationsformen weisen demgegenüber einen höheren Spezifitätsgrad auf, die es erlauben, gezielt einzelne Kundensegmente anzusprechen.

Ein großer Teil der Kommunikationsbudgets entfällt auf hochwertige, zum exklusiven Image der Marke kompatible **Anzeigentitel**. Diese sind gekennzeichnet durch eine Nähe zu distinktiven (zum Beispiel Wirtschaftsmagazine: Status, Prestige) und wertexpressiven Themenfeldern (zum Beispiel Modemagazine: Stil, Eleganz) auf. Die inhaltliche Gestaltung der **Anzeigen** zielt typischerweise auf die Vermittlung emotional-symbolischer Erlebniswelten durch die erlebnisorientierte, oftmals sinnlich-erotische Darstellung von Personen oder auf die unkommentierte Produktdarstellung ab. Die vermittelte Botschaft ist dabei weniger direkt als symbolisch im Vergleich zu herkömmlichen Marken, da der Sprachanteil deutlich geringer ausfällt und oft auf die reine Darstellung des Markenlogos beschränkt bleibt. Die Anzeigen spiegeln folglich stärker die Markenästhetik und -inszenierung (Diez 2001, S. 109 ff.) denn ein konkretes Nutzenversprechen wider (vgl. Abbildung 5).

Ebenfalls direkte, aber sogenannte nicht-klassische Kommunikationskanäle stellen **Sponsoringaktivitäten und Events** dar. Während mit dem Sponsoring die systematische Förderung von Personen, Organisationen oder Veranstaltungen gemeint ist, wird unter Events die eigenständige Inszenierung von Veranstaltungen durch ein Unternehmen verstanden (Lasslop 2003). Sponsoring wird von vielen Luxusmarken dazu genutzt, Internationalität, Exklusivität und kulturelle Kompetenz zu demonstrieren.

So engagiert sich Boss beispielhaft in der Formel 1 und im weltweit berühmten New Yorker Guggenheim-Museum (Joachimsthaler/Aaker 2001, S. 548). Selbstkonzipierte Events, bei denen im Gegensatz zum Sponsoring eine wesentlich enger gezielte Kommunikation zwischen Marke und Konsument angestrebt wird, finden sich dagegen häufig im Rahmen von Produktvorstellungen (insbesondere bei Kollektionspräsentationen der Haute-Couture-Häuser) statt. Durch Events lassen sich die besonders für Luxusmarken wichtigen emotional-symbolischen Markeninhalte in Form von multisensualen Erlebniswelten mit hoher Effektivität transportieren.

Abbildung 5: Beispielhafte Kommunikation von Luxusmarken

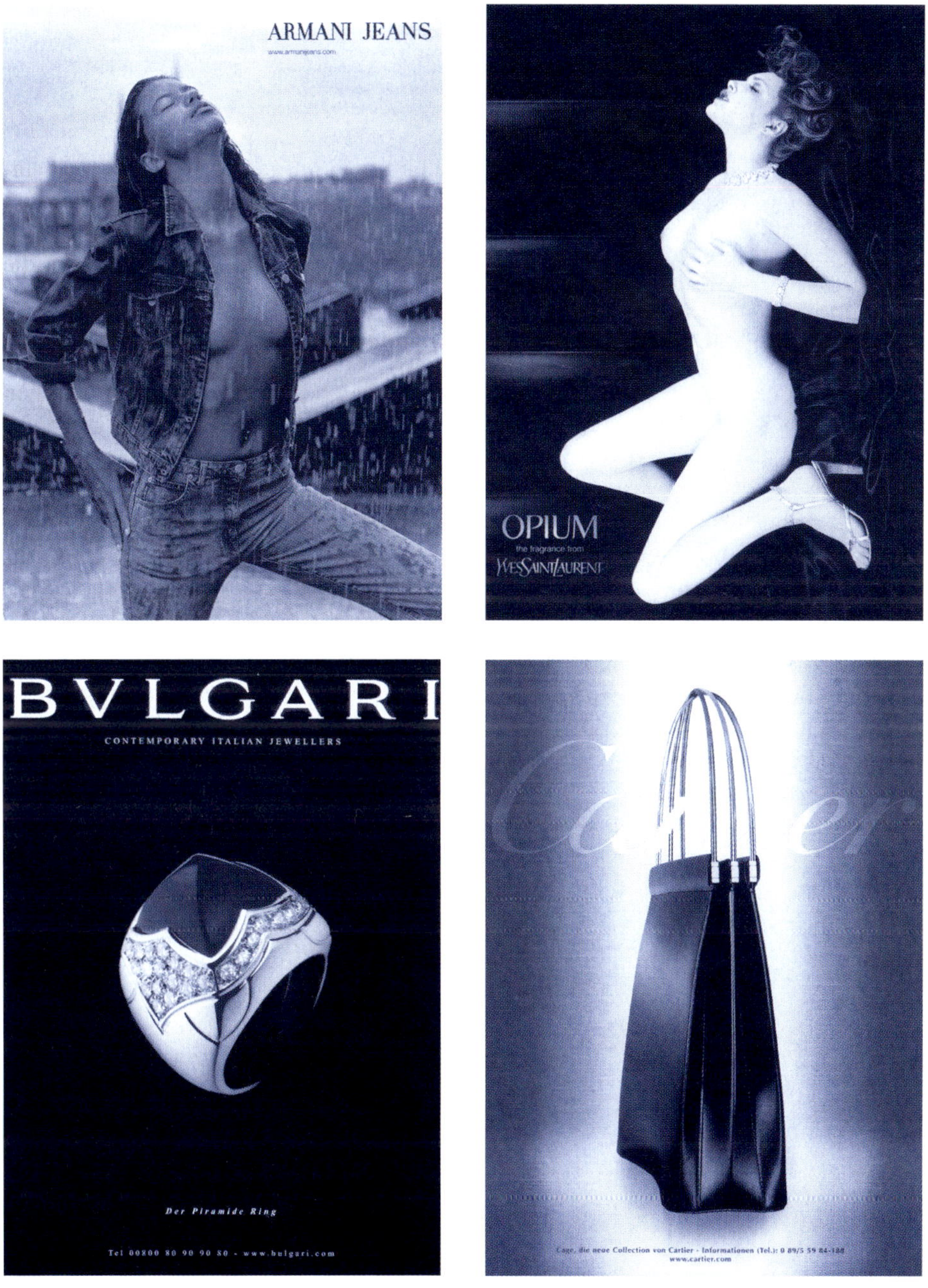

GABLER GRAFIK

Der Erfolg dieser ereignisbezogenen Maßnahmen hängt entscheidend davon ab, wer neben der direkten Zielgruppe (Teilnehmer, Besucher der Sponsoringveranstaltung/ des Events) an den Veranstaltungen teilnimmt und wie die Berichterstattung in den Medien ausfällt. Trotz einer vergleichsweise starken Präsenz in den Medien und einem damit höheren Anteil freier Berichterstattung („free editorial press“, Braun 1997, S. 34) kommt der planmäßigen Beziehungspflege zu Journalisten und prominenten Meinungsführern im Rahmen der **Public Relations** damit große Bedeutung zu.

In den letzten Jahren wird von einigen Luxusmarken verstärkt das Instrument des **Product Placements** eingesetzt. Dabei werden in der klassischen Form Markenprodukte deutlich sichtbar in Filmen und Serien eingesetzt (Meffert 2001, S. 734). Als besonders geeignetes Umfeld für Luxusmarken können wiederum Filme angesehen werden, die ein internationales und hochwertiges Image vermitteln. So fanden sich zum Beispiel im Rahmen des Films „James Bond: The world is not enough“ neben Bollinger (Champagner), Calvin Klein und Omega noch weitere Luxusmarken.

Zusätzlich ist die bestehende Kundenbasis als wichtiger Kommunikationsmultiplikator für die Marke gezielt und **direkt** anzusprechen. Hier bieten sich besonders der Aufbau von elitären Kundenclubs sowie die Herausgabe hochwertiger Kundenzeitschriften an (Belz 1994, S. 649). Diese Maßnahmen können den Charakter der Kennerschaft und des Netzwerkgedankens, der sich aus der Distinktionsfunktion der Luxusmarke ableitet, unter den bestehenden Kunden fördern und somit zu einer Stärkung der Markenbindung beitragen.

Generell ist auch bei Luxusmarken auf eine starke **Integration der Kommunikation** zu achten. Dies gilt neben der inhaltlichen, räumlichen und zeitlichen Abstimmung besonders für die Wahrung höchster qualitativer Standards aller Kommunikationsträger: „The magazines selected for advertising (…), the movies in which the brand appears, the celebreties and pop-icons seen wearing the brand – all contribute to the brand image.“ (Nueno/Quelch 1997, S. 64).

5. Fazit

Der Wandel in den wirtschaftlichen und sozio-kulturellen Rahmenbedingungen in den westlichen Industrienationen hat zu einer gestiegenen Bedeutung des Konsums von Luxusmarken geführt. Aus theoretischer Perspektive ermöglichen die Selbstkonzept- sowie die symbolische Interaktionsforschung eine differenzierte Analyse der Anziehungskraft von Luxusmarken. Luxusmarken dienen demnach als Symbol in einem sozialen oder individuellen Kommunikationsprozess und befriedigen Bedürfnisse nach Selbstverwirklichung, sozialer Abgrenzung und Anerkennung. Die hier gewonnenen Einsichten sind insbesondere hilfreich im Rahmen der operativen Gestaltung von Luxusmarken, begrenzen jedoch gleichzeitig die strategischen Möglichkeiten um eine breite Ausdehnung dieser Marken in untere Massensegmente.

Für die Führung von Luxusmarken ergibt sich die Notwendigkeit einer holistischen Betrachtung aller relevanten Gestaltungsparameter des Marketing unter markenpolitischen Gesichtspunkten, da das präferenzbildende Markenfremdbild im Kopf der Nachfrager weniger durch eigenen Gebrauch der Marken, sondern vor allem durch die Wahrnehmung der einzelnen Facetten des Vermarktungssystems entsteht. Nur durch konsistentes und kontinuierliches Management der Markenidentität kann daher letztlich eine für starke Luxusmarken kennzeichnende mythische Aufladung und daraus resultierende Begehrlichkeit der Marke entstehen.

Die Forschung hat den Schwerpunkt ihrer Bemühungen hinsichtlich vertikaler Markenstrategien in den letzten Jahren häufig auf Handelsmarken beschränkt. Vor dem Hintergrund eines weiter wachsenden Verlusts der Mitte in vielen Produktkategorien werden Fragestellungen, die sich mit den spezifischen Besonderheiten der Markenführung von Luxusmarken beschäftigen, in Zukunft weiter an Bedeutung gewinnen.

Literatur

Adlwarth, W. (1983), Formen und Bestimmungsgründe prestigegeleiteten Konsumentenverhaltens: Eine verhaltenstheoretisch-empirische Analyse, München.

Arnauld, B. (2000), Präsentation im Rahmen der Bilanzpressekonferenz von LVMH am 17.5.2000 in Paris, www.lvmh.com/finance/agm2000/ba_/ sld006.htm, Abruf vom 6.6.2001.

Bearden, W. O., Etzel, M. J. (1982), Reference Group Influence on Product and Brand Purchase Decisions, in: Journal of Consumer Research, September, S. 183–194.

Belk, R. W., Bahn, K. D., Mayer, R. N. (1982), Development recognition of consumption symbolism, in: Journal of Consumer Research, Juni, S. 4–17.

Belz, O. (1994), Luxusmarkenstrategie, in: Bruhn, M. (Hrsg.), Handbuch Markenartikel, Band 1, Stuttgart, S. 645–652.

Berry, C.J. (1994), The Idea of Luxury: A Conceptual and Historical Investigation, Cambridge.

Braitmayer, O. (1998), Die Lizensierung von Marken, Frankfurt/M.

Braun, M. (1997), Becoming an Institutional Brand. A long-Term-Strategy for Luxury Goods, St. Gallen.

Burmann, Ch.; Blinda, L.; Nitschke, A. (2003), Konzeptionelle Grundlagen des identitätsbasierten Markenmanagements, Arbeitspapier Nr. 1 des Lehrstuhls für innovatives Markenmanagement (LiM), Burmann, Chr. (Hrsg.) , Universität Bremen, Bremen.

Buß, E. (1998), Die Marke als soziales Symbol. Überlegungen zu einem neuen Markenverständnis, in: Public Relations Forum, Nr. 2, S. 96–100.

Chaudhuri, A. (1998), Product class effects on perceived risk: The role of emotion, in: International Journal of Research in Marketing, S. 157–168.

Dierickx, J., Cool, K. (1989), Asset Stock Accumulation and Sustainability of Competitive Advantage, in: Management Science, Vol. 35, Dezember, S. 1504–1513.

Diller, H. (2000), Preispolitik, Stuttgart.

Diez, W. (2001), Herausforderungen und Perspektiven im Premiummarkt für Automobile, Forschungsbericht Nr. 22/2001, Institut für Automobilwirtschaft (IFA) an der Fachhochschule Nürtigen.

Dubois, B., Paternault, C. (1995), Observations: Understanding the World of International Luxury Brands: The “Dream” Formula, in: Journal of Advertising Research, Juli/August, S. 69–76.

Dubois, B., Paternault, C. (1997), Does Luxury Have a Home Country?, in: Marketing and Research Today, Mai, S. 79–85.

Dubois, B., Duquesne, P. (1993), The Market für Luxury Goods: Income versus Culture, in: European Journal of Marketing, No. 1, S. 35–44.

Dubois, B., Laurent, G., Czellar, S. (2001), Consumer Rapport To Luxury: Analyzing Complex And Ambivalent Attitudes, Working Paper, Paris.

Esch, F.-R., Fuchs, M., Bräutigam S., Redler, J. (2001), Konzeption und Umsetzung von Markenerweiterungen, in: Esch, F. R. (Hrsg.), Moderne Markenführung, 3. Aufl., Wiesbaden. S. 755–791.

Grubb, E., Grathwohl, H. (1967), Consumer Self-Concept, Symbolism and Market Behaviour: A Theoretical Approach, in: Journal of Marketing, October, S. 22–27.

Grubb, E. L., Hupp, G. (1968), Perception of Self, Generalized Stereotypes, and Brand Selection, in: Journal of Marketing Research, Februar, S. 58–63.

Haas, A. (2000), Pemiummarke – Quo Vadis?, in: Markenartikel 3/2000, S. 36–42.

Haseloff, O. W. (2000), Personale und soziale Funktion des privaten Verbrauchs, in: Rosenberger, G. (Hrsg.), Konsum 2000, Frankfurt/M., S. 141–156.

Hogg, M. K., Michell, P. (1996), Identity, Self and Consumption: A Conceptual Framework, in: Journal of Marketing Management, S. 629–644.

Hogg, M. K., Cox, A. J, Keeling, K. (2000), The impact of self-monitoring on image congruence and product/brand evaluation, in: European Journal of Marketing, No.5/6, S. 641–666.
Holman, R. H. (1980), Clothing as communication: an empirical investigation, in: Advances in Consumer Research, S. 372–377.
Joachimsthaler, E., Aaker, D. (2001), Aufbau von Marken im Zeitalter der Post-Massenmedien, in: Esch, F. R. (Hrsg.), Moderne Markenführung, 3. Aufl., Wiesbaden. S. 539–563.
Kapferer, J. N. (2001), Luxusmarken, in: Esch, F.-R. (Hrsg.), Moderne Markenführung, 3. Aufl., Wiesbaden. S. 345–364.
Karmasin, H. (1998), Produkte als Botschaften, 2. Aufl., Wien.
Kemp, S. (1998), Perceiving luxury and necessity, in: Journal of Economic Psychology, S. 591–606.
Kirmani, A., Sood, S., Bridges, S. (1999), The Ownership effect in Consumers Responses to Brand Line Stretches, in: Journal of Marketing, Januar, S. 88–101.
Kisabaka, L. (2001), Marketing für Luxusprodukte, Köln.
Kroeber-Riel, W., Trommsdorff, V. (1973), Markentreue beim Kauf von Konsumgütern – Ergebnisse einer empirischen Untersuchnung, in: Kroeber-Riel, W. (Hrsg.), Konsumentenverhalten und Marketing, Opladen, S. 57–82.
Krünitz, D. J. G. (1801), Oekonomisch-technologische Encyclopädie, 82. Teil, Berlin.
Lee, D. H. (1990), Symbolic Interactionism: Some Implications for Consumer Self-Concept and Product Symbolism Research, in: Advances in Consumer Research, S. 386–393.
Levy, S. J. (1959), Symbols for Sale, in: Harvard Business Review, July/August, S. 117–124.
LVMH (2004), Documentation of the annual shareholders meeting.
Mayer, M. J. (1998), Luxus – ein Gefühl, in: Vogue, Dezember, S. 46–50.
McCracken, G. (1992), Die Geschichte des Konsums – ein Literaturüberblick und Leseführer, in: Rosenberger, G. (Hrsg.), Konsum 2000, Frankfurt/M., S. 25–51.
McKinsey (1990), The Luxury Industry: An Asset for France, Paris.
Meffert, H. (1994), Entscheidungsorientierter Ansatz der Markenpolitik, in: Bruhn, M. (Hrsg.), Handbuch Markenartikel, Band 1, Stuttgart, S. 173–197.
Meffert, H. (2000), Marketing. Grundlagen marktorientierter Unternehmensführung, 9. Aufl., Wiesbaden.
Meffert, H., Lasslop, I. (2004), Luxusmarkenstrategie, Arbeitspapier Nr. 164 der Wissenschaftlichen Gesellschaft für Marketing und Unternehmensführung, Münster.
Mühlmann, H. (1975), Luxus und Komfort. Wortgeschichte und Wortvergleich, Bonn.
Nueno, J. L, Quelch, J. A., (1998), The Mass Marketing of Luxury, in: Business Horizons, 11/12.
Piron, F. (2000), Consumers' perceptions of the country-of-origin effect on purchasing intentions of (in)conspicuous products, in: Journal of Consumer Marketing, No.4, S. 308–321.
Pöll, G. (1980), Luxus. Eine wirtschaftstheoretische Analyse, Berlin.
Rinsche, G. (1961), Der aufwendige Verbrauch – Sozialökonomische Besonderheiten geltungsbedingter Nachfrage, in: Kreikebaum, H., Rinsche, G., Das Prestigemotiv in Konsum und Investition, Berlin, S. 105–221.
Rosenberg, M. (1979), Conceiving the Self, New York.
Sattler, H. (2001), Markenpolitik, Stuttgart.
Schneider, H. (1999), Preisbeurteilung als Determinante der Verkehrsmittelwahl. Ein Beitrag zum Preismanagement im Verkehrsdienstleistungsbereich, Wiesbaden.
Sirgy, M. J. (1982), Self-concept in Consumer Behaviour: A critical Review, in: Journal of Consumer Research, December, S. 287–299.
Solomon, M. E. (1983), The Role of Products as Social Stimuli: A Symbolic Interactionism Perspective, in: Journal of Consumer Research, December, S. 319–329.
Tonbridge, H. (1995), Luxury Packaging, in: Packaging Week, November, S. 17–19.

Vishwanath, V., Mark, J. (1997), Premiummarken richtig führen, in: Harvard Business Manager, Nr. 4, S. 31–38.
Vukelic, S. (2000), Unternehmensidentität als Ressource. Zur Bedeutung eines identitätsorientierten Ressourcenmanagements für die Luxusgüterindustrie, Wiesbaden.
Wiswede, G. (1999), Groß-Engelmann, M., GfK-Trendsensor Konsum, Nürnberg.
Wölfer, U. (1994), Produktlinienerweiterung, in: Bruhn, M. (Hrsg.), Handbuch Markenartikel, Band 1, Stuttgart, S. 527–541.

Markenführung im professionellen Ligasport

Michael Welling

1.	**Bedeutungszuwachs der Markenführung im professionellen Ligasport als Folge einer veränderten Aufgabenumwelt**	**496**
2.	**Bedingungen und Herausforderungen einer identitätsorientierten Markenführung im Ligasport**	**500**
2.1	Leistungsbündelspezifische Besonderheiten des professionellen Ligasports als Ausgangspunkt	500
2.2	Multiple Zielgruppen der Markenführung als Konsequenz leistungsbündelspezifischer Besonderheiten	504
2.21	Leistungsabsatzbezogene Zielgruppen: Zuschauer als konsumtive und Sponsoren als investive Nachfrager	504
2.22	Leistungsaufteilungsbezogene Zielgruppen: Medien- und Agenturpartner sowie Netzwerkpartner im Dienstleistungszentrum Stadion	506
2.23	Leistungspotenzialbezogene Zielgruppen: Mitarbeiter im sportlichen und außersportlichen Bereich	508
3.	**Adaption des GAP-Modells der identitätsorientierten Markenführung für Ligasportklubs**	**510**
3.1	Harmonisierung von Selbst- und Fremdbildern als Leitidee für die Entwicklung eines GAP-Modells	510
3.2	Konzeption eines GAP-Modells für die Markenführung im Ligasport	511
3.3	Anwendung des GAP-Modells – ausgewählte Ergebnisse am Beispiel VfL Bochum 1848 e. V.	514
4.	**Fazit**	**518**

1. Bedeutungszuwachs der Markenführung im professionellen Ligasport als Folge einer veränderten Aufgabenumwelt

In der Ligasportindustrie wird Aktivitäten der Markenführung in den letzten Jahren von allen Beobachtern einhellig eine zunehmende Bedeutung beigemessen. Analog zur Entwicklung des Markenwesens in anderen Branchen (Meffert/Giloth 2002, S. 99 ff.) ist dies damit zu begründen, dass sich die Aufgabenumwelt von Organisationen des professionellen Ligasports durch dessen häufig skizzierten **ökonomischen Bedeutungszuwachs** verändert hat (Woratschek/Beier 2001, S. 209 ff.). Denn viele Sportarten befinden sich momentan im Übergang zur letzten Phase des Kommerzialisierungsprozesses nach Haase: Während in der Nullphase die ideellen Werte des Sports im Mittelpunkt stehen, die erste Instrumentalisierungsphase durch die Abkehr von diesen und die Hinwendung zu gesundheitsorientierten, aber auch politischen Interessen gekennzeichnet ist und sich die zweite Instrumentalisierungsphase durch die Vermarktung des Sports als Unterhaltung charakterisieren lässt, zeichnet sich die so genannte Produktionsphase durch die zunehmende Leistungserbringung durch sportfremde Investoren aus (Haase 1991, S. 6). Dieser Entwicklungsprozess ist vor allem durch Aspekte getrieben, die sich mit den Schlagworten Medialisierung und (teilweise dadurch begründet) Internationalisierung verbinden lassen.

Medialisierung bedeutet, dass Sportveranstaltungen von Medienunternehmungen als wichtiger Inputfaktor für die eigene Geschäftstätigkeit entdeckt wurden, um den Bedingungen der Aufmerksamkeitsökonomie (Franck 1998) zu begegnen. In Deutschland 1984 durch die Dualisierung des Rundfunksystems ausgelöst, mündete dies in einem Bieterwettbewerb für die medialen Distributionsrechte, der zu einem Großteil dafür verantwortlich ist, dass beispielsweise die 36 Profivereine der ersten und zweiten Fußballbundesliga in der Saison 2000/2001 erstmals mehr als eine Milliarde Euro Gesamtumsatz erzielen konnten, der in der folgenden Saison weiter auf 1,3 Milliarden Euro anstieg (vgl. Abbildung 1). Nach Angaben der DFL (Deutsche Fußball Liga GmbH) wurde dieser Umsatz zu 36,8 Prozent durch TV-Einnahmen, zu 23,8 Prozent durch Werbeeinnahmen und zu 16 Prozent durch Spieltageseinnahmen erlöst (DFL 2003, S. 8 f.).

Neben der Medialisierung ist die **Internationalisierung** ein entscheidender Veränderungstreiber der Aufgabenumwelt. Während die (Personal-)Beschaffungsprozesse bereits lange vor dem 1985 verabschiedeten Binnenmarktprogramm der Europäischen Kommission – das seit dem viel beachteten Bosman-Urteil des Europäischen Gerichtshofes 1995 endgültig auch auf den Sportbereich anzuwenden ist (Busche 2004, S. 89 f.) – schon globalen Charakter besaßen, findet die Internationalisierung inzwischen vermehrt Ausdruck in der Neukonzeption der Ligasportwettbewerbe (zum Beispiel die Etablierung so genannter Champions Leagues im Europäischen Fußball und Handball). Sie schafften die Vorraussetzung für die Ausweitung der Absatzmarkttätigkeiten über die angestammten nationalen Grenzen hinweg (Troisen 2001, S. 651 ff.).

Abbildung 1: **Entwicklung des Gesamtumsatzes im deutschen Lizenzfußball**

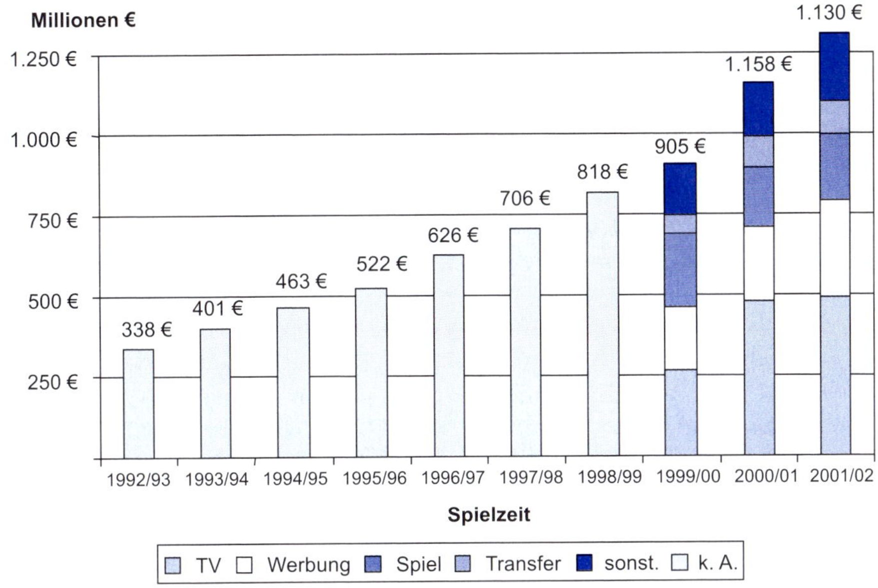

Quelle: DFL 2003, S. 15

So erreichte etwa die Fußballbundesliga im Jahr 2003 knapp 10,3 Millionen Zuschauer in den europäischen Kernmärkten (Deutschland, Frankreich, Italien, Spanien und England) außerhalb des eigenen Ländermarktes und konnte dadurch Einnahmen aus internationalen TV-Rechten von 15 Millionen Euro erzielen. Im Vergleich ist unter Berücksichtigung dieser Zahlen der Internationalisierungsprozess der englischen Premiere League noch weiter vorangeschritten, die es im gleichen Zeitraum auf 106,3 Millionen Zuschauer und 90 Millionen Euro Einnahmen bringen konnte (Klotz 2004, S. 27). Daneben kann die ausgedehnte Asienreise von Real Madrid im Rahmen der Saisonvorbereitung 2003/2004, deren kommerzieller Erfolg auch durch die Verpflichtung von David Beckham garantiert wurde, genauso als Indikator herangezogen werden, wie die erstmals im Sommer 2003 initiierte und im Sommer 2004 erweiterte „Champions World Series", eine auf dem nordamerikanischen Kontinent ausgetragene Reihe von Freundschaftsspielen, an der unter anderem Bayern München, Celtic Glasgow und Manchester United teilnahmen. Im globalen Ligen- und Klubwettbewerb zielen diese Aktivitäten darauf ab, sowohl dem Fußball insgesamt als auch den einzelnen Vereinen zu größerer Popularität zu verhelfen. Denn im Gegenzug wird der europäische Stammmarkt der Klubs bereits seit 1995 durch die National Football League (NFL) bearbeitet. Als umsatzstärkste Liga der Welt – 1998 wurde beispielsweise ein achtjähriger Fernsehvertrag mit einem Volumen von rund 17 Milliarden Euro abgeschlossen – investierte die NFL große Summen zur Etablierung der NFL Europe League, gründete Klubs wie Rhein Fire Düsseldorf, Amsterdam Admirals oder Scottish Claymores und lässt diese um die so genannte World Bowl spielen (Engels/Erdmann 2001, S. 220 f.).

Der Wandel der Aufgabenumwelt findet seinen Niederschlag darin, dass viele frühere „Idealvereine" Veränderungsprozesse mit dem Ziel initiierten, die Vereinsstrukturen den geänderten Anforderungen anzupassen. Die Ausgliederung von Lizenzspielerabteilungen in Kapitalgesellschaften als Reaktion auf den Vorwurf der Rechtsformverfehlung, in Deutschland von Borussia Dortmund mit einem viel beachteten und inzwischen kritisierten Börsengang verbunden (Paul/Sturm 2004), ist dabei das wohl offensichtlichste Beispiel für die **Professionalisierung** der Entscheidungsträger und damit der Entscheidungsprozesse. Ein weiteres, weniger bekanntes Beispiel ist die Einführung moderner Controlling-Systeme (Dörnemann 2002), etwa die Implementierung einer sportspezifischen Balanced Scorecard beim VfB Stuttgart, für die 30 Kriterien zur Steuerung einer Ligasportunternehmung isoliert wurden (Staudt 2004, S. 10). Wenngleich der derzeitige Entwicklungsstand dabei durch eine ausgeprägte Asymmetrie nicht nur zwischen den einzelnen Sportarten (zum Beispiel Fußball versus Handball versus Feldhockey), den unterschiedlichen Länderligen (zum Beispiel Premiere League versus Bundesliga versus Serie A) sowie zwischen einzelnen Klubs innerhalb einer Liga gekennzeichnet ist (zum Beispiel Bayern München versus VfL Bochum versus Arminia Bielefeld), darf angenommen werden, dass die Professionalisierung gleichzeitig dazu beiträgt, dass sich viele Strukturen, Prozesse und Leistungen der einzelnen Wettbewerber angleichen. Folglich wären gegenwärtige, zu Wettbewerbsvorteilen führende Differenzierungspotenziale nachhaltig in ihrem Bestand bedroht. Man denke etwa an die auch durch die Vergabe der Fußball-WM 2006 ausgelöste Entwicklung im Stadionbereich, die als Grund dafür anzusehen ist, dass in Deutschland inzwischen viele Klubs über wettbewerbsfähige Stadien verfügen.

Neben der Bewältigung weiterer Aufgaben wird vor diesem Hintergrund vor allem die **Notwendigkeit zur Professionalisierung der Markenführung** sowohl von Praktikern (Hoffmann, 2001; Zils 2002) als auch von Wissenschaftlern (Boone/Kochunny/Willkins 1995; Gladden/Milne/Sutton 1998) betont. Ausgangspunkt ist die in der Markenführungsliteratur ausgiebig erörterte Überlegung, dass durch starke Marken Differenzierungspotenziale realisierbar sind. Sie eröffnen die Chance, dass sich Klubs in ihrer Erlössituation vom sportlichen Erfolg abkoppeln und so die inhärente Erlösunsicherheit reduzieren. Für die im Sport tätigen Manager kommt dies einem neuen Selbstverständnis gleich. Denn bislang demonstrierten sie lediglich *„a consistently myopic view that winning is the only means to generate equity"* (Gladden/Irwin/Sutton, 2001, S. 301). Betrachtet man die von FutureBrand ermittelten Markenwerte europäischer Fußballklubs ist zwar die Korrelation zwischen sportlichem und wirtschaftlichem Erfolg nicht von der Hand zu weisen, unklar bleibt allerdings die Richtung des Zusammenhangs. Nach der FutureBrand-Methode wird der Markenwert von Manchester United, häufig als „reichster Fußballklub der Welt" apostrophiert, auf 288 Millionen Euro, der von Real Madrid auf 278 Millionen Euro, der vom AC Milan auf 197 Millionen Euro und der von Bayern München auf 149 Millionen Euro geschätzt. Die ersten vier Plätze dieser Rangliste nehmen also durchweg Klubs ein, die in den letzten Jahren auch sportliche Erfolge vorweisen konnten. Allerdings können bereits die Nummern 5 (FC Barcelona, 141 Millionen Euro), 10 (Liverpool FC, 84 Millionen Euro) und 14 (FC Schalke 04, 47 Millionen Euro) der Rangliste nur auf Erfolge blicken, die schon länger in der Vergangenheit liegen. Bayer Leverkusen, mit einem nach der FutureBrand-Methode ermittelten Markenwert von 40 Millionen Euro immerhin Nr. 15 im europäischen Vergleich, wartet hingegen noch immer auf den ersten sportlich bedeutsamen nationalen Titel der Vereinsgeschichte (vgl. Abbildung 2). Auch die Ligasportmarken mit dem nach einer früheren Studie höchsten Markenwert der Welt außerhalb des Fußballs (FutureBrand 2001), die Dallas Cowboys und die Washington Redskins (274 beziehungsweise 211 Millionen Dollar, beide NFL) scheinen es geschafft zu haben, den wirtschaftlichen vom sportlichen Erfolg abzukoppeln. Erste wissenschaftlich fundierte empirische Studien für die NBA, die NHL und die MLB (Gladden/Milne 1999) sowie für die Fußball-Bundesliga (Bauer/Sauer/Schmitt 2004) bestätigen diese Einschätzung.

Abbildung 2: **Markenwerte von Ligasportvereinen**

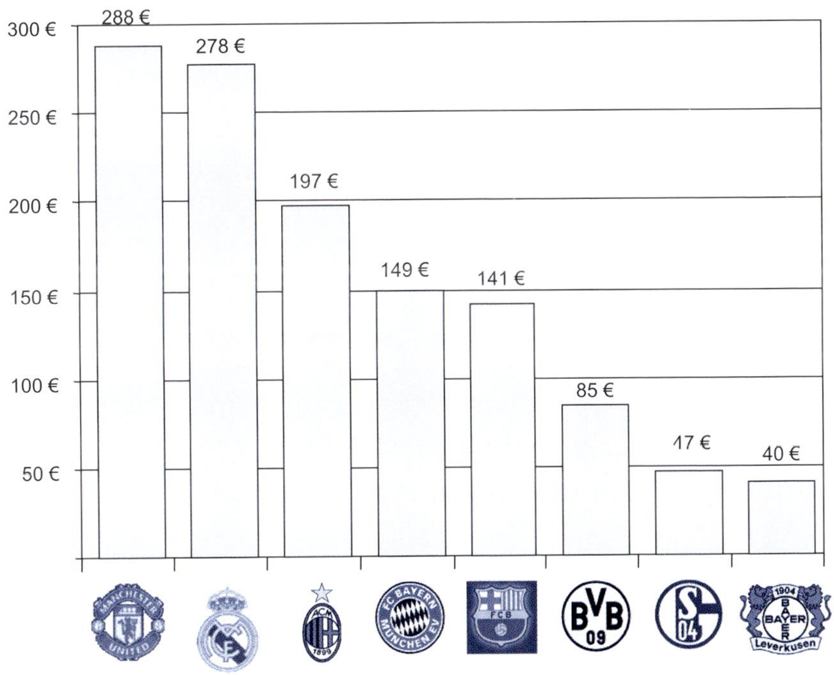

GABLER GRAFIK

Quelle: FutureBrand 2004

Für die Wertschaffung durch ein auf höchster Ebene zu initiierendes Markenführungskonzept bietet sich dabei die Grundidee der so genannten identitätsorientierten Markenführung an (Aaker 1992, Kapferer 1992; Meffert/Burmann 1996; Esch 2003), die im vorliegenden Sammelband ausführlich dokumentiert ist. Ohne auf die bereits an anderer Stelle herausgearbeiteten Unterschiede und Probleme der Konzeptionen der verschiedenen Autoren einzugehen (Welling 2003, S. 20 ff.), ist die **besondere Eignung der identitätsorientierten Markenführung** dadurch bedingt, dass Anbieter von Ligasportleistungen in ausgeprägter Form in einem vielschichtigen Beziehungsgeflecht agieren (müssen), das die Berücksichtigung unterschiedlichster interner und externer Zielgruppen erfordert, deren Interdependenzen bei der Markenführung zu berücksichtigen sind. Die identitätsorientierte Markenführung als funktionenübergreifender und somit ganzheitlicher Managementansatz betont aber gerade die interne und externe Perspektive gleichermaßen, wodurch das Management in die Lage versetzt wird, die Ansprüche unterschiedlicher Zielgruppen wertschaffend zu koordinieren (Meffert/Burmann/Koers 2002).

Das angesprochene Beziehungsgeflecht der unterschiedlichen Zielgruppen eines Ligasportklubs wird daher im folgenden Kapitel 2 herausgearbeitet und um die daraus resultierenden Besonderheiten der Markenführung im Ligasport ergänzt. Die auf leistungstheoretischen Überlegungen aufbauende Skizze und die gleichzeitig vorgenommene Ableitung der Interdependenzen zwischen den Zielgruppen dient dann als Grundlage für ein im Abschnitt 3 vorgestelltes GAP-Modell, das im Rahmen der Markenführung im Ligasport zum Einsatz kommen kann. Dass für das Anwendungsbeispiel auf empirische Belege aus dem Fußball zurückgegriffen wird und Beispiele aus diesem Bereich bei den Ausführungen dominieren, ist lediglich damit begründet, dass der Fußball in Europa die größte Bedeutung besitzt. Ohne weiteres sind die Aussagen aber auch auf Vereine anderer Ligasportarten übertragbar.

2. Bedingungen und Herausforderungen einer identitätsorientierten Markenführung im Ligasport

2.1 Leistungsbündelspezifische Besonderheiten des professionellen Ligasports als Augsangspunkt

In der wissenschaftlichen Literatur wird der 1956 im Journal of Political Economy veröffentlichte Beitrag von Simon Rottenberg für gewöhnlich als Beginn der sportökonomischen Forschungsarbeiten angegeben, in dem bereits die „eigenartige Ökonomie" (Neale 1964) des professionellen Ligasports herausgestellt wurde. Die auch als Louis-Schmeling-Paradox bezeichnete Eigenartigkeit wird vor allem darin gesehen, dass ein Akteur die entsprechende Leistung nicht alleine produzieren kann und somit nicht bestrebt sein wird, eine Monopolstellung einzunehmen (Kurscheidt 2004, S. 36 f.).

Die **Koproduktion** bezieht sich dabei vor allem auf die Kernleistungserstellung für den Teilhaber- beziehungsweise Zuschauermarkt, der sich dadurch auszeichnet, dass Nachfrager ihren Nutzen primär aus der sinnlichen Wahrnehmung des Sportspiels anderer ziehen. Dem Ligasport inhärent ist folglich, dass zwei wetteifernde Mannschaften erforderlich sind. Das führt dazu, dass auch ein Verein wie der FC Bayern München einen Partner wie den VfL Bochum für den Leistungserstellungsprozess benötigt. Generell sind somit alle Ligateilnehmer aufeinander angewiesen, um eine Meisterschaft als Summe einzelner Meisterschaftsspiele zu „produzieren". Die Nutzenstiftung für potenzielle Nachfrager nach Ligaspielen basiert deshalb auf Teilleistungen von zwei beziehungsweise n – bezogen auf die erste Fußballbundesliga von 18 – Anbietern. Für die Markenführung hat diese Besonderheit vor allem zwei, die Freiheitsgrade der Entscheidungsträger einschränkende Konsequenzen (Welling 2004a):

Erstens stellt jedes einzelne Ligaspiel eine Leistung dar für deren Absatz die **Markenform des Co-Branding konstitutiv** ist. Eine Leistung also, die zwei Marken zweier unterschiedlicher Anbieter trägt (Baumgarth 2003). Die Relevanz der (horizontalen) Doppelmarkierung für die Nachfrage der Leistungen verdeutlicht die erhöhte Zahlungsbereitschaft bei so genannten lokalen Derbys wie beispielsweise dem Old Firm in Glasgow, dem Stadtderby zwischen dem FC Bayern und dem TSV 1860 München oder auch Handballspielen zwischen der SG Flensburg-Handewitt und dem THW Kiel.

Zweitens ist für den Ligaspielbetrieb nicht nur diese (horizontale) Doppelmarkierung bedeutsam, sondern auch, dass die Ligaorganisationen selbst einen Markenaufbau anstreben. Für den nordamerikanischen Ligasport ist dieses Bestreben trotz des Closed-Shop-Systems (keine Auf- und Abstiege) besonders evident – man denke nur an die weltweit bekannten Marken NFL, NBA (National Basketball Association) oder MLB (Major League Baseball), die als Synonyme für American Football, Basketball und Baseball stehen und somit quasi Gattungsmarkencharakter besitzen. Doch auch die europäischen Sportligen sehen in der Intensivierung ihrer Markenführungsbemühungen eine Möglichkeit zur Schaffung einer eigener (Liga-)Reputation. Mit dem Markenaufbau wird dabei nicht nur der – durch die Auf- und Abstiegsregelungen bedingten – wechselnden Ligazusammensetzung begegnet. Eine starke Ligamarke dient auch dazu, im intra- und intersportartenbezogenen Ligenwettbewerb einen komparativen Konkurrenzvorteil zu generieren (Bieling/Eschweiler/Hardenacke 2004, S. 10 f.). Für die am Ligabetrieb teilnehmenden Klubs resultiert, dass sie die **Ligamarke als Markendach** eigener Markenführungsbemühungen begreifen müssen. Während die damit angesprochene (vertikale) Doppelmarkierung in den US-amerikanischen Major Leagues aufgrund der genossenschaftlichen Organisationsform durch die Franchiseverträge geregelt ist, fällt das resultierende Konfliktpotenzial in den bisher verbandsrechtlich organisierten Sportligen Europas größer aus, wie etwa die Auseinandersetzungen der in der so genannten G-14 zusammengeschlossenen europäischen Großklubs mit der UEFA (Union des Associations Européennes des Football) und der FIFA (Fédération Internationale de Football Association) zeigen (Hardenacke/Muhle 2004, S. 288 ff.).

Neben dem Merkmal der Koproduktion wird (Liga-)Sportleistungen ein **Dienstleistungscharakter** zugesprochen. Obwohl die Ausprägungen der für die Abgrenzung von Diensten und Sachen vereinfachend herangezogenen Merkmale Materialität und Integrativität (Engelhardt/Kleinaltenkamp/Reckenfelderbäumer 1993) von der konkreten Gestaltung der abzusetzenden Leistungsbündel abhängig sind – man denke etwa an die Unterschiede zwischen der Konzeption eines Live-Spiels und der Wahrnehmung der identischen Kernleistung über das Fernsehen (Welling 2004b, S. 273 f.) –, kann die **Ligasportmarke als Dienstleistungsmarke** eingeordnet werden. Denn die Anforderungen an die Führung von Dienstleistungsmarken (Graumann 1983; Stauss 1998; Burmann/Schleusener/Weers in diesem Buch) müssen – teilweise sogar in herausgehobener Weise – Berücksichtigung finden.

Aus den Materialitätsformen der Leistungsergebnisse resultiert etwa die Vermarktung von Leistungsversprechen, die vom Nachfrager in ihrer konkreten Ausprägung vor dem Tausch (Erfahrungs- beziehungsweise Vertrauenseigenschaftscharakter) nicht beurteilbar sind. Aus diesem Grund spielt die **Marke im Kaufentscheidungsprozess** eine große Rolle, die noch dadurch gesteigert wird, dass weniger eine funktionale, denn vielmehr eine emotionale beziehungsweise symbolische Nutzenstiftung der Leistungsergebnisse konstatiert werden kann (Burmann/Blinda/Nitschke 2003, S. 7). Eine weitere Konsequenz ist die bekannte Problematik der (Nicht-)Markierbarkeit der Leistungsergebnisse. Daher ist für die Kennzeichnung auf die **Markierung interner und externer Kontaktsubjekte und -objekte** zurückzugreifen (Meffert/Bruhn 2000, S. 317; Welling 2004a, S. 408).

Bedeutsamer für die Markenführung sind jedoch die aus den Integrativitätsformen resultierenden Aspekte. So stellt die **Sicherung konstanter Qualität** im Vergleich zu Sachleistungen bereits durch die Einflüsse der an der koproduktiven Kernleistungserstellung beteiligten Klubs eine Herausforderung dar, weil dadurch eine Standardisierung der Kernleistungen nicht möglich ist. Des Weiteren ist bei Live-Erlebnissen im Stadion aber die Kundenmitwirkung zu berücksichtigen, das heißt die Integration externer Faktoren in die Prozesse zur Erstellung angereicherter Leistungsbündel, wie sie zum Beispiel bei der eigenständigen Anreise oder dem selbständigen Getränkeholen erfolgt. Dies beeinflusst die Qualitätsausprägung und deren Wahrnehmung entscheidend. Nachfragern kommt bei Ligasportleistungen aber zugleich eine **doppelte Prosumer-Rolle** zu (Welling 2004b, S. 288). Denn beim integrativen Erstellungsprozess handelt es sich um eine Leistungserbringung von Personen für ein Personenkollektiv. Da die Interaktionen zwischen den Nachfragern nutzenerhöhenden (beispielsweise das atmosphäreschaffende Anfeuerungsverhalten), aber auch nutzenreduzierenden (beispielsweise das Ausleben von Aggression) Charakter haben können, sind Aspekte des Kompatibilitäts-Managements auch im Rahmen der Markenführung bedeutsam (Reckenfelderbäumer 2004, S. 361 ff.).

Die Einordnung des Ligaspiels als eine von Personen für Personen erbrachte Kollektivleistung verdeutlicht zudem die **Notwendigkeit zur Berücksichtigung der Ich-Identitäten der Nachfrager und Mitarbeiter im Rahmen der Markenführung** in prägnanter Weise. Denn für die Wirkung der Identifikationsfunktion von Ligasportmarken ist es notwendig, dass einzelne Individuen sich mit der Personengruppe der Leistungsanbieter und gleichzeitig der Personengruppe der Leistungsnachfrager identifizieren können. Die jeweiligen Gruppenidentitäten und Ich-Identitäten sind folglich aufeinander abzustimmen beziehungsweise bilden sich in wechselseitigen und reflexiven Selbstselektionsprozessen. Aus dieser Perspektive wird auch die Interpretation der Markenidentität als Gruppenidentität des die Marke führenden Personenkollektivs von Burmann, Blinda und Nitschke (2003, S. 16) verständlich. Typische Fans prägen die Wahrnehmung der Marke durch andere Nachfrager, haben aber auch Einfluss auf die Vereinsmitarbeiter. Exempla-

Abbildung 3: **Umsetzung der Markenherkunft in der Bildkommunikation (oben) und im Merchandising (unten) beim FC St. Pauli**

GABLER GRAFIK

Quelle: FC St. Pauli, Merchandising-Katalog Saison 2004/2005

risch sei auf die Markenherkunft des als alternativ, tolerant, politisch interessiert und kreativ geltenden FC St. Pauli verwiesen: Entstanden unter anderem aus dem Interesse der Besetzer der Hamburger Hafenstrasse am Fußballspiel, die ihre Symbole (Piratenflagge) als Ausdruck ihrer Gruppenidentität zum Stadionbesuch mitnahmen, entwickelte sich eine eigene alternative Fußballkultur, die immer mehr Sympathisanten anzog und später vom Verein aufgegriffen wurde. Dokumentiert werden kann dies etwa dadurch,

marktung aller Rechte durch eine einzelne Agentur, die mitunter auch durch eine Beteiligung am Eigenkapital begleitet werden kann. Ein steigender Agentureinfluss kann für die Markenführung dabei nicht nur positive Effekte durch die Professionalisierung der Vermarktungsbemühungen bedeuten (Parensen 2004, S. 320 ff.). Je größer der Umfang des an eine Agentur vergebenen Rechtepakets und je längerfristiger dessen Vergabe, desto ausgeprägter ist auch der **Verlust der Markenführungshoheit der Klubs**. Die negativen Folgen des Verlustes liegen auf der Hand, wenn beispielsweise unterschiedliche Vorstellungen über die konkrete Ausgestaltung der Markenpositionierung existieren. Negativen Folgen können aber auch aufgrund unterschiedlicher Zeithorizonte entstehen: Denn während Agenturen möglicherweise eine kurzfristige Exploitation der Klubmarke anstreben – ein Vorwurf, der gegenüber dem Engagement der Sportwelt hervorgebracht wurde –, muss es Ziel der Ligasportanbieter sein, ihren Markenwert dauerhaft hoch zu halten. Die Gefahr des Zielkonfliktes einer solchen Principal-Agenten-Beziehung wird dabei durch die Reputation der Agenturmarke verringert. Das kann als Grund für die derzeit feststellbaren Marktbereinigungstendenzen gesehen werden.

2.23 Leistungspotenzialbezogene Zielgruppen: Mitarbeiter im sportlichen und außersportlichen Bereich

Bereits bei der Darstellung der Ligasportleistungen als von einer Personenvielzahl für ein Kollektiv erbrachte Leistungsbündel wurde auf die Bedeutung der internen Markenführung hingewiesen. Tendenziell ist zu konstatieren, dass die interne Markenführung an Bedeutung gewinnt, je ausgeprägter die Adjunktivität der Leistungserstellung (Personendominanz) ist, je mehr unterschiedliche Personen auf Anbieterseite in Interaktionsprozesse mit Nachfragern eingebunden sind und je größer die Personenzahl ist, die mit diesen Leistungserbringern in Kontakt kommen.

Die Aufgabe der internen Markenführung besteht dabei darin, die Markenführungskompetenz zu erhöhen (Hammann 2002, S. 350 ff.) und auch dadurch ein **ausgeprägtes Brand Commitment** als Voraussetzung für ein konsistentes Mitarbeiterverhalten (Brand Citizenship Behavior) zu erreichen. Die Einflussmöglichkeiten der internen Markenführung zur Förderung des Brand Commitment lassen sich dabei in den Bereichen der personalpolitischen Aktivitäten, der gezielten (internen und externen) Kommunikationsmaßnahmen und im Führungsverhalten selbst verorten (Burmann/Zeplin 2004). Vor dem Hintergrund der vorherigen Ausführungen ist allerdings darauf zu verweisen, dass ein solches Commitment möglichst auch für die Mitarbeiter der Partner im Dienstleistungsnetzwerk anzustreben ist, wenngleich nicht nur die Einflussmöglichkeiten geringer sein dürften, sondern unter Umständen auch Zielkonflikte bestehen.

Personalpolitische Aktivitäten zur Erreichung eines hohen Brand Commitment beginnen bereits bei der zielgerichteten Personalauswahl: Ligasportklubs müssten zum Beispiel versuchen, die regionale Markenherkunft bei der Spielerverpflichtung zu berücksichtigen. Aufgrund der regionalen Nähe wird aus der Region stammenden Spielern häufig eine höhere Identifikation mit dem Klub unterstellt, die wiederum einen verstärkenden Effekt auf die Identifikationsfunktion der Marke für die Zuschauer besitzt. Deshalb achtet etwa Bayern München darauf, dass möglichst immer Spieler aus München beziehungsweise Bayern im Team stehen. Über die Personalauswahl hinweg werden solche identitätsstiftenden Maßnahmen aber auch durch die Lederhose als Antrittsgeschenk und den gemeinsamen Oktoberfestbesuch der Mannschaft initiiert. Daneben wurde bei Bayern München seit Jahren betont, neue Spieler müssten das Bayern-Gen, das heißt eine ausgesprochene Siegermentalität, mitbringen: Die Ich-Identität der Spieler muss in dieser Dimension kongruent zur Gruppenidentität bei Bayern München sein. Dieser Anspruch wird auch durch das Führungsverhalten von Franz Beckenbauer, Uli Hoeness und Karl-Heinz Rummenigge vorgelebt. Da jede an der Leistungserstellung beteiligte Person zur Außenwahrnehmung beiträgt, sind Medien- beziehungsweise Interviewschulungen für die Spieler und Trainer, aber auch interne Richtlinien für die Informationspolitik notwendig.

Während bislang vornehmlich Mitarbeiter im sportlichen Bereich im Fokus standen, die aufgrund der medialen Begleitung des Fußballs für das Markenerscheinungsbild hohe Relevanz besitzen, müssen Maßnahmen zur Förderung von Markenkompetenz und Brand Commitment auf alle Mitarbeitergruppen gleichermaßen zielen. Dazu zählen im Einzelnen:

- Klubrepräsentanten, die mit der Führung der Geschäfte beauftragt und somit als Initiatoren der Markenführung aufzufassen sind. Ohne dabei nach den spezifischen Rechtsformenbesonderheiten zu differenzieren, sind die **Mitglieder von Vorstand und Aufsichtsrat beziehungsweise Geschäftsführung und Beirat** zu nennen, die aufgrund ihrer Führungskompetenz gesondert zu berücksichtigen sind.
- **Mitarbeiter im außersportlichen Bereich**, wobei den mit der Umsetzung der Markenführungsmaßnahmen betrauten Mitarbeitern aufgrund ihrer (insbesondere operativen) Steuerungsfunktion ebenfalls eine gesonderte Stellung einzuräumen ist.
- **Klubmitglieder**, wobei fallweise zu untersuchen wäre, welchen Einfluss diese im Rahmen der Markenführung ausüben (können) und/oder ob diese Gruppe sich von unterschiedlichen Fangruppen wesentlich unterscheidet.
- **Eigenkapitalgeber**, wobei auch hier zu erarbeiten wäre, inwieweit Deckungsgleichheit mit anderen besteht, etwa, wie sich institutionelle Anleger zu Shareholdern verhalten, die als Fans investieren.

3. Adaption des GAP-Modells der identitätsorientierten Markenführung für Ligasportklubs

3.1 Harmonisierung von Selbst- und Fremdbildern als Leitidee für die Entwicklung eines GAP-Modells

Die Besonderheit der identitätsorientierten Markenführung, die sich im letzten Jahrzehnt des neunzehnten Jahrhunderts aus bisherigen Markenführungsansätzen heraus entwickelt hat, liegt in der „Betonung einer über Funktions- und Unternehmensgrenzen hinweg greifenden Vernetzung aller markenbezogenen Aktivitäten" (Meffert/Burmann 2002a, S. 29), durch die der häufig reinen Außenorientierung im Sinne des verhaltensorientierten beziehungsweise des technokratisch-strategieorientierten Ansatzes der Markenführung eine um interne Facetten erweiterte Sichtweise gegenübergestellt wird (siehe dazu in diesem Buch). Als **Imperativ einer zugleich innen- und außenorientierten Markenführung wird die Harmonisierung von Selbst- und Fremdbild betont**, wobei der Übereinstimmungsgrad als Ausmaß für die Markenstärke dient (Meffert/Burmann 1996, S. 38 f.). Stark vereinfacht sind die drei in Abbildung 5 dargestellten Fälle zu unterscheiden. Fall 1 steht idealtypisch für die Situation, in der überhaupt keine Deckung von Selbst- und Fremdbild vorhanden ist, während Fall 3 den gegensätzlichen Extrempol einer völligen Deckung von Selbst- und Fremdbild zeigt, die es aufgrund der Individualität der Bezugspersonen in der Realität nicht geben kann (Welling 2003, S. 33 ff.).

Folgt man dem Grundgedanken der identitätsorientierten Markenführung sind aber nicht nur die interne und die externe Ebene voneinander abzugrenzen. Die Ganzheitlichkeit des Ansatzes bezieht sich vielmehr auch darauf, innerhalb der internen und externen Ebene weitere Zielgruppen zu differenzieren, die sich in ihren Ansprüchen unterscheiden. Hieraus wurde eingangs die Eignung der identitätsorientierten Markenführung für Organisationen im Ligasport abgeleitet, weil Klubs als Anbieter von Sportleistungen in besonderer Weise in einem Beziehungsgeflecht interner und externer Zielgruppen agieren müssen. Da sich die Markenbilder auch innerhalb dieser Gruppen jeweils beträchtlich unterscheiden können ist es sinnvoll, auch die jeweiligen Lücken in der Markenwahrnehmung zwischen ihnen zu analysieren. Ein Gedanke, der von Meffert und Burmann (2002c, S. 90) für die Konzeption eines GAP-Modells aufgegriffen wurde, das sie in Analogie zu dem aus dem Dienstleistungsmarketing bekannten GAP-Modell von Parasuraman, Zeithaml und Berry (1985, S. 41 ff.) für die Zwecke der Markenführung modellierten. Neben den jeweiligen Ist-Bildern unterschiedlichster Gruppen werden darüber hinaus auch die jeweiligen Ideal-Bilder der Marke abgebildet und in Beziehung gesetzt. Denn es ist zu prüfen, ob die Zielgruppen ein Vorstellungsbild von der Marke besitzen, das ihren (Ideal-)Vorstellungen so nahe kommt, dass wiederholte (Kauf-)Entscheidungen getroffen werden. Das von Meffert und Burmann vorgeschlagene Modell wird im Folgenden unter Berücksichtigung des zuvor identifizierten Beziehungsgeflechts für die Markenführung im Ligasport adaptiert (Welling 2003, S. 44 ff.).

Abbildung 5: **Ausprägungsformen der Markenstärke**

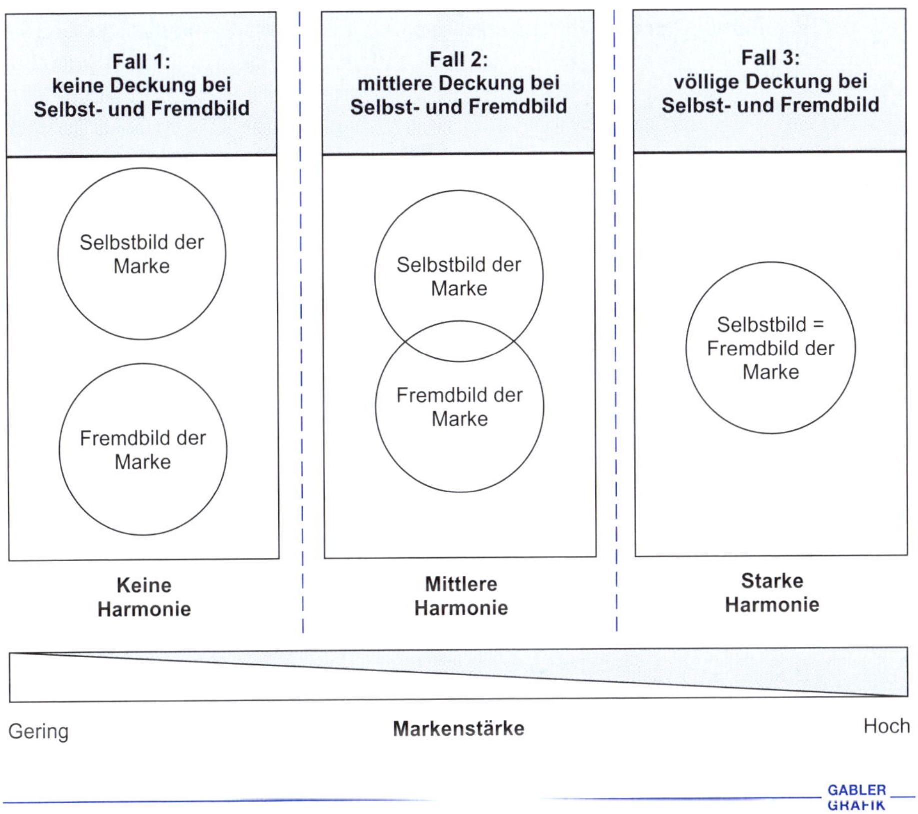

Quelle: Welling 2003, S. 35

3.2 Konzeption eines GAP-Modells für die Markenführung im Ligasport

Der erste Schritt zur Konzeption des dargestellten GAP-Modells der Markenführung im Ligasport wurde bereits durch die Identifikation der unterschiedlichen Zielgruppen, die sich durch eine möglichst große Intragruppenhomogenität und Intergruppenheterogenität auszeichnen sollten, vollzogen. Aus Gründen der Komplexitätsreduktion wird das hier vorgestellte Modell (vgl. Abbildung 6) dabei auf drei interne („Management", „Mitarbeiter im sportlichen Bereich" und „Mitarbeiter im außersportlichen Bereich") und drei externe Zielgruppen („Fangruppen eins bis drei", „Sponsoren" und „Medien") beschränkt. In der praktischen Anwendung müssen nach Möglichkeit aber alle Einflussgruppen Berücksichtigung finden, wobei etwa die interne Ebene um Eigenkapitalgeber, die externe um Fremdkapitalgeber, Vermarktungspartner, Netzwerkpartner oder auch Ligadachorganisation und weitere Klubs ergänzt werden könnte.

Nach der Bestimmung der relevanten Zielgruppen ist im Rahmen der Analyseaufgabe die oben herausgestellte Markenstärke festzustellen, indem die Ist-Selbst- und Ist-Fremdbilder erhoben und miteinander in Beziehung gesetzt werden. Wie ausgeführt ist die Markenstärke umso ausgeprägter, je größer die Übereinstimmungen zwischen den jeweiligen Selbst- und Fremdbildern sind. Im Umkehrschluss kann **GAP 1** daher als **Harmonie-GAP** bezeichnet werden. Da ein solches GAP, bei Meffert und Burmann 1996 als Kommunikationslücke bezeichnet, in der internen und externen Wahrnehmung der Marke darüber hinaus jeweils zwischen unterschiedlichen internen und externen Zielgruppen vorliegen kann, müssen als Sublücken auch die (internen) GAPs $1i_{1-n}$ und (externen) GAPs $1e_{1-n}$, das heißt die Lücken zwischen den einzelnen Gruppen selbst, erfasst werden. Sie geben als Kenngrößen die interne und externe Markenstärke wieder. Wenn beispielsweise Vorstand und Aufsichtsrat eines Vereins diesen als „innovativ", „erfolgsorientiert" und „familiär" verstehen, die bei diesem Klub angestellten Spieler mit der Marke aber vielleicht „nüchterne Professionalität" verbinden, existiert bereits auf der internen Ebene eine Differenz, die für die Außendarstellung kontraproduktiv ist und möglicherweise auch dort zu diffusen Vorstellungsbildern führt. Ebenfalls problematisch wäre eine Lücke zwischen der Sponsoren- und der Zuschauerwahrnehmung, da Sponsoren ihre angestrebten Ziele dann nicht erreichen würden. Für die Klubführung könnte sich das Problem darin äußern, dass sich die Sponsorengewinnung problematisch gestaltet.

Sind diese Harmonielücken aufgedeckt, ist es notwendig, auch die jeweiligen Ideal-Selbst- und -Fremdbilder der einzelnen Personen in den Zielgruppen und zwischen ihnen zu erheben und zu vergleichen. Durch die Ableitung von **GAP 2** (beziehungsweise wiederum der Sub-GAPs $2i_{1-n}$ und GAPs $2e_{1-n}$) als **Anforderungs-GAP** können Konflikte in den Idealvorstellungen identifiziert werden. Sollten diese zu groß ausfallen, könnte ihnen intern möglicherweise durch die Personalauswahl, extern durch eine veränderte Marktsegmentierung begegnet werden.

Auch der durch den **GAP 3** vorgenommene Vergleich der Ideal-Bilder mit den Ist-Bildern deckt Ansatzpunkte für die Markenführung auf. In Anlehnung an die Ausführungen von Meffert und Burmann (2002c) kann für diese **Identifikations-GAPs** konstatiert werden, dass die Markenbindung umso geringer ist, je größer die hier festgestellten Abweichungen sind. Auf der externen Ebene besteht etwa die Gefahr, dass sich Fans, bei denen sich die tatsächliche Wahrnehmung (Ist-Image) vom Idealbild immer weiter entfernt, von der Marke abwenden. Im Fall des oben ausgeführten Beispiels des FC St. Pauli könnten etwa Probleme entstehen, wenn die „Kommerzialisierung des Alternativen" noch größere Ausmaße annehmen würde und die inhärenten Konflikte offen zu Tage treten. Denn das alternative Idealbild korrespondiert zu großen Teilen damit, dass viele Fans die soziale Komponente über den monetären Erfolg stellen. Inzwischen wird etwa der Absatz von „Weltpokalsiegerbesieger-Retter" Utensilien kritisch gesehen und in Fanforen immer häufiger als „Ausverkauf der Identität" bezeichnet. Auch auf der internen Ebene sind Probleme zu konstatieren: je ausgeprägter die Lücken hier ausfallen, desto geringer wird das Brand Commitment sein. Die negativen Auswirkungen für das Brand Citizenship Behavior wurde oben beschrieben.

Abbildung 6: GAP-Modell der Markenführung im Ligasport

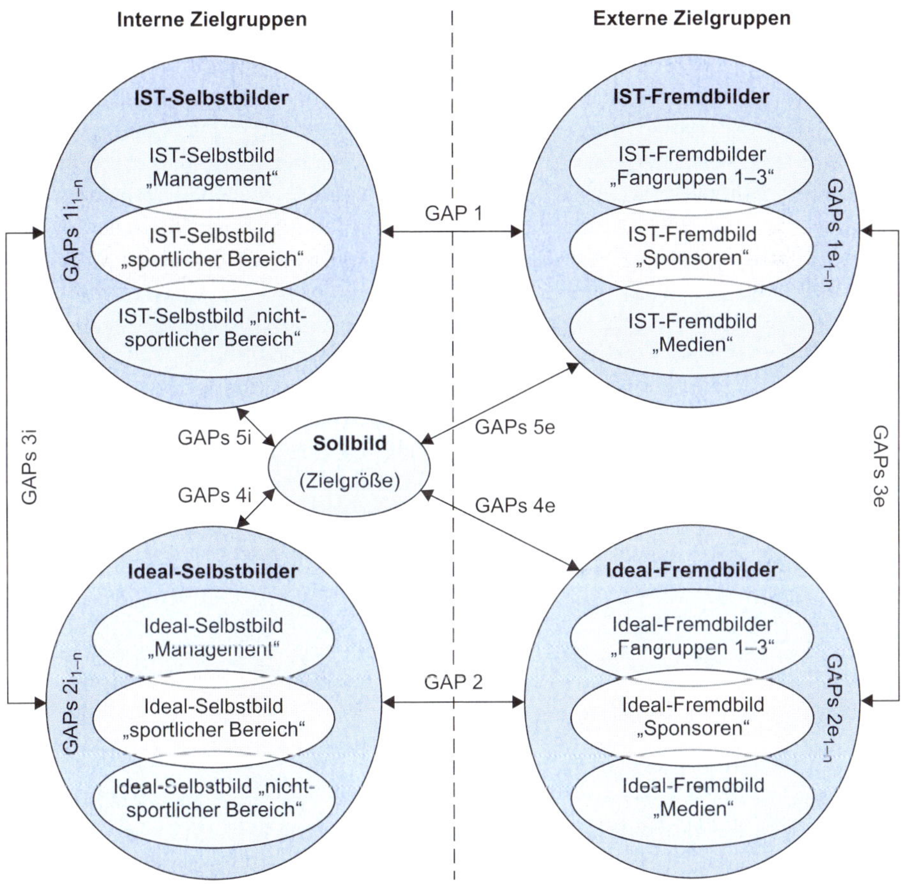

GABLER GRAFIK

Die Feststellung der Ideal- und Ist-Bilder ist aber auch wichtig, um die Zielsetzungen der Markenführung zu konkretisieren. Denn hier müssen die Erwartungen einerseits (Ideal Bilder) und die gegenwärtige Wahrnehmung anderseits (Ist-Bilder) genauso einfließen, wie etwa die Markenherkunft (als historische Basis der Markenidentität) sowie gegenwärtige und zukünftige Möglichkeiten der Ausrichtung der Markenführungsbemühungen, die durch Wettbewerberaktivitäten beeinflusst sind. Aus diesem Grund ist das hier vorgestellte GAP-Modell um ein Soll-Bild der Marke im Sinne einer Zielgröße der Markenführung ergänzt (Welling 2003, S. 50 ff.). Die Abweichungen dieser Zielgröße von den einzelnen Ideal-Bildern können als **GAPs 4** daher auch als **Zielbildungs-GAPs** bezeichnet werden. Denn gerade weil es zwischen den unterschiedlichen Zielgruppen Unterschiede in den jeweiligen Ideal-Bildern gibt, müssen diese Abweichungen von den Markenführenden bewusst geplant sein. In ihnen spiegeln sich die Managemententscheidungen bei der Zielbestimmung und folglich auch die Kenntnisse der Markenidentität wider.

Die so konkretisierte Zielvorgabe fließt dann wiederum in diejenigen Entscheidungen ein, die zur Zielerreichung führen sollen: Steht fest, wie die Marke intern und extern wahrgenommen werden soll, das heißt welche Assoziationen mit ihr bei den einzelnen Zielgruppen verbunden werden sollen, müssen Entscheidungen dahingehend getroffen werden, wie diese Assoziationen durch konkrete Umsetzungsmaßnahmen aufgebaut werden können, wobei die Markenidentität dabei als Instrument zu nutzen ist. Werden die Vorgaben nicht entsprechend der Ziele realisiert, könnte man eine Umsetzungslücke feststellen. Ein (sehr konstruiertes) Beispiel für eine solche wäre, wenn sich der SC Freiburg als „umweltfreundlich" sieht, aus ökonomischen Zwängen aber einen Sponsorenvertrag mit Yello statt mit Naturenergie abschließen würde oder sich Spieler abfällig über diese Zielsetzung äußern würden. Je größer vor diesem Hintergrund die Umsetzungsprobleme sind, desto größer werden tendenziell wiederum die **GAPs 5** ausfallen, die deshalb auch als **Zielerreichungs-GAPs** zu verstehen sind. In ihnen spiegeln sich die Unterschiede zwischen dem angestrebten Ziel-Bild und den tatsächlichen Ist-Bildern bei den einzelnen Zielgruppen und daher die Erfolge oder Misserfolge der Markenführungsbemühungen wider. Da für die Identifizierung dieses GAPs die jeweiligen Ist-Bilder zu erheben sind, kann wiederum die Markenstärke bestimmt und der Managementprozess von Neuem angestoßen werden.

3.3 Anwendung des GAP-Modells – ausgewählte Ergebnisse am Beispiel VfL Bochum 1848 e. V.

Das zuvor vorgestellte GAP-Modell wurde als Rahmen für ein Praxisprojekt verwendet, das an der Ruhr-Universität Bochum begonnen wurde und derzeit an der Universität Bremen in Zusammenarbeit mit dem VfL Bochum 1848 e. V. durchgeführt wird. Anlass der gemeinsamen Bemühungen war die festgestellte Bedeutung, die Fragen der Markenführung in Ligasportklubs beizumessen ist. Ohne auf die einzelnen Ergebnisse und insbesondere die aus ihnen abzuleitenden Implikationen detailliert einzugehen, sollen im folgenden einige Aspekte beleuchtet werden, die bereits aus dem Vergleich der jeweiligen Ist-Selbst- und Ist-Fremdbilder gewonnen werden können.

Grundlage zur Ableitung der Erkenntnisse war zunächst die Identifikation unterschiedlicher Zielgruppen der Markenführung, wie sie in den vorherigen Kapiteln dargestellt wurde. In den ausgewählten Gruppen waren dann die jeweiligen Ist- und Ideal-Bilder mit Hilfe standardisierter, zuvor geprüfter Fragebögen in persönlichen Interviews zu erheben. Von den im Frühjahr 2004 insgesamt befragten 375 Personen lassen sich 48 Personen als

„intern" kennzeichnen, die sich weiter in die Gruppen „Management" (n = 24), „Mitarbeiter im sportlichen" (n = 11) und „Mitarbeiter im nicht-sportlichen Bereich" (n = 13) aufteilen lassen. Die 327 „Externen" setzen sich aus der Gruppe „Medien" (n = 7), „Sponsoren" (n = 35) und „Zuschauer" (n = 285) zusammen. Die Gruppe der Zuschauer ist weiter danach differenzierbar, ob es sich um „traditionelle Fans" (Stehplatzbesucher, n = 174), um „Convenience Fans" (Sitzplatzbesucher, n = 75) oder um „VIP-Fans" (Besucher von Business Seats u. Ä., n = 36) handelt, da davon auszugehen ist, dass sich durch die unterschiedlichen Konsumgewohnheiten auch das Markenimage zwischen den jeweiligen Gruppen unterscheidet. Aus forschungsökonomischen Gründen konnte das Ist-Fremdbild allerdings bei lediglich 105 „traditionellen Fans" und 42 „Convenience Fans" erhoben werden. Für die restlichen Probanden dieser Gruppen wurde ausschließlich das Ideal-Bild identifiziert. Mit Hilfe einpoliger Skalen (1 = „stimme voll zu"; 5 = „stimme gar nicht zu") wurden im Rahmen persönlicher Interviews dazu Attribute abgefragt, die zuvor durch Literaturstudium und explorative Fokusgruppendiskussionen gewonnen werden konnten.[1]

Im Rahmen der momentan noch nicht vollständig abgeschlossenen Auswertung konnte ein erster Vergleich der erhobenen Daten mit den in einer früheren Studie veröffentlichten Werten (UFA Sports 2000) bestätigen, dass der VfL Bochum als „regional verwurzelt", „volksnah", und „familiär" wahrgenommen wird und über ausgesprochen hohe Sympathiewerte verfügt. Diese drücken sich auch darin aus, dass das Attribut „arrogant" nicht im Zusammenhang mit dem VfL Bochum gesehen wird.

Die detaillierte Umsetzung des GAP-Modells erfolgte anschließend durch statistische Mittelwertvergleiche zwischen den entsprechenden Gruppen. Auf der höchsten Aggregationsebene, bei der lediglich ein Ist-Selbstbild über alle internen Zielgruppen mit einem Ist-Fremdbild über alle externen Zielgruppen verglichen wurde, konnten dabei für den VfL Bochum nur wenige signifikante Lücken festgestellt werden. Bezogen auf die dargestellten Attribute könnte das ein erster Hinweis auf eine ausgeprägte Markenharmonie ein (vgl. Abbildung 7).

Als signifikante Lücken sind hier beispielhaft aufgeführt die Einschätzung des „Engagements", die auf einem hohen Niveau intern ausgeprägter ist als extern, sowie die Wahrnehmung der Attribute „selbstbewusst", „cool" und „spontan", bei denen die interne Wahrnehmung von der externen signifikant abweicht. Ob diese Lücken geschlossen werden sollen und wenn ja, in welche Richtung, ist dabei abhängig von den Markenzielen, auf die an dieser Stelle nicht eingegangen wird. Auffällig ist vor allem, dass bei den emotionalen, in der Fußballstudie von Sportfive als wichtig beziehungsweise sehr wichtig eingeschätzten Attributen „sympathisch", „traditionsreich" und „familiär" (Sportfive 2004, S. 18) keine signifikanten Unterschiede zwischen den aggregierten Ist-Selbst- und Ist-Fremdbildern ausgemacht werden können.

---

1 Die Erhebung wurde im Rahmen einer Diplomarbeit vorgenommen, die gegenwärtig von Arne Dirks, M.A. am Lehrstuhl für Mittelstand, Existenzgründung und Entrepreneurship (Prof. Dr. Jörg Freiling) an der Universität Bremen angefertigt und durch den Verfasser gemeinsam mit Vertretern des VfL Bochum 1848 e. V. betreut wird. Eine Veröffentlichung der Ergebnisse ist in Vorbereitung, in denen das empirische Vorgehen ausführlich dokumentiert wird.

Abbildung 7: **GAP 1 (Harmonie-GAP „intern/extern“) beim VfL Bochum 1848 e. V. (Auswahl)**

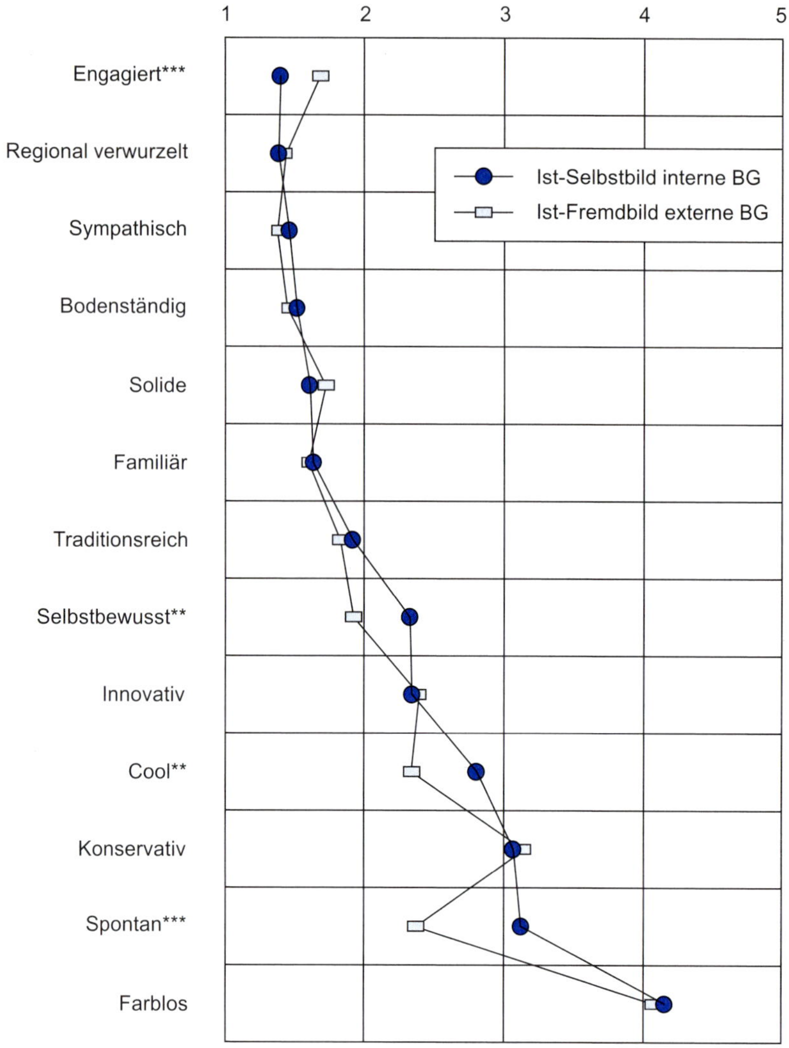

* signifikant, ** sehr signifikant, *** höchst signifikant

GABLER GRAFIK

Abbildung 8: **GAP 1e₁ (Harmonie-GAP „Zuschauer/Sponsoren") beim VfL Bochum 1848 e. V. (Auswahl)**

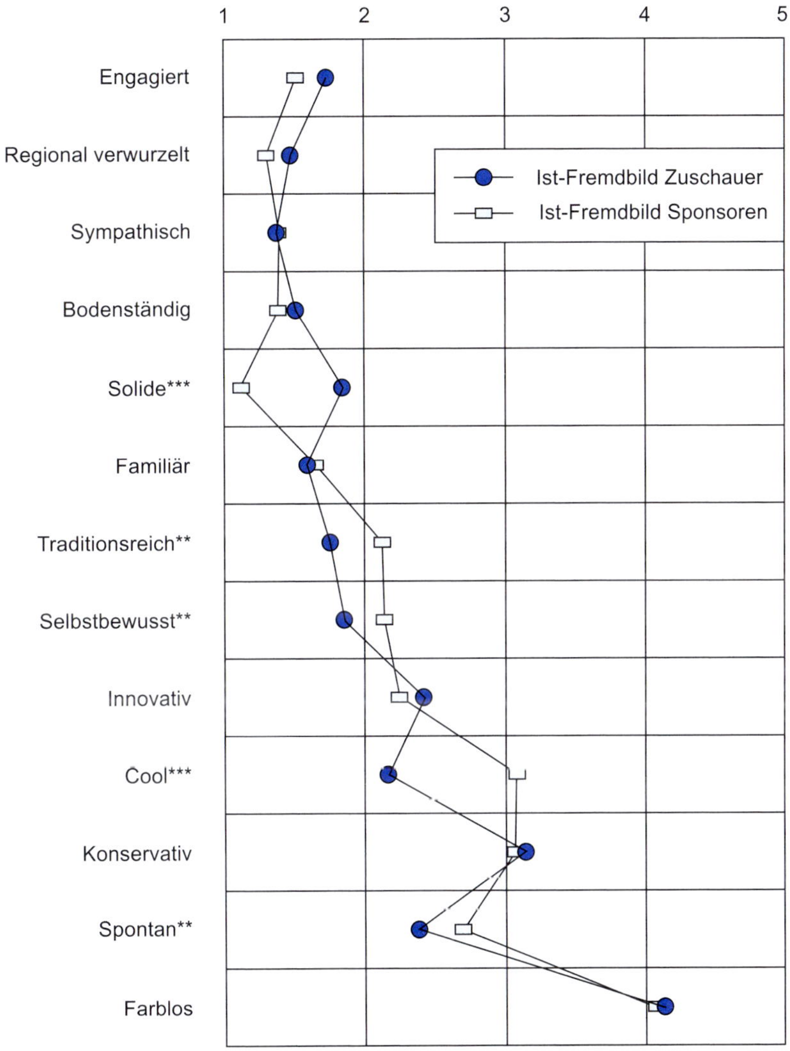

* signifikant, ** sehr signifikant, *** höchst signifikant

Bei diesen, aufgrund der für jeden Fußballklub konstatierten Wichtigkeit auch als Hygienefaktoren einzuschätzenden Attribute, zeigte sich vielmehr, dass sie dem VfL Bochum durchweg auf einem hohen Niveau zugesprochen werden (vgl. Abbildung 7). Das lange vor allem in den Medien kolportierte Bild von der „grauen Maus“ konnte hingegen in den befragten Zielgruppen abgelegt werden. Die hohen Werte bei „regionaler Verwurzelung“, „familiär“ und „traditionsreich“ zeigen zudem, dass die regionale, kulturelle und institutionelle Markenherkunft bei den Markenführungsbemühungen des VfL Bochum Berücksichtigung findet.

Auch die bei der theoretischen Herleitung des GAP-Modells betonte Notwendigkeit, nach Möglichkeit die aggregierten Ebenen zu verlassen und bei den Ist-Bildern auch Sub-GAPs aufzudecken, kann beispielhaft durch die Ergebnisse der Studie untermauert werden. Dazu zeigt die Abbildung 8 ergänzend das GAP $1e_1$, das heißt die externe Markenstärke bezogen auf die Zielgruppe der Sponsoren im Vergleich zu den aggregierten Werten der Fans. Vergleicht man diese Ist-Fremdbilder, ergeben sich Erkenntnisse, die für die Markenführung sowohl des VfL Bochum als auch für diejenige der Sponsoren relevant sein können. Dass die Zuschauer den VfL Bochum beispielsweise als „traditionsreicher“ und „cooler“ einschätzen als die Sponsoren, könnte in Abhängigkeit der angestrebten Imagetransfereffekte etwa dazu beitragen, dass für Sponsoren eine größere Zielerreichung möglich ist, als ursprünglich erwartet. Für den VfL Bochum könnte die festgestellte Lücke nach Maßgabe eigener Markenführungsziele aber einen Hinweis darauf geben, dass beispielsweise gegenüber Sponsoren stärker als bisher traditionelle Aspekte zu betonen sind. Der signifikante Unterschied bezüglich der Solidität wird daneben auch durch die zu differenzierenden Leistungsbeziehungen zwischen Klub und Sponsor sowie Klub und Zuschauer begründet sein. Das hohe Niveau, das die Gruppe der befragten Sponsoren dem VfL Bochum bezüglich der Solidität zuspricht, kann als Ausdruck für gesunde Geschäftsbeziehungen zwischen diesen Partnern interpretiert werden.

Die hier dargestellten Analyseergebnisse sollten aber nicht vorschnell für die Ableitung von Handlungsempfehlungen Verwendung finden. Wie die theoretischen Ausführungen zum GAP-Modell bei Ligasportorganisationen zeigen, sind dazu auch auf der internen Ebene weitere Differenzierungen bei den Gruppen notwendig, sind bei allen Gruppen ergänzend die Ideal-Bilder auszuwerten, untereinander zu vergleichen und mit den Ist-Bildern in Beziehung zu setzen, um schließlich auf dieser Basis die Markenführungsziele zu bestimmen.

4. Fazit

Das Management im (Liga-)Sport steht in den nächsten Jahren weiterhin vor der Aufgabe, das Spannungsfeld zwischen sportlichem und wirtschaftlichem Erfolg zu überbrücken, um das Überleben der eigenen Organisation nachhaltig zu sichern. Obwohl der sportliche Wettkampf für die Erlöserzielung eminent wichtig bleibt, wird der ökonomische Wettbewerb auch außerhalb der Spielfelder entschieden. Eine Möglichkeit, in der

„eigenartigen Ökonomie" des Ligasports Erlöse stärker von Sieg und Niederlage abzukoppeln, ist dabei in der Markenführung zu sehen. Die vorherigen Ausführungen haben verdeutlicht, dass die Markenführung in der Ligasportindustrie in einem besonderen Spannungsfeld zu erfolgen hat, das zusammenfassend in Abbildung 9 nochmals dargestellt ist.

Abbildung 9: Spannungsfeld der Markenführung im Ligasport

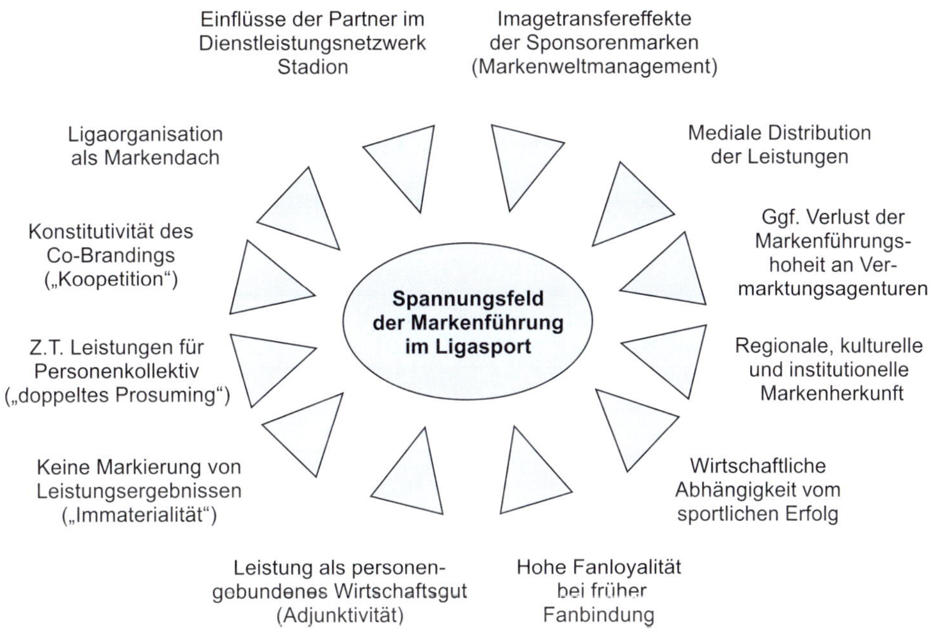

GABLER GRAFIK

Aufgrund der Heterogenität und Interdependenz der dabei zu berücksichtigenden Zielgruppen, der durch sie zum Teil eingeschränkten Freiheitsgrade und der starken Bedeutung von Regionalität, Tradition und eben sportlichem Erfolg, besitzt die identitätsorientierte Markenführung hohe Relevanz, um dieses Spannungsfeld erfolgreich zu überbrücken. Als Hilfsmittel wurde dazu ein GAP-Modell vorgestellt, das ein systematisches Vorgehen ermöglicht. Anhand zu identifizierender Ausprägungen der jeweiligen GAPs können praktische Anhaltspunkte für die Markenführung im Ligasport abgeleitet werden, wobei die konkrete Ausprägung der GAPs bei den einzelnen Klubs genauso differieren wird, wie die Bestimmung der jeweiligen Markenziele, die nur vor dem Hintergrund historischer und situativer Gegebenheiten hergeleitet werden können. Diese zu konkretisieren wird die entscheidende Aufgabe für Ligasportklubs sein.

Literatur

Aaker, D. A. (1992), Management des Markenwertes, Frankfurt/M. u.a.

Bauer, H. H., Sauer, N. E., Schmitt, P. (2004), Die Erfolgsrelevanz der Markenstärke in der 1. Fußball-Bundesliga, Wissenschaftliche Arbeitspapiere des IMU, Mannheim.

Baumgarth, C. (2003), Wirkungen des Co-Brandings, Wiesbaden.

Bieling, M., Eschweiler, M., Hardenacke, J. (2004), Business-to-Business-Marketing im Profifußball – Eine Einführung, in: Bieling, M., Eschweiler, M., Hardenacke, J. (Hrsg.), Business-to-Business-Marketing im Profifußball, Wiesbaden , S. 3–24.

Boone, L. E., Kochunny, C. M., Wilkins, D. (1995), Applying the Brand Equity Concept to Major League Baseball, in: Sport Marketing Quarterly, 4. Jg., Nr. 3, S. 33–42.

Burmann, Ch., Blinda, L., Nitschke, A. (2003), Konzeptionelle Grundlagen des identitätsbasierten Markenmanagements, Arbeitspapier Nr. 1 des Lehrstuhls für innovatives Markenmanagement (LiM), Burmann, Ch. (Hrsg.), Universität Bremen, Bremen.

Burmann, Ch., Zeplin, S. (2004), Innengerichtetes identitätsbasiertes Markenmanagement – State-of-the-Art und Forschungsbedarf, Arbeitspapier Nr. 7 des Lehrstuhls für innovatives Markenmanagement (LiM), Burmann, Ch. (Hrsg.), Universität Bremen, Bremen 2004.

Busch, W. (2004), Das Merchandisingkonzept von Bayer 04 Leverkusen, in: Hammann, P., Schmidt, L., Welling, M. (Hrsg.), Ökonomie des Fußballs – Grundlegungen aus volks- und betriebswirtschaftlicher Perspektive, Wiesbaden, S. 419–434.

Busche, A. (2004), Ökonomische Implikationen des Bosman-Urteils, in: Hammann, P., Schmidt, L., Welling, M. (Hrsg.), Ökonomie des Fußballs – Grundlegungen aus volks- und betriebswirtschaftlicher Perspektive, Wiesbaden, S. 87–104.

DFL, Deutsche Fußball Liga GmbH (2003), Die wirtschaftliche Situation im Lizenzfußball, Frankfurt/M.

Dörnemann, J. (2002), Elemente eines Controllingsystems für Profi-Sport-Organisationen, in: Controlling, Nr. 1, S. 31–40.

Engelhardt, W. H., Kleinaltenkamp, M., Reckenfelderbäumer, M. (1993), Leistungsbündel als Absatzobjekte, in: Zeitschrift für betriebswirtschaftliche Forschung, 45. Jg., S. 395–426.

Engels, K., Erdmann, M. (2001), Die Vermarktung von Sport und Entertainment: Das Beispiel Rhein Fire, in: Hermanns, A., Riedmüller, F. (Hrsg.), Management Handbuch Sport-Marketing, München, S. 217–230.

Esch, F.-R.(2003), Strategie und Technik der Markenführung, München.

Franck, G. (1998), Ökonomie der Aufmerksamkeit – Ein Entwurf, München,Wien.

FutureBrand (2001), Global Sports Teams – Brand Values, New York.

FutureBrand (2004), The most valuable football brands in Europe – The 2004 report, New York.

Gladden, J. M., Irwin, R. L., Sutton, W A. (2001), Managing North American Major Professional Sport Teams in the new Millenium, A Focus on Building Brand Equity, in: Journal of Sport Management, 15. Jg., S. 297–317.

Gladden, J. M., Milne, G. R., Sutton, W. A. (1998), A Conceptual Framework for Assessing Brand Equity in Division I College Athletics, in: Journal of Sport Management, 12. Jg., S. 1–19.

Gladden, J. M., Milne, G. (1999), Examining the Importance of Brand Equity in Professional Sport, in: Sport Marketing Quarterly, 8. Jg., Nr. 1, S. 21–29.

Graumann, J. (1983), Die Dienstleistungsmarke – Charakterisierung und Bewertung eines neuen Markentypus aus absatzwirtschaftlicher Sicht, München.

Haase, H. (1991), Sport und Kommerz, in: Leistungssport, Nr. 1, S. 5–8.

Hammann, P. (2002), Markenführung aus der Sicht des Strategischen Kompetenzmanagements, in: Böhler, H. (Hrsg.), Marketing-Management und Unternehmensführung – Festschrift für Professor Dr. Richard Köhler zum 65. Geburtstag, Stuttgart, S. 342–361.

Hammann, P. (2004), Eine zielgruppenorientierte Marketingkonzeption für Fußballklubs, in: Hammann, P., Schmidt, L., Welling, M. (Hrsg.), Ökonomie des Fußballs – Grundlegungen aus volks- und betriebswirtschaftlicher Perspektive, Wiesbaden, S. 331–356.

Hardenacke, J., Muhle, D. (2004), Kooperationsformen im Profifußball – Eine ökonomische Analyse der DFL und der europäischen G-14, in: Bieling, M., Eschweiler, M., Hardenacke, J. (Hrsg.), Business-to-Business-Marketing im Profifußball, Wiesbaden, S. 271–301.

Hermanns, A.; Bob Bomliz Group (Hrsg.) (2004), Sponsoring Trends 2004, Düsseldorf.

Hoffmann, B. (2001), Die Vermarktung von Rechten im Sport: Dargestellt am Beispiel des Fußballs, in: Hermanns, A., Riedmüller, F. (Hrsg.), Management Handbuch Sport-Marketing, München, S. 333–347.

Kapferer, J.–N. (1992), Die Marke – Kapital des Unternehmens, Landsberg/Lech.

Klotz, Ph. (2004), Konsolidierung geht weiter, in: Sponsors, Nr. 1, S. 26–27.

Kurscheidt, M. (2004), Stand und Perspektiven ökonomischer Forschung zum Fußball – eine dogmenhistorische Annäherung, in: Hammann, P., Schmidt, L., Welling, M. (Hrsg.), Ökonomie des Fußballs – Grundlegungen aus volks- und betriebswirtschaftlicher Perspektive, Wiesbaden, S. 25–58.

Meffert, H., Birkelbach, R. (1999), Qualitätsmanagement in Dienstleistungszentren – Konzeptionelle Grundlagen und typenspezifische Ausgestaltung, in: Bruhn, M., Stauss, B. (Hrsg.), Dienstleistungsqualität, 3. Aufl., Wiesbaden, S. 169–199.

Meffert, H., Bruhn, M. (2000), Dienstleistungsmarketing, 3. Aufl., Wiesbaden.

Meffert, H., Burmann, Ch. (1996), Identitätsorientierte Markenführung – Grundlagen für das Management von Markenportfolios, in: Meffert, H., Wagner, H., Backhaus, K. (Hrsg.), Arbeitspapier Nr. 100 der Wissenschaftlichen Gesellschaft für Marketing und Unternehmensführung e.V.

Meffert, H., Burmann, Ch. (2002a), Wandel in der Markenführung – vom instrumentellen zum identitätsorientierten Markenverständnis, in: Meffert, H., Burmann, Ch., Koers, M. (Hrsg.), Markenmanagement, Wiesbaden , S. 18–30.

Meffert, H., Burmann, Ch. (2002b), Theoretisches Grundkonzept der identitätsorientierten Markenführung, in: Meffert, H., Burmann, Ch., Koers, M. (Hrsg.), Markenmanagement, Wiesbaden, S. 35–72.

Meffert, H., Burmann, Ch. (2002c), Managementkonzept der identitätsorientierten Markenführung, in: Meffert, H., Burmann, Ch., Koers, M. (Hrsg.), Markenmanagement, Wiesbaden, S. 73–97

Meffert, H., Burmann, Ch., Koers, M. (2002), Stellenwert und Gegenstand des Markenmanagement, in: Meffert, H., Burmann, Ch., Koers, M. (Hrsg.), Markenmanagement, Wiesbaden, S. 3–15.

Meffert, H., Giloth, M. (2002), Aktuelle markt- und unternehmensbezogene Herausforderungen an die Markenführung, in: Meffert, H., Burmann, Ch., Koers, M. (Hrsg.), Markenmanagement, Wiesbaden, S. 99–132.

Neale, W. C. (1964), The Peculiar Economics of Professional Sports: A Contribution to the Theory of the Firm in Sporting Competition and in Market Competition, in: Quarterly Journal of Economics, 78. Jg., Nr. 1, S. 1–14.

Parasuraman, A., Zeithaml, V. A., Berry, L. L. (1985), A Conceptual Model of Service Quality and its Implications for Future Research, in: Journal of Marketing, Vol. 49, S. 41–50.

Parensen, A. (2004), Der Fußballmarkt in Deutschland und seine Bearbeitung durch Agenturen, in: Hammann, P., Schmidt, L., Welling, M. (Hrsg.), Ökonomie des Fußballs – Grundlegungen aus volks- und betriebswirtschaftlicher Perspektive, Wiesbaden, S. 307–329.

Paul, S., Sturm, S. (2004), Going Public von Fußballclubs, in: Hammann, P., Schmidt, L., Welling, M. (Hrsg.), Ökonomie des Fußballs – Grundlegungen aus volks- und betriebswirtschaftlicher Perspektive, Wiesbaden, S. 193–218.

Reckenfelderbäumer, M. (2004), Auswirkungen der Integrativität auf die Qualitätspolitik von Fußballclubs, in: Hammann, P., Schmidt, L., Welling, M. (Hrsg.), Ökonomie des Fußballs – Grundlegungen aus volks- und betriebswirtschaftlicher Perspektive, Wiesbaden, S. 357–389.

Rottenberg, S. (1956), The Baseball Players' Labor Market, in: Journal of Political Economy, 64. Jg., S. 242–258.

Sportfive (2004), Fußballstudie 2004, Hamburg .

Staudt, E. (2004), Fans erwarten mehr als Kunden, Interview mit Erwin Staudt, in: Absatzwirtschaft, Nr. 6, S. 6–11.

Stauss, B. (1998), Markierungspolitik bei Dienstleistungen – Die „Dienstleistungsmarke", in: Bruhn, M., Meffert, H. (Hrsg.), Handbuch Dienstleistungsmanagement, Wiesbaden, S. 559–580.

Troisen, G. (2001), Globalisierung des Sport-Marketings, in: Hermanns, A., Riedmüller, F. (Hrsg.), Management Handbuch Sport-Marketing, München , S. 651–672.

UFA Sports (2000), UFA Fussball Studie. Märkte, Events, Vereine, Medien, Marken. Hamburg.

Welling, M. (2003), Bausteine einer integrierten image- und identitätsorientierten Markenführung als Beitrag zur Markentheorie, Schriften zum Marketing Nr. 47, Bochum.

Welling, M. (2004a), Die (Fußball-)Vereinsmarke – Konzeptionelle Grundlagen und ausgewählte Besonderheiten der Markenführung von Fußballvereinen, in: Hammann, P., Schmidt, L., Welling, M. (Hrsg.), Ökonomie des Fußballs – Grundlegungen aus volks- und betriebswirtschaftlicher Perspektive, Wiesbaden, S. 391–418.

Welling, M. (2004b), Grundlagen der Absatz- und Produktionsprozesse bei Produkten der Teamsportindustrie – dargestellt am Beispiel des Gutes Fußballspiel, in: Hammann, P., Schmidt, L., Welling, M. (Hrsg.), Ökonomie des Fußballs – Grundlegungen aus volks- und betriebswirtschaftlicher Perspektive, Wiesbaden, S. 269–306.

Welling, M. (2004c), Absatzmarktbezogene Business-to-Business-Geschäftsbeziehungen von Fußballklubs, in: Bieling, M., Eschweiler, M., Hardenacke, J. (Hrsg.), Business-to-Business-Marketing im Profifußball, Wiesbaden, S. 25–50.

Woratschek, H. (2002), Theoretische Elemente einer ökonomischen Betrachtung von Sportdienstleistungen, in: Albach, H., Frick, B. (Hrsg.), Sportökonomie, Ergänzungsheft 4, 2002 der Zeitschrift für Betriebswirtschaft, Wiesbaden, 1–21.

Woratschek, H., Beier, K. (2001), Sportmarketing, in: Tscheulin, D., Helmig, B. (Hrsg.), Branchenspezifisches Marketing, Wiesbaden, S. 203–235.

Zils, O. (2002), Die neue Sachlichkeit, in: Horizont Sport Business, Nr. 9, S. 12–18.

Ausgestaltung einer identitätsorientierten Markenführung in der Politik

Helmut Schneider

1.	**Von der politischen Propaganda zur Markenführung – Entwicklungslinien und Perspektiven des Politikmarketing**	**524**
2.	**Relevanz und Funktionen von Marken in der Politik**	**526**
3.	**Identitätsorientierte Führung von Politikmarken**	**531**
3.1	Das GAP-Modell als Bezugsrahmen der identitätsorientierten Führung von Politikmarken	532
3.2	Ausgestaltung einer identitätsorientierten Führung von Politikmarken – dargestellt am Beispiel der SPD	536
4.	**Fazit**	**557**

1. Von der politischen Propaganda zur Markenführung – Entwicklungslinien und Perspektiven des Politikmarketing

Als Geburtsstunde eines systematischen Politikmarketing wird in der Literatur häufig der US-Präsidentschaftswahlkampf zwischen Kennedy und Nixon des Jahres 1960 angeführt, da für Kennedys Sieg in erster Linie seine durch PR-Berater unterstützten Erfolge in den TV-Rededuellen ausschlaggebend gewesen seien (Maarek 1995, S. 14).

Ausgehend von den USA ist mittlerweile in allen westlichen Demokratien mit unterschiedlicher Intensität ein **wachsender Stellenwert von Marketingaspekten** im politischen Wettbewerb zu beobachten (Beresford 1998, S. 29).

Offensichtlicher Ausdruck dieser Entwicklung sind unter anderem größere Wahlkampfbudgets und die gestiegene Zahl politischer Berater, der so genannten spin doctors, deren Einfluss in den Planungsstäben politischer Parteien zudem kontinuierlich zugenommen hat (Falter 1998; Kinsey 1999). In Deutschland zeugen nicht zuletzt die Art und Weise der erfolgreichen Wahlkampagne der SPD zur Bundestagswahl 1998 (Holtz-Bacha 1999; Müller 1999; Machnig 1999) oder die von der FDP zur Bundestagswahl 2002 beschlossene „Strategie 18" von einer stärkeren Marketingorientierung der Parteien. Als wesentliche Ursachen der vermehrten Bedeutung des Politikmarketing in der Praxis identifiziert Wring die steigende Volatilität des Wählerverhaltens sowie eine generelle Ökonomisierung der Gesellschaft (Wring 1999).

Kongruent zur empirischen Evidenz hat sich insbesondere im **anglo-amerikanischen Sprachraum** eine eigene Forschungsrichtung des Politikmarketing entwickelt. Der Begriff „Political Marketing" wurde dabei von Kelley bereits Mitte der 50er Jahre in die wissenschaftliche Diskussion eingeführt (Kelley 1956). Seinerzeit noch als Synonym für den diskreditierten Terminus der Propaganda benutzt (Scammell 1999, S. 723), hat sich das Verständnis über den Charakter des Politikmarketing im Zeitablaufgrundlegend gewandelt. Die Forschungsbemühungen sind dabei nicht auf die Marketingwissenschaft beschränkt, sondern umfassen auch politik- und kommunikationswissenschaftliche Arbeiten.

Der eher **politikwissenschaftlich** ausgerichtete Forschungszweig konzentriert sich auf die Analyse von Wahlkämpfen (beispielhaft Nimmo 1970; Farell/Wortmann 1987; Bowler/Farell 1992; Kavanagh 1995; Wring 1997). Im Zentrum der Forschung steht dabei die Ursachenanalyse einer ausgemachten Veränderung von Wahlkampagnen sowie deren Bedeutung für den Wahlausgang. Politikmarketing wird in dieser Perspektive auf eine erfolgreiche Kampagnengestaltung reduziert (Mauser 1983; Butler/Collins 1996, S. 32; Scammell 1999, S. 719).

Auch die **kommunikationswissenschaftliche** Forschung interpretiert Politikmarketing im wesentlichen als Kampagnenmanagement, richtet ihr Augenmerk aber auch auf die Konsequenzen veränderter politischer Kommunikation für den demokratischen Prozess

(Edelmann 1976; Dörner 2001; Meyer 2001; Jarren/Donges 2002). Wachsende soziale Komplexität wird dabei nicht nur als Ursache der beobachteten Veränderung von Parteien zu undifferenzierten, so genannte Catch-All-Parteien (Kirchheimer 1965) ausgemacht, sondern auch als Treiber der gestiegenen gesellschaftlichen Bedeutung von Medien identifiziert. Damit wird für Parteien die Kampagnengestaltung in immer stärkerem Maße zum zentralen Erfolgsfaktor und die Medien gleichermaßen zum wichtigsten Adressaten wie Instrument politischer Kommunikation (Swanson/Mancini 1996). In jüngster Zeit wird die so veränderte politische Kommunikation als wesentliche Ursache einer wachsenden Politikverdrossenheit ausgemacht (Cappella/Jamieson 1997; Caspari/Schönbach/Lauf 1999).

Pioniere der dritten, **marketingwissenschaftlich** ausgerichteten Forschungsrichtung waren Kotler und Shama (Kotler 1975; Shama 1976). Ihre Arbeiten fußen auf zwei grundlegenden wissenschaftlichen Entwicklungen. Einerseits auf der schon von Schumpeter in den 40er Jahren des vergangenen Jahrhunderts entwickelten, später von Downs (1957) und anderen vorangetriebenen **Analogie zwischen wirtschaftlichen und politischen Austauschprozessen.** In dieser Perspektive werden Parteien als Anbieter eines politischen Produktes verstanden, das im demokratischen Wettbewerb vom nutzenmaximierenden Wähler gegenüber alternativen Angeboten bevorzugt werden soll. Andererseits hat die Marketingwissenschaft ihr Erkenntnisinteresse im Rahmen des von Kotler und Levy 1969 initiierten **Broadening** auf nicht-erwerbswirtschaftlich ausgerichtete Organisationen ausgedehnt (Kotler/Levy 1969).

Im Gegensatz zur politik- und kommunikationswissenschaftlichen Forschung wird in der marketingwissenschaftlichen Perspektive Politikmarketing nicht auf politische Kommunikation oder Kampagnengestaltung beschränkt, sondern als ein umfassendes, eher strategisch ausgerichtetes Konzept zur Erreichung der Ziele politischer Parteien oder Kandidaten interpretiert. Stellvertretend für diese Auffassung sei hier auf die Arbeiten von Butler und Collins (1994, 1996, 1999), Lock und Harris (1996, 2001), Kotler (1999), Newman (1994, 1999), Niffenegger (1989), Egan (1999) und Lees-Marshment (2001) verwiesen.

Insgesamt hat sich die Forschung auf dem Gebiet des Politikmarketing mittlerweile als fester Bestandteil der Marketingforschung im anglo-amerikanischen Sprachraum etabliert. Davon zeugen nicht nur die Vielzahl von Beiträgen in einschlägigen Marketingfachzeitschriften (Advances in Consumer Research, Research in Marketing, European Journal of Marketing, Journal of Marketing Management, Journal of Marketing) sowie die umfassenden Sammelbände von Newman (Newman/Sheth 1985; Newman 1999a), sondern auch die Tatsache, dass diese Forschungsrichtung eigene Konferenzen abhält (Henneberg 1996) und Politikmarketing zum festen Bestandteil im Lehrprogramm US-amerikanischer Universitäten im Fach Marketing geworden ist. In **Deutschland** finden sich hingegen bislang nur vereinzelte Forschungsbemühungen zum Politikmarketing. In der betriebswirtschaftlichen Literatur sind abgesehen von Beiträgen in Handwörterbüchern (Eberlein 1978; Hasitschka 1995; Freter 2001) vor allem die Monografien von Wangen (1983), Oellerking (1988) und Dombrowski (1997) sowie die Beiträge von Hermann/Huber/Braunstein (1999), Bauer/Huber/Herrmann (1995) und Stoiber (1983) zu nennen. Im Gegensatz zum anglo-amerikanischen Sprachraum kann in Deutschland ein eigenständiges Forschungsgebiet Politikmarketing angesichts der im Vergleich zu den USA zeitlich nachgelagerten Forschungsinitiierung und infolgedessen vergleichsweise geringen Anzahl von Publikationen noch nicht ausgemacht werden.

Ungeachtet der vielfältigen, in unterschiedlichen Disziplinen beheimateten Forschungsbemühungen und dem hohen Stellenwert des Politikmarketing als Forschungsgegenstand im anglo-amerikanischen Sprachraum, hat die Forschung dem Aspekt der **Marke** im politischen Kontext bislang kaum Beachtung geschenkt (Reichel 1999; White/de Charnotey 2001; Arnold 2002; Meffert/Schneider 2003; Schneider 2004a; Schneider 2004b). Dies überrascht um so mehr, als dass der Markenführung seitens der Praxis im Politikmarketing in jüngster Zeit eine größere Aufmerksamkeit zuteil wird (in der Beeck/Halstrick/Richter 2000; HORIZONT Serie „Parteien vor der Wahl" 2001; Struckmeier 2002, o. V. 2002) und Kirchheimer bereits 1965 in seinen Thesen zum Wandel des westeuropäischen Parteiensystems die Rolle der Partei auf politischem Gebiet als das sieht, „was auf dem wirtschaftlichen Sektor ein überall gebrauchter Marken- und Massenartikel ist" (Kirchheimer 1965, S. 34).

Zentrales **marketingwissenschaftliches Erkenntnisinteresse** ist in diesem Kontext neben der Frage nach der Relevanz von Politikmarken für die politische Präferenzbildung insbesondere die Ableitung eines den Spezifika des politischen Austauschprozesses gerecht werdendes Markenführungskonzeptes.

2. Relevanz und Funktionen von Marken in der Politik

Bislang hat sich die Forschung eher sporadisch und oberflächlich mit dem Phänomen von Politikmarken auseinandergesetzt. Dabei lassen sich zwei verschiedene Perspektiven identifizieren.

Zum einen wird der Markenbegriff zur Bildung von Analogien zwischen Politik- und kommerziellem Marketing eingesetzt. Newman beispielsweise sieht den Ruf eines Politikers als ein Ergebnis desselben Prozesses, der auch für die Entwicklung der Identität einer Marke eine Rolle spielt. „A politician's reputation is percieved by people in the same way that products and services develop brand identities in the marketplace" (Newman 1999, S. 45). Auch in den Ausführungen von Kotler und Shama erfolgt eine Markenbetrachtung auf Basis einer semantischen Parallele. So sieht Kotler das Image eines politischen Kandidaten als vergleichbar mit dem Image einer Marke, Shama setzt die Ausdrücke „party loyalty" und „party manager" gleich mit „brand loyalty" und „brand manager" (Shama 1976, S. 765; Kotler 1978, S. 36).

Andererseits werden Politikmarken im Kontext des Zielsystems im Politikmarketing diskutiert. Butler und Collins verweisen etwa auf die Bedeutung von Marken als Eintrittsbarrieren für wichtige Themenfelder. „Strategists should attempt to brand policies and ideas and build barriers to entry in order to own an important issue" (Butler/Collins 1994,

S. 23). Eine Markierung politischer Produkte soll somit helfen, Parteien und Politikern spezifische Themengebiete und Kompetenzen zuzuordnen. O'Cass macht ergänzend auf den Bindungsaspekt von Politikmarken im Sinne von Markenloyalität aufmerksam. „The objective of meeting voter's needs through the party offering is to build brand loyalty" (O'Cass 1996, S. 59).

Vernachlässigt wurde in der bisherigen Forschung die Frage, welches Gewicht Marken im Kontext des Politikmarketing aus Wählerperspektive beizumessen ist. Die Bedeutung von Politikmarken, die sich letztlich aus ihrer Relevanz für Wahlentscheidungen ergibt, wird in der Regel gleichsam axiomatisch vorausgesetzt (vgl. zu dem Versuch einer konzeptionellen Begründung Schweiger/Adami 1999).

Hier wird der Standpunkt vertreten, dass sich die Verhaltensrelevanz von Politikmarken aus der Erfüllung bestimmter Funktionen für den Wähler ergibt. Eine solche Argumentation basiert auf einem sozialpsychologischen Markenverständnis. Im Kontext des For-Profit-Marketing bildet diese Sichtweise in der Regel die Grundlage für die Ermittlung eines konsumentenorientierten Markenwertes. **Typische Funktionen** von Marken sind eine erleichterte Identifikation von und mit der angebotenen Leistung, eine Orientierungshilfe in Form eines „information chunk", eine Risikoreduktionsfunktion im Sinne eines Vertrauenssurrogats sowie Image- beziehungsweise Prestigeaspekte (Meffert 2000, S. 847). Diese vielfältigen Markenfunktionen lassen sich zu den drei Dimensionen Informationseffizienz, Risikoreduktion und ideeller Nutzen zusammenfassen (Fischer/ Hieronimus/ Kranz 2002, S. 18). Analysiert man die Austauschbeziehung zwischen Parteien und Wählern unter dem Aspekt der Markenfunktionen, wird deutlich, dass alle drei Markenfunktionen auch für Politikmarken relevant sind.

Die Bedeutung der **Informationskosten** für die Erklärung von Wahlbeteiligung und -entscheidung ist im Kontext der empirischen Wahlforschung insbesondere von Vertretern der Rational-Choice-Theorie intensiv beleuchtet worden (Downs 1968, S. 110). Popkins et al. haben in diesem Zusammenhang den Begriff des „informational shortcut" geprägt:

„Because information is costly, most voters will save time and energy by using informational shortcuts to the vote decision" (Popkins et al. 1976, S. 789).

Angesichts der aus zunehmender politischer Komplexität resultierenden hohen Informationskosten für den Wähler (Dalton/Wattenberg 1993, S. 194) und dem öffentlichen Gut-Charakter des Wahlausgangs wird angenommen, dass Wähler zur Informationsbeschaffung auf Kosten senkende **informational shortcuts** zurückgreifen (Fuchs/Kühnel 1990, S. 315 f.). Derartige shortcuts sind neben Ideologien in erster Linie die Parteien (Popkins et al. 1976, S. 804). Politikmarken als fest verankerte, differenzierte Wissensstrukturen dienen dem Wähler in dieser Sichtweise als Informationsspeicher, aus dem er bei politischen Entscheidungen Kosten sparend Informationen abruft.

Der Stellenwert von Politikmarken bezüglich der **Risikoreduktion** ergibt sich aus den Spezifika des politischen Austauschprozesses, die in Summe zu einem hohen wahrgenommenen Risiko für den Wähler führen. Parteien und Kandidaten offerieren dem Wähler im Austausch für dessen Wahlstimme ein Versprechen der Werterealisierung sowie der Ideen- und Interessenvertretung (Hasitschka 1995, S. 2036). Angesichts der Immaterialität des Leistungsversprechens sowie einer zeitlichen Verzögerung zwischen dem Kauf- beziehungsweise Wahlakt und der eigentlichen Leistungserbringung (Harrop 1990, S. 278) weist das Politikmarketing mehr Parallelen zum Dienstleistungs- als zum Sachgütermarketing auf (O'Shaughnessy/Holbrook, 1989, S. 99). Für Dienstleistungen wird wegen des hohen Anteils von Erfahrungs- beziehungsweise Vertrauenseigenschaften (Kaas 1996), das heißt Leistungsbestandteilen, deren Nutzen vom Kunden erst nach Inanspruchnahme einer Leistung beziehungsweise gar nicht beurteilt werden können, generell ein höheres subjektives Kaufrisiko als bei Sachgütern konstatiert (Meffert/Bruhn 2003, S. 112). Die aus diesem Umstand abgeleitete besondere Bedeutung von Vertrauenskomponenten im Dienstleistungsmarketing (Stauss 2001, S. 556) erfährt im Politikmarketing durch weitere risikosteigernde Rahmenbedingungen eine herausragende Relevanz (Scammell 1999, S. 728).

Im Gegensatz zu Markttransaktionen besteht für die Anbieter politischer Leistungen zunächst keine vertragliche Verpflichtung zur Einlösung des gegenüber dem Wähler explizit oder implizit abgegebenen Leistungsversprechens, dessen Einhaltung durch den Wähler angesichts der Komplexität politischer Prozesse zudem mitunter gar nicht überprüft werden kann. Darüber hinaus zeichnet sich die vom Wähler „gekaufte" Dienstleistung durch Veränderlichkeit (mutability) aus. Butler und Collins (1999, S. 59) kennzeichnen damit den Umstand, dass die Regierungsbildung häufig Koalitionsverhandlungen notwendig macht, die mitunter das vor der Wahl abgegebene Leistungsversprechen vor dem Hintergrund erforderlicher Kompromisse erheblich verändern. Die Tatsache schließlich, dass Wahlen als demokratischer Sanktionsmechanismus nur in größeren zeitlichen Abständen stattfinden, erhöht das wahrgenommene Risiko des Wählers weiter. Insgesamt ist die Wahlentscheidung aus Sicht des Wählers also mit zahlreichen risikosteigernden Komponenten behaftet. Es kann somit angenommen werden, dass die daraus resultierende hohe Bedeutung der **Vertrauenskomponente** im politischen Bereich (Bauer/Huber/Herrmann 1995, S. 115; Schweer 2000) Politikmarken als Vertrauensanker eine Präferenz bildende Wirkung bei Wahlentscheidungen verleiht.

Obgleich die **ideelle Nutzenstiftung** von Marken im kommerziellen Kontext in erster Linie aus expressivem, das heißt nach außen sichtbarem Konsum abgeleitet wird (zum Beispiel Prestigeeffekt eines Rolls Royce), können auch Politikmarken einen ideellen Nutzen für den Wähler stiften. Ein solcher Nutzen resultiert zum Beispiel aus dem Gefühl der Zugehörigkeit zu einer Gruppe von gleich gesinnten Wählern im Sinne einer Wertegemeinschaft oder dem Gefühl der Identifikation mit der Partei oder dem Kandidaten.

Im Rahmen einer empirischen Analyse von Politikmarken aus Wähler- und Mitgliedersicht (Schneider 2004a) wurde unter anderem auch die Bedeutung der aufgezeigten **Markenfunktionen** für den Wähler **empirisch** analysiert. Dazu wurden die Markenfunktionen in Form von Statements operationalisiert, die von den Befragten auf einer 5er-Skala entweder als zutreffend oder nicht zutreffend gekennzeichnet werden sollten. Die Erfüllung der Markenfunktionen wurde dabei jeweils nur im Hinblick auf die präferierte Partei beziehungsweise den präferierten Kandidaten abgefragt. Die Ergebnisse dieser repräsentativen Studie sind in Abbildung 1 dargestellt. Als Interpretationshilfe für die Frage, inwieweit Politikmarken typische Markenfunktionen erfüllen, sind in der Abbildung die Ergebnisse einer am Marketing Centrum der Universität Münster in Kooperation mit McKinsey durchgeführten repräsentativen Untersuchung (n = 2.552) zu den Markenfunktionen im Konsumgüter- und Dienstleistungsbereich als Vergleichsmaßstab aufgeführt (Fischer/ Hieronimus/Kranz 2002, S. 29).

Abbildung 1: Funktionen von Politikmarken

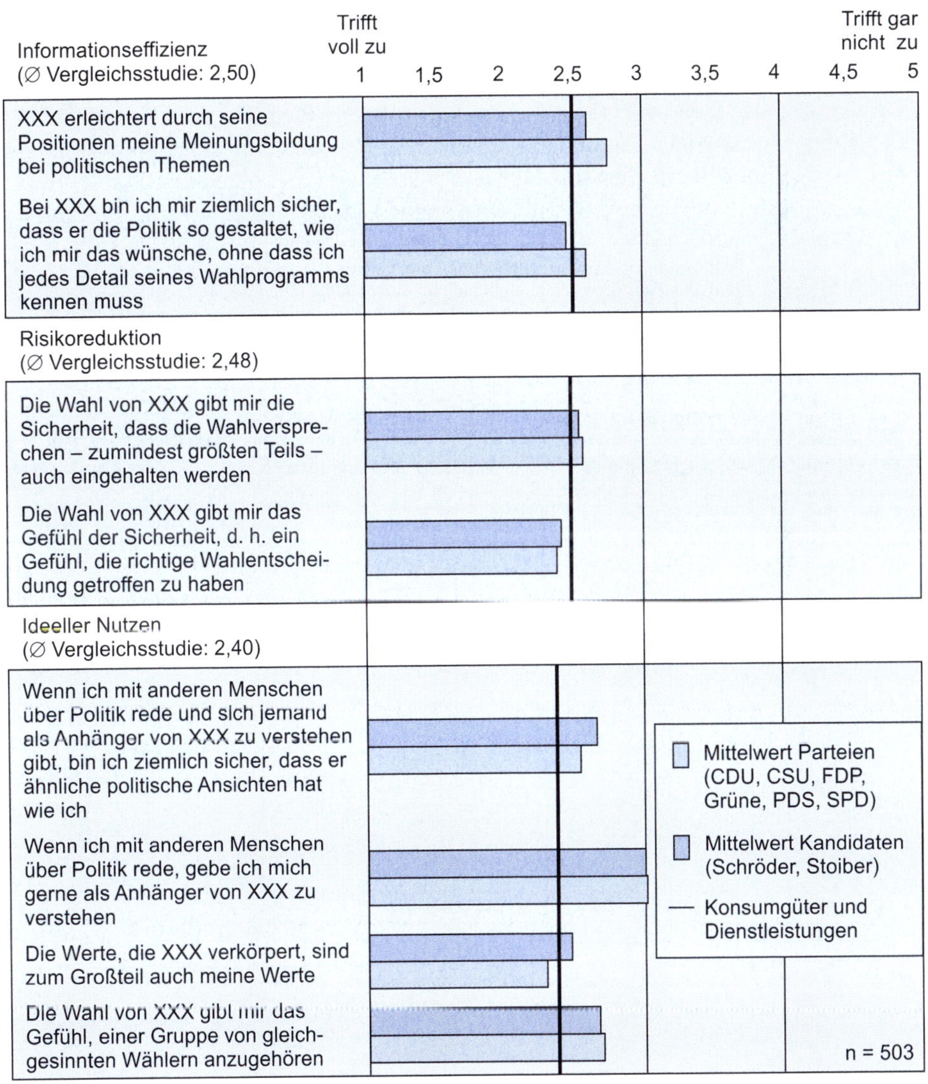

GABLER GRAFIK

Im Ergebnis zeigt sich, dass alle drei Markenfunktionen in der Politik für den Wähler relevant sind. Im Durchschnitt über alle Parteien und die Kanzlerkandidaten von CDU und SPD zur Bundestagswahl 2002 sind im Vergleich mit den Konsumgüter- und Dienstleistungsbranchen Informationseffizienz und ideeller Nutzen etwas weniger, die Risikoreduktion hingegen gleich wichtig (vgl. Abbildung 1).

Die aus den Markenfunktionen abgeleitete Bedeutung von Politikmarken für den Wähler soll abschließend an einem **Beispiel** illustriert werden. Im Rahmen der bereits angeführten empirischen Untersuchung wurde der in der Marketingwissenschaft zur Verdeutlichung der Markenrelevanz oft zitierte **Cola-Test** (de Chernatony/McDonald 1992, S. 9), bei dem Testpersonen ihre Präferenz für ein Cola-Getränk einmal ohne und einmal mit Darbietung der Marken abgeben, für Politikmarken **modifiziert**. Dazu wurden die Befragten in drei Gruppen eingeteilt, denen jeweils die gleiche politische Fragestellung (Abschaffung der Wehrpflicht) zur Beurteilung vorgelegt wurde. Einer Gruppe wurde das Statement jedoch ohne Parteimarke, einer Gruppe mit dem Markenstimulus SPD und einer Gruppe mit dem Markenstimulus CDU präsentiert (vgl. Abbildung 2).

Abbildung 2: **Relevanz von Politikmarken für die politische Präferenzbildung**

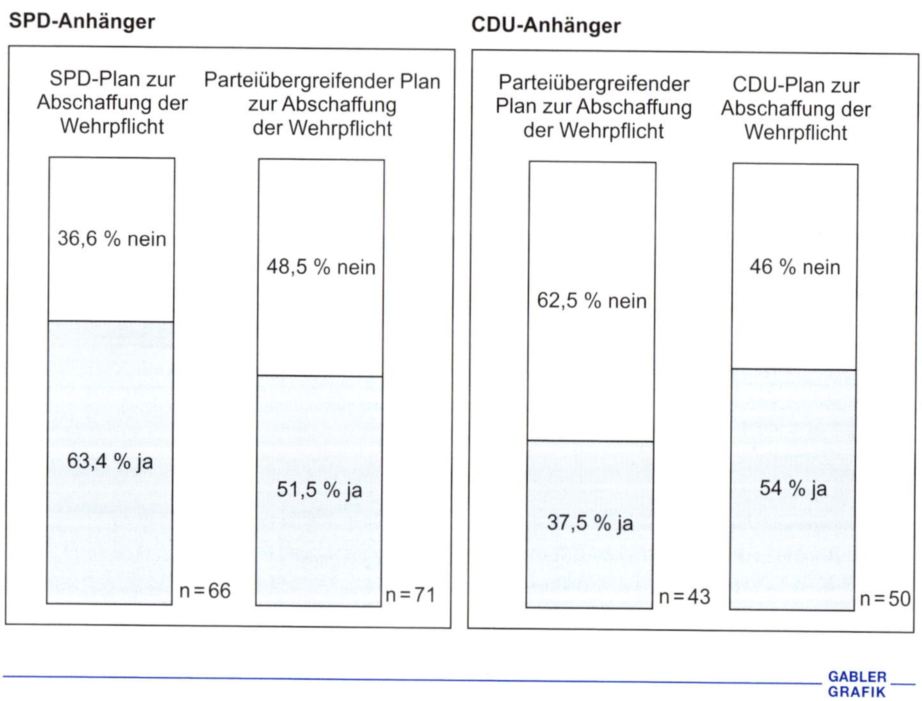

Das Ergebnis zeigt deutlich, dass Marken die politische Präferenzbildung verändern. Während die Anhänger der CDU die Abschaffung der Wehrpflicht ohne Darbietung des Markenstimulus noch zu 62,5 Prozent ablehnen, sinkt dieser Wert auf 46 Prozent, wenn es sich um einen Vorschlag der CDU handelt. Bei den SPD-Anhängern sind ohne Markenreiz 51,5 Prozent der Befragten für die Abschaffung der Wehrpflicht, handelt es sich um einen Vorschlag der SPD, wächst die Zahl der Befürworter auf 63,4 Prozent an.

Ausgehend von der aus den Markenfunktionen abgeleiteten Relevanz von Politikmarken für das Wählerverhalten stellt sich aus einer betriebswirtschaftlich-entscheidungsorientierten Perspektive die Frage nach einem adäquaten **Markenführungsansatz**.

3. Identitätsorientierte Führung von Politikmarken

Die Auswahl der von einer Partei zu ergreifenden Maßnahmen zur Sicherstellung der positiven Markenwirkungen hängt unmittelbar vom zugrunde liegenden Markenverständnis ab. In Konsequenz des wirkungsbezogenen Markenverständnisses fokussierte sich die Marketingwissenschaft lange Zeit auf die Wahrnehmung von Marken in den Augen der Nachfrager in unterschiedlichen Eigenschaftsdimensionen, das heißt auf das Markenfremdbild (Markenimage) als zentralem Erfolgsfaktor der Markenführung. In diesem Zusammenhang wurde eine Position im Markt angestrebt, die einerseits den Idealvorstellungen der Nachfrager möglichst nah kommen sollte, andererseits eine möglichst große Differenzierung zu den Konkurrenzprodukten aufweisen sollte.

Die Reduzierung der Markenführung auf den Imageaspekt erwies sich insbesondere unter zwei Gesichtspunkten als inadäquat. Einerseits führte der imagebezogene Ansatz zu einer Überbetonung von methodischen Aspekten der Markenführung und damit zu einer Vernachlässigung des für Marken essenziellen Integrationsaspektes **(Integrationsdefizit)**. „Die funktionsübergreifende Abstimmung und Vernetzung einzelner Maßnahmen zur Imagegestaltung blieb als Folge der zumeist partialanalytischen Vorgehensweise aus" (Meffert/Burmann 1996, S. 10).

Andererseits bewirkte die dominante Außenorientierung im Sinne eines „Wer soll ich sein?" eine Ausblendung der Innenperspektive im Sinne eines „Wer möchte ich sein?" beziehungsweise „Wer kann ich sein?" **(Identitätsdefizit)**. So birgt eine einseitige Ausrichtung der Marke an den mitunter rasch wechselnden Präferenzen potenzieller Abnehmer das Risiko von Inkonsistenzen und Diskontinuitäten im Markenbild, die einer Marke die Vertrauensbasis entziehen können. Der imageorientierte Ansatz der Markenführung wird damit den Anforderungen an die Führung von Politikmarken in besonderer Weise nicht gerecht, da im politischen Kontext die Innenorientierung, die sich etwa in programmatischen Grundsätzen und Leitlinien niederschlägt, ein außergewöhnliches Gewicht besitzt. Die beliebige Anpassung politischer Inhalte an die jeweils vom relevanten Wählersegment geforderte Position im Sinne einer reinen Außenorientierung scheidet im politischen Kontext als Ansatz der Markenführung nicht nur angesichts ethischer Bedenken, sondern auch vor dem Hintergrund der besonderen Sensibilität im Hinblick auf die politische Glaubwürdigkeit aus (Scammell 1994, S. 36 f.; O'Cass 1996, S. 59). Insofern bewegen sich Politikmarken in einem besonderen **Spannungsfeld einer Outside-in- und Inside-out-Orientierung** (Harrop 1990, S. 277; Delaney 1994, S. 48; Ormrod 2003).

Mit dem **identitätsorientierten Ansatz** der Markenführung wurde in der Marketingwissenschaft ein Markenführungskonzept entwickelt (Kapferer 1992; Meffert/Burmann 1996), das in seiner Zielsetzung mit dem Vertrauensaspekt die **wesentliche Anforderung an Marken im politischen Kontext aufgreift.** Darüber hinaus stellt der Ansatz über den Einbezug von Selbst- und Fremdbild einer Marke die Innen- und Außenperspektive der Markenführung in den erforderlichen integrativen Rahmen. Dieses im For-Profit-Bereich nicht zuletzt auch ressourcentheoretisch begründete Vorgehen (Koers 2001, S. 51 ff.) besitzt für mitgliederbasierte Organisationen – wie beispielsweise Parteien – eine besondere Relevanz. Insofern trägt der identitätsorientierte Ansatz der Markenführung sowohl in der Zieldimension als auch in seiner grundsätzlichen Bi-Perspektivität den Spezifika der Führung von Politikmarken auf besondere Weise Rechnung.

3.1 Das GAP-Modell als Bezugsrahmen der identitätsorientierten Führung von Politikmarken

In Anbetracht der Wechselseitigkeit des Identitätsbegriffes, die auch als Paradigma der Identitätsforschung charakterisiert wird (Frey/Haußer 1987, S. 17), wurde in der Literatur in Anlehnung an das im Kontext des Qualitätsmanagements konzipierte Modell von Parasuraman et al. (1985) ein GAP-Modell der identitätsorientierten Markenführung entwickelt (Meffert/Burmann 1996). Ausgehend von der sozialpsychologisch gestützten Grundannahme, dass die Identität und damit das Vertrauenspotenzial einer Marke durch das Maß der Übereinstimmung zwischen ihrem Fremd- und ihrem Selbstbild bestimmt werden, sind diese in der Situationsanalyse der identitätsorientierten Markenführung zu bestimmen und etwaige **Lücken** (GAPs) zwischen der Innen- und der Außenperspektive zu identifizieren. Um aus der Gegenüberstellung von Markenselbst- und -fremdbild differenzierte Implikationen für die Markenführung ableiten zu können, ist es dabei zweckmäßig, beide Perspektiven in eine Soll- und eine Ist-Komponente zu zerlegen, da etwaige Diskrepanzen zwischen Markenselbst- und -fremdbild sowohl auf Unterschieden hinsichtlich der Idealposition einer Marke als auch ihrer aktuellen Wahrnehmung mit jeweils jedoch unterschiedlichen Implikationen für die Markenführung beruhen können.

Die Bestimmung des **Markenfremdbildes** ist nur mit geringen Operationalisierungsproblemen verbunden. Angesichts der expliziten Erfassung der Soll- und Ist-Komponente soll hierzu auf das Konzept der Einstellungsmessung nach Trommsdorff (1975, S. 67 f.) zurückgegriffen werden. Diese Form der Erfassung des Markenfremdbildes geht konform mit den in der Literatur bislang vorgestellten Modellen von Meffert/Burmann (siehe Beitrag in diesem Band), Koers (2001, S. 166 f.) und Bierwirth (2003).

Hinsichtlich der Operationalisierung des **Markenselbstbildes** ergibt sich im Vergleich zu den im Kontext des For-Profit-Marketing entwickelten Modellen indes Modifikations- respektive Akzentuierungsbedarf, der aus den Spezifika des Untersuchungsgegenstandes Politikmarken resultiert. Meffert/Burmann (1996, S. 38) definieren als Kern der Markenidentität im Hinblick auf das Selbstbild die Markenphilosophie, „welche die Idee, den Inhalt und die zentralen Eigenschaften einer Marke in Form eines plastischen Markenleitbildes festlegt“. Die vielfältigen Komponenten der Markenphilosophie können in Anlehnung an Aaker (1996, S. 68 ff.) zu den vier Dimensionen Art der Produkte und Dienstleistungen, symbolische Eigenschaften, Persönlichkeitsmerkmale und Eigenschaften der Organisation verdichtet werden.

Schon im kommerziellen Kontext wird dabei insbesondere im Dienstleistungsbereich dem **Verhalten der Mitarbeiter** als Bestandteil der organisationalen Dimension eine zentrale Bedeutung für das Markenselbstbild zugebilligt, da alle anderen Facetten der Markenphilosophie letztlich durch das Verhalten und die Entscheidungen der in den Markenauftritt involvierten Personen determiniert werden (siehe Beitrag zum theoretischen Grundkonzept der identitätsorientierten Markenführung in diesem Buch). Dies gilt angesichts der demokratischen Willensbildungsprozesse in besonderem Maße für Parteien. Die Markenphilosophie einer Partei beruht ungeachtet des hohen Einflusses der Führungsgremien einer Partei – etwa in Form von Programm- oder Grundsatzkommissionen – in letzter Konsequenz auf dem mehrheitlichen Willen der Parteimitglieder, die Personalfragen und programmatische Entwürfe auf Parteitagen diskutieren, gegebenenfalls modifizieren und verabschieden (Niclauß 2002, S. 202 ff.). Demnach kommt den **Parteimitgliedern** in Bezug auf das Selbstbild einer Partei zentrale Bedeutung zu (Stöss 1997, S. 182 ff.). Damit entsteht die Markenidentität einer Partei im Wesentlichen im Wechselspiel zwischen Ist- und Soll-Bild in den Augen der Wähler (Markenfremdbild) auf der einen und der Parteimitglieder (Markenselbstbild) auf der anderen Seite.

Die nachfolgende exemplarische Offenlegung von Spannungsfeldern der identitätsorientierten Führung von Politikmarken im Rahmen eines GAP-Modells basiert daher auf einer symmetrischen Befragung der wahlberechtigten Gesamtbevölkerung[1] einerseits und von Mitgliedern der SPD andererseits. Bei beiden Zielgruppen wurde die Zerlegung in Soll- und Ist-Komponente auf Basis der Trommsdorffschen Einstellungsmessung durchgeführt. In Konsequenz der Differenzierung zwischen Selbst- und Fremdbild wurde dabei allerdings die zur Abbildung der Soll-Komponente eingesetzte Frage nach der Idealpartei zwischen beiden Gruppen modifiziert. Während die Wähler nach der idealen Regierungspartei gefragt wurden, sollten die Parteimitglieder Auskunft über die ideale SPD machen.

1 Im Hinblick auf die Abgrenzung des relevanten Marktes wurden dabei nur Wähler mit einer Wahlwahrscheinlichkeit von größer 0 Prozent berücksichtigt. So reduzierte sich die Stichprobe bei der Fremdbildanalyse von ursprünglich 503 auf n = 372. Eine Ausrichtung der Markenführung auf die Zielgruppe mit einer Wahlwahrscheinlichkeit von 0 Prozent für die jeweilige Partei erscheint angesichts der unvermeidbaren Ausstrahlungseffekte auf alle anderen Wählergruppen nicht sinnvoll.

Es kann angenommen werden, dass eine Modifikation des Markenprofils nicht auf diejenigen Wähler beschränkt bleibt, die dies positiv bewerten, sondern gleichermaßen von allen Wählern wahrgenommen wird. Wenn es der SPD beispielsweise durch die Verabschiedung eines Sonderprogramms „Sozialstaat 21" gelänge, in den Augen der Wähler sozialer zu sein, würde diese Veränderung eben nicht nur von den Wählern registriert, die eine solche Modifikation für vorteilhaft erachten, sondern von allen Wählern. Insofern kann aus der in Tabelle 1 dargestellten differenzierten Analyse von GAP 1 noch nicht unmittelbar auf ein Anforderungsprofil der Markenführung geschlossen werden. Zur Ermittlung dieses Referenzpunktes für die Markenführung aus der Fremdbildperspektive müssen zunächst die individuellen Abweichungen der einzelnen Befragten im Hinblick auf ihre Ursachen näher analysiert werden. Dazu wurden die absoluten Abweichungen in mögliche Kombinationen aus Idealvorstellung und Realeindruck von der SPD differenziert (vgl. Tabelle 2). Negative Werte sind angesichts der Berechnungsvorschrift „Realbild der SPD minus Idealanforderung" dabei dahingehend zu interpretieren, dass die Eigenschaft aus Sicht dieser Befragten zu stark ausgeprägt ist. Positive Werte hingegen signalisieren eine zu schwache Ausprägung der Eigenschaft bei der SPD.

Für die Simulation von Maßnahmen der Markenführung ist vor allem von Interesse, wie groß der Anteil der Befragten ist, deren Idealpunkt bei einem bestimmten Item an einem der Extrempunkte (1 = sehr gut beziehungsweise 5 = sehr schlecht) der Skala liegt. Für diese Gruppe von Befragten kann bei dem jeweiligen Item ein Nutzenverlauf nach dem Idealvektor- und nicht wie bei der Einstellungsmessung nach Trommsdorff grundsätzlich unterstellt – nach dem Idealpunktmodell angenommen werden. Dies ist insofern von Bedeutung, als dass für diese Gruppe die Veränderung einer bestimmten Eigenschaft auch über den aus der Differenz zwischen Ideal und Real abgeleiteten Änderungsbedarf hinaus nicht zu einer neuen Lücke zwischen Ideal und Real mit dann allerdings umgekehrtem Vorzeichen führt. Wenn ein Befragter beispielsweise das Item „sozial" als für eine Partei sehr gut angesehen hat (Antwort bei Ideal = 1), die SPD im Hinblick auf die Ist-Position aber nur mit 2 bewertet hat (1 = trifft voll und ganz zu) so wird auch eine über diese Lücke von +1 hinausgehende Stärkung der Eigenschaft „sozial" für diesen Befragten nicht zu einer Lücke zwischen Ideal und Real führen. Hat ein Befragter hingegen bei der Frage nach der Idealpartei in Bezug auf das Item „sozial" eine 2 angegeben und den Realzustand der SPD mit 3 bewertet, könnte eine Stärkung der Eigenschaft „sozial" über die Lücke von 1 hinaus erneut zu einer dann negativen Abweichung führen (Ideal = 2, Real = 1), für diesen Wähler wäre die SPD dann zu sozial.

Tabelle 2: Differenzierung der individuellen Lücken zwischen Realbild von der SPD und Anforderungen an eine Idealpartei

Eigenschaft ist aus Sicht der Wähler bei der SPD …

Zu stark ausgeprägt				Ideal	Zu schwach ausgeprägt			
Differenz zwischen Realbild von der SPD und Anforderung an Idealpartei								
–4*	–3	–2	–1	0	1	2	3	4
Real 1 – Ideal 5	Real 2 – Ideal 5	Real 3 – Ideal 5	Real 4 – Ideal 5	Real 5 – Ideal 5	Real 2 – Ideal 1	Real 3 – Ideal 1	Real 4 – Ideal 1	Real 5 – Ideal 1
	Real 1 – Ideal 4	Real 2 – Ideal 4	Real 3 – Ideal 4	Real 4 – Ideal 4	Real 3 – Ideal 2	Real 4 – Ideal 2	Real 5 – Ideal 2	
		Real 1 – Ideal 3	Real 2 – Ideal 3	Real 3 – Ideal 3	Real 4 – Ideal 3	Real 5 – Ideal 3		
			Real 1 – Ideal 2	Real 2 – Ideal 2	Real 5 – Ideal 4			
				Real 1 – Ideal 1				

Bezeichnung der Skalen:
Ideal: 5 = sehr schlecht; 1 = sehr gut; Real: 5 = trifft gar nicht zu; 1 = trifft voll und ganz zu

* Berechnungsvorschrift: Realbild von der SPD – Idealanforderung an eine Partei. Zum Beispiel europäisch zu sein ist für eine Partei sehr schlecht (Wert = 5); die SPD ist sehr europäisch (Wert = 1). Ergebnis = –4, Eigenschaft ist deutlich zu stark ausgeprägt

GABLER GRAFIK

Vor dem Hintergrund der in Tabelle 2 dargestellten Differenzierung wurde nun für jedes Item der Anteil der Befragten berechnet, deren Vorstellung von einer idealen Regierungspartei der Realvorstellung von der SPD bei einer Stärkung oder Schwächung der Eigenschaft von –4 (Eigenschaft wird geschwächt) bis +4 (Eigenschaft wird gestärkt)[8] ent-

8 Die Ausführungen sind dabei von dem Bewusstsein geprägt, dass komplexe Bewertungsvorgänge in der Psyche des Wählers nicht der hier unterstellten Metrik gehorchen. Darüber hinaus kann sicher in Frage gestellt werden, dass eine bestimmte Markenführungsmaßnahme einerseits aufgrund interpersoneller Unterschiede, andererseits aufgrund individuell verschiedener Ausgangssituationen bei allen Rezipienten die gleiche Wirkung erzielt. Ungeachtet dieser Limitationen können die Ergebnisse aber doch Tendenzrichtungen für die Führung von Politikmarken aufzeigen.

sprach. Die zu diesem Zweck jeweils erstellte Arbeitstabelle ist nachfolgend für das Item „europäisch" exemplarisch dargestellt (vgl. Tabelle 3).

Tabelle 3: Aufteilung der Befragten auf mögliche Real-Ideal-Kombinationen am Beispiel des Items „europäisch"

Eigenschaft „europäisch" ist aus Sicht der Wähler bei der SPD ...								
Zu stark ausgeprägt				**Ideal**	**Zu schwach ausgeprägt**			
Differenz zwischen Realbild von der SPD und Anforderung an Idealpartei								
–4	–3	–2	–1	0	1	2	3	4
n = 2	n = 2	n = 4	n = 0	n = 1	n = 56	n = 15	n = 5	n = 0
	n = 2	n = 6	n = 7	n = 2	n = 37	n = 6	n = 0	
		n = 12	n = 45	n = 28	n = 2	n = 0		
			n = 15	n = 90	n = 1			
				n = 32				n = 370

GABLER GRAFIK

Auf Basis dieser Arbeitstabellen konnte nun für jedes Item ermittelt werden, wie sich die Lücke zwischen Ideal und Real entwickelt, wenn es der SPD im Rahmen der Markenführung gelingt, das jeweilige Item in den Augen der Wähler zu stärken oder zu schwächen. Dabei stand in erster Linie die Frage im Mittelpunkt, wie sich der Anteil derjenigen Wähler verändert, deren modifiziertes Ist-Bild von der SPD ihrem Ideal entspricht. Die optimale Veränderungsrichtung und -intensität und damit **der Referenzpunkt für die Markenführung** sind dann erreicht, wenn dieser **Wähleranteil maximal** ist. Die Berechnungsvorschrift für diese Simulation ist in nachfolgender Tabelle erneut am Beispiel der Eigenschaft „europäisch" illustriert. Wenn beispielsweise die Eigenschaft „europäisch" bei der SPD in den Augen der Wähler um zwei Einheiten weniger stark ausgeprägt wäre, so würde für alle Wähler, welche die SPD bislang um zwei Einheiten zu „europäisch" empfunden haben (Differenz zwischen Real und Ideal = –2), die SPD ihrem Ideal entsprechen.

Tabelle 4: Simulationslogik am Beispiel des Items „europäisch" für die SPD

Wähler, für die die SPD bislang zu europäisch ist					Wähler, für die die SPD bislang zu wenig europäisch ist			
Maßnahmen der Markenführung – Eigenschaft „europäisch" wird bei der SPD …								
geschwächt				**nicht verändert**	**gestärkt**			
um –4	um –3	um –2	um –1	0	um 1	um 2	um 3	um 4
Ergebnis: Zahl der Wähler, deren Ist-Bild von der SPD nach erfolgter Veränderung der Anforderung an eine Idealpartei entspricht								
2+2+4+ 0+1 = 9	2+2+4+ 0+1 = 9	4+6+12 +0+1 = 23	0+7+45 +15+1 = 68	1+2+28+90+ 32 **= 153 (max.)**	56+37+ 2+1+32 = 128	15+6+0 +56+32 = 109	5+0+15 +56+32 = 108	0+5+15+ 5+6+32 = 108
n = 2	n = 2	n = 4 [1]	n = 0 [4]	n = 1 [5]	n = 56	n = 15	n = 5	n = 0
	n = 2	n = 6 [2]	n = 7	n = 2	n = 37	n = 6	n = 0	
		n = 12 [3]	n = 45	n = 28	n = 2	n = 0		
			n = 15	n = 90	n = 1			
				n = 32				n = 370

GABLER GRAFIK

In Tabelle 4 sind dies die Wähler mit den Ausprägungen Ideal 5, Real 3 (Zelle 1); Ideal 4, Real 2 (Zelle 2) und Ideal 3, Real 1 (Zelle 3). Hinzu kommen noch diejenigen Befragten, die „europäisch" als überhaupt nicht wünschenswerte Eigenschaft erachtet haben (Ideal = 5) **und** bislang eine Lücke **größer** –2 aufwiesen (Ideal 5, Real 4 [Zelle 4] und Ideal 5, Real 5 [Zelle 5]). Auch diese Befragten würden nach einer Schwächung der Eigenschaft „europäisch" um zwei Einheiten die SPD anschließend (Zelle 4) respektive nach wie vor (Zelle 5) als ideal ansehen. Im Ergebnis zeigt sich, dass es für die SPD nicht sinnvoll wäre, an ihrem derzeitigen Profil im Hinblick auf das Item „europäisch" etwas zu verändern. Bei jeder Stärkung oder Schwächung der Eigenschaft ist der Anteil der Wähler, deren Bild von der SPD ihrer Anforderung an eine Idealpartei entspricht, kleiner als in der Ausgangssituation (n = 153; 41,4 Prozent).

Auf Basis der vorgestellten Simulationslogik wurden für jedes Item Richtung und Ausmaß der Veränderung bestimmt, bei dem der Anteil der Wähler im Idealzustand maximal ist. Das Ergebnis dieser Berechnungen, das als Veränderungsaufforderung im Sinne eines **Referenzpunktes für die Markenführung** interpretiert werden kann, zeigt Tabelle 5.

Tabelle 5: Veränderung des Anteils der Wähler im Idealzustand in Abhängigkeit von Veränderungen des Ist-Bildes der SPD

	Eigenschaft wird bei der SPD...								
	Geschwächt					Gestärkt			
	um –4	um –3	um –2	um –1	0	um 1	um 2	um 3	um 4
Anteil der **Wähler** in Prozent, deren Ideal-Anforderung mit Realbild der SPD übereinstimmt									
1. Gruppe von Eigenschaften: keine Veränderung sinnvoll									
Europäisch	2,4	2,4	6,2	18,4	**41,4**	34,6[9]	29,5	29,2	29,2
Integrierend	0,8	0,8	1,9	12,9	**39,9**	35,8	25,6	25,3	25,3
Sympathisch	1,3	1,6	4,6	14,8	**39,0**	37,6	31,2	30,4	30,9
Traditionsbewusst	6,5	6,8	10,0	22,4	**38,6**	24,3	11,6	10,0	10,8
Diskussionsfreudig	1,1	1,1	6,2	16,7	**38,2**	37,4	34,4	34,7	34,7
2. Gruppe von Eigenschaften: begrenzte Stärkung sinnvoll									
Fortschrittlich	0,0	0,0	1,3	5,4	31,8	**44,2**	44,2	43,9	44,2
Konstruktiv	0,8	0,3	0,5	4,6	28,3	**43,2**	38,3	39,4	39,7
Kompromissfähig	0,3	0,5	2,2	11,7	30,6	**41,7**	36,6	36,6	36,3
Leistungsorientiert	0,5	0,3	1,6	7,6	34,5	**38,3**	29,6	29,1	29,6
3. Gruppe von Eigenschaften: deutliche Stärkung sinnvoll									
Ehrlich	3,2	3,2	3,5	6,7	13,7	28,5	58,1	71,5	**73,9**
Vertrauenswürdig	0,3	0,8	0,8	4,8	18,0	35,5	59,4	67,7	**69,9**
Regierungsfähig	0,0	0,0	1,1	7,3	26,9	45,4	65,1	68,0	**69,4**
Demokratisch	0,3	0,3	0,3	7,0	34,9	61,0	64,2	64,5	**65,1**
Kompetent	0,0	0,0	0,5	3,8	21,9	44,1	58,6	61,9	**62,2**
Packt die wichtigen polit. Probleme an	1,1	1,1	1,9	6,7	22,6	32,8	49,5	57,3	**59,9**
Zukunftsorientiert	0,8	0,5	1,6	4,8	29,0	47,6	51,6	54,8	**55,4**
Sozial	0,5	0,5	2,2	9,9	33,6	47,3	52,2	54,0	**55,1**
Menschlich	1,1	1,1	1,6	6,7	33,6	48,9	51,6	52,4	**53,5**
Transparent	0,5	1,1	0,5	7,3	25,8	29,6	36,7	38,9	**40,8**
In wichtigen politischen Fragen einig	2,2	1,9	3,8	12,2	27,6	33,6	33,1	34,1	**36,0**

GABLER GRAFIK

9 Lesebeispiel: Wenn es der SPD gelingt, in den Augen der Wähler „um eine Einheit" europäischer zu wirken, wäre für 34,6 Prozent der Wähler die Abweichung zwischen der Anforderung an eine Idealpartei und dem Ist-Bild der SPD bei der Eigenschaft „europäisch" gleich null.

Eine genauere Betrachtung der Ergebnisse zeigt zunächst, dass es für die SPD bei keinem der Items sinnvoll wäre, die Eigenschaft in den Augen der Wähler zu schwächen. Darüber hinaus lassen sich drei Gruppen von Eigenschaften identifizieren. **Erstens** solche – wie zuvor am Beispiel „europäisch“ dargestellt –, bei denen eine Veränderung nicht ratsam wäre, da der Anteil der Wähler, deren aktuelles Ist-Bild von der SPD ihrem Idealbild von einer Partei entspricht, im Status quo maximal ist. Im Einzelnen sind dies die Dimensionen „europäisch“, „integrierend“, „sympathisch“, „traditionsbewusst“ und „diskussionsfreudig“. **Zweitens** eine Gruppe von Eigenschaften, bei denen aus Wählersicht zwar eine Stärkung, allerdings nur in begrenztem Umfang, wünschenswert ist. Hierbei handelt es sich um die Items „fortschrittlich“, „konstruktiv“, „kompromissfähig“ und „leistungsorientiert“. Die **dritte** und größte Gruppe umfasst schließlich solche Eigenschaften, bei denen von einer Mehrheit der Wähler eine sehr deutliche Stärkung präferiert wird. Dies sind die Items „ehrlich“ „vertrauenswürdig“, „regierungsfähig“, „demokratisch“, „kompetent“, „zupackend“, „zukunftsorientiert“, „sozial“, „menschlich“, „transparent“ und „in wichtigen politischen Fragen einig“.

Der Anteil der Wähler, deren modifiziertes Ist-Bild von der SPD ihrer Vorstellung von einer Idealpartei entspricht, entwickelt sich bei diesen Eigenschaften jedoch nicht linear. So würde zum Beispiel eine Stärkung der Eigenschaft „menschlich“ um vier Einheiten zu einem Anteil von Wählern im Idealzustand von 53,5 Prozent führen, eine Stärkung der Eigenschaft um eine Einheit jedoch schon zu einem Anteil von 48,9 Prozent.

Angesichts stark sinkender Grenzerträge in Abhängigkeit der Intensität von Markenführungsmaßnahmen und den vermutlich mit dem Ausmaß der Veränderung steigenden Grenzkosten ergibt sich abschließend das in Tabelle 6 dargestellte „optimale“[10] Veränderungsprofil für die SPD.

In der bisherigen Argumentation zur Ableitung eines Anforderungsprofils an die Markenführung der SPD wurde in Konsequenz der Zielsetzung einer Maximierung des Anteils der Wähler, deren Anforderung an eine Idealpartei mit dem Realbild der SPD übereinstimmt, lediglich auf eine **Veränderung des Ist-Bildes** der SPD abgehoben. In Anbetracht der zugrunde liegenden Logik einer Differenzierung zwischen Soll- und Ist-Position ließe sich das gleiche Ergebnis über eine spiegelbildliche Veränderung der Wähleranforderungen an eine Idealpartei erzielen. Am Beispiel des Items „fortschrittlich“ bedeutet dies beispielsweise, dass eine Stärkung des Ist-Bildes der SPD um eine Einheit den gleichen Effekt hätte wie eine Schwächung der Soll-Vorstellungen um eine Einheit.

10 Streng genommen kann hier nicht von einem Optimum gesprochen werden, da dazu die exakte Kenntnis der Grenzzuwächse und Grenzkosten einer Veränderung des Ist-Profils der SPD erforderlich wäre. In Ermangelung von Informationen über die Grenzkosten wird hier primär auf Basis der über den Anteil der Wähler im Idealzustand abgeleiteten Grenzgewinne argumentiert. Als heuristisches Kriterium für in diesem Sinne stark abfallende Grenzgewinne diente eine dem Elbow-Kriterium der Cluster-Analyse entlehnte Vorgehensweise (Backhaus et al. 2003, S. 307 f.).

Tabelle 6: Fremdbildinduziertes Anforderungsprofil an die Markenführung der SPD

	Maximale Veränderung*	Anteil der Wähler (Ideal = Real) bei maximaler Veränderung	Zuwachs der Wähler im Ideal in Prozent im Vergleich zum Status quo	Optimale Veränderung	Anteil der Wähler (Ideal = Real) bei optimaler Veränderung	Zuwachs der Wähler im Ideal in Prozent im Vergleich zum Status quo
	1. Gruppe von Eigenschaften: keine Veränderung sinnvoll					
Europäisch	0	41,4 %	–	0	41,4 %	–
Integrierend	0	39,9 %	–	0	39,9 %	–
Sympathisch	0	39,0 %	–	0	39,0 %	–
Traditionsbewusst	0	38,6 %	–	0	38,6 %	–
Diskussionsfreudig	0	38,2 %	–	0	38,2 %	–
	2. Gruppe von Eigenschaften: begrenzte Stärkung sinnvoll					
Fortschrittlich	+1	44,2 %	39,0	+1	44,2 %	39,0
Konstruktiv	+1	43,2 %	52,7	+1	43,2 %	52,7
Kompromissfähig	+1	41,7 %	36,3	+1	41,7 %	36,3
Leistungsorientiert	+1	38,3 %	11,0	+1	38,3 %	11,0
	3. Gruppe von Eigenschaften: deutliche Stärkung sinnvoll					
Ehrlich	+4	73,9 %	439,4	+3	71,5 %	421,9
Regierungsfähig	+4	69,4 %	158,0	+2	65,1 %	142,0
Demokratisch	+4	65,1 %	86,5	+1	61,0 %	74,8
Vertrauenswürdig	+4	69,9 %	288,3	+2	59,4 %	230,0
Kompetent	+4	62,2 %	184,0	+2	58,6 %	167,6
Packt die wichtigen polit. Probleme an	+4	59,9 %	165,0	+3	57,3 %	153,5
Menschlich	+4	53,5 %	59,2	+1	48,9 %	45,5
Zukunftsorientiert	+4	55,4 %	91,0	+1	47,6 %	64,1
Sozial	+4	55,1 %	64,0	+1	47,3 %	40,8
Transparent	+4	40,8 %	58,1	+2	36,7 %	42,2
In wichtigen politischen Fragen einig	+4	36,0 %	30,4	+1	33,6 %	21,7

* Skala reicht von –4 bis +4. Positive Vorzeichen bedeuten: Eigenschaft (Ist-Position) stärken, negative Vorzeichen bedeuten: Eigenschaft schwächen; 0 bedeutet: Eigenschaft so belassen.

GABLER GRAFIK

Zur Beantwortung der Frage, ob es im Rahmen der Markenführung eher ratsam erscheint, die Ist- oder die Soll-Komponente der Wähler zu beeinflussen, ist eine Analyse der Lücken zwischen Wählern und Mitgliedern in Ist- und Soll-Komponente erforderlich, da beispielsweise der Versuch, die Anforderungen der Wähler an eine Idealpartei bei bestimmten Eigenschaften zu senken, kaum denkbar ist, wenn die Soll-Vorstellung der Mitglieder von ihrer Partei einer solchen Maßnahme entgegensteht. Vor dieser Analyse ist es jedoch zunächst notwendig, das Selbstbild der SPD-Mitglieder im Hinblick auf Soll- und Ist-Komponente – also GAP 2 – zu untersuchen, um so den **innerparteilichen Veränderungsbedarf** zu erfassen, der unabhängig von den Anforderungen der Wähler zu einer Veränderung des Ist-Selbstbildes führen kann. Analog zu den Berechnungen beim Fremdbild wurden auch die **Abweichungen der Mitglieder** zwischen dem Idealbild der SPD und dem Ist-Bild der Partei im Hinblick auf das Vorzeichen einer möglichen Differenz und den jeweiligen Anteil der Mitglieder mit positiver, negativer oder keinerlei Abweichung bei den einzelnen Items untersucht. Das Ergebnis dieser differenzierten Analyse von GAP 2 zeigt nachfolgende Tabelle 7. Der im Vergleich zum Fremdbild in Summe kleineren Abweichung zwischen Idealanforderung und Ist-Bild der SPD entsprechend, ist beim Selbstbild bis auf das Item „ehrlich" bei allen Eigenschaften die Mehrzahl der SPD-Mitglieder der Ansicht, dass die SPD ihre Anforderungen an die Partei erfüllt. Allerdings sind diese Mehrheiten bei einigen Eigenschaften, wie beispielsweise „packt die wichtigen politischen Probleme an", „transparent" oder „kompetent", sehr knapp.

Angesichts demokratischer Willensbildungsprozesse innerhalb einer Partei kann unterstellt werden, dass es bei Eigenschaften, die von einer vergleichsweise großen Minderheit der Partei als verbesserungswürdig angesehen werden, zu **innerparteilichem Veränderungsdruck** kommen wird. Die Erfolgswahrscheinlichkeit derartiger Bemühungen, die im Ergebnis das Ist-Selbstbild verändern, hängt davon ab, inwieweit eine solche Veränderung mehrheitsfähig ist. Aus diesem Grund wurde auch für das Selbstbild der SPD eine Simulation durchgeführt, bei der in Abhängigkeit der Stärkung oder Schwächung der in die Untersuchung einbezogenen Eigenschaften die Entwicklung des Anteils der Mitglieder untersucht wurde, deren Anforderung an die SPD dem dann veränderten Ist-Bild entspricht. Das Resultat dieser Berechnungen zeigt Tabelle 8.

Tabelle 7: Differenzierte Darstellung von GAP 2 (Selbstbild) bei der SPD

	Anteil der Mitglieder, ...	Ausmaß der gewünschten ...			
	Spalte 1	Spalte 2	Spalte 3	Spalte 4	Spalte 5
	die keine Veränderung wünschen	die eine Stärkung der Eigenschaft wünschen	die eine Schwächung der Eigenschaft wünschen	Stärkung	Schwächung
Regierungsfähig	**64,6 %**	22,2 %	13,2 %	1,34	-1,09
Demokratisch	**60,9 %**	32,0 %	7,10 %	1,19	-1,37
Europäisch	**58,7 %**	25,9 %	15,4 %	1,10	-1,22
Sympathisch	**57,9 %**	23,3 %	18,8 %	1,31	-1,12
Diskussionsfreudig	**56,4 %**	29,3 %	14,3 %	1,37	-1,34
Leistungsorientiert	**53,4 %**	29,3 %	17,3 %	1,42	-1,11
Integrierend	**53,2 %**	31,7 %	15,1 %	1,25	-1,13
Traditionsbewusst	**53,2 %**	18,9 %	27,9 %	1,40	-1,30
Zukunftsorientiert	**52,6 %**	38,0 %	9,4 %	1,32	-1,08
Menschlich	**51,9 %**	39,8 %	8,3 %	1,32	-1,23
Fortschrittlich	**50,8 %**	37,2 %	12,0 %	1,26	-1,03
Sozial	**50,0 %**	40,2 %	9,8 %	1,34	-1,27
Vertrauenswürdig	**49,2 %**	39,5 %	11,3 %	1,42	-1,13
Kompromissfähig	**48,1 %**	30,8 %	21,1 %	1,20	-1,21
Konstruktiv	**46,3 %**	43,2 %	10,5 %	1,30	-1,14
In wichtigen politischen Fragen einig	**45,5 %**	34,2 %	20,3 %	1,34	-1,13
Packt die wichtigen polit. Probleme an	**45,1 %**	43,2 %	11,7 %	1,57	-1,16
Transparent	**44,8 %**	43,2 %	12,0 %	1,60	-1,19
Kompetent	**44,4 %**	43,2 %	12,4 %	1,30	-1,09
Ehrlich	**43,3 %**	48,4 %	8,3 %	1,48	-1,14

GABLER GRAFIK

Tabelle 8: Ergebnisse einer Simulation für ein modifiziertes Selbstbild der SPD

	Eigenschaft wird bei der SPD ...								
	geschwächt				nicht verändert	gestärkt			
	um –4	um –3	um –2	um –1	0	um 1	um 2	um 3	um 4
Anteil der Mitglieder in Prozent, deren Anforderung an Idealpartei und Realbild von der SPD übereinstimmen									
	1. Gruppe von Eigenschaften: keine Veränderung zu erwarten								
Regierungsfähig	0,0	0,0	1,1	12,0	**64,7**	57,9	59,0	59,0	59,8
Europäisch	0,4	0,0	2,3	12,8	**58,6**	50,8	46,2	45,5	45,5
Sympathisch	0,0	0,0	2,3	16,5	**57,9**	45,1	40,2	41,7	42,1
Diskussionsfreudig	0,4	1,5	1,9	10,9	**56,4**	48,1	48,5	48,5	49,2
Leistungsorientiert	0,0	0,0	1,9	15,4	**53,4**	28,6	23,7	24,4	24,1
Integrierend	0,0	0,0	1,9	13,2	**53,2**	39,2	34,7	34,3	34,3
Traditionsbewusst	3,4	2,6	6,4	21,5	**53,2**	38,5	35,5	34,7	35,1
Zukunftsorientiert	0,0	0,0	0,8	8,6	**52,6**	48,9	49,6	50,0	50,4
Fortschrittlich	0,0	0,0	0,4	11,7	**50,8**	45,1	41,0	41,7	41,7
Konstruktiv	0,8	0,8	1,9	9,0	**46,2**	44,7	42,9	44,0	44,0
In wichtigen politischen Fragen einig	1,1	1,1	3,4	17,7	**45,5**	29,7	24,1	25,2	24,8
Kompromissfähig	0,4	0,4	4,5	16,5	**48,1**	38,3	30,8	30,5	30,5
Transparent	0,4	0,4	2,3	9,8	**44,7**	32,7	36,1	37,2	38,0
	2. Gruppe von Eigenschaften: Veränderung zu erwarten								
Demokratisch	0,4	0,0	1,5	5,3	60,9	69,5	72,2	**72,9**	**72,9**
Sozial	0,4	0,4	1,9	7,5	50,0	63,5	66,9	68,8	**69,2**
Kompetent	0,0	0,0	1,1	11,3	44,4	54,5	57,5	58,3	**58,6**
Menschlich	0,4	0,0	0,8	7,1	51,9	54,9	56,0	57,5	**57,9**
Vertrauenswürdig	1,9	1,9	1,9	10,5	49,2	47,4	50,4	53,8	**54,1**
Packt die wichtigen polit. Probleme an	0,8	0,8	2,6	9,8	45,1	44,4	50,8	53,4	**53,8**
Ehrlich	1,1	1,1	1,1	7,9	43,6	44,7	47,4	50,8	**51,1**

GABLER GRAFIK

Die Ergebnisse offenbaren, dass zunächst unabhängig vom Anforderungsprofil des Wählers den Spannungsfeldern des Selbstbildes **Veränderungstendenzen** für die SPD inhärent sind. So wäre der Anteil der Mitglieder, deren Ist-Bild von der Partei ihrer Vorstellung von einer idealen SPD entspräche, bei sieben der insgesamt 20 Eigenschaften nach einer Veränderung des Ist-Selbstbildes größer als im Status quo.

Für die Markenführung gilt es nun zu prüfen, in welchem Verhältnis diese mittelfristig zu erwartenden Veränderungen[11] des SPD-Selbstbildes zu den Anforderungen des Wählers stehen (vgl. Tabelle 9).

Es zeigt sich, dass die **innerparteiliche Veränderungstendenz** der SPD durchweg in die auch vom Wähler präferierte Richtung geht. Lediglich bei den in Tabelle 9 unten angeführten Items gibt es zwar beim Wähler den Wunsch nach einer Stärkung, nicht jedoch bei den Mitgliedern.

Für die Markenführung ist es nun entscheidend, welche Wirkungen die skizzierten möglichen innerparteilichen Veränderungen beim Fremdbild erzeugen. In diesem Zusammenhang ist zu berücksichtigen, dass die durch den innerparteilichen Veränderungsdruck ausgelöste Modifikation im Selbstbild der SPD zunächst einmal nur die Lücke zwischen Soll-Anforderung und Ist-Bild von der SPD **innerhalb** der Partei schließt. Wenn dieses veränderte Selbstbild keinen Niederschlag in der Ist-Wahrnehmung aufseiten des Wählers findet, wird sich die Lücke aufseiten des Fremdbildes (GAP 1) nicht verringern. Im Ergebnis wird sich also zunächst das innerparteiliche GAP 2 verkleinern, während GAP 4 als Ausdruck der Differenzen in der Ist-Wahrnehmung zwischen Wählern und Mitgliedern sogar wächst. Eine zum Zwecke der Quantifizierung dieser Konsequenzen durchgeführte Simulationsrechnung erbrachte das Ergebnis, dass sich unter Zugrundelegung der in Tabelle 9 dargestellten Veränderungen das innerparteiliche GAP 2 von 12,61 auf 11,72 geringfügig vermindert und die Lücke zwischen Ist-Wahrnehmung der Mitglieder und Ist-Wahrnehmung der Wähler (GAP 4) von 10,26 auf 16,26 deutlich anwächst.

11 Analog zur Argumentation beim Fremdbild wurde auch für die angesichts innerparteilicher Kontroversen mit Grenzkosten verbundene Veränderung des Selbstbildes der Grenzgewinn in Form der Veränderung des Anteils der Mitglieder, deren Idealbild von der SPD dem modifizierten Ist-Bild entspricht, als zusätzliche Information herangezogen. Insofern weichen die in Tabelle 9 dargestellten Anforderungen der Mitglieder von den in Tabelle 8 dargestellten Ergebnissen ab.

Tabelle 9: Anforderungen an die SPD von Wählern und SPD-Mitgliedern im Vergleich

	Anforderungen ...		Verhältnis der Wähler- und Mitgliederanforderungen
	der Wähler	der Mitglieder	
Ehrlich	+3	+3	Ausmaß und Richtung identisch
Demokratisch	+1	+1	Ausmaß und Richtung identisch
Sozial	+1	+1	Ausmaß und Richtung identisch
Menschlich	+1	+1	Ausmaß und Richtung identisch
Diskussionsfreudig	0	0	Ausmaß und Richtung identisch
Integrierend	0	0	Ausmaß und Richtung identisch
Europäisch	0	0	Ausmaß und Richtung identisch
Sympathisch	0	0	Ausmaß und Richtung identisch
Traditionsbewusst	0	0	Ausmaß und Richtung identisch
Kompetent	+2	+1	Richtung identisch
Vertrauenswürdig	+2	+3	Richtung identisch
Packt die wichtigen politischen Probleme an	+3	+2	Richtung identisch
Fortschrittlich	+1	0	Richtung unterschiedlich
Konstruktiv	+1	0	Richtung unterschiedlich
Leistungsorientiert	+1	0	Richtung unterschiedlich
Regierungsfähig	+2	0	Richtung unterschiedlich
Transparent	+2	0	Richtung unterschiedlich
In wichtigen polit. Fragen einig	+1	0	Richtung unterschiedlich
Zukunftsorientiert	+1	0	Richtung unterschiedlich
Kompromissfähig	+1	0	Richtung unterschiedlich

GABLER GRAFIK

Damit richtet sich nach Ermittlung möglicher durch Spannungen zwischen Soll- und Ist-Selbstbild induzierten Veränderungen des Ist-Selbstbildes der Blick der Markenführung erneut auf **Optionen zur Schließung von GAP 1**, also auf das Fremdbild. Mit der skizzierten Veränderung des Ist-Selbstbildes hat sich dieses nicht nur dem Soll-Selbst-, sondern auch dem Soll-Fremdbild angenähert, da zwischen den Soll-Vorstellungen der Mitglieder und den Soll-Vorstellungen der Wähler nur eine vergleichsweise kleine Lücke von insgesamt 3,33 besteht. Eine Schließung der Fremdbildlücke (GAP 1) über die Beeinflussung des Soll-Fremdbildes in Richtung des Soll-Selbstbildes erscheint in Anbetracht der ohnehin nur geringen Unterschiede zwischen Wählern und Parteimitgliedern nicht sehr viel versprechend. **Wesentlicher Stellhebel** für die Verkleinerung der Fremdbildlücke bleibt somit die **Beeinflussung des Ist-Fremdbildes**. Wähler und Mitglieder der SPD haben ähnliche Vorstellungen über eine ideale Partei, das Bild der Mitglieder ist aber deutlich positiver als dasjenige der Wähler, was durch die dargestellte mögliche Veränderung des Ist-Selbstbildes noch verstärkt wird. Das Potenzial für die Markenführung, das sich erschließt, wenn es gelingt, das Ist-Selbstbild respektive das modifizierte Ist-Selbstbild zum Wähler zu transportieren, verdeutlicht Abbildung 5.

In ihr ist einerseits in Dunkelblau das über die Simulation ermittelte Anforderungsprofil der Wähler als Referenzpunkt der Markenführung dargestellt. Darüber hinaus ist in hellblauer Farbe die ursprüngliche Abweichung zwischen Ist-Selbst- und Ist-Fremdbild sowie schließlich in Weiß die Abweichung zwischen Ist-Selbst- und Ist-Fremdbild nach erfolgter innerparteilicher Anpassung des Ist-Selbstbildes eingetragen.[12]

So würde ein dem Ist-Selbstbild entsprechendes Ist-Fremdbild bei den Eigenschaften „demokratisch“, „sozial“ und „menschlich“ genau dem aus der Wähleranalyse abgeleiteten Veränderungsbedarf des Ist-Fremdbildes entsprechen. So war der Veränderungsbedarf aufseiten der Wähler beim Item „demokratisch“ +1, das heißt, aus Sicht der Wähler ist die SPD im Vergleich mit den Anforderungen an eine Idealpartei zu wenig demokratisch. Im Durchschnitt ist die SPD nach Auffassung der Mitglieder genau um 1,05 Einheiten demokratischer als nach Meinung der Wähler (vgl. weißer Balken in Abbildung 5). Gelänge es also, den Wählern das gleiche Bild von der SPD zu vermitteln wie es die Mitglieder haben, würden die Wähler die SPD um 1,05 Einheiten demokratischer ansehen.

---

12 Diejenigen Items, bei denen eine mit der Annäherung des Ist-Fremdbildes an das Ist-Selbstbild verbundene Stärkung nicht wünschenswert ist, da dies den Anteil der Wähler, deren Anforderung an eine Idealpartei dem Ist-Bild der SPD entspricht, reduzieren würde, sind in der Abbildung nicht aufgeführt. Diese Eigenschaften werden der SPD zwar von den Parteimitgliedern in höherem Maße zugesprochen als seitens der Wähler, eine Betonung dieser Merkmale ist aber aus der Fremdbildperspektive kontraproduktiv, da der Wähler keine Akzentuierung wünscht. Hierbei handelt es sich um die Eigenschaften: „diskussionsfreudig“, „europäisch“, „traditionsbewusst“, „integrierend“ und „sympathisch“. Das Längenverhältnis des grauen respektive weißen Balkens, die das Kommunikationsgap ausdrücken, zum schwarzen Balken, der Ausdruck der Wähleranforderung ist, spiegelt das Potenzial einer Schließung des Kommunikationsgaps für die Attraktivierung der SPD beim Wähler wider. Dieses kommunikative Potenzial nimmt in Abbildung 5 von oben nach unten ab.

Abbildung 5: Ist-Selbstbild und Ist-Fremdbild der SPD (GAP 4)

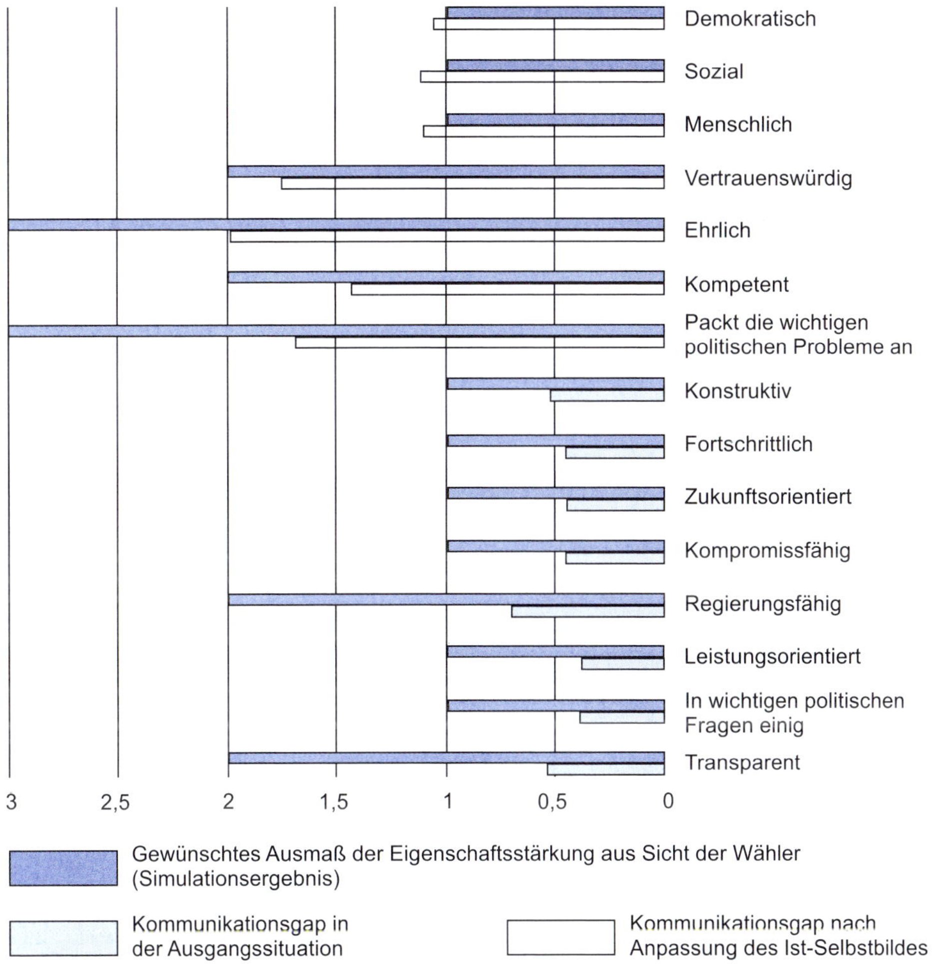

GABLER GRAFIK

Tabelle 10: **Simulation einer Annäherung des Ist-Fremdbildes an das Ist-Selbstbild am Beispiel der Eigenschaft „demokratisch"**

		Ausgangssituation				
		Idealausprägung				
		1	2	3	4	5
Trifft voll zu	1	n = 68; GAP = 0	n = 7; GAP = −1	n = 0; GAP = −2	n = 0; GAP = −3	n = 0; GAP = −4
	2	n = 122; GAP = 1	n = 44; GAP = 0	n = 16; GAP = −1	n = 1; GAP = −2	n = 1; GAP = −3
	3	n = 46; GAP = 2	n = 34; GAP = 1	n = 16; GAP = 0	n = 3; GAP = −1	n = 0; GAP = −2
	4	n = 4; GAP = 3	n = 3; GAP = 2	n = 2; GAP = 1	n = 2; GAP = 0	n = 0; GAP = −1
Trifft gar nicht zu	5	n = 2; GAP = 4	n = 0; GAP = 3	n = 0; GAP = 2	n = 1; GAP = 1	n = 0; GAP = 0

Mittelwert GAP Item demokratisch Ausgangssituation = [(68·0) + (122·1) + (46·2) + (4·3) + (2·4) + (7·1) + (44·0) + (34·1) + (3·2) + (0·3) + (0·2) + (16·1) + (16·0) + (2·1) + (0·2) + (0·3) + (1·2) + (3·1) + (2·0) + (1·1) + (0·4) + (1·3) + (0·2) + (0·1) + (0·0)] / 372 = **0,828**

1−1,05 = 1
2−1,05 = 1

		Realausprägung wird um Kommunikationsgap vermindert (1,05)				
		Idealausprägung				
		Sehr gut				Sehr schlecht
		1	2	3	4	5
Trifft voll zu	1	n = 68; GAP = 0	n = 7; GAP = −1	n = 0; GAP = −2	n = 0; GAP = −3	n = 0; GAP = −4
	1	n = 122; GAP = 0 ↓	n = 44; GAP = −1 ↑	n = 16; GAP = −2 ↑	n = 1; GAP = −3 ↑	n = 1; GAP = −4 ↑
	1,95	n = 46; GAP = 0,95 ↓	n = 34; GAP = −0,05 ↓	n = 16; GAP = −1,05 ↑	n = 3; GAP = −2,05 ↑	n = 0; GAP = −3,05 ↑
	2,95	n = 4; GAP = 1,95 ↓	n = 3; GAP = −0,95 ↓	n = 2; GAP = −0,05 ↓	n = 2; GAP = −1,05 ↑	n = 0; GAP = −2,05 ↑
Trifft gar nicht zu	3,95	n = 2; GAP = 2,95 ↓	n = 0; GAP = −1,95 ↓	n = 0; GAP = −0,95 ↓	n = 1; GAP = −0,05 ↓	n = 0; GAP = 1,05 ↑

Mittelwert GAP Item demokratisch nach Anpassung des Fremdbildes = [(68·0) + (122·0) + (46·0,95) + (4·1,95) + (2·2,95) + (7·1) + (44·1) + (34·0,05) + (3·0,95) + (0·1,95) + (0·2) + (16·2) + (16·1,05) + (2·0,05) + (0·0,95) + (0·3) + (1·3) + (3·2,05) + (2·1,05) + (1·0,05) + (0·4) + (1·4) + (0·3,05) + (0·2,05) + (0·1,05)]/372 = **0,625**

GABLER GRAFIK

Die Auswirkungen dieser Veränderungen bei den unterschiedlichen Kombinationen aus Ideal- und Realausprägungen auf die Lücke zwischen Soll- und Ist-Fremdbild von der SPD zeigt Tabelle 10 am Beispiel der Eigenschaft „demokratisch". Sie stellt im oberen Teil die Ausgangsituation und im unteren Teil die Konsequenzen einer Veränderung des Ist-Fremdbildes um 1,05 Einheiten dar.

Es zeigt sich, dass für Wähler, welche die Eigenschaft „demokratisch" als sehr gut ansehen, durch die Annäherung des Ist-Fremdbildes an das Ist-Selbstbild die Lücke zwischen der Anforderung an eine Idealpartei und dem Ist-Bild der SPD sinkt, umgekehrt für Wähler, die diese Eigenschaft als sehr schlecht ansehen, die Lücke jedoch wächst. Da der Anteil der erstgenannten Gruppe deutlich größer ist als derjenige der letztgenannten, reduziert sich GAP 1 beim Item „demokratisch" von 0,828 auf 0,625.

Insgesamt verdeutlicht Abbildung 5 das Potenzial einer Schließung der Kommunikationslücke für die Markenführung der SPD. Eine Berechnung[13], bei der diese Schließung nach der am Beispiel der Eigenschaft „demokratisch" vorgestellten Logik simuliert wurde, erbrachte im Ergebnis eine Verminderung von GAP 1 von ursprünglich 20,9 auf 16,1. Diese Einstellungsverbesserung[14] ist auf eine Reduktion der Differenz zwischen Ist-Selbst- und Ist-Fremdbild (GAP 4) von ursprünglich 16,26 auf 2,51 zurückzuführen.

Die nachfolgende Abbildung stellt das Vorgehen und die entsprechenden Ergebnisse im Hinblick auf die GAPs der identitätsorientierten Markenführung noch einmal zusammenfassend dar. Auf Basis der Ausgangssituation wurde zunächst ein **Anforderungsprofil** der Markenführung aus Wählersicht ermittelt. Grundlage der Berechnung dieses Referenzpunktes für die Markenführung war die Annahme, dass es für eine Partei optimal ist, wenn der Anteil der Wähler, deren Ist-Fremdbild ihrem Soll-Fremdbild entspricht, maximal ist. Um zu überprüfen, inwieweit die SPD diese Wähleranforderungen vor dem Hintergrund ihres Selbstbildes erfüllen kann, wurde anschließend das Verhältnis zwischen Soll- und Ist-Selbstbild analysiert.

Im Ergebnis zeigte sich, dass sich der Anteil der Mitglieder, deren Ist-Selbstbild ihrem Soll-Selbstbild entspricht, im Hinblick auf einzelne Eigenschaften bei einer **Veränderung des Ist-Selbstbildes** erhöhen würde. Aufgrund der demokratischen Willensbildungsprozesse innerhalb einer Partei wurde hieraus auf eine Veränderung des Ist-Selbstbildes in Richtung des Soll-Selbstbildes geschlossen. In Bezug auf die Anforderungen der Wähler zeigte sich, dass sich diese Veränderung des Ist-Selbstbildes aufgrund der geringen Divergenz zwischen Soll-Selbst- und Soll-Fremdbild gleichzeitig in Richtung des

13 Dabei wurde für jeden Befragten das Ist-Fremdbild um den Mittelwert der Abweichung zwischen Ist-Selbst- und Ist-Fremdbild (Kommunikationsgap) verändert. Für Befragte, deren so modifiziertes Fremdbild Werte kleiner 1 aufwies, wurde dieser anschließend auf 1 gesetzt (trifft voll zu). Abschließend wurde die Gesamteinstellung nach der Formel von Trommsdorff berechnet.

14 Diese Verminderung von GAP 1 kann als wesentlich gekennzeichnet werden. Eine zur Bewertung durchgeführte Simulationsrechnung, bei der das Ist-Fremdbild gemäß der ermittelten optimalen Verschiebung (vgl. Tabelle 6) verändert wurde, erbrachte im Ergebnis eine Lücke von 13,9. Durch die Annäherung des Ist-Fremdbildes an das modifizierte Ist-Selbstbild der SPD können also circa 69 Prozent [(20,87–16,1) / (20,87–13,9)] der möglichen Lückenschließung realisiert werden.

Soll-Fremdbildes vollzog. Demnach erweist sich abschließend die **Reduzierung der Lücke zwischen Ist-Selbst- und Ist-Fremdbild als Schlüssel der Markenführung**. Gelänge es der SPD, ihr in Richtung der Mitglieder- und damit auch Wählerwünsche verändertes Ist-Selbstbild dem Wähler zu kommunizieren, trüge dies wesentlich zur Annäherung des Ist-Fremdbildes an das Soll-Fremdbild und so zur Steigerung der Wahlwahrscheinlichkeit der SPD bei. Die verbleibenden Lücken sowohl beim Selbst- als auch beim Fremdbild resultieren im Wesentlichen aus der Varianz der Mitglieder- und Wähleranforderung und sind für eine Volkspartei mit ihrer sui generis undifferenzierten Marktbearbeitung kaum zu mindern.

Abbildung 6: Zusammenfassung des identitätsorientierten Markenführungsprozesses für die SPD

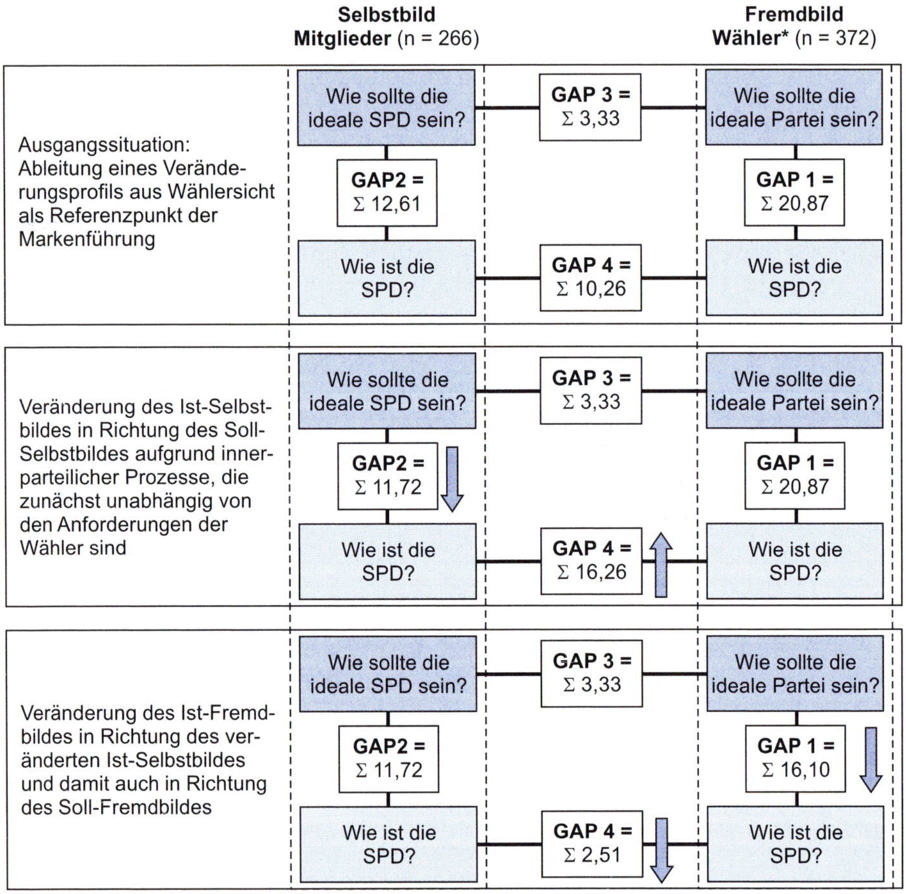

* Wahlwahrscheinlichkeit der SPD > 0 %

GABLER GRAFIK

4. Fazit

Angesichts einer insbesondere auf eine nachlassende Bindungskraft soziologischer Einflussgrößen der Wahlentscheidung zurückzuführenden wachsenden Volatilität des Wahlverhaltens wird die Bedeutung des Politikmarketing in Deutschland vermutlich zukünftig weiter zunehmen. Da Parteien und prominente Spitzenpolitiker Eigenschaften einer Marke in einem sozialpsychologischen Sinne besitzen und diese Politikmarken aufgrund der Erfüllung typischer Markenfunktionen für den Wähler wahlverhaltensrelevant sind, werden sich Forschung und Praxis des Politikmarketing dabei nicht zuletzt verstärkt mit Fragen der Markenführung auseinander zu setzen haben. Der identitätsorientierte Ansatz der Markenführung vermag hierbei aufgrund seines integrativen Charakters im Hinblick auf Selbst- und Fremdbild einer Marke dem zentralen Spezifikum der Markenführung im politischen Kontext auf besondere Weise gerecht zu werden. Für Parteien ist die Gewinnung von Marktanteilen im Sinne der Erlangung von politischer Gestaltungsfähigkeit kein Finalziel, sondern nur Modalziel zur Veränderung der Gesellschaft im Sinne ihrer Wertvorstellungen. Insofern bewegen sich Parteien in einem ausgeprägten Spannungsfeld aus Orientierung am Wählerwillen einerseits, die erforderlich ist, um politische Gestaltungsmöglichkeiten zu erlangen und programmatischen Grundsätzen andererseits, die normative Grundlage für die inhaltliche Ausgestaltung der politischen Gestaltungsmöglichkeiten sind und nicht beliebig an wechselnde Wählerpräferenzen angepasst werden können. Dies verdeutlicht gleichzeitig, dass eine identitätsorientierte Führung von Politikmarken nicht im Widerspruch zu demokratietheoretischen Anforderungen steht. Im Gegenteil offeriert eine identitätsorientierte Markenführung nicht nur den geeigneten Rahmen zum Management des handlungsrationalen Spannungsfeldes zwischen Outside-in- und Inside-out-Orientierung von Parteien, sondern ist gleichermaßen Ausdruck der demokratietheoretischen Polarität zwischen Responsivität gegenüber dem Wählerwillen einerseits und der Notwendigkeit zur politischen Führung andererseits (Schneider 2004a, S. 206 ff.).

Literatur

Aaker, D. A. (1996), Building Strong Brands, New York.

Arnold, M. (2002), Qualitative Politik- und Wahlforschung als Markenforschung, in: Planung und Analyse, 29. Jg., Nr. 1, S. 47–51.

Bauer, H. H., Huber, F., Herrmann, A. (1995), Politik-Marketing – Inhalt, Instrumente und Institutionen, in: Der Markt, 34. Jg., Nr. 4, S. 115–124.

Beresford, Q. (1998), Selling Democracy Short: Elections in the Age of the Market, in: Current Affairs Bulletin, Vol. 74, No. 5, S. 24–32.

Bierwirth, A. (2003), Die Führung der Unternehmensmarke. Ein Beitrag zum zielgruppenorientierten Corporate Branding, Frankfurt/M.

Bowler, S., Farrell, D. (Hrsg.) (1992), Electoral Strategies and Political Marketing, London u. a.

Butler, P., Collins N. (1999), A Conceptual Framework for Political Marketing, in: Newman, B. (Hrsg.), Handbook of Political Marketing, Thousand Oaks, S. 55–72.

Butler, P., Collins N. (1994), Political Marketing: Structure and Process, in: European Journal of Marketing, Vol. 28, No. 1, S. 19–34.

Butler, P., Collins, N. (1996), Strategic Analysis in Political Markets, in: European Journal of Marketing, Vol. 30, No. 10/11, S. 32–44.

Cappella, J., Jamieson, K. (1997), Spiral of Cynicism. The Press and the Public Good, Oxford.

Caspari, M., Schönbach, K., Lauf, E. (1999), Bewertung politischer Akteure in Fernsehnachrichten. Analyse der Berichterstattung in Bundestagswahlkämpfen der 90er Jahre, in: Media Perspektiven, 30. Jg., Nr. 5, S. 270–274.

Dalton, R., Wattenberg, M. (1993), The Not So Simple Act of Voting, in: Finifter, A. (Hrsg.), Political Science – The State of the Discipline II, Washington, S. 193–218.

de Chernatony, L., McDonald, M. H. (1992), Creating Powerful Brands, Oxford.

Delaney, B. (1994), Political Marketing, in: Contemporary Record, Vol. 8, No. 1, S. 44–48.

Dombrowski, I. (1997), Politisches Marketing in den Massenmedien, Wiesbaden.

Dörner, A. (2001), Politainment, Frankfurt/M.

Downs, A. (1968), Ökonomische Theorie der Demokratie, amerikanische Erstausgabe 1957, Tübingen.

Eberlein, K.-D. (1978), Marketing im politischen Bereich, in: Koinecke, J. (Hrsg.), Handbuch Marketing, Bd. 2, Gernsbach, S. 1567–1575.

Edelmann, M. (1976), Politik als Ritual – Die symbolische Funktion staatlicher Institutionen und politischen Handelns, Frankfurt/M., New York.

Egan, J. (1999), Political Marketing: Lessons from the Mainstream, in: Journal of Marketing Management, Vol. 15, No. 6, S. 495–503.

Falter, J. W. (1998), Alle Macht dem Spin Doctor, in: Frankfurter Allgemeine Zeitung vom 27.04.1998, S. 11–12.

Fischer, M., Hieronimus, F., Kranz, M. (2002), Markenrelevanz in der Unternehmensführung. Messung, Erklärung und empirische Befunde für B2C-Märkte, Backhaus, K., Meffert, H., Perrey, J., Schröder, J. (Hrsg.), MCM & McKinsey Arbeitspapier Nr. 1, Münster.

Freter, H. (2001), Polit-Marketing, in: Tscheulin, D., Helmig, B. (Hrsg.), Branchenspezifisches Marketing, Wiesbaden, S. 315–330.

Frey, H. P., Haußer, K. (1987), Entwicklungslinien sozialwissenschaftlicher Identitätsforschung, in: Frey, H. P., Haußer, K. (Hrsg.), Identität – Entwicklungslinien psychologischer und soziologischer Forschung, Stuttgart, S. 3–26.

Fuchs, D., Kühnel, St. (1994), Wählen als rationales Handeln: Anmerkungen zum Nutzen des Rational-Choice-Ansatzes in der empirischen Wahlforschung, in: Klingemann, H. D., Kaase, M. (Hrsg.), Wahlen und Wähler. Analysen aus Anlass der Bundestagswahl 1990, Opladen, S. 305–364.

Harris, P. (2001), Machiavelli, political marketing and reinventing government, in: European Journal of Marketing, Vol. 35, No. 9/10, S. 1136–1154.

Harrop, M. (1990), Political Marketing, in: Parliamentary Affairs, Vol. 43, No. 3, S. 277–292.

Hasitschka, W. (1995), Politik-Marketing, in: Tietz, B. (Hrsg.), Handwörterbuch des Marketing, 2. Aufl., Stuttgart, S. 2030–2041.

Henneberg, S. (1996), Second Conference on Political marketing: Judge Institute of Management Studies, University of Cambridge 27–29 March 1996, in: Journal of Marketing Management, Vol. 12, No. 8, S. 777–783.

Hermann, A., Huber, F., Braunstein, C. (1999), Wählerorientierte Positionierung von Politikern – Ergebnisse einer Untersuchung in Europa auf der Basis der Conjoint Analyse, in: Der Markt, 38. Jg., Nr. 2, S. 86–98.

Holtz-Bacha, C. (1999), Wahlkampf 1998 – Modernisierung und Professionalisierung, in: Holtz-Bacha, C. (Hrsg.), Wahlkampf in den Medien, Wahlkampf mit den Medien. Ein Reader zum Wahljahr 1998, Opladen, Wiesbaden, S. 9–24.

in der Beeck, N., Halstrick, J., Richter, K. (2000), Politik sucht Markenprofil, in: werben&verkaufen, Nr. 19, S. 146–149.

Horizont Serie „Parteien vor der Wahl", in: HORIZONT, Nr. 25, 2001, S. 18 (Interview mit Guido Westerwelle); HORIZONT, Nr. 30, 2001, S. 20 (Interview mit Matthias Machnig); HORIZONT, Nr. 34, 2001, S. 24 (Interview mit Thomas Goppel); HORIZONT, Nr. 38, 2001, S. 18 (Interview mit Laurenz Meyer).

Jarren, O., Donges, P. (2002), Politische Kommunikation in der Mediengesellschaft, Wiesbaden.

Kaas, K. P., Busch, A. (1996), Inspektions-, Erfahrungs- und Vertrauenseigenschaften von Produkten, in: Marketing ZFP, 18. Jg., Nr. 4, S. 243–252.

Kapferer, J. N. (1992), Die Marke. Kapital des Unternehmens, Landsberg/Lech.

Kavanagh, D. (1995), Election Campaigning. The new Marketing of Politics, Oxford.

Kelley, S. (1956), Professional Public Relations and Political Power, Baltimore.

Kinsey, D. (1999), Political Consulting. Bridging the Academic and Practical Perspectives in: Newman, B. (Hrsg.), Handbook of Political Marketing, Thousand Oaks, S. 113–127.

Kirchheimer, O. (1965), Wandel des westeuropäischen Parteiensystems, in: Politische Vierteljahresschrift, 6. Jg., Nr. 1, S. 20–41.

Koers, M. (2001), Steuerung von Markenportfolios – Ein Beitrag zum Mehrmarkencontrolling am Beispiel der Automobilwirtschaft, Frankfurt/M.

Kotler, P. (1975), Overview of Political Candidate Marketing, in: Advances in Consumer Research, Vol. 2, No. 1, S. 761–769.

Kotler, P. (1978), Marketing für Nonprofit Organisationen, Stuttgart.

Kotler, P, Kotler, N. (1999), Political Marketing, in: Newman, B. (Hrsg.), Handbook of Political Marketing, Thousand Oaks, S. 3–18.

Kotler, P., Levy, S. J. (1969), Broadening the concept of Marketing, in: Journal of Marketing, Vol. 33, No. 1, S. 10–15.

Lees-Marshment, J. (2001), Political Marketing and British Political Parties. The Party's Just Begun, Manchester.

Lees-Marshment, J. (2001), The product, sales and market-oriented party. How Labour learnt to market the product, not just the presentation, in: European Journal of Marketing, Vol. 35, No. 9/10, S. 1074–1084.

Lock, A., Harris, P. (1996), Political Marketing – Vive la Difference, in: European Journal of Marketing, Vol. 30, No. 10/11, S. 21–32.

Maarek, P. J. (1995), Political Marketing and Communication, London.

Machnig, M. (1999), Die Kampa als SPD-Wahlkampfzentrale der Bundestagswahl '98. Organisation, Kampagnenformen und Erfolgsfaktoren, in: Forschungsjournal NSB, 12. Jg., Nr. 3, S. 20–39.

Mauser, G. A. (1983), Political Marketing. An Approach to Campaign Strategy, New York.

Meffert, H. (2000), Marketing – Grundlagen marktorientierter Unternehmensführung, 9. Aufl., Wiesbaden.

Meffert, H., Bruhn, M. (2003), Dienstleistungsmarketing, 4. Aufl., Wiesbaden.

Meffert, H., Burmann, Ch. (1996), Identitätsorientierte Markenführung – Grundlagen für das Management von Markenportfolios, Meffert, H., Wagner, H., Backhaus, K. (Hrsg.), Arbeitspapier Nr. 100 der Wissenschaftlichen Gesellschaft für Marketing und Unternehmensführung e. V., Münster.

Meffert, H., Schneider, H. (2003), MarkenPolitik? Zur Bedeutung von Politikmarken für das Wählerverhalten, in: forum medienethik, 9. Jg., Nr. 1, S. 51–58.

Meyer, T. (2001), Mediokratie. Die Kolonialisierung der Politik durch die Medien, Frankfurt/M.

Müller, M. G. (1999), Parteienwerbung im Bundestagswahlkampf 1998. Eine qualitative Produktionsanalyse politischer Werbung, in: MP, 30. Jg., Nr. 5, S. 251–261.

Newman, B., Sheth, J. N. (Hrsg.) (1985), Political Marketing: Readings and Annotated Bibliography, Chicago.

Newman, B. (1994), The Marketing of the President. Political Marketing as Campaign Strategy, Thousand Oaks.

Newman, B. (1999), The Mass Marketing of Politics. Democracy in an Age of manufactured Images, Thousand Oaks.

Newman, B. (Hrsg.) (1999a), Handbook of Political Marketing, Thousand Oaks.

Niclauß, K. (2002), Das Parteiensystem der Bundesrepublik Deutschland, 2. Aufl., Paderborn.

Nieffenegger, P. B. (1989), Strategies for Success from the Political Marketers, in: Journal of Consumer Marketing, Vol. 6, No. 1, S. 45–51.

Nimmo, D. (1970), The Political Persuaders. The Techniques of Modern Election Campaigns, New Jersey.

o. V. (2002), „Politiker als Marken", gemeinsame Studie von equity und werben&verkaufen, Hamburg, August/September.

O'Cass, A. (1996), Political Marketing and the Marketing Concept, in: European Journal of Marketing, Vol. 30, No. 10/11, S. 45–61.

Ormrod, R. P. (2003), A Conceptual Model of Political Market Orientation, Working Paper presented at the Political marketing group panels, PSA conference.

O'Shaughnessy, N. J., Holbrook, M. (1989), What U.S. Business can learn from Political marketing, in: Journal of Applied Business Research, Vol. 4, No. 3, S. 98–109.

O'Shaughnessy, N. J. (1990), The Phenomenon of Political Marketing, Basingstoke.

Oellerking, C. (1988), Marketingstrategien für Parteien. Gibt es eine Technologie des legalen Machterwerbs?, Frankfurt/M.

Parasuraman, A., Zeithaml, V., Berry, L. L. (1985), A Conceptual Model of Service Quality and its Implications for Future Research, in: Journal of Marketing, Vol. 49, No. 4, S. 41–50.

Popkins, S. et al. (1976), Comment: What Have You Done for Me Lately? Toward An Investment Theory of Voting, in: American Political Science Review, Vol. 70, S. 779–805.

Reichel, P. (1999), Führen durch Ästhetisieren der Alltagswelt. „Führer" und „Volksgemeinschaft" als politische Markenartikel des NS-Staates, in: Brandmeyer, K., Deichsel, A. (Hrsg.), Jahrbuch Markentechnik 2000/2001, Frankfurt/M., S. 503–526.

Scammell, M. (1999), Political Marketing: Lessons for Political Science, in: Political Studies – Oxford, Vol. 47, No. 4, S. 718–739.

Scammelll, M. (1994), The Phenomenon of Political Marketing: The Thatcher Contribution, in: Contemporary Record, Vol. 8, No. 11, S. 23–43.

Schneider, H. (2004a), Marken in der Politik. Erscheinungsformen, Relevanz, identitätsorientierte Führung und demokratietheoretische Reflektion, Wiesbaden.

Schneider, H. (2004b), Branding in Politics – Manifestations, Relevance and Identity-Oriented Management, in: Journal of Political Marketing, Vol. 3, No. 3, S. 41-67.

Schumpeter, J. A. (1947), Kapitalismus, Sozialismus und Demokratie, Bern.

Schweer, M. K. W. (2000), Politisches Vertrauen. Theoretische Ansätze und empirische Befunde, in: Schweer, M. K. W. (Hrsg.), Politische Vertrauenskrise in Deutschland? Eine Bestandsaufnahme, Münster u. a., S. 9–26.
Schweiger, G., Adami, M. (1999), The Nonverbal Image of Politicians and Political Parties, in: Newman, B. (Hrsg.), Handbook of Political Marketing, Thousand Oaks, S. 347–364.
Shama, A. (1976), The Marketing of Political Candidates, in: Journal of the Academy of the Marketing Science, Vol. 4, No. 4, S. 764–777.
Stauss, B. (2001), Markierungspolitik bei Dienstleistungen, in: Bruhn, M., Meffert, H. (Hrsg.), Handbuch Dienstleistungsmanagement, 2. Aufl., Wiesbaden, S. 549–571.
Stoiber, E. (1983), Marketing und Politik, in: Marketing ZFP, 5. Jg., Nr. 2, S. 98–102.
Stöss, R. (1997), Stabilität im Umbruch, Opladen.
Struckmeier, O. (2002), Was können Politiker von Marken lernen, in: werben&verkaufen, Nr. 19, S. 43.
Swanson, D., Mancini, P. (Hrsg.) (1996), Politics, Media and Modern Democracy, Westport.
Trommsdorff, V. (1975), Die Messung von Produktimages für das Marketing. Grundlagen und Operationalisierung, Köln u. a.
Wangen, E. (1983), Polit-Marketing. Das Marketing Management der politischen Parteien, Opladen.
White, J., de Chernatony, L. (2001), New Labour: A Study of the Creation, Development and Demise of a Political Brand, Conference Paper, 8th International Public Relations Research Symposium, Bled, Slowenia.
Wring, D. (1997), Parties merging Politics and Marketing, in: Congressional quarterly weekly Report, Vol. 55, No. 33, S. 1967 - 1972.
Wring, D. (1999), The Marketing Colonization of Political Campaigning, in: Newman, B. (Hrsg.), Handbook of Political Marketing, Thousand Oaks, S. 41–54.

1. Markenführung als Herausforderung an das Stadtmarketing

Angesichts veränderter gesellschaftlicher, politischer und wirtschaftlicher Rahmenbedingungen sehen sich Städte und Kommunen seit längerer Zeit einem **kontinuierlichen Anpassungsdruck und wachsenden Wettbewerbsherausforderungen** ausgesetzt (Schückhaus/Graf/Dormeier 1993; Junghans 2001). Auf globaler Ebene findet die nachhaltige Veränderung der kommunalen Rahmenbedingungen ihren Ausdruck in der fortschreitenden EU-Integration und der sich wandelnden geopolitischen Lage in Osteuropa. Hinzu kommen dynamische Entwicklungen im Transport-, Informations- und Kommunikationssektor, die den Nachfragern kommunaler Leistungen erweiterte Alternativen der Standortwahl bieten. Neben diesen globalen Trends sind Städte angesichts eines Werte- und Einstellungswandels der Bevölkerung auch im lokalen Umfeld mit einem zunehmenden Handlungsdruck konfrontiert. Ein gestiegenes Demokratiebewusstsein und erhöhte Partizipationsanforderungen verdeutlichen die Notwendigkeit einer verstärkten Kommunikation mit den Bürgern. Veränderte Freizeitgewohnheiten tragen dazu bei, dass zunehmend „weichen“ Standortfaktoren (Grabow et al. 1995) wie Lebensqualität, Kultur- und Freizeitangebot verstärkte Aufmerksamkeit beigemessen wird. Rückläufige Bevölkerungszahlen sowie die Dekonzentration von Bevölkerung und Industrie verstärken den Anpassungsdruck auf lokaler Ebene (Pollotzek 1993, S. 26 ff.).

Als Reaktion auf diese Entwicklungen ist in der kommunalen Praxis seit geraumer Zeit ein **zunehmender Stellenwert von Marketingaspekten** zu beobachten. Parallel zur empirischen Evidenz entwickelte sich im deutschsprachigen Raum Mitte der 90er Jahre das Stadtmarketing zu einer eigenständigen Forschungsrichtung (Meffert 1989; Töpfer 1993; Helbrecht 1994; Funke 1994). Analog zum Verständnis des kommerziellen Marketing wird das Stadtmarketing dabei ganzheitlich interpretiert und bezweckt die Profilierung einer Stadt als Wirtschafts-, Wohn- oder Fremdenverkehrsstandort bei den relevanten Zielgruppen.

Die angestrebte Profilbildung wird durch zahlreiche **Spezifika des Stadtmarketing** im Vergleich zum kommerziellen Marketing erschwert (Meffert 1989, S. 274 f.). So muss eine Stadt heterogenen Zielgruppen (zum Beispiel Touristen, Unternehmen, Messebesucher etc.) mit teilweise divergierenden Ansprüchen gerecht werden, die jeweils nur ausgewählte kommerzielle beziehungsweise nicht-kommerzielle Leistungskomponenten nachfragen. Aufgrund dieser selektiven beziehungsweise rollenbezogenen Wahrnehmung kann eine klare Profilierung letztlich nur durch die Bündelung der kommunalen Einzelleistungen in einem zielgruppenübergreifenden Rahmen erfolgen.

Angesichts der Integration der Zielgruppen in den Leistungserstellungsprozess (zum Beispiel Bürgerberatung, Fremdenverkehr) und der zeitlichen Verzögerung zwischen Kauf und Inanspruchnahme einer regionalen Leistung lassen sich zahlreiche Gemeinsamkeiten des Stadtmarketing mit dem Dienstleistungsmarketing ausmachen. Analog zu Dienstleistungen zeichnet sich auch das kommunale Angebot durch einen hohen Anteil an Erfahrungs- und Vertrauenseigenschaften aus, das heißt Leistungen, deren Qualität sich erst während oder nach der Inanspruchnahme beziehungsweise gar nicht beurteilen lassen (Meffert/Bruhn 2000, S. 311). Die Immaterialität vieler Einzelleistungen trägt zu einer Erhöhung des wahrgenommenen Risikos für die Zielgruppen bei.

Da aufgrund ihrer vertrauensbildenden Eigenschaften der Marke im Dienstleistungsmarketing eine besondere Bedeutung zukommt, stellt sich die Frage, inwieweit der **Aufbau einer Marke** auch einen Beitrag für das Stadtmarketing leisten kann. Die Bedeutung einer Marke für die Austauschprozesse des Stadtmarketing ergibt sich in diesem Zusammenhang aus den mit ihr verbundenen Markenfunktionen. Vor dem Hintergrund der aufgezeigten Rahmenbedingungen erfüllt eine Stadt als Marke dabei auf der Anbieter- und Nachfragerebene dieselben Funktionen wie Sachgüter- und Dienstleistungsmarken (vgl. den Beitrag zur theoretischen Grundkonzeption des identitätsorientierten Markenmanagements in diesem Buch).

Die Spezifika des Stadtmarketing und die Markenfunktionen verdeutlichen, dass eine rein absatzmarktorientierte, wirkungsbezogene Interpretation einer Stadt als Marke jedoch zu kurz greift. Vielmehr ist diese externe Dimension der Markenführung um eine interne Dimension zu ergänzen. Dies geschieht im Rahmen des identitätsorientierten Markenverständnisses.

2. Identität einer Stadt als inhaltlicher Referenzpunkt der Markenführung im Stadtmarketing

2.1 Inhaltliche Präzisierung des Begriffs der Stadtidentität

Aspekte der räumlichen beziehungsweise raumbezogenen Identität werden seit Anfang der 90er Jahre in unterschiedlichen Teildisziplinen der Sozialwissenschaften diskutiert. Trotz der intensiven wissenschaftlichen Auseinandersetzung liegt den meisten Arbeiten jedoch **keine eindeutige Definition der Stadtidentität** zugrunde (Aschauer 1997, S. 3). Einzig die Gültigkeit der konstitutiven Identitätsmerkmale der Wechselseitigkeit, Konsistenz, Kontinuität und Individualität für Städte werden weitgehend akzeptiert (Ebert 2004, S. 75 ff.).

Ungeachtet der Existenz konstitutiver Identitätsmerkmale existiert in der Literatur eine Vielzahl unterschiedlicher Interpretationsformen stadtbezogener Identität. Wenngleich die Anzahl der genannten Bedeutungskomplexe in Abhängigkeit von der jeweiligen Verwendungsrichtung variiert, lassen sich in Anlehnung an die sozialwissenschaftlichen Identitätsauffassungen **zwei grundlegende Bedeutungsvarianten** unterscheiden (vgl. Abbildung 1).

und kommunizierbare Formel und dient damit als informatorische Bezugsgröße lokaler Aktivitäten. Neben diesem primär kognitiven Aspekt leistet die daraus resultierende emotionale Verbundenheit einen weiteren Beitrag zur Integration der Akteure. Dieses als Grundlage der Kooperation geltende Zugehörigkeitsgefühl beschreibt die am deutlichsten nachvollziehbare Funktion der Stadtidentität. Für die Bindung an eine Stadt muss dabei nicht zwingend ein tatsächlicher Interaktionszusammenhang vorliegen, vielmehr können auch Symbole das Identifikationsgefühl begründen (Schuhbauer 1996, S. 29).

In engem Zusammenhang mit der Integrationsfunktion beschreibt dabei die **Systemstabilisierungsfunktion** einen zweiten Wirkungsbereich der Stadtidentität. Als Bestandteil und Inhalt der Kommunikation der Handlungsträger bildet die Stadtidentität einen Orientierungsanker für ihr Handeln und bietet somit physische Sicherheit und Stabilität. Die Bedeutung eines inhaltlichen Bezugspunktes resultiert dabei aus dem komplexitätsreduzierenden Charakter der Identität. Im Sinne eines „kulturellen Erkennungscodes" (Buß 2002, S. 27) fungiert die Stadtidentität als vereinfachtes Grundraster für die Systemprozesse und trägt somit zur Verringerung von Unbestimmtheit und Unsicherheit bei. Gleichzeitig leistet die lokale Identität einen Beitrag zur Konfliktvermeidung auf der Trägerebene (Kerscher 1992, S. 120). Den unterschiedlichen Interessen der Handlungsträger des Stadtmarketing steht mit der Stadtidentität ein inhaltlicher Anker gegenüber, der als verbindliches Grundmuster Vorgabecharakter hat. Die Existenz geteilter Normen- und Wertevorstellungen auf der Basis der Identität trägt zu einer Harmonisierung der Interessenlagen und somit zur Vermeidung eines nachträglichen Konfliktmanagements bei.

Darüber hinaus übernimmt die stadtbezogene Identität eine spezifische Bedeutung im Rahmen ihrer **Motivationsfunktion** für die Beteiligten (Singer 1988, S. 277 f.). Identifizieren sich die Handlungsträger mit ihrer Stadt und erkennen daraus spezifische Nutzenpotenziale, so regt die Stadtidentität kommunal bezogene Aktivitäten oder Handlungen an. Es kann dabei von einem „Aufforderungscharakter" (Gibson 1977, S. 67 ff.) lokaler Identität gesprochen werden, der auf der aktiven Auseinandersetzung der Akteure mit ihrer Stadt beruht.

Neben den primär innengerichteten Teilleistungen der Integration, Systemstabilisierung und Motivation kann die Stadtidentität auch in der externen Perspektive des Stadtmarketing einen wichtigen Beitrag übernehmen. So lässt sich die Notwendigkeit eines Referenzpunktes für das Stadtmarketing auf das Fehlen eines einheitlichen Oberziels zurückführen (Rabe/Süß 1995, S. 15). Die parallel existierenden und teilweise substitutiven Zielvorstellungen wie zum Beispiel Steigerung der Übernachtungszahlen, Ansiedlung neuer Unternehmen oder Verbesserung der Lebensqualität werden einer gesamtstadtbezogenen Ausrichtung jedoch nicht gerecht. Hier kann die stadtbezogene Soll-Identität eine wichtige Funktion als zukunftsbezogenes **Zielsurrogat** für die Markenführung übernehmen. Ihr kann aufgrund ihres umfassenderen und integrativeren Charakters eine grundsätzlich bessere Eignung zur Ausrichtung einer Stadt zugesprochen werden als herkömmlichen Zielen. Die Facettenvielfalt einer Stadt wird im Rahmen der Identität auf die zentralen, stadtspezifischen Identitätskomponenten reduziert. Die Stadtidentität definiert somit das reflexive Selbstverständnis beziehungsweise die „strategische Mission“ einer Stadt und dient der akteursübergreifenden, einheitlichen und langfristigen Orientierung des Stadtmarketing.

Des Weiteren kann die Stadtidentität als inhaltlich-mentaler „Kern“ eine **Differenzierungsfunktion** gegenüber Konkurrenzstandorten übernehmen. Dies erfordert jedoch das aktive Bemühen der Handlungsträger, die Stadtidentität im Rahmen kommunikativer Maßnahmen nach außen darzustellen. In seltenen Fällen sind es nur einzelne Merkmale, die diese Abgrenzungsfunktion gegenüber anderen Städten erfüllen. In Frage kommen neben natur-historischen Komponenten insbesondere selbsterschaffene stadtspezifische Symbole (zum Beispiel Freiheitsstatue in New York). Häufig jedoch haben einzelne Merkmale oder Eigenschaften einen allgemeinen Charakter und treffen ebenso auf andere Städte zu (zum Beispiel Universitätsstadt, Kulturstadt). In solchen Fällen ist daher die kombinatorische Verknüpfung von Identitätsfaktoren entscheidend, um die Einzigartigkeit einer Stadt zu begründen.

3. Stadtbezogene Modifikation des identitätsorientierten Markenführungsansatzes

Vor dem Hintergrund der skizzierten Nutzenpotenziale der stadtbezogenen Identität erscheint ein identitätsbasierter Markenführungsansatz auch für das Stadtmarketing grundsätzlich zweckmäßig. Einer **Übertragbarkeit des identitätsorientierten Ansatzes der Markenführung** sind jedoch aufgrund stadtspezifischer Charakteristika auf der Ebene des Selbstbildes einige Grenzen gesetzt. Zunächst lassen sich mit dem Selbstbild der Stadtmarketing-Träger und dem Selbstbild der Bürger, welche die Identität einer Stadt in entscheidendem Maße prägen (Honert 1991, S. 395), zwei grundsätzliche Aussagenkonzepte unterscheiden. Diese Problematik weist jedoch Parallelen zu der Rolle der Mitarbeiter in einem Unternehmen auf und wird unter dem Begriff des „Corporate Branding“ seit einiger Zeit diskutiert (Bierwirth 2003).

Größerer Modifikationsbedarf resultiert demgegenüber aus der **heterogenen Zusammensetzung der Trägerschaft** des Stadtmarketing. So bleibt die Frage nach den Verantwortlichen des Stadtmarketing, das heißt dem Trägeräquivalent zum unternehmerischen Marketing, bislang weitgehend unbeantwortet. Dies liegt darin begründet, dass im Gegensatz zu den eindimensionalen Führungsstrukturen im Unternehmensbereich das Stadtmarketing durch zahlreiche Akteure mit oftmals divergierenden Interessen und ohne formale Entscheidungsstrukturen gekennzeichnet ist. Während die modellmäßige Erfassung dieser Trägerschaft durch den identitätsorientierten Ansatz der Markenführung für eine einzelne Stadt grundsätzlich denkbar ist, erfordert ein allgemeingültiger Markenführungsansatz für das Stadtmarketing die Berücksichtigung einer interkommunal variierenden Trägerstruktur.

Angesichts ähnlicher Akteursstrukturen bietet die aus dem Industriegütermarketing bekannte **Theorie des organisationalen Beschaffungsverhaltens** einige Ansatzpunkte zur modellmäßigen Erfassung der Trägerschaft des Stadtmarketing (Balderjahn 2000, S. 57). Ähnlich wie das Stadtmarketing ist auch das Industriegütermarketing durch eine multipersonale Problemlösungs- und Entscheidungsfindung mit einem potenziell hohen Interaktionsgrad der Beteiligten gekennzeichnet (Johnston/Lewin 1996). Auch in der kontextabhängigen Zusammensetzung und Ausgestaltung der Akteursstruktur lassen sich Ähnlichkeiten erkennen. Mit Blick auf diese variierende Akteursstruktur ist eine Reihe von Ansätzen entwickelt worden, die die modellmäßige Abbildung der vermuteten Erklärungszusammenhänge im Industriegütermarketing zum Ziel haben. Während Prozessmodelle des organisationalen Beschaffungsverhaltens den Kaufprozess in den Mittelpunkt rücken, fokussieren Strukturmodelle auf den Beziehungsaspekt der Prozessbeteiligten. Ziel dieser auch als „Buying Center" bezeichneten Ansätze ist die gedankliche Zusammenfassung der am Kaufprozess beteiligten Personen (Backhaus 1999, S. 59). Zur Festlegung von Umfang und Struktur des Buying Centers bedarf es dabei eines Kriteriums zur Bestimmung der Buying Center-Mitgliedschaft. Hierzu wird meistens das Kommunikationsverhalten der Handlungsträger herangezogen (McQuiston 1989). Aufbauend darauf können die am Entscheidungsprozess Beteiligten als Rollenträger mit jeweils unterschiedlichen Verhaltenserwartungen verstanden werden (Meffert/Dahlhoff 1980, S. 22 ff.).

Bei einem Transfer auf das Stadtmarketing darf jedoch nicht übersehen werden, dass das im organisationalen Beschaffungsverhalten etablierte Konzept des Buying Centers das Kaufverhalten und damit die Nachfragerseite betrachtet, während die abzubildende Trägerschaft die Anbieterebene zum Gegenstand hat. Statt von einem Buying Center erscheint es somit sinnvoller, bezogen auf das Stadtmarketing von einem **„Selling Center"** zu sprechen. In Anlehnung daran lassen sich sechs verschiedene Rollen innerhalb der Trägerschaft des Stadtmarketing unterscheiden (vgl. Abbildung 2).

Eine besondere Bedeutung kommt den **„Machern"** zu, die auch als Träger des Stadtmarketing im eigentlichen Sinne bezeichnet werden können. Die „Macher" sind zuständig für das Tagesgeschäft des Stadtmarketing, das heißt die Konzeptentwicklung, Erstellung von Maßnahmenplänen und das Anstoßen von Schlüsselprojekten. Neben der Öffentlichkeitsarbeit kommt ihnen die Aufgabe der Gesamtkoordination des Stadtmarketing zu.

Den Machern stehen oftmals **„Berater"** zur Seite, die diesen insbesondere in Fragen von strategischer Reichweite Beistand leisten. In Betracht kommen dabei Vertreter der Wissenschaft aufgrund ihres methodischen Know-hows sowie Fachleute, die das Stadtmarketing in inhaltlichen Fragen unterstützen. Neben internen „Beratern", die oftmals ehrenamtlich arbeiten, wird häufig auf externe Hilfe im Rahmen der Prozessbegleitung zurückgegriffen. Die Funktionen externer „Berater" reichen dabei von der Veranstaltungsmoderation über das Coaching einzelner Prozessphasen bis hin zur längerfristigen Betreuung des Gesamtprozesses des Stadtmarketing (Grabow/Hollbach-Grömig 1998, S. 108 f.).

Abbildung 2: Rollenbezogene Interpretation der Anbieterstruktur des Stadtmarketing

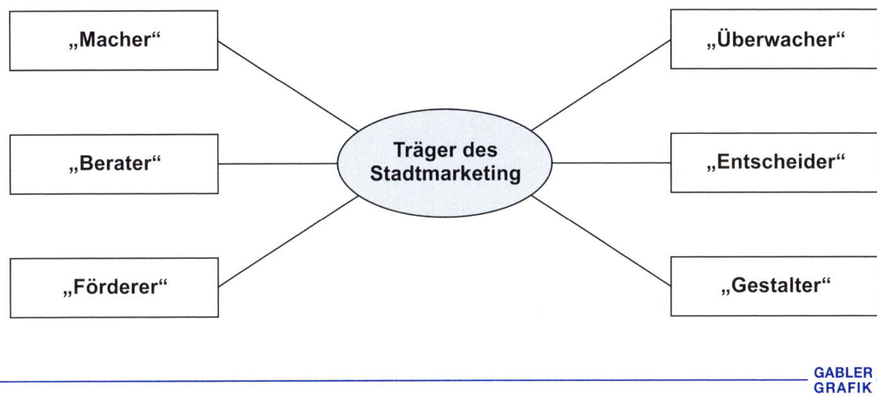

Während der Beitrag der Berater somit inhaltlicher Natur ist, unterstützen die **„Förderer“** das Stadtmarketing beziehungsweise einzelne Projekte materiell. Der finanziellen Förderung des Stadtmarketing muss eine besondere Bedeutung beigemessen werden, da viele Stadtmarketingprojekte an der Frage der Finanzierung scheitern (Weber 2000, S. 77 ff.). Aufgrund der Tatsache, dass die Fördermittel von Bund und Ländern oftmals nur einen geringen Anteil des erforderlichen Gesamtbudgets decken, erfolgt die finanzielle Absicherung häufig im Rahmen öffentlich-privater Kooperationen (Public-Private-Partnerships).

Die **„Überwacher“** sind dadurch gekennzeichnet, dass sie durch die Wahrnehmung ihrer Kontrollfunktion das Stadtmarketing passiv begleiten. Statt der aktiven Einbringung von Konzeptvorschlägen übernehmen sie in Fragen von größerer finanzieller beziehungsweise strategischer Reichweite die Aufgabe der Prüfung der von den Machern erarbeiteten Ideenvorschläge. Da in Stadtmarketing-Organisationen ein solches Aufsichtsgremium nur selten vorhanden ist, übernehmen in vielen Fällen Vertreter politischer Parteien diese Überwachungsfunktion.

Auch die **„Entscheider“** sind in der Regel politische Interessenvertreter. Sie lassen sich dadurch charakterisieren, dass sie aufgrund ihrer Machtposition letztlich über die Implementierung von Konzepten entscheiden. Aufgrund des strategischen Ausmaßes solcher Entscheidungen für eine Stadt kommt diese Aufgabe zumeist dem Stadtdirektor beziehungsweise Oberbürgermeister zu.

Die **„Gestalter“** schließlich sind solche Akteure des Stadtmarketing, die nach der Entscheidung über ein Projekt mit dessen Ausführung beauftragt sind. Ihr Tätigkeitsfeld ist somit abzugrenzen von dem der Macher, deren Aufgabe in der Konzeptionierung von Strategie- und Projektvorschlägen liegt. Im Stadtmarketing wird die Maßnahmenumsetzung häufig von Verwaltungsmitarbeitern der betroffenen Themenfelder durchgeführt.

Mit der allgemeingültigen Erfassung der Trägerschaft auf der Basis des „Selling Centers“ ist die Grundlage für eine Erfassung der Strukturzusammenhänge des Stadtmarketing gegeben. Eine wesentliche Voraussetzung für die dauerhafte Verankerung der Identität einer Stadt ist jedoch eine genaue Kenntnis der aktuell existierenden Selbst- und Fremdbilder der Stadt (Gröppel-Klein/Braun 2001, S. 355). Ausgehend von der sozialpsychologisch fundierten Annahme, dass die Verhaltensrelevanz der Stadt als Marke durch das Ausmaß der Übereinstimmung zwischen dem Selbst- und Fremdbild der Stadt, das heißt zwischen Stadtidentität und Stadtimage, determiniert wird, sind mögliche Lücken zwischen der Innen- und Außenperspektive aufzudecken. Aufgrund ähnlicher Problemstrukturen kann zur Analyse dieser Identitätslücken auf das **Marken-Gap-Modell** zurückgegriffen werden (vgl. den Beitrag zum Managementkonzept der identitätsorientierten Markenführung in diesem Buch). Dabei lassen sich **unterschiedliche Gaps des identitätsorientierten Stadtmarketing** unterscheiden (vgl. Abbildung 3):

Abbildung 3: Marken-Gap-Modell des identitätsorientierten Stadtmarketing

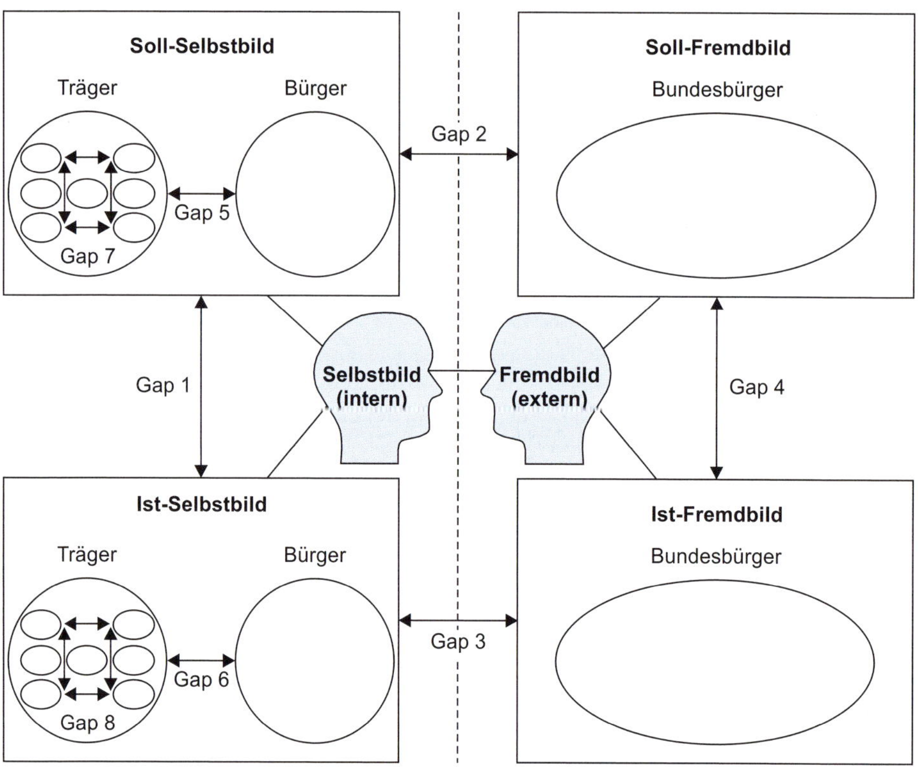

GABLER GRAFIK

Gap 1 kennzeichnet die Diskrepanz zwischen dem auf den existierenden Gegebenheiten einer Stadt aufbauenden Ist-Selbstbild und den aus Sicht der internen Anspruchsgruppen definierten Idealvorstellungen der Stadt. **Gap 2** ist Ausdruck einer Abweichung zwischen den Idealvorstellungen der externen Zielgruppen und den Erwartungen interner Bezugsgruppen an die Ausprägung der Identitätsdimensionen einer Stadt. **Gap 3** beschreibt Differenzen in der Wahrnehmung einer Stadt durch interne Anspruchsgruppen einerseits und auswärtige Bezugsgruppen anderseits. Wesentliche Ursache dieser Wahrnehmungsabweichungen ist die Qualität der persönlichen Erfahrungsgrundlage, da sich interne und externe Bezugsgruppen sowohl hinsichtlich ihres Informationsverhaltens als auch bezüglich ihrer stadtbezogenen Intentionen grundsätzlich unterscheiden. **Gap 4** schließlich charakterisiert Diskrepanzen zwischen den Idealvorstellungen externer Zielgruppen und dem tatsächlichen Bild, welches diese von einer Stadt haben.

Während die Gaps 1 bis 4 als zentrale Gaps der identitätsorientierten Markenführung gelten (Meffert/Burmann 1996), lassen sich mit den Gaps 5 bis 8 weitere Identitätslücken identifizieren, die in der stadtspezifischen Komplexität innerhalb des Selbstbildes begründet liegen:

Gap 5 steht für eine Differenz zwischen den Idealvorstellungen der Stadtmarketing-Träger und den Erwartungen der Bürger an ihre Stadt. Sie resultiert aus unterschiedlichen Interessenlagen von Bewohnern, die eine Stadt vornehmlich als Wohnstandort sehen und Entscheidern, die zudem wirtschaftliche und tourismusbezogene Motive verfolgen. **Gap 7** kennzeichnet unterschiedliche Soll-Anforderungen innerhalb der Trägerschaft des Stadtmarketing. Während **Gap 6** den Unterschied in der tatsächlichen Wahrnehmung einer Stadt zwischen Bewohnern und ortsansässigen Entscheidern charakterisiert, ist **Gap 8** Ausdruck heterogener Wahrnehmungen innerhalb der Trägerschaft. Ein wesentlicher Ursachenfaktor derartiger Diskrepanzen in der Innenperspektive ist ein unterschiedlicher Wissensstand der internen Anspruchsgruppen.

Zusammenfassend betrachtet verdeutlicht die konzeptionelle Skizzierung der Identitätslücken den **integrativen Charakter des identitätsorientierten Gap-Modells**, welches angesichts der differenzierten Betrachtung von Selbst- und Fremdbild ein hohes Transferpotenzial für das Stadtmarketing besitzt. Insgesamt steht mit dem identitätsorientierten Stadtmarketing und dem darauf aufbauenden modifizierten Gap-Modell somit ein zweckmäßiger Bezugsrahmen für die Markenführung im Stadtmarketing zur Verfügung, der jedoch für die Ableitung differenzierter Implikationen einer empirischen Fundierung bedarf.

4. Empirische Fundierung des identitätsorientierten Stadtmarketing

4.1 Tragfähigkeit der „Marke Münster" als Untersuchungsobjekt

Für die empirische Fundierung des identitätsorientierten Stadtmarketing wurden im Rahmen einer telefonischen Befragung von Juni bis September 2002 insgesamt 1.000 Bundesbürger und 296 Bewohner Münsters zum **Selbst- und Fremdbild der Stadt Münster** befragt. Im Mittelpunkt stand dabei die Erhebung der Soll- und Ist-Wahrnehmung der Befragten auf der Basis konkreter Angebotskomponenten anhand eines sechsseitigen Fragebogens. Im Unterschied zu diesen telefonischen Teilbefragungen erfolgte die Erhebung des Selbstbildes aus Sicht der Träger des Stadtmarketing schriftlich. Hierbei wurden zunächst 23 relevante Vertreter des Münsteraner Stadtmarketing identifiziert und im Mai 2003 angeschrieben. Gestützt durch Expertengespräche konnten die Befragten den zuvor abgeleiteten Rollen zugeordnet werden (Ebert 2004, S. 114 ff.).

Abbildung 4: **Identifikationsanker der Bewohner Münsters**

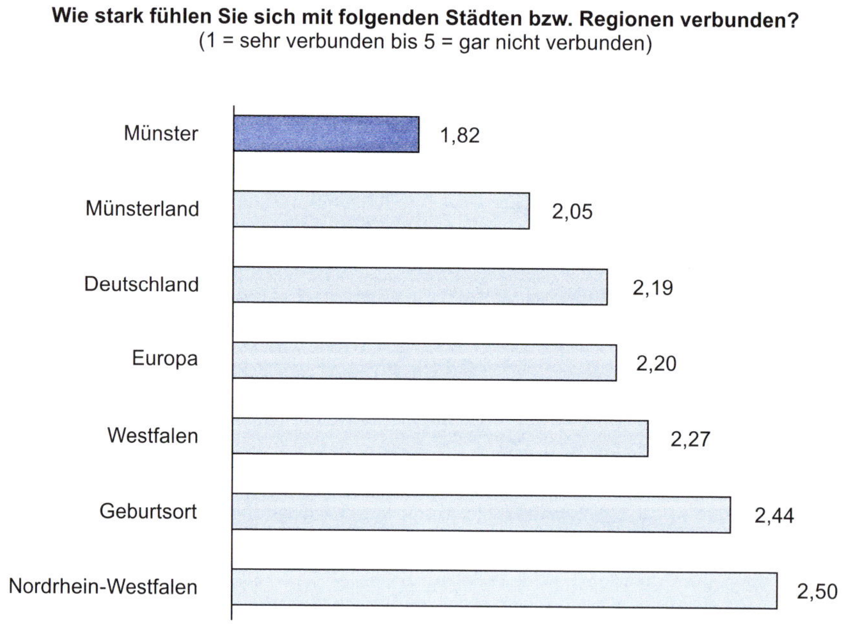

GABLER GRAFIK

Vor der Erfassung des **Selbst- und Fremdbildes der „Marke Münster"** war jedoch zunächst die Tragfähigkeit der Stadt Münster als Identitätsgrundlage empirisch zu überprüfen. Zu diesem Zweck wurden den Bewohnern Münsters unterschiedliche räumliche Hierarchiebenen zur Beurteilung als **Identifikationsalternativen** vorgelegt. Aufgrund der unklaren Definition des Begriffs „Region" wurden diesem Mesomaßstab drei konkrete Bezugsgrößen zugeordnet, die sich hinsichtlich ihrer Größe in eine aufsteigende Reihenfolge ordnen lassen: die flächenmäßig kleinste Sub-Region (zum Beispiel Münsterland), die Region Westfalen sowie das übergeordnete Bundesland Nordrhein-Westfalen. Zusätzlich wurde der Geburtsort der Befragten als lokale Bezugsgröße in die Analyse einbezogen (vgl. Abbildung 4).

Trotz einer überdurchschnittlichen Verbundenheit mit allen abgefragten Raumebenen bildet die **Stadt Münster für die eigenen Bewohner die stärkste Identifikationsbasis**. Nach der Sub-Region Münsterland an zweiter Stelle folgen Deutschland, Europa sowie die Mesoebene Westfalen. Noch hinter dem Geburtsort der Befragten rangiert das Bundesland Nordrhein-Westfalen als schwächste Identifikationsgrundlage. Dies erscheint vor dem Hintergrund der „künstlichen" Schaffung dieses Administrationsraumes sowie der damit verbundenen geringen Historie im Vergleich zu den anderen Bezugsebenen durchaus plausibel.

4.2 Ableitung eines Markenkerns als strategischer Ausgangspunkt des identitätsorientierten Stadtmarketing

Für die Konkretisierung von Identität und Image der „Marke Münster" war zunächst die grobe Bandbreite der Assoziationen innerhalb des Selbst- und Fremdbildes zu eruieren. Dabei wurden die Befragten zunächst um **spontane Assoziationen zu der Stadt Münster** gebeten, die zu übergeordneten Themenkomplexen verdichtet werden konnten (vgl. Abbildung 5).

Mit mehr als 13 Prozent entfallen die meisten Nennungen innerhalb des **Selbstbildes** (Identität von Münster) auf Assoziationen, die sich einem positiven Eigenschaftskomplex der Stadt Münster zuordnen lassen (zum Beispiel „schöne Stadt", „Gemütlichkeit"). In Kombinationen mit den an dritter Stelle genannten Begriffen „Grüne Stadt" beziehungsweise „Umgebung" deutet dies darauf hin, dass die Münsteraner mit ihrer Stadt in erster Linie eine **hohe Lebensqualität** verbinden. Eine ebenfalls starke assoziative Kraft entfaltet der Bedeutungskomplex **Studentenstadt** für die Münsteraner Bevölkerung. Mit den Begriffen „Fahrradstadt" sowie „Universität/Studenten" lässt sich nahezu ein Fünftel aller Nennungen diesem Themengebiet zuordnen. Neben der guten Lebensqualität und dem Image als Studentenstadt verbinden die Bürger Münsters zudem das **kulturell geprägte Stadtbild** in besonderem Maße mit ihrer Stadt. So entfallen auf die Assoziationen „Prinzipalmarkt", „Historische Altstadt", „Gebäude/Sehenswürdigkeiten", „Dom" und „Kirchen" insgesamt 28,9 Prozent aller Nennungen.

Abbildung 5: Spontanassoziationen mit der Stadt Münster (Selbstbild)

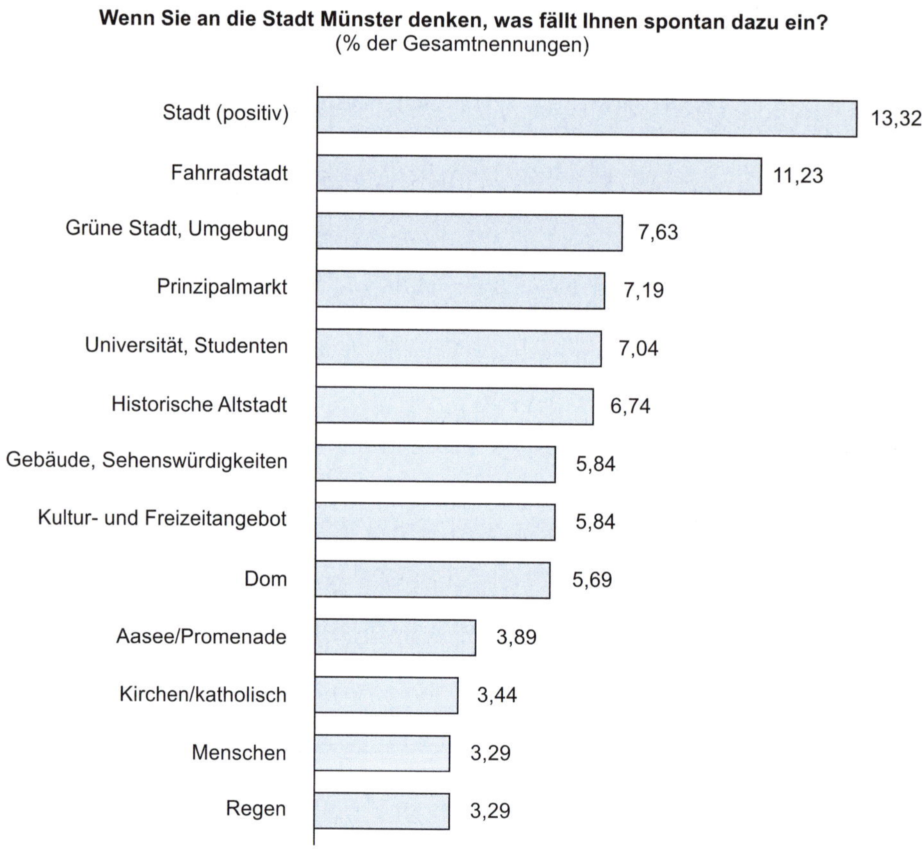

GABLER GRAFIK

Die analog zur Selbstbildanalyse durchgeführte Erhebung spontaner Assoziationen mit der Stadt Münster aus Sicht der Bundesbürger (Image von Münster) ist Abbildung 6 zu entnehmen. Bei inhaltlich ähnlichen Ergebnissen ergibt sich dabei eine andere Akzentuierung der unterschiedlichen Themenkomplexe. Die mit Abstand meisten Nennungen innerhalb des **Fremdbildes** beziehen sich auf die **Kultur** und das **Stadtbild** Münsters. Mit dem Dom, dem im Rahmen der externen Wahrnehmung eine Art „Leuchtturmfunktion" zuzuschreiben ist, sowie der Altstadt, den Kirchen und weiteren Sehenswürdigkeiten entfällt fast die Hälfte aller Nennungen auf diesen Themenkomplex. Während noch etwa 20 Prozent der Assoziationen das Image Münsters als **Studentenstadt** zum Gegenstand haben (Nennungen: „Universität/Studenten“ beziehungsweise „Fahrradstadt“) entfaltet der noch im Selbstbild dominante Faktor Lebensqualität eine geringere Assoziationskraft im Fremdbild. Stattdessen verbinden die befragten Bundesbürger in stärkerem Maße die Begriffe „Heimat“ und „Westfälischer Friede“ mit der Stadt Münster.

Abbildung 6: Spontanassoziationen mit der Stadt Münster (Fremdbild)

GABLER GRAFIK

Auf der Basis dieser ersten Ergebnisse lässt sich ein verdichteter **Identitätskern der „Marke Münster“** als strategischer Ausgangspunkt des identitätsorientierten Stadtmarketing wie folgt festhalten (vgl. Abbildung 7):

Abbildung 7: Identitätskern der „Marke Münster"

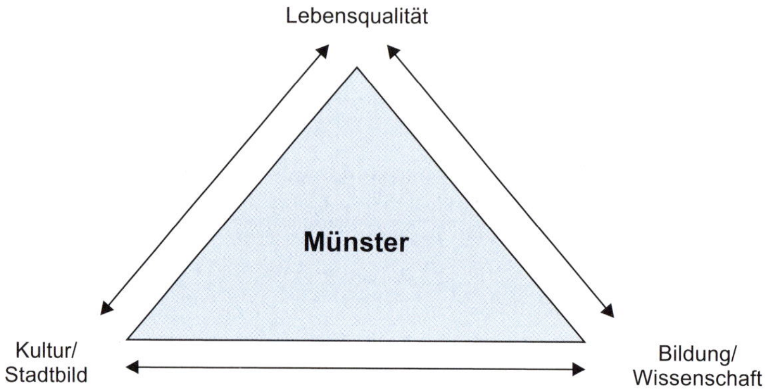

In besonderem Maße prägt der Bereich Bildung und Wissenschaft im Selbst- und Fremdbild die Wahrnehmung der Stadt Münster. Einerseits werden die Begriffe Universitäts- und Studentenstadt spontan mit Münster assoziiert, andererseits rangieren die Bildungseinrichtungen – mit der Westfälischen Wilhelms-Universität als „Aushängeschild" – hinsichtlich ihrer Bewertung auch bei der gestützten Abfrage stets an vorderster Stelle. Da die außergewöhnliche Anzahl und Qualität der Bildungseinrichtungen Münsters deutschlandweit ein besonderes Merkmal sind und dieser Bereich angesichts des Wandels zu einer Wissensgesellschaft an Bedeutung gewinnen wird, bildet der Faktor **„Bildung/Wissenschaft"** eine Komponente des Identitätskerns der „Marke Münster".

Insbesondere im Fremdbild kommt mit dem Dom, dem Prinzipalmarkt sowie der Altstadt den kulturellen Einrichtungen und Sehenswürdigkeiten ein starker assoziativer Charakter zu. Somit stellt der Faktor **„Kultur/Stadtbild"** als visuelle Verankerung der Münster-Identität eine zweite Komponente des Identitätskerns dar. Aus der münsterspezifischen Kombination guter Einkaufsmöglichkeiten in der City mit einer historischen Altstadtatmosphäre erwachsen besondere Differenzierungspotenziale gegenüber den Konkurrenzstädten des Ruhrgebiets.

Einen dritten Profilierungsfaktor bildet die im Selbst- und Fremdbild gleichermaßen wahrgenommene hohe **„Lebensqualität"** Münsters. Neben der atmosphärischen Altstadt wird diese durch die hohe Wohnqualität sowie die kulturelle Vielfalt und ein differenziertes Sport- und Freizeitangebot geprägt. Wenngleich den Lebensbedingungen isoliert nur ein geringes Profilierungspotenzial zugesprochen werden kann, so leisten sie in Kombination mit den beiden anderen Identitätsfaktoren einen wertvollen Beitrag für einen authentischen, individuellen und in sich konsistenten Identitätskern der Stadt Münster, den es durch geeignete leistungspolitische und kommunikative Maßnahmen gezielt zu entwickeln und an die internen und externen Zielgruppen zu vermitteln gilt.

4.3 Identifikation von Maßnahmenprioritäten

Im Hinblick auf die Ableitung von Implikationen für das Stadtmarketing sind aus zweierlei Gründen die in Abbildung 3 skizzierten **Gaps 1 und 4** einer näheren Betrachtung zu unterziehen (Ebert 2004, S. 134). Da diese als Differenz zwischen Soll- und Ist-Bild – und damit als stadtbezogene Einstellung – interpretiert werden, zeichnen sie sich gemäß der Dreikomponententheorie der Einstellungsforschung durch eine größere Verhaltensnähe als die Gaps 2 beziehungsweise 3 aus und beeinflussen demnach direkt die Verhaltensintentionen und indirekt das Verhalten der Zielgruppen (Trommsdorff 2003, S. 154). Auf eine Analyse der durch die Trägerschaft des Stadtmarketing induzierten Gaps 5 bis 8 wird aus Komplexitätsgründen an dieser Stelle verzichtet und somit der Fokus auf den Zielgruppenbezug der Markenführung gelegt (vgl. im Detail Ebert 2004, S. 128 ff.).

Aus ökonomischen Erwägungen erscheint es darüber hinaus sinnvoll, diejenigen Faktoren zu identifizieren, die einen besonderen Handlungsbedarf aufwerfen. Neben der Größe der Gaps, die einen Hinweis auf die Stärke des Anpassungsbedarfs bieten, ist hierzu die **Relevanz der Kriterien** für die internen und externen Zielgruppen zu erheben. Aus Objektivitäts- und Validitätsgründen wurde die Bedeutung der einzelnen Kriterien regressionsanalytisch anhand des Einflusses der Ist-Beurteilung einzelner Angebotskomponenten der Stadt Münster auf das Gesamturteil der Befragten erhoben. Die ermittelten Bedeutungsgewichte sowie die Größe der Gaps zwischen Soll- und Ist-Urteil der Befragten im Selbst- und Fremdbild sind in Tabelle 1 überblickartig dargestellt.

Mit Blick auf die Soll-Ist-Abweichungen weist der Faktor „Medizinische Versorgung" innerhalb des **Selbstbildes** die geringste Diskrepanz auf. Augenscheinlich kann die Stadt Münster die Anforderungen der eigenen Bewohner in Bezug auf diese Dimension am besten erfüllen. Demgegenüber liegen für die Dimensionen „Berufliche Perspektiven" und „Parkplätze" Soll-Ist-Differenzen von durchschnittlich über 1 vor, was auf einen besonders hohen Änderungsbedarf hindeutet. Im Unterschied zum Parkplatzangebot spielen die Berufsperspektiven für die Gesamtbeurteilung der Stadt Münster aus Sicht ihrer Bewohner jedoch keine signifikante Rolle. Die deutlich größte Bedeutung für die Beurteilung Münsters kommt hingegen dem Faktor „Wohnqualität" zu. Ähnlich wie im Selbstbild liegen auch im **Fremdbild** die größten Soll-Ist-Abweichungen bei den Dimensionen „Berufliche Perspektiven", „Parkplätze" und „Attraktiver Wirtschaftsstandort" vor. Diese besitzen jedoch aus Sicht der befragten Bundesbürger keine signifikante Relevanz für die Beurteilung Münsters. Neben der Wohnqualität kommt hier den Sehenswürdigkeiten und der Landschaft eine ähnlich hohe Bedeutung zu.

Tabelle 1: Ausprägungen der Gaps 1 und 4 sowie Relevanz der Angebotskomponenten für die internen und externen Zielgruppen der Stadt Münster

	Selbstbild		Fremdbild	
	Gap 1	Relevanz	Gap 4	Relevanz
Wohnqualität	0,61	0,270***	0,86	0,265***
Bildungseinrichtungen	0,56	0,122*	0,69	n. s.
Sehenswürdigkeiten	0,62	n. s.	0,73	0,255***
Berufliche Perspektiven	1,02	n. s.	1,14	n. s.
Freundl. des Menschen	0,92	0,191***	0,69	n. s.
Wetter	0,95	n. s.	0,76	–0,158**
Landschaft	0,56	n. s.	0,70	0,249***
Attr. Wirtschaftsstandort	0,77	n. s.	0,92	n. s.
Verkehrsanbindung	0,68	n. s.	0,82	n. s.
Sauberkeit	0,61	0,133*	0,66	0,121*
Einkaufsmöglichkeiten	0,56	0,159**	0,64	n. s.
Freizeitmöglichkeiten	0,60	n. s.	0,72	n. s.
Medizizinische Versorgung	0,47	n. s.	0,67	n. s.
Gaststätten und Restaurants	0,70	n. s.	0,56	n. s.
Parkplätze	1,01	0,114*	0,92	n. s.
Wohnungsangebot	0,84	n. s.	0,86	n. s.
Sportanlagen	0,60	n. s.	0,64	n. s.
Schulen und Kindergärten	0,64	n. s.	0,75	n. s.

Selbstbild: $r^2 = 0{,}388$
Fremdbild: $r^2 = 0{,}338$

Signifikanzniveau:
*** = $\alpha < 0{,}001$
** = $\alpha < 0{,}01$
* = $\alpha < 0{,}05$
n. s. = nicht signifikant

GABLER GRAFIK

Letztlich liegt nur für solche Angebotskomponenten ein Handlungsbedarf vor, die einen signifikanten Einfluss auf das Urteil der befragten Zielgruppen ausüben. Für die Priorisierung von Maßnahmen im Sinne eines effizienten Einsatzes des Marketing-Instrumentariums ist jedoch auch die Größe der korrespondierenden Lücken in die Beurteilung einzubeziehen. Stellt man Relevanz und Soll-Ist-Abweichung der Faktoren überblicksartig dar, so lassen sich die Maßnahmen in einem 4-Felder-Schema systematisieren (vgl. Abbildung 8).

Abbildung 8: Maßnahmenprioritäten für die identitätsorientierte Markenführung der Stadt Münster

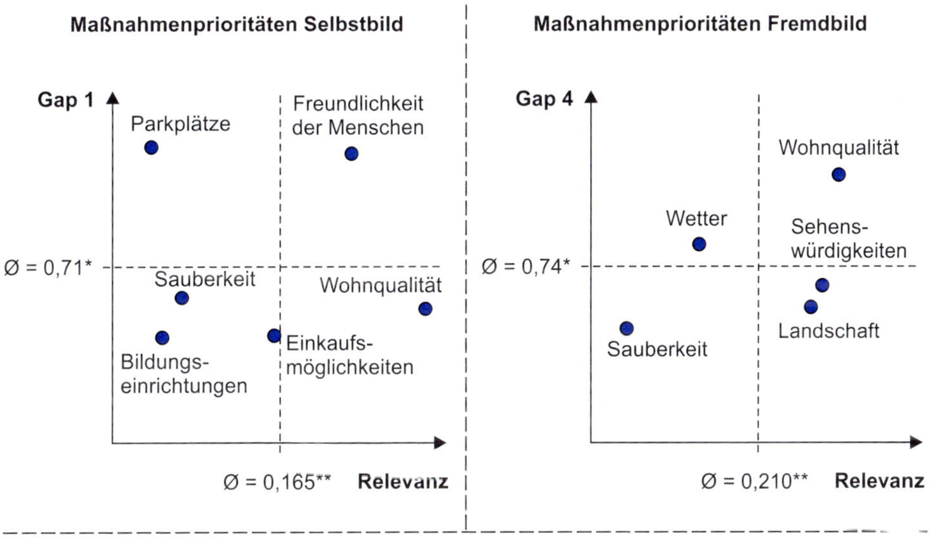

* Mittelwert der β-Faktoren aller signifikanten Items im Selbst- bzw. Fremdbild
** Mittelwert der Soll-Ist-Abweichungen aller signifikanten Items im Selbst- bzw. Fremdbild

GABLER GRAFIK

- Die höchste Priorität ist den Angebotsdimensionen im **rechten oberen Quadranten** einzuräumen. Diese Kriterien weisen eine überdurchschnittliche Differenz zwischen Ideal- und Realeindruck auf und besitzen gleichzeitig eine hohe Bedeutung für die Befragten. Für die Stadt Münster ist der Faktor „Freundlichkeit der Menschen" im Selbstbild und der Faktor „Wohnqualität" im Fremdbild diesem Feld zuzuordnen.
- Im **rechten unteren Quadranten** sind Faktoren angesiedelt, die zwar einen überdurchschnittlichen Einfluss auf das Urteil der Befragten haben, im Vergleich zu den anderen Dimensionen jedoch eine eher geringe Soll-Ist-Abweichung aufweisen. Be-

zogen auf die Stadt Münster sind das die Kriterien „Wohnqualität“ (Selbstbild) und „Landschaft“ bzw. „Sehenswürdigkeiten“ (Fremdbild). Aufgrund ihrer Bedeutung für die Zielpersonen ist diesen Komponenten grundsätzlich eine ebenfalls hohe Priorität beizumessen.

- Im **linken oberen Quadranten** befinden sich Angebotskomponenten, die aufgrund der Ausprägung des Gaps zwar einen großen Anpassungsbedarf mit sich bringen, gleichzeitig jedoch von untergeordneter Relevanz für die Befragten sind. Im Fall der Stadt Münster sind dies die Dimensionen „Parkplätze“ im Selbstbild sowie „Wetter“ im Fremdbild.
- Der **linke untere Quadrant** schließlich kennzeichnet Faktoren, denen eine vergleichsweise geringe Priorität beigemessen werden kann. Sowohl die Bedeutung für die Nachfrager als auch die Größe des Anpassungsbedarfs ist unterdurchschnittlich ausgeprägt. Im Selbstbild sind dies die Dimensionen „Sauberkeit“, „Einkaufsmöglichkeiten“ und „Bildungseinrichtungen“, im Fremdbild der Faktor „Sauberkeit“.

Die ermittelten Maßnamenprioritäten bilden die Grundlage für eine effiziente Ausgestaltung der identitätsorientierten Markenführung der Stadt Münster. Im Folgenden sollen die Ergebnisse eines identitätsorientierten Anpassungsprozesses am Beispiel der Stadt Münster überblickartig dargestellt werden.

4.4 Zusammenfassung des identitätsorientierten Anpassungsprozesses

Die Richtung beziehungsweise das Ausmaß der Anpassung einzelner Angebotskomponenten lässt sich mittels des Gap-Modells des identitätsorientierten Stadtmarketing simulativ ermitteln (Ebert 2004, S. 141 ff.). Dabei wird zunächst für jeden Faktor anhand der individuellen Differenz zwischen dem Soll- und Ist-Bild ermittelt, inwieweit die Zielgruppen eine Stärkung beziehungsweise Schwächung dieses Faktors wünschen. Anschließend kann mit einer schrittweisen Erhöhung beziehungsweise Verringerung der Soll- beziehungsweise Ist-Komponente dieses Faktors ermittelt werden, inwieweit hieraus eine Veränderung der zielgruppenübergreifenden Identitätslücke resultiert. Anhand dieser Simulationslogik lassen sich schließlich für sämtliche als relevant identifizierten Faktoren die **optimalen Anpassungsbedarfe**, welche zu einer Minimierung des entsprechenden Gaps führen, im Rahmen des identitätsorientierten Stadtmarketing ermitteln (vgl. Tabelle 2).

Tabelle 2: **Anforderungsprofil an das identitätsorientierte Stadtmarketing der Stadt Münster**

	Ausgangspunkt der Veränderung	Anpassungsbedarf	Ausmaß
Freundlichkeit der Menschen	Selbstbild	Reduktion der Soll-Vorstellungen	–1
Parkplätze	Selbstbild	Verbesserung der Ist-Wahrnehmung	+1
Bildungseinrichtungen	Selbstbild	Verbesserung der Ist-Wahrnehmung	+1
Wohnqualität	Selbstbild + Fremdbild	Verbesserung der Ist-Wahrnehmung	+1
		Selektive kommunikationspolitische Verbesserung der Ist-Wahrnehmung im Fremdbild	+3

GABLER GRAFIK

Es zeigt sich, dass der Veränderungsbedarf für das Stadtmarketing vornehmlich aus den **Anforderungen des Selbstbildes** resultiert. So basieren drei der in Tabelle 2 dargestellten Faktoren auf einem selbstbildinduzierten Änderungsbedarf, während für den Faktor „Wohnqualität" sowohl im Selbst- als auch im Fremdbild eine Anpassung als sinnvoll identifiziert wurde. Einzig für den Faktor „Freundlichkeit der Menschen" wurde dabei eine geringfügige Reduktion der Soll-Vorstellungen der Bürger als optimal identifiziert, für die anderen Faktoren hingegen ist eine ebenfalls nur geringe Stärkung der Ist-Wahrnehmung anzustreben. Für den Faktor „Wohnqualität" erwies sich darüber hinaus eine starke kommunikative Unterstützung der Wahrnehmung innerhalb des Fremdbildes als sinnvoll.

Die dargestellte Analyse der Auswirkungen des ermittelten Änderungsbedarfs fokussiert ausschließlich auf die itemspezifischen Effekte innerhalb des Selbst- beziehungsweise Fremdbildes. Zur **Bewertung der simulativ ermittelten Anpassungsmaßnahmen** ist jedoch diese Einzelkomponentenperspektive durch eine integrierte Betrachtung zu ergänzen. Hierzu wurde das Gap-Modell der Stadt Münster in der Ausgangssituation den Ergebnissen nach erfolgter Anpassung gegenübergestellt (vgl. Abbildung 9).

Abbildung 9: **Ergebnisse des identitätsorientierten Anpassungsprozesses für die Stadt Münster**

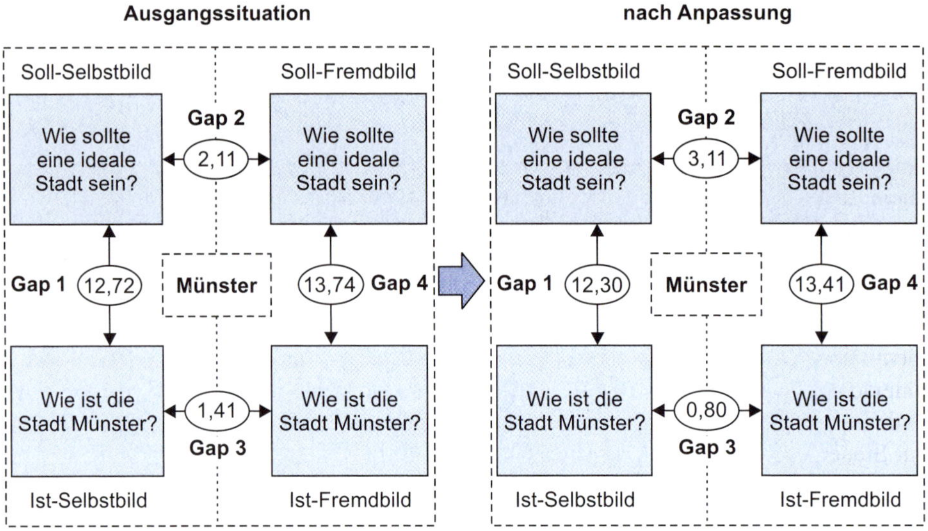

GABLER GRAFIK

Zunächst wird deutlich, dass sich einzig **Gap 2** im Vergleich zum Ausgangszustand vergrößert hat. Darüber hinaus konnte sowohl im Selbst- als auch im Fremdbild durch die simulierten Änderungsmaßnahmen eine Verringerung der Lücken und damit eine **Verbesserung der Einstellungen der Zielgruppen** erreicht werden. Absolut betrachtet erscheint die Verminderung der beiden Gaps zunächst unwesentlich. Allerdings ist zu berücksichtigen, dass aufgrund der Kriterienrelevanz nur für 4 von insgesamt 18 Angebotskomponenten, die das Gesamtgap determinieren, eine Anpassung durchgeführt wurde. Zudem ist darauf zu verweisen, dass eine vollständige Schließung der Lücken 1 und 4 aufgrund der Varianzen der internen und externen Zielgruppenanforderungen nicht möglich ist (Schneider 2004, S. 187).

Neben den Auswirkungen des Anpassungsprozesses auf die Gaps 1 und 4, die gemäß ihrer Interpretation als stadtbezogene Einstellungen primäre Bedeutung für das identitätsorientierte Stadtmarketing erlangen, ist der Effekt der Veränderungsmaßnahmen auf Divergenzen zwischen Ist-Selbstbild und Ist-Fremdbild von besonderem Interesse. Im vorliegenden Fall trägt die als optimal erachtete Einflussnahme auf die Identitätskomponenten im Selbst- und Fremdbild zu einer Reduktion von **Gap 3** um nahezu 50 Prozent auf 0,80 bei. Durch die **fast vollständige Angleichung der Ist-Wahrnehmung** der Stadt Münster im Selbst- und Fremdbild erzielt der identitätsorientierte Anpassungsprozess im Ergebnis somit einen Effekt, der als nahezu idealtypisch gekennzeichnet werden kann.

Die Ergebnisse verdeutlichen somit in der Ausgangssituation und insbesondere nach erfolgreicher Anpassung das Vorhandensein einer – am Verhältnis zwischen Selbst- und Fremdbild festgemachten – Stadtidentität für die „Marke Münster“.

5. Zusammenfassung und Implikationen

Analog zum Unternehmensbereich können der Aufbau und die Etablierung einer Marke auch für das Stadtmarketing einen Beitrag zur Profilierung im Wettbewerb leisten. Als inhaltlicher Referenzpunkt für das Stadtmarketing nimmt die Stadtidentität dabei angesichts ihrer internen und externen Nutzenpotenziale einen zentralen Stellenwert ein. Auf dieser Basis stellt das an die stadtspezifischen Charakteristika angepasste Marken-Gap-Modell des identitätsorientierten Stadtmarketing einen geeigneten Bezugsrahmen für die identitätsorientierte Führung einer Stadt als Marke dar. Das auf einer Differenzierung der unterschiedlichen Selbst- und Fremdbilder basierende Modell erlaubt sowohl die Analyse der resultierenden Lücken als auch die darauf aufbauende Ableitung von Maßnahmen zur Steuerung und Entwicklung von Identität und Image einer Stadt.

Ungeachtet der themenfeldbezogenen Ergebnisse einer quantitativen Modellanalyse ergeben sich für die kommunale Praxis weitere Gestaltungsparameter zur Förderung der Stadtidentität. Voraussetzung für die interne Verankerung der stadtbezogenen Identität ist zunächst die Festlegung einer situationsspezifisch adäquaten organisatorischen Verfestigung des Stadtmarketing. In engem Zusammenhang damit steht die Entwicklung einer „Stadtkultur“, das heißt die Förderung gemeinsamer Werte- und Normenvorstellungen sowie geteilter Denk- und Verhaltensmuster der Akteure. Eine besondere Rolle kommt dabei den Führungskräften einer Stadt (zum Beispiel Oberbürgermeister) zu, denen die Vermittlung von „shared values“ durch kommunikative und symbolische Handlungen obliegt. Als normatives Planungsinstrument des identitätsorientierten Stadtmarketing erlangt das Leitbild einer Stadt einen besonderen Stellenwert, welches einen internen Orientierungsrahmen bildet und gleichzeitig durch seinen kommunikativen Charakter zur externen Identitätsbildung beiträgt. Bei seiner Formulierung gilt es dabei, das Spannungsfeld zwischen Integrations- und Aussagekraft zu berücksichtigen, indem sich ein Leitbild angesichts seiner internen und externen Funktionen bewegt. Neben der **Identitätsermittlung** stellt schließlich die **Identitätsvermittlung** im Rahmen eines widerspruchsfreien Identitäts-Mix einen weiteren Baustein des identitätsorientierten Stadtmarketing dar. Als maßgebliche Ausdrucksform der Stadtidentität verlangt die City Behavior eine einheitliche und in Bezug auf die angestrebte Stadtidentität schlüssige Ausrichtung aller Verhaltensweisen der Akteure im Innen- und Außenverhältnis. Dabei ist zu beachten, dass nicht nur das Verhalten der Stadtmarketing-Träger, sondern insbesondere die Bürger einer Stadt die Identität in besonderem Maße prägen. Zentrale Aufgabe des City Designs ist die optisch-visuelle Umsetzung des auf der stadtbezogenen Identität basierenden Leitbildes. Es beinhaltet die ästhetische und symbolische Identitätsvermittlung durch den abgestimmten Einsatz aller von den internen und externen Zielgruppen visuell wahrnehmbaren Elemente einer Stadt (zum Beispiel Logo). Die City Communication schließlich umfasst den widerspruchsfreien Einsatz der Kommunikationsinstrumente des Stadtmarketing (zum Beispiel Slogan, Events etc.). Bei sämtlichen Gestaltungsparametern, insbesondere jedoch im Rahmen der Kommunikation, ist stets zu berücksichtigen, dass sich das identitätsorientierte Stadtmarketing in einem Spannungsfeld zwischen Identitätsvermittlung und Zielgruppenorientierung befindet, dem durch adäquate strategische Entscheidungen, wie etwa der Entwicklung einer Markenarchitektur, Rechnung zu tragen ist.

Literatur

Aschauer, W. (1997), Identität als Begriff und Realität, in: Heller, W. (Hrsg.), Identität – Regionalbewusstsein – Ethnizität, Potsdam.

Backhaus, K. (1999), Industriegütermarketing, 6. Aufl., München.

Balderjahn, I. (2000), Standortmarketing, Stuttgart.

Bierwirth, A. (2003), Die Führung der Unternehmensmarke. Ein Beitrag zum zielgruppenorientierten Corporate Branding, Frankfurt/M.

Birkigt, K., Stadler, M. M., Funck, H. J. (Hrsg.) (1998), Corporate Identity – Grundlagen, Funktionen, Fallbeispiele, 9. Aufl., Landsberg/Lech.

Buß, E. (2002), Regionale Identitätsbildung. Zwischen globaler Dynamik, fortschreitender Europäisierung und regionaler Gegenbewegung, Schriftenreihe der Stiftung Westfalen-Initiative, Band 2, Münster u. a.

Ebert, Ch. (2004), Identitätsorientiertes Stadtmarketing – Ein Beitrag zur Koordination und Steuerung des Stadtmarketing, Frankfurt/M.

Funke, U. (1994), Vom Stadtmarketing zur Stadtkonzeption, Stuttgart.

Gibson, J. J. (1979), The Theory of Affordances, in: Shaw, R., Bransford, J. (Hrsg.), Perceiving, Acting and Knowing – Toward an Ecological Psychology, New York u. a., S. 67–82.

Göschel, A. (1987), Lokale Identität: Hypothesen und Befunde über Stadtteilbindungen in Großstädten, in: Informationen zur Raumentwicklung, Nr. 3, S. 91–107.

Grabow, B. et al. (1995), Weiche Standortfaktoren, Stuttgart, Berlin, Köln.

Grabow, B., Hollbach-Grömig, B. (1998), Stadtmarketing – Eine kritische Zwischenbilanz, Difu-Beiträge zur Stadtforschung, Band 25, Berlin.

Gröppel-Klein, A., Braun, D. (2001), Stadtimage und Stadtidentifikation. Eine empirische Studie auf der Basis einstellungstheoretischer Erkenntnisse, in: Tscheulin, D. K. et al. (Hrsg.), Branchenspezifisches Marketing – Grundlage, Besonderheiten, Gemeinsamkeiten, Wiesbaden, S. 351–372.

Honert, S. (1991), Stadtmarketing und Stadtmanagement, in: der städtetag, 44. Jg., Nr. 6, S. 395.

Johnston, W. J., Lewin, J. E. (1996), Organizational buying behavior: Toward an integrative framework, in: Journal of Business Research, Vol. 35, No. 1, S. 1–16.

Junghans, K. (2001), Auf dem Prüfstand, in: Handelsblatt vom 16./17.03.2001, S. 60.

Kerscher, U. (1992), Raumabstraktionen und regionale Identität, Eine Analyse des regionalen Identitätsmanagements im Gebiet zwischen Augsburg und München, Kallmünz/Regensburg.

Luhmann, N. (2000), Vertrauen. Ein Mechanismus der Reduktion sozialer Komplexität, 4. Aufl., Stuttgart.

McQuiston, D. H. (1989), Novelty, Complexity and Importances as casual Determinants of Industrial Buying Behavior, in: Journal of Marketing, Vol. 53, No. 2, S. 66–79.

Meffert, H. (1989), Städtemarketing – Pflicht oder Kür?, in: Planung und Analyse, 16. Jg., Nr. 8, S. 273–280.
Meffert, H., Bruhn, M. (2003), Dienstleistungsmarketing. Grundlagen – Konzepte – Methoden, 4. Aufl., Wiesbaden.
Meffert, H., Burmann, Ch. (1996), Identitätsorientierte Markenführung – Grundlagen für das Management von Markenportfolios, Meffert, H., Wagner, H., Backhaus, K. (Hrsg.), Arbeitspapier Nr. 100 der Wissenschaftlichen Gesellschaft für Marketing und Unternehmensführung e. V., Münster.
Meffert, H., Dahlhoff, D. (1980), Kollektive Kaufentscheidungen und Kaufwahrscheinlichkeiten – Analysen und methodische Ergebnisse zu Basisproblemen der Käuferverhaltensforschung, Hamburg.
Pollotzek, J. (1993), Stadtmarketing – Notwendigkeiten, Möglichkeiten und Grenzen der kommunalen Marketingkonzeption, Nürnberg.
Rabe, H., Süß, W. (1995), Stadtmarketing zwischen Innovation und Krisendeutung, Berlin.
Rohrbach, C. (1999), Regionale Identität im Global Village – Chance oder Handicap für die Regionalentwicklung, Frankfurt/M.
Schneider, H. (2004), Markenführung in der Politik, Wiesbaden.
Schuhbauer, J. (1996), Wirtschaftsbezogene Regionale Identität, Mannheimer Geografische Arbeiten, Nr. 42, Mannheim.
Schückhaus, U., Graf, A.-H., Dormeier, C. (1993), Stadt- und Regionalmarketing – Einsatzmöglichkeiten und Nutzen, Kienbaum Unternehmensberatung GmbH, Düsseldorf.
Singer, C. (1988), Kommunale Imageplanung, in: AfK, Nr. 2, S. 271–279.
Töpfer, A. (Hrsg.) (1993), Stadtmarketing – Herausforderung und Chance für Kommunen, Baden-Baden.
Trommsdorff, V. (2003), Konsumentenverhalten, 5. Aufl., Stuttgart.
Weber, A. (2000), Stadtmarketing in bayerischen Städten und Gemeinden – Bestand und Ausprägungen eines kommunalen Instruments der neunziger Jahre, Maier, J. (Hrsg.), Arbeitsmaterialien zur Raumordnung und Raumplanung, Nr. 192, Bayreuth.
Weichhardt, P. (1990), Raumbezogene Identität – Bausteine zu einer Theorie räumlich-sozialer Kognition und Identifikation, Meynen, E., Kohlhepp, G., Leidlmair, A., (Hrsg.), Erdkundliches Wissen, Nr. 102, Schriftenreihe für Forschung und Praxis, Stuttgart.
Werthmöller, E. (1995), Räumliche Identität als Aufgabenfeld des Städte- und Regionenmarketing – ein Beitrag zur Fundierung des Placemarketing, Frankfurt/M.

Identitätsorientierter Aufbau und Gestaltung von Regionenmarken

Manfred Kirchgeorg

1.	**Stellenwert von Regionenmarken im Regionenmarketing**	**590**
1.1	Profilierung von Regionen im Wettbewerb	590
1.2	Funktionen und Besonderheiten von Regionenmarken	594
1.3	Gestaltung von Marken für Regionen	598
1.4	Erfassung von Einstellungen gegenüber Regionen und Regionenmarken	601
2.	**Empirische Analyse von Markennamen für Regionen**	**604**
2.1	Markenbildung für die Region „Mitteldeutschland"	604
2.2	Analyse der Assoziationen zum Regionennamen „Mitteldeutschland"	605
2.3	Bekanntheitsgrad von Aktivitäten der Region „Mitteldeutschland"	607
2.4	Räumliche Identifikation der Region „Mitteldeutschland"	607
2.5	Einstellungen zur Region „Mitteldeutschland" im Vergleich zum „Ruhrgebiet"	610
3.	**Implikationen für markenstrategische Entscheidungen im Regionenmarketing**	**612**

1. Stellenwert von Regionenmarken im Regionenmarketing

1.1 Profilierung von Regionen im Wettbewerb

Vor dem Hintergrund der rasanten Internationalisierung und Globalisierung der Weltwirtschaft verlieren nationale Grenzen an Bedeutung. Parallel zum Abbau zwischenstaatlicher administrativer und fiskalischer Mobilitätsbarrieren verlagert sich der Konkurrenzkampf um Arbeitskräfte, Investoren oder Touristen von der Ebene der Nationalstaaten auf die Regionenebene (Manschwetus 1995, S. 7). So spricht man angesichts des zusammenwachsenden europäischen Binnenmarktes immer weniger vom Wettbewerb der Nationen als vielmehr vom Wettbewerb der Regionen. Auch weltweit stehen Regionen angesichts ihrer Innovations- und Wirtschaftskraft heute mehr und mehr im Wettbewerb um qualifizierte Arbeitskräfte und Investoren. Damit verbundene Forschungsinteressen bemühen sich um die Identifikation allgemeingültiger Standortfaktoren, die es Regionen erlauben, über die Profilierung eigener Stärken Wettbewerbsvorteile gegenüber Konkurrenzregionen zu generieren (Kotler/Haider/Rein 1994). Neben der Intensivierung der Analyse so genannter harter Standortfaktoren (physisch, sozioökonomisch, demografisch und infrastrukturell) rücken „weiche" Faktoren wie die Soziokultur, Lebensqualität und Formen gesellschaftlicher Regulierung zunehmend in den Mittelpunkt der Betrachtungen (Fach et al. 1998, S. 13).

In diesem Zusammenhang hat das so genannte **Regionenmarketing** eine besondere Aufmerksamkeit erfahren. Im Mittelpunkt des Regionenmarketings steht die gezielte *„Gestaltung der Beziehungen zwischen Regionen und ihren Marktpartnern"* (Manschwetus 1995, S. 39; Meffert 1995, S. 21 f.) zur Profilierung von Regionen gegenüber relevanten Zielgruppen. Die Zielgruppenorientierung des Regionenmarketings ist sowohl innen- als auch außengerichtet zu interpretieren. Einerseits werden die in einer Region verfügbaren Leistungen durch die Bewohner und alle Leistungsträger sowie Entscheidungsträger aus den Bereichen Wirtschaft, Wissenschaft, Bildung, Kultur, Freizeit, Verwaltung und Politik in Anspruch genommen wie auch arbeitsteilig erstellt. Neben der Bindung der Bewohner an eine Region erlangt im Regionenmarketing andererseits die außengerichtete Profilierung bei potenziellen Investoren, qualifizierten Arbeitnehmern, Touristen und meinungsbildenden Multiplikatoren zentrale Bedeutung.

Bei der Übertragung des Marketinggedankens auf Regionen stellt sich die Frage, inwieweit die im Konsum-, Investitions- und Dienstleistungsmarketing praktizierten Markenkonzepte auch im Regionenmarketing erfolgreich eingesetzt werden können. Bei der Profilierung von Regionen können **Regionenmarken** eine wichtige Identifikations- und Orientierungsfunktion erfüllen und den visuellen Kristallisationskern des Leistungsspektrums einer Region bilden. In Deutschland sowie auch im internationalen Umfeld ist zunehmend die Etablierung von Regionenmarken zu beobachten (vgl. Abbildung 1).

Abbildung 1: **Etablierung von Regionenmarken in Deutschland (ausgewählte Beispiele)**

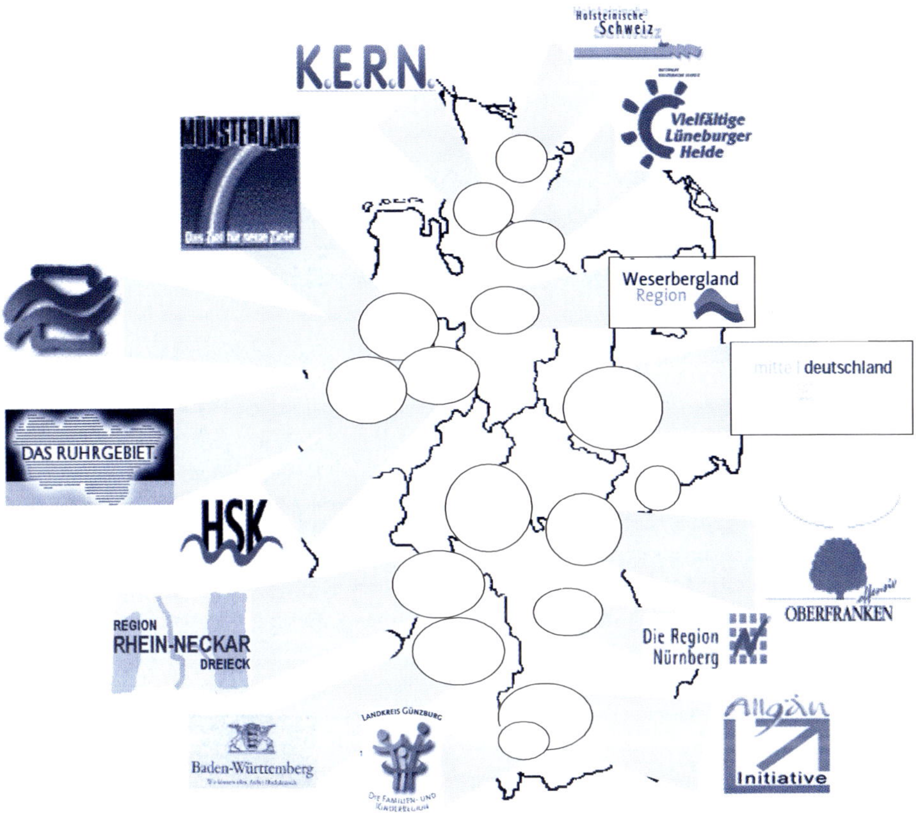

GABLER GRAFIK

Regionenmarken konkurrieren nicht nur untereinander um eine Vorzugsstellung in den Köpfen der Zielgruppe, sondern letztlich auch mit der gesamten „Markenflut", mit der die Bürger täglich konfrontiert werden. Neben den Marketingaktivitäten von Städten existieren in Deutschland bereits hunderte von Regionenlogos, die sich als Marke etablieren wollen. Aber nur profilierte Regionenmarken können als Leistungssurrogate und Identifikationsanker bei regionenbezogenen Entscheidungen (zum Beispiel Tourismus, Industrieansiedlungen, Tagungen, Wohnortwahl usw.) eine Identifikations- und Orientierungsfunktion für die jeweilige Zielgruppe erfüllen. Angesichts der sich abzeichnenden Markeninflation im Regionenwettbewerb erlangt deshalb die professionelle Markengestaltung und Markenführung auch in diesem Bereich zukünftig eine herausragende Bedeutung.

Wenngleich eine zunehmende Etablierung von Regionenmarken in der Praxis festzustellen ist, so wird diese Frage in der Literatur zum Regionenmarketing bisher kaum behandelt.[1] Dieser Sachverhalt verwundert zunächst, weil die Markentechnik seit Jahrzehnten als bedeutendes Marketinginstrument im Konsum-, Investitions- sowie Dienstleistungsmarketing gilt. Angesichts der Besonderheiten, die beim Aufbau von Regionenmarken zu berücksichtigen sind, erscheint eine tiefergehende Betrachtung des Markenphänomens in diesem Sektor jedoch angebracht.

Die Auseinandersetzung mit Regionenmarken erfordert zunächst die Präzisierung des Markenbegriffs. Im Marketing hat sich in den 80er Jahren die wirkungsbezogene Definition von Marken durchgesetzt. Betrachtet man die rechtliche Definition einer Marke nach dem Markengesetz, so kommt diese Sichtweise bereits zum Ausdruck. Hiernach können als Marken *„alle Zeichen, insbesondere Wörter einschließlich Personennamen, Abbildungen, Buchstaben, Zahlen, Hörzeichen, dreidimensionale Gestaltungen einschließlich der Form einer Ware oder ihrer Verpackung sowie sonstiger Aufmachungen geschützt werden, die geeignet sind, Waren oder Dienstleistungen eines Unternehmens von denjenigen anderer Unternehmen zu unterscheiden"* (Markengesetz § 3 (1); Berlit 2003, S. 269). Schließlich können Marken nur dann eine Identifikations- und Differenzierungsfunktion übernehmen, wenn sie diese Funktionen in den Köpfen der Nachfrager erfüllen.

Begrifflich ist zwischen regionalen Marken beziehungsweise Regionalmarken und Regionenmarken zu differenzieren (vgl. Tabelle 1). Hinsichtlich ihres Vermarktungsgebietes sind **Regionalmarken**, die vielfach auch als „Local Brands" bezeichnet werden, auf ein bestimmtes räumliches Gebiet begrenzt (Weinberg/Diehl 1999, S. 185 ff.; Meffert 2000, S. 874 f.; Geigenmüller 2001, S. 74 ff.). Regionalmarken werden gezielt auf die regionalen Bedürfnisse und Gewohnheiten der Zielgruppe ausgerichtet. Sie beziehen sich in der Regel auf Produkte wie auch Dienstleistungen, die nur in einer spezifischen Region angeboten und profiliert werden. Die konkrete Markenbezeichnung kann mit und ohne regionalen Bezug erfolgen, wobei in der Praxis zu beobachten ist, dass Regionalmarken (zum Beispiel Florena, Lammsbräu) keinen expliziten Hinweis auf das Absatzgebiet beinhalten (Berlit 2003, S. 65 ff.). Von der Markenstrategie können regionale Marken als Einzelmarken bis hin zu Dachmarken konzipiert werden. Anbieter starker Regionalmarken sehen häufig die Chance, durch eine Verbreiterung des Absatzgebietes Wachstumspotenziale zu erschließen. Eine Regionalmarke kann im Zeitablauf zu einer nationalen oder internationalen beziehungsweise globalen Marke entwickelt werden. Im Rahmen des Regionenmarketings stehen **Regionenmarken** hingegen für das gesamte Leistungsbündel (Infrastruktur, Wirtschaft, Kultur- und Bildungsangebote, Einwohner und andere) einer Region. Damit erlangen Regionenmarken immer den Charakter von Dachmarken, die ein komplexes Leistungsbündel einer Region repräsentieren. Vielfach wird der

---

1 Beispielsweise finden sich in aktuelleren Monographien keine Ausführungen zum Aufbau und zur Profilierung von Regionenmarken. Vgl. zum Beispiel Manschwetus, U., Regionalmarketing, a. a. O. oder Spieß, St., Marketing für Regionen, Wiesbaden 1998 sowie Wolfertz, K., Strategieentwicklung im kommunalen Standortmarketing, Göttingen 1999. Explizit findet die Markendiskussion bei Schmitz, H., Münsterland – Berge sind nicht unbedingt die Voraussetzung für Weitsicht, Münster 1999 statt.

Bezug zur Region bereits explizit in der Markenbezeichnung signalisiert. Die Funktionen von Regionenmarken sind sowohl auf die Zielgruppen innerhalb (zum Beispiel Bürger, Unternehmen, Meinungsbilder) wie auch außerhalb einer Region (zum Beispiel Investoren, Touristen, Arbeitskräfte, Politische Institutionen) ausgerichtet. Im Gegensatz zu traditionellen Regionalmarken werden Regionenmarken auch außerhalb der Region gegenüber internationalen Zielgruppen im Tourismus oder im Wirtschaftsbereich (Investoren) profiliert.

Tabelle 1: Abgrenzung von Regionalmarken und Regionenmarken

Kriterium	**Regionalmarken**	**Regionenmarken**
Markenobjekt	Produkte und/oder Dienstleistungen eines Anbieters bzw. einer Anbietergemeinschaft	Komplettes Leistungsbündel einer Region
Markenstrategische Ziele	Markenprofilierung für einzelne Produkte oder Dienstleistungen innerhalb der Region	Profilierung einer gesamten Region mit ausgewählten Leistungen, die gegenüber Wettbewerbsregionen einzigartig sind
Marktareal	Begrenzung des Absatzes auf ein regional begrenztes	Explizit nicht begrenzt
Zielgruppenbezug	Zielgruppen innerhalb eines regional begrenzten Marktareals	Zielgruppen innerhalb der Region (z. B. Bürger, Unternehmen, Medien) **und** außerhalb der Region (z. B. Investoren, Touristen, Arbeitskräfte)
Markenstrategie	Alle Formen der Markenstrategien möglich (Einzelmarken, Familienmarken, Dachmarken)	Dachmarkencharakter (zum Teil auch als Co-Branding)
Institutionelle Verankerung	In der Regel privatwirtschaftliche Anbieter bzw. Anbietergemeinschaften	In der Regel Kooperationsformen des Public Private Partnership
Beispiele	z. B. Biermarken wie Lammsbräu oder Marken wie Florena	Siehe Abbildung 1

GABLER GRAFIK

Da die für eine Region charakteristischen Merkmale und Leistungen für die relevanten Zielgruppen überwiegend standortgebunden sind und als Leistungspotenziale den Nachfragern bereit gestellt werden, ist das Regionenmarketing in hohem Maße als Dienstleistungsmarketing zu begreifen. Damit gestaltet sich die Markenführung im Rahmen eines Regionenmarketings sehr komplex. Deshalb erfordert der Aufbau einer Regionenmarke eine intensive Auseinandersetzung mit den Stärken und Schwächen einer Region, mit der Kennzeichnung des besonderen Charakters und ihrer einzigartigen Merkmale, die für die Bewohner innerhalb der Region sowie gegenüber den Zielgruppen außerhalb der Region wichtig, erfahrbar beziehungsweise kommunizierbar sind. Angesichts des zunehmenden Regionenwettbewerbs ist auf die Herausarbeitung der Einzigartigkeit regionaler Merkmale und deren Zielgruppenrelevanz besonderer Wert zu legen. Nur einzigartige Assoziationen haben die Chance, eine Marke in den Köpfen der Zielgruppe gegenüber Konkurrenzregionen abzugrenzen und zu profilieren.

Im Gegensatz zum klassischen Sachgüter- und Dienstleistungsmarketing von Unternehmen wird der Aufbau einer **Markenidentität** für eine Region einerseits durch das komplexe und zum Teil nur mittel- und langfristig gestaltbare Leistungsbündel und andererseits durch die Vielzahl unabhängiger Akteure, die das Leistungsprofil mitgestalten, erheblich erschwert. Als Markenidentität können diejenigen raum-zeitlich gleichartigen Merkmale einer Marke verstanden werden, die aus Sicht der internen Zielgruppen in nachhaltiger Weise den Charakter einer Marke prägen (Burmann/Blinda/Nitschke 2003, S. 5). Das Problem des Aufbaus der Identität für eine Regionenmarke liegt darin begründet, dass vielfach kein homogenes Leistungsbündel innerhalb einer Region vorliegt beziehungsweise aufgrund der Vielzahl der beteiligten Akteure eine gezielte Gestaltung des Leistungsspektrums besonders schwierig ist (Scheuch 2003, S. 46 f.). Zum Aufbau einer Identität für eine Regionenmarke ist es weiterhin notwendig, dass die Marke eine räumliche Ortung des Leistungsbündels fördert beziehungsweise eine exakte räumliche Abgrenzung der Region ermöglicht und ein wahrnehmbares und unterscheidbares Leistungsprofil gegenüber der Zielgruppe zum Ausdruck bringt. Erfolgreiche Regionenmarken zeichnen sich damit durch eine Synthese von inhaltlicher beziehungsweise leistungsbezogener und räumlicher Identität aus. Im Hinblick auf die Profilbildung kann die Herausbildung **regionaler Clusterstrukturen** dazu beitragen, gegenüber der Darstellung von fragmentierten Aktivitäten einzelner Akteure die Leistungsfähigkeit von regionalen Netzwerken zu dokumentieren (zum Clusterkonzept insbesondere Porter 1990), die wiederum durch ihre regionale Zusammenarbeit spezifische Agglomerationsvorteile (Transaktionskostensenkung, Umsatzvorteile, Informationsvorteile, Imagevorteile) erzielen können (Kirchgeorg/ Fiedler 2004). Die Agglomerationsvorteile können gegenüber anderen Regionen wiederum einzigartige Standortvorteile für die Ansiedlung neuer Unternehmen liefern. Die erfolgreiche Entwicklung regionaler Clusterstrukturen unterstützt somit die Prägnanz eines Leistungs- und Markenprofils einer Region.

Als weitere Besonderheit ist hervorzuheben, dass der Entscheidungsspielraum bei der Wahl der **Markenstrategie** sehr begrenzt ist, weil Regionenmarken ausschließlich als Dachmarken und kaum als Einzel- oder Mehrmarken konzipiert werden können. Damit sind die in der Literatur diskutierten Vorteile (zum Beispiel Synergienutzung, Goodwilltransfer) wie auch Nachteile (zum Beispiel Problem der Leistungsdifferenzierung, Badwilltransfer) einer Dachmarkenstrategie unweigerlich mit dem Aufbau von Regionenmarken verbunden. Da die in der Region ansässigen Unternehmen und Institutionen in der Regel eigene Marken für ihre Leistungen verwenden, sollten Regionenmarken für ein **Co-Branding** geeignet sein. Beispiele für den gemeinsamen Auftritt von Unternehmens- und Regionenmarke lassen sich vielfältig beobachten. Bei einer Akquisitionskampagne für qualifizierte Arbeitskräfte außerhalb einer Zielregion kann ein Co-Branding von Unternehmensmarke und Regionenmarke sowohl zur Identifikation der spezifischen Unternehmensleistung als auch der Leistung einer Region eingesetzt werden. Bei Marken im Konsum- und Dienstleistungsmarketing stellt der Zusatz „Made in Germany" beispielsweise auf die synergetische Nutzung von positiven Imagetransfereffekten einer Nation auf das Produkt- bzw. Unternehmensimage ab. Die Verwendung profilierter Regionenmarken als Herkunftsbezeichnung kann für Unternehmen der Region in gleicher Weise zu Imagetransfereffekten führen.

In zunehmendem Maße ist zu beobachten, dass fragmentierte Marketingaktivitäten von Teilregionen gebündelt werden und somit in Form von Co-Branding-Strategien (gemeinsamer Markenauftritt der kooperierenden Teilregionen) oder durch die Etablierung einer übergeordneten Dachmarke ein Profil für die gesamte Region geschaffen werden soll (Schnurrenberger 2000, S. 247 f.). In diesem Zusammenhang sind dann die Probleme der Gestaltung einer **regionalen Markenarchitektur** zu berücksichtigen, durch die der markenstrategische Auftritt der Teilregionen und der Gesamtregion zu definieren ist. Folgende grundlegenden Varianten der Markenarchitektur lassen sich in diesem Zusammenhang unterscheiden:

1. Dachmarke für die Gesamtregion („Branded Region"),
2. Co-Branding mit dominanter regionaler Dachmarke und gemeinsamer Auftritt mit den Marken der Teilregion,
3. Co-Branding mit dominanter Marke der Teilregion und Verwendung der Dachmarke zur Unterstützung (zum Beispiel Marke der Bundesländer wird mit Marken der Region innerhalb des Bundeslandes verwendet),
4. Unabhängiger Auftritt von Teilregionen mit eigenen Marken („Region of Brands").

Im Falle einer Region of Brands werden zwischen den Teilregionen keinerlei Synergien und Imagetransfereffekte erzielt, sodass jede Teilregion die Kosten der Markenprofilierung zu tragen hat. Insbesondere im Hinblick auf die internationale Profilierung von Regionen wird eine Strategie der „Region of Brands" vielfach ihre Grenzen zeigen.

Schließlich ist bereits auf die Vielzahl der im Regionenmarketing eingebundenen Akteure hingewiesen worden. Die Akteure prägen durch ihre Aktivitäten nach innen und außen die Leistungen und das Erscheinungsbild sowie den Charakter einer Region. Die **institutionelle Verankerung** des Regionenmarketings erfordert deshalb eine Einbindung der relevanten Leistungserbringer aus Politik, Wirtschaft, Gesellschaft und Wissenschaft. Hierzu stehen so genannte Public-Private-Partnership-Modelle zur Verfügung, in denen öffentliche und privatwirtschaftliche Entscheidungsträger gemeinsam Ziele, Strategien und Maßnahmen des Regionenmarketings festlegen. Trotz entsprechender Organisationskonzepte erweist sich der Aufbau und die kontinuierliche Führung von Regionenmarken als besondere Herausforderung.

1.3 Gestaltung von Marken für Regionen

Die konkrete Markengestaltung ist mit dem Einsatz von geeigneten **Markierungselementen** verbunden. Zu den am häufigsten verwendeten Markierungselementen von Produkten und Unternehmen zählen der Markenname und das Markenlogo. Grundsätzlich wird zwischen Bildlogos und Schriftlogos unterschieden (Esch/Langner 1999, S. 467 f.; Konken 2000, S. 327 ff.). Gegenüber einem Schriftlogo kommt dem Bildlogo die Aufgabe zu, visuelle Reize zu vermitteln, die schneller als verbale Reize im Gedächtnis abge-

Abbildung 3: Beispiele zur Markengestaltung ausgewählter Regionen

Region	Markenelemente	Inhalte
Baden-Württemberg	Markenoptik	Baden-Württemberg
	Art der Marke Slogan	Wort-Bild-Marke Wir können alles. Außer Hochdeutsch
Ruhrgebiet	Markenoptik	DAS RUHRGEBIET. ...mehr als eine Stadt.
	Art der Marke Slogan	Wort-Bild-Marke „... mehr als eine Stadt“
Mitteldeutschland	Markenoptik	mitte | deutschland
	Art der Marke Slogan	Wort-Marke „Hier geht was“
Münsterland	Markenoptik	MÜNSTERLAND® Das Ziel für neue Ziele
	Art der Marke Slogan	Wort-Bild-Marke „Das Ziel für neue Ziele“

GABLER GRAFIK

speichert werden können. Im Rahmen des Marketings wird deshalb bei der visuellen Markengestaltung vielfach eine Kombination aus Bild- und Schriftlogo gewählt und als Marke etabliert (vgl. Abbildung 3). Diese Form der Markengestaltung findet auch im Regionenmarketing häufig Anwendung. Als Zusatz zur Marke vermittelt ein Slogan in Kurzform eine Kernbotschaft, die der Zielgruppe die regionale Besonderheit bzw. Einzigartigkeit vermitteln soll. Im Gegensatz zur Marke, kann der Slogan im Zeitablauf häufiger auf neue Kernbotschaften ausgerichtet werden.

Der **Prozess der Namensgebung** für eine Region wird häufig nicht bewusst geplant und durchgeführt, womit ein erster wichtiger Schritt der Markenbildung vernachlässigt wird. Dies liegt darin begründet, dass Regionen häufig mit einem historisch gewachsenen Begriff belegt werden. Sie sind den Anwohnern einer Region in der Regel bekannt und sie werden mit gewissen räumlichen Vorstellungen verbunden. Inwieweit diese Regionennamen jedoch auch bei außenstehenden Zielgruppen im In- und Ausland eine Markenfunktion übernehmen können, wird häufig nicht explizit analysiert. Abbildung 4 zeigt anhand einer empirischen Untersuchung, welche Anforderungskriterien im Sachgütermarketing bei der Namensgebung für Marken besondere Berücksichtigung finden.

Abbildung 4: Kriterien zur Bewertung von Markennamen

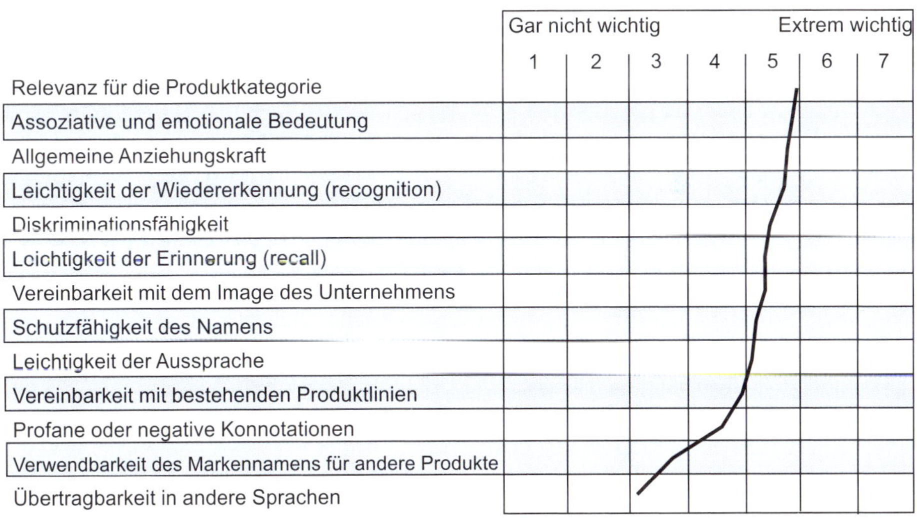

GABLER GRAFIK

Quelle: Kohli/LaBahn/Thakor 1999, S. 435

Nach den Ergebnissen wird die Eignung von Markennamen in der Unternehmenspraxis insbesondere anhand von folgenden Kriterien beurteilt (Kohle/LaBahn/Thakor 1999, S. 435 ff.):

- ihrer Relevanz für die Produktkategorien,
- ihrer assoziativen und emotionalen Bedeutung,
- ihrer allgemeinen Anziehungskraft,
- ihrer Einprägsamkeit,
- ihrer Differenzierungsfähigkeit,
- ihrer Vereinbarkeit mit dem Image des Unternehmens und
- ihrer rechtlichen Schutzfähigkeit.

Das erste Kriterium bezieht sich auf die grundsätzliche Vereinbarkeit eines Namens mit den generellen Eigenschaften einer Produktkategorie. Im Zusammenhang mit dem Regionenmarketing wäre die grundsätzliche Eignung eines Namens zur Kennzeichnung eines räumlichen Gebietes zu prüfen. Im Weiteren sind es Kriterien, die die Identifikations-, Orientierungs- und Imagefunktion von Marken betreffen und die nur durch Einbeziehung beziehungsweise Befragung der für das Regionenmarketing relevanten Zielgruppen erfasst werden können. Als Besonderheit für Regionenmarken ist hinsichtlich ihrer Differenzierungsfähigkeit insbesondere die gegenüber anderen Regionen zu erzielende räumliche Abgrenzung zu beachten, das heißt, eine Region sollte durch die Markierung einerseits eine geografische „Ortung" bei der Zielgruppe ermöglichen und andererseits bestimmte inhaltliche Charakteristika über die Region vermitteln. Überträgt man das Kriterium „Vereinbarkeit mit dem Image des Unternehmens", so kann für Regionenmarken hierunter die Kompatibilität mit dem mit der Region verbundenen Selbst- und Fremdimage verstanden werden. Bevor die Ansätze des Regionenmarketings entwickelt wurden, haben bestimmte Regionen bereits ein Selbst- und Fremdimage erlangt (zum Beispiel das Ruhrgebiet, Franken und andere). Wird angesichts des zunehmenden Regionenwettbewerbs über den professionellen Aufbau einer Regionenmarke in diesen Regionen nachgedacht, dann muss bei der Auswahl der Markennamen das im Zeitablauf bereits entstandene Image einer Region berücksichtigt werden.

Die Ausführungen verdeutlichen, dass bei der Auswahl und dem Aufbau einer geeigneten Marke im Regionenmarketing eine Reihe markentechnischer Anforderungen zu berücksichtigen sind. Wenngleich das Regionenmarketing ein vergleichsweise junges Feld der Marketingdisziplin ist, so sollten die in anderen sektoralen Marketingbereichen gewonnenen Erkenntnisse auch im Regionenmarketing unter Berücksichtigung der jeweiligen Besonderheiten verstärkt Anwendung finden. In Kapitel zwei wird anhand eines Fallbeispiels und empirischer Analysen verdeutlicht, welche Informationsgrundlagen Hilfestellungen bei der Auswahl von Markennamen und der Markengestaltung für eine Regionen liefern können.

1.4 Erfassung von Einstellungen gegenüber Regionen und Regionenmarken

Inwieweit bestehende Regionenmarken oder auszuwählende Regionennamen ihre markenspezifischen Funktionen erfüllen und eine Vorzugsstellung in den Köpfen der Zielgruppe erlangen, kann mit Hilfe von Zielgruppenbefragungen analysiert werden. Hierbei wird weitgehend auf die Erkenntnisse der Einstellungs- und Identitätsforschung sowie auf Positionierungsanalysen zurückgegriffen, wobei die zu betrachtenden Regionen den Einstellungsgegenstand bilden. Generell wird in der Diskussion regionaler Fragestellungen der Regionenbegriff im Sprachgebrauch häufig als „Akteur“ verwendet: eine Region wandelt sich, sie positioniert sich, Regionen wachsen etc. Dabei sind Regionen nicht von Natur aus als Einstellungsobjekt vorhanden, sondern entstehen erst als Ergebnis menschlicher Auseinandersetzung mit einem räumlich begrenzten Gebiet (Wollersheim 1999, S. 7).

Räumliche Identität als Spezialfall der sozialwissenschaftlichen Identitätsforschung beinhaltet nach Werthmöller zwei Perspektiven: die Sicht einer Person und die Sicht auf einen Raum (Werthmöller 1995, S. 47 ff.). Die personenbezogene Perspektive sieht Identität als Verbundenheit von Personen mit einer Region. Dieses Gefühl der Zugehörigkeit kommt dadurch zustande, dass Personen die mit einer Region assoziierten Merkmale als Bestandteil ihrer persönlichen Identität, ihrer Gruppenidentität oder einer sozialen Identität wahrnehmen.[2] In der Perspektive des Raumes versteht sich Identität hingegen als Individualisierung sowie Beschreibung eines Raumes auf der Basis von Merkmalen. Dies bedeutet auf der persönlichen Ebene, dass eine Region trotz der beschriebenen methodischen Unzulässigkeit als eigenständiges „Objekt“ betrachtet wird; auf der sozialen Ebene werden einer Region Eigenschaften in Form von Images zugeschrieben. Da die Operationalisierung der persönlichen Ebene eng mit der sozialen Ebene verknüpft ist,[3] werden nachfolgend beide Ebenen der räumlichen Perspektive als Beschreibung von Regionen anhand von Merkmalen (Images) zusammengefasst.

In den weiteren Betrachtungen zur räumlichen Identifikation[4] soll die Perspektive des Raumes um eine zusätzliche Ebene ergänzt werden. Räumliche Identifikation kann gleichzeitig bedeuten, dass Personen eine Region geografisch abgrenzen. Grundlegend ist bei diesem Ansatz das Wissen einer Person um die konkreten geografischen Ausmaße

2 Im Zusammenhang mit der Verbundenheit von Personen mit einer Region wird häufig der Heimatbegriff diskutiert. Durch die engere Interpretation von „Heimat“ soll jedoch in den folgenden Ausführungen weiterhin die Verbundenheit Basis der Betrachtungen sein. Vgl. ebenda, S. 57 ff.

3 Die Betrachtung einer Region als „Objekt“ bedingt, dass dieses Objekt über Merkmale charakterisiert werden muss.

4 Der Begriff der Identität vermittelt stärker den statischen Charakter dieses Konstruktes. Demgegenüber verdeutlicht Identifikation die Dynamik eines Prozesses. Aufgrund dieser Überlegungen soll im Folgenden von Identifikation anstelle Identität gesprochen werden. Vgl. Wollersheim, H.-W., Die Identifikationsjäger, a. a. O., S. 8.

einer Region.[5] Neben der Zuordnung von Merkmalen zu einem Raum und seiner Personifizierung als Individuum ist es für die Beurteilung von Regionen von hoher Bedeutung, dass Personen möglichst präzise die Grenzen einer Region bestimmen können. Der Fall einer diffusen räumlichen Abgrenzung führt ansonsten dazu, dass die Individualität der Region verloren geht und sich dies in einem wenig prägnanten Image widerspiegelt. Dies impliziert darüber hinaus die Gefahr einer Verringerung der persönlichen Verbundenheit mit der Region.

Die aufgezeigten Ebenen räumlicher Identifikation (Identifikation mit einer Region, Beschreibung einer Region über Merkmale, räumliche Abgrenzung der Region) verdeutlichen, dass die Analyse von Einstellungen gegenüber einer Region ein breites Band verschiedener Denkansätze miteinander verbinden sollte. Dies gelingt mit Hilfe der sogenannten *„geografischen Regionalbewusstseinsforschung"*, die von Blotevogel, Heinritz und Popp initiiert wurde (Briesen 1993, S. 769; Werthmöller 1995, S. 60). Der Begriff des **Regionalbewusstseins** beschreibt die raumbezogene Einstellung von Individuen oder Gruppen,[6] wobei unter Einstellung als Kernbegriff der Verhaltensforschung der *„Zustand einer gelernten und relativ dauerhaften Bereitschaft, in einer entsprechenden Situation gegenüber dem betreffenden Objekt regelmäßig mehr oder weniger stark positiv beziehungsweise negativ zu reagieren"* (Trommsdorff 1993, S. 139) zu verstehen ist.

Wie in der Dreikomponententheorie der Verhaltensforschung angewandt, kann auch die raumbezogene Einstellung in drei Dimensionen gegliedert werden: kognitiv, affektiv und konativ (beziehungsweise intentional). Die kognitive (das heißt wissensbasierte) Dimension fasst die generelle Wahrnehmung der Region zusammen. Die affektive (beziehungsweise gefühlsbasierte) Komponente beschreibt die Verbundenheit mit einer Region (Balderjahn 2000, S. 87 ff.). Durch die konative (beziehungsweise handlungsbezogene) Dimension werden regionale Handlungen ausgedrückt. Die drei Ausprägungen Wahrnehmung, Verbundenheit und Handlung verdeutlichen verschiedene Intensitätsstufen des Regionalbewusstseins. So sind die Wahrnehmungen bzgl. einer Region Voraussetzung dafür, dass Personen ein Gefühl der Verbundenheit aufbauen können. Ohne Verbundenheit wiederum werden Personen sich nicht langfristig durch Handlungen für eine Region engagieren. Andererseits muss zur Wahrnehmung von Regionen keinerlei gefühlsmäßige Bindung zum Raum aufgebaut werden, wie auch die regionale Bindung nicht zwingend eine Umsetzung in Aktivitäten für die Region nach sich zieht (vgl. Abbildung 5).

5 Grenzen stecken allerdings nicht nur faktisch den Raum für die Identitätsbildung ab, sondern sind selbst Teilaspekte dieses Prozesses. Vgl. Gans, R., Regionalbewusstsein und regionale Identität, in: Regionalgeschichte: ein Ansatz zur Erforschung regionaler Identität, Informationen zur Raumentwicklung, Nr. 11, 1993, S. 786.

6 Vgl. hierzu und zu den Ausführungen bzgl. der Komponenten des Regionalbewusstseins Blotevogel, H. H., Heinritz, G., Popp, H., „Regionalbewusstsein". Zum Stand der Diskussion um einen Stein des Anstoßes, in: Geografische Zeitschrift, H. 2, 1987, S. 65ff. zit. nach Werthmöller, E., Räumliche Identität als Aufgabenfeld des Städte- und Regionenmarketing, a. a. O., S. 63 ff.

Abbildung 5: Intensitätsstufen des Regionalbewusstseins

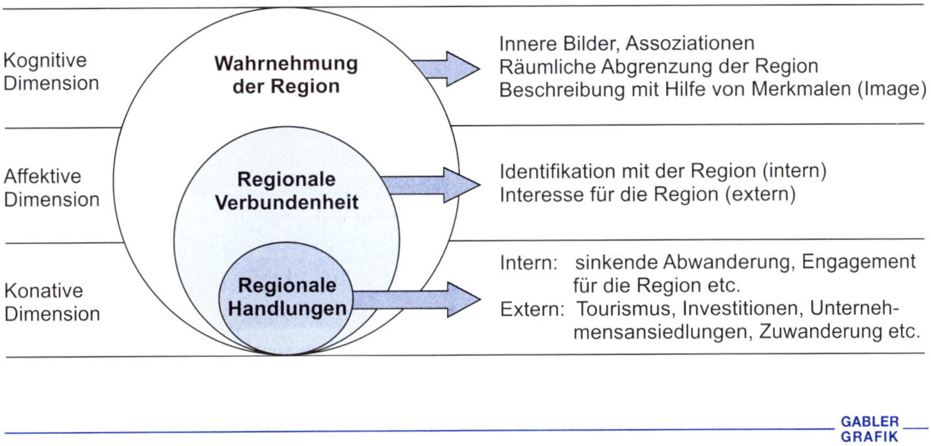

Quelle: in Anlehnung an Blotevogel/Heinritz/Popp 1987, S. 415

Die **Operationalisierung** der verschiedenen Dimensionen des Regionalbewusstseins setzt an den bereits beschriebenen Ebenen der räumlichen Identifikation an. Die Wahrnehmung einer Region kann über ihre Beschreibung mit Hilfe von Merkmalen ermittelt werden. Wichtig für die Wahrnehmung ist ebenso die geografische beziehungsweise räumliche Abgrenzung der Region. Darüber hinaus kann die Wahrnehmung über die Verdeutlichung innerer Bilder, zum Beispiel mittels Spontanassoziationen beurteilt werden. Die regionale Verbundenheit ist über den Grad der Identifikation beziehungsweise die emotionale Verbundenheit von Personen ermittelbar. Im Hinblick auf unterschiedliche Identitätsträger (Innen- und Außenperspektive beziehungsweise Selbst- und Fremdeinschätzung) lässt sich hierbei einerseits zwischen der Identifikation von Bewohnern einer Region und andererseits der Identifikation durch Personen, die außerhalb der Region angesiedelt sind, differenzieren. Diese Unterscheidung kommt insbesondere in unterschiedlichen Handlungsalternativen zum Tragen. Während Bewohner durch die Verringerung ihrer Abwanderung in andere Regionen regional handeln, verdeutlichen regionenexterne Personen mit der Zuwanderung ihre Verbundenheit. Der Einsatz für eine Region kann intern über das Engagement in regionalen Verbänden oder Aktionen zum Ausdruck kommen. Auswärtige fördern beispielsweise mittels Tourismus oder ihrem Investitionsverhalten eine Region.

2. Empirische Analyse von Markennamen für Regionen

2.1 Markenbildung für die Region „Mitteldeutschland"

Die bisherigen Ausführungen verdeutlichen, dass die Gestaltung und der Aufbau von Regionenmarken von besonderer Bedeutung für das Regionenmarketing sind. Anhand des Beispiels der Region Mitteldeutschland sollen im Folgenden ausgewählte Informationsgrundlagen, die zur Markenentwicklung erstellt wurden, dargestellt werden. Die Regionen in den neuen Bundesländern standen in den 90er Jahren im Vergleich zu den Regionen in den sogenannten alten Bundesländern vor besonderen Herausforderungen. Nach der Wiedervereinigung konnten sich die Regionen in Ostdeutschland aufgrund von Infrastrukturnachteilen oft nicht in offensiver Weise am Regionenwettbewerb beteiligen. Durch erhebliche Investitionen in den Aufbau und die Erneuerung der regionalen Infrastruktur haben die neuen Bundesländer ihre Ausgangsposition im internationalen Wettbewerb der Regionen um Investoren, Arbeitskräfte und Touristen wesentlich verbessert. Somit gewinnt ein offensives Regionenmarketing und die Profilierung von Regionenmarken für die neuen Bundesländer immer mehr an Bedeutung.

Die Region „Mitteldeutschland“ mit den Städten Leipzig, Halle und Dessau stellt einen historisch gewachsenen Wirtschafts- und Kulturraum dar, für den bereits Anfang der 90er Jahre erste Regionenmarketingaktivitäten entwickelt wurden. Im Jahre 2000 ist eine Bündelung und Zusammenführung der Regionenmarketingaktivitäten für Mitteldeutschland durch einen länderübergreifenden Schulterschluss zwischen Wirtschaft, Verwaltung und Politik initiiert worden. Angesichts der konzeptionellen und institutionellen Neuausrichtung des Regionenmarketings wurde der Entwicklung einer prägnanten Regionenmarke eine besondere Beachtung geschenkt. Insbesondere stellte sich die Frage, inwieweit der traditionelle Regionenname „Mitteldeutschland“ als Markenname Verwendung finden sollte. Einerseits ergaben sich Bedenken, dass der Name Mitteldeutschland zu sehr mit negativen Assoziationen wie Ost-Zone und ehemalige DDR bei Bürgern außerhalb der Region in Verbindung gebracht wird. Andererseits bestanden Zweifel darüber, ob mit dem Begriff „Mitteldeutschland“ auch tatsächlich die räumlich abgegrenzte Zielregion des Regionenmarketings verbunden wird. Gegebenenfalls könnte Mitteldeutschland für Zielgruppen außerhalb der Region auch als „Mitte von Deutschland“ räumlich abgegrenzt werden, sodass der Aufbau einer räumlichen Identität erschwert wird (Kirchgeorg/Kreller 2000).

Durch eine repräsentative Befragung von 2.139 Bundesbürgern innerhalb und außerhalb der Zielregion konnten Informationsgrundlagen zur Beantwortung der folgenden markenrelevanten Fragen generiert werden:

- Welche Assoziationen werden spontan mit dem Begriff „Mitteldeutschland“ verbunden und inwieweit geben sie Hinweise auf eine eher negative oder positive Belegung des Regionenbegriffs?

- Wie hoch ist der Bekanntheitsgrad von Aktivitäten der Region „Mitteldeutschland“?
- Welche räumliche Vorstellung (Identität) haben die Bundesbürger von der Region „Mitteldeutschland“?
- Welche Einstellungen haben die Bundesbürger gegenüber der Region „Mitteldeutschland“ im Vergleich zum Ruhrgebiet?

Diese Konstrukte wurden sowohl für die Zielregion „Mitteldeutschland“ als auch für die Referenzregion „Ruhrgebiet“ erhoben. Die Einbeziehung einer Referenzregion sollte als Benchmark darüber Auskunft geben, wie ein Regionenbegriff, der im Rahmen des Regionenmarketings des Ruhrgebietes[7] bisher bundesweite Verwendung findet, hinsichtlich der Markenstärke zu beurteilen ist.

Bei der Analyse der Ergebnisse wurde zwischen dem Selbstimage und Fremdimage der befragten Bundesbürger unterschieden. Beim Selbstimage (Innensicht) beziehen sich die Ergebnisse auf alle Befragten, die innerhalb der Region Mitteldeutschland beziehungsweise dem Ruhrgebiet wohnen. Hingegen sind beim Fremdimage die Befragungsergebnisse nur auf diejenigen Befragten bezogen worden, die außerhalb der jeweiligen Region wohnen.

2.2 Analyse der Assoziationen zum Regionennamen „Mitteldeutschland“

Die erste Frage zielte auf die Erfassung der spontanen Assoziationen der Befragten zum Begriff „Mitteldeutschland“ ab. Im **Gesamtdurchschnitt** verteilten sich die Antworten auf folgende Assoziationskategorien (vgl. Abbildung 6):

- Keine Assoziation beziehungsweise Begriff unbekannt 22 Prozent
- Räumliche Assoziation 58 Prozent
- Gefühlsbasierte Assoziation (positiv oder negativ) 15 Prozent
- Sonstige Assoziation 4 Prozent

Der Begriff „Mitteldeutschland“ wird von 22 Prozent der Bundesbürger mit keinerlei Inhalten verbunden und als unbekannt eingestuft. Hinsichtlich der inhaltlichen Nennungen wurden am häufigsten räumliche Assoziationen genannt, wobei die Assoziation „ehemalige DDR“ (13,4 Prozent) am stärksten vertreten war. 9,7 Prozent der Befragten nannten die Region „Sachsen“ (5,4 Prozent) oder „Sachsen-Anhalt“ (4,3 Prozent). Weitere Nen-

7 Vgl. zum Regionenmarketing des Ruhrgebietes zum Beispiel die Aktivitäten des Kommunalverbandes Ruhrgebiet, im Internet unter Adresse: http://www.ruhrgebiet.de Stand vom 21.9.2000 oder die Ausführungen bei Kunzmann, K. R., Nordrhein-Westfalen in Europa: eine Standorteinschätzung, in: Brunn, G. (Hrsg.), Neoliberalismus, die Entstehung des Maastrichter Vertrags und die Auswirkungen der Währungsunion auf Nordrhein-Westfalen, Schriftenreihe des Instituts für Europäische Regionalforschung, Band 4, Baden-Baden 1999, S. 137–151.

nungen, die zusammengefasst von 35,1 Prozent der Befragten erfolgten, bezogen sich auf Bundesländer oder Städte, die nicht dem Zielgebiet entsprechen. Vielmehr deuten diese Antworten eher auf ein diffuses Begriffsverständnis hin, das mit der räumlichen „Mitte von Deutschland" in Verbindung gebracht wird. Immerhin wird mit Mitteldeutschland in diesem Zusammenhang generell „Mitte" (6,1 Prozent), Hessen (6,1 Prozent), Thüringen (5,5 Prozent) und sogar Nordrhein-Westfalen (4,4 Prozent) oder Niedersachsen (2,0 Prozent) assoziiert.

Neben den räumlichen Assoziationen wurden bei den Spontannennungen von 12,3 Prozent Begriffe genannt, die mit positiven Attributen (schöne Gegend, Urlaub, Heimat) verbunden werden können. Direkte negative Spontanassoziationen konnten nur bei 2,9 Prozent der Bürger ermittelt werden. Unter den 4 Prozent der sonstigen Assoziationen wurden wertfreie Begriffe aus Wirtschaft und Politik sowie zum Mitteldeutschen Rundfunk (MDR) zusammengefasst. Obwohl der MDR über seine Programme bundesweit präsent ist und eine hohe begriffliche Nähe zum Regionennamen „Mitteldeutschland" aufweist, wird er nur von 1,9 Prozent der Befragten als spontane Assoziation genannt.

Abbildung 6: Kategoriale Aggregation der Spontanassoziationen

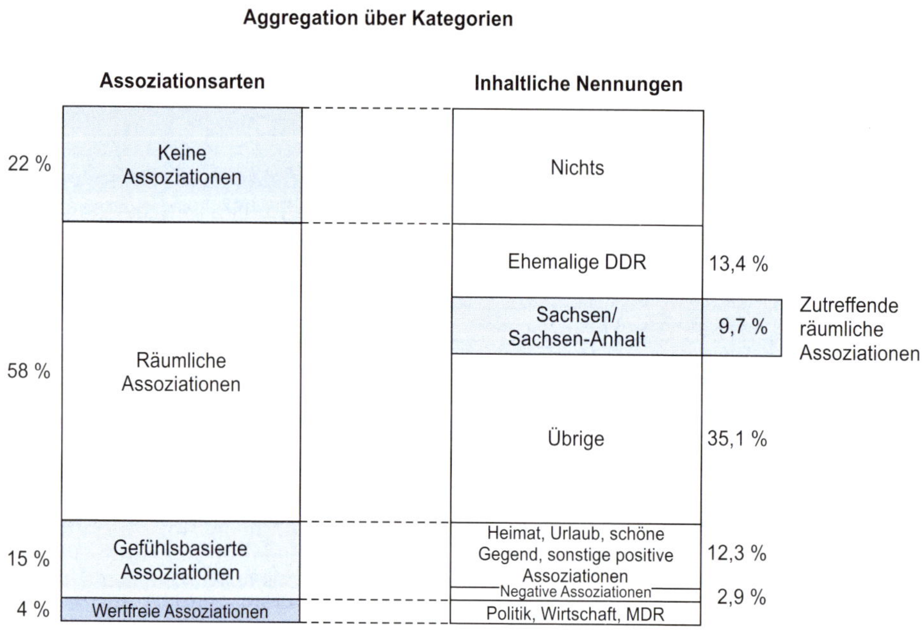

GABLER GRAFIK

2.3 Bekanntheitsgrad von Aktivitäten der Region „Mitteldeutschland"

Bei der Frage, ob den Bundesbürgern die Region „Mitteldeutschland" durch Werbung oder andere Regionenaktivitäten bekannt ist, wurde als Referenzregion das „Ruhrgebiet" mit einbezogen.

In der **Gesamtbeurteilung** haben 19,3 Prozent der Bundesbürger von Aktivitäten der Region „Mitteldeutschland" gehört, während der gestützte Bekanntheitsgrad von Aktivitäten des Ruhrgebiets bei 69,2 Prozent liegt.

Vergleicht man die Ergebnisse nach dem **Selbst- und Fremdimage**, so sind Aktivitäten der Region „Mitteldeutschland" nur bei 28,3 Prozent der Einwohner aus der Region bekannt, während nur 18,2 Prozent der Bürger, die außerhalb dieser Region wohnen, Regionenaktivitäten kennen. Im Vergleich zu den Ergebnissen des Ruhrgebietes wird deutlich, dass diese Region bundesweit in der Fremdeinschätzung bei 67,5 Prozent der Bundesbürger, die nicht im Ruhrgebiet wohnen und bei 75,4 Prozent der Bewohner des Landes Nordrhein-Westfalen einen hohen Bekanntheitsgrad durch die bisherigen Regionenmarketingaktivitäten erzielt.

Im Vergleich zum Ruhrgebiet ist die Region Mitteldeutschland durch Werbung und andere Aktivitäten bei Bürgern, die sowohl innerhalb als auch außerhalb von Mitteldeutschland wohnen, in weitaus geringerem Umfang bekannt.

2.4 Räumliche Identifikation der Region „Mitteldeutschland"

Während bei der Frage der Spontanassoziationen zunächst nur Nennungen zum Begriff „Mitteldeutschland" erfasst wurden, so sind die Bundesbürger im Weiteren danach befragt worden, welche Städte ihrer Auffassung nach zu einer Region „Mitteldeutschland" gehören. Hierzu wurden den Befragten zehn Städte vorgelesen, die sie der Region Mitteldeutschland zuordnen oder nicht zuordnen konnten. Von den vorgegebenen Städten liegen drei direkt in der Zielregion (Halle, Leipzig, Dessau), die weiteren genannten Städte liegen in den neuen (Magdeburg, Jena, Dresden, Berlin) wie auch alten Bundesländern (Kassel, Hannover, Frankfurt am Main). Da die Vermutung nahe lag, dass die Bürger mit Mitteldeutschland gegebenenfalls auch die „Mitte von Deutschland" verbinden, wurden Städte ausgewählt, die dieser geografischen Zuordnung am ehesten entsprechen würden.

Die Ermittlung der räumlichen Identifikation der Region „Mitteldeutschland" kann in einem ersten Schritt danach erfolgen, wie häufig die innerhalb und außerhalb der Region liegenden Städte der Zielregion „Mitteldeutschland" zugeordnet wurden. Werden Städte, die nicht der Zielregion angehören, auch in hohem Maße als „zugehörig" eingestuft, dann ist von einer geringen beziehungsweise diffusen räumlichen Identität auszugehen. In einem zweiten Schritt kann noch detaillierter ermittelt werden, welche Städtekombinationen die Befragten der Region „Mitteldeutschland" zuordnen. Durch diese Auswertung kann ein valideres Bild über die wahrgenommene räumliche Abgrenzung der Zielregion gewonnen werden.

Betrachtet man zunächst die Zuordnung einzelner Städte zu Mitteldeutschland anhand der absoluten Häufigkeiten, so zeigt sich auf den ersten Blick, dass die Region Mitteldeutschland von bis zu 60 Prozent der Befragten mit Städten in Verbindung gebracht wird, die nicht in der Zielregion liegen. Dies ist ein erster Indikator für eine diffuse räumliche Identität von Mitteldeutschland. Gemäß der Zuordnungshäufigkeiten im **Gesamtdurchschnitt** aller Befragten zeigt sich folgendes räumliches Profil (vgl. Abbildung 7). Den höchsten Anteil an Zustimmungen zur Zugehörigkeit zu Mitteldeutschland weist Halle (65,1 Prozent) gefolgt von Leipzig (64,1 Prozent) auf. Allerdings sind fast ebenso viele Befragte der Meinung, dass Jena zur Region Mitteldeutschland gehört. Weniger deutlich fällt dagegen die Zuordnung von Dessau aus, bei der sich über 15 Prozent der Befragten über die räumliche Identifikation der Stadt nicht sicher waren.

Abbildung 7: Gesamtnennungen der Städtezuordnungen zur räumlichen Identifikation der Region Mitteldeutschland in Prozent

Frage: „Wenn Sie an die Region Mitteldeutschland denken, welche der folgenden Städte gehören Ihrer Meinung nach zu dieser Region?"

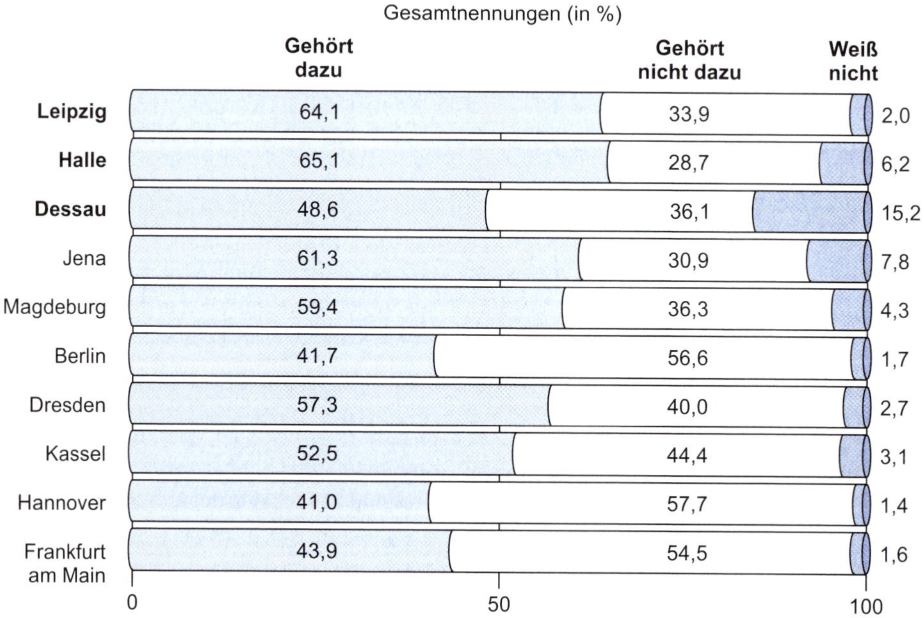

GABLER GRAFIK

Abbildung 8 verdeutlicht grafisch die ermittelte räumliche Identität von Mitteldeutschland aus Sicht der Befragten. Im Rahmen der Auswertung anhand der gewählten Städtekombinationen verbindet nahezu jeder Vierte den Begriff Mitteldeutschland mit den Städten der neuen Bundesländer. Spontan assoziiert gehören Berlin, Leipzig, Dresden und Hannover zur Region. Bei der direkten Städtezuordnung waren sich mindestens jeweils 50 Prozent sicher, dass neben Halle und Leipzig auch Jena, Magdeburg, Dresden und Kassel zu Mitteldeutschland zu zählen sind.

Abbildung 8: Räumliche Identität von Mitteldeutschland

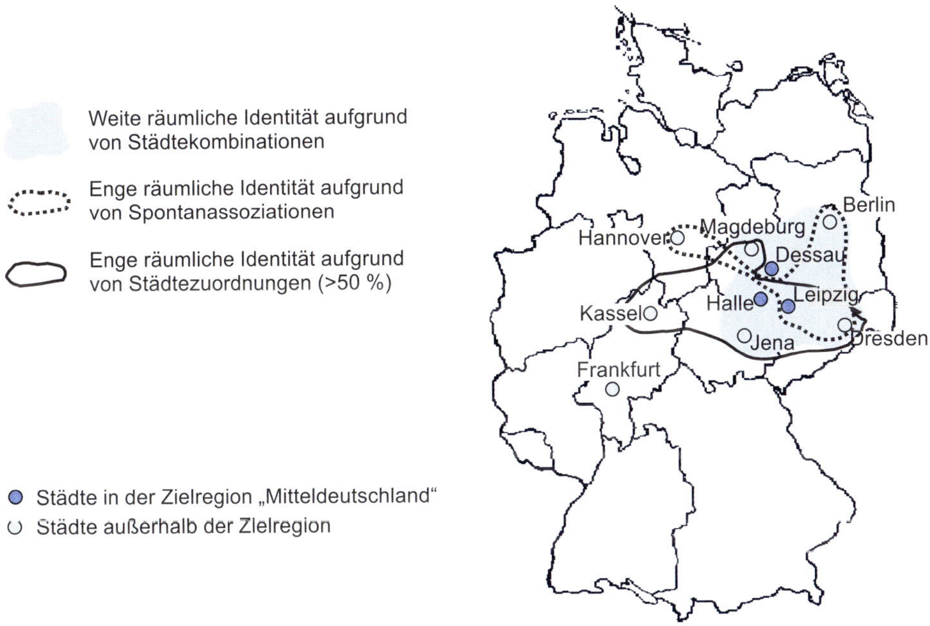

GABLER GRAFIK

Es ist festzustellen, dass die räumliche Wahrnehmung der Region „Mitteldeutschland“ als diffus zu beurteilen ist. Zwar werden in hohem Maße die Städte der Zielregion mit Mitteldeutschland verbunden, gleichzeitig aber ordnen die Bundesbürger zu einem hohen Anteil auch andere Städte aus Ostdeutschland und die berücksichtigten Städte aus den alten Bundesländern der Zielregion zu. Mit dem Begriff „Mitteldeutschland“ wird damit keine räumliche Prägnanz und Abgrenzung erzielt.

2.5 Einstellungen zur Region „Mitteldeutschland" im Vergleich zum „Ruhrgebiet"

Anhand von fünf Items wurde die Einstellung der Bundesbürger zur Region Mitteldeutschland und dem Ruhrgebiet erhoben. Hierzu wurden vorher festgelegte Attribute verwendet, denen auch für die Profilierung im Regionenmarketing eine wichtige Bedeutung zukommt und die damit auch für eine Positionierungsanalyse mit Konkurrenzregionen herangezogen werden können.[8] Entsprechende Analysen sollten für alle relevanten Zielgruppen einer Region durchgeführt werden, wobei je nach Anforderung der Zielgruppen (zum Beispiel Touristen im Vergleich zu Investoren) unterschiedliche Einstellungsattribute Entscheidungsrelevanz besitzen können. Für die Markenpositionierung sind dann die zielgruppenübergreifenden und zielgruppenspezifischen Anforderungen an eine Region zu identifizieren. Angesichts des begrenzten Fragebogenumfangs musste das Set an Kriterien in der vorliegenden Studie stark begrenzt werden. Bei der Beurteilung der Regioneneinstellung ist zu berücksichtigen, dass der Einstellungsmessung eine diffuse Regionenidentität von Mitteldeutschland zugrunde liegt. Die weite wahrgenommene räumliche Abgrenzung von Mitteldeutschland prägt somit auch das Einstellungsprofil der Befragten.

Im Gesamtdurchschnitt aller Bürger werden beide Regionen zunächst ohne besonders herausragende Eigenschaften gesehen, damit deuten die Ergebnisse eher auf eine „Profillosigkeit" der beiden Regionen hin (vgl. Abbildung 9). Im Vergleich ergibt sich ein etwas positiveres Einstellungsprofil des Ruhrgebiets bei den Eigenschaften „historisch gewachsen", „innovativ", „wachstumsstark" und „international orientiert". Mitteldeutschland wird hingegen als etwas sympathischer gegenüber der Region „Ruhrgebiet" eingestuft.[9]

In der Selbst- und Fremdwahrnehmung zeigen sich beim Einstellungsprofil für die Region „Mitteldeutschland" teilweise signifikante Unterschiede. Insbesondere die Wachstumsstärke von Mitteldeutschland wird von außen tendenziell besser eingeschätzt als von Bürgern der Region. Für sympathischer halten sich wiederum die Bewohner der Region selbst. In Bezug auf Innovativität und Internationalität unterscheidet sich die Selbst- und Fremdwahrnehmung hingegen nicht. Differenziert nach Bundesländern haben überwiegend die Bewohner aus Thüringen die positivsten Einstellungen zur Region „Mitteldeutschland". Hinsichtlich der Wachstumsstärke sind es sogar die Bewohner von Sachsen-Anhalt, die die Region Mitteldeutschland am schlechtesten bewerten. Die negativsten Einstellungen in Bezug auf die weiteren ermittelten Kriterien stammen von Befragungsteilnehmern aus Berlin und Hamburg.

---

8 Vgl. zum Beispiel die Betonung der Eigenschaft „historisch gewachsen", die aus der Definition des Regionenbegriffs hervorgeht.

9 Dabei unterscheiden sich die Mittelwerte der beiden Regionen voneinander signifikant auf einem Niveau von $p < 0{,}01$.

Abbildung 9: Gesamtdurchschnitt zur Regioneneinstellung Mitteldeutschland und Ruhrgebiet

Frage: „Bitte sagen Sie mir, welche der folgenden Eigenschaften Ihrer Meinung nach sehr gut oder gar nicht auf die Region Mitteldeutschland/Ruhgebiet zutreffen."

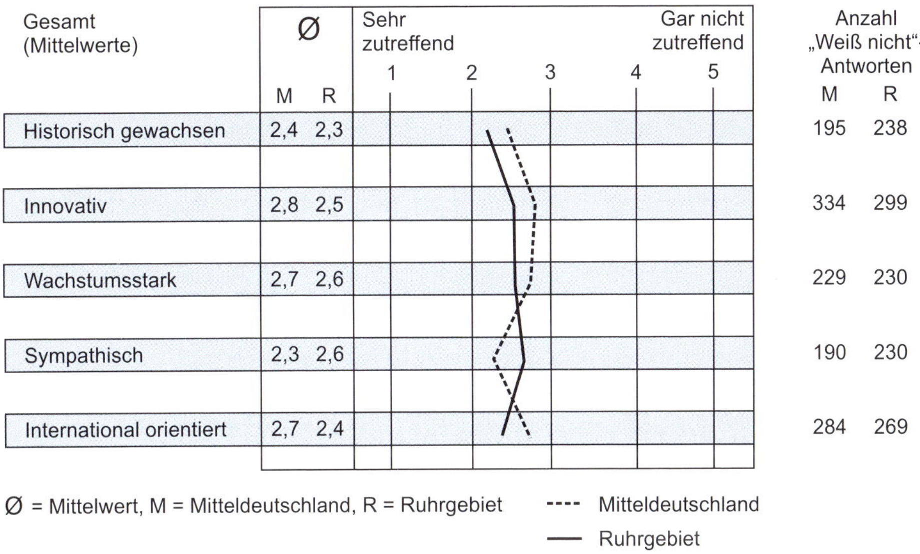

GABLER GRAFIK

Im Gegensatz zur geringen Differenzierung in der Selbst- und Fremdwahrnehmung der Region „Mitteldeutschland" demonstrieren die Einwohner des Ruhrgebietes durchgängig in allen Kriterien eine – bis auf die Internationalität signifikante – bessere Einstellung zu ihrer Region als die übrigen Befragungsteilnehmer. In der zusätzlichen Auswertung nach Bundesländern bestätigt sich dieses Bild. Mit Ausnahme der Einstellung zum Kriterium „innovativ" und „sympathisch" sind es jeweils die Bewohner von Nordrhein-Westfalen, die sich am besten bewerten. Hier hat sich eine hohe Markenidentität und Verbundenheit mit der Region herausgebildet.

Weiterführende Clusteranalysen führten zur Identifikation von Zielgruppen mit ähnlichen Einstellungen gegenüber der Zielregionen. Hier konnte ermittelt werden, dass nahezu 40 Prozent der Bundesbürger eine überdurchschnittlich positive Einstellung zu Mitteldeutschland haben, während bei weiteren Zielgruppensegmenten eine kritischere Einstellung zur Zielregion bestand. Diese zielgruppenspezifischen Erkenntnisse liefern für die Planung von Kommunikationsmaßnahmen des Regionenmarketings wichtige Hinweise.

3. Implikationen für markenstrategische Entscheidungen im Regionenmarketing

Angesichts der grundlegenden Bedeutung der Auswahl von Markennamen für den erfolgreichen Aufbau von Marken und Regionenmarken im Speziellen liefern die exemplarisch aufgezeigten Zielgruppenanalysen über Regionennamen eine wichtige Informationsgrundlage für die Markengestaltung im Regionenmarketing. Im Rahmen des dargestellten Fallbeispiels können folgende Argumente für die Verwendung des Namens „Mitteldeutschland“ angeführt werden:

- Der Begriff wird nicht mit grundlegenden negativen Assoziationen verbunden.
- Die Einstellungen zur Region „Mitteldeutschland“ weisen gegenüber der Referenzregion „Ruhrgebiet“ keine erheblichen Defizite auf. Die Dimension „sympathische Region“ wird sogar leicht besser eingeschätzt. Aufgrund der diffusen räumlichen Vorstellung beziehen sich diese Einstellungen allerdings nicht allein auf die von den Akteuren des Regionenmarketings definierte Zielregion.

Gegen die Verwendung des Namens „Mitteldeutschland“ spricht:

- Spontan wird Mitteldeutschland entweder mit der ehemaligen DDR oder mit einer diffusen räumlichen Vorstellung (Mitte von Deutschland) verbunden. Auch die Einwohner der Zielregion haben keine klare räumliche Vorstellung von Mitteldeutschland.
- Bei der Einstellung zur Leistungsfähigkeit wird die mit „Mitteldeutschland“ assoziierte Region „mittelmäßig“ und mit keinen Vorteilen gegenüber der Referenzregion „Ruhrgebiet“ empfunden.

Wenn für die Region ein Name als Marke etabliert werden soll, so müsste er den einleitend aufgeführten Funktionen und Anforderungen einer Marke gerecht werden.

Beurteilt man den Markencharakter des Begriffs „Mitteldeutschland“ danach, inwieweit er diese Funktionen übernehmen kann, dann ist folgendes festzustellen (vgl. Abbildung 10):

- Die Identifikations- und Orientierungsfunktion sind beim Begriff „Mitteldeutschland“ aufgrund der diffusen räumlichen Identität schwach ausgeprägt. Damit „Mitteldeutschland“ als Regionenmarke etabliert werden kann, wäre im Rahmen des Regionenmarketings durch eine Wort-Bild-Marke und entsprechende Kommunikationsmaßnahmen sowohl innen- als auch außengerichtet die Identifikations- und Orientierungsfunktion für die Zielgruppen der Region aufzubauen.
- Grundsätzlich zeigen sich im Einstellungsprofil keine grundlegenden Hindernisse, sodass der Begriff „Mitteldeutschland“ eine Vertrauensfunktion bei den innen- und außengerichteten Zielgruppen übernehmen kann.

- Die Kompetenzfunktion ist im Vergleich zur Referenzregion schwächer und mittelmäßig einzustufen.
- Die Imagefunktion einer Marke „Mitteldeutschland" könnte langfristig durch den weiteren Ausbau der „Sympathiedimension" innerhalb von Deutschland gewährleistet werden.

Abbildung 10: **Beurteilung des Regionennamens „Mitteldeutschland" als Bestandteil einer Regionenmarke**

Funktionen einer Marke	Erläuterung der Markenfunktion	Beurteilung der Eignung
Identifikationsfunktion	Markierung ermöglicht bei hinreichender Bekanntheit eine schnelle und prägnante Identifikation der Region.	–
Orientierungsfunktion	Bei der räumlichen und leistungsbezogenen Auswahl muss die Marke eine klare Orientierung bieten.	– –
Vertrauensfunktion	Der Marke wird aufgrund ihrer Bekanntheit und Reputation Vertrauen entgegengebracht.	–
Kompetenzfunktion	Die Marke wird mit spezifischen Kompetenzen der Region verbunden.	0
Imagefunktion	Die Marke der Region sollte eine positive Ausstrahlung auf interne und externe Zielgruppen haben.	0

Legende: +(+) = (sehr) gute Eignung/0 = mittelmäßige Eignung/–(–) = (sehr) geringe Eignung

GABLER GRAFIK

Dem Aufbau einer starken Regionenmarke „Mitteldeutschland" stehen somit die fehlende Identifikations- und Orientierungsfunktion besonders entgegen. Wenngleich grundlegende Einstellungsnachteile gegenüber der untersuchten Referenzregion nicht bestehen, so erschwert die diffuse räumliche Identifikation die prägnante Profilierung der von den Akteuren repräsentierten Zielregion.

INSERT 1 **Regionenmarke „Mitteldeutschland"**

Regionenmarke „Mitteldeutschland“

Ausgangssituation:

Die Analyse der Einstellungen der Bundesbürger zur Region „Mitteldeutschland“ bildet eine wichtige Grundlage der Entscheidungsträger des Regionenmarketing für die Entwicklung markenstrategischer Optionen. Aufgrund der bedeutenden Historie der Region Mitteldeutschland und der bei vielen Akteuren in Wirtschaft, Verwaltung und Politik entstandenen Identifikation mit „Mitteldeutschland“ wurde trotz der mit dem Regionenbegriff verbundenen räumlichen Unschärfe die Grundsatzentscheidung getroffen, den Regionenbegriff für die Markengestaltung zu verwenden. Hieraus ergab sich für die Markengestaltung die spezifische Anforderung, dass durch die Marke die räumliche Ortung der Region „Mitteldeutschland“ in Form von zusätzlichen Gestaltungselementen (Bild-/Wortelementen) gewährleistet werden sollte.

mitte | deutschland
Leipzig
Halle
Dessau

Markenentwicklung:

Auf der Grundlage eines Briefings gestaltete die Agentur McCann Erickson im Jahre 2001 das Markenkonzept für die Zielregion. Begleitet durch vertiefende Zielgruppenanalysen in den neuen und alten Bundesländern sowie im internationalen Umfeld und die Analyse von bestehenden Markenkonzepten anderer Regionen wurde die oben dargestellte Marke entwickelt.

Im Markenkonzept wird die Marke wie folgt charakterisiert:

„Mitteldeutschland ist mehr als eine Region in der Gegend Leipzig/Halle/Dessau. Es ist die Region, in der Investoren die besten Chancen für eine erfolgreiche Zukunft geboten werden. Es ist da, wo sich die Geschäftswelt trifft, wo Entscheidungen für die Zukunft getroffen werden. Und all das steht bereits im Namen der Region: Die zukünftige Mitte Deutschlands.

Mitteldeutschland muss nicht mit schönen Bildern oder Graphiken werben, muss sich nicht anbiedern - es steht einfach für sich und spricht damit klar die Sprache des Business: Einfach, selbstbewusst, konzentriert auf das Wesentliche, dabei seriös und intelligent.“

Quelle: Regionenmarketing Mitteldeutschland 2001

Auf der Grundlage der empirischen Erkenntnisse und weiterführender zielgruppenspezifischer Analyse wurden zwei Optionen für die Markengestaltung der Zielregionen als relevant erachtet:

1. Die Einbeziehung des Namens Mitteldeutschland in einer Wort-Marke oder Wort-Bild-Kombinationsmarke könnte eine Vorgehensweise darstellen, um durch grafische Elemente und/oder zusätzliche Namen eine prägnante optische beziehungsweise semantisch gestützte Ortung der Zielregion zu ermöglichen. Für die Kommunikationspolitik des Regionenmarketings ergibt sich für die ersten Phasen dann die Notwendigkeit, die räumlichen Bezüge **und** Leistungseigenschaften der Region nach innen und nach außen zu vermitteln. Die Wort-Bild-Marke könnte die Vermittlung der räumlichen Bezüge fördern und räumliche Prägnanz erzeugen.

2. Eine zweite Entscheidungsalternative besteht in der Einführung eines neuen Regionennamens beziehungsweise Kürzels für den Aufbau einer Regionenmarke. Für diese Alternative wäre zu prüfen, inwieweit ein bereits bestehender Begriff für die Regionenbenennung herangezogen oder ein völlig neuer Begriff eingeführt werden kann. Bei der Verwendung eines völlig neuen Namens wären Bekanntheitsgrad, räumliche Identität und Regioneneinstellung neu aufzubauen, wobei bereits bei der Namensfindung erneut die markenspezifischen Anforderungen einbezogen werden müssten.

Insgesamt verdeutlichen die Ausführungen, dass es zu den Aufgaben eines professionellen Regionenmarketings gehört, die Auswahl und den Aufbau von Regionenmarken in systematischer Form vorzunehmen. Ein Vergleich der Markenführungskonzepte im Sachgüter- und Dienstleistungsmarketing mit den praktischen Erfahrungen im Regionenmarketing zeigen deutliche Defizite bei der Entwicklung von Regionenmarken. Angesichts der Profilierungsnotwendigkeit von Regionen ist die Marke als „Waffe im Wettbewerb“ gleichermaßen wie in den traditionellen Bereichen des Marketings zu etablieren.

Literatur

Balderjahn, I., Aleff H.-J. (1996), Die Wirtschaftsregion Brandenburg: Grundlagen für ein Standortmarketing, Potsdam.

Balderjahn, I. (2000), Standort-Marketing, Stuttgart.

Berlit, W. (2003), Das neue Markengesetz, Berlin.

Blotevogel, H. H., Heinritz, G., Popp, H. (1987), „Regionalbewusstsein". Zum Stand der Diskussion um einen Stein des Anstoßes, in: Geografische Zeitschrift, H. 2, S. 65 ff.

Blotevogel, H. H., Heinritz, G., Popp, H. (1987), Regionalbewusstsein – Überlegungen zu einer geografisch landeskundlichen Forschungsinitiative, in: Informationen zur Raumentwicklung, H. 7/8, S. 409–418.

Blotevogel, H. H. (1996), Auf dem Weg zu einer „Theorie der Regionalität": die Region als Forschungsobjekt der Geografie, in: Brunn, G. (Hrsg.), Region und Regionsbildung in Europa. Konzeptionen der Forschung und empirische Befunde, Baden-Baden, S. 44–68.

Briesen, D. (1993), „Triviales" Geschichtsbewusstsein oder historische Elemente regionaler Identität?, in: Regionalgeschichte: ein Ansatz zur Erforschung regionaler Identität, Informationen zur Raumentwicklung, Nr. 11, S. 769–779.

Burmann, Ch.; Blinda, L.; Nitschke, A. (2003), Konzeptionelle Grundlagen des identitätsbasierten Markenmanagements, Arbeitspapier Nr. 1 des Lehrstuhls für innovatives Markenmanagement (LiM), Burmann, Ch. (Hrsg.) , Universität Bremen, Bremen.

Esch, F.-R., Langner, T. (1999), Gestaltung von Markenlogos, in: Esch, F.-R. (Hrsg.), Moderne Markenführung: Grundlagen – innovative Ansätze – praktische Umsetzungen, Wiesbaden, S. 465–490.

Fach, W., Köhnke, K.-C., Middell, M., Mühler, K., Siegrist, H., Tzschaschel, S., Wollersheim, H.-W. (1998), Regionenbezogene Identifikationsprozesse. Das Beispiel „Sachsen" – Konturen eines Forschungsprogramms, in: Wollersheim, H.-W., Tzschaschel, S., Middell, M. (Hrsg.), Region und Identifikation, Leipziger Studien zur Erforschung von regionenbezogenen Identifikationsprozessen, Bd. 1, Leipzig, S. 1–32.

Gans, R. (1993), Regionalbewusstsein und regionale Identität, in: Regionalgeschichte: ein Ansatz zur Erforschung regionaler Identität, Informationen zur Raumentwicklung, Nr. 11, S. 781–792.

Geigenmüller, A. (2001), Regionale Marken und Konsumentenverhalten – Konsequenzen für die Markenführung, Wiesbaden.

Kirchgeorg, M., Kreller, P. (2000), Etablierung von Marken im Regionenmarketing – Eine vergleichende Analyse der Regionennamen „Mitteldeutschland" und „Ruhrgebiet" auf der Grundlage einer repräsentativen Studie, Arbeitspapier Nr. 38 der Handelshochschule Leipzig, Leipzig.

Kirchgeorg, M., Fiedler, L. (2004), Profilierung von Regionen durch systematische Clusterentwicklung, Arbeitspapier der Handelshochschule Leipzig, Leipzig.

Kohli, Ch., LaBahn, D. W., Thakor, M. (1999), Prozess der Namensgebung, in: Esch, F.-R. (Hrsg.), Moderne Markenführung: Grundlagen – innovative Ansätze – praktische Umsetzungen, Wiesbaden, S. 421–444.

Konken, M. (2000), Stadtmarketing Handbuch für Städte und Gemeinden, Limburgerhof.

Kotler, P., Haider, D., Rein, I., (1994) Standort-Marketing: Wie Städte, Regionen und Länder gezielt Investitionen, Industrien und Tourismus anziehen, Düsseldorf [u.a.].

Kunzmann, K. R. (1999), Nordrhein-Westfalen in Europa: eine Standorteinschätzung, in: Brunn, G. (Hrsg.), Neoliberalismus, die Entstehung des Maastrichter Vertrags und die Auswirkungen der Währungsunion auf Nordrhein-Westfalen, Schriftenreihe des Instituts für Europäische Regionalforschung, Bd. 4, Baden-Baden, S. 137–151.

Manschwetus, U. (1995), Regionalmarketing, Marketing als Instrument der Wirtschaftsentwicklung, Wiesbaden.

Meffert, H. (1995), Einführung in das Thema Regionenmarketing, in: Regionenmarketing in Deutschland, Dokumentation zum Symposium am 6. September, Münster, S. 21–24.
Meffert, H. (2000), Marketing, 9. Aufl., Wiesbaden.
Meffert, H., Ebert, Chr. (2003), Marke Westfalen, Schriftenreihe der Stiftung Westfalen-Initiative, Band 5, Ibbenbüren.
o.V. (2000), Kommunalverband Ruhrgebiet, im Internet unter Adresse: http://www.ruhrgebiet.de (Stand vom 21.9.2000).
Porter, M. E. (1990), The Competitive Advantage of Nations, London.
Scheuch, F. (2003), Marketing für Regionen: Vom Grätzelfest zur Zielregion, in: der markt, 42. Jg., Nr. 164, S. 45–57.
Schmitz, H. (1999), Münsterland – Berge sind nicht unbedingt die Voraussetzung für Weitsicht, Münster.
Schnurrenberger, B. (2000), Standortwahl und Standortmarketing, Berlin.
Spieß, St. (1998), Marketing für Regionen, Wiesbaden.
Trommsdorff, V. (1993), Konsumentenverhalten, 2. Aufl., Stuttgart u.a.
Wardenga, U., Miggelbrink, J. (1998), Zwischen Realismus und Konstruktivismus: Regionenbegriffe in der Geografie und anderen Humanwissenschaften, in: Wollersheim, H.-W., Tzschaschel, S., Middell, M. (Hrsg.), Region und Identifikation, Leipziger Studien zur Erforschung von regionenbezogenen Identifikationsprozessen, Bd. 1, Leipzig, S. 33–46.
Weichhart, P. (1996), Die Region – Chimäre, Artefakt oder Strukturprinzip sozialer Systeme? in: Brunn, G. (Hrsg.), Region und Regionsbildung in Europa, Konzeptionen der Forschung und empirische Befunde, Baden-Baden, S. 25–43.
Weinberg, P., Diehl, S. (1999), Erlebniswelten für Marken, in: Esch, F.-R. (Hrsg.), Moderne Markenführung: Grundlagen – innovative Ansätze – praktische Umsetzungen, Wiesbaden, S. 185–207.
Werthmöller, E. (1995), Räumliche Identität als Aufgabenfeld des Städte- und Regionenmarketing, Frankfurt/M. u.a.
Wolfertz, K. (1999), Strategieentwicklung im kommunalen Standortmarketing, Göttingen.
Wollersheim, H.-W. (1999), Die Identifikationsjäger, in: ZHS/SFB-Info, Nr. 4, S.7–11.

KAPITEL

5 Best Practice im Markenmanagement

Markenführung im Spannungsfeld zwischen Tradition und Innovation: Persil – Da weiß man, was man hat 621

Klaus Morwind, Jörg P. Koppenhöfer und Peter Nüßler

Markenmonopol für Qualität – Das Beispiel Miele 649

Jürgen Plüss

Markenführung und Markentransfer der Zeitschrift GEO 667

Jürgen Althans und Gerd Brüne

Management von komplexen Markenportfolios – Markenführung in der World of TUI 693

Michael Lambertz

Erfolgreiche Markenpolitik bei homogenen Verbrauchsgütern – Das Beispiel JET 715

Heribert Meffert und Ingo Lasslop

Herausforderungen an die Markenführung bei produktpolitischer Standardisierung – Der Fall Ford Galaxy I und II 735

Martin Koers und Wolfgang Booms

High-speed-Aufbau einer neuen Marke – Das Beispiel Germanwings 763

Andreas Bierwirth/Volker Scheible

Markenmanagement als Motor der neuen Markenidentität DHL im Konzern Deutsche Post World Net 781

Wolfgang Giehl und Christoph Baumgarten

Lufthansa – Excellence in Branding 819

Harald W. Eisenächer

Markenführung in Stiftungen – Beispiel Bertelsmann Stiftung 837

Heribert Meffert

Markenführung im Spannungsfeld zwischen Tradition und Innovation: Persil – Da weiß man, was man hat

Klaus Morwind, Jörg P. Koppenhöfer und Peter Nüßler

1. Persil: Die bestimmende Marke im deutschen Waschmittelmarkt 623

2. Persil – von 1907 bis heute 626

2.1 Die Produkte 626
2.2 Die Kommunikation 628
2.3 Die Packung 629
2.4 Die Promotion 630
2.5 Der Vertrieb 631

3. Systematik einer erfolgreichen Produkteinführung – Der Launch von Persil Megaperls® 1994 631

3.1 Das System 631
3.2 Strategische Ausgangslage 633
3.3 Der Prozess der Neuproduktentwicklung und Einführung von Persil Megaperls® 635
3.31 Die Identifikation des Verbraucherbedürfnisses 635
3.32 Abgleich mit dem Markenimage und der Markenpositionierung 635
3.33 Entwicklung der Selling Proposition 636
3.34 Überprüfung der Produktleistung vor dem Hintergrund der Selling Proposition 637
3.35 Definition der Kommunikationsziele 639
3.36 Die Kommunikation 639
3.37 Überprüfung des gesamten Marketing-Mix und Ableitung des Marktpotenzials 641
3.4 Die Erfolgskontrolle nach der Produktneueinführung 642
3.41 Standardmarktbeobachtung 642
3.42 Effizienz- und Abweichungsanalysen 645

4. Es gibt nur ein Persil: Die Erfolgsfaktoren einer einzigartigen Marke 646

5. Grenzenloses Persil. Die internationale Verbreitung der Marke 647

Persil lebt nicht von Tradition allein. Im Gegenteil. Die „Weiße Dame“ ist heute so erfolgreich wie vor 90 Jahren. Persil vergrößert den Abstand zum Hauptwettbewerber immer deutlicher (vgl. Abbildung 3). 44 Millionen Kaufakte im Jahr 2003 sind der Beweis. Damit haben die Verbraucher fast doppelt so oft zu Persil gegriffen wie zum Hauptwettbewerber. Die Käuferreichweite von 26 Prozent und eine Wiederkaufrate von über 50 Prozent bestätigen die herausragende Stellung der Marke Persil.

Abbildung 3: **Entwicklung des Marktanteils von Persil und Hauptwettbewerber (in Prozent)**

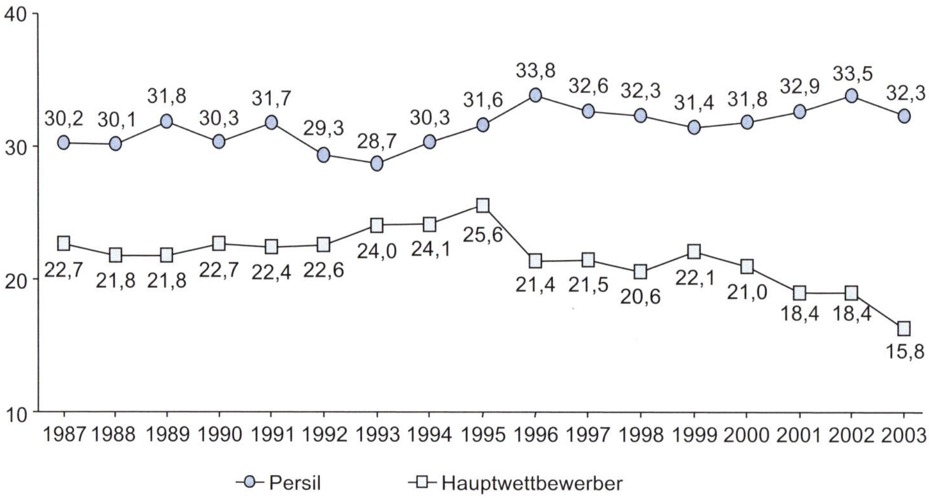

GABLER GRAFIK

Eine wichtige Basis dieser eindrucksvollen Marktdaten ist die überlegene Kraft der Marke.

Man kennt Persil. Das belegt die ungestützte Markenbekanntheit von 86 Prozent im Segment der Universalwaschmittel.

Man vertraut Persil. Das beweist die Wahl zur vertrauenswürdigsten Marke unter den Waschmitteln Deutschlands (vgl. Abbildung 4).

Nur wenige Marken haben eine so herausragende Stellung wie Persil.

Abbildung 4: **Deutschlands vertrauenswürdigste Marken in der Produktkategorie Waschmittel (Nennungen in Prozent, ungestützt)**

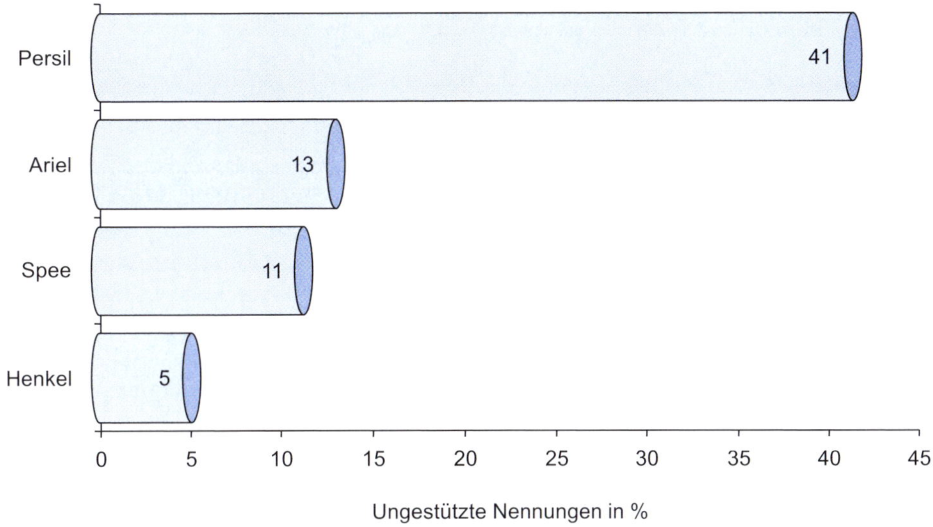

GABLER GRAFIK

Quelle: Reader's Digest: European Trusted Brands 2003

Und in den „Deutschen Standards" wird unter der Rubrik Vollwaschmittel ausschließlich Persil als „das Waschmittel" genannt.

Das Institut für Demoskopie, Allensbach, beschreibt das Markenbild von Persil im Vergleich zum Wettbewerb folgendermaßen: Persil verbindet Waschleistung, Spitzenqualität und Modernität. Gleichzeitig ist Persil voll Tradition und immer bodenständig geblieben. Diese Mischung ist kein Gegensatz, sondern definiert das einmalige Markenimage von Persil.

Aber wie konnte diese Marke ihre Spitzenposition über all die Jahrzehnte hinweg bewahren und immer weiter ausbauen? Wesentlicher Erfolgsfaktor ist die Tatsache, dass sich Produkt und Marke immer weiter entwickelt haben. Es gab und gibt niemals Stillstand. Produktleistung, Qualität, Verbraucheransprache und Aufmachung wurden ständig verbessert. In einer fast perfekten Kombination von Innovation und Tradition, von Veränderung und Kontinuität.

Es war ein langer Weg, und er ist noch lange nicht zu Ende.

2. Persil – von 1907 bis heute

2.1 Die Produkte

Persil hat durch neue Produktangebote den Markt bestimmt und vorangetrieben. Dabei waren die Bedürfnisse der Verbraucher immer der wichtigste Faktor.

1907 wurde von der 1876 gegründeten Firma Henkel & Cie das erste selbsttätige Waschmittel auf den Markt gebracht: *Persil.* Der Markenname leitet sich dabei aus den beiden wichtigsten chemischen Grundstoffen ab: *Per*borat und *Sil*icat. Das Produkt avancierte schnell zum Erfolg und fand rasch verschiedene Nachahmer. Frühzeitig erkannte Fritz Henkel, dass die kontinuierliche Weiterentwicklung der Produktqualität wesentlich den Erfolg der Marke bestimmt: „Sie werden sehen, dass es nicht besonders leicht ist, ein modernes Waschmittel herzustellen, und dass es außerordentlicher Mühe und sehr viel Arbeit bedarf, um ein solches Produkt auf der Höhe zu halten und es noch immer mehr zu verbessern."

Abbildung 5 **Zeitstrahl von 1907 bis heute mit den wesentlichen Launches und Re-Launches der letzten Jahre**

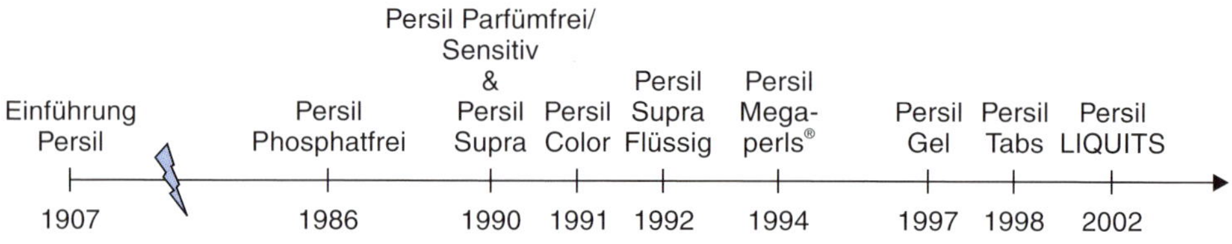

GABLER GRAFIK

Lange Zeit änderte sich an der Pulver-Form des Waschmittels nicht viel; es handelte sich vielmehr um rezepturtechnische Anpassungen oder Erneuerungen, die die Leistung des Produktes und die Schonung der Textilien während des Waschens verbesserten, begleitet von maschinentechnischen Innovationen, wie zum Beispiel den Waschvollautomaten.

Anfang der 80er Jahre wurde der Schutz der Umwelt immer wichtiger. Dabei übernahm Persil die Vorreiterrolle und führte 1986 das erste *phosphatfreie* Waschmittel ein. Vier Jahre später wurde mit *Persil Supra* eines der ersten Waschmittelkonzentrate eingeführt, welches 50 Prozent ergiebiger war als klassische Pulver und gleichzeitig Verpackungsmaterial sparte.

1990 wurde *Persil Parfümfrei* eingeführt und neun Jahre später in *Persil Sensitiv* umbenannt. Der Verzicht auf Duftstoffe entsprach den Bedürfnissen hautempfindlicher Personen.

1991 folgte mit *Persil Color* wieder eine Innovation auf dem Waschmittelmarkt: das erste Vollwaschmittel mit Farbschutz, der Farben vor dem Verblassen bewahrt. 1992 wurde das bereits im Jahr 1987 von Persil eingeführte Flüssigwaschmittel mit *Persil Supra Flüssig* und *Persil Color Flüssig* weiter verbessert. Produktneueinführungen, mit denen Persil eine neue konzentrierte Waschmittelform definierte und die Persil-Leistungsvorteile mit dem Nutzen vollständig löslicher Waschmittel kombinierte.

Mit der Verwendung von Plantaren®, einem Tensid-Komplex, der überwiegend auf Basis nachwachsender Rohstoffe wie Raps-, Palm-, Kokos- oder Palmkernöl hergestellt wird und vollständig biologisch abbaubar ist, leistet Persil 1993 einen weiteren wichtigen Beitrag zur Umweltentlastung.

1994 gelang mit der Entwicklung und Einführung der *Persil Megaperls®* eine der größten Innovationen in der Geschichte des Waschmittels. Dabei handelte es sich um eine doppelte Innovation:

Zum einen wurde das Waschmittel durch Anwendung eines neuen Produktionsverfahrens noch stärker konzentriert, mit allen Vorteilen bei Ergiebigkeit und Einsparung von Verpackungsmaterial. Zum anderen wurde durch die aus dem Extrusionsprozess entstehenden Waschmittelperlen die Form und das Aussehen des Pulverwaschmittels deutlich verändert. „Perlen statt Pulver" haben so zu einer deutlichen Differenzierung gegenüber den Wettbewerbsprodukten geführt.

Die Konzentration der Waschmittelprodukte fand 1997 ihre Fortsetzung mit der Einführung von *Persil Gel*. Mit *Persil Tabs* wurde 1998 der wichtige Convenience-Trend aufgegriffen – erstmals gab es ein konzentriertes Waschmittel in vordosierter Form. Dieser Produktnutzen ist auch Basis einer weiteren Innovation: *Persil LIQUITS* und *Persil Color LIQUITS*. *Persil LIQUITS* verbinden als erstes vorportioniertes Flüssig-Vollwaschmittel die Produktvorteile von Tabs und von Flüssigwaschmitteln.

Gleichzeitig werden Persil-Produkte parallel zu den Neuentwicklungen laufend verbessert und neuen Qualitätsanforderungen angepasst. Die daraus resultierende Sortimentsbreite – zur Zeit gibt es Persil in elf unterschiedlichen Angebotsformen – ermöglicht es, die verschieden ausgeprägten Konsumentenbedürfnisse perfekt abzudecken.

So kann das Versprechen „Persil bleibt Persil" eingehalten werden. Dieser Satz signalisiert das gleichbleibend hohe Qualitätsniveau auch 96 Jahre nach der Einführung von Persil. Helmut Sihler, früherer Vorstandsvorsitzender der Henkel KGaA, bringt es auf den Punkt: „Persil bleibt Persil, weil Persil nicht Persil bleibt." Allein der ständige Fokus auf die sich wandelnden Bedürfnisse der Konsumenten und die Anpassung an neue gesellschafts- und wettbewerbspolitische Rahmenbedingungen ermöglichen es, dass Persil stets der Qualitäts- und Innovationsführer am deutschen Waschmittelmarkt geblieben ist.

Doch zum Erfolg einer Marke zählt nicht nur die kontinuierliche Weiterentwicklung in technischer Hinsicht, sondern auch ihr öffentlicher Auftritt.

2.2 Die Kommunikation

Auch im öffentlichen Auftreten hat Persil immer wieder innovative Wege beschritten, sei es mit sogenannten „Sandwich“-Männern zu Beginn des 20. Jahrhunderts, mit Haushaltsberaterinnen, die in den 20er Jahren die Hausfrauen über die neue Anwendungsweise des Produkts aufklärten oder mit dem „Persil-Mann“, der den Werbeauftritt Mitte der 70er bis Mitte der 80er Jahre prägte.

Abbildung 6: Die Weiße Dame von 1922

GABLER GRAFIK

1922 entwarf Kurt Heiligenstaedt das Bild der „Weißen Dame“ (vgl. Abbildung 6). Dieses Bild hat sich über die Jahrzehnte allen gesellschaftlichen Entwicklungen und Moden angepasst und der Marke eine unverkennbare Identität gegeben. In ihrer Schönheit und Eleganz verkörpert die Weiße Dame eine Frau, die dank Persil von der beschwerlichen Arbeit der Wäschepflege befreit ist. Dadurch, dass Persil die ehemals mit der Wäsche verbundenen Probleme in den Hintergrund treten lässt, kann sich die moderne Frau voll und ganz auf das konzentrieren, was ihr wichtig ist.

Persil war auch stets eine der ersten Marken, die neue Medien genutzt hat, um den Menschen das Produkt und seinen Nutzen nahe zu bringen. In den Jahren zwischen 1927 und 1939 wurden beispielsweise zehn Persil-Filme gedreht, davon einer in der Länge von zwei Stunden mit bekannten Schauspielern. Diesen Film haben innerhalb von sechs Jahren circa 30 Millionen Zuschauer gesehen. Seit 1956 nutzt Persil neben Print und Plakat intensiv das Medium Fernsehen. Der erste TV-Spot im deutschen Fernsehen war ein Film von Persil. In diesem warben Beppo Brehm und Lisl Karlstadt für Persil.

Neue Formen der Zusammenarbeit mit den privaten TV-Sendern, die über die klassische TV-Werbung hinaus gehen, werden ebenfalls in die Kommunikationspolitik integriert. Bei der Einführung von Persil Tabs wurde durch ein breit angelegtes TV-Sponsoring in Kooperation mit allen großen Privatsendern in nur 6 Wochen eine gestützte Bekanntheit von 70 Prozent für das neue Produkt aufgebaut.

Und auch heute nutzt Persil die modernsten Medien der Kommunikation. Zum Beispiel das Internet: Persil entwickelt als erstes deutsches Waschmittel eine eigene Website mit speziellem Fleckenratgeber und Wasch-Center (www.persil.de). Dieser Schritt resultiert nicht zuletzt aus dem eigenen Anspruch, zum Thema Waschen in allen Fragen und über alle Kommunikationswege der kompetenteste Ansprechpartner für die Verbraucher zu sein. Es gibt eben nur ein Persil.

Typisch für Persil ist die Nutzung mehrerer Medien. Insbesondere das „öffentlichste" aller Medien, das Plakat, das kaum von anderen Waschmitteln genutzt wird, hat das Markenbild von Persil geprägt. Persil hat zudem als erste Marke auch die jüngste Innovation, die 3D-Plakate, im Rahmen des Kommunikations-Mix genutzt.

2.3 Die Packung

Über die direkte Kommunikation in den Massenmedien hinaus kommt der Entwicklung des Packungsbildes im Rahmen der kontinuierlichen Ansprache der Verbraucher große Bedeutung zu (vgl. Abbildung 7).

Trotz einzelner größerer Veränderungen bleiben wesentliche Gestaltungsmerkmale der Packung konstant beziehungsweise werden nur geringen Änderungen unterworfen, um die Kontinuität des Markenauftritts zu gewährleisten. In den ersten 50 Jahren hat sich die Packung nur marginal verändert. Der Farbcode wurde stets beibehalten. 1973 wurde das grüne Logo in einen roten Schriftzug umgewandelt. Seit Mitte der 80er Jahre wird das Design durch das grüne „Energiefeld" im unteren Bereich mitbestimmt und ist bis heute kontinuierlich weiterentwickelt worden. Dass die einzelnen Änderungen teilweise für den Verbraucher nicht oder nur kaum wahrnehmbar sind, liegt vor allem an der Tatsache, dass es sich um evolutionäre statt revolutionäre Schritte handelte. Eben die perfekte Kombination von Weiterentwicklung und Kontinuität als wichtige Basis für das Vertrauen der Verbraucher.

Genauso verhielt es sich mit den Imagefaktoren. Persil ist durch folgendes Image gekennzeichnet: „Der Marktführer mit dem überlegenen Produktangebot ist auch Innovations- und Qualitätsführer im gesamten Markt."

Auch hier war das Konzept von Persil Megaperls® ideal, um das Image der Marke Persil zu festigen und weiter auszubauen.

3.33 Entwicklung der Selling Proposition

Die Selling Proposition ist eine aus der Produktpositionierung abgeleitete Aussage (Benefit), die den Nutzen des Produktes beschreibt. Sie beschreibt auch den Vorteil, den der Verbraucher hat, wenn er ein bestimmtes Henkel Produkt anstelle eines Wettbewerbsproduktes verwendet. Die Selling Proposition dient damit auch der Differenzierung im Vergleich zum Wettbewerb und ist in der Regel mittel- bis langfristig gültig.

Wesentlich ist, dass die Selling Proposition folgende Erfolgskriterien erfüllt:

- Positionierungsadäquanz,
- Relevanz,
- Uniqueness,
- Glaubwürdigkeit und
- Newness.

Die Überprüfung des Konzepts hinsichtlich seiner Attraktivität und Relevanz für den Verbraucher kann in unterschiedlichen Stadien des Entwicklungsprozesses erfolgen. Dabei nimmt die Aussagefähigkeit hinsichtlich des tatsächlich am Markt zu realisierenden Erfolges mit jedem Schritt zu. Die Wahl der jeweils anzuwendenden Testmethode hängt davon ab, welche Marketing-Mix-Parameter bereits definiert beziehungsweise gestaltet sind. Die erste Stufe ist das anhand eines „Boards" visualisierte Konzept.

Bei der Entwicklung von Konzepten für eine Produktidee ist ein zunächst breites Vorgehen sinnvoll. Selbst kleine Unterschiede verschiedener konzeptioneller Ansätze haben oft einen großen Effekt, insbesondere auf die Glaubwürdigkeit. Frühzeitige Konzepttests haben auch den Vorteil, Ideen rechtzeitig zu prüfen und gegebenenfalls auch auszuscheiden, bevor die aufwendige Prüfung ihrer technischen Realisierbarkeit in Angriff genommen wird. Wichtig ist, dass die Entwicklung der Selling Proposition in Abstimmung zwischen Marketing, Produktentwicklung und Werbeagentur erfolgt.

Als Ergebnis dieser Phase wurde ein Konzept abgeleitet, das die Positionierung von Persil Megaperls® am Markt beschreibt: Persil Megaperls®: mehr Kraft durch hochkonzentrierte und einzigartige Form und daher mehr Leistung insbesondere bei hartnäckigen Verschmutzungen.

Im Rahmen der Konzeptentwicklung wurde zur Verdeutlichung der differenzierenden und vom Wettbewerb nicht kopierbaren Produktoptik auch ein einzigartiges Subbranding gesucht. Testsieger war der Begriff „Megaperls", welcher markenrechtlich geschützt wurde.

Wesentlich für die Einführung der Persil Megaperls® war es, alle Entwicklungen auf ihre Übereinstimmung mit der strategischen Leitidee der Marke Persil zu überprüfen: „Persil bietet stets die bestmögliche Lösung aller Waschprobleme." Oder mit anderen Worten: „Immer das beste Persil seiner Zeit."

3.34 Überprüfung der Produktleistung vor dem Hintergrund der Selling Proposition

Die wichtigsten Parameter für das zu entwickelnde Produkt sind

- die Rezeptur,
- der Duft,
- die Verpackung unter Handhabungsgesichtspunkten (zum Beispiel Transport, Lagerung, Dosierung),
- die Gestaltung der Packung sowie
- das Aussehen des Waschmittels.

Im Falle der Megaperls® gab es bereits 1991 erste Versuche auf Basis der in anderen Branchen eingesetzten Extrusions-Technologie, auf deren Grundlage mit Persil Megaperls® eine völlig neuartige, leistungsverbesserte Rezeptur entwickelt werden konnte. In der objektiven Überprüfung der Qualität unter Laborbedingungen konnte eine deutlich verbesserte Waschleistung im internen wie im Wettbewerbsvergleich bewiesen werden (vgl. Abbildung 12).

Abbildung 12: Laboranalysen zur Überprüfung der Waschkraft von Persil Megaperls®

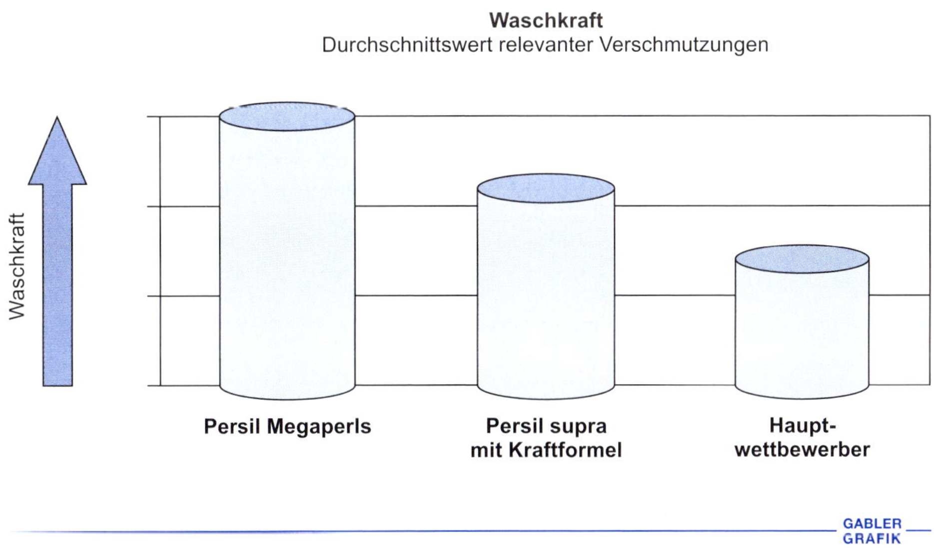

Neben internen Labor- und Lagertests wird auch zunehmend auf externe und unabhängige Testinstitute, wie zum Beispiel das Forschungsinstitut Hohenstein, zurückgegriffen, um die Produktleistung einer weiteren Beurteilung zu unterziehen.

Langfristig ist die Qualität des Produkts sicherlich der wichtigste Faktor im Markt, da der tägliche Einsatz beim Verbraucher zu einer ständigen kritischen Bewertung der Leistung führt. Leistungsdefizite gegenüber dem Wettbewerb können nicht durch andere Parameter, wie zum Beispiel Werbung, ausgeglichen werden. Daher ist die Überprüfung der Produktqualität durch den Verbraucher bei jeder Veränderung des Produktes zwingend notwendig. Dabei ist davon auszugehen, dass das Produktkonzept, welches dem Konsumenten über die Packungsgestaltung und auch via TV, Print und/oder Funk kommuniziert wird, seine Erwartungshaltung gegenüber dem Produkt und damit auch seine Wahrnehmung der Produktleistung beeinflusst. Die Abweichung von Erwartungen einerseits und Erleben andererseits bestimmen die Zufriedenheit des Konsumenten und damit letztlich seine Bereitschaft, das Produkt wiederzukaufen.

Die Überprüfung des subjektiven Erlebens beim Verbraucher in sogenannten Home-Use-Tests unter realen Verschmutzungs-, Dosierungs- und Anwendungsbedingungen war die wichtigste Entscheidungsbasis für die Einführung von Persil Megaperls®. Persil Megaperls® wurde von den meisten Testpersonen im Vergleich zu ihrer bisher verwendeten Stamm-Marke hinsichtlich der Waschkraft, der Wirtschaftlichkeit, der Fleckenentfernung und des Duftes bevorzugt (vgl. Abbildung 13).

Abbildung 13: Home-Use-Test-Ergebnisse zur Überprüfung der vom Verbraucher subjektiv wahrgenommenen Waschkraft von Persil Megaperls®

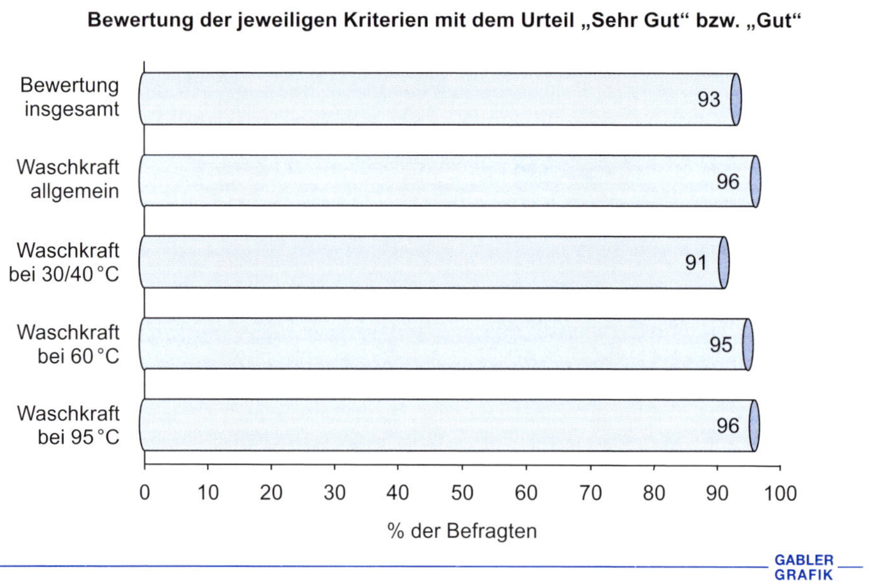

3.35 Definition der Kommunikationsziele

Um den Rahmen für die weitere Entwicklung zu bestimmen, gilt es, folgende Dimensionen des Kommunikationszieles festzulegen:

- die Zielgruppe, die durch die Kommunikation erreicht werden soll;
- die Verhaltensänderung der Verbraucher als Ergebnis der Kommunikation;
- das Ausmaß der Verhaltensänderung in einer operationalen, das heißt messbaren Größe.

3.36 Die Kommunikation

Die Kommunikation hat die Aufgabe, dem Verbraucher die Inhalte der Selling Proposition überzeugend zu vermitteln. Deshalb geht es im ersten Schritt darum, eine klare, einzigartige Selling Idea zu entwickeln.

Die Selling Idea ist in verschiedenen Medien darstellbar (TV, Print, Plakat). Sie passt zur Marke und ist unverwechselbar. Das heißt, die Kommunikation wird ganz klar dem Produkt und der Marke zugeordnet.

Durch die direkte Ansprache der Endverbraucher und die damit verbundene unmittelbare Marktwirksamkeit kommt der Verbraucherkommunikation als „Endprodukt" einer langen Testreihe besondere Bedeutung zu.

Die Kommunikationsbewertung lässt sich nach folgendem Methodenspektrum differenzieren:

- **Qualitative Aspekte:**
  Sind Bilder, Zeichensprache, Personen und Stimmungen kohärent mit der Kommunikationszielsetzung und schließen an das gelernte Zeichensystem an beziehungsweise gewährleisten sie eine ausreichende „Selbstähnlichkeit"?
- **Kommunikationsinhalte:**
  Welche Positionierungsinhalte werden kommuniziert? Stimmt das, was der Verbraucher durch die Werbebotschaft lernt, mit der strategischen Produktpositionierung und der Kommunikationsstrategie überein?
- **Impact:**
  Welche Durchsetzungsfähigkeit hat die Kommunikation? Hebt sie sich im Werbeumfeld deutlich genug ab?
- **Persuasion:**
  Welche Überzeugungskraft zum Spontankauf hat die Kommunikation? Ist der TV-Spot geeignet, die Käuferpenetration zu erhöhen?

Vor allem in wettbewerbsintensiven Märkten für Güter des täglichen Bedarfs ist der letzte Aspekt entscheidend, damit sich der Einsatz eines TV-Spots überhaupt lohnt.

Für die Einführungskommunikation der Megaperls® wurde die Selling Idea wie folgt definiert: Wenn Deutschlands Waschmittelmarke Nr. 1 statt herkömmlichen Pulvers Waschmittel in der neuen, einzigartigen Form der Perle anbietet, dann muss es sich um die neueste Waschmittelgeneration mit überragender Produktleistung handeln.

Der Announcement-Film „New Generation" erzielte eine deutlich über der Norm liegende Überzeugungsleistung. Die Norm definiert sich über die Wirksamkeit durchschnittlich arbeitender Spots im Wettbewerbsumfeld. Auch die Werbeerinnerung sowie die Erinnerung der zentralen Werbebotschaft lagen deutlich über der Norm (vgl. Tabelle 1). Erhoben wurde diese in einem sogenannten Persuasion-Shift-Testverfahren, welches die Fähigkeit des Spots testet, eine Person nach einmaligem Werbemittelkontakt zum Kauf des beworbenen Produktes zu führen.

Tabelle 1: Persuasion-Test-Ergebnisse für den TV-Spot Persil Megaperls® „New Generation"

	Norm	Persil Megaperls®
Überzeugungskraft	+ 7 %	+ 15 %
Werbeerinnerung	23 %	70 %
Erinnerung der zentralen Werbebotschaft	16 %	22 %

GABLER GRAFIK

Nach der Einführungsphase kam es zum Einsatz der sogenannten „Prominentenkampagne", in welcher unter anderem Manfred Krug, Heike Drechsler und Schalke 04 für Persil Megaperls® warben. Grundlage hierfür war die folgende Idee: Wenn große Persönlichkeiten ein neues Produkt testen und empfehlen, muss es ein überlegenes Produkt sein.

Da viele Kaufentscheidungen erst am Point of Sale erfolgen, kommt der Gestaltung der Packung eine sehr hohe Bedeutung zu. Die Packung muss primär auch ein optischer Ausdruck der Produktleistung sein und das Produktkonzept eigenständig kommunizieren. Gleichzeitig muss die Gestaltung die Kontinuität und das Vertrauen der Marke Persil ausstrahlen.

Das Design der Persil Megaperls® Packung wurde daher einerseits auf die Aspekte „Innovation" und „Waschkraft der Perle" abgestimmt, andererseits wurde die Familienzugehörigkeit zur Marke Persil beibehalten. Um die Kraft zum Ausdruck zu bringen, wurde das „Energiefeld" weiterentwickelt. Darüber hinaus wurde die Packung mit einem Sichtfenster ausgestattet, um die Perlenform als optisch wesentliches differenzierendes Merkmal der Megaperls® gegenüber der Pulverform der Wettbewerber darzustellen und diesen Unterschied bereits am Point of Sale eindrucksvoll zu visualisieren. Packungstests belegten dabei sowohl die Produkt- als auch die Konzeptadäquanz der Persil Megaperls®-Packung. Persil Megaperls® wurde von den Verbrauchern spontan deutlich gegenüber den Packungen anderer Wettbewerbsprodukte präferiert.

Ergänzend zu den genannten Maßnahmen wurden zeitlich und konzeptionell gekoppelte „Below-the-line-Aktivitäten" gewählt. Schwerpunkt lag unter anderem auf der Verteilung von Persil Megaperls®-Proben in ganz Deutschland, welche zeitlich und regional mit einem breit angelegten Einsatz von Werbedamen in großen Outlets abgestimmt wurde. Zusätzlich wurden Bodenstrahler mit Megaperls®-Schriftzug und outletspezifische Displays am Point of Sale eingesetzt.

3.37 Überprüfung des gesamten Marketing-Mix und Ableitung des Marktpotenzials

Erst die Ganzheit aus Produkt, Packung, Kommunikation und Preis ist die Grundlage für eine endgültige Beurteilung. Diese Beurteilung entscheidet, ob ein neues Produkt genügend Potenzial am Markt hat, um ein Erfolg zu werden. Da die mit der Einführung verbundenen Kosten in der Regel zu hoch sind, um ein Trial-and-Error-Verfahren zu riskieren, werden neue oder in wesentlichen Parametern geänderte Produkte zur Risikoabsicherung vor ihrer Markteinführung in einem oder mehreren Testmärkten überprüft. Hier werden die vorher jeweils einzeln getesteten Marketing-Mix-Elemente wie Produkt, Packung, TV-Spot nun erstmals als eine zusammenhängende Einheit beim Verbraucher erlebt und überprüft.

Aufgrund der herausragenden Bedeutung der Entscheidung für Persil, Megaperls® in Deutschland einzuführen, wurden zunächst reale Testmärkte in der Schweiz und in Österreich durchgeführt. In deren Verlauf wurden Probleme in der Rezeptur und in der Kommunikation aufgedeckt, die dann vor der Einführung in Deutschland aufgegriffen und gelöst werden konnten.

Bevor es jedoch zur endgültigen Einführungsentscheidung kam, wurde das gesamte optimierte Marketing-Mix für Persil Megaperls® auf dem deutschen Markt in einem simulierten Testmarkt nochmals überprüft. Die Ergebnisse sind Abbildung 14 zu entnehmen. Der signifikante Marktanteilsanstieg, der durch TESI prognostiziert wurde, war die Basis für die Entscheidung, Persil Megaperls® einzuführen.

Zu beachten bleibt, dass das standardisierte Vorgehen kein Garant dafür ist, dass die einzelnen Schritte innerhalb des Entwicklungsprozesses direkt zum gewünschten Erfolg führen. Nicht selten entsprechen die ersten Testergebnisse nicht den Erwartungen, was zu einer weiteren Optimierung der jeweiligen Inputfaktoren und deren erneuter Überprüfung führt. Wesentlich für den abschließenden Erfolg sind somit regelmäßige Konsistenzprüfungen zwischen den einzelnen Schritten im System. Nur über optimale Ergebnisse bei der Überprüfung der einzelnen Marketing-Mix-Elemente sind über TESI gemessene, überdurchschnittliche Werte zu erwarten.

Abbildung 14: Ergebnisse der Testmarktsimulation für Persil Megaperls®

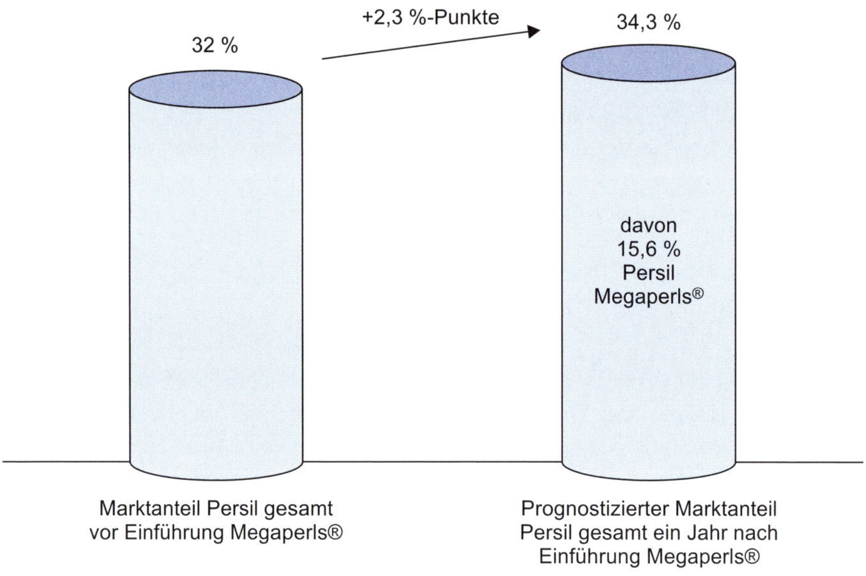

GABLER GRAFIK

3.4 Die Erfolgskontrolle nach der Produktneueinführung

3.41 Standardmarktbeobachtung

Die Vermarktungsstrategie als handels- und verbraucherbezogene Umsetzung der Markenstrategie enthält ein ganzes Bündel von Marketing-Mix-Elementen zur Steuerung des laufenden Geschäfts. Zur laufenden Bewertung der Steuerungsparameter werden umfassende Kennziffern erfasst und kontrolliert (vgl. Abbildung 15).

Abbildung 15: Erfolgskennziffern zur Bewertung einer Produktneueinführung

Handelspanel/Scannerdaten

- Wertmäßiger/mengenmäßiger Absatz
- Marktanteil
- Distributionsniveau
- Durchschnittlicher Endverbraucherpreis
- Zweitplatzierungsanteil

Interne Daten

- Absätze/Umsätze
- Ergebnisrechnung
- Verbraucherreklamationen

Haushaltspanel

- Wertmäßige/mengenmäßige Absätze
- Käuferreichweite
- Wiederkaufrate
- Imagedaten

Werbewirkungsdaten

- Werbeerinnerung
- Markenbekanntheit
- Markenverwendung

GABLER GRAFIK

Dass es sich bei der Einführung von Persil Megaperls® um einen der erfolgreichsten Launches aller Zeiten handelt, kann mit Hilfe folgender Kennziffern belegt werden:

- **Distributionsaufbau in Rekordzeit** (vgl. Abbildung 16)
- **Kommunikation**:
  Das Marktforschungsinstitut Millward Brown wies „die besten, jemals für eine Neueinführung gemessenen Werbewirkungsdaten" auf:
- → Gestützte Bekanntheit (November/Dezember 1994): 76 Prozent
- → Gestützte Werbeerinnerung (November/Dezember 1994): 65 Prozent
- **Leistung:**
  Stiftung Warentest veröffentlicht im Heft 8/95: Persil Megaperls®: Das Beste gegen Flecken
- **Verbraucherreaktion:**
  Mit der Einführung von Persil Megaperls® gelingt es, den Vorsprung der Gesamtmarke zum Hauptwettbewerber wieder deutlich auszubauen und mittelfristig Marktführer im strategisch wichtigen Kompaktsegment zu werden.
  Betrachtet man die Marktanteilsentwicklung der Persil Megaperls® (Abbildung 17), so wird deutlich, dass der mittels TESI prognostizierte Marktanteil nach einem Jahr auch tatsächlich erreicht wurde.

Abbildung 16: **Monatliche Entwicklung der gewichteten Distribution nach Einführung der Persil Megaperls®**

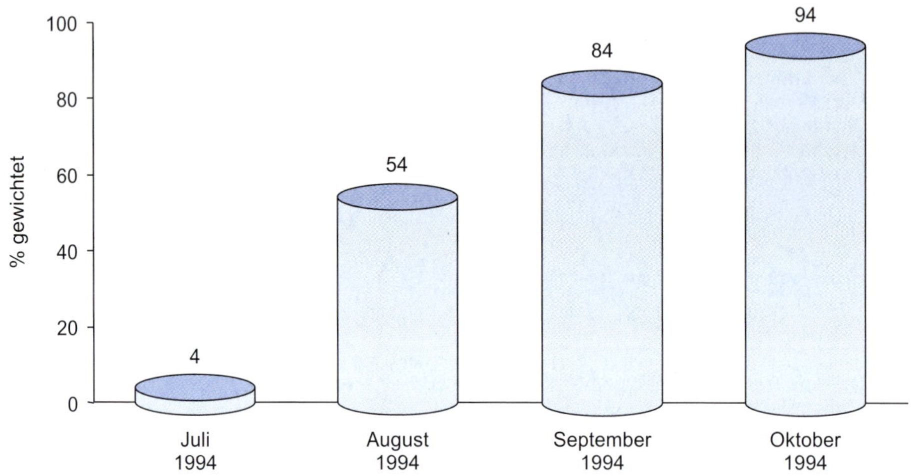

GABLER GRAFIK

Abbildung 17: **Entwicklung des wertmäßigen Marktanteils von Persil Megaperls® (in Prozent)**

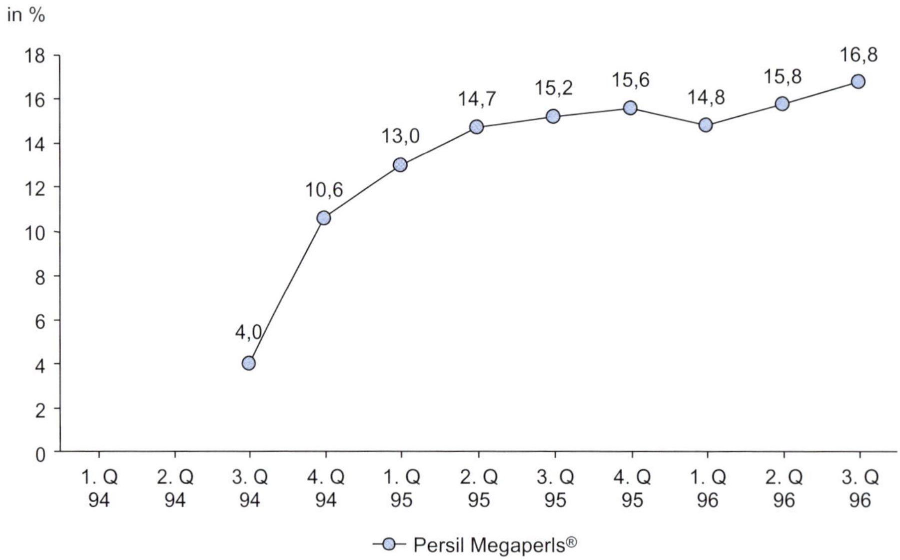

GABLER GRAFIK

Betrachtet man darüber hinaus die Marktstellung allein im Segment der Kompaktwaschmittel, so wird deutlich, dass mit der Einführung der Persil Megaperls® die zeitweilige Schwäche gegenüber dem Hauptwettbewerber ausgeglichen und die Marktführerschaft in diesem Segment erreicht werden konnte (vgl. Abbildung 18).

Abbildung 18: **Wertmäßiger Marktanteil von Persil versus Hauptwettbewerber im Segment der Kompaktwaschmittel (in Prozent)**

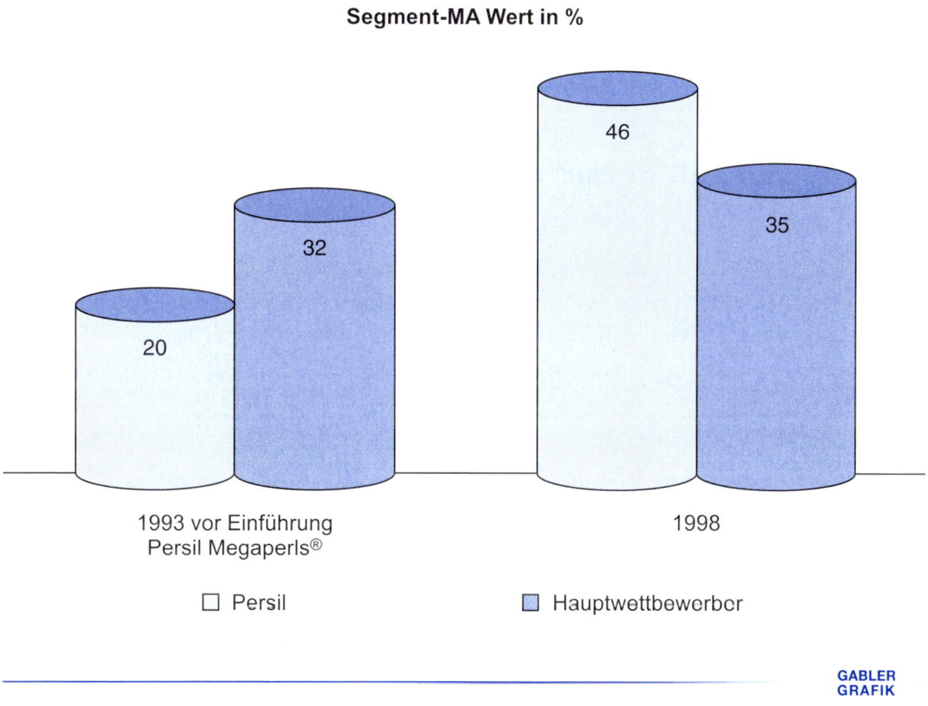

3.42 Effizienz- und Abweichungsanalysen

Bei der Bewertung der verbraucherorientierten Aktivitäten kommt vor allem dem Return-on-Investment (RoI) bezogen auf die Investitionen in die Kommunikation eine besondere Bedeutung zu. Diesbezügliche Effizienzanalysen belegen ebenfalls den Erfolg der Markteinführung von Persil Megaperls®.

Das RoI-Modell stellt dabei auf die kurzfristige Effektivität und Effizienz der Investitionen ab, indem den finanziellen Input-Faktoren einerseits, die durch die Kommunikation verursachte Änderung des Marktanteils andererseits gegenübergestellt wird. Wesentlich ist hierbei die Dekomposition des Marktanteils. Hintergrund ist die Überlegung, dass der Marktanteil nicht allein durch die Kommunikation, sondern darüber hinaus durch verschiedene andere Faktoren, wie zum Beispiel Distribution (betrifft vor allem Produkte, die sich in der Einführungsphase befinden), Promotion und Preis, beeinflusst wird. Von dem totalen Marktanteils-Effekt werden daher entsprechend zunächst die auf die genannten Faktoren zurückzuführenden Effekte extrahiert. Die verbleibende Änderung des Marktanteils kann somit auf die Kommunikation und die Investitionen in dieselbe zurückgeführt werden.

Im Falle der Einführung der Persil Megaperls® konnte auf Basis des beschriebenen Modellansatzes ein RoI von 19 Prozent ermittelt werden, welcher deutlich über der Benchmark lag.

4. Es gibt nur ein Persil: Die Erfolgsfaktoren einer einzigartigen Marke

Die Erfolgsstory von Persil ist das Ergebnis vieler Faktoren. Nur die Summe aller hat Persil zur bestimmenden Marke im deutschen Waschmittelmarkt gemacht:

- zu allen Zeiten überlegene Produktleistung: „Immer das beste Persil seiner Zeit“;
- Qualitätsgarantie von Henkel;
- Persil als Vorreiter im Markt durch kontinuierliche Entwicklung großer Produktinnovationen;
- Orientierung an den Bedürfnissen der Umwelt;
- gleich bleibend hohe Investitionen in Forschung und Technologie, um den Vorsprung in Produktleistung, Convenience und Umweltverträglichkeit durch ständige Weiterentwicklung zu garantieren;
- Positionierung mit dem Anspruch, Nr. 1 zu sein: „Das beste Waschmittel für Reinheit und Pflege“;
- Kontinuität in der Markenführung;
- Pflege der Stammverwender;
- Gewinnung von Neuverwendern, ohne dabei die Markenidentität zu verwässern.

Persil ist eine Marke mit Tradition und dennoch modern und zeitgemäß. Diese perfekte Kombination konnte nur gelingen, weil auch andere Faktoren berücksichtigt wurden:

- permanente Beobachtung der Verbraucher und das frühzeitige Erkennen ihrer Bedürfnisse;

- Umsetzung dieser Erkenntnisse in verbrauchergerechte Produktangebote und Problemlösungen;
- zeitgemäße Verbraucherkommunikation durch eine sensible Mischung aus vertrauter Kontinuität und moderner Ansprache, die die Menschen gewinnt und überzeugt;
- schnelle und flexible Anpassung an die Veränderungen im Handel;
- lückenloses System zur Prüfung aller Marketing-Mix-Faktoren;
- ständige Erfolgskontrolle aller Maßnahmen.

Wesentlicher Teil des Persil-Erfolges ist also der Blick auf den Verbraucher, das Erkennen seiner Bedürfnisse und die Entwicklung von Produktinnovationen, die seine Wünsche erfüllen. Der andere Teil ist ein Marketing-Mix, das die einmalige Tradition von Persil gezielt nutzt, ohne dabei unmodern zu werden.

Dieses einzigartige Spannungsfeld zwischen Tradition und Innovation sorgt jeden Tag dafür, dass Persil auch in Zeiten eines verschärften Wettbewerbs die große Marke bleibt. Nur Persil bleibt Persil.

5. Grenzenloses Persil. Die internationale Verbreitung der Marke

In seiner 125-jährigen Firmengeschichte hat sich Henkel vom deutschen Unternehmen zu einem weltweit operierenden Konzern gewandelt. Dies spiegelt sich auch in der Internationalisierung der „Flagship-Brand“ Persil wider:

Persil wurde bereits 1908 in der Schweiz, Österreich, den Niederlanden und Belgien eingeführt. 1909 folgte die Einführung via Lizenzvergabe in Großbritannien und in Frankreich. Die Markenrechte gingen jedoch durch Verkauf beziehungsweise Erlöschen 1919 beziehungsweise 1922 an den britischen Wettbewerber Lever Brothers, der die Marke noch heute in beiden Ländern führt und die Markenrechte in nahezu allen Ländern des ehemaligen Commonwealth besitzt. Hierin liegt ein wesentlicher Grund, weshalb die weitere Internationalisierung der Marke relativ spät erfolgte.

1990 wurde Persil in Portugal und in der Türkei eingeführt. Mit der durch den Zusammenbruch des Warschauer Pakts erfolgten politischen Neuordnung eröffneten sich neue Absatzmärkte in Osteuropa: Persil wurde in fast allen Staaten dieser Region eingeführt, zuletzt in Russland und den GUS Staaten. Darüber hinaus wurde mit China der erste außereuropäische Markt für Persil erschlossen.

Besonders starkes Wachstum konnte Persil in den Ländern des Nahen/Mittleren Ostens erzielen, wo die Marke seit Mitte der 90er Jahre eingeführt wurde. Chronologisch gesehen eine Ausnahme bildet der Libanon, wo Persil bereits seit über 50 Jahren mit über

40 Prozent Marktanteil eine marktführende Position innehat. Mit dem Launch von Persil in Saudi-Arabien und in den Golf-Staaten (1998) ist Persil in allen wichtigen Ländern des Nahen/Mittleren Ostens vertreten, unter anderem auch in Israel, Jordanien, Syrien. Inzwischen nimmt Persil in dieser Region die zweite Marktposition ein. In Ägypten verzeichnet Persil einen so großen Erfolg, dass sich dieses Land zum drittwichtigsten Persil-Absatzmarkt entwickelt hat.

Mit Finnland und Schweden wurden 2001 weitere „weiße Flecken“ auf der Persil-Landkarte geschlossen.

Ziel der Internationalisierungsstrategie von Persil ist es, das Wachstumspotenzial der Marke zu nutzen und dabei die Synergien zu nutzen, die sich bei der Führung einer großen Marke ergeben: das Erfolgskonzept sollte so weit wie möglich aus Deutschland beziehungsweise Europa in neue Märkte übertragen werden. Bei der Internationalisierung der Marke sind aber immer die länderspezifischen Besonderheiten berücksichtigt worden. So erlaubt zum Beispiel die oben angegebene markenrechtliche Situation in Frankreich Henkel nicht, die Marke Persil zu verwenden; als Folge wird in Frankreich das internationale Persil Konzept unter der Marke „Le Chat“, die 1986 akquiriert wurde, angeboten. Eine international vollständig standardisierte Markenführung ist aber auch aufgrund unterschiedlicher Verbraucherbedürfnisse, unterschiedlicher Waschgewohnheiten oder aufgrund differenzierender Marktentwicklungen ohnehin nicht möglich. So haben sich beispielsweise in vielen europäischen Märkten Produktangebotsformen entwickelt, die in vielen „Emerging Markets“ (noch) nicht existieren: konzentrierte und traditionelle Pulver, Flüssigprodukte und Tabletten charakterisieren europäische Märkte, während die Segmente der „Highfoams“ (hochschäumende Produkte primär für Handwäsche) und „Lowfoams“ (niedrigschäumende Produkte für Waschmaschinen) viele Emerging Markets kennzeichnen.

Der Qualitäts- und Führungsanspruch sowie die damit verbundene Premium-Positionierung der Marke Persil ist aber in allen Ländern gleich: Es gibt eben doch nur ein Persil.

Markenmonopol für Qualität – Das Beispiel Miele

Jürgen Plüss

1.	**Einleitung**	**650**
2.	**Das Umfeld der Markenführung im Hausgerätemarkt**	**650**
2.1	Hohe Marktsättigung	650
2.2	Distribution im Wandel	651
3.	**Die Miele Position: Qualitative und quantitative Marktführerschaft**	**651**
4.	**Miele: Die Erfolgsfaktoren**	**654**
4.1	Einzelmarkenstrategie	654
4.2	Markencode Qualität	655
4.3	Premiumposition in der Preispolitik	656
4.4	Innovation	657
4.5	Langlebiges Design	658
4.6	Guter Service beziehungsweise Kundendienst	660
4.7	Breite Distribution	661
4.8	Kommunikation: Kreativität reduziert auf das Produkt	662
4.9	Erfolgsfaktor „Erfolg“	664
4.10	Kontinuität	664
5.	**Ausblick**	**665**

1. Einleitung

Aktuelle Kennzeichen vieler Branchen und Märkte sind hohe Marktsättigung, Produktreife und intensiver Preiswettbewerb. Käufer sind zum Engpass geworden. Die strategischen Optionen von Unternehmen sind häufig immer die gleichen: kostengetriebene Volumenstrategien durch Übernahme von Wettbewerbern und Globalisierung von industriellen Aktivitäten einerseits oder Erlösoptimierung durch Premium- oder Qualitätsstrategien andererseits. Die Marke Miele ist ein gutes Beispiel für eine auf dem Faktor Qualität aufgebaute Differenzierungsstrategie mit dem Ergebnis einer einmaligen Marktposition, die sich durch qualitative als auch quantitative Marktführung in wesentlichen Segmenten des Hausgerätemarktes auszeichnet.

2. Das Umfeld der Markenführung im Hausgerätemarkt

2.1 Hohe Marktsättigung

Der Hausgerätemarkt ist durch eine hohe Marktsättigung beziehungsweise Haushaltssättigung geprägt. Für so genannte bedarfsnotwendige Produkte, also solche, ohne die nach heutigen Maßstäben kein zivilisatorisches Leben denkbar scheint, beträgt die Sättigung 95 Prozent und mehr. Zu solchen Produktgruppen gehören Kühlgeräte, Kochgeräte (Herde, Backöfen, Kochfelder) und Waschautomaten. Produktgruppen, deren Haushaltssättigung noch Wachstum zeigen, sind solche, die zusätzliche Lebensqualität und Komfort durch Zeitersparnis versprechen. Das sind zum Beispiel Geschirrspüler und Wäschetrockner, die in Deutschland erst in 50 beziehungsweise 35 Prozent aller Haushalte zu finden sind. Allerdings sind für diese Produkte Sättigungsraten von 95 Prozent, also ähnlich denen von so genannten bedarfsnotwendigen Produkten, nicht realistisch erreichbar, sodass das Wachstumstempo auch für diese Produktgruppen abnehmend sein wird. Aufgrund der haushaltsdemografischen Entwicklung dürften die Grenzen dafür bei etwa 70 beziehungsweise 50 Prozent liegen.

Demzufolge hat sich das Volumen des deutschen Hausgerätemarktes in den letzten Jahren nicht erhöht. Im Gegenteil, der Wettbewerb um Marktanteile hatte den Markt durch Preiserosionen leicht schrumpfen lassen. Reale Preisrückgänge Mitte der 90er Jahre wurden von nominalen Preisveränderungen, das heißt Leistungs- und Ausstattungsverbesserungen bei unveränderten Preisen, Ende der 90er Jahre abgelöst.

2.2 Distribution im Wandel

Ein weiteres Marktmerkmal, das die Wettbewerbsintensität erhöht, ist der Wandel in der Distribution. Der Hausgerätemarkt kennt im Wesentlichen drei Distributionskanäle: den Elektrohandel, den Küchen-/Möbelhandel und den Versandhandel. Alle drei Kanäle sind im Wandel begriffen, wobei insbesondere der Elektro- und der Versandhandel derzeit einen bedeutsamen Strukturwandel erleben, der durch das Wachsen von Großbetriebsformen (Fachmärkte) bestimmt wird. Fachmarktkonzepte mit den Leistungsfaktoren große Fläche, komplette Sortimente und aggressiver Preiswettbewerb greifen sowohl mittelständische Vertriebsformen als auch den Versandhandel an. Lediglich im Vertriebskanal Küchen-/Möbelhandel bleibt die Verteilung zwischen Großbetriebsformen und so genannten Küchenstudios nahezu gleich. Daran sollte sich auch in den nächsten Jahren nicht so viel ändern, da die große Dienstleistungsbreite, die hochwertige Küchen und Einbaugeräte verlangt, auf Sicht weiter von Spezialvertrieben besser abgedeckt werden kann als von Fachmärkten.

Der Hausgerätemarkt ist also durch einige Faktoren geprägt, die man durchaus als ungünstig bezeichnen kann. Wenn es einem Unternehmen dennoch gelingt, vor diesem Hintergrund Erträge zu erwirtschaften, Wachstum zu erzielen und mit Optimismus den weiteren Ausbau seiner Marktposition zu realisieren, dann muss die Frage gestellt werden, wie eine solche Position geschaffen werden konnte und welche Erfolgsfaktoren für weitere Wachstumsziele wirksam werden.

3. Die Miele Position: Qualitative und quantitative Marktführerschaft

Die Marke Miele ist in mehreren Produktsegmenten und in deren Hauptvertriebswegen mit großem Abstand qualitativer Marktführer und besitzt gleichzeitig die quantitative Marktführerschaft. Das hieße auf andere Gebrauchsgütermärkte übersetzt, dass zum Beispiel Mercedes Benz oder Bang & Olufsen, IWC oder interlübke im Pkw-, Unterhaltungselektronik-, Uhren- oder Möbelmarkt die quantitative Marktführerschaft besitzen würden. Eine zugegebenermaßen interessante Vorstellung, die für die Markenführung aber einen nicht vorstellbaren Spagat aus exklusivem Markenversprechen, hoher Erlöserwartung und demokratischer Öffnung bedeuten würde.

Diesen Spagat bewältigt die Marke Miele. Gemäß vieler Marken- und Kompetenzuntersuchungen stellt sie den exklusiven Höhepunkt der Markenhierarchie im Hausgerätemarkt dar. Miele Produkte erzielen dazu im Regelfall 50 Prozent und höhere Preise im Vergleich zum Durchschnitt aller anderen Wettbewerber. Andererseits ist die Distribution breit und schließt alle Fachhandelsstrukturen mit ein; die Marktanteile im Elektrohandel betragen für Kernerzeugnisse 20 bis 30 Prozent (GfK, Nürnberg).

Dieser Spagat zwischen qualitativer und quantitativer Marktführerschaft stellt die folgende Abbildung gut dar:

Abbildung 1: **Miele Marktposition**

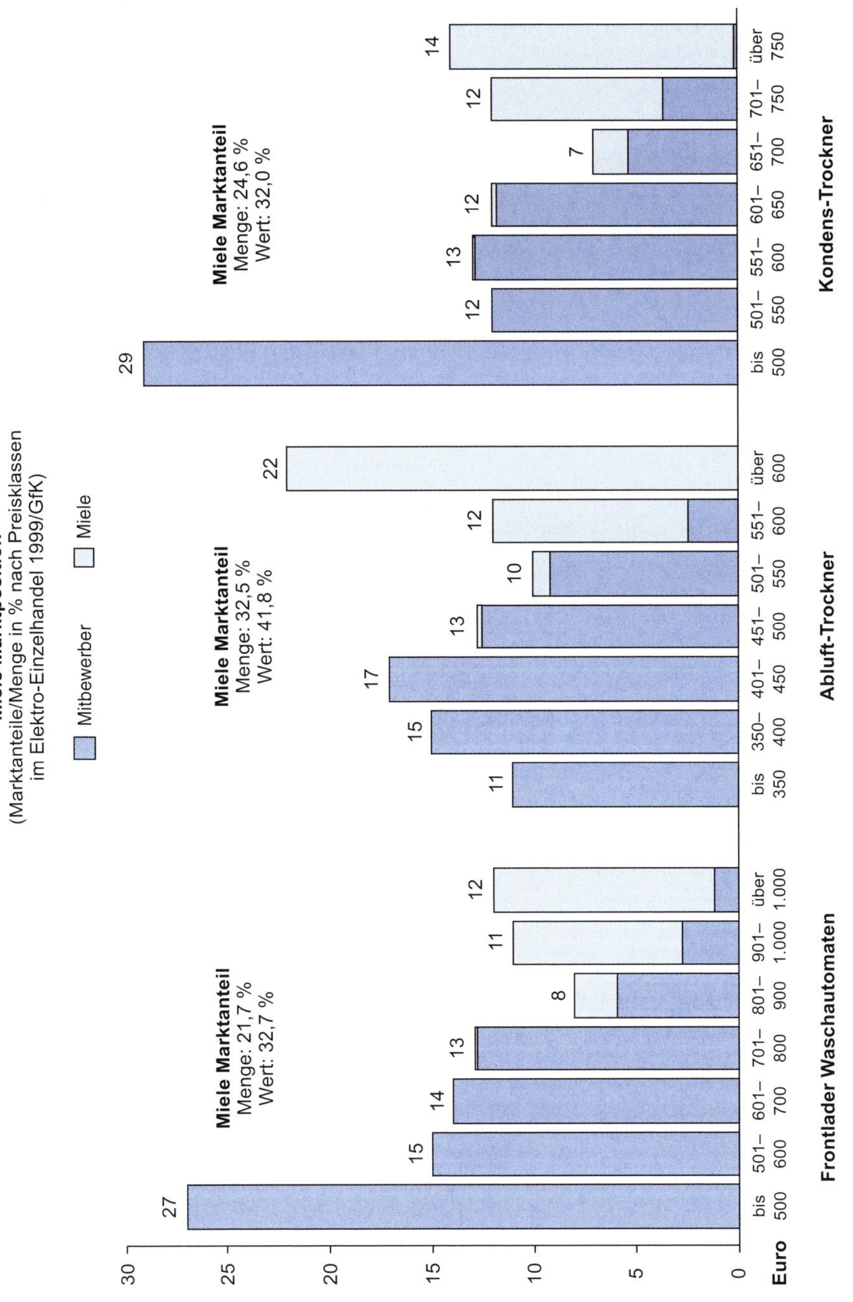

Am Beispiel der oben gezeigten Produktgruppen Frontlader, Waschautomaten und Wäschetrockner lässt sich die Miele Position gut illustrieren. Die Grafik zeigt die Preisklassenverteilung des Marktes und die von der Marke Miele belegten Segmente. Ablesbar daraus sind vier interessante Faktoren:

1. Der von Miele mitdefinierte Markt entspricht nicht der Lehre der klassischen Preis-Mengen-Funktion, nach der Nachfragesegmente mit zunehmendem Preis kleiner werden beziehungsweise sich die größte Nachfrage beim niedrigsten Preis einstellt.
2. Der Markt weist – selbst bei relativ homogenen Gütern – eine deutliche Nachfragespreizung auf, die auf unterschiedlich ausgeprägte Kaufmotive beziehungsweise darauf ausgelegte Angebote schließen lässt.
3. Der High-end-Markt ist ein geschlossener Miele Markt, der nahezu monopolistisch von der Marke Miele begründet und ausgeschöpft wird.
4. Der Wert-Marktanteil von bis zu 40 Prozent weist eine ungewöhnliche Dominanz in Form qualitativer und quantitativer Marktführung auf, die aus anderen Gebrauchsgütermärkten nicht vergleichbar bekannt ist.

Abbildung 2: **Preisabstand zum Wettbewerb**

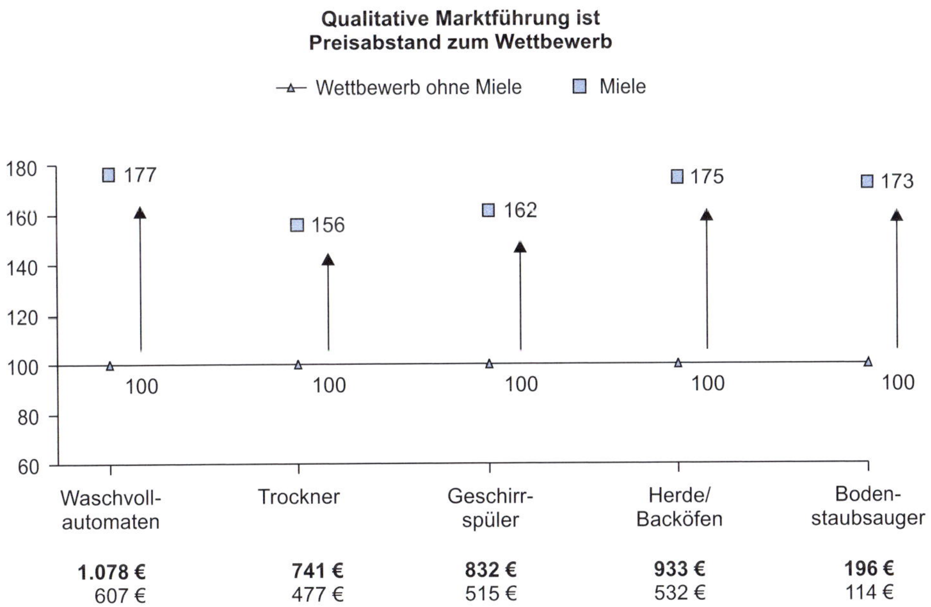

GABLER GRAFIK

Ursächlich für diese Marktposition ist die Fähigkeit der Marke Miele, deutlich über Wettbewerbsniveau liegende Preise für ihre Erzeugnisse zu erzielen, ohne dabei gleichzeitig als Randsegmentanbieter eingestuft zu werden. Die nebenstehende Grafik stellt die von der GfK ermittelten Preise für Miele Produkte als Index gegenüber dem Preisniveau des Wettbewerbs dar.

Wie ist das Markenphänomen Miele zu erklären? Wie gelingt es einer Marke, ein Markenversprechen zu kommunizieren und einzulösen, das in einem klassisch reifen Markt nicht nur deutlich höhere Preise, sondern teilweise auch die quantitative Marktführerschaft realisieren lässt. Es sind mehrere Erfolgsfaktoren, die im Falle der Marke Miele einen geschlossenen Wirkungskreis bedeuten.

4. Miele: Die Erfolgsfaktoren

4.1 Einzelmarkenstrategie

Der Kaufprozess für langlebige Gebrauchsgüter, wie zum Beispiel Hausgeräte (durchschnittliche Hausgeräte weisen eine Nutzungszeit von 10 bis 12 Jahren auf, Miele Hausgeräte dagegen von 20 Jahren), erfolgt nur wenige Male im Leben. Aus der Kaufmotivforschung für Hausgeräte weiß man, dass man eigentlich solche Geräte fürs Leben kauft. Elementare Markenwerte dafür sind Langlebigkeit, Zuverlässigkeit, Sicherheit. Diese Werte besetzt die Marke Miele mit hohem Abstand zu allen Wettbewerbern am stärksten und am glaubwürdigsten.

Die aus vielen Image- und Kompetenzstudien bekannten Werte sind stabile Wirkungsfaktoren, weil sie ihren Ursprung nicht aus Kommunikationsversprechen beziehen, sondern aus erlebten Erfahrungen beziehungsweise aus Beobachtung oder Empfehlung Dritter. Teilweise besteht im Fall Miele diese Erfahrung als eine über Generationen gewachsene Familienerfahrung. Die Marke Miele besitzt in den Köpfen der Käufer quasi ein Markenmonopol für den Erfolgsfaktor Qualität, ein wichtiges Basismotiv in der Kaufentscheidung von Hausgeräten.

Gerade bei langen Kaufzyklen, im Fall des Ersatzbedarfes teilweise mit recht kurzer Kaufvorbereitung, ohne Möglichkeit des Aufbaus warenkundlichen Wissens, stellen abrufbare Markenversprechen sichere Entscheidungshilfen für den Käufer dar. Die Inhalte der Marke Miele werden seit über 100 Jahren mit unverändertem Schwerpunkt – nämlich Qualität – kommuniziert.

Das Markenbild Miele basiert auf gewachsener Produkt- und Leistungskompetenz, die ursächlich für das Markenbild sind. Damit bestätigt Miele die These „Käufer kaufen Marken, aber Produkte müssen halten, was Marken versprechen.“ Verspricht eine Marke zu viel, produziert das Kundenirritation bis hin zu Kundenunzufriedenheit. Übertrifft die

Produktwahrnehmung das Markenversprechen, ist auch das irritierend, jedoch mit positiver Wirkung. Ein Produkterlebnis, das einem abgespeicherten Markenbild entspricht, wirkt dagegen am stärksten, nämlich in Form einer Bestätigung. Ein solches Erlebnis wird als Bestätigung eines positiven Vorurteils erlebt, das das vorhandene Markenbild verfestigt. Verfestigte Markenbilder sind eine Vertrauensbastion, die von anderen Wettbewerbern nur schwer eingenommen werden kann.

4.2 Markencode Qualität

Jede große Marke hat ihren Ruf durch ihren Faktor Qualität begründet. Langfristiger Erfolg kann nur durch langfristige positive Qualitätserlebnisse entstehen. Negative Qualitätserlebnisse verstoßen gegen das Ziel Kundenzufriedenheit. Mangelnde Kundenzufriedenheit führt zum Markenwechsel. Produkt- und Dienstleistungsqualität sind in heutigen gesättigten und reifen Märkten zu einer Selbstverständlichkeit geworden beziehungsweise werden als Selbstverständlichkeit angenommen. Erst eine besondere Form von Qualität wird als Leistungsdifferenz bemerkt. Auch der Faktor Qualität benötigt eine Differenzierung zu Wettbewerbsangeboten, ansonsten siegt bei qualitativ ähnlichen Produkten das preislich vermeindlich attraktivere.

Der Qualitäts-Mythos einer Marke lässt sich durch Kommunikation nicht aufbauen. Starke und stabile Markenwerte sind in erster Linie Ergebnis von gemachter, beobachteter oder übermittelter Erfahrung. Die sprichwörtliche Miele Qualität ist Basis für Kundenzufriedenheit, die von Besitzern wiederum allumfassend mit dem Begriff Qualität begründet wird.

Kundenzufriedenheit wird allgemein als Differenz zwischen Kundenerwartung und deren subjektiver Wahrnehmung ausgedrückt. Für Miele bedeutet das eine ständig hohe Herausforderung, denn einerseits ist die Kundenerwartung enorm hoch (man hat das Beste gekauft und einen höheren Preis bezahlt), und andererseits darf die Differenz zur erlebten Wahrnehmung maximal gering ausfallen.

Die Qualitätsdimensionen, an die Höchstforderungen gestellt werden, sind umfangreich und umfassend: zum Beispiel Langlebigkeit (20 Jahre), Zuverlässigkeit (keine überflüssigen Reparaturen), Funktionsgüte (beste Wasch- und Spülergebnisse), geringer Wasser- und Energieverbrauch (ökologische Kompetenz wird unterstellt), beste Bedienbarkeit (Einknopfbedienung, Klarschriftblenden statt Piktogramme), Geräuscharmut und visuelle Langlebigkeit (emaillierte Gehäuse, klassisches, alterloses Design).

Die Miele Qualitätsphilosophie ist ausschließlich an eigenen Normen und Ansprüchen gewachsen. Das Qualitäts-Know-how entsteht ständig durch intensiven Kundendialog und breites Engagement in gewerblichen Anwendungsmärkten, zum Beispiel in der Gastronomie, Hotellerie, in Krankenhäusern oder Waschsalons. Direkte Erfahrungstransfers aus dem Bereich der gewerblichen Anwendung für die Haushaltsanwendung sind ein qualitätstreibender Faktor, über den die meisten Hausgeräteanbieter nicht verfügen.

4.3 Premiumposition in der Preispolitik

Den Faktor Preis als Erfolgsfaktor zu beschreiben, heißt im Normalfall, dass ein Anbieter für ein vergleichbares Leistungspaket niedrigere Preispunkte als seine Wettbewerber bieten kann. Im Fallbeispiel Miele ist es das umgekehrte Beispiel, das zum Erfolgsfaktor wird.

Markenruf und Preis besitzen heute ein zwiespältiges Verhältnis. Vordergründig niedriger Preis und fairer Gegenwert für hohe Qualität scheinen im Widerspruch zu stehen. Auf der einen Seite ist in vielen Unternehmen der Trend zu beobachten, Angebote mit hoher Preisattraktivität in den Vordergrund zu stellen. Zugegeben, der niedrige Preis ist ein hochwirksames Mittel, um in kurzer Zeit Absatzsteigerungen zu realisieren. Diese Entwicklung bestätigt das Einkaufsverhalten vieler Käufer, zu allererst den Preis zu vergleichen. Gutes für weniger Geld zu erwerben, ist mittlerweile sozial akzeptiertes Verhalten geworden.

Hohe Preisattraktivität löst andererseits gegenteilige Empfindungen bei Käufern aus. Wäre das Produkt an anderer Stelle gegebenenfalls noch günstiger zu kaufen gewesen, ist eine Frage. Die generelle Unsicherheit, überhaupt das Richtige gekauft zu haben, ist eine andere. Dass es auch höherpreisige Angebote gibt, lässt den Schluss zu, dass auch qualitativ bessere Produkte verfügbar sind. Diese Erkenntnis mag bei kurzlebigen Produkten noch verschmerzbar sein, bei langlebigen Gebrauchsgütern jedoch löst das unter Umständen negative Gefühle aus, die auch an die jeweilige Marke gebunden sind.

Das von Erfahrung geprägte Wertgefühl, dass gute Qualität nie zu einem tiefen Preis und umgekehrt zu einem tiefen Preis nie Spitzenqualität realisierbar ist, hat natürlich Auswirkungen auf die Einstellungen zu einer Marke. Ein Markenbild, das Qualität als eine Kernkompetenz beinhaltet, kann durch einen tiefen Preis großen Irritationen ausgesetzt sein. Das positive Vorurteil – gute Qualität = hoher Preis – wird durch ein solches Erlebnis gestört. Andererseits bestätigt ein hoher Preis das akkumulierte Leistungsbild Qualität.

Marken, die für Qualität stehen und dafür auch objektive Mehrleistungen erbringen, die eine besondere Qualität bewirken, können aus wirtschaftlichen Gründen nie Preisführer sein, sie dürfen es auch ihrem Markenruf zuliebe nie sein. Markenführung, die dagegen verstößt, wird kurzfristig durchaus kommerziellen Erfolg verzeichnen können, langfristig jedoch den Markenkern Qualität durch Down-Trading verlieren und Wertschöpfungseffekte vernichten.

Preisvergleiche mit niedrigeren Wettbewerbsangeboten darf eine Marke deshalb nicht irritieren, da bei hinreichender Differenz ein echter Vergleich nicht möglich ist. Man kann eine vordergründig objektive, vergleichbare Ausstattung bewerten, aber was ist einem Kunden eine größere Langlebigkeit, der Komfort, diesen Produkterneuerungsprozess für viele Jahre vergessen zu können, die Ruhe und die Sicherheit wert? Was bedeutet einem Käufer die innere Zufriedenheit, das Beste gekauft zu haben? Was bedeutet ihm der soziale Fremdwirkungseffekt, ein Premiumprodukt zu besitzen? (In den USA fragt man sich dazu ganz offen: „What does a brand tell about me?") Wenn ein Preis einen Gegenwert für eine Leistung darstellt, muss ein niedriger Preis für ein Miele Produkt – gemessen an der Marken- und Leistungserwartung – irritieren. Provokativ ausgedrückt bedeutet der Umkehrschluss: ein hoher Preis stützt das Markenversprechen und die erwartete Leistung. Käufer wissen, dass das Beste nie das Billigste sein kann und dass die innere Zufriedenheit mit einem Schnäppchenkauf nie die gleiche ist wie die mit einem Produkt zu einem regulär bezahlten Gegenwert.

Diese Marken-Mehrwert-Theorie basiert im Fall Miele auf mehr Leistung in Form von intensiverer Entwicklung, Gestaltung und Erprobung, langlebigeren Bauteilen und flächendeckender Vertriebs- und Serviceunterstützung, die Aufwendungen bedeuten, die auf der einen Seite höhere Erlöse erfordern, auf der anderen Seite aber auch höhere Erlöse rechtfertigen. Die Höhe des Preises ist also ebenfalls ein Differenzierungsfaktor zum Wettbewerb, der selbstbewusst eine höhere Leistung übersetzt.

Die Durchgängigkeit eines Preises in einer breiten Distribution ist ein anderer Faktor, der ernsthaft zu beobachten und zu steuern ist. Marken- und Produktversprechen und der Preis als Gegenwert sind unteilbare Größen, deren Balance größte Aufmerksamkeit gewidmet werden muss. Die Marke würde sonst großen Irritationen ausgesetzt sein und der Handel sich selbst um die erforderliche Kostendeckung für Ausstellungsgestaltung, Beratung, Auslieferung und Anschluss eines hochwertigen Gerätes bringen.

4.4 Innovation

Marken leben von ihrem Ruf. Qualität stellt eine eher statische Basis des Rufes dar. Die dynamische Komponente dagegen ist die Innovation. Starke Marken sind deshalb auch immer innovative Marken, die ihren Markt oder ihr Erzeugnissegment nachvollziehbar weiterentwickelt haben.

Innovationen sind ein erheblicher Teil wahrgenommener Leistungsgeschichte. Abgesehen davon, dass Innovation einen wichtigen Baustein für Differenzierung und Wertschöpfung darstellt, besitzt Innovation einen hohen Wahrnehmungsgrad in der Öffentlichkeit. Immer wieder der Erste zu sein und einen Markt technisch voranzutreiben, verschafft einer Marke Respekt und Anerkennung. Marken, die als erfolgreiche Innovatoren bekannt sind, besitzen zudem Vertrauen in Form eines positiven Vorurteils. Das heißt neue Produkte von innovativ gesehenen Marken werden ohne Misstrauen oder Verzögerung angenommen, was geringere Marktwiderstände beziehungsweise geringere Produkteinführungsaufwendungen bedeutet.

Miele besitzt eine 100-jährige Innovationsgeschichte, die in wesentlichen Bereichen die Hausgeräteindustrie vorangetrieben hat. Historische Innovationsfelder waren der Waschmaschinen- und Geschirrspülerbereich. Neueste Beispiele sind die patentierte Besteckschublade in Geschirrspülern, die programmweit angebotene Update-Funktion für Steuerelektroniken, das als erstes eingeführte Handwaschprogramm für empfindliche Wolle oder Seide in der Waschmaschine oder der weltweit erste und einzige Einbau-Kaffeevollautomat (vgl. Abbildung 3).

Miele als unabhängiger und ausschließlicher Hausgerätespezialist – im Gegensatz zu vielen anderen spartengeführten Konzernmarken – lebt ausschließlich von Hausgeräten für den privaten und gewerblichen Einsatz. Die sich daraus ergebende Konzentration auf ein Kerngeschäft verschafft Miele eine hohe Auseinandersetzungsintensität mit den Bedürfnissen seiner Kunden und eine größere Umsetzungsschnelligkeit von Ideen als eher schwerfällig operierende Spartenorganisationen.

Abbildung 3: Beispiele für Miele Innovationen: Geschirrspüler und Einbau-Kaffeevollautomat

GABLER GRAFIK

4.5 Langlebiges Design

Design ist materialisiertes Markenbild. Das bedeutet, dass Markenführung und Design eng miteinander verzahnt werden müssen, um sicherzustellen, dass Markeninhalte durch Produktgestaltung keinen Irritationen ausgesetzt werden.

Produkte werden immer mehr nur noch über ihre äußere Form wahrgenommen. Die Produktgestaltung ist somit nicht nur ein Differenzierungsfaktor, der Qualität, Wert, Güte und Status darstellen soll, sondern auch ein Qualitätsfaktor, der als gute Ergonomie, leichte Bedienbarkeit, visuelle Langlebigkeit und Robustheit bestehen muss.

Das Miele Design ist an diesen Werten orientiert, ohne auf gewünschte emotionale Wirkungsfaktoren, so zum Beispiel bei Küchengeräten wie Backöfen oder Dunstabzugshauben, verzichten zu wollen. Kurzlebige modische Gestaltungselemente haben bei einer Produktlebenszeit von mehr als fünf Jahren mit einer Nutzungszeit in den Haushalten von bis zu über 20 Jahren keine Chance. Die weitgehende horizontale Designhomogenität des Miele-Designs sorgt für die störungsfreie Kombination von mehreren Produkten; die ebenfalls beachtete vertikale Designhomogenität lässt neue Miele-Produkte auch mit Vorgängerserien ohne große Brüche kombinieren. Bedienbarkeit, visuelle Ruhe, hohe Wertanmutung und internationale Gültigkeit sind Basiswerte des Miele-Designs, das häufig Vorlage für markttypische Gestaltungsstandards abgibt (vgl. Abbildung 4).

Abbildung 4: Beispiele für Miele-Design

GABLER GRAFIK

Markenbilder, deren Dimensionen zukünftig verändert werden sollen, können mit Hilfe des Instruments Design kommunikationsstark weiterentwickelt werden. Wichtig dabei ist, den Istzustand eines Markenbildes und seiner Kernkompetenzen zu ermitteln und geplante Weiterentwicklungen von Markeninhalten exakt zu beschreiben. Für die Marke Miele heißt das zum Beispiel, die besondere Markenkompetenz für Reinigungsgeräte (zum Beispiel Waschautomaten, Wäschetrockner, Geschirrspüler, Staubsauger) in Richtung einer Genuss- und Emotionalkompetenz gezielt zu erweitern. Eine zugeordnete Genusskompetenz ist für das Wachstumsziel des Unternehmens im Segment Kochgeräte unumgänglich. Innovationen und eine Vielzahl von emotional adäquaten Designlösungen für genussorientierte Kochgeräte haben geholfen, dass der Marke Miele mittlerweile auch auf diesem Gebiet hohe Kompetenz vom Handel und von Käufern zugeordnet wird.

4.6 Guter Service beziehungsweise Kundendienst

Service beziehungsweise Kundendienst besitzen für viele Konsumgüterbereiche keinen besonders herausragenden Stellenwert. Für langlebige Gebrauchsgüter stellt der Kundendienst aber ein enorm wichtiges Instrument dar, das Markenkompetenz stärken oder auch schwächen kann. Wenn Markenruf durch akkumulierte Leistungsgeschichte geschrieben wird, stellen Kundendiensterlebnisse unter Umständen die entscheidenden Kapitel dar. Servicefälle sind ärgerlich und schwächen die Markenloyalität. Wenn aber nach vielen Jahren ein Defekt auftritt, kann auch eine Stärkung der Beziehung eintreten. Ein Kundendienst, der leicht erreichbar, schnell verfügbar, freundlich, kompetent und sauber einen Defekt beseitigt, stützt positive Markenbilder. Das in diesem Zusammenhang häufiger gehörte Zitat von Sprechern der Automobilindustrie „Jeder Kundendienstfall gibt uns die Möglichkeit, die Leistungsfähigkeit unseres Unternehmens unter Beweis zu stellen“ ist so falsch nicht, wenn die Kundendienstabwicklung perfekt für den Kunden abläuft.

Kundendienstfälle sind ebenfalls Teil eines Beziehungsmanagements zwischen Unternehmen und Kundschaft. Die Intensität und Gestaltung der Beziehung zwischen beiden Partnern werden zukünftig von noch größerer Wichtigkeit sein als bereits heute. Mit zunehmender Serviceverknappung im Handel wird der direkte Kontakt zwischen Marke und Käufer wichtiger. Passive Medien, zum Beispiel die der klassischen Werbung, werden durch aktive dialogorientierte Medien, wie zum Beispiel Clubstrukturen oder auch das Internet, mehr und mehr ergänzt beziehungsweise zukünftig auch schrittweise ersetzt werden können. Eine hervorragende Kundendienststruktur ist Teil einer solchen Beziehungskette.

Ein guter Kundendienst erhöht die Kundenzufriedenheit und festigt die Kundenbindung. Miele legt auf dieses Instrument enorm hohen Wert und betrachtet dieses nicht nur als Profitcenter, sondern auch als Investition in Markenzufriedenheit und -vertrauen.

4.7 Breite Distribution

Marktführerschaft erfordert große Präsenz. Die numerische Miele Distribution umfasst nahezu 12.000 Kunden in allen hausgeräteführenden Vertriebswegen und Betriebstypen, sobald sie klassische Fachhandelsstrukturen aufweisen.

Im Gegensatz zu gängigen Premiumstrategien, die auf eine enge und selektive Distribution setzen – damit natürlich auch nur begrenzte Präsenz besitzen und Marktführerschaft ausschließen –, setzt die Miele Strategie immer auf eine breite Distribution. Die Chancen liegen auf der Hand, die Gefahren werden jedoch meist spontan als kritischer Faktor empfunden. Eine sehr breite Distribution heißt heute ein Parallelvertrieb über verschiedene Distributionskanäle (also zum Beispiel Elektrofachhandel, Warenhäuser, Küchen- und Möbelhandel, Sanitärfachhandel, Versandhandel) einerseits und verschiedene Einzelhandelsbetriebstypen andererseits (mittelständische Betriebsgrößen, Fachmärkte, national operierende und kommunizierende Großflächenanbieter).

Eine solche breit gefächerte Distributionsarchitektur ist im Regelfall für eine Premiumstrategie, die auch Preisdisziplin bedeutet, wenig geeignet. Sie bedarf einer jahrelang entwickelten und gepflegten Vertriebskultur, die auf Gleichberechtigung setzt und auf schnelles Volumenwachstum in neuen Betriebstypen bewusst verzichtet. Das Ergebnis ist eine im Markt einmalige Distributionsbalance, die bei größtmöglicher Breite den Nachfragefaktor der Marke Miele, die Produktqualität und die enge Fachhandelsbetreuung und -unterstützung vertriebswegeübergreifend als positive und stützende Markenleistung akzeptiert und honoriert.

Distributionsbreite und -qualität sind ohne Zweifel wesentliche Erfolgsbausteine der Marke Miele. Die Breite und Qualität der Handelslandschaft sind allerdings kein stabiler Zukunftsfaktor mehr. Markenführung und Wertschöpfung, die den Handel als Teil einer Leistungskette beinhaltet, müssen sich zukünftig neuen Herausforderungen stellen. Zwei Stichworte des Wandels sind Großbetriebsformen des Handels und Internet.

Qualitativ hochwertige Produkte benötigen qualifizierte Beratung und im Fall von großen elektrischen Hausgeräten ebenfalls qualifizierte Installation beziehungsweise im Fall von Küchen-Einbaugeräten auch den fachgerechten Einbau in Küchenmöbeln. Ein Handelsumfeld, das seine Haupterfolgsfaktoren in Form großer Fläche, hoher Bekanntheit und niedrigem Preis definiert, leistet sich in der Regel in Bezug auf generelle Warenkunde, spezifisches Produkt-Know-how und Verfügbarkeit von Beratungspersonal große Defizite. Der Claim einer großen, deutschen Elektro-Fachmarktkette „Wir können nur billig." ist entweder Konzept oder – was viel mehr zu vermuten ist – Resultat von Beratungsarmut. Welche Vernichtung von Wertschöpfung in Industrie und Handel auf der einen Seite und von Missachtung von Kundenbedürfnissen und daraus resultierender mangelhafter Kundenzufriedenheit auf der anderen Seite solche Konzepte bedeuten, wird mehr und mehr allen am Prozess Beteiligten deutlich.

Das Internet ist bester Ausdruck der heute so genannten Informations- oder Wissensgesellschaft. Nahezu alle bedeutenden Hausgeräteanbieter stellen breite Produktinformationen ins Netz. Der Markt war für Käufer noch nie so transparent wie heute. Die Prognosen, das Internet würde schnell die Rolle des stationären Handels einnehmen, sind – wie selbst Internetoptimisten einräumen – verfrüht, wenn nicht sogar, bezogen auf Hausgeräte, falsch. Richtig ist, dass es ausgesprochen Internet-geeignete Warengruppen gibt, deren Vertrieb über das Netz ständig steigt. Bücher, CDs, Wein, Reisen (Verkehrsmittel oder Hotels) sind Beispiele für solche Warengruppen. Beratungsintensive, langlebige Gebrauchsgüter hingegen, die zudem noch oft eingebaut oder besonders an Strom, Wasser und Abwasser angeschlossen werden müssen, benötigen den Kontakt zum Produkt, um zweifelsfreie Überzeugungen auszulösen, dass es sich im Vergleich zu anderen Produkten um die richtige Wahl für viele Jahre bedürfnisgerechter Nutzung handelt. Dazu gehört das Ausprobieren der Bedienung, das Vergleichen der Verarbeitung, der Vergleich von Materialoberflächen und vieles mehr.

Das Internet wird für Hausgeräte eine wichtige Informationsquelle sein. Viele kaufentscheidungsrelevante Elemente lassen sich jedoch nicht im Internet abbilden. Für den Handel bedeutet das, in Zukunft mehr vor- beziehungsweise teilinformierte Käufer anzutreffen und die Beratung darauf abzustellen.

Beide Elemente des Distributionswandels erfordern von Unternehmen beziehungsweise von Marken eine erweiterte Kommunikationsbreite beziehungsweise ein verbreitertes Kommunikationsmittelangebot. Virtuelle Beratungen im Internet, Beratungs-Call-Center, Ausstellungs- und Beratungszentren, Kundenmagazine oder -clubs beziehungsweise eine Intensivierung des Kundendienstes als Beratungsservice sind dazu einige Stichworte, die Miele verstärkt einsetzt.

Die Intensivierung des Instruments der klassischen Werbung reicht zur Kompensation einer bestehenden Beratungslücke im Handel nicht aus, zumal die Zunahme der Medienvielfalt und Fragmentierung des Medienkonsums eine Intensivierung dieses Instruments, bezogen auf seine Wirkung, zweifelhaft erscheinen lässt.

4.8 Kommunikation: Kreativität reduziert auf das Produkt

Marken werden häufig im Wesentlichen über Medien wahrgenommen. Der Faktor Kommunikation ist also ein wichtiges markenführendes Instrument.

Werbung löst allerdings heute ein durchaus widersprüchliches Meinungsbild aus. Auf der einen Seite wird Werbung als lästig oder falsches Versprechen abgelehnt, teilweise aber auch als Informationsmedium voll akzeptiert. Der Stellenwert der Werbung hat ohne Zweifel durch wenig differenzierende oder generische Inhalte verloren. Werbung für Bier oder Reinigungsmittel sind Beispiele dafür. Werbung, die unterhält, besitzt durchaus Publikumsakzeptanz, was sie aber für ihre Marke bewirkt, bleibt zweifelhaft, wie Werbung, die Testimonials in den Vordergrund stellt, das Produkt aber in den Hintergrund rückt.

Will Werbung Akzeptanz erzielen, muss sie Informationen transportieren, die den Menschen verständlich machen, welches Produkt mit welchem Vorteil von welcher Marke verfügbar ist. Beispiele dafür, dass das nicht langweilig sein muss, gibt es nur eben nicht viele. Kommunikation so verstanden konzentriert sich auf das Verstärken eines vorhandenen Inhaltes. Kommunikation kann damit für ein Produkt mit innovativen Leistungen, guter Gestaltung, hoher Qualität, einem guten und erfolgreichen Markenbild viel einfacher und überzeugender sein als für ein austauschbares Produkt ohne Differenzierungskraft. Marken, die so kommunizieren, schaffen und festigen Vertrauen. Gute Kommunikation ist ein Teil akkumulierter Leistungsgeschichte von Marken, die positive Vorurteile entstehen lassen.

In diesem Sinne folgt die Miele Kommunikation im ruhigen bis beruhigendem Stil dem Bild klassischer Bestätigungswerbung (vgl. Abbildung 5). Die stilistische Halbwertszeit von Kampagnen und Markenclaims bei Wettbewerbern im Hausgerätemarkt betrug in den letzten Jahren etwa zwei Jahre. Der Miele Stil wird – abgesehen von leichten Layout-Retuschen – seit gut zehn Jahren kontinuierlich eingesetzt und bestätigt in seiner blauen Grundstimmung technische Güte, Sauberkeit, Präzision und Verlässlichkeit. Der Markenclaim „Immer Besser" bestätigt die Erwartung einer besonderen Leistung und Qualität.

Abbildung 5: Anzeigenbeispiel der Miele-Kommunikation

4.9 Erfolgsfaktor „Erfolg"

Ein Faszinationselement von Marken ist Erfolg. Es überrascht allerdings immer wieder, wie selten in der Literatur der Faktor Erfolg für Markenbilder als nennenswert erwähnt wird.

Marken besitzen heute mehr denn je auch eine soziale Identifikationsfunktion. Mit der Wahl einer bestimmten Marke wird auch immer bewusst oder unbewusst die Frage beantwortet, was erzählt diese Marke über mich. Eine Marke, die wirtschaftlichen Erfolg hat und diesen auch kommuniziert, steigert ihre Attraktivität gegenüber erfolgsärmeren Wettbewerbern oder Wettbewerbern, die Erfolg nicht kommunizieren oder nicht kommunizieren können. Abgesehen von möglichen kurzzeitigen Mitleidseffekten präferieren Käufer erfolgreiche Marken. Wirtschaftliche Probleme können selbst emotionalen Marken, wie zum Beispiel die Marke Porsche, Faszination und Begehrlichkeit kosten, wie in der Phase des niedrigen US-Dollar-Kurses Mitte der 80er Jahre, der den seinerzeit dominanten US-Absatz einbrechen ließ. In der Folge litt auch das Erfolgsimage auf dem deutschen Markt.

Käufer verbinden sich gern mit erfolgreichen Marken. Marken, die Erfolg besitzen und kommunizieren, stützen ihre Faszination und damit ihren wirtschaftlichen Status.

4.10 Kontinuität

Kontinuität an sich ist natürlich kein Erfolgsfaktor. Unterstellt wird in dieser These, dass sich die Summe aller Erfolgsfaktoren zu einem geschlossenen Bild zusammenfügen und sich inhaltlich vom Standard kohärent entsprechen. Top-Qualität und niedriger Preis ergänzen sich nicht, Innovation ohne Servicekompetenz ebenso wenig wie modisches Design und 20 Jahre Lebensdauer. Alles muss zueinander passen, wie eine gute Kette, die ihre Qualität gleichstarken Gliedern verdankt.

In diesem Sinne ist das kontinuierliche Wiederholen von spezifischen Ausprägungen von Erfolgsfaktoren ein Wirkungsmodell, das erst die Durchsetzung einer Markenpositionierung ermöglicht. Markenkerne beziehungsweise Markenbilder sind Vorstellungswelten in den Köpfen von Käufern. Nur Kontinuität und das Wiederholen selbstähnlicher Botschaften lassen diese abrufbaren Bilder entstehen.

Die an der unternehmerischen Grundidee „Qualität" orientierten Instrumente werden bei Miele über 100 Jahre gelebt. Basis dieser Kontinuität ist die stabile Inhaberstruktur in Form eines Familienunternehmens, das keinen externen Führungseinflüssen unterliegt. Nur drei Inhabergenerationen haben das Unternehmen in über 100 Jahren von der Spitze her geführt, eine in dieser Form einmalige Kontinuität, die in Kumulation ihres Wirkens die Markenposition Miele in dieser besonderen Stärke mitbegründet.

5. Ausblick

Wachstum ist nicht endlich – diese These ist absolut gesehen nicht haltbar, soll aber Ausdruck eines unternehmerischen Optimismus sein, vermeintlich begrenzte Märkte oder Marktsegmente nicht als unüberwindbare Hindernisse anzusehen. Selbst für Unternehmen mit hoher Marktausschöpfung ergeben sich immer wieder strategische Optionen, Wachstum zu erzielen.

Ein Beispiel dafür ist das Unternehmen Miele, das trotz hoher Marktausschöpfung bis hin zur Marktführerschaft in wesentlichen Marktsegmenten weiter Wachstum zeigt. Für Miele sind das im Wesentlichen drei identifizierte und engagiert umgesetzte Wachstumsoptionen:

1. Qualitatives Wachstum durch Erweiterung des Leistungsumfangs von bestehenden Produkten (Vision: Qualitatives Wachstum ist unendlich).
2. Erhöhung der Ausschöpfung des eigenen Cross-Selling-Potenzials, das heißt die Steigerung der Haushaltsausstattung mit Miele Produkten (Vision: Der komplette Miele Haushalt).
3. Ausweitung der regionalen Präsenz, insbesondere in überseeischen Märkten beziehungsweise Osteuropa (Vision: Globale Präsenz und Einnahme der qualitativen Marktführerschaft in allen bedienten Märkten).

Basis dieses Strategiebündels ist Kontinuität in den Grunderfolgsfaktoren des Unternehmens Miele, das heißt Unabhängigkeit als langfristig denkendes Familienunternehmen, Konzentration auf eine Marke, auf einen Markt und auf eine Positionierung mit einem weltweit gleichen Angebot in Spitzenqualität. Das dafür errechenbare Potenzial ist mit der derzeitigen Unternehmensgröße von 2,15 Milliarden Euro Umsatz noch lange nicht ausgeschöpft.

Markenführung und Markentransfer der Zeitschrift GEO

Jürgen Althans und Gerd Brüne

1.	**Konzeptionelle Grundlagen der Markenführung von Zeitschriften**	**668**
2.	**Markenführung von GEO**	**669**
2.1	Markenführung im Lesermarkt	669
2.11	Produktpolitik	669
2.12	Kontrahierungspolitik	672
2.13	Distributionspolitik	672
2.14	Kommunikationspolitik	673
2.2	Markenführung im Anzeigenmarkt	674
2.21	Produktpolitik	674
2.22	Kontrahierungspolitik	675
2.23	Distributionspolitik	676
2.24	Kommunikationspolitik	676
3.	**Markentransferstrategien von GEO**	**677**
3.1	Transfer auf neue Zeitschriften im Inland	677
3.2	GEO-Nebenprodukte	681
3.3	Internationalisierung	683
3.4	Fernsehen und Internet	684
4.	**Erfolgskontrolle von Markenführung und Markentransfer bei GEO**	**685**
4.1	Messkriterien	685
4.2	Ökonomische Erfolgskontrolle	685
4.3	Erfolgskontrolle im Hinblick auf den Markenwert	686
4.4	Verbundeffekte	690
5.	**Zusammenfassung**	**691**

1. Konzeptionelle Grundlagen der Markenführung von Zeitschriften

In einer immer heterogener und zersplitterter werdenden Medienlandschaft kommt der Markierung von Medienprodukten – und damit auch von Zeitschriften – eine zentrale Bedeutung zu. Bei der Übertragung des Marketinggedankens auf das Verlagsgeschäft gilt es jedoch, die Besonderheiten von Medienprodukten zu beachten (Hensmann 1980, vgl. Abbildung 1):

Abbildung 1: **Besonderheiten des Verlagsmarketing**

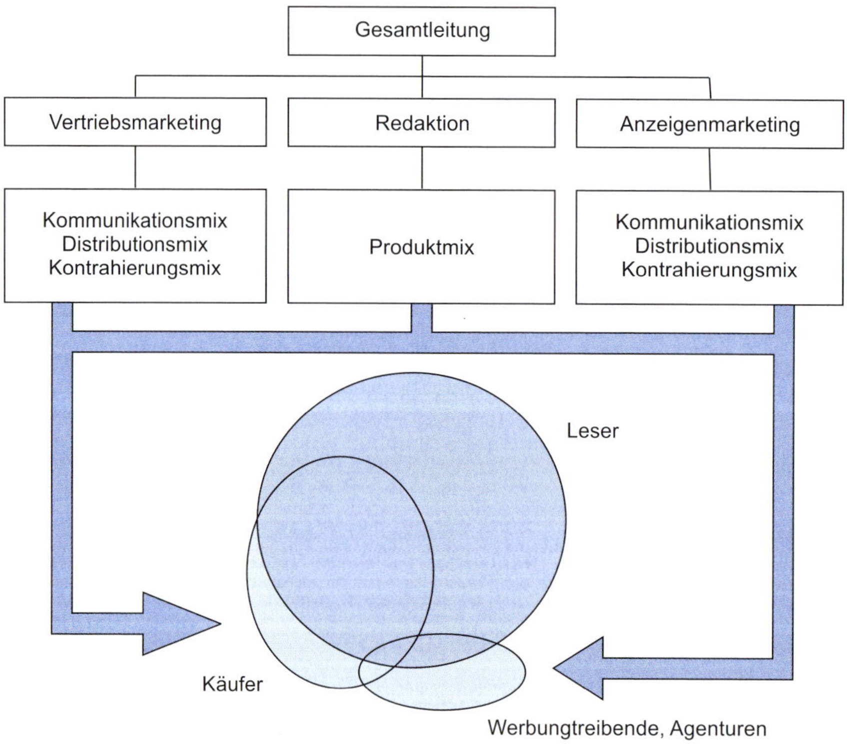

GABLER GRAFIK

- Das Produkt „Zeitschrift" wird zum einen dem Leser als Endverbraucher zur Information und Unterhaltung angeboten. Auf diesen „Käufer- beziehungsweise Leser-Markt" richten sich alle Aktivitäten des Vertriebsmarketing. Zum anderen wird das Produkt „Zeitschrift“ Werbungtreibenden und deren Agenturen als Werbeträger angeboten, um Kommunikationsbotschaften zu transportieren. Auf diesen „Inserentenmarkt“ zielt das Anzeigenmarketing. Zeitschriften sind damit grundsätzlich zugleich Konsumgut und investive Dienstleistung.

- Die Produktpolitik obliegt im Verlag nicht der Verlags- und Marketingleitung, sondern der Redaktion einer Zeitschrift unter einem verantwortlichen Chefredakteur. Somit hat die Marketingleitung keinen direkten Zugriff auf das wichtigste Element im Marketing-Mix: das Produkt. Umso mehr ist daher für den Markterfolg von Zeitschriften das Gespür der Journalisten für die Marke entscheidend, wie umgekehrt die Fähigkeit der Verlags- und Marketingleitung, „journalistisch“ zu denken. Ein konstruktives Zusammenspiel zwischen Verlagsleitung und Redaktion ist daher häufig der Schlüssel zum Erfolg einer Zeitschrift.
- Eine weitere Besonderheit des Marketing für Zeitschriften betrifft das Produkt selbst, da dieses nicht das konstituierende Marken-Merkmal „Homogenität“ aufweist. Jede Ausgabe einer Zeitschrift ist anders als die vorhergehende, stellt daher quasi ein jeweils neues Produkt dar. Doch auch hier verbleiben zumeist formal und inhaltlich konstante Parameter innerhalb einer geschlossenen Heftkonzeption, sodass man mit Fug und Recht von Zeitschriften-**Marken** reden kann.

2. Markenführung von GEO

2.1 Markenführung im Lesermarkt

2.11 Produktpolitik

Redaktionelles Selbstverständnis

Ausgangspunkt der Markenhistorie der GEO-Zeitschriftenfamilie ist das „grüne“ Reportage-Magazin GEO. 1976 wurde es als eines der aufwändigsten Printprodukte der Nachkriegszeit gegründet. Die möglichst besten Fotografen und Autoren sollten sich auf die Suche nach dem machen, was diese Zeitschrift im Untertitel trägt: Auf die Suche nach dem „neuen Bild der Erde“.

GEO-Chefredakteur Peter-Matthias Gaede begreift sein Blatt heute als „eine vitale und unverwechselbare Mischung aus der Kraft und Magie des Bildes und der Nachhaltigkeit gründlich und seriös recherchierter Texte. Mit neuen Ideen statt Schlagzeilenrecycling. Mit authentischen Reportagen statt Ex-und-Hopp-News. GEO sieht sich fern von thematischer Einseitigkeit und von der Nüchternheit mancher Fachmagazine.”

Reinhold Messner auf dem Mount Everest, Ulf Merbold an Bord des Space Shuttle, Hans Fricke in der Tiefe des Ozeans, Uwe George bei den Dinosaurier-Gräbern in der mongolischen Wüste und Oliver Sacks in den Labyrinthen der menschlichen Psyche – GEO-Reporter gehen besonders weite Wege, um für ihre Leser zu berichten. Dabei lassen sie sich bei ihrer Arbeit in der ganzen Welt von den Leitmotiven begleiten, die GEO als „Credo" mit auf den Weg gegeben wurden:

- Der Neugier auf alles Wissenswerte. Ob dies im Himalaya oder in der Tiefsee zu beobachten ist, im Kleinhirn des Menschen oder im Großrechner eines High-Tech-Labors.
- Der Aufgeschlossenheit gegenüber allem Fremden. Denn man versteht nur, was man kennen lernt, man lernt nur kennen, was man versteht.
- Dem Bewusstsein für das Bedrohte, Erhaltenswerte – für die Vielfalt menschlicher Kulturen, Träume und Pläne, für den Reichtum der Natur.

Heftkonzept und Positionierung

Das redaktionelle Konzept basierte von Beginn an auf klaren Objektleitlinien. Die frühe Niederlegung und Verfolgung dieser zentralen Leitlinien legte den Grundstein für den Aufbau einer starken Marke. Innerhalb eines Mindestumfanges von 126 Seiten Redaktion sollten die Themen ausführlich, kritisch und tiefgehend behandelt werden. Die Themenbereiche umfassten fremde Länder, Menschen, Kulturen, Gesichter einer Stadt, Abenteuer, Wissenschaft und Tiere.

Die Länge der Beiträge war vorgegeben, ebenso das formale und inhaltliche Informationsangebot. Hinsichtlich des Papiers und des Druckverfahrens wurde ebenfalls auf höchste Qualität Wert gelegt. Um die Länge, Geschlossenheit und Qualität der Beiträge in einem Heft zu gewährleisten, wurde der verfügbare Anzeigenraum beschränkt: nur zwischen den Geschichten und am Anfang und Schluss des Heftes waren Anzeigenplatzierungen vorgesehen.

Für den Aufbau einer wettbewerbsfähigen Position bot sich für GEO bei Markteinführung das Besetzen einer strategischen Nische an. Inhaltlich wurde das Blatt bei den Kultur- und Wissenszeitschriften angesiedelt, bezüglich der journalistischen Herangehensweise handelte es sich um ein Reportagemagazin.

Erst nachdem 1981 GEO Special und 1989 GEO SAISON das Licht der Zeitschriften-Welt erblickt hatten und sich seither vornehmlich Reisen, Ländern und fremden Kulturen widmen, hat sich das „grüne" GEO zum General-Interest-Reportage-Magazin weiterentwickelt und das Themenspektrum mehr und mehr vergrößert. Neue, zusätzliche Schwerpunkte wurden mit den Themenbereichen Naturwissenschaften, Medizin/Gesundheit, Psychologie, Politik und Historische Ereignisse gesetzt. Sowohl seine Leser als auch diejenigen, die GEO zumindest kennen, attestieren dem Titel, „einzigartig" zu sein. Somit besetzt GEO auch heute noch eine Marktnische.

Am ehesten vergleichbar ist GEO noch mit der deutschen Sprachausgabe von National Geographic, die 1999 gelauncht wurde. Gemeinsam ist diesen beiden Magazinen das starke Gewicht des journalistischen Stils „Reportage“. Darüber hinaus wird beiden Titeln vom Publikum bescheinigt, brillante Optik zu bieten. GEO deckt jedoch im Vergleich mit National Geographic ein breiteres Themen-Spektrum ab. Während zudem National Geographic dem deutschen Leser meist originalgetreue Übersetzungen des amerikanischen Mutterblattes bietet und damit die amerikanische Sicht der Dinge vermittelt, schreiben für die deutsche GEO-Ausgabe zumeist Autoren mit einem tiefen Einblick in die kulturellen Hintergründe der deutschen Leser (dies gilt analog auch für Frankreich, Spanien und Russland, wo es jeweils eigenständige Redaktionen gibt, die die entsprechenden Länderausgaben von GEO erstellen). Schließlich unterscheiden sich beide Magazine auch im Format – National Geographic ist, wie das amerikanische Mutterblatt, deutlich kleiner als GEO.

Abbildung 2: **GEO – Thematische Entwicklung von 1976 bis 2004**

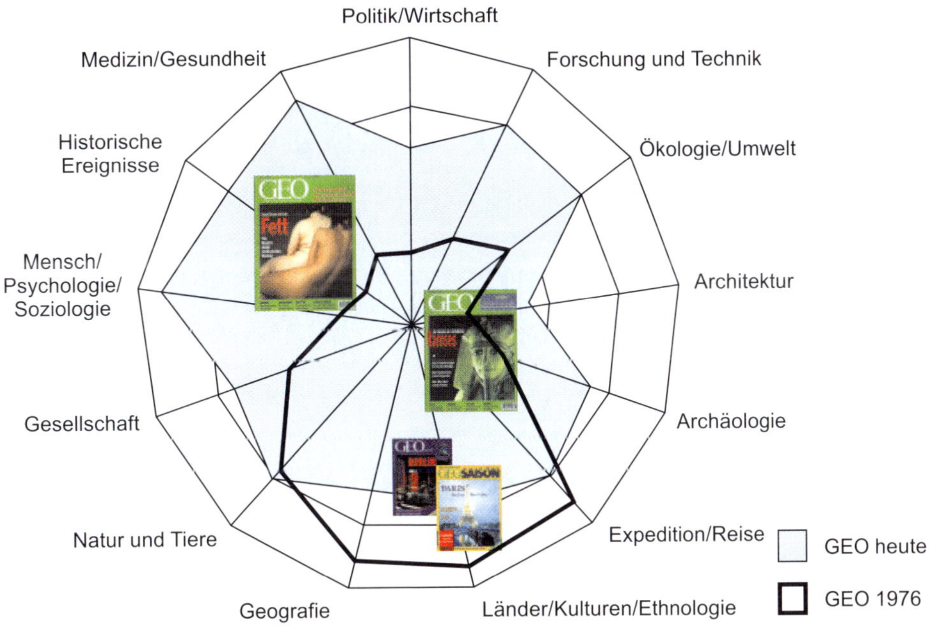

GABLER GRAFIK

Neben der Nähe zu National Geographic weist GEO jedoch auch Parallelen zu den aktuellen Wochenmagazinen auf: Mit dem Stern verbindet ihn die herausragende Fotografie, mit dem Spiegel (und vormals dem „Spiegel Reporter“) hervorragende Reportagen und mit Focus exzellente Informationsgrafiken. Darüber hinaus greifen die genannten aktuellen Wochenmagazine – nicht zuletzt bei ihren Titelgeschichten – oft Themen aus den Bereichen Wissenschaft, Medizin, Soziologie, Psychologie, Gesellschaft, Geschichte oder Geografie auf, die ähnlich auch von GEO behandelt werden (vgl. Abbildung 2).

2.12 Kontrahierungspolitik

Die Preispolitik für Zeitschriften ist in Deutschland von der grundsätzlichen Preisbindung der zweiten Hand geprägt. Dies bedeutet, dass Verlage – anders als die Anbieter vieler anderer Branchen – ihre Produkte zu einem fixen, vom Verlag festlegbaren Preis an die Leserbeziehungsweise Käufer abgeben. Der Einzelhandel hat keine Möglichkeit, den Preis von Zeitschriften individuell zu gestalten. Daher kommt der Preispolitik der Verlage im Zeitschriftenmarketing eine besondere Rolle zu.

Von Beginn an wurde GEO mit einer Hochpreispolitik auf den Markt gebracht. Zum einen lag dies zwingend in den hohen Kosten sowohl bei der redaktionellen Erarbeitung des Heftes als auch bei dessen Herstellung (Druck, Papier) begründet. Zum anderen führte auch die Selbstbeschränkung bezüglich der Anzahl beziehungsweise des Anteils von Anzeigen dazu, dass ein solches Blatt zu einem relativ hohen Copypreis angeboten werden konnte und musste.

Darüber hinaus erfolgte die hochpreisige Positionierung auch im Vertrauen darauf, dass Preise als Qualitätsindikatoren wahrgenommen werden. Ein Preistest vor der Einführung 1976 bewies, dass die potenziellen Käufer bereit waren, einen sehr hohen Preis zu bezahlen. Daher wurde GEO mit einem Copypreis von 8,00 DM im Einzelverkauf und von 6,50 DM im Abonnement eingeführt. Im Jahre 2004 betrug der Copypreis 5,80 Euro (Einzelverkauf) beziehungsweise 5,05 Euro (Abonnement).

2.13 Distributionspolitik

Der wichtigste Absatzweg für GEO und elementarer Bestandteil der GEO-Markenführung war von Anfang an der direkte Absatzkanal des **Abonnements**. Zum einen war GEO aufgrund seines besonderen Heftkonzeptes dazu prädestiniert, eine große „Community of interest“ zu erzeugen, die sich via Abonnement dauerhaft an das Magazin bindet. Zum anderen war es auch unter wirtschaftlichen Gesichtspunkten von großer Bedeutung, eine hohe Abonnentenzahl zu realisieren, da das Zeitschriftenabonnement aus Sicht eines Verlages die mit Abstand deckungsbeitragsstärkste Vertriebssparte ist.

Das Konzept ging auf: Schon zu Beginn gewann GEO rasch Abonnenten, und dieser Erfolg konnte auf hohem Niveau bis heute gehalten werden. Im Durchschnitt des Jahres 2003 hatten rund 338.000 Käufer GEO abonniert – das entspricht einem Abo-Anteil an der Gesamtauflage in Höhe von 71 Prozent. Angesichts steigender Wettbewerbsintensität im Zeitschriftenmarkt und zunehmender genereller Bindungsunwilligkeit der Leser ist zudem die von GEO erreichte durchschnittliche Abonnementdauer von rund fünf Jahren ebenfalls als sehr gut zu beurteilen.

Auch der **Einzelverkauf** über den Handel war durch die Auswahl und gezielte Selektion der Verkaufsstellen von Beginn an darauf angelegt, das Elitäre der Marke zu unterstützen. Zudem galt es, das Remissionsrisiko zu reduzieren; denn dem grundsätzlichen Vorteil der Verlage, dem Einzelhandel den Copypreis verbindlich vorzugeben, steht das Recht des Handels gegenüber, den Verlagen nicht verkaufte Hefte zurückgeben zu können. Gerade wegen der relativ hohen Produktionskosten von GEO (Druckqualität, Papier) war es daher wichtig, durch die gezielte Auswahl der belieferten Einzelhändler dafür zu sorgen, dass die Remissionsquote gering blieb. Der Einzelverkauf des GEO-Magazins erfolgt heute über circa 25.000 Verkaufsstellen des Einzelhandels – das sind nur rund ein Viertel aller Verkaufsstellen in Deutschland, in denen heute Presseprodukte angeboten werden. GEO verkaufte im Jahr 2003 durchschnittlich 89.000 Hefte auf diesem Vertriebsweg, was etwa 19 Prozent seiner Gesamt-Auflage entsprach.

Die dritte und im Zeitschriftengeschäft meist weniger erlösstarke Vertriebssparte der „sonstigen Verkäufe" (unter anderem Bordexemplare, Lesezirkel etc.) spielt bei GEO mit rund 10 Prozent der Gesamtverkäufe eine Nebenrolle. Insgesamt erzielte GEO im Durchschnitt des Jahres 2003 eine verkaufte Auflage von 474.000 Exemplaren – ein angesichts des relativ hohen Copypreises außerordentlich hoher Wert. Damit lag GEO im Übrigen auch klar vor seinem Wettbewerber National Geographic, der in diesem Zeitraum auf lediglich 278.000 Exemplare kam – trotz eines gegenüber GEO niedrigeren Copypreises von 3,95 Euro.

2.14 Kommunikationspolitik

Die Kommunikationspolitik ist schwerpunktmäßig auf die werbliche Umsetzung der Einzigartigkeit von GEO ausgerichtet. Dazu wurde eine Reihe von Gestaltungsgrundsätzen aufgestellt:

- Die zentrale Produktaussage „Das neue Bild der Erde" sowie der Claim „Die Welt mit anderen Augen sehen" sollen beim Leser verankert werden.
- Die eingesetzten Werbemittel sollen durch eine qualitativ hochwertige Gestaltung einen hohen Aufmerksamkeits- und Erinnerungswert besitzen und dabei zugleich die hohe Qualität von GEO repräsentieren.
- Durch einen konstanten Werbestil soll die Kontinuität des GEO-Auftritts auch bei der Erweiterung des Angebots im Sinne des Markentransfers sichergestellt werden.

Auch die Werbeträgerauswahl ist darauf ausgerichtet, markengerechte Umfelder zu finden und insbesondere die relevanten Zielgruppen zu erreichen. Hochwertige Zeitschriften mit gehobenen Zielgruppen stellen für die Marke GEO daher sowohl in der Einzelheft-Bewerbung wie auch in der Abonnentenwerbung die Basiswerbeträger dar. Der Einsatz von TV-Werbung dagegen ist für GEO aufgrund der insgesamt eher unterdurchschnittlich gebildeten Zielgruppen bei reichweitenstarken Sendungen sowie der nicht exakt planbaren Zielgruppen in Special-Interest-Sendungen ausgeschlossen worden.

Die Neukundengewinnung im Abonnentenbereich konzentriert sich primär auf Direktwerbemittel (Beilagen, Beihefter) in GEO selbst sowie in affinen anderen Zeitschriften. Die ständige Variation der Kreation, der Angebotsform, der Werbeträger und der Bestellmechanik führen zu einer anhaltenden Produktivität und Aktualität dieses Kommunikationsweges.

Die Bindung der so gewonnenen Abonnenten wird zum Beispiel über redaktionelle Preisausschreiben, einen sechsmal jährlich erscheinenden Newsletter (exklusiv für Abonnenten) und besondere Angebote kommunikativ gestärkt. Zu diesen besonderen Angeboten für Abonnenten zählen etwa preisreduzierte GEO-Produkte wie Bücher oder Kalender, rabattierte Eintrittspreise für spezielle, von GEO unterstützte Ausstellungen oder auch die Möglichkeit, exklusive Reisen mit GEO-Redakteuren erleben zu können.

Im Jahre 2001 wurde das gesamte Kommunikationskonzept der GEO-Familie grundlegend überarbeitet. In ein CI-Manual flossen Leitlinien ein, die allen für GEO-Titel tätigen Agenturen verbindliche Vorgaben für die Gestaltung von Kommunikationsmitteln setzen, ohne jedoch dadurch kreative Ansätze zu drosseln (vgl. Kapitel 3.1).

2.2 Markenführung im Anzeigenmarkt

2.21 Produktpolitik

Der Werbeträger GEO ist aus Sicht der Werbungtreibenden und Agenturen zum einen durch das redaktionelle Umfeld geprägt, das durch die Redaktion geschaffen wird. Zum anderen sind für die Anzeigenkunden die Media-Leistungsmerkmale von GEO relevant: Die verkaufte und verbreitete Auflage, die Zahl der Leser (die bei Qualitätszeitschriften wie GEO deutlich höher als die Zahl der verbreiteten Exemplare ist), die Zielgruppenqualität etc. spielen hier eine Rolle. Konkret bedeutet dies bei GEO, dass die hohe Auflage ein überaus wichtiges Argument für den Anzeigenverkauf darstellt. Hinzu tritt die Reichweite: die unabhängige „Media-Analyse" 2/2004 bescheinigt GEO, im Durchschnitt 3,11 Millionen Leser zu erreichen – womit GEO das reichweitenstärkste Monatsmagazin in Deutschland ist. Und da diese Leser zudem im Sinne der Werbungtreibenden überdurchschnittlich gute Zielgruppenqualitäten aufweisen (Alter, Einkommen, Bildung etc.), erfreut sich GEO im Anzeigenmarkt eines ausgezeichneten Rufs.

Alle oben genannten Merkmale sind eine Resultante der redaktionellen Umfelder sowie der Erfolge im Vertriebsmarketing. Das Anzeigenmarketing kann sie kommunikativ herausstellen, ist jedoch nicht selbst in der Lage, diese Daten zu beeinflussen. Gestaltungsparameter in der Anzeigen-Produktpolitik von Zeitschriften sind jedoch zum Beispiel besondere Anzeigenformate, Beilagemöglichkeiten (zum Beispiel regional differenziert), Beihefterofferten oder Anzeigen-Bundling-Angebote. Auch die Anzeigenplatzierung im Heft – also etwa die Fragen, in welchen redaktionellen Umfeldern die Anzeige platziert ist, ob sie auf einer der begehrten „Umschlagseiten" steht oder ob sie noch vor der jeweiligen Konkurrenz des Werbungtreibenden steht – stellt ein Gestaltungsmerkmal in der Produktpolitik dar.

Eine konsequente Markenführung verbietet bei GEO jedoch das Angebot bestimmter Anzeigenformate (zum Beispiel die „Inselanzeige", wie sie etwa der Spiegel akzeptiert – mitten im Text), da damit das hochwertige Layout und die fulminante redaktionelle Optik Schaden nehmen könnten. Dennoch gilt es, der Nachfrage nach neuen Anzeigenangeboten nicht grundsätzlich ablehnend gegenüber zu stehen, sondern sich evolutionär auf neue Trends auch in den Anzeigenformaten einzustellen – solange sie mit dem GEO-Konzept vereinbar erscheinen. Eine Entscheidung darüber fällt stets unter Einbeziehung der Chefredaktion.

2.22 Kontrahierungspolitik

GEO musste von Anfang an in der Anzeigenpreispolitik – ausgedrückt im absoluten Seitenpreis und dem Tausend-Leser-Preis (Anzeigenpreis geteilt durch Anzahl der Leser mal 1000) – den anspruchsvollen Gesamtauftritt unterstützen, gleichzeitig aber wettbewerbsorientiert sein und bleiben. Dies war in Abwägung zu dem begrenzt zur Verfügung stehenden Anzeigenraum ein besonderer „preispolitischer Drahtseilakt".

Im Vergleich mit Zeitschriften wie etwa Stern, Spiegel oder Focus ist GEO relativ teurer, was den Tausend-Leser-Preis betrifft. GEO vermag diesen Nachteil jedoch sowohl durch die sehr hohe Zielgruppenqualität (die allerdings auch bei den drei aktuellen Wochenmagazinen gegeben ist) als auch durch weitere Leistungsmerkmale auszugleichen. So sind die hohe Druck- und Papierqualität sowie die Berechenbarkeit der Leserschaft (hohe Abonnenten-Quote) Pluspunkte, die für Anzeigenbelegungen in GEO sprechen. Zudem schätzen Werbungtreibende auch den Vorteil, dass GEO aufgrund konzeptioneller Überlegungen nur einen gewissen Anteil an Anzeigen zulässt – die Wahrscheinlichkeit, mit einer Werbebotschaft wirklich zum Leser durchzudringen, steigt deshalb nach Auffassung der Anzeigenkunden.

Im Vergleich mit den Wettbewerbern National Geographic, Bild der Wissenschaft und Spektrum der Wissenschaft weist GEO ein attraktives Preis-Leistungs-Verhältnis auf. Hier aber ist zuweilen der relativ hohe absolute Anzeigenpreis (2004: rund 34.600 Euro für eine Vierfarbseite) ein Problem, wenn das Budget des Werbungtreibenden sehr begrenzt ist.

Mit dem Wachstum im Rahmen des Markentransfers von GEO wurde das „GEO First Class Package“ geschaffen, das die Einzeltitel GEO, GEO SAISON und GEO Special als jeweilige Markt- beziehungsweise Qualitätsführer in ihren Teilmärkten zusammenfasst und zu einem Kombinations-Preis anbietet, der rund 20 Prozent unter den Preisen der Einzeltitel liegt (Anzeigen-Bundling). Mittlerweile wurde auch ein „GEO Travel Package“ eingeführt, das in entsprechender Weise ein Bundling der beiden Reise-Titel GEO SAISON und GEO Special ist und einen Preisvorteil von zehn Prozent gegenüber der Summe der Einzelpreise mit sich bringt.

2.23 Distributionspolitik

Für die Distribution von Anzeigen sind bei Verlagen in aller Regel die Anzeigenabteilungen zuständig, die gemeinsam mit dem Anzeigenaußendienst – und/oder freien Handelsvertretern – den Markt bearbeiten. Der Verkauf selbst erfolgt zum einen über Mailings und telefonische Kontaktaufnahme, zum anderen und hauptsächlich in Form des persönlichen Verkaufsgesprächs. Für den GEO-Anzeigenverkauf sind im In- und Ausland Repräsentanten in regionalen Verkaufsbüros zuständig, die von der zentralen GEO-Anzeigenabteilung mit Verkaufsargumenten und -unterlagen ausgestattet und in ihren Aktivitäten gesteuert werden.

Eingehende Anzeigenaufträge werden in den Anzeigenabteilungen weiter bearbeitet. Da es sich bei Anzeigenschaltungen um investive Dienstleistungen des Verlages handelt, die nur durch die Bereitstellung der Druckvorlagen durch die Werbungtreibenden beziehungsweise deren Agenturen erbracht werden können, ergeben sich technisch anspruchsvolle Herausforderungen an alle Beteiligten, wenn unterschiedliche Druckverfahren und Druckereien mit den technischen Vorlagen der Anzeigenkunden in Einklang gebracht werden müssen, um optimale Druckergebnisse zu erzielen.

2.24 Kommunikationspolitik

Adressaten der Kommunikationspolitik im Anzeigenmarkt sind die Geschäftspartner im Media Buying Center, das aus Entscheidungsträgern auf Werbungtreibenden- und Agenturseite zusammengesetzt ist. Für die Kommunikationspolitik von GEO ist zu bedenken, dass das vorrangige Ziel – die Positionierung und „Aufladung“ der Marke GEO im Inserentenmarkt – teilweise bereits durch die Werbung im Lesermarkt erfolgt, da die Angehörigen des Media Buying Center zugleich potenzielle Zielgruppenmitglieder im Lesermarkt sind.

Traditionell ist im Anzeigengeschäft aufgrund der relativen Überschaubarkeit der Zielgruppen und der Erklärungsbedürftigkeit des angebotenen Produkts das persönliche Gespräch das dominante Kommunikationsinstrument. Durch die Möglichkeit, die Adressdatenbanken des Hauses G+J zu nutzen, spielen zudem gezielte, nach Kundengruppen selektierbare Mailings an aktuelle und potenzielle GEO-Kunden und deren Agenturen eine wichtige Rolle. Weiterhin sind Anzeigen in Fachzeitschriften der Branche ein probates Mittel, um wichtige GEO-Botschaften (etwa Auflagen- oder Reichweitenentwicklungen) schnell zu kommunizieren. Darüber hinaus sind Veranstaltungen und Events, wo Produkt und redaktionelle Qualität durch den persönlichen Auftritt des Chefredakteurs, spezielle Vorträge über die Entstehung von Reportagen („Story behind the story") und großzügige Diapräsentationen „erlebbar" gemacht werden, besonders effizient.

Inzwischen gewinnt zunehmend auch das Internet an Bedeutung, wenn es um die Interaktion mit Anzeigenkunden sowie die Bereitstellung der für diese relevanten Informationen geht (www.co.guj.de/titel/geo).

3. Markentransferstrategien von GEO

3.1 Transfer auf neue Zeitschriften im Inland

Im Zuge des raschen Auflagenwachstums von GEO seit 1976 entstanden bald Ideen, weitere Publikationen neben dem monatlichen „grünen" Magazin zu entwickeln. Diese Neuproduktideen waren die Ergebnisse kreativer Prozesse in Redaktion und Verlagsabteilungen – immer aus der GEO-Markenphilosophie heraus. Konkret wurden die Ideen in Form einer Markentransferstrategie zur Bildung einer heute veritablen Markenfamilie umgesetzt (vgl. Abbildung 3).

GEO Special

Die Familienbildung begann 1981 mit der Gründung von GEO Special. Ausgangspunkt war der Wunsch beziehungsweise die Überlegung, viele Reisethemen, die in GEO zu finden sind, noch umfassender zu behandeln, als es dort auf 20 bis 30 Seiten geschehen konnte.

Die „magische GEO-Formel" lautet beim Special: auf rund zwei Dritteln der Heftstrecke werden eine Stadt, eine Region oder ein Land porträtiert. Diese Porträts sind gekennzeichnet durch facettenreichen Journalismus, der ausführlich recherchierte, attraktive Reportagen und Essays in Text und Bild umsetzt. Im anderen Drittel des Heftes – dem „Infoteil" – finden sich Reise-Tipps und Trends, Orientierungshilfen und originelle „Seiteneingänge" in das Sujet.

Der Copypreis liegt höher als bei GEO: 2003 betrug er 7,80 Euro. GEO Special erscheint sechsmal pro Jahr und verkaufte im Durchschnitt des Jahres 2003 rund 126.000 Exemplare.

Abbildung 3: Positionierung der GEO-Familie

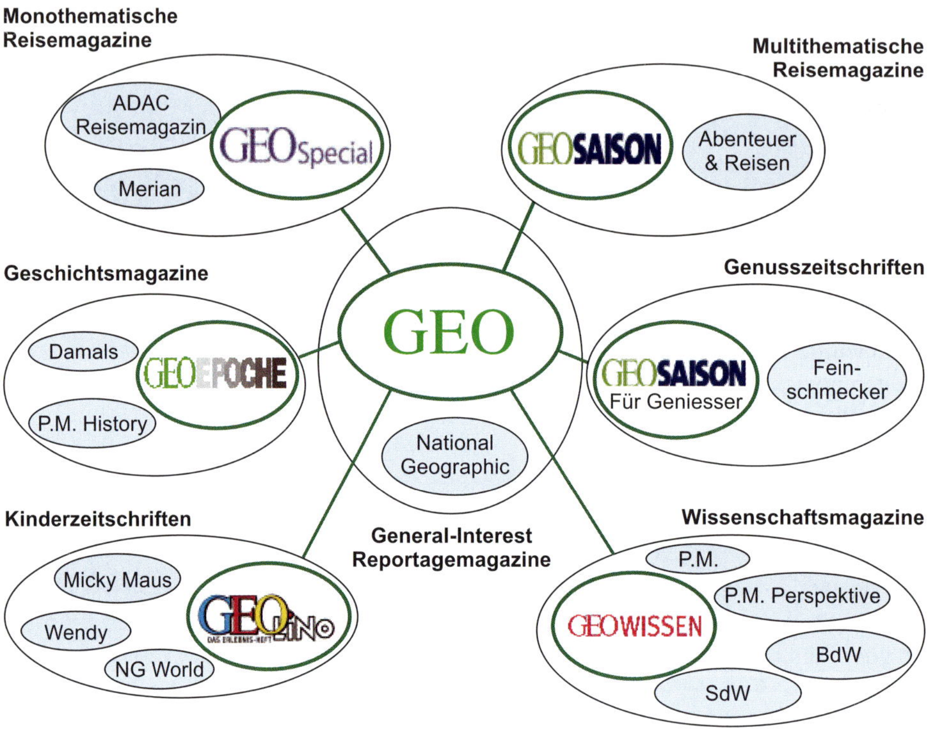

GABLER GRAFIK

GEO Wissen

In Analogie zum monothematischen GEO Special, das sich dem Thema „Reisen" widmet, wurde 1987 GEO Wissen als monothematisches Sonder-Heft zu bestimmten wissenschaftlichen Themen entwickelt und in den Markt eingeführt. GEO Wissen veranschaulicht mit Sachverstand und Gespür für Aktualität anspruchsvolle und komplexe Themen in Text- und Fotoreportagen. So berichtet GEO Wissen über Themen wie „Denken, Lernen, Schule", „Das Universum", „Sex, Geburt, Genetik" oder auch „Gesunde Ernährung".

Das lediglich zweimal pro Jahr erscheinende GEO Wissen verkaufte 2003 im Durchschnitt rund 160.000 Exemplare – zum Copypreis von acht Euro!

GEO SAISON

GEO SAISON erschien erstmals 1989 als ein multithematisches Reisemagazin. Es zeigt auf unterhaltsame Weise Wege zu einer neuen Kultur des Reisens, zu einem Tourismus, der nicht zerstört, was er entdeckt, sondern den Menschen anderer Kulturkreise mit Takt und Respekt begegnet. GEO SAISON gibt Anregungen und Orientierungshilfen – vor, während und nach der Reise.

GEO SAISON erscheint mit einem etwas geringeren Heftumfang als GEO Special und GEO Wissen und kostet daher „nur" 4,60 Euro. Das Heft erscheint zehnmal im Jahr und hatte im Durchschnitt des Jahres 2003 eine verkaufte Auflage von 151.000 Exemplaren.

GEOlino

1996 wurde die Kinder- und Jugendzeitschrift GEOlino gegründet. GEOlino stellt die Weiterentwicklung des GEO-Konzepts für junge Zielgruppen dar. Es ist ein General-Interest-Wissens-Magazin für Kinder und Jugendliche zwischen acht und 14 Jahren. Auch hier werden hohe Ansprüche an die Qualität der Optik und Inhalte gestellt, allerdings in einer zielgruppengerechten Umsetzung. Neuartige Themen aus den Bereichen Spiele, Basteln, Krimi, Rätsel etc. ergänzen das Produktkonzept.

Im Wettbewerb soll sich GEOlino durch die redaktionelle Aufbereitung und Präsentation der Themen gegenüber anderen deutschen Kinder- und Jugendzeitschriften deutlich abgrenzen. Zudem soll der Titel bereits bei jungen Zielgruppen das Markenbild von GEO prägen – um die kleinen Leser einige Jahre später auch als Leser der „erwachsenen" GEO-Titel begrüßen zu können.

GEOlino erscheint monatlich und verkaufte 2003 eine durchschnittliche Auflage von rund 227.000 Exemplaren bei einem Verkaufspreis von drei Euro.

GEO EPOCHE

Jede Ausgabe des 1999 gelaunchten Magazins GEO Epoche beschäftigt sich mit einer bestimmten geschichtlichen Periode. GEO EPOCHE enthält Geschichten über Alltag, Politik, Kultur, Gesellschaft und Wissenschaft ausgewählter zeitgeschichtlicher Perioden. In historischen Rekonstruktionen, Reportagen und Bildessays wird diese Epoche zum Leben erweckt, wird vor allem der Alltag jener Zeit sinnlich nacherzählt. „Das alte China", „Deutschland um 1900", „Amerikas Weg zur Weltmacht" oder „Das Reich der Zaren" sind typische Themen dieser Reihe.

GEO Epoche erscheint viermal pro Jahr und verkaufte 2003 im Schnitt rund 160.000 Exemplare – zum Copypreis von acht Euro.

GEO SAISON FÜR GENIESSER

Das erste Sonderheft von GEO SAISON erschien 1999. Das Heftkonzept besteht aus der Kombination von kompetenter Reiseberichterstattung und Lebensgenuss und widmet sich monothematisch einer bestimmten Region. Bisher wurden die Destinationen „Mallorca“, „Toskana“ und „Provence“ mehrfach fokussiert.

GEO SAISON FÜR GENIESSER erscheint dreimal pro Jahr und verkaufte 2003 rund 60.000 Exemplare zu einem Copypreis von 7,80 Euro.

GEOlino extra

Das erste Sonderheft von GEOlino befasste sich 2002 monothematisch mit dem Thema „Tiere“. In 2003 erschien ein weiteres Heft zum Thema „Ozeane“ – seit 2004 erscheint GEOlino extra regelmäßig zweimal pro Jahr.

GEOlino extra verkaufte bisher im Durchschnitt rund 70.000 Exemplare bei einem Copypreis von 5,90 Euro.

Von den acht Zeitschriften-Linien der GEO-Familie wurden 2004 insgesamt 51 einzelne Hefte publiziert. Im Herbst 2004 erschien unter der GEO-Dachmarke die Erstausgabe einer neunten Zeitschrift namens GEO kompakt, die sich monothematisch mit den „Grundlagen des Wissens“ befasst. Sie ist als Sammelreihe gedacht, die Lesern sukzessive den Aufbau einer „Bibliothek des Basiswissens“ ermöglicht – mit einem bis dahin einzigartigen journalistischen Ansatz. Das neue Heft wird 2005 mit insgesamt vier Ausgaben erscheinen.

In der Ausprägung der begleitenden Marketing-Instrumente finden sich bei allen GEO-Marken Identitäten beziehungsweise Ähnlichkeiten: neben den hohen Ansprüchen an die Produkt-(sprich: Text- und Bild-)Qualität zeichnen sich alle Titel durch hohe Copypreise, selektive Distributionspolitik (sprich ausgewählte Verkaufsstellen und – mit Ausnahme der vier jeweils nur zwei- bis viermal pro Jahr erscheinenden Sonderhefte – hohe Abonnenten-Anteile am Gesamtverkauf) und produktadäquate Kommunikationspolitik aus.

Im Rahmen der Überarbeitung des Kommunikationsauftritts von GEO wurde auch die Kommunikation für alle GEO-Zeitschriften insgesamt renoviert. Dies war nicht nur im Sinne stringenter Markenführung und konsequenten Markentransfers „logisch“, sondern auch „vernünftig“ aufgrund knapper Werbebudgets: Jede Einzelmarke zahlt fortlaufend auf das „Markenwertkonto“ der Markenfamilie ein (vgl. Abbildung 4).

Abbildung 4: Einzelverkaufs-Anzeigen für GEO-Titel

GABLER GRAFIK

3.2 GEO-Nebenprodukte

Die Stärke der Marke GEO erweckte rasch nach der Markteinführung 1976 den Wunsch, neben der Entwicklung neuer Zeitschriften auch andere Geschäftsfelder mit GEO-Produkten zu erschließen. Dabei wurde versucht, das Qualitätsimage, das sich GEO beim Käufer und Leser erwerben konnte, auf neue Sortimentsbereiche auszudehnen.

Die Gefahr bei dieser Strategie liegt darin, dass die neuen Geschäfte sowohl vom fachlichen Können als auch von der Kapazität durch Redaktion und Verlagsabteilungen nicht (mehr) bewältigt werden können. Auch stellt sich die Qualitätskontrolle bei dieser Form des Markentransfers – entspricht die Qualität der Nebenprodukte der Qualität der Zeitschriften? – als ein oft unüberwindbares Hindernis heraus.

Dennoch wurde der virtuelle „GEO-Shop“ entwickelt, dessen Angebote anfangs ausschließlich durch einen an die Abonnenten versandten Katalog kommuniziert wurden. Später wurden Produkte des Shops auch über Anzeigen in den GEO-Zeitschriften sowie über Mailings – auch an Nicht-Abonnenten – offeriert. Seit einigen Jahren ist der GEO-Shop auch im Internet (www.geowebshop.de) existent.

Zu den ersten Produkten zählten praktische Ergänzungen zur Sammlung der Hefte wie Sammel-Schuber oder Register. Schon bald aber erschienen die ersten GEO-Bücher, zunächst als spezifische Fortführung der Zeitschrifteninhalte und gemacht von denselben Autoren und Fotografen, die auch für die Zeitschriften verantwortlich zeichneten. Später kamen auch Bücher anderer Autoren und Fotografen hinzu; diese Bücher wurden in Kooperation mit Buchverlagen produziert oder als reine Lizenzprodukte auf den Markt gebracht. Mittlerweile erscheinen auch unter den Labels GEO SAISON und GEOlino entsprechende Produkte.

1980 wurde der GEO-Kalender eingeführt, ein Produkt, das die fotografische GEO-Kompetenz konsequent umsetzte. Heute werden pro Jahr rund 20.000 Exemplare allein dieses „Klassiker-Kalenders“ abgesetzt, zu einem Preis von 49 Euro. Konsequent wurde das Kalendergeschäft in den letzten Jahren ausgebaut. Im Jahre 2004 gab es neben dem „Klassiker-Kalender“ einen GEO-Panorama-Kalender im Riesenformat und zwei „GEO-Kunstkalender“ zu den Themen „Die Erde von oben“ sowie „Die rote Couch“. Des Weiteren erschienen ein GEOlino-Kalender (Thema „Spielende Tiere“), zwei GEO Special-Kalender („Himalaya“ und „Südafrika“), drei GEO SAISON-Kalender („Italiens Inseln“, „Toskana-Dörfer“ und „Provence“), ein GEO WISSEN- („Wasser “) sowie ein GEO Epoche-Kalender („Das alte China“). Insgesamt erzielten alle Kalender zusammen eine Verkaufsauflage von rund 80.000 Exemplaren.

Auch ein Kernproblem des Abonnement-Marketing wurde über den GEO-Shop – zumindest teilweise – „gelöst“: Abonnenten klagten zuweilen über den Platzbedarf beim Sammeln von GEOs – und begründeten damit manchmal ihre Kündigung. Nicht ganz ernsthaft wurde bei GEO daher über die Aufnahme eines GEO-Regals, genormt auf Format und Gewicht der GEO-Hefte, in das Shop-Angebot diskutiert. Und dann – umgesetzt. Mit erstaunlichem Erfolg: Über 4.000 gelabelte GEO-Regale wurden mittlerweile verkauft.

Inzwischen werden systematisch weitere Produktfelder geprüft, die für eine nochmalige Erweiterung des GEO-Produkt-Portfolios geeignet erscheinen. Ausgangspunkt ist dabei meist das Geschäftsmodell der Lizenzierung. So werden etwa 2004 unter dem GEO-Label Leuchtgloben, Puzzles und Postkarten angeboten, unter dem GEOlino-Label Mikroskopie-Kästen und Spiele. Und auch eine Reise nach China – unverwechselbar gemacht durch die Begleitung eines GEO-Reporters – sowie Fotografier-Kurse mit GEO-Fotografen in der Toskana stehen auf dem Programm.

Ziel der GEO-Nebengeschäfte ist die Festigung der Markenkompetenz sowie der Ausbau einer zusätzlichen Umsatz- und Ergebnisquelle. Das Marken-Controlling im Sinne der Auswahl ausschließlich markenkompatibler Produkte erfolgt nach der einfachen Philosophie „Wo GEO drauf steht, muss auch GEO drin sein“. Die GEO-Chefredaktion hat daher bei der Produktauswahl nicht nur ein Vorschlags-, sondern auch ein Vetorecht.

3.3 Internationalisierung

Aufgrund des hohen Reife- und Sättigungsgrades des deutschen Zeitschriftenmarktes wurde frühzeitig auch die Internationalisierung als Wachstumspfad erschlossen. Die bei GEO in Deutschland erarbeiteten Qualitätsstandards sowie das im Rahmen der Markteinführungsaktivitäten gewonnene Marketing-Know-how bildeten den Ausgangspunkt für die Auslandsaktivitäten. Bei der Analyse der für den ersten Internationalisierungsschritt ausgewählten Länder Frankreich und USA galt die These, dass die redaktionellen Inhalte von GEO in vielen Ländern auf Interesse stoßen müssten. Darüber hinaus galt die Annahme, dass GEO stark von seiner außerordentlichen optischen Wirkung lebt, die nicht an bestimmte Kulturkreise oder Sprachen gebunden ist.

Es zeigte sich jedoch schnell, dass es mit einer reinen Übersetzung der deutschen Ausgabe nicht getan war – nicht allein wegen formaler Probleme (so ist ein englischer Text kürzer als ein inhaltsgleicher deutscher). Vielmehr galt es, auch kulturell-gesellschaftliche Besonderheiten in den einzelnen Ländern zu berücksichtigen, um eine Zeitschrift wie GEO international erfolgreich einführen zu können. So muss eine Algerien-Reportage im französischen GEO einen anderen Duktus haben als im deutschen. Schon früh wurde die Notwendigkeit des „Re-writing" erkannt, häufig sogar unter Einsatz völlig neuer Autoren.

Aber auch in den Techniken des Verlagsmarketing wurden länderspezifische Adaptionen erforderlich. Die Ursprungsintention, die Markenpersönlichkeit weitgehend identisch auf die Auslandsmärkte zu übertragen, konnte daher nicht verwirklicht werden. Dies bedeutete aber nicht die Aufgabe der Qualitätsstandards.

1979 begann die Internationalisierung der Marke in Frankreich und den USA. Während die Einführung und Adaption in Frankreich gelang, endete das „Abenteuer USA" für GEO mit einem Flop: der Qualitätsanspruch, ausgedrückt in einem Jahresabonnement-Preis von 36 Dollar gegenüber 11 Dollar für den Hauptwettbewerber National Geographic, ließ sich nicht in eine tragfähige Auflagenzahl umwandeln. Auch gelang die Adaption der Reportageinhalte und der Erzählweise an die Erwartungen der Zielgruppe nicht. Gleichwohl waren die Lehren, die aus dem Scheitern in den USA gezogen werden konnten, für die weitere internationale Entwicklung von GEO wertvoll. Denn das Konzept in Frankreich wurde darauf hin optimiert, es entstand eine (noch) größere Eigenständigkeit der französischen Redaktion, was sich in Form stark steigender Auflagen auszahlte. Zwischenzeitlich konnte die französische Auflage diejenige in Deutschland sogar für einige Jahre überholen. Auf der Grundlage dieser Marktposition wurden auch in Frankreich Line Extensions durchgeführt. Zu einzelnen monothematischen Sonderheften gesellte sich im Jahr 2002 GEO Ado, das als monatliches Kinder- und Jugendmagazin für 10- bis 15jährige Leser zwar etwas älter als GEOlino positioniert ist, aber eine ähnliche Aufgabe hat: die Leser von morgen bereits heute auf die Marke GEO einzustimmen.

Die weitere Internationalisierung der Haupt-Marke GEO wurde schon zuvor 1987 in Spanien fortgeführt und erhielt einen neuen Schub im Jahre 1993, als Lizenzausgaben in Korea („Magazine of the year 1997") und Japan (jedoch Auslaufen der Lizenz aufgrund von Qualitätsmängeln 1998) erschienen.

Seit 1998 erscheint GEO auch in Russland, schwerpunktmäßig in den urbanen Zentren. Der Geschäfts-Partner, der bei der Einführung von GEO Russland Pate stand, ist ungewöhnlich: Die russisch-orthodoxe Kirche. Ob dies dazu führte, dass auf dem russischen GEO ein besonderer Segen lag? Jedenfalls konnte sich das Heft in Russland nicht nur im Vertriebs-, sondern vor allem im Anzeigenmarkt eine herausragende Position sichern. Diese starke Basis führte dazu, dass 2003 auch in Russland mit GEO-Focus eine Line Extension im Bereich der Wissensmagazine eingeführt wurde, inhaltlich in etwa vergleichbar mit dem deutschen PM-Magazin. Und auch GEOlino fand in Russland seine Entsprechung – mit GEOlenok wurde ebenfalls 2003 ein Kindermagazin eingeführt, das sich inhaltlich stark an seinem deutschen Pendant ausrichtet.

3.4 Fernsehen und Internet

Bereits in den 80er Jahren tauchte die Marke GEO auch im **Fernsehen** auf – lange etwa vor Spiegel-TV oder Stern-TV. Der inhaltliche und qualitative Markenkern von GEO wurde dabei in Expeditions- und Dokumentarreihen adäquat umgesetzt. Das erste in Zusammenarbeit mit GEO entstandene TV-Format war die vom ZDF ausgestrahlte populärwissenschaftliche Sendereihe „Querschnitte". Der Fernsehzuschauer konnte sich dabei über den Inhalt der Sendungen zusätzlich durch begleitende GEO-Reportagen informieren; der GEO-Leser wiederum wurde durch die Lektüre angeregt, sich den Bericht noch einmal mit bewegten Bildern erzählen zu lassen. Später produzierte Formate liefen unter dem Titel „GEO-Expeditionen", ebenfalls im ZDF und im Pay-TV-Kanal Premiere.

Seit 1999 gibt es die Dokumentationsreihe „360° – Die GEO-Reportage" mit jeweils rund 30 neuen Dokumentationen pro Jahr. Die Sendereihe wird unter direktem Mitwirken der GEO-Redaktion produziert und zunächst jeweils auf dem deutsch-französischen Gemeinschaftskanal arte ausgestrahlt, was nicht zuletzt auch mit Blick auf die französische GEO-Ausgabe sinnvoll ist. In der weiteren Verwertungskette werden die Dokumentationen alsdann im Discovery Channel (Pay-TV) und in den dritten Programmen der ARD ausgestrahlt.

Im **Internet** ist GEO seit April 1996 (www.geo.de) vertreten. Der Auftritt nimmt unter den deutschsprachigen Online-Angeboten von Monatsmagazinen eine Spitzenstellung ein. Qualitativ zählt die GEO-Site – so die einhellige Meinung vieler Experten – sowohl in Inhalt als auch in Gestaltung zum Besten, was das Netz in dieser Beziehung zu bieten hat. Auch quantitativ nimmt GEO.de unter den relevanten Wettbewerbern mit bis zu vier Millionen PageImpressions pro Monat (Stand: 2004) eine sehr gute Position ein. Die Refinanzierung des Auftritts gelingt weitgehend durch Bannerwerbung – denn die entsprechenden Zielgruppen sind aus Sicht der Werbungtreibenden sehr attraktiv – sowie die Gewinnung von Abonnenten für die GEO-Printprodukte über diesen Vertriebskanal.

4. Erfolgskontrolle von Markenführung und Markentransfer bei GEO

4.1 Messkriterien

Markenführung im Zeitschriftenmarketing ist dann erfolgreich, wenn es gelingt, sowohl unmittelbare **ökonomische Erfolge** zu erzielen als auch den **Markenwert** zu sichern und zu steigern. Zielgrößen für den ökonomischen Erfolg sind etwa

- Vertriebserlöse, Marktanteile im Vertriebsmarkt,
- Anzeigenerlöse, Marktanteile im Anzeigenmarkt,
- Merchandisingerlöse,
- Deckungsbeiträge,
- Umsatzrendite
- etc.

Der eigentliche Wert einer Marke ist jedoch nur bedingt aus oben genannten Kriterien abzulesen – er spiegelt sich vielmehr in den Köpfen der Nachfrager wider (Aaker 1992). Kurzfristig mag der Markenwert gegenüber reinen Rendite-Betrachtungen eine untergeordnete Rolle spielen – langfristig jedoch stellt er das eigentliche Kapital für das Unternehmen dar.

Wesentliche **Determinanten des Markenwertes** sind im Allgemeinen:

- Markenbekanntheit,
- Wahrgenommene Qualität,
- (Weitere) Assoziationen, die mit der Marke verbunden werden, zum Beispiel spontane Verbal-/Bild-Assoziationen,
- Sympathie,
- Vertrauen,
- Einzigartigkeit, Alleinstellung (Uniqueness),
- Persönlicher Nutzwert,
- Markentreue.

4.2 Ökonomische Erfolgskontrolle

Die Erlösstruktur der GEO-Familie in Deutschland spiegelt den strategischen Ansatz des Zeitschriftenkonzeptes – hohe Qualität, hoher Copypreis, dadurch konzeptionell bedingt geringer Anzeigenanteil – wider. Der Löwenanteil entfällt auf die Vertriebserlöse, die 2003 rund 63 Prozent der Gesamterlöse ausmachen. Die Anzeigenerlöse liefern mit rund 28 Prozent einen nicht einmal halb so großen Beitrag, der Rest entfiel vor allem auf die GEO Nebenprodukte.

Durch die Erlöse der sieben Zeitschriften-Submarken sowie der Nebenprodukte konnte der Gesamterlös des „grünen“ GEO-Magazins im Jahr 2003 um rund 85 Prozent ausgeweitet werden.

Interessant für die ökonomische Beurteilung des Marken-Transfers der Marke GEO erscheint zudem die Historie von GEO SAISON: Zunächst als eigenständige Marke SAISON gelauncht (mit dem dezenten Untertitel „Das Reisemagazin von GEO“), war der Titel wirtschaftlich nur bedingt erfolgreich. Erst nachdem im Jahr 1994 die Dachmarke GEO prominent in die Markenbezeichnung integriert und die Zeitschrift fortan als „GEO SAISON“ geführt wurde, entwickelte sich der Titel kontinuierlich positiv.

Eine wichtige strategische Rolle in der GEO-Zeitschriftenfamilie spielt auch GEOlino. Dieser Titel erzielt bereits selbst einen hohen positiven Deckungsbeitrag, was angesichts des (fast) nicht existenten Print-Werbemarkts für Produkte und Dienstleistungen für 8- bis 14-jährige Kinder und Jugendliche nicht selbstverständlich ist. Darüber hinaus erfüllt GEOlino jedoch noch weitere Funktionen:

- Mit GEOlino wird die Marke GEO bereits sehr frühzeitig bei Kindern und Jugendlichen verankert; es besteht daher die berechtigte Hoffnung, dass aus ihnen später auch Leser der erwachsenen GEO-Hefte werden.
- GEOlino erschließt zudem bereits heute neue Käufer-/Leserpotenziale für die erwachsenen GEO-Zeitschriften, da die Eltern (die zu rund 40 Prozent das Heft aus verschiedenen Gründen mitlesen!) zuweilen auf diesem Wege erstmals mit der Marke GEO in Kontakt kommen – und, so die Annahme, dadurch auch zu Käufern und Lesern der erwachsenen GEO-Titel werden. Es erfolgt also schon heute ein Rücktransfer auf die Marke GEO!

Neben diesen ökonomischen Kriterien interessiert insbesondere, inwiefern auch der **Markenwert** von GEO und seiner Zeitschriftenfamilie durch die Markenführung gesteigert werden konnte.

4.3 Erfolgskontrolle im Hinblick auf den Markenwert

Die einfache **Markenbekanntheit** von Zeitschriften wird regelmäßig unter anderem in den so genannten „Gemeinschaftsuntersuchungen“ gemessen (gestützte Abfrage). In der AWA (Allensbacher Werbeträger Analyse) werden GEO, GEO SAISON und GEO Special erhoben. Laut AWA 2004 verzeichnet GEO mit 62 Prozent eine gute Markenbekanntheit, GEO Special (30 Prozent) und GEO Saison (23 Prozent) erreichen insgesamt zufrieden stellende Werte.

Interessant ist das Gefälle des Bekanntheitsgrades der GEO-Zeitschriften, wenn man die von der AWA angebotene Unterteilung der Bevölkerung in sieben disjunkte wirtschaftlich-soziale Schichten zu Grunde legt: In der höchsten Schicht (Potenzial: 6,6 Millionen

Personen) erzielt GEO sogar eine Bekanntheit von 87 Prozent, während diese in der untersten Schicht auf 33 Prozent sinkt. Dieses Bild ergibt sich analog auch für GEO Special und für GEO SAISON.

Auch die Markenbekanntheit von GEOlino wurde in verschiedenen Studien gemessen, die sich auf die Zielgruppe der Kinder und Jugendlichen konzentrieren. Demnach kommt GEOlino in seiner Kernzielgruppe der 8- bis 14-jährigen Kinder und Jugendlichen auf einen Bekanntheitsgrad von gut 40 Prozent.

Die Markenbekanntheit kann gerade im Zeitschriftenmarkt noch stärker fokussiert werden, wenn man neben der reinen Bekanntheit der Marke die Frage untersucht, inwiefern die Zeitschriften **grundsätzlich** auch **gelesen** werden. Üblicherweise wird dabei mit dem WLK (weitester Leser-Kreis) gearbeitet, den man auch als **konkrete Markenbekanntheit** interpretieren könnte.

So sagen 24 Prozent der Gesamtbevölkerung (AWA 2004), dass sie „im letzten Jahr" zumindest eine GEO-Ausgabe gelesen haben; GEO Special kommt hier auf zehn Prozent, GEO SAISON auf sechs Prozent. Betrachtet man die sieben gesellschaftlich-wirtschaftlichen Statusgruppen, so ergibt sich erneut das bereits bei der einfachen Markenbekanntheit beobachtete deutliche Gefälle: Je höher der gesellschaftlich-wirtschaftliche Status einer Person, desto größer die Wahrscheinlichkeit, dass sie die GEO-Zeitschriften konkret kennt, also zum weitesten Leserkreis zählt.

Die – einfache und konkrete – Bekanntheit kann jedoch nur ein erstes Kriterium für die Positionierung von Marken in den Köpfen der (potenziellen) Leser sein; entscheidend sind tiefergehende Dimensionen des Markenimages. Dazu zählen die wahrgenommene **Markenqualität** in all seinen Ausprägungen sowie die **Assoziationen** (Aaker 1992; siehe oben), die die Marken des Weiteren auslösen.

Die Studie „Fame" der Verlagsgruppe Milchstrasse (zuletzt erschienen 2000) setzt hier an und befasst sich unter anderem mit den Images ausgewählter Zeitschriftenmarken. Die Titel wurden anhand von sechs Kriterien bewertet:

- Glaubwürdigkeit,
- Einzigartigkeit,
- Persönlicher Nutzwert,
- Sympathie,
- Modernität,
- Bedeutung in der Zukunft.

Bewertet wurden die Marken jeweils nur von denjenigen Personen, die zum „weitesten Leserkreis" zählten (mindestens eine der letzten zwölf Ausgaben gelesen). Diese Einschränkung auf Personen mit **konkreter Markenkenntnis** ist sinnvoll, da nur diese Personen Werturteile nach oben genannten Kriterien abgeben können.

Das Ergebnis von „Fame" (2000): **GEO hat das beste Image aller Zeitschriftenmarken in Deutschland.** In Bezug auf drei der sechs untersuchten Kriterien nimmt GEO unter allen untersuchten Zeitschriften die Nr. 1-Position ein, insbesondere auch im Hinblick auf die zentrale Dimension **Markenqualität**, die über die Kriterien „Glaubwürdigkeit" und „Einzigartigkeit" abgebildet wird (vgl. Abbildung 5).

Abbildung 5: GEO-Image im Vergleich

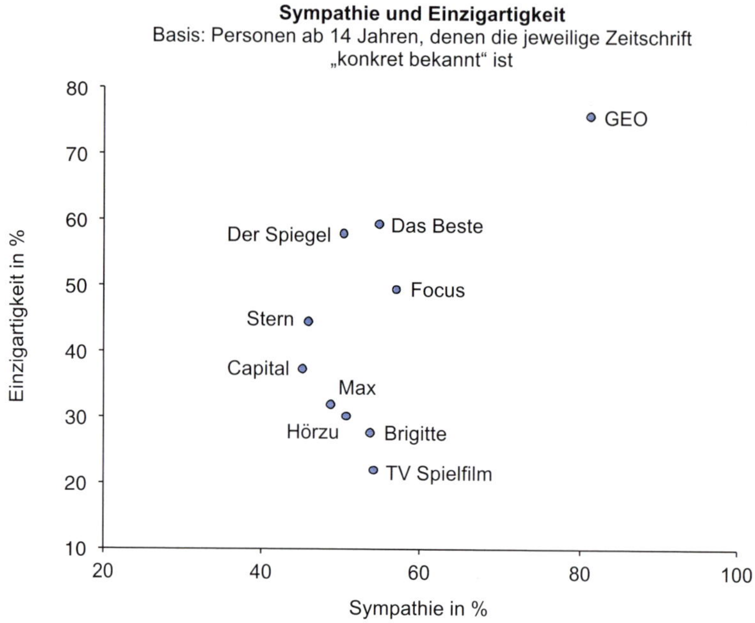

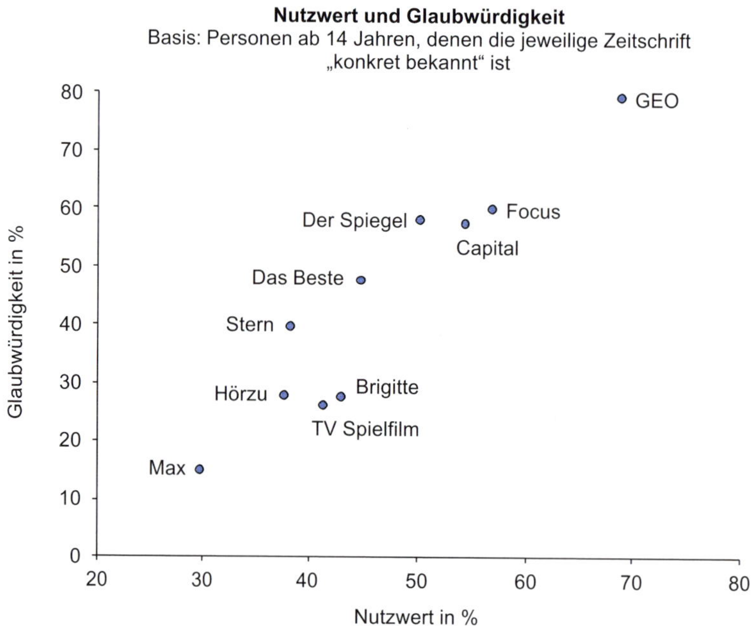

GABLER GRAFIK

Quelle: Fame 00/01

Wie aber steht es um die Markenwahrnehmung der anderen Zeitschriften der Familie, für die keine entsprechenden Daten vorliegen? Zur Beantwortung dieser Frage wurden im Herbst 1999 insgesamt 50 Leser der GEO-Zeitschriften in tiefenpsychologischen Einzel-Interviews zu ihren **Assoziationen** bezüglich der verschiedenen Zeitschriften der GEO-Familie befragt.

Nachteil dieser Vorgehensweise war die geringe Fallzahl, die jedoch dadurch relativiert wurde, dass die Probanden zugleich Käufer/Leser verschiedener GEO-Titel waren. Vorteil dieser Forschungsmethode ist die Möglichkeit, dass die Probanden ihre Marken-Assoziationen mit eigenen Worten beschreiben können, was gegenüber dem standardisierten Vorgehen in Studien wie „Fame" eine facettenreichere Erfassung des Markenbildes ermöglicht. Die Ergebnisse:

1. **GEO:** Beeindruckt die Leser mit hoher Text- und Bild-Qualität, macht Natur-/Weltgeschehen zum persönlichen Erlebnis. GEO steht für Themenvielfalt, dargeboten mit hoher Professionalität und mit hoher Glaubwürdigkeit. Einzigartige Darbietung durch die Kombination „Wissensvermittlung mit Leidenschaft", umfassend, berücksichtigt alle denkbaren Perspektiven. Fesselnde Lektüreerlebnisse, Bilder erzählen Geschichten. Hefte werden gesammelt als Wertgegenstand, Wertanlage.

2. **GEO Special:** Eigenständiger GEO-Ableger mit allen guten Anlagen. Auslösen von heftigem Fernweh durch Darbietung sinnlicher Kultur- und Landschaftswelten. Präpariert plastisch und facettenreich für eigene Erkundungen in der Fremde, ist aber auch geeignet für „Reisen im Kopf". Kann nur durch Hinreisen getoppt werden.

3. **GEO SAISON:** Etwas „wild-gereiste GEO-Verwandte". Lifestylige Welterkundung à la Reisebüro, durch GEO-Image „veredelt". Kunterbuntes Schwelgen in Urlaubsträumen, geeignet für die „kleinen Alltagsfluchten", ist wie „gedruckte Sonne".

4. **GEO Wissen:** Universaler Experte für speziellen Wissensdurst. Macht Erkenntnis zu ästhetischem Genuss, behält Gültigkeit und wirkt sinnstiftend bei der Auseinandersetzung mit der Zukunft. Spiegelt Stand der Forschung, ist Vorbild für lebenslanges Lernen. Ist das anspruchsvollste Magazin der Familie, verlangt „echten Aufwand".

5. **GEO Epoche:** GEO als Geschichtslehrer, erläutert „Sinn der Geschichte" beziehungsweise Konsequenzen für die heutige Zeit. Vertiefender Einblick in die Historie, locker dargeboten. GEO-würdiger Auftritt.

6. **GEOlino:** GEO Vielfalt für Sprößlinge bildungsbewusster Eltern und Paten. Wichtiges Pendant zu anderweitigen, weniger goutierten Freizeitbeschäftigungen der Kinder. Einzigartiger, wertvoller „Jugendbildner", erklärt die Welt ohne „Verkopfung". Heranführung an das große GEO, Inhalte können auch Erwachsene begeistern.

Zusammenfassend ist festzustellen, dass die GEO-Zeitschriften hinsichtlich der von Aaker benannten Kriterien **„Qualität"** und (positiven) **„Assoziationen"** allesamt gute Werte erzielen.

Darüber hinaus wurde auch untersucht, inwiefern die GEO-Zeitschriften-Ableger in ihrem Markenkern der Dachmarke GEO entsprechen (Distanzmessung). Ergebnis: Am nächsten zum Markenkern liegt GEO Special, gefolgt von GEO Wissen und – ein wenig überraschend – GEOlino, trotz der völlig anderen Zielgruppe (Kinder und Jugendliche zwischen acht und 14 Jahren). GEOlino wird von den Erwachsenen offenbar als eine gelungene und stimmige Adaption der Marke GEO gesehen. Bei allen drei Titeln ergeben sich nur relativ geringe konzeptionell wahrgenommene Distanzen zum Markenkern GEO – zugleich sind die Distanzen aber ausreichend groß, damit die Submarken überhaupt als „differenzierbar" erlebt werden können.

GEO Epoche weist bereits einen etwas größeren Abstand zum Markenkern von GEO auf, was allerdings auch dadurch bedingt sein könnte, dass zum Befragungszeitpunkt nur die Erstausgabe („Millenium") vorlag, die atypisch mit sehr vielen kleinen Beiträgen operierte und daher weniger „GEO-like" war. Die größte Distanz zu GEO weist schließlich GEO SAISON auf. GEO SAISON wird konzeptionell als relativ eigenständig gesehen – der empfundene Abstand zur Marke GEO ist allerdings nicht so groß, dass der erfolgte Markentransfer kritisch auf den Prüfstand zu stellen wäre.

4.4 Verbundeffekte

Neben der partiellen Erfolgskontrolle der einzelnen Zeitschriften ist es von Interesse, Verbundeffekte unter die Lupe zu nehmen. Die hier zunächst interessierende Frage bezieht sich auf eine etwaige Marktausweitung durch die Einführung der Zeitschriftenfamilie. Hierzu ist festzustellen:

- Eine Marktausweitung im Hinblick auf die Markenbekanntheit von GEO fand durch die Installation der Marken-Familie nicht statt. Dies ist allerdings auch ein hausgemachter Effekt, denn die Werbung für die Zeitschriften der GEO-Familie findet aus Gründen der Wirtschaftlichkeit vor allem in Form von Eigenwerbung in den Heften der Familie statt.
- Eine Marktausweitung kann jedoch bei den Lesern (+40 Prozent laut AWA 2004) und Käufern konstatiert werden. Die Kaufüberschneidungen sind zwar hoch, aber offenbar werden durch die verschiedenen GEO-Zeitschriften unterschiedliche Lesebedürfnisse angesprochen, was zu dieser Marktausweitung führt.
- Des Weiteren ist eine Marktausweitung auch insofern zu beobachten, als bei den „GEO-Afficinados" eine höhere Pro-Kopf-Wertschöpfung erzielt werden konnte, da diese „Fangemeinde" gar nicht genug von den verschiedenen GEO-Produkten bekommen kann.

Hinsichtlich der Frage der **wechselseitigen Stützung** der Zeitschriften der GEO-Familie ist davon auszugehen, dass eine solche stattfindet, und zwar in verschiedener Hinsicht:

- Eine unmittelbare Stützung findet durch die gegenseitige Bewerbung der Hefte statt. Davon ausgehend, dass es eine „GEO-Fangemeinde" gibt, ist diese werbliche Unterstützung eine kostengünstige und effiziente Kommunikation von Einzelausgaben der GEO-Zeitschriften.
- Darüber hinaus erfolgt eine Stützung auch in Bezug auf die Aufgabenverteilung gegenüber verschiedenen Konkurrenztiteln. Die beiden Reisetitel GEO SAISON und GEO Special schirmen das grüne Magazin vor der Konkurrenz der multi- und monothematischen Konkurrenz ab. Auch durch diese „Rückendeckung" war es GEO erst möglich, seine Themenfelder weiter aufzuspannen und zum heutigen „General-Interest-Reportage-Magazin" zu werden.
- Schließlich erfolgt eine Stützung fraglos – wenn auch heute im Größeneffekt noch nicht exakt abschätzbar – durch GEOlino. Denn das GEO für Kinder wird die Ausgangsposition von GEO bei jungen Lesern bereits in Kürze nachhaltig stärken.

Die Frage der gegenseitigen **Kannibalisierung** kann ebenfalls nur vage beantwortet werden. Es ist davon auszugehen, dass in einigen Fällen die Kauffrequenzen bei GEO-Käufern und -Lesern zugunsten der selektiven Nutzung der kompletten Angebotsbreite der GEO-Zeitschriften zurückgegangen sind. Dennoch: Die (bisher feststellbaren) Kannibalisierungseffekte in der GEO-Zeitschriftenfamilie sind gering – und im Vergleich mit den Vorteilen der Marktausweitung und der gegenseitigen Stützung innerhalb der Markenfamilie zu vernachlässigen.

5. Zusammenfassung

Der Erfolg von GEO beruht auf einer besonderen und dauerhaften Marketingleistung, deren Kern in der journalistischen Leistung und damit im Produkt-Mix liegt.

Die Kundenzufriedenheit – im Leser- wie im Inserentenmarkt – ist für GEO oberstes Gebot. Die von der Untersuchung „Fame" dokumentierte Nr.-1-Position ist daher Lohn und Ansporn zugleich. Der systematische Ausbau einer Zeitschriftenfamilie erfolgte stets unter Nutzung des hohen Markenkapitals von GEO, was Chance und Risiko zugleich war.

Alle vorliegenden Kontroll-Daten zeigen: **Der Markentransfer ist geglückt, und die Markenführung hat ihr Ziel, einen hohen Markenwert bei der Dachmarke GEO sowie den einzelnen Sub-Titeln aufzubauen, erreicht.**

Literatur

Aaker, D. A. (1992), Management des Markenwertes, Frankfurt/M.
Althans, J., Brüne, G. (2004), Markenführung im Zeitschriftenmarkt, in: Bruhn, M. (Hrsg.), Handbuch Markenführung, 2. Aufl., Wiesbaden, S. 2057–2080.
Esch, F.-R. (Hrsg.) (2001), Moderne Markenführung, 3. Aufl., Wiesbaden.
Hensmann, J. (1980), Verlagsmarketing, in: Marketing, Nr. 4, S. 239-249.
Meffert, H. (2000), Marketing – Grundlagen marktorientierter Unternehmensführung, 9. Aufl., Wiesbaden.

Management von komplexen Markenportfolios – Markenführung in der World of TUI

Michael Lambertz

1.	**Herausforderungen und Trends bei der Markenführung im Touristik-Markt**	**694**
1.1	Herausforderung der Markenführung im Tourismus	694
1.2	Zentrale Entwicklungstrends im Touristik-Markt	694
2.	**Ausgangssituation TUI AG**	**697**
3.	**Management von komplexen Markenportfolios über die touristische Wertschöpfungskette**	**700**
3.1	Ansatz einer mehrdimensionalen Markenführung	700
3.11	Horizontale Markenführung auf Veranstalterebene	700
3.12	Vertikale Markenführung über die Wertschöpfungskette	703
3.13	Internationale Markenführung über die Ländermärkte	706
3.2	Integration der Markenführung	709
4.	**Erfolge infolge der Einführung der Dachmarke „World of TUI"**	**710**
5.	**Ausblick**	**713**

1. Herausforderungen und Trends bei der Markenführung im Touristik-Markt

1.1 Herausforderung der Markenführung im Tourismus

Im Markt für Dienstleistungen steht die Markenführung aufgrund der Charakteristika von Dienstleistungen, wie Immaterialität und Integration des externen Faktors (vgl. den Beitrag zur Führung von Dienstleistungsmarken in diesem Buch), vor der spezifischen Herausforderung, das Bedürfnis des Nachfragers nach Identifikation mit der Marke zu befriedigen sowie den Aufbau von Vertrauen zu etablieren und durchzusetzen (zum Beispiel Meyer/Tostmann 1995, S. 12; Tomczak 1998, S. 7 ff.; Werner/Richter 1998, S. 29 ff.). Eine starke Marke, welche die Entwicklung und Stärkung des Vertrauens der Nachfrager in die Leistungen ermöglicht, kann gerade in diesem Umfeld einen wertvollen Beitrag zur Differenzierung im Wettbewerb und zur Kundenbindung leisten und damit Vorteile bei der Kaufentscheidung durch eine präferenzbildende Funktion bedeuten (Esch/Wicke 2001, S. 13). Tourismusleistungen stellen aufgrund ihres Dienstleistungscharakters sowie der ausgeprägten Prozesseigenschaft des touristischen Produktes innerhalb einer Dienstleistungskette besondere Anforderungen an die Markenführung. Die Qualitätswahrnehmung des Nachfragers wird neben dem eigentlichen Ergebnis in hohem Maße von der Prozessqualität des Leistungserstellungsprozesses beeinflusst. Auf der einen Seite ist die Signalwirkung der Marke als Vertrauensanker für das immaterielle Tourismusprodukt somit ungleich höher als in anderen Märkten, auf der anderen Seite bieten die integrierten Tourismus-Dienstleister ein teilweise diffuses Markenbild für den Nachfrager durch ein sehr komplexes Markenportfolio, welches historisch über verschiedene M&A-Aktivitäten entstanden ist. Tourismuskonzerne stehen somit vor der Herausforderung, eine klar und stark profilierte Marke über ein komplexes Markensystem aufzubauen, um das Vertrauen in eine gleichbleibende oder zunehmende Servicequalität zu erhöhen und Markenpräferenzen sowie Kundenbindung aufzubauen (Momberger 2000, S. 123).

Zielsetzung des vorliegenden Beitrags ist es, die Komplexität und Herausforderungen der Markenführung im Tourismus-Markt herauszuarbeiten und die strategische Ausgestaltung der Markenführung am Beispiel der TUI AG zu diskutieren.

1.2 Zentrale Entwicklungstrends im Touristik-Markt

Tourismusmärkte waren bis zum 11. September 2001 weltweit durch ein hohes Wachstum gekennzeichnet. Seitdem prägen widrige wirtschaftliche und politische Rahmenbedingungen die touristische Geschäftsentwicklung und führten zu erheblichen Umsatzeinbrüchen. Für die Zukunft wird jedoch mit einer Markterholung gerechnet. Das Zukunftsinstitut Prognos erwartet, dass – ohne weitere Schocks mit geopolitischem Ausmaß – die europäischen Touristen 2004 und 2005 zu ihrer gewohnten Reisefrequenz und -intensität zurückkehren (vgl. Abbildung 1). Betrug das Marktvolumen (gemessen an Reiseausgaben) in den wichtigsten europäischen Quellmärkten Westeuropas (EU15 + Norwegen, Schweiz) rund 153 Milliarden Euro im Jahr 2000, so dürfte es nach dem Einbruch in 2001 mittlerweile wieder bei deutlich über 154 Milliarden Euro liegen. Für die nächsten beiden Jahre wird mit einem realen Marktwachstum von fünf Prozent pro Jahr gerechnet, in den Folgejahren mit jährlichen Wachstumsraten von durchschnittlich drei bis vier Prozent.

Abbildung 1: Überproportionales Wachstum der Low-Cost-Airlines in Europa bis 2010

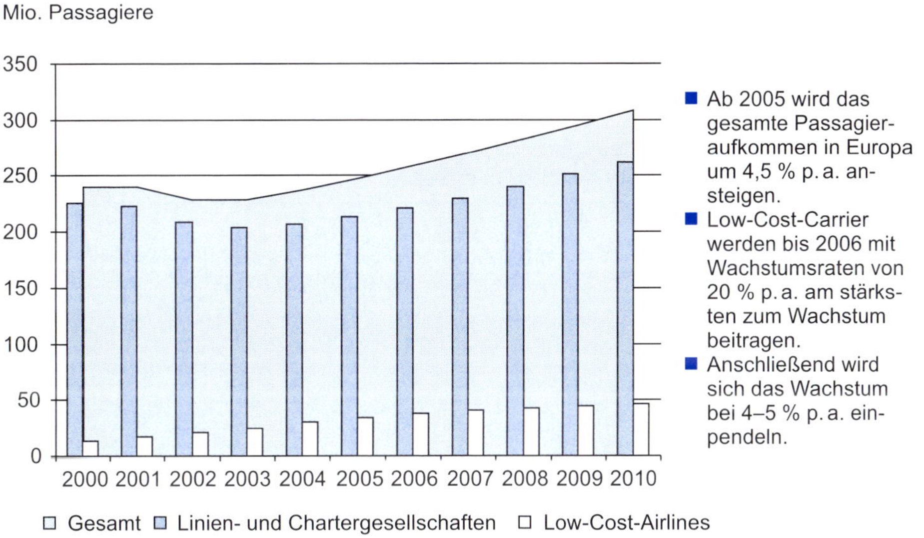

Quelle: TUI AG, Prognos AG 2004

Trends, wie die steigende Nachfrage nach kurzfristigen, flexiblen, preiswerten und immer vielfältigeren Angeboten, sorgen weiter für Dynamik. Eine Differenzierung der Vertriebslandschaft, die steigende Vielfalt von Produkten sowie erweiterte Angebote von Low-Cost-Carriern eröffnen den Nachfragern neue Möglichkeiten und führen in der Tourismuswirtschaft zu neuen Wachstumsimpulsen.

Die hohe Akzeptanz des Internets und der Trend zum „do it yourself" unterstützen auch in Zukunft die weitere Steigerung der Onlinebuchungen in der Tourismusindustrie. In Europa wird der Anteil der Onlinebuchungen von zwei Prozent im Jahr 2001 auf bis zu zehn Prozent im Jahr 2006 steigen (vgl. Abbildung 2). Spitzenreiter bei den Onlinebuchungen und wichtiger Treiber der Entwicklung sind die Low-Cost-Carrier – bereits heute erfolgen 80 bis 90 Prozent ihrer Buchungen online.

Die zunehmend individuellen Reiseansprüche beantworten die Anbieter mit der Flexibilisierung und Modularisierung ihres Angebots. Mittelfristig dürfte die Erfolg versprechende Zukunftsstrategie sein, alle Stufen der Wertschöpfungskette mit gesteigerter Flexibilität zu beherrschen. Dem Nachfrager können so gleichzeitig individuelle und komfortable Lösungen aus einer Hand geboten werden, was dem Wunsch nach einer bequemen und einfachen Buchung (one stop shopping) entgegen kommt. Die Pauschalreise der Zukunft bietet volle Flexibilität bei maximalem Komfort.

Eine hohe Dynamik auf dem Reisemarkt geht von Low-Cost-Carriern aus. Diese haben in den vergangenen drei bis vier Jahren ihre Kapazitäten erheblich vergrößert und durch eine attraktive Preisstruktur einen Nachfrageschub generiert. Ihr Angebot orientiert sich an den Bedürfnissen der hybriden Nachfrager und „Smart-Shopper" nach hoher Qualität und Sicherheit sowie einem dichten Verbindungsnetz zu einem ansprechenden Preis-Leistungs-Verhältnis.

Abbildung 2: **Entwicklungen im Online-Reisemarkt**

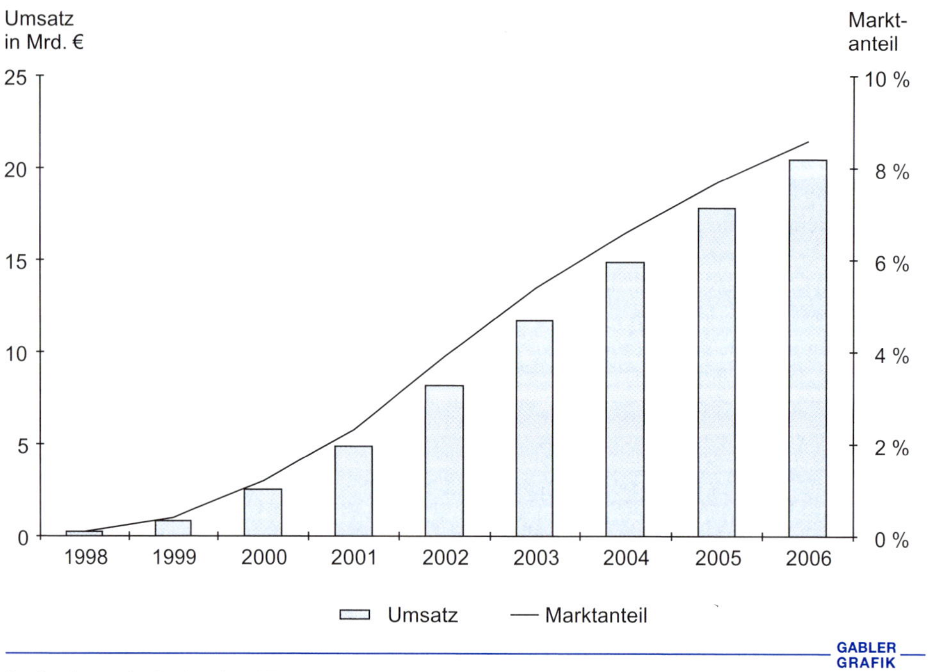

Quelle: Centre for Regional and Tourism Research, Dänemark 2004

Nach vorwiegend europäischen Städteverbindungen in der ersten Phase, erweitert die „zweite Generation“ der Low-Cost-Carrier nun ihr Angebot um klassische Tourismusdestinationen. Dies wird die Erschließung neuer Kundensegmente für Flugurlaubsreisen möglich machen. Kurz- bis mittelfristig darf hier mit Steigerungsraten von jährlich 20 Prozent gerechnet werden.

2. Ausgangssituation TUI AG

Kein deutsches Unternehmen hat jemals einen so deutlichen Wandel vollzogen wie die TUI AG, die aus der ehemaligen Preussag AG hervorgegangen ist. Innerhalb weniger Jahre hat sich der Konzern mit rund 65.000 Mitarbeitern vom Industriekonglomerat zum in Europa führenden Touristikkonzern entwickelt.

Mitte der 90er-Jahre, in einem schwierigen wirtschaftlichen Umfeld, traf das Management der Preussag AG die weit reichende Entscheidung, in den Wachstumsmarkt Dienstleistung mit dem Kerngeschäft Touristik einzusteigen. Ein rasanter Prozess, geprägt von Umstrukturierungen, Investitionen und Desinvestitionen, begann. 1997 wurde mit der Hapag-Lloyd AG ein starker Partner mit eigener Reisebürokette, Fluglinie und weltweiter Logistikdienstleistung erworben. Durch die vollständige Beteiligung an der TUI Deutschland sicherte sich der Konzern die Qualitätsmarke für Pauschalurlaub. Mit der Übernahme der First Reisebürokette und der Beteiligung an der Hotelkette Magic Life wurde die touristische Wertschöpfungskette abgerundet: Der integrierte Touristikkonzern war geboren.

Ein entscheidender Schritt auf den europäischen Markt war im Jahr 2000 die vollständige Übernahme der britischen Thomson Travel Group mit ihren starken Marken und Beteiligungen auch in Nordeuropa (Fritidsresor). Im selben Jahr beteiligte sich der Konzern am französischen Reisekonzern Nouvelles Frontières, dessen vollständige Übernahme mittlerweile erfolgt ist. Durch weitere Beteiligungen und Unternehmensgründungen zum Beispiel in Belgien, in der Schweiz, in Osteuropa, in China und Russland ist der Konzern zum führenden Touristikkonzern der Welt geworden.

Der Umbau des Konzerns ist heute nunmehr nahezu abgeschlossen. Von seinen industriellen Beteiligungen, deren Umsatz 1997 noch rund 93 Prozent des Gesamtumsatzes betrug, hat sich der Konzern in den letzten Jahren konsequent Schritt für Schritt getrennt und das Geschäftsportfolio neu strukturiert.

Im Kerngeschäft Touristik ist die TUI AG heute hervorragend positioniert. Mit einem Umsatz von rund 12,7 Milliarden Euro ist der Konzern mit deutlichem Vorsprung Marktführer in Europa.

Abbildung 3: Marktstellung der TUI AG in Europa im Jahr 2003

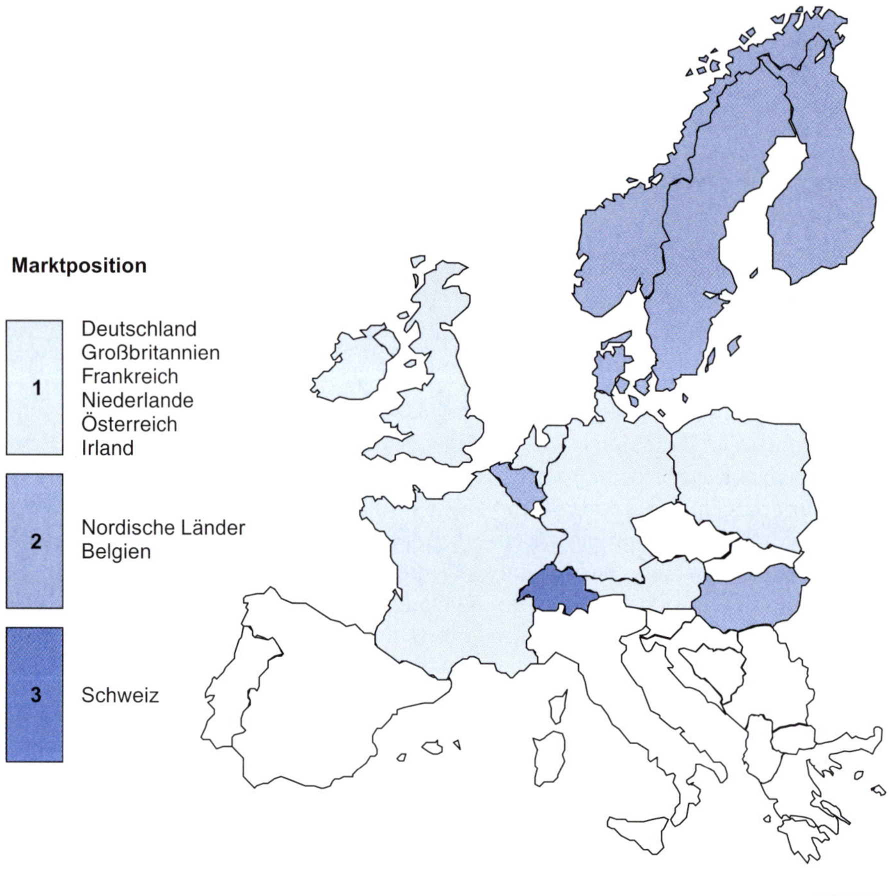

Quelle: TUI AG 2004

TUI bietet ihren Nachfragern Urlaub aus einer Hand – von der Reisebuchung, über den Flug bis hin zur Unterbringung in konzerneigenen Hotels sowie der Betreuung der Gäste durch eigene Reiseleiter. Durch diese Strategie der vertikalen Integration wird die gesamte Wertschöpfungskette im Absatzmarkt und in der Destination (Urlaubsgebiet) abgedeckt und dem Nachfrager eine durchgängige Qualität geboten (vgl. Abbildung 4).

Zum touristischen Geschäftsbereich der TUI gehören mehr als 3.600 Reisebüros. Insbesondere in Deutschland, Großbritannien, den Niederlanden und in Belgien ergibt sich dadurch mit den Marken TUI ReiseCenter, First Reisebüro, Hapag-Lloyd Reisebüro, TUI TravelCenter und Lunn Poly ein dichtes Netz und damit ein bedeutender Vertriebsweg für die Veranstalter.

Die TUI nutzt jedoch auch andere Vertriebskanäle für den Verkauf ihrer Produkte. So gewinnen beispielsweise die Direktvertriebsaktivitäten (zum Beispiel über die Marke Berge & Meer) und das Internet als Vertriebskanal zunehmend an Bedeutung. Der Nachfrager kann heute über verschiedenste Internetseiten der konzerneigenen Veranstalter und Fluggesellschaften sowie über das TUI-Hotelportal seine Reise buchen. Mit der Beteiligung am Reise-Fernseh-Kanal TV Travel Shop rundet TUI die umfangreichen Vertriebsaktivitäten ab.

Mit ihren rund 84 Veranstaltern ist die TUI in 18 europäischen Quellmärkten vertreten. Unter Quellmärkten versteht man in der Touristik Absatzmärkte, in denen das Produkt „Reise“ über die Veranstalter vertrieben wird. Zur Produktpalette der Veranstalter gehören neben der komplett gebündelten Pauschalreise auch individuelle Reisebausteine wie zum Beispiel Einzelflüge, Hotelunterkünfte, Ausflüge im Urlaubsgebiet und Mietwagen. Der Veranstalter handelt Konditionen mit den jeweiligen Vertragspartnern aus und bündelt die verschiedenen, individuell wählbaren Einzelbausteine einer Reise zu einem Gesamtprodukt und bietet diese dem Nachfrager an. Zu den bekanntesten Veranstaltermarken des Konzerns gehören unter anderem TUI, 1-2-Fly, Gebeco, Robinson, Airtours International, Thomson Holidays, Fritidsresor, Jetair, Gulet und Nouvelles Frontières.

Das touristische Portfolio der TUI-Gruppe umfasst 104 Flugzeuge unter Marken wie Hapag-Lloyd Flug, Britannia Airways UK, Britannia Airways SE und Corsair. Unter dem Markennamen Hapag-Lloyd-Express (HLX.com) ist die TUI Ende 2002 in den Markt der Low-Cost-Airlines eingestiegen. Auch die englische Konzerntochter Thomson ist seit Anfang 2004 mit der neuen Marke Thomsonfly.com im Low-Cost-Geschäft präsent.

In mehr als 70 Ländern werden die Gäste der TUI von Mitarbeitern der insgesamt 37 Zielgebietsagenturen und den Reiseleitern betreut. Mit ihrem Service unterstützen sie das Kerngeschäft der Veranstalter und leisten so einen wesentlichen Beitrag zur Qualitätssicherung der Programme.

Abbildung 4: Portfolio der World of TUI über die Wertschöpfungskette

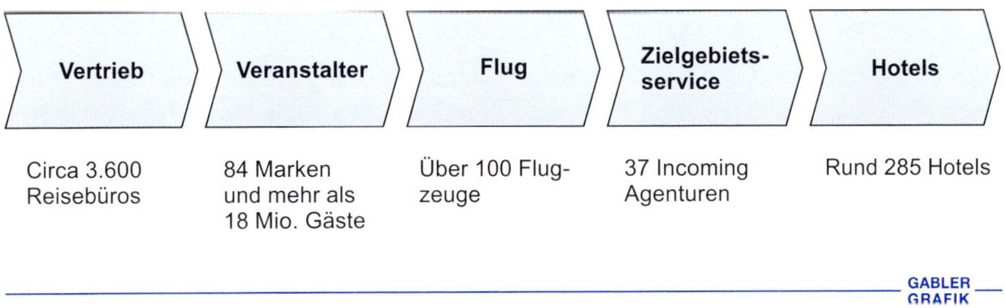

Quelle: TUI AG 2004

Mit 285 Hotels und mehr als 157.000 Betten ist TUI Hotels & Resorts größter Ferienhotelier Europas und rangiert auf Platz 14 im internationalen Ranking der größten Hotelketten. Hierzu gehören Marken wie zum Beispiel Riu, Grecotel, Grupotel, Iberotel, Dorfhotel, Robinson, Magic Life, Paladien und Nordotel.

3. Management von komplexen Markenportfolios über die touristische Wertschöpfungskette

3.1 Ansatz einer mehrdimensionalen Markenführung

Die TUI AG verfügt über ein komplexes Markenportfolio auf den einzelnen Wertschöpfungsstufen, sowie über die Wertschöpfungskette als auch über die Ländermärkte hinweg. Die Herausforderung des Management dieses Markensystems liegt folglich in einer integrierten und abgestimmten Markenführung in der horizontalen (das heißt auf der gleichen Wertschöpfungsstufe), der vertikalen (das heißt entlang der Wertschöpfungskette) sowie der internationalen Dimension (das heißt über die Ländermärkte hinweg). Eine Analyse entlang dieser drei Dimensionen ist Gegenstand der folgenden Ausführungen.

3.11 Horizontale Markenführung auf Veranstalterebene

Die Veranstalter der TUI AG bieten ihre Reiseprodukte in 18 europäischen Quellmärkten über mehr als 80 unterschiedliche Veranstaltermarken an. Im Rahmen dieser Mehrmarkenstrategie auf der Veranstalterstufe besteht die Zielsetzung darin, Partizipationseffekte durch eine gezieltere und bedarfsgerechtere Konsumentenansprache über spezifische Marken, eine breitere Marktabdeckung durch eine differenzierte Positionierung sowie eine Ausweitung der Kundengewinnung und Kundenbindung mit den jeweils bestgeeigneten Marken zu erreichen (vgl. in diesem Zusammenhang auch den Beitrag zur Mehrmarkenstrategie in diesem Band). Weiterhin kann eine Reduktion des Marktrisikos durch eine höhere Flexibilität bei der Reaktion auf neue Entwicklungen und Trends erzielt werden. Auf der anderen Seite sind Risiken der Mehrmarkenstrategie in horizontaler Richtung, wie zum Beispiel die Kannibalisierung der Marken durch eine gegenseitige Marktanteilssubstitution, hohe Kosten durch parallele Marktbearbeitung oder die Gefahr der Übersegmentierung, zu vermeiden.

Für die einzelnen Marken besteht auf der Veranstalterstufe in ihren jeweiligen Quellmärkten eine klare Positionierung. Die Aufteilung des Marktes erfolgt über alle Quellmärkte hinweg in ein Premium-, ein Spezialisten-, ein qualitatives Volumensegment, ein preisorientiertes Volumensegment und ein Last-Minute-Segment, wobei die spezifische Positionierung der einzelnen Veranstaltermarke auf die lokalen Konsumentenbedürfnisse im jeweiligen Markt ausgerichtet ist (vgl. Abbildung 5).

Abbildung 5: **Das Markenportfolio auf Veranstalterebene in ausgewählten Quellmärkten**

	Last-Minute/Direkt	Preis-attraktiver Massenmarkt	Qualitäts-orientierter Volumenmarkt	Premium-markt	Spezialisten
Deutschland	L'tur Last Minute Urlaub	1 2 Fly Bei diesen Preisen muss man reisen.	TUI	airtours Travel in Style; ROBINSON	Dr. Tigges; WOLTERS REISEN Das sichere Urlaubsgefühl
UK	Portland DIRECT	just	Thomson	something special villa holidays	Crystal Holidays; Simply Travel
Niederlande	KRAS SterVakanties	arke	Holland International	PANTA REIZEN	ZEETOURS CRUISES

GABLER GRAFIK

Quelle: TUI AG 2004

Auf dem deutschen Markt wird das Volumengeschäft vornehmlich durch die Generalistenmarke TUI, die als Qualitätsanbieter mit gutem Preis-Leistungs-Verhältnis positioniert ist, sowie durch 1-2-Fly, eine Marke, die das preisorientierte Volumensegment anspricht, bestritten. Daneben existieren die Premiummarke Airtours International sowie die Spezialveranstalter Dr. Tigges, der das Zielsegment der Studienreisen anspricht, Gebeco, eine Marke, die das Segment der Fern-/Erlebnisreisen anvisiert und Wolters Reisen, die den Ferienhausmarkt abdeckt. L'tur ist als Marke für das Segment der Last-Minute-Urlauber ausgerichtet. Robinson ist die Clubmarke der TUI in Deutschland, die im Clubsegment eine eher höherpreisige und hochqualitative Positionierung einnimmt.

Die Markenarchitektur der TUI AG lässt sich auf vier Hierarchieebenen darstellen. Für Deutschland sind dies die Unternehmensmarke TUI AG, die internationale Dachmarke World of TUI, die Konsumentenmarke im qualitätsorientierten Volumensegment TUI sowie Produktmarken als Einzelmarken (Keller 1998, S. 409 ff.). Aufgrund ihrer spezifischen Marktpositionierung werden die einzelnen Produktmarken unterschiedlich geführt: Die Länderprogramme sind unter der Konsumentenmarke TUI zusammengefasst. Weiterhin sind Submarken unter der Dachmarke entwickelt worden, die spezifische Kundenbedürfnisse ansprechen, der Zielgruppe der Marke TUI jedoch sehr nahe stehen. Hierzu zählen die Submarken TUI Stars mit exklusiven Luxusangeboten, TUI Vital, das auf das Wellness-Segment ausgerichtet ist und TUI Family als Produktmarke für qualitativ hochwertigen Familienurlaub.

Abbildung 6: Markenarchitektur der TUI AG in Deutschland (Ausschnitt)

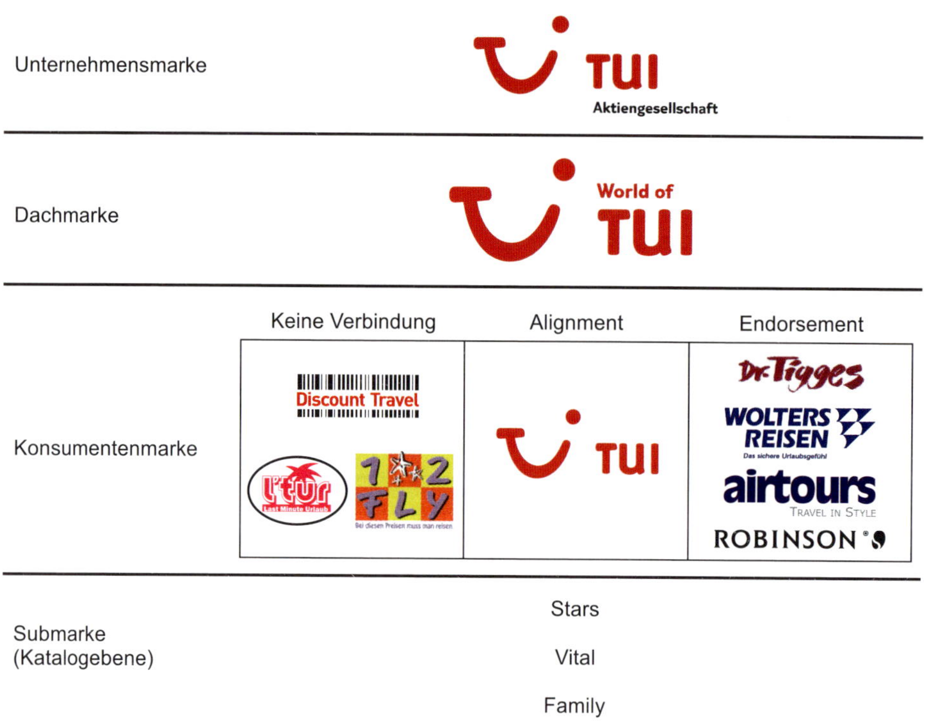

GABLER GRAFIK

Quelle: TUI AG 2004

Die Spezialistenmarken Oft Reisen, Dr. Tigges, Airtours International, Gebeco und Robinson werden als eigenständige Einzelmarken geführt, erfahren durch die übergeordnete Dachmarke World of TUI als Endorser jedoch eine Verstärkung, um Kompetenz und Glaubwürdigkeit zu signalisieren.

Für Marken wie 1-2-Fly, Discount Travel und L'tur, die auf das preisorientierte beziehungsweise das Last-Minute-Marktsegment ausgerichtet sind, wird eine Verbindung zur World of TUI explizit unterbunden, um die Eigenständigkeit der Marken zu fördern und eine Verwässerung der Markenpositionierung zu vermeiden. Zentrale Determinante zur Bestimmung der Beziehung zur Konsumentenmarke TUI, der Dachmarke World of TUI oder der Unternehmensmarke TUI AG ist das Markenimage. Liegt für die Marke ein eigenes, differenzierendes Markenimage vor und/oder ist ein Imagetransfer von der Konsumenten-, Dach- beziehungsweise der Unternehmensmarke nicht von Nutzen, so wird keine Beziehung zwischen den Markenebenen aufgebaut. Dies ist auch der Fall, wenn die Dachmarke selbst vor einem potenziellen negativen Imagetransfer geschützt werden soll.

3.12 Vertikale Markenführung über die Wertschöpfungskette

Ziel der vertikalen Integration ist zunächst eine Ausdehnung der Markenerlebniskette über alle Wertschöpfungsstufen hinweg. Der Nachfrager erlebt so von der Buchung, über die Reise bis zu seinem Hotelaufenthalt seinen Urlaub aus einer Hand. Hierbei wirkt das TUI Zeichen beziehungsweise das aligned Branding (vgl. Abbildung 8) als verbindende Klammer zwischen mehreren Marken.

Darüber hinaus ermöglicht die vertikale Integration über die Wertschöpfungskette eine stärkere Kontrolle knapper Ressourcen sowie ein besseres Kapazitäts- und Risikomanagement. Die Wertschöpfungsstufe Hotel stellt ein Kernelement des Pauschalreiseangebotes dar. Zu beobachten ist dabei eine zunehmende Knappheit an Hotels in Bestlagen, da die Nachfrage europaweit steigt und wesentliche Standorte bebaut sind. Zudem sind hochwertige Qualitätshotels hochprofitabel, da sich eine Preisprämie und eine hohe Auslastung realisieren lassen. Vor diesem Hintergrund versuchen die Veranstalter, durch zunehmende Beteiligungen an diesem Geschäft unmittelbar zu partizipieren. Die Wertschöpfungsstufe Flug ist durch große Auslastungsschwankungen und hohe Kapitalbindung gekennzeichnet. Durch ein integriertes Kapazitätsmanagement können unterjährige Steuerungsmaßnahmen integriert ausgeschöpft werden. Auf der Vertriebsstufe wird der Vorteil einer stärkeren vertikalen Integration vor allem im Erhalt der Verhandlungsmacht gesehen sowie in der Chance, die Vertriebseffizienz durch eine gezielte Steuerung auf die eigenen Produkte zu erhöhen. Die TUI AG verfügt zum einen über einen Eigenvertrieb, der die Steuerung der eigenen Reisebüros und Franchise-Betriebe zur Aufgabe hat, sowie einen Fremdvertrieb, der für den Vertrieb über Reisebüroketten und unabhängige Reisebüros zuständig ist. Als weiterer Vertriebskanal kommt der Internetvertrieb hinzu. Wichtigste Internetseite ist TUI.de. Daneben verfügen mittlerweile alle Veranstalter- und Vertriebsmarken über eigene E-Commerce-Internetauftritte, die von einer eigenen Gesellschaft, TUI Interactive, gesteuert werden. Ein vertikal integrierter Touristikkonzern wie die TUI AG besteht somit aus relationalen Märkten zwischen den verschiedenen Stufen der Wertschöpfung und ermöglicht ein integriertes Risikomanagement durch den Informationsaustausch zwischen allen Beteiligten.

Durch die vertikale Integration und den Zukauf verschiedener Marken und Markenportfolios ist ein komplexes vertikales Markensystem entstanden, welches in Auszügen für den deutschen Quellmarkt in Abbildung 7 dargestellt ist. Auf jeder einzelnen Stufe der

Wertschöpfungskette sind unterschiedliche Marken vertreten. So bestehen zum Beispiel im Reisebürovertrieb die TUI ReiseCenter, First Reisebüros oder Hapag-Lloyd Reisebüros, auf der Veranstalterstufe die Generalisten- und Spezialistenmarken, auf der Flugstufe die Marken Hapag-Lloyd Flug und Hapag-Lloyd Express, auf der Stufe der Zielgebietsagenturen, zum Beispiel TUI Hellas (Griechenland) und Travco (Ägypten) sowie die Marken RIU, Grecotel, Grupotel und Iberotel auf der Hotelstufe. Während der Urlaubsreise kommt der Nachfrager somit mit unterschiedlichen Marken auf den unterschiedlichen Stufen der Wertschöpfungskette in Berührung.

Abbildung 7: **Ausgewählte Marken im vertikalen Portfolio im deutschen Quellmarkt**

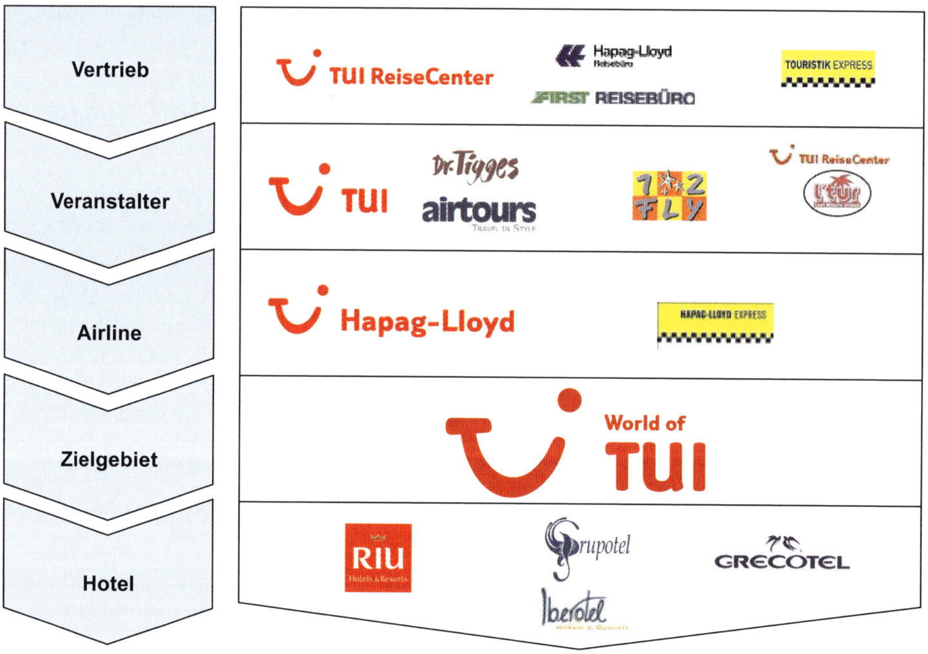

GABLER GRAFIK

Quelle: TUI AG 2004

Die beiden Stufen, die am stärksten über die Markenführung integriert sind, sind die Stufen Veranstalter und Eigenvertrieb, da die Marke TUI als Konsumentenmarke auch für die TUI ReiseCenter geführt wird. Durch einen positiven Imagetransfer konnte die Marke TUI dabei die TUI ReiseCenter in ihrer Profilierung unterstützen. Eine weitgehende Integration der Markenführung über die Vertikalisierung wurde im Jahr 2001 mit der Einführung der Dachmarke World of TUI vorgenommen, um ein Leverage der stärksten Marke im Markensystem zu erreichen. Sinn war, die Akzeptanz und Kompetenz der Marken in der Wahrnehmung der Verbraucher zu erhöhen (o. V. 2001, S. 24).

Mit dem Markenkonzept wurden die über 200 touristischen Marken der TUI AG unter einem Dach gebündelt. Ziel ist es, die Nachfrager auf allen Stufen der Wertschöpfungskette an den Konzern zu binden und die Markentreue zu erhöhen. Die touristischen Einzelmarken wurden dabei auf verschiedene Arten in das Markenkonzept integriert (vgl. Abbildung 8).

Abbildung 8: Das Dachmarkenkonzept der World of TUI

Dachmarkenkonzept der World of TUI
Die touristischen Einzelmarken wurden auf verschiedene Arten in das Markenkonzept integriert:
Alignment Bei der stärksten Form blieb der alte Markenname erhalten; Logo und Auftritt erhalten die World-of-TUI-Optik. Betroffen sind die Qualitätsvolumenmarken, zu denen zum Beispiel TUI und Hapag-Lloyd in Deutschland sowie Thomson, Lunn Poly und Britannia in Großbritannien gehören.
Endorsement Die Spezialanbieter behalten ihr Logo und ihren Auftritt, der jedoch um das World-of-TUI-Logo ergänzt wird. Diese Form der Anpassung wird auf circa 50 Marken angewendet, zum Beispiel auf die Veranstalter Robinson, Dr. Tigges, Airtours International oder die Hotelketten RIU und Grecotel.
Keine Verbindung Bei einigen Marken wie L'tur, Discount Travel und 1-2-Fly verzichtet die TUI AG bewusst auf den Verweis zur Dachmarke.

GABLER GRAFIK

Quelle: TUI AG 2004

Bei der offensichtlichsten Form der Anpassung, den Alignments, wurden die Marken relauncht. Der Name blieb bestehen, Logo und Auftritt bekamen aber das einheitliche Auftreten der World of TUI. Dies betraf die Volumenmarken, deren Kernzielgruppe die 25- bis 55-Jährigen mit einem mittleren bis gehobenen Qualitätsanspruch sind. In Deutschland sind dies im Vertrieb TUI ReiseCenter, der Veranstalter TUI und die Fluglinie Hapag-Lloyd Flug. Um Kannibalisierungseffekte zu vermeiden, ist in jedem Land jeweils maximal eine Marke pro Wertschöpfungsstufe aligned worden.

Im vertikalen Markenportfolio wird die Dachmarke World of TUI im Rahmen der Kommunikation auf allen Wertschöpfungsstufen als Endorsement genutzt. Durch diesen Schritt wird die Zielsetzung verfolgt, den Absender World of TUI als ein Qualitätssiegel auf den Stufen der Wertschöpfungskette zu kommunizieren, ohne die Werte der bestehenden Marken anzutasten. Die Nutzung der Marke World of TUI als Endorser erfolgt auf der Reisebürostufe bei den Vertriebsmarken First und Hapag-Lloyd, auf der Veranstalterstufe bei den Qualitätsmarken, wie zum Beispiel Dr. Tigges (vgl. auch Abbildung 6). Im Zielgebiet ist die Rolle der Dachmarke stärker im Vordergrund, indem die World of TUI als Servicemarke auftritt und die Veranstaltermarken als Co-Brands unter sich bündelt. Auf der Hotelstufe wird bei den eigenen Hotels im Katalog, in der Kommunikation sowie in der Außendarstellung ebenfalls der Zusatz World of TUI als Endorsement verwendet. Die Markenvertikalisierung über Endorsement ermöglicht somit ein dezentes Markenerlebnis über die einzelnen Stufen der Wertschöpfungskette. Der Grad der Vertikalisierung ist jedoch als relativ zurückhaltend zu bezeichnen, da sich das Auftreten der Absendermarke zum größten Teil auf die Kommunikation beschränkt und somit die Marke World of TUI im Rahmen des eigentlichen Urlaubserlebnisses über die einzelnen Stufen nur vereinzelt auftritt.

Aufgrund von potenziellen Gefahren, zum Beispiel im Rahmen eines negativen Imagetransfers auf einer anderen Wertschöpfungsstufe, und unter Berücksichtigung von Aspekten des Risikomanagements und der Aktionsflexibilität wurde bei einigen Marken wie Discount Travel, 1-2-Fly und Hapag-Lloyd Express, die im preisaggressiven Wettbewerbsumfeld agieren, auf eine sichtbare Verbindung zur Dachmarke World of TUI verzichtet.

3.13 Internationale Markenführung über die Ländermärkte

Die internationale Markenführung der TUI AG wurde durch die Akquisitionen im Tourismus ab 1998 und insbesondere durch die Akquisition der Thomson Travel Group im Jahr 2000 vor große Herausforderungen gestellt. Auf der Veranstalter- und Vertriebsseite ist die TUI AG heute in 18 Ländermärkten aktiv.

Im Folgenden sollen zunächst die grundlegenden Optionen bei der Findung von Internationalisierungsstrategien dargelegt werden. Grundsätzlich lassen sich Internationalisierungsstrategien in einer Matrix mit den Dimensionen Integrationsvorteile und Differenzierungsvorteile in vier strategische Optionen gliedern (Meffert/Bolz 1994, S. 25 ff.). Diese grundsätzlichen strategischen Optionen, die in Abbildung 9 dargestellt sind, können als Bezugsrahmen für die internationale Markenführung herangezogen werden.

Abbildung 9: **Systematisierung von Internationalisierungsstrategien der Markenführung**

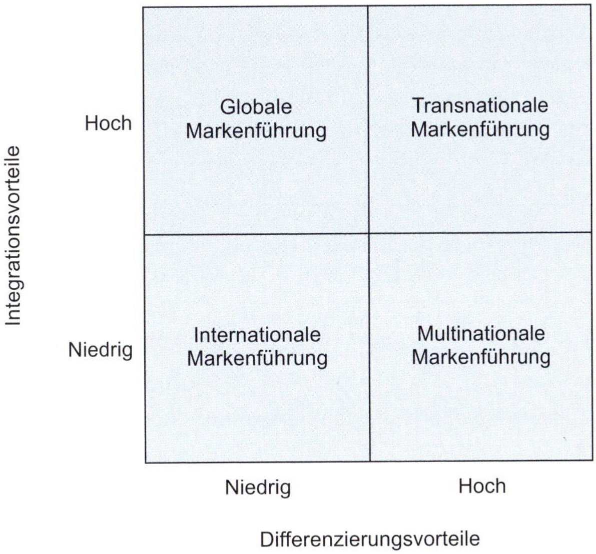

GABLER GRAFIK

Quelle: in Anlehnung an Meffert/Bolz, 1994, S. 27

Internationale Markenführung mit niedrigen Integrations- sowie Differenzierungsvorteilen weist eine hohe Konzentration auf einen Heimatmarkt auf und zeichnet sich dadurch aus, dass keine länderspezifischen Besonderheiten außerhalb des Heimatmarktes in der Markenführung berücksichtigt werden. Man könnte diese Option als das Anfangsstadium von Internationalisierungsstrategien bezeichnen. Die multinationale Markenführung weist niedrige Integrationsvorteile, aber hohe Differenzierungsvorteile auf. Internationale Tochtergesellschaften führen bei dieser Option quasi autonom eine nationale Markenstrategie. Die globale Markenstrategie mit hohen Integrations- und niedrigen Differenzierungsvorteilen beruht auf einer konsistenten Markenführung auf dem gesamten Weltmarkt ohne besondere Berücksichtigung nationaler Wünsche oder Bedürfnisse. Die transnationale Markenstrategie schließlich zeichnet sich durch hohe Integrations- und hohe Differenzierungsvorteile aus, bei der den länderspezifischen Bedürfnissen durch eine Differenzierungsstrategie Rechnung getragen wird, gleichzeitig aber eine hohe Integration der Markenführung über die einzelnen Ländermärkte vorliegt.

Die Grundherausforderung der TUI AG war letztlich in der Frage der Integration der beiden ehemaligen touristischen Holding-Gesellschaften TUI Group und Thomson Travel Group zu sehen. Bei großer Stärke der zugehörigen Konsumentenmarken in den jeweiligen Heimatmärkten schien prinzipiell die multinationale Markenführung mit geringer Integration der beiden Marken und relativ unabhängiger Markenführung in den jeweiligen Quellmärkten sinnvoll. Mit der Dachmarke World of TUI und dem damit verbundenen Alignment der Kernmarken wurde jedoch eine Option gewählt, die in der klassischen Theorie schwer zuzuordnen ist. Die World of TUI nutzt so die jeweiligen Stärken der Einzelmarken in den jeweiligen Ländern und bildet zusätzlich eine übergreifende Klammer mit gemeinsamen Markenwerten wie Qualität, Vertrauen, Sicherheit und Emotionen. So werden die Vorteile einer multinationalen Markenführung mit der Ausschöpfung und Weiterentwicklung der vorhandenen Markenidentität und dem existierenden Vertrauenskapital in den jeweiligen Heimatmärkten und damit einer Ausnutzung von lokalen Positionierungsvorteilen einer Marke umfassend ausgenutzt.

Dazu wird gezielt die wahrgenommene Positionierung der einzelnen Marken in den unterschiedlichen Ländermärkten nach und nach angeglichen, um die Vorteile einer globalen Markenführung zunehmend ausschöpfen zu können. Basis ist hier ein hoher Integrationsgrad über zum Beispiel eine gemeinsame Organisationseinheit zur strategischen Markenführung, um zum einen Synergievorteile zu nutzen und zum anderen lokale Bedürfnisse zu berücksichtigen.

Die globale Markenführung wird hier als die umfassende Ausprägung der Standardisierung im Vergleich zu einer transnationalen Markenführung betrachtet, bei der nur noch eine Dachmarke besteht, die über alle Ländermärkte geführt wird.

Abbildung 10: Internationalisierung und Vertikalisierung über die Wertschöpfungskette

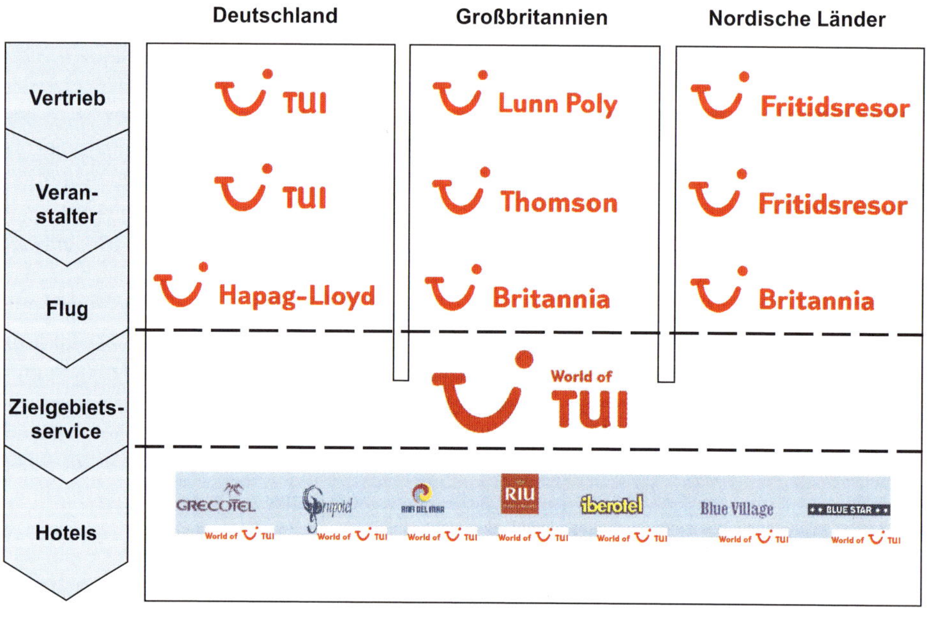

GABLER GRAFIK

Quelle: TUI AG 2004

Für die Marken unterhalb der Dachmarke World of TUI, die international geführt werden, stellt sich für die Zukunft die Frage nach einer transnationalen Markenstrategie, in der die Dachmarke als Integrationsanker dient, oder einer multinationalen Markenstrategie, bei der die Marken relativ autonom geführt werden. Die Frage der Internationalisierung ist somit auch auf den einzelnen Wertschöpfungsstufen von zentralem strategischen Interesse. Eine Internationalisierung ist insbesondere auf den Wertschöpfungsstufen, die sich nicht explizit auf den jeweiligen Quellmarkt beziehen, von hohem Stellenwert, also beim Flug, den Zielgebietsagenturen und den Hotels. Wie aus Abbildung 10 ersichtlich wird, sind die internationale und die vertikale Dimension der Markenführung nicht unabhängig voneinander zu betrachten. So hätte zum Beispiel eine mögliche Vertikalisierung der Marke TUI auf der Hotelstufe Auswirkungen auf den britischen Quellmarkt, da die Hotelmarken RIU, Grecotel, Grupotel und Iberotel neben den deutschen auch die britischen Urlaubsgäste bedienen. Hierbei scheint die Wahl eines Endorsements durch die Dachmarke World of TUI der richtige Schritt zu sein.

3.2 Integration der Markenführung

In den Ausführungen ist bereits deutlich geworden, dass die Markenführung in der horizontalen, vertikalen und internationalen Dimension nicht jeweils isoliert zu gestalten ist, sondern ein interdependentes Entscheidungsproblem darstellt. Insofern ist einer **integrierten Markenführung** über die drei Dimensionen ein zentraler Stellenwert beizumessen.

Im Rahmen einer integrierten Markenführung gründet bei der TUI AG jede Marke auf einer klaren Markenidentität, die sich vor allem aus der historischen Kompetenz der jeweiligen Marke ergibt und das Fundament für die Markenführung darstellt. Auf Basis dieser Markenidentität ergeben sich die Positionierung der jeweiligen Marken und die Formulierung der Markenstrategie. Fünf Pfeiler werden im TUI-Konzern als zentrale Stützpfeiler gesehen, um das Markenversprechen aus der Positionierung zu erfüllen und eine klare Profilierung der Marke zu erreichen:

1. die Corporate Identity, die das Dach der Markenführung darstellt und als Basis für die Markenarchitektur dient,
2. das Produkt- und Servicemanagement als eigentliche Erfüllung des Markenversprechens mit der Entwicklung von hochwertigen, innovativen und zielgruppengerechten Tourismusprodukten,
3. ein konsequentes Qualitätsmanagement zur Sicherstellung des Leistungsanspruchs,
4. die externe Kommunikation der Markenführung (Werbung, Vertriebskommunikation, Investor Relations und Pressearbeit) sowie
5. die interne Kommunikation mit Programmen zur Stärkung der Unternehmenskultur, Förderung der Beziehungen zwischen Führungskräften und Mitarbeiten und Sicherstellung einer konsistenten internen Servicequalität.

4. Erfolge infolge der Einführung der Dachmarke „World of TUI"

Drei Jahre nach dem Start des Dachmarkenkonzepts „World of TUI" bestätigen die Ergebnisse, dass das Konzept funktioniert (vgl. Abbildung 11). Das TUI-Logo als zentrale Klammer der Dachmarke stiftet für den Konzern international eine neue und innovative Identität (Lambertz 2003, S. 8 ff.).

Der Erfolg der Dachmarkenstrategie lässt sich an mehreren konkreten Indikatoren positiv ablesen:

- Bekanntheit und Image
- Marktanteile
- Synergien innerhalb des Konzerns
- Einsparungen in der Zusammenarbeit mit Werbepartnern
- Mitarbeiter-Identifikation
- Beurteilung in der Fachwelt
- Entwicklung des Markenwerts der TUI

Abbildung 11: **Vergleich der Wirkung des alten und neuen TUI-Logos für den Veranstalter in Deutschland**

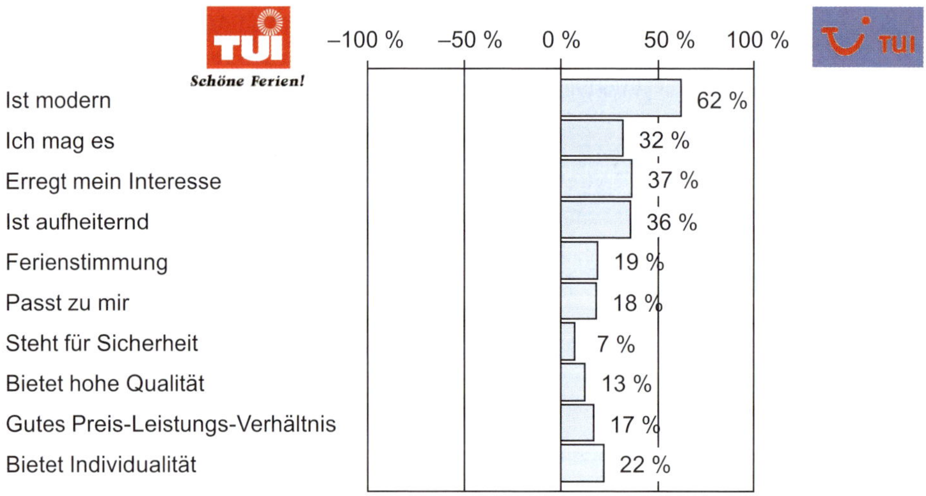

GABLER GRAFIK

Quelle: TUI AG 2003

Das neue Logo hat sich schnell durchgesetzt. Im Februar 2002, vier Monate nach der Einführung, kannten nach einer Untersuchung von Research International bereits 42 Prozent der „reiseaffinen" Verbraucher das Zeichen. Die GfK Nürnberg ermittelte ein Jahr später im Juni 2003 eine gestützte Bekanntheit von mittlerweile 90 Prozent. Diese Werte wurden erreicht, obwohl der 11. September den Zeitplan für die Strategieumsetzung verzögert hat. Nach den Ereignissen in New York wurden sämtliche Einführungs- und Werbemaßnahmen für das neue Outfit eingestellt und erst im Dezember wieder aufgenommen – mit einem von 100 Millionen Euro auf 70 Millionen Euro geschrumpften Budget. Ohne Unterbrechung und mit gleich bleibendem Etat wären die Ziele des Markenaufbaus und der Markenpersönlichkeit sogar noch schneller erreicht worden.

Untersuchungen dokumentieren auch international steigende Imagewerte. So wird zum Beispiel Thomson Holidays in Großbritannien seit der optischen Zugehörigkeit zur World of TUI von britischen Urlaubern als „moderner" und „frischer" bewertet. Zum alten Markenkern sind demnach neue Werte hinzugekommen. Thomson konnte mit dem neuen Logo Marktanteile hinzugewinnen.

Abbildung 12: Bekanntheit des TUI-Logos bei Urlaubern in Deutschland und Großbritannien

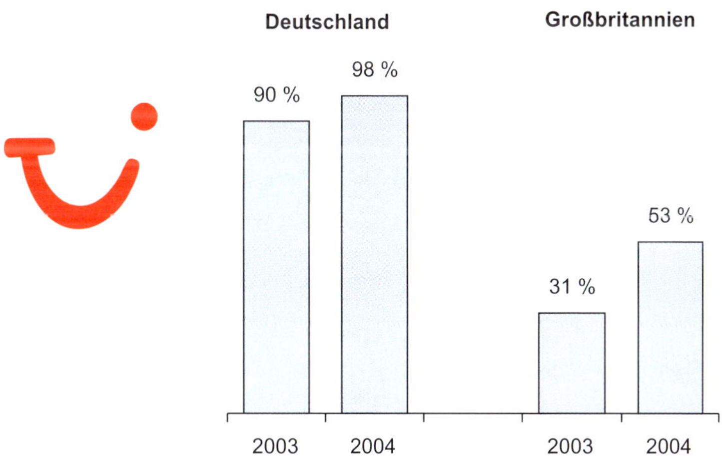

GABLER GRAFIK

Quelle: TUI AG 2004

Auch die finanzielle Rechnung geht auf. Dank multinationaler Zusammenarbeit konnten bereits Kommunikationssynergien in Höhe von 35 Millionen Euro realisiert werden. Durch eine gemeinsame Marketingplattform werden bei gleichzeitig höherem Wirkungsgrad die Kommunikationskosten um jährlich weitere zehn bis 15 Millionen Euro reduziert.

Die wichtigsten Maßnahmen, die bisher unternommen wurden, sind die einheitliche Kommunikation der Kernmarken mit nur einem Agenturnetzwerk, Jung von Matt/DDB, und die Internationalisierung bei der Produktion von Werbemitteln. Erhebliche Synergiepotenziale werden hier durch übergreifende Foto-Shootings, Spot-Produktionen und Kostensenkungen im Media-Einkauf realisiert.

Damit sind die Zusatzinvestitionen in Höhe von 70 Millionen Euro bereits nach rund fünf Jahren kompensiert. Und diese Rechnung ist ohne Marktanteilsgewinne und Markenwertsteigerungen gemacht. So hat sich beispielsweise allein der TUI Markenwert von 2001 auf 2003 um 3,988 Milliarden Euro erhöht (vgl. Abbildung 13).

Abbildung 13: Steigerung des TUI-Markenwerts von 2001 bis 2003

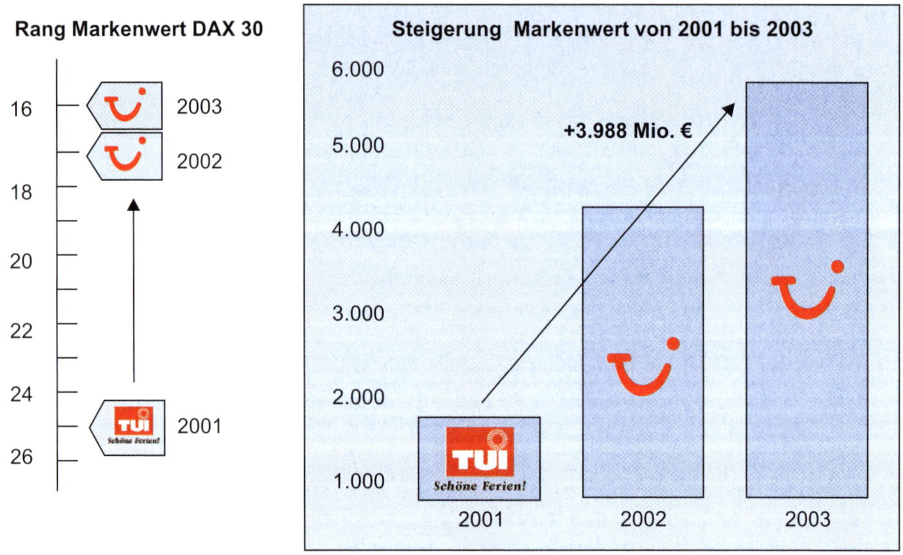

GABLER GRAFIK

Quelle: BBDO 2004

Der Aufbau der Marke war jedoch nur ein erster Schritt. Die World of TUI wird mit weiteren Werten aufgeladen, um noch stärker auf jeder Stufe der touristischen Wertschöpfungskette verankert zu sein und die Marke für neue Geschäftsmodelle tragfähig zu machen.

So sollen umfangreiche Sponsoringmaßnahmen, zum Beispiel im Fußball bei Hannover 96 in Deutschland und Tottenham Hotspur in England, und der gerade gestartete Verkauf von Merchandising- und Lizenzprodukten die Marke anfassbar machen und die Präsenz der Marke über den vergleichsweise kurzen Urlaubszeitraum hinaus auch während des übrigen Jahres erlebbar machen. Durch die gesteigerte Wahrnehmung der World of TUI bei den Nachfragern sollen in einem weiteren Schritt neue Geschäftsfelder abseits des klassischen Urlaubs erschlossen werden.

5. Ausblick

Im Rahmen des Beitrags wurde die hohe Komplexität der Markenführung von Tourismusmarken in horizontaler, vertikaler und internationaler Dimension aufgezeigt. Die zentralen Herausforderungen ergeben sich dabei in der horizontalen Dimension im Spannungsfeld zwischen **Kannibalisierung und Partizipation** im Rahmen einer Mehrmarkenstrategie, in der vertikalen Dimension im **Grad der Markenintegration über die Wertschöpfungskette** hinweg und in der internationalen Dimension im Spannungsfeld zwischen **Standardisierung und Differenzierung** in verschiedenen Ländermärkten.

Am Beispiel der Marke TUI konnte gezeigt werden, wie durch ein konsequentes Markenmanagement die hervorragende Position auf dem deutschen Markt erreicht werden konnte. Im Vergleich zu anderen Märkten und insbesondere Konsumgütermärkten ist jedoch festzustellen, dass die strategische Markenbildung von Tourismusleistungen erst in den letzten Jahren stark an Bedeutung gewonnen hat. Im Tourismusmarkt, der von einer zunehmenden Austauschbarkeit der objektiven Produktleistungen (zum Beispiel Angebot des gleichen Hotels durch mehrere Veranstalter) geprägt ist, ist daher eine große Chance fur Tourismuskonzerne zu sehen, sich aus dem preistreibenden Wettbewerb zu lösen und sich über eine starke Marke zu profilieren.

Die Fallstudie hat gezeigt, dass die Markenprofilierung integriert über die drei Dimensionen horizontal, vertikal und international erfolgt ist. Zukünftig könnte aber eine weitere Chance in der Einführung einer vierten Dimension liegen, nämlich in der lateralen Dimension. Diese bezeichnet die Aktivitäten in Geschäftsfeldern, die außerhalb der heutigen Wertschöpfung liegen. Hier wäre zum Beispiel eine theoretische Option in der weiteren Entwicklung der Dachmarke World of TUI in den Bereichen Freizeit oder Unterhaltung auf Basis des zentralen Markenwertes „Lebensfreude" zu sehen. Eine derartige Entwicklung bedarf jedoch einer differenzierten Betrachtung vor dem Hintergrund der Tragfähigkeit der Marke. Es bleibt daher sicherlich spannend zu beobachten, wohin sich die World of TUI in Zukunft entwickeln wird.

Literatur

Esch, F.-R., Wicke, A. (2001), Herausforderungen und Aufgaben des Markenmanagements, in: Esch, F.-R. (Hrsg.), Moderne Markenführung: Grundlagen – innovative Ansätze – praktische Umsetzungen, 3. Aufl., Wiesbaden, S. 3–55.

Keller, K. L. (1998), Strategic brand management: building, measuring, and managing brand equity, Upper Saddle River, N. J.

Lambertz, M. (2003), TUI wird die Coca-Cola des Tourismus, in: marketingjournal, Nr. 4, S. 8–12.

Meffert, H., Bolz, J. (1994), Internationales Marketing-Management, 2. Aufl., Stuttgart u. a.

Meyer, A., Tostmann, T. (1995), Die nur erlebbare Markenpersönlichkeit – Wie sich Dienstleistungsmarken aufbauen und pflegen lassen, in: Harvard Business Manager, Nr. 4, S. 9–15.

Momberger, W. (2000), Wertvolle Marken, in: Touristik Report, Jubiläumsausgabe zum 20-jährigen Bestehen, Oktober, S. 120–123.

o. V. (2001), Preussag fliegt in die schöne neue TUI-Welt, in: Horizont, Nr. 36, September, S. 24.

Werner, G., Richter, M. (1998), Marken im Bereich Dienstleistungen: Gibt es das überhaupt?, in: Tomczak, T., Schögel, M., Ludwig, E. (Hrsg.), Markenmanagement für Dienstleistungen, St. Gallen.

Erfolgreiche Markenführung bei homogenen Verbrauchsgütern – Das Beispiel JET

Heribert Meffert und Ingo Lasslop

1. Die Ausgangsposition der Marke JET **716**

2. Der deutsche Tankstellenmarkt **716**
2.1 Historische Branchenentwicklung 716
2.2 Veränderungen im Konsumentenverhalten 718
2.3 Veränderungen im Wettbewerbsumfeld 719
2.4 Die Bedeutung der Marke 723

3. Das Konzept zur Profilierung der Marke JET **724**
3.1 Die strategische Rolle der Markenpolitik für JET 724
3.2 Das Markenleitbild von JET 727
3.3 Durchsetzung des Markenleitbildes in der Preis-, Produkt- und Distributionspolitik 728
3.4 Durchsetzung des Markenleitbildes in der Kommunikationspolitik 728
3.5 Durchsetzung des Markenleitbildes nach Innen 732

4. Erfolg der Markenprofilierung bei JET **733**

1. Die Ausgangsposition der Marke JET

JET ist die Tankstellenmarke der CONOCO Mineraloel GmbH in Hamburg, einer 100-prozentigen Tochtergesellschaft des US-Mineraloelkonzerns CONOCO Inc. mit Sitz in Houston, Texas. Zu CONOCO gehören weltweit unter anderem rund 10.000 Tankstellen, Öl- und Gasfelder, eine Tankerflotte sowie einige Raffinerien. In Deutschland erlöste CONOCO 1998 im Tankstellen-, Großhandels- und Endverbrauchergeschäft (Handel mit industriellen Mineraloelprodukten) knapp 3 Milliarden Euro (CONOCO Mineraloel GmbH 1999).

In den 70er Jahren führte CONOCO die Tankstellenmarke JET in den deutschen Markt ein, die sich seitdem als preisgünstiger Anbieter von Kraftstoff etabliert hat. Obgleich der eigene Anspruch stets darin bestand, qualitativ hochwertigen Markenkraftstoff zu vertreiben, ist bis heute der Preisvorteil die primäre Profilierungsdimension im Wettbewerb geblieben. Ende 1998 wurden von der CONOCO Mineraloel GmbH 626 Tankstellen in Deutschland betrieben. In dieser Zahl sind neben den JET-Straßen- und Autobahntankstellen auch ca. 200 so genannte Supermarkttankstellen enthalten. Damit erreichte CONOCO einen Anteil von ca. 4 Prozent an allen deutschen Tankstellen. Betrachtet man die an den JET-Stationen und Supermarkttankstellen insgesamt verkaufte Menge an Kraftstoffen, so lag der volumenmäßige Marktanteil von CONOCO bei ca. 7 Prozent.

Obgleich die CONOCO Mineraloel GmbH 1998 das beste operative Ergebnis der Firmengeschichte feiern konnte, deutete die Entwicklung zentraler psychografischer Indikatoren auf Probleme im Bereich der Markenführung bei JET hin. So fiel die gestützte Markenbekanntheit in Westdeutschland von über 80 Prozent zu Beginn der 90er Jahre bis 1998 kontinuierlich auf unter 70 Prozent. Ähnlich, wenn auch weniger stark, verhielt es sich mit der wahrgenommenen Qualitätserwartung. Vor diesem Hintergrund sah sich das Unternehmen veranlasst, die Markenpolitik von JET neu auszurichten, um die Wettbewerbsposition zu festigen.

2. Der deutsche Tankstellenmarkt

2.1 Historische Branchenentwicklung

Die Entwicklung im deutschen Tankstellenmarkt wurde in den letzten drei Jahrzehnten durch einen Strukturwandel geprägt, der sich in einer deutlichen Netzreduktion widerspiegelt (vgl. Abbildung 1). So gab es 1970 noch 45.849 Tankstellen in Deutschland, deren primäre Erlösquelle im Vertrieb von Kraft- und Schmierstoffen bestand. Diese Zahl ging bis zum Jahre 2000 auf 16.404 Stationen zurück (vgl. EID 2001). Im Zuge der damit einhergehenden Um- und Ausbauten vieler Stationen stiegen die Fläche und auch der Umsatz pro

Tankstelle stark an: Betrug der durchschnittliche Umsatz an einer westdeutschen Tankstelle im Jahr 1980 ca. 180.000 Euro, so waren es im Jahr 1995 bereits 718.000 Euro (vgl. BTG 1995; Pauls 1998, S. 152).

Augenblicklich befindet sich der deutsche Tankstellenmarkt jedoch nicht nur hinsichtlich der absoluten Netzdichte in einer Stagnationsphase. Während für die Nachfrage nach Diesel in den nächsten Jahren zumindest mit einem leichten Plus gerechnet wird, prognostizieren die Experten für den Absatz von Ottokraftstoffen einen leichten Rückgang. Eine wesentliche Ursache hierfür liegt in der steten Weiterentwicklung der Motorentechnologie: Trotz eines weiter steigenden Verkehrsaufkommens auf deutschen Straßen führt ein tendenziell sinkender Kraftstoffverbrauch zu einem zunächst gleich bleibenden, langfristig dagegen rückläufigen Kraftstoffabsatz.

Abbildung 1: **Tankstellenbestand in Deutschland im Zeitablauf**

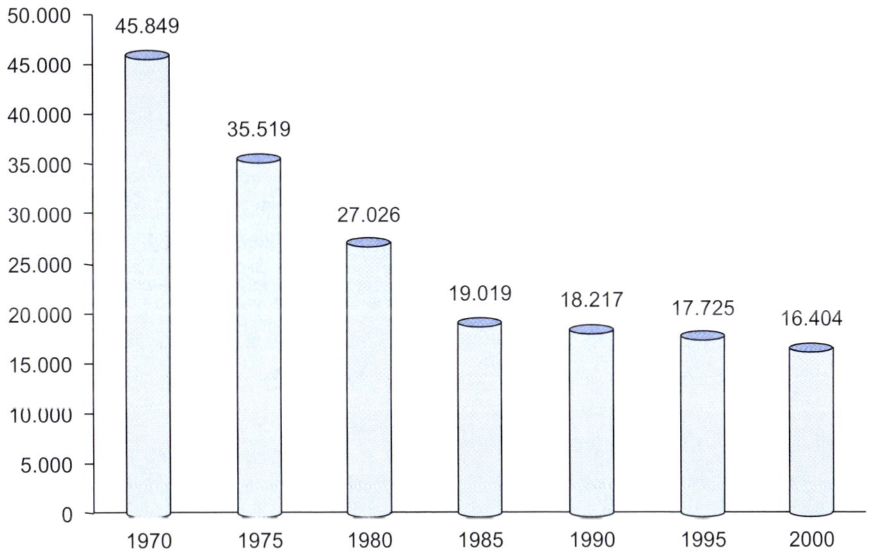

GABLER GRAFIK

Quelle: Pauls 1998, EID 2001

Gefördert wird diese Entwicklung durch staatliche Regelungen, welche zum Beispiel verbrauchsarme PKW steuerlich begünstigen oder auch die langfristige Entwicklung alternativer Antriebsstoffe, wie Wasserstoff, Brennstoffzellen oder die Solarenergie („Elektroauto"), durch diverse Programme fördern.

Nicht zuletzt auf Grund dieser Entwicklungen im technologischen und gesellschaftspolitischen Umfeld ist seit den späten 60er Jahren eine permanent breiter werdende Angebotspalette bei deutschen Tankstellen festzustellen. So gehörten bereits in den 70er Jahren neben dem traditionellen Verkauf von Kraftstoff diverse Dienstleistungen in den Bereichen Technik (insbesondere Reparaturen, Reifendienst, Ölwechsel) und Pflege (Waschstraßen, Innenpflege) zum Standard an vielen Tankstellen. Dazu kam die zunehmende Erweiterung des Angebots um branchenfremde Produkte, insbesondere aus den Bereichen Print (Tageszeitungen, Zeitschriften, Bücher) und Lebensmittel (Zigaretten, Süßwaren, Getränke). Diese Veränderungen im Angebot finden ihre Erklärung auch in einem gewandelten Konsumentenverhalten.

2.2 Veränderungen im Konsumentenverhalten

Betrachtet man zunächst die soziodemografische Struktur der Tankstellen-Kunden, so zeigt sich, dass ca. 60 Prozent jünger als 35 Jahren alt sind (35 bis 55 Jahre: ca. 30 Prozent) und ca. 70 Prozent männlich. Über die Hälfte der Kunden verfügt über ein monatliches Haushaltseinkommen von mehr als 1.500 Euro, wobei Einpersonen- (ca. 25 Prozent) und Zweipersonenhaushalte (ca. 40 Prozent) dominieren (vgl. Lekkerland 1998).

Die in den letzten Jahren zu beobachtende Ausweitung der Verkaufsfläche an vielen Tankstellen und die damit verbundene Ausdehnung kraftstofffremder Angebote ist neben dem Erlösdruck im traditionellen Kraftstoffgeschäft vor allem auf ein gewandeltes Verbraucherverhalten zurückzuführen, für das sich der Begriff Convenience etabliert hat (vgl. Swoboda 1999, S. 95 ff.). Kennzeichnend für diesen Verbrauchertrend ist ein Streben nach Annehmlichkeit, Bequemlichkeit und Verfügbarkeit beim Einkauf. Zurückzuführen ist dieser Trend insbesondere auf die wachsende Bedeutung, die dem Faktor Zeit bzw. Freizeit zugemessen wird. Immer mehr Menschen empfinden einen Mangel an Zeit, sodass die neben dem Beruf verbleibende Freizeit effektiv und möglichst stressfrei genutzt werden soll.

Dies zeigt sich zum einen in der gesteigerten Nachfrage nach vorgefertigten Produkten (Fertiggerichte, Schnellmahlzeiten) und zum anderen in dem Aufkommen neuer Vertriebsformen, den sog. Convenience-Shops (neben Tankstellen zum Beispiel Bahnhöfe, Poststellen, Bäcker, ...). Diese bieten lange Öffnungszeiten, gute Erreichbarkeit, Übersichtlichkeit und vor allem die Möglichkeit, verschiedene Bedürfnisse kombiniert und damit bequem und zeitsparend zu befriedigen. So zeigt sich inzwischen, dass nur noch ein knappes Drittel aller Kunden eine Tankstelle besucht, um ausschließlich zu tanken, während der Anteil der Tankstellenkunden, die mindestens einmal in der Woche auch vom Shop-Angebot Gebrauch machen, bei ca. 60 Prozent liegt (vgl. Abbildung 2).

Aus diesem Trend könnten in naher Zukunft weitere Geschäftsbereiche an Tankstellen entstehen, die dem Convenience-Gedanken Rechnung tragen. Neben dem Angebot von Finanzdienstleistungen in Form von Geldautomaten werden weitere Services, zum Beispiel in den Bereichen Reise, Post, Foto, Video und Ticketing (Konzert-, Theaterkarten), aktuell hinsichtlich ihrer Marktfähigkeit diskutiert (vgl. Volks- und Raiffeisenbank 1999).

Abbildung 2: Konsummuster an deutschen Tanksstellen

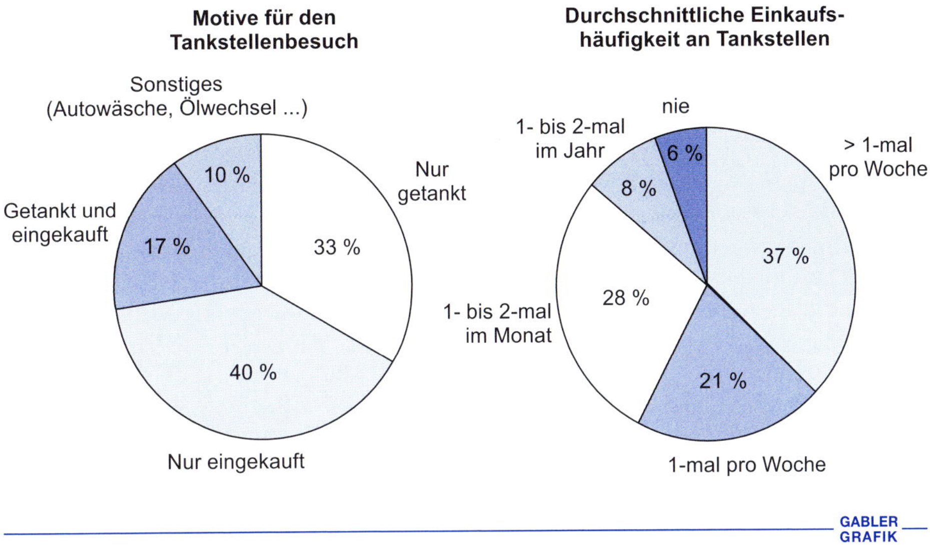

Quelle: Lekkerland 1998

In engem Zusammenhang damit steht die hohe Preisbereitschaft und geringe Preiselastizität der Nachfrage für convenienceorientierten Konsum. Kann dieser Aspekt bereits auf der Ebene der Sortimente identifiziert werden, so wird er auf der Ebene der Einkaufsstätten besonders deutlich: In convenienceorientierten Einkaufsstätten werden Preisbereitschaften abgeschöpft, die in der Regel deutlich über denen in anderen Einkaufsstätten liegen. Als Paradebeispiel dienen hier sicherlich die Tankstellen.

Trotz einer verstärkten Bedeutung des Convenience-Aspekts bleiben die Qualität und insbesondere der Preis des angebotenen Kraftstoffs wichtige Fakoren, die das Auswahlverhalten der Konsumenten und auch das Image einer Tankstellenmarke beeinflussen. Dies zeigt sich auch bei der Abgrenzung des Konkurrenzumfeldes der Marke JET.

2.3 Veränderungen im Wettbewerbsumfeld

Der deutsche Tankstellenmarkt gleicht einem klassischen Oligopol, in dem auf Grund der überschaubaren Anzahl relevanter Wettbewerber eine hohe Reaktionsverbundenheit, insbesondere hinsichtlich der Preisgestaltung, herrscht. Die Wettbewerber in diesem Markt werden traditionell in vier Kategorien aufgeteilt. Zentrale Unterscheidungsmerkmale sind primär die Preisstellung, die auf Grund der immer noch hohen absoluten Tankstellendichte äußerst transparent ist, sowie der Umfang kraftstofffremder Sortimentsbestandteile. Abbildung 3 verdeutlicht die Marktstruktur im Jahr 1998.

Die A-Marken Aral, DEA, Shell, Esso und BP besitzen jeweils ein in Deutschland flächendeckendes Tankstellennetz und sind dementsprechend bundesweit als Marken etabliert. Sie beherrschen das in Deutschland starre Preisgefüge insofern, als dass die Preisveränderungen dieser fünf Marken stets eine Reaktion bei den anderen Tankstellenbetreibern hervorruft, welche das gesamte Preisgefüge innerhalb kürzester Zeit wieder stabilisiert. Die Qualitäts- und Servicewahrnehmung dieser Gruppe ist am höchsten, wobei die Marke Aral auf Grund ihrer langjährigen Marktführerschaft eine klare Alleinstellung aufweist. Seit Mitte der 90er Jahre ist bei den A-Marken eine klare Tendenz erkennbar, sich primär über kraftstofffremde Leistungen zu profilieren, nicht zuletzt, um dem geschilderten Wandel im Verbraucherverhalten gerecht zu werden. Dies zeigt sich besonders in den seit Mitte der 90er Jahre geänderten Kommunikationsinhalten, die das Shop-Geschäft und Convenience-Aspekte stark hervorheben (zum Beispiel „Shell-Select“, „Wir bei DEA“). Für die Zukunft werden von einigen dieser Marken Geschäftsmodelle diskutiert, welche die Handels- und Standortkompetenz – und damit eine langfristige „Business-Migration“ in kraftstofffremde Branchen – noch stärker betonen (vgl. Pauls 1998; Heuskel 1999).

Abbildung 3: Struktur des deutschen Tankstellenmarktes 1998

Marke	Anzahl Tankstellen per 1.1.1999	Marktanteil (Tankstellen) per 1.1.1999	Marktanteil (Kraftstoffvolumen) 1998
Aral	2.418	14,55 %	18,9 %
Shell	1.616	9,72 %	11,9 %
DEA	1.623	9,77 %	9,4 %
Esso	1.440	8,67 %	10,1 %
BP	1.129	6,79 %	7,5 %
Avia	819	4,93 %	2,3 %
CONOCO[1]	626	3,77 %	7,0 %
Elf	603	3,63 %	6,1 %
Agip	403	2,43 %	1,7 %
Fina	323	1,94 %	0,9 %
Tamoil/HEM	212	1,28 %	n. v.
Total	186	1,12 %	1,0 %
Westfalen	174	1,05 %	0,7 %
BayWa	107	0,64 %	n. v.
Eggert Mineralöl (EM)	105	0,63 %	n. v.
Freie Tankstellen BFT	1.618	9,74 %	9,8 %
Supermarkt-Tankstellen	ca. 650	3,90 %	8,1 %[3]
Sonstige[2]	ca. 2.565	15,45 %	4,5 %[4]

1 JET und Supermarkt-Tankstellen der CONOCO
2 Übrige B-Marken und nicht organisierte Freie Tankstellen
3 Ohne CONCO-Supermarkttankstellen
4 Inklusive Tamoil/HEM, BayWa und Eggert Mineralöl

GABLER GRAFIK

Quelle: EID 1999; CONOCO; eigene Berechnungen

Die sogenannten B-Marken, zu denen neben JET auch Total, Fina, Elf, Avia, Agip oder Westfalen zählen, verfügen über ein vergleichsweise weitmaschiges Netz, welches in der Regel regional konzentriert ist. Auch sind die Tankstellen tendenziell kleiner als bei den A-Marken. Während die überwiegende Mehrzahl dieser B-Marken sich preislich den A-Marken anpasst, liegt der Preis bei JET immer genau einen halben Cent unter dem Preis der A-Marken. Die Mehrzahl der B-Marken versucht seit einigen Jahren, die Qualitäts- und Servicewahrnehmung in Richtung der etablierten A-Marken zu erhöhen. Dieses Trading-Up zeigt sich insbesondere in der Modernisierung älterer Tankstellen bei einer gleichzeitigen Ausweitung des Dienstleistungs- und Shopangebots.

Eine dritte strategische Gruppe bilden die freien Tankstellen. Sie haben sich je nach Lage bei einem Preis von 0,5 bis 1 Cent unter den A-Marken etabliert und verfügen meist über nur kleine Zusatzsortimente. Auch diese Gruppe versucht seit einiger Zeit eine gesteigerte Profilierung hinsichtlich der Qualitäts- und Servicedimension. So hatten sich Ende der 90er Jahre über 1.500 Betreiber von freien Tankstellen im „Bundesverband freier Tankstellen“ organisiert. Mit der Bezeichnung „BfT“ und einem dazu gehörigen einheitlichen Design und Auftritt eröffnet der Verband seinen Mitgliedern damit die Möglichkeit, sich unter einem gemeinsamen Markendach zu etablieren.

Abbildung 4: Positionierung der strategischen Gruppen im deutschen Tankstellenmarkt

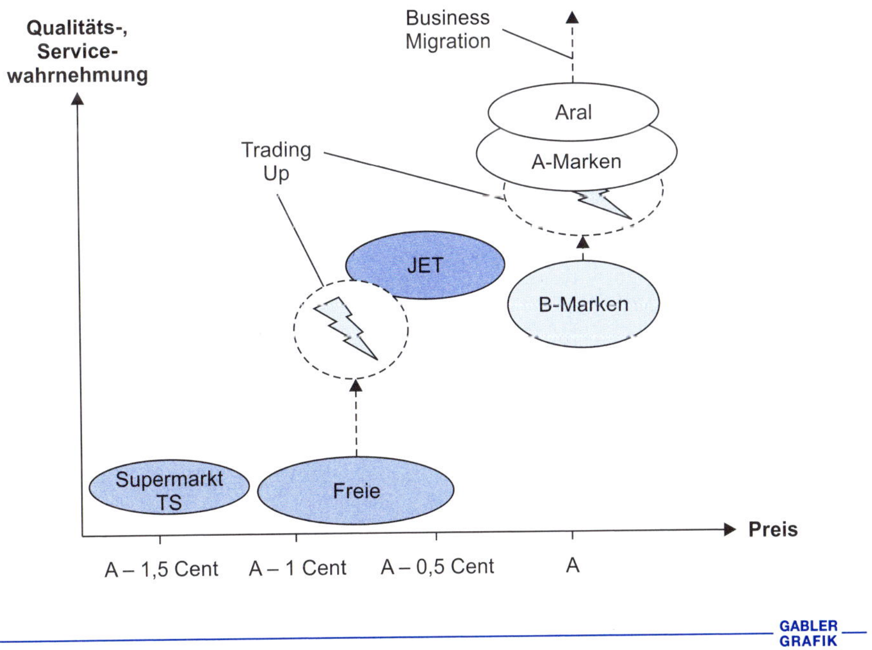

Die ca. 850 deutschen Supermarkttankstellen als vierter großer Block verkaufen ihren Kraftstoff in der Regel 1,5 Cent unter den A-Marken, weisen dafür aber auch nur ein minimales Angebot an zusätzlichen Leistungen auf. Auch hier sind erste Tendenzen eines Trading-Up erkennbar, allerdings stellt die Preisstellung auch weiterhin das primäre Differenzierungsmerkmal dar.

Generell fördert die Stagnation im Kerngeschäft Kraftstoff den Konkurrenzdruck sowohl zwischen als auch in den einzelnen strategischen Gruppen (vgl. Abbildung 4). Dies zeigt sich neben einigen aktuellen Zusammenschlüssen (zum Beispiel TotalFinaElf; Übernahme der Veba Oel AG und damit der Marke Aral durch BP) nicht zuletzt in den jährlich wachsenden Kommunikationsaufwendungen der einzelnen Marken („Markenwettbewerb"). Durch den erhöhten „Noise-Level" der Kommunikation wird es zunehmend schwieriger und kostenintensiver, die eigene Marke nachhaltig und differenziert zu positionieren. Dieses Spannungsfeld zwischen Kosten und Profilierung führt zu der Frage, inwieweit Investitionen in die Markenführung lohnenswert erscheinen beziehungsweise welche Rolle eine Marke im Rahmen des Tankstellengeschäfts besitzt.

Abbildung 5 gibt nochmals einen zusammenfassenden Überblick über die geschilderten Entwicklungsstufen im deutschen Tankstellenmarkt.

Abbildung 5: Zusammenfassende Entwicklungsstufen im deutschen Tankstellenmarkt

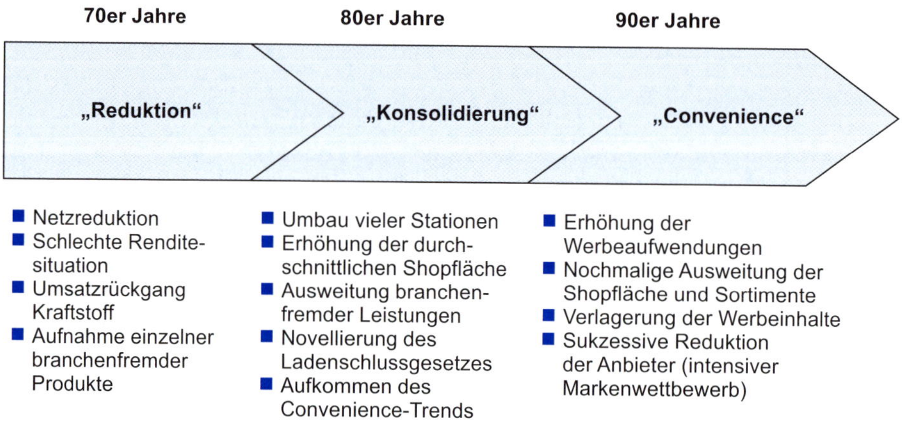

GABLER GRAFIK

Quelle: In Anlehnung an Pauls 1998

2.4 Die Bedeutung der Marke

Die Bedeutung der Markenführung im Tankstellenmarkt ist auf eine Reihe von unterschiedlichen Faktoren zurückzuführen.

- Zum einen handelt es sich bei dem noch im Mittelpunkt der Geschäftstätigkeit stehenden Kernprodukt Kraftstoff – trotz aller Convenience-Orientierung- um ein quasi-homogenes Verbrauchsgut. Durch die vorgeschriebene Oktanzahl sind die verschiedenen Kraftstofftypen (Super, Benzin, Diesel) hochstandardisiert.
- Der Besuch einer Tankstelle erfolgt im Rahmen einer größtenteils limitierten, später habitualisierten Auswahlentscheidung. Das Evoked Set der meisten Konsumenten ist in der Regel auf wenige Alternativen begrenzt. Die kognitive Aktivität bei der Kaufentscheidung ist eher gering und beschränkt sich auf interne, das heißt bereits bekannte und gespeicherte Erfahrungen. Dies zeigt sich auch darin, dass mit den Kriterien gute Erreichbarkeit der Station („liegt auf dem Weg zur Arbeit/zum Einkaufen"), gepflegter Gesamteindruck, freundliches Personal und günstige Öffnungszeiten vier leicht prüfbare Erfahrungseigenschaften die wiederholte Tankstellenwahl maßgeblich beeinflussen (vgl. Abbildung 6).
- Infolge der hohen Kaufhäufigkeit und der entsprechend großen Erfahrung bei der Auswahl einer Tankstelle ist das wahrgenommene Risiko und das Involvement des Konsumenten vergleichsweise gering. Die Suche und Verarbeitung von sachlichen Informationen über alternative Tankstellen ist daher bei weitem nicht so aufwendig wie bei anderen Produktkategorien.

Die Marke erfüllt vor diesem Hintergrund primär eine emotionale Vertrauens- und Sicherheitsfunktion. Da der Verbraucher in der Regel nicht nachprüfen kann, ob der Kraftstoff negative Auswirkungen auf die Funktionsfähigkeit seines Fahrzeugs hat, schafft die Marke hier ein emotionales Qualitätsvertrauen.

Hinsichtlich des Shop-Bereichs kann eine Marke vor allem die Sicherheit vermitteln, dass die relevanten Konsumentenbedürfnisse erfüllt werden. Dies gelingt insbesondere dann, wenn die Marke als Differenzierungsanker auch die positionierungsrelevanten Dimensionen der Tankstelle transportiert, wie im Falle DEA, wo die Marke stark mit einem umfassenden Shop- und Servicesortiment in Verbindung gebracht wird.

Darüber hinaus erfüllt die Marke aus Sicht des Anbieters auch eine Bindungsfunktion. So gaben bei einer direkten Befragung knapp 40 Prozent der Befragten an, dass die Marke einen wesentlichen Grund bei der Wahl einer Stammtankstelle darstellt. Nicht zuletzt vor diesem Hintergrund können die etablierten Markenanbieter von Kraftstoff ein Preispremium von zum Teil mehreren Cent pro Liter gegenüber der unmarkierten Konkurrenz realisieren.

Abbildung 6: Auswahlfaktoren für eine Tankstelle

Frage: Es gibt verschiedene Gesichtspunkte für die Wahl einer Tankstelle. Warum steuern Sie diese Tankstelle an?

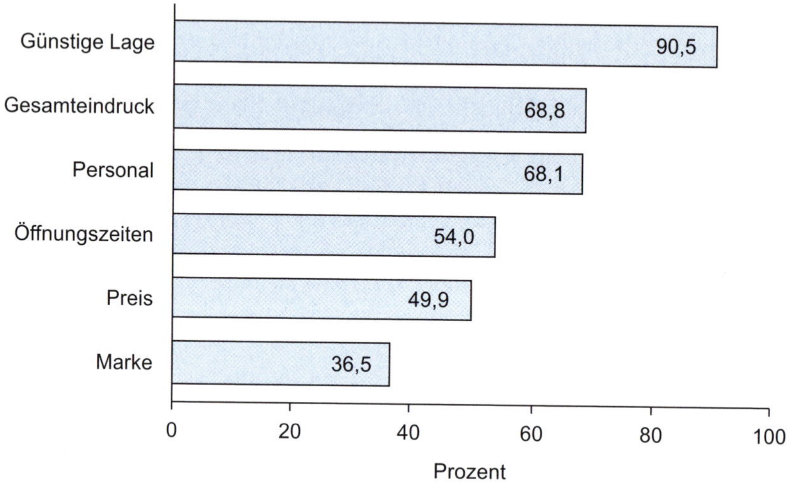

Quelle: CONOCO

GABLER GRAFIK

3. Das Konzept zur Profilierung der Marke JET

3.1 Die strategische Rolle der Markenpolitik für JET

Die strategische Ausrichtung von JET ist geprägt durch eine Kombination aus angestrebter Qualitätswahrnehmung und Preisgünstigkeit. Dabei erscheint diese Position im Wettbewerbsumfeld auf den ersten Blick als problematische „stuck-in-the-middle" Position, da JET weder das Preisniveau der billigen freien beziehungsweise Supermarkttankstellen realisiert, noch den Qualitätsstatus der etablierten A-Marken aufweist.

Die strategische Rolle der Marke wird allerdings bei Betrachtung einer von CONOCO durchgeführten Segmentierung des Tankstellenmarktes ersichtlich (vgl. Abbildung 7): So wird deutlich, dass JET zwar das Segment der „markenbewussten" Konsumenten nicht erreichen kann, bei den anderen Konsumententypen, die jeweils preis- und markenorientiert sind, jedoch stark vertreten ist. Um diese Position zu bewahren, hat die Marke vor dem Hintergrund der eingangs beschriebenen Markttendenzen zwei zentrale Funktionen zu erfüllen:

Abbildung 7: Segmentierung im deutschen Tankstellenmarkt

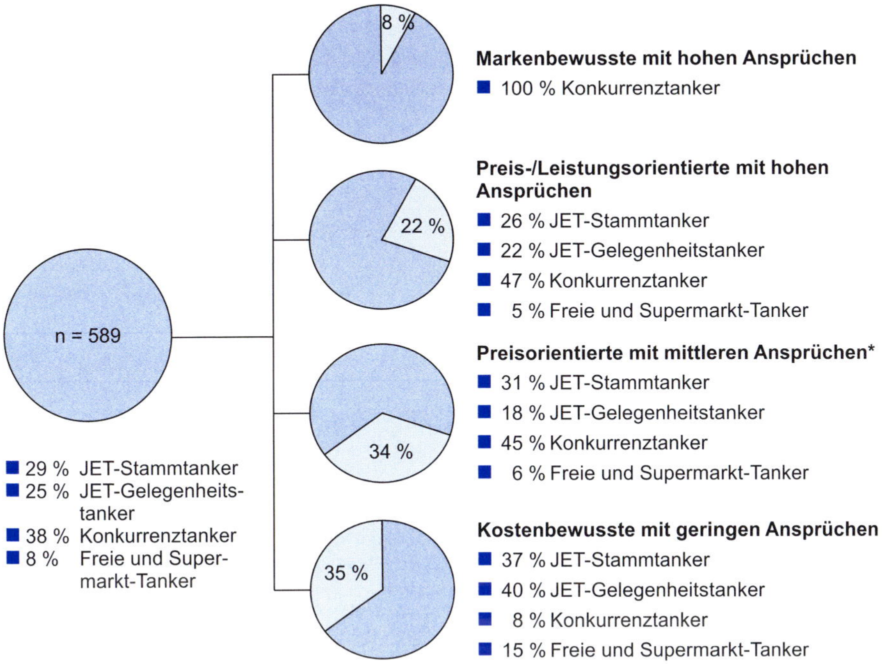

* Lesebeispiel: Von 589 Befragten bilden 22 % das Segment der Preisorientierten mit hohen Ansprüchen. Davon sind 26 % JET-Stammtanker, 22 % JET-Gelegenheitstanker, 47 % Tanker der markierten A- und B-Marken.

GABLER GRAFIK

Quelle: CONOCO

Ein beachtliches Gefährdungspotenzial geht zum einen von der Gruppe der aufstrebenden freien Tankstellen aus. Diese sind in der Regel in der relevanten Profilierungsdimension „Preis“ besser positioniert, was sich in einem überdurchschnittlichen Anteil dieser Wettbewerber im Segment der Kostenbewussten mit geringen Ansprüchen zeigt. Das primäre Differenzierungsmerkmal für JET stellt daher die Qualität des Angebots dar. Die Marke erfüllt hier insbesondere für die Kernleistung Kraftstoff die Funktion eines Qualitätsankers und schafft in der Wahrnehmung des Kunden Vertrauen und Sicherheit. Da diese Motive bei ähnlicher Erfüllung der Hygienefaktoren (Erreichbarkeit, Gesamteindruck, Personal, Öffnungszeiten) kaufentscheidend wirken, stellt die Marke den primären Wettbewerbsvorteil von JET gegenüber dem unterpreisigen, vielfach unmarkierten Wettbewerb dar.

- Auch im Wettbewerb mit den etablierten A-Marken und insbesondere mit aufstrebenden B-Marken ist die Marke ein erfolgsentscheidender Faktor. Dies gilt insbesondere für die Kundensegmente, die neben einer ausgeprägten Preisorientierung hohe und mittlere Ansprüche haben. JET ist hier in den wichtigen Profilierungsdimensionen Service- und Angebotsqualität und -umfang tendenziell gleich oder schlechter positioniert. Damit der Preisvorteil von JET gegenüber diesen Marken Relevanz für die Kaufentscheidung erlangt, muss die Marke JET auch hier ein Mindestmaß an Sicherheit und Vertrauen vermitteln – primär in Form einer Qualitätswahrnehmung des angebotenen Kraftstoffs, aber auch in ein zumindest angemessenes Shop- und Dienstleistungsangebot.

Betrachtet man die loyalen Stammtanker verschiedener Marken, so zeigen sich deutliche Unterschiede unter den einzelnen Wettbewerbern. Während Aral und Shell das angestrebte Qualitätsimage ebenso deutlich umsetzen wie die Freien- und Supermarkttankstellen das Preisimage, ist JET neben Avia die einzige Marke, die in der Kombination beider Entscheidungskriterien profiliert erscheint (vgl. Abbildung 8). Um diese Position langfristig zu sichern und auch bei Neukunden durchzusetzen, galt es im Rahmen der Markenstrategie, zunächst das Markenleitbild stärker zu fokussieren.

Abbildung 8: Positionierung der Marken bei Stammkunden

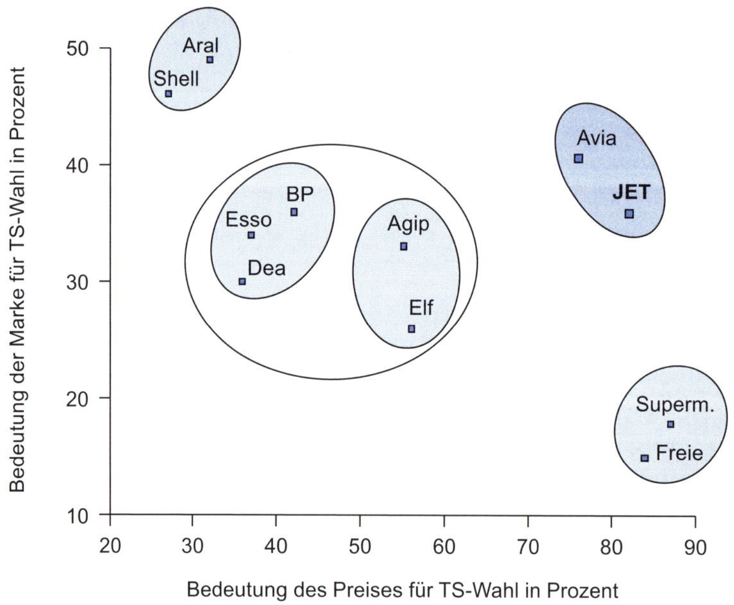

GABLER GRAFIK

Quelle: CONOCO

3.2 Das Markenleitbild von JET

Entsprechend der strategischen Rolle der Marke erfolgte im Zuge einer Neuformulierung der Markenziele eine Verfeinerung der Soll-Positionierung von JET. So sollte neben einer Verbesserung der Bekanntheit vor allem die Qualitäts- und Preiswahrnehmung nachhaltig gestützt werden. Auch wurde eine Verjüngung des Markenimages angestrebt. Konkret wurden daher für die Kernzielgruppe der 18- bis 35-jährigen Pkw-Fahrer folgende Ziele für das Jahr 2001 festgelegt:

Tabelle 1: Ziele der Markenstrategie (Angaben in Prozent)

	IST 1998	SOLL 2001
Markenbekanntheit (ungestützt)	21,8	28
Markenbekanntheit (gestützt)	69,6	77
Qualitätsimage[1]	51,3	57
Preisimage[2]	34,7	45
Markensympathie	26,3	30

1 „Wo kann man Kraftstoff mit Markenqualität tanken? [...]"

2 „Der Kraftstoff ist preiswerter als an anderen Tankstellen [...]"

GABLER GRAFIK

Quelle: CONOCO

Um die angedachte Profilierung als einzige nationale Marke mit Preisvorteil zu stärken, wurde ein Leitbild entwickelt, welches aus den Bausteinen „Günstig – Qualität – Basic – Jung" besteht: JET bietet Markenqualität, ist günstig, jung und konzentriert sich auf das, worauf es wirklich ankommt.

Damit das Markenleitbild nicht nur ein inhaltsleerer Merksatz bleibt, bedarf es einer konsequenten und konsistenten Umsetzung. Daher wurde dem Integrationsaspekt, das heißt der Abstimmung des Markenauftritts an allen Kundenkontaktpunkten, eine besondere Aufmerksamkeit gewidmet. Zudem ist das Image einer Tankstellenmarke erheblich von jeder einzelnen Station abhängig. Entsprechend wurden die Maßnahmen in den Bereichen in- und externe Kommunikation sowie Produkt-/Standortpolitik gemeinsam überarbeitet.

3.3 Durchsetzung des Markenleitbildes in der Preis-, Produkt- und Distributionspolitik

Im Rahmen der Preispolitik wurde an der bewährten Positionierung direkt unter den A-Marken festgehalten. Selbst im Zuge der teilweise dramatischen Preiserhöhungen für Kraftstoff zwischen 1998 und 2000 wurde eine bewusst reaktive Preispolitik betrieben, um nicht Gegenmaßnahmen der volumenmäßig weit größeren A-Wettbewerber herauszufordern. Daneben wurde der Markenbaustein „Günstig“ explizit auf die weiteren Bestandteile des Angebots (Öl, Autowäsche, Shop) ausgedehnt.

Die Umsetzung des Markenbausteins „Basic“ erfolgte im Rahmen der Produktpolitik zunächst durch eine im Vergleich zum A-Wettbewerb nur moderate Ausweitung der Sortimente. Angeboten wird daher nur, was dem Branchenstandard entspricht (Kraft- und Schmierstoffe, Waschanlagen und enges Shopangebot).

Um das Qualitätsimage der Marke zu verbessern, wurde bereits Ende 1997 ein neues, modernes Tankstellendesign für die Distribution konzipiert (vgl. Abbildung 9), dass in den beiden Folgejahren an knapp 300 JET-Tankstellen angepasst wurde. Um das neue Markendesign schnell im Straßenbild zu verankern, wurden 1998 in einem ersten Schritt 150 Tankstellen in nur 14 Wochen umgestellt. Wichtige Veränderungen betrafen dabei die Neugestaltung des Logos (welches zeitgleich auch in der Kommunikation geändert wurde) sowie die Entwicklung einer neuen Hausschrift und -farbe. Diese stilbildenden Elemente wurden insbesondere im Rahmen der Neugestaltung der sichtbaren Außenelemente (Preismasten, Dachstützen, Dachrandblenden, Zapfsäulen) als auch im Shop-Layout (Eingang, Auslagen) kombiniert. Darüber hinaus wurde die komplette Kommunikation am PoS (insbesondere Plakate und Salesfolder) an die gleichzeitig gestartete Imagekampagne angepasst.

3.4 Durchsetzung des Markenleitbildes in der Kommunikationspolitik

Nachdem Mitte der 90er Jahre nicht in klassische Werbung investiert worden war, wurde Ende 1997 wieder eine Imagekampagne gestartet, die das neue Leitbild bundesweit durchsetzen sollte. Der größte Teil des in den Jahren 1998 bis 2000 eingesetzten Mediabudgets von knapp 5 Millionen Euro entfiel dabei auf Printanzeigen in auflagenstarken Programmzeitschriften (TV Today, TV Spielfilm, TV Movie) und Publikumsmagazinen (Spiegel, Focus, Bild am Sonntag, Computer Bild). Unterstützt wurde diese Kampagne durch gezielte Funkspots in ausgewählten Schwerpunktregionen mit hoher JET-Tankstellendichte.

Abbildung 9: **Neues Tankstellen-Design von JET**

GABLER GRAFIK

Die inhaltliche Klammer stellte neben einem standardisierten Anzeigendesign (Farben, Seitenaufteilung) der stets mitaufgeführte Markenzusatz „JET. Den Rest können Sie sich sparen" dar. Durch diese starke formale Integration konnte eine hohe Wiedererkennung des Absenders sichergestellt werden.

Die Bausteine des Markenleitbilds „Günstig", „Qualität" und „Basic" wurden mit verschiedenen Slogans direkt kommuniziert (vgl. Abbildungen 10–12). Im Gegensatz zu vielen Wettbewerbern wurde bewusst auf Aktivitäten im Bereich Sponsoring verzichtet und dies explizit kommuniziert (vgl. Abbildung 12), um den Markenbaustein „Basic" nicht in Frage zu stellen.

Die zusätzlich avisierte Profilierungsdimension „jung" wurde primär durch eine dynamisch-aggressive Tonalität und die Wahl der Anzeigenmotive sichergestellt (vgl. Abbildung 13). Für Aufsehen sorgte in diesem Zusammenhang insbesondere eine Anzeigenserie, die den damaligen deutschen Finanzminister zunächst mit dem Slogan „Machen Sie es wie er, kassieren Sie beim Tanken ab", und später nach dessen Rücktritt mit den Worten „Wo würden Sie tanken, wenn Sie plötzlich aufs Geld achten müssen?" zeigte. CONOCO musste schließlich 50.000 Euro Schadensersatz zahlen, hatte aber nicht zuletzt auf Grund vielfältiger Kommentierungen der Anzeige in der Öffentlichkeit das Markenimage „jung und frech" von JET gestärkt. Abgerundet wurde die externe Kommunikation durch begleitende Maßnahmen im Bereich der Verkaufsförderung an den einzelnen Tankstellen, die thematisch eng an die Imagekampagne angelehnt waren.

Abbildung 10: Kommunikative Umsetzung des Markenbausteins „Günstig"

GABLER GRAFIK

Abbildung 11: Kommunikative Umsetzung des Markenbausteins „Qualität"

GABLER GRAFIK

Abbildung 12: Kommunikative Umsetzung des Markenbausteins „Basic"

GABLER GRAFIK

Abbildung 13: Kommunikative Umsetzung des Markenbausteins „Jung"

GABLER GRAFIK

3.5 Durchsetzung des Markenleitbildes nach Innen

Zur Vermittlung des Markenleitbildes wurde nicht nur die Kundenansprache forciert, sondern auch die Personen gezielt angesprochen, welche die Marke täglich repräsentieren: Die Pächter der einzelnen Tankstellen und deren Mitarbeiter (vgl. Abbildung 14). So wurde das neue Markenkonzept ausführlich im Rahmen von Kick-off-Veranstaltungen und in der Partnerzeitschrift der CONOCO („JET Kontakt") dargestellt. In diesem Zusammenhang wurde vor allem versucht, die Bedeutung eines konsistenten Verhaltens im Sinne des Markenleitbildes zu vermitteln. Durch diese Maßnahmen konnte eine hohe interne Akzeptanz für das Selbstbild der Marke geschaffen werden.

Zur Stärkung der Mitarbeiteridentifikation diente auch die neu entwickelte Bekleidungskollektion. Damit wurde sichergestellt, dass nicht nur die Ausstattung, sondern auch das Personal an der Tankstelle das avisierte Markenbild konsistent transportiert. Um auch gegenüber geschäftlichen Kunden das einheitliche Erscheinungsbild zu kommunizieren, wurde die Geschäftsausstattung (Formulare, Visitenkarten etc.) ebenfalls an das überarbeitete Corporate Design angepasst.

Abbildung 14: Vermittlung der Marke nach Innen

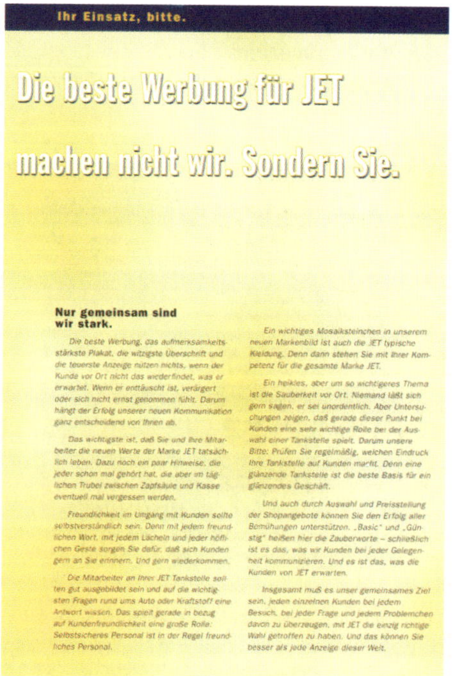
Ihr Einsatz, bitte.

Die beste Werbung für JET machen nicht wir. Sondern Sie.

Nur gemeinsam sind wir stark.

Die beste Werbung, das aufmerksamkeitsstärkste Plakat, die witzigste Überschrift und die teuerste Anzeige nützen nichts, wenn der Kunde vor Ort nicht das wiederfindet, was er erwartet. Wenn er enttäuscht ist, verärgert oder sich nicht ernst genommen fühlt. Darum hängt der Erfolg unserer neuen Kommunikation ganz entscheidend von Ihnen ab.

Das wichtigste ist, daß Sie und Ihre Mitarbeiter die neuen Werte der Marke JET tatsächlich leben. Dazu noch ein paar Hinweise, die jeder schon mal gehört hat, die aber im täglichen Trubel zwischen Zapfsäule und Kasse eventuell mal vergessen werden.

Freundlichkeit im Umgang mit Kunden sollte selbstverständlich sein. Denn mit jedem freundlichen Wort, mit jedem Lächeln und jeder höflichen Geste sorgen Sie dafür, daß sich Kunden gern an Sie erinnern. Und gern wiederkommen.

Die Mitarbeiter an Ihrer JET Tankstelle sollten gut ausgebildet sein und auf die wichtigsten Fragen rund ums Auto oder Kraftstoff eine Antwort wissen. Das spielt gerade in bezug auf Kundenfreundlichkeit eine große Rolle: Selbstsicheres Personal ist in der Regel freundliches Personal.

Ein wichtiges Mosaiksteinchen in unserem neuen Markenbild ist auch die JET typische Kleidung. Denn dann stehen Sie mit Ihrer Kompetenz für die gesamte Marke JET.

Ein heikles, aber um so wichtigeres Thema ist die Sauberkeit vor Ort. Niemand läßt sich gern sagen, er sei unordentlich. Aber Untersuchungen zeigen, daß gerade dieser Punkt bei Kunden eine sehr wichtige Rolle bei der Auswahl einer Tankstelle spielt. Darum unsere Bitte: Prüfen Sie regelmäßig, welchen Eindruck Ihre Tankstelle auf Kunden macht. Denn eine glänzende Tankstelle ist die beste Basis für ein glänzendes Geschäft.

Und auch durch Auswahl und Preisstellung der Shopangebote können Sie den Erfolg aller Bemühungen unterstützen. „Basic" und „Günstig" heißen hier die Zauberworte – schließlich ist es das, was wir Kunden bei jeder Gelegenheit kommunizieren. Und es ist das, was die Kunden von JET erwarten.

Insgesamt muß es unser gemeinsames Ziel sein, jeden einzelnen Kunden bei jedem Besuch, bei jeder Frage und jedem Problemchen davon zu überzeugen, mit JET die einzig richtige Wahl getroffen zu haben. Und das können Sie besser als jede Anzeige dieser Welt.

4. Erfolg der Markenprofilierung bei JET

Der Erfolg der Markenpolitik von JET lässt sich zunächst an der Entwicklung verschiedener Indikatoren in den Jahren 1998 bis 2001 ablesen (vgl. Tabelle 2):

Tabelle 2: Entwicklung ausgewählter Kennzahlen von 1998 bis 2001 (Angaben in Prozent bei 18- bis 35-jährigen Pkw-Fahrern)

	1998	1999	2000	2001	Veränderung 1998–2001
Bekanntheit (ungestützt)	21,8	22,5	30,9	38,1	**+ 16,3**
Bekanntheit (gestützt)	69,6	74,4	78,2	83,8	**+ 14,2**
Qualitätsimage	51,3	57,7	62,1	56,5	**+ 5,2**
Preisimage	34,7	48,6	43,1	47,9	**+ 13,2**
Markensympathie	26,3	34,0	25,9	31,0	**+ 4,7**
Werberecall	5,2	4,8	8,5	9,7	**+ 4,5**

GABLER GRAFIK

Quelle: CONOCO

- Die als zentrale Steuerungsgrößen definierten Zielgrößen (vgl. Tabelle 1) entwickeln sich seit 1998 deutlich positiv. Dabei zeigt sich zum einen der reine Bekanntheitseffekt der Kommunikationskampagne, da sich bei gleich bleibender Tankstellenzahl die Bekanntheit von JET zwischen 1998 und 2001 in der Zielgruppe der 18- bis 35-jährigen Pkw-Fahrer um 16,3 (ungestützt) beziehungsweise14,2 (gestützt) Prozentpunkte gesteigert hat. Gleichzeitig verdeutlichen die ebenfalls stark gestiegene Qualitäts- und Preiswahrnehmung auch den inhaltlichen Erfolg der Kampagne: So zeigt sowohl die Steigerung beim Qualitätsimage von 51,3 Prozent auf 56,5 Prozent als auch die gleichzeitige Ausweitung der Wahrnehmung „Preisgünstigkeit" von 34,7 Prozent auf 47,9 Prozent, dass die angestrebte Profilierung in den Dimensionen Preis und Qualität gelungen ist. Die positive Entwicklung der Preiswahrnehmung erstreckt sich dabei nicht nur auf den Kraftstoff, sondern überträgt sich auch auf den Shopbereich.

- Ebenfalls deutlich positiv wird ein jugendliches Image wahrgenommen: Glaubten 1998 nur 15,7 Prozent der 18- bis 35-jährigen Markenkenner, dass bei JET jüngere Leute tanken, so lag die Zustimmung zu dieser Aussage 2001 bei 36,9 Prozent. Auch das im Rahmen der Markenführung zentrale Kriterium des Markenvertrauens konnte in dieser Zielgruppe um über 10 Prozent gesteigert werden.

Teil 2: Segmentbehauptung und -abgrenzung durch zunehmende Differenzierung im reifenden Markt für Großraumlimousinen (Ford Galaxy II 2000–2004) **752**

1. **Erfahrungen aus Galaxy I sowie Marktsituation Ende der 90er Jahre** **752**

2. **Strategische Implikationen für den Galaxy II: horizontale Differenzierung bei verstärkter vertikaler Integration** **754**

3. **Auswirkungen der strategischen Umorientierung auf den Marketing-Mix des Galaxy II** **755**

3.1 Produkt- und Preispolitik 755

3.2 Kommunikations- und Distributionspolitik 758

4. **Zentrale Ergebnisse** **760**

Im Rahmen der folgenden Fallstudie wird der Lebenszyklus des Ford Galaxy als eine europäische Produktmarke der Dachmarke Ford eingehend betrachtet. Denn aus markenpolitischer Sicht sind mit dem Galaxy besondere Herausforderungen verbunden, deren Ursprünge vor allem in der Baugleichheit von Ford Galaxy und VW Sharan liegen. In chronologischer Folge werden hierzu in einem ersten Teil Segmenteinstieg und -eroberung (1990-2000) des Galaxy I sowie in einem zweiten Teil Segmentbehauptung und -abgrenzung des Galaxy II (2000–2004) erläutert.

Teil 1: Segmenteinstieg und -eroberung durch Produktstandardisierung im noch jungen Markt für Großraumlimousinen (Ford Galaxy I 1990–2000)

1. Zur Ausgangssituation bei der Entwicklung des Ford Galaxy

„Wer zu spät kommt, den bestraft bekanntlich das Leben" – eine Erkenntnis, die sich bei einigen in Europa operierenden Automobilherstellern bis Anfang der 90er Jahre zumindest auf einem Sektor nicht herumgesprochen hat: den weltweiten Trend zur Großraumlimousine (MPV: Multi Purpose Vehicle) aus den USA würdigten sie jahrelang keines Blickes. Erst zu Anfang der 90er Jahre entschieden sich die Verantwortlichen bei Ford und Volkswagen in Europa zum Start eines Gemeinschaftsprojektes in diesem Fahrzeugsegment. Das Ergebnis dieser Zusammenarbeit, die Fahrzeuge Ford Galaxy und VW Sharan, rollten 1995 mit Verspätung auf einen international schon agilen Markt. Der Renault Espace fuhr bereits seit 1984 als erster Van in Europa große Erfolge ein, der Chrysler Voyager dominierte seit Jahren den amerikanischen Markt. Die Eurovans aus der Fiat/Lancia/Peugeot/Citroen-Kooperation wurden 1994 eingeführt und der Honda Shuttle kurze Zeit später. Darüber hinaus waren einige japanische Wettbewerber zu dieser Zeit schon seit einigen Jahren in diesem Markt vertreten.

Großraumlimousinen versuchen, die Lücke zwischen Transporter und Pkw zu schließen, indem die Vorteile beider Konzepte miteinander verbunden werden. So vereint ein Van den limousinenhaften Komfort, die Fahreigenschaften (zum Beispiel gute Straßenlage) sowie die Handlichkeit und den Komfort eines Personenwagens mit dem großzügigen Raumangebot, der hohen Sitzposition und den vielfältigen Variationsmöglichkeiten eines Transporters.

Der europäische und deutsche Markt für Großraumlimousinen wurde bis Mitte der 90er Jahre mit der Ausnahme von Renault ausschließlich von kleinen Herstellern bedient und zeigte sich – gerade im internationalen Vergleich und hier insbesondere im Vergleich zu den USA – als unterentwickelt, ließ jedoch enorme Wachstumspotenziale vermuten. Abbildung 1 zeigt in diesem Zusammenhang die Entwicklung des Marktes für Großraumlimousinen in Deutschland und Europa sowie die dominierenden Anbieter im Jahr 1990 im deutschen Markt.

Abbildung 1: Entwicklung des Segments für Großraumlimousinen und Anteil zentraler Marken an diesem Segment in Deutschland

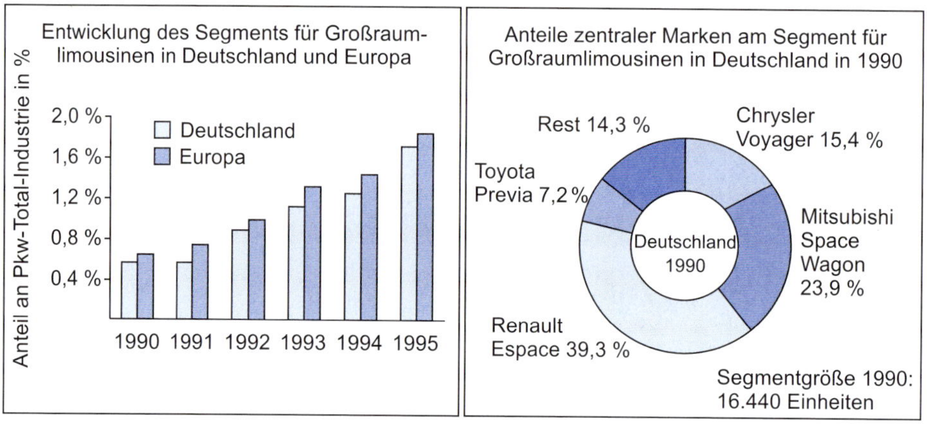

GABLER GRAFIK

Das Marktpotenzial des Großraumlimousinen-Segments veranlasste Ford in Europa Anfang der 90er Jahre, der Frage nachzugehen, auf welche Art und Weise dieses Segment mit einem eigenen Fahrzeug bearbeitet werden kann. Dabei wurde der Erfolg eines Einstiegs in das Großraumlimousinen-Segment mit einem eigenen Konzept bei den Planungsarbeiten aus mehreren Gründen kritisch hinterfragt:

- So herrschte Unsicherheit hinsichtlich der tatsächlichen Entwicklung des Segments, vor allem hinsichtlich der Preisbereitschaft der Nachfrager. Ein Vergleich mit den USA erschien hier vor dem Hintergrund der dort generell herrschenden geringeren Unterhaltskosten und anderer Nutzungsgewohnheiten als wenig hilfreich.
- Das Segment war zu Beginn der 90er Jahre durch kleine Hersteller oder exotische Fahrzeugkonzepte (zum Beispiel Kunststoff-Karosserien) dominiert. Es bot sich somit die Chance, als Volumenmarke mit einem starken Fahrzeugkonzept dieses Segment deutlich zu vergrößern.

- Internen Studien zufolge ging Ford langfristig von einem maximalen Absatz von 90.000 Fahrzeugen per annum aus. Selbst bei einer tatsächlich realisierten Menge in dieser Höhe stellte sich die Frage, inwieweit ein solches, komplett neu zu entwickelndes Fahrzeugkonzept dauerhaft rentabel gefertigt werden kann.
- Im Ford-Konzern selbst konnte zu Beginn der 90er Jahre nur in beschränktem Maße auf bereits etablierte Plattformen zurückgegriffen werden. Eine Fahrzeugneuentwicklung war unumgänglich.

Um das Segment mit einem sehr wettbewerbsfähigen Fahrzeug bedienen zu können, das in dieser Fahrzeugkategorie Maßstäbe setzen sollte, waren hohe Investitionen notwendig. Um dabei gleichzeitig jedoch die Entwicklungszeit und Produktionskosten sowie das eigene unternehmerische Risiko zu senken, entschloss sich Ford 1991, das Projekt nicht im Alleingang durchzuführen, sondern eine Entwicklungs- und Produktionspartnerschaft mit einem etablierten Hersteller einzugehen.

2. Ziele der horizontalen Kooperation zwischen Ford und Volkswagen

Ford legte bei der Selektion eines möglichen Kooperationspartners besonderen Wert auf einen Fit hinsichtlich der eigenen Kompetenzen sowie der Kompetenzen und Ziele des potenziellen Partners. Durch eine Kompetenzbündelung sollten innovative Lösungen für eine Großraumlimousine geschaffen werden, um so die angestrebte führende Position in diesem Segment innerhalb von nur kurzer Zeit zu verwirklichen. Vor diesem Hintergrund erwies sich der deutsche Hersteller Volkswagen als geeigneter Partner.

Volkswagen war wie Ford zur gleichen Zeit um einen Einstieg in das Großraumlimousinensegment bei gleichzeitiger Reduzierung des unternehmerischen Risikos bemüht. Zudem hatte auch VW das Ziel, ein solches Engagement in dem Segment aufgrund der internationalen Konkurrenz möglichst rasch zu realisieren. Wie Ford konnte jedoch auch VW auf keine geeignete Van-Plattform zurückgreifen. Zwar verfügten beide Hersteller über hinreichende Erfahrungen im Transportergeschäft, jedoch erwiesen sich weder die Plattform des VW Caravelle noch die des Ford Transit als brauchbar für einen angedachten Van. Durch Bündelung des jeweiligen Plattform Know-hows sollte mithin eine rasche Entwicklung einer spezifischen Van-Plattform realisiert werden.

Überdies ließ die Nähe der Marken Ford und Volkswagen zu einem Nachfragerkreis mit ähnlichen Erwartungen an Marke und Fahrzeug eine Kooperation beider Partner als sinnvoll erscheinen. Auf europäischer Ebene erwiesen sich beide Hersteller als gleichwertige und kompetente Partner mit unterschiedlichen regionalen Profilen, wobei sich beide Marken hinsichtlich ihrer Marktpräsenz in den verschiedenen europäischen Märkten ideal ergänzten. Während Volkswagen über eine große Handelsorganisation vor allem in Deutschland verfügte, die einen wesentlichen Beitrag zur Schaffung eines hohen Marktdrucks und damit zur weiteren Etablierung des Großraumkonzepts in Deutschland zu leisten schien, besaß und besitzt Ford eine solche Stellung vor allem in England. Entsprechend war auch davon auszugehen, dass sich die Fahrzeuge je nach Marktbedeutung des betrachteten Herstellers im jeweiligen Markt unterschiedlich verkaufen ließen.

Insgesamt ließ die Summe der Eigenschaften und Fähigkeiten beider Hersteller eine ideale Voraussetzung für eine herstellerseitige Kooperation vermuten, welche für beide Partner Vorteile beim Einstieg in das Großraumlimousinensegment versprach. Entsprechend beschlossen Ford und Volkswagen ein gleichberechtigtes Joint Venture für eine Dauer von zehn Jahren bis zum Jahr 2005. Im eigens errichteten Werk AutoEuropa nahe Lissabon in Portugal sollten ab 1995 Großraumlimousinen gemeinschaftlich produziert werden. Während Ford die leitende Verantwortung vor allem im Bereich der Produktion übernahm, spielte Volkswagen eine bedeutende Rolle im Rahmen der Fahrzeugentwicklung und -erprobung.

Insgesamt erhofften sich beide Unternehmen vielfältige Vorteile durch die Gemeinschaftsproduktion im Rahmen des so genannten „Badge Engineering“:

- Zeitvorteil durch Arbeitsteilung, sodass ein schneller Markteinstieg erfolgen kann,
- Teilung von Entwicklungskosten und Investitionen,
- Realisierung von Economies of Scale,
- Schnelles Erreichen des „Break-Even“-Produktionsvolumens,
- Komplettierung des Angebotsprogramms,
- Gegenseitiger Transfer von Know-how/Ressourcen.

Zielsetzung war es, eine Stärkung der Wettbewerbsfähigkeit der jeweiligen Unternehmen zu realisieren. Dabei war allen Beteiligten des Joint Ventures durchaus bewusst, dass Ford und Volkswagen innerhalb der coopetitiv ausgestalteten Wertschöpfungspartnerschaft Partner bei der Realisierung von Economies of Scale und der Schaffung sowie Erweiterung des Großraumlimousinensegments darstellen, jedoch Konkurrenten bei der Aufteilung dieses Marktpotenzials sind.

Mit anderen Worten: die Zusammenarbeit sollte sowohl für Ford als auch für Volkswagen durch Kooperation den Segmenteintritt beschleunigen und absichern, auf dem Fahrzeugmarkt war allerdings absehbar, dass diese Kooperation zum intensiven Wettbewerb zwischen den Volumenherstellern Ford und VW führen würde. Somit kann das Projekt auch idealtypisch als „COOPETITION“ im Sinne einer zeitgleichen „COOperation“ und „ComPETITION“ verstanden werden (vgl. Abbildung 2).

Entsprechend galt es, verschiedene Faktoren als Voraussetzung eines auch marktlich erfolgreichen Projekts zu berücksichtigen:

- Die Großraumlimousinen sollten mit dem jeweiligen Markenbild harmonieren.
- Durch eine Differenzierung im kommunikativen Marktauftritt sollten sich die Angebote möglichst weit voneinander abgrenzen.
- Die Handelsorganisation beider Hersteller hatte die Aufgabe, den Eintritt in das lukrative Fahrzeugsegment für sich zu nutzen und über ihre Dienstleistungen weiter zu differenzieren.

Abbildung 2: Coopetition im Rahmen des Badge-Engineering Ford-Volkswagen

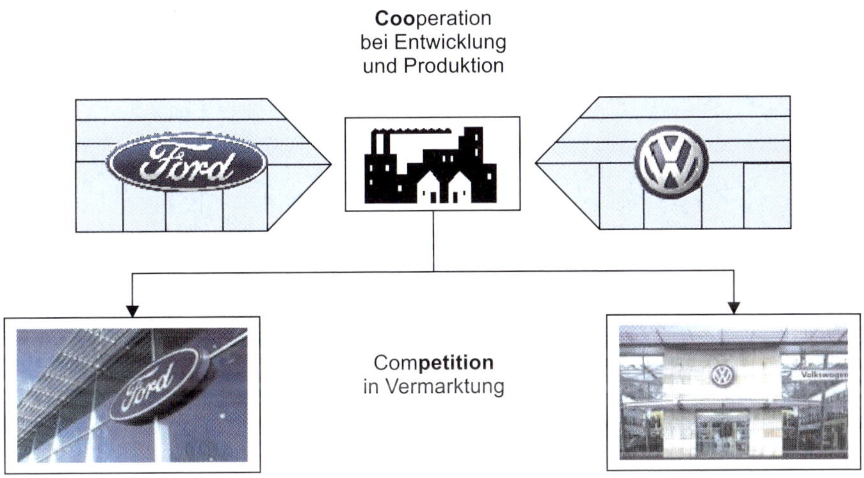

GABLER GRAFIK

In der Folge strebten Ford und Volkswagen bei der Vermarktung der gemeinschaftlich produzierten Großraumlimousine völlig getrennte Wege an. Da Volkswagen im Gegensatz zu Ford bereits seit Anfang der 90er Jahre mit VW, Audi, Skoda und Seat über unterschiedliche Marken verfügte, plante der Volkswagen-Konzern eine Einführung der Großraumlimousine nicht nur unter der Marke VW, sondern darüber hinaus auch unter der Marke Seat. Entsprechend lag die marktliche Herausforderung darin, das technische Gemeinschaftsprojekt mit unterschiedlichen „Badges“ unter den drei Marken Ford Galaxy, VW Sharan und Seat Alhambra getrennt zu vermarkten.

3. Maßnahmen im Rahmen des Badge Engineering auf Herstellerseite

3.1 Positionierung des Ford Galaxy: Room Needing, Image Concerned

Aus der Perspektive Fords galt es insbesondere, separate Überlegungen zur Positionierung des Galaxy im Vergleich zum VW Sharan und Seat Alhambra vorzunehmen. Aufgrund der technischen Gleichheit der Produkte war es in diesem Zusammenhang entscheidend, mit dem Galaxy einen primär psychologischen Zusatznutzen zu bieten. Während die zuvor eingeführten Vans der Konkurrenten Peugeot und Fiat mit unterschiedlicher Nuancierung auf die Familientauglichkeit des Fahrzeuges abhoben – Peugeot betonte mehr das Raumangebot, Fiat mehr die Flexibilität –, hob Citroen den Avantgardismus des Produktes besonders hervor.

Verbunden mit einer einzigartigen Gestaltung der werblichen Botschaft strebte Ford eine Alleinstellung des Galaxy im Sinne einer Unique Advertising Proposition an. Überlegungen zur Positionierung des Galaxy setzten dabei eine Analyse der Ford-Zielgruppen voraus, indem – ausgehend von den zentralen Kaufmotiven einer Großraumlimousine – die Frage beantwortet werden sollte, wodurch sich typische Galaxy Fahrer von potenziellen Sharan beziehungsweise Alhambra Besitzern unterscheiden sollen. Insbesondere die Auswertung von Sinus Milieus in Deutschland machte dabei deutlich, dass die Marke überdurchschnittlich im Arbeitermilieu, aber auch im konservativ technokratischen und modern bürgerlichen Milieu vertreten ist. Aus Marktforschungsstudien war überdies bekannt, dass sich die Käufer beim Erwerb einer Großraumlimousine primär an den Eigenschaften Platzangebot, Preis und Styling orientierten.

Aufgrund der vergleichsweise „breiten“ Milieupräsenz und in dem Bewusstsein, dass das Platzangebot das traditionelle Kaufmotiv einer Großraumlimousine darstellt, entschloss sich Ford, auch den Galaxy eher „breit“ zu positionieren. Während Volkswagen mit dem „Lebensabschnitt Familie“ eine spezifische, lifestage-orientierte Positionierung des Sharan vornahm, fokussierte Ford hingegen eine breitere, lifestyle-orientierte Zielgruppe, indem nicht nur die Familie, sondern auch Personen mit „platzintensiven“ Hobbys und sonstigem Raumbedarf bei gleichzeitigem Wunsch eines „luxury travels“ explizit angesprochen werden sollten. Unter dem Motto „Room needing, Image concerned“ sollte der Galaxy als „Die clevere Alternative“ vornehmlich jene Personen ansprechen, die eine automobile Raumnotwendigkeit besitzen, jedoch insbesondere die vor 1995 im Markt eingeführten Wettbewerber aufgrund von Imagedefiziten und dem damit verbundenen Kaufrisiko nicht präferierten.

Vor dem dargestellten Hintergrund wurde die Positionierung des Galaxy zusammenfassend wie folgt formuliert:

Ford Galaxy = Antwort auf Transport und Mobilität lifestyle-orientierter Trendsetter, Familien und Hobbytreibender.

Diese Positionierung galt es, im Rahmen des Marketing-Mix erfolgreich umzusetzen.

3.2 Operative Maßnahmen im Rahmen des Badge Engineering-Projekts

Im Rahmen des Badge Engineering unterliegen Produkte einer begrenzten autonomen Steuerung, sodass für Ford und Volkswagen als wesentliche Gestaltungsinstrumente im Marketing-Mix vor allem die Marketing-Kommunikation, die Vertriebswege beziehungsweise das After-Sales Marketing und in begrenztem Umfang die Preispolitik verblieben. Für Ford offenbarten sich somit nur in bestimmten Mix-Bereichen eigenständige Profilierungs- und Differenzierungsgrade gegenüber VW sowie dem sonstigen Wettbewerb.

3.21 Produktpolitik

Der Ford Galaxy wie auch der VW Sharan der ersten Generation wurden in vier unterschiedlichen Ausstattungslinien, der Seat Alhambra hingegen in nur drei Linien angeboten. Neben dem Markenlogo und Kühlergrill, den Front- und Rückleuchten sowie kleineren Details im Innnenraum weisen die Modelle keine sichtbaren Unterscheidungsmerkmale beim Verlassen der Werkshallen auf (vgl. Abbildung 3).

Allerdings ermöglichte die zum Teil unterschiedliche Ausstattung mit Motoren eine teilweise Differenzierung: das von Ford über Jahre meistverkaufte Modell, der Galaxy 2,3 l, profitierte unter anderem davon, dass es bei Volkswagen keinen vergleichbaren Motor mit ähnlich großem Hubraum gab. Überdies verfügt Ford im Gegensatz zu Volkswagen über ein zusätzliches Modifikationscenter als „verlängerte Werkbank der Serienfertigung“: Während nachfragerindividuell auszuwählende Zubehör-Details bei den meisten Marken von den Händlern vor Ort eingebaut werden, nimmt Ford eine solche Modifikation herstellerseitig in Modifikationscentern vor. Bevor die Automobile somit nach Verlassen der Werkshallen ihren Zielort erreichen, erfahren sie einen Zwischenstopp in Zeebrugge, um hier vom Hersteller angepasst zu werden. Ziel eines solchen Modifikationscenters ist es, mögliche „Differenzierungslücken“ zu decken, welche die Serienfertigung lässt. Über 30 Prozent der Galaxy-Serienfertigung werden in diesen Centern mit nachfragerindividueller Zusatzausstattung versehen.

Abbildung 3: Optische Produktdifferenzierung im Jahr 1995

Ford Galaxy
(Front und Innenraum)

VW Sharan
(Front und Innenraum)

Seat Alhambra
sowie Hintenansicht
Galaxy/Sharan

GABLER GRAFIK

3.22 Preispolitik

Bei preispolitischen Entscheidungen eines neuen Modells steht – trotz kurzfristig möglicher Preisanpassungen, um etwa bestimmte Aussagen in der Kommunikationspolitik (zum Beispiel „gleicher Preis wie der Vorgänger bei verbesserter Ausstattung“) treffen zu können – die langfristige strategische Orientierung im Vordergrund. Dabei gibt die grundsätzliche Positionierung der Marke den preispolitischen Korridor für die Preisfindung vor.

Als zentrale Stärke der Marke Ford kann die relative Preisführerschaft („most value for money“) genannt werden. Während die Basismodelle der Eurovans nahezu preisgleich sind, strebte Ford vor diesem Hintergrund trotz generell hoher Kaufkraft der Nachfrager im Großraumlimousinen-Segment (Vanbesitzer verfügen über ein überdurchschnittlich hohes Einkommen und sind zumeist Inhaber eines Zweitwagens) eine preisliche Positionierung unterhalb des VW Sharan an. Der Seat Alhambra sollte hingegen die Van-Palette des Volkswagen-Konzerns durch ein günstiges Einstiegsmodell nach unten abrunden. Abbildung 4 zeigt in diesem Zusammenhang die ausstattungsbedingte Preisleiter des Galaxy (vier Ausstattungslinien mit Basis CLX/Kool gefolgt von GLX und Sport sowie

Ghia als Highend-Version) im Vergleich zum Sharan (vier Ausstattungslinien Basis, Comfort, Trendline und Highline) und Alhambra (drei Ausstattungslinien Basis, Comfort und Exclusive) für 1997.

Abbildung 4: **Preisleiter Ford Galaxy versus VW Sharan/Seat Alhambra, Deutschland 1997 (in DM)**

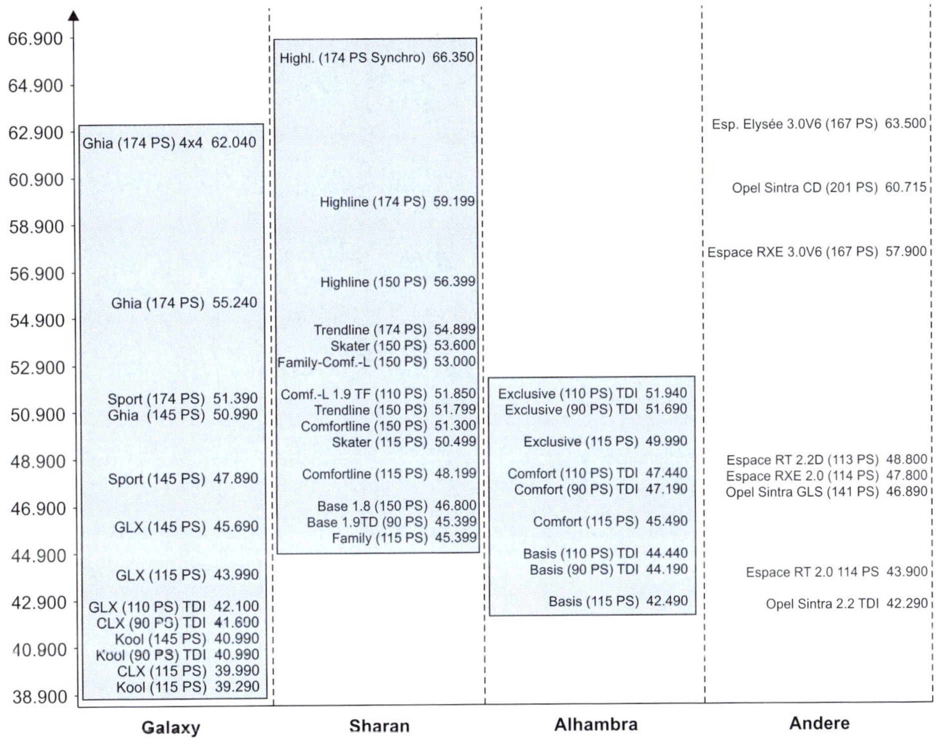

GABLER GRAFIK

Als grundsätzliche Orientierung strebte Ford eine Strategie „visuell günstiger Preise bei niedrigem Ausstattungsniveau“ an. So sind die unverbindlichen Preisempfehlungen ab Werk beim Galaxy auch durchgängig niedriger als beim Sharan, jedoch verfügt letzterer teilweise über ein deutlich höheres Ausstattungsniveau. Valide Aussagen über die relative Preispositionierung des Galaxy im Vergleich zum Sharan lassen sich somit nur unter Berücksichtigung der unterschiedlichen Ausstattungsmerkmale treffen. So liegt beispielsweise in 1998 der Preis des Galaxy-Sondermodells „Kool“ visuell 4.200 DM unterhalb des vergleichbaren Sharan, weist jedoch ausstattungsbereinigt nur noch einen Preisvorteil in Höhe von 3.330 DM auf (vgl. Tabelle 1). Ein entsprechender Vergleich bei den Top-Versionen Galaxy Ghia/Sharan Highline zeigt demgegenüber einen Preisnachteil des Ford-Modells in Höhe von 2.610 DM.

Tabelle 1: Preisvergleich Galaxy versus Sharan/Basisversion

	Galaxy Kool 1.9 l (90 PS)	Sharan Basis 1.9 l (90 PS)
Unverbindliche Preisempfehlung ab Werk	**42.600 DM**	**46.800 DM**
Galaxy über/(unter) Sharan	**(4.200 DM)**	
Ausstattungsmerkmale		S (= Serie)
2x Isofix-Vorbereitung (für Kindersitze)	200 DM	S
Zweiklanghorn	80 DM	S
Beheizbare Waschdüse	100 DM	S
Radiovorbereitung mit acht Lautsprechern	440 DM	S
Programmierbare Intervallschaltung	50 DM	S
Wert der zusätzlichen Ausstattung	**870 DM**	
Galaxy-Preisvorteil vergleichbarer Ausstattung	**3.330 DM**	

GABLER GRAFIK

3.23 Kommunikationspolitik

Die Positionierung des Ford Galaxy fand vor allem ihren Niederschlag in der Kommunikationspolitik. Während VW in seinen Kommunikationskampagnen mit Blick auf die lifestage-orientierte Positionierung des Sharan als Familienauto einen eindeutigen Bezug zur Familie betonte und eher emotionale Aspekte der angesprochenen Zielgruppe in den Vordergrund hob, indem vielfach gar auf eine Abbildung des Sharan in der Werbung nahezu gänzlich verzichtet wurde, betonte Ford eher rationale Aspekte im Rahmen der Botschaftsgestaltung, indem vor allem das Produkt selbst in den Vordergrund gestellt wurde (vgl. Abbildung 5).

Gerade in den Einführungskampagnen wurde der Galaxy als „Die clevere Alternative" präsentiert und dies „für alle, die etwas mehr haben wollen", sodass der breite Zielgruppenbezug durch Hervorhebung der Vielseitigkeit des Fahrzeugkonzepts auch in der

Kommunikation wiederzufinden war. Die Produkteigenschaften werden durch umfangreiche Textelemente erklärt. Einheitlich wurde der Slogan „Ford. Die Tun Was“ verwendet. Die Einführung der neuen Fahrzeugkonzepte erforderte einen entsprechenden Werbedruck, was mit hohen Werbeaufwendungen verbunden war. Es mag daher nicht verwundern, dass das MPV-Segment zur Einführung Galaxy/Sharan den höchsten Zuwachs im Werbeausgabevolumen aller Nischensegmente verzeichnete. Diese Werbeausgaben sind im MPV-Segment von 1994 bis 1997 – also kurz nach der Einführung von Galaxy und Sharan – um mehr als 100 Prozent gewachsen.

Abbildung 5: Anzeigenbeispiel VW Sharan und Ford Galaxy (1996)

GABLER GRAFIK

Gegenüber der Handelsorganisation hob Ford insbesondere das hohe Eroberungspotenzial des Galaxy hervor, betonte jedoch gleichzeitig den Händlern gegenüber die Notwendigkeit einer Differenzierung des Galaxy von den Händlerkollegen der Joint-Venture-Partner durch eigenständiges Händlermarketing und After Sales Service.

3.24 Distributionspolitik

Da die Zufriedenheit mit der Verkaufs- und Kundendienstleistung des Händlers als eine wesentliche Komponente in die Gesamtzufriedenheit des Nachfragers während sowie nach dem Kauf eingeht, kommt der Vertriebsorganisation und dem After Sales Marketing eine bedeutende präferenzbildende Funktion zu. Vor diesem Hintergrund war sich Ford bewusst, dass auch derjenige Hersteller einen Wettbewerbsvorteil realisieren kann, dem es gelingt, die gesamte Kundenkontaktkette von der Vorkaufphase bis hin zur Nachkaufphase mit positiven Erlebnissen anzureichern, um so eine umfassende Nachfragerzufriedenheit sicherzustellen.

Rein quantitativ weist Volkswagen in Deutschland allein aufgrund der höheren Netzdichte im Vergleich zu Ford einen Vorteil auf. Während Ford in Deutschland in 1995 über 2.562 Vertriebsstützpunkte verfügte, umfasste das Vertriebsnetz von Volkswagen/Audi 3.542 solcher Standorte. Während die Gesamtzufriedenheit der Sharan-Käufer mit ihren Händlern in 1997 auf einer Skala von 1 (= unzufrieden) bis 10 (= überaus zufrieden) bei 7,6 lag, wies Ford mit 8,0 einen im Segmentvergleich überdurchschnittlich hohen Wert aus (Segmentdurchschnitt: 7,8). Vor allem die Lieferzeit, aber auch die Sachkenntnis des Verkäufers stellten zentrale Vorteile in der Vertriebsorganisation von Ford dar.

Aufgrund der hohen Bedeutung qualifizierter Händler zur Markendifferenzierung am PoS streben sowohl VW als auch Ford eine qualitative Weiterentwicklung der Händlernetze an: in 1995 hat VW ein großes Umstrukturierungsprogramm für sein Händlernetz in Gang gesetzt, Ford stellte kurze Zeit später mit der flächendeckenden Kündigung aller Händlerverträge ebenfalls die Weichen für eine Neustrukturierung von Margensystem und Händlernetz.

Letztlich erhöht sich aufgrund der Baugleichheit der Produkte der Wettbewerb unter den Automobilhändlern. Letztere sind immer mehr gehalten, ihre Betriebe an die Corporate-Identity des jeweiligen Herstellers anzupassen, um das Markenerlebnis beim Nachfrager zu stärken und – im hier dargestellten Falle – die mangelnde technische Produktdifferenzierung am „Point of Sale“ zu kompensieren. In der Konsequenz bedeutet dies aber, dass die Kostensenkungseffekte in der Produktion aufgrund des Badge Engineering der Hersteller durch Kostensteigerungen im Vertrieb zumindest teilweise konterkariert werden. Hiermit verbunden sind ungleiche Kosteneffekte zwischen Hersteller und Händler: Während nämlich die Kostensenkungseffekte in der Produktion ausschließlich dem Hersteller und damit VW und Ford zugute kommen, haben Händler vielfach die Kosten der produktpolitischen Standardisierung in einem nicht unerheblichen Umfang durch verstärkte Differenzierungsbemühungen am PoS mitzutragen. So wird die Markendifferenzierung auf der Handelsseite auch durch markenspezifische Umbaukonzepte der Handelshäuser mehr und mehr sichtbar.

4. Zentrale Ergebnisse

Nach Einführung des Ford Galaxy und VW Sharan hat sich das Segment für Großraumlimousinen sowohl in Deutschland als auch in Europa sprunghaft entwickelt (vgl. Abbildung 6). Unmittelbar nach Einführung dominierten beide Fahrzeuge den deutschen Markt für Großraumlimousinen, wodurch die hohe Akzeptanz des Fahrzeugkonzepts prägnant verdeutlicht wird. 1996, ein Jahr nach ihrer Markteinführung, erreichten Ford Galaxy und VW Sharan in Deutschland zusammen 51,4 Prozent Segmentanteil im deutschen Markt.

Abbildung 6: Segmententwicklung in Deutschland und Europa sowie Stellenwert von Galaxy und Sharan im deutschen Wettbewerbsvergleich

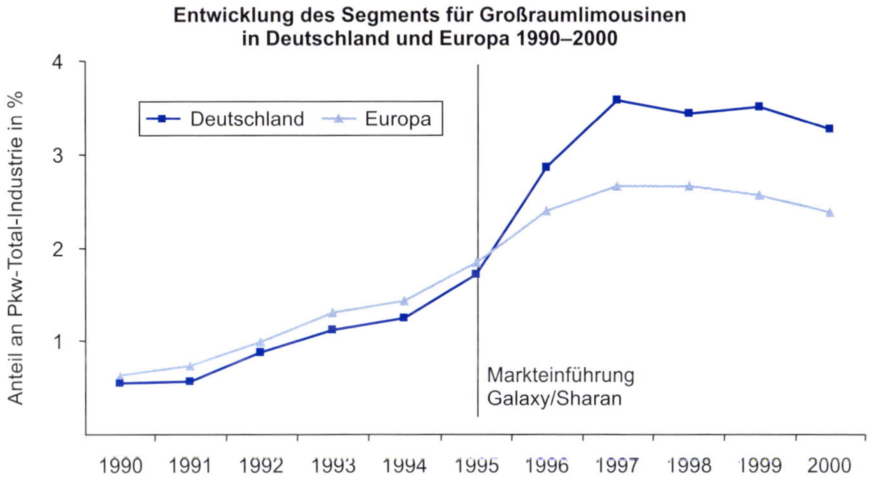

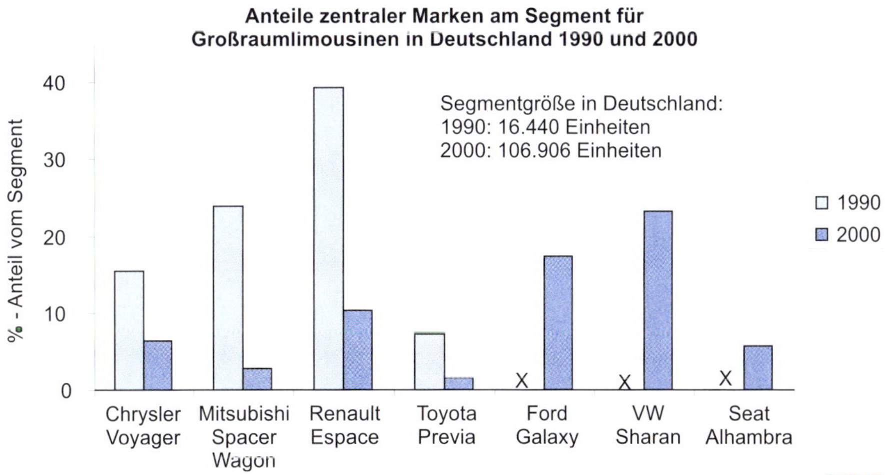

GABLER GRAFIK

Die Höhe des Verkaufsverhältnisses Galaxy/Sharan steht dabei in starker Beziehung zu den Kommunikationsausgaben, teilweise partizipieren die Hersteller auch gegenseitig an der jeweiligen Werbung. Mit 69 Prozent weist der Galaxy gegenüber dem Sharan (51 Prozent) jedoch eine enorme Fremdmarkeneroberungsrate auf: 69 Prozent der Galaxy-Neufahrzeugkäufer fuhren zuvor keinen Ford!

Abbildung 7: Ausgewählte psychografische Größen in 1997

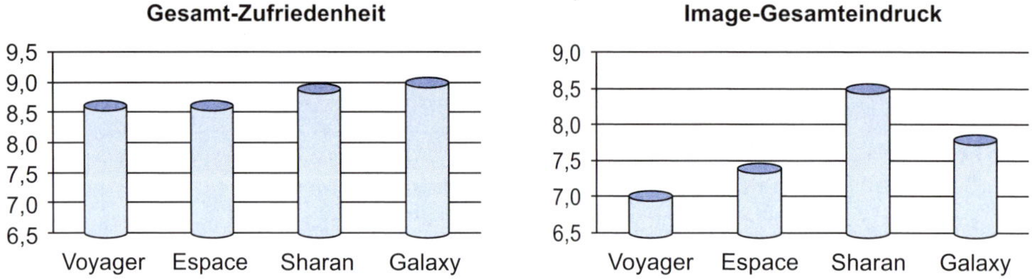

Imageitems [1 = schlechteste, 10 = beste Note]	**Voyager**	**Espace**	**Sharan**	**Galaxy**
Technisch fortgeschritten	7,3	7,3	**8,2**	7,8
Platzangebot	7,9	8,0	**8,6**	8,4
Sicherheit	7,7	7,6	**8,5**	8,3
Komfort	7,8	7,7	**8,3**	7,9
Qualität	7,1	7,2	**8,1**	8,0
Styling außen	7,4	7,3	**8,4**	7,8
Performance	7,2	7,2	**7,9**	7,7
Preis/Leistung	6,6	7,2	**7,8**	7,3
Verbrauch	5,5	6,5	**7,1**	6,6
Bekanntheit (in Prozent)	23	58	**69**	54

GABLER GRAFIK

Wie die Verkäufe selbst liegen auch die Werte der Galaxy-Erwägung in Deutschland bei etwa 90 Prozent der VW-Werte. Dies lässt sich neben der größeren VW-Handelsorganisation mit einem Imagevorteil der Marke Volkswagen im Heimatmarkt erklären. Das bessere Image der Marke VW färbt auf den VW Sharan ab. Ungeachtet der hohen Zufriedenheit der Galaxy-Nachfrager mit dem Fahrzeugkonzept weist der Sharan in sämtlichen Image-Items höhere Werte auf als der Galaxy (vgl. Abbildung 7), der Bekanntheitsgrad des Sharan liegt in Deutschland mit 69 Prozent über dem des Galaxy (54 Prozent).

In der Summe werden Eigenschaften beim Sharan besser beurteilt als beim Ford Galaxy, obwohl die Fahrzeuge nahezu baugleich sind. Selbst beim Preis-Leistungsverhältnis weist der Sharan einen Vorteil auf, obwohl der Preis neben dem Innenraum und dem Styling der Hauptkaufgrund der Galaxy-Käufer ist und die Marke Ford im Sinne des „most value for money“ die relative Preisführerschaft für sich beanspruchen kann. Obwohl der Kommunikationsschwerpunkt beim Galaxy nicht auf „Familie“ liegt, wird der Galaxy wie der Sharan zu 75 Prozent von Familien gekauft. Der Galaxy wird als „Familienauto zum Wohlfühlen“ eingestuft, junge Leute und Frauen sind als Käufer eher untypisch. Insgesamt erscheint der Ford Galaxy wie der Sharan erster Generation zwar als „risikoloser Kauf“, jedoch wird dem VW Sharan zusammenfassend mehr Persönlichkeit zugesprochen.

Teil 2: Segmentbehauptung und -abgrenzung durch zunehmende Differenzierung im reifenden Markt für Großraumlimousinen (Ford Galaxy II 2000–2004)

1. Erfahrungen aus Galaxy I sowie Marktsituation Ende der 90er Jahre

Das Kooperationsprojekt der ersten Generation hat die Erwartungen von Ford hinsichtlich des Markterfolges erfüllt. Das Joint Venture hat das Segment für Großraumlimousinen seit Einführung maßgeblich beeinflusst und etabliert. Ford und Volkswagen dominieren diesen Markt in Deutschland und Europa, sodass die Zielsetzungen hinsichtlich Verkaufsvolumen und Profit als erreicht gelten können.

Auch hinsichtlich der Wettbewerbspositionen der Unternehmen zueinander war VW der strategisch richtige Partner für Ford. Beide Marken bewegen sich als Volumenmarken im gleichen relevanten Markt und sind – mit durchaus unterschiedlichen regionalen Profilen – im europäischen Vergleich gleich stark. So hat die hohe Reputation VWs in Deutschland dem Ford Galaxy von Anfang an eine hohe Akzeptanz gebracht und damit zu dessen positiven Verkaufsergebnissen beigetragen.

Wie die Imageergebnisse zeigen, kann das primär technische Gemeinschaftsprojekt der ersten Generation aus psychografischer Perspektive jedoch auch kritisch gesehen werden. Zwar heben sich sowohl der Galaxy als auch der Sharan in der nachfragerseitigen Wahrnehmung und Beurteilung deutlich vom Wettbewerb ab, sodass die verfolgte Führungsrolle im Segment der Großraumlimousinen insgesamt realisiert werden konnte. Allerdings konnte weder der Ford Galaxy noch der VW Sharan der ersten Generation aufgrund der fehlenden Produktdifferenzierung einen wirklich entscheidenden Beitrag zur Identitätsstiftung der jeweils eigenen Herstellermarke leisten.

Auch hat das Fehlen einer echten Produktdifferenzierung den Druck auf die übrigen Marketing-Mix-Elemente maßgeblich erhöht. Werbung, Preispolitik und Differenzierung am PoS allein können jedoch die Eigenständigkeit und Unverwechselbarkeit eines Produktes in der Automobilindustrie nicht in vollem Umfang ersetzen. Nicht umsonst lautet in diesem Zusammenhang eine häufig zu hörende Aussage: „In diesem Geschäft konzentriert sich schlussendlich alles auf die Produkte".

In einer gesamthaften Würdigung ist das Kooperationsprojekt der ersten Phase aber vor dem Hintergrund der spezifischen Situation im Jahre 1990 zu betrachten. So scheint das Badge Engineering mit wenig Produktdifferenzierung zur Marktpenetration in neuen oder wachsenden Marktsegmenten aufgrund mangelnder Erfahrungen der Hersteller, kalkulierbarer Kosten und Risikoreduktion ein zunächst gangbarer Weg zur effizienten Erreichung von Markterfolg zu sein. In dieser ersten Phase stand der Eintritt in ein lukratives Fahrzeugsegment zu vertretbaren Kosten und bei absehbarem Risiko im Vordergrund. Allerdings erweist es sich als notwendig, mit voranschreitendem Marktlebenszyklus und hier vor allem in der Reifephase des Segmentes eine stärkere Produktdifferenzierung vorzunehmen.

Zusätzlich zu den Erfahrungen aus der ersten Generation des Gemeinschaftsprojektes hat sich auch die Wettbewerbssituation durch eine fortschreitende Markt-Fragmentierung weiterhin verschärft. Es haben sich weitere Van-Konzepte im deutschen und europäischen Markt entwickelt, die bei Einführung des Galaxy I noch wenig oder keine Relevanz besaßen. Abbildung 8 zeigt in diesem Zusammenhang die dramatische Entwicklung des Segments der Kompakt-Vans von 1995 bis 2004. Im Jahr 2004 repräsentiert dieses Segment (Opel Zafira, VW Touran, Ford Focus C-MAX, Renault Scenic etc.) mehr als zehn Prozent des deutschen Pkw-Marktes. Selbst das Kleinwagen-Segment ist mittlerweile mit Mini-Van-Konzepten bestückt (beispielsweise Opel Meriva oder Ford Fusion).

Abbildung 8: Entwicklung des Segments der Kompakt-Vans

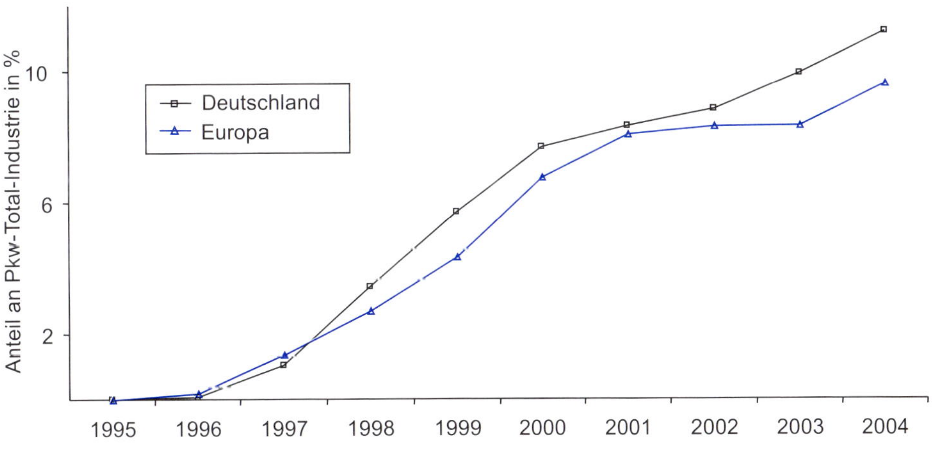

GABLER GRAFIK

Allein Ford bietet im Jahr 2004 zusätzlich zum Ford Galaxy den Ford Fusion, den Ford Focus C-MAX sowie den Ford Transit Connect und damit eine komplette Van-Familie an. Auch VW verfügt mit dem Touran über ein zusätzliches Van-Angebot im eigenen Produktportfolio. Diese zusätzlichen Van-Angebote bringen auch intern einen erhöhten Wettbewerb mit sich, sodass es in Zukunft zur Vermeidung hausinterner Kannibalisierungseffekte einer noch eindeutigeren Abgrenzung der Großraumlimousinen zu den sonstigen Van-Konzepten bedarf.

Unabhängig vom konkreten Fall wurden in einer explorativen Befragung von 400 Autofahrern in 1996 hinsichtlich identitätsprägender Bestandteile einer Automobilmarke die in Abbildung 9 dargestellten Ergebnisse erzielt. Hiernach konnten insbesondere der Motor mit 74 Prozent sowie die Karosserie des Fahrzeugs mit 66 Prozent als solche Produktmerkmale ermittelt werden, die wesentlich zur Eigenständigkeit von Automobilen in der Wahrnehmung der Nachfrager beitragen. Folglich können die jeweiligen Bauteile als maßgebliche Unterscheidungsmerkmale fungieren.

Abbildung 9: Nachfragerwahrnehmung der Eigenständigkeit von Automobilen

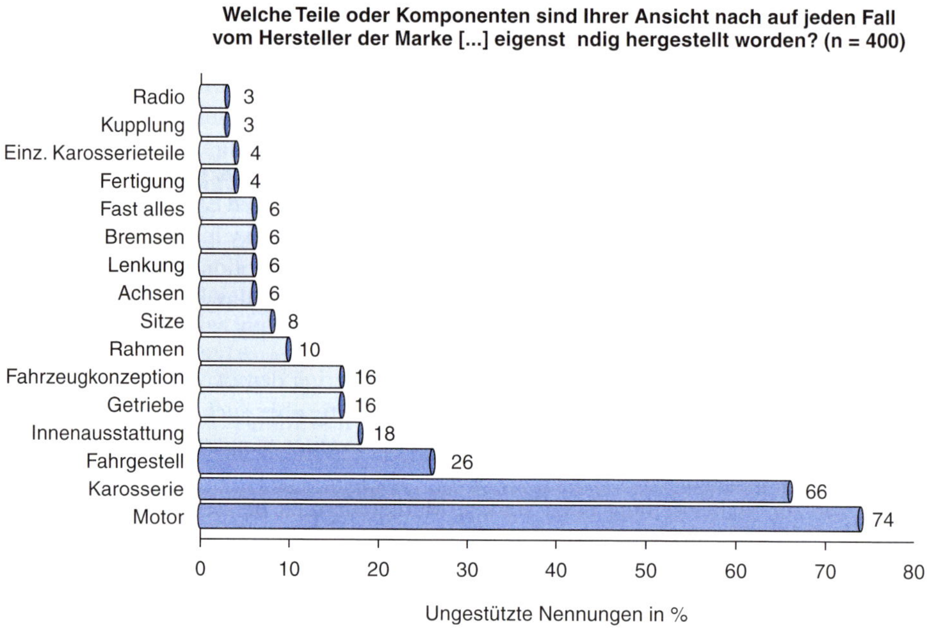

GABLER GRAFIK

Zur Bestimmung maßgeblicher Unterscheidungsmerkmale im Differenzierungsplan ist zu überprüfen, welche objektive Produkteigenschaft mit welcher Wahrnehmungsdimension korrespondiert. Soll der Ford-Galaxy als Lifestyle-Produkt wahrgenommen werden, der Sharan hingegen als Lifestage-Produkt im Sinne eines Familienautos, so sind die diesen Wahrnehmungsdimensionen zugrunde liegenden objektiven Produkteigenschaften zu konkretisieren. Sind diejenigen Produktmerkmale ermittelt, die wesentlich zur Eigenständigkeit der Vans in der Wahrnehmung der Nachfrager beitragen, lassen sich schließlich maßgebliche Unterscheidungsmerkmale im Rahmen des Differenzierungsplans festlegen sowie die aus kosteninduzierten Gründen zu standardisierenden Bauteile im Vereinheitlichungsplan bestimmen.

Vor dem Hintergrund der Wichtigkeit von Karosserie und vor allem Design als markenprägende Produktattribute wurden diese einer markenspezifischen Anpassung mittels einer umfangreichen Produktüberarbeitung (Front, Heck, Innenraum) unterzogen. Tropfenförmige Klarglas-Scheinwerfer, der elliptisch geformte Kühlergrill im Wabendesign, die V-förmige Prägung der Motorhaube sowie die schlanke Linienführung der Karosserie und das komplett neu entworfene Heck unterstreichen seither den fordtypischen Auftritt des Galaxy. Als Konsequenz zeigt der Galaxy ein fordtypisches Gesicht und unterscheidet sich deutlich vom VW Sharan. Abbildung 10 zeigt in diesem Zusammenhang die sichtbare Unterscheidung von VW Sharan bei gleichzeitiger vertikaler Integration in die Ford Produktfamilie.

Abbildung 10: Optische Produktdifferenzierung im Jahr 2000

GABLER GRAFIK

Die erhöhte Produktdifferenzierung ermöglicht dabei eine Entlastung der sonstigen Mix-Bereiche. So können im Rahmen der **Preispolitik** beim Galaxy II im Unterschied zum Galaxy I verstärkt Preisbereitschaften über die eigene Ford-Markenidentität realisiert werden, da nicht mehr allein der Wettbewerb, sondern vor allem die grundsätzliche

Preisphilosophie der Dachmarke Ford die Preispolitik dominiert. Hier gilt stets das Primat des Unternehmensgründers Henry Ford: „Ich will, dass sich jeder ein Auto leisten kann." In diesem Sinne hat auch der Galaxy preislich eine breite Käuferschicht anzusprechen.

Ford Galaxy und VW Sharan sind heute nahezu gleich gepreist, wobei der Ford Galaxy jedoch im Sinne der fordtypischen „value for money proposition" einen geringeren Einstiegspreis aufweist. Trotz des nach wie vor besseren VW-Images in Deutschland hat sich ein identisches Preisniveau für Ford als durchsetzbar erwiesen, da von vielen Nachfragern das Galaxy-Design und die Galaxy-Ausstattung schlichtweg präferiert werden.

3.2 Kommunikations- und Distributionspolitik

Wenngleich im Rahmen des **Kommunikations-Mixes** die grundsätzlichen Kommunikationsinhalte von beiden Herstellern beibehalten wurden, galt für den Ford Galaxy auch hier, einen stärkeren Bezug zur Dachmarke Ford zu schaffen. VW stellte auch beim Sharan der zweiten Generation das Familienthema eindeutig in den Vordergrund. Entsprechend wurde die Kampagne der ersten Generation mit neuen Motiven auf den VW Sharan der zweiten Generation übertragen (vgl. Abbildung 11). Dabei wurde mit Hilfe von Tierbildern versucht, die Eignung des Sharans zum außergewöhnlichen Familien-Transport besonders hervorzuheben: „Jede Spezies hat ihre besondere Art, ihren Nachwuchs zu transportieren." Als schwierig erweist sich dabei allerdings vor allem die Abgrenzung zum im Jahr 2003 eingeführten Kompakt-Van Touran, der kommunikativ ebenfalls die Familie anspricht.

Legte VW den kommunikativen Schwerpunkt abermals auf Familie, rückte Ford erneut die Vielseitigkeit des Fahrzeugkonzepts in den Vordergrund. Gleichzeitig wurde jedoch kommunikativ ein wesentlicher Schwerpunkt auf „luxury travel" gelegt, um hierdurch der gewünschten Emotionalisierung der Marke Rechnung zu tragen. Dabei sollten die verwendeten Text- und Bildelemente vor allem einen Bezug zur Business-Klasse schaffen, indem diese als „Galaxy Klasse" bezeichnet wurde. So wurde der Galaxy vielfach auf dem Rollfeld eines Flughafens oder am Bahnhof gezeigt, unterstützt durch Textelemente wie „Willkommen in der Galaxy Klasse: Wir freuen uns, Ihnen auf allen innerdeutschen Verbindungen ein reichhaltiges Programm bieten zu können." Hierdurch wurden „Business-Class-Assoziationen" und damit „luxury travel" hervorgehoben, gleichzeitig aber auch produktbezogene Optionen wie das Galaxy-Multimediasystem besonders betont. Ziel war es, das gerade im VW-Vergleich schlechtere Ansehen in den Bereichen Qualität und Persönlichkeit zu adressieren.

Abbildung 11: **Anzeigenbeispiel VW Sharan und Ford Galaxy 2003**

GABLER GRAFIK

Hierzu finden auch seit Ende 2000 die Markenwerte Verlässlichkeit, Zeitgemäß und Fahrvergnügen ihren Niederschlag in dem neu definierten Markenslogan „Besser ankommen“, der seither jede Kommunikationsbotschaft begleitet und den Anspruch der Marke verkörpern soll (vgl. rechte Anzeige oben in Abbildung 11). Das neue Leitbild „Ford. Besser ankommen“ drückt den Anspruch der Marke Ford aus: Besser ankommen mit und in verlässlichen und zeitgemäßen Produkten, die Fahrvergnügen bereiten!

Schließlich bringt die sichtbare Differenzierung des Galaxy II auch eine erhebliche Entlastung in der **Distribution** und damit für die Handelsorganisation, da das Produkt einen eigenständigeren Charakter hat und sich besser in die Ford-Produktpalette integiert. Gerade Design und sonstige fordindividuelle Optionen bieten Verkaufsargumente für die Händler im Ausstellungsraum, sodass das Fahrzeug im deutschen Handel nicht mehr „gegen“ das Joint Venture-Konkurrenzprodukt VW Sharan, sondern als Teil der fordeigenen Angebotspalette verkauft wird.

4. Zentrale Ergebnisse

Im Ergebnis wurden die mit dem Galaxy II gesteckten Ziele erreicht. Das Segment für Großraumlimousinen ist aufgrund des Aufkommens neuer Van-Konzepte einem intensiven Wettbewerb ausgesetzt. Die Wachstumsphase der 90er Jahre ist somit einer Reifephase gewichen. Abbildung 12 zeigt in diesem Zusammenhang die Entwicklung des Segments für Großraumlimousinen von 1990 bis 2004 in Deutschland und Europa.

Abbildung 12: Segmentanteil Großraumlimousinen in Deutschland und Europa 2004

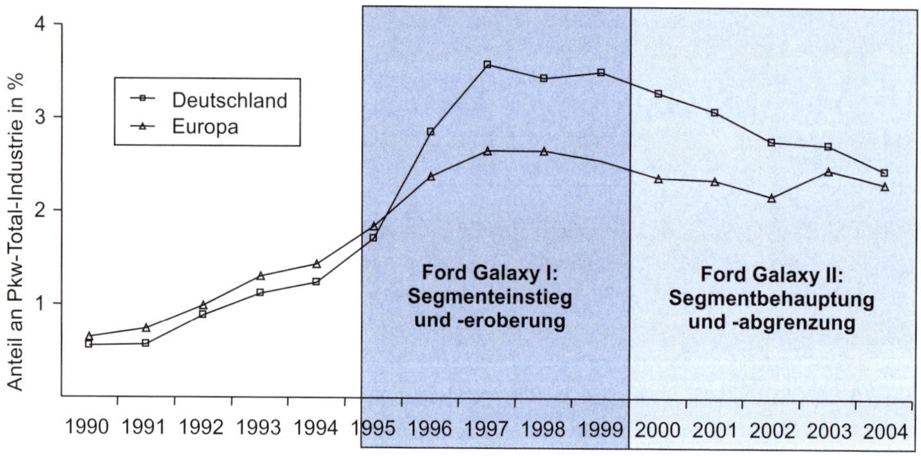

GABLER GRAFIK

Dabei dominiert weiterhin das Gemeinschaftskonzept von Ford und Volkswagen den Markt für Großraumlimousinen in Deutschland und Europa, wobei der deutsche Markt noch immer mit fast 50 Prozent Segmentanteil beherrscht wird. Der Phase des Segmenteinstiegs und der -eroberung folgte somit eine erfolgreiche Phase der Segmentbehauptung und -abgrenzung. Abbildung 13 zeigt in diesem Zusammenhang den Segmentanteil der Großraumlimousinen in Deutschland und Europa.

Abbildung 13: Segmentanteil Großraumlimousinen in Deutschland und Europa 2004

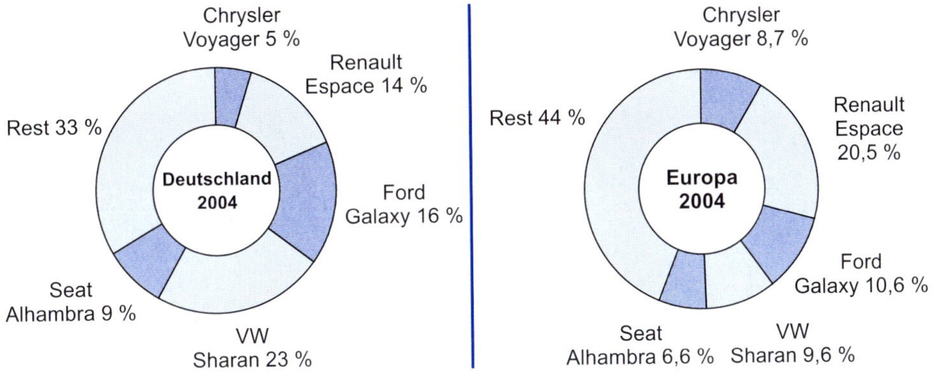

Neben den Verkaufsergebnissen erweisen sich aber auch die psychografischen Ergebnisse vor dem Hintergrund der Zielsetzung des Galaxy II, einen größeren Beitrag zur Aufladung der Dachmarke Ford zu leisten, als überaus positiv. Waren die Imagewerte des Ford Galaxy in Ford dominierten Ländern wie Großbritannien seit jeher aufgrund der positiven Beurteilung der Dachmarke Ford denen des VW Sharan überlegen, konnte der Image-Abstand zum VW Sharan auch in Deutschland seit Einführung des Galaxy II weiter verringert werden (vgl. Abbildung 14). Unter dem Bewusstsein, dass sich das Image einer Dachmarke nur sehr langsam ändert, ist die überaus starke Annäherung des Galaxy an den Sharan mit Einführung des Galaxy II ein Erfolg und Beweis sowohl für die Bedeutung der Marke allgemein als auch für die Richtigkeit der eingeschlagenen Ford-Strategie. So dominant die Marke Ford in Großbritannien ist, so stark ist die Marke VW im deutschen Markt. Folglich ist auch der Galaxy bei den Ford Markenwerten Verlässlichkeit, Zeitgemäß und Fahrvergnügen „Klassenbester" in Großbritannien, wohingegen der VW Sharan diesbezüglich in Deutschland dominiert.

Zusammenfassend ist festzuhalten, dass die Phase der Segmentbehauptung und -abgrenzung durch die strategische Umorientierung des Ford Galaxy erfolgreich bewältigt werden konnte. Trotz weiterer Nutzung von kostennotwendigen Produktionssynergien zwischen Ford und Volkswagen konnte dem nachfragerinduzierten Differenzierungserfordernis Rechnung getragen werden. Auch in Zukunft werden solche Synergien notwendig sein, um weiterhin Nischenfahrzeuge kostengünstig in den Markt einführen zu können. Ob hierzu jedoch weiterhin ein externer Partner vonnöten sein wird, muss im konkreten Fall beurteilt werden. Denn aufgrund des umfangreichen Markenportfolios mit den Marken Ford, Mazda, Mercury, Lincoln sowie Volvo, Jaguar, Land Rover und Aston Martin existieren bereits heute zahlreiche Synergiebereiche innerhalb der Ford Motor Company, die markenübergreifend genutzt werden können, ohne auf einen strategischen Partner zurückgreifen zu müssen. Inwieweit ein solches Vorgehen allerdings auch im Rahmen von Großraumlimousinen stattfinden kann, wird der Ford Galaxy der dritten Generation zeigen.

Abbildung 14: Ausgewählte psychografische Größen in 2003

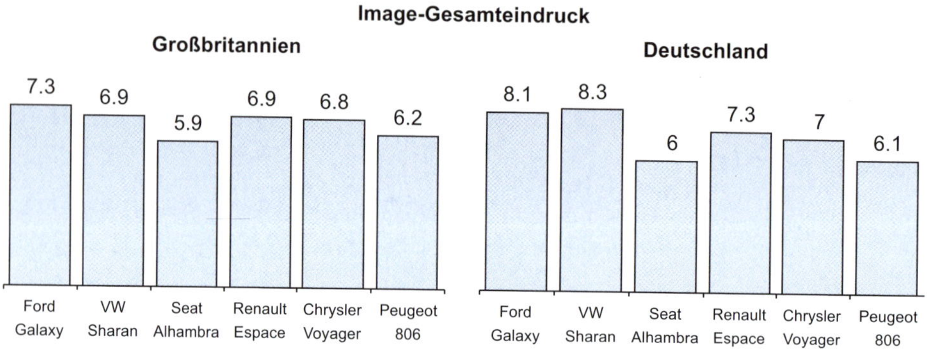

DCDQ-Image-Tracking	Best in Class Großbritannien	Best in Class Deutschland
Dependability (Verlässlichkeit)		
■ Sind Fahrzeuge, auf die man sich verlassen kann	Ford Galaxy	VW Sharan
■ Sind die sichersten in der Klasse	Ford Galaxy	VW Sharan
Contemporary (zeitgemäß) Sind modern	Ford Galaxy	VW Sharan
■ Machen Gebrauch von neusten Technologien	Ford Galaxy	VW Sharan
Driving Quality (Fahrvergnügen)		
■ Machen Spaß zu fahren	Ford Galaxy	VW Sharan
■ Sind komfortabler als andere Fahrzeuge der Klasse	Ford Galaxy	VW Sharan
Allgemein		
■ Sind Fahrzeuge, die stolz machen	Ford Galaxy	VW Sharan
■ Setzen Standards	Ford Galaxy	VW Sharan

GABLER GRAFIK

High-speed-Aufbau einer neuen Marke – Das Beispiel Germanwings

Andreas Bierwirth und Volker Scheible

1.	**Einleitung**	**764**
2.	**Die unternehmensstrategische Entscheidung: Einstieg in das Low-Cost-Segment**	**764**
3.	**Das Geschäftskonzept: Konsequente Umsetzung der Erfolgsfaktoren**	**766**
3.1	Preisstrategie: Königsdisziplin im preisdominierten Low-Cost-Segment	767
3.2	Marktstrategie und Streckennetz: Volumen und Vielfalt	768
4.	**Die Marke Germanwings als Fundament und Rahmen des unternehmerischen Vorgehens**	**770**
4.1	Identitätsorientierte Markenführung bei Germanwings	770
4.2	Die Positionierung der Marke Germanwings	770
4.3	Die Entwicklung und Gestaltung der Marke Germanwings	772
5.	**Produkt und Service an Bord und Boden: Qualität trotz „no-frills"**	**773**
6.	**Germanwings Vertrieb: Ein E-Commerce-Unternehmen**	**774**
7.	**Marketingkommunikation: Beschleuniger des Markenaufbaus**	**776**
8.	**Der Erfolg in Zahlen**	**777**
9.	**Ausblick**	**779**

1. Einleitung

Die europäische Airline Industrie befindet sich seit Anfang der 90er Jahre in einem stetigen Wandel, immer wieder forciert durch krisenbedingte Umbrüche konjunktureller und geopolitischer Natur. Die Privatisierung ehemals staatlicher Airlines, die Bildung von Allianzsystemen und auch erste Konsolidierungsschritte wie der aktuelle Merger von Air France und KLM kennzeichnen die Tragweite dieser Entwicklung. Im europäische Kontinental-Verkehr zeichnete sich seit den 90ern ausgehend von Großbritannien das Aufkommen eines neuen Geschäftssystems ab, das in den USA bereits seit den 70ern am Beispiel Southwest Airlines Markterfolge aufweisen konnte und das die Airline Branche nicht nur in Europa, sondern auch in Asien erheblich verändert: Die so genannten Low-Cost-Airlines, Billig-Airlines oder No-frills-Airlines. Diese begriffliche Vielfalt spiegelt die unterschiedlichen Ausprägungsformen dieses Geschäftssystems sehr gut wider. In Reinkultur geht es aber um Airlines, deren Unternehmensstruktur und -prozesse darauf ausgerichtet sind, auf Basis hoher Produktivität und geringer Stückkosten im Vergleich zu klassischen Airlines extrem günstige Tickets für ein reduziertes Kernprodukt, den Transport von A nach B in Volumenmärkten anzubieten, um bestehende Nachfrage abzuschöpfen aber vor allem um neue Nachfrage nach Flugleistungen in Zielgruppen, die bis dato nicht geflogen sind, zu generieren. Mit der Gründung und Entwicklung der Germanwings GmbH wurde dieser Markttrend erfolgreich aufgenommen und genutzt.

2. Die unternehmensstrategische Entscheidung: Einstieg in das Low-Cost-Segment

Im Sommer 2002 stand die Eurowings AG (Dortmund) vor einer Entscheidung mit erheblicher strategischer Tragweite: Die Charter-Division agierte mit fünf Airbus 319 in einem nachfrageschwachen Marktsegment mit ungünstigen Zukunftsperspektiven. Es stellten sich die Handlungsalternativen, das Geschäft fortzusetzen, einzustellen oder ein vielversprechenderes Marktsegment zu suchen. Das Low-Cost-Segment war das einzige Wachstumssegment im Luftverkehr und konnte spannende Perspektiven verschaffen. Es zeichnete sich damals mehr als deutlich ein fundamentaler Umbruch des europäischen Luftverkehrs ab, der bis heute anhält. Ausgehend von Großbritannien entwickelt sich auch in Deutschland ein erheblicher Angebotszuwachs von bereits existierenden und neuen Low-Cost-Carriern. Das Wachstum des europäischen Low-Cost-Marktes hatte 2002 jedoch gerade erst begonnen, zweistellige Wachstumsraten werden für die nächsten Jahre im Marktsegment prognostiziert. Nach einer kurzen aber intensiven Prüfung dieser Handlungsoption wurde der Business Plan entwickelt und der Einstieg vorbereitet.

Tabelle 1: Prognostizierte Entwicklung des Passagieraufkommens in Europa

	2001		2008		2016
Gesamtmarkt Euro außer Low Cost	280 Mio. Pax (89,6 %)	4 % p. a. →	368 Mio. Pax (82,9 %)	4 % p. a. →	504 Mio. Pax (77,6 %)
Euro Low Price	29,0 Mio. Pax (10,4 %)	19,9 % p. a. →	76,0 Mio. Pax (17,1 %)	8,5 % p. a. →	145,6 Mio. Pax (22,4 %)
Easy Jet Ryan Air	11,1 Mio. Pax 7,1 Mio. Pax		28,0 Mio. Pax 30,0 Mio. Pax		64,0 Mio. Pax 57,0 Mio. Pax
Sonstige	10,8 Mio. Pax		18,0 Mio. Pax		25,0 Mio. Pax

GABLER GRAFIK

Quelle: Goldman Sachs (2001)

Abbildung 1: Prognostizierter wert-/volumenmäßiger Anteil Low Cost am Gesamtmarkt

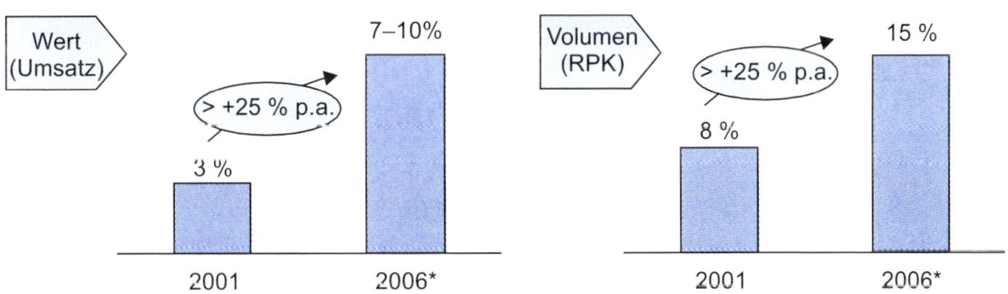

Vergleich mit Gesamtmarktwachstum = –45 %
* prognostiziert

GABLER GRAFIK

Quelle: Booz Allen Hamilton (OECD, Boeing)

Die Preisstrategie folgt dem Prinzip ansteigender Preislevel bei einem sinkenden Zeitraum vor dem Flug. Die Feinsteuerung erfolgt entsprechend Nachfragedruck und Wettbewerb auf den jeweiligen Strecken. Zu Vermarktungsbeginn des jeweiligen Flugplanes wird nach diesem Prinzip ein Set an Buchungsklassen pro Flug eingestellt, die mit entsprechenden Preisen verknüpft sind. Pro Flug wird ein Mindestkontingent von zehn bis 20 Prozent der extrem niedrigen Preisklassen ab 19 Euro eingestellt. Mit zeitlicher Annäherung an das Flugereignis steigt damit der Flugpreis, liegt aber auch sehr kurzfristig (bis wenige Stunden vor dem eigentlichen Flug) immer noch circa 50 Prozent unter den voll flexiblen Tarifen klassischer Airlines. Die Kunst des Pricings liegt nun darin, durch eine geschickte, nachfragebezogene Einstellung und Feinsteuerung der Buchungsklassen mit Ziel des Upsellings einen Durchschnittserlös von 70 bis 80 Euro pro Oneway-Ticket je nach Strecke und Sitzladefaktor und damit Streckenprofitabilität zu erreichen.

3.2 Marktstrategie und Streckennetz: Volumen und Vielfalt

Die Marktgröße am Ursprungs- und/oder Zielort einer Strecke sowie die jeweilige Wettbewerbssituation sind neben weiteren streckenspezifischen Kriterien (Flughafenkonditionen, Verfügbarkeit von Zeitfenster für Start/Landung etc.) sowie Faktoren, die den Flugplan in der Gesamtheit betreffen (Umlaufplanung, Fleet Utilization etc.) entscheidende Kriterien bei der Standortauswahl und Streckenplanung. Germanwings hat von Anbeginn die strategische Ausrichtung umgesetzt, durch einen großen Anteil an Strecken, die für Geschäfts- und Privatreisende sehr attraktiv sind, einen Streckenmix anzubieten, der auch im Low-Cost-Segment zahlungskräftigere Business-Kunden anzieht und saisonale Schwankungen ausgleichen kann. Dieses Bestreben setzt sich in der eigentlichen Zeitplanung des Flugplans fort, beispielsweise werden Strecken mit hohem Geschäftsreise-Anteil in Tagesrandverbindungen umgesetzt. Insgesamt werden Verbindungen hochfrequent (hoher Anteil täglich) angeboten. Es werden Primär- und Sekundärflughäfen in jeweiliger Nähe der Stadtzentren angeflogen. Zusätzliche attraktive touristische Verbindungen wie auch Angebote für ethnische Zielgruppen decken die Flugbedürfnisse einer breiten Zielgruppe ab und führen zu einem in toto stabilen Nachfrage-Mix.

Als erster Hauptstandort zum Markteinstieg wurde der Flughafen Köln/Bonn im Catchment Nordrhein-Westfalen gewählt. Mit 18 Millionen Einwohnern im größten Bundesland, starker Kauf- und Wirtschaftskraft, einer Unterversorgung mit Flugleistungen ex Köln im Vergleich zum Standort Düsseldorf, aber auch wegen der engen Nachbarschaft zu Rheinland-Pfalz und Hessen sowie den nah gelegenen EU Staaten Belgien und Niederlanden, ist dieser Markt sehr attraktiv. Bei einem vergrößerten Einzugsgebiet für ein Low-Cost-Angebot bis 150 km Umkreis zum Flughafen ist dieser Markt hinsichtlich des Potenzials vergleichbar mit den Großräumen London oder Paris.

Germanwings setzte sich das Ziel, als erster Low-Cost-Anbieter am Flughafen Köln/Bonn zu starten. So stand das Projekt von Anbeginn unter erheblichem Zeitdruck. Von Entwicklung des Business Plans, über die Entscheidung des Vorstandes bis zum letztendlichen Verkaufsstart vergingen lediglich fünf Monate.

Abbildung 4: **Streckennetz**

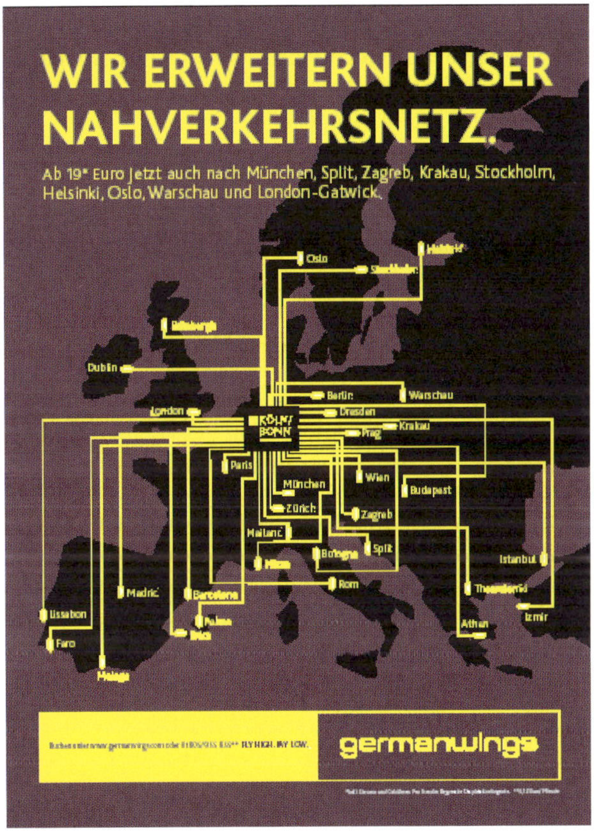

4. Die Marke Germanwings als Fundament und Rahmen des unternehmerischen Vorgehens

4.1 Identitätsorientierte Markenführung bei Germanwings

Die genannten Festlegungen in den Bereichen Preis- beziehungsweise Kostenmanagement, Strecken- und Flugplanung wurden und werden als Teilaspekte einer markenstrategischen Ausrichtung betrachtet. Die Umsetzung mit den Mitteln der Markentechnik und des Marketings im engeren Sinne musste dabei zwei grundsätzliche Stoßrichtungen berücksichtigen: Mit Blick auf interne Gegebenheiten war es eine Kernherausforderung, ein Unternehmen mit seinen Mitarbeitern in einem alten Geschäftsfeld (Eurowings Charter) auf ein neues Geschäftsfeld mit den entsprechenden Anforderungen auszurichten und weiterzuentwickeln. Germanwings ist eine neue Marke, aber kein neues Unternehmen. Die neue Marke muss den Mitarbeitern einen Ansatzpunkt für die Identifikation mit und die Begeisterung für das Unternehmen geben. Sie fungiert als Symbol für Innovationsgeist und Effizienzstreben, Neuanfang und dynamischer Zukunft, Low-Cost-Qualität und letztendlich auch Sicherheit des ursprünglich gefährdeten Arbeitsplatzes. Für das Management gelten die markenstrategischen Festlegungen als Leitbild für alle Entscheidungen in allen Funktionsbereichen (Netzplan, Vertrieb, Marketing, Produkt, Operations).

Mit Blick auf externe Zielgruppen musste durch die neue Marke den Stakeholdern ein Signal für Aufbruch, Innovation, unternehmerischer Mut und RoI (Return on Investment) in der Zukunft gegeben werden. Entscheidend war und ist, wie die neue Marke sich in Wahrnehmung und Verhalten bei den End-Kunden durchsetzen kann.

4.2 Die Positionierung der Marke Germanwings

Das Erfolgsrezept für Germanwings besteht in der exzellenten Umsetzung der Kernerfolgsfaktoren, zusammengefasst unter einer einzigartigen Marke mit einem ambitionierten Ziel: „Die" deutsche Günstigairline zu werden und die Marktführerschaft als deutsche Airline in diesem Segment zu erreichen. Germanwings positioniert und differenziert sich als die Airline mit sehr günstigen Tickets und einem Top-Kernprodukt (Netz, Flugplan, Flotte, Produkt/Service, Operations), das Vertrauen beim Nachfrager bewirkt. Dahinter steht das Bestreben, Qualität im Low-Cost-Segment neu zu definieren.

Bei der Entwicklung der Positionierungsidee wurde eine Vielzahl von Benchmarks vor allem auch außerhalb der Airline-Industrie untersucht. Marken wie IKEA oder H & M zeigen, wie auch in sehr preissensiblen Marktsegmenten Preisgünstigkeit und Qualitätswahrnehmung verknüpft und Marken zu einem Wettbewerbsvorteil werden können.

Qualität muss dabei den Kostenvorteil nicht mindern. Am Beispiel der Gestaltung des attraktiven Flugplans, der jungen Flotte von Germanwings (Airbus 319/320 beispielsweise mit Lederausstattung) oder eines attraktiven Produkt- und Servicekonzeptes kann aufgezeigt werden, dass Qualitätswahrnehmung und günstigste Preise nicht im Widerspruch stehen müssen. Nichtsdestotrotz ist im Low-Cost-Segment die Preiswahrnehmung neben dem Flugplanangebot der primäre Faktor für die Kaufentscheidung, insbesondere im Rahmen der Neukundengewinnung einer neuen Marke. Damit war und ist die Erreichung der wahrgenommenen Preisführerschaft das primäre Ziel bei jedem neuen Markteintritt, in Verbindung mit der Penetration des Streckenangebotes beziehungsweise des Flugplans. Längerfristiges Ziel ist jedoch, die Marke hinsichtlich der Qualitätsdimension differenzierend aufzuladen.

Abbildung 5: Markenpositionierung von Germanwings

GABLER GRAFIK

Um die Handlungsrelevanz der Markenpositionierung sicherzustellen, wurden in einem Markenhandbuch unter anderem die Kernwerte der Marke definiert. Im Rahmen interner Workshops in der Phase vor Markteintritt wurden alle Mitarbeiter über die Markenpositionierung und deren Umsetzung in den einzelnen Funktionsbereichen des Unternehmens informiert. Die Auseinandersetzung mit der Unternehmensmarke gehört heute zudem zum Inhalt der Schulung aller neuen Mitarbeiter.

Abbildung 6: **Kernwerte der Marke Germanwings**

- **Anerkannter Günstig-Preis-Führer**
- **Sicherheit, Verlässlichkeit, Pünktlichkeit**
- **Qualität des Kernproduktes/Innovative Services**
- **Tatenlust des Germanwings-Teams**

GABLER GRAFIK

4.3 Die Entwicklung und Gestaltung der Marke Germanwings

Die Entwicklung des Markennamens, der Markengestaltung und des Markenauftritts wurde mit dem in der Positionierung vorgegebenen Anspruch umgesetzt und bildete die Grundlage dafür, bei Markteintritt zügig ein spezifisches Markenbild in der Kundenwahrnehmung zu etablieren. Zunächst wurde der Markenname Germanwings bewusst dahingehend gewählt, Internationalität, Herkunft und Qualität gleichermaßen auszudrücken. Mit dem Wortbestandteil „wings“ wird eine schnelle Assoziation zum Fliegen geschaffen, zudem aber auch die Verbindung zum Mutterunternehmen Eurowings gehalten, was eine nicht unerhebliche Bedeutung für einen Teil der Mitarbeiter der Eurowings Charter zu Beginn des Transformationsprozesses Eurowings zu Germanwings hatte. Germanwings verzichtet – um die Einfachheit zu symbolisieren – bewusst auf eine Bildmarke.

Abbildung 7: **Logo der Marke Germanwings**

germanwings
Fly high, pay low.

GABLER GRAFIK

Der Claim des Unternehmens ergänzt die Wortmarke für den vollständigen Markenauftritt: Fly high. Pay low. Das bedeutet hohe Qualität, hohe Sicherheit, hohe Zuverlässigkeit – zu günstigen Preisen. Low-Cost-Airline also mit „Billigflieger" zu übersetzen wäre falsch.

Die Markenpositionierung und die Markenwerte wurden in eine Gestaltungssprache übersetzt, dem Germanwings Corporate Design. Es spiegelt durch die Farbwelt, Schriftschnitt, Formgebung, Materialwahl etc. die Positionierung wider. Das Design wurde in einem Corporate Design Manual detailliert dokumentiert und in allen gestaltungsrelevanten Anwendungen der Airline umgesetzt.

Abbildung 8: Germanwings Corporate Design

Silver: pared-down, simple, no frills, clean, reliable

Yellow: dynamic, cheeky, challenging, assertive

Aubergine: elegant, charming, safe, solid, warm

GABLER GRAFIK

5. Produkt und Service an Bord und Boden: Qualität trotz „no-frills"

Das Germanwings Produkt- und Servicekonzept ist klassen- beziehungsweise statuslos. Das Produkt an Bord und Boden wurde entsprechend der Qualitätspositionierung und der Designvorgaben entwickelt. Dabei wurde auf modische aber kurzlebige Elemente verzichtet, sondern die Anmutung und das Ambiente einer klassischen Premiumairline auf der Kurz- und Mittelstrecke übernommen. Komfortable Ledersitze mit einem breiteren Mittelsitz, klassische Uniformen der Mitarbeiter in Cockpit und Kabine, Sauberkeit und

Aufgeräumtheit an Bord und Boden u. v. m. kennzeichnen den Ansatz, eine Qualitätswahrnehmung beim Nachfrager auszulösen. An Bord wird dem Kunden ein umfangreiches Sortiment an Speisen, Getränken, Duty Free und Merchandising Produkten, zusammengefasst unter wechselnden Themen, kostenpflichtig angeboten, organisiert als Profit Center in Kooperation mit der Lufthansa Service Gesellschaft. Damit ist dem Prinzip no-frills dahingehend Rechnung getragen, dass der Kunde für das Kernprodukt bezahlt und sich individuelle Zusatzservices zukaufen kann. Ein Germanwings Bordmagazin sowie Zeitschriften können allen Passagieren gratis auf Basis von Verlagskooperationen wie bei klassischen Airlines angeboten werden.

Hinsichtlich der Serviceprozesse sind die prozessualen Vorgaben einer produktivitätsgetriebenen Low-Cost-Produktion sowie Kostenaspekte mit den Kundenerfordernissen in Einklang zu bringen. Beispielsweise ist kurze Verweildauer des Flugzeuges am Boden (Turnaround times) erfolgskritisch für eine hohe Produktivität der Flotte, maximal 25 Minuten sind der Richtwert. Die Nutzung einer Sitzplatzreservierung würde diesen Prozess gefährden und zudem zusätzliche Kosten verursachen. Folgerichtig wird ein Free-Seating angeboten, die Passagiere bekommen in der zeitlichen Reihenfolge beim Check-in eine Nummer, in dieser Reihenfolge wird dann auch an Bord gegangen und der Sitzplatz frei gewählt. Erfahrungswerte und Bordbefragungen zeigen die hohe Zufriedenheit der Kunden mit diesem Prozess, Kosten werden gespart und Prozesse beschleunigt. Low-Cost-Prozesse und Kundenzufriedenheit schließen sich nicht aus. Zudem spielt das Thema Service und Freundlichkeit bei der Ausbildung eine vorrangige Rolle, um in der Interaktion mit dem Nachfrager das Qualitätsversprechen jederzeit einlösen zu können. Durch ständige Innovationen, saisonale Produkt-Highlights und partnerfinanzierte Gratis-Zusatzleistungen wird versucht, auch im Bereich Produkt und Service Qualitätsstandards im Low-Cost-Segment zu setzen.

6. Germanwings Vertrieb: Ein E-Commerce-Unternehmen

Das Internet war von Anbeginn der Hauptvertriebskanal von Germanwings. Überschüssige Call Center Kapazitäten konnten nach Markteintritt sukzessive abgebaut werden. Der Internetkanal www.germanwings.com wurde stets den steigenden Auslastungskapazitäten angepasst. 94 Prozent aller Germanwings-Buchungen erfolgen über das Internet. An gewöhnlichen Wochentagen sind es zwischen 8000 und 10.000 Buchungen am Tag, bei speziellen Marketing-Aktionen wie den „Crazy Nights“ 15.000 Buchungen in der Stunde. Mit den „Crazy Nights“, bei denen mindestens 50.000 Tickets zu einem garantierten Günstig-Preis angeboten werden, setzte Germanwings europaweit Maßstäbe: Wettbewerber kopieren heute diese Aktionen. Mit 18 Millionen Seitenabrufen im Monat und 16 Millionen Clicks am Tag avancierte www.germanwings.com zu einem der beliebtesten Reiseportale in Deutschland. Die Website enthält überdies alle relevanten Informationen zu den Destinationen und Kooperationspartnern (Hotels, Autovermietungen etc.). Über Member Benefits wird ein Zusatznutzen für Germanwings-Passagiere geschaffen. Eine eigene Merchandising-Linie entstand. Produkte werden an Bord und im Online-Shop günstig angeboten. Außerdem wurde mit T-Mobile eine erste M-Commerce-Vereinbarung geschlossen: Flugtickets können via PDA (Personal Digital Assistent) bezahlt werden.

Neben dem Internet ist Germanwings auch über Call-Center und den Stationsverkauf buchbar. Zudem ist Germanwings auch im Reservierungssystem Amadeus integriert (Reisebüros), für Firmenkunden wurde ein spezifisches Angebot konzipiert, das deren Erfordernissen entgegenkommt (Firmenraten, Umbuchbarkeit, Abrechnungssysteme) und über einen spezifischen Internetauftritt angeboten wird. Das breite Spektrum der Vertriebskanäle soll die unterschiedlichen Anforderungen der Nachfrager treffen, die Dominanz des kostengünstigen Internets ist allerdings ein wesentlicher Baustein des Erfolges von Germanwings.

Abbildung 9: Vertriebskanäle bei Germanwings

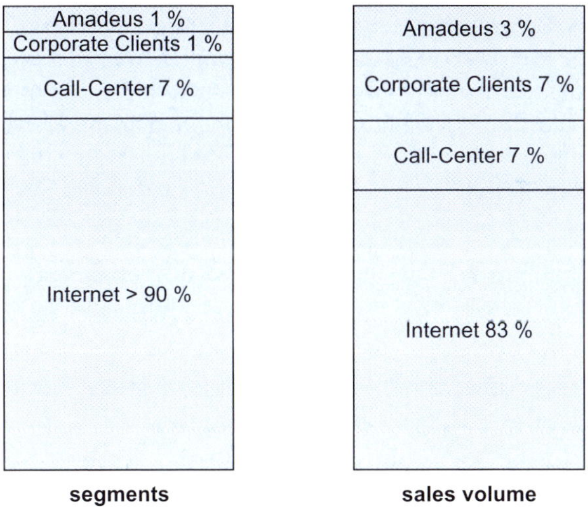

GABLER GRAFIK

7. Marketingkommunikation: Beschleuniger des Markenaufbaus

Die Marketingstrategie im engeren Sinne ist gekennzeichnet durch das zügige aber profitable Besetzen von Märkten unter rascher Durchsetzung der Preispositionierung und nachhaltiger Aufladung der Marke im Sinne der für Germanwings typischen Qualitätsdifferenzierung. Kommunikationsziele sind der zügigere Aufbau der Markenbekanntheit von Germanwings in den Zielgruppen der relevanten Catchments, die forcierte Bekanntmachung des Hauptvertriebskanals Internet und die Generierung entsprechenden Traffics, und damit die Sicherstellung der Absatzziele und Gewinnung von (Neu-)Kunden sowie die mittel- bis langfristige Durchsetzung der Markenpositionierung (Preis + Qualität) von Germanwings. Um diese Ziele zu erreichen, wurde im Rahmen der Markteinführung ein unkonventioneller, offensiver aber wertiger Markenauftritt mit Herausstellung der Preispositionierung „Fliegen ab 19 Euro“ gewählt. Der Aufbau von Markensympathie erfolgt durch die Ehrlichkeit in der Preiskommunikation (Inklusiv-Preise, gleiche Preislevel auf allen Strecken) und der Tonalität der Kundenansprache. Die Kosteneffizienz des Marketings wird durch hohen Anteil Marketing- und Medienkooperationen auf Barterbasis, Guerilla-Maßnahmen und Marketing-PR sichergestellt. In den europäischen Märkten stellen Marketing-und Medienkooperationen das kostengünstige Fundament der Marktbearbeitung dar. Medial wird auf die strategisch priorisierten Catchments fokussiert. Die Durchführung vielfältiger und regelmäßiger Preisaktionen stärkt die Preiswahrnehmung, setzt zusätzliche Akzente und unterstützt die taktische Absatzsteuerung streckenspezifisch.

Im Rahmen der kreativen Umsetzung werblicher Maßnahmen wurde ein unverwechselbarer Auftritt geschaffen, der Preis- und Netzangebot mit der Markenpositionierung verbindet, in allen Medien stark wirkt und das Potenzial für inhaltliche Weiterentwicklungen enthält. Folgende konzeptionelle Eckpunkte wurden definiert:

- Schaffung eines unverwechselbaren, merkfähigen Musters hinsichtlich Visualität und Tonalität auf Basis der Markenpositionierung und des Corporate Design,
- Signalisierung des Produktes (Airline) und des Eckpreises „ab 19 Euro“,
- Prominente Integration Marke und Claim,
- Crossmediale Umsetzbarkeit der Kernelemente des werblichen Auftritts,
- Plattform für Preis- und Netzangebote + Flexibilität für formale und inhaltliche Aufnahme weiterer Themen (Pünktlichkeit, Services etc.).

Die Mediastrategie zum Markteintritt setzte auf einen massiven durchgängigen Einsatz einer Vielzahl unterschiedlicher Medien, um die komplexe, breite Zielgruppenstruktur adäquat anzusprechen, eine Omnipräsenz der Marke/Angebote im Zielgebiet zu schaffen und eine breite positive Grunddisposition für die Marke und deren Angebot zu erreichen. Der Mediamix setzte auf eine mehrkanalig integrierte Kampagnenstruktur mit den Schwerpunkten Print und Outdoor sowie Funk und Promotions, ergänzt durch diverse

Online-Aktivitäten (zum Beispiel Banner, Pop-ups) auf reiseaffinen Websites. Flughafen-spezifische Kommunikationsmaßnahmen (Banner im Duty-Free-Bereich und Wartebereich etc.) sowie Flughafen-Events vervollständigen den medialen Auftritt.

Abbildung 10: **Marketingkommunikation bei Germanwings**

GABLER GRAFIK

8. Der Erfolg in Zahlen

Der Erfolg der Marke Germanwings lässt sich an unterschiedlichen Kennzahlen feststellen. Mit knapp drei Millionen Buchungen bis Ende 2003 wurde Germanwings zum Marktführer in Nordrhein-Westfalen und größter Anbieter am Standort Köln. Am Standort Stuttgart wird durch die Expansion zum Winterflugplan 2004/05 die Marktführerschaft im Marktsegment erreicht. Bis Ende 2003 wurden über 500.000 Kunden (Buchende) gewonnen, über 20 Prozent mit Wohnsitz im Ausland. In den relevanten Catchments

Nordrhein-Westfalen und Baden Württemberg wurde laut GfK (Gesellschaft für Konsumforschung) eine gestützte Markenbekanntheit von deutlich über 90 Prozent bei Privat- und Geschäftsreisenden erreicht. Der Anteil der Geschäftsreisenden beträgt über 40 Prozent. Hinsichtlich der Preiswahrnehmung als Airline mit einem günstigen Angebot liegt Germanwings jeweils auf Position Top 2 hinter Ryanair in den relevanten Märkten. Die Entwicklung der Berichterstattung seit November 2002 mit, laut Clipping-Analysen, 1.500 bis 2.000 Presseartikeln pro Monat im ersten Jahr nach Markteintritt zeigt die breite Presseresonanz für Germanwings.

PR und Unternehmenskommunikation sind ein fundamentaler Baustein für den effizienten Markenaufbau. Das Internet-Angebot www.germanwings.com konnte hinsichtlich Internet-Reichweite und Anzahl Unique Audience bereits bis Oktober 2003 Platz 2 hinter Lufthansa in der Kategorie Airlines erreichen, in 2004 sogar in einzelnen Monaten Platz 1 (Nielsen NetRatings).

Abbildung 11: **Entwicklung des Passagieraufkommens von Germanwings**

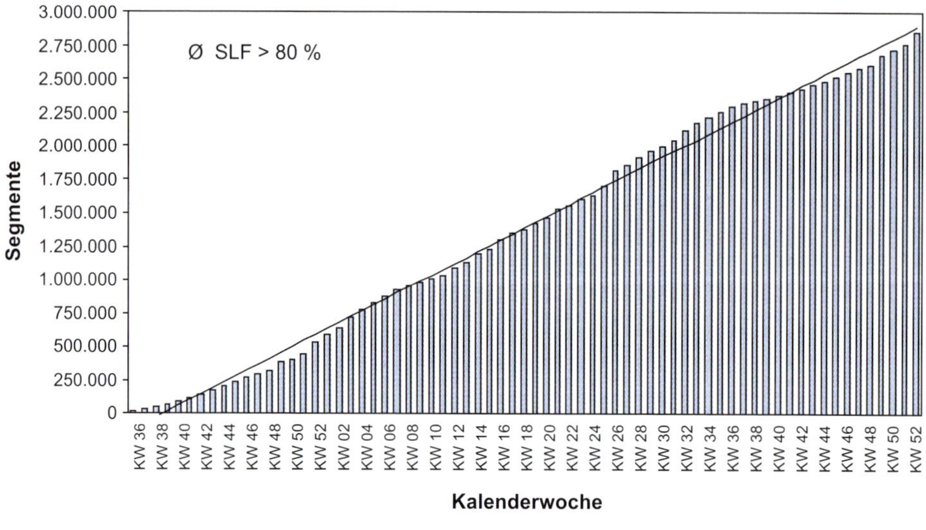

GABLER GRAFIK

9. Ausblick

Germanwings ist eine noch junge Marke, die in einem hart umkämpften Markt nicht nur überleben, sondern wachsen und eine führende Rolle einnehmen und auch im europäischen Ausland ihre Marktposition ausbauen will. Der Aufbau der neuen Marke, die Implementierung eines neuen Geschäftssystems in nur wenigen Monaten – sozusagen im Zeitraffer – wie auch das enorme aber nachhaltige und erfolgreiche Wachstum in den ersten zwei Jahren seit Markteintritt zeigt die Richtigkeit der strategischen Stoßrichtung und deren Umsetzung. Es zeigt auch, dass es sich auch in einem preissensiblen Markt unter hohem Zeit- und Wettbewerbsdruck lohnt, Energie und Geld in den systematischen, identitätsorientierten Markenaufbau zu investieren. Der Wettbewerbsdruck wird in den nächsten Monaten und Jahren noch einmal erheblich zunehmen, Konsolidierungen und das Verschwinden einiger Low-Cost-Anbieter vom Markt oder in eine Nische wird nicht ausbleiben. Germanwings ist durch die Bewährungsprobe der Launchphase gut gerüstet, der Optimierungsbedarf aber längst nicht gedeckt. Im Fokus steht dabei die Absicherung der Position als führender deutscher Low-Cost-Carrier, das nachhaltige und profitable Wachstum und die entschlossene Entwicklung neuer europäischer Märkte aus eigener Kraft oder durch Kooperationen. Die Erweiterung des Streckennetzes auf 34 Zielorte ab Köln und 16 Zielorte ab Stuttgart in 2004, die Entwicklung weiterer innerdeutscher Strecken (München und Hamburg), die forcierte Einbindung von touristischen Zielen im Sommerflugplan oder der Ausbau der führenden Position in den stark wachsenden osteuropäischen Märkten und in Skandinavien zeigt das Expansionsstreben von Germanwings. Mit der Erreichung des operativen Break-Even bereits im Sommer 2003, dem Break-Even zu Vollkosten im Frühjahr 2004 und dem realistischen Ziel eines positiven Ergebnisses für das Gesamtjahr 2004 beweist Germanwings sein Bekenntnis zu einem nachhaltigen, profitablen Wachstum.

Das Marktgeschehen wird weiterhin durch die Faktoren Preis und Flugplan dominiert werden. Jedoch werden langfristig Sättigungserscheinungen im Markt demjenigen einen Vorteil bieten, der Kunden nicht nur gewinnen, sondern zu regelmäßigen Wiederkäufern machen kann. Das ist alleine über den Preis nicht zu schaffen. Nur der Ausbau und die Neuentwicklung von weiteren kundenrelevanten Differenzierungselementen – symbolisiert durch die Marke – wird dies leisten können.

Markenmanagement als Motor der neuen Markenidentität DHL im Konzern Deutsche Post World Net

Wolfgang Giehl und Christoph Baumgarten

1.	**Einleitung**	**783**
2.	**Die Markenstrategie**	**783**
2.1	Ausgangslage	783
2.2	Von der Akquisition zur Integration	784
2.3	DHL wird zum Komplettanbieter	786
2.4	Corporate Design und Rebranding	787
2.41	Die Basics: DHL im Zeichen des Konzerns	787
2.42	Der Außenauftritt: Rebranding im großen Stil	789
2.43	Die Unternehmenskleidung: Marke hautnah	791
2.44	Die weltweite Umsetzung	793
2.5	Die Markenkampagne	794
2.6	Der Claim	794
2.7	Der Rollout-Plan	795
3.	**Die Markenkampagne im Detail**	**796**
3.1	TV-Spot international	796
3.2	Anzeigen international	798
3.21	Eine Botschaft geht um die Welt	798
3.22	Die Integration der Partner	800
3.23	Die Anzeigenschaltung	802
3.3	TV und Print speziell für Deutschland	802
3.4	Die Follow-up-Kampagne	803
3.5	Internet	804
3.6	Direktmarketing	805
3.7	Broschüren	805
3.8	Veranstaltungen	806

Die **Konzernfarbe Gelb** ist das prägnanteste Gestaltungsmerkmal von Deutsche Post World Net und spielt als visuelle Klammer die entscheidende Rolle. Konsequent wurde der DHL-Schriftzug farblich und typografisch verjüngt und auf das charakteristische Gelb gestellt.

Zu den prägnanten Merkmalen des Konzerns gehören neben der Unternehmensfarbe Gelb die **Leistungsfelder**. Sie beschreiben die Tätigkeitsbereiche der eigenständigen Leistungsmarken und sind ihnen grafisch klar und einheitlich zugeordnet. Auch DHL wurde konsequent in diese Systematik eingebunden. Die Bezeichnungen der vier Leistungsfelder der Marke DHL – Express, Freight, Danzas Air & Ocean und Solutions – erscheinen in den bekannten kursiven Versalien auf dem unverwechselbaren Hintergrund in Lamellenoptik (vgl. Abbildung 6).

Abbildung 5: **Das alte Logo**

GABLER GRAFIK

Abbildung 6: **Das neue Logo und seine Leistungsfelder**

GABLER GRAFIK

Das Erscheinungsbild der neuen DHL entspricht nun dem der beiden bestehenden Konzernmarken Deutsche Post und Postbank; **DHL wurde passgenau integriert** in das Corporate Design von Deutsche Post World Net.

Nach der Umstellung prüften weltweite Marktforschungen die internationale Akzeptanz des neuen Markenauftritts. Das Ergebnis: Erscheinungsbild und Farbkombination werden durchgehend positiv beurteilt. Die Kombination Rot/Gelb signalisiert Energie und Kraft und verstärkt die Dynamik des neuen DHL-Schriftzugs.

2.42 Der Außenauftritt: Rebranding im großen Stil

Das Rebranding ist überall da besonders wichtig, wo Nachfrager und Mitarbeiter in Kontakt mit der neuen DHL kommen – überall da, wo die **Marke konkret erlebbar** wird: an weltweit rund **75.000 Fahrzeugen, 250 Flugzeugen, 4.000 Gebäuden, an der Geschäftsausstattung und allen Verpackungen, an der Kleidung für 45.000 Mitarbeiterinnen und Mitarbeiter und auf über 100 Internet-Seiten** (vgl. Abbildung 7, 8 und 9).

Abbildung 7: Rebranding von Fahrzeugen und Flugzeugen

GABLER GRAFIK

Abbildung 8: **Das durchgängige Rebranding visualisiert die Markenintegration. Pünktlich zum Kampagnenstart war die neue DHL für Nachfrager und Mitarbeiter weltweit erlebbar.**

GABLER GRAFIK

Die Rebranding-Maßnahmen begannen am 1. April 2003. So war die neue Marke zum Startschuss der Werbekampagne am 1. Mai bereits in der Öffentlichkeit präsent. Von April bis Ende Mai 2003 wurden die Mitarbeiterinnen und Mitarbeiter von DHL, Danzas und Euro Express europaweit in internen Kick-off-Veranstaltungen auf die neue Marke eingestimmt, um angemessen auf Kundenfragen zum neuen Look, zum Leistungsportfolio und zur Konzernstruktur reagieren zu können.

Abbildung 9: **Zeitplan für die Umsetzung der Rebranding-Maßnahmen**

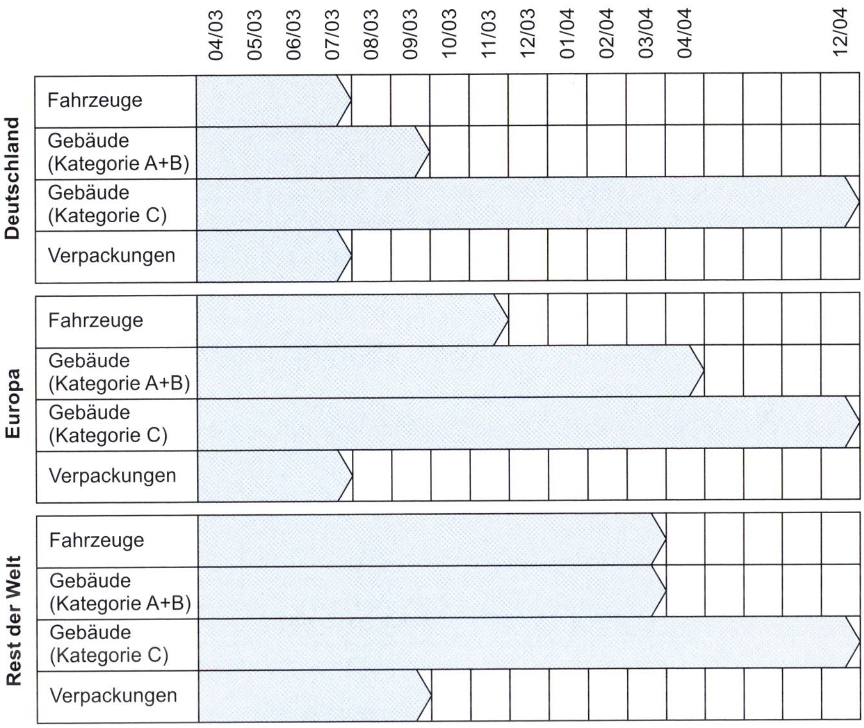

GABLER GRAFIK

2.43 Die Unternehmenskleidung: Marke hautnah

Unternehmenskleidung muss passen: zum Corporate Design, zum gesamten Markenauftritt und nicht zuletzt zu den Mitarbeiterinnen und Mitarbeitern, die sich darin wohl fühlen sollen, um ihr Unternehmen angemessen nach außen repräsentieren zu können. So trägt **Corporate Wear** entscheidend zum Unternehmenserfolg bei.

Neben dem Branding von Fahrzeugen und Gebäuden gehörte die Entwicklung einer neuen Unternehmenskleidung zu den Kernelementen des DHL-Relaunch. Zunächst gab es eine Übergangslösung: Bestimmte Mitarbeiterinnen und Mitarbeiter (vor allem der ehemaligen Deutschen Post Euro Express in den europäischen Ländern) erhielten ab Mai 2003 ein „Starter Pack" unter anderem mit T-Shirt, Jacke und Kappe im neuen Look. Ein **Übergangsdesign** kam in 54 Ländern weltweit zum Tragen. Mit der neuen Unternehmenskleidung schließlich wurde der durchgängig einheitliche Außenauftritt von DHL weltweit abgerundet (vgl. Abbildung 10). Bei der Realisierung standen als Ziele im Fokus:

- die Unterstützung von DHL-Markenattributen wie Modernität und Dynamik,
- die Stärkung von Bekanntheit und Vertrauen in DHL,
- die **Nutzung der täglich millionenfachen Kundenkontakte**, um den gemeinsamen Markenauftritt zu stärken,
- eine eindeutige Abgrenzung zum Wettbewerb sowie
- ein professioneller Außenauftritt.

Bei der Entwicklung (gestartet im Juni 2003) wurde auf langjährige Erfahrung zurückgegriffen. Es ging um die Ausgewogenheit zwischen Funktionalität, Qualität, Design und Kosten; außerdem mussten **kulturelle, klimatische und juristische Bedingungen** der einzelnen Ländern berücksichtigt werden. Ab Februar 2004 wurden die neuen Kleidungsstücke per Tragetest in acht Ländern auf ihre Eignung im Tagesgeschäft geprüft. Durch die Auswahl der Standorte (USA, Mexiko, Deutschland, Spanien, Schweden, Südkorea, Südafrika, Singapur) wurden unterschiedliche Klimazonen ebenso abgedeckt wie die integrierten Unternehmen Deutsche Post Euro Express, DHL, Danzas und Airborne.

Ab August 2004 wurden alle DHL-Mitarbeiterinnen und -Mitarbeiter weltweit mit der neuen Unternehmenskleidung ausgestattet. Erste Analysen bei Nachfragern zeigten positive Ergebnisse und unterstrichen die Bedeutung der Corporate Wear für den Markenauftritt der neuen DHL.

Abbildung 10: **Corporate Wear: die Marke DHL hautnah erleben**

GABLER GRAFIK

2.44 Die weltweite Umsetzung

Die reibungslose Realisierung des weltweiten Rebranding verlangt eine umfassende und zeitnahe Einbindung der betroffenen internen Abteilungen sowie der externen Dienstleister.

Für die weltweit synergetische Umsetzung der Rebranding-Maßnahmen wurden auf einer zentralen Website **Toolboxes online** bereitgestellt: eine Sammlung informativer und anschaulicher Design-Tools, die den korrekten Umgang mit dem neuen DHL-Design erläutern (vgl. Abbildung 11). Zu zwölf verschiedenen Themen – von der Gebäude-, Verpackungs- und Give-away-Gestaltung bis zur Erstellung von Internet-Seiten – gibt es Broschüren zum Download. Als zusätzliche Werkzeuge stehen Handbücher und CD-ROMs zur Verfügung, ergänzend aktuelles Bildmaterial. Außerdem wurden internationale Hotlines eingerichtet, um alle eventuellen Fragen zum neuen Corporate Design zu beantworten.

Der Erfolg: Bereits Ende 2003 war das DHL-Rebranding für die wichtigsten Bereiche weltweit abgeschlossen.

Abbildung 11: **Toolboxes für jede Maßnahme: praktische Unterstützung für die Umsetzung des neuen Designs**

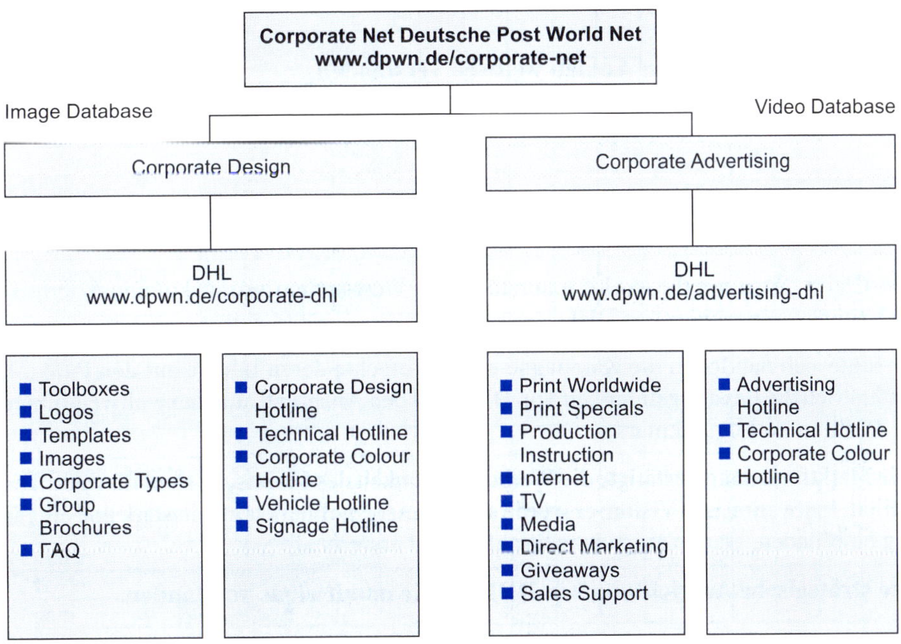

GABLER GRAFIK

Die Öffentlichkeit wurde über die Kampagne zur Neupositionierung von DHL am 30. April 2003 auf einer Pressekonferenz in Berlin informiert. Am nächsten Tag startete die weltweite TV-, Anzeigen- und Plakatkampagne. Direct Mailings erläuterten Geschäftskunden das neue DHL-Leistungsspektrum, Postwurfsendungen informierten Privatkunden. Die **DHL-Roadshow** begann ihren Weg durch ganz Europa und stellte die neue Marke Nachfragern, Journalisten und Entscheidern vor.

Die **internationale Anzeigenkampagne** wurde von Mai bis September 2003 in über 50 Ländern geschaltet. In Europa erreichten die „More"-Motive mehr als 110 Millionen, außerhalb Europas rund **240 Millionen Leserinnen und Leser**. Im gleichen Zeitraum lief der **TV-Spot „Pyramide"** weltweit in über 30 Ländern; insgesamt 674 Millionen Zuschauerinnen und Zuschauer wurden erreicht. Der Schwerpunkt der Schaltungen (für Print und TV) lag auf Europa und auf den Wachstumsmärkten im asiatisch-pazifischen Raum.

Für die Nachfrager in Deutschland, die den Paketdienst traditionell als Leistung der Deutschen Post kennen, wurden parallel zur „More"-Kampagne Anzeigen und TV-Spots entwickelt, die (mit den Gottschalk-Brüdern) die einfache Botschaft transportierten: Pakete bringt jetzt DHL.

3. Die Markenkampagne im Detail

3.1 TV-Spot international

Der internationale Spot thematisierte die erweiterte Leistungspalette von DHL: Die neue DHL bietet umfassende, individuelle Logistiklösungen. Dank ihrer Flexibilität, Schnelligkeit, Präzision und Zuverlässigkeit ist sie auch bei sehr ambitionierten Projekten die richtige Ansprechpartnerin.

Um diese Botschaften zu transportieren, bediente sich der Spot der Form großen **Hollywood-Kinos**. Am Beispiel einer der herausragenden architektonischen Leistungen der Menschheit, dem Bau der Pyramiden von Gizeh, demonstriert er die zentrale Rolle der Logistik. Und speziell der Logistiklösungen, wie DHL sie bietet (vgl. Abbildung 13).

Zwischen Mai und September 2003 lief der Spot in weltweit 30 Ländern sowie auf überregionalen Sendern in Asien und Lateinamerika (vgl. Abbildung 14). Der Schwerpunkt lag dabei auf Europa und dem asiatisch-pazifischen Raum. Dabei wurden **weltweit insgesamt 674 Millionen Zuschauerinnen und Zuschauer** erreicht (322 Millionen in Europa, außer Deutschland, 326 Millionen im asiatisch-pazifischen Raum und 26 Millionen in Osteuropa, dem Nahen Osten und Afrika).

Abbildung 13 **Im TV-Spot „Pyramid" liefert DHL auf dem See- und Luftweg Material für den Bau der Pyramiden von Gizeh.**

GABLER GRAFIK

Abbildung 14: Schaltplan des internationalen TV-Spots

	April		Mai				Juni					Juli				August					September			
Länder	21.04.	28.04.	04.05.	11.05.	18.05.	25.05.	01.06.	08.06.	15.06.	22.06.	29.06.	06.07.	13.07.	20.07.	27.07.	03.08.	10.08.	17.08.	24.08.	31.08.	07.09.	14.09.	21.09.	28.09.
Asiatisch-pazifischer Raum				■	■	■	■	■	■	■	■	■	■	■	■	■	■	■	■	■	■	■	■	
Europa				■	■	■	■	■	■	■	■	■	■											
Naher Osten und Afrika									■	■	■	■	■	■										

Länder, in denen Anzeigen geschaltet wurden

Asiatisch-pazifischer Raum
Gesamtregional, Australien, China (Städte-spezifisch), Hongkong, Indien, Indonesien, Japan, Korea, Malaysia, Philippinen, Singapur, Taiwan, Thailand

Europa
Dänemark, Finnland, Frankreich, Großbritannien, Island, Italien, Schweden, Slowakei, Spanien, Tschechische Republik, Türkei

Naher Osten und Afrika
Naher Osten, Südafrika

GABLER GRAFIK

3.2 Anzeigen international

3.21 Eine Botschaft geht um die Welt

Die Anzeigen visualisieren den strategischen Ansatz der Relaunch-Kampagne: DHL bietet jetzt mehr. Die knappen Headlines kreisen um den Kernbegriff „More" (vgl. Abbildung 15). Zusammen mit ausdrucksstarken Bildern bringen sie die Botschaft der Anzeigen auf den Punkt: DHL kann jetzt noch mehr als bisher. Und in vielen Bereichen mehr als der Wettbewerb.

Insgesamt zwölf verschiedene Motive für den internationalen Einsatz kommunizierten alle Facetten von „Mehr", der erweiterten Leistungsfähigkeit von DHL: Schnelligkeit, Flexibilität, Zuverlässigkeit, Sorgfalt, das weltweite Distributionsnetzwerk, die Kompetenz der Mitarbeiterinnen und Mitarbeiter, die Größe des Unternehmens sowie seiner Produkt- und Servicepalette. Zielgruppe dabei waren in erster Linie Geschäftskunden, Entscheider und Multiplikatoren.

Die Kernbotschaft der Relaunch-Kampagne funktionierte problemlos in allen weltweit eingesetzten Adaptionen (vgl. Abbildung 16). Die Motive wurden in jedem Land und in jeder Sprache sofort verstanden. Ohne großen Erklärungsbedarf transportierten sie die Vorteile der neuen Marke: im internationalen Umfeld (neben der erhöhten Leistungsfähigkeit) vor allem die globale Präsenz und die Flexibilität von DHL.

Abbildung 15: **Die zwölf „More"-Anzeigenmotive für internationalen Einsatz visualisieren eindrucksvoll die Strategie der Relaunch-Kampagne: DHL kann jetzt noch mehr.**

GABLER GRAFIK

Abbildung 16: **Die prägnant formulierte Kernbotschaft ließ sich problemlos international adaptieren und wurde überall verstanden – hier eine Anzeige für China.**

GABLER GRAFIK

3.22 Die Integration der Partner

In Belgien, Frankreich, Polen und Spanien gingen die Euro Express-Unternehmen Van Gend & Loos, Ducros, Servisco und Guipuzcoana in DHL über. In Skandinavien, im Baltikum, in Russland und der Ukraine wurde Danzas in DHL integriert. Um diesen Vorgang zu kommunizieren, wurden über die Basismotive der Kampagne hinaus weitere Anzeigenvarianten benötigt. Der flexible Ansatz der „More"-Kampagne bot auch hier reichlich Raum für speziell auf die europäische Situation zugeschnittene Umsetzungen. Mühelos visualisieren die adaptierten Motive die Integration der europäischen Partner in DHL (vgl. Abbildung 17).

Abbildung 17: **Die Partnerunternehmen wurden visuell und sprachlich in die neue Marke DHL eingebunden.**

3.23 Die Anzeigenschaltung

Der Startschuss der internationalen Kampagne fiel Ende April 2003 in Europa. Bis Ende September erschienen die „More"-Motive weltweit in über 50 Ländern. Auf dem Kampagnenschaltplan standen Titel der nationalen und supranationalen Tages-, Wirtschafts- und Fachpresse. Neben Europa lag der Schwerpunkt der Kampagne auf den Wachstumsmärkten im asiatisch-pazifischen Raum. Spezielle Motive unterstrichen die Präsenz und Leistungsfähigkeit der neuen DHL in diesen wichtigen Märkten. In Europa erreichten die Schaltungen der „More"-Motive mehr als 110 Millionen Leserinnen und Leser; dazu kamen rund 240 Millionen Rezipienten in der restlichen Welt.

3.3 TV und Print speziell für Deutschland

Auf dem Heimatmarkt von Deutsche Post World Net gehört der Paketdienst traditionell zu den Aufgaben der Deutschen Post. Mit dem Relaunch übernahm DHL diese Aufgabe. Speziell für Privatkunden in Deutschland wurde deshalb ein besonderer kommunikativer Ansatz neben der „More"-Kampagne notwendig. Die zentrale Botschaft hier: „Pakete bringt jetzt DHL".

Ein zusätzliches Ziel dieser Kampagne war die Steigerung der Bekanntheit von DHL und des Wissens über die Zugehörigkeit des Unternehmens zum Konzern Deutsche Post World Net. Die Privatkundenkampagne nutzte sowohl im Fernsehen als auch bei Anzeigen die Akzeptanz der etablierten Testimonials Thomas und Christoph Gottschalk.

Der TV-Spot „Speed" transportiert seine Botschaften in dynamischen Bildern. Thomas und Christoph Gottschalk sitzen im Auto und werden von einem Euro Express-Wagen überholt. Plötzlich erscheint ein Hubschrauber, Männer seilen sich ab und fangen an, den Wagen umzuspritzen. Innerhalb von Minuten wird aus Euro Express DHL. Die Botschaft: Postpakete bringt jetzt DHL, der weltweite Express-Dienstleister von Deutsche Post World Net. „Speed" startete im Mai 2003 bei den großen Privatsendern. Die Schaltungen erzielten eine Nettoreichweite von 37,6 Millionen oder 85 Prozent und generierten Kontakte von 464,4 Millionen.

Durch die besondere Situation im Paketdienst war auch im Printbereich eine eigene Anzeigenlinie für Deutschland nötig. Analog zur deutschen TV-Kampagne informierten die Brüder Gottschalk über die Neupositionierung von DHL. Zwei Anzeigen- und ein Plakatmotiv zeigten die Köpfe der Brüder und knappe Dialoge zur neuen Aufgabe von DHL beim Paketversand in Deutschland (vgl. Abbildung 18). Die Privatkundenlinie erschien als Anzeige in regionalen Tageszeitungen an drei Wochen zwischen Mitte Mai und Anfang Juni 2003. Im gleichen Zeitraum wurde das Plakat in Ballungsgebieten gehängt.

Ein großformatiger Beileger in der Frankfurter Allgemeinen Zeitung und dem Handelsblatt erschien am 7. Mai 2003, wenige Tage nach Beginn der Relaunch-Kampagne, und vermittelte Geschäftskunden die geballte Kraft von DHL, das Mehr an Kraft, Dynamik und Effizienz. Im imposanten DIN-A2-Format präsentierte der Beileger auf acht Seiten die neue DHL inklusive Daten und Fakten – und lieferte der Geschäftswelt damit einen umfassenden Eindruck von der internationalen Leistungsfähigkeit der neuen Marke.

Abbildung 18: **Die Anzeigen speziell für deutsche Privatkunden bringen Kerninformationen auf den Punkt.**

GABLER GRAFIK

3.4 Die Follow-up-Kampagne

Der deutsche **TV-Spot der Relaunch-Kampagne** hatte hervorragende Effizienzwerte erzielt, Gefühl und Verstand gleichermaßen angesprochen, die Bekanntheit der Marke DHL erhöht und das Vertrauen in sie gestärkt. An diese Erfolge knüpfte der Spot der Follow-up-Kampagne an, um die Markenpositionierung weiter auszubauen. Wieder lautete die Botschaft „Postpakete bringt jetzt DHL“. Vorrangig kommunizierte der zweite deutsche TV-Spot in actiongeladenen Sequenzen die weltweite Präsenz von DHL; Träger der

Botschaft blieben die Testimonials Thomas und Christoph Gottschalk. Im September und Oktober 2003 lief der TV-Spot auf klassischen Kanälen und Nachrichtensendern. Er kam auf rund **246 Millionen Kontakte** in der Zielgruppe der 14- bis 59-Jährigen.

Die Follow-up-Kampagne knüpfte an den konzeptionellen Ansatz der „More"-Motive an. Die zentrale Aussage „DHL bietet mehr" bekam einen neuen Schwerpunkt: Die vier Leistungsfelder Express, Freight, Danzas Air & Ocean und Solutions rückten in den Mittelpunkt, die Kommunikation dehnte sich aus auf die gesamte Bandbreite der Produkte und Leistungen und positionierte DHL als **One-stop-shopping-Partner**. Damit führte die Follow-up-Kampagne die Argumente der Relaunch-Kampagne fort und untermauerte den „Mehr"-Anspruch der neuen DHL in Express, Land-, Luft- und Seefracht sowie Logistik durch **konkretere Leistungsinformationen**. Unkonventionelle Bildmotive sorgten für hohe Aufmerksamkeit; die Headlines stellten einen engen Bezug zu den Angeboten der neuen DHL her.

Die Follow-up-Kampagne lief von Anfang September bis November 2003. Die Anzeigen wurden zunächst **für Deutschland und adaptiv für weitere 17 europäische Länder** eingesetzt. Eine Ausweitung auf die Zukunftsmärkte in Asien und Osteuropa war zu diesem Zeitpunkt bereits geplant. Schwerpunktmäßig wurde die Wirtschaftspresse (vor allem mit hoher Leserschaft im Mittelstand) bedient. Insgesamt erzielten die Anzeigen rund 1,5 Millionen Kontakte in Deutschland und rund 138 Millionen europaweit.

3.5 Internet

Einen Monat vor dem Start der internationalen Werbekampagne wurden die internationale .com-Website sowie die 76 alten DHL-Länder-Sites, die 28 Danzas-Länder-Sites und die zwölf Euro Express Länder-Sites in aller Welt in den neuen DHL-Webauftritt überführt. Ein zentrales **Corporate Portal Strategy Team** koordinierte die Neugestaltung und stellte sicher, dass www.DHL.com am 30. März 2003 mit neuer Struktur, neuen Inhalten und im neuen Design online gehen konnte.

Neben der Einheitlichkeit des Auftritts war ein zentrales Ziel der neuen Website der benutzerfreundliche Übergang zur neuen DHL: Nachfrager sollen gewohnte Funktionalitäten problemlos wiederfinden. So wurden die wichtigsten Anwendungen wie Track & Trace ins neue Design integriert, außerdem alle Produkte und Services der neuen DHL sowie ein Abriss der **Unternehmensgeschichten** von DHL, Danzas und Euro Express.

3.6 Direktmarketing

Weltweit erhielten DHL-Geschäftskunden ein aufmerksamkeitsstark gestaltetes Mailing mit Antwortcoupon und Rückumschlag. Basis für diese internationale Maßnahme war eine Masterversion in englischer Sprache. Sie stellte einen einheitlichen Auftritt in den Zielländern sicher. Das Mailing adaptierte die parallel laufende Anzeigenkampagne „More"; es informierte über den DHL-Relaunch und den Zusammenschluss von DHL, Danzas und Euro Express. Kommuniziert wurden die Vorteile dieser neuen Struktur. Insgesamt ging das Mailing an **rund eine Million Nachfrager in über 100 Ländern**. Die Responsequote in den verschiedenen Ländern war mit Werten zwischen 3,5 Prozent und 26,5 Prozent höchst unterschiedlich und entspricht einem Durchschnitt von acht Prozent.

In Deutschland wurden Privat- und Geschäftskunden ab der 19. Kalenderwoche (5. bis 11. Mai 2003) zielgruppenspezifisch über die neue DHL informiert. **Privatkunden** erhielten eine Postwurfsendung, die das neue Erscheinungsbild ihres Paket- und Expressdienstleisters vorstellte und das Unternehmen, die neue Marke und den Konzern erläuterte. Der Flyer beinhaltete darüber hinaus ein Gewinnspiel plus Antwortkarte. Auch in den Filialen der Deutschen Post lag eine Broschüre aus. **Geschäftskunden** informierte ein personalisiertes Mailing über die neue Marke und ihr Entstehen (vgl. Abbildung 19). Es enthielt ein sechsseitiges Faltblatt über die Vorteile der neuen DHL (internationale Reichweite, breites Produktportfolio) und ein Antwortfax zur Anforderung der DHL-Image-Broschüre. Für Geschäftskunden gab es außerdem einen Flyer, den die Mitarbeiterinnen und Mitarbeiter bei der Paketzustellung überreichten.

- **Die Postwurfsendung erreichte alle deutschen Haushalte.**
- **Das Geschäftskunden-Mailing wurde an rund 174.000 Ansprechpartner in Unternehmen geschickt und hatte eine Responserate von über acht Prozent.**
- **Der Geschäftskunden-Flyer wurde 300.000-mal überreicht.**

3.7 Broschüren

Auf 20 farbigen Seiten stellte die **Image-Broschüre** die neue DHL vor. Sie beschrieb die Unternehmen, die unter dem Dach der neuen Marke zusammengefasst wurden, und stellte die Vorteile dieser geballten Kompetenz heraus. Ausführlich wurden die vier Leistungsfelder, ihr Produkt- und Leistungsspektrum sowie der konkrete **Kundennutzen** dargestellt. Kundenaussagen belegten die Kompetenz von DHL in den Bereichen Express, Transport, Luft- und Seefracht und logistische Komplettlösungen. Die Image-Broschüre wurde zunächst in einer englischen und einer deutschen Basisversion erstellt und dann sukzessive in weitere Landessprachen übertragen.

Abbildung 19: Flyer für Geschäftskunden

GABLER GRAFIK

Mit dem neuen Markenauftritt von DHL mussten auch individuelle **Produktinformationen** und umfassende Informationen zu den einzelnen Leistungsfeldern dem neuen Design angepasst werden. So wurde in Deutschland speziell für Geschäftskunden eine umfangreiche Broschüre zum Leistungsfeld Express entwickelt – mit allen Produkten und Leistungen, die vorher von Euro Express angeboten wurden. Informationen zu Produkten wie POSTPAKET oder PLUSPÄCKCHEN erschienen ebenfalls im rot-gelben Design der neuen DHL.

3.8 Veranstaltungen

Die Marke DHL erlebbar machen durch die Inszenierung des neuen Markenauftritts: Das war das Ziel der DHL-Roadshow. Der **Kick-off** fand am 30. April 2003 im Flughafen Berlin-Tempelhof statt. Den geladenen Pressevertretern und Top-Kunden stellten Dr. Klaus Zumwinkel, Vorstandsvorsitzender von Deutsche Post World Net, und Dr. Peter E. Kruse, Vorstand DHL Express Europa, die geplanten Kommunikationsmaßnahmen zum DHL-Relaunch vor. Unterstützt wurden sie von Thomas und Christoph Gottschalk. Höhepunkt der Präsentation war die Premiere des deutschen TV-Spots.

Nach dem Kick-off in Berlin ging die **DHL-Show „on the road"**. Zwischen Mai und September 2003 gastierte sie in vier deutschen und 14 weiteren europäischen Städten. Jeweils 500 bis 800 Nachfrager, Entscheider und Pressevertreter erlebten ein umfassendes Programm aus Information, Unterhaltung und Show. In einem separaten Informationsbereich konnte man sich via Room-in-room-Installationen mit Multimedia-Terminals sowie Touchpad-Info-Terminals, Projektionsflächen und Performances über DHL und die geplanten Relaunch-Maßnahmen informieren. Eröffnet wurde die Veranstaltung mit der Begrüßungsansprache des jeweiligen Country Managers.

Neben der DHL-Relaunch-Tour boten **Messen** Gelegenheit, die neue Marke und ihre vier Leistungsfelder einem breiten Fachpublikum vorzustellen. Zwei internationale Logistikmessen kurz nach dem Relaunch der Marke DHL wurden dafür genutzt. Auf der „transport logistik" in München (20. bis 24. Mai 2003) erlebten rund 40.000 Besucher und 2.000 Aussteller die neue DHL mit ihren Leistungsfeldern Express, Freight, Danzas Air & Ocean und Solutions. Einen Monat später präsentierte sich die neue Marke erstmals im europäischen Ausland: auf der „SIL" in Barcelona/Spanien (17. bis 20. Juni 2003). Das Stand-Design in den Markenfarben Gelb und Rot ließ das Kampagnenmotto „Mehr Power" aus sechs Metern Höhe weit in die Messehallen leuchten. Der Stand, thematisch gegliedert in die vier Leistungsfelder, bot Raum für Information und Beratung ebenso wie für Emotion: eine Show, die Messe-Besucher auch atmosphärisch auf die neue Marke einstimmte – und gleichzeitig die Markenidentifikation des DHL-Teams stärkte.

4. Das Ergebnis: Mehr Wirkung

Der massive Werbedruck wurde belohnt. Die Marktforschung ergab eine **hohe Kampagneneffizienz**. Die Maßnahmen generierten Aufmerksamkeit, sprachen Gefühl wie Verstand an und transportierten die Kernbotschaft unmissverständlich: DHL bringt jetzt ein Mehr an Leistung. Das Vertrauen in die Marke wurde deutlich gestärkt; die Präsenz von DHL stieg signifikant im Bewusstsein der Zielgruppen. Ein Beispiel: Nach Ausstrahlung des TV-Spots „Speed" stieg das Wissen um die Konzernzugehörigkeit bei den Privatkunden um 35 Prozent auf 68 Prozent und bei den Geschäftskunden um 21 Prozent auf 76 Prozent. Die zentralen Image-Dimensionen Modernität, Schnelligkeit und Dynamik wurden durch den Spot positiv aufgeladen. Die gesamte Kampagne wurde durchgehend von Marktforschungs-Trackings begleitet. Die Ergebnisse:

- **Die Kunden haben die Botschaften verstanden und angenommen.**
- **Die intendierten Inhalte wurden von den Empfängern aufgenommen.**
- **Die Awareness für die neue Marke konnte erheblich gesteigert werden.**
- **Die Zugehörigkeit der Marke DHL zum Konzern Deutsche Post World Net wird wahrgenommen. Ein beidseitig positiver Image-Transfer findet statt.**

Die Presse reagierte entsprechend. In regionalen, überregionalen und internationalen Medien, in Tageszeitungen, Nachrichtenmagazinen, Finanz-, Wirtschafts- und Fachzeitschriften erschienen über 300 Abdrucke. Zwischen März und Juli 2003 berichteten mehr als 100 Internet-Seiten über den Relaunch. Vom British Brand Council wurde die neue Marke DHL zur **„Superbrand 2003“** gewählt. In Asien machte eine Kundenbefragung von Readers Digest im April 2004 DHL zur **„Gold Superbrand“**.

Fazit: Die Implementierung des neuen Designs, der neuen Markenoberfläche von DHL und die weltweite Kommunikationskampagne haben in kürzester Zeit eine starke neue Marke im Markt positioniert. Marktforschung und internationale Medienresonanz bestätigen den Markenerfolg von DHL und damit das konsequente Markenmanagement im Konzern Deutsche Post World Net.

Der Konzernfarbe Gelb als Gestaltungselement – im Feng Shui (der asiatischen Lehre des Wohnens) die Farbe der Langlebigkeit! – kam hierbei eine entscheidende Rolle zu: als Markensignal für Kunden, Meinungsbildner und Mitarbeiter.

5. Die interne Kommunikation

5.1 Information und Emotion

Innerhalb des Gesamtprojektes wird – in konzeptioneller Anlehnung an die externe Kampagne – eine eigenständige interne Kommunikationskampagne entwickelt. Die kommunikativen Intentionen: Mitarbeiterinnen und Mitarbeiter adäquat informieren, Ängste nehmen, **die Integration glaubhaft vermitteln** – auch hinsichtlich der Arbeitsplatzbedingungen. Um möglichst viele Menschen zu erreichen, wurden unterschiedliche Kommunikationswege genutzt. Die Kampagne enthielt sachliche Elemente mit Informationscharakter ebenso wie emotionale, dynamische und interaktive Elemente mit einem unterhaltsamen Schwerpunkt.

Die Mitarbeitermaßnahmen transportierten folgende Kernbotschaften:

- Persönliche und berufliche **Entwicklungschancen**,
- **Identifikation** mit dem globalen Unternehmen DHL,
- **Aufmerksamkeit** für die unterschiedliche Betroffenheit,
- **Selbstbewusstsein** als Marktführer und
- **Spaß** am Integrationsprozess.

Schon ab November 2002, also weit vor der offiziellen Markteinführung, berichteten die weltweiten Mitarbeitermedien umfassend über die bevorstehende Zusammenführung von Deutsche Post Euro Express, DHL und Danzas über **die Markenneugestaltung und ihre Hintergründe**. Im März und April 2003 folgte die Verteilung von zielgruppenspezifischen Broschüren, im Anschluss zwei Plakatmotive in elf Sprachen und ein Begrüßungspaket für alle Beschäftigten der neuen Marke DHL. Parallel dazu startete im April die erste von insgesamt 13 Kick-off-Veranstaltungen, die bis Anfang September in sieben europäischen Ländern die Mitarbeiterinnen und Mitarbeiter für die neue Marke DHL begeisterte.

5.2 Printmedien und -maßnahmen

Über die **regelmäßigen Mitarbeitermedien** Management *Mail*, The Network, PREMIUM Post (vgl. Abbildung 20), Partner Filiale und den STAR Newsletter wurde der Relaunch der Marke für alle Mitarbeiterinnen und Mitarbeiter direkt und konkret thematisiert und ihnen kontinuierlich näher gebracht.

Abbildung 20: Mitarbeiterzeitung PREMIUM Post, Ausgabe November 2002

Informationen zum Programm STAR auf den Seiten 1 bis 5!

Deutsche Post World Net
MAIL EXPRESS LOGISTICS FINANCE

PREMIUM Post

Die aktuelle Mitarbeiterzeitung — Nr. 11 / 2002

G 19205

SEITE 7

Polizeiuniform kommt im Paket

Die rund 25.000 Polizisten des Landes Baden-Württemberg erhalten ihre Dienstkleidung aus dem Logistik-Zentrum in Ditzingen mit Deutsche Post Euro Express.

AKTUELL

Neuer Konzernvorstand

Seit dem 1. November 2002 verantwortet Dr. Frank Appel als Konzernvorstand das neue Ressort »Corporate Services«. Hierzu gehören die Bereiche STAR, Konzernentwicklung, Recht, Konzerneinkauf, Konzerninformationsmanagement und IT-Infrastruktur. Dr. Appel leitete seit Juni 2000 den Bereich Konzernentwicklung von Deutsche Post World Net. (bee)

Kollegen im Konzern: Schon heute arbeiten Deutsche Post Euro Express, DHL und Danzas zusammen. STAR setzt mit der neuen gemeinsamen Marke DHL die Integration konsequent weiter fort.

Wir sind ein Team!

STAR-Maßnahmen vorgestellt – Marke DHL für Express und Logistik

Bereits heute arbeiten Vertrieb und Produktion von Deutsche Post Euro Express, DHL und Danzas in etlichen Projekten zusammen. Solche erfolgreichen Ansätze werden mit dem Programm STAR konsequent ausgebaut und in Zukunft viel einfacher. Der Zusammenschluss unter der neuen Marke DHL schafft die Voraussetzungen für einen einheitlichen Auftritt beim Kunden: eine Marke, ein klares Produktangebot, kundenorientierte Vertriebsprozesse und ein durchgehendes Produktionsnetz.

Der Startschuss für die Umsetzung des STAR-Programms ist gefallen. Dr. Klaus Zumwinkel, Vorstandsvorsitzender unseres Konzerns, informierte Mitarbeiterinnen und Mitarbeiter sowie Öffentlichkeit und Analysten über das Maßnahmenpaket zur Integration und Wertsteigerung. Wichtigste und weitreichendste STAR-Maßnahme ist der Zusammenschluss des gesamten Express- und Logistik-Geschäfts im Konzern weltweit unter der gemeinsamen starken Marke DHL. Dies gibt unserem Konzern Deutsche Post World Net zusätzlichen Schwung auf seinem Weg, weltweite Nummer 1 in Express und Logistik zu werden.

Dr. Zumwinkel betonte bei der Programmvorstellung die starke Kraft der Marke DHL und vor allem die Bedeutung eines erstklassigen Service: »Wir wollen mit der Marke sicherstellen, dass überall und jederzeit das Markenversprechen gilt: gleichmäßig gute Qualität – und das in der ganzen Welt. Das ist der Kern einer guten Marke.« Global und regional steht die Organisation der neuen DHL fest. Sie nimmt zum 1. Januar 2003 die Arbeit auf und wird nach und nach die jeweiligen Länderorganisationen planen. Deshalb steht heute auch noch nicht fest, was sich in einzelnen Ländern ändern wird.

Die neue Markenarchitektur wird ab 1. April 2003 umgesetzt. Für Kunden, Öffentlichkeit und Beschäftigte ist dies die auffälligste Veränderung. Der Vertrieb wird unter dem Markenzeichen DHL »mit einem Gesicht zum Kunden« auftreten.

Auf der Fahrzeugflotte wird die neue Marke DHL auf gelbem Grund nach und nach im Alltag sichtbar. Und für die Paket-/Expresszustellung in Deutschland gilt: Am gewohnt guten Service unserer Zustellerinnen und Zusteller wird sich nichts ändern. Sie stehen für die Verbindung von Deutscher Post und DHL.

Mehr zu STAR lesen Sie auf den Seiten 2, 3, 4 und 5. (ah)

STAR simply the best

IN DIESER AUSGABE

BRIEF Postfahrzeuge in den USA	S. 6
NACHRICHTEN Danke, Hochwasserhelfer!	S. 12
MARKT UND TECHNIK Surftipps für Ihre Gesundheit	S. 14
FIT IM JOB Sicher auf Winterstraßen	S. 15

SEITE 10

Fondsmanager bei der Postbank

Die Aktienkurse immer im Blick: Die Portfoliomanager in Frankfurt am Main betreuen verschiedene internationale Aktienfonds für die Kunden der Postbank.

AKTUELL

Zündende Ideen

Zigarrengenießer wissen, was gut schmeckt und duftet. Deswegen setzt der Hersteller Dannemann mit Mailings, die den Anspruch seiner Kunden erfüllen, auf die Deutsche Post – mehr auf Seite 6.

Zusammenarbeit im Konzern

One-Stop-Shopping pur: DPEED, das Euro Express-Netzwerk, Danzas und DHL bieten dem Kunden Busak+Shamban alles aus einer Hand – mehr auf Seite 7.

Gottschalk-Brüder werben für DHL

Zu Fuß in die USA: für die Gottschalk-Brüder kein Problem. Im neuen TV-Spot werben sie für unseren Express-Spezialisten DHL – mehr auf Seite 8.

Zehn Jahre Partner-Filialen

Es fing vor zehn Jahren mit dem ersten »Nachbarschaftsladen« in Bimöhlen an. Heute gibt es 7.500 Partner-Filialen – siehe Seite 10.

Riester-Rente aus einer Hand

Gemeinschaftsprojekt bietet Versicherungsbranche eine Komplettlösung – siehe Seite 14.

Die sachliche Darstellung des Relaunch, Hintergrundberichte, Perspektiven und die Aufbereitung bestimmter Einzelaspekte nahmen den Menschen im Konzern bereits im Vorfeld Ängste und bauten Vertrauen auf. Die regelmäßige, umfassende interne Informationsvermittlung begleitete ab November 2002 den gesamten Relaunch.

Vier verschiedene **Mitarbeiterzielgruppen** wurden in spezifischen Broschüren unter dem Titel „Start der neuen Marke DHL" informiert:

- **die Mitarbeiterinnen und Mitarbeiter der neuen Marke DHL,**
- **die Mitarbeiterinnen und Mitarbeiter der Deutschen Post,**
- **die Mitarbeiterinnen und Mitarbeiter der Partnerfilialen,**
- **die Zustellerinnen und Zusteller von DHL Deutschland.**

Die Broschüren für die ersten drei Zielgruppen umfassten jeweils acht Seiten. Sie erläutern zielgruppenspezifisch die Bedeutung einer starken Marke und deren Vorteile für die Mitarbeiterinnen und Mitarbeiter. Die Broschüren gaben eine **Vorschau** auf Rebranding, Werbekampagne und kommende Integrationsmaßnahmen. Sie beantworteten die wichtigsten konkreten Fragen der jeweiligen Zielgruppe zur neuen Marke.

Die **Broschüre an alle DHL-Mitarbeiterinnen und -Mitarbeiter in elf Landessprachen** wurde am 11. März 2003 weltweit versandt und parallel ins Intranet von Deutsche Post, DHL und Danzas gestellt. Kurz darauf folgten die Broschüren für die Mitarbeiterinnen und Mitarbeiter der Deutschen Post und der Partnerfilialen. Mitte April erhielten die Zustellerinnen und Zusteller von DHL Deutschland ein vierseitiges Faltblatt, das ihnen die erweiterten, vernetzten Leistungsmerkmale der Marke DHL speziell für den Standort Deutschland erläuterte.

Im Vordergrund der **Plakatserie** (vgl. Abbildung 21) stand der Teamgedanke. Das „Puzzle"-Motiv mit 18 Porträts repräsentiert die Internationalität der neuen Marke DHL und bot die Möglichkeit zur Identifikation. Das Motiv „Flotte" betont die Vielfalt und Leistungskraft der neuen Marke DHL: Die eindringliche visuelle Anordnung der Transportmittel Flugzeug und Schiff zusammen mit dynamischer „Manpower" spiegelt die Leistungsbündelung des Relaunch wider. Die Plakate wurden in elf Landessprachen produziert und weltweit an den Unternehmensstandorten präsentiert. Zusätzlich wurden sie ins **Intranet** von Deutsche Post, DHL und Danzas gestellt.

Abbildung 21: **Die Mitarbeiterplakate bilden die neue Situation kraftvoll und emotional ab.**

Brand Dynamics besteht aus zwei sich ergänzenden Modulen:

- **Modul 1 Brand Assessment** ermittelt die **Markenwahrnehmung** mit den relevanten Image-Dimensionen in Bezug auf Kaufentscheidungen.
- **Modul 2 Customer Interaction** ermittelt die **Leistungsperformance** der Marke beim Kunden.

Brand Dynamics bietet konkrete Aussagen, wie die Marke durch operative, kommunikative und/oder marketingstrategische Maßnahmen im Wettbewerb gestärkt werden kann. Damit ist Brand Dynamics den konzernweiten Unternehmensbereichen Operations, Marketing und Kommunikation ein äußerst hilfreiches und zudem **synergetisch wirkendes Werkzeug**.

Brand Dynamics beantwortet die Kernfragen des Marketing:

- Wie stark ist die Marke im Kaufprozess (Bekanntheit bis Loyalität)?
- Wo verliert die Marke Kunden?
- Wie wird die Marke im Wettbewerbsvergleich auf den Markentreibern wahrgenommen (Stärken und Schwächen)?
- Welches sind die wichtigsten Kundenkontaktpunkte, um die Markentreiber entscheidend positiv aufzuladen?
- Welche Maßnahmen können an den priorisierten Kundenkontaktpunkten zur Steuerung der Markenwahrnehmung ergriffen werden?

Das Marketing leitet aus Brand Dynamics Maßnahmen ab, die im Dialog mit operativen Einheiten priorisiert werden und in der Umsetzung nachhaltig auf die Marke einzahlen. Auf Basis der gewonnenen Ergebnisse wird parallel die laufende Markenkommunikation adjustiert. Markenführung wird so zu einer **ganzheitlichen Aufgabe von operativen und zentralen Bereichen**.

Über die Identifikation von Markenstatus und Markentreibern und die Ableitung von Maßnahmen an den Kundenkontaktpunkten hinaus werden via Brand Dynamics **Regelprozesse und Steuerungskennzahlen** implementiert. So sichert der Konzern Deutsche Post World Net die konsistente Markensteuerung in allen Leistungsbereichen. Von jeder Landesgesellschaft konzernweit ist Brand Dynamics für den gezielten Markenaufbau und die gezielte Markenpflege einsetzbar.

Brand Dynamics wird **zunächst für die Marke DHL in rund 20 Ländern** implementiert, davon zehn europäische und zehn weitere weltweit. Dabei wird Modul 1 Brand Assessment als Basismodul eingesetzt, während Modul 2 Customer Interaction individuell von den einzelnen Ländern ergänzt werden kann.

Brand Dynamics begleitet DHL auf dem Weg zur weltweiten Top-Logistik-Marke.

6.2 Nonstop zur weltweiten Top-Marke

Der Konzern Deutsche Post World Net führte die 2003 erfolgreich platzierte DHL-Markenkampagne im Jahr 2004 weltweit weiter, um die Position seiner Leistungsmarke DHL kontinuierlich auszubauen: als weltweit führendes Unternehmen im Bereich Express und Logistik. **Mittelpunkt der Werbemaßnahmen blieb die weltweit erfolgreiche „More"-Kampagne**. Die Markenattribute von DHL wie Verlässlichkeit, Geschwindigkeit und Effizienz wurden Privat- und Geschäftskunden, Entscheidungsträgern, Meinungsbildern und Multiplikatoren weiterhin nahe gebracht.

Ein **neuer TV-Spot** („Not to do") ergänzte die Printkampagne und veranschaulichte die logistische Leistungskraft von DHL. Er lief zu besten Sendezeiten auf Wirtschafts- und Nachrichtensendern wie CNN, CNBC und BBC.

Eine **Produktkampagne in 18 europäischen Ländern** zur Unterstützung des Domestic-Geschäfts von DHL lief im April 2004 an. Über Anzeigen in nationalen Wirtschaftstiteln sowie Funkspots und Online-Banner wurde die Position von DHL als führender Anbieter von Express- und Logistikleistungen sowie als kompetenter One-stop-shopping-Partner herausgestellt. Diese werbliche Unterstützung des Domestic-Geschäfts in den einzelnen Ländern war gerade für den europäischen Markt essenziell, da hier verschiedene regionale Partnerunternehmen integriert worden waren. Die Botschaft: DHL-Kunden erhalten auch lokal die gewohnt erstklassigen Services.

Die entsprechende **Produktkampagne für den asiatischen Markt** mit der Kernbotschaft „No one knows Asia like we do!" startete im Juni 2004. Zu diesem Zeitpunkt war DHL auf dem asiatischen Kontinent bereits die Nummer eins im Express- und Logistikgeschäft. Weiterführendes Ziel der Kampagne war, innerasiatisch das Umsatzvolumen zu steigern und die Marktführerschaft von DHL auszubauen.

In den USA wurde die nationale Kampagne „Momentum" (via Print, Direktmarketing und Internet) fortgesetzt, um DHL nach der Integration von Airborne im nordamerikanischen Express- und Logistikmarkt neu zu positionieren (vgl. Abbildung 23). Die Kommunikationsziele:

- die langjährige Erfahrung von DHL vermitteln,
- das Vertrauen in DHL stärken,
- DHL als US-Domestic-Marke etablieren.

Die Marschrichtung für das Markenmanagement des Konzerns Deutsche Post World Net – national, intereuropäisch und weltweit – wurde und wird konsequent weiterverfolgt. DHL hat auf dem europäischen Kontinent die stärkste Marktposition im Bereich der Kontraktlogistik, so das Ergebnis der Untersuchung „European Logistics Leaders 2004" von Transport Intelligence, einem der bedeutendsten Marktforschungsunternehmen für den europäischen Logistikmarkt – eine schöne Bestätigung für die **strategische Markenführung** bei Deutsche Post World Net. Alle Leistungsmarken im Konzern (Deutsche Post als

Marke für die Briefkommunikation, DHL als internationale Marke für Express und Logistik, Postbank als Marke für das Retail-Banking) operieren im **Konzernverbund**, um Synergien zu erzeugen und zu nutzen. Sie besitzen dabei aber auch ausreichend **individuelle Markenidentität**, um sich kraftvoll und eigenständig am Markt zu behaupten.

Der Weg von DHL zur internationalen Top-Logistik-Marke mit unverwechselbarer Identität ist vorgezeichnet.

Der neue Markenauftritt, die Etablierung von klaren und unverwechselbaren Markensignalen war Ende 2004 abgeschlossen. Doch Pflege und Ausbau der Flagship-Marke DHL sind ein kontinuierlicher, langfristiger Prozess, der nie zu Ende ist. Denn im Konzern Deutsche Post World Net versteht man **„Marke" als dynamisches Wertschöpfungssystem**, das mittels neuer Leistungen permanent aufgeladen wird.

Abbildung 23: **Motiv aus der Kampagne „Momentum": mit Emotion den amerikanischen Markt erobern**

GABLER GRAFIK

Abbildung 24: Motiv aus der DHL-Markenkampagne

GABLER GRAFIK

Lufthansa – Excellence in Branding

Harald W. Eisenächer

1. **Einführung** **820**

2. **Historie des Unternehmens und der Marke Lufthansa** **820**
2.1 Historie des Unternehmens 820
2.2 Markenhistorie und Entwicklung der Corporate Identity 821

3. **Prozess und Modell zur optimierten Markenführung** **826**

4. **Die Lufthansa Kommunikation im Zeichen des 11. September** **829**

5. **Neuer Markenauftritt und zunehmende Emotionalisierung** **832**

6. **Zusammenfassung und Konklusion** **835**

1. Einführung

Lufthansa ist die erfolgreichste Fluggesellschaft Europas und eine der erfolgreichsten Luftfahrtsmarken. Als Aviation Konzern betreibt Lufthansa seine Aktivitäten in sechs strategischen Geschäftsfeldern: Passage, Logistik, Technik, Catering, Touristik und IT-Services. Seit Beginn der 90er Jahre ist Lufthansa eine vollprivatisierte Aktiengesellschaft mit rund 400.000 Aktionären. Mit ihren Leistungsdaten belegt sie Spitzenplätze im IATA Ranking. Über die globale Positionierung mit einem weltweiten Streckennetz bedient Lufthansa derzeit mehr als 175 Zielorte in 75 Ländern. Als zentrale Drehscheiben im Lufthansa Steckennetz dienen Frankfurt und München. Hierüber werden die Hauptzielmärkte in Europa (inklusive Deutschland), Nordamerika sowie Asien/Pazifik bedient. Weitere wichtige Märkte befinden sich in Afrika, Südamerika und dem Nahen Osten. Darüber hinaus ist Lufthansa Mitglied der Star Alliance. Als Gründungsmitglied baute Lufthansa gemeinsam mit United Airlines, SAS, Thai Airways International und Air Canada 1997 das erste multilaterale Bündnis im Weltluftverkehr auf. Nach und nach wuchs das Bündnis. Mit dem neuen Partner US Airways wurde das Star Alliance Netz erneut ausgeweitet und bietet nun Zugang zu über 750 Flughäfen in 132 Ländern. Die Star Alliance vereint derzeit insgesamt neben Lufthansa 14 Fluggesellschaften: Air Canada, Air New Zealand, ANA (All Nippon Airways), Asiana Airlines, Austrian Airlines, bmi (British Midland), LOT (Polish Airlines), SAS, Singapore Airlines, Spanair, Thai Airways International, United Airlines, US Airways, und VARIG. Die Erfolgsgeschichte wird weitergehen. Ende 2004 beziehungsweise in 2005 ist der Beitritt von Blue 1, TAP (Air Portugal) und South African Airways vorgesehen.

2. Historie des Unternehmens und der Marke Lufthansa

2.1 Historie des Unternehmens

Im April 1926 erfolgte der Erstflug eines Lufthansa Flugzeuges. Schnell erwarb sich das junge Unternehmen ein guten Ruf: es hatte ein dichtes Netzwerk von Flügen innerhalb Europas aufgebaut und arbeitete intensiv an interkontinentalen Flugverbindungen. Asien und Südamerika (Postdienste) wurden für den Luftverkehr erschlossen. Nordatlantikflüge wurden mit Hilfe von Flugbooten und Wasserflugzeugen erprobt.

Der Zweite Weltkrieg bedeutete das Ende der Flugaktivitäten und 1945 auch das Ende der Lufthansa. Das Unternehmen wurde später liquidiert. 1953 entstand eine neue deutsche Luftverkehrsgesellschaft, die heutige Lufthansa. Im April 1955 startete erstmals wieder ein Flugzeug mit dem Kranich am Leitwerk. Als Pionier dieser neuen Luftfahrt-Ära galt die Super Constellation (Lockheed 1049). 1960 begann mit der Einführung der Boeing 707 das Jetzeitalter. 1970 flog der erste Jumbo Jet (Boeing 747-100). Der stetige Ausbau einer wirtschaftlichen Flotte war nicht mehr aufzuhalten. Derzeit verfügt Lufthansa über eine Flotte von 382 Flugzeugen. Weitere wichtige Meilensteine sind bereits vorhersehbar: für 2007 ist der Einsatz des größten zivilen Flugzeuges der Welt, des Airbus A380, geplant.

2.2 Markenhistorie und Entwicklung der Corporate Identity

Am 6. Januar 1926 entsteht durch den Zusammenschluss des Deutschen Aero Lloyd AG (DAL) mit dem Junkers Luftverkehr die „Deutsche Luft Hansa Aktiengesellschaft". Der Name wurde als gesellschaftsrechtliche Bezeichnung ab 1933 in der heute noch gebräuchlichen Schreibweise „Deutsche Lufthansa" genutzt. Flugzeuge, Fahrzeuge und alle übrigen von der Öffentlichkeit wahrgenommenen Unternehmensbestandteile waren zunächst weitgehend mit der Kurzbezeichnung Luft Hansa und ab 1933 mit der Wortmarke „Lufthansa" einheitlich gekennzeichnet. Auf den Leitwerken der Flugzeuge stand zusätzlich ein Bildsymbol in Form eines stilisierten Kranichs im Kreis. Der Grafiker Professor Otto Firle entwarf ihn für die Deutsche Luftreederei, die erste Fluggesellschaft der Welt – 1923 mit der Lloyd Gruppe in der Deutschen Aero Lloyd AG aufgegangen. Zum ersten Mal erschien der stilisierte Kranich 1920 vor einer größeren Öffentlichkeit auf einem Plakat. Diese Darstellung des Kranichs wurde zum Symbol für das 1926 in Berlin neugegründete Unternehmen. Die Unternehmensfarben Blau und Gelb bekam Lufthansa von der Junkers Luftverkehr AG.

Die Anfänge der Marke lebten von dem Spannungsfeld der für den Luftverkehr wichtigen Werte „Tradition" im Sinne der „Bewahrung gewonnener Erfahrungen" und „Pioniergeist". Die damals proklamierten Tugenden „Mut", „Pflichtbewusstsein" und „Zuverlässigkeit" bildeten schon immer für das Fliegen wichtige Attribute und kommen von der ersten Stunde an international agierenden deutschen Fluggesellschaften zugute. Vieles von dem, was heute unter „Corporate Design" bei Lufthansa zu verstehen ist, ist in den Grundzügen vorhanden: der Name Lufthansa als Wortmarke, das Bildsymbol des Kranichs und die Unternehmensfarben.

Nach dem Neustart 1953 benutzte Lufthansa ihr bewährtes Logo auch wieder als ihre neue Marke. Zu den ersten Abteilungen gehörte auch der Werbe- und Designbereich. Bei der Namenswahl besannen sich die Gründerväter wieder auf die bewährten legendären Werte, die bei einer Fluggesellschaft erwartet wurden: Sicherheit, Perfektion, Zuverlässigkeit. Die abstrakten Werte benötigen einen klaren und konkreten Markenauftritt. Die Wortmarke Lufthansa und insbesondere das Symbol des Kranichs sowie die Unternehmensfarben Blau und Gelb wurden wieder aufgegriffen. Die Wortmarke Lufthansa erschien in der Antiqua-Schriftart Schadow. Besondere Bedeutung kam natürlich der Außengestaltung der Flugzeuge zu. Der Kranich auf der in Flugrichtung gelegten Parabel wurde zur markanten Leitwerkgestaltung. Sie wurde auf allen Flugzeugmustern 1957 eingeführt. Damit war ein wieder erkennbarer Markenauftritt für die wichtigsten Anwendungsbereiche sichergestellt. Auf Werbeanzeigen, Plakaten, Displays, auf dem Flugplan, auf Beschilderungen und anderen ausgewählten Kommunikationsmitteln fand die Parabel Anwendung.

Der mit der Entwicklung vom Propeller zum Düsentriebwerk einhergehende Wertewandel erforderte auch einen Wandel im Unternehmensauftritt. 1962 beauftragte Lufthansa eine Entwicklungsgruppe um Otl Aicher mit der Ausarbeitung von Gestaltungsrichtlinien. Zum ersten Mal wurden Soll-Ist-Analysen für den Markenauftritt erstellt. Die gesellschaftliche Entwicklung und der Markt fordern neue Attribute wie Frische, Aufgeschlossenheit und Führungskompetenz. Die gestalterischen Grundlagen wurden verabschiedet und in einem Gestaltungsmanual dokumentiert; ein bewusst gesteuertes Erscheinungsbild war erstmalig aufgesetzt. Seine Grundzüge haben heute noch Gültigkeit. Der Schriftzug Lufthansa wurde in die zeitlose Schriftart Helvetica umgestaltet, der Kranich bekam den Kreis als festen Bestandteil und wurde der Wortmarke zugeordnet. Die Hausfarben wurden leicht modifiziert und ihr Einsatz systematisch geregelt. Lufthansa erhielt eine einheitliche Handschrift, funktional begründete Gestaltungsraster sowie Stilvorgaben für Fotoeinsatz und Illustrationen anhand praktischer Beispiele. Die konsistente Umsetzung der Gestaltungsrichtlinien auf alle als Identitätsträger ausgemachten internen wie externen Bereiche wurde von der internen Designabteilung weitergeführt. In Verbindung mit dem Unternehmenserfolg diente das funktionale Design als Auslöser für Assoziationen zu Präzision und Disziplin. Durch seine strenge Einhaltung wurde Kompetenz vermittelt. Der über das äußere Erscheinungsbild transportierte Anspruch wirkte nach innen wie nach außen und wurde als Unternehmensphilosophie verstanden.

Die 70er und 80er Jahre stellten Lufthansa und seine gefestigte Corporate Identity vor neue Herausforderungen. Bei einem stärker werdenden Wettbewerbsdruck im internationalen Luftverkehr erweiterte Lufthansa ihre Infrastruktur durch den Ausbau der für die Luftfahrt nötigen Zulieferdienste und den benachbarten Geschäftsfeldern. Mit der Wortmarke Lufthansa war nicht mehr nur die Fluggesellschaft zu bezeichnen. Ihre Identität ist vielschichtiger geworden.

Um dieser neuen Struktur gerecht zu werden, startete Lufthansa Ende der 70er Jahre unter Führung der beauftragten Züricher Corporate Identity Agentur Zintzmeyer & Lux einen zunächst internen Corporate Identity-Prozess. In zahlreichen Workshops wurden der Status quo der Unternehmensidentität ermittelt und auf Basis eines Soll-Profils die Ziele definiert. Neben dem Corporate Design wurden nun auch die Bereiche Corporate Culture und Corporate Communication bearbeitet. Es wurden zwölf Unternehmensleitsätze definiert, die in einem Manual festgeschrieben wurden. Sie bilden bis heute die Basis für alle sechs Konzerngeschäftsfelder. Die Grundelemente des Corporate Designs erfuhren auf Basis der neu festgeschriebenen Unternehmensidentität leichte Veränderungen. Die Bildmarke des Kranichs, bereits in den 80ern mit einem stärkeren Ring versehen, und die Wortmarke, von Otl Aicher aus der Helvetica entwickelt zu einem kräftigeren Schriftschnitt überarbeitet, bildeten von nun an eine fest definierte Einheit von Bild- und Wortmarke, wie sie bis heute gültig ist. Diese wurden Schlüsselelemente eines ausgeklügelten Farbkonzeptes mit dem Ziel des emotionaleren Markenauftritts und drückten zukünftig mit der Farbe Gelb mehr Kundenorientierung, Freundlichkeit und Wärme aus als in dem bis dahin verwendeten Blau. Gelb wurde zur Unterscheidungsfarbe im Wettbewerb. Konsequent wurde das Konzept der Entbuntung auch mit den Lufthansa Architekten umgesetzt. Gemäß der Forderung des Marktes nach Diversifizierung des Angebotes wurden auch die drei Klassen „First Class, Business Class und Economy Class" in Namen und Design an Bord und am Boden stärker ausgearbeitet. Fester Bestandteil der Weiterentwicklung war auch bei Zintzmeyer & Lux die Flugzeugaußenkennzeichnung. Das neue Design stand für die Symbiose von Innovationen und Tradition.

Immer stärker fordert der Wettbewerb die Umorientierung zu mehr Emotionalität und Kundennähe. Was bereits mit der gelben Bild-/Wortmarke bei Zintzmeyer & Lux begann, sollte nun besonders im dreidimensionalen Bereich mehr Ausdruck finden. 1996 wurde das heute existierende Produktdesign entwickelt. Eine Analyse der Kundenerwartungen ergab, dass eine ganzheitliche Anpassung des Flughafens und der Flugzeugkabine an die emotionalen Erwartungen der Passagiere vorzunehmen ist. Der „Retro Futurismus" wurde durch die Agentur frogdesign geboren. Durch den Einsatz von Wellblech, abgeleitet über das universell-historische Symbol der JU 52, finden liebevoll gestaltete Details im öffentlichen Bereich, zum Beispiel den Lounges, dem Check-in oder auch im Kabinen-Interieur der Interkont Flotte, Anwendung.

Abbildung 1: **Lufthansa-Corporate-Design-Entwicklung**

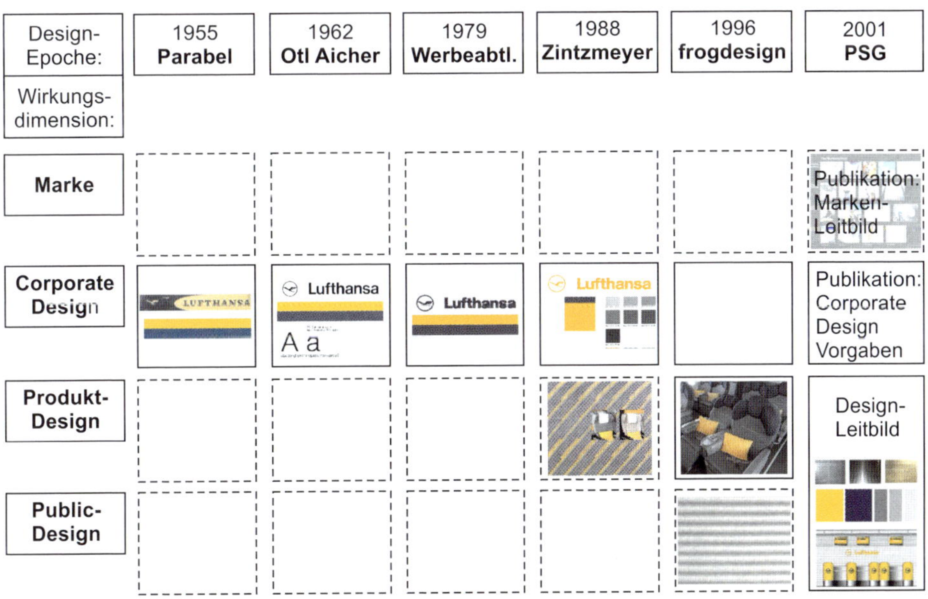

GABLER GRAFIK

Abbildung 2: Markenwerte der Lufthansa AG aus dem Jahre 1962

1. Gesellschaftlich ■ Lufthansa legt keinen Wert mehr auf Exklusivität ■ Fliegen ist kein Privileg mehr ■ Lufthansa ist gekennzeichnet durch soziale Offenheit	■ Verzicht auf Statussymbole ■ Zurückhaltung in der Präsentation ■ Statt Dekoration höchste Qualität im wirklichen Angebot
2. Technisch ■ Lufthansa repräsentiert Frische, Zuverlässigkeit, technischen Fortschritt ■ Das technische Personal steht nicht im Hintergrund: es ist Garant für Sicherheit und technische Dynamik.	■ Flugzeuge degenerieren nicht zu Werbeträgern. Sie sind zuerst in ihrer technischen Gestalt erkennbar. ■ Der Arbeitskleidung des technischen Personals ist mehr Bedeutung beizumessen.
3. National/International ■ Lufthansa repräsentiert ihr Herkunftsland, positive nationale Stereotype wie organisatorische Verlässlichkeit, technische Zuverlässigkeit, kulturelle Aufgeschlossenheit sollen Bestandteile bleiben ■ Höchste Zurückhaltung mit völkischer Argumentation	■ Größte Präzision und Exaktheit in der Anwendung aller visuellen Mittel ■ Verzicht auf nationale und völkische Embleme
4. Kaufmännisch ■ Lufthansa ist aufstrebendes Unternehmen innerhalb der Spitzengruppe der Luftfahrtgesellschaften ■ Ihr Platz ist im Bereich der Wirtschaft, nicht in der Verwaltung. Ihre Tradition ist Fortschritt.	■ Größte Sorgfalt, Betonung einer einheitlichen, konsequent angewandten Gestaltung ■ Staatliche Einrichtungen sind gegenüber ihrer visuellen Erscheinung gleichgültig, deshalb Betonung visueller Erscheinung. ■ Reduktion der traditionellen Werte, Anwendung heutiger Gestaltungsprinzipien
5. Marktpolitisch ■ Betonung des Services gegenüber der Konkurrenz	■ Direkte, unkomplizierte Anwendung ■ Keine Spielereien ■ Sorgfalt im Detail ■ Konsequente und alles umfassende Konzeption ■ Systematische Geschlossenheit ■ Entwicklung eines informatorischen, nicht dekorativen Systems

GABLER GRAFIK

Ende der 90er Jahre wurde eine strategische Ausrichtung des Unternehmens für die nächsten Jahre festgelegt. Durch die neuen erwähnten sechs Geschäftsfelder des Aviation Konzerns wird die Unternehmensstrategie folgerichtig für die unterschiedlichen Geschäftsfelder abgeleitet. Der Markenwert wird zur wichtigen Größe. Für die Markenführung sind die einzelnen Konzerngesellschaften jetzt selbst verantwortlich. Die Entwicklung der Marke Lufthansa wird beim Konzern und der Passage zwischen strategischer Zielsetzung und realistischer Machbarkeit gesteuert, ist von vielen Faktoren abhängig und unterliegt der Unternehmens- und Marketingstrategie. Entsprechende entwickelte Instrumente geben Aufschluss über die markenrelevanten Stellgrößen.

Die 1962 durch Otl Aicher definierten Markenwerte bilden die Grundlage für die heutige Design- und Kommunikationsentwicklung (vgl. Abbildung 2).

Es kann festgehalten werden, dass die „geschichtlichen" Kernwerte der Marke bis heute Bestand haben und die Basis des heutigen Erfolgs bilden. Lufthansa ist eine Traditionsmarke, sie hat sich in den Jahrzehnten stets weiterentwickelt, trotzdem ist sie im Kern gleich geblieben (vgl. Abbildung 3). Die Marke bildet auch zukünftig die Basis für die Unternehmensentwicklung.

Abbildung 3: Weiterentwicklung der Markenwerte

Damals	Heute
Unternehmen in Spitzengruppe	Führungsanspruch
Serviceorientiert	Persönliches Engagement
Höchste Qualität im Angebot	Streben nach Perfektion
Soziale Offenheit	Glaubwürdigkeit
Fortschritt ist Tradition	

CABLER GRAFIK

3. Prozess und Modell zur optimierten Markenführung

Für eine Differenzierung gegenüber dem Wettbewerb ist es unerlässlich, eine eindeutige Markenpositionierung im Markt zu erzielen. Die Premium Marke Lufthansa zeigt ein klares Profil: Sie gibt Orientierung, schafft Vertrauen, bildet emotionalen Mehrwert und vermittelt dem Nachfrager eine individualisierte Beziehungsqualität.

Die Marke spielt bei der Kaufentscheidung eine zunehmend bedeutsamere Rolle und ermöglicht Spielräume für preisliche Differenzierung oder Marktanteilsgewinne.

Qualitative Kaufentscheidungsgründe wie Flugplan, Preis oder Produktwahrnehmung werden zukünftig anteilig geringer.

Abbildung 4: Kaufentscheidende Faktoren der Marke Lufthansa

Relative Wichtigkeiten der kaufentscheidenden Faktoren variieren nach Flugdauer

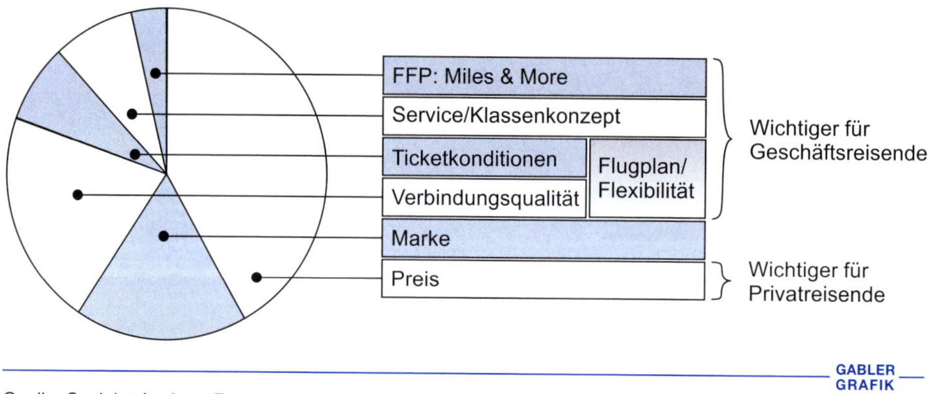

Quelle: Conjoint Analyse, Europa Verkehr, LH 2003/2004

Basis für die Marke und damit den Ausbau derselben ist daher zunächst ein kontinuierlicher Prozess im Markenmanagement (vgl. Abbildung 5). Ausgehend von einer Markenanalyse, einer Status-quo-Erhebung bezüglich Markenstatus, Kunden-, Marktbedürfnisse und Marktpotenzial werden die Markenziele in einem Markenleitbild aufgestellt. Das Soll-Markenleitbild definiert die Entwicklung und Umsetzung der Markenvision in alle Unternehmensbereiche (Produkt, Service, Vertrieb und Marketing). Hieran schließt sich die Bewertung der Marketinginstrumente zur konkreten Umsetzung und „Leben" des Markenkonzeptes an. Ein Markencontrolling ermittelt in regelmäßigen Abständen alle zwei bis drei Jahre den Markenstatus.

Abbildung 5: Managementprozess zur Steuerung der Markenidentität

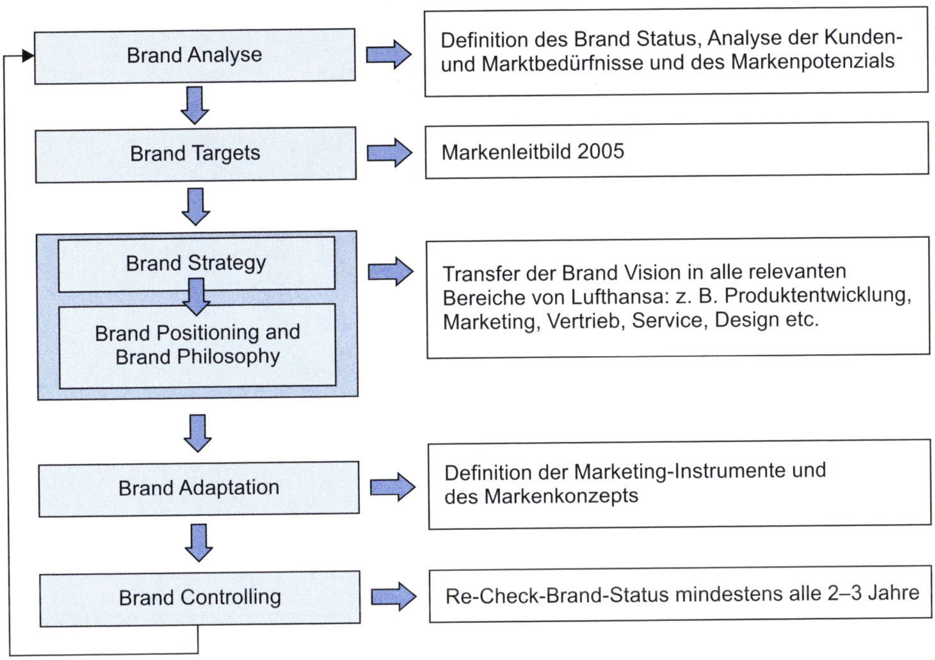

GABLER GRAFIK

Lufthansa arbeitet seit 2000 mit einem Markenleitbild, welches die Marken-Identität mit vier elementaren Facetten beschreibt (vgl. auch Abbildung 6):

- Wer bin ich?
- Wie bin ich?
- Was biete ich?
- Wie trete ich auf?

Damit lässt sich die Marke in Analogie zu einer Persönlichkeit hinsichtlich ihrer Eigenschaften analysieren, beschreiben und steuern. Spricht man von Markenidentität, beschreibt man den Status quo; spricht man von Markenprofilierung, beschreibt man die zukünftige Heraushebung beispielsweise zur eindeutigen Differenzierung zum Nachfrager.

Abbildung 6: Markenleitbild der Marke Lufthansa

Wer bin ich? Wo liegt die Kernkompetenz der Lufthansa passage? Wofür wollen wir stehen, was wollen wir erreichen? **Marke als Organisation**	**Wie** bin ich? Wie ist die Lufthansa Passage? Wie ist die Tonalität der Marke und ihres Auftritts? **Marke als Person**
Was biete ich? Was ist der Benefit für den Verbraucher? Welchen spezifischen Nutzen hat der Lufthansa Kunde? **Marke als Dienstleistung/Produkt**	**Wie** trete ich auf? Wie ist das Erscheinungsbild der Lufthansa Passage? Wie passt das zur Marke und zum Nutzen, den wir versprechen? **Marke als Symbol**

Quelle: ICON

GABLER GRAFIK

Wer bin ich?

– Marke als Organisation –

Wo liegt die Kernkompetenz der Lufthansa? Wofür steht Lufthansa, wo wird Lufthansa in der Zukunft stehen?

Lufthansa ist die Airline Nr. 1 in Europa für Geschäftsreisende, die sicher, zuverlässig, professionell ist und mit großer Netzkompetenz als starker Partner im erfolgreichsten Allianzsystem der Welt gute, innovative, individuelle Produkt- und Servicequalität liefert und die Chancen der neuen Technologien offensiv nutzt. Erkennbar am Kranich. Die klar profilierte Marke Lufthansa beschreibt die Kernaussage über ihre Identität im Kerngedanken, dem Claim „There's no better way to fly".

Wie bin ich?

– Die Identität der Marke Lufthansa als Person –

Wie ist die Tonalität der Marke Lufthansa und ihres Auftrittes? Welches sind die Kernmarkenwerte?

Die Werte „Streben nach Perfektion“ und „Glaubwürdigkeit“ werden aktiv genutzt und bewahrt. Perfektion macht sich an den Attributen Professionalität, Verantwortungsbewusstsein, Effizienz, Zuverlässigkeit und Disziplin bemerkbar. Glaubwürdigkeit spiegelt sich in Ehrlichkeit, Berechenbarkeit, Klarheit und Verständlichkeit wider. Der Führungsanspruch und das persönliche Engagement werden kommunikativ weiterentwickelt und ausgebaut.

Was biete ich?

– Marke als Produkt – Benefits & Reason why –

Die Identität der Marke Lufthansa wird über konkrete Eigenschaften in Service- und Produktmanagement beschrieben. Dem Nachfrager werden konkrete Nachweise für seinen individuellen Nutzen seiner Wahl zu Lufthansa aufgezeigt. Attribute wie technische Zuverlässigkeit, das weltweite Flugnetz, hohe Pünktlichkeit, saubere und gut gepflegte Flugzeuge sowie freundliche herzliche Flugbegleiter mit einer hohen Servicementalität beschreiben hier Marke die Lufthansa.

Wie trete ich auf?

– Marke als Symbol –

Wie ist das Erscheinungsbild, wie wird das Markenversprechen von Lufthansa zum Nachfrager kommuniziert?

Die Wort/Bild- Marke Lufthansa wird über das beschriebene Symbol des stilisierten Kranichs festgemacht. Die Unternehmensfarben Lufthansa gelb und Lufthansa blau verstärken hierbei die Markenwahrnehmung. Aufgezeigte Corporate Identity-Regeln steuern dabei die Markenführung.

4. Die Lufthansa Kommunikation im Zeichen des 11. September

Basierend auf dem beschriebenen Markenleitbild wurde in 2000 eine Lufthansa Image-Kampagne entwickelt (vgl. Abbildung 7). Ziel war es, die beschriebenen Markenwerte über konkrete „Leadership“ Attribute auszubauen, um den Markenwert der Lufthansa zu steigern. Ferner sollte der Leadership Anspruch durch die Implementierung der Kernaussage beziehungsweise des Claims: „There is no better way to fly“ unterstützt werden.

Wie reagiert Lufthansa kommunikativ auf die Extremsituation der Ereignisse des 11. September? Der verfolgte Leadership Anspruch war inhaltlich nicht mehr passend und wurde durch die Ereignisse in den USA fehlinterpretiert. Die Image-Kampagne wurde folglich gestoppt. Die wirtschaftliche Lage machte budgetseitige Umpriorisierungen notwendig.

Abbildung 7: Imagekampagne aus dem Jahr 2001

„Zugegeben, auch wir überlassen auch schon mal anderen die Führung"

„Wer seiner Linie treu bleibt, ist schneller oben"

GABLER GRAFIK

Aber die Extremsituation brachte auch große Chancen für den Lufthansa Konzern. Das Sicherheits- und Informationsbedürfnis der Nachfrager konnte in der Öffentlichkeit pro-aktiv aufgegriffen werden. Lufthansa trat hierzu in den aktiven Dialog und zeigte, dass es sich um seine Nachfrager kümmert und dazu bereit ist, gesellschaftliche Verantwortung zu übernehmen. Die Image-Kampagne wurde durch eine faktische Kommunikationskampagne ersetzt. Die faktische Kommunikation wurde in zwei Stufen aufgesetzt. Beginn war eine Informationskampagne zu nachfragerrelevanten Themen, wie Flugplanänderungen, Servicenummern oder Check-in-Zeiten. Hiermit wurden das Informationsbedürfnis der Nachfrager getroffen und herrschende Unsicherheiten abgebaut. In einem zweiten Schritt wurden mittels Testimonials (hier zum Beispiel Prof. Dr. Roman Herzog) die Vorteile und die Wichtigkeit des völkerverbindenden Fliegens kommuniziert (vgl. Abbildung 8). Es ist Lufthansa gelungen, durch eine schnelle Reaktion den neuen veränderten Kundenbedürfnissen nachzukommen (vgl. Abbildung 9).

Abbildung 8: **Faktische Kommunikationskampagne**

GABLER GRAFIK

Die weiteren Folgen der Extremsituation „11. September" und der wirtschaftliche Einbruch erforderten eine Konzentration der budgetären Mittel mit strategischem Fokus auf rein Umsatz generierende Maßnahmen.

Abbildung 9: **Weiterentwicklung der Marke Lufthansa**

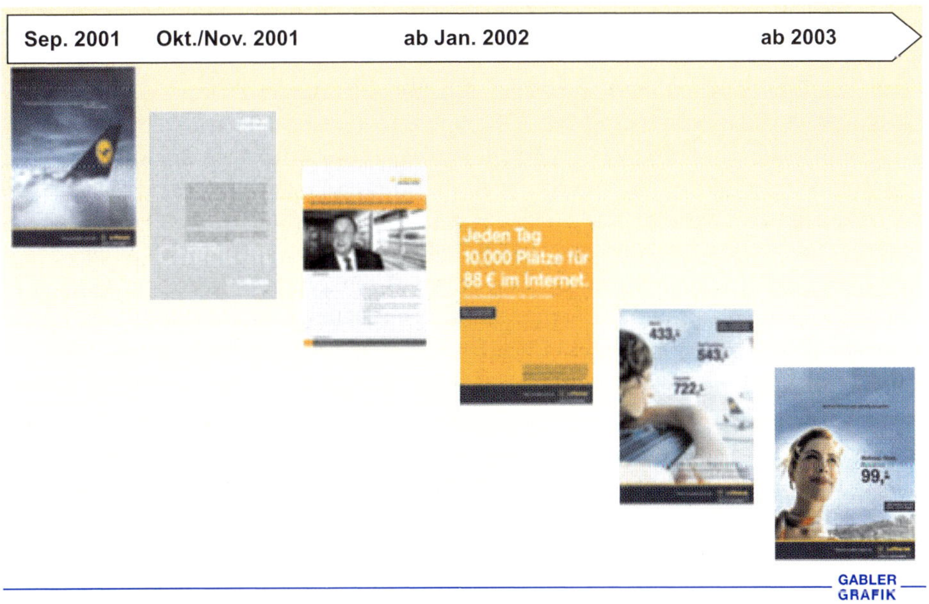

GABLER GRAFIK

Für die Marketingstrategie bedeutete dies, eine inhaltliche Reduzierung der Kommunikation auf „Preis“ vorzunehmen. Markenbildende Faktoren wie Innovation und Qualität traten in den Hintergrund. Die Tonalität der Kommunikation wurde durch den verstärkten Markteintritt und Preis-Wettbewerb der „No Frills Carrier“ verschärft. Der Gefahr des Markenwerteverfalls durch die inhaltliche Fokussierung auf Preis wurde durch die Entwicklung eines qualitativen Preiskommunikationskonzepts entgegengewirkt. Die reine taktische Preiskommunikation in Typoformat wurde durch ein neues ganzheitliches Kampagnenkonzept abgelöst. Durch den verstärkten Einsatz emotionaler Bildmotive unter Verwendung von „Consumer Insights“ wurde die Marke Lufthansa in ersten Schritten gemäß dem Markenleitbild emotional weiterentwickelt.

5. Neuer Markenauftritt und zunehmende Emotionalisierung

Die beschriebenen Rahmenbedingungen erforderten in den Jahren 2002/03 die Kommunikation von Preisangeboten. Qualitativ kaufentscheidende Faktoren, wie zum Beispiel Marke, Netz oder Produkt, wurden nur geringfügig beworben. Eine solch einseitige Konzentration auf Preiswerbung kann langfristig zu einem Werteverfall und Vertrauensverlust der Nachfrager in die Marke Lufthansa führen. Ergebnisse einer Lufthansa Markenuntersuchung im Jahr 2002 zeigten, dass Lufthansa im Vergleich zu den Wettbewerbern in wesentlichen Markenbestandteilen relativ verloren hat.

Ein weiteres Verbesserungspotenzial der Lufthansa Kommunikation bilden die in der Vergangenheit sehr vielschichtigen Auftritte und Botschaften. Diese führten zu einer nicht eindeutigen Wahrnehmung der Marke Lufthansa.

Im Herbst 2003 wurden mit der Kommunikation zur Einführung der neuen Business Class auf Langstrecken erste Schritte in Richtung einer neuen Fokussierung auf Produkt- und Qualitätsthemen begonnen. Im ersten Halbjahr 2004 erfolgten eine Reduktion der Preiskommunikation und eine inhaltliche Konzentration auf die klare Hervorhebung von differenzierenden USP’s im Produkt. Die Kampagne zur Einführung der neuen Business Class auf Langstrecken – mit dem längsten Bett seiner Klasse – wurde fortgeführt durch die Einführung der neuen Business Class im Kontinentalverkehr. Kernbotschaft war es hier, dass Lufthansa als einzige Airline Europas auf nationalen und europäischen Strecken den Mittelsitz in der Business Class frei hält. Im Mai 2004 wurde die Innovationsführerschaft von FlyNet®, dem Lufthansa Internetbreitbandportal an Bord der Interkontinental Flotte, gelauncht.

Marketingstrategisch bildet das Lufthansa „Marketing House" den Rahmen für einen integrierten Marketing-Auftritt zur Emotionalisierung der Marke Lufthansa. Die Maxime lautet „Creating value through integrated Marketing". Über fünf Säulen werden die strategischen Eckpfeiler verankert (vgl. Abbildung 10).

1. Premium-Positionierung,
2. Differenzierung/Segmentierung,
3. Internationalisierung,
4. Wachstumsperspektiven,
5. Kunden-Know-how.

Abbildung 10: **Premiumpositionierung „Marketing House"**

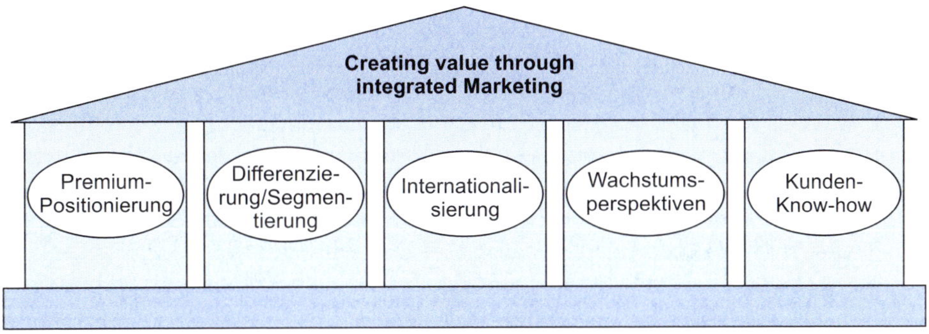

Die Premium Positionierung Lufthansa's wird durch Produkt- und Markenkommunikation kontinuierlich weiter ausgebaut.

Auf der Basis der Kommunikation der Produkt- und Qualitätsthemen wurde die neue internationale Markenkampagne „All for this one moment" entwickelt (vgl. Abbildung 11).

Der Kerngedanke der internationalen Markenkampagne ist Vertrauen. Vertrauen kann durch Kommunikation gesteigert werden, indem die Fähigkeiten und Taten „beim Kunden Gutes tun zu können" unter Beweis gestellt und zeitgleich aber auch Motivation und Ziele dahinter aufgezeigt werden, „Gutes tun zu wollen". Beides ist im beschriebenen Markenleitbild durch die Werte „Streben nach Perfektion", „Führungsanspruch", „Glaubwürdigkeit" und „Persönliches Engagement" verankert. Die Markenkampagne leitet daraus die Leitidee „Passion for Satisfaction" ab.

Abbildung 11: Internationale Markenkampagne

GABLER GRAFIK

Im Kreativkonzept dokumentiert Lufthansa Kundenorientierung und Nähe zum Fluggast. Sein positives Produkt- beziehungsweise Reiseerlebnis mit Lufthansa und der differenzierende Moment werden emotional inszeniert. Der Moment der besonderen Zufriedenheit der Nachfrager bildet den Mittelpunkt der neuen Kampagne „All for this one moment", im Bild festgehalten durch extreme Close-ups. Die Ansprache ist nicht distanziert und rein faktisch, sondern sie ist verbindlich und nah. Mittels eines starken visuellen Auftritts werden über den Text – ein Dreiklang – Vertrauen schaffende Leistungsaspekte kommuniziert und das persönliche Engagement herausgestellt. Die Steadyline „All for this one moment" wird in die jeweilige Landessprache übersetzt und bildet neben einer einheitlichen Bildauffassung die Kampagnenklammer.

Die Kampagne wurde in sieben strategischen Lufthansa Märkten getestet. Als Gesamtergebnis wurde die Kampagne für sehr gut, differenzierend und zielführend für Lufthansa bewertet.

Die Kampagne verfolgt dabei einen ganzheitlichen Ansatz, das heißt, für alle Themen (Marke, Produkt, Netz und Preis) und Medien wird ein integrativer Auftritt geschaffen, der Lufthansa einheitlich präsentiert. Ferner wurde die formale Anzeigengestaltung, die so genannte Bühne, überarbeitet, die durch teilweise Transparenz moderner und emotionaler wirkt (vgl. Abbildung 12). Bestehen bleibt der unverkennbare Absender: Lufthansa.

Abbildung 12: **Motiv „Sleeping Couple"**

GABLER GRAFIK

6. Zusammenfassung und Konklusion

Lufthansa – Die Marke als wesentlicher Wettbewerbsfaktor

Der Wert der Marke Lufthansa wird im Airline-Dienstleistungssektor zunehmend wichtiger. Eine starke und eindeutig positionierte Marke Lufthansa ist ein entscheidender Differenzierungsfaktor, insbesondere vor dem Hintergrund des zunehmenden Wachstums von No Frills Airlines.

Lufthansa stellt emotional aufgeladene Vermittlung von Innovationen und Qualitätsführerschaft in den Vordergrund der Markenkommunikation und baut somit gemäß dem Markenleitbild den Wert der Marke Lufthansa aus.

Eine verstärkte Emotionalisierung der Kernbenefits und eine eindeutige Premium-Positionierung stehen zukünftig noch stärker im strategischen Marketingfokus.

„There's no better way to fly"

Markenführung in Stiftungen – Beispiel Bertelsmann Stiftung

Heribert Meffert

1.	**Einführung**	**838**
2.	**Mission der Bertelsmann Stiftung – Leitbild als Fundament**	**838**
3.	**Bedeutung der Marke für die Arbeit der Bertelsmann Stiftung**	**840**
4.	**Genese des Markenkerns der Bertelsmann Stiftung**	**843**
4.1	Ausgangssituation	843
4.2	Entwicklung des Markenkerns	844
4.21	Inhaltlicher Markenkern	844
4.22	Definition der Arbeitsweise und des Anspruchs	846
4.3	Notwendigkeit einer Dachmarke	848
5.	**Fazit**	**851**

1. Einführung

Für nahezu alle Produkt- und Dienstleistungsbereiche haben sich Marken in ihrer Funktion als Orientierungs- und Vertrauensanker etabliert. Starke Marken bürgen für hochwertige Qualität und helfen damit den Nachfragern bei der Kaufentscheidung. Zunehmend findet der Markengedanke inzwischen auch im Non-Profit-Bereich Eingang, zumal auch NPOs großen Nutzen aus einer wertvollen Marke ziehen können. Hierzu soll im folgenden Beitrag der Nutzen der Marke für Stiftungen am Beispiel der Bertelsmann Stiftung dargestellt werden.

Als operative Stiftung ist die Bertelsmann Stiftung dann erfolgreich, wenn es ihr gelingt, die Entscheider in Politik und Gesellschaft zu beeinflussen. Das Vertrauen der Zielgruppen und Stakeholder in Kompetenz, Integrität und Unabhängigkeit der Bertelsmann Stiftung ist für die gesellschaftliche Wirkung der Stiftungsarbeit ausschlaggebend. Diese Faktoren bestimmen auch die Identität der Marke „Bertelsmann Stiftung“ und sie gehen aus ihrem Leitbild hervor.

2. Mission der Bertelsmann Stiftung – Leitbild als Fundament

Die Bertelsmann Stiftung engagiert sich in der Tradition ihres Gründers **Reinhard Mohn** für das Gemeinwohl. Fundament der Stiftungsarbeit ist die Überzeugung, dass Wettbewerb und bürgerschaftliches Engagement die Grundlage gesellschaftlichen Fortschritts bilden. Die Arbeit beruht auf der Einsicht Reinhard Mohns, dass unternehmerisches Denken und Handeln entscheidend dazu beitragen, gesellschaftliche Probleme zu lösen und starre Strukturen aufzubrechen. Das **Mission-Statement** lautet deshalb: „Die Bertelsmann Stiftung versteht sich als Förderin des gesellschaftlichen Wandels und unterstützt das Ziel einer zukunftsfähigen Gesellschaft. Die Stiftung will frühzeitig gesellschaftliche Herausforderungen und Probleme identifizieren sowie exemplarische Lösungsmodelle entwickeln und verwirklichen.“

Im **Leitbild** werden die normativen Grundhaltungen und Werte der Stiftung definiert. Das Leitbild gibt Orientierung nach innen, und es macht nach außen deutlich, wofür die Bertelsmann Stiftung steht. Es ist das **Fundament der Stiftung**, auf dem sie sich langfristig strategisch ausrichtet. Das Leitbild ist damit auch die Grundlage für die Inhalte der Projektarbeit und stellt sicher, dass Selbstbild und Fremdbild der Marke „Bertelsmann Stiftung“ übereinstimmen. Das Leitbild ist kein starrer Rahmen; es entwickelt sich evolutionär durch die Impulse neuer Projekte.

Um eine größere Wirkung der Arbeit der Bertelsmann Stiftung zu erreichen, wurde nach der Verabschiedung des Leitbildes ein umfangreicher Strategie- und Changeprozess angestoßen. Die Ziele des **Strategie-Prozesses** waren:

- Entwicklung einer **einheitlichen Stiftungsstrategie** mit einem konsistenten hierarchischen Zielsystem,
- Ableitung von **strategischen Zielen für die Themenfelder** aus den strategischen Zielen der Stiftung,
- **Fokussierung der Projektarbeit** der Bertelsmann Stiftung durch strategische Orientierung,
- **verbesserte Vernetzung** der Inhalte und Projekte,
- Entwicklung von **Leitprojekten** und themenfeldübergreifenden Großprojekten, um eine stärkere Entscheider-Orientierung zu erreichen und damit eine bessere Hebelwirkung,
- **Redesign der Kernprozesse** zur Effektivitäts- und Effizienzsteigerung sowie
- aus der Strategie abgeleitete **Profilierung der Marke** „Bertelsmann Stiftung".

Abbildung 1: Konzeption des strategischen Managements der Bertelsmann Stiftung

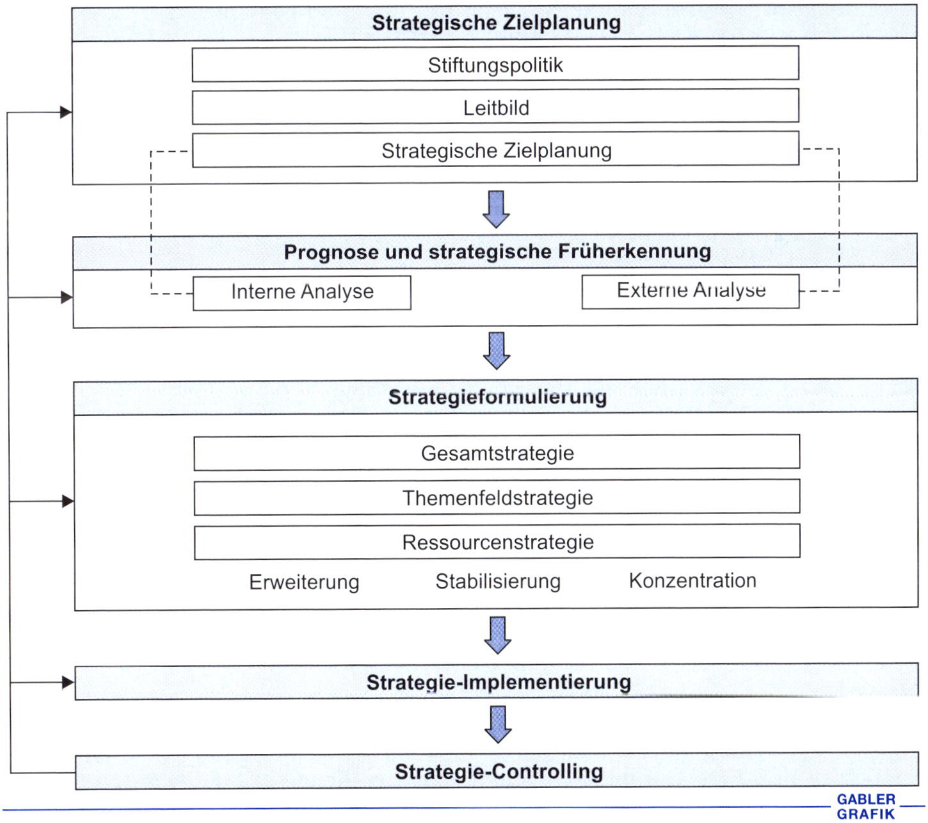

Durch den Strategieprozess wurde die Anzahl der Projekte deutlich reduziert und die Arbeit auf vier Themenfelder fokussiert: Bildung, Gesundheit, Internationale Verständigung sowie Wirtschaft & Soziales. Daneben bestehen Kompetenzfelder, die sich mit den Themen Stiftungsentwicklung, Unternehmenskultur und Führungsphilosophie sowie mit Kultur befassen.

Im Rahmen des Strategie-Prozesses wurde ein **Konzept zum strategischen Management der Bertelsmann Stiftung** entwickelt, das in seiner idealen Ausprägung in Abbildung 1 dargestellt ist.

3. Bedeutung der Marke für die Arbeit der Bertelsmann Stiftung

Aus dieser organisatorischen strategischen Grundausrichtung werden Projekte generiert und umgesetzt. Die entstehenden **gesellschaftlichen Innovationen** können im besten Sinne als Dienstleistungen für die Gesellschaft bezeichnet werden. Eine Innovation ist aus Stiftungsperspektive erfolgreich, wenn sie zur Zukunftsfähigkeit der Gesellschaft beiträgt. Die Generierung und Verbreitung gesellschaftlicher Innovationen erfolgt in der Bertelsmann Stiftung im Idealfall nach dem in Abbildung 2 dargestellten Schema.

Markenprofilierung als integraler Bestandteil der Projektarbeit

Eine klare und konsistente **Profilierung der Marke** „Bertelsmann Stiftung“ ist nicht Selbstzweck, sondern integrierender und integraler Bestandteil der Projektarbeit. Die Vertrauenssignale stützen sowohl die Zusammenarbeit mit Partnern als auch die Verbreitung der Innovationen.

Durch die strategische Neuausrichtung verwandelt sich die Stiftung immer mehr in einen „Think Tank“, der sich hauptsächlich mit der Entwicklung von Konzepten befasst. Es hat sich gezeigt, dass der Hebel von Modellprojekten oftmals nicht ausreicht, um den gesellschaftlichen Wandel zu unterstützen. Die wichtigste Zielgruppe der Stiftungsarbeit sind demnach **Entscheider in Politik und Wirtschaft**. Ein Beispiel für diese Neuausrichtung ist das Projekt „Demografischer Wandel“. Dort arbeitet die Stiftung mit Bundesministerien, gemeinnützigen Einrichtungen, Unternehmen und Medien zusammen. Mit Modellprojekten werden weiterhin aber auch Personengruppen in gesellschaftlichen Institutionen wie Schulen und Kindergärten angesprochen. Schließlich soll aber auch die breite Öffentlichkeit über gezielte Kampagnen erreicht werden.

Abbildung 2: **Projektarbeit als Innovationsgenerierung und Innovationsdiffusion**

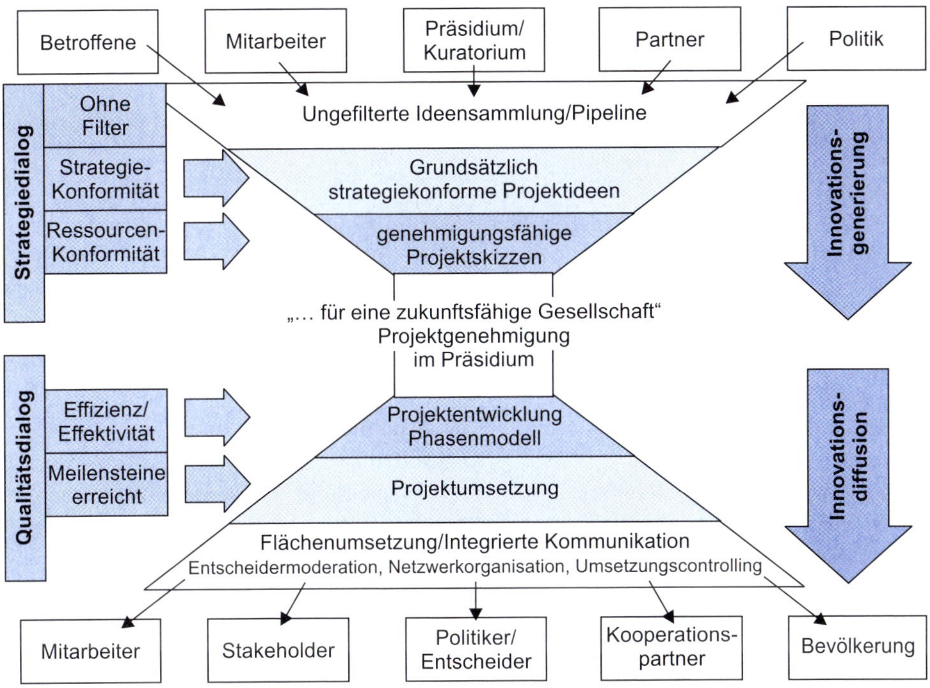

GABLER GRAFIK

Um die Adressaten der Stiftungsarbeit zu erreichen, kommt der **Marke „Bertelsmann Stiftung“** eine überragende Bedeutung zu. Die Marke erfüllt dabei **drei Funktionen**: Sie dient der **Risikoreduktion** beim Empfänger, indem sie Sicherheit, Kontinuität und **Vertrauen** schafft. Sie steigert die **Informationseffizienz**, da sie dem Empfänger eine schnelle Orientierung ermöglicht. Schließlich stiften Marken auch einen **ideellen Nutzen** als Prestige oder Gruppenzugehörigkeit (vgl. Abbildung 3).

Vertrauen ist für die Bertelsmann Stiftung von besonderer Bedeutung, da die **Produkte ihrer Arbeit immateriell** sind, sie sich also nicht unmittelbar messen lassen. Die positiven Effekte für die Gesellschaft wirken zudem langfristig, sodass ein direkter Erfolgsnachweis nicht einfach ist. Dass die Innovationen der Bertelsmann Stiftung weder kommerziellen Interessen noch den Interessen Dritter dienen, sondern allein dem Gemeinwohl – dieses Vertrauen kann nur durch eine starke Marke aufgebaut werden, welche die Identität der Stiftung authentisch widerspiegelt. Voraussetzung für eine **nachhaltig erfolgreiche Markenprofilierung** ist, dass das Image der Marke auch der gelebten Identität der Marke entspricht. Ein Ziel der Markenführung nach innen und außen ist die Übereinstimmung von **Selbstbild und Fremdbild**.

Abbildung 3: Funktionen der Marke „Bertelsmann Stiftung"

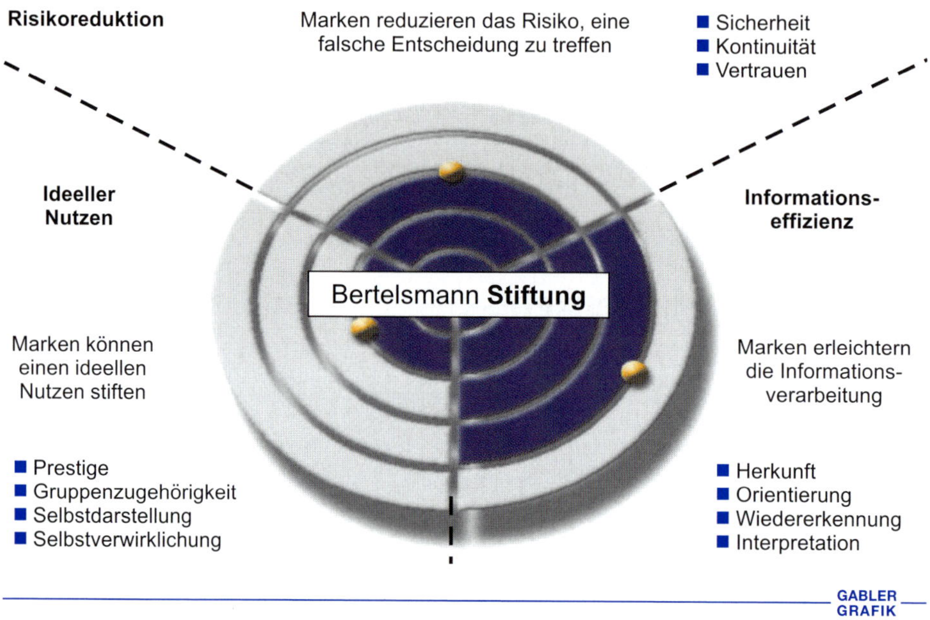

Bedeutung der Marke zur Differenzierung gegenüber den Wettbewerbern

Neben den Vertrauens- und Informationsfunktionen erfüllt die Marke „Bertelsmann Stiftung" eine wichtige **Differenzierungsfunktion** im Wettbewerb um die besten Ideen. Die Bertelsmann Stiftung sieht sich nicht nur im Wettbewerb mit anderen Stiftungen, sondern auch mit politischen Einrichtungen oder Partei-Stiftungen sowie Beratungsunternehmen des Profit-Sektors. Dabei ist unter Wettbewerb nicht die Verdrängung anderer Organisationen zu verstehen. Vielmehr ist die Bertelsmann Stiftung überzeugt, dass sich die besten Lösungen durchsetzen. Mit diesem Ziel sieht die Bertelsmann Stiftung die Beziehung zu Wettbewerbern eher als „cooptition-Beziehung" und sucht die **Kooperation mit anderen Organisationen**. Dadurch sollen nicht nur Doppelarbeiten vermieden, sondern Effizienzvorteile genutzt werden. Bei allem kommt es aber darauf an, einen Mehrwert für die Gesellschaft zu schaffen.

Interne Bedeutung der Marke

Nicht nur nach außen, sondern auch gegenüber den Mitarbeitern der Stiftung erfüllt die Marke eine wichtige, nämlich ideelle Funktion. Das Gefühl, an einer guten und sinnvollen Sache mitzuarbeiten, ist in einer Non-Profit-Organisation die Grundlage für ein hohes Identifikationspotenzial und für die Motivation der Mitarbeiter besonders wichtig.

Verantwortung für die Markenführung

Wegen der Bedeutung der Marke für die Erfüllung des Stiftungszwecks trägt die **oberste Führungsebene** die Verantwortung für Aufbau, Pflege und Implementierung der Marke. Die Bertelsmann Stiftung ist überzeugt davon, dass die Wirkung und damit der Erfolg der Stiftungsarbeit durch den Aufbau einer starken Marke gefördert werden. Die heterogenen Projekte machen eine übergreifende Steuerung der Marke notwendig.

Da eine Marke nur dann stark ist, wenn das **Selbstbild dem Fremdbild** entspricht, werden die Mitarbeiter in den Prozess der Markenprofilierung und -entwicklung einbezogen.

4. Genese des Markenkerns der Bertelsmann Stiftung

4.1 Ausgangssituation

Eine Umfrage im Jahr 2001 durch das F.A.Z.-Institut unter 514 Entscheidern ergab, dass nur 15 Prozent der Befragten mit der Stiftung konkrete (Projekt-)Inhalte verbinden (vgl. Abbildung 4).

Abbildung 4: **Einschätzung der Marke „Bertelsmann Stiftung"**

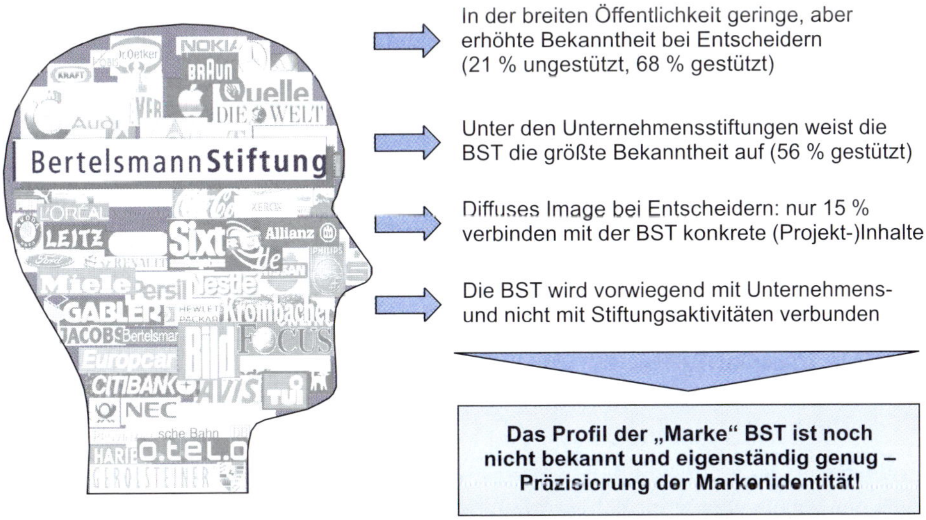

GABLER GRAFIK

Quelle: F.A.Z.-Institut

Chancen:

- Bislang existieren keine starken Marken im Wettbewerbsumfeld (andere Stiftungen).
- Es sind ausreichende finanzielle und personelle Ressourcen zum Aufbau einer starken Marke vorhanden.
- Generell besteht eine hohe Akzeptanz der Stiftungsarbeit in der Bevölkerung und bei Entscheidern. Dies eröffnet Chancen für den Aufbau einer starken Stiftungsmarke.
- Im relevanten Wettbewerbsumfeld existiert eine verhältnismäßig gute und ausbaufähige Wahrnehmung.

Risiken:

- Die Marke „Bertelsmann Stiftung“ besitzt ein diffuses Image.
- Die Heterogenität des Projektportfolios wird durch uneinheitliche Darstellung von Projekten verstärkt.
- Derzeit wird von der Bertelsmann Stiftung noch keine einheitliche Hauptbotschaft offensiv kommuniziert.
- Es wird derzeit kein einheitliches Corporate Design genutzt.
- Eine nicht abgestimmte Zielgruppenplanung führt zu Redundanzen in der Ansprache.
- Der Wettbewerb von Stiftungen und Institutionen um den Share of Mind bei Entscheidern steigt.

4.2 Entwicklung des Markenkerns

4.21 Inhaltlicher Markenkern

Um ein konsistentes Markenführungskonzept zu entwickeln, wurde zunächst das Selbstbild der Stiftung konkretisiert. Hierbei war das Stiftungsleitbild ein idealer Ausgangspunkt für die Entwicklung des **Markenleitbildes**. Im Leitbild sind die **zentralen Werte der Stiftung** verankert: Freiheit, Wettbewerb und Solidarität.

Freiheit: Die individuelle Freiheit, eigene Ziele und Lebensentwürfe zu verfolgen, ist nicht nur Voraussetzung für Selbstentfaltung und damit persönliches Glück. Sie ist auch Bedingung für die Zukunftsfähigkeit einer offenen Gesellschaft. Moderne, offene Gesellschaften zeichnen sich dadurch aus, dass die Menschen trotz unterschiedlicher individueller Ziele auf der Grundlage gemeinsamer Werte friedlich zusammenleben. Gerade in der Unterschiedlichkeit der Ziele sieht die Bertelsmann Stiftung die Chance für kreative Vielfalt und Innovation und damit für gesellschaftlichen Fortschritt.

Abbildung 5: **Vorgehen bei der Erarbeitung des Markenkerns in mehreren Workshops**

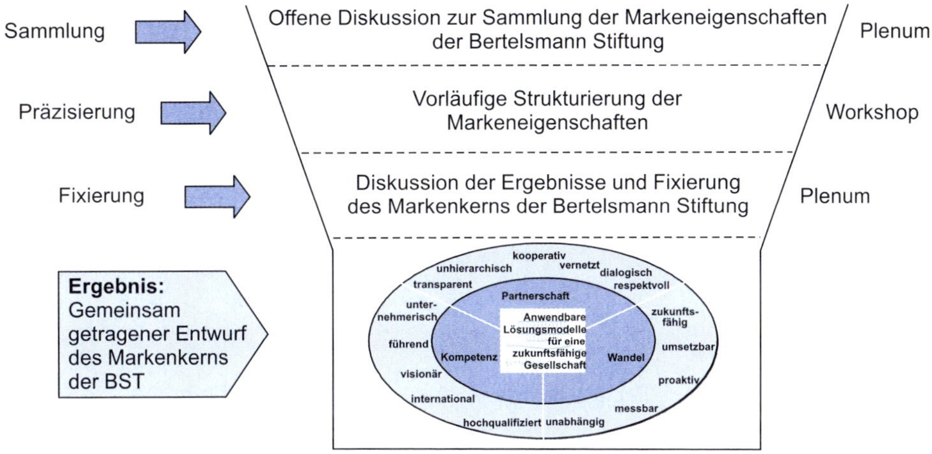

GABLER GRAFIK

Wettbewerb: Im Wettbewerb konkurrieren unterschiedliche Theorien, Ideen und Lösungskonzepte. Wettbewerb ist ein „Entdeckungsverfahren". Zugleich übernimmt der Wettbewerb eine wichtige Selektions- und Diffusionsfunktion: Erfolgreiche Theorien, Ideen und Lösungen setzen sich durch. Einziges Entscheidungskriterium ist dabei die Nützlichkeit für die Gesellschaft.

Solidarität: Eine Gesellschaft, in der Solidarität und Menschlichkeit nicht mehr zum Wertekanon gehören, untergräbt ihren eigenen Freiheitsspielraum. Wenn es keinen Konsens über Solidarität, Menschlichkeit und gesellschaftliche Verantwortung gibt, entsteht eine entsolidarisierte, bindungslose Gesellschaft, in der jeder rücksichtslos nur die eigenen Ziele verfolgt und in der sich der Staat veranlasst sehen könnte, Solidarität zu erzwingen.

Themenfelder und Projekte der Bertelsmann Stiftung zielen darauf ab, auf der Grundlage der Werte Freiheit, Wettbewerb und Solidarität einen Beitrag zur Zukunftsfähigkeit unseres Wirtschafts- und Gesellschaftssystems zu leisten. Damit ist der inhaltliche Markenkern definiert. Der **innerste Markenkern** – Freiheit, Wettbewerb und Solidarität – wird durch die Aussage **„Für eine zukunftsfähige Gesellschaft"** repräsentiert. Auch die Arbeitsweise der Stiftung prägt die Marke. Diese Charakterisierung findet sich in den Zonen, die den Markenkern umschließen.

4.22 Definition der Arbeitsweise und des Anspruchs

Nachdem der inhaltliche Kern der Marke definiert war, wurde auch die Arbeitsweise der Stiftung entlang dreier zentraler Fragen präzisiert (vgl. Abbildung 6):

1. Wo und wie suchen wir Themen?
2. Wie bearbeiten wir Themen?
3. Welchen Anspruch haben wir an unsere Ergebnisse?

Abbildung 6: Markenkern „Bertelsmann Stiftung"

GABLER GRAFIK

Die **erste Definitionszone des Markenkerns** wird durch die Adjektive unabhängig, operativ und unternehmerisch sowie wirkungsvoll charakterisiert.

Die **Unabhängigkeit** ist dadurch gesichert, dass die Bertelsmann Stiftung in keinerlei finanzieller Abhängigkeit von Dritten steht und inhaltlich nur ihrem Leitbild verpflichtet ist. Die Stiftung ist auf Initiative von Reinhard Mohn und in der Tradition des gesellschaftlichen Engagements der Familie entstanden. Als Stiftung der Familie ist die Bertelsmann Stiftung auch unabhängig von den Interessen der Bertelsmann AG.

Aus dem Geist des Leitbildes heraus generiert die Bertelsmann Stiftung Projekte, die sie selbst bearbeitet. Die Bertelsmann Stiftung will die Gesellschaft zukunftsfähig machen; die Ergebnisse der Projektarbeit sollen also stets **wirkungsvoll** sein.

Gegenüber den Wettbewerbern grenzt sich die Bertelsmann Stiftung durch ihre Unterscheidungskriterien **(Differenziatoren)** ab: Sie ist eine operative Stiftung, deren Projektarbeit unternehmerisch geprägt ist (vgl. Abbildung 7). Die Größe der Stiftung macht ein professionelles Management mit Zielhierarchie und strategischer Orientierung erforderlich. Die Bertelsmann Stiftung sieht sich nicht als Beratungsorganisation, sondern versteht sich als Partner der Politik und der gesellschaftlichen Entscheidungsträger. Dieser Anspruch unterscheidet sie von kommerziellen Beratern und unterstützt den Implementierungsanspruch der Projekte. Im Gegensatz zu parteinahen Stiftungen ist die Bertelsmann Stiftung politisch unabhängig und nicht interessengebunden.

Abbildung 7: Präzisierung und Fixierung des Markenkerns

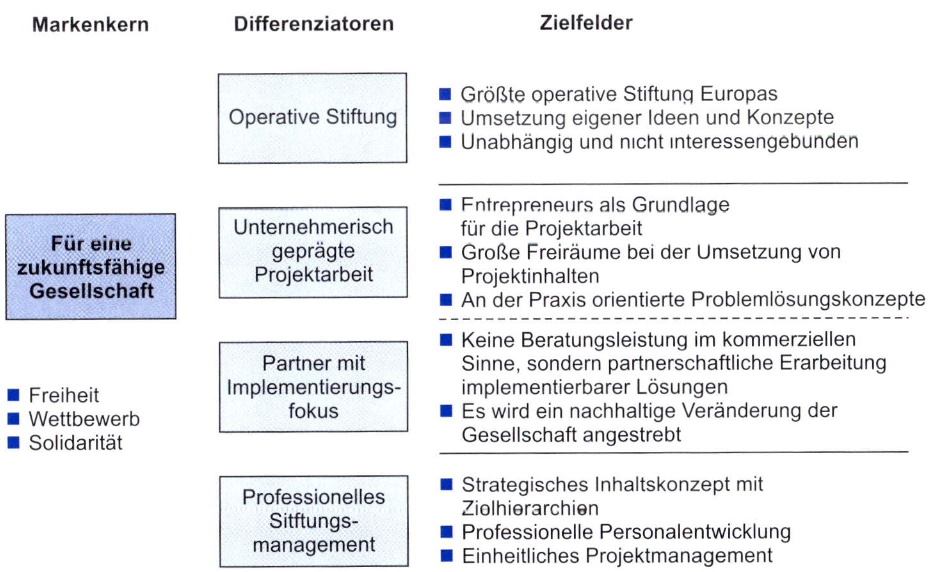

GABLER GRAFIK

4.3 Notwendigkeit einer Dachmarke

Die Profilierung der Marke ließ sich für die Bertelsmann Stiftung wegen des heterogenen Themenspektrums und der Vielzahl der Projekte nur durch eine konsequente **Dachmarkenarchitektur** erzielen. Weil die Bertelsmann Stiftung mit ihrem Leitbild und den darin verankerten Werten ein **solides Fundament** besitzt, können die vielfältigen Projekte konsistent unter einer Dachmarke vereint werden.

Da die Homogenisierung der Produkte immer mehr zunimmt und die Zahl der Anbieter für Produkte und Leistungen durch die Globalisierung in die Höhe geschnellt ist, ist die Marke zu einem der letzten Differenzierungsmerkmale geworden. Dies zwingt zu klarer Fokussierung der Kommunikationsaktivitäten, die nur mithilfe einer Dachmarkenstrategie gelingen kann. All dies gilt auch für den Non-Profit-Bereich, denn: Wer gesellschaftliche Wirkung erzielen will, muss **wahrgenommen** werden. Ist diese Hürde genommen, muss bewiesen werden, dass Leistungen die versprochene Qualität besitzen. Da diese **Qualität** bei **immateriellen Produkten** nur schwer messbar ist, ist Vertrauen eine wesentliche Voraussetzung für die Wirkung der Projektarbeit.

Abbildung 8: **Dynamik der Dachmarkenarchitektur der Bertelsmann Stiftung**

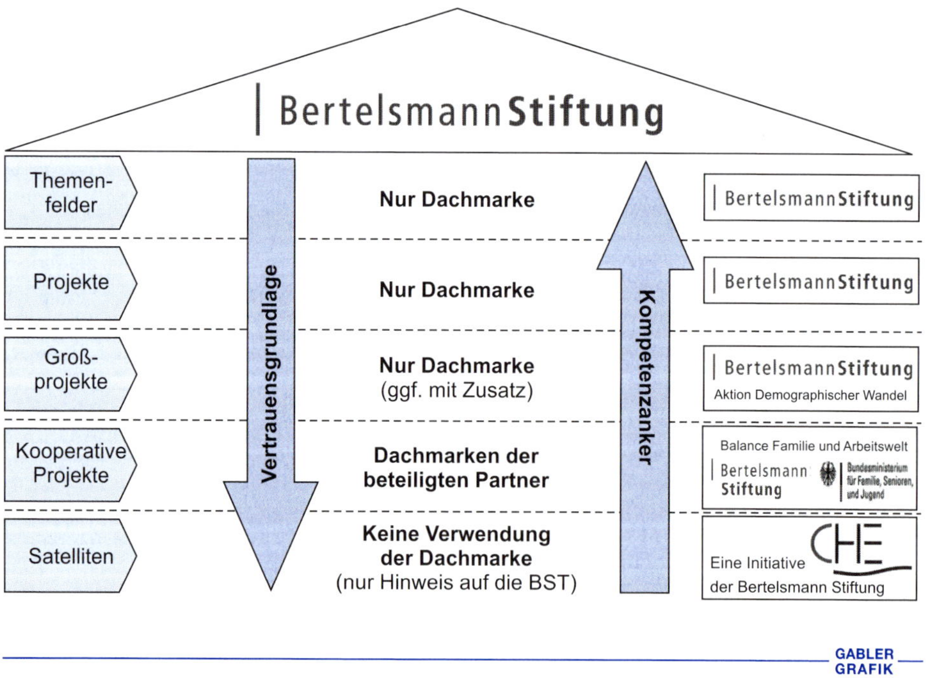

Durch das Dachmarkenkonzept erhält die Marke „Bertelsmann Stiftung" Klarheit, koordinierende Kraft und Stringenz. Die Dachmarke dient als **Türöffner** und **Vertrauensanker** für die Projekte. Diese Funktion kann sie nur erfüllen, wenn sie über die Inhalte der Projekte substanziell **aufgeladen** wird. Dabei muss der Auftritt der Einzelprojekte und Themenfelder das Image der Dachmarke untermauern. Die Integrität der Dachmarke strahlt auf die Projekte ab, die wiederum mit ihren substanziellen Ergebnissen die Dachmarke stärken (vgl. Abbildung 8).

Den Regeln entsprechend erfolgt die Markierung der Themenfelder und Kompetenzbereiche durch die Dachmarke „Bertelsmann Stiftung". Ausnahmen gibt es zum Beispiel bei sehr großen Projekten oder bei Projekten, die mit starken Kooperationspartnern gemacht werden. Hier kann die Dachmarke mit einem projektspezifischen Zusatz versehen werden. Die Projektpartner werden dann ebenfalls aufgeführt. Die Regeln zur Verwendung der Dachmarke stehen in einem **Dachmarken-Handbuch**.

Für die **Implementierung der Dachmarkenstrategie** ist eine Umsetzung in drei Schritten eingeleitet worden. Ein Corporate Design (CD) wird für sämtliche Formen der Stiftungskommunikation festgelegt. Da der Aufbau einer Marke durch das Corporate Design maßgeblich beeinflusst wird, wurde das Logo der Bertelsmann Stiftung weiterentwickelt. Eine Wortmarke ersetzt die bisherige Bildmarke (vgl. Abbildung 9).

Abbildung 9: **Weiterentwicklung des Logos von einer Bild- zu einer Wortmarke**

Altes Logo	Neues Logo
Bertelsmann Stiftung	BertelsmannStiftung

GABLER GRAFIK

Das **neue Logo** ist **klar** und in allen Medien und Zusammenhängen gut lesbar. Durch Fettdruck liegt die Betonung auf dem Wort „Stiftung". Mit dem **einheitlichen Corporate Design** werden nicht nur Logo, Schrifttyp und Farbklima, sondern auch die jeweiligen Internetauftritte der Projekte, Printprodukte bis hin zu Präsentationsvorlagen versehen. Als dritter Baustein wird die dachmarken-konforme Kommunikation zukünftig für alle Projekte bereits in der Planungsphase im Sinne eines **integrierten Kommunikationsansatzes** mitentwickelt (vgl. Abbildung 10).

Abbildung 10: Integrierter Kommunikationsfahrplan (IKF): Workflow und Verantwortlichkeiten

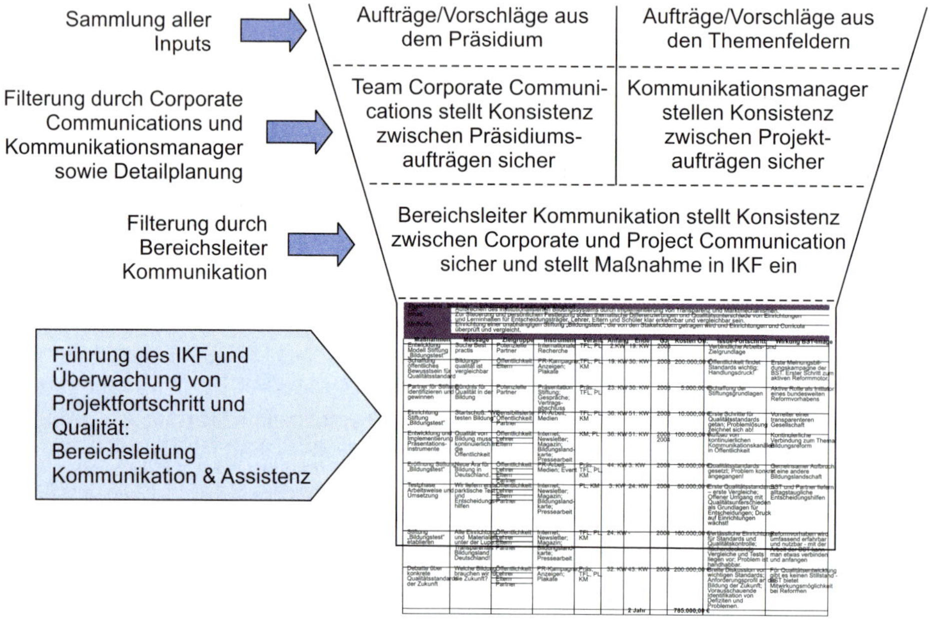

GABLER GRAFIK

Bei der integrierten Kommunikation sind neben der inhaltlichen Abstimmung der Themenfelder untereinander auch **Aspekte** des Timings zu berücksichtigen. Nicht nur die Zeitpunkte sind kommunikationsrelevant, zu denen konkrete Projektergebnisse vorliegen. Vielmehr müssen – dem Lebenszyklus gesellschaftlicher Anliegen entsprechend (vgl. Abbildung 11) – strategische Zeitfenster identifiziert werden, die eine effiziente Kommunikation ermöglichen.

Abbildung 11: Lebenszyklusmodell öffentlicher Anliegen

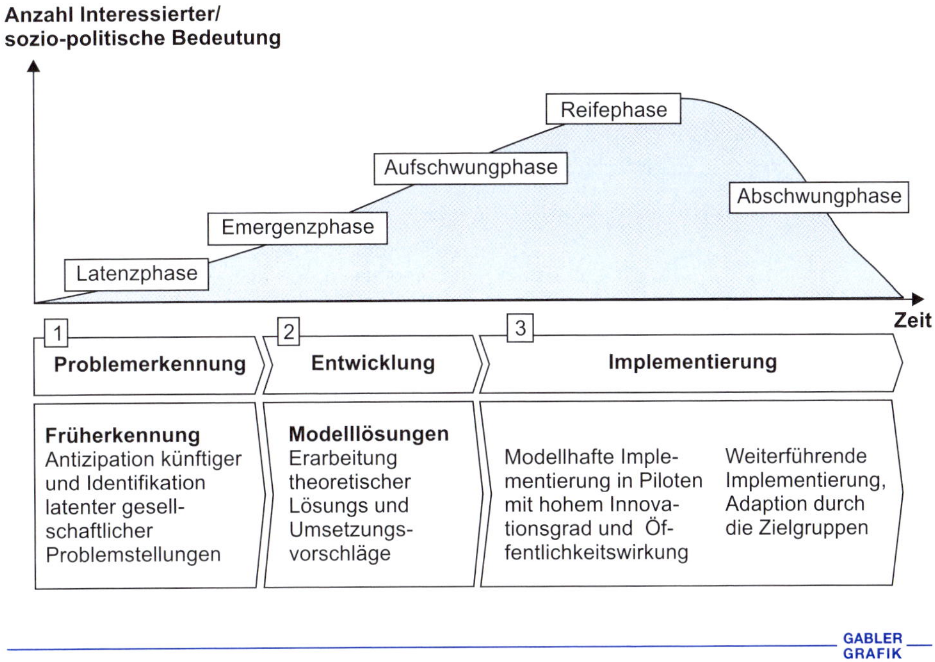

Neben den langfristig absehbaren Kommunikations-Zeitfenstern müssen auch aktuelle Ereignisse adaptiert und als Kommunikationsanlass berücksichtigt werden.

5. Fazit

Mit einer Marke, die externen und internen Anspruchsgruppen als Vertrauensanker dient, die regelmäßig über die konkrete Projektarbeit kompetenzorientiert aufgeladen wird und die auf Basis eines integrierten strategischen Kommunikationsfahrplans gesteuert wird, kann die Entwicklung und Verbreitung gesellschaftlicher Innovation in effizienter Form gelingen. Diesen handwerklichen Anforderungen übergeordnet bleibt jedoch die Forderung, die Marke „Bertelsmann Stiftung" auch zu leben und ihr dadurch Authentizität und Überzeugungskraft zu verleihen.

KAPITEL

6 Ausblick

Kritische Reflektion zum Markenmanagement 855
Christoph Burmann

Kritische Reflektion zum Markenmanagement

Christoph Burmann

Markenführung kommt von Marke. „Mensch, Du bist mir eine Marke", heißt es dazu im Volksmund. Was lehrt uns das?

Marken haben etwas mit besonderem Charakter zu tun, sei es bei Menschen oder „Artikeln". Sie stechen hervor aus der Masse. Das heißt zugleich, nicht jeder kann herausragen. Vordergründig für einen kurzen Moment vielleicht, aber nicht tief und nachhaltig.

Wer sind solche hervorstechenden Charaktere und wie **entstehen** sie?

Alleskönner? Everybody's Darling? Nein! Der Zehnkämpfer ist auch bei den Olympischen Sommerspielen eine Ausnahmeerscheinung. Führend ist man selten auf allen Gebieten. Die Ecken und Kanten der hier gesuchten Charaktere sind das Ergebnis von Konsequenz und klaren Prinzipien. Ohne Fokussierung auf Weniges sind klare Prinzipien weder für Dritte erkennbar noch mit Konsequenz realisierbar. Verzicht spielt also offenkundig eine große Rolle. Erst dadurch wird die Konzentration auf das, was einem wichtig ist, möglich. Auch Ideen vermögen immer dann Anhänger zu mobilisieren, wenn sie einfach und damit reduziert sind. Und was sind Marken zunächst anderes als großartige Ideen zur Generierung eines überlegenen Kundennutzens?

Hervorstechende Charaktere reifen über die Zeit. Sie sammeln Erfahrungen auf ihrem individuellen Lebensweg. Der Ressourcentheoretiker wurde sagen, sie akkumulieren spezifisches Know-how in einem pfadabhängigen Prozess. Ein langer Atem ist hier von entscheidender Bedeutung. Erst Zeit erzeugt Prägungstiefe beim Charakter. Auch die Perfektionierung herausragender Fähigkeiten braucht Zeit. Die Bereitschaft, diese Zeit auch in Marken zu investieren, setzt Geduld voraus. Eine Eigenschaft, die vielen Markenführenden heute abhanden gekommen zu sein scheint. In Führung gehen schafft man nicht über Nacht. Nachäffen geht schneller, braucht keine Geduld, hat deshalb auch nichts mit hervorstechendem Charakter zu tun.

Fokussierung durch Verzicht und Reifung durch Geduld führen jedoch nur dann zu hervorstechenden Charakteren, wenn dabei **vorhandene Begabungen** genutzt werden. Das Gesagte gilt im Übrigen für Individuen wie Kollektive. Bei Letzteren spricht man von organisationalen Fähigkeiten statt von Begabungen. Auch hier gilt, begabt ist der Mensch und die Gruppe nie in Allem, sondern in Wenigem. Schwierig ist nicht nur bei Kindern – die rechtzeitige und richtige Entdeckung der zunächst verborgenen Begabungen. Ist das gelungen, kann ebenso gezielt wie geduldig gefördert werden. Früchte ernten wird man dabei aber nur, wenn der Geförderte selbst ein hohes Maß an Motivation, gelebtem Engagement und Konsequenz mitbringt.

Was am Anfang stand, „Du bist mir eine Marke", lässt sich also recht gut erklären. Als Phänomen auf zwischenmenschlicher Ebene und als Marke in anderen Bereichen. Daher erneut gefragt, was lehrt uns das für die Markenführung?

Der Aufbau starker Marken erfordert Verzicht. Erst die konsequente Fokussierung auf einen klaren, einfach zu kommunizierenden Kundennutzen lässt starke Marken entstehen. Differenzierung als wichtigstes konstitutives Merkmal von Marken ist durch Konzentration auf Wesentliches besser erreichbar. Dieses Wesentliche muss in der Identität einer Marke zum Ausdruck kommen. Beim Versuch, es allen recht zu machen, jedem zu dienen, bleibt die Markenidentität diffus. Die Identität starker Marken bezieht Position. Positionierung von Marken hat deshalb viel mit klarer Standortbestimmung zu tun.

Unter der distinguierten englischen Luxusmarke Jaguar nun auch einen preiswerten Mittelklasse-Kombi für Kleingewerbetreibende anzubieten, ist das Gegenteil von klarer Standortbestimmung. Fahrzeuge des koreanischen Autoherstellers Daewoo dem Kunden einmal unter der „Marke" Chevrolet, ein anderes Mal unter der „Marke" Daewoo anzubieten, ist von klarer Standortbestimmung ebenso weit entfernt wie die Verwendung von drei verschiedenen „Marken" innerhalb weniger Jahre für das Privatkundengeschäft der Deutschen Bank. Auch der zurzeit „trendige" Multikanalvertrieb mit der anvisierten Omnipräsenz einer Marke, der damit meist einhergehenden hohen Preisspreizung und heterogenen PoS-Präsentation, dürfte langfristig eher zur Schwächung als zur Stärkung einer Marke beitragen. Klare Standortbestimmung und Markenidentitäten setzen kompetente Strategiearbeit voraus. Strategie bedeutet immer Langfristigkeit im Denken, klare Prinzipien und Konsequenz im Handeln. Hieran scheint es heute öfter denn je zu mangeln! Ohne dieses Fundament jedoch sind Marken auf Sand gebaut und ihre Tage gezählt.

Eine klare Markenidentität ist zugleich die Bedingung für die Entstehung einer dauerhaften **Marke-Kunde-Beziehung**. Diese Beziehung zu treuen und werthaltigen Kunden ist die Grundlage für den ökonomischen Wert einer Marke. Die Messung des Customer Equity auf Basis dieser Beziehungsqualität daher der vielversprechendste Weg zur Quantifizierung des ökonomischen Markenwertes. Auch hier gilt: Der Aufbau stabiler Marke-Kunde-Beziehungen erfordert Geduld und Kundenorientierung. Beziehungen müssen wachsen und Markenvertrauen über die Zeit erworben werden. Die Marke muss sich also immer wieder neu als **kompetenter Problemlöser** für die Kunden erweisen. Das setzt einerseits ein tiefes Verständnis der Kunden und ihrer manifesten wie latenten Wünsche voraus, ganz im Sinne echter Kundennähe, andererseits nachhaltige Innovationskraft, um tatsächlich nutzenstiftende Lösungen wiederholt entwickeln zu können.

Wenn sich global tätige Konzerne aus dem Konsumgüterbereich damit brüsten, bis zu 0,8 Prozent ihres Umsatzes in die Forschung & Entwicklung zu investieren, gleichzeitig aber mehr als den zehnfachen Betrag in klassische Werbung, dann ist es mit der nachhaltigen Problemlösungskompetenz der betroffenen Marken meist nicht gut bestellt. Zu derselben Schlussfolgerung gelangt, wer die Gewinn- und Verlustrechnung eines großen deutschen Automobilunternehmens analysiert und dabei feststellt, dass 2004 mehr Geld für Produktrückrufaktionen als für die Forschung und Entwicklung ausgegeben wurde. Hat man sich Problemlösungskompetenz einmal erarbeitet, sollte genauestens überlegt werden, ob dieses kostbare Know-how den Einzelhandelsketten für deren Handelsmarken zur Verfügung gestellt wird. Nachgiebigkeit führt hier nur zur Erhöhung der Nachfragemacht und langfristig zum „Tod“ der eigenen Marke.

Praktische Beispiele für erhebliche **Defizite bei Kundennähe und Innovationskraft** von Marken gibt es leider viele: Mineralwasser-Marken, deren Verschluss von Kindern, Senioren und manchen Frauen aufgrund des hohen Kraftaufwandes kaum geöffnet werden kann. Packt „mann“ dann kräftig zu und öffnet sich der Verschluss, spritzt das sprudelnde Wasser – dünnwandigen PET-Flaschen sei „Dank“ – auf die Kleidung. Oder Automobil-Marken, die zeitwertgerechte Reparaturen auch nach 15 Jahren Marktforschung mit dem an dieser Stelle immer gleichen Kundenwunsch nicht zu realisieren in der Lage sind. Oder die Fondsgesellschaften und andere Finanzdienstleister, die es trotz hervorragender Ausgangssituation (dezidierte Kundendaten sind vorhanden) bis heute selten geschafft haben, eine stabile, auf die Bedürfnisse der Kunden Rücksicht nehmende Beziehung zwischen Marke und Kunden aufzubauen. Der einmal jährlich eintreffende Standardbrief mit Geburtstagsglückwünschen begründet noch keine Beziehung zur Marke.

Damit keine Missverständnisse auftreten, Kundennähe und stabile Markenbeziehungen haben nichts mit oberflächlich-austauschbarer Gefühlsduselei durch die x-fache Wiederholung eines „emotional-aufgeladenen“ TV-Spots mit viel „Liebe“ zu tun. Im Gegenteil, es ist zumeist Ausdruck fehlender Kundennähe, weil beliebig und unglaubwürdig.

Ein erster Schritt, dieser Austauschbarkeit entgegenzutreten, ist das Sich-Bewusst-Machen der eigenen **Herkunft**. Sie ist für Kunden die erste wichtige Referenz zur Beurteilung der Authentizität einer Marke und damit auch der subjektiv empfundenen Nähe zu einer Marke. Unternehmensintern führt die Analyse der eigenen Herkunft oft zielsicher zu den „verborgenen Begabungen“ im Sinne der zu kultivierenden organisationalen Fähigkeiten einer Marke.

Zwei wichtige Ausprägungsformen dieser spezifischen Markenkompetenzen sind nachhaltige Innovationskraft und die Fähigkeit, den Kunden in seinem gesamten Lebenszyklus und allen Bedarfssituationen umfassend zu verstehen und ihm nahe zu sein. Letzteres bezieht sich nicht nur auf die Marktforschung, ersteres nicht nur auf die Forschungs- und Entwicklungsabteilung, sondern auf die gesamte Markenorganisation. An dieser Stelle ein letzter Bezug zu hervorstechenden Charakteren. Diese Personen sind sich meistens ihrer besonderen Fähigkeiten beziehungsweise Begabungen bewusst und „gestalten“ ihre Identität auf der Basis ihrer Begabungen. Davon sollte die Markenführung lernen.

Nachhaltig innovationsfähig kann eine Marke nur dort sein, wo ihren **Produkten und Dienstleistungen** ebenso spezifische wie werthaltige Kompetenzen zugrunde liegen. Werthaltigkeit ist das Ergebnis einer guten Passigkeit zwischen organisationalen Fähigkeiten und Kundenwünschen. Markenerweiterungsstrategien sind somit enge Grenzen gesetzt, wenn diese Kompetenzen nicht mehr oder nur noch in geringem Umfang genutzt werden können. Auch Mehrmarkenstrategien sind aus diesem Grund oft enge Grenzen gesetzt. Sie sind beim Automobilkonzern General Motors offenkundig überschritten. Die weltweite Zentralisation wichtiger Unternehmensfunktionen an jeweils einem Ort mit anschließender Nutzung dieser Funktionen durch mehrere Konzernmarken unterbindet die Entwicklung markenspezifischer Kompetenzen. Die Substanzschwäche der Mehrmarkenstrategie von GM zeigt sich nicht zuletzt an der seit sechs Jahren weltweit niedrigsten Umsatzrentabilität in der Automobilbranche. Hervorstechende Charaktere sind ohne spezifische Fähigkeiten nicht vorstellbar, der „schleichende Tod" so mancher GM-Marke daher vorgezeichnet, heißt sie nun Oldsmobile, Daewoo oder Saab.

Die spezifischen Markenkompetenzen, einmal identifiziert, determinieren die zukünftigen Entwicklungsoptionen einer Marke, das heißt deren **Vision**. Diese Kausalität ergibt sich vor allem, aber nicht nur aus der Ressourcentheorie. In diesem Sinne basierte die Vision von der „Welt AG" der Corporate Brand DaimlerChrysler offenkundig nicht auf den hierfür notwendigen Kompetenzen, sondern war schlicht Wunschdenken. Leider weisen die Visionen vieler Marken keinen Fit zu den jeweiligen Markenkompetenzen auf. Sie führen damit langfristig in die Irre und zu einer Erosion der Marke.

Die fortlaufende Evolution der Markenkompetenzen erfordert das volle Engagement aller Markenmitarbeiter. Zur Sicherung dessen muss zunächst klar sein, wohin die Reise geht. Das ist die notwendige Bedingung für die Stabilität einer (Marken-)Organisation. Die hinreichende Bedingung für Stabilität trotz Wandel und Veränderung bei der Führung von Marken ist die Vermittlung von **Werten**. Das schließt die gesellschaftliche Verantwortung von Marken mit ein.

Erst wenn den Markenmitarbeitern klar ist, woran ihre Marke glaubt und mit welcher **Persönlichkeit**, das heißt mit welchem verbalen und non-verbalen Kommunikationsstil die Marke auf ihre Zielgruppen zugeht und interagiert, kann der erwünschte „Corps-Geist" im Sinne eines gemeinsamen Engagements für die Marke entstehen. Ein von Stolz und innerer Überzeugung getragenes **Markencommitment** schafft es dann, Marken nachhaltig mit Leben zu erfüllen und so die wirksamste aller Imitationsbarrieren zu errichten. Wie bedeutsam der Fit von Werten und Persönlichkeit einer Marke zu ihrer Herkunft, ihren Kompetenzen und ihren Leistungen ist, zeigte viele Jahre lang der Bekleidungseinzelhändler C & A. Hier hat ein Missfit zwischen Persönlichkeit und Werten in der TV-Werbung und dem tatsächlichen Markenauftritt vor Ort die Marke intern und extern ausgehöhlt. Kreative und trendige Kommunikation, losgelöst vom Rest der Marke, wirkt meist destruktiv.

Wie es tatsächlich um die Güte der – im obigen Sinne – ganzheitlichen Markenführung bestellt ist, zeigt sich spätestens dann, wenn das Wachstum nachlässt, der Wettbewerbsdruck zunimmt und Restrukturierungen notwendig werden. Betrachtet man in diesem Zusammenhang den Zustand einiger großer deutscher Markenunternehmen, seien es nun Geschäftsbanken, Automobilhersteller oder andere, offenbaren sich erhebliche Defizite.

Zusammenfassend wird deutlich: Der nachhaltige Erfolg von Marken begründet sich auf einem professionellen Identitätsmanagement. Die ganzheitlich ausgerichtete, identitätsorientierte Markenführung umfasst das Management der Herkunft, der Kompetenzen, der Kernleistungen, der Vision, der Werte und der Persönlichkeit einer Marke. Ein solches integriertes und modernes Verständnis von Marken und ihrer Führung steht in diametralem Gegensatz zum Verhalten so mancher Top-Manager vor allem großer Unternehmen. Ihnen sei mit den Worten von Josef Hattig, dem jahrzehntelangem Geschäftsführer der Brauerei Beck & Co. zugerufen: „Die Marke ist der Boss, nicht der Boss die Marke."

Häufig beschränkt sich Markenmanagement in der Praxis auf das Anbringen von Markenlogos und die Gestaltung gefälliger Anzeigen und Verkaufsunterlagen. Was „hinter" einer Marke steckt, so der irreführende und gefährliche Glaube vieler verantwortlicher Manager, sei dem Kunden egal. Nur Preis und vordergründige Optik zähle. Ein derart verkürztes „Markenmanagement" erzieht sich seine „Geiz ist geil"-Kunden. Die vielerorts lauthals beklagte Preisorientierung und Handelsmarken-Affinität der Nachfrager ist **nicht die Ursache** für die Probleme vieler Markenunternehmen, sie ist **das Ergebnis** der Markenführungsprobleme dieser Unternehmen!

Der in diesem Buch entwickelte indentitätsorientierte Markenführungsansatz bietet vor diesem Hintergrund das erforderliche Rüstzeug für eine Neuorientierung des Markenmanagements.

Stichwortverzeichnis

A

A-Marke 29, 91, 186
Abnutzbarkeit von Marken 349
– rechtliche 349
– verhaltenstheoretische Perspektive 350
– wirtschaftliche 349
Absatzkanäle 95
Abschöpfungsstrategie 83, 187
Added Value 9
Akzeptanzkonzept 52 f., 285
Anreizsystem 120, 132, 322
Anthromorphisation 378
– markenbezogene 286
Arbeitgebermarketing 124
Aufgabenumwelt 496 ff.
Aufmerksamkeitsökonomie 497
Aufmerksamkeitspotentiale 505
Aussagenkonzept 56, 285
Austauschtheorie 120
Autarkiestrategie 84, 203, 208

B

B-Marken 169
Badge Engineering 740
Balanced Scorecard 282 f., 498
BASS s. *Brand Assessment System*
Bedürfnispyramide von Maslow 366
Bedürfnisstrukturen 360
Beziehungsgeflecht 500
Bilanzierung 321
Bosman-Urteil 497
Brand Ambassadors 134
Brand Architecture *s. Markenarchitektur*
Brand Assessment System (BASS) 333
Brand Champions 91
Brand Citizenship Behaviour 84, 107, 118, 421, 508, 513
Brand Commitment 120 ff., 421, 508, 513
Brand Communities *s. Markencommunities*
Brand Dynamics 813 f.
Brand Equity Meter 329
Brand Extension s. *Markenerweiterung*
Brand Hierarchy s. *Markenhierarchie*
Brand Icons 94
Brand Mantra 126
Brand Personality Gameboard Brand 381
Brand Personality Scale 373
Brand-Stretch s. *Markenausdehnung*
Brand Touch Points 77
Branded House 80, 170 f.
Branded Region 597
Broadening 33, 525
Budgetallokation 322

C

C-Marken 169
Cash-Cow-Brand 169
Category Extension s. *Markentransfer*
Category Management 91
Change Management 122
Civic virtue 118
Claim 794
Co-Branding 84, 206 ff., 501, 506, 519
– bei Klubmarken 501
– Definition 206
– Erfolgsfaktoren 207 f.
– horizontal 206
– vertikal 207

Cola-Test
– bei Politikmarken 530
Company Brand 167
Competence-Based View 42
Coopetition 740
Corporate Brand 167
Corporate Branding 144 ff.
Corporate Design 821 f.
Corporate Identity 50, 51
Corporate Wear 791 f.
Counter-Cultures-Ansatz 132
Country-of-Origin-Effekt 476
Country-of-Origin-Forschung 58
Customer Equity 75, 147, 330

D

Dachmarke 355
Dachmarkenstrategie 705 f.
Deepening 33
Demonstranz, soziale 367
Design *s. Marke*
Deutscher Marketing-Preis 215
Dienstleistungen
– Markenlebensdauer von 356
Dienstleistungsmarken 86, 412 ff., 501
Dienstleistungsmarketing 412 ff.
Dienstleistungsnetzwerk 506, 519
Dienstleistungszentrum 506
Differenzierungsstrategie 650 ff.
Direktkommunikation 447
Distribution *s. Markendistribution*
Doppelmarkierung 501
Dreikomponententheorie 602
Drittmarke 355
Dynamic Capability-Ansatz 42

E

E-Share 441
Economies of scale 224
Eigenimage 595
Eigenmarkenstrategie des Handels 81, 226
Einstellungsmessung nach Trommsdorff 532
Einzelmarke 355
Einzelmarkenstrategie *s. Markenstrategie*
Electronic Commerce 434
– Einkaufsverhalten 445
– Vertrauensmangel 440
Empathie 119
Empowerment 131
Endorsed Brand 170, 172
Endorsement-Branding 81, 155, 158, 483
Erfahrungseigenschaften 502
Erfolg
– sportlicher 498, 519
– wirtschaftlicher 498, 519
Erhebungsmethoden 460
– erlaubnisbasiert 460
– nicht-reaktive 460
– reaktive 461
Erinnerungsleistung 351
Erlebniswelten 92
Erlösmodell 505
Erlösunsicherheit 498
Eroberungsrate 9
Erstmarke 355
Event 388
– Attribution 397
– Controlling 399
– Definition 388
– Durchführung 397
– Marken-Event 391
– Planung 395
– Relevanz 388
– Typen 391
– Wert 400
– Wirkung 392
Executive Brand Council 133
Externalisierungsstrategie 424

F

Fair Value 335
Fighter-Brand 169
First Choice Buyer 333
Fit 395
– Event-Marken-Fit 395
Flaggschiff-Brand 168

Flagship-Stores 486 f.
Flanker-Brand 169
Franchisestrategie 84, 203, 205 ff.
Fremdbild 49, 53, 159, 510 ff., 513, 515 ff.
Fügsamkeit 120, 124
Führung
– transformationale 130
Functional Benefit Representation Model 380 f.
Funktionen von Marken 415 ff.
Fusionen 144, 321

G
Ganzheitliche Markenführung 42
Gap
– Analyse 78, 107
– Anforderungs-Gap 512
– Harmonie-Gap 512, 515 ff.
– Identifikationslücke 109 f., 512, 518f.
– Kommunikationslücke 109 f., 512
– Leistungslücke 108, 110
– Modell 107 ff., 510 ff.
– Umsetzungs-Gap 514
– Wahrnehmungslücke 108, 110
– Zielbildungs-Gap 514, 518 f.
– Zielerreichungs-Gap 514, 518 f.
Gattungsmarken 179, 501
Globalisierungsdruck 357 f., 471
Gruppenidentität 502
Goodwill 321

H
Handelsmarke 178, 186, 474
– Eigenmarke 179
– Premiummarke 180, 474
Handelsmarkenmangement 180
Helping behavior 118
Hersteller-Handel-Konflikt 507
Herstellermarke 178
– generische 474
– Premium- 474
– Luxus- 474
High-End-Prestige Brand 169
High-Involvement-Produkte 355
Hilfsbereitschaft 119
Home-Use-Test 638
House of Brands 80, 170, 172
Human Resource
– Integration neuer Mitarbeiter 422
– Management 124
– Mitarbeiterführung 423
– Personalauswahl 124, 421
– Personalentwicklung 422

I
Ich-Identität 502, 509
Idealbild 510
Idealverein 498
Identifikation
– mit der Markenidentität 120
Identität
– Begriff 43, 46, 49, 116 f., 500
– Merkmale 45 f.
– räumliche 601 f.
– Theorie der sozialen Identität 121
– Vertrauen 43
– von Dienstleistungsmarken 417 ff.
– von Gruppen 48, 121, 417
– von Kunden 418, 425 ff.
– von Mitarbeitern 417 ff., 502
– von Personen 44, 121, 417 ff., 502
– von Unternehmen 48
Identitätsdefizit 531
Identitätsfit
– Personen-Markenidentitäts-Fit 124 f.
Identitätsforschung
– sozialwissenschaftliche Ansätze 43, 57
Identitätskonstrukt 417
Identitätsorientierte Markenführung
– bei Dienstleistungsmarken 412 ff.
– bei Ligamarken 495 ff.
– Bezugsgruppen 504 ff., 510 ff.
– Managementprozess 75
– Spannungsfelder 74
– theoretische Grundlagen 43
– von Ligasportmarken 504 ff.
Identitätsverständnis 43, 46, 50, 500

Image 510 ff.
– Transfer 202, 223 f., 248 ff., 393, 506
– Image-Kongruenz Hypothese 425
Immaterialität 413 ff.
Impairment-Test 322
Individual initiative 118
Individualisierung 450
Information Chunk 11, 151, 594
Informational shortcuts 527
Informationskosten 527
Innovation 657 f.
– Innovationsdruck 471
– Innovationsfähigkeit 87
– Innovationskraft 88
Inside-out-Perspektive 8, 78, 451
Institution 50
Instrumentalstrategien 234 ff.
Integration des externen Faktors 413 ff.
Integrationsdefizit 531
Integrativität 501
Interaktion
– zwischen Nachfrager und Mitarbeiter 419
Interbrand 331
International Financial Reporting Standards 322
Internationalisierung 497 f.
Internetprägung 440
Investitionsgüter
– Markenlebensdauer von 356
Ist-Bild 510
Ist-Fremdbild 65, 510 ff.
Ist-Identität, Bestimmung 381
Ist-Selbstbild 65, 510 ff.

K

Kampagne
– Effizienz 807 f.
– Gestaltung 798 f.
Kannibalisierung 226
Kaufgründe 280 f.
Kaufverhaltensrelevanz 9
Kernkompetenz 41
Kernleistung 500
Klubmarke 507
Kommunikation *s. Markenkommunikation*
Kommunikationspolitik 629
Kommunikationswettbewerb 357 f.
Kompetenz 41, 87, 204
– quasi-soziale 453
Kongruenztheorie 379
Konkurrenz
– extra-medial 450
– intra-medial 450
Konsum
– gewandelte Funktion 470
– symbolischer 479
Kontaktpunkt
– Kunden-Marken 117
– Kontaktpunktanalyse 424
Kontaktsubjekt, -objekt 502
Konzernzugehörigkeit 86
Koopetition 500, 519
Koproduktion 500, 519
Kundenbindung 13, 85, 101, 222
– Kundenakquisition 102
– Kundendurchdringung 102
– Kundensicherung 102
Kundenfunktion
– Kontrollinstanz 416
Kundenkontaktpersonal 414 ff.
Kundennutzen 52
– beziehungsorientierter 452
– funktionaler 452
– internetspezifischer 450
– prozessualer 452
– symbolischer 62
Kundenstammwert *s. Customer Equity*
Kundenzufriedenheit 280 f., 416
Kundenzugang 426, 428
Kuppelprodukt 505 f.

L

Label 413
Labeln 47
Leadership based brand building 122
Lebenszyklus öffentlicher Anliegen 850 f.

Lebenszyklusanalyse 352
Leistungsbündel 501
Leistungsergebnisse 502
Leistungspotenziale 502
Leistungstreiber 287
Lernlandkarte 128
Lerntheorie, soziale 130
Lernvorgänge 10, 350
Lieferantenrolle, interne 117
Ligamarke 499 ff.
Ligasport 495 ff., 500 ff.
– Besonderheiten 500 ff.
– Markenführung im 496 ff.
Line-Extension s. *Markenausdehnung*
Lizensierungsstrategie 84, 203 ff.
Lizenzfußball 496
Logfile-Analyse 460
Louis-Schmeling-Paradox 500
Low-Cost-Segment 764 f.
Low-End-Entry-Level-Brand 169
Loyalität 116
Luxus 470 ff.
– Begriff 472 ff.
– Begriffsverwendung, objektbezogene 472 f.
– Begriffsverwendung, verhaltensorientierte 472
– Dachmarke 482
Luxusgüter 470 ff.
– Kennzeichnung, interkategoriale 472 f.
– Kennzeichnung, intrakategoriale 473
Luxusmarken 470 ff.
– Adaptionsfähigkeit 476
– Akquisitionsstrategie 482
– Besonderheiten im operativen Vermarktungssystem 470
– Definition 475
– Endorsed Branding 483
– Fremdbild 477 f.
– Gründerpersönlichkeiten 476
– Herkunftsland 476
– Identitätssystem 475 ff.
– Innovationsfähigkeit 476
– Kern, wahrgenommener 473 f.
– Line Extension 483
– Management von 481 ff.
– Markenbildung 484 ff.
– Mehrmarkenstrategie 482
– Motive der Wahl von 480 f.
– Neumarkenstrategie 482
– Revitalisierung 483
– Selbstbild 475 ff.
– Selbstkongruenz 477 ff.
– Sondereditionen 485
– Symbole, Bedeutung von 477
– Wertausdruck 477 ff.
Luxusverständnis
– qualitatives 472

M

Marke
– Abnutzbarkeit 349
– Abwertungsdruck 360
– als Eigentumszeichen 22
– als Merkmalskatalog 23
– als Nutzenbündel 7
– Austauschbarkeit 357
– Begriff 5 ff., 412 f.
– Begriffe im Electronic Commerce 435
– Design 88, 629 f., 657 f.
– Einzigartigkeit 85
– entgeltlich erworbene 348
– Funktion, extrinsische 478 ff.
– Funktion, intrinsische 479 ff.
– Homogenität 357
– Kernkompetenz 66
– Lebensdauerverteilung 354
– Merkmale s. *Markenmerkmale*
– Nutzenkomponenten 7
– Nutzungsdauer 352 ff.
– organisationale Verankerung 84
– Positionierung 52, 65, 232 ff.
– Profilierung 12
– rechtliche Absicherung 355 f.
– Relevanz im E-Commerce 442, 446
– Serviceorientierung 85
– Verhaltensrelevanz 350

– Werteverzehr 357 ff.
– Werthaltigkeit 350
Markenadaption 196
Markenakquisition 231
Markenarchitektur 80, 165, 453, 786 ff.
– Dimensionen 80
– Gestaltung 80, 155, 173
– handelsgerichtete Dimension 81
– horizontale 81
– Integrationsgrad 173
– vertikaler Integrationsgrad 80
Markenassoziationen 168
Markenaufbau 501
Markenausdehnung 84, 197, 199, 200 ff.
– Definition 84, 200, 248
– Line Extension 483
– Trading-down/up 201
Markenausweitung s. *Markenerweiterung*
Markenbekanntheit 9, 53, 66, 230, 280 f.
Markenbewertung
– Einsatzfelder 323
– Verfahren 326
Markenbewusstsein 119, 357
Markenbeziehungsqualität 282
Markenbilanz 332
Markenbildung 9
Markencommitment 10, 84, 107
Markencommunities 460
Markencontrolling 75, 101 ff., 274 ff.
– Anforderungen und Zielgrößen 278 ff.
– Aufgaben 75, 101, 277
– Begriff 75, 101, 275 f.
– Funktion, systemgestaltende 277
– Funktion, systemnutzende 277
– im Electronic Commerce 451, 460
– Image- und Positionierungsanalyse 111 f.
– Markenberichtswesen 103 ff.
– Markenerfolgsmessung 105 ff.
– Markenscorecard *s. Markenscorecard*
– ökonomische Zielgrößen 78, 280
– psychographische Zielgrößen 78, 280
– Stellenwert 274
– Ziele 101, 276 f.
Markendehnung s. *Markenerweiterung*
Markendistribution 95
Markendach 501, 519
Markeneigner 9
Markeneisberg 334
Markenelemente 506
Markenelimination 231
Markenentwicklung 119
Markenerinnerung 9
Markenerweiterung 83, 192, 196 ff., 246 ff.
– Begriff 83, 196, 248
– Bestimmungsfaktoren 259 ff.
– einstellungstheoretische Ansätze 254 ff.
– Erfolgsfaktoren 197 f.
– Erklärungsansätze 253 f.
– Fit 197
– gedächtnispsychologische Ansätze 258 f.
– Gegenstand 247 ff.
– kategorisierungstheoretische Ansätze 254
– Management 264 ff.
– Merkmale 247 ff.
– Modell von Meffert/Heinemann 257 f.
– Modell von Schweiger 255 ff.
– Zielsystem 251
Markenevolution 83, 184 ff.
– Definition 184
– Strategie 166, 181
Markenexpansion 83, 192 ff.
– geografisch 83, 193 f.
– global 195
– international 193, 196
– multinational 194
Markenfarbe 506
Markenform 501
Markenführung 9, 510 ff.
– Entwicklungsstufen 20 ff., 349
– fraktaler Ansatz 29 f., 367

– fremdbestimmt 453
– funktionsorientierter Ansatz 25
– identitätsorientierter Ansatz 30 ff.
– innengerichtete 116 ff.
– instrumenteller Ansatz 23
– internationale 648, 706
– interne 504
– Komplexität 420
– technokratisch-strategieorientierter Ansatz 27
– Verankerung im Management 84
– verhaltens-/ imageorientierter Ansatz 26
– zielgruppenspezifisch 155
Markenführungshoheit 508, 519
Markenfunktion 527, 841 f.
– bei Politikmarken 527 ff.
– Differenzierungsfunktion 368, 447
– Entlastungsfunktion 55
– Identifikationsfunktion 55, 502 f., 509
– Informationsfunktion 11, 55
– Orientierungsfunktion 11, 442
– Prestigefunktion 12, 55
– Risikoreduktionsfunktion 12, 55, 443
– Statusfunktion 55
– Vertrauensfunktion 11, 55
Markengesetz *s. Markenschutz*
Markenherkunft 57 f., 66, 79, 437, 476, 502 ff., 519
– kulturelle 58
– institutionelle 59
– wahrgenommene 59
Markenhierarchie 166 f.
– Strukturierungsansätze 169, 173
Markenhistorie 58, 476, 502 ff.
Markenidentität 8, 39, 42, 52, 65, 234, 368, 379, 479, 502
– Fremdbild 49, 107, 575 ff.
– Interpretationsformen
– Komponenten 57, 64, 79, 126
– Konsistenz 206
– Konzeption 79
– Managementprozess 75 ff.
– Selbstbild 8, 107, 575 ff.
– wirtschaftswissenschaftliche Interpretation 49
Markenimage 8, 52 f., 53, 280 f., 479, 635 f.
Markeninflation 357
Markeninitiative 119
Markenintegration 97
– inter-mediale 457
– intra-mediale 457
Markenkannibalisierung 298
– Partizipation 300
– Substitution 300
Markenkern 56, 575 ff., 845 ff.
Markenkommunikation 91 ff., 450, 504
– erlebnisorientierte 388
– Event-Kommunikation 388
– formell intern 123
– Formen interner 127
– horizontale 448, 459
– intern 187
– internetbasierte 458
– Push- und Pull-Prinzip 127
– Sponsoring 388
– symbolische 478 f., 488 ff.
Markenkompetenz 42, 57, 59, 79, 82, 178, 204, 437
Markenkonsolidierung 83, 185 ff.
– abgestufter Rückzug 83, 187
– Fokussierung 83, 190
– Gründe 185 f.
– sofortige Elimination 83, 186
Markenlebensdauer 353, 355
Markenleistungen 57, 60, 66, 79, 86, 438
Markenleitbild 234, 289 ff.
Markenlogo 378
Markenloyalität 230, 280 f., 310
Markenmanagement 8, 75, 166
– operatives 75, 86 ff.
– Prozess 76
– strategisches 75, 77 ff.
Markenmerkmale 51, 54 ff., 66
– akzidenzielle 56
– essenzielle 56
Markenmigration 83, 188

Markenmissionierung 119
Markennamen 191, 378, 599 f.
Markennutzen 13, 232 f., 349, 366, 474 f.
– Kundenbindung 13
– preispolitischer Spielraum 15
– Unternehmenswertsteigerung 13
– Wachstumspotenziale 15
Markenoptik 598
Markenorganisation 84
Markenpersönlichkeit 57, 63, 66, 79, 365 ff., 478
– Definition 370
– Determinanten 376 f.
– Dimensionen 375
– Fünf-Faktoren-Modell 372
– Messansätze 372 ff.
– Produktpersönlichkeit 373
– Steuerung 376 f.
Markenpiraterie 357 f.
Markenportfolio 85, 164, 216 ff., 291 ff., 305, 322
– Einstiegstiefen 237
– Gestaltung 230 ff.
– Loyalität 230
– Scorecard-Hierarchie 292 f.
– Zentralisationsgrade 237
Markenpositionierung 81
Markenpricing 90
Markenpyramide 632
Markenrecht 412
Markenschutz 97 ff.
– Markengesetz 6, 99, 205
– Markenüberwachung 99
– Rechtsordnungen 98
– Schutzfähigkeit 99
– Verkehrsgeltung 99
Markenscorecard 103 f., 284 ff.
– Ergebnisperspektive 287 f.
– Grundstruktur 284 f.
– Hierarchisierung 293
– interne Perspektive 287 f.
– Marktperspektive 287 f.
– Steuerungsgrößen 285 ff.
Markenspezifische Rolle 232
Markenstärke 9, 38, 106, 249 f., 260, 279 f., 324, 510 f.
– Analyse 106
Markenstrategie
– als Determinante der Markenlebensdauer 356
– Dachmarkenstrategie 705 f.
– duale 454
– Einzelmarkenstrategie 81, 175, 654 f.
– Fokussierungsstrategie 83, 190 ff.
– gemischte 196
– globale 195
– internationale 196
– Mehrmarkenstrategie *s. Mehrmarkenstrategie*
– multinationale 194
– Neumarkenstrategie 193
– Politikmarken 524 ff.
– Substitutionsstrategie 188
– virtuelle 454
– vollständig integrierte 454
Markensubstitution 303, 305
Markensympathie 280 f.
Markentechnik 23
Markentransfer 84, 197, 199, 201 ff., 209, 248
– Chancen 202, 209
– Erfolgsfaktoren 201
– Fit 197, 201
– Risiken 202, 209
Markentreue 9, 280 ff.
– sinkende 359
Markenverpackung 88
Markenverständnis 20 ff.
– verkürztes 349
Markenvertrautheit 280 f.
Markenvision 57, 61, 66, 79
Markenwahrnehmung 117, 129, 423
Markenwechselbereitschaft 357, 359
Markenwelt 506
Markenweltmanagement 519
Markenwert 38, 57, 62, 66, 219, 499
– Abschreibungen, planmäßige 355, 357
– Abwertungsrisiko 358

- Bilanzierung 321 f.
- einer Unternehmung 144 ff.
- erweiterter 325
- finanzorientierter 324 ff.
- finanzwirtschaftlicher 38
- monetärer 322
- Nachhaltigkeit 357
- ökonomischer 9, 279 f.
- psychographischer 9, 350
- verhaltensorientierter 324 ff.
- verhaltenstheoretischer 350 f.
- verhaltenswissenschaftlicher 38
- von Ligasportvereinen 498 f.
- zielgruppenspezifischer 147 ff.

Markenwerte 79
Markenwissen 381
Markenzeichen 189, 414 ff.
Markenziele 61
Market-Based-View 39
Marketing House 833
Markierung
- Anbringung einer 414

Markierungsobjekt 356
Marktabsicherung 219 f.
Marktdurchdringung 219
Markteintrittszeitpunkt 356
Markterschließung 220 ff.
Marktsättigung 185
Marktsegmente 15
Marktsegmentierung 229 f.
- Übersegmentierung 226

Marktzugangsschranke 416
Me-too-Marke 355
Medialisierung 497
Mehrmarkenstrategie 81, 175 f., 214 ff., 298, 304, 309
- Chancen 219 ff.
- Charakteristika 214 ff.
- Controlling 316
- organisatorische Verankerung 236 ff.
- Planungsprozess 227 ff.
- Risiken 219 ff.
- Spannungsfelder 239 ff.

Merchandising 506
Mergers & Acquisitions s. *Fusionen*
Metafunktion der Komplexitätsreduktion 567
Migrationsstrategie 83, 188 ff.
Moments of truth 424, 428
Mystery Shoppers 127

N

Netzwerk(partner) 506
Neue Institutionenökonomie 151
No-Frill Konzept 424
Nutzen, ideeller 475
Nutzenkomponenten
- physisch-funktionale 7, 54 f., 66
- symbolische 7, 54 f., 66

Nutzenversprechen 350, 476
Nutzungsdauer von Marken 352 ff.
- Bestimmung 352
- Determinanten zur Klassifikation 355
- Verteilungsfunktion 354

O

One-Stop-Shopping
Online-Einkauf
- Barrieren 444

Organisationale Fähigkeiten 41
Organizational Citizenship Behavior 118
Organizational compliance 118
Organizational loyalty 118
Outside-in-Perspektive 8, 78, 451

P

Part-time Marketer 117
Patentierbarkeit 415, 416
Permission Marketing s. *Erhebungsmethoden*
Personal s. *Human Resource*
Personalisierung 453
Perspektive, wirkungsorientierte 473
Pioniermarke 355
Point of Sale 95, 427
Points-of-Difference-Strategie 66
Politikmarken 524 ff.
- Fremdbild 532

– Führungsansatz 531 ff.
– GAP-Modell 532 ff.
– Selbstbild 533
Politikmarketing 524 ff.
– Inside-Out-Perspektive 532
– Outside-In-Perspektive 532
Portfoliomanagement 237 f.
Positionierung 232 ff.
– aktive 82
– erstarrte 416
– Ist 77
– reaktive 82
Potenzialfaktoren, visuelle Gestaltung 414
Präferenztest 5
Preis als Wettbewerbsinstrument 471
Preisbereitschaft 91
Preisbewusstsein 357, 360
Preisprämie 91, 327
Preispremium 474
Preisstellung 474
Preisstrategie 767 f.
Premiummarken 471
Primärleistungen 439
Problemlösungsfähigkeit 86
Product-Placement 490
Produkt
– markiertes 349
– High-Involvement- 355
– Low-Involvement- 355
Produktdesign 484
Produktgestaltung 86
Produkthomogenität 358
Produktlebensdauer 353
Produktmarke 167, 168
Prosuming/ Prosumer-Rolle 502, 519
Psychologie
– differenzielle 371
Pull-Wirkung 96
Purchase Price Allocation 321

Q

Qualität 650 ff.
Qualitätsbeurteilung
– preisorientierte 485
Qualitätskonstanz 415
Qualitätsmanagement 416

R

Rational-Choice-Theorie 527
Reaktanz 392
Rebranding 790 f.
Rechtsformverfehlung 498
Region „Mitteldeutschland" 604 ff.
Region of Brands 597
Regionalbewusstsein 602 f.
Regionalmarken 592 ff.
Regionenmarke „Mitteldeutschland" 614
Regionenmarken 590 ff.
– Co-Branding 597
– Dachmarken 595
– Funktionen 594
– Markenidentität 596
Regionenmarketing 590
– Markenarchitektur, regionale 597
– Markengestaltung 598 ff.
– markenstrategische Entscheidungen 596, 612 ff.
Regionennamen, Assoziationen zu 606 f.
Relationship Basis Model 380
Rentabilitätsdruck 185
Reputation 152, 501
Resource-Based-View 40
Resource-Conduct-Performance Paradigma 40
Ressourcen 40, 41
Return on Investment 645
Risikoempfinden 12
Rückzug (abgestuft) s. *Markenkonsolidierung*

S

Sättigungsrate 650
SBU-Brands 167
Schutzrecht, gewerbliches 349
Sekundärleistung 439
Selbstbild 510 ff.
Selbstentwicklung 119

Selbstimage 477 ff.
Selbstkonzept 121,124, 153, 379, 425, 477 ff.
– distinktives 481
– öffentliches 481
– privates 480
Selbstverwirklichung 366
Self-development 118
Self-stereotyping 121
Semantische Netze 381
Simulationslogik 543
Sinus-Milieus 742
Situationsanalyse 77
Snob-Effekt 378 f.
Soll-Bild 513 f.
Soziale Demonstranz 382
Sozialisationsprozess 125
Sponsoren 505
Sponsoring 388, 506
– Controlling 399
– Definition 389
– Durchführung 397
– Planung 395
– Relevanz 388
– Typen 390
– Wirkung 392
Sportsgeist 119
Sportsmanship 118
Stadtidentität 565 ff.
– Definition 565 ff.
Stadtmarken 565 ff.
– Führung 569 ff.
– GAP-Modell 572 ff.
Stadtmarketing 564 ff.
– Spezifika 564 f.
Standardisierung
– von Verhalten 420
Storytelling, organisationales 128
strategische Rolle 168
Sub-Branding 81, 170 f.
Substitute for leadership 423, 428
Substitutionsstrategie *s. Markenstrategie*
Sucheigenschaften 153
Symbole 478 ff.
Synergiepotenzial 220 ff.

T

Testimonial 377 f.
Theorie des organisationalen Beschaffungsverhaltens 570
Theory of Animism 370
Tobin's q 320
Trading-down/up 201

U

Unique Selling Proposition (USP) 232, 636 ff.
Uno-actu-Prinzip 416
Unternehmensbereichsmarke 168
Unternehmenshierarchie 167
Unternehmenskultur 131
Unternehmensmarke 50, 144 ff., 168
– Rationalisierungsfunktion 153
– Vertrauensfunktion 151
Unternehmenswert 320 ff.
USP s. *Unique Selling Proposition*

V

Value in Use 336
Variety seeking behavior 359
Veblen-Effekt 485
Vergessenswirkungen 350, 357
Verhaltensleitlinien 126
Verhaltensrelevanz 106
Verhaltensstandardisierung 420
Vermögenswerte 321
Verpackungen *s. Markenverpackungen*
Vertrauen 116, 445
– Vertrauenseigenschaften 11, 151, 356, 502
Vertrieb
– Multi-Kanal-Vertrieb 427
– Vertriebskanäle 699
– Vertriebsstärke 426
Vertriebskanäle 699
Virtuelle Communities 459
Vorstellungsbild 350

W
Wachstumskerne 595
Wahrnehmungsverzerrung, subjektive 354
Wanderungsanalyse 299, 303
– Kannibalisierungsanalyse 307
– Partizipationsanalyse 311
– Substitutionsanalyse 305
Wanderungsbilanzen 313
Warenzeichenrechte 349
Wertschöpfungskette 699 ff.
Wettbewerb
– horizontaler 357 f.
– Intensität in Premium-/Luxussegmenten 471
– vertikaler 357 f.

Z
Zielgruppenansprache
– differenzierte 155
– gemischte 155 f.
– undifferenzierte 155

Marken- und Firmenverzeichnis

A

Accenture 83, 189, 191
AC Milan 498
Adidas 92, 204
Agip 720
Aigner 203
Air France 764
Airbus 167, 821
Airtours 216
Aldi 9, 179, 328
Alfa 359
Alfa-Romeo 88
Alhambra 737
Allianz 94, 116, 129, 133, 145, 170, 416, 426
Amazon 436, 438, 453
AMB Generali 426
American Express 14
Amiga 186
Amsterdam Admirals 497
AOL Time Warner 439
Aral 720
Aramark 506
Armani 473, 478
Arminia Bielefeld 498
Arthur Andersen 83, 189, 191
AS 179
Ashton Martin 291, 482
Atari 186
Attika 186
Audi 87, 88, 90, 93, 218, 233, 302, 359
Avia 720
AXA 426

B

Bang & Olufson 88, 201, 484
BASF 188
Bayer Leverkusen 499
Bayern München 496, 498, 499, 501, 509
Becel 220
Beck's 88, 92, 93, 95, 130, 204, 859
Beiersdorf 167, 193
Bentley 93, 218, 482
Bertelsmann 156, 167, 170
Bertelsmann Stiftung 838 ff.
Bertolli 195, 220
BfG Bank AG 186
Bild 94
Bitburger 94
Blend-a-Med 175
BMW 14, 55, 95, 99, 133, 145, 170, 222, 231, 233, 359, 368, 482, 490
Boeing 820 f.
Bogner 195
Bollinger 490
Borussia Dortmund 498, 499
Boss 95, 169, 193, 201, 205, 488
BP 720
Braun 88
Bremen 401
Brigitte 688
Bugatti 218
Budweiser 14,
Burger King 205

C

C&A 116, 858
Cadillac 264
Calgon 94
Calvin Klein 170, 490
Camel 193, 201, 204
Capital 688
Cartier 473
Cathay Pacific Airlines 86
CDU 530 ff.
Celtic Glasgow 496
Champions League 497
Champions World Series 497
Chanel 195, 476 f., 484, 486
Charmin 173
Che Guevara 504
Chevrolet 856
Christian Lacroix 482
Chrysler 737, 761
Cisco 14
Citibank 14
Citroen 88, 359
Club Mediterranée 201
Coca Cola 4 f., 14, 88, 89, 92, 94, 96, 99, 195, 369, 459
Condor 216
CONOCO 716 ff.
Credit Suisse Group 426

D

Daewo 856, 858
Daihatsu 359
Daimler-Benz 359
Daimler Chrysler 132, 145, 215, 231, 233, 377, 482, 858
Dallas Cowboys 499
Daniel Hechter 95
Danzas 784
Das Beste 688
Dash 334
David Beckham 497
Dawn 190,
DEA 83, 186, 188, 720 f., 724
Dell 14
Deutsche Aerolloyd 821
Deutsche Bahn 133, 167, 216, 412
Deutsche Bank 86, 119, 130, 145, 426, 856
Deutsches Patent- und Markenamt 246
Deutsche Post 100, 145
Deutsche Post World Net 783 ff.
Deutsche Telekom 93, 133, 145
Dextro Energy 201, 246
DFL Deutsche Fußball Liga 496, 497
DHL 783 ff.
Diesel 169
Dior 473
Disney, *s. Walt Disney*
dit 80, 167, 170
Douglas 95
Dresdner Bank 80, 167, 170
Dr. Oetker 354
Dr. Tigges 216
Du Darfst 220
Duplo 217

E

EADS 167
easyJet 130, 771
eBay 43, 436
Eckes 214
Elf 720
EMTEC 188
E.ON 144, 274
ERGO Versicherungsgruppe 426
e-Sixt 439
Escada 95
Essanelle 205
Esso 720
EuroExpress 784
Eurowings AG 764
Extra 179

F

Fairy Ultra 190, 191
FC Barcelona 498, 499
FC Schalke 04 498, 499
FC St. Pauli 1910 503, 504, 512
Ferrari 477, 484, 506
Ferrero 175, 217, 231, 378

Fiat 233, 359
FIFA 501
Florena 592
FlyNet 832
Focus 672, 688
Ford 14, 85, 223, 233, 280, 289 ff., 303, 359, 482, 737 ff.
Fosters 58
Foto Quelle 205
Füllhorn 181
FutureBrand 498, 499

G
Galaxy 737 ff.
General Electric 14, 377
General Motors 215, 858
GEO 170, 668 ff.
Germania 169
Germanwings 763 ff.
Gesellschaft für Konsumforschung (GfK) 333, 336, 381
Gexx 169
Gillette 14, 170, 172
Giotto 175, 217
Gletscherkrone 180
Golf 167
Gruner + Jahr 156, 167, 170, 668 ff.
Gucci 202, 264

H
Hapag Lloyd 216
Hapag-Lloyd Express 169, 771
Haribo 94
Harley -Davidson 63, 93, 366, 376, 380
Hasseröder 193
Head 204
Heinz 89
Heisse Tasse 186
Henkel 81, 167 ff., 626 f., 380
Hermes 476, 482 f.
Hertz 292
Hewlett-Packard 14, 170 ff.
Hilcona 88
HiPP 454
HLX 216
H&M 770
HP Deskjet 81
Holsten 89
Honda 14, 233, 359, 737
Hörzu 688
Hugo Boss 169
Hyundai 58

I
IBM 14, 41, 80, 170,172, 188, 195
ICE 167
icon brand navigation 334
IKEA 770
Intel 14
Interbrand 331

J
Jaguar 60, 85, 94, 202, 291, 856
Jägermeister 92
JET 716 ff.
Jil Sander 204, 476, 478
Joop 193, 203, 476, 478
Junkers Luftverkehr 821

K
Karstadt 454
Kellogg's 207
Kia 95
KLM 764
Knorr 195
Kodak 133
KPMG 336
Kraft Foods 214, 220

L
l'tur 216
Lada 95
Lätta 220
Lagerfeld 476
Lamborghini 93, 218, 482
Lammsbräu 592
Lancia 359
Land Rover 291
Lange & Söhne 476
Langnese 81

Levi's 170, 195, 202
Lexus 170
Lincoln 291
Lipobay 186
Lipton 195
Liverpool FC 498, 499
Lotus 170
Louis Vuitton 476, 486
Lufthansa 92, 153, 169, 207, 216, 771, 820 ff.
Lux-Seife 169
LVMH 471, 482

M
M&Ms 378
Maggi 89, 354
Magnum 81
Manchester United 497, 498, 499
Mannesmann 189
Marks & Spencer 181
Marlboro 14, 93, 202, 204, 368, 506
Mars 188, 202
Maurice Lacroix 485
Max 688
Maybach 482
Mazda 223, 233, 291, 359
McDonald's 14, 80, 96, 172, 195, 205, 206
MCI 191
McKinsey&Company 86, 153, 329, 381
McMuffin 170
Mercedes 14, 132, 473
Mercury 291
Metropolitan 216
Michelin 202, 380
Microsoft 14, 99, 195
Miele 649 ff.
Milka 94, 201, 207
Milsani 179
Mini 63, 133, 231
Minnesota Mining & Manufacturing Company (3M) 133
Mitsubishi 359, 749
MLB 499, 501
Mon Chérie 217
Mövenpick 202, 205
Münster 574 ff.
MTV 92

N
National Geographic 671 ff.
Natreen 203
Naturenergie 514
NBA 499, 501
Nescafé 14, 171
Nesquik 171
Nestea 170 f.
Nestlé 172
NHL 499
NFL 497, 499, 501
NFL Europe League 497
Nike 126, 367
Nissan 233, 359
Nivea 88, 167, 192, 198 f., 201, 354
Nokia 14, 80, 99, 172
Nutella 175

O
O_2 117
OBI 206
Odol 89
Oldsmobile 858
Omega 485, 490
Opel 133, 233, 359, 753
Opel Manta 63
Otto 206

P
Pampers 170,175
Pantene 170
Paulaner 58
Pepsi 5, 14
Perrier 195
Persil 80, 167 f.,170, 354, 622 ff.
Peugeot 359, 762
Philip Morris 94, 214, 220
Porsche 199, 473, 483

Premier League 497
PriceWaterhouseCoopers 188, 336
Procter&Gamble 80, 170ff., 175, 190, 215, 219, 246

R

Raffaello 175, 217
Raider 188
Ralph Lauren 484, 486
Rama 220
Real Madrid 497, 498, 499
Red Bull 92
Renault 88, 233, 359, 473, 737 ff.
Rennie 94
REWE 179
Rhein Fire Düsseldorf 497
Ritz-Carlton 93, 422
Robinson Club 216
Rocher 217
Rolex 80, 96, 473, 476
Rolls-Royce 88, 133, 473, 476 f., 482, 484
RWE 145
Ryanair 771

S

Sainsburry 180
Salto 179
Sanella 220
Scion 220 ff.
Saab 858
Samsung 14
SAT.1 92
SC Freiburg 514
Schlecker 179
Schmitz Cargobull 190
Schneekoppe 180
Scotish Claymores 497
Scout 24 454
Seat 93, 176, 218, 220, 223, 233, 280, 298, 741 ff.
Securicor 506
SG Flensburg-Handewitt 501
Sharan 737 ff.
Shell 83, 188, 506, 720
Shouldice Hospital 424
Siemens 92, 126, 145
Sixt 439
Skoda 93, 176, 218, 220, 233, 298, 302
Smart 132, 220, 231
Smarties 206
SmartPrice 179
Sony 14, 41, 170, 195, 207
Southwest Airlines 424, 764
Sparkasse 94
SPD 530 ff.
Spee 81, 169, 334
SPIEGEL 439, 671, 688
Sport Bild 92
Sportive 515
Sportwelt 508
Sprite 92
Spüli 186
Star Alliance 207, 820
Starbucks 118, 195
Stern 170, 688
St. Michael 181
StyleLab 169
Subaru 359
Suzuki 359
Swatch 97

T

TAG Heuer 486
Tchibo 127
Tempo 175
Texaco 83, 186
The Body Shop 62
The Progressive Transportation Group 429
Thomas Cook 216
THW Kiel 501
Tipp 179
TotalFina 720
Toyota 14, 170, 220 ff., 233, 359, 749
TSV 1860 München 501
TUI 94, 201, 216, 220, 230, 693 ff.
TV Spielfilm 688
Twix 188

U

UEFA 501
UFA 515
Unilever 80, 165, 169, 172, 185, 220, 246
United Airlines Express 81, 169
United Technologies 156

V

Vendome 471
Verpoorten 95
VfB Stuttgart 498
VfL Bochum 1848 e.V. 498, 501, 506, 514 ff.
Virgin 156, 170,172
Virgin Express 771
Viva St. Pauli 504
Vodafone 133, 189
Volkswagen 56, 93, 145, 167, 176, 215, 218 f., 220, 223, 233, 240, 280, 298, 349, 359, 482, 737 ff.
Volvo 291, 303

W

Wal Mart 179, 190
Walt Disney 14, 126, 422
Warsteiner 94
Washington Redskins 499
Weißer Riese 169
Weltpokalsiegerbesieger 512
Werder Bremen 401
Westfalen 720
White Cloud 190
Wolters Reisen 216
World Bowl 497

Y

Yahoo 436
Yello 274, 514
Yves Saint Laurent 476

Z

Zintzmeyer & Lux 822 f.
Zürich Gruppe 426

Die Autoren

Prof. Dr. Jürgen Althans, am 8. Dezember 1950 in Jever/Friesland geboren, studierte nach Abitur, Bundeswehr und einer Auslandstätigkeit als Verkäufer und Reisender Betriebswirtschaftslehre in Münster mit dem Abschluss Diplom-Kaufmann. Von 1977 bis 1982 war er am Institut für Marketing der Universität Münster (Direktor: Prof. Dr. Dr. h. c. mult. Heribert Meffert) als Wissenschaftlicher Assistent, von 1981 bis 1982 als Geschäftsführer tätig und promovierte 1981 über das Thema „Die Übertragbarkeit von Werbekonzeptionen auf internationale Märkte". 1982 begann Althans als Trainee im Druck- und Verlagshaus Gruner + Jahr in Hamburg und war dann Assistent des Vorstandsvorsitzenden. Von 1986 bis 1994 war er als Verlagsleiter Stern, von 1994 bis 2000 als Verlagsgeschäftsführer der Verlagsgruppe GEO, von 2000 bis 2003 als Verlagsgeschäftsführer der Verlagsgruppe G+J-Wirtschaftspresse (Capital, Impulse, Börse Online, Bizz) tätig. Seit 2004 ist Althans Leiter der Personal- und Managemententwicklung von Gruner + Jahr. Seit 1992 ist Jürgen Althans zudem Lehrbeauftragter sowie seit 1998 Honorarprofessor für Marketing an der Universität Rostock.

Christoph Baumgarten wurde am 31.01.1972 in Hagen/ Westfalen geboren. Im Jahr 1995 schloss er sein Studium an der Fachhochschule des Bundes für öffentliche Verwaltung (Köln und Dieburg) als Diplom-Verwaltungswirt ab. Seit 1995 ist Christoph Baumgarten bei der Deutschen Post AG beschäftigt. Nach einigen Monaten Tätigkeit im Verwaltungsbereich eines Paketzentrums übernahm er in Dortmund die Aufgabe eines Pressesprechers im Bereich Öffentlichkeitsarbeit/Marktkommunikation. 1996 wechselte Christoph Baumgarten in die Zentrale des Konzerns zur Abteilung Konzernwerbung & Marken. Hier arbeitet er im Corporate Brand Management und ist mitverantwortlich für die Entwicklung der Konzern-Markenarchitektur und die Ausgestaltung der Positionierung der Marken des Konzerns Deutsche Post World Net.

Dr. Andreas Bierwirth, geboren 1971 in Lünen, absolvierte seine Ausbildung zum Bankkaufmann bei der Deutschen Bank AG. Anschließend durchlief er seine Ausbildung zum Berufsflugzeugführer unter anderem an der Verkehrsfliegerschule der Deutschen Lufthansa AG/ATTI in Bremen und Tuscon AZ/ USA. 1993 begann Andreas Bierwirth ein Studium der Betriebswirtschaftslehre an der Universität in Münster, welches er 2001 mit der Ernennung zum Dr. rer. pol. abschloss. Von April bis Oktober 2002 war Herr Bierwirth Manager Business Developement, Marketing & Sales bei der Eurowings Flug GmbH in Dortmund. Seit Oktober 2002 ist er tätig bei der Germanwings GmbH in Köln, zuerst als stellvertretender Geschäftsführer, im Januar 2005 folgte die Ernennung zum Geschäftsführer.

Lars Blinda, geboren am 16. Mai 1977 in Hannover, studierte Betriebswirtschaftslehre an der Universität Bremen und der University of Victoria (Kanada) mit den Schwerpunkten Internationales Marketing und strategisches Management. Während dieser Zeit absolvierte er in Deutschland und Kanada Praktika in der Lebensmittel-, IT-, und Beratungsbranche. Im Jahr 2001 nahm er parallel zur Betriebswirtschaftslehre ein englischsprachiges Studium zum Master of Arts in Business Studies an der Universität Bremen auf, welches er 2002 erfolgreich abschloss. Herr Blinda ist seit Oktober 2002 als wissenschaftlicher Mitarbeiter am Lehrstuhl für innovatives Markenmanagement (LiM) unter Leitung von Univ.-Prof. Dr. Christoph Burmann tätig und gehört damit zum Gründungsteam des LiM. Seine Forschungsschwerpunkte liegen in der identitätsorientierten Markenführung und hier vor allem in der Forschung zu Markenkompetenzen zur geographischen und institutionellen Markenherkunft sowie zur strategischen Markenführung.

Dr. Michael Bongartz arbeitet seit 2003 als Berater für The Boston Consulting Group GmbH in Düsseldorf. Seine Beratungsschwerpunkte liegen unter anderem im Bereich des Vertriebs von Industriegütern sowie Dienstleistungen. Zuvor war er von 1999 bis 2002 wissenschaftlicher Mitarbeiter von Prof. Dr. Dr. h. c. mult. Heribert Meffert am Institut für Marketing der Westfälischen Wilhelms-Universität Münster. Hier befasste sich Dr. Bongartz vor allem mit Fragestellungen der Markenführung sowie der Erfolgsfaktorenforschung und promovierte mit einer Arbeit zur Markenführung im Internet.

Wolfgang Booms (37) studierte Betriebswirtschaft an der Universität Münster. Nach seinem Abschluss als Diplom-Kaufmann begann er 1993 seine Laufbahn bei Ford als Graduate Trainee. Seither hatte er verschiedene Positionen in Marketing und Verkauf inne, darunter die Position des Produktmanagers Große Pkw für Ford Deutschland (1998 bis Jahresende 2000 und damit verantwortlich für die Einführung des Ford Galaxy II), Leiter Verkaufsplanung sowie Leiter Markenstrategie und Kommunikation Ford Deutschland. Gleichzeitig erwarb er einen Abschluss des Global Leadership 2020 Executive Programms der Tuck University in New Hampshire (USA) in 2001. Heute nimmt er die Position des Direktor European Vehicle Pricing war und ist verantwortlich für die Produktangebots- und Preisgestaltung aller Ford Pkw und Nutzfahrzeuge in Europa.

Dr. Gerd Brüne, geboren am 4. Juli 1957 in Remscheid, studierte nach dem Abitur von 1977 bis 1982 Wirtschaftswissenschaft an der Ruhr-Universität Bochum. Nach seinem Abschluss als Diplom-Ökonom wurde er 1983 Wissenschaftlicher Mitarbeiter am Lehrstuhl für Allgemeine Betriebswirtschaft IV: Marketing von Prof. Dr. Peter Hammann, ebenfalls an der Ruhr-Universität. Er schloss sein Promotionsstudium 1988 ab; seine Dissertation wurde mit dem Wissenschaftspreis der Deutschen Marketing Vereinigung ausgezeichnet. Seine berufliche Laufbahn führte Brüne ab 1989 beim Verlag Gruner + Jahr fort, zunächst als Leiter Projektmanagement im Fachbereich Anzeigen, später dann als stellvertretender Anzeigenleiter des Stern. Seit 1997 ist er für GEO tätig, zunächst als Anzeigenleiter und stellvertretender Verlagsleiter, seit 2000 als Verlagsleiter dieser Zeitschriften-Gruppe. Brüne ist zudem Mitglied der Jury, die alljährlich den Wissenschaftspreis der Deutschen Marketing Vereinigung vergibt und paritätisch aus Hochschullehrern und Praktikern zusammengesetzt ist.

Univ.-Prof. Dr. habil. Christoph Burmann, 1962 in Damme geboren, studierte Betriebswirtschaftslehre an der Universität Münster mit den Schwerpunkten Marketing und Bankbetriebslehre. Er arbeitete 1985 und 1986 bei der amerikanischen Werbeagentur Ogilvy & Mather in Kapstadt/Südafrika in der Marketingplanung und Marktforschung. Seit 1989 war er Mitarbeiter von Prof. Dr. Dr. h. c. mult. Heribert Meffert am Institut für Marketing des Marketing Centrum Münster (MCM), wo er 1993 promovierte. Im Februar 2002 schloss er seine Habilitation an der Universität Münster im Fach Betriebswirtschaftslehre ab. Neben Aufgaben in Forschung und Lehre hat er zahlreiche Fachbeiträge zu einem breiten Spektrum an Marketingfragestellungen publiziert. Darüber hinaus hat er seit Anfang der 90er Jahre an zahlreichen Beratungsprojekten mit mittelständischen Unternehmen und internationalen Konzernen in leitender Funktion mitgewirkt. Seit dem 1. Oktober 2002 ist Prof. Burmann Inhaber des Lehrstuhls für innovatives Markenmanagement (LiM) am Fachbereich Wirtschaftswissenschaft der Universität Bremen. Der Lehrstuhl wurde von den Markenartikelunternehmen Kraft Foods Deutschland, Brauerei Beck & Co, Masterfoods, Kelloggs Deutschland, Frosta und BaslerSecuritas Versicherungen gestiftet.

Dr. Mirko Caspar war nach dem Studium an der Westfälischen Wilhelms-Universität in Münster mit den Schwerpunkten Marketing und Finanzen ein Jahr lang als Produktmanager für Jive Records tätig. Im Anschluss daran arbeitete er fünf Jahre als Unternehmensberater bei McKinsey & Company, wobei er sich auf die Bereiche Marketing und Strategie spezialisierte. Während dieser Zeit war er als Projektleiter maßgeblich an der Entwicklung des neuen Markenführungsansatzes von McKinsey beteiligt. Parallel promovierte Herr Dr. Caspar als externer Doktorand bei Prof. Dr. Dr. h. c. mult. Heribert Meffert in Münster über das Thema Cross-Channel-Medienmarken. Gegenwärtig leitet er als Head of Strategic Business Development die Abteilung New Channels bei Universal Music, Deutschland.

Dr. Christian Ebert ist seit 2004 Referent Konzernmarketing bei der Deutschen Bahn AG in Berlin und beschäftigt sich dort schwerpunktmäßig mit Fragestellungen des strategischen Marketing, des Marketing-Controlling sowie der Markenführung. Zuvor war er von Juni 2000 bis März 2004 wissenschaftlicher Mitarbeiter von Prof. Dr. Dr. h. c. mult. Heribert Meffert am Marketing Centrum Münster der Westfälischen Wilhelms-Universität Münster. Seine Forschungsschwerpunkte lagen dabei unter anderem in den Bereichen (Verkehrs-)Dienstleistungsmarketing, Markenführung sowie Städte- und Regionenmarketing. Nach Fertigstellung seiner Dissertation zum Thema „Identitätsorientiertes Stadtmarketing" erfolgte im November 2003 die Promotion zum Dr. rer. pol.

Harald W. Eisenächer (37) ist als Hauptabteilungsleiter Marketing der Deutschen Lufthansa AG verantwortlich für die Marke und Markenmanagement, das Kundenbindungsprogramm Miles & More, Direktmarketing, Werbung, Marktforschung und Zielkundenmanagement. Von 1999 bis 2003 war Herr Eisenächer Bereichsleiter Marketing und Services bei der Lufthansa Cargo AG mit den Verantwortlichkeiten Produktmanagement, Pricing, Business Intelligence, Produktentwicklung, Revenue Management und Branding/Kommunikation. Herr Eisenächer hat einen Abschluss als Diplom-Kaufmann von der WHU Koblenz und zusätzlich den Abschluss „Master of Business Administration" von der University of Texas in Austin.

Wolfgang Giehl begann 1995 bei der Deutschen Post als Leiter Marktkommunikation und verantwortet heute die Abteilung Marken und Konzernwerbung von Deutsche Post World Net. Davor leitete er als Geschäftsführer die Robert Pütz GmbH. Seine berufliche Laufbahn begann er nach einem Studium zum Diplom-Betriebswirt als Berater bei Young & Rubicam in Frankfurt und als Etat-Direktor bei GGK Düsseldorf.

Dr. Fabian Hieronimus ist Engagement Manager im Frankfurter Büro der Unternehmensberatung McKinsey & Company. Seine Beratungsschwerpunkte liegen in den Bereichen Markenführung, Markenportfoliomanagement sowie Marketingeffektivität. Hauptsächlich berät er Unternehmen aus der Automobilindustrie sowie der Finanzdienstleistungsindustrie. Herr Dr. Hieronimus studierte Betriebswirtschaftslehre an der Universität Mannheim und der University of California at Berkeley und promovierte zu dem Thema „Persönlichkeitsorientiertes Markenmanagement" am Institut für Marketing der Westfälischen Wilhelms-Universität Münster.

Prof. Dr. Manfred Kirchgeorg ist Inhaber des Lehrstuhls Marketingmanagement an der HHL – Leipzig Graduate School of Management. In drei Competence Centern werden an seinem Lehrstuhl Forschungsprojekte auf die Bereiche „Holistic Branding", „Media Management" und „Sustainability Marketing" ausgerichtet. Vor zwanzig Jahren begann Prof. Kirchgeorg am Institut für Marketing der Westfälischen Wilhelms-Universität in Münster mit seinen ersten Forschungen zum Umweltmanagement und Öko-Marketing. Nach seiner Promotion über den „Einfluss der Ökologie auf das Unternehmensverhalten" beschäftigte er sich im Rahmen seiner Habilitationsschrift mit dem Themenkomplex des „Marktstrategischen Kreislaufmanagement". Er hat vielfältige Lehraufträge an verschiedenen Universitäten im In- und Ausland wahrgenommen und ist Mitglied in zahlreichen betriebswirtschaftlichen Verbänden und Vereinigungen.

Dr. Martin Koers (33) studierte Betriebswirtschaft an der Universität Münster und der University of Edinburgh in Schottland. Nach seinem Diplom 1996 arbeitete er als Doktorand am Institut für Marketing von Prof. Dr. Dr. h. c. mult Heribert Meffert. Er promovierte zum Themenbereich Markenführung und Controlling und arbeitete an unterschiedlichen markenbezogenen Beratungsprojekten mit. Im Jahr 2001 hatte er einen Lehrauftrag als Visiting Assistant Professor an der University of Illinois (USA) im Bereich „Branding and Communications" inne. Seit Januar 2003 ist er Assistent des Vorstandsvorsitzenden der Ford-Werke AG.

Jörg P. Koppenhöfer, Jahrgang 1943, Diplom-Kaufmann, arbeitete von 1970 bis 2003 in verschiedenen Marketing- beziehungsweise Vertriebspositionen der Henkel KGaA, Düsseldorf. 1982 wurde er Geschäftsführer der Thompson GmbH, in den Jahren 1990 bis 1992 der Henkel Austria, Wien, und ab 1993 der Henkel Wasch- und Reinigungsmittel GmbH, Düsseldorf. Sein wissenschaftliches Interesse liegt in den Prinzipien der Markenführung.

Marcel Kranz, geboren 1974, studierte Betriebswirtschaftslehre in Essen und Münster. Im Mai 2003 promovierte er am Marketing Centrum Münster über die Relevanz der Unternehmensmarke mit Auszeichnung. Marcel Kranz war zunächst im Markenmanagement der Volkswagen AG tätig und arbeitet seit Ende 2004 im zentralen Marketing der BMW Group, München.

Michael Lambertz, am 2. April 1961 in Tönisvorst geboren, studierte nach dem Abitur von 1982 bis 1987 Betriebswirtschaftslehre in Aachen mit dem Abschluss Diplom-Kaufmann. Seine berufliche Laufbahn begann Lambertz 1987 bis 1993 bei der Henkel KGaA, bei der er in verschiedenen Positionen, zuletzt als internationaler Marketing und Projekt Manager, tätig war. 1994 wechselte er zur Groupe Danone nach Paris. Von 1996 bis 1999 war Lambertz als Marketing- und Innovations-Managementberater für Unternehmen der Konsumgüter- und Dienstleistungsbranche tätig. Von 1999 bis 2002 war Michael Lambertz Direktor Marketing bei der TUI Deutschland GmbH. Zum 1. Januar 2001 ist Lambertz zusätzlich zum Direktor Konzernmarketing der TUI AG ernannt worden. Gemeinsam mit seinem multinationalen Team ist er für die strategische Positionierung und Führung der touristischen Marken des TUI Konzerns verantwortlich.

Dr. Ingo Lasslop war von 1998 bis 2003 wissenschaftlicher Mitarbeiter von Prof. Dr. Dr. h. c. mult. Heribert Meffert am Institut für Marketing der Universität Münster, wo er mit einer Arbeit zur Effektivität und Effizienz von Marketing-Events promovierte. Seit Juni 2003 ist Dr. Lasslop Mitarbeiter im Strategischen Marketing eines Automobilherstellers.

Philip Maloney, geboren am 26. Februar 1979 in Bremen, studierte Betriebswirtschaftslehre an der Universität Bremen und der St. Petersburg State University (Russland) mit den Schwerpunkten Internationales Management, Corporate Governance in Schwellenländern und Markenmanagement. Während dieser Zeit absolvierte er Praktika in der Automobil-, Chemie-, und Beratungsbranche. Nach Abschluss eines Parallelstudiums zum Master of Arts in Business Studies, begann er am 1. Januar 2004 seine Tätigkeit als wissenschaftlicher Mitarbeiter am Lehrstuhl für innovatives Markenmanagement (LiM) unter Leitung von Univ.-Prof. Dr. Christoph Burmann. Seine Forschungsschwerpunkte liegen in der identitätsorientierten Markenführung und hier vor allem in der Forschung zur Bedeutung organisationaler Fähigkeiten für den Erfolg von Marken.

Prof. Dr. Dr. h. c. mult. Heribert Meffert wurde 1937 in Oberlahnstein geboren. Er studierte Betriebswirtschaftslehre an der Universität München. 1968 habilitierte er über „Flexibilität in betriebswirtschaftlichen Entscheidungen". Im Jahr 1969 folgte er einem Ruf auf den Lehrstuhl für Betriebswirtschaftslehre an der Universität Münster. Dort baute er das erste Institut für Marketing an einer deutschen Hochschule auf. 1981 war er Gründungsmitglied der Wissenschaftlichen Gesellschaft für Marketing und Unternehmensführung e. V., Münster. Nach der Wende in Ostdeutschland übernahm er neben seiner Tätigkeit in Münster auch die wissenschaftliche Geschäftsführung (Rektorat) der wiedergegründeten privaten Handelshochschule (HHL) in Leipzig. An das Marketing Science Institute in Cambridge/Mass. folgte er einem Ruf als Visiting Research Professor. Im März 2004 wurde Heribert Meffert zudem in die Internationale Akademie für das Hochschulwesen (IHEAS) in Moskau aufgenommen.

Heribert Meffert erhielt zahlreiche Ehrungen und Ehrendoktorwürden. Am 31. Juli 2002 wurde Professor Meffert emeritiert. Er gehört mehreren Aufsichtsräten und Beiräten international tätiger Unternehmen an. Als Marketingwissenschaftler publizierte er mehr als dreihundert wissenschaftliche Schriften und mehr als dreißig Monographien. Am 1. Oktober 2002 wurde Heribert Meffert Vorsitzender des Präsidiums (seit 2005: Vorstand) der Bertelsmann Stiftung.

Dr. Klaus Morwind, Jahrgang 1943, ist Mitglied der Geschäftsführung und persönlich haftender geschäftsführender Gesellschafter der Henkel KGaA in Düsseldorf. Nach seinem Studium an der Hochschule für Welthandel in Wien und der TH Wien folgte eine dreijährige Tätigkeit an wissenschaftlichen Instituten. Nach seiner Promotion in Handelswissenschaften 1969 kam er zur Persilgesellschaft in Wien, einer Tochtergesellschaft der Henkel Gruppe. Er machte hier eine klassische Marketingkarriere vom Brand Manager zum Marketing Director, bevor er 1983 internationale Verantwortung in der Henkel-Zentrale in Düsseldorf übernahm. Seit 1991 ist er Mitglied der Geschäftsführung und zuständig für den Unternehmensbereich Wasch- und Reinigungsmittel. Dr. Klaus Morwind hat in der Marketingfachpresse zahlreiche Artikel veröffentlicht, die sich schwerpunktmäßig mit der Analyse moderner Business-Techniken im Verhältnis zur praktischen Umsetzung beschäftigen.

Axel Nitschke, geboren am 12. Februar 1977 in Düsseldorf, studierte von 1997 bis 2002 Betriebswirtschaftslehre an den Universitäten Münster und Aix-Marseille III mit den Schwerpunkten Marketing und Controlling. Während dieser Zeit absolvierte er Praktika bei der Deutschen Bank, der Unternehmensberatung A.T. Kearney sowie der Deutschen Bahn AG. Darüber hinaus war er bei verschiedenen Unternehmen im Bereich des Sportmanagements als freier Mitarbeiter tätig. Herr Nitschke ist seit November 2002 als wissenschaftlicher Mitarbeiter am Lehrstuhl für innovatives Markenmanagement (LiM) unter Leitung von Univ.-Prof. Dr. Christoph Burmann tätig und gehört damit zum Gründungsteam des LiM. Seine Forschungsschwerpunkte liegen in der identitätsorientierten Markenführung und hier vor allem in der Forschung zur Markenprofilierung mit Events und Sponsoring, zur strategischen Markenführung sowie zum Markencontrolling.

Peter Nüßler, Jahrgang 1962, Diplom-Kaufmann, arbeitet seit 1991 bei der Henkel Wasch- und Reinigungsmittel GmbH in Düsseldorf. Nach vierjähriger Tätigkeit im Vertrieb wechselte er 1995 ins Marketing, wo er zunächst die nationale Einführung der Marke Spee mitgestaltete. Nach Stationen als Produktmanager für Persil Megaperls, Projektmanager für Persil Tabs sowie einem einjährigen Einsatz im Marketing bei The Clorox Company, USA war er von Anfang 2000 bis Mitte 2003 als Director für die Führung der Marke Persil in Deutschland verantwortlich.

Dr. Jesko Perrey ist Partner bei McKinsey & Company im Düsseldorfer Büro und Leiter des europäischen Branding & Marketing Spend Effectiveness Funktionsbereichs. Seine Beratungsschwerpunkte sind Marketing- und Markenstrategien, Marktsegmentierung, Reorganisation und Funktionalstrategien. Seine Branchenschwerpunkte sind Konsumgüter und Einzelhandel sowie Automobilindustrie und Transportdienstleistungen. Zuvor war Dr. Perrey von 1995 bis 1999 wissenschaftlicher Mitarbeiter von Prof. Dr. Dr. h. c. mult. Heribert Meffert am Institut für Marketing der Universität Münster, wo er mit einer Arbeit zum Zielgruppenmarketing promovierte.

Jürgen Plüss studierte Betriebswirtschaft in Bremen und sammelte bei Rollei und der Blaupunkt/Bosch-Gruppe umfangreiche Marketingerfahrungen in der Gebrauchsgüterindustrie. Seit 1993 ist er beim Premiumanbieter der Hausgeräteindustrie Miele & Cie. KG für das Marketing verantwortlich und führt dort seit 2001 den Geschäftsbereich Küchengeräte International. Neben seiner beruflichen Aufgabe ist er in verschiedenen Kuratorien und Jurys zu den Themen Marketing, Markenführung und Design tätig.

Volker Scheible, geb. 1967, studierte Marketing und Kommunikationswissenschaften in Stuttgart und Berlin und ist Diplom-Wirtschaftsingenieur (FH) sowie Diplom-Kommunikationswirt (UdK). Nach verschiedenen Tätigkeiten bei Werbeagenturen in Stuttgart und Berlin folgte der Einstieg als Management Trainee bei Lufthansa. Nach der Wahrnehmung verschiedener Funktionen im nationalen und internationalen Marketing, unter anderem im Bereich Markenführung Konzern, Global Marketing Management Passage, war Volker Scheible zuletzt kommissarischer Leiter Werbung und Markenführung bei Lufthansa Passage. Seit 2002 ist Volker Scheible Leiter Marketing und Produktmanagement bei der Germanwings GmbH in Köln.

Dr. Michael Schleusener ist Senior Consultant bei SIMON ◆ KUCHER & PARTNERS Strategy & Marketing Consultants GmbH in Bonn. Er studierte Betriebswirtschaftslehre mit den Schwerpunkten Marketing und Internationales Management an der Universität Münster mit dem Abschluss Diplom-Kaufmann. Anschließend war er Wissenschaftlicher Mitarbeiter bei Prof. Dr. Dr. h. c. mult. Heribert Meffert am Institut für Marketing der Universität Münster. Dort leitete er unter anderem die am Institut bestehende Forschungskooperation mit der Deutschen Bahn AG.

PD Dr. Dr. Helmut Schneider ist Akademischer Oberrat am Marketing Centrum der Westfälischen Wilhelms-Universität Münster. Er studierte von 1988 bis 1995 zunächst Politik- und Kommunikationswissenschaft sowie ab 1990 zusätzlich Betriebswirtschaftslehre an der Universität Münster. Im Jahre 1996 promovierte er mit einer Arbeit zur Rationalität von Wirtschaftspolitik zum Dr. phil. 1999 folgte die Promotion zum Dr. rer. pol. mit einer Arbeit zur Preisbeurteilung im Verkehrsdienstleistungsbereich. Für seine Habilitationsschrift „Marken in der Politik" verlieh ihm die Wirtschaftswissenschaftliche Fakultät der Westfälischen Wilhelms-Universität Münster im Juli 2003 die venia legendi für das Fach Betriebswirtschaftslehre. Zu seinen Forschungsschwerpunkten zählen Dienstleistungsmarketing, Non-Profit-Marketing, Strategisches Marketing sowie Fragen der Markenführung und des Interaktiven Direktmarketing.

Jan-Philipp Weers wurde 1976 in Cuxhaven geboren. Nach Abitur und Wehrdienst studierte er an der Westfälischen Wilhelms-Universität in Münster Betriebswirtschaftslehre mit Auslandssemester an der State University in New York. Im Rahmen seiner Schwerpunktfächer Marketing und International Business Management absolvierte Herr Weers zahlreiche Praktika, u.a. bei SAT.1 in Berlin, bei der Deutsch-Arabischen Industrie- und Handelskammer in Kairo und bei Warner Bros. in New York City. Nach seinem Abschluss im Jahr 2003 arbeitete er als Unternehmensberater in Köln, bevor er im Mai 2004 als wissenschaftlicher Mitarbeiter an den Lehrstuhl für innovatives Markenmanagement (LiM) wechselte. Seine Forschungsschwerpunkte liegen in der identitätsbasierten Markenführung und hier insbesondere im Bereich der wertorientierten Steuerung von Marken, der Marke-Kunde Beziehung und dem Vertriebsmanagement.

Michael Welling (33) studierte Wirtschaftswissenschaft an der Ruhr-Universität Bochum und der University of Strathclyde in Glasgow mit den Schwerpunkten Marketing, Controlling und Umweltökonomie. Nach seinem Studium war er zunächst im Bereich Controlling & Strategic Planning bei der adidas-Salomon AG tätig und arbeitete anschließend als Wissenschaftlicher Mitarbeiter am Lehrstuhl für Angewandte Betriebswirtschaftslehre (Marketing) bei Prof. Dr. Peter Hammann an der Ruhr-Universität Bochum. Im Rahmen seiner Promotionsschrift beschäftigte er sich dabei mit einer ökonomisch-theoretischen Analyse der Markenführung. Seit Juli 2004 ist er am Lehrstuhl für Mittelstand, Existenzgründung und Entrepreneurship (Prof. Dr. Jörg Freiling) an der Universität Bremen beschäftigt. Zudem ist er Lehrbeauftragter der Fakultät für Sportwissenschaft der Ruhr-Universität Bochum für die Veranstaltung „Markenführung im Sport".

Sabrina Zeplin, Jahrgang 1975, studierte in Münster und Zaragoza (Spanien) Betriebswirtschaft und ist seit 2001 als Beraterin bei The Boston Consulting Group (BCG) in Hamburg angestellt. Sie war bei BCG bisher schwerpunktmäßig in den Bereichen Markenmanagement und Vertrieb in verschiedenen Branchen tätig, unter anderem im Maschinenbau, in der Medienbranche und im Tourismus. Derzeit promoviert sie als externe Mitarbeiterin am Lehrstuhl für innovatives Markenmanagement (LiM) in Bremen bei Prof. Dr. Burmann über innengerichtetes Markenmanagement.